READER'S DIGEST 1986

ALMANAC

AND YEARBOOK

PUBLISHED ANNUALLY BY
THE READER'S DIGEST ASSOCIATION, INC.
PLEASANTVILLE, NEW YORK 10570

Reader's Digest

1986
ALMANAC
AND YEARBOOK

A specially commissioned work
prepared by
David C. Whitney Associates, Inc.,
with the editors of
The Reader's Digest Association, Inc.
Editor: David C. Whitney

Library of Congress Catalog Card Number 66-14383

ISBN 0-89577-216-7
ISSN 0079-9831

CONTENTS

The main sections of the *Reader's Digest 1986 Almanac and Yearbook* are listed below along with the contents of each. To find specific information on persons, places, or subjects, turn to the alphabetical *Index* with its more than 9,000 references on pages 987–1024.

6 CONTENTS

MAJOR NEWS DEVELOPMENTS: 1985

For the convenience of the reader who seeks the year's news at a glance, following is a listing of some of 1985's major events and developments with references to the pages on which you can find information about them.

The many events and developments that affected the United States and the world in 1985 are examined in detail throughout the *Reader's Digest 1986 Almanac and Yearbook.*

For the reader who wishes to review the events of the year in the order in which they happened, pages 8–26 provide a month-by-month, day-by-day chronology.

Facing each monthly summary of events is a FOCUS page providing details of a major event or development.

The main body of the *Almanac* contains 38 sections arranged alphabetically from *Ac-* *cidents and Disasters* to *Women's Rights.* Within these sections other articles and features examine additional important happenings of 1985. Each section also contains the latest facts and statistics on relevant persons, places, and events.

To find a specific fact the reader should consult the alphabetical *Index* on pages 987–1024.

QUICK QUIZ questions at the bottom of right-hand pages in the sections *History* and *Nations of the World* guide the curious reader to interesting information throughout the *Reader's Digest 1986 Almanac and Yearbook.*

JANUARY

1 Airliner crash kills 29 in Bolivia: Eastern Airlines jet crashes into mountain southeast of La Paz, killing all aboard.

2 Japanese prime minister Nakasone meets with President Reagan: Talk in Los Angeles centers on need to open Japanese market to more American products.

3 U.S. Congress opens 99th session: After brief meeting, adjourns until presidential inauguration on Jan. 21.

3 President calls for $1 billion aid for Africa: Proposes $411 million increase in aid for drought victims.

5 Alaska buys federal railroad: State purchases Alaska Railroad from federal government for $22.7 million.

6 Pro football championships: Miami Dolphins defeat Pittsburgh Steelers 45-28 to win American Conference championship; San Francisco 49ers defeat Chicago Bears 23-0 to take National Conference.

7 Vietnamese troops attack Cambodian rebels: Destroy main rebel headquarters at Ampil, Cambodia.

7 Ferraro's husband guilty of fraud: John A. Zaccaro, husband of unsuccessful Democratic vice-presidential candidate Geraldine A. Ferraro, pleads guilty to giving false information in real estate deal; plea saves him from possibility of jail sentence.

8 GM will manufacture new line of cars: Announces plans to build subcompact cars under name Saturn; first new brand name in 67 years for giant automaker.

8 President Reagan switches top aides: Secretary of the Treasury Donald T. Regan will become White House chief of staff, replacing James A. Baker 3d, who takes over Regan's position as Treasury Secretary.

8 U.S. and Soviet Union agree to renew talks on limiting nuclear arms: Accord follows two days of discussions in Geneva, Switzerland, between Soviet Foreign Minister Gromyyko and U.S. Secretary of State George P. Shultz.

9 Unemployment rate rises: Labor Department reports unemployment rate rose to 7.1% in December from 7% in November.

9 Four killed in Ecuadorian violence: Police break up demonstrations during general strike protesting price increases.

10 President announces cabinet changes: Secretary of Energy Donald P. Hodel to replace William P. Clark as Secretary of the Interior; White House personnel director John S. Herrington to succeed Hodel as head of Department of Energy; William Bennett, head of the National Endowment for the Humanities, to become Secretary of Education.

11 Missile accident kills 3 U.S. soldiers: Unarmed Pershing 2 missile catches fire at Heilbronn, West Germany; 7 other soldiers injured.

12 France sends troops to New Caledonia: 1,000 soldiers sent to Pacific island after police kill rebel independence leader.

13 Train crash kills 392 in Ethiopia: Additional 370 injured when train falls off bridge.

14 Israel to withdraw from Lebanon: Cabinet approves plan to pull out troops in three stages during next 6 to 9 months.

14 U.S. cracks down on church sanctuary movement: 16 persons indicted, including 3 nuns, 2 priests, and 1 minister, on charges of smuggling illegal aliens from Central America.

15 Brazil chooses civilian president: Tancredo Neves, 74, chosen by electoral college to replace military rulers.

15-17 Riots kill 10 in Jamaica: Widespread violence in Caribbean island as demonstrators protest fuel price increases.

15 Student searches okayed: U.S. Supreme Court rules teachers and school authorities can search students suspected of wrongdoing without obtaining search warrant.

17 Cities spending more on police than on education: Census bureau reports cities spent $10.7 billion on police in 1982 with spending on education dropping to $9.8 billion.

17 TV networks to limit election projections: Agree not to use exit polls to project results in any state before its polls close.

18 U.S. walks out of World Court hearings: Refuses to take part in trial of Nicaragua charge U.S. trying to overthrow its government.

20-22 Worst cold wave of century in East: Sub-zero records set in many cities; cold damages citrus crops throughout Florida.

20 President sworn in for second term: Private ceremony in White House televised to nation; see opposite page.

20 Pro football Super Bowl: San Francisco 49ers win NFL championship by defeating Miami Dolphins 38-16 in Palo Alto, Calif.

21 Charter airliner crash kills 71: Lockheed Electra crashes after takeoff at Reno, Nev.

21 Inauguration Day outdoor ceremonies and parade cancelled by cold: See opposite page.

22 U.S. military transport crash kills 21: Hercules C-130A crashes on coast of Honduras on flight from Panama.

22 U.S. economy grew 6.8% in 1984: Commerce Department says growth rate was best since 1951; inflation held to 3.7% in 1984.

24 Time magazine wins major libel suit: Jury rules against former Israel defense minister Ariel Sharon in his effort to collect $50 million from Time for libeling him in its account of his role in 1982 massacre of Palestinians in Beirut.

24-27 Space shuttle Discovery flies military mission: 3-day mission launches spy satellite to listen in on Soviet communications.

25 Special assembly of Roman Catholic bishops called by Pope John Paul II: Meeting to be held in Rome Nov. 25 to Dec. 8 to review 20-year results of Second Vatican Council.

26 Pope begins 12-day Latin American tour: Arrives in Caracas, Venezuela, in 25th foreign trip since becoming pope in 1978.

28 Iraq launches ground attack on Iran: Iraq sends 40,000 troops into action to regain lost territory along border.

30 U.S. trade deficit sets record: Commerce Department reports trade deficit in 1984 was $123.3 billion, increase of $53.9 billion over 1983 deficit.

PRESIDENT SWORN IN FOR 2d TERM

Because the day specified by the Constitution for the presidential inauguration fell on a Sunday, President Ronald Reagan began his second term as 40th President of the United States with a brief ceremony in the White House on Jan. 20, 1985.

On Sunday morning the President and First Lady Nancy Reagan attended a prayer service conducted by the Rev. Billy Graham at the National Cathedral.

Then at noon, the 73-year-old President, the oldest man ever elected to the office, was sworn at the foot of the grand staircase of the White House. At his side was Mrs. Reagan wearing a red dress and holding the family Bible.

Chief Justice Warren E. Burger administered the oath of office.

The Cabinet and fewer than 100 guests were present at the brief ceremony. However, millions watched via television.

After Vice President George Bush also had been sworn in for a second term, Reagan and Bush stepped out of the White House to let photographers take their picture. Wearing no overcoats, they were quickly driven back inside by the below-zero wind chill of an icy wind.

Remaining at the White House, the President later in the day took part in televised opening ceremonies for pro football's Super Bowl XIX, tossing the coin that determined which goal each team would defend.

CURTAILED INAUGURAL ACTIVITIES

With artic cold gripping Washington, D.C., along with the eastern half of the nation, outdoor inaugural ceremonies on Monday, Jan. 21, were cancelled for the first time in history to prevent frostbite among participants.

Rather than the public inauguration planned to take place on the west front of the capital, the President and Vice President repeated their oaths shortly before noon in the rotunda of the Capitol before a crowd of about 1,000 government officials and friends.

Instead of the traditional inaugural parade down Pennsylvania Avenue, the President and Mrs. Reagan flew by helicopter in mid-afternoon to attend a party at the Capital Center in Landover, Md., for the 12,000 disappointed members of 57 bands that had planned to march in the parade.

In the evening the Reagans spent a few minutes at each of 10 galas and balls held throughout the capital that were attended by some 50,000 happy party-goers.

REAGAN'S 2d INAUGURAL ADDRESS

In an 18-minute address after the oath taking in the Capitol rotunda, President Reagan reviewed the accomplishments of his first term and previewed what he hoped to achieve during his second term.

"Four years ago I spoke to you of a new beginning," he said, "and we have accomplished that. . . . Tax rates have been reduced, inflation cut dramatically and more people are employed than ever before in our history. . . .

"My fellow citizens, our nation is poised for greatness. We must do what we know is right and do it with all our might. Let history say of us, these were golden years—when the American Revolution was reborn, when freedom gained new life and America reached for her best. . . .

"We must not repeat the well-intentioned errors of our past. We must never again abuse the trust of working men and women by sending their earnings on a futile chase after the spiraling demands of a bloated Federal establishment. You elected us in 1980 to end this prescription for disaster. And I don't believe you reelected us in 1984 to reverse course.

"The heart of our efforts is one idea vindicated by 25 straight months of economic growth:

"Freedom and incentives unleash the drive and entrepreneurial genius that are the core of human progress."

"We have begun to increase the rewards for work, savings and investment; reduce the increase in the cost and size of government and its interference in people's lives.

"We must simplify our tax system, make it more fair and bring the rates down for all who work and earn. We must think anew and move with a new boldness so every American who seeks work can find work; so the least among us shall have an equal chance to achieve the greatest things—to be heroes who heal our sick, feed the hungry, protect peace among nations and leave this world a better place.

"The time has come for a new American emancipation, a great national drive to tear down economic barriers and liberate the spirit of enterprise in the most distressed areas of our country. My friends, together we can do this, and do it we must, so help me God."

FEBRUARY

4 President submits $973.7 billion budget: Presents budget for 1986, calling for new cuts in domestic programs while continuing buildup of military forces.

4 New Zealand refuses visit by U.S. destroyer: New Zealand government bans visit of ships that are nuclear-powered or that carry nuclear weapons.

5 Military pensions called a "scandal": Budget Director David A. Stockman tells Senate committee that military "are more concerned about protecting their retirement benefits than they are about protecting the security of the American people."

6 President calls for "second American revolution": Outlines goals in State of the Union address; see opposite page.

7 Boston bank guilty of money laundring: First National Bank of Boston pleads guilty and fined $500,000 for not reporting deposits of $1.2 billion in cash in Swiss banks.

7 Four Polish police convicted of killing priest: Sentenced to long prison terms after 25-day trial for kidnapping and killing priest who was outspoken supporter of outlawed Solidarity movement.

8 New UN ambassador names: Gen. Vernon A. Walters named to succeed Jeane J. Kirkpatrick as U.S. chief delegate to UN.

8 Purchaser of Conrail chosen: U.S. Secretary of Transportation Elizabeth Dole announces selection of Norfolk Southern Corporation to buy government-controlled Conrail railroad for at least $1.2 billion; sale will require congressional approval.

11 Record-breaking balloonist killed: Ben Abruzzo, 54, who made first balloon flights across Atlantic and Pacific, dies in plane crash with five others in Albuquerque, N.M.

11 Jordan and PLO sign pact: King Hussein and Palestine Liberation Organization leader Yasir Arafat sign accord that calls for Israel to exchange territory it holds for Mideast peace.

14 Conservative Jews approve women as rabbis: Rabbinical Assembly approves action in 636–267 vote.

14 American hostage escapes in Lebanon: Jeremy Levin, Beirut bureau chief for Cable News Network, escapes from Muslim terrorists after being held prisoner for 11 months.

16 Israeli troops complete 1st stage of withdrawal from Lebanon: Leave city of Sidon; Shiite Muslims hold victory rally in Sidon, calling for establishment of fundamentalist Muslim nation in Lebanon.

16 President appeals for aid to Nicaraguan rebels: In radio address, calls rebels "our brothers" and compares them to American Revolutionary War patriots; says Nicaraguan government seeks to spread communism to Central American neighbors.

17 Postage rates increase: U.S. Postal Service increases cost of mailing first class letter from 20 cents to 22 cents; other increases go into effect for domestic and international mail.

17 U.S. halts economic aid to Sudan: State Department says Sudan must work out agreement to pay its foreign debts before· aid can be restored.

18 General drops $120 million CBS libel suit: Gen. William C. Westmoreland, commanding general in Vietnam in 1964–68, ends five-month jury trial in New York City without decision; he had accused CBS of libel in TV documentary that said he took part in conspiracy to deceive public and President Johnson as to strength of enemy forces in Vietnam War.

19 Local government employees subject to federal standards: Supreme Court rules 5–4 that 13 million state and local government employees must work under federal wage and hour standards; requires overtime pay for police, firemen, and others.

19 Spanish air crash kills 148: Iberia Air Lines Boeing 727 hits mountain near Bilbao, killing all aboard.

21 PBS in joint venture with corporations: Public Broadcasting Service announces plan to join with Merrill Lynch & Co. and International Business Machines Corp. to broadcast financial news to personal computer owners.

21 British Prime Minister Thatcher addresses U.S. Congress: Lauds Reagan's policies.

21 Israeli troops take prisoner hundreds of Shiite Muslims: Drive launched against resistance of Shiites in southern Lebanon.

23 Meese wins approval as U.S. Attorney General: Senate votes 63–31 in favor of nomination of Edwin Meese 3d to Cabinet post; appointment had been held up by 4-day filibuster and by long probe of his ethics.

24 Egypt calls for new Mideast peace talks: President Mubarak expresses willingness to host peace talks attended by U.S., Israel, Jordan, and PLO.

24 Governors call for federal spending freeze: Executive committee of National Governors' Association urges 1-year freeze on spending by federal government.

24 Chernenko appears on TV: Soviet president shown casting vote in parliamentary election; seen as effort to dispel rumors of illness.

25 Parliamentary election in Pakistan: Voters rebuff President Zia by defeating seven cabinet members and over 30 other of his appointees in election for national legislature.

25 Value of dollar reaches record highs: British pound valued at $1.056, German mark at $0.29, and French franc at $0.095.

26 Nine Mafia bosses indicted: Federal grand jury charges nine were members of commission that controls five organized-crime families in New York.

26 States must provide free psychiatrist to poor defendants: Supreme Court rules 8 to 1 that indigent criminal defendants must be given free assistance of psychiatrist to help prepare insanity plea.

28 Irish guerrillas kill 9 persons: Attack police headquarters at Newry, Northern Ireland, with mortar shells.

28 Louisiana governor indicted: Gov. Edwin Edwards and 6 others, including his brother, indicted by federal grand jury on 51 counts of racketeering; group said to have made $10 million in hospital scheme.

STATE OF THE UNION: 1985

FOCUS

In an evening appearance before a joint meeting of Congress on Feb. 6, President Reagan delivered his 4th State of the Union address, calling for "a second American Revolution of hope and opportunity."

Because the day marked the President's 74th birthday, the entire Congress joined in singing "Happy Birthday." The President responded by joking, "Thank you for making the 35th time I have been 39 the happiest of them all."

REVIEW OF ACCOMPLISHMENTS

"Four years ago, we said we would invigorate our economy by giving people greater freedom and incentives to take risks, and letting them keep more of what they earned," the President said. "We did what we promised, and a great industrial giant is reborn. Tonight we can take pride in 25 straight months of economic growth, the strongest in 34 years; a three-year inflation average of 3.9 percent, the lowest in 17 years; and 7.3 million new jobs in two years, with more of our citizens working than ever before. . . .

"We have begun well. But it's only a beginning. We are not here to congratulate ourselves on what we have done, but to challenge ourselves to finish what has not yet been done."

A SECOND AMERICAN REVOLUTION

"We are here to speak for millions in our inner cities who long for real jobs, safe neighborhoods and schools that truly teach," President Reagan said. "We are here to speak for the American farmer, the entrepreneur and every worker in industries fighting to modernize and compete. And, yes, we are here to stand, and proudly so, for all who struggle to break free from totalitarianism; for all who know in their hearts that freedom is the one true path to peace and human happiness. . . .

"My fellow citizens, this nation is poised for greatness. The time has come to proceed toward a great new challenge—a Second American Revolution of hope and opportunity; a revolution carrying us to new heights of progress by pushing back frontiers of knowledge and space; a revolution of spirit that taps the soul of America, enabling us to summon greater strength than we have ever known; and, a revolution that carries beyond our shores the golden promise of human freedom in a world at peace.

"Let us begin by challenging conventional wisdom: There are no constraints on the human mind, no walls around the human spirit, no barriers to our progress except those we ourselves erect. Already, pushing down tax rates has freed our economy to vault forward to record growth.

"In Europe, they call it "the American Miracle." Day by day, we are shattering accepted notions of what is possible.

"When I was growing up, we failed to see how a new thing called radio would transform our marketplace. Well, today many have not yet seen how advances in technology are transforming our lives. . . .

"We stand on the threshold of a great ability to produce more, do more, be more. Our economy is not getting older and weaker, it's getting younger and stronger; it doesn't need rest and supervision, it needs new callenge and greater freedom. And that word—freedom—is the key to the Second American Revolution we mean to bring about."

The Democractic Party replied to the President's address in a 30-minute TV program. The narrator, Gov. Bill Clinton of Arkansas, admitted the Democratic Party received a "resounding defeat" in the 1984 election and "has to change."

SPECIFIC PROPOSALS

The President made many specific recommendations to Congress, including:

—Tax simplification "for fairness and growth."

—Enterprise zones "to help those in the abandoned corners of our land find jobs, learn skills and build better lives."

—Reduction in minimum wages for teenagers to help them find summer jobs.

—A freeze on government spending to reduce the budget deficit.

—Reduce or eliminate government subsidies to railroads.

—A constitutional amendment to require a balanced federal budget.

—Further deregulation of natural gas, bus, trucking, and railroad industries.

—Expansion of the Superfund program to clean up hazardous waste sites.

—Build up of a strong military defense that "has influenced the Soviet Union to return to the bargaining table."

—Research for non-nuclear defense against ballistic missiles as a means of "eliminating the threat of nuclear war."

—Support for rebels fighting against the Marxist government of Nicaragua.

MARCH

1 Japanese auto export curbs to end: President Reagan announces he will not ask Japan to continue export restrictions that have protected U.S. auto industry for four years; curbs to end March 31.

1 Uruguay restores civilian rule: Elected President Julio Maria Sanguinetti sworn in, ending 12 years of military rule.

3 British coal miners end 357-day strike: Union calls off longest major strike in British history without reaching agreement with government; major victory for Prime Minister Thatcher who has resisted union demands.

3 Earthquake hits Chile: Kills 150 persons and injures over 2,000 in and around San Antonio and Melipilla.

4 U.S. and Israel agree on free trade pact: All tariffs would be ended within 10 years; Congress expected to approve treaty.

5 U.S. Agents arrest Caribbean leader in drug plot: Chief minister of British Turks and Caicos Islands arrested in Miami by federal undercover agents; charged with seeking to use islands as base to smuggle narcotics.

6 South Korea ends ban on political opponents: Ends restrictions imposed after military coup in November 1980.

7 President Reagan vetoes $1.85 billion farm credit measure: Says federal government cannot "bail out every farmer hopelessly in debt, or every bank which made imprudent or speculatives loans;" Democrats will not attempt to override veto.

8 New Yorker magazine sold: Publisher S. I. Newhouse buys magazine for $142 million.

8 Car-bomb kills 62 in Beirut, Lebanon: Explosion in Shiite Muslim suburb also wounds about 200.

10 Suicide bomber kills 12 Israeli soldiers: Terrorist crashes bomb-laden truck into Israeli army convoy in southern Lebanon.

10 Soviet President Chernenko dies: Succeeded by Mikhail S. Gorbachev. See opposite page.

12 Nuclear arms talks begin: U.S. and Soviet negotiators meet in Geneva, Switzerland, for new round of talks on ways to limit nuclear arms; Soviet Union broke off previous negotiations in December 1983.

13 Bush and Gorbachev meet in Moscow: Vice President George Bush, while attending funeral of late President Chernenko, meets with new Soviet leader Gorbachev; delivers letter from President Reagan proposing summit meeting.

15 Indicted U.S. Secretary of Labor resigns: Raymond J. Donovan quits post after New York judge refuses to dismiss charges of larceny and fraud against Donovan and 9 others.

15 Brazil restores civilian rule: Vice President Jose Sarney sworn in as Brazil's interim president because President-elect Tancredo Neves is too ill to take office; military had ruled nation since 1964 uprising.

15 Ohio closes 71 S&Ls to halt runs by depositors: Ohio Gov. Richard F. Celeste orders saving and loan associations to close after collapse of one S&L had caused depositors to begin withdrawing savings from others.

16–17 Fierce fighting in Iraq-Iran War: Iraq claims to have killed 15,000 Iranians in halting invasion of southeastern Iraq.

17–18 President Reagan visits Canada: Meets with Canadian Prime Minister Brian Mulroney; signs agreements on security, trade, law enforcement, and fishing rights; agrees to exchange of special envoys to study issue of acid rain pollution.

18 ABC TV Network purchased for $3.5 billion: Capital Cities Communications Inc. reaches agreement to buy network, which has 214 affiliated stations.

18 IBM ends production of home computer: International Business Machines Corp. says it will stop making PCjr computer because of poor sales.

20 New U.S. Secretary of Labor named: President Reagan picks former Tennessee U.S. Senator Bill Brock for cabinet post.

21 South African police kill 20 blacks: Fire into crowd of about 4,000 defying government ban on demonstrations; incident takes place near Uitenhage; police claim they were attacked by mob.

21 Israeli army in "iron fist" sweep of southern Lebanon: Israeli troops and tanks storm through Muslim villages, killing 21 suspected terrorists; two CBS News camera crew members killed and one wounded during action.

21 Ohio S&Ls permitted to reopen: Depositors allowed to make limited withdrawals for first time since state closed 71 saving and loan institutions on March 15.

23 Consumer prices rose slightly in February: Department of Labor reports Consumer Price Index increased only 0.3%, at rate of 3.5% for year.

23–24 South African blacks wreak vengeance: Black militants kill blacks suspected of supporting white government; burn homes of 18 black policemen.

25 U.S. army major slain by Soviet guard: Maj. Authur D. Nicholson Jr., shot near Ludwigslust, East Germany, while observing Soviet military installation.

26 G.E. indicted for defrauding government: General Electric Company, nation's fourth largest defense contractor, accused of falsifying $800,000 in claims against government.

27 Supreme Court restricts use of deadly force by police: Strikes down state laws giving police right to kill any fleeing suspect.

28 Additional MX missiles approved: House of Representatives votes 217 to 210 to purchase 21 more missiles for $1.5 billion; marks victory for President Reagan, who had lobbied Democratic congressmen to support measure; Senate had okayed legislation by 55 to 45 vote on March 19.

30 Spain and Portugal to join European Common Market in 1986: Agreement reached to prevent Greece from vetoing their membership when other nine members approve paying Greek farmers $2 billion in special subsidies.

31 President Duarte wins legislative election in El Salvador: His Christian Democratic Party upsets rightists to control national assembly.

GORBACHEV BECOMES NEW SOVIET LEADER

Soviet President Konstantin U. Chernenko, 73, died on March 10. Within a few hours Mikhail S. Gorbachev, 54, was named as his successor.

Chernenko had become leader of the Soviet Union only a little more than 13 months earlier upon the death of Yuri V. Andropov, 69, on Feb. 9, 1984. Throughout his brief tenure, Chernenko suffered from lung, liver, and heart ailments that repeatedly brought premature rumors of his death when he failed to attend important functions.

When Andropov's predecessor, Leonid I. Brezhnev died on Nov. 10, 1982, most observers had expected Chernenko (at that time Brezhnev's chief of staff) to succeed him. Instead, Andropov, head of the Soviet spy network KGB, took over as head of the Soviet Union. Chernenko finally achieved his ambition to become the supreme Soviet leader after Andropov's death.

During Chernenko's regime, the only major change in Soviet foreign policy came with agreement on Nov. 22, 1984, to resume talks with the U.S. on ways to limit nuclear arms—negotiations that had been broken off a year earlier during Andropov's administration. The new talks began in Geneva, Switzerland, on March 12, 1985, two days after Chernenko's death.

Gorbachev's accession obviously had been agreed upon much earlier because it was announced less than five hours after Chernenko died.

Born in 1931 in Privolnoye, a village near Stavropol, Gorbachev became a member of the Communist Party at the age of 21. He received a law degree from Moscow University in 1955. After studying agriculture, he rose in the party ranks until he was brought to Moscow as the Communist Party's secretary of agriculture. At the age of 49 he became the youngest member of the ruling Politburo. During Andropov's and Chernenko's regimes he served as the No. 2 man in the Kremlin, taking on much power delegated by the ailing leaders.

Western observers believed that Gorbachev was prepared to initiate many changes in Soviet policies.

In an acceptance speech upon being named general secretary of the Communist Party on March 11, Gorbachev indicated that he would like to improve relations with the United States.

"We value the successes of the relaxation of international tensions achieved in the 1970s and are ready to take part in carrying on with the process of establishing peaceful mutually beneficial cooperation between states on the basis of principles of equality, mutual respect, and non-intervention in the internal affairs. New steps along these lines could duly mark the 40th anniversary of the great victory over Hitler fascism and Japanese militarism.

"Never before has so terrible a threat loomed so far and dark over mankind as these days. The only reasonable way out of the existing situation is agreement of the confronting forces on an immediate termination of the race in arms, above all, nuclear arms, on earth and its prevention in space, an agreement on an honest and equitable basis without attempts at outplaying the other side and dictating terms to it, an agreement which would help all to advance toward the cherished goal—the complete elimination and prohibition of nuclear war. This is our firm conviction.

"Negotiations between the Soviet Union and the United States of America will open in Geneva tomorrow. The approach of the USSR to these negotiations is well known. I can only reaffirm that: we do not strive to acquire unilateral advantages over the United States, over NATO countries, for military superiority over them; we want termination, and not continuation, of the arms race, and, therefore, offer a freeze of nuclear arsenals, an end to further deployment of missiles; we want a real and major reduction of the arms stockpiles, and not the development of ever new weapon systems, be it in space or on earth.

"We would like our partners in the Geneva negotiations to understand the Soviet Union's position and respond in kind. Then agreement will be possible. The peoples of the world would sigh with relief."

Responding to the new Soviet leader's peaceful remarks, President Reagan sent an invitation for a meeting with Gorbachev in a letter that was delivered on March 13 by Vice President George Bush, who headed the U.S. delegation to Chernenko's funeral.

For the next several months there was much speculation as to whether or not a summit meeting could be arranged between the two superpower leaders. Then on July 2 the U.S. announced that Gorbachev had accepted the President's invitation. The summit meeting was scheduled to be held on Nov. 19–20 in Geneva, Switzerland.

APRIL

1 U.S. warns Iran on kidnapped Americans: Threatens military reprisals if harm comes to five Americans held by Shiite Muslims in Lebanon.

1 Villanova wins NCAA basketball title: Defeats Georgetown 66-64 in championship game in Lexington, Ky.

3 U.S. accuses Israel of violating Geneva pact: U.S. State Department and International Committee of Red Cross denounce Israel for violating rights of 1,100 Shiite Muslim prisoners by moving them out of Lebanon.

3 Congress approves $160 million in extended unemployment payments: Measure saves 339,000 long-term unemployed from being abruptly cut off from additional funds.

4 Tulane to drop basketball: Tulane University announces it will end participation in intercollegiate sport as result of gambling scandal that brought indictment of three of its players and five other persons.

4 President approves $52 billion budget cut: Agreement reached with Senate Republicans on plan to reduce $227 billion budget deficit to $175 billion.

5 Japan agrees to end whaling: Agrees to halt all commercial whaling by March 1988; Japan previously had fought international agreement to end whaling.

5 Government halts payments to General Dynamics: Refuses to pay for work on defense contracts until company repays $154 million in excess claims.

6 Military coup in Sudan: President Muhammed Nimeiri overthrown.

7 Gorbachev freezes missile deployment: Soviet leader announces halt in deployment of Soviet medium-range missiles in Europe; calls on U.S. to stop putting more missiles in Europe pending outcome of Geneva arms talks; U.S. rejects Soviet call for freeze on medium-range missiles, declaring Moscow merely wishes to preserve its 10–1 advantage in missiles.

8 Reagan to cut 80,000 federal jobs: Cabinet approves plan to freeze federal pay for one year and reduce work force by 4%.

8 India sues Union Carbide over Bhopal disaster: Suit filed in New York asks punitive damages for industrial accident that killed over 2,000 and injured 200,000.

9 Japan's prime minister urges more imports: Yasuhiro Nakasone in TV address calls on Japanese people to buy more foreign goods; appeal seeks to prevent U.S. Congress from adopting protectionist measures against Japanese trade.

10 Gorbachev calls for end to "ice age" in U.S.—Soviet relations: Reaffirms interest in summit conference with President Reagan; makes comments in meeting with U.S. congressmen in Moscow.

11 Long-term Albanian leader dies: Enver Hoxha, 76, led communist Albania since World War II.

11 Reagan reorganizes White House: Seven cabinet councils eliminated; Attorney General Meese to head council for development of domestic policies and Secretary of Treasury Baker to head council for economic policies.

12 U.S. Senator soars into space: Sen. Jake Garn (R-Utah) becomes first politician to fly in space as shuttle Discovery takes off on 7-day mission from Cape Canaveral, Fla.

12 Terrorist bomb kills 18 in Spain: 14 Americans among 82 persons injured in blast at restaurant.

15 South Africa to permit mixed marriages: Government announces plan to end legal barriers to marriages of whites to nonwhites.

17 Shiite Muslims win control of West Beirut: Defeat Sunni Muslim militia in night-long battle in Lebannon's capital; Lebanese cabinet resigns because of crisis.

18 Reagan defends plan to visit German military cemetery: Calls German soldiers "victims" of Nazis "just as surely as the victims in the concentration camps."

18 U.S. economy grows 1.3% in 1st quarter: Commerce Department reports growth slowed from 4.3% rate in 4th quarter of 1984.

19 Space shuttle Discovery completes 7-day mission: Lands safely at Cape Canaveral, Fla., but suffers major damage when brakes lock and tires blow out.

23 Coca-Cola's 99-year-old formula changed: Company says new formula for soft drink provides "smoother" taste.

23 Consumer Price Index rises in March: Labor Department says increase of 0.5% is largest in year.

23 First round of Geneva disarmament talks ends: Soviet leader Gorbachev accuses U.S. of violating agreement that set up talks by unwillingness to link discussions of space weapons to limitation of medium-range and strategic missiles.

24 Pope names 28 new cardinals: Archbishops of New York and Boston among those elevated.

24 Broadway musical wins Pulitzer drama prize: "Sunday in the Park with George" wins prize for Stephen Sondheim and James Lapine.

24 House kills Reagan request for aid to Nicaraguan rebels: Vote of 303-123 rejects President's efforts to help rebels fight against Marxist Nicaraguan government.

26 Senate calls for cancellation of Reagan visit to German military cemetery: Adopts resolution by voice vote opposing attendance by President at "reconcilliation" ceremonies at Bitburg, West Germany.

26 Fire kills 78 in Buenos Aires: Another 152 injured as fire destroys psychiatric hospital.

26 Communist nations extend Warsaw pact: Meeting of Soviet satellite nations in Warsaw agrees to extend military alliance for 20 more years.

29 Shuttle Challenger blasts off: Begins seven-day scientific mission in space; crew includes five scientists.

29 Robbers steal $8 million in New York City: Gunmen overpower guards at Wells Fargo building, escape with $8 million in cash, but leave behind another $12 million.

29 Israel completes second stage of Lebanon pull-out: Israeli troops leave Tyre, last major Lebanese city under Israeli military occupation.

BATTLE OVER AID TO NICARAGUAN REBELS FOCUS

In one of President Reagan's major battles with Democrats in the 99th Congress, he sought to provide aid to the "Contra" rebels fighting against the communist Sandinista government of Nicaragua.

In his weekly radio broadcast on Feb. 16, the President called the Nicaraguan rebels "our brothers." "There are over 15,000 freedom fighters struggling for liberty and democracy in Nicaragua and helping to stem subversion in El Salvador," the President said. "They are our brothers. How can we ignore them? How can we refuse them assistance when we know that ultimately their fight is our fight?"

Then, five days later, when asked in a nationally televised news conference if the objective of U.S. policy was to remove the Sandinista government, the President replied: "Well, removed in the sense of its present structure in which it is a communist, totalitarian state."

Less than a week later, Nicaragua's deputy foreign minister visited Washington, D.C., to lobby against aid to the rebels.

The President dug in his heels, calling the issue of aid to the Nicaraguan rebels "one of the greatest moral challenges" to the United States. He said it was a test of American will to fight communism. However, he offered a compromise to Democrats who opposed his request, assuring them that the aid would be used for humanitarian purposes rather than for military weapons.

The Republican-controlled Senate approved $14 billion in aid to the rebels with a 53–43 vote on April 23.

The President appeared to have suffered a major defeat, however, when on April 24 the House voted 123–303 to reject his request for $14 million in aid to the rebels. House Speaker Thomas P. O'Neill Jr. (D-Mass.), who led the fight against the measure, said the President would never be satisfied until American troops were fighting in Nicaragua.

But, just as all appeared lost, the President received help from a most unexpected source. Nicaragua's President Daniel Ortega erased all doubts about the policies of his regime by flying to Moscow on April 28 to ask for $200 million in Soviet aid.

The President on May 1 imposed a trade embargo and other economic sanctions on Nicaragua, effective May 7. Nicaraguan ships and aircraft were banned from using U.S. ports. However, diplomatic relations were not broken.

The Senate voted 55–42 on June 6 to provide $38 million for food, clothing, and other non-military aid to the rebels.

Shortly before the House voted on a similar measure, House Speaker O'Neill called on Democrats to vote against it, declaring the President seemed to view "victory" on the measure like "leading a contingent down Broadway, with a big smile on his face, kind of like a grade-B motion picture actor, coming home the conquering hero." But House Democrats joined Republicans on June 12 in a 271–156 vote to approve $27 million in non-military aid to the rebels.

During the next six weeks, a conference committee worked to reconcile differences between the House and Senate versions of the measure.

At the last minute before adjourning for a month's summer vacation on Aug. 1, Congress gave final approval to the conference committee's version, which provided $27 million for non-military aid to the "Contra" rebels. It was approved by voice votes in both the House and the Senate. The measure provided that the aid could not be distributed by the CIA or the Defense Department.

When President Reagan signed the measure into law on Aug. 16, he said:

"While the program that has been approved is more modest than I believe necessary, we have clearly won bipartisan support on this very critical issue as well as recognition and humanitarian support for those fighting the Sandinista dictatorship. This is an important element in our overall effort to assist neighboring countries to defend themselves against Nicaraguan attack and subversion. Unfortunately, the provision unduly and unnecessarily restricts efficient management and administration of the program. Nevertheless, I will continue to work with the Congress to carry out the program as effectively as possible and will take care to assure that the law is faithfully executed."

Robert W. Duemling, director of the State Department's Nicaraguan Humanitarian Assistance office, reported that the first shipment of $980,000 in supplies had been flown from New Orleans to the Contra rebels on Oct. 10. He said the shipment included boots, clothing, and medicine.

Bosco Matamoros, a spokesman for the main rebel army, the Nicaraguan Democratic Force, called the shipment "the beginning of what we hope will be a continuous flow of supplies to satisfy the basic needs of our forces."

MAY

1 U.S. embargos trade with Nicaragua: President Reagan orders action in effort to weaken Marxist regime; Nicaraguan planes and ships banned from U.S.

1 Disputed congressional seat given to Democrat: U.S. House of Representatives votes 236–190 to seat Frank McCloskey as representative of Indiana's 8th district; GOP contested his 4-vote victory over Richard D. McIntyre in November election.

1 President Reagan attends economic summit: At 7-nation meeting in Bonn, West Germany, France blocks his efforts to schedule talks to reduce trade barriers.

2 Brokerage firm pleads guilty to fraud: E. F. Hutton & Co. agrees to pay $2 million in fines and $750,000 in costs for defrauding banks in check kiting scheme.

3 Nigeria expels 700,000 aliens: Orders illegal immigrants to leave by May 10.

4 111th Kentucky Derby won by Spend a Buck: Finishes over 5 lengths ahead of Stephan's Odyssey; favorite Chief's Crown comes in third.

5 Reagan honors German war dead: Attends ceremony at German military cemetery despite opposition by Jewish groups.

6 Space shuttle Challenger completes 11-day mission: Makes perfect landing at Edwards Air Force Base in California; over 15 scientific experiments were conducted in shuttle's Spacelab scientific workshop.

6–7 President visits Spain: Agrees to negotiate eventual withdrawal of 12,000 U.S. troops from Spain.

7 New York City honors Vietnam vets with ticker tape parade: 25,000 veterans march as 1 million spectators cheer them, marking 10th anniversary of end of Vietnam War.

10–11 Sikh terrorist violence in India: Attacks and bombings in northern India kill 72 persons; police arrest 1,500.

11 Fire kills 53 at British soccer match: Flash fire sweeps grandstand in Bradford, England, as millions watch on TV.

13 Philadelphia police bomb radicals: 11 persons killed; fire destroys 53 homes in neighborhood, leaving 250 homeless; members of cult called Move defied police arrest warrants with gunfire.

13 FBI foils plot to assassinate Gandhi: Five Sikhs arrested on charges of planning to kill India's prime minister during his June visit to United States.

13 GE admits defrauding Air Force of $800,000: General Electric Co. pleads guilty to filing false payment claims on defense contracts; will repay sum plus $1.04 million fine.

17 United Airlines pilots begin strike: Walkout by 5,000 pilots causes nation's largest airline to cancel many flights.

17–19 Wildfires destroy about 200 Florida homes: Some 200,000 acres of woodland burn throughout drought-parched state.

20 Navy seaman and father arrested as Soviet spies: Michael Walker, 22, and John Walker, 47, retired Navy warrant officer, accused by FBI of selling defense secrets; two others later charged as members of spy ring; see page 169.

20 Soviets to supply Nicaragua with oil: Nicaraguan President Ortega, on return from 25-day trip to Moscow and other communist nations, says Soviet Union has agreed to provide 80% or more of nation's oil needs.

20 Israel trades 1,150 Muslim prisoners for 3 Israeli soldiers: Convicted Arab terrorists among those freed to obtain release of 3 Israelis held by Palestinians.

20 Stocks hit record high: Stock market soars with Dow Jones industrial average closing at record high of 1,304.85.

21 Navy fines contractor for gifts to admiral: Orders General Dynamics Corp. to pay $676,283 for presents given to former head of nuclear project, retired Adm. Hyman Rickover.

21 U.S. economy slowed in 1st quarter: Commerce Department reports gross national product grew only at annual rate of 0.7% in first three months of 1985.

22 Car-bomb kills 50 in East Beirut: Explosion in Christian section of city also wounds 172 persons.

23 Texan wins poker title and $1.4 million pot: Bill Smith, former oil worker from Texas, takes final hand in Las Vegas, Nev., tourney with 5s-high full house.

24 Director of OSHA resigns: Robert A. Rowland, who headed Occupational Safety and Health Administration for 10 months, announces resignation; had been under fire for conflict of interest in regulating companies in which he owned stock, but Office of Government Ethics reports no evidence of wrongdoing.

25 Ruler of Kuwait escapes assassination: Suicide terrorist rams car-bomb into motorcade of Sheik Jabir; 4 killed; ruler uninjured.

25 Over 10,000 killed in Bangladesh storm: Winds of 100 mph and waves 15 feet high sweep out of Bay of Bengal; about 275,000 homeless.

26 Two tankers explode in Spain: 16 killed in blasts as tankers sink while docked at refinery in Algeciras, Spain.

27 Race horse wins $2.6 million: Largest purse in racing history won by Spend a Buck in Jersey Derby at Cherry Hill, N.J.

28 President Reagan calls for tax "revolution": Outlines proposed income tax revision in TV address; see opposite page.

29 Mideast peace plan proposed by Jordan: King Hussein meets President Reagan in Washington; announces Jordan and Palestine Liberation Organization (PLO) would negotiate peace at international conference attended by Israel.

29 Soccer riot kills 38: British fans attack Italians at match in Brussels, Belgium; leads to ban on British soccer teams playing on European continent.

30 Admiral punished for costly ashtrays: Navy relieves rear admiral and two other officers from duties because their supply depot ordered 7 airplane ashtrays costing $659 each.

31 Tornadoes hit northeast region: Storms kill 86 persons in Ohio, Pennsylvania, and southern Canada; hundreds injured; over 1,000 homeless.

REAGAN CALLS FOR TAX "REVOLUTION"

FOCUS

President Reagan launched a campaign for overhaul of the federal income tax code with a TV appeal to the American people for support on May 28. He called the present tax system "unwise, unwanted, and unfair." He said his plan would "reduce tax burdens on the working people of the country."

In his 20-minute address, the President reviewed the success of the tax cut during his first administration, outlined the major aspects of his tax revision plan, and described the impact it would have on America's future.

For other details of the provisions of the tax plan, see page 913.

A CALL FOR RADICAL CHANGE

"No other issue goes so directly to the heart of our economic life," the President said. "No other issue will have more lasting impact on the well-being of your families and your future.

In 1981 our critics charged that letting you keep more of your earnings would trigger an inflationary explosion, send interest rates soaring and destroy our economy. Well, we cut your tax rates anyway by nearly 25 percent. And what that helped trigger was falling inflation, falling interest rates and the strongest economic expansion in 30 years.

"We have made one great dramatic step together. We owe it to ourselves now to take another. For the sake of fairness, simplicity and growth we must radically change the structure of a tax system that still treats our earnings as the personal property of the IRS; radically change a system that still treats people earning similar incomes much differently regarding the tax they pay and, yes, radically change a system that still causes some to invest their money, not to make a better mousetrap but simply to avoid a tax trap. . . ."

"LET'S GET STARTED"

"Death and taxes may be inevitable," the President continued, "but unjust taxes are not. The first American Revolution was sparked by an unshakable conviction: Taxation without representation is tyranny. Two centuries later a second American Revolution for hope and opportunity is gathering force again, a peaceful revolution but born of popular resentment against a tax system that is unwise, unwanted and unfair.

"I've spoken with and received letters from thousands of you, Republicans, Democrats and Independents. I know how hungry you are for change. Make no mistake, we, the sons and daughters of those first brave souls who came to this land to give birth to a new life in liberty, we can change America again; we can change America forever. So let's get started, let's change the tax code to make it fairer, and change tax rates so they are lower.

"The proposal I am putting forth tonight for America's future will free us from the grip of special interests and create a binding commitment to the only special interest that counts, you, the people who pay America's bills. It will create millions of new jobs for working people and it will replace the politics of envy with a spirit of partnership, the opportunity for everyone to hitch their wagon to a star and set out to reach the American dream. . . ."

"TAX RELIEF IS IN SIGHT"

After using charts to illustrate the main elements of his tax plan, the President made a final emotional appeal for support.

"The pessimists will give a hundred reasons why this historic proposal won't pass and can't work. Well, they've been opposing progress and predicting disaster for four years now. Yet here we are tonight, a stronger, more united, more confident nation than at any time in recent memory.

"Remember, there are no limits to growth and human progress when men and women are free to follow their dreams," he said. "The American dream belongs to you; it lives in millions of different hearts; it can be fulfilled in millions of different ways. And with you by our side we're not going to stop moving and shaking this town until that dream is real, for every American, from the sidewalks of Harlem to the mountaintops of Hawaii.

"My fellow citizens, let's not let this magnificent moment slip away. Tax relief is in sight. Let's make it a reality. Let's not let prisoners of mediocrity wear us down. Let's not let the special interest raids of the few rob us all of our dreams.

"In these last four years we've made a fresh start together. In these next four we can begin a new chapter in our history, freedom's finest hour. We can do it. If you help we will do it this year.

"Thank you, God bless you, and good night."

JUNE

2 Socialists win Greek election: Voters endorse anti-American government.

2 Cigarette company to buy Nabisco for $4.9 billion: Purchase by R. J. Reynolds Industries will create largest U.S. consumer goods company with annual sales of $19 billion.

4 Supreme Court outlaws silent prayer in schools: Rules 6–3 Alabama law unconstitutional because it offers moment of silence for "voluntary prayer."

5 General Motors to make $5 billion acquisition: Announces purchase of Hughes Aircraft Co., nation's 7th largest defense supplier.

6 Israel completes 3d phase of Lebanon pullout: All soldiers withdrawn from Lebanon except for few hundred left in narrow "security zone" along border.

7 U.S. Attorney General Meese awarded $472,190 to pay for his defense: Federal appeals court approves payment by government for charges by lawyers defending him against accusations of improprieties during controversy over his appointment.

9 Los Angeles Lakers win NBA championship: Defeat Boston Celtics 111-100 in Boston to win championship series 4 games to 2.

10 President declares U.S. will continue to abide by SALT II treaty: Although treaty never has been ratified by U.S. Senate, President says he will continue to honor it as show of good faith in arms negotiations.

10 Claus Von Bulow acquitted of attempting to murder wife: Rhode Island jury finds millionaire socialite not guilty in his second trial.

11 "Right to die" figure succumbs after 10-year coma: Karen Ann Quinlan, 31, dies in New Jersey; fell into coma April 15, 1975; controversy arose when parents obtained court order in 1976 to remove respirator to allow her to "die with dignity."

11 East and West exchange convicted spies: Spy swap carried out on bridge between East and West Berlin; four East European spies held by U.S. traded for 25 Western agents imprisoned in East Germany and Poland.

12 Terrorists blow up Jordanian jetliner: Shiite Muslims free passengers before destroying plane at Beirut airport.

12 Reagan wins victory on aid to Nicaraguan rebels: House of Representatives in 248-184 vote reverses itself to provide $27 million in nonmilitary aid to Nicaraguan rebels.

13 Trans World Airlines agrees to merger: Texas Air Corp., which also owns Continental Airlines and New York Air, will buy TWA for $794 million.

13 India's Prime Minister Gandhi addresses U.S. Congress: Supports political solution for Soviet invasion of Afghanistan to create sovereign non-aligned nation.

14 South Africa raids Botswana: South African commandos attack guerrilla stronghold in 40-minute raid on Gaborone; 16 persons reported killed; U.S. recalls ambassador from South Africa in protest over raid.

14-30 Muslim terrorists hijack TWA airliner: Kill one American; hold other hostages in 17-day ordeal; see opposite page.

15 Lebanese free 21 UN soldiers: Israeli-backed militia had held Finnish UN soldiers prisoners for 8 days in dispute about UN role in defection of 11 militiamen.

15 Pilots end 29-day strike against United Airlines: Strike by 5,000 pilots against nation's largest airline had severely curtailed operations.

16 U.S. Open golf championship won by Andy North: Wins with one-under-par 279 over 72 holes at Birmingham, Mich.

17 Arab prince soars into space: Space shuttle Discovery takes off from Cape Canaveral, Fla., on 7-day mission; Prince Sultan Salman al-Saud, nephew of Saudi Arabia's King Fahd, becomes first Arab astronaut as member of crew.

18 Banks lower prime rate to 9.5%: Interest rate on business loans lowest since 1978.

19 Car bomb kills 31 in Lebanon: Explosion in Tripoli slays Muslims celebrating end of holy month Ramadan.

20 Terrorists kill 6 Americans in El Salvador: 4 U.S. marines, 2 U.S. businessmen, and 7 other persons killed as terrorists blast sidewalk cafes with automatic rifles in San Salvador.

21 Body of Nazi doctor identified: Experts agree man who drowned in Brazil in 1979 was Dr. Josef Mengele, widely sought as war criminal who killed thousands in medical experiments at Auschwitz death camp.

23 Air crash kills 329 persons: Air-India Boeing 747 en route from Montreal to London crashes into Atlantic Ocean off Ireland, killing all abroad; authorities suspect terrorist bomb caused disaster.

23 Airport bomb kills 2 in Tokyo: Baggage handlers die when luggage from Canadian airliner explodes.

23 Brazilian airline crash kills 17: Taba Airlines plane falls in Amazon jungle.

24 Israel frees 36 Muslim prisoners: Release some of 766 prisoners whose freedom is demanded by hijackers holding Americans hostage in Beirut.

24 Space shuttle Discovery lands: Makes safe landing at Edwards Air Force Base, Calif., completing successful mission in which three satellites were launched.

25 Fireworks plant explodes: At least 21 persons killed in blast at Hallett, Okla.

25 IBM moves into phone business: Computermaker buys 18% share of MCI, second-largest long distance phone company.

27 Senate committee rejects Reagan appointee: Senate Judiciary Committee in 10-8 vote opposes nomination of William Bradford Reynolds to be Associate U.S. Attorney General in slap at President's civil rights policies; Reynolds has headed Justice Department's civil rights division since 1981.

28 U.S. economy turns up: Commerce Department's index of leading indicators estimates 3.1% growth rate in 2d quarter.

29-30 South African troops raid guerrillas in Angola: Kill 61 in two days of fighting.

30 Extra second added to year: Scientists at National Bureau of Standards add one second to standard for clock time to match actual solar time.

BRUTAL TERRORIST HIJACKING

Two Arab gunmen hijacked a Trans World Airlines (TWA) Boeing 727 jet airliner on June 14 after it took off from the airport at Athens, Greece, on a scheduled flight to Rome, Italy. There were 153 persons aboard, including 104 Americans. Thus began 17 days of terror and international crisis.

Under threat by the terrorists that they would kill the passengers and blow up the plane with hand grenades, the pilot, John L. Testrake, 57, of Richmond, Mo., flew the plane to Beirut, Lebanon. As the pilot pleaded by radio with the airport control tower for permission to land, the sound of a passenger being beaten could be heard in the background. The terrorists let 17 women and 2 children leave the plane in Beirut.

Identifying themselves as members of a group called Islamic Holy War, the terrorists outlined their demands in a statement that they read in Arabic over the plane's radio. They called for the release more than 700 Shiite Muslims imprisoned by Israel.

Later on the first day, the terrorists made the pilot fly to Algiers, Algeria, where they freed 21 more passengers. Then they forced the pilot fly the plane back to Beirut.

On their second stop in Beirut, the hijackers tortured and shot to death one of the American passengers, 23-year-old U.S. Navy diver Robert D. Stehem. About a dozen other Muslims joined the hijackers.

On June 15 the terrorists made the pilot fly the plane back to Algiers. There they declared they would kill all the Greek passengers aboard unless the Greek government freed one of their accomplices who had been arrested at the Athens airport. When Greece complied with the demand, the hijackers allowed an additional 61 passengers and 5 crew members to leave the plane in Algiers.

On June 16 the pilot was forced to fly the plane to Beirut for the third time.

In a televised news conference on June 18, President Reagan called the hijacking a "cowardly crime." He declared: "Let me further make it plain to the assassins in Beirut and their accomplices, wherever they may be, that America will never make concessions to terrorists. To do so would only invite more terrorism. Nor will we ask nor pressure any other government to do so. Once we head down that path, there would be no end to it—no end to the suffering of innocent people, no end to the bloody ransom all civilized nations must pay."

Three more hostages were freed on June 18. They included a Greek folk singer, his American secretary, and an American student of Greek descent. While the pilot and two other crewmembers remained prisoner on the plane, the remaining 37 passenger-hostages—all Americans—were taken to secret hiding places in Beirut.

Nabih Berri, Shiite Muslim leader of the Lebanese Amal militia and minister of justice in Lebanon's government, took charge of negotiating for the hijackers. He said the hostages would be freed only if Israel released its more than 700 Shiite prisoners.

On June 22 a U.S. naval task force of seven warships, including two aircraft carriers, two landing ships, and some 1,800 U.S. Marines rendezvoused off Lebanon's coast.

Two days later, on June 24, Israel freed 31 of its 766 Shiite prisoners. However, Shiite leader Berri declared that in addition to the freeing of all the Shiite prisoners by Israel, he now insisted on withdrawal of the American warships.

As diplomats worked secretly in negotiations with Berri and with Syria, Reagan administration spokesmen indicated on June 25 that the United States was considering a blockade of Lebanon to cut off shipping and close down Beirut's airport unless the hostages were released.

One more American hostage was released on June 26 because the man, Jimmy Palmer, 48, of Little Rock, Ark., had a heart ailment.

On June 28 officials said Berri had agreed to turn the hostages over to Syria on the following day. But on June 29 Berri demanded that before the release could take place the United States had to guarantee that it would not retaliate. The U.S. State Department responded by reissuing a previous statement that the United States reaffirmed its "longstanding support for the preservation of Lebanon."

Finally, on June 30, the 39 remaining hostages were driven to Damascus, Syria, and then flown to freedom in West Germany in a U.S. Air Force transport. Only 30 of the hostages decided to return immediately to the United States. They were personally greeted by President Reagan upon their arrival on July 2 at Andrews Air Force Base near Washington, D.C.

On July 3 Israel freed another 300 of its Shiite prisoners.

Meanwhile, seven Americans who had been kidnapped in Lebanon prior to the hijacking were still missing.

JULY

1 U.S. bans Beirut airport: Calls on allies to isolate Lebanon's airport until it is made secure from terrorist attacks.

1 Exxon fined $2 billion for overpricing: Federal court orders corporation to pay for violating price control laws in 1970s.

2 Gromyko becomes Soviet president: After 28 years as foreign minister, Andrei A. Gromyko, 75, chosen for ceremonial post of president.

2 President welcomes hostages home: President greets 30 American hostages freed by Lebanese terrorists as they arrive back in U.S. See page 19.

3 Summit meeting set: President Reagan and Soviet leader Gorbachev agree to meet in Geneva, Switzerland, in November.

5 Unemployment rate steady: Department of Labor reports unemployment rate remains 7.2% for fifth month.

7 Vietnam to return more U.S. bodies: Vietnamese government agrees to return bodies of 26 American servicemen who were killed in Vietnam War.

7 German teen wins Wimbledon title: Boris Becker, 17, wins men's tennis singles.

8 California fire destroys homes: About 10,000 flee from forest fire near San Luis Obispo, northwest of Los Angeles.

8 Five nations accused of terrorism: President Reagan calls Cuba, Iran, Libya, Nicaragua, and North Korea "terrorist states" that are "a new, international version of Murder, Inc."

9 Budget Director David Stockman resigns: Blunt-spoken director of Office of Management and Budget will leave office on Aug. 1 to join investment banking firm.

10 Coca-Cola brings back old Coke: Responding to complaints by thousands of customers, officials of Coca-Cola reversed their decision of April 23 to abandon the old formula of the soft drink; the old less sweet formula will be brought back under the name "Coca-Cola Classic."

11 CIA employee arrested for spying: Sharon Scranage, 29, charged with giving secrets to Ghanaian described as her lover.

12 President enters hospital for surgery: See opposite page.

12 Space flight aborted: Just 3 seconds before liftoff, computers abort flight of space shuttle *Challenger* because of failure of booster rockets.

13 Trans-Atlantic Live Aid rock concert: Musicians raise estimated $70 million for African famine relief with telethon that begins before live audience of 60,000 in London and ends 16 hours later before 90,000 in Philadelphia.

15 Supreme Court urged to overturn abortion ruling: Acting Solicitor General Charles Fried files brief with Supreme Court on behalf of Reagan administration arguing that its 1973 decision making abortion a constitutionally protected right was too broad.

15 Arms talks complete 2d round: Arms reduction talks between American and Soviet regotiators in Geneva, Switzerland, adjourned until Sept. 19; U.S. says Soviet offers have seemed vague; Soviets accuse Americans of "empty words and indefinite promises."

18 U.S. economy slows: Commerce Department reports gross national product (GNP) grew 1.7% in second quarter.

18 Pro basketball league suspends play: United States Basketball League (USBL) ends play in middle of inaugural season, saying National Basketball Association (NBA) has lured away more than 40% if its players.

19 New budget director named: President Reagan announces appointment of James C. Miller 3d, currently chairman of the Federal Trade Commission, to succeed David Stockman as head of the Office of Management and Budget.

19 Teacher chosen for space flight: Sharon Christa McAuliffe, 36, New Hampshire high school teacher and mother of two, chosen from 10 finalists to be "the first private citizen passenger in the history of space flight."

19 Dam collapse in Italy kills 197: Earthen dam gives way, destroying houses in path of flood of mud and water at Stava, Italy.

20 Emergency declared in South Africa: President Botha decrees state of emergency, expanding power of police; subsequently hundreds of black activists were jailed and scores died as police broke up black demonstrations.

20 Immense sunken treasure found: Divers find wreck of Spanish galleon *Nuestra Senorade Atocha* that sank off Florida coast in 1622; gold and silver hoard valued at $400 million.

23 U.S. and China sign nuclear pact: Agreement opens way to sale of U.S. nuclear reactors and other high technology; signing of pact comes during visit of China's President Li Xiannian with President Reagan.

24 France imposes sanctions on South Africa: Suspends all new investments and recalls ambassador in protest against treatment of blacks.

24 Mexico devalues peso: Government cuts value of monetary unit by 20% in effort to stabilize economy.

26 UN calls for sanctions on South Africa: UN Security Council adopts resolution calling on member states to impose voluntary sanctions against South Africa because of its racism; U.S. and Britain abstain in 13-0 vote.

27 Military coup in Uganda: Commander of armed forces Maj. Gen. Tito Okello overthrows President Milton Obote.

29 President rejects Senate budget plan: Reagan refuses deficit-reduction proposal by Republican Senate leaders because it calls for tax increase and reduced Social Security benefits.

29 Crippled space shuttle reaches orbit: Although one of its three main engines fails 5 minutes after takeoff, space shuttle *Challenger* manages to achieve space orbit.

29 U.S. and Soviet Union trade offers on nuclear tests: President Reagan offers to let Moscow send observers to U.S. underground nuclear tests in Nevada; Soviet leader Gorbachev counters with call for moratorium on all nuclear weapons tests; each rejects proposal of other.

31 Congress approves $25.4 billion in foreign aid: For first time in four years both houses agree on foreign aid measure; provides $12.7 billion for each of next two years.

REAGAN WEATHERS CANCER SURGERY

The White House announced on July 10 that President Reagan would enter the Bethesda Naval Medical center on July 12 to have a benign polyp removed from his lower intestine. The polyp had been discovered during a routine medical examination in March. A similar polyp had been removed in 1984. Doctors said the procedure was comparatively simple and would not require a general anesthetic. The President was expected to spend only one night in the hospital.

However, when the doctors examined the President on Friday July 12 they discovered a previously unknown tumor in his large intestine.

White House spokesman Larry Speakes announced that the President would undergo surgery the next day to have the tumor cut out. It was not known whether the tumor was cancerous or benign.

"The President was given the choice of waiting two or three weeks or would he like to proceed immediately," Speakes said. "The President made the decision, with Mrs. Reagan and the doctors present, to proceed immediately."

Because the operation required a general anesthetic, before undergoing the surgery on Saturday July 13, the President formally transferred the power and duties of his office to George Bush as Acting President in a five paragraph letter. The actual transfer of power came at 11:28 A.M. when anesthesia was administered to President Reagan.

The operation itself, conducted by a surgical team headed by Navy Captain Dale Oiler, lasted 2 hours and 53 minutes. The surgeons cut into the President's abdomen to remove a tumor about 2 inches long and a 2-foot section of the President's large intestine to which the polyp was attached. When the President awoke from anesthesia, White House Chief of Staff Donald T. Regan brought him a second letter to sign in which he resumed the powers and duties of the office at 7:22 P.M.

On Sunday the President's doctors said that the progress of his recovery was "spectacular," but that they would not know until the next day whether the tumor they had removed was cancerous.

The doctors reported at a news conference on Monday July 15 that the large tumor they had removed was cancerous. However, they said there was better than a 50% chance that no cancer cells remained in the President's body and that he would live out a normal life span. Dr. Steven Rosenberg, the chief of surgery at the National Cancer Institute, said that earlier in the day they had announced the results of their diagnosis to the President and Mrs. Reagan.

"The President was reading a book when we entered the room," Dr. Rosenberg said. "He indicated that he had been waiting to hear the results. When he heard the results, the President indicated that he was glad there was no evidence of tumor spread and that was basically the substance of the discussion."

Later that day the First Lady substituted for the President at a diplomatic reception on the South Lawn of the White House.

On the following day, Mrs. Reagan spent most of the afternoon with the President. She also distributed to children patients at the hospital some 500 balloons that had been contributed by comedienne Joan Rivers.

The President met with Vice President Bush in his hospital suite on Wednesday July 17 to discuss national and international affairs. The Vice President told reporters later that the President greeted him by joking about rumors that he had died, which had circulated in financial circles. "Somebody must be trying to make a buck," the President told Bush. That night President Reagan had his first full night's sleep since entering the hospital.

On July 18, the fifth day after his surgery, the President was removed from intravenous feeding and put on a liquid diet, including soup and fruit juices.

Looking fit and happy, the President returned to the White House on July 20, flown there by a U.S. Marine Corps helicopter. As he walked across the lawn holding the hand of Nancy Reagan, he was greeted by the cheers of about 2,000 balloon waving admirers, including the entire Cabinet. Members of the crowd carried signs that read: "The Gipper Is Home" and "The Gipper Comes Through (Again)."

"I'm feeling great," the President said, "but I'm getting a little restless. I'm eager to get back to work."

The President resumed public duties on July 23 when China's President Li Xiannian came to the White House for a visit that was marked by the signing of a nuclear agreement by China and the United States. The 74-year-old Reagan helped the somewhat feeble 76-year-old Li by putting his arm around him to help guide him to a seat.

AUGUST

1 Congress takes vacation: Congress adjourns for August vacation after adopting $967.6 billion budget for 1986 that projects $172 billion deficit.

2 Texas air crash kills 136: Delta Airlines Lockheed L-1011 widebody jet crashes while landing at Dallas in thunderstorm; 1 person on ground killed; 30 aboard plan survived.

2 Freak Wyoming storm kills 11: Cloudburst of 6 inches or rain in less than 4 hours sends 5-foot walls of water racing through Cheyenne; 70 persons injured.

2 Montgomery Ward to end mail-order catalog: Will issue last catalog in December 1985, phasing out mail-order sales in 1986; company says it lost $260 million on catalog sales since 1979; catalog begun in 1872 by Aaron Montgomery Ward was mainstay of farm families;

5 President reveals skin cancer operation: Tells reporters blemish removed from nose on July 30 was skin cancer.

6 Space shuttle completes 8-day mission: Shuttle *Challenger* lands at Edwards Air Force Base in California after scientific mission that studied sun and stars with array of telescopes.

6 Student loan deadbeats to lose tax refunds: Federal Education Department announces IRS will withhold income tax refunds from those who fail to repay student loans.

6 President of Guyana dies: Forbes Burnham, 62, dies after throat operation; succeeded as president by Prime Minister Desmond Hoyte.

6-7 Two-day strike by baseball players: See opposite page.

8 Terrorists kill 2 U.S. servicemen: Car bomb exploded by Red Army Faction terrorists outside headquarters of U.S. Rhein-Main Air Base in West Germany; 20 Americans and Germans injured by blast.

9 Navy spy convicted: Retired Navy Lt. Cmdr. Arthur Walker, 50, found guilty on seven counts in espionage trial at Norfolk, Va.; faces life sentence and fines up to $40,000 for his part in Soviet spy ring run by his brother.

9 Stealth bomber is flying wing: Sen. Barry Goldwater (R. Ariz.) reveals shape of supersecret bomber designed to evade radar detection.

11 Toxic chemical leak injures 120: Chemical used in making pesticides escapes at Union Carbide plant at Institute, W. Va.; new $5 million warning system fails to alert nearby residents.

12 Worst plan crash kills 520: Japan Air Lines Boeing 747 jumbo jet crashes into mountain northwest of Tokyo after losing tail section; 4 injured passengers survive.

15 South Africa reaffirms apartheid: South African President Botha declares in major speech that he will not lead whites "to abdication and suicide" by granting vote to blacks; Nobel laureate Bishop Desmond Tutu expresses disappointment, saying nation in on brink of "catastrophe."

17 Big Mexican drug bust: Agents seize 1,500 pounds of cocaine worth $191 million in Tijuana; 35 suspects arrested.

18 Stuntman barrels over Niagara Falls: Steve Trotter, 22, rides down 178-foot drop in pickle barrel craft; 7th person in 84 years to survive daring feat.

19 High West German spy official defects: Hans Joachim Tiedge, who had been in charge of hunting out communist spies, flees to East Germany; government fears he has given East Germany supersecret information about Western espionage network.

19 Sen. Paul Laxalt (R-Nev.) to retire: Announcement that close associate of President Reagan will not run again in 1986 raises Republican fears that they may not be able to retain majority in Senate.

21 Federal agents arrest 26 in crackdown on organized crime in New Jersey: U.S. Attorney Thomas W. Greelish says arrests halt operation of Luchese crime family in state.

21 U.S. accuses Soviets of using spy dust: State Department says chemical power sprinkled on Americans to trace their movements in Moscow might cause cancer.

21 AT&T to layoff 24,000 workers: American Telephone and Telegraph Co. to cutback over 20% of work force in division that makes computers, phones, and communication equipment.

22 British plane crash kills 54: British charter jet Boeing 737 catches fire on takeoff; 83 aboard escape flames.

23 MX missile passes test: MX "Peacekeeper" missile hits target in South Pacific with all 6 of its warheads after 4,100-mile flight from California; first time to be launched from underground silo.

25 Samantha Smith killed: 13-year-old schoolgirl, whose letter to Soviet leader brought her a trip to Soviet Union, dies with 7 others in crash of airplane at Auburn, Me.

26 Balloonists rescued: Three Dutch balloonists seeking to set record for transatlantic crossing crash into ocean 900 miles west of England; plucked from water by merchant ship.

27 Military coup in Nigeria: Maj. Gen. Ibrahim Babangida, army chief of staff, overthrows government of Maj. Gen. Mohammed Buhari.

27 Poverty declines: Census Bureau reports number of poor people in U.S. fell by 1.8 million from 1983 to 1984.

27 Bank fined $2.25 million: Treasury Department penalizes Crocker National Bank of San Francisco for failure to report $3.9 billion in cash transactions believed to have been involved in laundering of drug money.

27 $3 billion weapon system cancelled: Defense Secretary Caspar Weinberger stops purchases of Sergeant York antiaircraft weapon by U.S. Army; says it is not worth additional cost of $3 billion; some $1.8 billion previously had been spent on development of the weapon.

29 President calls for wage freeze: Asks Congress not to increase pay of federal civilian workers in 1986.

29 Artificial heart implanted: Michael Drummond, 25, becomes 9th person to receive artificial heart in operation in Tucson, Ariz.

31 Military recruits face AIDS test: Department of Defense announces prospective recruits will be rejected if they are found to have the fatal disease.

FOURTH STRIKE AND OUT!

FOCUS

For the fourth time in 13 years major league baseball players went on strike in 1985.

The first strike in 1972 began on April 1, just as spring training was ending and the regular season was about to start. The outgrowth of a pension dispute, the strike lasted 13 days. The players won about an 8% increase in their pensions, but the season was two weeks behind schedule and 84 games had to be canceled. Bowie Kuhn, who was then commissioner of baseball, said: "Everybody lost—the fans, the players, the owners, and baseball itself." For the 1972 season gate receipts were $1.8 million less than the previous year.

In 1980 a strike by the players passed almost unnoticed because it affected only a few days of the preseason exhibition schedule.

But the third strike in 1981—the longest strike in professional sports history—shut down the major league baseball parks for 50 days, from June 12 to July 31, wiping out 712 games from the regular season schedule. The owners lost an estimated $116 million, but part of the reason the strike lasted so long was that the owners had purchased strike insurance from Lloyd's of London that paid them about $44 million. The players lost some $28 million in salaries and the cities with the major league teams lost an estimated $200 million to $500 million in revenues. The main issue of the strike concerned the amount of compensation a baseball club should receive when one of its players signs as a free agent with another club. In the end baseball owners retained the right to hold players for up to six years before they could become free agents and sign with another club. Owners also won the right to receive as compensation players from another owner who signed one of the club's players who was a free agent.

Negotiations for a new contract between the players' association and the owners began on Nov. 14, 1984. Lee MacPhail headed the negotiating team for the owners and Donald Fehr represented the players. The old contract expired on Dec. 31, 1984. Calling for a salary cap on the spiraling multi-million dollar contracts of individual players, the owners claimed they lost $42 million during the 1984 season. After being given the opportunity of inspecting the books of the owners, the players' union claimed the owners actually had made a profit of $9 million in 1984. On July 15 the players set a strike deadline of Aug. 6. Baseball Commissioner Peter Uberroth, saying that he represented the fans, called on the players not to strike and for the owners to put disputed money in an escrow fund pending arbitration of the dispute.

But, after games were played on Aug. 5, the players—whose salaries averaged $360,000 a year—packed their bags and left the club houses locked behind them. Not knowing how long the strike might last, many already had been exploring other jobs they might find to keep income coming in for their families.

On the first day of the strike, Aug. 6, negotiators met together for 11 hours. When talks recessed for the night, Fehr told reporters that the union had "tried every avenue we know how to get through this dispute. My conclusion right now is that there's no possible way."

Then, shortly after noon on Aug. 7, Baseball Commissioner Ueberroth surprised news reporters with an announcement that a "tentative understanding" on a new 5-year agreement had been reached. Another 11 hours elapsed before the negotiators worked out the final contract language.

Ueberroth refused to take credit for settling the strike so quickly, saying that all credit should be given to the negotiators from each side. However, MacPhail said of Ueberroth: "He is a persuasive man. He has personality and is very intelligent. He perceived his role as the representative of the fan, and he did what he could."

The boys of summer returned to the ball parks on Aug. 8. All the missed games of Aug. 6-7 were soon made up.

The new contract eliminated the controversial requirement that when a team loses a player as a free agent it can draft a replacement from another team—one of the points won by the owners in the 1981 strike.

Players won a 50% increase in their minimum salaries, raising them from $40,000 to $60,000 a year. In addition the minimum salary was pegged to the cost of living index, providing automatic increases to keep up with inflation.

The union won a substantially improved pension plan for players. For example, a player with 10 years of major league experience can begin receiving more than $90,000 annually at age 62. However, the players agreed to reduce from 33% to 18% their pension plan share of TV revenue.

SEPTEMBER

2 Hurricane Elena hits Mississippi: See opposite page.

2 Wreck of *Titanic* found: U.S.—French team locates at depth of more than 2 miles British liner that sank in 1912, killing 1,502 of those aboard.

6 Unemployment rate falls to 6.9%: Labor Department reports August jobless rate is lowest since Reagan became President.

7 Canada refuses to join in "Star Wars" research: Joins Australia, Denmark, France, Greece, and Norway in turning down President Reagan's invitation to allies to participate in anti-missile defense program.

9 President Reagan imposes sanctions on South Africa: Announces economic measures to protest South Africa's racist policies.

9 Thai coup attempt: Military fails to overthrow Thailand government; 2 American TV newsmen among 5 persons killed; former Prime Minister Kriangsak Chamanand arrested.

10 Daughter of El Salvador president kidnapped: Leftist rebels take as hostages daughter of President Jose Napoleon Duarte and a woman friend after killing two bodyguards; demand government release rebel prisoners.

11 Comet's tail explored: U.S. unmanned spacecraft *International Cometary Explorer* flies through tail of comet Giacobini-Zinner about 44 million miles from Earth; finds comet is like giant "dirty snowball."

11 Pete Rose breaks Ty Cobb record: Cincinnati Reds player-manager makes 4,192d hit in baseball game against San Diego Padres.

12 Britain expels 25 Soviet spies: Officials reveal head of Soviet KGB spy network in Britain has defected to West revealing names of agents; Soviet Union ejects 25 Britons in reprisal on Oct. 13.

13 U.S. space weapon destroys satellite: Air Force conducts "flawless" test in which rocket launched from F-15 fighter plane hits satellite 345 miles above Earth.

14 One American hostage freed in Lebanon: Rev. Benjamin Weir, 61, Presbyterian minister kidnapped in Beirut, had been held hostage by Arab terrorists for 16 months; six other kidnapped Americans still missing.

15 Grenades kill 35 in movie theater: Thrown from balcony to lower floor of theater in Lala, Philippines; 100 wounded.

15 Socialists win reelection in Sweden: Prime Minister Olaf Palme leads Social Democrats to victory, winning majority control of parliament.

16 China shakes up leadership: 10 of 24 ruling Politburo members replaced by younger leaders.

16 South Africans invade Angola: About 500 South African troops attack guerrillas who seek independence for Namibia.

16 Chinese crime syndicate broken: FBI arrests 12 leaders of United Bamboo group charged with murder for hire and plan to war with other crime groups to take over sale of illegal drugs.

17 German spy scandal widens: Secretary of West Germany's Chancellor Kohl reported to have defected to East Germany to avoid arrest as communist spy.

19-20 Major earthquakes strike Mexico: See opposite page.

20 Koreas briefly open borders: For first time since 1945 division into two nations, North and South Korea let 100 separated relatives cross borders for weekend visits.

22 France admits sinking anti-nuke ship: France's prime minister confirms French government planted bombs that sank *Rainbow Warrior* in New Zealand on July 10, killing 1 crewmember; sought to prevent vessel belonging to anti-nuclear Greenpeace group from interfering with French atomic weapons tests in South Pacific.

23 Dollar drops sharply in value: Loses 4.29% of value in one day following agreement on Sept. 22 by United States, Britain, France, West Germany, and Japan to cooperate in driving down dollar's value to improve U.S. international trade balance.

23 President calls for subsidies to aid exports: Faced with demands by Congress for trade barriers to foreign goods, President proposes low-interest loans to industries to support certain exports.

23 Guidelines set for gene transplants: Scientists agree that both local and federal review panels must approve each case in which genes are transplanted into a human; first such operations expected to try to correct fatal hereditary diseases.

24 Inflation remains in check: Labor Department reports consumer prices rose only 0.2% in August, for an annual rate of 3.3%—lowest in two decades.

26 Tunisia breaks relations with Libya: Expells Libyan diplomats accused of mailing scores of letter bombs to Tunisian journalists.

26 Soviet spy official defects to U.S.: Vitaly Yurchenko, 50, described as "high up" Soviet KGB officer in Italy said to have named Soviet spies in Western countries including double agents in CIA.

27 Hurricane Gloria hits Long Island and Connecticut: See opposite page.

27 Soviet arms cut plan delivered to Regan: Soviet Foreign Minister Eduard A. Shevardnadze visits White House with letter from Soviet leader Gorbachev and details of proposal for mutual 50% nuclear arms reduction if U.S. gives up "Star Wars" defense plan.

27 New Soviet prime minister: Nikolai I. Ryzhkov, 56, replaces Nikolai A. Tikhonov, 80, said to have resigned because of illness; Ryzhkov had been chief administrator of Kremlin's economic policies.

28 Former CIA double agent eludes FBI: Edward L. Howard, charged with spying for Soviet Union while serving as CIA agent, flees from home in New Mexico that was under surveillance by FBI.

28 Panama president ousted: President Nicolas Ardito Barletta forced to resign by military commander Gen. Manuel A. Noriega; former vice president, Eric Arturo Delvalle, sworn in as new president.

29 South African businessmen call for end to apartheid: Leaders of nation's largest companies appeal to government to end its racial policies and to negotiate with black leaders.

30 President calls Western summit meeting: Invites leaders of Britain, Canada, France, West Germany, Italy, and Japan to meet with him in New York City on Oct. 23-24 to discuss strategy for his talks with Soviet leader Gorbachev in November.

30 Lebanese terrorists kidnap 4 Soviet diplomats: Threaten to kill them and blow up Soviet embassy in Beirut unless pro-communist forces halt fighting in port of Tripoli.

EARTHQUAKES ROCK MEXICO

FOCUS

Two large earthquakes struck Mexico City and Mexican states to the southwest in September. The first quake hit shortly after 7 o'clock on the morning of Sept. 19, measuring as a powerful 8.1 on the Richter scale. The second struck on the evening of Sept. 20, measuring 7.3 on the Richter scale.

U.S. Ambassador to Mexico John Gavin estimated that 10,000 or more persons were dead or missing, although estimates by the Mexican government were lower. Thousands of persons were injured and about 250,000 were left homeless. Thirty-four Americans were listed as dead or missing. Many had been staying in hotels that collapsed.

Property damage was estimated at $5 billion. More than 400 large buildings collapsed into heaps of debris, including three hospitals, two large apartment complexes, four hotels, and about 100 government buildings. About 700 other large buildings were severely damaged.

The United States and other nations rushed tons of relief supplies and equipment.

For more than a week, rescue workers dug tunnels into the rubble of buildings, sometimes finding infants or adults who had managed to survive.

When Ruben Vera Rodriguez was rescued after being buried for four days, he said: "Maybe I was blessed by God. I'm alive when I should have died. But if God had really liked me, he would have pulled me out on the first day."

Eight days after the quake, rescue workers still found a few survivors who had lived beneath the wreckage of Juarez hospital, including a nurse and two patients.

Ten days after the disaster all hope was given up on finding additional survivors.

"We will bury our dead with sadness," said Mexico's President Miguel de la Madrid, "but at the same time we will renew our will to live and to cure our wounds. The truth is that in the face of an earthquake of this magnitude, we do not have the resources to confront the tragedy with speed and sufficiency."

HURRICANES POUND UNITED STATES

FOCUS

HURRICANE ELENA

The worst storm to hit the Gulf Coast states since 1979, Hurricane Elena roared ashore on Sept. 2, causing damages estimated at more than $1 billion in Mississippi, Alabama, Louisiana, and Florida. Only four persons died because coastal residents heeded warnings to go to disaster shelters.

Packing winds up to 125 mph, the hurricane had followed a meandering course in the Gulf of Mexico. On Aug. 29 the hurricane seemed headed toward Louisiana, causing the evacuation of eastern parts of New Orleans. Then on Aug. 30 it headed for Florida as about a million people left their coastal homes along the central part of the state's western coast. On Sept. 1 the storm backed off and then moved toward Florida's panhandle region, forcing several hundred thousand people to leave their homes. Finally, the main force of the storm was unleashed on Mississippi, striking Pascagoula, Biloxi, and Gulfport.

HURRICANE GLORIA

On Sept. 25 Hurricane Gloria churned the ocean about 500 miles southeast of North Carolina with winds of 145 mph, described by Director of the National Hurricane Center Neil Frank as a "very dangerous hurricane."

The U.S. Navy ordered more than 60 of its ships to leave coastal ports to escape the coming storm.

The hurricane had closed to about 190 miles south of Cape Hatteras, N.C., by 6 p.m. on Sept. 26. Thousands of persons began leaving coastal areas from North Carolina to New York.

During the night of Sept. 26–27, the 300-mile-wide hurricane sideswiped North Carolina, Virginia, Pennsylvania, Delaware, and southern New Jersey. The storm seemed headed directly for the New York City metropolitan area.

Then, on the morning of Sept. 27 Hurricane Gloria smashed ashore on central Long Island, N.Y., with 130 mph winds. It tore across Long Island Sound and crashed into the coast of Connecticut with diminishing winds of about 92 mph. Tens of thousands of trees were blown down or uprooted, hundreds of buildings were damaged, and 1.7 million homes in New York and Connecticut lost electric power—some for a week or more.

Damages by the storm were estimated at more than $340 million and six persons died. However, because the storm hit the coast at low tide, damage was less than had been anticipated.

OCTOBER

1 Israelis bomb PLO headquarters in Tunis: Planes fly 1,500 miles to hit Palestine Liberation Organization (PLO) building; PLO says attack killed 67 persons and wounded nearly as many more; Israelis say raid was reprisal for terrorist killing of three Israelis in Cyprus on Sept. 25.

1 Federal tax on booze rises: Federal excise tax on distilled alcholic drinks, such as vodka, gin, and whiskey, raised to $12.50 per gallon from previous $10.50.

1 Heckler resigns: Secretary of Health and Human Services Margaret M. Heckler resigns at request of President to become ambassador to Ireland.

2 Lebanese terrorists kill Soviet hostage: Body of kidnapped Soviet aide found in Beirut; extremists threaten to kill three other Soviet hostages and blow up Soviet embassy unless pro-communist forces stop fighting to take Lebanese city of Tripoli.

3 New space shuttle launched: *Atlantis* begins maiden space voyage; details kept secret on flight to orbit military communications satellites.

3 Successful "Star Wars" test: Secretary of Defense Weinberger discloses laser beam able to lock onto moving rocket target.

3 Soviet leader asks for French support: Addresses French parliament, calling for ban on U.S. "Star Wars" defense weapons in return for 50% cut in nuclear offensive weapons.

4 France and Britain rebuff Soviets: French and British governments turn down proposal by Soviet Union for separate negotiations on limiting nuclear arms in Western Europe.

4 Earthquake rocks Tokyo: Registers 6.2 on Richter scale, but causes only minor damage.

6 Election in Portugal: Moderate Social Democrats win 30% of vote, led by Anibal Cavaco Silva, who is expected to become prime minister; defeat governing Socialist Party that won only 21%.

6 Riot between 500 police and armed mob in London slum: One policeman killed and dozens of others injured.

6 Senate fails to end budget filibuster: Meets in unusual Sunday session to increase nation's debt ceiling, but Democrats prevent action by in opposition to amendment requiring balanced federal budget by 1991.

7 Storm kills hundreds in Puerto Rico: Tropical storm Isabel causes floods and mudslides near Ponce, leaving estimated 150 dead and missing.

7 Poor nations to receive $2.7 billion: Joint meeting of leaders of World Bank and International Monetary Fund in Seoul, South Korea; agree on emergency loans to aid nations whose per capita income is below $410.

7 Palestinians hijack cruise ship: Kill American tourist. See opposite page.

10 Senate approves balanced budget measure: Votes 51-37 to raise national debt ceiling to $2.078 trillion and require balanced federal budget by 1991; legislation goes to House for consideration.

11 1985 Nobel Peace Prize awarded: Won by International Physicians for the Prevention of Nuclear War, organization founded jointly by U.S. and Soviet physicians in 1981 that campaigns for end to nuclear testing.

11 President reports minor cancer surgery: Tells news conference that additional skin cancer cells were removed from his nose; assures reporters "my nose is clean."

14 1985 Nobel Medicine Prize awarded: Two geneticist researchers at University of Texas Health Science Center at Dallas, Dr. Joseph L. Goldstein, 45, and Dr. Michael S. Brown, 44, win prestigious award for discovery in 1973 that deficiency of low density lipoprotein (LDL) receptors in cells (caused by inherited defective genes or by sedentary lifestyle and high-fat diets) produce high levels of cholesterol in blood, leading to hardening of arteries and heart attacks or strokes—condition estimated to affect 30 to 50 million Americans.

14 St. Lawrence Seaway closed: Wall collapse in Welland Canal traps scores of cargo ships; repairs expected to take several weeks.

15 U.S. economist wins Nobel Prize: Franco Modigliani, 67, professor at Massachusetts Institute of Technology, awarded prize for development in 1958 of theory that people primarily save for retirement and therefore stock values are based on prospective future earnings rather than on corporation's worth.

15 U.S. Marine helicopter crash kills 15: Aircraft falls into Atlantic Ocean off coast of North Carolina after takeoff from *USS Guadalcanal*; four survivors rescued.

16 St. Louis and K.C. win baseball playoffs: St. Louis Cardinals win National League pennant, defeating Los Angeles Dodgers 4 games to 2; Kansas City Royals win American League pennant 4 games to 3 over Toronto Blue Jays.

16 Auto workers strike against Chrysler: Over 80,000 workers in U.S. and Canada walk off jobs as contract expires; seek wages and benefits comparable to Ford and General Motors employees.

16 Two American chemists get Nobel Prize: Dr. Herbert A. Hauptman, 68, director of the Medical Foundation of Buffalo, N.Y., and Dr. Jerome Karle, 67, of the Naval Research Laboratory, awarded Nobel Chemistry Prize for their discovery in 1950s of mathematical method of determining three-dimensional structure of molecules by use of X-ray crystallography.

16 West German wins Nobel Physics Prize: Dr. Klaus von Klitzing, 42, of Max Planck Institute for Solid State Physics in Stuttgart, West Germany, receives award for his 1980 discovery of method of precisely measuring resistance of materials used in electronics components.

17 French author wins Nobel Prize: Claude Simon, 72, avant-garde writer receives Nobel Literature Prize for combining "the poet's and the painter's creativeness."

22 U.S. accuses Soviets of violating treaty: Secretary of Defense Weinberger says deployment by Soviet Union of portable SS-25 ICBM nuclear missile violates 1979 treaty limitations on strategic weapons.

24 President addresses UN: In speech honoring 40th anniversary of United Nations, President Reagan calls on Soviets to withdraw military forces from Afghanistan and four other developing nations as step toward world peace.

27 Kansas City wins baseball World Series: Defeats St. Louis 4 games to 3.

U.S. NAVY CAPTURES SHIP-HIJACKERS

FOCUS

After years of frustration while Mideast terrorists went unpunished for kidnapping, bombing, and murdering Americans, President Reagan struck back forcefully and triumphantly in October.

The incident that triggered American action began on Oct. 7. Four terrorists identifying themselves as members of the Palestine Liberation Organization (PLO) hijacked the 23,629-ton Italian cruise ship *Achille Lauro* in the Mediterranean Sea off coast of Egypt. Over 400 passengers and crew were aboard the vessel.

The terrorists had boarded the ship in Italy, planning to slip into Israel when the ship stopped there. But they changed their plans after one of the ship's stewards saw them polishing their weapons in their cabin.

After terrorizing the crew and passengers with bursts of machinegun fire, the hijackers ordered the captain to sail to Syria. They broadcast demands that Israel release 50 Palestinian prisoners on threat of killing the passengers one by one. Those marked for death were chosen in a lottery by shuffling their passports.

On the afternoon of Oct. 8 they killed disabled American tourist Leon Klinghoffer, 69, of New York and made crew members throw him and his wheelchair overboard. His body later washed ashore on the Syrian coast, providing evidence he had been shot.

After Syrian officials refused to let the ship enter the port of Taurus, it returned to the Egyptian coast. The terrorists forced the captain to broadcast assurances that all aboard were safe and unharmed, winning a guarantee of safe conduct from Egyptian officials. The terrorists left the ship on Oct. 9, waving happily to cameramen and to cheering and clapping Arab onlookers.

U.S. Ambassador to Egypt Nicholas A. Veliotes boarded the ship shortly after the terrorists had left, discovered that Klinghoffer had been slain, and broadcast an angry message to the Egyptian government demanding that the murderers be held for prosecution. However, Egypt proceeded with plans to fly the terrorists to safety.

On orders from President Reagan on Oct. 10, four U.S. Navy fighter planes from the aircraft carrier *USS Saratoga* intercepted the Egyptian airliner carrying the terrorists. They forced the plane to land at a NATO base in Sicily. The Egyptian pilot later said the U.S. fighter pilots had threatened to shoot down his plane unless he followed their instructions.

The President had given the order to intercept the hijackers' plane in an uncoded radio conversation with Defense Secretary Caspar Weinberger while aboard Air Force One returning to Washington from a speaking engagement in Deerfield, Ill. A ham radio operator who overheard the conversation said Weinberger argued against the decision, pointing out that it might harm relations with Egypt.

President Reagan praised the action of the U.S. Navy pilots, declaring they had "sent a message to terrorists everywhere: 'You can run, but you can't hide.'" Both Democrats and Republicans congratulated the President for his forceful action against terrorism.

The United States issued warrants for the terrorists and for two PLO officials accompanying them, asking Italy for their extradition. One of the PLO officials, Mohammed Abbas, was described as the "mastermind" of the hijacking.

Italian police arrested the four terrorists. However, Italian Prime Minister Bettino Craxi permitted the two PLO officials to leave Italy for Yugoslavia. He said he could not hold them because Abbas carried an Iraqi diplomatic passport. Yugoslavia also rejected a U.S. request to extradite Abbas for prosecution. Subsequently, Italian magistrates investigating the hijacking ordered the arrest of several additional persons as accomplices to the hijackers.

Egyptian President Mubarak, who said he had been unaware of Klinghoffer's murder when he guaranteed the terrorists safe conduct, denounced the United States for "an act of piracy." He demanded a public apology from President Reagan. But, when asked if he would apologize to Egypt, President Reagan gave a one-word reply: "Never." Second only to Israel as a recipient of U.S. foreign aid, Egypt has received $17.5 billion in U.S. economic and military grants since 1974.

Israel made public on Oct. 16 tape recordings as evidence that PLO official Mohammed Abbas had helped direct the ship hijacking. In the recording of ship-to-shore radio conversations between Abbas and the hijackers on Oct. 8, Abbas seemed well-acquainted with the terrorists and referred to "our objective" in relation to their mission.

The Italian government collapsed on Oct. 17 after Defense Minister Giovanni Spadolini resigned, withdrawing his small Republican Party from Craxi's coalition in protest against the release of Mohammed Abbas.

QUOTABLE QUOTES: 1985

MESSAGE TO TERRORISTS
"You can run but you can't hide."
—**President Reagan,** at press conference on Oct. 11, discussing message sent to terrorists by U.S. military action that captured hijackers of Italian cruise ship

MEXICAN EARTHQUAKE
"Oh, I was scared. It swayed and swayed and then people shouted, 'Run, run, the building will fall.' But oh, God, we didn't know where to run to."
—**Maria de los Angeles Lara Rivas,** telling of her experience in Mexico City earthquake

CLOUD OVER BASEBALL
"A cloud hangs over baseball. It's a cloud called drugs and it's permeated our game."
—**Baseball Commissioner Peter V. Ueberroth**

BOTHA ON APARTHEID
"I am not prepared to lead white South Africans and other minority groups on a road to abdication and suicide."
—**South African President P. W. Botha,** rejecting proposals that black majority be given voting rights

HURRICANE FORECASTS
"All our weather planes and radars create a false impression that we can do a great job forecasting. That's a myth. What we're doing is a great job observing."
—**Dr. Neil Frank,** director of the National Hurricane Center, while tracking Hurricane Gloria

ICE AGE RELATIONS
"The world situation is disquieting, even dangerous, and a kind of ice age is being observed in relations between the Soviet Union and the United States, at least it has been until recently."
—**Mikhail S. Gorbachev,** leader of Soviet Union

PARTY SWITCHING
"Finally I began to feel it was perfectly clear that I wasn't thinking like a Democrat, I wasn't acting like a Democrat, and I didn't feel like a Democrat anymore."
—**Jeane J. Kirkpatrick,** former U.S. ambassador to UN, explaining why she was formally switching to Republican Party

ON IMPROVING COCA-COLA
"The only way that I could figure they could improve Coca-Cola, one of life's most delightful elixirs, which studies prove will heal the sick and occasionally raise the dead, is to put rum or bourbon in it."
—**Lewis Grizzard,** Atlanta, Ga., columnist

CHINA'S OPEN DOOR
"No country can now develop by closing its door. We suffered from this and our forefathers suffered from this. Isolation landed China in poverty, backwardness, and ignorance."
—**China's leader Deng Xiaoping**

ON FREEDOM
"When freedom does not have a purpose, when it does not wish to know anything about the rule of law engraved in the hearts of men and women, when it does not listen to the voice of conscience, it turns against humanity and society."
—**Pope John Paul II**

ON THE HOLOCAUST
"Who could remain unsuspecting after the burning of the synagogues, the plundering, the stigmatization with the Star of David, the deprivation of rights, the ceaseless violation of human dignity? Whoever opened his eyes and ears and sought information could not fail to notice that Jews were being deported. When the unspeakable truth of the Holocaust then became known at the end of the war, all too many of us claimed they had not known anything about it or even suspected anything."
—**West Germany's President Richard von Weizsaecker**

FAVORITE JFK QUOTE
"We all share the same planet. We all breathe the same air. We all cherish our children's future and we are all mortal."
—**Caroline Kennedy,** reciting her favorite quotation from the speeches of her father, President John F. Kennedy

ON DEADLY FORCE
"The use of deadly force to prevent the escape of all felony suspects, whatever the circumstances, is constitutionally unreasonable. It is not better that all felony suspects die then that they escape."
—**Supreme Court Associate Justice Byron R. White**

ON DRUNK DRIVING
"I feel a special responsibility now, having had to face my own flawedness, to invite everyone, especially young people, to join me in promising God, that with his help, we will never again risk the consequences of drinking and driving."
—**Roman Catholic Archbishop of St. Paul-Minneapolis John Roach,** after pleading guilty to driving while drunk

Accidents and Disasters

DISASTROUS HURRICANES AND TYPHOONS

DATE	PLACE	DEATHS	REMARKS
1703, Nov. 26–27	England	8,000	Hurricane
1864, Oct. 5	Calcutta, India	50,000	Much of city stripped by cyclone
1876, Oct. 31	Bakarganj, India (now Bangladesh)	200,000	Storm surge inundates city
1881, Oct. 8	Indochina	300,000	Typhoon and storm surge
1882, June 5	Bombay, India	100,000	Cyclone and storm surge
1899, Aug. 8	Puerto Rico	3,369	San Ciriaco hurricane
1900, Aug. 27–Sept. 15	Texas	6,000	$25 million damage caused by storm tide that inundates Galveston island
1906, Sept. 18	Hong Kong	10,000	Typhoon
1909, Sept. 14–21	Louisiana and Mississippi	350	Wide extent of Louisiana coast inundated; $5 million damage
1915, Aug. 5–25	Texas and Louisiana	275	12-foot storm tide inundates Galveston to depth of 5–6 feet; $50 million damage
1915, Sept. 22–Oct. 1	Middle Gulf Coast	275	90% of buildings destroyed over large area of Louisiana south of New Orleans; $13 million damage
1919, Sept. 2–15	Florida, Louisiana, and Texas	287	Hurricane hits Florida and Texas; over 500 casualties in ships lost at sea; $22 million damage
1926, Sept. 11–22	Florida and Alabama	243	Very severe in Miami area and from Pensacola into southern Alabama; $73 million damage
1926, Oct. 20	Havana, Cuba	600	Hurricane strikes city and suburbs
1928, Sept. 6–20	Southern Florida	1,836	Wind-driven waters of Lake Okeechobee overflow into populated areas; $25 million damage
1930, Sept. 3	Santo Domingo, Dominican Rep.	2,000	Hurricane
1931, Sept. 10	British Honduras (Belize)	1,000	Hurricane and tidal wave destroys city of Belize
1934, Sept. 21	Honshu, Japan	4,000	Typhoon causes $50 million property damage
1935, Aug. 29–Sept. 10	Southern Florida	408	"Labor Day Storm"; barometer reading of 26.35 inches on Long Key lowest on record in Western Hemisphere; $6 million damage
1935, Oct. 21	Haiti	2,150	Hurricane
1938, Sept. 10–22	Long Island, New York; southern New England	600	Very heavy wind causes $306 million damage in New England
1940, Aug. 5–15	Georgia and Carolinas	50	Heavy flooding; $2 million damage
1942, Oct. 16	Bengal India	40,000	Cyclone
1944, Sept. 9–16	North Carolina to New England	46	$102 million damage
1944, Oct. 12–23	Florida	18	Warnings prevent heavier casualties; $10 million damage
1944, Dec. 18	South China Sea	800	Three U.S. ships lost in typhoon
1947, Sept. 4–21	Florida and Middle Gulf Coast	51	$55 million damage on east coast of Florida and in Louisiana and Mississippi
1947, Sept. 15–19	Honshu, Japan	1,000	Typhoon and floods
1949, Oct. 27	Southeastern India	1,000	Cyclone
1949, Oct. 31– Nov. 2	Philippines	1,000	Typhoon
1951, Dec. 9–10	Philippines	569	Typhoon leaves 60,000 homeless
1952, Oct. 22	Philippines	431	Southern Luzon hit by typhoon
1953, Sept. 26	Vietnam	1,000	Typhoon and floods
1954, Aug. 25–31	North Carolina to New England	60	Hurricane Carol causes $439 million property losses; greatest of any single storm to this date
1954, Sept. 2–14	New Jersey to New England	21	Edna causes $41 million damage in New England
1954, Sept. 26	Northern Japan	1,218	Typhoon causes train ferry to capsize
1954, Oct. 5–18	South Carolina to New York	505	Hurricane Hazel hits Haiti and then rakes East Coast of U.S. from South Carolina to New York; $200 million property damage
1955, Aug. 3–14	North Carolina	43	Hurricane Connie causes $46 million damage with heavy rains
1955, Aug. 16–20	North Carolina to New England	187	Hurricane Diane brings severe floods through Northeast; $714 million damage exceeds any prior storm
1955, Sept. 19	Tampico, Mexico	300	Hurricane Hilda
1955, Sept. 22–28	West Indies and Mexico	712	Hurricane Janet
1956, Aug. 1	China	2,161	Typhoon devastates Hopen and Honan provinces
1956, Sept. 21–30	Louisiana to Florida	15	Hurricane Flossy hits area from New Orleans and mouth of Mississippi to western Florida
1957, June 26–29	Texas to Alabama	390	Hurricane Audrey hits Louisiana coast with 12-foot storm surge; $138 million damage

DISASTROUS HURRICANES AND TYPHOONS (continued)

DATE	PLACE	DEATHS	REMARKS
1958, Sept. 27–28	Japan	679	Typhoon Ida strikes central Honshu
1958, Oct. 30–Nov. 5	East Pakistan (Bangladesh)	500	Cyclone
1959, Aug. 20	China	720	Typhoon Iris strikes coast of Fukien Province
1959, Sept. 17–19	South Korea	669	Typhoon Sarah
1959, Sept. 26–27	Japan	4,580	Typhoon Vera strikes central Honshu
1959, Oct. 27–28	Mexico	960	Hurricane, flood, and mud slides on Pacific coast
1960, Sept. 9–13	Florida to New England	50	Hurricane Donna's; first storm with hurricane winds to travel up Atlantic coast in 75 years; $1.3 billion damage
1960, Oct. 10, 31	East Pakistan (Bangladesh)	14,000	Two cyclones strike Bay of Bengal area
1961, May 9	East Pakistan (Bangladesh)	2,000	Cyclone and storm surge
1961, Sept. 11–14	Texas	46	Hurricane Carla causes $408 million damage along Texas coast
1961, Sept. 16–17	Japan	172	Typhoon strikes Honshu and other islands
1961, Oct. 31	British Honduras (Belize)	262	Hurricane Hattie devastates Belize
1961, Nov. 12	Southern Mexico	436	Hurricane Tara
1962, Sept. 1	Hong Kong	400	Typhoon Wanda
1962, Oct. 27	Thailand	769	Cyclone
1963, May 28–29	East Pakistan (Bangladesh)	22,000	Cyclone and storm surge leave 1 million homeless
1963, Oct. 1–9	Caribbean Sea	7,200	Hurricane Flora
1964, June 13–14	West Pakistan	250	High winds and floods
1964, Aug. 22	Caribbean Sea	214	Hurricane Cleo sweeps through Guadeloupe and Haiti
1964, Aug. 28–Sept. 16	Florida and Georgia	5	Dora is first hurricane to hit northeastern Florida during this century; $250 million damage
1964, Sept. 28–Oct. 5	Louisiana, Mississippi, Carolinas, and Georgia	38	Hurricane Hilda spawns 6 tornadoes; $125 million damage
1964, Dec. 22	Ceylon (Sri Lanka)	800	Cyclone hits east coast, principally Trincomalee
1965, May 12	East Pakistan (Bangladesh)	13,000	Cyclone and storm leaves 5–7 million homeless
1965, Sept. 7–12	Florida and Louisiana	87	Hurricane Betsy strikes Miami and devastates New Orleans; damage estimated at $1.42 billion
1965, Oct. 1–9	Northern Mariana Islands	208	Typhoon Carmen
1965, Dec. 15	East Pakistan (Bangladesh)	25,000	Cyclone and storm surge
1966, Sept. 25	Japan	318	Typhoon Ida strikes Japan with winds to 200 mph
1966, Sept. 25–Oct. 11	West Indies, Fla., Mexico	1,000	Hurricane Inez carries 135–145 mph winds
1967, July 9	Southwestern Japan	263	Typhoon Billie causes landslides and floods
1967, Sept. 5–22	Texas	15	Hurricane Beulah and its 115 tornadoes cause $208 million damage
1968, April 11	East Pakistan (Bangladesh)	200	Cyclone
1968, May 9–10	Burma	1,000	Cyclone leaves 17,200 homeless
1969, May 19–20	Andhra Pradesh, India	608	Cyclone leaves 20,000 homeless
1969, Aug. 17–20	Mississippi and Louisiana coasts	324	Powerful Hurricane Camille with winds up to 200 mph and tides up to 24 feet; thousands homeless; $1.42 billion damage
1970, Aug. 3–5	Texas	11	Port Aransas and Aransas Pass suffer worst destruction from Hurricane Celia
1970, Sept. 15	Philippines	300	Typhoon strikes Luzon
1970, Oct. 14	Philippines	575	Typhoon strikes Luzon Island; 193 missing
1970, Oct. 18	Philippines	631	Typhoon strikes Mindanao Island; 284 missing
1970, Nov. 12–13	East Pakistan (Bangladesh)	500,000	Cyclone and storm surge devastates coastal areas
1970, Nov. 20	Philippines	120	Typhoon strikes Manila
1971, Aug. 16–17	Hong Kong	100	Typhoon Rose
1971, Oct. 29–30	India	10,000	Cyclone and tidal wave strike Orissa State
1972, June 17–23	Florida to New York	105	Hurricane Agnes is costliest U.S. storm to date with over $4 billion in damage; Pennsylvania is hardest hit with $1.2 billion damage and 48 deaths
1973, April–June	Bangladesh	427	Storms and floods leave 10,000 homeless
1973, April 29–May 2	Indonesia	1,650	Storm and tidal wave hit Flores and Palue islands
1973, Nov. 8	Bangladesh	127	Cyclone in Bay of Bengal sinks fishing fleet
1974, March 25	Bangladesh	300	Storm hits coast Bay of Bengal
1974, June 11	Luzon, Philippines	71	Typhoon Dinah strikes Luzon
1974, July 6	Japan and South Korea	108	Typhoon Gilda causes over $300 million damages
1974, Sept. 7–8	Louisiana	1	Hurricane Carmen causes $150 million damage
1974, Sept. 19–20	Honduras	2,000	Hurricane Fifi leaves 115,000 homeless
1974, Nov. 28	Bangladesh	500	Cyclone hits Bay of Bengal coast
1974, Dec. 25	Darwin, Australia	48	Cyclone destroys port city; 35,000 homeless
1975, May 9	Northern Burma	130	Tropical storm damages 20 towns
1975, Sept. 15–27	Puerto Rico, Florida, Northeastern states	61	Hurricane Eloise hits Puerto Rico with 130 mph winds; floods in East Coast states; $420 million damage
1976, May 20–22	Philippines	215	Typhoon Olga leaves 630,000 homeless
1976, Aug. 9–10	Atlantic Coast, North Carolina to New England	1	Hurricane Belle hits Long Island, N.Y., with 90 mph winds; $250 million damage

DISASTROUS HURRICANES AND TYPHOONS (*continued*)

DATE	PLACE	DEATHS	REMARKS
1976, Sept. 8–13	Japan	104	Typhoon Fran causes flood; 325,000 homeless
1976, Oct. 1	Baja California, Mexico	630	Hurricane Liza breaks dam outside La Paz
1977, July 25	Southern Taiwan	28	Typhoon Thelma destroys 20,000 homes
1977, July 30	Taipei, Taiwan	45	Typhoon Vera hits northern Taiwan, steel bridge collapses in Taipei
1977, Nov. 12	Tamil Nadu, India	400	Cyclone strikes southern India
1977, Nov. 14	Phillipines	80	Typhoon whips fire in Manila hotel, killing 47
1977, Nov. 19	Andhra Pradesh, India	over 20,000	Cyclone causes flooding and tidal waves
1978, April 4	Bay of Bengal	1,000	Storm sinks about 100 boats
1978, April 16	Eastern India	173	Tornado hits 10 villages; over 600 injured
1978, Oct. 27	Luzon, Philippines	314	Typhoon Rita leaves 50,000 homeless and estimated $85.4 million damages
1978, Nov. 24	Sri Lanka	500	Cyclone strikes coastal area
1979, April 18	Philippines	29	Typhoon causes $3 million damage
1979, May 12	Andhra Pradesh, India	607	Cyclone leaves 2.5 million homeless and causes $850 million in damage
1979, Aug. 29–Sept. 7	Caribbean and eastern United States	1,380	Dominica and Dominican Republic hardest hit by Hurricane David; total damage more than $1 billion
1979, Sept. 12	Florida, Alabama, Mississippi	8	Evacuation of 500,000 people prevents high loss of life; $1.5 billion damage by Hurricane Frederic
1979, Oct. 19	Japan	52	Typhoon Tip ravages Japan; sets off gas-tank fire at U.S. Marine base, killing 12
1980, Aug. 4–11	Caribbean and U.S. Gulf Coast	272	Hurricane Allen, worst Caribbean storm in history, caused more than $1 billion damage
1980, Sept. 15	Central Vietnam	164	Typhoon Ruth wipes out rice crop
1981, July 1	Central Philippines	120	Tropical storm causes flash floods, mudslides
1981, Sept. 20	Northern Philippines	21	Typhoon wrecks Philippine Navy destroyer and sinks freighter
1981, Sept. 20	North Pacific coast of Mexico	65	Tropical storm breaks two dams
1981, Nov. 2	West Coast of India	1,300	Tropical storm sinks fishing fleet off Rajpara
1981, Nov. 24	Luzon, Philippines	204	Typhoon causes tidal waves, floods
1981, Nov. 29–Dec. 5	Thailand	37	Typhoon causes flash floods
1981, Dec. 11	India, Bangladesh	27	Typhoon batters coast
1981, Dec. 26–27	Philippines	185	Typhoon Lee destroys more than 24,000 houses
1982, March 27–28	Philippines	50	Typhoon Nelson causes high waves and flooding
1982, June 3	Orissa, India	200	Hurricane lashes coastal region, 200,000 left homeless
1982, Aug. 2	Central Japan	62	Typhoon Bess causes torrential rain
1982, Aug. 13–14	South Korea	38	Typhoon Cecil causes flooding and mudslides
1982, Sept. 12	Central Japan	26	Typhoon Judy causes flooding, landslides
1982, Sept. 17–20	Guatemala, El Salvador	1,315	Hurricane Olivia sweeps across Central America
1982, Nov. 9	Gujarat, India	275	Hurricane displaces 5,000,000 people
1982, Nov. 24	Hawaii	1	Hurricane Iwa causes $200 million damage
1983, July 15	Philippines	45	Typhoon Vera sweeps through southern part of Luzon Island
1983, Aug. 18	Texas	18	Hurricane Alicia devastates Galveston and Houston; $1.6 billion in damage
1984, Jan. 14	N. British Isles	7	100 mph winds sweep Britain and Ireland
1984, Sept. 2–3	Philippines	1,363	Typhoon Ike, fiercest in 15 years hits 7 major islands; 1.12 million homeless
1984, Sept. 11–13	North Carolina	2	Hurricane Diana rakes coast; more than $65 million damage
1984, Nov. 5	Philippines	515	Typhoon Agnes sweeps Panay Island; 100,000 homeless
1985, March 29	Bangladesh	300	Monsoon storm flattens villages
1985, May 25	Bangladesh	10,000 to 20,000	Cyclone and tidal wave hits Bay of Bengal coast; 275,000 homeless
1985, June 30	Luzon, Philippines	78	Typhoon Irma causes floods in Manila and surrounding region
1985, July 30	Zhejiang, China	177	Typhoon injures 1,400; destroys 20,000 homes
1985, Aug. 15	Gulf Coast of Louisiana	1	Hurricane Danny with 85 mph winds drives thousands from homes
1985, Sept. 27	Long Island, N.Y., and Connecticut	16	Hurricane Gloria with winds of 130 mph; over 280,000 flee coastal areas; widespread damage; 1.7 million homes lose electric power
1985, Oct. 19	Luzon, Philippines	31	Typhoon Dot hits Philippines with 150 mph winds; thousands left homeless

MAJOR U.S. TORNADOES SINCE 1900

Source: National Oceanic and Atmospheric Administration

DATE	PLACE	DEATHS	INJURED	DAMAGE
1900, Nov. 20	Arkansas, Mississippi, Tennessee	73	many	$ 500,000
1903, June 1	Gainesville, Georgia	98	190	$ 1,000,000
1905, May 10	Snyder, Oklahoma	87	49	$ 20,000
1908, April 24	Lamar and Wayne counties, Mississippi	100	649	$ 880,000
1909, March 8	Dallas and Monroe counties, Arkansas	64	671	$ 640,000
1913, March 23	Omaha, Nebraska	95	—	$ 3,500,000
1916, June 5	Arkansas (series of tornadoes)	83	400	millions
1917, March 23	New Albany, Indiana	45	—	$ 2,000,000
1917, May 26	Mattoon and Charleston, Illinois	101	638	$ 2,500,000
1917, May 27	Tennessee and Kentucky	70	—	$ 2,000,000
1919, June 22	Fergus Falls, Minnesota	59	—	$ 3,500,000
1920, March 28	Alabama and Georgia	50	—	$ 1,400,000
1920, March 28	Chicago, Illinois, and vicinity	28	—	$ 3,000,000
1920, April 20	Oktibbeha County, Mississippi, and Franklin County, Ala.	87	—	$ 1,500,000
1920, May 2	Rogers, Mayes, and Cherokee counties in Oklahoma	64	—	$ 180,000
1921, April 15	Cass County, Texas; Hempstead, Miller, Pike counties, Ark.	61	—	$ 1,300,000
1924, April 30	Central South Carolina	67	—	$ 1,000,000
1924, June 28	Lorain and Sandusky, Ohio	85	—	$ 12,000,000
1925, March 18	Missouri, Illinois, Indiana	689	1,980	$ 17,000,000
1926, Nov. 25	Belleville to Portland, Arkansas	53	—	$ 630,000
1927, April 12	Rock Springs, Texas	74	—	$ 1,200,000
1927, May 9	Randolph County, Arkansas; Poplar Bluff, Missouri	92	—	$ 2,300,000
1927, Sept. 29	St. Louis, Missouri	72	—	$ 22,000,000
1929, April 25	Southeastern and central Georgia	40	—	$ 850,000
1930, May 6	Hill and Ellis counties, Texas	41	—	$ 2,100,000
1932, March 21	Alabama (series of tornadoes)	268	1,874	$ 5,000,000
1933, May 1	Webster and Bienville Parishes, Louisiana	23	400	$ 1,300,000
1936, April 2	Cordele, Georgia	23	500	$ 3,000,000
1936, April 5	Tupelo, Mississippi	216	700	$ 3,500,000
1936, April 6	Gainesville, Georgia	203	934	$ 13,000,000
1938, Sept. 29	Charleston, South Carolina	32	150	$ 2,000,000
1939, April 16	Drew County, Arkansas	27	62	$ 20,000
1942, March 16	Central to northeastern Mississippi	75	525	$ 1,400,000
1942, April 27	Rogers and Mayes counties, Oklahoma	52	181	$ 2,000,000
1944, June 25	Ravenna, Ohio; Pennsylvania; West Virginia; Maryland	150	867	$ 4,200,000
1945, April 12	Oklahoma and Arkansas	102	689	$ 4,000,000
1946, Jan. 4	Northeastern Texas	30	335	$ 2,700,000
1947, April 9	Texas, Oklahoma, Kansas	169	983	$ 9,800,000
1948, March 19	Bunker Hill and Gillespie, Illinois	33	449	$ 3,800,000
1949, Jan. 3	Louisiana and Arkansas	58	439	$ 1,500,000
1949, May 21	Cape Girardeau, Missouri	23	130	$ 3,500,000
1952, March 21–22	Arkansas, Missouri, and Tennessee (series of tornadoes)	208	1,154	$ 14,000,000
1953, May 11	Waco, Texas	114	597	$ 41,000,000
1953, June 8	Flint to Lakeport, Michigan	116	867	$ 19,000,000
1953, June 9	Central and eastern Massachusetts	90	1,288	$ 52,000,000
1953, Dec. 5	Vicksburg, Mississippi	38	270	$ 25,000,000
1955, May 25	Blackwell, Oklahoma	20	280	$ 8,000,000
1955, May 25	Udall, Kansas	80	270	$ 2,200,000
1956, April 3	Southern Michigan	18	340	$ 11,000,000
1956, April 15	Birmingham, Alabama	25	200	$ 1,500,000
1957, May 20	Williamsburg, Kansas, to Ruskin Heights, Missouri	44	531	millions
1959, Feb. 10	St. Louis, Missouri	21	345	millions
1964, Oct. 3	Lafourche Parish, Louisiana	22	165	$ 500,000
1965, April 11	Illinois, Michigan, Indiana, and Ohio (series of tornadoes)	226	3,000	$620,500,000
1966, March 3	Mississippi and western Alabama	58	531	$ 18,500,000
1966, June 8	Topeka, Kansas, and Vicinity	16	406	$100,000,000
1967, April 21	Boone, McHenry, and Cook counties, Ill.; Kent County, Mich.	57	982	$ 18,000,000
1968, May 15–16	Arkansas, Illinois, Indiana, Iowa, Minnesota, Mississippi, Missouri, Nebraska, Ohio, Tennessee, and Wisconsin	72	1,000	$ 51,000,000
1969, Jan. 23	Jefferson to Newton counties, Mississippi	32	241	$ 500,000
1969, July 4	Northern Ohio (storm and tornadoes)	41	—	substantial
1970, April 17	Texas Panhandle	25	200	$ 5,000,000
1970, May 11	Lubbock, Texas	26	500	$135,000,000
1971, Feb. 21	Mississippi, Louisiana, Tennessee (series of tornadoes)	121	1,600	$ 19,000,000
1973, May 26–28	10 states in South and Midwest (series of 195 tornadoes)	47	—	$ 55,000,000
1974, April 3–4	13 states in South and Midwest (148 tornadoes)	329	6,142	$540,000,000
1974, June	Tulsa and Drumright, Okla., hit by about 20 tornadoes	26	294	$ 23,500,000
1975, Jan. 10	Series of tornadoes in Mississippi, Alabama, and Louisana	15	298	$ 5,000,000
1975, Feb. 22	Tornadoes, thunderstorms, and hail in Oklahoma	4	91	$ 5,000,000
1975, March 24	Atlanta, Ga., about 500 homes, including Governor's mansion, badly damaged	3	152	$ 56,500,000

MAJOR U.S. TORNADOES SINCE 1900 *(continued)*

DATE	PLACE	DEATHS	INJURED	DAMAGE
1975, March 28	Warren, Ark., tornado hits center of city	7	50	$ 5,000,000
1975, May 6	Omaha, Neb., 10 or more tornadoes destroy over 1,000 homes	3	133	$400,000,000
1976, March 26–29	Arkansas and Mississippi, series of tornadoes	8	249	$ 27,000,000
1977, April 4	Northwest of Birmingham, Alabama	22	130	$ 15,000,000
1977, Aug. 21	Lake Mattoon, Illinois, resort area	6	56	$ 5,000,000
1978, April 18	Series of tornadoes hits southeastern Mississippi	4	31	$ 500,000
1978, May 4	Hits elementary school in Pinellas County, Florida	3	94	$ 3,000,000
1978, July 4–5	Cuts 75-mile path in North Dakota and Minnesota	9	73	$ 5,000,000
1978, Sept. 16	Destroys businesses and farms near Grinnell, Iowa	6	45	$ 5,000,000
1978, Dec. 3	Three series of tornadoes in Arkansas and Louisiana	4	250	$100,000,000
1979, April 9–11	Series of tornadoes in Texas and Oklahoma	60	800	$300,000,000
1980, May 12–13	Series of tornadoes in Missouri, Pennsylvania, Michigan	7	—	$100,000,000
1980, June 3	Grand Island, Nebraska	4	134	$140,000,000
1981, April 4	Series of tornadoes in Wisconsin, neighboring states	8	125	$ 9,000,000
1981, June 13–15	Series of tornadoes in Midwest and East	20	99	$ 10,000,000
1982, April 2	Tornadoes hit Arkansas, Texas, Missouri	27	383	$ 50,000,000
1982, May 11–13	Tornadoes hit southwest U.S.	3	16	$220,000,000
1982, May 29	Tornado strikes southern Illinois	10	181	$100,000,000
1983, May 18–23	Series of tornadoes in Texas, Tennessee, Mississippi, and neighboring states cause floods	32	100	$ 41,000,000
1984, Mar. 28	North and South Carolina (over 24 tornadoes)	59	979	$120,000,000
1984, Apr. 21	Northern Mississippi	15	100+	millions
1984, Apr. 26–29	Midwest (more than 130 tornadoes)	17	107	millions
1984, May 2–3	7 Southern States (48 twisters)	5		substantial
1984, Jun. 8	Upper Midwest	16		substantial
1985, March 17	Venice, Florida	2	40	substantial
1985, April 6	Series of 25 tornadoes from Illinois to Georgia	4	30	substantial
1985, May 31	Series of 41 tornadoes hit New York, Ohio, Pennsylvania, Ontario	89	1,473	$639,000,000
1985, Aug. 13	Group of 6 tornadoes in Wisconsin	2	22	substantial
1985, Aug. 16	Series of 24 tornadoes in Alabama	2	20	substantial

MAJOR VOLCANIC DISASTERS

DATE	PLACE	DEATHS	REMARKS
A.D. 79, Aug. 24–26	Pompeii, Herculaneum, Italy	16,000	Mt. Vesuvius erupts; destroys these towns
1169	Sicily	15,000	Mt. Etna erupts
1631, Dec. 16	Italy	4,000	Mt. Vesuvius erupts; destroys five towns
1669	Sicily	20,000	Mt. Etna erupts for 40 days
1772	Java, Indonesia	3,000	Mt. Papandayan erupts
1783	Iceland	9,000	Mt. Hekla erupts; 20 villages obliterated
1815	Sumbawo, Indonesia	12,000	Tambora explodes, followed by tidal waves
1883, Aug. 26–28	Indonesia	35,000	Krakatau erupts, followed by tidal wave
1902, April 8	Guatemala	1,000	Santa Maria erupts
1902, May	Saint Vincent, West Indies	2,000	Soufrière volcano erupts
1902, May 8	Martinique, West Indies	40,000	Mt. Pelée erupts, wiping out city of St. Pierre
1911	Philippines	1,400	Mt. Taal, on Luzon, erupts
1919	Java, Indonesia	5,000	Mt. Kelud erupts, 100 villages destroyed
1951, Jan. 18–21	New Guinea	3,000	Mt. Lamington erupts
1963, March	Bali, Indonesia	1,500	Mt. Agung erupts, leaving 85,000 homeless
1965, Sept. 28	Philippines	500	Mt. Taal, on Luzon, erupts
1966, April 28	Java, Indonesia	1,000	Mt. Kelud erupts; nine villages destroyed
1968, July 29	Costa Rica	100	Mt. Arenal erupts for first time in 500 years
1973, Jan. 23	Heimaey, Iceland	—	Kirkjufell Volcano erupts; 5,000 homeless
1979, Feb. 20	Java, Indonesia	175	Mt. Sinila erupts; 6 villages destroyed
1979, Sept. 12	Catania, Sicily	9	Mt. Etna erupts, 24 injured
1980, May 18	Cascade Mtns., Washington	57	Mount St. Helens erupts; $1.6 billion in damages
1982, March 28	Pichucalco, Mexico	100	Chichón volcano erupts; 20,000 evacuated
1982, April 9	Java, Indonesia	30	Galunggung volcano erupts; 30,000 homeless

PRINCIPAL WORLD FLOODS

DATE	PLACE	DEATHS	REMARKS
1228	Holland	100,000	Sea flood in Friesland
1642	China	300,000	Yellow River dikes collapse at K'ai-feng
1787	Eastern India	10,000	Storm drives seawater inland 20 miles
1861	Sacramento, California	700	Sacramento River overflows banks
1874	Western Pennsylvania	220	River floods

PRINCIPAL WORLD FLOODS *(continued)*

DATE	PLACE	DEATHS	REMARKS
1874	Mill River Valley, Mass.	144	Dam bursts
1881	Mississippi and Ohio rivers ...	138	Rivers flood; $15,000,000 damage
1887	Honan, China	900,000	Yellow River overflows
1889, May 31	Johnstown, Pennsylvania.....	2,209	Dam bursts on South Fork Reservoir
1896	Sanriku, Japan	22,000	Tidal wave caused by earthquake
1900, Sept. 8	Galveston, Texas	6,000	Tidal wave caused by hurricane
1903, May–June	Kansas, Missouri, Miss. rivers	100	Rivers flood; $40,000,000 damage
1903, June 15	Heppner, Oregon	325	Flash flood following cloudburst
1911	China	100,000	Yangtze River overflows
1912, March	Bolivar County, Mississippi ...	200	Mississippi River floods; $70,000,000 damage
1913, March 25–27	Ohio and Indiana	732	$180,873,000 damage
1913, Dec. 1–5	Texas.....................	177	Brazos River floods; $9,000,000 damage
1915, Aug. 17	Galveston, Texas	300	Tidal wave caused by hurricane
1921, June	Pueblo, Colorado...........	120	Arkansas River floods
1921, September	Texas.....................	215	Rivers flood; $19,000,000 damage
1927, Spring	Mississippi River Valley	313	Mississippi River floods; $284,118,000 damage
1927, November	New England	88	Winooski River floods; $45,578,000 damage
1928, March 13	Santa Paula, California......	450	St. Francis Dam collapses
1928, Sept. 13	Lake Okeechobee, Florida	1,836	Flood caused by hurricane
1935, May–June	Kansas	110	Republican and Kansas rivers flood
1935, July	Pennsylvania	52	Susquehanna River tributaries flood
1936, March–April	New England, Pennsylvania..	107	Rivers flood; $270,000,000 damage
1937, Jan.–Feb.	Ohio and Miss. river valleys ..	137	1 million homeless; $417,685,000 damage
1938, March	Southern California.........	79	Streams flood; $24,500,000 damage
1939, July	Kentucky..................	78	Licking and Kentucky rivers flood
1939	China....................	1 million	Floods in north, followed by starvation
1940, August	Va., Tenn., N. and S. Carolina .	40	Floods cause $12,000,000 damage
1942, May	Pennsylvania	33	Delaware and Susquehanna rivers flood
1943, April–June	Midwest	60	Mississippi River and tributaries flood
1946, April 1	Hawaii	173	Tidal wave caused by earthquake in Alaska
1947	Honshu Island, Japan	2,000	Flooding after typhoon
1947, May–July	Middle West	29	Missouri and Upper Mississippi valleys flood; $235,000,000 damage
1948, May–June	Columbia River, Washington ..	35	$101,725,000 damage
1950, June	West Virginia	31	Rivers flood in central part of state
1951, June–July	Kansas and Missouri valleys ..	41	50,000 homeless in floods; $923,224,000 damage
1951, August	Manchuria	1,800	Flood; some estimates of dead as high as 5,000
1953, Feb. 1	Northwest Europe	1,850	Storm floods Netherlands and North Sea coast
1954, August	Iran	2,000	Flash flood
1955, Aug. 18–21	Northeastern U.S.	187	Hurricane-caused floods; $714,079,000 damage
1955, Oct. 7–12	Pakistan and India	1,700	Flood
1955, December	California, Oregon, Washington	61	Streams and rivers flood; $154,532,000 damage
1956, August	China....................	2,000	Three provinces flood after typhoon
1957	Kyushu Island, Japan	513	Flood
1957, April–June	Tex., Ark., Kan., La., Mo., Okla.	18	Floods cause $105,000,000 damage
1958, July	Iowa	19	Flash floods on E. Nishnabotna River cause $5,850,000 damage
1959, November	Western Mexico	2,000	Flood
1959, Dec. 2	Frejus, France	412	Collapse of dam and flood
1960, Feb. 29	Agadir, Morocco	12,000	Tidal wave caused by earthquake
1960, October	East Pakistan (Bangladesh) ..	10,000	Tidal wave
1961, July	Charleston, West Virginia	22	Flash floods on streams cause $3,238,000 damage
1962, Feb. 17	West Germany	342	Storm breaks North Sea dikes
1963, March	Ohio River Valley	26	Floods cause $97,600,000 damage
1963, Sept. 27	Barcelona, Spain	445	Flash flood west and north of city
1963, Oct. 9	Northern Italy	2,000	Vaiont Dam collapses
1963, Nov. 14–15	Haiti	500	Flood and landslides
1964, June 8–9	Northern Montana	31	Floods cause $54,279,000 damage
1964, December	California and Oregon	40	Floods cause $415,832,000 damage
1965, March–May	Midwest	16	Missouri, Upper Mississippi, and Red River of the North flood
1965, June	Nebraska	16	South Platte River floods; $415,076,000 damage
1965, June 18–19	Sanderson, Texas	26	Flash flood causes $2,715,000 damage
1965, June	Kansas and Missouri	16	Flood causes $58,340,000 damage
1966, Jan. 11–13	Rio de Janeiro, Brazil	405	Floods and landslides leave 50,000 homeless
1966, April–May	Texas....................	14	Sabine and Trinity rivers flood
1966, Nov. 3–4	Arno Valley, Italy	113	Art treasures in Florence damaged and destroyed
1967, Jan.–March	Brazil	1,200	Heavy rains in Rio de Janeiro and São Paulo states
1967, Nov. 26	Lisbon, Portugal	464	Record rainfall causes heavy flooding
1967, Nov. 30	Java, Indonesia	160	Irrigation dam collapses
1968, May	Northern New Jersey	—	Floods cause $166,690,000 damage
1968, Aug. 7–14	Western India..............	1,000	Widespread flooding kills 80,000 cattle

PRINCIPAL WORLD FLOODS (continued)

DATE	PLACE	DEATHS	REMARKS
1968, Oct. 3–7	Northeastern India	900	Torrential rains cause flooding
1969, Jan. 18–26	Southern California	91	Floods, mudslides cause $399,233,000 damage
1969, March–April	Upper Midwestern states	—	Snowmelt floods cause $151,000,000 damage
1969, March 16	Northeastern Brazil	218	Flash floods
1969, July 4	Ohio and Michigan	33	Flash floods cause $87,915,000 damage
1969, Aug. 20–22	Virginia and West Virginia	153	Floods caused by Hurricane Camille
1969, October	Tunisia	500	Heavy rains cause flash floods
1970, January	California	18	Sacramento River floods
1970, May–June	Romania	215	Danube River flood causes $500 million damages
1970, July	Uttar Pradesh, India	600	Buses swept away by flooding of Alaknanda River
1970, September	India	600	Floods from Bombay to Calcutta; 20,000 homeless
1970, September	Arizona	23	Floods cause $5,000,000 damage
1970, October	Puerto Rico	50	Floods cause $62,000,000 damage
1970, October	South Vietnam	193	Worst floods in six years leave 200,000 homeless
1970, November	Colombia	250–750	Heavy flooding on the Magdalena River
1971, Feb. 26	Rio de Janeiro, Brazil	130	Flash flood
1971, April 26–28	Salvador, Brazil	140	Flood from heavy rains
1971, July 29	Afghanistan	1,000	Flood caused by landslide into a reservoir
1972, Feb. 26	Buffalo Creek, West Virginia	125	Coal-waste dam collapses
1972, June 9–10	Rapid City, South Dakota	237	Canyon Lake Dam collapses in flash flood
1972, June 21–27	East Coast United States	105	Hurricane Agnes causes $4,019,721,000 damage
1972, July 1–Aug. 7	Philippines	454	Floods from heavy rains
1972, mid-July	Japan	370	Landslides and floods from heavy rains
1972, Aug. 18–19	Seoul, South Korea	296	Flash floods from worst rains in nation's history
1973, April–May	Mississippi, Ohio, Missouri rivers	33	Valley floods; $1,154,770,000 damage
1973, Aug. 19–31	Pakistan	1,500	Floods in Punjab destroys 3,000 villages
1973, Oct. 19–20	Spain	190	Floods and mudslides in southern Spain
1974, March–May	Brazil	2,000	Ten states devasted by floods; 300,000 homeless
1974, July–August	Bangladesh and India	2,750	Flood damage estimated at $2 billion
1974, Sept. 14	Nelson Landing, Nevada	14	Flash flood causes $1,000,000 damage
1976, June	Bangladesh	143	Floods result from monsoon rains
1976, July 31–Aug. 1	Big Thompson Canyon, Colorado	139	Flash flood causes $50,000,000 damage
1976, July	Mexico	120	Floods caused by two weeks of rain in central Mexico
1976, August	Pakistan	316	Flood waters flow from Himalayas
1976, November	Indonesia	136	Floods caused by torrential rains in East Java
1977, April 4–6	Southeastern U.S. states	40	Tornadoes cause flooding; $275,000,000 damage
1977, June 30	Karachi, Pakistan	400	Rains flood low-lying slum dwellings
1977, July 9	Anyang, South Korea	188	Heavy rains trigger floods and mudslides
1977, July 19–20	Johnstown, Pennsylvania	74	Rains cause dam to burst; $200,000,000 damage
1977, Sept. 12–13	Kansas City, Missouri	25	Flash floods cause $140,000,000 damage
1977, Nov. 2–3	Athens and Piraeus, Greece	25	Rivers flooded after torrential rains
1977, Nov. 6	Toccoa, Georgia	39	Dam bursts after 4 days of rain
1978, July 9	Afghanistan-Pakistan border	122	Torrential rains cause flooding
1978, Aug. 4–8	Southern and Central Texas	26	Flash flood cause $50,000,000 damage
1978, Aug. 13	Northern India	450	Monsoon rains cause flooding of Ganges River
1978, Aug. 18	Acajutla, El Salvador	100	Tidal wave strike summer resort town
1978, September	Northern India	1,500	Heavy rains trigger floods and mudslides
1979, Aug. 11	Morvi, India	1,335	Rain-soaked dam collapses
1979, October	Egypt	42	Worst floods in 25 years leave 25,000 homeless
1980, Feb. 13–22	Southern California, Arizona	36	Heavy rains bring $320,000,000 damage
1980, August	India	987	Floods from monsoon rains in Uttar Pradesh
1980, Aug. 31	Ibadan, Nigeria	240	Flood from 12-hour rainstorm
1980, Sept. 17	Orissa, India	203	Flash floods from overflow of Mahanadi River
1981, Jan. 26	Laingsburg, South Africa	130	Torrential rains flood Buffels River
1981, May 25	Austin, Texas	13	Rains cause flash floods; $20,000,000 damage
1981, July 12–15	Sichuan Province, China	753	Yangtze River overflows; $1,140,000,000 damage
1981, July 19–25	Northwest India	550	Swollen rivers overflow banks
1982, Jan. 3–6	San Francisco Bay Area	36	Floods cause $280 million damage
1982, Jan. 23–27	Peru	800	Chontayacu and Huallaga rivers flood
1982, March 26	Peru	220	Heavy rains cause floods, landslides
1982, May 12	Guangdong, China	430	Worst floods in 30 years leave 450,000 homeless
1982, May 24–28	Nicaragua, Honduras	226	Floods cause $200 million damage; 65,000 homeless
1982, June 3	Sumatra Island, Indonesia	176	Flooding destroys farmland; 2,500 homeless
1982, July 23	Nagasaki, Japan	307	Heaviest rains in 25 years cause floods
1982, Aug.–Sept.	Northeastern India	600	Torrential rains leave 2.2 million homeless
1982, Dec. 2–10	Mississippi Valley, U.S.	22	Floods cause $600,000,000 damage; 34,000 homeless
1983, March 20	Northern Peru and Bolivia	260	Floods and mudslides bury towns
1983, April 6–12	Southern states, United States	15	Floods cause $625 million damage

PRINCIPAL WORLD FLOODS (continued)

DATE	PLACE	DEATHS	REMARKS
1983, May 2	Pacasmayo, Peru	50	Flash floods sweep across Pan American Highway
1983, June 22–26	Gujarat, India	500	Heavy rains result in flooding
1983, July 23	Honshu, Japan	120	Floods cause landslides
1983, Oct. 14–15	Uttar Pradesh, India	42	Heavy rains bring flooding
1984, Feb. 2	Southern Africa	100	Torrential rains flood Mozambique, Swaziland, and South Africa
1984, May 6–8	Southern States, U.S.	17	Heavy rains flood rivers
1984, May 27	Tulsa, Oklahoma	13	Motorists swept away by floods
1984, Sept. 1–2	South Korea	200	Heavy rains cause floods; 200,000 homeless
1984, Nov. 6	Colombia	40	Heavy rains overflow rivers
1984, Nov.	Andrhra Pradish, India	393	Flooded river; 78,000 homeless
1985, Jan. 10–25	Southeastern Brazil	71	Floods from heavy rains
1985, April 1–17	Northeastern Brazil	100	Flash floods drive 1 million from homes
1985, May 31	Buenos Aires, Argentina	14	Floods caused by 12-inch rain drive 93,000 from homes
1985, July 19	Stava, Italy	261	Dam collapses; wall of mud and water floods resort area
1985, Aug. 2	Cheyenne, Wyoming	12	Cloudburst sends wall of water through city; 70 injured
1985, Aug. 6–7	Southern China	283	Flash floods from torrential rains
1985, Oct. 7	Mamayes, Puerto Rico	150	Mud slides bury shantytown
1985, Oct. 19	West Bengal, India	49	Floods destroy homes of 150,000

WORLD EARTHQUAKES AND AVALANCHES

The strength of an earthquake is measured by the 9-point Richter scale developed in the 1930s by Dr. Charles Francis Richter of the California Institute of Technology. Each point on the Richter scale stands for a magnitude 10 times greater than the previous number. Thus an earthquake with a Richter number of 9 would be 100,000,000 times as strong as a tremor with a Richter number of 1. No earthquake has yet been recorded with a Richter number of 9.

The great San Francisco earthquake of 1906 is calculated to have had a Richter number of 8.3.

DATE	PLACE	DEATHS	REMARKS
526, May 20	Antioch, Syria	250,000	Earthquake
551, July 9	Beirut, Lebanon	—	Destroyed by earthquake
856, December	Corinth, Greece	45,000	Earthquake
936	Constantinople	—	Destroyed by earthquake
1057	Hopeh Province near Peking, China	25,000	Earthquake
1268	Cilicia, Asia Minor	60,000	Earthquake
1290, Sept. 27	Hopeh Province near Peking, China	100,000	Earthquake
1293, May 20	Kamakura, Japan	30,000	Earthquake
1531, Jan. 26	Lisbon, Portugal	30,000	Earthquake
1556, Jan. 24	Shensi, China	830,000	Earthquake
1667, November	Shemakha, East Azerbaijan	80,000	Earthquake
1693, Jan. 11	Catania, Italy	60,000	Earthquake
1703, Dec. 30	Tokyo, Japan	200,000	Earthquake
1737, Oct. 11	Calcutta, India	300,000	Earthquake
1755, June 7	Northern Persia	40,000	Earthquake
1755, Nov. 1	Lisbon, Portugal	60,000	Earthquake destroys most of city
1783, Feb. 4	Southern Italy and Sicily	50,000	Wide-ranging earthquake; Messina ravaged
1797, Feb. 4	Cuzco, Peru, and Quito, Ecuador	40,000	Earthquakes destroy cities
1811, Dec. 15	New Madrid, Missouri	—	Heaviest recorded earthquake in North America
1822, Sept. 5	Aleppo, Syria	22,000	Earthquake
1828, Dec. 28	Honshu, Japan	30,000	Earthquake
1868, Aug. 13–15	Peru and Ecuador	25,000	Earthquakes razes towns; $300 million loss
1875, May 16	Venezuela and Colombia	16,000	Earthquake
1886, Aug. 31	Charleston, South Carolina	60	Earthquake severely damages city
1896, June 15	Sanriku coast, Japan	22,000	Earthquakes and seismic sea wave
1906, April 18	San Francisco, California	700	Earthquake followed by fire; $500 million loss
1906, Aug. 16	Chile	1,500	Earthquake; $100 million loss
1908, Dec. 28	Southern Italy and Sicily	75,000	Earthquake
1915, Jan. 13	Central Italy	30,000	Earthquake
1918, Oct. 11	Puerto Rico	116	Earthquake and tidal wave; $4 million damage
1920, Dec. 16	Kansu, China	180,000	Earthquake destroys 10 cities
1923, Sept. 1	Yokohama and Tokyo, Japan	143,000	Earthquake destroys all of Yokohama, half of Tokyo
1932, Dec. 26	Kansu, China	70,000	Earthquake
1933, March 10	Long Beach, California	115	Earthquake; about $40 million loss
1935, May 31	Quetta, Baluchistan, India	60,000	Earthquake
1939, Jan. 24	Chile	30,000	Earthquake
1939, Dec. 27	Anatolia, Turkey	23,000	Series of earthquakes followed by floods
1946, May 31	Eastern Turkey	1,300	Earthquake
1946, Dec. 21	Southern Japan	2,000	Earthquake and six seismic sea waves
1948, June 28	Fukui, Japan	5,131	Earthquake and fire destroys most of Fukui
1949, Aug. 5	Ecuador	6,000	Earthquake heavily damages 50 towns

WORLD EARTHQUAKES AND AVALANCHES *(continued)*

DATE	PLACE	DEATHS	REMARKS
1950, Aug. 15	Assam, India	1,500	Earthquake and widespread flooding
1953, Feb. 12	Eastern Iran	1,000	Earthquake destroys town of Trud
1953, March 18	Northwestern Turkey	1,200	Earthquake; 50,000 homeless
1954, Sept. 9–12	Algeria	1,600	Earthquake destroys most of Orléansville
1956, June 10–17	Northern Afghanistan	2,000	Series of earthquakes
1957, July 2	Iran	2,500	Earthquakes along shores of Caspian Sea
1957, Dec. 2	Outer Mongolia	1,200	Earthquake
1957, Dec. 13	Western Iran	2,000	Earthquake
1960, Feb. 29	Agadir, Morocco	12,000	Earthquake, seismic sea wave, and fire
1960, May 21–30	Chile	5,700	Earthquake and seismic sea waves
1962, Jan. 10	Peru	2,000	Avalanche on Huascarán, extinct volcano
1962, Sept. 1	Northwestern Iran	10,000	Earthquake
1963, July 26	Skoplje, Yugoslavia	1,100	Earthquake destroys most of city
1964, March 27	Alaska	131	Earthquake and seismic sea wave
1965, March 28	Near Santiago, Chile	400	Earthquake
1966, Jan. 11–13	Rio de Janeiro, Brazil	300	Landslide caused by record rain
1966, Aug. 19	Turkey	2,529	Earthquake; 100,000 homeless
1967, July 29	Venezuela	236	Earthquake extending from Andes to Caribbean Sea
1968, Jan. 15	Western Sicily	224	Series of earthquakes destroys several towns
1968, Aug. 2	Manila, Philippines	207	Earthquake
1968, Aug. 15	Donggala, Indonesia	200	Earthquake
1968, Aug. 31	Northeastern Iran	13,000	Earthquake, world's worst in 30 years
1969, Feb. 23	Celebes Island, Indonesia	600	Earthquake and seismic sea waves
1970, March 28	Western Turkey	1,089	Earthquakes
1970, May 31	Northern Peru	60,000	Earthquake and avalanche
1970, Dec. 12	Cauca Valley, Colombia	200	Avalanche
1971, Feb. 9	Southern California	64	Earthquake in San Fernando Valley
1971, July 9	North central Chile	90	Earthquake
1972, Jan. 26	Bogotá, Colombia	70	Torrential rains cause landslide
1972, April 10	Southwestern Iran	5,374	Earthquake
1972, Dec. 23	Managua, Nicaragua	10,000	Capital city destroyed by earthquake
1973, Jan. 30	Mexico	52	Earthquake makes 22,000 homeless
1973, Aug. 28	Mexico	527	Earthquake damages 67 villages
1974, April 25	Peru	750	Landslides destroy three villages
1974, June 28	Colombia	200	Landslide on eastern slope of Andes
1974, Sept. 30	Colombia	90	Landslide buries small town
1974, Oct. 3	Lima, Peru	78	Earthquake and tidal wave hit coast
1974, Dec. 28	Pakistan	5,300	Earthquake near Chinese border; 16,000 injured
1975, Feb. 4	Manchuria, China	Unknown	Widespread destruction by earthquake
1975, July 8	Pagan, Burma	—	Hundreds of ancient temples destroyed
1975, Sept. 6	Eastern Turkey	2,200	Village of Lice destroyed; 3,500 injured
1976, Feb. 4	Guatemala, Honduras	22,934	Earthquake leaves 1,277,000 homeless
1976, May 6	Northern Italy	968	Earthquake devastates Friuli area of northern Italy
1976, June 26	Western New Guinea	443	Earthquake results in mud and rock slides
1976, July 14	Bali, Indonesia	500	Earthquake
1976, July 28	Tientsin-Tangshan, China	242,000	Strongest quake since 1964; 164,000 injured
1976, Aug. 17	Philippines	8,000	Earthquake off southern island of Mindanao
1976, Oct. 29	West Iran, Indonesia	133	Earthquake hits remote jungle area
1976, Nov. 24	Turkey	3,790	Earthquake in eastern Turkey; 50,000 homeless
1977, March 4	Bucharest, Romania	1,541	Earthquake almost destroys central city
1977, March 22	Southern Iran	167	Earthquake causes heavy damage
1977, April 6	Western Iran	352	Destroys mountain villages
1977, Aug. 19	Indonesia	150	Quake causes tidal waves
1977, Nov. 23	Western Argentina	100	Earthquake destroys town of Caucete
1977, Dec. 20	Southeastern Iran	519	Earthquake near Zarand leaves thousands homeless
1978, Sept. 16	Northeastern Iran	25,000	Earthquake destroys whole villages
1979, Jan. 16	Qaen, Iran	199	Earthquake strikes three villages in northeast Iran
1979, April 15	Yugoslavia	235	Earthquake jolts Adriatic coast; 80,000 homeless
1979, April 30	West Sumatra, Indonesia	82	Landslide caused by burst of crater on Merapi volcano
1979, July 18	Lomblen Island, Indonesia	539	Landslide on Mt. Werung causes tidal wave
1979, Aug. 6	San Francisco, Calif.	—	Strong quake jolts northern California
1979, Sept. 12	Yapen Island, Indonesia	100	Earthquake causes tidal wave; 10,000 homeless
1979, Oct. 15	California–Mexico border	—	Earthquake causes property damage; injures 70
1979, Nov. 14	Northeastern Iran	248	Earthquake rocks 14 villages
1979, Nov. 23	Western Colombia	300	Earthquake causes $20 million damage
1979, Dec. 12	Colombia–Ecuador border	133	Six coastal towns flattened by earthquake
1980, Oct. 10	Algeria	2,950	Quake destroys Al Asnam; 300,000 homeless
1980, Nov. 23	Southern Italy	2,735	Quakes flatten 133 villages; 300,000 homeless
1981, Jan. 18	Irian Jaya, Indonesia	250	Earthquake destroys 14 villages
1981, Jan. 24	Sichuan, China	150	Earthquake disrupts communication
1981, May 20	Java, Indonesia	184	Landslide hits villages on Mt. Semeru

WORLD EARTHQUAKES AND AVALANCHES (continued)

DATE	PLACE	DEATHS	REMARKS
1981, June 11	Kerman, Iran	1,600	Quake flattens town of Golbaf
1981, July 28	Kerman, Iran	1,500	Second quake in 6 weeks devastates area
1981, Sept. 12–13	Gilgit, Northern Pakistan	212	Quake causes much damage
1982, Dec. 13	North Yemen	2,000	Many towns and villages destroyed
1982, Dec. 16	Afghanistan	500	Occurs in Hindu-Kush mountain range
1983, March 7	Northwest China	270	Landslide destroys villages
1983, March 12	Phupan, Pakistan	84	Landslide engulfs village
1983, March 31	Popayán, Colombia	240	Earthquake devastates town
1983, April 27	Ecuador	100	Landslide buries highway in Chimborazo province
1983, May 26	Honshu, Japan	102	Quake sets off tidal wave
1983, July 28	Gachalá, Colombia	160	Mudslide buries workers at hydroelectric project
1983, Oct. 30	Turkey	1,333	50 villages in eastern Turkey leveled
1983, Nov. 6	Shandong province, China	30	Measures 5.9 on Richter scale
1983, Dec. 21, Dec. 24	Guinea	443	Two quakes destroy score of villages
1984, April 29	Monte Urbino, Italy	—	Earthquake leaves 3,000 homeless
1984, Sept. 14	Otaki, Japan	29	Earthquake causes mud slide burying village
1985, Jan. 6–11	Albania	57	Heavy snows cause avalanches
1985, March 3	San Antonio, Chile, and vicinity	150	About 2,000 injured; much property damage
1985, April 24	Northern Philippines	6	Series of earthquakes shake islands destroys homes and schools
1985, Aug. 15	Southern China	22	Quake destroys homes and schools
1985, Sept. 19	Mexico City and vicinity	c.10,000	Biggest earthquake since 1980 measures 8.1 on Richter scale; many tall buildings collapse; damage estimated at $5 billion

WORLD'S WORST FIRES, EXPLOSIONS AND MINE DISASTERS

DATE	PLACE	DEATHS	REMARKS
1666, Sept. 2–6	London, England	—	Fire destroys many public buildings, 89 churches and over 13,200 houses; 200,000 homeless
1835, Dec. 16	New York, New York	—	Nearly 700 buildings burned; $20 million loss
1836, Feb. 14	St. Petersburg, Russia	700	Theater fire
1842, May 5–7	Hamburg, Germany	100	More than 4,000 buildings destroyed
1845, April 10	Pittsburgh, Pennsylvania	—	1,000 buildings destroyed in fire; $6 million loss
1846, June 12	Quebec, Canada	200	Theater fire
1851, May 4	St. Louis, Missouri	—	Much of city burned; $15 million loss
1863, Dec. 8	Santiago, Chile	2,000	Church burned while filled with worshipers
1866, July 4	Portland, Maine	—	City almost totally destroyed by fire; $10 million loss
1866, Oct. 13	Quebec, Canada	—	2,500 buildings burned
1871, Oct. 8–9	Chicago, Illinois	300	3½ square miles devastated by fire; 18,000 buildings lost; 100,000 homeless; $200 million loss
1871, Oct. 8–14	Michigan and Wisconsin	1,000	Great forest fire devastates large area
1872, Nov. 9–11	Boston, Massachusetts	—	Fire; 600 buildings ruined; $75 million loss
1876, Dec. 5	Brooklyn, New York	295	Conway's Theater fire
1877, June 20	St. John, New Brunswick, Canada	100	Fire; $12,500,000 property loss
1881, Dec. 8	Vienna, Austria	640	Ring Theater fire
1883, Jan. 13	Berdichev, Russia	270	Theater fire
1887, May 25	Paris, France	200	Opéra Comique fire
1887, Sept. 4	Exeter, England	200	Theater fire
1888, May 25	Oporto, Portugal	200	Baquet Theater fire
1889, June 6	Seattle, Washington	—	Fire loss about $10 million
1889, Aug. 4	Spokane, Washington	—	Fire destroys business district
1894, Sept. 1	Hinckley, Minnesota	418	160,000 forest acres burned; $25 million loss
1897, May 4	Paris, France	150	Fire at charity bazaar
1889, March 17	New York, New York	45	Windsor Hotel fire
1990, May 1	Scofield, Utah	200	Mine explosion
1900, June 30	Hoboken, New Jersey	300	Pier burned; property damage, $4,627,000
1902, Sept. 20	Birmingham, Alabama	115	Church fire
1903, Dec. 30	Chicago, Illinois	639	Iroquois Theater fire
1904, Feb. 7–8	Baltimore, Maryland	—	Fire; 75 city blocks destroyed; $85 million loss
1906, March 10	Courrières, France	1,060	Mine disaster
1906, April 18	San Francisco, California	700	Following earthquake, fire devastates 4 square miles; property damage about $500 million
1907, Dec. 6	Monongah, West Virginia	362	Coal-mine explosion
1907, Dec. 19	Jacobs Creek, Pennsylvania	239	Explosion in mine
1908, Jan. 13	Boyertown, Pennsylvania	173	Fire from motion-picture machine explosion
1908, March 4	Collinwood, Ohio	161	School fire
1908, April 12	Chelsea, Massachusetts	—	Destroyed by fire; $17 million loss
1909, Feb. 15	Acapulco, Mexico	250	Flores Theater fire
1909, Nov. 13	Cherry, Illinois	259	Coal-mine fire

WORLD'S WORST FIRES, EXPLOSIONS AND MINE DISASTERS (continued)

DATE	PLACE	DEATHS	REMARKS
1911, March 25	New York, New York.........	145	Triangle Shirtwaist Factory fire
1913, Oct. 22	Dawson, New Mexico........	263	Mine fire
1914, June 25–26	Salem, Massachusetts.......	—	1,700 buildings burned; $14 million loss
1914, Dec. 15	Fukuoka, Japan.............	687	Coal-mine disaster at Hojo Colliery
1916, July 30	Black Tom Island, Jersey City, N.J.	—	German war sabotage; $22 million loss
1917, April 10	Eddystone, Pennsylvania.....	133	Munitions plant explosion
1917, Dec. 6	Halifax, Nova Scotia........	1,500	Explosion of war material; $35 million damage
1918, Oct. 4–5	Morgan Station, New Jersey ..	64	Gillespie Loading Co. explosion
1918, Oct. 13–15	Minnesota and Wisconsin	1,000	Forest fires; $100 million loss
1919, June 20	San Juan, Puerto Rico	150	Mayaguez Theater fire
1921 Sept. 21	Oppau, Germany............	600	Ammonium-nitrate plant explosion
1922, Sept. 13	Smyrna, Turkey............	—	Fire almost totally destroys city; 100,000 homeless
1923, May 17	Kershaw County, N.C........	77	Fire in school during presentation of play
1928, May 19	Mather, Pennsylvania.......	194	Coal-mine explosion
1929, May 15	Crile Hospital, Cleveland, Ohio	125	Poisonous fumes cause mass suffocation
1930, April 21	Columbus, Ohio............	317	Fire at Ohio State Penitentiary
1934, March 22	Hakodate, Japan............	1,500	Fire destroys largest city north of Tokyo
1934, May 19	Chicago, Illinois	—	Union Stockyards burn; $10 million loss
1934, Sept. 22	Wrexham, Wales	265	Coal-mine explosion
1937, Feb. 13	Antung, Manchuria	658	Theater fire
1937, March 18	New London, Texas..........	413	Schoolhouse destroyed by natural-gas explosion
1938, Nov. 12–16	Changsha, China	2,000	Fire levels city
1939, March 1	Osaka, Japan..............	500	Munitions explosion destroys part of Osaka
1939, July 10	Peñaranda de Bracamonte, Spain	100	Town demolished by munitions factory explosion
1939, Nov. 14	Lagunillas, Venezuela........	500	Oil town built on Lake Maracaibo destroyed by fire
1940, April 23	Natchez, Mississippi.........	198	Dance-hall fire
1941, May 31	Jersey City, New Jersey	—	Waterfront fire; $25 million loss
1941, June 8	Smederevo, Yugoslavia	1,000	Explosion of ammunition plant; town destroyed
1942, April 26	Honkeiko Colliery, Manchuria .	1,549	Worst mine disaster in history
1942, May 1	Tessenderlo, Belgium........	250	Chemical works explosion
1942, Nov. 28	Boston, Massachusetts	493	Cocoanut Grove nightclub fire
1942, Dec. 13	St. John's, Newfoundland	100	Knights of Columbus Hostel fire panic
1943, May 7	Sandoná, Colombia..........	103	Municipal Palace demolished by fire
1944, April 14	Bombay, India	1,500	Ship's fire causes explosion of ammunition
1944, July 6	Hartford, Connecticut	168	Audience panics in circus "Big Top" fire
1944, July 17	Port Chicago, California	300	Two ammunition-dump explosions
1944, Oct. 20	Cleveland, Ohio	121	Liquid-gas tanks explode; fire burns 50 blocks
1946, June 5	Chicago, Illinois	60	La Salle Hotel fire
1946, Dec. 7	Atlanta, Georgia	119	Winecoff Hotel fire
1947, March 25	Centralia, Illinois	111	Coal-mine explosion
1947, April 16	Texas City, Texas	468	Explosion of French ship Grandcamp ruins city
1947, Aug. 20	Cádiz, Spain	400	Shipyard explosion
1947, Oct. 25	Bar Harbor, Maine	—	Forest fire; estimated loss at $30 million
1948, March 9	Tsingtao, China	200	Ammunition storehouse explosion
1948, July 28	Ludwigshafen, Germany	200	I. G. Farben Company explosions and fire
1948, Sept. 22	Hong Kong	135	Fire and chemical explosion in warehouse
1949, Sept. 4	Chungking, China	1,700	Central part of city burns; 100,000 homeless
1950, May 19	South Amboy, New Jersey	30	Munitions barges explode
1951, May 13	Kano, Nigeria	100	Movie house burns
1951, Dec. 21	West Frankfort, Illinois	119	Coal-mine explosion
1955, Feb. 17	Near Yokohama, Japan	97	Home for aged women burns
1956, Aug. 7	Cali, Colombia	1,100	Seven trucks carrying dynamite explode
1956, Aug. 8	Marcinelle, Belgium	263	Coal-mine fires
1957, Feb. 17	Warrenton, Missouri	72	Home for aged burns
1958, Feb. 19	Near Asansol, India..........	180	Coal-mine explosion
1958, June 23	Santo Amaro, Brazil	100	Fireworks explosion
1958, Dec. 1	Chicago, Illinois	93	Parochial-school fire
1958, Dec. 16	Bogotá, Colombia	84	Department-store fire
1960, Jan. 21	Coalbrook, South Africa......	437	Coal-mine cave-ins and explosion
1960, Feb. 22	Zwickau, East Germany	123	Explosion in Karl Marx Mine
1960, March 4	Havana, Cuba	75	French munitions ship explodes
1960, July 14	Guatemala City, Guatemala...	200	Hospital for insane swept by fire
1960, Nov. 13	Amude, Syria	152	Movie-house fire
1961, July 8	Dolna Suce, Czechoslovakia ..	108	Coal-mine gas explosion
1961, Dec. 17	Niteroi, Brazil...............	323	Circus-tent fire
1962, Feb. 7	Saar, Germany..............	298	Coal-mine explosion
1963, May 4	Diourbel, Senegal	64	Theater fire
1963, Oct. 31	Indianapolis, Indiana.........	73	Explosion at State Fair coliseum
1963, Nov. 9	Fukuoka, Japan.............	458	Coal-mine disaster
1963, Nov. 23	Fitchville, Ohio..............	63	Fire burns rest home
1964, July 23	Bone, Algeria	100	Explosion aboard Egyptian munitions ship

WORLD'S WORST FIRES, EXPLOSIONS AND MINE DISASTERS *(continued)*

DATE	PLACE	DEATHS	REMARKS
1965, May 28	Bihar, India	400	Mine disaster
1965, June 1	Fukuoka, Japan	237	Coal-mine disaster at Yamano Colliery
1965, June 8	Kakanj, Yugoslavia	108	Mine disaster
1965, Aug. 9	Searcy, Arkansas	53	Explosion in a Titan 11 missile silo
1967, May 22	Brussels, Belgium	322	Fire in L'Innovation department store
1968, April 6	Richmond, Indiana	43	Explosion and fire; nearly two city blocks wrecked
1968, Nov. 20	Mannington, West Virginia	78	Fire and explosions in coal mine
1969, March 31	Barroteran, Mexico	183	Coal-mine explosion
1969, Nov. 7	Buffelstein, South Africa	64	Explosion in gold mine
1970, Jan. 9	Marietta, Ohio	31	Private nursing-home fire
1970, April 9	Osaka, Japan	73	Gas-leak explosions at subway construction site
1970, Nov. 1	Saint-Laurent-du-Pont, France	144	Fire in dance hall
1970, Dec. 30	Wooton, Kentucky	38	Coal-mine explosion
1971, Dec. 25	Seoul, South Korea	163	Hotel fire
1972, March 11	Minsk, Soviet Union	100	Factory fire and/or explosion
1972, May 2	Kellogg, Idaho	91	Sunshine silver-mine fire
1972, May 13	Osaka, Japan	115	Nightclub fire
1972, June 6	Wankie, Rhodesia	427	Coal-mine explosion
1973, Feb. 10	Staten Island, New York City	40	Oil storage-tank explosion
1973, June 24	New Orleans, Louisiana	32	Nightclub fire
1973, Aug. 2	Douglas, Isle of Man, Britain	51	Amusement-park fire
1973, Sept. 1	Copenhagen, Denmark	35	Hotel fire; 20 Americans killed
1973, Nov. 29	Kumamoto, Japan	101	Department-store fire; 2,500 shoppers saved
1974, Feb. 1	São Paulo, Brazil	189	Fire in 25-story skyscraper; 293 injured
1974, June 17	Lahore, Pakistan	40	Store building destroyed by fire
1974, Dec. 27	Lievin, France	42	Explosion and fire in coal mine
1975, Jan. 22	Manila, Philippines	51	Factory fire; 79 injured
1975, Dec. 12	Mecca, Saudi Arabia	138	Muslim pilgrims' tent-city fire; 151 injured
1975, Dec. 27	Dhanbad, India	431	Explosion floods coal mine
1976, March 9–11	Oven Fork, Kentucky	26	Explosions in coal mine
1976, April 13	Lapua, Finland	40	Ammunition-factory explosion
1976, Dec. 31	Chlebovice, Czechoslovakia	43	Gas explosion in coal mine
1977, Feb. 25	Moscow, Soviet Union	45	Fire in Rossiya Hotel, world's largest hotel
1977, May 28	Southgate, Kentucky	164	Nightclub fire, more than 100 injuries
1977, June 9	Abidjan, Ivory Coast	41	Nightclub fire
1977, June 26	Columbia, Tennessee	42	Maurcy County Jail fire traps inmates and visitors
1977, Aug. 2	Moatize, Mozambique	150	Explosion in coal mine; 9 killed in later rioting
1977, Nov. 14	Manila, Philippines	47	Hotel fire fanned by winds of typhoon
1977, Dec. 22	Westwego, Louisiana	35	Explosion in grain elevator
1978, July 11	Tarragona, Spain	181	Tank truck explodes and falls into campsite
1978, Aug. 19	Abadan, Iran	430	Enemies of Shah set fire in movie theater
1978, Nov. 2	Huimanguillo, Mexico	52	Gas pipeline explodes
1978, Dec. 1	Klerksdorp, South Africa	41	Gold-mine fire
1979, Feb. 15	Warsaw, Poland	49	Explosion in savings bank; 110 injured
1979, July 12	Saragossa, Spain	71	Oil tank explodes in luxury hotel
1979, July 29	Tuticorin, India	104	Fire in movie theater
1979, Oct. 10	Bytom, Poland	34	Coal-mine fire
1979, Oct. 31	Czechowice-Dziedzice, Poland	63	Coal-mine fire
1980, Jan. 1	Chapais, Quebec	45	Fire in social club
1980, Jan. 31	Guatemala City, Guatemala	39	Fire in Spanish Embassy
1980, May 20	Kingston, Jamaica	157	Fire in home for poor and elderly
1980, Aug. 2	Bologna, Italy	81	Terrorist bomb explodes in railroad station
1980, Aug. 15	Baghdad, Iraq	59	Fire in movie theater
1980, Aug. 16	London, England	37	Fire in adjoining social clubs
1980, Oct. 24	Ortuella, Spain	51	Explosion in elementary school
1980, Nov. 2	Gorna Grupa, Poland	50	Fire in mental hospital
1980, Nov. 16	Bangkok, Thailand	60	Explosion in munitions plant
1980, Nov. 19	Kawaji, Japan	44	Fire in resort hotel
1980, Nov. 22	Las Vegas, Nevada	84	Fire in MGM Grand resort hotel and casino
1980, Nov. 24	Danaciobasi, Turkey	97	Explosion at village engagement party
1980, Dec. 3	Northern Romania	49	Explosion in Livezeni coal mine
1980, Dec. 4	Harrison, New York	26	Fire in motel conference center
1981, Jan. 9	Keansburg, New Jersey	31	Fire in nursing home
1981, Feb. 7	Bangalore, India	71	Circus tent catches fire
1981, Feb. 14	Dublin, Ireland	46	Fire in discotheque
1981, Sept. 3	Northern Czechoslovakia	65	Explosion in Zaluzi coal mine
1981, Oct. 16	Hokkaido, Japan	93	Explosion in coal mine caused by methane gas
1982, Feb. 8	Tokyo, Japan	32	Fire in luxury hotel
1982, April 25	Todi, Italy	34	Fire in antiques exhibit
1982, May 12	Zenica, Yugoslavia	39	Explosion in coal mine caused by methane gas
1982, Nov. 3	Salang Pass Tunnel, Afghanistan	c.1,100	Explosion caused by oil tank truck

WORLD'S WORST FIRES AND EXPLOSIONS *(continued)*

DATE	PLACE	DEATHS	REMARKS
1982, Nov. 11	Tyre, Lebanon	89	Explosion in Israeli army headquarters
1982, Dec. 19	Caracas, Venezuela	132	Fuel-tank fire and explosions at power plant
1983, Feb. 13	Turin, Italy	64	Fire in movie theater
1983, Feb. 16–17	Australia	71	Brush fires in two Australian southern states
1983, March 7	Eregli, Turkey	98	Coal-mine explosion
1983, April 18	Taegu, South Korea	25	Fire in disco
1983, May 7	Istanbul, Turkey	42	Hotel fire
1983, May 8	Tlapacoya, Mexico	34	Gunpowder explodes in church
1983, June 7	Serbia, Yugoslavia	21	Coal-mine explosion
1983, June 22	Oroszlay, Hungary	36	Coal-mine explosion
1983, Sept. 12	Natal, South Africa	64	Coal-mine explosion
1983, Dec. 17	Madrid, Spain	79	Fire in discotheque
1984, Jan. 14	Pusan, South Korea	38	Fire in tourist hotel
1984, Jan. 18	Kyushu, Japan	83	Fire in coal mine
1984, Feb. 25	Cubatao, Brazil	508	Oil pipeline explodes, destroys shantytown
1984, March 24	Mandalay, Burma	10	Fire destroys 2,700 homes and buildings
1984, Apr. 21	Vodna Mine, Yugoslavia	33	Coal mine explosion
1984, May 11	Jackson Township, N.J.	8	Fire in amusement park funhouse
1984, May 23	Abbeystead, England	15	Methane gas explodes in river pumping station
1984, May 28	Taipei, Taiwan	19	Fire in 14-story Time Hotel
1984, Jun. 20	Tucheng, Taiwan	74	Fire in Haishan coal mine
1984, July 4	Beverly, Mass.	14	Fire in rooming house
1984, Jul. 10	Juifang, Taiwan	102	Explosion at Mei-shan coal mine
1984, Jul. 23	Romeoville, Illinois	17	Explosion in oil refinery
1984, Oct. 18	Paterson, N.J.	13	Fire in Alexander Hamilton Hotel
1984, Oct. 22	Baguio, Philippines	23	Hotel fire; 8 Americans die
1984, Nov. 3	Medenec, Czechoslovakia	26	Fire in home for handicapped
1984, Nov. 17	Welkom, South Africa	4	Mud slide in gold mine
1984, Nov. 19	Mexico City, Mexico	452	Gas tank explodes in crowded neighborhood
1984, Dec. 3	Bhopal, India	over 2,000	Accident releases poison gas from Union Carbide chemical plant; about 2,000 injured
1984, Dec. 5	Haishan Yiken, Taiwan	95	Explosion in coal mine
1984, Dec. 19	Orangeville, Utah	27	Coal-mine fire
1985, Feb. 7	Castellanta, Italy	34	Collapse of apartment building
1985, Feb. 13	Manila, Philippines	30	Fire in 470-room Regent Hotel
1985, Feb. 25	Forbach, France	22	Explosion in coal mine; 180 injured
1985, March 13	Bahia Blanca, Argentina	19	Blast in grain elevator
1985, April 20	Harbin, China	10	Fire in 15-story Swan Hotel
1985, April 21	Tabaca, Philippines	44	Movie theater fire
1985, April 24	Nagasaki, Japan	11	Coal mine explosion
1985, April 26	Buenos Aires, Argentina	79	Fire in psychiatric hospital
1985, May 11	Bradford, England	53	Grandstand burns at soccer match
1985, May 17	Yubari, Japan	61	Explosion in coal mine
1985, May 20	Youngstown, Ohio	9	Unlicensed fireworks factory explodes
1985, May 29	San Antonio, Texas	4	Ammonia gas explosion in ice factory
1985, June 25	Hallett, Oklahoma	21	Fireworks plant explodes
1985, July 12	Guangdong province, China	55	Coal mine explosion
1985, Sept. 2	Passaic, N.J.	—	Fire destroys 40 acres of factories and homes; $400 million in damages
1985, Oct. 17	Port of Spain, Trinidad	10	Explosion on oil barge

WORLD'S WORST AIRCRAFT DISASTERS

DATE	AIRCRAFT	DEATHS	REMARKS
1921, Aug. 24	English dirigible R-38 (U.S. ZR-2)	62	Breaks in two over Hull, England
1928, Dec. 21	French dirigible *Dixmude*	52	Vanishes over Mediterranean Sea or Sahara Desert
1930, Oct. 5	English dirigible R-101	47	Crashes near Beauvais, France
1933, April 4	U.S. dirigible *Akron II*	73	Crashes off New Jersey coast
1935, May 18	Soviet aircraft *Maxim Gorky*	49	Collides with a small plane over Moscow
1937, May 6	German zeppelin *Hindenburg*	36	Burns at mooring in Lakehurst, N.J.
1938, July 24	Military stunt plane	53	Crashes into grandstand in Bogotá, Colombia
1944, Aug. 23	U.S. bomber	76	Crashes into school in Freckleton, England
1945, July 28	U.S. bomber	13	Crashes into Empire State Building
1949, Nov. 1	P-38 fighter and DC-4 airliner	55	Collide above airport in Washington, D.C.
1950, March 12	English airliner	80	Crashes near Cardiff, Wales
1952, March 27	Two Soviet planes	70	Collide over Tula Airport, Moscow
1952, Dec. 20	U.S. Air Force plane	87	Crashes at Larson Air Force Base, Wash.
1953, June 18	U.S. Air Force Globemaster	129	Crashes near Tokyo, Japan
1955, Oct. 6	Airliner, DC-4	66	Crashes in mountains near Laramie, Wyo.

WORLD'S WORST AIRCRAFT DISASTERS

DATE	AIRCRAFT	DEATHS	REMARKS
1956, June 20	Venezuelan airliner	74	Crashes in Atlantic 40 miles south of New York City
1956, June 30	Two airliners	128	Collide over Grand Canyon, Ariz.
1957, Aug. 11	Chartered Canadian airliner	79	Crashes near Quebec, Canada
1958, May 18	Belgian airliner	65	Crashes in Casablanca, Morocco
1958, Aug. 14	Dutch airliner	99	Crashes in ocean west of Ireland
1958, Oct. 17	Soviet jet airliner	75	Crashes in Kanash, Soviet Union
1959, Feb. 3	U.S. turboprop airliner	65	Crashes into East River, New York City
1959, June 26	U.S. luxury airliner	68	Explodes near Milan, Italy
1960, Feb. 25	U.S. Navy and Brazilian planes	61	Collide over Rio de Janeiro
1960, March 17	Turboprop airliner	63	Mid-air explosion over Tell City, Ind.
1960, Aug. 29	French airliner	63	Crashes into sea near Dakar, Senegal
1960, Sept. 18	U.S. DC-6AB	80	Crashes on takeoff from Guam
1960, Oct. 4	U.S. Electra	62	Crashes into harbor at takeoff in Boston, Mass.
1960, Dec. 16	U.S. DC-8 and U.S. Constellation	134	Collide over New York City
1961, Feb. 15	Belgian jet airliner	73	Crashes near Berg, Belgium
1961, May 10	French airliner	79	Crashes in Ghadames, Libya
1961, Sept. 1	U.S. Constellation	78	Crashes after takeoff in Chicago, Ill.
1961, Sept. 10	U.S. charter plane	83	Crashes in Shannon, Ireland
1961, Nov. 8	U.S. charter plane	77	Crashes in Richmond, Va.
1962, March 1	U.S. B-707	95	Explodes as it crashes into Jamaica Bay, N.Y. City
1962, March 4	English DC-7	111	Crashes in jungle near Douala, Cameroon
1962, March 16	U.S. Super Constellation	107	Crashes into western Pacific Ocean
1962, June 3	French B-707	130	Crashes at takeoff in Paris, France
1962, June 22	French B-707	113	Crashes near Guadeloupe, West Indies
1962, July 7	Italian DC-8	94	Crashes near Bombay, India
1962, Nov. 27	Brazilian jet airliner	97	Crashes and burns in Lima, Peru
1963, Feb. 1	British and Turkish planes	95	Collide over Ankara, Turkey
1963, June 3	U.S. military chartered airliner	101	Crashes in Pacific Ocean off British Columbia
1963, Nov. 29	Canadian airliner	118	Crashes after takeoff in Montreal, Canada
1963, Dec. 8	U.S. B-707/121	81	Crashes near Elkton, Md.
1964, Feb. 25	U.S. DC-8	58	Crashes in Lake Pontchartrain, La.
1964, Feb. 29	English Britannia	83	Crashes near Innsbruck, Austria
1964, March 1	U.S. Constellation	85	Crashes near Lake Tahoe, Calif.
1964, May 11	U.S. military C-135 transport	75	Crashes at Clark Air Force Base, the Philippines
1965, Feb. 6	Chilean DC-6B	87	Crashes in the Andes
1965, Feb. 8	U.S. DC-7B	84	Plunges into Atlantic ocean near Kennedy Airport, N.Y. City
1965, May 20	Pakistani jet airliner	119	Crashes near Cairo, Egypt
1965, June 25	U.S. Air Force transport	84	Crashes into mountains near Los Angeles, Calif.
1965, Nov. 8	U.S. B-727	58	Crashes during landing near Cincinnati, Ohio
1965, Dec. 11	U.S. Air Force transport C-123	85	Crashes into mountain near Nhatrang, South Vietnam
1966, Jan. 24	Indian B-707	117	Crashes into Mont Blanc, France
1966, Feb. 4	Japanese B-727	133	Plunges into Tokyo Bay during landing
1966, March 5	British B-707	124	Catches fire above Mt. Fuji and crashes on slopes
1966, April 22	U.S. Lockheed Electra	82	Crashes near Ardmore, Okla.
1966, Sept. 1	British turboprop	95	Crashes during landing in Belgrade, Yugoslavia
1966, Nov. 24	TABSO Airways, Ilyushin-18	82	Crashes at Bratislava, Czechoslovakia
1966, Dec. 24	Flying Tiger CL-44	111	Cargo flight crashes at Danang, South Vietnam
1967, April 20	Swiss jetliner	126	Crashes while landing at Nicosia, Cyprus
1967, June 3	British DC-6	88	Crashes on Mt. Canigou in French Pyrenees
1967, Nov. 20	U.S. Convair jetliner	69	Crashes on landing near Cincinnati, Ohio
1968, April 20	South African Boeing 707	122	Crashes near Windhoek, South West Africa
1968, May 3	U.S. jetliner	85	Crashes in central Texas during thunderstorm
1968, Sept. 11	French Caravelle jetliner	95	Catches fire and crashes off French Riveria
1969, March 16	Venezuelan DC-9	155	Crashes into suburb of Maracaibo, Venezuela
1969, March 20	Egyptian IL-18	91	Crashes on landing at Aswan airport, Egypt
1969, June 4	Mexican jet	79	Flies into mountain near Monterrey, Mexico
1969, Sept. 9	U.S. DC-9 and Piper Cherokee	83	Collide over Shelbyville, Ind.
1969, Sept. 20	U.S. Phantom and Vietnamese DC-4	77	Collide near Danang, South Vietnam
1969, Nov. 20	Nigerian VC-10	87	Crashes near Iju, Nigeria
1969, Dec. 8	Greek DC-6B	90	Crashes on mountain near Athens during storm
1970, Feb. 15	Dominican Airways DC-9	102	Crashes into sea after takeoff from Santo Domingo
1970, July 4	British four-engine Comet	112	Crashes into mountain in Spain
1970, July 5	Canadian DC-8	109	Crashes near Toronto airport
1970, Aug. 9	Peruvian Electra	101	Crashes near Cuzco
1970, Nov. 14	U.S. DC-9	75	Crashes near Kenova, W.Va.
1970, Dec. 31	Aeroflot Ilyushin-18	90	Crashes at takeoff from Leningrad
1971, May 23	Yugoslav TU-134A	78	Crashes and burns on island off Rijeka, Yugoslavia
1971, July 30	Japanese Boeing 727 and F-86	162	Collide over Morioka, Japan
1971, Sept. 4	Alaska Airlines Boeing 727	111	Crashes in Tongass National Forest, Alaska
1972, Jan. 7	Iberian Airlines Caravelle	104	Crashes near island of Ibiza, Spain
1972, March 14	Danish Sterling Airways charter	112	Crashes near Gulf of Oman

WORLD'S WORST AIRCRAFT DISASTERS *(continued)*

DATE	AIRCRAFT	DEATHS	REMARKS
1972, May 6	Alitalia DC-8	115	Crashes into mountain on Sicily
1972, June 18	BEA Trident-1	118	Crashes after takeoff at London
1972, June	Antonov-10	108	Crashes near Kharkov in the Ukraine
1972, Aug. 14	E. German Ilyushin-62	156	Crashes after takeoff from Schönefeld Airport
1972, Oct. 3	Soviet Ilyushin-18	106	Crashes near Black Sea resort of Sochi
1972, Oct. 13	Soviet Ilyushin-62	176	Crashes near Sheremetyevo Airport
1972, Dec. 3	Spanish charter jet	155	Crashes in Canary Islands
1972, Dec. 29	Eastern Airlines L-1011 jet	101	Crashes in Everglades near Miami, Fla.
1973, Jan. 22	Royal Jordanian Airways 707	176	Crashes in fog at Kano, Nigeria
1973, Feb. 19	Soviet jetline	77	Crashes in landing at Prague, Czechoslovakia
1973, Feb. 21	Libyan airliner	108	Shot down by Israeli jets near Suez Canal
1973, April 10	British charter flight	105	Hits mountain near Basel, Switzerland
1973, July 11	Brazilian 707 jet	122	Burns on mountain near Paris, France
1973, July 23	Pan American 707 jet	78	After takeoff, crashes near Tahiti
1973, July 31	Delta Air Lines DC-9	89	Hits seawall while landing in fog, Boston, Mass.
1973, Aug. 13	Aviaco Airline Caravelle	85	Hits trees while landing in fog, La Coriena, Spain
1973, Dec. 22	Charter Caravelle airliner	106	Crashes into mountain near Tangier, Morocco
1974, Jan. 31	Pan American 707 jet	92	Landing crash at Pago Pago, American Samoa
1974, March 3	Turkish Airlines DC-10	346	Falls near Paris after cargo door blows off
1974, April 4	Chartered DC-4	77	Takeoff crash at Francistown, Botswana
1974, April 22	Pan American 707	107	Crashes into mountainside on Bali, Indonesia
1974, April 27	Soviet turboprop airliner	118	Takeoff crash at Leningrad
1974, Sept. 8	TWA 707 airliner	88	Falls in Ionian Sea off Greece in storm
1974, Sept. 11	Eastern Airlines DC-9	72	Landing crash at Charlotte, N.C.
1974, Dec. 1	TWA 727 jet airliner	92	Crashes during landing at Washington, D.C.
1974, Dec. 4	Dutch DC-8 jet airliner	191	Falls during landing approach on Sri Lanka
1974, Dec. 22	Venezuelan airliner	77	Takeoff crash at Maturin, Venezuela
1975, April 4	Air Force C-5A Galaxy	155	Planeload of war orphans crashes in South Vietnam
1975, June 24	Eastern Airlines Boeing 727	113	Crashes at Kennedy Airport, New York City
1975, Aug. 3	Moroccan Boeing 707 airliner	188	Strikes mountain near Agadir, Morocco
1975, Aug. 20	Czechoslovak Ilyushin 62	126	Landing crash near Damascus, Syria, airport
1975, Oct. 25	Bolivian Air Force Convair 440	70	Hits mountain near La Paz, Bolivia
1975, Oct. 30	Yugoslav DC-9 airliner	68	Crashes landing in fog at Prague, Czechoslovakia
1976, Jan. 1	Lebanese Boeing 707 airliner	82	Explodes in storm over Arabian Desert
1976, July 28	Czechoslovak Ilyushin 18	70	Falls into lake near Bratislava, Czechoslovakia
1976, Sept. 4	Venezuelan Air Force transport	68	Crashes on landing at U.S. air base in Azores
1976, Sept. 10	British Trident and Yugoslav DC-9	176	Collide near Zagreb, Yugoslavia
1976, Sept. 19	Turkish Boeing 727	155	Strikes Karakaya Mountain in Turkey
1976, Oct. 6	Cuban DC-8 airliner	73	Explodes after takeoff from Barbados
1976, Oct. 12	Indian Airlines Caravelle	95	Crashes after takeoff from Bombay
1976, Oct. 13	Chartered Boeing 707	100	Falls into downtown street in Santa Cruz, Bolivia
1976, Nov. 28	Soviet Tupolev TU-104	72	Crashes after takeoff from Moscow
1976, Dec. 25	Egyptian Boeing 707	72	Crashes into factory at Bangkok, Thailand
1977, March 27	Pan Am 747 and KLM 747	581	Jets collide on airport runway at Santa Cruz de Tenerife, Canary Islands; aviation's worst disaster
1977, April 4	Southern Airways DC-9	71	Crashes in hailstorm at New Hope, Ga.
1977, May 27	Soviet IL-62	66	Crashes on landing at Havana, Cuba
1977, Nov. 19	Portuguese Boeing 727	130	Crashes on landing at Funchal, Madeira, airport
1977, Dec. 4	Malaysian jetliner	100	Explodes in southern Malaysia after being hijacked
1978, Jan. 1	Air India Boeing 747	213	Explodes and crashes in sea near Bombay, India
1978, March 16	Bulgarian Tupolev-134	73	Crashes after takeoff from Sofia, Bulgaria
1978, Sept. 25	Boeing 727 and Cessna 172	144	Collide over San Diego, Calif.
1978, Nov. 15	Icelandic Airlines DC-8	183	Crashes short of runway at Colombo, Sri Lanka
1978, Dec. 23	Alitalia Airlines DC-9	108	Crashes into sea short of Palermo, Italy, airport
1979, March 18	Soviet TU-104	90	Crashes after takeoff from Moscow's Vnukovo Airport
1979, May 25	American Airline DC-10	273	Crashes on takeoff from Chicago airport
1979, Aug. 11	Two Soviet TU-134 jets	173	Collide over Ukraine in bad weather
1979, Oct. 31	Western Airlines DC-10	73	Crashes on landing at Mexico City airport
1979, Nov. 26	Pakistan Int'l Airlines Boeing 707	156	Crashes after takeoff from Jidda, Saudi Arabia
1979, Nov. 28	Air New Zealand DC-10	257	Crashes in Antarctica during sightseeing flight
1980, Jan. 21	Iran Air Boeing 727	128	Crashes in mountains near Teheran, Iran
1980, March 14	Polish IL-62 jetliner	87	Crashes on landing in Warsaw, Poland
1980, April 25	British Boeing 727	146	Hits mountain in Tenerife, Canary Islands
1980, June 28	Itavia Airlines DC-9	81	Falls into Tyrrhenian Sea on flight to Sicily
1980, July 7	Soviet TU-154	163	Crashes on takeoff from Alma Ata, Soviet Union
1980, Aug. 19	Saudi Arabian Lockheed Tri-star	301	Flames trap passengers after landing at Riyadh
1980, Sept. 13	Florida Commuter Airlines DC-3	34	Crashes into Atlantic Ocean on flight to Bahamas
1980, Sept. 14	Saudi Arabian C-130 transport	89	Catches fire and plunges into desert near Medina
1980, Dec. 21	Colombian Caravelle Jet	68	Crashes in northern desert of Colombia
1981, Feb. 7	Soviet ILA26 jet	70	Crashes near Leningrad, Soviet Union
1981, Aug. 22	Taiwanese Boeing 737	110	Explodes and crashes near Sanyi, Taiwan

WORLD'S WORST AIRCRAFT DISASTERS (continued)

DATE	AIRCRAFT	DEATHS	REMARKS
1981, Dec. 1	Yugoslav DC-9 jetliner	174	Hits mountain near Ajaccio, Corsica
1982, Jan. 13	Air Florida Boeing 737	78	Crashes on takeoff from Washington, D.C.
1982, Feb. 3	French army aircraft	36	Crashes into mountain during training flight
1982, April 26	Chinese Trident jetliner	112	Strikes mountain near Guilin, China
1982, June 8	Brazilian Boeing 727	137	Crashes into mountain near Fortaleza, Brazil
1982, July 6	Soviet IL-62 jetliner	90	Burns after takeoff from Moscow
1982, July 9	Pan Am 727 jetliner	154	Crashes on takeoff from New Orleans, La.
1982, Sept. 13	Spantax Airlines DC-10	52	Crashes as pilot aborts takeoff from Málaga, Spain
1982, Dec. 9	Nicaraguan MI-8 helicopter	84	Crashes in mountains of Nicaragua
1983, Jan. 16	Turkish Airlines Boeing 727	47	Crashes on landing in Ankara, Turkey
1983, July 11	Ecuadorian Boeing 737	119	Explodes trying to land at Cuenca, Ecuador
1983, Sept. 1	Korean Air Lines Boeing 747	269	Shot down over Sea of Japan by Soviet Union
1983, Sept. 23	Gulf Air Boeing 737	111	Crashes on landing in Abu Dhabi
1983, Nov. 8	Angolan Boeing 737	126	Crashes on takeoff from Lubango, Angola
1983, Nov. 27	Colombian Boeing 747	183	Crashes on landing approach to Madrid, Spain, airport
1983, Nov. 28	Nigerian Fokker F-28	53	Crashes on landing at Lagos, Nigeria
1983, Dec. 7	Iberian Boeing 727 and Aviaco DC-9	93	Collide on runway at Madrid, Spain, airport
1984, Jan. 10	Bulgarian Tu 134 jetliner	50	Crashes on landing at Sofia, Bulgaria
1984, Feb. 19	Two Bell UH-1H helicopters	28	Collide after being fired on by guerrillas in northern El Salvador
1984, Feb. 28	U.S. Air Force C-130 Hercules	18	Crashes on mountain in northern Spain
1984, Mar. 24	U.S. Marine Corps helicopter	29	Hits mountain near Seoul, South Korea, during military exercises
1984, Aug. 5	Bangladesh Fokker airliner	49	Crashes on landing at Dhaka, Bangladesh
1984, Aug. 24	Wings West airliner and private plane	17	In-flight collision near San Luis Obispo, Calif.
1984, Sep. 13	Fokker airliner	27	Crashes in Bandundu province, Zaire
1984, Sep. 18	Ecuadorian DC-8 Cargo jet	60	Crashes during take off in Quito, Ecuador, killing 56 on ground
1984, Dec. 6	Provincetown-Boston airliner	13	Crashes after take off in Jacksonville, Fla.
1985, Jan. 1	Eastern Airlines Boeing 727	29	Crashes into mountain near La Paz, Bolivia
1985, Jan. 18	Chinese Soviet-made airliner	38	Crashed in landing at Jinan, China
1985, Jan. 19	Cuban jetliner	40	Crashes after takeoff from Havana, Cuba
1985, Jan. 21	Galaxy Airlines Lockheed Electra	71	Crashes on takeoff at Reno, Nev.
1985, Jan. 22	U.S. military C-130A transport	21	Crashes on coast of Honduras
1985, Feb. 1	Soviet Aeroflot TU-134	80	Crashed near Minsk, Soviet Union
1985, Feb. 19	Iberia Airlines Boeing 727	148	Hits mountain near Bilbao, Spain
1985, Feb. 22	Air Mali turboprop	50	Explodes during landing approach at Timbuktu, Mali
1985, March 28	Colombian Fokker 28 airliner	40	Hits mountain during storm in Colombia
1985, May 3	Soviet Aeroflot TU-134	80	Collides with military plane near Lvov, U.S.S.R.
1985, May 6	U.S. Marine Corps helicopter	17	Falls in Pacific Ocean off Japan's coast
1985, June 23	Air-India Boeing 747	329	Explodes and crashes into Atlantic Ocean off Ireland
1985, June 23	Taba Airlines plane	17	Falls in Brazil's Amazon jungle
1985, Aug. 2	Delta Airlines Lockheed L-1011	133	Crashes landing in storm at Dallas, Tex.
1985, Aug. 12	Japan Airlines Boeing 747	520	Hits mountain in Japan after losing tail; 4 passengers survive
1985, Aug. 22	British charter Boeing 737	54	Burns while taking off from Manchester, England; 83 aboard escape flames
1985, Sept. 6	Midwest Express Airlines DC-9	31	Crashes after takeoff from Milwaukee, Wis.
1985, Sept. 23	Henson Airlines Beech 99 Turboprop	14	Hit mountain near Weyers Cave, W.Va.
1985, Sept. 29	Single-engine Cessna 208 Caravan	17	Crash of plane filled with parachustists near Jenkinsburg, Ga.
1985, Oct. 15	U.S. Marine Corps helicopter	15	Falls in Atlantic off North Carolina

SHIPWRECKS AND MARINE DISASTERS

DATE	CRAFT	DEATHS	REMARKS
1831, July 19	*Lady Sherbrooke*	263	Sinks off Cape May, N.J.
1833, May 11	*Lady of the Lake*	215	Strikes iceberg while bound for Quebec
1840, Jan. 13	*Lexington*, steam ferry	146	Burned in Long Island Sound
1850, March 29	*Royal Adelaide*	400	Wrecked off Margate, England
1852, March 26	*Birkenhead*, troopship	454	Wrecked; bound for Cape of Good Hope
1853, Sept. 29	*Annie Jane*, immigrant vessel	348	Wrecked off Scotland
1854, March	*City of Glasgow*	450	Vanishes; bound for Philadelphia from Liverpool
1854, Sept. 27	*Arctic*	322	Sinks near Grand Banks, off Newfoundland
1857, Sept. 12	*Central America*	400	Sinks in storm; bound for New York from Havana
1858, Sept. 13	*Austria*	471	Burns on Hamburg–New York run
1859, April 27	*Pomona*	386	Wrecked off Ireland
1859, Oct. 25	*Royal Charter*	450	Wrecked in Irish Sea
1860, Sept. 8	*Lady Elgin*, excursion steamer	300	Collides with lumber ship on Lake Michigan

SHIPWRECKS AND MARINE DISASTERS *(continued)*

DATE	CRAFT	DEATHS	REMARKS
1865, April 27	*Sultana*, river steamer	1,450	Explodes and sinks in Memphis, Tenn.
1867, Oct. 29	*Rhone* and *Wye*, mail boats	1,000	Wrecked in storm; St. Thomas, West Indies
1870, Sept. 17	*Captain*, English warship	472	Founders off Finistère, France
1871, July 30	*Westfield*, Staten Island (N.Y.) ferry	104	Boiler explosion at slip in New York City
1873, April 1	*Atlantic*, English steamer	547	Wrecked off Nova Scotia
1878, Sept. 3	*Princess Alice*, English steamer	700	Collides and sinks in River Thames
1890, Sept. 19	*Ertogrul*, Turkish frigate	540	Burns off Japanese coast
1891, March 17	*Utopia*, British steamer	574	Collides and sinks off Gibraltar
1895, March 14	*Reina Regenta*, Spanish cruiser	400	Founders in Atlantic near Gibraltar
1898, Feb. 15	*Maine*, U.S. battleship	264	Blown up in Havana Harbor
1898, July 4	*Bourgogne* and *Cromartyshire*	560	Collide near Sable Island off Nova Scotia
1904, June 15	*General Slocum*	1,000	Burns in East River, New York City
1904, June 28	*Norge*	600	Wrecked on Rockall Reef off Scotland
1912, April 15	*Titanic*	1,502	Strikes iceberg and sinks in North Atlantic
1912, Sept. 28	*Kichemaru*	1,000	Sinks off coast of Japan
1914, May 29	*Empress of Ireland*	1,024	Strikes Norwegian collier in St. Lawrence River
1915, May 7	*Lusitania*	1,195	Sunk by German submarine off coast of Ireland
1915, July 24	*Eastland*, excursion steamer	812	Capsizes in Chicago River, Ill.
1916, Aug. 29	*Hsin Yu*	1,000	Sinks off coast of China
1917, July 9	*Vanguard*, English warship	800	Blown up at Scapa Flow dock off northern Scotland
1918, July 12	*Kawachi*, Japanese battleship	500	Explodes in Tokayama Bay, Japan
1919, Jan. 17	*Chaonia*	460	Wrecked in Strait of Messina, Italy
1921, March 18	*Hong Kong*	1,000	Wrecked on rocks off Swatow in South China Sea
1926, Oct. 16	Chinese troopship	1,200	Explodes in Yangtze River, China
1927, Oct. 25	*Principessa Mafalda*, Italian liner	326	Sinks off coast of Brazil
1928, Nov. 12	*Vestris*	113	Founders off Virginia Capes
1931, June 14	French excursion steamer	450	Overturns in Bay of Biscay storm off St. Nazaire
1934, Sept. 8	*Morro Castle*	137	Burns off coast of New Jersey near Asbury Park
1939, May 23	*Squalus*, U.S. submarine	26	Sinks off New Hampshire coast
1939, June 1	*Thetis*, British submarine	99	Sinks in Irish Sea
1939, June 15	*Phenix*, French submarine	63	Sinks off Indochina
1941, June 16	O-9, U.S. submarine	33	Sinks in test dive off Maine coast
1942, Feb. 9	*Normandie*, French liner	1	Burns at Hudson River pier, New York City
1942, Oct. 2	*Queen Mary* and *Curacao*	338	Liner rams and sinks British cruiser
1942, Oct. 26	Jewish refugee ship	200	Wrecked in Sea of Marmara, Turkey
1944, Dec. 17–18	Three U.S. Third Fleet destroyers	790	Capsize during typhoon in Philippine Sea
1945, Jan. 30	*Wilhelm Gustloff*, German ship	6,100	Sunk by Russian submarine in Baltic Sea
1945, April 9	U.S. Liberty ship	360	Explodes in harbor at Bari, Italy
1945, July 29	*Indianapolis*, U.S. cruiser	883	Sunk by Japanese torpedo in Pacific Ocean
1946, Aug. 2	*Vitya*	295	Sinks in Lake Nyasa, Tanganyika
1947, Jan. 19	*Himara*	392	Hits mine and sinks off Athens, Greece
1947, July 17	*Ramdas*, coastal steamer	550	Sinks off Bombay, India
1948, Jan. 28	*Joo Maru*, freighter	250	Hits mine and sinks in Inland Sea, Japan
1948, Feb. 28	Steamer	160	Sinks during pirate attack near Amoy, China
1948, June 11	*Kjoebenhavn*, Danish liner	140	Hits mine and sinks off coast of Jutland
1948, Dec. 3	Steamer	1,140	Explodes and sinks south of Shanghai
1949, Jan. 27	Chinese liner and collier	600	Collide and sink off south coast of China
1949, Sept. 17	*Noronic*, Great Lakes liner	130	Burns at pier in Toronto, Canada
1950, Jan. 12	*Truculent*, English submarine	65	Rammed by tanker in Thames Estuary
1951, April 16	*Affray*, English submarine	75	Sinks off Isle of Wight, near southern England
1952, April 26	*Hobson*, U.S. destroyer, and *Wasp*, aircraft carrier	176	Collide; *Hobson* sinks in Atlantic Ocean
1953, Jan. 9	South Korean passenger liner	249	Sinks in heavy seas off Pusan, South Korea
1953, Jan. 31	Ferry	132	Sinks in storm off Northern Ireland
1953, Aug. 1	*Monique*	120	Vanishes near New Caledonia in South Pacific
1954, May 26	*Bennington*, U.S. aircraft carrier	103	Explodes and burns off Quonset Point, R.I.
1954, Sept. 26	*Toya Maru*, Japanese ferry	1,172	Sinks in Tsugaru Strait, Japan
1956, June 3	Pakistani liner	199	Wrecked in storm in Bay of Bengal
1956, July 26	*Andrea Doria* and *Stockholm*	50	Collide; *Andrea Doria* sinks off Massachusetts
1957, April 10	Two pilgrimage boats	150	Sink in Godavari River, India
1957, July 14	Soviet ship	270	Runs aground in storm in Caspian Sea
1958, Jan. 26	Japanese ferry	170	Vanishes in Inland Sea
1958, March 1	Turkish ferry	238	Sinks near Istanbul, in Sea of Marmara
1959, May 8	Nile River excursion boat	150	Sinks north of Cairo, Egypt
1960, Dec. 19	*Constellation*, U.S. aircraft carrier	50	Burns in Brooklyn Navy Yard, New York
1961, April 8	*Dara*, English liner	212	Burns in Persian Gulf
1961, July 8	*Save*	259	Runs aground and explodes in Mozambique
1961, Sept. 3	*Vencedor*, excursion ship	150	Sinks near Buenaventura, Colombia
1963, April 10	*Thresher*, U.S. nuclear submarine	129	Sinks in North Atlantic
1963, May 4	Motor launch	206	Sinks in Upper Nile
1963, Aug. 17	*Midori Maru*, Japanese ferry	128	Sinks in East China Sea

SHIPWRECKS AND MARINE DISASTERS *(continued)*

DATE	CRAFT	DEATHS	REMARKS
1963, Dec. 23	*Lakonia*, Greek liner	155	Sinks after fire in Atlantic north of Madeira
1964, Feb. 11	*Voyager*, destroyer, and *Melbourne*, aircraft carrier	85	Collide; *Voyager* sinks near Ulladulla, Australia
1965, Feb. 11	Four fishing trawlers	100	Sink in Bering Sea
1965, May 24	African ferry	150	Capsizes in Shire River, Malawi
1965, Nov. 13	*Yarmouth Castle*, cruise ship	90	Catches fire and sinks in Caribbean
1966, Dec. 8	*Heraklion*, Greek ferry	217	Sinks in storm in Sea of Crete
1967, July 29	*Forrestal*, U.S. aircraft carrier	134	Crippled by fire off Vietnam
1968, Jan. 26	*Dakar*, Israeli submarine	69	Sinks in eastern Mediterranean Sea
1968, May 27	*Scorpion*, U.S. nuclear submarine	99	Sinks in Atlantic Ocean southwest of Azores
1969, June 2	*Frank E. Evans*, U.S. destroyer, and *Melbourne*, aircraft carrier	74	Collide; *Evans* breaks in half, bow section sinks
1970, March 4	*Eurydice*, French submarine	57	Sinks in Mediterranean near Toulon, France
1970, April 12	Soviet submarine	88	Sinks in Atlantic off Spain
1970, Aug. 1	*Christena*, motor launch	125	Capsizes and sinks in Caribbean off St. Kitts
1970, Dec. 15	South Korean ferry	308	Capsizes in Korea Strait
1971, Nov. 21	*Beethoven II*	106	Sinks off Philippines
1974, Feb. 22	South Korean tugboat	157	Capsizes in Chungmu harbor, South Korea
1974, May 1	Bangladesh motor launch	250	Capsizes in coastal waters off Bangladesh
1974, Sept. 12	Soviet guided-missile destroyer	350	Explodes and sinks in Black Sea
1975, Aug. 9	Two Chinese riverboats	500	Collide and sink in West River, near Canton
1975, Nov. 10	U.S. ore carrier *Edmund Fitzgerald*	29	Sank during storm on Lake Superior
1975, Dec. 18	Burmese coastal schooner	70	Capsizes in storm in Andaman Sea
1976, Oct. 20	Tanker and ferry *George Prince*	78	Collide in Mississippi River
1976, Dec. 23	Egyptian passenger ship *Patria*	170	311 rescued in Red Sea sinking
1976, Dec. 30	*Grand Zenith*, Panamanian tanker	38	Sinks off Cape Cod, Mass.
1977, Jan. 17	U.S. Navy launch and freighter	46	Collide in Barcelona, Spain, harbor
1977, Sept. 25	Egyptian ferry	50	Capsizes in Nile River near Cairo
1978, April 8	Burmese coastal transport	100	Capsizes in Bay of Bengal
1978, June 17	Steam showboat *Whippoorwill*	15	Overturned by tornado on Lake Pomona, Kans.
1978, Oct, 12	Liberian tanker *Spyros*	59	Explodes in Singapore harbor; 90 injured
1978, Dec. 2	Vietnamese refugee boat	143	Sinks in rough seas off Pasir Puteh, Malaysia
1979, Jan. 8	French oil tanker *Betelgeuse*	50	Explodes while unloading at Bantry, Ireland
1979, March 31	Vietnamese refugee boat	100	Capsizes while being towed to sea off Malaysia
1979, Nov. 15	Romanian tanker and Greek freighter	47	Collide in Bosporus off Istanbul, Turkey
1979, Nov. 25	Chinese drilling rig *Bo Hai #2*	72	Collapses while being towed in Bohai Gulf
1980, Feb. 27	Chinese ferry	276	Capsizes during storm in southern China river
1980, March 27	Oil rig platform *Alexander L Kielland*	128	Collapses, overturns in stormy North Sea
1980, April 22	Philippine ferry and oil tanker	300	Collide off Mindoro Island, Philippines
1980, May 9	Freighter *Summit Venture*	35	Rams into bridge at Tampa Bay, Fla.
1980, Aug. 22	Mexican ferry	50	Sinks off Ciudad del Carmen, Mexico
1980, Oct. 25	Freighter *S.S. Poet*	34	Disappears after leaving Philadelphia, Pa.
1981, Jan. 6	Brazilian ferry *Novo Amapo*	230	Sinks in Jari River
1981, Jan. 27	Indonesian ferry	374	Sinks in storm in Java Sea
1981, Feb. 26	Soviet freighter *Komsomolets Nakhodki*	38	Sinks in storm near Hakodate, Japan
1981, Sept. 19	Amazon riverboat *Sobral Santos*	252	Sinks at port of Obidos, Brazil
1981, Oct. 26	Haitian refugee boat	33	Breaks apart just off Hillsborough Beach, Fla.
1981, Dec. 29	Italian freighter *Marina d'Equa*	30	Sinks in storm in Bay of Biscay
1982, Feb. 15	Oil-drilling rig *Ocean Ranger*	84	Sinks in storm off Newfoundland, Canada
1982, Feb. 16	Soviet freighter *Mekhanik Tarasov*	33	Sinks near Halifax, Nova Scotia
1982, March 28	Burmese ferry	129	Capsizes in canal in Burma
1982, April 11	Burmese ferry	160	Capsizes near Henzada, Burma
1982, June 17	Philippine passenger ferry *Queen Helen*	36	Explodes in Sulu Sea, Philippines
1982, Aug. 8	Indonesian ferry	300	Capsizes off coast of Celebes, Indonesia
1982, Sept. 4	Indian ferry	35	Capsizes in swollen river in Orissa, India
1982, Oct. 17	Indonesian steamer *Karya Tambangan*	58	Sinks in Java Sea
1983, Feb. 11	Coal transport *Marine Electric*	31	Overturns off coast of Virginia
1983, March 1	Chinese ferry boat	150	Capsizes near Canton, China
1983, May 25	Egyptian ferry *10th of Ramadan*	317	Catches fire and sinks in Nile River
1983, June 5	Soviet river boat *Aleksandr Suvorov*	240	Rams railway bridge on Volga River
1983, June 16	Indonesian inter-island ferry	80	Lost in Banda Sea
1983, Aug. 5	Indonesian passenger boat *Sumber Wangi*	104	Sinks in Java Sea
1983, Sept. 28	Nicaraguan passenger ferry *Santa Elena*	127	Sinks in Lake Nicaragua
1983, Oct. 25	Drilling ship *Glomar Java Sea*	81	Disappears in South China Sea
1983, Nov. 21	Philippine ferry *Dona Cassandra*	200	Sinks in typhoon off Mindanao Island
1984, Jan. 22	Philippine ferry boat	54	Capsizes off Tawitawi Island, Philippines
1984, Jan. 24	Liberian cargo ship *Radiant Med*	17	Capsizes in English Channel
1984, Jun. 3	British bark *Marques*	18	Sinks in squall in tall ship transatlantic race
1984, Aug. 15	Malaysian ferry	200	Sinks off Malaysian coast
1984, Sept. 25	Passenger launch	31	Sinks near Tananarive, Madagascar
1984, Oct. 2	Yacht, *Martina*	19	Collision with tug towing barge at Hamburg, West Germany

SHIPWRECKS AND MARINE DISASTERS *(continued)*

DATE	CRAFT	DEATHS	REMARKS
1984, Oct. 13	Nigerian ferry	100	Sinks on Aiyela River in Nigeria
1984, Oct. 17	Bangladesh ferry	245	Sinks near Tarakindi, Bangladesh
1984, Oct. 28	Philippine ferry *Venus*	100	Sinks in storm off Luzon, Philippines
1985, March	Ferry	100	Capsizes in Buri Ganga River, Bangladesh
1985, May 21	Oil drilling barge *Tonkawa*	10	Capsizes near Morgan City, La.
1985, May 26	Tankers *Petragen-1* and *Camponavia*	31	Explode at dock in Algeciras, Spain
1985, May 26	Riverboat	74	Capsizes in Chambal River in central India
1985, Oct. 5	Ferry and fishing trawler	100	Collide on Karnaphuli River, Bangladesh

WORLD RAILROAD DISASTERS

DATE	PLACE	DEATHS	REMARKS
1856, July 17	Near Philadelphia, Pennsylvania	66	Train wrecked
1857, March 17	Near Hamilton, Ontario, Canada	60	Train derailed on bridge over Desjardins Canal
1864, July 15	Near Lackawaxen, Pennsylvania	65	Two trains collide
1876, Dec. 29	Ashtabula, Ohio	92	Bridge collapses in snowstorm
1879, Dec. 28	Dundee, Scotland	78	Train falls from Tay Bridge
1881, June 24	Cuautla, Mexico	200	Train falls into river
1882, July 13	Near Tchnery, Russia	150	Train derailed
1887, Aug. 10	Chatsworth, Illinois	81	Train wrecked as burning bridge collapsed
1888, Oct. 10	Mud Run, Pennsylvania	62	Locomotive hits standing excursion train
1889, June 12	Near Armagh, Ireland	80	Train collision
1891, June 14	Near Basel, Switzerland	100	Train collision
1896, July 30	Atlantic City, New Jersey	60	Train wrecked
1903, Dec. 23	Laurel Run, Pennsylvania	78	Train wrecked
1904, Aug. 7	Eden, Colorado	96	Train wrecked
1904, Sept. 24	New Market, Tennessee	56	Train wrecked
1906, Dec. 30	Washington, D.C.	53	Train wrecked
1910, March 1	Wellington, Washington	96	Avalanche throws two trains into canyon
1910, March 21	Green Mountain, Iowa	55	Passenger train wrecked
1915, May 22	Quintinshill, near Gretna, Scotland	227	Troop train collides with local train
1917, Dec. 12	Modane, France	543	Troop train derailed near Mont Cénis tunnel
1918, June 22	Ivanhoe, Indiana	68	Train rams circus train
1918, July 9	Near Nashville, Tennessee	101	Two trains collide head-on; 171 injured
1918, Nov. 1	Brooklyn, New York	92	Five-car rapid transit train derailed
1937, July 16	Near Patna, India	107	Delhi–Calcutta Express derailed
1938, Dec. 19	Babacena, Minas Gerais, Brazil	90	Freight and passenger trains collide head-on
1938, Dec. 25	Near Kishinev, Romania	100	Passenger trains collide
1939, Dec. 22	Near Magdeburg, Germany	132	Two express trains collide
1939, Dec. 22	Near Friedrichshafen, Germany	99	Train wrecked
1940, Jan. 29	Osaka, Japan	200	Passenger trains collide and burn
1943, Sept. 6	Philadelphia, Pennsylvania	79	Nine cars of Congressional Limited derailed
1943, Dec. 16	Rennert, North Carolina	72	Two streamliners collide
1944, Jan. 16	León Province, Spain	500	Train wrecked inside tunnel
1944, March 2	Salerno, Italy	426	Train stalls in tunnel; mass suffocation
1944, Dec. 31	Near Ogden, Utah	50	Two sections of Pacific Limited wrecked
1945, Feb. 1	Cazadero, Mexico	100	Train with religious pilgrims hit by freight train
1946, March 20	Near Aracaju, Brazil	185	Train wrecked
1947, Aug. 3	Sumatra, East Indies	400	Train wrecked
1948, March 31	Osaka, Japan	70	Express hits electric train
1949, April 28	Near Johannesburg, South Africa	73	Three trains collide
1949, Oct. 22	Nowy Dwor, Poland	200	Danzig–Warsaw Express derailed
1950, April 6	Near Tanguá, Brazil	108	Train falls into flooded Indios River
1950, May 7	Bihar State, India	81	Punjab mail train crashes near Jasidih
1950, Nov. 22	Jamaica, New York	78	Train collides with standing commuter train
1951, Feb. 6	Woodbridge, New Jersey	84	Commuter train falls through temporary overpass
1952, March 4	Near Rio de Janeiro, Brazil	119	Two passenger trains collide
1952, July 9	Near Rzepin, Poland	160	Train wrecked
1952, Oct. 8	Harrow, England	112	Commuter train hit by two express trains
1953, Dec. 24	Near Wairoa, New Zealand	155	Wellington–Auckland Express falls into stream
1954, Jan. 21	North of Karachi, Pakistan	60	Mail express wrecked
1954, Jan. 31	Near Seoul, South Korea	56	Train crashes
1954, Sept. 28	East of Hyderabad, India	137	Express falls from flood-damaged bridge
1955, April 3	Near Guadalajara, Mexico	300	Train falls into canyon
1956, Sept. 2	Near Secunderabad, India	121	Two coaches fall into river as bridge collapses
1956, Nov. 23	Marudaiyar River, India	143	Express train plunges down river embankment
1957, Sept. 1	Jamaica, British West Indies	178	Train pitches into ravine
1957, Sept. 29	Near Montgomery, West Pakistan	250	Express crashes into standing oil train
1957, Oct. 20	Near Instanbul, Turkey	89	Two trains collide at high speed
1957, Dec. 4	Near London, England	90	Commuter trains collide; bridge collapses

WORLD RAILROAD DISASTERS *(continued)*

DATE	PLACE	DEATHS	REMARKS
1958, March 7	Santa Cruz, Brazil	67	Three commuter trains collide
1958, May 8	Near Rio de Janeiro, Brazil	128	Two trains collide head-on
1958, Sept. 15	Newark Bay, Elizabethport, N.J.	48	Train plunges through lift bridge
1959, May 28	Java, Indonesia	92	Train plunges into ravine
1959, June 5	São Paulo, Brazil	60	Two trains collide head-on
1960, May 15	Leipzig, East Germany	59	Local train and express collide
1960, Nov. 14	Pardubìce, Czechoslovakia	110	Two passenger trains collide
1961, Dec. 23	Cantanzaro, Italy	69	Train car plummets into gorge
1962, Jan. 8	Woerden, Netherlands	91	Passenger trains collide
1962, May 3	Tokyo, Japan	163	Two commuter trains collide with freight train
1962, May 31	Voghera, Italy	63	Passenger train collide with freight train
1962, July 21	Dumraon, India	69	Passenger train and freight train collide
1964, Jan. 4	Jajinci, Yugoslavia	66	Commuter train hits stalled passenger train
1964, Feb. 1	Altamirano, Argentina	70	Express rams stalled freight train
1964, July 26	Oporto, Portugal	94	Train wrecked
1965, Oct. 5	Near Durban, South Africa	100	Passenger train derails
1965, Dec. 9	Burma	76	Two trains collide head-on near Toungoo
1966, June 13	Bombay, India	60	Two suburban trains collide
1967, July 6	Langenweddingen, East Germany	82	Train collides with gasoline truck
1969, July 14	Jaipur, India	85	Freight train collides with passenger train
1970, Feb. 1	Buenos Aires, Argentina	139	Two passenger trains collide
1970, Feb. 16	Northern Nigeria	81	Train wreck
1972, June 4	Jessore, Bangladesh	76	Two passenger trains collide in station
1972, June 16	Vierzy, France	107	Two trains collide in tunnel cave-in
1972, July 21	Lebrija, Spain	76	Two passenger trains collide head-on
1972, Oct. 6	Saltillo, Mexico	208	Speeding passenger train derails on curve
1972, Oct. 30	Chicago, Illinois	44	Commuter train crushed from behind by another
1974, March 27	Laurenço Marques, Mozambique	60	Head-on collision of two trains
1974, Aug. 30	Zagreb, Yugoslavia	153	Passenger train derails in station
1974, Nov. 7	Cotonou, Dahomey	80	Two passenger trains collide
1975, Feb. 28	London, England	41	Subway train crashes in blind tunnel; 70 injured
1977, Jan. 18	Granville, Australia	82	Commuter train derails on bridge, which collapses
1977, Oct. 10	Naini, India	61	Passenger train hits freight train stopped at station
1977, Nov. 11	Iri, South Korea	57	Freight train explodes at railroad station
1978, April 15	Bologna, Italy	45	Mudslide causes collision; 120 injured
1979, Jan. 5	Turkey	56	Two express trains crash in blizzard near Ankara
1979, Jan. 26	Chuadanga, Bangladesh	70	Express train derails
1979, Aug. 21	Tailing Chan, Thailand	65	Freight train rams commuter train
1979, Sept. 13	Stalac, Yugoslavia	60	Freight train crashes into express train
1979, Oct. 30	Djibouti	50	Train derails and crashes near Ethiopian border
1980, June 7	Empageni, South Africa	45	Freight train hits bus filled with shoppers
1980, Aug. 19	Northern Poland	62	Passenger train collides with freight train
1981, March 8	Coronel Brandsen, Argentina	45	Passenger train collides with two derailed freight cars
1981, May 14	Kyongsan, South Korea	54	Commuter train rams express train
1981, June 6	Bihar, India	268	Train goes off bridge into Bagmati River
1981, June 21	Gagry, Soviet Union	70	Express train and local train collide
1982, Jan. 27	Agra, India	66	Freight train collides with express train in fog
1982, Jan. 27	El Asnam, Algeria	130	Derails during trip from Algiers to Oran
1982, July 11	Tepic, Mexico	120	Train derails, plunges down 800-foot gorge
1983, Feb. 19	Empalme, Mexico	100	Two trains collide
1983, Aug. 31	Pojuca, Brazil	42	Tank cars explode
1984, Feb. 10	Bahadurgarh, India	43	Passenger train collides with mail train
1984, Jun. 18	Luanda, Angola	50	Passenger train derails
1984, Jul. 14	Divaca, Yugoslavia	31	Freight train rams passenger express stopped in station
1984, Jul. 30	Edinburgh, Scotland	14	Express derails after hitting cow
1984, Oct. 31	Buenos Aires, Argentina	43	Train hits bus at suburban crossing
1984, Nov. 22	Bombay, India	25	Commuter train derails
1984, Dec. 23	Florence, Italy	25	Explosion aboard passenger train in tunnel
1984, Dec. 24	Hwange, Zimbabwe	31	Passenger train plunges into ravine
1985, Jan. 13	Awash, Ethiopia	392	Train falls off bridge
1985, Jan. 13	Puradaha, Bangladesh	27	Fire aboard express passenger train
1985, Jan. 20	Sri Lanka	33	Bomb explodes aboard train
1985, Feb. 23	Musra, India	50	Fire aboard passenger train
1985, March 11	Rio de Janeiro, Brazil	10	Two passenger trains collide head-on
1985, June 13	Raja-Ki-Mandi, India	37	Trains collide
1985, Aug. 2	Westminster, Colorado	5	Freight trains collide
1985, Aug. 3	Flaugac-Gare, France	35	Express train collides with local train
1985, Aug. 14	Uluguney, Turkey	14	Freight trains collide
1985, Aug. 31	Argenton-Sur-Creuse, France	43	Passenger train derails
1985, Sept. 11	Viseu, Portugal	54	Passenger trains collide
1985, Oct. 1	Southwestern Sudan	13	Famine relief train derails

Animals in the News

USA 22 — Quarter horse

USA 22 — Morgan

USA 22 — Saddlebred

USA 22 — Appaloosa

U.S. Postal Service

A block of four stamps featuring American horses was issued by the U. S. Postal Service on Sept. 25 at the Parade of Breeds Barn in the state–operated Kentucky Horse Park in Lexington, Ky. The stamps, depicting Saddlebred, Morgan, Appaloosa, and Quarter horses, were designed by Roy Andersen of Sedona, Ariz.

HIGHLIGHTS: 1985

FISH BLOCK $4.2 BILLION ROAD

In 1974 a huge $4.2 billion project called Westway was proposed to redevelop the decaying West Side of New York City's Manhattan Island along the Hudson River. The project included the building of a new highway, partly underground, and the creation of waterside parks and new apartment developments on hundreds of acres of landfill. The federal government would pay 90% of the cost of the project from highway funds.

The project immediately became a major issue in New York politics. Motorists supported the project because of the bad condition of the West Side Highway—an elevated portion of which had collapsed in 1973, permanently closing much of the highway. On the other hand, subway riders and many residents of Manhattan's West Side opposed the

project, saying the money would be better spent to improve the city's transit system. Westway was supported both by New York Gov. Mario Cuomo and New York City's Mayor Edward Koch, largely because of the thousands of jobs the project would create.

The project officially got underway in 1981 when President Reagan delivered a check for $85 million to the city for the purchase of land.

Seeking some way to block the project, opponents of Westway went to court, claiming that the project would destroy the rotting, unused shipping piers of the Hudson River that protect a prime spawning area for striped bass—a commercial food fish species that has declined over 80% in commercial catches in northeastern waters in the past decade.

BREEDS OF CATS

Abyssinian: *Coat:* ruddy (brown) or red, banded or ticked with darker brown, black, or red: *Eyes:* gold, green hazel

American Short Hair: *Body:* heavily built; *Coat:* short and lustrous, same colors as Persian.

Angora, or **Turkish Angora:** *Body and Head:* more elongated than Persian; *Coat: long-haired, silky; Eyes:* blue, copper, odd (one blue, one copper).

Balinese, or **Long-haired Siamese:** *Body and Coat:* like Siamese except coat is long.

Himalayan: *Body:* like Persian; *Coat:* like Balinese.

Maine Coon: *Coat:* long-haired in all colors; *Body:* long and powerful; *Head:* medium to broad.

Manx, *Body:* tailless and often hops like rabbit; *Coat:* thick, double coat in variety of colors.

Persian: *Body:* Short and cobby, wide across shoulders; *Head:* wide with small ears; *Nose:* short; *Coat:* long, flowing, glossy; *Color:* there are five color divisions—Solid, Tabby and Tortie, Smoke, Silver, and Cameo.

Rex: *Coat:* curly, like lamb fleece; *Color:* all colors.

Russian Blue: *Body:* fine-boned, slender; *Coat:* double-coated, short, thick; *Eyes:* deep green; *Color:* blue with silver tipping.

Siamese: *Body:* long, slender with long tail; *Head:* triangular; *Eyes:* deep blue, almond-shaped; *Coat:* short-haired, sandy brown with points (darker colors on face, ears, paws, tail), which form darkest to lightest are called seal, chocolate, blue, lilac, and red. Points may be tortoise or striped.

HIGHLIGHTS: 1985 *(continued)*

In 1982 opponents succeeded in getting Federal Judge Thomas P. Griesa to issue an injunction against the project on grounds that the Army Corps of Engineers had not given sufficient consideration to the striped bass issue when a permit had been granted for dredging and landfill.

After holding public hearings on the environmental impact of the project on striped bass, the Army Corps of Engineers issued a new permit in February 1985 to resume the project.

Then on Aug. 8, 1985, Judge Griesa reinstated his injunction, declaring that the corps still had not given adequate consideration to the effect of the project on the striped bass.

In September Governor Cuomo and Mayor Koch conceded victory to the striped bass, agreeing to abort the Westway project and instead use the remaining funds for other mass transit and highway projects.

TEXAS TEAM SETS BIRDATHON RECORD

A team of Texas birdwatchers led by naturalist Roger Tory Peterson, 76, set a new United States record for a birdathon by identifying 244 birds in 24 hours on May 1. They broke a previous record of 243 birds set last year by a California team.

The birdathon, which took place in and around the Anahuac Wildlife Refuge east of Houston, Tex., was sponsored by the National Audubon Society and the American Birding Association.

Rules of the event call for 95% of the bird species to be identified by all members of a team, either by sighting or by recognizing the bird calls.

The world record for birds identified in a single 24 hour period was set in 1984 in Peru by a team of two Americans, Ted Parker and Scott Robinson, who found 331 birds.

TIGER PROBLEMS

Farmers and villagers near the Sunderbans Reserve Forest in India believe they are the endangered species rather than the Bengal tigers the government has protected from hunting for 11 years. The tigers have killed 659 people in the Sunderbans area near the border with Bangladesh in the past 15 years. Some 56 of the deaths took place in 1984, and 22 were killed by tigers in the first three months of 1985.

WOMAN WINS DOGSLED RACE

For the first time a woman, Libby Riddles, 28, and her 13 huskies, won the $50,000 prize for Alaska's 1,135-mile Anchorage-to-Nome Iditarod Trail International Race in March. Her time, just short of 18 days on the trail, was three hours faster than that of her nearest competitor. She explained that she won

LONGEVITY AND GESTATION PERIOD OF ANIMALS

ANIMAL	LONGEVITY (years)	GESTATION (days)	LITTER SIZE	ANIMAL	LONGEVITY (years)	GESTATION (days)	LITTER SIZE
Baboon	15–30	180–185	1–2	Kangaroo	6–20	32–40	1–2
Bear, black	15–40	210–215	1–4	Lion	10–20	100–110	1–4
Camel	10–25	365–400	1	Monkey	12–20	140–270	1–2
Cat	10–20	54–69	1–6	Mouse	1–3	18–30	1–9
Cattle	10–20	270–290	1–2	Pig	10–20	100–130	4–6
Deer	10–20	200–300	2	Rabbit	6–13	29–34	1–13
Dog	10–20	55–70	1–12	Sheep	10–15	140–155	1–3
Elephant	30–80	520–725	1	Squirrel	8–10	40–48	2–5
Fox	8–12	50–60	1–8	Tiger	15–30	100–108	2–4
Goat	10–15	140–160	1–3	Wolf	10–15	58–65	1–13
Hamster	2–8	16–19	2–12	Zebra	15–25	330–365	1
Horse	20–30	270–420	1				

BREEDS OF DOGS

The following chart compiled by the American Kennel Club (AKC) lists the 128 breeds that make up the 1,071,299 purebred dogs registered by the AKC for the year 1984.

1.	Cocker Spaniels	94,803	44.	Weimaraners	4,107	87.	Belgian Tervuren	422
2.	Poodles	87,750	45.	Norwegian Elkhounds	3,916	88.	Japanese Chin	402
3.	Labrador Retrievers	71,235	46.	St. Bernards	3,797	89.	Cardigan Welsh Corgis	360
4.	German Shepherd Dogs	59,450	47.	Fox Terriers (Smooth & Wire)	3,646	90.	Flat-Coated Retrievers	301
5.	Golden Retrievers	54,490	48.	Afghan Hounds	3,225	91.	Irish Terriers	299
6.	Doberman Pinschers	51,414	49.	Miniature Pinschers	2,784	92.	Kuvaszok	296
7.	Beagles	40,052	50.	Pembroke Welsh Corgis	2,768	93.	Lakeland Terriers	289
8.	Miniature Schnauzers	37,694	51.	Silky Terriers	2,567	94.	Staffordshire Bull Terriers	281
9.	Shetland Sheepdogs	33,164	52.	Newfoundlands	2,297	95.	Border Terriers	276
10.	Dachshunds	33,068	53.	Great Pyrenees	1,836	96.	American Water Spaniels	268
11.	Chow Chows	32,777	54.	Bouviers des Flandres	1,827	97.	Puli	265
12.	Yorkshire Terriers	29,342	55.	Schipperkes	1,747	98.	Briards	259
13.	Lhasa Apsos	27,910	56.	Vizslas	1,730	99.	Bedlington Terriers	254
14.	Shih Tzu	25,588	57.	American Staffordshire Terriers	1,659	100.	Norwich Terriers	248
15.	English Springer Spaniels	21,660	58.	Mastiffs	1,584	101.	French Bulldogs	240
16.	Pomeranians	21,207	59.	Rhodesian Ridgebacks	1,450	102.	Welsh Springer Spaniels	239
17.	Siberian Huskies	20,889	60.	Basenjis	1,421	103.	Greyhounds	222
18.	Collies	19,261	61.	English Cocker Spaniels	1,371	104.	Skye Terriers	204
19.	Basset Hounds	18,710	62.	Borzois	1,344	105.	Brussels Griffons	199
20.	Boxers	17,745	63.	Whippets	1,337	106.	Komondorok	192
21.	Pekingese	17,653	64.	Bloodhounds	1,247	107.	Black and Tan Coonhounds	191
22.	Chihuahuas	17,250	65.	Bull Terriers	1,191	108.	Portuguese Water Dogs	182
23.	Rottweilers	17,193	66.	Irish Setters	1,066	109.	Scottish Deerhounds	173
24.	Brittanys	17,046	67.	Soft-Coated Wheaten Terriers	1,066	110.	Dandie Dinmont Terriers	162
25.	Boston Terriers	12,205	68.	Bullmastiffs	1,050	111.	Norfolk Terriers	152
26.	Great Danes	10,403	69.	German Wirehaired Pointers	1,037	112.	Affenpinschers	140
27.	Maltese	9,367	70.	Irish Wolfhounds	1,018	113.	English Toy Spaniels	136
28.	German Shorthaired Pointers	9,018	71.	Gordon Setters	1,008	114.	Pharaoh Hounds	130
29.	Samoyeds	8,032	72.	Bearded Collies	858	115.	Tibetan Spaniels	113
30.	West Highland White Terriers	7,520	73.	Giant Schnauzers	802	116.	Sealyham Terriers	111
31.	Pugs	7,134	74.	Papillons	772	117.	Irish Water Spaniels	105
32.	Bulldogs	7,004	75.	Belgian Sheepdogs	710	118.	Clumber Spaniels	102
33.	Alaskan Malamutes	6,748	76.	Australian Cattle Dogs	708	119.	Ibizan Hounds	98
34.	Keeshonden	6,359	77.	Welsh Terriers	660	120.	Wirehaired Pointing Griffons	84
35.	Dalmatians	6,354	78.	Australian Terriers	652	121.	Belgian Malinois	74
36.	Airedale Terriers	6,169	79.	Salukis	642	122.	Field Spaniels	61
37.	Old English Sheepdogs	6,124	80.	Italian Greyhounds	609	123.	Curly-Coated Retrievers	54
38.	Cairn Terriers	5,892	81.	Bernese Mountain Dogs	594	124.	American Foxhounds	42
39.	Scottish Terriers	5,538	82.	Standard Schnauzers	561	125.	Otter Hounds	23
40.	Irish Setters	4,553	83.	Kerry Blue Terriers	558	126.	Sussex Spaniels	23
41.	Chesapeake Bay Retrievers	4,499	84.	Tibetan Terriers	552	127.	English Foxhounds	22
42.	Bichon Frises	4,439	85.	Pointers	439	128.	Harriers	19
43.	Akitas	4,235	86.	Manchester Terriers	429			

because she and her team plodded on through a heavy snowstorm that halted most of her 60 competitors. "I left those guys in the dust," she said.

What did the huskies get for winning? "I'm going to get a box of dog biscuits for each of the dogs," Riddles said.

TOP DOGS

A 6-year-old black Scottish terrier, Ch. Braeburn's Close Encounter, won top honors over 2,600 dogs representing 139 breeds in February at what is regarded as the most prestigious dog show in the United States, the Westminster Kennel Club Show. Before winning,

BEST-IN-SHOW CHAMPION DOGS AT THE WESTMINSTER KENNEL CLUB SHOW

YEAR	BREED	BEST-IN-SHOW CHAMPION	OWNER
1970	Boxer	Ch. Arriba's Prima Donna	Dr. and Mrs. P.J. Pagano and Dr. T.S. Fickles
1971–72	English Springer Spaniel	Ch. Chinoe's Adamant James	Dr. Milton Prickett
1973	Standard Poodle	Ch. Acadia Command Performance	Mrs. Jo Ann Sering and Edward B. Jenner
1974	German Shorthaired Pointer	Ch. Gretchenhof Columbia River	Dr. Richard P. Smith
1975	Old English Sheepdog	Ch. Sir Lancelot of Barvan	Mr. and Mrs. Ronald Vanword
1976	Lakeland Terrier	Ch. Jo-Ni's Red Baron of Crofton	Virginia Dickson
1977	Sealyham Terrier	Ch. Dersade Bobby's Girl	Dorothy Wimer
1978	Yorkshire Terrier	Ch. Cede Higgens	Barbara and Charles Switzer
1979	Irish Water Spaniel	Ch. Oak Tree's Aristocrat	Mrs. Ann Snelling
1980	Siberian Husky	Ch. Innisfree's Sierra Cinnar	Mrs. Trish Kanzler
1981	Pug	Ch. Dandy's Favorite Woodchuck	Robert A. Hauslohner
1982	Pekingese	Ch. St. Aubrey Dragonora	Anne Snelling
1983	Afghan	Ch. Kabik's The Challenger	Chris and Marguerite Terrell
1984	Newfoundland	Ch. Seaward's Blackbeard	Elinor Ayers
1985	Scottish Terrier	Ch. Braeburn's Close Encounter	Sonnie and Alan Novick

HIGHLIGHTS: 1985 *(continued)*

the Scottie already had collected a record 185 best-in-show awards.

Three new breeds, first recognized by the American Kennel Club in 1983, competed at the Westminster show: the Pharaoh Hound, believed to be the same kind of dog seen in carvings on the tombs of Egyptian rulers; the Portuguese Water Dog, once used to swim from ship to ship carrying messages; and the Tibetan Spaniel, said to be the predecessor breed to the Lhasa Apso and the Pekingese.

For the second year in a row, the Cocker Spaniel topped the list of the American Kennel Club registrations of purebred dogs as the most popular dog. The number of registered Cocker Spaniels increased by 2.1% since 1983. The Poodle, which was displaced as top dog in 1983, remained in second place but declined in numbers by 2.8%. Doberman Pinschers suffered the largest decline in numbers, falling by 22.3% from 66,184 to 51,414. The Doberman reached its peak in 1978 with 81,964 registrations.

The Cocker Spaniel, so-named when it was used for hunting woodcocks, previously had been the most popular dog in the United States from 1936 to 1952.

The total number of purebred dogs registered by the American Kennel Club has remained nearly constant since crossing the 1 million mark in 1970.

MURDER TRIAL FOR PRIZE DOG

King Boots, an 8-year-old shaggy Old English sheepdog, was placed on trial for murder in 1985. In the 5-day trial in Michigan District Court in Birmingham, Mich., the state charged that King Boots killed 87-year-old Gertrude Monroe by biting her in the neck and severing an artery.

Mrs. Monroe's daughter, Kathryn Schwarb, owner of King Boots, hired an attorney to defend the dog. She contended that King Boots, who had won 225 prizes in 371 dog shows, had merely been defending himself when the elderly woman suffered a heart attack and fell on top of the dog, stabbing him in the nose with a fork she was holding.

The Oakland County medical examiner, Dr. William Brooks, testified that an autopsy disclosed no evidence of a heart attack or a stroke. He said Mrs. Monroe died as a result of the dog's bite.

Judge Edward Sosnick found King Boots guilty. He gave the dog's owner the choice of having King Boots put to death or having him castrated and defanged. Mrs. Schwarb accepted the latter choice, preserving King Boots as a pet.

JAPAN TO END COMMERCIAL WHALING

Japan gave in to international pressure in 1985, agreeing to end commercial whaling by March 1988.

GROUP NAMES OF ANIMALS

band—apes
bed—clams, oysters, scallops
bevy—deer, larks, quail
brood—young birds or fish
cast—falcons, hawks
cete—badgers
charm—finches
cloud—gnats or other small flying insects
clowder—cats
clutch—young chickens
clutter—cats
colony—ants, beavers, coral
congregation—birds
covert—coots
covey—game birds, grouse, partridge
cry—hounds
drift—hogs
drove—cattle, hogs
exhaltation—larks
fall—woodcocks
flight—birds
flock—birds, goats, sheep
gaggle—geese
gam—whales
gang—buffalos, elk, wolves
herd—antelopes, buffalos, cattle, deer, elephants, elks, goats, hogs, horses, seals, whales
hive—bees
kennel—dogs, hounds

kindle—litter of kittens
leash—foxes, hounds
muster—peacocks
nide—pheasants
pack—dogs, grouse, hounds, wolves
plague—grasshoppers, locust
pod—seals, whales
pride—lions
rookery—crows, rooks
rout—wolves
school—fish, porpoises
shoal—fish, porpoises
shrewdness—apes
skein—wildfowl
skulk—foxes
sleuth—bears
sloth—bears
sord—mallard ducks
sounder—wild hogs
spring—teal ducks
stable—horses
string—horses
swarm—bees, flies, gnats, wasps, other insects
trip—goats, seals
troop—apes, kangaroos
volery—birds
warren—rabbits
watch—nightingales
wisp—snipe

The Arts

Broadbill Decoy

Mallard Decoy

Folk Art USA 22

Folk Art USA 22

Canvasback Decoy

Redhead Decoy

Folk Art USA 22

Folk Art USA 22

U.S. Postal/Service

As part of the U.S. Postal Service's Folk Art Series, a block of four duck decoy stamps were issued on March 22 in Shelburne, Vt., where two ot the decoys depicted are displayed at the Shelburne Museum. Two previous blocks of stamps have been issued in the series—Quilts in 1978 and Pennsylvania Toleware in 1979.

HIGHLIGHTS: 1985

FIRST U.S. ARTS MEDALS

The first 12 recipients of the National Medal of the Arts were honored at a White House luncheon in April for their contributions to American culture. Established by Congress in 1984, the medal can be awarded to no more than 12 recipients each year. The recommendations for those to be honored were made by the National Council on the Arts and final selections were made by President Reagan. Those receiving the medal were:

Elliott Carter, 76, composer, who has won two Pulitzer Prizes for his work.

Dorothy Chandler, 83, patron of the arts who endowed the Music Center of Los Angeles.

Ralph Ellison, 71, author, who wrote the novel *Invisible Man*.

Jose Ferrer, 73, Puerto Rican movie, TV, and stage actor and director.

Martha Graham, 90, dancer, choreographer, and founder-director of her own dance company.

Lincoln Kirstein, 77, organizer of the New York City Ballet and the School of American Ballet.

Paul Mellon, 77, patron of the arts and chairman of the National Gallery of Art in Washington, D.C.

Louise Nevelson, 85, Russian-born sculptor, who originated what is called "environmental sculpture."

Georgia O'Keefe, 97, painter, best known for her work depicting the American Southwest.

Leontyne Price, 58, operatic and concert soprano.

Alice Tully, 82, patron of the arts, whose donations to New York City's Lincoln Center are memorialized in its Alice Tully Hall.

Hallmark Cards, company that has sponsored TV's award-winning "Hallmark Hall of Fame" series and has contributed to many cultural institutions.

TOP ARCHITECTURAL AWARD

Austrian architect Hans Hollein, 51, won the most prestigious award in his field in 1985. He received the seventh annual Pritzker Architecture Prize, which includes $100,000 tax

HIGHLIGHTS: 1985 *(continued)*

free and a bronze sculpture by Henry Moore. The prize is named for its donors, the family that owns the Hyatt Hotels.

Hollein was cited as "an architect who is also an artist, one who with wit and eclectic gusto draws upon the traditions of the new world as readily as upon those of the old." He has designed many types of buildings in Europe, including an award-winning design for a new pyramid-like Museum of Modern Art in Frankfurt, West Germany.

Previous recipients of the award have included American architects Philip Johnson, Kevin Roche, I.M. Pei, and Richard Meier; British architect James Stirling; and Mexican architect Luis Barragan.

ARSONIST DESTROYS MASTERPIECE

An arsonist set fire to and destroyed a painting by Flemish artist Peter Paul Rubens on June 13 at the Kunsthaus Museum in Zurich, Switzerland. The 1628 painting of Spanish King Felipe IV was valued by the museum at $1.9 million. Police arrested a young man for the crime after an alarm automatically locked all the doors to the museum. However, police said that the man refused to tell them his motive for destroying the painting.

RECORD ART ENDOWMENT

Jacob Rothschild, chairman of the board of trustees of the British National Gallery, announced in June that the art museum had received the largest donation since it was founded in 1824. He said the endowment of $25.2 million came from John Paul Getty 2d, 52, heir to the Getty oil fortune who makes his home in Britain. Rothschild said that Getty also had promised to add another $38 million to the endowment fund "as soon as is practicable."

Rothschild said Getty's gift would make it possible for the museum "to continue to acquire and keep works of art through an endowment probably unparalleled by an one individual in the history of British public collections."

ART AUCTIONS

New York magazine publisher Malcolm Forbes outbid the Soviet government in June to acquire for $1.76 million an 11th Faberge

AMERICAN SYMPHONY ORCHESTRAS

Source: American Symphony Orchestra League

MAJOR ORCHESTRAS	DIRECTOR	OTHER INFORMATION
Atlanta Symphony Orchestra	Robert Shaw	Founded 1945; Shaw became director in 1966
Baltimore Symphony Orchestra	David Zinman	Founded 1916; Zinman became director in 1984
Boston Symphony Orchestra	Seiji Ozawa	Founded 1881; also performs as Boston Pops, under John Williams
Buffalo Philharmonic Orchestra	Julius Rudel	Founded 1935; Rudel became director in 1979
Chicago Symphony Orchestra	Sir Georg Solti	Founded 1891; Solti joined orchestra in 1969
Cincinnati Symphony Orchestra	Michael Gielen	Founded 1895; Gielen became director in 1980
Cleveland Orchestra	Christoph von Dohnanyi	Founded 1918; von Dohnanyi named director in 1983
Dallas Symphony Orchestra	Eduarto Mata	Founded 1900; Mata became director in 1977
Denver Symphony Orchestra	Gaetano Delogu	Founded 1933; Delogu became director in 1979
Detroit Symphony Orchestra	Gunther Herbig	Founded 1914; Herbig became director in 1984
Houston Symphony Orchestra	Sergiu Comissiona	Founded 1913; Comissiona became music advisor, 1979
Indianapolis Symphony Orchestra	John Nelson	Founded 1930; Nelson joined orchestra in 1976
Los Angeles Philharmonic	Andre Previn	Founded 1919
Milwaukee Symphony Orchestra	Lukas Foss	Founded 1930; Foss joined orchestra in 1980
Minnesota Orchestra	Neville Marriner	Founded 1903 as Minneapolis Symphony Orchestra; Marriner joined orchestra in 1979
National Symphony Orchestra	Mstislav Rostropovich	Founded 1931 as orchestra of Washington, D.C.; Rostropovich became director in 1977
New Orleans Symphony Orchestra	Philippe Entrement	Founded 1935; Entrement joined orchestra in 1980
New York Philharmonic	Zubin Mehta	America's oldest orchestra, founded in 1842; Leonard Bernstein is director emeritus; Mehta named director beginning 1978–79 season
Oregon Symphony Orchestra	James DePriest	Founded 1896; DePriest became director in 1980
Philadelphia Orchestra	Riccardo Muti	Founded 1900; Muti became director in 1980
Pittsburgh Symphony	Lorin Maazel	Founded 1927; Maazel became director in 1984
Rochester Philharmonic	David Zinman	Founded 1929; Zinman named music advisor in 1973
St. Louis Symphony Orchestra	Leonard Slatkin	Founded 1880; Slatkin named music director in 1979
St. Paul Chamber Orchestra	Pinchas Zukerman	Founded 1959; Zukerman became music director, 1980
San Antonio Symphony Orchestra	Lawrence Leighton Smith	Founded 1937; Smith joined orchestra in 1980
San Diego Symphony Orchestra	David Atherton	Founded 1927; became major orchestra in 1980
San Francisco Symphony	Herbert Blomstedt	Founded 1911; Blomstedt appointed in 1985
Seattle Symphony Orchestra	Gerard Schwarz	Founded 1903; Schwarz became conductor in 1983
Syracuse Symphony Orchestra	Christopher Keene	Founded 1924; Keene joined orchestra in 1975
Utah Symphony Orchestra	Joseph Silverstein	Founded 1926; Silverstein joined orchestra in 1983

LEADING U. S. OPERA COMPANIES

Source: Central Opera Service

MAJOR COMPANIES	DIRECTOR	OTHER INFORMATION
Baltimore Opera Company	Jay Holbrook	Founded 1941; Holbrook appointed in 1980
Cincinnati Opera Association	James de Blasis	Founded 1921; de Blasis appointed in 1973
Cleveland Opera Company	David Bamberger	Founded 1976, with Bamberger as director
Connecticut Opera Association	George Osborne	Founded 1942; Osborne appointed in 1979
Dallas Opera Company	Plato Karayanis	Founded 1957; Karayanis appointed in 1977
Fort Worth Opera Association	Dwight Bowes	Founded 1946; Bowes appointed in 1982
Greater Miami Opera Association	Robert Heuer	Founded 1941; Heuer appointed in 1985
Houston Grand Opera	David Gockley	Founded 1956; Gockley appointed in 1972
Kentucky Opera Assn. (Louisville)	Thomson Smillie	Founded 1952; Smillie appointed in 1981
Lyric Opera of Chicago	Ardis Krainik	Founded 1954; Krainik appointed in 1981
Lyric Opera of Kansas City	Russell Patterson	Founded 1958, with Patterson as director
Metropolitan Opera Association (N.Y.) .	Bruce Crawford	Founded 1883; Crawford appointed in 1985
Michigan Opera Theatre (Detroit)	David Di Chiera	Founded 1966, with Di Chiera as director
Minnesota Opera Company (St. Paul) ..	Wesley Balk	Founded 1964; Balk appointed in 1974
New Orleans Opera Association	Arthur Cosenza	Founded 1943; Cosenza appointed in 1966
New York City Opera	Beverly Sills	Founded 1944; Sills appointed in 1979
Opera Colorado (Denver)	Nathaniel Merrill	Founded 1982, with Merrill as director
Opera Company of Boston	Sarah Caldwell	Founded 1958, with Caldwell as director
Opera Company of Philadelphia	Margaret Everitt	Founded 1975; Everitt appointed in 1980
Opera Theatre of St. Louis	Richard Gaddes	Founded 1976, with Gaddes as director
Pittsburgh Opera	Tito Capobianco	Founded 1940; Capobianco appointed in 1983
Portland Opera Association	Robert Bailey	Founded 1951; Bailey appointed in 1982
San Diego Opera Association	Ian Campbell	Founded 1965; Campbell appointed in 1983
San Francisco Opera Association	Terence McEwen	Founded 1923; McEwen appointed in 1982
Santa Fe Opera	John Crosby	Founded 1957, with Crosby as director
Seattle Opera Association	Speight Jenkins	Founded 1962; Jenkins appointed in 1983
Tulsa Opera Inc.	Edward Purrington	Founded 1948; Purrington appointed in 1975
Virginia Opera Association (Norfolk) ...	Peter Mark	Founded 1974, with Mark as artistic director
Washington Opera Company	Martin Feinstein	Founded 1957; Feinstein appointed in 1979

Easter egg for his collection that is displayed in a museum adjacent to his Fifth Avenue offices. The Soviet representative dropped out of the bidding at $1.5 million. The Soviets had wanted to add it to their collection of 10 of the bejeweled eggs that. are displayed in Moscow at the Armory Museum. A total of 58 of the Easter eggs were made at the rate of one per year for the Russian imperial family by the goldsmith Faberge. The egg purchased by Forbes in June had belonged to California recording company executive Bernard Solomon, who had bought it in 1973 for $196,000, and was forced to sell it as part of a divorce settlement.

A 400-year-old Ming Dynasty jar was sold at a Sotheby's auction in New York in June for $1.2 million—believed to be the highest price ever paid in the United States for a Chinese work of art. The jar was purchased for a private collection in Hong Kong.

A 1932 painting called "Arbor Day" by the American artist Grant Wood sold for $1.375 million at a Sotheby's auction in May. The previous record price for one of the artist's works was $143,000 in 1983. At the same auction, a cowboy painting by Frederic Remington sold for $627,000—a record for one of that artist's works.

NOGUCHI MUSEUM

The 80-year-old Japanese-American sculptor Isamu Noguchi accomplished his dream of a lifetime in May 1985 by opening his own museum near his studio in Long Island City, N.Y. Called the Isamu Noguchi Garden Museum, it is a converted factory with 24,000 square feet of exhibition space and an outdoor sculpture garden. The museum displays the full range of Noguchi's 60 years of creativity, including sculptures, stage set designs, and industrial products.

MUSICIANS, COMPOSERS, SINGERS, DANCERS*

Licia Albanese (1913–), Italian soprano who was one of the principal singers at the Metropolitan Opera after her debut in 1940.

Marian Anderson (1902–), American contralto who achieved worldwide fame as a concert artist.

Johann Christian Bach (1735–82), German composer; J.S. Bach's 18th child. He spent much of his life in the court of England's George III, where he wrote operas and many symphonies.

Johann Sebastian Bach (1685–1750), German composer. A master of counterpoint, he was among the most influential composers of all time. His works include the six Brandenburg Concertos (1721), the B Minor Mass (1733–38), and many keyboard works.

Karl Philipp Emanuel Bach (1714–88), J.S. Bach's fifth child. With Haydn and Mozart, he helped develop the sonata form, which dominated instrumental music for two centuries.

* See pages 981–986 for 1985 deaths, and see pages 263–280 for popular musicians and composers.

MUSICIANS (continued)

George Balanchine (1904–83), Russian-American ballet dancer and choreographer; director of ballet at the Metropolitan Opera (1934–37) and the New York City Ballet (since 1948).

Samuel Barber (1910–81), American composer whose outstanding works include an overture to *The School for Scandal* (1931), *Adagio for Strings* (1936), and *Essays for Orchestra* (1937).

Sir John Barbirolli (1899–1970), English conductor who led the British National Opera (1926–27), the New York Philharmonic (1937–42), and the Houston Symphony.

Béla Bartók (1881–1945), Hungarian composer whose music combines folk elements with an extremely modern style. His works include three piano concertos (1926, 1931, 1945) and the *Concerto for Orchestra* (1944).

Mikhail Baryshnikov (1948–), Russian ballet dancer with Kirov Ballet who defected to the West in 1974; became guest artist for world's leading ballet companies; choreographed *The Nutcracker Suite* for American Ballet Theatre in 1976; made film debut in *The Turning Point* (1976); named director of American Ballet Theatre in 1980.

Sir Thomas Beecham (1879–1961), English conductor who organized the London Philharmonic Orchestra in 1932 and the Royal Philharmonic in 1946.

Ludwig van Beethoven (1770–1827), German composer who ranks among the greatest musical geniuses of all time. His masterpieces include 9 symphonies, 32 piano sonatas, 17 string quartets, and 5 piano concertos.

Alban Berg (1885–1935), Austrian atonal composer and pupil of Arnold Schoenberg. His opera *Wozzeck* (1914–1920) is considered his masterpiece.

Irving Berlin (1888–), American composer of popular songs, including *God Bless America*.

Hector Berlioz (1803–69), French composer and exponent of the Romantic movement. The *Symphonie Fantastique* (1830–31) and *Harold in Italy* (1834) are among his greatest works.

Leonard Bernstein (1918–), American conductor and composer (*Jeremiah Symphony*, 1941–44; *West Side Story*, 1957) who was musical director of the New York Philharmonic Orchestra (1958–69).

Georges Bizet (1838–75), French composer whose *Carmen* (1873–74) is one of the world's most popular operas.

Jussi Bjorling (1911–60), Swedish tenor who appeared in major European and American opera houses in over 50 leading roles.

Marc Blitzstein (1905–64), American composer of operas *The Cradle Will Rock* (1937) and *Regina* (1949).

Ernest Bloch (1880–1959), Swiss-American composer of the opera *Macbeth* (1903–09) and the *Israel Symphony* (1912–16).

Aleksandr Borodin (1833–87), Russian composer of nationalistic music, including the unfinished opera *Prince Igor*.

Johannes Brahms (1833–97), German composer of four symphonies (1855–76, 1877, 1883, 1884–85), *The Academic Festival Overture* (1880), *The Tragic Overture* (1880–81), one violin and two piano concertos, and much chamber music.

Alexander Brailowsky (1896–1976), Russian-born pianist noted for his playing of Chopin.

Benjamin Britten (1913–76), English composer whose opera *Peter Grimes* (1945) was one of few modern operas to achieve worldwide acclaim.

Anton Bruckner (1824–96), Austrian composer whose works utilize romantic themes in an expanded sonata structure. He wrote nine symphonies, the last unfinished, and four masses.

Ferruccio Busoni (1866–1924), Italian composer whose most popular compositions are the *Comedy Overture* (1897), the *Pianoforte Concerto* (1903–04), and *Doctor Faust* (1916–24).

William Byrd (1543–1623), English organist and composer called the father of English music for his masses, madrigals, chamber and keyboard music.

John Cage (1912–), American composer who employs random, nonmusical sounds to create highly experimental works.

Maria Callas (1923–77), Greek-American soprano who appeared in the major opera houses of Europe and the United States. Her greatest roles included Tosca and Norma.

Elliott Carter (1908–), American composer of the ballet *Pocahontas* (1939) and the Second String Quartet (1959), for which he received the 1960 Pulitzer Prize in music.

Enrico Caruso (1873–1921), Italian tenor and one of the world's most celebrated opera stars. He sang with the New York Metropolitan Opera from 1903 to 1920.

Robert Casadesus (1899–1972), French pianist who earned a reputation as a major artist.

Pablo Casals (1876–1973), Spanish cellist and conductor generally regarded as the world's greatest cellist. A distinguished conductor, he formed the Orquesta Pau Casals in Barcelona in 1919.

Feodor Chaliapin (1873–1938), Russian basso who sang in the major European opera houses and at the Metropolitan Opera (1907–08, 1921–29).

Lucia Chase (1907–), ballerina and co-director of the American Ballet Theatre (1945–80).

Frédéric Chopin (1810–49), Polish-French composer of highly romantic compositions for the piano. His works include 27 études, 25 preludes, 13 polonaises, and 2 concertos.

Van Cliburn (1934–), American pianist, gained worldwide fame by winning 1958 International Tchaikovsky Piano Competition in Moscow.

Aaron Copland (1900–), American composer whose highly successful works include *Music for the Theater* (1925), *Saga of the Prairie* (1937), *Billy the Kid* (1938), *Rodeo* (1942), *Appalachian Spring* (1944), and *Nonet* (1960).

Franco Corelli (1923–), Italian tenor who made his operatic debut at the Spoleto (Italy) Festival in 1952 and debuted with the New York Metropolitan Opera in 1961.

Henry Cowell (1897–1965), American composer whose unconventional music includes the five *Hymn-and-Fuguing Tunes* (1941–55).

George Crumb (1929–), American composer, received 1968 Pulitzer Prize for *Echoes of Time and The River*.

Merce Cunningham (1919–), American dancer and choreographer who performed with the Martha Graham Company (1940–45) before forming his own dance company in 1952.

Walter Damrosch (1862–1950), American conductor. Organized Damrosch Opera Company (1895) and led Metropolitan Opera Orchestra (1885–91, 1900–02) and New York Symphony (1903–27).

Alexandra Danilova (1906–), Russian ballerina and choreographer. She was the prima ballerina with the Ballet Russe de Monte Carlo (1938–58).

Claude Debussy (1862–1918), French composer and founder of the impressionistic school. His best works include *L'Après-midi d'un faune* (1892–94), *La Mer* (1905), the opera *Pelléas et Mélisande* (1902), and many pieces for piano solo.

Léo Delibes (1836–91), French composer best known for *Sylvia* (1876) and other ballets.

Frederick Delius (1862–1934), English composer whose best-known compositions include *A Village Romeo and Juliet* (1900–01), *Sea Drift* (1903), and *Mass of Life* (1904–05).

Victoria de Los Angeles (1923–), Spanish soprano

who sang in Madrid, Milan, and Paris before joining the Metropolitan Opera in 1950.

Agnes De Mille (1909–), ballerina and choreographer who created the first noteworthy American ballet, *Rodeo* (1938). She was the first to use ballet in musical comedies such as *Oklahoma!* (1943) and *Carousel* (1945).

Sergei Diaghilev (1872–1929), Russian ballet director who founded the famous Diaghilev's Ballet Russe in Paris in 1909.

David Diamond (1915–), American composer of dissonant, rhythmic music, including *Psalm* (1936), *Rounds* (1944).

Anton Dolin (1904–83), English ballet dancer and choreographer who performed with Diaghilev's Ballet Russe (1921–25) and the Ballet Theater in New York. He formed several ballet companies.

Placido Domingo (1941–), Spanish-born tenor: Operatic debut with Metropolitan Opera in 1968; also won wide audience for his recordings of popular music

Gaetano Donizetti (1797–1848), Italian composer of operas. *Lucia di Lammermoor* (1835) is his most popular creation.

Anton Dvořák (1841–1904), Czech composer whose works were strongly influenced by Bohemian folk music. He completed nine symphonies, including the New World Symphony.

Emma Eames (1865–1952), American soprano who starred at the Metropolitan Opera from 1891 to 1909. Her greatest performances were in *Tosca, Don Giovanni,* and *Aïda.*

André Eglevsky (1917–77), American ballet dancer who performed at the Ballet Russe de Monte Carlo (1939–42) and the Ballet Theater (1942–46). He was *premier danseur* at the New York City Ballet (1951–58).

Sir Edward Elgar (1857–1934), English composer whose distinctly British pieces include the five *Pomp and Circumstance* marches (1901–30) and *Enigma Variations* (1899).

Duke Ellington (1899–1974), American jazz musician and composer; best-known pieces are *Mood Indigo, Sophisticated Lady,* and *Harlem.*

Mischa Elman (1891–1967), Russian-American violinist who began his long and successful career at the age of twelve.

Manuel de Falla (1876–1946), Spanish composer whose nationalistic music includes *La Vida Breve,* (1903), *El Amor Brujo* (1915), and *Nights in the Gardens of Spain* (1916).

Geraldine Farrar (1882–1967), American soprano who enjoyed tremendous popularity during her career with the Metropolitan Opera (1906–22). Her most famous performances were in *Madame Butterfly* and *Carmen.*

Eileen Farrell (1920–), American soprano who sang on radio and in concerts before her successful opera debuts in San Francisco (1956) and at the Metropolitan Opera (1960).

Suzanne Farrell (1943–), American ballerina with the New York City Ballet in 1961–69 and since 1975.

Gabriel Fauré (1845–1924), French organist and composer whose works include the lyric drama *Pénélope* (1913).

Arthur Fiedler (1894–1979), American conductor, who led the Boston Pops Orchestra (1930–79).

Kirsten Flagstad (1895–1962), Norwegian soprano hailed as one of the greatest Wagnerian sopranos of this century. She sang at the Metropolitan Opera (1935–37; 1950–52).

Carlisle Floyd (1926–), American composer whose operas include *Susannah* (1953–54) and *The Passion of Jonathan Wade* (1962).

Mikhail Fokine (1880–1942), Russian choreographer and ballet dancer who is considered the founder of modern ballet.

Dame Margot Fonteyn (1919–), English ballerina who won international acclaim. She was *prima ballerina assoluta* of the Royal Ballet.

Lukas Foss (1922–), German-American composer of avant-garde music and a noted conductor.

Stephen Foster (1826–64), American composer of popular folk ballads, including *Oh! Susanna* (1848) and *Old Folks at Home* (1851).

Zino Francescatti (1905–), French violinist who has given concerts all over the world and is considered one of the greatest living musicians.

César Franck (1822–90), French composer and organist whose important works include the Symphony in D minor (1886–88).

Wilhelm Furtwängler (1886–1954), German conductor who led virtually all the great European orchestras as well as the New York Philharmonic.

Amelita Galli-Curci (1882–1963), Italian soprano who won wide U.S. acclaim at the Chicago (until 1942) and Metropolitan (1926–30) operas.

Mary Garden (1877–1967), Scottish soprano who became a sensational star as a result of her performances throughout Europe and with the Manhattan (1907–10) and Chicago (1910–31) operas.

George Gershwin (1898–1937), American composer of the popular song *Swanee* (1919), *Rhapsody in Blue* (1924), *Concerto in F* for piano and orchestra (1925), *An American in Paris* (1928), and the folk opera *Porgy and Bess* (1935).

Walter Gieseking (1895–1956), German pianist noted for his performances of Debussy.

Beniamino Gigli (1890–1957), Italian tenor who was regarded as Caruso's successor at the Metropolitan Opera (1920–32; 1938–39).

Mikhail I. Glinka (1804–57), Russian composer regarded as father of the Russian national school. His works include *Kamarinskaya* (1848).

Christoph Willibald von Gluck (1714–87), German composer and influential reformer of the opera. His greatest works are *Alceste* (1767) and *Iphigénie en Tauride* (1778).

Aleksandr Godunov (1949–) Russian-ballet dancer who starred with the Bolshoi Ballet of Moscow in 1971–79. He defected to the U.S. in 1979, joining the American Ballet Theatre.

Glenn Gould (1932–82), Canadian pianist best known as interpreter of keyboard music of Bach.

Morton Gould (1913–), American composer and pianist. His works, in the traditional vein, include *Latin American Symphonette* (1940).

Charles Gounod (1818–93), French composer of the well-known operas *Faust* (1859) and *Romeo and Juliette* (1867).

Martha Graham (1894–), American dancer, choreographer, director, and teacher of modern dance. She formed her own company in 1929.

Edvard Hagerup Grieg (1843–1907), Norwegian composer whose music was inspired by Norwegian folk tunes: the *Piano Concerto in A Minor* (1868) and the *Peer Gynt Suite* (1876).

Ferde Grofé (1892–1972), American composer of such works as *The Grand Canyon Suite* (1931) and *The Hudson River Suite* (1955).

Oscar Hammerstein II (1895–1960), American librettist for musicals. Wrote *The Desert Song* (1926) with Sigmund Romberg, *Show Boat* (1927) with Jerome Kern, and many with Richard Rodgers, such as *Oklahoma!* (1943), *South Pacific* (1949), *The King and I* (1951), and *The Sound of Music* (1959).

George Frideric Handel (1685–1759), German composer of baroque music. In addition to the *Messiah* (1741) and other oratorios, he wrote operas, cantatas, and chamber music.

Howard Hanson (1896–1981), American composer of

MUSICIANS *(continued)*
highly romantic works, the best known of which is the *Romantic Symphony* (1930).

Roy Harris (1898–1979), American composer whose best-known works are his *Third Symphony* (1939) and the *Cumberland Concerto* (1951).

Melissa Hayden (1923–), Canadian-born ballerina who starred with New York City Ballet in 1950–73.

Franz Joseph Haydn (1732–1809), Austrian composer who wrote the first important symphonies in the classical sonata-allegro form. He composed more than 100 symphonies and 80 string quartets.

Jascha Heifetz (1901–), Russian-American violinist and one of the foremost artists in his field. Before coming to New York (1917), he played in St. Petersburg, Kiev, Berlin, and Vienna.

Victor Herbert (1859–1924), Irish-American cellist, conductor, and composer best known for his operettas *Babes in Toyland* (1903), *Naughty Marietta* (1910), and *Sweethearts* (1913).

Paul Hindemith (1895–1963), German composer who employed highly advanced and varied methods of composition. His most important work is the symphony *Mathis der Maler* (1934).

Arthur Honegger (1892–1955), French composer whose best-known works include the tone poem *Pacific 231* (1923) and the oratorios *King David* (1921) and *Joan of Arc at the Stake* (1935).

Vladimir Horowitz (1904–), Russian-American pianist who has enjoyed great popularity during his career on the U.S. concert stage (since 1928).

Engelbert Humperdinck (1854–1921), German composer of the opera *Hansel and Gretel* (1893).

Doris Humphrey (1895–1958), dancer and choreographer who developed new dance approaches.

Vincent d'Indy (1851–1931), French composer; his masterpiece is the *Symphony Cévenole* (1886).

Charles Ives (1874–1954), American composer whose music captures the spirit of America. His works include the *Third Symphony* (1901–04) and the *Concord Sonata* (1909–15).

Robert Joffrey (1930–), American dancer, choreographer, and director of the Robert Joffrey Ballet Company, which he founded in 1956.

Um Kalthoum (1899–1975), Arab concert singer who was Egypt's most popular star from 1922 to 1972.

Herbert von Karajan (1908–), Austrian conductor who has directed the leading orchestras in Austria and Germany and has made highly successful guest appearances in the U.S.

Jerome David Kern (1885–1945), American composer of musicals, including *Show Boat* (1927).

Aram Khatchaturian (1903–78), Soviet-Armenian composer known for the lively "Sabre Dance" in his ballet *Gayane* (1924) and for his ballet *Spartacus* (1954).

Ralph Kirkpatrick (1911–), American harpsichordist and musicologist. He is an authority on the music of Domenico Scarlatti.

Zoltán Kodály (1882–1967), Hungarian composer whose music combines folk themes with a romantic style. His most famous works are the *Psalmus Hungaricus* (1923) for chorus, and the opera *Háry János* (1925–26).

André Kostelanetz (1901–80), Russian-American conductor. He directed orchestras on radio and TV for CBS and made many recordings.

Serge Koussevitzky (1874–1951), Russian conductor who directed the Russian State Symphony (1917–20), the Grand Opera of Moscow (1918–20), and the Boston Symphony Orchestra (1924–49).

Fritz Kreisler (1875–1962), Austrian-American violinist and composer who won international fame for his performances in Europe and the U.S.

Wanda Landowska (1877–1959), Polish-American harpsichordist, considered the greatest modern master

of that instrument. She is best remembered for her recording of Bach's *Well-Tempered Clavier.*

Leonid Lavrosky (1905–), Russian choreographer who directed the Leningrad Opera and Ballet (1938–44) and the Bolshoi Theater (1944–64).

Lilli Lehmann (1848–1929), German soprano and one of the foremost Wagnerian opera stars. She sang throughout Europe and with the Metropolitan Opera (1885–89; 1891–92).

Lotte Lehmann (1888–1976), German soprano who sang with the Hamburg (1909), the Vienna State (1914–38), and the New York Metropolitan (1934–45) operas. She later was stage director of the Metropolitan.

Erich Leinsdorf (1912–), Austrian-American conductor who led the New York Metropolitan Opera (1938–43; 1956–62), the Cleveland Orchestra (1943–44), the Rochester (N.Y.) Orchestra (1945–54), and the Boston Symphony (1962–69).

Ruggiero Leoncavallo (1858–1919), Italian composer whose best known work is *I Pagliacci* (1892).

Josef Lhévinne (1874–1944), Russian-American pianist and teacher who taught at the Moscow Conservatory (1902–06) and for many years at the Juilliard Graduate School in New York.

José Limón (1908–72), dancer, choreographer, and teacher who was with the Humphrey-Weidman Company and later formed his own dance group.

Jenny Lind (1820–87), Swedish soprano whose magnificent voice and dramatic ability made her the idol of opera lovers throughout Europe. She toured the U.S. from 1850 to 1852.

Franz Liszt (1811–86), Hungarian composer whose virtuosity as a pianist has never been equaled. His compositions include the *Faust Symphony* (1854–57), *Les Préludes* (1856), and 20 Hungarian rhapsodies (1851–86).

Jean Baptiste Lully (1632–87), French operatic composer who wrote the first French operas and founded the Paris Opera in 1672. His works include *Alceste* (1674), *Thésée* (1675), *Psyché* (1678), *Armide* (1686), and *Acis et Galatée* (1687).

Edward MacDowell (1861–1908), American composer whose best-known works are *Indian Suite* (1897) and the *Piano Concerto No. 2* (1890).

Gustav Mahler (1860–1911), Austrian composer and perhaps the last important member of the late Romantic school of symphonists. He wrote 10 great symphonies, the last unfinished, and the song cycle *Das Lied von der Erde* (1908).

Natalia Makarova (1940–), Russian ballerina who defected from Kirov Ballet in 1970; has since appeared with world's leading ballet companies.

Gian Francesco Malipiero (1882–), Italian composer of operas (*L'Orfeide,* 1918–21; *Guilio Cesare,* 1935), symphonies (*Impressions from Nature I, II, and III,* 1910–22), choral and chamber music.

Alicia Markova (1910–), English ballerina who achieved recognition for her performances with the Diaghilev Ballet Russe (1925–32); the Vic-Wells Ballet (1932–35), where she was prima ballerina; and the Ballet Russe de Monte Carlo (1938–41).

Giovanni Martinelli (1885–1969), Italian tenor who made his debut in Milan (1910) and sang at the Metropolitan Opera (1913–46) in over 50 leading roles.

Pietro Mascagni (1863–1945), Italian composer whose best-known work is *Cavalleria rusticana* (1890).

Jules Massenet (1842–1912), French composer of over 20 operas, including *Manon* (1884), *Werther* (1892), *Thaïs* (1894), and *Don Quichotte* (1910).

Léonide Massine (1896–1979), Russian-American ballet dancer and choreographer who worked with Diaghilev's Ballet Russe (1914–20), the Ballet Russe de Monte Carlo (1932–42), and the Ballet Theater in New York (1942–44).

Patricia McBride (1942–), American-born ballerina; principal dancer with New York City ballet since 1959.

John McCormack (1884–1945), Irish-American tenor. A major operatic star in London and New York, he confined his last years to concerts.

Zubin Mehta (1936–), Indian-American conductor of the New York Philharmonic Orchestra, appointed in 1978.

Dame Nellie Melba (1859–1931), Australian soprano who sang with tremendous success in Brussels (1887), London (1889), Paris (1889–91), and New York (1893–96; 1907–20).

Lauritz Melchior (1890–1973), Danish tenor who appeared in Copenhagen (1913–21), Bayreuth (1925–26), and at the Metropolitan Opera (1926–50), where he was the leading Wagnerian tenor.

Felix Mendelssohn (1809–47), German composer whose beautiful music includes the Overture to *A Midsummer Night's Dream* (1826), the *Scotch Symphony* (1830–42), a violin concerto (1844), the opera *Elijah* (1846), and chamber music.

Peter Mennin (1923–83), American composer who was president of the Juilliard School of Music since 1962. Among his works are seven symphonies and eight choral works.

Gian-Carlo Menotti (1911–), Italian-American composer best known for his operas *Amahl and the Night Visitors* (1951) and *The Saint of Bleecker Street* (1954), which won a Pulitzer Prize in 1955.

Yehudi Menuhin (1916–), American violinist who gave his first concert at the age of seven.

Robert Merrill (1917–), American baritone at the Metropolitan Opera since the early 1950s.

Giacomo Meyerbeer (1791–1864), German composer and master of the French grand opera. Among his works are *Les Huguenots* (1836) and *L'Africaine* (1838–63).

Darius Milhaud (1892–1974), French composer best known for his operas *Le Pauvre Matelot* (1926) and *Christophe Colombe* (1928).

Dimitri Mitropoulos (1896–1960), Greek conductor who led the Paris Symphony (1932), the Minneapolis Symphony (1937–49), and the New York Philharmonic (1950–58).

Igor Moiseyev (1906–), Russian dancer and choreographer who was with the Bolshoi Theatre (1924–39). In 1936 he organized the Moiseyev Dance Company.

Pierre Monteux (1875–1964), French conductor who directed the Metropolitan Opera (1917–19), the Boston Symphony (1919–24), the Paris Symphony (1928–35), the San Francisco Symphony (1935–52), and the London Symphony (1962–64).

Claudio Monteverdi (1567–1643), Italian composer credited with writing the first significant operas, including *Orfeo* (1607), *The Return of Ulysses* (1641), and *The Coronation of Poppea* (1642).

Grace Moore (1901–47), American soprano who sang at the Metropolitan Opera (1928–32, 1934–35, 1937–39) and made several films. She was killed in a plane crash at the height of her career.

Wolfgang Amadeus Mozart (1756–91), Austrian composer who epitomized the classical tradition with 41 symphonies, over 30 piano concertos, concertos for other instruments, chamber music, masses, and such operas as *Don Giovanni* (1787) and *The Magic Flute* (1791).

Charles Münch (1891–1968), French conductor who directed the Paris Philharmonic Orchestra (1938–46), the Boston Symphony (1949–62), and the Berkshire Music Center (1951–62).

Patrice Munsel (1925–), American soprano who made her debut at the Metropolitan Opera in 1943 and has also appeared in films.

Modest Mussorgsky (1839–81), Russian composer whose best-known work is the opera *Boris Godunov* (1874).

Bronislava Nijinska (1891–1971), Russian dancer and choreographer associated with the Diaghilev Ballet Russe until 1924.

Vaslav Nijinsky (1890–1950), Russian ballet dancer considered by many to be the greatest of all time. He began dancing at the age of 10. He performed with the Diaghilev Ballet Russe (1909–17) until he was committed to an insane asylum.

Birgit Nilsson (1918–), Swedish singer considered the greatest living Wagnerian soprano. Her triumphant debut at the Metropolitan Opera (1959) made front-page news.

Lillian Nordica (1857–1914), American soprano most famous for her Wagnerian roles. In addition to many appearances in Europe, she starred at the Metropolitan Opera from 1893 to 1909.

Rudolf Nureyev (1938–), Russian ballet dancer who has been called a second Nijinsky. He starred with the Kirov Ballet before defecting to the West in 1961 while on a trip to London. Since then Nureyev has been the principal dancer and choreographer for the Royal Ballet.

Jacques Offenbach (1819–80), French composer of over 100 operettas. His masterpiece is the opera *Tales of Hoffmann* (1877–80), which was not produced until after his death.

David Oistrakh (1908–74), Russian violinist hailed as one of the greatest 20th century musicians.

Carl Orff (1895–1982), German composer: best known for cantata *Carmina Burana* (1936).

Eugene Ormandy (1899–1985), Hungarian-American conductor who came to the U.S. in 1920. He led the Minneapolis Symphony (1931–35) and the Philadelphia Orchestra (1936–80).

Seiji Ozawa (1935–), Japanese conductor: conductor of Toronto Symphony in 1965–69; music director of San Francisco Symphony in 1968–76; artistic and music director of Boston Symphony Orchestra from 1973.

Ignace Jan Paderewski (1860–1941), Polish pianist and composer who enjoyed tremendous international popularity as a performer. His best-known composition is the *Minuet in G* for piano (1899).

Niccolò Paganini (1782–1840), Italian violinist considered the world's greatest violin virtuoso. He charmed audiences throughout Europe.

Giovanni Palestrina (1524–94), Italian composer of polyphonic sacred motets and masses and of secular madrigals. His works rank among the most important of the Italian Renaissance.

Luciano Pavarotti, (1935–), Italian tenor: Made operatic debut in Reggio Emilia, Italy, in 1961; debuted with the New York Metropolitan Opera on Nov. 23, 1968.

Anna Pavlova (1881–1931), Russian ballerina who won international recognition for her magnificent performances in Europe and America.

Jan Peerce (1904–84), American tenor who sang on radio and at the Radio City Music Hall (1932–37) before joining the Metropolitan Opera in 1941.

Roberta Peters (1930–), American operatic soprano: debuted with Metropolitan Opera in 1950; recorded operas; appeared in several motion pictures.

Gregor Piatigorsky (1903–76), Russian-born concert cellist, made his American debut in 1929. He became a U.S. citizen in 1942.

Ezio Pinza (1892–1957), Italian basso who sang at the Metropolitan Opera (1926–48). In 1949 he was featured in the Broadway musical *South Pacific.*

Walter Piston (1894–1976), American composer who was awarded two Pulitzer Prizes in music for his Third (1948) and Seventh (1961) symphonies.

Ildebrando Pizzetti (1880–1968), Italian composer whose operas *Fedra* (1909–12) and *Debora e Jaele* (1915–21) are his most popular works.

Lily Pons (1904–76), French soprano who sang at the Metropolitan Opera from 1931 to 1959.

Rosa Ponselle (1897–1981), American soprano who

MUSICIANS *(continued)*

gave outstanding performances at the Metropolitan Opera (1918–37) and in London (1929–31).

Cole Porter (1893–1964), American composer of musical comedies, including *Kiss Me, Kate* (1948) and *Silk Stockings* (1955), and the songs *Night and Day* and *Begin the Beguine.*

Francis Poulenc (1899–1963), French composer whose works include *Concert Champêtre* (1927–28) and the Mass in G (1937).

Andre Previn (1929–), American conductor, composer, pianist: conductor Houston Symphony Orchestra (1966–69), London Symphony Orchestra (1968–79), Los Angeles Philharmonic from 1985.

Leontyne Price (1927–), American soprano who has sung on Broadway and in major opera houses. She made her debut with the Metropolitan Opera in 1961.

William Primrose (1903–82), Scottish violist regarded as one of the world's finest.

Sergei Prokofiev (1891–1953), Russian composer and piano virtuoso. His distinctive works include the First (1916–17) and Fifth (1944) symphonies, *Peter and the Wolf* (1936), and the ballet *Romeo and Juliette* (1935–36).

Giacomo Puccini (1858–1924), Italian composer of the universally popular operas *La Bohème* (1896), *Tosca* (1900), and *Madame Butterfly* (1904).

Henry Purcell (1659–95), English composer believed by some authorities to be England's greatest. His works include the opera *Dido and Aeneas* (1689) and religious music.

Sergei Rachmaninov (1873–1943), Russian composer and pianist. Among his best works are the Second Piano Concerto (1901), the Second Symphony (1907), and Rhapsody on a Theme of Paganini (1934).

Maurice Ravel (1875–1937), French composer whose works include the ballet *Daphnis et Chloé* (1909–11) and *Rhapsodie Espagnole* (1907) and *Bolero* (1928) for orchestra.

Fritz Reiner (1888–1963), Hungarian conductor who directed the Cincinnati Orchestra (1922–31), the Pittsburgh Orchestra (1938–48), and the Chicago Orchestra (1953–62).

Ottorino Respighi (1879–1936), Italian composer known for his symphonic poems *The Fountains of Rome* (1917) and *The Pines of Rome* (1924).

Sviatoslav Richter (1914–), Russian pianist acclaimed as a distinguished virtuoso.

Wallingford Riegger (1885–1961), American composer of highly original works, including four symphonies and Music for Brass Choir (1948–49).

Nicholas Rimsky-Korsakov (1844–1908), Russian nationalist composer of the *Spanish Capriccio* (1887), *Scheherazade* (1888), and *Easter Overture* (1888).

Jerome Robbins (1918–), American dancer and choreographer who joined the Ballet Theater in New York (1940–44) and in 1959 became associate musical director of the New York City Ballet.

Paul Robeson (1898–1976), American black concert singer and actor, noted for his singing in *Showboat* (1936) and as the Moor in *Othello.*

Richard Rodgers (1902–79), American composer of musicals. Teamed with librettist Oscar Hammerstein II on many, including *Oklahoma!* (1943), *South Pacific* (1949), *The King and I* (1951), and *The Sound of Music* (1959).

Sigmund Romberg (1887–1951), American composer of operettas and musicals, including *The Student Prince* (1924) and *The Desert Song* (1926).

Gioacchino Rossini (1792–1868), Italian composer best known for his operas *The Barber of Seville* (1816) and *William Tell* (1829).

Anton Rubenstein (1829–94), Russian pianist and composer whose renowned mastery of the keyboard ranked second only to that of Liszt.

Arthur Rubinstein (1887–1982), Polish-American musician considered one of the greatest pianists.

Ruth St. Denis (1877–1968), American dancer, choreographer, and pioneer in the development of modern dance in the U.S.

Charles Camille Saint-Saëns (1835–1921), French composer of the opera *Samson et Dalila* (1868–75), three symphonies, and five piano concertos.

Alessandro Scarlatti (1660–1725), Italian composer of 115 operas.

Domenico Scarlatti (1685–1757), Italian composer and harpsichordist; son of A. Scarlatti. His roughly 500 sonatas are among the first important keyboard works written in this form.

Alexander Schneider (1908–), Russian-American violinist and conductor. A member of the Budapest String Quartet (1938–68), he is also a major participant in the Casals summer music festivals.

Arnold Schoenberg (1874–1951), Austrian composer and creator of the 12-tone (atonal) method. His works include *Verklärte Nacht* (1899), the Variations for Orchestra (1928), and an unfinished opera, *Moses und Aron* (1932–51).

Franz Schubert (1797–1828), Austrian composer of over 600 songs; nine symphonies, of which the "Unfinished" (1822) is best known; and the "Trout" Quintet in A Major (1819).

William Schuman (1910–), American composer; president of Lincoln Center in New York (1962–68). His works include the *American Festival Overture* (1939).

Robert Schumann (1810–56), German romantic composer of the Piano Concerto in A Minor (1841–45) and the Spring (1841) and Rhenish (1850) symphonies.

Ernestine Schumann-Heink (1861–1936), Austrian-American contralto. She appeared at the Chicago Opera (1898), the Metropolitan Opera (1899–1904), and in many concerts.

Antonio Scotti (1866–1936), Italian baritone who enjoyed great popularity as a member of the Metropolitan Opera (1899–1933).

Aleksandr Scriabin (1872–1915), Russian pianist whose notable works include *Divine Poem* (1903) and *Prometheus: A Poem of Fire* (1909–10).

Andrés Segovia (1893–), Spanish guitarist noted for his interpretation of classical works.

Marcella Sembrich (1858–1935), Polish soprano who sang in the great European opera houses and with the Metropolitan Opera (1898–1909).

Peter Serkin (1947–), American pianist and son of Rudolf Serkin. He is among the most accomplished of the younger keyboard artists.

Rudolf Serkin (1903–), Austrian-American pianist who ranks among the best contemporary artists. He has toured widely and since 1951 has directed the Marlboro (Vt.) School of Music.

Roger Sessions (1896–85), American composer: Orchestral Suite from *The Black Maskers* (1928) and four symphonies (1927, 1946, 1957, 1958); won 1982 Pulitzer Prize for *Concerts for Orchestra.*

Ted Shawn (1891–1972), American dancer, choreographer, and teacher. With Ruth St. Denis he founded the influential Denishawn School for Modern Dance.

Dimitri Shostakovich (1906–75), Russian composer who won international acclaim with such symphonies as the Fifth (1937) and Ninth (1945).

Jean Sibelius (1865–1957), Finnish composer of stirring nationalist music and seven symphonies.

Cesare Siepi (1923–), Italian bass and a member of the New York Metropolitan Opera since 1950.

Beverly Sills (1929–), American soprano, made her debut with the New York City Opera in 1955 and with the Metropolitan Opera in 1975; appointed director of New York City Opera in 1978.

Bedrich Smetana (1824–84), Czech nationalist composer whose well-known works include the opera *The*

Bartered Bride (1866) and the symphonic poem *My Country* (1874–79).

Sir Georg Solti (1912–), British conductor: born in Hungary; music director of Munich State Opera (1946–52); conductor of the British Royal Opera House from 1961; music director of the Chicago Symphony Orchestra from 1969; conductor of the London Philharmonic Orchestra from 1979.

Michael Somes (1917–), English ballet dancer who began his career with the Sadler's Wells Ballet Company in 1935 and was a leading dancer with the Royal Ballet in London.

John Philip Sousa (1854–1932), American band-master and composer of over 100 marches including *The Stars and Stripes Forever* (1897).

Eleanor Steber (1916–), American soprano who sang with the Metropolitan Opera from 1940.

William Steinberg (1899–1978), German–American conductor of the Pittsburgh Symphony (1952–75) and Boston Symphony (1969–71) orchestras.

Issac Stern (1920–), American violinist who has given outstanding performances throughout the world.

Risë Stevens (1913–), American mezzo-soprano who sang throughout the world and with the Metropolitan Opera from the 1930s through the 1950s.

Karlheinz Stockhausen (1928–), German composer whose avant-garde works include *Kontrapunkte* (1952) and *Koutackte* (1960) for electronic sounds, percussion, and piano.

Leopold Stokowski (1882–1977), American conductor who led the Cincinnati Symphony (1909–12), the Philadelphia Orchestra (1912–36), and the New York Philharmonic (1945–50). In 1962 he founded the American Symphony in New York.

Johann Strauss Jr. (1825–99), Austrian conductor and composer of more than 400 waltzes, including *The Blue Danube* (1866) and *Tales from the Vienna Woods* (1868).

Richard Strauss (1864–1949), German composer whose major works are the symphonic poems *Don Juan* (1888) and *Till Eulenspiegel* (1894–95) and the opera *Der Rosenkavalier* (1911).

Igor Stravinsky (1882–1971), Russian–French composer considered the father of modern music. Among his most important works are the ballets *The Firebird* (1910) and *The Rite of Spring* (1913).

Sir Arthur Sullivan (1842–1900), English composer (with W. S. Gilbert) of operettas, including *H.M.S. Pinafore* (1878) and *The Mikado* (1885).

Joan Sutherland (1926–), Australian soprano. In 1961 she made a spectacular debut at the Metropolitan Opera.

George Szell (1897–1970), Hungarian conductor who led the Berlin State Opera (1924–30), the Metropolitan Opera (1942–45), and the Cleveland Orchestra (1946–70).

Maria Tallchief (1925–), American ballerina who danced with the Ballet Russe de Monte Carlo (1942–47) and was the prima ballerina at the New York City Ballet (1954–55) and at the American Ballet Theatre (1960).

Deems Taylor (1885–1966), American composer: *Through the Looking Glass* (1922) for orchestra, and the opera *The King's Henchmen* (1927).

Paul Taylor (1930–), American dancer and choreographer who performed with the Martha Graham Company (1955–61) and the New York City Ballet (1959–61).

Peter Ilich Tchaikovsky (1840–93), Russian composer. His works include six symphonies, the *Romeo and Juliet Overture* (1870), the Piano Concerto in B Flat Minor (1875), the ballet *Swan Lake* (1876), and a concerto for violin and orchestra.

Renata Tebaldi (1922–), Italian soprano who has performed in Milan (1949–54, 1959), London (1950), San Francisco (1950), and at the Metropolitan Opera (since 1955).

Twyla Tharp (1941–), American choreographer who uses popular and jazz music to blend ballet with modern dance.

Virgil Thomson (1896–), American composer of the opera *Four Saints in Three Acts* (1928).

Lawrence Tibbett (1896–1960), American baritone who starred at the Metropolitan Opera (1923–50) and in several films.

Arturo Toscanini (1867–1957), Italian conductor renowned for his artistry. He led the orchestras at the La Scala Opera (1898–1903) and Metropolitan Opera (1908–15), and the New York Philharmonic (1927–36) and NBC Symphony (1937-54).

Helen Traubel (1899–1972), American soprano who excelled in Wagnerian roles at the Metropolitan Opera (1939–53), and sang with leading orchestras.

Richard Tucker (1914–75), American tenor who starred with the Metropolitan Opera (1945–75).

Antony Tudor (1909–), English dancer and choreographer who worked with the Rambert Ballet (1930–38), Sadler's Wells Ballet (1931–36), and American Ballet Theater (1939–56). He became ballet director of the Metropolitan Opera in 1957.

Galina Ulanova (1910–), Russian ballerina considered one of the greatest dancers since Anna Pavlova. She appeared with the Bolshoi Theatre from 1935, becoming prima ballerina in 1944.

Ralph Vaughan Williams (1872–1958), English composer. *Three Norfolk Rhapsodies* (1905–07) and the opera *Hugh the Drover* (1911–14).

Giuseppe Verdi (1813–1901), Italian composer of such well-known operas as *Rigoletto* (1851), *La Traviata* (1853), *Don Carlos* (1867), *Aïda* (1871), *Otello* (1886), and *Falstaff* (1893).

Heitor Villa-Lobos (1887–1959), Brazilian composer: *Amazonas* (1917), the *Bachiana brasileira* (1930), and the Chorós No. 11 (1941).

Antonio Vivaldi (1675–1741), Italian composer of over 40 operas who is best-known for his violin concertos *The Seasons* and the *Tempesta di Màre*.

Richard Wagner (1813–83), German romantic opera composer. *Tannhäuser* (1843–45), *Lohengrin* (1846–48), and *Die Meistersinger* (1862–67).

Bruno Walter (1876–1962), German conductor who directed the New York Philharmonic (1923–33, 1947–49).

Sir William Walton (1902–83), British composer whose works include the oratoria *Belshazzar's Feast* (1931) and the opera *Troilus and Cressida* (1954).

Leonard Warren (1911–60), American baritone who won acclaim at the Metropolitan Opera (1939–60), where he died onstage.

André Watts (1943–), American pianist who made his debut at the age of nine and has played with numerous major orchestras.

Carl Maria von Weber (1786–1826), German composer who began the Romantic movement in German opera. Among his operas are *Der Freischütz* (1821) and *Oberon* (1826).

Anton von Webern (1883–1945), Austrian composer and pupil of Arnold Schoenberg. A leading atonal composer, he is best known for *Five Pieces for Orchestra* (1911–13) and *Variations* (1940).

Charles Weidman (1901–75), American dancer, choreographer, and director who helped develop modern dance; founded own company in 1941.

Kurt Weill (1900–50), German composer for the stage. *The Threepenny Opera* (1928), *One Touch of Venus* (1943), and *Street Scene* (1947).

Hugo Wolf (1860–1903), Austrian composer known for more than 250 songs composed by setting the poems of others to music.

Igor Youskevitch (1912–), Russian ballet dancer with the Ballet Russe de Monte Carlo (1938) and the Ballet Theater in New York (1946–56).

FAMOUS PAINTERS, SCULPTORS, AND ARCHITECTS

Famous artists, sculptors, architects, and painters are included in the following list. Where it was thought helpful to the reader, the artist is described according to the movement or school to which he belonged. In most cases one or more works typical of each artist's output are mentioned. See pages 981–986 for 1985 deaths.

A glossary describing the artistic movements and schools mentioned in connection with many of the artists can be found on page 68.

Leone Battista Alberti (1404–72), Florentine architect and a pioneer in Renaissance church design: the Church of Sant'Andrea (1470) in Mantua.

Andrea del Sarto (1486–1531), Florentine painter of religious frescoes: *The Birth of the Virgin* (1514).

Fra Angelico (c.1400–55), Florentine painter of religious subjects: *Annunciation* (c.1440–50).

Alexander Archipenko (1887–1964), Ukrainian-American abstract sculptor: *Boxers* (1935).

Jean Arp (1887–1966), French surrealist and Dadaist painter and sculptor: *Constellation According to the Laws of Chance* (1932), wood relief.

John James Audubon (1785?–1851), American ornithologist and artist noted for his finely detailed illustrations of American wildlife: *The Birds of America* (1827–38).

Francis Bacon (1910–), English surrealist painter: *Study After Velázquez's Portrait of Pope Innocent X* (1953).

James Barry (1741–1806), Anglo-Irish painter: *The Progress of Human Culture* (1777–83).

Fra Bartolommeo (1475–1517), Italian painter of the High Renaissance: *Marriage of St. Catherine.*

Aubrey Vincent Beardsley (1872–98), English illustrator in black and white: *Isolde* (c.1890).

Max Beckmann (1884–1950), German expressionist painter: *Self-portrait with a Saxophone* (1930).

Giovanni Bellini (c.1430–1516), Venetian religious painter: *St. Francis in Ecstasy* (c.1485).

George Wesley Bellows (1882–1925), American realistic painter: *Stag at Sharkey's* (1907), *Up the Hudson* (1908).

Thomas Hart Benton (1889–1975), American regional painter: *Lonesome Road, Cotton Pickers.*

Giovanni Lorenzo Bernini (1598–1680), Italian baroque sculptor: *David* (1623), *Ecstasy of St. Teresa* (1645–52).

George Caleb Bingham (1811–79), American regional painter: *The County Election* (c.1851).

Umberto Boccioni (1882–1916), Italian futurist painter and sculptor: *The City Rises* (1910).

Giovanni da Bologna (1524–1608), French-born mannerist sculptor who worked in Florence: *The Rape of the Sabines* (1583).

Pierre Bonnard (1867–1947) French postimpressionist painter: *Man and Woman* (1900), *Nude Washing* (c.1922).

Francesco Borromini (1599–1677), Italian baroque architect: San Carlo alle Quattro Fontane, in Rome (begun in 1638).

Hieronymus Bosch or **Jerome Bos** (c.1450–1516), Flemish painter of bizarre fantasies: *The Garden of Delights* (1500).

Sandro Botticelli (Alessandro di Mariano dei Filipepi, c.1444–1510), Florentine religious and allegorical painter: *Primavera* (1477–78), *The Birth of Venus* (c.1480).

Edmé Bouchardon (1698–1762), French sculptor of religious subjects and portrait busts: *Christ Leaning on His Cross* (1745).

François Boucher (1703–70), French rococo painter: *The Triumph of Venus* (1740).

Constantin Brancusi (1876–1957), Romanian abstract sculptor: *The Kiss* (1908), *Bird in Space* (1919).

Georges Braque (1882–1963), French cubist painter: *Still Life, "Melody"* (1914), *The Bike* (1952).

Il Bronzino (Agnolo di Cosimo di Mariano, 1503–72), Florentine mannerist painter: *Eleanor de Toledo and Her Son* (c.1550).

Pieter Bruegel the Elder (c.1525–69), Flemish landscape painter: *The Return of the Hunters* (1565), *Peasant Wedding* (1565).

Filippo Brunelleschi (1377–1446), Florentine architect who produced the first important early Renaissance architecture: dome for the cathedral in Florence (1420–36).

Bernard Buffet (1928–), French painter whose work derives from several modern schools: *Landscape in Provence* (1957).

Charles Burchfield (1893–1967), American painter of landscapes and urban scenes, especially in watercolor: *Ice Glare* (1933).

Edward Coley Burne-Jones (1833–98), English Pre-Raphaelite painter: *Love Among the Ruins* (1894).

Alexander Calder (1898–1976), American abstract sculptor who introduced the mobile and the stabile forms: *Lobster Trap and Fish Tail* (1939).

Antonio Canova (1757–1822), Venetian neoclassic sculptor: *Pauline Bonaparte Borghese* (1808).

Michelangelo Merisi da Caravaggio (1573–1610), Italian baroque painter: *Calling of St. Matthew* (1598–99).

Jean Baptiste Carpeaux (1827–75), French romantic sculptor: *The Dance* (in Paris Opéra, 1865–69).

Mary Cassatt (1845–1926), American impressionist painter: *Mother and Child at a Boating Party.*

Andrea del Castagno (c.1423–57), Florentine religious painter: *Last Supper* (1445–50).

Benvenuto Cellini (1500–71), Italian mannerist sculptor: *Perseus with the Head of Medusa* (c.1545).

Paul Cézanne (1839–1906), French painter who began the postimpressionist movement: *Fruit Bowl, Glass and Apples* (1879–82), *Mont Sainte-Victoire Seen from Bibemus Quarry* (1898–1900).

Marc Chagall (1889–1985), Russian expressionist painter: *I and the Village* (1911), *The Grey House* (1917).

Jean Baptiste Chardin (1699–1779), French genre painter: *Return from Market* (1739).

Giorgio de Chirico (1888–1978), Italian surrealist painter: *The Anguish of Departure* (1913–14).

Frederick Edwin Church (1826–1900), American landscape painter: *Niagara Falls* (1857), *The Heart of the Andes* (1859); his *Icebergs* (1861) was sold in 1979 for record price of $2.5 million.

Giovanni Cimabue (Cenni di Pepo, c.1240–1302), Florentine painter of religious frescoes: *Madonna of St. Francis,* in the church at Assisi.

Claude Lorrain (1600–82), French landscape painter: *View of the Campagna* (c.1650).

Clodion (Claude Michel, 1738–1814), French rococo sculptor: *Bacchante and a Satyr, Montesquieu* (1779–83).

Thomas Cole (1801–48), American landscape painter and member of the Hudson River School: *The Oxbow of the Connecticut* (1836).

John Constable (1776–1837), English landscape painter: *Hampstead Heath* (1821).

John Singleton Copley (1738–1815), American painter of portraits (*Mrs. Thomas Boylston, 1766*) and romanticized historic works (*Watson and the Shark, 1778*).

Jean Baptiste Camille Corot (1796–1875), French romantic landscape painter: *The Bridge at Narni (1826), Homer and the Shepherds* (1845).

Correggio (Antonio Allegri, 1494–1534), Italian mannerist painter: *Assumption of the Virgin* (c.1525), *Jupiter and Io* (c.1532).

Gustave Courbet (1819–77), French realist painter: *The Stone Breakers* (1849), *Painter's Studio* (1855).

Lucas I. Cranach (1472–1553), German painter, etcher, and woodcut designer: Made portraits of notable contemporaries, including Martin Luther.

John Steuart Curry (1897–1946), American artist who painted scenes of Midwestern life: *Baptism in Kansas* (1928), *Tornado over Kansas* (1929).

Salvador Dali (1904–), Spanish surrealist painter: *Persistence of Memory* (1931).

Honoré Daumier (1808–79), French painter, sculptor, and caricaturist of the realist school: *The Third-Class Carriage* (1862), *Don Quixote Attacking the Windmills* (1866).

Jacques Louis David (1748–1825), French neoclassic painter: *The Death of Marat* (1793), *The Rape of the Sabines* (1799).

Leonardo da Vinci (1452–1519), Italian painter, architect, and sculptor: Was influential leader of Renaissance art. Paintings include *Last Supper* (c.1495–97) and *Mona Lisa* (c.1503–05). He was also an innovator and inventor in the physical sciences and engineering.

Stuart Davis (1894–1964), U.S. semiabstract painter: *The Barber Shop* (1930), *Visa* (1951).

Edgar Degas (1834–1917), French impressionist painter: *Prima Ballerina* (1876), *Absinthe Drinkers* (1876), *Ballet Class* (c.1878).

Willem de Kooning (1904–), Dutch-American abstract expressionist painter: *Woman I* (1950–52).

Ferdinand Victor Eugène Delacroix (1798–1863), French romantic painter: *Massacre of Scio* (1822–24), *Frédéric Chopin* (1838).

André Derain (1880–1954), French fauvist painter: *Seascape* and *Collioure* (both c.1905).

Donatello (Donato di Niccolò di Betto Bardi, c.1386–1466), Florentine sculptor of the Renaissance: statues include *St. Mark* (1411–13); panels include *St. George and the Dragon* (1415–17).

Jean Dubuffet (1901–85), French surrealist painter: *Landscape with Two Personages* (1952).

Marcel Duchamp (1887–1968), French cubist and Dadaist painter: *Nude Descending a Staircase* (1913).

Raoul Dufy (1877–1953), French painter influenced by the impressionists and fauvists: *Casino at Nice* (1927), *Deauville, Drying the Sails* (1933).

Albrecht Dürer (1471–1528), German Renaissance painter and engraver: *The Four Horsemen of the Apocalypse* (1497–98).

Thomas Eakins (1844–1916), American realist painter: *The Gross Clinic* (1875).

Charles Eames (1907-78), U.S. architect and designer: Responsible for first mass-produced molded plastic chair used in many public waiting rooms; his luxury lounge chairs regarded as ultimate in comfort.

Sir Jacob Epstein (1880–1959), American sculptor: the Oscar Wilde Memorial (1911), *Adam, Jacob and the Angel* (1939).

Max Ernst (1891–1976), German-American surrealist painter: *Two Children Are Threatened by a Nightingale* (1924), *Euclid* (1945).

Lyonel Feininger (1871–1956), American cubist painter: *Church in the Market Place* (1929).

Jean Honoré Fragonard (1732–1806), French rococo painter: *The Swing* (c.1765); *The Progress of Love* (c.1771), a series of painted panels.

Thomas Gainsborough (1727–88), English landscape and portrait painter: *Robert Andrews and His Wife* (c.1748–50), *The Mall* (1783).

Paul Gauguin (1848–1903), French postimpressionist painter: *The Yellow Christ* (1890).

Jean Louis André Théodore Géricault (1791–1824),

French romantic painter: *Mounted Officer of the Imperial Guard* (1812), *Raft of the Medusa* (1818–19).

Lorenzo Ghiberti (c.1378–1455), Florentine sculptor of religious subjects: *The Sacrifice of Isaac*, (1401–02), a set of bronze doors for the Baptistery in Florence.

Domenico Ghirlandaio (1449–94), Florentine painter of religious subjects: *Saint Jerome* (1480).

Alberto Giacometti (1901–66), Swiss sculptor, mainly of the surrealist school: *The Palace at 4 A.M.* (1932–33), *Man Pointing* (1947).

Giorgione (c.1478–1510), Venetian painter who influenced art in Venice: *The Tempest*.

Giotto (di Bondone, c.1266–1337), Florentine artist generally considered one of the founders of modern, naturalist painting: religious frescoes in the Arena Chapel in Padua (1305–06).

William James Glackens (1870–1938), American realist painter: *Chez Mouquin* (1905).

Arshile Gorky (1904–48), American abstract expressionist painter: *Agony* (1947).

Francisco José de Goya y Lucientes (1746–1828), Spanish painter, etcher, and lithographer whose work covers a wide range, from official portraits to satire: *The Family of Charles IV* (1800), *The Third of May, 1808* (1814–15).

El Greco (Domenikos Theotokopoulos, c.1541–1614), Greek mannerist painter who spent most of his career in Spain: *Burial of the Count of Orgaz* (1586), *View of Toledo*.

Juan Gris (1887–1927), Spanish cubist painter: *Still Life Before an Open Window* (1915).

George Grosz (1893–1959), German-American expressionist painter: *Germany, A Winter's Tale* (1918).

Mathias Grünewald (c.1480–1528), German Gothic painter: *Isenheim Altarpiece* (c.1510–15).

Francesco Guardi (1712–93), Venetian landscape painter, especially scenes of the city: *Venice, Piazza San Marco* (1765).

Frans Hals (c.1580–1666), Dutch portrait and genre painter: *The Jolly Toper* (1627), *Malle Bobbe* (c.1650).

William M. Hartnett (1848–92), American still-life painter: *The Social Club* (1879).

Meindert Hobbema (1638–1709), Dutch landscape painter: *Avenue at Middelharnis* (1689).

Hans Hofmann (1880–1966), German-American abstract expressionist painter: *Elegy* (1950).

William Hogarth (1697–1764), English painter and engraver who did satiric studies of English society: *The Rake's Progress* (c.1735).

Katsushika Hokusai (1760–1849), Japanese painter whose work influenced Western landscape art: *Views of Famous Bridges* (1823–35), *Hundred Views of Mount Fuji* (1835).

Hans Holbein the Younger (c.1497–1543), German portrait painter: *Erasmus of Rotterdam* (c.1523), *Sir Thomas More* (1527), *Henry VIII* (1540).

Winslow Homer (1836–1910), American romantic painter, especially of seascapes: *The Gulfstream* (1889), *Breaking Storm* and *Maine Coast* (1894).

Pieter de Hooch (c.1629–84), Dutch genre painter: *Delft After the Explosion* (1654).

Edward Hopper (1882–1967), American regional painter and engraver: *Early Sunday Morning* (1930), *Night Hawks* (1942).

Jean Antoine Houdon (1741–1828), French neoclassic sculptor: *Morpheus* (1777), *Girl Shivering* (1783).

Jean Auguste Dominique Ingres (1780–1867), French neoclassic painter: *Vow of Louis XIII* (1824).

George Inness (1825–94), American landscape painter: *Delaware Valley* (1865), *Niagara* (1889).

Augustus John (1878–1961), English landscape and portrait painter: *The Marchesa Casati* (1919), *An Irish Bay* (1911–14).

PAINTERS, SCULPTORS, AND ARCHITECTS *(continued)*

Jasper Johns (1930–), American pop artist: *Map* (1962).

Philip Cortelyou Johnson (1906–), American architect who helped plan the Seagram Building and Lincoln Center, both in New York City.

Inigo Jones (1573–1652), English architect deeply influenced by Italian Renaissance styles: the banquet hall at Whitehall Palace (1619–22).

Vasili Kandinsky (1866–1944), Russian painter who originated modern abstract painting, or tachisme: *Black Patch* (1921), *Movement I* (1935).

Rockwell Kent (1882–1971), American illustrator and painter: illustrated *Moby Dick, Beowulf,* and *The Canterbury Tales.*

Paul Klee (1879–1940), Swiss painter of fantastic, often humorous subjects: *The Twittering Machine* (1922), *Park Near Lucerne* (1938).

Franz Kline (1910–62), American abstract expressionist painter, best known for an extensive series of paintings which he numbered rather than giving them titles.

Oskar Kokoschka (1886–1980), Austrian expressionist painter: *Hans Tietze and His Wife* (1909).

Le Corbusier (Charles Edouard Jeanneret, 1887–1965), Franco-Swiss architect who was a major influence on modern architecture: Savoye House, Poissy, France (1929–31), Secretariat Building, Chandigarh, India (1952–56).

Doris Emrick Lee (1905–), American painter: *Thanksgiving* (1935).

Fernand Léger (1881–1955), French cubist painter: *The City* (1919), *Women in an Interior* (1922).

Emanuel Gottlieb Leutze (1816–68), German-American historical painter: *Washington Crossing the Delaware* (1851).

Roy Lichtenstein (1923–), American pop artist: *Step-on Can with Leg,* a diptych (1961).

Jacques Lipchitz (1891–1973), French-Lithuanian sculptor whose works bear cubist influences: *Man with a Guitar* (1915).

Fra Filippo Lippi (c.1406–69), Italian painter of religious subjects: *Madonna with Saints* (c.1432).

Richard Lippold (1915–), American abstract sculptor, best known for his elaborate wire constructions: *The Sun* (1953–56).

Aristide Maillol (1861–1944), French sculptor of the female nude: *Seated Woman* (c.1901).

Édouard Manet (1832–83), French painter usually associated with the impressionist movement: *Luncheon on the Grass* (1863), *The Fife Player* (1866).

John Marin (1870–1953), American expressionist painter best known for watercolors: *Maine Islands* (1922), *Gray Sea* (1924).

Masaccio (Tommaso Guidi, c.1401–28), Florentine painter of frescoes in Italian churches: *Madonna and Child* (1426).

Henri Matisse (1869–1954), French painter and leader of the fauvist movement: *The Joy of Life* (1905–06), *Harmony in Red* (1908–09).

Michelangelo Buonarroti (1475–1564), Italian painter, sculptor, and architect who was a leading figure in Renaissance art. His most famous paintings include the frescoes in the Sistine Chapel. Among his many statues are those of *David* (1501–04) and *Moses* (c.1513–15). He is generally considered the greatest sculptor and draftsman.

Ludwig Miës van der Rohe (1886–1969), German-American architect: Lake Shore apartments, Chicago (1950–52), Seagram Building, New York (with Philip Johnson, 1955–57).

John Millais (1829–96), English portrait and genre painter and, for a while, a key member of the Pre-Raphaelites: *The Carpenter's Shop* (1850).

Jean François Millet (1814–75), French romantic painter: *The Sower* (c.1850), *Angelus* (1859).

Joan Miró (1893–1983), Spanish surrealist painter: *Carnival of Harlequin* (1924–25).

Amedeo Modigliani (1884–1920), Italian painter who lived in France, and whose work combines influences from various schools: *Boy in a Blue Jacket* (1918), *Reclining Nude* (c.1919).

Piet Mondrian (1872–1944), Dutch abstract expressionist painter whose canvases are painted in simple horizontal and vertical stripes: *Composition with Red, Blue, and Yellow* (1930).

Claude Monet (1840–1926), French painter who was among the leaders of the impressionists: *Sailboat at Argenteuil* (1875).

Henry Moore (1898–), English abstract sculptor: *Recumbent Figure* (1938), *Locking Piece* (1963–65).

Grandma Moses (Anna Mary Robertson Moses, 1860–1961), American primitive painter of rural and domestic scenes: *Hurrah for Christmas* (1939).

Robert Motherwell (1915–), American abstract expressionist painter: *Elegy for the Spanish Republic* (1953–54).

Edvard Munch (1863–1944), Norwegian expressionist painter: *The Scream* (1893), *Dance of Life* (1900).

Bartolomé Esteban Murillo (1617?–82), Spanish portrait and religious painter: *Birth of the Virgin* (c.1655), *Marriage of St. Catherine* (1682).

Louise Nevelson (1900–), American sculptor in wood whose work shows cubist and surrealist influences: *Sky Cathedral* (1958).

Georgia O'Keeffe (1887–), American regional painter of the Southwest: *Black Cross, New Mexico* (1929).

Claes Oldenburg (1929–), American pop artist whose sculpture consists of rearranged junk and huge realistic objects, such as a giant lipstick, *Feasible Monument* (1969).

José Clemente Orozco (1883–1949), Mexican social-realist mural painter: *An Epic of American Civilization* (1934), at Dartmouth College.

Charles Willson Peale (1741–1827), American portrait painter: *George Washington* (1780).

I.M. (Ieoh Ming) Pei (1917–), Chinese-born architect: John Hancock Tower, Boston; National Gallery of Art East Building, Washington, D.C.; John F. Kennedy Library, Boston.

Claude Perrault (1613–88), French architect who designed much of the Louvre.

Perugino (Pietro Vannucci, c.1445–1523), Italian painter of religious subjects, and the teacher of Raphael: *Crucifixion with Saints* (1496).

Phidias of Athens (c.500–432 B.C.), Greek sculptor: *Athena* (c.447–439 B.C.) in the Parthenon, a building whose construction he may have supervised.

Pablo Picasso (1881–1973), Spanish painter and sculptor who helped found cubism and who produced major works in styles ranging from neoclassicism to surrealism. Paintings include *Woman in White* (1923), *The Three Dancers* (1925), *Guernica* (1937). Sculptures include *Woman's Head* (1909).

Piero della Francesca (c.1420–92), Italian painter of religious subjects: *The Flagellation of Christ* (c.1441–51), *The Story of the True Cross* (c.1452).

Camille Pissarro (1830–1903), French impressionist painter: *Le Fond de l'Hermitage* (1879), *The Boulevard Montmartre* (1897).

Jackson Pollock (1912–56), American abstract expressionist painter noted for his "action paintings": *Convergence* (1952).

Polycletus of Argos (400s B.C.), Greek sculptor whose *Doryphorus* or *Spear-Bearer* (c.450–440 B.C.) was held to represent ideal human proportions.

Nicolas Poussin (1594–1665), French painter noted for his heroic classic style: *The Rape of the Sabine Women* (c.1636–37).

Praxiteles (300s B.C.), Greek sculptor: *Hermes* (c.330–320 B.C.), *Aphrodite of Cnidus* (c.330 B.C.).

Maurice Prendergast (1859–1924), American impressionist painter: *Ponte della Paglia* (1899).

Pierre Proudhon (1758–1823), French romantic painter: *Empress Josephine* (1805).

Sir Henry Raeburn (1756–1823), Scottish portrait painter: *The Macnab* (c.1803), *Lord Newton* (c.1806).

Raphael Santi or **Sanzio** (1483–1520), Italian painter: numerous *Madonnas; The School of Athens* (1509–12), a fresco in the Vatican Palace.

Robert Rauschenberg (1925–), American pop artist: *Reservoir* (1961).

Odilon Redon (1840–1916), French symbolist painter and lithographer: *Cyclops* (1895–1900).

Rembrandt Harmenszoom van Rijn (1606–69), Dutch painter and greatest of the northern European Renaissance artists: *The Supper in Emmaus* (1648), *Aristotle Contemplating the Bust of Homer* (1653), *The Polish Rider* (1655), numerous *Self-Portraits*.

Frederic Remington (1861–1909), American painter and sculptor of cowboys and Indians: *The Bronco Buster* (1895), *The Cheyenne* (1901).

Pierre Auguste Renoir (1841–1919), French impressionist painter: *Moulin de la Galette* (1876), *Luncheon of the Boating Party* (1880–81).

Sir Joshua Reynolds (1723–92), English portrait painter: *Garrick Between Comedy and Tragedy* (1760–61), *Dr. Beattie (The Triumph of Truth)*. He was also a writer of considerable repute.

Diego Rivera (1886–1957), Mexican muralist and fresco painter.

Luca della Robbia (1400–82), Italian sculptor: *The Madonna of the Rose Garden* (c.1430).

Norman Rockwell (1894–1978), U.S. painter and illustrator: won popularity for realistic paintings of everyday life, many appearing as covers for *The Saturday Evening Post*.

Auguste Rodin (1840–1917), French impressionist sculptor: *The Thinker* (1879–89), *The Kiss* (1896–98), *Balzac* (1892–97).

Dante Gabriel Rossetti (1828–82), English romantic painter and poet, and leading member of the Pre-Raphaelites: *Girlhood of Mary Virgin* (1849), *Mary Magdalene* (1878).

Mark Rothko (1903–70), American abstract expressionist painter: *Orange, Red, Yellow* (1961), *Slate Blue and Brown on Plum* (1958) typify his studies in simple color contrasts.

Georges Rouault (1871–1958), French expressionist painter whose works often use dark lines to suggest stained glass: *Head of Christ* (1905), *Three Judges* (1913), *The Old King* (1916–37).

Henri Rousseau (1844–1910), French primitivist painter: *The Snake Charmer* (1907), *The Dream* (1910).

Peter Paul Rubens (1577–1640), Flemish baroque painter: *Raising of the Cross* (1609–10), *The Judgment of Paris* (1639).

Jacob van Ruisdael (c.1628–82), Dutch landscape painter: *The Jewish Graveyard* (c.1655).

Charles Marion Russell (1864–1926), American painter and sculptor of scenes of the West: *Bronc to Breakfast*.

Albert Pinkham Ryder (1847–1917), American painter of romantic and fantastic subjects: *Toilers of the Sea, Flying Dutchman, The Forest of Arden, The Race Track,* or *Death on a Pale Horse*.

Eero Saarinen (1910–61), Finnish-American architect: TWA Terminal, Kennedy Airport, New York; American Embassy, London.

Augustus Saint-Gaudens (1848–1907), American realist sculptor: Shaw Memorial, Boston; statue of General Sherman, New York City.

John Singer Sargent (1856–1925), American portrait and landscape painter: *Portrait of Madame X* (1884),

Robert Louis Stevenson (1887).

Georges Seurat (1859–91), French postimpressionist painter who used tiny dots of color to create mosaiclike effects in his works: *Sunday Afternoon on the Island of La Grande Jatte* (1884–86).

Ben Shahn (1898–1969), American expressionist painter: *The Passion of Sacco and Vanzetti* (1931–32).

Paul Signac (1863–1935), French neoimpressionist painter: *The Harbor at Saint-Tropez* (1893).

Alfred Sisley (1839–99), Anglo-French impressionist painter: *Square at Argenteuil* (1872).

John Sloan (1871–1951), American realist painter of everyday life: *McSorley's Bar* (1912).

David Smith (1906–65), American abstract sculptor best known for his works in welded metal: *Lectern Sentinel* (1961).

Chaim Soutine (1894–1943), Russian-French expressionist painter: *The Madwoman* (1920).

Jan Steen (1626–79), Dutch genre painter: *Grace Before Meat* (c.1665).

Philip Wilson Steer (1860–1940), English impressionist painter: *The Bridge, Etaples* (1887), *Chepstow Castle* (1905).

Frank Stella (1937–), American modernist painter best known for his "shaped canvases": *Sinjerli II* (1969).

Joseph Stella (1877–1946), U.S. semiabstract painter of subjects of the Industrial Age: *The Bridge* (1922).

Clyfford Still (1904–80), American abstract expressionist painter: *Jamais* (1944).

Edward Durell Stone (1902-78), U.S. architect: John F. Kennedy center in Washington, D.C.; General Motors building in New York City; U.S. embassy in New Delhi, India.

Gilbert Stuart (1755–1828), American portrait painter: *George Washington, John Adams*.

Louis Henry Sullivan (1856–1924), American architect and a pioneer in the design of skyscrapers: Roosevelt College building, Chicago (1887–89), Chicago Stock Exchange.

Lorado Taft (1860–1936), American sculptor: *Fountain of Time* (1922), *Solitude of the Soul* (1901), *Black Hawk* (1911).

Yves Tanguy (1900–55), French-American surrealist painter: *Mama, Papa Is Wounded* (1927).

Albert Bertel Thorvaldsen (1770–1844), Danish neoclassical sculptor: *Jason* (1802), *Cupid and Psyche* (1807).

Giovanni Battista Tiepolo (1696–1770), Venetian rococo painter of frescoes: several in Doge's Palace, Venice; Episcopal Palace, Würzburg.

Tintoretto (c.1518–94), Venetian mannerist painter: *Christ Before Pilate* (1566–67), *Bacchus and Ariadne* (1577), *The Last Supper* (1592–94).

Titian (Tiziano Vecellio, 1490?–1576), Venetian painter and one of the masters of Renaissance art: *Bacchanal* (1518), *Rape of Europa* (1559), *Christ Crowned with Thorns* (1570).

Henri de Toulouse-Lautrec (1864–1901), French postimpressionist painter and lithographer best known for his character studies: *Jane Avril* (1890), *At the Moulin Rouge* (1892).

John Trumbull (1756–1843), American painter of Revolutionary War scenes; his murals hang in U.S. Capitol.

Joseph Mallord William Turner (1775–1851), English romantic landscape painter: *The Grand Canal* (1835), *Rain, Steam, and Speed* (1844).

Maurice Utrillo (1883–1955), French painter of street scenes: *Rooftops at Sarcelle* (1909).

Sir Anthony Van Dyck (1599–1641), Flemish portrait and religious painter: *Portrait of Charles I Hunting* (c.1635), *The Vision of St. Augustine* and *Lamentation* (both 1634–35).

Jan Van Eyck (c.1390–1441), Flemish religious

PAINTERS, SCULPTORS, AND ARCHITECTS *(continued)*
painter: *Ghent Altarpiece* (1425–32).

Vincent Van Gogh (1853–90), Dutch postimpressionist painter who worked mainly in France: *The Sunflowers* (1888), *Starry Night* (1889), several self-portraits.

Jan Van Goyen (1596–1656), Dutch artist who was among the founders of the Dutch and Flemish school of landscape painting: *Windmill by the River* (1642).

Diego Velázquez (1599–1660), Spanish portrait painter: *Borrachos* (1629), *The Maids of Honor* (1656), *The Water-Carrier of Seville* (1619–21), *The Surrender of Breda* (1634–35).

Jan Vermeer (1632–75), Dutch genre painter: *Officer and Laughing Girl* (c.1655–60), *The Letter* (1666).

Paolo Veronese (1528–88), Venetian painter of religious and allegorical subjects: *Christ in the House of Levi* (1573), *The Rape of Europa* (1576), *Marriage at Cana* (1563).

Andrea del Verrocchio (1435–88), Florentine painter and sculptor: *Baptism of Christ* (c.1470), *Putto with a Dolphin* (c.1470).

Maurice de Vlaminck (1876–1958), French fauvist painter: *On the Banks of the Seine* (1906).

Andy Warhol (1927–), American pop artist: *Campbell's Soup Can.*

Antoine Watteau (1684–1721), French baroque painter: *Gilles* (c.1716), *Pilgrimage to Cythera* (1717), *The Fatigues of War* or *Troop March* (1712–15), *Gersaint's Shop Sign* (1720).

Max Weber (1881–1961), American abstract and cubist painter: *Chinese Restaurant* (1915).

Benjamin West (1738–1820), American painter of romantic and heroic scenes: *Death of General Wolfe* (1770).

Rogier van der Weyden (1399–1464), Flemish painter of religious subjects: *The Last Judgment* (c.1446).

James Abbott McNeill Whistler (1834–1903), American painter and etcher whose work shows influences both of French impressionists and English academic painters: *Arrangement in Gray and Black*; *The Artist's Mother* (1871), *The Falling Rocket* (1874).

Grant Wood (1891–1942), American painter of rural Midwest scenes: *American Gothic* (1930), *Daughters of the Revolution* (1932).

Sir Christopher Wren (1632–1723), English architect who worked in the neoclassic style: St. Paul's Cathedral, London.

Frank Lloyd Wright (1869–1959), American architect who pioneered in radical designs: Johnson Wax Building, Racine, Wis. (1936–39); the Guggenheim Museum, New York City (1946–59).

Andrew Wyeth (1917–), American romantic realist painter: *Winter* (1946), *Christina's World* (1948).

MAJOR ART MOVEMENTS

Abstract expressionism, American painting style that reached peak in 1940s and 1950s. Form and color are emphasized for their own sake, and works seldom contain identifiable objects. Earlier European movement producing similar results (for example, Kandinsky's paintings) was called *tachisme.*

Art nouveau, ornate style that originated in the late 1800s. Among best-known artists in style were Louis C. Tiffany and René Lalique.

Barbizon School, group of French artists in mid-1800s; including Millet, who painted romantic landscapes and pastoral scenes.

Baroque, predominantly Italian style of art and architecture that reached peak in the mid-1600s. Baroque works are ornate and dramatic.

Cubism, early movement in painting and, to lesser extent, in sculpture. It reduced all shapes to simple geometric forms, or distorted objects by simultaneously presenting them from several different angles. Founders of cubism were Braque and Picasso.

Dadaism, movement originating in 1916 in France, expressing nihilistic protest against all previous art and culture. One of its leaders, Marcel Duchamp, attached labels to ordinary commercial products (for example, bicycle wheels, drinking fountains) and called them art.

Expressionism, 20th century northern European movement in painting. Usually ordinary subjects were given distorted shapes, and colors were exaggerated to produce strong emotional effects.

Fauvism, French movement of painters who exhibited together in Paris from about 1903 to 1905. Their use of distorted design and wild colors caused them to be called *Les fauves* (beasts) by some critics. Their leaders included Matisse and Rouault.

Futurism, Italian art movement of early 1900s, glorifying mechanical age, speed, and motion.

Genre painting, type of picture, usually of small size, that represents everyday life in unidealized manner. Examples, which are found through ages, include many peasant and tavern and household scenes depicted by Dutch painters of 1600s.

Impressionism, most important art movement of 1800s, mainly centered around Paris. Impressionistic painters were primarily concerned with effects of natural light in their spontaneous and undetailed portrayals of subjects in their artwork.

Mannerism, movement between 1520 and 1600 mainly in Italy, although probably the greatest mannerist painter was Greek-Spanish El Greco. Human figure was central subject, but it was posed in dramatically strained positions, or its shape was elongated.

Minimal art, kind of abstract painting developed in 1960s, eliminating emotions or symbolism.

Neoclassicism, movement of 1700s that arose in reaction to excesses of baroque and rococo art. Painters, and especially sculptors, consciously imitated styles and subject matter of ancient Greek and Roman art.

New realism, movement of 1970s, in which paintings are executed with photographic realistic detail.

Op art, movement of 1960s, emphasizing optical illusion through creation of complex geometric constructions or designs.

Pop art, New York-centered movement of 1960s, in which everyday examples of graphic design are illustrated or reproduced, often greatly enlarged. Comic strips and advertising art are favorite subjects.

Postimpressionism, loosely knit movement of late 1800s, mainly in rejection of impressionism. Cézanne usually considered founder of movement, although work has little in common with other postimpressionists.

Pre-Raphaelite, English movement of mid-1800s emphasizing purity and use of moral and religious themes. Leaders included Millais and Rossetti.

Realism, movement begun by Courbet in mid-1800s, depicting real people in everyday situations.

Rococo, movement in art and architecture that began in France in 1700s and spread to Germany and Austria. Prettiness, gaiety, and ornate delicacy characterize rococo art.

Romanticism, movement of early 1800s reacting against neoclassicism by combining realistic details and expression of emotions. Constable and Turner were leaders of romanticism.

Surrealism, essentially an outgrowth from cubism; its subject matter consists of fantastic, dreamlike objects and scenes. Surrealism reached its peak in works by Picasso, Dali, and Ernst.

Awards and Prizes

NOBEL PRIZES

Nobel Prizes are awarded each year to persons who have made important contributions for the good of humanity.

The awards were established in the will of Alfred Bernhard Nobel (1833–96), a Swedish chemist who became wealthy from his invention of dynamite in 1867. He regretted that dynamite had been used as an instrument of war, and left a fund of about $9 million to establish the Nobel Prizes to encourage peace and progress.

Six prizes are awarded each year in chemistry, economics, literature, peace, physics, and physiology or medicine. The first prizes were awarded in 1901. The economics prize was added in 1969. Each prize in 1984 carried a monetary award of about $193,000, divided when there was more than one recipient.

The Royal Academy of Science in Sweden picks the prizewinners in physics, chemistry, and economics. The medical faculty of Stockholm's Caroline Institute chooses the winner in the field of physiology or medicine. The Swedish Academy of Literature names the literature winner. The Norwegian parliament elects a committee of five persons to select the winner of the prize for peace.

A total of 180 Americans have received Nobel Prizes through 1984. The British are second with 84. Some 58 Germans have won Nobel Prizes, French 44, Swedes 29, Russians 14, Swiss 14, Danes 12, Dutch 12, Italians 11, Austrians 9, Belgians 8, Norwegians 7, Japanese 6, Spanish 5, Argentinians 5, Canadians 4, Irish 4, Australians 3, Poles 3, and Indians 3. Two Nobel Prizes have been won by Israelis, Chileans, Hungarians, Finns, South Africans, Czechs, and Greeks. One each have been won by an Egyptian, an Icelander, a Yugoslav, a Guatemalan, a Vietnamese, a Portuguese, a Pakistani, a Bulgarian, a Mexican, and a Colombian.

NOBEL LITERATURE PRIZES

Year	Description
1901	Sully-Prudhomme (Renáe Prudhomme), French poet: *La Justice* (1878), *Le Bonheur* (1888)
1902	C. M. T. Mommsen, German historian: *History of Rome* (1854–56)
1903	Björnstjerne Björnson, Norwegian author: novel, *The Fisher Girl* (1868); poem, *Arnljot Gelline* (1870)
1904	Frédéric Mistral, French poet: *Miréio* (1859)
	José Echegaray, Spanish dramatist: *The Great Galeoto* (1881)
1905	Henryk Sienkiewicz, Polish novelist: *Quo Vadis?* (1895)
1906	Giosuè Carducci, Italian poet: *Odi barbari* (1877)
1907	Rudyard Kipling, British author: poetry, *Barrack-Room Ballads* (1892), *If* (1910); novel, *The Light That Failed* (1890)
1908	Rudolf C. Eucken, German philosopher: *The Truth of Religion* (1901)
1909	Selma Lagerlöf, Swedish novelist: *The Story of Gösta Berling* (1891)
1910	Paul J. L. Heyse, German novelist: *The Fury* (1855), *Children of the World* (1873)
1911	Count Maurice Maeterlinck, Belgian author: play, *The Blue Bird* (1909)
1912	Gerhart Hauptmann, German author: play, *Before Dawn* (1889); novel, *The Fool in Christ, Emanuel Quint* (1910)
1913	Rabindranath Tagore, Indian author: philosophy, *Sadhana, The Realization of Life* (1913)
1914	No award
1915	Romain Rolland, French author: novel, *Jean-Christophe* (1904–12)
1916	Carl G. von Heidenstam, Swedish author: poetry, *New Poems* (1915)
1917	Karl A. Gjellerup, Danish poet and novelist: *The Pilgrim Kamanita* (1906)
	Henrik Pontoppidan, Danish novelist: *Kingdom of the Dead* (1912–16)
1918	No award
1919	Carl F. G. Spitteler, Swiss poet: *Olympian Spring* (1900–06)
1920	Knut Hamsun, Norwegian novelist: *Growth of the Soil* (1920)
1921	Anatole France, French author: novel, *Penguin Island* (1908)
1922	Jacinto Benavente, Spanish dramatist: *Bonds of Interest* (1907), *The Passion Flower* (1913)
1923	William Butler Yeats, Irish poet and dramatist: poetry, *The Wild Swans at Coole* (1919)
1924	Wladyslaw S. Reymont, Polish author: novel, *The Peasants* (1902–09)
1925	George Bernard Shaw, British (Irish-born) author: plays, *Man and Superman* (1905), *Pygmalion* (1913)
1926	Grazia Deledda, Italian novelist: *After the Divorce* (1902), *Ashes* (1904)
1927	Henri Bergson, French philosopher: *Creative Evolution* (1907)
1928	Sigrid Undset, Norwegian (Danish-born) novelist: *Kristin Lavransdatter* (1920–22)
1929	Thomas Mann, German novelist: *Buddenbrooks* (1901), *The Magic Mountain* (1924)
1930	Sinclair Lewis, U.S. novelist: *Main Street* (1920), *Babbitt* (1922)
1931	Erik A. Karlfeldt, Swedish poet: *Songs of the Wilderness and of Love* (1895)
1932	John Galsworthy, British author: novels, *The Forsyte Saga* (1922), *A Modern Comedy* (1928)
1933	Ivan A. Bunin, French (Russian-born) author: novel, *The Village* (1910); short stories, *The Gentleman from San Francisco* (1916)
1934	Luigi Pirandello, Italian author: play, *Six Characters in Search of an Author* (1920)
1935	No award
1936	Eugene O'Neill, U.S. dramatist: *Mourning Becomes Electra* (1931), *Strange Interlude* (1927)
1937	Roger Martin du Gard, French novelist: *The World of the Thibaults* (1922–40)
1938	Pearl S. Buck, U.S. novelist: *The Good Earth* (1931)
1939	Frans E. Sillanpää, Finnish novelist: *Meek Heritage* (1919), *People in a Summer Night* (1934)
1940–43	No award

NOBEL LITERATURE PRIZES (continued)

1944	**Johannes V. Jensen**, Danish author: novel, *The Long Journey* (1908-22)
1945	**Gabriela Mistral**, Chilean poet: *Desolación* (1922), *Tala* (1938), *Lagar* (1954)
1946	**Hermann Hesse**, Swiss (German-born) author: novels, *Steppenwolf* (1927), *Death and the Lover* (1930)
1947	**André Gide**, French author: novels, *The Immoralist* (1902), *Strait is the Gate* (1909)
1948	**T. S. Eliot**, British (U.S.-born) poet: *The Waste Land* (1922), *Four Quartets* (1935-42)
1949	**William Faulkner**, U.S. novelist: *The Sound and the Fury* (1929), *Sanctuary* (1931)
1950	**Bertrand Russell**, British philosopher: *Marriage and Morals* (1929), *The Conquest of Happiness* (1930)
1951	**Pär F. Lagerkvist**, Swedish author: novels, *The Dwarf* (1944), *Barabbas* (1950)
1952	**François Mauriac**, French author: novels, *The Desert of Love* (1925), *Vipers' Tangle* (1932)
1953	**Sir Winston Churchill**, British statesman and historian: *The Second World War* (1948-53)
1954	**Ernest Hemingway**, U.S. novelist: *A Farewell to Arms* (1929), *For Whom the Bell Tolls* (1940)
1955	**Halldór K. Laxness**, Icelandic novelist: *Salka Valka* (1931-32), *Independent People* (1934-35)
1956	**Juan Ramón Jiménez**, Spanish poet: *Unidad* (1925), *Sucesión* (1932), *Presente* (1935)
1957	**Albert Camus**, French author: novels, *The Stranger* (1946), *The Plague* (1948)
1958	**Boris L. Pasternak**, Russian poet and novelist (Prize declined): novel, *Doctor Zhivago* (1957)
1959	**Salvatore Quasimodo**, Italian poet: *Acque E Terra* (1930)
1960	**Saint-John Perse**, French poet: *Éloges* (1911), *Anabase* (1924), *Exil* (1944)
1961	**Ivo Andrić**, Yugoslavian novelist: *The Bridge on the Drina* (1945), *Vizier's Elephant* (1960)
1962	**John Steinbeck**, U.S. novelist: *The Grapes of Wrath* (1939), *East of Eden* (1952)
1963	**George Seferis**, Greek poet: *Strophe* (1931), *Mithistorima* (1935)
1964	**Jean-Paul Sartre**, French author (Prize declined): novels, *The Age of Reason* (1945), *The Reprieve* (1945); play, *The Respectful Prostitute* (1947)
1965	**Mikhail Sholokhov**, Russian novelist: *The Silent Don* (1928-40)
1966	**Shmuel Yosef Agnon**, Israeli (Austrian-born) author: novels, *The Bridal Canopy* (1919), *A Guest for the Night* (1938) **Nelly Sachs**, Swedish (German-born) poet: *In the Apartments of Death* (1947)
1967	**Miguel Angel Asturias**, Guatemalan author: novels, *El señor presidente* (1946), *Strong Wind* (1950)
1968	**Yasunari Kawabata**, Japanese novelist: *The Izu Dancer* (1925), *Snow Country* (1956)
1969	**Samuel Beckett**, French (Irish-born) author: play, *Waiting for Godot* (1952); novels, *Murphy* (1938), *Molloy* (1951)
1970	**Aleksandr I. Solzhenitsyn**, Russian author: novel, *One Day in the Life of Ivan Denisovich* (1962); non-fiction, *The Gulag Archipelago* (1974)
1971	**Pablo Neruda**, Chilean poet: *Crepusculario* (1919), *Canto General* (1950), *Elementary Odes* (1954)
1972	**Heinrich Böll**, German author: novels, *Adam, Where Art Thou?* (1951), *Billiards at Half Past Nine* (1959)
1973	**Patrick White**, Australian novelist: *The Happy Valley* (1939), *Vivisector* (1970).
1974	**Eyvind Johnson**, Swedish novelist: *Romanen om Olov* (1934-37) **Harry Edmund Martinson**, Swedish author: poetry, *Aniara* (1956), *Flowering Nettle* (1936)
1975	**Eugenio Montale**, Italian poet: *Poesie* (1958), *The Butterfly of Dinard* (1960)
1976	**Saul Bellow**, U.S. (Canadian-born) novelist: *The Adventures of Augie March* (1953), *Herzog* (1964), *Humboldt's Gift* (1975)
1977	**Vicente Aleixandre**, Spanish poet: *Environment* (1928), *Swords of Lips* (1932)
1978	**Isaac Bashevis Singer**, U.S. (Polish-born) author: novels, *The Family Moskat* (1950), *Enemies: A Love Story* (1972)
1979	**Odysseus Elytis**, Greek poet: *The Sovereign Sun* (1974)
1980	**Czeslaw Milosz**, U.S. (Polish-born) author: novel, *The Issa Valley* (1981) poetry, *The Bells of Winter* (1978)
1981	**Elias Canetti**, Bulgarian author: novel, *Auto da fé* (1935)
1982	**Gabriel García Márquez**, Colombian novelist: *One Hundred Years of Solitude* (1967), *The Autumn of the Patriarch* (1975)
1983	**William Golding**, British novelist: *Lord of the Flies* (1954)
1984	**Jaroslav Seifert**, Czech poet: *The Plague Monument* (1980), *The Casting of Bells* (1983)
1985	See page 26.

NOBEL CHEMISTRY PRIZES

YEAR	NAME AND NATIONALITY	AWARDED FOR:
1901	Jacobus H. van't Hoff, Dutch	Discovery of laws of chemical dynamics and osmotic pressure in solutions.
1902	Emil Fischer, German	Work on sugar and purine syntheses.
1903	Svante A. Arrhenius, Swedish	Electrolytic theory of dissociation.
1904	Sir William Ramsay, British	Discovery of inert gaseous elements in air and determination of their place in periodic system.
1905	Johann von Baeyer, German	Work on organic dyes and hydroaromatic compounds.
1906	Henri Moissan, French	Study and isolation of element fluorine and development of electric furnace named after him.
1907	Eduard Buchner, German	Biochemical researches and discovery of cell-free fermentation.
1908	Ernest Rutherford, British	Studies of disintegration of elements, and chemistry of radioactive substances.
1909	Wilhelm Ostwald, German	Work on catalysis and studies of fundamental principles governing chemical equilibria and rates of reaction.
1910	Otto Wallach, German	Pioneer work in field of alicyclic compounds.
1910	Marie Curie, French (Polish-born)	Discovery of elements radium and polonium, isolation of radium and study of its nature and compounds.
1912	Victor Grignard, French	Discovery of Grignard reagent.
	Paul Sabatier, French	Method of hydrogenating organic compounds in presence of finely disintegrated metals.
1913	Alfred Werner, Swiss (German-born)	Work on linkage of atoms in molecules.
1914	Theodore W. Richards, U.S.	Determinations of atomic weight of many chemical elements.
1915	Richard M. Willstätter, German	Researches on plant pigments, especially chlorophyll.
1916	No award	
1917	No award	
1918	Fritz Haber, German	Synthesis of ammonia from its elements.
1919	No award	
1920	Walther H. Nernst, German	Work in thermochemistry.

1921	Frederick Soddy, British	Studies of chemistry of radioactive substances, and investigations into origin and nature of isotopes.
1922	Francis W. Aston, British	Discovery, by means of his mass spectrograph, of isotopes in a large number of nonradioactive elements.
1923	Fritz Pregl, Austrian	Invention of method of microanalysis of organic substances.
1924	No award	
1925	Richard A. Zsigmondy, German (Austrian-born)	Demonstration of heterogeneous nature of colloid solutions.
1926	Theodor Svedberg, Swedish	Work on dispersion systems and colloid chemistry.
1927	Heinrich O. Wieland, German	Studies of constitution of bile acids and related substances.
1928	Adolf O. R. Windaus, German	Research into constitution of sterols and their connection with vitamins.
1929	Arthur Harden, British Hans von Euler–Chelpin, Swedish (German-born)	Investigations on fermentation of sugar and fermentative enzymes.
1930	Hans Fischer, German	Researches into constitution of hemin and chlorophyll.
1931	Friedrich Bergius, German Carl Bosch, German	Contributions to invention and development of chemical high-pressure methods.
1932	Irving Langmuir, U.S.	Discoveries and investigations in surface chemistry.
1933	No award	
1934	Harold C. Urey, U.S.	Discovery of heavy hydrogen.
1935	Frédéric Joliot-Curie, French Irène Joliot-Curie, French	Synthesis of new radioactive elements.
1936	Peter J. W. Debye, Dutch	Knowledge of molecular structure by studies of dipole moments, diffraction of X rays, and electrons in gases.
1937	Walter N. Haworth, British Paul Karrer, Swiss (Russian-born)	Research on carbohydrates and vitamin C. Investigations on carotenoids, flavins, and vitamins A and B_2.
1938	Richard Kuhn, German (Austrian-born)	Work on carotenoids and vitamins. (Prize declined.)
1939	Adolf F. J. Butenandt, German Leopold Ruzička, Swiss	Work on sex hormones. (Prize declined under political pressure.) Work on polymethylenes and higher terpenes.
1940–42	No award	
1943	Georg de Hevesy, Hungarian	Work on use of isotopes as tracers in chemistry.
1944	Otto Hahn, German	Discovery of fission of heavy nuclei.
1945	Artturi I. Virtanen, Finnish	Research and inventions in agricultural and nutrition chemistry.
1946	James B. Sumner, U.S. John H. Northrop, U.S. Wendell M. Stanley, U.S.	Discovery that enzymes can be crystallized. Preparation of enzymes and virus proteins in pure form.
1947	Sir Robert Robinson, British	Investigation of plant products of biological importance.
1948	Arne W. K. Tiselius, Swedish	Research on electrophoresis and adsorption analysis.
1949	William F. Giauque, U.S.	Contributions in field of chemical thermodynamics, particularly behavior of substances at extremely low temperatures.
1950	Kurt Alder, German Otto P. H. Diels, German	Discovery and development of diene synthesis.
1951	Edwin M. McMillan, U.S. Glenn T. Seaborg, U.S.	Discoveries in chemistry of transuranium elements.
1952	Archer J. P. Martin, British Richard L. M. Synge, British	Invention of partition chromatography, method for analysis of mixtures.
1953	Hermann Staudinger, German	Discoveries in field of macromolecular chemistry.
1954	Linus C. Pauling, U.S.	Research into nature of chemical bond and its application.
1955	Vincent du Vigneaud, U.S.	Work on biochemically important sulfur compounds, especially for first synthesis of polypeptide hormone.
1956	Sir Cyril N. Hinshelwood, British Nikolai N. Semenov, Russian	Researches into mechanism of chemical reactions.
1957	Lord Todd (Alexander R. Todd), British	Work on nucleotides and nucleotide coenzymes.
1958	Frederick Sanger, British	Work on structure of proteins, especially of insulin.
1959	Jaroslav Heyrovsky, Czech	Discovery and development of polarographic methods of analysis.
1960	Willard F. Libby, U.S.	Method to use carbon-14 for age determination in archaeology, geology, geophysics, and other branches of science.
1961	Melvin Calvin, U.S.	Research on carbon dioxide assimilation in plants.
1962	Sir John C. Kendrew, British Max F. Perutz, British (Austrian-born)	Studies of structures of globular proteins.
1963	Giulio Natta, Italian Karl Ziegler, German	Discoveries in chemistry and technology of high polymers.
1964	Dorothy Crowfoot Hodgkin, British	Discovery by X-ray techniques of structure of important biochemical substances.
1965	Robert B. Woodward, U.S.	Techniques for syntheses of complicated organic compounds.
1966	Robert S. Mulliken, U.S.	Fundamental work on chemical bonds and electronic structure of molecules by molecular orbital method.
1967	Manfred Eigen, German Ronald G. W. Norrish, British Sir George Porter, British	Studies of extremely fast chemical reactions effected by disturbing equilibrium by means of very short pulses of energy.
1968	Lars Onsager, U.S. (Norwegian-born)	Discovery of reciprocal relations that bear his name, which are fundamental to thermodynamics of irreversible processes.
1969	Derek H. R. Barton, British Odd Hassel, Norwegian	Work to develop and apply concept of conformation in chemistry.
1970	Luis F. Leloir, Argentine (French-born)	Discovery of sugar nucleotides and their role in biosynthesis of carbohydrates.
1971	Gerhard Herzberg, Canadian (German-born)	Studies in electronic structure and geometry of molecules, particularly free radicals.
1972	Christian B. Anfinsen, U.S. Stanford Moore, U.S. William H. Stein, U.S.	Research relating to chemical structure and biologic reactions of protein ribonuclease.
1973	Ernest Otto Fischer, German Geoffrey Wilkinson, British	Research on merging of organic and metallic compounds, seeking solution to automobile exhaust pollution.

NOBEL CHEMISTRY PRIZES *(continued)*

1974	**Paul J. Flory**, U.S.	Pioneering analytical methods for studying long-chain molecules, leading to development of many plastics and synthetic materials.
1975	**John Warcus Cornforth**, British (Australian-born) **Vladimir Prelog**, Swiss (Yugoslav-born)	Research in field of stereochemistry, study of how properties of chemical compounds are affected by arrangement of their atoms.
1976	**William N. Lipscomb**, U.S.	Studies on structure and bonding of compounds called boranes, providing new insight into nature of chemical bonding.
1977	**Ilya Prigogine**, Belgian (Russian-born) ..	Lifetime contributions to nonequilibrium thermodynamics, particularly theory of dissipative structures that helps explain how living organisms use energy and how life originated.
1978	**Peter Mitchell**, British	Research on energy transformations in living cells and formulation of the chemiosmotic theory of how cells convert food into metabolic energy.
1979	**Herbert C. Brown**, U.S. (British-born) **Georg Wittig**, West German	Development of boron and phosphorus compounds linking large molecules, enabling mass production of many pharmaceuticals and industrial chemicals.
1980	**Paul Berg**, U.S. **Walter Gilbert**, U.S. **Frederick Sanger**, British	Pioneering work in gene-splicing or genetic engineering. Determining the chemical structure of nucleic acids in regard to DNA used in gene-splicing.
1981	**Roald Hoffman**, Swedish **Kenichi Fukui**, Japanese	Applying theories of quantum mathematics to predict course of chemical reactions.
1982	**Aaron Klug**, British (South African-born)	Developing three-dimensional electron microscope images revealing the structure of viruses and other tiny biological organisms.
1983	**Henry Taube**, U.S. (Canadian-born)	Discovery of the way electrons transfer between molecules in chemical reactions
1984	**R. Bruce Merrifield**, U.S.	Discovery of method making important new drugs faster and more economically by assembling amino acids into chains called peptides.
1985	See page 26.	

NOBEL PHYSICS PRIZES

1901	**Wilhelm C. Roentgen**, German	Discovery of Roentgen rays (X rays).
1902	**Hendrik A. Lorentz**, Dutch **Pieter Zeeman**, Dutch	Researches into influence of magnetism upon radiation phenomena.
1903	**Antoine Henri Becquerel**, French **Marie Curie**, French (Polish-born) **Pierre Curie**, French	Discovery of spontaneous radioactivity. Joint researches on radiation phenomena discovered by A. Henri Becquerel.
1904	**Lord Rayleigh (John W. Strutt)** British	Investigations of densities of most important gases and discovery of argon.
1905	**Philipp E. A. von Lenard**, German (Hungarian-born)	Work on cathode rays.
1906	**Sir Joseph John Thomson**, British	Theoretical and experimental investigations on conduction of electricity by gases.
1907	**Albert A. Michelson**, U.S. (German-born)	Optical precision instruments for spectroscopic and meteorological investigations.
1908	**Gabriel Lippmann**, French (Luxembourgian-born)	Method of reproducing colors photographically based on phenomenon of interference.
1909	**Guglielmo Marconi**, Italian **Carl F. Braun**, German	Development of radio (wireless telegraphy).
1910	**Johannes D. van der Waals**, Dutch	Work on equation of state for gases and liquids.
1911	**Wilhelm Wien**, German	Discoveries regarding laws of heat radiation.
1912	**Nils G. Dalén**, Swedish	Invention of automatic regulators to be used with gas accumulators for illuminating lighthouses and buoys.
1913	**Heike Kamerlingh-Onnes**, Dutch	Investigations on properties of matter at lower temperatures, which led to production of liquid helium.
1914	**Max von Laue**, German	Discovery of diffraction of X rays by crystals.
1915	**Sir William H. Bragg**, British **Sir William L. Bragg**, British	The analysis of crystal structure by means of X rays.
1916	No award	
1917	**Charles G. Barkla**, British	Discovery of characteristic Roentgen radiation of elements.
1918	**Max K. E. L. Planck**, German	Discovery of energy quanta.
1919	**Johannes Stark**, German	Discovery of Doppler effect in canal rays and splitting of spectral lines in electric fields.
1920	**Charles E. Guillaume**, French (Swiss-born)	Discovery of anomalies in nickel-steel alloys.
1921	**Albert Einstein**, U.S. (German-born)	Studies in theoretical physics, and especially for discovery of law of photoelectric effect.
1922	**Niels Bohr**, Danish	Investigation of atomic structure and radiation.
1923	**Robert A. Millikan**, U.S.	Work on elementary charge of electricity and on photoelectric effect.
1924	**Karl M. G. Siegbahn**, Swedish	Discoveries and research in field of X-ray spectroscopy.
1925	**James Franck**, German **Gustav Hertz**, German	Discovery of laws governing impact of electron upon atom.
1926	**Jean B. Perrin**, French	Work on discontinuous structure of matter, and especially for discovery of sedimentation equillibrium.
1927	**Arthur H. Compton**, U.S. **Charles T. R. Wilson**, British (Scottish-born)	Discovery of Compton effect concerning increase in wave length of X rays and gamma rays scattered by electrons. Method of making paths of electrically charged particles visible by condensation of vapor.

1928	Owen W. Richardson, British	Work on thermionics, phenomena associated with emission of electrically charged particles by heated body, and for discovery of Richardson's law.
1929	Prince Louis-Victor de Broglie, French . .	Discovery of wave nature of electrons.
1930	Sir Chandrasekhara V. Raman, Indian . .	Work on scattering of light and discovery of Raman effect.
1931	No award	
1932	Werner Heisenberg, German	Creation of quantum mechanics, which led to discovery of allotropic forms of hydrogen.
1933	Paul A. M. Dirac, British Erwin Schrödinger, Austrian	Extensions of atomic theory.
1934	No award	
1935	Sir James Chadwick, British	Discovery of neutron.
1936	Carl D. Anderson, U.S. Victor F. Hess, Austrian	Discovery of positron. Discovery of cosmic radiation.
1937	Clinton J. Davisson, U.S. George P. Thomson, British	Experimental discovery of diffraction of electrons by crystals.
1938	Enrico Fermi, U.S................... (Italian-born)	Demonstrations of existence of new radioactive elements produced by neutron irradiation, and discovery of nuclear reactions caused by slow neutrons.
1939	Ernest O. Lawrence, U.S.	Invention and development of cyclotron and results obtained from its use in investigation of artificial radioactive elements.
1940	No award	
1941	No award	
1942	No award	
1943	Otto Stern, U.S. (German-born)	Contribution to development of molecular-ray method and discovery of magnetic moment of proton.
1944	Isidor Isaac Rabi, U.S.	Resonance method for recording magnetism of atomic nuclei.
1945	Wolfgang Pauli, U.S.	Discovery of exclusion, or Pauli, principle in quantum physics.
1946	Percy Williams Bridgman, U.S.	Invention of apparatus to produce extremely high pressures, and resulting discoveries in field of high-pressure physics.
1947	Sir Edward V. Appleton, British	Investigations of physics of upper atmosphere and discovery of Appleton layer of ionosphere.
1948	Patrick M. S. Blackett, British	Development of Wilson cloud-chamber method and resulting discoveries in fields of nuclear physics and cosmic radiation.
1949	Hideki Yukawa, Japanese	Theoretical prediction of existence of mesons.
1950	Cecil F. Powell, British	Development of photographic method of studying nuclear processes and resulting discoveries regarding mesons.
1951	Sir John D. Cockcroft, British Ernest T. S. Walton, Irish	Research on transmutation of atomic nuclei by artificially accelerated atomic particles.
1952	Felix Bloch, U.S. (Swiss-born) Edward M. Purcell, U.S.	Development of new methods for nuclear-magnetic precision measurements and related discoveries.
1953	Frits Zernike, Dutch	Demonstration of phase-contrast method, and invention of phase-contrast microscope.
1954	Max Born, British (German-born) Walther Bothe, German	Fundamental research in quantum mechanics. Coincidence method of counting, used in nuclear and cosmic-ray research.
1955	Polykarp Kusch, U.S. (German-born) Willis E. Lamb, U.S.	Precise determination of magnetic moment of electron. Discoveries concerning fine structure of hydrogen spectrum.
1956	John Bardeen, U.S. Walter H. Brattain, U.S. William Shockley, U.S.	Research on semiconductors and discovery of transistor.
1957	Tsung-Dao Lee, U.S. (Chinese-born) ... Chen Ning Yang, U.S. (Chinese-born)	Investigation of parity laws, which led to important discoveries regarding elementary particles.
1958	Paval A. Cherenkov, Russian Ilya M. Frank, Russian Igor J. Tamm, Russian	Discovery and interpretation of Cherenkov effect.
1959	Owen Chamberlain, U.S. Emilio G. Segrè, U.S. (Italian-born)	Discovery of antiproton.
1960	Donald A. Glaser, U.S.	Invention of bubble chamber.
1961	Robert Hofstadter, U.S. Rudolf L. Mössbauer, German	Studies of electron scattering with resulting discoveries concerning structure of nucleons. Studies of resonance absorption of gamma radiation and resulting discovery of Mössbauer effect.
1962	Lev D. Landau, Russian	Theories of condensed matter, especially liquid helium.
1963	Maria Goeppert-Mayer, U.S. J. Hans D. Jensen, German Eugene P. Wigner, U.S................	Discoveries concerning nuclear shell structures. Contribution to theory of atomic nucleus and elementary particles.
1964	Nikolai G. Basov, Russian Aleksandr M. Prokhorov, Russian Charles H. Townes, U.S.	Fundamental work in field of quantum electronics, leading to construction of maser-laser oscillators and amplifiers.
1965	Richard P. Feynman, U.S............. Julian S. Schwinger, U.S. Sin-itiro Tomonaga, Japanese	Research in quantum electrodynamics, which contributed to understanding of elementary particles in high-energy physics.
1966	Alfred Kastler, French	Discovery and development of optical methods for studying Herzian resonances in atoms.
1967	Hans A. Bethe, U.S.................. (German-born)	Contributions to theory of nuclear reaction, especially discoveries concerning energy production of stars.
1968	Luis W. Alvarez, U.S.	Contributions to physics of subatomic particles, in particular discovery of large number of resonance states.
1969	Murray Gell-Mann, U.S...............	Contributions and discoveries concerning classification of elementary particles and their interactions.

NOBEL PHYSICS PRIZES *(continued)*

1970	Hannes O. G. Alfvén, Swedish	Contributions and discoveries in magnetohydrodynamics with applications in plasma physics.
	Louis E. F. Néel, French	Discoveries and work in ferromagnetism and antiferromagnetism with applications in solid-state physics.
1971	Dennis Gabor, British (Hungarian-born)	Invention of system of three-dimensional photography known as holography.
1972	John Bardeen, U.S.	Development of superconductivity theory of certain metals
	Leon N. Cooper, U.S.	at very low temperatures.
	John R. Schrieffer, U.S.	
1973	Ivar Giaever, U.S. (Norwegian-born) ...	Developments relating to miniature electronic semiconductors
	Leo Esaki, Japanese	and superconductors.
	Brian D. Josephson, British	Discovery of "Josephson effects" of electric supercurrent.
1974	Antony Hewish, British	Studies of universe using radiotelescopes; Dr. Hewish
	Sir Martin Ryle, British	discovered pulsars in 1967.
1975	L. James Rainwater, U.S.	Discovery and explanation of fact that nuclei of some atoms
	Aage Bohr, Danish	are not spherical because of connection between
	Ben Roy Mottelson, Danish (U.S.-born)	collective motion and particle motion in atomic nucleus.
1976	Burton Richter, U.S.	Independent discoveries of Psi or J particle, heavy ele-
	Samuel C. C. Ting, U.S.	mentary particle believed smallest building block of matter.
1977	John H. Van Vleck, U.S.	Founding modern magnetism by explaining magnetic properties of solids and how foreign ion or atom behaves in crystal.
	Philip W. Anderson, U.S.	Discoveries made separately in sold-state physics that led to
	Sir Nevill F. Mott, British	use of amorphous material, such as glass, in electronic switching and memory devices.
1978	Robert W. Wilson, U.S.	Discovery of cosmic microwave background radiation,
	Arno A. Penzias, U.S. (German-born)	confirming "big bang" theory of creation of universe.
	Pyotr Leontevitch Kapitsa, Russian	Basic research in low-temperature physics.
1979	Steven Weinberg, U.S.	Development of theory of weak interactions, regarded as a major
	Abdus Salam, Pakistani	step toward unifying knowledge of four major forces of nature:
	Sheldon L. Glashow, U.S.	gravity, electromagnetism, force that holds together atomic nuclei, and weak force that causes radioactive decay in some atomic nuclei.
1980	James W. Cronin, U.S.	Discovery in 1964 of asymmetry of subatomic particles,
	Val L. Fitch, U.S.	later used to explain "big bang" theory of birth of universe.
1981	Nicolaas Bloembergen, U.S.	Development of laser spectroscopy
	Arthur Schawlow, U.S.	and high-resolution electron spectroscopy.
	Kai M. Siegbahn, Swedish	
1982	Kenneth Geddes Wilson, U.S.	Solving the complex interactions that occur when matter changes from one form to another, as when water boils.
1983	Subrahmanyan Chandrasekhar, U.S. (India-born)	Research and theories concerning evolution of stars, especially white dwarf stars.
	William A. Fowler, U.S.	Study of nuclear reactions in stars and development of theory of formation of chemical elements in universe.
1984	Carlo Rubbia, Italian	Detection of three subatomic particles, a positive W particle, a
	Simon van der Meer, Dutch	negative W particle, and a neutral Z particle, confirming the existence of "weak force."
1985	See page 26.	

NOBEL PEACE PRIZES

1901	Jean H. Dunant, Swiss	1918	No award
	Frédéric Passy, French	1919	Woodrow Wilson, U.S.
1902	Elie Ducommun, Swiss	1920	Léon V. A. Bourgeois, French
	Charles A. Gobat, Swiss	1921	Karl H. Branting, Swedish
1903	Sir William R. Cremer, British		Christian L. Lange, Norwegian
1904	Institute of International Law	1922	Fridtjof Nansen, Norwegian
1905	Baroness Bertha von Suttner, Austrian	1923	No award
1906	Theodore Roosevelt, U.S.	1924	No award
1907	Ernesto T. Moneta, Italian	1925	Sir J. Austen Chamberlain, British
	Louis Renault, French		Charles G. Dawes, U.S.
1908	Klas P. Arnoldson, Swedish	1926	Aristide Briand, French
	Fredrik Bajer, Danish		Gustav Stresemann, German
1909	Auguste M. F. Beernaert, Belgian	1927	Ferdinand Buisson, French
	Paul H. B. B. d'Estournelles de Constant, French		Ludwig Quidde, German
		1928	No award
1910	Permanent International Peace Bureau	1929	Frank B. Kellogg, U.S.
1911	Tobias M. C. Asser, Dutch	1930	Lars O. N. Söderblom, Swedish
	Alfred H. Fried, Austrian	1931	Jane Addams, U.S.
1912	Elihu Root, U.S.		Nicholas Murray Butler, U.S.
1913	Henri Lafontaine, Belgian	1932	No award
1914-16	No award	1933	Sir Norman Angell, British
1917	International Committee of the Red Cross	1934	Arthur Henderson, British

1935	Carl von Ossietzky, German
1936	Carlos Saavedra Lamas, Argentinian
1937	Viscount Cecil of Chelwood, British
1938	International Office for Refugees
1939–43	No award
1944	International Committee of the Red Cross
1945	Cordell Hull, U.S.
1946	Emily G. Balch, U.S.
	John R. Mott, U.S.
1947	Friends Service Council, British
	American Friends Service Committee
1948	No award
1949	Lord John Boyd Orr of Brechin, British
1950	Ralph J. Bunche, U.S.
1951	Léon Jouhaux, French
1952	Albert Schweitzer, French (German-born)
1953	George C. Marshall, U.S.
1954	Office of UN High Commissioner for Refugees
1955	No award
1956	No award
1957	Lester B. Pearson, Canadian
1958	Georges Pire, Belgian
1959	Philip J. Noel-Baker, British
1960	Albert J. Luthuli, South African
1961	Dag Hammarskjöld, Swedish (posthumous)
1962	Linus C. Pauling, U.S.
1963	International Committee of the Red Cross
	Red Cross Societies League
1964	Martin Luther King Jr., U.S.
1965	United Nations Children's Fund (UNICEF)
1966	No award
1967	No award
1968	René Cassin, French
1969	International Labor Organization (ILO)
1970	Norman E. Borlaug, U.S.
1971	Willy Brandt, German
1972	No award
1973	Henry A. Kissinger, U.S. (German-born)
	Le Duc Tho, North Vietnamese
1974	Eisaku Sato, Japanese
	Sean MacBride, Irish
1975	Andrei D. Sakharov, Russian
1976	Betty Williams and Mairead Corrigan, organizers of peace movement to resist terrorist violence in Northern Ireland
1977	Amnesty International, organization that exposes governmental violations of human rights
1978	Anwar al-Sadat, president of Egypt, and Menachem Begin, prime minister of Israel, for Mideast peace initiative to end three decades of conflict
1979	Mother Teresa, Indian (Albanian-born), for charitable work in helping poor of Calcutta.
1980	Adolfo Pérez Esquivel, Argentinian, a leading human-rights advocate.
1981	Office of UN High Commissioner for Refugees
1982	Alfonso García Robles, Mexican, and Alva Reimer Myrdal, Swedish, for their work promoting disarmament
1983	Lech Walesa, Polish, for his avoidance of violence in labor struggle with Poland's communist government
1984	Desmond Tutu, South African Anglican bishop, for his campaign to end apartheid in South Africa.
1985	See page 26.

NOBEL PHYSIOLOGY OR MEDICINE PRIZES

1901	Emil A. von Behring, German	Work on serum therapy, especially for use against diphtheria.
1902	Sir Ronald Ross, British	Investigation of how malaria parasites enter the body.
1903	Niels R. Finsen, Danish	Contribution to treatment of tuberculous skin diseases, especially lupus vulgaris, with concentrated light radiation.
1904	Ivan P. Pavlov, Russian	Work on physiology of digestion.
1905	Robert Koch, German	Investigations and discoveries in relation to tuberculosis.
1906	Camillo Golgi, Italian; Santiago Ramón y Cajal, Spanish	Work on structure of nervous system.
1907	Charles L. A. Laveran, French	Work on role played by protozoa in causing diseases.
1908	Paul Ehrlich, German; Élie Metchnikoff, French (Russian-born)	Work on immunity.
1909	Emil T. Kocher, Swiss	Work on physiology, pathology, and surgery of thyroid gland.
1910	Albrecht Kossel, German	Contributions to knowledge of cell chemistry made through his work on proteins, including nucleic substances.
1911	Allvar Gullstrand, Swedish	Work on dioptrics of eye.
1912	Alexis Carrel, U.S.	Work on vascular suture and transplantation of blood vessels and organs.
1913	Charles R. Richet, French	Work on anaphylaxis and allergies.
1914	Robert Bárány, Hungarian	Work on physiology and pathology of inner ear.
1915–18	No award	
1919	Jules Bordet, Belgian	Discoveries relating to immunity.
1920	Schack A. S. Krogh, Danish	Discovery of capillary motor-regulating mechanism.
1921	No award	
1922	Archibald V. Hill, British	Discovery relating to production of heat in muscle.
	Otto F. Meyerhof, German	Discovery of fixed relationship between consumption of oxygen and metabolism of lactic acid in muscle.
1923	Frederick G. Banting, Canadian; John J. R. Macleod, Canadian	Discovery of insulin.
1924	Willem Einthoven, Dutch	Discovery of mechanism of electrocardiogram.
1925	No award	
1926	Johannes A. G. Fibiger, Danish	Experimental production of cancerlike growth in rats.
1927	Julius Wagner-Jauregg, Austrian	Use of malaria inoculation to treat paralysis and mental deterioration associated with syphilis.
1928	Charles J. H. Nicolle, French	Work on typhus.
1929	Christiaan Eijkman, Dutch	Discovery of health defects due to vitamin B_1 deficiency.
	Sir Frederick G. Hopkins, British	Discovery of growth-stimulating vitamins.
1930	Karl Landsteiner, U.S. (Austrian-born)	Discovery of human blood groups.
1931	Otto H. Warburg, German	Discovery of nature and mode of action of respiratory enzyme.
1932	Edgar D. Adrian, British; Sir Charles S. Sherrington, British	Discoveries regarding functions of nerve cells.
1933	Thomas H. Morgan, U.S.	Discoveries concerning role of chromosome in heredity.
1934	George R. Minot, U.S.; William P. Murphy, U.S.; George H. Whipple, U.S.	Discoveries concerning liver therapy in cases of anemia.

NOBEL PHYSIOLOGY OR MEDICINE PRIZES *(continued)*

Year	Name	Discovery
1935	Hans Spemann, German	Discovery of organizer effect in embryonic development.
1936	Sir Henry H. Dale, British Otto Loewi, U.S. (Austrian-born)	Discoveries relating to chemical transmission of nerve impulses.
1937	Albert Szent-Györgyi von Nagyrapolt U.S. (Hungarian-born)	Studies in body metabolism with special reference to role of vitamin C and fumaric acid.
1938	Corneille J. F. Heymans, Belgian	Discovery of role played by sinus and aortic mechanisms in regulation of respiration.
1939	Gerhard Domagk, German	Discovery of antibacterial effects of drug prontosil. (Prize declined under political pressure; awarded later.)
1940	No award	
1941	No award	
1942	No award	
1943	Henrik C. P. Dam, Danish Edward A. Doisy, U.S.	Discovery of vitamin K. Discovery of chemical nature of vitamin K.
1944	Joseph Erlanger, U.S. Herbert S. Gasser, U.S.	Discoveries relating to highly differentiated functions of single nerve fibers.
1945	Sir Alexander Fleming, British Ernst B. Chain, British (German-born) Sir Howard W. Florey, British (Australian-born)	Discovery of penicillin and its curative effect in various infectious diseases.
1946	Hermann J. Muller, U.S.	Discovery of production of mutations by means of X rays.
1947	Carl F. Cori, U.S. (Czech-born) Gerty T. Cori, U.S. (Czech-born) Bernardo A. Houssay, Argentine	Discovery of course of catalytic conversion of glycogen. Discovery of part played by hormone of anterior pituitary lobe in metabolism of sugar.
1948	Paul H. Müller, Swiss	Discovery of high efficiency of DDT as insecticide.
1949	Walter R. Hess, Swiss Antonio Moniz, Portuguese	Discovery of functional organization of interbrain as coordinator of activities of internal organs. Discovery of value of prefrontal lobotomy in certain psychoses.
1950	Philip S. Hench, U.S. Edward C. Kendall, U.S. Tadeus Reichstein, Swiss (Polish-born)	Discoveries relating to hormones of adrenal cortex, their structure and biological effects.
1951	Max Theiler, U.S. (S. African-born)	Discoveries concerning yellow fever and how to combat it.
1952	Selman A. Waksman, U.S.	Discovery of streptomycin, first antibiotic effective against TB.
1953	Hans A. Krebs, British (German-born) Fritz A. Lipmann, U.S. (German-born)	Discovery of citric acid cycle. Discovery of coenzyme A and its importance for intermediary metabolism.
1954	John F. Enders, U.S. Federick C. Robbins, U.S. Thomas H. Weller, U.S.	Discovery of ability of poliomyelitis viruses to grow in cultures of various types of tissue.
1955	Alex H. T. Theorell, Swedish	Discoveries concerning oxidation enzymes.
1956	Andrée F. Cournand, U.S. (French-born) Werner Forssmann, German Dickinson W. Richards Jr., U.S.	Discoveries concerning heart catheterization and pathological changes in circulatory system.
1957	Daniel Bovet, Italian (Swiss-born)	Discoveries relating to synthetic compounds that inhibit action of certain body substances.
1958	George W. Beadle, U.S. Edward L. Tatum, U.S. Joshua Lederberg, U.S.	Discovery that genes act by regulating definite chemical events. Discoveries concerning genetic recombination and organization of genetic material of bacteria.
1959	Arthur Kornberg, U.S. Severo Ochoa, U.S. (Spanish-born)	Discovery of mechanisms in biological synthesis of RNA and DNA.
1960	Sir F. Macfarlane Burnet, Australian Peter B. Medawar, British (Brazilian-born)	Discovery of acquired immunological tolerance.
1961	Georg von Békésy, U.S. (Hungarian-born)	Discoveries of physical mechanism of stimulation within cochlea of inner ear.
1962	Francis H. C. Crick, British James D. Watson, U.S. Maurice H. F. Wilkins, British	Discoveries concerning molecular structure of nuclear acids and its significance for information transfer in living material.
1963	Sir John C. Eccles, Australian Alan L. Hodgkin, British Andrew F. Huxley, British	Discoveries concerning nerve-cell membrane.
1964	Konrad E. Bloch, U.S. Feodor Lynen, German	Discoveries concerning mechanism and regulation of cholesterol and fatty-acid metabolism.
1965	François Jacob, French André Lwoff, French Jacques Monod, French	Discovery of regulatory processes in body cells that contribute to genetic control of enzymes and virus synthesis.
1966	Charles B. Huggins, U.S. Francis Peyton Rous, U.S.	Discoveries concerning hormonal treatment of cancer of prostate gland. Discovery of tumor-inducing viruses in chickens.
1967	Ragnar Granit, Swedish (Finnish-born) Haldan Keffer Hartline, U.S. George Wald, U.S.	Discoveries concerning primary chemical and physiological visual processes in eye.
1968	Robert W. Holley, U.S. Har Gobind Khorana, U.S. (Indian-born) Marshall W. Nirenberg, U.S.	Explanation of genetic code that determines function of cells.
1969	Max Delbrück, U.S. (German-born) Alfred D. Hershey, U.S. Salvador D. Luria, U.S. (Italian-born)	Discoveries concerning reproductive mechanism and genetic structure of viruses.

1970	Julius Axelrod, U.S. Ulf von Euler, Swedish Bernard Katz, British	Basic research in chemistry of nerve transmission.
1971	Earl W. Sutherland Jr., U.S.	Discoveries concerning mechanisms of action of hormones.
1972	Gerald M. Edelman, U.S. Rodney Porter, British	Determination of antibody's exact chemical structure.
1973	Karl von Frisch, Austrian Konrad Lorenz, Austrian Nikolaas Tinbergen, British (Dutch-born)	Discoveries in individual and social behavior patterns of birds and bees in relation to natural selection and survival of species.
1974	Albert Claude, U.S. (Luxembourgian-born) Christian Rene de Duve, Belgian George Emil Palade, U.S. (Romanian-born)	Founding science of cell biology, pioneering in use of electron microscope to study living cells, and discovering such cell parts as ribosomes and lysosomes.
1975	David Baltimore, U.S. Howard Martin Temin, U.S. Renato Dulbecco, U.S. (Italian-born)	Research discoveries concerning interaction between tumor viruses and genetic material of living cell.
1976	Baruch S. Blumberg, U.S. D. Carleton Gajdusek, U.S.	Research that led to test for hepatitis virus in donated blood and to experimental vaccine against hepatitis. Discovery of virus causing kuru disease among cannibals in New Guinea, transmitted through eating of human brains.
1977	Rosalyn S. Yalow, U.S. Roger C. L. Guillemin, U.S. (French-born) Andrew V. Schally, U.S. (Polish-born)	Development of radioimmunoassay, use of radioactive materials to measure hormones and other substances in blood and tissues. Discovery and synthesis of peptide hormones produced by hypothalmus in brain, providing greater understanding of brain's control of body's chemistry.
1978	Daniel Nathans, U.S. Hamilton O. Smith, U.S. Werner Arber, Swiss	Research that made possible gene splicing or recombinant DNA to create mutant life forms by discovering and using enzymes called *restriction endonucleases.*
1979	Allan McLeod Cormack, U.S. Godfrey Newbold Hounsfield, British ..	Development of computerized axial tomography (CAT), an X-ray scanning technique used in medical diagnosis of patients.
1980	George D. Snell, U.S. Baruj Benacerraf, U.S. (Venezuelan-born) Jean Dausset, French	Identification of the HLA antigens, or histocompatability system, in human cells, leading to more successful surgical transplants of human organs.
1981	David H. Hubel, U.S. Roger W. Sperry, U.S. Torsten N. Wiesel, U.S. (Swedish-born)	Research on human brain organization and function.
1982	Sune Bergstrom, Swedish Bengt Samuelsson, Swedish John R. Vane, British	Research on prostaglandins, explaining how the hormone-like substances are formed in human body and how they defend cells from disease.
1983	Barbara McClintock, U.S.	Discovery that genes of corn can move from one place in the chromosomes of a plant to another, changing the characteristics of future plants.
1984	Cesar Milstein, Argentinian Georges J.F. Koehler, German Niels K. Jerne, Danish	Discovery in 1975 of techniques for producing monoclonal antibodies used in immunology. Cited as the "Leading Theoretician in immunology during the last 30 years."
1985	See page 26.	

NOBEL ECONOMICS PRIZES

1969	Ragnar Frisch, Norwegian Jan Tinbergen, Dutch	Development of mathematical models for analyzing economic activity.
1970	Paul A. Samuelson, U.S.	Raising level of scientific analysis in economic theory.
1971	Simon Kuznets, U.S.	Determining country's gross national product.
1972	Kenneth J. Arrow, U.S. Sir John R. Hicks, British	Pioneering studies in theory of general economic equilibrium.
1973	Wassily Leontief, U.S. (Russian-born)	Development of "input-output" method of economic analysis used by most industrial nations.
1974	Gunnar Myrdal, Swedish Friedrich A. von Hayek, Austrian	Pioneering work in theory of money and economic fluctuations.
1975	Leonid V. Kantorovich, Russian Tjalling C. Koopmans, U.S. (Dutch-born)	Contributions to theory of optimum allocation of resources.
1976	Milton Friedman, U.S.	Achievements in consumption analysis, monetary history and theory, and demonstration of complexity of stabilization policy.
1977	Bertil Ohlin, Swedish James Edward Meade, British	For pathbreaking contributions to theory of international trade and international capital movement.
1978	Herbert Simon, U.S.	Pioneering research into how businesses and other organizations make economic decisions.
1979	Sir Arthur Lewis, British (St. Lucian-born) Theodore W. Schultz, U.S.	For efforts to solve economic problems of need and poverty in world and to find solutions for developing nations.
1980	Lawrence Klein, U.S.	For development of econometric models to analyze economic fluctuations.
1981	James Tobin, U.S.	Development of "portfolio selection theory."
1982	George J. Stigler, U.S.	Studies of industry and government regulation.
1983	Gerard Debreu, U.S. (French-born) ...	Refining and confirming Adam Smith's theory of supply and demand by use of mathematical models.
1984	Sir Richard Stone, British	Pioneering development of national accounting systems for governments to keep track of their finances.
1985	See page 26.	

PULITZER PRIZES

The Pulitzer Prizes are the most prestigious awards made each year in the United States for journalism, literature, and music. The prizes were established under terms of the will of Joseph Pulitzer (1847–1911), a Hungarian immigrant who in 1878 founded one of America's great newspapers, the *St. Louis* (Mo.) *Post-Dispatch,* and then in 1883 purchased New York City's *The World,* making it into a crusading newspaper with the largest circulation in the United States.

Upon his death in 1911, Pulitzer left $2 million to found a graduate school of journalism at Columbia University in New York City with the provision that after the school had operated for at least three years prizes should be awarded annually for the advancement of journalism, literature, music, and public service. The Columbia University School of Journalism was founded in 1912. The first Pulitzer Prizes began to be awarded in 1917.

Each prize carries an award of $1,000 except for the gold medal award to a newspaper for meritorious public service.

Prizes in journalism are awarded in 14 categories. Prizes in literature, drama, and music are awarded in seven areas. In addition, special awards are made from time to time.

LOCAL INVESTIGATIVE REPORTING

1953　Edward J. Mowery, *New York World-Telegram & Sun*
1954　Alvin S. McCoy, *Kansas City* (Mo.) *Star*
1955　Roland K. Towery, *Cuero* (Tex.) *Record*
1956　Arthur Daley, *New York Times*
1957　Wallace Turner and William Lambert, *Portland Oregonian*
1958　George Beveridge, *Washington Evening Star*
1959　John Harold Brislin, *Scranton* (Pa.) *Tribune and Scrantonian*
1960　Mariam Ottenberg, *Washington Evening Star*
1961　Edgar May, *Buffalo Evening News*
1962　George Bliss, *Chicago Tribune*
1963　Oscar O'Neal Griffin Jr., *Pecos* (Tex.) *Independent and Enterprise*
1964　James V. Magee, Albert V. Gaudiosi, and Frederick A. Meyer, *Philadelphia Bulletin*
1965　Gene Goltz, *Houston Post*
1966　John A. Frasca, *Tampa* (Fla.) *Tribune*
1967　Gene Miller, *Miami Herald*
1968　J. Anthony Lukas, *New York Times*
1969　Albert Delugach and Denny Walsh, *St. Louis Globe-Democrat*
1970　Harold E. Martin, *Montgomery* (Ala.) *Advertiser*
1971　William Hugh Jones, *Chicago Tribune*
1972　Ann DeSantis, S. A. Kurkjian, T. Leland, and G. M. O'Neill, *Boston Globe*
1973　*Sun* Newspapers, Omaha, Nebr.
1974　William Sherman, *New York Daily News*
1975　*Indianapolis Star*
1976　Staff of *Chicago Tribune*
1977　Acel Moore and Wendell Rawls Jr., *Philadelphia Inquirer*
1978　Anthony R. Dolan, *Stamford* (Conn.) *Advocate*
1979　Gilbert M. Paul and Elliot G. Jaspin, *Pottsville* (Pa.) *Republican*
1980　Stephen A. Kurkjian, Alexander B. Hawes Jr., Nils J. Bruzelius, Joan Vennochi, and Robert Porterfield, *Boston Globe*
1981　Clark Hallas and Robert B. Lowe, *Arizona Daily Star*
1982　Paul Henderson, *Seattle Times*
1983　Loretta Tofani, *Washington Post,* for articles on conditions in Maryland detention center
1984　*Boston Globe* for series on employment difficulties by members of minorities
1985　Lucy Morgan and Jack Reed, St. Petersburg, Fla., *Times,* series that led to indictment of sheriff; William K. Marimow, *Philadelphia Inquirer,* articles on city police dog attacks on civilians

LOCAL GENERAL REPORTING

1953　*Providence* (R.I.) *Journal and Evening Bulletin*
1954　*Vicksburg* (Miss.) *Sunday Post-Herald*
1955　Caro Brown, *Alice* (Tex.) *Daily Echo*
1956　Lee Hills, *Detroit Free Press*
1957　*Salt Lake Tribune*
1958　*Fargo* (N.D.) *Forum*
1959　Mary Lou Werner, *Washington Evening Star*
1960　Jack Nelson, *Atlanta Constitution*
1961　Sanche de Gramont, *New York Herald Tribune*
1962　Robert D. Mullins, *Deseret News,* Salt Lake City, Utah
1963　Sylvan Fox, Anthony Shannon, and William Longgood, *New York World-Telegram & Sun*
1964　Norman C. Miller, *Wall Street Journal*
1965　Melvin H. Ruder, *Hungry Horse* (Mont.) *News*
1966　Staff, *Los Angeles Times*
1967　Robert V. Cox, *Chambersburg* (Pa.) *Public Opinion*
1968　*Detroit Free Press*
1969　John Fretterman, *Louisville Courier-Journal*
1970　Thomas Fitzpatrick, *Chicago Sun-Times*
1971　*Akron* (Ohio) *Beacon Journal*
1972　R. I. Cooper and J. W. Machacek, *Rochester* (N.Y.) *Times-Union*
1973　*Chicago Tribune*
1974　Arthur M. Petacque and Hugh F. Hough, *Chicago Sun-Times*
1975　*Xenia* (Ohio) *Daily Gazette*
1976　Gene Miller, *Miami Herald*
1977　Margo Huston, *Milwaukee Journal*
1978　Richard Whitt, *Louisville* (Ky.) *Courier-Journal*
1979　Staff of *San Diego* (Calif.) *Evening Tribune*
1980　Staff of *Philadelphia Inquirer*
1981　Staff of *Longview* (Wash.) *Daily News* for reporting of Mount St. Helens volcanic eruption
1982　*Kansas City Star* and *Kansas City Times* for coverage of Hyatt Regency Hotel disaster
1983　Staff of *Ft. Wayne (Ind.) News-Sentinel* for coverage of 1982 flood
1984　*Newsday* (Long Island, N.Y.) for coverage of Baby Jane Doe case
1985　Thomas Turcol, Norfolk, Va., *Virginia-Pilot* and *Ledger-Star* articles on financial dealings of local official

NATIONAL REPORTING

1942　Louis Stark, *New York Times*
1943　No award
1944　Dewey L. Fleming, *Sun,* Baltimore
1945　James B. Reston, *New York Times*
1946　Edward A. Harris, *St. Louis Post-Dispatch*
1947　Edward T. Folliard, *Washington Post*
1948　Bert Andrews, *New York Herald Tribune,* and Nat S. Finney, *Minneapolis Tribune*
1949　Charles P. Trussell, *New York Times*
1950　Edwin O. Guthman, *Seattle Times*
1951　No award
1952　Anthony Leviero, *New York Times*
1953　Don Whitehead, Associated Press
1954　Richard Wilson, Cowles Newspapers

1955 Anthony Lewis, *Washington Daily News*
1956 Charles Bartlett, *Chattanooga* (Tenn.) *Times*
1957 James Reston, *New York Times*
1958 Relman Morin, Associated Press
1959 Howard Van Smith, *Miami News*
1960 Vance Trimble, Scripps-Howard
1961 Edward R. Cony, *Wall Street Journal*
1962 Nathan G. Caldwell and Gene S. Graham, *Nashville Tennessean*
1963 Anthony Lewis, *New York Times*
1964 Merriman Smith, United Press International
1965 Louis Kohlmeier, *Wall Street Journal*
1966 Haynes Johnson, *Washington Evening Star*
1967 Monroe W. Karmin and Stanley W. Penn, *Wall Street Journal*
1968 Howard James, *Christian Science Monitor,* and Nathan Kotz, *Register,* Des Moines, Iowa
1969 Robert Cahn, *Christian Science Monitor*
1970 William J. Seton, *Chicago Daily News*
1971 Lucinda Franks and Thomas Powers, United Press International
1972 Jack Anderson, syndicated columnist
1973 Robert Boyd and Clark Hoyt, the Knight. Newspapers
1974 James R. Polk, *Washington Star-News,* and Jack White, *Providence* (R.I.) *Journal-Bulletin*
1975 Donald L. Barlett and James B. Steel *Philadelphia Inquirer*
1976 James Risser, *Register,* Des Moines, Iowa
1977 Walter Mears, Associated Press
1978 Gaylord Shaw, *Los Angeles Times*
1979 James Risser, *Register,* Des Moines, Iowa
1980 Bette Swenson Orsini and Charles Stafford, *St. Petersburg* (Fla.) *Times*
1981 John H. Crewdson, *New York Times*
1982 Rick Atkinson, *Kansas City Times*
1983 Staff of *Boston Globe,* for "War and Peace in the Nuclear Age" supplement
1984 John Noble Wilford, *New York Times,* for science reporting
1985 Thomas J. Knudson, *Register,* Des Moines, Iowa, articles on dangers of farming

INTERNATIONAL REPORTING

1942 Laurence E. Allen, Associated Press
1943 Ira Wolfert, North American Newspaper Alliance
1944 Daniel DeLuce, Associated Press
1945 Mark S. Watson, *Sun,* Baltimore
1946 Homer W. Bigart, *New York Herald Tribune*
1947 Eddy Gilmore, Associated Press
1948 Paul W. Ward, *Sun,* Baltimore
1949 Price Day, *Sun,* Baltimore
1950 Edmund Stevens, *Christian Science Monitor*
1951 Keyes Beech and Fred Sparks, *Chicago Daily News,* Homer Bigart and Marguerite Higgins, *New York Herald Tribune,* Relman Morin and Don Whitehead, Associated Press
1952 John M. Hightower, Associated Press
1953 Austin Wehrwein, *Milwaukee Journal*
1954 Jim G. Lucas, Scripps-Howard Newspapers
1955 Harrison Salisbury, *New York Times*
1956 William Randolph Hearst Jr., Kingsbury Smith, and Frank Conniff, International News Service
1957 Russell Jones, United Press
1958 *New York Times*
1959 Joseph Martin and Philip Santora, *New York Daily News*
1960 A.M. Rosenthal, *New York Times*
1961 Lynn Heinzerling, Associated Press
1962 Walter Lippmann, New York Herald Tribune Syndicate
1963 Hal Hendrix, *Miami News,*
1964 Malcolm W. Browne, Associated Press David Halberstam, *New York Times*

1965 J.A. Livingston, *Philadelphia Bulletin*
1966 Peter Arnett, Associated Press
1967 R.J. Hughes, *Christian Science Monitor*
1968 Alfred Friendly, *Washington Post*
1969 William Tuohy, *Los Angeles Times*
1970 Seymour M. Hersh, Dispatch News Service
1971 Jimmie Lee Hoagland, *Washington Post*
1972 Peter R. Kann, *Wall Street Journal*
1973 Max Frankel, *New York Times*
1974 Hedrick Smith, *New York Times*
1975 William Mullen and Ovie Carter, *Chicago Tribune*
1976 Sydney H. Schanberg, *New York Times*
1977 No award
1978 Henry Kamm, *New York Times*
1979 Richard Ben Cramer, *Philadelphia Inquirer*
1980 Joel Brinkley and Jay Mather, *Louisville* (Ky.) *Courier-Journal* for Cambodia coverage
1981 Shirley Christian, *Miami Herald*
1982 John Darnton, *New York Times,* for reporting on Poland's crisis
1983 Thomas L. Friedman, *New York Times,* and Loren Jenkins, *Washington Post,* for reports on fighting in Lebanon
1984 Karen Elliott House, *Wall Street Journal,* for articles on U.S. policy in the Mideast
1985 Josh Friedman, Dennis Bell, Ozier Muhammad, *Newsday,* Long Island, N.Y., series on famine in Africa

FEATURE WRITING

1979 Jon D. Franklin, *Baltimore Evening Sun*
1980 Madeline Blais, *Miami Herald*
1981 Theresa Carpenter, *The Village Voice*
1982 Saul Pett, *Associated Press*
1983 Nan Robertson, *New York Times,* for account of her experience with toxic shock syndrome
1984 Peter Mark Rinearson, *Seattle Times*
1985 Alice Steinbach, *Baltimore Sun,* article about blind boy

EXPLANATORY JOURNALISM

1985 Jon Franklin, *Baltimore Evening Sun,* series on molecular psychiatry

SPECIALIZED REPORTING

1985 Randall Savage and Jackie Crosby, Macon, Ga., *Telegraph and News,* articles on athletics and academics at Georgia's universities

EDITORIAL WRITING

1917 *New York Tribune*
1918 *Courier-Journal,* Louisville, Ky.
1919 No award
1920 Harvey E. Newbranch, *Evening World-Herald,* Omaha
1921 No award
1922 Frank M. O'Brien, *New York Herald*
1923 William Allen White, *Emporia* (Kans.) *Gazette*
1924 *Boston Herald; Frank I. Cobb, New York World*
1925 *Charleston* (S.C.) *News and Courier*
1926 Edward M. Kingsbury, *New York Times*
1927 F.L. Bullard, *Boston Herald*
1928 Grover Cleveland Hall, *Montgomery* (Ala.) *Advertiser*
1929 Louis I. Jaffee, *Norfolk Virginian-Pilot*
1930 No award
1931 Charles S. Ryckman, *Fremont* (Nebr.) *Tribune*
1932 No award
1933 *Kansas City Star*
1934 E.P. Chase, *Atlantic* (Iowa) *News-Telegraph*
1935 No award
1936 Felix Morley, *Washington Post;* George B. Parker, Scripps-Howard

PULITZER PRIZES *(continued)*

1937 John W. Owens, *Baltimore Sun*
1938 W.W. Waymack, *Register and Tribune,*
Des Moines, Iowa
1939 Ronald G. Callvert, Portland *Oregonian*
1940 Bart Howard, *St. Louis Post-Dispatch*
1941 Reuben Maury, *New York Daily News*
1942 Geoffrey Parsons, *New York Herald Tribune*
1943 Forrest W. Seymour, *Register and Tribune,*
Des Moines, Iowa
1944 Henry J. Haskell, *Kansas City Star*
1945 George W. Potter, *Providence* (R.I.) *Journal-
Bulletin*
1946 Hodding Carter, *Delta Democrat-Times,*
Greenville, Miss.
1947 William Grimes, *Wall Street Journal*
1948 Virginius Dabney, *Richmond* (Va.) *Times-
Dispatch*
1949 John H. Crider, *Boston Herald*
Herbert Elliston, *Washington Post*
1950 Carl M. Saunders, *Jackson* (Mich.) *Citizen Patriot*
1951 William Fitzpatrick, *New Orleans States*
1952 Louis LaCoss, *St. Louis Globe-Democrat*
1953 Vermont Royster, *Wall Street Journal*
1954 Don Murray, *Boston Herald*
1955 Royce Howes, *Detroit Free Press*
1956 Lauren K. Soth, *Register and Tribune,* Des
Moines, Iowa
1957 Buford Boone, *Tuscaloosa* (Ala.) *News*
1958 Harry S. Ashmore, *Arkansas Gazette,* Little Rock
1959 Ralph McGill, *Atlanta Constitution*
1960 Lenoir Chambers, *Norfolk Virginian-Pilot*
1961 William J. Dorvillier, *San Juan* (P.R.) *Star*
1962 Thomas M. Storke, *Santa Barbara* (Calif.) *News-
Press*
1963 Ira B. Harkey Jr., *Pascagoula* (Miss.) *Chronicle*
1964 Hazel Smith, *Lexington* (Miss.) *Advertiser*
1965 John R. Harrison, *Gainesville* (Fla.) *Sun*
1966 Robert Lasch, *St. Louis Post-Dispatch*
1967 Eugene C. Patterson, *Atlanta Constitution*
1968 John S. Knight, Knight Newspapers
1969 Paul Greenberg, *Pine Bluff* (Ark.) *Commercial*
1970 Philip Geyelin, *Washington Post*
1971 Horance G. Davis Jr., *Gainesville* (Fla.) *Sun*
1972 J. Strohmeyer, *Bethlehem* (Pa.) *Globe-Times*
1973 Roger B. Linscott, *Berkshire Eagle,* Mass.
1974 F. Gilman Spencer, *Trenton Trentonian*
1975 John Daniell Maurice, *Charleston* (W.Va.) *Daily
Mail*
1976 Philip P. Kerby, *Los Angeles Times*
1977 Warren L. Lerude, Foster Church, Norman F.
Cardoza, *Reno Evening Gazette* and *Nevada State
Journal*
1978 Meg Greenfield, *Washington Post*
1979 Edwin M. Yoder Jr., *Washington Star*
1980 Robert L. Bartley, *Wall Street Journal*
1981 No award
1982 Jack Rosenthal, *New York Times*
1983 Editorial board, *Miami Herald*
1984 Albert Scardino, *Georgia Gazette* (Savannah, Ga.)
1985 Richard Aregood, *Philadelphia Daily News*

CARTOON PULITZER PRIZES

1922 Rollin Kirby, *New York World*
1923 No award
1924 Jay Norwood Darling, *New York Tribune*
1925 Rollin Kirby, *New York World*
1926 Daniel R. Fitzpatrick, *St. Louis Post-Dispatch*
1927 Nelson Harding, *Brooklyn Daily Eagle*
1928 Nelson Harding, *Brooklyn Daily Eagle*
1929 Rollin Kirby, *New York World*
1930 Charles R. Macauley, *Brooklyn Daily Eagle*
1931 Edmund Duffy, *Baltimore Sun*

1932 John McCutcheon, *Chicago Tribune*
1933 H.M. Talburt, *Washington Daily News*
1934 Edmund Duffy, *Baltimore Sun*
1935 Ross A. Lewis, *Milwaukee Journal*
1936 No award
1937 Clarence Daniel Batchelor, *N.Y. Daily News*
1938 Vaughn Shoemaker, *Chicago Daily News*
1939 Charles G. Werner, *Daily Oklahoman,* Oklahoma
City
1940 Edmund Duffy, *Baltimore Sun*
1941 Jacob Burck, *Chicago Times*
1942 Herbert L. Block (Herblock), Newspaper
Enterprise Association Service
1943 Jay Norwood Darling, *N.Y. Herald Tribune*
1944 Clifford K. Berryman, *Washington Evening Star*
1945 William (Bill) Mauldin, United Features
Syndicate, Inc.
1946 Bruce Russell, *Los Angeles Times*
1947 V. Shoemaker, *Chicago Daily News*
1948 Reuben L. (Rube) Goldberg, *New York Sun*
1949 Lute Pease, *Newark,* (N.J.) *Evening News*
1950 James T. Berryman, *Washington Evening Star*
1951 Reginald W. Manning, *Arizona Republic,* Phoenix,
Ariz.
1952 Fred L. Packer, *New York Mirror*
1953 Edward D. Kuekes, *Cleveland Plain Dealer*
1954 Herbert L. Block (Herblock), *Washington Post &
Times-Herald*
1955 Daniel R. Fitzpatrick, *St. Louis Post-Dispatch*
1956 Robert York, *Louisville Times*
1957 Tom Little, *Nashville Tennessean*
1958 Bruce M. Shanks, *Buffalo Evening News*
1959 William (Bill) Mauldin, *St. Louis Post-Dispatch*
1960 No award
1961 Carey Orr, *Chicago Tribune*
1962 E.S. Valtman, *Hartford* (Conn.) *Times*
1963 Frank Miller, *Des Moines Register*
1964 Paul Conrad, *Denver Post*
1965 No award
1966 Don Wright, *Miami News*
1967 Patrick B. Oliphant, *Denver Post*
1968 E. G. Payne, *Charlotte* (N.C.) *Observer*
1969 John Fischetti, *Chicago Daily News*
1970 Thomas Darcy, *Newsday,* Garden City, N.Y.
1971 Paul Conrad, *Los Angeles Times*
1972 J. K. MacNelly, *Richmond* (Va.) *News Leader*
1973 No award
1974 Paul Szep, *Boston Globe*
1975 Garry Trudeau, creator of "Doonesbury"
1976 Tony Auth, political cartoonist, *Philadelphia
Inquirer*
1977 Paul Szep, *Boston Globe*
1978 J. K. MacNelly, *Richmond* (Va.) *News Leader*
1979 Herbert L. Block (Herblock), *Washington Post*
1980 Don Wright, *Miami News*
1981 Mike Peters, *Dayton* (Ohio) *Daily News*
1982 Ben Sargent, *Austin* (Tex.) *American-Statesman*
1983 Richard Locher, *Chicago Tribune*
1984 Paul Conrad, *Los Angeles Times*
1985 Jeff MacNelly, *Chicago Tribune*

NEWS PHOTOGRAPHY PULITZER PRIZES

1942 Milton Brooks, *Detroit News*
1943 Frank Noel, Associated Press
1944 Frank Filan, Associated Press
1945 Joe Rosenthal, Associated Press
1946 No award
1947 Arnold Hardy, amateur photographer
1948 Frank Cushing, *Boston Traveler*
1949 Nathaniel Fein, *New York Herald Tribune*
1950 Bill Crouch, *Oakland* (Calif.) *Tribune*
1951 Max Desfor, Associated Press
1952 John Robinson and Don Ultang, *Des
Moines Register and Tribune*

1953 William M. Gallagher, *Flint* (Mich.) *Journal*
1954 Mrs. Walter M. Schau, photographer
1955 John L. Gaunt Jr., *Los Angeles Times*
1956 *New York Daily News*
1957 Harry A. Trask, *Boston Traveler*
1958 William C. Beall, *Washington Daily News*
1959 William Seaman, *Minneapolis Star*
1960 Andrew Lopez, United Press International
1961 Yasushi Nagao, Mainichi Newspapers, Tokyo, Japan
1962 Paul Vathis, Associated Press
1963 Hector Rondon, Caracas, Venezuela
1964 Robert H. Jackson, *Dallas Times Herald*
1965 Horst Faas, Associated Press
1966 Kyoichi Sawada, United Press International
1967 Jack R. Thornell, Associated Press
1968 Rocco Morabito, *Jacksonville* (Fla.) *Journal*
1969 Edward T. Adams, Associated Press
1970 Steve Starr, Associated Press
1971 John Paul Filo, amateur photographer
1972 H. Faas, M. Laurent, Associated Press
1973 Huynh Cong Ut, Associated Press
1974 Anthony K. Roberts, freelance
1975 Gerald H. Gay, *Seattle Times*
1976 Stanley Forman, *Boston Herald-American*
1977 Stanley Forman, *Boston Herald-American,* and Neal Ulevich, Associated Press
1978 John W. Blair, freelance
1979 Thomas J. Kelley III, *Pottstown* (Pa.) *Mercury*
1980 Unidentified photographer of Iranian firing squad
1981 Larry C. Price, *Fort Worth Star-Telegram*
1982 Ron Edmonds, Associated Press
1983 Bill Foley, Associated Press
1984 Stan Grossfeld, *Boston Globe*
1985 *Register,* Santa Ana, Calif.

FEATURE PHOTOGRAPHY PULITZER PRIZES

1968 Toshio Sakai, United Press International
1969 Moneta Sleet Jr., *Ebony* magazine
1970 Dallas Kinney, *Palm Beach* (Fla.) *Post*
1971 Jack Dykinga, *Chicago Sun-Times*
1972 Dave Kennerly, United Press International
1973 B. Lanker, *Topeka* (Kans.) *Capital-Journal*
1974 Slava Veder, Associated Press
1975 Matthew Lewis, *Washington Post*
1976 Photographic staff of *Louisville Courier-Journal and Times*
1977 Robin Hood, *News-Free Press,* Chattanooga, Tenn.
1978 J. Ross Baughman, freelance
1979 Staff of *The Boston Herald-American*
1980 Erwin H. Hagler, *Dallas Times Herald*
1981 Taro M. Yamasaki, *Detroit Free Press*
1982 John H. White, *Chicago Sun-Times*
1983 James B. Dickman, *Dallas Times Herald*
1984 Anthony Suau, *Denver Post*
1985 Stan Grossfeld, *Boston Globe;* Larry C. Price, *Philadelphia Inquirer*

MERITORIOUS PUBLIC SERVICE

1918 *New York Times*
1919 *Milwaukee Journal*
1920 No award
1921 *Boston Post*
1922 *World,* New York
1923 *Memphis Commercial Appeal*
1924 *World,* New York
1925 No award
1926 *Enquirer Sun,* Columbus, Ga.
1927 *Canton* (Ohio) *Daily News*
1928 *Indianapolis Times*
1929 *Evening World,* New York

1930 No award
1931 *Atlanta Constitution*
1932 *Indianapolis News*
1933 *New York World-Telegram*
1934 *Medford* (Oreg.) *Mail Tribune*
1935 *Sacramento* (Calif.) *Bee*
1936 *Cedar Rapids* (Iowa) *Gazette*
1937 *St. Louis Post-Dispatch*
1938 *Bismarck* (N.D.) *Tribune*
1939 *Miami Daily News*
1940 *Waterbury* (Conn.) *Republican and American*
1941 *St. Louis Post-Dispatch*
1942 *Los Angeles Times*
1943 *World-Herald,* Omaha, Nebr.
1944 *New York Times*
1945 *Detroit Free Press*
1946 *Scranton* (Pa.) *Times*
1947 *Baltimore Sun*
1948 *St. Louis Post-Dispatch*
1949 *Nebraska State Journal*
1950 *Chicago Daily News; St. Louis Post-Dispatch*
1951 *Miami Herald; Brooklyn Eagle*
1952 *St. Louis Post-Dispatch*
1953 *News Reporter,* Whiteville, N.C. *Tabor City* (N.C.) *Tribune*
1954 Newsday, Garden City, N.Y.
1955 *Columbus* (Ga.) *Ledger and Sunday Ledger-Enquirer*
1956 *Watsonville* (Calif.) *Register-Pajaronian*
1957 *Chicago Daily News*
1958 *Arkansas Gazette,* Little Rock
1959 *Utica* (N.Y.) *Observer-Dispatch Utica* (N.Y.) *Daily Press*
1960 *Los Angeles Times*
1961 *Amarillo* (Tex.) *Globe-Times*
1962 *Panama City* (Fla.) *News-Herald*
1963 *Chicago Daily News*
1964 *St. Petersburg* (Fla.) *Times*
1965 *Hutchinson* (Kans.) *News*
1966 *Boston Globe*
1967 *Louisville Courier-Journal; Milwaukee Journal*
1968 *Riverside* (Calif.) *Press*
1969 *Los Angeles Times*
1970 *Newsday,* Garden City, N.Y.
1971 *Winston-Salem* (N.C.) *Journal and Sentinel*
1972 *New York Times*
1973 *Washington Post*
1974 *Newsday,* Garden City, N.Y.
1975 *Boston Globe*
1976 *Anchorage* (Alaska) *Daily News*
1977 *Lufkin* (Tex.) *News*
1978 *Philadelphia Inquirer*
1979 *Point Reyes* (Calif.) *Light,* for Synanon exposé
1980 Gannett News Service, for exposing mismanagement of funds of Pauline Fathers
1981 *Charlotte* (N.C.) *Observer,* for exposure of "brown lung" disease among textile workers
1982 *Detroit News,* for exposure of Navy cover-ups of circumstances of shipboard deaths
1983 Jackson, Miss., *Clarion Ledger,* for investigation of Mississippi public school system
1984 *Los Angeles Times* for 27-part series on California Hispanics
1985 Fort Worth *Star-Telegram,* series on overpriced spare parts bought by military services

CRITICISM PULITZER PRIZES

1970 Ada Louise Huxtable, *New York Times*
1971 Harold C. Schonberg, *New York Times*
1972 Frank L. Peters Jr., *St. Louis Post-Dispatch*
1973 Ronald Powers, *Chicago Sun-Times*
1974 Emily Genauer, *Newsday* syndicate
1975 Roger Ebert, *Chicago Sun-Times*
1976 Alan M. Kriegsman, *Washington Post*

PULITZER PRIZES *(continued)*

1977 William McPherson, *Washington Post*
1978 Walter Kerr, *New York Times*
1979 Paul Gapp, *Chicago Tribune*
1980 William A. Henry III, TV critic, *Boston Globe*
1981 Jonathan Yardley, book critic, *Washington Star*
1982 Martin Bernheimer, music critic, *Los Angeles Times*
1983 Manuela Hoelterhoff, *Wall Street Journal*
1984 Paul Goldberger, *New York Times*
1985 Howard Rosenberg, *Los Angeles Times*

COMMENTARY PULITZER PRIZES

1970 Marquis Childs, *St. Louis Post-Dispatch*
1971 William A. Caldwell, *Record*, Hackensack, N.J.
1972 Mike Royko, *Chicago Daily News*
1973 David S. Broder, *Washington Post*
1974 Edwin A. Roberts Jr., *National Observer*
1975 Mary McGrory, *Washington Star*
1976 Walter W. (Red) Smith, sports columnist, *New York Times*
1977 George F. Will, syndicated columnist, Washington Post Writers Group
1978 William Safire, columnist, *New York Times*
1979 Russell Baker, columnist, *New York Times*
1980 Ellen H. Goodman, columnist, *Boston Globe*
1981 Dave Anderson, sports columnist, *N.Y. Times*
1982 Art Buchwald, *Los Angeles Times* syndicate
1983 Claude Sitton, Raleigh, N.C., *News & Observer*
1984 Vermont Royster, *Wall Street Journal*
1985 Murray Kempton, *Newsday*, Long Island, N.Y.

SPECIAL PULITZER PRIZE CITATIONS

1964 Gannett Newspapers, Rochester, N.Y., for their program *The Road to Integration*, a distinguished example of the use of a newspaper group's resources to complement the work of its individual newspapers
1973 James T. Flexner, for *George Washington*, a four-volume biography
1976 Scott Joplin (1868–1917), special Bicentennial year award for his contributions to American music with such compositions as *Maple Leaf Rag*
1976 John Hohenberg, for 22 years of service as administrator of the Pulitzer Prizes
1977 Alex Haley, for *Roots*, an "important contribution to the literature of slavery"
1978 E.B. White, for contributions to literature; Richard L. Strout, for contributions to journalism
1982 Milton Babbitt, for life work as distinguished composer
1984 Theodore Seuss Geisel (Dr. Seuss), for his many children's books

FICTION PULITZER PRIZES

1918 *His Family*, Ernest Poole
1919 *The Magnificent Ambersons*, Booth Tarkington
1920 No award
1921 *The Age of Innocence*, Edith Wharton
1922 *Alice Adams*, Booth Tarkington
1923 *One of Ours*, Willa Cather
1924 *The Able McLaughlins*, Margaret Wilson
1925 *So Big*, Edna Ferber
1926 *Arrowsmith*, Sinclair Lewis
1927 *Early Autumn*, Louis Bromfield
1928 *The Bridge of San Luis Rey*, Thornton Wilder
1929 *Scarlet Sister Mary*, Julia Peterkin
1930 *Laughing Boy*, Oliver LaFarge
1931 *Years of Grace*, Margaret Ayer Barnes
1932 *The Good Earth*, Pearl S. Buck
1933 *The Store*, T.S. Stribling
1934 *Lamb in His Bosom*, Caroline Miller
1935 *Now in November*, Josephine W. Johnson

1936 *Honey in the Horn*, Harold L. Davis
1937 *Gone with the Wind*, Margaret Mitchell
1938 *The Late George Apley*, John Phillips Marquand
1939 *The Yearling*, Marjorie Kinnan Rawlings
1940 *The Grapes of Wrath*, John Steinbeck
1941 No award
1942 *In This Our Life*, Ellen Glasgow
1943 *Dragon's Teeth*, Upton Sinclair
1944 *Journey in the Dark*, Martin Flavin
1945 *A Bell for Adano*, John Hersey
1946 No award
1947 *All the King's Men*, Robert Penn Warren
1948 *Tales of the South Pacific*, James Michener
1949 *Guard of Honor*, James Gould Cozzens
1950 *The Way West*, A. B. Guthrie Jr.
1951 *The Town*, Conrad Richter
1952 *The Caine Mutiny*, Herman Wouk
1953 *The Old Man and the Sea*, Ernest Hemingway
1954 No Award
1955 *A Fable*, William Faulkner
1956 *Andersonville*, MacKinlay Kantor
1957 No award
1958 *A Death in the Family*, James Agee
1959 *The Travels of Jaimie McPheeters*, Robert Lewis Taylor
1960 *Advise and Consent*, Allen Drury
1961 *To Kill a Mockingbird*, Harper Lee
1962 *The Edge of Sadness*, Edwin O'Connor
1963 *The Reivers*, William Faulkner
1964 No award
1965 *The Keepers of the House*, Shirley Ann Grau
1966 *The Collected Stories of Katherine Anne Porter*, Katherine Anne Porter
1967 *The Fixer*, Bernard Malamud
1968 *The Confessions of Nat Turner*, William Styron
1969 *House Made of Dawn*, N. Scott Momaday
1970 *Collected Stories*, Jean Stafford
1971 No award
1972 *Angle of Repose*, Wallace Stegner
1973 *The Optimist's Daughter*, Eudora Welty
1974 No award
1975 *The Killer Angels*, Michael Shaara
1976 *Humboldt's Gift*, Saul Bellow
1977 No award
1978 *Elbow Room*, James Alan McPherson
1979 *The Stories of John Cheever*, John Cheever
1980 *The Executioner's Song*, Norman Mailer
1981 *A Confederacy of Dunces*, John Kennedy Toole
1982 *Rabbit Is Rich*, John Updike
1983 *The Color Purple*, Alice Walker
1984 *Ironweed*, William Kennedy
1985 *Foreign Affairs*, Alison Lurie

DRAMA PULITZER PRIZES

1917 No award
1918 *Why Marry?*, by Jesse L. Williams
1919 No award
1920 *Beyond the Horizon*, By Eugene O'Neill
1921 *Miss Lulu Bett*, by Zona Gale
1922 *Anna Christie*, by Eugene O'Neill
1923 *Icebound*, by Owen Davis
1924 *Hell-Bent for Heaven*, by Hatcher Hughes
1925 *They Knew What They Wanted*, by Sidney Howard
1926 *Craig's Wife*, by George Kelly
1927 *In Abraham's Bosom*, by Paul Green
1928 *Strange Interlude*, Eugene O'Neill
1929 *Street Scene*, Elmer L. Rice
1930 *The Green Pastures*, Marc Connelly
1931 *Alison's House*, Susan Glaspell
1932 *Of Thee I Sing*, George S. Kaufman, Ira Gershwin, and Morris Ryskind

1933	*Both Your Houses*, Maxwell Anderson
1934	*Men in White*, Sidney Kingsley
1935	*The Old Maid*, Zoe Akins
1936	*Idiot's Delight*, Robert E. Sherwood
1937	*You Can't Take It with You*, Moss Hart and George S. Kaufman
1938	*Our Town*, Thornton Wilder
1939	*Abe Lincoln in Illinois*, Robert E. Sherwood
1940	*The Time of Your Life*, William Saroyan
1941	*There Shall Be No Night*, Robert E. Sherwood
1942	No award
1943	*The Skin of Our Teeth*, Thornton Wilder
1944	No award
1945	*Harvey*, Mary Chase
1946	*State of the Union*, Russel Crouse and Howard Lindsay
1947	No award
1948	*A Streetcar Named Desire*, Tennessee Williams
1949	*Death of a Salesman*, Arthur Miller
1950	*South Pacific*, Richard Rogers, Oscar Hammerstein II, and Joshua Logan
1951	No award
1952	*The Shrike*, Joseph Kramm
1953	*Picnic*, William Inge
1954	*The Teahouse of the August Moon*, John Patrick
1955	*Cat on a Hot Tin Roof*, Tennessee Williams
1956	*Diary of Anne Frank*, Albert Hackett and Frances Goodrich
1957	*Long Day's Journey Into Night*, Eugene O'Neill
1958	*Look Homeward, Angel*, Ketti Frings
1959	*J. B.*, Archibald MacLeish
1960	*Fiorello!* Jerome Weidman and George Abbott
1961	*All the Way Home*, Tad Mosel
1962	*How to Succeed in Business Without Really Trying*, Frank Loesser and Abe Burrows
1963–64	No award
1965	*The Subject Was Roses*, Frank Gilroy
1966	No award
1967	*A Delicate Balance*, Edward Albee
1968	No award
1969	*The Great White Hope*, Howard Sackler
1970	*No Place to Be Somebody*, Charles Gordone
1971	*The Effect of Gamma Rays on Man-in-the-Moon Marigolds*, Paul Zindel
1972	No award
1973	*That Championship Season*, Jason Miller
1974	No award
1975	*Seascape*, Edward Albee
1976	*A Chorus Line*, produced Joseph Papp
1977	*The Shadow Box*, Michael Cristofer
1978	*The Gin Game*, Donald L. Coburn
1979	*Buried Child*, Sam Shepard
1980	*Talley's Folly*, Lanford Wilson
1981	*Crimes of the Heart*, Beth Henley
1982	*A Soldier's Play*, Charles Fuller
1983	*'Night, Mother*, Marsha Norman
1984	*Glengarry Glen Ross*, David Mamet
1985	*Sunday in the Park with George*, Stephen Sondheim and James Lapine

HISTORY PULITZER PRIZES

1917	*With Americans of Past and Present Days*, J. J. Jusserand
1918	*A History of the Civil War, 1861–65*, James Ford Rhodes
1919	No award
1920	*The War with Mexico*, Justin H. Smith
1921	*The Victory at Sea*, William Sowden Sims and Burton J. Hendrick
1922	*The Founding of New England*, James Truslow Adams

1923	*The Supreme Court in United States History*, Charles Warren
1924	*The American Revolution—A Constitutional Interpretation*, Charles McIlwain
1925	*A History of the American Frontier*, Frederic L. Paxson
1926	*The History of the United States*, Edward Channing
1927	*Pinckney's Treaty*, Samuel Flagg Bemis
1928	*Main Currents in American Thought* (2 vols.), Vernon Louis Parrington
1929	*The Organization and Administration of the Union Army, 1861–1865*, Fred Albert Shannon
1930	*The War of Independence*, Claude H. Van Tyne
1931	*The Coming of the War: 1914*, Bernadotte E. Schmitt
1932	*My Experiences in the World War*, John J. Pershing
1933	*The Significance of Sections in American History*, Frederick J. Turner
1934	*The People's Choice*, Herbert Agar
1935	*The Colonial Period of American History*, Charles McLean Andrews
1936	*The Constitutional History of the United States*, Andrew C. McLaughlin
1937	*The Flowering of New England*, Van Wyck Brooks
1938	*The Road to Reunion, 1865–1900*, Paul Herman Buck
1939	*A History of American Magazines*, Frank Luther Mott
1940	*Abraham Lincoln: The War Years*, Carl Sandburg
1941	*The Atlantic Migration, 1607–1860*, Marcus Lee Hansen
1942	*Reveille in Washington*, Margaret Leech
1943	*Paul Revere and the World He Lived In*, Esther Forbes
1944	*The Growth of American Thought*, Merle Curti
1945	*Unfinished Business*, Stephen Bonsal
1946	*The Age of Jackson*, Arthur M. Schlesinger Jr.
1947	*Scientists Against Time*, James Phinney Baxter III
1948	*Across the Wide Missouri*, Bernard DeVoto
1949	*The Disruption of American Democracy*, Roy Franklin Nichols
1950	*Art and Life in America*, Oliver W. Larkin
1951	*The Old Northwest: Pioneer Period, 1815–1840*, R. Carlyle Buley
1952	*The Uprooted*, Oscar Handlin
1953	*The Era of Good Feelings*, George Dangerfield
1954	*A Stillness at Appomattox*, Bruce Catton
1955	*Great River: The Rio Grande in North American History*, Paul Horgan
1956	*Age of Reform*, Richard Hofstadter
1957	*Russia Leaves the War: Soviet-American Relations, 1917–1920*, George F. Kennan
1958	*Banks and Politics in America—From the Revolution to the Civil War*, Bray Hammond
1959	*The Republican Era: 1869–1901*, Leonard D. White, assisted by Jean Schneider
1960	*In the Days of McKinley*, Margaret Leech
1961	*Between War and Peace: The Potsdam Conference*, Herbert Feis
1962	*The Triumphant Empire: Thunder-Clouds Gather in the West*, Lawrence H. Gipson
1963	*Washington: Village and Capital, 1800–1878*, Constance McLaughlin Green
1964	*Puritan Village: The Formation of a New England Town*, Sumner Chilton Powell
1965	*The Greenback Era*, Irwin Unger
1966	*Life of the Mind in America: From the Revolution to the Civil War*, Perry Miller
1967	*Exploration and Empire: The Explorer and Scientist in the Winning of the American West*, William H. Goetzmann
1968	*The Ideological Origins of the American Revolution*, Bernard Bailyn

PULITZER PRIZES *(continued)*

1969 *Origins of the Fifth Amendment*, Leonard Levy
1970 *Present at the Creation: My Years in the State Department*, Dean G. Acheson
1971 *Roosevelt: The Soldier of Freedom, 1940–1945*, James MacGregor Burns
1972 *Neither Black Nor White*, C. N. Degler
1973 *People of Paradox: An Inquiry Concerning the Origin of American Civilization*, Michael Kammen
1974 *The Americans: The Democratic Experience*, Daniel J. Boorstin
1975 *Jefferson and His Time*, Dumas Malone
1976 *Lamy of Santa Fe*, Paul Horgan
1977 *The Impending Crisis*, David M. Potter
1978 *The Visible Hand: The Managerial Revolution in American Business*, Alfred D. Chandler Jr.
1979 *The Dred Scott Case*, Don E. Fehrenberger
1980 *Been in the Storm So Long*, Leon F. Litwack
1981 *American Education: The National Experience, 1783–1876*, Lawrence A. Cremin
1982 *Mary Chestnut's Civil War*, C. Vann Woodward, editor
1983 *The Transformation of Virginia, 1740–1790*, Rhys L. Isaac
1984 No Award
1985 *The Prophets of Regulation*, Thomas K. McCraw

BIOGRAPHY/AUTOBIOGRAPHY

1917 *Julia Ward Howe*, Laura E. Richards, Maude H. Elliot, and Florence H. Hall
1918 *Benjamin Franklin, Self-Revealed*, William Cabell Bruce
1919 *The Education of Henry Adams*, Henry Adams
1920 *The Life of John Marshall* (4 vols.), Albert J. Beveridge
1921 *The Americanization of Edward Bok*, Edward Bok
1922 *A Daughter of the Middle Border*, Hamlin Garland
1923 *The Life and Letters of Walter H. Page*, Burton J. Hendrick
1924 *From Immigrant to Inventor*, Michael Pupin
1925 *Barrett Wendell and His Letters*, M. A. DeWolfe Howe
1926 *The Life of Sir William Osler* (2 vols.), Harvey Cushing
1927 *Whitman*, Emory Holloway
1928 *The American Orchestra and Theodore Thomas*, Charles Edward Russell
1929 *The Training of an American: The Earlier Life and Letters of Walter H. Page*, Burton J. Hendrick
1930 *The Raven*, Marquis James
1931 *Charles W. Eliot*, Henry James
1932 *Theodore Roosevelt*, Henry F. Pringle
1933 *Grover Cleveland*, Allan Nevins
1934 *John Hay*, Tyler Dennett
1935 *R.E. Lee*, Douglas Southall Freeman
1936 *The Thought and Character of William James*, Ralph Barton Perry
1937 *Hamilton Fish*, Allan Nevins
1938 *Pedlar's Progress*, Odell Shepard *Andrew Jackson*, by Marquis James
1939 *Benjamin Franklin*, Carl Van Doren
1940 *Woodrow Wilson, Life and Letters, Volumes VII and VIII*, Ray Stannard Baker
1941 *Jonathan Edwards*, Ola E. Winslow
1942 *Crusader in Crinoline*, Forrest Wilson
1943 *Admiral of the Ocean Sea*, Samuel Eliot Morison
1944 *The American Leonardo: The Life of Samuel F. B. Morse*, Carleton Mabee
1945 *George Bancroft: Brahmin Rebel*, Russell Blaine Nye
1946 *Son of the Wilderness*, Linnie M. Wolfe

1947 *The Autobiography of William Allen White*, William Allen White
1948 *Forgotten First Citizen: John Bigelow*, Margaret Clapp
1949 *Roosevelt and Hopkins*, Robert E. Sherwood
1950 *John Quincy Adams and the Foundations of American Foreign Policy*, Samuel Bemis
1951 *John C. Calhoun: American Portrait*, Margaret Louise Coit
1952 *Charles Evans Hughes*, Merlo J. Pusey
1953 *Edmund Pendleton 1721–1803*, David J. Mays
1954 *The Spirit of St. Louis*, Charles A. Lindbergh
1955 *The Taft Story*, William S. White
1956 *Benjamin Henry Latrobe*, T. F. Hamlin
1957 *Profiles in Courage*, John F. Kennedy
1958 *George Washington, Volumes I-VI*, Douglas Southall Freeman; *Volume VII*, Mary Ashworth and John Carroll
1959 *Woodrow Wilson, American Prophet*, Arthur Walworth
1960 *John Paul Jones*, Samuel Eliot Morison
1961 *Charles Sumner and the Coming of the Civil War*, David Donald
1962 No award
1963 *Henry James*, Leon Edel
1964 *John Keats*, Walter Jackson Bate
1965 *Henry Adams*, Ernest Samuels
1966 *A Thousand Days*, Arthur Schlesinger Jr.
1967 *Mr. Clemens and Mark Twain*, Justin Kaplan
1968 *Memoirs (1925–1950)*, George F. Kennan
1969 *The Man from New York: George Quinn and His Friends*, Benjamin Reid
1970 *Huey Long*, T. Harry Williams
1971 *Robert Frost: The Years of Triumph, 1915–1938*, Lawrance R. Thompson
1972 *Eleanor and Franklin*, J. P. Lash
1973 *Luce and His Empire*, W. A. Swanberg
1974 *O'Neill, Son and Artist*, Louis Sheaffer
1975 *The Power Broker: Robert Moses and the Fall of New York*, Robert A. Caro
1976 *Edith Wharton: A Biography*, Richard Warrington Baldwin Lewis
1977 *A Prince of Our Disorder* (T. E. Lawrence), John E. Mack
1978 *Samuel Johnson*, Walter Jackson Bate
1979 *Days of Sorrow and Pain: Leo Baeck and the Berlin Jews*, Leonard Baker
1980 *The Rise of Theodore Roosevelt*, Edmund Morris
1981 *Peter the Great: His Life and World*, Robert K. Massie
1982 *Grant: A Biography*, William S. McFeely
1983 *Growing Up*, Russell Baker
1984 *Booker T. Washington*, Louis R. Harlan
1985 *The Life and Times of Cotton Mather*, Kenneth Silverman

GENERAL NONFICTION

1962 *The Making of the President 1960*, Theodore H. White
1963 *The Guns of August*, Barbara Tuchman
1964 *Anti-intellectualism in American Life*, Richard Hofstadter
1965 *O Strange New World*, Howard Mumford Jones
1966 *Wandering Through Winter*, Edwin Way Teale
1967 *The Problem of Slavery in Western Culture*, David Brion Davis
1968 *Rousseau and Revolution*, Will and Ariel Durant
1969 *So Human an Animal: How We Are Shaped by Surroundings and Events*, René Dubos
 The Armies of the Night, Norman Mailer
1970 *Gandhi's Truth*, Erik H. Erikson
1971 *The Rising Sun*, John Toland

1972	*Stilwell and the American Experience in China, 1911–1945*, Barbara W. Tuchman
1973	*Fire in the Lake*, by Frances FitzGerald *Children of Crisis*, Robert Coles
1974	*The Denial of Death*, Ernest Becker
1975	*Pilgrim at Tinker Creek*, Annie Dillard
1976	*Why Survive? Being Old in America*, Robert N. Butler
1977	*Beautiful Swimmers: Watermen, Crabs and the Chesapeake Bay*, William W. Warner
1978	*The Dragons of Eden*, Carl Sagan
1979	*On Human Nature*, Edward O. Wilson
1980	*An Eternal Golden Braid*, Douglas R. Hofstadter
1981	*Fin-de-Siecle Vienna: Politics and Culture*, Carl E. Schorske
1982	*The Soul of a New Machine*, Tracy Kidder
1983	*Is There No Place on Earth for Me?* Susan Sheehan
1984	*Social Transformation of American Medicine*, Paul Starr
1985	*The Good War: An Oral History of World War II*, Studs Terkel

POETRY PULITZER PRIZES

1918	*Love Songs*, Sara Teasdale
1919	*Corn Huskers*, Carl Sandburg
	Old Road to Paradise, Margaret Widdemer
1920–21	No awards
1922	*Collected Poems*, Edwin Arlington Robinson
1923	*The Ballad of the Harp-Weaver; A Few Figs from Thistles;* eight sonnets in *American Poetry, 1922, A Miscellany*, Edna St. Vincent Millay
1924	*New Hampshire: A Poem with Notes and Grace Notes*, Robert Frost
1925	*The Man Who Died Twice*, Edwin Arlington Robinson
1926	*What's O'Clock*, Amy Lowell
1927	*Fiddler's Farewell*, Leonora Speyer
1928	*Tristram*, Edwin Arlington Robinson
1929	*John Brown's Body*, Stephen Vincent Benét
1930	*Selected Poems*, Conrad Aiken
1931	*Collected Poems*, Robert Frost
1932	*The Flowering Stone*, George Dillon
1933	*Conquistador*, Archibald MacLeish
1934	*Collected Verse*, Robert Hillyer
1935	*Bright Ambush*, Audrey Wurdemann
1936	*Strange Holiness*, R. P. Tristram Coffin
1937	*A Further Range*, Robert Frost
1938	*Cold Morning Sky*, Marya Zaturenska
1939	*Selected Poems*, John Gould Fletcher
1940	*Collected Poems*, Mark Van Doren
1941	*Sunderland Capture*, Leonard Bacon
1942	*The Dust Which Is God*, William Benét
1943	*A Witness Tree*, Robert Frost
1944	*Western Star*, Stephen Vincent Benét
1945	*V-Letter and Other Poems*, Karl Shapiro
1946	No award
1947	*Lord Weary's Castle*, Robert Lowell
1948	*The Age of Anxiety*, W. H. Auden
1949	*Terror and Decorum*, Peter Viereck
1950	*Annie Allen*, Gwendolyn Brooks
1951	*Complete Poems*, Carl Sandburg
1952	*Collected Poems*, Marianne Moore
1953	*Collected Poems 1917–1952*, Archibald MacLeish
1954	*The Waking*, Theodore Roethke
1955	*Collected Poems*, Wallace Stevens
1956	*Poems—North & South*, Elizabeth Bishop
1957	*Things of This World*, Richard Wilbur
1958	*Promises: Poems 1954–56*, Robert Penn Warren
1959	*Selected Poems 1928–1958*, Stanley Kunitz
1960	*Heart's Needle*, W. D. Snodgrass
1961	*Times Three: Selected Verse from Three Decades*, Phyllis McGinley
1962	*Poems*, Alan Dugan

1963	*Pictures from Breughel*, William Carlos Williams
1964	*At the End of the Open Road*, Louis Simpson
1965	*77 Dream Songs*, John Berryman
1966	*Selected Poems*, Richard Eberhart
1967	*Live or Die*, Anne Sexton
1968	*The Hard Hours*, Anthony Hecht
1969	*Of Being Numerous*, George Oppen
1970	*Untitled Subjects*, Richard Howard
1971	*The Carrier of Ladders*, W. S. Merwin
1972	*Collected Poems*, James Wright
1973	*Up Country*, Maxine Winokur Kumin
1974	*The Dolphin*, Robert Lowell
1975	*Turtle Island*, Gary Snyder
1976	*Self-Portrait in a Convex Mirror*, John Ashbery
1977	*Divine Comedies*, James Merrill
1978	*Collected Poems*, Howard Nemerov
1979	*Now and Then*, Robert Penn Warren
1980	*Selected Poems*, Donald Rodney Justice
1981	*The Morning of the Poem*, James Schuyler
1982	*The Collected Poems*, Sylvia Plath
1983	*Selected Poems*, Galway Kinnell
1984	*American Primitive*, Mary Oliver
1985	*Yin*, Carolyn Kizer

MUSIC PULITZER PRIZES

1943	*Secular Cantata No. 2*, William Schuman
1944	*Symphony No. 4, opus 34*, Howard Hanson
1945	*Appalachian Spring*, Aaron Copland
1946	*The Canticle of the Sun*, Leo Sowerby
1947	*Symphony No. 3*, Charles Ives
1948	*Symphony No. 3*, Walter Piston
1949	*Louisiana Story*, Virgil Thomson
1950	*The Consul*, Gian-Carlo Menotti
1951	*Giants in the Earth*, Douglas S. Moore
1952	*Symphony Concertante*, Gail Kubik
1953	No award
1954	*Concerto for Two Pianos and Orchestra*, Quincy Porter
1955	*The Saint of Bleecker Street*, Gian-Carlo Menotti
1956	*Symphony No. 3*, Ernst Toch
1957	*Meditations on Ecclesiastes*, Norman Dello Joio
1958	The score of *Vanessa*, Samuel Barber
1959	*Concerto for Piano and Orchestra*, John La Montaine
1960	*Second String Quartet*, Elliott C. Carter Jr.
1961	*Symphony No. 7*, Walter Piston
1962	*The Crucible*, Robert Ward
1963	*Piano Concerto No. 1*, Samuel Barber
1964–65	No awards
1966	*Variations for Orchestra*, Leslie Bassett
1967	*Quartet No. 3*, Leon Kirchner
1968	*Echoes of Time and the River*, George Crumb
1969	*String Quartet No. 3*, Karel Husa
1970	*Time's Encomium*, Charles W. Wuorinen
1971	*Synchronisms No. 6*, Mario Davidovsky
1972	*Windows*, Jacob Druckman
1973	*String Quartet No. 3*, Elliott Carter
1974	*Notturno*, Donald Martino; special citation to Roger Sessions
1975	*From the Diary of Virginia Woolf*, D. Argento
1976	*Air Music*, 10 études for orchestra, Ned Rorem
1977	*Visions of Terror and Wonder*, by Richard Wernick
1978	*Déjà Vu for Percussion Quartet and Orchestra*, by Michael Colgrass
1979	*Aftertones of Infinity*, Joseph Schwantner
1980	*In Memory of a Summer Day*, David Del Tredici
1981	No award
1982	*Concerts for Orchestra*, Roger Sessions
1983	*Three Movements for Orchestra*, Ellen T. Zwilich
1984	*Canti del Sole*, Bernard Rands
1985	*Symphony, River Run*, Stephen Albert; special citation to William H. Schuman

HALL OF FAME FOR GREAT AMERICANS

The Hall of Fame for Great Americans was established in 1900 by Dr. Henry Mitchell MacCracken, chancellor of New York University, to honor United States citizens.

MEMBERS OF THE HALL OF FAME	ELECTED
Adams, John (1735–1826), 2d U.S. President	1900
Adams, John Quincy (1767–1848), 6th U.S. President	1905
Addams, Jane (1860–1935), reformer	1965
Agassiz, Louis (1807–73), naturalist	1915
Anthony, Susan B. (1820–1906), social reformer	1950
Audubon, John James (1785?–1851), ornithologist, artist	1900
Bancroft, George (1800–91), historian and diplomat	1910
Barton, Clara (1821–1912), founder of American Red Cross	1976
Beecher, Henry Ward (1813–87), theologian	1900
Bell, Alexander Graham (1847–1922), inventor	1950
Boone, Daniel (1734–1820), frontiersman	1915
Booth, Edwin (1833–93), actor	1925
Brandeis, Louis D. (1856–1941), jurist	1973
Brooks, Phillip (1835–93), theologian	1910
Bryant, William Cullen (1794–1878), writer	1910
Burbank, Luther (1849–1926), horticulturist	1976
Carnegie, Andrew (1835–1919), steelmaker and philanthropist	1976
Carver, George Washington (1859?–1943), chemist	1973
Channing, William Ellery (1780–1842), theologian	1900
Choate, Rufus (1799–1859), lawyer and legislator	1915
Clay, Henry (1777–1852), statesman	1900
Clemens, Samuel Langhorne (Mark Twain; 1835–1910), novelist	1920
Cleveland, Grover (1837–1908), 22d and 24th U.S. President	1935
Cooper, James Fenimore (1789–1851), novelist	1910
Cooper, Peter (1791–1883), philanthropist	1900
Cushman, Charlotte (1816–76), actress	1915
Eads, James (1820–87), engineer	1920
Edison, Thomas Alva (1847–1931), inventor	1960
Edwards, Jonathan (1703–58), theologian	1900
Emerson, Ralph Waldo (1803–82), poet and essayist	1900
Farragut, David Glasgow (1801–70), naval officer	1900
Foster, Stephen (1826–64), composer	1940
Franklin, Benjamin (1706–90), statesman and inventor	1900
Fulton, Robert (1765–1815), inventor	1900
Gibbs, Josiah (1839–1903), physicist	1950
Gorgas, William Crawford (1854–1920), physician	1950
Grant, Ulysses S. (1822–85), Union general and 18th U.S. President	1900
Gray, Asa (1810–88), botanist	1900
Hamilton, Alexander (1755?–1804), statesman	1915
Hawthorne, Nathaniel (1804–64), author	1900
Henry, Joseph (1797–1878), physicist	1915
Henry, Patrick (1736–99), statesman	1920
Holmes, Oliver Wendell (1809–94), writer	1910
Holmes, Oliver Wendell, Jr. (1841–1935), Supreme Court associate justice	1965
Hopkins, Mark (1802–87), educator	1915
Howe, Elias (1819–67), inventor	1915
Irving, Washington (1783–1859), author and diplomat	1900
Jackson, Andrew (1767–1845), 7th U.S. President	1910
Jackson, Stonewall (1824–63), Confederate general	1955
Jefferson, Thomas (1743–1826), 3d U.S. President	1900

MEMBERS OF THE HALL OF FAME	ELECTED
Jones, John Paul (1747–92), naval commander	1925
Kent, James (1763–1847), jurist	1900
Lanier, Sidney (1842–81), poet and musician	1945
Lee, Robert E. (1807–70), Confederate general	1900
Lincoln, Abraham (1809–65), 16th U.S. President	1900
Longfellow, Henry Wadsworth (1807–82), poet	1900
Lowell, James Russell (1819–91), poet	1905
Lyon, Mary (1797–1849), educator	1905
MacDowell, Edward Alexander (1861–1908), composer	1960
Madison, James (1751–1836), 4th U.S. President	1905
Mann, Horace (1796–1859), educator	1900
Marshall, John (1755–1835), Chief Justice of U.S.	1900
Maury, Matthew Fontaine (1806–73), naval officer and oceanographer	1930
Michelson, Albert (1852–1931), physicist	1970
Mitchell, Maria (1818–89), astronomer	1905
Monroe, James (1758–1831), 5th U.S. President	1930
Morse, Samuel F. B. (1791–1872), inventor	1900
Morton, William (1819–68), dentist	1920
Motley, John Lothrop (1814–77), historian	1910
Newcomb, Simon (1835–1909), astronomer	1935
Paine, Thomas (1737–1809), political writer	1945
Palmer, Alice (1855–1902), educator	1920
Parkman, Francis (1823–93), historian	1915
Peabody, George (1795–1869), philanthropist	1900
Penn, William (1644–1718), colonial leader	1935
Poe, Edgar Allan (1809–49), poet and author	1910
Reed, Walter (1851–1902), physician	1945
Roosevelt, Franklin Delano (1882–1945), 32d U.S. President	1973
Roosevelt, Theodore (1858–1919), 26th U.S. President	1950
Saint-Gaudens, Augustus (1848–1907), sculptor	1920
Sherman, William Tecumseh (1820–91), Union general	1905
Sousa, John Philip (1854–1932), bandleader	1973
Story, Joseph (1779–1845), Supreme Court associate justice	1900
Stowe, Harriet Beecher (1811–96), novelist	1910
Stuart, Gilbert (1755–1828), painter	1900
Thayer, Sylvanus (1785–1872), military educator	1965
Thoreau, Henry David (1817–62), essayist and poet	1960
Wald, Lillian (1867–1940), social worker	1970
Washington, Booker T. (1856–1915), educator	1945
Washington, George (1732–99), Revolutionary War general and 1st U.S. President	1900
Webster, Daniel (1782–1852), statesman	1900
Westinghouse, George (1846–1914), inventor	1955
Whistler, James A. McNeill (1834–1903), painter	1930
Whitman, Walt (1819–92), poet	1930
Whitney, Eli (1765–1825), inventor	1900
Whittier, John Greenleaf (1807–92), poet	1905
Willard, Emma (1787–1870), educator	1905
Willard, Frances Elizabeth (1839–98), reformer	1910
Williams, Roger (1603?–83), colonial leader	1920
Wilson, Woodrow (1856–1924), 28th U.S. President	1950
Wright, Orville (1871–1948), inventor	1965
Wright, Wilbur (1867–1912), inventor	1955

SPINGARN MEDAL

The highest award each year to blacks for achievement, the gold Spingarn Medal was established in 1914 by Elias Spingarn, chairman of the board of the National Association for the Advancement of Colored People (NAACP). Medals awarded since 1962 include:

YEAR	NAME	FIELD	YEAR	NAME	FIELD
1963	Medgar W. Evers	Civil rights	1974	Damon J. Keith	Law
1964	Roy Wilkins	Civil rights	1975	Henry Aaron	Sports
1965	Leontyne Price	Music	1976	Alvin Ailey	Dance
1966	John H. Johnson	Publishing	1977	Alex Haley	Literature
1967	Edward W. Brooke	Government	1978	Andrew Young	Government
1968	Sammy Davis Jr.	Entertainment	1979	W. Rayford Logan	Education
1969	Clarence M. Mitchell Jr.	Government	1980	Coleman A. Young	Government
1970	Jacob Lawrence	Painting	1981	Benjamin Elijah Mays	Education
1971	Leon H. Sullivan	Economic opportunity	1982	Lena Horne	Entertainment
1972	Gordon Parks	The Arts	1983	Thomas Bradley	Government
1973	Wilson C. Riles	Education	1984	Bill Cosby	Entertainment

Books

HIGHLIGHTS: 1985

BESTSELLERS

The bestselling hardcover book of 1984, *Iacocca: An Autobiography* by Lee Iacocca with William Novak, sold more than a million copies from its publication date in October 1984 to the beginning of 1985. It then continued to top the bestseller lists for the first seven months in 1985, until being displaced late in July by *Yeagar: An Autobiography* by Gen. Chuck Yeagar and Leo Janos. The autobiography of the first man to fly faster than sound already had 350,000 copies in print by the end of July.

Horror book writer Stephen King topped the fiction hardcover bestseller lists in mid-1985 with his newest novel, *Skeleton Crew*. He had won the fiction hardcover bestseller sweepstakes of 1984 with *The Talisman*, which he wrote in collaboration with Peter Straub.

After Iacocca's biography, the leading nonfiction hardcover bestsellers of 1984 were: *Loving Each Other* by Leo Buscaglia, *Eat to Win: The Sports Nutrition Bible* by Robert Haas, M.D., *Pieces of My Mind* by Andrew A. Rooney, *Weight Watchers Fast and Fabulous Cookbook* by Weight Watchers International, *What They Don't Teach You at Harvard Business School: Notes from a Street-Smart Executive* by Mark H. McCormack, *Women Coming of Age* by Jane Fonda with Mignon McCarthy, *Moses the Kitten* by James Herriot, *The One Minute Salesperson* by Spencer Johnson and Larry Wilson, *Weight Watchers Quick Start Program Cookbook* by Jean Nidetch, *Chef Paul Prudhomme's Louisiana Kitchen,* by Paul Prudhomme, *Putting the One Minute Manager to Work* by Kenneth Blanchard and Robert Lorder, *Tough Times Never Last, but Tough People Do!* by Robert H. Schuller, *The Bridge Across Forever* by Richard Bach, and *Dr. Burns' Prescription for Happiness* by George Burns.

Among the runners-up in hardcover nonfiction were *Motherhood: The Second Oldest Profession* by Erma Bombeck, *One Writer's Beginnings* by Eudora Welty, *The Kennedys: An American Drama* by Peter Collier and David Horowitz, *The Good War* by Studs Terkel, *Mayor* by Edward I. Koch with William Rauch, *The March of Folly* by Barbara W. Tuchman, *Wired: The Short Life and Fast Times of John Belushi* by Bob Woodward, and *Hey, Wait a Minute, I Wrote a*

A 14-cent stamp commemorating the centennial of the birth of novelist Sinclair Lewis was issued on March 21 in Sauk Centre, Minn., the author's birthplace. The stamp design by Bradbury Thompson is based on a charcoal portrait of Lewis by Soss Melik.

Book! by John Madden with Dave Anderson.

After Stephen King's *The Talisman,* the leading fiction hardcover bestsellers of 1984 were: *The Aquitaine Progression* by Robert Ludlum, *The Sicilian* by Mario Puzo, *Love and War* by John Jakes, *The Butter Battle Book* by Dr. Seuss, ... *And Ladies of the Club* by Helen Hoover Santmyer, *The Fourth Protocol* by Frederick Forsyth, *Full Circle* by Danielle Steel, *The Life and Hard Times of Heidi Abromowitz* by Joan Rivers, *Lincoln: A Novel* by Gore Vidal, *The Walking Drum* by Louis L'Amour, *The Haj* by Leon Uris, *Strong Medicine* by Arthur Hailey, *First Among Equals* by Jeffrey Archer, *The Dune Storybook* adapted by Joan D. Vinge, *Heretics of Dune* by Frank Herbert, *Crescent City* by Belva Plain, *God Knows* by Joseph Heller, *Nutcracker* by E.T.A. Hoffmen (translated by Ralph Manheim and illustrated by Maurice Sendak), *The Revenge of the Robins Family* by Bill Adler and Thomas Chastain, *Julie* by Catherine Marshall, *Indiana Jones and the Temple of Doom* adapted by Michael French, *Tough Guys Don't Dance* by Norman Mailer, *Job: A Comedy of Justice* by Robert A Heinlein, *Stillwatch* by Mary Higgins Clark, *The*

HIGHLIGHTS: 1985 *(continued)*

Passion of Molly T. by Lawrence Sanders, and *So Long, and Thanks for All the Fish* by Douglas Adams.

AWARDS

The $50,000 Ritz Paris Hemingway Award for literature, co-sponsored by the Sultan of Brunei and the Ritz Hotel in Paris was awarded in March to Peruvian novelist Mario Vargas Llosa for his historical novel *The War of the End of the World.*

The National Book Critics Circle Awards in 1985 were: fiction, *Love Medicine* by Louise Erdrich; general nonfiction, *Weapons and Hope* by Freeman Dyson; biography, *Dostoevsky: The Years of Ordeal, 1850-1859* by Joseph Frank; poetry, *The Dead and the Living* by Sharon Olds; criticism, *Twentieth Century Pleasures: Prose on Poetry,* by Robert Hass.

The American Library Association 1985 awards for children's books were:

The John Newberry Medal for the oustanding children's book of the year went to Robin McKinley, for *The Hero and the Crown.* The Randolph J. Caldecott Medal for the best American picture book for children to Trina Schart Hyman for her illustrations in *Saint George and the Dragon.*

Yale University's prestigious Bollingen Prize in Poetry was awarded in 1985 to John Ashbery, 56, of Brooklyn College and to Fred Chappell, 48, of the University of North Carolina.

U.S. BOOK TITLES PUBLISHED

Source: *Publishers Weekly*

CLASSIFICATION	1950	1955	1960	1965	1970	1975	1980	1983	1984
Agriculture	152	168	156	270	265	456	461	572	416
Art	357	347	470	971	1,169	1,561	1,691	1,896	1,463
Biography	603	833	879	685	1,536	1,968	1,891	2,135	1,674
Business	250	312	305	537	797	820	1,185	1,636	1,393
Education	256	274	348	954	1,178	1,038	1,011	1,059	831
Fiction	1,907	2,073	2,440	3,241	3,137	3,805	2,835	5,470	4,876
General Works	345	387	282	634	846	1,113	1,643	2,767	2,333
History	516	665	865	1,682	1,995	1,823	2,220	2,296	1,791
Home Economics	193	255	197	300	321	728	879	1,325	1,022
Juveniles	1,059	1,485	1,725	2,895	2,640	2,292	2,859	3,197	2,566
Language	148	168	228	527	472	438	529	669	551
Law	298	305	394	436	604	915	1,102	1,756	1,125
Literature	591	660	736	1,686	3,085	1,904	1,686	1,957	1,638
Medicine	443	534	520	1,218	1,476	2,282	3,292	4,002	2,502
Music	113	103	98	300	404	305	357	417	308
Philosophy, Psychology	340	314	480	979	1,280	1,374	1,429	1,578	1,242
Poetry, Drama	531	493	492	994	1,474	1,501	1,179	1,234	946
Religion	727	849	1,104	1,855	1,788	1,778	2,055	2,433	1,930
Science	705	801	1,089	2,562	2,358	2,942	3,109	3,620	2,564
Sociology, Economics	515	520	754	3,242	5,912	6,590	7,152	8,470	6,257
Sports, Recreation	188	200	286	591	799	1,225	971	1,335	1,072
Technology	497	477	698	1,153	1,141	1,720	2,337	2,974	2,139
Travel	288	366	466	883	1,394	794	504	582	441
TOTAL	11,022	12,589	15,012	28,595	36,071	39,372	42,377	53,380	41,380

U.S. BOOK PUBLISHING SALES

Source: Association of American Publishers

TYPE OF SALES	1975	1980	1983	1984	% change from '83
Trade (retail stores)	$ 549,200,000	$1,271,300,000	$1,595,200,000	$1,695,800,000	6.3%
Adult hardbound	313,400,000	695,900,000	807,600,000	833,400,000	3.2%
Adult paperback	111,200,000	364,600,000	531,600,000	582,100,000	9.5%
Juvenile	124,600,000	210,800,000	256,000,000	280,300,000	9.5%
Religious	154,600,000	351,400,000	454,900,000	461,700,000	1.5%
Professional	501,200,000	999,100,000	1,373,000,000	1,458,100,000	6.2%
Technical and scientific	175,500,000	334,800,000	491,000,000	526,400,000	7.2%
Business and other	242,300,000	424,400,000	561,200,000	589,100,000	5.0%
Medical	83,400,000	239,900,000	320,800,000	342,600,000	6.8%
Book clubs	303,400,000	538,300,000	654,400,000	660,900,000	1.0%
Mail-order books	279,800,000	566,900,000	554,500,000	573,900,000	3.5%
Mass-market paperbacks	356,200,000	653,300,000	706,100,000	732,900,000	3.8%
University presses	48,800,000	80,700,000	129,900,000	139,300,000	7.2%
Textbooks	1,173,700,000	1,893,000,000	2,378,300,000	2,589,700,000	8.8%
Elementary and secondary	643,100,000	940,300,000	1,149,700,000	1,310,700,000	14.0%
College	530,600,000	952,700,000	1,228,600,000	1,279,000,000	4.1%
Standardized tests	36,700,000	67,200,000	79,700,000	85,800,000	7.7%
Subscription reference	258,100,000	384,700,000	443,000,000	465,200,000	5.0%
Audio Visual and other	189,000,000	233,500,000	223,000,000	258,100,000	15.7%
TOTAL	$3,810,000,000	$7,039,400,000	$8,592,000,000	$9,121,400,000	6.2%

BESTSELLERS AND NOTEWORTHY BOOKS: 1985

Nonfiction and fiction books in the following table include most of those mentioned during 1985 on bestseller lists of the *New York Times* and *Publishers Weekly* as well as other noteworthy books published in 1985.

FICTION

The Accidental Tourist, Anne Tyler (Knopf, $16.95): Man obsessed with neatness falls in love with his uneducated dog trainer.

After the Reunion, Rona Jaffe (Delacorte, $17.95): Sequel to *Class Reunion* continues to probe lives of Radcliffe alumnae.

A Catskill Eagle, Robert B. Parker (Delacorte/ Seymour Lawrence, $14.95): Thriller about Boston private detective caught up in tangle with wealthy arms maker and CIA.

Chapterhouse: Dune, Frank Herbert (Putnam, $17.95): New desert world is created from ashes of Old Empire as Dune saga continues.

The Cider House Rules, John Irving (Morrow, $18.95): Author of *The World According to Garp* presents case for right to abortions in novel set in orphanage in rural Maine.

The Class, Erich Segal (Bantam, $17.95): Successes and failures of five members of Harvard class of 1958.

Confessional, Jack Higgins (Stein and Day, $17.95): Suspense novel about KBG agent who, while posing as village priest in Ireland, decides to kill the Pope.

Contact, Carl Sagan (Simon and Schuster, $17.95): Novel by notes scientist describes man's first encounter with intelligent life beyond the Earth.

A Creed for the Third Millennium, Colleen McCullough (Harper & Row, $17.95): Author of *Thorn Birds* tells story that looks into the near future of America.

Depths of Glory, Irving Stone (Doubleday, $17.95): Biographical novel about French impressionist artist Camille Pissarro.

The Double Man, William Cohen and Gary Hart (Morrow, $15.95): Two U.S. Senators team up to write espionage thriller.

Extravagant Gestures, Carole Bayer Sager (Arbor House/A Belvedere Book, $16,95): Bestselling author of books on mother/daughter relationships has difficulties overcoming problems with her own mother.

Family Album, Danielle Steel (Delacorte, $16.95): Woman escapes from poverty to develop film empire.

Fiskadoro, Denis Johnson (Knopf, $14.95): Teen-ager clings to life in remnants of civilization destroyed by atomic holocaust.

Footfall, Larry Niven and Jerry Pournelle (Del Rey/Ballantine, $17.95): America invaded by high tech aliens.

The Fourth Deadly Sin, Lawrence Sanders (Putnam, $17.95): Detective Edward X. Delaney returns to solve complex case.

The Good Terrorist, Doris Lessing (Knopf, $16.95): Heroine becomes emeshed in British terrorist activities.

Hold the Dream, Barbara Taylor Bradford (Doubleday, $17.95): Family saga continues from *A Woman of Substance* as Emily Harte turns over control of her empire to her grandchildren.

Honorable Men, Louis Auchincloss (Houghton Mifflin, $15.95): Exploration of effect of changing moral values in modern America.

The House of Spirits, Isabel Allende, translated by Magda Bogin (Knopf, $17.95): Novel by Chilean author tells rise and fall of wealthy family.

Hot Wire, James Brown (Arbor House, $15.95): Life on the seamy side in Los Angeles.

The Hunt for Red October, Tom Clancy (Naval Institute Press, $14.95): Lithuanian submariner defects to U.S., bringing with him Soviet nuclear secrets.

If Tomorrow Comes, Sidney Sheldon (Morrow, $17.95): Woman seeks revenge on crime bosses who sent her to prison.

The Immigrant's Daughter, Howard Fast (Houghton Mifflin, $17.95): Fifth novel in saga of Lavette family brings trying congressional campaign for Barbara Lavette.

Inside, Outside, Herman Wouk (Little, Brown, $19.95): Problems of traditionalist Jew in coping with modern America.

Joe Crown, Harold Robbins (Simon & Schuster, $17.95): Jewish kid from Brooklyn seeks to satisfy ambitions in Hollywood.

Jubal Sackett, Louis L'Amour (Bantam, $16.95): Hero explores the West from the Carolinas to what is now New Mexico.

The Lonely Silver Rain, John D. MacDonald (Knopf, $15.95): Detective Travis McGee tries to solve mystery of debutante's murder.

Lonesome Dove, Larry McMurty (Simon & Schuster, $18.95): Epic Western with cattle drive from Texas to Montana.

Love Always, Ann Beattie (Random House, $16.95): Trials and tribulations of post-1960s generation in Hollywood and New England.

The Loving Cup: The Tenth Poldark Novel, Winston Graham (Doubleday, $17.95): Saga of Poldark family continues in post-Napoleonic era.

Lucky, Jackie Collins (Simon & Schuster, $17.95): Sequel to *Chances* continues account of life and loves of rich Lucky Santangelo.

The Maggot, John Fowles (Little, Brown, $19.95): Author of *The French Lieutenant's Woman* delves into black magic and witchcraft in England in 1700s.

McKenzie's Hundred, Frank Yerby (Doubleday, $17.95): Sexy Civil War romance.

Playing Catch-up, A.B. Guthrie Jr. (Houghton Mifflin, $13.95): Search for killer of two girls in tiny Montana town.

Queenie, Michael Korda (Linden Press/Simon & Schuster, $17.95): Career of beautiful star in entertainment world.

The Road to Paradise Island, Victoria Holt (Doubleday, $16.95): Gothic romance in which heroine and her brother become caught up in searching for island shown on map left by an ancestor.

Robots and Empire, Isaac Asimov (Doubleday, $16.95): Intergalactic adventure interweaves au-

88 BOOKS

BESTSELLERS: 1985 *(continued)*
thor's three major science fiction series.
The Secrets of Harry Bright, Joseph Wambaugh (Morrow, $17.95): Detective's search for meaning of his son's death.
See You Later Alligator, William F. Buckley Jr. (Doubleday, $15.95): Fifth novel about CIA agent Blackford Oakes.
Skeleton Crew, Stephen King (Putnam $18.95): Collection of short stories.
Stanley and the Women, Kingsley Amis (Summit, $16.95): Stanley's son is going mad and the plot finds ways to blame the whole thing on the women in Stanley's life.
The Tenth Man, Graham Greene (Simon & Schuster, $14.95): French banker gives up fortune to save life from Nazi firing squad and later develops relationship with family of man who took his place.
Texas, James A. Michener (Random House, $19.95): Blockbuster novel spanning four and a half centuries of Texas history.
Thinner, Richard Bachman (pseudonym of Stephen King) (NAL Books, $12.95): Body of lawyer mysteriously grows weaker and weaker.
World's Fair, E.L. Doctorow (Random House, $17.95): New York of the 1930s as seen through eyes of a child.

NONFICTION

Agatha Christie, Janet Morgan (Knopf, $18.95): Biography of famed mystery writer.
"And I Was There": Pearl Harbor and Midway—Breaking the Secrets, Rear Adm. Edwin T. Layton with Captain Roger Pineau and John Costello (Morrow, $19.95): Former Pacific Fleet intelligence officer reveals facts about early days of war with Japan.
The Amateurs, David Halberstam (Morrow, $14.95): Study of sport of single-scull racing.
Are You Hungry? A Completely New Approach to Raising Children Free of Food and Weight Problems, Jane R. Hirschmann and Lela Zapiropoulos (Random House, $15.95): Blueprint of how to raise children without eating and weight problems by applying theory of self-demand feeding.
Dr. Berger's Immune Power Diet, Stuart M. Berger, M.D. (NAL Books, $14.95): How to lose weight and become more energetic.
Bob Hope's Confessions of a Hooker: My Lifelong Love Affair with Golf, Bob Hope as told to Dwayne Netland (Doubleday, $17.95): Witty anecdotes about comedian's half century of playing golf with celebrities.
Breaking with Moscow, Arkady N. Shevchenko (Knopf, $18.95): Prominent Soviet official tells own story of how and why he defected to the United States.
The Bridge Across Forever, Richard Bach (Morrow, $16.95): Author of *Jonathan Livingston Seagull* searches for love.
Common Ground: A Turbulent Decade in the Lives of Three American Families, J. Anthony Lukas (Knopf, $19.95): Detailed account of the effect of Boston's school integration crisis on three families.
The Courage of a Conservative, James Watt with Doug Wead (Simon & Schuster, $15.95):

Controversial former Secretary of the Interior issues conservative call to arms.
The Courage to Change, Dennis Wholey (Houghton Mifflin, $15.95): Interviews with celebrities and others about coping with alcoholism.
Dark Star, Leatrice Gilbert Fountain with John R. Maxim (St. Martin's, $14.95): Daughter recounts life of famous father John Gilbert, the Great Lover of the silent screen.
Eisenhower at War: 1943-1945, David Eisenhower (Random House, $25): First volume of biography of Allied supreme commander by his grandson, illustrated with photos and maps.
Elvis and Me, Priscilla Beaulier Presley with Sandra Harmon (Putnam, $16.95): A full account of the rock star's love life with Priscilla.
Frank Sinatra: My Father, Nancy Sinatra (Doubleday, $50.00): Pictorial biography of singing star with more than 700 photos, many in color.
The 4 Day Wonder Diet: Lose 10 pounds in 4 Days, Margaret Danbrot (Putnam's, $10.95): Plan for quick weight loss while eating three meals a day.
The Frugal Gourmet, Jeff Smith (Morrow, $14.95): Recipes for eating well without spending a fortune.
Hello Everybody, I'm Lindsey Nelson, Lindsey Nelson (Beech Tree Books/Morrow, 18.95): Lots of anecdotes for fans of the TV sportscaster.
The Holocaust: The History of the Jews of Europe During the Second World War, Martin Gilbert (Holt, Rinehart & Winston, $19.95): Definitive account of Nazi crimes against the Jews.
I, Koch: A Decidedly Unauthorized Biography of the Mayor of New York City, Edward I. Koch, Arthur Browne, Dan Collins, and Michael Goodwin (Dodd, Mead, $18.95): Three City Hall reporters seek to correct what they regard as distortions in Koch's autobiography.
I Never Played the Game, Howard Cosell with Peter Bonventre (Morrow, $18.95): Controversial TV sports caster expresses opinions on various aspects of sports.
Living with the Kennedys: The Joan Kennedy Story, Marcia Chellis (Simon & Schuster, $17.95): Family friend tells all about Ted and Joan and Jackie.
Made in America, Peter Ueberroth with Richard Levin and Amy Quinn (Morrow, $19.95): Autobiography of man who guided 1984 Olympics to success.
Married People: Staying Together in the Age of Divorce, Francine Klagsbrun (Bantam, $14.95): What it takes to make marriage work as learned from interviews with couples who found happiness in long-term marriages.
Martina, Martina Navratilova with George Vecsey (Knopf, $16.95): Candid autobiography of tennis star who defected from communist Czechoslovakia at 18.
Mountbatten, Phillip Ziegler (Knopf, $24.95): Biography of Earl Mountbatten of Burma—confidant of British royalty, World War II naval hero, and diplomat.
My Mother's Keeper, B.D. Hyman (Morrow, $19.95): Daughter of movie star Bette Davis

tells her version of living with tempestuous mother.

Nothing Down: How to Buy Real Estate with Little or No Money, Robert G. Allen (Simon and Schuster, $16.95): Up-dated version of 1980 book.

Nutcracker: Money, Madness, Murder—A Family Album, Shana Alexander (Doubleday $17.95): About the murder of Utah millionaire Franklin Bradshaw by his family.

On the Road with Charles Kuralt, Charles Kuralt (Putnam, $16.95): TV's explorer of America recounts interesting encounters with men and women throughout the nation.

On Your Own, Brooke Shields (Villard Books, $17.95): Autobiographical account about how to succeed at college while being beautiful.

Once Upon A Time: A True Story, Gloria Vanderbilt (Knopf, $16.95): Autobiographical account of turbulent childhood of poor little rich girl.

Orson Welles, Barbara Leaming (Viking, $19.95): Carefully researched biography of major entertainment personality's life.

A Passion for Excellence: The Leadership Difference, Thomas J. Peters and Nancy K. Austin (Random House, $19.95): Follow-up to *In Search of Excellence* tells managers how to inspire their subordinates.

Re-inventing the Corporation: Transforming Your Job and Your Company for the New Information Society, John Naisbitt and Patricia Aburdine (Warner, $17.50): Sequel to *Megatrends* outlines the way to achieve the good business life in the changing world.

A Remarkable Woman, Anne Edwards (Morrow, $18.95): Biography of star actress Katherine Hepburn.

Royal Feud, Michael Thornton (Simon & Schuster, $17.95): Authentic details of feud between Duchess of Windsor and George VI's Queen Elizabeth.

Savage Grace, Natalie Robins and Steven M.L.Aronson (Morrow, $17.95): True story of how and why heir to Bakelite plastics fortune murdered his mother in 1972.

Smart Cookies Don't Crumble: A Modern Woman's Guide to Living and Loving Her Own Life, Sonya Friedman (Putnam, $15.95): Advice on how to cope with dominating males.

Smart Women, Foolish Choices: Finding the Right Men and Avoiding the Wrong Ones, Dr. Connell Cowan and Dr. Melvyn Kinder (Clarkson N. Potter, $14.95): Clinical psychologists counsel women not to make foolish choices in relations with men.

Springsteen, Robert Hilburn (Rolling Stone Press/Scribners, $32.50): Portrait of rock and roll star complete with 16 pages of full color pictures and 180 black-and-white photos.

Stefanie Powers: Superlife!, Stefanie Powers and Judy Quine (Simon & Schuster, $17.95): Step-by-step account of how popular TV actress achieves beauty and fitness.

Thin Within: How to Eat and Live Like a Thin Person, Jody Wardell, in collaboration with Barbara Austin (Harmony Books, $14.95): How to use the power of positive thinking to become slimmer.

Through My Eyes: The Story of a Surgeon Who Dared Take On the Medical World, Charles D. Kelman, M.D. (Crown, $14.95): Autobiography of jazz-playing eye surgeon who discovered new method of safely removing cataracts.

Vital Lies, Simple Truths: The Psychology of Self-Deception, Daniel Goleman (Simon & Schuster, $17.95): How a person's mind works to protect one from admitting flaws and failures.

What Do You Really Want for Your Children, Dr. Wayne W. Dyer (Morrow, $17.95): Author of *Your Erroneous Zone* tells parents how to raise their children to be happy.

Yeager: An Autobiography, Gen. Chuck Yeager and Leo Janos (Bantam, $17.95): Adventurous life of first man to fly faster than sound, blazing way for space travel.

AUTHORS AND WRITERS

Authors, writers, poets, and dramatists whose works are of enduring interest are listed below in alphabetical order. Birth dates and nationalities are given, along with the titles of the authors' most famous works, and their major literary prizes.

See pages 981–986 for deaths of authors and writers in 1985.

George Abbott (1887–), American playwright and producer: won a Pulitzer Prize as coauthor of musical comedy *Fiorello!* (1959).

Henry Adams (1838–1918), American historian who idealized Middle Ages and deplored materialistic modern civilization: *Mont-Saint-Michel and Chartres* (1904); *The Education of Henry Adams* (1906) won Pulitzer Prize in 1919.

James Truslow Adams (1878–1949), American historian: won a Pulitzer Prize for *The Founding of New England* (1921).

Samuel Hopkins Adams (1871–1958), American writer. His articles about fraudulent patent medicines stirred enactment in 1906 of first Pure Food and Drug Act. Wrote several biographies and novels.

Joseph Addison (1672–1719), English essayist. His essays in the *Tatler, Spectator,* and *Guardian* periodicals were noted for excellence of style.

George Ade (1866–1944), American humorist and playwright: *Fables in Slang* (1899), *The Sultan of Sulu* (1902), *The College Widow* (1904).

Aeschylus (525–456 B.C.), Greek tragic poet. Of his estimated 90 dramas, only 7 survive, including *Prometheus Bound* and *Oresteia*, a trilogy.

James Agee (1909–55), American essayist and novelist: *Let Us Now Praise Famous Men* (1941) is a powerful documentary on Alabama sharecroppers; *A Death in the Family* (1955), a novel, won a 1958 Pulitzer Prize.

Conrad Aiken (1889–1973), American poet: *Selected Poems* (1929) won a Pulitzer Prize.

Edward Albee (1928–), American playwright: *Who's Afraid of Virginia Woolf?* (1962), *Tiny Alice* (1964); *A Delicate Balance* (1966) and *Seascape* (1974) both

AUTHORS AND WRITERS (continued)
won Pulitzer Prizes.

Louisa May Alcott (1832–88), American children's writer: *Little Women* (1868–69), *Little Men* (1871).

Horatio Alger (1832–99), American author: *Ragged Dick* (1867), *Tattered Tom* (1871).

Nelson Algren (1909–81), American novelist: *The Man with the Golden Arm* (1949), *A Walk on the Wild Side* (1956).

Hervey Allen (1889–1949), American author: *Anthony Adverse* (1933).

Hans Christian Andersen (1805–75), Danish writer of fairy tales: *The Emperor's New Clothes.*

Maxwell Anderson (1888–1959), American playwright: *Elizabeth the Queen* (1930), *Winterset* (1935), *Joan of Lorraine* (1946); *Both Your Houses* (1932) won a Pulitzer Prize.

Sherwood Anderson (1876–1941), American novelist: *Winesburg, Ohio* (1919), short stories.

Jean Anouilh (1910–), French playwright: *Waltz of the Toreadors* (1952), *Becket* (1959).

Aristophanes (c. 450–388 B.C.), Greek comic dramatist. Of his 40 or more plays, 11 are extant, including *Clouds, Lysistrata,* and *Frogs.*

Matthew Arnold (1822–88), English poet and critic. His romantic pessimism is expressed in such poems as "Dover Beach."

Sholem Asch (1880–1957), Polish-American novelist: *The Nazarene* (1939), *Moses* (1951), *The Prophet* (1955).

Isaac Asimov (1920–), Russian–American author: science-fiction trilogy *Foundation* (1951–53).

Louis Auchincloss (1917–), American novelist: *The Rector of Justin* (1964), *A World of Profit* (1968), *The Winthrop Covenant* (1976), *The Dark Lady* (1977).

W. H. (Wystan Hugh) Auden (1907–73), Anglo-American poet: *The Age of Anxiety* (1947) won a Pulitzer Prize.

Jane Austen (1775–1817), English novelist whose books often satirize manners: *Pride and Prejudice* (1813), *Emma* (1815).

Sir Francis Bacon (1561–1626), English essayist and philosopher: *The Advancement of Learning* (1605), an effort to summarize all science; *Novum Organum* (1620), an inductive analysis of knowledge; *History of Henry VII* (1622); and *Maxims of the Law* (1637).

James Baldwin (1924–), American novelist and essayist who portrays aspects of black problems: *Go Tell It on the Mountain* (1953), a novel.

Honoré de Balzac (1799–1850), French novelist and dramatist: *The Chouans* (1829), *Droll Stories* (1832–37), *Old Goriot* (1834).

George Bancroft (1800–91): American historian: 10-volume *History of the United States* (1834–74).

Imamu Amiri Baraka, formerly known as LeRoi Jones (1934–), American dramatist and essayist: *Dutchman* (1964) and *The Slave* (1966).

Sir James Matthew Barrie (1860–1937), Scottish playwright and novelist: best-known play was *Peter Pan* (1904). Novels include *The Little Minister* (1891).

Philip Barry (1896–1949), American playwright: *The Philadelphia Story* (1939).

John Barth (1930–), U.S. novelist: *The Sot-Weed Factor* (1960), *Giles Goat-Boy* (1966), *Letters* (1979).

John Bartlett (1820–1905), American bookseller and writer: *Familiar Quotations* (1855).

Charles Baudelaire (1821–67), French poet and leader of the French symbolist movement: *Les Fleurs du Mal* (1857).

Samuel Beckett (1906–), Irish-born French novelist and playwright: *Malone Dies* (1951), a novel; *Waiting for Godot* (1952), his best-known play. He won a Nobel Prize in 1969.

Sir Max Beerbohm (1872–1956), English parodist and critic: *Poet's Corner* (1904), satiric essay; *Zuleika Dobson* (1912), a novel.

S. N. Behrman (1893–1973), American playwright: *Brief Moment* (1931), *No Time for Comedy* (1939).

Saul Bellow (1915–), Canadian-born American novelist; awarded 1976 Nobel Prize: *The Adventures of Augie March* (1953), *Herzog* (1964), *Mr. Sammler's Planet* (1970), all of which won National Book Awards; *Humboldt's Gift* (1975) won 1976 Pulitzer Prize.

Robert C. Benchley (1889-1945), American humorist: *Inside Benchley* (1942).

Stephen Vincent Benét (1898–1943), American poet: *John Brown's Body* (1928) and *Western Star* (1943) won Pulitzer Prizes.

Arnold Bennett (1867–1931), English novelist: *The Old Wives' Tale* (1908), *Clayhanger* (1910).

John Berryman (1914–72), American poet: *77 Dream Songs* (1963) won a Pulitzer Prize, and *His Toy* (1968) won a National Book Award.

Ambrose Bierce (1842–1914?), American critic and short-story writer: *In the Midst of Life* (1898).

Josh Billings (real name Henry Wheeler Shaw, 1818–85), American humorist: *Josh Billings' Farmers' Allminax* (1869–80).

William Blake (1757–1827), English poet and mystic: *Songs of Innocence* (1789), *Songs of Experience* (1794).

Robert Bly (1926–), American poet: *The Light Around the Body* (1967) won a National Book Award.

Giovanni Boccaccio (1313–75), Italian poet: the *Decameron* (1348–53), the *Filostrato* (c. 1338).

James Boswell (1740–95), Scottish biographer and diarist: *Life of Samuel Johnson* (1791).

Elizabeth Bowen (1899–1973), Anglo-Irish novelist: *The Death of the Heart* (1938).

Ray Bradbury (1920–), American sci-fi author: *Martian Chronicles* (1950), *Fahrenheit 451* (1953).

Anne Bradstreet (c. 1612–1672), American poet: *The Tenth Muse Lately Sprung Up in America* (1650).

Bertolt Brecht (1898–1956), German dramatist and poet. Borrowing freely from past writers, he combined polemics and lyricism in such plays as *The Threepenny Opera* (1928), *Mother Courage* (1940).

Louis Bromfield (1896–1956): American novelist: *Early Autumn* (1926) won a Pulitzer Prize.

Charlotte Brontë (1816–55), English novelist: *Jane Eyre* (1847).

Emily Brontë (1818–48), English novelist: *Wuthering Heights* (1847).

Rupert Brooke (1887–1915), English poet: his work treats the horrors of World War I.

Gwendolyn Brooks (1917–), American poet: *Annie Allen* (1949) won a Pulitzer Prize.

Van Wyck Brooks (1886–1963), American critic and historian: *The Flowering of New England* (1936) won a Pulitzer Prize.

Elizabeth Barrett Browning (1806–61), English poet and translator who was the wife of Robert Browning.

Robert Browning (1812–89), English dramatic poet: *The Ring and the Book (1869).*

William Cullen Bryant (1794–1878), American poet: *Thanatopsis* (1817).

Pearl S. Buck (1892–1973), American novelist: *The Good Earth* (1931) won Pulitzer Prize in 1932 and Nobel Prize in 1938.

John Bunyan (1628–88), English allegorist: *Pilgrim's Progress* (1678).

Edmund Burke (1729–97), English essayist and orator: *American Taxation* (1774) and *Letter to the Sheriff of Bristol* (1777) pleaded cause of American colonists.

Robert Burns (1759–96), Scottish lyric poet and ballad writer: "The Cotter's Saturday Night."

Edgar Rice Burroughs (1875–1950), American adventure and science-fiction writer, best known for his many Tarzan jungle stories.

John Burroughs (1837–1921), American outdoors writer: *Camping and Tramping with Roosevelt* (1907),

Under the Apple-Trees (1916).

George Gordon, Lord Byron (1788–1824), English lyric poet: *Don Juan* (1819–24).

James Branch Cabell (1879–1958), American novelist: *Jurgen* (1919).

Caius Julius Caesar (100?–44 B.C.), Roman statesman and historian: *The Gallic Wars*.

James Mallahan Cain (1892–1977), American crime novelist: *The Postman Always Rings Twice* (1934), *Double Indemnity* (1936), *Mildred Pierce* (1941).

Erskine Caldwell (1903–), American novelist: *Tobacco Road* (1932), *God's Little Acre* (1933).

(Janet) Taylor Caldwell (1900–85), American novelist: *Dear and Glorious Physician* (1959), *Testimony of Two Men* (1968), *Captains and Kings* (1972).

Albert Camus (1913–60), French essayist and novelist. His *Myth of Sisyphus* (1955) was an existentialist essay. His novels include *The Stranger* (1946) and *The Plague* (1948). He won a Nobel Prize in 1957.

Karel Capek (1890–1938), Czech dramatist: *R.U.R.* (*Rossum's Universal Robots*, 1921).

Truman Capote (1924–84), American short-story writer and essayist: *Other Voices, Other Rooms* (1948); *In Cold Blood* (1965), a documentary; *Music for Chameleons* (1980).

Thomas Carlyle (1795–1881), Scottish critic and historical essayist: *The French Revolution* (1837).

Lewis Carroll (real name Charles Lutwidge Dodgson; 1832–98), British mathematician and author: *Alice's Adventures in Wonderland* (1865).

Joyce Cary (1888–1957), Anglo-Irish novelist: *The Horse's Mouth* (1944).

Giovanni Casanova (1752–98), Italian memoirist. His amorous and adventurous *Memoirs* were not published in their complete form until 1960–61.

Willa Cather (1873–1947), American novelist: *O Pioneers!* (1913), *My Antonia* (1918); *One of Ours* (1922) won a Pulitzer Prize.

Bruce Catton (1899–1978), American historian: *A Stillness at Appomattox* (1953) won a Pulitzer Prize.

Caius Valerius Catullus (84?–54 B.C.), Roman poet. Of his numerous lyric poems, 116 are extant.

Miguel de Cervantes Saavedra (1547?–1616), Spanish novelist: *Don Quixote* (1614).

Raymond Chandler (1888–1959), American mystery and detective novelist: *The Big Sleep* (1939).

François René de Chateaubriand (1768–1848), French essayist and novelist. Best known for his autobiography, *Mémoires d'outre-tombe* (1850).

Geoffrey Chaucer (1343?–1400), English poet: *Canterbury Tales* (c. 1387), *Troilus and Criseyde* (c. 1385).

John Cheever (1912–82), American novelist: *The Wapshot Chronicle* (1951), *Bullet Park* (1969), *Falconer* (1977); *The Stories of John Cheever* (1978) won a Pulitzer Prize.

Anton Chekhov (1860–1904), Russian dramatist and short-story writer. After achieving success in short fiction he produced several great plays, including *The Sea Gull* (1896) and *The Cherry Orchard* (1904).

G. K. (Gilbert Keith) Chesterton (1874–1936), English novelist, poet, and critic who created the "Father Brown" detective story series.

Agatha Christie (1891–1976), English mystery novelist: *The Murder of Roger Ackroyd* (1926) and more than 50 other crime novels.

Sir Winston Churchill (1874–1965), English statesman and historian: *History of the English-Speaking Peoples* (4 vols., 1956–58).

John Ciardi (1916–), American poet: *As If: Poems New and Selected* (1955).

Marcus Tullius Cicero (106–43 B.C.), Roman statesman and orator: wrote many essays.

Arthur C. Clarke (1917–), British science-fiction author: *Against the Fall of Night* (1953); coauthor of movie *2001: A Space Odyssey* (1968).

Jean Cocteau (1891–1963), French dramatist, novelist, and poet: *Les Enfants Terribles* (1929), a drama.

Robert Peter Tristram Coffin (1892–1955), American writer: *Strange Holiness* (1935) won a Pulitzer Prize.

Samuel Taylor Coleridge (1772–1834), English poet and critic: collaborated with Wordsworth in the book of verse *Lyrical Ballads* (1798); *Biographia Literaria* (1817), essays on criticism.

Colette (full name Sidonie Gabrielle Colette; 1873–1954), French novelist and a leading feminist: *Chéri* (1920), *Gigi* (1945).

Padraic Colum (1881–1972), Irish-American novelist, dramatist, and poet. He was a leader of the Irish literary revival during the early 20th century.

Ivy Compton-Burnett (1892–1969), English novelist: *Brother and Sister* (1929).

William Congreve (1670–1729), English comic dramatist: *The Way of the World* (1700).

Marc Connelly (1890–1980), American playwright: *Green Pastures* (1930) won a Pulitzer Prize.

Joseph Conrad (1857–1924), Polish-born British novelist and short-story writer: *Lord Jim* (1900), *Typhoon* (1903); *Tales of Hearsay* (1925), stories.

James Fenimore Cooper (1789–1851), American novelist: *The Last of the Mohicans* (1826).

Noel Coward (1899–1973), English playwright and composer: *Private Lives* (1930); *Blithe Spirit* (1941).

Malcolm Cowley (1898–), American literary critic: *Exile's Return* (1934), *The Literary Situation* (1954), *The Faulkner-Cowley File* (1966).

James Gould Cozzens (1903–78), American novelist: *Guard of Honor* (1948) won a Pulitzer Prize; *By Love Possessed* (1957).

Hart Crane (1899–1932), U.S. poet: *The Bridge* (1930).

Stephen Crane (1871–1900), American novelist: *The Red Badge of Courage* (1895).

A. J. Cronin (1896–1981), British author: *The Keys of the Kingdom* (1941).

Walter Cronkite (1916–), radio-TV news correspondent; winner numerous broadcast and journalism awards.

Russel Crouse, see Howard Lindsay.

E. E. (Edward Estin) Cummings (1894–1962), American poet. His books of lyric verse, including *Tulips and Chimneys* (1923), experimented with unusual typographical styles.

Richard Henry Dana Jr. (1815–1882), American author: *Two Years Before the Mast* (1840).

Gabriele D'Annunzio (1863–1938), Italian poet, novelist, playwright: *La città morta* (1898), a play.

Dante Alighieri (1265–1321), Italian epic poet. His *Divine Comedy* ranks as the most important literary work of the Middle Ages.

Owen Davis (1874–1956), American playwright: *Icebound* (1923) won a Pulitzer Prize.

Clarence S. Day Jr. (1874–1935), American author: *Life with Father* (1935).

Thomas De Quincey (1785–1859), English author: *Confessions of an English Opium Eater* (1821).

Daniel Defoe (1660–1731), English novelist and journalist: *Robinson Crusoe* (1720), *Moll Flanders* (1722), *Journal of the Plague Year* (1722).

Lester Del Rey (born 1915), American science fiction author: *Nerves* (1956), *Pstalemate* (1971).

Charles Dickens (1812–70), English novelist: *Pickwick Papers* (1836), *Oliver Twist* (1837–39), *David Copperfield* (1849–50), *Great Expectations* (1860–61).

James Dickey (1925–), American poet and novelist: *Into the Stone* (1960), poetry; *Deliverance* (1970).

Emily Dickinson (1830–86), American poet. Her lyric poems reflect solitude and preoccupation with death.

Denis Diderot (1713–84), French encyclopedist and novelist.

George Dillon (1906–68), American poet: *The Flowering Stone* (1931) won a Pulitzer Prize.

AUTHORS AND WRITERS *(continued)*
Isak Dinesen (real name **Karen Blixen**; 1885–1962), Danish novelist: *Seven Gothic Tales* (1934).
E. L. (Edgar Lawrence) Doctorow (1931–), American novelist: *The Book of Daniel* (1971), *Ragtime* (1975), *Loon Lake* (1980).
J. P. (James Patrick) Donleavy (1926–), American novelist: *The Ginger Man* (1955), *Schultz* (1979).
John Donne (1572–1631), English poet and preacher noted for his metaphysical and devotional poems.
Hilda Doolittle ("H. D."; 1886–1961), American poet of the American Imagist movement.
John Dos Passos (1896–1970), American novelist: *U.S.A.*, a trilogy consisting of *The 42d Parallel* (1930), *1919* (1932), and *The Big Money* (1936).
Feodor Dostoyevsky (1821–81), Russian novelist: *Memoirs from the House of the Dead* (1861–62), *Crime and Punishment* (1866), *The Idiot* (1868), *The Possessed* (1871–72), *The Brothers Karamazov* (1879–80).
Lloyd C. Douglas (1877–1951), American author: *Magnificent Obsession* (1929), *Green Light* (1935), *The Robe* (1942), *The Big Fisherman* (1948).
Sir Arthur Conan Doyle (1859–1930), Scottish mystery novelist and creator of Sherlock Holmes.
Theodore Dreiser (1871–1945), American novelist: *Sister Carrie* (1900), *An American Tragedy* (1925).
Allen Drury (1918–), U.S. novelist: *Advise and Consent* (1960) won a Pulitzer Prize; *Anna Hastings* (1977); *The Hill of Summer* (1981).
John Dryden (1631–1700), English poet, dramatist, and critic: *Fables, Ancient and Modern* (1699).
Alexandre Dumas, père (1802–70), French novelist and dramatist: *The Count of Monte Cristo* (1844) and *The Three Musketeers* (1844).
Alexandre Dumas, fils (1824–95), French dramatist: *Monsieur Alphonse* (1873), *Denise* (1885).
Will Durant (1885–1981), U.S. historian and philosopher: *The Story of Philosophy* (1926), *The Story of Civilization* (12 vols., begun in 1935); *Rousseau and Revolution* (1967) won a Pulitzer Prize for nonfiction.
Lawrence Durrell (1912–), English novelist: *The Alexandria Quartet* (1958–60), *Tunc* (1968).
Richard Eberhart (1904–), American poet: *Selected Poems* (1965) won a Pulitzer Prize.
Leon Edel (1907–), American literary historian and biographer: *Henry James* (1953–72), a 5-volume biography. The third volume, *Henry James: The Middle Years* (1962), won a Pulitzer Prize and a National Book Award.
Ilya Ehrenberg (1891–1967), Russian novelist: *A Street in Moscow* (1930), *Out of Chaos* (1934).
George Eliot (real name **Marian Evans**; 1819–80), English novelist: *Silas Marner* (1861).
T. S. (Thomas Stearns) Eliot (1888–1965), American-born English poet and critic: *The Lovesong of J. Alfred Prufrock* (1917), *The Wasteland* (1922). He won a Nobel Prize in 1948.
Ralph Ellison (1914–), American novelist: *Invisible Man* (1952).
Ralph Waldo Emerson (1803–82), American essayist and poet; developed transcendentalist philosophy.
Euripides (485?–406 B.C.), Greek tragic dramatist. Of about 92 plays 19 are extant, including *Medea* (431 B.C.) and *Electra* (413 B.C.).
James T. Farrell (1904–79), American novelist: *Studs Lonigan* (1932–35), a trilogy.
William Faulkner (1897–1962), American novelist: *The Sound and the Fury* (1929) and *Light in August* (1932). He won a Nobel Prize in 1949 and Pulitzer Prizes for *A Fable* (1954) and *The Reivers* (1962).
Edna Ferber (1885–1968), American novelist: *So Big* (1924) won a Pulitzer Prize; *Show Boat* (1926); *Cimarron* (1930); *Giant* (1952).
Lawrence Ferlinghetti (1919–), American beat-generation poet; *A Coney Island of the Mind* (1958).

Eugene Field (1850–95), American poet and journalist: best known for children's poems "Little Boy Blue" and "Wynken, Blynken, and Nod."
Henry Fielding (1707–54), English novelist and dramatist: *Joseph Andrews* (1742), *Tom Jones* (1749).
Edward Fitzgerald (1809–83), English poet, translated Omar Khayyam's *Rubaiyat* in 1859.
F. (Francis) Scott Fitzgerald (1896–1940), American novelist and short-story writer: *This Side of Paradise* (1920), *The Great Gatsby* (1925).
Gustave Flaubert (1821–80), French novelist: *Madame Bovary* (1857).
Ford Madox Ford (real name **Ford Madox Hueffer**; 1873–1939), English novelist and poet: *The Good Soldier* (1915), *Parade's End* (1924–28), a tetralogy published in one volume in 1950.
E. M. (Edward Morgan) Forster (1879–1970), English novelist and critic: *A Passage to India* (1924), a novel; *Aspects of the Novel* (1927), criticism.
John Fowles (1926–), English novelist: *The Collector* (1963), *The Magus* (1966), *The French Lieutenant's Woman* (1970), *Mantissa* (1982).
Anatole France (real name **Anatole Jacques Thibault**; 1844–1924), French novelist and satirist: *Balthasar* (1889), short stories; won a Nobel Prize in 1921.
Douglas Southall Freeman (1886–1953), American historian: *R. E. Lee*, 4 vols. (1934), and *George Washington*, 7 vols. (1948–57) won Pulitzer Prizes.
Robert Frost (1874–1963), American lyric poet captured much of the American rural spirit. He won four Pulitzer Prizes for *New Hampshire* (1923), *Collected Poems* (1930), *A Further Range* (1936), and *A Witness Tree* (1942).
Christopher Fry (1907–), English dramatist and translator: *The Lady's Not for Burning* (1949).
William Gaddis (1922–), American novelist: *The Recognitions* (1962).
John Galsworthy (1867–1933), English novelist and playwright: *The Forsyte Saga* (1922), a trilogy.
Erle Stanley Gardner (1889–1970), American detective-story writer: *The Case of the Velvet Claws* (1933) was his first novel featuring the lawyer Perry Mason.
William H. Gass (1924–), American novelist and critic: *Omensetter's Luck* (1966), a novel; *In the Heart of the Heart of the Country* (1968).
John Gay (1685–1732), English dramatist and poet: *The Beggar's Opera* (1728).
Jean Genet (1910–), French novelist and dramatist: *The Balcony* (1957) and *The Blacks* (1959), dramas; *Miracle of the Rose* (1951), a novel.
Edward Gibbon (1737–94), English historian: *The Decline and Fall of the Roman Empire* (1776–88).
André Gide (1869–1951), French novelist: *The Immoralist* (1902), *Strait Is the Gate* (1909); awarded 1947 Nobel Prize.
Allen Ginsberg (1926–), American poet of beat and hippie movements: *Howl and Other Poems* (1955). His *The Fall of America: Poems of These States* (1973) won a National Book Award.
Jean Giraudoux (1882–1944), French dramatist: *Tiger at the Gates* (1935).
Ellen Glasgow (1874–1945), American novelist: *In This Our Life* (1941) won a Pulitzer Prize.
Johann Wolfgang von Goethe (1749–1832), German poet and dramatist. His greatest work was the dramatic poem *Faust* (1808 and 1833).
Nikolai Vasilyevich Gogol (1809–52), Russian novelist, short-story writer, and playwright: *The Inspector General* (1836), a play; *Dead Souls* (1842), a novel.
William Golding (1911–), English novelist: *Lord of the Flies* (1954), *Darkness Visible* (1979), *The Paper Men* (1984); won 1983 Nobel Prize in Literature.
Oliver Goldsmith (1730?–74), Irish novelist, poet, and dramatist: *The Vicar of Wakefield* (1766), a novel; *She Stoops to Conquer* (1773), a drama.

Maxim Gorki (real name Aleksey Maximovich Pyeshkov; 1868–1936), Russian dramatist and novelist: *The Lower Depths* (1902), play; *Mother* (1907), novel.

Gunter Grass (1927–), German novelist: *The Tin Drum* (1959), *Local Anaesthetic* (1970), *The Meeting at Telgate* (1981).

Shirley Ann Grau (1929–), American novelist: *The Keepers of the House* (1964), which won a Pulitzer Prize; *The Condor Passes* (1971).

Robert Graves (1895–), English poet, novelist, and critic. Besides much lyric verse, he wrote such novels as *I, Claudius* (1934).

Thomas Gray (1716–71), English poet: "Elegy Written in a Country Churchyard" (1750).

Graham Greene (1904–), English novelist: *The Power and the Glory* (1940); *The Comedians* (1966); *A Sort of Life* (1971), autobiography; *The Honorary Consul* (1973); *The Human Factor* (1978); *Monsignor Quixote* (1982).

Lady Augusta Gregory (1852–1932), Irish dramatist and founder of Dublin's Abbey Theatre: her plays include *The Rising of the Moon* (1907).

Zane Grey (1872–1939), U.S. novelist of Old West: *The Last of The Plainsmen* (1908), *Riders of The Purple Sage* (1912).

John Gunther (1901–70), American author: *Inside Europe* (1936), *Inside Asia* (1939).

A. B. Guthrie Jr. (1901–), American novelist: *The Big Sky* (1947); *The Way West* (1949) won a Pulitzer Prize.

Arthur Hailey (born 1920), British-Canadian novelist: *Hotel* (1965), *Airport* (1968), *The Moneychangers* (1975), *Strong Medicine* (1984).

Alex Haley (1921–), American author: *Roots* (1976) won a special Pulitzer Prize.

James Norman Hall, see Charles Nordhoff.

Dashiell Hammett (1894–1961), U.S. detective-story writer: created Sam Spade in *The Maltese Falcon* (1930) and Nick and Nora Charles in *The Thin Man* (1934).

Knut Hamsun (1859–1952), Norwegian novelist: *Growth of the Soil* (1920), *Mysteries* (1927). He won a Nobel Prize in 1920.

Lorraine Hansberry (1930–65), American black playwright: *A Raisin in the Sun* (1959).

Thomas Hardy (1840–1928), English novelist, poet, and dramatist: *Tess of the D'Urbervilles* (1891) and *Jude the Obscure* (1895), novels.

Joel Chandler Harris (1848–1908), American novelist and short-story writer who recorded Southern dialect: *Uncle Remus: His Songs and His Sayings* (1881).

Moss Hart (1904–61), American playwright and stage director: co-winner of Pulitzer Prize for *You Can't Take It With You* (1936). Wrote many plays and musicals including *Lady in the Dark* (1941), *Winged Victory* (1943).

Bret Harte (1836–1902), American western author: *The Luck of Roaring Camp* (1870).

Gerhart Hauptmann (1862–1946), German dramatist, poet, and novelist: *Before Dawn* (1889), a play.

Nathaniel Hawthorne (1804–64), American novelist and short-story writer: *The Scarlet Letter* (1850), *The House of Seven Gables* (1851).

Heinrich Heine (1797–1856), German poet: His lyrics used in songs of Schubert, Liszt, and Schumann.

Robert A. Heinlein (1907–), American science-fiction author: *Stranger in a Strange Land* (1961), *The Past Through Tomorrow* (1967).

Joseph Heller (1923–), U.S. novelist: *Catch-22* (1961), *Something Happened* (1974), *Good as Gold* (1979), *God Knows* (1984).

Lillian Hellman (1907–84), American playwright: *The Children's Hour* (1934), *The Little Foxes* (1939), *Watch on the Rhine* (1941); *An Unfinished Woman* (1969), autobiography.

Ernest Hemingway (1899–1961), American novelist and short-story writer: *A Farewell to Arms* (1929); *For Whom the Bell Tolls* (1940); *The Old Man and the Sea* (1952) won a Pulitzer Prize. He was awarded a Nobel Prize in 1954.

O. Henry (William Sydney Porter; 1862–1910), U.S. short-story writer of about 300 stories memorable for concise plotting and surprise endings.

Frank Herbert (born 1920), American science fiction novelist: *Dune* (1965), *Dune Messiah* (1969), *Children of Dune* (1976), *The White Plaque* (1982), *Heretics of Dune* (1984).

Herodotus (484?–425 B.C.), Greek historian: *History of the Persian Wars.*

Robert Herrick (1591–1674), English poet. His highly polished verse reflects classical influences.

John Hersey (1914–), American novelist and journalist: *A Bell for Adano* (1944) won a Pulitzer Prize; *Hiroshima* (1946), *The Walnut Door* (1977).

Hermann Hesse (1877–1962), German poet and novelist: *Steppenwolf* (1927), *Magister Ludi* (1949). He won a Nobel Prize in 1946.

Robert Silliman Hillyer (1895–1961), American poet: *Collected Verse* (1933) won a Pulitzer Prize.

Laura Z. Hobson (1900–), U.S. novelist: *Gentleman's Agreement* (1947); *Over and Above* (1979); *Untold Millions* (1982).

Oliver Wendell Holmes (1809–94), American poet, essayist: "Old Ironsides" (1830), a poem; *Autocrat of the Breakfast Table* (1858), sketches.

Homer (c. 800–700 B.C.), Greek epic poet: the *Odyssey,* the *Iliad.*

Gerard Manley Hopkins (1844–89), English mystical poet: "The Windhover" (1918).

Horace (65–8 B.C.), Latin poet. He published three books of *Odes* and two books of *Satires.*

Paul Horgan (1903–), American author: won Pulitzer Prizes for *Great River* (1954) and *Lamy of Santa Fe* (1975).

A. E. (Alfred Edward) Housman (1859–1936), English poet: *A Shropshire Lad* (1896).

William Dean Howells (1837–1920), American novelist and critic: *The Rise of Silas Lapham* (1885), *A Hazard of New Fortunes* (1890).

Victor Hugo (1802–85), French novelist, poet, and dramatist: novels include *Notre Dame de Paris* (1831) and *Les Misérables* (1862).

Aldous Huxley (1894–1963), English novelist and essayist: *Brave New World* (1932).

Henrik Ibsen (1828–1906), Norwegian dramatist. He pioneered social realism in such plays as *A Doll's House* (1879) and *Rosmersholm* (1886).

William Inge (1913–73), American dramatist: *Come Back, Little Sheba* (1950); *Picnic* (1952) won a Pulitzer Prize; *The Dark at the Top of the Stairs* (1958).

Eugene Ionesco (1912–), French dramatist. A pioneer in the theater of the absurd, his plays include *The Chairs* (1952) and *Rhinoceros* (1960).

Washington Irving (1783–1859), American editor and short-story writer: "Rip Van Winkle" and "The Legend of Sleepy Hollow" (both 1820).

Christopher Isherwood (1904–), English dramatist and novelist. His collection of sketches, *Goodbye to Berlin* (1939), was adapted for the stage in 1951 by John Van Druten as *I Am a Camera,* as was the musical *Cabaret* in 1971.

Shirley Jackson (1919-65), American author of horror tales: novel, *Haunting of Hill House* (1959).

John Jakes (born 1932), American historical novelist: *The Rebels* (1975), *North and South* (1982), *Love and War* (1984).

Henry James (1843–1916), American novelist and short-story writer: *Wings of the Dove* (1902), *The Ambassadors* (1903), *The Golden Bowl* (1904).

Marquis James (1891–1955), American author: won Pulitzer Prizes for biographies *The Raven* (1929) and

AUTHORS AND WRITERS (continued)
Andrew Jackson (1937).

Randall Jarrell (1914–65), American poet: *Little Friend, Little Friend* (1945), poems of World War II.

Robinson Jeffers (1887–1962), American poet: *Give Your Heart to the Hawks* (1933).

Samuel Johnson (1709–84), English essayist, critic, poet, and lexicographer: his essays in *The Rambler* helped establish literary standards; famous for his witty *Dictionary of the English Language* (1755).

James Jones (1921–77), American novelist: *From Here to Eternity* (1951) won a National Book Award.

Ben Jonson (1573?–1637), English dramatist and poet: *Volpone* (1606), *The Alchemist* (1610).

James Joyce (1882–1941), Irish novelist, poet, and short-story writer. He applied poetic techniques to his novels, *A Portrait of the Artist as a Young Man* (1916), *Ulysses* (1922), and *Finnegans Wake* (1939). *Dubliners* (1914) is a short-story collection.

Juvenal (55?–135), Roman satirical poet.

Franz Kafka (1883–1924), Austrian novelist: *Amerika* (1927), *The Castle* (1930), *The Trial* (1937).

MacKinlay Kantor (1904–77), American novelist, won a Pulitzer Prize for *Andersonville* (1955).

George S. Kaufman (1889–1961), American playwright and director: co-recipient of Pulitzer Prizes for *Of Thee I Sing* (1931) and *You Can't Take It With You* (1936).

Nikos Kazantzakis (1883?–1957), Greek novelist: *Zorba the Greek* (1946).

Alfred Kazin (1915–), American critic: *On Native Grounds* (1942), *The Inmost Leaf* (1955).

John Keats (1795–1821), English poet: "Ode on a Grecian Urn" and "To a Nightingale" (both 1820).

George Edward Kelly (1887–1974), American playwright: *Craig's Wife* (1925) won a Pulitzer Prize.

Jack Kerouac (1922-69), American author of the "beat generation": *On the Road* (1957), *Big Sur* (1962).

Stephen King born 1947, American novelist, noted for horror stories: *Carrie* (1974), *The Shining* (1976), *Cujo* (1981), *The Talisman* (with Peter Straub; 1984), *Skeleton Crew* (1985).

Rudyard Kipling (1865–1936), English poet, novelist, and short-story writer: *The Light That Failed* (1890), *Barrack Room Ballads* (1892), *The Jungle Book* (1894), *Captains Courageous* (1897), *Kim* (1901), *Just So Stories* (1902); won a Nobel Prize in 1907.

George Lyman Kittredge (1860–1941), American literary scholar: *Shakespeare* (1916).

Arthur Koestler (1905–83), British-Hungarian political novelist: *Darkness at Noon* (1941).

Oliver La Farge (1901–63), American author: *Laughing Boy* (1929) won a Pulitzer Prize.

Jean de La Fontaine (1621–95), French fabulist and poet: *Fables choisies mises en vers* (1668–94) consists of about 230 fables.

Pär Lägerkvist (1891–1974), Swedish Nobel Prize-winning author: *Barabas* (1951).

Charles Lamb (1775–1834), English essayist and critic. With his sister Mary he wrote the children's book *Tales from Shakespeare* (1807).

Louis L'Amour (born 1908), American author of scores of novels about Western frontier life from *Westward the Tide* (1950) to *The Walking Drum* (1984).

Sidney Lanier (1842–81), American poet and critic: *Poems* (1887).

Ring Lardner (1885–1933), American satirist and short-story writer: *You Know Me, Al* (1916).

D. H. (David Herbert) Lawrence (1885–1930), English novelist, poet, and critic: *Sons and Lovers* (1913), *Lady Chatterley's Lover* (1928).

Harper Lee (1926–), American novelist: *To Kill a Mockingbird* (1960) won a Pulitzer Prize.

Cecil Day Lewis (1904–72), English essayist and novelist: *Overtures to Death* (1938), poems. He became

poet laureate of England in 1968.

C. S. (Clive Staples) Lewis (1898–1963), English religious essayist and poet: *The Allegory of Love* (1936), *The Screwtape Letters* (1942).

Sinclair Lewis (1885–1951), American novelist: *Main Street* (1920), *Babbitt* (1922), *Elmer Gantry* (1927); *Arrowsmith* (1925) won a Pulitzer Prize. He won a Nobel Prize in 1930.

Howard Lindsay (1889–1968) American playwright: coauthor with Russel Crouse (1893–1966) of Pulitzer Prize-winning *State of the Union* (1945) and long-running *Life with Father* (1939), in which Lindsay starred as actor.

Vachel Lindsay (1879–1931), American poet: *General William Booth Enters into Heaven* (1913).

Livy (59 B.C.–A.D. 17), Roman historian; 35 books of his 142-book *History of Rome* are extant.

Jack London (1876–1916), American novelist: *The Call of the Wild* (1903), *Martin Eden* (1909).

Henry Wadsworth Longfellow (1807–82), American poet: *Evangeline* (1847).

Federico García Lorca (1899–1936), Spanish poet and dramatist: *Blood Wedding* (1938).

Amy Lowell (1874–1925), American poet, pioneered free verse: *Sword Blades and Poppy Seeds* (1914); *What's O'Clock* (1925) won a Pulitzer Prize.

James Russell Lowell (1819–91), American poet and essayist: *A Fable for Critics* (1848).

Robert Lowell (1917–77), American poet and critic: *Lord Weary's Castle* (1946) and *The Dolphin* (1973) won Pulitzer Prizes.

Malcolm Lowry (1909–57), British novelist: *Under the Volcano* (1947).

Robert Ludlum (born 1927), American novelist: *The Matlock Paper* (1973), *The Rhinemann Exchange* (1974), *The Gemini Contenders* (1976), *The Chancellor Manuscript Contenders* (1976), *The Chancellor Manuscript* (1977), *The Holcroft Covenant* (1978), *The Matarese Circle* (1979), *The Bourne Identity* (1980), *The Parsifal Mosaic* (1982), and *The Aquitaine Progression* (1983).

John D. MacDonald (born 1916), American mystery writer, best known for stories about detective Travis McGee: *The Deep Blue Good-by* (1964), *The Green Ripper* (1979).

Ross Macdonald (pseudonym of **Kenneth Millar**; 1915–83), American mystery writer: *The Chill* (1964), *The Underground Man* (1971), *The Blue Hammer* (1976).

Niccolò Machiavelli (1469–1527), Italian essayist and dramatist: *The Prince* (1532).

Archibald MacLeish (1892–1982), American poet and dramatist. He won Pulitzer Prizes for poetry with *Conquistador* (1932) and *Collected Poems* (1952). His drama *J. B.* (1958) also won a Pulitzer Prize.

Norman Mailer (1923–), American novelist and essayist: *The Naked and the Dead* (1948), *Why Are We in Vietnam?* (1967). *The Armies of the Night* (1968) and *The Executioner's Song* (1979) won Pulitzer Prizes.

Bernard Malamud (1914–), American novelist: *The Natural* (1952), *The Assistant* (1957), *Dubin's Lives* (1979); *The Fixer* (1966) won a National Book Award and a Pulitzer Prize; *God's Grace* (1982).

Stéphane Mallarmé (1842–98), French poet: *L'Après-Midi d'un faune* (1887).

Sir Thomas Malory (died 1471), English writer of romances: *Morte D'Arthur* (1485).

André Malraux (1901–76), French novelist: *Man's Fate* (1933), *The Voices of Silence* (1953), essays.

Thomas Mann (1875–1955), German novelist: *The Magic Mountain* (1927) and *Joseph and His Brothers* (1934–44); won Nobel Prize in 1929.

Katherine Mansfield (1888–1923), British short-story writer: *The Garden Party* (1922).

Edwin Markham (1852–1940), American poet: "The

Man with the Hoe" (1899).

Christopher Marlowe (1564–93), English dramatist and poet: *Tamburlaine the Great* (1587?), *Dr. Faustus* (1588?).

John P. Marquand (1893–1960), American novelist: *The Late George Apley* (1937) won a Pulitzer Prize.

Gabriel Garcia Márquez, (1928–), Colombian novelist: *One Hundred Years of Solitude* (1967), *The Autumn of the Patriarch* (1975); won Nobel Prize for Literature in 1982.

John Masefield (1878–1967), English poet laureate (1930–67): *Salt Water Ballads* (1902).

Edgar Lee Masters (1869–1950), American poet: *Spoon River Anthology* (1915).

W. Somerset Maugham (1874–1965), English novelist and playwright: *Of Human Bondage* (1915), *The Moon and Sixpence* (1919), *The Razor's Edge* (1944).

Guy de Maupassant (1850–93), French novelist and short-story writer. *Une Vie* (1883) is his best novel. His 300 masterful short stories include "The Necklace" and "The Piece of String."

François Mauriac (1885–1970), French novelist: *The Desert of Love* (1925). He won a Nobel Prize in 1952.

André Maurois (1885–1967), French novelist and biographer: *Ariel* (1923), a life of Shelley; *Proust*, (1949); *Memoirs* (1970).

Mary McCarthy (1912–), American novelist and essayist: *The Groves of Academe* (1952), *The Group* (1963), *Cannibals and Missionaries* (1979), novels.

Carson McCullers (1917–67), American novelist and playwright: *Member of the Wedding* (1946).

Phyllis McGinley (1905–78), American poet: *Times Three: Selected Verse from Three Decades* (1961) won a Pulitzer Prize.

Herman Melville (1819–91), American novelist. His allegorical *Moby-Dick*, (1851) is his masterpiece. His last great book, *Billy Budd*, was published in 1924.

H. L. (Henry Louis) Mencken (1880–1956), American satirist, editor, and essayist: *Prejudices* (1919–27), *Treatise on Right and Wrong* (1934), *The American Language* (1919, 1946, 1948).

George Meredith (1828–1909), English novelist: *The Ordeal of Richard Feverel* (1859), *The Egoist* (1879).

W. S. Merwin (1927–), American poet: *The Carrier of Ladders* (1970) won a Pulitzer Prize.

James A. Michener (1907–), American novelist: *Tales of the South Pacific* (1947) won a Pulitzer Prize; *The Source* (1965), *Centennial* (1974), *Chesapeake* (1978), *The Covenant* (1980), *Space* (1982), *Poland* (1983).

John Stuart Mill (1806–73), English philosopher: *Essay on Liberty* (1859), *Utilitarianism* (1863).

Edna St. Vincent Millay (1892–1950), American poet best remembered for her sonnets. *The Ballad of the Harp-Weaver* (1922) won a Pulitzer Prize.

Arthur Miller (1915–), American playwright: *Death of a Salesman* (1949) won a Pulitzer Prize; *The Crucible* (1953), *A View From the Bridge* (1955), *After the Fall* (1964), *The Price* (1968).

Henry Miller (1891–1980), American novelist: *Tropic of Cancer* (1934), *Tropic of Capricorn* (1939).

Joaquin Miller (1839?–1913), American poet; *Song of the Sierras* (1871), *Life Among the Modocs* (1873).

A. A. (Alan Alexander) Milne (1882–1956), English poet and children's writer: *Winnie-the-Pooh* (1926).

Czeslaw Milosz (1911–), Polish-born American poet: *Postwar Polish Poetry* (1965), *Bells in Winter* (1978); won Nobel Prize in 1980.

John Milton (1608–74), English poet. His epic *Paradise Lost* (1667) is a literary landmark.

Margaret Mitchell (1900–49), American novelist: *Gone with the Wind* (1936) won a Pulitzer Prize.

Jean Baptiste Molière (1622–73), French dramatist and one of the great comic playwrights of all time. His works include *The Miser* (1668) and *The Doctor in Spite of Himself* (1666).

Michel Eyquem de Montaigne (1533–92), French essayist and one of the world's great literary stylists.

Marianne Moore (1887–1972), American poet: *Collected Poems* (1951) won a Pulitzer Prize; *O to Be a Dragon* (1959).

Alberto Moravia (1907–), Italian novelist: *Two Women* (1957), *The Empty Canvas* (1961).

Sir Thomas More (1478–1535), English essayist: *Utopia* (1516).

Samuel Eliot Morison (1887–1976), American historian: *Admiral of the Ocean Sea* (1942) and *John Paul Jones* (1959) won Pulitzer Prizes.

Christopher Morley (1890–1957), American novelist and editor: *Kitty Foyle* (1939), a novel.

Iris Murdoch (1919–), Anglo-Irish novelist: *The Bell* (1958), *A Severed Head* (1961), *The Sacred and Profane Love Machine* (1974).

Edward R. Murrow (1908-65), radio and TV newscaster, director of U.S. Information Agency in 1961-64.

Vladimir Nabokov (1899–1977), Russian-American novelist: *Lolita* (1955), *Pnin* (1957), *Pale Fire* (1962), *Ada* (1969).

Ogden Nash (1902–71), American humorous poet: *Hard Lines* (1931), *I'm a Stranger Here Myself* (1938), *You Can't Get There From Here* (1957).

Robert Nathan (1894–1985), American author: novel *Portrait of Jennie* (1940), poetry *The Green Leaf: Collected Poems* (1950).

Allan Nevins (1890–1971) American historian: won Pulitzer Prizes for *Grover Cleveland* (1933) and *Hamilton Fish* (1936).

Charles Bernard Nordhoff (1887–1947) and **James Norman Hall** (1887–1951), American writing team: *Lafayette Flying Corps* (1920), *Mutiny on the Bounty* (1932), *The Hurricane* (1935).

Frank Norris (1870–1902), American novelist: *McTeague* (1899), *The Octopus* (1901), *The Pit* (1902).

Joyce Carol Oates (1938–), American novelist and critic: *Them* (1969), a novel, won a National Book Award; *Childworld* (1976); *Unholy Loves* (1979); *Bellefleur* (1980), *Angel of Light* (1981), *Mysteries of Winterthurn* (1984).

Sean O'Casey (1884–1964), Irish playwright: *The Shadow of a Gunman* (1923), *Juno and the Paycock* (1924), *The Plough and the Stars* (1926).

Edwin O'Connor (1918–1968), American novelist: *The Last Hurrah* (1956); *The Edge of Sadness* (1961) won a Pulitzer Prize.

Flannery O'Connor (1925–64), American novelist and short-story writer: *Wise Blood* (1952); *The Violent Bear It Away* (1960); *Complete Stories* (1971).

Clifford Odets (1906–63), American playwright: *Waiting for Lefty* (1935), *Golden Boy* (1937).

Sean O'Faoláin (1900–), Irish author: *King of the Beggars* (1938), biographies of Irish statesmen; *I Remember! I Remember!* (1961), short stories.

Liam O'Flaherty (1897–1984), Irish novelist: *The Informer* (1925).

John O'Hara (1905–70), American novelist and short-story writer: *Appointment in Samarra* (1934), *Butterfield 8* (1935), *Pal Joey* (1940), novels.

Omar Khayyam (11th century), Persian poet: *The Rubaiyat*.

Eugene O'Neill (1888–1953), American dramatist: *Mourning Becomes Electra* (1931) and *The Iceman Cometh* (1946). Four of his plays won Pulitzer Prizes: *Beyond the Horizon* (1919), *Anna Christie* (1921), *Strange Interlude* (1927), and *Long Day's Journey Into Night* (1941); won Nobel Prize in 1936.

José Ortega y Gasset (1883–1955), Spanish essayist and critic: *Meditations on Quixote* (1914), *The Revolt of the Masses* (1930).

George Orwell (1903–50), English satirist: *Animal Farm* (1946), *Nineteen Eighty-Four* (1949).

AUTHORS AND WRITERS (continued)

Ovid (43 B.C.A.D. 18), Latin poet: *Metamorphoses.*

Thomas Paine (1737–1809), American political essayist. His pamphlet *Common Sense* (1776) promoted America's independence from Britain.

Dorothy Parker (1893–1967), American poet and short-story writer: *Enough Rope* (1926), verse; *After Such Pleasures* (1933), *Here Lies* (1939), stories.

Boris Pasternak (1890–1960), Soviet poet, novelist, and translator of Shakespeare into Russian: *Doctor Zhivago* (1957), a novel; forced by his government to decline 1958 Nobel Prize.

Samuel Pepys (1633–1703), English diarist; presents vivid picture of Restoration London.

St.-John Perse (real name **Marie R.A.A.S. Léger**; 1887–1975), French poet who won a Nobel Prize in 1960. One of his best-known works is the long poem *Anabase* (1924).

Francesco Petrarch (1304–74), Italian poet of the Latin and Italian languages. He was among the first and greatest of the Renaissance poets and a popularizer of the sonnet form.

Harold Pinter (1930–), English dramatist: *The Birthday Party* (1957), *The Caretaker* (1959).

Luigi Pirandello (1867–1936), Italian playwright: *Six Characters in Search of an Author* (1920).

Sylvia Plath (1932–63), American poet and novelist: *Ariel* (1965), poems; *The Bell Jar* (1971), a novel.

Plutarch (45?–125), Greek biographer and essayist. His *Parallel Lives* is a collection of 46 biographies of notable Greek and Roman figures.

Edgar Allan Poe (1809–49), American poet and short-story writer: "The Raven" (1845) and "The Bells" (1847), poems; "The Fall of the House of Usher" (1839), and "The Gold Bug" (1843), stories.

Alexander Pope (1688–1744), English poet. His *Essay on Criticism* (1711) and *Essay on Man* (1734) used rhymed couplets in popularizing dominant ideas of the time; *The Rape of the Lock* (1714) is a landmark among mock-heroic poems.

Katherine Anne Porter (1890–1980), American short-story writer and novelist: *Pale Horse, Pale Rider* (1939), short stories; *Ship of Fools* (1962), a novel. Her *Collected Stories* (1965) won a National Book Award and a Pulitzer Prize.

Ezra Pound (1885–1972), American expatriate poet. He dominated the imagism and vorticism movements of early 1900s; best known for his serial poems, *Cantos* (1925–60).

Anthony Powell (1905–), British author: *A Dance to the Music of Time* series (1951-76).

John Boynton Priestley (1894–1984), English novelist: *The Good Companions* (1929).

Marcel Proust (1871–1922), French novelist. From 1913 to 1922 he produced 16-volume masterpiece, *Remembrance of Things Past.*

Aleksandr Sergeyevich Pushkin (1799–1837), Russian poet: *Eugene Onegin* (1828).

Mario Puzo (born 1920), American novelist: *The Godfather* (1969), *The Sicilian* (1984).

Ernest Taylor Pyle (1900–45), World War II newspaper correspondent.

Thomas Pynchon (1937–), American novelist: *V* (1963), *Gravity's Rainbow* (1973) won a National Book Award.

Salvatore Quasimodo (1901–68), Italian poet. His poems, philosophical interpretations of man's history, won a Nobel Prize in 1959.

Ellery Queen, pen name of Frederic Dannay (1905–82) and Manfred Lee (1905–1971), American detective-story writing team: Books featured detective Ellery Queen.

Francois Rabelais (1494?–1553), French satirist: *Gargantua* and *Pantagruel* (both 1532).

Jean Baptiste Racine (1639–99), French dramatist:

Britannicus (1669) and *Bérénice* (1670).

Ayn Rand (1905–82), American novelist: *The Fountainhead* (1943), *Atlas Shrugged* (1957).

Marjorie Kinnan Rawlings (1896–1953), American novelist: *The Yearling* (1938) won a Pulitzer Prize.

Erich Maria Remarque (1897–1970), German-American novelist: *All Quiet on the Western Front* (1929), *Three Comrades* (1938).

Kenneth Rexroth (1905–82), American poet and critic: *Natural Numbers* (1963), poems; *Assays* (1961), essays; *The Morning Star* (1979).

Elmer Rice (1892–1967), American playwright: *Street Scene* (1929) won a Pulitzer Price; *Dream Girl* (1945).

I. A. (Ivor Armstrong) Richards (1893–1979), Anglo-American critic, pioneer in New Criticism movement: *Principles of Literary Criticism* (1925).

Samuel Richardson (1689–1761), English novelist: *Pamela* (1740), *Clarissa* (1747–48).

Conrad Richter (1890–1968), American novelist: *The Town* (1950) won a Pulitzer Prize.

James Whitcomb Riley (1849–1916), American poet best-known for Indiana dialect verse: *Rhymes of Childhood* (1890).

Rainer Maria Rilke (1875–1926), German poet; wrote on themes of spiritual isolation.

Arthur Rimbaud (1854–91), French poet: *A Season in Hell* (1873), *Les Illuminations* (1886).

Mary Roberts Rinehart (1876–1958), American mystery novelist: *The Circular Staircase* (1908).

Kenneth Roberts (1885–1957), American historical novelist: *Arundel* (1930), *Northwest Passage* (1937).

Edwin Arlington Robinson (1869–1935), American poet: *Collected Poems* (1921), *The Man Who Died Twice* (1924), and *Tristam* (1927) won Pulitzer Prizes.

Theodore Roethke (1908–63), American poet: *The Waking* (1953) won a Pulitzer Prize.

Romain Rolland (1866–1944), French novelist and biographer: biographies of Beethoven (1903) and Tolstoy (1911); 10-volume novel *Jean-Christophe* (1904–12) won a Nobel Prize in 1915.

Ole Edvart Rolvaag (1876–1931), Norwegian-American novelist: *Giants in the Earth* (1927).

Edmond Rostand (1868–1918), French dramatist and poet: *Cyrano de Bergerac* (1897).

Philip Roth (1933–), American novelist and short-story writer: *Goodbye Columbus* (1959), *Portnoy's Complaint* (1969), *The Ghost Writer* (1979).

Jean Jacques Rousseau (1712–78), French philosopher, novelist, and essayist: *The Social Contract* (1762), *Confessions* (1782).

John Ruskin (1819–1900), English critic and essayist: *The Seven Lamps of Architecture* (1849).

George Russell ("A.E."; 1867–1935), Irish poet: *Homeward: Songs by the Way* (1894).

Saki (real name **Hector Hugh Munro**; 1870–1916), English short-story writer. His stories are minor classics of satiric humor.

J. D. (Jerome David) Salinger (1919–), American novelist and short-story writer: *The Catcher in the Rye* (1951), *Franny and Zooey* (1961).

George Sand (real name **Amandine A. L. Dupin, Baronne Dudevant**; 1804–76), French novelist and playwright. She wrote about 80 novels that enjoyed wide popularity in their time.

Carl Sandburg (1878–1967), American poet and biographer. He wrote numerous poems celebrating America and an epic 6-volume biography of Abraham Lincoln (1926–39). *Cornhuskers* (1918), *Abraham Lincoln: The War Years* (1939), and *Complete Poems* (1950) won Pulitzer Prizes.

George Santayana (1863–1952), American poet and essayist. His *The Life of Reason* (1905–06) studied the development of human reason.

William Saroyan (1908–81), American novelist, dramatist, and short-story writer: *My Name Is Aram*

(1940), short stories; *The Human Comedy* (1943), a novel; *The Time of Your Life* (1939), a play, won a Pulitzer Prize.

Jean Paul Sartre (1905–80), French philosopher, novelist, and playwright: *Being and Nothingness* (1943), a treatise on existentialism; *No Exit* (1944) and *Dirty Hands* (1948), plays; declined a Nobel Prize in 1964.

Siegfried Sassoon (1886–1967), English poet. Much of his work derives from bitterness about World War I: *Counterattack* (1918).

Friedrich von Schiller (1759–1805), German dramatist, historian, and poet: *Wallenstein* (1798–99), a dramatic trilogy. His lyric "Ode to Joy" (1785) was used by Beethoven in his Ninth Symphony.

Delmore Schwartz (1913–66), American poet, critic, and editor: *Shenandoah* (1941).

Sir Walter Scott (1771–1832), British novelist and poet: *The Lady of the Lake* (1810), a poem; *Ivanhoe* (1820), a novel.

Lucius Annaeus Seneca (3 B.C.?–A.D. 65), Roman dramatist: *Phaedra* and *Thyestes*.

Robert Service (1874–1958), Canadian poet best known for popular Yukon ballads: *Songs of a Sourdough* (1907).

Dr. Suess (Theodor Seuss Geisel; born 1904), American author and illustrator of books for young readers: *The 500 Hats of Bartholomew Cubbins* (1938), *How the Grinch Stole Christmas* (1957), *The Cat in the Hat* (1957), *The Butter Battle Book* (1984).

William Shakespeare (1564–1616), English dramatist and poet. In addition to his purely poetic works such as *Venus and Adonis* (1593) and the *Sonnets* (1609), he wrote comic, tragic, and historical dramas, including *The Comedy of Errors* (1590–94), *Henry VI, Parts I, II, III* (1590–92), *Richard III* (1593), *The Taming of the Shrew* (1593), *Titus Andronicus* (1594), *The Two Gentlemen of Verona* (1594), *King John* (1594), *A Midsummer Nights Dream* (1595), *Richard II* (1595), *Love's Labor's Lost* (1596), *Romeo & Juliet* (1596), *The Merchant of Venice* (1597), *Henry IV* (two parts, 1597), *Hamlet* (1600–01), and *Macbeth* (1606?).

Karl Jay Shapiro (1913–), American writer: *V-Letter and Other Poems* (1944) won a Pulitzer Prize.

George Bernard Shaw (1856–1950), Irish-born dramatist, critic: *Man and Superman* (1903), *Major Barbara* (1905), *Pygmalion* (1912); won Nobel Prize in 1925.

Irwin Shaw (1913–84), American novelist: *The Young Lions* (1948), *Rich Man, Poor Man* (1970); *Beggarman, Thief* (1977); *Top of the Hill* (1979); *Acceptable Losses* (1982).

Wilfrid Sheed (1930–), Anglo-American critic and novelist: editor of *G. K. Chesterton's Essays and Poems* (1957); *Max Jamison* (1970), a novel; *Transatlantic Blues* (1978); *Clare Booth Luce* (1982).

Mary Wollstonecraft Shelley (1797–1851), English author: *Frankenstein* (1818).

Percy Bysshe Shelley (1792–1822), English romantic poet: *Prometheus Unbound* (1820).

Richard Brinsley Sheridan (1751–1816), English dramatist: *The Rivals* (1775), *The School for Scandal* (1777).

Robert E. Sherwood (1896–1955), American author: plays, *Waterloo Bridge* (1930), *Idiot's Delight* (1936), *Abe Lincoln in Illinois* (1938), and *There Shall Be No Night* (1940) all won Pulitzer Prizes. Biography *Roosevelt and Hopkins* (1947) also won a Pulitzer Prize.

William L. Shirer (1904–), American journalist: *The Rise and Fall of the Third Reich* (1960).

Mikhail Sholokhov (1905–84), Russian novelist: *The Silent Don* (1941); won Nobel Prize in 1965.

Neil Simon (1927–), American playwright: *Come Blow Your Horn* (1961); *Barefoot in the Park* (1963); *The Odd Couple* (1965); *Plaza Suite* (1968); *The Prisoner of Second Avenue* (1971); *California Suite* (1976); *They're Playing Our Song* (1979).

Upton Sinclair (1878–1968), American novelist: *The Jungle* (1906), *King Coal* (1917); *Dragon's Teeth* (1943) won a Pulitzer Prize.

Isaac Bashevis Singer (1904–), Polish-American author: won National Book Awards for *A Day of Pleasure: Stories of a Boy Growing Up in Warsaw* (1969) and *A Crown of Feathers* (1973); *Shosha* (1978); won 1978 Nobel Prize for Literature.

Dame Edith Sitwell (1887–1964), English poet and critic: *Rustic Elegies* (1927).

Aleksandr I. Solzhenitsyn (1918–), Russian novelist: *The Cancer Ward* (1968), *August 1914* (1972), *The Gulag Archipelago, 1918–1956* (1973). He won a Nobel Prize for literature in 1970.

Susan Sontag (1933–), American critic and novelist: *Against Interpretation* (1966), essays; *Death Kit* (1967), a novel.

Sophocles (496–406 B.C.), Greek dramatist: *Oedipus Rex* and *Electra*.

Muriel Spark (1918–), English novelist and short-story writer: *The Comforters* (1957), *The Prime of Miss Jean Brodie* (1961), *Territorial Rights* (1979).

Stephen Spender (1909–), English poet, critic, and editor. Much of his poetry is social protest.

Edmund Spenser (1552–99), English poet: *The Faerie Queene.*

Jean Stafford (1915–79), American novelist and short-story writer: *Boston Adventure* (1944). Her *Collected Stories* won a Pulitzer Prize in 1970.

Sir Richard Steele (1672–1729), English essayist and dramatist. With Joseph Addison he founded and contributed essays to the *Tatler* and the *Spectator.*

Wallace Stegner (1909–), American author: *Angle of Repose* (1971) won a Pulitzer Prize for fiction.

Gertrude Stein (1874–1946), American expatriate poet and critic: *Three Lives* (1908) and *The Autobiography of Alice B. Toklas* (1933).

John Steinbeck (1902–1968), American novelist: *The Grapes of Wrath* (1939) won a Pulitzer Prize; *East of Eden* (1952). He was awarded a Nobel Prize in 1962.

Stendhal (real name **Marie Henri Beyle;** 1783–1842), French novelist: *The Red and the Black* (1831), *The Charterhouse of Parma* (1839).

Laurence Sterne (1713–68), English novelist: *Tristram Shandy* (1760–67).

Wallace Stevens (1879–1955), American poet: *Harmonium* (1923); *Notes Toward a Supreme Fiction* (1942); *Collected Poems* (1954) won a Pulitzer Prize.

Robert Louis Stevenson (1850–94), Scottish novelist and poet: *Treasure Island* (1883), *A Child's Garden of Verses* (1885).

Irving Stone (1903–), American author: *Lust for Life* (1934), *The Agony and the Ecstasy* (1961), *The Origin* (1980).

Rex Todhunter Stout (1886–1975), American detective-story writer; wrote many books around fictional fat detective Nero Wolfe.

Harriet Beecher Stowe (1811–96), American novelist: *Uncle Tom's Cabin* (1852).

August Strindberg (1849–1912), Swedish dramatist and novelist: best known for such naturalistic dramas as *The Father* (1887) and *Miss Julie* (1888).

Jessee Hilton Stuart (1907–84), American author: *Taps for Private Tussie* (1965).

William Styron (1925–), American novelist: *Lie Down in Darkness* (1951); *The Confessions of Nat Turner* (1967), which won a Pulitzer Prize; *Sophie's Choice* (1979).

Jacqueline Susann (1921–74), American novelist: *Valley of the Dolls* (1966), which sold a record 17 million copies; *The Love Machine* (1969), *Once Is Not Enough* (1973), *Dolores* (1976).

Jonathan Swift (1667–1745), English satirist, poet, and essayist: *Tale of a Tub* (1704), *The Battle of the Books* (1704), *Gulliver's Travels* (1726), *A Modest Proposal* (1729).

AUTHORS AND WRITERS (continued)

Algernon Charles Swinburne (1837–1909), English poet and critic: *Songs Before Sunrise* (1871).

John Millington Synge (1871–1909), Irish dramatist and poet: *Riders to the Sea* (1904), *Playboy of the Western World* (1907).

Cornelius Tacitus (55?–117?), Roman historian who recorded contemporary history of Rome.

Booth Tarkington (1869–1946), American novelist: *The Magnificent Ambersons* (1918) and *Alice Adams* (1922) won Pulitzer Prizes.

Allen Tate (1899–1979), American poet and critic: *Mr. Pope and Other Poems* (1928).

Sara Teasdale (1884–1933), American poet: *Love Songs* (1917) won first Pulitzer Prize for poetry in 1918; *Flame and Shadow* (1920), *Strange Victory* (1933).

Alfred Lord Tennyson (1809–92), English poet: *In Memoriam* (1850), *Idylls of the King* (1859–85).

William Makepeace Thackeray (1811–63), English novelist: *Vanity Fair* (1847–48).

Dylan Thomas (1914–53), Welsh poet. A major 20th century lyric poet, he also wrote a drama for voices, *Under Milk Wood* (1954).

Lowell Thomas (1892–1981), radio and TV commentator, author of books on travel and adventure.

Henry David Thoreau (1817–62), American essayist and poet, champion of the individual against social organization: *Walden; or, Life in the Woods* (1854).

James Thurber (1894–1961), American humorist: *The Owl in the Attic and Other Perplexities* (1931), *My Life and Hard Times* (1934).

Alexis de Tocqueville (1805–59), French essayist and politician who studied and wrote extensively about the early days of the United States: *De la démocratie en Amérique* (4 vols., 1835–40).

J. R. R. Tolkien (1892–1973), British novelist: *The Hobbit* (1937), *Lord of the Rings* trilogy (1954–56), *The Silmarillion* (1977).

Leo Tolstoy (1828–1910), Russian novelist: *War and Peace* (1862–69), *Anna Karenina* (1875–77).

Arnold Toynbee (1889–1975), English historian: *A Study of History* (10 vols., 1934–54).

Lionel Trilling (1905–1975), American critic: *The Liberal Imagination* (1950).

Anthony Trollope (1815–82), English novelist: *The Warden* (1855), *Barchester Towers* (1857).

Thomas Tryon (1926–), American novelist: *The Other* (1971), *Lady* (1974).

Barbara Tuchman (1912–), American author: *The Guns of August* (1962) and *Stilwell and the American Experience in China, 1911–1945* (1971) both won Pulitzer Prizes; *A Distant Mirror: The Calamitous Fourteenth Century* (1978); *The March of Folly: From Troy to Vietnam* (1984).

Ivan Turgenev (1818–83), Russian novelist and dramatist: *Fathers and Sons* (1861), a novel.

Mark Twain (real name **Samuel Clemens;** 1835–1910), American author: *Tom Sawyer* (1876), *Huckleberry Finn* (1884).

Louis Untermeyer (1885–1977), American poet and anthologist. He edited *Modern American Poetry* (1919, frequently revised).

John Updike (1932–), American novelist: *Rabbit, Run* (1960), *The Centaur* (1963), *Couples* (1968), *Bech: A Book* (1970), *Rabbit Redux* (1971), *Rabbit Is Rich* (1981), *Bech is Bach* (1982).

Leon Uris (1924–), American novelist: *Exodus* (1958), *Trinity* (1976), *The Haj* (1984).

Paul Valéry (1871–1945), French poet and critic. *Charmes* (1922) is his best verse collection.

S. S. Van Dine (real name **Willard Huntington Wright;** 1888–1939), American detective-story author. His books featured the amateur detective Philo Vance.

Mark Van Doren (1894–1972), American poet and critic: *Collected Poems* (1939) won Pulitzer Prize.

Thorstein Veblen (1857–1929), American essayist and social scientist: *The Theory of the Leisure Class* (1899).

Jules Verne (1828–1905), French novelist and a pioneer in science fiction: *Twenty Thousand Leagues Under the Sea* (1870).

Gore Vidal (1925–), American author: *Visit to a Small Planet* (1956), a play for TV; *Washington, D.C.* (1967), *Burr* (1973), *1876* (1976), *Lincoln* (1984).

Virgil (70–19 B.C.), Roman poet. His masterpiece is the unfinished epic the *Aeneid.*

François Marie Arouet de Voltaire (1694–1778), French novelist, dramatist, critic, and poet. He was at his best in such short novels as *Candide* (1759).

Kurt Vonnegut Jr. (1922–), American novelist: *Mother Night* (1961), *Slaughterhouse-Five* (1969), *Jailbird* (1979), *Palm Sunday* (1981), *Deadeye Dick* (1982).

Alice Walker (1944–), American novelist: *The Color Purple* (1982) won Pulitzer Prize and National Book Award.

Horace Walpole (1717–97), English novelist: *The Castle of Otranto* (1764).

Robert Penn Warren (1905–), American novelist, poet, editor, and biographer. His novel *All the King's Men* (1946) won a Pulitzer Prize, as did *Promises: Poems 1954–1956* (1957), and *Now and Then* (1978).

Evelyn Waugh (1903–66), English novelist: *Decline and Fall* (1928), *Brideshead Revisited* (1945), *The Loved One* (1948).

Noah Webster (1758–1843), American lexicographer: *An American Dictionary of the English Language* (1800–28) set standard for American lexicography.

H. G. (Herbert George) Wells (1866–1946), English novelist and social historian: *The Time Machine* (1895), *The War of the Worlds* (1898).

Eudora Welty (1909–), American novelist and short-story writer: *Delta Wedding* (1946). *The Optimist's Daughter* (1972) won a Pulitzer Prize.

Franz Werfel (1890–1945), Austrian-born author: *The Song of Bernadette* (1941).

Jessamyn West (1902–84), American author: *The Friendly Persuasion* (1945).

Nathanael West (1902–40), American novelist: *The Day of the Locust* (1939).

Rebecca West (1892–1983), English novelist and journalist: *The Return of the Soldier* (1918).

Edith Wharton (1862–1937), American novelist and short-story writer: *Ethan Frome* (1911); *The Age of Innocence* (1920) won a Pulitzer Prize.

E. B. White (1899–1985), American author: *One Man's Meat* (1942), *The Points of My Compass* (1962); *Stuart Little* (1945) and *Charlotte's Web* (1952), children's classics.

Walt Whitman (1819–92), American poet: *Leaves of Grass* (1855).

John Greenleaf Whittier (1807–92), American poet: *Snowbound* (1866).

Oscar Wilde (1854–1900), Anglo-Irish dramatist, novelist, and poet: *The Picture of Dorian Gray* (1891), a novel; *The Importance of Being Earnest* (1899), a play; *Ballad of Reading Gaol* (1898), a poem.

Thornton Wilder (1897–1975), American novelist and dramatist. He won Pulitzer Prizes for the novel *The Bridge of San Luis Rey* (1927) and the plays *Our Town* (1938) and *Skin of Our Teeth* (1942).

Tennessee Williams (1911–83), American playwright: *The Glass Menagerie* (1944), *The Rose Tattoo* (1950); *A Streetcar Named Desire* (1947) and *Cat on a Hot Tin Roof* (1955) both won Pulitzer Prizes.

William Carlos Williams (1883–1963), American poet and novelist. *Paterson* (1946) is a long poem evoking the atmosphere of his native New Jersey; *Pictures from Breughel* (1962) won a Pulitzer Prize.

Edmund Wilson (1895–1972), American critic: *Axel's Castle* (1931), *The Scrolls from the Dead Sea* (1955;

revised edition 1969).

Thomas Wolfe (1900–38), American novelist: *Look Homeward, Angel* (1929), *Of Time and the River* (1935), *You Can't Go Home Again* (1940).

Virginia Woolf (1882–1941), English novelist: *Mrs. Dalloway* (1925), *To the Lighthouse* (1927).

William Wordsworth (1770–1850), English poet: "Tintern Abbey" (1800); "Ode: Intimations of Immortality" (1807).

Herman Wouk (1915–), American novelist: *The Caine Mutiny* (1951) won a Pulitzer Prize; *Marjorie Morningstar* (1955); *The Winds of War* (1971); *War and Remembrance* (1978).

Richard Wright (1908–60), American novelist: *Native Son* (1940); *Black Boy* (1945), autobiography.

Philip Gordon Wylie (1902–71), American author: *Generation of Vipers* (1942).

William Butler Yeats (1865–1939), Irish poet: *The Wild Swans at Coole* (1919); *The Tower* (1928); won a Nobel Prize in 1923.

Yevgeny Yevtushenko (1933–), Russian poet. His verse deals mainly with social protest.

Émile Zola (1840–1902), French novelist and critic, one of the most important novelists of the naturalist school. His works include the 20-volume series *Les Rougon-Macquart* (1871–93).

CHARACTERS IN FAMOUS BOOKS

How many of the characters listed below can you identify with the name of the book in which they appear? You can check whether you are right by noting the number of the character and then looking to see if that number follows the title of the book listed at the bottom of this page.

1. Roberta Alden	23. Chingachgook	45. Catherine Earnshaw	67. John Little
2. Fern Arable	24. Nick Chopper	46. Sondra Finchley	68. Jo March
3. Aunt Chloe	25. Christian	47. Robert Fitzooth	69. Mr. Micawber
4. Aunt Em	26. Angel Clare	48. Henry Fleming	70. Carol Milford
5. Aunt Polly	27. Jim Conklin	49. Phileas Fogg	71. William Morel
6. Sophia Baines	28. Nana Coupeau	50. Dr. Gibbs	72. Scarlett O'Hara
7. David Balfour	29. Ichabod Crane	51. Griffin	73. O-Lan
8. Horace Benbow	30. Bob Cratchit	52. Clyde Griffiths	74. Sugar-Boy O'Sheean
9. Jane Bennet	31. Art Croft	53. Griselda	75. Doctor Pangloss
10. Bernabò of Genoa	32. Sam Croft	54. Heathcliff	76. Sancho Panza
11. Pierre Bezúkhov	33. Edward Cummings	55. Uriah Heep	77. Passepartout
12. Leopold Bloom	34. Cunegonde	56. Captain Hook	78. Pilar
13. Raff Brinker	35. Edmond Dantès	57. Injun Joe	79. Popeye
14. John Brooke	36. Wendy Darling	58. Ishmael	80. Hester Prynne
15. Buck	37. Stephen Dedalus	59. Javert	81. Queequeg
16. Natty Bumppo	38. Arthur Dimmesdale	60. Miss Jessel	82. Peter Quint
17. Rhett Butler	39. Nicole Diver	61. Tom Joad	83. Mr. Rochester
18. Mr. By-Ends	40. Temple Drake	62. Robert Jordan	84. Mildred Rogers
19. Philip Carey	41. Dulcinea del Toboso	63. Will Kennicott	85. Rose of Sharon
20. Eppie Cass	42. C. Auguste Dupin	64. Kincaid	86. Nataly Rostóva
21. Holden Caulfield	43. Léon Dupuis	65. Elizabeth Lavenza	87. Emma Roualt
22. Harvey Cheyne	44. Tess Durbeyfield	66. Simon Legree	88. Evangeline St. Clare

WELL-KNOWN BOOKS AND THEIR AUTHORS

The Adventures of Tom Sawyer, Mark Twain (5, 57)
All the King's Men, Robert Penn Warren (74)
An American Tragedy, Theodore Dreiser (1, 46, 52)
Around the World in Eighty Days, Jules Verne (49, 77)
The Call of the Wild, Jack London (15)
Candide, François de Voltaire (34, 75)
Captains Courageous, Rudyard Kipling (22)
The Catcher in the Rye, J.D. Salinger (21)
Charlotte's Web, E.B. White (2)
A Christmas Carol, Charles Dickens (30)
The Count of Monte Cristo, Alexandre Dumas (35)
David Copperfield, Charles Dickens (55, 69)
Decameron, Giovanni Boccaccio (10, 53)
Don Quixote, Miguel de Cervantes Saavedra (41, 76)
For Whom the Bell Tolls, Ernest Hemingway (62, 78)
Frankenstein, Mary Wollstonecraft Shelley (65)
Gone With the Wind, Margaret Mitchell (17, 72)
The Good Earth, Pearl S. Buck (73)
The Grapes of Wrath, John Steinbeck (61, 85)
Hans Brinker, Mary Mapes Dodge (13)
The Invisible Man, H.G. Wells (51)
Jane Eyre, Charlotte Brontë (83)
Kidnapped, Robert Louis Stevenson (7)
The Last of the Mohicans, James Fenimore Cooper (16, 23)
Les Misérables, Victor Hugo (59)
Little Women, Louisa May Alcott (14, 68)
Madame Bovary, Gustave Flaubert (43, 87)

Main Street, Sinclair Lewis (63, 70)
The Merry Adventures of Robin Hood, Howard Pyle (47, 67)
The Murders in the Rue Morgue, Edgar Allan Poe (42)
Moby-Dick, Herman Melville (58, 81)
The Naked and the Dead, Norman Mailer (32, 33)
Nana, Emile Zola (28)
Of Human Bondage, W. Somerset Maugham (19, 84)
The Old Wives' Tale, Arnold Bennett (6)
Our Town, Thornton Wilder (50)
The Ox-Bow Incident, Walter Van Tilburg Clark (31, 64)
Peter and Wendy, Sir James Barrie (36, 56)
The Pilgrim's Progress, John Bunyan (18, 25)
Pride and Prejudice, Jane Austen (9)
The Red Badge of Courage, Stephen Crane (27, 48)
Sanctuary, William Faulkner (8, 40, 79)
The Scarlet Letter, Nathaniel Hawthorne (38, 80)
Silas Marner, George Eliot (20)
Sketchbook, Washington Irving (29)
Sons and Lovers, D.H. Lawrence (71)
Tender Is the Night, F. Scott Fitzgerald (39)
Tess of the D'Urbervilles, Thomas Hardy (26, 44)
The Turn of the Screw, Henry James (60, 82)
Ulysses, James Joyce (12, 37)
Uncle Tom's Cabin, Harriet Beecher Stowe (3, 66, 88)
War and Peace, Leo Tolstoy (11, 86)
The Wizard of Oz, Lyman Frank Baum (4, 24)
Wuthering Heights, Emily Brontë (45, 54)

BESTSELLERS OF THE PAST

The following were the bestselling books in the U.S. from 1921 to 1984. Sources for these lists are *70 Years of Best Sellers,* by Alice Payne Hackett (Bowker), and *Publishers Weekly.*

FICTION BESTSELLERS		NONFICTION BESTSELLERS	
1921	Main Street, Sinclair Lewis	1921	The Outline of History, H.G. Wells
1922	If Winter Comes, A.S.M. Hutchinson	1922	The Outline of History, H.G. Wells
1923	Black Oxen, Gertrude Atherton	1923	Etiquette, Emily Post
1924	So Big, Edna Ferber	1924	Diet and Health, Lulu Hunt Peters
1925	Soundings, A. Hamilton Gibbs	1925	Diet and Health, Lulu Hunt Peters
1926	The Private Life of Helen of Troy, John Erskine	1926	The Man Nobody Knows, B. Barton
1927	Elmer Gantry, Sinclair Lewis	1927	The Story of Philosophy, Will Durant
1928	The Bridge of San Luis Rey, Thornton Wilder	1928	Disraeli, André Maurois
1929	All Quiet on the Western Front, Erich Remarque	1929	The Art of Thinking, Ernest Dimnet
1930	Cimarron, Edna Ferber	1930	The Story of San Michele, Axel Munthe
1931	The Good Earth, Pearl S. Buck	1931	Education of a Princess, Grand Duchess Marie
1932	The Good Earth, Pearl S. Buck	1932	The Epic of America, James Truslow Adams
1933	Anthony Adverse, Hervey Allen	1933	Life Begins at Forty, Walter B. Pitkin
1934	Anthony Adverse, Hervey Allen	1934	While Rome Burns, Alexander Woollcott
1935	Green Light, Lloyd C. Douglas	1935	North to the Orient, Anne Morrow Lindbergh
1936	Gone with the Wind, Margaret Mitchell	1936	Man the Unknown, Alexis Carrel
1937	Gone with the Wind, Margaret Mitchell	1937	How to Win Friends . . ., Dale Carnegie
1938	The Yearling, Marjorie K. Rawlings	1938	The Importance of Living, Lin Yutang
1939	The Grapes of Wrath, John Steinbeck	1939	Days of Our Years, Pierre van Paassen
1940	How Green Was My Valley, Richard Llewellyn	1940	I Married Adventure, Osa Johnson
1941	The Keys of the Kingdom, A.J. Cronin	1941	Berlin Diary, William L. Shirer
1942	The Song of Bernadette, Franz Werfel	1942	See Here, Private Hargrove, Marion Hargrove
1943	The Robe, Lloyd C. Douglas	1943	Under Cover, John Roy Carlson
1944	Strange Fruit, Lillian Smith	1944	I Never Left Home, Bob Hope
1945	Forever Amber, Kathleen Winsor	1945	Brave Men, Ernie Pyle
1946	The King's General, Daphne du Maurier	1946	The Egg and I, Betty MacDonald
1947	The Miracle of the Bells, Russell Janney	1947	Peace of Mind, Joshua Loth Liebman
1948	The Big Fisherman, Lloyd C. Douglas	1948	Crusade in Europe, Dwight D. Eisenhower
1949	The Egyptian, Mika Waltari	1949	White Collar Zoo, Clare Barnes Jr.
1950	The Cardinal, Henry Morton Robinson	1950	Betty Crocker's Picture Cook Book
1951	From Here to Eternity, James Jones	1951	Look Younger, Live Longer, Gaylord Hauser
1952	The Silver Chalice, Thomas B. Costain	1952	The Holy Bible: Revised Standard Version
1953	The Robe, Lloyd C. Douglas	1953	The Holy Bible: Revised Standard Version
1954	Not as a Stranger, Morton Thompson	1954	The Holy Bible: Revised Standard Version
1955	Marjorie Morningstar, Herman Wouk	1955	Gift from the Sea, Anne Morrow Lindbergh
1956	Don't Go Near the Water, William Brinkley	1956	Arthritis and Common Sense, D. D. Alexander
1957	By Love Possessed, James Gould Cozzens	1957	Kids Say the Darndest Things, Art Linkletter
1958	Doctor Zhivago, Boris Pasternak	1958	Kids Say the Darndest Things, Art Linkletter
1959	Exodus, Leon Uris	1959	Twixt 12 and 20, Pat Boone
1960	Advise and Consent, Allen Drury	1960	Folk Medicine, D.C. Jarvis
1961	The Agony and the Ecstasy, Irving Stone	1961	The New English Bible: The New Testament
1962	Ship of Fools, Katherine Anne Porter	1962	Calories Don't Count, Dr. Herman Taller
1963	The Shoes of the Fisherman, Morris L. West	1963	Happiness Is a Warm Puppy, Charles M. Schultz
1964	The Spy Who Came in from the Cold, John Le Carré	1964	Four Days, American Heritage and UPI
1965	The Source, James A. Michener	1965	How to Be a Jewish Mother, Dan Greenburg
1966	Valley of the Dolls, Jacqueline Susann	1966	How to Avoid Probate, Norman F. Dacey
1967	The Arrangement, Elia Kazan	1967	Death of a President, William Manchester
1968	Airport, Arthur Hailey	1968	Better Homes and Gardens New Cook Book
1969	Portnoy's Complaint, Philip Roth	1969	American Heritage Dictionary of the English Language, ed. William Morris
1970	Love Story, Erich Segal	1970	Everything You Always Wanted to Know About Sex, David Reuben, M.D.
1971	Wheels, Arthur Hailey	1971	The Sensuous Man, "M"
1972	Jonathan Livingston Seagull, Richard Bach	1972	The Living Bible, Kenneth Taylor
1973	Jonathan Livingston Seagull, Richard Bach	1973	The Living Bible, Kenneth Taylor
1974	Centennial, James A. Michener	1974	The Total Woman, Marabel Morgan
1975	Ragtime, E.L. Doctorow	1975	Angels: God's Secret Agents, Billy Graham
1976	Trinity, Leon Uris	1976	The Final Days, Bob Woodward and Carl Bernstein
1977	The Silmarillion, J.R.R. Tolkien	1977	Roots, Alex Haley
1978	Chesapeake, James A. Michener	1978	If Life Is a Bowl of Cherries—What Am I Doing in the Pits?, Erma Bombeck
1979	The Matarese Circle, Robert Ludlum	1979	Aunt Erma's Cope Book, Erma Bombeck
1980	The Covenant, James Michener	1980	Crisis Investing, Douglas R. Casey
1981	Noble House, James Clavell	1981	The Beverly Hills Diet, Judy Mazel
1982	E.T. The Extra-Terrestrial Storybook, William Kotzwinkle	1982	Jane Fonda's Workout Book, Jane Fonda
1983	Return of the Jedi Storybook, Joan D. Vinge	1983	In Search of Excellence, Thomas J. Peters and Robert H. Waterman Jr.
1984	The Talisman, by Stephen King and Peter Straub	1984	Iacocca: An Autobiography by Lee Iacocca with William Novak

Calendars, Time and Holidays

FEDERAL, STATE, AND RELIGIOUS HOLIDAYS AND SPECIAL DAYS: 1986

JANUARY
1 New Year's Day (U.S. federal holiday) ... Wednesday
6 Epiphany (Armenian Christmas) Monday
8 Battle of New Orleans Day (Louisiana) .. Wednesday
19 Robert E. Lee's Birthday (born 1807)....... Sunday
20 Martin Luther King Jr. Day (U.S. federal holiday) Monday
26 Gen. Douglas MacArthur Day (Arkansas) Sunday
30 F.D. Roosevelt's Birthday (Ky.) (b. 1882) .. Thursday

FEBRUARY
1 National Freedom Day (120th anniversary of signing of resolution to end slavery) Saturday
2 Groundhog Day Sunday
8 Chinese New Year (Year of the Tiger) Saturday
11 Shrove Tuesday, Mardis Gras (Alabama, Florida, Louisiana) Tuesday
12 Ash Wednesday (Christian) Wednesday
12 Lincoln's 177th Birthday (born 1809) .. Wednesday
12 Georgia Day (Georgia) Wednesday
14 Valentine's Day Friday
14 Admission Day (Arizona).................. Friday
15 Susan B. Anthony's Birthday (born 1820).. Saturday
17 Washington's Birthday (U.S. fed. holiday) .. Monday
22 Washington's 254th Birthday (born 1732) Saturday

MARCH
1 World Day of Prayer (Christian) Saturday
2 Texas Independence Day (Texas) Sunday
4 Town Meeting Day (Vermont) Tuesday
15 Andrew Jackson's Birthday (TN) (b. 1767) . Saturday
17 St. Patrick's Day Monday
17 Evacuation Day (Massachusetts) Monday
20 Spring begins at 5:03 P.M. EST Thursday
23 Palm Sunday (Christian) Sunday
25 Maryland Day (Maryland) Tuesday
27 Maundy Thursday (Christian) Thursday
28 Good Friday (Christian) Friday
28 Kuhio Day (Hawaii) Friday
30 Easter (Christian) Sunday
31 Easter Monday (North Carolina) Monday
31 Seward's Day (Alaska) Monday

APRIL
1 April Fool's Day Monday
13 Thomas Jefferson's Birthday (born 1743) ... Sunday
14 Pan American Day Monday
21 Patriots' Day (Massachusetts, Maine) Monday
21 San Jacinto Day (Texas) Monday
22 Arbor Day (Nebraska) Tuesday
24 First Day of Passover, Pesach (Jewish) ... Thursday
25 Arbor Day (Utah) Friday
27 Daylight Saving Time begins (clocks set ahead one hour at 2 A.M.) Sunday
28 Fast Day (New Hampshire)................. Monday
28 Confederate Memorial Day (Ala., Miss.) Monday

MAY
1 May Day, Loyalty Day, Law Day Thursday
4 Orthodox Easter (Eastern Orthodox) Sunday
8 Harry Truman's Birthday (Mo.) (b. 1884) .. Thursday
8 Ascension Day, Holy Thursday (Christ.) ... Thursday
10 Confederate Memorial Day (South Carolina). Saturday
11 Minnesota Day (Minnesota) Sunday
11 Mother's Day Sunday
11 First Day of Ramadan (Islamic) Sunday
17 Armed Forces Day Saturday
18 Whitsunday, Pentecost (Christian) Sunday

19 Queen's Birthday (Canada) Monday
26 Memorial Day (U.S. federal holiday)........ Monday

JUNE
1 Corpus Christi (Christian) Sunday
2 Jefferson Davis' Birthday (So. States)...... Monday
3 Jefferson Davis' Birthday (actual—born 1808) Tuesday
11 Festival of the End of Ramadan (Islamic) Wednesday
13 Shavuot, Feast of Weeks (Jewish) Friday
14 Queen's Official Birthday (Britain) Saturday
14 Flag Day, 209th anniversary of U.S. Flag ... Saturday
15 Father's Day............................. Sunday
21 Summer begins at 12:30 P.M. EDT Saturday

JULY
1 Canada Day (119th anniv. of Canada)...... Tuesday
4 Independence Day (210th anniversary of U.S. Declaration of Independence) Friday
24 Pioneer Day (Utah) Thursday

AUGUST
11 Victory Day (Rhode Island) (41st anniversary of end of World War II) Monday
15 Admission Day (Hawaii) Friday
16 Bennington Battle Day (Vermont) Saturday
27 L. B. Johnson's Birthday (TX) (born 1908) Wednesday
30 Huey Long's Birthday (LA) (born 1893) ... Saturday

SEPTEMBER
1 Labor Day (U.S. federal holiday) Monday
5 Islamic New Year (Year 1407 of Islamic Era) . Friday
7 National Grandparents Day Sunday
9 Admission Day (California) Tuesday
12 Defenders' Day (Maryland) Friday
16 Mexico's Independence Day Tuesday
17 Citizenship Day Wednesday
23 Autumn begins at 3:59 A.M. EDT Tuesday
26 American Indian Day Friday
28 Gold Star Mother's Day................... Sunday

OCTOBER
4 Rosh Hashana, Jewish New Year, first day of year 5747 of Jewish Era Saturday
9 Leif Erikson Day (Minnesota) Thursday
13 Columbus Day (U.S. federal holiday) Monday
13 Pioneers' Day (South Dakota) Monday
13 Canadian Thanksgiving Day (Canada) Monday
13 Yom Kippur, Day of Atonement (Jewish) Monday
26 Standard Time begins (clocks set back 1 hour at 2 A.M.) Sunday
31 Halloween............................... Friday
31 Nevada Day (Nevada) Friday

NOVEMBER
1 All Saints' Day (Christian) Saturday
4 Will Rogers' Birthday (Okla.) (b. 1879)..... Tuesday
4 Election Day Tuesday
7 World Community Day..................... Friday
11 Veterans Day (U.S. federal holiday) Tuesday
27 Thanksgiving Day (U.S. federal holiday) ... Thursday
28 Day after Thanksgiving (Okla., Wash.) Friday
30 First Sunday in Advent (Christian) Sunday

DECEMBER
6 St. Nicholas Day (Orthodox) Saturday
10 Wyoming Day (Wyoming) Wednesday
15 Bill of Rights Day, 195th anniversary Monday
21 Winter begins at 11:02 P.M. EST Sunday
25 Christmas Day (Christian) Thursday
27 First day of Hanukkah (Jewish)........... Saturday
31 New Year's Eve (Watch Night) Wednesday

SPECIAL MONTHS, WEEKS, AND DAYS: 1986

The President of the United States regularly issues proclamations throughout the year designating certain months, weeks, and days for special observance.

JANUARY
- **1** New Year's Day, U.S. federal holiday.
- **13** Stephen Foster Memorial Day, since 1952.
- **20** Martin Luther King Jr. Day, U.S. federal holiday.

FEBRUARY
- **1–28** American Heart Month, since 1964.
- **1** National Freedom Day, 120th anniversary of resolution to end slavery, annually since 1949.
- **17** Washington's Birthday, U.S. federal holiday, third Monday in February; actual birthday on Feb. 22, 1732.

MARCH
- **1–31** Red Cross Month, since 1943.
- **2–8** Save Your Vision Week, first week, since 1963.
- **16–22** National Poison Prevention Week, third week of March since 1962.

APRIL
- **1–30** Cancer Control Month, since 1938.
- **13** Thomas Jefferson's Birthday (born 1743), observed annually since 1938.
- **13–19** Pan American Week, week that includes Pan American Day, since 1946.
- **14** Pan American Day, Pan American Union's 96th anniversary; observed annually since 1940.

MAY
- **1–31** Older Americans Month, since 1963, previously called Senior Citizens Month until 1974.
- **1–31** Steelmark Month, since 1967.
- **1** Law Day, issued each year since 1958.
- **1** Loyalty Day, proclaimed annually since 1959.
- **1** National Day of Prayer, issued since 1952.
- **11** Mother's Day, issued annually for second Sunday in May since congressional resolution in 1914.
- **11–17** Police Week, proclaimed since 1962 for week that includes Peace Officers Memorial Day.
- **11–17** National Transportation Week, since 1960.
- **15** Peace Officers Memorial Day, since 1962.
- **16** National Defense Transportation Day, issued each year for third Friday in May, since 1957.
- **17** Armed Forces Day, always third Saturday in May since 1950.
- **18–24** World Trade Week, week that includes National Maritime Day, since 1948.
- **22** National Maritime Day, since 1933.
- **26** Prayer for Peace, Memorial Day, U.S. federal holiday, last Monday in May since 1971.

JUNE
- **1–7** National Safe Boating Week, issued annually; week commencing with first Sunday in June.
- **8–14** National Flag Week, issued annually since 1966 for week that includes Flag Day.
- **9–15** National Little League Baseball Week, week beginning the second Monday in June, since 1959.
- **14** Flag Day, observes 209th anniversary of adoption of first national flag by Congress; proclaimed since 1941.
- **15** Father's Day, third Sunday in June, since 1971.

JULY
- **4** Independence Day, U.S. federal holiday, 210th anniversary of U.S. Declaration of Independence.
- **13–19** Captive Nations Week, third week of July, issued annually since 1959.

AUGUST
- **19** National Aviation Day, since 1939.
- **26** Women's Equality Day, 66th anniversary of adoption of 19th amendment, since 1973.

SEPTEMBER
- **1** Labor Day, U.S. federal holiday, always on first Monday in September.
- **7** National Grandparents Day, first Sunday after Labor Day, since 1979.
- **14–20** National Hispanic Heritage Week, since 1968.
- **14–20** National Farm Safety Week, issued since 1944; third week in September.
- **17** Citizenship Day, 199th anniversary of signing of U.S. Constitution, issued since 1952.
- **17–23** Constitution Week, week beginning Sept. 17, annual since 1955.
- **27** National Hunting and Fishing Day, fourth Saturday in September, since 1979.
- **28** Gold Star Mother's Day, last Sunday in September, since 1936.

OCTOBER
- **5–11** Fire Prevention Week, week that includes Oct. 9, since 1925.
- **5–11** National Employ the Handicapped Week, since 1945.
- **5–11** Minority Enterprise Development Week, since 1983.
- **6** Child Health Day, first Monday in October; since 1928.
- **9** Leif Erikson Day, issued annually since 1964.
- **11** General Pulaski Memorial Day, since 1929.
- **12–18** National School Lunch Week, week beginning second Sunday in October, since 1962.
- **13** Columbus Day, U.S. federal holiday, second Monday in October; proclaimed since 1934.
- **15** White Cane Safety Day, since 1964.
- **19–25** National Forest Products Week, week beginning with third Sunday in October, since 1960.
- **24** United Nations Day, always issued for Oct. 24 since 1948, by request of UN General Assembly.
- **31** National UNICEF Day, issued to fall on Halloween since 1967.

NOVEMBER
- **9–15** American Education Week, second week in November; since 1921.
- **11** Veterans Day, U.S. federal holiday, 68th anniversary of end of World War I in 1918.
- **21–27** National Farm-City Week, week ending on Thanksgiving Day, annually since 1955.
- **27** Thanksgiving Day, U.S. federal holiday; proclaimed for fourth Thursday in November.

DECEMBER
- **2** Pan American Health Day, since 1940.
- **10** Human Rights Day, since 1949.
- **10–16** Human Rights Week, week of Dec. 10–16, annually since 1958.
- **15** Bill of Rights Day, issued annually for Dec. 15 since 1962, observing 195th anniversary date of ratification of Bill of Rights in 1791.
- **17** Pan American Aviation Day, since 1940.
- **17** Wright Brothers Day, issued for Dec. 17 since 1959; 83d anniversary of first flight in 1903.
- **25** Christmas Day, U.S. federal holiday.

DATES OF EASTER: 1986–2009

1986	March 30	1990	April 15	1994	April 3	1998	April 12	2002	March 31	2006	April 16
1987	April 19	1991	March 31	1995	April 16	1999	April 4	2003	April 20	2007	April 8
1988	April 3	1992	April 19	1996	April 7	2000	April 23	2004	April 11	2008	March 23
1989	March 26	1993	April 11	1997	March 30	2001	April 15	2005	March 27	2009	April 12

UNITED STATES TIME ZONES

The map above shows time-zone boundaries (solid line), which in most places have moved westward somewhat from those that first went into effect on Jan. 1, 1919 (broken line).

Daylight-saving time begins at 2 A.M. on the last Sunday in April (April 27, 1986) and ends on the last Sunday in October (Oct. 26, 1986). Clocks are set ahead one hour in the spring and set back one hour in the fall.

If it had been possible to ask for the time at exactly the same moment in a number of U.S. towns in 1873, the variety of answers would have been puzzling: 12:12 P.M. in New York, 11:08 A.M. in Memphis, and so on across the nation. Yet each answer would have been right, for "Sun time" prevailed throughout much of the world until the late 1800s.

In November 1883, U.S. and Canadian rail companies agreed to set up zones for each 15 degrees of longitude with uniform time in each zone.

Most of the country went along quickly with this orderly system, but Congress did not pass a Standard Time Act until 1917. In 1966 Congress passed a Uniform Time Act urging all states to adopt daylight-saving time during half of the year from spring to fall.

As an energy conservation measure Congress passed a law in 1974 establishing year-round daylight-saving time. It was modified to eight months of daylight time in 1975, and reverted to six months in 1976.

Areas of the nation that do not observe daylight-saving time include Arizona, Hawaii, most of Indiana, Puerto Rico, the Virgin Islands, and American Samoa.

The longitudes of the standard meridians for U.S. standard time zones are Atlantic 60°W., Eastern 75°W., Central 90°W., Mountain 105°W., Pacific 120°W., Yukon 135°W., Alaska-Hawaii 150°W., and Bering 165°W.

PAST AND FUTURE CALENDARS: 1776–2014

Directions: Choose year you want in key below. Number opposite year is number of calendar to use for that year.

1776 .. 9	1795 .. 5	1814 .. 5	1833 .. 3	1852 .. 12	1871 .. 1
1777 .. 4	1796 .. 13	1815 .. 7	1834 .. 3	1853 ..	1872 .. 9
1777 .. 5	1797 .. 1	1816 .. 9	1835 .. 5	1854 .. 1	1873 .. 4
1779 .. 6	1798 .. 2	1817 .. 4	1836 .. 13	1855 .. 2	1874 .. 5
1780 .. 14	1799 .. 3	1818 .. 5	1837 ..	1856 .. 10	1875 .. 6
1781 .. 2	1800 ..	1819 .. 6	1838 ..	1857 ..	1876 .. 14
1782 .. 3	1801 .. 5	1820 .. 14	1839 .. 3	1858 .. 6	1877 .. 2
1783 .. 4	1802 .. 6	1821 .. 2	1840 .. 11	1859 .. 6	1878 .. 3
1784 .. 12	1803 .. 7	1822 .. 3	1841 ..	1860 .. 8	1879 ..
1785 .. 7	1804 ..	1823 .. 4	1842 ..	1861 ..	1880 .. 12
1786 .. 1	1805 ..	1824 .. 12	1843 ..	1862 .. 4	1881 ..
1787 .. 2	1806 .. 4	1825 .. 7	1844 .. 13	1863 ..	1882 .. 1
1788 .. 10	1807 ..	1826 ..	1845 ..	1864 ..	1883 ..
1789 ..	1808 .. 13	1827 ..	1846 ..	1865 ..	1884 .. 10
1790 .. 6	1809 .. 7	1828 .. 10	1847 .. 6	1866 ..	1885 ..
1791 .. 7	1810 .. 2	1829 .. 5	1848 .. 14	1867 .. 3	1886 ..
1792 ..	1811 ..	1830 ..	1849 .. 2	1868 ..	1887 ..
1793 .. 3	1812 .. 11	1831 .. 1	1850 ..	1869 ..	1888 ..
1794 .. 4	1813 ..	1832 .. 8	1851 .. 4	1870 .. 7	1889 ..

1890 .. 4	1915 .. 6	1940 .. 9	1965 .. 6	1990 .. 2
1891 .. 5	1916 .. 14	1941 .. 4	1966 .. 7	1991 .. 3
1892 .. 13	1917 .. 2	1942 .. 5	1967 .. 1	1992 .. 11
1893 ..	1918 ..	1943 ..	1968 ..	1993 .. 6
1894 .. 2	1919 .. 4	1944 .. 14	1969 .. 4	1994 .. 7
1895 .. 3	1920 .. 12	1945 .. 2	1970 .. 5	1995 .. 1
1896 .. 11	1921 ..	1946 ..	1971 ..	1996 .. 9
1897 ..	1922 ..	1947 .. 4	1972 .. 14	1997 .. 4
1898 .. 7	1923 .. 2	1948 .. 12	1973 .. 2	1998 .. 5
1899 ..	1924 .. 10	1949 .. 7	1974 .. 3	1999 .. 6
1900 .. 2	1925 ..	1950 .. 1	1975 .. 4	2000 .. 14
1901 ..	1926 ..	1951 ..	1976 .. 12	2001 ..
1902 .. 4	1927 ..	1952 .. 10	1977 .. 7	2002 .. 3
1903 ..	1928 ..	1953 .. 5	1978 .. 1	2003 .. 4
1904 .. 13	1929 ..	1954 ..	1979 ..	2004 ..
1905 ..	1930 ..	1955 .. 7	1980 .. 10	2005 ..
1906 ..	1931 .. 5	1956 .. 8	1981 .. 5	2006 .. 1
1907 ..	1932 .. 13	1957 .. 3	1982 .. 6	2007 .. 2
1908 .. 11	1933 .. 1	1958 ..	1983 ..	2008 .. 10
1909 ..	1934 .. 2	1959 ..	1984 .. 8	2009 ..
1910 ..	1935 ..	1960 .. 13	1985 ..	2010 .. 6
1911 .. 1	1936 ..	1961 .. 1	1986 ..	2011 .. 7
1912 ..	1937 ..	1962 .. 2	1987 .. 5	2012 ..
1913 ..	1938 .. 7	1963 .. 3	1988 .. 13	2013 .. 3
1914 .. 5	1939 ..	1964 .. 11	1989 .. 1	2014 .. 4

1 1989

JANUARY · FEBRUARY · MARCH · APRIL · MAY · JUNE · JULY · AUGUST · SEPTEMBER · OCTOBER · NOVEMBER · DECEMBER

2 1990

JANUARY · FEBRUARY · MARCH · APRIL · MAY · JUNE · JULY · AUGUST · SEPTEMBER · OCTOBER · NOVEMBER · DECEMBER

3 1985

JANUARY · FEBRUARY · MARCH · APRIL · MAY · JUNE · JULY · AUGUST · SEPTEMBER · OCTOBER · NOVEMBER · DECEMBER

4 1986

JANUARY · FEBRUARY · MARCH · APRIL · MAY · JUNE · JULY · AUGUST · SEPTEMBER · OCTOBER · NOVEMBER · DECEMBER

5 1987

JANUARY · FEBRUARY · MARCH · APRIL · MAY · JUNE · JULY · AUGUST · SEPTEMBER · OCTOBER · NOVEMBER · DECEMBER

6 1982

JANUARY · FEBRUARY · MARCH · APRIL · MAY · JUNE · JULY · AUGUST · SEPTEMBER · OCTOBER · NOVEMBER · DECEMBER

7 1983

JANUARY	FEBRUARY	MARCH	APRIL
S M T W T F S	S M T W T F S	S M T W T F S	S M T W T F S

MAY	JUNE	JULY	AUGUST

SEPTEMBER	OCTOBER	NOVEMBER	DECEMBER

8 (LEAP YEAR) 1984

JANUARY	FEBRUARY	MARCH	APRIL
MAY	JUNE	JULY	AUGUST
SEPTEMBER	OCTOBER	NOVEMBER	DECEMBER

9 (LEAP YEAR) 1996

JANUARY	FEBRUARY	MARCH	APRIL
MAY	JUNE	JULY	AUGUST
SEPTEMBER	OCTOBER	NOVEMBER	DECEMBER

10 (LEAP YEAR) 1980

JANUARY	FEBRUARY	MARCH	APRIL
MAY	JUNE	JULY	AUGUST
SEPTEMBER	OCTOBER	NOVEMBER	DECEMBER

11 (LEAP YEAR) 1992

JANUARY	FEBRUARY	MARCH	APRIL
MAY	JUNE	JULY	AUGUST
SEPTEMBER	OCTOBER	NOVEMBER	DECEMBER

12 (LEAP YEAR) 2004

JANUARY	FEBRUARY	MARCH	APRIL
MAY	JUNE	JULY	AUGUST
SEPTEMBER	OCTOBER	NOVEMBER	DECEMBER

13 (LEAP YEAR) 1988

JANUARY	FEBRUARY	MARCH	APRIL
MAY	JUNE	JULY	AUGUST
SEPTEMBER	OCTOBER	NOVEMBER	DECEMBER

14 (LEAP YEAR) 2000

JANUARY	FEBRUARY	MARCH	APRIL
MAY	JUNE	JULY	AUGUST
SEPTEMBER	OCTOBER	NOVEMBER	DECEMBER

WORLD TIME ZONES

The world is divided into 24 time zones, each 15° longitude wide. The longitudinal meridian passing through Greenwich, England, is the starting point, and is called the *prime meridian*.

Travelers heading west should set their watches back one hour for each time zone passed. Those going east must set their watches ahead one hour. The twelfth zone is divided by the 180th meridian (International Date Line). When the line is crossed going west, the date is advanced one day. When crossed going east, the date becomes a day earlier.

The table below gives the time in countries around the world when it is noon (Eastern Standard Time) in New York City. An asterisk (*) indicates that it is the next day.

COUNTRY	DIFFER-ENCE	TIME	COUNTRY	DIFFER-ENCE	TIME	COUNTRY	DIFFER-ENCE	TIME
Afghanistan	+ 9½	9:30 p.m.	Germany, West	+ 6	6:00 p.m.	Peru	− 0	12:00 noon
Albania	+ 6	6:00 p.m.	Ghana	+ 5	5:00 p.m.	Philippines	+13	1:00 a.m.*
Algeria	+ 5	5:00 p.m.	Greece	+ 7	7:00 p.m.	Poland	+ 6	6:00 p.m.
Angola	+ 6	6:00 p.m.	Grenada	+ 1	1:00 p.m.	Portugal	+ 5	5:00 p.m.
Argentina	+ 2	2:00 p.m.	Guam	+15	3:00 a.m.*	Puerto Rico	+ 1	1:00 p.m.
Australia			Guatemala	− 1	11:00 a.m.	Qatar	+ 8	8:00 p.m.
Perth	+14	2:00 a.m.*	Guinea	+ 5	5:00 p.m.	Romania	+ 7	7:00 p.m.
Adelaide	+15½	3:30 a.m.*	Guinea-Bissau	+ 4	4:00 p.m.	Rwanda	+ 7	7:00 p.m.
Sydney	+16	4:00 a.m.*	Guyana	+ 1¼	1:15 p.m.	Samoa	− 6	6:00 a.m.
Austria	+ 6	6:00 p.m.	Haiti	0	12:00 noon	San Marino	+ 6	6:00 p.m.
Azores	+ 4	4:00 p.m.	Honduras	− 1	11:00 a.m.	Saudi Arabia	Sun time	c.8:00 p.m.
Bahamas	0	12:00 noon	Hungary	+ 6	6:00 p.m.	Senegal	+ 5	5:00 p.m.
Bahrain	+ 8	8:00 p.m.	Iceland	+ 5	5:00 p.m.	Seychelles	+ 9	9:00 p.m.
Bangladesh	+10½	10:30 p.m.	India	+10½	10:30 p.m.	Sierra Leone	+ 5	5:00 p.m.
Barbados	+ 1	1:00 p.m.	Indonesia	+12	12:00 mid.	Singapore	+ 7½	12:30 a.m.*
Belgium	+ 6	6:00 p.m.	Iran	+ 8½	8:30 p.m.	Solomons	+16	4:00 a.m.*
Benin	+ 6	6:00 p.m.	Iraq	+ 8	8:00 p.m.	Somalia	+ 8	8:00 p.m.
Bermuda	+ 1	1:00 p.m.	Ireland	+ 5	5:00 p.m.	South Africa	+ 7	7:00 p.m.
Bolivia	+ 1	1:00 p.m.	Israel	+ 7	7:00 p.m.	Soviet Union		
Botswana	+ 7	7:00 p.m.	Italy	+ 6	6:00 p.m.	Moscow	+ 8	8:00 p.m.
Brazil (Rio)	+ 2	2:00 p.m.	Ivory Coast	+ 5	5:00 p.m.	Gorki	+ 9	9:00 p.m.
Britain	+ 5	5:00 p.m.	Jamaica	0	12:00 noon	Sverdlovsk	+10	10:00 p.m.
Bulgaria	+ 7	7:00 p.m.	Japan	+14	2:00 a.m.*	Tashkent	+11	11:00 p.m.
Burkinafaso	+ 5	5:00 p.m.	Jordan	+ 7	7:00 p.m.	Novosibirsk	+12	12:00 mid.
Burma	+11½	11:30 p.m.	Kenya	+ 8	8:00 p.m.	Irkutsk	+13	1:00 a.m.*
Burundi	+ 7	7:00 p.m.	Korea, North	+14	2:00 a.m.*	Yakutsk	+14	2:00 a.m.*
Cambodia	+12	12:00 mid.	Korea, South	+14	2:00 a.m.*	Vladivostok	+15	3:00 a.m.*
Cameroon	+ 6	6:00 p.m.	Kuwait	+ 8	8:00 p.m.	Spain	+ 6	6:00 p.m.
Canada			Laos	+12	12:00 mid.	Sri Lanka	+10½	10:30 p.m.
Victoria, B.C.	− 3	9:00 a.m.	Lebanon	+ 7	7:00 p.m.	Sudan	+ 7	7:00 p.m.
Edmonton, Alta.	− 2	10:00 a.m.	Lesotho	+ 7	7:00 p.m.	Suriname	+ 1½	1:30 p.m.
Winnipeg, Man.	− 1	11:00 a.m.	Liberia	+ 5	5:00 p.m.	Swaziland	+ 7	7:00 p.m.
Montreal, Que.	0	12:00 noon	Libya	+ 7	7:00 p.m.	Sweden	+ 6	6:00 p.m.
Halifax, N.S.	+ 1	1:00 p.m.	Liechtenstein	+ 6	6:00 p.m.	Switzerland	+ 6	6:00 p.m.
St. John's, Nfld.	+ 1½	1:30 p.m.	Luxembourg	+ 6	6:00 p.m.	Syria	+ 7	7:00 p.m.
Canary Is.	+ 5	5:00 p.m.	Madagascar	+ 8	8:00 p.m.	Taiwan	+13	1:00 a.m.*
Cape Verde	+ 3	3:00 p.m.	Malawi	+ 7	7:00 p.m.	Tanzania	+ 8	8:00 p.m.
Central Africa	+ 6	6:00 p.m.	Malaysia	+12½	12:30 a.m.*	Thailand	+12	12:00 mid.
Chad	+ 6	6:00 p.m.	Maldives	+10	10:00 p.m.	Togo	+ 5	5:00 p.m.
Chile	+ 2	2:00 p.m.	Mali	+ 5	5:00 p.m.	Tonga	− 6	6:00 a.m.
China	+13	1:00 a.m.*	Malta	+ 6	6:00 p.m.	Trinidad-Tobago	+ 1	1:00 p.m.
Colombia	0	12:00 noon	Mauritania	+ 5	5:00 p.m.	Tunisia	+ 6	6:00 p.m.
Comoros	+ 8	8:00 p.m.	Mauritius	+ 9	9:00 p.m.	Turkey	+ 7	7:00 p.m.
Congo	+ 6	6:00 p.m.	Mexico			Uganda	+ 8	8:00 p.m.
Costa Rica	− 1	11:00 a.m.	(Mexico City)	− 1	11:00 a.m.	United Arab Em.	+ 9	9:00 p.m.
Cuba	0	12:00 noon	Midway Is.	− 6	6:00 a.m.	United States		
Cyprus	+ 7	7:00 p.m.	Mongolia	+13	1:00 a.m.*	Honolulu	− 5	7:00 a.m.
Czechoslovakia	+ 6	6:00 p.m.	Morocco	+ 5	5:00 p.m.	Anchorage	− 4	8:00 a.m.
Denmark	+ 6	6:00 p.m.	Mozambique	+ 7	7:00 p.m.	Los Angeles	− 3	9:00 a.m.
Djibouti	+ 8	8:00 p.m.	Nauru	+16½	4:30 a.m.*	Denver	− 2	10:00 a.m.
Dominican Rep.	+ 1	1:00 p.m.	Nepal	+10½	10:30 p.m.	Chicago	− 1	11:00 a.m.
Ecuador	0	12:00 noon	Netherlands	+ 6	6:00 p.m.	New York	0	12:00 noon
Egypt	+ 7	7:00 p.m.	New Zealand	+18	6:00 a.m.*	Uruguay	+ 2	2:00 p.m.
El Salvador	− 1	11:00 a.m.	Nicaragua	− 1	11:00 a.m.	Venezuela	+ 1	1:00 p.m.
Equatorial Guinea	+ 6	6:00 p.m.	Niger	+ 6	6:00 p.m.	Vietnam	+12	12:00 mid.
Ethiopia	+ 8	8:00 p.m.	Nigeria	+ 6	6:00 p.m.	Virgin Islands	+ 1	1:00 p.m.
Fiji	+17	5:00 a.m.*	Norway	+ 6	6:00 p.m.	Yemen, North	+ 8	8:00 p.m.
Finland	+ 7	7:00 p.m.	Oman	+ 9	9:00 p.m.	Yemen, South	+ 8	8:00 p.m.
France	+ 6	6:00 p.m.	Pakistan	+10	10:00 p.m.	Yugoslavia	+ 6	6:00 p.m.
Gabon	+ 6	6:00 p.m.	Panama	0	12:00 noon	Zaire (Kinshasa)	+ 6	6:00 p.m.
Gambia	+ 5	5:00 p.m.	Papua New Guinea	+15	3:00 a.m.*	Zambia	+ 7	7:00 p.m.
Germany, East	+ 6	6:00 p.m.	Paraguay	+ 2	2:00 p.m.	Zimbabwe	+ 7	7:00 p.m.

Cities

HIGHLIGHTS: 1985

METROPOLITAN AREA GROWTH

The U.S. Census Bureau released new estimates of the population of U.S. metropolitan areas in June.

The new figures showed that a total of 55 of the nation's 277 largest metropolitan areas grew by at least 10% in the period 1980-1984. All were in the South and West. They include 17 in Florida, 15 in Texas, and seven in California.

The leaders, with 1984 population estimates and percent change from 1980 to 1984, were:

Midland, Texas, 113,600, up 38%; Anchorage, Alaska, 226,700, up 30%; Naples, Fla., 110,800, up 29%; Ocala, Fla., 155,600, up 27%; Fort Pierce, Fla., 190,200, up 26%; Bryan-College Station, Texas, 117,400, up 25%; Odessa, Texas, 144,500, up 25%; Fort Myers-Cape Coral, Fla., 252,900, up 23%; Melbourne-Titusville-Palm Bay, Fla., 329,500, up 21%; Austin, Texas, 645,400, up 20%; and West Palm Beach-Boca Raton-Delray Beach, Fla., 692,200, up 20%.

Five large metropolitan areas continued to lose population in the 1980s as they did in the 1970s—Buffalo, Cleveland, Detroit, Milwaukee, and Pittsburgh.

Three large metropolitan areas reversed their population trend by registering gains in the 1980s—New York, Philadelphia, and St. Louis.

THE BEST AND THE WORST

Rand McNally's *Places Rated Almanac* in 1985 ranked the 10 best metropolitan areas in which to live as Pittsburgh, Pa.; Boston, Mass.; Raleigh-Durham, N.C.; San Francisco, Calif., Philadelphia, Pa.; Nassau-Suffolk, N.Y.; St. Louis, Mo.; Louisville, Ky.; Norwalk, Conn.; and Seattle, Wash. The publication said the 10 worst were Yuba City, Calif.; Pine Bluff, Ark.; Modesto, Calif.; Dothan, Ala.; Albany, Ga.; Benton Harbor, Mich.; Gadsden, Ala.; Casper, Wyo.; Rockford, Ill.; and Anderson, Ind.

However, geography professor Robert Pierce, writing in the July issue of *American Demographics* magazine, disputed the rankings, saying greater weight should be given to economic factors and less weight to culture and recreation.

According to Pierce, the 10 best metropolitan areas in which to live are Nassau-Suffolk, N.Y., on Long Island; Raleigh-Dur-

ham, N.C.; Norwalk, Conn.; Knoxville, Tenn.; Asheville, N.C.; Pittsburgh, Pa.; Johnson City-Kingsport-Bristol, Tenn.; Charlottesville, Va.; Louisville, Ky., and Boston, Mass.

He said the 10 worst were Pine Bluff, Ark.; Flint, Mich.; Rockford, Ill.; Yuba City, Calif.; Peoria, Ill.; Benton Harbor, Mich.; Baton Rouge, La.; Janesville-Beloit, Wisc.; Casper, Wyo.; and Racine, Wisc.

POPULATION TRENDS IN CITIES

Dr. John G. Keane, director of the U.S. Census Bureau, addressed the U.S. Conference of Mayors in Anchorage, Alaska, on June 18, pointing out major population trends in cities.

In regard to the shift from an industrial society to an information society, Dr. Keane said that from 1970 to 1980 employment in manufacturing slid from 26% to 22% of the national total. But during the same period employment in service industries rose from 57% to 62%. The hardest hit manufacturing industries were primary metals (down 25%), textiles (down 24%), and apparel (down 13%). At the same time the winners were manufacturers of instruments and related products (up 37%), publishing (up 22%), and manufacturers of electric and electronic equipment (up 16%).

"Population shifts can be shifty," Dr. Keane said. "Pun aside, this observation is meant to convey the vulnerability of presum-

20 LARGEST CITIES IN U.S.

RANK	CITY AND STATE	POPULATION[1]
1	New York City, N.Y.	7,086,096
2	Los Angeles, Calif.	3,022,247
3	Chicago, Ill.	2,997,155
4	Houston, Tex.	1,725,617
5	Philadelphia, Pa.	1,665,382
6	Detroit, Mich.	1,138,717
7	Dallas, Tex.	943,848
8	San Diego, Calif.	915,956
9	Phoenix, Ariz.	824,230
10	San Antonio, Tex.	819,021
11	Baltimore, Md.	774,113
12	Indianapolis, Ind.	707,655
13	San Francisco, Calif.	691,637
14	San Jose, Calif.	659,181
15	Memphis, Tenn.	645,760
16	Washington, D.C. [2]	633,425
17	Milwaukee, Wis.	631,509
18	Columbus, Ohio	570,588
19	New Orleans, La.	564,561
20	Boston, Mass.	560,847

[1] U.S. Census Bureau 1982 estimates. [2] 1983 estimate is 623,000.

HIGHLIGHTS: 1985 *(continued)*

ing past trends as the prospective future. Here are several cases in point.

"Not all the sunshine is in the sunbelt. North Dakota, New Hampshire and Washington enjoyed growth rates above the national average during the 1980-1984 period. And, in fact, Alaska had the highest growth rate of any state . . . 24%.

"During the same period, several Southern states had population growth rates below the national average: West Virginia at 0.1%, Kentucky at 1.7%, Alabama at 2.5%, Tennessee and Arkansas at 2.7%, Mississippi at 3.1%. Western state Oregon checked in with 1.6%.

"In such large cities as New York City, San Francisco, Boston, and Denver, population increased from 1980 to 1984 following losses during the 1970s.

"And in Philadelphia, Baltimore, Washington, D.C., and St. Louis, the rate of population decline eased. In fact, according to Washington's school superintendent, the District expects its first public school enrollment increase in 14 years this fall.

"Nationally, the number of five-year-olds began to increase again in 1982. The total number of children of elementary school age will start to increase in 1986. The projected increase in the elementary school age population from 1985 to 1990 is 9%. This follows a 1970-1985 decline of 19%. In general, the outlook is for the elementary school age population to increase faster where it is already increasing and decline slower or even increase slightly where it is now declining."

In regard to immigration trends, Dr. Keane said, "In 1980, foreign-born persons were double the proportion of the population of metropolitan area central cities (10%) compared with the rest of the country (5%) Among cities with 500,000 or more population in 1980, three had 20% or more foreign-born: San Francisco 28%, Los Angeles 27%, and New York City 24%. Persons born in Latin America and Asia accounted for over one-half of the foreign-born population in each of these cities."

MORE BLACK MAYORS

According to the Joint Center for Political Studies the number of black mayors in the United States has risen steadily since 1970. In that year there were 48 black mayors. The number grew to 135 in 1975, to 182 in 1980, to 204 in 1981, to 223 in 1982, to 247 in 1983, to 255 in 1984, and to 286 in 1985.

Four of the 10 largest cities in the United States have black mayors: Tom Bradley of Los Angeles, Harold Washington of Chicago, W. Wilson Goode of Philadelphia, and Coleman A. Young of Detroit.

Among the new black mayors elected in 1984 were Richard E. Jackson Jr. in Peekskill, N.Y.; William A. Kent in South Boston, Va.; Maude J. Bristol in Battle Creek, Mich.; John W. Morrow Jr. in Gainesville, Ga.; Johnnie G. McGowan in Union Springs, Ala., and Joe W. Jackson in Pasco, Wash.

LARGEST U.S. METROPOLITAN AREAS

RANK	METROPOLITAN AREA	POPULATION[1]
1	New York City	17,807,100
2	Los Angeles	12,372,600
3	Chicago	8,035,000
4	Philadelphia	5,755,300
5	San Francisco	5,684,600
6	Detroit	4,577,100
7	Boston	4,026,600
8	Houston	3,565,700
9	Washington	3,429,400
10	Dallas-Fort Worth	3,348,000
11	Miami	2,799,300
12	Cleveland	2,788,400
13	St. Louis	2,398,400
14	Atlanta	2,380,000
15	Pittsburgh	2,372,000
16	Baltimore	2,244,700
17	Minneapolis-St. Paul	2,390,900
18	Seattle-Tacoma	2,207,800
19	San Diego	2,063,900
20	Tampa	1,810,900

WORLD'S LARGEST METROPOLITAN AREAS

RANK	METROPOLITAN AREA	POPULATION
1	New York City, U.S.A. [1]	17,807,100
2	Mexico City, Mexico [2]	14,750,182
3	Los Angeles, U.S.A. [1]	12,372,600
4	Tokyo, Japan [2]	11,634,428
5	Shanghai, China [2]	10,820,000
6	Buenos Aires, Argentina [2]	9,927,404
7	Calcutta, India [2]	9,165,650
8	Peking, China [2]	8,626,050
9	Paris, France [2]	8,612,531
10	Seoul, South Korea [2]	8,364,379
11	Moscow, Soviet Union [2]	8,302,000
12	Bombay, India [2]	8,227,332
13	Chicago, U.S.A. [1]	8,035,000
14	Sao Paulo, Brazil [2]	7,033,529
15	London, Britain [2]	6,696,008
16	Jakarta, Indonesia [2]	6,503,449
17	Philadelphia, U.S.A. [1]	5,755,300
18	Delhi, India [2]	5,713,581
19	San Francisco, U.S.A. [1]	5,684,600
20	Rio de Janeiro, Brazil [2]	5,093,232

[1] U.S. Census Bureau 1984 estimates. [2] 1982 UN Demographic Yearbook.

LARGEST METROPOLITAN AREAS OF THE WORLD

Source: Censuses and official estimates by national governments; *UN Demographic Year Book 1982*

More than two hundred of the world's largest metropolitan areas are shown below. The list includes 40 of the largest metropolitan areas in the United States.

CITY	POPULATION	CITY	POPULATION	CITY	POPULATION
Addis Ababa, Ethiopia	1,408,068	Havana, Cuba	1,924,886	Osaka, Japan	2,635,211
Ahmedabad, India	2,515,195	Ho Chi Minh City, Vietnam	1,825,297	Paris, France	8,612,531
Alexandria, Egypt	2,317,705	Houston, Texas	3,565,700	Peking, China	8,626,050
Alma-Ata, Soviet Union	1,001,000	Hyderabad, India	2,528,198	Perm, Soviet Union	1,028,000
Anaheim, California	2,075,800	Inchon, S. Korea	1,083,906	Philadelphia, Pa.	5,755,300
Ankara, Turkey	2,238,967	Indianapolis, Indiana	1,194,600	Phoenix, Arizona	1,714,800
Athens, Greece	2,101,103	Istanbul, Turkey	2,909,455	Pittsburgh, Pa.	2,372,000
Atlanta, Georgia	2,380,000	Izmir, Turkey	1,059,183	Poona, India	1,685,300
Baghdad, Iraq	1,657,424	Jaipur, India	1,004,000	Port Arthur, China	1,508,000
Baku, Soviet Union	1,616,000	Jakarta, Indonesia	6,503,449	Portland, Oreg.–Wash.	1,340,900
Baltimore, Maryland	2,244,700	Johannesburg, So. Af.	1,726,073	Porto, Portugal	1,314,794
Bandung, Indonesia	1,462,637	Kabul, Afghanistan	1,127,417	Pôrto Alegre, Brazil	1,108,883
Bangalore, India	2,913,537	Kanpur, India	1,688,242	Prague, Czechoslovakia	1,183,724
Bangkok, Thailand	3,077,361	Kansas City, Mo.–Kans.	1,476,700	Providence, R.I.	1,095,000
Barcelona, Spain	1,754,900	Karachi, Pakistan	3,498,634	Pusan, South Korea	3,159,766
Belo Horizonte, Brazil	1,442,483	Kawasaki, Japan	1,045,244	Quezon City, Philippines	1,165,865
Berlin (East), E. Ger.	1,157,557	Kazan, Soviet Union	1,023,000	Rangoon, Burma	2,276,000
Berlin (West), W. Ger.	1,888,669	Kharkov, Soviet Union	1,503,000	Recife, Brazil	1,184,215
Birmingham, Britain	2,358,980	Kiev, Soviet Union	2,297,000	Rio de Janeiro, Brazil	5,093,232
Bogotá, Colombia	2,855,065	Kinshasa, Zaire	2,242,297	Rochester, New York	989,000
Bombay, India	8,227,332	Kitakyushu, Japan	1,065,032	Rome, Italy	2,914,042
Boston, Massachusetts	4,026,600	Kobe, Japan	1,375,006	Rostov-on-Don, Sov. Un.	966,000
Brasília, Brazil	1,306,400	Konya, Turkey	1,425,910	Rotterdam, Netherlands	1,024,749
Brisbane, Australia	1,086,500	Kuibyshev, Soviet Union	1,243,000	Sacramento, California	1,219,600
Brussels, Belgium	1,008,715	Kyoto, Japan	1,477,028	St. Louis, Mo.–Ill.	2,398,400
Bucharest, Romania	1,934,025	Lagos, Nigeria	1,476,837	Salt Lake City, Utah	1,025,300
Budapest, Hungary	2,062,195	Lahore, Pakistan	2,165,372	Salvador, Brazil	1,496,276
Buenos Aires, Argentina	9,927,404	Leeds, Britain	1,735,700	San Antonio, Texas	1,188,500
Buffalo, New York	1,204,800	Leningrad, Soviet Union	4,722,000	San Diego, California	2,063,900
Cairo, Egypt	5,074,016	Lima, Peru	4,600,891	San Francisco, Calif.	5,684,600
Calcutta, India	9,165,000	Lisbon, Portugal	1,611,887	San Jose, California	1,371,500
Cali, Colombia	990,304	Liverpool, Britain	1,226,310	San Juan, Puerto Rico	1,541,500
Canton, China	1,840,000	London, Britain	6,696,000	Santiago, Chile	4,039,287
Cape Town, South Africa	1,490,935	Los Angeles, California	12,372,600	São Paulo, Brazil	7,033,529
Caracas, Venezuela	2,944,000	Lucknow, India	1,006,538	Sapporo, Japan	1,371,108
Casablanca, Morocco	1,753,400	Lyon, France	1,185,919	Seattle–Tacoma, Wash.	2,207,800
Changchun, China	975,000	Madras, India	4,276,635	Semarang, Indonesia	1,026,671
Chelyabinsk, Soviet Un.	1,066,000	Madrid, Spain	3,188,297	Seoul, South Korea	8,364,379
Chengtu, China	1,107,000	Manchester, Britain	2,389,260	Shanghai, China	10,820,000
Chicago, Illinois	8,035,000	Manila, Philippines	1,630,485	Shenyang, China	2,411,000
Chittagong, Bangladesh	1,388,476	Marseille, France	1,076,897	Sian, China	1,310,000
Chungking, China	2,121,000	Medan, Indonesia	1,378,955	Singapore, Singapore	2,390,800
Cincinnati, Ohio–Ky.	1,673,500	Medellín, Colombia	1,159,194	Sofia, Bulgaria	1,052,433
Cleveland, Ohio	2,788,400	Melbourne, Australia	2,803,600	Stockholm, Sweden	1,386,980
Cologne, W. Germany	971,403	Mexico City, Mexico	14,750,182	Supporo, Japan	1,433,355
Columbus, Ohio	1,279,000	Miami, Florida	2,799,300	Surabaja, Indonesia	2,027,913
Copenhagen, Denmark	1,379,473	Milan, Italy	1,666,354	Sverdlovsk, Soviet Un.	1,252,000
Cordoba, Argentina	982,018	Milwaukee, Wisconsin	1,567,600	Sydney, Australia	3,280,900
Dallas, Texas	3,348,000	Minneapolis, Minn.–Wis.	2,230,900	Taegu, South Korea	1,604,934
Damascus, Syria	1,251,028	Minsk, Soviet Union	1,370,000	Taipei, Taiwan	1,769,568
Delhi, India	5,713,518	Monterrey, Mexico	2,018,625	Taiyuan, China	1,020,000
Denver, Colorado	1,791,400	Montevideo, Uruguay	1,173,254	Tampa–St. Petersburg, Fla.	1,810,900
Detroit, Michigan	4,577,100	Montreal, Canada	2,828,349	Tashkent, Soviet Union	1,902,000
Dhaka, Bangladesh	1,730,253	Moscow, Soviet Union	8,302,000	Tbilisi, Soviet Union	1,110,000
Dnepropetrovsk, Sov. Un.	1,114,000	Munich, W. Germany	1,291,828	Teheran, Iran	4,589,201
Donetsk, Soviet Union	1,047,000	Nagoya, Japan	2,089,163	Tel Aviv–Yato, Israel	1,260,000
Erevan, Soviet Union	1,076,000	Nagpur, India	1,297,977	Tientsin, China	4,280,000
Fort Lauderdale, Florida	1,093,300	Nanking, China	1,419,000	Tokyo, Japan	11,634,428
Fortaleza, Brazil	1,306,800	Naples, Italy	1,221,295	Torino, Italy	1,181,567
Fukuoka, Japan	1,104,483	Netzahualcoyotl, Mexico	2,331,151	Toronto, Canada	2,998,947
Fushun, China	985,000	New Orleans, La.	1,318,800	Tsingtao, China	1,121,000
Giza, Egypt	1,230,446	New York, New York	17,807,100	Turin, Italy	1,151,974
Glasgow, Scotland	1,727,625	Newark, N.J.	1,875,300	Ufa, Soviet Union	1,023,000
Gorky, Soviet Union	1,373,000	Norfolk, Va.	1,261,200	Vancouver, Canada	1,268,183
Guadalajara, Mexico	2,467,657	Nova Ignacu, Brazil	1,183,600	Vienna, Austria	1,515,666
Guayaquil, Ecuador	1,278,908	Novosibirsk, Soviet Union	1,357,000	Warsaw, Poland	1,602,784
Hamburg, W. Germany	1,637,132	Oakland, Calif.	1,871,400	Washington, D.C.	3,429,400
Harbin, China	1,552,000	Odessa, Soviet Union	1,085,000	Wuhan, China	2,146,000
Hartford, Conn.	1,030,400	Omsk, Soviet Union	1,061,000	Yokohama, Japan	2,806,523

LARGEST U.S. CITIES

Source: U.S. Census Bureau 1982 estimates.

According to estimates by the U.S. Census Bureau, 176 U.S. cities had more than 100,000 population in 1982. New York remained in first place, but Los Angeles moved past Chicago to become the nation's second most populous city. Houston grew 8.2 percent between 1980 and 1982, becoming the fourth largest U.S. city.

CITY AND STATE	POPULATION	CITY AND STATE	POPULATION	CITY AND STATE	POPULATION
Abilene, Texas	104,302	Garland, Texas	148,975	Parma, Ohio	90,572
Akron, Ohio	231,659	Gary, Ind.	147,537	Pasadena, Calif.	120,954
Albany, N.Y.	100,048	Glendale, Ariz.	106,420	Pasadena, Texas	122,010
Albuquerque, N. Mex.	341,978	Glendale, Calif.	142,148	Paterson, N.J.	138,986
Alexandria, Va.	104,276	Grand Rapids, Mich.	182,774	Peoria, Ill.	122,261
Allentown, Pa.	104,324	Greensboro, N.C.	157,337	Philadelphia, Pa.	1,665,382
Amarillo, Texas	155,356	Hammond, Ind.	91,546	Phoenix, Ariz.	824,230
Anaheim, Calif.	226,467	Hampton, Va.	124,966	Pittsburgh, Pa.	414,936
Anchorage, Alaska	194,675	Hartford, Conn.	136,334	Pomona, Calif.	100,465
Ann Arbor, Mich.	104,880	Hayward, Calif.	96,287	Ponce, Puerto Rico	190,100
Arlington, Texas	182,975	Hialeah, Fla.	154,713	Portland, Oreg.	367,530
Atlanta, Ga.	428,153	Hollywood, Fla.	122,051	Portsmouth, Va.	105,807
Aurora, Colo.	184,372	Honolulu, Hawaii	365,048	Providence, R.I.	155,717
Austin, Texas	368,135	Houma, La.	100,346	Pueblo, Colo.	100,934
Bakersfield, Calif.	115,528	Houston, Texas	1,725,617	Raleigh, N.C.	154,211
Baltimore, Md.	774,113	Huntington Beach, Calif.	176,314	Reno, Nev.	106,748
Baton Rouge, La.	361,572	Huntsville, Ala.	145,421	Richmond, Va.	218,237
Bayamón, Puerto Rico	198,400	Independence, Mo.	111,617	Riverside, Calif.	174,023
Beaumont, Texas	123,477	Indianapolis, Ind.	707,655	Roanoke, Va.	100,187
Berkeley, Calif.	103,479	Inglewood, Calif.	97,416	Rochester, N.Y.	244,094
Birmingham, Ala.	283,239	Irving, Texas	114,305	Rockford, Ill.	138,334
Boise, Idaho	105,586	Jackson, Miss.	204,195	Sacramento, Calif.	288,597
Boston, Mass.	560,847	Jacksonville, Fla.	556,370	St. Louis, Mo.	437,354
Bridgeport, Conn.	143,745	Jersey City, N.J.	222,881	St. Paul, Minn.	270,443
Brockton, Mass.	96,538	Kansas City, Kans.	162,211	St. Petersburg, Fla.	241,214
Buffalo, N.Y.	348,035	Kansas City, Mo.	445,222	Salt Lake City, Utah	163,859
Caguas, Puerto Rico	199,200	Knoxville, Tenn.	175,298	San Antonio, Texas	819,021
Cambridge, Mass.	93,841	Koolaupoko, Hawaii	109,373	San Bernardino, Calif.	124,319
Canton, Ohio	93,077	Lakewood, Colo.	118,498	San Diego, Calif.	915,956
Carolina, Puerto Rico	168,400	Lansing, Mich.	128,338	San Francisco, Calif.	691,637
Cedar Rapids, Iowa	109,086	Las Vegas, Nev.	179,587	San Jose, Calif.	659,181
Charlotte, N.C.	323,972	Lexington, Ky.	207,668	San Juan, Puerto Rico	430,500
Chattanooga, Tenn.	168,016	Lincoln, Nebr.	177,340	Santa Ana, Calif.	217,219
Chesapeake, Va.	119,749	Little Rock, Ark.	167,974	Savannah, Ga.	145,699
Chicago, Ill.	2,997,155	Livonia, Mich.	101,366	Seattle, Wash.	490,077
Cincinnati, Ohio	380,118	Long Beach, Calif.	371,426	Shreveport, La.	210,881
Cleveland, Ohio	558,869	Los Angeles, Calif.	3,022,247	South Bend, Ind.	107,690
Colorado Springs, Colo.	231,699	Louisville, Ky.	293,531	Spokane, Wash.	171,903
Columbia, S.C.	101,457	Lowell, Mass.	92,774	Springfield, Ill.	100,054
Columbus, Ga.	174,348	Lubbock, Texas	176,588	Springfield, Mass.	151,586
Columbus, Ohio	570,588	Macon, Ga.	118,730	Springfield, Mo.	135,453
Concord, Calif.	104,061	Madison, Wis.	172,640	Stamford, Conn.	103,614
Corpus Christi, Texas	246,081	Mayaguez, Puerto Rico	99,800	Sterling Heights, Mich.	108,482
Dallas, Texas	943,848	Memphis, Tenn.	645,760	Stockton, Calif.	161,815
Davenport, Iowa	103,799	Mesa, Ariz.	171,695	Sunnyvale, Calif.	107,110
Dayton, Ohio	188,499	Miami, Fla.	382,726	Syracuse, N.Y.	166,187
Decatur, Ill.	92,733	Miami Beach, Fla.	93,702	Tacoma, Wash.	161,351
Denver, Colo.	505,563	Milwaukee, Wis.	631,509	Tallahassee, Fla.	102,579
Des Moines, Iowa	191,506	Minneapolis, Minn.	369,161	Tampa, Fla.	276,413
Detroit, Mich.	1,138,717	Mobile, Ala.	204,586	Tempe, Ariz.	112,514
Duluth, Minn.	90,311	Modesto, Calif.	114,076	Toledo, Ohio	350,565
Durham, N.C.	101,242	Montgomery, Ala.	182,406	Topeka, Kans.	120,269
East Los Angeles, Calif.	110,017	Nashville, Tenn.	455,252	Torrance, Calif.	130,213
El Paso, Texas	445,071	New Bedford, Mass.	98,478	Trenton, N.J.	92,124
Elizabeth, N.J.	106,803	New Haven, Conn.	125,348	Tucson, Ariz.	352,455
Erie, Pa.	118,493	New Orleans, La.	564,561	Tulsa, Okla.	375,300
Eugene, Oreg.	103,709	New York City, N.Y.	7,086,096	Virginia Beach, Va.	282,588
Evansville, Ind.	130,275	Newark, N.J.	320,512	Waco, Texas	102,200
Fall River, Mass.	93,126	Newport News, Va.	151,240	Warren, Mich.	156,131
Flint, Mich.	154,019	Norfolk, Va.	266,874	Washington, D.C.	633,425
Fort Lauderdale, Fla.	153,755	Oakland, Calif.	344,652	Waterbury, Conn.	102,940
Fort Wayne, Ind.	167,633	Odessa, Tex.	102,465	Wichita, Kans.	288,723
Fort Worth, Texas	401,402	Oklahoma City, Okla.	427,714	Wichita Falls, Texas	99,555
Fremont, Calif.	137,925	Omaha, Nebr.	328,557	Winston-Salem, N.C.	140,846
Fresno, Calif.	244,623	Orange, Calif.	94,606	Worcester, Mass.	161,049
Fullerton, Calif.	104,532	Orlando, Fla.	134,255	Yonkers, N.Y.	192,342
Garden Grove, Calif.	126,340	Oxnard, Calif.	115,657	Youngstown, Ohio	111,391

LARGEST U.S. METROPOLITAN AREAS

Source: U.S. Census Bureau 1984 estimates.

Among the largest metropolitan areas, those that grew at the fastest rate from 1980 to 1984 were Anchorage, AK (29.9%), Fort Myers, FL (23.2%), Melbourne-Titusville-Palm Bay, FL (20.7%), Austin, TX (20.3%), West Palm Beach, FL (20%), and McAllen-Edinburg, TX (19%).

METROPOLITAN AREA	POPULATION	METROPOLITAN AREA	POPULATION	METROPOLITAN AREA	POPULATION
Albany, NY	842,900	Hartford, CT	1,030,400	Peoria, IL	355,900
Albuquerque, NM	449,400	Hickory, NC	212,100	Philadelphia, PA–NJ–DE	5,755,300
Allentown–Bethlehem–Easton, PA–NJ	646,700	Honolulu, HI	805,300	Phoenix, AZ	1,714,800
Anaheim–Santa Ana, CA	2,075,800	Houston, TX	3,565,700	Pittsburgh, PA	2,372,000
Anchorage, AK	226,700	Huntington–Ashland, WV–KY–OH	334,000	Ponce, PR	233,000
Appleton–Oshkosh, WI	299,400	Huntsville, AL	210,000	Portland–Vancouver–OR–WA	1,340,900
Atlanta, GA	2,380,000	Indianapolis, IN	1,194,600	Portsmouth–Dover, NH	206,500
Atlantic City, NJ	290,400	Jackson, MS	382,400	Poughkeepsie, NY	253,100
Augusta, GA–SC	368,300	Jacksonville, FL	795,300	Providence–Pawtucket–Fall River, RI–MA	1,095,000
Aurora–Elgin, IL	331,000	Jersey City, NJ	559,900	Provo-Orem, UT	240,600
Austin, TX	645,400	Johnson City–Kingsport–Bristol, TN–VA	441,900	Raleigh-Durham, NC	609,300
Bakersfield, CA	462,400	Johnstown, PA	259,000	Reading, PA	317,200
Baltimore, MD	2,244,700	Joliet, IL	363,800	Reno, NV	211,500
Baton Rouge, LA	538,000	Kalamazoo, MI	215,200	Richmond, VA	796,100
Beaumont–Port Arthur–Orange, TX	391,900	Kansas City, MO–KS	1,476,700	Riverside–San Bernardino, CA	1,810,900
Bergen–Passaic, NJ	1,299,500	Killeen–Temple, TX	225,700	Roanoke, VA	222,700
Binghamton, NY	264,100	Knoxville, TN	589,400	Rochester, NY	989,000
Birmingham, AL	895,200	Lafayette, LA	215,900	Rockford, IL	278,800
Boston, MA–NH	4,026,600	Lakeland–Winter Haven, FL	354,600	Sacramento, CA	1,219,600
Bridgeport–Milford, CT	441,500	Lancaster, PA	381,300	Saginaw–Bay City–Midland, MI	411,900
Brownsville, TX	241,100	Lansing, MI	416,200	St. Louis, MO–IL	2,398,400
Buffalo–Niagra Falls, NY	1,204,800	Las Vegas, NV	536,500	Salem–Gloucester, MA	259,100
Caguas, PR	274,660	Lawrence-Haverhill, MA–NH	356,900	Salem, OR	255,200
Canton, OH	404,200	Lexington–Fayette, KY	327,200	Salinas–Monterey, CA	319,200
Charleston, SC	472,500	Lincoln, NE	203,000	Salt Lake City–Ogden, UT	1,025,300
Charleston, WV	267,000	Little Rock–North Little Rock, AR	492,700	San Antonio, TX	1,188,500
Charlotte–Gastonia, NC	1,031,400	Lorain–Elyria, OH	271,300	San Diego, CA	2,063,900
Chattanooga, TN–GA	422,500	Los Angeles, CA	12,372,600	San Francisco, CA	5,684,600
Chicago, IL	8,035,000	Louisville, KY–IN	962,600	San Jose, CA	1,371,500
Cincinnati, OH–KY–IN	1,673,500	Lowell, MA–NH	250,400	San Juan, PR	1,541,500
Cleveland–Akron, OH	2,788,400	Lubbock, TX	218,900	Santa Barbara, CA	322,800
Colorado Springs, CO	349,100	Macon, GA	277,900	Santa Rosa, CA	326,300
Columbia, SC	433,200	Madison, WI	333,000	Sarasota, FL	237,600
Columbus, GA–AL	244,500	Mayaguez, PR	207,800	Savannah, GA	232,900
Columbus, OH	1,279,000	McAllen–Edinburg–Misson, TX	337,100	Scranton–Wilkes Barre, PA	726,800
Corpus Christi, TX	361,300	Melbourne–Titusville–Palm Bay, FL	329,500	Seattle–Tacoma, WA	2,207,800
Dallas–Fort Worth, TX	3,348,000	Memphis, TN–AR–MS	934,600	Shreveport, LA	360,900
Davenport–Rock Island–Moline, IA–IL	380,900	Miami–Ft. Laud., FL	2,799,300	South Bend, IN	239,800
Dayton, OH	930,100	Middlesex–Somerset–Hunterdon, NJ	921,800	Spokane, WA	352,900
Daytona Beach, FL	300,300	Milwaukee–Racine, WI	1,567,600	Springfield, MO	217,200
Denver–Boulder, CO	1,791,400	Minneapolis–St. Paul, MN	2,230,900	Springfield, MA	515,900
Des Moines, IA	377,100	Mobile, AL	465,700	Stamford, CT	196,900
Detroit–Ann Arbor, MI	4,577,100	Modesto, CA	295,700	Stockton, CA	398,600
Duluth, MN–WI	253,800	Monmouth–Ocean, NJ	900,600	Syracuse, NY	650,500
El Paso, TX	526,500	Montgomery, AL	284,800	Tacoma, WA	515,800
Erie, PA	282,100	Nashville, TN	890,300	Tallahassee, FL	207,600
Eugene–Springfield, OR	266,400	Nassau–Suffolk, NY	2,653,400	Tampa–St. Petersburg, FL	1,810,900
Evansville, IN–KY	281,300	New Haven, CT	506,000	Toledo, OH	610,800
Fayetteville, NC	251,300	New London–Norwich, CT	257,000	Trenton, NJ	313,800
Flint, MI	434,100	New Orleans, LA	1,318,800	Tucson, AZ	594,800
Fort Lauderdale–Hollywood, FL	1,093,300	New York City, NY	17,807,100	Tulsa, OK	725,600
Fort Myers, FL	252,900	Newark, NJ	1,875,300	Utica-Rome, NY	321,400
Fort Wayne, IN	348,400	Norfolk–Newport News–Virginia Beach, VA	1,261,200	Vallejo–Napa, CA	367,600
Fresno, CA	564,900	Oakland, CA	1,871,400	Visalia–Tulare, CA	272,400
Galveston–Texas City, TX	215,400	Oklahoma City, OK	962,600	Washington, DC	3,429,400
Gary–Hammond, IN	629,600	Omaha, NE–IA	607,400	Waterbury, CT	208,200
Grand Rapids, MI	626,400	Orlando, FL	824,100	West Palm Beach, FL	692,200
Greensboro–Winston Salem–High Point, NC	886,100	Oxnard–Ventura, CA	584,700	Wichita, KS	428,600
Greenville, SC	592,900	Pensacola, FL	318,700	Wilmington, DE–NJ–MD	539,700
Hamilton–Middletown, OH	265,500			Worcester, MA	404,700
Harrisburg, PA	570,200			York, PA	391,400
				Youngstown–Warren, OH	518,100

U.S. CITIES, ZIP CODES, AND POPULATIONS

Cities and communities with 6,000 or more people and the ZIP CODES for these places are listed on the following pages.

Population figures for cities and communities are for the U.S. Census of April 1, 1980, or later

estimates as noted.

An asterisk (*) after a ZIP CODE number indicates the place has more than one code. So you should check a ZIP CODE directory for the code for a specific street address.

PLACE AND ZIP CODE	POP.[2]	PLACE AND ZIP CODE	POP.[2]	PLACE AND ZIP CODE	POP.[2]

ALABAMA (Ala or AL)

PLACE AND ZIP CODE	POP.	PLACE AND ZIP CODE	POP.	PLACE AND ZIP CODE	POP.
Alabaster 35007	7,605	Forestdale 35214	10,814[1]	Oxford 36203	9,220
Albertville....... 35950	12,520	Fort Payne 35967	11,877	Ozark 36360	13,628
Alexander City... 35010	14,286	Fultondale 35068	6,051	Pelham 35124	7,896
Andalusia 36420	10,586	Gadsden........ 35901*	47,030	Pell City 35125	6,796
Anniston........ 36201*	30,278	Gardendale 35071	8,572	Phenix City 36867	26,943
Arab 35016	6,126	Greenville....... 36037	7,887	Pleasant Grove .. 35127	7,294
Athens 35611	14,633	Guntersville 35976	6,852	Prattville....... 36067	19,088
Atmore 36502	8,819	Hartselle........ 35640	8,917	Prichard........ 36610	39,895
Attalla.......... 35954	7,705	Homewoood 35209	21,129	Rainbow City 35901	6,920
Auburn 36830	28,851	Hoover 35236	21,836	Roanoke 36274	5,951
Bay Minette 36507	7,537	Hueytown....... 35023	14,788	Russellville...... 35653	8,497
Bessemer....... 35020*	31,257	Huntsville....... 35813	145,421	Saraland........ 36571	10,521
Birmingham.... 35203*	283,239	Irondale 35210	7,142	Scottsboro 35768	14,996
Boaz 35957	7,046	Jackson........ 36545	6,229	Selma 36701	27,532
Brewton 36426	6,885	Jacksonville..... 36265	9,868	Sheffield........ 35660	11,460
Center Point 35220	23,317[1]	Jasper.......... 35501	12,031	Sylacauga 35150	12,858
Chickasaw 36611	7,402[1]	Lanett 36863	8,776	Talladega 35160	19,783
Cullman 35055	13,036	Leeds 35094	9,140	Tarrant City..... 35217	8,148[1]
Decatur 35602*	41,874	Midfield 35228	6,150	Theodore 36582	6,392[1]
Demopolis 36732	7,770	Mobile.......... 36601*	204,586	Tillman's Corner . —	15,941[1]
Dothan 36303*	51,288	Montgomery 36119*	182,406	Troy 36081	13,109
Enterprise 36330	19,439	Mountain Brook .. 35223	19,710	Tuscaloosa..... 35403*	73,743
Eufaula 36027	11,811	Muscle Shoals ... 35661	8,911[1]	Tuscumbia 35674	9,124
Fairfield 35064	12,946	Northport 35476	15,070	Tuskegee 36083	13,168
Fairhope 36532	7,469	Opelika 36801	23,589	Walley City..... —	9,126
Florence........ 35631*	37,467	Opp 36467	7,214	Vestavia Hills ... 35216	15,702

ALASKA (Alas. or AK)

PLACE AND ZIP CODE	POP.	PLACE AND ZIP CODE	POP.	PLACE AND ZIP CODE	POP.
Anchorage 99502*	194,675	Juneau 99801*	21,778	Kodiak 99615	5,809
Fairbanks....... 99701	26,860	Ketchikan....... 99901	7,660	Sitka 99835	7,875

ARIZONA (Ariz. or AZ)

PLACE AND ZIP CODE	POP.	PLACE AND ZIP CODE	POP.	PLACE AND ZIP CODE	POP.
Apache Junction . 85220	12,053	Glendale 85301*	106,420	Safford 85546	6,914
Avondale 85323	8,575	Globe 85501	7,309	Scottsdale 85251*	94,233
Bisbee.......... 85603	7,029	Kingman........ 86401	10,425	Sierra Vista 85635	27,895
Casa Grande 85222	15,503	Lake Havasu City. 86403	16,520	Somerton 85350	6,366
Chandler 85224	36,515	Mesa 85201*	171,695	South Tucson 85725	6,402
Coolidge 85228	7,047	Nogales 85621	16,249	Sun City 85351*	40,505[1]
Douglas 85607	13,424	Paradise Valley .. 85253	12,501	Tempe 85282	112,514
Eloy 85231	6,251	Peoria 85345	13,757	Tucson 85726*	352,455
Flagstaff........ 86001	34,895	Phoenix 85026*	824,230	Winslow 86047	7,994
Gilbert 85234	6,548	Prescott 86301	21,266	Yuma 85364	44,744

ARKANSAS (Ark. or AR)

PLACE AND ZIP CODE	POP.	PLACE AND ZIP CODE	POP.	PLACE AND ZIP CODE	POP.
Arkadelphia 71923	10,035	Hope 71801	10,395	Pine Bluff 71601*	56,107
Batesville 72501	8,694	Hot Springs 71909	36,060	Rogers 72756	19,113
Benton 72015	17,776	Jacksonville 72076	28,964	Russellville...... 72801	16,118
Bentonville...... 72712	9,346	Jonesboro 72401	31,143	Searcy 72143	13,554
Blytheville 72315	23,915	Little Rock 72231*	167,974	Sherwood 72116	11,461
Camden 71701	15,848	Magnolia 71753	12,143	Siloam Springs .. 72761	7,673
Conway......... 72032	20,445	Malvern 72104	10,014	Springdale...... 72764	24,185
Crossett 71635	6,831	Marianna 72360	6,306	Stuttgart 72160	11,004
Dumas 71639	6,196	Monticello 71655	9,073	Texarkana 75502	21,663
El Dorado 71730	25,291	Morrilton 72110	7,217	Trumann 72472	6,004
Fayetteville 72701	36,270	Mountain Home . 72653	8,192	Van Buren 72956	12,237
Forrest City 72335	13,909	Newport 72112	8,354	Warren 71671	7,538
Fort Smith 72901*	71,275	North Little Rock 72114*	64,322	West Helena 72390	11,215
Harrison........ 72601	9,801	Osceola 72370	8,981	West Memphis .. 72301	27,808
Helena 72342	9,317	Paragould 72450	15,491	Wynne 72396	7,970

[1] 1980 Census. [2] 1982 Census Bureau estimate.

PLACE AND ZIP CODE	POP.[2]	PLACE AND ZIP CODE	POP.[2]	PLACE AND ZIP CODE	POP.[2]

CALIFORNIA (Calif., Cal., or CA)

Place	ZIP	Pop.	Place	ZIP	Pop.	Place	ZIP	Pop.
Agoura Hills	91301	11,508	Cherryland	94541	9,425[1]	Foster City	94404	23,609
Alameda	94501	67,662	Chico	95926	27,924	Fountain Valley	92728	54,874
Alamo	94507	8,505[1]	Chico North	—	11,733[1]	Freedom	95019	6,416[1]
Albany	94706	15,120	Chino	91710	42,925	Fremont	94537*	137,925
Alhambra	91802*	67,170	Chula Vista	92010*	86,984	Fresno	93706*	244,768
Alondra Park	90249	12,096[1]	Citrus	—	12,450[1]	Fullerton	92631*	104,532
Altadena	91001	40,983[1]	Citrus Heights	95610	85,911[1]	Garden Grove	92640*	126,340
Alum Rock	95116	16,890[1]	Claremont	91711	32,389	Gardena	90247*	46,070
Anaheim	92803*	226,467	Clearlake	95422	9,217	Gilroy	95020	23,413
Anderson	96007	7,384	Clovis	93612	35,556	Glen Avon	—	8,444[1]
Antioch	94509	45,324	Coachella	92236	10,318	Glendale	91209*	142,148
Apple Valley	92307	14,305[1]	Coalinga	93210	7,003	Glendora	91740	39,090
Aptos	95003	7,039[1]	Colton	92324	22,227	Grand Terrace	92324	9,216
Arcadia	91006	46,096	Commerce	90040	11,542	Grass Valley	95945	7,759
Arcata	95521	13,522	Compton	90220*	84,685	Grover City	93433	9,523
Arden–Arcade	95825	87,570[1]	Concord	94520*	104,061	Hacienda Heights	91745	49,422[1]
Arroyo Grande	93420	12,232	Corcoran	93212	6,703	Half Moon Bay	94019	7,388
Artesia	90701	14,609	Corona	91720	40,089	Hanford	93230	22,396
Arvin	93203	7,305	Coronado	92118	19,798	Hawaiian Gdns.	90716	11,342
Ashland	94577	13,893[1]	Corte Madera	94925	8,149	Hawthorne	90250	57,770
Atascadero	93422	17,678	Costa Mesa	92626*	84,977	Hayward	94544*	96,287
Atherton	94025	7,655	Country Club	—	9,585[1]	Healdsburg	95448	7,468
Atwater	95301	18,276	Covina	91722*	38,749	Hemet	92343	25,272
Auburn	95603	7,991	Crestline	92325	6,715[1]	Hercules	94547	6,905
Avocado Heights	91745	11,721[1]	Cudahy	90201	19,080	Hermosa Beach	90254	18,032
Azusa	91702	31,269	Culver City	90230	38,054	Hesperia	92345	13,540[1]
Bakersfield	93302*	115,528	Cupertino	95014	37,461	Highland	92346	10,908[1]
Baldwin Park	91706	53,835	Cypress	90630	41,118	Hillsborough	94010	10,461
Banning	92220	14,912	Daly City	94015*	79,726	Hollister	95023	12,727
Barstow	92311	19,361	Dana Point	92629	10,602[1]	Huntington		
Baywood–Las Osas	—	10,933[1]	Danville	94526	26,871	Beach	92647*	176,314
Beaumont	92223	7,152	Davis	95616	37,433	Huntington Park	90255	48,495
Bell	90201	26,778	Del Aire	90250	8,487[1]	Imperial Beach	92032	23,497
Bell Gardens	90201	35,827	Delano	93215	17,754	Indio	92201	23,471
Bellflower	90706	55,242	Desert Hot Sprgs.	92240	6,913	Inglewood	90311*	97,416
Belmont	94002	24,427	Diamond Bar	91765	28,045[1]	Irvine	92713	71,446
Ben Lomond	95005	7,238[1]	Dinuba	93618	10,393	La Canada–		
Benicia	94510	17,724	Dixon	95620	8,534	Flintridge	91011	19,959
Berkeley	94704*	103,479	Downey	90241*	82,778	La Crescenta–		
Beverly Hills	90213*	31,728	Duarte	91010	18,853	Montrose	91214	16,531[1]
Big Bear	92314	11,151[1]	Dublin	94568	13,998	La Habra	90631	46,671
Bloomington	92316	12,781[1]	East Hemet	—	14,712[1]	La Mesa	92041	51,246
Blythe	92225	6,843	East La Mirada	90638	9,688[1]	La Mirada	90638	40,615
Bonita	92002	6,257[1]	East Los Angeles	90022	110,017[1]	La Palma	90623	15,543
Brawley	92227	16,749	East Palo Alto	94303	18,331	La Puente	91747*	31,394
Brea	92621	30,879	Edwards	93523	8,554[1]	La Riviera	—	10,906[1]
Broderick–Bryte	95605	10,194[1]	El Cajon	92020*	77,707	La Verne	91750	24,860
Buena Park	90622	64,323	El Centro	92243	25,539	Ladera Heights	94025	6,647[1]
Burbank	91505*	85,465	El Cerrito	94530	22,831	Lafayette	94549	22,819
Burlingame	94010	26,085	El Monte	91734*	84,797	Laguna Beach	92651*	18,172
Calexico	92231	15,683	El Paso de Robles	93446	10,758	Laguna Hills	92654	33,600[1]
Calwa	93745	6,640[1]	El Segundo	90245	13,874	Laguna Niguel	92677	12,237[1]
Camarillo	93010	40,346	El Sobrante	94803	10,535[1]	Lake Arrowhead	92352	6,272[1]
Camarillo Heights	93010	6,341[1]	El Toro	92630	38,153[1]	Lake Elsinore	92330	7,621
Campbell	95008	32,509	El Toro Station	92709	7,632[1]	Lakeside	92040	23,921[1]
Canyon Country	91351	15,728[1]	Elk Grove	95624	10,959[1]	Lakewood	90714	74,404
Capistrano Beach	92624	6,168[1]	Encinitas	92024	10,796[1]	Lamont	93241	9,616[1]
Capitola	95010	9,181	Escondido	92025	70,004	Lancaster	93534	50,890
Cardiff-by-the–			Eureka	95501	24,175	Larkspur	94939	11,213
Sea	92007	10,054[1]	Fair Oaks	95628	22,602[1]	Lawndale	90260	24,266
Carlsbad	92008	37,679	Fairfax	94930	7,324	Lemon Grove	92045	21,473
Carmichael	95608	43,108[1]	Fairfield	94533	61,742	Lemoore	93245	9,718
Carpinteria	93013	11,050	Fallbrook	92028	14,041[1]	Lennox	90304	18,445[1]
Carson	90749	83,326	Fillmore	93015	9,920	Leucadia	92024	9,478[1]
Casa de Oro–Mt. Helix	92077	19,651[1]	Florence–Graham	90001	48,662[1]	Linda	95901	10,225[1]
Castle Pk.–Otay	—	21,049[1]	Florin	95828	16,523[1]	Lindsay	93247	7,216
Castro Valley	94546	44,011[1]	Folsom	95630	12,993	Livermore	94550	49,564
Cathedral City	92234	12,890	Fontana	92335	43,253	Lodi	95240	36,985
Ceres	95307	14,767	Foothill Farms	95841	13,700[1]	Loma Linda	92354	10,969
Cerritos	90701	54,089	Fortuna	95540	7,717	Lomita	90717	19,285

[1] 1980 Census. [2] 1982 Census Bureau estimate.

PLACE AND ZIP CODE	POP.[2]	PLACE AND ZIP CODE	POP.[2]	PLACE AND ZIP CODE	POP.[2]
CALIFORNIA *(continued)*					
Lompoc 93436	28,128	Paradise 95969	23,374	San Marino 91108	13,280
Long Beach 90809*	371,426	Paramount 90723	38,885	San Mateo 94402*	77,918
Los Alamitos 90720	11,631	Parkway–Sacra-		San Pablo 94806	20,904
Los Altos 94022	26,137	mento South .. 95823	26,815[1]	San Rafael 94901*	44,392
Los Altos Hills ... 94022	7,500	Pasadena 91109*	120,954	San Ramon 94583	21,410
Los Angeles 90052*	3,022,247	Perris 92370	7,689	Sanger 93657	13,007
Los Banos 93635	10,955	Petaluma 94952	35,387	Santa Ana 92711*	217,219
Los Gatos....... 95030	27,122	Pico Rivera 90660	54,800	Santa Barbara .. 93102*	74,663
Lucas Valley-		Piedmont 94611	10,357	Santa Clara 95050*	88,171
Marinwood —	6,409[1]	Pinole 94564	14,475	Santa Cruz 95060*	42,352
Lynwood........ 90262	50,809	Pittsburg 94565	36,315	Santa Fe Springs 90670	14,630
Madera 93638*	23,933	Placentia 92670	36,523	Santa Maria 93456	42,181
Manhattan Beach. 90266	32,285	Placerville 95667	7,066	Santa Monica ... 90406*	89,187
Manteca 95336	27,216	Pleasant Hill ... 94523	26,672	Santa Paula 93060	21,394
Marina 93933	23,116	Pleasanton 94566	35,695	Santa Rosa 95402*	86,989
Marina del Ray .. 90292	6,336[1]	Pomona 91766	100,465	Santee 92071	43,854
Martinez........ 94553	23,715	Port Hueneme ... 93041	18,370	Saratoga 95070	29,289
Marysville 95901	10,159	Porterville 93257	21,905	Saugus-Bouquet	
Maywood 90270	23,414	Poway 92064	34,746	Canyon 91350	16,283[1]
McKinleyville ... 95521	7,772[1]	Quartz Hill 93534	7,421[1]	Sausalito 94965	7,595
Meiners Oaks-		Ramona 92065	8,173[1]	Scotts Valley 95066	7,220
Miramonte 93023	9,512[1]	Rancho Cordova . 95670	42,881[1]	Seal Beach 90740	25,567
Menlo Park 94025	26,160	Rancho Cucamonga 91730	59,315	Seaside 93955	37,789
Merced 95340	39,774	Rancho Mirage .. 92270	6,704	Selma 93662	11,512
Mill Valley 94941	12,797	Rancho Palos		Shafter 93263	7,297
Millbrae 94030	20,036	Verdes 90274	36,693	Sierra Madre 91024	10,775
Milpitas 95035	39,954	Red Bluff 96080	10,109	Simi Valley 93065*	81,385
Mira Loma 91752	8,707[1]	Redding 96001	43,687	Solana Beach ... 92075	13,047[1]
Mission Viejo 92675	50,666[1]	Redlands 92373	46,847	Soledad 93960	6,064
Modesto 95350*	114,076	Redondo Beach .. 90277*	58,872	Sonoma 95476	6,350
Monrovia 91016	30,982	Redwood City ... 94064*	54,948	Soquel 95073	6,212[1]
Montclair 91763	24,019	Reedley......... 93654	11,543	South El Monte .. 91733	17,786
Montebello 90640	54,594	Rialto 92376	41,713	South Gate 90280	72,015
Monterey 93940*	28,266	Richmond 94802*	75,927	South Laguna ... 92677	6,013[1]
Monterey Park .. 91754	56,599	Ridgecrest 93555	22,134	S. Lake Tahoe ... 95705	20,991
Moraga 94556	14,790	Rio del Mar —	7,067[1]	South Modesto .. 95350	12,492[1]
Morgan Hill 95037	18,352	Rio Linda 95673	7,359[1]	South Pasadena . 91030	22,855
Morro Bay 93442	9,257	Riverbank....... 95367	5,988	S. San Francisco . 94080	50,141
Mountain View .. 94042	60,050	Riverside 92507*	174,023	South San Jose Hl 91744	16,049[1]
Muscoy 92405	6,188[1]	Rocklin 95677	8,193	South Whittier .. 90605	43,815[1]
Napa 94558	52,562	Rodeo 94572	8,286[1]	South Yuba 95991	7,530[1]
National City ... 92050	53,687	Rohnert Park 94928	25,923	Spring Valley ... 92077	40,191[1]
Newark 94560	33,372	Rolling Hills Est. . 90274	7,757	Stanford 94305	11,045[1]
Newhall......... 91321	12,029[1]	Roseland 95407	7,915[1]	Stanton 90680	24,935
Newport Beach .. 92660*	64,754	Rosemead 91770	44,213	Stockton 95208*	161,815
Norco 91760	21,224	Rosemont —	18,882[1]	Suisun City 94585	12,785
North Auburn ... -	7,619[1]	Roseville 95678	26,453	Sun City 92381	8,460[1]
North Fair Oaks . 94025	10,308[1]	Rossmoor....... 90720	10,457[1]	Sunnymead 92388	11,554[1]
North Highlands . 95660	37,825[1]	Rowland Heights . 91748	28,252[1]	Sunnyvale 94086*	107,110
Norwalk 90650	86,317	Rubidoux 92519	17,048[1]	Susanville 96130	6,778
Novato 94947	45,005	Sacramento 95813*	288,597	Tamalpais–Home-	
Oakdale 95361	8,925	Salinas 93907*	84,443	stead Valley ... —	8,511[1]
Oakland 94615*	344,652	San Anselmo 94960	11,951	Tara Hills–Mt.	
Oceanside 92054*	84,082	San Bernardino .. 92403*	124,319	Manor —	9,471[1]
Oildale 93388	23,382[1]	San Bruno 94066	35,963	Temple City 91780	29,613
Ojai 93023	7,091	San Carlos 94070	25,008	Thousand Oaks.. 91360*	90,639
Olivehurst 95961	8,929[1]	San Clemente ... 92672	28,722	Tiburon 94920	6,664
Ontario......... 91761*	96,790	San Diego 92199*	915,956	Torrance........ 90510*	130,213
Orange 92667	94,606	San Dimas 91773	26,080	Tracy 95376	20,364
Orangevale 95662	20,585[1]	San Fernando ... 91346*	18,296	Tulare 93274	23,697
Orinda 94563	16,843[1]	San Francisco ... 94101*	691,637	Turlock 95380	28,681
Oroville 95965*	9,517	San Gabriel 91776	30,785	Tustin 92680	38,371
Oxnard 93030	115,657	San Jacinto 92383	7,981	Tustin–Foothills . 92705	26,174[1]
Pacific Grove.... 93950	15,853	San Jose........ 95101*	659,181	Twentynine Palms 92277	7,465[1]
Pacifica 94044	36,865	San Juan		Ukiah 95482	12,350
Palm Desert 92260	13,009	Capistrano 92690*	20,453	Union City 94587	42,413
Palm Springs 92263	33,799	San Leandro 94577*	64,606	Upland 91786	49,844
Palmdale 93550	14,298[1]	San Lorenzo 94580	20,545[1]	Vacaville 95688	46,945
Palo Alto 94303*	54,968	San Luis Obispo . 93401	34,252	Valencia 91355	12,163[1]
Palos Verdes Est. 90274	14,190	San Marcos 92069	18,576	Valinda 91744	18,700[1]

[1] 1980 Census. [2] 1982 Census Bureau estimate.

PLACE AND ZIP CODE	POP.[2]	PLACE AND ZIP CODE	POP.[2]	PLACE AND ZIP CODE	POP.[2]

CALIFORNIA (continued)

PLACE AND ZIP CODE	POP.	PLACE AND ZIP CODE	POP.	PLACE AND ZIP CODE	POP.
Vallejo......... 94590	85,824	Walnut Park..... 90255	11,811[1]	Westlake 94015	6,106
Ventura 93002*	80,759	Wasco.......... 93280	10,499	Westminster 92683	72,602
Victorville....... 92392	16,569	Watsonville 95076	24,563	Westmont 90047	27,916[1]
View Park–		West Athens 90044	8,531[1]	Whittier 90605*	69,059
Windsor Hills.. 90043	12,101[1]	West Carson 90502	17,997[1]	Willowbrook..... 90222	30,845
Villa Park 92667	7,099	West Covina 91793	86,530	Woodland....... 95695	31,498
Vine Hill–Pacheco —	6,129[1]	West Hollywood . 90069	35,703[1]	Yorba Linda..... 92686	31,275
Visalia 93277	53,238	W. Puente Valley. 91746	20,445[1]	Yreka 96097	6,386
Vista 92083	39,614	W. Sacramento .. 95691	10,875[1]	Yuba City 95991	19,890
Walnut 91789	13,578	West Whittier–		Yucaipa 92399	23,345[1]
Walnut Creek... 94596*	56,246	Los Nietos 90605	21,001[1]	Yucca Valley 92284	8,294[1]

COLORADO (Colo. or CO)

PLACE AND ZIP CODE	POP.	PLACE AND ZIP CODE	POP.	PLACE AND ZIP CODE	POP.
Alamosa 81101	6,854	Englewood 80110*	31,434	Longmont....... 80501	45,711
Applewood —	12,040[1]	Evergreen 80439	6,376[1]	Louisville 80027	6,081
Arvada 80001	88,478	Federal Heights.. 80221	8,103	Loveland........ 80537	32,340
Aurora 80010*	184,372	Fort Carson 80913	13,219[1]	Montrose 81401	9,494
Boulder......... 80302	78,178	Fort Collins 80521*	68,534	Northglenn...... 80233	30,201
Brighton 80601	13,473	Fort Morgan.... 80701	8,913	Pueblo 81003*	100,934
Broomfield...... 80020	22,244	Fountain 80817	9,201	Salida 81201	4,863
Canon City...... 81212	13,367	Golden 80401*	13,269	Security–Widefield 80931	18,768[1]
Castlewood —	16,413[1]	Grand Junction.. 81501	31,014	Sherrelwood —	17,629[1]
Colorado Springs 80901*	231,699	Greeley......... 80631	53,502	Southglenn 80161	37,787[1]
Columbine —	23,523[1]	Gunnison 81230	5,968	Sterling........ 80751	11,642
Commerce City.. 80022	16,558	Ken Caryl —	10,661[1]	Thornton 80229	44,417
Cortez.......... 81321	7,657	La Junta 81050	8,365	Trinidad 81082	9,785
Craig........... 81625	9,991	Lafayette 80026	10,457	Welby —	9,668[1]
Denver 80202*	505,563	Lakewood 80215	118,498	Westminster 80030	55,098
Derby —	8,578[1]	Lamar 81052	7,915	Westminister East 80030	6,002[1]
Durango 81301	12,389	Littleton 80120*	31,770	Wheat Ridge 80033	30,589

CONNECTICUT (Conn. or CT)

PLACE AND ZIP CODE	POP.	PLACE AND ZIP CODE	POP.	PLACE AND ZIP CODE	POP.
Ansonia 06401	19,114	Killingly † 06239	14,719	Rocky Hill † 06067	15,108
Avon † 06001	12,086	Ledyard † 06339	14,050	Seymour † 06483	13,674
Berlin 06037	15,351	Litchfield † 06759	7,580	Shelton 06484	32,328
Bethel † 06801	16,507	Madison † 06443	14,676	Simsbury † 06070	21,463
Bloomfield 06002	18,787	Manchester † .. 06040	49,483	Somers † 06071	8,959
Branford † 06405	6,011	Mansfield † 06250	20,409	South Windsor † . 06074	17,760
Bridgeport 06602*	143,745	Meriden 06450	57,871	Southbury † 06488	14,431
Bristol......... 06010	57,626	Middlebury † 06762	6,058	Southington † ... 06489	37,133
Brookfield † 06804	13,440	Middletown 06457	38,886	Stafford † 06075	9,367
Burlington † 06013	6,011	Milford 06460	49,678	Stamford 06904*	103,614
Canton † 06019	7,845	Monroe † 06468	14,529	Stonington † 06378	16,398
Cheshire † 06410	22,208	Montville † 06353	16,830	Storrs 06268	11,394[1]
Clinton † 06413	11,330	Naugatuck 06770	27,382	Stratford † 06497	50,752
Colchester † ... 06415	8,114	New Britain 06050	73,362	Suffield † 06078	9,599
Coventry † 06238	9,203	New Canaan † .. 06840	18,039	Thomaston † 06787	6,236
Cromwell † 06416	10,445	New Fairfield † . 06810*	12,269	Thompson † 06277	8,141[1]
Danbury 06810*	62,404	New Haven...... 06511*	125,348	Tolland † 06084	9,829
Darien † 06820	18,958	New London 06320	29,338	Torrington ..+... 06790	31,428
Derby 06418	12,272	New Milford † .. 06776	20,254	Trumbull † 06611	33,295
East Hampton † . 06424	8,687	Newington † 06111	28,939	Vernon † 06066	28,553
East Hartford † . 06108	51,906	Newtown † 06470	19,747	Wallingford † 06492	37,357
East Haven † ... 06512	25,078	North Branford † 06471	11,771	Waterbury 06701*	102,940
East Lyme † 06333	14,213	North Haven † ... 06473	21,963	Waterford † 06385	17,693
East Windsor † .. 06088	8,973	Norwalk 06856*	78,851	Watertown † 06795	19,537
Easton † 06612	6,472	Norwich 06360	38,526	West Hartford † . 06107	60,683
Ellington † 06029	9,990	Oakville 06779	8,737[1]	West Haven 06516	53,412
Enfield † 06082	42,564	Old Lyme † 06371	6,401	Weston † 06883	8,476
Fairfield † 06430	54,623	Old Saybrook † .. 06475	9,430	Westport † 06880	25,734
Farmington †.... 06032	16,643	Orange † 06477	13,059	Wethersfield † ... 06109	25,705
Glastonbury..... 06033	24,568	Oxford † 06483	6,881	Willimantic 06226	14,652
Granby † 06035	8,189	Plainfield † 06374	13,244	Wilton † 06897	15,457
Greenwich † 06830	60,122	Plainville † 06062	16,783	Winchester † 06094	10,891
Griswold † 06351	9,008	Plymouth † 06782	10,976	Windham † 06280	21,263
Groton 06340	40,341	Portland † 06480	8,226	Windsor † 06095	25,694
Guilford † 06437	17,880	Prospect † 06712	6,811	Windsor Locks † . 06096	12,069
Haddam † 06438	6,628	Putnam.......... 06260	7,007	Wolcott † 06716	12,841
Hamden † 06514	51,171	Redding † 06875	7,371	Woodbridge † .. 06525	7,856
Hartford 06101*	136,334	Ridgefield † 06877	20,727	Woodbury † 06798	7,312

1 1980 Census.　　2 1982 Census Bureau estimate.　　3 † Town or township (includes rural population).

PLACE AND ZIP CODE	POP.[2]	PLACE AND ZIP CODE	POP.[2]	PLACE AND ZIP CODE	POP.[2]
DELAWARE (Del. or DE)					
Brookside 19713	15,255[1]	Edgemoor 19809	7,397[1]	Talleyville 19803	6,880[1]
Claymont 19703	10,022[1]	Elsmere	6,493[1]	Wilmington 19850*	69,896
Dover 19901	23,125	Newark 19711*	25,228	Wilmington Manor	9,233[1]
FLORIDA (Fla. or FL)					
Altamonte Springs 32701	24,021	Fern Park 32730	8,890[1]	Lehigh Acres 33936	9,604[1]
Apopka 32703	6,661	Fernandina Beach 32034	7,754	Leisure City —	17,905[1]
Arcadia 33821	6,063	Ferry Pass 32504	16,910[1]	Leto 33614	9,003[1]
Atlantic Beach 32233	8,425	Florida City 33034	6,382	Lighthouse Point. 33064	11,347
Auburndale 33823	7,061	Forest City 32714	6,819[1]	Lindgren Acres —	11,986[1]
Aventura —	9,698	Fort Lauderdale 33310*	153,755	Live Oak 32060	7,019
Avon Park 33825	8,537	Fort Myers 33906*	38,271	Lockhart 32860	10,569[1]
Azalea Park 32857	8,301[1]	Fort Pierce 33454*	36,001	Longwood 32750	11,451
Bartow 33830	15,570	Ft. Walton Beach 32548	21,716	Lynn Haven 32444	7,283
Bayonet Point	14,945[1]	Gainesville 32602*	83,704	Maitland 32751	9,019
Bayshore Gdns. 33507	14,945[1]	Gladview —	18,919[1]	Mango-Seffner 33550	6,439[1]
Beacon Square —	6,513[1]	Glenvar Hts. —	13,216[1]	Marathon 33050	7,568[1]
Bellair–Mdwbrk. Terr.	12,144[1]	Golden Glades —	23,154[1]	Margate 33063	38,753
Belle Glade 33430	16,977	Goldenrod 32733	13,682[1]	Marianna 32446	7,132
Bellview 32620	15,439[1]	Gonzales 32560	6,084[1]	Melbourne 32901*	49,937
Boca Raton 33432*	53,615	Goulds 33170	7,078[1]	Merritt Island 32952	30,708[1]
Boynton Beach 33435	37,938	Greenacres City —	13,967	Miami 33152*	382,726
Bradenton 33506*	34,099	Gulf Gate Est. —	9,284[1]	Miami Beach 33139	93,702
Brandon 33511	41,826[1]	Gulfport 33737	11,414	Miami Gardens —	9,025[1]
Brent 32503	21,872[1]	Haines City 33844	11,757	Miami Lakes —	9,809[1]
Brooksville 33512	6,488	Hallandale 33009	36,517[1]	Miami Shores 33153	9,139
Browardale —	7,409[1]	Hialeah 33010*	154,713	Miami Springs 33266	12,095
Brownsville —	18,058[1]	Hobe Sound 33455	6,822[1]	Milton 32570	7,449
Callaway 32401	7,861	Holden Heights 32805	13,864[1]	Mims 32754	7,583[1]
Cape Canaveral 32920	6,248	Holiday 33590	18,392[1]	Miramar 33023	34,721
Cape Coral 33910	38,832	Holly Hill 32017	10,487	Mount Dora 32757	6,266
Carol City 33055	47,349[1]	Hollywood 33022*	122,051	Myrtle Grove 32506	14,238[1]
Casselberry 32707	16,929	Homestead 33030*	21,638	Naples 33941*	19,181
Century Village —	10,619[1]	Homestead Base 33039	7,594[1]	Naranja-Princeton 33032	10,381[1]
Clearwater 33575*	90,238	Immokalee 33934	11,038[1]	New Port Richey 33552*	12,329
Cocoa 32922	17,492	Indian Harbor Bch. 32937	6,469	New Smyrna Beach 32069	14,209
Cocoa Beach 32931	11,911	Inwood 33880	6,668[1]	Niceville 32578	9,475
Cocoa West 32922	6,432[1]	Ives Estates —	12,623[1]	Norland 33169	19,471[1]
Coconut Creek —	9,482	Jacksonville 32203*	556,370	N. Andrews Gardens —	8,967[1]
Collier City —	7,135[1]	Jacksonville Bch. 32240	16,662	North Fort Myers 33903	22,880[1]
Collier Manor —	7,045[1]	Jasmine Estates —	11,995[1]	North Lauderdale 33068	20,310
Conway 32809	24,027[1]	Jensen Beach 33457	6,639[1]	North Miami 33261	43,108
Cooper City 33328	11,868	Jupiter 33458	12,990	N. Miami Beach 33160	36,481
Coral Gables 33114	43,266	Kendale Lakes —	32,769[1]	North Naples 33940	7,950[1]
Coral Springs 33065	44,731	Kendall 33256	73,758[1]	N. Palm Beach 33408	11,670
Coral Terrace —	22,702	Kendall Green —	6,768[1]	North Port 33596	7,905
Crestview 32536	7,946	Key Biscayne 33149	6,313[1]	Oak Ridge —	15,477[1]
Crystal Lake —	6,827[1]	Key Largo 33037	7,447[1]	Oakland Park 33307	23,821
Cutler —	15,593[1]	Key West 33040	25,134	Ocala 32678*	40,722
Cutler Ridge 33157	20,886[1]	Killearn —	8,700[1]	Ocoee 32761	10,225
Cypress Gardens 33880	8,043[1]	Kings Point —	8,724[1]	Ojus 33163	17,344[1]
Cypress Lake —	8,721[1]	Kissimmee 32741	18,642	Olympia Hts. 33265	33,112[1]
Dania 33004	12,344	Lake Carroll —	13,012[1]	Oneco 33558	6,417[1]
Davie 33328	32,311	Lake City 32055	9,354	Opa–Locka 33054	15,312
Daytona Beach 32015*	55,504	Lake Lucerne —	9,762[1]	Orange Park 32073	9,485
De Land 32720	15,786	Lake Magdalene 33612	13,331[1]	Orlando 32802*	134,255
Deerfield Beach 33441	41,274	Lake Park 33403	7,049	Orlovista 32861	6,474[1]
Del Rio —	7,409[1]	Lake Wales 33853*	8,756	Ormond Beach 32074	23,535
Delray Beach 33444	39,628	Lake Worth 33461*	27,965	Ormond-by-the-Sea 32074	7,665[1]
Deltona 32728	15,710[1]	Lakeland 33802*	51,788	Pahokee 33476	6,441
Dunedin 33528	31,079	Lakeland Highlands —	10,426[1]	Palatka 32077	10,526
East Naples 33942	12,127[1]	Lakeside —	10,534[1]	Palm Bay 32906	26,421
Edgewater 32032	8,239	Lantana 33465	8,488	Palm Beach 33480	10,286
Egypt Lake 33614	11,932[1]	Largo 33540*	60,339	Palm Beach Gardens 33410	17,329
Elfers 33531	11,396[1]	Lauderdale Lakes 33313	26,749	Palm Springs —	9,015
Englewood 33533	9,663	Lauderhill 33313	38,963	Palmetto 33561	9,125
Ensley 32504	14,422[1]	Laurel 33545	6,368[1]	Palmetto Estates —	11,116[1]
Eustis 32726	10,188	Lealman —	19,873	Panama City 32401*	34,565
Fairview Shores —	10,174[1]	Leesburg 32748	13,844	Pembroke Pines 33084	41,791

[1] 1980 Census. [2] 1982 Census Bureau estimate.

PLACE AND ZIP CODE	POP.[1]	PLACE AND ZIP CODE	POP.[1]	PLACE AND ZIP CODE	POP.[1]

FLORIDA (continued)

PLACE AND ZIP CODE	POP.[1]	PLACE AND ZIP CODE	POP.[1]	PLACE AND ZIP CODE	POP.[1]			
Pensacola	32501*	58,967[2]	Satellite Beach	32937	9,652[2]	Titusville	32780	34,805[2]
Perrine	33257	16,129	Scott Lake	—	14,154	Town 'n' Country	33685	37,834
Perry	32347	8,563[2]	Sebring	33870	9,933[2]	Treasure Island	33740	6,570[2]
Pine Castle	32859	9,992	Siesta Key	33578	7,010	Union Park	32867	19,175
Pine Hills	32858	35,771	Sky Lake	—	6,692	University	33124	24,514
Pinellas Park	33565	35,565[2]	South Apopka	32703	5,687	Valparaiso	32580	6,232[2]
Pinewood	—	16,252	South Bradenton	—	14,297	Venice	33595*	13,180[2]
Plant City	33566	17,670[2]	South Daytona	32021	11,688[2]	Venice Gardens	—	6,568
Plantation	33317	51,487[2]	South Miami	33243	10,821[2]	Vero Beach	32960	17,488[2]
Pompano Beach	33060*	58,036[2]	South Miami Hts.	—	23,559	Villas	—	8,724
Pompano Beach Highlands	—	16,154	South Patrick Shores	—	9,816	Warrington	32507	15,792
Port Charlotte	33952	25,770	South Venice	33595	8,075	Washington Park	—	7,240
Port Orange	32029	22,742[2]	Southgate	34277	7,322	Wekiva Springs	—	13,386
Port St. Lucie	33485	22,563[2]	Spring Hill	33526	6,468	West Bradenton	—	8,767
Punta Gorda	33950*	7,772[2]	Springfield	32401	7,554[2]	West Little River	—	32,492
Quincy	32351	8,692[2]	Stuart	33494*	10,248[2]	West Miami	33174	6,373[2]
Richmond Hts.	—	8,577	Sunny Isles	33160	12,564	West Palm Beach	33401*	66,243[2]
Riviera Beach	33404	28,437[2]	Sunrise	33304	44,629[2]	West Pensacola	—	24,371
Rockledge	32955	12,566[2]	Sunset	—	13,531	Westchester	—	29,272
Safety Harbor	33572	7,891[2]	Sweetwater	—	9,280[2]	Westview	—	9,102
St. Augustine	32084	12,492[2]	Tallahassee	32301*	102,579[2]	Westwood Lakes	—	11,478
St. Cloud	32769	8,632[2]	Tamarac	33320	30,679[2]	Wilton Manors	33334	12,668[2]
St. Petersburg	33730*	241,214[2]	Tamiami	33144	17,607	Winston	—	9,315
St. Petersbg. Bch.	33736	9,397[2]	Tampa	33630*	276,413[2]	Winter Garden	32787	6,890[2]
Sanford	32771	25,572[2]	Tanglewood	—	8,229	Winter Haven	33880	21,762[2]
Sarasota	33578*	50,632[2]	Tarpon Springs	33589*	14,137[2]	Winter Park	32789*	22,357[2]
Sarasota Springs	—	13,860	Temple Terrace	33687	11,535[2]	Winter Springs	32708	13,292[2]
			Tice	33905	6,645	Wright	32548	13,011

GEORGIA (Ga. or GA)

PLACE AND ZIP CODE	POP.[1]	PLACE AND ZIP CODE	POP.[1]	PLACE AND ZIP CODE	POP.[1]			
Albany	31706*	74,425	East Point	30344	37,486	North Druid Hills	—	12,438
Americus	31709	16,120	Fair Oaks	30060	8,486	Panthersville	—	11,366
Athens	30603*	42,549	Fairview	—	6,558	Peachtree City	30269	6,429
Atlanta	30304*	428,153[2]	Fitzgerald	31750	10,187	Perry	31069	9,453
Augusta	30901*	47,532	Forest Park	30050	18,782	Riverdale	30274	7,121
Bainbridge	31717	10,553	Fort Benning S.	—	15,074	Rome	30161	29,654
Belvedere Park	—	17,776	Fort Gordon	30905	14,069	Roswell	30077	23,337
Blakely	31723	5,880	Fort Stewart	31314	15,031	St. Simons	31522	6,566
Brunswick	31520*	17,605	Fort Valley	31030	9,000	Sandersville	31082	6,137
Buford	30518	6,578	Gainesville	30501	15,280	Sandy Springs	30358	46,877
Cairo	31728	8,777	Garden City	31408	6,895	Savannah	31401*	145,699[2]
Camilla	31730	5,414	Gresham Park	—	6,232	Scottdale	30079	8,770
Candler-McAfee	—	27,306	Griffin	30223	20,728	Smyrna	30080	20,312
Carrollton	30117	14,078	Hapeville	30354	6,166	Snellville	30278	8,514
Cartersville	30120	9,247	Hinesville	31313	11,309	South Augusta	—	51,072
Cedartown	30125	8,619	Jesup	31545	9,418	Statesboro	30458	14,866
Chamblee	30341	7,137	La Fayette	30728	6,517	Swainsboro	30401	7,602
College Park	30354	24,632	La Grange	30240	24,204	Sylvester	31791	5,860
Conley	30027	6,033	Lawrenceville	30245	8,928	Thomaston	30286	9,682
Conyers	30207*	6,567	Lithia Springs	30057	9,145	Thomasville	31792	18,463
Cordele	31015	11,184	Mableton	30059	25,111	Thomson	30824	7,001
Covington	30209	10,586	Macon	31213*	118,730[2]	Tifton	31794	13,749
Dalton	30720	20,548	Marietta	30060	30,805	Toccoa	30577	9,104
Decatur	30030*	18,404	Martinez	30907	16,472	Tucker	30084	25,399
Dock Junction	—	6,189	Midway-Hardwick	31320	8,977	Valdosta	31603*	37,596
Doraville	30340	7,414	Milledgeville	31061	12,176	Vidalia	30474	10,393
Douglas	31533	10,980	Monroe	30655	8,854	Warner Robbins	31093	39,893
Douglasville	30134	7,641	Moultrie	31768	15,105	Waycross	31501	19,371
Druid Hills	30333	12,700	Mountain Park	—	9,425	Waynesboro	30830	5,760
Dublin	31021	16,083	Newnan	30263	11,449	West Augusta	—	24,242
Dunwoody	30338	17,768	North Atlanta	30319	30,521	Wilmington Is	31410	7,546
			North Decatur	30033	11,830	Winder	30680	6,705

HAWAII (HI)

PLACE AND ZIP CODE	POP.[1]	PLACE AND ZIP CODE	POP.[1]	PLACE AND ZIP CODE	POP.[1]			
Ahuimanu	—	6,238	Kaneohe	96744	29,919	Nanakuli	96792	8,185
Aiea	96701	32,879	Kihei	96753	5,644	Pearl City	96782	42,575
Ewa Beach	96706	14,369	Lahaina	96761	16,095	Schofield Barracks	96857	18,851
Hilo	96720	35,269	Makaha	—	6,582	Wahiawa	96786	16,911
Honolulu	96820*	365,048	Makakilo City	—	7,691	Waianae	96792	7,941
Kahului	96732	12,978	Mililani	96789	21,365	Wailuku	96793	10,260
Kailua	96734	35,812	Mokapu	—	11,615	Waipahu	96797	29,139

[1] 1980 Census. [2] 1982 Census Bureau estimate.

PLACE AND ZIP CODE	POP.[2]	PLACE AND ZIP CODE	POP.[2]	PLACE AND ZIP CODE	POP.[2]
IDAHO (Ida. or ID)					
Ammon 83401	4,598	Idaho Falls 83401	40,700	Payette 83661	5,390
Blackfoot 83221	10,082	Jerome 83338	7,102	Pocatello 83201	46,494
Boise City 83708*	104,586	Lewiston 83501	27,762	Post Falls 83854	6,030
Burley 83318	8,959	Meridian 83642	6,882	Rexburg 83440	12,084
Caldwell 83605	17,699	Moscow 83843	17,338	Rupert 83350	5,441
Chubbuck 83202	8,732	Mountain Home 83647	7,844	Twin Falls 83301	26,947
Coeur D'Alene 83814	21,855	Nampa 83651	26,242	Weiser 83672	4,743
ILLINOIS (Ill. or IL)					
Addison 60101	30,366	Dixon 61021	15,101	Lincolnwood 60645	11,883
Algonquin 60102	6,134	Dolton 60419	24,391	Lindenhurst —	6,465
Alsip 60658	17,414	Downers Grove 60515	42,801	Lisle 60532	14,999
Alton 62002	33,545	Du Quoin 62832	6,490	Litchfield 62056	7,033
Arlington Heights 60004*	66,457	East Alton 62024	6,876	Lockport 60441	8,988
Aurora 60507*	81,899	East Moline 61244	21,556	Lombard 60148	37,830
Barrington 60010	9,285	East Peoria 61611	22,494	Loves Park 61130	14,036
Bartlett 60103	14,288	East St. Louis 62201*	53,381	Lyons 60534	9,846
Bartonville 61607	6,140	Edwardsville 62025	12,484	Macomb 61455	20,526
Batavia 60510	12,782	Effingham 62401	11,228	Marion 62959	14,243
Beardstown 62618	6,180	Elgin 60120	64,407	Markham 60426	15,534
Belleville 62220*	41,496	Elk Grove 60007	29,572	Matteson 60443	10,852
Bellwood 60104	20,039	Elmhurst 60126	44,213	Mattoon 61938	19,203
Belvidere 61008	15,393	Elmwood Park 60635	23,672	Maywood 60153	27,766
Bensenville 60106	16,216	Evanston 60204*	73,056	McHenry 60050	11,913
Benton 62812	7,722	Evergreen Park 60642	21,706	Melrose Park 60160*	20,518
Berwyn 60402	45,905	Fairfield 62837	6,060	Mendota 61342	7,036
Bethalto 62010	8,570	Fairview Heights 62208	11,987	Metropolis 62960	7,020
Bloomingdale 60108	13,289	Flossmoor 60422	8,392	Midlothian 60445	14,233
Bloomington 61701	45,402	Forest Park 60130	15,375	Milan 61264	6,332
Blue Island 60406	21,818	Fox Lake 60020	7,152	Moline 61265	46,340
Bolingbrook 60439	38,866	Franklin Park 60131	17,515	Monmouth 61462	10,499
Bourbonnais 60914	13,606	Freeport 61032	26,184	Morris 60450	8,693
Bradley 60915	11,459	Galesburg 61401	34,112	Morton 61550	14,014
Bridgeview 60455	14,187	Geneseo 61254	6,091	Morton Grove 60053	23,554
Broadview 60153	8,749	Geneva 60134	9,850	Mount Carmel 62863	9,017
Brookfield 60513	19,229	Glen Ellyn 60137	23,872	Mount Prospect 60056	52,581
Buffalo Grove 60090	23,585	Glencoe 60022	9,040	Mount Vernon 62864	17,595
Burbank 60459	28,146	Glendale Heights 60139	24,788	Mundelein 60060	17,121
Cahokia 62206	18,553	Glenview 60025	33,319	Murphysboro 62966	9,927
Calumet City 60409	39,638	Glenwood 60425	10,497	Naperville 60566	45,769
Calumet Park 60643	8,733	Granite City 62040	35,990	Niles 60648	30,011
Canton 61520	14,166	Gurnee 60031	7,597	Normal 61761	35,635
Carbondale 62901	26,439	Hanover Park 60103	30,602	Norridge 60656	16,045
Carmi 62821	6,474	Harrisburg 62946	10,608	North Chicago 60064	40,882
Carol Stream —	17,639	Harvey 60426	35,609	North Riverside 60546	6,570
Carpentersville 60110	23,039	Harwood Heights 60656	7,925	Northbrook 60062	31,401
Cary 60013	6,797	Hazel Crest 60429	13,992	Northlake 60164	12,304
Centralia 62801	15,018	Herrin 62948	10,687	Oak Brook 60521	7,083
Centreville —	9,826	Hickory Hills 60457	13,982	Oak Forest 60452	26,799
Champaign 61820	59,011	Highland 62249	7,050	Oak Lawn 60454*	59,488
Charleston 61920	19,372	Highland Park 60035*	30,704	Oak Park 60301*	54,751
Chester 62233	8,134	Hillside 60162	8,195	O'Fallon 62269	12,991
Chicago 60607*	2,997,155	Hinsdale 60521	16,686	Olney 62450	9,617
Chicago Heights 60411	36,189	Hoffman Estates 60195	38,768	Orland Park 60462	24,405
Chicago Ridge 60415	14,112	Homewood 60430	19,304	Ottawa 61350	17,973
Chillicothe 61523	6,194	Hoopeston 60942	6,183	Palatine 60067	33,301
Cicero 60650	61,115	Itasca 60143	7,203	Palos Heights 60463	10,982
Clarendon Hills 60514	6,827	Jacksonville 62650	19,940	Palos Hills 60465	16,688
Clinton 61727	7,896	Jerseyville 62052	7,447	Pana 62557	5,715
Collinsville 62234	19,684	Joliet 60436*	76,678	Paris 61944	9,720
Country Club Hills 60477	15,000	Justice 60458	10,392	Park Forest 60466	26,378
Countryside —	6,568	Kankakee 60901	29,317	Park Forest South 60466	6,384
Crestwood —	11,407	Kewanee 61443	13,506	Park Ridge 60068	37,861
Creve Coeur 61611	6,711	La Grange 60525	15,625	Pekin 61554	33,602
Crystal Lake 60014	18,817	La Grange Park 60525	13,143	Peoria 61601*	122,261
Danville 61832	38,034	La Salle 61301	9,968	Peoria Heights 61614	7,460
Darien 60559	15,512	Lake Forest 60045	15,520	Peru 61354	10,570
De Kalb 60115	32,823	Lake Zurich 60047	8,682	Pontiac 61764	11,255
Decatur 62521*	92,733	Lansing 60438	28,480	Princeton 61356	7,269
Deerfield 60015	17,215	Libertyville 60048	16,827	Prospect Heights 60070	12,722
Des Plaines 60018*	55,945	Lincoln 62656	15,684	Quincy 62301*	42,335

1 1980 Census. 2 1982 Census Bureau estimate.

PLACE AND ZIP CODE		POP.[2]	PLACE AND ZIP CODE		POP.[2]	PLACE AND ZIP CODE		POP.[2]

ILLINOIS (continued)

Place	ZIP	Pop.	Place	ZIP	Pop.	Place	ZIP	Pop.
Rantoul	61866	21,215	Schaumberg	60194	55,962	Warrenville	60555	8,118
Richton Park	60471	9,917	Schiller Park	60176	11,579	Washington	61571	10,339
River Forest	60305	12,086	Silvis	61282	7,113	Washington Park	62204	8,365
River Grove	60171	10,127	Skokie	60076*	59,766	Waukegan	60085*	69,270
Riverdale	60627	13,040	South Elgin	60177	6,304	West Chicago	60185	13,094
Riverside	60546	9,086	South Holland	60473	24,263	West Frankfort	62896	9,594
Robbins	60472	8,801	Springfield	62703*	99,370	Westchester	60153	17,302
Robinson	62454	7,295	Steger	60475	8,826	Western Springs	60558	12,791
Rochelle	61068	8,444	Sterling	61081*	15,812	Westmont	60559	17,880
Rock Falls	61071	10,673	Streamwood	60103	23,858	Wheaton	60187	44,341
Rock Island	61201	46,623	Streator	61364*	14,257	Wheeling	60090	24,824
Rockford	61125*	138,334	Summit	60501	9,988	Wilmette	60091	27,655
Rolling Meadows	60008	20,763	Sycamore	60178	9,401	Winnetka	60093	12,699
Romeoville	60441	15,478	Taylorville	62568	10,944	Wood Dale	60191	11,408
Roselle	60194*	17,569	Tinley Park	60477	27,133	Wood River	62095	12,196
Round Lake Bch.	60073	13,449	Urbana	61801	35,764	Woodridge	60517	23,066
St. Charles	60174	17,782	Vandalia	62471	6,098	Woodstock	60098	11,907
Salem	62881	7,810	Vernon Hills	60061	10,973	Worth	60482	11,722
Sauk Village	60411	10,836	Villa Park	60181	22,865	Zion	60099	18,394

INDIANA (Ind. or IN)

Place	ZIP	Pop.	Place	ZIP	Pop.	Place	ZIP	Pop.
Alexandria	46001	5,730	Goshen	46526*	19,661	Mount Vernon	47620	7,878
Anderson	46018*	62,148	Greencastle	46135	8,426	Muncie	47302*	75,510
Auburn	46706	8,290	Greenfield	46140	11,363	Munster	46321	20,607
Bedford	47421	13,753	Greensburg	47240	9,272	New Albany	47150	37,869
Beech Grove	46107	12,942	Greenwood	46142	20,811	New Castle	47362	19,167
Bloomington	47401	53,045	Griffith	46319	16,462	New Haven	46774	7,046
Bluffton	46714	8,572	Hammond	46320*	91,546	Noblesville	46060	12,467
Boonville	47601	6,710	Hartford City	47348	7,551	Peru	46970	13,168
Brazil	47834	7,730	Highland	46322	25,165	Plainfield	46168	9,723
Brownsburg	46112	6,475	Hobart	46342	22,966	Plymouth	46563	7,920
Carmel	46032	18,588	Huntington	46750	15,503	Portage	46368	28,392
Cedar Lake	46303	8,932	Indianapolis	46206*	707,655	Portland	47371	6,828
Chesterton	46304	8,668	Jasper	47546	8,987	Princeton	47670	9,389
Clarksville	47130	14,988	Jeffersonville	47130	20,880	Richmond	47374	40,752
Columbus	47201	30,890	Kendallville	46755	7,333	Rushville	46173	5,824
Connersville	47331	16,646	Kokomo	46902	46,043	Schererville	46375	13,953
Crawfordsville	47933	13,037	La Porte	46350*	21,872	Seymour	47274	15,489
Crown Point	46307	16,487	Lafayette	47901*	43,914	Shelbyville	46176	14,894
Decatur	46733	8,496	Lake Station	46405	14,928	South Bend	46624*	107,690
Dyer	46311	9,672	Lawrence	46226	25,445	Speedway	46224	12,691
East Chicago	46312	38,458	Lebanon	46052	12,156	Tell City	47586	8,723
Elkhart	46515	41,005	Linton	47441	6,287	Terre Haute	47808*	60,297
Elwood	46036	10,471	Logansport	46947	17,645	Valparaiso	46383	22,773
Evansville	47708*	130,275	Madison	47250	11,962	Vincennes	47591	21,333
Fort Wayne	46802*	167,633	Marion	46952	34,698	Wabash	46992	12,455
Frankfort	46041	15,449	Martinsville	46151	11,578	Warsaw	46580	10,863
Franklin	46131	11,590	Merrillville	46410	27,526	Washington*	47501	11,596
Gary	46401*	147,537	Michigan City	46360	36,608	West Lafayette	47906	21,717
Gas City	46933	6,320	Mishawaka	46544	40,898			

IOWA (Ia. or IA)

Place	ZIP	Pop.	Place	ZIP	Pop.	Place	ZIP	Pop.
Algona	50511	6,285	Davenport	52802*	103,799	Mason City	50401	30,157
Altoona	50009	6,100	Decorah	52101	8,020	Mount Pleasant	52641	7,209
Ames	50010	45,747	Denison	51442	6,911	Muscatine	52761	24,218
Ankeny	50021	15,801	Des Moines	50318*	191,506	Newton	50208	15,162
Atlantic	50022	7,920	Dubuque	52001	61,209	Oelwein	50662	7,501
Bettendorf	52722	27,561	Estherville	51334	7,440	Oskaloosa	52577	10,995
Boone	50036	12,555	Fairfield	52556	9,459	Ottumwa	52501	26,950
Burlington	52601	29,090	Fort Dodge	50501	28,857	Pella	50219	8,500
Carroll	51401	9,607	Fort Madison	52627	13,192	Perry	50220	6,848
Cedar Falls	50613	36,206	Grinnell	50112	8,698	Red Oak	51566	6,702
Cedar Rapids	52401*	109,086	Independence	50644	6,463	Shenandoah	51601	6,220
Centerville	52544	6,492	Indianola	50125	10,760	Sioux City	51101*	82,095
Charles City	50616	8,678	Iowa City	52240	51,559	Spencer	51301	11,593
Cherokee	51012	6,788	Iowa Falls	50126	6,127	Storm Lake	50588	8,819
Clear Lake City	50428	7,529	Keokuk	52632	13,524	Urbandale	50322	19,010
Clinton	52732	32,437	Knoxville	50138	8,175	Washington	52353	6,739
Clive	50053	6,213	Le Mars	51031	8,045	Waterloo	50701*	76,399
Coralville	52241	7,878	Maquoketa	52060	6,407	Waverly	50677	8,506
Council Bluffs	51501	56,694	Marion	52302	19,897	Webster City	50595	8,817
Creston	50801	8,351	Marshalltown	50158	27,221	West Des Moines	50265	21,976

[1] 1980 Census. [2] 1982 Census Bureau estimate.

PLACE AND ZIP CODE	POP.[2]	PLACE AND ZIP CODE	POP.[2]	PLACE AND ZIP CODE	POP.[2]

KANSAS (Kan., Kans., or KS)

PLACE AND ZIP CODE	POP.[2]	PLACE AND ZIP CODE	POP.[2]	PLACE AND ZIP CODE	POP.[2]			
Abilene	67410	6,640	Great Bend	67530	17,697	Mission	66222	8,633
Arkansas City	67005	13,608	Hays	67601	17,554	Newton	67114	16,661
Atchison	66002	11,911	Haysville	67060	8,365	Olathe	66061	42,248
Augusta	67010	7,328	Hutchinson	67501	40,411	Ottawa	66067	10,987
Bonner Springs	66012	6,591	Independence	67301	11,131	Overland Park	66204	84,262
Chanute	66720	11,201	Iola	66749	6,981	Parsons	42340	13,052
Coffeyville	67337	15,575	Junction City	66441	20,381	Pittsburg	66762	18,749
Colby	67701	5,611	Kansas City	66110*	162,211	Prairie Village	66208	24,389
Concordia	66901	6,625	Lansing	66043	6,171	Pratt	67124	7,223
Derby	67037	10,504	Lawrence	66044	54,307	Roeland Park	66203	7,884
Dodge City	67801	18,775	Leavenworth	66048	33,621	Russell	67665	5,411
El Dorado	67042	11,835	Leawood	66206	13,905	Salina	67401	42,406
Emporia	66801	26,528	Lenexa	66215	20,610	Shawnee	66203	30,651
Fort Riley North	—	16,086[1]	Liberal	67901	16,076	Topeka	66603*	120,269
Fort Scott	66701	8,825	Manhattan	66502	33,294	Wellington	67152	8,308
Garden City	67846	20,082	McPherson	67460	12,030	Wichita	67276*	288,723
Goodland	67735	5,465	Merriam	66203	10,842	Winfield	67156	12,201

KENTUCKY (Ky., Ken., or KY)

PLACE AND ZIP CODE	POP.[2]	PLACE AND ZIP CODE	POP.[2]	PLACE AND ZIP CODE	POP.[2]			
Ashland	41101	26,450	Fort Mitchell	41017	6,713	Morehead	40351	7,164
Bardstown	40004	6,373	Fort Thomas	41075	15,685	Mount Sterling	40353	5,930
Bellevue	41073	7,560	Frankfort	40601	26,025	Murray	42071	14,048
Berea	40403	8,666	Franklin	42134	7,561	Newburg	—	5,876
Beuchel	—	6,855	Georgetown	40324	11,065	Newport	41071*	21,060
Bowling Green	42101	43,799	Glasgow	42141	12,662	Nicholasville	40356	11,173
Campbellsville	42718	9,195	Harrodsburg	40330	7,266	Owensboro	42301	54,898
Corbin	40701	8,196	Hazard	41701	5,404	Paducah	42001	29,207
Covington	41011*	48,319	Henderson	42420	25,035	Paris	40361	7,863
Cynthiana	41031	5,940	Hopkinsville	42240	28,308	Princeton	42445	6,937
Danville	40422	12,731	Independence	41051	9,698	Radcliff	40160	16,103
Dayton	41074	7,013	Jeffersontown	40299	15,626	Richmond	40475	21,752
Edgewood	41017	7,694	Lebanon	40033	6,489	Russellville	42276	7,383
Elizabethtown	42701	16,322	Lexington–Fayette	40511*	207,668	St. Matthews	40207	14,231
Elsmere	—	7,328	Louisville	40231*	293,531	Shively	40216	15,931
Erlanger	41018	14,535	Madisonville	42431	17,008	Somerset	42501	10,783
Flatwoods	41139	8,198	Mayfield	42066	10,294	Versailles	40383	6,598
Florence	41042	16,410	Maysville	41056	7,579	Villa Hills	—	6,051
Fort Knox	40121	31,055[1]	Middlesboro	40965	12,196	Winchester	40391	15,505

LOUISIANA (La. or LA)

PLACE AND ZIP CODE	POP.[2]	PLACE AND ZIP CODE	POP.[2]	PLACE AND ZIP CODE	POP.[2]			
Abbeville	70510	13,099	Harahan	70183	11,028	Port Allen	70767	6,193
Alexandria	71301	52,250	Harvey	70058	22,709[1]	Poydras	—	5,722[1]
Arabi	70032	10,248[1]	Houma	70360	100,346	Prien	—	6,224[1]
Avondale	—	6,699[1]	Jeanerette	70544	6,968	Raceland	70394	6,302[1]
Baker	70714	13,545	Jefferson	70181	15,550[1]	Rayne	70578	9,408
Bastrop	71220	15,536	Jennings	70546	12,444	Reserve	70084	7,288[1]
Baton Rouge	70821*	361,572	Kenner	70062	71,076	River Edge	—	17,146[1]
Bayou Cane	—	15,723[1]	Lafayette	70501*	85,593	Ruston	71270*	21,175
Bogalusa	70427	17,045	Lake Charles	70601*	76,396	St. Martinville	70582	8,345
Bossier City	71111*	54,641	Lake Providence	71254	6,250	Scotlandville	70897	15,113[1]
Broadmoor	70185	7,051[1]	Laplace	70068	16,112[1]	Shreveport	71102*	210,881
Brownsville–Bawcomville	—	7,252[1]	Leesville	71446	9,601	Slidell	70458	30,022
			Mandeville	70448	6,767	Springhill	71075	6,759
Bunkie	71322	5,473	Mansfield	71052	6,775	Sulphur	70663	20,746
Chalmette	70043	33,847[1]	Marrero	70072	36,548[1]	Tallulah	71282	11,378
Claiborne	—	6,278[1]	Metairie	70009*	164,160[1]	Terrytown	—	23,548[1]
Covington	70433	8,546	Minden	71055	15,341	Thibodaux	70301	16,695
Crowley	70526	16,492	Monroe	71203*	57,050	Timberlane	—	11,579[1]
De Ridder	70634	11,251	Morgan City	70380	16,298	Vidalia	71373	6,208
Denham Springs	70726	9,476	Moss Bluff	70612	7,004[1]	Ville Platte	70586	9,401
Donaldsonville	70346	7,934	Natchitoches	71457	16,688	Violet	70092	11,678[1]
Estelle	—	12,724[1]	New Iberia	70560	35,358	Waggaman	—	9,004[1]
Eunice	70535	13,247	New Orleans	70113*	564,561	West Monroe	71291	15,474
Franklin	70538	9,742	Oakdale	71463	7,058	Westwego	70094	12,475
Gonzales	70737	7,833	Opelousas	70570	19,640	Winnfield	71483	7,531
Gretna	70053	20,896	Pineville	71360	12,801	Winnsboro	71295	6,044
Hammond	70401	17,245	Plaquemine	70764	7,425	Zachary	70791	7,905

[1] 1980 Census. [2] 1982 Census Bureau estimate.

PLACE AND ZIP CODE	POP.²	PLACE AND ZIP CODE	POP.²	PLACE AND ZIP CODE	POP.²

MAINE (Me. or ME)

PLACE AND ZIP CODE	POP.²	PLACE AND ZIP CODE	POP.²	PLACE AND ZIP CODE	POP.²
Auburn 04210	23,128¹	Gardiner 04345	6,485¹	Rockland 04841	7,919¹
Augusta 04330	21,819¹	Gorham † 04038	10,101¹	Rumford 04276	6,256¹
Bangor 04401	31,643¹	Houlton † 04730	6,766¹	Saco 04072	12,921¹
Bath 04530	10,246¹	Kennebunk † 04043	6,621¹	Sanford 04073	10,268¹
Belfast 04915	6,243¹	Lewiston 04240	40,481¹	Scarborough † 04074	11,347¹
Biddeford 04005	19,638¹	Limestone † 04750	8,719¹	Skowhegan 04976	6,517¹
Brewer 04412	9,017¹	Lisbon † 04250	8,769¹	South Portland 04106	22,712¹
Brunswick 04011	10,990¹	Millinocket 04462	7,567¹	Waterville 04901	17,779¹
Cape Elizabeth † 04107	7,838¹	Old Orchard Beach 04064	6,023¹	Wells † 04090	8,211¹
Caribou 04736	9,916¹	Old Town 04468	8,422¹	Westbrook 04092	14,976¹
Fairfield † 04937	6,113¹	Orono 04473	9,981¹	Windham † —	11,282¹
Falmouth † 04105	6,853¹	Portland 04101*	61,572¹	Yarmouth † 04096	6,585¹
Farmington † 04938	6,730¹	Presque Isle 04769	11,172¹	York † 03909	8,465¹

MARYLAND (Md. or MD)

PLACE AND ZIP CODE	POP.²	PLACE AND ZIP CODE	POP.²	PLACE AND ZIP CODE	POP.²
Aberdeen 21001	11,600	Ferndale 21061	14,314¹	North Bethesda —	22,671¹
Adelphi 20783	12,530¹	Forestville 20747	16,401¹	North Kensington —	9,039¹
Andrews 20331	10,064¹	Fort Meade 20755	14,083¹	North Laurel —	6,093¹
Annapolis 21401*	31,910	Frederick 21701	30,629	Odenton 21113	13,270¹
Arbutus 21227	20,163¹	Friendly —	8,848¹	Olney 20832	13,026¹
Arnold 21012	12,285¹	Frostburg 21532	7,624	Overlea 21206	12,965¹
Aspen Hill 20906	47,455¹	Gaithersburg 20877	28,407	Owings Mills 21117	9,526¹
Baltimore 21233*	774,113	Germantown 20874	9,721¹	Oxon Hill 20745	36,267¹
Bel Air 21014	7,926	Glassmanor —	7,751¹	Palmer Park 20785	7,986¹
Bel Air South —	9,140¹	Glen Burnie 21061	37,263¹	Parkville 21234	35,159¹
Beltsville 20705	12,760¹	Goddard 20771	6,147¹	Pasadena 21122	7,439¹
Bethesda 20814*	63,022¹	Green Haven 21122	6,577¹	Perry Hall 21128	13,455¹
Bladensburg 20710	7,772	Greenbelt 20770	16,805	Pikesville 21208	22,555¹
Bowie 20715	34,274	Hagerstown 21740	33,310	Potomac 20854	40,402¹
Brooklyn Park 21225	11,508¹	Halfway —	8,659¹	Randallstown 21133	25,927¹
Calverton —	7,649¹	Havre De Grace 21078	8,670	Redland —	10,759¹
Cambridge 21613	11,388	Hillandale —	9,686¹	Reisterstown 21136	19,385¹
Camp Springs 20748	16,118¹	Hillcrest Heights 20031	17,021¹	Riviera Beach 21122	8,812¹
Cape St. Clair 21401	6,022¹	Hyattsville 20780*	12,187	Rockville 20850*	43,861
Carney —	21,488¹	Joppatowne 21085	11,348¹	Rosedale 21237	19,956¹
Catonsville 21228	33,208¹	Kentland 20785	8,596¹	Rossville —	8,646¹
Chevy Chase 20815	12,232¹	Kettering —	6,972¹	St. Charles —	13,921¹
Chillum 20783	32,775¹	Lake Shore 21122	10,181¹	Salisbury 21801	16,448
Clinton 20735	16,438¹	Langley Park 20787	14,038¹	Security —	29,453¹
Cockeysville 21030	17,013¹	Lanham–Seabr'k. 20706	15,814¹	Severn 21144	20,147¹
Colesville 20904	14,359¹	Lansdowne– 21227	16,759¹	Severna Park 21146	21,253¹
College Park 20740	23,000	Baltimore Hlds...		Silver Spring 20907*	72,893¹
Columbia 21045*	52,518¹	Laurel 20707	12,262	South Gate 21061	24,185¹
Coral Hills 20027	11,602¹	Lexington Park 20653	10,361¹	S. Kensington 20795	9,344¹
Crofton 21114	12,009¹	Linthicum 21090	7,457¹	South Laurel 20810	18,034¹
Cumberland 21502	25,233	Londontowne —	6,052¹	Suitl'd.–Silver Hill 20746	32,164¹
District Heights 20747	6,874	Lochearn —	26,908¹	Takoma Park 20912	15,282
Dundalk 21222	71,293¹	Lutherville– 21093	16,871¹	Tantallon —	9,945¹
East Riverdale —	14,117¹	Timonium...		Temple Hills 20748	6,630¹
Easton 21601	7,766	Maryland City —	6,949¹	Towson 21204	51,083¹
Edgemere 21219	9,078¹	Middle River 21220	26,756¹	Waldorf 20601	9,782¹
Edgewood 21040	19,455¹	Milford Mill —	20,354¹	Walker Mill 20028	10,651¹
Elkton 21921	6,685	Montgomery Vill. 20879	18,725¹	Westminster 21157	9,142
Ellicott City 21043	21,784¹	Mount Rainier 20712	7,487	Wheaton 20902	48,598¹
Essex 21221	39,614¹	New Carrollton 20784	12,474	White Oak 20903	13,700¹

MASSACHUSETTS (Mass. or MA)

PLACE AND ZIP CODE	POP.²	PLACE AND ZIP CODE	POP.²	PLACE AND ZIP CODE	POP.²
Abington † 02351	13,619	Barnstable † 02630	32,745	Burlington † 01803	23,130
Acton † 01720	17,420	Bedford † 01730	12,718	Cambridge 02140*	93,841
Acushnet † 02743	8,817	Belchertown † 01007	8,684	Canton † 02021	17,976
Adams † 01220	10,095	Bellingham † 02019	14,150	Carver † 02330	7,883
Agawam † 01001	26,646	Belmont † 02178	25,730	Charlton † 01507	7,129
Amesbury † 01913	14,250	Beverly † 01915	37,660	Chatham † 02633	6,202
Amherst † 01002	32,973	Billerica † 01821	37,436	Chelmsford † 01824	31,034
Andover † 01810	26,744	Blackstone † 01504	6,613	Chelsea 02150	25,534
Arlington 02174	46,859	Boston † 02205*	560,847	Chicopee 01021*	55,624
Ashland † 01721	9,836	Bourne † 02532	14,344	Clinton † 01510	12,499
Athol 01331	10,600	Braintree † 02184	36,027	Cochituate 01778	6,126¹
Attleboro 02703	34,123	Bridgewater † 02324	17,361	Cohasset † 02025	7,192
Auburn † 01501	14,597	Brockton † 02403	96,538	Concord † 01742	16,416
Ayer † 01432*	6,921	Brookline † 02146	54,205	Dalton † 01226	6,637

¹ 1980 Census. ² 1982 Census Bureau estimate. † Town or township.

PLACE AND ZIP CODE	POP.[2]	PLACE AND ZIP CODE	POP.[2]	PLACE AND ZIP CODE	POP.[2]

MASSACHUSETTS (continued)

Place	ZIP	Pop.	Place	ZIP	Pop.	Place	ZIP	Pop.
Danvers †	01923	23,733	Ludlow †	01056	18,148	Scituate †	02066	17,410
Dartmouth †	02714	24,597	Lynnfield †	01940	11,083	Seekonk †	02771	12,370
Dedham †	02026	24,757	Malden	02148	53,280	Sharon †	02067	13,832
Deerfield †	01342	4,511	Manchester †	01944	5,331	Shirley †	01464	5,361
Dennis †	02638	12,962	Mansfield †	02048	13,880	Shrewsbury †	01545	22,480
Dracut †	01826	22,154	Marblehead †	01945	19,891	Somerset †	02726	18,534
Dudley †	01570	8,787	Marlborough	01752	30,803	Somerville	02143	76,825
Duxbury †	02332	12,337	Marshfield †	02050	21,364	South Hadley †	01075	16,253
E. Bridgewater †	02333	9,990	Mattapoisett †	02739	5,664	South Yarmouth	02664	7,525[1]
E. Longmeadow †	01028	12,596	Maynard †	01754	9,583	Southborough †	01772	6,317
Easthampton †	01027	15,740	Medfield †	02052	10,328	Southbridge †	01550	16,683
Easton †	02334	17,214	Medford	02155	57,850	Southwick †	01077	7,478
Everett	02149	36,884	Medway †	02053	8,682	Spencer †	01562	10,979
Fairhaven †	02719	15,657	Melrose	02176	29,392	Springfield	01101*	151,586
Fall River	02722*	93,126	Methuen †	01844	37,261	Sterling †	01564	5,563
Falmouth †	02540*	24,294	Middleboro †	02346	16,732	Stoneham †	02180	21,816
Fitchburg	01420	39,843	Milford	01757	23,661	Stoughton †	02072	27,022
Fort Devens	01433	9,546[1]	Millbury †	01527	11,732	Stow †	01775	5,222
Foxborough †	02035	14,349	Millis †	02054	6,947	Sturbridge †	01566	6,186
Framingham †	01701	65,468	Milton †	02187	25,839	Sudbury †	01776	13,847
Franklin †	02038	18,450	Monson †	01057	7,281	Sutton †	—	6,012
Freetown †	—	7,405	Montague †	01351	7,964	Swampscott †	01907	13,585
Gardner	01440	17,881	Nantucket †	02554	5,281	Swansea †	02777	15,524
Gloucester	01930	27,855	Natick †	01760	29,709	Taunton	02780	45,561
Grafton †	01519	11,571	Needham †	02192	27,510	Templeton †	01468	6,047
Grt. Barrington †	01230	7,351	New Bedford	02741*	98,912	Tewksbury †	01876	24,476
Greenfield †	01301	18,239	Newburyport	01950	16,249	Topsfield †	01983	5,663
Groton †	01450	6,362	Newton	02158	82,791	Townsend †	01469	7,586
Groveland †	01834	5,028	Norfolk †	02056	6,876	Tyngsborough †	01879	6,076
Halifax †	02338	5,873	North Adams	01247	17,374	Uxbridge †	01569	8,441
Hamilton †	01936	6,983	North Andover †	01845	20,709	Wakefield †	01880	24,881
Hampden †	01036	4,713	N. Attleboro †	02760*	21,494	Walpole †	02081	19,080
Hanover †	02339	11,479	North Reading †	01864	11,240	Waltham	02154	58,234
Hanson †	02341	8,835	Northampton †	01060	29,024	Ware †	01082	8,981
Harvard †	01451	12,361	Northborough †	01532	10,493	Wareham †	02571	19,035
Harwich †	02645	9,176	Northbridge †	01534	12,185	Watertown †	02172	33,685
Haverhill	01830	47,165	Norton †	02766	12,779	Wayland †	01778	12,212
Hingham †	02043	20,253	Norwell †	02061	9,263	Webster †	01570	14,465
Holbrook †	02343	11,021	Norwood †	02062	29,183	Wellesley †	02181	26,868
Holden †	01520	13,413	Orange †	01364	6,933	West Boylston †	01583	5,993
Holliston †	01746	12,687	Orleans †	02653	5,532	W. Bridgewater †	02379	6,429
Holyoke	01040	43,446	Oxford †	01540	11,849	W. Springfield †	01089	27,025
Hopkinton †	01748	7,415	Palmer †	01069	11,520	Westborough †	01581	13,266
Hudson †	01749	16,808	Peabody	01960	46,227	Westfield	01085	36,794
Hull †	02045	9,814	Pembroke †	02359	13,924	Westford †	01886	13,915
Hyannis	02601	9,118[1]	Pepperell †	01463	8,382	Westminster †	01473	5,218
Ipswich †	01938	11,364	Pinehurst †	01866	6,588[1]	Weston †	02193	11,056
Kingston †	02364	7,430	Pittsfield	01201	50,615	Westport †	02790	13,817
Lakeville †	—	6,168	Plainville †	02762	5,936	Westwood †	02090	13,149
Lancaster †	01523	6,414	Plymouth †	02360	37,092	Weymouth †	02188	54,530
Lawrence	01842*	64,218	Quincy	02269	84,001	Whitinsville	01588	5,379[1]
Lee †	01238	6,101	Randolph †	02368	28,436	Whitman †	02382	13,726
Leicester †	01524	9,464	Raynham †	02767	9,120	Wilbraham †	01095	11,396
Lenox †	01240	6,511	Reading †	01867	22,747	Williamstown †	01267	8,350
Leominster	01453	34,627	Rehoboth †	02769	7,732	Wilmington †	01887	17,422
Lexington †	02173	29,126	Revere	02151	42,344	Winchendon †	01475	7,129
Lincoln †	01773	7,329	Rockland †	02370	15,771	Winchester †	01890	20,143
Littleton †	01460	7,074	Rockport †	01966	6,385	Winthrop †	02152	18,930
Longmeadow †	01106	16,192	Salem	01970	38,199	Woburn	01801	36,690
Lowell	01853*	92,774	Salisbury †	01950	6,193	Worcester	01613	161,049
Lunenburg †	01462	8,742	Sandwich †	02563	9,645	Wrentham †	02093	7,683
Lynn	01901*	79,258	Saugus †	01906	25,060	Yarmouth †	02675	18,946

MICHIGAN (Mich. or MI)

Place	ZIP	Pop.	Place	ZIP	Pop.	Place	ZIP	Pop.
Adrian	49221	20,871	Avon	—	40,779[1]	Berkley	48072	18,152
Albion	49224	10,867	Battle Creek	49016*	55,520	Beverly Hills	48009	11,351
Allen Park	48101	32,418	Bay City	48706*	40,834	Big Rapids	49307	14,072
Alma	48801	9,003	Beecher	—	17,178[1]	Birmingham	48012*	20,965
Alpena	49707	11,942	Benton Harbor	49022	14,211	Bloomfield	—	42,876[1]
Ann Arbor	48106*	104,880	Benton Heights	—	6,787[1]	Burton	—	29,238

[1] 1980 Census. [2] 1982 Census Bureau estimate. † Town or township.

MICHIGAN (continued)

PLACE AND ZIP CODE		POP.[2]	PLACE AND ZIP CODE		POP.[2]	PLACE AND ZIP CODE		POP.[2]
Cadillac	49601	10,368	Hazel Park	48030	20,645	Okemos	48864	8,882[1]
Carrollton †	48724	7,286	Highland Park	48203	25,733	Owosso	48867	15,822
Center Line	48015	8,916	Hillsdale	49242	7,385	Petoskey	49770	6,093
Charlotte	48813	8,205	Holland	49423*	26,833	Plymouth	48170	9,578
Clawson	48017	14,513	Holt	48842	10,097[1]	Pontiac	48056*	73,156
Clinton	49236	72,400	Houghton	49931	6,980	Port Huron	48060	33,539
Coldwater	49036	9,049	Howell	48843	7,018	Portage	49081	38,800
Cutlerville	49508	8,256[1]	Huntington Wds.	48070	6,552	River Rouge	48218	12,220
Davison	48423	5,955	Inkster	48141	33,786	Riverview	48192	14,117
Dearborn	48120*	86,544	Ionia	48846	5,825	Rochester	48308	7,387
Dearborn Heights	48127	64,702	Iron Mountain	49801	8,185	Romulus	48174	24,249
Detroit	48233*	1,138,717	Ironwood	49938	7,551	Roseville	48066	52,785
Dowagiac	49047	6,221	Ishpeming	49849	7,353	Royal Oak	48068*	68,390
East Detroit	48021	37,033	Jackson	49201*	38,514	Saginaw	48605*	75,377
E. Grand Rapids	49506	11,110	Jenison	49428	16,330[1]	St. Clair Shores	48080	73,450
East Lansing	48823	48,824	Kalamazoo	49001*	79,146	St. Johns	48879	7,393
Eastwood	—	7,186	Kentwood	49508	32,009	St. Joseph	49085	9,320
Ecorse	48229	13,956	Kingsford	49801	5,385	Saline	48176	6,511
Escanaba	49829	14,337	Lakeview	48850	13,345[1]	Sault Ste. Marie	49783	14,337
Fair Plain	—	8,289[1]	Lambertville	48144	6,341[1]	South Haven	49090	5,861
Farmington	48024	10,577	Lansing	48924*	128,338	Southfield	48037	73,311
Farmington Hills	48018	60,945	Lapeer	48446	5,870	Southgate	48195	30,679
Fenton	48430	8,095	Lincoln Park	48146	43,533	Springfield	—	5,807
Ferndale	48220	25,550	Livonia	48150*	101,366	Sterling Heights	48077	108,482
Flat Rock	48134	6,557	Ludington	49431	8,954	Sturgis	49091	9,540
Flint	48502*	154,019	Madison Heights	48071	34,609	Taylor	48180	73,796
Flushing	48433	8,467	Manistee	49660	7,441	Tecumseh	49286	7,251
Fraser	48026	14,233	Marquette	49855	22,438	Three Rivers	49093	7,568
Garden City	48135	33,811	Marshall	49068	7,152	Traverse City	49684	15,439
Grand Blanc	48439	6,583	Marysville	48040	7,426	Trenton	48183	21,680
Grand Haven	49417	11,791	Mason	48854	6,017	Troy	48099*	67,031
Grand Ledge	48837	6,954	Melvindale	48122	11,934	Walker	49504	15,337
Grand Rapids	49501*	182,774	Menominee	49858	9,818	Warren	48089	156,131
Grandville	49418	12,586	Midland	48640	37,372	Waterford †	48095	63,304
Greenville	48838	8,176	Monroe	48161	22,515	Wayne	48184	20,520
Grosse Ile †	48138	9,113	Mount Clemens	48046*	18,845	West Bloomfield †	48033	43,129
Grosse Pointe	48236	5,579	Mt. Pleasant	48858	22,904	Westland	48185	81,533
Grosse Pt. Farms	48236	10,254	Muskegon	49440*	39,995	Westwood	—	8,519[1]
Grosse Pointe Park	48236	13,761	Muskegon Heights	49444	14,091	Whitelake—		
Grosse Pointe Wds.	48236	18,219	Niles	49120	12,633	Seven Harbors	—	7,557[1]
Hamtramck	48212	20,071	Northview	—	11,662[1]	Wixom	48096	6,563
Harper Woods	48225	15,461	Northville	48167	5,748	Woodhaven	48183	10,807
Harrison	48625	23,649[1]	Norton Shores	49441	21,556	Wyandotte	48192	32,526
Haslett	48840	7,025[1]	Novi	48050	23,023	Wyoming	49509	60,419
Hastings	49058	6,391	Oak Park	48237	30,716	Ypsilanti	48197	23,846

MINNESOTA (Minn. or MN)

PLACE AND ZIP CODE		POP.[2]	PLACE AND ZIP CODE		POP.[2]	PLACE AND ZIP CODE		POP.[2]
Albert Lea	56007	19,108	Eagan	55121	23,947	Mendota Heights	55050	7,646
Alexandria	56308	7,827	East Bethel	55005	7,021	Minneapolis	55401*	369,161
Andover	—	9,842	East Grand Forks	56721	8,305	Minnetonka	55343	40,572
Anoka	55303	15,738	Eden Prairie	55344	18,982	Moorhead	56560	29,653
Apple Valley	55124	24,474	Edina	55424	45,817	Mound	55364	9,461
Arden Hills	—	8,623	Elk River	55330	7,336	Mounds View	55112	13,027
Austin	55912	22,497	Fairmont	56031	11,699	New Brighton	55190*	22,988
Bemidji	56601	11,034	Faribault	55021	16,536	New Hope	55428	23,322
Blaine	55433	30,849	Fergus Falls	56537	12,404	New Ulm	56073	13,923
Bloomington	55420	83,442	Fridley	55432	29,846	North Mankato	56001	9,626
Brainerd	56401	11,269	Golden Valley	55427	22,714	North St. Paul	55109	11,837
Brooklyn Center	55429	31,621	Grand Rapids	55744	8,044	Northfield	55057	13,124
Brooklyn Park	55444	46,596	Ham Lake	—	8,603	Oakdale	—	13,249
Burnsville	55337	38,075	Hastings	55033	13,180	Orono	—	6,865
Champlin	55316	9,647	Hibbing	55746	21,042	Owatonna	55060	18,494
Chanhassen	55317	6,896	Hopkins	55343	14,824	Plymouth	55447	36,605
Chaska	55318	8,895	Hutchinson	55350	9,570	Prior Lake	55372	7,930
Cloquet	55720	11,035	Inver Grove Hts.	55075	17,648	Ramsey	55303	10,586
Columbia Heights	55421	19,598	Lakeville	55044	15,479	Red Wing	55066	13,953
Coon Rapids	55433	38,684	Little Canada	—	7,751	Richfield	55423	37,200
Cottage Grove	55016	20,195	Little Falls	56345	7,188	Robbinsdale	55422	14,229
Crookston	56716	8,500	Mankato	56001*	28,529	Rochester	55901*	59,008
Crystal	55428	25,068	Maple Grove	—	24,473	Roseville	55113	35,539
Detroit Lakes	56501	6,960	Maplewood	55109	28,078	St. Anthony	55418	7,771
Duluth	55806*	90,311	Marshall	56258	11,238	St. Cloud	56301	42,549

[1] 1980 Census. [2] 1982 Census Bureau estimate. † Township.

PLACE AND ZIP CODE	POP.[2]	PLACE AND ZIP CODE	POP.[2]	PLACE AND ZIP CODE	POP.[2]
MINNESOTA *(continued)*					
St. Louis Park ... 55426	42,953	South St. Paul ... 55075	20,986	West St. Paul 55118	18,164
St. Paul 55101*	270,443	Spring L. Park ... 56680	6,468	White Bear Lake . 55110	23,087
St. Peter 56082	9,110	Stillwater 55082	12,590	Willmar 56201	16,265
Sauk Rapids 56,379	6,016	Thief River Falls . 56701	8,458	Winona 55987	24,807
Shakopee 55379	10,299	Virginia 55792	10,759	Woodbury 55125	12,113
Shoreview 55112	18,666	Waseca 56093	8,337	Worthington 56187	10,113
MISSISSIPPI (Miss. or MS)					
Aberdeen 39730	7,296	Greenwood 38930	20,507	N. Long Beach ... —	7,063[1]
Amory 38821	7,481	Grenada 38901	12,698	Ocean Springs... 39564	15,288
Bay St. Louis 39520	8,474	Gulfport 39503*	40,741	Orange Grove ... —	13,476[1]
Biloxi........... 39530*	50,476	Hattiesburg 39401	41,962	Oxford 38655	10,090
Booneville 38829	6,299	Holly Springs ... 38635	7,441	Pascagoula 39567	30,256
Brandon 39042	11,178	Indianola 38751	8,185	Pearl 39208	19,912
Brookhaven 39601	11,214	Jackson 39205*	204,195	Petal 39465	8,684
Canton 39046	10,763	Kosciusko 39090	7,121	Philadelphia...... 39350	6,434
Clarksdale 38614	21,858	Laurel 39440	22,599	Picayune 39466	10,913
Cleveland 38732	14,470	Leland 38756	6,799	Ridgeland 39157	7,784
Clinton 39056	15,004	Long Beach 39560	15,330	Southaven 38671	16,510
Columbia 39429	8,082	Louisville 39339	7,159	Starkville 39759	16,636
Columbus....... 39701	28,923	McComb 39648	12,263	Tupelo 38801	24,638
Corinth 38834	12,800	Meridian 39301	46,300	Vicksburg....... 39180	25,910
D'Iberville....... —	13,369[1]	Moss Point...... 39563	18,956	West Point 39773	9,020
Gautier 39553	8,917[1]	Natchez 39120	22,840	Winona 38967	5,969
Greenville....... 38701	41,022	New Albany 38652	6,862	Yazoo City 39194	11,982
MISSOURI (Mo. or MO)					
Affton 63123	23,181[1]	Festus.......... 63028	7,907	Monett 65708	6,127
Arnold.......... 63010	19,361	Florissant 63033*	55,301	Neosho 64850	9,530
Aurora 65605	6,401	Fulton 65251	10,547	Nevada 64772	9,001
Ballwin 63011	13,044	Gladstone....... 64118	25,302	O'Fallon 63366	9,258
Bellefontaine		Glendale 63122	5,982	Olivette......... 63132	7,895
Neighbors 63137	11,800	Grandview 64030	24,789	Overland 63114	19,060
Belton 64012	13,232	Hannibal........ 63401	19,073	Perryville 63775	7,303
Berkeley 63134	16,118	Harrisonville ... 64701	6,580	Pine Lawn 63120	6,704
Blue Springs 64015	27,698	Hazelwood 63042*	15,848	Poplar Bluff 63901	16,966
Bolivar 65613	6,059	Independence ... 64051*	111,617	Raytown 64133	31,369
Boonville 65233	6,962	Jackson 63755	8,061	Richmond Hts. .. 63117	11,302
Brentwood 63144	8,351	Jefferson City ... 65101	34,575	Rolla 65401	13,693
Bridgeton 63044	17,882	Jennings 63136	16,963	St. Ann 63074	15,323
Cape Girardeau.. 63701	34,483	Joplin 64801	39,449	St. Charles 63301	45,907
Carthage 64836	11,244	Kansas City 64108*	445,222	St. Johns 63114	7,926
Caruthersville ... 63830	8,212	Kennett 63857	10,230	St. Joseph 64501*	75,572
Chillicothe 64601	9,222	Kirksville 63501	17,191	St. Louis 63155*	437,354
Clayton 63105	14,047	Kirkwood 63122	27,841	St. Peters 63376	17,949
Clinton 64735	8,375	Ladue 63124	9,258	Sappington 63126	11,388[1]
Columbia 65201	63,305	Lebanon 65536	9,596	Sedalia 65301	20,356
Crestwood 63126	12,581	Lees Summit 64063	30,584	Sikeston 63801	17,547
Creve Coeur ... 63141	11,629	Lemay 63125	35,424[1]	Spanish Lake ... —	20,632[1]
Dellwood 63136	6,334	Liberty 64068	17,056	Springfield 65801*	134,453
De Soto......... 63020	6,203	Malden 63863	6,231	Trenton 64683	6,671
Des Peres 63131	8,089	Manchester 63011	6,353	University City .. 63130	42,728
Dexter 63841	7,060	Maplewood 63143	10,459	Warrensburg ... 64093	12,925
Ellisville —	6,589	Marshall 65340	12,869	Washington 63090	9,457
Excelsior Springs 64024	10,447	Maryville 64468	9,802	Webb City 64870	7,473
Farmington 63640	8,035	Mexico 65265	12,232	Webster Groves . 63119	23,236
Ferguson 63135	24,103	Moberly 65270	13,260	West Plains 65775	7,628
MONTANA (Mont. or MT)					
Anaconda–Deer		Great Falls 59403*	57,143	Miles City 59301	9,802
Lodge 59711	11,583	Havre 59501	11,290	Missoula 59806*	33,078
Billings 59101*	68,787	Helena 59601*	24,289	Missoula South .. —	5,557[1]
Billings Heights.. 59105	8,480[1]	Kalispell 59901*	10,558	Orchard Homes . —	10,837[1]
Bozeman 59715	22,532	Laurel 59044	5,816	Sidney.......... 59270	7,200
Butte-Silver Bow . 59701	35,753	Lewiston 59457	6,995		
Glendive........ 59330	6,526	Livingston 59047	7,168		
NEBRASKA (Neb., Nebr., or NE)					
Alliance......... 69301	10,263	Blair 68008	6,523	Fremont 68025	24,075
Beatrice 68310	12,830	Chadron 69337	5,868	Gering.......... 69341	7,810
Bellevue 68005	21,927	Columbus....... 68601	18,439	Grand Island 68801	34,548

[1] 1980 Census. [2] 1982 Census Bureau estimate.

PLACE AND ZIP CODE	POP.[1]	PLACE AND ZIP CODE	POP.[1]	PLACE AND ZIP CODE	POP.[1]

NEBRASKA (continued)

Place and ZIP	Pop.[1]	Place and ZIP	Pop.[1]	Place and ZIP	Pop.[1]
Hastings 68901	23,532[2]	McCook 69001	8,548[2]	Plattsmouth 68048	6,568[2]
Holdrege 68949	5,919[2]	Nebraska City 68410	6,995[2]	Ralston 68127	5,891[2]
Kearney 68847	22,376[2]	Norfolk 68701	19,955[2]	Scottsbluff 69361	14,191[2]
La Vista 68128	10,669[2]	North Platte 69101	23,146[2]	Sidney 69162	5,997[2]
Lexington 68850	7,216[2]	Omaha 68108*	328,557[2]	South Sioux City 68776	9,596[2]
Lincoln 68501*	177,340[2]	Papillion 68046	8,642[2]	York 68467	7,927[2]

NEVADA (Nev. or NV)

Place and ZIP	Pop.[1]	Place and ZIP	Pop.[1]	Place and ZIP	Pop.[1]
Boulder City 89005	10,696[2]	Incline Village 89450	6,225	Reno 89510*	106,748[2]
Carson City 89701	34,597[2]	Las Vegas 89114*	179,587[2]	Sparks 89431	45,335[2]
East Las Vegas 89112	6,449	Nellis A.F.B. 89191	7,476	Sunrise Manor —	44,155
Elko 89801	9,967[2]	North Las Vegas 89030	45,451[2]	Sun Valley 89431	8,222
Henderson 89015	32,506[2]	Paradise 89132	84,818	Winchester —	19,728

NEW HAMPSHIRE (N.H. or NH)

Place and ZIP	Pop.[1]	Place and ZIP	Pop.[1]	Place and ZIP	Pop.[1]
Amherst † 03031	8,427[2]	Hampton † 03842	10,875[2]	Nashua 03061	70,386[2]
Bedford † 03102	9,851[2]	Hanover † 03755	9,187[2]	Newport † 03773	6,439[2]
Berlin 03570	12,643[2]	Hooksett † 03106	7,732[2]	Pelham † 03076	8,328[2]
Claremont 03743	14,657[2]	Hudson † 03051	14,714[2]	Plaistow † 03865	5,651[2]
Concord 03301	30,706[2]	Keene 03431	21,560[2]	Portsmouth 03801	27,099[2]
Conway † 03818	7,481[2]	Laconia 03246	15,541[2]	Raymond † 03077	5,946[2]
Derry † 03038	19,947[2]	Lebanon 03766	11,338[2]	Rochester 03867	22,382[2]
Dover 03820	22,869[2]	Littleton † 03561	5,642[2]	Salem † 03079	24,099[2]
Durham † 03824	11,484[2]	Londonderry † 03053	14,273[2]	Seabrook † 03874	6,217[2]
Exeter † 03833	11,260[2]	Manchester 03103*	92,104[2]	Somersworth 03878	10,505[2]
Franklin 03235	7,877[2]	Merrimack † 03054	16,068[2]	Swanzey † —	5,375[2]
Goffstown † 03045	11,884[2]	Milford † 03055	8,923[2]	Windham † 03087	6,062[2]

NEW JERSEY (N.J. or NJ)

Place and ZIP	Pop.[1]	Place and ZIP	Pop.[1]	Place and ZIP	Pop.[1]
Aberdeen † —	17,235	Crestwood Village —	7,965	Hawthorne 07507	18,200
Absecon 08201	6,859	Dover 07801	14,681	Hazlet 07730	23,013
Asbury Park 07712	17,015	Dumont 07628	18,334	Highland Park 08904	13,396
Atlantic City 08401*	40,199	Dunellen 08812	6,593	Hillsdale 07642	10,495
Audubon 08106	9,533	East Brunswick † 08816	37,711	Hillside 07205	21,440
Barrington 08007	7,418	East Hanover 07936	9,319	Hoboken 07030	42,460
Bayonne 07002	65,047	East Orange 07019*	77,878	Holiday City—	
Beachwood 08722	7,687	East Rutherford 07073	7,849	Berkeley —	9,019
Belleville 07109	35,367	East Windsor † —	21,041	Hopatcong 07843	15,531
Bellmawr 08031	13,721	Eatontown 07724	12,703	Irvington 07111	61,493
Belmar 07719	6,771	Edgewater Park —	9,273	Jersey City 07303*	222,881[2]
Bergenfield 07621	25,568	Edison † 08818*	70,193	Keansburg 07734	10,613
Berkeley Heights 07922	12,549	Elizabeth 07207*	106,803[2]	Kearny 07032	35,735
Bernardsville 07924	6,715	Elmwood Park 07407	18,377	Kendall Park 08824	7,419
Bloomfield 07003	47,792	Emerson 07630	7,793	Kenilworth 07033	8,221
Bloomingdale 07403	7,867	Englewood 07631	23,701	Keyport 07735	7,413
Bogota 07603	8,344	Ewing Township —	34,842	Kinnelon 07405	7,770
Boonton 07005	8,620	Fair Lawn 07410	32,229	Lake Mohawk —	8,498
Bound Brook 08805	9,710	Fairfield † 07006	7,987	Lakewood 08701	22,863
Bridgeton 08302	18,795	Fairview 07022	10,519	Laurence Harbor 08879	6,737
Brigantine 08203	8,318	Fanwood 07023	7,767	Leonia 07605	8,027
Browns Mills 08015	10,568	Florence 08518	7,677	Lincoln Park 07035	8,806
Budd Lake 07828	6,523	Florham Park 07932	9,359	Linden 07036	37,836
Burlington 08016	10,246	Fort Lee 07024	32,449	Lindenwold 08021	18,196
Butler 07405	7,616	Franklin Lakes 07417	8,769	Linwood 08221	6,144
Caldwell 07006	7,624	Freehold 07728	10,020	Little Falls 07424	11,496
Camden 08101*	84,910	Garfield 07026	26,803	Little Ferry 07643	9,399
Candlewood —	6,166	Gilford Park —	6,528	Livingston 07039	28,040
Carlstadt 07072	6,166	Glassboro 08028	14,574	Lodi 07644	23,956
Carney's Point 08069	7,574	Glen Ridge 07028	7,855	Long Branch 07740	29,819
Carteret 07008	20,598	Glen Rock 07452	11,497	Lyndhurst 07071	20,326
Cedar Grove 07009	12,600	Gloucester City 08030	13,121	Madison 07940	15,357
Chatham 07928	8,537	Gordon's Corner —	6,320	Madison Park —	7,447
Cherry Hill † 08034*	68,785	Guttenberg 07093	7,340	Manville 08835	11,278
Cinnaminson 08077	16,072	Hackensack 07602*	36,039	Maple Shade 08052	20,525
Clark 07066	16,699	Hackettstown 07840	8,850	Maplewood 07040	22,950
Clayton 08312	6,013	Haddon Heights 08035	8,361	Margate City 08402	9,179
Cliffside Park 07010	21,464	Haddonfield 08033	12,337	Marlton 08053	9,411
Clifton 07015*	74,388	Haledon 07538	6,607	Matawan 07747	8,837
Closter 07624	8,164	Hammonton 08037	12,298	Maywood 07607	9,895
Collingswood 08108	15,838	Hanover Township —	11,846	Mercerville 08619	25,446
Cranford 07016	24,573	Harrison 07029	12,242	Metuchen 08840	13,762
Cresskill 07626	7,609	Hasbrouck Hts. 07604	12,166	Middlesex 08846	13,480

[1] 1980 Census. [2] 1982 Census Bureau estimate. † Town or township (includes rural population).

PLACE AND ZIP CODE	POP.[1]	PLACE AND ZIP CODE	POP.[1]	PLACE AND ZIP CODE	POP.[1]

NEW JERSEY (continued)

PLACE AND ZIP CODE	POP.[1]	PLACE AND ZIP CODE	POP.[1]	PLACE AND ZIP CODE	POP.[1]
Middletown 07748	62,298	Phillipsburg 08865	16,647	Stratford 08084	8,005
Midland Park 07432	7,381	Pine Hill 08021	8,684	Succasunna 07876	10,931
Millburn 07041	19,543	Piscataway 08854	42,223	Summit......... 07901	21,071
Milltown 08850	7,136	Pitman 08071	9,744	Teaneck 07666	39,007
Millville 08332	24,815	Plainfield 07061*	45,555	Tenafly 07670	13,552
Montclair 07042*	38,321	Pleasantville ... 08232	13,435	Tinton Falls 07724	7,740
Montvale 07645	7,318	Point Pleasant ... 08742	17,747	Toms River 08753	7,465
Moorestown..... 08057	13,695	Pompton Lakes.. 07442	10,660	Totowa 07511	11,448
Morristown ... 07960*	16,614	Princeton 08540	12,035	Trenton 08650*	92,124
Mt. Holly........ 08060	10,818	Rahway......... 07065*	26,723	Twin Rivers —	7,742
Mountainside... 07092	7,118	Ramblewood 08054	6,475	Union 07083	50,184
Neptune † —	28,336	Ramsey 07446	12,899	Union Beach 07735	6,354
New Brunswick .. 08901*	41,442	Raritan 08869	6,128	Union City 07087	55,593
New Milford 07646	16,876	Red Bank 07701	12,031	Upper Saddle R. . 07458	7,958
New Providence . 07974	12,426	Ridgefield....... 07657	10,294	Ventnor City 08406	11,704
Newark 07102*	320,512[2]	Ridgefield Park .. 07660	12,738	Verona 07044	14,166
Newton 07860	7,748	Ridgewood 07451*	25,208	Vineland 08360	53,753
North Arlington .. 07032	16,587	Ringwood 07456	12,625	Waldwick 07463	10,802
North Bergen † .. 07047	47,019	River Edge 07661	11,111	Wallington 07057	10,741
North Haledon .. 07508	8,177	River Vale....... 07675	9,489	Wanaque 07465	10,025
North Plainfield.. 07060	19,108	Riverside 08075	7,941	Washington 07882	6,429
Northfield....... 08225	7,795	Rockaway 07866	6,852	Washington † ... 07882	9,550
Nutley.......... 07110	28,998	Roselle 07203*	20,641	Watchung 07060	15,290
Oakland 07436	13,443	Roselle Park 07204	13,377	Wayne.......... 07470	46,474
Ocean City 08226	13,949	Rumson 07760	7,623	Weehawken 07087	13,168
Ocean Twnshp. † 07712	23,570	Runnemede 08078	9,461	West Caldwell ... 07006	11,407
Old Bridge † 08857	51,515	Rutherford 07070*	19,068	West Freehold ... —	9,929
Oradell 07649	8,658	Saddle Brook.... 07662	14,084	W. Long Branch .. 07764	7,380
Orange 07051*	31,136	Salem 08079	6,959	West New York .. 07093	39,194
Palisades Park .. 07650	13,732	Sayreville 08872	20,969	West Orange 07052	39,510
Palmyra 08065	7,085	Scotch Plains.... 07076	20,774	West Paterson ... 07424	11,293
Paramus........ 07652	26,474	Secaucus 07094	13,719	Westfield 07091*	30,447
Park Ridge 07656	8,515	Silverton —	7,236	Westwood 07675	10,714
Parsippany—		Somers Point.... 08244	10,330	White Horse —	10,098
Troy Hills 07054	49,868	Somerset 08873	21,731	White Meadow Lk. —	8,429
Passaic......... 07055	52,463	Somerville 08876	11,973	Williamstown 08094	5,768
Paterson........ 07510*	138,986[2]	South Amboy ... 08879	8,322	Willingboro 08046	39,912
Paulsboro....... 08066	6,944	South Orange † .. 07079	15,864	Wood-Ridge 07075	7,929
Pennsauken..... 08110	33,775	South Plainfield . 07080	20,521	Woodbridge † ... 07095	90,074
Pennsville † 08070	13,848	South River 08882	14,361	Woodbury 08096	10,353
Pequannock † 07440	13,776	Spotswood 08884	7,840	Wyckoff 07481	15,500
Perth Amboy ... 08861*	38,951	Springfield 07081	13,955	Yardville 08620	9,414

NEW MEXICO (N.M., N. Mex., or NM)

PLACE AND ZIP CODE	POP.[1]	PLACE AND ZIP CODE	POP.[1]	PLACE AND ZIP CODE	POP.[1]
Alamogordo..... 88310	25,475[2]	Farmington 87401	35,659[2]	Raton 87740	7,474[2]
Albuquerque ... 87101*	341,978[2]	Gallup 87301	20,440[2]	Rio Rancho 87174	11,169[2]
Artesia 88210	11,057[2]	Grants 87020	10,894[2]	Roswell 88201	42,296[2]
Aztec........... 87410	6,336[2]	Hobbs 88240	31,531[2]	Santa Fe........ 87501*	50,957[2]
Bloomfield 87413	5,911[2]	Las Cruces 88001*	46,476[2]	Shiprock........ 87420	7,237
Carlsbad 88220	26,559[2]	Las Vegas 87701	15,509[2]	Silver City 88061*	10,807[2]
Clovis 88101	32,513[2]	Los Alamos 87544	11,039	Socorro 87801	8,175[2]
Deming 88030	10,361[2]	Lovington 88260	10,562[2]	Tucumcari 88401	6,732[2]
Espanola 87532	6,910[2]	Portales 88130	10,184[2]	White Rock 87544	6,560

NEW YORK (N.Y. or NY)

PLACE AND ZIP CODE	POP.[1]	PLACE AND ZIP CODE	POP.[1]	PLACE AND ZIP CODE	POP.[1]
Albany 12212*	100,048[2]	Beacon 12508	13,378[2]	Center Moriches . 11934	5,703[1]
Albion 14411	4,960[2]	Bellmore 11710	18,431[1]	Centereach 11720	30,136[1]
Alfred 14802	5,015[2]	Bethpage 11714	18,555[1]	Centerport 11721	6,576[1]
Amityville 11701	8,989[2]	Binghamton 13902*	54,777[2]	Central Islip 11722	19,734[1]
Amsterdam 12010	21,371[2]	Bohemia 11716	9,308[1]	Cheektowaga ... 14225	92,145[1]
Arlington 12603	11,305[1]	Brentwood 11717	44,321[1]	Cobleskill 12043	5,075[2]
Auburn 13021	32,405[2]	Briarcliff Manor . 10510	7,027[2]	Cohoes 12047	18,111[2]
Babylon 11702*	12,333[2]	Brighton 11235	35,776[1]	Cold Spring Hbr.. 11724	5,336
Baldwin......... 11510	34,525[1]	Brockport 14420	9,433[2]	Colonie 12212	8,959[2]
Baldwinsville ... 13027	6,655[2]	Bronxville 10708	6,176[2]	Commack 11725	34,719[1]
Ballston Spa 12020	4,707[2]	Buffalo 14240*	348,035[2]	Congers 10920	7,123[1]
Batavia 14020	16,274[2]	Canandaigua 14424	10,761[2]	Copiague 11726	20,132[1]
Bath 14810	5,894[2]	Canastota 13032	4,676[2]	Coram 11727	24,752[1]
Bay Shore 11706	10,784[1]	Canton 13617	7,091[2]	Corning 14830	12,661
Bayport 11705	9,282[1]	Catskill 12414	4,638[2]	Cortland 13045	19,715[2]
Bayville 11709	7,236[2]	Cedarhurst 11516	6,082[2]	Croton-on-Hudson 10520	6,766[2]

[1] 1980 Census. [2] 1982 Census Bureau estimate. † Town or township (includes rural population).

PLACE AND ZIP CODE	POP.[2]	PLACE AND ZIP CODE	POP.[2]	PLACE AND ZIP CODE	POP.[2]

NEW YORK (continued)

PLACE AND ZIP CODE	POP.[2]	PLACE AND ZIP CODE	POP.[2]	PLACE AND ZIP CODE	POP.[2]
Dansville 14437	4,940	Ithaca 14850	28,212	N. Massapequa 11758	21,385[1]
De Witt 13214	9,024[1]	Jamestown 14701	35,721	North Merrick 11566	12,848[1]
Deer Park 11729	30,394[1]	Jefferson Valley–		North New Hyde	
Delmar 12054	8,423[1]	Yorktown 10535	13,380[1]	Park 11040	15,114[1]
Depew 14043	19,361	Jericho 11753	12,739[1]	N. Syracuse 13212	7,940
Dix Hills 11746	26,693[1]	Johnson City 13790	17,050	N. Tarrytown 10591	8,028
Dobbs Ferry 10522	9,912	Johnstown 12095	9,442	N. Tonawanda 14120	35,391
Dunkirk 14048	15,030	Kenmore 14217	17,925	North Valley	
East Aurora 14052	6,743	Kings Park 11754	16,131[1]	Stream 11580	14,530[1]
East Hills 11577	7,538	Kings Point 11024	5,191	North Wantagh 11793	12,677[1]
East Islip 11730	13,852[1]	Kingston 12401	24,248	Northport 11768	7,550
E. Massapequa 11758	13,987[1]	Lackawanna 14218	22,019	Norwich 13815	8,026
East Meadow 11554	39,317[1]	Lake Grove 11755	9,511	Nyack 10960	6,543
East Northport 11731	20,187[1]	Lake Ronkonkoma 11779	38,336[1]	Oakdale 11769	8,090[1]
East Patchogue 11772	18,139[1]	Lancaster 14086	13,091	Oceanside 11572	33,639[1]
East Rochester 14445	7,596[1]	Larchmont 10538	6,162	Ogdensburg 13669	12,011
East Rockaway 11518	10,763	Latham 12110	11,182[1]	Old Bethpage 11804	6,215[1]
Eastchester 10709	20,305[1]	Lawrence 11559	6,043	Olean 14760	18,121
Elmira 14901*	34,183	Levittown 11756	57,045[1]	Oneida 13421	10,517
Elmont 11003	27,592[1]	Lindenhurst 11757	26,662	Oneonta 13820	14,812
Elwood 11731	11,847[1]	Little Falls 13365	6,092	Ossining 10562	20,597
Endicott 13760	14,355	Lockport 14094	24,598	Oswego 13126	19,354
Endwell 13760	13,745[1]	Locust Grove 11791	9,670[1]	Oyster Bay 11771	6,497[1]
Fairmount 13219	13,415[1]	Long Beach 11561	33,744	Patchogue 11772	11,160
Fairport 14450	6,130	Loudonville 12211	11,480[1]	Pearl River 10965	15,893[1]
Farmingdale 11735	7,783	Lynbrook 11563	20,118	Peekskill 10566	18,505
Farmingville 11738	13,398[1]	Mahopac 10541	7,681[1]	Pelham 10803	6,665
Floral Park 11001*	16,808	Malone 12953	7,413	Pelham Manor 10803	6,146
Fort Salonga —	19,550[1]	Malverne 11565	9,264	Pitcher Hill —	6,063[1]
Franklin Square 11010	29,051[1]	Mamaroneck 10543	17,234	Plainedge 11714	9,629[1]
Fredonia 14063	11,111	Manhasset 11030	8,485[1]	Plainview 11803	28,037[1]
Freeport 11520	38,982	Manlius 13104	5,414	Plattsburgh 12901	20,449
Fulton 13069	13,179	Massapequa 11758	24,454[1]	Pleasantville 10570	6,882
Garden City 11530	22,565	Massapequa Park 11762	19,491	Port Chester 10573	23,162
Garden City Park 11530	7,712	Massena 13662	12,370	Port Jefferson 11777	6,685
Geneseo 14454	6,713	Mastic 11950	10,413[1]	Port Jefferson	
Geneva 14456	14,741	Mastic Beach 11951	8,318[1]	Station 11776	17,009[1]
Glen Cove 11542	24,294	Mattydale 13211	7,511[1]	Port Jervis 12771	8,699[1]
Glens Falls 12801	16,078	Mechanicville 12118	5,348	Port Washington 11050	14,521[1]
Gloversville 12078	17,435	Medford 11763	20,418[1]	Potsdam 13676	10,659
Great Neck 11022*	9,077	Medina 14103	6,511	Poughkeepsie 12601*	29,638
Greece 14616	16,177[1]	Melville 11747	8,139[1]	Rensselaer 12144	8,899
Greenlawn 11740	13,869[1]	Merrick 11566	24,478[1]	Ridge 11961	8,977[1]
Greenville 12083	8,706[1]	Middletown 10940	21,766	Riverhead 11901	6,339
Hamburg 14075	10,401	Miller Place 11764	7,877[1]	Rochester 14692*	244,094
Hampton Bays 11946	7,256[1]	Mineola 11501	20,475	Rockville Centre 11570	25,326
Harrison 10528	23,040	Monroe 10950	6,395	Rocky Point 11778	7,012[1]
Hartsdale 10530	10,216[1]	Monsey 10952	12,380[1]	Roessleville 12205	11,685[1]
Hastings-on-		Monticello 12701	6,041	Rome 13440	43,510
Hudson 10706	8,259	Mount Kisco 10549	7,755	Roosevelt 11575	14,109[1]
Hauppauge 11788	20,960[1]	Mount Sinai 11766	6,591[1]	Roslyn Heights 11577	6,546[1]
Haverstraw 10927	9,007	Mount Vernon 10551*	66,168	Rotterdam 12303	22,933
Hempstead 11551*	40,419	Nanuet 10954	12,578[1]	Rye 10580	15,266
Herkimer 13350	8,312	Nesconset 11767	10,706[1]	St. James 11780	12,122[1]
Herricks 11040	8,123[1]	New Cassel 11590	9,635[1]	Salamanca 14779	6,684
Hewlett 11557	6,986[1]	New Castle † 10514	15,425[1]	Saranac Lake 12983	5,469
Hicksville 11802*	43,245[1]	New City 10956	35,859[1]	Saratoga Springs 12866	23,906[1]
Holbrook 11741	24,382[1]	New Hyde Park 11040	9,634	Sayville 11782	12,013[1]
Holtsville 11742	13,515[1]	New Paltz 12561	5,112	Scarsdale 10583	17,490
Hornell 14843	9,987	New Rochelle 10802*	70,673	Schenectady 12301*	67,614
Horseheads 14845	7,192	New Windsor † 12550	19,534[1]	Scotchtown 10940	7,352[1]
Hudson 12534	8,127	New York 10001*	7,086,096	Scotia 12302	7,280[1]
Hudson Falls 12839	7,372	Newark 14513	9,979	Sea Cliff 11579	5,283
Huntington 11743	21,727[1]	Newburgh 12550	23,570	Seaford 11783	16,117[1]
Huntington Sta. 11746	28,769[1]	Niagara Falls 14302*	68,454	Selden 11784	17,259[1]
Ilion 13357	9,508	North Amityville 11701	13,140[1]	Seneca Falls 13148	7,332
Inwood 11696	8,228[1]	North Babylon 11703	19,019[1]	Setauket–East	
Irondequoit 14617	57,648[1]	North Bellmore 11710	20,630[1]	Setauket 11733	10,176[1]
Irvington 10533	5,691	N. Great River 11739	11,416[1]	Shirley 11967	18,072[1]
Islip 11751	13,438[1]	N. Lindenhurst 11757	11,511[1]	Smithtown 11787	30,906[1]

[1] 1980 Census. [2] 1982 Census Bureau estimate. † Township.

PLACE AND ZIP CODE	POP.[1]	PLACE AND ZIP CODE	POP.[1]	PLACE AND ZIP CODE	POP.[1]

NEW YORK (continued)

PLACE AND ZIP CODE	POP.[1]	PLACE AND ZIP CODE	POP.[1]	PLACE AND ZIP CODE	POP.[1]
Solvay 13209	7,105[2]	Troy 12180*	55,669[2]	West Haverstraw 10993	9,270[2]
Sound Beach 11789	8,071[1]	Tuckahoe 10707	6,046[2]	West Hempstead 11552	18,536[1]
S. Farmingdale 11735	16,439[1]	Uniondale 11553	20,016[1]	West Islip 11795	29,533[1]
S. Huntington 11746	14,854[1]	Utica 13504*	73,722[2]	West Nyack 10994	8,553[1]
S. Westbury 11590	9,732[1]	Valley Cottage 10989	8,214[1]	West Point 10996	8,105[1]
Southport 14904	8,329[1]	Valley Stream 11580*	35,085[2]	West Sayville 11796	8,185[1]
Spring Valley 10977	20,829[2]	Walden 12586	5,826[2]	West Seneca 14224	51,210[1]
Stony Brook 11790	16,155[1]	Wantagh 11793	19,817[1]	Westbury 11590*	13,618[2]
Stony Point 10980	8,686[1]	Wappinger Falls 12590	5,066[2]	White Plains 10602*	45,996[2]
Suffern 10901	10,814[2]	Waterloo 13165	5,165[2]	Williamsville 14221	5,886[2]
Syosset 11791	9,818[1]	Watertown 13601	27,332[2]	Williston Park 11596	8,210[2]
Syracuse 13220*	166,187[2]	Watervliet 12189	11,250[2]	Woodbury 11797	7,043[1]
Tappan 10983	8,267[1]	Webster 14580	5,544[2]	Woodmere 11598	17,205[1]
Tarrytown 10591	10,715[2]	Wellsville 14895	5,428[2]	Wyandanch 11798	13,215[1]
Thornwood 10594	7,197[1]	West Amityville —	6,623[1]	Yonkers 10701*	192,342[2]
Tonawanda 14150	18,470[2]	West Babylon 11704	41,699[1]	Yorktown Heights 10598	7,696[1]

NORTH CAROLINA (N.C. or NC)

PLACE AND ZIP CODE	POP.[1]	PLACE AND ZIP CODE	POP.[1]	PLACE AND ZIP CODE	POP.[1]
Albemarle 28001	15,110	Henderson 27536	13,522	Reidsville 27320	12,492
Asheboro 27203	15,252	Hendersonville 28739	6,862	Roanoke Rapids 27870	14,702
Asheville 28810*	53,583	Hickory 28601	20,757	Rockingham 28379	8,300
Boone 28607	10,191	High Point 27260*	63,808	Rocky Mount 27801	41,283
Burlington 27215	37,266	Jacksonville 28540*	18,259	Roxboro 27573	7,532
Carrboro 27510	7,336	Kannapolis 28081	34,564	St. Stephens —	10,797
Cary 27511	21,763	Kernersville 27284	6,802	Salisbury 28144	22,677
Chapel Hill 27514	32,421	King 27021	8,757	Sanford 27330	14,773
Charlotte 28228*	323,972[2]	Kings Grant —	6,562	Shelby 28150	15,310
Clemmons 27012	7,401	Kings Mountain 28086	9,080	Smithfield 27577	7,288
Clinton 28328	7,552	Kinston 28501	25,234	Southern Pines 28387	8,620
Concord 28025	16,942	Laurinburg 28352	11,480	Spring Lake 28390	6,273
Dunn 28334	8,962	Lenoir 28645	13,748	Statesville 28677	18,622
Durham 27701*	101,242[2]	Lexington 27292	15,711	Tarboro 27886	8,634
Eden 27288	15,672	Lumberton 28358	18,241	Thomasville 27360	14,144
Elizabeth City 27909	14,004	Mint Hill 28212	7,915	Trinity 27370	6,878
Fayetteville 28302*	59,507	Monroe 28110	12,639	Washington 27889	8,418
Forest City 28043	7,688	Mooresville 28115	8,575	Waynesville 28786	6,765
Garner 27529	10,073	Morganton 28655	13,763	West Concord —	5,859
Gastonia 28052*	47,333	Mount Airy 27030	6,862	White Oak 28399	6,058
Goldsboro 27530	31,871	New Bern 28560	14,557	Whiteville 28472	5,565
Graham 27253	8,674	Newton 28658	7,624	Williamston 27892	6,159
Greensboro 27420*	157,337[2]	North Belmont 28012	10,762	Wilmington 28402*	44,000
Greenville 27834	35,740	Oxford 27565	7,603	Wilson 27893	34,424
Havelock 28532	17,718	Raleigh 27611*	152,211[2]	Winston-Salem 27102*	140,846[2]

NORTH DAKOTA (N.D., or N. Dak., or ND)

PLACE AND ZIP CODE	POP.[1]	PLACE AND ZIP CODE	POP.[1]	PLACE AND ZIP CODE	POP.[1]
Bismarck 58501*	45,929[2]	Grand Forks 58201*	44,149[2]	Wahpeton 58075	9,519[2]
Devils Lake 58301	7,457[2]	Jamestown 58401	16,233[2]	West Fargo 58078	11,032[2]
Dickinson 58601	18,950[2]	Mandan 58554	16,057[2]	Williston 58801	16,660[2]
Fargo 58102	62,596[2]	Minot 58701	33,432[2]		
Grafton 58237	5,326[2]	Valley City 58072	7,760[2]		

OHIO (O. or OH)

PLACE AND ZIP CODE	POP.[1]	PLACE AND ZIP CODE	POP.[1]	PLACE AND ZIP CODE	POP.[1]
Akron 44309*	231,659[2]	Bedford Heights 44146	12,849[2]	Brooklyn 44144	12,148[2]
Alliance 44601	24,180[2]	Bellaire 43906	8,234[2]	Brunswick 44212	28,572[2]
Amherst 44001	10,597[2]	Bellefontaine 43311	11,990[2]	Bryan 43506	7,771[2]
Ashland 44805	20,130[2]	Bellevue 44811	8,201[2]	Bucyrus 44820	13,355[2]
Ashtabula 44004	22,894[2]	Belpre 45714	7,044[2]	Cambridge 43725	13,386[2]
Athens 45701	20,332[2]	Berea 44017	19,402[2]	Campbell 44405	11,286[2]
Aurora 44202	8,333	Bexley 43209	13,445[2]	Canton 44711*	90,868[2]
Austintown 44515	33,636[1]	Blacklick Estates 43004	11,223[1]	Celina 45822	9,214[2]
Avon 44011	7,256[2]	Blue Ash 45242	10,120[2]	Centerville 45459	19,202[2]
Avon Lake 44012	13,313[2]	Boardman 44512	39,161[1]	Cheviot 45211	9,993[2]
Barberton 44203	29,184[2]	Bowling Green 43402	25,352[2]	Chillicothe 45601	23,556[2]
Bay Village 44140	17,587[2]	Brecksville 44141	10,243[2]	Cincinnati 45234*	380,118[2]
Beachwood 44122	9,838[2]	Bridgetown —	11,460[1]	Circleville 43113	11,750[2]
Beavercreek —	32,700[2]	Broadview Heights 44147	10,903[2]	Cleveland 44101*	558,869[2]
Bedford 44146	14,838[2]	Brook Park 44142	25,591[2]	Cleveland Heights 44118	55,765[2]

[1] 1980 Census. [2] 1982 Census Bureau estimate. † Town or township (includes rural population).

PLACE AND ZIP CODE	POP.[2]	PLACE AND ZIP CODE	POP.[2]	PLACE AND ZIP CODE	POP.[2]

OHIO (continued)

PLACE AND ZIP CODE	POP.[2]	PLACE AND ZIP CODE	POP.[2]	PLACE AND ZIP CODE	POP.[2]
Columbus...... 43216*	570,588	Macedonia 44056	6,757	Salem 44460	12,888
Conneaut 44030	13,571	Madeira 45243	9,071	Sandusky 44870	30,996
Coshocton 43812	13,419	Mansfield 44901*	52,915	Sandusky South . —	6,548[1]
Cuyahoga Falls .. 44222*	43,368	Maple Heights ... 44137	29,100	Seven Hills...... 44131	13,352
Dayton 45401*	188,499	Marietta 45750	16,713	Shaker Heights .. 44120	31,776
Deer Park...... 45236	6,707	Marion 43302	36,755	Sharonville...... 45241	10,317
Defiance 43512	16,418	Martins Ferry ... 43935	9,276	Sheffield Lake ... 44054	10,451
Delaware 43015	19,229	Marysville....... 43040	7,569	Shelby.......... 44875	9,640
Delphos 45833	7,226	Mason.......... 45040	9,565	Sidney.......... 45365	17,819
Dover 44622	11,665	Massillon 44646	30,864	Silverton......... —	6,012
East Cleveland .. 44112	36,865	Maumee 43537	15,918	Solon........... 44139	14,947
East Liverpool ... 43920	16,548	Mayfield Heights. 44124	20,710	South Euclid 44121	25,353
Eastlake 44094	22,222	Medina 44256	15,764	Springboro...... 45066	5,419
Eaton 45320	6,987	Mentor 44060	42,636	Springdale 45246	10,367
Elyria.......... 44035*	57,338	Mentor–on–Lake. 44060	8,167	Springfield 45501*	71,344
Englewood 45322	11,224	Miamisburg 45342	15,783	Steubenville..... 43952	25,510
Euclid......... 44117	58,175	Middleburg Hts.. 44017	15,634	Stow 44224	25,518
Fairborn....... 45324	29,296	Middletown 45042	43,854	Streetsboro 44240	9,143
Fairfield 45014	31,655	Monfort Heights . —	9,745[1]	Strongsville 44136	29,847
Fairlawn 44313	6,155	Montgomery ... 45242	10,599	Struthers 44471	13,358
Fairview Park.... 44126	18,753	Mount Healthy .. 45231	7,530	Sylvania 43560	15,641
Findlay........ 45840	36,175	Mount Vernon... 43050	14,522	Tallmadge 44278	14,765
Forest Park 45405	18,700	Napoleon 43545	8,461	Tiffin............ 44883	19,212
Fort McKinley ... —	10,161[1]	New Carlisle 45344	6,704	Toledo 43601*	350,565
Fostoria 44830	15,758	New Philadelphia 44663	17,083	Toronto 43964	6,817
Franklin 45005	10,634	Newark 43055	41,893	Trenton 45067	6,451
Fremont 43420	17,532	Niles 44446	22,704	Trotwood 45426	7,838
Gahanna........ 43230	19,029	North Canton ... 44720	14,681	Troy 45373	19,332
Galion 44833	12,184	North College Hill 45239	11,001	Twinsburg 44087	8,105
Gallipolis 45631	5,162	North Madison ... —	8,741[1]	Uhrichsville 44683	6,129
Garfield Heights . 44125	34,308	North Olmsted .. 44070	36,117	University Heights 44118	15,277
Geneva 44041	6,615	North Ridgeville . 44039	21,768	Upper Arlington . 43221	35,449
Girard 44420	12,530	North Royalton .. 44133	18,407	Upper Sandusky . 43351	5,913
Grandview Hts... 43212	7,505	Northbrook —	8,357[1]	Urbana 43078	10,768
Greenville....... 45331	12,667	Northview —	9,973[1]	Van Wert 45891	10,649
Groesbeck 45239	9,594[1]	Norton 44203	12,004	Vandalia 45377	12,939
Grove City 43123	17,182	Norwalk 44857	14,325	Vermilion 44089	11,186
Hamilton 45012*	63,887	Norwood 45212	25,887	Wadsworth 44281	15,198
Heath 43056	7,115	Oakwood 45873	9,227	Wapakoneta..... 45895	8,572
Hilliard 43026	8,308	Oberlin 44074	8,417	Warren 44481*	55,778
Hillsboro 45133	6,512	Oregon 43616	18,552	Warrensville Hts.. 44122	16,447
Hubbard....... 44425	9,183	Orrville 44667	7,698	Washington 43160	12,806
Huber Heights... 45424	38,692	Overlook–Page		Wauseon 43567	6,310
Huron 44839	7,084	Manor 45431	14,825[1]	Wellston 45692	6,126
Independence ... 44131	6,449	Oxford 45056	17,467	West Carrollton .. 45449	13,475
Ironton 45638	13,672	Painesville 44077	16,821	Westerville 43081	24,199
Jackson 45640	6,715	Parma 44129	90,572	Westlake 44145	20,193
Kent 44240*	27,536	Parma Heights .. 44130	22,740	White Oak —	9,563[1]
Kenton 43326	8,571	Pepper Pike 44124	6,523	Whitehall 43213	21,874
Kenwood 43606	9,928[1]	Perry Heights ... —	9,206[1]	Wickliffe 44092	16,355
Kettering 45429	60,371	Perrysburg 43551	10,640	Willard 44890	5,823
Kirtland —	6,096	Piqua 45356	20,300	Willoughby 44094	19,614
Lakewood....... 44107	61,453	Pisgah.......... —	15,660[1]	Willoughby Hills . 44094	8,580
Lancaster....... 43130	35,234	Port Clinton 43452	7,162	Willowick 44094	17,352
Lebanon 45036	9,755	Portage Lakes ... —	11,310[1]	Wilmington 45177	10,572
Lima 45802*	46,909	Portsmouth 45662	25,093	Woodbourne–Hyde	
Lincoln Village... 43228	10,548[1]	Ravenna 44266	12,048	Park 45208	8,826[1]
Logan 43138	6,865	Reading 45215	12,464	Wooster 44691	19,687
London 43140	7,446	Reynoldsburg ... 43068	21,513	Worthington 43085	16,397
Lorain 44052*	74,707	Richmond Heights 44143	9,911	Wyoming 45215	8,326
Louisville 44641	7,910	Rittman 44270	5,902	Xenia 45385	24,732
Loveland 45140	9,249	Rocky River 44116	20,558	Youngstown 44501*	111,391
Lyndhurst 44124	17,325	St. Marys 45885	8,427	Zanesville....... 43701	28,717

OKLAHOMA (Okla. or OK)

PLACE AND ZIP CODE	POP.[2]	PLACE AND ZIP CODE	POP.[2]	PLACE AND ZIP CODE	POP.[2]
Ada............ 74820	16,525	Bartlesville....... 74003*	37,305	Chickasha 73018	17,160
Altus.......... 73521	23,273	Bethany 73008	22,357	Choctaw 73020	8,410
Alva............ 73717	6,363	Bixby........... 74008	7,943	Claremore 74017	13,198
Anadarko 73005	6,897	Blackwell 74631	8,701	Clinton 73601	10,502
Ardmore........ 73401	24,663	Broken Arrow ... 74012	42,302	Coweta 74429	5,123

[1] 1980 Census. [2] 1982 Census Bureau estimate.

PLACE AND ZIP CODE	POP.[2]	PLACE AND ZIP CODE	POP.[2]	PLACE AND ZIP CODE	POP.[2]

OKLAHOMA (continued)

PLACE AND ZIP CODE	POP.[2]	PLACE AND ZIP CODE	POP.[2]	PLACE AND ZIP CODE	POP.[2]
Cushing 74023	8,483	Marlow 73055	5,093	Sallisaw 74955	6,349
Del City......... 73155	28,757	McAlester....... 74501	17,532	Sand Springs.... 74063	14,051
Duncan 73533	24,293	Miami 74354	14,102	Sapulpa 74066	17,028
Durant 74701	12,282	Midwest City 73140	52,829	Seminole 74868	8,935
Edmond 73034	39,963	Moore 73103	38,791	Shawnee........ 74801*	27,533
El Reno 73036	17,011	Muskogee 74401	40,557	Stillwater 74074	39,459
Elk City........ 73644	13,094	Mustang 73064	8,689	Sulphur......... 73086	5,677
Enid............ 73701	54,441	Norman 73070*	73,077	Tahlequah 74464	9,918
Frederick 73542	6,081	Oklahoma City .. 73125*	427,714	The Village 73156	11,831
Guthrie 73044	10,738	Okmulgee....... 74447	16,552	Tulsa........... 74101*	375,300
Guymon 73942	8,572	Owasso......... 74055	7,516	Vinita 74301	6,875
Henryetta 74437	6,639	Pauls Valley 73075	5,898	Wagoner........ 74467	6,656
Hugo........... 74743	7,113	Perry........... 73077	6,037	Warr Acres 73123	10,410
Idabel 74745	7,456	Ponca City 74601	27,866	Weatherford 73096	11,459
Jenks 74037	6,336	Poteau 74953	7,156	Woodward 73801	16,349
Lawton 73501*	85,673	Pryor Creek 74361	8,878	Yukon 73099	19,990

OREGON (Ore., Oreg., or OR)

PLACE AND ZIP CODE	POP.[2]	PLACE AND ZIP CODE	POP.[2]	PLACE AND ZIP CODE	POP.[2]
Albany 97321	28,377	Grants Pass 97526	15,312	Ontario 97914	9,236
Ashland 97520	15,106	Gresham 97030	34,839	Oregon City 97045	14,929
Astoria 97103	9,914	Hazelwood —	25,541[1]	Parkrose........ 97230	21,108[1]
Baker 97814	9,604	Hayesville...... —	9,213[1]	Pendleton....... 97801	14,594
Beaverton 97005*	33,307	Hermiston 97838	9,932	Portland 97208*	366,968
Bend 97701	17,122	Hillsboro 97123	29,305	Powellhurst —	20,132[1]
Canby 97013	7,802	Keizer 97303	20,106	Raleigh Hills 97225	6,517[1]
Cedar Hills 97225	9,619[1]	Klamath Falls ... 97601*	17,361	Redmond 97756	6,495
Centennial —	22,118[1]	La Grande 97850	12,010	River Road —	10,370[1]
Central Point 97502	6,421	Lake Oswego.... 97034	23,048	Roseburg 97470	16,181
City of the Dalles . 97058	11,094	Lebanon 97355	10,680	St. Helens 97051	7,183
Coos Bay 97420	15,357	Lincoln City 97367	5,734	Salem 97301*	90,431
Cornelius 97113	5,000	McMinnville..... 97128	14,644	Santa Clara —	14,288[1]
Corvallis 97333	41,289	Medford 97501	40,411	Silverton 97381	5,279
Cottage Grove... 97424	7,180	Milton-Freewater . 97862	5,353	Springfield 97477	41,215
Cully —	10,569[1]	Milwaukie....... 97222	17,969	Sweet Home 97386	6,939
Dallas 97338	8,929	Monmouth 97361	5,425	Tigard.......... 97223	17,917
Errol Heights ... —	10,847	Newberg........ 97132	11,022	Troutdale....... 97060	6,583
Eugene 97401*	103,709	Newport 97365	7,776	Tualatin 97062	9,104
Forest Grove 97116	11,691	North Bend 97459	9,551	West Linn 97068	12,357
Four Corners.... 97301	11,331[1]	North Springfield . —	6,140[1]	Wilkes–Rockwood . —	23,216[1]
Gladstone....... 97027	9,829	Oak Grove 97268	11,640[1]	Woodburn 97071	11,207

PENNSYLVANIA (Pa., Penn., or PA)

PLACE AND ZIP CODE	POP.[2]	PLACE AND ZIP CODE	POP.[2]	PLACE AND ZIP CODE	POP.[2]
Aliquippa 15001	16,714	Carnegie........ 15106	9,890	Easton 18042	26,060
Allentown 18101*	104,324	Castle Shannon.. 15234	9,919	Economy........ —	9,577
Altoona......... 16603*	55,857	Catasauqua 18032	6,765	Edinboro 16412	6,854
Ambler 19002	6,807	Chambersburg .. 17201	16,460	Elizabethtown ... 17022	8,399
Ambridge....... 15003	9,335	Chester......... 19013*	44,987	Ellwood City..... 16117	9,757
Archbald 18403	6,299	Clairton 15025	12,215	Emmaus 18049	11,045
Arnold.......... 15068	6,773	Clarion 16214	5,997	Ephrata 17522	11,317
Avalon —	6,213	Clearfield....... 16830	7,412	Erie 16515*	118,493
Baldwin......... 15234	24,302	Clifton Heights .. 19018	7,219	Farrell 16121	8,313
Beaver Falls 15010	12,141	Coatesville 19320	10,876	Folcroft......... 19032	8,324
Bellefonte....... 16823	6,339	Collingdale 19023	9,569	Forest Hills 15540	8,161
Bellevue 15202	9,886	Columbia 17512	10,846	Franklin 16323	8,234
Berwick 18603	11,598	Connellsville 15425	10,056	Franklin Park.... —	6,282
Bethel Park 15102	34,667	Conshohocken .. 19428	8,528	Fullerton....... 18052	8,055[1]
Bethlehem 18016*	70,255	Coraopolis 15108	7,140	Gettysburg..... 17325	7,280
Blakely 18447	7,474	Corry........... 16407	7,395	Glassport 15045	6,054
Bloomsburg..... 17815	11,670	Crafton 15205	7,685	Glenolden 19036	7,523
Bradford 16701	10,853	Darby 19023	11,198	Greensburg 15601	17,440
Brentwood 15227	11,489	Dickson City 18519	6,581	Greenville...... 16125	7,699
Bridgeville 15017	6,112	Donora 15033	7,312	Grove City 16127	8,147
Bristol.......... 19007	10,880	Dormont........ 15216	11,116	Hanover 17331	14,701
Brookhaven 19015	7,795	Downingtown.... 19335	8,242	Harrisburg 17105*	52,501
Butler 16001	17,067	Doylestown 18901	8,795	Hatboro........ 19040	7,538
Camp Hill 17011	8,218	DuBois 15801	9,036	Hazleton 18201	26,560
Canonsburg..... 15317	10,279	Dunmore 18512	16,534	Hellertown 18055	6,011
Carbondale 18407	11,203	Duquesne 15110	9,877	Hershey 17033	13,249[1]
Carlisle 17013	18,608	E. Stroudsburg .. 18301	8,151	Huntingdon 16652	6,859

[1] 1980 Census. [2] 1982 Census Bureau estimate.

PENNSYLVANIA (cont.)

PLACE AND ZIP CODE		POP.[2]	PLACE AND ZIP CODE		POP.[2]	PLACE AND ZIP CODE		POP.[2]
Indiana	15701	15,876	New Cumberland	17070	8,028	Souderton	18964	6,786
Jeannette	15644	12,923	New Kensington	15068	17,637	S. Williamsport	17701	6,313
Jefferson	15344	8,612	Norristown	19401*	34,710	Springfield	19064	25,326[1]
Johnstown	15901*	34,088	North Braddock	15104	8,510	State College	16801*	35,287
Kingston	18704	15,638	North Versailles†	15137	13,050	Steelton	17113	6,478
Lancaster	17604*	55,518	Northampton	18067	8,594	Sunbury	17801	12,287
Lansdale	19446	16,999	Norwood	19074	6,508	Swarthmore	19081	5,706
Lansdowne	19050	11,670	Oakmont	15139	6,916	Swissvale	15218	11,301
Latrobe	15650	10,449	Oil City	16301	13,969	Tamaqua	18252	8,661
Lebanon	17042	26,251	Old Forge	18517	9,159	Tarentum	15084	6,480
Lehighton	18235	5,950	Palmyra	17078	7,399	Taylor	18517	7,244
Lewistown	17044	9,423	Penn Hills	15235	57,632[1]	Titusville	16354	6,840
Lititz	17543	7,863	Philadelphia	19104*	1,665,382	Turtle Creek	15145	6,865
Lock Haven	17745	9,401	Phoenixville	19460	14,165	Tyrone	16686	6,327
Lower Burrell	15068	12,945	Pittsburgh	15219*	414,936	Uniontown	15401	14,003
Mahanoy City	17948	6,015	Pittston	18640*	9,643	Upper Darby†	19082	83,371
McKees Rocks	15136	8,483	Pleasant Hills	15236	9,388	Upper Merion	—	26,138[1]
McKeesport	15134*	29,974	Plum	15239	25,706	Upper St. Clair	15241	19,083[1]
Meadville	16335	15,365	Plymouth	18651	7,363	Vandergrift	15690	6,527
Mechanicsburg	17055	9,630	Pottstown	19464	23,043	Warminster	18974	35,463[1]
Media	19063*	5,972	Pottsville	17901	17,799	Warren	16365	11,926
Middletown	17057	10,323	Prospect Park	19076	6,534	Washington	15301	18,422
Millersville	17551	7,445	Punxsutawney	15767	7,371	Waynesboro	17268	9,831
Milton	17847	6,787	Quakertown	18951	9,148	West Chester	19380	17,912
Monaca	15061	7,499	Reading	19603*	78,772	West Mifflin	15122	25,923
Monessen	15062	11,463	Red Lion	17356	5,943	West Pittston	18643	5,855
Monongahela	15063	5,854	Ridley Park	19078	7,792	West View	15229	7,649
Monroeville	15146	30,926	St. Marys	15857	6,301	Westmont	—	5,944
Moosic	18507	6,030	Sayre	18840	7,166	White Oak	15131	9,548
Morrisville	19067	10,038	Schuylkill Haven	17972	5,962	Whitehall	18052	14,922
Mount Carmel	17851	8,020	Scottdale	15683	5,734	Wilkes-Barre	18701*	50,677
Mount Joy	17552	5,764	Scranton	18505*	85,950	Wilkinsburg	15221	23,348
Munhall	15120	14,235	Shamokin	17872	10,185	Williamsport	17701	32,717
Murrysville	15668	16,369	Sharon	16146	17,632	Wilson	15025	7,564[1]
Nanticoke	18634	12,911	Sharon Hill	19079	6,107	Wyomissing	19610	6,526
New Brighton	15066	7,397	Shenandoah	17976	7,286	Yeadon	19050	12,057
New Castle	16101*	32,777	Somerset	15501	6,500	York	17405*	44,607

RHODE ISLAND (R.I. or RI)

PLACE AND ZIP CODE		POP.[2]	PLACE AND ZIP CODE		POP.[2]	PLACE AND ZIP CODE		POP.[2]
Barrington†	02806	16,073	Glocester †	—	8,058	Portsmouth †	02871	14,759
Bristol†	02809	20,085	Hopkinton †	02833	6,540	Providence	02940*	155,717
Burrillville †	02830	13,853	Johnston †	02919	25,112	Scituate †	02857	8,429
Central Falls	02863	17,168	Lincoln †	02865	16,986	Smithfield †	02917	17,000
Charlestown†	02813	5,087	Middletown †	02840	17,305	S. Kingstown †	02879	20,956
Coventry †	02816	27,907	Narragansett †	02882	12,226	Tiverton†	02878	13,788
Cranston	02910	71,622	Newport	02840	29,910	Warren †	02885	10,764
Cumberland †	02864	26,797	N. Kingstown †	02852	22,664	Warwick	02887*	86,832
East Greenwich †	02818	10,134	N. Providence	02908	29,871	West Warwick	02893	27,467
East Providence	02914	51,301	N. Smithfield †	02876	10,094	Westerly †	02891	18,753
Exeter†	02822	4,414	Pawtucket	02860*	71,829	Woonsocket	02895	45,297

SOUTH CAROLINA (S.C. or SC)

PLACE AND ZIP CODE		POP.[2]	PLACE AND ZIP CODE		POP.[2]	PLACE AND ZIP CODE		POP.[2]
Aiken	29801	15,570	Dorchester Terrace– Brentwood	29405	7,862[1]	Lancaster	29720	9,997
Anderson	29621*	27,721	Easley	29640	14,913	Laurens	29360	10,554
Beaufort	29902	8,840	Florence	29501*	30,465	Marion	29571	7,806
Belvedere	29841	6,859[1]	Forest Acres	29260	5,935	Mauldin	29662	8,480
Bennettsville	29512	8,916	Gaffney	29340	13,393	Mt. Pleasant	29464	16,574
Berea	29611	13,164[1]	Gantt	—	13,719[1]	Mullins	29574	5,934
Brookdale	—	6,123[1]	Georgetown	29440	10,347	Myrtle Beach	29577	20,074
Camden	29020	7,375	Goose Creek	29445	20,665	Newberry	29108	9,650
Capitol View	—	10,456[1]	Greenville	29602*	57,490	North Augusta	29841	14,306
Cayce	29033	11,751	Greenwood	29646	22,105	North Charleston	29406	67,633
Charleston	29423*	70,776	Greer	29651	10,874	North Trenholm	—	10,962[1]
Chester	29706	6,972	Hanahan	29410	13,675	Oak Grove	—	7,092[1]
Clemson	29631	7,870	Hartsville	29550	8,985	Orangeburg	29115	15,276
Clinton	29325	8,579	Hilton Head Is.	29928*	12,132	Parris Island	29905	7,752[1]
Columbia	29201*	101,457	Homeland Park	—	6,720[1]	Pinehurst–Sheppard Park	—	6,936[1]
Conway	29526	10,814	James Island	29412	24,124[1]	Rock Hill	29730	36,434
Darlington	29532	8,104	Ladson	29456	13,246[1]	St. Andrews		
Dentsville	29204	13,579[1]	Lake City	29560	6,685	(Charleston)	29417	9,908[1]
Dillon	29536	7,149						

1 1980 Census. 2 1982 Census Bureau estimate. † Town or township.

PLACE AND ZIP CODE		POP.[2]	PLACE AND ZIP CODE		POP.[2]	PLACE AND ZIP CODE		POP.[2]

SOUTH CAROLINA (continued)

PLACE AND ZIP CODE		POP.[2]	PLACE AND ZIP CODE		POP.[2]	PLACE AND ZIP CODE		POP.[2]
St. Andrews (Richland)	—	20,245[1]	South Sumter	—	7,096[1]	Wade Hampton	—	20,180[1]
Sans Souci	29609	8,393[1]	Spartanburg	29301*	43,522	Walterboro	29488	6,380
Seneca	29678	7,716	Summerville	29483	10,785	Welcome	—	6,922[1]
Seven Oaks	—	16,604[1]	Sumter	29150	25,649	West Columbia	29169	11,092
Simpsonville	29681	10,099	Taylors	29687	15,801[1]	Woodfield	—	9,588[1]
			Union	29379	10,429	York	29745	6,651

SOUTH DAKOTA (S.D., S.Dak., or SD)

PLACE AND ZIP CODE		POP.[2]	PLACE AND ZIP CODE		POP.[2]	PLACE AND ZIP CODE		POP.[2]
Aberdeen	57401	26,307	Mitchell	57301	13,847	Spearfish	57783	5,432
Brookings	57006	15,277	Pierre	57501	12,194	Vermillion	57069	10,068
Huron	57350	13,008	Rapid City	57701	48,122	Watertown	57201	16,359
Madison	57042	6,318	Sioux Falls	57101*	83,497	Yankton	57078	12,096

TENNESSEE (Tenn. or TN)

PLACE AND ZIP CODE		POP.[2]	PLACE AND ZIP CODE		POP.[2]	PLACE AND ZIP CODE		POP.[2]
Alcoa	37701	6,780	Franklin	37064	14,214	Memphis	38101*	645,760
Athens	37303	12,039	Gallatin	37066	17,712	Milan	38358	8,126
Bartlett	38134	21,049	Germantown	38138	24,361	Millington	38053	17,802
Bloomingdale	37660	12,088	Goodlettsville	37072	8,574	Morristown	37814	20,887
Bolivar	38008	6,490	Greeneville	37743	13,781	Mount Carmel	37642	5,108
Brentwood	37027	10,251	Harriman	37748	8,306	Murfreesboro	37130	34,642
Bristol	37620	23,850	Hendersonville	37075	27,441	Nashville–		
Brownsville	38012	9,588	Humboldt	38343	10,074	Davidson	37202*	455,252
Chattanooga	37422*	168,016	Jackson	38301	49,387	Newport	37821	7,555
Clarksville	37040*	59,715	Jefferson City	37760	5,656	Oak Ridge	37830	27,865
Cleveland	37311	26,565	Johnson City	37601	44,002	Paris	38242	10,769
Collierville	38017	8,340	Kingsport	37662*	31,959	Powell	37849	7,220
Colonial Heights	37663	6,744	Knoxville	37901*	175,298	Pulaski	38478	7,131
Columbia	38401	26,670	La Follette	37766	8,175	Red Bank	37415	13,273
Concord	37933	8,569	La Vergne	37086	6,030	Ripley	38063	6,168
Cookeville	38501	21,444	Lawrenceburg	38464	10,089	Rockwood	37854	5,765
Covington	38019	6,245	Lebanon	37087	11,767	Savannah	38372	7,093
Crossville	38555	6,489	Lenoir City	37771	5,819	Shelbyville	37160	13,554
Dayton	37321	5,817	Lewisburg	37091	8,888	Signal Mountain	37377	5,931
Dickson	37055	7,126	Lexington	38351	5,964	Smyrna	37167	10,003
Dyersburg	38024	15,862	Manchester	37355	7,357	Soddy–Daisy	37379	8,424
East Ridge	37412	20,888	Martin	38237	8,938	Springfield	37172	10,789
Elizabethton	37643	12,570	Maryville	37801	17,454	Tullahoma	37388	16,517
Farragut	37933	7,116	McKenzie	38201	5,306	Union City	38261	10,279
Fayetteville	37334	7,483	McMinnville	37110	10,462	Winchester	37398	6,184

TEXAS (Tex. or TX)

PLACE AND ZIP CODE		POP.[2]	PLACE AND ZIP CODE		POP.[2]	PLACE AND ZIP CODE		POP.[2]
Abilene	79604*	104,302	Bridge City	77611	8,038	Deer Park	77536	23,981
Alamo	78516	7,156	Brownfield	79316	10,896	Del Rio	78840	31,855
Alamo Heights	78209	6,133	Brownsville	78520*	91,440	Denison	75020	23,984
Alice	78332	21,974	Brownwood	76801	19,715	Denton	76201*	49,833
Allen	75002	10,252	Bryan	77801	53,107	Dickinson	77539	8,171
Alvin	77511	17,878	Burkburnett	76354	10,948	Donna	78537	10,511
Amarillo	79120*	155,356	Burleson	76028	13,064	Dumas	79029	12,737
Andrews	79714	12,400	Canyon	79015	10,885	Duncanville	75138	29,405
Angleton	77515	14,757	Carrizo Springs	78834	7,570	Eagle Pass	78852	23,282
Aransas Pass	78336	8,155	Carrollton	75006	48,694	Edinburg	78539	27,961
Arlington	76010*	182,975	Carthage	75633	6,972	El Campo	77437	10,812
Athens	75751	10,652	Cedar Hill	75104	7,606	El Paso	79910*	445,071
Atlanta	75551	6,356	Cleburne	76031	20,149	Ennis	75119	12,582
Austin	78710*	368,135	Cleveland	77327*	6,654	Euless	76039	26,799
Azle	76020	6,739	Clute	77531	9,517	Falfurrias	78355	6,264
Balch Springs	75180	14,833	College Station	77840	42,685	Farmers Branch	75234	25,694
Bay City	77414	17,172	Colleyville	76034	7,388	Fort Stockton	79735	9,649
Baytown	77520	61,375	Commerce	75428	7,910	Fort Worth	76101*	401,402
Beaumont	77704*	123,477	Conroe	77301*	20,117	Fredericksburg	78624	6,719
Bedford	76021	25,377	Converse	78109	6,332	Freeport	77541	13,103
Beeville	78102	15,096	Copperas Cove	76522	21,282	Friendswood	77546	12,103
Bellaire	77401	15,205	Corpus Christi	78408*	246,081	Gainesville	76240	14,421
Bellmead	76705	7,710	Corsicana	75110	22,666	Galena Park	77547	10,127
Belton	76513	11,029	Crockett	75835	7,563	Galveston	77553*	62,667
Benbrook	76126	14,996	Crowley	76036	6,256	Garland	75040*	148,975
Big Spring	79720	26,874	Crystal City	78839	8,501	Gatesville	76528	6,616
Bonham	75418	7,159	Cuero	77954	7,431	Georgetown	78626	10,716
Borger	79007	17,470	Dalhart	79022	6,781	Gladewater	75647	7,251
Breckenridge	76024	7,582	Dallas	75260*	943,848	Gonzales	78629	7,847
Brenham	77833	12,333	De Soto	75115	16,726	Graham	76046	9,786

[1] 1980 Census. [2] 1982 Census Bureau estimate.

PLACE AND ZIP CODE	POP.[2]	PLACE AND ZIP CODE	POP.[2]	PLACE AND ZIP CODE	POP.[2]

TEXAS (continued)

Place and ZIP	Pop.	Place and ZIP	Pop.	Place and ZIP	Pop.
Grand Prairie.... 75051	77,146	Lubbock 79402*	176,588	Round Rock 76664	15,691
Grapevine 76051	14,678	Lufkin 75901	30,126	Rowlett 75088	9,194
Greenville 75401	23,518	Mansfield 76063	9,107	Saginaw 76179	6,430
Groves 77619	17,226	Marlin 76661	6,803	San Angelo 76902*	79,214
Haltom City 76117	30,498	Marshall 75670	25,627	San Antonio 78284*	819,021
Harker Heights .. 76543	7,678	McAllen 78501	72,063	San Benito 78586	19,270
Harlingen 78551	47,083	McKinney 75069	17,433	San Juan 78589	8,398
Henderson 75652	11,357	Mercedes 78570	12,453	San Marcos 78666	23,903
Hereford 79045	15,076	Mesquite 75149	71,171	Santa Fe 77510	6,837
Hewitt 76643	6,175	Mexia 76667	7,165	Schertz 78154	7,358
Highland Park ... 75205	8,630	Midland 79701*	84,174	Seagoville....... 75159	7,910
Hillsboro 76645	7,196	Mineral Wells.... 76067	15,372	Seguin 78155	18,417
Hitchcock 77563	6,397	Mission 78572	25,443	Seminole 79360	6,456
Hondo 78861	6,009	Missouri City 77459	30,161	Sherman 75090	30,871
Houston 77201*	1,725,617	Monahans 79756	9,358	Silsbee 77656	7,913
Humble......... 77338	9,662	Mt. Pleasant 75455	11,573	Sinton 78387	6,323
Huntsville....... 77340	28,696	Nacogdoches ... 75961	28,074	Slaton 79364	6,971
Hurst 76053	32,764	Navasota 77868	6,515	Snyder 79549	13,796
Ingleside........ 78362	6,076	Nederland 77627	17,075	South Houston .. 77587	14,100
Iowa Park 76367	6,367	New Braunfels... 78130	23,839	Stephenville..... 76401	12,299
Irving 75061*	114,305	N. Richland Hills . 76118	32,992	Sugar Land 77478	11,662
Jacinto City 77029	9,203	Odessa 79760*	102,465	Sulphur Springs . 75482	13,379
Jacksonville 75766	12,512	Orange 77630	24,278	Sweetwater 79556	12,787
Jasper 75951	6,975	Palestine 75801	17,214	Taylor 76574	10,775
Katy............ 77450	8,159	Pampa 79065	22,822	Temple 76501	42,061
Kermit 79745	9,007	Paris 75460	25,483	Terrell 76160	13,491
Kerrville 78028	16,440	Pasadena 77501*	122,010	Texarkana 75501	31,777
Kilgore 75662	11,847	Pearland........ 77581	14,174	Texas City 77590	42,812
Killeen 76541*	50,559	Pearsall 78061	7,581	The Colony 75028	19,284
Kingsville 78363	29,870	Pecos 79772	13,429	Tyler 15712*	73,117
Kingwood 77339	16,261	Perryton 79070	9,188	Universal City ... 78148	10,908
Kirby 78280	7,369	Pharr 78577	22,770	University Park .. 78228	22,357
La Marque 77568	15,746	Plainview 79072	22,286	Uvalde 78801	14,557
La Porte 77571	19,528	Plano 75074	84,191	Vernon 76384	12,808
Lake Jackson ... 77566	19,846	Pleasanton 78064	6,643	Victoria......... 77901	54,947
Lamesa......... 79331	11,985	Port Arthur 77640*	65,128	Vidor 77662	13,440
Lampasas....... 76550	6,124	Port Lavaca 77979	11,773	Waco 76701*	102,200
Lancaster 75146	15,898	Port Neches 77651	14,542	Watauga 76148	12,533
Laredo 78041*	99,874	Portland 78374	12,734	Waxahachie 75165	14,993
League City 77573	19,843	Raymondville 78580	9,685	Weatherford 76086	13,119
Leon Valley	9,911	Richardson 75080*	76,074	Weslaco 78596	21,069
Levelland 79336	14,721	Richland Hills ... 76681	8,328	West Univ. Place . 77005	11,759
Lewisville 75067	25,131	Richmond....... 77469	13,324	Wharton 77488	9,432
Liberty 77575	8,501	River Oaks 77219	7,244	White Settlement . 76108	15,147
Littlefield 79339	7,556	Robinson 76706	6,075	Wichita Falls 76307*	89,555
Live Oak	8,578	Robstown 78380	12,948	Windcrest.......	6,163
Lockhart........ 78644	8,379	Rockwall 75087	6,970	Woodway 76710	7,260
Longview 75602*	69,038	Rosenberg 77471	19,254	Yoakum 77995	6,468

UTAH (Ut. or UT)

Place and ZIP	Pop.	Place and ZIP	Pop.	Place and ZIP	Pop.
American Fork .. 84003	14,091	Midvale 84047	10,918	South Cottonwood —	11,117[1]
Bennion —	9,575[1]	Mount Olympus .. —	16,068[1]	South Jordan —	8,855
Bountiful 84010	33,830	Murray 84107	26,850	South Ogden 84403	11,782
Brigham City 84302	15,986	North Ogden 84404	9,901	South Salt Lake .. 84115	11,251
Cedar City 84720	11,717	Ogden 84401*	66,215	Spanish Fork 84660	10,454
Centerville 84014	8,850	Orem 84057	56,418	Springville 84663	12,703
Clearfield 84015	20,187	Payson 84651	8,950	Sunset —	5,733[1]
Cottonwood 84121	11,554[1]	Pleasant Grove .. 84062	11,906	Taylorsville —	17,448[1]
Cottonwood Hts.. —	22,665[1]	Price 84501	9,860	Tooele.......... 84074	14,964
Holladay 84117	22,189[1]	Provo 84601*	77,475	Union–East Midvale —	9,665[1]
Kaysville........ 84037	10,903	Riverdale —	6,388	Val Verda —	6,422[1]
Kearns 84118	21,353[1]	Riverton 84065	8,100	Vernal.......... 84078	7,986
Layton 84041	28,915	Roy 84067	20,744	Washington Terrace 84403	8,320
Lehi 84043	7,422	St. George 84770	14,563	West Jordan 84084	32,507
Logan 84321	28,325	Salt Lake City ... 84119*	163,859	West Valley 84120	81,770
Magna.......... 84044	13,138[1]	Sandy City 84070	56,959	White City —	7,267[1]

VERMONT (Vt. or VT)

Place and ZIP	Pop.	Place and ZIP	Pop.	Place and ZIP	Pop.
Barre........... 05641	9,909	Burlington 05401*	37,737	Essex Junction .. 05452	7,272
Bennington 05201	16,064	Colchester † 05446	13,302	Hartford † 05047	8,209
Brattleboro† 05301	11,950	Essex † 05451	14,823	Middlebury† 05753	7,629

[1] 1980 Census. [2] 1982 Census Bureau estimate. † Town or township.

PLACE AND ZIP CODE	POP.[1]	PLACE AND ZIP CODE	POP.[1]	PLACE AND ZIP CODE	POP.[1]
VERMONT (*continued*)					
Milton † 05468	7,236²	Rutland 05701	17,908²	S. Burlington 05401	11,061²
Montpelier 05602	8,261²	St. Albans 05478	7,233²	Springfield 05156	10,200²
Northfield † 05663	5,498²	St. Johnsbury† 05819	7,795²	Winooski 05404	6,487²
VIRGINIA (Va. or VA)					
Alexandria 22313*	104,276²	Fredericksburg 22404*	15,523²	N. Springfield 22151	9,538
Annadale —	49,524	Front Royal 22630	11,203²	Oakton 22124	19,150
Arlington 22210*	152,599	Galax 24333	6,491²	Petersburg 23804*	40,234²
Bailey's Crossroads 22041	12,564	Glen Allen 23060	6,202	Pimmit Hills 22043	6,658
Bedford 24523	6,265²	Groveton —	18,860	Poquoson 23662	9,472²
Belle Haven 23306	6,520	Hampton 23670*	124,966²	Portsmouth 23705*	105,807²
Blacksburg 24060	30,596²	Harrisonburg 22801	25,398²	Pulaski 24301	9,899²
Bon Air 23235	16,224	Herndon 22070*	12,865²	Quantico Station 22134	7,121
Bristol 24201	18,765²	Highland Springs 23075	12,146	Radford 24141	13,132²
Buena Vista 24416	6,553²	Hollins 24019	12,295	Reston 22090	36,407
Burke 22015	33,835	Hopewell 23860	23,969²	Richlands 24641	6,063²
Cave Spring —	21,862	Hybla Valley —	15,333	Richmond 23232*	218,237²
Centreville 22020	7,473	Idylwood —	11,982	Roanoke 24022*	100,187²
Chantilly 22021	12,259	Jefferson —	24,342	Rose Hill 24281	11,926
Charlottesville 22906*	40,299²	Lake Barcroft —	8,725	Salem 24153	24,007²
Chesapeake 23320*	119,749²	Lake Ridge —	11,072	Seven Corners 22044	6,058
Chester 23831	11,728	Lakeside 23228	12,289	South Boston 24592	7,091²
Christiansburg 24073	11,016²	Laurel 23060	10,569	Springfield 22150*	21,435
Collinsville 24078	7,517	Leesburg 22075	8,557²	Staunton 24401	22,038²
Colonial Heights 23834	17,116²	Lexington 24450	7,087²	Sterling Park —	16,080
Covington 24426	8,395²	Lincolnia 22312	10,350	Suffolk 23434	47,522²
Culpeper 22701	6,725²	Lynchburg 24506*	67,315²	Timberlake 24502	9,697
Dale City 22193	33,127	Madison Heights 24572	14,146	Tuckahoe 23229	39,868
Danville 24541	44,813²	Manassas 22110	17,109²	Tyson's Corner 22103	10,065
Dumbarton —	8,149	Manassas Park 22111	6,604²	University Hts. —	6,736
Dunn Loring 22027	6,077	Mantua —	6,524	Vienna 22180	16,258²
East Highland Park —	11,797	Marion 24354	7,236²	Vinton 24179	8,013²
Fairfax 22030	20,454²	Martinsville 24112	18,124²	Virginia Beach 23450*	282,588²
Falls Church 22046*	9,357²	McLean 22101*	35,664	Waynesboro 22980	15,131²
Farmville 23901	6,338²	Mechanicsville 23111	9,269	West Springfield 22152	25,012
Fort Belvoir 22060	7,726	Merrifield 22116	7,525	Williamsburg 23185	10,068²
Fort Hunt —	14,294	Mount Vernon 22121	24,058	Winchester 22601	20,285²
Fort Lee 23801	9,784	Newington 22122	8,313	Wolf Trap —	9,875
Franconia 22310	8,476	Newport News 23607*	151,240²	Woodbridge 22191	24,004
Franklin 23851	6,951²	Norfolk 23501*	266,874²	Wytheville 24382	7,135
WASHINGTON (Wash. or WA)					
Aberdeen 98520	18,447²	Kenmore 98028	7,281	Puyallup 98371	18,738²
Alderwood Manor 98036	16,524	Kennewick 99336	38,260²	Redmond 98052	25,464²
Anacortes 98221	9,427²	Kent 98031	23,599²	Renton 98057	33,282²
Auburn 98002	29,170²	Kingsgate —	12,652²	Richland 99352	35,152²
Bellevue 98009*	74,095²	Kirkland 98033	19,260²	Richmond Highlands —	24,463
Bellingham 98225	45,312²	Lacey 98503	14,303²	Riverton —	14,182
Bothell 98011	7,444²	Lake Forest North —	7,995	Rose Hill 98033	7,616
Boulevard Park —	8,382	Lakeland North —	11,648	Seattle 98109*	490,077²
Bremerton 98310*	34,475²	Lakes District —	54,533	Sedro–Woolley 98284	6,469²
Burien 98148	23,189	Longview 98632	30,921²	Shelton 98584	7,782²
Cascade 98055	16,939	Lynnwood 98036	23,279²	Sheridan Beach —	6,873
Centralia 98531	12,047²	Martha Lake —	7,022	Silver Lake–Fircrest 98645	10,299
Chehalis 98532	6,088²	Mercer Island 98040	21,003²	Spanaway 98387	8,868
Cheney 99004	7,608²	Moses Lake 98837	10,432²	Spokane 99202*	171,903²
Clarkston 99403	6,891²	Mount Vernon 98273	13,867²	Sunnyside 98944	9,530²
Des Moines 98188	9,942²	Mountlake Terrace 98043	15,791²	Tacoma 98413*	161,351²
Dishman 99213	10,169	Newport Hills 98006	12,245	Toppenish 98948	6,584²
E. Renton Highlands —	12,033	North City 98155	13,551	Tumwater 98501	7,098²
E. Wenatchee Beach 98801	11,410	North Hill —	10,170	University Place 98466	20,381
Eastgate 98007	8,341	North Marysville —	15,159	Valley Ridge —	17,961
Edmonds 98020	27,166²	Oak Harbor 98277	12,111²	Vancouver 98661*	43,141²
Ellensburg 98926	11,717²	Olympia 98501*	27,980²	Veradale 99037	7,256
Esperance —	11,120	Opportunity 99214	21,241	Walla Walla 99362	25,693²
Everett 98201*	56,586²	Orchards 98662	8,828	Wenatchee 98801	17,444²
Fort Lewis 98433	23,761	Parkland 98444*	23,355	West Federal Way —	16,872
Hazel Dell 98665	15,386	Pasco 99301	19,339²	West Pasco —	5,729
Hoquiam 98550	9,420²	Port Angeles 98362	17,091²	White Center–	
Inglewood 98011	12,467	Port Townsend 98368	6,120²	Shorewood —	19,362
Juanita 98033	17,232	Poverty Bay —	8,353	Yakima 98903*	50,127²
Kelso 98626	11,071²	Pullman 99163	23,124²	Zenith–Saltwater —	8,982

1 1980 Census. 2 1982 Census Bureau estimate. † Town or township.

PLACE AND ZIP CODE	POP.[2]	PLACE AND ZIP CODE	POP.[2]	PLACE AND ZIP CODE	POP.[2]

WEST VIRGINIA (W. Va. or WV)

PLACE AND ZIP CODE	POP.[2]	PLACE AND ZIP CODE	POP.[2]	PLACE AND ZIP CODE	POP.[2]			
Beckley	25801	20,400	Huntington	25704*[d]	62,090	Princeton	24740	7,895
Bluefield	24701	15,926	Keyser	26726	6,645	St. Albans	25177	12,207
Bridgeport	26330	6,635	Martinsburg	25401	13,090	S. Charleston	25303	15,475
Buckhannon	26201	7,041	Morgantown	26505	28,482	Vienna	26105	11,633
Charleston	25301*	61,806	Moundsville	26041	12,306	Weirton	26062	24,398
Clarksburg	26301	22,070	New Martinsville	26155	7,036	Weston	26452	6,118
Dunbar	25064	9,291	Nitro	25143	7,900	Westover	26505	4,975
Elkins	26241	8,640	Oak Hill	25901	7,196	Wheeling	26003	42,609
Fairmont	26554	23,388	Parkersburg	26101	39,477	Williamson	25661	5,193
Grafton	26354	6,770	Point Pleasant	25550	5,559			

WISCONSIN (Wis., Wisc., or WI)

PLACE AND ZIP CODE	POP.[2]	PLACE AND ZIP CODE	POP.[2]	PLACE AND ZIP CODE	POP.[2]			
Antigo	54409	8,659	Janesville	53545	51,321	Portage	53901	7,913
Appleton	54911	60,553	Jefferson	53549	5,559	Prairie du Chien	53821	5,887
Ashland	54806	9,478	Kaukauna	54130	11,648	Racine	53401*	84,472
Ashwaubenon	54304	14,774	Kenosha	53141*	76,455	Reedsburg	53959	5,253
Baraboo	53913	8,065	Kimberly	54136	5,940	Rhinelander	54501	7,778
Beaver Dam	53916	14,092	La Crosse	54601	48,151	Rice Lake	54868	7,844
Beloit	53511	34,498	Lake Geneva	53147	5,609	Richland Center	53581	5,092
Berlin	54923	5,642	Little Chute	54140	8,372	Ripon	54971	7,078
Brookfield	53005	33,741	Madison	53707	172,640	River Falls	54022	9,134
Brown Deer	53209	12,953	Manitowoc	54220	32,801	St. Francis	53207	10,024
Burlington	53105	8,399	Marinette	54143	11,963	Shawano	54166	7,146
Cedarburg	53012	8,982	Marshfield	54449	18,755	Sheboygan	53081	48,321
Chippewa Falls	54729	12,508	Menasha	54952	14,702	Sheboygan Falls	53085	5,410
Cudahy	53110	19,380	Menomonee Falls	53051	27,469	Shorewood	53211	14,617
De Pere	54115	15,461	Menomonie	54751	12,951	S. Milwaukee	53172	21,007
Delavan	53115	5,660	Mequon	53092	16,335	Sparta	54656	7,082
Eau Claire	54702*	53,032	Merrill	54452	9,553	Stevens Point	54481	21,997
Elm Grove	53122	6,406	Middleton	53562	12,584	Stoughton	53589	7,926
Fond du Lac	54935	35,983	Milwaukee	53201*	631,509	Sturgeon Bay	54235	9,243
Fort Atkinson	53538	9,823	Monona	53716	8,817	Sun Prairie	53590	13,540
Fox Point	53217	7,472	Monroe	53566	10,133	Superior	54880	29,440
Franklin	53132	17,806	Muskego	53150	15,524	Tomah	54660	7,151
Germantown	53022	11,227	Neenah	54956	22,514	Two Rivers	54241	13,377
Glendale	53209	13,968	New Berlin	53151	30,493	Watertown	53094	18,249
Grafton	53024	8,378	New London	54961	6,409	Waukesha	53186	51,376
Green Bay	54305*	89,758	Oak Creek	53154	17,465	Waupun	53963	8,339
Greendale	53129	16,659	Oconomowoc	53066	9,845	Wausau	54401	32,107
Greenfield	53220	31,762	Onalaska	54650	9,950	Wauwatosa	53213	50,782
Hales Corners	53130	6,966	Oshkosh	54901	50,221	West Allis	53214	64,541
Hartford	53027	7,245	Platteville	53818	9,564	West Bend	53095	21,462
Hartland	53029	5,833	Plover	54467	5,630	Whitefish Bay	53217	14,760
Howard	54303	8,512	Plymouth	53073	6,164	Whitewater	53190	11,632
Hudson	54016	5,486	Port Washington	53074	8,661	Wisconsin Rapids	54494	18,506

WYOMING (Wyo., or WY)

PLACE AND ZIP CODE	POP.[2]	PLACE AND ZIP CODE	POP.[2]	PLACE AND ZIP CODE	POP.[2]			
Casper	82601*	53,392	Green River	82935	14,029	Riverton	82501	9,406
Cheyenne	82001*	49,216	Jackson	83001	5,224	Rock Springs	82901	21,732
Cody	82414	7,982	Lander	82520	8,174	Sheridan	82801	15,919
Douglas	82633	6,471	Laramie	82070	25,339	Torrington	82240	5,646
Evanston	82930	11,008	Powell	82435	6,005	Wheatland	82201	5,397
Gillette	82716	18,419	Rawlins	82301	11,924	Worland	82401	6,886

DIST. OF COLUMBIA (D.C. or DC) | GUAM (GU) | VIRGIN ISLANDS (V.I. or VI)

PLACE AND ZIP CODE	POP.[2]	PLACE AND ZIP CODE	POP.[2]	PLACE AND ZIP CODE	POP.[2]			
Washington	20013*	633,425	Tamuning	96911	13,527[1]	Charlotte Amalie	00801	11,756[1]

PUERTO RICO (P.R. or PR)

PLACE AND ZIP CODE	POP.[2]	PLACE AND ZIP CODE	POP.[2]	PLACE AND ZIP CODE	POP.[2]			
Aguada †	00602	32,500	Fajardo †	00648	33,600	Rio Grande †	00745	36,600
Aguadilla †	00603	54,300	Guayama †	00654	39,600	Salinas †	00751	25,800
Aibonito †	00609	22,800	Guaynabo †	00657	82,300	San German †	00753	34,100
Arecibo †	00612	86,600	Hatillo †	00659	29,300	San Juan †	00936*	430,500
Bayamon †	00619	198,400	Humacao †	00661	49,200	San Lorenzo †	00754	34,300
Cabo Rojo †	00623	35,100	Isabela †	00662	37,900	San Sebastian †	00755	36,200
Caguas †	00625	199,200	Juana Diaz †	00665	43,000	Toa Alta †	00758	33,800
Canovanas †	00629	33,200	Juncos †	00666	27,200	Toa Baja †	00759	82,100
Carolina †	00630	168,400	Lares †	00669	27,600	Trujillo Alto †	00760	52,500
Catano †	00632	25,900	Las Piedras †	00671	23,600	Utuado †	00761	35,000
Cayey †	00633	43,200	Manati †	00701	36,200	Vega Alta †	00762	29,100
Cidra †	00639	29,500	Mayaguez †	00708	99,800	Vega Baja †	00763	49,600
Coamo †	00640	31,700	Moca †	00716	30,400	Yabucoa †	00767	31,000
Corozal †	00643	29,700	Ponce †	00731*	190,100	Yauco †	00768	38,300

[1] 1980 Census. [2] 1982 Census Bureau estimate. † Town or township.

AREAS, LATITUDES, LONGITUDES, AND ELEVATIONS OF U.S. CITIES

Sources: National Oceanic and Atmospheric Administration (elevations of weather stations); Bureau of the Census

STATE AND CITY	AREA (sq. mi.)	LATITUDE °	LATITUDE ′	LONGITUDE °	LONGITUDE ′	ELEVATION (ft.)
ALABAMA						
Anniston........	20.7	33	35	85	51	599
Bessemer.......	15.1	33	22	87	01	540
Birmingham.....	98.5	33	34	86	45	620
Dothan.........	70.5	31	12	85	21	300
Florence........	21.4	34	48	87	41	578
Gadsden........	35.4	34	02	86	00	565
Huntsville.......	113.5	34	42	86	35	600
Mobile..........	123.0	30	41	88	15	211
Montgomery....	128.3	32	18	86	24	221
Tuscaloosa.....	43.2	33	14	87	37	170
ALASKA						
Anchorage......	1,732.0	61	10	150	01	114
Fairbanks.......	31.4	64	49	147	52	436
Juneau.........	2,626.0	58	22	134	35	12
Sitka...........	2,938.0	57	04	135	21	15
ARIZONA						
Flagstaff........	64.1	35	08	111	40	7,006
Mesa...........	67.6	33	25	111	52	1,230
Phoenix........	324.0	33	27	112	04	1,083
Scottsdale......	88.4	33	30	111	55	1,227
Tempe.........	37.9	33	26	111	56	1,150
Tucson.........	98.8	32	15	110	57	2,444
Yuma..........	18.4	32	44	114	37	240
ARKANSAS						
Fort Smith.....	46.4	35	39	94	09	793
Hot Springs.....	22.7	34	31	93	03	680
Little Rock.....	79.4	34	46	92	19	512
Pine Bluff.......	21.6	34	13	92	01	215
Texarkana......	13.6	33	27	94	00	361
CALIFORNIA						
Altadena........	8.5	34	11	118	08	1,127
Bakersfield.....	73.6	35	25	119	03	495
Berkeley........	10.9	37	52	122	15	345
Burlingame.....	4.3	37	35	122	21	10
Chula Vista.....	17.7	32	36	117	06	9
Concord........	29.3	37	58	121	59	195
El Centro.......	5.3	32	46	115	34	–30
Fairfield........	27.0	38	16	122	02	38
Fresno.........	65.6	36	46	119	43	328
Fullerton.......	22.1	33	53	117	55	330
Hayward........	39.0	37	39	121	59	715
Long Beach.....	49.8	33	49	118	09	34
Los Angeles.....	464.7	34	03	118	14	270
Modesto........	24.9	37	39	121	00	91
Oakland........	53.9	37	48	122	16	30
Oxnard.........	24.0	34	12	119	11	49
Palm Springs....	76.0	33	50	116	30	425
Palo Alto........	24.6	37	27	122	08	25
Pasadena.......	23.1	34	09	118	09	864
Pomona........	22.8	34	04	117	49	740
Redwood City ...	33.7	37	29	122	14	31
Richmond.......	32.8	37	56	122	21	55
Riverside.......	71.8	33	57	117	23	840
Sacramento.....	96.1	38	35	121	30	19
Salinas.........	15.1	36	40	121	36	85
San Bernardino..	53.2	34	08	117	16	1,125
San Diego.......	320.0	32	44	117	10	13
San Francisco ...	46.4	37	47	122	25	52
San Jose........	158.0	37	21	121	54	67
San Mateo......	11.7	37	32	122	18	21
Santa Ana......	27.4	33	45	117	52	115
Santa Barbara...	18.7	34	25	119	41	5
Santa Clara.....	19.1	37	21	121	56	88
Santa Monica ...	8.2	34	00	118	30	15
Santa Rosa.....	26.6	38	27	122	42	167
Stockton........	40.0	38	00	121	19	12
Torrance........	20.5	33	48	118	20	110
Ventura........	15.2	34	17	119	17	105
Whittier........	12.8	33	58	118	02	340
COLORADO						
Boulder.........	19.5	40	00	105	16	5,420
Colorado Springs	103.4	38	49	104	43	6,090
Denver.........	110.6	39	45	104	59	5,320
Lakewood.......	35.6	39	45	105	08	5,637
Pueblo	33.2	38	17	104	31	4,639
CONNECTICUT						
Bridgeport......	14.7	41	10	73	08	7
Danbury........	46.5	41	23	73	28	510
Hartford........	17.8	41	48	72	39	19
Manchester.....	27.4	41	46	72	29	420
Milford.........	23.4	41	12	73	05	30
New Haven......	18.9	41	18	72	56	24
Norwalk........	22.3	41	07	73	25	37
Norwich........	28.6	41	32	72	04	20
Stamford.......	38.1	41	08	73	33	190
DELAWARE						
Wilmington	10.5	39	40	75	36	74
DIST. OF COLUMBIA						
Washington.....	62.7	38	56	77	02	10
FLORIDA						
Clearwater......	22.4	27	58	82	46	65
Fort Lauderdale .	29.2	26	06	80	12	16
Gainesville......	32.2	29	38	82	22	92
Jacksonville.....	759.7	30	30	81	42	26
Key West	9.0	24	34	81	48	6
Miami..........	34.3	25	48	80	16	7
Orlando........	39.5	28	26	81	20	85
Pensacola.......	24.1	30	28	87	12	112
St. Petersburg...	55.5	27	46	82	38	8
Tampa.........	84.4	27	58	82	32	19
GEORGIA						
Albany.........	42.6	31	32	84	08	180
Atlanta.........	131.0	33	39	84	26	1,010
Augusta	16.8	33	22	81	58	148
Columbus.......	217.5	32	31	84	56	385
Macon..........	49.6	32	42	83	39	354
Savannah.......	56.8	32	08	81	12	46
HAWAII						
Hilo...........	54.3	19	43	155	04	27
Honolulu........	87.0	21	20	157	55	7
IDAHO						
Boise...........	39.3	43	34	116	13	2,838
Idaho Falls......	12.8	43	31	112	04	4,730
Lewiston........	16.1	46	23	117	01	1,413
Pocatello	22.4	42	55	112	36	4,454
ILLINOIS						
Aurora	25.5	41	45	88	21	690
Belleville.......	12.2	38	30	89	51	450
Bloomington	14.2	40	31	89	00	785
Chicago	228.1	41	47	87	45	607

STATE AND CITY	AREA (sq. mi.)	LATI-TUDE °	'	LONGI-TUDE °	'	ELEVA-TION (ft.)
Decatur	37.1	39	51	88	58	670
Elgin	19.3	42	02	88	16	758
Joliet	23.5	41	33	88	05	550
Peoria	41.0	40	40	89	41	652
Rockford	38.8	42	12	89	06	724
Springfield	39.8	39	50	89	40	588
Waukegan	20.3	42	21	87	53	700
INDIANA						
Evansville	37.3	37	58	87	33	384
Fort Wayne	52.6	41	00	85	12	791
Gary	39.4	41	37	87	23	597
Indianapolis	352.0	39	44	86	17	792
Muncie	21.9	40	11	85	21	957
South Bend	36.3	41	42	86	19	773
Terre Haute	26.3	39	21	87	25	555
IOWA						
Cedar Rapids	53.9	41	53	91	42	840
Davenport	59.5	41	31	90	34	568
Des Moines	66.1	41	32	93	39	938
Dubuque	22.7	42	24	90	42	1,056
Iowa City	21.7	41	39	91	32	640
Sioux City	51.5	42	24	96	23	1,103
Waterloo	62.0	42	33	92	24	868
KANSAS						
Dodge City	10.5	37	46	99	58	2,582
Emporia	8.4	38	20	96	12	1,209
Lawrence	19.1	38	58	95	16	1,000
Salina	18.9	38	48	97	38	1,257
Topeka	49.4	39	04	95	38	877
Wichita	101.4	37	39	97	26	1,321
KENTUCKY						
Bowling Green	26.1	37	00	86	26	536
Covington	14.7	39	04	84	40	869
Lexington-Fayette	284.7	38	02	84	36	966
Louisville	60.0	38	14	85	46	462
Owensboro	11.2	37	46	87	09	420
LOUISIANA						
Baton Rouge	61.6	30	32	91	09	64
Lafayette	27.1	30	13	92	01	37
Lake Charles	27.2	30	07	93	13	9
Monroe	24.5	32	33	92	07	80
New Orleans	199.4	29	56	90	08	6
Shreveport	80.9	32	28	93	49	254
MAINE						
Bangor	35.4	44	48	68	49	163
Lewiston	34.9	44	06	70	13	180
Portland	23.2	43	39	70	19	43
MARYLAND						
Baltimore	80.3	39	17	76	37	14
Rockville	11.8	39	07	77	06	400
Towson	14.0	39	23	76	34	390
MASSACHUSETTS						
Boston	47.2	42	22	71	02	15
Brockton	21.5	42	03	71	00	80
Fall River	33.7	41	43	71	08	190
Framingham	24.9	42	17	71	25	170
Haverhill	31.8	42	46	71	04	60
Holyoke	21.0	42	12	72	36	98
Lawrence	6.6	42	42	71	10	57
New Bedford	18.7	41	38	70	56	120
Provincetown	7.3	42	04	70	12	30
Springfield	31.7	42	07	72	35	190
Worcester	37.4	42	16	71	52	986

STATE AND CITY	AREA (sq. mi.)	LATI-TUDE °	'	LONGI-TUDE °	'	ELEVA-TION (ft.)
MICHIGAN						
Ann Arbor	24.6	42	18	83	43	900
Bay City	10.8	43	37	83	52	590
Dearborn	23.8	42	19	83	14	607
Detroit	135.6	42	25	83	01	623
Flint	32.4	42	58	83	44	770
Grand Rapids	43.4	42	53	85	31	784
Kalamazoo	24.6	42	18	85	34	760
Lansing	35.3	42	47	84	36	841
Pontiac	18.7	42	39	83	18	974
Saginaw	17.4	43	32	84	05	662
MINNESOTA						
Duluth	67.3	46	50	92	11	1,438
Minneapolis	55.1	44	53	93	13	834
Rochester	18.7	43	55	92	30	1,297
MISSISSIPPI						
Biloxi	19.7	30	24	88	54	15
Gulfport	20.0	30	23	89	08	35
Jackson	106.2	32	19	90	05	330
Meridian	35.4	32	20	88	45	290
MISSOURI						
Columbia	41.9	38	49	92	13	887
Independence	80.6	39	06	94	25	1,000
Jefferson City	24.0	38	34	92	11	640
Kansas City	316.3	39	00	94	32	870
St. Louis	61.4	38	37	90	11	446
Springfield	64.9	37	14	93	23	1,268
MONTANA						
Billings	20.3	45	46	108	29	3,097
Great Falls	16.1	47	29	111	22	3,662
Helena	13.3	46	36	112	00	3,828
NEBRASKA						
Lincoln	60.0	40	49	96	42	1,150
Omaha	90.9	41	22	96	01	1,309
NEVADA						
Carson City	145.6	39	09	119	46	4,651
Las Vegas	55.0	36	05	115	10	2,162
Reno	31.0	39	30	119	47	4,404
NEW HAMPSHIRE						
Concord	64.1	43	12	71	30	346
Manchester	32.1	43	00	71	28	170
Nashua	31.3	42	47	71	30	188
NEW JERSEY						
Atlantic City	10.7	39	23	74	26	11
Jersey City	13.2	40	44	74	03	135
Newark	24.1	40	42	74	10	11
Paterson	8.3	40	54	74	09	100
Trenton	7.0	40	13	74	46	56
NEW MEXICO						
Albuquerque	95.3	35	03	106	37	5,311
Santa Fe	31.5	35	39	105	58	6,800
NEW YORK						
Albany	21.6	42	45	73	48	275
Binghamton	10.4	42	13	75	59	1,590
Buffalo	41.8	42	56	78	44	705
New York	301.5	40	47	73	58	132
Rochester	34.2	43	07	77	40	547
Schenectady	10.2	42	50	73	55	225
Syracuse	23.8	43	07	76	07	410
Utica	16.8	43	09	75	23	718
White Plains	9.6	41	04	73	43	397

AREAS, LATITUDES, LONGITUDES, AND ELEVATIONS OF U.S. CITIES *(continued)*

STATE AND CITY	AREA (sq. mi.)	LATITUDE °	′	LONGITUDE °	′	ELEVATION (ft.)
NORTH CAROLINA						
Asheville	28.7	35	36	82	32	2,242
Charlotte	139.7	35	13	80	56	735
Durham	40.6	36	02	78	58	406
Fayetteville	33.0	35	13	80	56	735
Greensboro	60.3	36	05	79	57	897
High Point	31.5	35	58	79	59	912
Raleigh	53.8	35	47	78	42	400
Winston-Salem	60.7	36	05	80	13	770
NORTH DAKOTA						
Bismarck	18.8	46	51	100	33	1,720
Fargo	25.7	46	54	96	48	896
Grand Forks	13.1	47	56	97	05	830
Minot	12.9	48	16	101	17	1,713
OHIO						
Akron	57.5	41	05	81	31	1,007
Canton	19.5	40	46	81	23	1,020
Cincinnati	78.1	39	09	84	31	761
Cleveland	79.0	41	29	81	43	690
Columbus	180.9	39	57	83	07	875
Dayton	48.4	39	46	84	11	745
Hamilton	19.4	39	24	84	34	590
Lima	12.3	40	45	84	05	870
Mansfield	25.5	40	49	82	31	1,295
Toledo	84.2	41	39	83	32	595
Warren	14.8	41	09	80	49	900
Youngstown	34.5	41	16	80	40	1,178
OKLAHOMA						
Lawton	44.6	34	37	98	27	1,150
Oklahoma City	603.6	35	28	97	33	1,200
Tulsa	185.6	36	11	95	54	668
OREGON						
Eugene	32.5	44	07	123	13	364
Portland	103.3	45	36	122	36	21
Salem	36.8	44	55	123	01	195
PENNSYLVANIA						
Allentown	17.5	40	39	75	26	387
Altoona	9.1	40	30	78	28	1,320
Erie	21.7	42	05	80	11	732
Harrisburg	7.7	40	13	76	51	338
Lancaster	6.4	40	01	76	17	255
Philadelphia	136.0	39	57	75	09	35
Pittsburgh	55.4	40	27	80	00	747
Reading	9.6	40	19	75	56	270
Scranton	24.8	41	25	75	40	746
Wilkes-Barre	7.3	41	20	75	44	930
York	5.2	39	54	76	44	640
RHODE ISLAND						
Newport	7.7	41	31	71	19	20
Providence	18.9	41	44	71	26	51
Woonsocket	7.8	41	59	71	30	115
SOUTH CAROLINA						
Charleston	25.5	32	47	79	56	9
Columbia	107.1	33	59	81	01	242
Greenville	27.9	34	52	82	24	1,010
SOUTH DAKOTA						
Aberdeen	6.5	45	27	98	26	1,296
Huron	5.3	44	22	98	13	1,277
Pierre	12.7	44	23	100	17	1,734
Rapid City	22.0	44	04	103	16	3,370
Sioux Falls	40.7	43	34	96	44	1,418

STATE AND CITY	AREA (sq. mi.)	LATITUDE °	′	LONGITUDE °	′	ELEVATION (ft.)
TENNESSEE						
Chattanooga	123.8	35	02	85	12	665
Knoxville	77.1	35	57	83	55	895
Memphis	264.1	35	09	90	03	205
Nashville-Davidson	479.5	36	07	86	41	590
TEXAS						
Abilene	75.9	32	25	99	41	1,784
Amarillo	80.1	35	14	101	42	3,607
Arlington	79.1	32	44	97	07	630
Austin	116.0	30	18	97	42	597
Beaumont	72.9	30	06	94	06	20
Brownsville	27.8	25	54	97	26	19
Corpus Christi	104.0	27	46	97	30	44
Dallas	333.0	32	51	96	51	481
El Paso	239.2	31	48	106	24	3,918
Fort Worth	240.2	32	45	97	20	616
Galveston	48.2	29	18	94	48	7
Houston	556.4	29	45	95	22	96
Laredo	19.7	27	30	99	28	396
Odessa	29.4	31	53	102	24	2,910
San Antonio	262.7	29	32	98	28	788
Waco	74.1	31	37	97	13	500
Wichita Falls	49.2	33	58	98	29	994
UTAH						
Ogden	26.1	41	15	111	57	4,350
Provo	35.0	40	13	111	40	4,470
Salt Lake City	75.2	40	46	111	53	4,320
VERMONT						
Burlington	10.8	44	28	73	12	400
Montpelier	10.6	44	12	72	34	1,126
VIRGINIA						
Alexandria	15.0	38	48	77	05	70
Lynchburg	49.5	37	20	79	12	916
Newport News	65.3	37	01	76	27	50
Norfolk	53.0	36	54	76	12	22
Richmond	60.1	37	30	77	20	164
Roanoke	43.1	37	19	79	58	1,149
WASHINGTON						
Bellingham	22.5	48	45	122	29	140
Everett	23.3	47	59	122	11	60
Olympia	16.8	46	58	122	54	195
Seattle	144.6	47	39	122	18	19
Spokane	51.7	47	40	117	25	1,875
Tacoma	47.7	47	15	122	26	267
WEST VIRGINIA						
Charleston	28.0	38	21	81	39	600
Huntington	15.9	38	25	82	27	565
Wheeling	13.4	40	06	80	42	659
WISCONSIN						
Appleton	15.8	44	15	88	23	730
Green Bay	43.2	44	29	88	08	682
Kenosha	15.4	42	33	87	48	600
La Crosse	16.5	43	52	91	15	651
Madison	53.9	43	08	89	20	858
Milwaukee	95.8	42	57	87	54	672
Oshkosh	13.5	44	03	88	33	753
Racine	13.8	42	43	87	52	695
WYOMING						
Casper	13.9	42	51	106	18	5,195
Cheyenne	14.9	41	09	104	49	6,126
Laramie	9.7	41	19	105	35	7,173

Climate and Weather

HIGHLIGHTS: 1985

CRAZY WINTER WEATHER

If you think that the winters lately have had crazy weather, you are right according to a statistical analysis by climate researchers of the National Oceanic and Atmospheric Administration (NOAA)—Thomas Karl, Robert Livezey, and Edward Epstein.

The researchers reported that their calculations show the extreme fluctuations of weather experienced in winters since 1975 are unlikely to happen again for more than 1,000 years—not until some decade after the year 3000.

The researchers pointed out that considered alone the string of abnormally cold winters of 1976-77, 1977-78, and 1978-79 would be unlikely to happen again for more than 500 years.

But, when combined with the abnormally warm winters 1975-76, 1980-81, and 1982-83, odds on recurrence of the phenomena more than doubled.

The statistical model used in the research was based on the assumption that the climate was stable during the previous 89 years during which weather records have been kept. Using that data, a computer analysis generated random weather data for 2 million winters. A study of that long span indicated that 6 abnormal winters within a span of 8 years happened only about every 1,100 to 1,250 years on the average.

The researchers said, however, that if the extreme variability of recent winter weather continues, then it may indicate that the nation's climate is changing.

TIPS ON WATER CONSERVATION

Many areas of the United States were hit by drought in 1985. Authorities called on consumers to help conserve water supplies by observing the following tips:

1. Flush toilet only when essential—not to dispose of cigarettes, face tissues, and so on. Eliminating 2 flushes per day saves 7½ gallons of water.
2. Take a 3-minute shower. Saves 4 to 6 gallons of water.
3. Install water saver on bathroom shower head. Saves up to 60% of water usage.
4. Take a bath in less then half-full tub. Saves 10 gallons of water.
5. Don't let tap run while shaving. Shave in half-full sink. Saves 3 gallons of water.
6. Don't let tap run when washing dishes. Wash dishes once a day in sink or pan of water. Saves 7½ gallons of water.
7. Don't let tap run while brushing your teeth. Instead, use a glass of water. Saves 3 gallons of water.
8. Don't let tap run to get cool water to drink. Instead, keep container of drinking water in refrigerator. Saves 4 to 8 gallons of water each time.
9. When using dishwasher or washing machine, run only full load. Saves 4 to 8 gallons of water each time.
10. Fix dripping faucets or plumbing leaks. Saves huge amounts of water.

NAMES OF HURRICANES

Names chosen for hurricanes and tropical storms in the Atlantic, Caribbean, and Gulf of Mexico in 1985 were Ana, Bob, Claudette, Danny, Elena, Fabian, Gloria, Henri, Isabel, Juan, Kate, Larry, Mindy, Nicholas, Odette, Peter, Rose, Sam, Teresa, Victor, and Wanda.

Names for storms and hurricanes in the North Pacific in 1985 were Andres, Blanca, Carlos, Dolores, Enrique, Fefa, Guillermo, Holda, Ignacio, Jimena, Kevin, Linda, Marty, Nora, Olaf, Pauline, Rick, Sandra, Terry, Vivian, and Waldo.

Major storms in the central Pacific Ocean were given the names Nele, Oka, Peke, Uleki, Wila, Aka, Ekeka, Hali, and Iniki.

Storms with counter-clockwise circular rotation are named by the national hurricane centers when their wind speeds are 39 mph or more. They are designated hurricanes when the wind speeds reach 74 mph or more.

STORMS FORECAST FOR 1985-86

Based on a research study of the relationship of bad storms to phases of the Moon, the worst storms in 1985-86 may take place in the following periods.

1985	May 26–28
November 1–2	June 8–10
November 13–15	June 24–26
November 30	July 7–9
December 12–14	July 24–26
December 29–31	August 6–8
1986	August 22–24
January 11–13	September 5–7
January 28–30	September 21–23
February 9–11	October 4–6
February 27–28	October 20–22
March 11–13	November 3–5
March 28–30	November 19–21
April 10–12	December 2–4
April 27–29	December 19–21
May 9–11	December 31

HEAT DISCOMFORT APPARENT TEMPERATURES

The National Weather Service adopted in 1985 an index of apparent temperatures to describe the discomfort of summer heat in the same way that wind chill temperatures describe cold discomfort in the winter.

The apparent temperatures indicate the feelings of a person wearing light clothing and walking in the shade under varying conditions of temperature and moisture content in the air.

To use the table, find the outdoor temperature in the column at the left, then look across that row to the column headed by the day's relative humidity. For example, if an outdoor thermometer registers a temperature of 90° F. and the relative humidity is 70%, then you would feel as though the temperature is 104° F.

TEMPER-ATURE[1]	RELATIVE HUMIDITY (top row)																
	95%	90%	85%	80%	75%	70%	65%	60%	55%	50%	45%	40%	35%	30%	25%	20%	15%
115°	SD	SD	SD	SD	SD	SD	SD	SD	SD	SD	SD	SD	152°	138°	127°	120°	115°
114°	SD	SD	SD	SD	SD	SD	SD	SD	SD	SD	SD	161°	147°	134°	125°	118°	114°
113°	SD	SD	SD	SD	SD	SD	SD	SD	SD	SD	SD	158°	142°	131°	123°	116°	113°
112°	SD	SD	SD	SD	SD	SD	SD	SD	SD	SD	SD	152°	138°	128°	121°	115°	112°
111°	SD	SD	SD	SD	SD	SD	SD	SD	SD	SD	160°	147°	134°	125°	118°	113°	111°
110°	SD	SD	SD	SD	SD	SD	SD	SD	SD	SD	157°	142°	131°	123°	116°	112°	110°
109°	SD	SD	SD	SD	SD	SD	SD	SD	SD	151°	137°	128°	120°	115°	110°	109°	
108°	SD	SD	SD	SD	SD	SD	SD	SD	160°	145°	133°	124°	118°	113°	109°	108°	
107°	SD	SD	SD	SD	SD	SD	SD	SD	154°	140°	129°	122°	116°	111°	107°	107°	
106°	SD	SD	SD	SD	SD	SD	SD	159°	147°	135°	126°	119°	114°	109°	106°	106°	
105°	SD	SD	SD	SD	SD	SD	SD	156°	141°	130°	123°	116°	112°	108°	105°	105°	
104°	SD	SD	SD	SD	SD	SD	160°	149°	136°	127°	120°	114°	110°	106°	104°	104°	
103°	SD	SD	SD	SD	SD	SD	157°	142°	131°	123°	117°	112°	108°	105°	103°	103°	
102°	SD	SD	SD	SD	SD	160°	149°	136°	127°	120°	114°	110°	106°	103°	102°	102°	
101°	SD	SD	SD	SD	SD	156°	142°	131°	123°	117°	112°	108°	104°	102°	101°	101°	
100°	SD	SD	SD	SD	158°	148°	135°	126°	119°	114°	109°	106°	103°	100°	100°	100°	
99°	SD	SD	SD	SD	154°	140°	130°	122°	116°	111°	107°	104°	101°	99°	99°	99°	
98°	SD	SD	SD	160°	145°	133°	125°	118°	113°	109°	105°	102°	100°	98°	98°	98°	
97°	SD	SD	SD	161°	151°	137°	128°	120°	114°	110°	106°	103°	101°	98°	97°	97°	97°
96°	SD	SD	SD	156°	142°	131°	122°	116°	111°	107°	104°	101°	99°	97°	96°	96°	96°
95°	SD	SD	161°	146°	134°	125°	118°	113°	108°	105°	102°	100°	97°	96°	95°	95°	95°
94°	SD	160°	150°	137°	127°	120°	114°	109°	106°	103°	100°	98°	96°	94°	94°	94°	94°
93°	SD	155°	140°	129°	121°	115°	110°	106°	103°	100°	98°	96°	94°	93°	93°	93°	93°
92°	158°	143°	131°	123°	116°	111°	107°	104°	101°	98°	96°	95°	93°	92°	92°	92°	92°
91°	146°	133°	124°	117°	112°	107°	104°	101°	99°	97°	95°	93°	92°	91°	91°	91°	91°
90°	135°	125°	118°	112°	108°	104°	101°	99°	97°	95°	93°	92°	90°	90°	90°	90°	90°
89°	126°	118°	112°	108°	104°	101°	99°	97°	95°	93°	92°	90°	89°	89°	89°	89°	89°
88°	118°	113°	108°	104°	101°	99°	96°	95°	93°	91°	90°	89°	88°	88°	88°	88°	88°
87°	112°	108°	104°	101°	98°	96°	94°	93°	91°	90°	89°	88°	87°	87°	87°	87°	87°
86°	107°	103°	100°	98°	96°	94°	92°	91°	89°	88°	87°	86°	86°	86°	86°	86°	86°
85°	103°	100°	97°	95°	93°	92°	90°	89°	88°	87°	86°	85°	85°	85°	85°	85°	85°
84°	99°	96°	94°	93°	91°	90°	88°	87°	86°	86°	85°	84°	84°	84°	84°	84°	84°
83°	96°	94°	92°	90°	89°	88°	87°	86°	85°	84°	83°	83°	83°	83°	83°	83°	93°
82°	93°	91°	90°	88°	87°	86°	85°	84°	84°	83°	82°	82°	82°	82°	82°	82°	82°
81°	90°	89°	87°	86°	85°	84°	84°	83°	82°	82°	81°	81°	81°	81°	81°	81°	81°
80°	87°	86°	85°	84°	84°	83°	82°	82°	81°	80°	80°	80°	80°	80°	80°	80°	80°
79°	85°	84°	83°	83°	82°	81°	81°	80°	80°	79°	79°	79°	79°	79°	79°	79°	79°
78°	83°	82°	82°	81°	80°	80°	79°	79°	79°	78°	78°	78°	78°	78°	78°	78°	78°
77°	81°	81°	80°	80°	79°	79°	78°	78°	77°	77°	77°	77°	77°	77°	77°	77°	77°
76°	80°	79°	79°	78°	78°	77°	77°	77°	76°	76°	76°	76°	76°	76°	76°	76°	76°
75°	78°	78°	77°	77°	77°	76°	76°	75°	75°	75°	75°	75°	75°	75°	75°	75°	75°
74°	77°	76°	76°	76°	75°	75°	75°	74°	74°	74°	74°	74°	74°	74°	74°	74°	74°
73°	76°	75°	75°	75°	74°	74°	74°	73°	73°	73°	73°	73°	73°	73°	73°	73°	73°
72°	75°	74°	74°	74°	73°	73°	73°	72°	72°	72°	72°	72°	72°	72°	72°	72°	72°
71°	74°	73°	73°	72°	72°	72°	71°	71°	71°	71°	71°	71°	71°	71°	71°	71°	71°
70°	72°	72°	72°	71°	71°	71°	70°	70°	70°	70°	70°	70°	70°	70°	70°	70°	70°

[1] All temperatures are Fahrenheit. SD = Severe Discomfort.

RECORD HIGH AND LOW TEMPERATURES

Source: Environmental Data Service, NOAA, U.S. Department of Commerce

	RECORD HIGH TEMPERATURES			RECORD LOW TEMPERATURES		
	Temp. (F.)	Date	Location	Temp. (F.)	Date	Location
World	136°	Sept. 13, 1922	Al Aziziyah, Libya	−129°	July 21, 1983	Vostock Research Station, Antarctica
United States	134°	July 10, 1913	Greenland Ranch, California	−79.8°	Jan. 23, 1971	Prospect Creek Camp, Alaska
Alabama......	112°	Sept. 5, 1925	Centerville	−27°	Jan. 30, 1966	New Market
Alaska........	100°	June 27, 1915	Fort Yukon	−79.8°	Jan. 23, 1971	Prospect Creek Camp
Arizona.......	127°	July 7, 1905*	Parker	−40°	Jan. 7, 1971	Hawley Lake
Arkansas.....	120°	Aug. 10, 1936	Ozark	−29°	Feb. 13, 1905	Pond
California.....	134°	July 10, 1913	Greenland Ranch	−45°	Jan. 20, 1937	Boca
Colorado.....	118°	July 11, 1888	Bennett	−60°	Feb. 1, 1951	Taylor Park
Connecticut...	105°	July 22, 1926	Waterbury	−32°	Feb. 16, 1943	Falls Village
Delaware.....	110°	July 21, 1930	Millsboro	−17°	Jan. 17, 1893	Millsboro
Dist. of Columbia	106°	July 20, 1930*	Washington	−18°	Jan. 22, 1984	Washington
Florida........	109°	June 29, 1931	Monticello	− 2°	Feb. 13, 1899	Tallahassee
Georgia.......	113°	May 27, 1978	Greenville	−17°	Jan. 27, 1940	CCC Camp F-16
Hawaii........	100°	Apr. 27, 1931	Pahala	12°	May 17, 1979	Mauna Kea
Idaho.........	118°	July 28, 1934	Orofino	−60°	Jan. 16, 1943	Island Park Dam
Illinois........	117°	July 14, 1954	E. St. Louis	−35°	Jan. 22, 1930	Mt. Carroll
Indiana.......	116°	July 14, 1936	Collegeville	−35°	Feb. 2, 1951	Greensburg
Iowa	118°	July 20, 1934	Keokuk	−47°	Jan. 12, 1912	Washta
Kansas	121°	July 24, 1936*	Alton (near)	−40°	Feb. 13, 1905	Lebanon
Kentucky	114°	July 28, 1930	Greensburg	−34°	Jan. 28, 1963	Cynthiana
Louisiana	114°	Aug. 10, 1936	Plain Dealing	−16°	Feb. 13, 1899	Minden
Maine	105°	July 10, 1911*	North Bridgton	−48°	Jan. 19, 1925	Van Buren
Maryland	109°	July 10, 1936*	Cumberland & Frederick	−40°	Jan. 13, 1912	Oakland
Massachusetts	107°	Aug. 2, 1975	New Bedford and Chester	−34°	Jan. 18, 1957	Birch Hill Dam
Michigan	112°	July 13, 1936	Mio	−51°	Feb. 9, 1934	Vanderbilt
Minnesota	114°	July 6, 1936*	Moorhead	−59°	Feb. 16, 1903*	Pokegama Dam
Mississippi....	115°	July 29, 1930	Holly Springs	−19°	Jan. 30, 1966	Corinth 4 SW
Missouri	118°	July 14, 1954*	Warsaw & Union	−40°	Feb. 13, 1905	Warsaw
Montana	117°	July 5, 1937	Medicine Lake	−70°	Jan. 20, 1954	Rogers Pass
Nebraska	118°	July 24, 1936*	Minden	−47°	Feb. 12, 1899	Camp Clarke
Nevada	122°	June 23, 1954*	Overton	−50°	Jan. 8, 1937	San Jacinto
New Hampshire	106°	July 4, 1911	Nashua	−46°	Jan. 28, 1925	Pittsburg
New Jersey ...	110°	July 10, 1936	Runyon	−34°	Jan. 5, 1904	River Vale
New Mexico ...	116°	July 10, 1934*	Orogrande	−50°	Feb. 1, 1951	Gavilan
New York	108°	July 22, 1926	Troy	−52°	Feb. 9, 1934	Stillwater Reservoir
North Carolina	109°	Sept. 7, 1954*	Weldon	−29°	Jan. 30, 1966	Mt. Mitchell
North Dakota..	121°	July 6, 1936	Steele	−60°	Feb. 15, 1936	Parshall
Ohio	113°	July 21, 1934*	Gallipolis (near)	−39°	Feb. 10, 1899	Milligan
Oklahoma	120°	July 26, 1943*	Tishomingo	−27°	Jan. 18, 1930*	Watts
Oregon	119°	Aug. 10, 1938*	Pendleton	−54°	Feb. 10, 1933*	Seneca
Pennsylvania..	111°	July 10, 1936*	Phoenixville	−42°	Jan. 5, 1904	Smethport
Rhode Island ..	104°	Aug. 2, 1975	Providence	−23°	Jan. 11, 1942	Kingston
South Carolina	111°	June 28, 1954*	Camden	−20°	Jan. 18, 1977	Caesars Head
South Dakota .	120°	July 5, 1936	Gannvalley	−58°	Feb. 17, 1936	McIntosh
Tennessee	113°	Aug. 9, 1930*	Perryville	−32°	Dec. 30, 1917	Mountain City
Texas	120°	Aug. 12, 1936	Seymour	−23°	Feb. 8, 1933*	Seminole
Utah	116°	June 28, 1892	Saint George	−50°	Jan. 5, 1913*	Strawberry Tunnel
Vermont.......	105°	July 4, 1911	Vernon	−50°	Dec. 30, 1933	Bloomfield
Virginia	110°	July 15, 1954	Balcony Falls	−29°	Feb. 10, 1899	Monterey
Washington ...	118°	Aug. 5, 1961*	Ice Harbor Dam	−48°	Dec. 30, 1968	Mazama & Winthrop
West Virginia ..	112°	July 10, 1936*	Martinsburg	−37°	Dec. 30, 1917	Lewisburg
Wisconsin.....	114°	July 13, 1936	Wisconsin Dells	−54°	Jan. 24, 1922	Danbury
Wyoming	114°	July 12, 1900	Basin	−63°	Feb. 9, 1933	Moran

* Also on earlier dates at same or other places in the state.

WEATHER IN U.S. STATES, CITIES, AND TERRITORIES

Source: *Local Climatological Data*, Environmental Data Service, NOAA

PLACE	TEMPERATURE RECORDS				NUMBER OF HOT AND COLD DAYS[1]			NUMBER OF SUNNY AND CLOUDY DAYS[1]			NUMBER OF STORMY DAYS[1]		
	High	Date	Low	Date	Hot[2]	Freez- ing[3]	Below zero[4]	Clear	Partly cloudy	Over- cast	Rain[5]	Snow[6]	Fog[7]
ALABAMA													
Birmingham	107°	July 1930	−10°	Feb. 1899	50	46	2	—	—	—	128	2	7
Huntsville	104°	July 1966	−11°	Jan. 1966	30	59	3	70	106	189	153	2	23
Mobile	104°	July 1952	− 1°	Feb. 1899	61	23	0	91	119	155	128	0	45
Montgomery	107°	July 1881	− 5°	Feb. 1899	77	29	0	85	102	178	106	0	49
ALASKA													
Anchorage	86°	June 1953	−38°	Feb. 1947	4[6]	212	37	62	66	237	111	16	34
Barrow	78°	July 1927	−56°	Feb. 1924	0	254	185	59	60	180	94	8	52
Fairbanks	99°	July 1919	−66°	Jan. 1934	47[8]	218	113	76	66	223	133	28	15
Juneau	90°	July 1975	−22°	Jan. 1972	29[8]	71	12	—	—	194	29	14	
Kodiak	86°	June 1953	−12°	Feb. 1971	5[8]	133	2	77	81	207	189	16	14
Nome	86°	July 1977	−47°	Jan. 1919	11[8]	228	77	96	66	203	153	32	18
ARIZONA													
Flagstaff	97°	July 1973	−30°	Jan. 1937	0	217	5	167	98	100	10	32	—
Phoenix	118°	July 1958	16°	Jan. 1913	164	0	0	189	93	83	54	0	0
Tucson	112°	June 1902	6°	Jan. 1913	122	12	0	168	87	110	67	0	0
Winslow	109°	July 1971	−19°	Dec. 1898	57	118	2	179	97	89	64	4	—
Yuma	123°	Sept. 1950	22°	Jan. 1937	173	0	0	177	97	91	28	0	—
ARKANSAS													
Fort Smith	113°	Aug. 1936	−15°	Feb. 1899	62	70	2	101	94	170	90	5	17
Little Rock	110°	Aug. 1936	−13°	Feb. 1899	64	54	0	119	101	145	126	3	17
CALIFORNIA													
Bakersfield	118°	July 1908	13°	Dec. 1905	110	7	0	151	88	126	49	0	31
Fresno	115°	July 1905	17°	Jan. 1913	90	21	0	168	74	123	59	0	50
Long Beach	111°	Oct. 1961	25°	Jan. 1963	29	0	0	146	93	126	37	0	13
Los Angeles	110°	Sept. 1963	23°	Jan. 1937	6	0	0	133	115	117	47	0	14
Sacramento	115°	June 1961	17°	Dec. 1932	40	27	0	176	70	119	75	0	36
San Diego	111°	Sept. 1963	25°	Jan. 1913	3	0	0	116	106	143	56	0	14
San Francisco	106°	June 1961	20°	Dec. 1932	2	0	0	151	94	120	78	0	6
Stockton	114°	July 1972	19°	Jan. 1963	71	31	0	175	75	115	70	0	—
COLORADO													
Alamosa	93°	July 1971	−50°	Jan. 1948	0	225	33	147	137	81	74	10	—
Colorado Springs . .	100°	June 1954	−32°	Jan. 1883	12	174	8	114	118	133	103	9	22
Denver	105°	Aug. 1878	−30°	Feb. 1936	21	161	11	98	126	141	98	8	8
Grand Junction . .	105°	July 1976	−23°	Jan. 1963	57	115	4	110	100	155	73	3	7
Pueblo	106°	July 1981	−31°	Feb. 1951	65	153	8	140	120	105	69	9	8
CONNECTICUT													
Bridgeport	103°	July 1957	−20°	Feb. 1934	5	110	3	106	82	176	110	7	—
Hartford	102°	July 1966	−26°	Jan. 1961	11	138	6	87	105	173	117	12	34
DELAWARE													
Wilmington	107°	Aug. 1918	−15°	Feb. 1899	16	103	3	101	110	154	119	9	37
DIST. OF COLUMBIA													
Washington	106°	July 1930	−18°	Jan. 1984	22	67	1	88	96	181	106	6	9
FLORIDA													
Jacksonville	105°	July 1942	10°	Feb. 1899	92	12	0	79	148	138	136	0	52
Key West	97°	Aug. 1956	41°	Jan. 1886	53	0	0	125	145	95	99	0	3
Miami	100°	July 1942	26°	Dec. 1934	81	0	0	91	182	92	149	0	1
Orlando	103°	Sept. 1921	20°	Jan. 1977	109	3	0	67	151	147	121	0	30
Pensacola	106°	July 1980	5°	Jan. 1985	40	15	0	96	133	136	107	0	45
Tallahassee	104°	June 1933	− 2°	Feb. 1899	83	25	0	88	119	158	120	0	53
Tampa	98°	June 1977	18°	Dec. 1962	51	3	0	107	144	114	106	0	16
West Palm Beach .	101°	July 1942	27°	Jan. 1977	72	1	0	70	172	123	159	0	5
GEORGIA													
Athens	108°	July 1930	− 4°	Jan. 1985	67	40	1	92	106	167	119	2	71
Atlanta	105°	July 1980	− 9°	Feb. 1899	25	39	3	85	99	181	134	3	44
Augusta	107°	July 1980	− 2°	Jan. 1982	70	50	0	93	118	154	114	0	41
Columbus	106°	Sept. 1925	− 3°	Feb. 1899	87	47	0	121	97	147	95	0	7
Macon	108°	June 1980	− 6°	Jan. 1985	76	27	0	87	119	159	110	2	29
Savannah	105°	July 1879	4°	Jan. 1985	61	24	0	86	93	186	130	0	52
HAWAII													
Hilo	94°	May 1966	51°	May 1910	0	0	0	27	119	219	281	0	0
Honolulu	93°	Oct. 1979	53°	Feb. 1976	27	0	0	51	178	136	124	0	0

1 Average per year. 2 Highest temperature 90° F. or above. 3 Lowest temperature 32° F. or below. 4 Lowest temperature 0° F. or below. 5 Rain of 0.01 inch or more. 6 Snow of 1 inch or more. 7 Visibility of 1/4 mile or less. 8 Days 70° F. and above.

WEATHER IN U.S. STATES, CITIES, AND TERRITORIES (continued)

PLACE	High	Date	Low	Date	Hot[2]	Freezing[3]	Below zero[4]	Clear	Partly cloudy	Overcast	Rain[5]	Snow[6]	Fog[7]
IDAHO													
Boise	111°	July 1960	−23°	Dec. 1972	36	137	8	99	76	190	103	10	14
Lewiston	117°	July 1939	−23°	Dec. 1919	46	86	1	65	87	213	118	6	—
Pocatello	105°	July 1931	−31°	Jan. 1949	28	169	26	78	108	179	132	21	14
ILLINOIS													
Chicago	105°	July 1934	−27°	Jan. 1985	8	135	19	73	100	192	130	13	20
Moline	106°	Aug. 1936	−27°	Jan. 1979	8	135	22	89	90	186	132	12	16
Peoria	113°	July 1936	−27°	Jan. 1884	8	120	15	73	83	209	130	16	30
Rockford	112°	July 1936	−27°	Jan. 1982	3	142	26	81	98	186	130	15	22
Springfield	112°	July 1954	−24°	Feb. 1905	118	118	13	77	95	193	136	8	21
INDIANA													
Evansville	108°	July 1936	−23°	Feb. 1951	24	87	7	78	113	174	134	4	17
Fort Wayne	106°	July 1936	−24°	Jan. 1918	4	128	1.17	79	102	184	141	20	30
Indianapolis	107°	July 1934	−25°	Jan. 1884	7	114	14	67	100	198	138	10	24
South Bend	109°	July 1934	−22°	Jan. 1943	1	124	14	67	89	209	149	24	31
IOWA													
Des Moines	110°	July 1936	−30°	Jan. 1884	13	127	24	95	85	185	136	16	28
Sioux City	111°	July 1939	−35°	Jan. 1912	15	147	33	84	99	182	116	16	28
Waterloo	112°	Aug. 1936	−34°	Mar. 1962	9	150	36	73	90	202	122	14	21
KANSAS													
Concordia	116°	Aug. 1936	−25°	Feb. 1899	37	128	14	108	103	154	95	9	20
Dodge City	109°	July 1978	−26°	Feb. 1899	62	120	6	114	118	133	81	8	22
Topeka	114°	July 1936	−25°	Feb. 1899	20	124	11	96	94	175	110	6	17
Wichita..........	114°	Aug. 1936	−22°	Feb. 1899	60	114	9	110	114	141	84	5	21
KENTUCKY													
Lexington	108°	July 1936	−21°	Jan. 1963	7	87	4	61	106	198	141	3	23
Louisville	107°	July 1901	−20°	Jan. 1963	11	89	4	69	110	186	130	3	12
LOUISIANA													
Baton Rouge.....	110°	Aug. 1909	2°	Feb. 1899	101	18	0	90	137	138	121	0	34
Lake Charles	104°	Aug. 1951	12°	Jan. 1948	80	13	0	89	120	156	108	0	51
New Orleans	102°	June 1954	7°	Feb. 1899	89	8	0	71	124	170	123	0	27
Shreveport	110°	Aug. 1909	−5°	Feb. 1899	96	33	0	82	103	180	109	1	23
MAINE													
Caribou	96°	May 1977	−41°	Feb. 1955	4	184	48	67	100	198	142	30	—
Portland.........	103°	Aug. 1975	−39°	Feb. 1943	4	154	18	81	114	170	133	16	43
MARYLAND													
Baltimore........	107°	July 1936	−7°	Jan. 1963	18	100	1	109	98	158	124	8	28
MASSACHUSETTS													
Boston	104°	July 1911	−18°	Feb. 1934	7	96	1	94	100	171	119	16	26
Worcester	102°	July 1911	−24°	Feb. 1943	4	138	8	96	110	159	135	14	—
MICHIGAN													
Detroit	105°	July 1934	−24°	Dec. 1872	3	132	13	79	92	194	133	16	26
Flint	108°	July 1936	−28°	Feb. 1916	0	121	15	58	102	205	140	14	23
Grand Rapids	108°	July 1936	−24°	Feb. 1899	5	135	7	51	101	213	155	24	26
Lansing	102°	Aug. 1918	−33°	Feb. 1875	4	139	122	59	115	191	147	14	18
Marquette	108°	July 1901	−34°	Feb. 1979	0	183	45	—	—	—	179	45	44
Sault Ste. Marie ..	98°	Aug. 1947	−37°	Feb. 1934	0	183	45	64	71	230	174	45	30
MINNESOTA													
Duluth	106°	July 1936	−41°	Jan. 1885	1	180	64	75	88	202	145	26	55
International Falls	103°	July 1923	−49°	Jan. 1896	2	184	80	73	90	202	136	19	23
Minn.–St. Paul ...	108°	July 1936	−34°	Jan. 1970	17	148	38	85	104	176	122	19	7
Rochester	108°	July 1936	−42°	Jan. 1887	6	150	36	69	100	196	124	13	37
MISSISSIPPI													
Jackson	107°	July 1930	−5°	Jan. 1940	91	49	0	101	97	167	110	1	21
Meridian	105°	Aug. 1943	−7°	Jan. 1940	103	33	0	88	111	166	118	1	43
MISSOURI													
Columbia	113°	July 1954	−26°	Feb. 1899	21	111	7	90	102	173	127	6	25
Kansas City	113°	Aug. 1936	−22°	Feb. 1899	22	117	13	101	91	173	115	7	25
St. Louis	115°	July 1954	−23°	Jan. 1864	18	100	10	76	112	177	117	7	16
Springfield	113°	July 1954	−29°	Feb. 1899	46	96	9	81	109	175	107	5	30

[1] Average per year. [2] Highest temperature 90° F. or above. [3] Lowest temperature 32° F. or below. [4] Lowest temperature 0° F. or below. [5] Rain of 0.01 inch or more. [6] Snow of 1 inch or more. [7] Visibility of 1/4 mile or less.

WEATHER IN U.S. STATES, CITIES, AND TERRITORIES (continued)

PLACE	TEMPERATURE RECORDS				NUMBER OF HOT AND COLD DAYS[1]			NUMBER OF SUNNY AND CLOUDY DAYS[1]			NUMBER OF STORMY DAYS[1]		
	High	Date	Low	Date	Hot[2]	Freezing[3]	Below zero[4]	Clear	Partly cloudy	Overcast	Rain[5]	Snow[6]	Fog[7]
MONTANA													
Billings	112°	July 1901	−49°	Feb. 1899	29	147	26	74	106	185	115	23	20
Great Falls	107°	July 1933	−49°	Feb. 1936	7	178	35	67	107	191	121	34	16
Helena	105°	Aug. 1969	−42°	Jan. 1957	18	182	32	73	122	170	109	21	7
Missoula	105°	July 1973	−33°	Jan. 1957	10	171	16	63	98	204	148	17	22
NEBRASKA													
Grand Island	117°	July 1936	−34°	Feb. 1899	18	155	26	104	103	158	97	9	30
Lincoln	115°	July 1936	−33°	Jan. 1974	27	147	26	96	99	170	112	9	17
Omaha	114°	July 1936	−32°	Jan. 1884	16	147	29	113	107	145	97	8	23
NEVADA													
Elko	107°	July 1890	−43°	Jan. 1937	36	182	10	120	99	146	103	16	6
Las Vegas	117°	July 1942	8°	Jan. 1963	110	23	0	175	88	102	34	0	0
Reno	106°	July 1931	−19°	Jan. 1890	38	181	1	130	106	129	78	14	1
NEW HAMPSHIRE													
Concord	102°	July 1966	−37°	Feb. 1943	6	167	32	75	121	169	128	16	53
NEW JERSEY													
Atlantic City	106°	June 1969	−10°	Jan. 1977	11	100	4	91	121	153	105	8	46
Newark	105°	July 1966	−14°	Feb. 1934	12	86	4	101	92	172	117	6	18
NEW MEXICO													
Albuquerque	105°	June 1974	−17°	Jan. 1971	70	123	0	135	120	110	65	3	8
Roswell	110°	July 1958	−29°	Feb. 1905	91	86	1	167	114	84	49	11	8
NEW YORK													
Albany	104°	July 1911	−28°	Jan. 1971	4	143	16	68	118	179	120	14	21
Binghamton	103°	July 1936	−28°	Jan. 1893	1	143	11	70	87	208	141	20	54
Buffalo	99°	Aug. 1948	−21°	Feb. 1934	4	136	7	50	100	215	158	28	14
New York City	107°	July 1966	−15°	Feb. 1934	4	70	2	112	86	167	110	5	46
Rochester	102°	July 1936	−22°	Feb. 1934	4	137	12	67	89	209	161	29	15
Syracuse	102°	July 1936	−26°	Jan. 1966	4	137	16	59	103	203	164	28	5
NORTH CAROLINA													
Asheville	99°	July 1936	−16°	Jan. 1985	1	87	3	77	111	177	135	6	98
Cape Hatteras . . .	97°	June 1952	6°	Jan. 1985	0	20	0	102	110	153	112	0	23
Charlotte	104°	Sept. 1954	−5°	Feb. 1899	12	55	0	84	107	174	120	3	54
Greensboro	102°	July 1977	−8°	Jan. 1985	12	74	0	81	112	172	121	4	56
Raleigh	105°	July 1952	−9°	Jan. 1985	32	59	0	77	110	178	126	2	48
NORTH DAKOTA													
Bismarck	114°	July 1936	−45°	Feb. 1936	16	183	62	87	107	171	111	25	10
Fargo	114°	July 1936	−48°	Jan. 1887	13	177	61	72	110	183	113	16	11
OHIO													
Akron	104°	Aug. 1918	−22°	Jan. 1982	9	113	9	59	103	203	155	15	31
Cincinnati	109°	July 1934	−25°	Jan. 1977	10	99	9	60	99	206	133	6	29
Cleveland	103°	July 1941	−19°	Jan. 1963	6	121	10	54	98	213	136	21	11
Columbus	106°	July 1936	−20°	Feb. 1899	5	117	10	59	100	206	144	10	16
Dayton	108°	July 1901	−28°	Feb. 1899	8	123	9	53	108	204	146	10	28
Toledo	105°	July 1936	−17°	Jan. 1963	6	134	16	63	113	189	139	14	21
Youngstown	100°	July 1954	−20°	Jan. 1985	2	124	9	50	96	219	137	14	31
OKLAHOMA													
Oklahoma City . . .	113°	Aug. 1936	−17°	Feb. 1899	70	80	2	95	114	156	79	5	19
Tulsa	115°	Aug. 1936	−16°	Jan. 1930	83	69	1	119	112	134	87	2	15
OREGON													
Astoria	101°	July 1942	6°	Dec. 1972	1	39	0	57	79	229	175	2	27
Eugene	108°	Aug. 1981	−12°	Dec. 1972	10	93	0	67	79	219	140	3	62
Medford	115°	July 1946	−10°	Dec. 1972	49	99	0	121	77	167	106	3	50
Portland	107°	July 1965	−3°	Feb. 1950	14	37	0	75	77	213	157	2	23
Salem	108°	July 1941	−12°	Dec. 1972	14	90	0	86	73	206	139	2	22
PENNSYLVANIA													
Allentown	105°	July 1966	−12°	Jan. 1961	5	125	4	93	98	174	118	9	24
Erie	99°	Sept. 1953	−17°	Feb. 1979	1	125	8	64	100	201	171	25	17
Harrisburg	107°	July 1966	−14°	Jan. 1912	8	105	2	92	107	166	121	14	15
Philadelphia	106°	Aug. 1918	−11°	Feb. 1934	12	95	2	100	117	148	122	7	24
Pittsburgh	103°	July 1936	−20°	Feb. 1899	0	124	7	58	110	197	149	10	23

[1] Average per year. [2] Highest temperature 90°F. or above. [3] Lowest temperature 32°F. or below. [4] Lowest temperature 0°F. or below. [5] Rain of 0.01 inch or more. [6] Snow of 1 inch or more. [7] Visibility of 1/4 mile or less.

WEATHER IN U.S. STATES, CITIES, AND TERRITORIES (continued)

PLACE	High	Date	Low	Date	Hot[2]	Freezing[3]	Below zero[4]	Clear	Partly cloudy	Overcast	Rain[5]	Snow[6]	Fog[7]
	TEMPERATURE RECORDS				NUMBER OF HOT AND COLD DAYS[1]			NUMBER OF SUNNY AND CLOUDY DAYS[1]			NUMBER OF STORMY DAYS[1]		
RHODE ISLAND													
Providence	104°	Aug. 1975	–17°	Feb. 1934	4	107	5	89	105	171	126	13	31
SOUTH CAROLINA													
Charleston	104°	June 1944	6°	Jan. 1985	38	26	0	75	97	193	120	0	49
Columbia	107°	June 1954	– 2°	Feb. 1899	44	54	0	77	97	191	122	1	54
Greenville	101°	July 1977	– 6°	Jan. 1966	6	51	0	96	103	166	133	3	54
SOUTH DAKOTA													
Aberdeen	115°	July 1936	–46°	Jan. 1912	25	180	46	101	103	161	86	12	18
Rapid City	110°	July 1973	–33°	Feb. 1936	12	170	27	95	118	152	117	12	20
Sioux Falls	110°	July 1936	–42°	Feb. 1899	12	161	36	91	99	175	117	15	27
TENNESSEE													
Bristol	102°	July 1952	–21°	Jan. 1985	1	90	3	79	103	183	147	5	56
Chattanooga	106°	July 1952	–10°	Jan. 1966	31	65	1	72	116	177	128	2	30
Knoxville	104°	July 1930	–16°	Jan. 1884	7	70	3	80	116	169	137	5	50
Memphis	108°	July 1980	–13°	Dec. 1963	62	55	1	95	99	171	121	2	10
Nashville	107°	July 1952	–17°	Jan. 1985	28	80	4	87	103	175	143	2	23
TEXAS													
Abilene	111°	Aug. 1943	– 9°	Jan. 1947	103	52	0	129	108	128	73	2	4
Amarillo	108°	June 1953	–16°	Feb. 1899	65	116	3	117	128	120	72	6	21
Austin	109°	Aug. 1954	– 2°	Jan. 1949	125	19	0	106	109	150	86	1	28
Brownsville	104°	Sept. 1947	12°	Feb. 1899	159	5	0	100	121	144	59	0	31
Dallas–Fort Worth	112°	Aug. 1936	– 8°	Feb. 1899	103	43	0	99	134	132	90	0	14
El Paso	112°	July 1979	– 8°	Jan. 1962	123	54	0	174	89	102	54	4	3
Galveston	101°	July 1932	8°	Feb. 1899	23	6	0	—	—	—	80	0	—
Houston	108°	Aug. 1909	5°	Jan. 1940	125	14	0	85	118	162	98	0	34
San Antonio	107°	Aug. 1909	0°	Jan. 1949	114	29	0	88	117	160	87	0	25
UTAH													
Salt Lake City	107°	July 1960	–30°	Feb. 1933	39	129	1	94	112	159	112	20	6
VERMONT													
Burlington	101°	Aug. 1944	–30°	Jan. 1957	2	144	27	55	93	217	148	15	9
VIRGINIA													
Norfolk	105°	Aug. 1918	–3°	Jan. 1985	18	47	0	83	116	166	127	1	36
Richmond	107°	Aug. 1918	–12°	Jan. 1940	21	68	0	77	102	186	123	6	34
Roanoke	105°	July 1936	–12°	Dec. 1917	10	104	3	81	110	174	127	6	35
WASHINGTON													
Olympia	104°	Aug. 1981	– 7°	Jan. 1972	10	102	0	56	92	217	165	9	78
Seattle–Tacoma	100°	June 1955	0°	Jan. 1950	2	30	0	68	63	234	145	5	27
Spokane	108°	Aug. 1961	–30°	Jan. 1888	20	150	5	63	110	192	124	16	59
Walla Walla	113°	Aug. 1961	–29°	Jan. 1875	42	70	0	85	111	169	121	3	—
Yakima	111°	July 1928	–25°	Feb. 1950	29	150	2	113	99	153	75	8	17
WEST VIRGINIA													
Charleston	108°	July 1931	–17°	Dec. 1917	13	96	5	73	96	196	156	10	108
Huntington	108°	July 1930	–15°	Jan. 1963	1	99	5	46	85	234	152	7	92
WISCONSIN													
Green Bay	104°	July 1936	–36°	Jan. 1888	3	162	27	67	101	197	124	13	23
LaCrosse	108°	July 1936	–43°	Jan. 1873	16	151	27	95	97	173	110	13	20
Madison	107°	July 1936	–37°	Jan. 1951	3	154	29	74	95	196	126	11	33
Milwaukee	105°	July 1934	–26°	Jan. 1982	3	146	22	67	104	194	135	17	43
WYOMING													
Casper	104°	July 1954	–40°	Jan. 1972	42	172	24	76	110	179	121	35	11
Cheyenne	100°	June 1954	–38°	Jan. 1875	5	174	14	91	127	147	112	12	24
Sheridan	106°	July 1954	–41°	Dec. 1919	39	184	31	83	105	177	112	29	10
AMERICAN SAMOA													
Pago Pago	92°	Feb. 1977	62°	July 1964	8	0	0	8	143	214	226	0	0
GUAM													
Taguac	95°	Sept. 1957	54°	Mar. 1965	2	0	0	4	117	244	291	0	—
PACIFIC ISLANDS													
Johnston Island	89°	Nov. 1969	62°	Dec. 1964	0	0	0	109	147	109	165	0	0
Kwajalein Island	97°	Oct. 1958	69°	Dec. 1963	8	0	0	26	66	273	239	0	0
Wake Island	95°	Sept. 1980	64°	Dec. 1954	66	0	0	149	145	71	179	0	0
PUERTO RICO													
San Juan	98°	Oct. 1981	60°	Mar. 1957	121	0	0	89	202	74	189	0	0

[1] Average per year. [2] Highest temperature 90°F. or above. [3] Lowest temperature 32°F. or below. [4] Lowest temperature 0°F. or below. [5] Rain of 0.01 inch or more. [6] Snow of 1 inch or more. [7] Visibility of 1/4 mile or less.

WEATHER IN FOREIGN COUNTRIES AND CITIES

Source: Environmental Data Service, *Climates of the World*

COUNTRY AND CITY	TEMPERATURES (in degrees Fahrenheit)						RAINFALL (in inches)				
	Extremes		Daily Average Range								
	Low	High	Jan.	April	July	Oct.	Annual	Jan.	Apr.	July	Oct.
Afghanistan: Kabul	− 6	104	18–36	43–66	61–92	42–73	12.6	3.1	0.3	0.1	T
Algeria: Algiers	32	107	49–59	55–68	70–83	63–74	30.0	4.4	1.6	T	3.1
Angola: Luanda	58	98	74–83	75–85	65–74	71–79	12.7	1.0	4.6	T	0.2
Argentina: Buenos Aires	22	104	63–85	53–72	42–57	50–69	37.4	3.1	3.5	2.2	3.4
Australia: Canberra	14	109	55–82	44–67	33–52	43–68	23.0	1.9	1.6	1.8	2.2
Austria: Vienna	−14	98	26–34	41–57	59–75	44–55	25.6	1.5	2.0	3.0	2.0
Bahamas: Nassau	41	94	65–77	69–81	75–88	73–85	46.4	1.4	2.5	5.8	6.5
Bangladesh: Dhaka	43	108	56–77	74–92	79–88	75–88	73.9	0.3	5.4	13.0	5.3
Barbados: Bridgetown	61	95	70–83	72–86	74–86	73–86	50.3	2.6	1.4	5.8	7.0
Bermuda: Hamilton	40	99	58–68	59–71	73–85	69–79	57.6	4.4	4.1	4.5	5.8
Bolivia: La Paz	26	80	43–63	40–65	33–62	40–66	22.6	4.5	1.3	0.4	1.6
Brazil: Brasília	46	93	65–80	62–82	51–78	64–82	54.0	9.0	3.4	0.0	4.9
Rio de Janeiro	46	102	73–84	69–80	63–75	66–77	42.6	4.9	4.2	1.6	3.1
Britain: London	9	99	35–44	40–56	55–73	44–58	22.9	2.0	1.8	2.0	2.3
Bulgaria: Sofia	−17	99	22–34	41–62	57–82	42–63	25.0	1.3	2.3	2.4	2.1
Burkinafaso: Ouagadougou	48	118	60–92	79–103	74–91	74–95	35.2	T	0.6	8.0	1.3
Burma: Mandalay	44	111	55–82	77–101	78–93	73–89	32.6	0.1	1.2	2.7	4.3
Canada: Edmonton, Alta.	−57	99	−3–16	28–52	50–74	30–51	18.0	0.9	1.0	3.3	0.8
Montreal, Que.	−35	97	6–21	33–50	61–78	40–54	40.8	3.8	2.6	3.7	3.4
Ottawa, Ont.	−38	102	3–21	31–51	58–81	37–54	34.3	2.9	2.7	3.4	2.9
St. John, N.B.	−24	93	11–28	32–43	54–69	41–54	42.6	4.1	3.2	3.1	4.1
Vancouver, B.C.	2	92	32–41	40–58	54–74	44–57	57.4	8.6	3.3	1.2	5.8
Winnipeg, Man.	−54	108	−13–7	27–48	55–79	31–51	21.2	0.9	1.4	3.1	1.5
Canary Islands: Las Palmas	46	99	58–70	61–71	67–77	67–79	8.6	1.4	0.5	T	1.1
Central Africa: Bangui	57	101	68–90	71–91	69–85	69–87	60.8	1.0	5.3	8.9	7.9
Chad: N'Djamena	47	114	57–93	74–107	72–92	70–97	29.3	0.0	0.1	6.7	1.4
Chile: Santiago	24	99	53–85	45–74	37–59	45–72	14.2	0.1	0.5	3.0	0.6
China: Canton	31	101	49–65	65–77	77–91	67–85	63.6	0.9	6.8	8.1	3.4
Shanghai	−3	109	16–33	45–68	73–90	48–68	21.0	0.2	0.5	7.6	0.6
Tientsin	−30	112	−7–13	36–60	58–82	31–50	11.5	0.6	1.5	0.7	1.7
Colombia: Bogotá	30	75	48–67	51–67	50–64	50–66	41.8	2.3	5.8	2.0	6.3
Congo: Brazzaville	54	98	69–88	71–91	63–82	70–89	58.0	6.3	7.0	T	5.4
Costa Rica: San José	49	92	58–75	62–79	62–77	60–77	70.8	0.6	1.8	8.3	11.8
Cuba: Havana	43	104	65–79	69–84	75–89	73–85	48.2	2.8	2.3	4.9	6.8
Cyprus: Nicosia	23	116	42–58	50–74	69–97	58–81	14.6	2.9	0.8	T	0.9
Czechoslovakia: Prague	−16	101	25–34	40–55	58–74	44–54	19.3	0.9	1.5	2.6	1.2
Denmark: Copenhagen	− 3	91	29–36	37–50	55–72	42–53	23.3	1.6	1.7	2.2	3.2
Dominican R.: Santo Domingo	59	98	66–84	69–85	72–88	72–87	55.8	2.4	3.9	6.4	6.0
Ecuador: Quito	25	88	46–67	47–69	44–71	46–71	43.9	3.9	6.9	0.8	4.4
Egypt: Cairo	34	117	47–65	57–83	70–96	65–86	1.1	0.2	0.1	0.0	T
El Salvador: San Salvador	45	105	60–90	65–93	65–89	65–87	70.0	0.3	1.7	11.5	9.5
Ethiopia: Addis Ababa	32	94	43–75	50–77	50–69	45–75	48.7	0.5	3.4	11.8	0.6
Finland: Helsinki	−23	89	17–27	31–43	57–71	37–45	27.6	2.2	1.7	2.3	2.9
France: Marseille	9	101	38–53	41–59	58–78	57–76	23.2	1.9	2.0	0.6	3.7
Paris	1	105	32–42	41–60	55–76	44–59	22.3	1.5	1.7	2.1	2.2
Germany, East: Berlin	−15	96	26–35	38–55	55–74	41–55	23.1	1.9	1.7	3.1	1.7
Germany, West: Hamburg	− 4	92	28–35	39–51	56–69	44–53	28.9	2.1	1.8	3.4	2.6
Munich	−14	99	23–33	37–54	54–72	40–53	34.1	1.7	2.7	4.7	2.2
Ghana: Accra	59	100	73–87	76–88	73–81	74–85	28.5	1.3	3.2	1.8	2.5
Greece: Athens	20	109	42–54	52–67	72–90	60–74	15.8	2.2	0.8	0.2	1.7
Guadeloupe: Basse-Terre	54	92	64–77	65–79	68–81	68–81	140.4	9.2	7.3	17.6	12.4
Guam: Agana	54	95	72–84	73–86	72–87	73–86	88.5	4.6	3.0	9.0	13.1
Guatemala: Guatemala City	41	90	53–73	58–82	60–78	60–76	51.8	0.3	1.2	8.0	6.8
Guinea: Conakry	63	96	72–88	73–90	72–83	73–87	169.0	0.1	0.9	51.1	14.6
Haiti: Port-au-Prince	58	101	68–87	71–89	74–94	72–90	53.3	1.3	6.3	2.9	6.7
Honduras: Tegucigalpa	58	96	67–82	72–87	73–88	71–86	96.1	8.9	3.3	6.4	13.5
Hong Kong: Victoria	32	97	56–64	67–75	78–87	73–81	85.1	1.3	5.4	15.0	4.5
Hungary: Budapest	−10	103	26–35	44–62	61–82	45–61	24.2	1.5	2.0	2.0	2.1
Iceland: Reykjavík	4	74	28–36	33–43	48–58	36–44	33.9	4.0	2.1	2.0	3.4
India: Calcutta	44	111	55–80	76–97	79–90	74–89	63.0	0.4	1.7	12.8	4.5
New Delhi	31	115	43–71	68–97	80–95	64–93	25.2	0.9	0.3	7.1	0.4
Indonesia: Jakarta	66	98	74–84	75–87	73–87	74–87	70.8	11.8	5.8	2.5	4.4
Iran: Tehran	− 5	109	27–45	49–71	72–99	53–76	9.7	1.8	1.4	0.1	0.3
Iraq: Baghdad	18	121	39–60	57–85	76–110	61–92	5.5	0.9	0.5	T	0.1
Ireland: Dublin	8	86	35–47	38–54	51–67	43–57	29.7	2.7	1.9	2.8	2.7
Ireland, Northern: Belfast	14	82	34–42	38–53	52–65	44–55	38.2	4.2	2.4	3.5	3.8
Israel: Jerusalem	26	107	41–55	50–73	63–87	59–81	19.7	5.1	0.9	0.0	0.3

T = trace, less than 0.05 inch. [1] Average daily minimum and maximum temperatures.

COUNTRY AND CITY	TEMPERATURES (in degrees Fahrenheit)						RAINFALL (in inches)				
	Extremes		Daily Average Range								
	Low	High	Jan.	April	July	Oct.	Annual	Jan.	Apr.	July	Oct.
Italy: Rome..................	20	104	39–54	46–68	64–88	53–73	29.5	3.3	2.0	0.4	4.3
Jamaica: Kingston	56	97	67–86	70–87	73–90	73–88	31.5	0.9	1.2	1.5	7.1
Japan: Tokyo	17	101	29–47	46–63	70–83	55–69	61.6	1.9	5.3	5.6	8.2
Jordan: Amman	21	109	39–54	49–73	65–89	57–81	10.9	2.7	0.6	0.0	0.2
Kenya: Nairobi	41	87	54–77	58–75	51–69	55–76	41.8	1.5	8.3	0.6	2.1
Korea, South: Seoul	-12	99	15–32	41–62	70–84	45–67	49.2	1.2	3.0	14.8	1.6
Lebanon: Beirut	30	107	51–62	58–72	73–87	69–81	35.1	7.5	2.2	T	2.0
Liberia: Monrovia	62	97	71–89	72–90	72–80	72–86	174.9	0.2	11.7	24.2	25.2
Libya: Tripoli	33	114	47–61	57–72	71–85	65–80	15.1	3.2	0.4	T	1.6
Madagascar: Antananarivo	34	95	61–79	58–76	48–68	54–80	53.4	11.8	2.1	0.3	2.4
Malaysia: Kuala Lumpur	64	99	72–90	74–91	72–90	73–89	96.1	6.2	11.5	3.9	9.8
Mali: Bamako	47	117	61–91	76–103	71–89	71–93	44.1	T	0.6	11.0	1.7
Malta: Valletta	34	105	51–59	56–66	72–84	66–76	20.3	3.3	0.8	T	2.7
Martinique: Fort-de-France	56	96	69–83	71–86	74–86	73–87	80.4	4.7	3.9	9.4	9.7
Mauritania: Nouakchott	44	115	57–85	64–90	74–89	71–91	6.2	T	T	0.5	0.4
Mauritius: Port-Louis	50	95	73–86	70–82	62–75	64–80	50.6	8.5	5.0	2.3	1.6
Mexico: Acapulco	60	97	70–85	71–87	75–89	74–88	55.1	0.3	T	9.1	6.7
Chihuahua	12	102	36–65	51–81	66–89	51–79	15.4	0.2	0.2	3.6	0.9
Mexico City	24	92	42–66	52–78	54–74	50–70	23.0	0.2	0.7	4.5	1.6
Monterrey	25	107	48–68	62–84	71–90	64–80	22.9	0.6	1.3	2.4	3.0
Veracruz	53	98	66–77	72–83	74–87	73–85	65.7	0.9	0.8	4.1	6.9
Morocco: Rabat	32	118	46–63	52–71	63–82	58–77	19.8	2.6	1.7	T	1.9
Mozambique: Maputo	45	114	71–86	66–83	55–76	64–82	29.9	5.1	2.1	0.5	1.9
Netherlands: Amsterdam	3	95	34–40	43–52	59–69	48–56	25.6	2.0	1.6	2.6	2.8
New Zealand: Wellington ...	29	88	56–69	51–63	42–53	48–60	47.4	3.2	3.8	5.4	4.0
Nigeria: Lagos	60	104	74–88	77–89	74–83	74–85	72.3	1.1	5.9	11.0	8.1
Norway: Oslo	-21	93	20–30	34–50	56–73	37–49	26.9	1.7	1.6	2.9	2.9
Pakistan: Islamabad	25	118	38–62	59–86	77–98	57–89	36.5	2.5	1.9	8.1	0.6
Panama: Panama City	63	97	71–88	74–90	74–87	73–85	69.7	1.0	2.9	7.1	10.1
Papua N.G.: Port Moresby	64	98	76–89	75–87	73–83	75–86	39.8	7.0	4.2	1.1	1.4
Paraguay: Asunción	29	110	71–95	65–84	53–74	62–86	51.8	5.5	5.2	2.2	5.5
Peru: Lima	49	93	66–82	63–80	57–67	58–71	1.6	0.1	T	0.3	0.1
Philippines: Manila	58	101	69–86	73–93	75–88	74–88	82.0	0.9	1.3	17.0	7.6
Poland: Warsaw	-22	98	21–30	38–54	56–75	41–54	22.0	1.2	1.5	3.0	1.7
Portugal: Lisbon	29	103	46–56	52–64	63–79	57–69	27.0	3.3	2.4	0.2	3.1
Puerto Rico: San Juan	60	94	67–81	69–84	74–87	73–87	64.2	4.7	3.7	6.3	5.8
Romania: Bucharest	-18	105	20–33	41–63	61–86	44–65	22.8	1.5	1.6	2.3	1.6
Samoa, American: Pago Pago ...	67	98	75–87	76–87	74–83	75–85	193.6	24.5	16.5	10.0	14.9
Saudi Arabia: Riyadh	19	113	46–70	64–89	.78–107	61–94	3.2	0.1	1.0	0.0	0.0
Senegal: Dakar	53	109	64–79	65–81	76–88	76–89	21.3	T	T	3.5	1.5
Seychelles: Victoria	67	92	75–83	77–86	75–81	75–83	92.5	15.2	7.2	3.3	6.1
Singapore: Singapore	66	97	73–86	75–88	75–88	74–87	95.0	9.9	7.4	6.7	8.2
Solomons: Tulagi	68	96	76–88	76–88	76–86	76–87	123.4	14.3	10.0	7.6	8.7
Somalia: Mogadiscio	59	97	73–86	78–90	73–83	76–86	16.9	T	2.3	2.5	0.9
South Africa: Cape Town	28	103	60–78	53–72	45–63	52–70	20.0	0.6	1.9	3.5	1.2
Soviet Union: Leningrad	-36	91	12–23	31–45	57–71	37–45	19.2	1.0	1.0	2.5	1.8
Moscow	-49	96	9–21	31–47	55–76	34–46	24.8	1.5	1.9	3.0	2.7
Spain: Madrid	14	102	33–47	44–64	62–87	48–66	16.5	1.1	1.7	0.4	1.9
Sri Lanka: Colombo	59	99	72–86	76–88	77–85	75–85	92.3	3.5	9.1	5.3	13.7
Sudan: Khartoum	41	118	59–90	72–105	77–101	75–104	6.2	T	T	2.1	0.2
Suriname: Paramaribo	62	99	72–85	73–86	73–87	73–91	91.0	8.4	9.0	9.1	3.0
Sweden: Stockholm	-26	97	23–31	32–45	55–70	39–48	22.4	1.5	1.5	2.8	2.1
Switzerland: Bern	-9	96	26–35	39–56	56–74	42–55	38.5	1.9	3.0	4.4	3.5
Syria: Damascus	21	113	36–53	49–75	64–96	54–81	8.6	1.7	0.5	T	0.4
Tahiti: Papeete	61	93	72–89	72–89	68–86	70–87	74.7	13.2	6.8	2.6	3.4
Taiwan: Taipei	32	101	53–66	64–77	76–92	68–80	72.7	3.8	5.3	8.8	5.5
Tanzania: Dar es Salaam	59	96	77–83	73–86	66–83	69–85	41.9	2.6	11.4	1.2	1.6
Thailand: Bangkok	50	104	68–89	78–95	76–90	76–88	57.8	0.2	2.3	6.9	9.9
Togo: Lomé	58	94	72–85	74–86	71–80	72–83	31.0	0.6	4.6	2.8	2.4
Trinidad-Tob.: Port of Spain	52	101	69–87	69–90	71–88	71–89	64.2	2.7	2.1	8.6	6.7
Tunisia: Tunis	30	118	43–58	51–70	68–90	59–77	16.5	2.5	1.4	0.1	2.0
Turkey: Istanbul	17	100	36–45	45–61	65–81	54–67	31.5	3.7	1.9	1.7	3.8
Uganda: Kampala	53	97	65–83	64–79	62–77	63–81	46.2	1.8	6.9	1.8	3.8
Uruguay: Montevideo	25	109	62–83	53–71	43–58	49–68	37.4	2.9	3.9	2.9	2.6
Venezuela: Caracas	45	91	56–75	60–81	61–78	61–79	32.9	0.9	1.3	4.3	4.3
Vietnam: Hanoi	41	108	58–68	70–80	79–92	72–84	69.4	0.8	3.6	11.9	3.5
Virgin Is., U.S.: Charlotte Amalie ..	63	92	71–82	74–85	77–88	76–87	43.7	2.5	2.2	3.2	5.6
Yugoslavia: Belgrade	-14	107	27–37	45–64	61–84	47–65	24.6	1.6	2.2	1.9	2.7
Zaire: Kinshasa	58	97	70–87	71–89	64–81	70–88	53.3	5.3	7.7	0.1	4.7
Zambia: Lusaka	39	100	63–78	59–79	49–73	64–88	32.9	9.1	0.7	T	1.0
Zimbabwe: Harare	32	95	60–78	55–78	44–70	58–83	32.6	7.7	1.1	T	1.1

CAUSES OF CLIMATE AND WEATHER

Source: Environmental Data Service, U.S. Department of Commerce

The climate of a place is the long-term normal weather for a given day, month, season, or year. It is the weather we expect for spring in our hometown or for vacation time at our favorite camping grounds. These expectations are based on weather data collected over a relatively long period, usually several decades.

In contrast, weather is the current or recent state of the atmosphere. Both can be described in terms of temperature, pressure, humidity, sunshine, winds, clouds, and precipitation. For example, temperature in weather is the present temperature at a place, while temperature in climate is the average temperature for the location, determined from previous records.

The underlying causes of weather and climate are heat from the Sun and the rotation of the Earth. The radiant energy of the Sun and the constant rotation of the Earth about its axis serve to set up circulation patterns within the atmosphere. These circulation patterns carry heat and moisture from the equator to the poles, across land and sea, and over flat land and mountains. Patterns of winds, rainfall, cloudiness, and temperature tend to remain relatively steady at any given location on Earth. Weather tends to follow the same pattern year after year. These patterns determine the climate of a place.

Briefly, climate is controlled by latitude, land surfaces and sources of moisture, prevailing winds, ocean currents, elevation, and mountain barriers.

LATITUDE

Heat from the Sun reaches the Earth after passing through approximately 93 million miles of space. The rays reaching the equator appear to come from nearly directly overhead. At points nearer the poles, the Sun appears lower in the sky. The position of the Sun causes warm climates in the equatorial regions and successively cooler climates toward the poles—thus the higher the latitude, the cooler the climate.

Seasons modify the latitude effect because of the tilt of the axis of the Earth. The Earth's axis is tilted 23.5 degrees from a line perpendicular to the plane that contains the Sun and the Earth's oribt around the Sun. Beginning about September 21 and ending about March 21, the north end of the axis points away from the Sun, so the rays from the Sun are more slanting in the Northern Hemisphere and more directly overhead in the Southern Hemisphere.

The length of daylight, hence the length of time a location receives solar heat, increases as we move from the pole to the equator during winter. During summer, the length of daylight increases north of the equator, but the more slanted rays of the Sun keep the higher latitudes cooler than the low latitudes.

LAND SURFACES AND SOURCES OF MOISTURE

Land and water surfaces react differently to the incoming rays of the Sun. In general, land surfaces are heated rapidly by the Sun, but the heat does not penetrate deeply, so land surfaces also cool rapidly. On the other hand, water warms up slowly, holds a much larger quantity of heat than the land surface, and cools slowly.

As a result the surface layer of air over the continents is warmer in summer and colder in winter than that over the oceans. Because warm air rises, permitting air from cooler areas to flow in to replace it, there is a net inflow of cool ocean air onto continents in summer and an outflow from the continents in winter. Land and sea breezes result from a similar situation in coastal areas, where the land is colder than the water at night and early morning but warmer later in the day.

Sources of moisture—oceans, gulfs, lakes, and other large bodies of water—have a major influence on the climate of an area. Places in the interior of continents usually tend to be hotter and drier in summer and colder in winter than coastal areas, and usually have greater differences between daily high and low temperatures.

PREVAILING WINDS

The uneven heating of the Earth by the Sun is the main cause of wind systems. The equatorial regions receive considerably more solar heat per square mile than do the polar regions. Warm equatorial surface air rises and is replaced by cooler surface air flowing in from the poles. The unequal heating of the Earth's surface together with its rotation produces a general global movement of air.

The global air movement causes a worldwide pattern of prevailing winds. Surface winds in the Northern Hemisphere are arranged in three broad belts: the northeast trades (from the northeast) in the tropics and subtropics; the prevailing westerlies (from the west to southwest) in the middle latitudes; and the polar easterlies (from the northeast) in the polar region.

HIGH- AND LOW-PRESSURE AREAS

The rotation of the Earth about its axis causes winds to turn to the right (clockwise) in the Northern Hemisphere. For example, a wind blowing from south to north turns toward the east. Similarly, a north wind turns toward the west. The resulting huge whirling masses of air are called high-pressure areas (also called highs or anticyclones). Between these highs are low-pressure areas (also called lows or cyclones) that rotate to the left (counterclockwise). Air tends to flow inward toward low-pressure centers and outward from high-pressure areas.

AIR MASSES

When temperature and humidity are very much the same throughout any level in a high-pressure area, the high is called an *air mass*. Four general types of air masses are recognized in the United States: (1) cold dry air masses that move in from Canada, generally traveling south-eastward; (2) cool moist air masses that generally travel eastward across the states from the Pacific Ocean; (3) warm moist air masses that move in from the Pacific, the Gulf of Mexico, or the Atlantic; and (4) warm dry air masses that may move from the southwest.

STORMS

Most storms and active weather occur in and around the low-pressure areas between highs.

The Canadian highs bring cool dry conditions. As they move into an area, they usually are preceded by showers along or adjacent to a cold front. The Pacific highs, also preceded by fronts, are moister and somewhat warmer than the Canadian highs.

Lows bring in warm humid air from the Pacific, the Gulf of Mexico, or the Atlantic. Lows are usually accompanied by widespread rain or snow.

The migrating highs and lows occur more frequently, are more intense, and travel faster in winter than in summer. Average motion is 750 miles per day in winter and 500 in summer.

The air masses that prevail over an area determine its climate. For example, the southeastern states are dominated in summer by a moist tropical air mass associated with a high-pressure area located offshore. The southerly winds on the west side of this high bring moist air from the Gulf of Mexico into these states. In winter the southern states are invaded by Canadian air masses that bring cold fronts across the area about once every five days.

Severe local storms, such as thunderstorms and tornadoes, and tropical cyclones up to hurricane intensity are superimposed on the general climatic pattern.

Winds in the upper atmosphere tend to "steer" moving air masses at lower levels. The jet stream, a meandering current of air at 30,000 to 50,000 feet, moves air masses in a generally eastward direction.

SEMIPERMANENT HIGHS AND LOWS

Wind and storm patterns are strongly influenced by the locations and intensities of semipermanent high- and low-pressure areas.

The Aleutian low is the semipermanent pressure system that dominates the northern end of the North Pacific. This low intensifies and expands in winter and weakens and moves to the northwest in summer. Its average central pressure in February is 29.50 inches.

The Pacific high, another semipermanent pressure system, intensifies and expands in summer. The average summer pressure at the center of this high is 30.27 inches at its center, about 1,600 miles west of San Francisco. In its summer position, this semipermanent Pacific high effectively blocks the passage of storms into the California-Oregon-Washington coastal area, steering them instead to the coast of British Columbia. In autumn and winter this high becomes weak, and its center moves to the southwest. In this new position, it cannot block the movement of storms to the coast, so there is an increase in the frequency of storms reaching the Washington coast by September. By late November and December, storms reach the coast as far south as southern California.

The semipermanent pressure systems in the Atlantic are the Icelandic low and the Bermuda (or Azores) high. Many of the storms associated with migratory low-pressure areas in the central and eastern United States tend to drift toward the Icelandic low. The favored path of these storms is across the Great Lakes and along the valley of the St. Lawrence River.

During the summer, the Bermuda high has a marked effect on the eastern states. This high is strongest in summer when it lies off the East Coast and brings a southerly flow of warm moist maritime air from the Caribbean Sea. On occasion, this warm moist air is carried into the Arizona-New Mexico area, bringing welcome rainfall.

OCEAN CURRENTS

Well-established ocean currents have a great effect on the climates of coastal areas. Perhaps the best-known ocean current is the Gulf Stream that carries warm waters from the Florida Straits northward along the Atlantic coast and then northeastward and eastward to the British Isles. Winds blowing across the warm stream of water pick up heat and moisture and bring them over the East Coast.

The climate of the East Coast is also affected by the cold Labrador Current, which flows southward as far as Norfolk, Va. This current is responsible for frequent fogs over the coast.

The Japanese Current is the major ocean current affecting the West Coast. This current reaches the west coast of the continent at about the latitude of the United States-Canada border. Here it branches. One branch, the Alaska Current, turns northward bringing a milder warmer climate to coastal British Columbia and Alaska. The other branch, the California Current, turns southward bringing cooler water along the shore of Washington, Oregon, and California. During winter, the Davidson Current moves in from southeast of the California Current, bringing warmer weather to the coast.

ELEVATION

Temperature in the atmosphere decreases with increasing elevation, or altitude. The usual rate of decrease is 3.3°F. per 1,000 feet. The climatic mean temperature on a mountain generally is 3.3°F. lower per 1,000 feet of elevation than that of nearby lower altitude stations.

MOUNTAIN BARRIERS

Mountain ranges not only have colder temperatures at higher elevations but they also act as barriers to block the flow of prevailing winds and the movement of storms.

Air flowing upward on the slopes of a mountain barrier tends to drop much of its moisture on the windward side of the range. This is the reason deserts lie to the east of the Coast Ranges and the Cascade-Sierra Nevada ranges of California.

Because mountain ranges in the United States run north and south, they block the flow of the prevailing westerlies. Moisture-laden air from the Pacific is forced up the slopes of the Coast and Cascade-Sierra Nevada ranges where it dumps most of its moisture. In the east the Appalachian Mountains tend to block the flow of Atlantic air into the interior but permit the free passage of the cold arctic and polar air masses of Canada over the central and eastern two-thirds of the United States.

The lack of an east-west mountain barrier allows a northward flow of warm maritime tropical air far northward into the interior.

BE YOUR OWN WEATHER FORECASTER

Source: NOAA, U.S. Department of Commerce

You can forecast weather merely by observing the direction from which the wind blows and reading the level of air pressure on a barometer.

The following table summarizes wind and barometer indications of approaching weather that are generally applicable to most U.S. regions.

WIND DIRECTION	BAROMETER (reduced to sea level)	WEATHER FORECAST
SW to NW	30.10 to 30.20 and steady	Fair, with slight temperature changes for 1 to 2 days
SW to NW	30.10 to 30.20, rising rapidly	Fair, followed within 2 days by rain
SW to NW	30.20 and above, stationary	Continued fair with no decided temperature change
SW to NW	30.20 and above, falling slowly	Slowly rising temperature and fair for 2 days
S to SW	30.00 or below, rising slowly	Clearing within a few hours and fair for several days
S to E	29.80 or below, falling rapidly	Severe storm imminent, followed within 24 hours by clearing and in winter by colder temperatures
S to SE	30.10 to 30.20, falling slowly	Rain within 24 hours
S to SE	30.10 to 30.20, falling rapidly	Wind increasing in force; rain within 12 to 24 hours
SE to NE	30.10 to 30.20, falling slowly	Rain in 12 to 18 hours
SE to NE	30.10 to 30.20, falling rapidly	Increasing wind; rain within 12 hours
SE to NE	30.00 or below, falling slowly	Rain will continue 1 to 2 days
SE to NE	30.00 or below, falling rapidly	Rain with high wind, followed within 36 hours by clearing, and in winter by colder temperatures
E to NE	30.10 and above, falling slowly	In summer, with light winds, rain may not fall for several days; in winter, rain within 24 hours
E to NE	30.10 and above, falling rapidly	In summer, rain probable within 12 to 24 hours; in winter, rain or snow with increasing winds
E to N	29.80 or below, falling rapidly	Severe northeast gale; in summer, heavy rain; in winter, heavy snow followed by cold wave
Easterly	29.80 or below, rising rapidly	Clearing and colder

CLOUD FORMATIONS—AND WHAT THEY MEAN

FEET

32,000 —
28,000 —
24,000 —
20,000 —
16,000 —
12,000 —
8,000 —
4,000 —
0 —

Cumulus fair-weather clouds

Cumulonimbus

Altocumulus

Altocumulus

INTERMITTENT RAIN SHOWERS THUNDERSTORMS ADVANCING COLD FRONT WARM A MASS

WIND CHILL—WHY YOU FEEL COLDER THAN THE THERMOMETER

Source: Environmental Data Service, NOAA, U.S. Department of Commerce

In winter the stronger the wind the colder the weather seems. The wind causes the chill that you *feel* to be even colder than the temperature *shown* on your thermometer. The following wind-chill table prepared by the National Weather Service can help you find what the equivalent wind-chill temperature is when you know the thermometer temperature and the wind speed. For example, if the thermometer shows a temperature of 15° and you know that the wind speed is 10 mph, then look in the table and you will see that the wind-chill temperature you will feel is 3° below zero.

| WIND SPEED | THERMOMETER TEMPERATURES IN DEGREES FAHRENHEIT | | | | | | | | | | | | | |
	35°	30°	25°	20°	15°	10°	5°	0°	−5°	−10°	−15°	−20°	−25°	−30°
	EQUIVALENT WIND–CHILL TEMPERATURES (HOW COLD YOU SEEM TO FEEL)													
5 mph	32°	27°	22°	16°	11°	6°	0°	−5°	−10°	−15°	−21°	−26°	−31°	−36°
10 mph	22°	16°	10°	3°	−3°	−9°	−15°	−22°	−27°	−34°	−40°	−46°	−52°	−58°
15 mph	16°	9°	2°	−5°	−11°	−18°	−25°	−31°	−38°	−45°	−51°	−58°	−65°	−72°
20 mph	12°	4°	−3°	−10°	−17°	−24°	−31°	−39°	−46°	−53°	−60°	−67°	−74°	−81°
25 mph	8°	1°	−7°	−15°	−22°	−29°	−36°	−44°	−51°	−59°	−66°	−74°	−81°	−88°
30 mph	6°	−2°	−10°	−18°	−25°	−33°	−41°	−49°	−56°	−64°	−71°	−79°	−86°	−93°
35 mph	4°	−4°	−12°	−20°	−27°	−35°	−43°	−52°	−58°	−67°	−74°	−82°	−89°	−97°
40 mph	3°	−5°	−13°	−21°	−29°	−37°	−45°	−53°	−60°	−69°	−76°	−84°	−92°	−100°
45 mph	2°	−6°	−14°	−22°	−30°	−38°	−46°	−54°	−62°	−70°	−78°	−85°	−93°	−102°
50 mph	0°	−7°	−17°	−24°	−31°	−38°	−47°	−56°	−63°	−70°	−79°	−88°	−96°	−103°

BEAUFORT WIND SCALE

The Beaufort wind scale indicates wind strength by a series of numbers. it was developed in 1805 by a British admiral, Sir Francis Beaufort, to help gauge wind speed without an instrument.

BEAUFORT NUMBER	WIND NAME	SPEED (mph)	OBSERVED EFFECT OF WIND
0	Calm	0–1	Calm. Smoke rises straight up into the air.
1	Light Air	1–3	Weather vanes remain motionless. Smoke drifts slightly with wind.
2	Light Breeze	4–7	Weather vanes active. You can feel wind on your face. Leaves rustle.
3	Gentle Breeze	8–12	Light flags fill out with wind. Twigs on trees move.
4	Moderate Breeze	13–18	The wind picks up dust and loose paper. Small tree branches sway.
5	Fresh Breeze	19–24	Waves break on inland waters. Small trees sway in the wind.
6	Strong Breeze	25–31	Using an umbrella becomes difficult. Large tree branches sway.
7	Near Gale	32–38	Walking against the wind is difficult. Entire large trees sway.
8	Gale	39–46	Walking against the wind is almost impossible. Twigs break off trees.
9	Strong Gale	47–54	Shingles blown off house roofs. Some damage to buildings.
10	Storm	55–63	Entire trees blown over and uprooted. Much damage to buildings.
11	Violent Storm	64–72	Severe damage to crops, trees, and property.
12	Hurricane	73–82	Widespread violent destruction.

RECORD U.S. BLIZZARDS AND SNOWSTORMS

Source: Environmental Data Service, NOAA, U.S. Department of Commerce

DATE	PLACE	DEPTH	DESCRIPTION
1717, Feb. 19–24	New England	60–72 in.	The "great snow"; drifts cover many one-story houses
1888, March 11–14	Northeast States	40–50 in.	Snow and winds to 70 mph; over 400 deaths
1899, Feb. 11–14	Washington, D.C.	35.2 in.	Record snowfall in one month for capital
1901, April 19–21	Watertown, Ohio	45 in.	Greatest 24-hour snowfall in state
1911, Jan.	Tamarack, Calif.	390 in.	Greatest U.S. snowfall in one month
1921, April 14–15	Silver Lake, Colo.	95 in.	Record snowfall of 75.8 inches in 24 hours
1921, Nov. 17–20	The Dalles, Oreg.	54 in.	Record snowfall for state
1922, Jan. 27–29	Washington, D.C.	28 in.	Snow collapses Knickerbocker theater, killing 98
1928, April 27–28	Bayard, W. Va.	34 in.	Record 24-hour snowfall (34 inches) for state
1933, Jan. 18–19	Giant Forest, Calif.	60 in.	Record 24-hour snowfall for state
1935, Jan. 20–24	Winthrop, Wash.	52 in.	Record 24-hour snowfall for state
1940, Jan. 18–22	Watertown, N.Y.	69 in.	Record snowfall for state
1940, Jan. 23–24	Louisville, Miss.	15.5 in.	Record 24-hour snowfall for state
1940, Nov. 11–12	Iowa to Minnesota	—	144 deaths; subzero temperatures; high winds
1946, January	Stampede Pass, Wash.	192.9 in.	Record snowfall in one month
1946, Nov. 2–6	New Mexico	36 in.	Unprecedented heavy snowfall
1947, March 2–5	Readsboro, Vt.	50 in.	Record snowfall for state
1947, March 2–5	Peru, Mass.	47 in.	Record snowfall for state
1949, Jan. 1–6	Colorado to Dakotas	7–30 in.	39 deaths; severe blizzard; 70 mph winds
1950, March 25–27	Dumont, S.D.	60 in.	Record snowfall for state
1950, Nov. 23–28	Ohio, Pa., West Virginia	33–57 in.	Record snowfall for three states
1951, March 10–14	Iowa City, Iowa	27.2 in.	Record snowfall for state
1955, April 2–5	Colorado to Dakotas	30–52 in.	One of heaviest and latest spring snowstorms
1956, March 16–17	New England, New York, Pa.	20 in.	Crippling winds and snowstorm
1958, Feb. 13–19	North Carolina to New Jersey	36 in.	43 deaths; damage $500 million
1958, March 19–22	Virginia to New England	17–30 in.	Severe snowstorm; 49 deaths
1959, Feb. 13–19	Mt. Shasta Ski Bowl, Calif.	189 in.	Greatest U.S. snowfall in one storm
1959, March 11–13	New England, New York	20 in.	Blizzard conditions; transportation paralyzed
1960, Feb. 18–20	Maryland to New England	20–36 in.	Damage in millions of dollars
1961, Jan. 19–20	North Carolina to New York	10–30 in.	37 deaths; many cities paralyzed
1961, Feb. 3–5	North Carolina to New England	10–36 in.	73 deaths; drifts of 15 feet
1964, Feb. 2–5	N.M., Okla., Texas	18–36 in.	Second heaviest storm in Panhandle's history
1966, Jan. 29–31	Virginia to New England	12–36 in.	50 deaths; drifts to 20 feet
1966, March 2–5	Nebraska to Dakotas	12–36 in.	15 deaths; 100,000 cattle killed; drifts to 30 feet
1967, Jan. 26–27	Chicago and Midwest	23 in.	Record snow and ice storms; high winds
1969, Feb. 9–10	New York and New England	15 in.	Worst storm to hit New York City in 8 years
1969, February	Mt. Washington, N.H.	172.8 in.	State record for one-month snowfall
1973, Feb. 10–11	Georgia and Carolinas	15–21 in.	Worst storm in South in this century
1974, Dec. 1–2	Michigan, Ohio	17–20 in.	Record 19.2 in. of snow paralyzes Detroit
1975, Jan. 10–12	N.D., S.D., Neb., Kan., Mo., Iowa, Minn., Wis.	8–15 in.	Winds of 80 mph drift snow to 20 feet; over 60 killed; hundreds injured; over $15 million damage
1977, Jan. 1–31	West Virginia	104 in.	West Virginia record for one-month snowfall
1977, Jan. 28–Feb. 1	Ill., Ind., Ohio, N.Y., Pa.	12–71 in.	Blizzard with winds to 69 mph kills 75 persons
1978, Jan. 26–27	Midwestern and Eastern states	12–34 in.	Called "worst blizzard of century"; 100 killed; winds gust to 100 mph; snow drifts to 25 feet
1978, Feb. 6–7	Northeast states	18–38 in.	Winds to 100 mph cause 40-foot coastal waves
1979, Jan. 13–14	Chicago and Midwest	20.7 in.	Heavy snowfall paralyzes Chicago
1980, March 2	Middle Atlantic and Southern states	10–28 in.	Surprise blizzard paralyzes mid-Atlantic area; Florida citrus crop damaged; 36 killed
1982, Jan. 20–23	Northern Minnesota	38 in.	Blizzard paralyzes area
1982, Jan. 31	St. Louis, Mo., and Midwest	18–22 in.	Blizzard immobilizes area
1982, January	Muskegon, Mich.	89 in.	Record snow total for one month
1982, Dec. 24–25	Denver, Colo.	24 in.	Blizzard strands holiday travelers
1983, Feb. 11–12	Northeast states	17–35 in.	Record 22 in. of snow in Philadelphia
1983, Nov. 27–28	Rocky Mts. and Central Plains	15–22 in.	Blizzards blamed for over 50 deaths

U.S. AND WORLD RECORD RAINFALLS

DURATION	DEPTH	LOCATION	DATE
1 minute (world record)	1.50 in.	Barst, Guadeloupe	Nov. 26, 1970
1 minute (U.S. record)	1.23 in.	Unionville, Maryland	July 4, 1956
15 minutes (world record)	7.80 in.	Plumb Point, Jamaica	May 12, 1916
1 hour (U.S. record)	12.00 in.	Holt, Missouri	June 22, 1947
1 hour (U.S. record)	12.00 in.	Kilauea plantation, Kauai, Hawaii	Jan. 24–25, 1956
12 hours (world record)	52.76 in.	Belouve, Réunion	Feb. 28–29, 1964
24 hours (world record)	73.62 in.	Cilaos, Réunion	March 15–16, 1952
24 hours (U.S. record)	43.00 in.	Alvin, Texas	July 25–26, 1979
1 month (world record)	366.14 in.	Cherrapunji, India	July 1861
1 month (U.S. record)	107.00 in.	Puu Kukui, Maui, Hawaii	March 1942
1 year (world record)	1,041.78 in.	Cherrapunji, India	Aug. 1860–July 1861
1 year (U.S. record)	704.38 in.	Puu Kukui, Maui, Hawaii	1982

Computers

HIGHLIGHTS: 1985

FASTEST SUPERCOMPUTER

The world's fastest supercomputer, the Cray-2, was unveiled in June by Cray Research Inc. of Minneapolis, Minn. The computer is able to perform 1.2 billion arithmetic calculations in one second—about 3 to 5 times faster than the previous record holder, the Cray X-MP.

Comparatively, an IBM personal computer can perform about 1,000 arithmetic operations per second and a business mainframe computer can manage about 5 million per second.

The new supercomputer contains 240,000 silicon chips that are cooled with 200 gallons of liquid fluorocarbon.

The Cray company expects to build and sell about 40 of the supercomputers per year, each with a price tag of $17.6 million.

Altogether there are about 140 supercomputers in the world, 97 of which have been built by Cray. Most of the supercomputers are owned by government agencies and by large industries. They are used for such tasks as navigating spacecraft, breaking secret spy codes, testing the computer designs of aircraft, and sorting through geological data to find potential mineral resources.

Seymour Cray, 59, who founded the company in 1972, already is at work on the Cray-3, which is planned to perform 10 billion calculations per second. He hopes to achieve the increased speed by using chips made of gallium arsenide rather than silicon.

HEALTHY FOUR-YEAR-OLD

The International Business Machine Corporation (IBM) produced its first personal computer on Aug. 12, 1981. Four years later, the company celebrated the success of the IBM PC.

Some 1.7 million IBM PCs were sold in the first four years, bringing in about $3.8 billion in revenues. In all, IBM produces about 40% of all personal computers sold in the United States. The company's personal computer division now employs 10,000 workers in Boca Raton, Fla., and Austin, Tex.

POPULARITY POLL

A survey of 38,000 homes by market research firm Future Computing Inc. of Dallas, Tex., found that the Commodore home computer was the most popular, being owned by 30%

of those who responded. Runners-up were Apple 16%, Tandy 10%, Atari 10%, and IBM 8%.

However, the survey indicated that opinions of home computers may be changing because the largest number of persons considering buying a home computer—32%—gave preference to the Apple. Runners-up in the preference for a new purchase were IBM 26%, Commodore 19%, Tandy 3%, and Atari 2%.

COMPUTERIZED SHOPPING MACHINES

Hundreds of supermarkets throughout the United States began testing new computerized shopping machines produced by various companies.

A machine can display pictures of thousands of products to a potential purchaser. The consumer can choose the item desired by pressing a button and then insert a credit card in the machine to complete the transaction. The product then will be shipped to the consumer's home.

Among supermarket chains testing shopping machines were the 7-Eleven stores in Texas, The Marsh Supermarkets in Indiana, and Stop-n-Shop stores near Cleveland, Ohio.

BERNOULLI BOXES

One of the newest types of storage devices for personal computer users is the Bernoulli Box, named after Daniel Bernoulli, a Swiss mathematician who discovered the principles of fluid dynamics in the 1700s.

Promoters of the device say it has several advantages over a hard disk. The Bernoulli Box uses a removable disk that can contain millions of bytes of computer data, so backup copies of valuable data can be removed from the computer to be stored in a safe place. In a Bernoulli Box, the head that reads the disk cannot accidentally drop on the disk wiping out valuable information as sometimes happens with hard disk drives.

EYE STRAIN FROM COMPUTERS

The Occupational Safety and Health Administration (OSHA) reported that the majority of persons working with computers and computer terminals complain of eye problems. One of the most common problems comes from glare on the computer screen caused by overhead fluorescent lights and from other

HIGHLIGHTS: 1985 *(continued)*

lights reflected onto the viewing screen.

The Polaroid Corporation and several other manufacturers produce glass and plastic filters that can be attached to the computer's viewing screen to eliminate much of the glare.

BIG BROTHER IS WATCHING

Although 1984 came and went without George Orwell's predicted "Big Brother" turning up as head of the government, he seems to have turned instead to private business. This became apparent as scores of companies adopted computerized monitoring systems to check up on the work of their employees.

Computer monitors are mounted in trucks by some trucking companies to determine which drivers are exceeding speed limits.

Drivers who fail to comply get fired.

Computers collect data on typists in some companies, determining how many pages they produce each day. Raises go to those who turn out the most.

In manufacturing plants, computers monitor how fast each worker is completing the tasks assigned. Those who work the fastest receive a bonus.

Labor unions oppose such computer monitoring, declaring that it dehumanizes employees. Labor leaders have stimulated legislators in several states to consider laws outlawing or restricting computer monitoring.

Surveys by independent organizations have reported that employees in computer monitored companies have more health problems caused by additional stress than do employees in similar companies that do not have computer monitoring.

COMPUTER TERMS

accumulator—location within a computer's arithmetic/logic unit (ALU) where solution to a problem is accumulated

ADA—a high-level computer language developed for U.S. Department of Defense

address—a location within the computer's memory

ALU—abbreviation for **arithmetic/logic unit**

application program—a computer program that carries out a specific task, such as word processing

arithmetic/logic unit—part of a computer that solves arithmetic and logic problems; abbreviated as **ALU**

ASCII—abbreviation for American Standard Code for Information Interchange, a code agreed upon by computer manufacturers that standardizes the values assigned to each letter and other symbol shown on a computer viewing screen so that a computer can correctly interpret the meaning of letters and numbers input into the computer

assembler—a computer program that can translate an assembly language program into a machine language program

assembly language—a computer language used by programmers that can be translated into machine language by an assembler

Basic—a high-level language widely used in writing programs for personal computers; derived from name "Beginner's all-purpose symbolic instruction code"

baud rate—a standard measure in bits per second of the speed used in transmitting computer information over a phone line; most personal computers use modems with a baud rate of 300, or about six words per second; some modems used with business computers can run at 2,400 baud or 4,800 baud

binary number system—number system used within a computer to control the operation of its electronic switches; the binary number system has only two digits, 0 and 1, that tell the computer to turn a switch on or off; each digit

in a binary number to the left of the one's place has a place value two times that of the place value of the digit to its right, so the binary number 10 has a value of 2 in the decimal number system

bit—the smallest unit of computer memory; one bit is one binary digit in a binary number

bug—error within a computer program

byte—unit of measure of computer memory; one byte equals 8 bits (8 binary digits)

cathode ray tube—electronic vacuum tube used as the viewing screen of a computer or a television set; abbreviated as **CRT**

central processing unit—the main part within a computer that includes the computer's memory and its arithmetic/logic unit (ALU); abbreviated as **CPU**

chip—silicon chip that contains miniaturized electronic circuit

Cobol—high level computer language commonly used in business computers; derived from name "Common business oriented language"

code—a set of symbols and rules that can be used as a computer language in programming a computer

compatible—a computer that uses a microprocessor and operating system like that of another computer, so that computer programs are interchangeable between the two

compiler—type of computer program that can translate a program written in a high-level language into a machine language program

computer literacy—ability to understand computer terms and use a computer

CP/M—a widely used operating system for microcomputers; name derived from control program for microcomputers

CPU—abbreviation for **central processing unit**

CRT—abbreviation for **cathode ray tube**

cursor—symbol shown on the viewing screen of a computer that marks the place where the next character will be entered

daisy-wheel printer—device similar to a typewriter that prints material contained within a com-

puter; so-called because each character of type is at the end of a petal on a printing wheel, somewhat resembling a daisy

data—information that is fed into a computer to be saved or processed or information that is output by a computer

data base—large amount of information stored for use by a computer

data base management program—a computer program that enables the user to store a variety of information in a computer and retrieve it in the form of lists, reports, statistical research, and so on

data processing—manipulation of data within a computer to search for specific information or to solve problems

debug—to find and remove bugs, or errors, from a computer program

directory—a listing of the file names contained in a disk or other computer storage device; see **file** and **file name**

disk—plastic or metal disk used to store electronic signals on its magnetic surface; the signals stored may be computer programs or data

disk drive—a device somewhat like a record player that can read or record computer programs or data on a computer disk

diskette—a small disk; see **disk**

DOS—a computer program that controls the operation of a computer that uses a disk or disks to store programs and data; derived from disk operating system

dot-matrix printer—device somewhat like a typewriter used to print out material from a computer; each character is printed as a group of dots so close together that they appear to be joined together to form letters, numbers, and other symbols

dumb terminal—a viewing screen and a keyboard that can send information to a computer or receive information from a computer but can do little else; see also **smart terminal**

EDP—abbreviation for electronic data processing; see **data processing**

ENTER key—key on some computer keyboards that is used to tell the computer to carry out an instruction or to store information in its memory; see also **RETURN key**

file—a computer program or a collection of data

file name—the name of a specific file used in a computer; see **file** and **directory**

floppy disk—a small flexible disk; see **disk**

Fortran—a high-level computer language used by engineers, mathematicians, and scientists; derived from name "Formula translation"

glitch—an interruption of the electronic circuit of a computer or of a device it controls, usually causing an error

graphics—drawings or graphs produced with a computer

hacker—a computer enthusiast who spends much of his time working with and playing with a computer

hard disk—computer storage device that can contain many files of data and programs

hardcopy—material printed on paper from a computer

hardware—computers and electronic or mechanical devices used with computers

hex—abbreviation for **hexadecimal**

hexadecimal number system—number system used by computer programmers because large numbers can be stored using fewer digits than with the binary or decimal number systems; in addition to the digits 0-9, the hexadecimal number system uses the letters A to F as digits equivalent to the decimal numbers 10 to 15; in a hexadecimal number each digit to the left of the one's place has a place value 16 times the place value of the digit to its right, so the hexadecimal number 10 would have the same value as the decimal number 16

high-level language—a type of computer language that is easier to use in programming than assembly language or machine language

high-resolution—viewing screen of computer with many points of light, enabling screen to display illustrations with greater clarity than on an ordinary television set

incompatible—a computer that uses a different microprocessor or a different operating system than that of another computer so that computer programs are not interchangeable between the two

input—data or programs fed into a computer

input device—device, such as a computer keyboard, that can be used to put information into a computer

instruction—a command put into computer

instruction set—commands used in the internal design of a computer

interpreter—a type of computer program used in conjunction with a program written in high-level language, such as Basic, that translates and executes the instructions in machine language one step at a time

joy stick—device used to send signals to a computer's viewing screen; often used with computer games

K—abbreviation for **kilobyte**

keyboard—device similar to a typewriter keyboard that is used to put commands and information into a computer

kilobyte—unit of measure of computer memory; one kilobyte equals 1,024 bytes; abbreviated as **K**

language—code used in writing computer programs

large-scale integrated circuit—complicated electronic circuit usually miniaturized and printed on a silicon chip for use as part of a computer; abbreviated as **LSI**

LED—device used as a space-saving flat viewing screen for a portable computer, a pocket calculator, or a digital watch; derived from light-emitting diode

light pen—device used to put information into a computer by pointing the light pen at the computer's viewing screen

LSI—abbreviation for **large-scale integrated circuit**

M—abbreviation for **megabyte**

machine language—code used to communicate directly with a computer using its instruction set so that it can carry out commands instantly without having to translate the commands from a high-level language

mainframe—largest kinds of computers used to process large amounts of data

main memory—part of the computer used to

COMPUTER TERMS (*continued*)

store programs and data being used by the computer

megabyte—unit of measure of computer memory; one megabyte equals a thousand kilobytes or a million bytes; abbreviated as **M**

memory—part of a computer that stores commands, programs, or data

menu—the table of contents of a computer program displayed on the viewing screen to offer the user choices of ways to use the program

microcomputer—smallest kinds of computers

microprocessor—the central processing unit of a microcomputer printed on a silicon chip

minicomputer—medium-sized computer, smaller than a mainframe and larger than a microcomputer

modem—device used to translate computer electronic signals into audio signals for transmission over a telephone line; derived from **modulator/demodulator**

monitor—viewing screen of a computer

mouse—device used to put commands into a computer by moving the device on a flat surface

MS-DOS—the operating system used on IBM personal computers and IBM compatibles; see also **DOS**

nibble or **nybble**—unit of measure of computer memory; one nibble equals 4 bits or one-half a byte

on-line database—computer data that can be accessed at a distance by a consumer using a phone line connection to his own computer

operating system—a computer program that coordinates all the parts of the computer, enabling the user to control the computer; see also **DOS**

output—information sent out by the computer

parallel port—a channel through which a computer sends or receives data several bits at a time, or in parallel

Pascal—a high-level computer language sometimes used in helping beginners learn how to program; named for early inventor of a calculating machine, Blaise Pascal

PC—abbreviation for personal computer

peripheral—device used with a computer, such as a joystick or a printer

personal computer—a microcomputer used by an individual for such tasks as word processing

pixel—one point of light on the viewing screen of a computer; see also **high-resolution**

port—a channel through which a computer sends out or receives information; see also **serial port** and **parallel port**

printer—device used with computer to print out information; see also **daisy-wheel printer** and **dot-matrix printer**

printout—material from a computer that has been typed out on a printer; also called **hardcopy**

program—set of commands and information put into a computer so that it can carry out a task or solve a problem

programmer—a person who writes programs for computers

programming—the writing of computer programs

RAM—abbreviation for random access memory

random access memory—part of a computer's memory that can be accessed by a user to input programs or data for temporary storage while the computer is turned on; abbreviated as **RAM**

read only memory—the part of a computer's memory that permanently stores its designer's instructions and that cannot be used to store programs or data input by a user; abbreviated as **ROM**

register—a location within the computer's arithmetic/logic unit where information or a command is temporarily stored

RETURN key—key on some computer keyboards that is used to tell the computer to carry out an instruction or to store information in its memory; see also **ENTER key**

ROM—abbreviation for read only memory

screen—the viewing screen of a computer

serial port—a channel through which a computer sends or receives data one bit at a time, or serially

smart terminal—a computer-connected terminal that contains chips that enable it to perform additional functions beyond merely receiving or sending data; for example, it may be used to edit information received from the computer

software—programs and data used by a computer

spread sheet program—a computer program used for bookkeeping or for the processing of financial or statistical data; the program creates an electronic spread sheet within the computer like that in a bookkeeping ledger with many horizontal rows and vertical columns; the user can place labels, numbers, or formulas at the intersection of each row and column; when a number or formula is changed, the program automatically recalculates the numbers in other rows and columns that may be affected

string—a specially marked group of letters, words, or symbols that can be used repeatedly in the same form in a computer program

string variable—a variable used in a program to stand for a string; for example, H$ could be used to represent the word "Hello", then if you told the computer to print H$ it would display the word "Hello"

tape—magnetic tape used to store electronic signals that can be read by a computer as programs or as data

tape drive—device similar to a music tape recorder that can be used with a computer to store computer programs or data on magnetic tape

terminal—device connected to a computer, usually consisting of a keyboard and a viewing screen

UNIX—a computer operating system developed by Bell Laboratories, written in a computer language called C

variable—a symbol or group of symbols used in a program to represent a specific number or string

VDT—viewing screen of a computer; derived from video display terminal

video—viewing screen of a computer or a TV set

voice synthesizer—device used with a computer that produces computer output as human speech

word processing—use of a computer to produce business letters or other written documents

Congress of the United States

The U.S. Postal Service issued the *Help End Hunger* commemorative stamp in conjunction with "World Food Day," proclaimed for Oct. 16 by President Reagan. The stamp, designed by Jerry Pinkney of Croton-on-Hudson, N.Y., depicts the debilitated faces of an Oriental child, a Caucasian woman, and a black boy. Rep. Mickey Leland (D-Texas), chairman of the House Select Committee on Hunger, took part in the dedication ceremonies for the stamp held in the Rayburn House Office Building on Oct. 15.

Help End Hunger USA 22

U.S. Postal Service

HIGHLIGHTS: 1985

ASSESSMENT: MEDIOCRE

For the fifth year Congress remained politically divided between a Democratic-controlled House and a Republican-controlled Senate. Not since the period 1883–89, during the administrations of Presidents Arthur and Cleveland, had the two houses of Congress remained divided for so many years.

Because of the political division, attention focused on the party leaders—Democratic Speaker of the House Thomas P. O'Neill Jr. (D-Mass) and Senate Majority Leader Robert J. Dole (R-Kan.).

The 73-year-old O'Neill is presiding over the House in his fifth and last term as speaker, having announced that he does not intend to run for Congress again in 1986. He was first elected to Congress in 1952 and 25 years later first became speaker in 1977.

The 62-year-old Dole is serving his first term as majority leader of the Senate. A World War II hero, whose arm was permanently crippled in combat in Italy, Dole was elected to four consecutive terms in the House of Representatives from 1960 before winning election to the Senate in 1968, 1974, and 1980. He was the unsuccessful Republican candidate for Vice President on the ticket with President Ford in 1976 and four years later unsuccessfully campaigned for the Republican presidential nomination in 1980. He faces the question of whether to again seek the Republican presidential nomination for himself in 1988 or to give his support to his wife, 50-year-old Secretary of Transportation Elizabeth Hanford Dole, who also has been mentioned frequently as a possible contender for the party's presidential nomination.

When Congress adjourned for its summer recess in August, Senate Minority Leader Robert C. Byrd (D-W.Va.) was asked what he thought of the record so far of the 99th Congress.

"I would rate it as mediocre," he said. "There hasn't been anything in the way of new initiatives that I can see."

FOOD FOR STARVING AFRICANS

Reacting to worldwide concern for the famine-stricken peoples of Africa, Congress approved and the President signed in April measures raising to about $1.4 billion the amount of food and emergency aid for African nations appropriated since Oct. 1, 1984.

Although about $600 million in aid for Africa previously had been approved for fiscal 1985, President Reagan on Jan. 3, 1985, had asked Congress to provide an additional $235 million.

On March 20 the Senate approved by a 98-1 vote a measure providing $669 million in additional aid for Africa. The lone dissenter was Sen. Barry Goldwater (R-Ariz.), who declared:

"Why this Congress can send billions of dollars around this world to every little Godforsaken country and then not pay attention to our Indians in this country is beyond me."

The House had approved a measure on Feb. 28 that provided $880 million in new aid for Africa.

A House-Senate conference committee reached a compromise agreement on March 27 that gave $784 million additional African aid—$609 million for food and $175 million for other non-food aid.

Both the House and the Senate approved the compromise measure on April 2.

"We have once again shown the world that individual caring and giving is an American way of life," President Reagan said after signing the legislation two days later.

PRESIDENT WINS MX BATTLE

Despite concerted opposition by many legislators who wanted to cut Defense Department spending, President Reagan succeeded in winning congressional approval to spend $1.5 billion in 1985 for the construction of 21 new MX "Peacekeeper" intercontinental ballistic missiles.

The President used every trick in his bag of personal persuasion to achieve passage of the legislation—phoning individual senators and representatives and inviting others to the White House for arm-twisting chats, arguing that approval of the MX program was essential to strengthen the hand of American negotiators in arms limitation talks with the Soviet Union.

"Make no mistake about it, the power and popularity of the President is awesome," commented House Speaker O'Neill, who unsuccessfully led opposition to the MX missiles. "It's as awesome as the weapon itself."

The first leg of the President's victory came on March 19-20 when the Senate twice approved the MX program by votes of 55 to 45.

The scene of the controversy then shifted to the House, where the President called home from Geneva the chief arms negotiator for the U.S., Max M. Kampelman, who effectively persuaded doubting congressmen that defeat of the MX program would give the Soviet Union an undeserved victory in the arms talks.

The House finally approved the MX program in votes of 219-213 on March 26 and 217-210 on March 28.

BUDGET COMPROMISE

After months of wrangling about how the federal deficit might be reduced, a compromise budget resolution was approved on August 1 by the House 309-119 and by the Senate 67-32. Congress then adjourned for a month's vacation.

The resolution calls for federal outlays of $967.6 billion in 1986, $1.02 trillion in 1987,

and $1.07 trillion in 1987. Deficits would be $181 billion in 1986, $175 billion in 1987, and $161 billion in 1988.

$27.54 BILLION FOREIGN AID

At the end of July Congress approved a foreign aid bill that provided for the spending of $12.77 billion each year in fiscal 1986 and 1987 as well as $2 billion in emergency economic aid to Israel and Egypt in fiscal 1985. The measure was signed by President Reagan on August 8.

BITTER FIGHT FOR HOUSE SEAT

Democrats and Republicans bitterly denounced each other in a long fight for a contested seat in the Indiana 8th Congressional District.

Two days after the 1984 November election, an official tally showed that Democratic incumbent Rep. Frank McCloskey held a 72-vote lead over Republican challenger Richard D. McIntyre.

However, a recount of part of the vote in December gave McIntyre a 34-vote lead, and on Dec. 14 the Indiana secretary of state, a Republican, certified McIntyre as the winner.

On Jan. 22 Indiana completed the recount, giving McIntyre a 418-vote lead.

A House committee task force of two Democrats and one Republican made a new recount of the ballots and on April 22 its chairman announced McCloskey had won with 116,645 votes to McIntyre's 116,641. The Republican member of the group charged that the Democrats refused to count additional absentee ballots once McCloskey had gained a lead.

On May 1, the House voted 236 to 190 to seat McCloskey. Before McCloskey could be sworn in, Republicans marched out of the chamber, declaring they had been robbed. They later returned, vowing vengance on the Democratic leadership.

SPECIAL DAYS, WEEKS, AND MONTHS

Among the 75 public laws that won passage during the first seven months of the 99th Congress more than half established special days, special weeks, or special months for observance or commemoration. But the ponderous legislative process often resulted in these innocuous measures being signed into law after the day, week, or month already had come and gone. These public laws included:

The second measure passed by the 99th Congress, public law 99-2, named the week of Feb. 10-16, 1985, as *National DECA Week.* The legislation was introduced by Sen. Alan K. Simpson (R-Wyo.). It was signed by the President on Feb. 11.

The week of March 24-30, 1985, was named *National Skin Cancer Prevention and Detection Week* by public law 99-6, which was introduced by Rep. Richard C. Shelby (D-Ala.) and was signed by the President on March 22.

National Employ the Older Worker Week was designated for March 10-16, 1985, by public law 99-9. Introduced by Rep. Edward R. Roybal (D-Calif.), it received final passage by the Senate on March 28 and was signed by the President on April 3.

Public law 99-11 set *Fair Housing Month* for April 1985. Introduced by Sen. Charles McC. Mathias Jr. (R-Md.), it was signed by the President on April 4.

April 1985 also was named *Child Abuse Prevention Month* by public law 99-13. It was introduced by Sen. Slade Gorton (R-Wash.) and was signed by the President on April 4.

March 22, 1985, was designated *National Energy Education Day* by public law 99-14, introduced by Rep. W. J. Tausin (D-La.) on Feb. 21. The measure finally was approved by Congress on March 28 and was signed by the President on April 4.

World Health Week was set for April 1-7, 1985, and *World Health Day* was designated for April 7, 1985, by public law 99-16. Introduced by Sen. Donald W. Riegle Jr. (D-Mich.), it was signed by the President on April 4.

April 2, 1985, was named *Education Day U.S.A.* by public law 99-19. Introduced by Rep. Robert H. Michel (R-Ill.), it was signed by the President on April 4.

National Independent Retail Grocer Week was designated for the week of Sept. 8, 1985, by public law 99-20, introduced by Rep. Carroll Campbell Jr. (R-S.C.) and signed by the President on April 14.

April 21-27, 1985, was named *National Organ Donation Awareness Week* in public law 99-21. It was introduced by Sen. Slade Gorton (R-Wash.) and was signed by the President on April 14.

Jewish Heritage Week was set for April 21-28, 1985, by public law 99-26. It was introduced by Sen. Alfonse M. D'Amato (R-N.Y.) and was signed by the President on April 19.

The week beginning April 14, 1985, was named *Crime Victims Week* by public law 99-27. Introduced by Sen. Robert J. Dole (R-Kans.), it received final passage by the House on April 18 and was signed by the President on April 19.

The week of April 21-27, 1985, was named *National DES Awareness Week* in public law 99-28. It was introduced by Sen. Donald W. Riegle Jr. (D-Mich.). The President signed it on April 25.

May 7, 1985, was called *Helsinki Human Rights Day* by public law 99-29. Introduced by Sen. Dennis DeConconi (D-Ariz.), it was

HOW A BILL BECOMES A LAW

The process by which a bill becomes a law is long and complicated. Following is a summary of steps in the passage of legislation by Congress.

Introduction of Bill. The bill is introduced in the House by a representative or in the Senate by a senator. Sometimes to speed up action the same bill is introduced in both houses at the same time. All tax bills must be introduced in the House, but the Senate is free to amend them.

First Reading. The title of the bill is read to the House or Senate. It is given a number, and it is printed.

Assignment to Committee. The Speaker of the House, or the Vice President in the Senate, assigns each bill to a committee for consideration.

Committee Consideration. The committee may hold hearings on the bill, and then rewrite or amend it. The committee also can decide to table the bill, or kill it.

Committee Approval. If the committee approves the bill, it is sent to the floor to await its turn on the calendar. The bill can be pushed ahead of others in the House by the House Rules Committee or in the Senate by the majority leaders.

Second Reading. When the bill reaches the floor of the House or Senate, it is read in full and then debated. It may be amended or it may be returned to committee. The time for debate is limited in the House but is unlimited in the Senate unless a two-thirds majority votes to impose limits. At the end of the debate the House or Senate votes on the bill.

Third Reading. Only the title of the bill is read, and another vote is taken, usually by roll call.

Consideration by Other House of Congress. After a bill is passed by one house, it must go through the same process already described in the other house. If it is amended during the process by the other house and then is passed on

third reading by a majority vote, it is returned to the house that originated the bill.

Approval of Amendments by Originating House. When a bill is returned to the house of Congress in which it originated, it is debated and a vote is taken to decide whether the majority approves the amended version of the bill.

Conference Committee. If the majority of the house in which the bill originated rejects the other house's amendments, the bill is sent to a conference committee composed of both representatives and senators. The conference committee revises the bill to reconcile the differences between its two versions.

Final Approval by House and Senate. After the conference committee reports out its revised version of the bill, the House and the Senate each must vote again. If a majority in each house votes to approve the bill, it then is sent to the President.

Presidential Signature. If the President signs the bill, it immediately becomes law.

Becoming a Law Without Presidential Signature. If Congress is in session the bill automatically becomes law 10 days after the President receives it, excluding Sundays, even though he does not sign it.

Regular Veto. The President may within 10 days veto the bill by returning it to Congress with an explanation of why he refuses to approve it.

Pocket Veto. If Congress adjourns within the 10-day period of presidential consideration, the bill automatically is killed if the President does not sign it.

Overriding a Veto. If the President vetoes a bill, Congress can make it become law if both the House and the Senate again pass the bill, each by a two-thirds majority.

signed by the President on April 25.

Public law 99-30, signed by the President on April 30, authorized the proclaiming of May 1985 as *National Child Safety Awareness Month.* It was introduced by Rep. Tom Lewis (R-Fla.).

Public law 99-31, signed by the President on May 14, named the week beginning on May 5, 1985, as *National Correctional Officers Week.* It was introduced by Sen. Donald W. Riegle Jr. (D-Mich.).

Public law 99-32, introduced by Sen. Robert J. Dole (R-Kan.), named the week beginning May 5, 1985, as *National Asthma and Allergy Awareness Week.* It was signed by the President on May 14.

Public law 99-33, signed by the President on May 14, designated May 6, 1985, as *Dr. Jonas Salk Day.* It was introduced by Rep. James H. Scheuer (D-N.Y.).

May 1985 was named *Older Americans Month* by public law 99-34, which was introduced by Rep. Bill McCollum (R-Fla.) and was signed by the President on May 14.

Public law 99-35, introduced by Sen. Robert C. Byrd (D-W.Va.), designated May 7, 1985, as *Vietnam Veterans' Recognition Day.* It was signed by the President on May 14.

November 1985 was designated as *National Alzheimer's Disease Month* by public law 99-37, which was introduced by Sen. Thomas F. Eagleton (D-Mo.) and was signed by the President on May 15.

June 1985 was named *Youth Suicide Prevention Month* by public law 99-38, signed by the President on May 15. It was introduced by Sen. Jeremiah Denton (R-Ala.).

The week beginning May 12, 1985, was designated *National Digestive Diseases Awareness Week* by public law 99-39. Signed by the President on May 15, it had been introduced by Sen. Albert Gore Jr. (D-Tenn.).

Senior Center Week was designated for May 12-18, 1985, by public law 99-40, which was introduced by Sen. Sam Nunn (D-Ga.) and was signed by the President on May 15.

The week of May 12-18, 1985, also was named *National Science Week* by public law 99-41, introduced by Sen. Orrin G. Hatch (R-Utah) and signed on May 17.

National Osteoporosis Awareness Week was set for the week of May 20-26 by public law 99-42. It was introduced by Sen. Charles E. Grassley (R-Iowa) and was signed by the President on May 20.

Very Special Arts U.S.A. Month was designated for May 1985 by public law 99-43. It was introduced by Sen. Claiborne Pell (D.-R.I.) and was signed by the President on May 21.

Public law 99-48 also named May 1985 as *Better Hearing and Speech Month.* It had been introduced by Sen. Howard M. Metzenbaum (D-Ohio). It did not receive final passage by the House until June 4, and was signed by the President on June 12.

Baltic Freedom Day was named as June 14, 1985, by public law 99-49. It was introduced by Sen. Alfonse M. D'Amato (R-N.Y.) and was signed on June 13.

June 12, 1985, was named *Anne Frank Day* in public law 99-50. It was introduced by Sen. Carl Levin (D-Mich.) and was signed by the President on June 14.

Public law 99-51, designating the week beginning June 2, 1985, as *National Theatre Week,* received final passage on June 10. Signed on June 14, it had been introduced by Rep. S. William Green (R-N.Y.).

Family Reunion Month was the name given to the period May 12, 1985, *(Mother's Day)* to June 16, 1985 *(Father's Day)* by public law 99-52. Introduced by Rep. Richard Ray (D-Ga.), it was signed by the President on June 14.

The week of June 23-29, 1985, was designated *Helen Keller Deaf-Blind Awareness Week* in public law 99-56 signed by the President on June 26. It had been introduced by Sen. Patrick J. Leahy (D-Vt.).

July 19, 1985, was named *National P.O.W./M.I.A. Recognition Day* by public law 99-57, which was signed by the President on June 27. It was introduced by Sen. Frank H. Murkowski (R-Alaska).

Public law 99-60 was signed by the President on July 3. Calling for commemoration of the 75th anniversary of the Boy Scouts of America, it was introduced by Rep. Richard Stallings (D-Idaho).

Public law 99-61, signed by the President on July 9, provided for the minting of coins in commemoration of the centennial of the Statue of Liberty. It was introduced by Rep. Frank Annunzio (D-Ill.).

Public law 99-66, signed by the President on July 17, designated July 13, 1985, as *Live Aid Day.* It was introduced by Rep. M. Robert Carr (D-Mich.).

Public law 99-67 named July 20, 1985, as *Space Exploration Day.* Signed by the President on July 17, it was introduced by Sen. Jake Garn (R-Utah).

October 1985 was designated *National Down* (Down's) *Syndrome Month* by public law 99-72, signed by the President on July 24. It was introduced by Sen. Richard G. Lugar (R-Ind.).

The week of July 25-31, 1985, was designated *National Disability in Entertainment Week* by public law 99-74 signed by the President on July 29. It had been introduced by Sen. Pete Wilson (R-Calif.).

UNITED STATES SENATE

Republicans control the U.S. Senate in the 99th Congress, with 53 members to the Democrats' 47.

The U.S. Senate with 100 members is the smaller but the more influential of the two houses of Congress.

The Senate's presiding officer is Vice President Bush.

Senate officers chosen for the 99th Congress included:

President Pro Tempore Strom Thurmond (R-S.C.), Republican Majority Leader Robert J. Dole (R-Kan.), Democratic Floor Leader Robert C. Byrd (D-W. Va.), Republican Whip Alan K. Simpson (R-Wyo.), and Democratic Whip Alan Cranston (D-Calif.)

Thurmond is the senior Republican senator, having served since Nov. 7, 1956.

The senior Democratic senator is John D. Stennis of Mississippi, who has served since Nov. 5, 1947.

U.S. senators are elected for terms of 6 years. A senator must be at least 30 years of age, a citizen for 9 years, and a resident of the state he represents.

Senators' salaries were raised 3.5% to $75,100 on Jan. 1, 1985. Salaries of the president pro tem and majority and minority leaders were raised to $84,900.

In addition each senator receives free office space, staff salaries, travel expenses, and other allowances averaging $500,000 or more annually.

Dates in the table show when each senator took office. An asterisk (*) indicates a freshman (first-term) senator.

State	Senators
Alabama	Howell Heflin (D), Jan. 3, 1979
	*Jeremiah Denton (R), Jan. 2, 1981
Alaska	Theodore F. Stevens (R), Dec. 24, 1968
	*Frank H. Murkowski (R), Jan. 3, 1981
Arizona	Barry Goldwater (R), Jan. 3, 1969
	*Dennis DeConcini (D), Jan. 3, 1977
Arkansas	Dale Bumpers (D), Jan. 3, 1975
	David Pryor (D), Jan. 3, 1979
California	Alan Cranston (D), Jan. 3, 1969
	*Pete Wilson (R), Jan. 3, 1983
Colorado	Gary Hart (D), Jan. 3, 1975
	William L. Armstrong (R), Jan. 3, 1979
Connecticut	Lowell P. Weicker Jr. (R), Jan. 3, 1971
	*Christopher J. Dodd (D), Jan. 3, 1981
Delaware	William V. Roth Jr. (R), Jan. 1, 1971
	Joseph R. Biden Jr. (D), Jan. 3, 1973
Florida	Lawton Chiles (D), Jan. 3, 1971
	*Paula Hawkins (R), Jan. 3, 1981
Georgia	Sam Nunn (D), Nov. 8, 1972
	*Mack Mattingly (R), Jan. 3, 1981
Hawaii	Daniel K. Inouye (D), Jan. 3, 1963
	Spark M. Matsunaga (D), Jan. 3, 1977
Idaho	James A. McClure (R), Jan. 3, 1973
	*Steven D. Symms (R), Jan. 3, 1981
Illinois	*Alan J. Dixon (D), Jan. 3, 1981
	*Paul Simon (D), Jan. 3, 1985
Indiana	Richard G. Lugar (R), Jan. 3, 1977
	*Dan Quayle (R), Jan. 3, 1981
Iowa	*Charles E. Grassley (R), Jan. 3, 1981
	*Tom Harkin (D), Jan. 3, 1985
Kansas	Robert J. Dole (R), Jan. 3, 1969
	Nancy L. Kassebaum (R), Dec. 23, 1978
Kentucky	Wendell H. Ford (D), Dec. 28, 1974
	*Mitchell McConnell (R), Jan. 3, 1985
Louisiana	Russell B. Long (D), Dec. 31, 1948
	J. Bennett Johnston Jr. (D), Nov. 14, 1972
Maine	William S. Cohen (R), Jan. 3, 1979
	George J. Mitchell (D), May 8, 1980
Maryland	Charles McC. Mathias Jr. (R), Jan. 3, 1969
	Paul S. Sarbanes (D), Jan. 3, 1977
Massachusetts	Edward M. Kennedy (D), Nov. 7, 1962
	*John F. Kerry (D), Jan. 2, 1985
Michigan	Donald W. Riegle Jr. (D), Dec. 30, 1976
	Carl Levin (D), Jan. 3, 1979
Minnesota	David Durenberger (R), Nov. 8, 1978
	Rudy Boschwitz (R), Dec. 30, 1978
Mississippi	John Stennis (D), Nov. 5, 1947
	Thad Cochran (R), Dec. 27, 1978
Missouri	Thomas F. Eagleton (D), Dec. 28, 1968
	John C. Danforth (R), Dec. 27, 1976
Montana	John Melcher (D), Jan. 3, 1977
	Max Baucus (D), Dec. 15, 1978
Nebraska	Edward Zorinsky (D), Dec. 28, 1976
	J. James Exon (D), Jan. 3, 1979
Nevada	Paul Laxalt (R), Dec. 18, 1974
	*Chic Hecht (R), Jan. 3, 1983
New Hampshire	Gordon Humphrey (R), Jan. 3, 1979
	*Warren Rudman (R), Jan. 3, 1981
New Jersey	Bill Bradley (D), Jan. 3, 1979
	*Frank R. Lautenberg (D), Jan. 3, 1983
New Mexico	Pete V. Domenici (R), Jan. 3, 1973
	*Jeff Bingaman (D), Jan. 3, 1983
New York	Daniel P. Moynihan (D), Jan. 3, 1977
	*Alfonse M. D'Amato (R), Jan. 3, 1981
North Carolina	Jesse A. Helms (R), Jan. 3, 1973
	*John P. East (R), Jan. 3, 1981
North Dakota	Quentin N. Burdick (D), Aug. 8, 1960
	*Mark Andrews (R), Jan. 3, 1981
Ohio	John H. Glenn (D), Dec. 24, 1974
	Howard M. Metzenbaum (D), Dec. 29, 1976
Oklahoma	David L. Boren (D), Jan. 3, 1979
	*Don Nickles (R), Jan. 3, 1981
Oregon	Mark O. Hatfield (R), Jan. 10, 1967
	Robert W. Packwood (R), Jan. 3, 1969
Pennsylvania	H. John Heinz III (R), Jan. 3, 1977
	*Arlen Specter (R), Jan. 3, 1981
Rhode Island	Claiborne Pell (D), Jan. 3, 1961
	John H. Chafee (R), Dec. 29, 1976
South Carolina	Strom Thurmond (R), Nov. 7, 1956
	Ernest F. Hollings (D), Nov. 9, 1966
South Dakota	Larry Pressler (R), Jan. 3, 1979
	*James Abdnor (R), Jan. 3, 1981
Tennessee	James R. Sasser (D), Jan. 3, 1977
	*Albert Gore Jr. (D), Jan. 3, 1985
Texas	Lloyd M. Bentsen Jr. (D), Jan. 3, 1971
	*Phil Gramm (R), Jan. 3, 1985
Utah	Jake Garn (R), Dec. 21, 1974
	Orrin G. Hatch (R), Jan. 3, 1977
Vermont	Robert T. Stafford (R), Sept. 16, 1971
	Patrick J. Leahy (D), Jan. 3, 1975
Virginia	John W. Warner (R), Jan. 2, 1979
	*Paul S. Trible Jr. (R), Jan. 3, 1983
Washington	*Daniel J. Evans (R), Sept. 12, 1983
	*Slade Gorton (R), Jan. 3, 1981
West Virginia	Robert C. Byrd (D), Jan. 3, 1959
	*J. D. Rockefeller 4th (D), Jan. 3, 1985
Wisconsin	William Proxmire (D), Aug. 28, 1957
	*Robert W. Kasten Jr. (R), Jan. 3, 1981
Wyoming	Malcolm Wallop (R), Jan. 3, 1977
	Alan K. Simpson (R), Jan. 1, 1979

U.S. HOUSE OF REPRESENTATIVES

Democrats control the U.S. House of Representatives in the 99th Congress, with 253 votes to the Republicans' 182.

The chief officers of the House in the 98th Congress include: Speaker of the House Thomas P. O'Neill Jr. (D-Mass.), Democratic Floor Leader Jim Wright (D-Texas), Republican Floor Leader Robert H. Michel (R-Ill.), Democratic Whip Thomas S. Foley (D-Wash.), and Republican Whip Trent Lott (R-Miss.).

The senior Democrat is Jamie L. Whitten of Mississippi, who has served since Nov. 4, 1941. The senior Republicans are Michel and Rep. William S. Broomfield (R-Mich.); both have served since Jan. 3, 1957.

The larger house of Congress (435 members) represents the people more directly than the Senate. Three powers are delegated exclusively to the House: (1) it originates all bills for raising revenue, (2) it elects the President if there is no electoral majority, and (3) it impeaches federal officials.

A representative must be at least 25 years of age, a citizen of the U.S. for 7 years, and a resident of the state he represents.

The salaries of representatives were raised 3.5% to $75,100 on Jan. 1, 1985. At the same time the salaries of the chief officers of the House were raised to $84,900.

In addition each representative receives other allowances.

An asterisk (*) in the table below indicates a freshman member (one serving his first term in the House).

Congressional districts within a state are indicated by numerals. A representative-at-large is shown as AL.

ALABAMA
1. H. L. Callahan (R)*
2. William L. Dickinson (R)
3. William Nichols (D)
4. Tom Bevill (D)
5. Ronnie G. Flippo (D)
6. Ben Erdreich (D)
7. Richard C. Shelby (D)
ALASKA
AL Donald E. Young (R)
ARIZONA
1. John McCain (R)
2. Morris K. Udall (D)
3. Bob Stump (R)
4. Eldon D. Rudd (R)
5. Jim Kolbe (R)*
ARKANSAS
1. Bill Alexander Jr. (D)
2. Tommy Robinson (D)*
3. John Hammerschmidt (R)
4. Beryl F. Anthony Jr. (D)
CALIFORNIA
1. Douglas H. Bosco (D)
2. Eugene A. Chappie (R)
3. Robert T. Matsui (D)
4. Vic Fazio (D)
5. Sala Burton (D)
6. Barbara Boxer (D)
7. George Miller III (D)
8. Ronald V. Dellums (D)
9. Fortney H. Stark (D)
10. Don Edwards (D)
11. Tom Lantos (D)
12. Ed Zschau (R)
13. Norman Y. Mineta (D)
14. Norman D. Shumway (R)
15. Tony Coelho (D)
16. Leon E. Panetta (D)
17. Charles Pashayan Jr. (R)
18. Richard Lehman (D)
19. R. J. Lagomarsino (R)
20. William Thomas (R)
21. Bobbi Fiedler (R)
22. Carlos J. Moorhead (R)
23. Anthony Beilenson (D)
24. Henry A. Waxman (D)
25. Edward R. Roybal (D)
26. Howard L. Berman (D)
27. Mel Levine (D)

28. Julian C. Dixon (D)
29. Augustus F. Hawkins (D)
30. Matthew G. Martinez (D)
31. Mervyn M. Dymally (D)
32. Glenn M. Anderson (D)
33. David Dreier (R)
34. Esteban Torres (D)
35. Jerry Lewis (R)
36. George E. Brown Jr. (D)
37. Al McCandless (R)
38. Robert K. Dornan (R)*
39. William Dannemeyer (R)
40. Robert E. Badham (R)
41. Bill Lowery (R)
42. Dan Lungren (R)
43. Ron Packard (R)
44. Jim Bates (D)
45. Duncan L. Hunter (R)
COLORADO
1. Patricia Schroeder (D)
2. Timothy E. Wirth (D)
3. Michael L. Strang (R)*
4. Hank Brown (R)
5. Ken Kramer (R)
6. Daniel L. Schaefer (R)
CONNECTICUT
1. Barbara B. Kennelly (D)
2. Samuel Gejdenson (D)
3. Bruce A. Morrison (D)
4. Stewart B. McKinney (R)
5. John G. Rowlands (R)*
6. Nancy L. Johnson (R)
DELAWARE
AL Thomas R. Carper (D)
FLORIDA
1. Earl Hutto (D)
2. Don Fuqua (D)
3. Charles E. Bennett (D)
4. Bill Chappell Jr. (D)
5. Bill McCollum (R)
6. Kenneth MacKay (D)
7. Sam Gibbons (D)
8. C.W. Young (R)
9. Michael Bilirakis (R)
10. Andrew P. Ireland (R)
11. Bill Nelson (D)
12. Tom Lewis (R)
13. Connie Mack (R)
14. Daniel Mica (D)

15. E. Clay Shaw Jr. (R)
16. Larry Smith (D)
17. William Lehman (D)
18. Claude Pepper (D)
19. Dante B. Fascell (D)
GEORGIA
1. Lindsay Thomas (D)
2. Charles F. Hatcher (D)
3. Richard Ray (D)
4. Pat Swindall (R)*
5. Wyche Fowler Jr. (D)
6. Newt Gingrich (R)
7. George Darden (D)
8. J. Roy Rowland (D)
9. Ed Jenkins (D)
10. Doug Barnard Jr. (D)
HAWAII
1. Cecil Heftel (D)
2. Daniel Akaka (D)
IDAHO
1. Larry Craig (R)
2. Richard Stallings (D)*
ILLINOIS
1. Charles A. Hayes (D)
2. Gus Savage (D)
3. Martin A. Russo (D)
4. George M. O'Brien (R)
5. William Lipinski (D)
6. Henry J. Hyde (R)
7. Cardiss Collins (D)
8. Dan Rostenkowski (D)
9. Sidney R. Yates (D)
10. John E. Porter (R)
11. Frank Annunzio (D)
12. Philip M. Crane (R)
13. Harris W. Fawell (R)*
14. John E. Grotberg (R)*
15. Edward R. Madigan (R)
16. Lynn M. Martin (R)
17. Lane Evans (D)*
18. Robert H. Michel (R)
19. Terry L. Bruce (D)*
20. Richard J. Durbin (D)
21. Melvin Price (D)
22. Kenneth J. Gray (D)*
INDIANA
1. Peter J. Visclosky (D)*
2. Philip R. Sharp (D)
3. John Hiler (R)

4. Daniel R. Coats (R)
5. Elwood H. Hillis (R)
6. Daniel L. Burton (R)
7. John T. Myers (R)
8. Francis X. McCloskey (D)
9. Lee H. Hamilton (D)
10. Andrew Jacobs Jr. (D)
IOWA
1. James Leach (R)
2. Tom Tauke (R)
3. Cooper Evans (R)
4. Neal Smith (D)
5. J. R. Lightfoot (R)*
6. Berkley Bedell (D)
KANSAS
1. Pat Roberts (R)
2. Jim Slattery (D)
3. Jan Meyers (R)*
4. Dan Glickman (D)
5. Robert Whittaker (R)
KENTUCKY
1. Carroll Hubbard Jr. (D)
2. William H. Natcher (D)
3. Romano L. Mazzoli (D)
4. M. G. (Gene) Snyder (R)
5. Harold Rogers (R)
6. Larry J. Hopkins (R)
7. Carl C. Perkins (D)
LOUISIANA
1. Robert L. Livingston Jr. (R)
2. Lindy Boggs (D)
3. W.J. (Billy) Tauzin (D)
4. Buddy Roemer (D)
5. Jerry Huckaby (D)
6. Henson Moore (R)
7. John B. Breaux (D)
8. Cathy Long (D)
MAINE
1. John R. McKernan Jr. (R)
2. Olympia Snowe (R)
MARYLAND
1. Roy Dyson (D)
2. H. Delich Bentley (R)*
3. Barbara A. Mikulski (D)
4. Marjorie S. Holt (R)
5. Steny H. Hoyer (D)
6. Beverly Byron (D)
7. Parren J. Mitchell (D)
8. Michael Barnes (D)

MASSACHUSETTS
1. Silvio O. Conte (R)
2. Edward P. Boland (D)
3. Joseph D. Early (D)
4. Barney Frank (D)
5. Chester G. Atkins (D)*
6. Nicholas Mavroules (D)
7. Edward J. Markey (D)
8. Thomas P. O'Neill Jr. (D)
9. John (Joe) Moakley (D)
10. Gerry E. Studds (D)
11. Brian J. Donnelly (D)

MICHIGAN
1. John Conyers Jr. (D)
2. Carl D. Pursell (R)
3. Howard Wolpe (D)
4. Mark Siljander (R)
5. Paul B. Henry (R)*
6. M. Robert Carr (D)
7. Dale E. Kildee (D)
8. Bob Traxler (D)
9. Guy A. Vander Jagt (R)
10. Bill Schuette (R)*
11. Robert W. Davis (R)
12. David E. Bonior (D)
13. G. W. Crockett Jr. (D)
14. Dennis M. Hertel (D)
15. William D. Ford (D)
16. John D. Dingell (D)
17. Sander Levin (D)
18. William S. Broomfield (R)

MINNESOTA
1. Timothy J. Penny (D)
2. Vin Weber (R)
3. Bill Frenzel (R)
4. Bruce F. Vento (D)
5. Martin O. Sabo (D)
6. Gerry Sikorski (D)
7. Arlan Stangeland (R)
8. James L. Oberstar (D)

MISSISSIPPI
1. Jamie L. Whitten (D)
2. Webb Franklin (R)
3. G. V. Montgomery (D)
4. Wayne Dowdy (D)
5. Trent Lott (R)

MISSOURI
1. William L. Clay (D)
2. Robert A. Young (D)
3. Richard A. Gephardt (D)
4. Ike Skelton (D)
5. Alan Wheat (D)
6. E. Thomas Coleman (R)
7. Gene Taylor (R)
8. Bill Emerson (R)
9. Harold L. Volkmer (D)

MONTANA
1. Pat Williams (D)
2. Ron Marlenee (R)

NEBRASKA
1. Douglas K. Bereuter (R)
2. Hal Daub (R)
3. Virginia Smith (R)

NEVADA
1. Harry Reid (D)
2. Barbara Vucanovich (R)

NEW HAMPSHIRE
1. Robert C. Smith (R)*
2. Judd Gregg (R)

NEW JERSEY
1. James J. Florio (D)
2. William J. Hughes (D)
3. James J. Howard (D)
4. Christopher H. Smith (R)
5. Marge Roukema (R)
6. Bernard J. Dwyer (D)
7. Matthew J. Rinaldo (R)
8. Robert A. Roe (D)
9. Robert Torricelli (D)
10. Peter W. Rodino Jr. (D)
11. Dean A. Gallo (R)*
12. Jim Courter (R)
13. H. James Saxton (R)*
14. Frank J. Guarini (D)

NEW MEXICO
1. Manuel Lujan Jr. (R)
2. Joe Skeen (R)
3. Bill Richardson (D)

NEW YORK
1. William Carney (R)
2. Thomas J. Downey (D)
3. Robert J. Mrazek (D)
4. Norman F. Lent (R)
5. Raymond J. McGrath (R)
6. Joseph P. Addabbo (D)
7. Gary Ackerman (D)
8. James H. Scheuer (D)
9. T. J. Manton (D)*
10. Charles E. Schumer (D)
11. Edolphus Towns (D)
12. Major R. Owens (D)
13. Stephen J. Solarz (D)
14. Guy V. Molinari (R)
15. S. William Green (R)
16. Charles B. Rangel (D)
17. Theodore S. Weiss (D)
18. Robert Garcia (D)
19. Mario Biaggi (D)
20. Joseph D. DioGuardi (R)*
21. Hamilton Fish Jr. (R)
22. Benjamin A. Gilman (R)
23. Samuel S. Stratton (D)
24. Gerald Solomon (R)
25. Sherwood Boehlert (R)
26. David O'B. Martin (R)
27. George Wortley (R)
28. Matthew F. McHugh (D)
29. Frank Horton (R)
30. Fred J. Eckert (R)*
31. Jack F. Kemp (R)
32. John J. LaFalce (D)
33. Henry J. Nowak (D)
34. Stanley N. Lundine (D)

NORTH CAROLINA
1. Walter B. Jones (D)
2. I. T. Valentine Jr. (D)
3. Charles Whitley (D)
4. W. W. Cobey Jr. (R)
5. Stephen L. Neal (D)
6. Howard Coble (R)
7. Charles G. Rose III (D)
8. W. G. (Bill) Hefner (D)
9. J. Alex McMillan (R)*
10. James T. Broyhill (R)
11. W. M. Hendon (R)*

NORTH DAKOTA
AL Byron L. Dorgan (D)

OHIO
1. Thomas A. Luken (D)
2. Bill Gradison (R)
3. Tony P. Hall (D)
4. Michael Oxley (R)
5. Delbert L. Latta (R)
6. Bob McEwen (R)
7. Michael DeWine (R)
8. Thomas N. Kindness (R)
9. Marcy Kaptur (D)
10. Clarence E. Miller (R)
11. Dennis E. Eckart (D)
12. John R. Kasich (R)
13. Donald J. Pease (D)
14. John F. Seiberling Jr. (D)
15. Chalmers P. Wylie (R)
16. Ralph S. Regula (R)
17. J. A. Traficant Jr. (D)*
18. Douglas Applegate (D)
19. Edward F. Feighan (D)
20. Mary Rose Oakar (D)
21. Louis Stokes (D)

OKLAHOMA
1. James R. Jones (D)
2. Mike Synar (D)
3. Wes Watkins (D)
4. Dave McCurdy (D)
5. Mickey Edwards (R)
6. Glenn English (D)

OREGON
1. Les AuCoin (D)
2. Bob Smith (R)
3. Ron Wyden (D)
4. James Weaver (D)
5. Denny Smith (R)

PENNSYLVANIA
1. Thomas M. Foglietta (D)
2. William H. Gray III (D)
3. Robert A. Borski (D)
4. Joseph P. Kolter (D)
5. Richard T. Schulze (R)
6. Gus Yatron (D)
7. Robert W. Edgar (D)
8. Peter H. Kostmayer (D)
9. E. G. (Bud) Shuster (R)
10. Joseph M. McDade (R)
11. Paul E. Kanjorski (D)*
12. John P. Murtha (D)
13. Lawrence Coughlin (R)
14. William J. Coyne (D)
15. Donald L. Ritter (R)
16. Robert S. Walker (R)
17. George W. Gekas (R)
18. Doug Walgren (D)
19. William F. Goodling (R)
20. Joseph M. Gaydos (D)
21. Thomas J. Ridge (R)
22. Austin J. Murphy (D)
23. William Clinger Jr. (R)

RHODE ISLAND
1. F. J. St. Germain (D)
2. Claudine Schneider (R)

SOUTH CAROLINA
1. Thomas F. Hartnett (R)
2. Floyd D. Spence (R)
3. Butler D. Derrick Jr. (D)
4. Carroll Campbell Jr. (R)
5. John Spratt (D)
6. Robin Tallon (D)

SOUTH DAKOTA
AL Tom Daschle (D)

TENNESSEE
1. James H. Quillen (R)
2. John J. Duncan (R)
3. Marilyn Lloyd (D)
4. Jim Cooper (D)
5. Bill Boner (D)
6. Bart Gordon (D)*
7. Don Sundquist (R)
8. Ed Jones (D)
9. Harold E. Ford (D)

TEXAS
1. Jim Chapman (D)
2. Charles Wilson (D)
3. Steve Bartlett (R)
4. Ralph M. Hall (D)
5. John Bryant (D)
6. Joe Barton (R)*
7. Bill Archer (R)
8. Jack Fields (R)
9. Jack Brooks (D)
10. J. J. Pickle (D)
11. Marvin Leath (D)
12. James C. Wright Jr. (D)
13. Beau Boulter (R)
14. Mac Sweeny (R)*
15. Eligio de la Garza (D)
16. Ronald Coleman (D)
17. Charles Stenholm (D)
18. Mickey Leland (D)
19. Larry Combest (R)*
20. Henry B. Gonzalez (D)
21. Tom Loeffler (R)
22. Tom DeLay (R)*
23. A. G. Bustamente (D)*
24. Martin Frost (D)
25. Mike Andrews (D)
26. Richard Armey (R)*
27. Solomon P. Ortiz (D)

UTAH
1. James V. Hansen (R)
2. David S. Monson (R)
3. Howard C. Nielson (R)

VERMONT
AL James M. Jeffords (R)

VIRGINIA
1. Herbert Bateman (R)*
2. G. William Whitehurst (R)
3. Thomas J. Bliley Jr. (R)
4. Norman Sisisky (D)
5. W. C. (Dan) Daniel (D)
6. James Olin (D)
7. D. F. Slaughter (R)*
8. Stanford E. Parris (R)
9. Frederick Boucher (D)
10. Frank R. Wolf (R)

WASHINGTON
1. John Miller (R)*
2. Al Swift (D)
3. Don Bonker (D)
4. Sid Morrison (R)
5. Thomas S. Foley (D)
6. Norman D. Dicks (D)
7. Mike Lowry (D)
8. Rodney Chandler (R)

WEST VIRGINIA
1. Alan B. Mollohan (D)
2. Harley O. Staggers Jr. (D)
3. Robert E. Wise (D)
4. Nick J. Rahall II (D)

WISCONSIN
1. Les Aspin (D)
2. Robert W. Kastenmeier (D)
3. Steve Gunderson (R)
4. G. D. Kleczka (D)
5. James Moody (D)
6. Thomas E. Petri (R)
7. David R. Obey (D)
8. Tobias A. Roth (R)
9. F. J. Sensenbrenner Jr. (R)

WYOMING
AL Richard Cheney (R)

COMMITTEES OF CONGRESS

The fate of legislation introduced in Congress depends to a large extent on what happens to it in House or Senate committees. Before a bill goes back to either house for a vote, the committee can revise it, change it beyond recognition, or simply bottle it up.

Committee chairmen, who achieve their positions largely through seniority, have considerable influence in determining which measures will or will not become law. They also can use pressure to get their favorite bills passed.

A committee's importance is determined by the kind of legislation it handles. The House Ways and Means Committee and the Senate Finance Committee are responsible for all tax, tariff, and Social Security legislation.

The House Rules Committee decides which bills will go to the floor of the House. The House and Senate Appropriations Committees consider appropriation measures, and the House and Senate Budget Committees establish the federal budget for each fiscal year.

Listed below are the permanent committees, their chairmen, and members by party (D-Democrat; R-Republican) during the 99th Congress.

COMMITTEE, CHAIRMAN, AND MEMBERSHIP SENATE	JURISDICTION	COMMITTEE, CHAIRMAN, AND MEMBERSHIP HOUSE
Agriculture, Nutrition, and Forestry Jesse A. Helms (R-N.C.) R-9, D-8	All matters dealing with agriculture, including farm credit and security, crop insurance, soil conservation, and rural electrification; **and (Senate only) forestry; human nutrition, including school nutrition programs**	**Agriculture** E. de la Garza (D-Tex.) D-26, R-17
Appropriations Mark O. Hatfield (R-Oreg.) R-15, D-14	All matters pertaining to the appropriations of government revenues	**Appropriations** Jamie L. Whitten (D-Miss.) D-35, R-22
Armed Services Barry Goldwater (R-Ariz.) R-10, D-9	Military affairs, including aeronautical and space activities concerned with weapons systems; **and (Senate only) Panama Canal and Canal Zone**	**Armed Services** Les Aspin (D-Wis.) D-27, R-19
Banking, Housing, and Urban Affairs Jake Garn (R-Utah) R-8, D-7	All financial matters other than taxes and appropriations, particularly those concerned with banking and currency, including public and private housing matters; urban affairs	**Banking, Finance, and Urban Affairs** Fernand J. St. Germain (D-R.I.) D-28, R-19
Budget Pete V. Domenici (R-N.M.) R-12, D-10	Reviews presidential budget proposals; considers advice of congressional budget office and other committees regarding federal expenditures	**Budget** William H. Gray 3d (D-Pa.) D-20, R-13
Commerce, Science, and Commerce John Danforth (R-Mo.) R-9, D-8	Interstate transportation and communications, inland waterways, civil aeronautics; **(Senate only)** science; weather; **(House only) foreign commerce, railroad labor, securities and exchanges, interstate oil compacts, natural gas and public health, regulation of interstate transmission of power (except between government projects)** Merchant Marine, Coast Guard, Coast and Geodetic Survey, fisheries and wildlife Maintenance and operation of Panama Canal and administration of Canal Zone	**Energy and Commerce** John D. Dingell (D-Mich.) D-25, R-17 **Merchant Marine and Fisheries** Walter B. Jones (D-N.C.) D-25, R-17
Energy and Natural Resources James A. McClure (R-Idaho) R-10, D-8	Energy regulation, conservation; research and development; solar energy; oil and gas; hydroelectric power; coal; naval petroleum; mining; public parks; recreation areas; public lands	**Interior and Insular Affairs** Morris K. Udall (D-Ariz.) D-22, R-15
Environment and Public Works Robert T. Stafford (R-Vt.) R-8, D-7	Environment in general; environmental research; fisheries and wildlife; ocean dumping; solid waste disposal; pollution; public works; dams and bridges; federal buildings	(In House split among several committees)

SENATE COMMITTEE, CHAIRMAN, AND MEMBERSHIP	JURISDICTION	HOUSE COMMITTEE, CHAIRMAN, AND MEMBERSHIP
Ethics Warren Rudman (R-N.H.) R-3, D-3	Standards and conduct of members and employees; recommends remedies for unethical conduct	**Standards of Official Conduct** Julian C. Dixon (D-Calif.) D-6, R-6
Finance Robert W. Packwood (R-Ore.) R-11, D-9	All matters pertaining to taxes, tariffs, import quotas, social security, and social welfare	**Ways and Means** Dan Rostenkowski (D-Ill.) D-23, R-13
Foreign Relations Richard G. Lugar (R-Ind.) R-9, D-8	Relations of the United States with foreign nations and international organizations, including the Red Cross, diplomatic service, United Nations, foreign loans, and (Senate only) treaties	**Foreign Affairs** Dante B. Fascell (D-Fla.) D-25, R-17
Governmental Affairs William V. Roth Jr. (R-Del.) R-7, D-6	Reorganization of the Executive Branch, and governmental relationships between federal, state, and local governments; civil service; and (Senate only) between U.S. and international organizations; District of Columbia	**Government Operations** Jack Brooks (D-Texas) D-23, R-16
Judiciary Strom Thurmond (R-S.C.) R-10, D-8	Federal courts and judges, civil rights, civil liberties, constitutional amendments, interstate compacts, immigration and naturalization, apportionment of representatives, meetings of Congress, and members' attendance; (Senate only) claims against the United States; (House only) presidential succession and impeachment	**Judiciary** Peter W. Rodino Jr. (D-N.J.) D-21, R-14
Labor and Human Resources Orrin G. Hatch (R-Utah) R-9, D-7	Health, education, public welfare, labor, arts, child development, migratory labor, handicapped, health research, aging	**Education and Labor** Augustus F. Hawkins (D-Calif.) D-19, R-13
Rules and Administration Charles McC. Mathias Jr. (R-Md.) R-8, D-7	General administration of the Senate and management of the Library of Congress and the Smithsonian Institution; (House only) rules and orders of business of the House	**Rules** Claude D. Pepper (D-Fla.) D-9, R-4
Indian Affairs Mark Andrews (R-N.D.) R-5, D-4	All legislation on Indian affairs; Indian problems in education, health, and other areas; Indian claims against the United States	(Indian affairs under House Interior and Insular Affairs Committee)
Small Business Lowell P. Weicker Jr. (R-Conn.) R-10, D-9	Study and investigation of the problems of small business and of legislation affecting small business	**Small Business** Parren J. Mitchell (D-Md.) D-25, R-17
Veterans Affairs Frank H. Murkowski (R-Alaska) R-7, D-5	Veterans pensions, armed forces life insurance, rehabilitation, education, medical care and treatment of veterans, veterans hospitals	**Veterans Affairs** G.V. Montgomery (D-Miss.) D-20, R-14
(see Senate Governmental Affairs Committee)	Operation of all municipal affairs of the District of Columbia except for the appropriation of money for its operation	**District of Columbia** Ronald V. Dellums (D-Calif.) D-7, R-4
—	House administration; printing and correction of the Congressional Record; federal elections; and management of the Library of Congress; supervision of the Smithsonian Institution	**House Administration** Frank Annunzio (D-Ill.) D-12, R-7
—	All matters pertaining to the postal and civil services; the census; the National Archives	**Post Office and Civil Service** William D. Ford (D-Mich.) D-15, R-9
—	Public buildings and roads; flood control, improvement of rivers and harbors; stream pollution; waterpower; and transportation	**Public Works and Transportation** James J. Howard (D-N.J.) D-30, R-18
—	Nonmilitary scientific research, development, and administration of all matters in energy and space and aeronautical activities; National Science Foundation; National Weather Service	**Science and Technology** Don Fuqua (D-Fla.) D-24, R-17
Aging John Heinz (R-Pa.) R-10, D-9	Investigation of problems of aged.; (Senate only) cannot send legislation to floor	**Select Aging** Claude Pepper (D-Fla.) D-38, R-22
Select Intelligence Barry Goldwater (R-Ariz.) R-8, D-7	Legislation, and budgets of CIA, FBI, and other intelligence agencies of the federal government	**Select Intelligence** Edward P. Boland (D-Mass.) D-9, R-5

POLITICAL MAKEUP OF CONGRESS: 1789–1986

CONGRESS	YEARS	PRESIDENT AND PARTY	HOUSE OF REPRESENTATIVES			SENATE		
			Majority Party	Minority Party	Other	Majority Party	Minority Party	Other
1st	1789–1791	G. Washington Fed	Fed-38	AF-26	—	Fed-17	AF-9	—
2d	1791–1793	G. Washington Fed	Fed-37	DR-33	—	Fed-16	DR-13	—
3d	1793–1795	G. Washington Fed	DR-57	Fed-48	—	Fed-17	DR-13	—
4th	1795–1797	G. Washington Fed	Fed-54	DR-52	—	Fed-19	DR-13	—
5th	1797–1799	J. Adams Fed	Fed-58	DR-48	—	Fed-20	DR-12	—
6th	1799–1801	J. Adams Fed	Fed-64	DR-42	—	Fed-19	DR-13	—
7th	1801–1803	T. Jefferson DR	DR-69	Fed-36	—	DR-18	Fed-13	—
8th	1803–1805	T. Jefferson DR	DR-102	Fed-39	—	DR-25	Fed-9	—
9th	1805–1807	T. Jefferson DR	DR-116	Fed-25	—	DR-27	Fed-7	—
10th	1807–1809	T. Jefferson DR	DR-118	Fed-24	—	DR-28	Fed-6	—
11th	1809–1811	J. Madison DR	DR-94	Fed-48	—	DR-28	Fed-6	—
12th	1811–1813	J. Madison DR	DR-108	Fed-36	—	DR-30	Fed-6	—
13th	1813–1815	J. Madison DR	DR-112	Fed-68	—	DR-27	Fed-9	—
14th	1815–1817	J. Madison DR	DR-117	Fed-65	—	DR-25	Fed-11	—
15th	1817–1819	J. Monroe DR	DR-141	Fed-42	—	DR-34	Fed-10	—
16th	1819–1821	J. Monroe DR	DR-156	Fed-27	—	DR-35	Fed-7	—
17th	1821–1823	J. Monroe DR	DR-158	Fed-25	—	DR-44	Fed-4	—
18th	1823–1825	J. Monroe DR	DR-187	Fed-26	—	DR-44	Fed-4	—
19th	1825–1827	J. Q. Adams Co	Co-105	Ja-97	—	Co-26	Ja-20	—
20th	1827–1829	J. Q. Adams Co	Ja-119	Co-94	—	Ja-28	Co-20	—
21st	1829–1831	A. Jackson D	D-139	NR-74	—	D-26	NR-22	—
22d	1831–1833	A. Jackson D	D-141	NR-58	14	D-25	NR-21	2
23d	1833–1835	A. Jackson D	D-147	AM-53	60	D-20	NR-20	8
24th	1835–1837	A. Jackson D	D-145	W-98	—	D-27	W-25	—
25th	1837–1839	M. Van Buren D	D-108	W-107	24	D-30	W-18	4
26th	1839–1841	M. Van Buren D	D-124	W-118	—	D-28	W-22	—
27th	1841–1843	W. H. Harrison W J. Tyler W	W-133	D-102	6	W-28	D-22	2
28th	1843–1845	J. Tyler W	D-142	W-79	1	W-28	D-25	1
29th	1845–1847	J. K. Polk D	D-143	W-77	6	D-31	W-25	—
30th	1847–1849	J. K. Polk D	W-115	D-108	4	D-36	W-21	1
31st	1849–1851	Z. Taylor W M. Filmore W	D-112	W-109	9	D-35	W-25	2
32d	1851–1853	M. Fillmore W	D-140	W-88	5	D-35	W-24	3
33d	1853–1855	F. Pierce D	D-159	W-71	4	D-38	W-22	2
34th	1855–1857	F. Pierce D	R-108	D-83	43	D-42	R-15	5
35th	1857–1859	J. Buchanan D	D-131	R-92	14	D-39	R-20	5
36th	1859–1861	J. Buchanan D	R-113	D-101	23	D-38	R-26	2
37th	1861–1863	A. Lincoln R	R-106	D-42	28	R-31	D-11	7
38th	1863–1865	A. Lincoln R	R-103	D-80	—	R-39	D-12	—
39th	1865–1867	A. Lincoln U A. Johnson U	U-145	D-46	—	U-42	D-10	—
40th	1867–1869	A. Johnson U	R-143	D-49	1	R-42	D-11	—
41st	1869–1871	U. S. Grant R	R-170	D-73	—	R-61	D-11	2
42d	1871–1873	U. S. Grant R	R-139	D-104	—	R-57	D-17	—
43d	1873–1875	U. S. Grant R	R-203	D-88	2	R-54	D-19	1
44th	1875–1877	U. S. Grant R	D-181	R-107	5	R-46	D-29	1
45th	1877–1879	R. B. Hayes R	D-156	R-137	—	R-39	D-36	1
46th	1879–1881	R. B. Hayes R	D-150	R-128	15	D-43	R-33	—
47th	1881–1883	J. A. Garfield R C. A. Arthur R	R-152	D-130	11	R-37	D-37	2
48th	1883–1885	C. A. Arthur R	D-200	R-119	6	R-40	D-36	—
49th	1885–1887	G. Cleveland D	D-182	R-140	3	R-41	D-34	1
50th	1887–1889	G. Cleveland D	D-170	R-151	4	R-39	D-37	—
51st	1889–1891	B. Harrison R	R-173	D-156	1	R-47	D-37	—
52d	1891–1893	B. Harrison R	D-231	R-88	14	R-47	D-39	2

CONGRESS	YEARS	PRESIDENT AND PARTY	HOUSE OF REPRESENTATIVES			SENATE		
			Majority Party	Minority Party	Other	Majority Party	Minority Party	Other
53d......	1893–1895	G. Cleveland D	D-220	R-126	10	D-44	R-38	6
54th......	1895–1897	G. Cleveland D	R-246	D-104	7	R-44	D-39	5
55th......	1897–1899	W. McKinley....... R	R-206	D-134	17	R-46	D-34	10
56th......	1899–1901	W. McKinley....... R	R-185	D-163	9	R-53	D-26	11
57th......	1901–1903	W. McKinley....... R / T. Roosevelt........ R	R-198	D-153	6	R-56	D-29	5
58th......	1903–1905	T. Roosevelt........ R	R-207	D-178	1	R-58	D-32	—
59th......	1905–1907	T. Roosevelt....... R	R-250	D-136	—	R-58	D-32	—
60th......	1907–1909	T. Roosevelt....... R	R-222	D-164	—	R-61	D-29	2
61st......	1909–1911	W. H. Taft......... R	R-219	D-172	—	R-59	D-32	1
62d......	1911–1913	W. H. Taft......... R	D-228	R-162	1	R-49	D-42	1
63d......	1913–1915	W. Wilson D	D-290	R-127	18	D-51	R-44	1
64th......	1915–1917	W. Wilson D	D-231	R-193	11	D-56	R-39	1
65th......	1917–1919	W. Wilson D	D-210 [1]	R-216	9	D-53	R-42	1
66th......	1919–1921	W. Wilson D	R-237	D-191	7	R-48	D-47	1
67th......	1921–1923	W. G. Harding R	R-300	D-132	3	R-59	D-37	—
68th......	1923–1925	W. G. Harding R / C. Coolidge R	R-225	D-207	3	R-51	D-43	2
69th......	1925–1927	C. Coolidge R	R-247	D-183	5	R-54	D-40	2
70th......	1927–1929	C. Coolidge R	R-237	D-195	3	R-48	D-47	1
71st......	1929–1931	H. Hoover......... R	R-267	D-163	5	R-56	D-39	1
72d......	1931–1933	H. Hoover......... R	D-216 [2]	R-218	1	R-48	D-47	1
73d......	1933–1935	F. D. Roosevelt D	D-313	R-117	5	D-59	R-36	1
74th......	1935–1937	F. D. Roosevelt D	D-322	R-103	10	D-69	R-25	2
75th......	1937–1939	F. D. Roosevelt D	D-333	R-89	13	D-75	R-17	4
76th......	1939–1941	F. D. Roosevelt D	D-262	R-169	4	D-69	R-23	4
77th......	1941–1943	F. D. Roosevelt D	D-267	R-162	6	D-66	R-28	2
78th......	1943–1945	F. D. Roosevelt D	D-222	R-209	4	D-57	R-38	1
79th......	1945–1947	F. D. Roosevelt D / Harry S. Truman... D	D-243	R-190	2	D-57	R-38	1
80th......	1947–1949	Harry S. Truman... D	R-246	D-188	1	R-51	D-45	—
81st......	1949–1951	Harry S. Truman... D	D-263	R-171	1	D-54	R-42	—
82d......	1951–1953	Harry S. Truman... D	D-234	R-199	2	D-48	R-47	1
83d......	1953–1955	D. D. Eisenhower .. R	R-221	D-213	1	R-48	D-46	2
84th......	1955–1957	D. D. Eisenhower .. R	D-232	R-203	—	D-48	R-47	1
85th......	1957–1959	D. D. Eisenhower .. R	D-234	R-201	—	D-49	R-47	—
86th......	1959–1961	D. D. Eisenhower .. R	D-283	R-153	—	D-64	R-34	—
87th......	1961–1963	John F. Kennedy ... D	D-262	R-175	—	D-64	R-36	—
88th......	1963–1965	John F. Kennedy ... D / Lyndon B. Johnson . D	D-258	R-176	1	D-67	R-33	—
89th......	1965–1967	Lyndon B. Johnson. D	D-295	R-140	—	D-68	R-32	—
90th......	1967–1969	Lyndon B. Johnson. D	D-248	R-187	—	D-64	R-36	—
91st......	1969–1971	Richard Nixon R	D-243	R-192	—	D-58	R-42	—
92d......	1971–1973	Richard Nixon R	D-255	R-180	—	D-54	R-44	2
93d......	1973–1975	Richard Nixon R / Gerald Ford R	D-242	R-192	1	D-56	R-42	2
94th......	1975–1977	Gerald Ford R	D-291	R-144	—	D-60	R-37	2
95th......	1977–1979	Jimmy Carter D	D-292	R-143	—	D-61	R-38	1
96th......	1979–1981	Jimmy Carter D	D-277	R-158	—	D-58	R-41	1
97th......	1981–1983	Ronald Reagan ... R	D-242	R-192	1	R-53	D-46	1
98th......	1983–1985	Ronald Reagan ... R	D-267	R-167	1	R-55	D-45	—
99th......	1985–1987	Ronald Reagan R	D-253	R-182	—	R-53	D-47	—

Political party abbreviations: AF—Antifederalist; AM—Anti-Masonic; Co—Coalition; D—Democrat; DR—Democratic-Republican; Fed—Federalist; Ja—Jacksonian; NR—National Republican; R—Republican; U—Unionist; W—Whig.
[1] Democrats organized House with help of other parties. [2] Democrats organized House because of Republican deaths.

SPEAKERS OF THE HOUSE OF REPRESENTATIVES: 1789–1986

The speaker of the U.S. House of Representatives is the third most important position in the federal government after President and Vice President. He presides over the House and is the recognized leader of the majority party in the House of Representatives.

There are several ways in which the speaker can become President without being elected to that office, including:

If both the office of President and Vice President should become vacant as a result of the deaths or resignations of the incumbents.

If the office of Vice President is vacant and the incumbent President should die or resign before a new Vice President is sworn in.

If the President-elect and the Vice President-elect are found not to be qualified to take office on Inauguration Day.

Rep. Thomas P. O'Neill Jr. (D-Mass.) was chosen speaker without opposition in December 1976 after the retirement of Rep. Carl Albert (D-Okla.), who had held the position since 1971. O'Neill has served in Congress since 1953 from the same district once represented by President John Kennedy.

Only one speaker ever has become President: James K. Polk of Tennessee, who served in the position in 1835–39.

CONGRESS	SPEAKER	PARTY
1st (1789–91)	Frederick A. C. Muhlenberg	Federalist
2d (1791–93)	Jonathan Trumbull	Federalist
3d (1793–95)	Frederick A. C. Muhlenberg	Federalist
4th (1795–97)	Jonathan Dayton	Federalist
5th (1797–99)	Jonathan Dayton	Federalist
	George Dent	Dem.-Rep.
6th (1799–1801)	Theodore Sedgwick	Federalist
7th (1801–03)	Nathaniel Macon	Dem.-Rep.
8th (1803–05)	Nathaniel Macon	Dem.-Rep.
9th (1805–07)	Nathaniel Macon	Dem.-Rep.
10th (1807–09)	Joseph B. Varnum	Dem.-Rep.
11th (1809–11)	Joseph B. Varnum	Dem.-Rep.
12th (1811–13)	Henry Clay	Dem.-Rep.
13th (1813–15)	Henry Clay	Dem.-Rep.
	Langdon Cheves	Dem.-Rep.
14th (1815–17)	Henry Clay	Dem.-Rep.
15th (1817–19)	Henry Clay	Dem.-Rep.
16th (1819–21)	Henry Clay	Dem.-Rep.
	John W. Taylor	Dem.-Rep.
17th (1821–23)	Philip P. Barbour	Dem.-Rep.
18th (1823–25)	Henry Clay	Dem.-Rep.
19th (1825–27)	John W. Taylor	Dem.-Rep.
20th (1827–29)	Andrew Stevenson	Democrat
21st (1829–31)	Andrew Stevenson	Democrat
22d (1831–33)	Andrew Stevenson	Democrat
23d (1833–35)	Andrew Stevenson	Democrat
	John Bell	Whig
24th (1835–37)	James K. Polk	Democrat
25th (1837–39)	James K. Polk	Democrat
26th (1839–41)	Robert M. T. Hunter	Democrat
27th (1841–43)	John White	Whig
28th (1843–45)	John W. Jones	Democrat
29th (1845–47)	John W. Davis	Democrat
30th (1847–49)	Robert C. Winthrop	Whig
31st (1849–51)	Howell Cobb	Democrat
32d (1851–53)	Linn Boyd	Democrat
33d (1853–55)	Linn Boyd	Democrat
34th (1855–57)	Nathaniel P. Banks	American
35th (1857–59)	James L. Orr	Democrat
36th (1859–61)	William Pennington	Whig
37th (1861–63)	Galusha A. Grow	Republican
38th (1863–65)	Schuyler Colfax	Republican
39th (1865–67)	Schuyler Colfax	Republican
40th (1867–69)	Schuyler Colfax	Republican
	Theodore M. Pomeroy	Republican
41st (1869–71)	James G. Blaine	Republican
42d (1871–73)	James G. Blaine	Republican
43d (1873–75)	James G. Blaine	Republican
44th (1875–77)	Michael C. Kerr	Democrat
	Samuel S. Cox	Democrat
	Milton Sayler	Democrat
	Samuel J. Randall	Democrat
45th (1877–79)	Samuel J. Randall	Democrat
46th (1879–81)	Samuel J. Randall	Democrat
47th (1881–83)	J. Warren Keifer	Republican

CONGRESS	SPEAKER	PARTY
48th (1883–85)	John G. Carlisle	Democrat
49th (1885–87)	John G. Carlisle	Democrat
50th (1887–89)	John G. Carlisle	Democrat
51st (1889–91)	Thomas B. Reed	Republican
52d (1891–93)	Charles F. Crisp	Democrat
53d (1893–95)	Charles F. Crisp	Democrat
54th (1895–97)	Thomas B. Reed	Republican
55th (1897–99)	Thomas B. Reed	Republican
56th (1899–1901)	David B. Henderson	Republican
57th (1901–03)	David B. Henderson	Republican
58th (1903–05)	Joseph G. Cannon	Republican
59th (1905–07)	Joseph G. Cannon	Republican
60th (1907–09)	Joseph G. Cannon	Republican
61st (1909–11)	Joseph G. Cannon	Republican
62d (1911–13)	Champ Clark	Democrat
63d (1913–15)	Champ Clark	Democrat
64th (1915–17)	Champ Clark	Democrat
65th (1917–19)	Champ Clark	Democrat
66th (1919–21)	Frederick H. Gillett	Republican
67th (1921–23)	Frederick H. Gillett	Republican
68th (1923–25)	Frederick H. Gillett	Republican
69th (1925–27)	Nicholas Longworth	Republican
70th (1927–29)	Nicholas Longworth	Republican
71st (1929–31)	Nicholas Longworth	Republican
72d (1931–33)	John N. Garner	Democrat
73d (1933–35)	Henry T. Rainey	Democrat
74th (1935–37)	Joseph W. Byrns	Democrat
	William B. Bankhead	Democrat
75th (1937–39)	William B. Bankhead	Democrat
76th (1939–41)	William B. Bankhead	Democrat
	Sam Rayburn	Democrat
77th (1941–43)	Sam Rayburn	Democrat
78th (1943–45)	Sam Rayburn	Democrat
79th (1945–47)	Sam Rayburn	Democrat
80th (1947–49)	Joseph W. Martin Jr.	Republican
81st (1949–51)	Sam Rayburn	Democrat
82d (1951–53)	Sam Rayburn	Democrat
83d (1953–55)	Joseph W. Martin Jr.	Republican
84th (1955–57)	Sam Rayburn	Democrat
85th (1957–59)	Sam Rayburn	Democrat
86th (1959–61)	Sam Rayburn	Democrat
87th (1961–63)	Sam Rayburn	Democrat
88th (1963–65)	John W. McCormack	Democrat
89th (1965–67)	John W. McCormack	Democrat
90th (1967–69)	John W. McCormack	Democrat
91st (1969–71)	John W. McCormack	Democrat
92d (1971–73)	Carl Albert	Democrat
93d (1973–75)	Carl Albert	Democrat
94th (1975–77)	Carl Albert	Democrat
95th (1977–79)	Thomas P. O'Neill Jr.	Democrat
96th (1979–81)	Thomas P. O'Neill Jr.	Democrat
97th (1981–83)	Thomas P. O'Neill Jr.	Democrat
98th (1983–85)	Thomas P. O'Neill Jr.	Democrat
99th (1985–87)	Thomas P. O'Neill Jr.	Democrat

Crime

HIGHLIGHTS: 1985

ESPIONAGE FLOURISHES

More than a dozen Americans, including a U.S. marine, an FBI agent, a CIA employee, former U.S. Navy officers, and various businessmen were jailed in 1985 in what FBI officials said was the largest outbreak of spy cases in the nation's history. They said the increase in espionage was being caused by stepped up efforts by the Soviet Union and its allies to steal or buy American technology and military secrets.

Defense Secretary Caspar W. Weinberger called on June 12 for a change in the code of military justice to permit the execution in peacetime of military personnel found guilty of espionage. Two weeks later the U.S. House of Representatives approved such a change.

The biggest spy ring was uncovered with the arrest on May 20 in Washington, D.C., of retired Navy Chief Warrant Officer John Anthony Walker Jr., 47. FBI officials said Walker had conducted a spy ring for the Soviet Union for as long as 20 years, passing along secret information gathered from members of his family and friends. Two days later, his son, seaman Michael Lance Walker, 22, was arrested aboard the aircraft carrier USS Nimitz. A week later the senior Walker's brother, retired Navy Lt. Cmdr. Arthur J. Walker, 50, was arrested. On June 3, Jerry A. Whitworth, 45, a retired Navy chief petty officer who had been a shipmate of John Walker, was taken into custody in California.

Arthur Walker was brought to trial in Norfolk, Va., in August and was found guilty on seven counts of espionage, conspiracy, and unauthorized possession of classified information. He faces up to three life sentences and fines of $40,000. Trials for the others were scheduled later in year.

The FBI broke the case after receiving a telephone call in November 1984 from Barbara Walker, 47, who was divorced from John Walker in 1976. She said her former husband had been a spy for the Soviets since the 1960s, while he still was on active duty with the Navy. She estimated that her former husband had received about $1 million for passing secrets to the Soviets. She told news reporters that after turning her husband in to the FBI, she had phoned Arthur Walker to tell him what she had done. She said she did so thinking he would tip off his

brother to flee to the Soviet Union.

In July two Soviet emigres, Nikolai Ogorodnikov, 52, and his wife Svetlana, 35, were sentenced to long prison terms after they pleaded guilty to espionage. They changed their pleas from not guilty to guilty after they had been on trial for two months in Los Angeles. The government had charged Svetlana lured FBI agent Richard W. Miller, 48, into a love affair as part of a plot to get him to sell U.S. secrets to the Soviet Union. Miller, who is married and has eight children, was the first FBI agent ever charged with betraying his country. At a separate trial for Miller, which began in August, he claimed he merely was trying to infiltrate the Soviet spy network to win promotion from his superiors.

Navy Petty Officer Third Class Michael Tobias, 21, was found guilty by a federal jury in San Diego, Calif., on Aug. 14, of stealing secret government codes and trying to blackmail the Secret Service into buying them back for $100,000. His roommate, Francis Xavier Pizzo, pleaded guilty a week earlier to helping in the scheme.

In May Thomas Patrick Cavanagh, 40, an aerospace engineer, was sentenced to life imprisonment after he pleaded guilty to espionage in a Los Angeles federal court. He admitted he had tried to sell blueprints of the supersecret Stealth bomber to Soviet agents for $55,000. Cavanagh was arrested after the FBI intercepted phone calls he made to Soviet officials. Then FBI agents posing as Soviet spies contacted him and paid him for the secret papers.

On July 11 the FBI arrested CIA employee Sharon M. Scranage, 29, charging her with passing secret information to her Ghanaian lover, who also was jailed for espionage. Scranage pleaded guilty to two counts of revealing the names of U.S. secret agents, but declared she was not guilty of 16 of the charges.

In February an East German physicist, Alred Zehe, 45, was sentenced to prison after he pleaded guilty in a federal court in Boston to having paid $21,800 to an unnamed U.S. Navy civilian employee for U.S. military secrets. Zehe had been arrested in November 1983 while attending a scientific meeting in Boston. Unknown to Zehe the Navy employee was cooperating with the FBI.

HIGHLIGHTS: 1985 *(continued)*

The FBI revealed in January 1985 that in a previously undisclosed spy case a U.S. marine private, Robert E. Cordrey, 23, had been sentenced to 12 years in prison by a secret court-martial in August 1984. Cordrey was found guilty of making contact with Soviet and East European spies while trying to sell military secrets. The FBI said the case had been kept secret because it was part of an "extremely sensitive investigation."

THE "NIGHT STALKER"

The most intensive police hunt in California in the 1980s led to the arrest on Aug. 31 of a man accused as the "night stalker" who had terrorized the state with 14 murders and 20 rapes and assaults during the first seven months of 1985.

The criminal was called the "night stalker" because he followed a pattern of entering homes at night through unlocked doors or windows and then killing his victims for no apparent reason. Some householders were shot, some had their throats slashed, women were raped and then beaten to death, and others were strangled. The homes struck were mostly in Los Angeles suburbs but also including some in the San Francisco area. For months terrorized homeowners lived in fear as to where the killer might strike next.

The suspect, Richard Ramirez, 27, was captured and beaten by residents of East Los Angeles when they saw him trying to steal a car. Police said Ramirez' fingerprints matched those found in a stolen car known to have been used by the "night stalker."

A former roommate of Ramirez told newspapers that Ramirez had been obsessed with a song "Night Prowler" by the rock band AC-DC that said in part:

"Was that a noise out your window
Or a shadow on your blind?
And you lie there naked
Like a body in a tomb;
Suspended animation
As I slip into your room."

NAZI DEATH DOCTOR'S BODY FOUND

After a search of more than 40 years, Nazi war criminal hunters tracked down the elusive Dr. Josef Mengele, who had been known as the "Angel of Death" at the Auschwitz concentration camp because of his sadistic experiments on inmates. He was blamed for some 400,000 deaths.

In June a body was exhumed at Embu, Brazil, and an international team of forensic scientists announced on June 21 that the skeleton had been positively identified as that of Mengele, who had drowned while swimming at the age of 67 in February 1979. He had been living in Brazil under the assumed name of Wolfgang Gerhard.

The United States, Israel, and West Germany had cooperated in the search for Mengele, who had believed to be hiding in South America. Rewards of more than $2.5 million had been announced for his capture.

After Mengele's body was found, his family in Germany admitted they had always known where he was hiding and had regularly sent him money for his support.

U.S. CRIME RATE

Source: Federal Bureau of Investigation

YEAR	REPORTED CRIMES		VIOLENT CRIMES [2]		PROPERTY CRIMES [3]		MURDERS		ROBBERIES	
	Total	Rate [1]	Total	Rate [1]	Total	Rate [1]	Total	Rate [1]	Total	Rate [1]
1960	3,384,200	1,887.2	288,460	160.9	3,095,700	1,726.3	9,110	5.1	107,840	60.1
1963	4,109,500	2,180.3	316,970	168.2	3,792,500	2,012.1	8,640	4.6	116,470	61.8
1964	4,564,600	2,388.1	364,220	190.6	4,200,400	2,197.5	9,360	4.9	130,390	68.2
1965	4,739,400	2,449.0	387,390	200.2	4,352,000	2,248.8	9,960	5.1	138,690	71.7
1966	5,223,500	2,670.8	430,180	220.0	4,793,300	2,450.9	11,040	5.6	157,990	80.8
1967	5,903,400	2,989.7	499,930	253.2	5,403,500	2,736.5	12,240	6.2	202,910	102.8
1968	6,720,200	3,370.2	595,010	298.4	6,125,200	3,071.8	13,800	6.9	262,840	131.8
1969	7,410,900	3,680.0	661,870	328.7	6,749,000	3,351.3	14,760	7.3	298,850	148.4
1970	8,098,000	3,984.5	738,820	363.5	7,359,200	3,621.0	16,000	7.9	349,860	172.1
1971	8,588,200	4,164.7	816,500	396.0	7,771,700	3,768.8	17,780	8.6	387,700	188.0
1972	8,248,800	3,961.4	834,900	401.0	7,413,900	3,560.4	18,670	9.0	376,290	180.7
1973	8,718,100	4,154.4	875,910	417.4	7,842,200	3,737.0	19,640	9.4	384,220	183.1
1974	10,253,448	4,850.4	974,716	461.1	9,278,732	4,389.3	20,711	9.8	442,397	209.3
1975	11,256,566	5,281.7	1,026,284	481.5	10,230,282	4,800.2	20,505	9.6	464,973	218.2
1976	11,304,788	5,266.4	986,578	459.6	10,318,210	4,806.8	18,784	8.8	420,214	195.8
1977	10,935,777	5,055.1	1,009,499	466.6	9,926,278	4,588.4	19,121	8.8	404,847	187.1
1978	11,141,334	5,109.3	1,061,826	486.9	10,079,508	4,622.4	19,555	9.0	417,038	191.3
1979	12,152,730	5,521.5	1,178,539	535.5	10,974,191	4,986.0	21,456	9.7	466,881	212.1
1980	13,295,400	5,899.9	1,308,898	580.8	11,986,501	5,319.1	23,044	10.2	548,809	243.5
1981	13,290,256	5,799.9	1,321,906	576.9	11,968,350	5,223.0	22,516	9.8	574,134	250.6
1982	12,933,674	5,586.1	1,301,497	562.1	11,632,177	5,024.0	21,012	9.1	546,204	235.9
1983	12,108,630	5,175.0	1,258,087	537.7	10,850,543	4,637.4	19,308	8.3	506,567	216.5
1984	11,881,755	5,031.3	1,273,282	539.2	10,608,473	4,492.1	18,692	7.9	485,008	205.4

[1] Crimes per 100,000 population. [2] Violent crimes include murder, forcible rape, robbery, and aggravated assault.
[3] Property crimes include burglary, larceny, and auto theft.

STATE AND FEDERAL PRISONERS

Source: U.S. Department of Justice, Bureau of Justice Statistics

From 1980 to 1984 the number of prisoners held by federal and state authorities increased by 134,045—a rise of 40.6% in the 4-year period.

The prison rate, the number of prisoners per 100,000 population, rose from 179 to 188 between 1983 and 1984. The number of female prisoners increased by 8.9%, much higher than the rise in number of men prisoners.

REGION AND STATE	TOTAL			LONG TERM PRISONERS [1]			PRISON RATE [2]
	1984	1983	Percent change	1984	1983	Percent change	
United States, total	463,866	437,248	6.1	445,381	419,731	6.1	188
Federal prisons	34,263	31,926	7.3	27,602	26,331	4.8	12
State prisons	429,603	405,322	6.0	417,779	393,400	6.2	176
Male	443,013	418,104	6.0	425,986	402,120	5.9	369
Female	20,853	19,144	8.9	19,395	17,611	10.1	16
Northeast	70,537	64,671	9.1	67,835	61,977	9.5	136
Maine	1,025	1,082	−5.3	840	861	−2.4	72
New Hampshire	561	479	17.1	561	479	17.1	57
Vermont	515	497	3.6	392	378	3.7	74
Massachusetts	4,890	4,482	9.1	4,890	4,372	11.8	84
Rhode Island	1,220	1,157	5.4	888	878	1.1	92
Connecticut	5,718	5,474	4.5	3,748	3,577	4.8	119
New York	33,155	30,541	8.6	33,155	30,541	8.6	187
New Jersey	10,363	9,192	12.7	10,363	9,192	12.7	138
Pennsylvania	13,090	11,767	11.2	12,998	11,699	11.1	109
Midwest	85,859	81,917	4.8	85,429	81,365	5.0	144
Ohio	18,694	18,007	3.8	18,694	18,007	3.8	174
Indiana	9,328	9,296	0.3	9,063	8,973	1.0	165
Illinois	17,187	15,595	10.2	17,187	15,522	10.7	149
Michigan	14,604	14,382	1.5	14,604	14,382	1.5	161
Wisconsin...........	5,023	4,865	3.2	5,023	4,865	3.2	105
Minnesota	2,167	2,113	2.6	2,167	2,113	2.6	52
Iowa	2,836	2,814	0.8	2,836	2,814	0.8	97
Missouri	8,808	8,275	6.4	8,808	8,275	6.4	175
North Dakota........	434	410	5.9	374	350	6.9	54
South Dakota	917	826	11.0	900	808	11.4	127
Nebraska	1,623	1,629	−0.4	1,535	1,551	−1.0	95
Kansas	4,238	3,705	14.4	4,238	3,705	14.4	173
South	193,286	185,677	4.1	187,925	179,963	4.4	231
Delaware	2,200	2,198	0.1	1,615	1,579	2.3	263
Maryland	13,124	12,617	4.0	12,442	11,979	3.9	285
District of Columbia..	4,834	4,344	11.3	4,031	3,465	16.3	649
Virginia	10,667	10,093	5.7	10,493	9,855	6.5	185
West Virginia	1,599	1,624	−1.5	1,599	1,624	−1.5	82
North Carolina	16,371	15,395	6.3	15,219	14,257	6.7	246
South Carolina	10,035	9,576	4.8	9,434	9,076	3.9	284
Georgia.............	15,731	15,358	2.4	14,944	14,935	0.1	254
Florida	27,106	26,334	2.9	26,933	25,393	6.1	242
Kentucky	4,793	4,752	0.9	4,793	4,752	0.9	128
Tennessee	7,302	8,201	−11.0	7,302	8,201	−11.0	154
Alabama	10,482	9,856	6.4	10,246	9,641	6.3	256
Mississippi..........	6,115	5,586	9.5	5,974	5,481	9.0	229
Arkansas	4,454	4,244	4.9	4,427	4,226	4.8	188
Louisiana	13,919	12,812	8.6	13,919	12,812	8.6	310
Oklahoma	7,872	7,428	6.0	7,872	7,428	6.0	236
Texas	36,682	35,259	4.0	36,682	35,259	4.0	226
West	79,921	73,057	9.4	76,590	70,095	9.3	166
Montana	1,005	903	11.3	1,005	901	11.5	121
Idaho...............	1,282	1,192	7.6	1,282	1,192	7.6	127
Wyoming	740	721	2.6	740	721	2.6	143
Colorado	3,364	3,244	3.7	3,347	3,244	3.2	104
New Mexico	2,129	1,977	7.7	1,908	1,708	11.7	133
Arizona.............	7,845	7,251	8.2	7,638	7,115	7.4	247
Utah	1,419	1,274	11.4	1,407	1,261	11.6	84
Nevada	3,510	3,188	10.1	3,510	3,188	10.1	380
Washington	6,821	6,659	2.4	6,821	6,659	2.4	156
Oregon	4,563	3,941	15.8	4,563	3,941	15.8	170
California	43,314	39,373	10.0	41,780	38,025	9.9	162
Alaska..............	1,995	1,634	22.1	1,290	1,075	20.0	252
Hawaii..............	1,934	1,700	13.8	1,299	1,065	22.0	124

[1] Prisoners sentenced to 1 year or more. [2] Number of prisoners per 100,000 population.

CRIME IN THE STATES

Source: Federal Bureau of Investigation, 1984 data

An estimated 11,881,755 criminal offenses were reported to law-enforcement agencies in 1984, down 1.9% from 1983. Property crimes decreased 2.2%, while the number of violent crimes increased by 1.2%.

Florida had the highest crime rate among the states, with 6,821.2 per 100,000 population.

Nevada was second with 6,561.0 and Michigan third with 6,556.0. California continues to lead the nation with the largest number of crimes—1,657,320.

West Virginia had the lowest crime rate—2,335.9. North Dakota reported the fewest number of crimes—17,722.

STATE	REPORTED CRIMES Total	Rate[1]	VIOLENT CRIMES [2] Total	Rate[1]	PROPERTY CRIMES [3] Total	Rate[1]	MURDERS Total	Rate[1]	ROBBERIES Total	Rate[1]
U.S. TOTAL ..	11,881,755	5,031.3	1,273,282	539.2	10,608,473	4,492.1	18,692	7.9	485,008	205.4
Alabama	155,691	3,902.0	17,204	431.2	138,487	3,470.9	374	9.4	3,833	96.1
Alaska	30,576	6,115.2	3,108	621.6	27,468	5,493.6	58	11.6	547	109.4
Arizona	198,426	6,499.4	15,756	516.1	182,670	5,983.3	238	7.8	4,003	131.1
Arkansas	79,103	3,367.5	7,549	321.4	71,554	3,046.1	176	7.5	1,587	67.6
California ...	1,657,320	6,468.3	195,589	763.4	1,461,731	5,705.0	2,717	10.6	83,924	327.5
Colorado.....	205,652	6,471.1	14,548	457.8	191,104	6,013.3	184	5.8	1,238	39.0
Connecticut ..	145,995	4,628.9	12,422	393.8	133,573	4,235.0	122	3.9	6,009	190.5
Delaware	30,692	5,006.9	2,671	435.7	30,692	5,006.9	25	4.1	711	116.0
Florida.......	748,699	6,821.2	95,270	868.0	748,699	6,821.2	1,264	11.5	30,311	276.2
Georgia	262,556	4,498.1	27,935	478.6	262,556	4,498.1	546	9.4	8,414	144.1
Hawaii	56,982	5,484.3	2,409	231.9	54,573	5,252.5	34	3.3	1,204	115.9
Idaho........	36,753	3,671.6	2,355	235.3	34,398	3,436.4	34	3.4	244	24.4
Illinois	610,565	5,304.2	83,441	724.9	527,124	4,579.3	1,033	9.0	34,965	303.8
Indiana	216,039	3,929.4	16,781	305.2	199,258	3,624.2	303	5.5	5,435	98.9
Iowa.........	110,566	3,799.5	5,781	198.7	104,785	3,600.9	59	2.0	1,114	38.3
Kansas	105,793	4,339.3	8,147	334.2	97,646	4,005.2	89	3.7	1,745	71.6
Kentucky	110,145	2,958.5	10,342	277.8	99,803	2,680.7	244	6.6	2,631	70.7
Louisiana	228,029	5,110.5	30,251	678.0	197,778	4,432.5	575	12.9	8,501	190.5
Maine	40,776	3,527.3	1,832	158.5	38,944	3,368.9	20	1.7	305	26.4
Maryland	226,780	5,214.5	34,455	792.3	192,325	4,422.3	354	8.1	13,097	301.1
Massachusetts	266,037	4,588.4	30,362	523.7	235,675	4,064.8	211	3.6	10,122	174.6
Michigan.....	594,958	6,556.0	68,979	760.1	525,979	5,795.9	879	9.7	27,832	306.7
Minnesota ...	159,884	3,841.5	8,802	211.5	151,082	3,630.0	74	1.8	2,960	71.1
Mississippi ...	79,495	3,059.9	7,326	282.0	72,169	2,777.9	252	9.7	1,572	60.5
Missouri	215,194	4,297.0	23,071	460.7	192,123	3,836.3	358	7.1	7,053	140.8
Montana	38,338	4,652.7	1,958	237.6	36,380	4,415.0	36	4.4	226	27.4
Nebraska	56,153	3,496.5	3,627	225.8	52,526	3,270.6	54	3.4	381	23.7
Nevada	59,771	6,561.0	5,726	628.5	54,045	5,932.5	98	10.8	2,542	279.0
New Hampshire	30,655	3,137.7	1,308	133.9	29,347	3,003.8	10	1.0	227	23.2
New Jersey...	364,890	4,855.5	39,659	527.7	325,231	4,327.8	402	5.3	18,218	242.4
New Mexico ..	88,906	6,243.4	9,798	688.1	79,108	5,555.3	130	9.1	1,856	130.3
New York	989,126	5,577.3	162,157	914.3	826,969	4,662.9	1,786	10.1	89,900	506.9
North Carolina	249,322	4,044.2	24,855	403.6	224,437	3,640.5	539	8.7	4,612	74.8
North Dakota .	17,722	2,583.4	368	53.6	17,354	2,529.7	8	1.2	53	7.7
Ohio	459,441	4,273.1	41,430	385.3	418,011	3,887.8	551	5.1	15,656	145.6
Oklahoma....	161,355	4,892.5	13,438	407.5	147,917	4,485.1	258	7.8	3,668	111.2
Oregon	166,956	6,243.7	13,533	506.1	153,423	5,737.6	128	4.8	4,508	168.6
Pennsylvania .	364,114	3,059.5	38,154	320.6	325,960	2,738.9	538	4.5	17,656	148.4
Rhode Island .	45,926	4,744.0	3,220	334.7	42,706	4,439.3	33	3.4	1,091	113.4
South Carolina	153,877	4,662.9	20,607	624.5	133,270	4,038.5	305	9.2	3,408	103.3
South Dakota .	18,444	2,612.5	1,041	147.5	17,403	2,465.0	13	1.8	105	14.9
Tennessee ...	183,472	3,889.6	21,010	445.4	162,462	3,444.2	394	8.4	7,867	166.8
Texas	964,128	6,029.9	80,737	505.0	883,391	5,525.0	2,093	13.1	28,540	178.5
Utah	78,738	4,766.2	4,035	244.2	74,703	4,522.0	47	2.8	958	58.0
Vermont	21,030	3,967.9	769	145.1	20,261	3,822.8	12	2.3	122	23.0
Virginia	213,241	3,783.6	16,660	295.6	196,581	3,488.0	434	7.7	5,765	102.3
Washington ..	265,963	6,101.7	17,676	406.4	247,687	5,695.3	202	4.6	5,247	120.6
West Virginia .	45,596	2,335.9	3,283	168.2	42,313	2,167.7	86	4.4	744	38.1
Wisconsin....	198,851	4,172.3	9,367	196.5	189,484	3,975.7	117	2.5	3,167	66.4
Wyoming	18,819	3,682.8	1,237	242.1	17,582	3,440.7	17	3.3	118	23.1

[1] Crimes per 100,000 population. [2] Violent crimes include murder, forcible rape, robbery, and aggravated assault.
[3] Property crimes include burglary, larceny of $50 or more, and auto theft.

CRIME IN U.S. METROPOLITAN AREAS

Source: Federal Bureau of Investigation

Atlantic City, N.J., once again was the metropolitan area with the highest crime rate in the United States in 1984, counting 9,997.9 crimes per 100,000 population. Miami, Fla., was in second place with a rate of 9,893.3. Lubbock, Tex., was third with a rate of 9,121.3; West Palm Beach, Fla., was fourth with a rate of 8,253.1; and Dallas, Tex., was fifth with a rate of 8,247.0.

Other metropolitan areas with a crime rate of more than 8,000 per 100,000 population were Fort Worth, Tex., with 8,169.3, Flint, Mich., 8,102.6, Albuquerque, N.M., 8,059.9, and Portland, Ore., 8,038.6.

Others with high crime rates were Detroit, Mich., 7,997.2; Stockton, Calif., 7,801.7; New York City, 7,742.7; Tucson, Ariz., 7,662.6; Las Vegas, Nev., 7,571.2; San Antonio, Tex., 7,567.5; Denver, Colo., 7,545.9; Oakland, Calif., 7,499.0; Shreveport, La., 7,306.5; Los Angeles, Calif, 7,291.0.

	TOTAL CRIMES		VIOLENT CRIMES[2]		PROPERTY CRIMES[3]		MURDERS		ROBBERIES	
	Number	Rate[1]	Total	Rate[1]	Total	Rate[1]	Total	Rate[1]	Total	Rate[1]
Akron, Ohio	30,062	4,598.9	2,269	347.1	27,793	4,251.8	23	3.5	649	99.3
Albany-Schenectady, N.Y.	29,065	3,450.4	2,301	273.2	26,764	3,177.3	12	1.4	671	79.7
Albuquerque, N. Mex.	36,506	8,059.9	4,118	909.2	32,388	7,150.8	35	7.7	1,299	286.8
Allentown, Pa.-N.J.	19,034	2,956.2	1,151	178.8	17,883	2,777.4	12	1.9	390	60.6
Amarillo, Tex.	10,665	5,639.2	770	407.1	9,895	5,232.0	22	11.6	169	89.4
Anaheim-Santa Ana, Calif.	120,708	5,761.4	8,939	426.7	111,769	5,334.8	102	4.9	3,652	174.3
Appleton-Oshkosh, Wis.	10,818	3,654.2	235	79.4	10,583	3,574.8	6	2.0	28	9.5
Asheville, N.C.	6,442	3,844.0	482	287.6	5,960	3,556.3	12	7.2	110	65.6
Atlanta, Ga.	136,744	5,891.5	16,027	690.5	120,717	5,201.0	215	9.3	5,723	246.6
Atlantic City, N.J.	28,425	9,997.9	1,902	669.0	26,523	9,328.9	26	9.1	790	277.9
Austin, Tex.	42,390	6,943.4	2,463	403.4	39,927	6,540.0	71	11.6	865	141.7
Bakersfield, Calif.	31,242	6,923.4	3,088	684.3	28,154	6,239.1	38	8.4	904	200.3
Baltimore, Md.	137,052	6,066.2	24,593	1,088.5	112,459	4,977.7	268	11.9	9,731	430.7
Baton Rouge, La.	36,226	6,823.6	5,008	943.3	31,218	5,880.3	54	10.2	845	159.2
Battle Creek, Mich.	8,226	5,919.1	721	518.8	7,505	5,400.3	8	5.8	171	123.0
Beaumont-Port Arthur, Tex.	18,875	4,609.9	1,849	451.6	17,026	4,158.3	43	10.5	646	157.8
Bergen-Passaic, NJ	52,974	4,040.3	4,146	316.2	48,828	3,724.1	62	4.7	2,132	162.6
Binghamton, N.Y.	7,336	2,751.6	231	86.6	7,105	2,665.0	5	1.9	53	19.9
Birmingham, Ala.	45,708	5,072.4	5,006	555.5	40,702	4,516.8	91	10.1	1,591	176.6
Boise, Idaho	8,184	4,397.3	593	318.6	7,591	4,078.7	5	2.7	73	39.2
Boston, Mass.	148,727	5,247.5	17,757	626.5	130,970	4,621.0	116	4.1	7,534	265.8
Bradenton, Fla.	11,517	6,805.0	1,463	864.4	10,054	5,940.5	16	9.5	305	180.2
Bridgeport-Milford, Conn.	24,778	5,452.4	2,670	587.5	22,108	4,864.8	28	6.2	1,411	310.5
Brockton, Mass.	8,383	4,267.9	903	459.7	7,480	3,808.2	6	3.1	238	121.2
Brownsville, Tex.	13,934	5,898.0	1,213	513.4	12,721	5,384.6	13	5.5	212	89.7
Buffalo, NY	44,990	4,459.7	5,131	508.6	39,859	3,951.1	41	4.1	1,626	161.2
Canton, Ohio	15,913	3,947.2	1,166	289.2	14,747	3,658.0	14	3.5	396	98.2
Cedar Rapids, Iowa	8,834	5,226.4	322	190.5	8,512	5,035.9	6	3.5	90	53.2
Charleston, S.C.	24,968	5,339.2	3,512	751.0	21,456	4,588.2	46	9.8	877	187.5
Charleston, W. Va.	10,509	3,925.1	665	248.4	9,844	3,676.7	7	2.6	252	94.1
Charlotte-Gastonia, N.C.	62,935	6,123.3	7,058	686.7	55,877	5,436.6	103	10.0	1,582	153.9
Chattanooga, Tenn.-Ga.	19,522	4,486.6	1,890	434.4	17,632	4,052.3	40	9.2	422	97.0
Chicago, Ill.	405,191	6,688.0	67,434	1,113.0	337,757	5,574.9	818	13.5	31,189	514.8
Cincinnati, Ohio-Ky.-Ind.	66,139	4,696.2	5,811	412.6	60,328	4,283.6	61	4.3	1,920	136.3
Cleveland, Ohio	86,197	4,605.8	9,650	515.6	76,547	4,090.2	192	10.3	4,823	257.7
Colorado Springs, Colo.	21,040	6,129.1	1,384	403.2	19,656	5,725.9	15	4.4	418	121.8
Columbia, S.C.	25,065	5,764.7	3,514	808.2	21,551	4,956.5	39	9.0	759	174.6
Columbus, Ga.-Ala.	12,025	4,797.6	1,192	475.6	10,833	4,322.0	34	13.6	393	156.8
Columbus, Ohio	71,160	5,637.4	6,130	485.6	65,030	5,151.8	76	6.0	2,755	218.3
Corpus Christi, Tex.	23,164	6,365.5	1,453	399.3	21,711	5,966.2	43	11.8	397	109.1
Dallas, Tex.	175,951	8,247.0	15,471	725.1	160,480	7,521.9	382	17.9	5,606	262.8
Danbury, Conn.	4,695	3,053.6	305	198.4	4,390	2,855.3	2	1.3	91	59.2
Dayton-Springfield, Ohio	47,087	5,036.6	4,824	516.0	42,263	4,520.6	43	4.6	2,156	230.6
Daytona Beach, Fla.	19,916	6,750.8	1,739	589.5	18,177	6,161.3	26	8.8	464	157.3
Denver, Colo.	118,942	7,545.9	8,913	565.5	110,029	6,980.4	120	7.6	2,755	174.8
Des Moines, Iowa	25,161	6,777.2	1,518	408.9	23,643	6,368.3	20	5.4	466	125.5
Detroit, Mich.	348,042	7,997.2	41,951	963.9	306,091	7,033.2	648	14.9	23,373	537.1
El Paso, Tex.	31,954	6,045.8	3,890	736.0	28,064	5,309.8	27	5.1	1,076	203.6
Erie, Pa.	8,510	3,022.8	702	249.4	7,808	2,773.5	6	2.1	235	83.5
Eugene-Springfield, Oreg.	16,257	5,963.9	790	289.8	15,467	5,674.1	11	4.0	228	83.6
Evansville, Ind.-Ky.	11,576	4,125.9	1,001	356.8	10,575	3,769.1	21	7.5	174	62.0
Fall River, Mass.-R.I.	7,597	4,772.7	776	487.5	6,821	4,285.2	6	3.8	204	128.2
Fayetteville, N.C.	15,171	5,917.6	1,569	612.0	13,602	5,305.6	26	10.1	360	140.4
Flint, Mich.	35,487	8,102.6	4,775	1,090.3	30,712	7,012.3	58	13.2	1,137	259.6
Ft. Collins-Loveland, Col.	8,618	5,254.5	619	377.4	7,999	4,877.1	5	3.0	41	25.0
Ft. Lauderdale-Hollywood, Fla.	76,685	6,826.4	7,834	697.4	68,851	6,129.1	117	10.4	3,258	290.0

[1] Crimes per 100,000 population. [2] Violent crimes includes murder, forcible rape, robbery, and aggravated assault. [3] Property crimes include burglary, larceny of $50 or more, and auto theft.

CRIME IN U.S. METROPOLITAN AREAS (continued)

	TOTAL CRIMES		VIOLENT CRIMES ²		PROPERTY CRIMES ³		MURDERS		ROBBERIES	
	Number	Rate¹	Total	Rate¹	Total	Rate¹	Total	Rate¹	Total	Rate¹
Fort Wayne, Ind.	15,704	4,477.3	851	242.6	14,853	4,234.7	8	2.3	307	87.5
Fort Worth, Tex.	95,042	8,169.3	7,819	672.1	87,223	7,497.2	172	14.8	2,713	233.2
Fresno, Calif.	42,796	7,682.0	3,674	659.5	39,122	7,022.5	71	12.7	1,436	257.8
Gainesville, Fla.	12,889	6,743.2	1,517	793.7	11,372	5,949.5	16	8.4	246	128.7
Galveston-Texas City, Tex.	12,790	5,889.7	1,008	464.2	11,782	5,425.6	23	10.6	269	123.9
Gary-Hammond, Ind.	32,483	5,085.9	3,186	498.8	29,297	4,587.1	107	16.8	1,236	193.5
Grand Rapids, Mich.	30,183	4,922.0	2,751	448.6	27,432	4,473.4	30	4.9	656	107.0
Green Bay, Wis.	7,838	4,350.9	300	166.5	7,538	4,184.4	3	1.7	44	24.4
Greensboro-Winston-Salem-High Point, N.C.	35,721	4,009.2	4,062	455.9	31,659	3,553.3	59	6.6	677	76.0
Greenville-Spartanburg, S.C.	29,863	4,995.8	3,350	560.4	26,513	4,435.4	45	7.5	542	90.7
Hagerstown, Md.	2,799	2,458.8	276	242.5	2,523	2,216.4	5	4.4	64	56.2
Hamilton-Middletown, Ohio	12,994	4,958.6	1,000	381.6	11,994	4,577.0	6	2.3	231	88.2
Harrisburg-Lebanon-Carlisle, Pa.	18,025	3,187.5	1,466	259.2	16,559	2,928.2	19	3.4	543	96.0
Hartford, Conn.	38,520	5,265.5	3,622	495.1	34,898	4,770.4	29	4.0	1,871	255.8
Honolulu, Hawaii	44,560	5,496.0	1,950	240.5	42,610	5,255.5	25	3.1	1,117	137.8
Houston, Texas	218,810	6,814.0	20,139	627.2	198,671	6,186.9	609	19.0	10,799	336.3
Huntington-Ashland W.Va.-Ky.-O.	11,672	3,483.4	1,268	378.4	10,404	3,105.0	12	3.6	216	64.5
Huntsville, Ala.	12,265	6,017.9	802	393.5	11,463	5,624.4	17	8.3	259	127.1
Indianapolis, Ind.	57,908	4,888.1	6,152	519.3	51,756	4,368.8	68	5.7	2,417	204.0
Jackson, Miss.	18,732	4,976.6	1,929	512.5	16,803	4,464.2	44	11.7	558	148.2
Jacksonville, Fla.	53,425	6,749.8	7,389	933.5	46,036	5,816.2	117	14.8	2,369	299.3
Jersey City, N.J.	33,247	5,865.9	4,602	812.0	28,645	5,054.0	52	9.2	2,294	404.7
Johnson City, Tenn.	11,866	2,657.0	731	163.7	11,135	2,493.3	18	4.0	123	27.5
Johnstown, Pa.	4,139	1,584.8	347	132.9	3,792	1,451.9	4	1.5	59	22.6
Joliet, Ill.	16,116	4,256.3	1,414	373.4	14,702	3,882.9	13	3.4	283	74.7
Kankakee, Ill.	4,613	4,501.2	412	402.0	4,201	4,099.2	12	11.7	119	116.1
Kansas City, Mo.-Kans. ...	92,034	6,260.9	11,268	766.5	80,766	5,494.4	140	9.5	3,332	226.7
Killeen-Temple, Tex.	9,055	3,988.8	542	238.8	8,513	3,750.0	18	7.9	155	68.3
Knoxville, Tenn.	19,005	3,233.5	1,427	242.8	17,578	2,990.7	30	5.1	408	69.4
Lake County, Ill.	19,331	4,194.7	1,448	314.2	17,883	3,880.5	11	2.4	392	85.1
Lakeland-Winter Haven, Fla.	23,920	6,687.7	2,631	735.6	21,289	5,952.2	35	9.8	554	154.9
Lancaster, Pa.	9,343	2,508.6	559	150.1	8,784	2,358.5	6	1.6	179	48.1
Lansing-E. Lansing, Mich. ..	20,949	5,069.8	1,661	402.0	19,288	4,667.8	30	7.3	282	68.2
Las Vegas, Nev.	40,151	7,571.2	4,009	756.0	36,142	6,815.2	74	14.0	2,020	380.9
Lexington-Fayette, Ky.	15,767	4,845.9	1,268	389.7	14,499	4,456.2	16	4.9	337	103.6
Lima, Ohio	7,374	4,831.3	559	366.2	6,815	4,465.1	7	4.6	121	79.3
Lincoln, Nebr.	11,127	5,541.9	552	274.9	10,575	5,267.0	5	2.5	84	41.8
Little Rock, Ark.	28,152	5,732.7	3,405	693.4	24,747	5,039.3	60	12.2	964	196.3
Los Angeles-Long Beach...	582,407	7,291.0	94,754	1,186.2	487,653	6,104.8	1,301	16.3	47,252	591.5
Louisville, Ky.-Ind.	42,109	4,358.4	3,524	364.7	38,585	3,993.7	63	6.5	1,571	162.6
Lowell, Mass.-N.H.	9,038	3,631.8	1,038	417.1	8,000	3,214.7	7	2.8	166	66.7
Lubbock, Tex.	20,443	9,121.3	1,805	805.4	18,638	8,315.9	29	12.9	354	157.9
Madison, Wis.	18,518	5,670.3	669	204.9	17,849	5,465.4	6	1.8	199	60.9
Manchester, N.H.	6,721	5,060.9	429	323.0	6,292	4,737.9	2	1.5	91	68.5
McAllen-Edinburg, Tex.	15,893	4,898.7	965	294.4	14,928	4,601.2	17	5.2	108	33.3
Melbourne-Titusville, Fla. .	18,403	5,797.9	1,703	536.5	16,700	5,261.4	14	4.4	349	110.0
Memphis, Tenn.-Ark.-Miss.	61,585	6,575.9	9,745	1,040.6	51,840	5,535.4	127	13.6	4,967	530.4
Miami-Hialeah, Fla.	177,778	9,893.3	29,056	1,617.0	148,722	8,276.4	425	23.7	12,519	696.7
Milwaukee, Wis.	74,925	5,350.2	4,360	311.3	70,565	5,038.9	49	3.5	2,121	151.5
Minneapolis-St. Paul, Minn.	108,108	-4,907.1	7,415	336.6	100,693	4,570.5	50	2.3	2,765	125.5
Mobile, Ala.	26,195	5,658.5	3,599	777.4	22,596	4,881.1	61	13.2	922	199.2
Montgomery, Ala.	11,938	4,209.8	729	257.1	11,209	3,952.7	34	12.0	201	70.9
Muskegon, Mich.	10,161	6,563.4	1,409	910.1	8,752	5,653.3	5	3.2	178	115.0
Nashville, Tenn.	41,328	4,714.8	4,064	463.6	37,264	4,251.1	95	10.8	1,594	181.8
New Haven-Meriden, Conn.	28,142	5,253.8	2,626	490.2	25,516	4,763.5	21	3.9	1,412	263.6
New London-Norwich, Conn.	9,126	3,401.9	538	200.6	8,588	3,201.4	11	4.1	165	61.5
New Orleans, La.	88,824	6,696.6	13,180	993.7	75,644	5,702.9	298	22.5	6,042	455.5
New York, N.Y.	648,891	7,742.7	136,698	1,631.1	512,193	6,111.6	1,492	17.8	81,605	973.7
Newark, N.J.	102,091	5,380.1	16,592	874.4	85,499	4,505.7	132	7.0	8,496	447.7
Niagara Falls, N.Y.	9,908	4,408.3	814	362.2	9,094	4,046.1	4	1.8	278	123.7
Norfolk-Va. Bch-N. News, Va.	65,222	5,277.7	5,481	443.5	59,741	4,834.2	117	9.5	2,009	162.6
Oakland, Calif.	141,687	7,499.0	15,858	839.3	125,829	6,659.7	231	12.2	6,522	345.2
Oklahoma City, Okla.	65,014	6,865.6	5,888	621.8	59,126	6,243.8	90	9.5	1,968	207.8
Omaha, Nebr.-Iowa	29,372	4,892.7	2,776	462.4	26,596	4,430.3	33	5.5	591	98.4
Orlando, Fla.	52,577	6,588.9	6,470	810.8	46,107	5,778.1	48	6.0	1,741	218.2
Oxnard-Ventura, Calif.	24,023	4,136.1	1,827	314.6	22,196	3,821.6	29	5.0	604	104.0
Parkersburg-Marietta, W.Va.-O.	4,618	2,931.6	198	125.7	4,420	2,805.9	3	1.9	57	36.2

¹ Crimes per 100,000 population. ² Violent crimes includes murder, forcible rape, robbery, and aggravated assault.
³ Property crimes include burglary, larceny of $50 or more, and auto theft.

	TOTAL CRIMES		VIOLENT CRIMES [2]		PROPERTY CRIMES [3]		MURDERS		ROBBERIES	
	Number	Rate[1]	Total	Rate[1]	Total	Rate[1]	Total	Rate[1]	Total	Rate[1]
Pensacola, Fla.	17,989	5,570.9	2,632	815.1	15,357	4,755.8	19	5.9	460	142.5
Peoria, Ill.	14,772	4,043.1	1,542	422.1	13,230	3,621.1	8	2.2	268	73.4
Philadelphia, Pa.-N.J.	198,191	4,162.8	26,612	559.0	171,579	3,603.9	368	7.7	12,937	271.7
Phoenix, Ariz.	119,331	7,022.8	9,350	550.3	109,981	6,472.6	139	8.2	2,687	158.1
Pittsburgh, Pa.	71,414	3,243.8	7,409	336.5	64,005	2,907.3	88	4.0	4,186	190.1
Portland, Maine	12,183	5,704.3	667	312.3	11,516	5,392.0	2	0.9	137	64.1
Portland, Oreg.	90,967	8,038.6	9,672	854.7	81,295	7,183.9	62	5.5	3,746	331.0
Poughkeepsie, N.Y.	7,266	2,922.0	752	304.4	6,514	2,619.6	5	2.0	203	81.6
Providence, R.I.	33,784	5,312.1	2,530	397.8	31,254	4,914.3	25	3.9	914	143.7
Provo-Orem, Utah	9,154	3,737.2	216	88.2	8,938	3,649.1	7	2.9	23	9.4
Pueblo, Colo.	8,251	6,333.6	891	683.9	7,360	5,649.6	7	5.4	137	105.2
Racine, Wis.	10,608	6,105.4	980	564.0	9,628	5,541.3	2	1.2	311	179.0
Raleigh-Durham, N.C.	31,573	5,321.2	2,273	383.1	29,300	4,938.1	41	6.9	647	109.0
Reading, Pa.	9,113	2,891.8	664	210.7	8,449	2,681.1	6	1.9	250	79.3
Reno, Nev.	14,142	6,543.2	1,177	544.6	12,965	5,998.6	11	5.1	427	197.6
Richmond-Petersburg, Va.	41,407	5,175.5	4,062	507.7	37,345	4,667.7	118	14.7	1,730	216.2
Riverside, Calif.	115,616	6,615.5	12,309	704.3	103,307	5,911.2	197	11.3	4,061	232.4
Roanoke, Va.	11,187	4,910.8	566	248.5	10,621	4,662.3	18	7.9	178	78.1
Rochester, N.Y.	46,412	4,688.9	3,749	378.8	42,663	4,310.2	54	5.5	1,214	122.6
Rockford, Ill.	17,420	6,207.6	1,319	470.0	16,101	5,737.6	13	4.6	444	158.2
Sacramento, Calif.	87,567	7,222.0	7,137	588.6	80,430	6,633.4	104	8.6	3,031	250.0
Saginaw-Bay City, Mich. ...	21,671	5,242.1	2,471	597.7	19,200	4,644.4	20	4.8	482	116.6
St. Cloud, Minn.	4,738	2,806.6	168	99.5	4,570	2,707.1	3	1.8	35	20.7
St. Louis, Mo.-Ill.	96,158	5,180.4	11,245	605.8	84,913	4,574.6	171	9.2	3,919	211.1
Salem, Oreg.	15,340	6,029.2	821	322.7	14,519	5,706.5	8	3.1	229	90.0
Salem-Gloucester, Mass. ..	7,918	3,045.3	463	178.1	7,455	2,867.3	19	7.3	96	36.9
Salt Lake City-Ogden, Utah	58,150	5,675.2	3,214	313.7	54,936	5,361.5	28	2.7	886	86.5
San Antonio, Tex.	89,843	7,567.5	6,343	534.3	83,500	7,033.2	186	15.7	2,836	238.9
San Diego, Calif.	114,177	5,594.1	10,719	525.2	103,458	5,068.9	162	7.9	4,114	201.6
San Francisco, Calif.	97,586	6,231.0	12,651	807.8	84,935	5,423.3	105	6.7	6,231	397.9
San Jose, Calif.	71,442	5,165.9	5,502	397.8	65,940	4,768.1	75	5.4	1,772	128.1
Santa Rosa, Calif.	16,797	5,154.3	1,140	349.8	15,657	4,804.4	18	5.5	245	75.2
Sarasota, Fla.	13,198	5,802.8	1,171	514.9	12,027	5,287.9	16	7.0	242	106.4
Savannah, Ga.	16,523	6,968.0	1,418	598.0	15,105	6,370.0	45	19.0	653	275.4
Scranton-Wilkes Barre, Pa.	16,995	2,333.9	938	128.8	16,057	2,205.1	18	2.5	292	40.1
Seattle, Wash.	119,828	7,077.7	8,573	506.4	111,255	6,571.3	90	5.3	3,220	190.2
Shreveport, La.	25,798	7,306.5	2,507	710.0	23,291	6,596.4	44	12.5	522	147.8
Sioux City, Iowa-Nebr.	6,605	5,589.4	353	298.7	6,252	5,290.7	3	2.5	70	59.2
Sioux Falls, S.D.	4,179	3,659.2	192	168.1	3,987	3,491.1	3	2.6	25	21.9
South Bend, Ind.	14,388	5,986.0	1,018	423.5	13,370	5,562.5	13	5.4	361	150.2
Spokane, Wash.	20,505	5,781.8	1,189	335.3	19,316	5,446.6	13	3.7	294	82.9
Springfield, Ill.	10,835	5,742.8	910	482.3	9,925	5,260.5	7	3.7	204	108.1
Springfield, Mo.	10,702	5,023.2	461	216.4	10,451	4,806.8	13	6.1	138	64.8
Springfield, Mass.	22,964	4,383.0	3,681	702.6	19,283	3,680.4	17	3.2	604	115.3
Stamford, Conn.	9,290	4,607.8	458	227.2	8,832	4,380.7	9	4.5	247	122.5
Stockton, Calif.	30,156	7,801.7	2,167	560.6	27,989	7,241.1	50	12.9	883	228.4
Syracuse, N.Y.	25,595	3,959.8	1,393	215.5	24,202	3,744.3	16	2.5	635	98.2
Tacoma, Wash.	36,501	7,040.3	3,322	640.7	33,179	6,399.6	37	7.1	1,003	193.5
Tallahassee, Fla.	12,562	5,950.8	1,268	600.7	11,294	5,350.1	11	5.2	267	126.5
Tampa-St. Petersburg, Fla.	116,640	6,474.7	14,723	817.3	101,917	5,657.4	155	8.6	3,758	208.6
Terre Haute, Ind.	5,870	4,304.4	290	212.7	5,580	4,091.8	8	5.9	47	34.5
Texarkana, Tex.-Ark.	5,522	4,643.3	448	376.7	5,074	4,266.6	11	9.2	80	67.3
Toledo, Ohio	35,257	5,745.2	2,854	465.1	32,403	5,280.1	40	6.5	1,188	193.6
Topeka, Kans.	9,463	5,393.3	820	467.3	8,643	4,925.9	5	2.8	221	126.0
Trenton, N.J.	17,459	5,582.7	1,728	552.5	15,731	5,030.1	15	4.8	945	302.2
Tuscson, Ariz.	45,944	7,662.6	3,661	610.6	42,283	7,052.0	45	7.5	964	160.8
Tulsa, Okla.	41,922	5,824.7	3,625	503.7	38,297	5,321.0	55	7.6	1,027	142.7
Utica-Rome, N.Y.	7,765	2,413.8	393	122.2	7,372	2,291.6	10	3.1	117	36.4
Vancouver, Wa.	10,182	4,949.6	596	289.7	9,586	4,659.9	9	4.4	157	76.3
Waco, Tex.	11,870	6,490.8	897	490.5	10,973	6,000.3	15	8.2	264	144.4
Washington, D.C.-Md.-Va. .	174,000	5,131.1	22,375	659.8	151,625	4,471.3	285	8.4	10,797	318.4
West Palm Beach, Fla. ...	55,923	8,253.1	6,548	966.4	49,375	7,286.8	87	12.8	1,898	280.1
Wichita, Kans.	26,055	5,994.1	1,703	391.8	24,352	5,602.3	17	3.9	487	112.0
Williamsport, Pa.	3,366	2,864.9	154	131.1	3,212	2,733.8	3	2.6	26	22.1
Wilmington, Del.-N.J.-Md. .	26,760	4,951.9	2,330	431.2	24,430	4,520.8	16	3.0	689	127.5
Wilmington, N.C.	7,267	6,609.1	494	449.3	6,773	6,159.8	9	8.2	155	141.0
Worcester, Mass.	15,082	3,694.5	1,665	407.9	13,417	3,286.7	9	2.2	577	141.3
Yakima, Wash.	12,386	6,918.4	684	382.1	11,702	6,536.3	10	5.6	157	87.7
York, Pa.	10,453	2,695.8	428	110.4	10,025	2,585.4	12	3.1	180	46.4
Youngstown-Warren, Ohio .	19,076	3,647.3	1,998	382.0	17,078	3,265.3	28	5.4	641	122.6

[1] Crimes per 100,000 population. [2] Violent crimes includes murder, forcible rape, robbery, and aggravated assault.
[3] Property crimes include burglary, larceny of $50 or more, and auto theft.

HISTORIC ASSASSINATIONS

44 B.C. (March 15) Julius Caesar, Roman general and dictator, stabbed to death in Roman Senate by Brutus, Cimber, Cassius, Casca and others.

1792 (March 16) Gustavus III, king of Sweden, shot at masked ball by assassin hired by nobles.

1793 (July 13) Jean Marat, French Revolutionary leader, stabbed by Charlotte Corday.

1801 (March 24) Paul I, czar of Russia, slain by Russian nobles after he refused to abdicate.

1865 (April 14) Abraham Lincoln, 16th U.S. President, shot by John Wilkes Booth in Ford's Theater in Washington, D.C. Died next day.

1881 (March 13) Alexander II, czar of Russia, assassinated by Russian terrorist.

1881 (July 2) James A. Garfield, 20th U.S. President, shot by disappointed job seeker Charles J. Guiteau. Died Sept. 19, 1881.

1898 (Sept. 10) Elizabeth, empress of Austria, assassinated in Geneva by Italian anarchist.

1900 (July 29) Humbert I, king of Italy, killed by Gaetano Bresci in Monza, Italy.

1901 (Sept. 6) William McKinley, 25th U.S. President, shot by anarchist Leon Czolgosz in Buffalo, N.Y. Died eight days later.

1903 (June 11) Alexander I, king of Serbia, and his wife, assassinated in Belgrade.

1908 (Feb. 1) Carlos I, king of Portugal, and his son, the crown prince, shot in Lisbon.

1913 (Feb. 22) Francisco I. Madero, president of Mexico, shot in coup by Gen. Victoriano Huerta.

1913 (March 18) George I, king of Greece, assassinated during second Balkan War.

1914 (June 28) Francis Ferdinand, archduke of Austria-Hungary, and his wife, shot by Serbian nationalist in Sarajevo, starting World War I.

1916 (Dec. 30) Grigori Rasputin, Russian monk, poisoned, stabbed, and shot by nobles who hated his influence on Czar Nicholas II.

1918 (July 16) Nicholas II, czar of Russia, his wife, and children, shot in Ekaterinburg.

1919 (April 10) Emiliano Zapata, Mexican revolutionary and reformer, killed in ambush by agents of President Venustiano Carranza.

1923 (July 20) Pancho Villa, Mexican revolutionary, assassinated at his estate in Durango.

1928 (July 17) Alvaro Obregón, president of Mexico, killed by Roman Catholic fanatic.

1934 (July 25) Engelbert Dollfuss, Austrian chancellor, assassinated by Nazis.

1934 (Oct. 9) Alexander I, king of Yugoslavia, killed by terrorist in Marseille, France.

1935 (Sept. 8) Huey P. Long, U.S. senator from Louisiana and candidate for Democratic presidential nomination, shot by Dr. Carl A. Weiss. Died two days later.

1940 (Aug. 20) Leon Trotsky, Russian revolutionary exile, stabbed by Stalinist agent Ramón Mercader in Mexico City. Died next day.

1948 (Jan. 30) Mohandas Gandhi, leader of India, shot by Nathuram Godse, Hindu who blamed Gandhi for partition of India.

1951 (July 20) Abdullah ibn Hussein, king of Jordan, assassinated in Jerusalem.

1955 (Jan. 2) José Antonio Remón, president of Panama, killed by machine-gunner.

1956 (Sept. 21) Anastasio Somoza, president of Nicaragua, shot. Died eight days later.

1957 (July 26) Carlos Castillo Armas, president of Guatemala, shot by a palace guard.

1958 (July 14) Faisal II, king of Iraq, killed in revolt by Abdul Karim Kassem.

1959 (Sept. 25) Solomon Bandaranaike, prime minister of Ceylon, shot by Buddhist monk.

1960 (Aug. 29) Hazza Majali, premier of Jordan,

killed by time bomb in his office.

1961 (May 30) Rafael L. Trujillo, dictator and president of the Dominican Republic, slain.

1963 (Jan. 13) Sylvanus Olympio, president of Togo, killed by former soldiers in Lomé.

1963 (Nov. 1-2) Ngo Dinh Diem, president of South Vietnam, and his brother slain.

1963 (Nov. 22) John F. Kennedy, U.S. President, shot by Lee Harvey Oswald in Dallas.

1966 (Sept. 6) Hendrik F. Verwoerd, prime minister of South Africa, stabbed in parliament in Cape Town by Dimitrio Stifanos.

1968 (April 4) Martin Luther King Jr., U.S. civil-rights leader, shot by ex-convict James Earl Ray in Memphis.

1968 (June 5) Robert F. Kennedy, U.S. senator from New York, shot by Sirhan Sirhan in Los Angeles while celebrating California presidential primary victory. Died next day.

1969 (Oct. 15) A. A. Shermarke, president of Somalia, assassinated in Las Anos, Somalia.

1973 (March 2) Cleo A. Noel Jr., U.S. ambassador, slain in Khartoum, Sudan, by Arab terrorists.

1974 (Aug. 19) Rodger P. Davies, U.S. ambassador, slain by Greek Cypriots in embassy at Nicosia, Cyprus.

1975 (Feb. 11) Madagascar head of state Col. Richard Ratsimandrava slain in ambush.

1975 (March 25) King Faisal of Saudi Arabia shot by nephew during palace reception.

1975 (April 13) President N'Garta Tombalbaye of Chad slain in military coup.

1975 (Aug. 15) Bangladesh President Mujibur Rahman killed by army officers in coup.

1976 (Feb. 13) Nigeria's head of state, Gen. Murtala Ramat Muhammed, killed in unsuccessful coup.

1976 (June 16) U.S. Ambassador to Lebanon Francis Meloy Jr. assassinated by terrorists.

1976 (July 21) British Ambassador to Ireland Christopher Biggs slain in Ireland.

1977 (Feb. 3) Ethiopia's chief of state Gen. Teferi Bante assassinated in coup, reportedly by Mengistu Haile Mariam, who became dictator.

1977 (March 18) Congo's President Marien Ngouabi assassinated in Brazzaville.

1977 (Oct. 11) North Yemen's President Ibrahim al-Hamdi and his brother assassinated in Sana.

1978 (April 27) Afghanistan's President Mohammad Daoud slain in communist coup in Kabul.

1978 (June 24) North Yemen's President Ahmed Hussein al-Ghashmi assassinated by South Yemen envoy.

1978 (Nov. 18) U.S. Rep. Leo J. Ryan and 4 other Americans assassinated in Guyana by California religious sect; then its 914 members kill selves.

1978 (Nov. 27) San Francisco's Mayor George Moscone assassinated by former official Dan White.

1979 (Feb. 14) Adolph Dubs, U.S. Ambassador to Afghanistan, killed in police shootout with terrorists.

1979 (Aug. 27) Britain's Earl Mountbatten of Burma assassinated by Irish terrorists.

1979 (Sept. 14) Afghanistan's President Noor Taraki slain by his prime minister, Hafizullah Amin.

1979 (Oct. 26) South Korean President Park Chung Hee assassinated at dinner by intelligence chief.

1981 (May 30) Bangladesh President Ziaur (Zia) Rahman slain in unsuccessful coup by army officers.

1981 (Aug. 30) Iran's President Mohammed Ali Rajai, Prime Minister Mohammed Jad Bahonar, and 3 others assassinated by bomb planted in office by opponents.

1981 (Oct. 6) Egyptian President Anwar al-Sadat assassinated at military parade by Muslim fanatics.

1982 (Sept. 14) Lebanon's President-elect Bashir Gemayel killed with 25 others in Beirut bomb blast.

1984 (Oct. 31) India's Prime Minister Indira Gandhi slain by two Sikh members of personal bodyguard.

Earth

HIGHLIGHTS: 1985

DEEPEST HOLE PLANNED

West Germany's government announced plans in 1985 to dig the world's deepest hole.

Heinz Riesenhuber, minister of research and technology said the project—to drill about nine miles below the surface—would cost about $138 million.

He said drilling would begin in 1988 and would take until about 1995 to complete.

When completed, the hole would be about 2 feet wide at the top and about 8 inches wide at the bottom.

Riesenhuber said the site of the hole would be either in the Black Forest or in Bavaria.

Over a 15-year period the Soviet Union has drilled what is currently the world's deepest hole—about 7.6 miles in depth—on the Kola Peninsula near Murmansk.

Drilling to such great depths requires a different technology than that used in ordinary oil well drilling in which the entire drilling pipe turns as the hole goes deeper. The Soviet scientists developed a drill in which only the bit at the end of the pipe turns.

The purpose of digging such deep holes has the practical benefit of enabling geologists to learn more about how mineral resources have been formed, thus helping them determine better ways to find locations for minerals and petroleum. On the more theoretical level, it aids scientists in determining how the continents were formed.

Although for many years American geologists have wanted to undertake such a deep hole project, they have been delayed by lack of funds. Test sites for deep holes have been planned for the southern Appalachian mountains and near Creede, Colo.

EARTHQUAKE FORECAST

In its first such forecast, the U.S. Geological Survey announced in April 1985 that an earthquake with a magnitude of 6 on the Richter scale would occur near the sparsely populated area of Parkfield, Calif., northwest of Los Angeles, probably early in 1988. The earthquake is expected to strike somewhere along a 16-mile portion of the San Andreas Fault.

The last time an earthquake of that intensity hit the Parkfield region was in 1966. Earlier large earthquakes in the area were recorded in 1857, 1881, 1901, 1922, and 1934.

Scientists said that although it is possible that the expected earthquake might extend southeast toward Los Angeles there was not sufficient data to make such a prediction. Earlier studies by the National Security Council and the Federal Emergency Management Agency have said that a major earthquake in the range of 8.3 on the Richter scale is likely to strike the Los Angeles region sometime before the year 2010. Property damage from such a quake is expected to be $69 billion with from 3,000 to 16,000 deaths, depending on the time of day the earthquake hits.

In hope that they can obtain early warning before a quake occurs, scientists have placed radio monitors at intervals along the San Andreas Fault to record even the smallest movement of the earth.

FACTS ABOUT THE EARTH

Age of Earth: 4.6 to 5 billion years.

Area of Earth: *Total area,* 196,940,000 square miles; *Land area,* 30%, 57,506,000 square miles; *Water area,* 70%, 139,434,000 square miles.

Atmosphere of Earth: Extends about 1,000 miles above surface; *Chemical composition,* nitrogen 78%, oxygen 21%, argon and other gases 1%.

Circumference of Earth: *Polar circumference* (distance around Earth at poles), 24,859.82 miles; *Equatorial circumference* (distance at equator), 24,901.55 mi.

Density of Earth: 5.52 (water has density of 1).

Diameter of Earth: *Polar diameter* (through Earth from pole to pole), 7,899.83 miles; *Equatorial diameter* (through Earth at equator), 7,926.41 miles.

Distance of Moon from Earth: *Closest distance,* 221,456 miles; *Farthest distance,* 252,711 miles; *Average distance,* 238,875 miles.

Distance of Sun from Earth: *Closest distance,* 91.4 million miles; *Farthest distance,* 94.5 million miles; *Average distance,* 92.9 million miles.

Escape Velocity from Earth: 7 miles per second.

Inclination of Earth on Axis: 23° 27′.

Interior of Earth: *Crust,* made up of igneous, sedimentary, and metamorphic rock, extends 20 miles deep under continents and about 5 miles deep under oceans; *Mantle,* layer of solid rock about 1,800 miles thick beneath Earth's crust, has temperatures of 1600° to 4400°F.; *Outer Core,* 1,400-mile thick layer of molten iron and nickel between mantle and inner core, has temperatures of 4000° to 9000°F.; *Inner Core,* ball of solid iron and nickel at Earth's center with diameter of about 1,600 miles, with temperature of about 9,000°F.

Period of Revolution of Earth around Sun: 1 year (or 365 days, 6 hours, 9 minutes, 9.54 seconds).

Period of Rotation of Earth on Axis: 1 day (or 23 hours, 56 minutes, 4.09 seconds).

Speed of Earth in Orbit around Sun: 18.5 miles per second.

Volume of Earth: 260 billion cubic miles.

Weight or Mass of Earth: 6,586,000,000,000,000,000,000 tons (or 6.586 sextillion tons).

EXTREMES OF THE EARTH

Source: National Geographic Society

Highest mountain	Mt. Everest, Nepal–China; 29,028 feet	Deepest lake	Baykal, U.S.S.R.; 5,315 ft.
Lowest point on surface	Dead Sea, Israel–Jordan; –1,312 feet below sea level	Driest spot	Atacama Desert, Chile; rainfall barely measurable
Greatest ocean depth ..	Mariana Trench, Pacific Ocean; 35,810 feet	Northernmost town ...	Ny Alesund, Spitsbergen, Norway
Highest volcano	Chimborazo, Ecuador; 20,561 feet	Southernmost town ...	Puerto Williams, Chile
Largest desert	Sahara, North Africa; over 3 million square miles	Lowest town	Villages along Dead Sea; 1,299 feet below sea level
Largest island	Greenland; 840,000 square miles	Largest gorge	Grand Canyon, Colorado River, Arizona; 277 miles long, 600 feet to 18 miles wide, 1 mile deep
Longest river	Nile, Africa; 4,145 miles		
Highest waterfall	Angel Falls, Venezuela; 3,212 feet	Deepest gorge	Hells Canyon, Snake River, Idaho; 7,900 feet deep
Largest lake	Caspian Sea, Asia; 143,244 square miles	Strongest wind	231 mph; record in 1934 at Mt. Washington, New Hampshire
Rainiest spot	Mt. Waialeale, Hawaii; average 460 inches a year	Greatest tides	Bay of Fundy, Nova Scotia; 53 feet

SEVEN CONTINENTS

Source: National Geographic Society

NAME	AREA (in square miles)	% OF WORLD'S LAND	HIGHEST POINT (in feet)	LOWEST POINT (feet below sea level)	TEMPERATURE RECORDS HIGHEST (with date)	LOWEST (with date)
Asia	16,999,000	29.7	Mt. Everest Nepal–China (29,028)	Dead Sea, Israel–Jordan (1,312)	Tirat Zevi, Israel 129.0° F. (June 21, 1942)	Oymyakon, Soviet Union –89.9° F. (Feb. 6, 1933)
Africa	11,688,000	20.4	Mt. Kilimanjaro, Tanzania (19,340)	Lake Assal, Djibouti (512)	Al Aziziyah, Libya 136.0° F. (Sept. 13, 1922)	Ifrane, Morocco –11.2° F. (Feb. 11, 1935)
North America	9,366,000	16.3	Mt. McKinley, Alaska (20,320)	Death Valley, California (282)	Death Valley, California 134.0° F. (July 10, 1913)	Snag, Yukon, Canada –81.0° F. (Feb. 3, 1947)
South America	6,881,000	12.0	Mt. Aconcagua, Argentina (22,834)	Valdes Peninsula, Argentina (131)	Rivadavia, Argentina 120.0° F. (Dec. 11, 1905)	Sarmiento, Argentina –27.4° F. (June 1, 1907)
Antarctica ...	5,100,000	8.9	Vinson Massif (16,864)	Not known	Esperanza Station 58.3° F. (Oct. 20, 1956)	Vostok –127.0° F. (Aug. 24, 1960)
Europe	4,017,000	7.0	Mt. Elbrus, Soviet Union (18,510)	Caspian Sea, Soviet Union (92)	Seville, Spain 122.0° F. (Aug. 4, 1881)	Ust' Schchugor, Soviet Union –67.0° F.
Australia	2,966,000	5.2	Mt. Kosciusko, New South Wales (7,310)	Lake Eyre, South Australia (52)	Cloncurry, Queensland 127.6° F. (Jan. 16, 1889)	Charlotte Pass, New S. Wales –8.0° F. (July 22, 1947)

OCEANS OF THE EARTH AND THEIR GREATEST DEPTHS

Source: National Geographic Society

OCEANS	AREA (in sq. mi.)	PERCENT OF WORLD'S WATER	GREATEST DEPTH IN OCEANS Location	Feet
Pacific Ocean	64,186,000	46.0%	Mariana Trench, off the Mariana Islands	35,810
Atlantic Ocean	33,420,000	23.9%	Puerto Rico Trench, off Puerto Rico	28,374
Indian Ocean	28,350,000	20.3%	Java Trench, off Java	23,376
Arctic Ocean	3,662,000	2.6%	Eurasia Basin	16,804

SEAS OF THE EARTH AND THEIR AVERAGE DEPTHS

SEAS	AREA (sq. mi.)	AVERAGE DEPTH (feet)	SEAS	AREA (sq. mi.)	AVERAGE DEPTH (feet)
South China Sea....	1,148,500	4,802	East China Sea	256,600	620
Caribbean Sea	971,400	8,448	Andaman Sea	218,100	3,667
Mediterranean Sea :	969,100	4,926	Black Sea	196,100	3,906
Bering Sea	873,000	4,893	Red Sea	174,900	1,764
Gulf of Mexico	582,100	5,297	North Sea	164,900	308
Sea of Okhotsk.....	537,500	3,192	Baltic Sea	147,500	180
Sea of Japan	391,100	5,468	Yellow Sea	113,500	121
Hudson Bay	281,900	305			

EARTH HISTORY

The rocks of the Earth's crust tell scientists the history of our planet. Because the rocks form layers, or *strata*, the dating of various eras and periods of Earth history relates to the age of these rocks.

AZOIC ERA

The Earth began during this era, about 4.6 to 5 billion years ago when the solar system formed around the Sun. The oldest rocks found on the Moon, dated as 4.66 billion years old, are believed to be from this era. Meteorites, thought to have formed at the same time as the Earth, have been dated by the radioactive technique as being 4.7 billion years old. The air and the oceans formed.

ARCHEOZOIC ERA

Beginning about 3.5 billion years ago, life originated in the warm seas in the form of bacteria and algae. Some kinds of chert, slate, and marble formed in this period contain fossils of these early types of life.

PROTEROZOIC ERA

About 1.2 billion years ago, the first animals began to live in the oceans. These were invertebrates, or animals without backbones. They included sponges, jellyfish, and worms. Rocks that formed in this era included many metal ores, such as iron and copper. Land thrust up as continents.

PALEOZOIC ERA

Much more is known of this era than of earlier eras because of the plentiful supply of fossils that have been found. The era is divided into six major periods.
Cambrian Period began about 600 million years ago and lasted about 120 million years. Most of North America was covered with seas. Mountains formed in Vermont. Fossils of small sea animals called trilobites date from this period. The first fish appeared.
Ordovician Period began about 500 million years ago and lasted about 45 million years. Corals and animals with shells developed in the seas.
Silurian Period began about 435 million years ago and lasted 30 million years. Gas, oil, and salt deposits formed. The first animals that breathed air appeared.
Devonian Period began about 405 million years ago and lasted 60 million years. Sharks and other large fish lived in the seas. The first amphibian animals crawled onto the land. Forests covered the swampy land.
Carboniferous Period began 345 million years ago and lasted about 70 million years. It is often divided into two equal-length periods called the *Mississippian* and *Pennsylvanian*. The first land animals with backbones, the reptiles, appeared. Huge coal deposits formed.
Permian Period began about 275 million years ago and lasted about 50 million years. The Appalachian Mountains formed in North America. The first plants with seeds developed—trees with cones.

MESOZOIC ERA

This was the era of the dinosaurs.
Triassic Period began about 225 million years ago and lasted 45 million years. The first dinosaurs and turtles appeared.
Jurassic Period began 180 million years ago and lasted about 50 million years. The mountains of the Sierra Nevada and California Coast ranges were formed. Dinosaurs reached their biggest size. Small mammals began living on the land. Birds began to fly.
Cretaceous Period began about 130 million years ago and lasted about 65 million years. The Rocky Mountains formed in North America. The huge dinosaurs died out. Plants with flowers appeared.

CENOZOIC ERA

Tertiary Period began about 65 million years ago and lasted about 62 million years.
Paleocene Epoch began 65 million years ago and lasted about 10 million years. Erosion formed soil in which flowering plants flourished. The earliest primates appeared.
Eocene Epoch began about 55 million years ago and lasted about 15 million years. Modern mammals appeared, including whales, camels, and monkeys.
Oligocene Epoch began 40 million years ago and lasted 14 million years. Large grazing animals appeared, as did primitive apes.
Miocene Epoch began 26 million years ago and lasted about 12 million years. Dogs, elephants, and apes became common throughout Asia and Africa.
Pliocene Epoch began 14 million years ago and lasted about 11 million years. The Cascade Mountains formed in North America. Most modern kinds of animals appeared, as well as the first men.
Quaternary Period began about 3,100,000 years ago and lasts to the present day.
Pleistocene Epoch lasted over 3,000,000 years. During this Ice Age, glaciers formed over most of North America and Eurasia four times. Prehistoric man hunted, made tools, tamed animals, and began farming.
Holocene Epoch covers the most recent 10,000 years, since the retreat of the last glaciers. Civilization developed.

U.S. GEOGRAPHIC CENTERS AND HIGHEST AND LOWEST POINTS

Source: Geological Survey, U.S. Department of the Interior

STATE	GEOGRAPHIC CENTER [1] County and Locality	HIGHEST POINT [2] Name and Elevation (in feet)	LOWEST POINT Name and Elevation (in feet)
UNITED STATES	Butte Co., S.D. (West of Castle Rock)	Mt. McKinley (20,320)	Death Valley (−282)
Alabama	Chilton (12 mi. SW of Clanton)	Cheaha Mountain (2,407)	Gulf of Mexico [3]
Alaska	63° 50′ N, 152° 00′ W, 60 miles NW of Mt. McKinley	Mt. McKinley (20,320)	Pacific Ocean [3]
Arizona	Yavapai (55 mi. ESE of Prescott)	Humphreys Peak (12,633)	Colorado River(70)
Arkansas	Pulaski (12 mi. NW of Little Rock)	Magazine Mountain (2,753)	Ouachita River (55)
California	Madera (38 mi. E of Madera)	Mt. Whitney (14,494)	Death Valley (−282)
Colorado	Park (30 mi. NW of Pikes Peak)	Mt. Elbert (14,433)	Arkansas River (3,350)
Connecticut	Hartford (at East Berlin)	Mt. Frissell, on south slope (2,380)	Long Island Sound [3]
Delaware	Kent (11 mi. S of Dover)	Ebright Road (442)	Atlantic Ocean [3]
District of Columbia . .	Near 4th and L Streets NW	Tenleytown (410)	Potomac River (1)
Florida	Hernando (12 mi. NNW of Brooksville)	Sec. 30, T6N, R20′W, Walton Co. (345)	Atlantic Ocean [3]
Georgia	Twiggs (18 mi. SE of Macon)	Brasstown Bald (4,784)	Atlantic Ocean [3]
Hawaii	Hawaii (20° 15′ N, 156° 20′ W, off Maui Island)	Mauna Kea (13,796)	Pacific Ocean [3]
Idaho	Custer (at Custer, SW of Challis)	Borah Peak (12,662)	Snake River (710)
Illinois	Logan (28 mi. NE of Springfield)	Charles Mound (1,235)	Mississippi River (279)
Indiana	Boone (14 mi. NNW of Indianapolis)	Franklin T, Wayne Co. (1,257)	Ohio River (320)
Iowa	Story (5 mi. NE of Ames)	Sec. 29, T100N, R41W, Osceola Co. (1,670)	Mississippi River (480)
Kansas	Barton (15 mi. NE of Great Bend)	Mt. Sunflower (4,039)	Verdigris River (680)
Kentucky	Marion (3 mi. NNW of Lebanon)	Black Mountain (4,145)	Mississippi River (257)
Louisiana	Avoyelles Parish (3 mi. SE of Marksville)	Driskill Mountain (535)	New Orleans (−5)
Maine	Piscataquis (18 mi. N of Dover)	Mt. Katahdin (5,268)	Atlantic Ocean [3]
Maryland	Prince Georges (4½ miles NW of Davidsonville)	Backbone Mountain (3,360)	Atlantic Ocean [3]
Massachusetts .	Worcester (north part of city of Worcester)	Mt. Greylock (3,491)	Atlantic Ocean [3]
Michigan	Wexford (5 mi. NNW of Cadillac)	Mt. Arvon (1,979)	Lake Erie (572)
Minnesota	Crow Wing (10 mi. SW of Brainerd)	Eagle Mountain, Cook Co. (2,301)	Lake Superior (602)
Mississippi	Leake (9 mi. WNW of Carthage)	Woodall Mountain (806)	Gulf of Mexico [3]
Missouri	Miller (20 mi. SW of Jefferson City)	Taum Sauk Mountain (1,772)	St. Francis River (230)
Montana	Fergus (11 mi. W of Lewistown)	Granite Peak (12,799)	Kootenai River (1,800)
Nebraska	Custer (10 mi. NW of Broken Bow)	Johnson T. Kimball Co. (5,426)	SE corner of state (840)
Nevada	Lander (26 mi. SE of Austin)	Boundary Peak (13,143)	Colorado River (470)
New Hampshire .	Belknap (3 mi. E. of Ashland)	Mt. Washington (6,288)	Atlantic Ocean [3]
New Jersey	Mercer (5 mi. SE of Trenton)	High Point (1,803)	Atlantic Ocean [3]
New Mexico	Torrance (12 mi. SSW of Willard)	Wheeler Peak (13,161)	Red Bluff Reservoir (2,817)
New York	Madison (12+ mi. S of Oneida and 26+ mi. SW of Utica)	Mt. Marcy (5,344)	Atlantic Ocean [3]
North Carolina . . .	Chatham (10 mi. NW of Sanford)	Mt. Mitchell (6,684)	Atlantic Ocean [3]
North Dakota . . .	Sheridan (5 mi. SW of McClusky)	White Butte, Slope Co. (3,506)	Red River (750)
Ohio	Delaware (25 mi. NNE of Columbus)	Campbell Hill (1,550)	Ohio River (433)
Oklahoma	Oklahoma (8 mi. N of Oklahoma City)	Black Mesa (4,973)	Little River (287)
Oregon	Crook (25 mi. SSE of Prineville)	Mt. Hood (11,239)	Pacific Ocean [3]
Pennsylvania . . .	Centre (2½ mi. SW of Bellefonte)	Mt. Davis (3,213)	Delaware River [3]
Rhode Island . . .	Kent (1 mi. SSW of Crompton)	Jerimoth Hill (812)	Atlantic Ocean [3]
South Carolina . .	Richland (13 mi. SE of Columbia)	Sassafras Mountain (3,560)	Atlantic Ocean [3]
South Dakota . . .	Hughes (8 mi. NE of Pierre)	Harney Peak (7,242)	Big Stone Lake (962)
Tennessee	Rutherford (5 mi. NE of Murfreesboro)	Clingmans Dome (6,643)	Mississippi River (182)
Texas	McCulloch (15 mi. NE of Brady)	Guadalupe Peak (8,749)	Gulf of Mexico [3]
Utah	Sanpete (3 mi. N of Manti)	Kings Peak (13,528)	Beaverdam Creek (2,000)
Vermont	Washington (3 mi. E of Roxbury)	Mt. Mansfield (4,393)	Lake Champlain (95)
Virginia	Buckingham (5 mi. SW of Buckingham)	Mt. Rogers (5,729)	Atlantic Ocean [3]
Washington	Chelan (10 mi. WSW of Wenatchee)	Mt. Rainier (14,410)	Pacific Ocean [3]
West Virginia . . .	Braxton (4 mi. E of Sutton)	Spruce Knob (4,863)	Potomac River (240)
Wisconsin	Wood (9 mi. SE of Marshfield)	Timms Hill, Price Co. (1,952)	Lake Michigan (581)
Wyoming	Fremont (58 mi. ENE of Lander)	Gannett Peak (13,804)	Belle Fourche River (3,100)

[1] Approximate [2] Sec. = section; T = township; R = range; N = north; W = west; S = south; [3] Sea level.

PREHISTORIC MAN

In the 1600s people believed that man had lived on Earth for less than 6,000 years. But with Charles Darwin's publication of the theory of evolution in 1859, anthropologists began searching for a "missing link" that might prove man had evolved from a lower primate.

The most ancient complete human skull was found by anthropologist Richard Leakey in Kenya in 1972. It has been dated as 2.9 million years old. His parents, anthropologists Louis and Mary Leakey, first proved in 1959–63 that man had lived over 1 million years ago.

Anthropologists classify prehistoric humans into several genera based largely on brain shape and size.

HOMO SAPIENS—500,000 B.C. TO PRESENT

Two general types of prehistoric men have skulls about the size of modern men, and are classified as *Homo sapiens.*

Cro-Magnon Man was like modern man, standing about 6 feet tall. He was named after fossils found at Cro-Magnon, France, by Edouard Larter in 1868. The oldest remains of Cro-Magnon Man have been dated as about 35,000 years old.

Neanderthal Man had a brain the size of modern man's, but was somewhat shorter and had heavier bones. Fossils of Neanderthal Man were the first remains of prehistoric man to be found, creating a scientific sensation at the time of their discovery in 1856 in the Neander Valley near Düsseldorf, Germany, by Johann C. Fuhlrott.

Neanderthals are believed to have lived from about 500,000 to 25,000 B.C. in many parts of the world. Fossil remains of this type were found in Zambia (then Northern Rhodesia) in 1921 and called Rhodesian Man. Similar fossil remains found in Java, Indonesia, from 1931 to 1936 were called Solo Man. Other Neanderthaloid fossils were found by anthropologists at Steinheim, Germany, in 1933; at Swanscombe, England, in 1935–36; in caves at Mount Carmel (now in Israel) from 1929 to 1934; and at Shanidar, Iraq, in 1957.

HOMO ERECTUS—1,700,000 TO 500,000 B.C

Homo erectus was a smaller type of man about 5 feet tall with a brain about three-fourths the size of the brain of modern man.

Heidelberg Man. A fossil jaw discovered near Heidelberg, Germany, in 1907 by Otto Schoetensack dates to about 500,000 B.C. Identification has been difficult because no other parts of the skull were found.

Java Man, who made tools, hunted, and used fire, lived from about 1,000,000 to 500,000 B.C. Fossil remains of this primitive man were discovered in Java, Indonesia, by Eugène Dubois in 1891.

Peking Man. Several 500,000-year-old skulls were found near Peking, China, in 1927 by Davidson Black. They are believed to be of the type *Homo erectus,* although at least one skull was as large as that of a modern man.

Kenya Man. Richard Leakey discovered a skull identified as *Homo erectus* near Lake Turkana (Rudolf) in Kenya in 1975. It was dated as 1.5 million years old.

Yuanmou Man. Fossil teeth discovered in China in 1965 have been dated as 1.7 million years old.

HOMO HABILIS—3,750,000 TO 1,500,000 B.C.

Scientists disagree as to whether certain fossils found in Africa should be classified as early man or as primates. They were called *Homo habilis* (skilled man) by their discoverers, the Leakeys, because they used stone tools.

Olduvai Man. The first skulls of an early type of man that used stone tools were found at Olduvai Gorge in Tanganyika in 1959–63 by the Leakeys. These remains have been dated as 1.8 million years old. The discovery provided the first evidence that man had lived more than a million years ago.

Laetolil Man. Jaws and teeth of 11 adults and children were discovered by Mary Leakey in the Laetolil area of Tanzania in 1975. The fossils were dated as between 3.35 and 3.75 million years old.

HOMINOIDS—18,000,000 TO 1,300,000 B.C.

Hominoids are extinct primates that had features similar both to apes and to man.

The earliest, called *Sivapithecus,* that lived about 18 million years ago, have been found in Africa. Others, called *Ramapithecus,* found in Africa, Europe, Pakistan, and India, are up to 14 million years old.

The hominoid *Australopithecus,* a small apelike creature, lived in Africa 5.5 million to 1.3 million years ago. It stood about 4 feet tall with a brain about one-third that of modern man. The first fossils of this type were found at Taung, South Africa, in 1924 by Raymond A. Dart.

Parts of jawbones, teeth, and leg bones were found in 1973–77 by American anthropologist Donald Johanson in Ethiopia. They were dated as 2.9 to 3.6 million years old and identified as a new species named *Australopithecus afarensis,* or Afar ape-man.

HIGHEST MOUNTAINS

Source: National Geographic Society

Mountain ranges were formed when land-masses were pushed up. As time passed, the mountains wore away by weathering and erosion.

The Himalaya range in Asia includes Mt. Everest, the highest peak in the world.

The highest mountains in Europe lie in the Caucasus, a range in the Soviet Union that divides Europe and Asia.

In western Europe the tallest peaks are the Alps, which are located in Switzerland, Italy, France, West Germany, and Austria.

NAME	LOCATION	FEET	NAME	LOCATION	FEET
Highest Peaks in North America			**Highest Peaks in South America**		
McKinley	Alaska	20,320	Aconcagua	Argentina	22,834
Logan	Canada	19,850	Ojos del Salado	Argentina–Chile	22,572
Pico de Orizaba	Mexico	18,700	Bonete	Argentina	22,546
St. Elias	Alaska–Canada	18,008	Tupungato	Argentina–Chile	22,310
Popocatépetl	Mexico	17,887	Pissis	Argentina	22,241
Foraker	Alaska	17,400	Mercedario	Argentina	22,211
Iztaccihuatl	Mexico	17,343	Huascarán	Peru	22,205
Lucania	Canada	17,147	Llullaillaco	Argentina–Chile	22,057
King	Canada	16,971	El Libertador	Argentina	22,047
Steele	Canada	16,644	Cachi	Argentina	22,047
Bona	Alaska	16,421	Yerupaja	Peru	21,709
Blackburn	Alaska	16,390	Galán	Argentina	21,654
Sanford	Alaska	16,237	El Muerto	Argentina–Chile	21,457
South Buttress	Alaska	15,885	Sajama	Bolivia	21,391
Wood	Canada	15,885	Nacimiento	Argentina	21,302
Vancouver	Alaska–Canada	15,700	Illimani	Bolivia	21,201
Churchill	Alaska	15,638	Coropuna	Peru	21,083
Fairweather	Alaska	15,300	Laudo	Argentina	20,997
Zinantecatl (Toluca)	Mexico	15,016	Ancohuma	Bolivia	20,958
Hubbard	Alaska–Canada	15,015	Ausangate	Peru	20,945
Bear	Alaska	14,831	Toro	Argentina–Chile	20,932
Walsh	Canada	14,780	Illampu	Bolivia	20,873
East Buttress	Alaska	14,730	Tres Cruces	Argentina–Chile	20,853
Matlalcueyetl	Mexico	14,636	Huandoy	Peru	20,852
Hunter	Alaska	14,573	Parinacota	Bolivia–Chile	20,768
Alverstone	Alaska–Canada	14,565	Tórtolas	Argentina–Chile	20,745
Browne Tower	Alaska	14,530	Ampato	Peru	20,702
Whitney	California	14,494	Cóndor	Argentina	20,669
Elbert	Colorado	14,433	Salcantay	Peru	20,574
Massive	Colorado	14,421	Chimborazo	Ecuador	20,561
Harvard	Colorado	14,420	Huancarhuas	Peru	20,531
Rainier	Washington	14,410	Famatina	Argentina	20,505
Williamson	California	14,375	Pumasillo	Peru	20,492
Blanca Peak	Colorado	14,345	Solo	Argentina	20,492
La Plata Peak	Colorado	14,336	Polleras	Argentina	20,456
Uncompahgre Peak	Colorado	14,309	Pular	Chile	20,423
Crestone Peak	Colorado	14,294	Chañi	Argentina	20,341
Lincoln	Colorado	14,286	Aucanquilcha	Chile	20,295
Grays Peak	Colorado	14,270	Juncal	Argentina–Chile	20,276
Antero	Colorado	14,269	Negro	Argentina	20,184
Torreys Peak	Colorado	14,267	Quela	Argentina	20,128
Castle Peak	Colorado	14,265	Condoriri	Bolivia	20,095
Quandary Peak	Colorado	14,265	Palermo	Argentina	20,079
Evans	Colorado	14,264	Solimana	Peru	20,068
Longs Peak	Colorado	14,255	San Juan	Argentina–Chile	20,049
McArthur	Canada	14,253	Sierra Nevada	Argentina–Chile	20,023
Wilson	Colorado	14,246	Antofalla	Argentina	20,013
White	California	14,246	Marmolejo	Argentina–Chile	20,013
North Palisade	California	14,242	Chachani	Peru	19,931
Shavano Peak	Colorado	14,229	Chaupi Orko	Peru–Bolivia	19,682

Highest Peaks in Asia

NAME	LOCATION	FEET
Everest	Nepal–China (Tibet)	29,028
K2 (Godwin–Austen)	Pakistan (Kashmir)	28,250
Kanchenjunga	Nepal–India (Sikkim)	28,208
Lhotse I	Nepal–China (Tibet)	27,923
Makalu I	Nepal–China (Tibet)	27,824
Lhotse II	Nepal–China (Tibet)	27,560
Dhaulagiri	Nepal	26,810
Manaslu I	Nepal	26,760
Cho Oyu	Nepal–China (Tibet)	26,750
Nanga Parbat	Pakistan (Kashmir)	26,660
Annapurna	Nepal	26,504
Gasherbrum	Pakistan (Kashmir)	26,470
Broad	Kashmir	26,400
Gosainthan	China (Tibet)	26,287
Annapurna II	Nepal	26,041
Gyachung Kang	Nepal–China (Tibet)	25,910
Disteghil Sar	Pakistan (Kashmir)	25,858
Himalchuli	Nepal	25,801
Nuptse	Nepal–China (Tibet)	25,726
Masherbrum	Pakistan (Kashmir)	25,660
Nanda Devi	India	25,645
Rakaposhi	Pakistan (Kashmir)	25,550
Kamet	India–China (Tibet)	25,447
Namcha Barwa	China (Tibet)	25,445
Gurla Mandhata	China (Tibet)	25,355
Ulugh Muz Tagh	China (Tibet-Sinkiang)	25,340
Kungur	China (Sinkiang)	25,325
Tirich Mir	Pakistan	25,230
Makalu II	Nepal–China (Tibet)	25,120
Minya Konka	China	24,900
Kula Gangri	Bhutan–China (Tibet)	24,784
Changtzu	Nepal–China (Tibet)	24,780
Muz Tagh Ata	China (Sinkiang)	24,757
Skyang Kangri	Pakistan (Kashmir)	24,750
Communism Peak	Soviet Union	24,590
Jongsang Peak	Nepal–India (Sikkim)	24,472
Pobedy Peak	Soviet Union–China	24,406
Sia Kangri	Pakistan (Kashmir)	24,350
Haramosh Peak	Pakistan	24,270
Istoro Nal	Pakistan	24,240
Tent Peak	Nepal–India (Sikkim)	24,165
Chomo Lhari	Bhutan–China (Tibet)	24,040
Chamlang	Nepal	24,012
Kabru	Nepal–India (Sikkim)	24,002
Alung Gangri	China (Tibet)	24,000
Baltoro Kangri	Pakistan (Kashmir)	23,990
Mussu Shan	China (Sinkiang)	23,890
Mana	India	23,860
Baruntse	Nepal	23,688
Nepal Peak	Nepal–India (Sikkim)	23,500
Amne Machin	China	23,490
Gauri Sankar	Nepal–China (Tibet)	23,440
Badrinath	India	23,420
Nunkun	Pakistan (Kashmir)	23,410
Lenina Peak	Soviet Union	23,405
Pyramid	Nepal–India (Sikkim)	23,400
Api	Nepal	23,399
Pauhunri	India–China (Tibet)	23,385
Trisul	India	23,360
Kangto	India–China (Tibet)	23,260
Nyenchhen Thanglha	China (Tibet)	23,255
Trisuli	India	23,210
Dunagiri	India	23,184
Lombo Kangra	China (Tibet)	23,165

Highest Peaks in Europe

NAME	LOCATION	FEET
Elbrus	Soviet Union	18,510
Shkara	Soviet Union	17,064
Dykh Tau	Soviet Union	17,054
Kashtan Tau	Soviet Union	16,877
Dzhangi Tau	Soviet Union	16,565
Kazbek	Soviet Union	16,558
Mont Blanc	France–Italy (Alps)	15,771
Monte Rosa	Italy–Switzerland (Alps)	15,203
Dom	Switzerland (Alps)	14,911
Liskamm	Switzerland (Alps)	14,852
Weisshorn	Switzerland (Alps)	14,780
Täschhorn	Switzerland (Alps)	14,733
Matterhorn	Switzerland (Alps)	14,690
Dent Blanche	Switzerland (Alps)	14,293
Nadelhorn	Switzerland (Alps)	14,196
Grand Combin	Switzerland (Alps)	14,154
Lenzspitze	Switzerland (Alps)	14,088
Finsteraarhorn	Switzerland (Alps)	14,022
Castor	Switzerland (Alps)	13,865
Zinalrothorn	Switzerland (Alps)	13,849
Hohberghorn	Switzerland (Alps)	13,842
Alphubel	Switzerland (Alps)	13,799
Rimpfischhorn	Switzerland (Alps)	13,776
Aletschhorn	Switzerland (Alps)	13,763
Strahlhorn	Switzerland (Alps)	13,747
Dent d'Hérens	Switzerland (Alps)	13,686
Breithorn	Switzerland (Alps)	13,665
Bishorn	Switzerland (Alps)	13,645
Jungfrau	Switzerland (Alps)	13,642

Highest Peaks in Africa

NAME	LOCATION	FEET
Kilimanjaro (2 peaks):		
Kibo	Tanzania	19,340
Mawenzi	Tanzania	16,896
Kenya	Kenya	17,058
Margherita	Uganda–Zaire	16,763
Ras Dashan	Ethiopia	15,158
Meru	Tanzania	14,979
Karisimbi	Rwanda–Zaire	14,787
Elgon	Kenya–Uganda	14,178
Batu	Ethiopia	14,131
Guge	Ethiopia	13,780
Toubkal	Morocco	13,655
Birhan	Ethiopia	13,628

Highest Peaks in the Pacific and Southeast Asia

NAME	LOCATION	FEET
Jaya	Indonesia (Irian Jaya)	16,500
Pilimsit	Indonesia (Irian Jaya)	15,748
Trikora	Indonesia (Irian Jaya)	15,585
Mandala	Indonesia (Irian Jaya)	15,420
Wilhelm	Papua New Guinea	14,793

Highest Peaks in Antarctica

NAME	LOCATION	FEET
Vinson Massif		16,864
Tyree		16,290
Shinn		15,750
Gardner		15,375
Epperly		15,100

MAJOR VOLCANOES

About 600 active and 10,000 inactive or dormant volcanoes are found along three belts, closely matching the earthquake regions of the world.

The "ring of fire" includes the Pacific coasts of North and South America and Asia.

A second belt extends from the Mediterranean to the East Indies, and a third lies along the midocean ridges of the major oceans.

Volcanic activity is deceptively sporadic—brief periods of outgassing or eruption, followed by unpredictably longer dormant periods.

Many volcanoes began their eruptions on the bed of the sea. Italy's Etna and Vesuvius were submarine volcanoes originally.

Cones are inevitably modified by eruptions. Thus some heights are approximate.

See also *Major Volcanic Disasters*, page 38.

NAME	LOCATION	HEIGHT
AFRICA AND INDIAN OCEAN		
Kilimanjaro	Tanzania	19,340
Cameroon Mt.	Cameroon	13,350
Teide	Tenerife Island	12,198
Nyiragongo	Zaire	11,400
Nyamlagira	Zaire	10,028
Fogo	Cape Verde	9,281
Piton de la Fournaise	Réunion	8,630
Tristan da Cunha	Atlantic Ocean	6,760
ANTARCTICA		
Erebus	Rosa Island	12,450
ASIA AND PACIFIC OCEAN		
Klyuchevskaya	Soviet Union	15,584
Mauna Kea	Hawaii	13,796
Mauna Loa	Hawaii	13,680
Kerinci	Indonesia	12,467
Fuji	Japan	12,388
Rinjani	Indonesia	12,224
Tolbachik	Soviet Union	12,080
Semeru	Indonesia	12,060
Ichinskaya	Soviet Union	11,880
Kronotskaya	Soviet Union	11,575
Koryakskaya	Soviet Union	11,339
Slamet	Indonesia	11,247
Raung	Indonesia	10,932
Shiveluch	Soviet Union	10,771
Dempo	Indonesia	10,364
Welirang	Indonesia	10,354
Agung	Indonesia	10,308
Sundoro	Indonesia	10,285
Plosky Tolbachik	Soviet Union	10,121
Ciremay	Indonesia	10,098
Ontake	Japan	10,049
Gede	Indonesia	9,705
Merapi	Indonesia	9,548
Bezymyannaya	Soviet Union	9,514
Apo	Philippines	9,369
Tambora	Indonesia	9,353
Ruapehu	New Zealand	9,175
Peuetsagoe	Indonesia	9,121
Bromo	Indonesia	9,088
Avachinskaya	Soviet Union	9,026
Api Siau	Indonesia	8,856
Mayon	Philippines	7,943
Ngauruhoe	New Zealand	7,516
Sarychev	Kurile Islands	4,910
Karimsky	Soviet Union	4,875
Kilauea	Hawaii	4,077
Sakurazima	Kyushu, Japan	3,657
Suwanosezima	Ryukyus	2,620
Usu	Hokkaido, Japan	2,385
Shin-dake	Ryukyus	2,100
EUROPE		
Etna	Italy	10,791
Beeren Berg	Norway	7,470
Askja	Iceland	4,954

NAME	LOCATION	HEIGHT
Europe (continued)		
Hekla	Iceland	4,892
Vesuvius	Italy	4,190
Katla	Iceland	3,182
Stromboli	Italy	3,038
Leirhnukur	Iceland	2,132
NORTH AMERICA		
Citlaltepec	Mexico	18,700
Popocatépetl	Mexico	17,887
Wrangell	Alaska	14,163
Colima	Mexico	12,988
Torbert	Alaska	11,413
Spurr	Alaska	11,069
Baker	Washington	10,778
Lassen	California	10,457
Redoubt	Alaska	10,197
Iliamna	Alaska	10,016
Mount St. Helens	Washington	9,671*
Shishaldin	Alaska (Aleutians)	9,387
Pavlof	Alaska	8,261
Veniaminof	Alaska	8,225
Griggs	Alaska	7,600
Paricutín	Mexico	7,451
St. Augustine	Alaska	3,969
CENTRAL AMERICA AND CARIBBEAN SEA		
Tajumulco	Guatemala	13,845
Tacaná	Guatemala	13,428
Acatenango	Guatemala	12,992
Fuego	Guatemala	12,582
Santa María	Guatemala	12,372
Atitlán	Guatemala	11,565
Irazú	Costa Rica	11,260
San Pedro	Guatemala	9,921
Póas	Costa Rica	8,859
Pacaya	Guatemala	8,346
San Miguel	El Salvador	6,988
San Cristóbal (El Viejo)	Nicaragua	5,842
Arenal	Costa Rica	5,092
La Soufrière	Guadeloupe	4,812
SOUTH AMERICA		
Chimborazo	Ecuador	20,561
Guallatiri	Chile	19,882
Lascar	Chile	19,652
Cotopaxi	Ecuador	19,347
Misti	Peru	19,098
Cayambe	Ecuador	18,996
Tupungatito	Chile	18,504
Sangay	Ecuador	17,159
Tungurahua	Ecuador	16,512
Cotacachi	Ecuador	16,204
Pichincha	Ecuador	15,696
Puracé	Colombia	15,604
Reventador	Ecuador	11,431
Lautaro	Chile	11,090
Llaima	Chile	10,239
Villarrica	Chile	9,318

* Estimated 1,500 feet sheared off during 1980 eruption.

PRINCIPAL DESERTS

Once simply used for an uninhabited, or "deserted" place, the term *desert* is now commonly applied to regions that have little rainfall, scanty vegetation, and limited human use.

Of the three types of deserts commonly recognized, only a few *tropical* deserts, such as the Libyan part of the Sahara, resemble the popular image of a hot, dry, sandy expanse.

Middle latitude deserts lie in the "rainshadow" of a mountain barrier (as deserts in the southwestern U.S.), or deep within the moisture-starved interiors of continents (the Gobi).

Polar deserts occur because moisture is "locked up" as ice and snow.

Desert landscapes range from flat, sandy plains to mountainous plateaus. The rocks of deserts are typically eroded into fantastic shapes by the action of wind-driven sand.

DESERT	LOCATION	SIZE	REMARKS
NORTH AMERICA			
Black Rock	Humboldt and Pershing counties, Nevada	An area of 1,000 square miles	A barren plain practically devoid of vegetation; from its surface, alkaline dust is blown into vast clouds by the summer winds.
Colorado	Arid region of southeastern California	200 miles long; maximum width of 50 miles	The soil of its Imperial Valley is highly productive when irrigated.
Death Valley	Eastern California and Southwestern Nevada	2,936 square miles	Yielded much borax in the 19th century.
Mohave	Southern California; northeast of Los Angeles extends into Mohave County, Arizona	15,000 square miles	Needles, on the Arizona-California boundary, is one of the hottest towns in the United States.
Painted Desert	Coconino and Navajo counties in northern Arizona	200 miles long; 15–30 miles wide	Within the desert are seven Hopi villages; the Painted Desert is so called because of its coloring, caused by centuries of erosion exposing brilliantly colored rock formations.
SOUTH AMERICA			
Atacama	Northern Chile	600 miles long	An area of rich nitrate and copper deposits.
AFRICA			
Kalahari	South Africa; the Orange River marks its southern limit	120,000 square miles	Hottentots and Bushmen inhabit the area.
Namib	Namibia	800 miles long; 30–100 miles wide	Long, narrow desert plain along Atlantic coast.
Sahara	North Africa; on the west the desert extends to the Atlantic coast	Over 3,000,000 square miles	Nomadic herding is still an important activity in the desert, but in recent years there has been petroleum extraction; the Libyan and Nubian deserts are part of the Sahara.
ASIA			
Dasht i Kavir	Iran, from the Caspian Sea to the Persian Gulf	300 miles long; 100 miles wide	Saline swamps and dry salt areas.
Gobi	Extends 1,500 miles from Manchuria to Sinkiang Province, China	500,000 square miles	Many paleontological finds, including dinosaur eggs, have been made there.
Kara Kum	Asiatic Soviet Union	110,000 square miles	The Kara Kum has a number of "old river beds" that may have been either channels or tributaries of the Amu.
Kizil-Kum	Asiatic Soviet Union	370 by 220 miles	The surface is characterized by stationary sands with sparse vegetation.
Negev	Southern Israel	4,700 square miles	Barren expanses of sand, now dotted with prosperous farms, orchards, and towns; has King Solomon's mines and the Dead Sea.
An Nafud	Northern Saudi Arabia	An average width of 200 miles	Huge area of sand dunes, populated only by a few nomads.
Rub al-Khali (Empty Quarter)	Southern Saudi Arabia	300,000 square miles	Practically unexplored; it may contain large tracts of hard gravel or limestone deposits.
Syrian	Northernmost Saudi Arabia, extending into Jordan, Syria, and Iraq	——	The oasis of Al Jawf has extensive palm groves and a population of more than 10,000.
Taklamakan	Central Asia, in the Chinese province of Sinkiang	125,000 square miles	Ancient trade routes cross this desert, and there are reports of buried cities; the Chinese exploded their first atomic bomb there in 1964.
Thar (Indian)	Northwestern India, between the Gulf of Cutch and the Arabian Sea on the south	100,000 square miles	Camel caravans still traverse the desert; parts of the Thar are disputed between India and Pakistan.
AUSTRALIA			
Great Australian	Much of central and western Australia	——	Primitive Bushmen live in this area, which Australians prefer to call "Sparselands."

MAJOR ISLANDS

Source: National Geographic Society

Islands are bodies of land surrounded by water. Continents are islands in the strict sense of the word, differing from other islands only in size.

The largest islands in the world are, in square miles: Greenland (840,000); New Guinea (306,000); Borneo (280,100); Madagascar (226,658); Baffin (195,928); Sumatra (165,000); Honshu (87,805); Great Britain (84,200); Victoria (83,896); and Ellesmere (75,767).

The largest islands of the United States, in square miles, are: Hawaii (4,037); Kodiak (3,670); and Puerto Rico (3,515).

Islands in minor waters (in square miles): Manitoulin (Canada), Lake Huron (1,068); Singapore, Singapore Strait (239); Isle Royale, Mich., Lake Superior (209); Pinang (Malaysia), Strait of Malacca (110); Staten Island, N.Y. (59); Manhattan, N.Y. (22).

NAME	AREA (in sq. miles)
ARCTIC OCEAN	
Canadian	
Axel Heiberg	16,671
Baffin	195,928
Banks	27,033
Devon	21,331
Ellesmere	75,767
Melville	16,274
Prince of Wales	12,872
Southampton	15,913
Victoria	83,896
Soviet Union	
Franz Josef Land	8,000
Novaya Zemlya	35,000
Wrangel	2,800
Norwegian	
Svalbard	23,940
Nordaustlandet	5,410
Spitsbergen	15,060
ATLANTIC OCEAN	
British Isles	
Great Britain, mainland	84,200
Hebrides	2,744
Ireland	32,599
Man	227
Orkney Is.	390
Shetland Is.	567
Skye	670
Other Atlantic Islands	
Anticosti (Canada)	3,066
Azores (Portugal)	902
Bahamas	5,353
Bermuda Is. (Britain)	20
Canary Is. (Spain)	2,808
Cape Breton (Canada)	3,981
Cape Verde Is.	1,750
Faeroe Is. (Denmark)	540
Falkland Is. (Britain)	4,700
Fernando Po (Equatorial Guinea)	785
Greenland (Denmark)	840,000
Iceland	39,769
Long Island (New York)	1,396
Madeira Is. (Portugal)	307
Marajó (Brazil)	15,528
Martha's Vineyard (Massachusetts)	91
Nantucket (Massachusetts)	46
Newfoundland (Canada)	42,030
Prince Edward (Canada)	2,184
South Georgia (Britain)	1,450
Tierra del Fuego (Chile and Argentina)	17,800

NAME	AREA (in sq. miles)
BALTIC SEA	
Aland (Finland)	581
Bornholm (Denmark)	227
Gotland (Sweden)	1,164
CARIBBEAN SEA	
Antigua	108
Barbados	166
Cuba	44,218
Isle of Youth	1,182
Dominica	290
Guadeloupe (France)	687
Hispaniola (Haiti and Dominican Republic)	29,530
Jamaica	4,244
Martinique (France)	425
Puerto Rico (U.S.)	3,515
Trinidad	1,864
Virgin Is. (U.S.)	132
INDIAN OCEAN	
Andaman Is. (India)	2,500
Madagascar	226,658
Mauritius	720
Pemba (Tanzania)	380
Réunion (France)	969
Seychelles	107
Sri Lanka	25,332
Zanzibar (Tanzania)	640
Persian Gulf	
Bahrain	258
MEDITERRANEAN SEA	
Balearic Is. (Spain)	1,936
Corfu (Greece)	229
Corsica (France)	3,365
Crete (Greece)	3,186
Cyprus	3,572
Elba (Italy)	86
Euboea (Greece)	1,409
Malta	122
Rhodes (Greece)	542
Sardinia (Italy)	9,262
Sicily (Italy)	9,822
PACIFIC OCEAN	
Aleutian Is. (Alaska)	6,821
Caroline (U.S. Trust Territory)	473
Galápagos Is. (Ecuador)	3,043
Guadalcanal (Britain)	2,500
Guam (U.S.)	209
Hainan (China)	13,000
Hawaiian Is. (U.S.)	6,450
Hawaii	4,037
Oahu	593

NAME	AREA (in sq. miles)
Hong Kong (Britain)	29
Japan	145,809
Hokkaido	30,144
Honshu	87,805
Iwo Jima	8
Kyushu	14,114
Okinawa	459
Shikoku	7,049
Kodiak (Alaska)	3,670
Marquesas Is. (France)	492
Marshall Is. (U.S. Trust)	70
Nauru	8
New Caledonia (France)	6,530
New Guinea (Indonesia–Papua New Guinea)	306,000
New Zealand	103,883
North	44,035
South	58,305
Northern Mariana Is. (U.S.)	184
Philippines	115,831
Leyte	2,787
Luzon	40,880
Mindanao	36,775
Mindoro	3,790
Negros	4,907
Palawan	4,554
Panay	4,446
Samar	5,050
Quemoy	56
Sakhalin (Soviet Union)	29,500
Samoa Islands	1,177
American Samoa	77
Tutuila	52
Western Samoa	1,101
Savaii	670
Upolu	429
Tahiti (France)	402
Taiwan	13,823
Tasmania (Australia)	26,178
Vancouver (Canada)	12,079
Vanuatu	5,700
Viti Levu (Fiji)	4,109
Indonesia	
Bali	2,147
Borneo (with Malaysia–Britain)	280,100
Celebes	69,000
Java	48,900
Moluccas	28,766
Sumatra	165,000
Timor	11,570
Papua New Guinea	
New Britain	14,093
New Ireland	3,707

LONGEST RIVERS

Source: National Geographic Society

RIVER	EMPTIES INTO	MILES
NORTH AMERICA		
Albany (Canada)	James Bay	610
Arkansas (Colo.–Ark.)	Mississippi River	1,459
Athabasca (Canada)	Lake Athabasca	765
Back (Canada)	Chantrey Inlet	605
Brazos (Texas)	Gulf of Mexico	1,210
Canadian (N.M.–Okla.)	Arkansas River	906
Churchill (Canada)	Hudson Bay	1,000
Cimarron (Colo.–Okla.) ...	Arkansas River	600
Colorado (Colo.–Mexico) ..	Gulf of California	1,450
Colorado (Texas)	Matagorda Bay	840
Columbia (U.S.–Canada) ..	Pacific Ocean	1,243
Cumberland (Ky.–Tenn.) ..	Ohio River	720
Fraser (Brit. Col.)	Strait of Georgia	850
Green (Utah–Wyo.)	Colorado River	730
James (N.D.–S.D.)	Missouri River	710
Kuskokwim (Alaska)	Kuskokwim Bay	800
Mackenzie (Canada)	Beaufort Sea	2,635
Mississippi (Minn.–La.)....	Gulf of Mexico	2,348
Mississippi–Missouri–Red Rock (Mont.–La.)	Gulf of Mexico	3,870
Missouri (Mont.–Mo.)	Mississippi River	2,315
Missouri–Red Rock (Mont.–Mo.)	Mississippi River	2,533
Nelson (Canada)	Hudson Bay	1,600
North Canadian (Okla.) ...	Canadian River	760
North Platte (Wyo.–Nebr.) .	Platte River	680
Ohio (Pa.–Ill.)	Mississippi River	981
Ohio–Allegheny (Pa.–Ill.) ..	Mississippi River	1,306
Ottawa (Canada)	St. Lawrence River	790
Peace (Canada)	Slave River	1,195
Pecos (N.M.–Tex.)	Rio Grande	735
Red (Okla.–Tex.–La.)	Mississippi River	1,270
Rio Grande (Colo.–Mexico)	Gulf of Mexico	1,885
Saguenay (Canada)	St. Lawrence River	434
St. Lawrence (N.Y.–Canada)	Gulf of St. Lawrence	800
Saskatchewan (Canada)...	Lake Winnipeg	1,205
Snake (Wyo.–Wash.)	Columbia River	1,038
Tennessee–French Broad (N.C.–Ky.)	Ohio River	900
Trinity (Canada)	Trinity Bay	715
Usumacinta (Mexico)	Gulf of Mexico	270
White (Ark.–Mo.)	Mississippi River	720
Yukon (Alaska–Canada) ...	Bering Sea	1,979
SOUTH AMERICA		
Amazon (Brazil)	Atlantic Ocean	4,000
Japura (Colombia–Brazil) .	Amazon River	1,750
Madeira (Brazil)	Amazon River	2,013
Magdalena (Colombia)	Caribbean Sea	956
Negro (Brazil)	Amazon River	1,400
Orinoco (Venezuela)	Atlantic Ocean	1,600
Paraguay (Paraguay)	Paraná River	1,584
Paraná (Argentina)	Rio de la Plata	2,485
Pilcomayo (Arg.-Paraguay)	Paraguay River	1,000
Purus (Peru–Brazil)	Amazon River	2,100
Rio Theodore Roosevelt (Brazil)	Aripciana River	400
São Francisco (Brazil)	Atlantic Ocean	1,988
Tocantins (Brazil)	Pará River	1,677
Uruguay (Arg.–Uruguay) ..	Rio de la Plata	1,000

RIVER	EMPTIES INTO	MILES
EUROPE		
Bug S. (Poland–Soviet Union)	Dnieper River	532
Bug W. (Soviet Union– Poland)	Wisla River	481
Danube (W. Germany– Romania)	Black Sea	1,776
Daugava–Dvina (Soviet Union)	Gulf of Riga	634
Dnieper (Soviet Union)	Black Sea	1,420
Dniester (Soviet Union) ...	Black Sea	877
Don (Soviet Union)	Sea of Azov	1,224
Drava (Yugoslavia)	Danube River	447
Ebro (Spain)	Mediterranean Sea	565
Elbe (E. Germany)	North Sea	724
Loire (France)	Bay of Biscay	634
Meuse (Belgium–France) ..	North Sea	580
Oder (E. Germany–Poland)	Baltic Sea	567
Rhine (Switz.–Netherlands)	North Sea	820
Rhone (France–Switz.)	Mediterranean Sea	505
Seine (France)	English Channel	496
Tajo or Tagus (Spain–Port.)	Atlantic Ocean	626
Tisza (Hungary)	Danube River	600
Ural (Soviet Union)	Caspian Sea	1,575
Volga (Soviet Union)	Caspian Sea	2,194
Weser (W. Germany)	North Sea	454
Wisla (Poland)	Baltic Sea	675
AFRICA		
Gambia (Gambia)	Atlantic Ocean	700
Niger (Nigeria)	Gulf of Guinea	2,590
Nile (Sudan–Egypt)	Mediterranean Sea	4,160
Orange (South Africa)	Atlantic Ocean	1,300
Zaire or Congo (Zaire–Congo)	Atlantic Ocean	2,900
Zambezi (Zambia– Mozambique)	Indian Ocean	1,700
ASIA		
Amu (Soviet Union)	Aral Sea	1,578
Amur (Soviet Union)	Tatar Strait	2,744
Angara (Soviet Union)	Yenisey River	1,151
Brahmaputra	Bay of Bengal	1,800
Euphrates (Syria–Iraq)	Persian Gulf	2,235
Ganges (India–Bangladesh)	Bay of Bengal	1,560
Hsi (China)	South China Sea	1,200
Indus (Pakistan)	Arabian Sea	1,800
Irrawaddy (Burma)	Bay of Bengal	1,337
Lena (Soviet Union)	Laptev Sea	2,734
Mekong (SE Asia)	South China Sea	2,600
Ob–Irtysh (Soviet Union) ..	Gulf of Ob	3,362
Salween (Burma)	Gulf of Martaban	1,500
Sungari (China)	Amur River	1,150
Syr Darya (Soviet Union) ..	Aral Sea	1,370
Tigris (Iraq)	Euphrates River	1,180
Chang Jiang or Yangtze (China)	East China Sea	3,964
Huang or Yellow (China) ..	Yellow Sea	2,903
Yenisey (Soviet Union)	Kara Sea	2,543
AUSTRALIA		
Murray–Darling	Indian Ocean	2,310

FAMOUS WATERFALLS

Source: National Geographic Society

There are tens of thousands of waterfalls scattered over the Earth, hundreds of them of considerable magnitude. The highest waterfalls in the world are: Angel (Venezuela), 3,212 feet; Yosemite (California), 2,425 feet; Southern Mardalsfossen (Norway), 2,149 feet; Tugela (South Africa), 2,014 feet; Cuquenán (Venezuela), 2,000 feet; Sutherland (New Zealand), 1,904 feet.

On the basis of annual flow combined with considerable height, Guaira, between Brazil and Paraguay, is the world's greatest waterfall; its estimated annual flow is 470,000 cusecs (cubic feet per second). A greater volume of water passes over Boyoma Falls, in Zaire, the former Democratic Republic of the Congo, but not one of its seven falls, spread over a distance of 60 miles, is higher than 10 feet.

The estimated annual flows of other great waterfalls are: Niagara (Canada and United States), 212,200 cusecs; Paulo Afonso (Brazil), 100,000; Urubupunga (Brazil), 97,000; Iguazú (Argentina and Brazil), 61,600; Patos-Maribondo (Brazil), 53,000; Victoria (Zambia and Zimbabwe), 35,400; and Kaieteur (Guyana), 23,400.

LOCATION AND NAME	FEET HIGH[1]
AFRICA	
Angola	
Duque de Braganca	344
Ruacana, Cuene R.	406
Ethiopia	
Del Verme, Dawa R.	98
Fincha	508
T'Is Isat, Blue Nile	140
Lesotho	
Maletsunyane [2]	630
South Africa	
Aughrabies [2], Orange R.	480
Howick, Umgeni R.	311
Tugela [3]	2,014
Highest single fall	597
Tanzania–Zambia	
Kalambo [2]	726
Uganda	
Kabalega (Murchison) Victoria Nile R.	130
Zambia	
Chirombo	880
Zimbabwe and Zambia	
Victoria [2], Zambezi R.	343
ASIA	
India	
Cauvery [2]	330
Gokak [2], Ghataprabha R.	170
Jog [2] (Gersoppa), Sharavathi R.	830
Japan	
Kegon [2], Daiya R.	330
Laos	
Khon Cataracts [4], Mekong R.	70
AUSTRALASIA	
Australia	
New South Wales	
Wentworth [3]	614
Wollomombi	1,100
Queensland	
Coomera	210
Tully	885
Wallaman [3]	1,137
New Zealand	
Bowen	540
Helena	890
Stirling	505
Sutherland [3], Arthur R.	1,904

LOCATION AND NAME	FEET HIGH[1]
EUROPE	
Austria	
Gastein [3]	492
Golling [2, 3], Schwarzbach R.	250
Krimml [3]	1,312
France	
Gavarnie [3]	1,385
Great Britain	
Scotland: Glomach	370
Wales: Rhaiadr	240
Iceland	
Detti	144
Italy	
Frua [4], Toce R.	470
Norway	
Mardalsfossen (Northern)	1,535
Mardalsfossen [3] (Southern)	2,149
Skjeggedal [3, 5], Nybuai R.	1,378
Skykkje [5]	984
Vetti	900
Võring, Bjoreio R.	597
Sweden	
Handöl [3]	427
Tannforsen, Are R.	120
Switzerland	
Diesbach [3]	394
Giessbach [4]	984
Handegg, Aare R.	150
Iffigen	120
Pissevache, Salanfe R.	213
Reichenbach [3]	656
Simmen [3]	459
Staubbach	984
Trümmelbach [3]	1,312
NORTH AMERICA	
Canada	
Alberta	
Panther, Nigel Cr.	600
British Columbia	
Della	1,443
Takakkaw, Daly Glacier	1,200
Northwest Territories	
Virginia, S. Nahanni R.	294
Quebec	
Montmorency	274
Canada–United States	
Niagara [6]	
American	182
Horseshoe	173
Mexico	
El Salto	218
United States	
California	
Feather [2], Fall R.	640

LOCATION AND NAME	FEET HIGH[1]
Yosemite Natl. Park:	
Bridal Veil [2]	620
Nevada [2], Merced R.	594
Ribbon [5]	1,612
Silver Strand [5], Meadow Br.	1,170
Yosemite [3, 5]	2,425
Colorado	
Seven [3], S. Cheyenne Cr.	300
Hawaii	
Akaka	442
Idaho	
Shoshone [5], Snake R.	212
Twin, Snake R.	120
New York	
Taughannock [2]	215
Oregon	
Multnomah [3]	620
Tennessee	
Fall Creek	256
Washington	
Mt. Rainier Natl. Park:	
Narada, Paradise R.	168
Sluiskin, Paradise R.	300
Palouse	197
Snoqualmie [5]	268
Wisconsin	
Big Manitou [2, 4], Black R.	165
Wyoming	
Yellowstone Natl. Park:	
Tower	132
Yellowstone (upper) [2]	109
Yellowstone (lower) [2]	308
SOUTH AMERICA	
Argentina–Brazil	
Iguazú	230
Brazil	
Glass	1,325
Herval	400
Patos-Maribondo	115
Grande R. Paulo Afonso, São Francisco R.	275
Urubupunga, Paraná R.	40
Colombia	
Catarata de Candelas, Cusiana R.	984
Tequendama, Bogotá R.	427
Guyana	
Kaieteur, Potaro R.	741
Great Kamarang R.	1,600
Marina [3], Ipobe R.	500
Venezuela	
Angel [2, 3]	3,212
Cuquenán	2,000

[1] Height means total drop whether in one or more leaps. [2] Falls greatly diminish seasonally. [3] Falls consist of more than one leap. [4] Cascade-type falls. [5] Falls dry part of year. [6] Niagara's cataract is divided by Goat Island into two waterfalls.

LARGEST LAKES IN EACH U.S. STATE

Source: National Geographic Society

STATE	LAKE	AREA (sq. miles)	MAX. DEPTH (feet)	SHORE-LINE (miles)
Alabama	Guntersville [1,3,5]	106	68	949
	Eufaula [2,3,5]	71	90	640
Alaska	Iliamna [1,4]	1,115	987	—
Arizona	Theodore Roosevelt [1,3]	27	280	88
	Powell [2,3]	252	580	1,800
Arkansas	Ouachita [1,3]	75	207	975
	Bull Shoals [2,3]	71	250	740
California	Salton Sea [1,4]	375	50	—
	Tahoe [2,4]	191	1,645	71
Colorado	Blue Mesa [1,3,5]	14	342	96
	Navajo [2,3,5]	24	388	150
Connecticut	Candlewood [1,3]	8	85	65
	Colebrook River [2,3]	2	140	13
Delaware	Lum's Pond [1,3]	0.3	10	7
Florida	Okeechobee [1,4]	700	15	96
	Seminole [2,3]	59	27	—
Georgia	Sidney Lanier [1,3]	59	156	540
	Clark Hill [2,3]	109	145	1,200
Hawaii	Waita [1,3,5]	0.7	29	4
Idaho	Pend Oreille [1,4]	148	1,237	226
Illinois	Carlyle [3,5]	41	40	83
	Michigan [2,4]	22,300	923	1,660
Indiana	Monroe [1,3,5]	17	70	150
	Michigan [2,4]	22,300	923	1,660
Iowa	Rathbun [1,3,5]	17	102	180
Kansas	Tuttle Creek [1,3,5]	25	90	112
Kentucky	Cumberland [1,3]	79	183	1,255
	Kentucky [2,3]	250	71	2,380
Louisiana	Pontchartrain [1,4]	621	18	112
	Toledo Bend [2,3,5]	284	92	1,200
Maine	Moosehead [1,4]	117	246	190
Maryland	Deep Creek [1,3]	7	72	65
	Youghiogheny [2,3,5]	4	115	38
Massachusetts	Quabbin [1,3,5]	39	150	118
Michigan	Houghton [1,4]	31	20	30
	Superior [2,4]	31,700	1,333	2,980
Minnesota	Red [1,4]	451	31	123
	Superior [2,4]	31,700	1,333	2,980
Mississippi	Ross Barnett [1,3,5]	52	55	105
	Pickwick [2,3]	67	—	496
Missouri	Harry S. Truman [1,3,5]	87	125	958
	Bull Shoals [2,3,5]	71	250	740
Montana	Fort Peck [1,3,5]	389	210	1,650
	Koocanusa [2,3]	73	350	224
Nebraska	McConaughy [1,3]	55	142	105
	Lewis and Clark [2,3]	27	50	90
Nevada	Pyramid [1,4]	169	330	66
	Mead [2,3]	247	432	550
New Hamp.	Winnipesaukee [1,4]	70	180	240
	Umbagog [2,4]	12	—	—
New Jersey	Hopatcong [1,4]	4	58	32
	Greenwood [2,4]	3	52	14
New Mexico	Elephant Butte [1,3,5]	58	157	250
	Navajo [2,3,5]	24	388	150
New York	Oneida [1,4]	79	55	58
	Erie [2,4]	9,910	210	856
North Carolina	Mattamuskeet [1,4]	67	5	—
	John H. Kerr [2,3,5]	76	105	800
North Dakota	Sakakawea [1,3]	575	180	1,600
	Oahe [2,3,5]	556	200	2,250
Ohio	Grand [1,2]	22	10	60
	Erie [2,4]	9,910	210	856
Oklahoma	Eufaula [1,3]	160	87	600
	Texoma [2,3]	139	142	580
Oregon	Upper Klamath [1,4]	143	50	165
	Goose [2,4]	194	24	90
Pennsylvania	Raystown [1,3,5]	13	186	115
	Erie [2,4]	9,910	210	856
Rhode Island	Scituate [1,3,5]	5	94	38
South Carolina	Marion [1,3]	173	40	330
	Clark Hill [2,3]	123	150	1,200
South Dakota	Francis Case [1,3,5]	159	140	540
	Oahe [2,3,5]	556	200	2,250
Tennessee	Watts Bar [1,3]	61	61	771
	Kentucky [2,3]	250	71	2,380
Texas	Sam Rayburn [1,3,5]	179	73	560
	Toledo Bend [2,3,5]	284	92	1,200
Utah	Great Salt [1,4]	1,680	34	335
	Powell [2,3]	252	560	1,960
Vermont	Bomoseen [1,4]	4	65	22
	Champlain [2,4]	437	400	379
Virginia	Smith Mountain [1,3]	31	200	500
	John H. Kerr [2,3,5]	76	105	800
Washington	F.D. Roosevelt [1,3]	123	375	151
West Virginia	Summersville [1,3]	4	267	65
Wisconsin	Winnebago [1,4]	215	21	85
	Superior [2,4]	31,700	1,333	2,980
Wyoming	Yellowstone [1,4]	137	309	110
	Flaming Gorge [2,3,5]	66	437	—

[1] Entirely within state. [2] Shared with another state or states. [3] Man-made. [4] Natural. [5] Reservoir.

WORLD'S LARGEST LAKES

Source: National Geographic Society

LAKE AND LOCATION	AREA (sq. miles)	LENGTH (miles)	MAX. DEPTH (feet)
Caspian Sea (U.S.S.R.-Iran)	143,244	760	3,363
Superior (U.S.-Canada)	31,700	350	1,333
Victoria (Uganda-Tanzania-Kenya)	26,828	250	270
Aral Sea (U.S.S.R.)	24,904	280	220
Huron (U.S.-Canada)	23,000	206	750
Michigan (U.S.)	22,300	307	923
Tanganyika (Zaire-Burundi-Tanzania-Zambia)	12,700	420	4,823
Baykal (U.S.S.R.)	12,162	395	5,315
Great Bear (Canada)	12,096	192	1,463
Nyasa or Malawi (Tanzania-Mozambique-Malawi)	11,150	360	2,280
Great Slave (Canada)	11,031	298	2,015
Erie (U.S.-Canada)	9,910	241	210
Winnipeg (Canada)	9,417	266	60
Ontario (U.S.-Canada)	7,550	193	802
Balkhash (U.S.S.R.)	7,115	376	85
Ladoga (U.S.S.R.)	6,835	124	738
Chad (Chad-Niger-Nigeria)	6,300	175	24
Maracaibo (Venezuela)	5,217	133	115
Onega (U.S.S.R.)	3,710	145	328
Eyre (Australia)	3,600	90	4
Volta (Ghana)	3,276	250	—
Titicaca (Peru-Bolivia)	3,200	122	922
Nicaragua (Nicaragua)	3,100	102	230
Athabasca (Canada)	3,064	208	407
Reindeer (Canada)	2,568	143	—
Turkana (Kenya-Ethiopia)	2,473	154	240
Issyk Kul (U.S.S.R.)	2,355	115	2,303

COAST AND SHORELINE OF THE UNITED STATES

Source: National Ocean Service, National Oceanic and Atmospheric Administration

STATE	GENERAL COASTLINE [1]	TIDAL SHORELINE [2]	STATE	GENERAL COASTLINE [1]	TIDAL SHORELINE [2]
United States	12,383	88,633	South Carolina	187	2,876
Atlantic Coast	2,069	28,673	Virginia	112	3,315
Connecticut	—	618	Gulf Coast	1,631	17,141
Delaware	28	381	Alabama	53	607
Florida (Atlantic only)	580	3,331	Florida (Gulf only) ...	770	5,095
Georgia	100	2,344	Louisiana	397	7,721
Maine	228	3,478	Mississippi	44	359
Maryland	31	3,190	Texas	367	3,359
Massachusetts	192	1,519	Pacific Coast	7,623	40,298
New Hampshire	13	131	Alaska	5,580	31,383
New Jersey	130	1,792	California	840	3,427
New York	127	1,850	Hawaii..............	750	1,052
North Carolina	301	3,375	Oregon	296	1,410
Pennsylvania	—	89	Washington	157	3,026
Rhode Island	40	384	Arctic Coast, Alaska ...	1,060	2,521

[1] Statute mile length of general outline of seacoast. Measurements made with unit measure of 30 minutes of latitude on charts as near scale of 1:1,200,000 as possible. [2] Statute mile length of shoreline of outer coast, offshore islands, sounds, bays, rivers, and creeks to the head of tidewater or to point where tidal waters narrow to 100 feet wide.

TIDE RANGES IN THE UNITED STATES

Source: National Ocean Service, National Oceanic and Atmospheric Administration

Listed below are the average tidal ranges for 1986. "Mean range" is the difference in height between mean high and low tides. "Spring range" is the average range occurring semimonthly due to a new or full moon. "Diurnal range" is the difference in height between average higher high tide and average lower low tide.

EAST COAST LOCATION	MEAN RANGE	SPRING RANGE	WEST COAST LOCATION	MEAN RANGE	DIURNAL RANGE
Portland, Maine	9.1 ft.	10.4 ft.	Seattle, Washington	7.7 ft.	11.4 ft.
Boston, Massachusetts	9.5 ft.	11.0 ft.	Coos Bay, Oregon................	5.6 ft.	7.3 ft.
New London, Connecticut	2.6 ft.	3.0 ft.	Crescent City, California	5.1 ft.	7.0 ft.
The Battery, New York City	4.6 ft.	5.5 ft.	San Francisco, California	4.1 ft.	5.8 ft.
Atlantic City, New Jersey	4.1 ft.	5.0 ft.	Santa Barbara, California	3.6 ft.	5.4 ft.
Hampton Roads, Virginia	2.5 ft.	2.9 ft.	Los Angeles, California	3.8 ft.	5.5 ft.
Charleston, South Carolina......	5.3 ft.	6.1 ft.	San Diego, California	4.0 ft.	5.7 ft.
Savannah, Georgia	7.4 ft.	8.6 ft.	Honolulu, Hawaii................	1.3 ft.	2.0 ft.
Miami, Fla. (E. end of causeway) .	2.0 ft.	2.4 ft.	Cordova, Alaska	10.1 ft.	12.5 ft.

GREAT LAKES SYSTEM OF NORTH AMERICA

Source: National Ocean Service, National Oceanic and Atmospheric Administration

GENERAL LAKE DIMENSIONS	LAKE SUPERIOR	LAKE MICHIGAN	LAKE HURON	LAKE ST. CLAIR	LAKE ERIE	LAKE ONTARIO
Length in miles	350	307	206	26	241	193
Breadth in miles	160	118 [1]	183 [2]	24	57	53
Length of coastline in miles (including islands)	2,726	1,638	3,827 [3]	257	871	712
Areas in square miles:						
Total water surface	31,700 [4]	22,300 [5]	23,000 [6]	490 [7]	9,910	7,550 [8]
Water surface, United States	20,600 [4]	22,300 [5]	9,100 [6]	198 [7]	4,980	3,560 [8]
Water surface, Canada..................	11,100 [4]		13,900 [6]	292 [7]	4,930	3,990 [8]
Drainage basin (land) total	49,300 [4]	45,600 [5]	51,700 [6]	6,930 [7]	22,720	27,300 [8]
Drainage basin land, United States	16,900 [4]	45,600 [5]	16,200 [6]	2,850 [7]	18,000	15,200 [8]
Drainage basin land, Canada.............	32,400 [4]		35,500 [6]	4,080 [7]	4,720	12,100 [8]
Drainage basin (land and water) total	81,000 [4]	67,900 [5]	74,700 [7]	7,420 [7]	32,630 [8]	34,850 [8]
Maximum depth, feet...........................	1,330	923	750	21 [9]	210	802
Average depth, feet............................	489	279	195	10	62	283
Volume of water in cubic miles	2,900	1,180	850	1	116	393
Length of outflow river (shown under lake from which it flows), approximate miles:						
St. Marys	70					
St. Clair			27			
Detroit				32		
Niagara					37	
St. Lawrence						502

[1] Measured at wide point through Green Bay. [2] Measured at wide point through Georgian Bay. [3] Includes Georgian Bay and North Channel. [4] Including St. Marys River above Brush Point. [5] Lake Michigan including Green Bay. [6] Including St. Marys River below Brush Point, North Channel, and Georgian Bay. [7] Lake St. Clair and St. Clair and Detroit Rivers. [8] Lake Ontario including Niagara River and St. Lawrence River above Iroquois Dam. [9] Maximum natural depth; dredged navigation channel has 27.5-foot depth.

Ecology and Environment

YMCA Youth Camping USA **22**

Boy Scouts USA **22**

Big Brothers Big Sisters USA **22**

Campfire USA **22**

U.S. Postal Service

A block of four stamps honoring youth organizations that emphasize outdoor activities was issued by the U.S. Postal Service in Chicago, Ill., on Oct. 7 during the International Youth Services Conference. The year was designated "International Youth Year" by proclamation of the United Nations General Assembly. The youth groups featured in the block of four stamps are Young Men's Christian Association (YMCA) Youth Campers, the Boy Scouts, Big Brothers/Big Sisters, and Campfire. The stamps were designed by Dennis Luzak of Redding Ridge, Conn.

HIGHLIGHTS: 1985

LEAD IN GASOLINE CUT

The Environmental Protection Agency (EPA) on March 4 ordered the lead content of automobile gasoline reduced by 90% by Jan. 1, 1986. The ruling permits only 0.1 grams of lead per gallon of gasoline after that date. Previously the permitted amount of lead has been 1.1 grams per gallon.

Lee M. Thomas, head of the EPA, said the agency was considering a complete ban on lead in gasoline by 1988.

"There is no doubt in my mind that lead in the environment is still a national health problem and that gasoline is a major contributor to lead exposure, Thomas said. "These standards will significantly reduce the adverse health effects that result from lead in gasoline and will reduce the misuse of leaded gasoline in vehicles designed for unleaded fuel."

Thomas estimated that the new rules would add about 2 cents to the cost of producing a gallon of gasoline.

The EPA has research studies that show there is a direct relationship between the amount of lead in gasoline and the levels of lead found in the average person's blood. The studies indicate that lead in gasoline has been a leading cause of high blood pressure. Therefore the EPA expects that the reduced level of lead will save about 5,000 lives a year from death by heart attack, strokes, and other heart and blood vessel diseases and will reduce the number of cases of high blood pressure by 1.8 million or more.

Research studies also have shown that high levels of lead in blood cause mental retardation in children and permanent damage to the nervous system.

Most automobiles made in the United States since 1975 and all since 1980 are designed to use gasoline that does not include lead. However, the EPA said many motorists have been using leaded gasoline because it has been less expensive than unleaded.

Lead has been the cheapest additive that can be used to increase the octane rating of gasoline to improve automobile performance.

HIGHLIGHTS: 1985 *(continued)*

However, octane also can be increased with other more expensive additives, such as ethanol or methanol.

Automotive authorities said that older cars that were not designed to use unleaded gasoline were likely to have more valve wear from using gasoline without lead but would have less frequent spark plug changes, oil changes, and repairs or replacement of mufflers and exhaust pipes.

INDOOR POLLUTANTS

The EPA released results of a study that shows indoor exposure to pollutants in the home is much greater than in the outdoors.

Four sites were used in the test: Elizabeth and Bayonne, N.J., which have chemical plants and refineries that discharge pollutants into the air; Greensboro, N.C., which has light industry but no chemical plants; and Devils Lake, N.D., a rural community.

The 11 pollutants studied were benzene, carbon tetrachloride, chloroform, ethylebenze, meta-para-dichlorobenzene, meta-para-xylene, orthoxylene, perchloroethylene, 111 trichloroethane, trichloroethylene, and styrene.

A surprising result of the study, according to Dr. Bernard Goldstein, the EPA's assistant administrator for research and development, was that people living far away from chemical plants and people living near chemical plants had equivalent amounts of the chemicals in their blood.

The report on the study said in some cases indoor pollution was 70 times greater than outdoor pollution. The major sources of the indoor pollutants were believed to be such consumer products as cleansers, cosmetics, paints, plastics, and building materials.

SULFITE PRESERVATIVE BAN

The Food and Drug Administration (FDA) issued rules in August banning six sulfite preservatives from use on fresh vegetables and fruits. The compounds had been used especially on fresh fruits and vegetables used in salad bars in supermarkets and restaurants to prevent them from turning brown after being cut or peeled.

The FDA said the rules were issued because of a study by the Federation of American Societies for Experimental Biology which cited 13 deaths and 500 "adverse reactions" by persons who had eaten foods treated with sulfide compounds.

An FDA official, William Grigg, said:

"The FDA concluded that sulfites pose no danger to the general population, but cause reactions in up to a million sulfite-sensitive people, mostly asthmatics. Reactions range from nausea and diarrhea, to hives and shortness of breath, to fatal shock."

The new ruling did not apply to the use of sulfite preservatives in other products, such as dried fruits, frozen potatoes, or wine and beer.

Consumer groups applauded the FDA's action, but some complained that it did not go far enough.

A spokesman for the Center for Science in the Public Interest, which has lobbied for a total ban on sulfite preservatives said: "While a ban on fresh fruits and vegetables is a step in the right direction, it is not an adequate response to the hazards posed by sulfites. We would hope that the FDA will move quickly to ban all other uses of sulfites in food and drugs."

Legislation has been introduced in both houses of Congress to completely ban the use of sulfites.

WORLD'S POPULATION GROWTH: 1975–2000

Source: U.S. Census Bureau

Estimates of how large the world's population will be by the year 2000 depend on how widely and how quickly the world's people accept family planning methods to reduce population growth.

	World	Africa	Asia and Oceania	Latin America	Soviet Union and Eastern Europe	Northern America, Western Europe Japan, Australia, and New Zealand
Total population (millions):						
1975	4,090	399	2,274	324	384	708
2000	6,350	814	3,630	636	460	809
Net growth, 1975 to 2000:						
Persons (millions)	2,260	415	1,356	312	76	101
Percent	55%	104%	60%	96%	20%	14%
Birthrate (per 1,000 persons):						
1975	30.4	46.7	33.7	37.2	17.7	14.8
2000	25.6	38.5	25.9	28.7	15.9	14.5
Death rate (per 1,000 persons):						
1975	12.3	19.0	13.0	8.9	9.7	9.6
2000	9.1	11.3	8.7	5.7	10.5	10.5
Rate of natural increase:						
1975	1.8%	2.8%	2.1%	2.8%	0.8%	0.5%
2000	1.7%	2.7%	1.7%	2.3%	0.5%	0.4%

WORDS IN ECOLOGY AND ENVIRONMENT

abiotic environment—nonliving parts of environment, including air, soil, water, climate, weather, and nonliving nutrients .

acclimatization—way plant or animal adjusts to changes of climate

acid fog—fog laden with sulfuric acid droplets released by industrial or oil-refining operations

acid rain—rainfall containing acids produced by emissions from power plants, smelters, and motor vehicles, considered toxic to wildlife and natural resources

action grants—federal funds for distribution to cities that compete for them by submitting urban-development plans; cities must also obtain commitment to projects by private investment sector

adaptation—way plant or animal adjusts to live in certain environment

aerosol—fine particles of liquids, dust, smoke, or solids that remain suspended in air for long periods of time

Agent Orange—code name for dioxin, toxic chemical spray, released by military planes to defoliate enemy croplands or jungle areas, as in Vietnam War

air pollution—poisoning of air by ash, bacteria, dust gases, pollen, smoke, and other substances, both man-made and natural

algeny—upgrading of existing organisms and design of wholly new ones with intent of perfecting their performance

aseptic packaging—method of packaging fruit juices, milk, and other beverages in specially treated containers of paper, polyethylene, and aluminum foil that require no refrigeration; contents and containers are sterilized separately and have shelf life of about six months

aspartame—sweetener many times sweeter than sugar; made from two amino acids, L-aspartic acid and L-phenylalanine, found in protein-bearing foods such as bananas and beans

bad actor—waste product from high-level fission in nuclear power plant; including cesium 137, strontium 90, and plutonium

balance of nature—stability of population of each of many kinds of animals and plants living in certain environment

biodegradable—easily decomposed by normal biological processes without environmental damage

biome—large community of animals and plants living together in specific climate and region, as in tropical rain forest

biosphere—life-sustaining part of world, including soil, rock, bodies of water, and lower atmosphere

biotic environment—living plants, animals, and microorganisms and their interaction in certain area

Bone Valley—five-county area in central Florida where phosphate is mined and turned into fertilizer

bregoil—waste product of pulp-and-paper industry used for cleaning oil spills by absorbing petroleum, forming hardened mass that later can be used for fuel

co-generation—production of power by combined combustion of fuels, offering higher efficiency than conventional methods by recycling exhaust fumes and excess steam

community—animals and plants that live together and depend upon each other

conservation—protection and management of environment to preserve resources and basic ingredients needed for life

defoliant—chemical agent that causes leaves to fall from trees and plants

ecocide—destruction of natural environment by massive use of herbicides

ecological allergy—allergic reaction from exposure to chemicals in plastics, petroleum-based products or pesticides

ecology—study of relationship of plants, animals, and people to each other and to their environments

ecosystem—system of relationships within given community that supports life of each kind of plant and animal in area

effluent—liquid or gaseous waste discharged into environment

emission standard—legal limit for discharge of waste material

endangered species—animal in danger of extinction

enterprise zone—blighted area in city in which government controls, restrictions, and taxes are reduced or eliminated to encourage rehabilitation by private enterprise

environment—living and nonliving things in certain area and forces and conditions that affect them

Environmental Protection Agency (EPA)—federal agency responsible for protecting environment by controlling pollution

ergonomics—science of designing equipment for maximum user comfort; also known as human-factors engineering

erosion—gradual wearing away of natural resource, such as soil by wind and floods, or rock by freezing and thawing

eutrophication—unwholesome condition of fresh-water, marked by decrease in oxygen, caused by sewage or chemical-fertilizer runoff

fallout—dropping to earth of dust or particles carried in air, such as radioactive fallout resulting from explosion of atomic bomb

flood control—building of dams, dikes, and reservoirs in effort to prevent destruction by floods and water erosion

fluorocarbon—aerosol gas propellant, considered harmful to atmosphere

food chain—series or chain of plants and animals that depend upon each other for food supply to live; for example, man eats fish, which eat shrimp, which eat algae

footprint—area of major destruction produced by nuclear weapon

fugitive air emission—pollutant inadvertently released into atmosphere

gasohol—motor-fuel mixture consisting of 90% unleaded gasoline and 10% 200-proof ethyl alcohol

gentrification—upgrading of property values in town or city district by widespread renovation and improvement of deteriorated residential or commercial buildings

WORDS IN ECOLOGY *(continued)*

grant lands—designated areas granted by state or federal authority to private companies for exploitation of natural resource, such as oil or gas, with exemption from paying production royalties

green vote—voters concerned with environmental issues, considered as bloc

greenhouse effect—warming of atmosphere by buildup of carbon dioxide, water vapor, and ozone, preventing normal dissipation of heat from earth surface

greeny—slang for environmentalist or conservationist

grid lock—complete stoppage of vehicular traffic in city resulting from tie-ups at intersections within given area

habitat—area in which plant or animal lives

herbicide—chemical agent for controlling or destroying weeds and unwanted plant growth

hortitherapy—therapy of growing plants and flowers that aids persons in overcoming physical and emotional problems

hydrasorter—device that separates useful solid materials, such as metals and glass, from liquid garbage for recovery and recycling while also producing steam for generating electricity

infill—construction of building on vacant lot in mainly built-up area

inversion—condition in atmosphere that occurs when warm layer of air is trapped between two cooler layers of air, sometimes causing smog to linger over area

meltdown—disintegration of reactor core in nuclear power plant resulting from cooling-system failure, with possible release of toxic radioactivity

natural selection—process that results in specific kinds of animals and plants surviving in particular environment

noise pollution—unwanted, disagreeable sounds

ozone layer—region of ozone gas in stratosphere serving as shield against solar radiation

particulates—tiny particles of dust or soot in air

pesticide—chemical agent for controlling or destroying unwanted animals, insects, or plants

pH—symbol with scale of numbers from 0 to 14 to indicate whether water or soil is acid or alkaline; pH 7 is neutral, while pH numbers below 7 are acid and pH numbers above 7 are alkaline

pollutant—any substance that adversely affects natural environment

pollution—discharge of waste materials that cause adverse and unpleasant effects to environment

population density—relationship of total number of plants, animals, or people to area of region where they live, such as number of people per square mile

predacide—chemical agent for killing or warding off predator animals

primary consumer—animal that eats plants and then is eaten by another kind of animal

primary producer—plant that produces engery from Sun and then provides energy to animal that eats it

rain radar—radar technique for measuring number and size of falling raindrops

recycling—process to convert waste materials into useful materials, such as recycling of waste paper, glass, and aluminum

runoff—water from rain, snow, or industrial waste that flows over ground surface and discharges into streams

secondary consumer—animal that depends upon eating primary consumer for its energy; for example, fish that lives on shrimp for food is secondary consumer because shrimp is primary consumer, deriving its energy from eating algae

smokeout—campaign whereby persons voluntarily stop smoking for entire day as step toward permanent abstention

soil pollution—damage to soil, such as destruction of microscopic organisms in the soil by pesticides

solar index—amount of sunshine available for operating solar water heaters on given day, rated on scale of 0 to 100; data compiled by U.S. Energy Department and National Weather Service

space junk—debris in outer space, fallen from or jettisoned by spacecraft or other objects

Steel Valley—area of industrial suburbs southeast of Pittsburgh, Pa., along Monongahela River, with high concentration of steel mills

stream walker—one of group of volunteers who patrol designated stream or creek to monitor water for pollution by illegal discharge of industrial waste

survival suit—flotation suit of neoprene rubber covering entire body, including feet, hands, and forehead, to enable shipwrecked mariners to survive immersion in chilling waters

third kingdom—class of primitive organisms, simpler than bacteria, that use salts and acids as food; called *archaebacteria*, they include methanogens, halophiles, and thermoacidophiles

tight-sands gas—natural gas trapped in sandy rock, considered potential source of fuel

transit mall—system of enclosed shelters within city for convenience of persons waiting for buses, especially in bad weather

trashformation—transformation of discarded trash, junk, or other found objects into useful or artistic articles

urban amenity zone—area in city designed to attract private enterprise by provision of improved housing, transportation, and shopping facilities

urban nomads—inner-city residents displaced from older, moderate-priced dwellings by developers who renovate them for sale or lease to more affluent persons

value engineering—review of proposed engineering projects by independent consultants to evaluate whether plans and specifications are reliable and economically sound

waste disposal—process of getting rid of waste materials such as garbage or sewage

water pollution—discharge of waste materials into body of water

web of life—dependence of living things upon each other for survival

yellow rain—yellow powder released by plane in chemical warfare; derived from highly toxic fungi, it causes convulsions, hemorrhaging, and agonizing death within minutes of exposure

Social Security Act 1935-1985 USA 22

U.S. Postal Service

A commemorative stamp marking the 50th anniversary of the Social Security Act of 1935 was issued by the U.S. Postal Service on Aug. 14. The Social Security Act brought millions of Americans under a retirement plan for the first time. The Act and later amendments created essential protection for workers, including old age, survivor, disability, and health insurance; compensation for unemployment; public assistance; and health and welfare services. Altogether about $15 billion in benefits are paid each month to about 37 million people—a total of about $180 billion a year. Some 122 million persons work at jobs covered by Social Security—95% of all jobs in the U.S. economy.

HIGHLIGHTS: 1985

By mid-year in 1985 growth of the economy of the United States had slowed. During the second quarter of the year, from April through June, the gross national product (GNP) rose to an annualized rate of $3.85 trillion dollars—an increase of 5.2% over 1984, compared with a 10.8% rise in the previous year. When adjusted for inflation, the real increase in GNP in 1985 was expected by government economists to amount to an annual growth rate of about 1½%.

The Department of Labor's Bureau of Labor Statistics reported that the rate of unemployment fell to 6.9% in August—the lowest level since April 1980. The number of unemployed workers decreased by about 325,000 to 8.1 million in August. At the same time, civilian employment rose by 310,000 in August to a total of more than 107 million with jobs—over 60% of the entire population. Jobless rates declined for teenagers to 17.3% and for adult men to 6.0%. The unemploy-

ment rate for adult women, at 6.7% showed little change during the year. The jobless rate for black teenagers dipped to 34.4% in August.

Because of a reduction in the total size of the youth population, only about 3.6 million young people aged 16-to-24 years entered the labor force between April and July of 1985 to find summer jobs, according to the Labor Department. This was a smaller number than the 3.9 million young summer job seekers in 1984 and the 4.2 million in 1983. About 4 out of 5 young job-seekers found summer jobs in 1985.

Inflation remained under control in 1985. By July the Consumer Price Index (CPI) had increased only 3.6% during the previous 12 months. Costs of medical care continued to increase at a higher rate—6.2%. Prices for fuel oil continued to decline—falling to an average of $1.04 per gallon, 16.6% below their peak level of April 1981. Likewise, gas-

HIGHLIGHTS: 1985 *(continued)*

oline prices had fallen to an average of $1.23 per gallon—11.4% below their peak level of March 1981. Food and beverage prices rose at a lower rate than the overall index, increasing 2.1% in the 12 months ending in July. Decreases in grocery store prices for beef and poultry offset increases in prices for pork, fish, and eggs. In July beef prices stood at 7.4% below their December 1984 level.

Americans had more to spend in 1985. The Labor Department reported that in August weekly earnings for the average worker rose 86 cents to $302.32. This amounted to $7.67 more than the average weekly earnings of $294.65 in August 1984—an increase of 2.6%.

The Census Bureau reported that in 1984 real median family income increased 3.3% to $26,430. Real median income of white families grew by 3.3% to $27,690, and that of Spanish heritage families by 6.8% to $18,830. The black family median income of $15,430 showed no statistically significant change. Families with a householder completing four or more years of college had a median income of $43,170, up by 2.2%. Those with four years of high school had an income of $26,530, up 3.9%. Two-earner families—which accounted for about 42% of all families—had a median income of $31,710 compared with $20,290 for one-earner families.

The Census Bureau reported that the number of people below the poverty level declined from 35.5 million in 1983 to 33.7 million in 1984. The poverty rate for whites dropped from 12.2% in 1983 to 11.5% in 1984, and rate for blacks fell from 35.7% to

U.S. GROSS NATIONAL PRODUCT

Source: U.S. Bureau of Economic Analysis

The gross national product (GNP) is the total national output of goods and services valued at market prices. It includes all consumer purchases of goods and services, private investment expenditures, the net value of exports less imports, and government purchases of goods and services. The United States has the highest GNP of any country in the world. The following amounts are in $ billions (add 000,000,000).

YEAR	GNP	GROWTH RATE	YEAR	GNP	GROWTH RATE
1910	$ 35.3	2.8%	1964	$ 637.7	6.9%
1915	$ 40.0	0.8%	1965	$ 691.1	8.4%
1920	$ 91.5	4.3%	1966	$ 756.0	9.4%
1925	$ 93.1	8.4%	1967	$ 799.6	5.8%
1930	$ 90.4	9.8%	1968	$ 873.4	9.2%
1932	$ 58.0	14.7%	1969	$ 944.0	8.1%
1933	$ 55.6	1.8%	1970	$ 992.7	5.2%
1935	$ 72.2	9.9%	1971	$1,077.6	8.6%
1940	$ 99.7	16.1%	1972	$1,185.9	10.1%
1945	$211.9	1.7%	1973	$1,326.4	11.8%
1950	$286.2	10.9%	1974	$1,434.2	8.1%
1952	$348.0	5.2%	1975	$1,549.2	8.0%
1953	$366.8	5.4%	1976	$1,718.0	10.9%
1954	$366.8	0%	1977	$1,918.3	11.7%
1955	$400.0	9.0%	1978	$2,163.9	12.8%
1956	$421.7	5.4%	1979	$2,417.8	11.7%
1957	$444.0	5.3%	1980	$2,631.7	8.8%
1958	$449.7	1.3%	1981	$2,957.8	12.4%
1959	$487.9	8.5%	1982	$3,069.3	3.8%
1960	$506.5	3.8%	1983	$3,304.8	7.7%
1961	$524.6	3.6%	1984	$3,662.8	10.8%
1962	$565.0	7.7%	1985*	$3,853.5	5.2%
1963	$596.7	5.6%			

* Data annualized for 2nd quarter 1985.

33.8%. The poverty rate among children under 18 declined from 22.2% in 1983 to 21.3% in 1984. The poverty rate among people aged 65 and over decreased by 1.8% to 12.4%. The poverty threshold for a family of four in 1984 was $10,609.

EMPLOYEES[1] IN U.S. INDUSTRIES: 1900–1985

Source: U.S. Bureau of Labor Statistics

Year	Total	Mining	Construction	Manufacturing	Transportation & Public Utilities	Wholesale & Retail Trade	Finance, Insurance, and Real Estate	Services	Government Federal	Government State & Local
1900	15,178	637	1,147	5,468	2,282	2,502	308	1,740	1,094	
1910	21,697	1,068	1,342	7,828	3,366	3,570	483	2,410	1,630	
1920	27,434	1,180	850	10,702	4,317	4,012	902	3,100	2,371	
1930	29,424	1,009	1,372	9,562	3,685	5,797	1,475	3,376	526	2,622
1934	25,953	883	862	8,501	2,750	5,281	1,319	3,058	652	2,647
1940	32,376	925	1,294	10,985	3,038	6,750	1,502	3,681	996	3,206
1950	45,197	901	2,364	15,241	4,034	9,386	1,888	5,357	1,928	4,098
1960	54,189	712	2,926	16,796	4,004	11,391	2,629	7,378	2,270	6,083
1970	70,880	623	3,588	19,367	4,515	15,040	3,645	11,548	2,731	9,823
1975	76,945	752	3,525	18,323	4,542	17,060	4,165	13,892	2,748	11,937
1976	79,382	779	3,576	18,997	4,582	17,755	4,271	14,551	2,733	12,138
1977	82,471	813	3,851	19,682	4,713	18,516	4,467	15,303	2,727	12,399
1978	86,697	851	4,229	20,505	4,923	19,542	4,724	16,252	2,753	12,919
1979	89,823	958	4,463	21,040	5,136	20,192	4,975	17,112	2,773	13,147
1980	90,406	1,027	4,346	20,285	5,146	20,310	5,160	17,890	2,866	13,375
1981	91,156	1,139	4,188	20,170	5,165	20,547	5,298	18,619	2,772	13,259
1982	89,566	1,128	3,905	18,781	5,082	20,457	5,341	19,036	2,739	13,097
1983	90,196	952	3,948	18,434	4,954	20,881	5,468	19,694	2,774	13,098
1984	94,461	974	4,345	19,412	5,171	22,134	5,682	20,761	2,807	13,246
1985[2]	97,466	976	4,649	19,382	5,318	23,201	5,909	21,891	2,846	13,294

[1] All figures in thousands (add 000). Excludes farm workers, proprietors, self-employed, domestics.　[2] June 1985 data.

U.S. EMPLOYMENT AND UNEMPLOYMENT: 1900–1985

Source: U.S. Bureau of Labor Statistics

Year	Potential Labor Force [1]	Not in Labor Force [2]	Armed Services	Total Civil Employed	Employed in Agriculture	Employed in Nonfarm jobs	Unemployed	Percent Unemployed
1900	57,950,000	28,877,000	124,000	28,376,000	11,050,000	15,906,000	1,420,000	5.0%
1910	71,580,000	33,413,000	141,000	36,709,000	11,260,000	23,299,000	2,150,000	5.9%
1920	82,739,000	41,125,000	380,000	41,340,000	10,440,000	28,768,000	2,132,000	5.2%
1930	98,723,000	49,893,000	260,000	48,523,000	10,340,000	33,843,000	4,340,000	8.9%
1933	99,150,000	48,019,000	250,000	50,882,000	10,090,000	27,962,000	12,830,000	25.2%
1940	100,147,000	47,136,000	540,000	55,640,000	9,540,000	37,980,000	8,120,000	14.6%
1950	106,164,000	42,787,000	1,169,000	58,918,000	7,160,000	51,758,000	3,288,000	5.2%
1955	111,747,000	44,660,000	2,064,000	62,170,000	6,450,000	55,722,000	2,852,000	4.3%
1960	119,106,000	46,617,000	1,861,000	65,778,000	5,458,000	60,318,000	3,852,000	5.4%
1965	128,459,000	52,058,000	1,946,000	71,088,000	4,361,000	66,726,000	3,366,000	4.4%
1969	136,573,000	53,602,000	2,238,000	77,902,000	3,606,000	74,296,000	2,832,000	3.4%
1970	139,203,000	54,315,000	2,118,000	78,678,000	3,463,000	75,215,000	4,093,000	4.8%
1972	145,939,000	57,091,000	1,813,000	82,153,000	3,484,000	78,669,000	4,882,000	5.5%
1973	148,870,000	57,667,000	1,774,000	85,064,000	3,470,000	81,594,000	4,355,000	4.8%
1974	151,841,000	58,171,000	1,721,000	86,794,000	3,515,000	83,279,000	5,166,000	5.5%
1975	154,831,000	59,377,000	1,678,000	85,845,000	3,408,000	82,438,000	7,929,000	8.3%
1976	157,818,000	59,991,000	1,668,000	88,752,000	3,331,000	85,421,000	7,406,000	7.6%
1977	160,689,000	60,025,000	1,656,000	92,017,000	3,283,000	88,734,000	6,991,000	6.9%
1978	153,541,000	59,659,000	1,631,000	96,048,000	3,387,000	92,661,000	6,202,000	6.0%
1979	166,460,000	59,900,000	1,597,000	98,824,000	3,347,000	95,477,000	6,137,000	5.8%
1980	169,349,000	60,806,000	1,604,000	99,303,000	3,364,000	95,938,000	7,637,000	7.0%
1981	171,775,000	61,460,000	1,645,000	100,397,000	3,368,000	97,030,000	8,723,000	7.5%
1982	173,939,000	62,067,000	1,668,000	99,526,000	3,401,000	96,125,000	10,578,000	9.5%
1983	175,891,000	62,665,000	1,676,000	100,834,000	3,383,000	97,450,000	10,717,000	9.6%
1984	178,080,000	62,839,000	1,697,000	105,005,000	3,321,000	101,685,000	8,539,000	7.5%
1985 [3]	179,798,000	61,524,000	1,702,000	107,819,000	3,138,000	103,232,000	8,753,000	7.5%

[1] Americans 16 years and older not in institutions, such as prisons and mental hospitals. [2] Includes dependent wives and husbands, and full-time students. [3] June 1985 data.

CONSUMER AND PRODUCER PRICE INDEXES: 1955–1985

Source: U.S. Department of Labor, Bureau of Labor Statistics

YEAR	CONSUMER PRICES (1967 = 100) All items		Commodities		Services		PRODUCER PRICES (1967 = 100) All commodities		Farm products, food, and feeds		Industrial commodities	
	Index	Percent change	Index	Percent change	Index	Percent change	Index	Percent change	Index	Percent change	Index	Percent change
1955	80.2	−0.4%	85.1	−0.9%	70.9	2.0%	87.8	0.2%	91.2	−4.7%	86.9	2.2%
1960	88.7	1.6%	91.5	0.9%	83.5	3.3%	94.9	0.1%	93.7	0.2%	95.3	0%
1961	89.6	1.0%	92.0	0.5%	85.2	2.0%	94.5	−0.4%	93.7	0.0%	94.8	−0.5%
1962	90.6	1.1%	92.8	0.9%	86.8	1.9%	94.8	0.3%	94.7	1.1%	94.8	0%
1963	91.7	1.2%	93.6	0.9%	88.5	2.0%	94.5	−0.3%	93.8	−1.0%	94.7	−0.1%
1964	92.9	1.3%	94.6	1.1%	90.2	1.9%	94.7	0.2%	93.2	−0.6%	95.2	0.5%
1965	94.5	1.7%	95.7	1.2%	92.2	2.2%	96.6	2.0%	97.1	4.2%	96.4	1.3%
1966	97.2	2.9%	98.2	2.6%	95.8	3.9%	99.8	3.3%	103.5	6.6%	98.5	2.2%
1967	100.0	2.9%	100.0	1.8%	100.0	4.4%	100.0	0.2%	100.0	−3.4%	100.0	1.5%
1968	104.2	4.2%	103.7	3.7%	105.2	5.2%	102.5	2.5%	102.4	2.4%	102.5	2.5%
1969	109.8	5.4%	108.4	4.5%	112.5	6.9%	106.5	3.9%	108.0	5.5%	106.0	3.4%
1970	116.3	5.9%	113.5	4.7%	121.6	8.1%	110.4	3.7%	111.7	3.4%	110.0	3.8%
1971	121.3	4.3%	117.4	3.4%	128.4	5.6%	114.0	3.3%	113.9	2.0%	114.1	3.7%
1972	125.3	3.3%	120.9	3.0%	133.3	3.8%	119.1	4.5%	122.4	7.5%	117.9	3.3%
1973	133.1	6.2%	129.9	7.4%	139.1	4.4%	134.7	13.1%	159.1	30.0%	125.9	6.8%
1974	147.7	11.0%	145.5	12.0%	152.1	9.3%	160.1	18.9%	177.4	11.5%	153.8	22.2%
1975	161.2	9.1%	158.4	8.9%	166.6	9.5%	174.9	9.2%	184.2	3.8%	171.5	11.5%
1976	170.5	5.8%	165.2	4.3%	180.4	8.3%	182.9	4.6%	183.1	−0.6%	182.3	6.3%
1977	181.5	6.5%	174.7	5.8%	194.3	7.7%	194.2	6.1%	188.8	3.1%	195.1	7.0%
1978	195.3	7.6%	187.1	7.1%	210.9	8.5%	209.3	7.8%	206.6	9.4%	209.4	7.3%
1979	217.7	11.5%	219.4	17.3%	249.3	18.2%	249.7	19.3%	234.6	13.6%	253.1	20.9%
1980	246.8	13.4%	233.9	6.6%	270.3	8.4%	268.8	7.6%	244.7	4.3%	274.8	8.6%
1981	272.3	10.2%	253.6	8.4%	305.7	13.1%	293.4	9.2%	251.5	2.8%	304.1	10.6%
1982	288.6	6.0%	263.8	4.0%	333.3	9.0%	299.3	2.0%	248.9	−1.0%	312.3	2.7%
1983	297.4	3.0%	271.5	2.9%	344.9	3.5%	303.1	1.3%	253.9	2.0%	315.7	1.1%
1984	307.6	3.4%	280.7	3.4%	363.0	5.2%	310.3	2.4%	262.4	3.3%	322.6	2.2%
1985*	318.7	3.6%	286.9	2.2%	381.3	5.0%	309.5	−0.3%	249.1	−5.0%	325.2	0.8%

* Data for June 1985.

WORLD TRADE BY NATIONS: 1970–1984

Source: United Nations

The value of exports and imports rose in 1984 as the world began to recover from economic recession. U.S. exports increased to $217.9 billion and U.S. imports increased to $341.2 billion.

In 1984 the U.S. continued as the leading exporting nation in foreign trade, followed by Japan, West Germany, Britain, France, Soviet Union, Canada, Italy, and Netherlands.

	IMPORTS[1]				EXPORTS[1]			
	1970	1980	1983	1984	1970	1980	1983	1984
WORLD	$328,597	$2,054,047	$1,908,650	$1,995,524	$314,309	$1,999,589	$1,908,650	$1,914,299
Afghanistan ...	112	552	—	—	86	705	—	—
Algeria	1,257	10,544	10,395	—	1,009	15,618	11,116	—
Argentina	1,694	10,541	4,490	—	1,773	8,021	7,836	—
Australia	4,543	20,337	19,393	23,424	4,770	26,393	24,901	27,794
Austria	3,549	24,449	19,364	19,612	2,856	17,493	15,431	15,724
Bahamas	337	5,507	3,230	3,025	90	4,906	2,581	2,383
Bahrain	247	3,484	3,342	—	274	3,598	3,200	—
Bangladesh	—	1,973	1,716	2,042	—	738	690	934
Barbados......	118	522	621	659	40	226	321	391
Belgium-Luxembourg .	11,413	71,874	55,314	55,287	11,600	64,664	51,939	51,690
Bolivia	159	665	532	631	190	1,037	818	773
Brazil	2,849	24,141	16,311	15,210	2,739	20,132	21,899	27,005
Britain	21,689	115,566	100,072	105,616	19,346	110,140	91,711	94,538
Brunei	—	565	728	—	—	4,519	3,386	—
Bulgaria	1,831	9,650	12,283	—	2,004	10,372	12,130	—
Burkina Faso...	49	358	288	—	—	90	57	—
Burma	169	353	268	239	108	471	378	310
Burundi	22	168	194	187	24	65	76	148
Cameroon	242	1,602	1,217	1,106	232	1,384	939	879
Canada	13,360	59,227	61,325	73,933	16,119	65,123	73,797	86,817
Central Africa ..	34	81	—	—	31	115	—	—
Chad.........	61	74	—	—	30	71	—	—
Chile..........	930	5,124	2,754	3,191	1,234	4,671	3,836	3,657
China	2,331	19,550	21,324	28,516	2,260	18,270	22,150	25,760
Colombia	843	4,663	4,968	—	727	3,945	3,081	—
Congo	57	562	806	—	31	911	1,066	—
Costa Rica.....	317	1,524	988	1,121	231	1,002	866	941
Cuba..........	1,311	6,457	7,213	8,144	1,049	5,536	6,407	6,172
Cyprus........	235	1,202	1,219	1,364	108	533	494	575
Czechoslovakia	3,695	15,148	16,325	17,070	3,792	14,891	16,522	17,173
Denmark	4,407	19,742	16,265	16,975	3,356	17,217	16,059	16,334
Dominican Rep.	278	1,498	1,279	—	214	962	785	690
Ecuador.......	274	2,253	1,465	1,717	190	2,481	2,203	2,569
Egypt.........	787	4,860	10,274	—	762	3,046	3,215	—
El Salvador	214	962	892	—	228	1,074	735	—
Ethiopia	172	721	875	942	122	425	403	416
Fiji............	104	562	484	450	68	377	240	256
Finland........	2,636	15,641	12,856	12,443	2,306	14,153	12,519	13,507
France	19,114	135,082	105,395	103,735	17,935	111,114	91,231	93,312
Gambia	18	163	116	—	17	31	48	—
Germany, East .	4,847	19,082	21,524	22,940	4,581	17,312	23,793	24,836
Germany, West.	29,814	188,001	152,899	151,232	34,189	192,930	169,425	169,777
Ghana	411	1,057	2,534	—	458	1,257	2,049	—
Greece	1,958	10,531	9,632	9,434	642	5,142	4,459	4,811
Guatemala.....	284	1,598	1,135	1,277	299	1,520	1,159	876
Guyana	134	396	—	601	133	389	—	91
Haiti	52	354	314	—	41	226	187	—
Honduras	221	1,019	767	—	179	822	692	—
Hungary.......	2,506	9,235	8,503	8,109	2,316	8,677	8,696	8,592
Iceland	157	1,000	816	820	147	931	749	728
India	2,124	14,090	13,234	13,215	2,026	8,378	8,713	8,294
Indonesia	1,002	10,834	16,352	13,882	1,108	23,950	21,146	21,888
Iran..........	1,662	12,250	—	—	2,623	14,160	20,247	13,220
Iraq..........	509	—	—	—	1,100	26,278	9,785	—
Ireland	1,573	10,607	9,189	9,663	1,039	8,399	8,620	9,629
Israel	1,422	7,878	8,370	—	734	5,292	4,894	—

[1] All figures in millions of U.S. dollars (add 000,000).

THE ECONOMY 199

	IMPORTS[1]				EXPORTS[1]			
	1970	1980	1983	1984	1970	1980	1983	1984
Italy	$14,970	$99,639	$80,367	84,215	$13,206	$77,659	$72,681	$73,303
Ivory Coast	388	3,015	1,808	1,340	469	3,124	2,067	—
Jamaica	525	1,171	1,530	1,176	347	963	732	177
Japan	18,881	140,524	126,392	136,492	19,318	129,812	146,668	170,132
Jordan	184	2,394	3,030	2,784	34	573	579	678
Kenya	442	2,588	1,361	—	305	1,389	980	—
Korea, South	1,984	22,292	26,192	30,631	835	17,505	24,445	29,094
Kuwait	625	6,531	—	—	1,901	19,854	11,305	10,568
Lebanon	567	3,813	—	—	198	868	—	—
Liberia	150	534	415	—	213	589	429	—
Libya	554	6,777	—	—	2,366	16,085	11,957	11,076
Madagascar	170	600	387	—	145	402	296	—
Malawi	86	440	311	279	60	285	229	293
Malaysia	1,490	12,139	—	—	1,763	14,345	—	—
Mali	47	440	344	—	33	205	167	—
Malta	161	938	733	—	39	483	363	394
Mauritania	56	286	227	194	89	194	305	294
Mauritius	76	619	440	472	69	431	368	373
Mexico	2,320	19,416	8,201	—	1,282	15,301	21,012	—
Morocco	684	4,185	3,599	—	488	2,403	2,062	—
Mozambique	324	800	635	—	156	281	132	—
Netherlands	13,426	76,618	60,803	62,136	11,774	73,952	64,830	65,874
New Zealand	1,245	5,470	5,333	6,194	1,225	5,418	5,284	5,511
Nicaragua	198	887	799	808	179	450	411	393
Niger	58	594	—	—	32	566	—	—
Nigeria	1,059	15,025	13,440	—	1,239	24,999	11,317	14,125
Norway	3,702	16,928	13,541	13,890	2,457	18,545	18,015	18,920
Oman	18	1,732	2,492	—	495	3,748	4,248	—
Pakistan	1,171	5,350	5,341	5,884	723	2,588	3,074	3,219
Panama	357	1,289	1,412	1,423	106	353	304	256
Papua New Guinea	268	1,023	720	—	103	1,033	654	890
Paraguay	64	517	506	—	64	310	284	—
Peru	619	3,062	2,147	1,870	1,048	3,916	3,027	3,131
Philippines	1,286	8,295	7,980	—	1,142	5,788	5,005	—
Poland	3,608	19,089	9,995	10,324	3,548	16,997	10,951	11,408
Portugal	1,582	9,447	8,259	7,797	949	4,627	4,601	5,184
Qatar	—	1,446	1,456	—	236	5,698	3,384	4,513
Romania	1,960	13,201	9,959	—	1,851	11,401	13,241	—
Rwanda	29	243	279	—	25	76	79	83
Saudi Arabia	692	30,221	39,206	—	2,424	109,111	46,941	46,869
Senegal	193	1,052	1,039	—	152	477	543	—
Sierra Leone	116	414	166	166	101	204	92	148
Singapore	2,461	23,589	28,158	6,836	1,554	19,376	21,833	24,108
Solomons	11	74	61	—	8	73	61	—
Somalia	45	348	—	—	31	133	—	—
South Africa	3,566	18,553	14,528	—	2,151	12,548	9,672	9,334
Soviet Union	11,732	68,522	80,412	80,624	12,800	76,449	91,343	91,649
Spain	4,716	34,081	29,194	28,812	2,388	20,721	19,735	23,544
Sri Lanka	389	2,035	1,787	1,846	342	1,042	1,066	1,449
Sudan	284	1,576	1,354	—	298	543	624	—
Suriname	115	504	446	—	135	514	345	—
Sweden	7,004	33,526	26,120	26,345	6,792	30,969	27,468	29,340
Switzerland	6,486	36,356	29,119	29,474	5,152	29,634	25,595	25,864
Syria	357	4,124	4,542	4,114	203	2,108	1,923	1,854
Tanzania	318	1,226	822	—	259	508	366	—
Thailand	1,299	9,213	9,159	10,235	710	6,505	6,368	7,414
Togo	65	550	284	—	55	335	162	—
Trinidad-Tobago	542	3,194	2,582	—	480	4,085	2,353	1,633
Tunisia	306	3,527	3,117	3,171	182	2,235	1,872	1,793
Turkey	894	7,538	9,348	10,817	588	2,911	5,694	7,098
Uganda	172	293	—	—	282	345	372	399
United Arab Emir.	267	8,752	—	—	550	20,678	14,596	14,103
UNITED STATES	39,756	256,984	269,878	341,177	42,590	220,786	200,538	217,888
Uruguay	231	1,680	788	—	233	1,059	1,045	—
Vanuatu	13	71	63	67	12	35	29	44
Venezuela	1,641	10,671	6,667	6,310	3,197	19,919	15,002	—
Western Samoa	14	63	56	50	5	17	19	20
Yemen, North	32	1,853	—	—	3	779	—	—
Yemen, South	200	652	—	—	135	—	—	—
Yugoslavia	2,874	18,279	11,104	11,996	1,679	10,770	9,038	10,255
Zaire	533	842	498	—	781	1,639	1,134	—
Zambia	477	1,111	690	566	1,001	1,299	831	648
Zimbabwe	329	1,290	1,052	959	367	1,423	1,128	1,088

WORLD PRODUCTION: 1970–1984

Source: United Nations

	1970	1975	1980	1982	1983	1984
POPULATION						
World total	3,610,000,000	4,033,000,000	4,453,000,000	4,607,000,000	4,685,000,000	4,763,000,000
AGRICULTURE						
Barley [1]	139,426,000	153,000,000	159,000,000	162,000,000	168,000,000	173,000,000
Cocoa beans [1] (chocolate)	1,507,000	1,544,000	1,658,000	1,597,000	1,609,000	1,642,000
Corn (maize) [1]	261,548,000	326,000,000	397,000,000	448,000,000	347,000,000	450,000,000
Cotton [1]	11,738,000	12,294,000	13,900,000	14,800,000	14,400,000	17,100,000
Eggs (hen) [1]	21,132,000	23,600,000	26,700,000	29,842,800	28,800,000	29,400,000
Livestock						
Cattle [2]	1,086,955,000	1,194,749,000	1,201,810,000	1,226,432,000	—	—
Hogs [2]	545,565,000	682,899,000	797,957,000	763,813,000	—	—
Horses [2]	64,227,000	66,102,000	65,784,000	65,044,000	—	—
Sheep [2]	1,075,322,000	1,063,316,000	1,117,964,000	1,157,690,000	—	—
Milk [1]	396,054,000	430,000,000	471,000,000	476,000,000	495,000,000	496,000,000
Peanuts [1]	18,300,000	19,300,000	18,400,000	18,500,000	18,600,000	18,300,000
Potatoes [1]	312,134,000	285,000,000	264,000,000	288,000,000	287,000,000	314,000,000
Rice [1]	308,578,000	360,000,000	399,000,000	423,000,000	450,000,000	467,000,000
Tobacco [1]	4,678,000	5,416,000	5,287,000	6,886,000	5,837,000	6,133,000
Wheat [1]	318,319,000	356,000,000	446,000,000	455,000,000	497,000,000	519,000,000
Wool [1]	2,768,000	2,638,000	2,773,000	2,852,000	2,861,000	2,910,000
FISHING						
Total catch [1]	70,000,000	68,600,000	72,300,000	76,800,000	—	—
ENERGY						
Coal [1]	1,774,000,000	1,889,000,000	2,732,000,000	2,829,000,000	2,829,000,000	2,997,000,000
Electricity [3]	4,846,000,000	6,331,000,000	8,228,000,000	8,477,000,000	8,797,000,000	8,976,000,000
Natural gas	2,241,198[4]	11,106,503[4]	13,117,660[4]	54,665[5]	54,451[5]	58,959[5]
Petroleum [1]	2,253,000,000	2,575,000,000	2,975,000,000	2,674,000,000	2,648,000,000	2,716,000,000
FOOD AND BEVERAGES						
Coffee [1]	3,869,000	4,652,000	4,774,000	4,910,000	5,610,000	5,387,000
Flour (wheat) [1]	121,450,000	125,700,000	137,200,000	139,100,000	—	—
Meat [1]	84,567,000	122,800,000	141,000,000	137,000,000	141,000,000	143,000,000
Sugar [1]	72,896,000	81,600,000	84,000,000	102,600,000	97,800,000	99,100,000
Tea [1]	1,078,000	1,547,000	1,853,000	1,954,000	2,087,000	2,213,000
FOREST PRODUCTS						
Natural Rubber [1]	3,100,000	3,315,000	3,845,000	3,755,000	4,025,000	4,200,000
Paper (newsprint) [1]	21,535,000	20,948,000	25,400,000	25,600,000	26,400,000	—
Sawnwood	404,425[6]	404,000[6]	439,000[6]	26,000,000[1]	27,500,000[1]	—
Wood pulp [1]	104,445,000	81,100,000	95,200,000	89,800,000	96,000,000	—
MINERALS AND METALS						
Aluminum [1]	9,445,000	11,856,000	16,653,000	18,581,000	18,642,000	18,740,000
Copper [1]	6,221,000	7,250,000	8,389,000	8,542,000	8,603,000	8,589,000
Iron (pig iron) [1]	439,300,000	456,000,000	527,000,000	465,000,000	495,000,000	504,000,000
Iron ore [1]	424,100,000	483,000,000	743,000,000	695,000,000	675,000,000	689,000,000
Lead [1]	3,146,000	3,150,000	4,729,000	4,781,000	4,788,000	4,737,000
Steel (crude) [1]	576,000,000	615,000,000	703,000,000	626,000,000	665,000,000	678,000,000
Tin [1]	183,600	176,000	227,000	229,000	230,000	237,000
Zinc [1]	4,664,000	4,700,000	5,820,000	5,717,000	5,828,000	5,887,000
MANUFACTURED PRODUCTS						
Automobiles [2]	22,550,000	25,220,000	28,990,000	30,020,000	—	—
Buses and trucks [2]	6,780,000	7,960,000	9,870,000	10,700,000	—	—
Cement [1]	569,000,000	703,000,000	867,000,000	876,000,000	880,000,000	889,000,000
Fertilizer (nitrogenous) [1]	30,200,000	42,500,000	124,900,000	120,800,000	—	—
Ships (merchant) [7]	21,690,000	34,200,000	13,570,000	17,170,000	14,620,000	—

[1] Metric tons [2] Units [3] Megawatts. [4] Tetracalories. [5] Petajoules. [6] Cubic meters. [7] Gross tons launched.

As part of a celebration marking the 350th anniversary of the Boston Latin School, the U.S. Postal Service first displayed on April 26 the design of a commemorative stamp honoring public education. The multicolor stamp, designed by Uldis Purins of Newton, Mass., features an illustration of objects associated with a typical teacher's desk in the early years of public education in the United States. Those items include a quill pen and holder, an apple, a pair of glasses, and a penmanship practice paper.

U.S. Postal Service

HIGHLIGHTS: 1985

The U.S. Supreme Court ruled in 1985 that public school teachers and administrators can conduct searches of students without a warrant if there are "reasonable grounds" for believing the search will find evidence of violation of school rules or public laws.

The Court's 6-3 ruling on Jan. 15 came in

a case in which a Piscataway, N.J., school administrator searched the purse of a 14-year-old student in 1980 and found evidence that indicated the girl was using marijuana. The school's order expelling the student was suspended while the case remained in litigation. The girl already had graduated by the

U.S. ELEMENTARY AND SECONDARY SCHOOL ENROLLMENT: 1955–1993

Source: National Center for Educational Statistics, U.S. Department of Education; U.S. Census Bureau

YEAR [1]	TOTAL PUBLIC AND NONPUBLIC			PUBLIC			PRIVATE [2]		
	K-12	K-8	9-12	K-12	K-8	9-12	K-12	K-8	9-12
1955	35,280,000	27,717,000	7,563,000	30,680,000	23,917,000	6,763,000	4,600,000	3,800,000	800,000
1960	42,181,000	32,492,000	9,689,000	36,281,000	27,692,000	8,589,000	5,900,000	4,800,000	1,100,000
1965	48,473,000	35,463,000	13,010,000	42,173,000	30,563,000	11,610,000	6,300,000	4,900,000	1,400,000
1970	51,272,000	36,629,000	14,643,000	45,909,000	32,577,000	13,332,000	5,363,000	4,052,000	1,311,000
1974	50,028,000	34,596,000	15,432,000	45,053,000	30,921,000	14,132,000	4,975,000	3,675,000	1,300,000
1975	49,834,000	34,211,000	15,623,000	44,791,000	30,487,000	14,304,000	5,043,000	3,724,000	1,319,000
1976	49,484,000	33,831,000	15,653,000	44,317,000	30,006,000	14,311,000	5,167,000	3,825,000	1,342,000
1977	48,716,000	33,133,000	15,583,000	43,577,000	29,336,000	14,240,000	5,140,000	3,797,000	1,343,000
1978	47,636,000	32,060,000	15,576,000	42,550,000	28,328,000	14,223,000	5,085,000	3,732,000	1,353,000
1979	46,679,000	31,585,000	15,094,000	40,984,000	27,665,000	13,319,000	5,100,000	3,700,000	1,360,000
1980	46,318,000	31,666,000	14,652,000	40,987,000	27,674,000	13,313,000	5,330,000	3,992,000	1,339,000
1981	45,600,000	31,345,000	14,255,000	40,099,000	27,245,000	12,855,000	5,550,000	4,100,000	1,400,000
1982	45,252,000	31,356,000	13,896,000	39,652,000	27,156,000	12,496,000	5,600,000	4,200,000	1,400,000
1983 [2]	45,043,000	31,288,000	13,754,000	39,328,000	26,973,000	12,354,000	5,715,000	4,315,000	1,400,000
1984 [2]	44,625,000	30,946,000	13,679,000	38,925,000	26,646,000	12,279,000	5,700,000	4,300,000	1,400,000
1985 [2]	44,677,000	30,936,000	13,741,000	38,977,000	26,636,000	12,341,000	5,700,000	4,300,000	1,400,000
1986 [2]	44,775,000	31,187,000	13,588,000	39,075,000	26,887,000	12,188,000	5,700,000	4,300,000	1,400,000
1987 [2]	44,873,000	31,693,000	13,180,000	39,173,000	27,293,000	11,880,000	5,700,000	4,400,000	1,300,000
1988 [2]	44,944,000	32,183,000	12,761,000	39,244,000	27,783,000	11,461,000	5,700,000	4,400,000	1,300,000
1989 [2]	45,244,000	32,809,000	12,435,000	39,444,000	28,309,000	11,135,000	5,800,000	4,500,000	1,300,000
1990 [2]	45,669,000	35,525,000	12,144,000	39,869,000	28,925,000	10,944,000	5,800,000	4,600,000	1,200,000
1991 [2]	46,341,000	34,157,000	12,184,000	40,441,000	29,457,000	10,984,000	5,900,000	4,700,000	1,200,000
1992 [2]	47,078,000	34,825,000	12,253,000	41,078,000	30,025,000	11,053,000	6,000,000	4,800,000	1,200,000
1993 [2]	47,913,000	35,376,000	12,537,000	41,713,000	30,476,000	11,237,000	6,200,000	4,900,000	1,300,000

HIGHLIGHTS: 1985 *(continued)*

time the Supreme Court ruled in favor of the school.

Associate Justice Byron R. White wrote the majority opinion, which was joined by Chief Justice Warren E. Burger and by Associate Justices Lewis F. Powell Jr., William H. Rehnquist, and Sandra Day O'Connor. Associate Justice Harry A. Blackmun concurred in a separate opinion.

White's majority opinion said in part:

"Under ordinary circumstances, a search of a student by a teacher or other school official will be 'justified at its inception' when there are reasonable grounds for suspecting that the search will turn up evidence that the student has violated or is violating either the law or the rules of the school.

"Such a search will be permissible in its scope when the measures adopted are reasonably related to the objectives of the search and not excessively intrusive in light of the age and sex of the student and the nature of the infraction.

"This standard will, we trust, neither unduly burden the efforts of school authorities to maintain order in their schools nor authorize unrestrained intrusions upon the privacy of schoolchildren. By focusing attention on the question of reasonableness, the standard will spare teachers and school administrators the necessity of schooling themselves in the niceties of probable cause and permit them to regulate their conduct according to the dictates of reason and common sense. At the same time, the reasonableness standard should insure that the interests of students will be invaded no more than is necessary to achieve the legitimate end of preserving order in the schools."

Associate Justices William J. Brennan Jr., John Paul Stevens, and Thurgood Marshall dissented from the Court ruling.

U.S. HIGH SCHOOL GRADUATES: 1869–1994

Source: National Center for Educational Statistics, U.S. Department of Education

YEAR	GRADUATES	YEAR	GRADUATES	YEAR	GRADUATES	YEAR	GRADUATES
1869–70	16,000	1957–58	1,513,000	1970–71	2,937,000	1982–83 [2]	2,890,000
1879–80	23,634	1959–60	1,864,000	1971–72	3,001,000	1983–84 [2]	2,741,000
1889–90	43,731	1960–61	1,971,000	1972–73	3,036,000	1984–85 [2]	2,656,000
1899–1900	94,883	1961–62	1,925,000	1973–74	3,074,000	1985–86 [2]	2,595,000
1909–10	156,429	1962–63	1,950,000	1974–75	3,133,000	1986–87 [2]	2,663,000
1919–20	311,266	1963–64	2,290,000	1975–76	3,148,000	1987–88 [2]	2,739,000
1929–30	666,904	1964–65	2,665,000	1976–77	3,154,000	1988–89 [2]	2,742,000
1939–40	1,221,475	1965–66	2,632,000	1977–78	3,127,000	1989–90 [2]	2,491,000
1949–50	1,199,700	1966–67	2,679,000	1978–79	3,101,000	1990–91 [2]	2,408,000
1951–52	1,196,500	1967–68	2,702,000	1979–80	3,043,000	1991–92 [2]	2,323,000
1953–54	1,276,100	1968–69	2,829,000	1980–81	3,020,000	1992–93 [2]	2,378,000
1955–56	1,421,000	1969–70	2,896,000	1981–82	3,001,000	1993–94 [2]	2,339,000

[1] Fall enrollment. [2] Estimated.

U.S. COLLEGES AND UNIVERSITIES: 1985-1986

Source: Adapted from *College Facts Chart 85-86* by National Beta Club, Box 730, Spartanburg, SC 29304

Information in the following table provides a general guide to attending more than 3,400 specific colleges and universities.

The chart includes information collected by The National Beta Club, founded in 1934, a nonprofit leadership-service organization for secondary school students throughout the U.S. Membership is selected by each school administration from students who demonstrate worthy character, good mentality, creditable achievement, and commendable attitude.

No reference to accreditation is made or implied. Inclusion of an institution does not constitute approval or endorsement of that institution.

Following are explanations of the main column headings in the table:

Name and Address. The schools are grouped by states to make it easier for you to locate them.

Level. Two-year programs—Junior (J); four-year programs—Senior (S); graduate program (G); professional degree program (P); technical (T).

Type. Most colleges are now coordinate or coeducational (C), but some are for women only (W) and some are for men only (M).

Affiliation. Schools supported by taxes are **Public**, **Community (Comm)**, or **State**.

Private schools largely without church support are independent (**Ind**). The listing of a church may indicate indirect support or direct control.

Enrollment and Teachers figures are for the 1984–1985 school year.

Tuition and Fees are the estimated cost for the 1985–1986 school year. For variations, including nonresident costs, consult the institution directly.

Board and Room. These are average costs for housing and food available *on the campus.* A dash (—) means room and board are *not available on the campus* or that the school did not provide this information.

Total Cost. These are average costs for state residents. In most cases the cost does not include laundry or other personal expenses.

NAME	ADDRESS	FOUN-DED	AFFIL-IATION	LEVEL/TYPE	ENROLL-MENT	TEACH-ERS	TUITION & FEES	BOARD & ROOM	TOTAL COST
ALABAMA									
Alabama A.&M. University...	Normal, AL 35762	1875	State	S-G/C	4,111	236	$ 880	$1,710	$ 2,590
Alabama Christian College ..	Montgomery, AL 36193 .	1942	C of Chr	S/C	449	28	$ 3,100	$2,500	$ 5,600
Alabama State University ...	Montgomery, AL 36195 .	1874	State	S-G/C	3,786	239	$ 960	$1,620	$ 2,580
Alexander City St. Jr. College	Alexander City, AL 35010	1965	State	J/C	1,098	42	$ 450	—	$ 450
Athens State College	Athens, AL 35611	1822	State	S/C	1,220	40	$ 900	$1,380	$ 2,280
Auburn University	Auburn, AL 36849	1856	State	S-G/C	18,888	1,579	$ 1,080	$2,300	$ 3,380
At Montgomery	Montgomery, AL 36193 .	1969	State	S-G/C	5,142	188	$ 855	$2,570	$ 3,425
Birmingham School of Law ..	Birmingham, AL 35203..	1915	Independ	P/C	250	25	$ 1,000	—	$ 1,000
Birmingham-Southern College	Birmingham, AL 35254..	1856	Methodist	S/C	1,570	111	$ 5,120	$2,375	$ 7,896
Brewer State Jr. College ...	Fayette, AL 35555	1969	State	J/C	724	40	$ 450	—	$ 450
Chattahoochee Val. Comm. Col.	Phenix City, AL 36867 ..	1973	State	J/C	1,400	42	$ 450	—	$ 450
Comm. College of the Air Force	Maxwell AFB, AL 36112 .	1972	Federal	J/C	219,601	9,345	—	—	—
Concordia College	Selma, AL 36701	1922	Lutheran	J/C	307	16	$ 1,403	$1,271	$ 2,674
Enterprise State Jr. College .	Enterprise, AL 36331 ...	1965	State	J/C	2,076	108	$ 450	—	$ 450
Faulkner State Jr. College ...	Bay Minette, AL 36502 ..	1965	State	J/C	1,710	81	$ 450	$1,665	$ 2,115
Gadsden State Jr. College ..	Gadsden, AL 35999.....	1965	State	J/C	2,990	108	$ 450	$1,395	$ 1,845
Geo. C. Wallace St. Comm. Col.	Dothan, AL 36303	1965	State	J/C	2,885	95	$ 450	—	$ 450
Geo. C. Wallace St. Comm. Col.	Selma, AL 36702	1965	State	J-T/C	1,368	53	$ 600	—	$ 600
Huntingdon College	Montgomery, AL 36194 .	1854	Un. Meth	S/C	774	63	$ 3,450	$2,600	$ 6,050
Jacksonville State University	Jacksonville, AL 36265..	1883	State	S-G/C	6,744	350	$ 800	$1,600	$ 2,250
Jefferson Davis St. Jr. College	Brewton, AL 36427	1965	State	J/C	903	31	$ 450	—	$ 450
Jefferson State Jr. College .	Birmingham, AL 35215..	1963	State	J/C	6,030	294	$ 465	—	$ 465
John C. Calhoun St. Comm. C.	Decatur, AL 35602	1965	State	J/C	5,482	266	$ 450	—	$ 450
Judson College	Marion, AL 36756	1838	Baptist	S/W	409	33	$ 2,895	$2,620	$ 5,515
Lawson State Comm. College	Birmingham, AL 35221..	1949	State	J/C	1,597	82	$ 152	—	$ 152
Livingston University	Livingston, AL 35470 ...	1835	State	S-G/C	1,500	83	$ 1,008	$1,560	$ 2,658
Lurleen B. Wallace St. Jr. Col.	Andalusia, AL 36420 ...	1969	State	J/C	774	27	$ 450	—	$ 450
Marion Military Institute.....	Marion, AL 36756	1842	Independ	J/M	343	32	$ 4,590	$2,500	$ 7,090
Miles College	Birmingham, AL 35208..	1905	CME	S/C	582	42	$ 3,300	$1,850	$ 5,150
Mobile College	Mobile, AL 36613	1961	Baptist	S-G/C	884	65	$ 2,890	$2,275	$ 5,165
Northeast Ala. St. Jr. College	Rainsville, AL 35986	1965	State	J/C	1,003	50	$ 450	—	$ 450
Northwest Ala. St. Jr. College	Phil Campbell, AL 35581	1963	State	J/C	1,086	74	$ 450	—	$ 450
Oakwood College	Huntsville, AL 35896....	1896	7-D Adv	S/C	1,331	104	$ 4,290	$2,295	$ 6,585
Patrick Henry St. Jr. College .	Monroeville, AL 36460 ..	1963	State	J/C	692	24	$ 450	—	$ 450
Samford University.........	Birmingham, AL 35229..	1841	Baptist	S-G/C	4,007	250	$ 3,936	$2,290	$ 6,226
S.D. Bishop St. Jr. College ...	Mobile, AL 36690	1936	State	J/C	1,587	49	$ 450	—	$ 450
Selma University	Selma, AL 36701	1878	Baptist	S/C	351	15	$ 1,330	$1,620	$ 2,950
Shelton State Comm. College	Tuscaloosa, AL 35405 ..	1979	State	J/C	2,500	60	$ 450	—	$ 450
Snead State Jr. College	Boaz, AL 35957	1935	State	J/C	1,114	62	$ 450	$1,350	$ 1,800
Southeastern Bible College ..	Birmingham, AL 35256..	1935	Independ	S-G/C	200	21	$ 2,720	$2,070	$ 4,900
Southern Union St. Jr. College	Wadley, AL 36276	1922	State	J/C	1,801	100	$ 450	$1,470	$ 1,920
Spring Hill College........	Mobile, AL 36608	1830	Catholic	S-G/C	1,045	85	$ 6,000	$2,950	$ 8,950
Stillman College..........	Tuscaloosa, AL 35403 ...	1876	Presby	S/C	730	62	$ 2,450	$2,153	$ 4,603
Talladega College	Talladega, AL 35160	1867	Independ	S/C	524	49	$ 2,967	$2,030	$ 4,997
Troy State University	Troy, AL 36082	1887	State	S-G/C	3,568	175	$ 990	$1,740	$ 2,730
Fort Rucker/Dothan	Dothan, AL 36302	1959	State	S-G/C	1,600	50	$ 900	—	$ 900
Montgomery Branch	Montgomery, AL 36195 .	1965	State	S-G/C	2,000	125	$ 1,260	—	$ 1,260
Tuskegee Institute........	Tuskegee Inst., AL 36088	1881	Independ	S-G/C	3,291	240	$ 3,900	$2,050	$ 5,950
University of Alabama	University, AL 35486	1831	State	S-G/C	15,145	940	$ 1,200	$2,300	$ 3,500
Birmingham	Birmingham, AL 35294..	1966	State	S-G/C	14,200	1,648	$ 1,476	—	$ 1,476
Huntsville...............	Huntsville, AL 35899....	1966	State	S-G/C	5,908	285	$ 1,815	$ 975	$ 2,890
University of Montevallo	Montevallo, AL 35115...	1895	State	S-G/C	2,782	170	$ 1,030	$1,860	$ 2,890
University of North Alabama	Florence, AL 35632	1872	State	S-G/C	5,197	223	$ 1,000	$1,920	$ 2,920
University of South Alabama	Mobile, AL 36609	1963	State	S-G/C	9,342	356	$ 1,485	$1,935	$ 3,420
Walker College	Jasper, AL 35501	1938	Independ	J/C	739	48	$ 1,400	$1,600	$ 3,000

NAME	ADDRESS	FOUN-DED	AFFILI-ATION	LEVEL/TYPE	ENROLL-MENT	TEACH-ERS	TUITION & FEES	BOARD & ROOM	TOTAL COST
ALASKA									
Alaska Bible College	Glennallen, AK 99588 ...	1966	Independ	S/C	75	12	$ 1,800	$3,000	$ 4,800
Alaska Pacific University	Anchorage, AK 99508 ...	1959	Un. Meth	S-G/C	1,200	80	$ 4,220	$3,650	$ 8,230
Sheldon Jackson College	Sitka, AK 99835	1878	Independ	S/C	272	34	$ 3,976	$3,500	$ 7,476
University of Alaska									
Anchorage	Anchorage, AK 99508 ...	1976	State	S-G/C	4,208	156	$ 768	—	$ 768
Anchorage Comm. College	Anchorage, AK 99508 ...	1954	State	J/C	9,656	146	$ 638	—	$ 638
Chukchi Comm. College ...	Kotzebue, AK 99752	1978	State	J/C	132	6	$ 600	—	$ 600
Fairbanks	Fairbanks, AK 99701	1917	State	S-G/C	5,278	240	$ 958	$2,370	$ 3,328
Islands Community College	Sitka, AK 99835	1962	State	J/C	892	6	$ 600	—	$ 600
Juneau.................	Juneau, AK 99801	1978	State	S-G/C	2,315	63	$ 744	$ 810	$ 1,554
Kenai Peninsula Comm. Col.	Soldotna, AK 99669	1964	State	J/C	1,609	28	$ 636	—	$ 636
Ketchikan Community Col.	Ketchikan, AK 99901	1954	State	J/C	731	9	$ 610	—	$ 610
Kodiak Community College	Kodiak, AK 99615	1968	State	J/C	855	5	$ 600	—	$ 600
Kuskokwim Community Col.	Bethel, AK 99559	1972	State	J/C	653	13	$ 630	$ 925	$ 1,555
Matanuska–Susitna Comm. Col.	Palmer, AK 99645	1957	State	J/C	1,257	11	$ 612	—	$ 612
Northwest Community Col.	Nome, AK 99762	1975	State	J/C	302	4	$ 600	—	$ 600
Prince William Sound Comm.	Valdez, AK 99686	1978	State	J/C	694	7	$ 620	—	$ 620
Rural Education	Anchorage, AK 99503...	1975	State	J/C	1,660	2	$ 450	—	$ 450
Tanana Valley Comm. College	Fairbanks, AK 99701 ...	1974	State	J/C	2,192	20	$ 838	—	$ 838
ARIZONA									
American Grad. Sch. Int. Man.	Glendale, AZ 85306	1946	Independ	G/C	1,082	95	$ 6,475	$2,975	$ 9,450
American Indian Bible College	Phoenix, AZ 85021	1957	A of God	S/C	70	8	$ 1,584	$1,726	$ 3,310
Arizona State University	Tempe, AZ 85287	1885	S-G/C		40,563	2,379	$ 950	$2,135	$ 3,103
Arizona Western College	Yuma, AZ 85364	1961	State	J/C	3,718	220	$ 384	$2,040	$ 2,424
Central Arizona College	Coolidge, AZ 85228	1967	State	J/C	3,477	211	$ 450	$1,920	$ 2,370
Cochise College	Douglas, AZ 85607	1962	State	J/C	4,194	286	$ 384	$1,928	$ 2,312
College of Ganado	Ganado, AZ 86505	1970	Independ	J/C	266	18	$ 1,164	$3,458	$ 4,622
Devry Inst. of Technology ...	Phoenix, AZ 85016	1967	Independ	S/C	3,851	82	$ 3,658	—	$ 3,658
Eastern Arizona College	Thatcher, AZ 85552	1888	State	J/C	3,403	248	$ 416	$2,175	$ 2,591
Embry-Riddle Aeronautical Univ.	Prescott, AZ 86301	1926	Independ	S/C	917	55	$ 3,750	$2,500	$ 6,250
Grand Canyon College	Phoenix, AZ 85061	1949	Baptist	S/C	1,380	60	$ 2,500	$2,000	$ 4,500
Jan Hus University	Scottsdale, AZ 85251 ...	1972	Independ	P/C	—	—	$ 3,000	$2,000	$ 5,000
Maricopa County Comm. Col.	Phoenix, AZ 85001	1920	County	J/C					
Glendale Comm. College ..	Glendale, AZ 85301	1965	County	J/C	13,013	494	$ 336	—	$ 336
Maricopa Tech. Comm. Col.	Phoenix, AZ 85034	1968	County	J/C	2,877	164	$ 336	—	$ 336
Mesa Comm. College	Mesa, AZ 85202	1965	County	J/C	14,915	692	$ 336	—	$ 336
Phoenix College	Phoenix, AZ 85013	1920	County	J/C	11,798	467	$ 336	—	$ 336
Rio Salado Comm. College .	Phoenix, AZ 85003	1978	County	J/C	12,501	636	$ 336	—	$ 336
Scottsdale Comm. College .	Scottsdale, AZ 85253 ...	1967	County	J/C	7,324	296	$ 336	—	$ 336
South Mountain Comm. Col.	Phoenix, AZ 85040	1980	County	J/C	1,154	110	$ 336	—	$ 336
Mohave Comm. College	Kingman, AZ 86401	1970	State	J/C	3,211	315	$ 290	—	$ 290
Navajo Community College ..	Tsaile, AZ 86556	1968	Private	J/C	1,801	235	$ 730	$2,320	$ 3,610
Northern Arizona University .	Flagstaff, AZ 86011	1899	State	S-G/C	11,826	489	$ 950	$1,960	$ 4,560
Northland Pioneer College ..	Holbrook, AZ 86025	1973	State	J/C	4,535	285	$ 120	—	$ 120
Ottawa University	Phoenix, AZ 85015	1977	Baptist	S/C	565	45	$ 1,920	—	$ 1,920
Pima Community College	Tucson, AZ 85702	1967	State	J/C	20,882	968	$ 408	—	$ 408
Prescott College	Prescott, AZ 86301	1966	Private	S/C	187	20	$ 3,700	—	$ 3,700
Southwestern College	Phoenix, AZ 85032	1960	Baptist	S/C	147	16	$ 2,840	$2,200	$ 5,040
University of Arizona	Tucson, AZ 85721	1885	State	S-G/C	30,306	1,652	$ 990	$2,400	$ 3,390
University of Phoenix	Phoenix, AZ 85004	1978	Independ	S-G/C	2,400	380	$ 3,450	—	$ 3,450
Western International Univ...	Phoenix, AZ 85021	1978	Independ	S-G/C	884	49	$ 3,420	—	$ 3,420
Yavapai College	Prescott, AZ 86301	1970	State	J/C	5,290	372	$ 550	$1,900	$ 2,450
ARKANSAS									
Arkansas Baptist College	Little Rock, AR 72202 ...	1884	Baptist	S/C	175	21	$ 1,350	$ 900	$ 2,250
Arkansas College	Batesville, AR 72501 ...	1872	Presby	S/C	724	60	$ 4,100	$2,000	$ 6,100
Arkansas State University ...	State Univ., AR 72467 ...	1909	State	S-G/C	8,319	335	$ 790	$1,850	$ 2,640
Beebe Campus...........	Beebe, AR 72012	1927	State	J/C	754	29	$ 300	$ 635	$ 935
Arkansas Tech University ...	Russellville, AR 72801 ...	1909	State	S-G/C	3,575	170	$ 840	$1,736	$ 2,576
Central Baptist College	Conway, AR 72032	1952	Baptist	S-G/C	238	18	$ 1,000	$1,280	$ 2,280
College of the Ozarks	Clarksville, AR 72830 ...	1834	Presby	S/C	723	46	$ 1,870	$1,610	$ 3,480
Crowley's Ridge College	Paragould, AR 72450 ...	1964	C of Chr	J/C	111	13	$ 2,230	$1,768	$ 1,998
East Arkansas Comm. College	Forrest City, AR 72335 ..	1974	State	J/C	1,266	46	$ 288	—	$ 3,600
Garland County Comm. College	Hot Springs, AR 71913..	1973	State	J/C	1,536	38	$ 504	—	$ 504
Harding University	Searcy, AR 72143	1924	C of Chr	S-G/C	2,828	180	$ 3,087	$2,126	$ 5,213
Henderson State University..	Arkadelphia, AR 71923..	1890	State	S-G/C	2,625	145	$ 830	$1,500	$ 2,300
Hendrix College	Conway, AR 72032	1884	Un. Meth	S/C	975	68	$ 4,299	$1,965	$ 6,264
John Brown University	Siloam Springs, AR 72761	1919	Independ	S/C	831	55	$ 3,200	$2,400	$ 5,600
Mississippi County Comm. Col.	Blytheville, AR 72315 ...	1975	State	J/C	1,214	61	$ 630	—	$ 630
North Arkansas Comm. College	Pioneer Ridge, AR 72601	1974	State	J/C	939	50	$ 600	$1,800	$ 2,400
Ouachita Baptist University ..	Arkadelphia, AR 71923..	1886	Baptist	S-G/C	1,401	98	$ 3,100	$1,700	$ 4,900
Philander Smith College	Little Rock, AR 72202 ...	1877	Un. Meth	S/C	505	44	$ 1,587	$2,000	$ 3,587
Phillips County Comm. College	Helena, AR 72342	1965	State	J/C	1,476	89	$ 464	—	$ 464
Shorter College	N. Little Rock, AR 72114	1886	AME	J/C	78	7	$ 1,400	$1,890	$ 3,290
Southern Arkansas University	Magnolia, AR 71753	1909	State	S-G/C	2,165	140	$ 790	$1,580	$ 2,370
El Dorado Campus	El Dorado, AR 71730. ...	1975	State	J/C	640	40	$ 600	—	$ 600
Tech-Camden	East Camden, AR 71701	1967	State	J/C	683	60	$ 600	$1,575	$ 2,175
Southern Baptist College	Walnut Ridge, AR 72476	1941	Baptist	S/C	477	30	$ 2,368	$1,644	$ 4,012
University of Arkansas	Fayetteville, AR 72701 ..	1871	State	S-G/C	13,982	812	$ 900	$2,000	$ 2,900
Little Rock	Little Rock, AR 72204 ...	1927	State	S-G/C	10,236	450	$ 900	—	$ 900
Medical Sciences Campus .	Little Rock, AR 72205 ...	1879	State	P/C	1,365	428	$ 2,130	$2,200	$ 4,330
Monticello..............	Monticello, AR 71655 ...	1909	State	S/C	1,921	98	$ 850	$1,600	$ 2,450
Pine Bluff	Pine Bluff, AR 71601 ...	1873	State	S/C	2,605	146	$ 820	$1,670	$ 2,490

NAME	ADDRESS	FOUN-DED	AFFILI-ATION	LEVEL/TYPE	ENROLL-MENT	TEACH-ERS	TUITION & FEES	BOARD & ROOM	TOTAL COST
ARKANSAS *(continued)*									
University of Central Arkansas	Conway, AR 72032	1907	State	S-G/C	6,241	293	$ 720	$1,688	$ 2,408
Westark Community College .	Fort Smith, AR 72913 ...	1928	State	J/C	3,709	99	$ 522	—	$ 522
CALIFORNIA									
Allan Hancock College	Santa Maria, CA 93454..	1920	Public	J/C	6,672	108	$ 140	—	$ 140
Ambassador College........	Pasadena, CA 91129	1947	C of God	S/C	635	58	$ 1,500	$2,300	$ 3,800
American College of Law	Anaheim, CA 92805	1972	Independ	G/C	90	22	$ 3,000	—	$ 3,000
American River College	Sacramento, CA 95841 ..	1955	State	J/C	19,451	527	$ 50	$3,120	$ 3,170
Anaheim Christian College ..	Anaheim, CA 92802	1980	Independ	S/C	60	7	$ 2,000	—	$ 2,000
Antelope Valley Comm. Col.	Lancaster, CA 93534	1929	Public	J/C	6,894	265	$ 100	—	$ 100
Antioch University West									
Los Angeles	Venice, CA 90291	1852	Independ	S-G/C	367	16	$ 4,650	—	$ 4,650
San Francisco	San Francisco, CA 94108	1852	Independ	S-G/C	300	16	$ 4,650	—	$ 4,650
Santa Barbara	Santa Barbara, CA 93101	1852	Independ	S-G/C	77	5	$ 4,650	—	$ 4,650
Armstrong College	Berkeley, CA 94704	1918	Independ	S-G/C	466	42	$ 2,500	—	$ 2,500
Art Center Col. of Design	Pasadena, CA 91103....	1930	Independ	S/C	1,180	168	$ 5,500	—	$ 5,500
Azusa Pacific College	Azusa, CA 91702	1899	Independ	S-G/C	2,100	150	$ 5,600	$2,700	$ 8,300
Bakersfield College	Bakersfield, CA 93305 ..	1913	Public	J/C	10,270	448	$ 2,219	$2,200	$ 4,419
Barstow College...........	Barstow, CA 92311	1959	State	J/C	1,428	75	$ 100	—	$ 100
Berean Bible College.......	San Diego, CA 92105 ...	1970	Independ	T/C	100	18	$ 990	—	$ 990
Bethany Bible College......	Santa Cruz, CA 95066 ..	1919	A of God	S/C	500	47	$ 3,686	$2,283	$ 5,969
Biola University	La Mirada, CA 90639 ...	1908	Independ	S-G/C	3,025	253	$ 5,308	$2,874	$ 8,192
Brooks College...........	Long Beach, CA 90804 ..	1970	Independ	J/C	854	74	$ 4,380	$3,180	$ 7,560
Brooks Institute	Santa Barbara, CA 93108	1946	Independ	S-G/C	733	28	$ 5,250	—	$ 5,250
Butte College	Oroville, CA 95965	1967	State	J/C	9,000	117	$ 47	—	$ 47
Cabrillo College	Aptos, CA 95003	1959	State	J/C	9,953	184	$ 142	—	$ 142
California Baptist College ...	Riverside, CA 92504	1950	Baptist	S-G/C	597	63	$ 4,174	$2,600	$ 7,412
California Christian College .	Fresno, CA 93703	1955	Baptist	S/C	30	6	$ 1,200	$1,600	$ 2,800
California Coast University ..	Santa Ana, CA 92701 ...	1973	Independ	S-G/C	5,000	—	$ 3,000	—	$ 3,000
Calif. Col. of Arts & Crafts..	Oakland, CA 94618	1907	Private	S-G	1,038	130	$ 5,990	$3,750	$ 9,740
California Col. of Commerce .	Long Beach, CA 90813 ..	1921	Independ	S-G/C	150	10	$ 1,650	—	$ 1,650
Calif. Col. of Podiatric Med...	San Francisco, CA 94115	1912	Independ	G/C	399	55	$11,200	—	$11,200
Calif. Graduate Institute ..	Los Angeles, CA 90024..	1968	Independ	G/C	450	75	$ 3,500	—	$ 3,500
Calif. Inst. of the Arts	Valencia, CA 91355	1961	Independ	S/C	843	179	$ 7,303	$3,635	$10,938
California Institute of Tech...	Pasadena, CA 91125.....	1891	Independ	S-G/C	1,765	332	$ 9,900	$2,700	$12,600
Calif. International University	Los Angeles, CA 90017..	1974	Independ	S-G/C	200	12	$ 2,430	—	$ 2,430
Calif. Lutheran College	Thousand Oaks, CA 91359	1959	Lutheran	S-G/C	2,370	232	$ 6,200	$2,700	$ 8,900
Calif. Maritime Academy ...	Vallejo, CA 94590	1929	State	S/C	456	26	$ 1,008	$3,379	$ 4,387
Calif. Missionary Baptist Inst.	Bellflower, CA 90706 ...	1957	Baptist	G/C	44	13	$ 500	$ 500	$ 250
Calif. Polytechnic State Univ.	San Luis Obispo, CA 93407	1901	State	S-G/C	15,967	950	$ 696	$3,138	$ 3,834
California School of Professional Psychology	Berkeley, CA 94704	1970	Independ	G/C	242	82	$ 7,960	$4,880	$12,848
Calif. Sch. of Prof. Psychology	Fresno, CA 93721	1973	Independ	G/C	145	33	$ 7,960	$4,760	$12,720
Calif. Sch. of Prof. Psychology	Los Angeles, CA 90057..	1970	Independ	G/C	265	78	$ 7,960	$5,070	$13,030
Calif. Sch. of Prof. Psychology	San Diego, CA 92121 ...	1972	Independ	G/C	320	89	$ 7,960	$6,310	$14,270
Calif. State College									
Bakersfield	Bakersfield, CA 93311 ...	1965	State	S-G/C	3,613	167	$ 615	$2,900	$ 3,515
Stanislaus	Turlock, CA 95380	1957	State	S-G/C	4,184	288	$ 679	$2,670	$ 3,349
California State Polytechnic University	Pomona, CA 91768	1938	State	S-G/C	17,024	1,062	$ 642	$2,970	$ 3,612
California State University									
Chico	Chico, CA 95929	1887	State	S-G/C	14,196	877	$ 708	$2,484	$ 3,192
Dominguez Hills..........	Carson, CA 90747	1960	State	S-G/C	7,927	489	$ 650	$2,800	$ 3,450
Fresno	Fresno, CA 93740	1911	State	S-G/C	16,293	1,048	$ 716	$2,466	$ 3,182
Fullerton	Fullerton, CA 92634	1959	State	S-G/C	23,399	1,388	$ 694	—	$ 694
Hayward	Hayward, CA 94542	1967	State	S-G/C	11,978	625	$ 670	—	$ 670
Long Beach	Long Beach, CA 90840 ..	1949	State	S-G/C	32,034	1,686	$ 700	$3,200	$ 3,900
Los Angeles.............	Los Angeles, CA 90032..	1947	State	S-G/C	20,000	1,300	$ 184	—	$ 184
Northridge	Northridge, CA 91330....	1958	State	S-G/C	27,736	1,597	$ 703	—	$ 703
Sacramento	Sacramento, CA 95819 ..	1947	State	S-G/C	21,671	1,225	$ 671	$2,601	$ 3,272
San Bernadino	San Bernadino, Calif. 95819	1947	State	S-G/C	22,483	1,261	$ 650	$2,756	$ 3,406
Canada College	Redwood City, CA 94061	1968	State	J/C	7,195	226	$ 100	—	$ 100
Casa Loma College	Lake View Terrace, CA 91342	1966	Independ	V/C	98	7	$ 5,450	—	$ 5,450
Center for Early Education ..	Los Angeles, CA 90048..	1939	Independ	S/C	35	11	$ 2,640	—	$ 2,640
Cerritos College	Norwalk, CA 90650	1956	State	J/C	18,485	246	$ 350	—	$ 350
Cerro Coso Comm. College .	Ridgecrest, CA 93555...	1973	State	J/C	3,299	196	$ 75	—	$ 75
Chabot College	Hayward, CA 94545	1961	Public	J/C	18,755	735	$ 137	—	$ 137
Chaffey College	Alta Loma, CA 91701	1883	State	J/C	10,500	315	$ 102	—	$ 102
Chapman College	Orange, CA 92666	1861	D of Chr	S-G/C	1,900	179	$ 7,200	$3,250	$10,450
Christian Heritage College ..	El Cajon, CA 92021	1970	Baptist	S/C	445	18	$ 3,770	$2,210	$ 5,980
Christian Life College	Stockton, CA 95205	1953	Un Pent	P/C	202	20	$ 1,400	$2,000	$ 3,400
Church Div. Sch. of Pacific .	Berkeley, CA 94709	1893	Episcopal	G/C	97	16	$ 3,700	$3,300	$ 7,000
Citrus Belt Law School	Riverside, CA 92506	1971	Independ	P/C	160	15	$ 2,160	—	$ 2,160
Citrus College	Glendora, CA 91740	1915	State	J/C	8,936	373	$ 125	—	$ 125
City College of San Francisco	San Francisco, CA 94112	1935	State	J/C	23,000	1,022	$ 50	—	$ 50
City Univ. Los Angeles	Los Angeles, CA 90017..	1974	Independ	S-G/C	400	—	$ 3,350	$2,350	$ 5,700
City Univ. School of Law....	Los Angeles, CA 90017..	1976	Independ	P/C	135	—	$ 1,900	—	$ 1,900
Claremont Graduate School .	Claremont, CA 91711 ...	1925	Independ	G/C	1,775	80	$ 7,380	—	$ 7,380
Claremont McKenna College .	Claremont, CA 91711 ...	1946	Independ	S/C	830	105	$ 9,300	$3,565	$12,865
Cleveland Chiropractic College	Los Angeles, CA 90004..	1908	Independ	P/C	408	42	$ 7,200	—	$ 7,200
Coast. School of Deep Sea Diving, Inc.	Oakland, CA 94601	1950	Independ	T/C	280	6	$ 1,595	$1,500	$ 3,095
Cogswell College	Cupertino, CA 95104 ..	1887	Independ	S/C	292	21	$ 5,000	—	$ 5,000
Coleman College	La Mesa, CA 92041	1963	Independ	S-G/C	940	62	$ 5,900	—	$ 5,900

NAME	ADDRESS	FOUN-DED	AFFILI-ATION	LEVEL/TYPE	ENROLL-MENT	TEACH-ERS	TUITION & FEES	BOARD & ROOM	TOTAL COST
CALIFORNIA *(continued)*									
College of Alameda	Alameda, CA 94501	1970	State	J/C	5,728	171	$ 100	—	$ 100
College of the Canyons	Valencia, CA 91355	1969	State	J/C	3,584	105	$ 120	—	$ 120
College of the Desert	Palm Desert, CA 92260	1958	State	J/C	9,687	342	$ 100	—	$ 100
College of Marin	Kentfield, CA 94904	1926	Public	J/C	8,086	253	$ 100	—	$ 100
College of Notre Dame	Belmont, CA 94002	1851	Catholic	S-G/C	1,051	85	$ 5,830	$3,300	$ 8,600
College of the Redwoods	Eureka, CA 95501	1964	State	J/C	6,214	494	$ 100	$2,960	$ 3,060
College of San Mateo	San Mateo, CA 94402	1922	State	J/C	12,836	407	$ 100	—	$ 100
College of the Sequoias	Visalia, CA 93277	1925	State	J/C	7,200	139	$ 100	$2,450	$ 2550
College of the Siskiyous	Weed, CA 96094	1957	State	J/C	2,984	144	$ 100	$2,550	$ 2,650
Columbia College	Columbia, CA 95310	1968	State	J/C	2,736	35	$ 100	—	$ 100
Columbia College-Hollywood	Hollywood, CA 90038	1952	Independ	J-S/C	350	38	$ 3,000	—	$ 3,000
Columbia Pacific University	San Rafael, CA 94901	1978	Independ	S-G/C	4,000	400	$ 3,500	—	$ 3,500
Common College	Woodside, CA 94062	1971	Independ	S/C	5	10	$ 4,000	—	$ 4,000
Compton Community College	Compton, CA 90221	1927	Public	J/C	3,439	171	$ 75	—	$ 75
Contra Costa College	San Pablo, CA 94806	1950	Public	J/C	6,973	250	$ 100	—	$ 100
Cosumnes River College	Sacramento, CA 95823	1970	Public	J/C	5,400	177	$ 100	—	$ 100
Crafton Hills College	Yucaipa, CA 92399	1972	Public	J/C	3,245	49	$ 100	—	$ 100
Cuesta College	San Luis Obispo, CA 93403	1965	State	J/C	5,893	185	$ 100	$ 200	$ 300
Cuyamaca College	El Cajon, CA 92020	1978	State	J/C	2,330	93	$ 100	—	$ 100
Cypress College	Cypress, CA 90630	1966	State	J/C	12,893	181	$ 100	—	$ 100
De Anza College	Cupertino, CA 95014	1967	Public	T/C	26,262	729	$ 118	—	$ 118
Deep Springs College	Deep Springs, CA 89010	1917	Independ	J/M	20	7	—	—	—
Devry Institute Tech	City of Indust, CA 91744	1983	Independ	S/C	1,680	—	$ 3,658	—	$ 3,658
Diablo Valley College	Pleasant Hill, CA 94523	1949	District	J/C	15,043	587	$ 100	—	$ 100
Dominican Col. of San Rafael	San Rafael, CA 94901	1890	Catholic	S-G/C	725	141	$ 6,300	$3,850	$10,150
Dominican School of Philosophy and Theology	Berkeley, CA 94709	1932	Catholic	S-G/C	118	18	$ 3,000	—	$ 3,000
Don Bosco Technical Institute	Rosemead, CA 91770	1969	Catholic	J/M	287	40	$ 2,000	—	$ 2,000
D-Q University	Davis, CA 95617	1970	Independ	J/C	209	20	$ 3,030	$3,343	$ 6,373
East Los Angeles College	Monterey Park, CA 91754	1945	State	J/C	20,534	624	—	—	—
El Camino College	Torrance, CA 90506	1947	Public	J/C	25,434	716	$ 100	—	$ 100
Empire College	Santa Rosa, CA 95401	1959	Independ	P/C	210	9	$ 4,000	—	$ 4,000
Empire College Sch. of Law	Santa Rosa, CA 95401	1959	Independ	P/C	111	24	$ 2,280	—	$ 2,280
Ernest Holmes College School of Ministry	Los Angeles, CA 90020	1972	Church	P/C	60	17	$ 2,700	—	$ 3,000
Eubanks Cons. of Music & Arts	Los Angeles, CA 90043	1951	Independ	S-G/C	400	32	$ 2,100	—	$ 2,100
Evergreen Valley College	San Jose, CA 95135	1975	State	J/C	10,147	400	$ 10	—	$ 10
Feather River College	Quincy, CA 95971	1968	State	J/C	1,550	60	$ 150	$3,500	$ 4,000
Fielding Institute	Santa Barbara, CA 93105	1974	Independ	G/C	458	38	$ 5,220	—	$ 5,940
Foot Hills College	Los Altos Hills, CA 94022	1958	State	J/C	13,798	450	$ 100	—	$ 100
Fresno City College	Fresno, CA 93741	1910	State	J/C	13,576	452	$ 50	—	$ 50
Fresno Pacific College	Fresno, CA 93702	1944	Church	S-G/C	1,025	40	$ 5,000	$2,600	$ 7,600
Fuller Theological Seminary	Pasadena, CA 91101	1947	Independ	G/C	2,900	196	$ 4,500	$5,000	$ 9,500
Fullerton College	Fullerton, CA 92634	1913	State	J/C	16,652	616	$ 100	—	$ 100
Gavilan College	Gilroy, CA 95020	1919	State	J/C	2,805	71	$ 112	—	$ 112
Glendale College	Glendale, CA 91208	1927	State	J/C	11,294	463	$ 100	—	$ 100
Glendale Univ. Col. of Law	Glendale, CA 91206	1967	Independ	P/C	113	15	$ 4,800	—	$ 4,800
Gold. Gate Bapt. Theol. Sem.	Mill Valley, CA 94941	1944	Baptist	G/C	670	33	$ 750	$3,250	$ 4,000
Golden Gate University	San Francisco, CA 94105	1901	Independ	S-G/C	10,500	850	$ 3,328	—	$ 3,328
Golden State University	San Diego, CA 92101	1977	Independ	S-G/C	3,497	371	$ 2,940	—	$ 2,940
Grace Bible Institute	Long Beach, CA 90807	1974	Church	S/C	212	23	$ 4,725	—	$ 4,725
Grace Graduate School	Long Beach, CA 90807	1974	Church	G/C	84	17	$ 8,100	—	$ 8,100
Graduate Theol. Union	Berkeley, CA 94709	1962	Independ	G/C	324	125	$ 5,900	—	$ 5,900
Grantham Col. of Engineering	Los Angeles, CA 90034	1951	Independ	P/C	715	—	—	—	—
Grossmont College	El Cajon, CA 92020	1961	Public	J/C	14,590	420	$ 150	—	$ 150
Hartnell College	Salinas, CA 93901	1920	State	J/C	6,471	215	$ 100	—	$ 100
Harvey Mudd College	Kingston Hall, CA 91711	1955	Independ	S-G/C	522	65	$ 9,500	$4,110	$13,610
Hebrew Union College	Los Angeles, CA 90007	1875	Jewish	G/C	74	27	$ 4,900	—	$ 4,900
Holy Names College	Oakland, CA 94619	1868	Catholic	S-G/C	655	91	$ 5,720	$3,000	$ 8,720
Humboldt State University	Arcata, CA 95221	1913	State	S-G/C	6,113	502	$ 681	$2,930	$ 3,611
Humphreys College	Stockton, CA 95207	1896	Independ	S/C	400	45	$ 2,394	$2,700	$ 2,394
Humphreys Col. School of Law	Fresno, CA 93721	1896	Independ	P/C	17	8	$ 1,950	—	$ 1,950
Imperial Valley College	Imperial, CA 92251	1922	State	J/C	3,370	192	$ 120	—	$ 120
Indian Valley College	Novato, CA 94947	1971	Public	J/C	3,500	67	—	—	—
Inst. of Buddhist Studies	Berkeley, CA 94704	1966	Buddhist	G/C	7	8	$ 2,400	—	$ 2,400
International College	Los Angeles, CA 90024	1970	Independ	S-G/C	605	175	$ 4,600	—	$ 4,600
Jesuit School of Theology	Berkeley, CA 94709	1934	Catholic	P/C	211	27	$ 3,600	—	$ 3,600
John F. Kennedy University	Orinda, CA 94563	1964	Independ	P/C	1,894	200	$ 3,100	$6,000	$ 9,100
Kings River Comm. College	Reedley, CA 93654	1926	State	J/C	3,254	149	$ 100	$2,000	$ 2,100
Lake Tahoe Comm. College	Lake Tahoe, CA 95702	1974	Public	J/C	1,800	78	$ 100	—	$ 100
Laney College	Oakland, CA 94607	1953	State	J/C	9,882	351	$ 50	—	$ 50
Lassen College	Susanville, CA 96130	1925	State	J/C	2,600	160	$ 100	$2,600	$ 2,700
Laurence University	Santa Barbara, CA 93101	1973	Independ	G/C	105	15	$ 2,250	—	$ 4,950
L.I.F.E. Bible College	Los Angeles, CA 90026	1925	4 Square	S/C	453	28	$ 2,178	$2,025	$ 4,203
Lincoln University	San Francisco, CA 94118	1919	Independ	S-G/C	400	58	$ 2,970	—	$ 2,970
Linda Vista Bapt. Bible College	El Cajon, CA 92021	1946	Ind. Bapt.	S-G/C	85	9	$ 1,630	$1,575	$ 3,205
Living Word Bible College	Pasadena, CA 91107	1971	Gospel	S/C	50	10	$ 1,245	—	$ 1,245
Loma Linda University	Loma Linda, CA 92350	1905	7-D Adv	S-G/C	4,610	—	$ 6,150	$2,616	$ 8,766
Long Beach City College	Long Beach, CA 90808	1927	Public	J/C	22,340	900	$ 100	—	$ 100
Los Angeles Baptist College	Newhall, CA 91321	1927	Baptist	S/C	308	48	$ 4,260	$2,750	$ 7,010
Los Angeles City College	Los Angeles, CA 90029	1929	Public	J/C	17,000	750	$ 100	—	$ 100
Los Ang. Col. of Chiropractic	Whittier, CA 90609	1911	Independ	P/C	708	48	$ 6,150	—	$ 6,150
Los Angeles Cultural Center	Los Angeles, CA 90006	1966	Independ	P/C	350	35	$ 1,575	—	$ 1,575

NAME	ADDRESS	FOUN-DED	AFFILI-ATION	LEVEL/TYPE	ENROLL-MENT	TEACH-ERS	TUITION & FEES	BOARD & ROOM	TOTAL COST
CALIFORNIA (continued)									
Los Angeles Harbor College .	Wilmington, CA 90744 ..	1949	Public	J/C	9,558	317	$ 100	—	$ 100
Los Angeles Pierce College ..	Woodland Hills, CA 91371	1947	State	J/C	21,260	583	$ 100	—	$ 100
Los Angeles Southwest College	Los Angeles, CA 90047..	1967	State	J/C	4,400	96	$ 150	—	$ 150
Los Angeles Trade-Tech. Col.	Los Angeles, CA 90015..	1925	Public	J/C	12,577	639	$ 100	—	$ 100
Los Angeles Valley College ..	Van Nuys, CA 91401	1949	State	J/C	18,500	550	$ 100	—	$ 100
Los Medanos College	Pittsburg, CA 94565 ...	1973	Public	J/C	6,000	200	$ 25	—	$ 300
Loyola Marymount University	Los Angeles, CA 90045..	1911	Catholic	S-G/C	5,138	226	$ 6,625	$2,930	$ 9,555
Magna Carta University	San Francisco, CA 94080	1974	Independ	P/C	65	6	$ 1,000	$4,800	$ 5,800
Marymount Palos Verdes College ...	Rancho Palos Verdes, CA 90274	1933	Catholic	J/C	755	62	$ 5,100	$4,320	$ 9,420
Melodyland School of Theology	Anaheim, CA 92802	1971	Independ	G/C	10	4	$ 2,500	$3,402	$ 5,902
Mendocino College	Ukiah, CA 95482	1972	State	J/C	3,149	216	$ 100	$3,402	$ 3,502
Menlo College	Atherton, CA 94025 ...	1927	Independ	J-S/C	645	63	$ 8,030	$4,320	$12,350
Mennonite Brethren Biblical Seminary	Fresno, CA 93727	1955	Mennon	G-P/C	161	20	$ 2,752	—	$ 2,752
Merced College	Merced, CA 95348......	1962	Public	J/C	6,119	325	$ 138	—	$ 138
Merritt College...........	Oakland, CA 94602	1954	State	J/C	6,800	125	$ 100	—	$ 100
Mills College.............	Oakland, CA 94613	1852	Independ	S-G/W	938	146	$ 8,400	$4,100	$12,500
Miracosta College	Oceanside, CA 92056 ..	1934	State	J/C	10,845	235	$ 116	—	$ 116
Modesto Junior College	Modesto, CA 95350.....	1921	State	J/C	11,033	302	$ 100	—	$ 100
Monterey Institute of International Studies	Monterey, CA 93940 ...	1955	Independ	S-G/C	473	75	$ 6,250	$3,600	$ 9,850
Monterey Peninsula College .	Monterey, CA 93940 ...	1947	State	J/C	5,585	306	$ 120	—	$ 120
Moorpark College	Moorpark, CA 93021 ...	1967	State	J/C	9,300	125	$ 150	—	$ 150
Mount St. Mary's College ...	Los Angeles, CA 90049..	1925	Catholic	S-G/W	1,222	141	$ 6,000	$3,700	$ 9,700
Mt. San Antonio Community College	Walnut, CA 91789	1946	State	J/C	20,693	647	$ 110	—	$ 110
Mt. San Jacinto Comm. College	San Jacinto, CA 92383 ..	1963	State	J/C	2,840	45	$ 50	—	$ 100
Music and Arts Institute of San Francisco	San Francisco, CA 94115	1934	Independ	S-G/C	64	16	$ 2,875	$3,000	$ 2,875
Napa Valley College	Napa, CA 94558........	1942	Public	J/C	8,789	327	$ 100	—	$ 100
National Technical Schools ..	Los Angeles, CA 90037..	1905	Independ	J/C	850	51	$ 4,500	—	$ 4,500
National University	San Diego, CA 92108 ...	1971	Independ	S-G/C	9,107	621	$ 4,350	—	$ 4,350
Naval Postgraduate School ..	Monterey, CA 93940 ...	1909	Federal	G/C	1,680	200	—	—	—
New College of California ..	San Francisco, CA 94110	1971	Independ	S-G/C	650	45	$ 3,200	—	$ 3,200
Northern Calif. Bible College .	San Jose, CA 95122	1971	Church	S/C	120	10	$ 700	—	$ 750
Northrop University	Inglewood, CA 90306 ..	1942	Independ	S-G/C	2,200	153	$ 5,463	$1,500	$ 6,963
Nyingma Institute	Berkeley, CA 94709	1973	Buddhist	P/C	200	25	$ 1,500	$1,200	$ 1,700
Occidental College	Los Angeles, CA 90041..	1887	Independ	S-G/C	1,578	126	$ 9,659	$3,705	$13,364
Ohlone College............	Fremont, CA 94539	1966	Public	J/C	7,501	383	$ 100	—	$ 100
Orange Coast College	Costa Mesa, CA 92628 .	1948	Public	J/C	23,887	774	$ 100	—	$ 100
Otis Art Institute	Los Angeles, CA 90057..	1918	Independ	S-G/C	661	124	$ 5,990	$3,082	$ 9,072
Oxnard College	Oxnard, CA 93033......	1975	Public	J/C	4,662	193	$ 130	—	$ 130
Pacific Christian College	Fullerton, CA 92631 ...	1928	Christian	S-G/C	504	24	$ 2,830	$2,600	$ 5,430
Pacific Coast Baptist Bible College	San Dimas, CA 91773 ..	1967	Baptist	S/C	278	20	$ 1,360	$2,400	$ 3,760
Pacific Oaks College	Pasadena, CA 91103 ...	1945	Independ	S-G/C	300	30	$ 3,840	—	$ 3,840
Pacific School of Religion ..	Berkeley, CA 94709	1866	Independ	G/C	289	14	$ 3,630	$3,600	$ 7,230
Pacific States University ...	Los Angeles, CA 90006..	1928	Independ	S-G/C	700	45	$ 1,920	—	$ 1,920
Pacific Union College	Angwin, CA 94508	1882	7-D Adv	S-G/C	1,403	117	$ 6,225	$2,235	$ 8,460
Pacific Western University ..	Encino, CA 91436	1976	Independ	S-G/C	3,000		$ 1,900	—	$ 1,900
Palo Verde Comm. College ..	Blythe, CA 92225.......	1947	Public	J/C	710	32	$ 20	—	$ 40
Palomar College	San Marcos, CA 92027 .	1946	Public	J/C	16,500	638	$ 100	—	$ 100
Pasadena City College	Pasadena, CA 91001....	1924	Public	J/C	18,071	343	$ 100	—	$ 100
Pasadena Col. of Chiropractic	Pasadena, CA 91103....	1976	Independ	P/C	250	26	$ 6,600	—	$ 6,600
Patten College	Oakland, CA 94601	1944	Church	S/C	190	19	$ 2,512	$2,417	$ 4,929
Peninsula Univ. Col. of Law .	Mountain View, CA 94043	1975	Independ	P/C	150	15	$ 1,400	—	$ 1,400
Pepperdine University	Malibu, CA 90265	1937	C of Chr	S-G/C	6,894	465	$ 9,440	$4,188	$13,628
Pitzer College.............	Claremont, CA 91711 ..	1963	Independ	S/C	771	52	$ 8,822	$3,482	$12,304
Point Loma College	San Diego, CA 92106 ..	1902	Nazarene	S-G/C	1,917	96	$ 4,806	$2,430	$ 7,236
Pomona College...........	Claremont, CA 91711 ..	1887	Independ	S-G/C	1,338	151	$ 9,407	$3,852	$13,259
Porterville College	Porterville, CA 93257 ...	1927	State	J/C	1,983	164	$ 110	—	$ 110
Rancho Arroyo Voc. Tech. Institute................	Sacramento, CA 95826 .	1965	Independ	T/C	48	9	$ 4,000	—	$ 4,000
Rand Graduate Institute....	Santa Monica, CA 90406	1970	Independ	G/C	57	39	$10,000	$8,000	$18,000
Rio Hondo Comm. College ..	Whittier, CA 90608	1960	State	J/C	12,547	317	$ 100	—	$ 100
Riverside City College	Riverside, CA 92506 ...	1916	State	J/C	13,809	491	$ 100	—	$ 100
Sacramento City College ...	Sacramento, CA 95822 .	1916	State	J/C	13,710	275	$ 100	—	$ 100
Saddleback College........	Mission Viejo, CA 92692	1968	State	J/C	22,000	700	$ 100	—	$ 100
St. Joseph's College	Mountain View, CA 94039	1925	Catholic	S/M	119	20	$ 4,500	$1,000	$ 5,500
St. Mary's College of Calif...	Moraga, CA 94566	1863	Catholic	S-G/C	3,206	231	$ 6,477	$3,382	$ 9,895
St. Stephens Univ. & Seminary	Los Angeles, CA 90003..	1952	Baptist	S-G/C	381	68	$ 3,778	—	$ 3,778
San Bernardino Valley College	San Bernardino, CA 92410	1926	Public	J/C	11,061	360	$ 100	—	$ 325
San Diego City College	San Diego, CA 92101 ...	1914	Public	J/C	12,211	374	$ 100	—	$ 100
San Diego Mesa College ...	San Diego, CA 92111 ...	1962	State	J/C	17,137	692	$ 100	—	$ 100
San Diego State University ..	San Diego, CA 92182 ...	1897	State	S-G/C	33,611	2,075	$ 661	$2,800	$ 3,461
Imperial Valley Campus ..	Calexico, CA 92231	1960	State	S-G/C	300	15	$ 661	—	$ 661
San Francisco Art Institute ..	San Francisco, CA 94133	1871	Independ	S-G/C	638	74	$ 6,200	—	$ 6,200
San Fran. Bapt. Theol. Sem. .	San Francisco, CA 94109	1958	Baptist	G/C	20	7	$ 1,650	—	$ 1,650
San Francisco College of Mortuary Science	San Francisco, CA 94109	1932	Independ	J/C	50	8	$ 3,600	—	$ 3,600

NAME	ADDRESS	FOUN-DED	AFFILI-ATION	LEVEL/TYPE	ENROLL-MENT	TEACH-ERS	TUITION & FEES	BOARD & ROOM	TOTAL COST
CALIFORNIA *(continued)*									
San Francisco Cons. of Music	San Francisco, CA 94122	1917	Independ	P/C	219	66	$ 6,000	—	$ 6,000
San Francisco State University	San Francisco, CA 94132	1899	State	S-G/C	24,170	1,729	$ 672	$1,400	$ 2,072
San Joaquin College of Law	Fresno, CA 93726	1969	Independ	P/C	205	30	$ 2,600	—	$ 2,600
San Joaquin Delta College	Stockton, CA 95207	1963	State	J/C	16,000	250	$ 100	—	$ 100
San Jose Bible College	San Jose, CA 95108	1939	Church	S/C	178	21	$ 2,880	$1,950	$ 4,830
San Jose City College	San Jose, CA 95128	1921	State	J/C	11,788	179	$ 100	—	$ 100
San Jose State University	San Jose, CA 95192	1857	State	S-G/C	25,000	1,800	$ 594	$2,688	$ 3,282
Santa Ana College	Santa Ana, CA 92706	1915	State	J/C	20,225	996	$ 50	—	$ 50
Santa Barbara City College	Santa Barbara, CA 93109	1908	Public	J/C	10,700	438	$ 100	—	$ 100
Santa Monica College	Santa Monica, CA 94045	1929	State	J/C	22,111	700	$ 100	—	$ 100
Santa Rosa Junior College	Santa Rosa, CA 95401	1918	Public	J/C	20,178	812	$ 103	$3,000	$ 3,103
School of Theol. at Claremont	Claremont, CA 91711	1885	Church	G/C	382	56	$ 4,050	$5,200	$ 9,250
Scripps College	Claremont, CA 91711	1926	Independ	S/W	564	81	$ 9,370	$4,330	$13,700
Shasta College	Redding, CA 96099	1949	State	J/C	9,259	121	$ 112	$2,532	$ 2,644
Shiloh Bible College	Oakland, CA 94602	1967	Church	S-G/C	211	38	$ 500	—	$ 500
Sierra Bible Institute	Fresno, CA 93726	1985	Church	S/C	—	—	—	—	—
Sierra Comm. College	Rocklin, CA 95677	1914	State	J/C	10,000	123	$ 100	$2,660	$ 2,760
Simpson College	San Francisco, CA 94134	1921	Mission	S-G/C	302	24	$ 3,650	$2,100	$ 5,800
Skyline College	San Bruno, CA 94066	1969	State	J/C	7,063	144	$ 100	—	$ 100
Solano Community College	Suisun City, CA 94585	1945	State	J/C	9,500	420	$ 100	—	$ 100
Sonoma State University	Rohnert Park, CA 94928	1960	State	S-G/C	5,370	365	$ 679	$2,800	$ 3,479
South Bay College	Hawthorne, CA 90250	1965	Independ	T/C	1,248	60	$ 4,500	—	$ 4,500
Southern Calif. Bible College	San Diego, CA 92115	1970	Independ	S/C	79	13	$ 2,055	—	$ 2,055
Southern Calif. College	Costa Mesa, CA 92626	1927	Church	S-G/C	917	67	$ 4,160	$2,600	$ 6,760
Southern California College of Optometry	Fullerton, CA 92631	1904	Independ	P/C	384	85	$ 8,300	$3,700	$12,000
So. Calif. Comm. Bible College	Norwalk, CA 90650	1971	Non-Den	S-G/C	190	22	$ 795	—	$ 795
So. Calif. Conserv. of Music	Sun Valley, CA 91352	1972	Independ	S-G/C	117	16	$ 900	—	$ 900
So. Calif. Inst. of Architecture	Santa Monica, CA 90404	1972	Independ	S-G/C	375	65	$ 2,400	—	$ 2,400
Southwestern College	Chula Vista, CA 92010	1960	State	J/C	10,324	165	$ 130	—	$ 130
S.W. Univ. School of Law	Los Angeles, CA 90005	1911	Independ	G/C	1,010	64	$ 7,095	—	$ 7,095
Stanford University	Stanford, CA 94305	1885	Independ	S-G/C	6,593	1,219	$10,476	$4,417	$14,893
Starr King School for the Ministry	Berkeley, CA 94709	1904	Unitarian	G/C	57	10	$ 3,050	—	$ 3,050
Taft College	Taft, CA 93268	1921	State	J/C	1,123	70	$ 100	$2,078	$ 2,178
Thomas Aquinas College	Santa Paula, CA 93060	1969	Catholic	S/C	125	14	$ 5,795	$2,935	$ 8,730
Union University	Los Angeles, CA 90033	1973	Independ	S-G/C	300	26	$ 2,535	—	$ 2,535
United College of Business	Hollywood, CA 90028	1969	Independ	S/G	800	40	$ 5,000	—	$ 5,000
U.S. International University	San Diego, CA 92131	1952	Independ	S-G/C	3,500	230	$ 6,000	$3,270	$ 9,870
University of California									
Berkeley Campus	Berkeley, CA 94720	1868	State	S-G/C	31,008	1,600	$ 1,407	$4,009	$ 6,803
Davis Campus	Davis, CA 95616	1905	State	S-G/C	18,971	1,366	$ 1,353	$2,800	$ 4,153
Irvine Campus	Irvine, CA 92717	1960	State	S-G/C	12,684	805	$ 1,335	$3,586	$ 4,921
Los Angeles Campus	Los Angeles, CA 90024	1919	State	S-G/C	34,503	3,200	$ 1,290	$2,741	$ 4,031
Riverside Campus	Riverside, CA 92521	1954	State	S-G/C	4,855	375	$ 1,338	$3,145	$ 4,483
San Diego Campus	La Jolla, CA 92093	1964	State	S-G/C	14,303	1,542	$ 1,330	$4,011	$ 5,341
Santa Barbara Campus	Santa Barbara, CA 93106	1944	State	S-G/C	16,936	850	$ 1,299	$2,972	$ 4,271
Santa Cruz Campus	Santa Cruz, CA 95064	1965	State	S-G/C	7,137	436	$ 1,388	$3,504	$ 4,892
University of Judaism	Los Angeles, CA 90077	1947	Independ	S-G/C	166	51	$ 4,500	$3,350	$ 7,850
University of La Verne	La Verne, CA 91750	1891	Independ	S-G/C	1,224	101	$ 7,300	$2,710	$10,010
University of Redlands	Redlands, CA 92374	1907	Independ	S-G/C	1,287	110	$ 8,346	$3,477	$11,823
University of San Diego	San Diego, CA 92110	1949	Catholic	S-G/C	5,264	326	$ 6,840	$3,684	$10,524
University of San Francisco	San Francisco, CA 94117	1855	Catholic	G/C	7,000	411	$ 5,920	$1,662	$ 7,582
University of Santa Clara	Santa Clara, CA 95053	1851	Catholic	S-G/C	7,448	450	$ 6,663	$3,588	$10,251
University of Southern California	Los Angeles, CA 90089	1880	Independ	S-G/C	30,369	1,549	$ 9,436	$3,714	$13,332
University of the Pacific	Stockton, CA 95211	1851	Independ	S-G/C	5,806	560	$ 9,200	$3,636	$12,836
Univ. of West Los Angeles	Los Angeles, CA 90066	1966	Independ	S-G/C	675	41	$ 2,500	—	$ 2,500
Ventura College	Ventura, CA 93003	1925	State	J/C	11,837	170	$ 180	—	$ 180
Ventura College of Law	Ventura, CA 93003	1969	Independ	P/C	150	15	$ 2,200	—	$ 2,200
Victor Valley College	Victorville, CA 92392	1961	State	J/C	4,149	198	$ 100	—	$ 100
West Coast University	Los Angeles, CA 90020	1909	Independ	S-G/C	1,500	250	$ 5,580	—	$ 5,580
West Hills Community College	Coalinga, CA 93210	1932	State	J/C	1,965	120	$ 50	$2,170	$ 2,220
West Los Angeles College	Culver City, CA 90230	1968	District	J/C	8,000	289	$100	—	$ 100
West Valley College	Saratoga, CA 95070	1964	Public	J/C	13,000	430	$ 124	—	$ 124
Western State College of Engineering	Inglewood, CA 90301	1946	Independ	S/C	112	14	$ 2,300	—	$ 2,300
Western State University College of Law	Fullerton, CA 92631	1966	Independ	P/C	1,561	56	$ 6,030	—	$ 6,030
Western State University College of Law	San Diego, CA 92101	1969	Independ	P/C	624	32	$ 6,030	—	$ 6,030
Westminster Theol. Sem.	Escondido, CA	1979	Independ	G/C	101	13	—	$3,420	$ 3,420
Westmont College	Santa Barbara, CA 93108	1940	Independ	S-C	1,208	80	$ 6,905	$3,440	$10,345
Whittier College	Whittier, CA 90608	1887	Independ	S-G/C	1,608	143	$ 8,186	$3,130	$11,316
Woodbury University	Los Angeles, CA 90017	1884	Independ	S-G/C	1,000	85	$ 5,190	—	$ 5,190
World College West	Petaluma, CA 94952	1973	Independ	S/C	100	12	$ 5,550	$2,916	$ 8,466
Wright Institute	Berkeley, CA 94704	1968	Independ	G/C	160	18	$ 6,900	—	$ 6,900
Yeshiva Univ. of Los Angeles	Los Angeles, CA 90035	1977	Jewish	S/M	70	13	$ 2,300	$2,500	$ 4,800
Yuba College	Marysville, CA 95901	1927	State	J/C	8,600	430	$ 100	$2,292	$ 2,392
COLORADO									
Adams State College	Alamosa, CO 81102	1921	State	S-G/C	2,116	88	$ 1,048	$2,110	$ 3,158
Aims Community College	Greeley, CO 80634	1967	Public	J/C	6,656	649	$ 396	—	$ 396

NAME	ADDRESS	FOUN-DED	AFFILI-ATION	LEVEL/TYPE	ENROLL-MENT	TEACH-ERS	TUITION & FEES	BOARD & ROOM	TOTAL COST
COLORADO *(continued)*									
Arapahoe Community College	Littleton, CO 80120	1965	State	J/C	5,719	134	$ 812	—	$ 812
Baptist Bible Col. of Denver .	Broomfield, CO 80020 ..	1952	Church	S-G/C	121	16	$ 2,880	$2,520	$ 5,400
Belleview College	Westminster, CO 80030 .	1921	P/Fire	S/C	25	5	$ 1,800	$1,250	$ 3,050
Colorado Christian College ..	Lakewood, CO 80226 ..	1914	Church	S/C	300	25	$ 4,240	$1,660	$ 5,900
Colorado College	Colorado Spgs., CO 80903	1874	Independ	S/C	1,895	139	$ 8,190	$2,720	$10,910
Colorado Mountain College .	Glenwood Spgs., CO 81602	1965	Public	J/C	10,830	700	$ 1,125	$2,580	$ 3,705
Colorado Northwest. Comm. College	Rangely, CO 81648	1962	Public	J/C	1,211	220	$ 610	$2,030	$ 2,640
Colorado School of Mines ..	Golden, CO 80401	1874	State	S-G/C	2,734	200	$ 2,940	$3,100	$ 6,040
Colorado State University ..	Fort Collins, CO 80523 ..	1870	State	S/C	18,094	956	$ 1,562	$2,610	$ 4,172
Colorado Technical College ..	Colorado Spgs., CO 80907	1965	Independ	S/C	787	43	$ 2,970	—	$ 2,970
Community College of Denver	Denver, CO 80218	1967	State	J/C			—		—
Auraria Campus	Denver, CO 80204	1970	State	J/C	3,687	293	$ 735	—	$ 735
Fort Range Campus	Westminster, CO 80030	1968	State	J/C	5,449	260	$ 773	—	$ 773
Red Rocks Campus	Golden, CO 80401	1969	State	J/C	4,791	87	$ 768	—	$ 768
Denver Conservative Baptist Theological Seminary ..	Denver, CO 80210	1950	Baptist	G/C	544	49	$ 3,060	—	$ 5,500
Fort Lewis College	Durango, CO 81301	1933	State	S/C	3,708	150	$ 902	$2,078	$ 2,980
Iliff School of Theology	Denver, CO 80210	1892	Methodist	G-P/C	377	25	$ 3,120		$ 3,120
Lamar Comm. College	Lamar, CO 81052	1937	State	J/C	464	21	$ 922	$1,998	$ 2,920
Loretto Heights College	Denver, CO 80236	1918	Independ	S/C	711	106	$ 5,850	$3,100	$ 8,950
Mesa College	Grand Junction, CO 81502	1925	State	S/C	3,568	144	$ 1,038	$2,166	$ 3,204
Metropolitan State College .	Denver, CO 80204	1965	State	S/C	14,388	668	$ 922	—	$ 922
National College—									
Colorado Springs Campus .	Colorado Spgs., CO 80932	1974	Private	S/C	237	33	$ 2,667	—	$ 2,667
Denver Campus	Denver, CO 80221	1974	Private	S/C	125	13	$ 2,577	—	$ 2,577
Pueblo Campus	Pueblo, CO 81004	1975	Private	S/C •	187	23	$ 2,613	—	$ 2,613
Northeastern Junior College .	Sterling, CO 80751	1941	District	J/C	1,660	64	$ 735	$2,200	$ 2,935
Otero Junior College	La Junta, CO 81050	1941	State	J/C	651	61	$ 852	$2,280	$ 3,132
Pikes Peak Comm. College ..	Colorado Spgs., CO 80906	1967	State	J/C	5,673	426	$ 753	—	$ 753
Pueblo Comm. Col.	Pueblo, CO 81004	1933	State	T/C	1,299	116	$ 732	—	$ 732
Regis College	Denver, CO 80221	1877	Catholic	S/C	947	69	$ 6,650	$3,310	$ 9,960
St. Thomas Theol. Seminary .	Denver, CO 80210	1907	Catholic	G/C	122	26	$ 2,550	$2,520	$ 5,070
Trinidad State Junior College	Trinidad, CO 81082......	1925	State	J/C	1,328	51	$ 900	$2,500	$ 3,400
U.S. Air Force Academy	USAF, CO 80840	1955	Federal	S/C	4,425	574	—	—	—
University of Colorado	Boulder, CO 80309	1876	State	S-G/C	22,299	1,301	$ 1,444	$2,606	$ 4,050
Colorado Springs Campus .	Colorado Spgs., CO 80933	1965	State	S-G/C	5,207	309	$ 800	3,429	$ 4,229
Denver..................	Denver, CO 80202	1938	State	S-G/C	10,831	600	$ 1,010		$ 1,010
University of Denver	Denver, CO 80208	1864	Independ	S-G/C	7,269	616	$ 7,920	$3,500	$11,420
University of Northern Colo. .	Greeley, CO 80639	1889	State	S-G/C	9,247	387	$ 1,480	$2,520	$ 4,000
University of Southern Colo. .	Pueblo, CO 81001	1933	State	S-G/C	4,796	164	$ 1,066	$2,422	$ 3,488
Western Bible College	Morrison, CO 80465	1948	Int-Den	S/C	164	11	$ 3,200	$2,000	$ 5,200
Western State College of Colo.	Gunnison, CO 81230.....	1911	State	S-G/C	2,700	130	$ 1,100	$1,880	$ 2,980
CONNECTICUT									
Albertus Magnus College ...	New Haven, CT 06511 ..	1925	Independ	S/W	500	56	$ 6,530	$3,640	$10,170
Bridgeport Engineering Inst. .	Bridgeport, CT 06606 ...	1924	Independ	S/C	869	104	$ 2,810	—	$ 2,810
Central Conn. State University	New Britain, CT 06050 ..	1849	State	S-G/C	13,333	641	$ 1,174	$2,601	$ 3,775
Connecticut College	New London, CT 06320 .	1911	Independ	S-G/C	1,911	231	$10,300	$2,930	$13,230
Eastern Conn. State University	Willimantic, CT 06226 ..	1889	State	S-G/C	3,873	257	$ 1,170	$2,658	$ 3,828
Fairfield University	Fairfield, CT 06430	1924	Catholic	S-G/C	5,104	355	$ 6,700	$3,700	$11,400
Greater Hartford Comm. Col.	Hartford, CT 06105.....	1967	State	J/C	3,430	241	$ 604	—	$ 604
Hartford College For Women	Hartford, CT 06105.....	1939	Independ	J/W	206	36	$ 5,365	$3,240	$ 8,605
Hartford Graduate Center ...	Hartford, CT 06120.....	1955	Independ	G/C	2,243	87	—		—
Hartford State Tech. College.	Hartford, CT 06106.....	1946	State	T/C	1,835	82	$ 768	—	$ 768
Holy Apostles Sem./College .	Cromwell, CT 06416	1957	Catholic	S-G/C	172	26	$ 2,600	$2,400	$ 5,000
Housatonic Community Col. .	Bridgeport, CT 06608 ...	1966	State	J/C	2,386	94	$ 560	—	$ 560
Manchester Community Col. .	Manchester, CT 06040 ..	1963	State	J/C	6,600	180	$ 604	—	$ 604
Mattatuck Community College	Waterbury, CT 06708 ...	1967	State	J/C	3,584	232	$ 560	—	$ 560
Middlesex Community College.	Middletown, CT 06457 ..	1966	Independ	J/C	2,690	120	$ 604	—	$ 604
Mitchell College	New London, CT 06320 .	1938	Independ	J/C	506	28	$ 6,475	$3,275	$ 9,750
Morse School of Business ...	Hartford, CT 06103......	1860	Independ	J/C	—	—	—	—	—
Mount Sacred Heart College .	Hamden, CT 06514	1954	Catholic	J/W	—	—	—	—	—
Northwest Conn. Comm. Col.	Winsted, CT 06098	1965	State	J/C	2,343	75	$ 604	—	$ 604
Norwalk Comm. College	Norwalk, CT 06854	1961	State	J/C	3,357	73	$ 580	—	$ 580
Norwalk State Tech. College .	Norwalk, CT 06854	1961	State	T/C	1,770	69	$ 768	—	$ 768
Post College	Waterbury, CT 06708 ...	1890	Independ	S/C	1,438	61	$ 5,500	$3,100	$ 8,600
Quinnipiac College	Hamden, CT 06518	1929	Independ	S-G/C	3,139	312	$ 6,630	$3,050	$ 9,680
Sacred Heart University	Bridgeport, CT 06606 ...	1963	Catholic	S-G/C	5,014	350	$ 4,550	$	$ 4,550
St. Alphonsus College	Suffield, CT 06078	1963	Catholic	S/M	52	18	$ 2,700	$1,800	$ 4,500
St. Basil College	Stamford, CT 06902	1939	Catholic	S/M	16	10	$ 5,000	$3,000	$ 8,000
St. Joseph College..........	West Hartford, CT 06117	1932	Catholic	S-G/W	1,223	120	$ 5,225	$3,190	$ 8,415
South Central Comm. Col. ...	New Haven, CT. 06515 ..	1968	State	J/C	2,245	111	$ 604	—	$ 604
Southern Conn. State Univ. ..	New Haven, CT 06515 ..	1893	State	S-G/C	10,733	615	$ 1,075	$2,690	$ 3,765
Thames Valley State Technical College	Norwich, CT 06360	1963	State	T/C	749	41	$ 741	—	$ 741
Trinity College	Hartford, CT 06106......	1823	Private	S-G/C	1,800	137	$ 9,700	$3,350	$13,050
Tunxis Community College ..	Farmington, CT 06032 ..	1970	State	J/C	3,043	123	$ 560	—	$ 560
U.S. Coast Guard Academy ..	New London, CT 06320 .	1876	Federal	S/C	764	105	—		—
University of Bridgeport.....	Bridgeport, CT 06601 ...	1927	Independ	S-G/C	6,337	264	$ 7,100	$3,600	$10,700
University of Connecticut ...	Storrs, CT 06268	1881	State	S-G/C	22,976	1,150	$ 1,657	$2,362	$ 4,019

NAME	ADDRESS	FOUN-DED	AFFILI-ATION	LEVEL/TYPE	ENROLL-MENT	TEACH-ERS	TUITION & FEES	BOARD & ROOM	TOTAL COST
CONNECTICUT *(continued)*									
University of Hartford	West Hartford, CT 06117	1877	Independ	S-G/C	7,613	300	$ 7,030	$3,905	$10,935
University of New Haven	West Haven, CT 06516..	1920	Independ	S-G/C	7,044	440	$ 5,900	$3,300	$ 9,200
Waterbury State Tech. College	Waterbury, CT 06708 ...	1964	State	T/C	1,653	105	$ 642	—	$ 642
Wesleyan University	Middletown, CT 06457 ..	1831	Independ	S-G/C	2,766	250	$10,513	$3,920	$15,358
Western Conn. State Univ....	Danbury, CT 06810	1903	State	S-G/C	5,778	258	$ 1,150	$2,472	$ 3,700
Yale University	New Haven, CT 06520 ..	1701	Independ	S-G/C	10,920	1,766	$10,700	$4,500	$15,200
DELAWARE									
Delaware State College......	Dover, DE 19901	1891	State	S-G/C	2,209	138	$ 700	$1,980	$ 2,680
Delaware Technical and Community College.	Dover, DE 19903	1966	State	T/C	7,160	218	$ 627	—	$ 627
Goldey Beacom College	Wilmington, DE 19808 ..	1886	Independ	S/C	1,918	89	$ 3,210	$1,950	$ 5,160
University of Delaware	Newark, DE 19716......	1833	State	S-G/C	18,083	1,147	$ 1,919	$2,405	$ 4,324
Wesley College..............	Dover, DE 19901	1873	Methodist	S/C	1,000	78	$ 5,600	$2,700	$ 8,300
Widener University									
Brandywine College	Wilmington, DE 19803 ..	1965	Independ	J/C	738	66	$ 4,650	$3,180	$ 7,830
Delaware Law School	Wilmington, DE 19803 ..	1971	Independ	P/C	870	57	$ 6,700	—	$ 6,700
School of Hotel & Restaurant Management	Wilmington, DE 19803 ..	1981	Independ	S/C	416	12	$ 5,200	$3,180	$ 8,380
University College	Wilmington, DE 19803 ..	1980	Independ	S/C	848	75	$ 1,200	—	$ 1,200
Wilmington College.........	New Castle, DE 19720 ..	1967	Independ	S-G/C	1,060	120	$ 3,420	$1,260	$ 4,680
DISTRICT OF COLUMBIA									
American University	Washington, DC 20016 ..	1893	Methodist	S-G/C	11,062	1,062	$ 8,270	$3,956	$12,226
Antioch School of Law	Washington, DC 20009..	1852	Independ	G-P/C	490	17	$ 6,930	—	$ 6,930
Beacon College	Washington, DC 20005..	1971	Independ	S-G/C	16	—	$ 3,300	—	$ 3,300
Catholic University of America	Washington, DC 20064..	1887	Catholic	P/C	6,780	454	$ 6,900	$3,800	$10,700
Gallaudet College	Washington, DC 20002..	1864	Private	S-G/C	2,000	271	$ 2,154	$2,946	$ 5,100
George Washington University	Washington, DC 20052..	1821	Independ	S-G/C	19,332	1,679	$ 7,515	$4,305	$11,820
Georgetown University	Washington, DC 20057..	1789	Catholic	S-G/C	11,989	1,555	$ 9,380	$3,500	$14,000
Howard University..........	Washington, DC 20059..	1867	Independ	S-G/C	11,480	1,968	$ 3,045	$5,330	$ 8,375
Mount Vernon College	Washington, DC 20007..	1875	Independ	S/W	463	61	$ 6,400	$4,100	$10,500
Sch. of Ad. Inter. Stud.-J.H.U.	Washington, DC 20036..	1943	Independ	G/C	383	117	$ 9,000	$6,500	$15,500
Southeastern University.....	Washington, DC 20024..	1879	Independ	S-G/C	1,247	175	$ 3,750	—	$ 3,750
Strayer College	Washington, DC 20005..	1904	Independ	S/C	1,800	75	$ 2,640	—	$ 2,640
Trinity College	Washington, DC 20017..	1897	Catholic	S-G/W	824	82	$ 6,500	$4,180	$10,680
USDA Graduate School	Washington, DC 20250..	1921	Federal	G-C	10,000	1,000	$ 345	—	$ 345
Univ. of the Dist. of Columbia	Washington, DC 20008 ..	1976	Public	S-G/C	12,832	558	$ 462	—	$ 462
Washington Musical Institute	Washington, DC 20016..	1928	Independ	S-G/C	120	5	—	—	—
Wesley Theological Seminary	Washington, DC 20016..	1882	Un. Meth	G/C	412	36	$ 4,000	$1,900	$ 5,900
FLORIDA									
Art Inst. of Fort Lauderdale ..	Fort Lauderdale, FL 33316	1968	Independ	J/C	1,167	55	$ 5,025	$2,325	$ 7,350
Baptist Bible Institute	Graceville, FL 32440	1943	Baptist	S/C	362	24	$ 929	$2,990	$ 3,919
Barry University.............	Miami Shores, FL 33161.	1940	Catholic	S-G/C	4,240	320	$ 5,165	$3,350	$ 8,515
Bethune-Cookman College ..	Daytona Beach, FL 32015	1904	Un. Meth	S/C	1,708	126	$ 3,537	$2,212	$ 5,749
Brevard Community College .	Cocoa, FL 32922	1960	State	J/C	10,709	233	$ 608	—	$ 608
Central Fla Comm. College	Ocala, FL 32678.........	1957	State	J/C	2,567	96	$ 456	—	$ 456
Chipola Junior College	Marianna, FL 32446	1947	State	J/C	1,232	48	$ 576	$1,142	$ 1,718
Clearwater Christian College.	Clearwater, FL 33519 ...	1965	Independ	S/C	201	18	$ 2,400	$2,400	$ 4,800
College of Boca Raton	Boca Raton, FL 33431 ..	1963	Independ	S/C	780	45	$ 6,200	$3,500	$ 9,700
College of the Palm Beaches .	W. Palm Beach, FL 33401	1926	Independ	S-G/C	285	18	$ 2,000	—	$ 2,000
Daytona Beach Comm. College	Daytona Beach, FL 32015	1957	State	J/C	18,596	168	$ 720	—	$ 720
Eckerd College..............	St. Petersburg, FL 33712	1958	Church	S/C	1,573	113	$ 7,200	$3,000	$10,200
Edison Community College ..	Fort Myers, FL 33907 ...	1962	State	J/C	6,022	249	$ 600	—	$ 600
Edward Waters College	Jacksonville, FL 32209 ..	1866	AME	S/C	746	53	$ 2,500	$3,400	$ 5,900
Embry-Riddle Aero. University	Bunnell, FL 32010	1926	Independ	S/C	4,798	265	$ 3,750	$2,500	$ 6,250
Evangel Bible School	Lakeland, FL 33801	1934	Independ	G/C	20	7	$ 140	—	$ 140
Evangelical Bible Seminary, Inc.	Lakeworth, FL 33463	1975	Church	S-G/C	22	4	$ 600	—	$ 600
Faith Bible College	Milton, FL 32570	1974	Baptist	S/C	64	20	$ 800	—	$ 800
Flagler College	St. Augustine, FL 32084 .	1968	Independ	S/C	1,050	87	$ 3,300	$2,100	$ 5,400
Florida A&M University	Tallahassee, FL 32307 ..	1887	State	S-G/C	5,295	394	$ 894	$2,232	$ 3,081
Florida Atlantic University ..	Boca Raton, FL 33431 ..	1961	State	S-G/C	10,200	500	$ 900	$2,450	$ 3,350
Florida Baptist College	Lakeland, FL 33802	1968	Baptist	S-G/C	91	14	$ 680	$ 900	$ 1,580
Florida Beacon Bible College.	Largo, FL 33541.........	1947	Independ	S/C	50	15	$ 960	$1,200	$ 2,160
Florida Bible College;	Kissimmee, FL 32741 ...	1962	Independ	S/C	150	16	$ 2,800	$1,000	$ 3,800
Florida Christian College ..	Orlando, FL 32856.......	1975	Church	S/C	130	10	$ 2,273	$2,068	$ 4,341
Florida College	Temple Terrace, FL 33617	1946	Independ	J/C	389	36	$ 2,800	$2,000	$ 4,800
Florida Inst. of Technology ..	Melbourne, FL 32901 ...	1958	Independ	S-G/C	4,500	220	$ 5,000	$2,610	$ 7,610
Florida International University	Miami, FL 33199	1965	State	S-G/C	15,875	776	$ 870	$3,300	$ 4,170
Fla. Jr. Col. at Jacksonville .	Jacksonville, FL 32202 ..	1966	State	J/C	13,962	348	$ 540	—	$ 540
Florida Keys Comm. College .	Key West, FL 33040	1965	State	J/C	1,568	35	$ 456	$4,260	$ 4,716
Florida Memorial College ...	Miami, FL 33054	1879	Baptist	S/C	1,634	111	$ 2,950	$2,250	$ 5,200
Florida Southern College ...	Lakeland, FL 33802	1885	Methodist	S/C	2,402	214	$ 4,255	$2,745	$ 7,000
Florida State University	Tallahassee, FL 32306 ..	1857	State	S-G/C	21,320	1,500	$ 942	$2,374	$ 3,316
Fort Lauderdale College	Fort Lauderdale, FL 33301	1940	Independ	S/C	950	40	$ 2,500	—	$ 2,500
Freedom Seminary	Orlando, FL 32819.......	1973	Independ	S-G/C	1,200	85	$ 1,200	—	$ 1,200
Gulf Coast Comm. College ..	Panama City, FL 32401 .	1957	State	J/C	3,952	184	$ 450	—	$ 450
Heritage College	Orlando, FL 32808.......	1976	Baptist	S/C	70	10	$ 1,000	$1,700	$ 2,700
Hillsborough Comm. College.	Tampa, FL 33622........	1968	State	J/C	12,644	196	$ 600	—	$ 600
Hobe Sound Bible College ..	Hobe Sound, FL 33455..	1960	Independ	S/C	220	21	$ 1,800	$1,650	$ 3,450

NAME	ADDRESS	FOUN-DED	AFFILI-ATION	LEVEL/TYPE	ENROLL-MENT	TEACH-ERS	TUITION & FEES	BOARD & ROOM	TOTAL COST
FLORIDA (continued)									
Indian River Comm. College .	Fort Pierce, FL 33450 ..	1959	State	J/C	13,298	145	$ 500	—	$ 500
International Fine Arts College	Miami, FL 33132	1965	Independ	J/C	295	24	$ 5,985	$1,905	$ 7,890
Jacksonville University......	Jacksonville, FL 32211 ..	1934	Independ	S-G/C	2,117	183	$ 4,750	$2,580	$ 7,330
Jones College...............	Jacksonville, FL 32211 ..	1918	Independ	S/C	1,331	44	$ 2,584	—	$ 2,584
Lake City Comm. College	Lake City, FL 32055	1947	State	J/C	1,949	177	$ 576	$ 820	$ 1,396
Lakeland College...........	Lakeland, FL 33803	1977	Independ	J/C	250	12	$ 3,600	—	$ 3,600
Lake-Sumter Comm. College.	Leesburg, FL 32748	1962	State	J/C	1,772	89	$ 1,756	—	$ 1,756
Landmark Baptist College ...	Haines City, FL 33844 ...	1979	Baptist	S-G/C	50	12	$ 1,522	$1,372	$ 2,894
Liberty Bible College........	Pensacola, FL 32506	1966	S-G/C		351	18	$ 1,200	$1,700	$ 2,900
Luther Rice Seminary........	Jacksonville, FL 32207 ..	1962	Independ	S/G	1,800	14	$ 1,500	—	$ 1,500
Manatee Comm. College	Bradenton, FL 33506 ...	1957	State	J/C	6,025	257	$ 663	—	$ 663
Miami Christian College	Miami, FL 33167	1949	Int-Den	S/C	321	18	$ 3,320	$2,420	$ 5,740
Miami-Dade Comm. College .	Miami, FL 33176	1960	State	J/C	41,427	781	$ 675	—	$ 675
Nassau Baptist College	Yulee, FL 32097	1974	Church	G/C	25	4	$ 250	—	$ 250
Nat'l Education Center	Ft. Lauderdale, FL 33334	1964	Independ	J/C	825	51	$ 4,700	$2,035	$ 6,735
Nat'l Educ. Center	Tampa, FL 33610......	1948	Independ	J/C	1,730	52	$ 4,200	—	$ 4,200
North Florida Junior College .	Madison, FL 32340	1958	State	J/C	900	42	$ 520	—	$ 520
Nova University	Ft. Lauderdale, FL 33314	1964	Independ	S-G/C	6,641	82	$ 3,710	$3,530	$ 7,240
Okaloosa-Walton Jr. College .	Niceville, FL 32578	1963	State	J/C	6,029	189	$ 638	—	$ 638
Orlando College	Orlando, FL 32810......	1953	Independ	S/C	917	47	$ 2,448	—	$ 2,448
Palm Beach Atlantic College .	W. Palm Beach, FL 33401	1968	Baptist	S/C	990	52	$ 3,500	$3,500	$ 7,000
Palm Beach Junior College ..	Lake Worth, FL 33461 ..	1933	State	J/C	11,225	547	$ 680	—	$ 680
Pasco-Hernando Comm. Col.	Dade City, FL 33525.....	1967	State	J/C	2,881	181	$ 580	—	$ 580
Pensacola Christian College .	Pensacola, FL 32523 ...	1974	Independ	S-G/C	800	50	$ 1,600	$1,600	$ 3,200
Pensacola Junior College ...	Pensacola, FL 32504....	1948	State	J/C	16,300	876	$ 528	—	$ 528
Polk Community College	Winter Haven, FL 33881	1964	State	J/C	4,531	178	$ 673	—	$ 673
Prospect Hall College	Hollywood, FL 33020 ...	1929	Independ	J/C	493	25	$ 3,900	—	$ 3,900
Ringling School of Art & Design	Sarasota, FL 33580	1931	Independ	S/C	417	31	$ 4,050	$2,700	$ 6,750
Rollins College.............	Winter Park, FL 32789 ..	1885	Independ	S-G/C	1,360	101	$ 5,936	$2,640	$ 8,576
St. John Vianney Col. Sem. .	Miami, FL 33165	1959	Catholic	S/M	66	10	$ 2,500	$2,500	$ 5,000
St. John's River Comm. College	Palatka, FL 32077	1958	State	J/C	1,463	102	$ 576	—	$ 576
St. Leo College.............	Saint Leo, FL 33574	1889	Catholic	S/C	1,083	65	$ 4,515	$1,500	$ 6,015
St. Petersburg Junior College	St. Petersburg, FL 33733	1927	State	J/C	15,865	292	$ 652	—	$ 652
St. Thomas of Villanova U...	Miami, FL 33054	1962	Church	S-G/C	3,400	125	$ 4,650	$3,150	$ 7,800
St. Vincent De Paul Rg. Sem.	Boynton Beach, FL 33435	1963	Church	P/M	121	27	$ 1,500	$3,400	$ 5,900
Santa Fe Comm. College	Gainesville, FL 32601 ...	1966	State	J/C	7,296	220	$ 570	—	$ 570
Sarasota Theological Sem. .	Sarasota, FL 33579	1979	Independ	G/C	—	—	$ 500	—	$ 500
Seminole Community College	Sanford, FL 32771......	1965	State	J/C	4,692	116	$ 640	—	$ 640
S. E. Col. of the Assem. of God	Lakeland, FL 33801.....	1935	A of God	S/C	1,023	52	$ 2,000	$ 700	$ 2,700
South Florida Comm. College	Avon Park, FL 33825 ...	1965	State	J/C	967	30	$ 476	—	$ 476
Southern College	Orlando, FL 32807......	1968	Independ	J/C	757	42	$ 2,300	—	$ 2,300
Spurgeon Baptist Bible College	Mulberry, FL 33860.....	1970	Baptist	S/C	44	9	$ 2,142	$ 950	$ 3,092
Stetson University	Deland, FL 32720	1883	Baptist	S-G/C	2,739	215	$ 5,690	$2,400	$ 8,090
Tallahassee Comm. College .	Tallahassee, FL 32304 ..	1965	State	J/C	4,885	203	$ 540	—	$ 540
Talmudic College of Florida ..	Miami Beach, FL 33139 .	1974	Jewish	S-G/M	88	7	$ 2,400	$3,000	$ 5,400
Trinity Baptist College	Jacksonville, FL 32205 ..	1974	Baptist	S/C	351	29	$ 1,900	$2,100	$ 4,000
Trinity College	Dunedin, FL 33528	1932	Independ	S-G/C	83	22	$ 1,330	$1,500	$ 2,830
United Bible Col. & Seminary	Orlando, FL 32808......	1979	Independ	P/C	250	9	$ 1,440	—	$ 1,800
United Electronics Institute ..	Tampa, FL 33607.......	1967	Independ	J/C	1,029	24	$ 4,500	—	$ 4,500
University of Central Florida .	Orlando, FL 32816......	1963	State	S-G/C	15,846	441	$ 993	$2,521	$ 3,514
University of Florida	Gainesville, FL 32611 ...	1853	State	S-G/C	35,449	3,179	$ 970	$3,000	$ 3,970
University of Miami	Coral Gables, FL 33124 .	1925	Independ	S-G/C	13,708	1,269	$ 7,774	$3,404	$11,178
University of North Florida ..	Jacksonville, FL 32216 ..	1965	State	S-G/C	5,800	185	$ 850	$2,235	$ 3,085
University of Sarasota	Sarasota, FL 33580	1973	Independ	S-G/C	200	10	$ 4,500	—	$ 4,500
University of South Florida ..	Tampa, FL 33620.......	1956	State	S-G/C	27,815	1,089	$ 979	$2,328	$ 3,307
New College	Sarasota, FL 33580	1960	State	S/C	400	48	$ 1,064	$2,440	$ 3,504
Sarasota	Sarasota, FL 33580	1975	State	S-G/C	1,000	74	$ 950	—	$ 950
University of Tampa	Tampa, FL 33606.......	1931	Independ	S-G/C	2,047	168	$ 6,876	$3,034	$10,210
University of West Florida ...	Pensacola, FL 32514 ...	1963	State	S-G/C	6,031	356	$ 888	$2,367	$ 3,255
Valencia Community College .	Orlando, FL 32802......	1967	State	J/C	11,432	428	$ 637	—	$ 637
Walden University	Naples, FL 33940......	1970	Independ	G/C	259	20	$11,000	$1,000	$12,000
Warner Southern College....	Lake Wales, FL 33853 ..	1968	C of God	S/C	338	50	$ 4,050	$2,070	$ 6,120
Webber College	Babson Park, FL 33827 .	1927	Independ	S-G/C	407	23	$ 3,800	$2,380	$ 6,180
Yeshiva Gedolah Rabbin. Col.	Miami Beach, FL 33139 .	1973	Jewish	S-G/M	60	3	$ 2,000	$2,000	$ 4,000
GEORGIA									
Abraham Baldwin Agri. College	Tifton, GA 31793	1908	State	J/C	1,979	96	$ 804	$1,710	$ 2,514
Agnes Scott College	Decatur, GA 30030	1889	Independ	S/W	539	78	$ 7,275	$2,850	$10,125
Albany Junior College	Albany, GA 31707	1963	State	J/C	1,770	78	$ 684	—	$ 684
Albany State College........	Albany, GA 31705	1903	State	S-G/C	1,893	133	$ 1,194	$1,770	$ 2,964
Amer. Col. for Applied Arts .	Atlanta, GA 30342......	1975	Independ	S/C	330	25	$ 4,650	$4,200	$ 8,850
Andrew College	Cuthbert, GA 31740	1854	Un. Meth	J/C	300	21	$ 716	$ 770	$ 1,486
Armstrong State College	Savannah, GA 31406 ...	1935	State	S-G/C	2,750	190	$ 1,000	—	$ 1,300
Atlanta Area Tech. School ...	Atlanta, GA 30310......	1959	State	T/C	2,300	150	$ 150	—	$ 300
Atlanta Christian College ..	East Point, GA 30344 ...	1937	Christian	S/C	147	20	$ 2,016	$2,047	$ 4,036
Atlanta College of Art	Atlanta, GA 30309	1928	Independ	S/C	250	46	$ 4,900	$2,400	$ 7,300
Atlanta Junior College	Atlanta, GA 30310......	1974	State	J/C	1,460	67	$ 675	—	$ 675
Atlanta University	Atlanta, GA 30314......	1867	Independ	S-G/C	1,038	134	$ 3,940	$1,300	$ 5,240
Augusta Area Tech. School ..	Augusta, GA 30906	1961	State	T/C	3,100	130	$ 500	—	$ 500
Augusta College	Augusta, GA 30910	1925	State	S-G/C	4,091	155	$ 972	—	$ 972
Bainbridge Junior College ...	Bainbridge, GA 31717 ..	1973	State	J/C	575	31	$ 675	—	$ 675
Berry College	Mt. Berry, GA 30149	1902	Independ	S-G/C	1,394	103	$ 4,380	$2,595	$ 6,975
Brenau College	Gainesville, GA 30501 ...	1878	Independ	S-G/W	643	98	$ 4,300	$3,600	$ 7,900
Brewton-Parker College	Mt. Vernon, GA 30445 ..	1904	Baptist	J/C	1,277	128	$ 2,140	$1,620	$ 3,760

NAME	ADDRESS	FOUN-DED	AFFILI-ATION	LEVEL/TYPE	ENROLL-MENT	TEACH-ERS	TUITION & FEES	BOARD & ROOM	TOTAL COST
GEORGIA (continued)									
Brunswick Junior College ...	Brunswick, GA 31523 ..	1961	State	J/C	1,243	50	$ 735	—	$ 735
Carver Bible College	Atlanta, GA 30313	1943	Church	S/C	54	13	$ 1,348	$1,904	$ 3,252
Clark College	Atlanta, GA 30314	1869	Un. Meth	S/C	1,879	133	$ 3,969	$1,978	$ 5,945
Clayton Junior College	Morrow, GA 30260	1969	State	J/C	3,360	149	$ 675	—	$ 675
Columbia Theological Sem. .	Decatur, GA 30031	1828	Presby	P/C	472	28	$ 3,000	$2,800	$ 5,800
Columbus College	Columbus, GA 31993 ...	1958	S-G/C	3,985	182	$ 1,068	—	$ 1,068	
Dalton Junior College	Dalton, GA 30720	1963	State	J/C	1,616	68	$ 675	—	$ 675
DeKalb Community College .	Clarkston, GA 30021	1964	County	J/C	16,848	319	$ 1,115	—	$ 1,115
DeVry Inst. of Technology ...	Atlanta, GA 30341	1969	Independ	S/C	2,625	127	$ 3,658	—	$ 3,658
Draughon's Junior College ..	Savannah, GA 31406	1899	Independ	J/C	715	46	$ 2,655	—	$ 2,655
Emanuel County Jr. College .	Swainsboro, GA 30401 ..	1973	State	J/C	416	23	$ 690	—	$ 690
Emmanuel College	Franklin Spgs., GA 30639	1919	Pent H	J/C	352	28	$ 2,335	$1,935	$ 4,290
Emory University	Atlanta GA 30322	1836	Methodist	S-G/C	8,533	1,191	$ 7,630	$3,200	$10,830
Floyd Junior College	Rome, GA 30163	1970	State	J/C	1,275	52	$ 675	—	$ 675
Fort Valley State College	Fort Valley, GA 31030 ...	1895	State	S-G/C	1,873	165	$ 1,101	$1,710	$ 2,811
Gainesville Junior College ..	Gainesville, GA 30503...	1964	State	J/C	1,744	69	$ 708	—	$ 708
Gammon Theological Seminary	Atlanta, GA 30314	1883	Un. Meth	G/C	137	33	$ 3,000	$1,300	$ 4,300
Georgia College	Milledgeville, GA 31061 .	1889	State	S-G/C	3,554	143	$ 876	$1,730	$ 2,606
Georgia Institute of Technology	Atlanta, GA 30332	1885	State	S-G/C	10,958	515	$ 1,416	$2,775	$ 4,191
Georgia Military College	Milledgeville, GA 31061 .	1879	Independ	J/C	1,403	110	$ 1,782	$3,462	$ 5,244
Georgia Southern College ...	Statesboro, GA 30460 ...	1906	State	S-G/C	6,526	373	$ 1,086	$1,890	$ 2,976
Georgia Southwestern College	Americus, GA 31709	1906	State	S-G/C	2,259	116	$ 1,155	$1,806	$ 2,961
Georgia State University	Atlanta, GA 30303	1913	State	S-G/C	21,366	755	$ 1,185	—	$ 1,185
Gordon Junior College	Barnesville, GA 30204 ..	1852	State	J/C	1,365	43	$ 710	$1,500	$ 2,210
Immanuel Baptist Schools ...	Atlanta, GA 30316	1952	Baptist	S-G/C	48	3	$ 590	—	$ 590
Interdenominational Theological Center	Atlanta, GA 30314	1958	Independ	G/C	310	34	$ 2,580	$2,200	$ 4,780
Kennesaw College	Marietta, GA 30061	1963	State	S-G/C	5,821	175	$ 890	—	$ 890
Lagrange College	Lagrange, GA 30240	1831	Methodist	S-G/C	947	55	$ 2,805	$1,680	$ 4,485
Life Chiropractic College ...	Marietta, GA 30060	1974	Independ	P/C	1,596	102	$ 5,658	—	$ 5,658
Macon Junior College	Macon, GA 31297	1968	State	J/C	2,821	89	$ 675	—	$ 675
Medical College of Georgia ..	Augusta, GA 30912	1828	State	P/C	2,320	596	$ 3,171	$ 250	$ 3,421
Mercer University	Macon, GA 31207	1833	Baptist	S-G/C	2,776	230	$ 5,000	$2,500	$ 7,500
Mercer Univ. in Atlanta	Atlanta, GA 30341	1903	Baptist	S-G/C	2,326	115	$ 3,800	—	$ 3,800
Middle Georgia College	Cochran, GA 31014	1884	State	J/C	1,293	85	$ 849	$1,635	$ 2,484
Morehouse College	Atlanta, GA 30314	1867	Independ	S-G/M	2,054	129	$ 3,760	$2,560	$ 6,320
Morris Brown College	Atlanta, GA 30314	1881	AME	S/C	1,257	100	$ 3,600	$2,000	$ 5,600
North Georgia College	Dahlonega, GA 30597 ...	1873	State	S-G/C	1,979	104	$ 1,140	$1,645	$ 2,805
North Ga. Tech. & Voc. School	Clarkesville, GA 30523 ..	1943	State	T/C	650	48	$ 60	$1,348	$ 1,408
Oglethorpe University	Atlanta, GA 30319	1835	Independ	S-G/C	1,029	66	$ 5,430	$2,980	$ 8,410
Oxford College of Emory Univ.	Oxford, GA 30267	1836	Methodist	J/C	477	36	$ 5,700	$2,740	$ 8,440
Paine College	Augusta, GA 30901	1882	Methodist	S/C	724	63	$ 3,435	$1,700	$ 5,135
Phillips College	Augusta, GA 30902	1948	Independ	S/W	203	25	$ 3,575	—	$ 3,575
Phillips College	Columbus, GA 31901	1954	Independ	J/C	700	35	$ 1,350	—	$ 1,350
Piedmont College	Demorest, GA 30535	1897	Congreg	S/C	450	38	$ 2,112	$2,400	$ 4,512
Reinhardt College	Waleska, GA 30183	1883	Methodist	J/C	318	23	$ 2,775	$2,100	$ 4,875
Savannah State College	Savannah, GA 31404	1890	State	S-G/C	1,983	133	$ 2,448	$2,772	$ 5,220
Shorter College	Rome, GA 30161	1873	Baptist	S/C	730	68	$ 3,640	$2,240	$ 5,880
South Georgia College	Douglas, GA 31533	1906	State	J/C	1,059	54	$ 720	$1,725	$ 2,445
Southern Technical Institute .	Marietta, GA 30064	1948	State	S/C	3,610	173	$ 1,100	$2,700	$ 3,800
Spelman College	Atlanta, GA 30314	1881	Independ	S/W	1,604	142	$ 4,200	$3,000	$ 7,200
Thomas County Comm. College	Thomasville, GA 31792 .	1950	Independ	J/C	391	31	$ 1,896	—	$ 1,896
Tift College	Forsyth, GA 31029	1849	Baptist	S/W	610	70	$ 2,700	$2,625	$ 5,325
Toccoa Falls College	Toccoa Falls, GA 30598 .	1907	Private	S/C	642	49	$ 3,100	$1,990	$ 5,090
Truett-McConnell College ...	Cleveland, GA 30528	1946	Baptist	J/C	902	60	$ 2,580	$1,830	$ 4,410
University of Georgia	Athens, GA 30602	1785	State	S-G/C	25,230	1,380	$ 1,577	$2,166	$ 3,743
Valdosta State College	Valdosta, GA 31698	1906	State	S-G/C	6,093	237	$ 1,185	$1,770	$ 2,955
Waycross Junior College	Waycross, GA 31501.....	1976	State	J/C	469	23	$ 678	—	$ 678
Wesleyan College	Macon, GA 31297	1836	Methodist	S/W	404	51	$ 3,950	$2,700	$ 6,650
West Georgia College	Carrollton, GA 30118 ...	1933	State	S-G/C	6,250	244	$ 1,092	$1,581	$ 2,673
Woodrow Wilson Col. of Law .	Atlanta, GA 30308	1933	Independ	P/C	250	15	$ 2,160	—	$ 2,160
Young Harris College	Young Harris, GA 30582	1886	Un. Meth	J/C	382	25	$ 2,550	$2,205	$ 4,755
HAWAII									
Brig. Young U./Hawaii Camp.	Laie, HI 96762	1955	Mormon	S/C	1,912	96	$ 1,200	$1,960	$ 3,160
Chaminade Univ. of Honolulu	Honolulu, HI 96816	1955	Catholic	S-G/C	2,389	165	$ 3,940	$2,580	$ 6,790
Hawaii Loa College	Kaneone, HI 96744	1967	Ecumen.	S/C	430	33	$ 4,850	$3,000	$ 7,850
University of Hawaii									
At Manoa	Honolulu, HI 96822	1907	State	S-G/C	19,965	1,624	$ 910	$2,150	$ 3,060
At Hilo	Hilo. HI 96720	1947	State	S/C	3,234	239	$ 790	$2,140	$ 2,930
West Oahu College	Pearl City, HI 96701	1976	State	S/C	435	18	$ 630	—	$ 630
Honolulu Community College	Honolulu, HI 96817	1920	State	J/C	4,549	198	$ 240	—	$ 240
Kaiolaini Community College.	Honolulu, HI 96814	1946	State	J/C	5,264	182	$ 240	—	$ 240
Kauai Community College	Lihue, HI 96766	1928	State	J/C	1,159	70	$ 240	—	$ 240
Leeward Community College .	Pearl City, HI 96782	1968	State	J/C	5,753	217	$ 240	—	$ 240
Maui Community College	Kahului, HI 96732	1931	State	J/C	2,087	107	$ 248	$1,128	$ 1,376
Windward Community College	Kaneohe, HI 96744	1972	State	J/C	1,363	59	$ 240	—	$ 240
IDAHO									
Boise State University	Boise, ID 83725	1932	State	S-G/C	10,435	528	$ 1,016	$2,222	$ 3,238
College of Idaho...........	Caldwell, ID 83605	1891	Presby	S-G/C	876	70	$ 5,124	$2,556	$ 7,680

NAME	ADDRESS	FOUN-DED	AFFILI-ATION	LEVEL/TYPE	ENROLL-MENT	TEACH-ERS	TUITION & FEES	BOARD & ROOM	TOTAL COST
IDAHO *(continued)*									
College of Southern Idaho	Twin Falls, ID 83301	1965	State	J/C	4,674	124	$ 750	$1,980	$ 2,730
Idaho State University	Pocatello, ID 83209	1901	State	S-G/C	11,555	447	$ 1,010	$1,900	$ 2,910
Lewis-Clark State College	Lewiston, ID 83501	1893	State	S/C	2,026	95	$ 928	$1,980	$ 2,908
North Idaho College	Coeur d'Alene, ID 83814	1933	Independ	J-T/C	2,274	171	$ 630	$2,250	$ 2,880
Northwest Nazarene College	Nampa, ID 83651	1913	Nazarene	S-G/C	1,007	87	$ 4,200	$2,200	$ 6,400
Ricks College	Rexburg, ID 83440	1888	Mormon	J/C	6,318	250	$ 1,100	$2,160	$ 3,260
University of Idaho	Moscow, ID 83843	1889	State	S-G/C	8,970	588	$ 970	$2,160	$ 3,130
ILLINOIS									
American Academy of Art	Chicago, IL 60604	1923	Independ	J/C	944	48	$ 4,100	—	$ 4,100
American Conserv. of Music	Chicago, IL 60603	1886	Independ	G/C	224	108	$ 4,000	—	$ 4,000
Augustana College	Rock Island, IL 61201	1860	Lutheran	S-G/C	2,193	143	$ 6,162	$2,568	$ 8,730
Aurora College	Aurora, IL 60506	1893	Independ	S/C	1,615	65	$ 5,005	$2,725	$ 7,730
Barat College	Lake Forest, IL 60045	1907	Catholic	S/C	669	80	$ 5,310	$2,700	$ 8,010
Belleville Area College	Belleville, IL 62221	1948	State	J/C	12,480	657	$ 690	—	$ 690
Bethany Theological Seminary	Oak Brook, IL 60521	1905	Brethren	G/C	138	22	$ 2,700	$1,215	$ 3,915
Blackburn College	Carlinville, IL 62626	1837	Presby	S/C	543	49	$ 4,360	$1,470	$ 5,830
Black Hawk College									
East Campus	Kewanee, IL 61443	1967	State	J/C	1,362	62	$ 885	—	$ 885
Quad Cities Campus	Moline, IL 61265	1946	State	J/C	5,379	134	$ 885	—	$ 885
Bradley University	Peoria, IL 61625	1897	Independ	S-G/C	5,366	428	$ 6,300	$2,950	$ 9,250
Carl Sandburg College	Galesburg, IL 61401	1966	State	J/C	4,200	178	$ 705	—	$ 705
Catholic Theological Union	Chicago, IL 60615	1968	Catholic	G/C	303	51	$ 4,200	$3,800	$ 8,000
Chicago Col. of Osteo. Med.	Chicago, IL 60615	1900	Independ	P/C	396	300	$ 9,650	—	$ 9,650
Chicago State University	Chicago, IL 60628	1867	State	S-G/C	7,404	279	$ 1,114	—	$ 1,114
Chicago Theol. Seminary	Chicago, IL 60637	1855	C of Chr	G/C	166	13	$ 3,200	$1,470	$ 4,670
City Colleges of Chicago	Chicago, IL 60601	1911	State	J/C					
Chicago City-Wide College	Chicago, IL 60601	1975	State	J/C	19,049	63	$ 562	—	$ 562
Chicago Urban Skills Inst.	Chicago, IL 60609	1970	State	J/C	35,129	2,351	$ 40	—	$ 40
Daley College	Chicago, IL 60652	1960	State	J/C	11,092	138	$ 562	—	$ 562
Kennedy-King College	Chicago, IL 60621	1934	State	J/C	9,171	264	$ 562	—	$ 562
Loop College	Chicago, IL 60601	1962	State	J/C	9,496	182	$ 562	—	$ 562
Malcolm X College	Chicago, IL 60612	1911	State	J/C	7,142	148	$ 562	—	$ 562
Olive-Harvey College	Chicago, IL 60628	1957	State	J/C	9,343	152	$ 562	—	$ 562
Truman College	Chicago, IL 60645	1956	State	J/C	13,075	230	$ 562	—	$ 562
Wright College	Chicago, IL 60634	1934	State	J/C	9,627	178	$ 562	—	$ 562
College of Dupage	Glen Ellyn, IL 60137	1966	State	J/C	26,281	1,167	$ 765	—	$ 765
College of Lake County	Grayslake, IL 60030	1967	State	J/C	12,284	552	$ 695	—	$ 695
College of St. Francis	Joliet, IL 60435	1930	Catholic	S-G/C	3,850	233	$ 4,750	$2,550	$ 7,300
Columbia College Chicago	Chicago, IL 60605	1890	Independ	S-G/C	4,257	375	$ 3,500	—	$ 3,500
Concordia College	River Forest, IL 60305	1864	Lutheran	S-G/C	1,366	101	$ 3,552	$2,355	$ 5,907
Danville Area Comm. College	Danville, IL 61832	1946	Public	J/C	4,100	70	$ 700	—	$ 700
De Lourdes College	Des Plaines, IL 60016	1927	Catholic	S/W	194	27	$ 1,800	—	$ 1,800
DePaul University	Chicago, IL 60604	1898	Catholic	S-G/C	12,326	911	$ 5,382	$3,250	$ 8,632
DeVry Institute of Technology	Chicago, IL 60618	1931	Independ	S/C	3,384	178	$ 3,658	—	$ 3,658
DeVry Institute of Technology	Lombard, IL 60148	1982	Independ	S/C	2,798	50	$ 3,658	—	$ 3,658
Dr. William M. Scholl College									
of Podiatric Medicine	Chicago, IL 60610	1912	Independ	P/C	520	60	$ 9,900	—	$ 9,900
Eastern Illinois University	Charleston, IL 61920	1895	State	S-G/C	10,419	550	$ 1,426	$2,150	$ 3,576
Elgin Community College	Elgin, IL 60120	1949	State	J/C	5,906	89	$ 900	—	$ 900
Elmhurst College	Elmhurst, IL 60126	1871	C of Chr	S/C	1,913	104	$ 4,972	$2,560	$ 7,532
Eureka College	Eureka, IL 61530	1855	Church	S/C	527	36	$ 3,700	$2,500	$ 6,200
Felician College	Chicago, IL 60659	1926	Catholic	J/C	325	36	$ 2,000	—	$ 2,000
Garrett-Evang. Theol. Sem.	Evanston, IL 60201	1853	Un. Meth	G/C	353	40	$ 3,600	$2,325	$ 5,925
George Williams College	Downers Grove, IL 60515	1890	Independ	S-G/C	1,186	104	$ 4,650	$2,400	$ 7,050
Governors State University	Park Forest S., IL 60466	1969	State	S-G/C	4,921	288	$ 1,107	—	$ 1,107
Greenville College	Greenville, IL 62246	1892	Fr. Meth	S/C	650	47	$ 5,336	$2,540	$ 7,876
Hebrew Theological College	Skokie, IL 60077	1922	Jewish	P-G/C	70	20	$ 1,900	$2,795	$ 4,695
Highland Community College	Freeport, IL 61032	1962	State	P/C	2,663	114	$ 608	—	$ 3,458
Illinois Benedictine College	Lisle, IL 60532	1887	Catholic	S-G/C	1,486	127	$ 5,396	$2,715	$ 8,111
Illinois Central College	East Peoria, IL 61635	1966	Public	J/C	12,400	608	$ 700	—	$ 700
Illinois College	Jacksonville, IL 62650	1829	Presby	S/C	785	82	$ 3,850	$2,350	$ 6,200
Illinois College of Optometry	Chicago, IL 60616	1955	Independ	P/C	531	73	$11,000	$1,455	$12,455
Ill. Eastern Comm. Colleges									
Frontier Comm. College	Fairfield, IL 62837	1977	Public	J/C	3,853	436	$ 384	—	$ 384
Lincoln Trail College	Robinson, IL 62454	1969	Public	J/C	1,514	232	$ 384	—	$ 384
Olney Central College	Olney, IL 62450	1962	Public	J/C	2,449	368	$ 384	—	$ 384
Wabash Valley College	Mt. Carmel, IL 62863	1960	Public	J/C	2,354	240	$ 384	—	$ 384
Illinois Inst. of Technology	Chicago, IL 60616	1890	Independ	S-G/C	6,441	485	$ 7,380	$3,330	$10,710
Chicago-Kent Col. of Law	Chicago, IL 60606	1888	Independ	P/C	1,090	103	$ 7,500	$4,200	$11,700
Illinois State University	Normal, IL 61761	1857	State	S-G/C	20,134	1,405	$ 500	$2,200	$ 2,700
Illinois Valley Comm. College	Oglesby, IL 61348	1924	State	J/C	3,940	162	$ 420	—	$ 420
Illinois Wesleyan University	Bloomington, IL 61702	1850	Methodist	S/C	1,641	126	$ 6,660	$2,750	$ 9,410
John A. Logan College	Carterville, IL 62918	1967	State	J/C	2,396	94	$ 444	—	$ 444
John Marshall Law School	Chicago, IL 60604	1899	Independ	P/C	1,509	119	$ 6,650	$6,050	$12,700
Joliet Junior College	Joliet, IL 60436	1901	State	J/C	9,845	504	$ 610	—	$ 610
Judson College	Elgin, IL 60120	1963	Baptist	S/C	411	50	$ 5,300	$2,840	$ 8,140
Kankakee Community College	Kankakee, IL 60901	1966	State	J/C	3,964	56	$ 585	—	$ 585
Kaskaskia College	Centralia, IL 62801	1940	State	J/C	2,894	64	$ 638	—	$ 638
Kendall College	Evanston, IL 60201	1934	Independ	S/C	325	31	$ 4,500	$2,500	$ 7,000
Kishwaukee College	Malta, IL 60150	1968	Public	J/C	3,444	209	$ 704	—	$ 5,230
Knox College	Galesburg, IL 61401	1837	Independ	S/C	910	91	$ 7,923	$2,637	$10,560
Lake Forest College	Lake Forest, IL 60045	1857	Presby	S/C	1,125	83	$ 8,800	$2,500	$11,300

NAME	ADDRESS	FOUN-DED	AFFILI-ATION	LEVEL/TYPE	ENROLL-MENT	TEACH-ERS	TUITION & FEES	BOARD & ROOM	TOTAL COST
ILLINOIS *(continued)*									
LakeLand College	Mattoon, IL 61938	1966	Public	J/C	3,389	100	$ 864	—	$ 864
Lewis & Clark Comm. College	Godfrey, IL 62035	1970	State	J/C	4,743	265	$ 658	—	$ 658
Lewis University	Romeoville, IL 60441 ...	1932	Catholic	S-G/C	2,820	174	$ 5,056	$2,360	$ 7,416
Lincoln Christian College	Lincoln, IL 62656	1944	Christian	S-G/C	473	26	$ 3,040	$1,890	$ 4,930
Lincoln College	Lincoln, IL 62656	1865	Independ	J/C	1,594	93	$ 4,700	$2,650	$ 7,350
Lincoln Land Comm. College .	Springfield, IL 62708	1967	State	J/C	6,646	370	$ 749	—	$ 749
Loyola Univ. of Chicago	Chicago, IL 60611	1870	Catholic	S-G/C	14,557	1,266	$ 5,190	$3,086	$ 8,276
Niles College	Chicago, IL 60631	1961	Catholic	S/M	181	28	$ 5,158	$1,500	$ 6,658
Lutheran School of Theology.	Chicago, IL 60615	1860	Lutheran	P/C	342	58	$ 2,000	—	$ 2,000
MacCormac College	Chicago, IL 60604	1904	Independ	J/C	714	53	$ 3,750	—	$ 3,750
MacMurray College	Jacksonville, IL 62650 ..	1846	Un. Meth.	S/C	632	75	$ 4,870	$1,330	$ 7,200
Mallinckrodt College	Wilmette, IL 60091	1918	Catholic	S/C	285	25	$ 2,730	—	$ 2,730
McCormick Theological Sem.	Chicago, IL 60615	1829	Presby	G/C	551	25	$ 2,940	$3,320	$ 6,260
McHenry County College	Crystal Lake, IL 60014 ..	1967	State	J/C	3,536	182	$ 840	—	$ 840
McKendree College	Lebanon, IL 62254	1828	Un. Meth.	S/C	1,155	50	$ 4,266	$2,310	$ 6,576
Meadville/Lombard Theol. School	Chicago, IL 60637	1844	Unit. Univ.	P/C	35	4	$ 7,500	—	$ 7,500
Midwest Col. of Engineering .	Lombard, IL 60148	1967	Independ	S-G/C	263	45	$ 4,550	—	$ 4,550
Midwest Montessori Teach. Tr. Ctr.	Chicago, IL 60622	1964	Independ	P/C	112	16	$ 2,300	—	$ 2,300
Millikin University	Decatur, IL 62522	1901	Presby	S/C	1,605	140	$ 6,111	$2,700	$ 8,811
Monmouth College	Monmouth, IL 61462.....	1853	Presby	S/C	618	77	$ 7,440	$2,490	$ 9,930
Moody Bible Institute	Chicago, IL 60610	1886	Independ	S/C	1,350	59	$ 550	$3,100	$ 3,600
Moraine Valley Comm. College	Palos Hills, IL 60465 ...	1969	Public	J/C	13,990	575	$ 766	—	$ 766
Morton College	Cicero, IL 60650	1924	State	J/C	3,492	185	$ 570	—	$ 570
Mundelein College	Chicago, IL 60660	1929	Catholic	S-G/W	1,171	135	$ 5,443	$2,549	$ 7,992
Nat. College of Chiropractic .	Lombard, IL 60148	1906	Independ	P/C	908	72	$ 5,010	$2,710	$ 7,720
North Central College	Naperville, IL 60566	1861	Un. Meth.	S/C	1,656	115	$ 6,000	$2,700	$ 8,700
North Park College	Chicago, IL 60625	1891	Evang	S/C	1,396	86	$ 6,162	$2,795	$ 8,957
Northeastern Illinois Univ. ...	Chicago, IL 60625	1961	State	S-G/C	10,075	533	$ 900	—	$ 900
No. Baptist Theological Sem.	Lombard, IL 60148	1913	Baptist	G/C	230	12	$ 3,080	—	$ 3,080
Northern Illinois University ..	DeKalb, IL 60115	1895	State	S-G/C	23,689	1,230	$ 1,360	$2,220	$ 3,560
Northwestern University	Evanston, IL 60201	1851	Independ	S-G/C	15,300	1,780	$10,380	$3,735	$15,315
Oakton Community College...	Des Plaines, IL 60016 ...	1969	State	J/C	8,871	510	$ 622	—	$ 622
Olivet Nazarene College	Kankakee, IL 60901.....	1907	Nazarene	S/C	1,771	115	$ 4,142	$2,274	$ 6,416
Parkland College	Champaign, IL 61821 ...	1966	Public	J/C	8,525	505	$ 720	—	$ 720
Parks Col. of St. Louis Univ. .	Cahokia, IL 62206	1927	Catholic	S/C	1,112	78	$ 1,985	$1,295	$ 3,280
Prairie State College	Chicago Hgts, IL 60411 .	1958	State	J/C	5,073	173	$ 825	—	$ 825
Principia College	Elsah, IL 62028	1898	Independ	S/C	711	72	$ 7,125	$3,747	$10,872
Quincy College	Quincy, IL 62301	1859	Catholic	S/C	1,502	96	$ 4,900	$2,240	$ 7,140
Reid Col. of Detect. of Deception	Chicago, IL 60606	1947	Independ	G/C	10	4	$ 3,000	—	$ 3,000
Rend Lake College..........	Ina, IL 62846	1967	State	J/C	2,418	54	$ 540	—	$ 540
Richland Community College	Decatur, IL 62526	1971	State	J/C	3,138	132	$ 630	—	$ 630
Robert Morris College	Carthage, IL 62321	1965	Independ	S/C	575	34	$ 6,800	$3,600	$10,400
Chicago Branch	Chicago, IL 60601	1965	Independ	J/C	1,030	69	$ 6,800	—	$ 6,800
Rock Valley College	Rockford, IL 61101	1964	State	J/C	10,483	604	$ 780	—	$ 780
Rockford College	Rockford, IL 61108	1847	Independ	S-G/C	1,450	115	$ 5,490	$2,500	$ 7,990
Roosevelt University	Chicago, IL 60605	1945	Independ	S-G/C	6,286	481	$ 4,725	$3,150	$ 7,825
Rosary College	River Forest, IL 60305 ..	1918	Catholic	S-G/C	1,650	137	$ 5,200	$2,700	$ 7,900
Saint Xavier College	Chicago, IL 60655	1847	Catholic	S-G/C	2,269	140	$ 5,100	$3,463	$ 8,563
Sangamon State University ..	Springfield, IL 62708 ...	1969	State	S-G/C	3,027	194	$ 1,044	$1,400	$ 2,444
Sauk Valley College........	Dixon, IL 61021.......	1965	Public	J/C	2,685	175	$ 864	—	$ 864
Sch. of the Art Inst. of Chicago	Chicago, IL 60603	1866	Independ	S-G/C	1,691	190	$ 6,150	$2,500	$ 8,650
Seabury-Western Theol. Sem.	Evanston, IL 60201	1933	Episcopal	P/C	97	12	$ 4,030	$2,300	$ 9,500
Sherwood Music School	Chicago, IL 60605	1895	Independ	S-G/C	50	30	$ 2,500	—	$ 2,500
Southeastern Illinois College .	Harrisburg, IL 62946 ...	1960	State	J/C	2,753	65	$ 540	—	$ 2,710
Southern Illinois University ..	Carbondale, IL 62901 ..	1869	State	S-G/C	22,874	1,296	$ 1,520	$2,472	$ 3,992
So. Ill. Univ. at Edwardsville .	Edwardsville, IL 62026 ..	1957	State	S-G/C	10,820	635	$ 1,290	$2,534	$ 3,824
Spertus College of Judaica ..	Chicago, IL 60605	1925	Independ	S-G/C	300	12	$ 2,680	—	$ 2,680
Spoon River College	Canton, IL 61520	1959	Public	J/C	1,993	122	$ 864	—	$ 864
Springfield College in Illinois .	Springfield, IL 62702 ...	1929	Catholic	J/C	507	39	$ 3,200	—	$ 3,200
State Community College ...	St. Louis, IL 62201......	1969	State	J/C	1,357	45	$ 665	—	$ 665
Thornton Community College	South Holland, IL 60473.	1927	State	J/C	10,217	292	$ 825	—	$ 825
Trinity Christian College	Palos Heights, IL 60463 .	1959	Independ	S/C	510	50	$ 5,090	$2,290	$ 7,380
Trinity College	Deerfield, IL 60015	1897	Independ	S/C	580	51	$ 5,200	$2,520	$ 7,720
Triton College	River Grove, IL 60171 ...	1964	State	J/C	25,057	1,064	$ 800	—	$ 800
University of Chicago	Chicago, IL 60637	1891	Independ	S-G/C	8,118	1,121	$ 8,670	$4,100	$12,770
University of Illinois	Urbana, IL 61801.......	1867	State	G-P/C					
Chicago Campus	Chicago, IL 60680	1896	State	S-G/C	24,067	2,305	$ 1,764	$3,261	$ 5,025
Health Sciences Campus ..	Chicago, IL 60680	1896	State	G/C	4,244	1,208	$ 1,833	$3,650	$ 5,483
Urbana-Champaign Campus	Urbana, IL 61801......	1867	State	S-G/C	34,760	2,336	$ 1,722	$2,910	$ 4,632
Vandercook College of Music	Chicago, IL 60616	1909	Independ	S-G/C	141	36	$ 4,840	$3,290	$ 8,130
Waubonsee Community Col. .	Sugar Grove, IL 60554 ..	1966	State	J/C	5,773	295	$ 800	—	$ 800
Western Illinois University ..	Macomb, IL 61455......	1899	State	S-G/C	11,750	700	$ 1,328	$2,070	$ 3,398
Wheaton College	Wheaton, IL 60187	1860	Independ	S/C	2,571	150	$ 6,000	$2,700	$ 8,700
William Rainey Harper College	Palatine, IL 60067	1965	State	J/C	21,684	708	$ 786	—	$ 786
INDIANA									
Ancilla College	Donaldson, IN 46513 ...	1937	Catholic	J/C	467	24	$ 1,300	—	$ 1,300
Anderson College	Anderson, IN 46012	1917	C of God	S-G/C	2,070	160	$ 4,490	$1,790	$ 6,280
Ball State University	Muncie, IN 47306	1918	State	S-G/C	18,321	842	$ 1,550	$2,150	$ 3,700
Bethel College	Mishawaka, IN 46545 ...	1947	Mission	S-G/C	550	40	$ 4,200	$2,140	$ 6,340
Butler University	Indianapolis, IN 46208 ..	1855	Independ	S-G/C	3,861	260	$ 6,340	$1,360	$ 7,700
Calumet College	Whiting, IN 46394	1951	Catholic	S/C	1,130	60	$ 3,400	—	$ 3,400
Christian Theol. Seminary ...	Indianapolis, IN 46208 .	1924	D of Chr	G/C	365	32	$ 3,000	—	$ 3,000

NAME	ADDRESS	FOUN-DED	AFFILI-ATION	LEVEL/TYPE	ENROLL-MENT	TEACH-ERS	TUITION & FEES	BOARD & ROOM	TOTAL COST
INDIANA *(continued)*									
Concordia Theol. Seminary ..	Fort Wayne, IN 46825 ...	1846	Lutheran	G/M	516	35	$ 3,840	$2,100	$ 5,940
DePauw University	Greencastle, IN 46135 ...	1837	Methodist	S-G/C	2,282	201	$ 7,670	$3,090	$10,760
Earlham College	Richmond, IN 47374	1847	Friends	S/C	980	99	$ 7,875	$2,700	$10,575
Elkhart Inst. of Technology ..	Elkhart, IN 46516	1882	Independ	T/C	80	6	$ 2,025	$1,400	$ 3,425
Fort Wayne Bible College ...	Fort Wayne, IN 46807 ...	1904	Mission	S/C	405	43	$ 3,760	$2,290	$ 6,050
Franklin College	Franklin, IN 46131	1834	Baptist	S/C	705	64	$ 5,930	$2,480	$ 8,410
Goshen Biblical Seminary ...	Elkhart, IN 46517	1946	Mennon	G/C	134	11	$ 2,304	$2,170	$ 4,470
Goshen College	Goshen, IN 46526	1894	Mennon	S/C	1,043	96	$ 5,280	$2,285	$ 7,565
Grace College	Winona Lake, IN 46590..	1948	Brethren	S/C	846	65	$ 4,271	$2,460	$ 6,731
Grace Theological Seminary .	Winona Lake, IN 46590..	1937	Brethren	G/C	407	21	$ 3,364		$ 3,364
Hanover College	Hanover, IN 47243	1827	Presby	S/C	1,020	71	$ 4,150	$2,250	$ 6,400
Herron School of Art of Ind. Univ.	Indianapolis, IN 46202 ..	1902	State	S-G/C	381	31	$ 1,488	$3,140	$ 4,628
Holy Cross Junior College ...	Notre Dame, IN 46556 ...	1966	Catholic	J/C	364	25	$ 2,325		$ 2,325
Huntington College	Huntington, IN 46750 ...	1897	Brethren	S-G/C	418	60	$ 5,070	$2,180	$ 7,250
Indiana Central University ...	Indianapolis, IN 46227 ..	1902	Independ	S-G/C	3,042	139	$ 5,490	$2,360	$ 7,850
Indiana Inst. of Technology ..	Fort Wayne, IN 46803 ...	1930	Independ	S/C	800	43	$ 4,100	$2,000	$ 6,000
Indiana State University	Terre Haute, IN 47809 ..	1865	State	S-G/C	11,638	660	$ 1,454	$2,006	$ 3,460
Ind. State Univ. Evansville ..	Evansville, IN 47712	1965	State	S/C	3,848	175	$ 1,350		$ 1,350
Indiana University	Bloomington, IN 47405..	1820	State						
Bloomington.............	Bloomington, IN 47405..	1820	State	S-G/C	32,715	1,418	$ 1,534	$2,164	$ 3,698
East	Richmond, IN 47374	1946	State	J/C	1,326	31	$ 1,311	—	$ 1,311
Kokomo	Kokomo, IN 46902	1945	State	S/C	2,499	55	$ 1,285	—	$ 1,285
Northwest	Gary, IN 46408	1922	State	S-G/C	4,686	138	$ 1,281	—	$ 1,281
Purdue Univ. at Fort Wayne	Fort Wayne, IN 46805 ...	1964	State	S-G/C	4,910	148	$ 1,274	—	$ 1,274
Purdue Univ. at Indianapolis	Indianapolis, IN 46202 ..	1969	State	S-G/C	23,368	1,266	$ 1,400	—	$ 1,400
South Bend	South Bend, IN 46634...	1922	State	S-G/C	5,442	145	$ 1,293	—	$ 1,293
Southeast	New Albany, IN 47150 ...	1941	State	S-G/C	4,399	98	$ 1,315	—	$ 1,315
Indiana Vocational Tech. Coll.									
Central Indiana	Indianapolis, IN 46202 ..	1966	State	T/C	4,631	228	$ 1,107	—	$ 1,107
Columbus	Columbus, IN 47201	1967	State	T/C	1,891	58	$ 1,107	—	$ 1,107
East Central	Muncie, IN 47302	1968	State	T/C	1,918	94	$ 1,107	—	$ 1,107
Kokomo	Kokomo, IN 46901	1968	State	T/C	1,415	89	$ 1,107	—	$ 1,107
Lafayette	Lafayette, IN 47903	1968	State	T/C	1,343	83	$ 1,107	—	$ 1,107
North Central	South Bend, IN 46619...	1967	State	T/C	2,407	139	$ 1,107	—	$ 1,107
Northeast	Fort Wayne, IN 46805 ...	1968	State	T/C	3,402	209	$ 1,107	—	$ 1,107
Northwest	Gary, IN 46408	1948	State	T/C	3,637	202	$ 1,107	—	$ 1,107
Southcentral	Sellersburg, IN 47172...	1968	State	T/C	1,388	89	$ 1,107	—	$ 1,107
Southeast	Madison, IN 47250	1968	State	T/C	729	57	$ 1,107	—	$ 1,107
Southwest	Evansville, IN 47710	1968	State	T/C	2,103	133	$ 1,107	—	$ 1,107
Wabash Valley	Terre Haute, IN 47802 ..	1966	State	T/C	1,784	85	$ 1,107	—	$ 1,107
Whitewater	Richmond, IN 47374	1968	State	T/C	1,044	88	$ 1,107	—	$ 1,107
Manchester College	Manchester, IN 46962 ..	1889	Brethren	S-G/C	1,027	91	$ 5,590	$2,160	$ 7,750
Marian College	Indianapolis, IN 46222 ..	1851	Catholic	S/C	1,044	95	$ 4,130	$2,215	$ 6,345
Marion College	Marion, IN 46952	1920	Wesleyan	S-G/C	1,058	95	$ 4,964	$2,316	$ 7,280
Mennonite Biblical Seminary .	Elkhart, IN 46517	1946	Mennon	G/C	91	13	$ 2,300	$2,170	$ 4,470
Oakland City College	Oakland City, IN 47660 ..	1885	Church	S-G/C	734	36	$ 4,410	$1,998	$ 6,408
Purdue University	West Lafayette, IN 47907	1869	State	S-G/C	46,789	3,071	$ 1,629	$2,500	$ 4,129
Calumet	Hammond, IN 46323	1946	State	S-G/C	7,442	325	$ 1,600	—	$ 1,600
North Central Campus	Westville, IN 46391	1946	State	S-G/C	2,616	150	$ 1,300	—	$ 1,300
Rose-Hulman Institute of Technology	Terre Haute, IN 47803 ..	1874	Independ	S-G/M	1,347	93	$ 6,765	$2,670	$ 9,435
St. Francis College	Fort Wayne, IN 46808 ...	1890	Catholic	S-G/C	1,310	85	$ 3,892	$2,400	$ 6,292
St. Joseph's College	Rensselaer, IN 47978 ...	1889	Catholic	S/C	933	72	$ 5,300	$2,470	$ 7,770
St. Mary-of-The-Woods College	St. Mary/Woods, IN 47876	1840	Catholic	S/W	670	85	$ 5,290	$2,510	$ 7,800
St. Mary's College	Notre Dame, IN 46556 ..	1844	Catholic	S/W	1,799	177	$ 6,982	$3,052	$10,034
St. Meinrad College	St. Meinrad, IN 47577 ...	1861	Catholic	S/M	164	36	$ 2,774	$3,168	$ 5,942
Taylor University	Upland, IN 46989	1846	Independ	S/C	1,473	111	$ 5,306	$2,494	$ 7,800
Tri-State University	Angola, IN 46703	1884	Independ	S/C	1,012	74	$ 4,944	$2,400	$ 7,344
Union Bible Seminary	Westfield, IN 46074	1911	Int-Den	S/C	137	14	$ 1,323	$1,980	$ 3,303
University of Evansville	Evansville, IN 47702	1854	Methodist	S-G/C	4,208	240	$ 6,160	$2,696	$ 8,856
University of Notre Dame ...	Notre Dame, IN 46556 ...	1842	Catholic	S-G/C	9,350	923	$ 6,850	$2,459	$ 9,309
Valparaiso Technical Institute	Valparaiso, IN 46383 ...	1874	Independ	T/C	220	14	$ 3,400	$3,550	$ 6,950
Valparaiso University	Valparaiso, IN 46383 ...	1859	Independ	P/C	3,958	266	$ 5,790	$2,410	$ 8,200
Vincennes University	Vincennes, IN 47591	1801	State	J/C	6,688	393	$ 1,124	$2,060	$ 3,184
Wabash College	Crawfordsville, IN 47933	1932	Independ	S/M	787	76	$ 6,300	$2,575	$ 8,875
IOWA									
American Institute of Business	Des Moines, IA 50321 ...	1921	Independ	J/C	1,062	50	$ 2,940	$1,240	$ 4,180
Briar Cliff College	Sioux City, IA 51104	1930	Catholic	S/C	1,307	64	$ 4,800	$2,100	$ 6,900
Buena Vista College	Storm Lake, IA 50588 ...	1891	Presby	S/C	1,500	54	$ 5,885	$2,109	$ 7,994
Central University of Iowa ...	Pella, IA 50219..........	1853	Reformed	S/C	1,548	78	$ 6,000	$2,450	$ 8,450
Clarke College	Dubuque, IA 52001	1843	Church	S-G/C	927	80	$ 5,400	$2,105	$ 7,505
Coe College	Cedar Rapids, IA 52402 ..	1851	Presby	S/C	1,311	85	$ 6,310	$2,180	$ 8,490
Cornell College	Mt. Vernon, IA 52314 ...	1853	Methodist	S/C	1,084	71	$ 7,009	$2,642	$ 9,651
Des Moines Area Comm. Col.	Ankeny, IA 50021	1966	State	J/C	6,429	294	$ 973	—	$ 973
Boone Campus	Boone, IA 50036	1927	State	J/C	693	26	$ 973	—	$ 973
Urban Campus	Des Moines, IA 50314 ...	1972	State	J/C	934	23	$ 973	—	$ 973
Divine Word College	Epworth, IA 52045.......	1912	Catholic	S/M	89	24	$ 3,500	$1,200	$ 4,700
Dordt College	Sioux Center, IA 51250...	1955	Reformed	S-G/C	1,103	73	$ 4,650	$1,690	$ 6,350
Drake University	Des Moines, IA 50311....	1881	Independ	S-G/C	5,751	305	$ 6,630	$2,970	$ 9,600
Eastern Iowa Comm. Col. Dist.	Davenport, IA 53803								
Clinton Community College	Clinton, IA 52732.......	1946	State	J/C	1,014	59	$ 917	—	$ 917
Muscatine Community College	Muscatine, IA 52761	1929	State	J/C	850	50	$ 917	—	$ 917

NAME	ADDRESS	FOUN-DED	AFFILI-ATION	LEVEL/TYPE	ENROLL-MENT	TEACH-ERS	TUITION & FEES	BOARD & ROOM	TOTAL COST
IOWA *(continued)*									
Scott Community College .	Bettendorf, IA 52722 ...	1966	State	J/C	2,606	162	$ 911	—	$ 911
Ellsworth Community College	Iowa Falls, IA 50126 ...	1890	State	J/C	925	56	$ 1,030	$1,890	$ 2,920
Emmaus Bible College	Dubuque, IA 52001	1941	Church	S/C	170	14	$ 1,390	$2,400	$ 3,790
Faith Baptist Bible College...	Ankeny, IA 50021	1924	Baptist	S-G/C	347	26	$ 3,170	$2,200	$ 5,370
Graceland College	Lamoni, IA 50140	1895	R.L.D.S.	S/C	998	82	$ 5,145	$1,955	$ 7,100
Grand View College	Des Moines, IA 50316 ...	1896	Lutheran	S/C	1,323	112	$ 4,260	$1,900	$ 6,160
Grinnell College	Grinnell, IA 50112 ...	1846	Independ	S/C	1,251	125	$ 8,436	$2,544	$10,980
Hawkeye Inst. of Technology.	Waterloo, IA 50704 ...	1966	State	T/C	1,948	140	$ 807	—	$ 807
Indian Hills Comm. College .	Ottumwa, IA 52501	1966	State	J/C	2,212	124	$ 630	$1,500	$ 2,130
Iowa Central Comm. College	Fort Dodge, IA 50501 ...	1966	State	J/C	2,889	104	$ 904	$1,995	$ 2,899
Iowa Lakes Comm. College .	Estherville, IA 51334	1967	State	J/C	1,687	80	$ 785	$2,115	$ 2,900
Iowa State University	Ames, IA 50011	1858	State	S-G/C	26,321	1,703	$ 1,304	$1,900	$ 3,204
Iowa Wesleyan College	Mt. Pleasant, IA 52641 ..	1842	Methodist	J/C	721	56	$ 5,300	$2,270	$ 7,570
Iowa Western Comm. College	Council Bluffs, IA 51502.	1966	State	J/C	2,865	278	$ 960	$1,188	$ 2,148
Clarinda Campus.........	Clarinda, IA 51632	1966	State	J/C	364	26	$ 1,065	—	$ 1,065
Kirkwood Comm. College ...	Cedar Rapids, IA 52406 .	1966	State	J/C	6,340	418	$ 800	—	$ 800
Loras College	Dubuque, IA 52004	1839	Catholic	S-G/C	1,995	138	$ 5,700	$2,350	$ 8,050
Luther College	Decorah, IA 52101 ...	1861	Lutheran	S/C	2,137	155	$ 6,500	$2,100	$ 8,600
Marshalltown Comm. College	Marshalltown, IA 50158 .	1927	State	J/C	1,400	90	$ 900	—	$ 900
Marycrest College	Davenport, IA 52804	1939	Catholic	S-G/C	1,200	90	$ 4,730	$2,150	$ 6,880
Morningside College	Sioux City, IA 51106	1894	Methodist	G/C	1,292	89	$ 5,575	$1,950	$ 7,525
Mount Mercy College	Cedar Rapids, IA 52402 .	1928	Catholic	S/C	1,287	90	$ 4,950	$2,175	$ 7,125
Mount St. Clare College	Clinton, IA 52732	1928	Catholic	J-S/C	366	36	$ 3,850	$2,150	$ 6,000
North Iowa Area Comm. Col. .	Mason City, IA 50401 ...	1918	State	J/C	2,096	87	$ 950	$1,900	$ 2,850
Northeast Iowa Tech. Institute	Calmar, IA 52132.......	1967	Public	T/C	1,100	110	$ 1,233	—	$ 1,233
Northwest Iowa Tech. Col. ..	Sheldon, IA 51201	1966	State	T/C	472	36	$ 1,200	—	$ 1,200
Northwestern College	Orange City, IA 51041 ...	1882	Church	S/C	900	58	$ 4,752	$1,868	$ 6,620
Palmer Col. of Chiropractic ..	Davenport, IA 52803	1895	Independ	P/C	1,975	120	—	—	$12,000
Saint Ambrose College	Davenport, IA 52803	1882	Catholic	S-G/C	2,236	158	$ 6,015	$2,394	$ 8,409
Simpson College	Independianola, IA 50125	1860	Un. Meth	S/C	1,244	70	$ 6,165	$2,195	$ 8,360
Sioux Empire College	Hawarden, IA 51023 ...	1965	Independ	J/C	151	30	$ 3,030	$1,550	$ 4,580
Southeastern Comm. College	W. Burlington, IA 52655 .	1966	State	J/C	1,962	81	$ 880	—	$ 920
Southwestern Comm. College	Creston, IA 50801	1966	State	J/C	667	48	$ 870	$1,900	$ 2,770
University of Dubuque	Dubuque, IA 52001	1852	Presby	S/C	986	79	$ 5,050	$2,000	$ 7,250
University of Iowa	Iowa City, IA 52242	1847	State	S-G/C	29,712	1,634	$ 1,304	$2,127	$ 3,431
University of Northern Iowa .	Cedar Falls, IA 50613 ...	1876	State	S-G/C	11,161	720	$ 1,242	$1,812	$ 3,054
Univ. of Ost. Med. & Hlth. Sci.	Des Moines, IA 50312 ...	1898	Independ	P/C	897	88	$12,775	—	$12,775
Upper Iowa University	Fayette, IA 52142	1857	Independ	S/C	716	30	$ 5,280	$2,420	$ 7,700
Vennard College	University Park, IA 52595	1910	Independ	P/C	201	17	$ 2,550	$1,840	$ 4,390
Waldorf College	Forest City, IA 50436 ...	1903	Lutheran	J/C	423	37	$ 5,750	$2,050	$ 7,800
Wartburg College	Waverly, IA 50677	1852	Lutheran	S/C	1,199	82	$ 6,060	$2,310	$ 8,370
Wartburg Theological Sem. .	Dubuque, IA 52001	1854	Lutheran	P/C	247	18	$ 1,850	$1,715	$ 3,565
Western Iowa Tech. Comm. Col	Sioux City, IA 51102	1967	State	J/C	1,279	95	$ 920	$ 900	$ 1,820
Westmar College	LeMars, IA 51031	1890	Un. Meth	S/C	514	34	$ 5,180	$2,403	$ 7,583
William Penn College	Oskaloosa, IA 52577	1873	Quaker	S/C	472	37	$ 5,670	$2,180	$ 7,850
KANSAS									
Allen County Comm. College .	Iola, KS 66749	1923	State	J/C	2,012	90	$ 440	$1,600	$ 2,040
Baker University	Baldwin City, KS 66006 .	1858	Un. Meth	S-G/C	749	53	$ 4,150	$2,200	$ 6,350
Barton Co. Comm. College .	Great Bend, KS 67530 ..	1965	State	J/C	4,446	78	$ 555	$1,850	$ 2,405
Benedictine College	Atchison, KS 66002.....	1858	Catholic	S/C	898	92	$ 4,523	$2,270	$ 6,793
Bethany College	Lindsborg, KS 67456 ...	1881	Lutheran	S/C	816	59	$ 4,150	$2,450	$ 6,600
Bethel College	North Newton, KS 67117	1887	Mennon	S/C	643	80	$ 4,500	$2,392	$ 6,892
Butler County Comm. College	El Dorado, KS 67042.....	1927	State	J/C	3,569	229	$ 704	$1,902	$ 2,606
Central Baptist Theol. Sem...	Kansas City, KS 66102 ..	1901	Baptist	P/C	167	18	$ 1,650	$ 855	$ 2,505
Central College	McPherson, KS 67460 ..	1884	Methodist	J/C	293	25	$ 4,100	$2,250	$ 6,350
Cloud County Comm. College	Concordia, KS 66901 ...	1965	State	J/C	2,066	200	$ 700	$1,790	$ 2,490
Coffeyville Comm. College .	Coffeyville, KS 67337 ...	1923	State	J/C	1,598	34	$ 464	$1,590	$ 2,054
Colby Community College ..	Colby, KS 67701	1964	State	J/C	1,818	91	$ 650	$1,850	$ 2,500
Cowley County Comm. College	Arkansas City, KS 67005	1922	County	J/C	1,697	87	$ 408	$1,980	$ 2,388
Dodge City Comm. College .	Dodge City, KS 67801....	1935	State	J/C	1,379	82	$ 520	$1,720	$ 2,240
Donnelly College	Kansas City, KS 66102 ..	1949	Catholic	J/C	779	57	$ 1,500	—	$ 1,500
Emporia State University ..	Emporia, KS 66801	1863	State	S-G/C	5,498	294	$ 1,090	$2,060	$ 3,150
Fort Hays State University ..	Hays, KS 67601	1902	State	S-G/C	5,399	288	$ 1,020	$1,960	$ 2,980
Fort Scott Comm. Jr. College	Fort Scott, KS 66701....	1919	State	J/C	1,239	41	$ 510	$1,904	$ 2,414
Friends Bible College	Haviland, KS 67059.....	1917	Friends	S/C	135	18	$ 4,200	$1,600	$ 5,800
Friends University	Wichita, KS 67213	1898	Friends	S/C	882	55	$ 3,990	$3,580	$ 7,570
Garden City Comm. College .	Garden City, KS 67846 ..	1919	State	J/C	2,076	65	$ 584	$1,850	$ 2,434
Haskell Indian Jr. College ..	Lawrence, KS 66044....	1884	Federal	J/C	800	65	$ 935	—	$ 935
Hesston College	Hesston, KS 67062.....	1909	Mennon	J/C	520	50	$ 4,400	$2,300	$ 6,700
Highland Comm. College ...	Highland, KS 66035	1858	Public	J/C	1,305	102	$ 620	$1,900	$ 2,520
Hutchinson Comm. College .	Hutchinson, KS 67501....	1928	State	J/C	3,439	197	$ 550	$1,875	$ 2,425
Independence Comm. College	Independence, KS 67301	1925	State	J/C	907	65	$ 510	$1,875	$ 2,385
Johnson County Comm. Col. .	Overland Park, KS 66210	1967	County	J/C	8,103	243	$ 565	$3,256	$ 4,556
Kansas City Kans. Comm. Col.	Kansas City, KS 66112 ..	1923	State	J/C	3,800	101	$ 510	—	$ 510
Kansas Newman College ..	Wichita, KS 67213	1933	Catholic	S/C	891	60	$ 4,050	$2,140	$ 6,190
Kansas State University ...	Manhattan, KS 66502 ...	1863	State	S-G/C	18,092	2,188	$ 1,081	$1,980	$ 3,061
Kansas Technical Institute ..	Salina, KS 67401	1965	State	T/C	629	38	$ 695	$1,940	$ 2,635
Kansas Wesleyan	Salina, KS 67401	1886	Methodist	S/C	528	43	$ 3,977	$2,449	$ 6,426
Labette Comm. Jr. College .	Parsons, KS 67357	1923	Public	J/C	2,407	182	$ 480	$1,750	$ 2,230
Manhattan Christian College .	Manhattan, KS 66502 ...	1927	Independ	S/C	191	18	$ 1,848	$2,020	$ 3,868
Marymount College of Kansas	Salina, KS 67401	1922	Catholic	S/C	670	52	$ 4,200	$2,400	$ 6,600

NAME	ADDRESS	FOUN-DED	AFFILI-ATION	LEVEL/TYPE	ENROLL-MENT	TEACH-ERS	TUITION & FEES	BOARD & ROOM	TOTAL COST
KANSAS (continued)									
McPherson College	McPherson, KS 67460 ..	1887	Brethren	S/C	505	50	$ 4,150	$2,350	$ 6,500
Mid-America Nazarene College	Olathe, KS 66061.....	1966	Nazarene	S/C	1,115	63	$ 3,500	$2,300	$ 5,800
Neosho Cnty. Comm. Col. ...	Chanute, KS 66720	1936	State	J/C	960	49	$ 450	$1,700	$ 2,150
Ottawa University	Ottawa, KS 66067	1865	Baptist	S/C	440	35	$ 4,080	$2,228	$ 6,308
Kansas City Center	Overland Park, KS 66210	1974	Baptist	S/C	966	7	—	—	—
Pittsburg State University ..	Pittsburg, KS 66762	1903	State	S-G/C	4,927	284	$ 1,028	$2,152	$ 3,180
Pratt Community College....	Pratt, KS 67124	1938	State	J/C	3,001	130	$ 566	$2,120	$ 2,686
St. John's College	Winfield, KS 67156	1893	Lutheran	S/C	258	29	$ 3,950	$2,440	$ 6,390
St. Mary College	Leavenworth, KS 66048 .	1923	Catholic	S/W	1,009	84	$ 4,340	$2,400	$ 6,740
St. Mary of the Plains College	Dodge City, KS 67801....	1952	Catholic	S/C	705	65	$ 4,090	$2,200	$ 6,290
Seward County Comm. College	Liberal, KS 67901	1967	State	J/C	1,557	104	$ 510	$1,850	$ 2,360
Southwestern College.......	Winfield, KS 67156	1885	Methodist	S/C	585	65	$ 3,740	$2,400	$ 6,140
Sterling College	Sterling, KS 67579	1887	Presby	S/C	345	34	$ 4,150	$2,200	$ 6,350
Tabor College	Hillsboro, KS 67063	1908	Mennon	S/C	399	46	$ 4,142	$2,190	$ 6,332
University of Kansas	Lawrence, KS 66045	1864	State	S-G/C	24,436	1,305	$ 1,148	$2,014	$ 3,162
Medical Center Campus ..	Kansas City, KS 66103 ..	1905	State	S-G/C	2,310	649	—	—	—
Washburn University	Topeka, KS 66621......	1865	City	S-G/C	7,088	263	$ 1,800	$2,475	$ 4,275
Wichita State University	Wichita, KS 67208	1895	State	S-G/C	17,021	818	$ 943	$2,211	$ 3,154
KENTUCKY									
Alice Lloyd College	Pippa Passes, KY 41844	1923	Independ	S/C	548	31	$ 2,660	$1,650	$ 4,310
Asbury College............	Wilmore, KY 40390	1890	Independ	S/C	1,074	96	$ 4,191	$2,451	$ 6,642
Ashland Comm. College	Ashland, KY 41101	1957	State	J/C	1,997	54	$ 468	—	$ 468
Bellarmine College	Louisville, KY 40205	1950	Catholic	S-G/C	2,710	160	$ 4,200	$2,110	$ 6,310
Berea College.............	Berea, KY 40404	1955	Independ	S/C	1,554	132	$ 120	$1,836	$ 1,956
Brescia College	Owensboro, KY 42301 ..	1950	Catholic	S/C	815	70	$ 3,750	$2,080	$ 5,830
Campbellsville College	Campbellsville, KY 42718	1906	Baptist	S/C	573	43	$ 3,630	$2,430	$ 5,790
Centre College	Danville, KY 40422	1819	Independ	S/C	748	65	$ 6,650	$2,775	$ 9,425
Cumberland College	Williamsburg, KY 40769.	1889	Baptist	S-G/C	2,106	100	$ 2,864	$1,776	$ 5,000
Eastern Kentucky University .	Richmond, KY 40475	1906	State	S-G/C	12,357	650	$ 950	$1,900	$ 2,850
Elizabethtown Comm. College	Elizabethtown, KY 42701	1963	State	J/C	2,096	55	$ 468	—	$ 468
Georgetown College	Georgetown, KY 40324 ..	1829	Baptist	S-G/C	1,298	93	$ 3,760	$2,480	$ 6,240
Hazard Community College ..	Hazard, KY 41701	1968	State	J/C	629	21	$ 468	—	$ 468
Henderson Community Col. ..	Henderson, KY 42420....	1960	State	J/C	1,434	32	$ 468	—	$ 468
Hopkinsville Comm. College .	Hopkinsville, KY 42240 ..	1965	State	J/C	1,113	30	$ 468	—	$ 468
Jefferson Comm. College....	Louisville, KY 40202	1968	State	J/C	6,767	159	$ 468	—	$ 468
Kentucky Christian College ..	Grayson, KY 41143	1919	Christian	S/C	820	29	$ 4,200	—	$ 4,200
Kentucky State University ...	Frankfort, KY 40601	1886	State	S-G/C	2,066	140	$ 880	$1,858	$ 2,738
Kentucky Wesleyan College .	Owensboro, KY 42301 ..	1858	Methodist	S/C	851	56	$ 3,960	$2,340	$ 6,300
Lees College	Jackson, KY 41339	1883	Presby	J/C	329	25	$ 2,520	$1,800	$ 4,320
Lexington Comm. College ...	Lexington, KY 40506	1965	State	J/C	2,573	72	$ 1,124	—	$ 1,124
Lexington Theol. Seminary ..	Lexington, KY 40508	1865	D of Chr	P/C	137	12	$ 1,510	$3,000	$ 4,510
Lindsey Wilson College.....	Columbia, KY 42728	1903	Methodist	J/C	564	40	$ 3,200	$2,588	$ 5,788
Louisville Presby. Theol. Sem.	Louisville, KY 40205	1853	Presby	G/C	264	17	—	$3,200	$ 8,000
Madisonville Community Col.	Madisonville, KY 42431 .	1968	State	J/C	1,417	30	$ 468	—	$ 468
Maysville Comm. College ...	Maysville, KY 41056.....	1968	State	J/C	654	26	$ 468	—	$ 468
Midway College	Midway, KY 40347......	1847	D of Chr	J/W	354	50	$ 3,400	$2,400	$ 5,800
Morehead State University ..	Morehead, KY 40351	1922	State	S-G/C	6,700	320	$ 890	$1,970	$ 2,860
Murray State University.....	Murray, KY 42071.......	1923	State	G/C	7,392	348	$ 890	$1,690	$ 2,580
Northern Kentucky University	Highland Hgts., KY 41076	1968	State	S-G/C	8,879	480	$ 944	$1,140	$ 2,084
Paducah Community College .	Paducah, KY 42001......	1932	State	J/C	1,916	47	$ 468	—	$ 468
Pikeville College	Pikeville, KY 41501	1889	Presby	S/C	511	40	$ 3,300	$1,900	$ 5,400
Prestonsburg Comm. College	Prestonsburg, KY 41653	1964	State	J/C	1,267	34	$ 468	—	$ 468
St. Catharine College	Springfield, KY 40069...	1931	Catholic	J/C	200	23	$ 2,690	$2,000	$ 4,690
Somerset Community College	Somerset, KY 42501	1965	State	J/C	1,153	39	$ 468	—	$ 468
Southeast Community College	Cumberland, KY 40823 .	1960	State	J/C	726	26	$ 468	—	$ 468
Southern Baptist Theol. Sem.	Louisville, KY 40280	1859	Baptist	P/C	2,829	137	$ 710	$2,000	$ 2,710
Spaulding College	Louisville, KY 40203	1814	Catholic	S-G/C	1,150	107	$ 3,752	$2,360	$ 6,112
Sue Bennett College	London, KY 40741.......	1897	Methodist	J/C	330	26	$ 1,930	$1,360	$ 3,290
Thomas More College	Crestview Hills, KY 41017	1921	Catholic	S/C	1,319	111	$ 4,200	$2,600	$ 6,800
Transylvania University	Lexington, KY 40508.....	1780	D of Chr	S/C	749	64	$ 5,700	$2,450	$ 8,150
Union College	Barbourville, KY 40906 .	1879	Methodist	S-G/C	879	56	$ 3,950	$1,930	$ 5,880
University of Kentucky	Lexington, KY 40506.....	1865	State	S-G/C	20,637	1,542	$ 1,124	$2,382	$ 3,506
University of Louisville	Louisville, KY 40292	1798	State	S-G/C	19,794	1,300	$ 1,239	$2,000	$ 3,239
Western Kentucky University	Bowling Green, KY 42101	1906	State	S-G/C	11,771	551	$ 954	$2,270	$ 3,224
LOUISIANA									
Baptist Christian College	Shreveport, LA 71115...	1961	Baptist	S/C	360	15	$ 2,300	$2,000	$ 4,300
Bossier Parish Comm. College	Bossier City, LA 71111..	1967	State	J/C	1,706	74	$ 394	—	$ 394
Centenary Col. of Louisiana..	Shreveport, LA 71134...	1825	Methodist	S/C	1,295	110	$ 4,320	$2,530	$ 6,850
Delgado Comm. College	New Orleans, LA 70119 ..	1921	State	J/C	8,405	282	$ 440	—	$ 440
Dillard University	New Orleans, LA 70122 .	1869	Methodist	S/C	1,212	100	$ 3,700	$2,600	$ 6,300
Grambling State University ..	Grambling, LA 71245 ...	1901	State	S-G/C	4,767	257	$ 310	$ 931	$ 1,241
Louisiana College	Pineville, LA 71359	1906	Baptist	S/C	1,477	82	$ 1,834	$1,780	$ 3,614
Louisiana State Univ. System	Baton Rouge, LA 70893 .								
Agricultural & Mech. College	Baton Rouge, LA 70803 .	1855	State	S-G/C	29,863	2,154	$ 971	$1,954	$ 2,925
Alexandria	Alexandria, LA 71303 ...	1959	State	J/C	1,985	85	$ 500	—	$ 500
Cent. for Agri. Sci. & Rur. Dev.	Baton Rouge, LA 70803 .	1972	State	—	—	—	—	—	—
Eunice	Eunice, LA 70535	1967	State	J/C	1,650	70	$ 450	—	$ 450
Medical Center...........	New Orleans, LA 70112 .	1931	State	P/C	2,552	517	$ 700	$1,000	$ 1,700
Paul M. Herbert Law Center	Baton Rouge, LA 70803 .	1906	State	P/C	800	53	$ 1,188	$1,876	$ 3,064

NAME	ADDRESS	FOUN-DED	AFFILI-ATION	LEVEL/TYPE	ENROLL-MENT	TEACH-ERS	TUITION & FEES	BOARD & ROOM	TOTAL COST
LOUISIANA (continued)									
School of Medicine	Shreveport, LA 71130 . .	1965	State	P/C	403	300	$ 2,200	—	$ 2,200
Shreveport	Shreveport, LA 71105 . .	1965	State	S-G/C	4,690	215	$ 780	—	$ 780
University of New Orleans .	New Orleans, LA 70148 .	1958	State	S-G/C	16,660	687	$ 984	$2650	$ 3,634
Louisiana Tech University . . .	Ruston, LA 71272	1894	State	S-G/C	10,825	450	$ 1,700	$1,000	$ 2,700
Loyola University	New Orleans, LA 70118 .	1912	Catholic	S-G/C	4,873	327	$ 4,923	$3225	$ 8,148
McNeese State University . . .	Lake Charles, LA 70609 .	1939	State	S-G/C	7,981	386	$ 781	$1,584	$ 2,365
Nicholls State University	Thibodaux, LA 70301 . . .	1948	State	S-G/C	7,429	325	$ 800	$1,800	$ 4,000
Northeast Louisiana Univ. . . .	Monroe, LA 71209	1931	State	S-G/C	11,558	444	$ 762	$1,620	$ 2,382
Northwest State Univ. of La. .	Natchitoches, LA 71457 .	1884	State	S-G/C	6,178	379	$ 838	$1,820	$ 2,658
Notre Dame Seminary Grad									
School of Theology	New Orleans, LA 70118 .	1923	Catholic	P/C	98	18	$ 2,450	$2,030	$ 4,480
Our Lady of Holy Cross Col. .	New Orleans, LA 70114 .	1916	Catholic	S/C	621	60	$ 3,050	—	$ 3,050
St. Bernard Parish Comm. Col.	Chalmette, LA 70043 . . .	1968	State	J/C	1,115	26	$ 105	—	$ 105
St. Joseph Seminary College.	St. Benedict, LA 70457 .	1891	Catholic	S/M	102	31	$ 2,500	$2,800	$ 5,300
Southeastern Louisiana Univ.	Hammond, LA 70402 . . .	1925	State	S-G/C	9,019	285	$ 797	$1,404	$ 2,201
Southern University System .	Baton Rouge, LA 70813 .								
Baton Rouge Campus	Baton Rouge, LA 70813 .	1880	State	S-G/C	9,938	464	$ 662	$2,264	$ 2,826
New Orleans Campus	New Orleans, LA 70126 .	1959	State	S/C	2,826	111	$ 626	—	$ 626
Shreveport Campus	Shreveport, LA 71107 . .	1967	State	J/C	458	40	$ 237	—	$ 237
Tulane University	New Orleans, LA 70118 .	1834	Independ	S-G/C	10,232	879	$ 8,000	$3,660	$12,740
Newcomb College	New Orleans, LA 70118 .	1886	Independ	S/W	1,662	139	$ 6,500	$2,620	$ 9,120
University of Southwest La. . .	Lafayette, LA 70504 . . .	1898	Independ	S-G/C	16,351	667	$ 729	$1,687	$ 2,416
Xavier Univ. of Louisiana	New Orleans, LA 70125 .	1925	Catholic	S-G/C	2,090	158	$ 4,000	$2,600	$ 6,600
MAINE									
Andover College	Portland, ME 04103 . . .	1966	Independ	J/C	601	25	$ 2,600	—	$ 2,600
Bangor Theological Seminary	Bangor, ME 04401	1814	Independ	P/C	155	23	$ 3,500	$2,325	$ 5,825
Bates College	Lewiston, ME 04240 . . .	1855	Independ	S/C	1,435	135	$ 9,560	$2,640	$12,200
Beal College	Bangor, ME 04401	1891	Independ	J/C	429	43	$ 2,850	$1,600	$ 4,450
Bowdoin College	Brunswick, ME 04011 . . .	1794	Independ	S/C	1,390	130	$ 9,980	$3,615	$13,595
Casco Bay College	Portland, ME 04101 . . .	1863	Independ	J/C	264	21	$ 2,975	$2,300	$ 5,275
Central Maine Voc. Tech. Inst.	Auburn, ME 04210	1964	State	T/C	420	42	$ 900	$1,905	$ 2,805
Colby College	Waterville, ME 04901 . .	1813	Independ	S/C	1,675	143	$ 9,800	$3,560	$13,360
College of the Atlantic	Bar Harbor, ME 04609 .	1969	Private	S/C	120	18	$ 6,975	$2,650	$ 9,625
Eastern Maine Voc. Tech. Inst.	Bangor, ME 04401	1966	State	T/C	529	58	$ 800	$1,905	$ 2,705
Husson College	Bangor, ME 04401	1898	Independ	S-G/C	1,493	80	$ 5,600	$3,000	$ 8,600
Kennebec Valley Vocational									
Tech. Inst.	Fairfield, ME 04937 . . .	1970	State	T/C	320	30	$ 800	—	$ 800
Maine Maritime Academy . . .	Castine, ME 04420	1941	State	S/C	621	64	$ 2,720	$2,955	$ 5,675
Mid-State College	Auburn, ME 04210	1916	Independ	J/C	400	30	$ 2,400	—	$ 2,400
New England Bapt. Bible Col.	Portland, ME 04105 . . .	1980	Baptist	S/C	35	5	$ 1,575	—	$ 1,575
North. Maine Voc. Tech. Inst.	Presque Isle, ME 04769 .	1961	State	T/C	1,150	54	$ 800	$1,905	$ 2,705
Portland School of Art	Portland, ME 04046 . . .	1882	Independ	P/C	250	31	$ 5,590	$1,700	$ 7,290
St. Joseph's College	North Windham, ME 04062	1912	Catholic	S/C	798	80	$ 4,725	$2,700	$ 7,425
South. Maine Voc. Tech. Inst.	South Portland, ME 04106	1946	State	J/C	1,342	98	$ 800	$1,905	$ 2,705
Thomas College	Waterville, ME 04901 . .	1894	Independ	S-G/C	850	23	$ 5,455	$3,150	$ 8,605
Unity College	Unity, ME 04988	1965	Independ	J-S/C	283	36	$ 5,455	$2,970	$ 8,425
University of Maine									
Augusta	Augusta, ME 04330	1965	State	J/C	3,368	183	$ 1,530	—	$ 1,530
Bangor Comm. College . . .	Bangor, ME 04401	1974	State	J/C	850	73	$ 1,509	$2,921	$ 4,430
Farmington	Farmington, ME 04938 . .	1864	State	S/C	2,041	120	$ 1,463	$2,740	$ 4,203
Fort Kent	Fort Kent, ME 04743 . . .	1878	State	S/C	656	29	$ 1,443	$2,630	$ 4,073
Machias	Machias, ME 04654	1909	State	S/C	834	38	$ 1,413	$2,650	$ 4,063
Orono	Orono, ME 04469	1865	State	S-G/C	11,180	511	$ 1,509	$2,921	$ 4,430
Presque Isle	Presque Isle, ME 04769 .	1903	State	S/C	1,210	59	$ 1,483	$2,692	$ 4,175
School of Law	Portland, ME 04102 . . .	1961	State	G/C	227	16	$ 2,220	—	$ 2,220
University of New England . .	Biddeford, ME 04005 . . .	1978	Independ	S-G/C	898	72	$ 5,515	$2,900	$ 8,415
University of So. Maine	Gorham, ME 04103 . . .	1878	State	S-G/C	8,769	492	$ 1,533	$2,460	$ 3,993
Wash. County Voc. Tech. Inst.	Calais, ME 04619	1969	State	T/C	275	35	$ 830	$ 992	$ 1,822
Westbrook College	Portland, ME 04103 . . .	1831	Independ	J-S/C	1,138	112	$ 6,400	$3,200	$ 9,600
MARYLAND									
Allegany Community College .	Cumberland, MD 21502 .	1961	State	J/C	2,134	136	$ 836	—	$ 836
Anne Arundel Comm. College	Arnold, MD 21012 . . .	1961	State	J/C	8,894	512	$ 875	—	$ 875
Baltimore Hebrew College . . .	Baltimore, MD 21215 . . .	1919	Independ	G/C	1,500	25	$ 552	—	$ 552
Bowie State College	Bowie, MD 20715	1865	State	S-G/C	2,357	101	$ 1,451	$2,588	$ 4,039
Capitol Inst. of Technology . .	Laurel, MD 20708	1964	Independ	S/C	1,046	70	$ 4,400	—	$ 4,400
Catonsville Comm. College . .	Catonsville, MD 21228 . .	1956	County	J/C	9,793	431	$ 654	—	$ 654
Cecil Comm. College	North East, MD 21901 . .	1968	County	J/C	1,494	60	$ 600	—	$ 600
Charles County Comm. College	La Plata, MD 20646	1958	State	J/C	4,462	225	$ 900	—	$ 900
Chesapeake College	Wye Mills, MD 21679 . . .	1965	Public	J/C	2,005	172	$ 480	—	$ 480
Col. of Notre Dame of Md. . .	Baltimore, MD 21210 . . .	1896	Independ	S-G/W	1,745	81	$ 5,500	$3,300	$ 8,800
Columbia Union College	Takoma Park, MD 20912 .	1904	7-D Adv	S/C	940	62	$ 4,311	$1,800	$ 6,111
Comm. College of Baltimore .	Baltimore, MD 21215 . . .	1947	City & St.	J/C	10,000	530	$ 700	—	$ 700
Coppin State College	Baltimore, MD 21216 . . .	1900	State	S-G/C	2,433	166	$ 1,300	—	$ 1,300
Dundalk Community College .	Baltimore, MD 21222 . . .	1971	Local	J/C	3,203	183	$ 680	—	$ 680
Eastern Christian College . . .	Bel Air, MD 21014	1959	Christian	S/C	65	8	$ 1,385	$1,490	$ 2,875
Essex Community College . . .	Baltimore, MD 21237 . . .	1957	State	J/C	9,861	494	$ 640	—	$ 640
Frederick Comm. College . . .	Frederick, MD 21701 . . .	1957	State	J/C	3,190	188	$ 810	—	$ 810
Frostburg State College	Frostburg, MD 21532 . . .	1898	State	S-G/C	3,572	230	$ 1,472	$2,826	$ 4,298
Garrett Community College . .	McHenry, MD 21541 . . .	1967	Local	J/C	569	58	$ 750	—	$ 750

NAME	ADDRESS	FOUN-DED	AFFILI-ATION	LEVEL/TYPE	ENROLL-MENT	TEACH-ERS	TUITION & FEES	BOARD & ROOM	TOTAL COST
MARYLAND *(continued)*									
Goucher College	Towson, MD 21204	1885	Independ	S-G/W	982	125	$ 8,300	$4,270	$12,570
Hagerstown Business College	Hagerstown, MD 21740	1938	Independ	J/C	260	20	$ 3,150	$1,980	$ 5,130
Hagerstown Junior College	Hagerstown, MD 21740	1946	Public	J/C	2,497	148	$ 900	—	$ 900
Harford Community College	Bel Air, MD 21014	1957	Public	J/C	4,285	231	$ 776	—	$ 776
Hood College	Frederick, MD 21701	1893	C of Chr	S-G/W	1,735	157	$ 7,648	$3,883	$11,531
Howard Community College	Columbia, MD 21044	1969	Local	J/C	3,534	208	$ 900	—	$ 900
Johns Hopkins University	Baltimore, MD 21218	1876	Independ	S-G/C	3,300	350	$ 9,600	$4,500	$14,100
Loyola College	Baltimore, MD 21210	1852	Catholic	S-G/C	5,173	284	$ 5,030	$2,870	$ 7,900
Maryland Institute of Art	Baltimore, MD 21217	1826	Independ	S-G/C	911	81	$ 5,300		
Montgomery College	Germantown, MD 20874	1946	State	J/C	2,554	88	$ 1,089	—	$ 1,089
Montgomery College	Rockville, MD 20850	1946	State	J/C	12,682	540	$ 1,089	—	$ 1,089
Montgomery College	Takoma Park, MD 20912	1946	State	J/C	4,650	196	$ 1,089	—	$ 1,089
Morgan State University	Baltimore, MD 21239	1867	State	S-G/C	4,248	249	$ 1,304	$1,534	$ 2,839
Mount St. Mary's College	Emmitsburg, MD 21727	1808	Catholic	S/C	1,675	110	$ 5,150	$2,950	$ 8,600
Ner Israel Rabbinical College	Baltimore, MD 21208	1933	Jewish	S-G/M	295	12	$ 2,000	$2,500	$ 4,500
Peabody Institute J.H.U.	Baltimore, MD 21202	1857	Independ	S-P/C	374	112	$ 7,865	$3,300	$11,165
Prince George's Comm. Col.	Largo, MD 20772	1958	Public	J/C	14,083	561	$ 1,000	—	$ 1,000
St. John's College	Annapolis, MD 21404	1784	Independ	S/G	400	51	$ 8,850	$3,000	$11,850
St. Mary's Col. of Maryland	St. Mary's City, MD 20686	1839	State	S/C	1,302	110	$ 1,840	$3,400	$ 5,240
St. Mary's Sem. & University	Baltimore, MD 21210	1791	Catholic	G-P/C	570	33	$ 3,730	$2,800	$ 6,530
Salisbury State College	Salisbury, MD 21801	1922	State	S-G/C	4,485	190	$ 1,472	$2,560	$ 4,032
Sojourner-Douglass College	Baltimore, MD 21205	1972	Independ	S/C	600	60	$ 3,970		$ 3,970
Towson State University	Baltimore, MD 21204	1866	State	S-G/C	15,106	866	$ 1,509	$3,443	$ 4,952
United States Naval Academy	Annapolis, MD 21402	1845	Federal	S/C	4,600	500	—		—
University of Baltimore	Baltimore, MD 21201	1925	State	S-G/C	5,177	27	$ 1,252		$ 1,252
University of Maryland	Adelphi, MD 20783		State						
Baltimore County Campus	Catonsville, MD 21228	1963	State	S-G/C	8,153	501	$ 1,518	$2,890	$ 4,408
Baltimore Prof. Schools	Baltimore, MD 21201	1807	State	P/C	4,633	914	$ 1,274	$1,770	$ 3,044
College Park Campus	College Park, MD 20742	1856	State	S-G/C	1,039	135	$ 3,450	—	$ 3,450
Eastern Shore Campus	Princess Anne, MD 21853	1886	State	S-G/C	1,230	90	$ 1,350	$2,810	$ 4,160
University College	College Park, MD 20742	1947	State	S-G/C	11,640	563	$ 2,303		$ 2,303
Villa Julie College	Stevenson, MD 21153	1952	Independ	J/C	1,039	135	$ 3,450		$ 3,450
Washington Bible College	Lanham, MD 20706	1938	Independ	S-G/C	514	35	$ 3,314	$2,670	$ 5,984
Washington College	Chestertown, MD 21620	1782	Independ	S/C	850	75	$ 6,800	$2,940	$ 9,800
Western Maryland College	Westminster, MD 21157	1867	Independ	S-G/C	1,585	171	$ 7,275	$2,680	$ 9,955
Wor-Wic Tech. Comm. College	Salisbury, MD 21801	1976	State	J/C	856	65	$ 702		$ 702
MASSACHUSETTS									
American International College	Springfield, MA 01109	1885	Private	S-G/C	1,585	86	$ 5,000	$2,500	$ 7,500
Amherst College	Amherst, MA 01002	1821	Independ	S/C	1,543	140	$ 9,521	$3,000	$12,521
Andover Newton Theol. Sch.	Newton Centre, MA 02159	1807	Independ	P/C	458	63	$ 3,738	$2,374	$ 6,112
Anna Maria College	Paxton, MA 01612	1946	Catholic	S-G/C	1,749	146	$ 5,450	$3,100	$ 8,550
Aquinas Junior College	Milton, MA 02186	1956	Catholic	J/W	400	27	$ 3,500		$ 3,500
Aquinas Junior College-Newton	Newton, MA 02158	1961	Catholic	J/W	253	23	$ 4,100		$ 4,100
Arthur D. Little Mgt. Ed. Inst.	Cambridge, MA 02140	1972	Independ	G/C	67	40	$13,000		$13,000
Assumption College	Worcester, MA 01609	1904	Catholic	S-G/C	2,000	125	$ 6,000	$3,200	$ 9,200
Atlantic Union College	South Lancaster, MA 01561	1882	7-D Adv	S/C	600	56	$ 5,968	$2,114	$ 8,082
Babson College	Babson Park, MA 02157	1919	Independ	S-G/C	3,180	135	$ 8,420	$3,270	$11,690
Bay Path Junior College	Longmeadow, MA 01106	1897	Independ	J/W	658	30	$ 5,000	$3,600	$ 8,600
Bay State Junior College	Boston, MA 02116	1946	Independ	J/C	650	35	$ 3,750	$3,050	$ 6,800
Becker Jr. Col.–Leicester	Leicester, MA 01524	1887	Independ	J/C	529	37	$ 3,500	$2,600	$ 6,100
Becker Jr. Col.–Worcester	Worcester, MA 01609	1887	Independ	J/C	734	47	$ 3,500	$2,600	$ 6,100
Bentley College	Waltham, MA 02254	1917	Independ	S-G/C	10,900	351	$ 6,640	$3,490	$10,130
Berklee College of Music	Boston, MA 02215	1945	Independ	S/C	2,425	214	$ 4,510	$3,650	$ 8,160
Berkshire Christian College	Lenox, MA 01240	1897	Adv Chr	S/C	127	21	$ 5,100	$2,600	$ 7,700
Berkshire Community College	Pittsfield, MA 01201	1960	State	J/C	3,017	127	$ 810	—	$ 810
Blue Hills Tech. Institute	Canton, MA 02021	1963	Public	T/C	465	38	$ 3,000	—	$ 3,000
Boston College	Chestnut Hill, MA 02167	1863	Catholic	S-G/C	14,210	705	$ 8,400	$4,280	$12,680
Boston Conserv.	Boston, MA 02215	1867	Independ	S-G/C	420	122	$ 5,800	$3,200	$ 9,000
Boston University	Boston, MA 02215	1839	Independ	S-G/C	27,633	2,800	$ 8,420	$3,780	$12,200
Bradford College	Bradford, MA 01830	1803	Independ	S/C	425	47	$ 7,495	$3,845	$11,340
Brandeis University	Waltham, MA 02254	1948	Independ	S-G/C	3,393	357	$10,485	$4,385	$14,870
Bridgewater State College	Bridgewater, MA 02324	1840	State	S-G/C	8,308	376	$ 880	$2,175	$ 3,055
Bristol Community College	Fall River, MA 02720	1965	State	J/C	4,718	254	$ 802	—	$ 802
Bunker Hill Comm. College	Boston, MA 02129	1973	State	J/C	3,423	153	$ 748	—	$ 748
Cambridge College	Cambridge, MA 02138	1971	Independ	G/C	300	36	$ 5,600	—	$ 5,600
Cape Cod Community College	West Barnstable, MA 02668	1960	State	J/C	4,251	276	$ 901	—	$ 901
Central New Eng. Col.	Worcester, MA 01610	1888	Independ	J-S/C	2,146	137	$ 4,800	—	$ 4,800
Chamberlayne Junior College	Boston, MA 02116	1892	Independ	J/C	800	52	$ 4,190	$3,730	$ 7,920
Clark University	Worcester, MA 01610	1887	Independ	S-G/C	3,282	250	$ 8,650	$2,830	$11,480
College of the Holy Cross	Worcester, MA 01610	1843	Jesuit	S/C	2,506	185	$ 8,400	$3,700	$12,100
Col. of Our Lady of the Elms	Chicopee, MA 01013	1928	Catholic	S/W	909	85	$ 5,500	$2,850	$ 8,350
Curry College	Milton, MA 02186	1879	Independ	S-G/C	1,530	102	$ 6,850	$3,700	$10,550
Dean Junior College	Franklin, MA 02038	1865	Independ	J/C	2,524	157	$ 5,790	$2,560	$ 8,350
Eastern Nazarene College	Quincy, MA 02170	1918	Nazarene	S-G/C	951	60	$ 4,388	$2,425	$ 6,813
Emerson College	Boston, MA 02116	1880	Independ	S-G/C	2,287	196	$ 8,000	$4,900	$12,900
Emmanuel College	Boston, MA 02115	1919	Catholic	S-G/W	1,146	90	$ 6,200	$3,300	$ 9,500
Endicott College	Beverly, MA 01915	1939	Independ	J/W	700	68	$ 5,950	$3,600	$ 9,550
Episcopal Divinity School	Cambridge, MA 02138	1857	Episcopal	G/C	107	24	$ 5,000	$2,250	$ 7,250
Fisher Junior College	Boston, MA 02116	1903	Independ	J/C	4,640	50	$ 4,850	$4,250	$ 9,100
Fitchburg State College	Fitchburg, MA 01420	1894	State	S-G/C	6,692	292	$ 1,094	$2,090	$ 3,184
Forsyth Sch. For Den. Hygienists	Boston, MA 02115	1916	Independ	J/C	200	20	$ 6,300	$4,000	$10,300

NAME	ADDRESS	FOUN-DED	AFFILI-ATION	LEVEL/TYPE	ENROLL-MENT	TEACH-ERS	TUITION & FEES	BOARD & ROOM	TOTAL COST
MASSACHUSETTS *(continued)*									
Framingham State College ..	Framingham, MA 01701 .	1839	State	S-G/C	5,652	393	$ 1,250	$2,000	$ 3,250
Franklin Institute of Boston .	Boston, MA 02116......	1908	Independ	J/C	430	38	$ 5,100	$4,300	$ 9,400
Gordon College	Wenham, MA 01984	1889	Independ	S/C	1,073	75	—		$ 9,700
Gordon-Conwell Theol. Sem.	So. Hamilton, MA 01982	1884	Independ	G/C	861	68	$ 4,240	$2,350	$ 6,590
Greenfield Comm. College ..	Greenfield, MA 01301 ...	1962	State	J/C	2,396	132	$ 827		$ 827
Hampshire College	Amherst, MA 01002	1965	Independ	S/C	1,000	95	$11,000	$2,950	$13,950
Harvard University	Cambridge, MA 02138 ..	1636	Independ	S-G/C	24,782	1,934	$10,590	$4,510	$15,100
Hebrew College	Brookline, MA 02146 ...	1921	Independ	S-G/C	185	7	$ 1,500		$ 1,500
Hellenic College/Holy Cross .	Brookline, MA 02146 ...	1937	Orthodox	S-G/C	230	40	$ 3,750	$2,570	$ 6,320
Holyoke Community College .	Holyoke, MA 01040	1946	State	J/C	3,027	191	$ 812		$ 812
Laboure Junior College	Boston, MA 02124......	1971	Catholic	J/C	681	65	$ 5,275	$2,200	$ 7,475
Lasell Junior College........	Newton, MA 02166	1851	Independ	J/C	465	75	$ 5,980	$4,000	$ 9,980
Lesley College	Cambridge, MA 02238 ..	1909	Independ	S/W	600	55	$ 6,600	$4,150	$11,750
Mass. Bay Comm. College ..	Wellesley Hills, MA 02181	1961	State	J/C	4,931	243	$ 877		$ 877
Mass. College of Art	Boston, MA 02215......	1873	State	S-G/C	1,100	107	$ 1,200	$4,300	$ 5,500
Mass. College of Pharmacy .	Boston, MA 02115......	1823	Independ	S-G/C	900	69	$ 5,660	$4,000	$ 9,660
Mass. Inst. of Technology ..	Cambridge, MA 02139 ..	1861	Independ	S-G/C	9,626	1,900	$10,300	$4,200	$14,500
Mass. Maritime Academy ...	Buzzards Bay, MA 02532	1891	State	S/C	800	72	$ 1,400	$2,600	$ 5,000
Massasoit Commmunity Col.	Brockton, MA 02402.....	1966	State	J/C	6,227	182	$ 840	—	$ 840
Merrimack College	North Andover, MA 01845	1947	Catholic	S/C	2,232	139	$ 6,200	$3,500	$ 9,700
Middlesex Community College	Bedford, MA 01730	1970	State	J/C	2,258	145	$ 801		$ 801
Mount Holyoke College	South Hadley, MA 01075	1837	Independ	S/W	1,929	218	$10,350	$3,200	$13,550
Mount Ida Junior College ...	Newton Centre, MA 02159	1899	Independ	J-S/C	825	72	$ 5,624	$3,710	$ 9,334
Mount Wachusett Comm. Col.	Gardner, MA 01440	1963	State	J/C	1,733	72	$ 794		$ 794
New Eng. Col. of Optometry .	Boston, MA 02115......	1894	Private	P/C	329	50	$ 9,480	$6,000	$15,480
New Eng. Conser. of Music ..	Boston, MA 02115......	1867	Independ	S-G/C	740	160	$ 7,550	$3,870	$11,420
New Eng. Inst. of App. Arts & Sci.	Boston, MA 02115......	1907	Independ	J/C	130	14	$ 6,705	—	$ 6,705
New England School of Law..	Boston, MA 02116......	1908	Independ	P/C	950	32	$ 5,600		$ 5,600
Newbury Junior College	Boston, MA 02115......	1962	Private	J/C	3,848	298	$ 4,605	$2,800	$ 7,405
Nichols College	Dudley, MA 01570......	1815	Independ	S-G/C	1,092	60	$ 5,020	$2,910	$ 7,930
North Adams State College ..	North Adams, MA 01247	1894	State	S/C	2,185	128	$ 1,233	$1,100	$ 2,333
North Shore Comm. College .	Beverly, MA 01915	1965	State	J/C	8,047	400	$ 739		$ 739
Northeastern University	Boston, MA 02115......	1898	Independ	S-G/C	36,219	820	$ 5,900	$2,790	$ 8,690
Northern Essex Comm. Col. .	Haverhill, MA 01830	1961	State	J/C	6,110	231	$ 870		$ 870
Pine Manor College	Chestnut Hill, MA 02167	1911	Independ	S/W	537	61	$ 8,280	$4,660	$12,940
Quincy Junior College	Quincy, MA 02169......	1958	Public	J/C	2,829	140	$ 785		$ 785
Quinsigamund Comm. College	Worcester, MA 01606 ..	1963	State	J/C	2,465	188	$ 857		$ 857
Radcliffe College	Cambridge, MA 02138 ..	1879	Independ	S/W	2,691	—	$11,340	$3,760	$15,100
Regis College	Weston, MA 02193	1927	Catholic	S-G/W	1,240	96	$ 6,500	$3,300	$ 9,800
Roxbury Community College .	Roxbury, MA 02115	1973	State	J/C	1,290	95	$ 800		$ 800
St. Hyacinth Col. Seminary .	Granby, MA 01033	1927	Catholic	S/M	41	21	$ 3,000	$3,000	$ 6,000
St. John's Seminary College .	Brighton, MA 02135....	1968	Catholic	S/M	80	25	$ 2,400	$2,200	$ 4,600
Salem State College	Salem, MA 01970	1854	State	S-G/C	5,481	328	$ 745	$1,600	$ 2,345
Sch. of the Mus. of Fine Arts .	Boston, MA 02115......	1876	Private	S-G/C	612	79	$ 6,300		$ 6,300
Simmons College	Boston, MA 02115......	1899	Independ	S-G/W	3,138	268	$ 8,604	$3,920	$12,524
Simon's Rock of Bard College	Gt. Barrington, MA 01230	1966	Independ	S/C	312	50	$ 8,580	$2,960	$11,540
Smith College............	Northampton, MA 01063	1871	Independ	S-G/W	2,464	266	$ 9,170	$3,570	$12,740
Southeastern Mass. University	No. Dartmouth, MA 02747	1895	State	S-G/C	5,618	350	$ 1,185	$3,200	$ 4,385
Springfield College	Springfield, MA 01109 ..	1885	Independ	S-G/C	2,219	124	$ 5,723	$2,674	$ 8,397
Springfield Tech. Comm. Col.	Springfield, MA 01105 ..	1967	State	J/C	3,505	218	$ 982		$ 982
Stonehill College	North Easton, MA 02357	1948	Catholic	S/C	2,786	220	$ 5,975	$3,150	$ 9,125
Suffolk University	Boston, MA 02108......	1906	Private	S-G/C	6,203	346	$ 5,095		$ 5,095
Swain School of Design	New Bedford, MA 02740	1881	Independ	P/C	150	18	$ 5,100	$2,900	$ 8,000
Swedenborg Sch. of Religion.	Newton, MA 02158	1866	Swed	G/C	11	5	$ 1,200	$3,000	$ 4,200
Tufts University	Medford, MA 02155	1852	Independ	S-G/C	7,379	944	$ 9,600	$4,600	$14,200
Flet. Sch. of Law and Dip. .	Medford, MA 02155	1933	Independ	G/C	285	31	$ 9,600	$4,600	$14,200
University of Lowell	Lowell, MA 01854	1894	State	S-G/C	10,314	621	$ 1,400	$2,700	$ 4,100
Univ. of Mass./Amherst	Amherst, MA 01003	1863	State	S-G/C	25,906	1,324	$ 1,657	$2,368	$ 4,025
Wellesley College	Wellesley, MA 02181....	1875	Independ	S/W	2,296	314	$10,000	$3,953	$13,953
Wentworth Inst. of Tech. ...	Boston, MA 02115......	1904	Independ	S/C	3,710	170	$ 5,050	$3,500	$ 8,550
Western New England College	Springfield, MA 01119 ..	1919	Independ	S-G/C	5,176	319	$ 5,550	$3,490	$ 9,040
Westfield State College	Westfield, MA 01086....	1838	State	S-G/C	3,022	190	$ 1,250	$2,000	$ 3,250
Weston School of Theology .	Cambridge, MA 02138 ..	1922	Catholic	P/C	212	37	$ 4,200	—	$ 4,200
Wheaton College	Norton, MA 02766......	1834	Independ	S/W	1,112	~113	$ 9,980	$3,800	$13,780
Wheelock College	Boston, MA 02215......	1888	Independ	G/C	652	80	$ 7,240	$3,500	$10,740
Williams College	Williamstown, MA 01267	1793	Independ	S/C	2,009	226	$10,050	$3,360	$13,410
Woods Hole Oceanog. Inst. .	Woods Hole, MA 02543 .	1930	Independ	G/C	110	20	$13,750	—	$13,750
Worcester Polytechnic Inst. .	Worcester, MA 01609 ...	1865	Independ	S-G/C	3,871	234	$ 9,008	$3,410	$12,418
Worcester State College.....	Worcester, MA 01602 ...	1874	State	S-G/C	3,331	165	$ 1,084	$1,936	$ 3,020

MICHIGAN

NAME	ADDRESS	FOUN-DED	AFFILI-ATION	LEVEL/TYPE	ENROLL-MENT	TEACH-ERS	TUITION & FEES	BOARD & ROOM	TOTAL COST
Adrian College	Adrian, MI 49221........	1859	Methodist	S/C	1,220	75	$ 6,126	$2,094	$ 8,220
Albion College	Albion, MI 49224	1835	Methodist	S/C	1,635	118	$ 6,310	$3,052	$ 9,362
Alma College	Alma, MI 48801	1886	Presby	S/C	1,048	85	$ 5,980	$2,516	$ 8,496
Alpena Community College ..	Alpena, MI 49707	1952	State	J/C	1,918	50	$ 660	—	$ 660
Andrews University	Berrien Springs, MI 49104	1874	7-D Adv	S-G/C	3,034	210	$ 5,985	$3,012	$ 8,997
Aquinas College	Grand Rapids, MI 49506	1922	Catholic	S-G/C	2,831	170	$ 5,600	$2,786	$ 8,386
Baker Jr. College of Business	Flint, MI 48507........	1911	Independ	J/C	2,500	130	$ 3,000	$1,500	$ 4,500
Bay De Noc Comm. College ..	Escanaba, MI 49829 ...	1962	State	J/C	1,806	91	$ 950	$2,500	$ 3,450
Calvin College	Grand Rapids, MI 49506	1876	Reformed	S-G/C	3,971	243	$ 4,980	$2,220	$ 7,200
Calvin Theological Seminary .	Grand Rapids, MI 49506	1876	Reformed	P/C	240	23	$ 2,600		$ 2,640
Center for Creative Studies ..	Detroit, MI 48202	1906	Private	S/C	1,195	183	$ 5,500	$1,900	$ 7,400

MICHIGAN (continued)

NAME	ADDRESS	FOUNDED	AFFILIATION	LEVEL/TYPE	ENROLLMENT	TEACHERS	TUITION & FEES	BOARD & ROOM	TOTAL COST
Central Michigan University .	Mt. Pleasant, MI 48859 .	1892	State	S-G/C	15,922	680	$ 1,555	$2,350	$ 3,905
Cleary College	Ypsilanti, MI 48197	1883	Independ	S/C	973	50	$ 3,420	—	$ 3,420
Concordia College . . .	Ann Arbor, MI 48105 ...	1963	Lutheran	S/C	490	53	$ 4,118	$2,778	$ 6,896
Cranbrook Academy of Art .	Bloomfield Hills, MI 48013	1932	Independ	G/C	147	9	$ 6,100	$2,750	$ 8,850
Davenport College of Business	Grand Rapids, MI 49503	1866	Independ	J/C	4,219	220	$ 4,820	$2,500	$ 7,320
Delta College	Univ. Center, MI 48710 .	1961	State	J/C	10,015	420	$ 868	$2,420	$ 3,288
Detroit College of Business .	Dearborn, MI 48126	1962	Independ	S/C	3,318	190	$ 3,261	—	$ 3,261
Detroit College of Law	Detroit, MI 48201	1891	Private	P/C	809	75	$ 4,800	—	$ 4,800
Eastern Michigan University .	Ypsilanti, MI 48197	1849	State	S-G/C	20,257	597	$ 1,502	$2,618	$ 4,120
Faithway Baptist College	Belleville, MI 48111 ...	1974	Baptist	S-G/C	88	16	$ 1,580	$2,300	$ 3,880
Ferris State College	Big Rapids, MI 49307 ...	1884	State	S-G/C	10,350	570	$ 1,671	$2,453	$ 4,124
Gen. Motors Eng. & Mgmt. Inst.	Flint, MI 48502	1919	Private	S/C	2,667	140	$ 5,264	$2,100	$ 7,364
Glen Oaks Community College	Centreville, MI 49032 ...	1965	Public	J/C	1,382	90	$ 780	—	$ 780
Gogebic Community College .	Ironwood, MI 49938	1932	Public	J/C	1,203	37	$ 725	$1,500	$ 2,225
Grace Bible College	Grand Rapids, MI 49509	1939	Gospel	S/C	145	18	$ 2,300	$2,150	$ 4,450
Grand Rapids Baptist College	Grand Rapids, MI 49505	1941	Baptist	S/C	727	52	$ 3,730	$2,628	$ 6,358
Grand Rapids Baptist Sem. . .	Grand Rapids, MI 49505	1941	Baptist	P/C	224	12	$ 2,890	—	$ 2,890
Grand Rapids Junior College .	Grand Rapids, MI 49503	1914	State	J/C	8,922	355	$ 1,200	—	$ 1,200
Grand Valley State Colleges .	Allendale, MI 49401	1960	State	S-G/C	7,153	370	$ 1,502	$2,630	$ 4,132
Great Lakes Bible College . .	Lansing, MI 48901	1949	C of Chr	S/C	149	17	$ 2,325	$2,152	$ 4,477
Henry Ford Community College	Dearborn, MI 48128	1938	Public	J/C	15,828	196	$ 1,010	—	$ 1,010
Highland Park Comm. College	Highland Park, MI 48203	1918	State	J/C	2,500	152	$ 950	—	$ 950
Hillsdale College	Hillsdale, MI 49242	1844	Independ	S/C	1,040	75	$ 6,400	$3,000	$ 9,400
Hope College	Holland, MI 49423	1866	Reformed	S/C	2,519	180	$ 6,280	$2,770	$ 9,050
Jackson Community College .	Jackson, MI 49201	1928	State	J/C	7,100	340	$ 930	—	$ 930
Jordan College	Cedar Springs, MI 49319	1967	Independ	S/C	1,928	115	$ 3,000	$1,800	$ 4,800
Kalamazoo College	Kalamazoo, MI 49007 ...	1833	Independ	S/C	1,110	80	$ 7,713	$2,883	$11,300
Kalamazoo Valley Comm. Col.	Kalamazoo, MI 49009 ...	1966	State	J/C	8,773	88	$ 630	—	$ 630
Kellogg Community College .	Battle Creek, MI 49016 .	1956	State	J/C	7,378	255	$ 759	—	$ 759
Kendall School of Design . . .	Grand Rapids, MI 49503	1928	Independ	S/C	687	65	$ 4,500	$3,708	$ 8,208
Kirtland Community College .	Roscommon, MI 48653 . .	1966	State	J/C	1,400	75	$ 700	—	$ 700
Lake Michigan College	Benton Harbor, MI 49022	1946	State	J/C	3,050	253	$ 1,600	—	$ 1,600
Lake Superior State College .	Sault Ste. Marie, MI 49783	1946	State	S/C	2,783	115	$ 1,530	$2,700	$ 4,230
Lansing Community College .	Lansing, MI 48901	1957	State	J/C	19,157	1,082	$ 637	—	$ 637
Lawrence Inst. of Technology .	Southfield, MI 48075....	1932	Independ	S/C	6,121	302	$ 2,604	—	$ 2,604
Lewis College of Business ...	Detroit, MI 48235	1929	Private	J/C	328	10	$ 3,500	—	$ 3,500
Macomb County Comm. College	Warren, MI 48093	1954	State	J/C	30,410	814	$ 945	—	$ 945
Madonna College	Livonia, MI 48150	1947	Catholic	S-G/C	3,896	216	$ 2,510	$2,320	$ 4,830
Marygrove College	Detroit, MI 48221	1910	Catholic	S-G/C	1,188	101	$ 4,412	$2,230	$ 6,642
Mercy College of Detroit	Detroit, MI 48219	1941	Catholic	S-G/C	2,280	173	$ 3,590	$1,600	$ 5,190
Michigan Christian College . .	Rochester, MI 48063	1959	C of Chr	J/C	372	35	$ 2,740	$2,216	$ 4,956
Michigan State University . . .	East Lansing, MI 48824 . .	1855	State	S-G/C	42,193	2,794	$ 1,727	$2,259	$ 3,986
Michigan Technical Institute .	Ann Arbor, MI 48107 ...	1915	Independ	T/C	300	22	$ 4,500	—	$ 4,500
Michigan Tech. University . . .	Houghton, MI 49931	1885	State	S-G/C	6,935	450	$ 1,764	$2,438	$ 4,202
Mid Michigan Comm. College	Harrison, MI 48625	1965	State	J/C	1,968	83	$ 754	—	$ 754
Midrasha College of Jewish Studies	Southfield, MI 48076....	1948	Independ	S/C	707	20	$ 900	—	$ 900
Midwestern Baptist College .	Pontiac, MI 48053	1953	Baptist	S-G/C	243	33	$ 1,728	$1,400	$ 3,184
Monroe County Comm. College	Monroe, MI 48161	1964	State	J/C	2,880	138	$ 456	—	$ 456
Montcalm Community College	Sidney, MI 48885.......	1965	State	J/C	1,488	25	$ 613	—	$ 613
Mott Community College	Flint, MI 48502	1923	State	J/C	11,158	210	$ 1,012	—	$ 1,012
Muskegon Business College .	Muskegon, MI 49442 ...	1888	Independ	J/C	1,453	45	$ 2,340	$1,900	$ 4,240
Muskegon Community College	Muskegon, MI 49442 ...	1926	Public	J/C	5,000	100	$ 875	—	$ 875
Nazareth Col. at Kalamazoo .	Nazareth, MI 49074	1924	Catholic	S/G	821	68	$ 5,430	$2,530	$ 7,960
North Central Michigan College	Petoskey, MI 49770.....	1958	State	J/C	1,754	80	$ 780	$2,634	$ 3,600
Northeastern School of Com. .	Bay City, MI 48706	1880	Independ	T/C	200	8	$ 2,000	—	$ 2,000
Northern Michigan University .	Marquette, MI 49855 ...	1899	State	S-G/C	8,532	321	$ 1,472	$2,176	$ 3,648
Northwestern Michigan College	Traverse City, MI 49684 .	1951	State	J/C	3,223	160	$ 1,035	$2,175	$ 3,210
Northwood Institute	Midland, MI 48640	1959	Private	S/C	1,850	75	$ 4,545	$2,550	$ 7,095
Oakland Community College .	Bloomfield Hills, MI 48013	1964	State	J/C	28,000	700	$ 800	—	$ 800
Oakland University	Rochester, MI 48063....	1957	State	S-G/C	11,971	555	$ 1,877	$1,397	$ 3,274
Olivet College	Olivet, MI 49076	1844	Church	S/C	683	51	$ 5,080	$2,350	$ 7,430
Reformed Bible College	Grand Rapids, MI 49506	1939	Independ	S/C	223	14	$ 3,000	$2,200	$ 5,200
Sacred Heart Seminary College	Detroit, MI 48206	1919	Catholic	S/C	260	18	$ 2,625	$1,600	$ 4,245
Saginaw Valley State College .	Univ. Center, MI 48710 . .	1963	State	S-G/C	4,857	259	$ 1,676	$2,503	$ 4,179
St. Clair County Comm. College	Port Huron, MI 48060 ...	1923	County	J/C	3,883	199	$ 672	—	$ 672
St. John's Provincial Sem.	Plymouth, MI 48170	1949	Catholic	P/C	198	25	$ 2,100	$3,900	$ 6,000
St. Mary's College	Orchard Lake, MI 48033 .	1885	Catholic	S/C	288	47	$ 2,250	$2,225	$ 4,475
Schoolcraft College	Livonia, MI 48152	1961	State	J/C	8,512	365	$ 885	—	$ 885
Siena Heights College	Adrian, MI 49221	1919	Catholic	S-G/C	1,468	97	$ 4,380	$2,600	$ 6,980
Southwestern Michigan College	Dowagiac, MI 49047 ...	1964	State	J/C	3,000	200	$ 837	—	$ 837
Spring Arbor College	Spring Arbor, MI 49283 .	1873	Methodist	S/C	1,046	115	$ 5,290	$2,208	$ 7,498
Saints Cyril & Methodius Sem.	Orchard Lake, MI 48033	1885	Catholic	G/C	55	20	$ 2,100	$3,000	$ 5,100
Suomi College	Hancock, MI 49930	1896	Lutheran	J/C	681	60	$ 6,000	$2,500	$ 8,500
Thomas M. Cooley Law School	Lansing, MI 48901	1972	Independ	P/C	1,136	31	$ 5,271	—	$ 5,271
University of Detroit	Detroit, MI 48221	1877	Catholic	S-G/C	6,125	425	$ 5,800	$2,500	$ 8,300
University of Michigan	Ann Arbor, MI 48109 ...	1817	State	S-G/C	34,347	2,392	$ 2,475	$2,911	$ 5,386
Dearborn Campus	Dearborn, MI 48128	1959	State	S-G/C	6,321	174	$ 1,666	—	$ 1,666
Flint Campus	Flint, MI 48502	1956	State	S-G/C	5,596	156	$ 1,472	—	$ 1,472
Walsh College of Accounting .	Troy, MI 48007.........	1922	Independ	S-G/C	2,052	90	$ 2,862	—	$ 2,862
Washtenaw Community College	Ann Arbor, MI 48106 ...	1965	State	J/C	7,858	447	$ 1,426	—	$ 1,426
Wayne County Comm. College	Detroit, MI 48226	1969	State	J/C	12,000	506	$ 836	—	$ 836
Wayne State University	Detroit, MI 48202	1868	State	S-G/C	29,070	1,200	$ 1,990	—	$ 1,990

NAME	ADDRESS	FOUN-DED	AFFILI-ATION	LEVEL/TYPE	ENROLL-MENT	TEACH-ERS	TUITION & FEES	BOARD & ROOM	TOTAL COST
MICHIGAN *(continued)*									
West Shore Community College	Scottsville, MI 49454	1967	State	J/C	1,078	61	$ 775	—	$ 775
Western Michigan University	Kalamazoo, MI 49008	1903	State	S-G/C	18,237	865	$ 1,550	$2,475	$ 4,025
William Tyndale College	Farmington Hls, MI 48018	1945	Independ	S/C	321	37	$ 2,580	$2,310	$ 4,890
MINNESOTA									
Anoka-Ramsey Comm. College	Coon Rapids, MN 55433	1965	State	J/C	3,776	175	$ 1,500	—	$ 1,500
Arrowhead Comm. College ..									
Hibbing Campus	Hibbing, MN 55746	1916	State	J/C	912	46	$ 1,100	—	$ 1,100
Itasa Campus	Grand Rapids, MN 55744	1922	State	J/C	1,103	60	$ 1,176	—	$ 1,176
Vermillion Campus	Ely, MN 55731	1922	State	J/C	570	36	$ 1,176	—	$ 1,176
Augsburg College	Minneapolis, MN 55454 .	1869	Lutheran	S/C	1,707	159	$ 6,190	$2,500	$ 8,690
Austin Community College ..	Austin, MN 55912	1940	State	J/C	993	49	$ 1,102	—	$ 1,102
Bemidji State University	Bemidji, MN 56601	1919	State	S-G/C	4,318	250	$ 1,588	$1,750	$ 3,338
Bethany Lutheran College ...	Mankato, MN 56001	1927	Lutheran	J/C	225	23	$ 4,150	$2,010	$ 6,160
Bethel College & Seminary ..	St. Paul, MN 55112	1871	Baptist	S/C	1,861	150	$ 5,395	$2,445	$ 7,840
Brainerd Community College	Brainerd, MN 56401	1938	State	J/C	653	35	$ 1,102	—	$ 1,102
Carleton College	Northfield, MN 55057....	1866	Independ	S/C	1,845	186	$ 9,343	$2,482	$11,825
College of Saint Benedict ...	St. Joseph, MN 56374 ...	1913	Catholic	S/W	1,779	130	$ 5,825	$2,355	$ 8,180
College of St. Catherine ...	St. Paul, MN 55105	1905	Catholic	S-G/W	2,458	197	$ 5,805	$2,470	$ 8,275
College of St. Scholastica....	Duluth, MN 55811	1912	Catholic	S-G/C	1,431	127	$ 5,802	$2,483	$ 8,285
College of St. Teresa........	Winona, MN 55987	1907	Catholic	S/W	474	60	$ 5,850	$2,100	$ 7,950
College of St. Thomas	St. Paul, MN 55105	1885	Catholic	S-G/C	6,435	379	$ 5,900	$2,425	$ 8,325
Concordia College	Moorhead, MN 56560 ...	1891	ALC	S/C	2,464	182	$ 6,000	$2,000	$ 6,000
Concordia College	St. Paul, MN 55104	1893	Lutheran	S/C	746	53	$ 4,575	$1,980	$ 6,555
Crosier Seminary Jr. College .	Onamia, MN 56359	1922	Catholic	J/M	22	15	$ 5,135	$3,650	$ 8,785
Dr. Martin Luther College ..	New Ulm, MN 56073	1884	Lutheran	S/C	558	64	$ 1,845	$1,620	$ 3,465
Fergus Falls Community College	Fergus Falls, MN 56537 .	1960	State	J/C	706	32	$ 1,173	$2,300	$ 4,600
Golden Valley Lutheran College	Minneapolis, MN 55422 .	1967	Independ	J/C	429	37	$ 5,580	$2,414	$ 7,994
Gustavus Adolphus College ..	St. Peter, MN 56082	1862	Lutheran	S/C	2,183	146	$ 7,250	$2,200	$ 9,450
Hamline University	St. Paul, MN 55104	1854	Methodist	S-G/C	1,875	140	$ 6,910	$2,680	$ 9,590
Inver Hills Comm. College ..	Inver Grove Hts., MN 55075	1970	State	J/C	3,624	190	$ 1,102	—	$ 1,102
Itasca Community College ...	Grand Rapids, MN 55744	1922	State	J/C	1,100	70	$ 1,175	—	$ 1,175
Lakewood Community College	White Bear La., MN 55110	1967	State	J/C	4,100	146	$ 1,100	—	$ 1,100
Luther Northwestern Seminary	St. Paul, MN 55108	1869	Lutheran	G-P/C	834	54	$ 1,930	$2,200	$ 4,130
Macalester College	St. Paul, MN 55117	1885	Presby	S/C	1,696	174	$ 8,155	$2,800	$10,955
Mankato State University....	Mankato, MN 56001	1867	State	S-G/C	12,350	550	$ 1,485	$1,620	$ 3,150
Mayo Foundation	Rochester, MN 55905....	1915	Independ.	G/C	1,300	827	—	—	—
Mesabi Community College ..	Virginia, MN 55792	1918	State	J/C	1,245	42	$ 1,200	—	$ 1,200
Metropolitan State University	St. Paul, MN 55101	1971	State	J-S/C	3,696	175	$ 1,333	—	$ 1,333
Minneap. Col. of Art & Design	Minneapolis, MN 55404 .	1886	Independ	S/C	513	62	$ 6,100	$2,500	$ 8,600
Minneapolis Comm. College .	Minneapolis, MN 55403 .	1965	State	J/C	2,984	122	$ 5,000	—	$ 5,000
Minnesota Bible College	Rochester, MN 55901 ...	1913	Christian	S/C	89	12	$ 2,100	$2,065	$ 4,165
Moorhead State University ...	Moorhead, MN 56560 ...	1887	State	S-G/C	7,520	326	$ 1,482	$1,641	$ 3,123
National Col.–St. Paul Ext. ...	St. Paul, MN 55104	1974	Private	S/C	283	24	$ 2,617	—	$ 2,617
Normandale Community College	Bloomington, MN 55431	1968	State	J/C	6,349	240	$ 1,102	—	$ 1,102
North Central Bible College ..	Minneapolis, MN 55404 .	1930	A of God	J-S/C	1,130	51	$ 3,230	$1,752	$ 4,562
North Hennepin Comm. College	Minneapolis, MN 55445 .	1966	State	J/C	4,555	170	$ 883	—	$ 883
Northland Community College	Thief Riv. Falls, MN 56701	1965	State	J/C	694	20	$ 1,150	—	$ 1,150
Northwestern College	Roseville, MN 55113	1902	Independ	S/C	994	86	$ 5,400	$2,175	$ 7,575
Pillsbury Baptist Bible College	Owatonna, MN 55060 ...	1854	Baptist	S/C	448	37	$ 2,440	$2,042	$ 4,482
Rainy River Comm. College ..	Intl. Falls, MN 56649 ...	1967	State	J/C	590	39	$ 1,200	$1,100	$ 2,300
Rochester Community College	Rochester, MN 55904	1915	State	J/C	3,158	140	*	—	$ 1,100
St. Cloud State University ...	St. Cloud, MN 56301	1869	State	S-G/C	12,430	546	$ 1,493	$1,674	$ 3,167
St. John's University	Collegeville, MN 56321 .	1857	Catholic	S-G/M	2,024	161	$ 5,200	$2,480	$ 7,680
St. Mary's College	Winona, MN 55987	1912	Catholic	S-G/C	1,480	102	$ 5,650	$2,420	$ 8,070
St. Mary's Junior College ...	Minneapolis, MN 55454 .	1964	Catholic	J/C	780	93	$ 3,672	—	$ 3,672
St. Olaf College	Northfield, MN 55057....	1874	Lutheran	S/C	3,027	320	$ 7,150	$2,300	$ 9,450
St. Paul Bible College	Bible College, MN 55375	1916	Church	S/C	638	45	$ 3,884	$2,500	$ 6,384
St. Paul Seminary	St. Paul, MN 55105	1894	Catholic	G/M	93	18	$ 4,658	$3,580	$ 8,236
Southwest State University ..	Marshall, MN 56258	1963	State	S/C	2,234	108	$ 1,513	$1,600	$ 3,113
United Theological Seminary	New Brighton, MN 55112	1960	UC Chr	G/C	219	19	$ 3,600	—	$ 7,000
University of Minnesota ...	Minneapolis, MN 55455 .								
Duluth Campus	Duluth, MN 55812	1947	State	S-G/C	7,461	458	$ 2,141	$2,488	$ 4,629
Morris Campus	Morris, MN 56267	1960	State	S/C	1,665	133	$ 2,088	$2,392	$ 4,480
Technical College, Crookston	Crookston, MN 56716....	1966	State	T/C	1,145	81	$ 1,830	$2,432	$ 4,235
Technical College, Waseca..	Waseca, MN 56093	1971	State	T/C	1,120	70	$ 1,780	$2,220	$ 4,000
Twin Cities Campus	Minneapolis, MN 55455 .	1851	State	S-G/C	44,659	4,592	$ 1,969	$2,488	$ 4,457
Walden University	Minneapolis, MN 55401 .	1970	Independ	G/C	251	—	$ 6,600	—	$ 6,600
Wm. Mitchell College of Law .	St. Paul, MN 55105	1900	Independ	P/C	1,110	86	$ 6,000	—	$ 6,000
Willmar Community College ..	Willmar, MN 56201	1962	State	J/C	897	55	$ 1,103	—	$ 1,103
Winona State University	Winona, MN 55987	1858	State	S-G/C	5,376	250	$ 1,482	$1,638	$ 3,120
Worthington Comm. College .	Worthington, MN 56187 .	1936	State	J/C	615	30	$ 1,102	—	$ 1,102
MISSISSIPPI									
Alcorn State University	Lorman, MS 39096	1871	State	S-G/C	2,400	157	$ 975	$1,625	$ 2,600
Belhaven College	Jackson, MS 39202	1883	Presby	S/C	762	65	$ 3,670	$1,830	$ 5,500
Blue Mountain College	Blue Mountain, MS 38610	1873	Baptist	S/W	375	34	$ 2,454	$1,730	$ 4,184
Coahoma Junior College	Clarksdale, MS 38614....	1949	State	J/C	1,762	59	$ 935	$1,261	$ 2,196
Copiah-Lincoln Junior College	Wesson, MS 39191	1915	State	J/C	1,722	128	$ 500	$1,300	$ 1,800
Natchez Campus	Natchez, MS 39120	1971	State	J/C	444	32	$ 540	—	$ 540
Delta State University	Cleveland, MS 38733 ...	1924	State	S-G/C	3,445	212	$ 1,000	$1,450	$ 2,450
East Central Junior College ..	Decatur, MS 39327	1928	State	J/C	969	50	$ 500	$1,200	$ 1,800¹

NAME	ADDRESS	FOUNDED	AFFILIATION	LEVEL/TYPE	ENROLLMENT	TEACHERS	TUITION & FEES	BOARD & ROOM	TOTAL COST
MISSISSIPPI (*continued*)									
East Mississippi Jr. College..	Scooba, MS 39358	1927	State	J/C	1,645	60	$ 420	$1,010	$ 1,430
Hinds Junior College......	Raymond, MS 39154	1917	State	J/C	10,462	375	$ 702	$1,320	$ 2,022
Holmes Junior College......	Goodman, MS 39079 ...	1925	State	J/C	1,112	71	$ 500	$1,200	$ 1,700
Itawamba Junior College....	Fulton, MS 38843	1948	Public	J/C	5,950	156	$ 480	$1,470	$ 1,950
Jackson State University....	Jackson, MS 39217....	1877	State	S-G/C	6,088	353	$ 1,072	$1,984	$ 2,818
Jones County Junior College.	Ellisville, MS 39437	1927	State	J/C	2,462	120	$ 460	$1,400	$ 1,860
Magnolia Bible College	Kosciusko, MS 39090 ...	1976	C of Chr	S/C	116	10	$ 610	$2,200	$ 2,810
Mary Holmes College	West Point, MS 39773 ..	1892	Presby	J/C	703	34	$ 1,450	$1,550	$ 3,000
Meridian Junior College	Meridian, MS 39305 ...	1937	Public	J/C	2,550	160	$ 225	—	$ 225
Mid South Christian College .	Senatobia, MS 38668 ...	1959	C of Chr	S/C	41	8	$ 1,700	$1,850	$ 3,550
Millsaps College............	Jackson, MS 39210	1890	Methodist	S-G/C	1,301	96	$ 5,575	$2,310	$ 7,885
Mississippi Baptist Seminary	Jackson, MS 39209	1942	Baptist	S-G/C	550	30		$ 800	$ 800
Mississippi College	Clinton, MS 39058	1826	Baptist	S-G/C	3,208	138	$ 3,348	$1,890	$ 5,238
Clarke College	Newton, MS 39345	1908	Baptist	J/C	153	23	$ 2,290	$1,840	$ 4,130
Mississippi Delta Jr. College .	Moorhead, MS 38761 ...	1926	State	J/C	1,754	101	$ 500	$1,095	$ 1,595
Miss. Gulf Coast Jr. College									
Jackson County Campus ..	Gautier, MS 39553	1965	State	J/C	3,878	96	$ 544	—	$ 544
Jefferson Davis Campus ..	Gulfport, MS 39501	1965	State	J/C	3,762	108	$ 544	—	$ 544
Perkinston Campus	Perkinston, MS 39573 ..	1925	State	J/C	1,282	61	$ 544	$1,400	$ 1,944
Mississippi State University .	Mississippi State, MS 39762	1878	State	S-G/C	11,720	840	$ 1,358	$2,090	$ 3,448
Mississippi Univ. for Women	Columbus, MS 39701 ...	1884	State	S-G/C	2,234	164	$ 925	$1,660	$ 2,585
Mississippi Valley State Univ.	Itta Bena, MS 38941 ...	1950	State	S-G/C	2,575	145	$ 850	$1,350	$ 2,200
Natchez Junior College	Natchez, MS 39120....	1885	Baptist	J/C	133	14	$ 810	$ 800	$ 1,600
Northeast Mississippi Jr. Col.	Booneville, MS 38829 ...	1948	State	J/C	2,200	125	$ 550	$1,380	$ 1,930
Northwest Mississippi Jr. Col.	Senatobia, MS 38668 ...	1927	State	J/C	3,240	165	$ 754	$1,308	$ 2,062
Pearl River Junior College ..	Poplarville, MS 39470 ..	1909	State	J/C	2,785	113	$ 450	$ 535	$ 985
Prentiss Normal & Indust. Inst.	Prentiss, MS 39474.....	1907	Independ	J/C	90	12	$ 2,492	$1,654	$ 4,146
Reformed Theo. Sem........	Jackson, MS 39209	1963	Church	G/C	306	20	$ 2,225	—	$ 2,225
Rust College	Holly Springs, MS 38635	1866	Methodist	S/C	870	42	$ 2,109	$1,800	$ 3,909
Southeastern Baptist College	Laurel, MS 39440	1948	Baptist	S/C	89	16	$ 1,200	$1,250	$ 2,450
Southwest Mississippi Jr. Col.	Summit, MS 39666	1918	State	J/C	1,475	60	$ 400	$1,100	$ 1,500
Tougaloo College...........	Tougaloo, MS 39174....	1869	D of Chr	S/C	606	55	$ 3,160	$1,500	$ 4,660
University of Mississippi	University, MS 38677	1844	State	S-G/C	8,715	525	$ 1,401	$2,229	$ 3,630
Medical Center..........	Jackson, MS 39216	1955	State	S-G/C	1,737	529	$ 3,205	$6,210	$ 9,415
University of Southern Miss.	Hattiesburg, MS 39406 .	1910	State	S-G/C	11,169	646	$ 1,266	$1,910	$ 3,176
Utica Junior College........	Utica, MS 39175	1903	State	J/C	675	37	$ 265	$ 660	$ 925
Wesley Biblical Seminary ...	Jackson, MS 39206......	1974	Independ	G/C	67	15	$ 1,965	—	$ 1,965
Wesley College	Florence, MS 39073	1944	Methodist	S/C	81	14	$ 3,050	$1,700	$ 4,750
William Carey College.......	Hattiesburg, MS 39401 .	1906	Baptist	S-G/C	3,044	103	$ 2,770	$1,900	$ 4,670
Wood Junior College........	Mathiston, MS 39752 ...	1886	Methodist	J/C	400	40	$ 1,440	$1,950	$ 3,390
MISSOURI									
Avila College	Kansas City, MO 64145 ..	1916	Catholic	S-G/C	1,600	150	$ 4,500	$2,100	$ 6,600
Calvary Bible College	Kansas City, MO 64147 .	1932	Independ	S-G/C	429	33	$ 2,450	$2,160	$ 4,610
Cardinal Glennon College ...	St. Louis, MO 63119	1900	Catholic	S/M	83	28	$ 4,135	$1,500	$ 5,635
Central Bible College	Springfield, MO 65802 ..	1922	A of God	S/C	903	58	$ 2,100	$2,240	$ 4,340
Central Christian College ...	Moberly, MO 65270	1957	Christian	S/C	132	13	$ 1,600	—	$ 1,600
Central Methodist College ..	Fayette, MO 65248	1854	Methodist	S/C	629	72	$ 4,690	$2,260	$ 6,950
Central Missouri State Univ.	Warrensburg, MO 64093 .	1871	State	S-G/C	9,112	480	$ 992	$2,070	$ 3,062
Cleveland Chiropractic College	Kansas City, MO 64131 .	1922	Independ	P/C	380	53	$ 4,100		$ 4,100
Columbia College	Columbia, MO 65216 ...	1851	D of Chr	S/C	2,745	160	$ 4,975	$2,400	$ 7,275
Conception Seminary College	Conception, MO 64433..	1886	Catholic	S/M	104	26	$ 2,500	$2,500	$ 5,000
Concordia Seminary	St. Louis, MO 63105	1839	Lutheran	P/C	616	40	$ 2,925	$2,385	$ 5,310
Cottey College	Nevada, MO 64772	1884	Independ	J/W	346	32	$ 2,400	$1,800	$ 4,200
Covenant Theological Sem. .	St. Louis, MO 63141	1956	Presby	P/C	154	19	$ 3,175	$ 540	$ 3,715
Crowder College	Neosho, MO 64850	1963	State	J/C	1,236	45	$ 400	$1,500	$ 1,900
Culver-Stockton College.....	Canton, MO 63435	1853	D of Chr	S/C	728	51	$ 4,600	$1,900	$ 6,500
Devry Institute of Technology	Kansas City, MO 64131 .	1969	Independ	S/C	1,916	—	$ 3,658		$ 3,658
Drury College	Springfield, MO 65802 ..	1873	D of Chr	S/C	2,500	140	$ 4,500	$1,350	$ 5,850
East Central Junior College ..	Union, MO 63084	1968	Public	J/C	2,336	98	$ 532		$ 532
Eden Theological Seminary ..	St. Louis, MO 63119	1850	UC Chr	G/C	250	20	$ 3,000	$1,000	$ 4,000
Evangel College	Springfield, MO 65802 ..	1955	A of God	S/C	1,777	126	$ 3,260	$2,300	$ 5,560
Fontbonne College	St. Louis, MO 63105	1917	Catholic	S-G/C	952	113	$ 5,000	$2,800	$ 7,800
Hannibal-Lagrange College ..	Hannibal, MO 63401	1858	Baptist	S/C	756	58	$ 3,440	$1,670	$ 4,710
Harris-Stowe State College ..	St. Louis, MO 63103	1857	State	S/C	1,775	84	$ 780		$ 780
Jefferson College	Hillsboro, MO 63050....	1963	State	J/C	3,054	145	$ 420		$ 420
Kansas City Art Institute	Kansas City, MO 64111 .	1885	Independ	S/C	475	50	$ 7,200	$3,075	$10,275
Kemper Military Sch. and Col.	Boonville, MO 65233....	1844	Independ	S/C	85	13	$ 5,950	$1,800	$ 7,750
Kirksville Col. of Osteo. Med.	Kirksville, MO 63501.....	1892	Independ	P/C	523	67	$14,000	$4,225	$18,225
Lincoln University of Missouri	Jefferson City, MO 65101.	1866	State	S-G/C	2,951	150	$ 825	$2,524	$ 3,349
Lindenwood College	St. Charles, MO 63301 ..	1827	Independ	S-G/C	1,755	158	$ 4,950	$2,800	$ 7,750
Logan College of Chiropractic	Chesterfield, MO 63017 .	1935	Independ	P/C	632	62	$ 7,560		$ 7,560
Maryville College	St. Louis, MO 63141	1872	Independ	S-G/C	2,299	155	$ 4,890	$2,510	$ 7,400
Metropolitan Comm. College .	Kansas, MO 64111	1915	Local	J/C					
Longview Comm. College ..	Lee's Summit, MO 64063	1969	Public	J/C	7,413	141	$ 660	—	$ 660
Maple Woods Comm. College	Kansas City, MO 64156 .	1969	Public	J/C	3,545	63	$ 660	—	$ 660
Penn Valley Comm. College	Kansas City, MO 64111 .	1969	Public	J/C	9,295	151	$ 660	—	$ 660
Pioneer Comm. College ...	Kansas City, MO 64111 .	1976	Public	J/C	2,068	28	$ 660	—	$ 660
Midwestern Bapt. Theol. Sem.	Kansas City, MO 64118 .	1957	Baptist	P/C	578	24	$ 600	$2,850	$ 3,450
Mineral Area College	Flat River, MO 63601	1965	State	J/C	1,675	75	$ 480		$ 480
Missouri Baptist College	St. Louis, MO 63141	1963	Baptist	S/C	574	27	$ 3,470	$1,900	$ 5,370
Missouri Southern State Col.	Joplin, MO 64801	1937	State	S/C	4,323	193	$ 770	$1,560	$ 2,330
Missouri Valley College	Marshall, MO 65340....	1889	Presby	S/C	461	27	$ 4,200	$2,370	$ 6,570

NAME	ADDRESS	FOUN-DED	AFFILI-ATION	LEVEL/TYPE	ENROLL-MENT	TEACH-ERS	TUITION & FEES	BOARD & ROOM	TOTAL COST
MISSOURI (continued)									
Missouri Western St. College	St. Joseph, MO 64507 ..	1915	State	S/C	4,077	203	$ 880	$1,566	$ 2,446
Moberly Junior College	Moberly, MO 65270	1927	Public	J/C	997	28	$ 450	—	$ 450
National College	Kansas City, MO 64138 .	1975	Private	S/C	81	11	$ 2,599	—	$ 2,599
Nazarene Theological Sem. .	Kansas City, MO 64131 .	1945	Nazarene	P/C	436	24	$ 1,190	—	$ 1,190
Northeast Missouri St. Univ.	Kirksville, MO 63501 ...	1867	State	S-G/C	6,875	305	$ 770	$1,590	$ 2,360
Northwest Missouri St. Univ.	Maryville, MO 64468 ...	1905	State	S-G/C	4,974	245	$ 900	$1,850	$ 2,750
Ozark Bible College.........	Joplin, MO 64801.......	1942	Christian	S/C	523	48	$ 1,650	$1,610	$ 3,260
Park College	Parkville, MO 64152....	1875	RLDS	S-G/C	869	45	$ 4,480	$2,240	$ 6,720
Rockhurst College	Kansas City, MO 64110 .	1910	Catholic	S-G/C	2,869	186	$ 4,960	$2,735	$ 7,695
St. Louis College of Pharmacy	St. Louis, MO 63110 ...	1864	Independ	P/C	685	43	$ 4,260	$2,400	$ 6,660
St. Louis Comm. College	St. Louis, MO 63110 ...	1962	Public	J/C					
Florissant Valley	St. Louis, MO 63135 ...	1963	Public	J/C	11,297	445	$ 720	—	$ 720
Forest Park..............	St. Louis, MO 63110 ...	1963	Public	J/C	6,965	470	$ 720	—	$ 720
Meramec................	St. Louis, MO 63122 ...	1963	Public	J/C	12,103	568	$ 720	—	$ 720
St. Louis Conserv. of Music ..	St. Louis, MO 63130 ...	1923	Independ	S-G/C	110	35	$ 5,515	—	$ 5,515
St. Louis University	St. Louis, MO 63103 ...	1818	Catholic	S-G/C	10,170	2,275	$ 5,710	$3,000	$ 8,710
St. Mary's College of O'Fallon	O'Fallon, MO 63366	1921	Catholic	J/C	674	45	$ 2,300	—	$ 2,300
St. Paul School of Theology ..	Kansas City, MO 64127	1958	Methodist	P/C	229	20	$ 3,650	$2,500	$ 6,150
St. Paul's College	Concordia, MO 64020 ..	1883	Lutheran	J/C	61	20	$ 2,830	$2,410	$ 5,240
School of the Ozarks	Point Lookout, MO 65726	1906	Independ	S/C	1,236	87	$ 90	—	$ 90
Southeast Missouri State Univ.	Cape Girardeau, MO 63701	1873	State	S-G/C	9,093	424	$ 850	$1,700	$ 2,600
Southwest Baptist Univ.....	Bolivar, MO 65613	1878	Baptist	S-G/C	1,963	104	$ 3,800	$1,550	$ 5,350
Southwest Missouri St. Univ. .	Springfield, MO 65804 .	1905	State	S-G/C	15,121	689	$ 1,104	$1,950	$ 3,054
State Fair Community College	Sedalia, MO 65301......	1966	Public	J/C	1,614	51	$ 400	—	$ 400
Stephens College..........	Columbia, MO 65215 ...	1833	Independ	S/W	1,094	107	$ 7,100	$3,100	$10,200
Tarkio College	Tarkio, MO 64491......	1883	Presby	S/C	880	60	$ 4,500	$2,800	$ 7,300
Three Rivers Comm. College .	Poplar Bluff, MO 63901	1966	State	J/C	1,785	118	$ 600	—	$ 600
Trenton Junior College	Trenton, MO 64683	1925	Public	J/C	650	45	$ 804	—	$ 804
University of Health Sciences	Kansas City, MO 64124 .	1916	Independ	P/C	610	64	$12,350	$10,170	$22,520
University of Missouri System	Columbia, MO 65211 ...								
Columbia Campus.........	Columbia, MO 65211 ...	1839	State	P/C	23,585	1,741	$ 1,457	$2,096	$ 3,553
Kansas City Campus......	Kansas City, MO 64110	1933	State	P/C	11,464	802	$ 1,489	$2,353	$ 3,842
Rolla Campus............	Rolla, MO 65401	1870	State	S-G/C	6,967	357	$ 1,579	$2,693	$ 4,272
St. Louis Campus........	St. Louis, MO 63121 ...	1963	State	P/C	11,596	391	$ 1,489	—	$ 1,489
Washington University	St. Louis, MO 63130 ...	1853	Private	S-G/C	10,610	2,589	$ 9,200	$3,579	$12,779
Webster University	St. Louis, MO 63119 ...	1915	Independ	S-G/C	6,057	954	$ 4,800	$2,720	$ 7,520
Wentworth Mil. Acad. & Jr. Col.	Lexington, MO 64067 ..	1880	Independ	J/M	115	12	—	—	$ 7,800
Westminster College	Fulton, MO 65251	1851	Independ	S/C	627	60	$ 5,300	$2,500	$ 7,800
William Jewell College	Liberty, MO 64068	1849	Baptist	S/C	1,991	173	$ 4,450	$2,182	$ 6,632
William Woods College	Fulton, MO 65251.......	1870	D of Chr	S/W	781	60	$ 5,800	$2,300	$ 8,100
MONTANA									
Carroll College	Helena, MT 59625	1909	Catholic	S/C	1,520	103	$ 3,410	$2,232	$ 5,642
College of Great Falls	Great Falls, MT 59405 ..	1932	Catholic	S-G/C	1,339	87	$ 3,300	$1,800	$ 5,100
Dawson Community College .	Glendive, MT 59330	1940	State	J/C	911	50	$ 450	$2,420	$ 3,070
Eastern Montana College ...	Billings, MT 59101	1927	State	S-G/C	4,207	276	$ 930	$2,600	$ 3,530
Flathead Valley Comm. College	Kalispell, MT 59901	1967	State	J/C	1,940	114	$ 383	—	$ 383
Miles Community College ...	Miles City, MT 59301 ...	1939	State	J/C	867	52	$ 390	$1,980	$ 2,370
Mont. Col. of Min. Sci. & Tech.	Butte, MT 59701.......	1893	State	G/C	2,128	136	$ 883	$2,250	$ 3,133
Montana State University ...	Bozeman, MT 59717 ...	1893	State	S-G/C	11,035	682	$ 992	$2,730	$ 3,722
Northern Montana College ..	Havre, MT 59501	1913	State	S-G/C	1,811	121	$ 751	$2,272	$ 3,023
Rocky Mountain College	Billings, MT 59102	1878	Int-Den	S/C	513	51	$ 4,022	$2,612	$ 6,633
University of Montana	Missoula, MT 59812....	1893	State	S-G/C	9,150	450	$ 1,131	$2,380	$ 3,511
Western Montana College ...	Dillon, MT 59725	1893	State	S-G/C	900	35	$ 413	$ 785	$ 1,198
NEBRASKA									
Bellevue College	Bellevue, NE 68005	1965	Independ	S-G/C	2,604	86	$ 1,350	—	$ 1,350
Central Comm. Col. Area ..	Grand Island, NE 68802	1973	Local	T/C	—	—	—	—	—
Grand Island Campus.....	Grand Island, NE 68802	1976	Local	T/C	1,281	17	$ 720	—	$ 720
Hastings Campus	Hastings, NE 68901	1966	Local	T/C	1,306	78	$ 720	$1,350	$ 2,070
Platte Campus	Columbus, NE 68601 ...	1969	Local	T/C	1,314	36	$ 720	$1,350	$ 2,070
Chadron State College	Chadron, NE 69337	1911	State	S-G/C	2,270	92	$ 825	$1,768	$ 2,593
College of Saint Mary	Omaha, NE 68124	1923	Catholic	S/W	1,061	116	$ 4,700	$2,200	$ 6,900
Concordia Teachers College .	Seward, NE 68434	1894	Lutheran	S-G/C	968	82	$ 4,069	$2,100	$ 6,169
Creighton University	Omaha, NE 68178	1878	Independ	S-G/C	5,913	991	$ 4,800	$2,420	$ 7,220
Dana College	Blair, NE 68008........	1884	Lutheran	S/C	469	46	$ 4,810	$2,200	$ 7,010
Doane College	Crete, NE 68333	1872	UCC Chr	S/C	657	55	$ 5,150	$2,000	$ 7,150
Grace College of the Bible ...	Omaha, NE 68108	1943	Independ	S/C	272	16	$ 2,990	$2,000	$ 4,990
Hastings College	Hastings, NE 68901	1882	Presby	S/C	811	56	$ 5,190	$2,130	$ 7,320
Kearney State College	Kearney, NE 68849	1903	State	S-G/C	8,392	257	$ 959	$1,676	$ 2,635
McCook Community College .	McCook, NE 69001	1929	State	J/C	847	50	$ 560	$1,460	$ 2,020
Met. Tech. Comm. College ..	Omaha, NE 68103	1974	State	T/C	6,018	290	$ 749	—	$ 749
Midland Lutheran College ..	Fremont, NE 68025	1883	Lutheran	S/C	853	60	$ 5,000	$1,200	$ 7,200
Mid-Plains Community College	North Platte, NE 69101 .	1968	Public	J/C	1,989	50	$ 580	—	$ 580
Nebraska Christian College ..	Norfolk, NE 68701	1945	C of Chr	S/C	151	12	$ 1,510	$1,750	$ 3,260
Nebraska Wesleyan Univ. ...	Lincoln, NE 68504	1887	Methodist	S/C	1,365	113	$ 5,136	$2,050	$ 7,186
Northeast Tech. Comm. Col. .	Norfolk, NE 68701	1928	State	T/C	2,298	105	$ 772	$1,800	$ 2,572
Peru State College.........	Peru, NE 68421........	1867	State	S/C	1,409	50	$ 955	$1,790	$ 2,745
Platte Valley Bible College ..	Scottsbluff, NE 69361 ..	1951	C of Chr	S/C	50	5	$ 960	$1,200	$ 2,160
Southeast Community College	Lincoln, NE 68520	1973	Public	T/C					
Fairbury Campus	Fairbury, NE 68352	1941	Public	T/C	302	15	$ 622	$1,700	$ 2,322

NAME	ADDRESS	FOUN-DED	AFFILI-ATION	LEVEL/TYPE	ENROLL-MENT	TEACH-ERS	TUITION & FEES	BOARD & ROOM	TOTAL COST
NEBRASKA *(continued)*									
Lincoln Campus	Lincoln, NE 68520	1967	Public	T/C	3,497	105	$ 618		$ 618
Milford Beatrice Campus	Milford, NE 68405	1941	Public	T/C	1,072	98	$ 618	$1,492	$ 2,110
Union College	Lincoln, NE 68506	1891	7-D Adv	S/C	898	60	$ 5,800	$2,135	$ 7,935
University of Nebraska	Lincoln, NE 68583								
Lincoln	Lincoln, NE 68588	1869	State	S-G/C	24,217	1,025	$ 1,472	$1,925	$ 3,397
Medical Center	Omaha, NE 68105	1902	State	S-G/C	2,495	207	$ 3,208	—	$ 3,208
Omaha	Omaha, NE 68132	1908	State	S-G/C	14,037	392	$ 1,345	—	$ 1,345
Sch. of Tech. Agriculture	Curtis, NE 69025	1965	State	T/C	285	30	$ 1,068	$2,220	$ 3,288
Wayne State College	Wayne, NE 68787	1910	State	S-G/C	2,836	134	$ 956	$1,914	$ 2,870
Western Tech. Comm. College	Scottsbluff, NE 69361	1973	Public	J/C	—	—	—	—	—
Nebraska Western College	Scottsbluff, NE 69361	1929	Public	J/C	1,550	49	$ 660	$1,890	$ 3,750
West. Nebraska Technical College	Sidney, NE 69162	1965	State	T/C	700	25	$ 720	$2,070	$ 2,790
York College	York, NE 68467	1890	C of Chr	J/C	395	30	$ 2,900	$2,400	$ 5,300
NEVADA									
Northern Nevada Comm. Col.	Elko, NV 89801	1968	State	J/C	1,746	110	$ 600	—	$ 600
Reno Business College	Reno, NV 89503	1902	Independ	S/C	200	15	$ 2,610	—	$ 2,610
Sierra Nevada College	Incline Village, NV 89450	1969	Independ	S/C	200	20	$ 2,500	—	$ 2,500
Univ. of Nevada, Las Vegas	Las Vegas, NV 89154	1957	State	S-G/C	10,989	533	$ 1,080	$2,469	$ 3,549
Univ. of Nevada, Reno	Reno, NV 89557	1864	State	S-G/C	9,458	503	$ 1,080	$2,298	$ 3,378
NEW HAMPSHIRE									
Antioch/New Eng. Grad. Cen.	Keene, NH 03431	1852	Independ	G/C	483	32	$ 5,000	—	$ 5,000
Castle Junior College	Windham, NH 03087	1963	Catholic	J/W	143	12	$ 2,150	—	$ 2,150
Colby-Sawyer College	New London, NH 03257	1837	Independ	S/W	500	48	$ 7,610	$3,130	$10,740
Daniel Webster College	Nashua, NH 03063	1965	Independ	S/C	442	32	$ 6,620	$2,950	$ 9,570
Dartmouth College	Hanover, NH 03755	1769	Independ	S-G/C	4,628	369	$10,670	$4,190	$14,860
Franklin Pierce College	Rindge, NH 03461	1962	Independ	S/C	2,293	150	$ 6,950	$3,150	$10,100
Hesser College	Manchester, NH 03101	1900	Independ	J/C	1,983	143	$ 3,500	$1,200	$ 4,700
Keene State College	Keene, NH 03431	1909	State	S-G/C	3,861	200	$ 2,060	$2,225	$ 5,280
Lebanon College	Lebanon, NH 03766	1957	Independ	J/C	1,800	120	—	—	—
Magdalen College	Bedford, NH 03102	1973	Catholic	S/C	70	7	$ 4,000	$2,500	$ 6,500
McIntosh College	Dover, NH 03820	1896	Independ	J/C	600	22	$ 2,300	—	$ 2,300
Merrimack Valley College	Manchester, NH 03102	1967	State	J/C	365	36	$ 1,210	—	$ 1,210
Nathaniel Hawthorne College	Antrim, NH 03440	1962	Independ	S/C	646	55	$ 6,050	$2,850	$ 8,900
New England College	Henniker, NH 03242	1946	Independ	S-G/C	1,150	95	$ 7,110	$3,140	$10,250
New Hampshire College	Manchester, NH 03104	1932	Independ	S-G/C	1,785	83	$ 6,740	$3,600	$10,340
New Hampshire Tech. Inst.	Concord, NH 03301	1965	State	T/C	826	76	$ 1,500	$2,000	$ 3,500
N.H. Voc. Tech. College	Berlin, NH 03570	1966	State	T/C	275	36	$ 1,350	—	$ 1,350
N.H. Voc. Tech. College	Claremont NH 03743	1967	State	T/C	345	35	$ 1,430	—	$ 1,430
N.H. Voc. Tech. College	Laconia, NH 03246	1967	State	J/C	215	20	$ 1,350	—	$ 1,350
N.H. Voc. Tech. College	Manchester, NH 03102	1945	State	J/C	448	46	$ 1,350	—	$ 1,350
N.H. Voc. Tech. College	Nashua, NH 03063	1967	State	T/C	1,080	83	$ 1,350	$2,350	$ 3,700
N.H. Voc. Tech. College	Stratham, NH 03885	1945	State	T/C	673	74	$ 1,467	—	$ 1,467
Notre Dame College	Manchester, NH 03104	1950	Catholic	S-G/W	763	82	$ 4,300	$2,800	$ 7,100
Plymouth State College	Plymouth, NH 03264	1870	State	S/C	3,577	148	$ 1,711	$2,198	$ 3,909
Rivier College	Nashua, NH 03060	1933	Catholic	S-G/W	2,285	172	$ 4,300	$2,700	$ 7,000
St. Anselm College	Manchester, NH 03102	1889	Catholic	S/C	1,917	159	$ 5,600	$2,900	$ 8,500
University of New Hampshire	Durham, NH 03824	1866	State	S-G/C	12,168	617	$ 2,474	$2,450	$ 4,924
White Pines College	Chester, NH 03036	1965	Independ	J/C	202	19	$ 3,800	$2,600	$ 6,400
NEW JERSEY									
Assumption College for Sisters	Mendham, NJ 07945	1953	Catholic	J/W	18	10	$ 1,200	$1,100	$ 2,300
Atlantic Community College	Mays Landing, NJ 08330	1964	County	J/C	4,019	140	$ 805	—	$ 805
Bergen Community College	Paramus, NJ 07652	1968	County	J/C	11,800	506	$ 850	—	$ 850
Berkeley School	Little Falls, NJ 07424	1931	Independ	J/C	568	19	$ 5,125	$2,700	$ 7,825
Bloomfield College	Bloomfield, NJ 07003	1868	Independ	S/C	1,636	142	$ 5,300	$2,730	$ 8,030
Brookdale Community College	Lincroft, NJ 07738	1967	State	J/C	11,048	391	$ 1,400	—	$ 1,400
Burlington County College	Pemberton, NJ 08068	1966	County	J/C	5,800	150	$ 885	—	$ 885
Caldwell College	Caldwell, NJ 07006	1939	Catholic	S/W	725	68	$ 4,890	$3,100	$ 7,990
Camden County College	Blackwood, NJ 08012	1967	Public	J/C	8,148	327	$ 650	—	$ 650
Centenary College	Hackettstown, NJ 07840	1867	Independ	S/W	1,436	130	$ 5,000	$3,800	$ 8,800
College of Saint Elizabeth	Convent Sta., NJ 07961	1899	Catholic	S/W	932	93	$ 5,650	$2,800	$ 8,450
County College of Morris	Randolph, NJ 07869	1968	Public	J/C	11,000	199	$ 840	—	$ 840
Cumberland County College	Vineland, NJ 08360	1963	County	J/C	2,366	96	$ 750	—	$ 750
Devry Technical Institute	Woodbridge, NJ 07095	1969	Independ	T/C	2,689	100	$ 3,658	—	$ 3,658
Don Bosco College	Newton, NJ 07860	1928	Catholic	S/M	66	19	$ 2,860	$1,925	$ 4,785
Drew University	Madison, NJ 07940	1866	Methodist	S-G/C	2,389	175	$ 9,174	$3,000	$12,174
Essex County College	Newark, NJ 07102	1968	Public	J/C	6,796	200	$ 700	—	$ 700
Fairleigh Dickinson Univ.									
Edward Williams College	Hackensack, NJ 07601	1942	Independ	J/C	1,059	55	$ 4,900	$3,500	$ 8,400
Florham-Madison Campus	Madison, NJ 07940	1942	Independ	S-G/C	4,273	231	$ 5,900	$3,500	$ 9,400
Rutherford Campus	Rutherford, NJ 07070	1942	Independ	S-G/C	3,089	203	$ 5,900	$3,500	$ 9,400
Teaneck-Hackensack	Teaneck, NJ 07666	1942	Independ	S-G/C	7,011	700	$ 5,900	$3,500	$ 9,400
Felician College	Lodi, NJ 07644	1942	Catholic	S/W	609	71	$ 3,460	—	$ 3,460
Georgian Court College	Lakewood, NJ 08701	1908	Catholic	S-G/W	1,555	111	$ 4,500	$2,570	$ 7,070
Glassboro State College	Glassboro, NJ 08028	1923	State	S-G/C	9,200	347	$ 932	$1,730	$ 2,662
Gloucester County College	Sewell, NJ 08080	1968	Public	J/C	3,400	78	$ 750	—	$ 750
Hudson County Comm. Col.	Jersey City, NJ 07306	1975	State	J/C	3,477	180	$ 700	—	$ 700
Immaculate Conception Sem.	So. Orange, NJ 07079	1861	Catholic	G/C	151	30	$ 2,650	$2,700	$ 5,350

NAME	ADDRESS	FOUN-DED	AFFILI-ATION	LEVEL/TYPE	ENROLL-MENT	TEACH-ERS	TUITION & FEES	BOARD & ROOM	TOTAL COST
NEW JERSEY *(continued)*									
Jersey City State College	Jersey City, NJ 07305 ...	1927	State	S-G/C	7,343	271	$ 1,280	$2,750	$ 4,030
Kean College of New Jersey .	Union, NJ 07083	1855	State	P/C	12,760	705	$ 1,305	$2,700	$ 4,005
Mercer County Comm. College	Trenton, NJ 08690	1966	County	J/C	9,171	418	$ 750	—	$ 750
Middlesex County College ...	Edison, NJ 08818	1966	County	J/C	11,200	430	$ 750	—	$ 750
Monmouth College	W. Long Branch, NJ 07764	1933	Independ	S-G/C	4,225	259	$ 6,332	$2,945	$ 9,277
Montclair State College	Upper Montclair, NJ 07043	1908	State	S-G/C	14,374	757	$ 1,400	$3,360	$ 4,760
New Brunswick Theol. Sem. .	New Brunswick, NJ 08901	1784	Reformed	P/C	90	21	$ 3,200	$1,200	$ 4,400
New Jersey Inst. of Tech. ...	Newark, NJ 07102	1881	State	S-G/C	7,235	289	$ 2,236	$3,046	$ 5,282
Northeastern Bible College ..	Essex Falls, NJ 07021 ...	1950	Independ	S/C	266	18	$ 3,790	$2,500	$ 6,290
Ocean County College	Toms River, NJ 08753 ...	1964	County	J/C	5,712	253	$ 855	—	$ 855
Passaic County Comm. College	Paterson, NJ 07509	1968	County	J/C	2,987	189	$ 816	—	$ 816
Princeton Theol. Seminary ..	Princeton, NJ 08540	1812	Presby	P/C	859	78	$ 3,000	$2,555	$ 5,555
Princeton University	Princeton, NJ 08544	1746	Private	S-G/C	6,169	738	$10,960	$3,980	$14,940
Rabbinical Col. of America ..	Morristown, NJ 07960 ...	1956	Jewish	S/M	230	14	$ 3,000	$2,500	$ 5,500
Ramapo Col. of New Jersey ..	Mahwah, NJ 07430	1969	State	S/C	4,000	190	$ 1,020	$2,700	$ 3,720
Rider College	Lawrenceville, NJ 08648	1865	Independ	S-G/C	5,062	282	$ 5,550	$2,889	$ 8,439
Rutgers, State Univ. of N.J..	New Brunswick, NJ 08903	1766	State	S-G/C					
Camden Col. of Arts & Sci.	Camden, NJ 08102	1927	State	S/C	3,632	162	$ 1,776	—	$ 1,776
College of Engineering ..	New Brunswick, NJ 08903	1864	State	S/C	2,727	86	$ 1,980	$2,498	$ 4,478
College of Nursing........	Newark, NJ 07102	1956	State	S/C	508	44	$ 1,775	—	$ 1,775
College of Pharmacy	New Brunswick, NJ 08903	1892	State	S/C	711	30	$ 1,980	$2,498	$ 4,478
Cook College	New Brunswick, NJ 08903	1921	State	S/C	3,096	125	$ 1,886	$2,498	$ 4,384
Douglass College	New Brunswick, NJ 08903	1918	State	S/W	3,344	224	$ 1,884	$2,498	$ 4,382
Livingston College	New Brunswick, NJ 08903	1965	State	S/C	3,510	204	$ 1,898	$2,498	$ 4,396
Mason Gross Sch. of the Arts	New Brunswick, NJ 08903	1976	State	S-G/C	526	12	$ 1,884	$2,498	$ 4,382
Newark Col. of Arts & Sci.	Newark, NJ 07105	1946	State	S/C	3,648	214	$ 1,786	—	$ 1,786
Rutgers College	New Brunswick, NJ 08903	1766	State	S/C	8,270	506	$ 1,898	$2,498	$ 4,396
Univ. College—Camden ...	Camden, NJ 08102	1935	State	S/C	1,069		—	—	—
Univ. College—New Brunswick	New Brunswick, NJ 08903	1934	State	S/C	3,411	101	—	—	—
Univ. College—Newark ...	Newark, NJ 07102	1934	State	S/C	1,753	36	—	—	—
Saint Peter's College........	Jersey City, NJ 07306....	1872	Catholic	S-G/C	4,022	443	$ 5,012	—	$ 5,012
Salem Comm. College........	Penns Grove, NJ 08069 .	1972	State	J/C	1,177	45	$ 750	—	$ 750
Seton Hall University	So. Orange, NJ 07079...	1856	Catholic	S-G/C	7,915	549	$ 5,450	$3,200	$ 8,650
Seton Hall Univ. Sch. of Law .	Newark, NJ 07102	1951	Catholic	P/C	1,050	106	$ 6,160	—	$ 6,160
Shelton College	Cape May, NJ 08204	1907	Church	S/C	35	9	$ 1,940	$1,750	$ 3,690
Somerset County College.....	Somerville, NJ 08876	1966	Public	J/C	4,626	235	$ 805	—	$ 805
Stevens Inst. of Technology ..	Hoboken, NJ 07030	1870	Independ	S-G/C	3,300	200	$ 8,850	$3,310	$12,160
Stockton State College	Pomona, NJ 08240	1969	State	S/C	5,708	227	$ 1,280	$2,100	$ 4,642
Thomas A. Edison State Col. .	Trenton, NJ 08625	1972	State	S/C	4,112		$ 105	—	$ 500
Trenton State College.......	Trenton, NJ 08625	1855	State	S-G/C	8,826	380	$ 1,550	$3,150	$ 4,700
Union County College	Cranford, NJ 07016	1933	Public	J/C	8,572	402	$ 875	—	$ 875
Univ. of Med. & Dent. of N.J.	Newark, NJ 07103	1956	State	P/C	2,345	735	$ 5,500	—	$ 5,500
Upsala College	East Orange, NJ 07019 .	1893	Lutheran	S-G/C	1,417	65	$ 5,700	$3,000	$ 8,700
Wirths Campus	Sussex, NJ 07461	1978	Lutheran	J/C	313	37	$ 750	—	$ 750
Westminster Choir College ..	Princeton, NJ 08540	1926	Independ	S-G/C	397	60	$ 6,330	$2,930	$ 9,260
William Paterson Col. of N.J.	Wayne, NJ 07470	1855	State	S-G/C	10,023	369	$ 1,298	$2,575	$ 3,873
NEW MEXICO									
Armand Hammer United World College	Montezuma, NM 87731 .	1982	Independ	J/C	197	28	$10,000	—	$10,000
College of Santa Fe	Santa Fe, NM 87501	1947	Catholic	S/C	957	62	$ 3,600	$2,800	$ 6,400
College of the Southwest	Hobbs, NM 88240	1956	Independ	S/C	241	28	$ 1,250	$1,500	$ 2,750
Eastern New Mexico Univ. ..	Portales, NM 88130	1934	State	S-G/C	3,549	199	$ 800	$1,750	$ 2,550
Clovis Campus	Clovis, NM 88101	1961	State	J/C	1,848	96	$ 162	—	$ 162
Roswell Campus	Roswell, NM 88201	1958	State	J/C	1,285	78	$ 512	$1,800	$ 2,312
Inst. of Amer. Indian Arts ..	Santa Fe, NM 87501	1962	Federal	J/C	184	20	—		
National College Albuquerque Branch	Albuquerque, NM 87198	1975	Private	S/C	278	33	$ 2,678	—	$ 2,678
New Mexico Highlands Univ.	Las Vegas, NM 87701 ...	1893	State	S-G/C	2,105	124	$ 556	$2,033	$ 2,569
N. M. Inst. of Min. & Tech.	Socorro, NM 87801	1889	State	S-G/C	1,256	116	$ 660	$2,720	$ 3,380
New Mexico Junior College ..	Hobbs, NM 88240	1965	Public	J/C	2,570	79	$ 164	—	$ 164
New Mexico Military Inst. ...	Roswell, NM 88201	1891	State	J/C	925	65	$ 750	$2,000	$ 2,750
New Mexico State University .	Las Cruces, NM 88033 ..	1888	State	S-G/C	12,786	710	$ 870	$2,000	$ 2,870
Alamogordo Campus	Alamogordo, NM 88310 .	1958	State	J/C	1,441	73	$ 384	—	$ 384
Carlsbad Campus	Carlsbad, NM 88220 ...	1950	State	J/C	1,002	53	$ 400	—	$ 400
Grants Campus	Grants, NM 87020	1968	State	J/C	518	45	$ 370	—	$ 370
St. John's College	Santa Fe, NM 87501	1784	Independ	S/C	301	47	$ 8,750	$3,000	$11,750
S.W. Indian Polytechnic Inst.	Albuquerque, NM 87184	1971	Federal	T/C	565	41	—		
University of Albuquerque....	Albuquerque, NM 87140	1920	Catholic	S/C	1,200	70	$ 3,700	$2,600	$ 6,300
University of New Mexico	Albuquerque, NM 87131	1889	State	S-G/C	24,309	1,810	$ 857	$2,175	$ 3,032
Western New Mexico Univ. ..	Silver City, NM 88061 ...	1893	State	S-G/C	1,843	83	$ 650	$1,920	$ 2,570
NEW YORK									
Academy of Aeronautics	Flushing, NY 11371	1932	Independ	J/T-C	1,485	76	$ 4,100	—	$ 4,100
Adelphi University	Garden City, NY 11530..	1896	Independ	S-G/C	10,717	835	$ 5,990	$3,300	$ 9,290
Albany Business College	Albany, NY 12210	1857	Independ	J/C	375	15	$ 3,600	—	$ 3,600
Albany College of Pharmacy .	Albany, NY 12208	1881	Independ	S/C	625	44	$ 4,450	$2,900	$ 7,350
Albany Law School of Union Univ.	Albany, NY 12208	1851	Independ	P/C	697	40	$ 6,500	—	$ 6,500
Albany Medical Coll. of Union Univ.	Albany, NY 12208	1839	Independ	P/C	576		$14,200	$6,900	$21,000
Alfred Univ.	Alfred, NY 14802........	1836	Independ	S-G/C	2,423	204	$ 8,000	$3,000	$11,000
American Acad. of Drama Arts	New York, NY 10016....	1884	Independ	J/C	539	32	$ 3,925	—	$ 3,900
Amer. Acad. McAllister Inst. .	New York, NY 10003....	1926	Independ	J/C	155	16	$ 3,500	—	$ 3,500
Bank Street College of Ed....	New York, NY 10025....	1916	Independ	G/C	700	48	$ 6,000	—	$ 6,000
Bard College..............	Ann'dal.-on-Hud., NY 12504	1860	Independ	S-G/C	733	85	$ 9,330	$3,170	$12,500
Barnard College............	New York, NY 10027....	1889	Independ	S/W	2,187	239	$10,546	$4,700	$15,246

NEW YORK (continued)

NAME	ADDRESS	FOUN-DED	AFFIL-IATION	LEVEL/TYPE	ENROLL-MENT	TEACH-ERS	TUITION & FEES	BOARD & ROOM	TOTAL COST
Berkeley School	Hicksville, NY 11801	1970	Independ	J-T/C	350	13	$ 5,100	—	$ 5,100
Berkeley School	New York, NY 10174	1936	Independ	T/C	548	16	$ 4,200	—	$ 4,200
Berkeley School	White Plains, NY 10604	1931	Independ	J/C	731	24	$ 5,100	$3,300	$ 8,400
Beth Israel School of Nursing	New York, NY 10003	1904	Independ	J/C	184	34	$ 3,300	$1,200	$ 4,500
Boricua College	New York, NY 10032	1973	Independ	S/C	10,000	102	$ 3,800	—	$ 3,800
Bramson ORT Tech. Institute	New York, NY 10010	1977	Independ	J/C	200	16	$ 3,771	—	$ 3,771
Briarcliffe Sec. School	Hicksville, NY 11801	1966	Independ	J/W	600	37	$ 4,000	—	$ 4,000
Brooklyn Law School	Brooklyn, NY 11201	1901	Independ	G/C	1,200	61	$ 7,300	—	$ 7,300
Bryant & Stratton Bus. Inst.	Buffalo, NY 14202	1854	Independ	J/C	4,282	222	$ 3,610	—	$ 3,610
Bryant & Stratton Bus. Inst.	Rochester, NY 14604	1973	Independ	J/C	948	32	$ 3,390	—	$ 3,390
Bryant & Stratton Bus. Inst.	Williamsville, NY 14221	1854	Independ	J/C	1,658	69	$ 3,390	—	$ 3,390
Bryant & Stratton Bus. Inst.	Syracuse, NY 13202	1926	Independ	J/C	1,565	90	$ 3,588	$1,335	$ 4,923
Canisius College	Buffalo, NY 14208	1870	Independ	S-G/C	4,600	297	$ 5,530	$2,830	$ 8,360
Cathedral College	Douglaston, NY 11362	1914	Catholic	S/M	91	27	$ 3,800	$2,000	$ 5,800
Cazenovia College	Cazenovia, NY 13035	1824	Independ	J/C	800	76	$ 5,324	$2,626	$ 7,950
Central City Business Institute	Syracuse, NY 13203	1904	Independ	J/C	1,057	64	$ 3,025	—	$ 5,025
Christ the King Seminary	East Aurora, NY 14052	1855	Catholic	G/M	138	21	$ 5,250	—	$ 5,250
City University of New York									
Bernard M. Baruch College	New York, NY 10010	1968	Public	S-G/C	15,581	780	$ 1,318	—	$ 1,318
Borough of Manhat. Comm. Col.	New York, NY 10007	1963	Public	J/C	9,867	579	$ 1,074	—	$ 1,074
Bronx Community College	Bronx, NY 10453	1957	Public	J/C	7,209	481	$ 1,295	—	$ 1,295
Brooklyn College	Brooklyn, NY 11210	1930	City	S-G/C	14,607	1,237	$ 1,325	—	$ 1,325
City College of New York	New York, NY 10031	1847	City	S-G/C	13,000	650	$ 1,291	—	$ 1,300
College of Staten Island	Staten Island, NY 10301	1976	City	S-G/C	11,400	365	$ 1,328	—	$ 1,328
Grad. Sch. and Univ. Center	New York, NY 10036	1961	City	G/C	3,384	700	$ 1,916	—	$ 1,916
Herbert H. Lehman College	Bronx, NY 10468	1931	City	S-G/C	9,850	660	$ 1,250	—	$ 1,250
Hostos Community College	Bronx, NY 10472	1970	City	J/C	4,094	327	$ 1,250	—	$ 1,250
Hunter College	New York, NY 10021	1870	City	S-G/C	17,944	1,501	$ 1,275	—	$ 1,275
John Jay Col. of Crim. Justice	New York, NY 10019	1964	City	S-G/C	6,500	447	$ 1,315	—	$ 1,315
Kingsborough Comm. College	Brooklyn, NY 11235	1964	City	J/C	10,106	545	$ 1,295	—	$ 1,295
LaGuardia Comm. College	L.I.C., NY 11101	1971	City	J/C	7,163	394	$ 1,306	—	$ 1,306
Medgar Evers College	Brooklyn, NY 11225	1969	City	J-S/C	2,458	157	$ 1,266	$5,384	$ 6,650
New York City Tech Col.	Brooklyn, NY 11201	1946	City	T/C	11,608	1,111	$ 1,250	—	$ 1,250
Queens College	Flushing, NY 11367	1937	City	S-G/C	16,369	1,420	$ 1,418	—	$ 1,418
Queensborough Comm. Col.	Bayside, NY 11364	1958	City	J/C	13,620	653	$ 1,245	—	$ 1,245
York College	Jamaica, NY 11451	1966	City	S/C	4,261	282	$ 1,275	—	$ 1,275
Clarkson University	Potsdam, NY 13676	1896	Independ	S-G/C	4,183	252	$ 8,500	$3,739	$12,239
Colgate Roch./Bexley/ Crozer	Rochester, NY 14620	1817	Independ	P/C	281	20	$ 3,700	$2,125	$ 5,825
Colgate University	Hamilton, NY 13346	1819	Independ	S-G/C	2,615	253	$ 9,790	$3,490	$13,280
College for Human Services	New York, NY 10014	1964	Independ	S-G/C	550	25	$ 5,400	—	$ 5,400
College of Insurance	New York, NY 10038	1962	Independ	S-G/C	1,494	121	$ 4,500	$4,130	$ 8,830
College of Mt. Saint Vincent	Riverdale, NY 10471	1847	Independ	S/C	1,079	74	$ 5,650	$3,450	$ 9,100
College of New Rochelle	New Rochelle, NY 10801	1904	Independ	S-G/C					
Graduate School	New Rochelle, NY 10801	1969	Independ	G/C	942	71	$ 4,320	—	$ 4,320
School of Arts & Sciences	New Rochelle, NY 10801	1904	Independ	S/W	675	106	$ 5,610	$3,400	$ 9,010
School of New Resources	New Rochelle, NY 10801	1972	Independ	S/C	2,917	431	$ 3,510	—	$ 3,510
School of Nursing	New Rochelle, NY 10801	1976	Independ	S-G/C	292	18	$ 5,760	$3,400	$ 9,160
College of Saint Rose	Albany, NY 12203	1920	Independ	S-G/C	2,840	194	$ 5,140	$3,000	$ 8,140
Colum. Mem. Hosp. Sch. of Nur.	Hudson, NY 12534	1900	Independ	J/C	75	7	$ 2,600	—	$ 2,600
Columbia University	New York, NY 10027	1754	Independ	S-G/C					
Columbia College	New York, NY 10027	1754	Independ	S/C	2,918	530	$ 8,942	$3,808	$12,751
Sch. of Eng. & Ap. Sci.	New York, NY 10027	1754	Independ	S-G/C	2,200	150	$ 9,450	$3,900	$13,350
Sch. of General Studies	New York, NY 10027	1947	Independ	S/C	2,950	420	$ 9,330	$3,600	$12,930
Teachers College	New York, NY 10027	1889	Independ	G/C	4,126	265	$ 7,312	—	$ 7,312
Concordia College	Bronxville, NY 10708	1881	Lutheran	J-S/C	560	45	$ 4,785	$2,945	$ 7,730
Cooper Union	New York, NY 10003	1859	Independ	S/C	1,065	179	$ 300	—	$ 300
Cornell University									
Endowed Division	Ithaca, NY 14853	1865	Independ	S-G/C	10,139	1,059	$10,500	$3,600	$14,100
Statutory Division	Ithaca, NY 14853	1865	State	S-G/C	6,784	775	$ 4,360	$3,600	$ 7,960
Medical College	New York, NY 10021	1865	Independ	G/C	532	526	$13,660	—	$13,660
Culinary Inst. of America	Hyde Park, NY 12538	1946	Independ	J/C	1,869	89	$ 5,850	$1,662	$ 7,512
Daemen College	Amherst, NY 14226	1947	Independ	S/C	1,441	125	$ 5,120	$2,600	$ 7,720
Dominican College of Blauvelt	Orangeburg, NY 10962	1952	Independ	S/C	1,643	129	$ 3,500	$3,000	$ 6,500
Dowling College	Oakdale, NY 11769	1959	Independ	S-G/C	2,550	181	$ 4,645	$2,791	$ 7,436
D'Youville College	Buffalo, NY 14201	1908	Independ	S-G/C	1,319	87	$ 4,670	$2,470	$ 7,230
Elizabeth Seton College	Yonkers, NY 10701	1960	Independ	J/C	1,343	163	$ 4,150	$3,000	$ 7,150
Elmira College	Elmira, NY 14901	1855	Independ	S/C	2,090	159	$ 6,440	$2,500	$ 8,940
Five Towns College	Seaford, NY 11783	1972	Independ	J/C	358	31	$ 3,750	—	$ 3,750
Fordham University	Bronx, NY 10458	1841	Independ	S-G/C	13,000	860	$ 6,450	$3,500	$ 9,950
Friends World College	Huntington, NY 11743	1965	Independ	S/C	152	20	$ 5,000	$3,650	$ 8,650
General Theological Seminary	New York, NY 10011	1817	Episcopal	P/C	150	19	$ 5,000	$7,000	$12,000
Grumman Data Systems Institute	Woodbury, NY 11797	1970	Independ	T/C	900	41	$ 3,755	—	$ 3,755
Grumman Data Systems Institute	Bohemia, NY 11716	1970	Independ	T/C	900	41	$ 3,755	—	$ 3,755
Hamilton College	Clinton, NY 13323	1812	Independ	S/C	1,626	155	$ 9,800	$3,200	$13,000
Hartwick College	Oneonta, NY 13820	1928	Independ	S/C	1,444	105	$ 8,050	$2,925	$10,975
Helene Fuld Sch. of Nursing	New York, NY 10035	1975	Independ	P/C	153	18	$ 4,230	—	$ 4,230
Hilbert College	Hamburg, NY 14075	1957	Independ	J/C	709	58	$ 3,340	$2,400	$ 5,740
Hobart College	Geneva, NY 14456	1822	Church	S/C	1,062	126	$ 9,690	$3,600	$13,290
Hofstra University	Hempstead, NY 11550	1935	Independ	S-G/C	11,414	732	$ 5,830	$2,870	$ 8,700
Houghton College	Houghton, NY 14744	1883	Wesleyan	S/C	1,325	85	$ 5,350	$2,200	$ 7,660
Buffalo Suburban Campus	West Seneca, NY 14224	1969	Wesleyan	S/C	136	18	$ 4,510	$1,870	$ 6,380
Institute of Design and Con.	Brooklyn, NY 11201	1947	Independ	T/C	250	25	$ 2,130	—	$ 2,130
Iona College	New Rochelle, NY 10801	1940	Independ	S-G/C	6,140	369	$ 5,150	$3,350	$ 8,500
Ithaca College	Ithaca, NY 14850	1892	Independ	S-G/C	5,493	426	$ 7,046	$3,140	$10,186

NAME	ADDRESS	FOUN-DED	AFFILI-ATION	LEVEL/TYPE	ENROLL-MENT	TEACH-ERS	TUITION & FEES	BOARD & ROOM	TOTAL COST
NEW YORK (continued)									
Jamestown Business College	Jamestown, NY 14701	1886	Independ	J/C	307	11	$ 2,760	$1,800	$ 4,560
Jewish Theol. Sem. of America	New York, NY 10027....	1886	Jewish	S-G/C	382	104	$ 3,740	$2,200	$ 5,940
Juilliard School	New York, NY 10023....	1905	Independ	S-G/C	874	200	$ 6,100	—	$ 6,100
Katherine Gibbs School	New York, NY 10166	1911	Independ	T/C	5,000	200	$ 5,750	—	$ 5,750
Keuka College	Keuka Park, NY 14478 . .	1890	Independ	S/C	420	55	$ 5,970	$2,370	$ 8,340
King's College	Briarcliff Man., NY 10510	1938	Independ	S/C	716	70	$ 7,750	—	$ 7,750
Laboratory Inst./Merchandising	New York, NY 10022....	1939	Independ	S/C	259	34	$ 5,435	—	$ 9,935
LeMoyne College	Syracuse, NY 13214	1946	Independ	S/C	2,144	182	$ 4,380	$2,200	$ 6,580
Long Island University									
Brooklyn Center	Brooklyn, NY 11201	1926	Independ	S-G/C	5,795	400	$ 5,900	$2,730	$ 8,630
C. W. Post Center	Greenvale, NY 11548	1954	Independ	S-G/C	12,400	705	$ 6,300	$3,300	$ 9,600
Southampton College	Southampton, NY 11968	1963	Independ	S-G/C	1,288	95	$ 6,470	$3,740	$10,210
L.I. Col. Hosp. Sch. of Nursing	Brooklyn, NY 11201	1883	Independ	J/C	143	14	$ 2,600	—	$ 2,600
Manhattan College	Riverdale, NY 10471....	1853	Independ	S-G/C	4,737	345	$ 5,030	$3,500	$ 8,530
Manhattan School of Music ..	New York, NY 10027....	1917	Independ	S-G/C	804	195	$ 6,100	—	$ 6,100
Manhattanville College	Purchase, NY 10577	1841	Independ	S-G/C	1,275	142	$ 7,700	$3,800	$11,500
Mannes College of Music	New York, NY 10021....	1916	Independ	S-G/C	160	50	$ 5,500	—	$ 9,500
Maria College	Albany, NY 12208	1958	Independ	J/C	957	78	$ 2,680	—	$ 2,680
Maria Regina College	Syracuse, NY 13208	1961	Catholic	J/W	598	40	$ 2,970	$2,000	$ 4,970
Marist College	Poughkeepsie, NY 12601	1946	Independ	S-G/C	3,744	325	$ 5,350	$3,300	$ 8,650
Maryknoll Sch. of Theology ..	Maryknoll, NY 10545 ...	1912	Catholic	G/C	149	23	$ 3,750	$5,248	$ 8,998
Marymount College	Tarrytown, NY 10591 ...	1907	Independ	S/W	1,202	125	$ 6,280	$3,860	$10,140
Marymount Manhattan College	New York, NY 10021....	1936	Independ	S/W	1,894	187	$ 4,890	—	$ 4,890
Mater Dei College	Ogdensburg, NY 13669 .	1960	Catholic	J/C	550	70	$ 2,666	$2,000	$ 4,666
Medaille College	Buffalo, NY 14214	1875	Independ	S/C	787	62	$ 4,140	—	$ 4,140
Mercy College	Dobbs Ferry, NY 10522 .	1950	Independ	S-G/C	8,767	793	$ 3,360	—	$ 3,360
Yorktown Campus	Yorktown Hghts., NY 10598	1978	Independ	S/C	967	—	$ 3,360	—	$ 3,360
Molloy College	Rockville Centre, NY 11570	1955	Catholic	S/C	1,654	183	$ 4,120	$2,000	$ 6,120
Monroe Business Institute ..	Bronx, NY 10468	1933	Independ	J/C	2,251	107	$ 2,700	—	$ 2,700
Mount Saint Alphonsus Sem.	Esopus, NY 12429	1907	Catholic	P/M	30	21	$ 2,400	—	$ 2,400
Mount Saint Mary College ...	Newburgh, NY 12550 ...	1959	Independ	S/C	1,131	92	$ 4,255	$2,332	$ 6,587
Nazareth Col. of Rochester ..	Rochester, NY 14610 ...	1924	Independ	S-G/C	2,480	98	$ 5,300	$3,050	$ 8,350
New School for Social Res. ..	New York, NY 10011.....	1919	Independ	S-G/C	13,200	1,300	$ 6,870	$4,175	$11,045
New York Chiropractic Col. ..	Glen Head, NY 11545 ...	1919	Independ	P/C	650	102	$ 9,125	—	$ 9,125
New York Col. of Pod. Med. .	New York, NY 10035....	1911	Independ	P/C	533	95	$10,911	—	$10,911
New York Inst. of Technology	Old Westbury, NY 11568	1955	Independ	S-G/C	14,338	1,064	$ 4,185	$3,200	$ 7,385
New York Law School	New York, NY 10013.....	1891	Independ	P/C	1,200	130	$ 7,300	—	$ 7,300
New York Medical College ..									
Medical School..........	Valhalla, NY 10595	1860	Independ	P/C	756	2,500	$17,700	$6,000	$23,700
Graduate School	Valhalla, NY 10595	1860	Independ	G/C	434	210	$ 4,500	—	$ 4,500
New York Sch. of Int. Design .	New York, NY 10022....	1916	Independ	S/C	767	72	$ 5,090	—	$ 5,090
New York Theol. Seminary ..	New York, NY 10011.....	1900	Independ	P/C	400	35	$ 2,000	—	$ 2,000
New York University	New York, NY 10003....	1831	Independ	S-G/C	46,390	4,700	$ 8,714	$4,580	$13,294
Niagara University..........	Niagara Univ., NY 14109	1856	Independ	S-G/C	3,596	267	$ 4,790	$2,800	$ 7,590
Nyack College	Nyack, NY 10960	1882	Christian	S-G/C	848	70	$ 4,822	$2,440	$ 7,262
Pace University									
College of White Plains....	White Plains, NY 10603 .	1923	Independ	S-G/C	3,259	159	$ 5,020	$3,220	$ 8,240
New York City Campus	New York, NY 10038....	1906	Independ	S-G/C	13,701	588	$ 5,020	$3,220	$ 8,240
Plsntville/Briarcliff Cam. ..	Pleasantville, NY 10570 .	1963	Independ	S-G/C	5,939	418	$ 5,020	$3,220	$ 8,240
Parsons School of Design ...	New York, NY 10011.....	1896	Independ	S-G/C	1,700	300	$ 7,530	—	$ 7,530
Paul Smith's Col. of Arts & Sci.	Paul Smith, NY 12970 ...	1946	Independ	J/C	891	77	$ 5,110	$2,815	$ 7,925
Polytechnic Institute of N.Y.	Brooklyn, NY 11201	1854	Independ	S-G/C	3,181	231	$ 8,470	$2,850	$11,550
Graduate Center	White Plains, NY 10605 .	1845	Independ	G/C	470	231	$ 8,470	$2,850	$11,550
Long Island Center	Farmingdale, NY 11735 .	1854	Independ	S-G/C	1,397	231	$ 8,470	$2,850	$11,550
Pratt Institute..............	Brooklyn, NY 11205	1887	Independ	S-G/C	3,603	437	$ 7,364	$3,465	$10,829
Rensselaer Polytechnic Inst. .	Troy, NY 12181	1824	Independ	S-G/C	6,595	390	$10,290	$3,500	$13,790
Roberts Wesleyan College ...	Rochester, NY 14624 ...	1866	Methodist	S/C	680	57	$ 5,354	$2,440	$ 7,794
Rochester Business Institute	Rochester, NY 14604 ...	1863	Independ	J/C	340	16	$ 3,300	—	$ 3,300
Rochester Institute of Tech. .	Rochester, NY 14623 ...	1829	Independ	S-G/C	15,231	1,238	$ 6,837	$3,553	$10,390
Rockefeller University	New York, NY 10021....	1901	Independ	G/C	104	—	$ 528	$ 528	$ 528
Russell Sage College	Troy, NY 12180	1916	Independ	S-G/W	1,424	182	$ 6,800	$2,872	$ 9,672
Evening Division	Albany, NY 12208	1949	Independ	S-G/C	2,600	150	—	—	—
Junior Col. of Albany	Albany, NY 12208	1957	Independ	J/C	1,222	93	$ 4,400	—	$ 4,400
St. Anthony-on-Hudson Seminary	Rensselaer, NY 12144 ..	1912	Catholic	P/M	38	20	$ 2,800	$2,200	$ 5,000
St. Bonaventure University ...	St. Bonaventure, NY 14778	1858	Catholic	S-G/C	2,685	194	$ 4,990	$2,765	$ 7,755
St. Francis College	Brooklyn, NY 11201	1884	Catholic	S/C	2,422	133	$ 3,900	—	$ 3,900
St. John Fisher College	Rochester, NY 14618 ...	1948	Independ	S/C	2,113	193	$ 5,591	$3,035	$ 8,626
St. John's University	Jamaica, NY 11439	1870	Catholic	S-G/C	19,123	905	$ 4,250	—	$ 4,250
St. Joseph's College	Brooklyn, NY 11205	1916	Independ	S/C	928	241	$ 3,725	—	$ 3,725
Suffolk Branch Campus ...	Patchogue, NY 11772 ...	1916	Independ	S/C	1,440	158	$ 3,725	—	$ 3,725
St. Joseph's Seminary	Yonkers, NY 10704	1896	Catholic	P/M	99	27	—	—	—
St. Lawrence University	Canton, NY 13617	1856	Independ	S/C	2,217	196	$ 9,225	$3,125	$13,450
St. Thomas Aquinas College ..	Sparkill, NY 10976	1952	Independ	S/C	2,000	100	$ 3,900	$1,650	$ 5,500
St. Vladimir's Orth. Theo. Sem.	Tuckahoe, NY 10701.....	1938	E Orth	G/C	80	19	$ 1,700	$1,900	$ 3,600
Sarah Lawrence College	Bronxville, NY 10708	1928	Independ	S/W	965	136	$10,879	$4,506	$15,385
School of Visual Arts	New York, NY 10010.....	1947	Independ	S-G/C	2,600	650	$ 6,200	$2,600	$10,920
Sem. of the Im. Conception ..	Huntington, NY 11743 ...	1930	Catholic	P/C	199	30	—	—	—
Siena College	Loudonville, NY 12211...	1937	Independ	S/C	3,473	201	$ 5,565	$3,270	$ 8,835
Skidmore College	Saratoga Spgs., NY 12866	1911	Independ	S/C	2,254	209	$ 9,720	$3,780	$13,500
State University of N.Y.									
Adirondack Comm. College	Glen Falls, NY 12801 ...	1960	State	J/C	2,878	146	$ 976	—	$ 976
Agricultural & Tech. College	Alfred, NY 14802........	1908	State	T/C	3,837	218	$ 1,464	$2,830	$ 4,294
Agricultural & Tech. College	Canton, NY 13617	1906	State	T/C	2,326	119	$ 1,555	$2,840	$ 4,395
Agricultural & Tech. College	Cobleskill, NY 12043....	1916	State	T/C	2,927	139	$ 1,350	$2,770	$ 4,120

NAME	ADDRESS	FOUN-DED	AFFILI-ATION	LEVEL/TYPE	ENROLL-MENT	TEACH-ERS	TUITION & FEES	BOARD & ROOM	TOTAL COST
NEW YORK (continued)									
Agricultural & Tech. College	Delhi, NY 13753	1913	State	T/C	2,389	137	$ 1,500	$2,800	$ 4,300
Agricultural & Tech. College	Farmingdale, NY 11735 . . .	1912	State	T/C	12,987	541	$ 1,496	$2,890	$ 4,386
Agricultural & Tech. College	Morrisville, NY 13408 . . .	1908	State	T/C	3,054	165	$ 1,515	$2,930	$ 4,445
Broome Community College	Birmingham, NY 13902 . .	1946	State	J/C	6,334	484	$ 1,400	—	$ 1,400
Cayuga County Comm. Col.	Auburn, NY 13021	1953	State	J/C	3,218	162	$ 1,056	—	$ 1,056
Clinton Comm. College	Plattsburgh, NY 12901 . . .	1966	State	J/C	1,600	80	$ 1,100	—	$ 1,100
Columbia-Greene Comm. C	Hudson, NY 12534	1969	State	J/C	3,000	55	$ 1,181	—	$ 1,181
Comm. Col. of Finger Lakes	Canandaigua, NY 14424 . .	1965	State	J/C	2,952	235	$ 1,334	—	$ 1,334
Corning Community College	Corning, NY 14830	1957	State	J/C	3,507	137	$ 1,350	—	$ 1,350
Downstate Medical Center .	Brooklyn, NY 11203	1860	State	P/C	1,424	793	$ 4,300	$1,600	$ 5,900
Dutchess Community Col. .	Poughkeepsie, NY 12601	1957	State	J/C	7,084	440	$ 1,150	—	$ 1,150
Empire State College	Saratoga Spgs., NY 12866	1971	State	S-G/C	5,661	269	$ 2,080	—	$ 2,080
Erie Community College . . .	Buffalo, NY 14623	1948	State	J/C	9,250	400	$ 1,000	—	$ 1,000
South Campus	Orchard Park, NY 14127	1946	State	J/C	11,312	769	$ 965	—	$ 965
Fashion Institute of Tech. .	New York, NY 10001	1944	State	S-G/C	10,732	669	$ 1,350	$3,200	$ 4,550
Fulton-Montgomery Comm. Col.	Johnstown, NY 12095 . . .	1963	State	J/C	1,824	65	$ 1,025	$1,300	$ 2,325
Genesee Comm. College . .	Batavia, NY 14020	1966	State	J/C	2,631	178	$ 1,080	—	$ 1,080
Herkimer Co. Comm. Col. .	Herkimer, NY 13350	1966	State	J/C	2,011	92	$ 940	—	$ 940
Hudson Valley Comm. Col.	Troy, NY 12180	1953	State	J/C	8,174	282	$ 1,275	—	$ 1,275
Jamestown Comm. College	Jamestown, NY 14701 . .	1950	State	J/C	4,200	125	$ 1,100	—	$ 1,100
Jefferson Comm. College . .	Watertown, NY 13601 . . .	1961	State	J/C	1,750	100	$ 1,200	—	$ 1,200
Maritime College	Bronx, NY 10465	1874	State	S-G/C	904	76	$ 2,240	$3,014	$ 5,254
Mohawk Valley Comm. Col.	Utica, NY 13501	1946	State	J/C	6,359	312	$ 1,300	$2,530	$ 3,830
Monroe Community College	Rochester, NY 14623 . . .	1961	State	J/C	11,479	605	$ 1,220	—	$ 1,220
Nassau Community College	Garden City, NY 11530 . .	1959	State	J/C	21,094	1,307	$ 1,220	—	$ 1,220
N.Y. St. Col. of Agr. & Life Sci.	Ithaca, NY 14850	1904	State	S-G/C	4,000	400	$ 3,740	—	$ 3,740
N.Y. St. Col. of Ceramics . .	Alfred, NY 14802	1900	State	S-G/C	780	48	$ 2,650	$2,880	$ 5,530
N.Y. State College of Human Eco. at Cornell Univ.	Ithaca, NY 14853	1925	State	G/C	1,336	142	$ 4,360	$3,600	$ 7,960
N.Y. State Col. of Optometry	New York, NY 10010	1971	State	P/C	260	100	$ 5,500	—	$ 5,500
N.Y. St. Col. of Technology	Utica, NY 13502	1966	State	S-G/C	2,500	156	$ 1,750	—	$ 1,750
N.Y. St. Col. of Vet. Med. . .	Ithaca, NY 14853	1894	State	P/C	405	116	$ 6,980	$4,150	$11,130
Niagara County Comm. Col.	Sanborn, NY 14132 . . .	1962	State	J/C	4,657	170	$ 1,100	—	$ 1,100
North Country Comm. Col.	Saranac Lake, NY 12983	1968	State	J/C	1,687	49	$ 1,100	—	$ 1,100
Onondaga Comm. College .	Syracuse, NY 13215 . . .	1962	State	J/C	7,642	520	$ 1,200	—	$ 1,200
Orange County Comm. Col.	Middletown, NY 10940 . .	1950	State	J/C	5,245	140	$ 1,252	—	$ 1,252
Rockland Comm. College . .	Suffern, NY 10901	1959	State	J/C	8,949	419	$ 1,160	—	$ 1,160
Schenectady Co. Comm. Col.	Schenectady, NY 12305	1967	State	J/C	3,216	168	$ 1,196	—	$ 1,196
State U. College	Brockport, NY 14420 . . .	1867	State	S-G/C	7,100	380	$ 1,475	$2,800	$ 4,275
State U. College	Buffalo, NY 14222	1871	State	S-G/C	11,637	544	$ 1,453	$2,850	$ 4,303
State U. College	Cortland, NY 13045	1868	State	S-G/C	6,430	371	$ 1,470	$2,394	$ 3,864
State U. College	Fredonia, NY 14063	1826	State	S-G/C	4,985	305	$ 1,375	$2,750	$ 4,125
State U. College	Geneseo, NY 14454	1867	State	S-G/C	5,282	284	$ 1,475	$2,498	$ 3,973
State U. College	New Paltz, NY 12561 . . .	1885	State	S-G/C	7,344	324	$ 1,473	$2,820	$ 4,293
State U. College	Old Westbury, NY 11568	1968	State	S/C	1,174	139	$ 1,425	$4,297	$ 5,722
State U. College	Oneonta, NY 13820	1889	State	S-G/C	5,884	375	$ 1,460	$2,740	$ 4,200
State U. College	Oswego, NY 13126	1861	State	S-G/C	7,751	403	$ 1,350	$2,660	$ 5,425
State U. College	Plattsburgh, NY 12901 . .	1889	State	S-G/C	6,044	370	$ 1,468	$2,864	$ 4,332
State U. College	Potsdam, NY 13676	1816	State	S-G/C	4,416	233	$ 1,465	$2,650	$ 4,115
State U. College	Purchase, NY 10577 . . .	1967	State	S-G/C	3,868	179	$ 1,475	$2,535	$ 4,010
State U. Col. of Env. Sc. & For.	Syracuse, NY 13210 . . .	1911	State	S-G/C	1,498	100	$ 1,400	$1,600	$ 3,000
State University of N.Y. . . .	Albany, NY 12222	1844	State	S-G/C	15,938	916	$ 1,467	$2,583	$ 4,050
State University of N.Y. . . .	Binghamton, NY 13901 . .	1946	State	S-G/C	11,964	686	$ 1,495	$2,800	$ 4,295
State University of N.Y. . . .	Buffalo, NY 14260	1846	State	S-G/C	26,160	1,854	$ 1,590	$2,980	$ 4,570
State University of N.Y. . . .	Stony Brook, NY 11794 .	1957	State	S-G/C	16,248	1,345	$ 1,475	$2,938	$ 4,413
Suffolk County Comm. Col.	Selden, NY 11784	1960	State	J/C	20,132	361	$ 1,110	—	$ 1,110
Sullivan County Comm. Col.	Loch Sheldrake, NY 12759	1963	State	J/C	1,656	116	$ 1,322	—	$ 1,322
Tompkins Cort. Comm. Col.	Dryden, NY 13053	1968	State	J/C	2,803	62	$ 1,244	—	$ 1,244
Ulster County Comm. Col. .	Stone Ridge, NY 12484 .	1963	State	J/C	3,197	180	$ 1,300	—	$ 1,300
Upstate Medical Center . .	Syracuse, NY 13210 . . .	1834	State	P/C	836	158	$ 1,350	$2,760	$ 4,110
Westchester Comm. College	Valhalla, NY 10595	1946	State	J/C	7,736	176	$ 1,324	—	$ 1,324
Stenotype Institute	New York, NY 10019	1937	Independ	J/C	602	17	$ 5,000	—	$ 5,000
Stenotype Institute	Hicksville, NY 11802	1969	Independ	J/C	106	9	$ 3,300	—	$ 3,300
Syracuse University	Syracuse, NY 13210	1870	Independ	S-G/C	21,044	2,058	$ 7,779	$3,730	$11,509
Utica College	Utica, NY 13502	1946	Independ	S/C	2,352	192	$ 6,350	$2,750	$ 9,100
Technical Career Institute . .	New York, NY 10001	1909	Independ	J/C	2,300	75	$ 6,600	—	$ 6,600
Tobe-Coburn Sch. of Fashion	New York, NY 10012	1937	Independ	S/C	500	15	$ 6,730	—	$ 6,730
Touro College	New York, NY 10036	1971	Independ	S-G/C	3,300	242	$ 3,600	$4,000	$ 7,600
Trocaire College	Buffalo, NY 14220	1958	Independ	S-G/C	1,219	79	$ 2,850	—	$ 2,850
Union College	Schenectady, NY 12308 .	1795	Independ	S-G/C	3,288	201	$ 9,573	$3,290	$12,863
Union Theological Seminary .	New York, NY 10027	1836	Independ	G/C	471	32	$ 6,250	$3,535	$ 9,785
U.S. Merchant Marine Acad. .	Kings Point, NY 11024 . .	1942	Federal	S/C	990	86	—	—	—
U.S. Military Academy	West Point, NY 10996 . .	1802	Federal	S/C	4,500	650	—	—	—
University of Rochester . . .	Rochester, NY 14627 . . .	1850	Independ	S-G/C	8,415	—	$ 9,400	$3,777	$13,177
Utica School of Commerce .	Utica, NY 13501	1896	Independ	J/C	400	20	$ 2,900	$2,820	$ 5,720
Vassar College	Poughkeepsie, NY 12601	1861	Independ	S-G/C	2,258	210	$ 9,680	$3,900	$13,580
Villa Maria College of Buffalo	Buffalo, NY 14225	1960	Catholic	J/C	671	55	$ 3,260	—	$ 3,260
Wadhams Hall Seminary-College	Ogdensburg, NY 13669 .	1924	Catholic	S/M	65	15	$ 2,695	$2,600	$ 5,295
Wagner College	Staten Island, NY 10301 .	1883	Independ	S-G/C	2,235	163	$ 6,310	$3,720	$10,030
Webb Inst. of Naval Arch . . .	Glen Cove, NY 11542 . . .	1889	Independ	S/C	87	14	—	$2,870	$ 2,870
Wells College	Aurora, NY 13026	1868	Independ	S/W	500	60	$ 8,145	$2,930	$11,075
Westchester Business Inst. .	White Plains, NY 10602 . .	1915	Independ	J/C	800	24	$ 5,050	—	$ 5,050
William Smith College	Geneva, NY 14456	1908	Independ	S/C	758	126	$ 9,690	$3,600	$13,290
Wood School	New York, NY 10016	1879	Independ	J/W	459	19	$ 5,400	—	$ 5,400

NAME	ADDRESS	FOUN-DED	AFFILI-ATION	LEVEL/TYPE	ENROLL-MENT	TEACH-ERS	TUITION & FEES	BOARD & ROOM	TOTAL COST
NEW YORK *(continued)*									
Yeshiva University.........	New York, NY 10033....	1886	Independ	P/C	4,146	892	$ 6,430	$3,320	$ 9,750
Rabbi Elchanan Theol. Sem.	New York, NY 10033....	1897	Jewish	P/M	236	33	$ 3,125	$3,320	$ 6,445
NORTH CAROLINA									
Appalachian State University	Boone, NC 28608	1899	State	S-G/C	9,507	556	$ 800	$1,500	$ 2,300
Ashevll.-Buncombe Tech. Col.	Asheville, NC 28801	1959	State	T/C	2,700	150	$ 220	—	$ 220
Atlantic Christian College ...	Wilson, NC 27893	1902	D of Chr	S/C	1,353	102	$ 3,700	$1,800	$ 5,500
Barber-Scotia College	Concord, NC 28025.....	1867	Presby	S/C	389	44	$ 3,130	$2,287	$ 5,417
Beaufort County Comm. Col.	Washington, NC 27889..	1967	State	J/C	1,112	73	$ 200	—	$ 200
Belmont Abbey College	Belmont, NC 28012	1876	Catholic	S/C	892	57	$ 3,500	$2,000	$ 5,500
Bennett College	Greensboro, NC 27401..	1873	Methodist	S/W	575	42	$ 3,400	$1,500	$ 4,900
Brevard College	Brevard, NC 28712	1853	Methodist	J/C	692	66	$ 3,360	$2,330	$ 5,690
Caldwell Community College.	Hudson, NC 28645	1964	State	J/C	1,645	80	$ 224	—	$ 224
Campbell University	Buies Creek, NC 27506	1887	Baptist	S-G/C	3,627	166	$ 4,421	$1,685	$ 6,106
Cape Fear Technical Inst....	Wilmington, NC 28401 ..	1959	State	T/C	1,813	87	$ 204	—	$ 204
Carteret Technical College ..	Morehead City, NC 28557	1963	State	T/C	1,057	42	$ 204	—	$ 204
Catawba College	Salisbury, NC 28144 ...	1851	UC Chr	S/C	910	68	$ 4,700	$2,280	$ 6,980
Catawba Valley Tech. College	Hickory, NC 28601	1960	State	T/C	2,329	80	$ 234	—	$ 234
Cecils Junior College	Asheville, NC 28806	1905	Independ	J/C	350	15	$ 2,112	—	$ 2,112
Central Carolina Tech. College	Sanford, NC 27330	1962	State	T/C	1,950	115	$ 165	—	$ 165
Central Piedmont Comm. Col.	Charlotte, NC 28235....	1963	State	J/C	25,887	798	$ 156	—	$ 156
Chowan College	Murfreesboro, NC 27855	1848	Baptist	J/C	911	68	$ 3,220	$2,170	$ 5,390
Coastal Carolina Comm. Col..	Jacksonville, NC 28540 ..	1964	State	J/C	3,073	123	$ 168	—	$ 168
College of the Albemarle ...	Elizabeth City, NC 27909	1960	State	J/C	1,487	46	$ 181	—	$ 181
Craven Community College ..	New Bern, NC 28560 ...	1965	State	J/C	1,961	81	$ 240	—	$ 240
Davidson College	Davidson, NC 28036	1837	Presby	S/C	1,373	117	$ 7,355	$2,640	$ 9,995
Davidson County Comm. Col.	Lexington, NC 27293 ...	1958	State	J/C	2,134	80	$ 160	—	$ 160
Duke University	Durham, NC 27706	1838	Methodist	S-G/C	10,479	1,422	$ 8,460	$3,799	$12,259
Durham Technical Institute ..	Durham, NC 27703	1961	State	T/C	3,772	195	$ 224	—	$ 224
East Carolina University	Greenville, NC 27834 ...	1907	State	S-G/C	13,826	957	$ 746	$2,010	$ 2,756
Cherry Point Center	Cherry Point, NC 28533.	1965	State	S-G/C	550	35	$ 1,525	—	$ 1,525
Elizabeth City State University	Elizabeth City, NC 27909	1891	State	S/C	1,557	110	$ 864	$1,900	$ 2,764
Elon College	Elon College, NC 27244 .	1889	UC Chr	S/C	2,800	165	$ 3,500	$2,270	$ 5,770
Fayetteville State University .	Fayetteville, NC 28301 ..	1867	State	S-G/C	2,679	141	$ 786	$2,506	$ 3,292
Fayetteville Technical Inst. ..	Fayetteville, NC 28303 ..	1961	State	J/C	5,473	182	$ 159	—	$ 159
Forsyth Technical Institute ..	Winston Salem, NC 27103	1960	State	T/C	3,066	104	$ 228	—	$ 228
Gardner-Webb College	Boiling Springs, NC 28017	1905	Baptist	S/C	1,855	85	$ 4,100	$2,315	$ 6,415
Gaston College	Dallas, NC 28034......	1963	State	J/C	3,013	99	$ 161	—	$ 161
Greensboro College	Greensboro, NC 27401..	1838	Methodist	S/C	524	53	$ 4,400	$2,300	$ 6,700
Guilford College	Greensboro, NC 27410..	1837	Quaker	S/C	1,461	89	$ 5,480	$2,660	$ 8,140
Guilford Technical Institute ..	Jamestown, NC 27282 ..	1958	Public	J/C	5,146	131	$ 248	—	$ 248
Haywood Technical College ..	Clyde, NC 28721.......	1965	State	T/C	1,000	75	$ 156	—	$ 156
High Point College.........	High Point, NC 27262 ...	1924	Methodist	S/C	1,332	70	$ 4,215	$1,800	$ 6,015
Isothermal Community College	Spindale, NC 28160	1964	State	J/C	2,490	55	$ 181	—	$ 181
Johnson C. Smith University	Charlotte, NC 28216	1867	Independ	S/C	1,200	90	$ 3,228	$1,744	$ 4,972
King's College	Charlotte, NC 28204	1901	Private	T/C	402	15	$ 5,000	$2,500	$ 7,500
Lees-McRae College	Banner Elk, NC 28604 ..	1900	Presby	J/C	670	35	$ 3,389	$2,022	$ 5,311
Lenoir Community College ..	Kinston, NC 28501	1958	State	J/C	1,978	71	$ 240	—	$ 240
Lenoir-Rhyne College	Hickory, NC 28603	1891	Church	S/C	1,475	128	$ 4,800	$1,900	$ 6,700
Livingstone College	Salisbury, NC 28144	1879	AME Zion	S/C	750	52	$ 2,900	$1,900	$ 4,800
Louisburg College	Louisburg, NC 27549 ...	1787	Methodist	J/C	729	40	$ 3,450	$1,900	$ 5,350
Mars Hill College	Mars Hill, NC 28754	1856	Baptist	S/C	1,357	113	$ 4,100	$1,800	$ 5,900
Martin Community College ..	Williamston, NC 27892 ..	1968	State	J/C	778	28	$ 224	—	$ 224
Meredith College	Raleigh, NC 27607......	1891	Baptist	S-G/W	1,761	116	$ 3,925	$1,725	$ 5,650
Methodist College	Fayetteville, NC 28301 ..	1956	Methodist	S/C	800	50	$ 4,200	$2,200	$ 6,400
Mitchell Community College .	Statesville, NC 28677 ...	1852	State	J/C	1,332	48	$ 180	—	$ 180
Montreat-Anderson College..	Montreat, NC 28757.....	1916	Presby	S/C	366	28	$ 3,128	$2,370	$ 5,498
Mount Olive College	Mount Olive, NC 28365 .	1951	Baptist	J/C	678	37	$ 3,350	$2,550	$ 5,900
N.C. A. & T. State University .	Greensboro, NC 27411..	1891	State	S-G/C	5,397	386	$ 888	$1,772	$ 2,660
N.C. Central University	Durham, NC 27707	1910	State	S-G/C	4,552	258	$ 760	$1,913	$ 2,673
N.C. School of the Arts	Winston-Salem, NC 27107	1965	State	S-G/C	511	90	$ 732	$2,252	$ 2,984
N.C. State University	Raleigh, NC 27695......	1887	State	S-G/C	22,632	1,269	$ 796	$2,300	$ 3,096
N.C. Wesleyan College	Rocky Mount, NC 27801	1956	Methodist	S/C	1,142	93	$ 4,130	$2,180	$ 6,310
Peace College	Raleigh, NC 27604......	1857	Presby	J/W	513	35	$ 3,030	$2,610	$ 5,640
Pembroke University	Pembroke, NC 28372 ...	1887	State	S/C	2,192	116	$ 1,450	$ 765	$ 2,215
Pfeiffer College	Misenheimer, NC 28109.	1885	Methodist	S/C	811	75	$ 4,380	$2,160	$ 6,540
Piedmont Bible College	Winston-Salem, NC 27101	1945	Baptist	S/C	322	23	$ 2,460	$1,830	$ 4,290
Pitt Comm. College	Greenville, NC 27834 ...	1962	State	J/C	2,710	175	$ 242	—	$ 242
Queens College	Charlotte, NC 28274	1857	Presby	S-G/W	1,236	146	$ 5,200	$3,055	$ 8,255
Randolph Technical College .	Asheboro, NC 27204....	1962	State	T/C	1,144	75	$ 219	—	$ 219
Richmond Technical Institute	Hamlet, NC 28345......	1964	State	T/C	983	83	$ 228	—	$ 228
Rockingham Community Col.	Wentworth, NC 27375 ...	1966	Public	T/C	1,568	52	$ 180	—	$ 180
Rowan Technical College ...	Salisbury, NC 28144	1963	State	T/C	1,196	52	$ 225	—	$ 225
Rutledge Col. of Charlotte ..	Charlotte, NC 28202	1977	Independ	J/C	400	20	$ 2,016	—	$ 2,016
Sacred Heart College	Belmont, NC 28012	1892	Catholic	S/C	379	45	$ 3,489	$2,225	$ 5,723
St. Andrews Presbyterian Col.	Laurinburg, NC 28352 ..	1896	Presby	S/C	737	51	$ 5,350	$2,645	$ 7,995
St. Augustine's College	Raleigh, NC 27611......	1867	Episcopal	S/C	1,716	75	$ 3,230	$2,000	$ 5,230
St. Mary's College	Raleigh, NC 27603......	1842	Episcopal	J/W	473	49	$ 4,390	$3,450	$ 7,840
Salem College	Winston-Salem, NC 27108	1772	Moravian	S/W	724	71	$ 5,700	$3,800	$ 9,500
Sandhills Community College	Carthage, NC 28327	1964	State	J/C	1,932	104	$ 177	—	$ 177
Shaw University	Raleigh, NC 27611......	1865	Baptist	S/C	1,774	102	$ 1,310	$1,540	$ 4,160
Southeast. Bapt. Theol. Sem.	Wake Forest, NC 27587 .	1951	Baptist	G/C	1,117	35	$ 650	$ 480	$ 1,130
Southeastern Comm. College	Whiteville, NC 28472 ...	1965	State	J/C	1,714	97	$ 229	—	$ 229

NAME	ADDRESS	FOUN-DED	AFFILI-ATION	LEVEL/TYPE	ENROLL-MENT	TEACH-ERS	TUITION & FEES	BOARD & ROOM	TOTAL COST
NORTH CAROLINA *(continued)*									
Southwestern Technical Col.	Sylva, NC 28779	1964	State	T/C	1,215	48	$ 167	—	$ 167
Surry Community College	Dobson, NC 27030	1964	State	J/C	2,715	98	$ 175	—	$ 175
Technical Inst. of Alamance	Haw River, NC 27258	1958	State	T/C	2,169	55	$ 216	—	$ 216
Univ. of N.C. at Asheville	Asheville, NC 28814	1927	State	S/C	2,651	102	$ 712	$1,900	$ 2,612
Univ. of N.C. at Chapel Hill	Chapel Hill, NC 27514	1789	State	S-G/C	21,612	1,886	$ 773	$2,375	$ 3,148
Univ. of N.C. at Charlotte	Charlotte, NC 28223	1946	State	S-G/C	10,459	689	$ 700	$2,096	$ 2,796
Univ. of N.C. at Greensboro	Greensboro, NC 27412	1891	State	S-G/C	10,090	628	$ 842	$2,121	$ 2,963
Univ. of N.C. at Wilmington	Wilmington, NC 28406	1947	State	S-G/C	5,535	329	$ 716	$2,140	$ 2,856
Wake Forest University	Winston-Salem, NC 27109	1834	Baptist	S-G/C	4,961	652	$ 5,550	$2,300	$ 7,850
Wake Technical College	Raleigh, NC 27603	1963	State	T/C	4,332	126	$ 140	—	$ 140
Warren Wilson College	Swannanoa, NC 28778	1894	Presby	S-G/C	467	62	$ 5,150	—	$ 5,500
Wayne Community College	Goldsboro, NC 27530	1957	State	J/C	2,002	98	$ 228	—	$ 228
Western Carolina University	Cullowhee, NC 28723	1889	State	S-G/C	6,131	364	$ 775	$1,570	$ 2,345
Western Piedmont Comm. Col.	Morganton, NC 28655	1964	State	J/C	2,055	70	$ 171	—	$ 171
Wilkes Community College	Wilkesboro, NC 28697	1965	State	J/C	2,935	58	$ 232	—	$ 232
Wilson County Tech. Institute	Wilson, NC 27893	1958	State	T/C	1,369	46	$ 230	—	$ 230
Wingate College	Wingate, NC 28174	1896	Baptist	S-G/C	1,562	73	$ 3,200	$2,090	$ 5,290
Winston-Salem State Univ.	Winston-Salem, NC 27110	1892	State	S/C	2,443	155	$ 705	$1,985	$ 2,690
NORTH DAKOTA									
Bismarck Junior College	Bismarck, ND 58501	1939	State	J/C	2,406	89	$ 960	$1,406	$ 2,420
Dickinson State College	Dickinson, ND 58601	1918	State	S/C	1,249	85	$ 1,032	$1,650	$ 2,682
Jamestown College	Jamestown, ND 58401	1883	Presby	S/C	586	49	$ 5,700	$1,930	$ 7,630
Lake Region Junior College	Devils Lake, ND 58301	1941	State	J/C	621	38	$ 960	$1,520	$ 2,480
Mary College	Bismarck, ND 58501	1959	Catholic	S/C	1,180	73	$ 3,570	$1,830	$ 5,400
Mayville State College	Mayville, ND 58257	1889	State	S/C	728	56	$ 1,023	$1,626	$ 2,649
Minot State College	Minot, ND 58701	1913	State	S-G/C	3,000	150	$ 969	$1,380	$ 2,349
North Dakota State Sch. of Sci.	Wahpeton, ND 58075	1903	State	J/C	2,932	174	$ 831	$1,800	$ 2,631
North Dakota State University	Fargo, ND 58105	1890	State	S-G/C	9,453	450	$ 1,008	$1,845	$ 2,853
Bottineau Branch	Bottineau, ND 58318	1907	State	J/C	502	29	$ 771	$1,690	$ 2,461
Northwest Bible College	Minot, ND 58701	1934	C of God	S/C	151	12	$ 2,775	$1,730	$ 4,505
University of North Dakota	Grand Forks, ND 58202	1883	State	S-G/C	11,063	613	$ 1,080	$1,764	$ 2,844
Williston Center	Williston, ND 58801	1957	State	J/C	666	42	$ 1,094	$1,600	$ 2,694
Valley City State College	Valley City, ND 58072	1890	State	S/C	1,046	64	$ 965	$1,875	$ 2,840
OHIO									
Air Force Inst. of Technology	Wright-Pat. AFB, OH 45433	1919	Federal	G/C	752	127	—	—	—
Antioch University	Yellow Springs, OH 45387	1852	Independ	S-G/C	—	—	—	—	—
Antioch College	Yellow Springs, OH 45387	1852	Independ	S/C	537	46	$ 6,980	$2,900	$ 9,880
Antioch International	Yellow Springs, OH 45387	1852	Independ	S-G/C	206	10	$ 3,775	—	$ 3,775
Art Academy of Cincinnati	Cincinnati, OH 45202	1887	Independ	S/C	225	28	$ 3,950	—	$ 3,950
Ashland College	Ashland, OH 44805	1878	Brethren	S-G/C	3,215	106	$ 6,060	$2,540	$ 8,600
Athenaeum of Ohio	Cincinnati, OH 45230	1829	Catholic	G/C	185	29	$ 2,900	$3,300	$ 6,200
Baldwin-Wallace College	Berea, OH 44017	1845	Methodist	S-G/C	3,702	205	$ 6,474	$2,971	$ 9,445
Bliss College	Columbus, OH 43214	1899	Independ	T/C	525	30	$ 2,400	$ 225	$ 2,625
Bluffton College	Bluffton, OH 45817	1899	Mennonite	S/C	573	48	$ 4,968	$2,094	$ 7,062
Borromeo College of Ohio	Wickliffe, OH 44092	1954	Catholic	S/M	111	28	$ 3,450	$1,725	$ 5,175
Bowling Green State Univ.	Bowling Green, OH 43403	1910	State	S-G/C	16,690	859	$ 1,878	$1,888	$ 3,766
Firelands College	Huron, OH 44839	1969	State	J/C	1,136	70	$ 1,492	—	$ 1,492
Capital University	Columbus, OH 43209	1830	Lutheran	P/C	2,560	208	$ 6,900	$2,800	$ 9,700
Case Western Reserve Univ.	Cleveland, OH 44106	1826	Independ	S-G/C	8,352	1,534	$ 8,650	$3,370	$12,020
Cedarville College	Cedarville, OH 45314	1887	Independ	S/C	1,793	129	$ 3,702	$2,370	$ 6,072
Central Ohio Technical Col.	Newark, OH 43055	1971	State	T/C	1,306	90	$ 1,098	—	$ 1,098
Central State University	Wilberforce, OH 45384	1887	State	S/C	2,501	146	$ 1,413	$2,868	$ 4,281
Cincinnati Bible Seminary	Cincinnati, OH 45204	1924	Church	S-G/C	937	45	$ 2,234	$2,200	$ 4,434
Cincinnati Coll. of Mort. Sci.	Cincinnati, OH 45206	1882	Independ	P/C	111	11	$ 3,720	$3,910	$ 7,630
Cincinnati Technical College	Cincinnati, OH 45223	1966	State	T/C	3,920	224	$ 990	—	$ 990
Circleville Bible College	Circleville, OH 43113	1948	Christian	S/C	186	18	$ 2,650	$1,850	$ 4,500
Clark Technical College	Springfield, OH 45505	1962	State	T/C	2,509	52	$ 1,250	—	$ 1,250
Cleveland Institute of Art	Cleveland, OH 44106	1882	Independ	S/C	840	100	$ 5,500	$3,300	$ 9,000
Cleveland Institute of Music	Cleveland, OH 44106	1920	Independ	S-G/C	210	65	$ 7,820	$3,260	$11,080
Cleveland State University	Cleveland, OH 44115	1964	State	S-G/C	18,033	722	$ 1,943	—	$ 1,943
College of Mount St. Joseph	Mt. St. Joseph, OH 45051	1920	Catholic	S-G/W	2,200	166	$ 4,827	$2,792	$ 7,619
College of Wooster	Wooster, OH 44691	1866	Presby	S/C	1,700	135	—	—	$11,245
Columbus Col. of Art & Design	Columbus, OH 43215	1879	Independ	S/C	964	74	$ 5,100	$3,280	$ 8,380
Columbus Tech. Institute	Columbus, OH 43216	1963	State	T/C	8,600	500	$ 1,152	—	$ 1,152
Cuyahoga Community College	Cleveland, OH 44115	1963	State	J/C	—	—	—	—	—
Eastern Campus	Warrensv. Twp., OH 44122	1971	State	J/C	5,792	235	$ 900	—	$ 900
Metropolitan Campus	Cleveland, OH 44115	1963	State	J/C	7,570	476	$ 900	—	$ 900
Western Campus	Parma, OH 44130	1966	State	J/C	12,058	446	$ 900	—	$ 900
Defiance College	Defiance, OH 43512	1850	UC Chr	S/C	903	71	$ 4,820	$2,200	$ 7,020
Denison University	Granville, OH 43023	1831	Independ	S/C	2,100	159	$ 8,110	$2,710	$10,820
Devry Institute of Technology	Columbus, OH 43209	1952	Independ	S/C	3,604	174	$ 3,658	—	$ 3,658
Dyke College	Cleveland, OH 44115	1848	Independ	S/C	1,310	50	$ 3,400	—	$ 3,400
Findlay College	Findlay, OH 45840	1882	C of God	S/C	1,168	87	$ 5,430	$2,500	$ 7,930
Franklin University	Columbus, OH 43215	1902	Private	S/C	4,881	221	$ 2,730	—	$ 2,730
Hebrew Union College	Cincinnati, OH 45220	1875	Jewish	G/C	145	30	$ 4,900	$2,675	$ 7,575
Heidelberg College	Tiffin, OH 44883	1850	UC Chr	S/C	1,022	75	$ 6,930	$2,500	$ 9,430
Hiram College	Hiram, OH 44234	1850	D Chr	S/C	1,109	75	$ 7,915	$2,510	$10,425
Hocking Technical College	Nelsonville, OH 45764	1968	State	T/C	3,650	198	$ 1,050	$2,325	$ 3,375
Jefferson Technical College	Steubenville, OH 43952	1966	State	T/C	1,449	104	$ 685	—	$ 685
John Carroll University	Univ. Hts., OH 44118	1886	Catholic	S-G/C	3,900	223	$ 5,344	$3,100	$ 8,444
Kent State University	Kent, OH 44242	1910	State	S-G/C	20,066	1,034	$ 2,016	$2,288	$ 4,304
Ashtabula Campus	Ashtabula, OH 44004	1958	State	J/C	848	55	$ 1,652	—	$ 1,652

NAME	ADDRESS	FOUN-DED	AFFILI-ATION	LEVEL/TYPE	ENROLL-MENT	TEACH-ERS	TUITION & FEES	BOARD & ROOM	TOTAL COST
OHIO *(continued)*									
East Liverpool Campus ...	East Liverpool, OH 43920	1965	State	J/C	343	39	$1,652	—	$ 1,652
Geauga Campus	Burton, OH 44021	1964	State	J/C	212	16	$1,652	—	$ 1,652
Salem Campus	Salem, OH 44460	1962	State	J/C	567	33	$1,652	—	$ 1,652
Stark Campus	Canton, OH 44720......	1946	State	J/C	1,622	70	$1,652	—	$ 1,652
Trumbull Campus	Warren, OH 44483	1954	State	J/C	1,077	76	$1,652	—	$ 1,652
Tuscarawas Campus......	New Phila., OH 44663 ..	1962	State	J/C	828	53	$1,652	—	$ 1,652
Kenyon College	Gambier, OH 43022	1824	Episcopal	S/C	1,458	149	$9,333	$2,767	$12,100
Kettering Col. of Med. Arts ..	Kettering, OH 45429	1967	Church	J/C	463	53	$3,629	$1,980	$ 5,609
Lake Erie College...........	Painesville, OH 44077..	1865	Independ	S-G/W	1,001	90	$6,100	$2,995	$ 9,095
Lakeland Community College	Mentor, OH 44060......	1967	State	J/C	9,209	450	$1,035	—	$ 1,035
Lima Technical College	Lima, OH 45804........	1971	State	T/C	1,885	125	$1,035	—	$ 1,035
Lorain County Comm. College	Elyria, OH 44035	1963	State	J/C	6,495	113	$1,012	—	$ 1,012
Lourdes College............	Sylvania, OH 43560.....	1958	Catholic	J-S/C	841	60	$2,630	—	$ 2,630
Malone College	Canton, OH 44709......	1892	Friends	S/C	919	40	$5,067	$2,510	$ 7,570
Marietta College	Marietta, OH 45750	1835	Independ	S-G/C	1,187	100	$7,500	$2,450	$ 9,950
Methodist Theol. Sch. of Ohio	Delaware, OH 43015....	1958	Methodist	P/C	253	25	$3,180	$1,575	$ 4,755
Miami-Jacobs Junior College	Dayton, OH 45401......	1860	Independ	J/C	680	35	$3,000	—	$ 3,000
Miami University	Oxford, OH 45056......	1809	State	S-G/C	15,134	803	$2,220	$2,225	$ 4,445
Hamilton Campus	Hamilton, OH 45011....	1968	State	J/C	1,750	50	$ 930	—	$ 930
Middletown Campus	Middletown, OH 45042..	1965	State	J/C	1,738	61	$1,865	—	$ 1,865
Mount Union College	Alliance, OH 44601......	1846	Methodist	S/C	938	69	$7,660	$2,330	$ 9,990
Mount Vernon Bible College .	Mt. Vernon, OH 43050 ..	1957	4 Square	S/C	81	13	$1,470	$1,785	$ 3,225
Mount Vernon Nazarene Col.	Mt. Vernon, OH 43050 ..	1966	Nazarene	S/C	1,065	72	$3,844	$2,150	$ 5,994
Muskingum Area Tech. Col...	Zanesville, OH 43701 ...	1969	State	T/C	1,441	85	$ 990	—	$ 990
Muskingum College.........	New Concord, OH 43762	1837	Presby	S/C	1,004	66	$7,420	$2,550	$ 9,950
Northwest Technical College .	Archbold, OH 43502....	1968	State	T/C	907	48	$1,080	—	$ 1,080
Notre Dame College of Ohio .	Cleveland, OH 44121....	1922	Catholic	S/W	741	79	$3,850	$2,280	$ 6,130
Oberlin College	Oberlin, OH 44074	1833	Independ	S/C	2,752	224	$9,445	$3,340	$12,785
Ohio Col. of Podiatric Med. ..	Cleveland, OH 44106....	1916	Independ	P/C	551	84	$9,500	—	$ 9,500
Ohio Dominican College....	Columbus, OH 43219....	1911	Catholic	S/C	1,053	81	$4,960	$2,820	$ 7,780
Ohio Northern University	Ada, OH 45810	1871	Methodist	S-G/C	2,445	160	$5,925	$2,400	$ 8,325
Ohio State University	Columbus, OH 43210 ...	1870	State	S-G/C	52,434	6,020	$1,641	$2,709	$ 4,350
Agricul. Tech. Institute ...	Wooster, OH 44691.....	1972	State	T/C	564	55	$1,593	$2,745	$ 4,338
Lima Campus	Lima, OH 45804	1960	State	S/C	939	58	$1,593	—	$ 1,593
Mansfield Campus	Mansfield, OH 44906 ...	1958	State	S/C	1,089	47	$1,593	—	$ 1,593
Marion Campus	Marion, OH 43302	1957	State	J/C	795	62	$1,593	—	$ 1,593
Newark Campus	Newark, OH 43055	1957	State	S/C	935	66	$1,593	—	$ 1,593
Ohio University	Athens, OH 45701......	1804	State	S-G/C	14,600	703	$1,917	$2,685	$ 4,602
Belmont County Campus ..	St. Clairsville, OH 43950	1957	State	J/C	1,075	60	$1,545	—	$ 1,545
Chillicothe Campus	Chillicothe, OH 45601...	1946	State	J/C	1,186	70	$1,545	—	$ 1,545
Southern Campus	Ironton, OH 45638	1956	State	J/C	1,012	80	$1,425	—	$ 1,425
Zanesville Campus	Zanesville, OH 43701 ...	1946	State	J/C	1,076	69	$1,545	—	$ 1,545
Ohio Wesleyan University ...	Delaware, OH 43015....	1842	Methodist	S/C	1,510	129	$7,800	$3,100	$10,900
Otterbein College	Westerville, OH 43081 ..	1847	Methodist	S/C	1,385	109	$6,750	$2,721	$ 9,471
Owens Technical College	Toledo, OH 43699	1965	State	T/C	4,535	250	$ 936	—	$ 936
Penn-Ohio College.........	Youngstown, OH 44507 .	1941	Independ	B/C	225	15	$1,818	—	$ 1,818
Pontifical Col. of Josephinum	Columbus, OH 43085 ...	1888	Catholic	S-G/M	196	51	$2,736	$1,870	$ 4,150
Ray. Walters Gen. & Tech. Col.	Cincinnati, OH 45236...	1967	State	J/C	3,213	140	$1,911	—	$ 1,911
Rio Grande Col. & Comm. Col.	Rio Grande, OH 45674 ..	1876	State	J-T/C	1,607	115	$1,107	$2,445	$ 3,552
St. Mary Seminary	Cleveland, OH 44108 ...	1848	Catholic	P/C	97	21	$3,510	$1,900	$ 5,410
Shawnee State Comm. College	Portsmouth, OH 45662 .	1975	State	J/C	2,314	120	$ 990	—	$ 990
Sinclair Community College .	Dayton, OH 45402......	1887	State	J/C	17,267	802	$ 792	—	$ 792
Southern Ohio College	Cincinnati, OH 45237 ...	1927	Independ	J/C	1,392	72	$4,540	—	$ 4,540
Southern State Comm. College	Hillsboro, OH 45133	1975	State	J/C	1,404	78	$1,080	—	$ 1,080
Tiffin University	Tiffin, OH 44883	1888	Independ	S/C	582	36	$3,350	$1,975	$ 5,325
United Theological Seminary .	Dayton, OH 45406......	1871	Methodist	P/C	307	44	$3,603	$2,530	$ 6,133
University of Akron	Akron, OH 44325.......	1870	State	S-G/C	26,566	1,477	$1,560	$2,406	$ 4,056
Wayne General & Tech. Col.	Orrville, OH 44667	1972	State	J/C	983	91	$1,650	—	$ 1,650
University of Cincinnati	Cincinnati, OH 45221 ...	1819	State	S-G/C	35,249	3,061	$1,911	$3,066	$ 4,977
University of Dayton	Dayton, OH 45469......	1850	Catholic	S-G/C	10,555	682	$4,760	$2,588	$ 7,348
University of Steubenville ..	Steubenville, OH 43952 .	1946	Catholic	S-G/C	946	53	$4,920	$2,750	$ 7,670
University of Toledo	Toledo, OH 43606......	1872	State	S-G/C	21,039	1,112	$1,606	$2,418	$ 4,024
Urbana College	Urbana, OH 43078	1850	Sweden	S/C	573	26	$4,500	$2,700	$ 7,200
Ursuline College	Pepper Pike, OH 44124 .	1871	Catholic	S-G/W	1,563	123	$4,000	$2,390	$ 6,390
Walsh College.............	Canton, OH 44720......	1958	Catholic	S/C	1,225	92	$3,900	$2,350	$ 6,250
Wilberforce University	Wilberforce, OH 45384..	1856	AME	S/C	904	61	$4,000	$2,160	$ 6,160
Wilmington College	Wilmington, OH 45177 ..	1870	Quaker	S/C	833	57	$5,700	$2,500	$ 8,200
Wittenberg University	Springfield, OH 45501 ..	1845	Lutheran	S/C	2,134	152	$8,445	$2,760	$11,205
Wright State University	Dayton, OH 45435......	1967	State	S-G/C	14,625	790	$1,623	$2,622	$ 4,245
Piqua Campus	Piqua, OH 45356	1969	State	S-G/C	26	3	$1,350	—	$ 1,350
Western Ohio Campus ..	Celina, OH 45822	1969	State	J/C	901	54	$1,449	—	$ 1,449
Xavier University	Cincinnati, OH 45207 ...	1831	Catholic	S-G/C	6,785	388	$5,080	$2,780	$ 7,860
Youngstown State University	Youngstown, OH 44555 .	1908	State	S-G/C	15,254	577	$1,335	$2,190	$ 3,525
OKLAHOMA									
Bacone College	Muskogee, OK 74401 ...	1880	Baptist	J/C	434	31	$1,900	$2,050	$ 3,950
Bartlesville Wesleyan College	Bartlesville, OK 74006 ..	1909	Wesleyan	S/C	652	80	$3,650	$2,150	$ 5,800
Bethany Nazarene College..	Bethany, OK 73008	1899	Nazarene	S-G/C	1,287	105	$3,404	$2,318	$ 5,722
Cameron University	Lawton, OK 73505......	1908	State	S/C	5,549	195	$ 590	$1,800	$ 2,390
Carl Albert Junior College ..	Poteau, OK 74953......	1934	State	J/C	2,044	52	$ 450	—	$ 450
Central State University ...	Edmond, OK 73034.....	1890	State	S-G/C	13,102	436	$ 433	$1,245	$ 1,678
Connors State College	Warner, OK 74469......	1908	State	J/C	1,423	64	$ 450	$1,300	$ 1,750
East Central Okl. St. Univ. ..	Ada, OK 74820.........	1909	State	S-G/C	4,144	175	$ 640	$1,788	$ 2,428
Eastern Okla. State College ..	Wilburton, OK 74578 ...	1909	State	J/C	1,907	58	$ 800	$1,700	$ 2,500

NAME	ADDRESS	FOUN-DED	AFFILI-ATION	LEVEL/TYPE	ENROLL-MENT	TEACH-ERS	TUITION & FEES	BOARD & ROOM	TOTAL COST
OKLAHOMA *(continued)*									
El Reno Junior College	El Reno, OK 73036	1938	State	J/C	1,653	84	$ 475	—	$ 475
Hillsdale Free Will Baptist Col.	Moore, OK 73153	1959	Baptist	J-S/C	156	23	$ 1,700	$1,950	$ 3,650
Langston University	Langston, OK 73050	1897	State	S/C	2,001	72	$ 459	$1,840	$ 3,000
Murray State College	Tishomingo, OK 73460	1908	State	J/C	1,463	38	$ 453	$2,130	$ 2,583
Northeastern Okla. A&M Col.	Miami, OK 74354	1919	State	J/C	2,629	98	$ 443	$1,692	$ 2,135
Northeastern State University	Tahlequah, OK 74464	1846	State	S-G/C	7,318	258	$ 591	$1,648	$ 2,239
Northern Oklahoma College	Tonkawa, OK 74653	1901	State	J/C	1,644	58	$ 470	$1,350	$ 1,820
Northwestern Okla. State Univ.	Alva, OK 73717	1897	State	S-G/C	1,817	81	$ 600	$1,480	$ 2,080
Oklahoma Baptist University	Shawnee, OK 74801	1910	Baptist	S/C	1,590	121	$ 2,700	$1,900	$ 4,600
Oklahoma Christian College	Oklahoma City, OK 73111	1950	C of Chr	S/C	1,522	77	$ 2,844	$1,950	$ 4,794
Oklahoma City Comm. College	Oklahoma City, OK 73159	1970	State	J/C	7,709	274	$ 450	—	$ 450
Oklahoma City University	Oklahoma City, OK 73106	1904	Methodist	S-G/C	3,231	222	$ 3,542	$2,570	$ 6,112
Okla. Col. of Osteo. Med. & Surg.	Tulsa, OK 74101	1972	State	P/C	318	32	$ 2,525	—	$ 2,525
Okla. Missionary Baptist Col.	Marlow, OK 73055	1954	Baptist	S-P/C	131	10	$ 350	—	$ 350
Okla. Panhandle State Univ.	Goodwell, OK 73939	1909	State	S/C	1,230	69	$ 644	$1,600	$ 2,264
Oklahoma State University	Stillwater, OK 74078	1890	State	S-G/C	21,931	1,071	$ 820	$2,106	$ 2,926
Okla. St. U. Sch. of Tech. Train.	Okmulgee, OK 74447	1946	State	T/C	3,043	155	$ 624	$2,159	$ 2,783
Okla. State U. Tech. Institute	Oklahoma City, OK 73107	1961	State	J/C	2,925	193	$ 710	—	$ 710
Oral Roberts University	Tulsa, OK 74171	1963	Independ	S-G/C	4,600	405	$ 3,886	$2,424	$ 6,310
Oscar Rose Junior College	Midwest City, OK 73110	1969	State	J/C	10,166	324	$ 385	—	$ 385
Phillips University	Enid, OK 73702	1906	Christian	S/C	1,039	72	$ 3,846	$2,000	$ 5,846
Rogers State College	Claremore, OK 74017	1909	State	J/C	2,669	121	$ 535	$2,000	$ 2,535
St. Gregory's College	Shawnee, OK 74801	1875	Catholic	J/C	320	35	$ 2,400	$2,200	$ 4,600
Sayre Junior College	Sayre, OK 73662	1938	State	J/C	494	15	$ 430	—	$ 430
Seminole Junior College	Seminole, OK 74868	1931	State	J/C	1,575	55	$ 392	$1,700	$ 2,092
Southeastern Okla. State Univ.	Durant, OK 74701	1909	State	S-G/C	4,032	202	$ 591	$1,800	$ 2,391
Southwestern Okla. State Univ.	Weatherford, OK 73096	1901	State	S-G/C	4,965	210	$ 620	$1,250	$ 1,870
Spartan School of Aeronautics	Tulsa, OK 74158	1928	Independ	T/C	1,738	92	$ 5,760	—	$ 5,760
Tulsa Junior College	Tulsa, OK 74135	1968	State	J/C	15,786	550	$ 350	—	$ 350
University of Oklahoma	Norman, OK 73019	1890	State	S-G/C	19,958	886	$ 858	$2,293	$ 3,151
Health Sciences Center	Oklahoma City, OK 73190	1890	State	S-G/C	3,308	714	—	—	$ 7,250
Univ. of Sci. and Arts of Okla.	Chickasha, OK 73018	1908	State	S/C	1,189	60	$ 585	$1,500	$ 2,085
University of Tulsa	Tulsa, OK 74104	1894	Independ	S-G/C	5,500	354	$ 4,770	$2,600	$ 7,370
Western Okla. State College	Altus, OK 73521	1926	State	J/C	2,000	56	$ 450	—	$ 450
OREGON									
Blake College	Eugene, OR 97405	1961	Independ	S/C	14	3	$ 3,000	$1,400	$ 4,400
Blue Mountain Comm. College	Pendleton, OR 97801	1962	State	J/C	1,390	71	$ 540	—	$ 540
Central Oregon Comm. College	Bend, OR 97701	1949	Public	J/C	1,968	61	$ 540	$2,346	$ 2,886
Chemeketa Comm. College	Salem, OR 97309	1969	County	J/C	7,354	250	$ 600	—	$ 600
Clackamas Comm. College	Oregon City, OR 97045	1966	State	J/C	4,204	156	$ 600	—	$ 600
Clatsop Community College	Astoria, OR 97103	1958	State	J/C	2,555	200	$ 576	—	$ 576
Columbia Christian College	Portland, OR 97220	1956	C of Chr	S/C	270	29	$ 3,600	$ 940	$ 4,540
Concordia College	Portland, OR 97211	1905	Lutheran	S/C	440	40	$ 4,260	$2,790	$ 7,050
Eastern Oregon State College	La Grande, OR 97850	1929	State	S-G/C	1,666	120	$ 1,419	$2,384	$ 3,803
George Fox College	Newberg, OR 97132	1891	Quaker	S/C	624	72	$ 5,770	$2,595	$ 9,365
Judson Baptist College	The Dalles, OR 97058	1956	Baptist	S/C	247	34	$ 3,900	$2,200	$ 6,100
Lane Community College	Eugene, OR 97405	1965	Local	J/C	7,262	323	$ 594	—	$ 594
Lewis and Clark College	Portland, OR 97219	1867	Independ	S-G/C	3,012	278	$ 8,023	$3,219	$11,242
Linfield College	McMinnville, OR 97128	1849	Baptist	S-G/C	1,518	115	$ 6,740	$2,394	$ 9,134
Linn-Benton Community Col.	Albany, OR 97321	1967	Local	J/C	9,615	537	$ 648	—	$ 648
Mount Angel Seminary	St. Benedict, OR 97373	1887	Catholic	S-G/M	120	27	$ 2,500	$2,000	$ 4,500
Mt. Hood Community College	Gresham, OR 97030	1965	State	J/C	9,098	575	$ 645	—	$ 645
Multnomah Sch. of the Bible	Portland, OR 97220	1936	Independ	S-G/C	765	42	$ 3,680	$2,060	$ 5,740
Northwest Christian College	Eugene, OR 97401	1895	D of Chr	S/C	236	19	$ 3,690	$2,168	$ 5,838
Oregon Graduate Center	Beaverton, OR 97006	1963	Independ	G/C	105	31	$ 6,200	—	$ 6,200
Oregon Inst. of Technology	Klamath Falls, OR 97601	1947	State	S/C	2,750	180	$ 1,403	$2,400	$ 3,803
Oregon State University	Corvallis, OR 97331	1868	State	S-G/C	15,636	1,570	$ 1,410	$2,300	$ 3,710
Pacific N.W. College of Art	Portland, OR 97205	1909	Independ	S/C	200	30	$ 4,075	—	$ 4,075
Pacific University	Forest Grove, OR 97116	1849	Private	S-G/C	1,065	82	$ 6,400	$2,400	$ 8,800
Portland Community College	Portland, OR 97219	1961	Public	J/C	27,042	1,737	$ 585	—	$ 585
Portland State University	Portland, OR 97207	1955	State	S-G/C	14,390	680	$ 1,450	—	$ 1,450
Reed College	Portland, OR 97202	1909	Independ	S-G/C	1,080	110	$ 9,000	$2,950	$11,950
Rogue Community College	Grants Pass, OR 97527	1971	State	J/C	4,190	303	$ 768	—	$ 768
Southern Oregon State Col.	Ashland, OR 97520	1926	State	S-G/C	4,433	231	$ 1,470	$2,392	$ 3,862
Southw. Oregon Comm. Col.	Coos Bay, OR 97420	1961	State	J/C	3,900	190	$ 660	—	$ 660
Treasure Valley Comm. Col.	Ontario, OR 97914	1961	State	J/C	1,435	65	$ 660	$ 500	$ 1,160
Umpqua Community College	Roseburg, OR 97470	1964	State	J/C	4,847	200	$ 725	—	$ 725
University of Oregon	Eugene, OR 97403	1876	State	S-G/C	15,840	1,457	$ 1,440	$2,300	$ 3,740
School of Dentistry	Portland, OR 97201	1898	State	P/C	324	168	$ 3,485	$6,375	$ 9,860
University of Portland	Portland, OR 97203	1901	Catholic	S-G/C	2,861	194	$ 5,580	$2,590	$ 8,170
Warner Pacific College	Portland, OR 97215	1937	C of God	S-G/C	412	55	$ 4,915	$2,400	$ 7,315
Western Baptist College	Salem, OR 97301	1935	Baptist	S/C	282	34	$ 3,945	$2,340	$ 6,285
Western Cons. Baptist Sem.	Portland, OR 97215	1927	Baptist	G/C	571	32	$ 3,000	—	$ 3,000
Western Evangelical Sem.	Portland, OR 97222	1945	Int-Den	G/C	208	16	$ 3,450	—	$ 3,450
Western Oregon State College	Monmouth, OR 97361	1856	State	S-G/C	2,820	233	$ 1,420	$2,195	$ 3,615
Western States Chirop. Col.	Portland, OR 97230	1907	Independ	P/C	397	35	$ 6,175	$ —	$ 6,175
Willamette University	Salem, OR 97301	1842	Methodist	S-G/C	1,865	167	$ 6,950	$2,950	$ 9,900
PANAMA CANAL									
Panama Canal College	APO, Miami 34002	1933	Federal	J/C	1,750	81	—	—	—
PENNSYLVANIA									
Academy of the New Church	Bryn Athyn, PA 19009	1876	Church	J-S/C	151	34	$ 1,950	$1,857	$ 3,807

NAME	ADDRESS	FOUN-DED	AFFILI-ATION	LEVEL/TYPE	ENROLL-MENT	TEACH-ERS	TUITION & FEES	BOARD & ROOM	TOTAL COST
PENNSYLVANIA *(continued)*									
Albright College............	Reading, PA 19604......	1856	Methodist	S/C	2,049	123	$ 7,575	$2,725	$10,300
Allegheny College	Meadville, PA 16335 ...	1815	Methodist	S/C	1,954	160	$ 7,815	$2,550	$10,365
Allentown Col. of St. F. De S..	Center Valley, PA 18034	1964	Catholic	S/C	800	80	$ 4,990	$2,940	$ 7,930
Alliance College	Cambrdg. Spgs., PA 16403	1912	Independ	J-S/C	300	31	$ 3,000	$2,300	$ 5,300
Alvernia College..........	Reading, PA 19607......	1958	Catholic	S/C	726	54	$ 3,290	$2,770	$ 6,060
American College	Bryn Mawr, PA 19010 ..	1927	Independ	P/C	50,000	40	$ 350	—	$ 350
Antioch Univ., Philadelphia ..	Philadelphia, PA 19108 .	1852	Independ	S-G/C	703	79	$ 4,000	—	$ 4,000
Baptist Bible College	Clarks Summit, PA 18411	1932	Baptist	S-G/C	711	38	$ 3,860	$2,106	$ 5,966
Beaver College	Glenside, PA 19038	1853	Presby	S-G/C	2,146	158	$ 6,750	$3,000	$ 9,750
Biblical Theological Seminary	Hatfield, PA 19440	1971	Independ	G/C	160	9	$ 2,400	—	$ 2,400
Bloomsburg Univ. of PA.....	Bloomsburg, PA 17815 .	1839	State	S-G/C	6,189	325	$ 1,570	$1,592	$ 3,162
Bryn Mawr College	Bryn Mawr, PA 19010 ..	1885	Independ	S-G/W	1,785	195	$ 9,700	$4,135	$13,835
Bucknell University	Lewisburg, PA 17837 ...	1846	Independ	S-G/C	3,438	227	$ 9,865	$2,450	$12,315
Bucks County Comm. College	Newtown, PA 18940	1965	Public	J/C	9,681	194	$ 1,144	—	$ 1,144
Butler County Comm. College	Butler, PA 16001	1965	State	J/C	1,176	93	$ 1,050	—	$ 1,050
Cabrini College	Wayne, PA 19087.......	1957	Catholic	S-G/C	900	90	$ 4,200	$3,300	$ 7,500
California Univ. of PA	California, PA 15419 ...	1852	State	S-G/C	5,058	265	$ 1,720	$1,800	$ 3,520
Carlow College	Pittsburgh, PA 15213 ..	1929	Catholic	S-G/W	1,246	133	$ 6,286	$3,444	$ 9,730
Carnegie-Mellon University ..	Pittsburgh, PA 15213 ..	1900	Private	S-G/C	6,251	467	$ 9,460	$3,600	$13,060
Cedar Crest College	Allentown, PA 18104 ...	1867	UCC	S/W	1,051	136	$ 6,920	$3,050	$ 9,970
Chatham College	Pittsburgh, PA 15232 ..	1869	Independ	S/W	536	74	$ 6,800	$3,400	$10,200
Chestnut Hill College	Philadelphia, PA 19118 .	1924	Catholic	S-G/W	1,124	110	$ 4,500	$2,670	$ 7,170
Cheyney Univ. of Penna.	Cheyney, PA 19319	1837	State	S-G/C	1,795	153	$ 1,730	$ 942	$ 2,672
Christ the Saviour Seminary .	Johnstown, PA 15906 ..	1940	Church	S-G/M	7	8	$ 865	$1,200	$ 2,065
Clarion University	Clarion, PA 16214	1867	State	S/C	5,297	240	$ 1,760	$1,970	$ 3,730
Venango Campus ..	Oil City, PA 16301	1961	State	S/C	591	34	$ 1,760	$1,970	$ 3,730
College Misericordia	Dallas, PA 18612	1924	Catholic	S-G/C	1,292	110	$ 4,350	$2,600	$ 6,950
Combs College of Music...	Bryn Mawr, PA 19010 ..	1885	Independ	S-G/C	80	27	$ 4,190	$2,350	$ 6,540
Comm. Col. of Allegheny Co.	Pittsburgh, PA 15233 ..	1966	Public	J/C	98,000	2,194	$ 792	—	$ 792
Allegheny Campus ..	Pittsburgh, PA 15212 ..	1966	Public	J/C	7,474	149	$ 871	—	$ 871
Boyce Campus............	Monroeville, PA 15146 .	1966	Public	J/C	4,736	80	$ 871	—	$ 871
North Campus	Pittsburgh, PA 15237 ..	1972	Public	J/C	3,303	41	$ 871	—	$ 871
South Campus	West Mifflin, PA 15122 .	1967	Public	J/C	5,197	83	$ 871	—	$ 871
Comm. Col. of Beaver County	Monaca, PA 15061......	1966	Public	J/C	2,377	135	$ 1,100	—	$ 1,100
Comm. Col. of Philadelphia .	Philadelphia, PA 19130 .	1964	State	J/C	19,596	659	$ 946	—	$ 946
Curtis Institute of Music....	Philadelphia, PA 19103 .	1924	Independ	P/C	184	68	$ 125	—	$ 125
Delaware County Comm. Col.	Media, PA 19063	1967	Public	J/C	7,254	498	$ 816	—	$ 816
Del. Val. Col. of Sci. & Agri..	Doylestown, PA 18901..	1896	Independ	S/C	1,534	89	$ 5,200	$2,500	$ 7,700
Dickinson College	Carlisle, PA 17013	1773	Independ	S/C	1,888	135	$ 9,130	$3,000	$12,130
Dickinson School of Law	Carlisle, PA 17013	1834	Independ	P/C	525	47	$ 5,500	$2,600	$ 8,100
Drexel University	Philadelphia, PA 19104 .	1891	Independ	S-G/C	12,566	860	$ 3,870	$2,285	$ 6,155
Dropsie Col. for Hebrew & Cognate	Merion, PA 19066......	1907	Independ	G/C	50	12	$ 4,700	—	$ 4,700
Dubois Business College	Dubois, PA 15801......	1883	Independ	S/C	285	27	$ 3,200	—	$ 3,200
Duquesne University	Pittsburgh, PA 15282 ..	1878	Catholic	S-G/C	6,598	276	$ 5,850	$2,842	$ 8,692
East Stroudsburg Univ.	E. Stroudsburg, PA 18301	1893	State	S-G/C	4,235	207	$ 1,650	$1,800	$ 3,450
Eastern Baptist Theol. Sem. .	Philadelphia, PA 19151 .	1925	Baptist	P/C	391	31	$ 3,776	$1,000	$ 4,776
Eastern College	St. Davids, PA 19087 ..	1953	Baptist	S-G/C	938	94	$ 5,570	$2,120	$ 7,690
Edinboro Univ. of PA	Edinboro, PA 16444 ...	1857	State	S/C	6,053	348	$ 1,570	$1,852	$ 3,422
Elizabethtown College	Elizabethtown, PA 17022	1899	Brethren	S/C	1,463	103	$ 6,765	$2,850	$ 9,615
Evangelical Sch. of Theology .	Myerstown, PA 17067 ..	1953	Evangel	G/C	75	9	$ 3,000	—	$ 3,300
Franklin and Marshall College	Lancaster, PA 17604 ...	1787	Independ	S/C	1,983	134	$ 9,150	$3,160	$12,310
Gannon University..........	Erie, PA 16541	1933	Catholic	S-G/C	4,184	225	$ 4,400	$2,300	$ 6,700
Geneva College	Beaver Falls, PA 15010 .	1848	Presby	S/C	1,214	91	$ 4,990	$2,480	$ 7,470
Gettysburg College	Gettysburg, PA 17325 ..	1832	Lutheran	S/C	1,925	170	$ 7,695	$2,500	$10,195
Gratz College	Philadelphia, PA 19141 .	1895	Independ	S/C	303	19	$ 550	—	$ 550
Grove City College	Grove City, PA 16127 ..	1876	Presby	S/C	2,196	120	$ 3,060	$1,800	$ 4,860
Gwynedd-Mercy College	Gwynedd Valley, PA 19437	1948	Catholic	S-G/C	2,210	209	$ 4,400	$2,600	$ 7,000
Hahnemann University	Philadelphia, PA 19102 .	1848	Independ	S-G/C	2,109	485	$ 8,500	—	$ 8,500
Harcum Junior College	Bryn Mawr, PA 19010 ..	1915	Independ	J/W	811	79	$ 4,105	$2,860	$ 6,965
Harrisburg Area Comm. Col..	Harrisburg, PA 17110 ..	1964	State	J/C	6,866	270	$ 768	—	$ 768
Haverford College	Haverford, PA 19041 ...	1833	Independ	S/C	1,080	110	$ 9,990	$3,700	$13,690
Holy Family College........	Philadelphia, PA 19114 .	1954	Catholic	S/C	1,528	152	$ 3,900	—	$ 3,900
Immaculata College	Immaculata, PA 19345 .	1920	Catholic	S/W	1,836	130	$ 3,950	$2,900	$ 6,850
Indiana Univ. of Pennsylvania	Indiana, PA 15705	1875	State	S-G/C	12,006	660	$ 1,778	$1,924	$ 3,702
Armstrong Campus...	Kittanning, PA 16201...	1963	State	J/C	511	13	$ 1,778	$1,872	$ 3,650
Punxsutawney Campus ...	Punxsutawney, PA 15767	1862	State	J/C	289	11	$ 1,710	$1,872	$ 3,582
Juniata College	Huntingdon, PA 16652 .	1876	Independ	S/C	1,214	90	$ 7,260	$2,634	$ 9,894
Keystone Junior College.....	La Plume, PA 18440.....	1868	Independ	J/C	1,068	82	$ 3,950	$2,500	$ 6,450
King's College	Wilkes-Barre, PA 18711	1946	Catholic	S/C	2,271	88	$ 5,150	$2,770	$ 7,920
Kutztown State College	Kutztown, PA 19530 ...	1866	State	S-G/C	6,014	298	$ 1,708	$1,760	$ 3,468
La Roche College	Pittsburgh, PA 15237 ..	1963	Catholic	S-G/C	1,780	109	$ 4,370	$2,600	$ 6,970
La Salle College	Philadelphia, PA 19141 .	1863	Catholic	S-G/C	6,333	294	$ 5,590	$3,070	$ 8,660
Lackawanna Junior College ..	Scranton, PA 18505....	1894	Independ	J/C	956	82	$ 2,820	—	$ 2,820
Lafayette College	Easton, PA 18042	1826	Presby	S/C	2,029	161	$ 9,250	$3,275	$12,525
Lancaster Bible College	Lancaster, PA 17601 ...	1933	Independ	S/C	359	23	$ 4,300	$2,260	$ 6,560
Lancaster Theological Sem..	Lancaster, PA 17603 ...	1825	UC Chr	G/C	244	26	$ 3,650	$2,500	$ 6,150
Lebanon Valley College	Annville, PA 17003	1866	Methodist	S/C	1,186	97	$ 6,600	$3,000	$ 9,600
Lehigh County Comm. College	Schnecksville, PA 18078	1966	Public	J/C	3,306	116	$ 1,080	—	$ 1,080
Lehigh University	Bethlehem, PA 18015 ..	1865	Independ	S-G/C	6,277	426	$ 9,550	$3,400	$12,950
Lincoln University	Lincoln Univ., PA 19352	1854	State	S-G/C	1,185	107	$ 1,830	$2,250	$ 4,080
Lock Haven U. of Penna.	Lock Haven, PA 17745 ..	1870	State	S/C	2,661	162	$ 1,480	$1,702	$ 3,182
Lutheran Theol. Sem.	Gettysburg, PA 17325 ..	1826	Lutheran	P/C	270	20	$ 1,932	$1,625	$ 3,557
Lutheran Theol. Sem.	Philadelphia, PA 19119 .	1864	Lutheran	P/C	259	29	$ 1,805	$2,380	$ 4,185

PENNSYLVANIA (continued)

NAME	ADDRESS	FOUN-DED	AFFILI-ATION	LEVEL/TYPE	ENROLL-MENT	TEACH-ERS	TUITION & FEES	BOARD & ROOM	TOTAL COST
Luzerne County Comm. Col. ..	Nanticoke, PA 18634 ...	1967	State	J/C	2,600	70	$ 990	—	$ 990
Lycoming College	Williamsport, PA 17701 .	1812	Methodist	S/C	1,286	80	$ 6,800	$2,670	$ 9,470
Lyon School of Business	New Castle, PA 16101 ..	1894	Independ	J/C	120	12	$ 2,640	$2,175	$ 4,815
Manor Junior College	Jenkintown, PA 19046..	1947	Church	J/W	340	46	$ 3,660	$1,860	$ 5,220
Mansfield Univ.	Mansfield, PA 16933 ...	1857	State	S-G/C	2,934	189	$ 1,650	$1,906	$ 3,556
Mary Immaculate Seminary..	Northampton, PA 18067	1939	Catholic	P/M	48	12	$ 2,350	$2,300	$ 4,650
Marywood College..........	Scranton, PA 18509	1915	Catholic	S-G/W	3,207	223	$ 4,500	$2,650	$ 7,150
Medical Col. of Pennsylvania .	Philadelphia, PA 19129 .	1850	Independ	P/C	454	282	$12,425	—	$12,425
Mercyhurst College	Erie, PA 16546	1926	Catholic	S-G/C	1,750	132	$ 5,560	$2,265	$ 7,825
Messiah College............	Grantham, PA 17027 ...	1909	Brethren	S/C	1,761	137	$ 5,200	$2,610	$ 7,810
Millersville University	Millersville, PA 17551 ..	1855	State	S-G/C	6,583	350	$ 1,570	$1,880	$ 3,450
Montgomery Co. Comm. Col..	Blue Bell, PA 19422	1964	County	J/C	7,239	350	$ 900	—	$ 900
Moore College of Art........	Philadelphia, PA 19103 .	1844	Independ	S/W	527	81	$ 6,600	$3,000	$ 9,600
Moravian College	Bethlehem, PA 18018 ...	1742	Moravian	S/C	1,747	134	$ 7,575	$2,625	$10,200
Moravian Theological Sem. ..	Bethlehem, PA 18018 ...	1807	Moravian	G/C	105	18	$ 3,750	$2,760	$ 6,510
Mount Aloysius Jr. College ..	Cresson, PA 16630......	1939	Catholic	J/C	751	91	$ 4,400	$2,400	$ 6,800
Muhlenberg College	Allentown, PA 18104 ...	1848	Lutheran	S/C	2,353	135	$ 6,585	$2,165	$ 8,750
Neumann College	Aston, PA 19014.......	1965	Catholic	S/C	982	86	$ 3,534	—	$ 3,534
New School of Music	Philadelphia, PA 19103 .	1942	Independ	S/C	51	31	$ 5,550	$3,250	$ 8,800
Nrthmptn Co. Area Comm. Col.	Bethlehem, PA 18017 ..	1966	Public	J/C	4,168	219	$ 1,200	—	$ 1,200
Northeastern Chrstn. Jr. Col.	Villanova, PA 19085....	1959	C of Chr	J/C	207	28	$ 3,806	$2,624	$ 6,430
Pendle Hill	Wallingford, PA 19086..	1930	Quaker	S-G/C	37	6	$ 6,350	—	$ 6,350
Pennco Tech.	Bristol, PA 19007	1961	Independ	T/C	608	40	$ 6,464	—	$ 6,464
Pa. College of Optometry ...	Philadelphia, PA 19141 .	1919	Independ	P/C	585	64	$11,166	$2,156	$13,322
Pa. College of Podiatric Med.	Philadelphia, PA 19107 .	1963	Independ	P/C	456	153	$10,800	$4,056	$14,856
Pennsylvania State Univ.	Univ. Park, PA 16802..	1855	State	S-G/C	34,401	1,782	$ 2,562	$2,620	$ 5,182
Allentown Campus	Fogelsville, PA 18057...	1912	State	J/C	482	22	$ 2,246	—	$ 2,246
Altoona Campus	Altoona, PA 16603	1929	State	J/C	2,081	90	$ 2,246	$2,620	$ 4,866
Beaver Campus	Monaca, PA 15061.....	1964	State	J/C	1,142	60	$ 2,246	$2,620	$ 4,866
Behrend College	Erie, PA 16563	1926	State	S-G/C	1,989	124	$ 2,562	$2,620	$ 5,182
Berks Campus	Reading, PA 19608......	1924	State	J/C	1,092	55	$ 2,246	—	$ 2,246
Capitol Campus	Middletown, PA 17057 .	1966	State	S-G/C	2,595	149	$ 2,562	$2,620	$ 5,182
Delaware County Campus .	Media, PA 19063	1966	State	J/C	1,504	78	$ 2,246	—	$ 2,246
DuBois Campus	DuBois, PA 15801	1935	State	J/C	868	41	$ 2,246	—	$ 2,246
Fayette Campus........	Uniontown, PA 15401 ..	1934	State	J/C	835	39	$ 2,246	—	$ 2,246
Hazleton Campus	Hazleton, PA 18201	1934	State	J/C	1,105	53	$ 2,246	$2,620	$ 4,866
Hershey Medical Center ..	Hershey, PA 17033	1964	State	P/C	757	333	$ 2,730	—	$ 2,730
King of Prussia Ctr. for Grad. Studies .	King of Prussia, PA 19406	1968	State	G/C	533	10	$ 2,520	—	$ 2,520
McKeesport Campus	McKeesport, PA 15132 .	1947	State	J/C	1,449	62	$ 2,246	$2,620	$ 4,866
Mont Alto Campus	Mont Alto, PA 17237 ...	1929	State	J/C	797	42	$ 2,246	$2,620	$ 4,866
New Kensington Campus ..	New Kensington, PA 15068	1958	State	J/C	1,270	71	$ 2,246	—	$ 2,246
Ogontz Campus	Abington, PA 19001	1950	State	J/C	3,492	114	$ 2,246	—	$ 2,246
Schuylkill Campus	Schuylkill, PA 17972 ...	1934	State	J/C	951	42	$ 2,246	—	$ 2,246
Shenango Valley Campus .	Sharon, PA 16146	1965	State	J/C	1,067	34	$ 2,246	—	$ 2,246
Wilkes-Barre Campus	Wilkes-Barre, PA 18708	1916	State	J/C	686	50	$ 2,246	—	$ 2,246
Worthington Scrntn. Camp.	Dunmore, PA 18512.....	1923	State	J/C	1,202	70	$ 2,246	—	$ 2,246
York Campus	York, PA 17403	1926	State	J/C	1,111	58	$ 2,246	—	$ 2,246
Philadelphia College of Bible .	Langhorne, PA 19047 ..	1913	Independ	S/C	573	31	$ 3,850	$2,500	$ 6,300
Phila. Col. of Osteo. Medicine	Philadelphia, PA 19131 .	1899	Independ	P/C	832	105	$11,250	—	$11,250
Phila. Col. of Perform. Arts .	Philadelphia, PA 19102 .	1870	Independ	S-G/C	400	157	$ 6,000	$2,000	$ 8,000
Phila. Col. of Pharm. and Sci.	Philadelphia, PA 19104 .	1821	Independ	S-G/C	1,111	150	$ 5,800	$2,650	$ 8,450
Phila. Col. of Textiles & Sci..	Philadelphia, PA 19144 .	1884	Private	S-G/C	2,746	178	$ 4,900	$2,750	$ 7,650
Pierce Junior College	Philadelphia, PA 19102 .	1865	Independ	J/C	1,642	81	$ 4,000	$1,500	$ 5,500
Pinebrook Junior College ...	Coopersburg, PA 18036	1969	Fellow	J/C	116	23	$ 3,575	$2,410	$ 5,985
Pittsburgh Theol. Seminary ..	Pittsburgh, PA 15206 ..	1794	Presby	G/C	436	34	$ 3,474	$2,425	$ 5,899
Point Park College	Pittsburgh, PA 15222 ..	1960	Private	S-G/C	2,594	161	$ 5,080	$2,510	$ 7,590
Reading Area Comm. College	Reading, PA 19603.....	1971	Public	J/C	1,384	30	$ 999	—	$ 999
Reconstructionist Rab. Col. .	Wyncote, PA 19095.....	1968	Jewish	G/C	45	20	$ 4,000	—	$ 4,000
Reformed Presby. Theol. Sem.	Pittsburgh, PA 15208 ..	1810	Presby	G/C	112	7	$ 1,650	$1,275	$ 2,925
Robert Morris College	Coraopolis, PA 15108 ..	1921	Independ	S-G/C	5,940	226	$ 3,240	$2,150	$ 5,390
Rosemont College	Rosemont, PA 19010 ...	1921	Catholic	S/W	565	84	$ 5,465	$3,395	$ 8,860
St. Francis College	Loretto, PA 15940	1847	Catholic	S-G/C	1,634	91	$ 5,360	$2,780	$ 8,140
St. Joseph's University	Philadelphia, PA 19131 .	1851	Catholic	S-G/C	6,000	350	$ 5,000	$3,200	$ 8,200
St. Vincent College	Latrobe, PA 15650	1846	Catholic	S/C	1,163	87	$ 5,488	$2,505	$ 7,993
Seton Hill College	Greensburg, PA 15601 .	1883	Catholic	S/W	870	77	$ 5,990	$2,800	$ 8,790
Shippensburg University	Shippensburg, PA 17257	1871	State	S-G/C	6,136	316	$ 1,962	$1,780	$ 3,742
Slippery Rock Univ.	Slippery Rock, PA 16057	1889	State	S-G/C	6,479	350	$ 1,570	$1,754	$ 3,324
Spring Garden College	Chestnut Hill, PA 19118	1851	Independ	S/C	1,268	91	$ 4,700	—	$ 4,700
Susquehanna University	Selinsgrove, PA 17870..	1858	Lutheran	S/C	1,459	121	$ 7,100	$2,870	$ 9,970
Swarthmore College	Swarthmore, PA 19081 .	1864	Indepen	S-G/C	1,326	153	$10,220	$3,880	$14,100
Temple University	Philadelphia, PA 19122 .	1884	State	S-G/C	30,559	1,679	$ 5,780	$1,600	$ 7,380
Theol. Sem. of Ref. Epis. Ch .	Philadelphia, PA 19104 .	1886	Episcopal	G/C	55	6	$ 1,740	$1,350	$ 3,050
Thiel College	Greenville, PA 16125 ...	1866	Lutheran	S/C	875	70	$ 5,600	$2,600	$ 8,200
Thomas Jefferson University	Philadelphia, PA 19107 .	1824	Private	P/C	2,028	96	$ 7,400	$1,560	$ 8,960
U.S. Army War College	Carlisle Bar, PA 17013 ..	1901	Federal	P/C	690	58	—	—	—
United Wesleyan College ...	Allentown, PA 18103 ...	1921	Wesleyan	S/C	225	13	$ 3,500	$2,000	$ 5,500
University of Pennsylvania ..	Philadelphia, PA 19104 .	1740	Independ	S-G/C	20,017	3,415	$ 8,000	$3,614	$11,614
University of Pittsburgh	Pittsburgh, PA 15260 ..	1787	State	S-G/C	29,197	2,765	$ 2,758	$2,732	$ 5,490
Bradford Campus	Bradford, PA 16701	1963	State	S/C	974	79	$ 2,760	$2,730	$ 5,490
Greensburg Campus......	Greensburg, PA 15601 .	1963	State	J/C	1,471	68	$ 2,640	$1,990	$ 4,630
Johnstown Campus......	Johnstown, PA 15904 ..	1927	State	S/C	3,223	177	$ 2,730	$2,426	$ 5,156
Titusville Campus	Titusville, PA 16354 ...	1963	State	J/C	323	36	$ 2,590	$2,460	$ 5,050
University of Scranton	Scranton, PA 18510	1888	Catholic	S-G/C	4,685	287	$ 4,800	$2,670	$ 7,470

236 EDUCATION

NAME	ADDRESS	FOUNDED	AFFILIATION	LEVEL/TYPE	ENROLLMENT	TEACHERS	TUITION & FEES	BOARD & ROOM	TOTAL COST
PENNSYLVANIA *(continued)*									
Ursinus College	Collegeville, PA 19426 ..	1869	C of Chr	S/C	1,142	103	$ 6,625	$3,000	$ 9,625
Valley Forge Christian College	Phoenixville, PA 19460..	1939	A of God	S/C	601	30	$ 2,810	$2,328	$ 5,138
Valley Forge Military Jr. Col..	Wayne, PA 19087	1935	Independ	J/M	144	31	$ 4,110	$4,395	$ 9,300
Villa Maria College	Erie, PA 16505.........	1925	Catholic·	S/W	671	74	$ 5,070	$2,600	$ 7,670
Villanova University	Villanova, PA 19085	1842	Catholic	S-G/C	11,665	819	$ 6,465	$3,990	$10,455
Washington and Jefferson Col.	Washington, PA 15301 ..	1781	Independ	S-G/C	1,322	100	$ 7,720	$2,490	$10,210
Waynesburg College	Waynesburg, PA 15370 ..	1849	Presby	S-G/C	824	62	$ 5,570	$2,410	$ 7,980
West Chester University of Pennsylvania	West Chester, PA 19383	1871	State	S-G/C	9,528	534	$ 1,570	$1,944	$ 3,514
Westminster College	New Wilmington, PA 16142	1852	Presby	S-G/C	1,345	95	$ 6,100	$2,320	$ 8,420
Westminster Theol. Seminary	Glenside, PA 19038......	1929	Independ	G/C	470	28	$ 3,040	$2,850	$ 5,890
Westmoreland Co. Comm. Col.	Youngwood, PA 15697 ..	1970	County	J/C	3,496	169	$ 854	—	$ 854
Widener University	Chester, PA 19013	1821	Independ	S-G/C	4,168	238	$ 6,700	$3,020	$ 9,720
University College	Chester, PA 19013	1980	Independ	S/C	1,109	70	$ 1,440	—	$ 1,440
Wilkes College	Wilkes-Barre, PA 18766 .	1933	Independ	S-G/C	1,860	150	$ 5,500	$2,650	$ 8,150
Williamsport Area Comm. Col.	Williamsport, PA 17701 .	1965	State	J/C	4,084	259	$ 2,768	—	$ 2,768
Wilson College	Chambersburg, PA 17201	1869	Presby	S/W	318	59	$ 6,676	$2,674	$ 9,350
Yorktown Business Institute .	York, PA 17404	1976	Independ	J/C	197	21	$ 3,580	—	$ 3,580
York Col. of Pennsylvania	York, PA 17405	1787	Independ	S-G/C	4,570	249	$ 3,290	$2,122	$ 5,412
PUERTO RICO									
Catholic. Univ. of Puerto Rico	Ponce, PR 00732	1948	Catholic	S-G/C					
Ponce Campus	Ponce, PR 00732	1948	Catholic	S-G/C	9,045	403	$ 1,765	$1,200	$ 2,965
Arecibo Branch Campus ..	Arecibo, PR 00612	1960	Catholic	S/C	1,444	57	$ 1,765	—	$ 1,765
Guayma Branch Campus ..	Guayama, PR 00654	1959	Catholic	S/C	1,144	49	$ 1,765	—	$ 1,765
Mayaguez Branch Campus	Mayaguez, PR 00709 ...	1975	Catholic	S/C	1,409	82	$ 1,765	—	$ 1,765
School of Law	Ponce, PR 00732	1961	Catholic	P/C	306	37	$ 3,800	$1,200	$ 5,000
Inter Amer. Un. of Puerto Rico	San Juan, PR 00936								
Aquadilla Regional College	Aquadilla, PR 00603	1957	Independ	J/C	2,760	153	$ 1,800	—	$ 1,850
Arecibo Regional College ..	Arecibo, PR 00612	1957	Independ	J/C	3,531	228	$ 1,800	—	$ 1,800
Barranquitas Regional Col.	Barranquitas, PR 00615..	1957	Independ	S/C	1,458	85	$ 1,800	—	$ 1,800
Bayamon Univ. College...	Bayamon, PR 00619	1984	Independ	S/C	3,343	191	$ 1,800	—	$ 1,800
Fajardo Regional College ..	Fajardo, PR 00648	1965	Independ	J/C	1,861	108	$ 1,800	—	$ 1,800
Guayama Regional College	Guayama, PR 00654	1958	Independ	J/C	1,374	100	$ 1,800	—	$ 1,800
Metropolitan Campus	Hato Rey, PR 00919	1962	Independ	S-G/C	13,249	672	$ 1,800	—	$ 1,800
Ponce Regional College ...	Ponce, PR 00731	1962	Independ	J/C	2,788	155	$ 1,800	—	$ 1,800
San German Campus	San German, PR 00753 .	1912	Independ	S-G/C	6,727	317	$ 1,800	$1,250	$ 3,050
School of Law	Santurce, PR 00910	1961	Independ	P/C	890	64	$ 3,850	—	$ 3,850
Metropolitan University College	Rio Piedras, PR 00928 ..	1980	Independ	S/C	5,017	118	$ 1,710	—	$ 1,710
Puerto Rico Junior College .	Rio Piedras, PR 00928 ..	1949	Independ	J/C·	4,853	80	$ 1,710	—	$ 1,710
University of Puerto Rico	San Juan, PR 00936	1903	State						
Aquadilla Reg. Col.	Ramey, PR 00604	1972	State	J/C	1,335	74	$ 625	$1,500	$ 2,325
Arecibo Tech. U. Col.	Arecibo, PR 00613	1967	State	S/C	3,569	171	$ 625	$1,500	$ 2,325
Bayamon Tech. U. Col. ...	Bayamon, PR 00620	1971	State	S/C	3,569	171	$ 625	$1,500	$ 2,325
Carolina Reg. Col.	Carolina, PR 00630	1974	State	J/C	1,409	87	$ 625	$1,500	$ 2,325
Cayey U. College	Cayey, PR 00633	1967	State	S/C	3,411	176	$ 620	$1,500	$ 2,320
Humacao U. College	Humacao, PR 00661 ...	1962	State	S/C	3,451	243	$ 620	$1,500	$ 2,320
La Montana Reg. Col.	Utuado, PR 00761	1979	State	J/C	529	40	$ 625	$1,500	$ 2,325
Mayaguez Campus	Mayaguez, PR 00708 ...	1911	State	S-G/C	9,673	586	$ 670	$2,700	$ 3,370
Medical Sciences Campus .	San Juan, PR 00936	1926	State	G/C	3,391	823	$ 2,860	$2,800	$ 5,660
Ponce Tech. U. Col.	Ponce, PR 00732	1970	State	J-S/C	1,867	118	—	—	
Rio Piedras Campus	Rio Piedras, PR 00931 ..	1903	State	S-G/C	20,996	1,384	$ 610	$2,800	$ 3,410
Univ. of the Sacred Heart ...	Santurce, PR 00914	1935	Catholic	S/C	8,019	130	$ 1,424	$1,000	$ 2,424
University of Turabo	Caguas, PR 00625	1972	Independ	S-G/C	7,435	92	$ 1,710	—	$ 1,710
RHODE ISLAND									
Brown University	Providence, RI 02912 ...	1767	Independ	S-G/C	7,117	510	$10,825	$3,695	$14,765
Bryant College	Smithfield, RI 02917	1863	Independ	S-G/C	6,457	250	$ 5,100	$3,320	$ 8,420
Comm. Col. of RI	Warwick, RI 02886	1964	State	J/C	12,317	490	$ 740	—	$ 740
Johnson & Wales College ..	Providence, RI 02903 ...	1914	Independ	S/C	4,750	160	$ 4,980	$2,900	$ 7,880
New England Inst. of Tech. .	Providence, RI 02907 ...	1940	Independ	S/C	1,500	80	$ 4,665	—	$ 4,665
Providence College	Providence, RI 02918 ...	1917	Catholic	S/C	5,663	252	$ 7,003	$3,700	$10,703
Rhode Island College	Providence, RI 02908 ...	1854	State	S-G/C	8,580	376	$ 1,234	$3,100	$ 4,334
Rhode Island Sch. of Design .	Providence, RI 02915 ...	1877	Independ	P/C	1,792	199	$ 7,600	$3,250	$10,850
Roger Williams College	Bristol, RI 02809	1948	Independ	S-G/C	3,723	271	$ 5,412	$3,596	$ 9,008
Salve Regina Coll.	Newport, RI 02840	1934	Catholic	S-G/C	2,065	203	$ 6,210	$3,600	$ 9,810
University of Rhode Island ..	Kingston, RI 02881	1888	State	S-G/C	13,685	733	$ 1,972	$3,185	$ 5,157
SOUTH CAROLINA									
Aiken Technical College	Aiken, SC 29802	1969	State	T/C	1,771	105	$ 680	—	$ 680
Allen University	Columbia, SC 29204 ...	1870	Church	S/C	200	25	$ 2,710	$1,870	$ 4,580
Anderson College	Anderson, SC 29621 ...	1911	Baptist	J/C	1,165	57	$ 3,300	$2,100	$ 5,400
Baptist College at Charleston	Charleston, SC 29411 ...	1960	Baptist	S/C	1,660	77	$ 4,874	$2,560	$ 7,434
Beaufort Technical College .	Beaufort, SC 29902.....	1972	State	T/C	2,168	75	$ 585	—	$ 585
Benedict College	Columbia, SC 29204 ...	1870	Independ	S/C	1,494	99	$ 3,320	$1,950	$ 5,270
Bob Jones University	Greenville, SC 29614 ...	1927	Independ	S/C	5,733	400	$ 2,378	$2,430	$ 4,808
Central Wesleyan College ..	Central, SC 29630	1906	Wesleyan	S/C	397	34	$ 4,460	$2,130	$ 6,590
Chesterfield-Marlb. Tech. Col.	Cheraw, SC 29520	1968	State	T/C	608	47	$ 660	—	$ 660
Citadel	Charleston, SC 29409 ..	1842	State	S-G/M	3,005	197	$ 1,630	$1,780	$ 3,410
Claflin College	Orangeburg, SC 29115..	1869	Methodist	S/C	648	56	$ 2,902	$1,700	$ 4,602
Clemson University	Clemson, SC 29631	1889	State	S-G/C	12,000	1,080	$ 1,652	$2,090	$ 3,742
Clinton Junior College	Rock Hill, SC 29731 ...	1894	Methodist	J/C	103	8	$ 1,050	$1,260	$ 2,310
Coker College	Hartsville, SC 29550 ...	1908	Independ	S/C	320	47	$ 5,140	$2,645	$ 7,785
College of Charleston	Charleston, SC 29424...	1770	State	S-G/C	5,395	325	$ 1,470	$2,390	$ 3,860

NAME	ADDRESS	FOUN-DED	AFFILI-ATION	LEVEL/TYPE	ENROLL-MENT	TEACH-ERS	TUITION & FEES	BOARD & ROOM	TOTAL COST
SOUTH CAROLINA *(continued)*									
Columbia Bible College	Columbia, SC 29203	1923	Int-Den	S-G/C	885	51	$ 3,300	$2,175	$ 5,475
Columbia College	Columbia, SC 29203	1854	Methodist	S-G/W	1,192	77	$ 5,500	$2,400	$ 7,900
Columbia Junior College	Columbia, SC 29203	1935	Independ	J/C	515	36	$ 1,850	—	$ 1,850
Converse College	Spartanburg, SC 29301	1889	Independ	S-G/W	1,037	77	$ 5,000	$3,200	$ 8,200
Denmark Tech. College	Denmark, SC 29042	1948	State	T/C	684	40	$ 740	$2,080	$ 2,820
Erskine College	Due West, SC 29639	1839	Church	S/G	633	57	$ 5,540	$2,550	$ 8,090
Florence-Darl. Tech. College	Florence, SC 29501	1963	State	T/C	1,986	219	$ 800	—	$ 800
Francis Marion College	Florence, SC 29501	1970	State	S-G/C	3,232	109	$ 1,020	$2,375	$ 3,395
Furman University	Greenville, SC 29613	1826	Baptist	S-G/C	2,611	171	$ 5,984	$3,048	$ 9,032
Greenville Technical College	Greenville, SC 29606	1962	State	T/C	6,383	362	$ 620	—	$ 620
Holmes Col. of the Bible	Greenville, SC 29601	1898	Church	S/C	175	14	—	—	—
Horry-Georgetown Tech. Col.	Conway, SC 29526	1966	State	T/C	3,249	112	$ 175	—	$ 175
Lander College	Greenwood, SC 29646	1872	State	S-G/C	2,283	125	$ 1,270	$1,820	$ 3,090
Limestone College	Gaffney, SC 29340	1845	Independ	S/C	1,075	129	$ 5,000	$2,500	$ 7,500
Lutheran Theol. South. Sem.	Columbia, SC 29203	1830	Lutheran	P/C	170	18	$ 1,765	$2,365	$ 4,130
Medical Univ. of S. Carolina	Charleston, SC 29425	1824	State	P/C	2,131	702	$ 2,256	$2,500	$ 4,756
Midlands Technical College	Columbia, SC 29202	1974	State	T/C	4,980	350	$ 750	—	$ 750
Morris College	Sumter, SC 29150	1908	Baptist	S/C	584	49	$ 2,722	$1,784	$ 4,506
Newberry College	Newberry, SC 29108	1856	Lutheran	S/C	628	71	$ 5,000	$2,300	$ 7,300
Nielsen Electronics Institute	Charleston, SC 29405	1965	Independ	T/C	310	10	$ 1,701	$ 783	$ 2,484
North Greenville College	Tigerville, SC 29688	1892	Baptist	J/C	501	51	$ 3,200	$2,120	$ 5,320
Orangeburg-CalhounTech.Col.	Orangeburg, SC 29115	1968	State	T/C	1,314	117	$ 700	—	$ 700
Piedmont Technical College	Greenwood, SC 29646	1966	State	T/C	1,645	120	$ 555	—	$ 555
Presbyterian College	Clinton, SC 29325	1880	Presby	S/C	914	74	$ 5,588	$2,324	$ 7,930
Rutledge College	Charleston, SC 29406	1911	Independ	J/C	588	15	$ 2,544	—	$ 2,544
Rutledge College	Columbia, SC 29202	1911	Independ	J/C	430	16	$ 2,544	—	$ 2,544
Rutledge College	Spartanburg, SC 29303	1910	Independ	J/C	370	30	$ 1,908	—	$ 1,908
Sherman Col. of Strgt. Chiro.	Spartanburg, SC 29304	1973	Independ	P/C	346	28	$ 5,600	—	$ 5,600
South Carolina State College	Orangeburg, SC 29117	1896	State	S-G/C	4,226	224	$ 1,050	$1,998	$ 3,048
Southern Methodist College	Orangeburg, SC 29115	1956	Methodist	S/C	37	7	$ 1,470	$1,700	$ 3,170
Spartanburg Methodist College	Spartanburg, SC 29301	1911	Methodist	J/C	1,005	72	$ 3,200	$2,150	$ 5,350
Spartanburg Tech. College	Spartanburg, SC 29306	1962	State	T/C	1,894	149	$ 405	—	$ 405
Sumter Area Tech. College	Sumter, SC 29150	1963	State	T/C	1,624	152	$ 540	—	$ 540
Tri-County Tech. College	Pendleton, SC 29670	1962	State	T/C	2,162	83	$ 700	—	$ 700
Trident Tech. College	Charleston, SC 29411	1964	State	T/C	4,785	470	$ 700	—	$ 700
Univ. of South Carolina	Columbia, SC 29208	1801	State	S-G/C	23,053	1,247	$ 1,440	$2,300	$ 3,740
Aiken Campus	Aiken, SC 29801	1961	State	S/C	1,939	151	$ 1,000	—	$ 1,000
Beaufort Campus	Beaufort, SC 29902	1959	State	J/C	753	53	$ 920	—	$ 920
Coastal Carolina College	Conway, SC 29526	1959	State	S/C	2,627	154	$ 1,000	—	$ 1,000
Lancaster Campus	Lancaster, SC 29720	1959	State	J/C	847	65	$ 940	—	$ 940
Salkehatchie Campus	Allendale, SC 29810	1965	State	J/C	446	32	$ 920	—	$ 920
Spartanburg Campus	Spartanburg, SC 29303	1967	State	S/C	2,610	158	$ 1,000	—	$ 1,000
Sumter Campus	Sumter, SC 29150	1966	State	J/C	1,160	53	$ 920	—	$ 920
Union Campus	Union, SC 29379	1965	State	J/C	324	31	$ 920	—	$ 920
Voorhees College	Denmark, SC 29042	1897	Episcopal	S/C	550	31	$ 4,884	$2,142	$ 7,026
Williamsburg Tech.	Kingstree, SC 29556	1969	State	J/C	400	37	$ 500	—	$ 500
Winthrop College	Rock Hill, SC 29733	1886	State	S-G/C	5,055	321	$ 1,272	$1,697	$ 2,968
Wofford College	Spartanburg, SC 29301	1854	Methodist	S/C	1,056	78	$ 5,255	$2,745	$ 8,000
York Technical College	Rock Hill, SC 29730	1962	State	T/C	2,070	150	$ 360	—	$ 360

SOUTH DAKOTA

NAME	ADDRESS	FOUN-DED	AFFILI-ATION	LEVEL/TYPE	ENROLL-MENT	TEACH-ERS	TUITION & FEES	BOARD & ROOM	TOTAL COST
Augustana College	Sioux Falls, SD 57197	1860	Lutheran	S-G/C	1,914	174	$ 6,075	$1,075	$ 7,150
Black Hills State College	Spearfish, SD 57783	1883	State	S/C	2,280	96	$ 1,193	$1,665	$ 2,858
Dakota State College	Madison, SD 57042	1881	State	S/C	980	64	$ 1,280	$1,560	$ 2,840
Dakota Wesleyan University	Mitchell, SD 57301	1885	Methodist	S/C	571	51	$ 4,020	$2,100	$ 6,120
Freeman Junior College	Freeman, SD 57029	1900	Mennon	J/C	69	15	$ 3,375	$1,800	$ 5,175
Huron College	Huron, SD 57350	1883	Presby	S/C	370	20	$ 4,100	$1,200	$ 5,300
Lake Area Voc. Tech. Inst.	Watertown, SD 57201	1965	State	T/C	936	76	$ 1,230	$2,310	$ 3,540
Mount Marty College	Yankton, SD 57078	1936	Catholic	S-G/C	605	70	$ 4,020	$2,010	$ 6,030
National College	Rapid City, SD 57701	1941	Private	S/C	850	43	$ 4,598	$2,787	$ 7,385
Rapid City Division	Rapid City, SD 57709	1974	Private	S/C	99	12	$ 2,624	—	$ 2,624
'Sioux Falls Extension	Sioux Falls, SD 57101	1974	Private	S/C	237	25	$ 2,631	—	$ 2,631
North Amer. Baptist Seminary	Sioux Falls, SD 57105	1858	Baptist	G/C	291	13	$ 2,800	—	$ 2,800
Northern State College	Aberdeen, SD 57401	1901	State	S-G/C	2,718	118	$ 1,324	$1,474	$ 2,798
Presentation College	Aberdeen, SD 57401	1951	Catholic	J/C	356	28	$ 3,780	$1,600	$ 5,380
Sioux Falls College	Sioux Falls, SD 57105	1883	Baptist	S-G/C	872	67	$ 4,600	$2,296	$ 6,896
S. D. School of Mines & Tech.	Rapid City, SD 57701	1885	State	S-G/C	2,583	132	$ 1,373	$1,684	$ 3,057
South Dakota State University	Brookings, SD 57007	1881	State	S-G/C	6,940	318	$ 1,260	$1,500	$ 2,760
University of South Dakota	Vermillion, SD 57069	1881	State	S-G/C	5,758	403	$ 1,164	$1,662	$ 2,826

TENNESSEE

NAME	ADDRESS	FOUN-DED	AFFILI-ATION	LEVEL/TYPE	ENROLL-MENT	TEACH-ERS	TUITION & FEES	BOARD & ROOM	TOTAL COST
American Baptist College	Nashville, TN 37207	1924	Baptist	S/C	133	14	$ 1,525	$1,100	$ 2,625
Aquinas Junior College	Nashville, TN 37205	1961	Catholic	J/C	365	35	$ 2,150	—	$ 2,150
Austin Peay State University	Clarksville, TN 37040	1927	State	S-G/C	5,493	192	$ 945	$2,004	$ 2,949
Belmont College	Nashville, TN 37203	1951	Baptist	S/C	2,147	180	$ 3,100	$2,550	$ 5,650
Bethel College	McKenzie, TN 38201	1842	Presby	S/C	520	45	$ 2,850	$1,815	$ 4,665
Bristol College	Bristol, TN 37621	1895	Independ	S/C	625	35	$ 2,400	—	$ 2,400
Bryan College	Dayton, TN 37321	1930	Independ	S/C	506	51	$ 3,950	$2,880	$ 6,830
Carson-Newman College	Jefferson City, TN 37760	1851	Baptist	S/C	1,707	134	$ 4,050	$1,840	$ 5,990
Chatta. St. Tech. Comm. Col.	Chattanooga, TN 37406	1965	State	J/C	4,858	109	$ 518	—	$ 518
Christian Brothers College	Memphis, TN 38104	1871	Catholic	S/C	1,502	123	$ 4,400	$2,856	$ 7,256
Cleveland State Comm. College	Cleveland, TN 37311	1967	State	J/C	3,102	148	$ 516	—	$ 516
Columbia State Comm. College	Columbia, TN 38401	1966	State	J/C	2,948	116	$ 516	—	$ 516

NAME	ADDRESS	FOUNDED	AFFILIATION	LEVEL/TYPE	ENROLLMENT	TEACHERS	TUITION & FEES	BOARD & ROOM	TOTAL COST
TENNESSEE (continued)									
Covenant College	Lookout Mtn., TN 37350	1955	Presby	S/C	515	44	$ 4,800	$2,570	$ 7,370
Cumberland University	Lebanon, TN 37087	1842	Independ	S/C	624	63	$ 2,900	$2,150	$ 5,050
David Lipscomb College.....	Nashville, TN 37203 ...	1891	C of Chr	S-G/C	2,270	142	$ 2,832	$2,085	$ 5,067
East Tennessee State Univ...	Johnson City, TN 37614	1911	State	S-G/C	9,646	431	$ 880	$1,200	$ 2,080
Emmanuel School of Religion	Johnson City, TN 37601 .	1961	Christian	G/C	160	10	$ 2,490		$ 2,490
Fisk University	Nashville, TN 37203	1866	Independ	S-G/C	553	72	$ —	$ —	$ 6,400
Freed-Hardeman College	Henderson, TN 38340 ...	1869	C of Chr	S/C	1,131	84	$ 3,040	$2,260	$ 5,450
Free Will Baptist Bible College	Nashville, TN 37205	1942	Baptist	S-G/C	417	26	$ 1,900	$2,020	$ 4,010
Hiwassee College	Madisonville, TN 37354 .	1849	Methodist	J/C	508	34	$ 2,310	$2,190	$ 4,500
Jackson State Comm. College	Jackson, TN 38301	1967	State	J/C	2,732	72	$ 516	—	$ 516
John A. Gupton College	Nashville, TN 37203	1946	Independ	J/C	43	13	—	—	$ 2,530
Johnson Bible College	Knoxville, TN 37920	1893	Christian	S/C	374	24	$ 2,000	$2,040	$ 4,040
King College	Bristol, TN 37620	1867	Presby	S/C	544	52	$ 3,890	$2,640	$ 6,530
Knoxville College	Knoxville, TN 37921	1875	Presby	S/C	560	32	$ 3,317	$2,034	$ 5,451
Lambuth College	Jackson, TN 38301	1843	Methodist	S/C	647	72	$ 3,890	$2,070	$ 5,960
Lane College	Jackson, TN 38301	1882	CME	S/C	691	44	$ 2,899	$1,810	$ 4,709
Lee College	Cleveland, TN 37311	1918	C of God	S/C	1,128	70	$ 2,400	$1,700	$ 4,100
LeMoyne-Owen College	Memphis, TN 38126	1870	UC of Chr	S/C	960	65	$ 3,000	—	$ 4,500
Lincoln Memorial University .	Harrogate, TN 37752 ...	1897	Private	S-G/C	1,425	101	$ 2,700	$2,000	$ 4,700
Martin College	Pulaski, TN 38478	1870	Methodist	J/C	290	22	$ 2,850	$2,125	$ 4,975
Maryville College	Maryville, TN 37801	1819	Presby	S/C	594	52	$ 4,685	$2,548	$ 7,233
Meharry Medical College ...	Nashville, TN 37208	1876	Independ	P/C	715	265	$11,000	$5,500	$16,500
Memphis Academy of Arts ..	Memphis, TN 38112	1936	Independ	S/C	207	26	$ 4,600	$3,045	$ 7,645
Memphis State University ...	Memphis, TN 38152	1912	State	S-G/C	21,295	1,171	$ 956	$1,950	$ 2,906
Middle Tenn. State University	Murfreesboro, TN 37132 .	1911	State	S-G/C	11,228	670	$ 846	$1,799	$ 2,645
Milligan College	Milligan Col., TN 37682 .	1866	Christian	S/C	628	67	$ 3,600	$2,400	$ 6,000
Morristown College	Morristown, TN 37814 ..	1881	Methodist	J/C	178	12	$ 2,150	$3,110	$ 4,260
Motlow State Community Col.	Tullahoma, TN 37388 ...	1969	State	J/C	2,427	137	$ 518	—	$ 518
Nashville State Tech. Institute	Nashville, TN 37209	1970	State	T/C	5,075	209	$ 564	—	$ 564
Rhodes College	Memphis, TN 38112	1848	Presby	S/C	1,024	109	$ 6,990	$3,130	$10,120
Scarritt Graduate School	Nashville, TN 37203	1892	Methodist	G/C	98	10	$ 4,940	$2,780	$ 7,720
Southern College	Collegedale, TN 37315 ..	1892	7-D Adv	S/C	1,622	110	$ 4,840	$2,260	$ 7,100
Southern Col. of Optometry .	Memphis, TN 38104	1932	Independ	P/C	426	44	$ 6,864	—	$ 6,864
State Tech. Inst. at Memphis.	Memphis, TN 38134	1967	State	T/C	6,780	422	$ 688	—	$ 688
Tennessee State University ..	Nashville, TN 37203	1912	State	S-G/C	7,651	364	$ 954	$1,878	$ 2,832
Tennessee Tech. University ..	Cookeville, TN 38501 ...	1915	State	S-G/C	7,494	400	$ 960	$2,095	$ 3,055
Tennessee Temple University	Chattanooga, TN 37404 .	1946	Baptist	S-G/C	2,354	125	$ 2,590	$2,425	$ 5,015
Tennessee Wesleyan College.	Athens, TN 37303	1857	Methodist	S/C	434	28	$ 3,624	$2,610	$ 6,234
Tomlinson College	Cleveland, TN 37311.....	1966	CofG Proph	J/C	247	27	$ 2,510	$2,290	$ 4,800
Trevecca Nazarene College ..	Nashville, TN 37203	1901	Nazarene	S/C	921	73	$ 3,330	$2,130	$ 5,460
Tusculum College	Greeneville, TN 37743 ..	1794	Presby	S/C	391	39	$ 3,900	$2,684	$ 6,584
Union University	Jackson, TN 38301	1825	Baptist	S/C	1,458	98	$ 2,890	$1,870	$ 4,760
University of Tennessee	Knoxville, TN 37996								
Center for the Health Sci. .	Memphis, TN 38163	1850	State	P/C	1,883	650	$ 1,976	$1,000	$ 2,976
Chattanooga Campus	Chattanooga, TN 37402 .	1886	State	S-G/C	7,474	260	$ 1,320	$2,286	$ 3,606
Knoxville Campus	Knoxville, TN 37996	1794	State	S-G/C	26,158	1,245	$ 1,108	$1,925	$ 3,033
Martin Campus	Martin, TN 38238	1927	State	S-G/C	5,366	250	$ 1,264	$1,900	$ 3,164
University of the South	Sewanee, TN 37375	1857	Episcopal	S-G/C	1,158	120	$ 8,445	$2,200	$10,645
Vanderbilt University	Nashville, TN 37240	1875	Independ	S-G/C	9,035	1,071	$ 8,200	$3,600	$11,800
Walters State Comm. College	Morristown, TN 37814 ..	1970	State	J/C	4,023	77	$ 636	—	$ 636
TEXAS									
Abilene Christian University .	Abilene, TX 79799	1906	C of Chr	S-G/C	4,617	235	$ 3,450	$2,150	$ 5,600
Alvin Community College....	Alvin, TX 77511	1949	State	J/C	3,937	193	$ 200	—	$ 200
Amarillo College	Amarillo, TX 79178	1929	State	J/C	6,151	314	$ 240	—	$ 240
Amber University	Garland, TX 75041	1971	Independ	S-G/C	1,000	40	$ 2,000	—	$ 2,000
American Technological Univ.	Killeen, TX 76540	1973	Independ	S-G/C	492	26	$ 2,600	$4,178	$ 6,856
Angelina College	Lufkin, TX 75902	1966	State	J/C	2,471	144	$ 260	$1,864	$ 2,124
Angelo State University	San Angelo, TX 76909 ..	1928	State	S-G/C	6,183	200	$ 510	$2,912	$ 3,422
Arlington Baptist College	Arlington, TX 76012	1939	Baptist	S/C	247	20	$ 1,200	$1,800	$ 3,000
Austin College	Sherman, TX 75090	1849	Presby	S/C	1,174	95	$ 5,540	$2,700	$ 8,240
Austin Community College ...	Austin, TX 78768	1972	State	J/C	17,807	727	$ 447	—	$ 447
Austin Presbyterian Theo. Sem.	Austin, TX 78705	1902	Presby	G/C	198	15	$ 3,615	$2,250	$ 5,865
Bauder Fashion College	Arlington, TX 76010	1967	Independ	T/C	510	35	$ 4,510	$3,080	$ 7,590
Baylor College of Dentistry ..	Dallas, TX 75246	1905	Independ	P/C	607	223	$ 800	—	$ 800
Baylor College of Medicine ..	Houston, TX 77030	1903	Independ	P/C	899	1,250	$ 1,077	—	$ 1,077
Baylor University	Waco, TX 76798........	1845	Baptist	S-G/C	10,990	596	$ 3,672	$2,694	$ 6,366
Bee County College	Beeville, TX 78102......	1965	Public	J/C	2,240	121	$ 304	$2,080	$ 2,384
Bishop College	Dallas, TX 75241	1881	Baptist	S/C	1,107	70	$ 3,000	$2,220	$ 5,220
Blinn College	Brenham, TX 77833	1883	Independ	J/C	3,588	144	$ 466	$1,800	$ 2,266
Brazosport College	Lake Jackson, TX 77566	1968	State	J/C	3,609	106	$ 150	—	$ 150
Central Texas College	West Killeen, TX 76542 .	1967	State	J/C	5,973	223	$ 250	$2,300	$ 2,550
Cisco Junior College	Cisco, TX 76437........	1909	State	J/C	1,747	62	$ 310	$1,550	$ 1,860
Clarendon College	Clarendon, TX 79226 ...	1898	Public	J/C	1,058	29	$ 98	$1,300	$ 1,398
College of the Mainland	Texas City, TX 77591 ...	1967	State	J/C	3,008	62	$ 108	—	$ 108
Commonwealth Col. of Fun. Serv.	Houston, TX 77006	1936	Independ	T/C	100	4	$ 3,200	—	$ 3,200
Concordia Lutheran College .	Austin, TX 78705.......	1926	Lutheran	S/C	463	42	$ 2,900	$2,600	$ 5,500
Cooke County College	Gainesville, TX 76240 ..	1924	Public	J/C	1,750	63	$ 324	$2,016	$ 2,340
Corpus Christi State Univ. ...	Corpus Christi, TX 78413	1973	State	S-G/C	3,710	146	$ 328	—	$ 328
Dallas Baptist College........	Dallas, TX 75211	1898	Baptist	S-G/C	1,551	66	$ 3,190	$2,290	$ 5,480
Dallas Christian College	Dallas, TX 75234	1950	Christian	S/C	125	18	$ 1,764	$1,880	$ 3,564
Dallas Theological Seminary .	Dallas, TX 75204	1924	Independ	G/C	1,471	66	$ 3,410	$2,200	$ 5,610

NAME	ADDRESS	FOUN-DED	AFFILI-ATION	LEVEL/TYPE	ENROLL-MENT	TEACH-ERS	TUITION & FEES	BOARD & ROOM	TOTAL COST
TEXAS *(continued)*									
Del Mar College	Corpus Christi, TX 78404	1935	State	J/C	9,574	550	$ 280	—	$ 280
Devry Inst. of Technology	Irving, TX 75062	1967	Independ	S/C	1,996	86	$ 3,658	—	$ 3,658
East Texas Baptist College	Marshall, TX 75670	1912	Baptist	S/C	718	59	$ 2,600	$2,270	$ 4,870
East Texas State University	Commerce, TX 75428	1889	State	S-G/C	7,135	315	$ 500	$2,200	$ 2,700
Texarkana	Texarkana, TX 75501	1972	State	S-G/C	1,254	36	$ 260	—	$ 260
Eastfield College	Mesquite, TX 75150	1970	Public	J/C	8,594	320	$ 200	—	$ 200
El Centro College	Dallas, TX 75202	1966	State	J/C	5,500	187	$ 250	—	$ 250
El Paso Comm. College Dist.	El Paso, TX 79998	1969	State	T/C	13,930	837	$ 273	—	$ 273
Episc. Theol. Sem. of the S.W.	Austin, TX 78768	1951	Episcopal	G/C	86	15	$ 3,600	—	$ 3,600
Frank Phillips College	Borger, TX 79007	1948	State	J/C	931	26	$ 382	$1,190	$ 1,572
Galveston College	Galveston, TX 77550	1967	State	J/C	1,649	99	$ 150	—	$ 150
Grayson County College	Denison, TX 75020	1965	State	J/C	5,045	204	$ 240	$1,820	$ 2,060
Gulf-Coast Bible College	Houston, TX 77270	1953	Ch of God	S/C	299	24	$ 3,380	$ 970	$ 4,350
Hardin-Simmons University	Abilene, TX 79698	1891	Baptist	S-G/C	1,834	120	$ 3,426	$2,250	$ 5,676
Henderson County Jr. College	Athens, TX 75751	1946	State	J/C	4,229	176	$ 230	$1,600	$ 1,830
Hill Junior College	Hillsboro, TX 76645	1962	State	J/C	1,500	45	$ 600	$2,400	$ 3,000
Houston Baptist University	Houston, TX 77074	1960	Baptist	S-G/C	2,962	130	$ 3,795	$2,163	$ 5,958
Houston Comm. Col. System	Houston, TX 77270	1971	State	J/C	40,122	1,301	$ 440	—	$ 440
Howard Co. Jr. College Dist.	Big Spring, TX 79720								
Howard College	Big Spring, TX 79720	1945	State	J/C	1,144	99	$ 250	$1,825	$ 2,075
Southw. Col. Inst. for the Deaf	Big Spring, TX 79720	1979	State	J/C	113	25	$ 250	$1,825	$ 2,075
Howard Payne University	Brownwood, TX 76801	1889	Baptist	S/C	1,134	76	$ 2,450	$2,146	$ 4,596
Huston-Tillotson College	Austin, TX 78702	1876	UC Chr	S/C	569	46	$ 3,000	$2,300	$ 5,400
Incarnate Word College	San Antonio, TX 78209	1881	Catholic	S-G/C	1,350	128	$ 8,520	$4,168	$12,688
Jacksonville College	Jacksonville, TX 75766	1899	Baptist	J/C	240	25	$ 2,000	$2,000	$ 4,000
Jarvis Christian College	Hawkins, TX 75765	1912	Christian	S/C	533	46	$ 3,400	$1,919	$ 5,319
Kilgore College	Kilgore, TX 75662	1935	State	J/C	4,469	150	$ 360	$1,700	$ 2,060
Lamar University	Beaumont, TX 77710	1923	State	S-G/C	15,835	262	$ 490	$2,074	$ 2,564
Orange Campus	Orange, TX 77630	1969	State	S/C	1,065	55	$ 550	—	$ 550
Laredo Junior College	Laredo, TX 78040	1946	Public	J/C	4,038	120	$ 307	—	$ 307
Laredo State University	Laredo, TX 78040	1970	State	S-G/C	928	57	$ 407	—	$ 407
Lee College	Baytown, TX 77520	1934	State	J/C	6,211	188	$ 250	—	$ 250
LeTourneau College	Longview, TX 75607	1946	Independ	S/C	906	60	$ 4,646	$2,590	$ 7,236
Lon Morris College	Jacksonville, TX 75766	1854	Methodist	J/C	340	24	$ 2,700	$2,500	$ 5,200
Lubbock Christian College	Lubbock, TX 79407	1957	C of Chr	S/C	997	96	$ 3,386	$2,044	$ 5,430
McLennan Community College	Waco, TX 76708	1965	State	J/C	4,733	225	$ 240	—	$ 240
McMurry College	Abilene, TX 79697	1923	Methodist	S/C	1,482	126	$ 3,330	$2,160	$ 5,490
Midland College	Midland, TX 79705	1969	State	J/C	3,504	194	$ 260	—	$ 260
Midwestern State University	Wichita Falls, TX 76308	1922	State	S-G/C	4,907	151	$ 465	$1,750	$ 2,215
Mountain View College	Dallas, TX 75211	1970	State	J/C	5,295	205	$ 250	—	$ 250
Navarro College	Corsicana, TX 75110	1946	State	J/C	2,359	118	$ 280	$1,012	$ 1,292
North Harris County College	Houston, TX 77060	1972	State	J/C	11,000	460	$ 160	—	$ 160
North Texas State University	Denton, TX 76203	1890	State	S-G/C	21,414	745	$ 1,008	$2,774	$ 3,782
Northwood Institute of Texas	Cedar Hill, TX 75104	1959	Independ	J/C	200	17	$ 4,300	$2,500	$ 6,800
Oblate Sch. of Theology	San Antonio, TX 78216	1903	Catholic	G/C	174	20	$ 3,748	—	$ 3,748
Odessa College	Odessa, TX 79764	1946	State	J/C	4,986	138	$ 388	$2,600	$ 2,988
Our Lady of the Lake Univ.	San Antonio, TX 78285	1911	Catholic	S-G/C	1,648	98	$ 3,960	$2,300	$ 6,260
Pan American University	Edinburg, TX 78539	1927	State	S-G/C	8,473	311	$ 316	$2,080	$ 2,440
Brownsville Campus	Brownsville, TX 78520	1973	State	S-G/C	1,206	87	$ 316	—	$ 316
Panola Junior College	Carthage, TX 75633	1947	State	J/C	1,370	48	$ 228	$1,750	$ 1,978
Paris Junior College	Paris, TX 75460	1924	Local	J/C	2,199	82	$ 308	$1,071	$ 1,379
Paul Quinn University	Waco, TX 76704	1872	AME	S/C	355	40	$ 2,429	$2,550	$ 5,098
Prairie View A&M University	Prairie View, TX 77445	1876	State	P/C	4,436	286	$ 480	$2,610	$ 3,090
Ranger Junior College	Ranger, TX 76470	1926	State	J/C	850	26	$ 350	$1,950	$ 2,300
Rice University	Houston, TX 77251	1891	Independ	S-G/C	3,851	441	$ 4,325	$3,650	$ 7,975
Richland College	Dallas, TX 75243	1972	State	J/C	14,000	308	$ 240	—	$ 240
St. Edward's University	Austin, TX 78704	1885	Catholic	S-G/C	2,355	121	$ 4,146	$3,678	$ 7,824
St. Mary's Univ. of San Antonio	San Antonio, TX 78284	1852	Catholic	S-G/C	3,296	193	$ 4,695	$2,390	$ 7,085
St. Philip's College	San Antonio, TX 78203	1898	District	J/C	6,702	439	$ 256	—	$ 256
Sam Houston State University	Huntsville, TX 77341	1879	State	S-G/C	10,472	428	$ 520	$2,390	$ 2,910
San Antonio College	San Antonio, TX 78247	1925	State	J/C	23,559	522	$ 200	—	$ 200
San Jacinto College, Central	Pasadena, TX 77505	1961	State	J/C	13,155	426	$ 206	—	$ 206
San Jacinto College, North	Houston, TX 77049	1974	State	J/C	3,578	75	$ 206	—	$ 206
Schreiner College	Kerrville, TX 78028	1923	Presby	S/C	489	48	$ 4,060	$2,800	$ 6,860
South Plains College	Levelland, TX 79336	1957	State	J/C	3,677	130	$ 300	$1,800	$ 2,100
South Texas College of Law	Houston, TX 77002	1923	Private	P/C	1,186	58	$ 4,198	—	$ 4,198
Southern Methodist Univ.	Dallas, TX 75275	1911	Methodist	S-G/C	9,265	570	$ 6,880	$3,670	$10,550
Southwestern Adventist Col.	Keene, TX 76059	1893	7-D Adv	S/C	683	41	$ 5,120	$2,666	$ 7,786
Southw. Assembly of God Col.	Waxahachie, TX 75165	1927	A of God	S/C	579	27	$ 1,987	$2,478	$ 4,465
Southw. Baptist Theol. Sem.	Fort Worth, TX 76122	1908	Baptist	G/C	4,296	190	$ 700	$2,500	$ 3,200
Southwest Christian College	Terrell, TX 75160	1949	C of Chr	S/C	282	18	$ 2,302	$1,506	$ 3,808
Southwest Texas Junior Col.	Uvalde, TX 78801	1946	State	J/C	2,483	131	$ 306	$1,800	$ 2,106
Southwest Texas State Univ.	San Marcos, TX 78666	1899	State	S-G/C	19,202	747	$ 442	$2,129	$ 2,571
Southwestern University	Georgetown, TX 78626	1840	Methodist	S/C	1,001	89	$ 5,500	$3,322	$ 8,822
Stephen F. Austin State Univ.	Nacogdoches, TX 75962	1923	State	S-G/C	12,668	639	$ 500	$2,500	$ 3,000
Sul Ross State University	Alpine, TX 79832	1917	State	S-G/C	1,708	73	$ 480	$2,000	$ 2,480
Uvalde Study Center	Uvalde, TX 78801	1973	State	S/C	484	35	$ 480	—	$ 480
Tarleton State University	Stephenville, TX 76402	1899	State	S-G/C	4,624	150	$ 480	$2,193	$ 2,673
Tarrant County Junior College	Fort Worth, TX 76102	1965	State	J/C					
Northeast Campus	Hurst, TX 76039	1965	State	J/C	11,010	443	$ 120	—	$ 120
Northwest Campus	Fort Worth, TX 76179	1965	State	J/C	4,753	186	$ 120	—	$ 120
South Campus	Fort Worth, TX 76102	1965	State	J/C	10,606	367	$ 120	—	$ 120
Temple Junior College	Temple, TX 76501	1926	State	J/C	2,507	117	$ 268	$3,083	$ 3,351
Texarkana Community College	Texarkana, TX 75501	1927	State	J/C	4,061	121	$ 115	—	$ 115

NAME	ADDRESS	FOUNDED	AFFILIATION	LEVEL/TYPE	ENROLLMENT	TEACHERS	TUITION & FEES	BOARD & ROOM	TOTAL COST
TEXAS *(continued)*									
Texas A&I University	Kingsville, TX 78363	1917	State	S-G/C	5,507	219	$ 480	$2,220	$ 2,700
Texas A&M University	College Station, TX 77843	1876	State	S-G/C	36,827	2,218	$ 480	$3,380	$ 3,860
Galveston Campus	Galveston, TX 77553	1971	State	S/C	586	71	$ 369	$2,810	$ 3,179
Texas Chiropractic College	Pasadena, TX 77505	1908	Independ	P/C	36,127	2,093	$ 452	$2,433	$ 2,885
Texas Christian University	Fort Worth, TX 76129	1873	Christian	S-G/C	6,747	385	$ 5,010	$1,962	$ 6,972
Texas College	Tyler, TX 75702	1894	CME	S/C	573	45	$ 2,415	$1,982	$ 4,397
Texas College of Osteo. Med.	Fort Worth, TX 76107	1966	State	P/C	395	150	$ 626	—	$12,207
Texas Lutheran College	Seguin, TX 78155	1891	Lutheran	S/C	1,014	73	$ 3,600	$2,100	$ 5,700
Texas Southern University	Houston, TX 77004	1947	State	S-G/C	8,914	457	$ 520	$2,250	$ 2,770
Texas Southmost College	Brownsville, TX 78520	1926	State	J/C	5,700	128	$ 400	$1,100	$ 1,856
Texas State Tech. Institute	Waco, TX 76705	1965	State	T/C					
Amarillo Campus	Amarillo, TX 79111	1970	State	T/C	1,118	89	$ 382	$2,220	$ 2,602
Harlingen Campus	Harlingen, TX 78850	1969	State	T/C	2,359	151	$ 386	$2,860	$ 3,246
Sweetwater Campus	Sweetwater, TX 79556	1970	State	T/C	591	54	$ 382	$2,860	$ 3,242
Waco Campus	Waco, TX 76705	1965	State	T/C	4,561	342	$ 492	$2,790	$ 3,232
Texas Tech. University	Lubbock, TX 79409	1924	State	S-G/C	23,500	994	$ 500	$2,500	$ 3,000
Texas Tech. University Health Science Center	Lubbock, TX 79430	1969	State	P/C	1,054	280	$ 480	—	$ 480
Texas Wesleyan College	Fort Worth, TX 76105	1891	Methodist	S/C	1,310	79	$ 3,650	$2,600	$ 6,250
Texas Woman's University	Denton, TX 76204	1901	State	S-G/W	8,259	380	$ 404	$2,283	$ 2,687
Trinity University	San Antonio, TX 78284	1869	Independ	S-G/C	2,925	229	$ 6,240	$3,125	$ 9,365
Tyler Junior College	Tyler, TX 75701	1926	State	J/C	6,988	353	$ 130	$1,736	$ 1,836
University of Dallas	Irving, TX 75061	1956	Catholic	S-G/C	2,466	166	$ 4,950	$2,850	$ 7,800
Univ. of Houston Central Camp.	Houston, TX 77004	1927	State	S-G/C	31,114	1,871	$ 400	$3,000	$ 3,400
Clear Lake Campus	Houston, TX 77058	1974	State	S-G/C	6,500	310	—	—	—
Downtown Campus	Houston, TX 77002	1974	State	S/C	7,339	301	$ 610	$2,680	$ 3,160
Victoria Campus	Victoria, TX 77901	1973	State	S-G/C	927	59	$ 464	—	$ 464
Univ. of Mary Hardin-Baylor	Belton, TX 76513	1845	Baptist	S-G/C	1,176	69	$ 3,040	$2,080	$ 5,120
University of St. Thomas	Houston, TX 77006	1947	Catholic	S-G/C	1,983	190	$ 3,500	$2,990	$ 6,490
Univ. of Texas at Arlington	Arlington, TX 76019	1895	State	S-G/C	23,397	1,363	$ 514	—	$ 514
Univ. of Texas at Austin	Austin, TX 78712	1883	State	S-G/C	47,973	2,278	$ 475	$2,989	$ 3,464
Univ. of Texas at Dallas	Richardson, TX 75083	1969	State	S-G/C	7,442	428	$ 454	—	$ 454
Univ. of Texas at El Paso	El Paso, TX 79968	1913	State	S-G/C	15,322	640	$ 424	$2,600	$ 3,024
Univ. of Texas at San Antonio	San Antonio, TX 78285	1969	State	S-G/C	12,612	482	$ 420	—	$ 420
Univ. of Texas at Tyler	Tyler, TX 75701	1971	State	S-G/C	3,456	212	$ 500	—	$ 500
Univ. of Tex. Health Sci. Center	Dallas, TX 75235	1943	State	S-G/C	1,368	646	$ 300	—	$ 300
Univ. of Tex. Health Sci. Center	Houston, TX 77225	1972	State	S-G/C	2,972	—	$ 1,600	$6,600	$ 8,200
Univ. of Tex. Health Sci. Center	San Antonio, TX 78284	1959	State	P/C	2,332	709	$ 480	—	$ 480
Univ. of Texas Med. Branch	Galveston, TX 77550	1891	State	P/C	1,729	873	$ 569	—	$ 9,764
Univ. of Texas of Permian Bas.	Odessa, TX 79762	1969	State	S-G/C	2,003	105	$ 348	—	$ 348
Vernon Regional Jr. College	Vernon, TX 76384	1970	State	J/C	1,863	57	$ 300	$ 740	$ 1,040
Victoria College	Victoria, TX 77901	1925	State	J/C	2,828	125	$ 150	—	$ 150
Wayland Baptist College	Plainview, TX 79072	1906	Baptist	S-G/C	1,809	148	$ 2,100	$2,184	$ 4,284
Weatherford College	Weatherford, TX 76086	1869	State	J/C	1,876	—	$ 400	$2,000	$ 2,400
West Texas State University	Canyon, TX 79016	1910	State	S-G/C	6,474	360	$ 475	$2,300	$ 2,775
Western Texas College	Snyder, TX 79549	1969	Public	J/C	1,319	42	$ 350	$1,550	$ 1,900
Wharton County Junior College	Wharton, TX 77488	1946	Public	J/C	2,535	140	$ 300	$1,380	$ 1,680
Wiley College	Marshall, TX 75670	1873	Methodist	S/C	540	50	$ 2,430	$1,754	$ 4,184
Woodcrest	Lindale, TX 75771	1940	Independ	S/C	216	20	$ 3,060	$2,280	$ 5,340
UTAH									
Brigham Young University	Provo, UT 84602	1875	Mormon	S-G/C	26,700	1,300	$ 1,480	$2,200	$ 3,680
College of Eastern Utah	Price, UT 84501	1938	State	J/C	1,215	48	$ 700	$1,800	$ 2,500
Dixie College	St. George, UT 84770	1911	State	J/C	1,930	85	$ 717	$1,600	$ 2,317
Snow College	Ephraim, UT 84627	1888	Independ	J/C	1,318	66	$ 723	$1,850	$ 2,573
Southern Utah State College	Cedar City, UT 84720	1897	State	S-G/C	2,642	146	$ 852	$ 770	$ 2,622
Stevens Henager College	Ogden, UT 84401	1891	Independ	J/C	397	20	$ 2,347	—	$ 2,347
Provo	Provo, UT 84001	1891	Independ	J/C	369	29	$ 2,820	$ 330	$ 3,150
University of Utah	Salt Lake City, UT 84112	1850	State	S-G/C	24,172	1,422	$ 1,085	$2,967	$ 4,052
Utah State University	Logan, UT 84322	1888	State	S-G/C	11,544	720	$ 1,092	$2,300	$ 3,392
Utah Technical Col. at Provo	Provo, UT 84603	1941	State	T/C	6,000	230	$ 747	—	$ 747
Utah Tech. Col. at Salt Lake	Salt Lake City, UT 84131	1948	Independ	T/C	8,288	532	$ 732	—	$ 732
Weber State College	Ogden, UT 84408	1889	State	S/C	10,116	593	$ 874	$2,457	$ 3,331
Westminster College	Salt Lake City, UT 84105	1875	Independ	S-G/C	1,234	82	$ 4,550	$3,220	$ 7,770
VERMONT									
Bennington College	Bennington, VT 05201	1925	Independ	S-G/C	584	73	$12,830	$2,980	$15,810
Burlington College	Burlington, VT 05401	1972	Independ	S/C	166	35	$ 4,350	—	$ 4,350
Castleton State College	Castleton, VT 05735	1787	State	S-G/C	2,043	136	$ 1,974	$2,896	$ 4,870
Champlain College	Burlington, VT 05402	1878	Independ	J/C	1,832	104	$ 4,435	$3,360	$ 7,795
Col. of St. Joseph the Provider	Rutland, VT 05701	1954	Independ	S/C	367	45	$ 4,442	$2,741	$ 7,160
Community Col. of Vermont	Montpelier, VT 05602	1970	State	J/C	2,344	346	$ 1,000	—	$ 1,000
Ethan Allen Community Col.	Manchester Ctr., VT 05255	1973	Independ	J/C	100	18	$ 1,510	—	$ 1,510
Goddard College	Plainfield, VT 05667	1938	Independ	S-G/C	251	20	$ 6,700	$2,400	$ 9,100
Green Mountain College	Poultney, VT 05764	1834	Independ	S/C	358	38	$ 5,741	$3,278	$ 9,019
Johnson State College	Johnson, VT 05656	1828	State	S-G/C	1,128	80	$ 1,984	$2,896	$ 4,880
Lyndon State College	Lyndonville, VT 05851	1911	State	S-G/C	1,014	85	$ 2,015	$2,896	$ 4,911
Marlboro College	Marlboro, VT 05344	1946	Independ	S-G/C	182	37	$ 8,750	$3,355	$12,360
Middlebury College	Middlebury, VT 05753	1800	Independ	S-G/C	1,900	189			$12,600
Norwich University									
Military Col. of Vermont	Northfield, VT 05663	1819	Independ	S-G/C	1,400	161	—	—	$10,250
Vermont Campus	Montpelier, VT 05602	1834	Independ	S-G/C	400	58	—	—	$10,150
St. Michael's College	Winooski, VT 05404	1903	Catholic	S-G/C	1,925	143	$ 7,500	$2,800	$10,300
School for Int. Training	Brattleboro, VT 05301	1964	Independ	S-G/C	400	28	$ 6,500	$2,300	$10,000

NAME	ADDRESS	FOUN-DED	AFFILI-ATION	LEVEL/TYPE	ENROLL-MENT	TEACH-ERS	TUITION & FEES	BOARD & ROOM	TOTAL COST
VERMONT *(continued)*									
Southern Vermont College	Bennington, VT 05201 ..	1924	Independ	S/C	482	43	$ 1,150	$2,320	$ 3,470
Trinity College	Burlington, VT 05401 ...	1925	Catholic	S/W	950	70	$ 5,590	$3,050	$ 8,640
University of Vermont...	Burlington, VT 05405 ..	1791	State	S-G/C	10,908	774	$ 2,783	$2,902	$ 5,685
Vermont Law School	South Royalton, VT 05068	1972	Independ	G/C	375	34	$ 6,250	—	$ 6,250
Vermont Technical College	Randolph Ctr., VT 05061	1957	State	T/C	755	59	$ 2,380	$2,950	$ 5,330
VIRGINIA									
Apprentice School	Newport News, VA 23607	1919	Independ	T/C	900	17	$ 91	—	$ 91
Averett College	Danville, VA 24541	1859	Baptist	S-G/C	1,000	65	$ 4,125	$2,800	$ 6,925
Bluefield College	Bluefield, VA 24605	1922	Baptist	S/C	406	42	$ 2,800	$2,380	$ 5,180
Bridgewater College	Bridgewater, VA 22812 .	1880	Church	S/C	803	68	$ 5,370	$2,880	$ 8,250
CBN University	Virginia Beach, VA 23463	1977	Independ	G/C	510	36	$ 4,000	—	$ 4,000
Christendom Col.	Front Royal, VA 22630 ..	1977	Catholic	S/C	128	15	$ 5,320	$2,600	$ 7,920
Christopher Newport College	Newport News, VA 23606	1960	State	S/C	4,268	110	$ 1,545	—	$ 1,545
College of William and Mary	Williamsburg, VA 23185.	1693	State	S-G/C	6,640	504	$ 2,000	$2,993	$ 4,993
Richard Bland College	Petersburg, VA 23805 ..	1960	State	J/C	978	45	$ 1,000	—	$ 1,000
Eastern Mennonite College	Harrisonburg, VA 22801	1917	Mennon	S/C	848	74	$ 5,250	$2,328	$ 7,578
Eastern Mennonite Seminary	Harrisonburg, VA 22801	1948	Mennon	G/C	89	19	$ 2,198	$2,328	$ 4,526
Eastern Virginia Medical Sch.	Norfolk, VA 23501......	1973	Independ	P/C	355	167	$10,520	$7,800	$18,320
Emory & Henry College .	Emory, VA 24327........	1836	Methodist	S/C	768	60	$ 4,551	$2,400	$ 6,951
Ferrum College	Ferrum, VA 24088	1913	Methodist	J-S/C	1,578	80	$ 4,750	$2,200	$ 6,950
George Mason University	Fairfax, VA 22030	1957	State	S-G/C	15,548	808	$ 1,608	$3,562	$ 5,170
Hampden-Sydney College	Hampden-Sdny, VA 23943	1776	Presby	S/M	750	64	$ 7,620	$2,380	$10,000
Hampton Institute	Hampton, VA 23668	1868	Independ	S-G/C	4,260	291	$ 4,020	$1,880	$ 5,900
Hollins College	Hollins Col., VA 24020 ..	1842	Independ	S/W	986	91	$ 7,800	$3,400	$11,200
Institute of Textile Tech.	Charlottesville, VA 22902	1944	Independ	G/C	16	21	—	—	—
James Madison University	Harrisonburg, VA 22807	1908	State	S-G/C	9,320	542	$ 2,006	$2,496	$ 4,502
Liberty Baptist College ..	Lynchburg, VA 24505 ...	1971	Baptist	S-G/C	4,566	184	$ 2,800	$2,800	$ 5,600
Longwood College	Farmville, VA 23901	1839	Public	S-G/C	2,719	155	$ 2,058	$2,325	$ 4,383
Lynchburg College	Lynchburg, VA 24501....	1903	D of Chr	S/C	2,150	157	$ 6,250	$3,200	$ 9,450
Mary Baldwin College ...	Staunton, VA 24401	1842	Presby	S/W	853	83	$ 6,000	$4,450	$10,450
Mary Washington College	Fredericksburg, VA 22401	1908	State	S-G/C	3,034	149	$ 1,578	$2,742	$ 4,320
Marymount Col. of Virginia	Arlington, VA 22207	1950	Catholic	S/C	2,070	150	$ 5,550	$3,360	$ 8,910
National Grad. University	Arlington, VA 22201	1967	Private	G/C	12	5	$ 3,850	—	$ 3,850
Norfolk State University .	Norfolk, VA 23504......	1935	State	S-G/C	7,400	398	$ 1,435	$1,648	$ 3,082
Old Dominion University	Norfolk, VA 23508......	1930	State	S-G/C	14,590	583	$ 1,464	$2,990	$ 4,454
Presby. Sch. of Christian Ed.	Richmond, VA 23227 ...	1914	Presby	G/C	138	17	$ 3,000	$2,231	$ 5,231
Protestant Episc. Theol. Sem.	Alexandria, VA 22304 ..	1823	Episcopal	G/C	218	18	$ 3,600	$2,560	$ 6,160
Radford University	Radford, VA 24142	1910	State	S-G/C	6,802	320	$ 1,675	$2,936	$ 4,611
Randolph-Macon College	Ashland, VA 23005	1830	Methodist	S/C	965	95	$ 6,500	$3,000	$ 9,500
Randolph-Macon Woman's Col.	Lynchburg, VA 24503 ...	1891	Methodist	S/W	777	90	$ 7,600	$3,500	$11,100
Roanoke College	Salem, VA 24153	1842	Lutheran	S/C	1,462	71	$ 6,500	$2,750	$ 9,250
St. Paul's College	Lawrenceville, VA 23868	1888	Episcopal	S/C	701	52	$ 3,190	$2,475	$ 5,725
Shenandoah C. & Cons. Music	Winchester, VA 22601 ..	1875	Methodist	S-G/C	932	125	$ 6,000	$2,800	$ 8,800
Southern Seminary Jr. College	Buena Vista, VA 24416 .	1867	Independ	J/W	248	35	$ 5,290	$2,700	$ 7,990
Sweet Briar College	Sweet Briar, VA 24595 ..	1901	Independ	S/W	732	72	$ 7,850	$2,650	$10,500
Union Theol. Sem. in Virginia	Richmond, VA 23227 ...	1812	Presby	G/C	273	23	$ 3,200	—	$ 3,200
University of Richmond .	Richmond, VA 23173 ...	1840	Baptist	S-G/C	2,700	200	$ 6,750	$2,235	$ 9,000
University of Virginia ...	Charlottesville, VA 22903	1819	State	S-G/C	17,143	1,697	$ 2,080	$2,445	$ 4,525
Clinch Valley College .	Wise, VA 24293	1954	State	S/C	1,191	70	$ 1,200	$2,160	$ 3,360
Falls Church Regl. Center	Falls Church, VA 22042 .	1952	State	S-G/C	2,500	200	—	—	—
Virginia Commonwn. Univ.	Richmond, VA 23284 ...	1838	State	S-G/C	19,984	1,876	$ 1,800	$2,880	$ 4,680
Virginia Community College System									
Blue Ridge Comm. College	Weyers Cave, VA 24486 .	1967	State	J/C	2,016	48	$ 686	—	$ 686
Central Virginia Comm. Col.	Lynchburg, VA 24502 ...	1967	State	J/C	3,565	69	$ 686	—	$ 686
Dabney S. Lancaster Com. Col.	Clifton Forge, VA 24422 .	1967	State	J/C	1,213	31	$ 686	—	$ 686
Danville Comm. College	Danville, VA 24541	1968	State	J/C	2,012	71	$ 686	—	$ 686
Eastern Shore Comm. College	Melfa, VA 23410	1971	State	J/C	378	14	$ 686	—	$ 686
Germanna Comm. College	Locust Grove, VA 22508	1970	State	J/C	1,758	32	$ 686	—	$ 686
John Tyler Comm. College	Chester, VA 23831	1967	State	J/C	3,904	71	$ 686	—	$ 686
J. S. Reynolds Comm. College	Richmond, VA 23241 ...	1972	State	J/C	9,190	156	$ 686	—	$ 686
Lord Fairfax Comm. College	Middletown, VA 22645 ..	1970	State	J/C	1,679	34	$ 686	—	$ 686
Mountain Emp. Comm. Col.	Big Stone Gap, VA 24219	1972	State	J/C	2,501	46	$ 686	—	$ 686
New River Comm. College	Dublin, VA 24084........	1970	State	J/C	2,737	60	$ 686	—	$ 686
Northern Va. Comm. College	Annandale, VA 22003 ...	1966	State	J/C	32,053	513	$ 686	—	$ 686
Patrick Henry Comm. College	Martinsville, VA 24112 ..	1971	State	J/C	1,598	30	$ 686	—	$ 686
Paul D. Camp Comm. College	Franklin, VA 23851	1971	State	J/C	1,154	28	$ 686	—	$ 686
Piedmont Va. Comm. College	Charlottesville, VA 22901	1972	State	J/C	3,644	58	$ 686	—	$ 686
Rappahannock Comm. Col.	Glenns, VA 23149	1970	State	J/C	1,318	29	$ 686	—	$ 686
Southside Va. Comm. College	Alberta, VA 23821......	1970	State	J/C	1,465	42	$ 686	—	$ 686
Southwest Va. Comm. College	Richlands, VA 24641.....	1967	State	J/C	3,520	61	$ 686	—	$ 686
Thomas Nelson Comm. Col.	Hampton, VA 23670	1968	State	J/C	6,151	116	$ 686	—	$ 686
Tidewater Comm. College	Portsmouth, VA 23703 ..	1968	State	J/C	14,976	277	$ 686	—	$ 686
Va. Highlands Comm. College	Abingdon, VA 24210	1969	State	J/C	1,595	54	$ 686	—	$ 686
Va. Western Comm. College	Roanoke, VA 24015.....	1966	State	J/C	5,722	111	$ 686	—	$ 686
Wytheville Comm. College	Wytheville, VA 24382 ...	1967	State	J/C	1,548	45	$ 686	—	$ 686
Virginia Intermont College	Bristol, VA 24201	1884	Baptist	S/C	517	64	$ 4,200	$2,600	$ 6,800
Virginia Military Institute	Lexington, VA 24450....	1839	State	S/M	1,338	120	$ 2,915	$2,115	$ 5,030
Virginia Poly. Inst. & St. Univ.	Blacksburg, VA 24061 ..	1872	State	S-G/C	21,454	2,065	$ 1,875	$1,758	$ 3,633
Virginia State University .	Petersburg, VA 23803 ..	1882	State	S-G/C	4,108	245	$ 1,800	$2,200	$ 4,000

NAME	ADDRESS	FOUN-DED	AFFILI-ATION	LEVEL/TYPE	ENROLL-MENT	TEACH-ERS	TUITION & FEES	BOARD & ROOM	TOTAL COST
VIRGINIA *(continued)*									
Virginia Union University	Richmond, VA 23220 ...	1865	Baptist	S-G/C	1,319	61	$ 3,520	$ 2,310	$ 5,830
Virginia Wesleyan College ...	Norfolk, VA 23502......	1961	Methodist	S/C	974	82	$ 5,200	$ 2,950	$ 8,150
Washington and Lee Univ.	Lexington, VA 24450....	1749	Independ	S-G/M	1,714	169	$ 7,200	$ 2,984	$10,194
WASHINGTON									
Antioch Seattle	Seattle, WA 98109	1852	Independ	S/C	2,576	208	$ 284	$ 1,133	$ 1,417
Bellevue Comm. College	Bellevue, WA 98007 ...	1966	State	J/C	9,000	412	$ 580	—	$ 580
Big Bend Comm. College	Moses Lake, WA 98837 .	1963	State	J/C	1,963	44	$ 696	$ 2,355	$ 3,051
Central Washington University	Ellensburg, WA 98926 ..	1890	State	S-G/C	7,377	316	$ 1,242	$ 2,565	$ 3,807
City University	Bellevue, WA 98008 ...	1973	Independ	S-G/C	3,000	250	$ 2,920	—	$ 2,920
Clark College	Vancouver, WA 98663 ..	1937	State	J/C	10,000	150	$ 581	—	$ 2,100
Columbia Basin College	Pasco, WA 99301	1955	State	J/C	5,700	200	$ 589	—	$ 589
Cornish Institute of Allied Arts	Seattle, WA 98102......	1914	Independ	S/C	535	125	$ 4,850	—	$ 4,850
Eastern Washington University	Cheney, WA 99004	1882	State	S-G/C	8,017	380	$ 1,017	$ 2,280	$ 3,297
Edmonds Community College	Lynnwood, WA 98036...	1867	State	J/C	6,944	262	$ 581	—	$ 581
Everett Community College ..	Everett, WA 98201	1941	State	J/C	6,569	225	$ 580	—	$ 580
Evergreen State College	Olympia, WA 98505	1967	State	S-G/C	2,826	173	$ 1,017	$ 2,610	$ 3,627
Fort Steilacoom Comm. College	Tacoma, WA 98498	1967	State	J/C	7,998	255	$ 580	—	$ 580
Gonzaga University	Spokane, WA 99258 ...	1887	Catholic	S-G/C	3,500	280	$ 6,160	$ 2,820	$ 8,980
Grays Harbor College	Aberdeen, WA 98520 ...	1930	State	J/C	2,544	132	$ 579	—	$ 579
Green River Comm. College ..	Auburn, WA 98002	1965	State	J/C	5,635	101	$ 581	—	$ 581
Griffin College	Seattle, WA 98121.....	1909	Independ	S/C	750	50	$ 4,000	—	$ 4,000
Heritage College	Toppenish, WA 98948...	1907	Ecum Chr	S-G/C	339	100	$ 2,400	—	$ 2,400
Highline Community College .	Midway, WA 98032	1961	State	J/C	8,052	360	$ 581	—	$ 581
Lower Columbia Comm. College	Longview, WA 98632....	1934	State	J/C	4,079	88	$ 573	—	$ 573
Northwest College	Kirkland, WA 98033 ...	1934	A of God	S/C	690	30	$ 3,491	$ 1,825	$ 5,315
Olympic College	Bremerton, WA 98310 ..	1946	State	J/C	6,399	337	$ 580	—	$ 580
Pacific Lutheran University ..	Tacoma, WA 98447.....	1890	Lutheran	S-G/C	3,694	253	$ 6,538	$ 2,985	$ 9,520
Peninsula College	Port Angeles, WA 98362	1961	State	J/C	2,764	158	$ 567	$ 2,270	$ 2,837
Puget Sound Christian Col. ..	Edmonds, WA 98020 ...	1950	Christian	S/C	122	14	$ 2,412	$ 2,025	$ 4,437
St. Martin's College	Lacey, WA 98503......	1895	Catholic	S-G/C	567	61	$ 6,000	$ 2,900	$ 8,900
Seattle Comm. Col. District ..	Seattle, WA 98119.....	1966	State	J/C	19,555	800	$ 600	—	$ 600
Seattle Pacific University	Seattle, WA 98119.....	1891	Methodist	S-G/C	2,935	188	$ 5,997	$ 3,090	$ 9,087
Seattle University	Seattle, WA 98122.....	1891	Catholic	S-G/C	4,653	197	$ 6,120	$ 2,934	$ 9,054
Shoreline Comm. College	Seattle, WA 98133.....	1964	State	J/C	6,980	263	$ 572	—	$ 572
Skagit Valley College	Mount Vernon, WA 98273	1926	State	J/C	4,725	248	$ 580	—	$ 580
South Puget Sound Com. Col.	Olympia, WA 98502	1970	State	J/C	3,612	54	$ 600	—	$ 600
Spokane Community College	Spokane, WA 99207	1963	State	J/C	5,299	335	$ 573	—	$ 573
Spokane Falls Comm. College	Spokane, WA 99204	1970	State	J/C	4,944	307	$ 573	—	$ 573
Tacoma Comm. College	Tacoma, WA 98465.....	1965	State	J/C	5,775	298	$ 573	—	$ 573
University of Puget Sound	Tacoma, WA 98416.....	1888	Methodist	S-G/C	2,951	179	$ 6,860	$ 3,240	$10,200
University of Washington	Seattle, WA 98195.....	1861	State	S-G/C	34,452	1,800	$ 1,455	$ 2,900	$ 4,355
Walla Walla College	College Pl., WA 99324 ..	1892	7-D Adv	S-G/C	1,660	135	$ 5,706	$ 2,295	$ 8,001
Walla Walla Community College	Walla Walla, WA 99362..	1967	State	J/C	4,421	198	$ 580	—	$ 580
Washington State University ..	Pullman, WA 99164.....	1890	State	S-G/C	16,459	1,049	$ 1,308	$ 2,520	$ 3,828
Wenatchee Valley College ...	Wenatchee, WA 98801 ..	1939	State	J/C	2,438	150	$ 699	—	$ 699
Western Washington University	Bellingham, WA 98225 ..	1893	State	S-G/C	9,144	446	$ 1,017	$ 2,400	$ 3,417
Whatcom Community College	Bellingham, WA 98226 ..	1967	State	J/C	2,224	114	$ 560	—	$ 560
Whitman College	Walla Walla, WA 99362..	1859	Independ	S/C	1,219	113	$ 7,370	$ 3,140	$10,510
Whitworth College	Spokane, WA 99251	1890	Presby	S-G/C	1,764	95	$ 6,755	$ 2,550	$ 9,305
Yakima Valley Comm. College	Yakima, WA 98907	1928	State	J/C	4,703	261	$ 583	$ 2,333	$ 2,916
WEST VIRGINIA									
Alderson-Broaddus College ..	Philippi, WV 26416	1871	Baptist	S/C	791	81	$ 5,054	$ 1,804	$ 6,858
Appalachian Bible College ..	Bradley, WV 25818	1950	Independ	J/C	188	20	$ 3,130	$ 2,230	$ 5,360
Beckley College	Beckley, WV 25801	1933	Independ	J/C	1,663	60	$ 1,080	—	$ 1,080
Bethany College............	Bethany, WV 26032....	1840	Christian	S/C	785	69	$ 7,160	$ 2,500	$ 9,660
Bluefield State College	Bluefield, WV 24701	1895	State	S/C	2,600	88	$ 800	—	$ 800
Concord College	Athens, WV 24712.....	1872	State	S/C	2,217	84	$ 840	$ 2,326	$ 3,166
Davis & Elkins College	Elkins, WV 26241.......	1904	Presby	S/C	1,018	53	$ 5,161	$ 2,660	$ 7,821
Fairmont State College......	Fairmont, WV 26554....	1867	State	S/C	5,005	306	$ 800	$ 2,200	$ 3,000
Glenville State College	Glenville, WV 26351	1872	State	S/C	1,807	75	$ 800	$ 2,386	$ 3,186
Marshall University	Huntington, WV 25701 ..	1837	State	S-G/C	11,318	629	$ 922	$ 2,643	$ 3,565
Ohio Valley College	Parkersburg, WV 26101 .	1958	C of Chr	S/C	299	34	$ 2,790	$ 2,300	$ 5,090
Parkersburg Community Col.	Parkersburg, WV 26101 .	1971	State	J/C	2,954	150	$ 520	—	$ 520
Salem College	Salem, WV 26426	1888	Independ	S-G/C	1,200	52	$ 4,800	$ 2,640	$ 7,440
Shepherd College	Shepherdstown, WV 25443	1871	State	S/C	3,534	108	$ 800	$ 2,200	$ 3,000
Southern West Va. Comm. Col.	Logan, WV 25601	1971	State	J/C	2,359	51	$ 520	—	$ 520
University of Charleston	Charleston, WV 25304 ..	1888	Independ	S/G-C	1,229	146	$ 4,750	$ 2,700	$ 7,450
West Liberty State College...	West Liberty, WV 26074 .	1837	State	S/C	2,521	178	$ 800	$ 2,226	$ 3,026
West Va. Col. of Grad. Studies	Institute, WV 25313	1972	State	G/C	2,715	196	$ 660	—	$ 660
West Va. Inst. of Technology .	Montgomery, WV 25136.	1895	State	S/C	3,210	196	$ 800	$ 2,675	$ 3,457
West Va. Northern Comm. Col.	Wheeling, WV 26003 ...	1972	State	J/C	2,540	235	$ 570	—	$ 570
West Va. Sch. of Osteo. Med.	Lewisburg, WV 24901 ...	1972	State	P/C	234	30	$ 1,892	$10,568	$12,460
West Virginia State College ..	Institute, WV 25112	1891	State	S/C	4,315	177	$ 880	$ 2,475	$ 3,355
West Virginia University	Morgantown, WV 26506 .	1867	State	S-G/C	19,071	2,265	$ 1,160	$ 2,801	$ 3,961
Potomac State College ..	Keyser, WV 26726......	1901	State	J/C	1,062	63	$ 800	$ 2,049	$ 2,849
West Virginia Wesleyan College	Buckhannon, WV 26201 .	1890	Methodist	S-G/C	1,539	112	$ 5,542	$ 2,675	$ 8,217
Wheeling College	Wheeling, WV 26003 ...	1954	Catholic	S-G/C	1,088	87	$ 5,120	$ 2,775	$ 7,895
WISCONSIN									
Alverno College	Milwaukee, WI 53215 ...	1887	Catholic	S/W	1,511	141	$ 4,625	$ 2,015	$ 6,640
Beloit College..............	Beloit, WI 53511	1846	Independ	S-G/C	976	78	$ 7,910	$ 2,464	$10,274

NAME	ADDRESS	FOUN-DED	AFFILI-ATION	LEVEL/TYPE	ENROLL-MENT	TEACH-ERS	TUITION & FEES	BOARD & ROOM	TOTAL COST
WISCONSIN (continued)									
Blackhawk Technical Institute	Janesville, WI 53545	1968	State	T/C	2,299	81	$ 700	—	$ 700
Cardinal Stritch College	Milwaukee, WI 53217	1937	Catholic	S-G/C	1,982	173	$ 4,640	$2,500	$ 7,140
Carroll College	Waukesha, WI 53186	1846	Presby	S/C	1,567	120	$ 7,100	$2,440	$ 9,540
Carthage College	Kenosha, WI 53141	1847	Lutheran	S-G/C	1,514	175			$ 7,777
Concordia College Wisconsin	Mequon, WI 53092	1881	Lutheran	S/C	851	61	$ 4,400	$2,590	$ 6,990
District One Tech. Institute	Eau Claire, WI 54701	1911	Public		3,742	210	$ 725	—	$ 725
Edgewood College	Madison, WI 53711	1927	Catholic	S/C	816	69	$ 4,800	$2,340	$ 7,140
Fox Valley Technical Institute	Appleton, WI 54913	1967	State	T/C	5,254	246	$ 775	—	$ 775
Gateway Technical Institute	Kenosha, WI 53141	1911	Independ	T/C	5,830	187	$ 615	$1,190	$ 1,805
Immanuel Lutheran College	Eau Claire, WI 54701	1959	Lutheran	S/C	136	13	$ 740	$1,300	$ 2,040
Institute of Paper Chemistry	Appleton, WI 54912	1929	Independ	G/C	100	32	$ 3,000	$2,500	$ 5,500
Lakeland College	Sheboygan, WI 53082	1862	UC Chr	S/C	965	34	$ 5,265	$2,400	$ 7,665
Lawrence University	Appleton, WI 54912	1847	Independ	S/C	1,080	109	$ 8,325	$2,475	$10,800
Madison Area Tech. College	Madison, WI 53703	1912	State	J/C	8,712	349	$ 750	—	$ 750
Marian College of Fond du Lac	Fond du Lac, WI 54935	1936	Independ	S/C	500	62	$ 4,500	$1,500	$ 6,000
Marquette University	Milwaukee, WI 53233	1881	Independ	S-G/C	11,690	929	$ 5,620	$3,000	$ 8,620
Medical College of Wisconsin	Milwaukee, WI 53226	1970	Independ	G/C	1,051	563	$ 7,291	—	$ 7,291
Mid-State Tech. Institute	Wis. Rapids, WI 54494	1911	State	T/C	1,800	70	$ 700	—	$ 700
Milwaukee Area Tech. College	Milwaukee, WI 53203	1912	State	T/C	38,552	1,629	$ 881	—	$ 881
Milwaukee Sch. of Engineering	Milwaukee, WI 53201	1903	Independ	S-G/C	2,553	125	$ 5,950	$2,700	$ 8,650
Moraine Park Tech. Institute	Fond du Lac, WI 54935	1967	Independ	T/C	4,846	145	$ 642	—	$ 642
Mount Mary College	Milwaukee, WI 53222	1913	Catholic	S-G/W	1,290	109	$ 4,500	$2,000	$ 6,500
Mount Senario College	Ladysmith, WI 54848	1963	Independ	S/C	494	53	$ 4,200	$2,200	$ 6,400
Nashotah House	Nashotah, WI 53058	1842	Episcopal	P/C	74	8	$ 3,630	$2,760	$ 6,390
Nicolet College	Rhinelander, WI 54501	1968	Public	J/C	1,167	65	$ 820	—	$ 820
North Central Tech. Institute	Wausau, WI 54401	1912	Public	T/C	2,500	100	$ 750	$2,000	$ 2,750
Northeast Wis. Tech. Institute	Green Bay, WI 54303	1913	State	T/C	4,376	173	$ 800	—	$ 800
Northland College	Ashland, WI 54806	1892	UC Chr	S/C	586	52	$ 5,395	$2,700	$ 8,095
Northwestern College	Watertown, WI 53094	1865	Lutheran	S/M	240	20	$ 1,650	$1,500	$ 3,150
Ripon College	Ripon, WI 54971	1851	Independ	S/C	868	94	$ 8,200	$2,200	$10,400
St. Norbert College	De Pere, WI 54115	1898	Catholic	S/C	1,763	115	$ 5,845	$2,370	$ 8,215
Silver Lake College	Manitowoc, WI 54220	1935	Catholic	S/C	426	61	$ 4,400	$2,365	$ 6,765
Univ. of Wisconsin System	Madison, WI 53706	1971	State	S-G/C	161,783	6,951			
UW—Eau Claire	Eau Claire, WI 54701	1816	State	S-G/C	10,757	503	$ 1,156		$ 3,070
UW—Green Bay	Green Bay, WI 54301	1965	State	S-G/C	4,906	233	$ 1,170	$2,240	$ 3,410
UW—La Crosse	La Crosse, WI 54601	1909	State	S-G/C	9,109	425	$ 1,166	$1,736	$ 2,902
UW—Madison	Madison, WI 53706	1848	State	S-G/C	44,055	2,342	$ 1,278	$2,313	$ 3,591
UW—Milwaukee	Milwaukee, WI 53211	1885	State	S-G/C	26,464	860	$ 1,335	$2,250	$ 3,585
UW—Oshkosh	Oshkosh, WI 54901	1871	State	S-G/C	11,103	530	$ 1,170	$1,840	$ 3,010
UW—Parkside	Kenosha, WI 53141	1968	State	S-G/C	5,544	345	$ 1,144		$ 1,144
UW—Platteville	Platteville, WI 53818	1866	State	S-G/C	5,293	270	$ 1,170	$1,800	$ 2,970
UW—River Falls	River Falls, WI 54022	1874	State	S-G/C	5,287	260	$ 1,155	$1,974	$ 3,129
UW—Stevens Point	Stevens Point, WI 54481	1894	State	S-G/C	9,008	565	$ 1,179	$1,154	$ 2,333
UW—Stout	Menomonie, WI 54751	1893	State	S-G/C	7,383	379	$ 1,169	$1,830	$ 2,999
UW—Superior	Superior, WI 54880	1893	State	S-G/C	2,095	120	$ 1,164	$2,135	$ 3,299
UW—Whitewater	Whitewater, WI 53190	1868	State	S-G/C	10,737	584	$ 1,154	$1,760	$ 2,914
Univ. of Wis. Centers	Madison, WI 53703	1971	State	J/C	10,042	430			
Baraboo/Sauk County	Baraboo, WI 53913	1968	State	J/C	504	21	$ 945	$ 976	$ 1,921
Barron County	Rice Lake, WI 54868	1966	State	J/C	346	25	$ 945	$ 929	$ 1,874
Fond du Lac	Fond du Lac, WI 54935	1933	State	J/C	643	28	$ 945	—	$ 945
Fox Valley	Menasha, WI 54952	1933	State	J/C	1,194	42	$ 945	—	$ 945
Manitowoc County	Manitowoc, WI 54220	1933	State	J/C	500	33	$ 945	—	$ 945
Marathon County	Wausau, WI 54401	1933	State	J/C	1,232	62	$ 945	$ 922	$ 1,867
Marinette County	Marinette, WI 54143	1936	State	J/C	427	21	$ 945	—	$ 945
Marshfield/Wood County	Marshfield, WI 54449	1964	State	J/C	628	30	$ 945	$ 931	$ 1,876
Richland	Richland Center, WI 53581	1967	State	J/C	283	23	$ 945	$ 988	$ 1,933
Rock County	Janesville, WI 53545	1966	State	J/C	1,026	42	$ 945	—	$ 945
Sheboygan County	Sheboygan, WI 53081	1933	State	J/C	673	33	$ 945	—	$ 945
Washington County	West Bend, WI 53095	1933	State	J/C	764	37	$ 945	—	$ 945
Waukesha County	Waukesha, WI 53186	1966	State	J/C	2,230	88	$ 945	—	$ 945
Viterbo College	La Crosse, WI 54601	1931	Catholic	S/C	1,092	110	$ 4,480	$1,900	$ 6,380
Waukesha County Tech. Inst.	Pewaukee, WI 53072	1923	State	T/C	4,863	139	$ 700	—	$ 700
Western Wisconsin Tech. Inst.	La Crosse, WI 54601	1912	State	T/C	3,750	190	$ 800	$1,800	$ 2,600
Wisconsin Cons. of Music	Milwaukee, WI 53208	1899	Independ	S-G/C	110	20	$ 5,050		$10,089
Wis. Independianhead Tech. Inst.	Shell Lake, WI 54871	1972	State	T/C					
Ashland	Ashland, WI 54806	1929	State	T/C	691	29	$ 627	—	$ 627
New Richmond	New Richmond, WI 54017	1967	State	T/C	2,001	34	$ 593	—	$ 593
Rice Lake	Rice Lake, WI 54868	1941	State	T/C	1,884	47	$ 610	—	$ 610
Superior Campus	Superior, WI 54880	1912	State	T/C	1,860	46	$ 632	—	$ 632
Wisconsin Lutheran College	Milwaukee, WI 53226	1973	Lutheran	J/C	110	20	$ 4,400	$2,275	$ 6,675
Wisconsin Luth. Seminary	Mequon, WI 53092	1863	Lutheran	G/M	224	16	$ 1,380	$1,620	$ 3,000

WYOMING

NAME	ADDRESS	FOUN-DED	AFFILI-ATION	LEVEL/TYPE	ENROLL-MENT	TEACH-ERS	TUITION & FEES	BOARD & ROOM	TOTAL COST
Casper College	Casper, WY 82601	1945	State	J/C	4,578	206	$ 414	$2,030	$ 2,444
Central Wyoming College	Riverton, WY 82501	1966	State	J/C	1,864	69	$ 432	$2,095	$ 2,527
Eastern Wyoming College	Torrington, WY 82240	1948	State	J/C	1,267	102	$ 360	$1,700	$ 2,060
Laramie County Comm. College	Cheyenne, WY 82007	1968	State	J/C	6,323	210	$ 445	—	$ 445
Northwest Comm. College	Powell, WY 82435	1946	State	J/C	1,920	74	$ 460	$1,900	$ 2,360
Sheridan College	Sheridan, WY 82801	1948	State	J/C	1,545	55	$ 408	$1,964	$ 2,372
University of Wyoming	Laramie, WY 82071	1886	State	S-G/C	10,045	850	$ 460	$1,235	$ 1,995
Western Wyoming College	Rock Springs, WY 82902	1959	State	J/C	1,300	64	$ 400	$2,100	$ 2,500

ENROLLMENTS IN SCHOOLS, COLLEGES, AND UNIVERSITIES: 1983–1984

Source: U.S. Department of Education; National Center for Education Statistics

	ELEMENTARY AND SECONDARY SCHOOLS[1]		COLLEGES AND UNIVERSITIES[2]		ELEMENTARY AND SECONDARY SCHOOLS[1]		COLLEGES AND UNIVERSITIES[2]
	K-8	9-12	Total		K-8	9-12	Total
UNITED STATES	26,636,000	12,341,000	12,415,586	Missouri	537,000	247,000	248,329
Alabama	501,000	211,000	171,381	Montana	110,000	45,000	37,877
Alaska	67,000	29,000	26,045	Nebraska	185,000	79,000	95,162
Arizona	348,000	157,000	213,437	Nevada	102,000	50,000	43,768
Arkansas	304,000	128,000	76,702	New Hampshire	103,000	53,000	53,143
California	2,822,000	1,309,000	1,730,847	New Jersey	739,000	374,000	314,468
Colorado	373,000	173,000	172,650	New Mexico	194,000	78,000	66,094
Connecticut	320,000	143,000	164,344	New York	1,689,000	912,000	1,022,521
Delaware	61,000	28,000	31,945	North Carolina	747,000	332,000	301,675
Dist. of Col.	59,000	25,000	80,367	North Dakota	86,000	33,000	37,591
Florida	1,042,000	464,000	443,436	Ohio	1,205,000	569,000	535,592
Georgia	737,000	317,000	201,453	Oklahoma	427,000	173,000	174,171
Hawaii	111,000	53,000	52,065	Oregon	302,000	142,000	141,172
Idaho	150,000	60,000	42,911	Pennsylvania	1,097,000	591,000	545,112
Illinois	1,233,000	567,000	673,084	Rhode Island	85,000	47,000	70,811
Indiana	658,000	308,000	256,470	South Carolina	422,000	182,000	134,532
Iowa	329,000	161,000	152,968	South Dakota	87,000	35,000	34,879
Kansas	283,000	124,000	141,709	Tennessee	577,000	237,000	207,777
Kentucky	447,000	193,000	146,503	Texas	2,180,000	888,000	795,741
Louisiana	564,000	220,000	179,647	Utah	297,000	105,000	103,324
Maine	142,000	63,000	53,347	Vermont	62,000	27,000	31,306
Maryland	446,000	224,000	239,232	Virginia	656,000	295,000	288,588
Massachusetts	555,000	285,000	423,348	Washington	496,000	239,000	229,639
Michigan	1,094,000	593,000	515,760	West Virginia	261,000	109,000	83,202
Minnesota	455,000	230,000	214,219	Wisconsin	491,000	266,000	277,751
Mississippi	323,000	140,000	109,728	Wyoming	75,000	28,000	23,844

[1] Public schools, Fall 1985 estimate. [2] Public and private, Fall 1983 data.

LARGEST U.S. UNIVERSITY AND COLLEGE LIBRARIES

Source: U.S. Department of Education; National Center for Education Statistics

RANK	INSTITUTION OR BRANCH	VOLUMES	STAFF	OPERATING COSTS		
				Total	Salaries	Books
1	Harvard University (Massachusetts)	10,409,228	802	$24,525,046	$15,128,979	$5,782,416
2	Yale University (Connecticut)	8,178,741	587	16,870,675	10,489,365	3,750,284
3	University of Michigan—Ann Arbor	6,561,427	449	13,839,587	8,412,124	3,643,519
4	University of Illinois (Urbana Campus)	6,240,615	408	12,528,142	7,383,435	4,019,841
5	University of California—Berkeley	6,117,424	388	20,189,652	14,027,167	3,662,962
6	University of California—Los Angeles	5,269,667	443	23,431,994	14,483,920	4,837,147
7	Columbia University (New York)	5,192,448	416	12,280,201	8,358,524	2,672,123
8	University of Texas at Austin	4,846,764	459	15,725,380	9,433,523	4,847,047
9	Stanford University (California)	4,658,033	522	18,537,416	11,781,649	4,723,935
10	University of Chicago (Illinois)	4,565,591	250	8,007,810	4,553,911	2,019,816
11	University of Wisconsin—Madison	4,184,038	339	13,038,168	7,976,374	3,384,052
12	Univ. of Minnesota—Minneapolis-St. Paul	3,945,397	288	11,908,116	7,722,330	2,781,213
13	Ohio State University, Main Campus	3,554,217	271	9,193,283	5,596,577	2,220,789
14	Cornell University, Endowed Colleges (New York)	3,552,452	300	9,485,109	5,549,040	2,586,195
15	Princeton University (New Jersey)	3,430,242	339	10,127,485	6,310,903	2,911,000
16	Indiana University at Bloomington	3,403,309	313	9,555,349	5,960,615	2,689,608
17	Duke University (North Carolina)	3,106,259	243	7,975,293	4,606,784	2,533,700
18	University of Pennsylvania	3,054,234	231	8,998,967	5,816,932	1,915,557
19	University of Washington	3,035,229	318	10,503,735	7,103,833	2,750,266
20	University of North Carolina at Chapel Hill	3,032,509	289	10,284,105	5,713,702	3,520,919
21	Northwestern University (Illinois)	2,889,402	258	8,367,411	5,316,907	2,244,989
22	New York University	2,698,879	266	9,437,605	5,808,832	2,344,351
23	University of Virginia, Main Campus	2,466,733	262	8,461,821	4,908,498	2,575,328
24	University of Iowa	2,412,577	171	7,057,759	3,811,817	2,794,902
25	Johns Hopkins University (Maryland)	2,260,219	174	5,428,882	2,875,201	1,695,551
26	University of Florida	2,231,509	172	8,482,904	4,834,992	2,468,646
27	University of Southern California	2,180,580	219	8,539,793	4,929,933	2,546,932
28	University of Georgia	2,141,617	223	6,946,855	3,756,668	2,590,782
29	University of Utah	2,119,959	241	4,724,848	2,620,391	1,469,126
30	University of Kansas, Main Campus	2,117,187	161	6,792,461	3,604,035	2,390,836
31	University of Missouri—Columbia	2,117,156	153	5,124,404	2,677,060	1,873,419
32	Michigan State University	2,099,099	193	7,396,874	3,142,141	2,296,850
33	University of Pittsburgh, Main Campus (PA)	2,026,135	238	7,442,539	4,781,972	1,992,216
34	Syracuse University, Main Campus (New York)	2,010,009	201	5,767,464	3,395,097	1,600,356
35	Louisiana State University and A&M College	1,965,311	144	6,865,066	3,238,880	2,951,934
36	University of Hawaii at Manoa	1,947,481	166	7,151,319	4,222,289	2,271,865

Energy and Resources

A stamp commemorating the 50th anniversary of the Rural Electrification Administration (REA) was issued by the U.S. Postal Service in Madison, S.D., on May 11. President Franklin D. Roosevelt created the REA by executive order on May 11, 1935, when only 10% of farms had electricity. Since then the agency has helped bring electricity to about 12 million rural consumers by making loans of nearly $60 billion to farm cooperatives for construction of rural networks. The stamp was designed by Howard Koslow of East Norwich, N.Y.

U.S. Postal Service

HIGHLIGHTS: 1985

ENERGY INDEPENDENCE ABANDONED

Spurred by the Arab oil boycott of the 1970s that brought soaring gasoline prices and short supplies, the federal government under Presidents Nixon, Ford, and Carter pushed forward plans to make the United States independent of imported oil.

One aspect of the plans called for the use of the huge coal reserves of the United States to produce synthetic fuels.

The most grandiose project undertaken to produce synthetic fuel was construction of a $2.1 billion coal gasification plant near Beulah, N.D. The plant, authorized in 1978, finally began production on July 28, 1984, and soon was providing 137 million cubic feet per day of natural gas to millions of customers in the Middle West.

ENERGY RESERVES OF THE WORLD AND OF THE UNITED STATES

Source: U.S. Department of Energy, Energy Information Administration, 1985

At current rates of consumption, the world's reserves of petroleum could be used up in 37 years—by 2021; natural-gas reserves could be used up in 63 years—by 2047; and uranium reserves in 35 years—by 2017; according to data released in 1985 by the U.S. Department of Energy.

ENERGY SOURCES	WORLD	UNITED STATES	U.S. % OF WORLD TOTAL
PETROLEUM[1] (in barrels):			
Estimated recoverable petroleum reserves, 1984	698,700,000,000	27,300,000,000	3.91%
Annual petroleum production	18,909,440,000	3,083,520,000	16.31%
Years remaining that known petroleum reserves would last at present rate of production	37 years	9 years	—
NATURAL GAS (in cubic feet):			
Estimated recoverable natural-gas reserves, 1984 ...	3,402,000,000,000,000	198,000,000,000,000	5.82%
Annual natural-gas production, 1982	53,726,000,000,000	17,758,000,000,000	33.052%
Years remaining that known natural-gas reserves would last at present rate of production	63 years	11 years	—
URANIUM[2] (short tons):			
Known recoverable uranium reserves, 1983	1,455,800	131,300	9.0%
Annual uranium production, 1982	41,290	10,300	25.0%
Years remaining known uranium reserves would last at present rate of production	35 years	13 years	—
COAL (in short tons):			
Estimated recoverable coal reserves, 1980	986,540,000,000	283,410,000,000	28.7%
Annual coal production, 1983	4,349,000,000	785,000,000	18.05%
Years remaining known coal reserves would last at present rate of production	226.84 years	316 years	—

[1] Including natural-gas plant liquids. [2] Containing U_3O_8. [3] 1981 data.

HIGHLIGHTS: 1985 *(continued)*

Meanwhile, however, a worldwide oil glut reduced oil and natural gas prices. By 1985 the synthetic gas produced by the plant in Beulah was costing three times that of natural gas. The consortium of five private companies operating the Beulah plant said they needed federal subsidies of $720 million in price supports and deferral of $673 million in payments due on government-guaranteed loans.

On July 30, 1985, Energy Secretary John S. Herrington refused to approve federal price supports for the project. On the following day the U.S. House of Representatives voted to cut off funds for the U.S. Synthetic Fuels Corporation which had financed the project. On Aug. 1, the consortium of five companies announced in a letter to Herrington that with no further federal support they were forced to abandon the project.

NUCLEAR POWER INCREASE

The International Atomic Energy Agency (IAEA) reported that 33 new atomic reactor units went into production in 1984, bringing the total capacity of nuclear generating plants to 31,000 megawatts of electricity—about 13% of the world's total production of electricity.

The IAEA said 180 more nuclear plants are under construction that will add about 163,000 megawatts of capacity.

According to the IAEA, France leads other nations in the percentage of electricity produced by nuclear power—58.7%. Belgium is second with 50.8%, followed by Finland 41.1%, Sweden 40.6%, Switzerland 36.5%, Bulgaria 28.6%, West Germany 23.2%, Japan 22.9%, Hungary 22.2%, Spain 19.3%, Britain 17.3%, United States 13.5%, Canada 11.6%, Soviet Union 9%, Czechoslovakia 8.5%, and Netherlands 5.8%.

The IAEA pointed out that nuclear power reactors have accumulated more than 3,500 operating years of experience with no accident having had significant harmful effects.

URANIUM DEPRESSION

The uranium mining industry sank into depression in 1985 with most mines closed in New Mexico, Wyoming, and Utah. The industry reached its peak in 1980 with 22,000 workers, who turned out nearly 44 million pounds of uranium oxide used as fuel for nuclear energy plants. However, only about one-fourth that amount of uranium will be produced in 1985 in the United States.

The decline in uranium production has been caused by delays and cancellations in the construction of nuclear power plants and by the development of lower cost uranium mines in other countries, such as Canada.

U.S. ENERGY PRODUCTION: 1940–1984

Source: U.S. Department of Energy, Energy Information Administration; All figures in quadrillion BTUs.

YEAR	TOTAL	COAL	NATURAL GAS[1]	OIL[2]	OTHER
1940	25.09	13.37	2.99	7.85	.88
1950	33.99	14.07	6.23	11.45	2.24
1960	41.50	10.83	12.66	14.93	3.08
1970	62.08	14.61	21.67	20.40	5.40
1975	59.87	15.00	19.64	17.73	7.50
1979	63.81	17.55	20.08	18.18	8.00
1980	64.76	18.60	19.91	18.25	8.00
1981	64.42	18.38	19.70	18.15	8.19
1982	63.89	18.64	18.25	18.31	8.69
1984[3]	65.51	19.70	17.75	18.59	9.47

[1] Dry natural gas. [2] Crude oil and lease condensates. [3] Preliminary data. Note: 1 quadrillion Btu equals approximately: 974 billion cubic feet of natural gas (dry); 172 million barrels of crude oil; 45.9 million short tons of coal; 500,000 barrels per day of crude oil for 1 year; or 8.0 billion gallons of gasoline.

In the 1960s analysts predicted that the United States would build 1,000 nuclear power plants by the year 2000. However, soaring costs and opposition by environmentalist groups have caused such plans to be scaled down greatly. Only 33 new nuclear plants remained under construction in the United States in 1985. Construction was halted on nine plants in 1984.

Because of declining demand for nuclear fuel, the federal government decided in 1985 to abandon construction of a $5 billion uranium processing plant in Portsmouth, Ohio. Some $2.6 billion already had been spent in building the facility.

WHAT IS IN A BARREL OF OIL?

Although most people know that gasoline is refined from crude oil, they generally are unaware of the other products that are refined. The Energy Information Administration provided the following table to explain the average annual yield from the 42 gallons of oil contained in one barrel.

PRODUCT	NO. OF GALLONS
Automobile gasoline	19.40
Aviation gasoline	0.08
Liquefied gas and ethane	0.92
Naphtha-type jet fuel	0.71
Kerosene-type jet fuel	2.69
Distillate fuel oil	9.03
Residual fuel oil	3.70
Petrochemical feedstocks	1.51
Special naphthas	0.17
Lubricants	0.50
Wax	0.04
Petroleum coke	1.43
Asphalt and road oil	1.13
Gases	1.85

Because the crude oil expands in volume in the refining of some products, the refined products total 43.83 gallons, an output of 1.83 gallons more than in the original barrel of crude oil.

WORLD CRUDE OIL PRODUCTION[1]

Source: Energy Information Administration, *International Energy Annual*

REGION AND COUNTRY	1975	1977	1978	1979	1980	1981	1982	1983*
North America	**10,519**	**10,546**	**11,229**	**11,509**	**11,968**	**12,170**	**12,769**	**12,824**
Canada	1,439	1,320	1,313	1,496	1,435	1,285	1,372	1,450
Mexico	705	981	1,209	1,461	1,936	2,313	2,748	2,686
United States	8,375	8,245	8,707	8,552	8,597	8,572	8,649	8,688
Central and South America	**3,581**	**3,546**	**3,550**	**3,802**	**3,644**	**3,650**	**3,456**	**3,387**
Argentina	395	431	453	473	491	496	491	491
Brazil	177	161	160	166	182	213	260	328
Colombia	157	138	131	124	126	125	141	151
Ecuador	161	183	202	214	204	211	211	237
Peru	70	102	151	195	195	193	195	171
Trinidad and Tobago	205	230	232	215	211	240	180	162
Venezuela	2,346	2,238	2,165	2,356	2,168	2,102	1,895	1,768
Other	69	63	57	59	67	70	83	79
Western Europe	**598**	**1,419**	**1,817**	**2,355**	**2,530**	**2,704**	**3,025**	**3,398**
Norway	189	280	356	403	528	501	520	614
Britain	12	768	1,082	1,568	1,622	1,811	2,065	2,291
Other	397	371	379	384	380	392	440	493
Eastern Europe	**10,024**	**11,082**	**11,570**	**11,813**	**12,109**	**12,248**	**12,430**	**12,405**
Romania	302	303	284	255	238	241	234	245
Soviet Union	9,625	10,682	11,185	11,460	11,773	11,909	12,080	12,034
Other	97	97	101	97	98	98	116	126
Middle East	**19,522**	**22,255**	**21,101**	**21,558**	**18,408**	**15,731**	**12,641**	**11,608**
Iran	5,350	5,663	5,242	3,168	1,662	1,380	2,214	2,426
Iraq	2,262	2,348	2,563	3,477	2,514	1,000	1,012	1,005
Kuwait	2,084	1,969	2,131	2,500	1,656	1,125	823	1,064
Qatar	438	445	487	508	472	405	330	295
Saudi Arabia	7,075	9,245	8,301	9,532	9,900	9,815	6,483	5,086
Syria	170	188	170	166	164	166	160	167
United Arab Emirates	1,664	1,999	1,831	1,831	1,709	1,474	1,250	1,147
Other	480	399	378	376	331	366	369	418
Africa	**4,965**	**6,228**	**5,966**	**6,524**	**6,031**	**4,575**	**4,456**	**4,425**
Algeria	983	1,152	1,161	1,154	1,012	805	710	675
Angola	165	194	131	147	150	130	122	177
Egypt	235	415	485	525	595	598	670	727
Gabon	223	222	209	203	175	151	156	157
Libya	1,480	2,063	1,983	2,092	1,787	1,140	1,150	1,076
Nigeria	1,783	2,085	1,897	2,302	2,055	1,433	1,295	1,241
Other	96	96	101	101	257	318	353	372
Far East and Oceania	**3,672**	**4,609**	**4,823**	**4,974**	**4,848**	**4,822**	**4,681**	**4,934**
Australia	409	431	432	441	380	394	370	416
Brunei	181	210	205	234	235	163	154	155
China	1,490	1,874	2,082	2,122	2,114	2,012	2,045	2,120
India	165	199	226	245	182	325	390	406
Indonesia	1,307	1,686	1,635	1,591	1,577	1,605	1,339	1,385
Malaysia	98	184	217	283	283	264	306	365
Other	23	25	25	58	77	59	77	87
WORLD TOTAL	**52,880**	**59,685**	**60,057**	**62,535**	**59,538**	**55,900**	**53,458**	**52,981**

[1] Data in thousands of barrels per day (add 000 to figures). * Preliminary Data.

U.S. CONSUMPTION OF ENERGY AND ENERGY RESOURCES

Source: Energy Information Administration, U.S. Department of Energy

YEAR	COAL (tons)	NATURAL GAS (cu. ft.)	PETROLEUM (barrels)[2]	ELECTRICITY Hydro and geothermal power (megawatt hrs.)	ELECTRICITY Nuclear power (megawatt hrs.)
1950	494,100,000	5,770,000,000,000	2,357,000,000	102,700,000	—
1955	447,000,000	8,690,000,000,000	3,086,000,000	120,300,000	—
1960	398,000,000	11,970,000,000,000	3,586,000,000	153,700,000	500,000
1961	390,300,000	12,490,000,000,000	3,641,000,000	157,600,000	1,700,000
1962	402,200,000	13,270,000,000,000	3,796,000,000	172,300,000	2,300,000
1963	423,500,000	13,970,000,000,000	3,921,000,000	169,300,000	3,200,000
1964	445,700,000	14,810,000,000,000	4,034,000,000	182,500,000	3,300,000
1965	472,000,000	15,280,000,000,000	4,202,000,000	197,000,000	3,700,000
1966	497,700,000	16,450,000,000,000	4,411,000,000	199,200,000	5,500,000
1967	491,400,000	17,390,000,000,000	4,585,000,000	224,900,000	7,700,000
1968	509,800,000	18,630,000,000,000	4,902,000,000	225,600,000	12,500,000
1969	516,400,000	20,060,000,000,000	5,106,000,000	261,100,000	13,900,000
1970	523,200,000	21,140,000,000,000	5,364,000,000	253,400,000	21,800,000
1971	501,600,000	21,790,000,000,000	5,553,000,000	273,600,000	38,100,000
1972	524,200,000	22,100,000,000,000	5,990,000,000	284,100,000	54,100,000
1973	562,600,000	22,050,000,000,000	6,317,000,000	291,700,000	83,500,000
1974	558,400,000	21,220,000,000,000	6,078,000,000	319,400,000	114,000,000
1975	562,600,000	19,540,000,000,000	5,958,000,000	312,500,000	172,500,000
1976	603,800,000	19,950,000,000,000	6,391,000,000	299,100,000	191,100,000
1977	625,300,000	19,520,000,000,000	6,727,000,000	244,600,000	250,900,000
1978	625,200,000	19,630,000,000,000	6,879,000,000	306,200,000	276,400,000
1979	680,500,000	20,240,000,000,000	6,757,000,000	307,300,000	255,200,000
1980	702,710,000	19,877,000,000,000	6,243,000,000	282,000,000	251,100,000
1981	735,600,000	19,404,000,000,000	5,861,000,000	267,000,000	272,700,000
1982	706,900,000	18,001,000,000,000	5,583,000,000	314,000,000	282,800,000
1983	736,600,000	16,835,000,000,000	5,559,000,000	338,000,000	294,000,000
1984*	792,800,000	17,489,000,000,000	5,749,000,000	330,000,000	325,000,000

U.S. CONSUMPTION OF ENERGY IN TRILLIONS OF BTUs[1]

Source: Energy Information Administration, U.S. Department of Energy

YEAR	COAL Anthracite	COAL Bituminous and Lignite	NATURAL GAS	PETROLEUM[2]	ELECTRICITY Hydro	ELECTRICITY Geothermal and other	ELECTRICITY Nuclear	TOTAL ENERGY USAGE Total BTUs	TOTAL ENERGY USAGE % Change From Prior Year
1950	991	11,900	5,970	13,320	1,440	—	—	33,621	+8.2
1955	579	10,940	9,000	17,260	1,410	—	—	39,170	+9.6
1960	426	9,690	12,390	19,920	1,660	—	10	43,750	+3.2
1962	346	9,830	13,730	21,050	1,820	—	27	46,480	+4.7
1963	336	10,360	14,400	21,700	1,770	—	38	48,270	+3.8
1964	344	10,900	15,290	22,300	1,910	—	39	50,440	+4.5
1965	309	11,580	15,770	23,250	2,060	—	44	52,620	+4.3
1966	271	12,210	17,000	24,130	2,070	—	64	55,590	+5.7
1967	251	11,990	17,940	25,280	2,340	—	90	57,500	+3.4
1968	234	12,420	19,210	26,980	2,340	—	141	60,940	+6.0
1969	203	12,520	20,680	28,340	2,660	—	153	64,120	+5.2
1970	190	12,470	21,790	29,520	2,650	20	240	66,440	+3.4
1971	170	11,840	22,470	30,560	2,860	10	413	67,820	+2.0
1972	136	12,310	22,700	32,950	2,940	30	584	71,190	+5.0
1973	129	13,170	22,510	34,840	3,010	50	910	74,290	+4.4
1974	120	12,760	21,730	33,450	3,310	60	1,270	72,550	−2.3
1975	111	12,710	19,950	32,730	3,220	70	1,900	70,550	−2.8
1976	112	13,620	20,350	35,170	3,070	80	2,110	74,370	+5.4
1977	115	14,000	19,930	37,120	2,510	80	2,700	76,290	+2.6
1978		13,770	20,000	37,970	3,140	70	3,020	78,090	+2.4
1979		15,040	20,670	37,120	3,140	90	2,780	78,900	+1.0
1980		15,430	20,390	34,200	3,120	110	2,740	75,960	−3.7
1981		15,910	19,930	31,930	3,110	130	3,010	73,990	−2.6
1982		15,320	18,510	30,230	3,560	110	3,130	70,840	−4.3
1983		15,900	17,360	30,050	3,870	130	3,200	70,500	−0.5
1984*		17,200	18,030	31,000	3,780	170	3,550	73,730	+4.6

* Preliminary. [1] One British Thermal Unit (BTU) is the quantity of heat required to raise the temperature of 1 pound of water 1 degree Fahrenheit at or near 39.2 °F. [2] Including liquids from natural-gas plants.

ENERGY PRICES: 1951–1984

Source: Energy Information Administration

YEAR	CRUDE OIL[1]	GASOLINE[2]	HEATING OIL[1]	ELECTRICITY[3]	BITUMINOUS COAL[4]	ANTHRACITE COAL[5]	NATURAL GAS[6]
1951	$ 2.53	$0.272	—	$0.0281	$ 4.92	$ 9.94	$0.76
1953	2.68	0.287	—	0.0274	4.92	9.87	0.87
1954	2.78	0.290	—	0.0270	4.52	8.76	0.89
1955	2.77	0.291	—	0.0265	4.50	8.00	0.89
1956	2.79	0.299	$0.152	0.0261	4.82	8.33	0.91
1957	3.09	0.310	0.160	0.0256	5.08	9.11	0.93
1958	3.01	0.304	0.151	0.0254	4.86	9.14	0.98
1959	2.90	0.305	0.153	0.0251	4.77	8.55	1.01
1960	2.88	0.311	0.150	0.0262	4.69	8.01	1.03
1961	2.89	0.308	0.156	0.0260	4.58	8.26	1.07
1962	2.90	0.306	0.156	0.0256	4.48	7.99	1.04
1963	2.89	0.304	0.160	0.0251	4.39	8.64	1.05
1964	2.88	0.304	0.161	0.0245	4.45	8.93	1.05
1965	2.86	0.312	0.160	0.0239	4.44	8.51	1.05
1966	2.88	0.321	0.164	0.0234	4.54	8.08	1.04
1967	2.92	0.332	0.169	0.0231	4.62	8.15	1.04
1968	3.17	0.337	0.174	0.0225	4.67	8.78	1.04
1969	3.29	0.348	0.178	0.0221	4.99	9.91	1.05
1970	3.40	0.357	0.185	0.0222	6.26	11.03	1.09
1971	3.60	0.364	0.196	0.0232	7.07	12.08	1.15
1972	3.58	0.361	0.197	0.0242	7.66	12.40	1.21
1973	4.15	0.388	0.228	0.0254	8.53	13.65	1.29
1974	9.07	0.532	0.360	0.0310	15.75	22.19	1.43
1975	10.38	0.567	0.377	0.0351	19.23	32.26	1.71
1976	10.89	0.590	0.406	0.0373	19.43	33.92	1.98
1977	11.96	0.622	0.460	0.0405	19.82	34.86	2.35
1978	12.46	0.626	0.494	0.0431	21.78	35.25	2.56
1979	17.72	0.857	0.704	0.0464	23.65	41.06	2.98
1980	28.07	1.191	0.974	0.0536	24.52	42.51	3.68
1981	35.24	1.311	1.194	0.0620	26.29	44.28	4.29
1982	31.87	1.222	1.160	0.0686	27.14	49.85	5.17
1983	28.99	1.157	1.078	0.0718	25.85	52.29	6.06
1984	28.63	1.129	1.091*	0.0756	27.00	55.00	—

[1] Refiners' cost per barrel. [2] Cost per gallon of leaded regular, including tax. [3] Cost per kwh (residential). [4] Cost per short ton F.O.B. mines to electric utilities. [5] Cost at preparation plants. [6] Residential cost per thousand cubic feet. *Preliminary data.

HOW TO SAVE ENERGY AND MONEY ON HOME APPLIANCES

Source: U.S. Department of Energy; Edison Electric Institute

If you let a single 100-watt light bulb burn steadily all year long, it would use 876 kilowatt-hours (kwh) of electricity. At a cost of 8.23¢ per kwh, this would add $71.27 to your electric bill. If you substituted a 60-watt bulb, *you would save $28.84.*

The average annual energy use and annual energy cost of common electrical appliances in a typical American home are shown in the following table.

ELECTRIC APPLIANCE	ANNUAL ENERGY USE	ANNUAL COST	ELECTRIC APPLIANCE	ANNUAL ENERGY USE	ANNUAL COST
Air conditioner	860 kwh	$ 70.78	Iron	60 kwh	$ 9.94
Broiler	85 kwh	7.00	Lighting	1,100 kwh	90.53
Can opener	3 kwh	0.30	Microwave oven	190 kwh	15.64
Clock	17 kwh	1.40	Radio	86 kwh	7.08
Clothes dryer	993 kwh	81.72	Radio-phonograph	109 kwh	8.97
Coffee maker	140 kwh	11.52	Range	730 kwh	60.08
Dishwasher	903 kwh	79.38	Refrigerator (17.5 cu. ft.)	2,250 kwh	185.18
Electric blanket	147 kwh	12.10	Sewing machine	11 kwh	0.91
Fan (attic)	290 kwh	23.87	Shaver	1 kwh	0.08
Fan (furnace)	650 kwh	54.00	Television (black and white)	100 kwh	8.23
Fluorescent light	260 kwh	21.40	Television (color)	320 kwh	26.34
Food freezer (16 cu. ft.)	1,820 kwh	149.79	Toaster	39 kwh	3.21
Food mixer	2 kwh	0.17	Vacuum cleaner	46 kwh	3.79
Food waste disposer	7 kwh	0.58	Waffle iron	20 kwh	1.70
Frying pan	100 kwh	8.23	Washer (clothes)	1,250 kwh	102.88
Hair dryer	25 kwh	2.06	Water heater (all-electric)	5,422 kwh	446.23
Hot plate	90 kwh	7.91			

* 8.23¢ per kwh was the 1985 national estimated average for residential users.

WORLD'S LARGEST HYDROELECTRIC GENERATING PLANTS

Source: *Water Power & Dam Construction;* In part, U.S. Bureau of Reclamation, Department of the Interior

RANK	DAM	LOCATION	CAPACITY (in megawatts) Present	Ultimate	BEGAN OPERATION
1	Itaipú (Paraná River)	Brazil–Paraguay	2,800	12,600	1983
2	Guri (Caroni River)	Venezuela	2,800	10,000	1968
3	Tucuruí (Tocantins River)	Brazil	3,960	8,000	1984
4	Grand Coulee (Columbia River)	Washington	6,494	6,494	1942
5	Sayano-Shushensk (Yenisei River)	Soviet Union	6,400	6,400	1980
6	Corpus Posadas (Paraná River)	Argentina–Paraguay	—	6,000	UC
7	Krasnoyarsk (Yenisei River)	Soviet Union	6,000	6,000	1968
8	La Grande 2 (La Grande River)	Quebec, Canada	2,000	5,328	1982
9	Churchill Falls (Churchill River)	Newfoundland, Canada	5,225	5,225	1971
10	Bratsk (Angara River)	Soviet Union	4,500	4,500	1964
11	Ust-Ilim (Angara River)	Soviet Union	3,675	4,500	1974
12	Yacyretá-Apipe (Paraná River)	Argentina–Paraguay	2,700	4,050	UC
13	Cabora Bassa (Zambezi River)	Mozambique	2,000	4,000	1975
14	Rogun (Vakhsh River)	Soviet Union	—	3,600	UC
15	Paulo Afonso I (São Francisco River)	Brazil	1,524	3,409	1979
16	Ilha Solteira (Paraná River)	Brazil	3,200	3,200	1955
17	Chapetón (Paraná River)	Argentina	—	3,000	UC
18	Gezhouba (Changjiang River)	China	2,715	2,715	1982
19	Bennett W.A.C. (Peace River)	British Columbia, Canada	2,700	2,700	1968
20	John Day (Columbia River)	Oregon–Washington	2,160	2,700	1969
21	Nurek (Vakhsh River)	Soviet Union	900	2,700	1976
22	Revelstoke (Columbia River)	British Columbia, Canada	900	2,700	1983
23	São-Simao (Paranaiba River)	Brazil	2,680	2,680	1979
24	Mica (Columbia River)	British Columbia, Canada	1,736	2,610	1976
25	Volgograd 22d Congress (Volga R.)	Soviet Union	2,563	2,563	1958
26	Itaparica (São Francisco River)	Brazil	—	2,500	UC
27	Chicoasen (Grijalva River)	Mexico	2,400	2,400	1981
28	Ataturk (Euphrates River)	Turkey	—	2,400	UC
29	Volga–V.I. Lenin (Volga River)	Soviet Union	2,300	2,300	1958
30	Iron Gates (Danube River)	Romania–Yugoslavia	2,300	2,300	1970
31	La Grande 3 (La Grande River)	Quebec, Canada	1,200	2,300	1982
32	Foz Do Areia (Iguacu River)	Brazil	2,250	2,250	1983
33	Bath County (Bath Creek)	Virginia	—	2,100	UC
34	High Aswan (Nile River)	Egypt	2,100	2,100	1967
35	Tarbela (Indus River)	Pakistan	1,400	2,100	1977
36	Chief Joseph (Columbia River)	Washington–Oregon	2,069	2,069	1955

WORLD'S HIGHEST DAMS

Source: *Water Power & Dam Construction;* in part, U.S. Bureau of Reclamation

RANK	NAME, LOCATION	TYPE	HEIGHT (feet)	COMPLETED
1	Rogun, Soviet Union	E	1,099	UC
2	Nurek, Soviet Union	E	984	1980
3	Grand Dixence, Switz.	G	935	1962
4	Inguri, Soviet Union	A	892	1985
5	Boruca, Costa Rica	E	876	UC
6	Vaiont, Italy	A	860	1961
7	Chicoasén, Mexico	R	856	1981
8	Tehri, India	E	856	UC
9	Alvaro Obregon, Mexico	G	853	1946
10	Kishau, India	E,R	830	UC
11	Sayano-Shushensk, USSR	A	803	1980
12	Guavio, Colombia	E	797	UC
13	Mica, Canada	E,R	794	1973
14	Mauvoisin, Switzerland	A	778	1957
15	Chivor, Colombia	R	778	1975
16	Chirkei, Soviet Union	A	764	1977
17	Oroville, California	E	755	1968
18	Bhakra, India	G	742	1963
19	El Cajón, Honduras	A	742	UC
20	Hoover, Arizona–Nevada	A,G	725	1936
21	Contra, Switzerland	A	722	1965
22	Dabaklamm, Austria	A	722	UC
23	Mratinje, Yugoslavia	A	722	1975
24	Dworshak, Idaho	G	719	1974
25	Glen Canyon, Arizona	A	709	1964

WORLD'S LARGEST DAMS

Source: *Water Power & Dam Construction;* in part, U.S. Bureau of Reclamation

RANK	NAME, LOCATION	VOLUME (cubic yds.)	COMPLETED
1	Chapetón, Argentina	379,305,670	UC
2	New Cornelia Tailings, Ariz.	274,016,000	1973
3	Tarbela, Pakistan	159,204,000	1976
4	Fort Peck, Montana	125,627,000	1940
5	Lower Usuma, Nigeria	121,639,000	UC
6	Ataturk, Turkey	111,176,000	UC
7	Yacyretá-Apipe, Arg.–Para.	105,944,000	UC
8	Guri, Venezuela	99,012,000	UC
9	Rogun, Soviet Union	92,995,000	UC
10	Oahe, South Dakota	92,000,000	1960
11	Gardiner, Canada	85,592,000	1968
12	Mangla, Pakistan	85,512,000	1967
13	Tucuruí, Brazil	84,101,000	1984
14	Afsluitdijk, Netherlands	82,963,000	1932
15	Oroville, California	78,005,000	1968
16	San Luis, California	77,669,000	1967
17	Nurek, Soviet Union	75,861,000	1980
18	Garrison, North Dakota	66,503,000	1956
19	Cochiti, New Mexico	65,698,000	1975
20	Oosterschelde, Netherlands	65,389,000	UC
21	Tabqua, Syria	60,166,000	1976
22	High Aswan, Egypt	57,981,000	1970
23	Bennett W.A.C., Canada	57,157,000	1967
24	Boruca, Costa Rica	56,242,000	UC
25	Kiev, Soviet Union	55,457,000	1964

E = Earth; UC = Under Construction; G = Gravity; A = Arch; R = Rockfill; MA = Multi-arch.

ELECTRICITY GENERATED BY ATOMIC POWER
Source: International Atomic Energy Agency

In 1985 a total of 26 countries had 345 operating reactors producing 219,718 megawatts of electricity. A total of 180 more were under construction or planned with an additional power output of 163,448 megawatts. Only 30 years earlier, in 1954, there were just two atomic reactors in the world that could generate electricity. They had a total output of 7.4 megawatts of electricity.

RANK	COUNTRY	NUMBER OF REACTORS	ELECTRICITY OUTPUT[1]	RANK	COUNTRY	NUMBER OF REACTORS	ELECTRICITY OUTPUT[1]
1	United States ..	85	68,867	15	East Germany..	5	1,694
2	France	41	32,993	16	Bulgaria	4	1,632
3	Soviet Union ...	46	22,997	17	Italy	3	1,273
4	Japan	31	21,751	18	India	5	1,020
5	West Germany .	19	16,133	19	Czechoslovakia.	3	1,194
6	Canada	16	9,521	20	Argentina	2	935
7	Britain	37	9,564	21	South Africa ...	1	921
8	Sweden	10	7,355	22	Hungary.......	2	820
9	Spain	7	4,690	23	Yugoslavia.....	1	632
10	Taiwan	5	4,011	24	Brazil	1	626
11	Belgium	6	3,474	25	Netherlands ...	2	508
12	Switzerland	5	2,882	26	Pakistan.......	1	125
13	Finland	4	2,310		TOTAL	345	219,718
14	South Korea ...	3	1,790				

WORLD'S LARGEST OPERATING ATOMIC ELECTRIC POWER REACTORS
Source: International Atomic Energy Agency

RANK	NAME	LOCATION	TYPE OF REACTOR*	ELECTRICITY NET OUTPUT[1]	BEGAN COMMERCIAL OPERATION
1	Ignalino–1	Soviet Union	LWGR	1,450	1984
2	KWG-Grohnde	West Germany	PWR	1,319	1985
3	Paluel–1	France	PWR	1,290	—
4	Paluel–2..............	France	PWR	1,290	—
5	Philippsburg–1	West Germany	BWR	1,268	1985
6	KKK Kruemmel.........	West Germany	BWR	1,250	1985
7	KRB-Gundremmingen-B .	West Germany	BWR	1,244	1984
8	KRB-Gundremmingen-C .	West Germany	BWR	1,244	1985
9	Biblis–B	Biblis, Hesse, West Germany	PWR	1,240	1977
10	KKU Unterweser	Stadland, West Germany	PWR	1,230	1979
11	Grand Gulf–1	Port Gibson, Mississippi	BWR	1,225	1983
12	KKG-Grafenrheinfeld....	Grafenrheinfeld, Bayern, W. Germany ..	PWR	1,225	1982
13	Callaway	Missouri	PWR	1,185	1985
14	McGuire–1	Cornelius, North Carolina	PWR	1,180	1982
15	McGuire–2.............	Cornelius, North Carolina	PWR	1,180	1983
16	Sequoyah–1	Daisy, Tennessee	PWR	1,148	1981
17	Sequoyah–2	Daisy, Tennessee	PWR	1,148	1982
18	Biblis–A	Biblis, Hesse, West Germany	PWR	1,146	1975
19	Ohi–1	Ohi, Fukui, Japan	PWR	1,120	1979
20	Ohi–2	Ohi, Fukui, Japan	PWR	1,120	1979
21	Salem–2..............	Salem, New Jersey	PWR	1,106	1981
22	WPPSS–2	South Carolina	BWR	1,103	1984
23	Diablo Canyon	California	PWR	1,084	1985
24	Tokai–2	Tokaimura, Ibaraki, Japan	BWR	1,080	1978
25	Trojan	Prescott, Oregon	PWR	1,080	1976
26	Salem–1..............	Salem, New Jersey	PWR	1,079	1977
27	LaSalle–1.............	Seneca, Illinois	BWR	1,078	1984
28	LaSalle–2.............	Seneca, Illinois	BWR	1,078	1984
29	San Onofre–2	San Clemente, California.............	PWR	1,070	1983
30	San Onofre–3	San Clemente, California.............	PWR	1,070	1984
31	Browns Ferry–1	Decatur, Alabama...................	BWR	1,067	1974
32	Browns Ferry–2	Decatur, Alabama...................	BWR	1,067	1975
33	Browns Ferry–3	Decatur, Alabama...................	BWR	1,067	1977
34	Fukushima I–6	Futaba, Fukushima, Japan	BWR	1,067	1979
35	Fukushima II–1	Naraha, Fukushima, Japan	BWR	1,067	1982
36	Fukushima II–2	Naraha, Fukushima, Japan	BWR	1,067	1984
37	Fukushima II–3	Fukushima, Japan	BWR	1,067	1985
38	Donald C. Cook–2	Bridgman, Michigan.................	PWR	1,060	1978
39	Susquehanna–2	Salem, Pennsylvania	BWR	1,052	1984
40	Peach Bottom–2.......	York County, Pennsylvania	BWR	1,050	1974
41	Zion–1	Zion, Illinois	PWR	1,040	1973
42	Zion–2................	Zion, Illinois	PWR	1,040	1974
43	Peach Bottom–3........	York County, Pennsylvania	BWR	1,035	1974

[1]Megawatts.*PWR = Pressurized light-water-moderated and cooled reactor. BWR = Boiling light-water-cooled and moderated reactor. LWGR = Light-water-cooled, graphite-moderated reactor.

LEADING PRODUCERS OF ENERGY AND RESOURCES

Source: United Nations, *1982 Statistical Yearbook*

The 8 leading producing nations are listed for each of 24 major types of energy or resources. The U.S. ranks among the 8 top producers in 19 of the following basic resources and leads in 8.

BAUXITE (Aluminum Ore)[1]

Country	Amount
World	77,267,000
Australia	24,690,000
Guinea	11,828,000
Jamaica	8,514,000
Brazil	4,186,000
Soviet Union	4,600,000
Yugoslavia	3,668,000
Suriname	3,060,000
Greece	2,853,000

CEMENT[1]

Country	Amount
World	875,972,000
Soviet Union	123,681,000
China	95,200,000
Japan	80,686,000
United States	58,369,000
Italy	40,245,000
W. Germany	30,079,000
Spain	29,604,000
France	26,141,000

COAL[3]

Country	Amount
World	2,299,842,000
United States	601,142,000
China	453,571,000
Soviet Union	409,241,000
Poland	153,344,000
Britain	103,261,000
South Africa	102,281,000
Australia	96,786,000
India	91,657,000

COPPER ORE[1]

Country	Amount
World	8,283,100
Chile	1,255,100
Soviet Union	1,180,000
United States	1,139,600
Zambia	693,300
Canada	606,200
Zaire	503,000
Peru	369,500
Poland	366,700

DIAMONDS[2]

Country	Amount
World	41,674,000
Soviet Union	10,600,000
Zaire	10,000,000
South Africa	9,154,000
Botswana	7,769,000
Namibia	1,014,000
Ghana	684,000
Venezuela	600,000
Liberia	433,000

ELECTRICITY[3]

Country	Amount
World	1,040,439
United States	283,418
Soviet Union	168,153
Japan	71,481
Canada	47,658
W. Germany	42,126
China	40,305
Britain	33,476
France	32,706

FISH CATCHES[1,6]

Country	Amount
World	74,760,400
Japan	10,656,500
Soviet Union	9,545,900
China	4,605,000
United States	3,767,400
Chile	3,393,400
Peru	2,750,500
Norway	2,551,500
India	2,415,400

FORESTRY (Roundwood)[4]

Country	Amount
World	2,958,500
United States	393,900
Soviet Union	358,200
China	224,600
India	228,300
Brazil	216,500
Canada	142,300
Indonesia	128,400
Nigeria	83,200

GAS, LPG[3]

Country	Amount
World	189,403,000
United States	74,382,000
Saudi Arabia	17,646,000
Soviet Union	14,763,000
Canada	13,092,000
Japan	11,839,000
Mexico	5,868,000
Britain	3,807,000
Brazil	3,695,000

GAS, NATURAL[3]

Country	Amount
World	1,853,520
United States	601,708
Soviet Union	594,193
Canada	96,375
Netherlands	76,961
Romania	55,958
Britain	47,561
Mexico	43,349
Norway	35,488

GOLD[5,6]

Country	Amount
World	954,000
South Africa	656,300
Canada	47,060
United States	42,860
Japan	37,757
Philippines	23,435
Papua, N.G.	18,010
Brazil	17,276
Australia	16,485

IRON ORE[1]

Country	Amount
World	482,888,000
Soviet Union	132,885,000
Brazil	81,559,000
Australia	54,886,000
China	53,660,000
India	26,458,000
United States	23,005,000
Canada	21,742,000
South Africa	15,370,000

LEAD[1]

Country	Amount
World	4,272,800
United States	799,000
Soviet Union	650,000
Japan	296,000
Britain	288,000
Australia	240,400
Canada	173,000
Mexico	128,800
Bulgaria	118,000

LIGNITE (Brown Coal)[3]

Country	Amount
World	403,498,000
E. Germany	84,231,000
Soviet Union	79,663,000
Czechoslov.	40,933,000
W. Germany	37,405,000
United States	22,950,000
Yugoslavia	22,594,000
Bulgaria	15,971,000
Australia	12,219,000

NICKEL[1]

Country	Amount
World	588,196
Soviet Union	169,600
Canada	88,740
Australia	81,424
New Caledonia	60,101
Indonesia	39,382
Cuba	37,606
South Africa	22,000
Botswana	17,756

PAPER (Newsprint)[1]

Country	Amount
World	25,966,000
Canada	8,117,000
United States	4,574,000
Japan	2,715,000
Soviet Union	1,532,000
Finland	1,501,000
Sweden	1,323,000
China	1,040,000
W. Germany	680,000

PETROLEUM[3]

Country	Amount
World	3,848,087,000
Soviet Union	890,721,000
United States	618,810,000
Saudi Arabia	467,796,000
Mexico	207,733,000
Britain	150,703,000
China	148,483,000
Venezuela	145,969,000
United A. Emir.	85,859

RUBBER, NATURAL[1]

Country	Amount
World	3,750,000
Malaysia	1,516,600
Indonesia	880,000
Thailand	552,200
India	165,900
Sri Lanka	152,200
Philippines[7]	72,000
Liberia	67,500
Nigeria	45,500

RUBBER, SYNTHETIC[1]

Country	Amount
World	5,735,000
United States	1,832,000
Japan	930,700
France	479,400
W. Germany	383,800
Brazil	228,100
Italy	210,000
Netherlands	202,700
Britain	190,200

SILVER[1]

Country	Amount
World	12,385
Peru	1,668
Mexico	1,550
Soviet Union	1,459
Canada	1,291
United States	1,252
France	964
Australia	888
Poland	657

STEEL (Crude)[1]

Country	Amount
World	616,869,000
Soviet Union	147,165,000
Japan	99,548,000
United States	67,656,000
China	37,120,000
W. Germany	35,880,000
Italy	24,188,000
France	18,402,000
Czechoslovakia	14,992,000

TIN CONCENTRATES[1]

Country	Amount
World	190,900
Malaysia	52,342
Indonesia	33,800
Bolivia	26,773
Thailand	26,207
Australia	12,615
Brazil	8,300
Britain	4,180
South Africa	3,035

URANIUM[1]

Country	Amount
World	41,290
United States	10,331
Canada	8,080
South Africa	5,815
Australia	4,453
Niger	4,259
Namibia	3,776
France	2,859
Gabon	970

ZINC[1]

Country	Amount
World	5,717,200
Soviet Union	875,000
Japan	606,200
Canada	505,000
Australia	301,000
United States	282,200
Belgium	240,900
France	240,000
West Germany	235,000

[1] In metric tons. [2] In metric carats. [3] In thousands of metric tons of coal equivalent. [4] In thousands of cubic meters. [5] In kilograms. [6] 1981 data. [7] June 30, 1981.

HIGHLIGHTS: 1985

WE ARE THE WORLD

British musicians formed an organization called Band Aid and put out a record "Do They Know It's Christmas," for the benefit of African famine victims. Following up on the idea, singer Harry Belafonte and producer Ken Kragen formed USA for Africa (United Support of Artists for Africa) for a similar project.

Michael Jackson and Lionel Richie teamed up to write the song "We Are the World," with an inspirational chorus:

"We are the world, we are the children.
"We are the ones to make a brighter day.
"So let's start giving.
"There's a choice we're making.
"We're saving our own lives.
"It's true we'll make a better day, just you and me."

In January about 45 American musicians gathered in Los Angeles to tape the recording, including Cyndi Lauper, Bruce Springsteen, Ray Charles, Dionne Warwick, Kenny Rogers, Huey Lewis, and Bob Dylan.

Upon release of the single in March, it immediately became a best-seller. An album with additional songs was released in April. Altogether the project was expected to raise $50 million or more. The first relief supplies bought from proceeds of the record were sent to Ethiopa and Sudan in June.

Later, American and British musicians teamed up on July 13 to put on a transatlantic concert and telethon for African relief. The Live Aid concert began in London before a live audience of 60,000 and ended 16 hours later before a crowd of 90,000 in Philadelphia. Among show stoppers of the concert was the first live broadcast of a Soviet rock group and reunions of such former popular rock groups as Who, Led Zepplin, and Crosby, Stills, Nash, and Young. An estimated 1.5 billion persons viewed the show on television in some 152 countries. It was expected to raise about $70 million.

APOLLO THEATER REOPENS

The legendary Apollo Theater on 125th Street in the middle of New York City's Harlem first opened in 1934. It became the main showcase of black performers, such as Duke Ellington, Melba Moore, Redd Fox, Pearl Bailey, Sammy Davis Jr., Stevie Wonder, Marvin Gaye, and many others. But as

A stamp commemorating the 100th anniversary of the birth of composer Jerome Kern (1885–1945) was issued on Jan. 23. Known as the "King of the American Musical Stage," Kern composed more than a thousand songs and over a hundred complete theatrical scores. He won two motion picture Oscar awards for his songs "The Way You Look Tonight" and "The Last Time I Saw Paris." His most successful Broadway musical was "Show Boat." The stamp was designed by Jim Sharpe of Westport, Conn.

blacks won acceptance in the general entertainment industry in the 1960s and 1970s, the theater fell on hard times and finally closed its doors in 1976.

After a $10.4 million renovation, the Apollo reopened on May 4, 1985, with a celebration that featured superstar performers who either had once performed at the Apollo or wished they had.

NBC taped a 3-hour special *Motown Returns to the Apollo*, hosted by comedian Bill Cosby, which won an Emmy Award as the best variety program of the 1984–85 TV season. Among the 60 featured performers were Little Richard, Diana Ross, Sarah Vaughan, Stevie Wonder, El DeBarge, and Patti LaBelle.

STAGE PLAYS ON AND OFF BROADWAY: 1985

As Is: Effect of disease AIDS on homosexual couple; author, William M. Hoffman; director, Marshall W. Mason; cast includes Jonathan Hadary, Jonathan Hogan, Ken Kliban, Lily Knight, Claris Erickson, Lou Liberatore; opened March 10, 1985.

Big River: The Adventures of Huckleberry Finn: Winner of seven 1985 Tony awards, including best Broadway musical; based on Mark Twain's novel; music and lyrics by country music composer Roger Miller; book by William Hauptman; directed by Des McAnuff; cast includes Seth Allen, William Youmans, Susan Browning, Patti Cohenour, Jennifer Leigh Warren, Bob Gunton, Ron Richardson, Daniel Jenkins, and Aramis Estevez; opened April 25, 1985.

Biloxi Blues: Neil Simon's comedy about an aspiring young writer undergoing basic training at an army camp in Mississippi during World War II; won 1985 Tony award as best play; directed by Gene Saks; cast includes Bruce Norris, Randall Edwards, Mark Nelson, Penelope Ann Miller, Jim Fyfe, Mark McDermott; opened March 28, 1985.

Brighton Beach Memoirs: 1983 New York Drama Critics Circle award as best play; comedy-drama by Neil Simon about Jewish families living in Brooklyn during Depression; cast includes Verna Bloom, Jennifer Blanc, Dick Latessa, Dorothy Holland, Wendy Gazelle, Brian Drillinger; directed by Gene Saks, who won 1983 Tony award as best director; opened March 27, 1983.

Cats: Musical based on poems of T.S. Eliot about cats; won seven 1983 Tony awards, including best musical and best director; music by Andrew Lloyd Webber; directed by Trevor Nunn; cast of 23 singers and dancers; opened Oct. 7, 1982.

A Chorus Line: Broadway's longest running show; winner of 1976 Tony award as best musical; about director picking dancers for chorus line; conceived, choreographed, and directed by Michael Bennett; music, Marvin Hamlisch; lyrics, Edward Kleban; book, James Kirkwood; opened on July 25, 1975.

Curse of the Starving Class: Revival of Sam Shepard's comedy about a battling family; directed by Robin Lynn Smith; cast includes Kathy Bates, Eddie Jones, Bradley Whitford, Karen Tull; opened May 23, 1985.

Dames at Sea: Revival of 1968 musical about smalltown girl waiting for a break as a Broadway dancer; book and lyrics by George Haimsohn and Robin Miller; music by Jim Wise; directed and choreographed by Neal Kenyon; opened June 12, 1985.

42nd Street: Won 1981 Tony awards for best musical and choreography; based on 1932 film about chorus girl who achieves stardom on Broadway; director and choreographer, Gower Champion; music and lyrics, Harry Warren and Al Dubin; book, Michael Stewart and Mark Bramble; cast includes, Millicent Martin, Don Chastain, Lisa Brown, and Lee Roy Reams; opened Aug. 25, 1980.

The Iceman Cometh: Revival of Eugene O'Neill play about failures who hang out in saloons; with Jason Robards, Barnard Hughes, Donald Moffat; directed by Jose Quintero; opened Sept. 29, 1985.

I'm Not Rappaport: Comedy by Herb Gardner starring Judd Hirsch and Cleavon Little as old men clowning in Central Park; directed by Daniel Sullivan; opened June 6, 1985.

La Cage Aux Folles: Won six 1984 Tony awards, including best musical; musical comedy about homosexual love affair; written by Harvey Fierstein, based on French comedy by Jean Poiret; music by Jerry Herman; directed by Arthur Laurents; starring Van Johnson and Walter Charles; opened on Aug. 21, 1983.

Mayor: Musical comedy about New York City's Mayor Ed Koch; music and lyrics by Charles Strouse; book by Warren Leight; cast includes Lenny Wolpe, Douglas Bernstein, Kathryn McAteer, Marion Caffey, Ilene Kristen, Keith Curran, Ken Jennings, and Nancy Giles; opened May 13, 1985.

The News: Rock Musical about New York tabloid editor, starring Jeff Conaway; music and lyrics by Paul Schierhorn; directed by David Rotenberg; opened Oct. 31, 1985.

The Odd Couple: Neil Simon's 1965 classic comedy revived and revised to change apartmentmates Oscar and Felix into Olive and Florence, starring Rita Moreno and Sally Struthers; directed by Gene Saks; opened June 11, 1985.

Orphans: Drama by Lyle Kessler about two orphan brothers and their encounter with a Chicago mobster; directed by Gary Sinise; cast includes Kevin Anderson, Terry Kinney, and John Mahoney; opened May 7, 1985.

The Search for Signs of Intelligent Life in the Universe (A Cozmic Soup Opera): One-person show by comedienne Lily Tomlin; opened Sept. 26, 1985.

Singin' in the Rain: Musical based on 1952 movie that starred Gene Kelly; screenplay and adaptation by Betty Comden and Adolph Green; directed and choreographed by Twyla Tharp; songs by Nacio Herb Brown and Arthur Freed; cast includes Don Correia, Mary D'Arcy, Faye Grand; opened July 2, 1985.

Song and Dance: Musical about amorous adventures of young Englishwoman in America; music by Andrew Lloyd Webber; lyrics by Don Black; directed by Richard Maltby Jr.; choreographed by Peter Martins; starring Bernadette Peters and Christoper d'Ambroise; opened Sept. 18, 1985.

Sunday in the Park with George: Won 1984 Pulitzer Prize and 1984 New York Drama Critics Circle award for best musical; about French painter Georges Seurat; music and lyrics by Stephen Sondheim; book and direction by James Lapine; starring Mandy Patinkin and Maryann Plunkett; opened on May 2, 1984.

Vampire Lesbians of Sodom: Charles Busch's laugh-a-minute comedy about vampires, Dracula, and everything else; directed by Kenneth Elliott; the author heads a large cast that includes Meghan Robinson, Tom Aulino, Andy Halliday; opened July 19, 1985.

MOVIES: 1985

After Hours (R): Bizarre comedy about trials of single man trying to score in New York City; with Griffin Dunne, Rosanna Arquette, Linda Fiorentino, John Heard, Teri Garr, Richard Cheech Marin, Thomas Chong; director, Martin Scorsese.

Agnes of God (PG-13): Based on Broadway play by John Pielmeier, about psychiatrist investigating whether nun killer her own newborn baby; with Jane Fonda, Ann Bancroft, Meg Tilley; director, Norman Jewison.

American Flyers (PG 13): Emotional and scenic view of America while bicycle racing; with Kevin Costner and David Grant; director, John Badham.

American Ninja (R): U.S. soldier in Philippines fights with martial-arts experts; with Michael Dudikoff, Steve James, Junie Aronson, Guich Koock, John Fujioka; director, Sam Firstenberg.

Back to the Future (PG): Good comedy about teenager sent backward in time to 1950s where he finds his parents as unmarried teenagers and becomes embroiled in trying to get them to meet and fall in love with each other; with Michael J. Fox, Crispin Glover, Lea Thompson; director, Robert Zemeckis.

The Black Cauldron (PG): Animated fantasy adventure from Walt Disney Pictures, based on Lloyd Alexander's series of books *The Chronicles of Prydain;* directors, Ted Berman and Richard Rich.

Brewster's Millions (PG): Comedy about young man who must spend $30 million in 30 days by terms of inheritance; with Richard Pryor, Lonette McKee, John Candy; director, Walter Hill.

The Bride (PG-13) Baron Frankenstein creates a bride for his monster, but proceeds to fall in love with her himself; with Sting, Jennifer Beals, Clancy Brown, David Rappaport, Anthony Higgins, Geraldine Page, Quentin Crisp, Verushka; director, Franc Roddam.

Cocoon (PG-13): Comedy about group of retirees rejuvenated by their accidental contact with cocoons placed in a swimming pool by beings from outer space; with Jessica Tandy, Maureen Stapleton, Gwen Verdon, Hume Cronyn, Don Ameche, Wilford Brimley, Jack Gilford; director, Ron Howard.

Compromising Positions (R): Comedy about housewife trying to track down murderer of dentist who seduced his female patients; with Susan Sarandon, Joe Mantegna, Edward Herrmann, Raul Julia, Judith Ivey, Joan Allen, Deborah Rush; director, Frank Perry.

Dance with a Stranger (R): True story about last woman to be hanged for murder in Britain and why she killed her lover; with Miranda Richardson, Rupert Everett, Ian Holm; director, Mike Newell.

Desperately Seeking Susan (PG-13): Comedy in which downtrodden housewife trades roles with liberated streetwise single; with Madonna, Rosanna Arquette, Aidan Quinn; director, Susan Seidelman.

Dim Sum: A Little Bit of Heart (PG): Comedy about Chinese family in San Francisco; with Kim Chew, Laureen Chew, and Victor Wong; director, Wayne Wang.

The Emerald Forest (R): American boy is kidnapped by Amazon Indians, grows up with them, and prefers living with tribe than returning to civilization; with Charley Boorman, Powers Boothe, Rui Polonah; director, John Boorman.

Eureka (R): Lucky strike makes poor gold prospector suddenly wealthy in 1920s; with Gene Hackman, Theresa Russell, Rutger Hauer, Mickey Rourke, Jane Lapotaire, and Joe Pesci; director, Nicolas Roeg.

Fletch (PG): Comedy about investigative reporter who assumes many identities to gather information; with Chevy Chase, Tim Matheson; director, Michael Ritchie.

Fright Night (R): Both funny and grisly things happen when teenager finds out neighbor is a vampire; with Chris Sarandon, William Ragsdale, Amanda Bearse, Stephen Geoffreys, Roddy McDowall; director, Tom Holland.

Godzilla 1985 (R): Monster of 1950s again returns to smash cities; with Raymond Burr, who also starred in first Godzilla film three decades ago; directors, Kohji Hashimoto and R.J. Kizer.

Goonies (PG): Scary comedy in which group of kids on treasure hunt in cave run into gangsters and have narrow escapes; director, Richard Donner.

Insignificance (R): Senator, professor, actress, and athlete confront each other in 1950s with thought-provoking consideration of social issues; with Tony Curtis, Michael Emil, Theresa Russell, and Gary Busey; director, Nicolas Roeg.

James Joyce's Women (R): Six of James Joyce's most famous and erotic women are played by actress-author-producer Fionnula Flanagan; director, Michel Pearce.

Joshua Then and Now (R): Adapted from novel by Mordecai Richler, about popular writer reviewing his life and loves; with James Woods, Gabrielle Lazure, Michael Sarrazin, and Alan Arkin; director, Ted Kotcheff.

Key Exchange (R): Not-so-funny comedy about yuppie man and woman New Yorkers try to decide whether to exchange keys to their apartments; with Ben Masters, Brooke Adams; director, Barnet Kellman.

Kiss of the Spider Woman (R): Homosexual convict seduces his cellmate with his retelling of old movie plots; with William Hurt, Raul Julia, Sonia Braga; director, Hector Babenco.

Lifeforce (R): Based on Colin Wilson's novel *The Space Vampires,* scientists exploring comet bring frozen aliens back to Earth where they revive with frightening results; with Steve Railsback, Peter Firth, Frank Finlay, and Mathilda May; director Tobe Hooper.

Mad Max Beyond Thunderdome (PG-13): Australian futuristic fantasy sequel to *Mad Max, The Road Warrior;* with Mel Gibson, Tina Turner; directors, George Miller and George Ogilvie.

Mishima: A Life in Four Chapters (R): About life and suicide of Japan's leading post-World War II author, Yukio Mishima; with Ken Ogata, Kenji Sawada, Yasosuke Bando, Toshiyuki Nagashima; director, Paul Schrader.

Morons from Outer Space (PG-13): Slapstick

sci-fi comedy about bumbling tourists from outer space who land on Earth; with Mel Smith, Griff Rhys Jones, James B. Sikking, Dinsdale Landen, Jimmy Nail, Joanne Pearce, Paul Bown; director, Mike Hodges.

My Other Husband (PG-13): Comedy about woman married to two husbands; with Miou-Miou, Roger Hanin, Eddy Mitchell, Dominique Lavanant, and Charlotte de Turckheim; director, Georges Lautner.

National Lampoon's European Vacation (PG-13): Slapstick adventure with lots of jokes; with Chevy Chase, Beverly D'Angelo, Dana Hill, Jason Lively, Victor Lanoux, and Eric Idle; director, Amy Heckerling.

Pale Rider (R): Western in which preacher protects gold prospectors from greedy big mining company; with Clint Eastwood, Michael Moriarty, Christopher Penn, Carrie Snodress; director, Cling Eastwood.

Pee-Wee's Big Adventure (PG): Entertaining comedy as Pee-Wee Herman searches for his bicycle; with Elizabeth Daily, Hark Holton, Diane Salinger, Judd Omen; director, Jim Burton.

Plenty (R): Adaptation of David Hare's Broadway play about Englishwoman haunted by memories of her work with the French Resistance in World War II; with Meryl Streep, Charles Dance, Tracey Ullman, John Gielgud; director, Fred Schepisi.

Prizzi's Honor (R): Satire on gangster movies, about complexity of life for matter-of-fact hit man who falls in love with beautiful hit woman; with Jack Nicholson, Kathleen Turner, Lee Richarson, Robert Loggia, William Hickey, Anjelica Huston; director, John Huston.

The Purple Rose of Cairo (PG): Comedy in which movie actor steps right off the screen to romance fantasy-starved waitress; with Mia Farrow, Jeff Daniels; director, Woody Allen.

Rambo: First Blood II (R): Adventurer searching for missing American prisoners of war in Vietnam takes bloody revenge on Vietnamese and Russians; with Sylvester Stallone, Charles Napier, Richard Crenna; director, George P. Cosmatos.

Real Genius (PG): Genuinely funny comedy about teenage physics genius in conflict with an ambitious professor; with Val Kilmer, Gabe Jarret, William Atherton, Michelle Meyrink, Robert Prescott; director, Martha Coolidge.

Return to Oz (PG): Based on L. Frank Baum's Oz books, takes Dorothy and friends on further adventures in Oz; with Fairuza Balk, Nicol Williamson, Jean Marsh, Piper Laurie, Matt Clark; director, Walter Murch.

St. Elmo's Fire (R): Drama about seven recent college graduates and their problems; with Judd Nelson, Demi Moore, Andrew McCarthy, Ally Sheedy, Mare Winningham, Rob Lowe, Emilio Estevez; director, Joel Schumacher.

Sesame Street Presents: Follow that Bird (G): Human actors and the Muppet puppets join together in a good-humored romp centered on helping Big Bird; with Jim Henson, Caroll Spinney, Frank Oz, Sandra Berhard, John Candy, Chevy Chase, Joe Flaherty, Waylon Jennings, Dave Thomas; director, Ken Kwapis.

Silverado (PG-13): Old fashioned Western with familiar plot; with Kevin Kline, Linda Hunt, Scott Glenn, Kevin Costner, Brian Dennehy; director, Lawrence Kasdan.

Sudden Death (R): Rape turns young woman into vigilante gun gal; with Denise Coward, Frank Runyeon; director, Sig Shore.

Summer Rental (PG): Comedy about man who gets more than he bargained for when he rents beach house for his family's summer vacation; with John Candy, Richard Crenna, Karen Austin, Rip Torn; director, Carl Reiner.

Teen Wolf (PG): Comedy about teenager who wins celebrity by turning into a wolf; with Michael J. Fox, James Hampton, Scott Paulin, Susan Ursitti, Jerry Levine, Jay Tarses; director, Rod Daniel.

A View to Kill (PG): Another James Bond film in which he saves the world from evil; with Roger Moore, Christopher Walken, Grace Jones; director, John Glen.

Volunteers (R): Slapstick comedy about wealthy young man who inadvertently joins the Peace Corps; with Tom Hanks, John Candy; director, Nicholas Meyer.

Weird Science (PG-13): Comedy tarnished with profanity, concerning two teenage scientists who among other things construct their concept of a perfect woman with their computer; with Anthony Michael Hall, Kelly LeBrock, Ilan Mitchell-Smith; director, John Hughes.

Wetherby (R): Bleak drama that searches for reason youth kills himself at home of schoolteacher; with Vanessa Redgrave, Tim McInnerny; director, David Hare.

Year of the Dragon (R): Violent drama about cop pitted against organized crime in New York City's Chinatown; with Mickey Rourke, John Lone; director, Michael Cimino.

Movie ratings: G = general, all ages admitted; PG = Parental guidance suggested; PG-13 = Parents cautioned to give guidance to children under 13; R = restricted, no one under 17 admitted unless with parent or guardian; X = no one under 17 admitted.

MOVIE OSCAR AWARDS

Source: American Academy of Motion Picture Arts and Sciences

BEST MOTION PICTURE

1927-28	Wings	1938	You Can't Take It with You
1928-29	Broadway Melody	1939	Gone with the Wind
1929-30	All Quiet on the Western Front	1940	Rebecca
1930-31	Cimarron	1941	How Green Was My Valley
1931-32	Grand Hotel	1942	Mrs. Miniver
1932-33	Cavalcade	1943	Casablanca
1934	It Happened One Night	1944	Going My Way
1935	Mutiny on the Bounty	1945	The Lost Weekend
1936	The Great Ziegfeld	1946	The Best Years of Our Lives
1937	The Life of Emile Zola	1947	Gentleman's Agreement

MOVIE OSCAR AWARDS: BEST MOTION PICTURE *(continued)*

1948 Hamlet	1967 In the Heat of the Night
1949 All the King's Men	1968 Oliver!
1950 All About Eve	1969 Midnight Cowboy
1951 An American in Paris	1970 Patton
1952 The Greatest Show on Earth	1971 The French Connection
1953 From Here to Eternity	1972 The Godfather
1954 On the Waterfront	1973 The Sting
1955 Marty	1974 The Godfather, Part II
1956 Around the World in 80 Days	1975 One Flew Over the Cuckoo's Nest
1957 The Bridge on the River Kwai	1976 Rocky
1958 Gigi	1977 Annie Hall
1959 Ben-Hur	1978 The Deer Hunter
1960 The Apartment	1979 Kramer vs. Kramer
1961 West Side Story	1980 Ordinary People
1962 Lawrence of Arabia	1981 Chariots of Fire
1963 Tom Jones	1982 Gandhi
1964 My Fair Lady	1983 Terms of Endearment
1965 Sound of Music	1984 Amadeus
1966 A Man for All Seasons	

BEST ACTOR

1927–28 Emil Jannings, The Last Command, The Way of All Flesh	1956 Yul Brynner, The King and I
	1957 Alec Guinness, The Bridge on the River Kwai
1928–29 Warner Baxter, In Old Arizona	1958 David Niven, Separate Tables
1929–30 George Arliss, Disraeli	1959 Charlton Heston, Ben-Hur
1930–31 Lionel Barrymore, A Free Soul	1960 Burt Lancaster, Elmer Gantry
1931–32 Wallace Berry, The Champ	1961 Maximilian Schell, Judgment at Nuremberg
1932–33 Frederic March, Dr. Jekyll and Mr. Hyde	1962 Gregory Peck, To Kill a Mockingbird
1934 Clark Gable, It Happened One Night	1963 Sidney Poitier, Lilies of the Field
1935 Victor McLaglen, The Informer	1964 Rex Harrison, My Fair Lady
1936 Paul Muni, The Story of Louis Pasteur	1965 Lee Marvin, Cat Ballou
1937 Spencer Tracy, Captains Courageous	1966 Paul Scofield, A Man for All Seasons
1938 Spencer Tracy, Boys Town	1967 Rod Steiger, In the Heat of the Night
1939 Robert Donat, Goodbye, Mr. Chips	1968 Cliff Robertson, Charly
1940 James Stewart, The Philadelphia Story	1969 John Wayne, True Grit
1941 Gary Cooper, Sergeant York	1970 George C. Scott, Patton
1942 James Cagney, Yankee Doodle Dandy	1971 Gene Hackman, The French Connection
1943 Paul Lukas, Watch on the Rhine	1972 Marlon Brando, The Godfather
1944 Bing Crosby, Going My Way	1973 Jack Lemmon, Save the Tiger
1945 Ray Milland, The Lost Weekend	1974 Art Carney, Harry and Tonto
1946 Frederic March, The Best Years of Our Lives	1975 Jack Nicholson, One Flew Over the Cuckoo's Nest
1947 Ronald Colman, A Double Life	1976 Peter Finch, Network
1948 Laurence Olivier, Hamlet	1977 Richard Dreyfuss, The Goodbye Girl
1949 Broderick Crawford, All the King's Men	1978 Jon Voight, Coming Home
1950 Jose Ferrer, Cyrano de Bergerac	1979 Dustin Hoffman, Kramer vs. Kramer
1951 Humphrey Bogart, The African Queen	1980 Robert De Niro, Raging Bull
1952 Gary Cooper, High Noon	1981 Henry Fonda, On Golden Pond
1953 William Holden, Stalag 17	1982 Ben Kingsley, Gandhi
1954 Marlon Brando, On the Waterfront	1983 Robert Duvall, Tender Mercies
1955 Ernest Borgnine, Marty	1984 F. Murray Abraham, Amadeus

BEST ACTRESS

1927–28 Janet Gaynor, Seventh Heaven, Street Angel, Sunrise	1950 Judy Holliday, Born Yesterday
	1951 Vivien Leigh, A Streetcar Named Desire
1928–29 Mary Pickford, Coquette	1952 Shirley Booth, Come Back, Little Sheba
1929–30 Norma Shearer, The Divorcee	1953 Audrey Hepburn, Roman Holiday
1930–31 Marie Dressler, Min and Bill	1954 Grace Kelly, The Country Girl
1931–32 Helen Hayes, The Sin of Madelon Claudet	1955 Anna Magnani, The Rose Tattoo
1932–33 Katharine Hepburn, Morning Glory	1956 Ingrid Bergman, Anastasia
1934 Claudette Colbert, It Happened One Night	1957 Joanne Woodward, The Three Faces of Eve
1935 Bette Davis, Dangerous	1958 Susan Hayward, I Want to Live
1936 Luise Rainer, The Great Ziegfeld	1959 Simone Signoret, Room at the Top
1937 Luise Rainer, The Good Earth	1960 Elizabeth Taylor, Butterfield 8
1938 Bette Davis, Jezebel	1961 Sophia Loren, Two Women
1939 Vivien Leigh, Gone with the Wind	1962 Anne Bancroft, The Miracle Worker
1940 Ginger Rogers, Kitty Foyle	1963 Patricia Neal, Hud
1941 Joan Fontaine, Suspicion	1964 Julie Andrews, Mary Poppins
1942 Greer Garson, Mrs. Miniver	1965 Julie Christie, Darling
1943 Jennifer Jones, The Song of Bernadette	1966 Elizabeth Taylor, Who's Afraid of Virginia Woolf?
1944 Ingrid Bergman, Gaslight	1967 Katharine Hepburn, Guess Who's Coming to Dinner?
1945 Joan Crawford, Mildred Pierce	1968 Katharine Hepburn, The Lion in Winter; Barbra Streisand, Funny Girl
1946 Olivia de Havilland, To Each His Own	1969 Maggie Smith, The Prime of Miss Jean Brodie
1947 Loretta Young, The Farmer's Daughter	1970 Glenda Jackson, Women in Love
1948 Jane Wyman, Johnny Belinda	1971 Jane Fonda, Klute
1949 Olivia de Havilland, The Heiress	

MOVIE OSCAR AWARDS: BEST ACTRESS (continued)

1972	Liza Minnelli, *Cabaret*	1979	Sally Field, *Norma Rae*
1973	Glenda Jackson, *A Touch of Class*	1980	Sissy Spacek, *Coal Miner's Daughter*
1974	Ellen Burstyn, *Alice Doesn't Live Here Anymore*	1981	Katharine Hepburn, *On Golden Pond*
1975	Louise Fletcher, *One Flew Over the Cuckoo's Nest*	1982	Meryl Streep, *Sophie's Choice*
1976	Faye Dunaway, *Network*	1983	Shirley MacLaine, *Terms of Endearment*
1977	Diane Keaton, *Annie Hall*	1984	Sally Field, *Places in the Heart*
1978	Jane Fonda, *Coming Home*		

BEST DIRECTOR

1927–28	Frank Borzage, *Seventh Heaven;* Lewis Milestone, *Two Arabian Knights*	1956	George Stevens, *Giant*
		1957	David Lean, *The Bridge on the River Kwai*
1928–29	Frank Lloyd, *The Divine Lady*	1958	Vincente Minnelli, *Gigi*
1929–30	Lewis Milestone, *All Quiet on the Western Front*	1959	William Wyler, *Ben-Hur*
1930–31	Norman Taurog, *Skippy*	1960	Billy Wilder, *The Apartment*
1931–32	Frank Borzage, *Bad Girl*	1961	Jerome Robbins, Robert Wise, *West Side Story*
1932–33	Frank Lloyd, *Cavalcade*	1962	David Lean, *Lawrence of Arabia*
1934	Frank Capra, *It Happened One Night*	1963	Tony Richardson, *Tom Jones*
1935	John Ford, *The Informer*	1964	George Cukor, *My Fair Lady*
1936	Frank Capra, *Mr. Deeds Goes to Town*	1965	Robert Wise, *Sound of Music*
1937	Leo McCarey, *The Awful Truth*	1966	Fred Zinnemann, *A Man for All Seasons*
1938	Frank Capra, *You Can't Take It with You*	1967	Mike Nichols, *The Graduate*
1939	Victor Fleming, *Gone with the Wind*	1968	Sir Carol Reed, *Oliver!*
1940	John Ford, *The Grapes of Wrath*	1969	John Schlesinger, *Midnight Cowboy*
1941	John Ford, *How Green Was My Valley*	1970	Franklin J. Chaffner, *Patton*
1942	William Wyler, *Mrs. Miniver*	1971	William Friedkin, *The French Connection*
1943	Michael Curtiz, *Casablanca*	1972	Bob Fosse, *Cabaret*
1944	Leo McCarey, *Going My Way*	1973	George Roy Hill, *The Sting*
1945	Billy Wilder, *The Lost Weekend*	1974	Francis Ford Coppola, *The Godfather, Part II*
1946	William Wyler, *The Best Years of Our Lives*	1975	Milos Forman, *One Flew Over the Cuckoo's Nest*
1947	Elia Kazan, *Gentleman's Agreement*	1976	John Avildsen, *Rocky*
1948	John Huston, *Treasure of Sierra Madre*	1977	Woody Allen, *Annie Hall*
1949	Joseph L. Mankiewicz, *A Letter to Three Wives*	1978	Michael Cimino, *The Deer Hunter*
1950	Joseph L. Mankiewicz, *All About Eve*	1979	Robert Benton, *Kramer vs. Kramer*
1951	George Stevens, *A Place in the Sun*	1980	Robert Redford, *Ordinary People*
1952	John Ford, *The Quiet Man*	1981	Warren Beatty, *Reds*
1953	Fred Zinnemann, *From Here to Eternity*	1982	Richard Attenborough, *Gandhi*
1954	Elia Kazan, *On the Waterfront*	1983	James L. Brooks, *Terms of Endearment*
1955	Delbert Mann, *Marty*	1984	Milos Forman, *Amadeus*

BEST SUPPORTING ACTOR

1936	Walter Brennan, *Come and Get It*	1961	George Chakiris, *West Side Story*
1937	Joseph Schildkraut, *The Life of Emile Zola*	1962	Ed Begley, *Sweet Bird of Youth*
1938	Walter Brennan, *Kentucky*	1963	Melvyn Douglas, *Hud*
1939	Thomas Mitchell, *Stagecoach*	1964	Peter Ustinov, *Topkapi*
1940	Walter Brennan, *The Westerner*	1965	Martin Balsam, *A Thousand Clowns*
1941	Donald Crisp, *How Green Was My Valley*	1966	Walter Matthau, *The Fortune Cookie*
1942	Van Heflin, *Johnny Eager*	1967	George Kennedy, *Cool Hand Luke*
1943	Charles Coburn, *The More the Merrier*	1968	Jack Albertson, *The Subject Was Roses*
1944	Barry Fitzgerald, *Going My Way*	1969	Gig Young, *They Shoot Horses, Don't They?*
1945	James Dunn, *A Tree Grows in Brooklyn*	1970	John Mills, *Ryan's Daughter*
1946	Harold Russell, *The Best Years of Our Lives*	1971	Ben Johnson, *The Last Picture Show*
1947	Edmund Gwenn, *Miracle on 34th Street*	1972	Joel Grey, *Cabaret*
1948	Walter Huston, *The Treasure of Sierra Madre*	1973	John Houseman, *The Paper Chase*
1949	Dean Jagger, *Twelve O'Clock High*	1974	Robert De Niro, *The Godfather, Part II*
1950	George Sanders, *All About Eve*	1975	George Burns, *The Sunshine Boys*
1951	Karl Malden, *A Streetcar Named Desire*	1976	Jason Robards, *All the President's Men*
1952	Anthony Quinn, *Viva Zapata!*	1977	Jason Robards, *Julia*
1953	Frank Sinatra, *From Here to Eternity*	1978	Christopher Walken, *The Deer Hunter*
1954	Edmond O'Brien, *The Barefoot Contessa*	1979	Melvyn Douglas, *Being There*
1955	Jack Lemmon, *Mister Roberts*	1980	Timothy Hutton, *Ordinary People*
1956	Anthony Quinn, *Lust for Life*	1981	Sir John Gielgud, *Arthur*
1957	Red Buttons, *Sayonara*	1982	Louis Gossett Jr., *An Officer and a Gentleman*
1958	Burl Ives, *The Big Country*	1983	Jack Nicholson, *Terms of Endearment*
1959	Hugh Griffith, *Ben-Hur*	1984	Haing S. Ngor, *The Killing Fields*
1960	Peter Ustinov, *Spartacus*		

BEST SUPPORTING ACTRESS

1936	Gale Sondergaard, *Anthony Adverse*	1944	Ethel Barrymore, *None But the Lonely Heart*
1937	Alice Brady, *In Old Chicago*	1945	Anne Revere, *National Velvet*
1938	Fay Bainter, *Jezebel*	1946	Anne Baxter, *The Razor's Edge*
1939	Hattie McDaniel, *Gone with the Wind*	1947	Celeste Holm, *Gentleman's Agreement*
1940	Jane Darwell, *The Grapes of Wrath*	1948	Claire Trevor, *Key Largo*
1941	Mary Astor, *The Great Lie*	1949	Mercedes McCambridge, *All the King's Men*
1942	Teresa Wright, *Mrs. Miniver*	1950	Josephine Hull, *Harvey*
1943	Katina Paxinou, *For Whom the Bell Tolls*	1951	Kim Hunter, *A Streetcar Named Desire*

MOVIE OSCAR AWARDS: BEST SUPPORTING ACTRESS *(continued)*

1952	Gloria Grahame, *The Bad and the Beautiful*	1969	Goldie Hawn, *Cactus Flower*
1953	Donna Reed, *From Here to Eternity*	1970	Helen Hayes, *Airport*
1954	Eva Marie Saint, *On the Waterfront*	1971	Cloris Leachman, *The Last Picture Show*
1955	Jo Van Fleet, *East of Eden*	1972	Eileen Heckart, *Butterflies Are Free*
1956	Dorothy Malone, *Written on the Wind*	1973	Tatum O'Neal, *Paper Moon*
1957	Miyoshi Umeki, *Sayonara*	1974	Ingrid Bergman, *Murder on the Orient Express*
1958	Wendy Hiller, *Separate Tables*	1975	Lee Grant, *Shampoo*
1959	Shelley Winters, *The Diary of Anne Frank*	1976	Beatrice Straight, *Network*
1960	Shirley Jones, *Elmer Gantry*	1977	Vanessa Redgrave, *Julia*
1961	Rita Moreno, *West Side Story*	1978	Maggie Smith, *California Suite*
1962	Patty Duke, *The Miracle Worker*	1979	Meryl Streep, *Kramer vs. Kramer*
1963	Margaret Rutherford, *The V.I.P.'s*	1980	Mary Steenburgen, *Melvin and Howard*
1964	Lila Kedrova, *Zorba the Greek*	1981	Maureen Stapleton, *Reds*
1965	Shelley Winters, *A Patch of Blue*	1982	Jessica Lange, *Tootsie*
1966	Sandy Dennis, *Who's Afraid of Virginia Woolf?*	1983	Linda Hunt, *The Year of Living Dangerously*
1967	Estelle Parsons, *Bonnie and Clyde* —	1984	Dame Peggy Ashcroft, *A Passage to India*
1968	Ruth Gordon, *Rosemary's Baby*		

TELEVISION EMMY AWARDS

Source: National Academy of Television Arts and Sciences

OUTSTANDING COMEDY SERIES

1969–70	*My World and Welcome to It* (NBC)	1977–78	*All in the Family* (CBS)
1970–71	*All in the Family* (CBS)	1978–79	*Taxi* (ABC)
1971–72	*All in the Family* (CBS)	1979–80	*Taxi* (ABC)
1972–73	*All in the Family* (CBS)	1980–81	*Taxi* (ABC)
1973–74	*M*A*S*H* (CBS)	1981–82	*Barney Miller* (ABC)
1974–75	*The Mary Tyler Moore Show* (CBS)	1982–83	*Cheers* (NBC)
1975–76	*The Mary Tyler Moore Show* (CBS)	1983–84	*Cheers* (NBC)
1976–77	*The Mary Tyler Moore Show* (CBS)	1984–85	*The Cosby Show* (NBC)

OUTSTANDING SPECIAL—DRAMA OR COMEDY

1969–70	*A Storm in Summer* (NBC)	1977–78	*The Gathering* (ABC)
1970–71	*The Andersonville Trial* (PBS)	1978–79	*Friendly Fire* (ABC)
1971–72	*Brian's Song* (ABC)	1979–80	*The Miracle Worker* (NBC)
1972–73	*A War of Children* (CBS)	1980–81	*Playing for Time* (CBS)
1973–74	*The Autobiography of Miss Jane Pittman* (CBS)	1981–82	*A Woman Called Golda* (SYN)
1974–75	*The Law* (NBC)	1982–83	*Special Bulletin* (NBC)
1975–76	*Eleanor and Franklin* (ABC)	1983–84	*Something About Amelia* (ABC)
1976–77	*Eleanor and Franklin: The White House Years* (ABC) *Sybil* (NBC) (tie)	1984–85	*Do You Remember Love* (CBS)

OUTSTANDING DRAMA SERIES

1971–72	*Elizabeth R* (PBS)	1978–79	*Lou Grant* (CBS)
1972–73	*The Waltons* (CBS)	1979–80	*Lou Grant* (CBS)
1973–74	*Upstairs, Downstairs* (PBS)	1980–81	*Hill Street Blues* (NBC)
1974–75	*Upstairs, Downstairs* (PBS)	1981–82	*Hill Street Blues* (NBC)
1975–76	*Police Story* (NBC)	1982–83	*Hill Street Blues* (NBC)
1976–77	*Upstairs, Downstairs* (PBS)	1983–84	*Hill Street Blues* (NBC)
1977–78	*The Rockford Files* (NBC)	1984–85	*Cagney & Lacey* (CBS)

OUTSTANDING VARIETY, MUSIC, OR COMEDY PROGRAM

1971–72	*Jack Lemmon in 'S Wonderful, 'S Marvelous* (NBC)	1978–79	*Steve & Eydie Celebrate Irving Berlin* (NBC)
1972–73	*Singer Presents Liza with a 'Z'* (NBC)	1979–80	*IBM Presents Baryshnikov on Broadway* (ABC)
1973–74	*Lily* (CBS)	1980–81	*Lily Sold Out* (CBS)
1974–75	*An Evening with John Denver* (ABC)	1981–82	*Night of 100 Stars* (ABC)
1975–76	*Gypsy in My Soul* (CBS)	1982–83	*Motown 25: Yesterday, Today, Forever* (NBC)
1976–77	*The Barry Manilow Special* (ABC)	1983–84	*A Celebration of the Performing Arts* (CBS)
1977–78	*Bette Midler—Old Red Hair is Back* (NBC)	1984–85	*Motown Returns to the Apollo* (NBC)

OUTSTANDING ACTOR IN A DRAMA SERIES

1971–72	Peter Falk, *Columbo* (NBC)	1978–79	Ron Leibman, *Kaz* (CBS)
1972–73	Richard Thomas, *The Waltons* (CBS)	1979–80	Ed Asner, *Lou Grant* (CBS)
1973–74	Telly Savalas, *Kojak* (CBS)	1980–81	Daniel J. Travanti, *Hill Street Blues* (NBC)
1974–75	Robert Blake, *Baretta* (ABC)	1981–82	Daniel J. Travanti, *Hill Street Blues* (NBC)
1975–76	Peter Falk, *Columbo* (NBC)	1982–83	Ed Flanders, *St. Elsewhere* (NBC)
1976–77	James Garner, *The Rockford Files* (NBC)	1983–84	Tom Selleck, *Magnum P.I.* (CBS)
1977–78	Ed Asner, *Lou Grant* (CBS)	1984–85	William Daniels, *St. Elsewhere* (NBC)

OUTSTANDING ACTOR IN LIMITED SERIES OR SPECIAL

1971–72	Keith Michell, *Catherine Howard* (CBS)	1978–79	Peter Strauss, *The Jericho Mile* (ABC)
1972–73	Laurence Olivier, *A Long Day's Journey* (ABC)	1979–80	Powers Boothe, *Guyana Tragedy* (CBS)
1973–74	Hal Holbrook, *Pueblo* (ABC)	1980–81	Anthony Hopkins, *The Bunker* (CBS)
1974–75	Laurence Olivier, *Love Among the Ruins* (ABC)	1981–82	Mickey Rooney, *Bill* (CBS)
1975–76	Hal Holbrook, *Sandburg's Lincoln* (NBC)	1982–83	Tommy Lee Jones, *The Executioner's Song* (NBC)
1976–77	Christopher Plummer, *The Moneychangers* (NBC)	1983–84	Laurence Olivier, *Laurence Olivier's King Lear* (SYN)
1977–78	Michael Moriarty, *Holocaust* (NBC)	1984–85	Richard Crenna, *The Rape of Richard Beck* (ABC)

TV EMMY AWARDS (continued)

OUTSTANDING ACTRESS IN A DRAMA SERIES

1971–72	Glenda Jackson, *Elizabeth R* (PBS)
1972–73	Michael Learned, *The Waltons* (CBS)
1973–74	Michael Learned, *The Waltons* (CBS)
1974–75	Jean Marsh, *Upstairs, Downstairs* (PBS)
1975–76	Michael Learned, *The Waltons* (CBS)
1976–77	Lindsay Wagner, *The Bionic Woman* (ABC)
1977–78	Sada Thompson, *Family* (ABC)
1978–79	Mariette Hartley, *The Incredible Hulk* (CBS)
1979–80	Barbara Bel Geddes, *Dallas* (CBS)
1980–81	Barbara Babcock, *Hill Street Blues* (NBC)
1981–82	Michael Learned, *Nurse* (CBS)
1982–83	Tyne Daly, *Cagney & Lacey* (CBS)
1983–84	Tyne Daly, *Cagney & Lacey* (CBS)
1984–85	Tyne Daly, *Cagney & Lacey* (CBS)

OUTSTANDING ACTRESS IN LIMITED SERIES OR SPECIAL

1970–71	Lee Grant, *The Neon Ceiling* (NBC)
1971–72	Glenda Jackson, *Shadow in the Sun* (PBS)
1971–72	Cloris Leachman, *A Brand New Life* (ABC)
1973–74	Cicely Tyson, *The Autobiography of Miss Jane Pittman* (CBS)
1974–75	Katharine Hepburn, *Love Among the Ruins* (ABC)
1975–76	Rosemary Harris, *Notorious Woman* (PBS)
1976–77	Patty Duke Astin, *Captains and the Kings* (NBC)
1977–78	Meryl Streep, *Holocaust* (NBC)
1978–79	Bette Davis, *Strangers* (CBS)
1979–80	Patty Duke Astin, *The Miracle Worker* (NBC)
1980–81	Vanessa Redgrave, *Playing for Time* (CBS)
1981–82	Ingrid Bergman, *A Woman Called Golda* (SYN)
1982–83	Barbara Stanwyck, *The Thorn Birds, Part 1* (ABC)
1983–84	Jane Fonda, *The Dollmaker* (ABC)
1984–85	Joanne Woodward, *Do You Remember Love* (CBS)

THEATER: TONY AWARDS

Source: Antoinette Perry awards by the American Theatre Wing and the League of N.Y. Theatres

BEST PLAY

1969–70	Frank McMahon, *Borstal Boy*
1970–71	Anthony Shaffer, *Sleuth*
1971–72	David Rabe, *Sticks and Stones*
1972–73	Jason Miller, *That Championship Season*
1973–74	Joseph A. Walker, *The River Niger*
1974–75	Peter Shaffer, *Equus*
1975–76	Tom Stoppard, *Travesties*
1976–77	Michael Cristofer, *The Shadow Box*
1977–78	Hugh Leonard, *Da*
1978–79	Bernard Pomerance, *The Elephant Man*
1979–80	Mark Medoff, *Children of a Lesser God*
1980–81	Peter Shaffer, *Amadeus*
1981–82	David Edgar, (based on Charles Dickens novel) *The Life and Adventures of Nicholas Nickleby*
1982–83	Harvey Fierstein, *Torch Song Trilogy*
1983–84	Tom Stoppard, *The Real Thing*
1984–85	Neil Simon, *Biloxi Blues*

BEST MUSICAL

1969–70	*Applause,* music and lyrics by Betty Comden and Adolph Green
1970–71	*Company,* music and lyrics by Stephen Sondheim
1971–72	*Two Gentlemen of Verona,* music and lyrics by Mel Shapiro and John Guare
1972–73	*A Little Night Music,* music and lyrics by Stephen Sondheim
1973–74	*Raisin,* producer: Robert Nemiroff
1974–75	*The Wiz,* music and lyrics by William F. Brown and Charlie Smalls
1975–76	*A Chorus Line,* music by Marvin Hamlisch, lyrics by Edward Kleban
1976–77	*Annie,* music by Charles Strouse, lyrics by Martin Charnin
1977–78	*Ain't Misbehavin',* based on songs associated with Fats Waller
1978–79	*Sweeney Todd,* music and lyrics by Stephen Sondheim
1979–80	*Evita,* musical score by Andrew Lloyd Webber and Tim Rice
1980–81	*42nd Street,* music and lyrics by Harry Warren and Al Dubine
1981–82	*Nine,* musical score by Maury Yeston
1982–83	*Cats,* musical score by Andrew Lloyd Webber
1983–84	*La Cage aux Folles,* music and lyrics by Jerry Herman
1984–85	*Big River,* music by Roger Williams

BEST DRAMATIC ACTRESS

1969–70	Tammy Grimes, *Private Lives*
1970–71	Maureen Stapleton, *The Gingerbread Lady*
1971–72	Sada Thompson, *Twigs*
1972–73	Julie Harris, *The Last of Mrs. Lincoln*
1973–74	Colleen Dewhurst, *A Moon for the Misbegotten*
1974–75	Ellen Burstyn, *Same Time, Next Year*
1975–76	Irene Worth, *Sweet Bird of Youth*
1976–77	Julie Harris, *The Belle of Amherst*
1977–78	Jessica Tandy, *The Gin Game*
1978–79	Constance Cummings, *Wings;* Carole Shelley, *The Elephant Man*
1979–80	Phyllis Frelich, *Children of a Lesser God*
1980–81	Jane Lapotaire, *Piaf*
1981–82	Zoe Caldwell, *Medea*
1982–83	Jessica Tandy, *Foxfire*
1983–84	Glenn Close, *The Real Thing*
1984–85	Stockard Channing, *Joe Egg*

BEST DRAMATIC ACTOR

1969–70	Fritz Weaver, *Child's Play*
1970–71	Brian Bedford, *The School for Wives*
1971–72	Cliff Gorman, *Lenny*
1972–73	Alan Bates, *Butley*
1973–74	Michael Moriarty, *Find Your Way Home*
1974–75	Jon Kani and Winston Nishona, *Sizwe Banzi* and *The Island*
1975–76	John Wood, *Travesties*
1976–77	Al Pacino, *The Basic Training of Pavlo Hummel*
1977–78	Bernard Hughes, *Da*
1978–79	Tom Conti, *Whose Life Is It Anyway?*
1979–80	John Rubinstein, *Children of a Lesser God*
1980–81	Ian McKellen, *Amadeus*
1981–82	Roger Rees, *The Life and Adventures of Nicholas Nickleby*
1982–83	Harvey Fierstein, *Torch Song Trilogy*
1983–84	Jeremy Irons, *The Real Thing*
1984–85	Derek Jacobi, *Much Ado About Nothing*

BEST MUSICAL ACTRESS

1969–70	Lauren Bacall, *Applause*
1970–71	Helen Gallagher, *No, No, Nanette*
1971–72	Alexis Smith, *Follies*
1972–73	Glynis Johns, *A Little Night Music*
1973–74	Virginia Capers, *Raisin*
1974–75	Angela Lansbury, *Gypsy*

TONY AWARDS: BEST MUSICAL ACTRESS (continued)

1975–76	Donna McKechnie, *A Chorus Line*	1980–81	Lauren Bacall, *Woman of the Year*
1976–77	Dorothy Laudon, *Annie*	1981–82	Jennifer Holliday, *Dreamgirls*
1977–78	Liza Minelli, *The Act*	1982–83	Natalia Makarova, *On Your Toes*
1978–79	Angela Lansbury, *Sweeney Todd*	1983–84	Chita Rivera, *The Rink*
1979–80	Patti LuPone, *Evita*	1984–85	No award

BEST MUSICAL ACTOR

1969–70	Cleavon Little, *Purlie*	1977–78	John Cullum, *On the Twentieth Century*
1970–71	Hal Linden, *The Rothschilds*	1978–79	Len Cariou, *Sweeney Todd*
1971–72	Phil Silvers, *A Funny Thing Happened on the Way to the Forum*	1979–80	Jim Dale, *Barnum*
		1980–81	Kevin Kline, *The Pirates of Penzance*
1972–73	George S. Irving, *Irene*	1981–82	Ben Harney, *Dreamgirls*
1973–74	Christopher Plummer, *Cyrano*	1982–83	Tommy Tune, *My One and Only*
1974–75	John Cullum, *Shenandoah*	1983–84	George Hearn, *La Cage aux Folles*
1975–76	George Rose, *My Fair Lady*	1984–85	No award
1976–77	Barry Bostwick, *The Robber Bridegroom*		

MUSIC: GRAMMY AWARDS

Source: National Academy of Recording Arts and Sciences

BEST RECORD

1958	Domenico Modugno, *Nel Blu Dipinto Di Blu*	1971	Carole King, *It's Too Late*
1959	Bobby Darin, *Mack the Knife*	1972	Roberta Flack, *The First Time Ever I Saw Your Face*
1960	Percy Faith, *Theme from A Summer Place*	1973	Roberta Flack, *Killing Me Softly with His Song*
1961	Henry Mancini, *Moon River*	1974	Olivia Newton-John, *I Honestly Love You*
1962	Tony Bennett, *I Left My Heart in San Francisco*	1975	Captain & Tennille, *Love Will Keep Us Together*
1963	Henry Mancini, *The Days of Wine and Roses*	1976	George Benson, *This Masquerade*
1964	Stan Getz and Astrud Gilberto, *The Girl from Ipanema*	1977	Eagles, *Hotel California*
		1978	Billy Joel, *Just the Way You Are*
1965	Herb Alpert, *A Taste of Honey*	1979	The Doobie Brothers, *What a Fool Believes*
1966	Frank Sinatra, *Strangers in the Night*	1980	Christopher Cross, *Sailing*
1967	5th Dimension, *Up, Up and Away*	1981	Kim Carnes, *Bette Davis Eyes*
1968	Simon & Garfunkel, *Mrs. Robinson*	1982	Toto, *Rosanna*
1969	5th Dimension, *Aquarius/Let the Sunshine In*	1983	Michael Jackson, *Beat It*
1970	Simon & Garfunkel, *Bridge Over Troubled Waters*	1984	Tina Turner, *What's Love Got to Do With It*

BEST ALBUM

1958	Henry Mancini, *The Music from Peter Gunn*	1972	*The Concert for Bangla Desh*
1959	Frank Sinatra, *Come Dance With Me*	1973	Stevie Wonder, *Innervisions*
1960	Bob Newhart, *Button Down Mind*	1974	Stevie Wonder, *Fulfillingness' First Finale*
1961	Judy Garland, *Judy At Carnegie Hall*	1975	Paul Simon, *Still Crazy After All These Years*
1962	Vaughn Meader, *The First Family*	1976	Stevie Wonder, *Songs in the Key of Life*
1963	Barbara Streisand, *The Barbara Streisand Album*	1977	Fleetwood Mac, *Rumours*
1964	Stan Getz and Astrud Gilberto, *Getz/Gilberto*	1978	Bee Gees, *Saturday Night Fever*
1965	Frank Sinatra, *September of My Years*	1979	Billy Joel, *52nd Street*
1966	Frank Sinatra, *A Man and His Music*	1980	Christopher Cross, *Christopher Cross*
1967	The Beatles, *Sgt. Pepper's Lonely Hearts Club Band*	1981	John Lennon and Yoko Ono, *Double Fantasy*
1968	Glen Campbell, *By the Time I Get To Phoenix*	1982	Toto, *Toto IV*
1969	Blood, Sweat and Tears, *Blood, Sweat and Tears*	1983	Michael Jackson, *Thriller*
1970	Simon & Garfunkel, *Bridge Over Troubled Waters*	1984	Lionel Richie, *Can't Slow Down*
1971	Carole King, *Tapestry*		

BEST MALE POP VOCALIST

1958	Perry Como, *Catch a Falling Star*	1972	Harry Nilsson, *Without You*
1959	Frank Sinatra, *Come Dance With Me*	1973	Stevie Wonder, *You Are the Sunshine of My Life*
1960	Ray Charles, *Georgia On My Mind*	1974	Stevie Wonder, *Fulfillingness' First Finale*
1961	Jack Jones, *Lollipops and Roses*	1975	Paul Simon, *Still Crazy After All These Years*
1962	Tony Bennett, *I Left My Heart in San Francisco*	1976	Stevie Wonder, *Songs in the Key of Life*
1963	Jack Jones, *Wives and Lovers*	1977	James Taylor, *Handy Man*
1964	Louis Armstrong, *Hello, Dolly!*	1978	Barry Manilow, *Copacabana*
1965	Frank Sinatra, *It Was a Very Good Year*	1979	Billy Joel, *52nd Street*
1966	Frank Sinatra, *Strangers in the Night*	1980	Kenny Loggins, *This Is It*
1967	Glen Campbell, *By the Time I Get to Phoenix*	1981	Al Jarreau, *Breaking Away*
1968	Jose Feliciano, *Light My Fire*	1982	Lionel Richie, *Truly*
1969	Harry Nilsson, *Everybody's Talkin'*	1983	Michael Jackson, *Thriller*
1970	Ray Stevens, *Everything Is Beautiful*	1984	Phil Collins, *Against All Odds*
1971	James Taylor, *You've Got a Friend*		

BEST FEMALE POP VOCALIST

1958	Ella Fitzgerald, *The Irving Berlin Song Book*	1963	Barbra Streisand, *The Barbra Streisand Album*
1959	Ella Fitzgerald, *But Not For Me*	1964	Barbra Streisand, *People*
1960	Ella Fitzgerald, *Mack the Knife*	1965	Barbra Streisand, *My Name is Barbra*
1961	Judy Garland, *Judy At Carnegie Hall*	1966	Eydie Gorme, *If He Walked into My Life*
1962	Ella Fitzgerald, *Ella Swings Brightly with Nelson Riddle*	1967	Bobbie Gentry, *Ode to Billie Joe*
		1968	Dionne Warwick, *Do You Know the Way to San Jose*

GRAMMY AWARDS: BEST FEMALE POP VOCALIST *(Continued)*

1969	Peggy Lee, *Is That All There Is*	1978	Anne Murray, *You Needed Me*
1970	Dionne Warwick, *I'll Never Fall in Love Again*	1979	Dionne Warwick, *I'll Never Love This Way Again*
1971	Carole King, *Tapestry*	1980	Bette Midler, *The Rose*
1972	Helen Reddy, *I Am Woman*	1981	Lena Horne, *Lena Horne: The Lady and Her Music*
1973	Roberta Flack, *Killing Me Softly with His Song*	1982	Melissa Manchester, *You Should See How She*
1974	Olivia Newton-John, *I Honestly Love You*		*Talks About You*
1975	Janis Ian, *At Seventeen*	1983	Irene Cara, *Flashdance*
1976	Linda Ronstadt, *Hasten Down the Wind*	1984	Tina Turner, *What's Love Got to Do With It*
1977	Barbra Streisand, *Evergreen*		

BEST POP DUO OR GROUP

1958	Louis Prima & Keely Smith, *That Old Black Magic*	1972	Roberta Flack & Donny Hathaway, *Where is the Love*
1959	Mormon Tabernacle Choir, *Battle Hymn of the Republic*	1973	Gladys Knight & The Pips, *Neither One of Us (Wants to be the First to Say Goodbye)*
1960	Steve Lawrence & Eydie Gorme, *We Got Us*	1974	Paul McCartney & Wings, *Band on the Run*
1961	Lambert, Hendricks and Ross, *High Flying*	1975	Eagles, *Lyin' Eyes*
1962	Peter, Paul and Mary, *If I Had a Hammer*	1976	Chicago, *If You Leave Me Now*
1963	Peter, Paul and Mary, *Blowin' in the Wind*	1977	Bee Gees, *How Deep is Your Love*
1964	The Beatles, *A Hard Day's Night*	1978	Bee Gees, *Saturday Night Fever*
1965	Anita Kerr Singers, *We Dig Mancini*	1979	The Doobie Brothers, *Minute by Minute*
1966	Anita Kerr Singers, *A Man and A Woman*	1980	Barbra Streisand & Barry Gibb, *Guilty*
1967	5th Dimension, *Up, Up and Away*	1981	Manhattan Transfer, *Boy from New York City*
1968	Simon & Garfunkel, *Mrs. Robinson*	1982	Joe Cocker & Jennifer Wames, *Up Where We Belong*
1969	5th Dimension, *Aquarius/Let the Sunshine In*		
1970	The Carpenters, *Close to You*	1983	Police, *Every Breath You Take*
1971	The Carpenters, *The Carpenters*	1984	Pointer Sisters, *Jump (for My Love)*

ACADEMY OF COUNTRY MUSIC AWARDS

Source: Academy of Country Music

TOP MALE VOCALIST

1965	Buck Owens	1970	Merle Haggard	1975	Conway Twitty	1980	George Jones
1966	Merle Haggard	1971	Freddie Hart	1976	Mickey Gilley	1981	Merle Haggard
1967	Glen Campbell	1972	Merle Haggard	1977	Kenny Rogers	1982	Ronnie Milsap
1968	Glen Campbell	1973	Charlie Rich	1978	Kenny Rogers	1983	Lee Greenwood
1969	Merle Haggard	1974	Merle Haggard	1979	Larry Gatlin	1984	George Strait

TOP FEMALE VOCALIST

1965	Bonnie Owens	1970	Lynn Anderson	1975	Loretta Lynn	1980	Dolly Parton
1966	Bonnie Guitar	1971	Loretta Lynn	1976	Crystal Gayle	1981	Barbara Mandrell
1967	Lynn Anderson	1972	Donna Fargo	1977	Crystal Gayle	1982	Sylvia
1968	Cathie Taylor	1973	Loretta Lynn	1978	Barbara Mandrell	1983	Janie Fricke
1969	Tammy Wynette	1974	Loretta Lynn	1979	Crystal Gayle	1984	Reba McEntire

TOP NEW MALE VOCALIST

1965	Merle Haggard	1970	Buddy Alan	1975	Freddy Fender	1980	Johnny Lee
1966	Billy Mize	1971	Tony Booth	1976	Moe Bandy	1981	Ricky Skaggs
1967	Jerry Inman	1972	Johnny Rodrigues	1977	Eddie Rabbitt	1982	Michael Murphey
1968	Ray Sanders	1973	Dorsey Burnette	1978	John Conlee	1983	Jim Glaser
1969	Freddy Weller	1974	Mickey Gilley	1979	R.C. Bannon	1984	Vince Gill

TOP NEW FEMALE VOCALIST

1965	Kaye Adams	1970	Sammi Smith	1975	Crystal Gayle	1980	Terri Gibbs
1966	Cathie Taylor	1971	Barbara Mandrell	1976	Billie Jo Spears	1981	Juice Newton
1967	Bobbie Gentry	1972	Tanya Tucker	1977	Debby Boone	1982	Karen Brooks
1968	Cheryl Poole	1973	Olivia Newton-John	1978	Cristy Lane	1983	Gus Hardin
1969	Donna Fargo	1974	Linda Ronstadt	1979	Lacy J. Dalton	1984	Nicolette Larson

TOP VOCAL GROUP AND/OR DUET

1965	Bonnie Owens & Merle Haggard	1974	No Award
1966	Bonnie Owens & Merle Haggard (Duet)/Bob Morris & Faye Hardin (Group)	1975	Loretta Lynn & Conway Twitty
		1976	Loretta Lynn & Conway Twitty
1967	Bonnie Owens & Merle Haggard/Sons of the Pioneers	1977	The Statler Bros.
		1978	The Oak Ridge Boys
1968	Johnny & Jonie Mosby	1979	Moe Bandy & Joe Stampley
1969	Kimberly's	1980	David Frizzell & Shelly West
1970	Kimberly's	1981	Alabama
1971	Loretta Lynn & Conway Twitty	1982	David Frizzell & Shelly West/Alabama
1972	The Statler Bros.	1983	Kenny Rogers & Dolly Parton/Alabama
1973	Brush Arbor	1984	The Judds (Duet)/Alabama

ENTERTAINER OF THE YEAR

1970	Merle Haggard	1974	Mac Davis	1978	Kenny Rogers	1982	Alabama
1971	Freddie Hart	1975	Loretta Lynn	1979	Willie Nelson	1983	Alabama
1972	Roy Clark	1976	Mickey Gilley	1980	Barbara Mandrell	1984	Alabama
1973	Roy Clark	1977	Dolly Parton	1981	Alabama		

SONG OF THE YEAR

1966 Bobby Austin, *Apartment #9*	1976 Mickey Gilley, *Don't The Girls Get Prettier At*
1967 Wynn Stewart, *It's Such A Pretty World Today*	*Closing Time*
1968 Glen Campbell, *Wichita Lineman*	1977 Kenny Rogers, *Lucille*
1969 Merle Haggard, *Okie From Muskogee*	1978 Anne Murray, *You Needed Me*
1970 Ray Price, *For The Good Times*	1979 Moe Bandy, *It's A Cheatin' Situation*
1971 Freddie Hart, *Easy Lovin'*	1980 George Jones, *He Stopped Loving Her Today*
1972 Donna Fargo, *Happiest Girl*	1981 David Frizell & Shelly West, *You're The Reason God*
1973 Charlie Rich, *Behind Closed Doors*	*Made Oklahoma*
1974 Cal Smith, *Country Bumpkin*	1982 Merle Haggard, *Are The Good Times Really Over*
1975 Glen Campbell, *Rhinestone Cowboy*	1983 Gary Morris, *The Wind Beneath My Wings*
	1984 The Judds, *Why Not Me*

SINGLE RECORD OF THE YEAR

1968 Roger Miller, *Little Green Apples*	1977 Kenny Rogers, *Lucille*
1969 Merle Haggard, *Oakie From Muskogee*	1978 Don Williams, *Tulsa Time*
1970 Ray Price, *For The Good Times*	1979 Larry Gatlin, *All The Gold In California*
1971 Freddie Hart, *Easy Lovin'*	1980 George Jones, *He Stopped Loving Her Today*
1972 Donna Fargo, *Happiest Girl*	1981 The Oak Ridge Boys, *Elvira*
1973 Charlie Rich, *Behind Closed Doors*	1982 Willie Nelson, *Always On My Mind*
1974 Cal Smith, *Country Bumpkin*	1983 Kenny Rogers & Dolly Parton, *Islands In The Stream*
1975 Glen Campbell, *Rhinestone Cowboy*	1984 Willie Nelson & Julio Iglesias, *To All The Girls I've*
1976 Mickey Gilley, *Bring It On Home*	*Loved Before*

ALBUM OF THE YEAR

1967 Glen Campbell, *Gentle On My Mind*	1976 Mickey Gilley, *Gilley's Smoking*
1968 Glen Campbell & Bobbie Gentry, *Glen Campbell &*	1977 Kenny Rogers, *Kenny Rogers*
Bobbie Gentry	1978 The Oak Ridge Boys, *Ya'll Come Back Saloon*
1969 Merle Haggard, *Okie From Muskogee*	1979 Larry Gatlin, *Straight Ahead*
1970 Ray Price, *For The Good Times*	1980 Urban Cowboy (Soundtrack)
1971 Freddie Hart, *Easy Lovin'*	1981 Alabama, *Feels So Right*
1972 Donna Fargo, *Happiest Girl*	1982 Willie Nelson, *Always On My Mind*
1973 Charlie Rich, *Behind Closed Doors*	1983 Alabama, *The Closer You Get*
1974 John Denver, *Back Home Again*	1984 Alabama, *Roll On*
1975 Loretta Lynn & Conway Twitty, *Feeling's*	

SHOW BUSINESS PERSONALITIES

Personalities of the theater, film, TV, and entertainment world are included in the following list. Real names follow show business names.

Members of the Theater Hall of Fame, are marked with (T). Members of the Entertainment Hall of Fame, elected by the nation's entertainment editors, are marked with (E). American

Academy of Motion Picture Arts and Sciences award winners are indicated with (A) and the year for which the Oscar was given.

See also *Musicians, Composers, Singers, Dancers*, pages 56–61; *Authors and Writers*, pages 90–99. See pages 981–986 for 1985 deaths of show business personalities.

Abbott and Costello: Bud Abbott (1895–1974), Lou Costello (1906–59), comedy team
George Abbott (1887–), theatrical producer, T
Philip Abbott (1924–), actor
Walter Abel (1898–), actor
Bettye Ackerman (1928–), actress, wed to Sam Jaffe
Roy Acuff (1903–), country music singer, bandleader
Brooke Adams (1949–), actress
Don Adams (1927–), actor
Edie Adams (Elizabeth Edith Enke; 1929–), singer
Joey Adams (1911–), comedian
Julie Adams (1927–), actress
Mason Adams (1919–), actor
Pepper Adams (1930–), jazz saxophonist, clarinetist
Stanley Adams (1907–), lyricist (*La Cucaracha*)
Maude Adams (Maude Kiskadden; 1872–1953), actress, T
Charles Addams (1912–), cartoonist (*The Addams Family*)
Dawn Addams (1930–85), actress
Cannonball Adderley (1928–75), jazz saxophonist
Larry Adler (1914–), harmonica virtuoso
Luther Adler (1903–84), actor
Richard Adler (1921–), composer, lyricist
John Agar (1921–), actor
Brian Aherne (1902–), British actor
Charles Aidman (1926–), actor
Alvin Ailey (1931–), dancer and choreographer
Anouk Aimee (Françoise Sorya; 1932–), actress
Claude Akins (1918–), actor
Toshiko Akiyoshi (1929–), jazz composer, pianist, bandleader
Edward Albee (1928–), playwright, T
Anna Maria Alberghetti (1936–), Italian-born singer
Eddie Albert (Eddie Heimberger; 1908–), actor
Edward Albert (1951–), actor, son of Eddie Albert
Jack Albertson (1907–81), actor, A-1968
Lola Albright (1924–), actress

Alan Alda (1936–), actor, son of Robert Alda
Robert Alda (Alphonso d'Abruzzo; 1914–), actor
Robert Aldrich (1918–1983), film director
Denise Alexander (1945–), actress
Jane Alexander (Jane Quigley; 1939–), actress
Duane David Allen (1943–), gospel singer, songwriter
Fred Allen (John F. Sullivan; 1894–1956), actor, comedian
Gracie Allen (1906–64), comedienne, wife of George Burns
Karen Jane Allen (1951–), actress
Mel Allen (1913–), sportscaster
Phillip Richard Allen (1939–), actor
Red Allen (1900–67), Dixieland trumpet player
Steve Allen (1921–), entertainer
Viola Allen (1867–1948), actress, T
Woody Allen (Allen Konigsberg; 1935–), comedian, writer, director, A-1977
Fran Allison (1924–), actress
Allman Brothers: Duane (1946–71), Gregg (1947–), rock musicians
June Allyson (Ella Geisman; 1923–), actress
Herb Alpert (1937–), pop-jazz trumpeter, singer
Robert Altman (1925–), film director
Don Ameche (Dominic Amici; 1908–), actor
Ames Brothers: Joe (1924–), Gene (1925–), Vic (1926–78), Ed (1927–), singing group
Leon Ames (Leon Waycoff; 1903–), actor
Nancy Ames (1937–), singer
Morey Amsterdam (1912–), actor and comedian
Bradley Jay Anderson (1924–), cartoonist (*Marmaduke*)
Eddie "Rochester" Anderson (1905–77), actor
Ian Anderson (1947–), British rock singer, guitarist
James William Anderson III (1937–), country music songwriter, entertainer
Dame Judith Anderson (Frances Margaret Anderson; 1898–), Australian actress, T
Lynn Anderson (1947–), country music singer

SHOW BUSINESS PERSONALITIES *(continued)*

Richard Anderson (1926–), actor
Robert Woodruff Anderson (1917–), playwright, T
Bibi Andersson (1935–), Swedish actress
Ursula Andress (1936–), Swiss-born actress
Andrews Sisters: LaVerne (1913–67), Maxine (1916–), Patty (1918–), singing group in 1940s
Dana Andrews (Carver Daniel Andrews; 1909–), actor
Julie Andrews (Julia Wells; 1935–), British actress and singer, A-1964, wed to Blake Edwards
Pier Angeli (1933–71), Italian-born actress
Philip Anglim (1953–), actor
Margaret Anglin (1876–1958), actress, T
Paul Anka (1941–), singer and composer
Ann-Margret (Ann-Margret Olsson; 1941–), Swedish-born actress
Michael Ansara (1922–), actor
Michelangelo Antonioni (1912–), Italian film director
Roscoe "Fatty" Arbuckle (1887–1933), comedian
Eve Arden (Eunice Guedens; 1912–), actress
Alan Arkin (1934–), actor and director
Harold Arlen (1905–), composer (*Stormy Weather*)
Richard Arlen (1899–1976), actor, T
George Arliss (1868–1946), British actor, A-1929–30, T
Louis Armstrong (1900–71), jazz trumpeter and singer
Desi Arnaz (1915–), Cuban-born actor and producer
Desi Arnaz Jr. (1953–), actor, son of Desi
Lucie Arnaz (1951–), actress, daughter of Desi
James Arness (James Aurness; 1923–), actor, brother of Peter Graves
Eddy Arnold (1918–), country music singer
Edward Arnold (1890–1956), actor
Beatrice Arthur (Bernice Frankel; 1926–), actress
Jean Arthur (Gladys Greene; 1905–), actress
Jane Asher (1945–), actress
Elizabeth Ashley (1941–), actress
Edward Asner (1929–), actor
Fred Astaire (Frederick Austerlitz; 1899–), dancer and actor, T, E, A-1949
Nils Asther (1897–1981), Swedish film actor
John Astin (1930–), actor, director
Mary Astor (1906–), actress, A-1941
Chet Atkins (1924–), country music guitarist
Sir Richard Attenborough (1923–), actor, director (A-1982)
Lionell Atwill (1885–1946), British actor
René Auberjonois (1940–), actor
Mischa Auer (1905–67), Russian-born actor
Jean-Pierre Aumont (1911–), French actor
Gene Autry (1907–), singer and cowboy star
Frankie Avalon (1939–), singer
Bob Avian (1937–), choreography, producer
John Avildsen (1935–), director, A-1976
Hoyt Axton (1938–), country singer, songwriter
Dan Aykroyd (1952–), Canadian-born comedic actor, writer
Lew Ayres (1908–), actor
Charles Aznavour (1924–), French singer, actor
Candy Azzara (1947–), actress
Lauren Bacall (Betty Joan Perske; 1924–), actress
Catherine Bach (1954–), actress
Burt Bacharach (1929–), musician and composer (*Raindrops Keep Falling on My Head*)
Jim Backus (1913–), actor
John Badham (1943–), film director
Buddy Baer (1915–), actor, brother of Max
Max Baer (1909–59), boxer and actor
Max Baer, Jr. (1937–), actor and producer
Joan Baez (1941–), folk singer
Pearl Bailey (1918–), blues singer
Barbara Bain (1934–), actress, wed to Martin Landau
Conrad Bain (1923–), Canadian-born actor
Fay Bainter (1892–1968), actress, A-1938
Scott Baio (1961–), actor
Bil Baird (1904–), puppeteer
Carroll Baker (1932–), actress
Ginger Baker (1940–), British rock drummer
Joe Don Baker (1936–), actor
Josephine Baker (1906–75), singer, dancer
George Balanchine (1904–83), choreographer, E
Ina Balin (1937–), actress
Ernest Ball (1878–1927), songwriter (*When Irish Eyes Are Smiling*)
Lucille Ball (1911–), comedienne
Kaye Ballard (Catherine Balotta; 1926–), actress and comedienne
Martin Balsam (1919–), actor, A-1965

Anne Bancroft (Anne Italiano; 1931–), actress, A-1962, wed to Mel Brooks
Kenneth Banghart (1910–80), radio-TV newscaster
Tallulah Bankhead (1903–68), actress, T
Vilma Banky (1903–), silent-film star
Theda Bara (1890–1955), actress, first "vamp"
Brigitte Bardot (1934–), French actress
Bobby Bare (1935–), country singer, songwriter
Lynn Bari (1917–), actress
Bob Barker (1923–), TV quiz show host
Phineas T. Barnum (1810–91), circus showman
Barbara Barrie (1931–), actress
Bernard Barrow (1927–), actor
Gene Barry (Eugene Klass; 1922–), actor
John Barry (1933–), British composer
Ethel Barrymore (1879–1959), actress, A-1944, T
John Barrymore (John Blythe; 1882–1942), actor, T
Lionel Barrymore (1878–1954), actor, A-1930–31, T
Richard Barthelmess (1895–1963), actor
Freddie Bartholomew (1924–), British-born child actor in 1930s
Eva Bartok (1926–), actress
James Barton (1890–1962), actor
Richard Basehart (1914–84), actor
Count Basie (1904–84), jazz pianist, composer
Shirley Bassey (1937–), British singer
Alan Bates (1934–), British actor
Jon Bauman (1947–), entertainer (Bowzer, with Sha Na Na)
Charita Bauer (1923–85), actress
Anne Baxter (1923–), actress, A-1946
Les Baxter (1922–), musical arranger and composer
Warner Baxter (1889–1951), actor, A-1928–29
Nora Bayes (1880–1928), vaudeville entertainer, T
Beach Boys: Brian Wilson (1942–), Dennis Wilson (1944–83), Carl Wilson (1946–), Alan Jardine (1942–), Mike Love (1941–), rock band formed in 1961
Orson Bean (Dallas Frederick Burrows; 1928–), actor and comedian
The Beatles: George Harrison (1943–), John Lennon (1940–80), Paul McCartney (1942–), Ringo Starr (1940–), British rock group
Cecil Beaton (1904–80), British photographer, designer
Ned Beatty (1937–), actor
Warren Beatty (1938–), actor, director, A-1981
Sidney Bechet (1897–1959), jazz sax musician
Bonnie Bedelia (1948–), actress
Brian Bedford (1935–), British actor
Bee Gees, British rock trio: Barry Gibb (1946–), Robin Gibb (1949–), Maurice Gibb (1949–)
Noah Beery (1884–1946), actor
Noah Beery Jr. (1916–), actor
Wallace Beery (1889–1949), actor, A-1931–32
Ed Begley (1901–70), actor, A-1962
Leon Bix Beiderbecke (1903–31), jazz cornetist
Harry Belafonte (1927–), singer and actor
David Belasco (1854–1931), impresario, T
Barbara Bel Geddes (1922–), actress
Norman Bel Geddes (1900–58), scenic designer, T
Ralph Bellamy (1904–), actor
Jean-Paul Belmondo (1933–), French actor
John Belushi (1950–82), comedian, actor
Pat Benatar (1953–), rock singer
Robert C. Benchley (1889–1945), humorist and author
Gary Bender (1940–), TV sportscaster
William Bendix (1906–64), actor
Dirk Benedict (1945–), actor, singer
Paul Benedict (1938–), actor
Richard Benjamin (1938–), actor
Constance Bennett (1905–65), actress, sister of Joan
Joan Bennett (1910–), actress, sister of Constance
Michael Bennett (1943–), director, choreographer
Richard Bennett (1873–1944), actor, T, father of Constance and Joan
Tony Bennett (1926–), singer
Jack Benny (Joseph Kubelsky; 1894–1974), comedian, E
George Benson (1943–), blues guitarist and singer
Robby Benson (1957–), actor
Robert Benton (1932–), director, A-1979
John Beradino (1917–), actor
Gertrude Berg (1899–1966), actress
Candice Bergen (1946–), actress, daughter of Edgar
Edgar Bergen (1903–78), ventriloquist
Polly Bergen (1930–), singer
Senta Berger (1941–), Austrian actress
Ingmar Bergman (1918–), Swedish film director, A-1956, E

Ingrid Bergman (1915–82), Swedish actress, A-1944, 1956, 1974
Bunny Berigan (1909–42), swing bandleader, trumpeter
Busby Berkeley (1895–1976), dance director
Milton Berle (Milton Berlinger; 1908–), comedian
Irving Berlin (Israel Balline; 1888–), Russian-born composer (*God Bless America*)
Warren Berlinger (1937–), actor
Shelley Berman (1926–), comedian
Herschel Bernardi (1923–), actor
Sarah Bernhardt (Rosine Bernard; 1844–1923), French actress, T
Ben Bernie (1893–1943), bandleader
Leonard Bernstein (1918–), conductor, composer (*West Side Story*)
Chuck Berry (1926–), rock singer and composer
Ken Berry (c. 1939–), actor
Bernardo Bertolucci (1940–), Italian film director
James Knowland Best (1926–), actor
Forrest Betts (1943–), guitarist, composer ("Rambling Man")
Bill Beutel (1930–), TV newscaster
Richard Beymer (1939–), actor
Charles Bickford (1889–1967), actor
Barney Bigard (1906–80), jazz clarinetist
Theodore Bikel (1924–), Austrian-born actor, singer
David Birney (1940–), actor
Joey Bishop (Joseph Gottlieb; 1919–), comedian
Stephen Bishop (1952–), singer, songwriter ("Everybody Needs Love")
Jacqueline Bisset (1946–) British-born actress
Bill Bixby (1934–), actor
Cilla Black (Priscilla White; 1943–), British singer
Karen Black (1942–), actress
Honor Blackman (1929–), actress
Sidney Blackmer (1895–1973), actor
Harry Blackstone Jr. (1934–), magician
James Blackwood (c. 1914–), gospel singer
Vivian Blaine (Vivienne Stapleton; 1921–), singer, actress
Janet Blair (1921–), actress
Linda Blair (1959–), actress
Amanda Blake (Beverly Louise Neill; 1931–), actress
Eubie Blake (1883–1983), jazz pianist, composer
Ran Blake (1935–), jazz pianist, composer
Robert Blake (Michael Gubitosi; 1933–), actor
Ronee Blakely (1946–), actress
Art Blakey (1919–), jazz drummer
Mel Blanc (1908–), cartoon voiceman (Bugs Bunny)
Jimmy Blanton (1921–42), jazz bass player
Carla Bley (1938–), jazz pianist, composer
Paul Bley (1932–), jazz pianist, composer
Ray Bloch (1902–82), band conductor, pianist
Joan Blondell (1909–79), actress
Claire Bloom (1931–), British actress
Ben Blue (1900–75), comedian
Monte Blue (1890–1963), actor
Ann Blyth (1928–), actress
Bob & Ray: Bob Elliott (1923–), Ray Goulding (1922–), comedy team
Jerry Bock (Jerrold Lewis; 1928–), couposer of musicals (*Fiorello*)
Dirk Bogarde (Derek Van den Bogaerde; 1921–), British actor
Humphrey Bogart (1899–1957), actor, A-1951, E
Peter Bogdanovich (1939–), film director
Mary Boland (1880–1965), actress
Buddy Bolden (1868–1931), first jazz band leader (1895); cornetist
John Boles (1895–1969), singer and actor
Ray Bolger (1904–), dancer and actor, T
Robert Bolt (1924–), playwright
Ward Bond (1903–60), actor in westerns
Sonny Bono (1935–), singer, teamed with Cher
Sorrell Booke (1930–), actor
Debby Boone (1956–), singer, daughter of Pat Boone
Pat Boone (Charles Eugene Boone; 1934–), singer
Richard Boone (1917–81), actor
John Boorman (1933–), film director
Edwin Booth (1833–93), actor, T
Shirley Booth (1907–), actress, A-1952, T
Victor Borge (1909–), Danish-born pianist and comedian
Ernest Borgnine (Ermes Borgnino 1917–), actor, A-1955
Frank Borzage (1893–1962), director, A-1927–28, 1931–32
Philip Bosco (1930–), actor
Tom Bosley (1927–), actor
Connee Boswell (1907–76), singer
Timothy Bottoms (1951–), actor

Clara Bow (1905–65), actress, known as "It Girl"
Major Edward Bowes (1874–46), radio amateur hour host
David Bowie (David Jones; 1947–), British rock singer
Lee Bowman (1914–79), actor
Stephen Boyd (1928–77), Irish-born actor
William Boyd (1898–1972), cowboy actor (Hopalong Cassidy)
Charles Boyer (1899–1978), French actor
Peter Boyle (1933–), actor
Eddie Bracken (1920–), comedian and actor
Ed Bradley (c. 1944–), TV newscaster
Alice Brady (1893–1939), actress, T, A-1937
Scott Brady (Gerald Tierney; 1924–85), actor
Neville Brand (1921–), actor
Marlon Brando (1924–), actor, A-1954, 1972
Keefe Brasselle (1923–), actor
Rossano Brazzi (1916–), Italian actor
Jacques Brel (1929–78), singer, composer
Eileen Brennan (1935–), actress
Walter Brennan (1894–1974), actor, A-1936, 1938, 1940
David Brenner (1945–), comedian
George Brent (1904–79), Irish-born actor
Teresa Brewer (1931–), singer
Fanny Brice (Fannie Borach; 1891–1951), actress and singer, T
Jack Brickhouse (1916–), TV sportscaster
Beau Bridges (1941–), actor, son of Lloyd Bridges
Jeff Bridges (1949–), actor, son of Lloyd
Lloyd Bridges (1913–), actor
David Brinkley (1920–), TV newscaster
Frederick Brisson (1915–84), Danish-born producer
May Britt (Maybritt Wilkins; 1936–), Swedish-born actress
Barbara Britton (1920–80), actress
Helen Broderick (1891–1959), actress; mother of Broderick Crawford
John Brodie (1935–), TV sportscaster
James Brolin (1942–), actor
Charles Bronson (Charles Butchinsky; 1922–), actor
Peter Brook (1925–), British director
Albert Brooks (1947–), actor, writer, director
Geraldine Brooks (Geraldine Stroock, 1925–77), actress
James L. Brooks (1940–), director, writer, A-1983
Mel Brooks (Melvin Kaminsky; 1926–), comedian
Thomas J. Brookshier (1931–), TV sportscaster
James Brown (1928–), soul singer
Jim Brown (1936–), actor and football star
Jim Ed Brown (1934–), country singer
Joe E. Brown (1892–1973), comedian
Johnny Mack Brown (1904–74), actor
Les Brown (1912–), bandleader, songwriter
Jackson Browne (1947–), folk rock musician and composer
Leslie Browne (1957–), dancer, actress
Roscoe Lee Browne (1925–), actor, writer
Dave Brubeck (1920–), jazz pianist, combo leader
Lenny Bruce (1926–66), comedian
Nigel Bruce (1895–1953), British actor, ("Dr. Watson" in Sherlock Holmes films)
Virginia Bruce (1910–82), actress
Anita Bryant (1940–), singer
Yul Brynner (1920–85), Russian-born actor, A-1956
Edgar Buchanan (1902–79), actor
Horst Buchholz (1933–), German actor
Genevieve Bujold (1942–), French-Canadian actress
Luis Buñuel (1900–83), Spanish director
Victor Buono (1938–82), actor
Gary Burghoff (1953–), actor
Billie Burke (1885–1970), actress, T
Johnny Burke (1908–64), songwriter (*Swinging on a Star*)
Carol Burnett (1936–), comedienne
George Burns (Nathan Birnbaum, 1896–), comedian, A-1975
Raymond Burr (1917–), Canadian-born actor
Kenny Burrell (1931–), jazz guitarist
Abe Burrows (1910–85), playwright and director
Ellen Burstyn (Edna Gilhooley; 1932–), actress, A-1974
Richard Burton (Richard Jenkins; 1925–84), Welsh actor, T
Gary Busey (1944–), actor, jazz drummer
Francis X. Bushman (1883–1966), actor
Charles Butterworth (1896–1946), actor
Red Buttons (Aaron Schwatt; 1919–), actor and comedian, A-1957
Ruth Buzzi (1936–), comedienne
Spring Byington (1893–1971), actress
Edd Byrnes (1933–), actor
James Caan (1940–), actor

SHOW BUSINESS PERSONALITIES (continued)

Bruce Cabot (1904–73), actor
Sebastian Cabot (1918–77), British actor
Sid Caesar (1922–), comedian
James Cagney (1899–), actor, A-1942, E
Jeanne Cagney (1919–), actress, sister of James
Sammy Cahn (1913–), lyricist ("Love and Marriage")
Michael Caine (Maurice Micklewhite; 1933–), British actor
Zoe Caldwell (1933–), Australian actress
Louis Calhern (Carl Vogt; 1895–1956), actor
Rory Calhoun (Francis Durgin; 1922–), actor
Michael Callan (Martin Caliniff; 1935–), actor
Cab Calloway (1907–), jazz musician, bandleader
Corinne Calvet (1925–), French actress
Godfrey Cambridge (1933–76), comedian and actor
Rod Cameron (1912–83), actor
Joseph Campanella (1927–), actor
Glen Campbell (1938–), country-rock singer
Mrs. Patrick Campbell (1865–1940), British actress, T
Milton Caniff (1907–), cartoonist (Steve Canyon)
Dyan Cannon (Samille Friesen; 1937–), actress
J.D. Cannon (1922–), actor
Judy Canova (1916–83), actress, singer
Cantinflas (Mario Moreno; 1913–), Mexican comedian
Eddie Cantor (Edward Iskowitz; 1892–1964), comedian and singer, T
Lana Cantrell (1943–), Australian-born singer
Frank Capra (1897–), Italian-born film director, A-1934, 1936, 1938
Captain and Tennille; Daryl Dragon (1942–), and Toni Tennille (1943–), husband-wife pop-rock singing duo
Capucine (1935–), French actress
Claudia Cardinale (1939–), Italian actress
Harry Carey (1878–1947), actor
Harry Carey Jr. (1921–), actor
MacDonald Carey (1913–), actor
Ron Carey (Ronald J. Cicenia; 1935–), actor, comedian
Len Cariou (1939–), actor, director
Kitty Carlisle (Catherine Holzman; 1915–), actress
Richard Carlson (1912–77), actor
Hoagy Carmichael (1899–1981), songwriter (Stardust)
Judy Carne (Joyce Botterill; 1939–), British-born comedienne, singer
Art Carney (1918–), actor, A-1974
Leslie Caron (1931–), French actress and dancer
Karen (1950–83) and Richard (1945–) Carpenter, singing team
Vikki Carr (Florencia Bisenta de Casillas; 1941–), singer
David Carradine (1940–), actor, son of John
John Carradine (1906–), actor
Keith Carradine (1949–), actor, singer, songwriter, son of John
Leo Carrillo (1880–1961), actor
Diahann Carroll (1935–), singer and actress
John Carroll (1907–79), actor (Zorro)
Leo G. Carroll (1892–1972), British actor
Madeleine Carroll (1906–), British actress
Nancy Carroll (1905–1965), actress
Pat Carroll (1927–), comedienne
Jack Carson (1910–63), comedian and actor
Johnny Carson (1925–), television personality
D'Oyle Carte (1844–1901), British impressario
Betty Carter (Lillie Mae Jones; 1929–), jazz singer, songwriter
Jack Carter (1923–), comedian
June Carter (1929–), country singer; wed to Johnny Cash
Mrs. Leslie Carter (1862–1937), actress, T
Lynda Carter (1951–), actress
Maybelle Carter (1909–78), country music singer
Nell Carter (1948–), actress, singer
Terry Carter (John E. Decoste; 1928–), actor, director
Johnny Cash (1932–), country music singer
Rosanne Cash (1955–), country-pop singer, daughter of Johnny Cash
Peggy Cass (1926–), comedienne
John Cassavetes (1929–), actor and director
David Cassidy (1950–), singer and actor
Jack Cassidy (1927–76), actor, father of David and Shaun
Shaun Cassidy (1958–), singer and actor
Richard Castellano (1933–) actor
Irene Castle (Irene Foote; 1893–1969) and Vernon Castle (Vernon Blythe; 1885– 1918), wife-husband dance team
Mary Jo Catlett (c. 1940–) actress
Sidney Catlett (1910–51), jazz drummer
Joan Caulfield (1922–), actress

Dick Cavett (1936–), television personality
Bennett Cerf (1898–1971), television panelist, publisher
George Chakiris (1933–), actor, A-1961
Richard Chamberlain (1935–), actor
Gower Champion (1921–80), T, and Marge Champion (1923–), husband-wife dance team
John Chancellor (1927–), television commentator
Jeff Chandler (1918–61), actor
Lon Chaney (1883–1930), actor
Lon Chaney Jr. (1907–73), actor
Carol Channing (1923–), actress, singer, T
Stockard Channing (Susan Stockard; 1944–), actress
Harry Chapin (1942–81), folk-rock singer
Sir Charles Chaplin (1889–1977), British comic actor, A-1971
Geraldine Chaplin (1944–), actress, daughter of Charles
Sydney Chaplin (1926–), actor, son of Charles
Cyd Charisse (Tula Finklea; 1923–), actress and dancer
Ray Charles (1930–), singer, songwriter
Charley Chase (1893–1940), comedian and director
Chevy Chase (Cornelius Crane; 1943–), comedian, writer
Ruth Chatterton (1893–1961), actress, T
Paddy Chayefsky (1923–81), playwright, A-1976
Chubby Checker (Ernest Evans; 1941–), singer, popularized "twist" dance in 1960s
Cheech & Chong: Tommy Chong (1938–), Cheech Marin (1946–); comedy team
Cher (Cherilyn LaPierre; 1946–), singer, TV personality
Maurice Chevalier (1888–1972), French actor, A-1958
Julia Child (1912–), television personality
Julie Christie (1940–), British actress, A-1965
Jordan Christopher (1941–), actor and musician
William Christopher (1932–), actor
Edwin P. Christy (1815–62), showman and minstrel
June Christy (1925–), singer
Michael Cimino (1943–), director, A-1978
Ina Claire (Ina Fagan; 1892–1985), actress, T
Eric Clapton (1945–), British rock singer, composer
Bobby Clark (1888–1960), comedian, T
Dane Clark (Bernard Zanville; 1913–), actor
Dave Clark (1942–), British rock singer, drummer
Dick Clark (1929–), television personality
Petula Clark (1932–), British singer and actress
Roy Clark (1933–), country music singer, guitarist
Susan Clark (Nora Goulding; 1944–), Canadian-born actress
Stanley Clarke (1951–), jazz bassist, composer
Jill Clayburgh (1944–), actress
Jan Clayton (1925–83), actress
James Cleveland (1931–), gospel singer, composer
Jimmy Cliff (James Chambers; 1948–), Jamaican reggae singer, composer
Montgomery Clift (1920–66), actor
Rosemary Clooney (1928–), singer
Lee J. Cobb (Leo Jacob; 1911–76), actor, T
Charles Coburn (1877–1961), actor, A-1943
D.L. Coburn (1938–), playwright (The Gin Game; 1976)
James Coburn (1928–), actor
Imogene Coca (1920–), comedienne
Joe Cocker (John Robert Cocker; 1944–), British rock singer
James Coco (1930–), actor and comedian
Iron Eyes Cody (1915–), actor
George M. Cohan (1878–1942), musician, composer, (I'm a Yankee Doodle Dandy and Over There)T
Myron Cohen (1902–), comedian
Claudette Colbert (Lily Claudette Chauchoin; 1905–), French-born actress, A-1934
Cozy Cole (1909–81), jazz drummer
Nat King Cole (1919–65), singer and musician
Natalie Cole (1950–), singer, daughter of Nat King Cole
Cy Coleman (1929–), pianist, composer of musicals (Sweet Charity; 1973)
Dabney Coleman (1932–), actor
Gary Coleman (1968–), actor
Constance Collier (1878–1955), British actress, T
Charles Collingwood (1917–), radio and TV news commentator
Dorothy Collins (1926–), singer
Joan Collins (1933–), British-born actress
Judy Collins (1939–), singer
Ray Collins (1890–1965), actor
Bud Collyer (1908–69), actor and TV personality
Ronald Colman (1891–1958), British actor, A-1947
Jerry Colonna (1904–), comedian
Jessie Colter (Miriam Johnson; 1947–), country-pop

singer, wed to Waylon Jennings
Anita Colton (1919–), singer, entertainer
John Coltrane (1926–67), jazz sax musician
Russ Columbo (1908–34), singer
Betty Comden (1919–), lyricist. T
Anjanette Comer (1941–), actress
Perry Como (1912–), singer
Forrest Compton (1925–), actor
Eddie Condon (1905–73), dixieland bandleader
Chester Conklin (1886–71), silent-film comedian
Sean Connery (1930–), Scottish-born actor
Ray Conniff (1916–), jazz trombonist, composer
Chuck Connors (1921–), actor
Mike Connors (1925–), actor
Robert Conrad (Conrad Robert Falk; 1935–), actor
William Conrad (1920–), actor
Hans Conreid (1915–82), actor
Michael Constantine (Constantine Efstration; 1927–), actor
Richard Conte (1915–75), Italian-born actor
Tom Conti (1941–), Scottish-born actor
Bert Convy (1939–), TV game show host
Kevin Conway (1942–), actor, director
Tim Conway (1933–), comedian
Rita Coolidge (1944–), singer
Jackie Coogan (1914–84), child star in silent movies
Alistair Cooke (Alfred Alistaire; 1908–), British author, television personality
Sam Cooke (1935–64), soul singer
Alice Cooper (Vincent Furnier; 1948–), rock singer
Gary Cooper (1901–61), actor, A-1941, 1952, 1960
Jackie Cooper (1922–), child movie star in 1930s, actor, director
Joan Copeland (c. 1929–), actress
Francis Ford Coppola (1939–), director, writer, A-1974
Ellen Corby (1913–), actress
Alex Cord (Alexander Viespi; 1931–), actor
Chick Corea (1941–), jazz pianist, composer
Jeff Corey (1914–), actor, drama coach
Wendell Corey (1914–68), actor
Katharine Cornell (1898–1974), stage actress, T
Charles Correll (1890–1972), radio actor, "Andy"
Bill Cosby (1937–), actor and comedian
Howard Cosell (Howard William Cohen; 1920–), TV sportscaster
Dolores Costello (1905–79), actress, wed John Barrymore
Joseph Cotten (1905–), actor
Tom Courtenay (1937–), British actor
Franklin Cover (1928–), actor
Noel Coward (1899–1973), British playwright, actor, and composer, T, A-1941
Jane Cowl (1890–1950), actress, T
Wally Cox (1924–73), comic actor
Buster Crabbe (1907–83), actor, Olympic swim champion
Jeanne Crain (1925–), actress
Bob Crane (1928–78), TV star of *Hogan's Heroes*
Broderick Crawford (1911–), actor, A-1949
Joan Crawford (Lucille le Sueur; 1908–77), actress, A-1945
Michael Crawford (1942–), actor
Richard Crenna (1927–), actor
Michael Crichton (1942–), film director, screenwriter
Donald Crisp (1880–1974), British actor, A-1941
Linda Cristal (1936–), actress
Michael Cristofer (1945–), actor and playwright
Jim Croce (1943–73), rock singer, composer
Walter Cronkite (1916–), newscaster
Hume Cronyn (1911–), Canadian actor, director, T, wed to Jessica Tandy
Bing Crosby (Harry Lillis Crosby; 1904–77), singer and actor, E, A-1944
Bob Crosby (1913–), bandleader, brother of Bing
David Crosby (1941–), rock musician
Kathy Crosby (1933–), actress, wed to Bing
Norm Crosby (1927–), comedian
Christopher Cross (1951–), singer, songwriter
Scatman Crothers (1910–), actor
Andrae Crouch (1942–), gospel singer, composer
Russel Crouse (1893–1966), playwright, T
Brandon Cruz (1962–), actor
Billy Crystal (1947–), actor, comedian
Xavier Cugat (1900–), Spanish-born bandleader
George Cukor (1899–1983), director, A-1964
Bill Cullen (1920–), television personality
John Cullum (1930–), actor, singer, director
Robert Culp (1930–), actor
Constance Cummings (Constance Halverstadt; 1910–), actress
Robert Cummings (1910–), actor

Jane Curtin (1947–), actress
Keene Curtis (1923–), actor
Tony Curtis (Bernard Schwarz; 1925–), actor
Michael Curtiz (1888–1962), Hungarian-born director, A-1943
Peter Cushing (1913–), British actor
Charlotte Cushman (1816–75), Shakespearean actress, T
Arlene Dahl (1928–), actress
Dan Dailey (1915–78), actor and dancer
Irene Dailey (1920–), actress
Jim Dale (1935–), British actor
Abby Dalton (1935–), actress
Arnold Daly (1875–1927), actor
Augustin Daly (1838–99), playwright, theater manager, T
James Daly (1918–78), actor
John Daly (1914–), newscaster, TV personality
Vic Damone (Vito Farinola; 1928–), singer
Bill Dana (1924–), comedian
Dorothy Dandridge (1923–65), actress
Rodney Dangerfield (Jack Roy; 1922–), comedian
Bebe Daniels (1901–71), actress, wife of Ben Lyon
Charlie Daniels (1936–), country musician, songwriter
Blythe Danner (1943–), actress
Ray Danton (1931–), actor
Kim Darby (1948–), actress
Denise Darcel (1925–), actress
Bobby Darin (1936–73), singer
Joe Darion (1917–), lyricist (*The Man of La Mancha;* 1965)
Linda Darnell (1923–65), actress
James Darren (1936–), actor
Danielle Darrieux (1917–), French actress
Jane Darwell (1880–1967), actress, A-1940
Howard Da Silva (1909–), actor
Jules Dassin (1911–), director, actor, and writer
Claude Dauphin (1905–78), French actor
John Davidson (1941–), singer, actor
Marion Davies (Marion Douras; 1898–1961), actress
Ann Bradford Davis (1926–), actress
Bette Davis (1908–), actress, A-1935, 1938
Billy Davis Jr. (1940–), singer
Danny Davis (George Nowlan; 1925–), jazz trumpist, bandleader
Eddie Davis (1921–), jazz saxophonist
James Davis (1945–), cartoonist ("Garfield")
Joan Davis (1908–61), comedienne
Mac Davis (1942–), country-western singer-composer
Miles Davis (1926–), jazz trumpet player
Ossie Davis (1917–), playwright and actor
Paul Davis (1948–), country-rock singer
Sammy Davis Jr. (1925–), actor, singer, and dancer
Pam Dawber (1951–), actress
Anthony Dawson (1916–), British actor
Leonard Dawson (1935–), sportscaster
Richard Dawson (1932–), British-born actor, TV game-show host
Dennis Day (1917–), singer
Doris Day (Doris Kappelhoff; 1924–), actress and singer
Laraine Day (Laraine Johnson; 1920–), actress
James Dean (1931–55), actor
Jimmy Dean (1928–), singer and entertainer
Rosemary De Camp (1910–), actress
Yvonne De Carlo (Peggy Middleton; 1922–), Canadian actress
Frances Dee (1907–), actress
Kiki Dee (Pauline Matthews; 1947–), rock singer
Ruby Dee (Ruby Ann Wallace; 1923–), actress
Sandra Dee (Alexandra Zuck; 1942–), actress
Don Defore (1917–), actor
Gloria De Haven (1925–), actress
Olivia de Havilland (1916–), British-born actress, sister of Joan Fontaine, A-1946, 1949
Jack DeJohnette (1942–), jazz drummer
Albert Dekker (1905–68), Dutch-born actor
Dino De Laurentiis (1919–), Italian producer
Alain Delon (1935–), French actor
Dolores Del Rio (1905–83), Mexican actress
Dom DeLuise (1933–), actor and comedian
William Demarest (1892–1983), actor
Agnes De Mille (1909–), choreographer, T
Cecil B. De Mille (1881–1959), director
Carol Dempster (1902–), actress
Catherine Deneuve (Catherine Dorleac; 1943–), French actress
Robert De Niro (1945–), actor, A-1974, 1980
Richard Denning (1914–), actor
Sandy Dennis (1937–), actress, A-1966
Bob Denver (1935–), comedian

SHOW BUSINESS PERSONALITIES *(continued)*

John Denver (Henry John Deutschendorf Jr.; 1943–), singer, composer, actor
Brian DePalma (1940–), film director
Bo Derek (Mary Cathleen Collins; 1957–), actress
John Derek (Derek Harris; 1926–), actor
Bruce Dern (1936–), actor
Vittorio De Sica (1902–74), Italian actor and director
William Devane (1937–), actor
Andy Devine (1905–77), actor and comedian
Colleen Dewhurst (1926–), Canadian-born actress, T
Brandon de Wilde (1942–72), child actor
Joyce DeWitt (1949–), actress
Billy De Wolfe (1907–74), comedian
Susan Dey (1952–), actress
Neil Diamond (1941–), singer and songwriter
Angie Dickinson (Angeline Brown; 1931–), actress
Bo Diddley (1928–), singer, songwriter
Marlene Dietrich (Maria von Losch; 1901–), German-born actress
Howard Dietz (1896–1983), lyricist for musicals and songs (*Dancing in the Dark*)
Dudley Digges (1879–1947), Irish actor, T
Phyllis Diller (Phyllis Driver; 1917–), comedienne
Bradford Dillman (1930–), actor
Matt Dillon (1964–), actor
Dion (Dion Dimucci; 1939–), rock singer
Bob Dishy (c. 1935–), actor, director
Walt Disney (1901–66), cartoonist and producer, creator of Mickey Mouse (1928), E
Richard Dix (Ernest Brimmer; 1894–1949), actor
Ivan Dixon (1931–), actor
Dolly Sisters: Rosie (1892–1970), Jenny (1892–1941), Hungarian-born twin dancers
Fats Domino (1928–), jazz musician and composer
Phil Donahue (1935–), TV personality, wed to Marlo Thomas
Troy Donahue (Merle Johnson; 1937–), actor
James Donald (1917–), British actor
Peter Donald (1918–), actor
Robert Donat (1905–58), British actor, A-1939
Brian Donlevy (1899–1972), Irish-born actor
Donovan (Donovan Leitch; 1946–), Scottish rock singer, songwriter
Diana Dors (Diana Fluk; 1931–84), British actress
Fifi D'Orsay (1908–83), Canadian actress
Jimmy Dorsey (1904–57), bandleader, brother of Tommy
Tommy Dorsey (1905–56), trombonist and bandleader
Kirk Douglas (Issur Demsky; 1918–), actor
Melvyn Douglas (Melvyn Hesselburg; 1901–81), actor, A-1963, 1979, T
Michael Douglas (1944–), actor, producer, son of Kirk
Mike Douglas (Michael D. Dowd Jr.; 1925–), television personality
Paul Douglas (1907–59), actor
Morton Downey (1902–), bandleader and singer
Hugh Downs (1921–), television personality
Jessica Dragonette (1905–80), singer
Alfred Drake (Alfredo Capurro; 1914–), Italian-born singer and actor, T
Marie Dressler (Leila Koeber; 1869–1934), Canadian actress, A-1930–31, T
John Drew (1853–1927), actor, T, uncle of Barrymores
Richard Dreyfuss (1947–), actor, A-1977
Joanne Dru (1923–), actress
James Drury (1934–), actor
Don Drysdale (1936–), sports broadcaster
Eddy Duchin (1905–51), pianist, father of Peter
Peter Duchin (1937–), pianist, bandleader
Howard Duff (1917–), actor, wed to Ida Lupino
Patrick Duffy (1949–), actor
Val DuFour (1927–), actor
Andrew Duggan (1923–), actor
Patty Duke (1946–), actress, A-1962; wed to John Astin
Keir Dullea (1936–), actor
Faye Dunaway (1941–), actress, A-1976
Isadora Duncan (1877–1927), dancer
Sandy Duncan (1946–), actress
James Dunn (1905–67), actor, A-1945
Michael Dunn (Gary Neil Miller; 1934–73), dwarf actor
Irene Dunne (1904–), actress
Mildred Dunnock (1904–), actress, T
Jimmy Durante (1893–1980), comedian
Deanna Durbin (1922–), Canadian actress, singer, A-1938
Charles Durning (1923–), actor
Dan Duryea (1907–68), actor
Eleanora Duse (1858–1924), Italian actress, T
Robert Duvall (1931–), actor, A-1983

Shelley Duvall (1949–), actress
Ann Dvorak (1912–79), actress
Bob Dylan (Robert Zimmerman; 1941–), folk-rock singer, composer
Jeanne Eagels (1894–1929), actress, T
Clint Eastwood (1930–), actor
Shirley Eaton (1936–), British actress
Ray Eberle (1919–79), singer, bandleader
Buddy Ebsen (Christian Rudolph Ebsen; 1908–), comedian, actor
Billy Eckstine (1914–), singer
Duane Eddy (1938–), rock guitarist, songwriter
Nelson Eddy (1901–67), singer and actor
Barbara Eden (Barbara Huffman; 1934–), actress
Blake Edwards (1922–), director, producer
Cliff Edwards (1897–1971), vaudeville entertainer "Ukelele Ike"
Gus Edwards (1879–1945), songwriter (*By the Light of the Silvery Moon*)
Douglas Edwards (1917–), news broadcaster
Ralph Edwards (1913–), entertainer
Vince Edwards (1928–), actor
Richard Egan (1921–), actor
Samantha Eggar (1939–), British actress
Sergei Eisenstein (1898–1948), Russian film director
Anita Ekberg (1931–), Swedish actress
Britt Ekland (1942–), Swedish actress
Jack Elam (1916–), actor
Florence Eldridge (Florence McKechnie; 1901–), actress, wed to Fredric March, T
Roy Eldridge (1911–), jazz trumpeter, bandleader
Larry Elgart (1922–), jazz altosaxophonist, bandleader
Yvonne Elliman (1953–), rock singer
Duke Ellington (Edward Kennedy Ellington; 1899–1974), jazz pianist, bandleader and composer, E
Mercer Ellington (1919–), jazz trumpeter, bandleader, son of Duke
Cass Elliott (1941–74), pop-rock singer
Faye Emerson (1918–83), TV personality
Daniel Decatur Emmett (1815–1904), organized first minstrel show (1843), songwriter (*Dixie*)
Dick Enberg (c. 1937–), sportscaster
Georgia Engel (1948–), actress
Leif Erickson (1914–), actor
Stuart Erwin (1903–67), comedian
Erik Estrada (1949–), actor
Ruth Etting (1898–1978), dancer and singer
Dale Evans (Frances Butts; 1912–), singer, actress, wed to Roy Rogers
Dame Edith Evans (1888–1976), British actress
Linda Evans (1942–), actress
Michael Evans (1949–), actor
Maurice Evans (1901–), Welsh actor, T
Chad Everett (Raymond Cramton; 1937–), actor
Everly Brothers: Don (1937–) and Phil (1939–), country music singers
Tom Ewell (S. Yewell Tompkins; 1909–), comic actor
Fabian (Fabian Forte; 1942–), singer
Nanette Fabray (Nanette Fabares; 1920–), actress
Sammy Fain (1902–), songwriter, composer (*Love Is a Many-Splendored Thing*)
Douglas Fairbanks (Julius Ullman; 1883–1939), actor, husband of Mary Pickford.
Douglas Fairbanks Jr. (1909–), actor and producer
Percy Faith (1908–76), orchestra conductor
Peter Falk (1927–), actor
Jinx Falkenburg (1919–), TV personality
Barry Farber (1930–), radio personality
James Farentino (1938–), actor
Donna Fargo (1945–), country music singer, songwriter
Donald Farmer (1938–), TV news anchorman
Francis Farmer (1915–70), actress
Felicia Farr (1932–), actress
Jamie Farr (1936–), actor ("Corporal Klinger" in TV's MASH series)
Geraldine Farrar (1882–1967), opera singer and actress
Charles Farrell (1901–), actor
Glenda Farrell (1904–71), actress
Mike Farrell (1939–), actor
Sharon Farrell (1949–), actress
Mia Farrow (1945–), actress, daughter of Maureen O'Sullivan
Farrah Fawcett (1947–), actress
Alice Faye (Alice Leppert; 1915–), singer, actress, wed to Phil Harris
Jules Feiffer (1929–), cartoonist, writer
Marty Feldman (1933–82), British comic actor
Barbara Feldon (1941–), actress

Tovah Feldshun (1952–), actress
Jose Feliciano (1945–), Puerto Rican singer, composer
Norman Fell (1925–), actor
Federico Fellini (1920–), Italian writer and director
Edith Fellows (1923–), actress
Maynard Ferguson (1928–), jazz trumpet player
Fernandel (1903–71), French comedian
Conchata Ferrell (1943–), actress
José Ferrer (1912–), Puerto Rican actor and director,
 A-1950, T
Mel Ferrer (1917–), actor and director
Stepin Fetchit (Lincoln Perry; 1902–), comedian
Fibber McGee and Molly: Jim Jordan (1896–), Marian
 Jordan (1897-1961), husband-wife comedy team
Betty Field (1918–73), actress
Sally Field (1946–), actress, A-1979
Dorothy Fields (1905–74), lyricist (The Way You Look
 Tonight)
Gracie Fields (Grace Stansfield; 1898–1979), British singer
 and comedienne
Totie Fields (1931–78), comedienne
W. C. Fields (William Dukinfield; 1879–1946), comedian
 and actor, T
Peter Finch (William Mitchell; 1916–77), British actor,
 A-1976
Albert Finney (1936–), British actor
Peter Firth (1953–), British actor
Carrie Fisher (1956–), actress, daughter of Eddie
 Fisher and Debbie Reynolds
Eddie Fisher (1928–), singer
Minnie Maddern Fiske (1865–1932), actress, T
Clyde Fitch (1865–1932), playwright, T
Barry Fitzgerald (William Shields; 1888–1961), Irish
 actor, A-1944
Ella Fitzgerald (1918–), jazz singer
Geraldine Fitzgerald (1912–), Irish actress
Roberta Flack (1939–), rock singer
Ed Flanders (1934–), actor
Lester Flatt (1914–79), bluegrass guitarist
Dave Fleischer (1895–1979), film animator, creator of
 cartoons characters Betty Boop, Popeye the Sailor, Koko
 the Clown
Arthur Fleming (1924–), actor, TV host
Peggy Fleming (1948–), Olympic ice skater
Rhonda Fleming (Marilyn Louis; 1923–), actress
Victor Fleming (1883–1949), director, A-1939
Louise Fletcher (1936–), actress, A-1975
Errol Flynn (1909–59), Australian-born actor
Nina Foch (1924–), Dutch-born actress
Dan Fogelberg (1951–), rock singer
John Fogerty (1946–), rock singer, songwriter
Red Foley (1910–68), country music singer
Henry Fonda (1905–82), actor, T, A-1981, father of Jane
 and Peter
Jane Fonda (1937–), actress, A-1971, 1978
Peter Fonda (1940–), actor
Frank Fontaine (1920–78), singer and comedian
Joan Fontaine (Joan de Havilland; 1917–), British-born
 actress, A-1941, sister of Olivia de Havilland
Lynn Fontanne (1887–1983), actress, T, wife of Alfred Lunt
Bryan Forbes (1926–), actor, writer, and director
Glenn Ford (Gwyllyn Ford; 1916–), Canadian-born actor
Harrison Ford (1942–), actor
John Ford (Sean O'Feeney; 1895–1973), director, A-1935,
 1940, 1941, 1952
Mary Ford (1928–), singer
Paul Ford (1901–76), actor
Ruth Ford (1920–), actress
Tennessee Ernie Ford (1919–), country music singer
Milos Forman (1932–), Czech-born director, A-1975
Edwin Forrest (1806–72), actor, T
Steve Forrest (1925–), actor
John Forsythe (John Freund; 1918–), actor
Bob Fosse (1927–), director, A-1972, T
Jodie Foster (1962–), actress
Phil Foster (1914–), comedian
Preston Foster (1904–70), actor
Stephen Collins Foster (1826–64), songwriter (My Old
 Kentucky Home; Oh, Susanna)
Pete Fountain (1930–), jazz clarinetist, bandleader
Redd Foxx (John Sanford; 1922–), actor, comedian
Eddie Foy Jr. (1905–83), actor and dancer
Marshall Frady (1940–), TV newscaster
Peter Frampton (1950–), British rock singer
Anthony Franciosa (Anthony Papaleo; 1928–), actor
Anne Francis (1932–), actress
Arlene Francis (1908–), television personality
Connie Francis (Constance Franconero; 1938–), singer

Kay Francis (Katherine Gibbs; 1899–1968), actress
James Franciscus (1934–), actor
John Frankenheimer (1930–), director
Aretha Franklin (1942–), rhythm and blues singer
Bonnie Franklin (1944–), actress
William Frawley (1887–1966), actor and comedian
Dallas Frazier (1939–), country singer, songwriter
Bert Freed (1919–), actor
Al Freeman Jr. (1934–), actor
Bud Freeman (1906–), musician
Mona Freeman (Monica Freeman; 1926–), actress
William Friedkin (1939–), director, A-1973
Rudolf Friml (1879–1972), Czech-born composer of
 operettas, T
Charles Frohmann (1860–1815), producer, T
Jane Froman (1911–80), singer
David Frost (1939–), television personality
David Frye (1934–), impressionist, comedian
Annette Funicello (1942–), actress
Allen Funt (1914–), TV Candid Camera personality
Betty Furness (1916–), television personality
Martin Gabel (1912–), actor and producer
Jean Gabin (1904–76), French actor
Clark Gable (1901–60), actor, A-1934
Eva Gabor (1921–), actress, sister of Zsa Zsa
Zsa Zsa Gabor (Sari Gabor; 1923–), Hungarian-born
 actress
Max Gail (1943–), actor
Don Galloway (1937–), actor
Rita Gam (1927–), actress
Joe Garagiola (1926–), television personality
Greta Garbo (Greta Gustafson; 1905–), Swedish-born
 actress, A-1954
Jerry Garcia (1942–), rock guitarist with Grateful Dead
Vincent Gardenia (1923–), actor
Ava Gardner (Lucy Johnson; 1922–), actress
John Garfield (Julius Garfinkle; 1913–52), actor
Art Garfunkel (1941–), folk-rock singer and composer
William Gargan (1905–79), actor
Judy Garland (Frances Gumm; 1922–69), singer and
 actress, E, A-1939, mother of Liza Minnelli
Erroll Garner (1923–77), jazz pianist, composer
James Garner (James Baumgarner; 1928–), actor
Peggy Ann Garner (1931–84), child star in 1940s, A-1945
Leif Garrett (1961–), actor, singer
Dave Garroway (1913–82), entertainer
Greer Garson (1908–), Irish-born actress, A-1942
John Gary (1932–), singer
Vittorio Gassman (1922–), Italian actor
David Gates (1948–), rock singer, songwriter
Larry Gatlin (1948–), country music singer, songwriter
Dick Gautier (1937–), actor
John Gavin (1932–), actor
William Gaxton (1894–1963), actor
Marvin Gaye (1939–84), rhythm and blues singer
Crystal Gayle (Brenda Gayle Webb; 1951–), singer
Gloria Gaynor (1949–), singer
Janet Gaynor (Laura Gainer; 1906–84), actress, A-1927-28
Mitzi Gaynor (Francesca Mitzi von Gerber; 1930–),
 dancer, actress, and singer
Ben Gazzara (Biago Anthony Gazzara; 1930–), actor
Will Geer (1902–78), actor
Judy Geeson (1950–), British actress
Larry Gelman (1930–), actor
Leo Genn (1905–), British actor
Bobbie Gentry (Roberta Streeter; 1944–), singer
Grace George (1879–1961), actress, T
Phyllis George (1949–), TV personality
Richard Gere (1949–), actor
George Gershwin (1898–1937), composer (Rhapsody in
 Blue)
Ira Gershwin (1896–1983), lyricist, T, brother of George
Stan Getz (1927–), jazz saxophonist
Alice Ghostley (1926–), actress
Giancarlo Giannini (1942–), Italian actor
Andy Gibb (1958–), British rock singer
Barry Gibb. See Bee Gees.
Georgia Gibbs (1926–), singer
Marla Gibbs (1931–), actress
Henry Gibson (1935–), actor
Hoot Gibson (1892–1962), cowboy actor
Mel Gibson (1956–), actor
Sir John Gielgud (1904–), British actor, T, A-1981
Billy Gilbert (1894–1971), actor and musician
John Gilbert (1897–1936), silent film actor
Jack Gilford (Jacob Gellman; 1907–), actor, comedian
Dizzy Gillespie (John Birks Gillespie; 1917–), jazz
 trumpeter, developed bop

SHOW BUSINESS PERSONALITIES *(continued)*

Anita Gillette (1938–), actress
William Gillette (1855–1937), actor, T
Mickey Gilley (1936–), country singer
Hermione Gingold (1897–), British comedienne
Dorothy Gish (1898–1968), actress, sister of Lillian
Lillian Gish (Lillian de Guiche; 1896–), actress, T
George Givot (1903–), actor
Ron Glass (1945–), actor
Jackie Gleason (1916–), comedian, actor
James Gleason (1886–1959), actor
Carlin Glynn (Carlin Masterson; 1940–), actress
George Gobel (1920–), comedian
Jean Luc Godard (1930–), French film director
Paulette Goddard (Marion Levy; 1915–), actress
Arthur Godfrey (1903–83), radio and TV personality
John Golden (1874–1955), playwright and producer, T
Richard Goldman (1911–80), band leader, composer
Bobby Goldsboro (1941–), country music singer
Sam Goldwyn (Samuel Goldfish; 1882–1974), director, producer, A-1946
Benny Goodman (1909–), jazz clarinetist, bandleader
Dody Goodman (1929–), actress, comedienne
Leo Gorcey (1917–69), actor
Dexter Gordon (1923–), jazz saxophonist
Ruth Gordon (1896–1985), actress, playwright, A-1968, T
Lesley Gore (1946–), rock singer
Cliff Gorman (1936–), actor
Eydie Gormé (1932–), singer, wed to Steve Lawrence
Frank Gorshin (1934–), actor, comedian
Marjoe Gortner (1945–), actor
Freeman Gosden (1899–1982), radio actor, "Amos"
Louis Gossett Jr. (1936–), actor, A-1982
Chester Gould (1900–85), cartoonist *(Dick Tracy)*
Elliott Gould (Elliott Goldstein; 1938–), actor
Morton Gould (1913–), composer
Ray Goulding. See Bob & Ray.
Robert Goulet (1933–), singer, actor
Curt Gowdy (1919–), sportscaster
Betty Grable (1916–73), actress
Martha Graham (1894–), dancer
Gloria Grahame (Gloria Hallward; 1924–81), actress, A-1952
Farley Granger (1925–), actor
Stewart Granger (James Stewart; 1913–), British actor
Cary Grant (Archibald Leach; 1904–), British-born actor, A-1969
Kathryn Grant (1933–), actress
Lee Grant (Lyova Rosenthal; 1931–), actress, A-1975
Bonita Granville (1923–), actress and producer
Karen Grassle (c. 1944–), actress
Ben Grauer (1908–77), radio and television announcer
Peter Graves (Peter Aurness; 1926–), actor, brother of James Arness
Gilda Gray (Marianna Michalska; 1901–1959), dancer, invented "shimmy"
Linda Gray (1940–), actress
Kathryn Grayson (Zelma Hedrick; 1929–), actress and singer
Buddy Greco (1926–), singer
José Greco (1918–), Italian-born dancer
Adolph Green (1915–), playwright, lyricist, T
Al Green (1946–), soul-gospel singer
Lorne Greene (1915–), Canadian-born actor
Shecky Greene (1926–), comedian
Sidney Greenstreet (1879–1954), British-born actor
Charlotte Greenwood (1893–78), comedienne, dancer, T
Joan Greenwood (1921–), British actress and director
Dick Gregory (1932–), comedian
James Gregory (1911–), actor
Joyce Grenfell (Joyce Phipps; 1910–79), British actress
Joel Grey (Joel Katz; 1932–), actor, A-1972
Merv Griffin (1925–), television entertainer
Andy Griffith (1926–), actor
Corinne Griffith (1906–79), silent film star
D.W. Griffith (1875–1948), 1st major U.S. film director, E
Hugh Griffith (1912–80), Welsh actor, A-1959
Tammy Grimes (1936–), actress
George Grizzard (1928–), actor
Charles Grodin (1935–), actor, writer, director
Ferde Grofé (1892–1972), composer *(Grand Canyon Suite;* 1931)
Harry Guardino (1925–), actor
Sir Alec Guinness (1914–), British actor, A-1957
Sacha Guitry (1885–1957), French writer-director
Tito Guizar (1908–), Mexican actor, singer, composer
Bryant Gumbel (1948–), TV broadcaster
Moses Gunn (1929–), actor, director

Arlo Guthrie (1947–), folk-rock singer, actor, son of Woody Guthrie
Sir Tyrone Guthrie (1900–71), British director, T
Woody Guthrie (1912–67), folk singer and composer
Edmund Gwenn (1875–1959), British actor, A-1947
Fred Gwynne (1926–), actor
Bobby Hackett (1915–76), jazz coronetist
Buddy Hackett (Leonard Hacker; 1924–), comedian
Joan Hackett (1934–83), actress
Gene Hackman (1930–), actor, A-1971
Charles Haden (1937–), jazz bassist, composer
Uta Hagen (1919–), German-born actress, T
Merle Haggard (1937–), country music singer, songwriter
Dan Haggerty (1941–), actor
Larry Hagman (1931–), actor, son of Mary Martin
Alan Hale (Rufus Alan McKahan; 1892–1950), actor
Alan Hale Jr. (1918–), actor, son of Alan
Bill Haley (1925–81), singer and songwriter, said to have coined phrase "rock and roll"
Jack Haley (1902–79), comedian
James Hall (1941–), jazz guitarist, composer
Monty Hall (1925–), Canadian-born TV personality
Mark Hamill (1951–), actor
George Hamilton (1939–), actor
Marvin Hamlisch (1944–), composer and pianist
Oscar Hammerstein II (1895–1960), lyricist, T
Walter Hampden (1879–1955), actor, T
Susan Hampshire (1942–), British actress
Lionel Hampton (1913–), jazz vibraphonist, combo leader
Herbie Hancock (1940–), jazz pianist, composer
W. C. Handy (1873–1958), blues composer (St. Louis Blues)
Carol Haney (1924–64), dancer and choreographer
Otto Harbach (1873–1963), playwright, librettist, T
Ann Harding (1902–81), actress
Sir Cedric Hardwicke (1893–1964), British actor
Oliver Hardy (1892–1957), comedian with Stan Laurel
Earl of Harewood (1923–), British impresario
Jean ("platinum blonde") Harlow (Harlean Carpenter; 1911–37), actress
Merle Harmon (1927–), sportscaster
Sheldon Harnick (1924–), lyricist *(Fiddler on the Roof;* 1964)
Valerie Harper (1940–), actress
Pat Harrington Jr.(1929–), actor
Barbara Harris (1935–), actress
Emmylou Harris (1947–), country music singer
Julie Harris (1925–), actress, T
Phil Harris (1906–), actor and comedian
Richard Harris (1933–), Irish actor
Rosemary Harris (1930–), British actress
Sam H. Harris (1872–1941), producer, T
George Harrison (1943–), singer, musician (Beatles)
Gregory Harrison (1950–), actor
Rex Harrison (Reginald Carey; 1908–), British actor, A-1964, T
Deborah Harry (1945–), rock singer
Lorenz Hart (1895–1943), lyricist (The Lady Is a Tramp), T
William S. Hart (1870–1946), silent-screen cowboy star
John Hartford (1937–), singer, songwriter ("Gentle on My Mind")
Mariette Hartley (Mariette Boyriven; 1940–), actress
David Hartman (1935–), television personality
Elizabeth Hartman (1945–), actress
Laurence Harvey (1928–73), Lithuanian-born actor
Paul Harvey (1918–), news commentator
Peter Haskell (1934–), actor
David Hasselhoff (1952–), actor
Signe Hasso (1915–), Swedish actress
Donald Hastings (1934–), actor
Hurd Hatfield (1918–), actor
Donny Hathaway (1945–72), singer, composer
Henry Hathaway (Henri Leopold de Fiennes; 1898–1985), director
June Haver (1926–), actress, wife of Fred MacMurray
June Havoc (June Hovick; 1916–), Canadian-born actress, sister of Gypsy Rose Lee
Coleman Hawkins (1904–69), jazz saxophonist
Jack Hawkins (1910–73), British actor
Howard Hawks (1896–77), director, A-1975
Goldie Hawn (1945–), comedienne, A-1969
Jill Haworth (1946–), British actress
Sessue Hayakawa (1890–1973), Japanese actor
Sterling Hayden (1916–), actor
Bill Hayes (1925–), actor
Gabby Hayes (1885–1969), actor in westerns

Helen Hayes (Helen Brown; 1900–), actress, A-1931–32, 1970, T
Isaac Hayes (1942–), soul singer, composer
Peter Lind Hayes (1915–), actor
Susan Seaforth Hayes (1928–), actress, wed to Bill Hayes
Dick Haymes (1918–80), singer, actor
Leland Hayward (1902–71), producer
Louis Hayward (1909–85), South African-born actor
Susan Hayward (1919–75), actress, A-1958
Rita Hayworth (Marguerite Cansino; 1918–), actress
Edith Head (1907–81), costume designer, A-1949, 1951, 1952, 1973
Mary Healy (1918–), singer, actress, wed to Peter Lind Hayes
Percy Heath (1923–), jazz bassist
Joey Heatherton (1944–), actress and dancer
Eileen Heckart (1919–), actress
David Hedison (1930–), actor
Van Heflin (Emmet Evan Heflin; 1910–71), actor, A-1942, 1972
Fred Hellerman (1927–), folksinger (Weavers), composer
Lillian Hellman (1905–84), playwright, T
David Hemmings (1942–), British actor
Sherman Hemsley (1938–), actor
Fletcher Henderson (1898–1952), jazz bandleader
Florence Henderson (1934–), singer and actress
Skitch Henderson (Lyle Russell Cedric; 1918–), pianist, bandleader
Jimi Hendrix (1943–70), acid rock singer
Sonja Henie (1913–69), Norwegian ice skater and actress
Doug Henning (1947–), Canadian-born magician
Paul Henreid (1908–), Austrian-born actor
Jim Henson (1936–), puppeteer, creator of Muppets (1954)
Audrey Hepburn (1929–), Belgian-born actress, A-1953
Katharine Hepburn (1909–), actress, A-1932–33, 1967, 1968, 1981, E, T
Hugh Herbert (1897–1952), comedian
Victor Herbert (1859–1924), Irish-American composer, T
Jerry Herman (1932–), composer of musicals (Hello Dolly)
Woody Herman (1913–), jazz clarinetist, bandleader
James A. Herne (1839–1901), playwright and actor, T
Edward Herrmann (1943–), actor
Jean Hersholt (1886–1956), Danish-born actor
Howard Hesseman (1940–), actor
Charlton Heston (1924–), actor, A-1959
Eddie Heywood (1926–), jazz musician
Jay Higginbotham (1906–73), jazz trombonist, singer
Hildegarde (Loretta Sell; 1906–), singer
Arthur Hill (1922–), Canadian actor
George Roy Hill (1922–), director, A-1973
Wendy Hiller (1912–), British actress, A-1958
John Hillerman (1932–), actor
Earl (Fatha) Hines (1906–83), jazz pianist, bandleader
Gregory Hines (1946–), actor
Mimi Hines (1933–), actress and singer
Pat Hingle (1924–), actor
Judd Hirsch (1935–), actor
Al Hirt (1922–), jazz trumpeter
Alfred Hitchcock (1899–1980), British director, E
Raymond Hitchcock (1865–1929), actor, T
Robert Hite (1943–81), rock singer
Don Ho (1930–), Hawaiian singer
Eddie Hodges (1947–), actor
Johnny Hodges (1906–70), jazz saxophonist
John Hodiak (1914–55), actor
Dustin Hoffman (1937–), actor, A-1979
Hal Holbrook (1925–), actor and impersonator
William Holden (William Beedle; 1918–81), actor, A-1953
Geoffrey Holder (1930–), choreographer
Billie Holiday (1915–59), jazz-blues singer
Judy Holliday (Judith Tuvim; 1923–65), actress, A-1950
Polly Holliday (1937–), actress
Earl Holliman (Anthony Numkena; 1928–), actor
Stanley Holloway (1890–1982), British actor
Sterling Holloway (1905–), actor
Buddy Holly (1936–59), country and rock singer
Celeste Holm (1919–), actress, A-1947
Jack Holt (1888–1951), cowboy actor
Tim Holt (1918–73), actor, son of Jack
Oscar Homolka (1901–78), Austrian-born actor
John Lee Hooker (1917–), folk-blues singer, guitarist, songwriter
Bob Hope (Leslie Townes Hope; 1903–), British-born comedian, E, A-1940, 1944, 1952 (honorary awards)

Mary Hopkin (1950–), singer
Anthony Hopkins (1937–), Welsh actor
Arthur Hopkins (1878–1950), producer, T
Miriam Hopkins (1902–72), actress
Sam Hopkins (1912–), singer, songwriter
Dennis Hopper (1936–), actor
De Wolf Hopper (1858–1935), actor, T
Hedda Hopper (1890–1966), columnist, wife of De Wolf
William Hopper (1915–70), actor, son of Hedda
Lena Horne (1917–), singer and actress
Lee Horsley (1956–), actor
Edward Everett Horton (1888–1970), actor
Johnny Horton (1929–60), country singer, songwriter
Harry Houdini (Ehrich Weiss; 1874–1926), magician
John Houseman (Jacques Haussmann; 1902–), Romanian-born actor, director, producer, T, A-1973
Eugene Howard (1881–1965), vaudevillian, T
Joe Howard (1867–1961), vaudevillian
Ken Howard (1944–), actor
Leslie Howard (Leslie Stainer; 1893–1943), British actor, T
Ron Howard (1954–), actor
Trevor Howard (1916–), British actor
Willie Howard (1886–1949), vaudevillian, T
Sally Ann Howes (1934–), actress and singer
Freddie Hubbard (1938–), jazz trumpeter
Rock Hudson (Roy Fitzgerald; 1925–85), actor
Barnard Hughes (1915–), actor
Howard Hughes (1905–76), movie producer, director
Henry Hull (1890–1977), actor, T
Josephine Hull (1886–1957), actress, A-1950
Mart Hulswit (1940–), Venezuelan-born actor
Engelbert Humperdinck (Arnold Dorsey; 1936–), British singer
Gayle Hunnicutt (1947–), actress
Linda Hunt (?–), actress, A-1983
Marsha Hunt (1917–), actress
Jeffrey Hunter (1925–69), actor
Kim Hunter (Janet Cole; 1922–), actress, A-1951
Tab Hunter (Art Gelian; 1931–), actor
Chet Huntley (1911–74), newscaster
Sol Hurok (1888–1974), impresario
John Hurt (1940–), British actor
Olivia Hussey (1952–), actress
Ruth Hussey (Ruth Carol O'Rourke; 1917–), actress
Angelica Huston (1952–), actress, daughter of John
John Huston (1906–), writer, director, actor, A-1948
Walter Huston (Walter Houghston; 1884–1950), Canadian-born actor, T, A-1948, father of John
Betty Hutton (Betty Thornburg; 1921–), actress
Lauren Hutton (Mary Hutton; 1944–), actress
Timothy Hutton (1960–), actor, A-1980
Janis Ian (1951–), folk-rock singer
Julio Iglesias (1943–), Spanish singer
Marty Ingels (1936–), comedian
Rex Ingram (1895–1969), actor
Jill Ireland (1941–), actress, wed to Charles Bronson
John Ireland (1915–), Canadian actor
Jeremy Irons (1948–), British actor
José Iturbi (1895–1980), Spanish-born pianist, actor
Burl Ives (Burl Iele Ivanhoe; 1909–), actor and folk singer, A-1958
Anne Jackson (1926–), actress, wife of Eli Wallach
Glenda Jackson (1936–), British actress, A-1970, 1973
Kate Jackson (1949–), actress
Keith Jackson (1928–), TV sportscaster
Mahalia Jackson (1911–72), spiritual singer
Jacksons: Jackie (1952–), Tito (1955–), Jermaine (1956–), Michael (1958–), Marlon (1959–), Randy (1960– ,) rock musical group
Sam Jaffe (1891–84), actor
Dean Jagger (1903–), actor, A-1949
Mick Jagger (1943–), rock musician, leader of Rolling Stones group
Dennis James (1917–), television personality
Harry James (1916–83), trumpeter and bandleader
Joni James (1930–), singer
Conrad Janis (1928–), actor, jazz trombonist
Elsie Janis (1889–1956), musical-comedy star, T
Leon Janney (1917–80), actor
Emil Jannings (1886–1950), German actor, A-1927–28
David Janssen (David Meyer; 1930–80), actor
Al Jarreau (1940–), singer
Renée Jeanmaire (1924–), French dancer and actress
Joseph Jefferson (1829–1905), actor, T
Anne Jeffreys (1923–), actress
Bruce Jenner (1949–), TV sportscaster
Peter Jennings (1938–), Canadian-born TV anchorman

SHOW BUSINESS PERSONALITIES *(continued)*

Waylon Jennings (1937–), country music singer
George E. Jessel (1898–1981), comedian
Billy Joel (1949–), rock singer
Elton John (Reginald Dwight; 1947–), British rock singer
Glynis Johns (1923–), South African-born actress
Arte Johnson (1934–), comedian
Ben Johnson (1918–), actor, A-1971
Bunk Johnson (1879–1949), jazz coronetist, trumpeter
Celia Johnson (1908–82), British actress
Chic Johnson (1892–1962), comedian with Ole Olsen
Rafer Johnson (1935–), actor, Olympic athlete
Van Johnson (1916–), actor
Al Jolson (Asa Yoelson; 1880–1950), singer, starred in first talking picture, "The Jazz Singer," T
Allan Jones (1907–), singer, actor
Buck Jones (1889–1942), cowboy actor
Carolyn Jones (1929–83), singer and actress
Dean Jones (1935–), actor
Elvin Ray Jones (1927–), jazz drummer, composer
George Jones (1931–), country singer, songwriter
Henry Jones (1912–), actor
Jack Jones (1938–), singer
James Earl Jones (1931–), actor, T
Jennifer Jones (Phyllis Isley; 1919–), actress, A-1943
Quincy Jones (1933–), jazz trumpeter, composer, conductor
Robert E. Jones (1887–1954), designer and director, T
Shirley Jones (1934–), actress and singer, A-1960
Spike Jones (Lindley Armstrong Jones; 1911–65), musician and comedian
Tom Jones (Thomas Jones Woodward; 1940–), Welsh rock singer
Tommy Lee Jones (1946–), actor
Janis Joplin (1943–70), rock singer
Scott Joplin (1868–1917), ragtime composer
Hamilton Jordan (1944–), TV commentator
Victor Jory (1902–82), Canadian actor
Louis Jourdan (Louis Gendre; 1921–), French actor
Raul Julia (1944–), actor
Curt Jurgens (1915–82), German actor
Madeline Kahn (1942–), actress
Marvin Kalb (1930–), TV commentator
Ida Kaminska (1899–1980), Polish-born actress
Steven Kanaly (1946–), actor
Carol Kane (1952–), actress
Garson Kanin (1912–), playwright, director, T
Gabriel Kaplan (1945–), comedian
Boris Karloff (William Pratt; 1885–1969), British-born actor
Alex Karras (1935–), actor, former football player
Danny Kaye (David Kaminsky; 1913–), comedian and actor, A-1954
Sammy Kaye (1910–), musician and bandleader
Elia Kazan (1909–), Turkish-born director and writer, T, A-1947, 1954
Lainie Kazan (1942–), singer
Stacy Keach (1941–), actor
Buster Keaton (Joseph Francis Keaton; 1895–1966), comedian and actor, A-1959
Diane Keaton (1946–), actress, A-1977
Lila Kedrova (1918–), Russian-French actress, A-1964
Howard Keel (1919–), actor and singer
Ruby Keeler (Ethel Keeler; 1910–), Canadian-born actress, dancer
Laura Keene (1820–73), actress and theater manager, T
Bob Keeshan (1927–), TV personality *(Captain Kangaroo)*
Garrison Keillor (1944–), humorist *(Prairie Home Companion)*
Harvey Keitel (1947–), actor
Brian Keith (1921–), actor
Cecil Kellaway (1893–1973), South African-born actor
Marthe Keller (1945–), Swiss-born actress
Sally Kellerman (1937–), actress
Jackson Kelley (1920–), actor
Emmett Kelly (1898–79), circus clown
Gene Kelly (1912–), dancer and actor, A-1951
Grace Kelly (1929–82), actress, A-1954
Patsy Kelly (1910–81), comedienne
Kay Kendall (1926–59), British actress
Eddie Kendricks (1940–), singer
Arthur Kennedy (1914–), actor
George Kennedy (1926–), actor, A-1967
Stan Kenton (Stanley Newcomb; 1912–79), jazz pianist and bandleader
Ken Kercheval (1935–), actor
Jerome Kern (1885–1945), composer of musicals, T

Deborah Kerr (1921–), British actress
John Kerr (1931–), actor
J. Warren Kerrigan (1889–1947), silent film star
Larry Kert (1930–), actor, singer
Hank Ketcham (1920–), cartoonist *(Denniss the Menace)*
Evelyn Keyes (1919–), actress
Michael Kidd (1919–), dancer, choreographer
Margot Kidder (1948–), Canadian-born actress
Richard Kiley (1922–), actor and singer
Alan King (Irwin Alan Kniberg; 1927–), comedian
B.B. King (1925–), blues singer
Carole King (1942–), folk-rock singer and composer
Dennis King (1897–1971), British-born actor
Wayne King (1901–85), bandleader
Ben Kingsley (1943–), British actor, A-1982
Sidney Kingsley (1906–), playwright, T
Durwood Kirby (1912–), actor and TV announcer
Lisa Kirk (1925–), actress and singer
Phyllis Kirk (Phyllis Kirkegaard; 1930–), actress
Dorothy Kirsten (1919–), singer
Eartha Kitt (1928–), singer
Werner Klemperer (1920–), German-born actor
Robert Kline (1942–), comedian
Kevin Kline (1947–), actor
Jack Klugman (1922–), actor
Evel Knievel (Robert Craig, 1938–), daredevil motorcyclist
Gladys Knight (1944–), soul singer
Shirley Knight (1936–), actress, T
Ted Knight (Tadeus Konopka; 1923–), actor
Don Knotts (1924–), actor, comedian
Al Kooper (1944–), rock guitarist, singer
Ted Koppel (c.1941–), British-born TV anchorman
Sir Alexander Korda (1893–1956), Hungarian-British movie producer
Harvey Korman (1927–), actor, comedian
André Kostelanetz (1901–80), Russian-born conductor
Apollonia Kotero (1960–), actress
Yaphet Kotto (1944–), actor
Ernie Kovacs (1919–62), comedian and comic actor
Stanley Kramer (1913–), director
Kris Kristofferson (1936–), actor, singer, songwriter
Otto Kruger (1885–1974), actor
Gene Krupa (1909–73), jazz drummer
Stanley Kubrick (1928–), producer and director
Nancy Kulp (1921–), comedienne
Charles Kuralt (1934–), TV commentator
Akira Kurosawa (1910–), Japanese director
Bill Kurtis (1940–), TV commentator
Swoosie Kurtz (1944–), actress
Kay Kyser (1905–85), musician and bandleader
Patti Labelle (1944–), rock singer
Jerry Lacy (Gerald Leroy; 1936–), actor
Alan Ladd (1913–64), actor
Cheryl Ladd (1951–), actress
Bert Lahr (Irving Lahrheim; 1895–1967), comedian, T
Frankie Laine (Frank Paul Lo Vecchio; 1913–), singer
Veronica Lake (Constance Ockleman; 1919–73), actress
Hedy Lamarr (Hedwig Kiesler; 1915–), Austrian-born actress
Fernando Lamas (1915–82), Argentinian actor
Dorothy Lamour (Dorothy Kaumeyer; 1914–), actress
Burt Lancaster (1913–), actor, A-1960
Elsa Lanchester (Elizabeth Sullivan; 1902–), British actress; wed to Charles Laughton
Martin Landau (1934–), actor
Ann Landers (Esther P. Lederer; 1918–), columnist
Michael Landon (Eugene Maurice Orowitz; 1937–), actor and director
Abbe Lane (1932–), singer, wed to Xavier Cugat
Fritz Lang (1890–1976), Austrian-born director
Walter Lang (1898–1972), director
Harry Langdon (1884–1944), comedian
Hope Lange (1931–), actress
Jessica Lange (1949–), actress, A-1982
Frank Langella (1940–), actor
Francis Langford (1914–), singer
Lily Langtry (Emily Charlotte Le Breton; 1856–1929), British actress, T
Angela Lansbury (1925–), British-born actress, T
Robert Lansing (Robert H. Brown; 1928–), actor
Mario Lanza (Alfredo Cocozza; 1921–59), singer and actor
Julius La Rosa (1930–), singer
Jesse L. Lasky (1880–1958), producer
Louise Lasser (1939–), actress
Sir Harry Lauder (1870–1950), Scottish comedian
Charles Laughton (1889–1962), British-American actor, A-1932–33, wed to Elsa Lanchester
Cindy Lauper (1953–), rock singer

Stan Laurel (Arthur Jefferson; 1890–1965), British-born comedian, teamed with Oliver Hardy
Piper Laurie (Rosetta Jacobs; 1932–), actress
Linda Lavin (1937–), actress
Peter Lawford (1923–84), British-born actor
Carol Lawrence (Carol Maria Laraia; 1935–), singer and actress
Gertrude Lawrence (Gertrude Klasen; 1898–1952), British actress, singer, T
Steve Lawrence (Steve Liebowitz; 1935–), singer, wed to Eydie Gormé
Vicki Lawrence (1949–), actress, singer
Cloris Leachman (1926–), actress, A–1971
David Lean (1908–), British director, A–1957, 1962
Norman Lear (1922–), producer, director
Michael Learned (1939–), actress
Led Zeppelin British rock group founded in 1968: John Bonham (1947–), John Paul Jones (1946–), Jimmy Page (1945–), Robert Plant (1947–)
Huddie "Lead Belly" Ledbetter (1888–1949), folk singer
Brenda Lee (1944–), singer
Canada Lee (1907–1952), actor
Christopher Lee (1922–), British actor
Gypsy Rose Lee (Louise Hovick; 1914–70), burlesque dancer, sister of June Havoc
Michele Lee (Michele Dusiak; 1942–), singer, actress
Peggy Lee (Norma Egstrom; 1920–), singer
Eva Le Gallienne (1899–), British-born actress, T
Ron Leibman (1937–), actor
Janet Leigh (Jeanette Morrison; 1927–), actress
Vivien Leigh (Vivien Hartley; 1913–67), British actress, A–1939, 1951
Margaret Leighton (1922–76), British actress
Jack Lemmon (1925–), actor, A–1955, 1973
John Lennon (1940–80), British rock-and-roll singer, musician (Beatles)
Lennon Sisters: Dianne (1939–), Janet (1946–), Kathy (1943–), Peggy (1941–), singing group
Lotte Lenya (Caroline Blamauer; 1898–1981), Austrian-born actress and singer
Jack E. Leonard (1911–73), comedian
Sheldon Leonard (Sheldon Bershad; 1907–), actor and comedian
Eugenie Leontovich (1894–), Russian-born actress
Alan Jay Lerner (1918–), librettist and lyricist (My Fair Lady)
Mervyn LeRoy (1900–), actor and director
Joan Leslie (1925–), actress
Jerry Lester (1911–), comedian
David Letterman (1947–), comedian
Oscar Levant (1906–72), musician and comedian
Sam Levene (1906–80), actor
Sam Levenson (1911–80), humorist
Joseph E. Levine (1905–), producer
George Q. Lewis (1914–79), comedian
Jerry Lewis (Joseph Levitch; 1926–), comedian, teamed with Dean Martin
Jerry Lee Lewis (1935–), country music singer, songwriter
Joe E. Lewis (1902–71), comedian
Ramsey Lewis (1935–), jazz pianist, songwriter
Shari Lewis (Shari Hurwitz; 1934–), puppeteer
Ted Lewis (1892–1971), bandleader, clarinetist
Wladziu Valentino Liberace (1920–), pianist
Judith Light (c.1949–), actress
Gordon Lightfoot (1939–), Canadian folk-rock singer, songwriter
Beatrice Lillie (Constance Sylvia Munston; 1898–), British comedienne, T
Elmo Lincoln (Otto Elmo Linkenhelter; 1889–1952), actor, first film Tarzan
Jenny Lind (1820–87), Swedish singer
Hal Linden (Harold Lipshitz; 1931–), actor
Viveca Lindfors (1920–), Swedish-born actress
Margaret Lindsay (1910–81), actress
Audra Lindley (1925–), actress
Pia Lindstrom (1938–), newscaster, daughter of Ingrid Bergman
Art Linkletter (1912–), TV entertainer
Virna Lisi (1937–), Italian actress
Cleavon Little (1939–), actor
Rich Little (1938–), Canadian-born comedian
Little Richard (Richard Penniman; 1935–), rock singer
Jay Livingston (1915–), composer (Buttons and Bows)
Mary Livingstone (1909–83), comedienne, wed to Jack Benny
Christopher Lloyd (1938–), actor
Frank Lloyd (1888–1960), Scottish-born director,

A–1928–29, 1932–33
Harold Lloyd (1893–1971), comedian, A–1952
Tony Lobianco (1936–), actor
Sondra Locke (1947–), actress
Gene Lockhart (1891–1957), Canadian actor
June Lockhart (1925–), actress, daughter of Gene
Margaret Lockwood (Margaret Day; 1916–), British actress
Frank Loesser (1910–69), composer of musicals (Guys and Dolls)
Frederick Loewe (1901–), German-born composer of musicals (My Fair Lady)
Ella Logan (1913–69), singer and actress
Joshua Logan (1908–), director and producer, T
Robert Loggia (1930–), actor
Kenny Loggins (1947–), rock musician, songwriter
Gina Lollobrigida (1928–), Italian actress
Herbert Lom (1917–), Czech-born actor
Carole Lombard (Jane Peters; 1908–42), actress, wed to Clark Gable
Guy Lombardo (1902–77), Canadian-born bandleader
Julie London (Julie Peck; 1926–), singer and actress
Priscilla Lopez (1948–), actress
Trini Lopez (1937–), singer
Jack Lord (1930–), actor, director, producer
Pauline Lord (1890–1950), actress, T
Sophia Loren (Sophia Scicoloni; 1934–), Italian actress, A–1961
Gloria Loring (1946–), singer, actress
Marion Lorne (1888–1968), actress
Peter Lorre (Laszlo Löewenstein; 1904–64), Hungarian-born actor
Dorothy Loudon (1933–), actress
Anita Louise (1915–70), actress
Tina Louise (1936–), actress
Bessie Love (1898–), actress
Frank Lovejoy (1912–62), actor
Edmund Lowe (1892–1971), actor
Myrna Loy (Myrna Williams; 1905–), actress
Ernst Lubitsch (1892–1947), German-born producer
George Lucas (1944–), director, producer
Laurence Luckinbill (1934–), actor
Allen Ludden (1919–81), TV game show host
Bela Lugosi (Arisztid Olt, 1888–1956), Hungarian-born actor
Paul Lukas (1895–1971), Hungarian-born actor, A–1943
Keye Luke (1904–), Chinese-born actor
Sidney Lumet (1924–), director
Jimmie Lunceford (1902–47), jazz clarinetist, bandleader
William Lundigan (1914–75), actor
Alfred Lunt (1893–1977), actor, wed to Lynn Fontanne, T
Ida Lupino (1918–), British actress and director
Patti LuPone (1949–), actress
Paul Lynde (1927–82), comedian
Carol Lynley (1942–), actress
Diana Lynn (1924–71), actress
Jeffrey Lynn (1909–), actor
Loretta Lynn (1935–), country music singer
Ben Lyon (1901–79), actor, husband of Bebe Daniels
James MacArthur (1937–), actor, son of Helen Hayes
Jeanette MacDonald (1907–65), singer and actress
Jack MacGouran (1918–73), Irish actor
Ali MacGraw (1939–), actress
Ted Mack (1904–76), television personality
Gisele MacKenzie (Marie LaFeche; 1927–), Canadian-born singer
Shirley MacLaine (Shirley Beatty; 1934–), actress, sister of Warren Beatty, A–1983
Barton MacLane (1900–69), actor
Gavin MacLeod (1930–), actor
Fred MacMurray (1908–), actor
Patrick MacNee (1922–), British actor
Gordon MacRae (1921–), singer and actor
Meredith MacRae (1945–), actress, daughter of Gordon and Sheila
Sheila MacRae (1924–), comedienne, wed to Gordon
George Macready (1909–73), actor
Bill Macy (1922–), actor
Donald Madden (1933–83), actor
John Madden (1936–), TV sportscaster
Guy Madison (Robert Moseley; 1922–), actor
Madonna (Madonna Louise Ciccone; 1958–), rock singer
Patrick Magee (1924–82), British actor
Anna Magnani (1908–73), Italian actress, A–1955
Marjorie Main (1890–1975), actress
Lee Majors (1940–), actor
Miriam Makeba (1932–), jazz singer

SHOW BUSINESS PERSONALITIES *(continued)*

Karl Malden (Malden Sekulovich; 1914–), actor, A-1951
John Malkovich (1954–), actor, director
Louis Malle (1932–), French film director
Dorothy Malone (Dorothy Maloney; 1925–), actress, A-1956
Rouben Mamoulian (1897–), Russian-born director, T
Melissa Manchester (1951–), singer
Henry Mancini (1924–), pianist and composer
Barbara Mandrell (1948–), soul-gospel singer
Barry Manilow (1946–), singer and composer
Joseph L. Mankiewicz (1909–), director, writer, and producer, A-1949, 1950
Delbert Mann (1920–), director, A-1955
Herbie Mann (1930–), jazz flutist
Jayne Mansfield (Vera Jane Palmer; 1932–67), actress
Richard Mansfield (1857–1907), German-Amer. actor, T
Robert B. Mantell (1854–1928), actor, T
Marcel Marceau (1923–), French pantomimist
Fredric March (Frederick Bickel; 1897–1975), actor, A-1931–32, 1946, T
Nancy Marchand (1928–), actress
Janet Margolin (1943–), actress
Cheech Marin See Cheech and Chong
Johnny Marks (1909–85), songwriter (*Rudolph the Red-Nosed Reindeer*)
Bob Marley (1945–81), reggae singer
Hugh Marlowe (Hugh Hipple; 1914–82), actor
Julia Marlowe (Sarah Frances Frost; 1865–1950), Shakespearean actress, T
Jean Marsh (1934–), British actress
E. G. Marshall (1910–), actor
Herbert Marshall (1890–1966), British actor
Penny Marshall (1943–), actress
Tully Marshall (William Phillips; 1864–1943, actor
Dean Martin (Dino Crocetti; 1917–), singer and actor, teamed with Jerry Lewis
Dick Martin (1922–), television comedian
Freddy Martin (1907–83), band leader
Mary Martin (1913–), singer and actress, T
Ross Martin (1920–81), actor
Steve Martin (1945–), comedian
Strother Martin (1920–80), character actor
Tony Martin (Alvin Morris; 1913–), singer
Al Martino (1927–), singer
Lee Marvin (1924–), actor, A-1965
Marx Brothers: Chico (1886–1961), Harpo (1888–1964), Groucho (1890–1977), Gummo (1897–1977), Zeppo (1901–1979), comedy team
James Mason (1909–84), British actor
Marsha Mason (1942–), actress, wed to Neil Simon
Pamela Mason (1922–), British actress, wed to James Mason
Raymond Massey (1896–1983), Canadian-born actor
Marcello Mastroianni (1924–), Italian actor
Johnny Mathis (1935–), singer
Walter Matthau (Walter Matasschanskayasky; 1920–), actor, A-1966
Victor Mature (1916–), actor
Marilyn Maxwell (Marvel Maxwell; 1922–72), actress
Elaine May (1932–), comedienne and writer
John Mayall (1933–), British rock musician songwriter
Louis B. Mayer (1885–1957), producer, A-1950
Curtis Mayfield (1942–), singer and songwriter
Virginia Mayo (Virginia Jones; 1922–), actress
Paul Mazursky (1930–), film writer, director
Andrea McArdle (1964–), actress and singer
Mary Margaret McBride (1899–1976), radio personality
David McCallum (1933–), Scottish-born actor
Mercedes McCambridge (1918–), actress, A-1949
Leo McCarey (1898–1969), director, A-1937, 1944
Kevin McCarthy (1914–), actor
Paul McCartney (1942–), British singer (Beatles)
Mary McCarty (1924–80), actress
Doug McClure (1935–), actor
Marilyn McCoo (1943–), singer
Kent McCord (1942–), actor
Patty McCormack (1945–), actress
Myron McCormick (1907–62), actor
Tim McCoy (1891–1978), cowboy actor
Joel McCrea (1905–), actor
Hattie McDaniel (1895–1952), actress, A-1939
Marie McDonald (1924–65), comedienne
Roddy McDowall (1928–), British-born actor
Malcolm McDowell (1943–), British actor
George McFarland (1928–), "Spankey" in "Our Gang" comedies
Darren McGavin (1925–), actor

Fibber McGee (1896–), comedian
Molly McGee (1898–1961), comedienne
John McGiver (1913–1975), actor
Patrick McGoohan (1928–), actor
Maureen McGovern (1949–), folk singer
Dorothy McGuire (1918–), actress
Jimmy McHugh (1894–1969), songwriter (*I Can't Give You Anything but Love, Baby*)
Frank McHugh (1899–1981), actor
Donna Ruth McKechnie (1942–), dancer, star of broadway musicals
Siobhan McKenna (1922–), Irish actress
Rod McKuen (1933–), singer, poet, composer
Victor McLaglen (1883–1959), British-born actor, A-1935
Emily McLaughlin (1940–), actress
Don McLean (1945–), folk-rock singer, songwriter
Allyn McLerie (1926–), Canadian-born actress
Ed McMahon (1923–), actor and television personality
Jimmy McNichol (1961–), actor
Kristy McNichol (1962–), actress
Jimmy McPartland (1907–), jazz coronetist
Butterfly McQueen (1911–), actress
Steve McQueen (1932–80), actor
Audrey Meadows (1924–), actress, sister of Jayne
Jayne Meadows (1926–), actress
Anne Meara (1929–), comedienne, wed to Jerry Stiller
Kay Medford (1921–80), comedienne
Donald Meek (1880–1946), Scottish-born actor
Ralph Meeker (Ralph Rathgeber; 1920–), actor
Melanie (Melanie Sofka; 1947–), rock singer
Sergio Mendes (1941–), jazz musician
Adolphe Menjou (1890–1963), actor
Helen Menken (1901–66), actress, T
Johnny Mercer (1909–76), lyricist (*I'm an Old Cowhand*)
Marian Mercer (1935–), actress
Melina Mercouri (1915–), Greek actress
Burgess Meredith (George Burgess; 1909–), actor, T
Lee Meriwether (1935–), actress
Una Merkel (1903–), actress
Ethel Merman (Ethel Zimmerman; 1908–84), singer and actress, T
David Merrick (1912–), stage producer, T
Dina Merrill (Nedenia Hutton; 1925–), actress, wed to Cliff Robertson
Gary Merrill (1914–), actor
Jim Messina (1947–), country-rock musician
Otto Messmer (1892–1983), film animator; created "Felix the Cat" (1919)
Bette Midler (1945–), singer and comedienne
Jo Mielziner (1901–76), scenic designer, T
Toshiro Mifune (1920–), Japanese actor
Joanna Miles (1940–), French-born actress
Sarah Miles (1941–), British actress
Sylvia Miles (1932–), actress
Vera Miles (Vera Ralston; 1930–), actress
Lewis Milestone (1895–1980), director, A-1927–28, 1929–30
Ray Milland (Reginald Truscott-Jones; 1905–), Welsh-born actor, A-1945
Ann Miller (Lucille Ann Collier; 1923–), dancer
Arthur Miller (1915–), playwright
Glenn Miller (1909–44), jazz trombonist and bandleader
Henry Miller (1860–1926), actor and theater manager, T
Jason Miller (1939–), playwright
Marilyn Miller (Mary Reynolds; 1898–1936), actress, T
Mitch Miller (1911–), musician, conductor
Roger Miller (1936–), country music singer
Steve Miller (1943–), rock guitarist
Hayley Mills (1946–), British actress, daughter of Sir John
Sir John Mills (1908–), British actor, A-1970
Juliet Mills (1941–), actress, daughter of John
Mills Brothers: Herbert (1912–), Harry (1913–82), Donald (1915–), singing group.
Martin Milner (1927–), actor
Ronnie Milsap (1943–), blind country-western singer
Yvette Mimieux (1942–), actress
Sal Mineo (1939–76), actor
Charles Mingus (1922–79), jazz bass player
Liza Minnelli (1946–), singer and actress, A-1972, daughter of Judy Garland and Vincente Minnelli
Vincente Minnelli (1910–), director, A-1958
Carmen Miranda (1914–55), Portuguese-born singer
Cameron Mitchell (Cameron Mizell; 1918–), actor
Joni Mitchell (Roberta Joan Anderson; 1943–), folk singer
Thomas Mitchell (1898–1962), actor, A-1939
Robert Mitchum (1917–), actor
Tom Mix (1880–1940), cowboy actor

Helena Modjeska (1845–1909), Polish-American actress, T
Donald Moffat (1930–), actor
Ferenc Molnar (1878–1952), Hungarian-born playwright, T
Thelonious Monk (1918–82), bop jazz pianist, composer
Marilyn Monroe (Norma Jean Baker Mortenson; 1926–62), actress, sex symbol of 1960s
Vaughn Monroe (1911–73), singer, bandleader
Ricardo Montalban (1920–), Mexican actor
Yves Montand (Ivo Levi; 1921–), French singer, actor
Elizabeth Montgomery (1933–), actress
George Montgomery (George Letz; 1916–), actor
Robert Montgomery (1904–81), actor, father of Elizabeth
Wes Montgomery (1925–68), jazz guitarist
Colleen Moore (Kathleen Morrison; 1900–), actress
Garry Moore (Thomas Garrison Morfit; 1915–), television personality
Grace Moore (1902–47), operatic singer and film actress
Mary Tyler Moore (1937–), actress
Melba Moore (Beatrice Moore; 1945–), actress and singer
Roger Moore (1927–), British actor
Terry Moore (Helen Koford; 1932–), actress
Victor Moore (1876–1962), vaudeville comedian, actor, T
Agnes Moorehead (1906–74), actress
Jeanne Moreau (1928–), French actress
Rita Moreno (Rosita Dolores Alverio; 1931–), actress, A-1961
Dennis Morgan (Stanley Morner; 1910–), actor
Frank Morgan (Francis Wupperman; 1890–1949), actor
Harry Morgan (Harry Bratsburg; 1915–), actor
Helen Morgan (1900–41), actress and singer
Henry Morgan (1915–), comedian
Jane Morgan (Florence Currier; 1916–), singer
Michael Moriarty (1941–), actor
Robert Morley (1908–), British actor
Chester Morris (1901–70), actor
Greg Morris (1934–), actor
Wayne Morris (1914–59), actor
Jim Morrison (1943–71), rock singer
Vic Morrow (1931–82), actor
Robert Morse (1931–), actor
Jelly Roll Morton (1885–1941), jazz pianist, composer
Arnold Moss (1910–), actor, director
Zero Mostel (1915–77), actor, singer, and comedian
Roger Mudd (1928–), newcaster
Maria Muldaur (1942–), folk singer
Edward Mulhare (1921–), British actor
Martin Mull (1943–), comedian
Gerry Mulligan (1927–), jazz saxophonist, songwriter
Richard Mulligan (1932–), actor
Paul Muni (1896–1967), actor, A-1936, T
Patrice Munsel (1925–), singer
Audie Murphy (1924–71), actor, World War II hero
Ben Murphy (1942–), actor
Eddie Murphy (1961–), comedian, actor
George Murphy (1904–), actor and dancer
Michael Murphy (1938–), actor
Anne Murray (1947–), country singer
Arthur Murray (1895–), dancer, husband of Kathryn
Bill Murray (1950–), actor, writer
Don Murray (1929–), actor
Jan Murray (1917–), comedian
Kathryn Murray (1906–), dancer, wife of Arthur
Ken Murray (1903–), comedian
Mae Murray (Marie Adrienne Koenig; 1885–1965), actress
Edward R. Murrow (1908–65), radio and TV newscaster
Tony Musante (1936–), actor
Brent Musburger (1939–), TV sportscaster
Bess Myerson (1924–), TV personality, author
Jim Nabors (1933–), comedian and singer
Conrad Nagel (1897–1970), actor
J. Carrol Naish (1900–73), actor
Graham Nash (1942–), rock musician
George Jean Nathan (1882–1958), drama critic, author, T
Mildred Natwick (1908–), actress
Theodore "Fats" Navarro (1923–50), bop jazz trumpeter
Alla Nazimova (1879–1945), Russian-born actress, T
Patricia Neal (1926–), aetress, A-1963
Pola Negri (1899–), Polish-born actress
Barry Nelson (Robert Neilson; 1920–), actor
David Nelson (1936–), actor, son of Ozzie
Ed Nelson (1928–), actor
Harriet Hilliard Nelson (Peggy Lou Snyder; 1914–), actress, wife of Ozzie
Ozzie Nelson (1906–75), actor and bandleader
Rick Nelson (1940–), actor and singer, son of Ozzie
Willie Nelson (1933–), country singer, songwriter
Peter Nero (1934–), pianist

Cathleen Nesbitt (1889–82), British actress
Bob Newhart (1929–), comedian
Anthony Newley (1931–), British actor and writer
Barry Newman (1938–), actor
Edwin Newman (1919–), news commentator
Paul Newman (1925–), actor and director
Phyllis Newman (1935–), actress
Randy Newman (1943–), rock singer
Julie Newmar (Julia Newmeyer; 1933–), actress
Robert Newton (1905–56), British character actor
Wayne Newton (1942–), singer
Olivia Newton-John (1948–), British rock singer
Mike Nichols (Michael Peschkowsky; 1931–), German-born comedian and director, A-1967
Red Nichols (1905–65), jazz cornetist and combo leader
Jack Nicholson (1937–), actor, A-1975, 1983
Stevie Nicks (1948–), rock singer
Leslie Nielson (1926–), Canadian-born actor
Harry Nilsson (1941–), folk-rock singer, songwriter
Leonard Nimoy (1931–), actor
David Niven (1909–83), Scottish-born actor, A-1958
Kathleen Nolan (1933–), actress
Kathy Nolan (1934–), actress
Lloyd Nolan (1903–85), actor
Nick Nolte (1940–), actor
Jimmie Noone (1895–1944), jazz clarinetist
Mabel Normand (Mabel Fortescue; 1894–1930), silent-movie comedienne
Chuck Norris (1942–), actor
John Ringling North (1903–), circus owner
Sheree North (Dawn Bethel; 1933–), actress
Judy Norton-Taylor (1958–), actress
Red Norvo (1908–), jazz xylophonist, vibraphonist
Kim Novak (Marilyn Novak; 1933–), actress
Ramon Novarro (1899–1968), Mexican actor
Elliott Nugent (1900–80), director and writer
Rudolf Nureyev (1938–), Russian-born dancer
Laura Nyro (1947–), rock singer, songwriter
Jack Oakie (Lewis D. Offield; 1903–78), comedian
Annie Oakley (1860–1926), Wild West performer, T
John Oates (1948–), singer, songwriter
Warren Oates (1932–82), actor
Merle Oberon (1911–79), British actress
Hugh O'Brian (Hugh Krampke; 1930–), actor
Edmond O'Brien (1915–85), actor, A-1954
Margaret O'Brien (1937–), child actress, A-1944
Pat O'Brien (1899–1983), actor
Arthur O'Connell (1908–81), character actor
Helen O'Connell (1920–), singer
Carroll O'Connor (1924–), actor
Donald O'Connor (1925–), actor and dancer
Una O'Connor (1893–1959), Irish actress
Clifford Odets (1906–63), playwright, T
Odetta (1930–), folk singer and actress
Maureen O'Hara (Maureen Fitzsimmons; 1920–), Irish-born actress
Dan O'Herlihy (1919–), Irish actor
Dennis O'Keefe (1908–68), actor
Warner Oland (1880–1938), Swedish-born actor, best known for Charlie Chan roles
Edna May Oliver (1883–1942), actress
King Oliver (1885–1938), jazz trumpeter, bandleader
Susan Oliver (1937–), actress
Lord Laurence Olivier (1907–), British actor and director, A-1944, 1948, T, E
Merlin Olsen (1940–), sportscaster, actor
Ole Olsen (1892–1963), vaudeville star with Chic Johnson
Patrick O'Neal (1927–), character actor
Ryan O'Neal (1941–), actor, father of Tatum
Tatum O'Neal (1963–), actress, A-1973
Eugene O'Neill (1888–1953), playwright, T, E
James O'Neill (1849–1920), Irish-born actor, father of Eugene
Jennifer O'Neill (1948–), Brazilian-born actress
Jerry Orbach (1935–), singer and actor
Roy Orbison (1936–), country music singer
Tony Orlando (1944–), singer
Kid Ory (1886–1973), jazz trombonist, bandleader
Donny Osmond (1957–), singer, brother of Marie
Marie Osmond (1959–), singer, sister of Donny
Maureen O'Sullivan (1911–), Irish-born actress
Peter O'Toole (1932–), Irish actor
Reginald Owen (1887–1972), British actor
Buck Owens (1929–), country music singer
Gary Owens (1936–), radio-TV personality
Frank Oz (c. 1942–), British-born puppeteer (*Muppets*)
Jack Paar (1918–), television personality
Al Pacino (1940–), actor

SHOW BUSINESS PERSONALITIES (continued)

Geraldine Page (1924–), actress, T
Patti Page (Clara Anne Fowler; 1927–), singer
Janis Paige (1922–), actress
Jack Palance (Walter Palanuik; 1920–), actor
Betsy Palmer (1929–), actress
Lilli Palmer (1914–), German-born British actress
Franklin Pangborn (1894–1958), comedian
Irene Papas (1926–), Greek actress
Joseph Papp (Joseph Papirofsky; 1921–), producer
Charlie "Bird" Parker (1920–55), jazz sax musician
Eleanor Parker (1922–), singer and actress
Fess Parker (1926–), actor
Bert Parks (Bert Jacobson; 1914–), television personality
Larry Parks (1914–75), actor
Michael Parks (1938–), actor
Estelle Parsons (1927–), actress, A-1967
Dolly Parton (1946–), country music singer
Joseph Pasternak (1901–), Hungarian-born producer
Mandy Patinkin (1952–), actor
Gail Patrick (1911–80), actress
Dick Patterson (1929–), actor
Les Paul (1915–), singer, guitarist
Jane Pauley (1950–), TV journalist
Katina Paxinou (1900–73), Greek actress, A-1943
Johnny Paycheck (Don Lytle; 1941–), country singer, songwriter
Freda Payne (1945–), singer
John Payne (1912–), actor
Pamela Payton-Wright (1941–), actress
Jack Pearl (1894-1982), comedian
Minnie Pearl (Sarah Ophelia Colley Cannon, 1912–), country music singer
Gregory Peck (1916–), actor, A-1962
Sam Peckinpah (1925–84), film director
Teddy Pendergrass (1950–), pop singer, drummer, songwriter
Austin Pendleton (1940–), actor, director
Arthur Penn (1922–), director
Sean Penn (1960–), actor
Joe Penner (Joseph Pinter; 1905–41), Hungarian-born comedian
George Peppard (1928–), actor
Anthony Perkins (1932–), actor
Osgood Perkins (1892–1937), actor, T
Valerie Perrine (1943–), actress
Nehemiah Persoff (1920–), character actor
Peter, Paul and Mary, singing group in 1960: Peter Yarrow (1935–), Noel Paul Stookey (1937–), Mary Travers (1937–)
Bernadette Peters (Bernadette Lazzara; 1948–), actress
Brock Peters (1927–), actor, singer
Jean Peters (1926–), actress
Oscar Peterson (1925–), Canadian jazz pianist
Edith Piaf (1915–63), French singer
Slim Pickens (1919–83), character actor
Wilson Pickett (1941–), rhythm and blues singer
Mary Pickford (Gladys Smith; 1893–79), Canadian-born actress, A-1928–29, 1976
Molly Picon (1898–), actress, T
Walter Pidgeon (1897–1984), Canadian-born actor
Harold Pinter (1930–), British playwright
Joe Piscopo (1951–), comedian, actor
Gene Pitney (1941–), folk-rock singer, songwriter
Zasu Pitts (1898–1963), comedienne and actress
Mary Kay Place (c. 1949–), actress, singer
Donald Pleasence (1919–), British actor
Suzanne Pleshette (1937–), actress
Joan Plowright (1929–), British actress
Christopher Plummer (1929–), Canadian actor
Sidney Poitier (1927–), actor, A-1963
Roman Polanski (1933–), Polish director
Michael Pollard (1939–), actor
Carlo Ponti (1910–), Italian producer, wed to Sophia Loren
Iggy Pop (James Osterberg; 1947–), punk rock singer, songwriter
Cole Porter (1893–1964), composer of musicals (Kiss Me Kate) and songs (Begin the Beguine), T, E
Tom Poston (1927–), actor
Bud Powell (1924–66), bop jazz pianist
Dick Powell (1904–63), actor, director, and producer
Eleanor Powell (1912–82), dancer and actress
Jane Powell (Suzanne Burce; 1929–), dancer and singer
Randolph Powell (1950–), actor
William Powell (1892–1984), actor
Tyrone Power (1913–58), actor
Stefanie Powers (Stefania Federkiewicz; 1943–), actress
Otto Preminger (1906–), Austrian-born producer

Paula Prentiss (Paula Ragusa; 1939–), actress
Elvis Presley (1935–77), singer, actor
Robert Preston (Robert Messervey; 1918–), actor, T
Andre Previn (1929–), composer and music arranger
Ray Price (1926–), country music singer
Vincent Price (1911–), actor
Charley Pride (1939–), country music singer
Louis Prima (1912–78), singer, trumpeter, bandleader
Prince (Prince Rogers Nelson; 1960–), rock singer
Harold Prince (1928–), producer, T
Victoria Principal (1950–), actress
Andrew Prine (1936–), actor
Freddie Prinze (1954–77), actor
Dorothy Provine (1937–), actress
Juliet Prowse (1937–), South African-born actress
Richard Pryor (1940–), comedian
Flora Purim (1942–), Brazilian-born singer, songwriter
Denver Pyle (1920–), actor
Dennis Quaid (1954–), actor
Randy Quaid (1953–), actor
Anthony Quayle (1913–), British actor and director
Mae Questel (1908–), actress, cartoon voices (Betty Boop and Olive Oyl)
Richard Quine (1920–), actor and director
Anthony Quinn (1915–), Mexican-born actor, A-1952, 1956
Ellis Rabb (1930–), actor, director, writer
Eddie Rabbitt (1941–), singer, songwriter
David Rabe (1940–), playwright, wed to Jill Clayburgh
Gilda Radner (1946–), comediennne
Charlotte Rae (1946–), actress
Deborah Raffin (1953–), actress
George Raft (George Ranft; 1895–1980), actor
Luise Rainer (1912–), Austrian actress, A-1936, 1937
Ma Rainey (Gertrude Pridgett; 1886–1939), blues and jazz singer
Claude Rains (1889–1967), British actor
Bonnie Raitt (1950–), singer
John Raitt (1917–), singer, actor, producer
Marjorie Rambeau (1889–1970), actress
Gustavus Ramsay (1937–), actor
Sally Rand (1904–79), striptease fan dancer
Tony Randall (Leonard Rosenberg; 1920–), actor
J. Arthur Rank (1888–1972), British producer
Basil Rathbone (1892–1967), South African-born actor
Dan Rather (1931–), newscaster
Gregory Ratoff (1897–1961), Russian-born actor, director
Lou Rawls (1935–), rhythm and blues singer
Aldo Ray (1926–), Character actor
Johnny Ray (1927–), singer
Gene Rayburn (1917–), TV game show host
Martha Raye (Margaret Yvonne Reed; 1916–), actress
Gene Raymond (1908–), actor
Ronald Reagan (1911–), actor and U.S. President
Harry Reasoner (1923–), newscaster
Otis Redding (1941–67), blues singer
Helen Reddy (1941–), Austalian singer
Robert Redford (1937–), actor, director, A-1980
Lynn Redgrave (1943–), British actress
Sir Michael Redgrave (1908–85), British actor, father of Lynn and Vanessa
Vanessa Redgrave (1937–), British actress, A-1977
Sir Carol Reed (1906–76), British director, A-1968
Donna Reed (1921–), actress, A-1953
Jerry Reed (1937–), country-rock singer, songwriter
Oliver Reed (1938–), British actor
Robert Reed (1932–), actor
Della Reese (Delloreese Patricia Early; 1931–), singer
Christopher Reeve (1952–), actor
Jim Reeves (1923–64), country music singer
Phil Regan (1908–), actor, singer
Ada Rehan (1860–1916), actress, T
Kate Reid (1930–), British-born actress
Wallace Reid (1890–1923), silent film star
Charles Nelson Reilly (1931–), comedy actor, director
Carl Reiner (1923–), actor, writer, and director
Robert Reiner (1947–), actor, son of Carl
Max Reinhardt (1873–1943), Austrian producer
Ann Reinking (1950–), actress, dancer
Lee Remick (1935–), actress
Duncan Renaldo (1904–80), actor (Cisco Kid)
Michael Rennie (1909–71), British actor
Jean Renoir (1894–1979), French film director
Alain Resnais (1922–), French director
Anne Revere (1903–), actress, A-1945
Burt Reynolds (1936–), actor
Debbie Reynolds (Mary Frances Reynolds; 1932–), actress, singer, and dancer

Frank Reynolds (1924–83), TV newscaster
Buddy Rich (1917–), jazz drummer and bandleader
Charlie Rich (1932–), country music singer
Irene Rich (Irene Luther; 1897–), actress
Sir Ralph Richardson (1902–83), British actor, T
Tony Richardson (1929–), British director, A-1963
Lionel Richie (1950–), singer, songwriter
Harry Richman (1895–1972), vaudeville singing star
Peter Richman (1927–), actor, painter
Marty Robbins (1925–82), country-western singer
Don Rickles (1926–), comedian
Nelson Riddle (1921–85), bandleader
Diana Rigg (1938–), British actress
Jack Riley (1935–), actor, writer
Ringling Bros.: Albert (1852–1916), Otto (1858–1911),
 Alfred (1861–1919), Charles Edward (1863–1926),
 John (1866–1936), circus managers
Minnie Riperton (1948–79), soul singer
Cyril Ritchard (1896–1977), British actor
John Ritter (1948–), actor, son of Tex
Tex Ritter (1907–74), country music singer
Thelma Ritter (1905–69), actress
Ritz Brothers: Al (1901–65), Jim (1903–), Harry
 (1906–), comedy team
Chita Rivera (1933–), singer, dancer, actress
Geraldo Rivera (1943–), newscaster
Joan Rivers (Joan Molinsky; 1937–), comedienne
Johnny Rivers (John Ramistella; 1942–), country-rock
 singer-songwriter
Hal Roach (1892–), director and producer
Jason Robards Jr. (1922–), actor, A-1976, 1977, T
Gale Robbins (1922–80), actress, singer
Jerome Robbins (1918–), dancer and choreographer, T,
 A-1961
Marty Robbins (1925–82), country-western singer
Doris Roberts (1930–), actress
Pernell Roberts (1930–), actor
Tony Roberts (1939–), actor
Cliff Robertson (1925–), actor, A-1968
Dale Robertson (1923–), actor
Paul Robeson (1898–1976), singer and actor, T
Bill "Bojangles" Robinson (1878–1949), dancer
Edward G. Robinson (Emanuel Goldenberg; 1893–1973),
 actor, A-1972
Smokey Robinson (1940–), singer, songwriter
May Robson (Mary Robinson; 1865–1942), Australian-
 born actress
Rochester (Eddie Anderson; 1905–77), actor best-known
 for role as Jack Benny's butler
Jimmie Rodgers (1897–1933), country music singer
Richard Rodgers (1902–79), composer of musicals (South
 Pacific), T, E
Buddy Rogers (1904–), actor, wed to Mary Pickford
Ginger Rogers (Virginia McMath; 1911–), actress and
 dancer, A-1940
Kenny Rogers (1941–), country-rock musician
Paul Rogers (1917–), British actor
Roy Rogers (Leonard Sly; 1912–), singer, cowboy actor
Wayne Rogers (1933–), actor
Will Rogers (1879–1935), humorist, T
Eric Rohmer (1920–), French director
Gilbert Roland (1905–), Mexican-born actor
Esther Rolle (1933–), actress
Rolling Stones, British rock group: Mick Jagger
 (1943–), Keith Richard (1943–), Brian Jones
 (1942–69), William Wyman (1941), Charles Watts
 (1941–)
Cesar Romero (1907–), actor
Linda Ronstadt (1946–), singer
Mickey Rooney (Joe Yule, Sr.; 1920–), actor, A-1938
Pat Rooney (1880–1962), dancer and songwriter
Casper Roos (1925–), actor
Billy Rose (1899–1966), showman
George Rose (1920–), British actor, T
Rose Marie (1925–), comedienne
Diana Ross (1944–), singer, actress
Katharine Ross (1943–), actress
Marion Ross (1928–), actress
Roberto Rossellini (1906–77), Italian director
Robert Rossen (1908–66), film writer, director, producer
Lillian Roth (1910–80), singer
Richard Roundtree (1942–), actor
Dan Rowan (1922–), television comedian
Gena Rowlands (1936–), actress, wed to John Cassavetes
Paul Rudd (1940–), actor
Charles Ruggles (1890–1970), actor
Louis Rukeyser (1933–), TV commentator
Janice Rule (1931–), actress

Todd Rundgren (1949–), rock singer, guitarist
Barbara Rush (1930–), actress
Harold Russell (1914–), actor, A-1946
Jane Russell (1921–), actress
Ken Russell (1927–), British director
Kurt Russell (1951–), actor
Lillian Russell (1861–1922), singer, actress, T
Mark Russell (1932–), comedian
Nipsey Russell (1924–), comedian
Pee Wee Russell (1906–69), jazz clarinetist
Rosalind Russell (1912–76), actress
Ann Rutherford (1924–), Canadian-born actress
Margaret Rutherford (1892–1972), British actress, A-1963
Irene Ryan (1903–73), actress
Peggy Ryan (1924–), comedienne
Robert Ryan (1913–73), actor
Bobby Rydell (1942–), singer
Mort Sahl (1927–), Canadian-born comedian
Eva Marie Saint (1924–), actress, A-1954
Raymond St. Jacques (1930–), actor
Susan Saint James (Susan Miller; 1946–), actress
Jill St. John (1940–), actress
Buffy Sainte-Marie (1941–), Canadian folk singer
Gene Saks (1921–), director, actor
Soupy Sales (Milton Hines; 1926–), comedian
Pierre Salinger (1925–), TV journalist
Sal Salvador (1925–), jazz guitarist
Paul Sand (Pablo Sanchez; 1935–), dancer, actor,
 director
Dominique Sanda (1951–), French actress
George Sanders (1906–), British actor, A-1950
Richard Sanders (1940–), actor
Diana Sands (1934–73), actress
Tommy Sands (1937–), singer
Isabel Sanford (1917–), actress
Samantha Sang (1953–), singer
Carlos Santana (1947–), Mexican-born jazz guitarist
Susan Sarandon (1946–), actress
Michael Sarrazin (1940–), Canadian actor
Telly Savalas (1926–), actor
John Saxon (1935–), actor
Leo Sayer (1948–), rock musician
Boz Scaggs (William Royce Scaggs; 1944–), rhythm and
 blues singer
Franklin Schaffner (1922–), director, A-1970
William Schallert (1922–), actor
Dore Schary (1905–80), writer and producer
Roy Scheider (1935–), actor
Maria Schell (1926–), Austrian actress, sister of
 Maximilian
Maximilian Schell (1930–), Austrian actor, A-1961
Joseph M. Schenck (1878–1961), Russian-born producer,
 founder of 20th Century-Fox, A-1950
Chris Schenkel (1924–), sportscaster
Joseph Schildkraut (1895–1964), Austrian actor, A-1937
Murray Schisgal (1926–), playwright
John Schlesinger (1926–), British director, A-1969
Stephan Schnabel (1912–), German-born actor
John Schneider (1954–), actor
Romy Schneider (Rose-Marie Albach-Retty; 1938–82),
 Austrian actress
Avery Schreiber (1935–), comedian
Charles Schulz (1922–), cartoonist (Peanuts, Charlie
 Brown, Snoopy)
Arthur Schwartz (1900–84), composer of musicals and
 songs (That's Entertainment; Dancing in the Dark)
Arnold Schwarzenegger (1947–), actor, body-building
 champion
Paul Scofield (1922–), British actor, A-1966
Martin Scorsese (1942–), director
George C. Scott (1927–), actor and director, A-1970
Lizabeth Scott (Emma Matso; 1922–), actress
Martha Scott (1914–), actress
Randolph Scott (Randolph Crane; 1903–), actor
Zachary Scott (1914–65), actor
Alexander Scourby (1913–85), actor
Earl Scruggs (1924–), country music singer
Vin Scully (1927–), TV sportscaster
John Sebastian (1944–), singer and composer
Jean Seberg (1938–79), actress
Neil Sedaka (1939–), rock singer and composer
Pete Seeger (1919–), folk singer, composer
George Segal (1934–), actor
Bob Seger (1945–), rock musician
Tom Selleck (1945–), actor
Peter Sellers (1925–80), British comedian and actor
David O. Selznick (1902–65), producer
Mack Sennett (1884–1960), producer, director, A-1937

SHOW BUSINESS PERSONALITIES (continued)

Rod Serling (1924–75), writer and producer
Bola Sete (1923–), Brazilian-born jazz guitarist
Eric Sevareid (1912–), television commentator
Doc Severinson (1927–), bandleader, trumpeter
Anne Seymour (1909–), actress
Jane Seymour (1951–), British-born actress
Ted Shackelford (1946–), actor
Bob Shane (1934–), singer (*Kingston Trio*)
Ravi Shankar (1920–), sitar player
Omar Sharif (Michael Shalhoub; 1932–), Egyptian actor
William Shatner (1931–), Canadian-born actor
Artie Shaw (Arthur Arshawsky; 1910–), jazz clarinetist and bandleader
Robert Shaw (1927–78), British actor and writer
Woody Shaw (1944–), jazz trumpeter, composer
Dick Shawn (1929–), actor
Moira Shearer (1926–), Scottish-born dancer
Norma Shearer (1904–83), Canadian-born actress, A-1929-30
George Shearing (1920–), British-born blind jazz pianist and composer
Martin Sheen (Ramon Estevez; 1940–), actor
Carole Shelley (1939–), British-born actress
Reid Shelton (1924–), actor
Sloane Shelton (1934–), actress
Sam Shepard (Samuel Shepard Rogers; 1943–), playwright, actor
Cybill Shepherd (1950–), actress
Ann Sheridan (1915–67), actress
Allan Sherman (1924–73), comedian
Brooke Shields (1965–), actress
Talia Shire (1946–), actress, sister of Francis Ford Coppola
Dinah Shore (Frances Rose Shore; 1917–), singer and TV personality
Bobby Short (1924–), jazz pianist
Herb Shriner (1918–70), comedian
Lee Shubert (1883–1953) and J. J. Shubert (1880–1963), theater managers and producers, T
Sarah Siddons (Sarah Kemble; 1756–1831), Welsh actress
Sylvia Sidney (Sophia Kossow; 1910–), actress
Simone Signoret (Simone Kaminker; 1921–85), German-born actress, A-1959
Phil Silvers (Philip Silversmith; 1912–), actor
Stephen Sills (1945–), rock musician
Alastair Sim (1900–76), Scottish actor
Gene Simmons (1949–), Israeli-born singer, actor, songwriter (founder singing group *Kiss*)
Jean Simmons (1929–), British actress
Carly Simon (1945–), rock singer, wife of James Taylor
Neil Simon (1927–), playwrite, T
Paul Simon (1940–), folk-rock singer and composer
Simone Simon (1914–), French actress
Nina Simone (1933–), jazz vocalist
Zoot Sims (1925–85), jazz saxophonist
Frank Sinatra (1915–), singer and actor, A-1953, E
Frank Sinatra Jr. (1944–), singer, son of Frank
Nancy Sinatra (1940–), actress, daughter of Frank
Zutty Singleton (1898–1975), jazz drummer
Red Skelton (1910–), comedian
Cornelia Otis Skinner (1901–79), actress and writer
Otis Skinner (1858–1942), actor, T, father of Cornelia
Alison Skipworth (1870–1952), comedienne
Spyros Skouras (1893–1971), Greek-born film executive
Walter Slezak (1902–83), Austrian-born actor
Grace Slick (1939–), rock singer
Charlie Smalls (1943–), composer and lyricist (*The Wiz*)
Alexis Smith (1921–), Canadian-born actress, wed to Craig Stevens
Sir C. Aubrey Smith (1863–1948), British actor
Bessie Smith (1898?–1937), blues singer
Howard K. Smith (1914–), television commentator
Jaclyn Smith (1948–), actress
Kate Smith (1907–), singer
Keely Smith (1932–), jazz-pop singer, wed Louis Prima
Lois Smith (1930–), actress
Maggie Smith (1934–), British actress, A-1969, 1978
Patti Smith (1945–), punk rock singer, songwriter
Pinetop Smith (1904–29), boogie-woogie jazz pianist
Roger Smith (1932–), actor
Smothers Brothers: Tom (1937–) and Dick (1939–), comedians and singers
Carrie Snodgress (1945–), actress
Hank Snow (1914–), Canadian country music singer
Phoebe Snow (1951–), rock singer
Suzanne Somers (Suzanne Mahoney; 1946–), actress

Elke Sommer (Elke Schletz; 1941–), German actress
Gale Sondergaard (1899–1985), actress, A-1936
Stephen Sondheim (1930–), composer and lyricist for musicals (*West Side Story*) T
Jack Soo (Goro Suzuki; 1917–79), character actor
Paul Sorvino (1939–), actor
Ann Sothern (Harriette Lake; 1909–), actress
E. A. Sothern (1826–81), British actor, T
E. H. Sothern (1859–1933), actor, T, son of E. A. Sothern, husband of Julia Marlowe
David Soul (David Solberg; 1943–), actor, singer
John Philip Sousa (1854–1932), bandleader, composer (*Semper Fidelis, Stars and Stripes Forever*)
Sissy Spacek (1950–), actress, A-1980
Muggsy Spanier (1906–67), dixieland jazz coronetist
Danielle Spencer (1965–), actress
Sam Spiegel (1901–), producer
Phil Spitalny (1890–1970), Russian-born leader of all-female orchestra
Charlie Spivak (1905–82), bandleader
Steven Spielberg (1947–), TV and film director
Dusty Springfield (Mary O'Brien; 1939–), British singer
Bruce Springsteen (1949–), rock singer, songwriter
Robert Stack (1919–), actor
Jo Stafford (1918–), singer
Sylvester Stallone (1946–), actor, writer, director
Terrence Stamp (1940–), British actor
Lionel Stander (1908–), actor
Arnold Stang (1925–), comedian
Konstantin Stanislavsky (1863–1938), Russian director, created "method" theory of acting
Kim Stanley (Patricia Reid; 1925–), actress, T
Barbara Stanwyck (Ruby Stevens; 1907–), actress
Jean Stapleton (Jeanne Murray; 1923–), actress
Maureen Stapleton (1925–), actress, T, A-1981
Kay Starr (1924–), singer
Ringo Starr (Richard Starkey; 1940–), British singer, musician (Beatles)
Tommy Steele (1936–), British singer
Mary Steenburgen (1952–), actress, A-1980
Rod Steiger (1925–), actor, A-1967
David Steinberg (1942–), Canadian-born comedian
Richard Sterban (1943–), country western singer
Jan Sterling (1923–), actress
Andrew Stevens (1955–), actor, producer
Cat Stevens (Steven Georgion; 1947–), folk-rock singer
Connie Stevens (Concetta Ingolia; 1938–), actress and singer
Craig Stevens (1921–), actor, wed to Alexis Smith
George Stevens (1904–75), director, A-1951, 1956
Stella Stevens (1938–), actress
Warren Stevens (1919–), actor
James Stewart (1908–), actor, A-1940
Rod Stewart (1945–), British-born rock singer
Slam Stewart (1914–), jazz bassist
Dorothy Stickney (1900–), stage actress, T
David Odgen Stiers (1942–), actor
Jerry Stiller (1929–), comedian, actor, wed to Ann Meara
Stephen Stills (1945–), rock musician
Sonny Stitt (1924–82), jazz saxophonist
Dean Stockwell (1936–), actor
Fred Stone (1873–1959), comedian, T
Leonard Stone (1923–), actor
Lewis Stone (1879–1953), actor
Sly Stone (1944–), rock singer
Three Stooges: Curly Howard (1906–52), Shemp Howard (1895?–1955), Moe Howard (1897–75), Larry Fine (1902–75), comedy team
Tom Stoppard (1937–), Czech-born playwright
Larry Storch (1925–), comedian
Gale Storm (1922–), actress
Beatrice Straight (1918—), actress, A-1976
Lee Strasberg (1901–82), director, T
Susan Strasberg (1938–), actress, daughter of Lee
Robin Strasser (1945–), actress
Charles E. (Tom Thumb) Stratton (1838–1883), midget
Peter Strauss (1947–), actor
Meryl Streep (1949–), actress, A-1979, 1982
Barbra Streisand (1942–), singer and actress, A-1968
Elaine Stritch (1922–), actress
Hunt Stromberg (1894–1968), producer
Charles Strouse (1928–), composer of Broadway musicals (*Annie*)
Sally Struthers (1948–), actress
Mary Stuart (c.1926–), actress
Preston Sturges (1898–1959), producer
Jules Styne (1905–), British-born composer, T

Margaret Sullavan (1911–60), actress, T
Barry Sullivan (Patrick Barry; 1912–), actor
Ed Sullivan (1902–74), columnist and TV personality
Susan Sullivan (c. 1944–), actress
Yma Sumac (1927–), Peruvian-born singer, actress
Donna Summer (1948–), rock singer
Slim Summerville (1892–1946), comedian and director
David Susskind (1920–), producer and TV personality
Donald Sutherland (1934–), Canadian-born actor
Bo Svenson (1941–), Swedish-born actor
Gloria Swanson (Josephine Swenson; 1899–1983), actress
John Cameron Swayze (1906–), newscaster
Blanche Sweet (1895–), silent film actress
Raymond Gram Swing (1887–1968), radio news
 commentator
Loretta Swit (1937–), actress
Mr. T (Lawrence Tero; 1952–), actor
Lewis Tabackin (1940–), jazz saxophonist, flutist,
 bandleader
Lyle Talbot (1904–), actor
Nita Talbot (1930–), actress
Norma Talmadge (1897–1957), silent-film actress
William Talman (1917–68), actor
Russ Tamblyn (1935–), actor
Akim Tamiroff (1899–1972), Russian-born actor
Jessica Tandy (1909–), British-born actress, wed to
 Hume Cronyn, T 1981
Fran Tarkenton (1940–), sportscaster, former pro
 football player
Lilyan Tashman (1899–1934), silent-film star
Art Tatum (1910–56), jazz pianist
Norman Taurog (1899–1981), director, A-1930–31
Vic Tayback (Victor Tabback; 1929–), actor
Billy Taylor (1921–), jazz pianist, composer
Cecil Taylor (1933–), jazz pianist, composer
Elizabeth Taylor (1932–), actress, A-1960, 1966
Estelle Taylor (Estelle Boylan; 1899–1958), silent-film
 actress
James Taylor (1948–), rock singer, composer
Kent Taylor (Louis Weiss; 1907–), actor
Laurette Taylor (Laurette Cooney; 1884–1946), actress, T
Robert Taylor (Spangler Brough; 1911–69),
 Australian-born actor
Rod Taylor (1930–), Australian-born actor
Jack Teagarden (1905–64), jazz trombonist and singer
Conway Tearle (Frederick Levy; 1878–1938), silent-film
 star
Sir Godfrey Tearle (1884–1953), British actor,
 half-brother of Conway
Shirley Temple (1928–), child star in 1930s, A-1934
Alec Templeton (1910–63), musician
Ellen Terry (1848–1928), British actress, T
Terry-Thomas (Thomas Terry Hoar-Stevens; 1911–),
 British comedian
Irving Thalberg (1899–1936), producer
Phyllis Thaxter (1921–), actress
Roy Thinnes (1938–), actor
B.J. Thomas (1942–), pop singer
Danny Thomas (Amos Jacobs; 1914–), comedian
Marlo Thomas (1943–), actress, daughter of Danny
Richard Thomas (1951–), actor
Sada Thompson (1929–), actress
Dame Sybil Thorndike (1882–1976), British actress
Ingrid Thulin (1929–), Swedish actress
Cheryl Tiegs (1947–), model, TV personality
Gene Tierney (1920–), actress
Pamela Tiffin (1943–), actress
Mel Tillis (1932–), country western musician,
 songwriter
Burr Tillstrom (1917–), puppeteer, (Kukla and Ollie)
Tiny Tim (Herbert Khaury; 1923–), singer
George Tobias (1901–80), actor
Ann Todd (1909–), British actress
Michael Todd (1907–58), film producer
Richard Todd (1919–), British actor
Thelma Todd (1908–35), film comedienne
Sidney Toler (1874–1974), character actor, known for role
 as "Charlie Chan" in film series
Lily Tomlin (1939–), comedienne
David Tomlinson (1917–), Scottish actor
Frank Tomlinson (1928–), TV journalist
Franchot Tone (1906–68), actor
Regis Toomey (1902–), actor
Mel Torme (1925–), singer
Rip Torn (1931–), actor, director
Audrey Totter (1923–), actress
Peter Townshend (1945–), British rock singer,
 composer, guitarist (co-founder The Who)

Lee Tracy (1898–1968), actor
Spencer Tracy (1900–67), actor, A-1937, 1938
Maria Augusta von Trapp (1905–), Austria-born leader
 Trapp Family Singers
Daniel John Travanti (1940–), actor
Mary Travers (1936–), singer
John Travolta (1954–), actor, singer
Arthur Treacher (1894–1975), British actor
Sir Herbert Beerbohm Tree (1853–1917), British actor
Claire Trevor (1909–), actress, A-1948
Ernest Truex (1889–1973), actor
François Truffaut (1932–84), French director
Forrest Tucker (1919–), actor
Sophie Tucker (Sophia Abuza; 1884–1966), singer
Tanya Tucker (1958–), singer, actress
Sonny Tufts (Bowen Charleston Tufts; 1911–70), actor
Tommy Tune (1939–), dancer, choreographer, director
Big Joe Turner (1911–), blues singer
Ike Turner (1931–), rock musician
Lana Turner (Julia Turner; 1920–), actress
Tina Turner (Annie Mae Bullock; 1941–), pop-rock
 singer
Ben Turpin (1847–1940), comedian
Rita Tushingham (1940–), British actress
Twiggy (Leslie Hornsby; 1949–), British actress
Conway Twitty (1933–), country music singer,
 songwriter
Cicely Tyson (1933–), actress
Earl Ubell (1926–), TV science commentator
Leslie Uggams (1943–), singer and actress
Liv Ullman (1939–), Norwegian actress
Myoshi Umeki (1929–), Japanese actress, A-1957
Robert Urich (1947–), Canadian-born actor
Peter Ustinov (1921–), British actor and director,
 A-1960, 1964
Brenda Vaccaro (1939–), actress
Roger Vadim (1927–), French director
Jerry Vale (1931–), singer
Caterina Valente (1931–), French singer
Jack Valenti (1921–), president, Motion Picture Assn.,
 1996-
Karen Valentine (1947–), actress
Rudolph Valentino (Rodolpho d'Antonguolla; 1895–1926),
 Italian born actor
Rudy Vallee (Hubert Vallee; 1901–), singer and actor
Frankie Valli (Frank Castelluccio; 1937–), singer
Bobby Van (1933–80), comedian, dancer
Lee Van Cleef (1925–), actor
Trish Van Devere (1943–), actress wed to George C.
 Scott
Mamie Van Doren (Joan Lucille Olander; 1933–),
 actress
Dick Van Dyke (1925–), actor
Jerry Van Dyke (1932–), actor, brother of Dick
Jo Van Fleet (1922–), actress, A-1955
Jimmy Van Heusen (1913–), songwriter ("Love and
 Marriage")
Nina Van Pallandt (1932–), Danish singer, actress
Dick Van Patten (1928–), actor
Vivian Vance (1912–79), actress
Gloria Vanderbilt (1924–), actress, TV personality
Diane Varsi (1938–), actress
Sarah Vaughan (1924–), jazz singer
Robert Vaughn (1932–), actor
Conrad Veidt (1893–1943), German character actor
Gwen Verdon (1927–), singer and dancer, T
Ben Vereen (1946–), dancer, actor, singer
Sid Vicious (1958–79), punk-rock musician
Martha Vickers (1925–71), actress
King Vidor (1895–1982), director
Abe Vigoda (1922–), actor
Herve Villechaize (1943–), French actor
Jan Michael Vincent (1944–), actor
Bobby Vinton (1935–), pop-rock singer, actor
Luchino Visconti (1906–76), Italian film director
Jon Voight (1932–), actor, A-1978
Betsy Von Fuerstenberg (1932–), German-born actress
Joseph von Sternberg (1894–1969), Austrian-born director
Erich Von Stroheim (1885–1957), Austrian-born actor,
 director
Max Von Sydow (1929–), Swedish actor
Harry Von Zell (1906–81), actor and radio-TV announcer
Lyle Waggoner (1935–), actor
Porter Wagoner (1927–), country singer, composer
Lindsay Wagner (1949–), actress
Robert Wagner (1930–), actor, wed to Natalie Wood
Ralph Waite (1929–), actor
Robert Walden (1943–), actor

SHOW BUSINESS PERSONALITIES *(continued)*

Christopher Walken (1943–), actor, A-1978
Clint Walker (1927–), actor
Nancy Walker (Ann Swoyer; 1922–), comedienne
Robert Walker (1919–51), actor
Mike Wallace (1918–), television newscaster
Eli Wallach (1915–), actor
James Wallack (1795–1864), British-American actor, T
Lester Wallack (1820–1888), actor, T, son of James
Fats Waller (1904–43), jazz pianist and singer
Hal B. Wallis (1899–), producer
Ray Walston (1914–), actor
Jessica Walter (1944–), actress
Barbara Walters (1931–), television commentator
Henry B. Walthall (1878–1936), silent-film star
Sam Wanamaker (1919–), actor, director
Walter Wanger (1894–1968), producer
Charles Ward (1952–), actor, singer, dancer
Simon Ward (1941–), British actor
Jack Warden (1920–), actor
David Warfield (1866–1951), actor, T
William Warfield (1920–), singer, actor, wed to
 Leontyne Price
Andy Warhol (1927–), producer and director
Fred Waring (1900–84), musician and bandleader
Jack L. Warner (1892–1978), producer (Warner Brothers)
Ruth Warrick (1916–), actress
Dionne Warwick (1941–), singer
Dinah Washington (1924–63), blues singer
Grover Washington Jr. (1943–), jazz saxophonist
Ethel Waters (1900–77), actress, T
Muddy Waters (McKinley Morganfield; 1915–83),
 country music singer
Sam Waterston (1940–), actor
Larkin Douglass Watson III (1921–), actor
Lucile Watson (1879–1962), character actress
Albert Waxman (1935–), Canadian-born actor, director
David Wayne (Wayne McKeekan; 1916–), actor
John Wayne (Marion Morrison; 1907–79), actor, director,
 producer, A-1969
Charlie Weaver (Cliff Arquette; 1905–74), comedian
Dennis Weaver (1924–), actor
Fritz Weaver (1926–), actor
Chick Webb (1909–39), jazz drummer
Clifton Webb (Webb Hollenbeck; 1896–1966), actor, T
Jack Webb (1920–82), actor, director, and producer
Joe Weber (1867–1942) and Lew Fields (1867–1941),
 vaudeville comedians, T
Margaret Webster (1905–72), theatrical producer, T
Johnny Weissmuller (1904–84), actor (Tarzan),
 Olympic swimmer
Raquel Welch (Raquel Tejada; 1940–), actress
Tuesday Weld (Susan Ker Weld; 1943–), actress
Lawrence Welk (1903–), musician and bandleader
Orson Welles (1915–85), actor, producer, director, T, E
Kitty Wells (Muriel Deason; 1917–), country music
 singer
Oskar Werner (Josef Schliessmayer; 1922–84), actor
Lina Wertmuller (1926–), Italian film director
Adam West (William Anderson; 1929–), actor
Dottie West (c.1932–), country music singer
Mae West (1892–1980), actress, T
Jack Weston (1915–), actor
Randy Weston (1926–), jazz pianist
Wheeler and Woolsey: Bert Wheeler (1895–1968), Rob-
 ert Woolsey (1889–1938), comedy team
Barry White (1944–), pop-soul singer, songwriter
Betty White (1924–), actress
Jesse White (1919–), actor
Maurice White (1941–), singer, drummer, founder
 musical group *Earth, Wind and Fire*
Pearl White (1889–1938), actress, queen of silent serials
Robert Whitehead (1916–), theatrical producer, T
Paul Whiteman (1890–1967), jazz bandleader
Margaret Whiting (1924–), singer
Stuart Whitman (1926–), actor
James Whitmore (1921–), actor
Richard Widmark (1914–), actor
Larry Wilcox (1947–), actor
Cornel Wilde (1918–), actor, producer, and director
Billy Wilder (1906–), Austrian-born producer and
 director, A-1945, 1960
Gene Wilder (Jerry Silberman; 1935–), actor, director
Michael Wilding (1912–79), British actor
Andy Williams (1930–), singer
Bert Williams (1877–1922), comedian, T
Billy Dee Williams (1937–), actor
Cindy Williams (1948–), actress

Don R. Williams (1939–), country singer, songwriter
Emlyn Williams (1905–), Welsh actor playwright
Esther Williams (1923–), actress, swimming champion
Hank Williams (1923–53), country music singer,
 songwriter (*Jumbalaya*)
Hank Williams Jr. (1949–), country singer, songwriter
Mary Lou Williams (1910–81), jazz pianist
Paul Williams (1940–), pop-rock singer, songwriter
Robin Williams (1952–), actor, comedian
Roger Williams (1926–), pianist
Tony Williams (1945–), jazz drummer
Nicol Williamson (1938–), Scottish-born actor
Chill Wills (1903–78), actor
Meredith Willson (1902–84), composer of musicals (*The
 Music Man*)
Don Wilson (1900–82), radio and television announcer
Flip Wilson (1933–), comedian
Julie Wilson (1924–), singer
Lanford Wilson (1937–), playwright
Marie Wilson (1916–72), actress
Nancy Wilson (1937–), singer
Phil Wilson (1937–), jazz trombonist, composer
Paul Winchell (1924–), ventriloquist
William Windom (1923–), actor
Paul Winfield (1941–), actor
Debra Winger (1953–), actress
Henry Winkler (1945–), actor
Charles Winninger (1884–1969), character actor
Jonathan Winters (1925–), comedian
Shelley Winters (Shirley Schrift; 1922–), actress,
 A-1959, 1965
Robert Wise (1914–), director, A-1961, 1965
Jane Withers (1926–), actress, child star in 1930s
Stevie Wonder (Steveland Hardaway; 1950–), blind
 rock-blues singer and composer
Anna May Wong (1902–60), Chinese-American actress
Natalie Wood (Natasha Gurdin; 1938–81), actress
Peggy Wood (1892–1978), actress, T
Phil Woods (1931–), jazz saxophonist, clarinetist,
 bandleader
Joanne Woodward (1930–), actress, A-1957; wed to
 Paul Newman
Monty Woolley (1888–1963), actor
Jo Anne Worley (1937–), comedienne
Irene Worth (1916–), actress, T
Fay Wray (1907–), actress
Teresa Wright (1918–), actress, A-1942
Earl Wrightson (1916–), singer
Jane Wyatt (1912–), actress
William Wyler (1902–81), director, A-1942, 1946, 1959
Jane Wyman (Sarah Jane Fulks; 1914–), actress, A-1948
Tammy Wynette (Wynette Pugh; 1942–),
 country-western singer
Ed Wynn (Isaiah Leopold; 1886–1966), comedian, T
Keenan Wynn (1916–), actor, son of Ed Wynn
Dana Wynter (1930–), British actress
Glenn Yarborough (1930–), country-western singer
Peter Yarrow (1938–), folk singer
Jack Yellen (1892–), Polish-born lyricist ("Happy Days
 Are Here Again")
Michael York (1942–), British actor
Susannah York (1942–), British actress
Bud Yorkin (1926–), director, producer
Vincent Youmans (1898–1946), composer ("Tea for
 Two")
Alan Young (1919–), British-born actor
Burt Young (1940–), actor
Faron Young (1932–), country singer
Gig Young (Byron Barr; 1917–78), actor, A-1969
Lester Young (1909–59), jazz saxophonist
Loretta Young (Gretchen Belzer; 1913–), actress, A-1947
Neil Young (1945–), Canadian rock musician,
 songwriter
Robert Young (1907–), actor
Roland Young (1887–1953), British-born actor
Henny Youngman (1906–), British-born comedian
Darryl Zanuck (1902–79), producer
Frank Zappa (1940–), rock musician, songwriter,
 founder of group *Mothers of Invention* (1964)
Josef Zawinful (1932–), Austrian-born jazz synthesizer,
 composer, bandleader
Franco Zeffirelli (1923–), Italian director
Florenz Ziegfeld (1869–1932), showman, T
Efrem Zimbalist Jr. (1923–), actor
Fred Zinnemann (1907–), Austrian-born direct-
 or, A-1953, 1966
Adolph Zukor (1873–1976), Hungarian-born producer,
 brought first major movie to U.S. (1912), A-1948

History

HOW TIME FLIES!

Today's headlines soon become history as time slips by with frightening rapidity. In the following tables, events are recalled that happened 10, 25, 50, 100, and 200 years ago.

EVENTS OF 10 YEARS AGO—1976

International Bill of Human Rights goes into effect on *Jan. 3*: UN treaty ratified by 35 nations.
Pittsburgh Steelers win Super Bowl in Miami, Fla., on *Jan. 18*: Defeat Dallas Cowboys 21–17.
Newspaper heiress Patty Hearst convicted of bank robbery on *March 20*: In 39-day trial she claimed kidnappers made her do it.
U.S. extends offshore control to 200 miles on *April 13*: Previous limit had been 12 miles.
Nationwide swine flu vaccination program signed into law on *April 15*: To prevent feared epidemic, federal government underwrites $135 million cost; program suspended on *Dec. 16.*
Nuclear treaty signed on *May 28*: In separate ceremonies in Moscow and Washington Soviet leader Leonid Brezhnev and President Ford sign treaty limiting size of underground nuclear blasts.
Economic slump begins in *June*: Worsening economy contributes to President Ford's election defeat. Unemployment rises to rate of 8.1% by November.
U.S. ambassador assassinated in Lebanon on *June 16*: Ambassador Francis Meloy Jr. slain; killers escape.
First women admitted to U.S. Air Force Academy on *June 28*: Three women enrolled.
Israeli commandos raid Entebbe Airport in Uganda on *July 3*: In midnight attack Israelis free over 100 passengers from hijacked airliner.
U.S. celebrates bicentennial on *July 4* with parades, fireworks, and other festivities.
First photos from Mars reveal lifeless planet on *July 20*: U.S. robot spaceship Viking I sends TV pictures showing Mars as sandy red desert.
Worst earthquake of century destroys Chinese city on *July 28*: About 242,000 killed in Tientsin-Tangshan; another 164,000 injured.
China's 82-year-old Communist leader Mao Ze-dong dies on *Sept. 29*: Sets off power struggle.
Incumbent President debates challenger for first time on *Sept. 23, Oct. 6, and Oct. 22*: Both President Ford and Democratic presidential nominee Jimmy Carter claim victory in TV debates.
Death penalty okayed by Supreme Court on *Oct. 4*: Lifts stay that had blocked executions.
New copyright law signed on *Oct. 19*: First major revision of copyright law since 1909 gives authors protection for life plus 50 years. Previously, copyright expired after 56 years.
Democrat Jimmy Carter wins presidency on *Nov. 2*: Defeats Republican President Gerald Ford by narrow margin. Democrats retain control of both houses of Congress.
Syrian army takes control of Beirut, Lebanon, on *Nov. 15*: Syria's intervention to end Lebanon's civil war approved by Arab League.

EVENTS OF 25 YEARS AGO—1961

President Eisenhower breaks diplomatic relations with Cuba on *Jan. 3* because Cuba refuses to pay for confiscated U.S. property.
Presidential farewell address on *Jan. 17*: Eisenhower warns "military-industrial complex" poses potential for "disastrous rise of misplaced power."
John F. Kennedy inaugurated as 35th U.S. President on *Jan. 20*: Calls on Americans to "ask not what your country can do for you—ask what you can do for your country."
Peace Corps created on *March 1* by executive order of President Kennedy.
Amendment 23 to U.S Constitution officially proclaimed on *April 3*: Gives Washington, D.C., residents right to vote for President.
First man orbits Earth in space on *April 12*: Soviet Maj. Yuri Gagarin accomplishes feat.
Unsuccessful Bay of Pigs invasion of Cuba on *April 17*: Authorized by President Kennedy, force of 1,600 Cuban exiles led by U.S. CIA fails in attempt to overthrow communist government of Fidel Castro.
South Africa declares independence as republic on *May 31*: Ends membership in British Commonwealth.
"Freedom riders" head South to integrate bus terminals on *May 4*: Demonstrators meet violence in Alabama and Mississippi. Attorney General Robert Kennedy sends federal marshals to protect group from hostile mobs.
First American astronaut flies in space on *May 5*: Alan Shepard Jr. makes 300-mile suborbital flight.
Space race to moon begins on *May 25*: President Kennedy in address to Congress pledges U.S. to "landing a man on the moon and returning him safely to earth" by end of 1960s.
Summit meeting on *June 3–4*: President Kennedy and Soviet leader Khrushchev meet in Vienna.
Berlin Wall built on *Aug. 13*: Fortified wall constructed by communists to prevent East Germans from escaping to West Berlin.
Minimum wage raised to $1.15 per hour on *Sept. 1*: Increased by new Fair Labor Standards Act.
New York Yankees win baseball World Series on *Oct. 9*: Defeat Cincinnati Reds 4 games to 1.
First direct U.S. military intervention in South Vietnam ordered by President Kennedy on *Dec. 11*: Two U.S. helicopter units to help fight communists.
India seizes Portuguese colonies on *Dec. 18–19*: Takes control of Goa, Damao, and Diu.

QUICK QUIZ: What college football team was national champion in 1929-30? See page 814.

EVENTS OF 50 YEARS AGO—1936

First unemployment insurance begins on *Jan. 1*: Financed by 1% payroll tax.

Agricultural Adjustment Act (AAA) declared unconstitutional on *Jan. 6* by Supreme Court.

Congress grants cash bonuses to World War I veterans on *Jan. 24*: Overrides President Roosevelt's veto of measure for distribution of $1.5 billion to veterans.

Soil Conservation and Domestic Allotment Act passed by Congress on *Feb. 29*: Provides subsidies to farmers to overcome practices that turned huge area of Midwest into "Dust Bowl."

Second Neutrality Act approved by Congress on *Feb. 29*: Forbids shipment of arms or granting of loans and credits to any belligerents.

Italian troops capture Addis Ababa, capital of Ethiopia, on *May 5*: Emperor Haile Selassie flees to Europe where he appeals unsuccessfully to League of Nations to help recover his nation from Italy.

First scheduled transatlantic passenger flight by dirigible completed on *May 9*: German zepplin

Hindenburg lands at Lakehurst, N.J.

Spanish civil war begins on *July 17*: Army revolt against leftist government led by General Francisco Franco, who wins control after disastrous fighting lasts until 1939. Italy and Germany support Franco while Soviet Union aids leftist Spanish government.

U.S. black track star Jesse Owens wins four gold medals in *July* at Summer Olympic Games held in Berlin, Germany.

Berlin-Rome Axis formed on *Oct. 27*: German dictator Adolf Hitler and Italian dictator Benito Mussolini agree on working partnership.

President Franklin D. Roosevelt wins reelection to second term in landslide on *Nov. 3*.

British king abdicates on *Dec. 10*: Edward VIII gives up throne to marry American divorcee Wallis Warfield Simpson. They receive titles: Duke and Duchess of Windsor.

First major "sit down strike" begins on *Dec. 30*: United Auto Workers (UAW) wins recognition from General Motors after strike lasts 44 days.

EVENTS OF 100 YEARS AGO—1886

Presidential Succession Act adopted on *Jan. 19*: Provided cabinet officers in order of creation of their offices would succeed President. Action hastened by death in November 1885 of Vice President Thomas A. Hendricks.

Invention of process to manufacture aluminum on *Feb. 23*: Discovered almost simultaneously by Charles Martin Hall in the U.S. and by Paul L.T. Heroult in France. Two years later aluminum produced in commercial quantities.

Railroad workers begin strike on *March 6*: Two-month strike by Knights of Labor ties up transcontinental Missouri-Pacific railroad; hungry workers end strike in May with no gains.

First presidential message to Congress devoted to problems of labor on *April 22*: President Grover Cleveland asks Congress to establish three-member commission to mediate labor-management disputes. Labor unions and anarchists in nationwide strike of 50,000 to 300,000 workers on *May 1*, calling for 8-hour work day.

Haymarket Riot on *May 4*: As police arrive to

break up anarchist-labor demonstration at Haymarket Square in Chicago, bomb is thrown, killing 7 policemen. Police and demonstrators shoot at each other with 10 civilians killed and many wounded. Eight anarchists were arrested and convicted of conspiracy; four were hanged.

First White House marriage of a President on *June 2*: President Grover Cleveland, 49, marries Frances Folsom, 21, daughter of his former law partner. Apache Indian War in Southwest ends on *Sept. 4* with capture of Apache Chief Geronimo by General Nelson A. Miles.

Statue of Liberty dedicated on *Oct. 28* in New York Harbor by President Grover Cleveland. Statue by Frederic Bartholdi was gift of people of France.

Former President Chester A. Arthur dies on *Nov. 18*.

American Federation of Labor (AFL) organized on *Dec. 8*: Convention held in Columbus, Ohio, under leadership of Samuel Gompers and Adolph Strasser.

EVENTS OF 200 YEARS AGO—1786

Religious freedom law adopted by Virginia legislature on *Jan. 16*: Act written by Thomas Jefferson and introduced by James Madison. Later became basis for first amendment to United States Constitution.

Virginia issues invitations to Annapolis Convention on *Jan. 21*: Asks other states to attend meeting in Maryland to decide what can be done to end protective trade barriers between states that are hurting the economy.

New Jersey refuses to pay its share of financial support to national government on *Feb. 20*: Highlights lack of power of U.S. government under Articles of Confederation.

George Washington calls for revision of Articles of Confederation in *May*: In letter to John Jay of New York, then serving as U.S. Secretary of Foreign Affairs, Washington declares, ". . . it is necessary to revise and amend the Articles of Confederation . . . something must be done, or

the fabric must fall, for it certainly is tottering."

Morocco agrees to end piracy of U.S ships in treaty on *June 28*: U.S. pays $10,000 for gifts to Morocco's king to obtain treaty.

Angry farmers close court in Northhampton, Mass., on *Aug. 31* to prevent foreclosure of mortgages. As unrest continues, mobs close courts in other Massachusetts towns.

Annapolis Convention meets on *Sept. 11-14*: Because only five states send delegates, convention can take no binding action to solve nation's problems. However, those present adopt resolution written by Alexander Hamilton of New York that invites all states to attend a constitutional convention in Philadelphia in May 1787.

Shays' Rebellion begins on *Sept. 26*: Former Revolutionary War Capt. Daniel Shays leads several hundred armed farmers in forcing state supreme court to adjourn at Springfield, Mass. Rebellion continues into 1787.

KEY EVENTS IN WORLD HISTORY

Many of the important events and developments in world history from the time of the first civilizations are arranged in chronological order on the following pages.

For other important events, see the tables: *How Time Flies!*, pages 281–282; *Key Events*

in *American History*, pages 301–309; *Important Dates in the History of American Women*, page 980; *History of the Middle East*, page 420; *History of the United Nations*, page 422; *Highlights of the Vietnam War*, page 679; and *World in Review*, pages 7–27.

DEVELOPMENT OF EARLY CIVILIZATIONS: 12,000–550 B.C.

c.12,000 B.C. Domestication of dogs: Evidence of dogs kept as household pets found in cave dwellings near Kirkuk, Iraq, in 1975.

c.9000–8000 B.C. End of Ice Age: Glaciers began receding in Europe, Asia, and North America.

c.8000–6000 B.C. Cultivation of grain: Wheat and barley grown for flour to make bread in Middle East; grain farming spreads to Greece about 6000 B.C.

c.7000–6000 B.C. Farm villages and towns develop in Middle East: Remains of villages of this period found in Iran, Turkey, and Israel.

c.4500–3100 B.C. Egyptians build villages along Nile River; begin to use hieroglyphics (picture writing); earliest recorded date believed 4241 B.C., marking beginning of Egyptian calendar; copper and glass come into use.

c.4000–3000 B.C. Sumerians build cities in valleys of Tigris and Euphrates rivers (now in Iraq); develop cuneiform writing; use wheel and bronze.

c.3100–2890 B.C. Egyptian kingdom formed by King Mena (or Menes) and successors of first dynasty; kings buried in stone tombs.

c.3100–2100 B.C. Elamites build city of Susa, now in western Iran; men ride horses.

c.3000–1720 B.C. Seafaring Phoenicians from city of Byblos (now in Lebanon) begin trading with Egypt and other areas around Mediterranean Sea.

c.3000–1450 B.C. Minoans develop city of Knossos on island of Crete; use earliest form of written Greek.

c.2900–1460 B.C. Hittites build city of Hattusas (now Bogazkoy) in eastern Turkey.

c.2650–2500 B.C. Great pyramids built by Egyptians as tombs for kings, including Great Pyramid of Giza for King Cheops.

c.2500–1500 B.C. Indus River valley people build cities of Harappa and Mohenjo-Daro (now in Pakistan); use script writing.

c.2360–2305 B.C. King Sargon I of Akkad conquers Sumerians in what is now Iraq.

c.2130–2112 B.C. Sumerian King Ur-Nammu builds ziggurat (tower) at city of Ur (in Iraq).

c.1813–1783 B.C. Assyrians rise to power with cities of Ashur, Nineveh, and Kalhu (in Iraq).

c.1800 B.C. Stonehenge monument of huge blocks of sandstone built in England.

c.1800 B.C. Father of Hebrews and Arabs, Abraham, begins journey from birthplace Ur, eventually leading his people to Egypt.

c.1792–1750 B.C. Babylonian King Hammurabi the Great issues code of laws; Babylonian scholars use advanced mathematics.

c.1766–1123 B.C. Chinese civilization develops under Shang dynasty of kings along Hwang Ho (Yellow River); script writing used; bronze tools and weapons made.

c.1650–1125 B.C. Mycenaean civilization in Greece centers on city of Mycenae; mythology of Greek gods develops.

c.1531 B.C. Hittites conquer Babylonians, destroying Babylon.

c.1500 B.C. Aryans from central Asia destroy Indus River valley civilization in Pakistan.

c.1457 B.C. Egyptians extend empire to include Syria as Thutmose III defeats Hittites.

c.1379–1362 B.C. Worship of single god, Aton, ordered by Egyptian Pharaoh Akhenaton; after his death, Egyptians resume worship of many gods.

c.1375–1335 B.C. Hittite King Suppiluliumas drives Egyptians out of Syria and Palestine; Hittites begin using some iron weapons.

c.1350 B.C. British Isles said to have been visited by Phoenicians, trading for tin used in making bronze.

c.1250–1232 B.C. Moses leads Israelites out of Egypt, giving them Ten Commandments of God; Israelites take southern Palestine from Phoenicians (Canaanites).

c.1200–100 B.C. Olmec civilization develops in southern Mexico; Olmecs build stone monuments, use picture writing.

c.1194–1184 B.C. Trojan War: Greeks of Mycenae capture city of Troy (now in Turkey).

c.1122–256 B.C. Chinese kings of Chou dynasty develop advanced civilization using mathematics, astronomy, silk textiles, copper coins, and some iron tools and weapons.

c.1116–1078 B.C. Assyrian King Tiglath-pileser I conquers Hittites; rules most of Middle East.

c.1100 B.C. End of Mycenaean civilization in Greece; Mycenae destroyed by invasion of Dorians from north.

c.1078–935 B.C. Assyria and Babylonia fall to invasion of Aramaeans and Chaldeans from north and east.

c.1000 B.C. Israel's first king, Saul, killed in battle with Philistines; succeeded by King David, who defeats Philistines and makes Jerusalem capital of Israel; about this time Hebrew elders begin to put Old Testament books of Bible into writing, based on oral traditions.

c.1000–950 B.C. Spain colonized by Phoenicians with settlement at Cádiz.

c.961–922 B.C. King Solomon of Israel constructs Jewish temple and palace in Jerusalem.

c.935–913 B.C. Assyrian King Assurdan II reestablishes dominance of Assyrians in what is now Iraq.

c.814–750 B.C. Phoenicians found Carthage in North Africa (now Tunisia).

c.800–700 B.C. Greek poet Homer believed to have composed *Iliad* and *Odyssey.*

c.800–300 B.C. Hinduism develops in India, with worship of many gods; society divides into caste system.

c.776 B.C. First Olympic Games held by Greeks to honor god Zeus.

c.753 B.C. Rome founded by twin brothers Romulus and Remus, according to legend.

c.745–728 B.C. Assyrian Empire extended to include Babylonia, Syria, and Palestine by King Tiglath-pileser III.

c.736–715 B.C. Greek Spartans under King Theopompus conquer Messenians of southwestern Greece.

c.725–722 B.C. Destruction of Israel as nation for next 2,600 years: Assyrian King Sargon II subdues rebelling Israelites, enslaving 27,000.

c.715 B.C. Egypt conquered by Ethiopia.

c.683–682 B.C. City-state Athens abolishes hereditary monarchy, establishing rule by archons chosen annually by council of nobles.

c.680–547 B.C. King of Lydia rules in what is now Turkey, with capital at Sardis (near present-day Izmir); first Western people to use coins as money; last king is Croesus.

c.663 B.C. Assyria conquers Egypt, driving out last Ethiopian pharaoh, Tanutamon.

c.660 B.C. Japanese Emperor Jimmu Tenno founds first dynasty, according to legend.

c.658–675 B.C. Byzantium (now Istanbul, Turkey) founded by Greek colonists.

c.626–561 B.C. Chaldeans of Babylonia conquer Assyrians; rebuild Babylon as capital of new Babylonian empire; construct hanging gardens of Babylon.

c.600 B.C. Southern France colonized by Greeks at Massalia (now Marseille).

c.587–582 B.C. Jews taken in captivity to Babylon: Babylonian King Nebuchadnezzar II captures Jerusalem; destroys Solomon's temple, ending kingdom of Judah.

QUICK QUIZ: Who was chosen male Athlete of the Year by the Associated Press in 1955? See page 766.

KEY EVENTS IN WORLD HISTORY *(continued)*

c.563–483 B.C. **Buddha** (Prince Siddartha Gautama) founds Buddhism in Nepal and India.

c.551–479 B.C. **Confucius** develops philosophy-reli-gion of Confucianism in China, providing rules of mor-als and ethics.

c.550 B.C. **Taoism** founded in China by Lao Tzu, ac-cording to legend.

RISE OF ANCIENT PERSIAN EMPIRE TO FALL OF ROME: 550 B.C.–A.D. 476

c.550–530 B.C. **Persian Empire** founded by Cyrus the Great, who conquers Lydians and Babylonians to con-trol most of Middle East.

c.550–500 B.C. **Carthage grows as military power:** Phoenician colony of Carthage in what is now Tunisia becomes major power in western Mediterranean Sea.

c.550–100 B.C. **City of Teotihuacán develops in Mexi-co:** City grows to cover about 3 square miles.

c.539–516 B.C. **Jews freed from captivity** as Persians conquer Babylon; Solomon's temple rebuilt in Jerusa-lem with aid from Persians.

c.530–486 B.C. **Persian Empire extended** to include Egypt and Pakistan under leadership of Cambyses and Darius I.

c.510–506 B.C. **Democracy begins in Athens** with gov-ernment controlled by 500-man legislative council; Athens fights off attempt by Sparta's King Cleomenes to restore aristocrats.

c.509 B.C. **Romans establish republic;** overthrow Etruscan King Tarquin the Proud.

c.499–478 B.C. **Greeks preserve independence** by de-feating invasions of Persian armies of Darius I and Xerxes I.

c.460–429 B.C. **Age of Pericles in Athens:** Art, sci-ence, and democracy flourish under leadership of Peri-cles; Parthenon is built.

c.447–445 B.C. **First history published in Greece:** Greek historian Herodotus writes 9-volume history of known world after travel through Persian empire.

c.431–404 B.C. **Spartans defeat Athens** in Peloponne-sian War; force Athens to surrender navy and tear down fortified walls.

c.404–399 B.C. **Egypt regains independence** from Per-sia under Pharaoh Amyrtaeus of Sais.

338 B.C. **Greece conquered by King Philip II** of Mace-donia, defeating allied armies of Thebes and Athens in Battle of Chaeronea.

336–323 B.C. **Alexander the Great** of Macedonia con-solidates rule of Greece, destroying Thebes; conquers Persian Empire, Egypt, and Pakistan; makes Babylon his capital.

c.321–184 B.C. **Northern India united** under Maurya dynasty founded by Emperor Chandragupta.

305–64 B.C. **Seleucid Empire** rules Middle East; founded by Seleucus I, one of Alexander's generals, who builds new capital cities of Antioch in Syria and Seleucia in Iraq.

305–30 B.C. **Egypt ruled by Greek dynasty** founded by Ptolemy I, one of Alexander's generals; capital Alex-andria becomes center of Greek learning with great library.

279 B.C. **Gauls** from northern Europe invade Macedo-nia, Greece, and found kingdom of Galatia in what is now Turkey.

276–167 B.C. **Macedonia and Greece** ruled by kings of Antigonid dynasty, descended from Antigonus, one of Alexander's generals.

264–146 B.C. **Punic Wars** fought between Roman re-public and Carthage, ending with destruction of Car-thage, Roman dominance of Mediterranean Sea, and establishment of Roman provinces in North Africa and Spain.

c.250–139 B.C. **Greeks found and rule kingdom of Bactria** in what is now Afghanistan; capital at Kabul.

c.221–210 B.C. **Great Wall of China** built by Chinese Emperor Shih Huang Ti, who centralizes rule of China, founds Ch'in dynasty; books written on silk scrolls.

c.165 B.C. **Jews revolt** (under leadership of Judas Maccabeus) against Seleucids; found independent king-dom of Judea.

c.146–121 B.C. **Roman armies conquer** Macedonia, Greece, Turkey, Balearic Islands, and southern France.

c.108 B.C. **Korea** conquered by China.

c.105 B.C. **Paper** invented in China.

c.100 B.C. **India invaded by Scythians** from central Asia, founding Kushana dynasty.

c.100 B.C.–A.D. **200** **Mayan civilization** develops in Central America.

c.66–62 B.C. **Seleucid Empire conquered** by Roman general Pompey; Syria and Judea become provinces of Rome.

58–44 B.C. **Roman general Julius Caesar** conquers all of France (Gaul); invades Germany, Britain, and Egypt; makes himself dictator of Rome until assassinat-ed (March 15, 44 B.C.) by senators led by Cassius and Brutus.

44–30 B.C. **Civil war among Roman generals:** Won by Julius Caesar's heir Octavian (Gaius Octavius), who in Battle of Actium (Sept. 2, 31 B.C.) defeats fleet of Ro-man general Mark Antony and Queen Cleopatra of Egypt; Octavian makes Egypt possession of Rome, fol-lowing suicides of Antony and Cleopatra.

27 B.C.–A.D. **14** **Roman Empire** established and ruled by Octavian, who takes title *Emperor Augustus*; art and science flourish during reign, known as *Augustan Age*; Roman literature develops with Virgil, Horace, Ovid, Livy.

c.5 B.C.–A.D. **30** **Jesus Christ** lives in Roman province of Judea, founding Christian religion; sentenced to death by crucifixion by Roman governor Pontius Pilate.

—All dates following in chronology are A.D.

25–57 **Chinese Emperor Kuang Wu Ti** founds Eastern Han dynasty; Buddhism introduced to China; Vietnam conquered by Chinese army.

43–122 **England conquered** by Roman army; Emper-or Hadrian builds wall between England and Scotland in 122–127.

64 **Persecution of Christians** begun by Roman Em-peror Nero, who accuses them of starting fire that de-stroys much of Rome; St. Peter and St. Paul are be-lieved to have been executed in 67 or 68.

70 **Romans destroy Jewish temple** in Jerusalem; out-law Jewish priesthood; disperse many Jews throughout Roman Empire as punishment for Jewish revolt against Roman rule.

71–80 **Colosseum** built in Rome.

c.78–96 **Kushan Empire** in Afghanistan and northern India ruled by King Kanishka, who sends Buddhist missionaries to China.

98–117 **Roman Emperor Trajan** extends Roman Em-pire to include Arabia, Iraq, Armenia, and what is now Romania and Hungary.

117–138 **Roman Emperor Hadrian** codifies laws of Rome; establishes postal system throughout empire; constructs many buildings, including Parthenon in Rome.

132–135 **New revolt by Jews** in Jerusalem leads to final Diaspora (dispersion) of Jews.

c.224–226 **Persian Empire reestablished** by Ardashir I, founding dynasty of Persian shahs called *Sassanids*, who rule until 642.

c.250–800 **Mayan civilization** in Central America de-velops writing, astronomy, and mathematics; builds great pyramids.

251–270 **Plague** kills about one-fourth of people throughout Roman Empire; German tribes invade em-pire from north.

306–337 **Roman Emperor Constantine I** builds new capital at Constantinople (previously Byzantium, now Istanbul); becomes Christian; issues Edict of Milan (c.313), legalizing Christianity throughout Roman Empire.

313 **Koreans win independence** from China.

c.320 **Gupta dynasty** founded in northern India by Chandragupta I.

c.376 **Huns** (Mongols) from central Asia establish Hunnic Empire in what is now Hungary.

380 **Christianity made official religion** of Roman Em-pire by Emperor Theodosius the Great.

395 **Roman Empire permanently divided:** western em-pire ruled from Rome; eastern empire ruled from Constantinople.

395–476 **Western Roman Empire disintegrates** under series of weak emperors; Visigoths led by Alaric cap-ture and sack Rome in 410; Huns led by Attila ravage Rome's provinces in 435–453; Rome again sacked in 455 by Vandals led by Genseric; in 476 last Roman emperor of west, Romulus Augustus, overthrown by Odoacer, leader of German Heruli.

BYZANTINE EMPIRE, ARAB EMPIRE, AND EUROPEAN MIDDLE AGES: 481–1294

481 Kingdom of Franks established by Clovis I in northern France and southern Germany with capital at Paris.

484–490 Hephthalites, or White Huns, invade Persia and India: Asian tribesmen loot wealthy cities; dominate region until defeated in India in 528 and in Afghanistan in 557.

493 Ostrogoth Kingdom of Italy established by Theodoric the Great.

c.500–542 King Arthur and Knights of Round Table rule in England, according to legend.

502–549 Buddhism becomes official religion in China: Emperor Liang Wu-ti adopts Buddhism; persecutes Taoists.

527–565 Byzantine Empire (Eastern Roman Empire) reaches height under Macedonian Emperor Justinian I the Great; conquers North Africa, Italy, and southeastern Spain.

c.550 Silk manufacture begins in Byzantine Empire after Christian missionaries to China smuggle out silkworm eggs and mulberry seeds.

568–586 Visigoths conquer Spain: Byzantine armies driven out of Spain by Visigoth King Leovigild.

c.587 Japanese Emperor Yomei converts to Buddhism.

589 Chinese Empire reunited by armies of Sui dynasty; Great Wall of China rebuilt.

590–640 Papal States founded in Italy: Pope Gregory takes charge of government as well as religious affairs in central and southern Italy.

c.597–605 English King Ethelbert I converts to Christianity; St. Augustine becomes first archbishop of Canterbury (Ethelbert's capital).

622–632 Mohammed founds Islamic religion; launches holy war by Arabs on nonbelievers.

630–648 Chinese armies conquer Turkestan (now part of Soviet Union).

634–644 Arab Empire expands by conquest of Iraq, Syria, Iran, Palestine, and Egypt by Muslim armies of caliph Omar.

661–680 Arab armies of caliph Muawiya make new conquests, adding North Africa, Afghanistan, Pakistan, and Turkestan to Arab Empire.

675–681 Slavic tribes invade Balkan region.

711–732 Spain and southern France invaded and conquered by Arabs and Berbers from Africa.

712–756 Chinese culture rises to new heights under Emperor Hsuan Tsung; porcelain made; paper printed with wooden blocks; mechanical clock invented.

768–814 Charlemagne, king of Franks, expands empire by conquest of Germany and northern Italy; attempts to revive Western Roman Empire by having Pope Leo III crown him emperor in 800.

c.787–794 Danish and Norse Vikings raid England and Scotland.

c.820–1431 Cambodia (Khmer) rules southeast Asia from magnificent capital at Angkor Thom.

841–856 Danish Vikings raid France, sacking Paris in 845 and 856.

c.855–879 Russian nation founded by Vikings under Prince Rurik, establishing capital at Novgorod.

866 Normandy region of France colonized by Viking Northmen (Normans).

867 Christianity splits Rome and Constantinople as Eastern Orthodox Church rejects control by Roman Catholic pope.

878 Alfred the Great prevents Danish Vikings from conquering all of England.

912–961 Muslim Spain becomes Europe's main center of learning and science under caliph AbdarRahman III.

962 Holy Roman Empire founded by Otto I, king of Germany since 936, crowned by Pope John XII.

976–1025 Byzantine Empire's power revived by Emperor Basil II, conquering Bulgaria and Armenia.

981 Greenland colonized by Norse Vikings.

987 Hugh Capet elected king of France, founding Capetian dynasty that rules until 1328.

c.1000 North America discovered by Norse Vikings, who call it *Vinland.*

1003–14 England conquered by Denmark's King Sven.

1055 Seljuk Turks from central Asia under Tughril Beg capture Baghdad, capital of Arab Empire.

1066 England invaded by Normans led by William the Conqueror, who defeats King Harold II at Battle of Hastings (Oct. 14).

1068–84 Southern Italy conquered by Normans led by Robert Guiscard; Rome sacked in 1084.

1071–85 Seljuk Turks extend empire, conquering Asiatic Turkey and Syria.

1096–99 First Crusade: Answering call by Pope Urban II to rescue Holy Land from control of Muslims, about 30,000 French and Italian crusaders invade Seljuk Turkish Empire, capturing Jerusalem and Turkey; establish Latin States of the Crusaders in Middle East.

c.1100 Timbuktu founded in West Africa, becoming center of learning for black Muslims.

1106 Northern France invaded and conquered by England's King Henry I, imprisoning his brother, who had been ruler of Normandy.

1147–49 Second Crusade: Because Muslims had reconquered most of Asiatic Turkey, new crusade is organized by kings of France and Germany, but is defeated by Turks.

c.1150–67 Universities of Paris and Oxford founded in France and England.

1167–71 Ireland claimed by England's King Henry II as Normans colonize Ireland.

1175–1206 Central India conquered by Muslim ruler of Persia.

1187 Jerusalem captured by Saladin, Muslim sultan of Syria and Egypt.

1189–92 Third Crusade: Kings of England, France, and Germany lead armies in unsuccessful effort to recapture Jerusalem; however, agreement is made with Saladin to let Christians visit Jerusalem.

c.1200–1438 Inca civilization develops in Peru; builds great cities and road system.

c.1200–1450 Mayan civilization in Central America ruled from Mayapán in Yucatán, following overthrow of rulers of Chichén-Itzá.

1202–04 Northern France recovered by France's King Philip II from England's King John.

1202–04 Fourth Crusade: Setting off to invade Arab Egypt, French knights divert to attack Byzantine Empire; capture Constantinople and massacre its people; Roman Catholics replace Greeks on throne of Byzantine Empire.

1203–23 Denmark raids and conquers many coastal areas of Baltic Sea.

1206–27 Genghis Khan leads Mongols in conquest of northern China and central Asia.

1212 Children's Crusade: Thousands of French and German children march toward Holy Land but die or are enslaved along way.

1215 (June 15–19) Magna Carta (Great Charter) agreed to by England's King John; sets first limits on monarch's absolute power by requiring assent of barons to special taxes.

1218–21 Fifth Crusade: Crusaders invade Egypt but are driven off.

1228–29 Sixth Crusade: Holy Roman Emperor Frederick II leads Teutonic Knights to Holy Land; acquires Jerusalem from sultan of Egypt, crowning himself its king.

1230–55 Mali Empire founded in West Africa by King Sundiata.

1237–41 Mongol armies conquer Russia and devastate Hungary; for next two centuries Russian princes pay tribute to Mongol Golden Horde that occupies southern Russia.

1244 Jerusalem recaptured by Muslims.

1245–65 Seljuk Turkish Empire destroyed by Mongols, who conquer Iran, Iraq, and Syria, sacking Baghdad in 1258.

1248–54 Seventh Crusade: France's King Louis IX leads attack on Egypt; captured by Muslims and held captive until ransom is paid.

1260–94 Kublai Khan rules China and Mongol Empire from Pacific Ocean to Mediterranean Sea, with capital at Peking; builds roads, canals, hospitals; encourages art and science.

1261 Greek rule of Byzantine Empire restored by Greek army that overthrows Roman Catholic Emperor Baldwin II.

1265 First English parliament meets under leader-

KEY EVENTS IN WORLD HISTORY *(continued)*
ship of Simon de Montfort.
1269–73 Gunpowder explosives first used in war: Chinese defenders of cities in Yangtze River Valley use explosives against Mongol invaders.
1270 Eighth Crusade: Kings of England and France attack Carthage in North Africa; French King Louis IX dies of plague; nothing accomplished.
1271–95 Marco Polo of Venice travels throughout Mongol Empire; upon return writes book describing wonders of Chinese civilization.
1272–1307 Great Britain unified for first time as English King Edward I conquers Wales and Scotland.

1276–78 Austria conquered by Holy Roman Emperor Rudolf I, founder of Hapsburg dynasty that rules Austria until 1918.
1281 Typhoon saves Japan from Mongol invasion; invading army of 150,000 Mongols halted when typhoon wrecks their fleet.
1287 Mongols conquer Burma: Capital city Pagan looted; Burma made part of Kublai Khan's empire.
1291 Last Christian crusaders driven from Middle East by Muslims.
1294 First Roman Catholic missionary travels to China: Franciscan friar Giovanni di Monte Covino reaches Peking; made first archbishop of China in 1307.

RENAISSANCE, EXPLORATION, AND REFORMATION: 1300–1599

c.1300 European Renaissance begins in Florence, Italy, with painter Giotto and writers Dante, Petrarch, and Boccaccio.
1300–26 Ottoman Turkish Empire founded by Osman I: Launches holy war against non-Muslims in Middle East.
1307–08 William Tell helps Switzerland win independence from Austria, legend says.
1312–37 Mali Empire reaches height in Africa under King Mansa Musa; said to have visited Cairo with caravan of 100 camels, each carrying 300 pounds of gold, and 500 slaves, each carrying staff made of gold.
1314 Scotland wins independence from England as Robert Bruce defeats English army at Battle of Bannockburn (June 24).
1325–1519 Mexico ruled by Aztecs from capital city of Tenochtitlán (now Mexico City).
1326–61 Ottoman Turkish Empire under Sultan Orkhan I conquers northeastern Greece.
1337–1453 Hundred Years War: English and French kings fight for control of France; by 1453 England holds only French city of Calais, but English claim throne of France until 1801.
1340–41 Portuguese explorers first visit Canary Islands off coast of northwest Africa.
1346 (Aug. 26) England's King Edward III wins Battle of Crécy over French, proving superiority of longbowmen over armored knights and crossbowmen of France; cannon fired by gunpowder possibly introduced then.
1347–52 Black Death (bubonic plague) sweeps across Europe, killing about one-fourth of estimated 100 million population.
1361–89 Ottoman Turkish Empire expands under Sultan Murad I with conquest of most of what is now Yugoslavia and Bulgaria.
1368–98 Ming dynasty founded in China by Emperor Hung-wu, whose armies drive Mongols into central Asia.
1369–1405 Mongol ruler Tamerlane conquers Afghanistan, Iran, Iraq, eastern Turkey, and northern India.
c.1376–82 Bible translated into English by John Wycliffe and his followers.
1378–1417 Rival popes in Rome and at Avignon, France, contend for control of Roman Catholic Church.
1381 Peasant Revolt in England led by Wat Tyler unsuccessfully demands end to feudal system of forced labor and high land rents.
1387–1412 Denmark, Norway, and Sweden united under Queen Margrethe of Denmark.
1399 Revolt in England: King Richard II imprisoned for reasserting absolute power; parliament elects Henry IV to throne.
c.1400–1500 Muslim Arabs conquer islands of Indonesia, Malaya, and south Philippines.
1414–17 Roman Catholics reunified with election of Pope Martin V; Council of Constance condemns and executes as heretics John Huss (Jan Hus) and Jerome of Prague for questioning validity of various church doctrines.
1418–60 Portugal's Prince Henry the Navigator sponsors exploration of Africa's coast.
c.1422–26 Technical improvements in arts: Oil painting developed by Flemish artist Jan Van Eyck; bronze statues cast by Florentine sculptor Donatello; perspective used to show depth by Florentine painter Masaccio.
1427–31 Azores Islands discovered by Portuguese explorer Diogo de Sevilla.
1429 (May 7) Joan of Arc, 17, leads French army at

Battle of Orléans, forcing English to lift siege of city; saves France from being conquered; burned as witch by English at Rouen on May 31, 1431.
1453 (May 29) Byzantine Empire comes to end as Ottoman Turks capture Constantinople.
c.1454 Johann Gutenberg invents printing with movable metal type at Mainz, Germany.
1455–85 Wars of the Roses: Civil war in England between rival families of York and Lancaster for throne of England; ends with marriage of King Henry VII (of Lancaster) to Elizabeth (of York), founding Tudor dynasty.
1462–1505 Ivan III the Great rules Russia as first czar; ends payment of tribute to Mongols; seizes part of Lithuania from Poland.
1479 Spain unified by joint rule of Queen Isabella of Castile and King Ferdinand II of Aragon; they complete conquest of Moorish Spain with capture of Granada in 1492.
1487–88 Portuguese explorer Bartolomeu Dias sails around southern tip of Africa.
1492–93 Christopher Columbus makes first voyage of discovery to America; lands at Bahamas island of San Salvador on Oct. 12, 1492; discovers Cuba; establishes settlement on Santo Domingo.
1493 Line of Demarcation established by Pope Alexander VI to prevent disputes between Portugal and Spain; gives Africa and Brazil to Portugal, rest of Americas to Spain.
c.1495–1519 Leonardo da Vinci paints Renaissance masterpieces *Last Supper* and *Mona Lisa;* produces many other works of art, science, and engineering in Italy.
1497–99 Portuguese explorer Vasco da Gama sails around Africa to India and back; gives Portugal opportunity to establish monopoly on trade in spices from Far East to Europe.
1501 First black slaves in America brought to Spanish colony of Santo Domingo.
1505–15 Portugal fortifies India's southwest coast; destroys Arab ships in Arabian Gulf to cut off Arab trade with Far East; establishes Goa in India as capital of Portuguese possessions in Asia.
1506–1626 St. Peter's Church built in Rome; designed and decorated by such Renaissance artists and architects as Donato Bramante, Michelangelo, Raphael, Leonardo da Vinci, and Gian Lorenzo Bernini.
1512–20 Ottoman Turks conquer Syria, Arabia, and Egypt under leadership of Sultan Selim I.
1513 (Sept. 9) Scotland's King James IV invades England; defeated and killed at Battle of Flodden Field.
1517 (Oct. 31) Reformation begins in Germany as Martin Luther posts on door of church in Wittenberg his *Ninety-Five Theses,* denouncing abuses by Roman Catholic Church.
1519–21 Spanish conquistador Hernándo Cortés conquers Mexico; defeats Aztec Indians at their capital, Tenochtitlán; sends back treasures of gold to Spain.
1519–22 First voyage around world: Begun in 1519 by Spanish explorer Ferdinand Magellan, killed in Philippines in 1521; one of his ships, under command of Juan Sebastián del Cano, continues around world to Spain, arriving in 1522.
1520–23 Sweden declares independence from Denmark; leader of revolt takes throne as King Gustavus I.
1520–66 Ottoman Turkish Empire expands with conquests of Yugoslavia, Hungary, Iraq, Iran, Arabia, and North Africa by Sultan Suleiman I the Magnificent.
1521 Martin Luther excommunicated by Pope Leo X; declared outlaw punishable by death by Holy Roman Emperor Charles V; before Luther's death, in 1546, thousands in Europe turn to Protestantism.

1526 (Aug. 29) Hungary conquered by Turks: In Battle of Mohács, armies of Sultan Suleiman I defeat Hungarian King Lajos II; over 100,000 Hungarian Christians enslaved by Turks.

1526–30 Mogul Empire in India founded by Babar, descendant of Gengis Khan.

1527–46 Mayan civilization of Yucatán conquered by Spaniards, who burn Mayan bark-cloth books, calling them "works of the Devil."

1529 (April 22) Portugal and Spain divide Eastern Hemisphere: Sign Treaty of Saragossa establishing boundary between possessions in Far East, recognizing Portugal's control of Indonesia and Spain's possession of Philippines and Pacific Islands.

1530–31 Schmalkaldic League formed by German states and cities ruled by Protestants.

1531 Commercial tobacco farming begun in America: Rising demand for tobacco in Spain, where it had been introduced by Christopher Columbus, causes colonists in what is now Dominican Republic to begin raising tobacco for export.

1531–35 Inca empire of Peru conquered by Spanish conquistador Francisco Pizarro, who loots their gold and sends it to Spain.

1534 Reformation begins in England as King Henry VIII makes himself head of church after being excommunicated for divorcing Catherine of Aragon.

1534–64 Presbyterian Protestantism, developed by John Calvin in Switzerland, gains English Puritans and French Huguenots as adherents.

1536–40 Denmark, Norway, and Sweden adopt Lutheranism as national religion.

1538 First university in Americas founded in Santo Domingo (now Dominican Republic).

1542 First European visits Japan; believed to be Portuguese explorer Antonio da Mota.

1542–51 Roman Catholicism introduced to India and Japan by Jesuit missionary St. Francis Xavier.

1543 Theory that Earth revolves around Sun published by Polish scholar Nicolaus Copernicus; later suppressed by Roman Catholic Church as denial of biblical teaching.

1546–55 Schmalkaldic War: Holy Roman Emperor Charles V tries to force Protestant states and cities of Germany to return to Roman Catholicism; Peace of Augsburg in 1555 gives Lutherans freedom of worship.

1547–84 Russia's Czar Ivan IV the Terrible conquers Tatars (Mongols) to acquire Volga River region, but loses western Russia to Poland and Sweden.

c.1550 Muskets first developed in Spain.

1553–58 Roman Catholicism restored in England by Queen Mary I; about 300 Protestant leaders burned at stake, including Archbishop of Canterbury Thomas Cranmer.

1558–1603 England ruled by Queen Elizabeth I, who restores Protestantism, establishes Church of England (Episcopalian), and persecutes Roman Catholics, Unitarians, and radical Puritans; Renaissance reaches

height in England with such writers as William Shakespeare, Edmund Spenser, and Christopher Marlowe.

1562–68 British slave trade begins with voyages of John Hawkins carrying slaves from Africa to Spanish colonies in Caribbean.

1562–98 Religious wars in France rage between Roman Catholics and Protestants (Huguenots); Roman Catholics slaughter thousands of Huguenots (Protestants) in St. Bartholomew's Day Massacre on Aug. 24, 1572; fighting ends with Edict of Nantes on April 15, 1598, giving Huguenots political rights but not full freedom of worship.

1568–1648 Protestant Netherlands wins independence from Catholic Spain in series of revolts; Renaissance reaches height in Netherlands with work of such Dutch masters as Peter Paul Rubens, Anthony Van Dyck, Franz Hals, and Rembrandt van Rijn.

1568–82 Central Japan unified by warrior-dictator Oda Nobunaga; Nagasaki becomes important port for trade with Portugal.

1571 (Oct. 7) Turkish fleet defeated by Spanish and Italian fleets in Mediterranean Sea in Battle of Lepanto, ending threat of further Turkish expansion.

1571 Manila founded by Spanish colonists in Philippines.

1571–1603 Muslim Empire of Kanem in central Africa reaches height of power under King Idris III, who rules from walled capital of N'gazargamu; wealth comes from slaves captured in south and sold in North Africa.

1574 Colony of Angola founded by Portuguese in Africa at mouth of Congo River.

1577–80 Sir Francis Drake of England sails around world after looting Spanish ships along South American coast.

1580 Spain conquers Portugal, placing Spanish Hapsburg ruler on throne.

1587 (Feb. 8) Mary Queen of Scots beheaded after being found guilty of plotting to kill England's Queen Elizabeth I.

1588 (July 31–Aug. 8) Defeat of Spanish Armada: King Philip II of Spain sends armada of 130 ships to invade England and restore Roman Catholicism; Spaniards defeated by English fleet of about 200 ships led by Adm. Lord Howard; many Spanish ships driven on Irish coast in storm.

1589–1610 France's King Henry IV comes to throne as Protestant but converts to Roman Catholicism in 1593 in effort to end religious wars; founds Bourbon dynasty that rules France to 1792.

1597 Christian persecution begins in Japan; Japan's dictator Hideyoshi executes nine Portuguese and Spanish missionaries.

1598–1605 Serfdom established in Russia by Czar Boris Godunov.

c.1599 Renaissance reaches height in Spain with work of painter El Greco, novelist Miguel de Cervantes, playwright Lope de Vega.

EUROPE'S MONARCHS MANEUVER FOR POWER AND TERRITORY: 1600–1757

1600 English East India Company founded to establish English colonies and expand trade.

1602 Dutch East India Company established to manage Netherlands' colonization and trade.

1605 (Nov. 5) Gunpowder plot: In retaliation for their persecution, English Roman Catholics try to blow up England's parliament and King James II; plot uncovered and leader Guy Fawkes hanged.

1607 First permanent English colony in North America founded at Jamestown, Virginia.

1608 French colony of Quebec established in Canada by explorer Samuel de Champlain.

1611 Protestant colony of Northern Ireland founded by England's King James I.

1611 King James Version of Bible published in England after translation by group of scholars appointed by King James I.

1611–32 Sweden becomes powerful under Gustavus II Adolphus, winning wars with Russia, Poland, and Holy Roman Empire.

1612 England establishes colony in India at Surat after defeating Portuguese fleet.

1612–14 Bermuda colonized by English.

1618–48 Thirty Years War: Protestants in Holy Roman Empire rebel against oppression by Roman Catholics; Denmark, Sweden, and France invade Germany;

great loss of life and property hinders Germany's development for next two centuries.

1619–23 Dutch found Batavia (now Jakarta) on Java as center of Far Eastern spice trade; massacre English traders in East Indies.

1623–51 Japanese isolation for next two centuries begun by shogun Iemitsu; foreign traders expelled, except for few Chinese and Dutch; Christianity ruthlessly stamped out.

1627–44 Manchus invade and conquer China, founding Manchu, or Ch'ing, dynasty that rules until 1912.

1632–52 Taj Mahal built in India by Shah Jahan.

1633 Italian astronomer Galileo tried by Roman Catholic court; forced to recant belief in Copernican theory.

1634 Dutch capture Curaçao in Caribbean Sea; Peter Stuyvesant becomes first governor.

1635 French settlers colonize Guadeloupe in Caribbean Sea.

1637 First public opera house opened in Venice, Italy: New art form of musical dramas had previously been performed only in palaces of nobility.

1637 Africa's Gold Coast (Ghana) seized by Dutch from Portugal as base for slave trade.

1640 Portugal regains independence in revolt against Spanish rulers.

QUICK QUIZ: Who won the Indianapolis 500 in 1920? See page 770.

KEY EVENTS IN WORLD HISTORY *(continued)*

1642–49 Puritan revolution in England: Puritan general Oliver Cromwell leads supporters of parliament in defeating royalist armies; King Charles I convicted of treason and beheaded on Jan. 30, 1649; Cromwell rules as military dictator, suppressing Church of England and decreeing Puritanical laws.

1642–59 France attacks Spain, taking Spain's northeastern provinces.

1648 Bahamas settled by British colonists from Bermuda; islands become haven for pirates.

1650–52 Tea and coffee introduced in England: Beverages quickly win popularity with opening of public coffeehouses.

1652 (April 7) Dutch establish colony in South Africa: Settlement at Cape Town becomes supply station for Dutch ships sailing on East Indies route around Africa.

1652–74 England and Netherlands fight three naval wars, ending with England winning command of seas; Netherlands gives up colony of New Netherland (New York) to England in exchange for Surinam in South America.

1655 British capture Jamaica from Spain in Caribbean Sea.

1656 Dutch capture Sri Lanka: Take main Portuguese settlement at Colombo.

1660 Monarchy restored in England as Charles II becomes king; Church of England reestablished; other Protestant faiths and Roman Catholicism suppressed.

1661 Palace of Versailles construction begun by France's King Louis XIV.

1665–66 Plague and fire devastate London; about 75,000 persons die of plague; fire (Sept. 2–6, 1666) destroys much of London.

1682–99 War between Austria and Ottoman Turks: Vienna withstands 2-month siege by Turks; Austria captures Hungary from Turks.

1685 Protestantism outlawed in France as Edict of Nantes of 1598 is revoked; thousands of Protestants flee to other countries.

1687 (Sept. 26) Parthenon in Athens demolished: In war fought in Greece between Turks and Venetians, artillery of Venetians hits ancient temple, exploding gunpowder stored there by Turks.

1687–88 Thailand drives out foreigners: Thai people force English traders and French missionaries to leave country, closing it to foreign influence for next two centuries.

1688–89 Glorious Revolution in England: Fearing King James II plans to restore Roman Catholicism, parliamentary leaders ask Dutch Prince William of Orange to protect Protestants; when William lands with army, James flees to France; monarchy given to William and his wife, who then rule as King William III and Queen Mary II; parliament adopts Bill of Rights (Dec. 16, 1689) to protect citizens from government.

1688–97 War of the League of Augsburg (called King William's War in America): France invades Germany, attacks English colonies in America; England, Netherlands, Spain, Sweden, and German states fight against France; Treaty of Ryswick (Sept. 30, 1697) ends war with few territorial changes.

1689–1725 Czar Peter I the Great rules Russia; carries out reforms to westernize nation; establishes Russia as major military power, defeating Sweden in Great Northern War in 1700–21.

1690 (July 11) Battle of the Boyne: England's King William III defeats rebellion in Ireland led by former King James II.

1698 First practical steam engine invented by Thomas Savery in England; used to pump water from mines and to pump water supply for homes; begins era of Industrial Revolution.

1698 Arab sultan of Oman seizes control of east coast of Africa from Portuguese.

1701 Kingdom of Prussia founded in eastern Germany by King Frederick I.

1701–14 War of the Spanish Succession (called Queen Anne's War in America): France's King Louis XIV preserves his grandson on throne of Spain as King Philip V; fights against alliance of England, Netherlands, Austria, and Savoy (Sardinia); at war's end France and Spain promise not to unite as single monarchy; Austria wins control of Luxembourg and Belgium; France gives England northeastern Canada (Acadia); Spain gives England Gibraltar and 30-year contract to supply slaves to Spain's American colonies.

1707 (May 1) United Kingdom of Great Britain: Parliaments of the Kingdom of England and Wales and of the Kingdom of Scotland each pass Act of Union, forming one government under Queen Anne.

1717–20 War of the Quadruple Alliance: Spain invades and captures Sardinia and Sicily; alliance of Britain, France, Netherlands, and Austria defeats Spain; Sardinia given independence under prince of Savoy.

1721–42 British cabinet system of government established as Sir Robert Walpole serves as chief minister of George I and George II.

1733–35 War of the Polish Succession: Russia and Austria fight against France, Spain, and Sardinia, winning right to place weak kings on Polish throne, paving way for partition.

1736–39 Ottoman Turks win most of Yugoslavia in war with Austria and Russia.

1738–40 Persians led by Nadir Shah invade and conquer northern India, forcing Mogul emperor to pay tribute to remain on throne.

1740–48 War of the Austrian Succession (called King George's War in America): Austria and Britain fight against France, Spain, Prussia, and German states that refuse to recognize Maria Theresa's claim to throne of Holy Roman Empire; at war's end she and husband, Francis I, retain throne but give up province of Silesia to Prussia.

1741–43 Sweden attacks Russia but is defeated; forced to give Russia control of Finland.

1756–63 Seven Years War (called French and Indian War in America): Britain and Prussia defeat France, Austria, Spain, and Russia; France loses colonial empire in North America and India to Britain; Prussia retains Silesia; Spain cedes Florida to Britain in exchange for Cuba.

1757 (June 23) Britain wins control of Bengal in India: under leadership of Robert Clive, 3,200 troops of English East India Company defeat 50,000 Indian soldiers in Battle of Plassey.

SOCIAL, POLITICAL, AND INDUSTRIAL REVOLUTIONS: 1760–1850

1762 *The Social Contract* by Jean Jacques Rousseau influences leaders of American and Franch revolutions with idea government requires contract between ruler and governed.

1764–69 Machines to spin yarn invented in England by James Hargreaves and Richard Arkwright, initiating first textile factories.

1768–74 War between Russia and Ottoman Turks: Russia conquers Crimean peninsula.

1768–82 Improved steam engine to operate machinery developed by James Watt.

c.1770–1830 German literature and music enriched by writers Goethe and Schiller and composers Bach, Mozart, and Beethoven.

1772 (June 22) Slavery ruled illegal in Britain by Chief Justice William Lord Mansfield, but ruling does not affect status of slaves in colonies.

1772–95 Partition of Poland: In three steps in 1772, 1793, and 1795, Austria, Russia, and Prussia divide land and people of Poland, ending its independence.

1775–83 American Revolutionary War: France, Spain, and Netherlands aid Americans in defeating Britain; in Treaty of Paris, Britain recognizes U.S. independence, gives up Tobago and Senegal to France, and Minorca and Florida to Spain.

1782 Thailand wins independence from Burma.

1787 Freetown, Sierra Leone, founded by British abolitionists as haven for freed slaves.

1788 (Jan. 26) Sydney, Australia, settled by British colonists.

1789 (April 30) George Washington takes office as first U.S. President under Constitution.

1789 (July 14) Storming of Bastille: Paris mob captures prison, symbol of royal power.

1789–99 French Revolution: Assembly adopts constitution limiting powers of king and nobles in 1789–90; republic declared on Sept. 21, 1792; King Louis XVI beheaded on Jan. 21, 1793; Reign of Terror with thousands guillotined in 1793–95; rule by 5-man directory in 1795–99.

1790 First American textile factory opened by Samuel Slater in Pawtucket, R.I.

1791–1803 Revolt by slaves in Haiti overthrows French rule.

1792–97 War of the First Coalition: In effort to restore nobility in France, coalition of Austria, Prussia, Britain, Netherlands, Spain, and Sardinia fight against France; at war's end France controls northern Italy, Netherlands, Belgium, Switzerland, and southern Germany.

1794 Polish revolt led by Tadeusz Kościuszko; defeated by Russia and Prussia.

1795–96 Britain takes advantage of France's conquest of Netherlands to take over Dutch colonies in Sri Lanka and South Africa.

1795–99 France ruled by directory: New constitution gives 5-man directory dictatorial power over France.

1798 Mass production of muskets with interchangeable parts developed by U.S. inventor Eli Whitney.

1798 Prediction that world population would outstrip food supply published by English economist Thomas Malthus in *Essay on the Principle of Population.*

1798–99 Egypt invaded and conquered by French troops led by Napoleon Bonaparte.

1798–1800 U.S. and France fight naval war.

1798–1802 War of the Second Coalition: Britain, Austria, Russia, Portugal, and Ottoman Turks fight against France; French armies win in Europe but are driven out of Egypt.

1799 (Nov. 9) Napoleon Bonaparte becomes dictator of France, naming himself first consul.

1800 China bans imports of opium: Decree by Emperor Chia-ch'ing has reverse of intended effect as corrupt officials accept bribes by foreign traders who increase flow of opium into China.

1801 (Jan. 1) United Kingdom of Great Britain and Ireland estalished with one monarch, one parliament, and one Protestant Episcopal Church; Catholics excluded from voting.

1804 (Jan. 1) Haiti declares independence from France; first black nation to gain freedom from European colonial rule.

1804 Napoleon I becomes emperor of France, placing crown on own head (Dec. 2).

1804–13 Russia defeats Persia, taking control of Georgia between Black and Caspian seas.

1805 (Oct. 21) Battle of Trafalgar: British fleet under Horatio Lord Nelson wins command of seas, defeating Napoleon's combined French-Spanish fleet at Strait of Gibralter, enabling Britain to blockade Napoleonic France.

1805–09 Napoleon I conquers continental Europe.

1806 (Aug. 6) Holy Roman Empire ends, Austria having lost German states to Napoleon.

1810–15 Unsuccessful revolutions in Mexico and Venezuela put down by Spanish troops.

1811 (Aug. 14) Paraguay declares independence from Spain; becomes dictatorship in 1814 under José Rodríguez de Francia.

1812 Napoleon meets disaster in Russia: After occupying Moscow, which was burned, lack of supplies forces Napoleon to retreat in winter; most of army of 600,000 desert or die.

1812–14 War of 1812: U.S. fights Britain.

1813–14 War of Liberation of Europe: Allies (Britain, Austria, Russia, Prussia, Sweden, and Portugal) defeat Napoleon, capturing Paris, March 31, 1814; Napoleon abdicates and is exiled to island of Elba off coast of Italy.

1814–24 France restores Bourbon monarchy under King Louis XVIII.

1815 Napoleon I escapes from Elba; defeated by Allies led by Duke of Wellington at Battle of Waterloo in Belgium (June 18); exiled to island of St. Helena in South Atlantic.

1815 Congress of Vienna: Victorious Allies redraw map of Europe, returning France to pre-Napoleonic borders; Switzerland guaranteed perpetual neutrality; Sweden acquires Norway; Russia gets Poland; Netherlands obtains Belgium; Britain receives Malta, protectorate over Ionian Islands, and several French and Dutch colonies.

1816–24 South American nations win independence from Spain with patriot armies led by José de San Martín and Simón Bolívar.

1820–23 Revolt in Spain: Troops refuse to go to America to reconquer Spain's colonies; put down by intervention of French army.

1821 (Feb. 24) Mexico declares independence from Spain; ruled as monarchy by Gen. Agustín de Iturbide

as Emperor Agustín I (1822–23); becomes republic on Oct. 4, 1824.

1821–31 Greece wins independence from Ottoman Turkish Empire.

1822 Liberia (then called Monrovia) established in Africa by American Colonization Society as settlement for freed American slaves.

1822 (Sept. 7) Brazil declares independence from Portugal as constitutional monarchy under Emperor Pedro I, son of Portugal's king.

1823 (July 1) United Provinces of Central America declare independence from Mexico with Manuel José Arce as first president.

1823 (Dec. 2) Monroe Doctrine issued by U.S., warning Europe against interfering in Western Hemisphere.

1825 (Sept. 27) First public railroad using steam locomotive completed in England.

1825–28 Uruguay wins independence as result of war between Argentina and Brazil.

1825–28 Russia defeats Persia and wins control of Armenia and Caspian Sea.

1828–29 Russia defeats Ottoman Turks, occupying Bulgaria and Romania.

1829 Britain grants Roman Catholics right to vote and hold public office.

1830 (July 5) France invades Algeria; takes 40 more years to conquer interior of Algeria.

1830 (July 28) Revolution in France: Charles X overthrown; replaced by Louis Philippe.

1830 (Aug. 25) Belgium begins revolt against Netherlands; national congress chooses Leopold I as king in 1831; Dutch refuse to recognize independence until 1839.

c.1830–1910 Russian literature and music reach golden age with such writers as Gogol, Turgenev, Dostoyevsky, Tolstoy, and Chekhov, and such composers as Glinka, Borodin, Mussorgsky, Tchaikovsky, and Rimsky-Korsakov.

1832–33 Egypt's ruler Mohammed Ali conquers Syria and southern Turkey, defeating Ottoman Turkish main army; intervention by Britain, France, and Russia prevents overthrow of Ottoman Empire.

1833 (Aug. 23) Britain abolishes slavery in colonies; pays compensation to owners of 700,000 slaves freed.

1837–38 Egypt captures most of Arabia from Ottoman Turkish Empire.

1838–40 Antarctica proven to be continent by U.S. Navy Lt. Charles Wilkes.

1838–41 Costa Rica, El Salvador, Guatemala, Honduras, and Nicaragua become independent.

1839–40 War between Egypt and Ottoman Turkish Empire: Turks defeated in attack on Syria and forced to surrender fleet to Egypt; intervention by Britain forces Egypt to return Turkish fleet and give up claims to Syria.

1839–42 Opium War between Britain and China: China seizes illegally smuggled opium; Britain retaliates with attacks on cities; China forced to give Hong Kong to Britain and to open other ports to trade.

1840 (Jan. 22) New Zealand settled by British.

1840 (May 6) First postage stamps issued by Britain; U.S. follows on July 1, 1847.

1844 (Feb. 27) Dominican Republic wins independence in revolt from Haiti.

1845–47 Irish potato famine and typhus kill about 750,000; about 2 million others emigrate from Ireland to U.S. and other countries.

1846–48 Mexican War: U.S. defeats Mexico.

1847 (July 26) Liberia declares independence; first black colony in Africa to gain freedom.

1848 *Communist Manifesto* published in Germany by Karl Marx and Friedrich Engels, calling for workers to overthrow middle class.

1848 Switzerland becomes federal union: New constitution provides centralized national government.

1848 (Feb. 24) Revolution in France: Monarchy overthrown, establishing republic; voters on Dec. 10 elect as president Prince Louis Napoleon, nephew of Napoleon I.

1848–49 Revolutions put down by royal troops in Austria, Hungary, Czechoslovakia, Germany, and Italy.

1850–64 T'ai P'ing rebellion in China: Rebel believers in Chinese form of Puritan Protestantism win control of central provinces; subdued by Manchus with aid of foreign mercenaries; about 20 million die in fighting.

QUICK QUIZ: Who was the NBA scoring leader in 1959-66? See page 794.

ITALIAN AND GERMAN UNIFICATION AND COLONIAL EXPANSION: 1852–1914

1852 (Dec. 2) France restores monarchy: President Louis Napoleon becomes Emperor Napoleon III.

1853 France annexes New Caledonia: Penal colony established in Pacific island possession.

1853–56 Crimean War: Begins as dispute over control of Christian holy places in Jerusalem; Russia attacks Ottoman Turkish Empire; Britain and France come to aid of Turks; Russia defeated in battles on Crimean peninsula; Florence Nightingale establishes modern nursing, supervising British army hospitals; in Treaty of Paris, Russia agrees to remove forts and warships from Black Sea.

1854 Japan forced to open two ports to trade by U.S. Commodore Matthew C. Perry; in following two years Britain, Russia, and Netherlands obtain similar treaties.

1854 Slavery abolished in Venezuela: Government pays compensation to former owners; freed slaves denied civil rights.

1855 Thailand opens ports to foreign trade: Britain persuades King Rama IV to allow imports for first time since 1600s.

1855–68 Ethiopia unified: Emperor Theodore brings local chiefs under control, establishing centralized government for nation, then called Abyssinia.

1856 Persia invades Afghanistan, but Britain intervenes to force Persian withdrawal and recognition of Afghanistan's independence.

1856–70 Christians persecuted in Korea with execution of missionaries.

1857–58 Britain takes over government of India from British East India Company after exiling last Mogul emperior of India.

1857–58 Second Opium War in China: Britain and France force China to legalize opium imports and open more ports to foreign trade.

1858 France conquers Cochin China (South Vietnam), occupying Saigon.

1858 (Aug. 5) First transatlantic telegraph cable completed by Cyrus W. Field; Britain's Queen Victoria exchanges greetings with U.S. President James Buchanan.

1859 Theory of evolution published by Charles Darwin in *On the Origin of Species by Means of Natural Selection.*

1859–61 Unification of Italy: Sardinia annexes most of northern Italy, defeating Austrian troops with aid of France in 1859–60; army of "red shirts" led by Giuseppi Garibaldi conquers Sicily and southern Italy in 1860–61, whose people vote to unite with northern Italy; on March 17, 1861, independent kingdom of Italy is proclaimed under King Victor Emmanuel II, who had ruled Sardinia since 1849.

1860 (Oct. 12) British and French troops capture Peking, China: Because Chinese government reneges on observing terms of treaties, foreign troops seize capital, burning royal palace.

1861 (March 3) Serfdom abolished in Russia by Czar Alexander II.

1861–65 Civil War in United States.

1863 Cambodia made French protectorate.

1863 (June 7) Mexico City captured by French troops.

1863–65 Japan's emperor orders expulsion of all foreign traders, but bombardment of Japan by U.S., British, French, and Dutch warships forces him to approve foreign trade treaties.

1864 Austria and Prussia fight Denmark, taking Danish provinces.

1864 (April 10) Mexican monarchy established by French with Austrian Archduke Maximilian as emperor of Mexico.

1865–70 Paraguayan War: Argentina, Brazil, and Uruguay invade Paraguay; about three-fourths of nation's people killed or flee to other countries; about one-fourth of Paraguay's land taken by its neighbors.

1865–76 Russia conquers Turkestan east of Caspian Sea.

1866 Seven Weeks War: Austria defeated by Prussia and Italy, both of which gain territory at Austria's expense.

1867 Malaysian Straits Settlement becomes British colony.

1867 (June 19) Mexican Emperor Maximilian executed; Mexicans restore republic.

1867 (July 1) Dominion of Canada established by Britain with confederation of Ontario, Quebec, New Brunswick, and Nova Scotia.

1867 (Sept. 9) Luxembourg becomes independent neutral nation.

1868 Japan's Emperor Mutsuhito assumes direct rule, ending 700 years of feudal rule by shoguns (military dictators); capital moved to Tokyo.

1869 (Nov. 17) Suez Canal opens.

1870 (Oct. 2) Italy annexes Rome and Papal States from pope, making Rome capital of Italy.

1870–71 Franco-Prussian War: Prussians force surrender of Emperor Napoleon III at Battle of Sedan, Sept. 2, 1870; after four-month siege, capture Paris, Jan. 28, 1871; force France to pay indemnity of 5 billion francs; France again becomes republic.

1871 (Jan. 18) New German Empire proclaimed by Kaiser Wilhelm I, who had ruled as king of Prussia since 1861.

1873–74 France conquers Tonkin (North Vietnam), capturing Hanoi.

1874 Britain conquers Ashanti kingdom in Ghana, later establishing Gold Coast colony.

1874 Britain annexes Fiji.

1875–79 Egypt takes Red Sea coastal area (Eritrea) from Ethiopia.

1877–78 Russia attacks Ottoman Turkish Empire; threat of British intervention prevents Russian capture of Constantinople; Turks grant independence to Romania, Montenegro, and Serbia; Russia occupies Bulgaria.

1878 Berlin Congress of European powers settles issues remaining from Russia's defeat of Ottoman Turks; Britain acquires Cyprus; France gains Tunisia; Austria obtains Bosnia and Herzegovina (now in Yugoslavia).

1879–84 War of the Pacific: Chile defeats Peru and Bolivia, taking Bolivia's entire coast and Peru's southern region.

1880 France founds Brazzaville, Congo, making region French protectorate.

1881–82 Persecution of Jews begins in Russia, forcing many to flee to other lands.

1882 Italy invades Red Sea coast of Ethiopia in region that later became Italian colony of Eritrea.

1882 (May 20) Triple Alliance defense pact signed by Germany, Austria, and Italy.

1882 (Sept. 13) Britain invades Egypt: Establishes military occupation.

1883 Germany begins settlement of Southwest Africa.

1883–96 France conquers Madagascar, exiling Queen Ranavalona III to island of Réunion.

1884 Eastern New Guinea divided between Britain and Germany (Dutch keep western New Guinea).

1884–85 France forces China to recognize French protectorate over Indochina.

1884–88 France and Britain take control of Somalia coast of East Africa.

1885 Serbia attacks Bulgaria, but is defeated as Bulgarians take eastern region of Serbia.

1885 Germany takes Marshall and Solomon islands in Pacific and Tanganyika in Africa.

1885 (Jan. 26) Massacre at Khartoum: British Gen. Charles Gordon and his troops slain by Sudanese.

1885 (May 2) Congo Free State (now Zaire) established by Belgium's King Leopold II.

1885–86 British troops conquer Burma.

1885–96 Britain takes control of Kenya in East Africa.

1885–98 French troops gain control of most of West Africa, defeating local rulers.

1889 Brazil becomes republic with overthrow of Emperor Pedro II by conservatives angered by his abolition of slavery in 1888.

1889 Eiffel Tower completed in Paris; at 954 feet, then highest structure in world.

1890 Zanzibar made British protectorate.

1894 (Jan. 4) France and Russia agree to defense alliance if attacked by Germany, Austria, or Italy.

1894 Uganda made British protectorate.

1894–95 War between China and Japan: Japan wins control of Korea, Formosa (now Taiwan), and Pescadores Islands.

1895–96 Italian troops invade Ethiopia but are defeated, forcing Italy to recognize Ethiopia's independence.

1896 First modern Olympic Games held at Athens, Greece.

1896–98 Sudan conquered by British troops.

1897 Germany seizes Chinese city of Tsingtao, forcing China to sign 99-year lease on port.

1897 Greece attacks Ottoman Turkish Empire but is defeated, losing territory to Turks.

1898 Spanish-American War: U.S. ends Spanish rule of Cuba, Puerto Rico, and Philippines.

1898 (Aug. 12) Hawaii annexed by U.S.

1898–1902 Rebellion in Philippines put down by U.S. troops, establishing American rule.

1899 Nigeria made British protectorate.

1899 Persian Gulf Arab Sheikdoms made British protectorate.

1899 Open Door for China notes sent to world powers by U.S. Secretary of State John Hay, obtaining assurances that leased Chinese ports would be open to U.S. trade.

1899 First Hague Peace Conference: Adopts rules of war and treatment of war prisoners; establishes permanent court of arbitration to settle international disputes.

1899–1902 Boer War in South Africa: Britain defeats Dutch settlers in South Africa to annex previously independent republics of Orange Free State and South African Republic.

1900 Psychoanalysis as treatment of mental disease promoted by publication of Sigmund Freud's *The Interpretation of Dreams.*

1900–01 Boxer War in China: China attempts to end its exploitation by killing foreigners and destroying foreign installations; U.S., Russian, British, French, and German troops subdue Chinese, capturing and looting Peking on Aug. 14, 1900, and forcing China to pay for damages to foreign property.

1901 (Jan. 1) Commonwealth of Australia established by Britain.

1902 Russia forces China to turn over control of Manchuria (northern China).

1902 Australia grants women right to vote in federal elections.

1902 Cuba gains independence with election of first president; U.S. troops withdraw.

1902 (Jan. 20) Britain and Japan sign defense treaty: Britain recognizes Japan's right to control Korea.

1903 (Nov. 3) Panama declares independence from Colombia; U.S. obtains rights to Canal Zone to build Panama Canal.

1904–05 Russo-Japanese War: Japan attacks and defeats Russia, winning Russian ports in China, control of Korea, and southern Sakhalin Island; Russia withdraws from Manchuria.

1905 Physics revolutionized by Albert Einstein's theory of relativity, quantum theory, and formula for relationship of mass and energy ($E = mc^2$).

1905 Russian czar's troops crush revolt led by V.I. Lenin, but continued turmoil forces czar to agree to establishment of nation's first parliament, called Duma.

1905 (June 7) Norway declares independence from Sweden.

1906 (May 3) British-controlled Egypt takes Sinai peninsula from Ottoman Turkish Empire.

1906–09 U.S. troops occupy Cuba to put down rebellion by opponents of President Tomás Estrada Palma.

1907 Second Hague Peace Conference: World powers agree on detailed rules of war.

1907 Morocco invaded and occupied by French troops.

1907 Japan makes Korea protectorate: Japanese troops occupy nation, force abdication of Korea's emperor.

1908 Austria annexes Bosnia and Herzegovina: Take Balkan regions from Ottoman Turkish Empire.

1908 (Oct. 5) Bulgaria declares independence from Ottoman Turkish Empire.

1908 (Oct. 7) Crete unites with Greece.

1909 (April 6) North Pole reached by American explorers Robert E. Peary and Matthew Henson.

1910 (May 31) Union of South Africa established by Britain from former Boer states.

1910 (Oct. 5) Portugal becomes republic with overthrow of monarchy.

1911 (Dec. 16) South Pole first reached by Norwegian explorer Roald Amundsen.

1911–1912 China becomes republic with overthrow of Manchu emperor.

1911–1912 Italy invades and takes Libya from Ottoman Turkish Empire.

1911–1917 Russia invades and takes control of Persia.

1912 (April 14–15) British ocean liner *Titanic* strikes iceberg and sinks in Atlantic Ocean on maiden voyage; 1,517 lives lost.

1912 (Nov. 28) Albania declares independence from Ottoman Turkish Empire, becoming kingdom under Prince Wilhelm of Wied in 1914.

1912–1913 First Balkan War: Bulgaria, Serbia, Montenegro, and Greece join in defeating Ottoman Turkish Empire; division of spoils by great powers dissatisfies victors, leading to second Balkan War.

1913 (June 29–Aug. 10) Second Balkan War: Serbia, Greece, Montenegro, Romania, and Ottoman Turks join in defeating Bulgaria, taking some of territory Bulgaria had been awarded in first Balkan War.

1914 (April 21–Nov. 23) U.S. Marines occupy Veracruz, Mexico, intervening in civil war to protect American interests.

PERIOD OF WORLD WAR I THROUGH WORLD WAR II: 1914–1945

1914 (June 28) Assassination of Austria's Archduke Francis Ferdinand and his wife at Sarajevo in Austrian province of Bosnia: Austria believes Serbians responsible, issuing ultimatum to Serbia that leads to World War I.

1914 (July 28) World War I begins as Austria-Hungary declares war on Serbia; Germany declares war on Russia on Aug. 1, invades Luxembourg on Aug. 2, declares war on France on Aug. 3, and invades neutral Belgium on Aug. 4, causing Britain to declare war on Germany the same day; later, Central Powers of Germany and Austria are aided by Ottoman Turkish Empire and Bulgaria, while 24 other nations join as Allies to defeat them.

1914 (Aug. 15) Panama Canal opens.

1914 (Aug. 26–30) Battle of Tannenberg: Germans defeat Russian army in east Prussia, eliminating threat of Russian invasion.

1914 (Sept. 6–8) Battle of the Marne: Germans advance to within 15 miles of Paris, but French-British counterattack forces them to pull back; Western Front stabilizes with neither side being able to make breakthrough.

1915 (May 7) British ocean liner *Lusitania* sunk by German submarine with loss of 1,198 lives.

1915 (July 3) U.S. Marines land in Haiti to preserve order; remain until 1934.

1916 (March 15) U.S. troops invade Mexico in pursuit of Mexican revolutionary Francisco (Pancho) Villa; withdraw on Feb. 5, 1917.

1916 (April 24–29) Easter Rebellion in Ireland put down by British troops; 15 Irish leaders executed, others imprisoned.

1916 (Nov. 29) U.S. Marines land in Dominican Republic; remain until 1924.

1916–28 Civil war rages in China.

1917 Russian Revolution: Riots and revolt by troops bring abdication of Czar Nicholas II on March 15; Bolsheviks (Communists) overthrow moderate provisional government on Nov. 6, making V.I. Lenin dictator.

1917 (April 6) U.S. declares war on Germany.

1917 (Dec. 6) Finland declares independence from Russia.

1918 (March 3) Russia withdraws from World War I; signs Treaty of Brest-Litovsk with Central Powers, giving up claims to Finland, Latvia, Estonia, Lithuania, Poland, and other territories.

1918 (July 16) Murder of Czar Nicholas II and his family by Bolsheviks (Communists).

1918 (Oct. 28) Czechoslovakia declares independence.

1918 (Nov. 3) Poland proclaims independence.

1918 (Nov. 9) Germany's Kaiser Wilhelm II abdicates; flees to Netherlands.

1918 (Nov. 11) Armistice ends World War I; fighting stops at 11 A.M. on Western Front.

1918–19 Flu epidemic around world kills estimated 5–20 million persons.

QUICK QUIZ: How many medals did the U.S. win in the 1984 Summer Olympics? See page 836.

KEY EVENTS IN WORLD HISTORY *(continued)*

1918–20 Russian Civil War: Fighting rages across Russia between Communists (Reds) and anti-Communists (Whites); U.S., British, and French troops intervene on side of Whites but are withdrawn in 1919.

1919 (May 16–27) First transatlantic airplane flight: U.S. Navy NC-4 flying boat with 5-man crew flies from Newfoundland to Lisbon, Portugal.

1919 (June 28) Treaty of Versailles signed, setting peace terms with Germany and establishing League of Nations; U.S. Senate later refuses to ratify treaty or join League.

1919 (Sept. 10) Treaty of Saint-Germain signed, setting peace terms for Austria and recognizing independence of Czechoslovakia, Hungary, Poland, and Yugoslavia.

1920 (Aug. 10) Treaty of Sèvres signed, setting World War I peace terms with Ottoman Turkish Empire; Turkish nationalists object to severity of treaty and refuse to accept it.

1920 (Nov. 15) League of Nations holds first meeting at Geneva, Switzerland.

1920 (Dec. 17) Japan receives mandate over Caroline, Marshall, and Mariana islands in Pacific Ocean.

1920 (Dec. 23) Britain divides Ireland into northern and southern parts, each with own parliament.

1920–23 Greece attacks Turkish nationalists, but is driven out of Turkey; victorious Turkish nationalists get Allies to sign Treaty of Lausanne modifying World War I penalties.

1921 (Feb. 20) Riza Khan Pahlevi seizes control of Iran: After ruling as dictator for four years, makes himself shah in 1925.

1921 (Dec. 6) Irish Free State formed in southern Ireland as self-governing dominion of British Empire; Northern Ireland remains part of United Kingdom.

1922 (Feb. 6) Washington naval arms limitation treaty signed, setting size of navies of U.S., Britain, France, Italy, and Japan, and requiring scrapping of many warships.

1922 (Feb. 28) Egypt regains sovereignty under King Fuad I as Britain ends protectorate, but British troops remain in Egypt.

1922 (Oct. 31) Benito Mussolini becomes premier of Italy; *Il Duce,* as he is called by Fascist followers, becomes dictator on Nov. 25.

1922 (Nov. 1) End of Ottoman Turkish Empire: Turkish nationalist leader Mustapha Kemal (Kemal Atatürk) abolishes sultanate and (in 1923) becomes first president.

1923 French troops occupy Germany's Ruhr area: France acts after Germany defaults on war reparations.

1923 (Nov. 8–11) Munich beer-hall putsch: Unsuccessful attempt by Nazi leader Adolf Hitler to overthrow state government of Bavaria; imprisoned, Hitler writes *Mein Kampf,* blueprint for new German empire.

1924 (Jan. 21) Death of Lenin: Joseph Stalin wins struggle for power, ruling as Soviet dictator until his death in 1953.

1926 (Jan. 8) Independent Kingdom of Hejaz and Nejd (now Saudi Arabia) proclaimed by King Ibn Saud.

1927 (Dec. 14) Iraq granted independence by Britain, but British troops remain in nation.

1928 Nationalist government of China established by Chiang Kai-shek with capital at Nanking after long civil war.

1928 (April 9) Turkey disestablishes Islam as state religion.

1928 (Aug. 27) Kellogg-Briand Pact signed, outlawing war, but provides no means of enforcement.

1929 (June 7) Vatican City becomes independent nation with signing of Lateran treaties between Italy and Roman Catholic Church.

1929–40 Worldwide Great Depression brings severe unemployment and economic chaos.

1930 (April 22) London naval treaty signed, providing further reductions in size of navies of U.S., Britain, and Japan.

1931 British Commonwealth of Nations established, giving dominions such as Australia and Canada complete independence with only formal allegiance to crown.

1931 (April 14) Spain becomes republic with overthrow of King Alfonso XIII.

1931–33 Japan invades and conquers Manchuria (northern China).

1932–35 Chaco War: Paraguay and Bolivia fight over possession of oil-rich Chaco region; treaty in 1938 awards two-thirds of region to Paraguay.

1933 (Jan. 30) Adolf Hitler becomes chancellor of Germany; *Der Führer,* as he is called by followers, becomes dictator on March 23.

1934–36 Italian-Ethiopian War: Italy invades and conquers Ethiopia.

1935 (March 16) Rearmament of Germany ordered by Hitler, renouncing Versailles Treaty's ban on German armament.

1936 (Oct. 27) Berlin-Rome Axis formed as Germany and Italy agree on working partnership; Japan later joins Axis powers with pact on Sept. 27, 1940.

1936 (Dec. 10) Britain's King Edward VIII abdicates to marry American-born divorcée.

1936–38 Soviet trials and executions of hundreds of Communist and military leaders strengthen Stalin's hold on dictatorship.

1936–39 Spanish Civil War: Army revolt led by Gen. Francisco Franco restores monarchy; Italy and Germany support Franco while Soviet Union aids Spanish republicans; about 1 million die in three years of fighting; Franco establishes himself as dictator.

1937–45 War between Japan and China: Japan attacks China, taking most of coastal region by 1938; China's government retreats inland, continuing fight through World War II.

1938 (March 12–13) Austria invaded and annexed by Germany.

1938 (Sept. 29) Munich agreement: Britain, France, and Italy agree to let Germany partition Czechoslovakia.

1938 (Oct. 1) Germany annexes Sudetenland, about one-third of Czechoslovakia's area.

1939 (March 15) Most of remainder of Czechoslovakia taken by Germany.

1939 (April 7) Albania annexed by Italy.

1939 (Aug. 24) Germany and Soviet Union sign 10-year peace pact; agreement frees Hitler to start World War II.

1939 (Sept. 1) World War II begins as Germany invades Poland without warning; Britain and France declare war on Germany on Sept. 3; Soviet Union invades Poland on Sept. 17; Hitler and Stalin partition Poland on Sept. 29.

1939–40 Russo-Finnish War: Soviet Union invades Finland, forcing nation to give up about one-tenth of its territory.

1939–45 German slave labor and extermination of Jews: Germany enslaves millions of conquered people, forcing them to work for German war effort; Hitler's Nazis kill about 60% of Europe's 10 million Jews.

1940 (April 9–May 3) Norway and Denmark conquered by Germany.

1940 (May 10–June 22) German blitzkrieg conquers Luxembourg, Netherlands, Belgium, and France; about 340,000 British and French troops escape to Britain in Dunkirk evacuation, May 28–June 4.

1940 (July 21) Estonia, Latvia, and Lithuania annexed by Soviet Union.

1940–41 Germany conquers Romania, Bulgaria, Yugoslavia, and Greece.

1941 (June 22) German troops invade Soviet Union, but meet stiff resistance and bog down in winter of 1941–42.

1941 (Dec. 7) Japan makes surprise air attacks on U.S. and British bases in Pacific, bringing U.S. into World War II.

1942–45 War in Africa and Europe: Under command of Gen. Dwight D. Eisenhower, Allied forces defeat Axis troops in Africa by May 1943, invade Italy on Sept. 3, 1943, and land in France on June 6, 1944; Russian troops advance across eastern Europe in 1944–45, while Eisenhower's armies liberate western Europe and roll across Germany; German military leaders sign unconditional surrender on May 7, 1945; fighting ends at 12:01 A.M. on May 9.

1942–45 War in Pacific: U.S. Navy's defeat of Japanese fleet at Battle of Midway on June 4–7, 1942, marks turning point of war in Pacific; U.S. begins offensive with landing of Marines on Guadalcanal in Solomon Islands on Aug. 7, 1942; series of amphibious landings in 1943–45 capture Japanese island strongholds from Gilbert Islands to Okinawa; on Oct. 19, 1944, U.S. troops under Gen. Douglas MacArthur land in Philippines; atomic bombs dropped on Japan on Aug. 6 and 9, 1945, bring Japan's capitulation on Aug. 14, with formal surrender signed on Sept. 2.

END OF COLONIAL EMPIRES, COLD WAR, AND ENERGY PROBLEMS: 1945–1983

1945–48 Communist Iron Curtain: After World War II Soviet Union keeps its troops in eastern European nations it had "liberated" from Germany; Latvia, Estonia, and Lithuania incorporated into Soviet Union; British leader Winston Churchill warns on March 5, 1946, "an Iron Curtain has descended across Europe"; communist governments establish dictatorships In Yugoslavia, Albania, Bulgaria, Romania, Poland, East Germany, Hungary, and Czechoslovakia, all as satellites of Soviet Union.

1945–49 Indonesian War for Independence: Indonesian nationalists declare independence on Aug. 17, 1945; Dutch troops fight rebels in effort to reimpose colonial rule until Netherlands finally recognizes independence of Indonesia on Dec. 27, 1949.

1945–54 Indochina War: Nationalist leaders in 1945 declare independence in Cambodia (March), Laos (April), and Vietnam (September); France determines to reimpose colonial rule; for over eight years French troops supplied by U.S. battle guerrillas aided by Soviet Union and communist China; French will to fight breaks after Battle of Dien Bien Phu when after 55-day siege French army of 10,000 surrenders on May 7, 1954; at conference in Geneva, France agrees on July 21, 1954, to end fighting, recognizing independence of North and South Vietnam; earlier, in 1953, independence to Laos (Oct. 22) and Cambodia (Nov. 9) granted by France.

1946 (Jan. 1) Japan's Emperor Hirohito disclaims his divinity, ending his worship as god.

1946 (Jan. 10) UN General Assembly meets for first time; delegates of 51 nations hold meeting in London.

1946 (March 22) Transjordan (now Jordan) granted independence by Britain.

1946 (June 2) Italy votes to become republic, ending monarchy.

1946 (July 4) Philippines granted independence by United States.

1946 (Oct. 16) Ten Nazi leaders hanged as war criminals after 10-month trial at Nuremberg; chief Hitler aide Hermann Goering kills himself a few hours before execution.

1946 (Nov. 3) Japan adopts new constitution under guidance of Allied Supreme Commander Gen. Douglas MacArthur, giving all emperor's power to parliament.

1946–49 Civil War in Greece: Greece votes to restore monarchy on Sept. 1, 1946; communist guerrillas supported by Soviet Union begin struggle to overthrow government; Truman Doctrine announced by U.S. in 1947 provides aid to Greek government, enabling it to defeat guerrillas by October 1949.

1947 (Aug. 15) India and Pakistan granted independence within British Commonwealth.

1948 (Jan. 4) Burma granted independence.

1948 (Feb. 4) Ceylon (now Sri Lanka) given independence by Britain.

1948 (April 3) European Recovery Program (Marshall Plan) enacted by U.S. at urging of President Truman to provide aid to European nations to save them from communism; over $12 billion given in four years.

1948 (April 30) Organization of American States (OAS) Charter signed at Bogotá, Colombia (effective Dec. 13, 1951).

1948 (Dec. 23) Seven wartime Japanese leaders hanged for war crimes, including former Japanese prime minister Hideki Tojo.

1948–49 First Arab-Israeli War: Israel proclaims independence on May 14, 1948, upon withdrawal of British troops from Palestine; six Arab nations attack Israel; U.S. supports Israel with military supplies; UN mediation brings truce in 1949; over 900,000 Arabs flee Israel.

1948–49 Berlin blockade and Berlin airlift: Soviet Union blockades roads to West Berlin beginning on June 24, 1948; U.S. starts airlift, delivering over 2 million tons of supplies in next 16 months to prevent city from falling to communists; blockade ends on May 12, 1949.

1949 (April 4) NATO treaty signed to provide military defense of western Europe.

1949 (April 18) Ireland declares independence from Britain.

1949 (Aug. 29) Soviet Union test-explodes its first atomic bomb, setting off fears in West that communists

would launch surprise A-bomb attack to destroy U.S. and western Europe.

1949 (Dec. 7) Communists win control of mainland China after 3-year civil war.

1950–53 Korean War: Begins on June 25, 1950; North Korea invades South Korea; UN calls for aid to South Korea; U.S. begins sending troops on June 27; 15 other UN nations send troops; Gen. Douglas MacArthur becomes UN supreme commander; over 1 million die in war, including 54,000 U.S. servicemen; ends with truce signed on July 27, 1953.

1950–53 Communist atomic spy ring: Members arrested in Britain and U.S. in 1950, convicted in 1951; U.S. citizens Julius and Ethel Rosenberg executed for treason on June 19, 1953.

1951 (Sept. 8) Japanese peace treaty signed in San Francisco by 49 nations: treaty goes into effect on April 28, 1952.

1951 (Dec. 24) Libya becomes independent kingdom.

1953 (June 18) Egypt becomes republic.

1954–62 Algerian War of Independence: Arab nationalists attack French outposts in November 1954; over 500,000 French troops fight for 7 years to maintain colonial rule; France agrees to Algeria's independence (effective July 3, 1962).

1955 (March 25) East Germany granted full sovereignty by Soviet Union.

1955 (May 5) West Germany becomes independent under Chancellor Konrad Adenauer.

1955 (July 27) Austria regains independence as peace treaty guaranteeing its neutrality becomes effective (signed May 15).

1956 (Oct. 23–Nov. 4) Hungarian Revolution: Revolt overthrows communist government but is suppressed by Soviet army; about 150,000 Hungarians flee to U.S. and other nations.

1956 (Oct. 29–Nov. 6) Second Arab-Israeli War: Israel with support of France and Britain attacks Egypt; Suez Canal seized; U.S. and Soviet Union condemn action; UN arranges cease-fire on Nov. 6; British and French troops withdraw on Dec. 22; Israel withdraws from Egypt on March 1, 1957.

1956–77 End of French colonial empire: Begins with Indochina War of 1945–54, in which Laos, Cambodia, and Vietnam win independence, but accelerates as following nations gain independence: 1956, Morocco, Tunisia; 1958, Guinea; 1960, Cameroon, Togo, Malagasy, Dahomey, Niger, Upper Volta, Ivory Coast, Chad, Central African Republic, Congo, Gabon, Senegal, Mali, Mauritania; 1962, Algeria, after 7 years of war; 1977, Djibouti.

1956–84 Breakup of British Empire: Begins in 1947–48 with independence of India, Pakistan, Ceylon, and Burma, but accelerates as following nations gain independence: 1956, Sudan; 1957, Ghana, Malaysia; 1960, Somalia, Cyprus, Nigeria; 1961, Sierra Leone, South Africa, Kuwait, British Cameroons, Tanganyika; 1962, Jamaica, Trinidad and Tobago, Uganda; 1963, Zanzibar, Kenya; 1964, Malawi, Malta, Zambia; 1965, Gambia, Maldive Islands; 1966, Guyana, Botswana, Lesotho, Barbados; 1967, South Yemen; 1968, Mauritius, Swaziland; 1970, Tonga, Fiji; 1971, Bahrain, Qatar, United Arab Emirates; 1973, Bahamas; 1974, Grenada; 1976, Seychelles; 1978, Solomons, Tuvalu, Dominica; 1979, St. Lucia, St. Vincent, Kiribati; 1980, Vanuatu, Zimbabwe; 1981, Antigua, Belize; 1983, St. Christopher and Nevis; 1984, Brunei.

1957 (Jan. 5) Eisenhower Doctrine proposed for U.S. to send troops to aid any Middle East nation to fight communist aggression; approved by U.S. Senate resolution on March 7.

1957 (Oct. 4) First man-made satellite orbits Earth: *Sputnik I* launched by Soviet Union.

1958 (Jan. 1) European Common Market begins, including Belgium, France, West Germany, Italy, Luxembourg, and Netherlands.

1958 (July 15) U.S. troops land in Lebanon under Eisenhower Doctrine; withdraw Oct. 15.

1958 (May 31) France's Gen. Charles de Gaulle becomes premier with emergency powers; becomes president on Jan. 8, 1959.

1959 (Jan. 1) Fidel Castro overthrows Cuban dictator Fulgencio Batista after 3-year civil war.

QUICK QUIZ: Who holds the men's high jump record? See page 869.

KEY EVENTS IN WORLD HISTORY (continued)

1959 (June 26) St. Lawrence Seaway formally opens, linking Atlantic Ocean and Great Lakes.

1960 Communist China and Soviet Union split in controversy over communist ideology.

1960 Soviet Premier Khrushchev cancels Paris summit meeting with President Eisenhower after Soviet Union shoots down U.S. U-2 spy plane and U.S. admits sending regular spy flights over Soviet territory.

1960 OPEC (Organization of Petroleum Exporting Countries) holds first meeting, forcing Standard Oil of New Jersey to retract an announced decrease in oil prices; OPEC's charter members were Iran, Iraq, Kuwait, Qatar, and Saudi Arabia.

1960 (Feb. 13) France becomes atomic power, exploding first A-bomb in desert of Algeria.

1960 (June 23) U.S.-Japanese mutual security treaty becomes effective.

1960–62 Belgium ends its African colonial empire, giving independence to Belgian Congo (now Zaire) on June 30, 1960, and to Rwanda and Burundi in 1962.

1960–67 Revolts in Congo (now Zaire): Immediately after Congo receives independence from Belgium, fighting breaks out as provinces of Katanga and Kasai seek independence; UN sends troops to aid government, 1960–64; rebellion ends in November 1967.

1961 (Jan. 3) U.S. breaks diplomatic relations with Cuba over refusal by Fidel Castro's government to pay for confiscated U.S. property.

1961 (April 12) First man orbits Earth in space: Soviet cosmonaut Maj. Yuri Gagarin.

1961 (April 17–20) Cuba defeats U.S.-supported Bay of Pigs invasion: Cuban troops overwhelm force of 1,600 Cuban exiles trained by U.S. CIA.

1961 (May 31) South Africa becomes independent republic: Severs ties with British Commonwealth of Nations because of criticism of its racial policies.

1961 (Aug. 13) Berlin Wall built by Soviet Union to prevent escape of East Germans to West Berlin.

1961 (Dec. 18–19) India seizes Portuguese colonies of Goa, Damao, and Diu.

1962 (Jan. 1) Western Samoa granted independence by New Zealand.

1962 (May 31) Israel executes Hitler aide Adolf Eichmann, convicted of directing World War II German extermination of Jews.

1962 (Oct. 20–Nov. 22) China invades India, but ends fighting on Nov. 22 and withdraws.

1962 (Oct. 22–28) Cuban missile crisis: U.S. blockades Cuba, forcing Soviet Union to withdraw nuclear missiles from island.

1963 (Jan. 22) France and Germany sign treaty of friendship, ending 400 years of conflict.

1964 (March 27) UN troops land in Cyprus to prevent fighting between Greeks and Turks.

1964–73 U.S. intervention in Vietnam War: U.S. begins bombing of North Vietnam on Aug. 5, 1964, in retaliation for reported attack on U.S. destroyers; on Aug. 7, U.S. Congress votes President authority "to prevent further aggression"; first U.S. ground combat authorized on June 28, 1965; over 541,000 U.S. troops fighting in Vietnam by 1969; U.S. begins withdrawing in 1969; cease-fire begins on Jan. 28, 1973; last U.S. troops leave Vietnam on March 29, 1973.

1966 (July 1) France withdraws from NATO.

1967 (June 5–10) Third Arab-Israeli War: Israel launches surprise attack; captures Egypt's Sinai peninsula to east bank of Suez Canal; takes Jordan territory west of Jordan River; seizes Golan Heights from Syria; additional 750,000 Arab refugees displaced.

1967–70 Nigerian Civil War: Attempted secession of eastern region of Biafra put down.

1968 (Aug. 20–21) Invasion of Czechoslovakia by about 650,000 troops of Soviet Union and Warsaw Pact nations ousts liberal communist regime.

1968–74 African drought south of Sahara: thousands of persons and millions of cattle die.

1970 (Sept. 4) Chile elects communist as president, first to head any nation as result of free election; later overthrown in military revolt, Sept. 11, 1973.

1970 (Dec. 12–20) Riots in Poland put down by Soviet troops; communist dictator Gomulka resigns.

1971 (Feb. 11) Seabed treaty outlawing installation of atomic weapons on ocean floor signed by U.S., Soviet Union, Britain, and others; effective on May 18, 1972.

1971 (March 25–Dec. 16) Bangladesh wins independence from Pakistan in civil war.

1971 (Oct. 25) Communist China admitted to UN as U.S. ends 22 years of opposition.

1972 (Sept. 29) China and Japan end state of war that began in 1937.

1973 (Jan. 1) European Common Market adds Britain, Denmark, and Ireland.

1973 (June 1) Greece ends monarchy as military dictator deposes King Constantine II.

1973 (June 16–24) End of Cold War between U.S. and Soviet Union hailed by spirit of détente at summit meeting of President Nixon and Soviet leader Leonid I. Brezhnev in U.S.

1973 (July 17) Afghanistan becomes republic.

1973 (Aug. 15) All U.S. combat operations end in Southeast Asia by congressional order.

1973 (Oct. 6–24) Fourth Arab-Israeli War: Egypt and Syria launch surprise attack on Israel; Israel counterattacks, crossing Suez Canal into Egypt and invading Syria; UN cease-fire ends fighting on Oct. 24.

1973 (Oct. 17) Oil embargo begun by Arab nations against U.S. and other nations in effort to force support of Arab policies against Israel; causes energy shortages; Arabs end embargo in 1974 (with U.S. on March 18).

1974 (May 18) India becomes sixth nuclear nation with atomic test explosion.

1974 (July 15–Aug. 16) Civil War in Cyprus: Greek-led national guard overthrows government; on July 20, Turkey intervenes, landing 40,000 troops.

1974 (Nov. 17) Democracy restored in Greece with first free national election in 10 years.

1974–76 End of Portugal's dictatorship and colonial empire in Africa: Military coup on April 25, 1974, overthrows 40-year dictatorship; colonies given independence; socialists win parliamentary elections in 1976.

1974–76 Worldwide inflation and recession rage when Organization of Petroleum Exporting Countries (OPEC) raises crude-oil prices nearly 500% above 1973 levels.

1975 (April 17) Cambodia falls to communists; red troops capture Phnom Penh.

1975 (April 30) 16-year Vietnam War end: Saigon captured by North Vietnamese troops.

1975 (Aug. 1) Helsinki Pact signed by U.S., Canada, Soviet Union, and 32 European nations guaranteeing national boundaries.

1975 (Nov. 6) Invasion of Spanish Sahara by thousands of unarmed Moroccans; Spain agrees to give up region to Morocco and Mauritania.

1975–76 Civil war rages in Lebanon between rightist Christians and leftist Muslims; ends when Syrian army occupies nation.

1976 (March 23) International Bill of Rights goes into effect with ratification by 35 nations.

1976 (July 28) Earthquake devastates Tientsin-Tangshan area of China; 655,237 reported dead.

1977 (Sept. 7) U.S. and Panama sign treaties to turn Canal over to Panama on Dec. 31, 1999.

1977 (Nov. 19) Egypt's President Sadat becomes first Arab national leader to visit Israel, launching drive to achieve peace in Middle East.

1978 (Oct. 23) China and Japan sign treaty: End 40 years of hostility with peace pact.

1979 (Jan. 16) Revolt overthrows shah of Iran, who flies to exile; Muslim leader Ayatollah Ruhollah Khomeini creates Islamic state with himself as ruler for life.

1979 (March 26) Egypt-Israel peace treaty signed at White House after mediation by President Carter; goes into effect on April 25.

1979 (Dec. 27) Soviet troops invade Afghanistan; overthrow communist ruler, replacing him with pro-Soviet leader; guerrillas fight Soviet troops.

1979–81 U.S.-Iranian crisis: Iranians capture U.S. embassy in Teheran on Nov. 4, 1979; hold 52 Americans hostage until Jan. 20, 1981.

1980–85 Iraq-Iran War in Middle East: Iraq attacks Iran on Sept. 22, 1980, seeking control of Shatt Al Arab waterway at head of Persian Gulf.

1982 (April 2–June 14) Falkland Islands War: Britain defeats Argentine invasion of British colony.

1983 (Oct. 23) Terrorist bomb kills 241 U.S. Marines of U.S. peacekeeping force in Lebanon.

1983 (Oct. 25) U.S. Troops land in Grenada: Oust Communists who had overthrown and killed Grenada's president.

1983 (Nov. 23–Dec. 15) Soviet Union breaks off arms limitation talks: Denounces arrival of new U.S. missiles in Europe.

1985 For events of 1985, see pages 7–27.

KINGS, QUEENS, AND RULERS

AUSTRIA [1]
Hapsburg Dynasty
Franz II [2] 1792–1835
Ferdinand I 1835–1848
Franz Josef I 1848–1916
Karl I 1916–1918
First Republic, 1918–1938
Part of Germany, 1938–1945
Second Republic, 1945–

BELGIUM
House of Coburg
Leopold I 1831–1865
Leopold II 1865–1909
Albert I 1909–1934
Leopold III 1934–1951
Baudouin 1951–

BRITAIN
Saxons and Danes
Egbert827–839
Ethelwulf839–858
Ethelbald858–860
Ethelbert860–866
Ethelred II866–871
Alfred the Great871–901
Edward the Elder901–925
Athelstan925–940
Edmund940–946
Edred .946–955
Edwy .955–959
Edgar .959–975
Edward the Martyr975–978
Ethelred II978–1016
Edmund Ironside1016
Canute the Dane1016–1035
Harold I1035–1040
Hardicanute1040–1042
Edward the Confessor1042–1066
Harold II1066
Norman
William I1066–1087
William II1087–1100
Henry1100–1135
Stephen1135–1154
Plantagenet
Henry II1154–1189
Richard I1189–1199
John1199–1216
Henry III1216–1272
Edward I1272–1307
Edward II1307–1327
Edward III1327–1377
Richard II1377–1399
Lancaster
Henry IV1399–1413
Henry V1413–1422
Henry VI1422–1461, 1470–1471
York
Edward IV1461–1470, 1471–1483
Edward V.1483
Richard III1483–1485
Tudor
Henry VII1485–1509
Henry VIII1509–1547
Edward VI1547–1553
Jane (14 days)1553

Mary I1553–1558
Elizabeth I1558–1603
Stuart
James I1603–1625
Charles I1625–1649
Commonwealth
Long Parliament1649–1653
Protectorate
Oliver Cromwell1653–1658
Richard Cromwell1658–1659
Stuart Restoration
Charles II1660–1685
James II1685–1688
Orange
William III1689–1702
 and Mary II1689–1694
Stuart
Anne1702–1714
Hanover
George I1714–1727
George II1727–1760
George III1760–1820
George IV1820–1830
William IV1830–1837
Victoria1837–1901
Saxe-Coburg–Gotha
Edward VII1901–1910
Windsor
George V1910–1936
Edward VIII (325 days)1936
George VI1936–1952
Elizabeth II1952–

BULGARIA
Saxe-Coburg–Gotha
Ferdinand I [3]1908–1918
Boris III1918–1943
Simeon II1943–1946
Communist state, 1946–

CHINA
Hsia Dynasty, c.2200–1766 B.C.
Shang Dynasty, c.1766–1123 B.C.
Chou Dynasty, c.1122–256 B.C.
Ch'in Dynasty, 221–207 B.C.
Han Dynasty, 202 B.C.–A.D. 220
Disorder, 220–589
T'ang Dynasty, 618–907
Sung Dynasty, 960–1279
Yuan Dynasty, 1260–1368
Ming Dynasty, 1368–1644
Manchu (Ch'ing) Dynasty
Shun-chih1644–1661
K'ang-hsi1661–1722
Yung-cheng1723–1735
Chien-lung1736–1796
Chia-ch'ing1796–1820
Tao-kuang1821–1851
Hsien-feng1851–1862
T'ung-chih1862–1875
Kuang-hsü1875–1908
Hsüan-t'ung1909–1912
Republic, 1912–1949
Sun Yat-sen1912
Yüan Shih-k'ai1912–1916
Chiang Kai-shek1928–1949
Communist state, 1949–

DENMARK
Waldemarian Dynasty
Waldemar the Great1157–1182
Knut VI1182–1202
Waldemar II1202–1241
Eric Plowpenny1241–1250
Abel1250–1252
Kristoffer1252–1259
Eric V1259–1286
Eric VI1286–1319
Kristoffer II1320–1332
Waldemar IV1340–1375
Olaf [4]1376–1387
Margrethe I [5]1387–1412
Eric [5]1412–1439
Kristoffer [5]1439–1448
House of Oldenburg
Kristian I of Oldenburg [5] . . .1448–1481
Hans [5]1481–1513
Kristian II [5]1513–1523
Frederik I [6]1523–1533
Kristian III [6]1534–1559
Frederik II [6]1559–1588
Kristian IV [6]1588–1648
Frederik III [6]1648–1670
Kristian V [6]1670–1699
Frederik IV [6]1699–1730
Kristian VI [6]1730–1746
Frederik V [6]1746–1766
Kristian VII [6]1766–1808
Frederik VI [6]1808–1839
Kristian VIII1839–1848
Frederik VII1848–1863
House of Glücksborg
Kristian IX1863–1906
Frederik VIII1906–1912
Kristian X1912–1947
Frederik IX1947–1972
Margrethe II1972–

EGYPT [7]
Protodynastic Period
Dynasty Ic. 3110–2884 B.C.
 Mena (Menes)c. 3110–3080 B.C.
Dynasty IIc. 2883–2811 B.C.
Old Kingdom
Dynasty IIIc. 2664–2180 B.C.
 Djoserc. 2663–2645 B.C.
Dynasty IVc. 2614–2502 B.C.
 Snefruc. 2614–2591 B.C.
 Khufu (Cheops) . . .c. 2590–2568 B.C.
 Menkaurec. 2534–2508 B.C.
Dynasty Vc. 2501–2342 B.C.
 Userkafc. 2501–2491 B.C.
 Sahurec. 2490–2476 B.C.
 Unisc. 2371–2342 B.C.
Dynasty VIc. 2341–2180 B.C.
 Tetic. 2341–2328 B.C.
 Pepi Ic. 2327–2278 B.C.
 Pepi IIc. 2272–2182 B.C.
First Intermediate Period
Dynasty VIIc. 2180–2175 B.C.
Dynasty VIIIc. 2174–2155 B.C.
Dynasty IXc. 2154–2100 B.C.
Dynasty Xc. 2100–2052 B.C.
Dynasty XIc. 2134–1999 B.C.
 Mentuhotep IIc. 2061–2011 B.C.

[1] From 1273 members of the Hapsburg dynasty ruled Austria as part of the German Holy Roman Empire; see list under Germany. [2] Franz II took title emperor of Austria in 1804 and gave up title Holy Roman emperor in 1806. [3] Ruled as prince from 1887 to 1908. [4] King of Denmark and Norway after 1380. [5] Ruler of Denmark, Norway, and Sweden. [6] Ruler of Denmark and Norway. [7] Listing does not include lesser-known Egyptian rulers.

EGYPT (continued)

Middle Kingdom
Dynasty XIIc. 1991–1786 B.C.
 Amenemhet Ic. 1991–1962 B.C.
 Senusert Ic. 1971–1928 B.C.
 Amenemhet IIc. 1929–1895 B.C.
 Senusert IIc. 1897–1879 B.C.
 Amenemhetc. 1842–1797 B.C.

Second Intermediate Period
Dynasty XIIIc. 1785–1660 B.C.
Dynasty XIVc. 1715–1650 B.C.
Dynasty XVc. 1652–1544 B.C.
Dynasty XVIc. 1650–1550 B.C.
Dynasty XVIIc. 1600–1554 B.C.

New Kingdom
Dynast XVIIIc. 1554–1529 B.C.
 Ahmosec. 1554–1529 B.C.
 Amenhotep Ic. 1529–1509 B.C.
 Thutmose Ic. 1509–1497 B.C.
 Thutmose IIc. 1497–1490 B.C.
 Hatshepsutc. 1489–1469 B.C.
 Thutmose IIIc. 1490–1436 B.C.
 Amenhotep IIc. 1438–1412 B.C.
 Thutmose IVc. 1412–1403 B.C.
 Amenhotep IIIc. 1403–1366 B.C.
 Akhenatonc. 1366–1349 B.C.
 Tutankhamenc. 1339–1335 B.C.
 Horemhebc. 1335–1304 B.C.
Dynasty XIXc. 1304–1192 B.C.
 Ramses Ic. 1304–1303 B.C.
 Seti Ic. 1303–1290 B.C.
 Ramses IIc. 1290–1223 B.C.
 Merneptahc. 1223–1211 B.C.
Dynasty XXc. 1192–1190 B.C.
 Ramses IIIc. 1190–1158 B.C.

Late Dynastic Period
Dynasty XXIc. 1075–940 B.C.
 Smendesc. 1075–1048 B.C.
Dynasty XXIIc. 940–730 B.C.
 (Libyan kings)
Dynasty XXIIIc. 761–715 B.C.
Dynasty XXIVc. 725–710 B.C.
Dynasty XXVc. 736–657 B.C.
 (Ethiopian kings)
Dynasty XXVIc. 664–525 B.C.
 Necho Ic. 664–663 B.C.
 Psamtik Ic. 663–609 B.C.
 Necho IIc. 609–594 B.C.

Ruled by Persian Empire
Dynasty XXVIIc. 525–404 B.C.

Independence regained
Dynasty XXVIIIc. 404–399 B.C.
 Amyrtaeusc. 404–399 B.C.
Dynasty XXIXc. 399–378 B.C.
Dynasty XXXc. 378–341 B.C.

Persian rule restored
Dynasty XXXIc. 341–332 B.C.

Conquest by Alexander the Great
and rule by Greeks, 332–30 B.C.
 Ptolemy I Soterc. 305–283 B.C.
 Ptolemy IIc. 285–246 B.C.
 Ptolemy IIIc. 246–221 B.C.
 Cleopatrac. 47–30 B.C.

Conquest by Romans, 30 B.C.

Conquest by Arabs, 639–642

Fatimid Caliphate of Egypt
Al-Mahdi 909–934
Al-Qaim 934–945
Al-Mansur 945–952

Al-Aziz 952–975
Al-Hakim 996–1021
Az-Zahir 1021–1036
Al-Mustansir 1036–1094
Al-Mustadi 1094–1101
Al-Amir 1101–1130
Al-Hafiz 1130–1149
Az-Zafir 1149–1154
Al-Faiz 1154–1160
Al-Adid 1160–1171

Ayyubid Caliphate, 1171–1250
Salah al-Din (Saladin)1171–1193

Mameluke Sultans, 1250–1517

Ottoman Turkish conquest and rule, 1517–1914

British protectorate, 1914–1922

Independent monarchy restored
Fuad I1922–1936
Faruk I1936–1952
Faruk II1952–1953

Republic, 1953–

FRANCE

Carolingian Dynasty
Charlemagne768–814
Louis I the Pious814–840
WEST FRANCIA
Charles the Bald840–877
Louis II877–879
Louis III879–882
Carloman879–884
Eudes .888–898
Charles the Simple893–923
Rudolph923–936
Louis IV936–954
Lothair954–986
Louis V986–987
MIDDLE KINGDOMS
Lothair, Emperor840–855
Louis (Italy), Emperor855–875
Charles (Provence), King855–863
Lothair II (Lorraine), King855–869

Capetian Kings
Hugh Capet987–996
Robert II996–1031
Henri I1031–1060
Philippe I1060–1108
Louis VI1108–1137
Louis VII1137–1180
Philippe II (August)1180–1223
Louis VIII1223–1226
Louis IX1226–1270
Philippe III1270–1285
Philippe IV1285–1314
Louis X1314–1316
Jean I . 1316
Philippe V1316–1322
Charles IV1322–1328

House of Valois
Philippe VI1328–1350
Jean II1350–1364
Charles V1364–1380
Charles VI1380–1422
Charles VII1422–1461
Louis XI1461–1483
Charles VIII1483–1498
Louis XII1498–1515
François I1515–1547
Henri II1547–1559
François II1559–1560

Charles IX1560–1574
Henri III1574–1589

Bourbon Dynasty
Henri IV1589–1610
Louis XIII1610–1643
Louis XIV1643–1715
Louis XV1715–1774
Louis XVI1774–1792

First Republic, 1792–1799

Napoleon Bonaparte
First Consul1799–1804
Napoleon I, Emperor1804–1814
Hundred Days 1815

Bourbon Restoration
Louis XVIII1814–1824
Charles X1824–1830
Louis Philippe1830–1848

Second Republic, 1848–1852

Napoleon III, Emperor, 1852–1870

Third Republic, 1870–1940

Pétain regime, 1940–1944

Provisional government, 1944–1946

Fourth Republic, 1946–1958

Fifth Republic, 1958–
Charles de Gaulle1958–1969
Georges Pompidou1969–1974
Valéry Giscard d'Estaing1974–1981
François Mitterrand1981–

GERMANY [1]

Carolingian Dynasty
Charlemagne768–814
Louis (Ludwig I) the Pious814–840
Lothair I840–855
Ludwig II the German843–876
Karl II the Bald875–877
Karl III the Fat876–887
Arnulf887–899
Ludwig III the Child899–911

Franconian House
Konrad I911–918

Saxon House
Heinrich I the Fowler919–936
Otto I the Great936–973
Otto II973–983
Otto III983–1002
Heinrich II the Saint1002–1024

Franconian (Salian) House
Konrad II1024–1039
Heinrich III1039–1056
Heinrich IV1056–1106
Heinrich V1106–1125
Lothair II1125–1137

Hohenstaufen House
Konrad III1138–1152
Friedrich I Barbarossa1152–1190
Heinrich VI1190–1197
Philipp of Swabia1198–1208
Otto IV of Brunswick1198–1215
Friedrich II1215–1250
Konrad IV1250–1254

Great Interregnum, 1254–1273

Rulers of Various Houses
Rudolf I of Hapsburg1273–1291
Adolf of Nassau1292–1298
Albrecht I of Austria1298–1308

[1] Most rulers of Germany were Holy Roman emperors from 800 through Franz II in 1792.

GERMANY (continued)

Heinrich VII of Luxembourg	1308–1313
Ludwig IV of Bavaria	1314–1347
Friedrich of Austria	1314–1326
Karl IV of Luxembourg	1346–1378
Wenzel of Bohemia	1378–1400
Ruprecht of Palatinate	1400–1410
Sigismund of Luxembourg	1411–1437

Hapsburg Dynasty

Albrecht II	1438–1439
Friedrich III	1440–1493
Maximilian I	1493–1519
Karl V (of Spain)	1519–1556
Ferdinand I	1556–1564
Maximilian II	1564–1576
Rudolf II	1576–1612
Matthias	1612–1619
Ferdinand II	1619–1637
Ferdinand III	1637–1657
Leopold I	1657–1705
Josef I	1705–1711
Karl VI	1711–1740
Maria Theresia	1740–1780
Franz I	1745–1765
Josef II	1765–1790
Leopold II	1790–1792
Franz II [2]	1792–1806

Hohenzollern Dynasty

Friedrich I [3]	1701–1713
Friedrich Wilhelm I [3]	1713–1740
Friedrich II the Great [3]	1740–1786
Friedrich Wilhelm II [3]	1786–1797
Friedrich Wilhelm III [3]	1797–1840
Friedrich Wilhelm IV [3]	1840–1861
Wilhelm I [4]	1861–1888
Friedrich III	1888
Wilhelm II	1888–1918

Weimar Republic, 1918–1933

Third Reich (Nazi Dictatorship)

Adolf Hitler	1933–1945

Allied occupation, 1945–1952

Division into Federal Republic of Germany (West) and German Democratic Republic (East), 1949–

GREECE

Otto I	1832–1862

Danish House

George I	1863–1913
Constantine I	1913–1917
Alexander I	1917–1920
Constantine I	1920–1922
George II	1922–1923

First Greek Republic, 1924–1935

Monarchy restored, 1935–1973

George II	1935–1947
Paul I	1947–1964
Constantine II	1964–1973

Second Greek Republic, 1973–

HUNGARY

Arpád Dynasty

St. István I	997–1038
Peter Orseolo	1038–1046
András I	1047–1060
Béla I	1061–1063
Solomon	1063–1074
Geza I	1074–1077
St. László	1077–1095
Coloman	1095–1116

István II	1116–1131
Béla II	1131–1141
Geza II	1141–1161
István III	1161–1173
István IV	1162–1163
Béla III	1173–1196
Emeric I	1196–1204
László III	1204–1205
András II	1205–1235
Béla IV	1235–1270
István V	1270–1272
László IV	1272–1290
András III	1290–1301
Carobert	1308–1342
Lajos I the Great	1342–1382
Maria	1382–1395
Sigismund	1387–1437
Albrecht	1437–1439
Ulászló I	1439–1444
László V	1444–1457
Mátyás Hollos	1458–1490
Ulászló II	1490–1516
Lajos II	1516–1526

Hungary Partitioned and Ruled by Turkey and Austria, 1526–1918

Revolution and Disorder, 1918–1920

Regency, Admiral Nicholas Horthy, 1920–1945

Communist state, 1945–

INDIA

Mogul Emperors

Babar	1526–1530
Humayun	1530–1556
Akbar the Great	1556–1605
Jahangir	1605–1627
Shah Jahan	1628–1658
Aurangzeb	1658–1707
Bahadur Shah I	1707–1712
Jahandar Shah	1712–1713
Farruk-Siar	1713–1719
Mohammed Shah	1719–1748
Ahmed	1748–1754
Alamgir	1754–1759
Shah Alam	1759–1806
Mohammed Akbar II	1806–1837
Bahadur Shah II	1837–1857

British rule, 1857–1947

British dominion, 1947–1950

Republic, 1950–

IRAN (PERSIA)

Achaemenid Empire

Cyrus II	559–530 B.C.
Cambyses II	530–522 B.C.
Smerdis	522 B.C.
Darius I	522–486 B.C.
Xerxes I	486–465 B.C.
Artaxerxes I	465–424 B.C.
Xerxes II	424–423 B.C.
Sogdianus	424–423 B.C.
Darius II	423–404 B.C.
Artaxerxes II	404–359 B.C.
Artaxerxes III	359–338 B.C.
Arses	338–336 B.C.
Darius III	336–330 B.C.

Conquest by Alexander the Great and rule by Seleucid Greeks, 331–187 B.C.

Parthian Empire, c.171 B.C.–A.D. 224

Sasanian Empire, c.224–651

Rule by Arabs, 651–892

Samanid Dynasty, 892–999

Ghaznavid Dynasty, 999–1037

Conquest and rule by Seljuk Turks, 1037–1157

Disorder, 1157–1260

Conquest and rule by Mongol Il-khans, 1260–1353

Conquest by Mongol Timur (Tamerlane) and rule by Timurid Dynasty, 1369–1469

Safavid Dynasty

Ismail I	1502–1524
Tahmasp I	1524–1576
Ismail II	1576–1578
Mohammed Khudabanda	1578–1587
Abbas I	1587–1629
Safi I	1629–1642
Abbas II	1642–1667
Suleiman	1667–1694
Husain	1694–1722
Tahmasp II	1722–1731
Abbas III	1731–1736

Nadir Shah, 1736–1747

Zand Dynasty, 1750–1794

Kajar Dynasty

Aga Mohammed	1794–1797
Fath Ali	1797–1835
Mohammed	1835–1848
Nasir ud-Din	1848–1896
Muzaffar ud-Din	1896–1907
Mohammed Ali	1907–1909
Ahmed Mirza	1909–1925

Pahlevi Dynasty

Riza Shah Pahlevi	1925–1941
Mohammed Riza Pahlevi	1941–1979

Republic, 1979–

ISLAMIC ARAB EMPIRE

Mohammed	622–632
Abu Bakr	632–634
Omar	634–644
Othman	644–656
Ali	656–661

Omayyad Caliphate

Muawiya I	661–680
Yasid I	680–682
Muawiya II	683
Marwan I	684–685
Abdalmalik	685–705
Walid I	705–715
Sulaiman	715–717
Omar ibn Abdul-Aziz	717–720
Yazid II	720–724
Hisham	724–743
Walid II	743–744
Yazid III	744
Ibrahim	744
Marwan II	744–750

Abbasid Caliphate

Abu-l-Abbas al-Saffah	750–754
Al-Mansur	754–775
Al-Mahdi	775–785
Al-Hadi	785–786
Harun Al-Rashid	786–809
Al-Amin	809–813
Al-Mamun	813–833
Al-Mu'tasim	833–842
Al-Wathiq	842–847
Al-Mutawakkil	847–861

[1] Most rulers of Germany were Holy Roman emperors from 800 through Franz II in 1792. [2] After giving up title Holy Roman emperor in 1806, he continued to rule Austria until 1835. [3] King of Prussia. [4] Emperor of Germany after 1871.

ISLAMIC ARAB EMPIRE (cont.)

Al-Muntasir	861–862
Al-Musta'in	862–866
Al-Mu'tazz	866–869
Al-Muqtadi	869–870
Al-Mu'tamid	870–892
Al-Mu'tadid	892–902
Al-Muqtafi	902–908
Al-Muqtadir	908–932
Al-Qahir	932–934
Al-Radi	934–940
Al-Muttaqi	940–944
Al-Mustaqfi	944–946
Al-Muti	946–974
Al-Ta'i	974–991
Al-Qadir	991–1031
Al-Qa'im	1031–1075
Al-Muqtadi	1075–1094
Al-Mustazhir	1094–1118
Al-Mustarshid	1118–1135
Al-Rashid	1135–1136
Al-Muqtafi	1136–1160
Al-Mustanjid	1160–1170
Al-Mustadi	1170–1180
Al-Nasir	1180–1225
Al-Zahir	1225–1226
Al-Mustansir	1226–1242
Al-Musta'sim	1242–1258

Mongols destroy Baghdad and overthrow Arab Empire, 1258

ITALY

Vittorio Emanuele II	1849–1878
Umberto I	1878–1900
Vittorio Emanuele III	1900–1946
Umberto II	1946

Fascist Dictatorship
Benito Mussolini	1922–1943

Italian Republic, 1946–

JAPAN

Legendary period, 660 B.C.–A.D. 710
Emperor Jimmu Tenno 660–585 B.C.

Nara Period, 710–784
Heian Period, 794–1185
Kamakura Period, 1185–1333
Ashikaga Period, 1336–1568
Unification Period, 1568–1603

Tokugawa Shoguns
Ieyasu	1603–1605
Hidetada	1605–1623
Iemitsu	1623–1651
Ietsuna	1651–1680
Tsunayoshi	1680–1709
Ienobu	1709–1713
Ietsugu	1713–1716
Yoshimune	1716–1745
Ieshige	1745–1760
Ieharu	1760–1786
Matsudaira Sadanobu	1787–1793
Ienari	1793–1838
Ieyoshi	1838–1853
Iesada	1853–1858
Iemochi	1858–1866
Yoshinobu	1866–1867

Meji Era
Emperor Mutsuhito	1867–1912

Taisho Era
Emperor Yoshihito	1912–1926

Showa Era
Emperor Hirohito	1926–

JORDAN

Abdullah	1946–1951
Talal	1951–1952
Hussein	1952–

LIECHTENSTEIN

Prince Johann II	1858–1929
Prince Franz I	1929–1938
Prince Franz Josef II	1938–

LUXEMBOURG

Duke Adolf of Nassau	1890–1905
William	1905–1912
Marie Adelaide	1912–1919
Charlotte	1919–1961
Prince Jean	1961–

NETHERLANDS

Houses of Orange and Nassau
Willem I (the Silent)	1581–1584
Maurice of Nassau	1584–1625
Frederik Heinrich	1625–1647
Willem II	1647–1650
Jan de Witt	1650–1672
Willem III [1]	1672–1702
Willem IV	1711–1751
Willem V	1751–1795

Batavian Republic, 1795–1806

French rule, 1806–1813
Louis Bonaparte	1806–1810

House of Orange-Nassau
Willem I	1813–1840
Willem II	1840–1849
Willem III	1849–1890
Wilhelmina	1890–1948
Juliana	1948–1980
Beatrix	1980–

NORWAY [2]

Harold I Fairhair	872–930
Haakon I the Good	935–961
Harold II Graycloak	961–970
Haakon, Jarl	970–995
Olav I Trygvesson	995–1000
Olav II (Saint Olav)	1016–1028
Magnus I the Good	1035–1047
Harold III Hardruler	1046–1066
Olav III the Quiet	1066–1093
Magnus II Bareleg	1093–1103
Sverre	1184–1202
Haakon IV the Old	1217–1263
Magnus V Lawmender	1263–1280
Erik II Priest-Hater	1280–1299
Haakon V	1299–1319

Governed by rulers of Denmark or Sweden, 1319–1905

Independence restored
Haakon VII	1905–1957
Olav V	1957–

POLAND

Piast Dynasty
Mieszko I	c. 960–992
Boleslaw I the Brave	992–1025
Mieszko II	1025–1034
Kazimierz I	1038–1058

Boleslaw II the Bold	1058–1079
Wladyslaw I	1079–1102
Boleslaw III	1102–1138
Wladyslaw II	1138–1146
Boleslaw IV	1146–1173
Mieszko III	1173–1177
Kazimierz II the Just	1177–1194
Leszek I the White	1194–1227
Boleslaw V the Chaste	1227–1279
Lezek II the Black	1279–1288
Przemyslaw II	1290–1296

Rule by Bohemia
Wenceslaus I	1300–1305

Piast Dynasty restored
Wladyslaw IV	1305–1333
Kazimierz III the Great	1333–1370

Elected Monarch
Louis of Anjou	1370–1382

Jagiellonian Dynasty
Jadwiga	1384–1399
Wladyslaw V Jagiello	1386–1434
Wladyslaw VI	1434–1444
Kazimierz IV	1447–1492
Jan I	1492–1501
Aleksandr I	1501–1506
Zygmunt I	1506–1548
Zygmunt II	1548–1572

Elected Monarchs
Henri of Valois	1573–1574
Stefan Bathory	1575–1586
Zygmunt III	1587–1632
Wladyslaw VII	1632–1648
Jan I Kazimierz	1648–1668
Michal Wisniowiecki	1669–1673
Jan III Sobieski	1674–1696
Augustus II	1697–1704
Stanislaw Leszczynski	1704–1709
Augustus II	1709–1733
Stanislaw Leszczynski	1733–1734
Augustus III	1734–1763
Stanislaw Poniatowski	1764–1795

Partition among Austria, Russia, and Prussia, 1795–1918

Republic of Poland, 1918–1939

Partition between Germany and Soviet Union, 1939–1945

Soviet occupation, 1945–1948

Communist state, 1948–

PORTUGAL

Burgundian Dynasty
Afonso Henriques	1139–1185
Sancho I	1185–1211
Afonso II	1211–1223
Sancho II	1223–1245
Afonso III	1245–1279
Diniz	1279–1325
Afonso IV	1325–1357
Pedro I	1357–1367
Fernando I	1367–1383

Avis Dynasty
João I	1385–1433
Duarte I	1433–1438
Afonso V	1438–1481
João II	1481–1495
Manuel I	1495–1521

[1] Willem III also ruled as King William III of England and Scotland in 1689–1702. [2] Does not include claimants to Norway's throne during many periods of civil war.

João III1521–1557
Sebastião I1557–1578
Henrique1578–1580
Spanish rule, 1580–1640
House of Braganza
João IV1640–1656
Afonso VI1656–1667
Pedro II...............1667–1706
João V.................1706–1750
José Manuel1750–1777
House of Coburg-Braganza
Maria I and Pedro III.......1777–1786
Maria I1786–1816
João VI1816–1826
Pedro IV 1826
Maria II1826–1828
Miguel.................1828–1833
Maria II1833–1853
Pedro V1853–1861
Luis I1861–1889
Carlos I1889–1908
Manuel II1908–1910
1st Portuguese Republic, 1910–1928
Fascist Dictatorship
Antonio Salazar.........1928–1968
Marcelo Caetano1968–1974
2d Portuguese Republic, 1974–

ROMANIA
Carol I1881–1914
Ferdinand I1914–1927
Michael................1927–1930
Carol II1930–1940
Michael................1940–1947
Communist state, 1947–

RUSSIA
Grand Princes of Moscow
Vsevolod III1176–1212
Yuri II1212–1216
Konstantin1216–1219
Yuri II1219–1238
Yaroslav II1238–1246
Andrei II1246–1252
Aleksandr Nevski1252–1263
Yaroslav III1263–1272
Vasili1272–1277
Dmitri1277–1294
Andrei III1294–1304
Mikhail1304–1319
Yuri III1319–1325
Dmitri1325–1326
Aleksandr..............1326–1328
Ivan I.................1328–1340
Simeon1340–1353
Ivan II1353–1359
Dmitri Donskoi1359–1389
Vasili I1389–1425
Vasili II1425–1462
Czars of Russia
Ivan III the Great1462–1505
Vasili III..............1505–1533
Ivan IV the Terrible1533–1584
Fedor I1584–1598
Boris Godunov1598–1605
Fedor II 1605
Dmitri I1605–1606
Vasili IV1606–1610
Romanov Dynasty
Mikhail1613–1645
Aleksei1645–1676
Fedor III1676–1682

Ivan V1682–1689
Peter I the Great1682–1725
Ekaterina Alekseevna I ...1725–1727
Peter II Alekseevich1727–1730
Anna Ioannovna1730–1740
Ivan VI................1740–1741
Elizaveta Petrovna1741–1762
Peter III Fedorovich 1762
Ekaterina Alekseevna II
 (the Great)............1762–1796
Pavel Petrovich1796–1801
Aleksandr I Pavlovich1801–1825
Nikolai I Pavlovich1825–1855
Aleksandr II Nikolaevich ...1855–1881
Aleksandr III
 Aleksandrovich1881–1894
Nikolai II Aleksandrovich ...1894–1917
Provisional Government
Aleksandr Kerensky 1917
Bolshevik Revolution, 1917
Soviet Union, 1917–

SAUDI ARABIA
Ibn Saud1932–1953
Saud1953–1964
Faisal1964–1975
Khalid1975–1982
Fahd1982–

SPAIN
Houses of Aragon and Castile
Fernando II of Aragon and
 Isabel I of Castile1479–1504
Fernando II and Felipe I1504–1506
Fernando II and
 Carlos II1506–1516
Spanish Hapsburgs
Carlos I (as Holy Roman
 Emperor, Karl V).......1516–1556
Felipe II...............1556–1598
Felipe III1598–1621
Felipe IV1621–1665
Carlos II1665–1700
Spanish Bourbons
Felipe V1700–1746
Fernando VI1746–1759
Carlos III1759–1788
Carlos IV..............1788–1808
French King of Spain
Joseph Bonaparte1808–1813
1st Bourbon Restoration
Fernando VII1813–1833
Isabel II1833–1868
House of Savoy
Amadeo I1868–1873
1st Spanish Republic, 1873–1875
2d Bourbon Restoration
Alfonso XII1875–1885
Alfonso XIII1886–1931
2d Spanish Republic, 1931–1939
Fascist Dictatorship
Francisco Franco1939–1975
3d Bourbon Restoration
Juan Carlos I1975–

SWEDEN
House of Vasa
Gustaf I1523–1560
Eric XIV1560–1568
Johan III1568–1592
Sigismund1592–1599

Karl IX................1604–1611
Gustaf II Adolf1611–1632
Christina1644–1654
Karl X Gustaf1654–1660
Karl XI1660–1697
Karl XII1697–1718
Ulrika Eleonora1718–1720
Fredrik I1720–1751
Adolf Fredrik1751–1771
Gustaf III1771–1792
Gustaf IV Adolf1792–1809
Karl XIII..............1809–1818
House of Bernadotte
Karl XIV Johan1818–1844
Oskar I1844–1859
Karl XV1859–1872
Oskar II1872–1907
Gustaf V1907–1950
Gustaf VI Adolf1950–1973
Karl XVI Gustaf1973–

TURKEY
Seljuk Sultans
Tughril I1055–1063
Alp Arslan1063–1072
Malik Shah I1073–1092
Mahmud1092–1094
Barkyaruk1094–1104
Malik Shah II.......... 1104
**Seljuk Turkish Empire
 divided** 1104
Ottoman Sultans
Osman Ic.1299–1326
Orkhan1326–1359
Murad I1359–1389
Bajazet I1389–1403
Suleiman I1403–1411
Musa1411–1413
Mohammed I1413–1421
Murad II1421–1451
Mohammed II1451–1481
Bajazet II1481–1512
Selim I1512–1520
Suleiman II1520–1566
Selim II1566–1574
Murad III1574–1595
Mohammed III1595–1603
Ahmed I1603–1617
Mustafa I1617–1618
Osman II1618–1622
Mustafa I1622–1623
Murad IV1623–1640
Ibrahim1640–1648
Mohammed IV1648–1687
Suleiman III1687–1691
Ahmed II1691–1695
Mustafa II1695–1703
Ahmed III1703–1730
Mahmud I1730–1754
Osman III1754–1757
Mustafa III1757–1774
Abdul-Hamid I1774–1789
Selim III1789–1807
Mustafa IV1807–1808
Mahmud II1808–1839
Abdul-Medjid I1839–1861
Abdul-Aziz1861–1876
Murad V 1876
Abdul-Hamid II1876–1909
Mohammed V1909–1918
Mohammed VI..........1918–1922
Republic, 1923–

ROMAN AND BYZANTINE EMPERORS AND EMPRESSES

Octavian, the grandnephew and adopted son of Julius Caesar, founded the Roman Empire. He became emperor in 27 B.C., called himself Augustus, and took complete control of military and governmental powers. At the death of Theodosius the Great in 395, the empire was divided into east and west.

The large-scale barbarian invasions of the 400s caused the empire in the west to crumble. In 476 Odoacer, a German leader, entered Rome and forced Emperor Romulus Augustulus to abdicate.

In the east the Roman Empire continued to exist for nearly 10 more centuries under Greek rulers as the Byzantine Empire.

Where dates overlap in the following list, the title of emperor was shared.

ROMAN EMPERORS

Augustus	27 B.C.-A.D. 14
Tiberius	14–37
Caligula	37–41
Claudius	41–54
Nero	54–68
Galba	68–69
Otho	69
Vitellius	69
Vespasian	69–79
Titus	79–81
Domitian	81–96
Nerva	96–98
Trajan	98–117
Hadrian	117–138
Antoninus Pius	138–161
Marcus Aurelius	161–180
Lucius Verus	161–169
Commodus	180–192
Pertinax	193
Didius Julianus	193
Septimius Severus	193–211
Geta	209–211
Caracalla	211–217
Macrinus	217–218
Heliogabalus (Elagabalus)	218–222
Alexander Severus	222–235
Maximinus Thrax	235–238
Gordian I Africanus	238
Gordian II	238
Balbinus	238
Pupienus Maximus	238
Gordian III Pius	238–244
Philip the Arab	244–249
Decius	249–251
Hostilian	251
Gallus	251–253
Aemilian	253
Valerian	253–259
Gallienus	259–268
Claudius II Gothicus	268–270
Quintillus	270
Aurelian	270–275
Tacitus	275–276
Florian	276
Probus	276–282
Carus	282–283
Carinus	283–285
Numerian	283–284
Diocletian	284–305
Maximian	286–305; 306–308
Constantius I Chlorus	305–306
Galerius	305–311
Severus	306–307
Maxentius	306–312
Maximinus Daia	308–313
Licinius	311–324
Constantine I the Great	311–337
Constantine II	337–340
Constans	337–350
Constantius II	337–361
Julian the Apostate	361–363
Jovian	363–364
Valentinian I (in the West)	364–375
Valens (in the East)	364–378
Gratian (in the West)	375–383
Valentinian II (in the West)	375–392
Theodosius I the Great	379–395
Magnus Maximus	383–388
Eugenius	392–394

ROMAN EMPERORS IN WEST

Honorius	395–423
Constantius III	421
Johannes	423–425
Valentinian III	425–455
Petronius Maximus	455
Avitus	455–456
Majorian	457–461
Libius Severus	461–465
Anthemius	467–472
Olybrius	472
Glycerius	473
Julius Nepos	473–475
Romulus Augustulus	475–476

ROMAN EMPERORS IN EAST

Arcadius	395–408
Theodosius II	408–450
Marcian	450–457
Leo I	457–474
Leo II	473–474
Zeno	474–491

BYZANTINE RULERS IN EAST

Anastasius I	491–518
Justin I	518–527
Justinian the Great	527–565
Justin II	565–578
Tiberius II	578–582
Maurice	582–602
Phocas I	602–610
Heraclius I	610–641
Constantine III	641
Heracleon	641
Constans II	641–668
Constantine IV	668–685
Justinian II	685–695
Leontius	695–698
Tiberius III	698–705
Justinian II	705–711
Philippicus	711–713
Anastasius II	713–715
Theodosius III	715–717
Leo III	717–741
Constantine V	741–775
Leo IV	775–780
Constantine VI	780–797
Irene	797–802
Nicephorus I	802–811
Stauracius	811
Michael I	811–813
Leo V	813–820
Michael II	820–829

Theophilus I	829–842
Michael III	842–867
Basil I	867–886
Leo VI	886–912
Alexander II	912–913
Constantine VII	912–959
Romanus I	920–944
Romanus II	959–963
Basil II	963–1025
Nicephorus II	963–969
John I	969–976
Constantine VIII	1025–1028
Zoë	1028–1050
Romanus III	1028–1034
Michael IV	1034–1041
Michael V	1041–1042
Constantine IX	1042–1055
Theodora	1055–1056
Michael VI	1056–1057
Isaac I	1057–1059
Constantine X	1059–1067
Romanus IV	1068–1071
Michael VII	1071–1078
Nicephorus III	1078–1081
Alexius I	1081–1118
Andronicus I	1183–1185
Isaac II	1185–1195
Alexis III	1195–1203
Isaac II	1203–1204
Alexius IV	1203–1204
Alexius V	1204

LATIN RULERS

Baldwin I	1204–1205
Henry	1205–1216
Peter of Courtenay	1216–1217
Yolande	1217–1219
Robert of Courtenay	1219–1228
Baldwin II	1228–1261
John of Brienne	1231–1237

NICAEAN EMPERORS

Theodore I	1204–1222
John III	1222–1254
Theodore II	1254–1258
John IV	1258–1261

PALEOLOGI EMPERORS

Michael VIII	1259–1282
Andronicus II	1282–1328
Michael IX	1295–1320
Andronicus III	1328–1341
John V	1341–1347
John VI	1347–1354
John V	1355–1376
Andronicus IV	1376–1379
John V	1379–1391
John VII	1390
Manuel II	1391–1425
John VIII	1425–1448
Constantine XI	1448–1453

KEY EVENTS IN AMERICAN HISTORY

Presented here in chronological order are many of the important events in American history from the time of the early explorers to the present day. For the convenience of the reader, the table of events has been divided into 10 broad periods of history.

PERIOD OF EXPLORATION AND COLONIZATION: 1000–1763

c.1000 Norse Vikings discover North America; Leif Ericson lands at Vinland (probably Newfoundland).

1492 (Oct. 12) Christopher Columbus discovers America for Spain; after sailing 33 days out of sight of land, goes ashore on San Salvador (Watling) Island in Bahamas, believing he has reached East Indies.

1492 (Dec. 26) First Spanish settlement in Western Hemisphere founded by Columbus at La Navidad in what is now Haiti; later destroyed by Indians.

1496 First Permanent Spanish city in Western Hemisphere founded by Bartholomew Columbus: Santo Domingo, now in Dominican Republic.

1497 (June 24) English claim for North America established by John Cabot, landing on either Newfoundland or Nova Scotia.

1508 First Spanish settlement in Puerto Rico founded by Juan Ponce de León.

1513 (April 2) Florida discovered and claimed for Spain by Juan Ponce de León.

1513 (Sept. 25) Pacific Ocean discovered and all lands bordering it claimed for Spain by Vasco de Balboa, after crossing Isthmus of Panama.

1524 French claim for North America established by Giovanni da Verrazano; explored Atlantic coast and sailed into New York harbor.

1538 First university in Western Hemisphere, University of St. Thomas Aquinas, founded in Santo Domingo, now in Dominican Republic.

1540–42 Francisco Vásquez de Coronado explores American southwest, going as far north as Kansas and claiming region for Spain.

1541 (May 8) Mississippi River discovered by Spanish explorer Hernando de Soto near present-day Memphis, Tenn.

1562 First French settlement in what is now the U.S. founded by Jean Ribaut; called Charlesfort, on Port Royal Sound in South Carolina; later abandoned.

1564 (June) First French colony in Florida founded by René de Laudonnière; called Fort Caroline, near present-day Jacksonville; later destroyed by Spaniards.

1565 (Sept. 8) First permanent European settlement in what is now continental U.S. established at St. Augustine, Fla., by Pedro Menéndez de Avilés of Spain.

1585 First English colony settled on Roanoke Island, N.C.; survived only 10 months.

1587 (Aug. 18) First English child, Virginia Dare, born in what is now U.S., in second Roanoke settlement—the "Lost Colony."

1607 (May 14) First permanent English settlement in what is now U.S. established at Jamestown, Va.

1609 Hudson River explored and claimed for Dutch by explorer Henry Hudson.

1610 Santa Fe established as capital of Spanish colony of New Mexico, oldest capital city in U.S.

1614 New Netherland (New York) founded by Dutch with building of fort at what is now Albany, N.Y.

1619 First black slaves in North America arrive at Jamestown in Dutch ship.

1619 (July 30) First legislature, Virginia's House of Burgesses, convenes at Jamestown.

1620 (Nov. 21) Mayflower Compact signed by Pilgrims aboard *Mayflower* in Provincetown, Mass., harbor.

1620 (Dec. 21) Pilgrims land to found colony at Plymouth, Mass.

1626 Manhattan Island, N.Y., bought by Dutch from Indians for about $24.

1628 (Sept. 6) Puritans land at Salem founding Massachusetts Bay Colony (royal charter granted March 14, 1629); Boston founded in 1630.

1634 (March 25) Maryland founded with landing of English Roman Catholics led by Gov. Leonard Calvert, brother of Lord Baltimore.

1636 Providence, R.I., founded by Roger Williams to provide religious freedom for all faiths.

1636 (Oct. 28) Harvard College founded in Massachusetts; first institution of higher learning in U.S.

1638 First printing press in English colonies set up by Stephen Day at Cambridge, Mass.; publishes first book, *Bay Psalm Book,* in 1640.

1639 (Jan. 24) Fundamental Orders of Connecticut adopted; provides for elected governor and legislature.

1649 (April 21) Maryland's Toleration Act passed, granting religious freedom to all Christian faiths.

1660 (Dec. 1) First Navigation Act passed by British parliament to regulate colonial trade.

1664 (Sept. 8) New Amsterdam (now New York City) captured by British from Dutch.

1670 (April) Colony of South Carolina begun with settlement established at Charleston.

1673 (July 17) Père Jacques Marquette and Louis Joliet explore Mississippi River as far south as Arkansas for France.

1675–78 King Philip's War fought between colonists and Indians in Massachusetts.

1676 (Sept. 19) Nathaniel Bacon burns Jamestown in rebellion against Virginia's British governor.

1677 First charter separating church and state framed for Quaker colony of West Jersey.

1681 (March 14) Pennsylvania proprietary charter granted William Penn by Charles II.

1682 (April 9) Sieur de La Salle paddles down Mississippi River to its mouth, claiming Louisiana for France.

1684 (Oct. 18) Massachusetts Bay Colony charter annulled by British court.

1685–89 Dominion of New England created by Britain's King James II to include all New England colonies plus New York, New Jersey, and Pennsylvania; rebellions by colonists and overthrow of James II in England ends scheme.

1689 (April 18) Rebellion in Boston overthrows British royal governor of New England, Sir Edmund Andros.

1689 (Aug. 1) Protestant rebellion in Maryland overthrows governor of Roman Catholic proprietors; Maryland restored to Baltimore family proprietors in 1715 after their conversion to Protestantism.

1689–91 Rebellion in New York: Jacob Leisler overthrows British governor and establishes elective assembly; arrested for treason and hanged in 1691.

1689–97 King William's War fought by British and French in New York, New England, and Canada.

1691 (Oct. 17) New Massachusetts royal charter issued, incorporating Plymouth Colony and Maine into Massachusetts.

1692 Witch trials in Salem, Mass., result in execution of 14 women and 6 men; 55 more plead guilty and accuse others.

1702–13 Queen Anne's War, in which British fight against French and Spaniards in New England, Florida, and South Carolina; France loses Hudson Bay region, Newfoundland, and Nova Scotia to Britain.

1704 (April 24) First successful newspaper in colonies established: *Boston News-Letter.*

1721 (May 29) South Carolina formally incorporated as royal colony.

1729 (July 25) North Carolina becomes royal colony under British king.

1732 (June 9) Royal charter for Georgia granted to James Edward Oglethorpe.

1735 (Aug. 4) Freedom of the press trial of John Peter Zenger ends as jury acquits him of libel, asserting that truth is not libelous.

1739–42 War of Jenkins' Ear fought between Georgia colonists and Spaniards in Florida.

1744–48 King George's War fought between British and French colonists; ends with no changes in territory by either side.

1749 (May 19) Ohio Company granted charter by

QUICK QUIZ: Who was heavyweight boxing champion in 1932-33? See page 796.

KEY EVENTS IN AMERICAN HISTORY (continued)

King George II to settle Ohio Valley.
1753 George Washington sent to Ohio Valley by Virginia's Gov. Robert Dinwiddie to warn French to leave.
1754 (May 28) French defeated by 22-year-old Lt. Col. George Washington in first skirmish of French and Indian War, at Great Meadows, Pa.; Washington surrenders Fort Necessity to French on July 4.
1755 (July 9) British Maj. Gen. Edward Braddock killed and his army routed by French near Fort Duquesne (Pittsburgh), Pa.; Braddock's aide, Col. George

Washington, escapes capture.
1759 (Sept. 18) French surrender Quebec to British.
1761 (Feb. 24) Massachusetts patriot James Otis in court suit denounces several warrants, known as writs of assistance, used by British customs officers.
1763 Indian Chief Pontiac kills hundreds of settlers along frontier in 7 months of warfare.
1763 (Feb. 10) Treaty of Paris ends French and Indian War; France loses to Britain all lands east of Mississippi River and Canada; Spain gives up Florida to Britain in exchange for Cuba.

ERA OF THE AMERICAN REVOLUTION: 1763–1783

1763 (Oct. 7) British government orders all settlers out of Ohio Valley and forbids settlement west of Appalachian Mountains.
1765 (March 22) Stamp Act passed by British parliament levying direct taxes on American colonists for first time.
1765 (March 24) Quartering Act passed by British parliament requires American colonists to provide living quarters and supplies for British troops.
1765 (Oct. 7–25) Stamp Act Congress held in New York City with delegates from nine colonies protesting British taxation without representation.
1766 (March 18) Repeal of Stamp Act approved by British parliament and king, bowing to American refusal to import taxed goods.
1766 (March 18) Declaratory Act passed by British parliament asserting its right to make laws binding on American colonists "in all cases whatsoever."
1767 Daniel Boone makes first journey over Appalachians into Kentucky.
1767 (June 29) Townshend Acts passed by British parliament, putting new import duties on glass, lead, paint, paper, and tea used by American colonists.
1767–69 Nonimportation by colonists of taxes goods cuts British trade by about 50%.
1770 (March 5) Boston Massacre: British troops fire on crowd of patriots protesting quartering of soldiers in Boston; 5 colonists killed and 8 wounded.
1770 (April 12) Repeal of Townshend Acts taxes, except those on tea, approved by King George.
1771 (May 16) Battle of Alamance fought in North Carolina between militia, led by Gov. William Tryon, and western Regulators, protesting lack of representation in legislature.
1772 (June 9) British customs schooner *Gaspée* burned by patriots near Providence, R.I.
1772 (Nov. 2) Committee of Correspondence elected by Boston town meeting with James Otis as chairman to circulate patriotic information.
1773 (May 10) Tea Act passed by British parliament giving East India Company right to undersell American tea merchants.
1773 (Dec. 16) Boston Tea Party: Sons of Liberty dressed as Indians dump tea from East India Company ships into Boston Harbor.
1774 (March 31) Boston Port Bill passed by British parliament closing Boston Harbor to trade in retaliation for Boston Tea Party.
1774 (May 20) Massachusetts Government Act: British parliament puts limits on powers of Massachusetts legislature and forbids town meetings without consent of governor.
1774 (May 20) Quebec Act approved by British parliament extends Canada's boundaries to Ohio River, ignoring claims to region by Connecticut, Massachusetts, and Virginia.
1774 (Sept. 5–Oct. 26) First Continental Congress meets in Philadelphia with delegates from 12 colonies, protesting British measures and calling for boycott on imports of all British goods.
1775 (March 30) New England Restraining Act passed by British parliament and approved by king forbids other colonies of New England from trading with any other nation than Britain or its colonies in West Indies.
1775 (April 19) Battles of Lexington and Concord signal beginning of American Revolution.
1775 (June 15) George Washington elected commander in chief of Continental Army by Second Conti-

nental Congress.
1775 (June 17) Battle of Bunker Hill won by British at Boston, but more than twice as many British troops are killed and wounded than are Americans.
1775 (Aug. 23) Britain's King George III declares American colonies in open rebellion; follows on Dec. 23 with decree forbidding all trade with colonies.
1776 (Jan. 9) Thomas Paine publishes *Common Sense*, rallying Americans to cause of independence.
1776 (March 4–17) British troops evacuate Boston, sailing to Halifax, Nova Scotia.
1776 (June 1–28) Charleston, S.C., successfully beats off British attack.
1776 (July 2) British army of 10,000 lands on Staten Island for invasion of New York.
1776 (July 4) Declaration of Independence adopted by Continental Congress.
1776 (Sept. 15) British take New York City: After being defeated by British troops in Battle of Long Island on Aug. 27, George Washington decides to evacuate New York City, fighting rearguard action while withdrawing.
1776 (Oct. 28) Battle of White Plains, N.Y.: Washington's troops inflict heavy casualties on British army.
1776 (Dec. 26) Battle of Trenton, N.J.: Washington crosses Delaware River for surprise attack, capturing 918 Hessians with loss of only 5 Americans.
1777 (June 14) U.S. flag design resolved by Congress: "thirteen stripes, alternate red and white; that the Union be thirteen stars, white in a blue field."
1777 (July 2–8) Vermont becomes first state to abolish slavery and provide universal male suffrage in its constitution.
1777 (Sept. 11) Battle of Brandywine, Pa.: British defeat Washington's army, opening way for capture of Philadelphia on Sept. 26.
1777 (Sept. 19 and Oct. 17) Battles of Saratoga: First major American victory in Revolutionary War; Gen. Horatio Gates' American troops defeat invasion from Canada led by British Gen. John Burgoyne south of Saratoga, N.Y.; Burgoyne surrenders entire army of about 5,000.
1778 (Feb. 6) France signs treaty of alliance with U.S. to defeat Britain.
1778 (June 18–28) British army evacuates Philadelphia, marches across New Jersey, fighting Battle of Monmouth against Washington's troops.
1778 (Dec. 29) British capture Savannah, Ga.
1779 (Sept. 23) John Paul Jones, commanding *Bonhomme Richard,* captures British 44-gun frigate *Serapis* in sea battle; replies "I have not yet begun to fight" when asked to surrender.
1780 (May 12) British capture Charleston, S.C., after 4-week siege; 5,500 American troops surrender.
1780 (Aug. 16) Battle of Camden, S.C.: British defeat American Gen. Horatio Gates; about half of American army of 4,000 are killed or captured.
1780 (Sept. 25) Maj. Gen. Benedict Arnold defects to British when his plans to surrender West Point go awry; British spy Maj. John André hanged on Oct. 2 at Tappan, N.Y.
1781 (March 1) Articles of Confederation ratified providing new U.S. national government.
1781 (Oct. 19) Surrender at Yorktown, Va., of 8,000-man British army of Gen. Charles Cornwallis after 10-day siege by American and French forces.
1783 (Sept. 3) Peace treaty signed with Britain ending Revolutionary War; effective on May 12, 1784.

EARLY YEARS OF THE NEW U.S. GOVERNMENT: 1787–1819

1787 (Feb. 4) Shays' Rebellion of dissident farmers put down by Massachusetts militia.
1787 (May 25–Sept. 17) U.S. Constitution written

by Constitutional Convention presided over by George Washington at Philadelphia.
1787 (July 13) Northwest Ordinance passed by Con-

gress of the Confederation, providing government and prohibiting slavery in territory north of Ohio River.
1787 (Dec. 7) Delaware becomes first state to ratify new U.S. Constitution.
1788 (June 21) U.S. Constitution goes into effect as New Hampshire becomes 9th state to ratify.
1789 (April 1–6) First U.S. Congress begins session in New York City.
1789 (April 30) Inauguration of George Washington as 1st President of the United States at Federal Hall in New York City.
1789 (Sept. 26) John Jay becomes 1st Chief Justice of the United States.
1790 First U.S. census shows population of 3,929,625, including 697,624 slaves.
1790 Capital of United States moved to Philadelphia from New York City.
1790 (May 29) Rhode Island joins Union as 13th state.
1791 (Feb. 25) Bank of the United States chartered.
1791 (March 4) Vermont becomes 14th state.
1791 (Dec. 15) Bill of Rights Amendments to U.S. Constitution become effective.
1791–94 Two political parties form: Democratic-Republicans led by Thomas Jefferson, and Federalists headed by Alexander Hamilton.
1792 (June 1) Kentucky becomes 15th state.
1793 (April 22) Neutrality proclamation issued by President Washington in war between Britain and France growing out of French Revolution.
1793 (Oct. 28) Eli Whitney files patent claim for his invention of cotton gin.
1794 Whisky Rebellion in western Pennsylvania by farmers protesting federal tax on whisky.
1796 (June 1) Tennessee becomes 16th state.
1796 (Sept. 17) Farewell Address by George Washington, declining third term as President.
1797 (March 4) John Adams inaugurated as 2d President of the United States.
1798 (Jan. 8) Amendment 11 to U.S. Constitution proclaimed: Provides that state cannot be sued by citizen of another state or country.
1798 (June 25) Alien Act authorizes President to expel aliens suspected of treasonable activities.
1798 (July 2) George Washington commissioned as commanding general of U.S. Army to prepare for possible war with France.
1798 (July 14) Sedition Act provides fines and jail terms for persons publishing "false, scandalous and malicious" writing about the President or U.S. government.
1798 (Nov. 16) Kentucky Resolution by Thomas Jefferson adopted by state legislature declaring Alien and Sedition Acts unconstitutional.
1798 (Nov. 20) In undeclared naval war with France, French capture U.S. schooner *Retaliation* (former French *La Croyable*); sea battles continue into 1800.
1798 (Dec. 24) Virginia Resolution by James Madison passed by state legislature declaring Alien and Sedition Acts unconstitutional.
1800 (Nov. 1) President John Adams moves into White House in Washington, D.C.
1800 (Nov. 21) Congress meets in Washington, D.C., for first time.
1801 (March 4) Thomas Jefferson inaugurated as 3d President of the United States after constitutional crisis caused by tie in electoral votes between Jefferson and Aaron Burr.
1801–05 Tripoli War between U.S. and North African pirates; ends when U.S. agrees to pay tribute.
1802 (March 16) U.S. Military Academy at West Point established by act of Congress.
1803 (Feb. 24) Supreme Court first declares act of Congress unconstitutional in *Marbury* v. *Madison.*

1803 (March 1) Ohio becomes 17th state.
1803 (April 30) Louisiana Purchase: U.S. pays about $15 million to France for vast territory nearly doubling size of U.S.
1804 (July 11) Vice President Aaron Burr fatally wounds Alexander Hamilton in duel at Weehawken, N.J.
1804 (Sept. 25) Amendment 12 to U.S. Constitution proclaimed: Provides that President and Vice President should be voted on separately by electors to prevent recurrence of tie vote between Jefferson and Burr in election of 1800.
1804–06 Lewis and Clark explore Missouri River and Pacific Northwest.
1807 (Aug. 17) Robert Fulton's steamboat *Clermont* begins first successful voyage up Hudson River.
1807 (Sept. 1) Aaron Burr acquitted of treason in jury trial on charges of plotting to build western empire.
1807 (Dec. 22) Embargo Act stops all U.S. trade with foreign nations to avoid conflict with Britain and France during Napoleonic wars.
1808 (Jan. 1) Importation of slaves forbidden by act of Congress urged by President Jefferson.
1809 (March 4) James Madison inaugurated as 4th President of the United States.
1810 (Oct. 27) Annexation of West Florida from Spain proclaimed by President Madison.
1811 (Nov. 7) Battle of Tippecanoe: Gen. William Henry Harrison defeats Shawnee Prophet in major Indian fight in Indiana Territory.
1812 (April 30) Louisiana becomes 18th state.
1812 (June 18) Declaration of war on Britain approved by Congress after many incidents of British interference with U.S. ships.
1812 (Aug. 16) Detroit surrendered by Gen. William Hull to Canadian-Indian army.
1813 (Sept. 10) Battle of Lake Erie: Capt. Oliver Perry defeats British lake squadron; reports, "We have met the enemy and they are ours."
1814 (March 27) Battle of Horseshoe Bend: Gen. Andrew Jackson defeats Creek Indians (in what is now Alabama).
1814 (Aug. 24–25) Washington, D.C., captured and burned by British.
1814 (Dec. 24) Treaty of Ghent signed to end War of 1812, with no gains for either side.
1815 (Jan. 8) Battle of New Orleans: Gen. Andrew Jackson severely defeats larger British army; unaware that peace treaty had already been signed.
1815 Barbary pirate states of North Africa defeated by U.S. fleet led by Capt. Stephen Decatur, ending U.S. tribute to pirates.
1816 (April 10) Second Bank of the United States chartered.
1816 (Dec. 11) Indiana becomes 19th state.
1817 (March 4) James Monroe inaugurated as 5th President of the United States.
1817 (April 29) Disarmament of Great Lakes and Canadian border initiated by Rush-Bagot Agreement between U.S. and Britain.
1817 (Dec. 10) Mississippi becomes 20th state.
1818 (April–May) East Florida captured from Spain by troops under Gen. Andrew Jackson in First Seminole War.
1818 (Oct. 20) Northern boundary of Louisiana Purchase set at 49th parallel in agreement by U.S. and Britain; ratified Jan. 19, 1819.
1818 (Dec. 3) Illinois becomes 21st state.
1819 Panic of 1819 causes many bank failures.
1819 (Feb. 22) Adams-Onís Treaty signed; Spain gives up East Florida and all lands east of Mississippi River for $5 million.
1819 (Dec. 14) Alabama becomes 22d state.

FROM MISSOURI COMPROMISE THROUGH CIVIL WAR: 1820–1865

1820 (March 3) Missouri Compromise approved by Congress to exclude slavery from territory north of 36°30′ latitude, with exception of Missouri to be admitted as slave state.
1820 (March 15) Maine becomes 23d state.
1821 (Aug. 10) Missouri becomes 24th state.
1823 (Dec. 2) Monroe Doctrine warns European nations against interference in Western Hemisphere.
1825 (March 4) John Quincy Adams inaugurated as

6th President after being elected by House of Representatives because no candidate had majority of electoral votes.
1825 (Oct. 26) Erie Canal opens, connecting Hudson River with Great Lakes.
1828 Democratic Party formed.
1828 First *American Dictionary of the English Language* published by Noah Webster.
1829 (March 4) Andrew Jackson inaugurated as 7th

QUICK QUIZ: What baseball pitcher had the best won-lost percentage in 1951? See page 784.

KEY EVENTS IN AMERICAN HISTORY *(continued)*
President of the United States.

1830 (May 28) Indian Removal Act gives President power to move eastern Indians to land west of the Mississippi River; in next 10 years some 70,000 Indians are forced to move west to reservations.

1831 Mechanical reaper first demonstrated by Cyrus McCormick.

1831 (Aug. 13–23) Slave uprising led by Nat Turner in Virginia; 57 whites and about 100 blacks killed; 20 blacks including Turner executed.

1832 (April 6–Aug. 2) Black Hawk War fought by settlers and Indians along upper Mississippi River.

1832 (July 10) Recharter of U.S. Bank vetoed by President Jackson, who detested bank.

1832 (Dec. 10) Nullification Proclamation issued by President Jackson warning that any effort by South Carolina to leave Union by force would be treason.

1834 Whig Party formed to oppose President Jackson.

1835–43 Seminole War fought between Indians and settlers in Florida.

1836 First state child-labor law by Massachusetts forbids employment of children under 15 in factories.

1836 (Feb. 23–March 6) Siege of the Alamo: 187 Texans and frontiersmen fight to death in San Antonio against 3,000-man Mexican army.

1836 (March 2) Texas declaration of independence adopted at Washington, Texas.

1836 (April 21) Battle of San Jacinto: Gen. Sam Houston defeats Mexicans and captures Mexican Gen. Santa Anna.

1836 (June 15) Arkansas becomes 25th state.

1836 (Oct. 22) Independent Republic of Texas installs Sam Houston as president.

1837 Panic of 1837 strikes nation with bank closings and unemployment.

1837 (Jan. 26) Michigan becomes 26th state.

1837 (March 3) Supreme Court membership increased to nine: Act of Congress adds two associate justices to Court.

1837 (March 4) Martin Van Buren inaugurated as 8th President of the United States.

1837 (Oct. 6) Samuel F. B. Morse files patent for his invention of the telegraph.

1837 (Nov. 7) Murder of abolitionist editor Elijah P. Lovejoy at Alton, Ill., by mob that also destroys his press.

1839 Process of vulcanizing rubber discovered by Charles Goodyear.

1839 Mormons settle Nauvoo, Ill.: Having been driven out of Missouri, about 10,000 Mormons travel to new home, making Nauvoo largest town in Illinois.

1840 (July 4) Independent Treasury Act gives federal government right to care for own funds.

1841 (March 4) William Henry Harrison inaugurated as 9th President of the United States.

1841 (April 6) John Tyler sworn in as 10th President two days after death of Harrison.

1841 (Aug. 9) Webster-Ashburton Treaty signed, settling dispute with Britain over boundary of Maine.

1841 (Aug. 13) Repeal of Independent Treasury Act by Whig-controlled Congress.

1845 (March 3) Florida becomes 27th state.

1845 (March 4) James K. Polk inaugurated as 11th President of the United States.

1845 (Dec. 29) Texas becomes 28th state.

1846 (April 25) Mexican troops attack U.S. soldiers stationed on Rio Grande in Texas.

1846 (May 13) Congress declares war on Mexico; House votes 174–14, Senate 40–2.

1846 (June 15) Oregon Treaty settling boundary with Canada at 49th parallel approved by Senate; becomes effective Aug. 5, 1846.

1846 (Dec. 28) Iowa becomes 29th state.

1847 Mormons found Salt Lake City and establish State of Deseret with Brigham Young as governor.

1847 (Sept. 14) Mexico City captured by U.S. troops led by Gen. Winfield Scott.

1848 (Jan. 24) Gold discovered in California by James W. Marshall at Sutter's Mill.

1848 (Feb. 2) Treaty of Guadalupe Hidalgo ends Mexican War; California and Southwest ceded to U.S. for payment of $15 million.

1848 (May 29) Wisconsin becomes 30th state.

1848 (July 19–20) First women's rights convention: Held at Seneca Falls, N.Y., under leadership of Elizabeth Cady Stanton and Lucretia Coffin Mott.

1849 (March 5) Zachary Taylor inaugurated as 12th President of the United States.

1850 (July 10) Millard Fillmore sworn in as 13th President after death of President Taylor.

1850 (Sept. 9) California becomes 31st state.

1850 (Sept. 9–20) Compromise of 1850 between slavery and antislavery forces in Congress admits California as free state.

1850 (Sept. 18) Fugitive Slave Act requires federal government to capture runaway slaves and punish persons who aid them.

1850 (Sept. 20) Slave trade abolished in District of Columbia by Congress, but slavery allowed to continue.

1852 (March 20) *Uncle Tom's Cabin* by Harriet Beecher Stowe published in Boston; over 1,200,000 copies sold during first two years.

1853 (March 4) Franklin Pierce inaugurated as 14th President of the United States.

1854 (Feb. 28) Republican Party founded at Ripon, Wis.

1854 (March 31) Japan forced to open its ports to U.S. trade by Commodore Matthew Perry.

1854 (May 30) Kansas-Nebraska Act repeals Missouri Compromise; "popular sovereignty" to decide slavery issue in Kansas and Nebraska.

1854 (June 29) Gadsden Purchase by the United States adds southern Arizona and New Mexico from Mexico for $10 million.

1855–56 Warfare in Kansas between slavery and antislavery factions.

1857 (March 4) James Buchanan inaugurated as 15th President of the United States.

1858 (May 11) Minnesota becomes 32d state.

1858 (Aug. 21–Oct. 15) Lincoln-Douglas debates in Illinois race for U.S. Senate; Lincoln loses election but becomes national figure.

1859 (Feb. 14) Oregon becomes 33d state.

1859 (Oct. 16–18) John Brown's raid seizes federal arsenal at Harpers Ferry, Va.

1859 (Dec. 2) John Brown hanged after being found guilty of trying to incite slave revolt.

1860 (Dec. 20) South Carolina secedes from Union, followed by 10 other Southern states in 1861: Miss. Jan. 9, Fla. Jan. 10, Ala. Jan. 11, Ga. Jan. 19, La. Jan. 26, Texas Feb. 23, Va. April 17, Ark. May 6, N.C. May 20, and Tenn. June 8.

1861 (Jan. 29) Kansas becomes 34th state.

1861 (Feb. 8) Confederate States of America organized in convention at Montgomery, Ala.; Jefferson Davis elected provisional president on Feb. 9.

1861 (March 4) Abraham Lincoln inaugurated as 16th President of the United States.

1861 (April 12) Civil War begins as South Carolina troops attack federal Fort Sumter at Charleston, S.C.; fort surrenders on April 14.

1862 (May 20) Homestead Act provides cheap land for settlement of West.

1863 (Jan. 1) Emancipation Proclamation issued by President Lincoln freeing slaves in areas controlled by Confederacy.

1863 (June 20) West Virginia becomes 35th state.

1863 (July 1–3) Battle of Gettysburg: Lee's invasion of Pennsylvania turned back by General Meade's Union army.

1864 (Oct. 31) Nevada becomes 36th state.

1865 (April 9) Lee surrenders at Appomattox Court House, Va., ending Civil War.

1865 (April 14) President Lincoln shot by John Wilkes Booth; dies on April 15.

FROM RECONSTRUCTION TO THE 20TH CENTURY: 1865–1900

1865 (April 15) Andrew Johnson sworn in as 17th President of the United States.

1865 (Dec. 18) Slavery abolished by 13th Amendment to U.S. Constitution.

1866–67 Ku Klux Klan organized; led by ex-Confederate Gen. Nathan B. Forrest.

1867 (March 1) Nebraska becomes 37th state.

1867 (March 2) Reconstruction Act passed over President Johnson's veto organizes Southern states into five military districts.

1867 (Oct. 18) Alaska purchased from Russia for $7.2 million.

1868 (Feb. 24) President Johnson impeached by 126–47 vote in House. After trial in Senate, key vote (May 16) is one short of two-thirds needed for conviction.

1868 (May 30) First Memorial Day honors war dead.

1868 (July 28) Citizenship granted former slaves by 14th Amendment to U.S. Constitution.

1869 First state board of health: Established by act of Massachusetts legislature.

1869 (March 4) Ulysses S. Grant inaugurated as 18th President of the United States.

1869 (May 10) First transcontinental railroad completed with driving of golden spike at Promontory Point, Utah.

1869 (Dec. 10) First law giving women right to vote and hold office in U.S. passed by Wyoming territorial legislature.

1870 First blacks in U.S. Congress: Black U.S. senator and U.S. representative sworn in.

1870 Last four Confederate States restored to Union: Georgia, Mississippi, Virginia, and Texas readmitted; previously 1 had been readmitted in 1866 and 6 in 1868.

1870 (March 30) Deprivation of voting rights because of race, color, or previous servitude prohibited by 15th Amendment to U.S. Constitution.

1871 (Oct. 8–9) Chicago fire destroys $3\frac{1}{2}$ square miles of city; kills 300; 100,000 made homeless.

1873 (Sept. 18) Panic of 1873 triggered by failure of Jay Cooke's banking firm.

1875 Whisky Ring scandals rock President Grant's administration with indictments of 239 persons.

1876 (March 2) Impeachment and resignation of Secretary of War William W. Belknap on bribery charges; Senate later votes to acquit.

1876 (March 10) Telephone invented by Alexander Graham Bell as it carries first words: "Mr. Watson, come here. I want you!"

1876 (June 25) Gen. George A. Custer's troops massacred by Sioux Indians of Chief Crazy Horse and Chief Sitting Bull at Battle of Little Bighorn in Montana.

1876 (Aug. 1) Colorado becomes 38th state.

1876 (Nov. 7) Disputed presidential election causes constitutional crisis.

1877 (March 5) Rutherford B. Hayes inaugurated as 19th President of the United States.

1877 (April 10–24) Reconstruction of South ends as federal troops withdraw from occupation.

1878 (Feb. 28) Bland-Allison Act passed over President Hayes' veto bases monetary system on gold and silver, with silver valued at ratio of 16–1.

1879 (Oct. 19–20) Incandescent electric light invented by Thomas A. Edison at Menlo Park, N.J.

1881 (March 4) James A. Garfield inaugurated as 20th President of the United States.

1881 (July 2) President Garfield shot by assassin in Washington, D.C.; dies on Sept. 19.

1881 (Sept. 20) Chester A. Arthur sworn in as 21st President of the United States.

1882 Standard Oil Trust formed by John D. Rockefeller, controlling 90% of nation's oil refining.

1883 (Jan. 16) Pendleton Act creates basis of present federal civil service system.

1883 (Nov. 18) Standard time zones established by U.S. and Canadian railroads.

1885 (March 4) Grover Cleveland inaugurated as 22d President of the United States.

1886 (May 4) Haymarket Riot: Bomb thrown during anarchist-labor demonstration in Chicago kills 7 policemen, wounds 70.

1886 (Sept. 4) Apache Indian War in Southwest ends with capture of Apache Chief Geronimo.

1886 (Dec. 8) American Federation of Labor (AFL) organized at convention in Columbus, Ohio.

1887 (Feb. 4) Interstate Commerce Act establishes federal regulation of railroads, beginning control of interstate commerce.

1889 (March 4) Benjamin Harrison inaugurated as 23d President of the United States.

1889 (April 22) Oklahoma land rush officially opens former Indian territory to settlement.

1889 (Nov. 2) North Dakota and South Dakota become 39th and 40th states.

1889 (Nov. 8) Montana becomes 41st state.

1889 (Nov. 11) Washington becomes 42d state.

1890 (July 2) Sherman Antitrust Act prohibits industrial monopolies, called trusts; leads to "trust-busting" suits.

1890 (July 3) Idaho becomes 43d state.

1890 (July 10) Wyoming becomes 44th state.

1890 (Dec. 29) Wounded Knee, S.D., massacre by federal troops of 300 captive Sioux Indians ends last Indian war in West.

1892 (July 6) Homestead Massacre: Strikers at Carnegie Steel Co. at Homestead, Pa., fire on strikebreakers, killing 7.

1893 Panic of 1893: Over 15,000 businesses bankrupted.

1893 First successful gasoline-powered automobile built in U.S. by Charles and Frank Duryea at Springfield, Mass.

1893 (March 4) Grover Cleveland inaugurated as 24th President of the United States.

1894 (April 30) Coxey's Army of about 500 unemployed men marches on Washington, D.C., to demand relief.

1894 (June 21–July 20) Pullman Strike: President Cleveland uses federal troops to restore order; federal court issues strike injunction.

1896 Segregation of blacks upheld by "separate but equal" doctrine of Supreme Court in *Plessy* v. *Ferguson* decision.

1896 (Jan. 4) Utah becomes 45th state.

1896 (Aug. 16) Klondike gold rush to Alaska begins with discovery of gold on Bonanza Creek just east of Alaska's border with Canada.

1897 (March 4) William McKinley inaugurated as 25th President of the United States.

1898 (Feb. 15) U.S. battleship *Maine* explodes in harbor of Havana, Cuba, killing 260 of crew.

1898 (April 25) U.S. declares war on Spain, demanding independence of Cuba.

1898 (Aug. 12) Hawaii annexed to U.S.

1898 (Dec. 10) Spanish-American War ends with signing of treaty; Spain frees Cuba, cedes Puerto Rico and Guam islands to U.S., and sells Philippines to U.S. for $20 million.

1899 Wake Island claimed by U.S.

1900 (March 14) Gold Standard Act establishes gold as standard for U.S. currency.

FROM TRUST–BUSTING THROUGH WORLD WAR I: 1901–1918

1901 (Sept. 6) President McKinley shot by assassin in Buffalo, N.Y.; dies on Sept. 14.

1901 (Sept. 14) Theodore Roosevelt sworn in as 26th President of the United States.

1902 First state workmen's compensation law adopted by Maryland.

1902 (March 10) Trust-busting begun by President Roosevelt with suit against J.P. Morgan's Northern Securities Co.

1902 (June 2) First statewide initiative and referendum law adopted by Oregon.

1903 First law limiting workday to 10 hours for women adopted by Oregon.

1903 (May 3) First direct-primary election law adopted by Wisconsin.

1903 (Dec. 17) First airplane flight by Orville and Wilbur Wright at Kitty Hawk, N.C.

1904 (Feb. 23) Panama Canal Zone control acquired by U.S. for $10 million from Panama with ratification of Hay–Bunau-Varilla Treaty.

1906 (April 18) San Francisco earthquake destroys 4 square miles of city; kills 700.

1906 (June 29) Panama Canal Act authorizes construction of canal with locks across Panama.

1906 (June 30) Pure Food and Drug Act provides federal regulation of food and drugs.

1906 (June 30) Meat Inspection Act provides federal regulation of interstate meat-packing industry.

1907 Panic of 1907: Stock market crash and many business failures follow collapse of Knickerbocker Trust Co. in New York.

1907 (Feb. 20) Immigration Act directed against Japanese authorizes President to exclude from U.S. immigrants from any other country.

1907 (Nov. 16) Oklahoma becomes 46th state.

1909 (Jan. 11) First inventory of U.S. natural resources submitted to President Roosevelt by National Conservation Commission.

QUICK QUIZ: Who won the women's giant slalom in the 1984 winter olympics? See page 854.

KEY EVENTS IN AMERICAN HISTORY (continued)

1909 (March 4) **William Howard Taft inaugurated** as 27th President of the United States.

1909 **First Model T car** manufactured by Henry Ford using assembly line.

1911 **First state welfare law** for mothers with dependent children adopted by Illinois.

1911 (May 15) **Standard Oil Co. of New Jersey** ordered dissolved by Supreme Court in antitrust suit against Rockefeller-owned company.

1912 **Massachusetts adopts first minimum-wage law.**

1912 (Jan. 6) **New Mexico** becomes 47th state.

1912 (Feb. 14) **Arizona** becomes 48th state.

1913 Feb. 25) **Federal income tax** authorized by 16th Amendment to U.S. Constitution.

1913 (March 4) **Woodrow Wilson inaugurated** as 28th President of the United States.

1913 (May 31) **Popular election of U.S. senators** required by 17th Amendment to U.S. Constitution.

1913 (Dec. 23) **Federal Reserve Act** reorganizes national banking system.

1914 (Aug. 15) **Panama Canal opened** to first crossing by ship.

1914 (Sept. 26) **Federal Trade Commission** established to regulate interstate commerce.

1915 **U.S. population reaches 100 million.**

1916 (March 15) **U.S. troops invade Mexico** to pursue revolutionary Gen. Pancho Villa; withdraw on Feb. 5, 1917.

1917 (Jan. 17) **Virgin Islands purchase** by U.S. from Denmark for $25 million ratified; becomes effective on March 31.

1917 (Feb. 3) **U.S. breaks relations with Germany** because of its sinking of U.S. ships.

1917 (April 6) **U.S. declares war on Germany;** first U.S. troops land in France on June 26; over 2 million soldiers sent to France before armistice ends World War I on Nov. 11, 1918.

1918 **First official U.S. airmail flights:** Route flown between Washington, D.C., and New York City.

FROM PROHIBITION TO THE GREAT DEPRESSION: 1919–1932

1919 (Jan. 29) **Prohibition** of sale and manufacture of alcoholic beverages by 18th Amendment to U.S. Constitution; goes into effect Jan. 16, 1920.

1919 (Feb. 25) **First state gasoline tax:** Established by act of Oregon legislature.

1919 (June 28) **Versailles Treaty signed** embodying peace settlement for World War I and establishing League of Nations.

1919 (Oct. 2) **President Wilson paralyzed** by stroke, making him invalid for rest of life.

1919 (Nov. 19) **Rejection of Versailles Treaty and League of Nations** by U.S. Senate.

1919–20 **Mass arrests** of thousands of anarchists, communists, and labor agitators by agents of U.S. Department of Justice; hundreds deported to Russia.

1920 **First commercial radio** begun by KDKA in Pittsburgh and WWJ in Detroit.

1920 **U.S. becomes urban nation:** For first time more than half of U.S. population lives in urban instead of rural areas.

1920 **Grand Canyon National Park established** in Arizona, including much of spectacular Colorado River canyon.

1920 (Aug. 26) **Women win right to vote** with 19th Amendment to U.S. Constitution.

1920–21 **Business recession** with high unemployment and some 20,000 business failures.

1921 (March 4) **Warren G. Harding inaugurated** as 29th President of the United States.

1921 (May 19) **Immigration quotas set:** Congress acts after nearly 1 million immigrate to U.S. in year.

1921 (June 10) **Budget and Accounting Act** creates General Accounting Office and Bureau of the Budget.

1922 (Feb. 6) **Naval arms-limitation pact** signed by U.S., Britain, France, Italy, and Japan, scrapping many existing warships.

1923 (Aug. 3) **Calvin Coolidge sworn in** as 30th President following death on Aug. 2 of President Warren G. Harding in San Francisco.

1923 (Oct. 25) **Investigation of Teapot Dome** scandals of Harding administration begun by U.S. Senate, leading to conviction of many former officials for bribery and conspiracy.

1923–26 **Ku Klux Klan reign of terror** against minority groups reaches peak with many lynchings.

1925 **Clarence Birdseye invents quick-frozen food process** to preserve food.

1925 (July 21) **Evolution trial:** John Scopes convicted in Dayton, Tenn., of teaching evolution; defended by Clarence Darrow; prosecuted by William Jennings Bryan.

1925 (Dec. 17) **Court-martial convicts Brig. Gen. William (Billy) Mitchell** of unmilitary conduct in criticizing superiors for ignoring importance of military air power.

1926 (March 16) **First liquid-fuel rocket successfully launched** by Dr. Robert H. Goddard near Auburn, Mass.; invention later makes space travel possible.

1927 (May 21) **First solo nonstop flight across Atlantic** completed by Charles A. Lindbergh; lands in Paris 33½ hours after taking off from Long Island, N.Y.

1927 (Aug. 23) **Sacco-Vanzetti case:** Anarchists Nicola Sacco and Bartolomeo Vanzetti executed in Charlestown, Mass., for 1920 murder; protesters claim conviction was on political grounds rather than on evidence.

1928 (Aug. 27) **War outlawed** by Kellogg-Briand Peace Pact; signed by U.S. and France; 62 nations eventually sign.

1929 (Feb. 20) **American Samoa** organized as territory of United States.

1929 (March 4) **Herbert Hoover inaugurated** as 31st President of the United States.

1929 (Oct. 24) **Great Depression** triggered by stock market crash; unemployed number 12 million; more than 37,000 banks, corporations, and other businesses fail by 1931.

1932 (Feb. 2) **Reconstruction Finance Corporation (RFC)** established to loan $2 billion to businesses, banks, and farm credit groups.

1932 (March 1) **Kidnap-murder** of son of aviation hero Charles A. Lindbergh at Hopewell, N.J.; after sensational trial, Bruno Richard Hauptmann is convicted of crime and executed in April 1936.

1932 (July 22) **Federal Home Loan Bank Act** provides $125 million for first federal mortgage loans.

1932 (July 28) **Bonus army** of unemployed veterans, who had marched on Washington seeking immediate bonus payment, dispersed by federal troops and tanks.

FROM THE NEW DEAL THROUGH WORLD WAR II: 1933–1945

1933 (Feb. 6) **"Lame Duck" 20th Amendment** to U.S. Constitution changes date of presidential inaugurations after 1933 to January 20.

1933 (March 4) **Franklin Delano Roosevelt inaugurated** as 32d President of the United States.

1933 (March 6–9) **Bank holiday** proclaimed by President Roosevelt with all bank operations halted; only financially sound banks allowed to open after holiday; measure taken to stop hoarding of money by persons fearing bank failures.

1933 (March 9–June 16) **Hundred Days** special session of 73d Congress passes New Deal legislation to provide relief to banks, manufacturers, farmers, labor, and unemployed.

1933 (Dec. 5) **Prohibition repealed** by 21st Amendment to U.S. Constitution.

1934 "Dust bowl" created in Midwest by extended drought and lack of conservation measures.

1935 (May 27) **Supreme Court** declares National Recovery Act (NRA) unconstitutional.

1935 (Aug. 14) **Social Security Act** provides first federal-state unemployment and old-age insurance.

1935 (Aug. 31) **Neutrality Act** provides measures intended to keep U.S. from becoming involved in Italian-Ethiopian War.

1935 (Nov. 9) **CIO labor organization** formed; begins organizing unions in auto and steel industries using "sit-down" strikes.

1936 (Jan. 6) **Supreme Court** rules Agricultural Adjustment Act (AAA) unconstitutional.

1937 (May 1) **Neutrality Act** adopted to prevent U.S. involvement in Spanish civil war.

1937 (July 22) **Court-packing legislation** killed by U.S. Senate; had been sought by President Roosevelt to liberalize Supreme Court.

1938 (June 25) **Wages and Hours Law** provides mini-

mum wages of 40¢ an hour and maximum workweek of 40 hours (effective in 1940); labor by children under 16 outlawed.

1939 (April 20) First commercial TV broadcasts by Radio Corporation of America.

1939 (Aug. 2) Hatch Act forbids federal employees below policy level from taking part in political campaigns.

1939 (Sept. 5) Neutrality of U.S. in World War II proclaimed by President Roosevelt (Germany had invaded Poland on Sept. 1).

1939 (Nov. 4) New Neutrality Act permits "cash and carry" sales of arms to belligerents.

1940 (Sept. 3) U.S. gives Britain 50 destroyers in exchange for military bases in West Indies and Newfoundland.

1940 (Sept. 16) First U.S. peacetime draft for compulsory military service enacted.

1941 (March 11) Lend-Lease Act enables President to supply materials to Britain and Soviet Union.

1941 (Aug. 9–12) Atlantic Charter of postwar goals set in shipboard meetings off Newfoundland by President Roosevelt and British Prime Minister Churchill.

1941 (Dec. 7) Japanese bomb Pearl Harbor naval base in Hawaii.

1941 (Dec. 8) Declaration of war on Japan approved by Congress with only one dissenting vote.

1941 (Dec. 11) Germany and Italy declare war on U.S.

1942 (Aug. 13) Secret Manhattan Project to develop atomic bomb initiated; first nuclear chain reaction achieved by Enrico Fermi in Chicago on Dec. 2.

1944 (June 6) D-Day landing by U.S. troops on Normandy coast of German-occupied France.

1944 (June 22) GI Bill of Rights authorizes educational and other benefits for World War II veterans.

1945 (Feb. 4-11) Big Three meeting at Yalta in the Soviet Union of Roosevelt, Churchill, and Stalin sets postwar plans, including formation of United Nations.

1945 (April 12) Harry S. Truman sworn in as 33d President upon death of President Roosevelt at Warm Springs, Ga.

1945 (May 8) V-E Day, formal end of war in Europe; Germany had signed unconditional surrender on May 7.

1945 (June 26) United Nations Charter signed in San Francisco by delegates of 50 nations.

1945 (July 16) First atomic bomb successfully exploded near Alamogordo, N.M.

1945 (July 17–Aug. 2) Potsdam Conference in Germany attended by Truman, Stalin, and Churchill (succeeded by Clement Attlee) decides on four-power rule of Germany and issues surrender ultimatum to Japan.

1945 (Aug. 6) Atomic bomb dropped on Hiroshima; on Japan's refusal to surrender, another bomb is dropped on Nagasaki on Aug. 9.

1945 (Aug. 14) Japan agrees to surrender.

1945 (Sept. 2) V-J Day: formal surrender of Japan aboard battleship USS *Missouri* at Tokyo.

FROM COLD WAR TO PRESIDENT KENNEDY'S ASSASSINATION: 1946–1963

1946 (March 5) Communist "Iron Curtain" has descended across Europe, former British Prime Minister Churchill warns in commencement address at Fulton, Mo.

1946 (July 4) Philippines granted independence.

1947 (March 12) Truman Doctrine announced by President to resist Soviet aggression and subversion with aid for Greece and Turkey.

1947 (June 5) Marshall Plan proposed by Secretary of State George C. Marshall calling for U.S. aid to rebuild Europe and preserve its freedom; aid begun with enactment of European Recovery Program on April 3, 1948.

1947 (June 23) Taft-Hartley Act passed by Congress over President Truman's veto bans closed shop and places other restrictions on labor unions.

1947 (July 18) Pacific Islands Trust Territory placed under U.S. administration by UN.

1947 (July 26) Defense Department created to coordinate U.S. military services.

1948 (June) Berlin airlift begun by U.S. and Britain, carrying 2 million tons of supplies to West Berlin in 16 months to break Soviet blockade of city.

1949 (April 4) North Atlantic Treaty creating NATO defense force signed by U.S. and 11 other nations.

1949 (Oct. 21) U.S. Communist Party's 11 top leaders sentenced to prison for advocating overthrow of U.S. government.

1950 (Jan. 21) Alger Hiss, former State Department official, convicted of perjury for denying membership in communist spy ring.

1950 (June 27) Korean War: President Truman orders U.S. forces to aid South Korea, invaded by communist North Korea on June 25.

1950 (Aug. 1) Guam organized as U.S. territory.

1950 (Aug. 27) U.S. railroads seized by President Truman to prevent general strike; returned to private ownership on May 23, 1952.

1950 (Dec. 11) Supreme Court rules that under 5th Amendment no one can be forced to testify against himself.

1951 (March 1) President limited to two terms by 22d Amendment to U.S. Constitution.

1951 (April 11) Gen. Douglas MacArthur relieved of command in Korea by President Truman for disregarding orders (MacArthur had sought to extend war into communist China).

1951 (Sept. 4) First transcontinental TV broadcast by President Truman at Japanese peace-treaty conference in San Francisco.

1952 (April 8) Nation's steel mills seized by President Truman to prevent strike; ruled as unconstitutional by Supreme Court on June 2.

1952 (July 25) Puerto Rico becomes self-governing commonwealth of U.S.

1952 (Nov. 1) First hydrogen bomb exploded by U.S. at Enewetak atoll in Pacific.

1953 (Jan. 20) Dwight D. Eisenhower inaugurated as 34th President of the United States.

1953 (June 19) Execution of Julius and Ethel Rosenberg at Ossining, N.Y., convicted of giving atomic secrets to Soviet Union.

1953 (July 27) Korean War armistice signed at Panmunjom, Korea, ending fighting.

1954 (Jan. 21) First atomic-powered submarine, USS *Nautilus,* launched at Groton, Conn.

1954 (April 22–June 17) Televised public hearings of charges by Sen. Joseph McCarthy of communist subversion in U.S. Army; U.S. Senate votes to condemn McCarthy on Dec. 2.

1954 (May 17) Racial segregation in public schools banned by Supreme Court.

1954 (Sept. 8) Southeast Asia Treaty Organization (SEATO) defense pact signed by U.S.

1955 (Feb. 12) President Eisenhower sends U.S. military advisers to train South Vietnam's army in Indochina war.

1955 (July 18–23) Summit meeting of U.S., Britain, Soviet Union, and France at Geneva, Switzerland, confirms independence of East and West Germany.

1955 (Dec. 1) Bus boycott in Montgomery, Ala., begun by blacks under leadership of Rev. Martin Luther King Jr.; leads to Supreme Court ruling on Nov. 13, 1956, against segregation on buses.

1955 (Dec. 5) AFL and CIO merge, with George Meany becoming president.

1956 (June 29) Federal-Aid Highways Act provides $32.5 billion to build 41,000-mile interstate highway system over next 13 years.

1957 (Sept. 24) President Eisenhower orders federal troops to Little Rock, Ark., to protect black students desegregating high school.

1958 (Jan. 31) *Explorer I,* first U.S. space satellite, launched from Cape Canaveral, Fla.

1958 (Dec. 10) First jet service in U.S. begun by National Airlines on New York–Miami run.

1959 (Jan. 3) Alaska becomes 49th state.

1959 (July 21) First atomic merchant ship, *Savannah,* launched at Camden, N.J.

1959 (Aug. 21) Hawaii becomes 50th state.

1959 (Sept. 15–27) Summit meeting at Camp David, Md., between President Eisenhower and Soviet Premier Nikita Khrushchev calls for "peaceful coexistence."

1959 (Dec. 1) Antarctica Treaty signed by U.S. and 11 other nations guaranteeing continent's neutrality.

1960 (Jan. 19) U.S. and Japan sign mutual-defense treaty for military assistance.

KEY EVENTS IN AMERICAN HISTORY *(continued)*

1960 (May 1) U.S. U-2 spy plane shot down over Soviet Union.

1960 (May 16) Summit conference in Paris broken off by Khrushchev over U-2 incident despite apology by President Eisenhower.

1961 (Jan. 3) President Eisenhower ends diplomatic relations with communist Cuba.

1961 (Jan. 20) John F. Kennedy inaugurated as 35th President of the United States.

1961 (March 1) Peace Corps created by President Kennedy to help developing nations.

1961 (April 3) Washington, D.C., residents given vote for President by 23d Amendment.

1961 (April 17) Unsuccessful Bay of Pigs invasion of Cuba led by U.S. CIA and Cuban exiles with authorization of President Kennedy.

1961 (June 3–4) Summit meeting by Kennedy and Khrushchev at Vienna, Austria, unsuccessfully discusses reunification of Germany.

1961 (Dec. 11) U.S. provides South Vietnam with armed helicopters and crews to fight communists; U.S. forces in Vietnam total 3,200.

1962 (Feb. 20) First U.S. astronaut to orbit Earth: Lt. Col. John H. Glenn Jr.

1962 (May 17) U.S. troops sent to Thailand to prevent possible communist invasion.

1962 (June 27) U.S. defense of Taiwan against attack by communist China pledged by President Kennedy.

1962 (Oct. 22–28) Cuban missile crisis: President Kennedy imposes naval and air blockade on Cuba, forcing Soviet Union to withdraw nuclear missiles.

1963 (June 17) Bible reading or prayers cannot be required in public schools, Supreme Court rules.

1963 (Aug. 28) Black equal-rights demonstration in Washington by 200,000 persons led by Rev. Martin Luther King Jr.

1963 (Aug. 30) Hot-line telephone set up between White House and Kremlin.

1963 (Sept. 14) First quintuplets in U.S. born to Mrs. Andrew Fischer in Aberdeen, S.D.

1963 (Oct. 10) Treaty bans atomic tests in atmosphere; signed by U.S., Britain, and Soviet Union.

1963 (Nov. 22) President Kennedy assassinated in Dallas, Texas, by former U.S. marine Lee Harvey Oswald.

ERA OF VIETNAM WAR, WATERGATE, AND ENERGY PROBLEMS: 1963–1983

1963 (Nov. 22) Lyndon B. Johnson sworn in as 36th President of the United States.

1964 (Feb. 4) Poll tax outlawed by 24th Amendment to U.S. Constitution.

1964 (July 2) Civil Rights Act forbids racial discrimination in hotels, motels, and restaurants, and by labor unions and businesses engaged in interstate commerce.

1964 (Aug. 7) Gulf of Tonkin Resolution gives President authority "to prevent further aggression" in Vietnam after reported North Vietnamese attack on U.S. destroyers on Aug. 2–4; first U.S. bombings of Vietnam on Aug. 5.

1964 (Aug. 20) War on Poverty program enacted.

1965 (April 28) U.S. Marines land in Dominican Republic to prevent communist takeover.

1965 (June 28) First ground combat by U.S. troops in Vietnam authorized by President Johnson; U.S. forces in Vietnam, 74,000.

1965 (Aug. 6) Voting Rights Act gives government power to force local communities to register blacks and allow them to vote.

1965 (Aug. 11–16) Riots by blacks in Watts area of Los Angeles result in 35 deaths.

1966 (May 30) First U.S. Moon landing by unmanned spaceship.

1966 (July 1) Medicare goes into effect, with medical insurance for persons 65 or older.

1967 (Jan. 27) Space Treaty signed banning military use of nuclear weapons in space.

1967 (Feb. 23) Presidential succession established by 25th Amendment to Constitution.

1967 (June 23–25) Summit meeting at Glassboro, N.J., by President Johnson and Soviet Premier Aleksei Kosygin.

1967 (July 23–30) Detroit riots by blacks put down by federal troops and National Guardsmen; 40 killed, more than 2,000 injured.

1968 U.S. population reaches 200 million.

1968 (Jan. 23) North Koreans seize USS *Pueblo* crew as spies; release them on Dec. 22.

1968 (April 4) Assassination of Rev. Martin Luther King Jr. in Memphis, Tenn.; followed by racial riots in more than 100 cities.

1968 (June 5) Sen. Robert F. Kennedy shot in Los Angeles; dies on June 6.

1968 (June 26) Iwo Jima and Bonin Islands returned to Japan by U.S.

1968 (July 1) Treaty on Nonproliferation of Nuclear Weapons signed by U.S., Britain, and Soviet Union; effective on March 5, 1970.

1968 (Aug. 26–30) Anti–Vietnam War demonstration during Democratic national convention in Chicago put down by police and troops.

1969 (Jan. 20) Richard M. Nixon inaugurated as 37th President of the United States.

1969 (March) U.S. troops in Vietnam reach peak level of 541,500.

1969 (June 8) Plans to reduce U.S. troops in Vietnam announced by President Nixon.

1969 (July 20) First man to walk on Moon: U.S. astronaut Neil Armstrong.

1969 (Oct. 15) Vietnam Moratorium Day brings out many antiwar demonstrators across nation.

1970 (April 30) President Nixon orders U.S. troops into Cambodia.

1970 (May 4) Four Kent State University students killed in Ohio when National Guard fires into war-protest demonstration.

1971 (March 29) Lt. William L. Calley Jr. convicted by court-martial of murder of 22 Vietnamese men, women, and children in 1968 My Lai massacre (Calley freed in 1974 after federal court overturns conviction).

1971 (April 20) Busing to achieve racially balanced schools upheld by Supreme Court.

1971 (May 2–5) Over 13,400 antiwar demonstrators arrested in Washington, D.C.

1971 (June 13) Secret Pentagon Papers study of Vietnam War begins to be published in series in *New York Times* and *Washington Post;* federal government obtains injunction on June 15 against further publication, but Supreme Court on June 30 throws out injunction.

1971 (July 5) Voting age lowered to 18 by 26th Amendment to U.S. Constitution.

1971 (Aug. 15) Freeze on wages and prices to combat inflation announced by President Nixon.

1972 (Feb. 21–28) Visit to communist China by President Nixon reverses U.S. policy on China.

1972 (May 15) Okinawa and Ryukyu Islands returned to Japan after 27-year U.S. rule.

1972 (May 15) Alabama Gov. George Wallace wounded and paralyzed from waist down in attempted assassination at Laurel, Md.; Arthur H. Bremmer convicted on Aug. 4 of attempted assassination and sentenced to 63 years in prison.

1972 (May 22–30) Summit meeting in Moscow between President Nixon and Soviet leader Leonid I. Brezhnev achieves first agreement limiting production of atomic weapons; ratified by U.S. Senate on Aug. 3.

1972 (June 17) Watergate offices of Democratic National Committee in Washington, D.C., secretly wiretapped; police arrest five men in act of burglarizing offices; on June 22, Nixon tells press conference, "There is no involvement by the White House."

1972 (June 17–23) Hurricane Agnes rakes East Coast from Florida to New York; storm and floods kill 122, cause $2.1 billion in damages.

1972 (June 19) Government practice of wiretapping without court order is illegal, Supreme Court rules.

1972 (July 31) Democratic vice-presidential candidate withdraws: Sen. Thomas F. Eagleton quits as candidate after disclosure he had been treated for psychiatric problems; former Peace Corps director Sargent Shriver chosen to succeed him on Democratic ticket on Aug. 5.

1972 (Sept. 15) First Watergate indictments: Seven persons indicted for break-in at Democratic national headquarters; later, White House counsel John Dean III tells Senate committee that President Nixon congratulated him on that day for keeping indictments from reaching higher in Nixon administration.

1972 (Nov. 7) President Nixon wins election to second term by landslide 60.7% of vote.

1973 (Jan. 28) Cease-fire ends U.S. participation in Vietnam War; last troops leave Vietnam on March 29.

1973 (Jan. 30) Watergate burglary trial ends with conviction of seven men; two were former officials of Committee to Reelect the President and one a former White House consultant.

1973 (Feb. 7) Senate Watergate investigating committee established by unanimous vote of Senate; leads to conviction of three cabinet officers and Nixon's two chief White House aides.

1973 (Feb. 27) Siege of Wounded Knee, S.D., begun by Indians protesting treatment by government; two Indians killed in gunfights with federal officers; siege ends on May 8.

1973 (May 11) Pentagon Papers espionage trial of Dr. Daniel Ellsberg dismissed by federal judge after disclosure that White House agents committed burglary in seeking evidence.

1973 (June 16–24) Summit meeting between President Nixon and Soviet leader Brezhnev in U.S. achieves nine agreements for U.S.-Soviet cooperation.

1973 (July 1) Congress orders halt to U.S. bombing of Cambodia and all U.S. military action in Indochina by Aug. 15.

1973 (July 16) Existence of White House tapes revealed: Witness tells Senate Watergate hearing that conversations in White House have been taped since 1970; after long court battle, President Nixon gives up tapes to investigators; tapes show President took part in effort to cover up Watergate scandals.

1973 (Oct. 10) Vice President Spiro Agnew resigns, accepts conviction for income-tax evasion to avoid trial on charges of accepting bribes.

1973 (Oct. 17) Arab nations cut oil exports to U.S. in retaliation for U.S. aid to Israel.

1973 (Nov. 7) Limitations on President's war-making powers voted by Congress over veto.

1973 (Nov. 25) Emergency restrictions on use of fuel and energy announced by President Nixon.

1973 (Dec. 6) Gerald R. Ford sworn in as Vice President: first Vice President appointed under 25th Amendment to U.S. Constitution.

1973 (Dec. 8) President Nixon discloses tax records; he paid less than $6,000 in income taxes for 1970–73 on income over $1 million.

1974 (Feb. 4) Nation's first political kidnapping: Patricia Hearst, 19-year-old granddaughter of publisher William Randolph Hearst, taken from apartment in Berkeley, Calif.; she later joins captors in terrorist activities and eludes FBI for 19 months until surrendering on Sept. 18, 1975; jury finds her guilty of bank robbery in 1976; sentenced to 7 years in prison.

1974 (July 24) U.S. Supreme Court rules President Nixon must turn over White House tapes and documents to special Watergate prosecutor.

1974 (Aug. 9) President Nixon resigns to avoid impeachment and removal by Congress because of role in Watergate scandals.

1974 (Aug. 9) Gerald R. Ford becomes 38th President of the United States.

1974 (Sept. 8) Full pardon granted to Nixon by President Ford.

1974 (Sept. 16) Conditional amnesty plan for Vietnam War draft evaders and deserters announced by President Ford.

1974 (Oct. 15) Presidential election campaign public financing law signed by President Ford.

1974 (Nov. 23–24) Summit meeting in Vladivostok, Soviet Union; Ford and Brezhnev agree in principle to "put cap on arms race."

1975 (Jan. 1) Watergate cover-up convictions: After 3-month trial, jury finds guilty President Nixon's top aides H.R. Haldeman and John D. Ehrlichman, and former Attorney General John N. Mitchell.

1975 (May) Unemployment rises to 9.2% with 8.5 million Americans out of work; highest unemployment rate since Great Depression.

1975 (May 7) End of Vietnam War Era announced by President Ford one week after South Vietnam surrenders to communists.

1975 (May 14–15) *Mayaguez* incident: U.S. Marines rescue U.S. freighter from Cambodians.

1975 (July 1) New York City financial crisis causes layoff of 40,000 city workers.

1975 (July 17) U.S. and Soviet spaceships link up for Apollo-Soyuz handshake in space.

1975 (Aug. 1) President Ford signs Helsinki pact endorsing post-World War II European boundaries and endorsing human rights.

1975 (Sept. 5 and 22) Two assassination attempts on President Ford made in California.

1975 (Dec. 20) Vietnam refugee program completed with resettlement of 130,000 in U.S.

1976 U.S. military service academies for first time admit women for officer training.

1976 (June 5) 300-foot-high Teton Dam collapses in Idaho; kills 69; estimated damage $1 billion.

1976 (June 20) U.S. closes last military bases in Thailand at request of Thai government.

1976 (July 4) U.S. celebrates 200th birthday with parades, picnics, fireworks, and prayers.

1976 (Sept. 23) First face-to-face presidential public debate in history held on TV between incumbent President Ford and challenger, Democratic presidential candidate Jimmy Carter.

1976 (Oct. 4) Death penalty for murder upheld by Supreme Court; lifts stay that blocked state executions for 10 years.

1977 (Jan. 20) Jimmy Carter inaugurated as 39th President of the United States.

1977 (March 1) U.S. extends coastal limit to 200 miles for control of fishing.

1977 (June 20) Trans-Alaska $7.7 billion pipeline begins carrying oil 789 miles from Prudhoe Bay oil field to Valdez, Alaska.

1977 (Sept. 7) President Carter signs Panama treaties, agreeing to turn over Panama Canal to Panama on Dec. 31, 1999; ratified April 18, 1978.

1977 (Oct. 1) U.S. Department of Energy becomes 12th cabinet-level executive department, with James R. Schlesinger as first U.S. secretary of energy.

1978 (Jan. 27) Nation's GNP (gross national product) reaches $2 trillion mark: economy first reached $1 trillion level in 1972.

1978 (June 6) California voters begin tax revolt; Referendum approves Proposition 13, cutting local property taxes in state from $12 billion to $5 billion; sets off nationwide efforts to put lids on federal, state, and local government spending.

1978 (Dec. 1) National Park System doubled: President Carter adds 56 million acres of Alaskan land, designating 17 new national monuments.

1979 (Jan. 1) U.S. and China establish diplomatic relations: For first time since communists seized power in China in 1949, U.S. and China exchange full ambassadors; at same time U.S. breaks formal relations with nationalist Chinese government on Taiwan.

1979 (Feb. 5) U.S. population reaches 220 million: Mark registered by census clock in Washington, D.C.

1979 (Feb. 12) President Carter asks for voluntary energy conservation: Cut-off of oil imports from Iran brings gasoline shortages to nation in next several months.

1979 (March 28) First major atomic accident in U.S.: Malfunction in reactor at Three Mile Island near Harrisburg, Pa., releases radioactive steam and starts meltdown of uranium fuel rods.

1979 (June 8) MX missile system approved: President Carter gives go-ahead to $30 billion plan to deploy about 200 new intercontinental missiles underground.

1979 (June 13) Sioux Indians win $100 million in land claim: Court awards compensation for land confiscated in 1877.

1979 (Oct. 1) Panama Canal Zone returned to Panama: U.S. turns over control of 553-square-mile area that had been under American jurisdiction since 1904.

1979 (Oct. 17) U.S. Department of Education approved in legislation signed by President Carter; becomes 13th cabinet-level department of federal government; Shirley M. Hufstedler appointed as first secretary of education.

1979 (Oct. 23) Emergency gasoline rationing approved: Congress gives President power to invoke rationing when necessary.

1981 (Jan. 20) Ronald Reagan inaugurated as 40th President of the United States.

1981 (Aug. 13) Reagan's New Economic Program becomes law; provides 25% income-tax cuts for 1981–84.

1982-83 Worst Recession since 1930s: U.S. unemployment soars to 10.8% of labor force with over 10 million out of work.

1984 Economic Recovery: GNP (gross national product) increases by 6.9%—highest rise since 1951.

1985 For events of 1985, see pages 7–27.

QUICK QUIZ: Who won the Wimbledon men's singles championship in 1939? See page 865.

DECLARATION OF INDEPENDENCE

Although the colonists had been openly fighting the British since the battles of Lexington and Concord in 1775, many members of the Continental Congress still sought a compromise. However, such patriots as John Hancock, John Adams, and Samuel Adams demanded complete independence from Britain. On June 7, 1776, Richard Henry Lee of Virginia called for a resolution on independence.

The actual drafting of the document was entrusted to Thomas Jefferson.

On July 4, 1776, Congress adopted the Declaration of Independence.

In Congress, July 4, 1776,
The unanimous Declaration of the thirteen united States of America,

When in the Course of human events, it becomes necessary for one people to dissolve the political bands which have connected them with another, and to assume among the Powers of the earth, the separate and equal station to which the Laws of Nature and of Nature's God entitle them, a decent respect to the opinions of mankind requires that they should declare the causes which impel them to the separation.

We hold these truths to be self-evident, that all men are created equal, that they are endowed by their Creator with certain unalienable Rights, that among these are Life, Liberty and the pursuit of Happiness. That to secure these rights, Governments are instituted among Men, deriving their just powers from the consent of the governed. That whenever any Form of Government becomes destructive of these ends, it is the Right of the People to alter or to abolish it, and to institute new Government, laying its foundation on such principles and organizing its powers in such form, as to them shall seem most likely to effect their Safety and Happiness. Prudence, indeed, will dictate that Governments long established should not be changed for light and transient causes; and accordingly all experience hath shown, that mankind are more disposed to suffer, while evils are sufferable, than to right themselves by abolishing the forms to which they are accustomed. But when a long train of abuses and usurpations, pursuing invariably the same Object evinces a design to reduce them under absolute Despotism, it is their right, it is their duty, to throw off such Government, and to provide new Guards for their future security.—Such has been the patient sufferance of these Colonies; and such is now the necessity which constrains them to alter their former Systems of Government. The history of the present King of Great Britain is a history of repeated injuries and usurpations, all having in direct object the establishment of an absolute Tyranny over these States. To prove this, let Facts be submitted to a candid world.

He has refused his Assent to Laws, the most wholesome and necessary for the public good.

He has forbidden his Governors to pass Laws of immediate and pressing importance, unless suspended in their operation till his Assent should be obtained; and when so suspended, he has utterly neglected to attend to them.

He has refused to pass other Laws for the accommodation of large districts of people, unless those people would relinquish the right of Representation in the Legislature, a right inestimable to them and formidable to tyrants only.

He has called together legislative bodies at places unusual, uncomfortable, and distant from the depository of their Public Records, for the sole purpose of fatiguing them into compliance with his measures.

He has dissolved Representative Houses repeatedly, for opposing with manly firmness his invasions on the rights of the people.

He has refused for a long time, after such dissolutions, to cause others to be elected; whereby the Legislative Powers, incapable of Annihilation, have returned to the People at large for their exercise; the State remaining in the mean time exposed to all the dangers of invasion from without, and convulsions within.

He has endeavoured to prevent the population of these States; for that purpose obstructing the Laws of Naturalization of Foreigners; refusing to pass others to migration hither, and raising the conditions of new Appropriations of Lands.

He has obstructed the Administration of Justice, by refusing his Assent to Laws for establishing Judiciary Powers.

He has made Judges dependent on his Will alone, for the tenure of their offices, and the amount and payment of their salaries.

He has erected a multitude of New Offices,

DECLARATION OF INDEPENDENCE *(continued)*
and sent hither swarms of Officers to harass our People, and eat out their substance.

He has kept among us, in times of peace, Standing Armies without the Consent of our legislatures.

He has affected to render the Military independent of and superior to the Civil Power.

He has combined with others to subject us to a jurisdiction foreign to our constitution, and unacknowledged by our laws; giving his Assent to their acts of pretended legislation:

For quartering large bodies of armed troops among us:

For protecting them, by a mock Trial, from Punishment for any Murders which they should commit on the Inhabitants of these States:

For cutting off our Trade with all parts of the world:

For imposing taxes on us without our Consent:

For depriving us in many cases, of the benefits of Trial by Jury:

For transporting us beyond Seas to be tried for pretended offences:

For abolishing the free System of English Laws in a neighbouring Province, and establishing therein an Arbitrary government, and enlarging its Boundaries so as to render it at once an example and fit instrument for introducing the same absolute rule into these Colonies:

For taking away our Charters, abolishing our most valuable Laws, and altering fundamentally the Forms of our Governments:

For suspending our own legislature, and declaring themselves invested with Power to legislate for us in all cases whatsoever.

He has abdicated Government here, by declaring us out of his Protection and waging War against us.

He has plundered our seas, ravaged our Coasts, burnt our towns, and destroyed the lives of our people.

He is at this time transporting large armies of foreign mercenaries to complete the works of death, desolation and tyranny, already begun with circumstances of Cruelty & perfidy scarcely paralleled in the most barbarous ages, and totally unworthy the Head of a civilized nation.

He has constrained our fellow Citizens taken Captive on the high Seas to bear Arms against their Country, to become the executioners of their friends and Brethren, or to fall themselves by their Hands.

He has excited domestic insurrections amongst us, and has endeavoured to bring on the inhabitants of our frontiers, the merciless Indian Savages, whose known rule of warfare, is an undistinguished destruction of all ages, sexes and conditions.

In every stage of these Oppressions We have Petitioned for Redress in the most humble terms: Our repeated Petitions have been answered only by repeated injury. A Prince, whose character is thus marked by every act which may define a Tyrant, is unfit to be the ruler of a free People.

Nor have We been wanting in attention to our British brethren. We have warned them from time to time of attempts by their legislature to extend an unwarrantable jurisdiction over us. We have reminded them of the circumstances of our emigration and settlement here. We have appealed to their native justice and magnanimity, and we have conjured them by the ties of our common kindred to disavow these usurpations, which, would inevitably interrupt our connections and correspondence. They too have been deaf to the voice of justice and of consanguinity. We must, therefore, acquiesce in the necessity, which denounces our Separation, and hold them, as we hold the rest of mankind, Enemies in War, in Peace Friends.

We, therefore, the Representatives of the United States of America, in General Congress, Assembled, appealing to the Supreme Judge of the world for the rectitude of our intentions, do, in the Name, and by Authority of the good People of these Colonies, solemnly publish and declare, That these United Colonies are, and of Right ought to be Free and Independent States; that they are Absolved from all Allegiance to the British Crown, and that all political connection between them and the State of Great Britain, is and ought to be totally dissolved; and that as Free and Independent States, they have full Power to levy War, conclude Peace, contract Alliances, establish Commerce, and to do all other Acts and Things which Independent States may of right do. And for the support of this Declaration, with a firm reliance on the protection of Divine Providence, we mutually pledge to each other our Lives, our Fortunes and our sacred Honor.
 John Hancock

New Hampshire
Josiah Bartlett
Wm. Whipple
Matthew Thornton
Massachusetts-Bay
Saml. Adams
John Adams
Robt. Treat Paine
Elbridge Gerry
Rhode Island
Step. Hopkins
William Ellery
Connecticut
Roger Sherman
Sam'el Huntington
Wm. Williams
Oliver Wolcott
Georgia
Button Gwinnett
Lyman Hall
Geo. Walton
Maryland
Samuel Chase
Wm. Paca
Thos. Stone
Charles Carroll
 of Carrollton
Virginia
George Wythe
Richard Henry Lee
Th. Jefferson
Benja. Harrison
Ths. Nelson, Jr.
Francis Lightfoot Lee
Carter Braxton

New York
Wm. Floyd
Phil. Livingston
Frans. Lewis
Lewis Morris
Pennsylvania
Robt. Morris
Benjamin Rush
Benja. Franklin
John Morton
Geo. Clymer
Jas. Smith
Geo. Taylor
James Wilson
Geo. Ross
Delaware
Caesar Rodney
Geo. Read
Tho. M'Kean
North Carolina
Wm. Hooper
Joseph Hewes
John Penn
South Carolina
Edward Rutledge
Thos. Heyward, Junr.
Thomas Lynch, Junr.
Arthur Middleton
New Jersey
Richd. Stockton
Jno. Witherspoon
Fras. Hopkinson
John Hart
Abra. Clark

QUICK QUIZ: Who won the NCAA golf championship in 1961? See page 823.

CONSTITUTION OF THE UNITED STATES

The Constitution of the United States embodies the fundamental principles upon which the American republic rests. A *living* instrument of government, the Constitution has been kept abreast of the times through the process of amendment, by federal laws that elaborate its clauses, and by judicial interpretation by the U.S. Supreme Court.

The original constitution of the American states, the Articles of Confederation, was ratified in 1781. Although the Articles established a kind of national unity, it did not provide for a strong central government. The individual states still held power.

When it became apparent that government under the Articles was, in the words of George Washington, "little more than the shadow without substance," agitation for a strong federal government began. This resulted in the Constitutional Convention of 1787, which met in Philadelphia to revise the Articles of Confederation.

The convention, presided over by George Washington, was torn by sharp conflict over the apportionment of power between the smaller states and the larger states.

Finally, a compromise measure won approval. This measure provided for a lower house to be elected according to population (the House of Representatives) and an upper house to be chosen by the state legislatures (the Senate). This provision for the

Senate held true until 1913, when the 17th Amendment provided for the direct popular election of senators.

After the Constitution was issued, the struggle for ratification was bitter, especially over the conferring of new powers on the central government. Alexander Hamilton, John Jay, and James Madison, in a series of newspaper essays now known as the *Federalist Papers,* did much to promote the acceptance of the Constitution. Delaware, on Dec. 7, 1787, became the first state to ratify the new Constitution. On June 21, 1788, by a vote of 57 to 46, New Hampshire became the ninth state to ratify.

By the terms of the Constitution, ratification by nine states was enough for its establishment. But the government could not succeed without the addition of New York and Virginia, neither of which had ratified. On June 25, 1788, Virginia ratified, over many objections. Finally, on July 26, 1788, New York ratified, with a recommendation that a bill of rights be appended.

With 11 states having thus ratified the Constitution, the Congress of the Confederation passed a resolution on Sept. 13, 1788, to put the new Constitution into operation. On April 1–6, 1789, the first session of the 1st U.S. Congress convened. Later, North Carolina added its ratification on Nov. 21, 1789, and Rhode Island on May 29, 1790.

PREAMBLE

We the People of the United States, in Order to form a more perfect Union, establish Justice, insure domestic Tranquility, provide for the common defence, promote the general Welfare, and secure the Blessings of Liberty to ourselves and our Posterity, do ordain and establish this Constitution for the United States of America.

ARTICLE I (Legislative Branch)

Section 1. All legislative Powers herein granted shall be vested in a Congress of the United States, which shall consist of a Senate and House of Representatives.

Section 2. The House of Representatives shall be composed of Members chosen every second Year by the People of the several States, and the Electors in each State shall have the Qualifications requisite for Electors of the most numerous Branch of the State Legislature.

No Person shall be a Representative who shall not have attained to the Age of twenty five Years, and been seven Years a Citizen of the United States, and who shall not, when elected, be an Inhabitant of that State in which he shall be chosen.

Representatives and direct Taxes shall be apportioned among the several States which may be included within this Union, according to their respective Numbers, [which shall be determined by

adding to the whole Number of free Persons, including those bound to Service for a Term of Years, and excluding Indians not taxed, three fifths of all other Persons.] [1] The actual Enumeration shall be made within three Years after the first Meeting of the Congress of the United States, and within every subsequent Term of ten Years, in such Manner as they shall by Law direct. The Number of Representatives shall not exceed one for every thirty Thousand, but each State shall have at Least one Representative; and until such enumeration shall be made, the State of New Hampshire shall be entitled to chuse three, Massachusetts eight, Rhode-Island and Providence Plantations one, Connecticut five, New-York six, New Jersey four, Pennsylvania eight, Delaware one, Maryland six, Virginia ten, North Carolina five, South Carolina five, and Georgia three.

When vacancies happen in the Representation from any State, the Executive Authority thereof shall issue Writs of Election to fill such Vacancies.

The House of Representatives shall chuse their speaker and other Officers; and shall have the sole Power of Impeachment.

Section 3. The Senate of the United States shall be composed of two Senators from each state, [chosen by the Legislature thereof,] [2] for six Years; and each Senator shall have one Vote.

Immediately after they shall be assembled in

[1] Changed by 14th Amendment, section 2. [2] Changed by 17th Amendment, section 1.

Consequence of the first Election, they shall be divided as equally as may be into three Classes. The Seats of the Senators of the first Class shall be vacated at the Expiration of the second Year, of the second Class at the Expiration of the fourth Year, and of the third Class at the Expiration of the sixth Year, so that one third may be chosen every second Year; [and if Vacancies happen by Resignation, or otherwise, during the Recess of the Legislature of any State, the Executive thereof may make temporary Appointments until the next Meeting of the Legislature, which shall then fill such Vacancies.] [3]

No Person shall be a Senator who shall not have attained to the Age of thirty Years, and been nine Years a Citizen of the United States, and who shall not, when elected, be an Inhabitant of that State for which he shall be chosen.

The Vice President of the United States shall be President of the Senate, but shall have no Vote, unless they be equally divided.

The Senate shall chuse their other Officers, and also a President pro tempore, in the Absence of the Vice President, or when he shall exercise the Office of President of the United States.

The Senate shall have the sole Power to try all Impeachments. When sitting for that Purpose, they shall be on Oath or Affirmation. When the President of the United States is tried, the Chief Justice shall preside: And no Person shall be convicted without the Concurrence of two thirds of the Members present.

Judgment in Cases of Impeachment shall not extend further than to removal from Office, and disqualification to hold and enjoy any Office of honor, Trust or Profit under the United States: but the Party convicted shall nevertheless be liable and subject to Indictment, Trial, Judgment and Punishment, according to Law.

Section 4. The Times, Places and Manner of holding Elections for Senators and Representatives, shall be prescribed in each State by the Legislature thereof; but the Congress may at any time by Law make or alter such Regulations, except as to the Places of chusing Senators.

[The Congress shall assemble at least once in every Year, and such Meeting shall be on the first Monday in December, unless they shall by Law appoint a different Day.] [4]

Section 5. Each House shall be the Judge of the Elections, Returns and Qualifications of its own Members, and a Majority of each shall constitute a Quorum to do Business; but a smaller Number may adjourn from day to day, and may be authorized to compel the Attendance of absent Members, in such Manner, and under such Penalties as each House may provide.

Each House may determine the Rules of its Proceedings, punish its Members for disorderly Behaviour, and, with the Concurrence of two thirds, expel a Member.

Each House shall keep a Journal of its Proceedings, and from time to time publish the same, excepting such Parts as may in their Judgment require Secrecy; and the Yeas and Nays of the Members of either House on any question shall, at the Desire of one fifth of those Present be entered on the Journal.

Neither House, during the Session of Congress, shall without the Consent of the other, adjourn for more than three days, nor to any other Place than that in which the two Houses shall be sitting.

Section 6. The Senators and Representatives shall receive a Compensation for their Services, to be ascertained by Law, and paid out of the Treasury of the United States. They shall in all Cases, except Treason, Felony and Breach of the Peace, be privileged from Arrest during their Attendance at the Session of their respective Houses, and in going to and returning from the same; and for any Speech or Debate in either House, they shall not be questioned in any other Place.

No Senator or Representative shall, during the Time for which he was elected, be appointed to any civil Office under the Authority of the United States, which shall have been created, or the Emoluments whereof shall have been encreased during such time; and no Person holding any Office under the United States, shall be a Member of either House during his Continuance in Office.

Section 7. All Bills for raising Revenue shall originate in the House of Representatives; but the Senate may propose or concur with Amendments as on other Bills.

Every Bill which shall have passed the House of Representatives and the Senate, shall, before it become a Law, be presented to the President of the United States; If he approve he shall sign it, but if not he shall return it, with his Objections to that House in which it shall have originated, who shall enter the Objections at large on their Journal, and proceed to reconsider it. If after such Reconsideration two thirds of that House shall agree to pass the Bill, it shall be sent together with the Objections, to the other House, by which it shall likewise be reconsidered, and if approved by two thirds of that House, it shall become a Law. But in all such Cases the Votes of both Houses shall be determined by Yeas and Nays, and the Names of the Persons voting for and against the Bill shall be entered on the Journal of each House respectively. If any Bill shall not be returned by the President within ten Days (Sundays excepted) after it shall have been presented to him, the Same shall be a Law, in like Manner as if he had signed it, unless the Congress by their Adjournment prevent its Return, in which Case it shall not be a Law.

Every Order, Resolution, or Vote to which the Concurrence of the Senate and House of Representatives may be necessary (except on a question of Adjournment) shall be presented to the President of the United States; and before the Same shall take Effect, shall be approved by him, or being disapproved by him, shall be repassed by two thirds of the Senate and House of Representatives, according to the Rules and Limitations prescribed in the Case of a Bill.

Section 8. The Congress shall have Power To lay and collect taxes, Duties, Imposts and Excises, to pay the Debts and provide for the common Defence and general Welfare of the United States; but all Duties, Imposts and Excises shall be uniform throughout the United States;

To Borrow Money on the Credit of the United States;

To regulate Commerce with foreign Nations, and among the several States, and with the Indian Tribes;

[3] Changed by 17th Amendment, clause 2. [4] Changed by 20th Amendment, section 2.

CONSTITUTION OF U.S. *(continued)*

To establish an uniform Rule of Naturalization, and uniform Laws on the subject of Bankruptcies throughout the United States;

To coin Money, regulate the Value thereof, and of foreign Coin, and fix the Standard of Weights and Measures;

To provide for the Punishment of counterfeiting the Securities and current Coin of the United States;

To establish Post Offices and post Roads;

To promote the Progress of Science and useful Arts, by securing for limited Times to Authors and Inventors the exclusive Right to their respective Writings and Discoveries;

To constitute Tribunals inferior to the supreme Court;

To define and punish Piracies and Felonies committed on the high Seas, and Offences against the Law of Nations;

To declare War, grant Letters of Marque and Reprisal, and make Rules concerning Captures on Land and Water;

To raise and support Armies, but no Appropriation of Money to that Use shall be for a longer Term than two Years;

To provide and maintain a Navy;

To make Rules for the Government and Regulation of the land and naval Forces;

To provide for calling forth the Militia to execute the Laws of the Union, suppress insurrections and repel Invasions;

To provide for organizing, arming, and disciplining, the Militia, and for governing such Part of them as may be employed in the Service of the United States, reserving to the States respectively, the Appointment of the Officers, and the Authority of training the Militia according to the discipline prescribed by Congress;

To exercise exclusive Legislation in all Cases whatsoever, over such District (not exceeding ten Miles square) as may, by Cession of Particular States, and the Acceptance of Congress, become the Seat of the Government of the United States, and to exercise like Authority over all Places purchased by the Consent of the Legislature of the State in which the Same shall be for the Erection of Forts, Magazines, Arsenals, dock-Yards, and other needful Buildings;—And

To make all Laws which shall be necessary and proper for carrying into Execution the foregoing Powers, and all other Powers vested by this Constitution in the Government of the United States, or in any Department or Officer thereof.

Section 9. The Migration or Importation of such Persons as any of the States now existing shall think proper to admit, shall not be prohibited by the Congress prior to the Year one thousand eight hundred and eight, but a Tax or duty may be imposed on such Importation, not exceeding ten dollars for each Person.

The Privilege of the Writ of Habeas Corpus shall not be suspended, unless when in Cases of Rebellion or Invasion the public Safety may require it.

No Bill of Attainder or ex post facto Law shall be passed.

[No Capitation, or other direct Tax shall be laid, unless in Proportion to the Census or Enumeration herein before directed to be taken.] [5]

No Tax or Duty shall be laid on Articles exported from any State.

No Preference shall be given by any Regulation of Commerce or Revenue to the Ports of one State over those of another: nor shall Vessels bound to, or from, one State, be obliged to enter, clear, or pay Duties in another.

No Money shall be drawn from the Treasury, but in Consequence of Appropriations made by Law; and a regular Statement and Account of the Receipts and Expenditures of all public Money shall be published from time to time.

No Title of Nobility shall be granted by the United States: And no Person holding any Office of Profit or Trust under them, shall, without the Consent of the Congress, accept of any present, Emolument, Office, or Title, of any kind whatever, from any King, Prince, or foreign State.

Section 10. No State shall enter into any Treaty, Alliance, or Confederation; grant Letters of Marque and Reprisal; coin Money; emit Bills of Credit; make any Thing but gold and silver Coin a Tender in Payment of Debts; pass any Bill of Attainder, ex post facto Law, or Law impairing the Obligation of Contracts, or grant any Title of Nobility.

No State shall, without the Consent of the Congress, lay any Imposts or Duties on Imports or Exports, except what may be absolutely necessary for executing its inspection Laws: and the net Produce of all Duties and Imposts, laid by any State on Imports or Exports, shall be for the Use of the Treasury of the United States; and all such Laws shall be subject to the Revision and Controul of the Congress.

No State shall, without the Consent of Congress, lay any Duty of Tonnage, keep Troops, or Ships of War in time of Peace, enter into any Agreement or Compact with another State, or with a foreign Power, or engage in War, unless actually invaded, or in such imminent Danger as will not admit of delay.

ARTICLE II (Executive Branch)

Section 1. The executive Power shall be vested in a President of the United States of America. He shall hold his Office during the Term of four Years, and, together with the Vice President,[6] chosen for the same term, be elected, as follows

Each State shall appoint, in such Manner as the Legislature thereof may direct, a Number of Electors, equal to the whole Number of Senators and Representatives to which the State may be entitled in the Congress: but no Senator or Representative, or Person holding an Office of Trust or Profit under the United States, shall be appointed an Elector.

[The Electors shall meet in their respective States, and vote by Ballot for two Persons, of whom one at least shall be an Inhabitant of the same State with themselves. And they shall make a List of all the Persons voted for, and of the Number of Votes for each; which List they shall sign and certify, and transmit sealed to the Seat of the Government of the United States, directed to the President of the Senate. The President of the Senate shall, in the Presence of the Senate and House of Representa-

5 See also 16th Amendment. 6 Superseded by 12th Amendment.

tives, open all the Certificates, and the Votes shall then be counted. The Person having the greatest Number of Votes shall be the President, if such Number be a Majority of the whole Number of Electors appointed; and if there be more than one who have such Majority, and have an equal Number of Votes, then the House of Representatives shall immediately chuse by Ballot one of them for President: and if no Person have a Majority, then from the five highest on the list the said House shall in like Manner chuse the President. But in chusing the President, the Votes shall be taken by States, the Representation from each State having one Vote; a quorum for this Purpose shall consist of a Member or Members from two thirds of the States, and a Majority of all the States shall be necessary to a Choice. In every Case, after the Choice of the President, the Person having the greatest Number of Votes of the Electors shall be the Vice President. But if there should remain two or more who have equal Votes, the Senate shall chuse from them by Ballot the Vice President.] [7]

The Congress may determine the Time of chusing the Electors, and the Day on which they shall give their Votes: which Day shall be the same throughout the United States.

No Person except a natural born Citizen, or a Citizen of the United States, at the time of the Adoption of this Constitution, shall be eligible to the Office of President; neither shall any Person be eligible to that Office who shall not have attained to the Age of thirty five Years, and been fourteen Years a Resident within the United States.

In Case of the Removal of the President from Office, or of his Death, Resignation, or Inability to discharge the Powers and Duties of the said Office, the Same shall devolve on the Vice President, and the Congress may by Law provide for the Case of Removal, Death, Resignation or Inability, both of the President and Vice President, declaring what Officer shall then act as President, and such Officer shall act accordingly, until the Disability be removed, or a President shall be elected. [8]

The President shall, at stated Times, receive for his Services, a Compensation, which shall neither be encreased nor diminished during the Period for which he shall have been elected, and he shall not receive within that Period any other Emolument from the United States, or any of them.

Before he enter on the Execution of his Office, he shall take the following Oath or Affirmation:—"I do solemnly swear (or affirm) that I will faithfully execute the Office of President of the United States, and will to the best of my Ability, preserve, protect and defend the Constitution of the United States."

Section 2. The President shall be Commander in Chief of the Army and Navy of the United States, and of the Militia of the several States, when called into the actual Service of the United States; he may require the Opinion, in writing, of the principal Officer in each of the executive Departments, upon any Subject relating to the Duties of their respective Offices, and he shall have Power to grant Reprieves and Pardons for Offences against the United States, except in Cases of Impeachment.

He shall have Power, by and with the Advice and Consent of the Senate, to make Treaties, provided two thirds of the Senators present concur; and he

shall nominate, and by and with the Advice and Consent of the Senate, shall appoint Ambassadors, other public Ministers and Consuls, Judges of the supreme Court, and all other Officers of the United States, whose Appointments are not herein otherwise provided for, and which shall be established by Law: but the Congress may by Law vest the Appointment of such inferior Officers, as they think proper, in the President alone, in the Courts of Law, or in the Heads of Departments.

The President shall have Power to fill up all Vacancies that may happen during the Recess of the Senate, by granting Commissions which shall expire at the End of their next Session.

Section 3. He shall from time to time give to the Congress Information of the State of the Union, and recommend to their Consideration such Measures as he shall judge necessary and expedient; he may, on extraordinary Occasions, convene both Houses, or either of them, and in Case of Disagreement between them, with Respect to the Time of Adjournment, he may adjourn them to such Time as he shall think proper; he shall receive Ambassadors and other public Ministers; he shall take Care that the Laws be faithfully executed, and shall Commission all the Officers of the United States.

Section 4. The President, Vice President and all civil Officers of the United States, shall be removed from Office on Impeachment for, and Conviction of, Treason, Bribery, or other High Crimes and Misdemeanors.

ARTICLE III (Judicial Branch)

Section 1. The judicial Power of the United States, shall be vested in one supreme Court, and in such Inferior Courts as the Congress may from time to time ordain and establish. The Judges, both of the supreme and inferior Courts, shall hold their Offices during good Behaviour, and shall, at stated Times, receive for their Services, a Compensation, which shall not be diminished during their Continuance in Office.

Section 2. The judicial Power shall extend to all Cases, in Law and Equity, arising under this Constitution, the Laws of the United States, and Treaties made, or which shall be made, under their Authority;—to all Cases affecting Ambassadors, other public Ministers and Consuls;—to all Cases of admiralty and maritime Jurisdiction;—to Controversies to which the United States shall be a Party;—to Controversies between two or more States; [between a State and Citizens of another State;] [9]—between Citizens of different States;—between Citizens of the same State claiming Lands under Grants of different States, and between a State, or the Citizens thereof, and foreign States, [Citizens or Subjects] [9].

In all Cases affecting Ambassadors, other public Ministers and Consuls, and those in which a State shall be Party, the Supreme Court shall have original Jurisdiction. In all the other Cases before mentioned, the supreme Court shall have appellate Jurisdiction, both as to Law and Fact, with such Exceptions, and under such Regulations as the Congress shall make.

The Trial of all Crimes, except in Cases of Impeachment, shall be by Jury; and such Trial shall be held in the State where the said Crimes shall

[7] Superseded by 12th Amendment. [8] Affected by 25th Amendment. [9] Affected by 11th Amendment.

CONSTITUTION OF U.S. *(continued)*

have been committed; but when not committed within any State, the Trial shall be at such Place or Places as the Congress may by Law have directed.

Section 3. Treason against the United States, shall consist only in levying War against them, or in adhering to their Enemies, giving them Aid and Comfort. No Person shall be convicted of Treason unless on the Testimony of two Witnesses to the same overt Act, or on Confession in open Court.

The Congress shall have Power to declare the Punishment of Treason, but no Attainder of Treason shall work Corruption of Blood, or Forfeiture except during the Life of the Person attainted.

ARTICLE IV (Relations of States)

Section 1. Full Faith and Credit shall be given in each State to the public Acts, Records, and judicial Proceedings of every other State. And the Congress may by general Laws prescribe the Manner in which such Acts, Records and Proceedings shall be proved, and the Effect thereof.

Section 2. The Citizens of each State shall be entitled to all Privileges and Immunities of Citizens in the several States.

A Person charged in any State with Treason, Felony, or other Crime, who shall flee from Justice, and be found in another State, shall on Demand of the executive Authority of the State from which he fled, be delivered up, to be removed to the State having Jurisdiction of the Crime.

No Person held to Service or Labour in one State, under the Laws thereof, escaping into another, shall in Consequence of any Law or Regulation therein, be discharged from such Service or Labour, but shall be delivered up on Claim of the Party to whom such Service or Labour may be due.

Section 3. New States may be admitted by the Congress into this Union; but no new State shall be formed or erected within the Jurisdiction of any other State; nor any State be formed by the Junction of two or more States, or Parts of States, without the Consent of the Legislatures of the States concerned as well as of the Congress.

The Congress shall have Power to dispose of and make all needful Rules and Regulations respecting the Territory or other Property belonging to the United States; and nothing in this Constitution shall be so construed as to Prejudice any Claims of the United States, or of any particular State.

Section 4. The United States shall guarantee to every State in this Union a Republican Form of Government, and shall protect each of them against invasion; and on Application of the Legislature, or of the Executive (when the Legislature cannot be convened) against domestic Violence.

ARTICLE V (Amending the Constitution)

The Congress, whenever two thirds of both Houses shall deem it necessary, shall propose Amendments to this Constitution, or, on the Application of the Legislatures of two thirds of the several States, shall call a convention for proposing Amendments, which, in either Case, shall be valid to all Intents and Purposes, as Part of this Constitution, when ratified by the Legislatures of three fourths of the several States, or by Conventions in three fourths thereof, as the one or the other Mode of Ratification

may be proposed by the Congress; Provided that no Amendment which may be made prior to the Year One thousand eight hundred and eight shall in any Manner affect the first and fourth Clauses in the Ninth Section of the first Article: and that no State, without its Consent, shall be deprived of its equal Suffrage in the Senate.

ARTICLE VI (National Debts)

All Debts contracted and Engagements entered into, before the Adoption of this Constitution, shall be as valid against the United States under this Constitution, as under the Confederation.

This Constitution, and the Laws of the United States which shall be made in Pursuance thereof; and all Treaties made, or which shall be made, under the Authority of the United States, shall be the supreme Law of the Land; and the Judges in every State shall be bound thereby, any Thing in the Constitution or Laws of any State to the Contrary notwithstanding.

The Senators and Representatives before mentioned, and the Members of the several State Legislatures, and all executive and judicial Officers, both of the United States and of the several States, shall be bound by Oath or Affirmation, to support this Constitution; but no religious Test shall ever be required as a Qualification to any Office or public Trust under the United States.

ARTICLE VII (Ratification)

The ratification of the Conventions of nine States, shall be sufficient for the Establishment of this Constitution between the States so ratifying the Same.

DONE in Convention by the Unanimous Consent of the States present the Seventeenth Day of September in the Year of our Lord one thousand seven hundred and Eighty seven and of the Independence of the United States of America the Twelfth **IN WITNESS** whereof we have hereunto subscribed our Names [1]

Gº Washington—Presidᵗ
and deputy from Virginia

Delaware	**New Hampshire**
Geo: Read	John Langdon
Gunning Bedford jun	Nicholas Gilman
John Dickinson	**Massachusetts**
Richard Bassett	Nathaniel Gorham
Jaco: Broom	Rufus King
Maryland	**Connecticut**
James McHenry	Wᵐ Samˡ Johnson
Dan of Sᵗ Thoˢ Jenifer	Roger Sherman
Danl Carroll	**New York**
Virginia	Alexander Hamilton
John Blair—	**New Jersey**
James Madison Jr	Wil: Livingston
North Carolina	David Brearley
Wᵐ Blount	Wᵐ Paterson
Richᵈ Dobbs Spaight	Jona: Dayton
Hu Williamson	**Pennsylvania**
South Carolina	B Franklin
J. Rutledge	Thomas Mifflin
Charles Cotesworth Pinckney	Robᵗ Morris
Charles Pinckney	Geo. Clymer
Pierce Butler	Thoˢ FitzSimons
Georgia	Jared Ingersoll
William Few	James Wilson
Abr Baldwin	Gouv Morris

[1] The order of signing was geographical, beginning in the right column with New Hampshire.

AMENDMENTS TO THE CONSTITUTION

BILL OF RIGHTS
The first 10 amendments to the Constitution of the United States were ratified on Dec. 15, 1791, and form what is known as the Bill of Rights.

AMENDMENT 1 (Freedoms, Assembly, Petitions)
Congress shall make no law respecting an establishment of religion, or prohibiting the free exercise thereof; or abridging the freedom of speech, or of the press; or the right of the people peaceably to assemble, and to petition the Government for a redress of grievances.

AMENDMENT 2 (Right to Bear Arms)
A well regulated Militia, being necessary to the security of a free State, the right of the people to keep and bear Arms, shall not be infringed.

AMENDMENT 3 (Quartering of Soldiers)
No Soldier shall, in time of peace be quartered in any house, without the consent of the Owner, nor in time of war, but in a manner to be prescribed by law.

AMENDMENT 4 (Search and Arrest)
The right of the people to be secure in their persons, houses, papers, and effects, against unreasonable searches and seizures, shall not be violated, and no Warrants shall issue, but upon probable cause, supported by Oath or affirmation, and particularly describing the place to be searched, and the persons or things to be seized.

AMENDMENT 5 (Rights in Criminal Cases)
No person shall be held to answer for a capital, or otherwise infamous crime, unless on a presentment or indictment of a Grand Jury, except in cases arising in the land or naval forces, or in the Militia, when in actual service in time of War or public danger; nor shall any person be subject for the same offence to be twice put in jeopardy of life or limb; nor shall be compelled in any criminal case to be a witness against himself, nor be deprived of life, liberty, or property, without due process of law; nor shall private property be taken for public use, without just compensation.

AMENDMENT 6 (Right to Fair Trial)
In all criminal prosecutions, the accused shall enjoy the right to a speedy and public trial, by an impartial jury of the State and district wherein the crime shall have been committed, which district shall have been previously ascertained by law, and to be informed of the nature and cause of the accusation; to be confronted with the witnesses against him; to have compulsory process for obtaining witnesses in his favor, and to have the Assistance of Counsel for his defence.

AMENDMENT 7 (Rights in Civil Cases)
In Suits at common law, where the value in controversy shall exceed twenty dollars, the right of trial by jury shall be preserved, and no fact tried by a jury, shall be otherwise re-examined in any Court of the United States, than according to the rules of the common law.

AMENDMENT 8 (Bail, Fines, and Punishment)
Excessive bail shall not be required, nor excessive fines imposed, nor cruel and unusual punishments inflicted.

AMENDMENT 9 (Rights Retained by People)
The enumeration in the Constitution, of certain rights, shall not be construed to deny or disparage others retained by the people.

AMENDMENT 10 (States' Rights)
The powers not delegated to the United States by the Constitution, nor prohibited by it to the States, are reserved to the States respectively, or to the people.

AMENDMENT 11 (Lawsuits Against States)
(*Proclaimed Jan. 8, 1798*)
The Judicial power of the United States shall not be construed to extend to any suit in law or equity, commenced or prosecuted against one of the United States by Citizens of another State, or by Citizens or Subjects of any Foreign State.

AMENDMENT 12 (Presidential Elections)
(*Proclaimed Sept. 25, 1804*)
The Electors shall meet in their respective states and vote by ballot for President and Vice-President, one of whom, at least, shall not be an inhabitant of the same state with themselves; they shall name in their ballots the person voted for as President, and in distinct ballots the person voted for as Vice-President, and they shall make distinct lists of all persons voted for as President, and of all persons voted for as Vice-President, and of the number of votes for each, which lists they shall sign and certify, and transmit sealed to the seat of the government of the United States, directed to the President of the Senate;— The President of the Senate shall, in the presence of the Senate and House of Representatives, open all the certificates and the votes shall then be counted;—The person having the greatest number of votes for President, shall be the President, if such number be a majority of the whole number of Electors appointed; and if no person have such majority, then from the persons having the highest numbers not exceeding three on the list of those voted for as President, the House of Representatives shall choose immediately, by ballot, the President. But in choosing the President, the votes shall be taken by states, the representation from each state having one vote; a quorum for this purpose shall consist of a member or members from two-thirds of the states, and a majority of all the states shall be necessary to a choice.

And if the House of Representatives shall not choose a President whenever the right of choice shall devolve upon them, before the fourth day of March next following, then the Vice-President shall act as President, as in the case of the death or other constitutional disability of the President.—The person having the greatest number of votes as Vice-President, shall be the Vice-President, if such number be a majority of the whole number of Electors appointed, and if no person have a majority, then from the two highest numbers on the list, the Senate shall choose the Vice-President; a quorum

CONSTITUTIONAL AMENDMENTS (continued)

for the purpose shall consist of two-thirds of the whole number of Senators, and a majority of the whole number shall be necessary to a choice. But no person constitutionally ineligible to the office of President shall be eligible to that of Vice-President of the United States.

AMENDMENT 13 (Abolition of Slavery)
(Proclaimed Dec. 18, 1865)
Section 1. Neither slavery nor involuntary servitude, except as a punishment for crime whereof the party shall have been duly convicted, shall exist within the United States, or any place subject to their jurisdiction.
Section 2. Congress shall have power to enforce this article by appropriate legislation.

AMENDMENT 14 (Civil Rights)
(Proclaimed July 28, 1868)
Section 1. All persons born or naturalized in the United States, and subject to the jurisdiction thereof, are citizens of the United States and of the State wherein they reside. No State shall make or enforce any law which shall abridge the privileges or immunities of citizens of the United States, nor shall any State deprive any person of life, liberty, or property, without due process of law; nor deny to any person within its jurisdiction the equal protection of the laws.
Section 2. Representatives shall be apportioned among the several States according to their respective numbers, counting the whole number of persons in each State, excluding Indians not taxed. But when the right to vote at any election for the choice of electors for President and Vice President of the United States, Representatives in Congress, the Executive and Judicial officers of a State, or the members of the Legislature thereof, is denied to any of the male inhabitants of such State, being twenty-one years of age, and citizens of the United States, or in any way abridged, except for participation in rebellion, or other crime, the basis of representation therein shall be reduced in the proportion which the number of such male citizens shall bear to the whole number of male citizens twenty-one years of age in such State.
Section 3. No person shall be a Senator or Representative in Congress, or elector of President and Vice President, or hold any office, civil or military, under the United States, or under any State, who, having previously taken an oath, as a member of Congress, or as an officer of the United States, or as a member of any State legislature, or as an executive or judicial officer of any State, to support the Constitution of the United States, shall have engaged in insurrection or rebellion against the same, or given aid or comfort to the enemies thereof. But Congress may by a vote of two-thirds of each House, remove such disability.
Section 4. The validity of the public debt of the United States, authorized by law, including debts incurred for payment of pensions and bounties for services in suppressing insurrection or rebellion, shall not be questioned. But neither the United States nor any State shall assume or pay any debt or obligation incurred in aid of insurrection or rebellion against the United States, or any claim for the loss or emancipation of any slave; but all such debts, obligations and claims shall be held illegal and void.

Section 5. The Congress shall have power to enforce, by appropriate legislation, the provisions of this article.

AMENDMENT 15 (Black Suffrage)
(Proclaimed March 30, 1870)
Section 1. The right of citizens of the United States to vote shall not be denied or abridged by the United States or by any State on account of race, color, or previous condition of servitude.
Section 2. The Congress shall have power to enforce this article by appropriate legislation.

AMENDMENT 16 (Income Taxes)
(Proclaimed Feb. 25, 1913)
The Congress shall have power to lay and collect taxes on incomes, from whatever source derived, without apportionment among the several States, and without regard to any census or enumeration.

AMENDMENT 17 (Senatorial Election)
(Proclaimed May 31, 1913)
The Senate of the United States shall be composed of two Senators from each State, elected by the people thereof, for six years; and each Senator shall have one vote. The electors in each State shall have the qualifications requisite for electors of the most numerous branch of the State legislatures.

When vacancies happen in the representation of any State in the Senate, the executive authority of such State shall issue writs of election to fill such vacancies: Provided, That the legislature of any State may empower the executive thereof to make temporary appointments until the people fill the vacancies by election as the legislature may direct.

This amendment shall not be so construed as to affect the election or term of any Senator chosen before it becomes valid as part of the Constitution.

AMENDMENT 18 (Prohibition of Liquor)
(Proclaimed Jan. 29, 1919)
(Repealed by 21st Amendment)
Section 1. After one year from the ratification of this article the manufacture, sale, or transportation of intoxicating liquors within, the importation thereof into, or the exportation thereof from the United States and all territory subject to the jurisdiction thereof for beverage purposes is hereby prohibited.
Section 2. The Congress and the several States shall have concurrent power to enforce this article by appropriate legislation.
Section 3. This article shall be inoperative unless it shall have been ratified as an amendment to the Constitution by the legislatures of the several States, as provided in the Constitution, within seven years from the date of the submission hereof to the States by the Congress.

AMENDMENT 19 (Woman Suffrage)
(Proclaimed Aug. 26, 1920)
The right of citizens of the United States to vote shall not be denied or abridged by the United States or by any State on account of sex.

Congress shall have power to enforce this article by appropriate legislation.

AMENDMENT 20 (Terms of Office)
(Proclaimed Feb. 6, 1933)
Section 1. The terms of the President and Vice-

EARLY CAPITALS OF THE UNITED STATES: 1774 to 1789

The Continental Congress and its successor, the Congress of the Articles of Confederation, met in eight different cities as the seat of the national government during and after the American Revolution.

Philadelphia, Pennsylvania:
Sept. 5, 1774, to Oct. 26, 1774
May 10, 1775, to Dec. 12, 1776

Baltimore, Maryland:
Dec. 20, 1776, to March 4, 1777

Philadelphia, Pennsylvania:
March 5, 1777, to Sept. 18, 1777

Lancaster, Pennsylvania:
Sept. 27, 1777 (one day only)

York, Pennsylvania:
Sept. 30, 1777, to June 27, 1778

Philadelphia, Pennsylvania:
July 2, 1778, to June 21, 1783

Princeton, New Jersey:
June 30, 1783, to Nov. 4, 1783

Annapolis, Maryland:
Nov. 26, 1783, to June 3, 1784

Trenton, New Jersey:
Nov. 1, 1784, to Dec. 24, 1784

New York City, New York:
Jan. 11, 1785, to Nov. 4, 1785
Nov. 7, 1785, to Nov. 3, 1786
Nov. 6, 1786, to Oct. 30, 1787
Nov. 5, 1787, to Oct. 21, 1788
Nov. 3, 1788, to March 2, 1789

President shall end at noon on the 20th day of January, and the terms of Senators and Representatives at noon on the 3d day of January, of the years in which such terms would have ended if this article had not been ratified; and the terms of their successors shall then begin.

Section 2. The Congress shall assemble at least once in every year, and such meeting shall begin at noon on the 3d day of January, unless they shall by law appoint a different day.

Section 3. If, at the time fixed for the beginning of the term of the President, the President-elect shall have died, the Vice-President-elect shall become President. If a President shall not have been chosen before the time fixed for the beginning of his term, or if the President-elect shall have failed to qualify, then the Vice-President-elect shall act as President until a President shall have qualified; and the Congress may by law provide for the case wherein neither a President-elect nor a Vice-President-elect shall have qualified, declaring who shall then act as President, or the manner in which one who is to act shall be selected, and such person shall act accordingly until a President or Vice-President shall have qualified.

Section 4. The Congress may by law provide for the case of the death of any of the persons from whom the House of Representatives may choose a President whenever the right of choice shall have devolved upon them, and for the case of the death of any of the persons from whom the Senate may choose a Vice-President whenever the right of choice shall have devolved upon them.

Section 5. Sections 1 and 2 shall take effect on the 15th day of October following the ratification of this article.

Section 6. This article shall be inoperative unless it shall have been ratified as an amendment to the Constitution by the legislatures of three-fourths of the several States within seven years from the date of its submission.

AMENDMENT 21 (Repeal of Prohibition)
(*Proclaimed Dec. 5, 1933*)

Section 1. The eighteenth article of amendment to the Constitution of the United States is hereby repealed.

Section 2. The transportation or importation into any State, Territory, or possession of the United States for delivery or use therein of intoxicating liquors, in violation of the laws thereof, is hereby prohibited.

Section 3. This article shall be inoperative unless it shall have been ratified as an amendment to the Constitution by conventions in the several States, as provided in the Constitution, within seven years from the date of the submission hereof to the States by the Congress.

AMENDMENT 22 (Limit on Presidential Terms)
(*Proclaimed March 1, 1951*)

Section 1. No person shall be elected to the office of the President more than twice, and no person who has held the office of President, or acted as President, for more than two years of a term to which some other person was elected President shall be elected to the office of the President more than once. But this Article shall not apply to any person holding the office of President when this Article was proposed by the Congress, and shall not prevent any person who may be holding the office of President, or acting as President, during the term within which this Article becomes operative from holding the office of President or acting as President during the remainder of such term.

Section 2. This article shall be inoperative unless it

PRESIDENTS OF CONGRESS: 1774 to 1789

NAME	STATE	ELECTED	REMARKS
1. Peyton Randolph	Virginia	Sept. 5, 1774	Resigned: Speaker of Virginia legislature 1766–75
2. Henry Middleton	South Carolina	Oct. 22, 1774	Defected to British 1780
3. Peyton Randolph	Virginia	May 10, 1775	Resigned because of ill health
4. John Hancock	Massachusetts	May 24, 1775	First to sign Declaration of Independence
5. Henry Laurens	South Carolina	Nov. 1, 1777	Held prisoner by British 1780–81
6. John Jay	New York	Dec. 10, 1778	First Chief Justice of U.S. 1789–95
7. Samuel Huntington	Connecticut	Sept. 28, 1779	Governor of Connecticut 1786–96
8. Thomas McKean	Delaware	July 10, 1781	First President elected under Articles of Confederation
9. John Hanson	Maryland	Nov. 5, 1781	Gave Washington Congress' thanks for Yorktown victory
10. Elias Boudinot	New Jersey	Nov. 4, 1782	Signed peace treaty ending American Revolutionary War
11. Thomas Mifflin	Pennsylvania	Nov. 3, 1783	Governor of Pennsylvania 1790–99
12. Richard Henry Lee	Virginia	Nov. 30, 1784	U.S. Senator from Virginia 1789–92
13. John Hancock	Massachusetts	Nov. 23, 1785	Resigned without serving because of illness
14. Nathaniel Gorham	Massachusetts	June 6, 1786	Signer of U.S. Constitution
15. Arthur St. Clair	Pennsylvania	Feb. 2, 1787	Governor of Northwest Territory 1789–1802
16. Cyrus Griffin	Virginia	Jan. 22, 1788	U.S. district judge for Virginia 1789–1810

CONSTITUTIONAL AMENDMENTS *(continued)*

shall have been ratified as an amendment to the Constitution by the legislatures of three-fourths of the several States within seven years from the date of its submission to the States by the Congress.

AMENDMENT 23 (Washington, D.C., Suffrage)

(Proclaimed April 3, 1961)

Section 1. The District constituting the seat of Government of the United States shall appoint in such manner as the Congress may direct:

A number of electors of President and Vice President equal to the whole number of Senators and Representatives in Congress to which the District would be entitled if it were a State, but in no event more than the least populous State; they shall be in addition to those appointed by the States, but they shall be considered, for the purposes of the election of President and Vice President, to be electors appointed by a State; and they shall meet in the District and perform such duties as provided by the twelfth article of amendment.

Section 2. The Congress shall have power to enforce this article by appropriate legislation.

AMENDMENT 24 (Abolition of Poll Taxes)

(Proclaimed Feb. 4, 1964)

Section 1. The right of citizens of the United States to vote in any primary or other election for President or Vice President, for electors for President or Vice President, or for Senator or Representative in Congress, shall not be denied or abridged by the United States or any State by reason of failure to pay any poll tax or other tax.

Section 2. The Congress shall have power to enforce this article by appropriate legislation.

AMENDMENT 25 (Presidential Succession)

(Proclaimed Feb. 23, 1967)

Section 1. In case of the removal of the President from office or of his death or resignation, the Vice President shall become President.

Section 2. Whenever there is a vacancy in the office of the Vice President, the President shall nominate a Vice President who shall take office upon confirmation by a majority vote of both houses of Congress.

Section 3. Whenever the President transmits to the President pro tempore of the Senate and the Speaker of the House of Representatives his written declaration that he is unable to discharge the powers and duties of his office, and until he transmits to them a written declaration to the contrary, such powers and duties shall be discharged by the Vice President as Acting President.

Section 4. Whenever the Vice President and a majority of either the principal officers of the executive departments or of such other body as Congress may by law provide, transmit to the President pro tempore of the Senate and the Speaker of the House of Representatives their written declaration that the President is unable to discharge the powers and duties of his office, the Vice President shall immediately assume the powers and duties of the office as Acting President.

Thereafter, when the President transmits to the President pro tempore of the Senate and the Speaker of the House of Representatives his written declaration that no inability exists, he shall resume the powers and duties of his office unless the Vice President and a majority of either the principal officers of the executive department or of such other body as Congress may by law provide, transmit within four days to the President pro tempore of the Senate and the Speaker of the House of Representatives their written declaration that the President is unable to discharge the powers and duties of his office. Thereupon Congress shall decide the issue, assembling within forty-eight hours for that purpose if not in session. If the Congress, within twenty-one days after receipt of the latter written declaration, or, if Congress is not in session, within twenty-one days after Congress is required to assemble, determines by two-thirds vote of both houses that the President is unable to discharge the powers and duties of his office, the Vice President shall continue to discharge the same as Acting President; otherwise, the President shall resume the powers and duties of his office.

AMENDMENT 26 (18-Year-Old Suffrage)

(Proclaimed July 5, 1971)

Section 1. The right of citizens of the United States, who are eighteen years of age or older, to vote shall not be denied or abridged by the United States or by any State on account of age.

Section 2. The Congress shall have power to enforce this article by appropriate legislation.

CONSTITUTIONAL AMENDMENTS NOT RATIFIED

Six amendments submitted to the states have failed to be ratified by them.

In 1791, of the 12 proposed amendments to the Constitution, Articles III-XII were ratified and became the Bill of Rights, the first 10 amendments to the Constitution. But the proposed Articles I and II were not ratified. They would have provided that as the population grew there could be a representative in Congress for every 50,000 people and would have prevented Congress from raising its own salaries during the term in session.

The 11th Congress proposed an amendment forbidding acceptance by U.S. citizens of foreign titles "of nobility or honour."

On March 2, 1861, President James Buchanan signed a proposed amendment that would have forbidden any amendments to the Constitution giving Congress the power to abolish or interfere with slavery. It was not ratified.

Congress approved an amendment in 1924 giving it power to regulate child labor. It was not ratified.

In 1972 an equal rights for women amendment was approved by Congress but failed to be ratified by three-fourths of the states. It stated: "Equality of rights under the law shall not be denied or abridged by the United States or any state on account of sex."

An amendment to give Washington, D.C., voting representation in Congress was approved by Congress in 1978 and sent to the states for ratification.

U.S. TERRITORIAL EXPANSION

The total gross area (land and water) of the U.S. and its outlying areas was 3,623,420 square miles in the 1980 census. The table below outlines the nation's physical growth since independence was declared in 1776.

The area figures are precise determinations of specific territories first made by a special government committee in 1912 and subsequently adjusted to bring them into agreement with later remeasurements.

In 1979 the U.S. gave up claims to several Pacific islands including Canton and Enderbury, which became part of the nation Kiribati (formerly the Gilbert Islands).

On Oct. 1, 1979, the United States restored to Panama sovereignty over the 553-square-mile Panama Canal Zone that had been governed by the U.S. since 1904.

DATE	ACQUISITION	GROSS AREA (in sq. miles)	HOW ACQUIRED	ACQUISITION PRICE
—	Original territory	888,685	Treaty with Britain	—
1803	Louisiana	827,192	Purchase from France	$15,000,000
1819	Florida (and other areas)	72,003	Treaty with Spain	$ 5,000,000
1845	Texas	390,143	Independent republic annexed	—
1846	Oregon	285,580	Treaty with Britain	—
1848	Mexican cession	529,017	Conquest from Mexico	$15,000,000
1854	Gadsden Purchase	29,640	Purchase from Mexico	$10,000,000
1867	Alaska	586,412	Purchase from Russia	$ 7,200,000
1898	Hawaiian Islands	6,471	Independent republic annexed	—
1898	Puerto Rico	3,515	Conquest from Spain	—
1898	Guam	209	Conquest from Spain	—
1899	American Samoa	77	Division with Germany and Britain	—
1917	Virgin Islands	132	Purchase from Denmark	$25,000,000
1947	Trust Territory of the Pacific Islands. . . . (Marshall and Caroline Islands)	533	UN Trusteeship	—
1978	Northern Mariana Islands	184	Conquest from Japan in World War II (achieved Commonwealth status in 1978). . .	
—	All other [1]	15		—

[1] Includes following islands with gross areas (in square miles) as indicated: Midway (2); Wake (3); Palmyra (4); Navassa (2); Baker, Howland, and Jarvis (combined, 3); Johnston and Sand (combined, less than ½ sq. mi.); Kingman Reef (less than ½ sq. mi.).

U.S. GOVERNMENT LANDHOLDINGS, BY STATE

Source: General Services Administration, Sept. 30, 1983

STATE	TOTAL AREA Acres	FEDERALLY OWNED Acres	%	STATE	TOTAL AREA Acres	FEDERALLY OWNED Acres	%
U.S. TOTAL ...	2,271,343,360	732,042,392.4	32.230	Missouri	44,248,320	2,177,561.9	4.921
Alabama	32,678,400	1,142,140.8	3.495	Montana	93,271,040	27,409,203.2	29.387
Alaska	365,481,600	321,527,546.9	87.974	Nebraska	49,031,680	650,736.6	1.327
Arizona	72,688,000	32,067,271.6	44.116	Nevada	70,264,320	60,049,674.3	85.463
Arkansas	33,599,360	3,474,463.3	10.341	New Hampshire	5,768,960	738,227.3	12.797
California	100,206,720	45,889,894.5	45.795	New Jersey	4,813,440	150,639.3	3.130
Colorado	66,485,760	23,919,232.3	35.977	New Mexico	77,766,400	25,920,578.4	33.331
Connecticut	3,135,360	10,464.0	0.334	New York	30,680,960	247,599.8	0.807
Delaware	1,265,920	40,744.8	3.219	North Carolina	31,402,880	2,158,585.7	6.874
Dist. of Col.	39,040	12,559.8	32.172	North Dakota	44,452,480	2,246,945.5	5.055
Florida	34,721,280	4,157,321.4	11.973	Ohio	26,222,080	365,565.4	1.394
Georgia	37,295,360	2,291,219.3	6.143	Oklahoma	44,087,680	1,600,947.5	3.631
Hawaii	4,105,600	691,053.6	16.832	Oregon	61,598,720	32,235,306.7	52.331
Idaho	52,933,120	34,480,886.1	65.141	Pennsylvania	28,804,480	694,724.5	2.412
Illinois	35,795,200	622,623.2	1.739	Rhode Island	677,120	5,804.9	0.857
Indiana	23,158,400	501,876.1	2.167	South Carolina	19,374,080	1,198,295.7	6.185
Iowa	35,860,480	228,048.7	0.636	South Dakota	48,881,920	3,148,093.2	6.440
Kansas	52,510,720	733,172.8	1.396	Tennessee	26,727,680	1,862,629.0	6.969
Kentucky	25,512,320	1,419,314.3	5.563	Texas	168,217,600	3,549,410.4	2.110
Louisiana	28,867,840	1,166,296.6	4.040	Utah	52,696,960	33,372,935.4	63.330
Maine	19,847,680	135,952.9	0.685	Vermont	5,936,640	319,700.2	5.385
Maryland	6,319,360	186,200.0	2.947	Virginia	25,496,320	2,429,066.4	9.527
Massachusetts	5,034,880	85,743.4	1.703	Washington	42,693,760	12,154,702.4	28.470
Michigan	36,492,160	3,613,649.2	9.903	West Virginia	15,410,560	1,117,425.0	7.251
Minnesota	51,205,760	3,450,423.8	6.738	Wisconsin	35,011,200	1,899,920.4	5.427
Mississippi	30,222,720	1,759,086.2	5.820	Wyoming	62,343,040	30,730,927.7	49.293

QUICK QUIZ: Who won the Heisman trophy in 1974 and 1975? See page 820.

THE STAR-SPANGLED BANNER

Oh! say, can you see, by the dawn's early light,
What so proudly we hailed at the twilight's last gleaming?
Whose broad stripes and bright stars thro' the perilous fight,
O'er the ramparts we watched, were so gallantly streaming?
And the rockets' red glare, the bombs bursting in air,
Gave proof thro' the night that our flag was still there.
Oh! say, does that star-spangled banner yet wave
O'er the land of the free and the home of the brave?

On the shore, dimly seen thro' the mist of the deep,
Where the foe's haughty host in dread silence reposes,
What is that which the breeze, o'er the towering steep,
As it fitfully blows, half conceals, half discloses?
Now it catches the gleam of the morning's first beam,
In full glory reflected, now shines on the stream,
'Tis the star-spangled banner. Oh! long may it wave
O'er the land of the free and the home of the brave!

And where is that band who so vauntingly swore,
That the havoc of war and the battle's confusion
A home and a country should leave us no more?
Their blood has washed out their foul footstep's pollution.
No refuge could save the hireling and slave
From the terror of flight or the gloom of the grave,
And the star-spangled banner in triumph doth wave
O'er the land of the free and the home of the brave.

Oh! thus be it ever when freemen shall stand
Between their loved home and the war's desolation,
Blest with vict'ry and peace may the Heav'n-rescued land
Praise the Pow'r that hath made and preserved us a nation.
Then conquer we must, when our cause it is just,
And this be our motto "In God is our trust."
And the star-spangled banner in triumph shall wave
O'er the land of the free and the home of the brave.

A naval bombardment during the War of 1812 led to the writing of the American national anthem.

Francis Scott Key, a successful Washington lawyer, visited the flagship of the British fleet in Chesapeake Bay, accompanying Col. John S. Skinner on an official mission to secure the release of a prisoner.

Detained on board the tender on which they had come out to the flagship, the two watched the bombardment of Fort McHenry at Baltimore, Md., on the night of Sept. 13–14, 1814.

Seeing the American flag still aloft at dawn, Key was inspired to write a poem.

The poem was first printed as a broadside and then, on Sept. 20, 1814, was published in the Baltimore *Patriot*. The next day, the Baltimore *American* also printed it with the title *Defence of Fort M'Henry*.

On Oct. 19, 1814, the poem was first sung in public and for the first time given the title *The Star-Spangled Banner*. As entertainment following a performance in Baltimore of the play *Count Benyowski*, the words were sung to a tune, *Anacreon in Heaven*, then widely known in America as the melody for a political song called "Adams and Liberty." Key had composed his poem in obvious imitation of this song. He borrowed not only the melody but meter and verse form as well.

President Wilson proclaimed *The Star-Spangled Banner* as the national anthem of the United States in 1916, but Congress did not confirm this action until 1931.

In Key's honor, the U.S. flag flies continuously over his grave at Frederick, Md.

There is no official act of Congress setting the exact wording of the national anthem, and several versions—differing only in detail—remain in use today.

PLEDGE OF ALLEGIANCE

I pledge allegiance to the flag of the United States of America and to the Republic for which it stands, one Nation under God, indivisible, with liberty and justice for all.

The Pledge of Allegiance to the flag was written by Francis Bellamy for the National Public School Celebration of Columbus Day in 1892. Bellamy was working for *The Youth's Companion,* a journal published in Boston. He had been appointed chairman of a committee to develop a program for the celebration of the 400th anniversary of the discovery of America.

Bellamy wrote the pledge in two hours on an August evening. It was published in *The Youth's Companion* on Sept. 8, 1892, and in the official program of the celebration. No one knows where the pledge was first used, although it is known to have been recited at the World's Columbian Exposition in Chicago on Oct. 21, 1892.

Originally, the pledge read: "I pledge allegiance to my flag and to the Republic for which it stands, one Nation indivisible, with liberty and justice for all."

In 1923, at the First National Flag Conference in Washington, D.C., the words "my flag" were changed to "the flag of the United States."

In the following year, at the Second National Flag Conference, the words "of America" were added to the phrase.

In 1954 the words "under God" were inserted.

Although the pledge became popular throughout the nation, it was not until 1942 that its words were included in federal legislation about flag use and customs. The pledge was given official congressional sanction in 1945.

HISTORY OF THE AMERICAN FLAG

Banners of the American Revolution: the Moultrie, Rhode Island, Bunker Hill, and Bennington flags.

Before American independence became a reality, there were colonial or regimental flags by the score. Many local banners carried such slogans as "Don't Tread On Me."

The Moultrie flag—the first distinctive American flag displayed in the South—flew over the fort on Sullivan's Island, outside Charleston, S.C., when a British fleet attacked on June 28, 1776. The garrison, under Col. William Moultrie, forced the British to withdraw—and the flag became known by his name. The design of this blue flag with a white crescent was suggested by the garrison's blue uniforms and the silver crescents worn by the men on their caps, inscribed with *Liberty or Death*.

Rhode Island had its own flag, carried at Brandywine, Trenton, and Yorktown. It bore an anchor, 13 stars, and the word *Hope*. Its white stars in a blue field are believed to have suggested the "starry blue field" displayed on our national flag.

Among famous New England banners was the Bunker Hill. This flag—one of the first to include the pine tree—was carried by American colonial troops at the Battle of Bunker Hill on June 17, 1775.

The Bennington flag was carried by the Green Mountain Boys at the Battle of Bennington on Aug. 16, 1777.

On Jan. 1, 1776, at a ceremony at Gen. George Washington's Prospect Hill headquarters in Cambridge (now part of Somerville), Mass., the Grand Union flag was raised as the standard of the Continental Army. It was similar to the Meteor flag of Great Britain, modified by red and white stripes signifying the 13 original colonies. Retention of the British Union in the canton, with its crosses of St. George and St. Andrew, indicated continued loyalty—as the colonists saw it—to the "mother country." This flag soon became known by various names, including the Grand Union flag, the

Union flag, the Cambridge flag, and the Colours of the United Colonies.

On June 14, 1777, the Continental Congress adopted this resolution proposed by John Adams: "Resolved: that the flag of the United States be made of thirteen stripes, alternate red and white; that the Union be thirteen stars, white in a blue field representing a new constellation." Thus was born the Stars and Stripes. It appears to have been designed primarily for use at sea, not as a battle flag on land. On a voyage that began on Sept. 30, 1787, Capt. Robert Gray in the *Columbia* carried the flag around the world for the first time.

The original flag, with its 13 stripes and 13 stars, remained in use only a few years. On Dec. 26, 1793, after the admission of two new states to the Union, Stephen R. Bradley of Vermont introduced a bill in Congress "for altering the Flag of the United States." It provided, in less than four lines of print, that beginning on May 1, 1795, the Flag of the United States should be "fifteen stripes, alternate red and white, with a union of fifteen stars white in a blue field." This was passed on Jan. 13, 1794.

Peter H. Wendover, representative to Congress from New York, was responsible for the Flag Act of April 4, 1818, which is still in effect. This act specified "thirteen horizontal stripes, alternate red and white." It provided that the "union have 20 stars, white on a blue field" and "on the admission of every new state into the Union," one star would be added on the following July 4.

On June 24, 1912, President William Howard Taft issued an executive order officially prescribing the relative proportions of the flag and the arrangement of the stars.

By an executive order of President Eisenhower, dated Aug. 21, 1959, a banner with 50 stars became the official flag of the United States on July 4, 1960.

Left to right: Grand Union Flag; original Stars and Stripes; flag of 1795–1818; flag since 1960.

HONORING THE AMERICAN FLAG

The U.S. flag code adopted by Congress provides rules for displaying and honoring the flag. The code states: "The flag represents a living country and is itself considered a living thing."

The code was amended in 1976 with Public Law 94–344 to clarify misunderstandings regarding rules that should be observed.

Below is a summary of the rules.

Raising and Lowering: The flag should be hoisted briskly and lowered ceremoniously.

When to Display: A flag made of weather-resistant material can be flown around the clock in any weather if properly illuminated.

It should be displayed especially on New Year's Day, Inauguration Day, Lincoln's Birthday, Washington's Birthday, Easter Sunday, Mother's Day, Armed Forces Day, Memorial Day, Flag Day, Independence Day, Labor Day, Constitution Day, Columbus Day, Navy Day, Veterans Day, Thanksgiving Day, Christmas Day, on other days proclaimed by the President, on the birthdays of states, and on state holidays.

Public Buildings: The flag should be displayed daily on or near the main administration building of every public institution, in or near every polling place on election days, and in or near every schoolhouse on school days.

In a Procession: When carried in a procession with another flag or flags, it should be either on the marching right (the flag's own right) or, if there is a line of other flags, in front of the center of that line (see Figure 1 above). It should not be carried on a parade float except flat or from a staff.

On a Vehicle: The flag should not be draped on or over any part of a vehicle, railroad train, or boat. When displayed on an automobile, the staff should be firmly clamped to the right front fender.

With Other Flags: No other flag or pennant should be placed above or, if on the same level, to the United States flag's right.

When it is displayed with another flag against a wall from crossed staffs, it should be on the right (the flag's own right) and its staff should be in front of that of the other flag (see Figure 2).

The U.S. flag should be at the center and at the highest point of the group when a number of flags of states or localities or society pennants are grouped and displayed from staffs (see Figure 3).

When state, city, local flags, or society pennants are flown on the same halyard with the U.S. flag, the latter should always be at the peak (see Figure 4). When such other

flags are flown from adjacent staffs, the U.S. flag should be hoisted first and lowered last.

When flags of two or more nations are displayed, they are to be flown from separate staffs of the same height *(see Figure 5)*. The flags should be of about equal size.

Within the United States or any U.S. territory or possession no person is permitted to display the United Nations flag or any other national or international flag equal, above, or in a position of superior prominence or honor to, or in place of, the U.S. flag. However, this does not apply to the practice at UN headquarters in New York City of displaying the flag of the UN in a position of superior prominence or honor, and other national flags in a position of equal prominence or honor.

At Half-Staff: The flag, when flown at half-staff, should first be hoisted momentarily to the peak and then lowered to one-half the distance between the top and bottom of the staff. It should be again raised to the peak before it is lowered *(see Figure 6)*.

From a Building: When displayed from a staff projecting horizontally or at an angle from the windowsill, balcony, or front of a building, the union (blue field) of the flag should be placed at the peak of the staff, unless the flag is at half-staff *(see Figure 7)*.

Not on a Staff: When the flag is displayed other than by being flown from a staff, indoors or out, it should either be displayed flat or suspended so that its folds fall freely as though it were staffed. When displayed flat (either horizontally or vertically) against a wall or window, the union should be uppermost and to the flag's own right (to the observer's left) *(see Figure 8)*.

Over a Street: When displayed over the middle of a street, the flag should be suspended vertically with the union to the north in an east-west street or to the east in a north-south street *(see Figure 9)*.

In an Auditorium: When used on a speaker's platform, the flag, if displayed flat, should be above and behind the speaker. When displayed from a staff in a church or public auditorium, the flag should hold the position of superior prominence, in advance of the audience, and in the position of honor at the clergyman's or speaker's right as he faces the audience. Any other flag so displayed should be placed at the clergyman's or speaker's left or to the right of the audience.

At an Unveiling: The flag should never be used as covering for the statue or monument.

At a Funeral: When the flag is used to cover a casket, it should be placed so that the union is at the head and over the left shoulder.

It should not be lowered into the grave or allowed to touch the ground.

Saluting the Flag: During the hoisting or lowering of the flag, when it is passing in a parade or in a review, or during rendition of the national anthem, all persons present should face the flag and stand at attention.

Those in uniform should give the military salute.

When not in uniform, men should remove their hats, holding them at their left shoulder with the right hand over the heart. Men without hats should salute by placing the right hand over the heart. Aliens should stand at attention. The salute to the flag in a moving column should be made at the moment the flag passes.

Some Flag Don'ts: The flag should:

Never be dipped in salute to any person or thing.

Never be displayed with the union down *except as a signal of dire distress.*

Never touch anything beneath it, such as the ground, the floor, or water.

Never be carried flat or horizontally, but always aloft and free.

Never be used as a ceiling covering.

Never have placed upon it, nor on any part of it, nor attached to it any mark, insignia, letter, word, figure, design, picture, or drawing of any nature.

Never be used as a receptacle for receiving, holding, carrying, or delivering anything.

Never be used as wearing apparel, bedding, or drapery.

Never be festooned, drawn back, or up, in folds, but always be allowed to fall free.

Never be fastened, displayed, used or stored in such a manner as to permit it to be easily torn, soiled, or damaged in any way.

Never be used for advertising purposes in any manner whatsoever.

Never be embroidered on such articles as cushions or handkerchiefs and the like, printed or impressed on paper napkins or boxes or anything designed for temporary use and discard.

Advertising signs should not be fastened to a staff or halyard from which the flag flies.

No part of the flag should ever be used as a costume or athletic uniform. However, a flag patch may be affixed to the uniform of military personnel, firemen, policemen, and members of patriotic organizations. The lapel flag pin, being a replica, should be worn on the left lapel near the heart.

It is a federal crime to knowingly cast contempt on the flag by "publicly mutilating, defacing, defiling, burning, or trampling upon it."

FAMOUS PERSONS IN AMERICAN HISTORY

Brief biographies of famous persons in American history on the following pages include statesmen, political leaders, heroes, reformers, and others.

Biographies of *U.S. Presidents and First Ladies* appear on pages 338–386.

For biographical information on other famous Americans, see the following tables: *Authors and Writers*, pages 90–99; *Musicians, Composers, Singers, and Dancers*, pages 56–61; *Show Business Personalities*, pages 263–280; *Painters, Sculptors, and Architects*, pages 62–66; *Pioneers in Medicine*, pages 454–456; *Scientists and Inventors*, pages 719–725; *Theologians and Philosophers*, pages 714–716; and obituaries of American men and women who died in 1985, pages 981–986.

Dean Gooderham Acheson (1893–1971): Played major role in developing U.S. foreign policy during and after World War II under Presidents F.D. Roosevelt and Truman; served as assistant secretary of state, 1941–45, under- secretary of state, 1945–47, secretary of state, 1949–53; became target of Sen. Joseph McCarthy (R-Wis.) and his followers, who accused Acheson of being "soft on communism" and of "coddling" communists as members of State Department; born in Middletown, Conn.

Samuel Adams (1722–1803): Patriot leader in period of American Revolution; helped organize Sons of Liberty to oppose British Stamp Act, 1765; began committee of correspondence in Massachusetts, 1772, to inform other colonies of patriot actions; organized Boston Tea Party, 1773; delegate to Continental Congress, 1774–82; voted for and signed Declaration of Independence, 1776; lieutenant governor of Massachusetts, 1789–93; governor of Massachusetts, 1793–97; born in Boston.

Jane Addams (1860–1935): Founded first settlement house (or neighborhood center) in Chicago, called Hull House, with Ellen Gates Starr, 1889; became first woman president of National Conference of Charities and Corrections, 1909; as pacifist, was president of Women's International League for Peace and Freedom, 1915–29; co-recipient of Nobel Peace Prize with Nicholas Murray Butler, 1931; born in Cedarville, Ill.

Spiro Theodore Agnew (born 1918): 39th Vice President of U.S., 1969–73; first ever forced to resign; accepted conviction for income tax evasion, 1973, to avoid prosecution on bribery charges; Republican governor of Maryland, 1967–69; nominated Richard M. Nixon for President at national convention, 1968, and became his running mate; born in Towson, Md.

Ethan Allen (1738–89): Led Vermont's Green Mountain Boys in capture of British Fort Ticonderoga, May 10, 1775, in first American victory of Revolutionary War; during Battle of Montreal in September 1775, was captured and imprisoned, 1775–78; upon return, worked to achieve recognition of Vermont's independence; born in Litchfield, Conn.

Richard Allen (1760–1831): Founded first black religious denomination in U.S., Bethel African Methodist Episcopal Church, 1794, in Philadelphia; born a slave in Philadelphia; gained freedom, 1786.

Susan Brownell Anthony (1820–1906): Early advocate of women's rights, temperance, and abolition; with Elizabeth Cady Stanton founded National Woman Suffrage ⸺⸺⸺⸺ 1869, and was its president, 1892–1900; arrested for voting in 1872; trial brought attention to women's rights movement; born in Adams, Mass.

Johnny Appleseed (John Chapman; 1774–1845): Legendary pioneer who planted apple trees in Ohio and Indiana along route of migrating settlers during westward movement in early 1800s; born in Leominster, Mass.

Neil Alden Armstrong (born 1930): First man to set foot on Moon as commander of *Apollo 11* mission, 1969, declaring: "That's one small step for a man, one giant leap for mankind"; performed first manual docking in space with astronaut David R. Scott in *Gemini 8*, 1966; flew 78 combat missions in Korean War as Navy pilot; born near Wapakoneta, Ohio.

Benedict Arnold (1741–1801): Revolutionary War traitor; as Continental Army major general displayed heroism in American victory at Battles of Saratoga, 1777; as military commander of Philadelphia, 1778–80, was convicted by court-martial of using position for personal gain, but received only reprimand; as commander of West Point, N.Y., 1780, bargained with British to surrender fort for large bonus, but plot was uncovered by capture of British spy Maj. John André; Arnold escaped to British lines and fought against Americans for rest of Revolutionary War; born in Norwich, Conn.

John Jacob Astor (1763–1848): Became one of richest men in U.S. by monopolizing fur trade with Europe and China; established American Fur Co., 1808, and Pacific Fur Co., 1810; founded Astoria, Ore., 1811; sold fur holdings, 1834, and invested in farmland that became heart of New York City; fortune was estimated at $20 million; born in Waldorf, Germany.

Stephen Fuller Austin (1793–1836): Established first American settlement in Texas, on Brazos River, 1821; initiated demands for Texas independence from Mexico; became first secretary of state of independent Texas Republic, 1836; born in Wythe County, Va.

George Bancroft (1800–91): Historian and public official; wrote 10-volume *History of the United States*, 1834–76; as secretary of the navy, 1845–46, founded U.S. Naval Academy at Annapolis, Md.; served as U.S. minister to Britain, 1846–49, and to Germany, 1867–74; born in Worcester, Mass.

Benjamin Banneker (1731–1806): Black mathematician and astronomer; helped survey District of Columbia, 1791; published annual astronomical almanac, 1791–1802, used by abolitionists to prove blacks were as capable as whites; born in Ellicott, Md.

Henry Barnard (1811–1900): First U.S. commissioner of education, 1867–70; published *American Journal of Education*, 1855–82; did much to develop U.S. public-school system; born in Hartford, Conn.

Phineas Taylor ("P.T.") Barnum (1810–91): Showman known for his claim "There's a sucker born every minute"; opened circus *Greatest Show on Earth*, 1871; combined with major rival to form Barnum & Bailey Circus, 1881; born in Bethel, Conn.

Clara Barton (1821–1912): Known as "Angel of the Battlefield"; organized nursing services for Union Army during Civil War, 1861–65; served in Europe as nurse during Franco-Prussian War, 1870; founded American Red Cross, 1881, and was its first president, 1882–1904; initiated Red Cross help for peacetime disasters; born near Oxford, Mass.

Bernard Baruch (1870–1965): Financier and adviser to eight Presidents from Woodrow Wilson to John F. Kennedy; prepared first plan for international development and control of atomic energy as U.S. representative to UN Atomic Energy Commission, 1946; made fortune as speculator in securities; born in Camden, S.C.

Henry Ward Beecher (1813–87): Popular Protestant preacher and reformer; advocated women's rights, abolition of slavery, and civil-service reform; pastor of Plymouth Congregational Church in Brooklyn, N.Y., 1847–87; sought to reconcile evolution and religion; charged with adultery in sensational trial, 1874–75, but jury could not arrive at verdict; brother of Harriet Beecher Stowe; born in Litchfield, Conn.

Thomas Hart Benton (1782–1858): Hot-tempered Democratic U.S. senator from Missouri for 30 consecutive years, 1821–51; shot Andrew Jackson in frontier brawl in 1813 but later became Jackson's firm friend and supporter; because of personal dislike of slavery, opposed Compromise of 1850 and lost Senate seat as result; U.S. representative (D-Mo.), 1853–55; born near Hillsborough, N.C.

Billy the Kid (William H. Bonney; 1859–81): Western outlaw said to have killed 21 men, first when he was only 12; led cattle rustlers in series of slayings in New Mexico; sentenced to hang in 1881, killed two sheriff's deputies and escaped; tracked down and killed by Sheriff Pat Garrett, 1881; born in New York City.

Black Hawk (1767–1838): Indian chief of Sauk tribe; refused to honor treaty giving up lands, claiming chiefs had been made drunk before signing it; fought Black Hawk War against settlers in Illinois, 1832; Black Hawk and two sons were captured and jailed; born at Rock River, Ill.

James Gillespie Blaine (1830–93): U.S. secretary of state, 1881 and 1889–92; initiated first Pan American Conference, 1889; U.S. representative (R-Me.), 1863–76, speaker of the House, 1869–75; U.S. senator (R-Me.), 1876–81; as Republican candidate for President, 1884, was defeated largely because New York voters were angered by Blaine supporter labeling Democrats as party of "rum, Romanism and rebellion";

born in West Brownsville, Pa.

Daniel Boone (1734–1820): Pioneer frontiersman; explored Kentucky, 1767; blazed Wilderness Road through Cumberland Gap and built Boonesborough, Ky., 1775; famous as Indian fighter; born near Reading, Pa.

John Wilkes Booth (1838–65): Assassin of President Lincoln, 1865; a Shakespearean actor, he escaped after shooting Lincoln but was tracked down and killed 12 days later in barn near Port Royal, Va.; born in Bel Air, Md.

James Bowie (1796–1836): Hero of Texas War for Independence; among those who fought to death against Mexicans in Battle of the Alamo, 1836; invented frontier hunting knife, called Bowie knife; born in Burke County, Ga.

William Bradford (1590–1657): Pilgrim leader; came to America on *Mayflower* and helped found Plymouth Colony; elected colony's governor, 1621, he served for 30 of next 35 years; wrote *History of Plymouth Plantation*, 1651; born in Yorkshire, England.

Omar Nelson Bradley (1893–1981): Commander of U.S. ground forces in Normandy invasion of France, 1944; then led about 1 million U.S. troops in 12th Army Group that conquered German-occupied Europe, 1944–45; U.S. Army chief of staff, 1948–49; first chairman Joint Chiefs of Staff, 1949–53; promoted to 5-star General of the Army, 1950; wrote *A Soldier's Story*, 1951; graduated from West Point, 1915; born in Clark, Mo.

Mathew B. Brady (c.1823–96): Photographer of U.S. Civil War; took more than 3,500 photos; born in Warren County, N.Y.

Louis Dembitz Brandeis (1856–1941): Associate justice of U.S. Supreme Court, 1916–39; during most of period court was controlled by conservatives, so that Brandeis often dissented from rulings, issuing his own more liberal opinions; born in Louisville, Ky.

John Cabell Breckinridge (1821–75): 14th Vice President of U.S., 1857–61; was unsuccessful Southern Democratic candidate for President against Lincoln, 1860; served several months in 1861 as Democratic U.S. senator from Kentucky, voting against Lincoln's war measures; escaped to South to become Confederate general and then secretary of war, 1865; after war fled to Cuba, then to England, returning home in 1868; born near Lexington, Ky.

James Bridger (1804–81): Frontiersman; explored Rocky Mountains as fur trapper; was first white man to discover Great Salt Lake, 1824, and one of first to describe wonders of Yellowstone region; built Fort Bridger in Wyoming, 1843, as supply station on Oregon Trail; born in Richmond, Va.

John Brown (1800–59): Radical abolitionist; led raid on proslavery settlers at Pottawatomie Creek in Kansas, 1856, killing five; with followers, captured federal arsenal at Harpers Ferry, Va., Oct. 16, 1859, planning to use arms to start slave revolt in South; U.S. Marines led by Col. Robert E. Lee forced Brown and followers to surrender; convicted of murder and treason against Virginia, Brown was hanged on Dec. 2, 1859; born in Torrington, Conn.

QUICK-QUIZ: What horse holds the world one-mile record for trotting? See page 835.

FAMOUS PERSONS IN AMERICAN HISTORY *(continued)*

Blanche Kelso Bruce (1841–98): First black to serve full term as U.S. senator (R-Miss.), 1875–81; register of U.S. treasury, 1881–85, 1897–98; born in slavery near Farmville, Va.

William Jennings Bryan (1860–1925): Three-time loser as Democratic candidate for President, 1896, 1900, 1908; as secretary of state, 1913–15, tried to keep U.S. out of World War I, resigning when President Wilson insisted on sending strong notes of protest to Germany about submarine attacks; originally won fame with "Cross of Gold" speech at Democratic convention, 1896, calling for free coinage of silver; a believer in fundamental religion, Bryan aided prosecution at Scopes evolution trial, 1925; born in Salem, Ill.

Ralph Johnson Bunche (1904–71): First black American awarded Nobel Peace Prize, 1950; UN mediator in first Arab-Israeli War, 1948–49; undersecretary of state of United Nations, 1955–71; born in Detroit, Mich.

Warren Earl Burger (born 1907): 15th Chief Justice of U.S., appointed 1969 by President Nixon; though known as conservative, surprised many by liberal rulings favoring busing to end school segregation, 1971; overturning state laws restricting abortions during first six months of pregnancy, 1973; and denying President Nixon's claim to executive privilege in Watergate investigation, 1974; judge of U.S. Court of Appeals in Washington, D.C., 1956–69; born in St. Paul, Minn.

Aaron Burr (1756–1836): 3d Vice President of U.S., 1801–05; after winning tie electoral vote for President, U.S. House of Representatives decided in favor of Thomas Jefferson; killed Alexander Hamilton in duel, 1804; tried for treason for plotting independent empire in West, but acquitted, 1807; served as U.S. senator (D-R.-N.Y.), 1791–97; born in Newark, N.J.

George Bush (born 1924): 43d Vice President of U.S., 1981– ; oil company executive, 1953–66; U.S. representative (R-Tex.), 1967–71; U.S. ambassador to UN, 1971–72; chairman, Republican National Committee, 1973–74; director, CIA, 1976–77; defeated by Ronald Reagan in campaign for Republican presidential nomination, 1980; born in Milton, Mass.

Richard Evelyn Byrd (1888–1957): Made first flight over North Pole, with pilot Floyd Bennett, 1926; established "Little America" base in Antarctica, 1928–30, 1933–35; made first flight over South Pole, 1929; promoted to rear admiral in U.S. Navy, 1930; born in Winchester, Va.

Saint Frances Xavier Cabrini (1850–1917): First U.S. citizen to be made saint by Roman Catholic Church, 1946; founded Missionary Sisters of the Sacred Heart, 1880; aided poor Italians in U.S., founding orphanages, schools, and hospitals; born in Lombardy, Italy.

John Caldwell Calhoun (1782–1850): 7th Vice President of U.S., 1825–32, resigning to lead nullification fight against President Jackson; felt South Carolina could nullify federal protective tariffs that it disapproved, but wilted when Jackson threatened to use force to enforce tariff; served as secretary of war, 1817–25, and secretary of state, 1844–45; as U.S. representative (D-S.C.), 1811–17, was "war hawk" in favor of

War of 1812; as U.S. senator (D-S.C.), 1832–43, 1845–50, opposed Mexican War and Compromise of 1850; born in what is now Mount Carmel, S.C.

Hattie Wyatt Caraway (1878–1950): First woman elected to U.S. Senate; was appointed U.S. senator (D-Ark.) on Nov. 13, 1931, to fill vacancy caused by death of husband, Sen. Thaddeus H. Caraway; elected to U.S. Senate on Jan. 12, 1932; reelected to full terms in 1932 and 1938; born in Bakerville, Tenn.

Benjamin Nathan Cardozo (1870–1938): Associate justice of U.S. Supreme Court, 1932–38; on principle that Constitution was flexible to permit social change, wrote ruling upholding Social Security Act, 1937; born in New York City.

Andrew Carnegie (1835–1919): Industrialist and philanthropist; starting work as telegraph messenger boy at 15, he amassed fortune estimated at $500 million; developed Carnegie Steel Company, which he sold to U.S. Steel for $225 million in 1901; contributed money to build 2,500 public libraries in English-speaking countries; endowed various foundations and institutions to promote peace and education; born in Dunfermline, Scotland.

Christopher ("Kit") Carson (1809–68): Explored West as frontiersman and fur trapper in 1820s and 1830s; guide for John C. Frémont on expeditions to Colorado, Oregon, and California, 1842–48; organized volunteer force to check Indian raids on settlers in New Mexico during Civil War; born in Madison County, Ky.

Salmon Portland Chase (1808–73): 6th Chief Justice of U.S., 1864–73; presided over Senate impeachment trial of President Johnson in 1868; as Lincoln's secretary of the treasury, 1861–64, financed Union expenses in Civil War through loans and issuing "greenbacks"; as antislavery U.S. senator from Ohio, 1849–55, 1861, fought Compromise of 1850 and Kansas-Nebraska Act; first Republican governor of Ohio, 1856–60; born in Cornish, N.H.

Cesar Estrada Chavez (born 1927): Labor organizer of migrant farm workers, especially Mexican-Americans; formed farm workers union, 1962; a believer in nonviolence, Chavez organized nationwide boycotts against grape and lettuce growers in 1960s and 1970s to force producers to agree to union contracts; born near Yuma, Ariz.

George Rogers Clark (1752–1818): Frontiersman-soldier during Revolutionary War; led about 200 militia down Ohio River and across wilderness to capture British forts at Kaskaskia, Ill., 1778, and at Vincennes, Ind., 1779; destroyed Shawnee village of Chillicothe, Ohio, 1780, putting an end to Indian raids on settlers in Kentucky; born near Charlottesville, Va.

William Clark (1770–1838): With Meriwether Lewis, explored Missouri and Columbia rivers of new Louisiana Territory, 1804–06; governor of Missouri Territory, 1813–20; younger brother of George Rogers Clark; born in Caroline County, Va.

Henry Clay (1777–1852): Whig leader; three-time loser for President, 1824, 1832, 1844; mediated Missouri Compromise of 1820 and sponsored Compromise of 1850; advocated protective tariff and federal aid for internal improvements; U.S. secretary of state, 1825–29; U.S.

senator from Kentucky, 1806–07, 1810–11, 1831–42, 1849–52; U.S. representative from Kentucky, 1811–14, 1815–21, 1823–25, also serving as Speaker of the House during most of those terms; led "war hawks" in favor of War of 1812; born in Hanover County, Va.

De Witt Clinton (1769–1828): Father of Erie Canal, linking Hudson River with Great Lakes; private secretary to uncle, New York Gov. George Clinton, 1790–95; U.S. senator (D-R–N.Y.), 1802–03; mayor of New York City, 1803–07, 1810–11, 1813–14; unsuccessful Federalist and Peace Party candidate for President, 1812; headed commission presenting plans for Erie Canal to legislature, 1815; as governor of New York, 1817–21, 1825–28, broke ground for beginning Erie Canal, 1817, and officially opened canal, 1825; born in Napanock, N.Y.

George Clinton (1739–1812): 4th Vice President of U.S., 1805–12, serving under Presidents Jefferson and Madison; first state governor of New York, 1777–95, 1801–04, elected to record seven terms; as delegate to Continental Congress, 1775–76, voted for Declaration of Independence but was unable to sign it, having been called to duty as brigadier general of militia on July 8, 1776; born in Little Britain, N.Y.

William Frederick ("Buffalo Bill") Cody (1846–1917): Frontiersman and showman; as buffalo hunter, claimed to have killed over 4,000 in 1867–68 as food for railroad construction crews; became nationally known in 1870s as result of dime novels about him written by E.Z.C. Judson (Ned Buntline); organized traveling "Wild West" show, 1883, with which he toured U.S. and Europe for rest of life; show featured markswoman Annie Oakley and, for a while, Indian Chief Sitting Bull; born in Scott County, Iowa.

Crazy Horse (c.1844–77): Sioux Indian chief who helped lead Sioux War of 1876–77, protesting federal government orders that Indians remain on reservations; defeated Gen. George Crook in Battle of Rosebud; massacred Gen. George A. Custer and troops in Battle of Little Bighorn; surrendered voluntarily but was killed while being forced into prison cell.

Davy Crockett (1786–1836): Frontiersman and congressman; served as scout for Gen. Andrew Jackson in Creek War, 1813–14, becoming colonel in Tennessee militia; represented Tennessee in Congress, first as Democrat, 1827–31, then as Whig, 1833–35; died in Battle of the Alamo, 1836; born in Greene County, Tenn.

George Armstrong Custer (1839–76): Union cavalry officer whose daring and skill won him promotion to brigadier general at age 23 during Civil War; in Battle of Little Bighorn in Montana, June 25, 1876, led U.S. cavalry attack on Sioux Indians of Crazy Horse and Sitting Bull, but he and entire column of about 225 men were slain in what became known as "Custer's Last Stand"; graduated last in his class at West Point, 1861; born in New Rumley, Ohio.

George Mifflin Dallas (1792–1864): 11th Vice President of U.S., under President Polk, 1845–49; mayor of Philadelphia, 1829; U.S. senator (D-Pa.), 1831–33; U.S. minister to Russia, 1837–39, and to Britain, 1856–61; born in Philadelphia.

Clarence Seward Darrow (1857–1938): Criminal and labor lawyer noted for his defense of underdog and unpopular causes; earned first fame for defense of labor leader Eugene V. Debs in Pullman strike of 1894; initiated use of psychiatric evidence in Leopold-Loeb murder trial, saving clients from death penalty, 1924; opposed William Jennings Bryan in Scopes trial, 1925; born in Kinsman, Ohio.

Jefferson Davis (1808–89): President of Confederate States of America during Civil War, 1861–65; imprisoned 1865–67 on charges of treason; finally released on bond signed by Horace Greeley and others and never brought to trial; served as U.S. representative (D-Miss.), 1845–46, resigning to fight as colonel in Mexican War; won acclaim in Battles of Monterrey and Buena Vista, 1846–47; U.S. senator (D-Miss.), 1847–51, opposing Compromise of 1850; U.S. secretary of war under President Pierce, 1853–57; born in Christian (now Todd) County, Ky., on June 3, 1808.

Charles Gates Dawes (1865–1951): 30th Vice President of U.S., under President Coolidge, 1925–29; co-recipient of Nobel Peace Prize in 1925 for Dawes Plan, scheduling payments of $33 billion in World War I reparations by Germany; U.S. ambassador to Britain, 1929–32; first chairman of Reconstruction Finance Corporation, 1932; born in Marietta, Ohio.

Benjamin Henry Day (1810–89): Founded New York *Sun* in 1833 as first penny newspaper hawked on streets by newsboys; circulation of 30,000 was largest of any newspaper at that time; born in West Springfield, Mass.

Stephen Day (c.1594–1668): First printer in what is now U.S.; established press in Cambridge, Mass; printed first broadside, *The Freeman's Oath*, 1639; first book, *The Bay Psalm Book*, 1640; born in Cambridge, England.

Eugene Victor Debs (1855–1926): Socialist labor leader; established American Railway Union (ARU), 1893; jailed for disobeying federal injunction against ARU boycott on moving Pullman cars to support striking Pullman workers, 1894; ran for President five times as candidate of Social Democratic (Socialist) Party, 1900–20; jailed under wartime Espionage Act, 1918–21; born in Terre Haute, Ind.

Stephen Decatur (1779–1820): U.S. Navy officer; gained first fame with daring raid in harbor of Tripoli, Libya, burning U.S. frigate *Philadelphia* that had been captured by Barbary Coast Arab pirates, 1804; in War of 1812 commanded squadron that captured British warship *Macedonian;* as commodore, 1815, led squadron to Mediterranean that forced Arab pirates to give up attacks on U.S. ships; upon return gave toast: "Our country: In her intercourse with foreign nations may she always be right; but our country, right or wrong"; born in Sinepuxent, Md.

George Dewey (1837–1917): Admiral in Spanish-American War; destroyed Spanish Pacific fleet in Manila Bay on May 1, 1898, after giving captain of lead ship of his squadron famous command: "You may fire when you are ready, Gridley"; victory assured U.S. conquest of Philippines; graduated from Annapolis, 1858; born in Montpelier, Vt.

QUICK QUIZ: Who was winner in the Cotton Bowl in 1974? See page 813.

FAMOUS PERSONS IN AMERICAN HISTORY *(continued)*

John Dewey (1859–1952): Philosopher and educator; was pragmatist, believing ideas can only be judged on basis of how well they work; developed philosophy, called instrumentalism, that man can overcome obstacles by using experience and intelligence; taught at University of Chicago, 1894–1904, and at Columbia, 1904–30; opposed traditional memorization of facts, in favor of learning through activities to stimulate thought; born in Burlington, Vt.

Thomas Edmund Dewey (1902–71): Unsuccessful Republican candidate for President, 1944, 1948; three-term governor of New York, 1943–54; gained fame as district attorney and special prosecutor in New York City, convicting such gangsters as Waxey Gordon and Lucky Luciano, 1931–38; born in Owosso, Mich.

John Dickinson (1732–1808): Called "Penman of the Revolution" because of many important documents he wrote in early U.S. history; as Pennsylvania delegate to Stamp Act Congress, wrote *Declaration of Rights and Grievances of the Colonists of America*, 1765; published *Letters from a Farmer in Pennsylvania to Inhabitants of the British Colonies*, 1767; opposed and refused to sign Declaration of Independence, believing colonies should remain part of British Empire; wrote Articles of Confederation, 1776; fought in Revolutionary War, 1777–78; president of Delaware, 1781–82; president of Pennsylvania, 1782–85; presided at Annapolis Convention, 1786; delegate to Constitutional Convention, 1787; born near Trappe, Md.

Dorothea Lynde Dix (1802–87): Crusaded for building of separate hospitals for mentally ill patients, who in 1840s were confined in prisons with criminals; succeeded in getting such hospitals built in 15 states, Canada, Europe, and Japan; superintendent of nurses for Union Army during Civil War; born in Hampden, Me.

Stephen Arnold Douglas (1813–61): Unsuccessful Democratic candidate for President against Abraham Lincoln in 1860; as U.S. senator (D-Ill.), 1847–61, helped pass Compromise of 1850 and sponsored Kansas-Nebraska Act of 1854 that replaced Missouri Compromise with "popular sovereignty" in territories on slavery issue; defeated Lincoln in Illinois Senate race in 1858, featuring seven famous Lincoln-Douglas debates; born in Brandon, Vt.

Frederick Douglass (1817–95): Black abolitionist; escaped from slavery in Maryland in 1838, settling in Massachusetts; published autobiography, 1845, and fled to England until friends arranged for purchase of his freedom; founded abolitionist newspaper *North Star*, 1847; recruited black troops for Union Army during Civil War, 1861–65; U.S. minister to Haiti, 1889–91; born in Tuckahoe, Md.

W.E.B. Du Bois (1868–1963): Black civil-rights leader and scholar; helped found National Association for the Advancement of Colored People (NAACP), 1909; edited NAACP magazine *The Crisis*, 1910–34; head of sociology department, Atlanta University, 1932–44; joined Communist Party, 1961, and emigrated to Ghana, 1962; born in Great Barrington, Mass.

John Foster Dulles (1888–1959): U.S. secretary of state under President Eisenhower, 1953–59; in Cold War period, developed policy of "brinksmanship," going almost to point of war with communist nations, and threatened "massive retaliation" for communist aggressions; delegate to UN, 1945–50; U.S. senator (R-N.Y.), 1949; main author of Japanese peace treaty, 1951; born in Washington, D.C.

Eleuthére Irénée du Pont de Nemours (1771–1834): Built gunpowder plant near Wilmington, Del., 1802, providing basis for later Du Pont industrial empire developed by his descendants; learned how to make gunpowder as student of French chemist Antoine Lavoisier; born in Paris.

Amelia Earhart (1897–1937): First woman pilot to fly solo across Atlantic, 1932; first to fly solo from Hawaii to mainland, 1935; vanished in Pacific Ocean while attempting around-the-world flight, 1937; born in Atchison, Kan.

Mary Baker Eddy (1821–1910): Founded Christian Science about 1870; wrote *Science and Health*, 1875, describing belief that prayer can overcome illness; chartered Church of Christ, Scientist, 1879; established *Christian Science Monitor*, 1908; born in Bow, N.H.

Oliver Ellsworth (1745–1807): 3d Chief Justice of U.S., 1796–1800; as special envoy to Paris he negotiated treaty ending undeclared naval war between U.S. and France, 1800; as U.S. senator (Fed.-Conn.), 1789–96, largely responsible for drafting Federal Judiciary Act of 1789, laying basis for U.S. court system; Connecticut delegate to Continental Congress, 1777–84, and to Constitutional Convention, 1787; born in Windsor, Conn.

James Leonard Farmer (born 1920): Black civil-rights leader; helped found Congress of Racial Equality (CORE), 1942, to end racial discrimination by passive resistance; under his guidance as national director, CORE began lunch-counter sit-ins and freedom rides in Southern states in 1960s that often touched off mass arrests of demonstrators; assistant secretary of Health, Education, and Welfare, 1969–70; born in Marshall, Texas.

David Glasgow Farragut (1801–70): U.S. Navy admiral in Civil War; best remembered for command "Damn the torpedoes. Full steam ahead!" in his victorious attack on Mobile, Ala., in August 1864; earlier became Union hero when his fleet forced surrender of New Orleans on May 1, 1862; first U.S. Navy officer to hold ranks of rear admiral (1862), vice admiral (1864), and full admiral (1866); born near Knoxville, Tenn.

Marshall Field (1834–1906): Merchant and philanthropist; beginning as $8-a-week sales clerk, became multimillionaire developer of largest department store in Chicago; innovated marking products with firm prices; coined slogan "Give the Lady What She Wants"; gave land and millions of dollars to establish University of Chicago and Field Museum of Natural History; born in Conway Township, Mass.

Nathan Bedford Forrest (1821–77): Confederate cavalry leader in Civil War; despite lack of formal education, rose from private to lt. general; led troops in many successful raids and battles; attributed success to ability "to git thar fustest with the mostest men"; reputedly was first Grand Wizard of Ku Klux Klan; born at Chapel Hill, Tenn.

Benjamin Franklin (1706–90): Helped draft and signed Declaration of Independence, 1776, alliance with France, 1778, treaty of peace with Britain, 1783, and U.S. Constitution, 1787; edited and published *Pennsylvania Gazette*, 1729–1766, and *Poor Richard's Almanack*, 1732–57; invented Franklin stove, 1740, and proved lightning was electricity, 1752; deputy postmaster of American colonies, 1753–74; wrote Albany Plan for uniting American colonies, 1754; Pennsylvania representative in London, 1757–75; member of Continental Congress and first postmaster general, 1775–76; ambassador to France, 1776–85; governor of Pennsylvania, 1785–88; born in Boston.

John Charles Frémont (1813–90): First Republican candidate for President, 1856; led military expeditions that explored territory from Rocky Mountains to California, 1842–44; on third expedition, 1845–47, helped capture California in Mexican War and served briefly as territory's first governor; in dispute with Maj. Gen. Stephen W. Kearny, was found guilty of insubordination by court-martial and resigned from Army; gold discovered on land he owned made him millionaire overnight; upon California's admission as state, served six months as Free-Soil Democrat U.S. senator, 1850–51; major general in Union Army in West during Civil War, 1861–64; governor of Arizona Territory, 1878–81; born in Savannah.

Albert Gallatin (1761–1849): U.S. secretary of the treasury under Presidents Jefferson and Madison, 1802–14; as member of War of 1812 peace commission, negotiated Treaty of Ghent, 1814; minister to France, 1815–23, and to Britain, 1826–27; born in Geneva, Switzerland.

William Lloyd Garrison (1805–79): Abolitionist leader; published abolitionist newspaper *Liberator*, 1831–65, promising, "I will be heard!"; helped organize American Anti-Slavery Society, 1833, and served as president in 1840s and 1850s; after Civil War, crusaded for prohibition and women's rights; born in Newburyport, Mass.

Horatio Gates (c.1728–1806): Revolutionary War major general; commanded American army at Battle of Saratoga, 1777, forcing surrender of over 5,000 British troops; reputation shattered at Battle of Camden (S.C.), 1780, when his army of 4,000 was destroyed by British General Cornwallis and Gates fled in retreat; born in Maldon, England.

Henry George (1839–97): Promoted "single tax" on land use to replace all other taxes to let economic laws operate freely; published ideas in *Progress and Poverty*, 1879; twice defeated as candidate for mayor of New York City, 1886, 1897; born in Philadelphia.

Geronimo (1829–1909): Apache Indian medicine-man; his tribe raided settlers in Mexico, New Mexico, and Arizona; surrendered in 1886; imprisoned for life but allowed to make brief appearances at St. Louis World's Fair, 1904, and in Theodore Roosevelt's inaugural procession, 1905; born in southern Arizona.

Elbridge Gerry (1744–1814): 5th U.S. Vice President, 1813–14, dying in office; Massachusetts delegate to Continental Congress, 1776–85, signing both Declaration of Independence and Articles of Confederation; delegate to Constitutional Convention, 1787, but refused to sign U.S. Constitution because he disagreed with some of its provisions; Antifederalist U.S. representative from Massachusetts, 1789–93; governor of Massachusetts, 1810–12; born in Marblehead, Mass.

John Herschel Glenn Jr. (born 1921): First U.S. astronaut to orbit Earth in space, Feb. 20, 1962; U.S. Marine fighter pilot in World War II and Korean War, flying 122 combat missions; retired as astronaut, 1964; elected U.S. senator (D-Ohio), 1974; born in Cambridge, Ohio.

George Washington Goethals (1858–1928): U.S. Army engineer who directed building of Panama Canal, 1907–14; governor of Panama Canal Zone, 1914–16; born in Brooklyn, N.Y.

Barry Morris Goldwater (born 1909): Unsuccessful Republican candidate for President, 1964; called "Mr. Conservative" because of political views; U.S. senator (R-Ariz.), 1953–65, 1969– ; born in Phoenix.

Samuel Gompers (1850–1924): Labor leader who helped found and was president of American Federation of Labor (AFL), 1886–94, 1896– 1924; opposed formation of independent labor political party or union affiliations with political parties; established system of labor-management negotiations for written union contracts; born in London.

Billy (William Franklin) Graham (born 1918): Protestant evangelist; ordained as Southern Baptist minister, 1939; in four-month crusade in New York City's Madison Square Garden in 1957, nearly 2 million persons attended, resulting in more than 50,000 conversions; born near Charlotte, N.C.

Horace Greeley (1811–72): Unsuccessful Democratic and Liberal Republican candidate for President against U.S. Grant, 1872; founded and edited influential New York *Tribune*, 1841–72; helped Lincoln win Republican presidential nomination, 1860; supported abolition, prohibition, and protective tariffs; popularized phrase "Go west, young man" but did not originate it; born near Amherst, N.H.

Nathanael Greene (1742–86): Revolutionary War major general who liberated Southern states from British military occupation in series of daring battles, 1781; earlier in war, distinguished himself in Battles of Trenton, Brandywine, and Germantown; quartermaster general of Continental Army, 1778–80; born in Potowomut (now Warwick), R.I.

Alexander Meigs Haig Jr. (born 1924): U.S. secretary of state under President Reagan, 1981–82; supreme allied commander of NATO forces in Europe, 1974–78; White House chief of staff under President Nixon, 1973–74; brigade commander in Vietnam War 1966–67; graduated from West Point, 1947; born in Philadelphia, Pa.

Nathan Hale (1755–76): During Revolutionary War, while on volunteer spy mission for George Washington, was captured on Long Island, N.Y., and hanged by British, Sept. 22, 1776; remembered for heroic last words: "I only regret that I have but one life to lose for my country"; born in Coventry, Conn.

QUICK QUIZ: Who holds the college career record for most touchdown passes? See page 817.

FAMOUS PERSONS IN AMERICAN HISTORY *(continued)*
Alexander Hamilton (c.1757–1804): As first
U.S. secretary of the treasury, 1789–95, put new
government on sound financial basis; helped initi-
ate political system of two major political parties
as leader of conservative Federalists in opposition
to Thomas Jefferson's liberal Democratic-Repub-
licans; served in Revolutionary War as aide-de-
camp to George Washington, 1777–81; com-
manded regiment at Battle of Yorktown, 1781;
represented New York in Continental Congress,
1782–83; signer of U.S. Constitution, 1787; wrote
most essays in *The Federalist*, urging ratification
of Constitution, 1787–88; appointed major gener-
al of new U.S. Army, second in command to
George Washington, 1798; killed in duel with
Vice President Aaron Burr, 1804; born on island
of Nevis in British West Indies.
John Hancock (1737–93): President of Conti-
nental Congress, 1775–77, 1785–86; first signer
of Declaration of Independence, 1776; was joint
leader with Samuel Adams of Massachusetts co-
lonial resistance after British seized one of his
merchant ships on charges of illegal trading,
1768; first state governor of Massachusetts,
1780–85, 1787–93; born in North Braintree
(now Quincy), Mass.
Patrick Henry (1736–99): Virginia patriot
leader; best remembered for call for colonial re-
sistance in 1775: "I know not what course oth-
ers may take; but as for me, give me liberty, or
give me death!"; commanded Virginia's militia,
1775–76; delegate to Continental Congress,
1774–76; first state governor of Virginia,
1776–79, 1784–86; opposed adoption of U.S.
Constitution because it lacked Bill of Rights,
1787–88; born in Hanover County, Virginia.
Oliver Wendell Holmes Jr. (1841–1935): As
associate justice of U.S. Supreme Court,
1902–32, became known as "the Great Dissent-
er" because he disagreed so often with conserva-
tive majority; believed court should not upset
social legislation unless it specifically violated
Constitution; born in Boston.
J. Edgar Hoover (1895–1972): Director of
Federal Bureau of Investigation (FBI), 1924–72;
developed FBI into efficient crime-fighting orga-
nization free of politics; initiated services to local
police, such as fingerprint file for identifying
criminals; born in Washington, D.C.
Mark Hopkins (1802–87): Educator; president
of Williams College, 1836–72; gained fame when
President James Garfield described his effective-
ness as a teacher, saying, "Give me a log hut, with
only a simple bench, Mark Hopkins on one end and
I on the other"; born in Stockbridge, Mass.
Samuel Houston (1793–1863): Commander of
army of American settlers in Texas War of Inde-
pendence, 1836; defeated Mexicans in Battle of
San Jacinto, April 21, 1836; president of Texas
Republic, 1836–38, 1841–44; U.S. senator (D-
Texas), 1846–59; as Texas governor, 1859–61,
deposed for opposition to secession; U.S. repre-
sentative (D-Tenn.), 1823–27; Tennessee gover-
nor, 1827–29; born near Lexington, Va.
Charles Evans Hughes (1862–1948): 12th
Chief Justice of U.S., 1930–41; fought President
F.D. Roosevelt's effort at "court packing" to
end court's reversals of New Deal legislation; as-
sociate justice of U.S. Supreme Court, 1910–16,

resigning to run, unsuccessfully, as Republican
candidate for President, 1916; secretary of state
under Presidents Harding and Coolidge,
1921–25; born in Glens Falls, N.Y.
Cordell Hull (1871–1955): U.S. secretary of
state, 1933–44; initiated "good neighbor" policy
with Latin America, 1933; was negotiating with
Japanese envoys in Washington when Pearl Har-
bor was bombed, 1941; developed plans for
United Nations, 1944; awarded Nobel Peace
Prize, 1945; U.S. representative (D-Tenn.),
1907–21, 1923–31; U.S. senator (D-Tenn.),
1931–33; born in Overton County, Tenn.
Hubert Horatio Humphrey (1911–78): 38th
Vice President of U.S., under President L.B.
Johnson, 1965–69; unsuccessful Democratic can-
didate for President, 1968; U.S. senator (D-
Minn.), 1949–65, 1971–78; mayor of Minneapo-
lis, Minn., 1945–49; born in Wallace, S.D.
Thomas Jonathan ("Stonewall") Jackson
(1824–63): Confederate general; twice defeated
Union Army at Bull Run, 1861, 1862; led Shenan-
doah Valley campaign, 1862; forced Union retreat
at Chancellorsville, 1863; accidentally killed by
own troops; graduated from West Point, 1846; born
in Clarksburg, W.Va. (then in Va.).
Jesse Woodson James (1847–82): Western out-
law; led gang that included his brother Frank,
Cole Younger, and others in bank and train rob-
beries; killed by gang member Robert Ford for
$5,000 reward; born in Clay County, Mo.
John Jay (1745–1829): 1st Chief Justice of U.S.,
1790–95; New York delegate to Continental Con-
gress, 1774–79; president of Congress, 1778–79;
helped negotiate and signed treaty of peace with
Britain, 1783; U.S. secretary of foreign affairs,
1784–89; authored five essays in *The Federalist*,
urging ratification of U.S. Constitution, 1787–88;
negotiated Jay's Treaty settling outstanding dis-
putes with Britain, 1794; governor of New York,
1795–1801; born in New York City.
John Paul Jones (1747–92): U.S. naval hero
in Revolutionary War; commanded *Bonhomme
Richard*, forcing surrender of more heavily
armed British frigate *Serapis*, 1779; during bat-
tle, reputed to have replied to British demand
for surrender: "I have not yet begun to fight!";
only Continental Navy officer to receive gold
medal from Congress, 1787; rear admiral in
Russian Navy, 1788–89, in war with Turks;
born in Kirkcudbrightshire, Scotland.
Edward Moore ("Ted") Kennedy (born 1932):
Brother of President Kennedy; U.S. senator (D-
Mass.), 1962– ; unsuccessfully opposed Presi-
dent Carter for Democratic presidential nomina-
tion in 1980; withdrew as candidate for Demo-
cratic presidential nomination in 1972 after re-
ceiving suspended sentence for leaving scene of
fatal automobile accident on Chappaquiddick
Island, Mass., 1969; born in Boston, Mass.
Robert Francis Kennedy (1925–68): Brother of
President Kennedy; U.S. attorney general,
1961–64; U.S. senator (D-N.Y.), 1965–68; as-
sassinated in Los Angeles while campaigning for
Democratic presidential nomination, 1968; born
in Brookline, Mass.
Ernest Joseph King (1878–1956): Admiral in
command of U.S. fleet during World War II,
1941–45, and chief of naval operations, 1942–45;
born in Lorain, Ohio.

Martin Luther King Jr. (1929–68): Black civil-rights leader; awarded Nobel Peace Prize, 1964; ordained as Baptist minister, 1947; began nonviolent crusade for black rights with boycott of buses in Montgomery, Ala., to end racial discrimination in seating on buses, 1955; founder of Southern Christian Leadership Conference (SCLC), 1957; at demonstration of more than 200,000 persons in Washington, D.C., 1963, made address *I Have a Dream*; assassinated by white escaped convict James Earl Ray in Memphis, Tenn., on April 4, 1968; assassination caused riots in 125 cities; born in Atlanta.

Rufus King (1755–1827): Unsuccessful Federalist candidate for President, 1816; Massachusetts delegate to Congress, 1784–87; signer of U.S. Constitution, 1787; U.S. senator (Fed.-N.Y.), 1789–96, 1813–25; U.S. minister to Britain, 1796–1803, 1825–26; born in Scarboro, Me. (then part of Massachusetts).

Henry Alfred Kissinger (born 1923): U.S. secretary of state under Presidents Nixon and Ford, 1973–77, promoting policy of détente that relaxed tensions of Cold War with Soviet Union; helped restore diplomatic relations with China, 1971–72; co-winner of Nobel Peace Prize in 1973 for negotiating cease-fire that ended American participation in Vietnam War; became naturalized U.S. citizen, 1943; on faculty of Harvard University 1951–69; born in Fuerth, Germany.

Robert Marion La Follette (1855–1925): Leader of Progressive movement; U.S. senator (Prog.-Wis.), 1906–25; U.S. representative (R-Wis.), 1885–91; governor of Wisconsin, 1901–05; opposed U.S. entry into World War I, 1917; opposed U.S. participation in League of Nations or World Court, 1918–19; unsuccessful Progressive candidate for President, 1924; born in Primrose, Wis.

Alfred Mossman Landon (born 1887): Unsuccessful Republican candidate for President, 1936; as wildcat oil prospector, became millionaire by age of 40; as governor of Kansas, 1933–37, managed state finances to maintain balanced budget while other states were going deeply into debt; born in West Middlesex, Pa.

Richard Henry Lee (1732–94): Virginia delegate to Continental Congress, 1774–79; introduced resolution for Declaration of Independence on June 7, 1776; as delegate to Congress, 1784–87, opposed U.S. Constitution, promoted adoption of Bill of Rights; U.S. senator (D-R-Va.), 1789–92; born in Westmoreland County, Va.

Robert Edward Lee (1807–70): In Civil War, commanded Confederate Army of Northern Virginia, 1862–65, after declining President Lincoln's offer to command Union Army; his master strategies gave smaller Confederate forces such victories as Seven Days Battle, Second Battle of Bull Run, Fredericksburg, and Chancellorsville; defeated at Gettysburg, 1863; appointed general in chief of Confederate armies, 1865; surrendered at Appomattox Court House, 1865; president of Washington College (now Washington and Lee University), 1865–70; born in Westmoreland County, Va.

John Llewellyn Lewis (1880–1969): Labor leader; president of United Mine Workers (UMW), 1920–60; organized Committee for Industrial Or-

ganizations (CIO), 1935; after CIO unions were expelled from AFL in 1938, Lewis served as CIO president until 1942; withdrew UMW from CIO in 1942 in policy dispute; born in Lucas, Iowa.

Meriwether Lewis (1774–1809): Leader with William Clark of expedition exploring Louisiana Purchase, 1804–06; governor of Louisiana Territory, 1807–09; born in Albemarle County, Va.

Charles Augustus Lindbergh (1902–74): American hero of 1920s for his courage in making first solo flight across Atlantic Ocean, on May 20–21, 1927; called "the Lone Eagle"; became semirecluse after sensational kidnap-murder of his baby son, 1932; opposed President F.D. Roosevelt's moves toward U.S. entry in World War II, but flew 50 combat missions against Japanese as civilian; born in Detroit.

Robert R. Livingston (1746–1813): New York delegate to Continental Congress, 1775–77, 1779–81; first U.S. secretary of foreign affairs, 1781–83; as chancellor (chief judge) of New York, 1777–1801, administered presidential oath to George Washington, 1789; U.S. minister to France, 1801–04, negotiating Louisiana Purchase from France; financed Robert Fulton's steamboat, 1803–07; born in New York City.

Henry Cabot Lodge (1850–1924): U.S. senator (R-Mass.), 1893–1924; pressed for U.S. entry in World War I in 1915; organized Senate opposition to Versailles Treaty and League of Nations, 1919–20; born in Boston.

Henry Cabot Lodge Jr. (1902–85): Unsuccessful Republican candidate for Vice President in 1960 as running mate of Richard M. Nixon; U.S. ambassador to UN, 1953–60; ambassador to South Vietnam, West Germany, and Vatican, 1963–77; U.S. senator (R-Mass.), 1937–44, 1947–53; born in Nahant, Mass.

Elijah Parish Lovejoy (1802–37): Abolitionist martyr; while editor of antislavery Alton (Ill.) *Observer*, was attacked and killed by proslavery mob, 1837; born in Albion, Me.

Mary Lyon (1797–1849): Founded first women's college, Mount Holyoke Seminary (later College) in South Hadley, Mass., and served as its president, 1837–49; born in Buckland, Mass.

Douglas MacArthur (1880–1964): Commanding general of U.S. Far East forces during World War II, 1941–45; commanded occupation forces in Japan, 1945–51; supreme commander of UN forces in Korean War, 1950–51, until relieved by President Truman because of outspoken desire to invade communist China; commanded 42d Division in World War I, 1917–18; U.S. Army chief of staff, 1930–35; born in Little Rock, Ark.

Horace Mann (1796–1859): Led establishment of free public schools in U.S.; as secretary of new Massachusetts state board of education, 1837–48, set standards adopted by other states as well; founded first teacher-training school, in Lexington, Mass., 1839; U.S. representative (Whig-Mass.), 1848–53; president of Antioch College, 1853–59; born in Franklin, Mass.

George Catlett Marshall (1880–1959): Commander of all U.S. armies in World War II as chief of staff, 1939–45; as U.S. secretary of state, 1947–49, initiated Marshall Plan to rebuild Europe; awarded Nobel Peace Prize, 1953; unsuc-

FAMOUS PERSONS IN AMERICAN HISTORY *(continued)*
cessfully attempted to mediate civil war in China, 1946; secretary of defense under President Truman during first years of Korean War, 1950–51; born in Uniontown, Pa.

John Marshall (1755–1835): 4th Chief Justice of U.S., 1801–35; established power of Supreme Court to declare laws unconstitutional in case of *Marbury* v. *Madison*, 1803; broadened scope of federal government with doctrine of implied powers, including all those necessary to carry out specific powers mentioned in U.S. Constitution; U.S. representative (Fed.-Va.), 1799–1800; U.S. secretary of state, 1800–01; born in Germantown (now Midland), Va.

Thurgood Marshall (born 1908): First black appointed as associate justice of U.S. Supreme Court, 1967; as head of legal services of National Association for the Advancement of Colored People (NAACP), 1940–61, won major Supreme Court decisions desegregating public schools, transportation, and housing; judge of U.S. Court of Appeals, 1961–65; U.S. solicitor general, 1965–67; born in Baltimore.

Matthew Fontaine Maury (1806–76): Pioneer oceanographer; headed U.S. Navy's Depot of Charts and Instruments (later Naval Observatory and Hydrographic Office), 1842–61; developed uniform system of recording oceanographic data; joined Confederate Navy during Civil War, commanding coast and harbor defenses; professor of meteorology at Virginia Military Institute, 1868–73; born near Fredericksburg, Va.

Joseph Raymond McCarthy (1908–57): U.S. senator (R-Wis.), 1947–57; charges that communists had infiltrated U.S. government and Army bred public hysteria; tactic of making unsupported charges came to be called *McCarthyism*; U.S. Senate censured McCarthy in 1954, ending his influence; born in Grand Chute, Wis.

George Brinton McClellan (1826–85): In Civil War, commanded Union Army of Potomac, 1861–62; reorganized Union forces after Bull Run defeat, 1861; failed to capture Richmond after forcing General Lee to retreat at Antietam, Md., causing Lincoln to relieve him of command, 1862; unsuccessful Democratic candidate for President, 1864; governor of New Jersey, 1878–81; graduated second in class from West Point, 1846; born in Philadelphia.

John Cardinal McCloskey (1810–85): First American cardinal of Roman Catholic Church, 1875–85; as archbishop of New York, 1864–85, responsible for building St. Patrick's Cathedral, opened 1879; born in Brooklyn, N.Y.

George Stanley McGovern (born 1922): Unsuccessful Democratic candidate for President, 1972; during campaign called Nixon administration "most corrupt in history," but majority of voters regarded this as political oratory until full extent of Watergate scandals was revealed in 1973–74; U.S. representative (D-S.D.), 1957–61; Democratic U.S. senator from South Dakota, 1963–81; born in Avon, S.D.

George Gordon Meade (1815–72): In Civil War, commanded Union Army of the Potomac, 1863–65; defeated Confederate General Lee at Battle of Gettysburg, 1863, in turning point of war; graduated from West Point, 1835; born in Cádiz, Spain.

William ("Billy") Mitchell (1879–1936): U.S. Army general who demonstrated obsolescence of battleship by sinking several with aerial bombs in experiments in 1921–23; defying superior officers, he urged developing air force independent of U.S. Army and U.S. Navy; court-martialed and convicted of insubordination, 1925; born in Nice, France.

Walter Frederick Mondale (born 1928): 42d Vice President of U.S., 1977–81; Democratic presidential candidate, 1984; U.S. senator (D-Minn.), 1964–77; attorney general of Minnesota, 1960–64; born in Ceylon, Minn.

John Pierpont Morgan (1837–1913): Multimillionaire banker who managed financing of many large U.S. corporations; powerful banking firm, J.P. Morgan & Company, halted gold drain on U.S. treasury by selling $62 million in bonds, 1895; organized U.S. Steel Corporation as world's largest corporation at time, 1901; helped end Panic of 1907 by loaning money to banks short of cash; born in Hartford, Conn.

Robert Morris (1734–1806): "Financier of the American Revolution"; pledged personal credit to supply Washington's army for Battles of Trenton and Princeton, 1776; appointed by Congress superintendent of finance, 1781–84; as Pennsylvania delegate to Continental Congress, 1776–78, signed Declaration of Independence and Articles of Confederation; as delegate to Constitutional Convention, signed U.S. Constitution, 1787; served Pennsylvania as U.S. senator, 1789–95; lost fortune and jailed for debt, 1798–1801; born in Liverpool, England.

Lucretia Coffin Mott (1793–1880): Abolitionist and women's rights leader; with Elizabeth Cady Stanton, organized first women's rights convention, at Seneca Falls, N.Y., 1848; aided escape of slaves through "underground railroad"; born on Nantucket, Mass.

Carry Amelia Moore Nation (1846–1911): Prohibitionist; conducted violent attacks on saloons in Kansas, using hatchet to smash liquor bottles and chop up furnishings in 1890s and early 1900s; born in Garrard County, Ky.

Chester William Nimitz (1885–1966): Admiral in command of U.S. Pacific Fleet in World War II, 1941–45; directed island-hopping campaign that led to Japan's surrender aboard his flagship, battleship USS *Missouri*, on Sept. 2, 1945; promoted to rank of 5-star fleet admiral, 1944; chief of naval operations, 1945–47; born in Fredericksburg, Texas.

Sandra Day O'Connor (born 1930): First woman appointed U.S. Supreme Court associate justice by President Reagan, 1981; Republican Arizona state senator, 1969–75, becoming first woman majority leader of any state senate, 1972–74; Arizona state court judge, 1975–81; graduated from Stanford University law school, 1952; married John Jay O'Connor 3d, 1952, having three children; born in El Paso, Texas.

James Otis (1725–83): Boston lawyer who paved way for American Revolution; his denunciation in 1761 of British writs of assistance (kind of search warrant) as illegal inspired patriots to stand up for rights; headed Massachusetts delegation to Stamp Act Congress, 1765; worked with Samuel Adams in protesting Townshend Acts and quartering of troops in Boston; born in West Barnstable, Mass.

Thomas Paine (1737–1809): Influenced adoption of Declaration of Independence by pamphlet *Common Sense,* January 1776; supported cause of freedom with series of essays, called *Crisis,* beginning in December 1776; after war, went to Europe where he wrote *The Rights of Man,* 1791–92, and *The Age of Reason,* 1794–96; returned to U.S., 1802; born in Thetford, England.

Nathaniel Brown Palmer (1799–1877): First explorer to sight Antarctica, on Nov. 18, 1820, while in command of 45-ton sloop *Hero*; first went to sea at age 14; commanded clipper ships trading with China, until retiring in 1850; born in Stonington, Conn.

George Smith Patton Jr. (1885–1945): In World War II, commanded U.S. Third Army in Europe, spearheading liberation of France, Germany, Czechoslovakia, and Austria, 1944–45; won nickname "Old Blood and Guts"; born in San Gabriel, Calif.

Robert Edwin Peary (1856–1920): First explorer to reach North Pole, April 6, 1909; promoted to rear admiral U.S. Navy, 1911, and retired; born in Cresson, Pa.

William Penn (1644–1718): Founded Pennsylvania as Quaker colony with religious freedom for other faiths, 1681; made treaty with Indians, paying for land granted to him by King Charles II, 1682; returned to England, 1684; visited Pennsylvania and wrote new constitution giving elective assembly complete lawmaking power, 1699–1701; born in London.

Frances Perkins (1882–1965): First woman member of presidential cabinet; U.S. secretary of labor under Presidents F.D. Roosevelt and Truman, 1933–45; U.S. civil service commissioner, 1946–53; born in Boston.

Matthew Calbraith Perry (1794–1858): U.S. naval officer who forced Japan to open two of its ports to U.S. trade, 1854; younger brother of Oliver Hazard Perry; born in Newport, R.I.

Oliver Hazard Perry (1785–1819): In War of 1812, commanded U.S. fleet on Lake Erie; after defeating British in Battle of Lake Erie, 1813, sent famous message: "We have met the enemy and they are ours"; born in South Kingston, R.I.

John Joseph ("Black Jack") Pershing (1860–1948): In World War I, commanding general of U.S. troops in Europe, 1917–19; U.S. Army chief of staff, 1921–24; awarded Pulitzer Prize for history in 1932 for book *My Experiences in the World War;* born near Laclede, Mo.

Charles Cotesworth Pinckney (1746–1825): Twice loser as Federalist candidate for President, 1804, 1808; also lost as President John Adams' running mate for Vice President, 1800; South Carolina delegate to Constitutional Convention and signer of U.S. Constitution, 1787; as special envoy to France, 1796, became famous for his reply to French official who asked for bribe: "It is no, no! Not a sixpence!"; major general in new U.S. Army, formed in 1798, third in command after Washington and Hamilton; born in Charleston, S.C.

Pontiac (c. 1720–69): Ottawa Indian chief who led attacks called "Pontiac's Conspiracy" on British colonial settlements west of Appalachian Mountains, 1763–66, killing hundreds of frontier families; signed peace treaty, 1766, receiving pardon from British.

Edmund Randolph (1753–1813): First U.S. attorney general under President Washington, 1789–94; U.S. secretary of state, 1794–95, resigning after being falsely charged with accepting bribe from France; as counsel, won acquittal for Aaron Burr in treason trial, 1807; as governor of Virginia, 1786–88, attended Constitutional Convention but refused to sign U.S. Constitution; born in Williamsburg, Va.

Sam Rayburn (1882–1961): Speaker of U.S. House of Representatives, 1940–47, 1949–53, 1955–61; as Texas Democrat, won election to Congress 25 consecutive times, serving 1913–61, under eight Presidents from Wilson to Kennedy; played major role in carrying out legislative programs of Presidents F.D. Roosevelt and Truman; born in Roane County, Tenn.

Paul Revere (1735–1818): Patriot and craftsman; on night of April 18–19, 1775, rode from Boston to Lexington, Mass., warning that the British were coming to arrest Samuel Adams and John Hancock for treason and to destroy patriot supplies; during Revolutionary War, made gunpowder, cannon, engraved and printed Continental currency, and served as lieutenant colonel of militia; designed many beautiful objects as silversmith; founded Revere Copper Co., at Canton, Mass., smelting copper and rolling it in sheets; born in Boston.

John Davison Rockefeller (1839–1937): Billionaire industrialist; made fortune in oil, founding Standard Oil Co., 1870; monopoly on oil broken by U.S. Supreme Court order, 1911; endowed University of Chicago, 1892, Rockefeller Institute of Medical Research, 1901, Rockefeller Foundation, 1913; born in Richford, N.Y.

Nelson Aldrich Rockefeller (1908–79): Appointed 41st Vice President of U.S. by President Ford, serving 1974–77; governor of New York four times, 1959–73; held variety of positions in federal government, 1940–45, 1953–55; unsuccessfully sought Republican presidential nomination in 1964 and 1968; grandson of John D. Rockefeller; born in Bar Harbor, Me.

Carl Schurz (1829–1906): German-American editor, statesman, general; immigrated to U.S., 1852; as leader in Wisconsin Republican Party, backed Lincoln's presidential nomination, 1860; U.S. minister to Spain, 1861–62; general in Union Army, 1862–63; editor, Detroit *Post,* 1866–67; editor-founder, St. Louis *Westliche Post,* 1867–69; U.S. senator (R-Mo.), 1869–75; as U.S. secretary of the interior, 1877–81, reformed treatment of Indians and established civil-service merit system in Interior Department; editor, New York *Evening Post,* 1881–83; chief editorial writer, *Harper's Weekly,* 1892–98; born in Liblar, Prussia.

Margaretha Meyer Schurz (1834–76): Founded first kindergarten in U.S., in Watertown, Wis., 1856; immigrated to U.S. with husband, Carl Schurz, 1852; born in Prussia.

Winfield Scott (1786–1866): General and unsuccessful Whig candidate for President in 1852; became national hero for courage displayed as fighting general in War of 1812 Battles of Chippewa and Lundy's Lane, 1814; as commanding

QUICK QUIZ: Who holds the men's 100-meter freestyle swimming record? See page 861.

FAMOUS PERSONS IN AMERICAN HISTORY *(continued)*

general of U.S. Army, 1841–61, became known to troops as "Old Fuss and Feathers" because of his plumed hat; in Mexican War, commanded amphibious invasion at Veracruz, captured Mexico City, 1847; commanded Union Army at beginning of Civil War, but retired at age 75 on Nov. 1, 1861; born near Petersburg, Va.

William Henry Seward (1801–72): U.S. secretary of state under Presidents Lincoln and Andrew Johnson, 1861–69; arranged purchase of Alaska from Russia for $7.2 million, known at time as "Seward's Folly"; forced France to withdraw troops from Mexico after Civil War; first Whig governor of New York, 1839–42; as U.S. senator (Whig-N.Y.), 1849–55, (R-N.Y.), 1855–61, opposed slavery, Compromise of 1850, and Kansas-Nebraska Act; wounded by accomplice of John Wilkes Booth on night of Lincoln's assassination, 1865; born in Florida, N.Y.

Philip Henry Sheridan (1831–1888): General in Union Army in Civil War; gained fame leading successful charge on Missionary Ridge in Battle of Chattanooga, 1863; as commander of cavalry of Army of Potomac under U.S. Grant, 1864, drove Confederate troops of Gen. Jubal Early out of Virginia's Shenandoah Valley; commanding general of U.S. Army, 1884–88; believed born in Somerset, Ohio.

William Tecumseh Sherman (1820–91): Commander of Union armies of West in Civil War: captured Atlanta, Sept. 1, 1864; led "March to the Sea" across Georgia with army of over 60,000, pillaging plantations and towns, capturing Savannah, Dec. 21, 1864; marching north, accepted surrender of Confederate Gen. J.E. Johnston at Durham, N.C., April 26, 1865; famed for statement "War is hell"; commanding general of U.S. Army, 1869–1884; when asked to run for President, he said, "I will not accept if nominated and will not serve if elected"; born in Lancaster, Ohio.

Sitting Bull (c.1834–90): Sioux Indian chief; battled U.S. Army and white settlers in 1860s and 1870s in Montana and Dakotas; led followers to Canada, 1877, but returned and surrendered, 1881; on Standing Rock Reservation in South Dakota, began Ghost Dance unrest among Sioux, 1890; police and soldiers sent to arrest him killed him and a son; born in South Dakota.

Samuel Slater (1768–1835): Brought Industrial Revolution to U.S.; to monopolize textile industry, Britain had forbidden export of machines or emigration of persons familiar with them; having memorized details of machinery, Slater in disguise left Britain for U.S., 1789; with Moses Brown, built first successful cotton-spinning mill in U.S., in Pawtucket, R.I., 1790; opened own textile mills in New England; born in Belper, England.

Alfred Emanuel Smith (1873–1944): Unsuccessful Democratic presidential candidate, 1928; as first Roman Catholic to run for President, was opposed by Ku Klux Klan; also controversial because he favored repeal of prohibition; elected four times as governor of New York, serving in 1919–20; 1923–28; born in New York City.

Jedediah Strong Smith (c.1799–1831): Fur trader and explorer; in 1820s, mapped routes from Rockies to California and along Pacific coast; born in Bainbridge, N.Y.

John Smith (1580–1631): Helped found Jamestown, Va., first permanent English colony in America, 1607; captured by Indians but saved from execution by Pocahontas, daughter of chief; elected president of Virginia, 1608–09; explored and named New England, 1614; born in Willoughby, England.

Edwin McMasters Stanton (1814–69): U.S. secretary of war during and after Civil War, 1862–68; fired by President Andrew Johnson for harsh treatment of militarily occupied South, leading Stanton's Radical Republican supporters in Congress to bring about Johnson's impeachment and trial; U.S. attorney general, 1860–61; born in Steubenville, Ohio.

Elizabeth Cady Stanton (1815–1902): Leader in women's rights, abolition, and temperance movements; graduated from Troy (N.Y.) Female Seminary, 1832; married Henry B. Stanton, 1840; with Lucretia C. Mott, sponsored first U.S. women's rights convention, at Seneca Falls, N.Y., 1848; with Susan B. Anthony, organized National Woman Suffrage Association, 1869; was its first president, 1869–90; born in Johnstown, N.Y.

Alexander Hamilton Stephens (1812–83): Vice President of Confederate States of America during Civil War; represented Confederacy in peace conference with President Lincoln at Hampton Roads, Va., February 1865; U.S. representative (Whig-Ga.) 1843–52, (D-Ga.) 1852–59, 1873–82; imprisoned after Civil War; elected by Georgia to U.S. Senate, 1866, but not allowed to serve; governor of Georgia, 1882–83; born near Crawfordsville, Ga.

Thaddeus Stevens (1792–1868): Led Radical Republicans in Congress demanding harsh treatment of South after Civil War; managed impeachment of President Andrew Johnson, 1868; U.S. representative (Whig-Pa.), 1849–53, (R-Pa.), 1859–68; born in Danville, Vt.

Adlai Ewing Stevenson (1835–1914): 23d Vice President, 1893–97, under President Cleveland; U.S. representative (D-Ill.), 1875–77, 1879–81; unsuccessful Democratic candidate for Vice President, 1900, and for governor of Illinois, 1908; born in Christian County, Ky.

Adlai Ewing Stevenson (1900–65): Unsuccessful Democratic candidate for President, 1952, 1956; governor of Illinois, 1949–53; U.S. ambassador to UN, 1961–65; grandson of Vice President Adlai E. Stevenson; born in Los Angeles.

Harlan Fiske Stone (1872–1946): 11th Chief Justice of U.S., 1941–46; associate justice of Supreme Court, 1925–41; as U.S. attorney general, 1924–25, cleaned up Justice Department from effects of Teapot Dome scandals; supported New Deal legislation while on Supreme Court; born in Chesterfield, N.H.

James Ewell Brown ("Jeb") Stuart (1833–64): Confederate cavalry general in Civil War; called "eyes of the army" by General Lee; daringly circled entire Union Army to gather information; killed in battle for Richmond at Yellow Tavern, Va.; graduated from West Point, 1854; born in Patrick County, Va.

Peter Stuyvesant (c.1610–72): Last Dutch governor of New Netherland (now New York), 1647–64; captured New Sweden (now Delaware, New Jersey, and part of Pennsylvania), 1655; ruled as dictator, forbidding sale of liquor to

Indians, tolerating no religions other than Dutch Reformed; surrendered colony to British, Sept. 6, 1664; lost leg in military expedition against Caribbean island of St. Martin, 1644; born in Scherpenzeel, Netherlands.

Roger Brooke Taney (1777–1864): 5th Chief Justice of U.S., 1836–64; ruling in Dred Scott case, 1857, that Congress could not outlaw slavery in U.S. territories invalidated Missouri Compromise and Compromise of 1850, helping to bring on Civil War; served under President Jackson as attorney general, 1831–33, and as secretary of the treasury, 1833–34; because he opposed Second Bank of the U.S., Senate refused to confirm him as secretary of the treasury, 1834, and as associate justice of Supreme Court, 1835; born in Calvert County, Md.

Samuel Jones Tilden (1814–86): Democratic candidate for President, 1876; won majority of popular vote but Republican-controlled election commission awarded presidency to Rutherford B. Hayes; led reform group ousting corrupt Tweed ring from control of New York City government, 1872; governor of New York, 1875–76; founded New York Public Library with bequest; born in New Lebanon, N.Y.

Harriet Tubman (c.1820–1913): Black abolitionist; escaped slavery in Maryland, 1849; during 1850s helped hundreds of slaves escape to North on "underground railroad"; born in Dorchester County, Md.

Nat Turner (1800–31): Led slave uprising in Virginia in August 1831, killing about 60 whites; Turner and about 100 other blacks captured and killed; uprising led to severe slave restrictions in South; born in Southampton County, Va.

Cornelius Vanderbilt (1794–1877): Multimillionaire steamship and railroad magnate; quit school at 11; began operating sailboat ferry between Staten Island and New York City at 16; in 1850s began operating steamship service to Europe and San Francisco; formed New York Central Railroad, becoming its first president, 1867; donated $1 million to Central University in Nashville, Tenn., which changed its name to Vanderbilt University; fortune estimated at $100 million; born on Staten Island, N.Y.

Lillian D. Wald (1867–1940): Social worker; established city-wide visiting-nurse service in connection with New York City's Henry Street Settlement, which she founded and headed, 1895–1933; started first public-school nurse program, 1902; militantly campaigned against sweatshops and child labor; born in Cincinnati.

Earl Warren (1891–1974): 14th Chief Justice of U.S., 1953–69; liberal rulings included outlawing racial segregation in public schools (1954), liberalizing definition of obscenity (1957), banning required prayers or religious services in public schools (1962), establishing "one man, one vote" rule (1962), increasing freedom of press by limiting news media's liability for libel (1964), and improving legal protection of persons accused of crimes (1966); headed Warren Commission investigating assassination of President Kennedy, 1963–64; Republican governor of California, 1943–53; unsuccessful Republican candidate for Vice President, 1948;

unsuccessful candidate for Republican presidential nomination, 1952; born in Los Angeles.

Booker Taliaferro Washington (1856–1915): Black educator and reformer; born a slave at Hales Ford, Va.; attended Hampton Institute, 1872–75; taught there, 1878–81; first president of Tuskegee Institute, Ala., 1881–1915; opposed political action for black civil rights; counseled blacks to work hard and acquire education; wrote *Up From Slavery,* 1901.

Daniel Webster (1782–1852): U.S. secretary of state, 1841–43, 1850–52; negotiated Webster-Ashburton Treaty settling Maine boundary dispute with Britain, 1842; unsuccessful Whig candidate for President, 1836; opposed War of 1812 and supported protective tariffs as Federalist U.S. representative from New Hampshire, 1813–17, and as U.S. representative from Massachusetts, 1823–27; as U.S. senator (Whig-Mass.), 1827–41, 1845–50, opposed Mexican War and supported Compromise of 1850; born in Salisbury (now Franklin), N.H.

Charles Wilkes (1798–1877): Discovered and named Antarctic continent on Jan. 30, 1840, while leading exploration mission for U.S. Navy; as rear admiral during Civil War, instigated Trent affair when he removed two Confederate commissioners from British ship, causing protest; born in New York City.

Emma Hart Willard (1787–1870): Established first college-level school for women in U.S.— Troy (N.Y.) Female Seminary, 1821; wrote poem "Rocked in the Cradle of the Deep," 1830; born in Berlin, Conn.

Frances Elizabeth Caroline Willard (1839–98): Educator and temperance reformer; president, Evanston (Ill.) College for Ladies, 1871–73; dean of women, Northwestern University, 1873–74; president, Woman's Christian Temperance Union (WCTU), 1879–98; founder and president of first international women's organization, World Woman's Christian Temperance Union, 1883; born in Churchville, N.Y.

Roger Williams (c.1603–83): Founder of Rhode Island; banished by Puritans from Massachusetts for belief in religious freedom and separation of church and state, 1635; founded first settlement at Providence, R.I., 1636; obtained charter for colony of Rhode Island, 1644; president of Rhode Island, 1654–57; born in London.

Wendell Lewis Willkie (1892–1944): Unsuccessful Republican candidate for President, 1940; president of electric utility company, 1933–40; wrote *One World,* 1943, promoting global unity; born in Elwood, Ind.

John Winthrop (1588–1649): Led Puritans to found Massachusetts Bay Colony and Boston, 1630; served as governor all but four years during 1630s and 1640s, sternly prohibiting practice of religions other than Congregationalist faith he established; born in Edwardstone, England.

John Witherspoon (1723–94): Only clergyman to sign Declaration of Independence; New Jersey delegate to Continental Congress, 1776–82; president, College of New Jersey (now Princeton University), 1768–94; Presbyterian pastor of Paisley, Scotland, 1757–68; born in Yester, Scotland.

QUICK QUIZ: When was the first USGA amateur women's championship held? See page 824.

PROFILES OF OUR PRESIDENTS AND FIRST LADIES

The President and Vice President of the United States are the only officials elected by the American people as a whole.

The nation has had 40 Presidents, but only 39 men have been Chief Executive. One of them, Grover Cleveland, served nonconsecutive terms and thus was both the 22d and 24th President. Ronald Reagan became the 40th President upon taking office in 1981.

The U.S. presidency is a unique institution. Few other democratic nations have a single leader perform both the symbolic role of chief of state and at the same time the job of administering the government.

The President is simultaneously chief of state, chief executive, chief legislator, party leader, chief diplomat, and commander in chief of the armed forces. The action of the President in any one role materially affects the others, because the President is the mainspring of the governmental system.

The manner in which the President exercises his several functions generally determines his place in history.

The President may supply creative leadership and seek positively to change the shape of public opinion. Or he may assume the role of a charismatic leader by inspiring the people to greater heights of action. But the President must assume the ultimate responsibility for the nation's successes and failures during his administration.

The highlights of the Presidents' lives, including information on the women who served as First Lady, appear below and on the following pages.

GEORGE WASHINGTON

1st President
(1789–97)

As commander of the Continental forces during the Revolutionary War and as the first President of the United States, George Washington became "father of his country."

In the eight years of his presidency the nation's basic institutions were established. Washington's personal qualities were remarkable.

Thomas Jefferson wrote that "his integrity was the most pure, his justice the most flexible, I have ever known. He was, indeed, in every sense of the word, a wise, a good and a great man."

EARLY LIFE

Washington was the son of Augustine Washington, a moderately wealthy planter, and his second wife, Mary Ball. He was born on the family's Virginia estate (now known as Wakefield) on Feb. 22, 1732. His father died in 1743. George's half-brother Lawrence then became head of the family. George displayed an early talent for mathematics, and at the age of 15 began earning small fees by surveying. In 1748 he assisted George Fairfax in making an extensive survey of Thomas Lord Fairfax's lands in the wilderness country west of Virginia's Blue Ridge Mountains.

In 1751–52 he accompanied Lawrence, who was suffering from tuberculosis, to Barbados. There George survived a case of smallpox, becoming immune to the disease that was to plague his troops during the Revolutionary War. Lawrence died soon after returning to his Mount Vernon home. George inherited part of his estate. At 20 he obtained a commission as major in the militia.

Washington first gained public notice in 1753 when he was entrusted with a dangerous mission before the French and Indian War. He volunteered to deliver a message from Virginia Gov. Robert Dinwiddie to the French in Ohio country, warning them to leave the British-claimed territory. His two-and-a-half-month journey took him across hundreds of miles of unmapped wilderness to the shore of Lake Erie. When he returned he was commissioned lieutenant colonel.

Washington was then sent back to the frontier in command of a militia unit. In May 1754 he fought the first skirmish of the French and Indian War. He built Fort Necessity near present-day Uniontown, Pa., but was forced to surrender it to the French on July 4, 1754.

A year later, as aide-de-camp to British Gen. Edward Braddock in the disastrous expedition against Fort Duquesne, Washington established his reputation as a military leader by rallying the survivors for an orderly retreat. In 1758, commanding colonial forces supporting British regulars, he distinguished himself anew in the final capture of the French fort.

Washington, not yet 27, retired to private life when peace returned. A tall, well-built man, he was amiable, just, and immensely vital. In 1759 he married Mrs. Martha Custis, a wealthy widow with two children. He then settled down to the life of a Virginia gentleman on his plantation, Mount Vernon.

Washington was a member of the Virginia House of Burgesses (1759–74), where he became a leader in opposing British colonial policy. He served in 1774–75 as a delegate to the Continental Congress.

COMMANDER OF THE CONTINENTAL ARMY

After the Revolution began, Washington became commander of the Continental Army, largely through the efforts of John Adams. Washington took command on July 3, 1775. His troops, unorganized and poorly disciplined, were mostly militia. Short terms of enlistment during the first years of the war kept his armies in a continuous state of disbandment and retraining.

Congress failed to provide essential equipment, supplies, and soldiers' pay. Washington was also beset with the jealousies and intrigues of insubordinate officers.

Washington's strategy was successful in forcing the British evacuation of Boston in March 1776. He was then compelled by Congress to defend New York City. Due to the poor condition of his men and the tactical error of deploying part of his forces to Brooklyn, Washington met defeat.

But he rescued his army in a withdrawal that eventually carried them to southeastern Pennsylvania.

From there, on Christmas night 1776, he and his men crossed the Delaware, a masterful move that led to the rout of the British at Trenton and Princeton.

Washington's efforts to defend Philadelphia ended in defeat at Brandywine in September 1777 and at Germantown in October.

Washington and his 9,000 men wintered at Valley Forge, Pa., 1777–78. Seldom have a general and his army endured such extended deprivation and misery.

Washington's essential greatness matched every problem and intrigue, however, and in the spring he emerged with increased powers from Congress and a well-trained force (despite 3,000 desertions).

When the British evacuated Philadelphia to return to New York, Washington attacked the British column in the Battle of Monmouth on June 28, 1778. But the battle was lost by the cowardice of one of his officers, Maj. Gen. Charles Lee.

Three years later Charles Lord Cornwallis and his English army were trapped at Yorktown, Va., by Washington with the support of French land and sea forces. Cornwallis surrendered on Oct. 19, 1781, virtually ending the Revolutionary War.

In 1783 Washington retired from the Army and returned to Mount Vernon.

He and other patriots, becoming dissatisfied with the weakness of the government under the Articles of Confederation, joined to reorganize it. In 1787 he presided over the Constitutional Convention, which wrote the Constitution of the United States.

FIRST PRESIDENT OF THE UNITED STATES

After the new government was organized, Washington was unanimously chosen as the first President. He took office on April 30, 1789, in New York City.

Washington's own views were Federalist. But in staffing his administration he was above partisanship. It was mainly his capacity for conciliation that kept the American Revolution free of terrorism, purges, and arbitrary seizures of power that have marked other revolutions.

He brought both Alexander Hamilton and Thomas Jefferson, leaders of opposing factions, into his cabinet.

Washington's poise, prestige, and dignity made the new government of the United States respected at home and abroad.

While President, Washington traveled extensively throughout the country.

Factions developed into political parties, and the strain put upon Washington as conciliator led to his refusal to accept a third term.

In public life Washington combined modesty with self-assurance. In his first inaugural address he acknowledged "deficiencies" in natural endowments and administrative experience. Characteristically, he set about overcoming them by study, as he had fitted himself for managing his plantations by studying agriculture.

Many precedents were set during his terms of office. The "advise and consent" role of the Senate evolved into the right of that body to approve or disapprove the President's actions but never to give him formal advice beforehand.

Chief among the vigorously debated issues of his administration were taxation and banking policies, the assumption of state debts, and the

WASHINGTON'S PRESIDENTIAL ADMINISTRATION

Congresses in Session:
1st, 2d, 3d, 4th

Vice President:
John Adams, 1789–97

Secretary of the Treasury:
Alexander Hamilton, 1789–95
Oliver Wolcott Jr., 1795–97

Secretary of State:
Thomas Jefferson, 1789–93
Edmund Randolph, 1794–95
Timothy Pickering, 1795–97
Secretary of War:
Henry Knox, 1789–95
Timothy Pickering, 1795–96
James McHenry, 1796–97

Attorney General:
Edmund Randolph, 1789–94
William Bradford, 1794–95
Charles Lee, 1795–97
Postmaster General:
Samuel Osgood, 1789–91
Timothy Pickering, 1791–95
Joseph Habersham, 1795–97

PRESIDENTIAL ELECTION OF 1789

Nominations: Washington, the most popular man in the nation, was chosen by the Continental Congress. **Campaign Issues:** In this first U.S. presidential election party division was at a minimum, for only those who supported the new Constitution took part. **Remarks:** Most of the 11 states that had recently ratified the Constitution had their state legislatures choose presidential electors. New York failed to do so. Rhode Island and North Carolina had not yet ratified the new United States Constitution.

PRESIDENTIAL CANDIDATES	PARTY	ELECTORAL VOTES
George Washington	None	69
John Adams	None	34
John Jay.............	None	9
Other candidates	None	26
Votes not cast	—	4

PRESIDENTIAL ELECTION OF 1792

Nominations: Washington and Adams, the incumbents, received the nomination of those who advocated a strong central government. Clinton was chosen by Antifederalist congressional leaders. **Campaign Issues:** The fiscal policy and strong centralization advocated by Alexander Hamilton, then secretary of the treasury and a staunch Federalist, provided the issues. **Remarks:** Washington's popularity could not be eclipsed. The Antifederalists had merely hoped to elect Clinton as Vice President.

PRESIDENTIAL CANDIDATES	PARTY	ELECTORAL VOTES
George Washington	Federalist	132
John Adams	Federalist	77
George Clinton	Antifederalist	50
Thomas Jefferson	—	4
Aaron Burr...........	—	1

QUICK QUIZ: Who was Pacific Ten football champion in 1970–71? See page 816.

GEORGE WASHINGTON (continued)

jurisdiction of federal courts. During his second administration he was severely criticized by the Jeffersonians, especially for Jay's Treaty with England. In the war between England and France, Washington proclaimed neutrality and urged it as basic U.S. policy. In his Farewell Address, he warned against "entangling alliances."

Washington died on Dec. 14, 1799. Over 178 years later, on March 13, 1978, in accord with a resolution of Congress, the U.S. Army promoted Washington to General of the Armies of the United States to preserve his seniority.

Martha Dandridge (Custis) Washington was born in 1731. At 18 she married Daniel Parke Custis, a wealthy plantation owner who died in 1757. She married Washington two years later, on Jan. 6, 1759.

The Washingtons had no children of their own, but Washington adopted Martha's two children, John Parke Custis and Martha Parke Custis.

Besides wealth and beauty Mrs. Washington was noted for her common sense, charm, and aristocratic graciousness She was a devoted wife. She died in 1802 and was buried beside her husband at Mount Vernon.

JOHN ADAMS

The second President, John Adams disliked political parties and had a stormy term of office marred by factional intrigues. Although considered aloof, he was praised for his abilities even by those who disliked him.

Adams was born on Oct. 30, 1735, in Braintree (later Quincy), Mass., the son of John and Susanna (Boylston) Adams. He graduated from Harvard at 20, taught school for a time, and was admitted to the bar in 1758.

2d President
(1797–1801)

He was an outspoken opponent of the Stamp Act, arguing the principle of taxation without representation. He gained fame as a defense attorney for the British soldiers accused of murder in the Boston Massacre of 1770.

Becoming a zealous advocate of independence, Adams was sent by Massachusetts to the Continental Congress. There he distinguished himself as a forceful leader. He proposed George Washington as commander in chief of the Continental Army and promoted adoption of the Declaration of Independence. In 1777 Adams presented the resolution establishing the design of the U.S. flag.

He next had a successful career as a diplomat for the embattled new nation. In 1777 he was sent as a commissioner to join Benjamin Franklin in France. In 1780–81 he persuaded the Netherlands to recognize the United States and lend it money. In 1782 he returned to France and helped draw up the Treaty of Paris to end the Revolutionary War. As the first U.S. envoy

to Britain in 1785, Adams and his wife were met with hostility.

In 1789 he was chosen Vice President—in his opinion, "the most insignificant office that ever the invention of man contrived or his imagination conceived." A Federalist, he served under Washington for two terms.

In the 1796 presidential election, Adams won by only three electoral votes. The runner-up, Democratic-Republican leader Thomas Jefferson, became Vice President.

The United States fought an undeclared naval war with France during his administration. He did not wholeheartedly endorse the despotic Alien and Sedition Acts of 1798, but he signed them. These acts, aimed essentially at Thomas Jefferson and other critics of the Federalists, earned him the hatred of the Jeffersonians.

Defeated by Jefferson for reelection in 1800, Adams did not attend the inauguration of his successor. He retired to Quincy, issuing political statements and writing.

Later, he carried on a long correspondence with his former rival, Jefferson.

By extraordinary coincidence, both Adams and Jefferson died on the 50th anniversary of the Republic they had done so much to establish—July 4, 1826.

Abigail Smith Adams (1744–1818) was the daughter of a minister. She and Adams were married on Oct. 25, 1764. Lively and intelligent, she was one of the most distinguished First Ladies. The Adamses had two daughters and three sons—one, John Quincy Adams, became the sixth President.

On Nov. 1, 1800, the Adamses became the first presidential family to live in the White House, although at the time it was called the Executive Mansion and had not yet been painted white.

JOHN ADAMS' PRESIDENTIAL ADMINISTRATION

Congresses in Session: 5th, 6th
Vice President:
Thomas Jefferson, 1797–1801
Secretary of State:
Timothy Pickering, 1797–1800
John Marshall, 1800–01

Secretary of the Treasury:
Oliver Wolcott Jr., 1797–1800
Samuel Dexter, 1801
Secretary of War:
James McHenry, 1797–1800
Samuel Dexter, 1800

Attorney General:
Charles Lee, 1797–1801
Postmaster General:
Joseph Habersham, 1797–1801
Secretary of the Navy:
Benjamin Stoddert, 1798–1801

PRESIDENTIAL ELECTION OF 1796

Nominations: Congressional leaders of the two parties chose their respective candidates. **Campaign Issues:** Foreign policy dominated the campaign; the Federalists supported closer ties with England, while the Democratic–Republicans sought France's friendship. **Remarks:** Because of a split in the Federalist Party—between Hamilton and Adams—many Federalist electors gave their second vote to Jefferson.

PRESIDENTIAL CANDIDATES	PARTY	ELECTORAL VOTES
John Adams	Federalist	71
Thomas Jefferson	Dem.–Rep.	68
Thomas Pinckney	Federalist	59
Aaron Burr	Dem.-Rep.	30
Other candidates	—	48

THOMAS JEFFERSON

3d President
(1801–09)

Jefferson was rivaled among Americans only by Benjamin Franklin in the range of his interests, the quality of his intellectual contribution, and his faith in human progress.

As President he sought to curb the growing power of the U.S. Supreme Court, in which he felt the Federalists were attempting to entrench their philosophy. Jefferson believed that the federal government should be concerned mostly with foreign affairs, leaving the states free to administer local matters.

The son of Peter and Jane (Randolph) Jefferson, he was born on April 13, 1743, at Shadwell, the family estate in Virginia. His father, a tobacco plantation owner and a surveyor, died when Jefferson was 14. The boy took over management of Shadwell. He graduated from the College of William and Mary at 19 and was admitted to the bar in 1767. Five years later he married and settled at Monticello, a mansion he had personally designed.

He entered politics by winning election to Virginia's House of Burgesses in 1769 at the age of 26. There he became acquainted with Patrick Henry and other patriot leaders.

Jefferson was one of the organizers of the Virginia branch of the Committees of Correspondence, the chief medium of revolutionary agitation in the colonies.

His brilliantly written pamphlet *A Summary View of the Rights of British America* called attention to his logic, legal knowledge, and literary gifts.

He was chosen to write the Declaration of Independence in June 1776 at the Second Continental Congress, which he attended as an alternate. John Adams, who also was on the committee to write the Declaration, said he deferred to Jefferson because "I had a great opinion of the elegance of his pen."

He returned to Virginia to carry out some of his political and social principles in the newly established state. Serving in its legislature (1776–79) and as its governor (1779–81), he removed feudal vestiges from the landholding system. He framed a statute on religious freedom that became a model for the rest of the country. His proposals for public education, public libraries, and a liberal university, although not then adopted, anticipated later developments.

In 1784 Jefferson served on a special diplomatic assignment in Europe, and in 1785 he succeeded Benjamin Franklin as minister to France. His absence until October 1789 prevented him from directly participating in drafting the U.S. Constitution, but his pressure contributed to the addition of the first 10 amendments, the Bill of Rights.

Jefferson entered President Washington's cabinet as secretary of state in 1790. At first he subordinated his views to preserve the unity of the new nation, backing the trade and banking measures of Secretary of the Treasury Alexander Hamilton. However, he soon became convinced that Hamilton and his group—the Federalist Party—sought to establish a monarchy, or at least an oligarchy of wealth. Jefferson opposed this and began rallying like-minded men, who came to call themselves Republicans—a group from which the present Democratic Party traces

JEFFERSON'S PRESIDENTIAL ADMINISTRATION

Congresses in Session:
7th, 8th, 9th, 10th

Vice President:
Aaron Burr, 1801–05
George Clinton, 1805–09

Secretary of State:
James Madison, 1801–09

Secretary of the Treasury:
Samuel Dexter, 1801
Albert Gallatin, 1801–09

Secretary of War:
Henry Dearborn, 1801–09

Secretary of the Navy:
Robert Smith, 1801–09

Attorney General:
Levi Lincoln, 1801–05
Robert Smith, 1805
John Breckinridge, 1805–07
Caesar Rodney, 1807–09
Postmaster General:
Joseph Habersham, 1801
Gideon Granger, 1801–09

PRESIDENTIAL ELECTION OF 1800

Nominations: Jefferson and Adams were the acknowledged leaders of their parties. **Campaign Issues:** Both parties debated an undeclared naval war with France and Federalist repression of opponents through the Alien and Sedition Acts. **Remarks:** Electoral voting caused a tie between Jefferson and Burr. The House of Representatives decided the contest. On the 36th ballot Jefferson was chosen President.

PRESIDENTIAL CANDIDATES	PARTY	ELECTORAL VOTES
Thomas Jefferson	Dem.–Rep.	73
Aaron Burr	Dem.–Rep.	73
John Adams	Federalist	65
Charles C. Pinckney	Federalist	64
John Jay	Federalist	1

PRESIDENTIAL ELECTION OF 1804

Nominations: At the first regular political caucuses, the congressional delegates of both parties unanimously nominated their respective candidates. **Campaign Issue:** Debate centered on the territorial expansion of the United States through the Louisiana Purchase, which had been achieved in the preceding year. **Remarks:** This was the first presidential election carried out under the 12th Amendment to the Constitution of the United States.

PRESIDENTIAL CANDIDATES	PARTY	ELECTORAL VOTES	VICE-PRESIDENTIAL CANDIDATES	PARTY	ELECTORAL VOTES
Thomas Jefferson	Dem.–Rep.	162	George Clinton	Dem.–Rep.	162
Charles C. Pinckney	Federalist	14	Rufus King	Federalist	14

QUICK QUIZ: What is the largest roosterfish ever caught? See page 804.

THOMAS JEFFERSON *(continued)*

its origin. Jefferson and Hamilton became openly antagonistic. Washington was unable to reconcile them. In 1793 Jefferson left the cabinet.

He spent the next two years remodeling his Monticello home and experimenting with scientific agriculture. He was also active in building up the Democratic-Republican Party. He became its presidential nominee in 1796. He lost by only three electoral votes to Washington's Vice President, John Adams.

As runner-up Jefferson became Vice President in 1797 under a constitutional provision then in effect. He opposed Federalist policies, particularly the Alien and Sedition Acts that were aimed at the Antifederalists. In protest against the repressive acts, Jefferson drafted the Kentucky Resolutions, the earliest statement of the states' rights interpretation of the Constitution.

Jefferson and his party were convinced that Adams and the Federalists wanted to go to war against the revolutionary government of France.

In 1800 the Democratic-Republicans nominated Jefferson and Aaron Burr. They easily triumphed over John Adams and the Federalists. However, Burr and Jefferson received the same number of electoral votes, and the choice of President was left to the House of Representatives. Burr tried to win the presidency. But after a long deadlock Jefferson was elected, largely because Alexander Hamilton advised Federalist congressmen to support Jefferson.

The chief foreign problem throughout Jefferson's two terms was maintaining neutrality in the conflict between England and France, both of which preyed upon U.S. shipping. Seeking to bring pressure by withholding needed goods, Jefferson sponsored acts suspending trade, especially the Embargo Act of 1807. These finally became effective, causing loss and suffering to many citizens and arousing such protest that Jefferson relaxed enforcement attempts.

One of Jefferson's major achievements was the acquisition in 1803 of the Louisiana Territory from France for $15 million. This new territory doubled the size of the U.S. In the interest of exploration and settlement, Jefferson sponsored the Lewis and Clark Expedition that blazed the pioneer trail to the Pacific Northwest.

Jefferson ordered the arrest of former Vice President Burr for treason in 1807. He regarded Burr's acquittal by Chief Justice John Marshall as a personal affront.

Jefferson retired in 1809 but remained active. He kept up a voluminous correspondence with many public figures, including his former adversary John Adams. Jefferson was instrumental in founding the University of Virginia. He also designed its buildings and served as rector in 1819–26, helping the university become one of the most advanced institutions of its time.

Jefferson died on July 4, 1826, within a few hours of his presidential predecessor and friend, John Adams—on the 50th anniversary of the Declaration of Independence. His epitaph expressed the accomplishments for which he most wanted to be remembered: "Here was buried Thomas Jefferson, author of the Declaration of American Independence, of the Statute of Virginia for Religious Freedom, and father of the University of Virginia."

Martha Wayles (Skelton) Jefferson (1748–82) became Jefferson's wife in 1772 but died 10 years later. He did not remarry after her death. Only two of their six children survived to maturity: Martha and Mary (Maria). Jefferson had been a widower for about 18 years when he became President. Both his daughters served as his official hostesses, aided by Dolley Madison, wife of his secretary of state.

JAMES MADISON

Physically small and unimpressive, Madison stood about five feet six inches tall and weighed perhaps only about 100 pounds. But he was a formidable figure in the founding period of the nation.

He was the father of the Constitution, a founder of the Democratic-Republican Party, a congressman, au-

4th President
(1809–17)

thor of the Virginia Resolutions and of much of the *Federalist Papers*, and the fourth President of the United States.

The first of nine children of James and Nelly (Conway) Madison, he was born on March 16, 1751, in Port Conway, Va. Much of his early education was at home. He later attended the College of New Jersey (now Princeton), from which he graduated at 20. Like George Washington and others of the Virginia planter aristocracy, he supported the agitation against British colonial administration.

Madison's profound knowledge of government was first proved in 1776 when he helped draft a constitution for Virginia. In 1776 and 1777 he was a member of the executive council directing Virginia's participation in the Revolutionary War.

As a delegate to the Continental Congress for four years, Madison grew increasingly apprehensive as he watched the Congress flounder under the ineffective Articles of Confederation. After much thought he became convinced of the need for a strong national government.

In 1786 he was instrumental in the calling of a constitutional convention. At the convention in 1787 he became the leading spokesman for a strong federal government. Madison's political knowledge and persuasive logic helped secure adoption of the Constitution. The notes he kept on the sessions are the main reference source on the debates during the convention.

Madison fought for ratification of the Constitution by the states. In his own state he overcame the opposition of Patrick Henry. In the national campaign his contributions to the brilliant *Federalist Papers*, along with those of Hamilton and John Jay, had a powerful effect.

Elected to the House of Representatives in the newly established Congress (where he served for four terms), Madison led in winning passage of

the Bill of Rights and in creation of the executive departments.

During Washington's presidency, Madison became a steadfast enemy of Hamilton and an ardent supporter of his friend Thomas Jefferson. It was during this time that he became one of the principal organizers of the opposition party, the Democratic-Republicans.

When John Adams became President in 1797, Madison retired to Montpelier, his Virginia plantation. In 1798 Madison framed the Virginia Resolutions, protesting the repressive Alien and Sedition Acts inspired by Hamilton. By asserting the right of individual states to decide on the constitutionality of the acts, these resolutions (along with the Kentucky Resolutions penned by Jefferson) became the theoretical base for the states' rights doctrine.

When Jefferson became President in 1801, Madison was named secretary of state. He worked closely with Jefferson in negotiations for the purchase of the Louisiana Territory and in keeping the United States out of the Napoleonic wars in Europe. In 1808, following the tradition of Washington, Jefferson declined a third term. Madison became the successful candidate of the Democratic-Republicans.

He began his administration by following Jefferson's policy of neutrality in the Napoleonic wars. Finally, however, he was bullied by the "war hawks," led by John C. Calhoun and Henry Clay, into the indecisive War of 1812 against England, which began as a protest against Britain's blockade of U.S. ships trading with France.

To pay war bills and rehabilitate the economy, Madison resorted to such Federalist measures as the funding of the national debt, establishment of a national bank, and a protective tariff.

The war, which Federalist opponents called "Mr. Madison's war," went badly. New England merchants and industrialists openly opposed American participation. Even friends and supporters of his administration became discouraged by repeated setbacks suffered by American forces. Even so, Madison won reelection in 1812.

In 1814 a British fleet entered Chesapeake Bay. British troops landed in Maryland and proceeded to defeat the American militia assigned to defend Washington, D.C., at the Battle of Bladensburg on Aug. 24, 1814. The enemy set fire to the Capitol, the White House, and other public buildings, while Madison and other members of the government fled to safety. Dolley Madison saved a painting of George Washington as she fled.

The Treaty of Ghent, signed on Dec. 24, 1814, ended the war. But because of slow communications, the Battle of New Orleans was fought two weeks later, on Jan. 8, 1815.

After the war the westward movement began in earnest. Steamboat navigation opened on the Mississippi River.

In 1817 Madison retired once more to Montpelier. Besides being a gentleman farmer, he wrote extensively, succeeded Thomas Jefferson as rector of the University of Virginia in 1826, and was a delegate to the Virginia Constitutional Convention of 1829.

Madison died at Montpelier on June 28, 1836.

Dolley Payne (Todd) Madison (1768–1849) a 26-year-old widow and the daughter of a North Carolina planter, became Madison's wife in 1794, when he was 43. An attractive, vivacious, intelligent woman, Dolley Madison was a popular First Lady. After her husband's death she was voted an honorary seat in the House of Representatives by a unanimous congressional resolution.

MADISON'S PRESIDENTIAL ADMINISTRATION

Congresses in Session:
11th, 12th, 13th, 14th
Vice President:
George Clinton, 1809–12
Elbridge Gerry, 1813–14
Secretary of War:
William Eustis, 1809–13
John Armstrong, 1813–14
James Monroe, 1814–15
William Crawford, 1815–17

Secretary of State:
Robert Smith, 1809–11
James Monroe, 1811–17
Secretary of the Navy:
Paul Hamilton, 1809–12
William Jones, 1813–14
Benjamin Crowninshield, 1815–17
Postmaster General:
Gideon Granger, 1809–14
Return J. Meigs Jr., 1814–17

Secretary of the Treasury:
Albert Gallatin, 1809–14
George Campbell, 1814
Alexander Dallas, 1814–16
William H. Crawford, 1816–17

Attorney General:
Caesar Rodney, 1809–11
William Pinkney, 1811–14
Richard Rush, 1814–17

PRESIDENTIAL ELECTION OF 1808

Nominations: Congressional caucuses nominated respective party candidates. **Campaign Issue:** Jefferson's Embargo Act. **Remarks:** A faction of the Democratic–Republicans supported Clinton for President.

PRESIDENTIAL CANDIDATES	PARTY	ELECTORAL VOTES	VICE-PRESIDENTIAL CANDIDATES	PARTY	ELECTORAL VOTES
James Madison	Dem.–Rep.	122	George Clinton	Dem.–Rep.	113
Charles C. Pinckney	Federalist	47	Rufus King	Federalist	47
George Clinton	Dem.–Rep.	6	Other candidates	—	15
Votes not cast	—	1	Votes not cast	—	1

PRESIDENTIAL ELECTION OF 1812

Nominations: A congressional caucus nominated the Democratic–Republican ticket. **Campaign Issue:** The War of 1812. **Remarks:** This was the first presidential election carried out while the nation was formally at war.

PRESIDENTIAL CANDIDATES	PARTY	ELECTORAL VOTES	VICE-PRESIDENTIAL CANDIDATES	PARTY	ELECTORAL VOTES
James Madison	Dem.–Rep.	128	Elbridge Gerry	Dem.–Rep.	131
DeWitt Clinton	Federalist	89	Charles J. Ingersoll	Federalist	86
Votes not cast	—	1	Votes not cast	—	1

QUICK QUIZ: Who was flyweight boxing champion in 1954-60? See page 798.

JAMES MONROE

5th President
(1817–25)

Although he did not rank in imagination or in brilliance with the Democratic-Republican Presidents who served before him, Monroe has been judged an abler administrator of his high office than either Jefferson or Madison.

The fourth Virginian to become Chief Executive, he was born in Westmoreland County on April 28, 1758. He was the son of Spence and Elizabeth (Jones) Monroe, landowning farmers.

Monroe left the College of William and Mary in 1776 to become a lieutenant in a Virginia regiment, saw action in several Revolutionary War battles, and achieved the rank of major. When the war ended he studied law under Thomas Jefferson.

In 1782 he was elected to the Virginia legislature. Then for three years he served in the Continental Congress, where he opposed a centralized federal government.

Under the new government Monroe served in the U.S. Senate and became a leading spokesman for Jefferson and the Democratic-Republicans.

Monroe was minister to France (1794–96). Because of his enthusiastic support of the French Revolution, he was the only ambassador of a foreign power invited to sit in the revolutionary legislature.

In 1799 Monroe was elected governor of Virginia. Jefferson sent him to assist Robert Livingston in 1803 during the Louisiana Purchase negotiations, which were virtually completed by the time he arrived.

As Madison's secretary of state (1811–17),

Monroe also served a short-term appointment as secretary of war.

In 1816 Monroe obtained his party's presidential nomination and was easily elected.

Because of political calm, the first years of his administration were known as the Era of Good Feelings. He made a long tour of the Northern states in 1817 and a similar journey through the Southern states in 1819. Monroe was reelected in 1820 without opposition, winning all but one electoral vote.

The good feelings, however, were only apparent. Seething dissensions erupted in North-South disputes over extension of slavery into new states to be formed from the territories. The conflict was temporarily eased in 1820 by the first Missouri Compromise. Maine was admitted as a free state and Missouri as a slave state. A boundary was drawn between future free and slave states in the Louisiana Territory.

Other events in Monroe's presidency included the acquisition of Florida (1819); recognition of the Latin American republics (1822); and promulgation of the Monroe Doctrine (1823) to protect the Western Hemisphere. In 1822 Liberia was founded in Africa as a colony for freed American slaves with its capital, Monrovia, named for Monroe.

At the end of his term Monroe retired to his home in Loudoun County, Va. He served as regent of the University of Virginia in 1826 and presided over the Virginia Constitutional Convention in 1829. He died on July 4, 1831, and was buried in New York City. In 1858 his body was removed to Richmond, Va.

Elizabeth Kortright Monroe (1768–1830) married Monroe in 1786. The daughter of a New York businessman, she bore him a son (who died in infancy) and two daughters.

Their home, near Jefferson's Monticello in Virginia, was called Ash Lawn.

MONROE'S PRESIDENTIAL ADMINISTRATION

Congresses in Session:
15th, 16th, 17th, 18th

Vice President:
Daniel Tompkins, 1817–25

Secretary of State:
John Quincy Adams, 1817–25

Secretary of the Treasury:
William H. Crawford, 1817–25
Secretary of War:
John Calhoun, 1817–25
Attorney General:
Richard Rush, 1817
William Wirt, 1817–25

Secretary of the Navy:
Benjamin Crowninshield, 1817–18
Smith Thompson, 1818–23
Samuel Southard, 1823–25
Postmaster General:
Return J. Meigs Jr., 1817–23
John McLean, 1823–25

PRESIDENTIAL ELECTION OF 1816

Nominations: A congressional caucus nominated the Democratic–Republican ticket. **Campaign Issue:** None. The Democratic–Republican Party by this time had adopted most of the Federalist program. **Remarks:** This was the last election in which the Federalist Party nominated candidates for the offices of President and Vice President.

PRESIDENTIAL CANDIDATES	PARTY	ELECTORAL VOTES	VICE-PRESIDENTIAL CANDIDATES	PARTY	ELECTORAL VOTES
James Monroe	Dem.–Rep.	183	Daniel D. Tompkins	Dem.–Rep.	183
Rufus King	Federalist	34	John E. Howard	Federalist	22
Votes not cast	—	4	Other candidates	—	12
			Votes not cast	—	4

PRESIDENTIAL ELECTION OF 1820

No one contested Monroe's second term because of his popularity. The Federalist Party was dead. William Plumer of New Hampshire voted against Monroe allegedly because he believed only Washington's election should be unanimous.

PRESIDENTIAL CANDIDATES	PARTY	ELECTORAL VOTES	VICE-PRESIDENTIAL CANDIDATES	PARTY	ELECTORAL VOTES
James Monroe	Dem.–Rep.	231	Daniel D. Tompkins	Dem.–Rep.	218
John Quincy Adams	Independent	1	Other candidates	—	14
Votes not cast	—	3	Votes not cast	—	3

JOHN QUINCY ADAMS

A high-minded man with little popular support and no political party, John Quincy Adams entered the presidency with gloomy prospects. He was charged with stealing the White House from the popular Andrew Jackson by making a political bargain with Henry Clay.

6th President
(1825–29)

As President, Adams alienated politicians by advocating a professional civil service free of patronage. And the one important act passed by Congress with Adams' approval—raising the protective tariff rates—angered farmers.

Born on July 11, 1767, in Braintree (now Quincy), Mass., Adams was the eldest son of President John Adams.

At the age of 10 he went to France with his father. He was educated in France and the Netherlands during his father's diplomatic service. At the age of 14 he went to Moscow where he served for two years as the private secretary of American ambassador Francis Dana. He graduated from Harvard in 1787 and was admitted to the bar in 1790.

Adams served as minister to the Netherlands (1794–97) under President Washington and as minister to Prussia (1797–1801) during his father's administration.

As a Massachusetts state senator in 1802, he demonstrated his disregard for partisan politics, though he was the son of a Federalist President and was elected by the Federalists.

Elected to the U.S. Senate in 1803, he acted so independently that the Federalists maneuvered him out of office in 1808.

In 1809 he was sent as minister to Russia, where he was held in esteem. He was in Russia during Napoleon's invasion in 1812. While there he was named and confirmed to the U.S. Supreme Court, but turned down the appointment.

In 1814 Adams negotiated the Treaty of Ghent, which ended the War of 1812.

As Monroe's secretary of state (1817–25) Adams gained great respect. He negotiated the 1819 treaty with Spain that added Florida to the United States, negotiated with Britain for the settlement of a U.S.-Canadian border dispute, and firmly dealt with Russian plans to penetrate America's West Coast. But Adams won his greatest praise as the chief architect of the Monroe Doctrine.

None of the candidates for the presidency in 1824—Adams, Jackson, William H. Crawford, Henry Clay—ran with a political party designation. Jackson received the most electoral votes but not the required majority, so the election had to be decided in the House of Representatives. Because Clay had the fewest electoral votes, he was dropped from consideration by the House. After a private meeting with Adams, Clay threw his support to Adams. In turn, Adams made Clay his secretary of state.

In 1828, running on the National Republican ticket, Adams was defeated by Andrew Jackson in his bid for reelection.

He was elected to Congress in 1830, where for 17 years he distinguished himself by his untiring and conscientious service.

In Congress, he actively opposed the extension of slavery, the annexation of Texas, and war with Mexico. He succeeded in 1844 in ending the "gag rules" in congressional debate on slavery.

Adams also sponsored the advancement of science. The Smithsonian Institution owes its development largely to him.

At the age of 80 Adams suffered a stroke while at his desk in the House of Representatives. He died two days later, on Feb. 23, 1848.

Louisa Catherine Johnson Adams (1775–1852), daughter of an American diplomat, married Adams in London in 1797. She made the White House a center for cultured and animated social life during her tenancy. The couple had three sons and a daughter. Their youngest son, Charles Francis Adams, served as U.S. minister to Britain during the Civil War.

JOHN QUINCY ADAMS' PRESIDENTIAL ADMINISTRATION

Congresses in Session:
 19th, 20th
Vice President:
 John Calhoun, 1825–29
Secretary of State:
 Henry Clay, 1825–29

Secretary of the Treasury:
 Richard Rush, 1825–29

Secretary of War:
 James Barbour, 1825–28
 Peter Porter, 1828–29

Attorney General:
 William Wirt, 1825–29
Secretary of the Navy:
 Samuel Southard, 1825–29
Postmaster General:
 John McLean, 1825–29

PRESIDENTIAL ELECTION OF 1824

Nominations: The disintegration of the Democratic–Republican Party led to presidential nominations by state legislatures. There were several "favorite son" candidates. **Campaign Issues:** The candidates supported domestic improvements and a higher protective tariff.

Remarks: No candidate received a majority of the electoral vote. The House of Representatives finally chose Adams after Clay was eliminated because he had the fewest electoral votes. Before 1824, records of popular votes are virtually nonexistent. State legislatures usually chose the presidential electors.

PRESIDENTIAL CANDIDATES	PARTY	ELECTORAL VOTES	POPULAR VOTE Total	Percentage	VICE-PRESIDENTIAL CANDIDATES AND ELECTORAL VOTES		PARTY
John Quincy Adams	None	84	108,740	30.6	John C. Calhoun ...	182	None
Andrew Jackson	None	99	153,544	43.1	Nathan Sanford ...	30	None
William H. Crawford	None	41	46,618	13.1	Nathaniel Macon ...	24	None
Henry Clay	None	37	47,136	13.2	Other candidates ..	25	—

QUICK QUIZ: Who won the James E. Sullivan Memorial Trophy in 1965? See page 767.

ANDREW JACKSON

7th President
(1829–37)

Although a man of personal dignity, Andrew Jackson was feared by many established citizens of his day as a dangerous upstart and the one who brought "rabble" into the White House. A leader of the movement toward increased popular participation in government, he came to symbolize the democratic sentiments of the period. Jackson's administration, which strengthened the role of the Executive Office, has been ranked as one of the most important in U.S. history.

The first "log cabin" President, Jackson was born on March 15, 1767, in Waxhaw Settlement on the border between North and South Carolina. He was the son of Irish immigrants Andrew and Elizabeth (Hutchinson) Jackson. His father died shortly before Andrew was born.

At 13 he and his brother were imprisoned by the British during the Revolutionary War. The boys caught smallpox and were released to the care of their mother. His brother and mother both died.

The orphaned Andrew Jackson lived with relatives and friends. He was admitted to the North Carolina bar in 1787 at the age of 20.

In 1788 Jackson moved west to Nashville, which later became the capital of Tennessee. He prospered in law and land speculation.

In 1797–98 Jackson served briefly in Congress, first in the House and then in the Senate. Before the War of 1812, he spent six years as a judge of the Tennessee superior court.

In 1802 Jackson was elected major general of the Tennessee state militia, a position considered next in importance to the governorship.

In the War of 1812, troops under his command crushed the Creek Indians, allies of the British, in the Battle of Horseshoe Bend in Alabama and forced them to make peace. This brought him the rank of major general in the U.S. Army. In one campaign he captured British strongholds in Florida. He then was given command of an expedition against a British army marching on New Orleans. Although outnumbered at that battle, he gained the victory that made him a national hero — even though the Battle of New Orleans was of no real military importance, having taken place a few weeks after Britain and the U.S. had signed the Treaty of Ghent, ending the War of 1812.

Jackson had acquired the reputation for personal toughness symbolized by his nickname "Old Hickory." According to some sources his duels and brawls numbered nearly 100.

JACKSON'S PRESIDENTIAL ADMINISTRATION

Congresses in Session:
21st, 22d, 23d, 24th

Vice President:
John Calhoun, 1829–32
Martin Van Buren, 1833–37

Secretary of State:
Martin Van Buren, 1829–31
Edward Livingston, 1831–33
Louis McLane, 1833–34
John Forsyth, 1834–37

Secretary of the Treasury:
Samuel Ingham, 1829–31
Louis McLane, 1831–33
William J. Duane, 1833
Roger Taney, 1833–34
Levi Woodbury, 1834–37

Attorney General:
John Berrien, 1829–31
Roger Taney, 1831–33
Benjamin Butler, 1833–37

Secretary of War:
John Eaton, 1829–31
Lewis Cass, 1831–36
Benjamin Butler, 1836–37

Secretary of the Navy:
John Branch, 1829–31
Levi Woodbury, 1831–34
Mahlon Dickerson, 1834–37

Postmaster General:
John McLean, 1829
William Barry, 1829–35
Amos Kendall, 1835–37

PRESIDENTIAL ELECTION OF 1828

Nominations: The Tennessee legislature nominated Jackson for the presidency. Adams was the incumbent. **Campaign Issues:** Jackson and his followers charged that the government was in the hands of an "aristocratic minority." His supporters charged the election of 1824 had been stolen from him by Adams. **Remarks:** Jackson was a popular hero.

PRESIDENTIAL CANDIDATES	PARTY	ELECTORAL VOTES	POPULAR VOTE Total	Percentage	VICE-PRESIDENTIAL CANDIDATES AND ELECTORAL VOTES		PARTY
Andrew Jackson ...	Democratic	178	647,286	56.0	John C. Calhoun ...	171	Democratic
John Quincy Adams	Natl. Rep.	83	508,064	44.0	Richard Rush	83	Natl. Rep.
					William Smith	7	Democratic

PRESIDENTIAL ELECTION OF 1832

Nominations: The modern political convention system dates from Sept. 26, 1831. Wirt was nominated on the first ballot by the Anti-Masonic Party. The National Republican Party convention met in Baltimore, Dec. 12–15, 1831, and chose Clay and Sergeant. At the Democratic Party convention in Baltimore, May 21–23, 1832, Jackson unanimously received the nomination. The Independents nominated Floyd and Lee. **Campaign Issue:** The Democrats fought the rechartering of the Second Bank of the United States. **Remarks:** The Anti-Masonic Party was the first legitimate third party.

PRESIDENTIAL CANDIDATES	PARTY	ELECTORAL VOTES	POPULAR VOTE Total	Percentage	VICE-PRESIDENTIAL CANDIDATES AND ELECTORAL VOTES		PARTY
Andrew Jackson ...	Democratic	219	687,502	52.2	Martin Van Buren ..	189	Democratic
Henry Clay	Natl. Rep.	49	530,189	40.2	John Sergeant	49	Natl. Rep.
John Floyd	Independent	11	—	—	Henry Lee	11	Nullifiers
William Wirt	Anti-Masonic	7	101,051	7.6	Amos Ellmaker ...	7	Anti-Masonic
Votes not cast	—	2	—	—	William Wilkins	30	Independent
					Votes not cast.....	2	—

In 1818 he was ordered to punish some Seminole Indians who had been raiding across the Alabama-Georgia border. He crossed over into Spanish Florida, captured Pensacola, and ordered executed two British subjects accused of inciting the raids. His unauthorized move involved the U.S. in serious trouble with both Spain and Britain, but when Florida became U.S. territory he was named its first governor—an appointment Jackson considered vindication.

The greatest popular hero of his time, a man of action, and an expansionist, Jackson by 1821 was being actively promoted as Monroe's successor in the White House.

In 1824 Jackson was nominated for the presidency by one of the four factions into which the ruling Democratic-Republicans had split.

Jackson won a plurality of the electoral votes, but not the required majority. The election was thrown into the House of Representatives, where supporters of one of the candidates, Henry Clay, gave their votes to John Quincy Adams, who became President. The angry Jacksonians called this "bargain and corruption."

In the election of 1828 Jackson easily defeated Adams' bid for reelection.

Jackson strengthened the authority of the presidency, taking leadership from most members of his official cabinet. His "kitchen cabinet"—an unofficial group of favorite advisers—wielded great influence. Party loyalty was intense. Members were rewarded with government posts in the spoils system.

In the nullification crisis of 1832, when South Carolina declared null and void the Tariff Act of that year, Jackson took a strong pro-Union stand. He indicated he would use troops if the state tried to secede, warning: "Our Federal Union, it must be preserved." However, he felt that the South had a real grievance and ordered a compromise tariff act.

In other respects Jackson supported the doctrine of states' rights, especially when he fought against the Bank of the United States. He finally removed the funds from this national bank and deposited them in chosen state banks.

Jackson probably could have won a third term in 1836, but instead he chose to put Vice President Martin Van Buren, a New York party politician, into the White House.

Jackson retired to The Hermitage, his Tennessee estate, but his voice was heard throughout Van Buren's administration. Because Van Buren opposed the annexation of Texas, Jackson helped James Polk win the presidency in 1844. Jackson died on June 8, 1845.

Rachel Donelson (Robards) Jackson (1767–1828), a divorcée, married Jackson in 1791. A mistake in her divorce proceedings made it necessary for them to be remarried three years later. This long-lived "scandal" made Jackson the butt of slurs, one of which led to a duel in which he killed his opponent. The Jacksons had no children of their own, but they adopted the son of Mrs. Jackson's brother. He was named Andrew Jackson Jr.

Mrs. Jackson died just before her husband became President. Her niece, Emily Donelson, and Jackson's daughter-in-law, Sarah Yorke Jackson, served as White House hostesses.

MARTIN VAN BUREN

8th President
(1837–41)

Political skill and native intelligence earned Martin Van Buren the nickname "Red Fox." As a Jacksonian Democrat he proclaimed himself a champion of the people.

But he lost popular support in the financial panic of 1837 by opposing federal aid to alleviate distress. He resisted the extension of slavery, and his stand against the annexation of Texas probably cost him the Democratic nomination in 1844.

The son of Abraham Van Buren, a farmer and innkeeper, and Maria (Hoes) Van Alen Van Buren, he was born on Dec. 5, 1782, in Kinderhook, N.Y. As a boy he waited on tables in his father's tavern. Though he never attended college, he trained in law offices and was admitted to the bar in 1803.

Van Buren's first public office was surrogate of Columbia County, N.Y., in 1808. He served as a state senator (1812–20) and during that time was state attorney general (1816–19).

As a U.S. senator (1821–28) he was inconsistent on the issues of states' rights and slavery. Van Buren was far more important as a political leader than as a legislator. He became one of the principal figures in a powerful political clique known as the Albany Regency. He swung his support to Andrew Jackson.

He won election as governor of New York in 1828, but resigned after serving only two months to accept appointment by Jackson as U.S. secretary of state.

Probably the most influential of Jackson's advisers, Van Buren was nominated for Vice President by the Democratic Party in 1832 and was elected along with President Jackson.

In 1836, supported by Jackson, he was chosen as Democratic candidate for President and was swept into office.

To combat the Panic of 1837, Van Buren called a special session of Congress. He asked for the establishment of an independent treasury system so that the government could control the money collected from taxes rather than deposit it in private banks. He also proposed that the government issue paper money in the form of treasury notes. However, Congress did not pass the Independent Treasury Act until July 1840.

As a friend of labor, he reduced the workday for federal employees to 10 hours.

His opponents criticized Van Buren for spending government money to install the first hot-water tank in the White House to warm his bathwater.

QUICK QUIZ: When was the last time a Chicago team won baseball's World Series? See page 772.

MARTIN VAN BUREN (*continued*)
Van Buren was defeated in his campaign for re-election as President in 1840. He then was denied renomination as his party's candidate in 1844, largely because he had angered Andrew Jackson by opposing the annexation of Texas.

Running on the antislavery Free Soil Party ticket in 1848, Van Buren failed to receive a single electoral vote.

Bitterly disappointed, he retired to his home in Kinderhook, where he died on July 24, 1862. **Hannah Hoes Van Buren** (1783–1819), who became his wife in 1807, was his boyhood sweetheart. They had four sons. She died while Van Buren was New York's attorney general. He never remarried. His daughter-in-law Angelica Singleton Van Buren served as White House hostess during his presidency.

VAN BUREN'S PRESIDENTIAL ADMINISTRATION

Congresses in Session:
25th, 26th

Vice President:
Richard M. Johnson, 1837–41

Secretary of State:
John Forsyth, 1837–41

Secretary of the Treasury:
Levi Woodbury, 1837–41
Secretary of War:
Joel Poinsett, 1837–41
Secretary of the Navy:
Mahlon Dickerson, 1837–38
James Paulding, 1838–41

Attorney General:
Benjamin Butler, 1837–38
Felix Grundy, 1838–40
Henry Gilpin, 1840–41
Postmaster General:
Amos Kendall, 1837–40
John Niles, 1840–41

PRESIDENTIAL ELECTION OF 1836

Nominations: At the Democratic convention in Baltimore, May 20–22, 1836, Van Buren was backed by Jackson and was nominated unanimously. The Whigs, who held no national convention, nominated several strong sectional candidates. **Campaign Issues:** The campaign centered on Andrew Jack-son, his policies, and when Van Buren should succeed him. **Remarks:** This was the only election in which none of the vice-presidential candidates received the required majority vote. The U.S. Senate chose Richard M. Johnson, who had been Van Buren's running mate, over Francis Granger.

PRESIDENTIAL CANDIDATES	PARTY	ELECTORAL VOTES	POPULAR VOTE Total	Percentage	VICE-PRESIDENTIAL CANDIDATES AND ELECTORAL VOTES		PARTY
Martin Van Buren ..	Democratic	170	765,483	50.9	Richard M. Johnson	147	Democratic
William H. Harrison	Whig	73	550,816	36.6	Francis Granger ...	77	Whig
Hugh L. White	Whig	26	146,107	9.7	John Tyler	47	Democratic
Daniel Webster	Whig	14	41,201	2.7	William Smith	23	Independent
W.P. Mangum	Anti-Jackson	11	—	—			

WILLIAM HENRY HARRISON

The Whigs in 1840 presented Harrison, their presidential candidate, as a cider-drinking, homespun, log-cabin-born, hardworking plow pusher. This was a fable, but it helped make the hero of the Battle of Tippecanoe an easy victor over Martin Van Buren.

What sort of a President Harrison would have been will never be known because of his

9th President
(1841)

early death after taking office.

Harrison's administration augured well because of the distinguished cabinet he assembled, which included Daniel Webster as secretary of state. However, Harrison died of pneumonia on April 4, 1841, a month after his inauguration—the first U.S. Chief Executive to die in the White House.

Harrison's birthplace actually was a brick mansion at "Berkeley," his family's estate in Charles City County, Va. He was born on Feb. 9, 1773, the son of Benjamin and Elizabeth (Bassett) Harrison. His father, a wealthy planter, had been one of the signers of the Declaration of Independence.

He was privately tutored and then attended

HARRISON'S PRESIDENTIAL ADMINISTRATION

Congresses in Session:
27th
Vice President:
John Tyler, 1841

Secretary of State:
Daniel Webster, 1841
Secretary of the Treasury:
Thomas Ewing, 1841

Secretary of War:
John Bell, 1841
Attorney General:
John Crittenden, 1841

Postmaster General:
Francis Granger, 1841
Secretary of the Navy:
George Badger, 1841

PRESIDENTIAL ELECTION OF 1840

Nominations: The Whigs met in Harrisburg, Pa., in December 1839, choosing Harrison and Tyler. The Democrats met in Baltimore in May 1840, and chose Van Buren without dissent.

The Liberty Party met in Albany in April 1840, nominating James G. Birney and Thomas Earle—the first effort by the abolitionists to win national political power.

PRESIDENTIAL CANDIDATES	PARTY	ELECTORAL VOTES	POPULAR VOTE Total	Percentage	VICE-PRESIDENTIAL CANDIDATES AND ELECTORAL VOTES		PARTY
William H. Harrison	Whig	234	1,274,624	53.1	John Tyler	234	Whig
Martin Van Buren ..	Democratic	60	1,127,781	46.9	Richard M. Johnson	48	Democratic
James G. Birney ...	Liberty	—	7,053	—	Thomas Earle	—	Liberty
					L.W. Tazewell	11	Independent
					James K. Polk	1	Democratic

Hampden-Sydney College. He went on to study medicine briefly in Philadelphia under Dr. Benjamin Rush, a signer of the Declaration of Independence.

In 1791 Harrison joined the Army. He resigned his commission in 1798 to become secretary of the Northwest Territory. In 1799, at the age of 26, he became its first delegate to Congress. There his proposal to divide the territory into Ohio and Indiana was approved.

As governor of Indiana Territory (1800–12), Harrison induced the Indians to cede vast tracts of land.

When the Shawnee Indians attacked encroaching settlers in 1811, Harrison led an expedition that defeated the Indians in the Battle of Tippecanoe. Harrison won national fame with the battle and settled the territory's claim to 3 million acres of Indian land.

In the War of 1812 he was appointed supreme commander of the Army of the Northwest. Marching into Canada, he defeated the British and their Indian allies at the Battle of the Thames River on Oct. 5, 1813.

After resigning from the Army, he became a farmer at North Bend, Ohio. He then entered politics, winning election as a U.S. congressman (1817–19), state senator (1819–25), and U.S. senator from Ohio (1825–28). President John Quincy Adams appointed him as minister to Colombia (1828–29).

In 1834 Harrison was given the lucrative post of court clerk in Hamilton County, Ohio.

Dissident Whigs nominated Harrison for President in 1836. He came in second in a field of five, losing to Martin Van Buren.

In 1840 the Whig Party nominated him with John Tyler as his running mate. This second campaign, a successful one against Van Buren, is memorable for its slogan "Tippecanoe and Tyler too" and for its demagogy.

Anna Tuthill Symmes Harrison (1775–1864), the 20-year-old daughter of a well-to-do Ohio landowner, married Harrison in 1795. They had 10 children. A grandson, Benjamin Harrison, became the 23d U.S. President.

JOHN TYLER

10th President
(1841–45)

Tyler was the first Vice President to succeed to the presidency because of the death of the incumbent, William Henry Harrison.

Never did a President prove more disappointing to the party that had placed him in office.

An ex-Democrat and a cultured Virginian, Tyler was nominated to run on Harrison's ticket as Vice President to attract Southern votes.

But when he became President, Tyler soon showed that all he had in common with Whig regulars was his antagonism to Jacksonian Democrats.

Tyler was born on March 29, 1790, in Charles City County, Va., the son of a prominent lawyer-politician. He graduated from the College of William and Mary at 17, was admitted to the bar at 19, and entered politics at 21 as a member of Virginia's state legislature. He served in Congress and as governor of Virginia before being elected Vice President. Exactly one month after taking office he succeeded Harrison, who died on April 4, 1841.

Within five months Tyler had twice vetoed a keystone measure of the Whigs—a bill to reestablish the national bank. As a result, his entire cabinet resigned, with the exception of Daniel Webster, secretary of state. Webster negotiated the Webster-Ashburton Treaty in 1842, settling a serious Canadian boundary dispute. Tyler was denounced by the Whigs and had few friends among the Democrats.

Despite strong opposition, Tyler advanced the annexation of Texas, which had won its independence from Mexico and was applying for statehood. An antislavery bloc in the Senate delayed ratification of the annexation treaty, but Tyler outmaneuvered them. Three days before his term ended, an annexation resolution was passed.

Whigs turned their backs on Tyler in 1844, choosing Clay as their presidential nominee. Tyler remained in virtual retirement for years, but in 1861 he presided over an unsuccessful Washington conference called to avert civil war. He then threw his support to the Confederacy. Tyler died on Jan. 18, 1862, in Richmond, Va.

Letitia Christian Tyler (1790–1842), who married Tyler in 1813, was an invalid when he became President. She died during his second year in office.

Julia Gardiner Tyler (1820–89), who was 30 years his junior, became his second wife in 1844. The first President to marry while in office, Tyler had 15 children, eight by his first wife. All but one lived to maturity. The last died in 1947.

TYLER'S PRESIDENTIAL ADMINISTRATION

Congresses in Session:
27th, 28th
Vice President:
Vacant
Secretary of State:
Daniel Webster, 1841–43
Abel Upshur, 1843–44
John Calhoun, 1844–45
Postmaster General:
Francis Granger, 1841
Charles Wickliffe, 1841–45

Secretary of the Treasury:
Thomas Ewing, 1841
Walter Forward, 1841–43
John Spencer, 1843–44
George Bibb, 1844–45

Secretary of War:
John Bell, 1841
John Spencer, 1841–43
James Porter, 1843–44
Williams Wilkins, 1844–45

Attorney General:
John Crittenden, 1841
Hugh Legaré, 1841–43
John Nelson, 1843–45

Secretary of the Navy:
George Badger, 1841
Abel Upshur, 1841–43
David Henshaw, 1843–44
Thomas W. Gilmer, 1844
John Mason, 1844–45

QUICK QUIZ: Who won the senior men's U.S. road bicycling championship in 1984? See page 795.

JAMES KNOX POLK

11th President
(1845–49)

At the 1844 Democratic convention a deadlock was broken when James K. Polk, supported by Andrew Jackson, was proposed as the nominee who could unite the opposing factions. His selection on the ninth ballot made him the first "dark horse" presidential candidate. As Jackson's protégé, Polk was called "Young Hickory" by his supporters.

An avowed expansionist in the age of "manifest destiny," Polk campaigned on promises of annexing Texas and expanding the Oregon Territory in the northwest. He narrowly defeated Whig candidate Henry Clay.

Born on Nov. 2, 1795, in Mecklenburg County, N.C., he was the son of Samuel Polk, a well-to-do farmer, and Jane Knox Polk. The family moved to Tennessee in 1806. Polk graduated from the University of North Carolina in 1818 and began to practice law in Columbia, Tenn., two years later.

He entered politics as a Jacksonian Democrat. His fiery campaigning won him the nickname "Napoleon of the Stump" and got him elected to the Tennessee legislature.

He then served seven consecutive terms in Congress (1825–39). He became chairman of the powerful Ways and Means Committee and then majority leader of the Democratic Party. During his last four years in Congress he was Speaker of the House. In 1839 he was elected governor of Tennessee, serving until 1841.

After Polk took office as President in 1845, he sent a personal emissary, John Slidell, to Mexico to try to buy New Mexico and California. When the Mexican government refused to receive Slidell, Polk sent troops under Gen. Zachary Taylor to the disputed Rio Grande boundary. Mexican troops attacked, and Polk claimed war had begun "by act of Mexico."

Congress declared war on Mexico on May 13, 1846. A succession of American victories culminated in the capture of the Mexican capital.

The Mexican War ended with the Treaty of Guadalupe Hidalgo, signed Feb. 2, 1848. Mexico accepted payment of $15 million for territory that was to become California, New Mexico, Arizona, Nevada, Utah, and parts of Colorado and Wyoming—the largest accession of territory since the Louisiana Purchase. Polk blocked the Wilmot Proviso, an attempt to exclude slavery from the new acquisitions.

In the meantime he had negotiated a Canadian boundary agreement with Britain in the Oregon Treaty of June 15, 1846. Ignoring his campaign slogan—"54°40' or Fight!"—Polk accepted the 49th parallel as the boundary with Canada.

Polk also tried to purchase Cuba from Spain for $100 million, but his offer was rejected.

Life in the White House was straitlaced during the Polk administration. Polk was a pious Methodist, and his wife was a strict Presbyterian. They banned dancing, card playing, and alcoholic beverages from the White House. And they installed the first gas lighting, replacing candles and oil lamps.

During the negotiations that led to Texas joining the Union and becoming the 28th state in 1845, Sam Houston remarked that the only thing wrong with Polk was that he drank too much water.

Former President John Quincy Adams wrote of Polk: "He has no wit, no literature, no point of argument, no gracefulness of delivery, no elegance of language, no philosophy, no pathos, no felicitous impromptus; nothing that can constitute an orator, but confidence, fluency, and labor."

Under constant harassment in Congress, not only from the Whig opposition but from resentful Northern Democrats, Polk labored strenuously to the detriment of his health. He refused renomination and died on June 15, 1849.

Sarah Childress Polk (1803–91) married Polk in 1824. They had no children of their own, but Mrs. Polk later adopted a daughter.

POLK'S PRESIDENTIAL ADMINISTRATION

Congresses in Session:
29th, 30th

Vice President:
George Dallas, 1845–49

Secretary of State:
James Buchanan, 1845–49

Secretary of the Treasury:
Robert Walker, 1845–49

Secretary of War:
William Marcy, 1845–49

Secretary of the Navy:
George Bancroft, 1845–46
John Mason, 1846–49

Attorney General:
John Mason, 1845–46
Nathan Clifford, 1846–48
Isaac Toucey, 1848–49

Postmaster General:
Cave Johnson, 1845–49

PRESIDENTIAL ELECTION OF 1844

Nominations: At the Whig convention in Baltimore, May 1, 1844, Clay was chosen on the first ballot by acclamation. On the third ballot Frelinghuysen received 155 out of 275 votes, and then his vice-presidential nomination was made unanimous. The Democrats met in Baltimore, May 27–30, 1844. Although Van Buren had a majority of the votes, he could not obtain the necessary two-thirds majority. On the ninth ballot Polk was nominated. Dallas received the vice-presidential nomination on the second ballot, after Silas Wright had declined the nomination. The Liberty Party met in Buffalo, N. Y., Aug. 30, 1843, and unanimously nominated its candidates, Birney and Morris. **Campaign Issues:** Foreign and domestic issues included whether Texas should be annexed to the U.S. as a slave state, whether the tariff should be lowered, and what steps should be taken to settle the Oregon boundary dispute with Britain.

PRESIDENTIAL CANDIDATES	PARTY	ELECTORAL VOTES	POPULAR VOTE Total	Percentage	VICE-PRESIDENTIAL CANDIDATES
James K. Polk	Democratic	170	1,338,464	49.6	George M. Dallas
Henry Clay	Whig	105	1,300,097	48.1	Theodore Frelinghuysen
James G. Birney	Liberty	—	62,300	2.3	Thomas Morris

ZACHARY TAYLOR

12th President
(1849–50)

Taylor's path to the White House was paved during the Mexican War, some two years before the 1848 Whig convention nominated him. In May 1846, soon after two victories by General Taylor's forces, it was predicted he would be elected President. Taylor scoffed at the idea, but within two years the nonpolitical hero accepted the Whig presidential nomination.

Zachary Taylor was born on Nov. 24, 1784, in Orange County, Va., while his family was on its way to a new home in Kentucky. His parents were Richard and Sarah Dabney Strother Taylor.

In 1808 he was commissioned a first lieutenant in the Army. Following his victory over the Seminoles at Lake Okeechobee, Fla., Taylor was promoted to brigadier general in 1837. He earned the nickname "Old Rough and Ready" in the Florida campaign.

In 1845 he was given command of the army in Texas. During the Mexican War he was at times defiant to the point of insubordination. An armistice Taylor granted after seizing Monterrey in 1846 created serious friction with President Polk, who thought the terms were too lenient. Taylor ignored orders to hold his position. Instead, in February 1847 he led his troops a few miles south, where he defeated numerically superior Mexican forces at Buena Vista. Taylor returned home to national acclaim.

Although a slaveholder and a conservative, Taylor was under the influence of Sen. William H. Seward (New York), leader of the antislavery Whigs. Taylor campaigned on his war record.

Taylor became the first person to win the presidency without having been previously elected to public office. Because March 4 fell on Sunday, Taylor postponed his inauguration to March 5.

Taylor's call in 1850 for admission to statehood of antislavery California alienated his Southern Whig supporters.

When Southern leaders threatened to drive federal troops from New Mexico to prevent it from becoming an antislavery state, Taylor warned he would take command of the Army.

Sen. Henry Clay offered the Compromise of 1850 in an effort to placate both North and South. President Taylor probably would have vetoed the Compromise, but he died of cholera on July 9, 1850.

Margaret Mackall Smith Taylor (1788–1852) married Taylor in 1810. They had six children.

TAYLOR'S PRESIDENTIAL ADMINISTRATION

Congress in Session:
31st
Vice President:
Millard Fillmore, 1849–50
Secretary of State:
John Clayton, 1849–50

Secretary of the Treasury:
William M. Meredith, 1849–50
Secretary of War:
George Crawford, 1849–50
Attorney General:
Reverdy Johnson, 1849–50

Postmaster General:
Jacob Collamer, 1849–50
Secretary of the Navy:
William B. Preston, 1849–50
Secretary of the Interior:
Thomas Ewing, 1849–50

PRESIDENTIAL ELECTION OF 1848

Nominations: The Democratic convention in Baltimore, May 22–26, 1848, chose Lewis Cass on the fourth ballot. Butler was chosen on the second ballot with 169 out of 253 votes cast. The Whig convention in Philadelphia, June 7–9, 1848, chose Taylor by a majority vote on the fourth ballot. Fillmore was chosen on the second ballot. The Free Soil Party convention in Buffalo, N.Y., Aug. 9–10, 1848, unanimously nominated Van Buren and Adams.

PRESIDENTIAL CANDIDATES	PARTY	ELECTORAL VOTES	POPULAR VOTE Total	Percentage	VICE-PRESIDENTIAL CANDIDATES
Zachary Taylor	Whig	163	1,360,967	47.3	Millard Fillmore
Lewis Cass	Democratic	127	1,222,342	42.5	William O. Butler
Martin Van Buren	Free Soil	—	291,263	10.1	Charles Francis Adams

MILLARD FILLMORE

13th President
(1850–53)

Fillmore took office on July 10, 1850, the day after President Taylor died. During his administration he sought to preserve the Union by conciliating the South. But the nation had become too deeply divided on the slavery issue, and his attempt to carry out the Compromise of 1850 alienated both sides. In particular, his strict enforcement of the Fugitive Slave Law of 1850 aroused the wrath of the antislavery wing of the Whig Party.

Two measures he did not initiate are also associated with Fillmore's administration. One was the dispatch of Commodore Perry to Japan to open that country's ports to U.S. trade. The other was the reorganization of the postal department to provide cheaper mail rates.

Fillmore was born on Jan. 7, 1800, in Locke, N.Y., the son of Nathaniel Fillmore, a farmer, and Phoebe Millard Fillmore.

As a youth he worked at odd jobs to earn a living, and was largely self-educated. He read law in his spare time, winning admission to the bar in 1823. After practicing briefly in East Aurora, N.Y., he moved to Buffalo.

Fillmore's political career began in 1828 when he was elected to the New York assembly. He went on to serve four terms in Congress, beginning in 1833. A Whig, he became chairman of the

MILLARD FILLMORE *(continued)*

powerful House Ways and Means Committee in 1841–43.

Defeated as the Whig candidate for governor of New York in 1844, Fillmore became state comptroller.

Because of the strong stand Fillmore had taken against the extension of slavery into the territories, Henry Clay backed him for the vice presidency on the successful Whig ticket in 1848. His position was intended to offset the supposed proslavery sympathies of presidential candidate Zachary Taylor.

Fillmore lost the Whigs' support in 1852, and their presidential nomination went to Gen. Winfield Scott, who favored a more radical antislavery program.

Fillmore attempted to regain the presidency in 1856 when he accepted the presidential nomination of the anti-Catholic, antiforeigner American (Know-Nothing) Party. In the election he won only eight electoral votes. Fillmore died in Buffalo, N.Y., on March 8, 1874.

Abigail Powers Fillmore (1798–1853), daughter of a Baptist clergyman, married Fillmore in 1826. They had two children. She was too ill to preside at White House functions. During her tenancy the first cooking stove was installed in the White House kitchen, replacing fireplace cookery. She died a month after Fillmore completed his presidential term.

Caroline Carmichael (McIntosh) Fillmore (1813–81), a wealthy widow, became Fillmore's second wife in 1858.

FILLMORE'S PRESIDENTIAL ADMINISTRATION

Congresses in Session:
31st, 32d

Vice President:
Vacant

Secretary of State:
Daniel Webster, 1850–52
Edward Everett, 1852–53

Secretary of the Treasury:
Thomas Corwin, 1850–53

Secretary of War:
Charles Conrad, 1850–53

Postmaster General:
Nathan Hall, 1850–52
Samuel Hubbard, 1852–53

Attorney General:
John J. Crittenden, 1850–53

Secretary of the Navy:
William Graham, 1850–52
John Kennedy, 1852–53

Secretary of the Interior:
T.M.T. McKennan, 1850
Alexander Stuart, 1850–53

FRANKLIN PIERCE

Pierce began his presidency under an emotional strain. Shortly before his term began, he and his wife saw their only surviving son killed in a train wreck. Mrs. Pierce, who disliked both Washington and her husband's involvement in politics, became withdrawn and was infrequently seen in public.

14th President
(1853–57)

A Northern Democrat, Pierce misjudged the nation's growing animosity to slavery. In the presidential election campaign, he had promised to prevent slavery from becoming a divisive political issue. But his willingness to aid Southern Democrats in the extension of slavery to new states added new fuel to the flames of the slavery controversy.

Born on Nov. 23, 1804, in Hillsboro, N.H., he was the son of Anna Kendrick Pierce and Benjamin

Pierce, a Revolutionary War general and twice New Hampshire governor. He attended Bowdoin College and was admitted to the bar in 1827.

Pierce entered politics as a Jacksonian Democrat and served two terms as a congressman in 1833–37. In 1836, at 32, he became one of the youngest men elected to the U.S. Senate. He resigned eight years later because of his wife's ill health. Pierce practiced law in Concord, N.H., and became leader of the state's Democratic Party. He served as a brigadier general of New England volunteers in the Mexican War.

Pierce was chosen president of the New Hampshire constitutional convention in 1850.

A delegate to the Democratic convention in 1852, Pierce emerged as a dark-horse presidential contender. His nomination on the 49th ballot broke a hopeless deadlock among the front-runners. As a Northerner with pro-South sympathies, he was deemed acceptable to both sides. Pierce went on to defeat the Whig candidate, Winfield Scott, his Mexican War commander.

Believing that conciliation of the South would preserve the Union, he endorsed the Southern doctrine that the constitutional provisions on

PIERCE'S PRESIDENTIAL ADMINISTRATION

Congresses in Session
33d, 34th

Vice President:
William King, 1853

Secretary of State:
William Marcy, 1853–57

Secretary of the Treasury:
James Guthrie, 1853–57

Secretary of War:
Jefferson Davis, 1853–57

Attorney General:
Caleb Cushing, 1853–57

Postmaster General:
James Campbell, 1853–57

Secretary of the Navy:
James Dobbin, 1853–57

Secretary of the Interior:
Robert McCleland, 1853–57

PRESIDENTIAL ELECTION OF 1852

Nominations: At the Whig convention in Baltimore, June 17–20, 1852, Scott received a majority on the 53d ballot. The Democratic convention in Baltimore, June 1–5, 1852, deadlocked between James Buchanan and Lewis Cass. Pierce was entered as a dark horse on the 35th ballot and won on the 49th ballot. **Campaign Issues:** Personalities.

PRESIDENTIAL CANDIDATES	PARTY	ELECTORAL VOTES	POPULAR VOTE		VICE-PRESIDENTIAL CANDIDATES
			Total	Percentage	
Franklin Pierce	Democratic	254	1,601,117	50.9	William R. King
Winfield Scott	Whig	42	1,385,453	44.1	William A. Graham
John P. Hale	Free Soil	—	155,825	5.0	George Julian

property rights meant a guarantee of slavery.

He helped push through the Kansas-Nebraska Act in 1854 that repealed the Missouri Compromise of 1820, giving settlers in the Kansas Territory the opportunity to vote on the slavery issue. Guerrilla warfare broke out between opposing forces in "Bleeding Kansas," heightening national tensions in 1855–56.

In his expansionist drive Pierce made premature and unsuccessful attempts to buy Alaska from Russia and to annex Hawaii. Another failure was the Ostend Manifesto of 1854. Issued by the American ministers to England, France, and Spain, it proposed annexation of Cuba, presumably as a slave state. Although repudiated by the State Department and the Senate, it raised protests both at home and abroad.

Pierce was more successful with two other enterprises in foreign policy. The Gadsden Purchase for $10 million from Mexico of the southern parts of Arizona and New Mexico was rati-

fied by the Senate on June 29, 1854. That same year Commodore Matthew C. Perry signed a treaty that opened Japan's ports to shippers.

Pierce had expected to be renominated by the 1856 Democratic national convention. Instead, he was humiliatingly rejected because of his support of the Kansas-Nebraska Act.

At the end of his term Pierce toured Europe and then returned to Concord.

In 1860 Pierce supported Jefferson Davis, his former secretary of war, as the man the Democrats should nominate for President. His opposition to the Civil War and to Lincoln's administration increased his unpopularity. He died in obscurity on Oct. 8, 1869.

Jane Means Appleton Pierce (1806–63), Pierce's wife, was the daughter of a president of Bowdoin College. None of the couple's three sons survived to maturity. While she was First Lady, the White House was equipped for the first time with a coal-burning furnace for central heating.

JAMES BUCHANAN

15th President
(1857–61)

Buchanan was the last President chosen because it was believed he would compromise and keep the slavery issue from tearing apart the nation.

He was born on April 23, 1791, in Cove Gap, Pa., the son of James and Elizabeth (Speer) Buchanan. After attending Dickinson College, he was admitted to the bar in 1812. He then built up a lucrative law practice in Lancaster, Pa.

Buchanan served in his state's legislature in both houses of Congress (first as a Federalist, then as a Jacksonian Democrat), as Polk's secretary of state, and as minister to England and Russia. In England he was involved in the notorious Ostend Manifesto proposing annexa-

tion of Cuba, even as a slave state. This permanently discredited Buchanan among large groups in the North.

In 1844, 1848, and 1852 Buchanan sought the Democratic presidential nomination.

In 1856 he became the Democratic candidate and defeated John C. Frémont, first candidate of the new Republican Party, as well as Millard Fillmore, candidate of the Whig and American (Know-Nothing) parties. He was the fourth President to enter office with less than a majority of the popular vote.

To meet the growing North-South crisis, Buchanan could only propose preservation of the "sacred balance" between the regions. He avowed personal disapproval of slavery, yet recommended the admission of Kansas as a slave state.

He deplored secession but took no steps to check it by garrisoning federal forts in the South. Even when a U.S. ship was fired on by South Carolina shore batteries, he took no action.

Buchanan's moderate views were disliked and mistrusted by extremists both in the North and in

BUCHANAN'S PRESIDENTIAL ADMINISTRATION

Congresses in Session:
35th, 36th

Vice President:
John C. Breckinridge, 1857–61

Secretary of State:
Lewis Cass, 1857–60
Jeremiah S. Black, 1860–61

Secretary of the Treasury:
Howell Cobb, 1857–60
Philip F. Thomas, 1860–61
John A. Dix, 1861

Secretary of War:
John Floyd, 1857–61
Joseph Holt, 1861

Secretary of the Navy:
Isaac Toucey, 1857–61

Attorney General:
Jeremiah Black, 1857–60
Edwin M. Stanton, 1860–61

Postmaster General:
Aaron Brown, 1857–59
Joseph Holt, 1859–61
Horatio King, 1861

Secretary of the Interior:
Jacob Thompson, 1857–61

PRESIDENTIAL ELECTION OF 1856

Nominations: The Republican convention was held in Philadelphia, June 17–19, 1856. On the first official ballot Frémont got 520 out of 558 votes. Dayton's nomination came on the first ballot. At the Democratic convention in Cincinnati, June 2–6, 1856, Buchanan was chosen on the 17th ballot. The vice-presidential nomination of Breckinridge was unanimous. **Campaign Issue:** Slavery in the Kansas-Nebraska territories was the main issue.

PRESIDENTIAL CANDIDATES	PARTY	ELECTORAL VOTES	POPULAR VOTE Total	Percentage	VICE-PRESIDENTIAL CANDIDATES
James Buchanan	Democratic	174	1,832,955	45.3	John C. Breckinridge
John C. Frémont	Republican	114	1,339,932	33.1	William L. Dayton
Millard Fillmore	American	8	871,731	21.6	Andrew J. Donelson

QUICK QUIZ: Who was Harness Horse of the Year in 1970? See page 835.

JAMES BUCHANAN *(continued)*
the South. He did not seek renomination.

In the last months of his administration, seven Southern states seceded and formed the Confederate States of America.

When he was 27, Buchanan had been engaged to Ann Caroline Coleman of Lancaster, but she broke the engagement because she believed he only wanted her fortune. So Buchanan became the first bachelor President.

Buchanan's niece Harriet Lane served as White House hostess during his administration.

Seven years after leaving office, Buchanan died in Lancaster on June 1, 1868.

ABRAHAM LINCOLN

16th President
(1861–65)

When Lincoln became President, the nation was divided. In the four months between his election as President and the time he took office, seven Southern states had seceded from the Union and formed the Confederate States of America with Jefferson Davis as President.

On April 12, 1861, Fort Sumter in South Carolina was bombarded by the Confederates, and the Civil War began. Lincoln became the leader of the people of the North.

EARLY YEARS

Lincoln's father, Thomas, was a farmer and carpenter who moved his family first from Kentucky to Indiana to Illinois. Abraham was born in a log cabin in Hardin County, Ky., on Feb. 12, 1809. His mother, Nancy Hanks Lincoln, died when he was nine, and his father married Mrs. Sarah Bush Johnston, a widow.

Providing for himself at an early age, Lincoln did handyman jobs, split rails, clerked in a store, surveyed land, delivered merchandise downstream on flatboats to New Orleans, and put his hand to other tasks. In 1831 he settled in the little village of New Salem, Ill., near Springfield. There he became a partner in a grocery store that failed. His partner's death left him with a burden of debts—all of which he eventually paid.

Lincoln grew into a tall, gaunt, muscular man six feet four inches tall, with a ruggedly homely face. Possessed of great physical strength, he often put down bullies. This, along with his talent for pointed storytelling, brought him popularity in the frontier villages where he spent his young manhood.

When Lincoln answered a call for volunteers in the Black Hawk War, he was unanimously elected captain by the men of the New Salem troop. By 1834 he had gathered such a following that he was elected, as a Whig, to the Illinois legislature, where he achieved prominence during his four terms. He was admitted to the bar in 1836 and moved to nearby Springfield. He built up a prosperous law practice in a succession of partnerships, the last with William H. Herndon, who later became his biographer.

Lincoln reentered politics in 1846, again as a Whig, and was overwhelmingly elected to Congress. There his opposition to the Mexican War cost him the backing of expansionist-minded constituents. He served only one term.

In 1854, however, he was goaded out of retirement by indignation over the Kansas-Nebraska Act favoring the extension of slavery, which had been sponsored by Illinois Democratic Sen. Stephen A. Douglas. Lincoln ran for the Senate on the Whig ticket but was defeated. The next year he joined the newly formed Republican Party. He was among the candidates for its vice-presidential nomination, polling an impressive though not winning vote.

In 1858 Lincoln became his party's candidate for U.S. senator. One of the ringing phrases in his acceptance speech, "A house divided against itself cannot stand," helped spread his renown. His debates with Douglas, his Democratic opponent, drew nationwide attention. Lincoln asserted he was not an abolitionist, but that he regarded slavery as an injustice and an evil. He was adamantly opposed to its extension. Although Douglas won the close election, Lincoln, through his masterful exposition, had made his mark and had become widely known.

At the Republican convention in 1860, William H. Seward was the leading contender. But there was an early swing to Lincoln, who was nominated on the third ballot. With the Democrats split between Northern and Southern wings, Republican victory was inevitable. After Lincoln's election, the Southern states began seceding from the Union.

CIVIL WAR PRESIDENT

From the beginning of hostilities Lincoln faced staggering difficulties, but he attacked the vast problems with vigor and surpassing skill. Lincoln pressed onward with the war, but even when prosecuting Southern sympathizers in the North—for which he was criticized—he sought to temper punishment with mercy.

On April 14, 1861, two days after the Confederate attack on Fort Sumter, Lincoln called for 75,000 volunteers to fight the rebels. He also ordered a blockade of Southern ports to cut them off from supplies the South needed.

Hopes by Northerners for a quick victory were dashed by the Union defeat in the First Battle of Bull Run in Virginia on July 21, 1861.

Lincoln was beset not only by the difficulties of the war but by opposition from men on his own side. Radical abolitionists condemned him as weak. Conservatives accused him of dictatorship. Jealousies and hatreds caused continual friction in his cabinet. In the midst of all this strife Lincoln continued his course with wisdom and patience, sometimes standing nearly alone.

Lincoln had offered command of the Union Army to Gen. Robert E. Lee. But Lee turned the appointment down, deciding to help his native state of Virginia by accepting command of Confederate forces. Lee inflicted a series of defeats on Northern troops while Lincoln searched for a Union general who could fight.

The dubious Northern victory at Antietam in

1862 gave Lincoln the opportunity to make a great stroke by issuing the Emancipation Proclamation, which proclaimed freedom for slaves in Confederate-controlled states.

The proclamation caused renewed enthusiasm for the war. But the fighting progressed without a decisive success until the Confederacy's defeat in 1863 at Gettysburg, Pa., where Lincoln later delivered his famous Gettysburg Address.

In 1864, after Ulysses S. Grant became commander of the Union Army and William T. Sherman took Atlanta, Lincoln's perseverance seemed vindicated.

With victory clearly in sight, the Republican Party, which had been on the point of abandoning him, rallied to Lincoln. He was renominated and reelected in 1864, defeating former Union army commander George McClellan.

In his celebrated second inaugural address, Lincoln outlined his postwar program. He would show "malice toward none" and grant "charity for all." His policy would be based on peace without retribution.

A month after Lincoln's second inauguration Lee surrendered on April 9, 1865, to Grant at Appomattox Court House, Va.

But Lincoln's dream of restoring the Union in harmony was brought to an abrupt end on April 14, 1865, when actor John Wilkes Booth, a Southern fanatic, shot him at Ford's Theater in Washington. Lincoln died the next day.

Mary Todd Lincoln (1818–82) of Kentucky became Lincoln's wife in 1842 after a troubled courtship. Their marriage was not an easy one, but Mrs. Lincoln served capably as White House hostess. Because she had several relatives in the Confederate Army, her loyalty to the North was questioned.

The Lincolns had four sons: Robert Todd Lincoln (1843–1926), Edward Baker Lincoln (1846–50), William Wallace Lincoln (1850–62), and Thomas "Tad" Lincoln (1853–71).

Only one son, Robert Todd Lincoln, lived to manhood, becoming secretary of war under Presidents Garfield and Arthur.

One of their sons died at the age of four in Springfield, another in the White House at the age of 12.

The first two deaths of her sons, her husband's assassination while at her side, and the death of their youngest son at age 18 in 1871 are said to have affected Mrs. Lincoln's mind. She was temporarily committed to a private sanatorium in Batavia, Ill., in 1875.

LINCOLN'S PRESIDENTIAL ADMINISTRATION

Congresses in Session:
37th, 38th, 39th

Vice President:
Hannibal Hamlin, 1861–65
Andrew Johnson, 1865

Secretary of State:
William Seward, 1861–65

Secretary of the Treasury:
Salmon Chase, 1861–64
William Fessenden, 1864–65
Hugh McCulloch, 1865

Secretary of War:
Simon Cameron, 1861–62
Edwin McM. Stanton, 1862–65

Secretary of the Navy:
Gideon Welles, 1861–65

Attorney General:
Edward Bates, 1861–64
James Speed, 1864–65

Postmaster General:
Montgomery Blair, 1861–64
William Dennison, 1864–65

Secretary of the Interior:
Caleb Smith, 1861–63
John Usher, 1863–65

PRESIDENTIAL ELECTION OF 1860

Nominations: The Democrats met in Charleston, S.C., April 23–May 3, 1860. They failed to choose a candidate, and many Southerners bolted the party. The convention reassembled in Baltimore on June 18 and met through June 23. Finally, after more Southerners had left, Douglas was nominated. The vice-presidential nominee, Benjamin Fitzpatrick of Alabama, declined the honor, and the party national committee chose Johnson. Many of the "bolters," who called themselves National Democrats, met in Baltimore, June 23, 1860, and chose Breckinridge and Lane. The Republicans met in Chicago, May 16–18, 1860. Sen. William H. Seward of New York was favored to win the nomination. On the third ballot Lincoln received a majority, and the nomination was then made unanimous. Hamlin was chosen on the second ballot. The Constitutional Union Party met in Baltimore, May 9–10, 1860, choosing former Secretary of War John Bell as their candidate. **Campaign Issues:** The campaign centered on slavery and the status of the Union.

PRESIDENTIAL CANDIDATES	PARTY	ELECTORAL VOTES	POPULAR VOTE Total	Percentage	VICE-PRESIDENTIAL CANDIDATES
Abraham Lincoln	Republican	180	1,865,593	39.8	Hannibal Hamlin
John C. Breckinridge	Southern Democratic	72	848,356	18.1	Joseph Lane
Stephen A. Douglas	Democratic	12	1,382,713	29.5	Herschel V. Johnson
John Bell	Constitutional Union	30	592,906	12.6	Edward Everett

PRESIDENTIAL ELECTION OF 1864

Nominations: The Republicans, who had been joined by the prowar Democrats (Johnson was one), met as the National Union Party in Baltimore, June 7–8, 1864. Lincoln on a roll-call vote on the first ballot received all but 22 votes (which went to U.S. Grant), and his nomination was then made unanimous. By the end of the first ballot, after switching had taken place, Johnson had received 494 out of 500 votes and the vice-presidential nomination. The Democratic convention met in Chicago, Aug. 29–31, 1864, and McClellan, the former Union Army commanding general who had been dismissed by Lincoln, was chosen on the third ballot. Pendleton was selected as the vice-presidential candidate on the first ballot. **Campaign Issue:** Democrats criticized Lincoln's conduct of the Civil War.

PRESIDENTIAL CANDIDATES	PARTY	ELECTORAL VOTES	POPULAR VOTE Total	Percentage	VICE-PRESIDENTIAL CANDIDATES
Abraham Lincoln	Republican	212	2,206,938	55.0	Andrew Johnson
George McClellan	Democratic	21	1,803,787	45.0	George Pendleton
Votes not cast	—	81	—	—	—

QUICK QUIZ: Who won bowling's U.S. Men's Open Championship in 1980? See page 795.

ANDREW JOHNSON

17th President
(1865–69)

Succeeding to the presidency on the death of Lincoln, Andrew Johnson was a Southerner and a Democrat. The political split that developed between Johnson and the powerful Radical Republicans led to the first effort to remove a President of the United States by impeachment. Born on Dec. 29, 1808, in Raleigh, N.C., Johnson was the son of Jacob and Mary McDonough Johnson. His father died when Andrew was three. At the age of 13 Johnson was apprenticed to a tailor. In 1826 he moved to Greeneville, Tenn.

EARLY CAREER

Unable to write or do arithmetic when he married at the age of 18, Johnson learned how with the help of his wife. He prospered as a tailor, and his shop became well known. Many other craftsmen, as well as laborers and farmers, met there to discuss community and general public affairs. The best debater in Greeneville, Johnson was frequently in the public eye.

At 19 Johnson won office as town alderman, and at 21 became mayor of Greeneville. He next served six years in the state legislature. He was elected to the U.S. House of Representatives (1843–53), governor of Tennessee (1853–57), and to the U.S. Senate (1857–62).

Although a slaveowner, Johnson vigorously opposed secession. Alone among Southern senators, he did not resign when secession began. In 1862 Lincoln appointed him military governor of Tennessee, and by 1864 Johnson had organized a loyal government there. For this achievement he was named Lincoln's running mate on the Republican ticket in 1864.

At the inauguration, March 4, 1865, when he was sworn in as Vice President, Johnson seemed to be drunk. President Lincoln cut off criticism with the remark, "He ain't no drunkard."

When he assumed the presidency on April 15, 1865, Johnson reverted to his earlier Democratic positions on tariffs, banking, internal improvements, and other issues, in opposition to the Republican Party. But the chief issue in his conflict with the Radical Republicans was their harsh Reconstruction policy.

Johnson intended to follow Lincoln's program of reconciliation with the South. He extended full amnesty to participants in the secession. But he opposed extension of full civil rights to Negroes on constitutional grounds and, in general, manifested Southern sympathies. Political attacks on Johnson became increasingly harsh.

When Congress passed a series of acts over his veto, including the Civil Rights Act of 1866, he appealed to the electorate in the congressional elections. Baited by mobs and slandered by the press, he lashed out at his political enemies in such harsh terms that he did great harm to his own cause. The Radicals won, and the conflict between Congress and the President intensified.

Although the problems of the postwar South dominated Johnson's administration, there were successes in foreign affairs, notably the 1867 purchase of Alaska from Russia negotiated by Secretary of State William Seward for the price of $7,200,000.

PRESIDENTIAL IMPEACHMENT

In 1867 Congress passed, over Johnson's veto, the Tenure of Office Act, which forbade the removal of any official appointed with the confirmation of the Senate. Johnson believed the act was unconstitutional (and 59 years later the U.S. Supreme Court upheld his judgment). He defied Congress by firing Secretary of War Edwin M. Stanton, replacing him with Gen. Ulysses S. Grant, who gave the office back to Stanton in February 1868. Johnson fired Stanton again, appointing Lorenzo Thomas to the post.

The Radical Republicans, led by Thaddeus Stevens, brought impeachment charges against Johnson for violation of the Tenure of Office Act. This first try failed, but on Feb. 24, 1868, the House passed a resolution of impeachment by a vote of 126 to 47.

On March 5, 1868, the Senate was organized as a court to hear the charges. The Senate on May 16 voted 35 to 19 against President Johnson, one vote shy of the required two-thirds majority needed to convict him. The vote that saved him was cast by Edmund G. Ross, a freshman Radical Republican senator from Kansas.

Despite a series of disappointments that might have deterred another man, Johnson continued his political activity. He sought and failed to win the nomination for President on the Democratic ticket in 1868, for U.S. senator in 1869, and for representative in 1872. But in 1874 he became the first former President to be elected to the U.S. Senate. A few months after reentering the Senate to represent Tennessee, he died on July 31, 1875.

Eliza McCardle Johnson (1810–76) married Andrew Johnson in 1827 when she was 16. She helped him learn to write and do arithmetic. They had three sons and two daughters. She was an invalid during her husband's term. Their daughter Martha served as the President's chief White House hostess.

ANDREW JOHNSON'S PRESIDENTIAL ADMINISTRATION

Congresses in Session:
39th, 40th

Vice President:
Vacant

Secretary of State:
William Seward, 1865–69

Secretary of the Treasury:
Hugh McCulloch, 1865–69

Attorney General:
James Speed, 1865–66
Henry Stanbery, 1866–68
William Evarts, 1868–69

Postmaster General:
William Dennison, 1865–66
Alexander Randall, 1866–69

Secretary of the Navy:
Gideon Welles, 1865–69

Secretary of War:
Edwin M. Stanton, 1865–67, 1868
Ulysses S. Grant, 1867–68
Lorenzo Thomas, 1868
John Schofield, 1868–69

Secretary of the Interior:
John P. Usher, 1865
James Harlan, 1865–66
Orville Browning, 1866–69

ULYSSES SIMPSON GRANT

18th President
(1869–77)

Grant's administrations were characterized by bitter politics and notorious corruption. A punitive Reconstruction policy gave supremacy to Northern bankers, speculators, and industrialists. It also encouraged the "carpetbaggers" who moved south to exploit both recently freed slaves and the defeated whites, helping to prolong the sectional division of the country between North and South.

Grant allowed himself to become the dupe of the "robber barons" of his time and of the shady politicians associated with them. During his two terms scandals were exposed involving cabinet members, his own secretary, and a number of congressmen. His administrations were characterized by bitter politics and corruption.

EARLY CAREER

He was born on April 27, 1822, in Point Pleasant, Ohio, the son of Jesse Root and Hannah (Simpson) Grant. He switched his given names, Hiram Ulysses, when still a boy. Then "Hiram" became "Simpson" through a clerical error when he applied for admission to West Point. Grant accepted the name change. He graduated in 1843, served with distinction in the Mexican War, and was promoted twice.

In 1854 Grant was forced to resign from the Army because of excessive drinking. He unsuccessfully tried farming, real estate, and storekeeping.

The Civil War proved his opportunity. Responding to President Lincoln's call for volunteers, he was eventually given command of a detachment of Illinois trainees. He showed outstanding ability in minor military actions and was promoted to brigadier general.

After training and mobilizing a force of 17,000 men, he conducted a bold operation against two

GRANT'S PRESIDENTIAL ADMINISTRATION

Congresses in Session:
41st, 42d, 43d, 44th
Vice President:
Schuyler Colfax, 1869–73
Henry Wilson, 1873–75
Secretary of State:
Elihu B. Washburne, 1869
Hamilton Fish, 1869–77
Postmaster General:
John Creswell, 1869–74
James W. Marshall, 1867
Marshall Jewell, 1874–76
James Tyner, 1876–77

Secretary of the Treasury:
Alexander T. Stewart, 1869
George Boutwell, 1869–73
William Richardson, 1873–74
Benjamin Bristow, 1874–76
Lot Morrill, 1876–77

Attorney General:
Ebenezer Hoar, 1869–70
Amos Akerman, 1870–71
George Williams, 1871–75
Edwards Pierrepont, 1875–76
Alphonso Taft, 1876–77

Secretary of War:
John Rawlins, 1869
William T. Sherman, 1869
William Belknap, 1869–76
Alphonso Taft, 1876
James Cameron, 1876–77
Secretary of the Navy:
Adolph Borie, 1869
George Robeson, 1869–77
Secretary of the Interior:
Jacob Cox, 1869–70
Columbus Delano, 1870–75
Zachariah Chandler, 1875–77

PRESIDENTIAL ELECTION OF 1868

Nominations: The Republican convention met in Chicago, May 20–21, 1868, and chose Grant. The Democratic Party met in New York City, July 4–9, 1868, nominated Seymour on the 22d ballot, and declared the nomination unanimous.

Campaign Issues: A paramount issue was Reconstruction of the Confederate states, with the Republicans in favor of harsh measures. **Remarks:** Mississippi, Texas, and Virginia did not participate in the presidential election.

PRESIDENTIAL CANDIDATES	PARTY	ELECTORAL VOTES	POPULAR VOTE Total	Percentage	VICE-PRESIDENTIAL CANDIDATES
Ulysses S. Grant	Republican	214	3,013,421	52.7	Schuyler Colfax
Horatio Seymour	Democratic	80	2,703,829	47.3	Francis P. Blair Jr.
Votes not cast	—	23	—	—	—

PRESIDENTIAL ELECTION OF 1872

Nominations: Liberal Republicans, who had defected from the Republican Party because they were dissatisfied with Grant, met in Cincinnati, May 1, 1872, and nominated Greeley and Brown on the sixth ballot. Democrats, meeting in Baltimore, July 9–10, 1872, accepted Greeley and Brown on the first ballot. The Republican convention in Philadelphia, June 5–6, 1872, chose Grant and Wilson. **Campaign Issues:** Besides Reconstruction and the "bloody shirt" (as vengeance against the South was called), other important is-

sues were corruption in government and the desirability of issuing paper money, which many debtors thought would aid them. Republicans ridiculed Greeley as a lifelong opponent of Democrats who now ran on their ticket. **Remarks:** Greeley died after the election but before the Electoral College met. His electoral votes went to: Thomas A. Hendricks (42); Benjamin G. Brown (18); Charles J. Jenkins (2); David Davis (1); and 3 Greeley votes were not counted. Congress rejected Greeley votes from Arkansas, Louisiana, and Georgia.

PRESIDENTIAL CANDIDATES	PARTY	ELECTORAL VOTES	POPULAR VOTE Total	Percentage	VICE-PRESIDENTIAL CANDIDATES	ELECTORAL VOTES
Ulysses S. Grant	Republican	286	3,596,745	55.6	Henry Wilson	286
Horace Greeley	Democratic– Liberal Rep.	—	2,843,446	44.0	Benjamin G. Brown	47
Charles O'Connor	Straight Dem.	—	29,489	0.4	John Quincy Adams ...	—
Other candidates	—	63	—	—	Other candidates......	—
Votes not cast	—	17	—	—	Votes not cast	—

QUICK QUIZ: What country won the tennis Davis Cup in 1984? See page 866.

ULYSSES S. GRANT (continued)

Confederate strongholds, Fort Henry and Fort Donelson, on the Tennessee and Cumberland rivers. It was the first major Union victory. From that time on, his military career was an almost continuous succession of triumphs, the most brilliant being the capture of Vicksburg in 1863, which cleared the Mississippi down to the sea and split the Confederacy in two.

Satisfied that he had at last found his general, Lincoln in 1864 put Grant in supreme command of the Union armies.

Grant pushed the Confederate Army south into Virginia while Gen. William T. Sherman advanced from the west to Atlanta, Ga. On April 9, 1865, Grant accepted the surrender of Gen. Robert E. Lee at Appomattox Court House, Va. His surrender terms to Lee and his treatment of the defeated Confederates were compassionate and magnanimous.

18th PRESIDENT OF THE UNITED STATES

A national hero, Grant was the Republican choice in the presidential election of 1868. He was nominated on the first ballot and easily won the presidency. At 46 he was the youngest man to become President to that time. His first term was tinged with scandal when his brother-in-law conspired with New York financier Jay Gould to corner the gold market.

In 1869 Grant approved a treaty with the Dominican Republic to annex that country. But the Senate rejected the treaty.

Grant's renomination for a second term was unanimous, and he was reelected by another landslide. His second term was wracked with scandals, leading to the resignations of two of his cabinet officers and the conviction of many government officials.

In 1880 his backers, the Stalwarts, led by Sen. Roscoe Conkling, failed to obtain Grant's nomination for a third term.

Moving to New York City, among his new financier associates, Grant invested his funds in a fraudulent banking firm. When it went bankrupt in 1884, Congress granted him some relief by reappointing him general at full pay and later by adding retirement pay.

Determined to provide for his family, Grant set to work on his memoirs. Although suffering from cancer of the throat, he kept on indomitably, finishing the two-volume book four days before his death. He died on July 23, 1885, and is interred in New York City.

Julia Dent Grant (1826–1902) was the daughter of a judge in St. Louis, Mo., and a sister of one of Grant's West Point classmates. She and Grant were married in 1848. They had three sons and a daughter, all surviving to maturity. As First Lady she was admired for her graces.

RUTHERFORD BIRCHARD HAYES

The election of 1876 pitted Hayes, the Republican nominee, against Samuel J. Tilden, the Democratic candidate. It was a significant election, marking the political reentry of the South into the Union and the resurgence of the Democrats. The Republicans lost decisively in the congressional elections, and Hayes received nearly 250,000 fewer popular votes than Tilden.

A special electoral commission with a Repub-

19th President
(1877–81)

lican majority gave the office to Hayes by a margin of only one electoral vote.

Hayes was born on Oct. 4, 1822, in Delaware, Ohio. He was the son of Rutherford Hayes, a storekeeper, and Sophia Birchard Hayes. Young Hayes attended Kenyon College and Harvard.

He practiced law in Lower Sandusky and then in 1849 moved to Cincinnati. From 1858 to 1861 he served as Cincinnati solicitor.

At the outbreak of the Civil War, Hayes enlisted and was commissioned a major. He was wounded four times, rising in rank to major general.

Elected to Congress in 1865 as a Republican, Hayes supported the Radicals' Reconstruction program. In 1867 he was elected governor of Ohio and served three terms.

HAYES' PRESIDENTIAL ADMINISTRATION

Congresses in Session:
45th, 46th
Vice President:
William Wheeler, 1877–81
Secretary of War:
George McCrary, 1877–79
Alexander Ramsey, 1879–81

Secretary of State:
William Evarts, 1877–81
Secretary of the Treasury:
John Sherman, 1877–81
Postmaster General:
David Key, 1877–80
Horace Maynard, 1880–81

Attorney General:
Charles Devens, 1877–81
Secretary of the Navy:
Richard Thompson, 1877–80
Nathan Goff Jr., 1881
Secretary of the Interior:
Carl Schurz, 1877–81

PRESIDENTIAL ELECTION OF 1876

Nominations: The Republican convention in Cincinnati, June 14–16, 1876, nominated Hayes on the seventh ballot. Wheeler was nominated by acclamation. The Democrats, meeting in St. Louis, June 27–29, 1876, nominated Tilden on the second ballot. **Campaign Issues:** Reconstruction and corruption in government. **Remarks:** An electoral commission composed of eight Republicans and seven Democrats awarded disputed votes to Hayes.

PRESIDENTIAL CANDIDATES	PARTY	ELECTORAL VOTES	POPULAR VOTE Total	Percentage	VICE-PRESIDENTIAL CANDIDATES
Rutherford B. Hayes	Republican	185	4,036,572	48.0	William A. Wheeler
Samuel J. Tilden	Democratic	184	4,284,020	51.0	Thomas A. Hendricks
Peter Cooper	Greenback	—	81,737	1.0	Samuel F. Carey

Facing a hostile Democratic majority in Congress, Hayes could not obtain passage of his legislative program.

His most outstanding act, withdrawal of the last federal troops from the South, antagonized extremists in his party. His efforts to reform the civil service also angered Republican bosses.

The economic depression during Hayes' administration brought the first nationwide strike by rail workers in 1877. When strike riots broke out in several states, Hayes sent in federal troops.

In an effort to halt Indian wars in the West, Hayes banned sale of firearms to Indians.

Hayes declined renomination and devoted his last years to education and philanthropy. He died in Fremont, Ohio, on Jan. 17, 1893.

Lucy Ware Webb Hayes (1831–89), who married Hayes in 1852, was the first college graduate to become First Lady.

Mrs. Hayes, a cheerful woman, was nicknamed "Lemonade Lucy" because she served only soft drinks in the White House. Both she and Hayes were total abstainers. Hayes' last executive order as President was to ban the sale of whisky on army posts. The Hayes' family life—they had eight children—was a happy one.

Hayes installed the first telephone in the White House, in 1877.

JAMES ABRAM GARFIELD

The second U.S. President killed by an assassin, Garfield served too short a time for anyone to know what sort of Chief Executive he might have been.

Born on Nov. 19, 1831, in Orange Township, Ohio, Garfield was the son of Abram and Eliza Ballou Garfield. He was left fatherless at two and

20th President
(1881)

spent his early years in poverty. He worked as a farmer and carpenter to support his mother. At 18 he entered Western Reserve Eclectic Institute (now Hiram College). He went on to Williams College, graduating in 1856. Garfield then returned to Hiram, where he became its president. He was also a lay preacher of the Disciples of Christ. He became a state senator in 1859 and was admitted to the bar in 1860.

During the Civil War he began service as an officer of an Ohio volunteer regiment. He was promoted to the rank of major general because of his bravery at the Battle of Chickamauga.

On his election to Congress in 1863 he resigned from the Army to take his seat in the House, where he served until 1880. He was a staunch advocate of Radical Reconstruction.

Garfield was one of the members of the electoral commission that awarded the presidential election of 1876 to Hayes. He then served as Republican minority leader of the House during Hayes' administration.

As leader of the Ohio delegation to the Republican national convention in 1880, Garfield was present at his own presidential nomination as a dark-horse candidate. Top runners at the convention that year were ex-President Grant and James G. Blaine. Up to the 34th ballot Garfield never drew more than two votes, but on the 36th ballot he won the nomination. Grant and his political sponsor, Sen. Roscoe Conkling of New York, were disgruntled. An effort was made to appease them by giving second place on the ticket to Chester Arthur, one of the Stalwarts—as Grant's supporters called themselves.

One of President Garfield's immediate problems on beginning his administration was the open break forced by Senator Conkling over the distribution of political spoils. Garfield was a brilliant orator and a man of integrity and charm. His conflict with Conkling and the political machine remained unresolved, however.

Before Garfield could make his mark as President, he was killed. Charles Guiteau, a disappointed office seeker who proclaimed himself a Stalwart, shot him on July 2, 1881. Garfield lingered until his death on Sept. 19, 1881.

Lucretia Rudolph Garfield (1832–1918), his wife, had been a schoolmate. They were married in 1858. The Garfields had seven children, two of whom died in childhood.

GARFIELD'S PRESIDENTIAL ADMINISTRATION

Congress in Session:
47th
Vice President:
Chester A. Arthur, 1881
Secretary of State:
James Blaine, 1881

Secretary of the Treasury:
William Windom, 1881
Secretary of War:
Robert Todd Lincoln, 1881
Attorney General:
Wayne MacVeagh, 1881

Postmaster General:
Thomas James, 1881
Secretary of the Navy:
William Hunt, 1881
Secretary of the Interior:
Samuel Kirkwood, 1881

PRESIDENTIAL ELECTION OF 1880

Nominations: The Republicans met in Chicago, June 2–8, 1880, and on the 36th ballot Garfield received the nomination. Arthur was chosen as the vice-presidential candidate on the first ballot. The Democrats met in Cincinnati, June 22–24, 1880, and nominated Hancock and English. **Campaign Issues:** The parties based their campaigns on the personalities of their candidates. Republicans favored high tariffs and Democrats opposed them.

PRESIDENTIAL CANDIDATES	PARTY	ELECTORAL VOTES	POPULAR VOTE Total	Percentage	VICE-PRESIDENTIAL CANDIDATES
James A. Garfield	Republican	214	4,453,295	48.5	Chester A. Arthur
Winfield S. Hancock	Democratic	155	4,414,082	48.1	William English
James B. Weaver	Greenback	—	308,578	3.4	B. J. Chambers
Neal Dow	Prohibition	—	10,305	—	H. A. Thompson

QUICK QUIZ: What yacht won the America's Cup in 1964? See page 872.

CHESTER ALAN ARTHUR

21st President
(1881–85)

Chester Arthur became President on Sept. 20, 1881, after the death of President Garfield from wounds by an assassin. A New York Republican machine politician, Arthur had been given the vice-presidential nomination in 1880 to appease supporters of ex-President Grant, who had hoped for a third-term nomination. Members of Arthur's Republican clique were called Stalwarts. Those who supported Garfield were called Half-Breeds.

Arthur was born on Oct. 5, 1829, in Fairfield, Vt., the son of William Arthur, a clergyman, and Malvina Stone Arthur. He graduated from Union College in 1848 and began teaching while studying law. Arthur was admitted to the New York bar in 1854 and developed a successful law practice. An abolitionist, Arthur took many cases defending fugitive slaves and other blacks.

He helped organize the New York militia during the Civil War and then served as quartermaster general.

In 1871 President Grant rewarded him with the post of collector of the New York Custom House, a much-sought political prize. He administered the office with personal honesty but, in the style of the time, openly dispensed political patronage to members of the powerful New York Republican machine. In 1879 President Hayes, a fellow Republican determined to reform civil service, removed Arthur from office.

As President, Arthur was stigmatized as a machine politician of dubious integrity and nicknamed "the Gentleman Boss" for his courtly manners and his taste for fine foods and expensive clothes. He had the White House redecorated in *art nouveau* style by New York designer Louis Tiffany, and he installed an elevator.

To the dismay of his political associates, Arthur's presidential administration proved honest and efficient. Arthur supported the Civil Service Reform Act of 1883, which limited the spoils system. He fought the passage of the Chinese Exclusion Act. He prosecuted corruption in the postal service, and he aided the passage of a new protective tariff.

A little more than a year after Arthur succeeded to office, his kidney trouble was diagnosed as Bright's disease. Only one or two of his closest friends were permitted to know the seriousness of his ailment. He thus lived throughout his term in the White House with the secret knowledge that he was a dying man. It is believed for this reason alone he refused to seek the 1884 nomination, to the bewilderment of his supporters.

Arthur returned to New York City and resumed his law practice. He died there on Nov. 18, 1886, a year after leaving office.

Ellen Lewis Herndon Arthur (1837–80) married Arthur in 1859 but died before he became President. Arthur's vivacious sister, Mary (Mrs. John McElroy), served as official White House hostess during his term.

ARTHUR'S PRESIDENTIAL ADMINISTRATION

Congresses in Session:
47th, 48th

Vice President:
Vacant

Secretary of State:
James G. Blaine, 1881
Frederick Frelinghuysen, 1881–85

Secretary of War:
Robert Todd Lincoln, 1881–85

Secretary of the Treasury:
William Windom, 1881
Charles Folger, 1881–84
Walter Q. Gresham, 1884
Hugh McCulloch, 1884–85

Postmaster General:
Thomas L. James, 1881
Timothy Howe, 1881–83
Walter Q. Gresham, 1883–84
Frank Hatton, 1884–85

Attorney General:
Wayne MacVeagh, 1881
Benjamin Brewster, 1881–85

Secretary of the Navy:
William Hunt, 1881–82
William Chandler, 1882–85

Secretary of the Interior:
Samuel Kirkwood, 1881–82
Henry Teller, 1882–85

GROVER CLEVELAND

22d and 24th President
(1885–89, 1893–97)

The first Democrat elected President after the Civil War, Grover Cleveland won office as a champion of honesty and reform. Cleveland became the only President to serve two nonconsecutive terms, losing a bid for reelection in 1888 and then regaining the office in the election of 1892.

The son of Richard Falley and Ann Neal Cleveland, Stephen Grover Cleveland was born on March 18, 1837, in Caldwell, N.J. The family moved to upstate New York when Cleveland was a child. His father, a Presbyterian minister, died when the boy was 16. He worked in a store in Clinton, N.Y., and later taught school. After deciding to move west as a pioneer, he stopped in Buffalo to visit an uncle and settled there. He clerked in a law office, becoming a lawyer in 1859.

Cleveland began his political career as a Democrat. After filling minor posts, he was elected sheriff of Erie County, N.Y. (1871–73). While sheriff he sprang the trap to hang two convicted murderers, giving him the later distinction of being the only President to have hanged a man. Cleveland was elected mayor of Buffalo in 1882. Known as the "veto mayor," he drove corruption from his administration and acquired renown for honesty and efficiency.

He then was elected governor of New York (1883–84). As governor he fought the corruption of New York's Democratic Tammany machine. He cooperated with Republican reformer Theodore Roosevelt, who was then in the state legislature.

During the mud-slinging presidential cam-

paign of 1884, opponents disclosed Cleveland had fathered an illegitimate child. Voters gave him extra points for refusing to deny the story, which was true. A further attack on the Democrats as the party of "rum, Romanism, and rebellion" boomeranged, costing Republican candidate James G. Blaine the Roman Catholic vote. Cleveland also received support from reform-minded Republicans, known as Mugwumps.

In his first term as President, Cleveland faced an unyielding Republican majority in the Senate. This opposition kept him from carrying through any planned policy.

Among the few significant acts of Cleveland's first term were his appointment of an Interstate Commerce Commission and passage of the Interstate Commerce Act of 1887.

Although he was forced to temper with expediency his own instinct for civil-service reform, he was adamant against graft, extravagance, and excessive tariffs.

In the presidential election of 1888 Cleveland won a plurality of the popular vote over Republican Benjamin Harrison, but he lost the electoral vote by a substantial margin.

During the period between his two administrations, Cleveland practiced law in New York City.

He helped the Democrats win control of Congress in the 1890 elections by his attacks on extravagant spending by the Republicans.

In 1892 Cleveland regained the White House for a second term, becoming the only defeated President ever to be reelected.

Inheriting the financial panic of 1893, he forced repeal of the Sherman Silver Purchase Act and sponsored issuance of government bonds to protect the gold reserve. By these measures he alienated the Populists and the silver advocates among the Democrats.

Determined to prevent interruption of postal service because of the 1894 strike of Pullman workers in Chicago, he sent federal troops to restore order. His action was against the wishes of the Democratic governor of Illinois and alienated organized labor.

Cleveland also felt that tendencies toward

CLEVELAND'S ADMINISTRATION AS 22d PRESIDENT

Congresses in Session:
49th, 50th
Vice President:
Thomas Hendricks, 1885
Secretary of State:
Thomas Bayard, 1885–89
Secretary of War:
William Endicott, 1885–89

Secretary of the Treasury:
Daniel Manning, 1885–87
Charles Fairchild, 1887–89
Attorney General:
Augustus Garland, 1885–89
Secretary of the Navy:
William Whitney, 1885–89

Postmaster General:
William Vilas, 1885–88
Don Dickinson, 1888–89
Secretary of the Interior:
Lucius Lamar, 1885–88
William Vilas, 1888–89
Secretary of Agriculture:
Norman Colman, 1889

PRESIDENTIAL ELECTION OF 1884

Nominations: The Republicans met in Chicago, June 3–6, 1884, and Blaine was nominated on the fourth ballot, receiving 541 of 813 votes. The Democrats met in Chicago, July 8–11, 1884, and on the second ballot Cleveland received 683 of 820 votes before the nomination was made unanimous. **Campaign Issues:** Charges that Cleveland had fathered an illegitimate child and that Blaine's vote in Congress had been bought several times.

PRESIDENTIAL CANDIDATES	PARTY	ELECTORAL VOTES	POPULAR VOTE Total	Percentage	VICE-PRESIDENTIAL CANDIDATES
Grover Cleveland	Democratic	219	4,879,507	48.5	Thomas A. Hendricks
James G. Blaine	Republican	182	4,850,293	48.2	John A. Logan
Benjamin F. Butler	Greenback	—	175,370	1.7	A.M. West
John P. St. John	Prohibition	—	150,369	1.5	William Daniel

CLEVELAND'S ADMINISTRATION AS 24th PRESIDENT

Congresses in Session:
53d, 54th
Vice President:
Adlai E. Stevenson, 1893–97
Secretary of the Treasury:
John Carlisle, 1893–97
Secretary of War:
Daniel Lamont, 1893–97

Secretary of State:
Walter Gresham, 1893–95
Richard Olney, 1895–97
Attorney General:
Richard Olney, 1893–95
Judson Harmon, 1895–97
Secretary of the Navy:
Hilary Herbert, 1893–97

Postmaster General:
Wilson Bissell, 1893–95
William Wilson, 1895–97
Secretary of the Interior:
Hoke Smith, 1893–96
David Francis, 1896–97
Secretary of Agriculture:
Julius Morton, 1893–97

PRESIDENTIAL ELECTION OF 1892

Nominations: The Republicans met in Minneapolis, June 7–10, 1892. Harrison received 535⅙ votes on the first roll call with 369⅙ against him. The Democrats met in Chicago, June 21–23, 1892. Cleveland received 617⅓ votes, barely more than the two-thirds necessary for the nomination. The Populists met in Omaha, July 2–5, 1892, where Weaver won the nomination on the first ballot. **Campaign Issues:** Discontent among farmers and tariff reform, the Democrats favoring a lower tariff. Populists drew off many votes from the Republicans.

PRESIDENTIAL CANDIDATES	PARTY	ELECTORAL VOTES	POPULAR VOTE Total	Percentage	VICE-PRESIDENTIAL CANDIDATES
Grover Cleveland	Democratic	277	5,555,426	46.0	Adlai E. Stevenson
Benjamin Harrison	Republican	145	5,182,690	43.0	Whitelaw Reid
James B. Weaver	Populist	22	1,029,846	8.5	James G. Field
Other candidates	—	—	285,297	2.5	

QUICK QUIZ: Who won the NCAA outstanding wrestler award in 1969? See page 871.

GROVER CLEVELAND *(continued)*

U.S. imperialism were beginning to grow. He refused to permit aid to a rebel movement in Cuba and prevented the annexation of Hawaii. Almost the only popular act of Cleveland's second term was his invocation of the Monroe Doctrine in 1895, which led Britain to arbitrate a boundary dispute with Venezuela.

Cleveland's personal fortitude was manifested by the manner with which he underwent major surgery in 1893. Stricken by a cancerous growth on his jaw, he accepted the advice of friends and was operated on in secret to prevent public alarm. The operation, necessitating removal of his upper left jaw, was performed aboard a yacht.

Blaming Cleveland for the continuing depression, voters elected a Republican majority to Congress in the 1894 elections. Cleveland was further humiliated in 1896 when the Democratic convention refused him a third term.

After leaving the White House, Cleveland retired to Princeton, N.J.. He participated little in public life. In 1901 he became a trustee of Princeton University. He later became a spokesman for insurance companies against government regulation.

Cleveland died on June 24, 1908, at his home in Princeton.

Frances Folsom Cleveland (1864–1947) became the bachelor President's wife in 1886. She was the 21-year-old daughter of his late law partner, as well as Cleveland's ward. Cleveland became the only President to be married in a White House wedding. Immensely popular, Mrs. Cleveland officiated at White House functions with poise and skill. The Clevelands' second child, Esther, born in 1893, was the first child of a President to be born in the White House.

BENJAMIN HARRISON

23d President
(1889–93)

A grandson of President W. H. Harrison, Benjamin Harrison campaigned in 1888 to the tune of "Grandfather's Hat Fits Ben." The Republicans stirred anti-British sentiment against President Cleveland by tricking the British ambassador into endorsing him. Although Harrison defeated Cleveland with a majority of the electoral votes, he received 90,728 fewer popular votes.

A comparatively colorless President, Harrison followed regular Republican policies. He supported the McKinley protective tariff and the lavishly liberal Disability Pension Act. An outstanding event of his administration was the formation of what was later to become the Pan American Union.

The Sherman Antitrust Act was passed to counteract popular feeling that the Republicans were the party of "big business." This proved insufficient to win popular support, and the congressional elections of 1890 gave the Democrats control of the House.

Harrison was born on Aug. 20, 1833, at North Bend, Ohio. He was the son of Rep. John Scott Harrison and Edith Erwin Harrison.

He graduated from Miami (Ohio) University, passed the bar in 1853, and began law practice in Cincinnati. In 1854 he moved to Indianapolis, where he became a reporter for the Indiana supreme court.

When the Civil War began Harrison helped recruit a regiment of volunteers, of which he became a colonel in 1862. Achieving an outstanding war record, he attained the rank of brigadier general.

After the war, he built a prosperous practice as a corporation lawyer. From 1881 to 1887 Harrison served as U.S. senator from Indiana.

During his administration, President Harrison installed the first electric lights in the White House, replacing gas lighting.

HARRISON'S PRESIDENTIAL ADMINISTRATION

Congresses in Session:
51st, 52d

Vice President:
Levi Morton, 1889–93

Secretary of State:
James Blaine, 1889–92
John Foster, 1892–93

Secretary of the Treasury:
William Windom, 1889–91
Charles Foster, 1891–93

Secretary of War:
Redfield Proctor, 1889–91
Stephen Elkins, 1891–93

Attorney General:
William Miller, 1889–93

Postmaster General:
John Wanamaker, 1889–93

Secretary of the Navy:
Benjamin Tracy, 1889–93

Secretary of the Interior:
John Noble, 1889–93

Secretary of Agriculture:
Jeremiah Rusk, 1889–93

PRESIDENTIAL ELECTION OF 1888

Nominations: The Democrats met in St. Louis, June 5–7, 1888, and nominated Cleveland by acclamation. Thurman was a unanimous vice-presidential choice on the first roll-call vote. The Republicans met in Chicago, June 19–25, 1888. On the eighth ballot Harrison received 544 of 830 votes. Morton won the vice-presidential nomination with 592 votes on the first ballot. **Campaign:** Cleveland had approved restoring the Confederate battle flags to the South, and the Republicans made much of this. Also, a Republican politician managed to get the British ambassador to write in a letter that Cleveland would best serve the interests of Britain, arousing anti-British sentiment. **Remarks:** Opposed by New York's Tammany machine, Cleveland lost that state's 36 electoral votes, throwing the election to Harrison.

PRESIDENTIAL CANDIDATES	PARTY	ELECTORAL VOTES	POPULAR VOTE Total	Percentage	VICE-PRESIDENTIAL CANDIDATES
Benjamin Harrison	Republican	233	5,447,129	47.9	Levi P. Morton
Grover Cleveland	Democratic	168	5,537,857	48.6	Allen G. Thurman
Clinton B. Fisk	Prohibition	—	249,506	2.2	John A. Brooks
Alson J. Streeter	Union Labor	—	146,935	1.3	C.E. Cunningham

Defeated by Cleveland in his bid for reelection in 1892, Harrison resumed his law practice. He also served as counsel for Venezuela in the Venezuela-British boundary dispute. In 1899 he represented the U.S. at the Hague Peace Conference.

He died in Indianapolis on March 13, 1901.

Caroline Lavinia Scott Harrison (1832–92), his first wife, was proficient in music and painting and brought cultural distinction to her role as First Lady. The Harrisons had two children. Mrs. Harrison became ill in 1891, dying a few months before Harrison's term ended.

Mary Scott Lord (Dimmick) Harrison (1858–1948), was Harrison's second wife. They married in 1896 and had one child. A niece of his first wife, she had served as White House hostess during her aunt's illness.

WILLIAM McKINLEY

McKinley's assassination in the first year of the 20th century marked the closing of an era. He was the last President to have served in the Civil War, and the last to embark on a war of territorial expansion—the Spanish-American War. The Western frontier had been tamed. A new industrial society was being created, and with it came a change from the 19th century pattern of life.

25th President
(1897–1901)

McKinley was born on Jan. 29, 1843, in Niles, Ohio, the son of William and Nancy (Allison) McKinley.

In 1861, at 18, he enlisted as a private in the Civil War. As a mess sergeant he received a battlefield commission for serving hot food to troops under fire. He later rose to major.

After the Civil War he passed the bar in 1867, establishing a law practice in Canton, Ohio.

After serving two years as a county prosecuting attorney, McKinley was elected to Congress in 1876. Except for one term, he remained there until 1891. While a House member he sponsored the restrictive McKinley Tariff Act of 1890 that pleased financial and business interests.

With the backing of Mark Hanna, a wealthy Ohio industrialist, McKinnley won election and reelection as governor of Ohio (1892–96). In the panic of 1893, he gained popularity by providing free food for the Ohio unemployed.

Through Hanna's astute management, McKinley won the Republican presidential nomination in 1896. The party platform emphasized higher tariffs and an expansionist foreign policy.

During McKinley's administration tariffs

McKINLEY'S PRESIDENTIAL ADMINISTRATION

Congresses in Session:
55th, 56th, 57th

Vice President:
Garret Hobart, 1897–99
Theodore Roosevelt, 1901

Secretary of State:
John Sherman, 1897–98
William Day, 1898
John Hay, 1898–1901

Secretary of the Treasury:
Lyman Gage, 1897–1901

Secretary of War:
Russell Alger, 1897–99
Elihu Root, 1899–1901

Attorney General:
Joseph McKenna, 1897–98
John Griggs, 1898–1901
Philander Knox, 1901

Postmaster General:
James Gary, 1897–98
Charles Smith, 1898–1901

Secretary of the Navy:
John Long, 1897–1901

Secretary of the Interior:
Cornelius Bliss, 1897–98
Ethan Hitchcock, 1898–1901

Secretary of Agriculture:
James Wilson, 1897–1901

PRESIDENTIAL ELECTION OF 1896

Nominations: The Republicans met in St. Louis, June 16–18, 1896, and McKinley with 661½ of 907 votes was nominated on the first ballot. The Democrats met in Chicago, July 7–11, 1896, and Bryan was nominated on the fifth ballot with 652 of 768 votes. The Populists supported Bryan. The National Democrats were so-called Gold Democrats, conservatives who opposed Bryan. **Campaign Issues:** The Democrats came out for "free and unlimited coinage of silver."

PRESIDENTIAL CANDIDATES	PARTY	ELECTORAL VOTES	POPULAR VOTE Total	Percentage	VICE-PRESIDENTIAL CANDIDATES
William McKinley	Republican	271	7,102,246	51.0	Garret Hobart
William Jennings Bryan	Democrat	176	6,492,559	46.7	{ Arthur Sewall / Thomas E. Watson
John M. Palmer	Natl. Dem.	—	133,148	1.0	Simon Buckner
Other candidates	—	—	182,250	1.3	

PRESIDENTIAL ELECTION OF 1900

Nominations: The Republicans, meeting in Philadelphia, June 19–21, 1900, made McKinley's nomination unanimous. The Democrats, meeting in Kansas City, Mo., July 4–6, 1900, chose Bryan unanimously on the first ballot. **Campaign:** Democrats accused McKinley of imperialism in Cuba and the Philippines and of being the tool of big business.

PRESIDENTIAL CANDIDATES	PARTY	ELECTORAL VOTES	POPULAR VOTE Total	Percentage	VICE-PRESIDENTIAL CANDIDATES
William McKinley	Republican	292	7,218,491	51.7	Theodore Roosevelt
William Jennings Bryan	Democrat	155	6,356,734	45.5	Adlai E. Stevenson
John G. Woolley	Prohibition	—	208,914	1.5	Henry B. Metcalf
Other candidates	—	—	189,126	1.3	

QUICK QUIZ: Who won the NCAA outstanding basketball player award in 1972-73? See page 790.

WILLIAM McKINLEY *(continued)*

were raised and Hawaii was annexed.

The Caribbean took the spotlight after Cubans rebelled against Spain in 1895. Ruthless Spanish repression followed, and U.S. property losses on the island were substantial. An unexplained explosion on the U.S. battleship *Maine* in Havana harbor (Feb. 15, 1898) was the final push needed to bring about war.

At McKinley's request, Congress declared war on Spain on April 25, 1898. The war lasted just four months. With U.S. victory, Cuba was placed under American military rule, and Puerto Rico, the Philippines, and Guam became U.S. possessions.

In 1900 McKinley was reelected. Less than a year later, he was shot by Leon Czolgosz, an anarchist, in Buffalo, N.Y., on Sept. 6, 1901. He died eight days later, on Sept. 14.

Ida Saxton McKinley (1847–1907) married McKinley in 1871. They had two daughters, both of whom died in childhood. She was an epileptic and an invalid during her husband's administration. But she insisted on accompanying McKinley everywhere and was with him in Buffalo where he was assassinated.

THEODORE ROOSEVELT

26th President
(1901–09)

Roosevelt entered the White House at the age of 42—the youngest man ever to attain the presidency. His vivid personality and his enthusiasm immediately made him a popular incumbent. His intellectual interests elevated the overall tone of American politics, although his glorification of military power and force drew considerable criticism.

Neither Republican boss Mark Hanna nor President McKinley had wanted Roosevelt as the vice-presidential candidate. Hanna's reaction on learning of McKinley's death was reportedly, "Now look, that damned cowboy is President of the United States."

EARLY LIFE

The first son of Theodore and Martha Bulloch Roosevelt, he was born on Oct. 27, 1858, in New York City. The scion of a wealthy family, he was educated by private tutors, traveled widely, graduated from Harvard (1880), and attended Columbia Law School.

As a youth Roosevelt's health was poor. His efforts to build up his physical strength by "roughing it" helped make him a sportsman, hunter, horseman, rancher, and explorer.

At the same time he retained wide cultural interests and was a prolific author, writing his first book in 1882, *The Naval War of 1812*.

POLITICAL AND MILITARY CAREER

Throughout his life, Roosevelt's major interest was politics, which he entered as a "young insurgent" Republican advocating reforms. Roosevelt served in the New York legislature from 1881 to 1884.

At the 1884 Republican presidential convention he opposed the nomination of James G. Blaine because of Blaine's connection with a stock-rigging scandal. This cost Roosevelt the support of the New York Republican boss, Thomas Platt. In turn, when Roosevelt, a loyal Republican, campaigned for Blaine, he lost the support of the young insurgents of his party.

Considering his political career at an end, and bereaved by the deaths of his mother and his wife on the same day in 1884, Roosevelt retired for the next two years to his North Dakota ranch. There he acquired many picturesque Western mannerisms of speech and gesture. He wrote many magazine articles about life in the West.

In 1886 Roosevelt was called back to New York City to run for mayor against powerful Democratic candidates. Although he was defeated, he attracted so much attention that President Harrison appointed him to the U.S. Civil Service Commission (1889–95), on which he became the dominant figure.

A reform mayor of New York City appointed Roosevelt head of the Board of Police Commissioners in 1895. Roosevelt proceeded vigorously to clean up the corruption-ridden police force. However, his zealous enforcement of Sunday blue laws, closing saloons, angered many of the city's residents.

In 1897 President McKinley reluctantly appointed him assistant secretary of the navy. In this post, anticipating war with Spain, he was instrumental in placing the Navy on a war footing.

At the outbreak of the Spanish-American War he resigned as assistant secretary of the navy. Then, with Leonard Wood, he organized the volunteer cavalry regiment known as the Rough Riders.

On July 1, 1898, Col. Roosevelt led the Rough Riders in a charge up Cuba's San Juan Hill, an event he always continued to regard as "the great day of my life."

Roosevelt returned from Cuba a military hero. New York's "Boss" Platt, though personally averse to him, supported him for the governorship of New York. Roosevelt won and served from 1899 to 1901.

His administration as governor of New York antagonized Platt and the other Republican bosses. It was in his relations with the New York Republican political machine that he first used the term that became one of his trademarks: "Speak softly and carry a big stick, you will go far."

In 1900 New York Republican leaders decided to dispose of Roosevelt, for at least the next four years, by backing his nomination for Vice President. The McKinley-Roosevelt slate was easily elected.

26th PRESIDENT OF THE UNITED STATES

Roosevelt served only a few months as Vice President before the assassination of McKinley made him President on Sept. 14, 1901.

This was the era of "muckraking" and reform,

and Roosevelt embodied the period. He strengthened government controls over big business through a reinvigorated Interstate Commerce Commission, directed "trust-busting" actions against big corporations, and supported passage of the Meat Inspection Act and the Pure Food and Drug Act. He also advocated conservation of forestlands and irrigation of wastelands.

Roosevelt's "big stick" policy toward Latin America contributed to anti-American feeling. When Colombia refused to give him permission to build a canal across its province Panama, Roosevelt backed a revolution in Panama. He immediately recognized the rebel regime, secured from it the desired agreement, and began construction of the canal. In 1906 he visited Panama—the first President to travel outside the U.S. while in office.

Through his mediation the Russo-Japanese War was ended in 1905 at the Portsmouth (N.H.) Peace Conference.

He helped avert war between France and Germany over Morocco by sponsoring the Algeciras Conference.

His advocacy of the Hague Tribunal raised hopes for international peace.

For his activities to improve international relations, he became in 1906 the first American awarded the Nobel Peace Prize.

Roosevelt was the first President to ride in a gasoline-powered automobile (Aug. 22, 1902). He also was the first to fly in an airplane (Oct. 11, 1910), a year after leaving the White House.

LATER ACTIVITIES

At the close of his second term Roosevelt chose as his successor William Howard Taft, his secretary of war. Roosevelt successfully backed Taft at the 1908 Republican convention and in the ensuing campaign.

After leaving the White House, Roosevelt went off on exploring and big-game expeditions and a tour of European capitals.

On his return in 1910, he broke with Taft. At the 1912 Republican convention Roosevelt sought the nomination for a third term. When Taft was selected, Roosevelt took the progressive Republicans out of the party. He organized them into a new Progressive, or "Bull Moose," Party. He then ran as the Progressive Party's presidential candidate.

During the ensuing campaign, a would-be assassin fired a shot that struck Roosevelt shortly before he was to make an address in Milwaukee, Wis., on Oct. 14, 1912. Although the bullet penetrated Roosevelt's chest, he insisted on completing his speech before going to a hospital.

The split in the Republican Party in 1912 enabled the Democratic candidate, Woodrow Wilson, to win. Roosevelt came in second, with Taft a poor third.

In addition to politics, Roosevelt engaged in what would have been separate careers for other men—exploration and writing. A former "River of Doubt" in the Brazilian jungle, which he traced to its outlet, was given the name Rio Roosevelt. He wrote nearly 40 books.

Roosevelt was deeply disappointed when President Wilson refused his offer to organize and lead a division of volunteers to fight in France in World War I.

On Jan. 6, 1919, Roosevelt died in his sleep.

Alice Hathaway Lee Roosevelt (1861–84) was his first wife. She died two days after the birth of their daughter, Alice.

Edith Kermit Carow Roosevelt (1861–1948) became Roosevelt's second wife in 1886. They had four sons and one daughter. One son died in action during World War I and two others died in World War II. As First Lady, Edith Roosevelt made the White House the social center of Washington.

THEODORE ROOSEVELT'S PRESIDENTIAL ADMINISTRATION

Congresses in Session:
57th, 58th, 59th, 60th

Vice President:
The vice-presidential office remained vacant during Roosevelt's first administration.
Charles Fairbanks, 1905–09

Secretary of State:
John Hay, 1901–05
Elihu Root, 1905–09
Robert Bacon, 1909

Secretary of War:
Elihu Root, 1901–04
William Taft, 1904–08
Luke Wright, 1908–09

Secretary of the Treasury:
Lyman Gage, 1901–02
Leslie Shaw, 1902–07
George Cortelyou, 1907–09

Attorney General:
Philander Knox, 1901–04
William Moody, 1904–06
Charles Bonaparte, 1906–09

Secretary of the Navy:
John Long, 1901–02
William Moody, 1902–04
Paul Morton, 1904–05
Charles Bonaparte, 1905–06
Victor Metcalf, 1906–08
Truman H. Newberry, 1908–09

Postmaster General:
Charles E. Smith, 1901–02
Henry Payne, 1902–04
Robert Wynne, 1904–05
George Cortelyou, 1905–07
George Meyer, 1907–09

Secretary of the Interior:
Ethan Hitchcock, 1901–07
James Garfield, 1907–09

Secretary of Agriculture:
James Wilson, 1901–09

Secretary of Commerce and Labor:
George Cortelyou, 1903–04
Victor Metcalf, 1904–06
Oscar Straus, 1906–09

PRESIDENTIAL ELECTION OF 1904

Nominations: Republicans met in Chicago, June 21–23, 1904, and chose Roosevelt unanimously. Democrats met in St. Louis, July 6–9, 1904, and nominated Parker on the first ballot.

Remarks: Roosevelt received a larger percentage of the popular vote than any previous President since tabulation of the vote had begun in 1824.

PRESIDENTIAL CANDIDATES	PARTY	ELECTORAL VOTES	POPULAR VOTE Total	Percentage	VICE-PRESIDENTIAL CANDIDATES
Theodore Roosevelt	Republican	336	7,628,461	56.4	Charles W. Fairbanks
Alton B. Parker	Democratic	140	5,084,223	37.6	Henry G. Davis
Eugene V. Debs	Socialist	—	402,283	3.0	Benjamin Hanford
Other candidates	—	—	407,968	3.0	

QUICK QUIZ: Who was baseball's American League Rookie of the Year in 1969? See page 788.

WILLIAM HOWARD TAFT

27th President
(1909–13)

The weightiest President, William Howard Taft stood six feet two inches tall and weighed over 300 pounds. An easygoing man, Taft presided over a prosperous nation more concerned with industrial growth than world affairs. He became the only President to later serve on the Supreme Court.

Taft was born on Sept. 15, 1857, in Cincinnati, Ohio, the son of Alphonso and Louise Maria Torrey Taft. His father had served as secretary of war and attorney general under President Grant. As a youth, "Willie," as he was called, won a reputation to be feared as a wrestler and boxer. Taft graduated from Yale in 1878 and from Cincinnati Law School in 1880.

EARLY CAREER

After practicing law in Cincinnati, he served successively as assistant prosecutor, assistant county solicitor, and superior court judge. He then received federal appointments as solicitor general of the U.S. (1890–92), U.S. circuit judge (1892–1900), president of the Philippine Commission (1900–01), and governor of the Philippines (1901–04).

President Roosevelt, his close friend, appointed him secretary of war (1904–08) and entrusted him with special missions to Cuba, Panama, the Philippines, and Japan.

Roosevelt chose Taft as his successor, and the Republicans nominated him as their presidential candidate in the election of 1908. Taft defeated Democrat William Jennings Bryan, who was making his third try for the White House.

PRESIDENTIAL ADMINISTRATION

Never having been elected to office before running for President, Taft had difficulty dealing with politicians and acting as leader of the Republican Party.

As President, Taft continued Roosevelt's policies, but the emphasis became more conservative. Republicans who favored progressive policies grew increasingly restive.

During his administration Arizona and New Mexico were admitted to the Union, bringing the number of U.S. states to 48.

Taft sought to conciliate the progressives by approving laws to institute postal savings and the parcel post. He also endorsed constitutional amendments authorizing direct election of senators and enactment of a federal income tax. Both were ratified by the states and were proclaimed in 1913. Taft also approved the Paine-Aldrich Act, which reduced duties on imports and opened the door to free trade with the Philippines.

These bids failed to placate the progressives, however. Led by Theodore Roosevelt, they bolted the Republican Party when it renominated Taft in 1912. They organized their own party, with Roosevelt as their candidate. The bitter split gave the election to the Democratic candidate, Gov. Woodrow Wilson of New Jersey.

Taft came in third, after Roosevelt. He was not unhappy, however, at the prospect of private life. Soon after Wilson's election he wrote, "The nearer I get to the inauguration of my successor the greater the relief I feel."

In his retirement Taft taught at Yale. During World War I he served as co-chairman of the National War Labor Board. He was among the Republicans who advocated U.S. entry into the League of Nations.

In 1921 he was appointed Chief Justice of the United States by President Harding, serving on the Supreme Court until a few weeks before his death, on March 8, 1930. He was the first President buried in Arlington National Cemetery.

Helen Herron Taft (1861–1943), his wife, was the daughter of a Cincinnati judge. She was a musician, and her White House musicales were highly regarded. She was ill during part of her husband's administration, so her sister, Mrs. Louise More, presided in her place.

The Tafts' children carried on the distinction of the family: Robert Alphonso was an influential senator. Charles Phelps was the first layman president of the Federal Council of Churches of Christ in America. Mrs. Helen Herron Taft Manning won note as an educator.

TAFT'S PRESIDENTIAL ADMINISTRATION

Congresses in Session:
61st, 62d

Vice President:
James Sherman, 1909–12

Secretary of State:
Philander Knox, 1909–13

Secretary of the Treasury:
Franklin MacVeagh, 1909–13

Secretary of War:
Jacob Dickinson, 1909–11
Henry Stimson, 1911–13

Attorney General:
George Wickersham, 1909–13

Secretary of the Interior:
Richard Ballinger, 1909–11
Walter Fisher, 1911–13

Postmaster General:
Frank Hitchcock, 1909–13

Secretary of the Navy:
George von L. Meyer, 1909–13

Secretary of Agriculture:
James Wilson, 1909–13

Secretary of Com. and Labor:
Charles Nagel, 1909–13

PRESIDENTIAL ELECTION OF 1908

Nominations: Republicans met in Chicago, June 16–19, 1908, and on the first ballot ratified by acclamation Roosevelt's choice of Taft as his successor. Democrats, meeting in Denver, July 8–10, 1908, selected Bryan on the first ballot.

Campaign: Roosevelt campaigned for Taft. Republicans promised tariff revision. Democrats called for lower tariffs, stringent antitrust enforcement, and relaxation of federal injunctions against labor strikes.

PRESIDENTIAL CANDIDATES	PARTY	ELECTORAL VOTES	POPULAR VOTE Total	Percentage	VICE-PRESIDENTIAL CANDIDATES
William H. Taft	Republican	321	7,675,320	51.6	James S. Sherman
William Jennings Bryan ...	Democratic	162	6,412,294	43.1	John W. Kern
Eugene V. Debs.	Socialist	—	420,793	2.8	Benjamin Hanford
Other candidates	—	—	379,833	2.5	—

WOODROW WILSON

28th President
(1913–21)

An idealist, Wilson carried out many liberal domestic reforms, establishing new government controls on business to prevent abuses of workers. He then led the nation into World War I "to make the world safe for democracy." His greatest disappointment came when an isolationist U.S. Senate rejected U.S. participation in the postwar League of Nations he had conceived to preserve world peace.

EARLY CAREER

Thomas Woodrow Wilson was born in Staunton, Va., on Dec. 29, 1856, the son of Joseph Ruggles Wilson, a Presbyterian minister, and Janet "Jessie" Woodrow Wilson. He graduated from the College of New Jersey (later Princeton) in 1879 and attended the University of Virginia Law School in 1881. Admitted to the Georgia bar in 1882, he practiced law for a year in Atlanta.

Deciding to become an educator, he took his Ph.D. at Johns Hopkins. Wilson then taught history and political science at Bryn Mawr and Wesleyan. In 1890 he joined Princeton's faculty. Twelve years later he became president of Princeton University, a post he held for eight years. He initiated many educational reforms and became a popular public speaker.

Wilson was nominated and elected Democratic governor of New Jersey in 1910. Despite resistance from regular Democrats, Wilson forced many progressive policies through the state legislature.

28th PRESIDENT OF THE UNITED STATES

At the 1912 Democratic national convention Wilson won the nomination on the 46th ballot. A split in the Republican Party was instrumental in sending him to the White House with a huge electoral-vote majority but less than 42% of the popular vote.

Wilson's first term was notable for its vigor. He became the first President to initiate frequently scheduled press conferences to keep the people informed on government activities. Liberal measures, carried out under the slogan "the New Freedom," included the Federal Reserve Act, which centralized the banking system of the country; the Keating-Owen Child Labor Act; the

WILSON'S PRESIDENTIAL ADMINISTRATION

Congresses in Session:
63d, 64th, 65th, 66th
Vice President
Thomas Marshall, 1913–21
Secretary of State:
William J. Bryan, 1913–15
Robert Lansing, 1915–20
Bainbridge Colby, 1920–21
Secretary of the Treasury:
William McAdoo, 1913–18
Carter Glass, 1918–20
David Houston, 1920–21

Secretary of War:
Lindley Garrison, 1913–16
Newton Baker, 1916–21
Attorney General:
James McReynolds, 1913–14
Thomas Gregory, 1914–19
A. Mitchell Palmer, 1919–21
Postmaster General:
Albert Burleson, 1913–21
Secretary of the Navy:
Josephus Daniels, 1913–21

Secretary of the Interior:
Franklin Lane, 1913–20
John Payne, 1920–21
Secretary of Agriculture:
David Houston, 1913–20
Edwin Meredith, 1920–21
Secretary of Commerce:
William Redfield, 1913–19
Joshua Alexander, 1919–21
Secretary of Labor:
William Wilson, 1913–21

PRESIDENTIAL ELECTION OF 1912

Nominations: Republicans met in Chicago, June 18–22, 1912. Taft won, but 344 delegates did not vote. Sherman died during the campaign and was replaced by Butler. The Progressive ("Bull Moose") Party, in Chicago, Aug. 5–7, 1912, nominated Roosevelt by acclamation. The Democrats, meeting in Baltimore, June 25–July 2, 1912, took 46 ballots to decide on Wilson. **Campaign:** The Republican split between Roosevelt and Taft gave Wilson an easy victory.

PRESIDENTIAL CANDIDATES	PARTY	ELECTORAL VOTES	POPULAR VOTE Total	Percentage	VICE-PRESIDENTIAL CANDIDATES
Woodrow Wilson.........	Democratic	435	6,296,547	41.9	Thomas R. Marshall
Theodore Roosevelt......	Progressive	88	4,118,571	27.4	Hiram Johnson
William H. Taft..........	Republican	8	3,486,720	23.2	James S. Sherman / Nicholas M. Butler
Eugene V. Debs..........	Socialist	—	901,255	6.0	Emil Seidel
Other candidates........	—	—	235,025	1.5	—

PRESIDENTIAL ELECTION OF 1916

Nominations: The Republican convention in Chicago, June 7–10, 1916, chose Hughes on the third ballot when he received 949½ votes of 986. The Democratic convention in St. Louis, June 14–16, 1916, renominated its previous ticket by acclamation, with only one delegate opposed to Wilson. **Remarks:** Hughes went to bed before the California returns had come in, believing he had won a close election. By morning the West Coast results showed Wilson the winner.

PRESIDENTIAL CANDIDATES	PARTY	ELECTORAL VOTES	POPULAR VOTE Total	Percentage	VICE-PRESIDENTIAL CANDIDATES
Woodrow Wilson.........	Democratic	277	9,127,695	49.4	Thomas R. Marshall
Charles E. Hughes.......	Republican	254	8,533,507	46.2	Charles W. Fairbanks
Allan L. Benson..........	Socialist	—	585,113	3.2	George R. Kirkpatrick
Other candidates........	—	—	233,909	1.2	—

QUICK QUIZ: Who was men's world figure skating champion in 1969–70? See page 857.

WOODROW WILSON *(continued)*

Farm Loan Act; the Clayton Antitrust Act; the Adamson Eight-Hour Law, reducing the working hours of trainmen; the La Follette Seamen's Act; and a lowered tariff.

To promote tariff reform, Wilson became the first President since John Adams to address Congress personally on the subject.

Wilson also favored equal rights for women. He welcomed the election in 1916 of America's first congresswoman, Jeannette Rankin of Montana. He aided the passage of the 19th Amendment, enfranchising women. Wilson also created a precedent by appointing the first woman to a subcabinet post, Annette Abbott Adams as assistant attorney general.

Opposed to prohibition, he vetoed the Volstead Act. Congress overrode his veto.

He disappointed many liberals by maintaining the "big stick" policy toward Latin America. On March 15, 1916, he sent U.S. troops into Mexico in pursuit of the revolutionary Pancho Villa. The United States purchased the Virgin Islands from Denmark in 1915 for $25 million.

The war in Europe that began in 1914 overshadowed all other foreign problems. Wilson sought to maintain U.S. neutrality, but went further in his warnings to Germany than Secretary of State William Jennings Bryan considered proper for a neutral. Bryan resigned after Wilson insisted on sending strong notes to Germany protesting the U-boat sinking of the *Lusitania* on May 7, 1915.

Under the slogan "He kept us out of war," Wilson barely won reelection in 1916 over Republican Charles Evans Hughes, who had resigned from the Supreme Court to run.

When Germany announced in 1917 that it would resume all-out submarine operations to impose its own blockade against the Allies, Wilson took America into the world conflict with public opinion behind him. Congress declared war on Germany on April 6, 1917.

Wilson's conduct of the war was vigorous. His stated war objectives were to "make the world safe for democracy" and to promote the "ultimate peace of the world." His program was embodied in the famous "Fourteen Points" of Jan. 8, 1918. These called for open diplomacy, adjustment of colonial claims, self-determination of peoples, and formation of a "general association of nations."

After the Allies achieved victory on Nov. 11, 1918, Wilson went to France to attend the Versailles Peace Conference. There he met fierce resistance from Lloyd George, Georges Clemenceau, and other European premiers, who made secret agreements among themselves.

Wilson finally agreed to what he considered the best treaty obtainable, acceptable chiefly because it provided for the League of Nations.

Wilson had broken irreconcilably at Versailles with his longtime friend and closest adviser Col. Edward M. House, whom he had once described as his "second personality."

En route home in 1919 he became the first President to make a radio broadcast when he addressed U.S. troops from shipboard.

Wilson was dismayed upon his return home when the League was attacked by various senators. Despite opposition led by Henry Cabot Lodge, the Senate might have ratified the Versailles treaty if reservations protecting U.S. sovereignty had been incorporated. But Wilson refused to compromise.

While stumping the country to gain support for the treaty, Wilson became ill.

A stroke on Oct. 2, 1919, paralyzed Wilson's left side. For months he was seen by only a few people. Many believed Mrs. Wilson was acting in his stead.

Although repudiated at home, Wilson was eulogized abroad. He was awarded the Nobel Peace Prize for 1919.

Nearly three years after completing his term of office, Wilson died in Washington, D.C., on Feb. 3, 1924. Entombed in the National Cathedral, he became the only President buried in Washington, D.C.

Ellen Louise Axson Wilson (1860–1914) married Wilson in 1885. They had three daughters. Mrs. Wilson died during her husband's second year in office.

Edith Bolling Galt Wilson (1872–1961), a widow, became his second wife in 1915.

WARREN GAMALIEL HARDING

29th President
(1921–23)

Harding was a handsome man who looked like the romantic ideal of a statesman. But he was ill equipped for the presidency. His administration is remembered for the Teapot Dome scandal and other corruption, although these did not become public until after his death.

Harding was born on Nov. 2, 1865, on a farm near what is now Blooming Grove, Ohio, the son of Dr. George Tryon and Phoebe Dickerson Harding.

He graduated from Ohio Central College, worked as a teacher, and studied law.

In 1884 he and two friends invested $300 to buy the bankrupt Marion (Ohio) *Star*. As its editor and eventual full owner, he became influential in local affairs and active in Republican politics.

Harding was elected a state senator (1898–1902) and lieutenant governor (1904–06). He failed in two subsequent tries for the Ohio governorship.

Harding received national attention in 1912 when he made the address nominating President Taft for a second term at the Republican national convention.

Under the guidance of Harry M. Daugherty, an able machine politician, he was elected to the U.S. Senate in 1914.

When the Republican national convention in 1920 reached a deadlock between the two main contenders for the presidential nomination, Daugherty arranged a deal in a "smoke-filled" hotel room that won Harding the nomination.

He was elected by a landslide after a "front-

porch" campaign that had "back to normalcy" as its major slogan.

During his administration the nation suffered a deep postwar depression. Taxes were reduced and tariffs were raised. Immigration was restricted for the first time with quotas.

In foreign relations, Harding called the Washington Disarmament Conference in 1921–22 that put limits on the size of navies.

While Harding was returning home from a trip to Alaska, he became ill, dying in San Francisco on Aug. 2, 1923.

Harding's wife refused to let doctors perform an autopsy, leading to later speculation that he may have been poisoned. She also burned his papers and correspondence, so no one has ever been able to learn how much Harding knew about the corruption of his associates.

After Harding's death, Senate investigations revealed many scandals of his administration. These included custodianship of alien property, sale of government-owned cargo ships, mismanagement of the Veterans Bureau, corruption of the Justice Department under Attorney General Daugherty, and the leasing of naval oil reserves (Teapot Dome) to private oil interests for a bribe.

Two of his cabinet members, Daugherty and Secretary of the Interior Albert B. Fall, were indicted and tried. Fall was sent to prison, but Daugherty was freed by a hung jury.

Mrs. Florence Kling DeWolfe Harding (1860–1924), a divorcée, became his wife in 1891. They had no children. After Harding's death, gossip alleged that he had carried on several illicit romances.

HARDING'S PRESIDENTIAL ADMINISTRATION

Congresses in Session:
67th, 68th

Vice President:
Calvin Coolidge, 1921–23

Secretary of State:
Charles Evans Hughes, 1921–23

Secretary of the Interior:
Albert Fall, 1921–23
Hubert Work, 1923

Secretary of the Treasury:
Andrew Mellon, 1921–23

Secretary of War:
John Weeks, 1921–23

Attorney General:
Harry Daugherty, 1921–23

Postmaster General:
Will Hays, 1921–22
Hubert Work, 1922–23
Harry New, 1923

Secretary of the Navy:
Edwin Denby, 1921–23

Secretary of Agriculture:
Henry C. Wallace, 1921–23

Secretary of Commerce:
Herbert Hoover, 1921–23

Secretary of Labor:
James Davis, 1921–23

PRESIDENTIAL ELECTION OF 1920

Nominations: The Republican convention, in Chicago, June 8–12, 1920, deadlocked in voting on the two main contenders, Gen. Leonard Wood and Illinois Gov. Frank Lowden, but finally selected Harding on the 10th ballot. The Democrats, in San Francisco, June 28–July 6, 1920, were deadlocked until the 44th ballot. Cox then received 732½ votes, or 3½ more than the necessary 729, but a motion was carried to make the nomination unanimous. **Campaign:** Democrats attempted to make approval of the League of Nations an issue. Harding called for a return to "normalcy."

PRESIDENTIAL CANDIDATES	PARTY	ELECTORAL VOTES	POPULAR VOTE Total	Percentage	VICE-PRESIDENTIAL CANDIDATES
Warren G. Harding	Republican	404	16,143,407	60.4	Calvin Coolidge
James M. Cox	Democratic	127	9,130,328	34.2	Franklin D. Roosevelt
Eugene V. Debs	Socialist	—	919,799	3.4	Seymour Stedman
Other candidates	—	—	540,371	2.0	—

CALVIN COOLIDGE

Coolidge had qualities and a program that appealed to the Americans of his day, a period of almost wild national prosperity. Spare of words, his nickname was "Silent Cal." He was straightforward and honest, and helped liquidate the scandals of the Harding administration. His program included economy in government, tax cuts, and reduction of the national debt.

30th President
(1923–29)

Born on July 4, 1872, at Plymouth, Vt., he was the son of John Calvin Coolidge, a storekeeper and justice of the peace, and Victoria Josephine Moor Coolidge.

He graduated from Amherst in 1895 and was admitted to the bar two years later.

In many ways the antithesis of the back-slap-

ping politician, Coolidge nonetheless rose swiftly in public life. He held minor offices in Northampton, Mass., where he had practiced law. He served in the state legislature (1912–15), as lieutenant governor (1916–18), and then as governor of Massachusetts (1919–20).

As governor he won national fame in 1919 when he sent state militia to break a strike by Boston police.

The 1920 Republican convention chose Coolidge as Harding's running mate. He became President on Harding's death, and in 1924 he was elected to a full term.

During Coolidge's administration speakeasies flourished in the cities despite efforts by government agents to enforce the national prohibition on sales of alcoholic beverages. Gangsters controlled the flow of illegal alcoholic beverages, leading to frequent gang wars.

Women's fashions changed drastically as "flappers" wore short skirts.

The Ku Klux Klan terrorized minority groups.

In 1927 the nation waited breathlessly as Charles A. Lindbergh made his dramatic solo flight across

QUICK QUIZ: Who won the NCAA women's team gymnastics championship in 1982–84? See page 825.

CALVIN COOLIDGE (*continued*)
the Atlantic from New York to Paris.

The Kellogg-Briand Peace Pact in 1928 outlawed war (but made no provision for enforcement).

Coolidge probably could have won another term, but he refused to seek renomination in 1928 in his famous laconic message, "I do not choose to run."

On his retirement Coolidge occupied himself mainly with writing newspaper and magazine articles and with his autobiography. The former President died on Jan. 5, 1933, in Northampton. **Grace Anna Goodhue Coolidge** (1879–1957), who married Coolidge in 1905, was a graduate of the University of Vermont. She was highly regarded for her gracious and cultured manner. However, White House social activities were curtailed during Coolidge's administration by the deaths of the younger of their two sons (at 16) and of the President's father.

COOLIDGE'S PRESIDENTIAL ADMINISTRATION

Congresses in Session:
68th, 69th, 70th
Vice President:
Charles Dawes, 1925–29
Secretary of State:
Charles Hughes, 1923–25
Frank Kellogg, 1925–29
Secretary of the Treasury:
Andrew Mellon, 1923–29
Postmaster General:
Harry New, 1923–29

Secretary of War:
John Weeks, 1923–25
Dwight Davis, 1925–29
Attorney General:
Harry Daugherty, 1923–24
Harlan Stone, 1924–25
John Sargent, 1925–29
Secretary of Agriculture:
Henry C. Wallace, 1923–24
Howard M. Gore, 1924–25
William Jardine, 1925–29

Secretary of the Navy:
Edwin Denby, 1923–24
Curtis Wilbur, 1924–29
Secretary of the Interior:
Hubert Work, 1923–28
Roy O. West, 1928–29
Secretary of Commerce:
Herbert Hoover, 1923–28
William Whiting, 1928–29
Secretary of Labor:
James Davis, 1923–29

PRESIDENTIAL ELECTION OF 1924

Nominations: The Republicans, meeting in Cleveland, June 10–12, 1924, chose Coolidge on the first ballot with 1,065 of 1,109 votes. Dawes was chosen after Frank Lowden had declined the vice-presidential nomination given him on the second ballot. The Democrats met in New York City in the longest of nominating conventions—it lasted from June 24 to July 9, 1924, with 60 candidates nominated for the presiden- cy. Southern Democrats fought against the nomination of New York Gov. Al Smith, a Roman Catholic. On the 103d ballot Davis finally received the nomination. **Campaign Issues:** The main issues were the Harding administration scandals. **Remarks:** The Progressive Party was formed as a result of left-wing dissatisfaction with the major candidates as well as with the contemporary social scene.

PRESIDENTIAL CANDIDATES	PARTY	ELECTORAL VOTES	POPULAR VOTE Total	Percentage	VICE-PRESIDENTIAL CANDIDATES
Calvin Coolidge	Republican	382	15,718,211	54.0	Charles G. Dawes
John W. Davis	Democratic	136	8,385,283	28.8	Charles W. Bryan
Robert M. LaFollette	Progressive	13	4,831,289	16.6	Burton K. Wheeler
Other candidates	—	—	155,883	0.5	—

HERBERT CLARK HOOVER

31st President
(1929–33)

While campaigning for the presidency in August 1928, Hoover said, "We are nearer to the final triumph over poverty than ever before in the history of any land. The poorhouse is vanishing from among us. We have not yet reached the goal, but we shall soon be in sight of the day when poverty will be banished from this nation." There seemed little reason then for Americans to disagree with this rosy appraisal of the nation's future, and Hoover was elected by a landslide.

Less than a year later, however, the stock market crashed, beginning the Great Depression.

Hoover was born on Aug. 10, 1874, in West Branch, Iowa, the son of Jesse Clark Hoover, a blacksmith, and Hulda Randall Minthorn Hoover. He graduated from Stanford University in 1895.

Hoover became a mining engineer, prospector, and businessman, accumulating a fortune through wide-ranging operations that took him all over the world. Because of his Quaker beliefs, he worked as organizer of relief operations during World War I. His administration of relief agencies attracted worldwide attention and respect.

In 1921 Hoover was appointed secretary of commerce by President Harding. He reorganized and expanded the department, sponsored conferences on unemployment, initiated programs to conserve fisheries, and constructed public works.

Chosen the Republican presidential nominee in 1928, Hoover won election in a campaign marred by bigotry directed at the Democratic candidate, Alfred E. Smith, because of his Roman Catholic religion.

The Great Depression deepened throughout Hoover's administration. To counter it he called for an extensive public-works program to restore business and employment.

In an effort to revive the economy, Hoover established the Reconstruction Finance Corporation, set up the Home Loan Bank, expanded the Farm Loan Bank, and supported legislation to relieve states and municipalities unable to bear the burden of the economic crisis. These measures proved ineffective, however, and Hoover's popularity waned drastically.

In foreign affairs he faced the problems of Japanese aggression in China, disarmament, and uncollected war debts.

In the presidential election of 1932, Hoover was defeated by Franklin D. Roosevelt.

In 1946 President Truman appointed Hoover coordinator of food supplies to dozens of countries devastated by World War II.

His long life in public service was further extended in 1947–49 and again in 1953–55, when he headed the Hoover Commission to reorganize the federal government.

Hoover died on Oct. 20, 1964, at the age of 90. **Lou Henry Hoover** (1875–1944), who was his college sweetheart, married Hoover in 1899. They had two sons. She was a charming White House hostess.

HOOVER'S PRESIDENTIAL ADMINISTRATION

Congresses in Session:
71st, 72d
Vice President:
Charles Curtis, 1929–33
Secretary of State:
Frank B. Kellogg, 1929
Henry Stimson, 1929–33
Secretary of the Treasury:
Andrew Mellon, 1929–32
Ogden Mills, 1932–33

Secretary of War:
James Good, 1929
Patrick Hurley, 1929–33
Attorney General:
William D. Mitchell, 1929–33
Postmaster General:
Walter Brown, 1929–33
Secretary of the Navy:
Charles Francis Adams, 1929–33

Secretary of the Interior:
Ray Lyman Wilbur, 1929–33
Secretary of Agriculture:
Arthur Hyde, 1929–33
Secretary of Commerce:
Robert Lamont, 1929–32
Roy D. Chapin, 1932–33
Secretary of Labor:
James Davis, 1929–30
William Doak, 1930–33

PRESIDENTIAL ELECTION OF 1928

Nominations: The Republicans met in Kansas City, Mo., June 12–15, 1928. On the first ballot, Hoover received 837 of 1,089 votes. The Democrats, meeting in Houston, Texas, June 26–29, 1928, chose Smith on the first ballot with 849⅔ of 1,097½ votes. **Campaign Issues:** Smith's Catholicism, prohibition, and farm relief.

PRESIDENTIAL CANDIDATES	PARTY	ELECTORAL VOTES	POPULAR VOTE Total	Percentage	VICE-PRESIDENTIAL CANDIDATES
Herbert C. Hoover	Republican	444	21,391,993	58.2	Charles Curtis
Alfred E. Smith	Democratic	87	15,016,169	40.9	Joseph T. Robinson
Norman M. Thomas	Socialist	—	267,385	0.7	James Maurer
Other candidates	—	—	69,180	0.2	

FRANKLIN DELANO ROOSEVELT

32d President
(1933–45)

Few people in the nation ever were neutral about Franklin Roosevelt. His followers loved him and his opponents hated him with remarkable vigor.

His secretary of the interior, Harold L. Ickes, said that Roosevelt seemed "either to inspire a mad devotion that can see no flaw or to kindle a hatred of an intensity that will admit of no virtue."

Roosevelt was a tradition breaker from the time he was selected as the Democrats' standard-bearer in 1932. He upset custom by flying to the national political convention to accept its nomination in person.

Taking office at the height of a national economic crisis, Roosevelt soon brought hope to a discouraged nation with his concern for the "forgotten man" and his promise of a "New Deal" for Americans.

EARLY POLITICAL CAREER

Roosevelt was born on Jan. 30, 1882, at Hyde Park, N.Y. His parents were James and Sara Delano Roosevelt, a wealthy and socially prominent family.

He graduated from Harvard in 1904 and married his cousin Eleanor Roosevelt the following year. He attended Columbia Law School and was admitted to the bar in 1907.

After practicing law for four years, he won a Democratic seat in the New York state senate (1911–12). He established himself as leader of the reform Democrats by opposing a Tammany nominee for the U.S. Senate.

In 1912 he campaigned for Woodrow Wilson, who appointed him assistant secretary of the navy (1913–20).

The Democratic Party chose Roosevelt as their vice-presidential candidate in the unsuccessful 1920 election campaign against Harding.

In 1921 he was stricken with polio that permanently crippled him from the waist down. But by indomitable effort he learned to walk again using leg braces and crutches.

Roosevelt was urged to resume his political career by his wife and New York's Gov. Alfred E. Smith. At 46 he won election in 1928 as New York's governor, while the national Democratic ticket headed by Smith went down to defeat.

As governor, Roosevelt achieved renown for his competence. The stock market crash of 1929 brought with it the Great Depression. Roosevelt, advised by a small group of intellectuals and experts called the "Brain Trust," undertook extensive relief measures.

Roosevelt also struck at corruption in New York City politics, forcing the resignation of Mayor James J. Walker.

32d PRESIDENT OF THE UNITED STATES

Roosevelt was chosen by the Democrats in 1932 to oppose President Hoover, whose administration had seen the start of this period of disaster and despair. Roosevelt was elected by a wide margin and buoyantly set out to create a peaceful social revolution.

The new Congress, overwhelmed by the magnitude of the Depression and by the forceful personality of Roosevelt, surrendered much power to

QUICK QUIZ: Who won the Mallory Cup in 1978–79? See page 872.

FRANKLIN D. ROOSEVELT *(continued)*
the President. He immediately launched a series of emergency measures to reorganize industry and agriculture—under government controls—and to revive the faltering economy by a great expenditure of public funds.

Between March 9 and June 16, 1933, in the famous "hundred days" session, Congress enacted, under Roosevelt's guidance, more decisive legislation than in any previous congressional session in history.

This vast and many-faceted New Deal program encountered bitter opposition. Roosevelt's critics accused him of having too many radical schemes for social betterment. Among conservatives he was disparagingly referred to as "that man in the White House."

Nonetheless, in 1936 Roosevelt was reelected

FRANKLIN D. ROOSEVELT'S PRESIDENTIAL ADMINISTRATION

Congresses in Session:
73d, 74th, 75th, 76th, 77th, 78th, 79th

Vice President:
John Garner, 1933–41
Henry A. Wallace, 1941–45
Harry Truman, 1945

Secretary of State:
Cordell Hull, 1933–44
Edward Stettinius Jr., 1944–45

Secretary of War:
George Dern, 1933–36
Harry Woodring, 1936–40
Henry Stimson, 1940–45

Secretary of the Treasury:
William Woodin, 1933–34
Henry Morgenthau Jr., 1934–45

Attorney General:
Homer Cummings, 1933–39
Frank Murphy, 1939–40
Robert Jackson, 1940–41
Francis Biddle, 1941–45

Postmaster General:
James Farley, 1933–40
Frank Walker, 1940–45

Secretary of Agriculture:
Henry A. Wallace, 1933–40
Claude Wickard, 1940–45

Secretary of Commerce:
Daniel Roper, 1933–38
Harry Hopkins, 1938–40
Jesse Jones, 1940–45
Henry A. Wallace, 1945

Secretary of Labor:
Frances Perkins, 1933–45

Secretary of the Navy:
Claude Swanson, 1933–40
Charles Edison, 1940
Frank Knox, 1940–44
James Forrestal, 1944–45

Secretary of the Interior:
Harold Ickes, 1933–45

PRESIDENTIAL ELECTION OF 1932

Nominations: The Republicans held their convention in Chicago, June 14–16, 1932. On the first ballot Hoover received 1,126½ of 1,150 votes. The Democrats met in Chicago, June 27–29, 1932. Roosevelt on the fourth ballot received 945 of 1,148½ votes. **Campaign Issues:** The major issues dealt with methods of meeting and alleviating the economic depression. **Remarks:** Roosevelt broke tradition by flying to Chicago to accept the nomination.

PRESIDENTIAL CANDIDATES	PARTY	ELECTORAL VOTES	POPULAR VOTE Total	Percentage	VICE-PRESIDENTIAL CANDIDATES
Franklin D. Roosevelt.....	Democratic	472	22,809,638	57.4	John Nance Garner
Herbert C. Hoover	Republican	59	15,758,901	39.7	Charles Curtis
Norman M. Thomas	Socialist	—	881,951	2.2	James Maurer
Other candidates	—	—	278,534	0.7	—

PRESIDENTIAL ELECTION OF 1936

Nominations: The Republicans convened in Cleveland, June 9–12, 1936. Landon was the only candidate placed in nomination, although 19 votes went to Senator Borah. The Democrats, meeting in Philadelphia, June 23–27, 1936, renominated Roosevelt by acclamation. **Remarks:** Roosevelt won 60.8% of the vote, a record to that time.

PRESIDENTIAL CANDIDATES	PARTY	ELECTORAL VOTES	POPULAR VOTE Total	Percentage	VICE-PRESIDENTIAL CANDIDATES
Franklin D. Roosevelt.....	Democratic	523	27,752,869	60.8	John Nance Garner
Alfred M. Landon	Republican	8	16,674,655	36.5	Frank Knox
William Lemke...........	Union	—	882,479	1.9	Thomas C. O'Brien
Other candidates	—	—	318,502	0.8	—

PRESIDENTIAL ELECTION OF 1940

Nominations: The Republicans met in Philadelphia, June 24–28, 1940. Willkie won on the sixth ballot. The Democrats met in Chicago, July 15–18, 1940. Roosevelt was nominated by acclamation. **Campaign Issues:** American neutrality and the effects of New Deal reforms. **Remarks:** Roosevelt broke tradition by running for a third term.

PRESIDENTIAL CANDIDATES	PARTY	ELECTORAL VOTES	POPULAR VOTE Total	Percentage	VICE-PRESIDENTIAL CANDIDATES
Franklin D. Roosevelt.....	Democratic	449	27,307,819	54.8	Henry A. Wallace
Wendell L. Willkie	Republican	82	22,321,018	44.8	Charles L. McNary
Other candidates	—	—	218,312	0.4	—

PRESIDENTIAL ELECTION OF 1944

Nominations: The Republicans convened in Chicago, June 26–28, 1944. Dewey was the only presidential candidate nominated. The Democrats, at their convention in Chicago, July 19–21, 1944, gave Roosevelt 1,086 of 1,176 votes on first ballot. **Remarks:** Democrats campaigned on the basis that leadership should not be changed in the middle of a war.

PRESIDENTIAL CANDIDATES	PARTY	ELECTORAL VOTES	POPULAR VOTE Total	Percentage	VICE-PRESIDENTIAL CANDIDATES
Franklin D. Roosevelt.....	Democratic	432	25,606,585	53.5	Harry S. Truman
Thomas E. Dewey	Republican	99	22,014,745	46.0	John W. Bricker
Other candidates	—	—	200,612	0.5	—

by an awesome majority over his Republican opponent, Alfred M. Landon, who won only the electoral votes of Maine and Vermont.

The Supreme Court's action in declaring unconstitutional several New Deal measures slowed the pace of reform. In 1937 Roosevelt attempted to "pack the court," but was unable to reorganize it to his advantage. He failed, too, in attempting to "purge" members of Congress who had opposed New Deal measures.

By 1938 the international skies were black with the shadow of impending war. As the power of Nazi Germany grew, Roosevelt spoke out against aggression and international greed. In 1939 he personally appealed for peace to the German and Italian dictators, Hitler and Mussolini.

Roosevelt was bitterly opposed by isolationist and conservative forces. In the 1940 presidential election an acrimonious issue was made of his breaking the third-term tradition. Although Roosevelt's majority was reduced, he decisively defeated the Republican candidate, Wendell Willkie.

The history of Roosevelt's third term is that of World War II.

The Japanese attack on Pearl Harbor, Hawaii, on Dec. 7, 1941 finally drew the U.S. directly into the conflict. War production multiplied beyond the most optimistic estimates.

In the European-African theater, U.S. Gen. Dwight D. Eisenhower was made supreme commander. U.S. forces landed in North Africa and followed with the invasion of Sicily, Italy, and finally Normandy.

In the Pacific the U.S. Navy carried marines and soldiers in a series of amphibious operations against Japanese-held islands. U.S. superiority in the air brought the war to Japan itself.

In the election of 1944 Roosevelt won an unprecedented fourth term with Harry Truman as his Vice President.

Roosevelt participated in a series of conferences with Winston Churchill, Joseph Stalin, and other Allied leaders to discuss plans for the postwar world. He planned to lay the foundations of lasting peace through formation of the United Nations.

On April 12, 1945, however, Roosevelt died of a massive cerebral hemorrhage before the war had been won.

Anna Eleanor Roosevelt Roosevelt (1884–1962), his wife, was the niece of Theodore Roosevelt as well as a distant cousin of her husband. As a young woman she had been a volunteer social worker. She continued her civic activities after her marriage, even though she bore five sons and one daughter.

Mrs. Roosevelt also gave her husband substantial assistance in his political career. During her husband's administrations she established a precedent as a First Lady famous in her own right. In doing so, she subjected herself to controversy and criticism. She traveled widely, making numerous speeches and reporting her observations in the press.

After Roosevelt's death she devoted herself to humanitarian causes. From 1949 to 1952 she was a U.S. delegate to the United Nations.

HARRY S. TRUMAN

Unexpectedly finding himself at the helm of the world's first atomic power, President Truman used the A-bomb to bring World War II to a quick conclusion. He then magnanimously extended American help both to friends and former foes in rebuilding their war-devastated economies. Under his leadership the United States became the protector of the free world from communist subversion and aggression in the postwar years. His accomplishments were hailed in these words by British leader Winston Churchill: "You, more than any other man, have saved Western Civilization."

33d President
(1945–53)

EARLY LIFE

Truman was born on May 8, 1884, in Lamar, Mo., the son of John Anderson Truman, a farmer, and Martha Ellen Young Truman. He began working in a local drugstore at the age of 11 and graduated from high school at 17. He clerked and farmed until World War I, when he helped organize a field artillery unit. He rose to major by the end of the war.

Civilian life seemed bleak to Truman after the failure of his haberdashery business in Kansas City in 1921. However, he had attracted the notice of the local Democratic boss, Thomas Pendergast, who helped him win election as a Jackson County official. During this time Truman studied law.

Elected U.S. senator from Missouri in 1934, Truman served for 10 years as a sometime supporter of the New Deal. He became a national figure as chairman of the Special Senate Committee to Investigate the National Defense Program (the Truman Committee). His fair and energetic inquiry into inefficiency and bungling on war-production contracts won wide praise.

In 1944 Truman was elected Vice President as Franklin D. Roosevelt's running mate.

33d PRESIDENT OF THE UNITED STATES

When Roosevelt died on April 12, 1945, Truman became the first President to take office in the midst of a war.

He was immediately confronted with the problems of ending World War II and preparing for postwar readjustment. Germany surrendered in May. After Truman authorized the atomic bombing of Hiroshima and Nagasaki, Japan capitulated in August.

Nominated in 1948 as the Democratic presidential candidate, he upset all those who had forecast his certain defeat by the Republican nominee, Thomas E. Dewey. By his vigorous railroad "whistle-stop" campaigning, he not only countered a nationwide Republican swing but overcame splits in his own party. On the right, Sen. J.

QUICK QUIZ: Who was world chess champion in 1969–72? See page 800.

HARRY S. TRUMAN (continued)

Strom Thurmond of South Carolina led a new States' Rights (Dixiecrat) Party of Southern Democrats antagonized by Truman's advocacy of civil rights for blacks. On the left, Henry A. Wallace led "progressive" groups at odds with Truman's anti-Soviet stand.

In his postwar domestic policy Truman faced strong congressional opposition from a coalition of Republicans and Southern Democrats.

The conservative coalition in Congress overrode his veto of the Labor-Management Relations Act (Taft-Hartley Law), enacted the McCarran-Walter Immigration Bill over his opposition, withheld support from his efforts to initiate government-sponsored health insurance, frustrated his attempts to maintain price controls, and blocked his civil-rights program.

In domestic affairs, however, he did achieve public housing projects, an increase in the minimum wage, civilian control of nuclear energy, and desegregation of the armed forces.

In foreign affairs, threatening communist advances in 1946–47 in Europe and the Middle East resulted in the Cold War. Congress backed Truman's foreign policy, which concentrated on containing communism.

The establishment of the UN was affirmed in 1945. Congress fully supported the "Truman Doctrine" in 1947, a program of economic and military assistance to nations threatened by communism. This was expanded later in 1947 by the Marshall Plan (European Recovery Program), and was supplemented by the Point Four Program in 1949 for aid to developing nations.

A victory in the Cold War was achieved in 1948–49 when an Anglo-American airlift frustrated the communists' Berlin blockade.

To safeguard Western Europe from possible communist attack, Truman pushed through the formation in 1950 of the North Atlantic Treaty Organization (NATO), an anticommunist military alliance.

The Cold War turned hot when communist North Korea attacked South Korea in 1950. Truman sent in U.S. troops under command of World War II hero Gen. Douglas MacArthur. But their advance to the Yalu River on the Chinese border brought China into the field, and the conflict became a stalemate. In 1951 Truman raised a storm of controversy when he relieved MacArthur of his Far Eastern command for failure to obey orders.

President Truman made the first coast-to-coast TV broadcast when he opened the Japanese Peace Conference in San Francisco in 1951.

The final years of his administration were shadowed by the stalemated Korean War, unsubstantiated charges by Sen. Joseph R. McCarthy of communist infiltration in the Department of State and the U.S. Army, plus partisan claims that U.S. failure to support Gen. Chiang Kaishek had lost China to the communists.

Refusing to consider renomination in 1952, Truman went into retirement, giving much time to writing and to the establishment of the Harry S. Truman Library at Independence, Mo., where his official papers are housed. Truman died in his 88th year on Dec. 26, 1972, in Kansas City, Mo.

Elizabeth Virginia "Bess" Wallace Truman, (1885–1982), was a high school classmate who married Truman in 1919. She was retiring in nature and avoided publicity. Their daughter, Margaret, was a concert singer. During most of Truman's administration, he and his wife lived in Blair House, across the street from the White House, while the Executive Mansion was completely rebuilt with a steel framework.

TRUMAN'S PRESIDENTIAL ADMINISTRATION

Congresses in Session:
79th, 80th, 81st, 82d

Vice President:
Alben Barkley, 1949–53

Secretary of State:
Edward R. Stettinius Jr., 1945
James Byrnes, 1945–47
George Marshall, 1947–49
Dean Acheson, 1949–53

Secretary of the Treasury:
Henry Morgenthau Jr., 1945
Fred Vinson, 1945–46
John Snyder, 1946–53

Secretary of War:
Henry L. Stimson, 1945
Robert Patterson, 1945–47
Kenneth Royal, 1947

Secretary of Defense:
James Forrestal, 1947–49
Louis Johnson, 1949–50
George Marshall, 1950–51
Robert Lovett, 1951–53

Attorney General:
Francis Biddle, 1945
Tom Clark, 1945–49
J. Howard McGrath, 1949–52
James McGranery, 1952–53

Postmaster General:
Frank C. Walker, 1945
Robert Hannegan, 1945–47
Jesse Donaldson, 1947–53

Secretary of the Navy:
James Forrestal, 1945–47

Secretary of the Interior:
Harold Ickes, 1945–46
Julius Krug, 1946–49
Oscar Chapman, 1949–53

Secretary of Agriculture:
Claude R. Wickard, 1945
Clinton Anderson, 1945–48
Charles Brannan, 1948–53

Secretary of Commerce:
Henry A. Wallace, 1945–46
W. Averell Harriman, 1946–48
Charles Sawyer, 1948–53

Secretary of Labor:
Frances Perkins, 1945
Lewis Schwellenbach, 1945–48
Maurice Tobin, 1948–53

PRESIDENTIAL ELECTION OF 1948

Nominations: Republicans met in Philadelphia, June 21–25, 1948, and on the third ballot gave Dewey a unanimous vote. Democrats convened in Philadelphia, July 12–14, 1948. Truman won on the first ballot. **Campaign Issues:** Truman capitalized on attacking the "do-nothing" Republican-controlled 80th Congress, winning a surprising upset victory.

PRESIDENTIAL CANDIDATES	PARTY	ELECTORAL VOTES	POPULAR VOTE Total	Percentage	VICE-PRESIDENTIAL CANDIDATES
Harry S. Truman	Democratic	303	24,105,812	49.5	Alben W. Barkley
Thomas E. Dewey	Republican	189	21,970,065	45.1	Earl Warren
J. Strom Thurmond	States' Rights	39	1,169,063	2.4	Fielding L. Wright
Henry A. Wallace	Progressive	—	1,157,172	2.4	Glenn Taylor
Other candidates	—	—	285,495	0.6	—

DWIGHT DAVID EISENHOWER

34th President
(1953–61)

The victorious commander of allied forces that defeated Germany in World War II, "Ike" Eisenhower was sought as a presidential candidate by both major political parties. At first he rejected the overtures. But he finally succumbed, resigning from the Army in 1952 to become the Republican presidential nominee. He chose as his running mate Sen. Richard M. Nixon.

With the campaign slogan "I like Ike," the hero general easily defeated his Democratic opponent, Gov. Adlai E. Stevenson of Illinois, both in 1952 and 1956.

As President, Eisenhower quickly settled the Korean War. Then, after a brief recession, the nation enjoyed a high level of prosperity, clouded only by fears of a possible atomic war with the Soviet Union.

The Space Age began as the Soviets and the U.S. first launched satellites into orbit in 1957–58. Alaska and Hawaii were admitted to the Union as the 49th and 50th states in 1959.

Eisenhower was born on Oct. 14, 1890, in Denison, Texas, the son of David Jacob and Ida Elizabeth Stover Eisenhower. When he was a child his family moved to Abilene, Kan.

MILITARY CAREER

Eisenhower graduated from West Point in 1915 as a U.S. Army second lieutenant.

In World War I, Eisenhower was commanding officer of a training camp for the new U.S. Army tank corps, near Gettysburg, Pa. After the war he was posted, successively, to the Panama Canal Zone, the office of the assistant secretary of war, and from 1935 to 1940 to the Philippines. There he learned to fly in 1939, later making him the first President to hold a pilot's license.

During World War II, Eisenhower commanded U.S. forces in the North African landings, and in 1943 became chief of Allied forces in North Africa. After directing the invasions of Sicily and Italy, he was appointed supreme commander of Allied Expeditionary Forces.

In 1944 Eisenhower was made a 5-star general. His genial nature helped achieve essential cooperation among the Allied forces in the Normandy invasion and in the momentous battle that won victory in Europe in 1945.

After the war, he became Army chief of staff. He wrote *Crusade in Europe* (1948), an account of World War II.

Eisenhower resigned from the Army to become president of Columbia University (1948–50), but donned his uniform again to accept appointment as Supreme Commander of Allied Forces in

EISENHOWER'S PRESIDENTIAL ADMINISTRATION

Congresses in Session:
83d, 84th, 85th, 86th
Vice President:
Richard M. Nixon, 1953–61
Secretary of State:
John Foster Dulles, 1953–59
Christian Herter, 1959–61
Secretary of the Treasury:
George Humphrey, 1953–57
Robert Anderson, 1957–61
Postmaster General:
Arthur Summerfield, 1953–61

Secretary of Defense:
Charles Wilson, 1953–57
Neil McElroy, 1957–59
Thomas Gates Jr., 1959–61
Attorney General:
Herbert Brownell Jr., 1953–57
William Rogers, 1957–61
Secretary of the Interior:
Douglas McKay, 1953–56
Frederick Seaton, 1956–61
Secretary of Agriculture:
Ezra Taft Benson, 1953–61

Secretary of Commerce:
Sinclair Weeks, 1953–58
Lewis Strauss, 1958–59
Frederick Mueller, 1959–61
Secretary of Labor:
Martin Durkin, 1953
James Mitchell, 1953–61
Secretary of Health, Education, and Welfare
Oveta Culp Hobby, 1953–55
Marion Folsom, 1955–58
Arthur Flemming, 1958–61

PRESIDENTIAL ELECTION OF 1952

Nominations: The Republicans met in Chicago, July 7–11, 1952. Despite opposition by conservative Sen. Robert A. Taft (R-Ohio), Eisenhower received 845 of 1,206 votes on the first ballot, and his nomination was made unanimous. The Democrats convened in Chicago, July 21–26, 1952. Stevenson won on the third ballot. **Campaign Issues:** Conduct of the Korean War, the stalemate in the Cold War, corruption in the Democratic administration, and McCarthyism. **Remarks:** Stevenson was the first presidential nominee since Garfield to be drafted by his party.

PRESIDENTIAL CANDIDATES	PARTY	ELECTORAL VOTES	POPULAR VOTE		VICE-PRESIDENTIAL CANDIDATES
			Total	Percentage	
Dwight D. Eisenhower	Republican	442	33,936,234	55.1	Richard M. Nixon
Adlai E. Stevenson	Democratic	89	27,314,992	44.4	John J. Sparkman
Other candidates	—	—	290,959	0.5	—

PRESIDENTIAL ELECTION OF 1956

Nominations: The Democrats met in Chicago, Aug. 13–17, 1956. On the first ballot Stevenson had 905½ of 1,372 votes, and his nomination was made unanimous. The Republicans, meeting in San Francisco, Aug. 20–23, 1956, renominated Eisenhower by acclamation. **Campaign Issues:** Conduct of the Cold War, atomic testing, and Eisenhower's health.

PRESIDENTIAL CANDIDATES	PARTY	ELECTORAL VOTES	POPULAR VOTE		VICE-PRESIDENTIAL CANDIDATES
			Total	Percentage	
Dwight D. Eisenhower	Republican	457	35,590,472	57.4	Richard M. Nixon
Adlai E. Stevenson	Democratic	73	26,022,752	42.0	Estes Kefauver
Other candidates	—	1	414,000	0.6	—

QUICK QUIZ: Who hold's the men's all-distance American Casting Association record? See page 804.

DWIGHT D. EISENHOWER *(continued)*

Europe (1951–52). There he organized the NATO (North Atlantic Treaty Organization) defense forces.

34th PRESIDENT OF THE UNITED STATES

During the presidential election campaign of 1952, Eisenhower had pledged to personally go to Korea to end the war there.

After winning the election, Eisenhower flew to Korea. He brought the war to an end six months after taking office.

In domestic affairs President Eisenhower restricted the role of the federal government. However, he approved extension of Social Security to millions of self-employed Americans, increased aid to farmers, and raised the minimum hourly wage to $1. He initiated construction of the 42,500-mile Interstate Highway System.

In 1956 Eisenhower refused to aid a revolt in Hungary that was crushed by Soviet troops. He also denounced an attempt by Britain, France, and Israel to seize the Suez Canal from Egypt, forcing them to withdraw their troops.

In 1957 he used federal troops to back up the Supreme Court's 1954 ruling that public schools must be racially integrated.

The President promulgated the "Eisenhower Doctrine" in 1957, promising military and economic aid to any Middle Eastern nation resisting communist subversion. The following year U.S. Marines were sent to aid Lebanon.

Late in his second term the President was embarrassed by a scandal involving his confidential aide, Sherman Adams.

President Eisenhower was frustrated in his efforts to achieve better relations with Soviet leaders by the revelation of U-2 espionage flights over the Soviet Union.

During his administration Eisenhower suffered several serious illnesses.

After leaving Washington he retired to his farm in Gettysburg, Pa., but he remained active, campaigning for Republican candidates, writing books, and commenting on national issues.

He died on March 28, 1969, and was buried in Abilene, Kan.

Mary "Mamie" Geneva Doud Eisenhower (1896–1979) became his wife in 1916. She was a reserved and unassuming White House hostess who avoided unnecessary publicity. The Eisenhowers had two sons: Doud Dwight, who died when he was 3, and John Sheldon Doud Eisenhower, who was born in 1923.

JOHN FITZGERALD KENNEDY

The youngest elected President at 43, John F. Kennedy inspired the confidence of American youth. His inaugural address touched a national urge to aid mankind with its appeal: "Ask not what your country can do for you; ask what you can do for your country."

Before Kennedy had achieved most of his planned goals for the nation, he became the fourth U.S. President to be assassinated.

35th President
(1961–63)

EARLY YEARS

Kennedy was born on May 29, 1917, in Brookline, Mass., the son of Joseph P. Kennedy, a prominent and wealthy businessman, and Rose Fitzgerald Kennedy, daughter of a former mayor of Boston.

Kennedy studied briefly at Princeton and the London School of Economics. He graduated from Harvard with honors in 1940, and in the same year published his first book, the bestselling *Why England Slept.*

During World War II, Kennedy commanded a Navy PT-boat in the Pacific. In action off the Solomon Islands, his boat was sunk by an enemy destroyer. He became a hero to his crew by his courage in securing their rescue.

He was elected to Congress in 1946 and was

KENNEDY'S PRESIDENTIAL ADMINISTRATION

Congresses in Session:
87th, 88th

Vice President:
Lyndon B. Johnson, 1961–63

Secretary of State:
Dean Rusk, 1961–63

Secretary of the Treasury:
C. Douglas Dillon, 1961–63

Secretary of Defense:
Robert S. McNamara, 1961–63

Attorney General:
Robert F. Kennedy, 1961–63

Postmaster General:
J. Edward Day, 1961–63
John A. Gronouski Jr., 1963

Secretary of the Interior:
Stewart L. Udall, 1961–63

Secretary of Agriculture:
Orville L. Freeman, 1961–63

Secretary of Commerce:
Luther H. Hodges, 1961–63

Secretary of Labor:
Arthur J. Goldberg, 1961–62
W. Willard Wirtz, 1962–63

Secretary of Health, Education, and Welfare:
Abraham A. Ribicoff, 1961–62
Anthony J. Celebrezze, 1962–63

PRESIDENTIAL ELECTION OF 1960

Nominations: Democrats met in Los Angeles, July 11–15, 1960. Kennedy was nominated on the first ballot. Republicans, meeting in Chicago, July 25–28, 1960, nominated Nixon on the first ballot. **Campaign Issues:** The Democrats charged there was a "missile gap," that U.S. prestige was declining abroad, and that the Soviets had forged ahead militarily. **Remarks:** Unpledged Alabama and Mississippi electors cast their votes for Sen. Harry F. Byrd (D-Va.).

PRESIDENTIAL CANDIDATES	PARTY	ELECTORAL VOTES	POPULAR VOTE Total	Percentage	VICE-PRESIDENTIAL CANDIDATES
John F. Kennedy	Democratic	303	34,227,096	49.5	Lyndon B. Johnson
Richard M. Nixon	Republican	219	34,108,546	49.4	Henry Cabot Lodge
Unpledged electors	—	15	638,822	0.9	
Other candidates	—	—	138,559	0.2	

reelected with ease in 1948 and 1950. In 1952, despite the Republican landslide, Kennedy ran against and defeated the incumbent U.S. senator, Henry Cabot Lodge (R-Mass.).

In 1954–55 Kennedy underwent operations to repair a spinal injury, suffered during the war. While recuperating, he wrote *Profiles in Courage,* for which he won a 1957 Pulitzer Prize.

In 1958 Kennedy was overwhelmingly reelected to the Senate.

The Massachusetts senator then began a campaign for the 1960 Democratic presidential nomination. Several important primary victories in 1960 helped ensure his nomination at the convention. Kennedy chose Sen. Lyndon B. Johnson of Texas as his running mate.

Kennedy campaigned against his Republican opponent, Richard M. Nixon, partly on the issue that the country's prestige had declined greatly during the Eisenhower administration. His cause was helped by his performance in a series of TV debates with Nixon.

Kennedy won the election in the closest presidential race of the 20th century. He became the first President who was a Roman Catholic, and the first President born in the 20th century.

35th PRESIDENT OF THE UNITED STATES

The Kennedy administration's program, called the New Frontier, pressed for U.S. aid to education, enlargement of civil rights, aid to economically depressed areas, medical care for the aged, and an accelerated space program. Major accomplishments in foreign affairs were the establishment of the Peace Corps, the Alliance for Progress with Latin American countries, and the nuclear test-ban treaty.

In 1961, when the CIA-led anti-Castro invasion of communist Cuba at the Bay of Pigs failed, Kennedy and the nation suffered deep humiliation.

Confidence in American power was restored in 1962 when the President's order of a naval blockade of Cuba compelled the Soviet Union to dismantle its missile bases in Cuba and remove its bombing planes from the island.

Deeply concerned with culture, Kennedy did much to foster public interest in literature and the arts. The White House guest list included many scientists, writers, artists, and musicians.

The march toward the New Frontier was brutally halted when Kennedy was assassinated in Dallas, Texas, on Nov. 22, 1963, by Lee Harvey Oswald, a former U.S. marine who believed in communism. Kennedy was buried in Arlington National Cemetery.

Jacqueline Lee Bouvier Kennedy, born in 1929, married Kennedy in 1953. As First Lady she redecorated the White House interior. She was noted for her charm and command of foreign languages. Widespread admiration was evoked by her courage at the time of her husband's death (she was at his side when he was killed). The Kennedys had three children: Caroline Bouvier, born in 1957; John Fitzgerald, born in 1960; and Patrick Bouvier, who died two days after his birth in 1963.

Five years after Kennedy's death, she married Greek ship-owner Aristotle Onassis in 1968. She was again widowed when Onassis died in 1975.

LYNDON BAINES JOHNSON

36th President
(1963–69)

Within hours after Kennedy's death, Johnson was sworn in as President. He entered office with the handicap of having to take over from a man who had won adulation for himself and a new respect abroad for the nation.

Johnson's years as President increasingly filled with controversy over the Vietnam War, but both friends and foes agreed he was a persuasive man and a brilliant politician.

Johnson was born on Aug. 27, 1908, on a ranch near Stonewall, Texas, the son of Samuel Ealy Johnson, a schoolteacher and state legislator, and Rebekah Baines Johnson. He graduated from Southwest Texas State College in 1930 and then taught school. In 1932 he became secretary to a Texas congressman. An ardent New Dealer, he was named National Youth Administration director for Texas in 1935.

Johnson was elected to Congress in 1937 to fill an unexpired term, and he held the seat until 1948. He served on active duty in the U.S. Navy in 1941–42 and then returned to Congress. In 1948 he won the Democratic nomination for U.S. senator from Texas by a scant 87 votes.

In the Senate he became Democratic whip in 1951 and Senate minority leader in 1953. Democrats won control of the Senate in 1954 and Johnson, elected to a second term, became majority leader, a post he held until 1960—despite suffering a serious heart attack in 1955. As majority leader Johnson was a powerful figure.

In 1960, after a vain try for the presidential nomination, Johnson accepted second place on the Kennedy ticket. By keeping the Southern states within the party, Johnson made a major contribution in the Democrats' victory.

In filling out the remaining 14 months of Kennedy's term, President Johnson used his legislative skill to win congressional passage of his slain predecessor's program, especially in his skillful handling of the Civil Rights Act of 1964 and the Economic Opportunity Act, which declared "war on poverty."

In the 1964 election Johnson won over Sen. Barry Goldwater, the Republican candidate, by the largest percentage of the popular vote ever recorded. He strove tirelessly to push through Congress his social reform program that he called the Great Society.

Drawing on his experience as Senate leader, Johnson succeeded in getting his massive domestic program passed. In a whirlwind of activity he initiated tax cuts, gained passage of a voting rights act, instituted the Medicare plan, obtained increased federal aid for education, and approved a new immigration law.

QUICK QUIZ: Who won the NCAA fencing foil championship in 1979? See page 800.

LYNDON B. JOHNSON (continued)

During 1965 Johnson dispatched U.S. troops to fight communist forces trying to take over South Vietnam. At the same time he spurred intensified diplomatic efforts aimed at negotiating settlement of the war.

By 1967 President Johnson's popularity took a downward turn as the Vietnam conflict intensified. According to public-opinion polls, Americans were dissatisfied with the President's handling of the war and deeply concerned about urban riots, rising taxes, and inflation.

On March 31, 1968, Johnson announced he would not run for a second full term. His last year in office was one of still more tragedy: the assassination on April 4 of the respected black leader and Nobel Peace Prize-winner Dr. Martin Luther King Jr.; the resultant city riots; the assassination of Sen. Robert F. Kennedy in June; and the strife-blemished Democratic convention in August.

After leaving the presidency in 1969, Johnson retired to his ranch near Johnson City, Texas. He died there at the age of 64 on Jan. 22, 1973. **Claudia "Lady Bird" Alta Taylor Johnson,** his wife, was born in 1912. They were married in 1934 and had two daughters: Lynda Bird (born in 1944) and Luci Baines (born in 1947). As First Lady, Mrs. Johnson spearheaded projects to beautify the national environment.

JOHNSON'S PRESIDENTIAL ADMINISTRATION

Congresses in Session:
88th, 89th, 90th
Vice President:
Hubert H. Humphrey, 1965–69
Secretary of State:
Dean Rusk, 1963–69
Secretary of the Treasury:
C. Douglas Dillon, 1963–65
Henry H. Fowler, 1965–68
Joseph W. Barr, 1968–69
Secretary of Defense:
Robert S. McNamara, 1963–68
Clark M. Clifford, 1968–69
Secretary of the Interior:
Stewart L. Udall, 1963–69

Attorney General:
Robert F. Kennedy, 1963–64
Nicholas deB. Katzenbach, 1964–66
Ramsey Clark, 1967–69
Secretary of Agriculture:
Orville L. Freeman, 1963–69
Secretary of Commerce:
Luther H. Hodges, 1963–64
John T. Connor, 1965–67
A. B. Trowbridge, 1967–68
C. R. Smith, 1968–69
Secretary of Labor:
W. Willard Wirtz, 1963–69

Postmaster General:
John A. Gronouski Jr., 1963–65
Lawrence F. O'Brien, 1965–68
W. Marvin Watson, 1968–69
Secretary of Health, Education, and Welfare:
Anthony J. Celebrezze, 1963–65
John W. Gardner, 1965–68
Wilbur J. Cohen, 1968–69
Secretary of Housing and Urban Development:
Robert C. Weaver, 1965–68
Robert C. Wood, 1968–69
Secretary of Transportation:
Alan S. Boyd, 1966–69

PRESIDENTIAL ELECTION OF 1964

Nominations: Republicans met in San Francisco, July 13–16, 1964, and chose Goldwater on the first ballot. Democrats met in Atlantic City, N.J., Aug. 24–27, 1964, and nominated President Johnson by acclamation. **Campaign Issues:** Direct issues concerned the Vietnam War, some of the Great Society programs of the incumbent administration, and the far right-wing support that was attracted by Goldwater. **Remarks:** President Johnson received the largest popular-vote majority and greatest percentage of the total vote than ever before won by a presidential candidate.

PRESIDENTIAL CANDIDATES	PARTY	ELECTORAL VOTES	POPULAR VOTE Total	Percentage	VICE-PRESIDENTIAL CANDIDATES
Lyndon B. Johnson.......	Democratic	486	43,129,484	61.1	Hubert H. Humphrey
Barry Goldwater	Republican	52	27,178,188	38.5	William E. Miller
Other candidates	—	—	336,838	0.4	

RICHARD MILHOUS NIXON

37th President
(1969–74)

Richard Nixon became the first President to resign, giving up his administration when it became clear he was about to be impeached and convicted by Congress as a result of his misuse of presidential power in the Watergate scandals. Many of his closest associates were convicted and jailed in the affair. His administration was further stained by the resignation and conviction for income tax evasion of Vice President Spiro Agnew, who avoided trial on charges of accepting bribes.

Despite Nixon's misuse of power, he was acclaimed for achievements in the area of foreign affairs. He brought an end to U.S. participation in the Vietnam War—the longest and costliest war in U.S. history. And he moved boldly to end the Cold War with communist China and the Soviet Union.

He was born on Jan. 9, 1913, in Yorba Linda, Calif., the son of Francis Anthony and Hannah Milhous Nixon, a devout Quaker. When he was nine years old the family moved to Whittier, Calif.

Nixon graduated from Whittier College and the Duke University Law School. During World War II he worked in the Office of Price Administration and then served as a naval officer in the Pacific.

EARLY POLITICAL CAREER

In 1946 Republicans in Nixon's California congressional district were seeking a candidate for Congress. Nixon gained their endorsement and was elected.

National fame came quickly. Serving on the House Un-American Activities Committee, Nixon pressed an investigation of charges that Alger Hiss, a former State Department official, had supplied secret documents to the Soviets. His adroit questioning discredited Hiss, who later was

convicted of perjury. The case established Nixon as an articulate foe of communism. He was elected to the Senate in 1950, but by then his use of the communist issue against political opponents was provoking criticism.

In 1952 Dwight Eisenhower chose Nixon as his running mate. During the campaign Nixon was accused of accepting large sums of money from wealthy contributors. Eisenhower told him he must come "clean as a hound's tooth," so Nixon went on TV to explain. His emotional "Checkers" speech—he referred in it to a dog of that name that he had accepted as a gift—turned the issue to his advantage, and the Eisenhower-Nixon ticket was elected.

Many Vice Presidents have languished in obscurity, but not the energetic Nixon. Eisenhower had little interest in partisan politics, and Nixon welcomed the chance to speak and campaign nationally. When Eisenhower became ill on three separate occasions, Nixon acted in his behalf with confidence and restraint.

After the Republican slate was reelected in 1956, Nixon became the almost unanimous choice of his party for the presidential nomination in 1960.

Nixon narrowly lost the 1960 presidential election to Sen. John F. Kennedy when the more articulate Kennedy gained votes in a series of TV debates with him.

He ran for governor of California in 1962 and lost. Blaming biased journalists, he announced his retirement from politics and said angrily, "You won't have Nixon to kick around anymore."

But in 1968 he was awarded the Republican presidential nomination on the first ballot. The Democrats were bitterly divided over U.S. involvement in Vietnam.

Nixon won with less than a majority of the popular vote in one of the closest elections in American history. He defeated the Democratic candidate, Vice President Hubert H. Humphrey, by less than 1% of the vote.

FIRST TERM AS PRESIDENT

As President, Nixon cut U.S. troop strength in

NIXON'S PRESIDENTIAL ADMINISTRATION

Congresses in Session:
91st, 92d, 93d

Vice President:
Spiro T. Agnew, 1969–73
Gerald R. Ford, 1973–74

Secretary of State:
William P. Rogers, 1969–73
Henry A. Kissinger, 1973–74

Secretary of the Treasury:
David M. Kennedy, 1969–71
John B. Connally Jr., 1971–72
George P. Shultz, 1972–74
William E. Simon, 1974

Secretary of Defense:
Melvin R. Laird, 1969–73
Elliot L. Richardson, 1973
James R. Schlesinger, 1973–74

Attorney General:
John N. Mitchell, 1969–72
Richard G. Kleindienst, 1972–73
Elliot L. Richardson, 1973
William B. Saxbe, 1974

Secretary of the Interior:
Walter J. Hickel, 1969–70
Rogers C. B. Morton, 1971–74

Secretary of Agriculture:
Clifford M. Hardin, 1969–71
Earl L. Butz, 1971–74

Postmaster General:
(abolished as cabinet post, 1971)
Winton M. Blount, 1969–71

Secretary of Transportation:
John A. Volpe, 1969–73
Claude S. Brinegar, 1973–74

Secretary of Commerce:
Maurice H. Stans, 1969–72
Peter G. Peterson, 1972–73
Frederick B. Dent, 1973–74

Secretary of Labor:
George P. Shultz, 1969–70
James D. Hodgson, 1970–73
Peter J. Brennan, 1973–74

Secretary of Health, Education, and Welfare:
Robert H. Finch, 1969–70
Elliot L. Richardson, 1970–73
Caspar W. Weinberger, 1973–74

Secretary of Housing and Urban Development:
George W. Romney, 1969–73
James T. Lynn, 1973–74

PRESIDENTIAL ELECTION OF 1968

Nominations: Republicans in Miami Beach, Fla., Aug. 5–8, 1968, named Nixon on the first ballot. Agnew's nomination was made unanimous. The Democratic convention in Chicago, Aug. 26–29, was marred by violence both in and out of the convention hall. Humphrey and Muskie were each a first-ballot choice. **Campaign Issues:** The war in Vietnam.

Remarks: Nixon's popular vote share—43.4%—was the lowest for a winning presidential candidate since Wilson's election in 1912. Earlier concern proved groundless that the electoral votes cast for third-party candidate Gov. George C. Wallace of Alabama might be enough to throw the election into the House of Representatives.

PRESIDENTIAL CANDIDATES	PARTY	ELECTORAL VOTES	POPULAR VOTE Total	Percentage	VICE-PRESIDENTIAL CANDIDATES
Richard M. Nixon	Republican	301	31,785,480	43.4	Spiro T. Agnew
Hubert H. Humphrey	Democratic	191	31,275,165	42.7	Edmund S. Muskie
George C. Wallace	American	46	9,906,473	13.5	Curtis E. LeMay
Others	—	—	244,444	0.4	—

PRESIDENTIAL ELECTION OF 1972

Nominations: Democrats met in Miami Beach, Fla., July 13–14, and named Sen. George McGovern of South Dakota and Sen. Thomas F. Eagleton of Missouri. When the press revealed Eagleton had received psychiatric treatment, McGovern asked him to withdraw. Sargent Shriver, brother-in-law of President Kennedy, replaced Eagleton on Aug. 8. Republicans met in Miami Beach, Aug. 22–23, nominating Nixon and Agnew for a second term. **Campaign Issues:** War in Vietnam, welfare reform. **Remarks:** One Virginia elector switched his vote from Nixon to a minor-party candidate.

PRESIDENTIAL CANDIDATES	PARTY	ELECTORAL VOTES	POPULAR VOTE Total	Percentage	VICE-PRESIDENTIAL CANDIDATES
Richard M. Nixon	Republican	520	47,169,911	60.7	Spiro T. Agnew
George McGovern	Democratic	17	29,170,383	37.5	Sargent Shriver
John G. Schmitz	American	0	1,098,482	1.4	Thomas J. Anderson
Other candidates	—	1	278,778	0.4	—

QUICK QUIZ: Who won the 1975 Orange Bowl football game? See page 812.

RICHARD NIXON *(continued)*

Vietnam from 550,000 to 27,000 by December 1972, but he increased U.S. air and naval power in Southeast Asia. In 1972, after North Vietnam invaded in force, Nixon ordered mining of the North Vietnamese ports and air attacks on land supply routes from China.

Antiwar protests were widespread but ineffective. The fatal shooting of four students by Ohio National Guardsmen during a demonstration at Kent State University in 1970 was the darkest hour of the Vietnam controversy.

The U.S. economy, plagued by government budgetary deficits, sagged in 1970. The President found it impossible to control inflation.

Many white parents opposed court-ordered busing of their children to achieve racial balance in public schools, and Nixon unsuccessfully sought a legal means of limiting such busing.

Environmentalists applauded his moves to eliminate water and air pollution, but they worked through Congress to block his plan to construct a supersonic transport plane that critics considered ecologically harmful.

President Nixon moved dramatically to end the Cold War with communist China and the Soviet Union. With U.S. support, the UN in 1971 admitted communist China and expelled the nationalist Chinese of Taiwan. In February 1972 Nixon became the first U.S. President ever to visit China while in office.

The President flew to Moscow in May 1972 for a summit meeting with leaders of the Soviet Union. Several agreements were signed, the most important being the strategic arms limitation (SALT) treaties, setting limits on the production and deployment of atomic weapons.

In the 1972 election campaign for a second term, the President sought the support of young voters going to the polls for the first time since a 1971 constitutional amendment lowered the voting age to 18. During the campaign Nixon supporters raised an unprecedented $60 million for expenses, leading to abuses later revealed in the Watergate investigations in 1973-74.

Twelve days before the election, presidential adviser Henry Kissinger, who had been conducting secret negotiations in Paris with the North Vietnamese, announced "peace is at hand."

A record of over 77 million voters cast ballots, giving the President a landslide victory over his Democratic opponent, Sen. George McGovern of South Dakota.

When Vietnam truce negotiations broke down late in 1972, Nixon ordered heavy bombing of North Vietnam until the communists returned to the talks.

SECOND TERM AND RESIGNATION

In his inaugural address in January 1973, the President promised to work for a "peace which can endure for generations to come." A week later, on Jan. 28, 1973, a Vietnam cease-fire agreement was signed in Paris, enabling all U.S. troops to be withdrawn from Vietnam by March 29. However, U.S. planes continued to bomb communist forces in Cambodia. Despite Nixon's opposition, the Democrat-controlled Congress forced an end to all U.S. military action in Southeast Asia on Aug. 15, 1973. Two years later communist military forces took over the governments of South Vietnam, Laos, and Cambodia.

Just as President Nixon seemed about to lead the nation into a new era of peace and harmony, the Watergate scandals engulfed his administration.

The affair had begun when police on June 17, 1972, arrested five men who had broken into and installed wiretapping devices in the headquarters of the Democratic National Committee at the Watergate office building in Washington, D.C.

A Senate investigation in 1973 revealed evidence that the Watergate break-in was only part of a pattern of crimes by Nixon aides in 1972 aimed at ensuring his reelection. Nixon denied he was involved in the scandals.

On Oct. 10, 1973, Vice President Agnew resigned and accepted conviction for income tax evasion to avoid being tried on charges of accepting bribes. For the first time in the nation's history Amendment 25 to the U.S. Constitution was used as President Nixon appointed Gerald R. Ford to succeed Agnew.

President Nixon ordered the firing of special Watergate prosecutor Archibald Cox on Oct. 30, 1973, because Cox had refused to drop a court suit against the President calling for the release of White House tapes and documents relating to the Watergate scandals.

A resulting public outcry caused the House of Representatives to institute hearings to determine if Nixon should be impeached.

Nine months later, in July 1974, the House Judiciary Committee voted to recommend Nixon's impeachment on three counts: obstructing justice in covering up the Watergate scandals, violating his presidential oath of office, and defying the committee's subpoenas for evidence.

Also in July 1974 the Supreme Court by a unanimous decision ordered the President to turn over evidence subpoenaed by the new Watergate special prosecutor, Leon Jaworski.

The White House on Aug. 5, 1974, made public some of the evidence ordered released by the Supreme Court. It showed that President Nixon had obstructed the FBI investigation of the Watergate break-in to protect associates and to ensure his reelection. Republican leaders told Nixon they could not prevent his impeachment and conviction.

President Nixon resigned on Aug. 9, 1974, and retired. He was succeeded by Ford.

A month later, on Sept. 8, 1974, President Ford granted Nixon a "full, free and absolute pardon for all offenses" during his administration, thus eliminating the possibility of his indictment or trial for his role in the scandals.

In subsequent months three cabinet officers, Nixon's two top White House aides, and many other administration officials and election campaign supporters were convicted on charges growing out of the scandals.

Thelma Catherine Patricia Ryan Nixon, born in 1912, was a popular White House hostess. She revealed considerable skill in person-to-person diplomacy during her trips abroad. She and Nixon were married in 1940 and had two daughters. Tricia Nixon (1946–) married Edward Cox in the White House in 1971. Julie Nixon (1948–) married President Eisenhower's grandson David Eisenhower in 1968.

GERALD RUDOLPH FORD

The first nonelected President, Gerald R. Ford became Chief Executive when Richard Nixon resigned to avoid impeachment and conviction by Congress in the Watergate scandal. Ford had been appointed Vice President 10 months earlier, following the resignation of Spiro T. Agnew.

38th President
(1974–77)

As President, Ford was confronted with the worst recession since the Great Depression of the 1930s. Ford served as President only 29 months, losing his bid for a full term to Democratic candidate Jimmy Carter.

EARLY LIFE

Ford was born on July 14, 1913, in Omaha, Neb. The son of Dorothy Gardner King and Leslie King, a wool trader, he was named Leslie Lynch King at birth. His parents were divorced in 1915. He and his mother returned to her parents' home in Grand Rapids, Mich., where she soon met and married Gerald Rudolf Ford, a young paint salesman. The boy was adopted by his stepfather and renamed Gerald Rudolph Ford Jr.

Ford went to the University of Michigan on an athletic scholarship, playing center on the Michigan football team.

Upon graduation he accepted an offer to become assistant football line coach and boxing coach at Yale University so that he could attend the Yale law school. After receiving his law degree in 1941 he returned to Grand Rapids.

After the United States entered World War II, Ford joined the U.S. Navy in April 1942, receiving a commission as an ensign. He served aboard the light aircraft carrier USS *Monterey* in the Pacific fighting against Japan, attaining the rank of lieutenant commander.

CONGRESSMAN AND VICE PRESIDENT

Upon his return to Grand Rapids in 1946, Jerry Ford resumed his law practice. At the age of 35 he won election in 1948 as U.S. representative from Michigan's 5th District.

For the next quarter of a century Ford won 12 more elections to Congress, each time by a large majority. A conservative Republican, Ford followed the party line in Congress.

When Vice President Agnew resigned in October 1973 to avoid being tried on charges of bribery, President Nixon nominated Ford to fill the vacancy. After lengthy hearings, Ford was sworn in as Vice President on Dec. 6, 1973—the first to attain the office under Amendment 25 to the U.S. Constitution.

During his eight months as Vice President, Ford toured the country speaking in 40 states in an effort to preserve confidence in the national government while Congress was holding hearings to consider the possible impeachment of President Nixon in the Watergate scandals.

PRESIDENTIAL ADMINISTRATION

Ford became President following Nixon's resignation on Aug. 9, 1974. Calling on the nation to "bind up the internal wounds of Watergate," he promised "openness and candor."

Ford's popularity took a nose dive when without consulting Congress he pardoned Nixon on Sept. 8, 1974, and eight days later announced a program of conditional amnesty for Vietnam War draft evaders and military deserters.

In the early months of Ford's administration skyrocketing inflation, caused largely by price increases for foreign oil, gripped the economy. Ford attacked inflation as "our domestic public enemy No. 1," urging consumers to buy less.

As consumers slowed their purchases, the automobile industry was hit first by a drop in sales and began closing plants in November and December 1974. The recession deepened in 1975 with unemployment soaring to more than 8.2 million persons or 8.9% of the work force in May—the highest unemployment rate since the Great Depression. To help stimulate the economy, Ford asked Congress early in 1975 to reduce income taxes. At the same time he submitted a $350 billion federal budget, and had a record deficit of more than $66 billion.

Ford asserted his conservative leadership by repeatedly vetoing spending measures passed by the Democratic-controlled Congress. Most of his 66 vetoes were upheld because of disunity in the Democratic Party. However, Congress overrode his veto 12 times—more than for any President since Andrew Johnson.

U.S. prestige in international affairs suffered in the spring of 1975 as South Vietnam and Cambodia surrendered to communist troops. When victorious Cambodian communists seized the U.S.

FORD'S PRESIDENTIAL ADMINISTRATION

Congresses in Session:
93d, 94th

Vice President:
Nelson A. Rockefeller, 1974–77

Secretary of State:
Henry A. Kissinger, 1974–77

Secretary of Defense:
James R. Schlesinger, 1974–75
Donald H. Rumsfeld, 1975–77

Secretary of Commerce:
Frederick B. Dent, 1974–75
Rogers C. B. Morton, 1975–76
Elliot L. Richardson, 1976–77

Secretary of the Treasury:
William E. Simon, 1974–76

Attorney General:
William B. Saxbe, 1974–75
Edward H. Levi, 1975–77

Secretary of the Interior:
Rogers C. B. Morton, 1974–75
Stanley K. Hathaway, 1975
Thomas S. Kleppe, 1975–77

Secretary of Labor:
Peter J. Brennan, 1974–75
John T. Dunlop, 1975–76
William J. Usery Jr., 1976–77

Secretary of Agriculture:
Earl L. Butz, 1974–76
John A. Knebel, 1976–77

Secretary of Health, Education, and Welfare:
Caspar W. Weinberger, 1974–75
F. David Mathews, 1975–77

Secretary of Housing and Urban Development:
James T. Lynn, 1974–75
Carla Anderson Hills, 1975–77

Secretary of Transportation:
Claude S. Brinegar, 1974–75
William T. Coleman Jr., 1975–77

QUICK QUIZ: Where were the Winter Olympics held in 1968? See page 837.

GERALD FORD (continued)

freighter *Mayaguez* in May, President Ford moved quickly to reaffirm American power by sending U.S. Marines to recapture the ship.

Ford continued Nixon's policy of détente with the Soviet Union. He held his first summit meeting with Soviet leader Leonid Brezhnev at Vladivostok on Nov. 23-24, 1974, but achieved no substantive new agreements.

President Ford had further meetings with Brezhnev at Helsinki, Finland, in 1975, where he signed the Helsinki Pact that formally recognized the European border changes imposed by the Soviet Union after World War II and guaranteed human rights for the peoples of Europe.

During Ford's administration, Secretary of State Henry Kissinger used "shuttle diplomacy" involving countless jet airplane flights to cool tense international situations.

Women made two separate attempts to assassinate President Ford in September 1975. On Sept. 5, Secret Service men grabbed a pistol from the hand of Lynette Alice Fromme, 27, as she pointed it at Ford from a crowd in Sacramento, Calif. She was a follower of convicted murderer Charles Manson. On Sept. 22, Sara Jane Moore, 45, a civil-rights activist, fired a pistol at Ford as he left a San Francisco hotel, but an alert bystander deflected her aim. Both women were sentenced to life imprisonment.

At the beginning of the 1976 presidential election campaign, public opinion polls showed the Democratic nominee Jimmy Carter the clear favorite with a 10% popularity lead over Ford. To combat this advantage, Ford challenged Carter to a series of TV debates, the first in history between a President and an opponent for the office.

In the national election in November, Ford lost to Carter in a close vote.

Elizabeth Bloomer (Warren) Ford (1918–), his wife, was a former professional dancer. They were married on Oct. 15, 1948, and had four children: Michael Gerald, John Gardner, Steven Meigs, and Susan Elizabeth. She strongly supported adoption of the women's equal rights amendment to the U.S. Constitution.

JIMMY CARTER

Defeating President Ford in the closely contested 1976 election, Jimmy Carter became the first former governor of a state of the Old Confederacy to be elected President since James Polk in 1844. His achievement was possible because his advancement of civil rights won him the support of Northern liberals and blacks.

39th President
(1977–81)

Because of Carter's weak leadership as President, U.S. prestige declined abroad, while at home the nation slid into an economic recession with high rates of inflation and unemployment. As a result, he was soundly defeated by Ronald Reagan in the election of 1980, becoming the first Democratic President to lose a bid for a second term since 1888.

EARLY LIFE

James Earl Carter Jr. was born on Oct. 1, 1924, in Plains, Ga., the first future President to be born in a hospital. He was the eldest son of James Earl and Lillian Gordy Carter. His father was a struggling farmer and storekeeper. His mother worked as a community nurse. Carter later attributed much of his success to his remarkable mother, who at the age of 68 in 1966 joined the Peace Corps and spent two years helping lepers in India.

After graduation from high school at 16 in 1941, Carter attended Georgia Southwestern College and Georgia Tech before appointment to the U.S. Naval Academy in 1943. Graduating from Annapolis in 1946, he ranked 59th in a class of 820.

As a naval officer Carter spent several years on submarine duty and did postgraduate work in nuclear physics at Union College in Schenectady, N.Y. He helped commission one of the na-tion's earliest atomic submarines.

After his father's death in 1953, Carter resigned from the U.S. Navy to return to his Georgia home. Over the next 10 years he became wealthy as a peanut farmer and wholesaler.

GOVERNOR AND PRESIDENTIAL CANDIDATE

Carter won election to the Georgia senate in 1962, serving two terms until 1966 when he made an unsuccessful bid for the Democratic nomination for governor. Stung by his loss to racial segregationist Lester G. Maddox, Carter campaigned across Georgia for four years, winning election as governor in 1970.

At his inauguration as governor in January 1971, Carter became a national celebrity as the first chief executive of a Southern state to declare: "The time for racial discrimination is over." As governor he promoted civil rights for blacks and reformed the state bureaucracy, cutting state departments and agencies from 300 to 22.

Carter announced his candidacy in December 1974 for the Democratic presidential nomination. His vigorous campaign culminated in a first-ballot win at the party's national convention in New York City in July 1976.

PRESIDENTIAL ADMINISTRATION

The 1976 election campaign was highlighted by three face-to-face TV debates with President Ford, the Republican nominee. Carter's success in the debates contributed to his victory in the November election. Perhaps of even greater importance was voter mistrust of the Republican Party because of the Watergate scandals. Voters also believed Carter would restore integrity to the federal government.

In his inaugural address on Jan. 20, 1977, the soft-spoken Carter pledged his administration to "the affirmation of our nation's continuing moral strength and our belief in an undiminished, ever-expanding American dream."

In his first major act he pardoned about 10,000 draft evaders of the Vietnam War.

To improve relations with Latin America, his

administration negotiated treaties to give up U.S. control of the Panama Canal in 1999, winning Senate ratification in 1978 despite conservative opposition.

Carter achieved his greatest triumph in international relations as a mediator with the leaders of Egypt and Israel, reconciling differences to enable them to sign a peace treaty in 1979. Later in 1979, he signed a new SALT II treaty with the Soviet Union, but failed to obtain Senate ratification.

In the 1976 presidential election campaign Carter had promised to reorganize the federal government to make it more efficient. Congress gave him the power to do so in April 1977. A major accomplishment was the reform of the Civil Service system in 1978 to allow greater latitude in the promotion and discharge of the 2.8 million federal employees. A new Department of Energy was created in 1977 and a separate Department of Education in 1980.

Confronted by a growing energy crisis from the nation's dependence on foreign oil, Carter urged strong measures to reduce the use of oil and gas as fuel. He called for a multibillion-dollar effort to develop new energy sources, financing the program with a tax on windfall profits of the major oil companies. Congress adopted much of his program in 1980.

The soaring price of oil, caused by the international OPEC cartel of oil-exporting nations, weakened the U.S. economy. A huge trade deficit caused the U.S. dollar to fall in value.

Although Carter had promised to balance the federal budget, government deficit spending grew year by year. The nation fell into recession in 1980 with high rates of unemployment and inflation.

When Soviet troops invaded Afghanistan in December 1979 to prop up a puppet communist government, President Carter sought to punish the Soviet Union with economic sanctions and a boycott of the summer Olympic Games held in Moscow.

The nation suffered humiliation in foreign affairs after anti-American Iranian militants captured the U.S. embassy in Teheran on Nov. 4, 1979, holding more than 50 Americans prisoner for more than a year while the Carter administration was unable to free them.

Carter had to fight for the Democratic nomination for a second term, overcoming efforts by Sen. Edward Kennedy (D-Mass.) to oust him.

In the 1980 election campaign he sought to portray his Republican opponent Ronald Reagan as a racist and a warmonger. But in a face-to-face TV debate with Reagan in October, viewers judged the President the loser and voted him out of office in November. He retired to Plains, Ga., to write his memoirs.

Rosalynn Smith Carter (born Aug. 18, 1927) married Carter on July 7, 1946. They had four children: John William in 1947, James Earl III ("Chip") in 1950, D. Jeffrey in 1952, and Amy Lynn in 1967. Mrs. Carter worked tirelessly in Carter's election campaigns and aided him as a trusted adviser in public office.

CARTER'S PRESIDENTIAL ADMINISTRATION

Congresses in Session:
95th, 96th
Vice President:
Walter F. Mondale, 1977–81
Secretary of State:
Cyrus R. Vance, 1977–80
Edmund S. Muskie, 1980–81
Secretary of the Treasury:
W. Michael Blumenthal, 1977–79
G. William Miller, 1979–81
Secretary of Defense:
Harold Brown, 1977–81
Attorney General:
Griffin B. Bell, 1977–79
Benjamin R. Civiletti, 1979–81

Secretary of the Interior:
Cecil D. Andrus, 1977–81
Secretary of Agriculture:
Robert S. Bergland, 1977–81
Secretary of Commerce:
Juanita M. Kreps, 1977–79
Philip Klutznick, 1979–81
Secretary of Labor:
F. Ray Marshall, 1977–81
Secretary of Health, Education, and Welfare:
Joseph A. Califano Jr., 1977–79
Patricia Roberts Harris, 1979

Secretary of Health and Human Services:
Patricia Roberts Harris, 1979–81
Secretary of Housing and Urban Development:
Patricia Roberts Harris, 1977–79
Moon Landrieu, 1979–81
Secretary of Transportation:
Brock Adams, 1977–79
Neil E. Goldschmidt, 1979–81
Secretary of Energy:
James R. Schlesinger, 1977–79
Charles W. Duncan Jr., 1979–81
Secretary of Education:
Shirley M. Hufstedler, 1979–81

PRESIDENTIAL ELECTION OF 1976

Nominations: Democrats met in New York City on July 12–15, 1976. Carter easily won the Democratic presidential nomination on the first ballot with 2,238.5 votes to 769.5 for other candidates. Mondale received the Democratic vice-presidential nomination on the first ballot, 2,817 to 191. Republicans met in Kansas City, Mo., on Aug. 16–19, 1976. Ford narrowly won the Republican presidential nomination on the first ballot, defeating Ronald Reagan, 1,187 to 1,070. Dole was selected as the GOP vice-presidential nominee on the first ballot, 1,921 to 338. **Campaign Issues:** Democrats denounced Ford's pardon of President Nixon and promised programs to end high levels of unemployment, to reduce taxes for low-income families, and to reorganize the federal government bureaucracy. **Remarks:** McCarthy, a liberal Democrat running as an independent, won enough votes in four states (Iowa, Maine, Oklahoma, and Oregon) to throw their 26 electoral votes to Ford. For the first time, an incumbent President debated his challenger face to face.

PRESIDENTIAL CANDIDATES	PARTY	ELECTORAL VOTES	POPULAR VOTE Total	Percentage	VICE-PRESIDENTIAL CANDIDATES
Jimmy Carter	Democratic	297	40,825,839	50.02	Walter F. Mondale
Gerald R. Ford	Republican	240	39,147,770	47.97	Robert Dole
Eugene J. McCarthy	Independent	0	680,390	0.83	
Roger Lea MacBride	Libertarian	0	171,627	0.21	David Bergland
Lester G. Maddox	American I.	0	168,264	0.21	William Dyke
Other candidates	—	1	609,456	0.75	—

QUICK QUIZ: Who was men's skiing World Cup Champion in 1981–83? See page 858.

RONALD REAGAN

A conservative Republican, Ronald Reagan won the White House in an electoral landslide over President Jimmy Carter, promising to lift the country out of economic stagnation and restore the U.S. to world leadership.

40th President
(1981–)

A former movie actor, Reagan was only the 9th President to reach the office by defeating an incumbent Chief Executive. At 69 he was the oldest to be elected to a first term, the first who had been a labor-union leader, and the first who ever had been divorced.

The nation plunged into its worst recession in 1981–82 since the Great Depression. However, in 1983–84 the nation's economy recovered with reduced inflation and a falling rate of unemployment.

At 73 he won a second term in a landslide victory over former Vice President Walter F. Mondale.

EARLY LIFE

Ronald Wilson Reagan was born in Tampico, Ill., on Feb. 6, 1911. He was the second son of Nelle Wilson Reagan and John Edward Reagan. His brother Neil was two years older. The Reagans moved to Dixon, Ill., where the father earned a meager living as a shoe salesman.

The future President, nicknamed "Dutch" by his father, was popular in high school, being elected president of the student body.

Working his way through school by washing dishes, Reagan graduated in 1932 from Eureka (Ill.) College, where he played football, captained the swimming team, and acted in plays. He then was a radio sports announcer in Des Moines, Ia., until 1937.

MOVIE STAR, GOVERNOR, AND PRESIDENT-ELECT

Having always wanted to become a professional actor, he leaped at the offer of a Hollywood movie contract in 1937. In his acting career he appeared in some 50 movies and many TV shows. An active member of the Screen Actors Guild, he headed the labor union in 1947–52 and 1959–60.

He married movie star Jane Wyman on Jan. 25, 1940. They had two children, Maureen (born 1941), and an adopted son Michael (born 1945). They were divorced in 1948.

After winning acclaim for his speeches in support of Barry Goldwater in the 1964 presidential campaign, he turned to a career in politics.

Reagan won election as governor of California in 1966 and reelection in 1970. During his administration in 1967–75 state taxes were reformed, ending deficit spending and rebating $4.7 billion to property-tax payers.

Reagan was an unsuccessful candidate for the Republican presidential nomination in 1968 and 1976. But in 1980 he won in the state primaries and was nominated at the GOP convention. He then triumphed over Carter.

FIRST TERM AS PRESIDENT

At the presidential inauguration on Jan. 20, 1981, Reagan and other dignitaries dressed formally, in contrast to the informality of the ceremony four years earlier when Carter took office. In his inaugural address, Reagan emphasized his plans for a "new beginning" for the national economy.

"These United States are confronted with an economic affliction of great proportions," he said, "Our present troubles parallel and are proportionate to the intervention and intrusion in our lives that result from unnecessary and excessive growth of government.

"It is time to reawaken this industrial giant," he said, "to get government back within its means and to lighten our punitive tax burden."

Within minutes after taking office, President Reagan ordered a freeze on the hiring of civilian employees by all departments and agencies of the federal government.

Although Reagan's election victory over Carter had helped Republicans win control of the U.S. Senate, Democrats still held the majority in the House of Representatives. Thus, faced with a divided Congress, he knew that to get his program enacted he must persuade the public to bring pressure to bear on their representatives.

Less than three weeks after his inauguration, President Reagan addressed the nation on TV on Feb. 5, 1981 declaring that the U.S. was confronted with "the worst economic mess since the Great Depression." He called for the cooperation of Congress to adopt his economic plan.

He unveiled details of his "Program for Economic Recovery" in an address on Feb. 18, 1981, to a joint meeting of Congress. He asked for a $41.4 billion reduction in the budget for 1982 and income tax cuts spread over the next three years. Many of his proposed reductions in government expenses

REAGAN'S PRESIDENTIAL ADMINISTRATION

Congresses in Session:
97th, 98th, 99th
Vice President:
George Bush, 1981–
Secretary of State:
Alexander M. Haig Jr., 1981–82
George P. Shultz, 1982–
Secretary of the Treasury:
Donald T. Regan, 1981–85
James A Baker 3d, 1985–
Secretary of Defense:
Caspar W. Weinberger, 1981–
Attorney General:
William French Smith, 1981–85
Edwin Meese 3d, 1985–

Secretary of the Interior:
James G. Watt, 1981–83
William P. Clark, 1983–85
Donald P. Hodel, 1985–
Secretary of Agriculture:
John R. Block, 1981–
Secretary of Commerce:
Malcolm Baldrige, 1981–
Secretary of Labor:
Raymond J. Donovan, 1981–85
William E. Brock 3d, 1985–
Secretary of Health and Human Services:
Richard S. Schweiker, 1981–83
Margaret M. Heckler, 1983–

Secretary of Housing and Urban Development:
Samuel R. Pierce Jr., 1981–
Secretary of Transportation:
Andrew L. Lewis Jr., 1981–82
Elizabeth Dole, 1983–
Secretary of Energy:
James B. Edwards, 1981–82
Donald P. Hodel, 1982–85
John S. Herrington, 1985–
Secretary of Education:
Terrel H. Bell, 1981–84
William J. Bennett, 1985–

PRESIDENTIAL ELECTION OF 1980

Nominations: Republicans met in Detroit, Mich., on July 14–17. Reagan, who had defeated nine other contenders in state primaries, received the nomination on the first ballot on July 16 with 1,939 of the convention's 1,994 votes. At the last minute Reagan failed to persuade former President Ford to join the ticket as vice-presidential candidate. He then named Bush as his choice of running mate, and the delegates ratified the decision on July 17. The Democratic National Convention met in New York City on Aug. 11–14. Carter had battled Sen. Edward Kennedy (D–Mass.) for the nomination in state primaries, winning a majority of the del-

egates. Although Kennedy formally withdrew as a candidate shortly after the convention opened, the party remained divided. Carter won renomination on the first ballot with 2,123 votes to Kennedy's 1,150.5. Mondale again was chosen as the vice-presidential candidate. **Campaign:** Both candidates stressed their differences in personalities rather than issues. Reagan was judged winner in a TV debate with Carter on Oct. 28, giving him momentum to win an electoral landslide a week later. **Remarks:** Rep. John B. Anderson (R–Ill.) waged a liberal independent campaign for the presidency, winning over 6% of the popular vote.

PRESIDENTIAL CANDIDATES	PARTY	ELECTORAL VOTES	POPULAR VOTE Total	Percentage	VICE-PRESIDENTIAL CANDIDATES
Ronald Reagan	Republican	489	43,904,153	50.75	George Bush
Jimmy Carter	Democratic	49	35,483,883	41.02	Walter Mondale
John B. Anderson	Independent	0	5,719,222	6.61	Patrick Lucey
Ed Clark	Libertarian	0	920,049	1.06	David Koch
Barry Commoner	Citizens	0	232,533	0.27	LaDonna Harris
Other candidates		0	245,329	0.29	—

pared social programs benefiting the poor.

President Reagan narrowly escaped death on March 30, 1981, when he was severely wounded by a would-be assassin, John Hinckley Jr. A jury found Hinckley not guilty by reason of insanity on June 21, 1982, and he was confined to a mental institution.

Over the next several months Reagan demonstrated great skill in persuading reluctant members of Congress to support his program, which came to be termed "Reaganomics." And on Aug. 13, 1981, he signed the economic legislation into law.

However, the United States was hard hit by a worldwide recession in 1981–1982 with unemployment rising to more than 10%—the highest since the Great Depression of the 1930s. The President's economic program was credited with bringing down the rate of inflation from more than 13% in 1981 to about 5% in 1982. But reduced revenues for the federal government and increased spending brought the greatest U.S. budget deficits in history—reaching $195 billion in 1983 and $175 billion in 1984.

A decline in President Reagan's popularity was reflected in losses by Republican congressional and gubernatorial candidates in the 1982 midterm elections. Although the Republicans managed to hang onto their 54–46 majority in the U.S. Senate, they lost 26 seats in the U.S. House of Representatives as the Democrats increased their majority to 269–166. In elections for governors, the GOP had a net loss of 7, giving the Democrats 34 governorships to 16 for the Republicans.

The nation's economy began to turn around in 1983 as consumer spending and industrial production rose, inflation held to a low rate, and unemployment fell.

Marking his first 1,000 days in office in October 1983, the President declared:

"We're witnessing an industrial renaissance, and this is only Act I."

The President pressed forward on the deployment of new nuclear cruise missiles in Western Europe in 1983. In reaction the Soviet Union broke off talks that had been seeking an agreement on reducing the nuclear arms race.

President Reagan used U.S. troops to oust a communist government on the island of Grenada

in 1983 and opposed leftist forces in Central America.

In the Middle East, the Reagan administration tried unsuccessfully to achieve a peaceful solution to problems in the region. Diplomatic efforts were overshadowed in 1983–84 by terrorist bombings in Lebanon that killed 241 U.S. marines and damaged U.S. embassy buildings.

After a hard-fought series of presidential primaries, former Vice President Walter F. Mondale won the Democratic presidential nomination at the party's national convention in San Francisco in July 1984. For the first time a major party placed a woman on its national ticket as the Democrats approved Mondale's choice of Rep. Geraldine Ferraro (D-N.Y.) as his running mate.

President Reagan and Vice President Bush received by acclamation the Republican nomination for a second term at the party's convention in Dallas, Texas, in August 1984. Highlights of the presidential election campaign were two TV debates between Reagan and Mondale and one between Bush and Ferraro.

Mondale attacked Reagan for having cut government spending on social programs while increasing military expenditures. Mondale declared that if elected he would raise taxes to reduce the federal budget deficits and would do more to help the poor and minorities.

The President credited his administration with reviving prosperity and renewing U.S. prestige in international affairs. He promised that the expanding economy would reduce the federal deficit without the need for higher taxes.

In an electoral landslide, 73-year-old President Reagan was reelected to a second term on Nov. 6, 1984. He won a record 525 electoral votes to his opponent's 13, carrying 49 states. Mondale won only the electoral votes of his home state, Minnesota, and of the District of Columbia. Although Republicans retained control of the U.S. Senate, the President's popularity was not enough to win a GOP majority in the House of Representatives.

SECOND TERM AS PRESIDENT

Because Jan. 20, 1985, fell on a Sunday, President

PRESIDENTIAL ELECTION OF 1984

Nominations: The Democrats had a hard-fought presidential primary campaign in the spring of 1984. Eight major candidates sought the Democratic presidential nomination at the beginning of the contest, but by March only three remained in the race: former Vice President Walter F. Mondale, the front runner because of his close ties to leaders of the party and because of his support by labor unions; Sen. Gary Hart (D-Colo.), who represented young Democratic liberals; and Rev. Jesse Jackson, a civil rights leader who became the first black to wage a serious nationwide campaign in an effort to win a major party's nomination for the nation's highest office. In the 29 Democratic primaries in which the voters had a chance to chose among the major candidates, Hart won the highest percentage of the popular vote in 16, Mondale in 11, and Jackson in 2. Before the Democratic National Convention met in San Francisco on July 16–19, 1984, Mondale announced he had accumulated enough delegate votes to win the nomination and that he would choose for his running mate Rep. Geraldine A. Ferraro (D–N.Y.) as the first woman to run on the national ticket of a major political party. Mondale won the Democratic presidential nomination on the first ballot with 2,191 votes, to 1,200.5 for Hart, and 465.5 for Jackson. Ferraro won the vice-presidential nomination by acclamation.

From the time 73-year-old President Reagan had formally announced on Jan. 29, 1984, that he and Vice President Bush would seek second terms, no major Republican made an effort to challenge them. The Republican National Convention was held in Dallas, Tex., on Aug. 20–23, 1984. Reagan won the Republican presidential nomination on the first ballot, receiving 2,233 votes, with two delegates abstaining. The vice-presidential nomination easily went to Bush, who received all but four of the delegates' votes.

Campaign: In his speech accepting the Democratic presidential nomination on July 19, Mondale called his program the "new realism" and declared he would raise taxes to reduce the federal budget deficit—a declaration that many political observers believed seriously hurt his chances to win the election. Mondale charged that President Reagan had a secret plan to raise taxes if reelected. The President denied Mondale's claim, declaring his economic policies would bring increasing prosperity with no need to raise taxes. Highlights of the campaign were two face-to-face TV debates between Reagan and Mondale and one between Bush and Ferraro. Mondale was generally regarded as having won the first presidential debate on Oct. 7 because Reagan appeared tired, confused, and unable to remember statistics that he wished to use. In the ensuing weeks, Democrats questioned whether the President was too old to competently serve a second term.

A relaxed President Reagan put the age issue to rest in the second TV debate on Oct. 27 with a joke about his 56-year-old opponent, saying, "I will not make age an issue of this campaign. I am not going to exploit, for political purposes, my opponent's youth and inexperience."

Remarks: In the election on Nov. 6, 1984, President Regan won election to a second term in a landslide, capturing 58.77% of the popular vote and a record 525 electoral votes of 49 states. Mondale received only the electoral votes of his home state of Minnesota and of the District of Columbia.

PRESIDENTIAL CANDIDATES	PARTY	ELECTORAL VOTES	POPULAR VOTE Total	Percentage	VICE-PRESIDENTIAL CANDIDATES
Ronald Reagan	Republican	525	54,455,074	58.77	George Bush
Walter F. Mondale	Democratic	13	37,577,137	40.56	Geraldine A. Ferraro
David Bergland	Libertarian	0	228,314	00.25	Jim Lewis
Lyndon H. LaRouche Jr.	Independent	0	78,807	00.09	Billy Davis
Sonia Johnson	Citizens	0	72,200	00.08	Richard Walton
Other candidates	—	0	241,261	00.26	—

RONALD REAGAN *(continued)*

Reagan and Vice President Bush took the oath of office for their second term before the Cabinet and a few invited guests in the White House. The brief ceremony was broadcast by TV so the entire nation could look on.

An outdoor inauguration ceremony on the steps of the Capitol and an elaborate parade had been planned for Monday Jan. 21, but a severe cold wave forced both to be cancelled for the first time in the nation's history. Instead, the President and Vice President were sworn in for the second time at an indoor televised ceremony in the rotunda of the Capitol.

In his Inaugural Address, President Reagan reviewed the accomplishments of his first term and previewed what he hoped to achieve during his second term. See page 9.

On the President's 74th birthday, Feb. 6, the entire Congress joined in singing "Happy Birthday" before he delivered his 4th State of the Union address. See page 11.

The first year of the President's second term saw some improvement in relations with the Soviet Union. Kremlin leaders resumed negotiations with the United States in an effort to reach agreement on a new treaty to limit nuclear arms. Mikhail S. Gorbachev became the new leader of the Soviet Union after the death of Soviet President Konstantin U. Chernenko on March 10, 1985. In July Gorbachev and President Reagan agreed to a summit meeting in November 1985 in Geneva, Switzerland—the first such discussion with a Soviet leader during Reagan's presidency. See page 13.

President Reagan launched a major campaign in May 1985 to get Congress to reform the federal income tax code to make it fairer and simpler (see pages 17, 913).

A crisis reminiscent of the Iranian hostage affair during President Carter's administration developed in June when Muslim terrorists hijacked a TWA airliner and held 39 Americans hostage for 17 days. See page 19.

The President underwent major surgery in July for removal of a cancer in his large intestine, but quickly resumed his duties. He revealed in August that he also had a minor operation to remove a patch of skin cancer from his nose. See page 21.

President Reagan won acclaim in Oct. 1985 when he used military force to capture 4 Palestinian terrorists who had hijacked a Mediterranean cruise ship and killed an American tourist. See page 26.

Nancy Davis Reagan (born July 6, 1923), a movie actress, became Reagan's second wife on March 4, 1952. They had two children: Patricia (born 1953) and Ronald Prescott (born 1958). First Lady Nancy Reagan supervised extensive redecoration of the White House and devoted efforts to fighting drug abuse.

PRESIDENTIAL ELECTION RESULTS: 1984 vs. 1980

Official returns for the 1984 presidential election showed that over 92.6 million Americans went to the polls, the largest number in history.

President Reagan won about 58.8% of the popular vote in the 1984 election compared to 50.8% in 1980.

In losing the elections in 1984 and 1980, Walter Mondale and Jimmy Carter each received about 41% of the vote.

Third party candidates won about 8% of the vote in 1980 and less than 1% in 1984.

States	1984 PRESIDENTIAL ELECTION POPULAR VOTE		1984 PRESIDENTIAL ELECTION ELECTORAL VOTE		1980 PRESIDENTIAL ELECTION POPULAR VOTE		1980 PRESIDENTIAL ELECTION ELECTORAL VOTE	
	Reagan	Mondale	Reagan	Mondale	Reagan	Carter	Reagan	Carter
Alabama	872,849	551,899	9	—	654,192	636,730	9	—
Alaska	138,377	62,007	3	—	86,112	41,842	3	—
Arizona	681,416	333,584	7	—	529,688	246,843	6	—
Arkansas	534,774	338,646	6	—	403,164	398,041	6	—
California	5,467,009	3,922,519	47	—	4,524,858	3,083,661	45	—
Colorado	821,817	454,975	8	—	652,264	367,973	7	—
Connecticut	890,877	569,597	8	—	677,210	541,732	8	—
Delaware	152,190	101,656	3	—	111,252	105,754	3	—
Dist. of Col.	29,009	180,408	—	3	23,545	131,113	—	3
Florida	2,730,350	1,448,816	21	—	2,046,951	1,419,475	17	—
Georgia	1,068,722	706,628	12	—	654,168	890,733	—	12
Hawaii	185,050	147,154	4	—	130,112	135,879	—	4
Idaho	297,523	108,510	4	—	290,699	110,192	4	—
Illinois	2,707,103	2,086,499	24	—	2,358,049	1,981,413	26	—
Indiana	1,377,230	841,481	12	—	1,255,656	844,197	13	—
Iowa	703,088	605,620	8	—	676,026	508,672	8	—
Kansas	677,296	333,149	7	—	566,812	326,150	7	—
Kentucky	821,702	539,539	9	—	635,274	616,417	9	—
Louisiana	1,037,299	651,586	10	—	792,853	708,453	10	—
Maine	336,500	214,515	4	—	238,522	220,974	4	—
Maryland	879,918	787,935	10	—	680,606	726,161	—	10
Massachusetts	1,310,936	1,239,606	13	—	1,057,631	1,053,802	14	—
Michigan	2,251,571	1,529,638	20	—	1,915,225	1,661,532	21	—
Minnesota	1,032,603	1,036,364	—	10	873,268	954,174	—	10
Mississippi	582,377	352,192	7	—	441,089	429,281	7	—
Missouri	1,274,188	848,583	11	—	1,074,181	931,182	12	—
Montana	232,450	146,742	4	—	206,814	118,032	4	—
Nebraska	460,054	187,866	5	—	419,937	166,851	5	—
Nevada	188,770	91,655	4	—	155,017	66,666	3	—
New Hampshire	267,050	120,347	4	—	221,705	108,864	4	—
New Jersey	1,933,630	1,261,323	16	—	1,546,557	1,147,364	17	—
New Mexico	307,101	201,769	5	—	250,779	167,826	4	—
New York	3,664,763	3,119,609	36	—	2,893,831	2,728,372	41	—
North Carolina	1,346,481	824,287	13	—	915,018	875,635	13	—
North Dakota	200,336	104,429	3	—	193,695	79,189	3	—
Ohio	2,678,560	1,825,440	23	—	2,206,545	1,752,414	25	—
Oklahoma	861,530	365,080	8	—	695,570	402,026	8	—
Oregon	685,700	536,479	7	—	571,044	456,890	6	—
Pennsylvania	2,584,323	2,228,131	25	—	2,261,872	1,937,540	27	—
Rhode Island	212,080	197,106	4	—	154,793	198,342	—	4
South Carolina	615,539	344,459	8	—	441,841	430,385	8	—
South Dakota	200,267	116,113	3	—	198,343	103,855	4	—
Tennessee	990,212	711,714	11	—	787,761	783,051	10	—
Texas	3,433,428	1,949,276	29	—	2,510,705	1,881,147	26	—
Utah	469,105	155,369	5	—	439,687	124,266	4	—
Vermont	135,865	95,730	3	—	94,628	81,952	3	—
Virginia	1,337,078	796,250	12	—	989,609	752,174	12	—
Washington	1,051,670	807,352	10	—	865,244	650,193	9	—
West Virginia	405,483	328,125	6	—	334,206	367,462	—	6
Wisconsin	1,198,584	995,740	11	—	1,088,845	981,584	11	—
Wyoming	133,241	53,370	3	—	110,700	49,427	3	—
TOTALS	54,455,074	37,577,137	525	13	43,904,153	35,483,883	489	49

ELECTORAL VOTE BY STATES FOR PRESIDENT: 1936–1984

	1936	1940	1944	1948	1952	1956	1960	1964	1968	1972	1976	1980	1984
Democratic ...	523	449	432	303	89	73	303	486	191	17	297	49	13
Republican....	8	82	99	189	442	457	219	52	301	520	240	489	525
Other[1]	—	—	—	39	—	1	15	—	46	1	1	—	—
Alabama	D–11	D–11	D–11	O–11	D–11	D–10	D–5	R–10	O–10	R–9	D–9	R–9	R–9
Alaska	—	—	—	—	—	—	R–3	D–3	R–3	R–3	R–3	R–3	R–3
Arizona	D–3	D–3	D–4	D–4	R–4	R–4	R–4	R–5	R–5	R–6	R–6	R–6	R–7
Arkansas........	D–9	D–9	D–9	D–9	D–8	D–8	D–8	D–6	O–6	R–6	R–6	R–6	R–6
California	D–22	D–22	D–25	D–25	R–32	R–32	R–32	D–40	R–40	R–45	R–45	R–45	R–47
Colorado	D–6	R–6	R–6	D–6	R–6	R–6	R–6	D–6	R–6	R–7	R–7	R–7	R–8
Connecticut	D–8	D–8	D–8	R–8	R–8	R–8	D–8	D–8	D–8	R–8	R–8	R–8	R–8
Delaware	D–3	D–3	D–3	R–3	R–3	R–3	D–3	D–3	R–3	R–3	R–3	R–3	R–3
Dist. of Col......								D–3	D–3	D–3	D–3	D–3	D–3
Florida	D–7	D–7	D–8	D–8	R–10	R–10	R–10	D–14	R–14	R–17	R–17	R–17	R–21
Georgia	D–12	D–12	D–12	D–12	D–12	D–12	D–12	R–12	O–12	R–12	D–12	D–12	R–12
Hawaii	—	—	—	—	—	—	D–3	D–4	D–4	R–4	D–4	D–4	R–4
Idaho	D–4	D–4	D–4	D–4	R–4	R–4	R–4	D–4	R–4	R–4	R–4	R–4	R–4
Illinois	D–29	D–29	D–28	D–28	R–27	R–27	D–27	D–26	R–26	R–26	R–26	R–26	R–24
Indiana	D–14	R–14	R–13	R–13	R–13	R–13	R–13	D–13	R–13	R–13	R–13	R–13	R–12
Iowa	D–11	R–11	R–10	D–10	R–10	R–10	R–10	D–9	R–9	R–8	R–8	R–8	R–8
Kansas	D–9	R–9	R–8	R–8	R–8	R–8	R–8	D–7	R–7	R–7	R–7	R–7	R–7
Kentucky........	D–11	D–11	D–11	D–11	D–10	R–10	R–10	D–9	R–9	R–9	D–9	R–9	R–9
Louisiana	D–10	D–10	D–10	O–10	D–10	D–10	D–10	R–10	O–10	R–10	D–10	R–10	R–10
Maine...........	R–5	R–5	R–5	R–5	R–5	R–5	R–5	D–4	D–4	R–4	R–4	R–4	R–4
Maryland........	D–8	D–8	D–8	R–8	R–9	R–9	D–9	D–10	D–10	R–10	D–10	D–10	R–10
Massachusetts...	D–17	D–17	D–16	D–16	R–16	R–16	D–16	D–14	D–14	D–14	D–14	D–14	R–13
Michigan........	D–19	R–19	D–19	R–19	R–20	R–20	D–20	D–21	D–21	R–21	R–21	R–21	R–20
Minnesota.......	D–11	D–11	D–11	D–11	R–11	R–11	D–11	D–10	D–10	D–10	D–10	D–10	D–10
Mississippi	D–9	D–9	D–9	O–9	D–8	D–8	O–8	R–7	O–7	R–7	D–7	R–7	R–7
Missouri	D–15	D–15	D–15	D–15	R–13	R–13	D–13	D–12	R–12	R–12	D–12	R–12	R–11
Montana	D–4	D–4	D–4	D–4	R–4	R–4	R–4	D–4	R–4	R–4	R–4	R–4	R–4
Nebraska	D–7	R–7	R–6	R–6	R–6	R–6	R–6	D–5	R–5	R–5	R–5	R–5	R–5
Nevada	D–3	D–3	D–3	D–3	R–3	R–3	D–3	D–3	R–3	R–3	R–3	R–3	R–4
New Hampshire ..	D–4	D–4	D–4	R–4	R–4	R–4	R–4	D–4	R–4	R–4	R–4	R–4	R–4
New Jersey	D–16	D–16	D–16	R–16	R–16	R–16	D–16	D–17	R–17	R–17	R–17	R–17	R–16
New Mexico	D–3	D–3	D–4	D–4	R–4	R–4	D–4	D–4	R–4	R–4	R–4	R–4	R–5
New York	D–47	D–47	D–47	R–47	R–45	R–45	D–45	D–43	D–43	R–41	D–41	R–41	R–36
North Carolina ...	D–13	D–13	D–14	D–14	D–14	D–14	D–14	D–13	D–12	R–13	R–13	R–13	R–13
North Dakota	D–4	R–4	R–4	R–4	R–4	R–4	R–4	D–4	R–4	R–3	R–3	R–3	R–3
Ohio............	D–26	D–26	D–25	D–25	R–25	R–25	R–25	D–26	R–26	R–25	D–25	R–25	R–23
Oklahoma........	D–11	D–11	D–10	D–10	R–8	R–8	R–7	D–8	R–8	R–8	R–8	R–8	R–8
Oregon	D–5	D–5	D–6	R–6	R–6	R–6	R–6	D–6	R–6	R–6	R–6	R–6	R–7
Pennsylvania	D–36	D–36	D–35	R–35	R–32	R–32	D–32	D–29	D–29	R–27	D–27	R–27	R–25
Rhode Island	D–4	D–4	D–4	D–4	R–4	R–4	D–4	D–4	D–4	D–4	D–4	D–4	R–4
South Carolina ...	D–8	D–8	D–8	O–8	D–8	D–8	D–8	R–8	R–8	R–8	R–8	R–8	R–8
South Dakota ...	D–4	R–4	R–4	R–4	R–4	R–4	R–4	D–4	R–4	R–4	R–4	R–4	R–3
Tennessee	D–11	D–11	D–12	D–11	R–11	R–11	R–11	D–11	R–11	R–10	D–10	R–10	R–11
Texas...........	D–23	D–23	D–23	D–23	R–24	R–24	D–24	D–25	D–25	R–26	D–26	R–26	R–29
Utah...........	D–4	D–4	D–4	D–4	R–4	R–4	R–4	D–4	R–4	R–4	R–4	R–4	R–5
Vermont	R–3	R–3	R–3	R–3	R–3	R–3	R–3	D–3	R–3	R–3	R–3	R–3	R–3
Virginia	D–11	D–11	D–11	D–11	R–12	R–12	R–12	D–12	R–12	R–11	R–12	R–12	R–12
Washington	D–8	D–8	D–8	D–8	R–9	R–9	R–9	D–9	R–9	R–9	R–9	R–9	R–10
West Virginia	D–8	D–8	D–8	D–8	D–8	R–8	D–8	D–7	D–7	R–6	D–6	D–6	R–6
Wisconsin	D–12	D–12	R–12	D–12	R–12	R–12	R–12	D–12	R–12	R–11	R–11	R–11	R–11
Wyoming........	D–3	D–3	R–3	R–3	R–3	R–3	R–3	D–3	R–3	R–3	R–3	R–3	R–3

D=Democratic; R=Republican; O=Other[1].

1936: Roosevelt (D), Landon (R); **1940:** Roosevelt (D), Willkie (R); **1944:** Roosevelt (D), Dewey (R); **1948:** Truman (D), Dewey (R); **1952:** Eisenhower (R); Stevenson (D); **1956:** Eisenhower (R), Stevenson (D); **1960:** Kennedy (D), Nixon (R); **1964:** Johnson (D), Goldwater (R); **1968:** Nixon (R), Humphrey (D); **1972:** Nixon (R), McGovern (D); **1976:** Carter (D), Ford (R); **1980:** Reagan (R), Carter (D); **1984:** Reagan (R), Mondale (D).

[1] In **1948:** 39 electoral votes cast for States' Rights Democratic candidates: Ala. 11; La. 10; Miss. 9; S.C. 8; Tenn. 1. In **1956:** 1 electoral vote cast for Walter B. Jones. In **1960:** 15 electoral votes cast for Harry F. Byrd: Ala. 6; Miss. 8; Okla. 1. In **1968:** 46 electoral votes cast for George C. Wallace: Ala. 10; Ark. 6; Ga. 12; La. 10; Miss. 7; N.C. 1. In **1972:** 1 Virginia electoral vote cast for John Hospers. In **1976:** 1 Washington electoral vote cast for Ronald Reagan.

ELECTING OR REPLACING A PRESIDENT

PRIMARY ELECTIONS

The first step in choosing a President comes in state primary elections or party caucuses in which voters choose delegates to attend a national political party convention. The candidates for delegate may or may not be bound to vote for a certain presidential candidate.

Many states hold *presidential preference primaries* in which voters can choose between several hopeful presidential candidates who are listed on the ballot.

PRESIDENTIAL NOMINATING CONVENTIONS

Since the 1830s the major political parties have held presidential nominating conventions. For many years the delegates were chosen by party leaders, and so the selection of presidential candidates was largely controlled by political bosses. Today most delegates are chosen in state primary elections. By winning a majority of state primaries, a presidential hopeful can be assured of selection as the party's presidential candidate by the national convention.

THE ELECTORAL COLLEGE

When you vote in a November presidential election, you vote for a slate of electors who in turn vote in December in the Electoral College for the candidate of your choice.

If no candidate for President wins a majority of the 538 electors' votes, the House of Representatives decides (with each state having one vote) who shall be President from among the three candidates having the largest number of votes in the Electoral College. But if the House fails to choose a President by January 20, the Vice President-elect acts as President until the House selects a President. (Two Presidents were chosen by the House of Representatives: Thomas Jefferson and John Quincy Adams.)

If no candidate for Vice President wins a majority of the electors' votes, the Senate decides between the two candidates who received the largest number of votes in the electoral college. (One Vice President was chosen by the Senate: Richard M. Johnson.)

IF A NOMINEE OR PRESIDENT-ELECT DIES

If a presidential or vice-presidential nominee dies between the adjournment of the nominating convention that chose him and Election Day: Democratic Party rules provide that their national committee can fill the vacancy, with each state or territory's delegation eligible to cast the same number of votes it had at that year's nominating convention. Republican national conventions have always authorized their national committee to do the same.

If a President-elect or a Vice President-elect dies between Election Day and the mid-December Electoral College meeting: In theory, the electors are free to vote for anyone they please. But national party rules for filing vacancies still would be in effect, and each elector probably would respect his national committee's decision. But in a close contest, just a few defecting electors could change the outcome.

If a President-elect or a Vice President-elect dies between the electors' meeting and January 6, when Congress counts the vote: Most constitutional experts believe that the 12th Amendment compels Congress to count all electoral votes cast if the person voted for was alive when the electors cast their ballots. Section 3 of the 20th Amendment would then become applicable: "If, at the time fixed for the beginning of the term of the President, the President-elect shall have died, the Vice-President-elect shall become President."

Upon becoming President, he then would be authorized under the 25th Amendment to nominate a new Vice President (who must be confirmed by Congress). Similarly, if the Vice President-elect should die, he would still be declared the winner, and the new President would be able to nominate his replacement.

If a President-elect or a Vice President-elect dies between the vote count in Congress Inauguration Day: If a President-elect dies, the same 20th Amendment provisions would elevate the Vice President-elect to the presidency. Should a Vice President-elect die, the 25th Amendment authorizes the new President to name a Vice President, subject to congressional approval.

If neither a President-elect nor a Vice President-elect is qualified on Inauguration Day: The order of succession follows the sequence that is listed in the next paragraph.

IF A PRESIDENT DIES, RESIGNS, OR IS REMOVED

When a President dies, resigns, or is removed from office, the Vice President becomes President. If the office of Vice President is vacant, the order of succession is Speaker of the House, President pro tempore of the Senate, and then the members of the cabinet in this order: State; Treasury; Defense; Justice; Interior; Agriculture; Commerce; Labor; Health and Human Services; Housing and Urban Development; Transportation; Energy; and Education.

IF A PRESIDENT CANNOT PERFORM HIS DUTIES

When the President cannot exercise the powers and duties of his office for any reason, such as physical or mental illness, the Vice President can become Acting President in one of three ways:

1. The President himself may notify in writing the President pro tempore of the Senate and the Speaker of the House of his incapacity.

2. The Vice President and a majority of the principal officers of the executive departments can notify in writing the heads of both houses of Congress of the President's incapacity.

3. If the President declares in writing that no inability exists, but the Vice President and a majority of the executive department heads disagree, Congress decides the issue. The President continues or resumes the powers of office unless within 21 days (23 days if Congress is not in session at the time of notification) two-thirds of both houses of Congress vote that the President is unable to discharge his duties.

U.S. VICE PRESIDENTS

The Vice President of the United States holds the second most important office in the executive branch of the U.S. government. The Vice President automatically becomes Chief Executive if the President dies, resigns, or is removed from office. If the President cannot perform his duties because of illness or some other reason, the Vice President becomes *acting President* until the President can resume his office.

The only official duty that the U.S. Constitution provides for the Vice President is that of being president of the U.S. Senate. As such he presides over Senate sessions and can vote only to break a tie. The President may assign other responsibilities to the Vice President.

The Vice President receives an annual salary of about $91,000, an expense allowance of $10,000, and about $400,000 for administrative and clerical help. The Vice President and his family also are provided with an official residence in Washington, D.C., called Admiral's House.

Thirteen of the 43 Vice Presidents became President—eight because of the death of a President, one because of the resignation of a President, and four by being elected President in their own right. Seven died in office.

NAME AND POLITICAL PARTY	YEARS IN OFFICE AND AGE AT INAUGURATION	SERVED UNDER PRESIDENT	BIRTHPLACE AND DATE	DEATH DATE	HIGHLIGHTS OF CAREER
1. John Adams [1] (Federalist)	1789–1797 (53)	Washington	Braintree, Mass. Oct. 30, 1735	July 4, 1826	Delegate to Continental Congress 1774–77; Commissioner to France 1778–79; wrote Massachusetts constitution 1779; diplomat in Europe 1780–88; 2d President 1797–1801
2. Thomas Jefferson [1] (Democratic-Republican)	1797–1801 (53)	J. Adams	Albemarle County, Va. April 13, 1743	July 4, 1826	Delegate to Continental Congress 1775–76; wrote Declaration of Independence 1776; Governor of Virginia 1779–81; delegate to Congress 1783–84; Secretary of State 1789–93; 3d President 1801–09
3. Aaron Burr (Democratic-Republican)	1801–1805 (45)	Jefferson	Newark, N.J. Feb. 6, 1756	Sept. 14, 1836	Attorney general N.Y. 1789–90; U.S. Senator 1791–97; killed Alexander Hamilton in duel 1804; organized expedition against Spanish colonies and Mexico; indicted for treason but acquitted 1807
4. George Clinton [2] (Democratic-Republican)	1805–1812 (65)	Jefferson and Madison	Little Britain, N.Y. July 26, 1739	April 20, 1812	Delegate to Continental Congress 1775–76; brig. general of militia 1776–77; Governor of New York 1777–95, 1801–04
5. Elbridge Gerry [2] (Democratic-Republican)	1813–1814 (68)	Madison	Marblehead, Mass. July 17, 1744	Nov. 23, 1814	Delegate to Congress 1776–85; delegate to Constitutional convention 1787; U.S. Representative (R-Mass.) 1789–93; Governor of Massachusetts 1810–12
6. Daniel D. Tompkins (Democratic-Republican)	1817–1825 (42)	Monroe	Scarsdale, N.Y. June 21, 1774	June 11, 1825	N.Y. State Supreme Court 1804–07; Governor of N.Y. 1807–17; put through state law ending slavery in New York
7. John C. Calhoun [3] (Democratic)	1825–1832 (42)	J. Q. Adams and Jackson	Abbeville District, S.C. March 18, 1782	March 31, 1850	First Vice President to resign; U.S. Rep. (D-S.C.) 1811–17; Secretary of War 1817–25; U.S. Senator (D-S.C.) 1832–43, 1845–50; Secretary of State 1844–45
8. Martin Van Buren [1] (Democratic)	1833–1837 (50)	Jackson	Kinderhook, N.Y. Dec. 5, 1782	July 24, 1862	U.S. Senator (D-N.Y.) 1821–28; Governor of New York 1829; Secretary of State 1829–31; minister to Britain 1831–32; 8th President 1837–41
9. Richard M. Johnson (Democratic)	1837–1841 (56)	Van Buren	Beargrass, Ky. Oct. 17, 1780	Nov. 19, 1850	Only Vice President ever elected by U.S. Senate; U.S. Rep. (D-Ky.) 1807–19, 1829–37; U.S. Senator (D-Ky.) 1819–29
10. John Tyler [4] (Whig)	1841 (50)	W. H. Harrison	Charles City Co., Va. March 29, 1790	Jan. 18, 1862	U.S. Rep. (D-R-Va.) 1816–21; Governor of Virginia 1825–27; U.S. Senator (D-Va.) 1827–36; 10th President 1841–45
11. George M. Dallas (Democratic)	1845–1849 (52)	Polk	Philadelphia, Pa. July 10, 1792	Dec. 31, 1864	Mayor of Philadelphia 1829; U.S. Senator (D-Pa.) 1831–33; minister to Russia 1837–39; minister to Britain 1856–61
12. Millard Fillmore [4] (Whig)	1849–1850 (49)	Taylor	Locke, N.Y. Jan. 7, 1800	March 8, 1874	U.S. Rep. (W-N.Y.) 1833–35, 1837–43; 13th President 1850–53

[1] Elected President. [2] Died in office. [3] Resigned as Vice President. [4] Succeeded to presidency on death of President.

U.S. VICE PRESIDENTS (continued)

NAME AND POLITICAL PARTY	YEARS IN OFFICE AND AGE AT INAUGURATION	SERVED UNDER PRESIDENT	BIRTHPLACE AND DATE	DEATH DATE	HIGHLIGHTS OF CAREER
13. William R. King [2] (Democratic)	1853 (66)	Pierce	Sampson County, N.C. April 7, 1786	April 18, 1853	U.S. Rep. (D-R.N.C.) 1811–16; U.S. Senator (D-Ala.) 1819–44, 1848–52; minister to France 1844–46; took vice-presidential oath in Havana, Cuba; died only a month later
14. John C. Breckinridge (Democratic)	1857–1861 (36)	Buchanan	Lexington, Ky. Jan. 15, 1821	May 17, 1875	Youngest Vice President; U.S. Rep. (D-Ky.) 1851–55; U.S. Senator (D-Ky.) 1861; Confederate general 1861–64; Confederate secretary of war 1865
15. Hannibal Hamlin (Republican)	1861–1865 (51)	Lincoln	Paris Hill, Me. Aug. 27, 1809	July 4, 1891	U.S. Rep. (D-Me.) 1843–47; U.S. Senator (D-Me.) 1848–57; Governor of Maine 1857; U.S. Senator (R-Me.) 1857–61, 1869–81; minister to Spain 1881–82
16. Andrew Johnson [4] (Democratic)	1865 (56)	Lincoln	Raleigh, N.C. Dec. 29, 1808	July 31, 1875	U.S. Rep. (D-Tenn.) 1843–53; Governor of Tennessee 1853–57, 1862–64; U.S. Senator (D-Tenn.) 1857–62, 1874–75; 17th President 1865–69
17. Schuyler Colfax (Republican)	1869–1873 (45)	Grant	New York, N.Y. March 23, 1823	Jan. 13, 1885	U.S. Rep. (R-Ind.) 1855–69; Speaker of House 1863–69
18. Henry Wilson [2] (Republican)	1873–1875 (61)	Grant	Farmington, N.H. Feb. 16, 1812	Nov. 22, 1875	Born Jeremiah Jones Colbaith; U.S. Senator (Free Soil-Mass.) 1855–73
19. William Wheeler (Republican)	1877–1881 (57)	Hayes	Malone, N.Y. June 30, 1819	June 4, 1887	U.S. Rep. (R-N.Y.) 1861–63, 1869–77
20. Chester Arthur [4] (Republican)	1881 (51)	Garfield	Fairfield, Vt. Oct. 5, 1829	Nov. 18, 1886	Collector, Port of New York 1871–79; 21st President 1881–85
21. Thomas A. Hendricks [2] (Democratic)	1885 (65)	Cleveland	Zanesville, Ohio Sept. 7, 1819	Nov. 25, 1885	U.S. Rep. (D-Ind.) 1851–55; U.S. Senator (D-Ind.) 1863–69; Governor of Indiana 1872
22. Levi P. Morton (Republican)	1889–1893 (64)	Harrison	Shoreham, Vt. May 16, 1824	May 16, 1920	Wall Street banker; U.S. Rep. (R-N.Y.) 1879–81; minister to France 1881–85; Governor of New York 1889–93
23. Adlai E. Stevenson (Democratic)	1893–1897 (57)	Cleveland	Christian County, Ky. Oct. 23, 1835	June 14, 1914	U.S. Rep. (D-Ill.) 1875–77, 1879–81; Assistant Postmaster General 1885–89
24. Garret A. Hobart [2]	1897–1899 (52)	McKinley	Long Branch, N.J. June 3, 1844	Nov. 21, 1899	Member New Jersey legislature 1872–81; member Republican National Committee 1884–96
25. Theodore Roosevelt [4] (Republican)	1901 (42)	McKinley	New York, N.Y. Oct. 27, 1858	Jan. 6, 1919	Police Commissioner, New York City 1895–97; Assistant Secretary of Navy 1897–98; colonel in Spanish–American War 1898; Governor of New York 1899–1900
26. Charles W. Fairbanks (Republican)	1905–1909 (52)	T. Roosevelt	Unionville Center, Ohio May 11, 1852	June 4, 1918	U.S. Senator (R-Ind.) 1897–1905
27. James Sherman [2] (Republican)	1909–1912 (53)	Taft	Utica, N.Y. Oct. 24, 1855	Oct. 30, 1912	Mayor of Utica, N.Y., 1884; U.S. Rep. (R-N.Y.) 1887–91, 1893–1909
28. Thomas R. Marshall (Democratic)	1913–1921 (58)	Wilson	North Manchester, Ind. March 14, 1854	June 1, 1925	Governor of Indiana 1909–13
29. Calvin Coolidge [4] (Republican)	1921–1923 (48)	Harding	Plymouth, Vt. July 4, 1872	Jan. 5, 1933	Massachusetts lieutenant governor 1916–18; Governor of Massachusetts 1919–20; 30th President 1923–29
30. Charles G. Dawes (Republican)	1925–1929 (59)	Coolidge	Marietta, Ohio Aug. 27, 1865	April 23, 1951	U.S. Comptroller of Currency 1898–1901; director Bureau of the Budget 1921–24; won Nobel Peace Prize in 1925 for German reparations plan; ambassador to Britain 1929–32; Chicago banker 1932–51
31. Charles Curtis (Republican)	1929–1933 (69)	Hoover	N. Topeka, Kan. Jan. 25, 1860	Feb. 8, 1936	U.S. Rep. (R-Kan.) 1893–1907; U.S. Senator (R-Kan.) 1907–13, 1915–29; majority leader U.S. Senate 1924–29
32. John N. Garner (Democratic)	1933–1941 (64)	F. Roosevelt	Red River Co., Tex. Nov. 22, 1868	Nov. 7, 1967	U.S. Rep. (D-Tex.) 1903–33; Speaker of House 1931–33
33. Henry A. Wallace (Democratic)	1941–1945 (52)	F. Roosevelt	Adair County, Iowa Oct. 7, 1888	Nov. 18, 1965	Secretary of Agriculture 1933–40; Secretary of Commerce 1945–46

[1] Elected President. [2] Died in office. [3] Resigned as Vice President. [4] Succeeded to presidency on death of President.

U.S. VICE PRESIDENTS (continued)

NAME AND POLITICAL PARTY	YEARS IN OFFICE AND AGE AT INAUGURATION	SERVED UNDER PRESIDENT	BIRTHPLACE AND DATE	DEATH DATE	HIGHLIGHTS OF CAREER
34. Harry S. Truman [4] (Democratic)	1945 (60)	F.D. Roosevelt	Lamar, Mo. May 8, 1884	Dec. 26, 1972	U.S. Senator (D-Mo.) 1935–45; 33d President 1945–53
35. Alben W. Barkley (Democratic)	1949–1953 (71)	Truman	Lowes, Graves County, Ky. Nov. 24, 1877	April 30, 1956	U.S. Rep. (D-Ky.) 1913–27; U.S. Senator (D-Ky.) 1927–49, 1955–56; majority leader U.S. Senate 1937–47
36. Richard M. Nixon [1] (Republican)	1953–1961 (40)	Eisenhower	Yorba Linda, Cal. Jan. 9, 1913	—	U.S. Rep. (R-Calif.) 1947–50; U.S. Senator (R-Calif.) 1950–53; 37th President 1969–74
37. Lyndon B. Johnson [4] (Democratic)	1961–1963 (52)	Kennedy	Stonewall, Tex. Aug. 27, 1908	Jan. 22, 1973	U.S. Rep. (D-Tex.) 1937–48; U.S. Senator (D-Tex.) 1949–60; majority leader U.S. Senate 1955–60; 36th President 1963–69
38. Hubert H. Humphrey Jr. (Democratic)	1965–1969 (53)	L.B. Johnson	Wallace, S.D. May 27, 1911	Jan. 13, 1978	Mayor of Minneapolis 1945–48; U.S. Senator 1949–65, 1971–78; proposed first medical care for aged bill; helped pass civil rights bills
39. Spiro T. Agnew [3] (Republican)	1969–1973 (50)	Nixon	Baltimore, Md. Nov. 9, 1918	—	Governor of Maryland 1967–69; forced to resign as Vice President and convicted of income tax evasion 1973
40. Gerald R. Ford [4] (Republican)	1973–1974 (60)	Nixon	Omaha, Neb. July 14, 1913	—	U.S. Rep. (R-Mich.) 1949–73; minority leader U.S. House 1965–73; 38th President 1974–77
41. Nelson Rockefeller [5] (Republican)	1974–1977 (66)	Ford	Bar Harbor, Me. July 8, 1908	Jan. 26, 1979	Assistant Secretary of State 1944–45; Under Secretary Health, Education, and Welfare 1953–54; Governor N.Y. 1958–73
42. Walter F. Mondale (Democratic)	1977–1981 (49)	Carter	Ceylon, Minn. Jan. 5, 1928	—	Attorney general of Minnesota 1960–64; U.S. Senator (D-Minn.) 1964–77
43. George Bush (Republican)	1981– (56)	Reagan	Milton, Mass. June 12, 1924	—	U.S. Rep. (R-Tex.) 1967–71; ambassador to UN 1971–72; director CIA 1976–77

PRESIDENTS ELECTED WITH MINORITY OF POPULAR VOTE

ELECTION	PRESIDENT	PARTY	POPULAR VOTE	ELECTION	PRESIDENT	PARTY	POPULAR VOTE
1824	John Quincy Adams ...	Independent	30.60%	1888	Benjamin Harrison	Republican	47.90%
1844	James K. Polk	Democrat	49.56%	1892	Grover Cleveland	Democrat	46.04%
1848	Zachary Taylor	Whig	47.31%	1912	Woodrow Wilson	Democrat	41.85%
1856	James Buchanan	Democrat	45.30%	1916	Woodrow Wilson	Democrat	49.40%
1860	Abraham Lincoln	Republican	39.79%	1948	Harry S. Truman	Democrat	49.51%
1876	Rutherford B. Hayes ..	Republican	47.94%	1960	John F. Kennedy	Democrat	49.50%
1880	James A. Garfield	Republican	48.50%	1968	Richard M. Nixon	Republican	43.40%
1884	Grover Cleveland	Democrat	48.50%				

UNCOMPLETED TERMS OF PRESIDENTS

PRESIDENT	UNCOMPLETED TERM	SUCCESSOR
William H. Harrison [2]	March 4, 1841–April 4, 1841	John Tyler
Zachary Taylor [2]	March 5, 1849–July 9, 1850	Millard Fillmore
Abraham Lincoln [6]	March 4, 1865–April 15, 1865 (second term)	Andrew Johnson
James A. Garfield [6]	March 4, 1881–Sept. 19, 1881	Chester A. Arthur
William McKinley [6]	March 4, 1901–Sept. 14, 1901 (second term)	Theodore Roosevelt
Warren G. Harding [2]	March 4, 1921–Aug. 2, 1923	Calvin Coolidge
Franklin D. Roosevelt [2] ...	Jan. 20, 1945–April 12, 1945 (fourth term)	Harry S. Truman
John F. Kennedy [6]	Jan. 20, 1961–Nov. 22, 1963	Lyndon B. Johnson
Richard M. Nixon [3]	Jan. 20, 1973–Aug. 9, 1974 (second term)	Gerald R. Ford

VETOES BY THE PRESIDENTS *

PRESIDENT	Vetoes Regular	Vetoes Pocket	PRESIDENT	Vetoes Regular	Vetoes Pocket	PRESIDENT	Vetoes Regular	Vetoes Pocket	PRESIDENT	Vetoes Regular	Vetoes Pocket
Washington	2	–	Polk	2	1	Arthur	4	8	Hoover	21	16
Adams	–	–	Taylor	–	–	Cleveland [7]	304	110	F. Roosevelt	372	263
Jefferson	–	–	Fillmore	–	–	B. Harrison	19	25	Truman	180	70
Madison	5	2	Pierce	9	–	Cleveland [8]	42	128	Eisenhower	73	108
Monroe	1	–	Buchanan	4	3	McKinley	6	36	Kennedy	12	9
J. Q. Adams	–	–	Lincoln	2	4	T. Roosevelt	42	40	L. Johnson	16	14
Jackson	5	7	A. Johnson	21	8	Taft	30	9	Nixon	27	16
Van Buren	–	1	Grant	45	48	Wilson	33	11	Ford	55	11
W. Harrison	–	–	Hayes	12	1	Harding	5	1	Carter	18	13
Tyler	6	4	Garfield	–	–	Coolidge	20	30	Reagan [9]	19	21

[1] Elected President. [2] Died in office. [3] Resigned. [4] Succeeded to presidency. [5] Appointed Vice President. [6] Assassinated. [7] 1st term. [8] 2d term. [9] To Sept. 1, 1985. * Source: U.S. Senate Library.

Home and Family

HIGHLIGHTS: 1985

THE GREAT COKE WAR

Coke sippers who believed in "the real thing" were shocked on April 23 when Coca-Cola Company officials announced they were changing the 99-year-old formula that had made the soft drink a symbol of America around the world and had built the company into a $7 billion a year business.

Robert C. Goizueta, chairman of Coca-Cola described the new Coke as "smoother, rounder, yet bolder . . . more harmonious." Those who tasted it said it was sweeter, like Coke's major rival Pepsi. In a 12-ounce can the new Coke had 154 calories, compared to 144 in the old Coke.

Ironically, the company had just completed a six-month advertising campaign that cost millions of dollars, in which TV actor Bill Cosby boosted the "less sweet" taste of Coke compared to Pepsi.

"We have chosen to reach out and seek the promise of our future because the time is right," said Brian Dyson, president of Coca-Cola USA in explaining the change.

Dyson did not mention that he had been helped in choosing the words by Pat Caddell, the political strategist in Sen. Gary Hart's unsuccessful bid for the Democratic presidential nomination, who had been employed by Coca-Cola for guidance in making the world-shaking announcement.

Julian Bond, a state senator from Atlanta, home base of the Coca-Cola company, expressed the outrage of Coke drinkers when he said:

"I think this will rank with the day a cake of Ivory soap sank at Procter & Gamble. You don't tug on Superman's cape, you don't spit in the wind, you don't pull the mask off the old Lone Ranger, and you don't change the formula of Coke."

Officials of Pepsi-Cola USA were jubilant. They gave their employees a holiday on April 26 and bought newspaper advertising that said:

"For 87 years Coke and Pepsi have been eyeball to eyeball. It looks to us like they just blinked."

Retired businessman Gay Mullins of Seattle was so angry about the change in the Coca-Cola formula that he founded the Old Cola Drinkers of America to bring pressure on the company. Soon the phones at Coca-Cola headquarters were receiving over 1,500 calls a day from irate customers demanding return of the old Coke.

Then on July 10 the Coca-Cola officials seemed to reverse their previous decision, announcing that the old Coke would return under the label "Coca-Cola Classic" to be on grocery shelves alongside the new Coke.

Pepsi-Cola officials again expressed happiness, saying they could now compete "with one product that lost to Pepsi in millions of taste tests and against one product that the public hates. That doesn't seem to be too tough a challenge."

But some business observers speculated that the entire sequence of events might have been planned by Coca-Cola management in

U.S. HOUSEHOLD AND FAMILIES:

Source: U.S. Bureau of the Census

	1940	1950	1960	1970	1980	1984
Total households	34,949,000	43,554,000	52,799,000	63,401,000	80,776,000	85,407,000
Family households	31,491,000	38,838,000	44,905,000	51,456,000	59,550,000	61,997,000
Married-couple family	26,571,000	34,075,000	39,254,000	44,728,000	49,112,000	50,090,000
Other family, male householder	1,510,000	1,169,000	1,228,000	1,228,000	1,733,000	2,030,000
Other family, female householder	3,410,000	3,594,000	4,422,000	5,500,000	8,705,000	9,878,000
Nonfamily households	3,458,000	4,716,000	7,895,000	11,945,000	21,226,000	23,410,000
Male householder	1,599,000	1,668,000	2,716,000	4,063,000	8,807,000	9,752,000
Female householder	1,859,000	3,048,000	5,179,000	7,882,000	12,419,000	13,658,000
Living alone	2,684,000	3,954,000	6,896,000	10,851,000	18,296,000	19,954,000
Total families	32,166,000	39,303,000	45,111,000	51,586,000	59,550,000	61,997,000
Married-couple family	26,971,000	34,440,000	39,329,000	44,755,000	49,112,000	50,090,000
Male householder and others	1,579,000	1,184,000	1,275,000	1,239,000	1,733,000	2,030,000
Female householder and others	3,616,000	3,679,000	4,507,000	5,591,000	8,705,000	9,878,000
Total married couples	28,517,000	36,091,000	40,200,000	45,373,000	49,714,000	50,864,000
With own household	26,571,000	34,075,000	39,254,000	44,728,000	49,112,000	50,090,000
Without own household	1,946,000	2,016,000	946,000	645,000	602,000	775,000
Total households of unrelated individuals	9,277,000	9,136,000	11,092,000	14,988,000	26,426,000	29,497,000
Male	4,942,000	4,209,000	4,462,000	5,693,000	11,813,000	13,283,000
Female	4,335,000	4,927,000	6,630,000	9,296,000	14,613,000	16,214,000

HIGHLIGHTS: 1985 *(continued)*

order to have both a New Coke and an Old Coke too.

FOOD HAZARDS

A consumer watchdog organization, Public Voice for Food and Health Policy, declared in 1985 that consumers should be aware of the following major hazards in food:

Antibiotics in meat from cattle, hogs, and poultry that eat thousands of tons of tetracycline and penicillin in their feed.

Fish and seafood that has not been inspected for chemical contaminants from polluted water.

Lead that may cause brain damage from foods preserved in cans sealed with solder.

Pesticide residues in fresh fruits and vegetables.

Red Dye No. 3, which has been linked to cancer in animals, but which continues to be used in gelatin desserts and bakery goods.

SUPERSWEET

While conducting research to find out exactly why some substances taste sweet, a scientist reported in March that he had determined the molecular structure of the sweetest natural substance that is known.

In a report to the National Academy of Sciences, Dr. Sung-Hou Kim, a chemistry professor at the University of California at Berkeley, said the supersweet substance was *thaumatin,* a substance that comes from the katemfe bush of West Africa. He said that it is 100,000 times sweeter than sugar and 600 times sweeter than the artificial sweetener aspartame. He also analyzed the second sweetest substance, *monellin,* which comes from the serendipity berry that also grows in West Africa.

END OF A TRADEMARK

Procter & Gamble announced in April that it was going to eliminate using on its products its 103-year-old trademark that shows a bearded man in the moon and 13 stars. The design has sparked countless rumors in recent years that claimed the logo was connected with devil worship.

TOLL-FREE PHONING

The Consumer Services Department of the Direct Marketing Association suggests that before phoning any business organization a consumer should find out whether it has a toll-free phone number. To find such information, you need only phone the toll-free number 800-555-1212 for information on

CONSUMER PRICE INDEX: 1940–1985

Source: U.S. Department of Labor, Bureau of Labor Statistics

The Consumer Price Index of the U.S. Department of Labor is based on the amount of goods and services a consumer could buy for $1 in 1967, so the Index for all items in 1967 is 100. It shows you would have spent 42¢ in 1940 or $3.16 in 1984 for goods and services that cost $3.22 in 1985.

YEAR	ALL ITEMS	MEDICAL CARE	FOOD	APPAREL AND UPKEEP	HOUSING	TRANS- PORTA- TION	PERSONAL CARE	ENTERTAINMENT	ALL SERVICES
1940	42.0	36.8	35.2	42.8	52.4	42.7	40.2	46.1	43.6
1945	53.9	42.1	50.7	61.5	59.1	47.8	55.1	62.4	48.7
1950	72.1	53.7	74.5	79.0	72.8	68.2	68.3	74.4	58.9
1955	80.2	64.8	81.6	84.1	82.3	77.4	77.9	76.7	70.5
1960	88.7	79.1	88.0	89.6	90.2	89.6	90.1	87.3	83.8
1965	94.5	89.5	94.4	93.7	94.9	95.9	95.2	95.9	92.2
1966	97.2	93.4	99.1	96.1	97.2	97.2	97.1	97.5	95.8
1967	100.0	100.0	100.0	100.0	100.0	100.0	100.0	100.0	100.0
1968	104.2	106.1	103.6	105.4	104.2	103.2	104.2	104.7	105.2
1969	109.8	113.4	108.9	111.5	110.8	107.2	109.3	108.7	112.5
1970	116.3	120.6	114.9	116.1	118.9	112.7	113.2	113.4	121.6
1971	121.3	128.4	118.4	119.8	124.3	118.6	116.8	119.3	128.4
1972	125.3	132.5	123.5	122.3	129.2	119.9	119.8	122.8	133.3
1973	133.1	137.7	141.4	126.8	135.0	123.8	125.2	125.9	139.1
1974	147.7	150.5	161.7	136.2	150.6	137.7	137.3	133.8	152.1
1975	161.2	168.6	175.4	142.3	166.8	150.6	150.7	144.4	166.6
1976	170.5	197.1	180.8	147.6	177.2	165.5	160.5	151.2	180.4
1977	181.5	202.4	188.0	154.2	186.5	177.2	172.1	167.7	172.2
1978	195.4	219.4	211.4	159.6	202.8	185.5	182.0	176.6	210.9
1979	217.4	239.7	234.5	166.6	227.6	212.0	195.8	188.5	234.2
1980	246.8	265.9	254.6	178.4	263.3	249.7	213.1	205.3	270.3
1981	272.3	294.5	274.6	186.9	293.5	280.0	239.1	221.4	305.7
1982	288.6	328.7	285.7	191.8	314.6	291.5	248.1	235.5	333.3
1983	303.5	366.2	286.5	199.3	327.4	306.3	266.3	249.5	351.6
1984	315.5	388.5	297.2	203.2	341.2	315.8	276.6	260.1	370.6
1985*	322.3	401.7	301.4	204.6	350.4	321.8	281.7	264.8	381.3

* 1985 data for June.

how to obtain a directory of toll-free numbers.

The organization also has a free booklet entitled *Guidelines for Telephone Shopping* that can be obtained by writing to Consumer Services Department, Direct Marketing Association, 6 East 43d Street, New York, N.Y. 10017.

ASCEPTIC FOOD PROCESSING

A new way to preserve foods may lead to better tasting food on grocery shelves. Called *asceptic processing*, the method enables the food and its container to be sterilized separately.

The process, which involves the use of hydrogen peroxide to sterilize the containers, was approved by the Food and Drug Administration in 1981. Since then it has had its most widespread use in the United States in the packaging of fruit juices in cardboard or plastic containers that do not require refrigeration.

For many years Europeans have used the process to package milk, eliminating the need for grocery stores to refrigerate the milk.

TRANSFORMERS TOP CABBAGE KIDS

Toy & Hobby World reported in May that Cabbage Patch Kid dolls had fallen from first place in the best-selling toys after leading the list for 16 months. The popular soft-sculpture dolls were nosed out by the toy robots called Transformers that can be manipulated to change them into such objects as toy cars and toy guns.

Officials of Hasbro Bradley Inc., the manufacturer of Transformers, estimated that about 30 million of the robot toys would be sold in 1985, twice as many as in the previous year.

Coleco Industries Inc., manufacturer of Cabbage Patch Kids dolls, said that about 20 million of the dolls would be sold in 1985.

Meanwhile, Xavier Roberts, who created the original Cabbage Patch Kids dolls, was busy promoting his latest toys, a line of teddy bears called the Furskin Family from the mythical village of Moody Hollow, Ga. The family includes Dudley, Hattie, Farrell, and Boone Furskin. They sell for $60 each.

Another contender in the toy race is the Dreeble, a computerized stuffed toy invented by a Silicon Valley, Calif., computer engineer, Glenn Keller. A Dreeble has long hair and wide-set eyes. Its built-in sensor makes the Dreeble purr when petted and squeal when squeezed. Prrrl Ventures, manufacturer of the Dreeble, expects to sell about half a million in 1985.

NEW INSTANT COLOR FILM

Polaroid Corp. introduced a new high-quality instant-developing color film in May, which it hopes will revitalize sales of its instant cameras. The new Polaroid pictures rival the quality of color and clarity achieved with photographs taken by 35-mm cameras.

BIGGER BURGERS

The Burger King fast-food chain announced

CONSUMER HOTLINE PHONE NUMBERS

The following U.S. government telephone hotlines were in effect at the time the Almanac went to press. Toll-free numbers may be changed, however. If you have difficulty reaching any of the following, you can dial 800-555-1212 to obtain the correct number.

Most of these toll-free numbers are not available in Alaska and Hawaii.

Abuse, Waste, and Fraud Hotline 800-424-5454
To report federal abuse, waste, and fraud.
ACTION AND PEACE CORPS 800-424-8580
Information for potential volunteers.
Army Retirement Benefits 800-336-4909
For inquiries about Army benefits.
Auto Recall Hotline 800-424-9393
To find out if your car has been recalled.
Basic Education Grants Program . (toll) 301-984-4070
General information on education grants.
Conservation and Renewable Energy Inquiry and Referral Service 800-523-2929
Information on energy and conservation.
Consumer Product Safety Commission .. 800-638-2772
To inquire about or report on safety of products.
Department of Defense 800-424-9098
To report fraud or waste in defense program.
Export-Import Bank 800-424-5201
Export information for small businesses.
Fair Housing and Equal Opportunity ... 800-424-8590
For housing and discrimination problems.

Federal Crime Insurance 800-638-8780
Information on insurance in high-risk areas.
Federal Election Commission 800-424-9530
Regulates campaign financing.
Library of Congress 800-424-8567
National Library Service for the Blind and Handicapped.
Lost Children 800-843-5678
For information or assistance about lost children.
National Solar Heating and Cooling Information Center 800-523-2929
Information on solar installations.
Product Safety 800-638-2772
To inquire about or report on product safety.
Social Welfare Fraud Hotline 800-368-5779
For abuses in Medicare, Medicaid, Social Security.
Tax Hotline 800-555-1212
Phone to get your state's toll-free IRS number.
VD Hotline (Operation Venus) 800-227-8922
General information on venereal disease.
Veterans' Information 800-555-1212
Phone to get your state's toll-free VA number.

HIGHLIGHTS: 1985 *(continued)*

in May that it was increasing the size of the meat in its Whopper hamburger to 4.2 ounces while reducing the size of its bun from 5 inches to 4.5 inches.

Officials of Burger King said the change makes their hamburgers 5% larger than those of McDonald's and Wendy's, but they denied the move was a result of Wendy's "Where's the Beef?" advertising campaign.

COPYPROOF PAPER

Ever since photocopiers became popular pieces of office equipment in the 1950s, inventors have tried to develop some kind of paper that could be used for secret or confidential documents to prevent copies from falling into the hands of unauthorized persons.

The Boise Cascade paper manufacturing corporation began selling such copyproof paper in 1985. The paper provides a range of security levels in colors that range from pink (hard to read when copied) to deep burgundy (impossible to read when copied).

The paper contains a red dye that reflects as black in a photo copying machine.

Boise Cascade obtained a license to use the dye from Nocopi Inc., a corporation formed by two Canadian inventors, Norman Gardner and Michael Voticky.

GROWTH IN ONE-PARENT HOMES

The Census Bureau reported that the number of one-parent homes with children has grown to 26% of all households, up from 22% in 1980 and from 13% in 1970.

Among white families, 20% with children have only one parent, an increase from 17.1% in 1980 and 10.1% in 1970.

The Census Bureau said the average number of persons per household had reached an alltime low of 2.7, a reduction from the 3.1 person average in 1970.

CONSUMER ORGANIZATIONS

The following consumer organizations are among those actively working for and with consumers at national, state and local levels to affect public policy as it relates to inflation.

Association of Community Organizations for Reform Now (ACORN): Works for advancement of low-to-moderate-income people.
628 Barrone St., New Orleans, LA 70113 or
523 W. 15th St., Little Rock, AR 72202
Center for Community Change: Provides technical assistance to community organizations on housing, manpower, economic development, and other grass-roots concerns.
1000 Wisconsin Ave., NW, Washington, D.C. 20007
Center for Science in the Public Interest: Research and education activities focus on nutrition, food programs, and the food industry.
1755 S St., NW, Washington, D.C. 20009
Common Cause: Nonpartisan public-affairs lobbying organization concerned mainly with government reform and accountability.
2030 M Street, NW, Washington, D.C. 20036
Community Nutrition Institute: Resource center on food and nutrition policy issues; provides technical assistance to community programs.
1146 19th St., NW, Washington, D.C. 20036
Congress Watch: Lobbying arm of Public Citizen; active in many areas of national energy and consumer legislation policymaking.
133 C St., SE, Washington, D.C. 20003
Consumer Coalition for Health: Coalition of national and local organizations and individuals across the country that develops programs designed to increase public awareness of health-planning issues.
1511 K St., NW, Suite 220, Washington, D.C. 20005
Consumer Federation of America: Federation of 225 national, state, and local nonprofit groups that advocates consumer interests on food, energy, credit and banking and health issues.
1012 14th St., NW, Washington, D.C. 20005
Consumers Union of the U.S., Inc.: Independent nonprofit product-testing organization that conducts research and prepares education materials on wide variety of consumer concerns.
256 Washington St., Mt. Vernon, NY 10550
Cooperative League of the U.S.A.: National organization of cooperatives of all types; lobbies, conducts research, publishes educational materials, including "how-to" pamphlets on broad range of subjects such as farm/rural issues, housing, and health.
1828 L St., NW, Washington, D.C. 20036.
Energy Action Committee: Nonprofit public-interest organization that monitors government and industry actions in the energy field.
1523 L St., NW, Washington, D.C. 20005
Environmental Action Foundation: Education and research organization; publishes information on citizen action in environmental areas including solid waste, electric-utility rate structure and reform, and transportation.
724 Dupont Circle Building, Washington, D.C. 20036
Environmental Defense Fund: Nationwide legal-action organization working to protect the public interest in environmental quality, energy, conservation, public health, and consumer welfare.
1525 18th St., NW, Washington, D.C. 20036
Food Research and Action Center: Provides legal assistance, organizing aid, training, and information to low-income people and others working to expand and improve federal food programs.
2011 Eye St., NW, Washington, D.C. 20006
Gray Panthers: National activist organization that lobbies, advocates in court, and organizes around issues involving health care, nursing homes, age discrimination, and housing.
3700 Chestnut St., Philadelphia, PA 19104
Health Research Group: Ralph Nader-affiliated consumer advocacy organization working on consumer-health issues.
2000 P St., NW, Washington, D.C. 20036
National Consumers League: Sponsors variety of consumer-education programs and lobbies for consumer rights.
1028 Connecticut Ave., NW, Washington, D.C. 20036
The National Commission on Neighborhoods: Presidential advisory group investigates causes of neighborhood decline.
2000 K St., NW, Suite 350, Washington, D.C. 20006

ADDRESSES OF FEDERAL CONSUMER OFFICES

When corresponding with a federal consumer office, be sure to include photocopies all documents pertinent to your request or complaint.

ADVERTISING
Director, Bureau of Consumer Protection, Federal Trade Commission, Washington, D.C. 20580.
AIR TRAVEL
Routes and Service: Director, Office of Consumer Protection, Department of Transportation, Washington, D.C. 20590.
Safety: Community and Consumer Liaison Division, Federal Aviation Administration, APA–430, Washington, D.C. 20591.
ALCOHOLISM, DRUG ABUSE, AND MENTAL ILLNESS
Office of Public Affairs, Alcohol, Drug Abuse, and Mental Health Service, 5600 Fishers Lane, Rockville, MD 20857.
BANKS
Federal Credit Unions: National Credit Union Administration, Washington, D.C. 20456.
Federally Insured Savings and Loans: Consumer Division, Office of Community Investment, Federal Home Loan Bank Board, Washington, D.C. 20552.
Federal Reserve Banks: Office of Saver and Consumer Affairs, Federal Reserve System, Washington, D.C. 20551.
National Banks: Consumer Affairs, Office of the Comptroller of the Currency, Washington, D.C. 20219.
State Chartered Banks: Office of Bank Customer Affairs, Federal Deposit Insurance Corporation, Washington, D.C. 20429.
BOATING
Chief, Information and Administrative Staff, U.S. Coast Guard, Washington, D.C. 20590.
BUS TRAVEL
Consumer Affairs Office, Interstate Commerce Commission, Washington, D.C. 20423.
BUSINESS
General: Office of the Ombudsman, Department of Commerce, Washington, D.C. 20230.
Women: Director, Women-in-Business and Consumer Affairs, Small Business Administration, 1441 L St., NW, Washington, D.C. 20416.
CHILD ABUSE
National Center on Child Abuse and Neglect, P.O. Box 1182, Washington, D.C. 20013.
CREDIT
Director, Bureau of Consumer Protection, Federal Trade Commission, Washington, D.C. 20580.
CUSTOMS
Public Information Division, U.S. Customs, Washington, D.C. 20229.
DISCRIMINATION
U.S. Commission on Civil Rights, 1121 Vermont Ave., Washington, D.C. 20425.
Equal Employment Opportunity Commission, 2401 E St., NW, Washington, D.C. 20506.
DRUGS AND COSMETICS
Consumer Inquiry Section, Food and Drug Administration, 5600 Fishers Lane, Rockville, MD 20857.
ELDERLY
Administration on Aging, Washington, D.C. 20201.
ENERGY
General: Director, Office of Consumer Affairs, Department of Energy, Washington, D.C. 20585.
Energy Efficiency: Information Office, National Bureau of Standards, Washington, D.C. 20234.
ENVIRONMENT
Office of Public Awareness, Environmental Protection Agency, Washington, D.C. 20460.

FISH AND WILDLIFE
Fish and Wildlife Service, Office of Public Affairs, Washington, D.C. 20240.
FOOD
Assistant Secretary for Food and Consumer Services, U.S. Department of Agriculture, Washington, D.C. 20250.
Consumer Inquiry Section, Food and Drug Administration, 5600 Fishers Lane, Rockville, MD 20857.
FRAUD
Director, Bureau of Consumer Protection, Federal Trade Commission, Washington, D.C. 20580.
HANDICAPPED
Director, Division of Public Information, Office of Human Development Services, Department of Health and Human Services, Washington, D.C. 20201.
IMMIGRATION AND NATURALIZATION
Information Services, Immigration and Naturalization Service, 425 Eye St., NW, Washington, D.C. 20536.
JOB SAFETY
Office of Information, Occupational Safety and Health Administration, Department of Labor, Washington, D.C. 20210.
MAIL ORDERS
Federal Trade Commission, Office of the Secretary, Washington, D.C. 20580.
MAIL SERVICE
Consumer Advocate, U.S. Postal Service, Washington, D.C. 20260.
MEDICAID AND MEDICARE
Health Care Financing Administration, in the Department of Health and Human Services, Washington, D.C. 20201.
MEDICAL RESEARCH
Division of Public Information, National Institutes of Health, 9000 Rockville Pike, Bethesda, MD 20014.
Center for Disease Control, Attention, Public Inquiries, Atlanta, GA 30333.
MOVING COMPANIES, INTERSTATE
Consumer Assistance Office, Interstate Commerce Commission, Washington, D.C. 20423.
PARKS AND RECREATION AREAS
National Forests: Forest Service, U.S. Department of Agriculture, Washington, D.C. 20250.
National Parks and Historic Sites: National Park Service, Washington, D.C. 20240.
PASSPORTS
Passport Office, Department of State, 1425 K St., NW, Washington, D.C. 20524.
PATENTS AND TRADEMARKS
Patents: Commissioner, Patent Office, Department of Commerce, Washington, D.C. 20231.
Trademarks: Commissioner, Trademark Office, Department of Commerce, Washington, D.C. 20231.
PENSIONS
Office of Communications, Pension Benefit Guaranty Corporation, 2020 K St., NW, Washington, D.C. 20006.
Labor Management Standards Administration, Department of Labor, Washington, D.C. 20210.
RADIO AND TELEVISION BROADCASTING AND INTERFERENCE
Consumer Assistance Office, Federal Communications Commission, Washington, D.C. 20554.
STOCKS AND BONDS
Office of Consumer Affairs, Securities and Exchange Commission, Washington, D.C. 20549.
WAGES AND WORKING CONDITIONS
Employment Standards Administration, Department of Labor, Washington, D.C. 20210.
WARRANTIES
Division of Special Statutes, Federal Trade Commission, Washington, D.C. 20580.

NUTRITION

A basic knowledge of good nutrition is essential for maintaining health. Poor diet in early life may impair both mental and physical development and in later years contribute to heart disease, strokes, and other disorders. Eating wisely also helps to keep desirable body weights.

There are at least 50 known nutrients necessary for health—vitamins, minerals, amino acids (protein), fatty acids, and glucose. No single food can adequately supply all of them. Hence, everyone should eat a varied menu taken from the four basic food groups below:

(1) **The meat group** includes not only beef, pork, lamb, and the like, but also poultry, fish, eggs, dried peas and beans, and nuts. All of these are high in protein.

(2) **The dairy group,** rich in calcium and proteins, includes milk and milk products.

(3) **The cereal group,** which supplies carbohydrates and some protein, consists of breakfast foods and breadstuffs made from oats, barley, wheat, and corn.

(4) **The fruit and vegetable group,** high in vitamins and minerals, includes fruits, berries, leafy and other green vegetables, and the "yellow" vegetables, such as carrots, squash, sweet potatoes, and the like.

A good diet should include two to four servings daily from each of the four groups. Avoid excessive use of sugar and fats.

RECOMMENDED DAILY DIETARY ALLOWANCES

Source: *Recommended Dietary Allowances,* revised 1980, National Academy of Sciences

	Age (years)	Weight (kg)	Weight (lbs)	Height (cm)	Height (in)	Energy (calories)	Protein (grams)	Ascorbic Acid*	Folacin†	Niacin*	Riboflavin*	Thiamin*	Vitamin B_6*	Vitamin B_{12}†
Infants	0.0-0.5	6	13	60	24	kg x 115	kg x 2.2	35	30	6	0.4	0.3	0.3	0.5
	0.5-1.0	9	20	71	28	kg x 105	kg x 2.0	35	45	8	0.6	0.5	0.6	1.5
Children	1-3	13	29	90	35	1,300	23	45	100	9	0.8	0.7	0.9	2.0
	4-6	20	44	112	44	1,700	30	45	200	11	1.0	0.9	1.3	2.5
	7-10	28	62	132	52	2,400	34	45	300	16	1.4	1.2	1.6	3.0
Boys	11-14	45	99	157	62	2,700	45	50	400	18	1.6	1.4	1.8	3.0
	15-18	66	145	176	69	2,800	56	60	400	19	1.7	1.4	2.0	3.0
Men	19-22	70	154	177	70	2,900	56	60	400	18	1.7	1.5	2.2	3.0
	23-50	70	154	178	70	2,700	56	60	400	16	1.6	1.4	2.2	3.0
	51+	70	154	178	70	2,400	56	60	400	15	1.4	1.2	2.2	3.0
Girls	11-14	46	101	157	62	2,200	46	50	400	14	1.3	1.1	1.8	3.0
	15-18	55	120	163	64	2,100	46	60	400	14	1.3	1.1	2.0	3.0
Women	19-22	55	120	163	64	2,100	44	60	400	13	1.3	1.1	2.0	3.0
	23-50	55	120	163	64	2,000	44	60	400	13	1.2	1.0	2.0	3.0
	51+	55	120	163	64	1,800	44	60	400	13	1.2	1.0	2.0	3.0
Pregnant mothers						+300	+30	+20	+400	+2	+0.3	+0.4	+0.6	+1.0
Nursing (lactating) mothers						+500	+20	+40	+100	+5	+0.5	+0.5	+0.5	+1.0

	Age (years)	Weight (kg)	Weight (lbs)	Height (cm)	Height (in)	Energy (calories)	Protein (grams)	Vitamin A (RE)[1]	Vitamin D[2]	Vitamin E[2]	Calcium*	Phosphorus*	Iodine†	Iron*	Magnesium*	Zinc*
Infants	0.0-0.5	6	13	60	24	kg x 115	kg x 2.2	420	400	3	360	240	40	10	50	3
	0.5-1.0	9	20	71	28	kg x 105	kg x 2.0	400	400	4	540	360	50	15	70	5
Children	1-3	13	29	90	35	1,300	23	400	400	5	800	800	70	15	150	10
	4-6	20	44	112	44	1,700	30	500	400	6	800	800	90	10	200	10
	7-10	28	62	132	52	2,400	34	700	400	7	800	800	120	10	250	10
Boys	11-14	45	99	157	62	2,700	45	1,000	400	8	1,200	1,200	150	18	350	15
	15-18	66	145	176	69	2,800	56	1,000	400	10	1,200	1,200	150	18	400	15
Men	19-22	70	154	177	70	2,900	56	1,000	300	10	800	800	150	10	350	15
	23-50	70	154	178	70	2,700	56	1,000	200	10	800	800	150	10	350	15
	51+	70	154	178	70	2,400	56	1,000	200	10	800	800	150	10	350	15
Girls	11-14	46	101	157	62	2,200	46	800	400	8	1,200	1,200	150	18	300	15
	15-18	55	120	163	64	2,100	46	800	400	8	1,200	1,200	150	18	300	15
Women	19-22	55	120	163	64	2,100	44	800	300	8	800	800	150	18	300	15
	23-50	55	120	163	64	2,000	44	800	200	8	800	800	150	18	300	15
	51+	55	120	163	64	1,800	44	800	200	8	800	800	150	10	300	15
Pregnant mothers						+300	+30	+200	+200	+2	+400	+400	+25	+30[3]	+150	+25
Nursing (lactating) mothers						+500	+20	+400	+200	+3	+400	+400	+50	+30[3]	+150	+50

* In milligrams. † In micrograms. [1] In retinol equivalents. [2] In International units. [3] Supplemental iron recommended.

CALORIES AND WEIGHT

The weight of an adult man or woman reflects the extent to which he or she balances the intake of energy in food with the expenditure of energy in activity and growth.

Weight will stay the same when the number of calories brought into the body by food equals the number of calories used by the body. Similarly, the body loses weight when it receives fewer calories from food than it uses. It gains weight when it receives more calories than are used.

Weight can be controlled by regulating either the amount of food eaten or the extent of physical activity, or both, so that the balance of calories is in the desired direction.

Overweight is a problem shared by more than 60 million Americans of all ages. There are a number of available low-calorie, nutritionally sound diets which, if faithfully followed, will take off excess pounds and help to keep them off. However, it is wise for anyone planning to lose more than a few pounds to consult a doctor.

DESIRABLE WEIGHTS FOR MEN AGE 25–59 [1]
Weight in pounds according to frame (in indoor clothing)

HEIGHT [2] Feet	Inches	SLENDER FRAME	MEDIUM FRAME	LARGE FRAME
5	2	128-134	131-141	138-150
5	3	130-136	133-143	140-153
5	4	132-138	135-145	142-156
5	5	134-140	137-148	144-160
5	6	136-142	139-151	146-164
5	7	138-145	142-154	149-168
5	8	140-148	145-157	152-172
5	9	142-151	148-160	155-176
5	10	144-154	151-163	158-180
5	11	146-157	154-166	161-184
6	0	149-160	157-170	164-188
6	1	152-164	160-174	168-192
6	2	155-168	164-178	172-197
6	3	158-172	167-182	176-202
6	4	162-176	171-187	181-207

DESIRABLE WEIGHTS FOR WOMEN AGE 25–59 [1]
Weight in pounds according to frame (in indoor clothing)

HEIGHT [2] Feet	Inches	SLENDER FRAME	MEDIUM FRAME	LARGE FRAME
4	10	102-111	109-121	118-131
4	11	103-113	111-123	120-134
5	0	104-115	113-126	122-137
5	1	106-118	115-129	125-140
5	2	108-121	118-132	128-143
5	3	111-124	121-135	131-147
5	4	114-127	124-138	134-151
5	5	117-130	127-141	137-155
5	6	120-133	130-144	140-159
5	7	123-136	133-147	143-163
5	8	126-139	136-150	146-167
5	9	129-142	139-153	149-170
5	10	132-145	142-156	152-173
5	11	135-148	145-159	155-176
6	0	138-151	148-162	158-179

[1] Men wearing five pounds of clothing; women wearing three. [2] In shoes with one-inch heels.

AVERAGE HEIGHTS AND WEIGHTS OF BOYS AND GIRLS

PHYSICAL GROWTH OF BOYS
(from age 1 month to 18 years; without clothing)

AGE (Month or year)	AVERAGE HEIGHT Centimeters	Inches	AVERAGE WEIGHT Kilograms	Pounds
1 mo.	54.6	21.5	4.29	9.5
3 mo.	61.1	24.1	5.98	13.2
6 mo.	67.8	26.7	7.85	17.3
9 mo.	72.3	28.5	9.18	20.2
12 mo.	76.1	30.0	10.15	22.4
18 mo.	82.4	32.4	11.47	25.3
2 yrs.	86.8	34.2	12.34	27.2
3 yrs.	94.9	37.4	14.62	32.2
4 yrs.	102.9	40.5	16.69	36.8
5 yrs.	109.9	43.3	18.67	41.2
6 yrs.	116.1	45.7	20.69	45.6
7 yrs.	121.7	47.9	22.85	50.4
8 yrs.	127.0	50.0	25.30	55.8
9 yrs.	132.2	52.1	28.13	62.0
10 yrs.	137.5	54.1	31.44	69.3
11 yrs.	143.3	56.4	35.30	77.8
12 yrs.	149.7	58.9	39.78	87.7
13 yrs.	156.5	61.6	44.95	99.1
14 yrs.	163.1	64.2	50.77	111.9
15 yrs.	169.0	66.5	56.71	125.0
16 yrs.	173.5	68.3	62.10	136.9
17 yrs.	176.2	69.4	66.31	146.2
18 yrs.	176.8	69.6	68.88	151.9

PHYSICAL GROWTH OF GIRLS
(from age 1 month to 18 years; without clothing)

AGE (Month or year)	AVERAGE HEIGHT Centimeters	Inches	AVERAGE WEIGHT Kilograms	Pounds
1 mo.	53.5	21.1	3.98	8.8
3 mo.	59.5	23.4	5.40	11.9
6 mo.	65.9	25.9	7.21	15.9
9 mo.	70.4	27.7	8.56	18.9
12 mo.	74.3	29.3	9.53	21.0
18 mo.	80.9	31.9	10.82	23.8
2 yrs.	86.8	34.2	11.80	26.0
3 yrs.	94.1	37.0	14.10	31.0
4 yrs.	101.6	40.0	15.96	35.2
5 yrs.	108.4	42.7	17.66	38.9
6 yrs.	114.6	45.1	19.52	43.0
7 yrs.	120.6	47.5	21.84	48.1
8 yrs.	126.4	49.8	24.84	54.8
9 yrs.	132.2	52.0	28.46	62.7
10 yrs.	138.3	54.4	32.55	71.8
11 yrs.	144.8	57.0	36.95	81.5
12 yrs.	151.5	59.6	41.53	91.6
13 yrs.	157.1	61.9	46.10	101.6
14 yrs.	160.4	63.1	50.28	110.8
15 yrs.	161.8	63.7	53.68	118.3
16 yrs.	162.4	63.9	55.89	123.2
17 yrs.	163.1	64.2	56.69	125.0
18 yrs.	163.7	64.4	56.62	124.8

Sources: Metropolitan Life Insurance Company; National Academy of Sciences.

CALORIE COUNT AND MAIN NUTRIENTS OF BASIC FOODS

Source: U.S. Department of Agriculture. T = trace.

In nutrition *calorie* expresses the energy-producing value of food. For the average American adult, energy is expended at about the following rates: running, 19.4 calories per minute; swimming, 11.2 calories per minute; bicycle riding, 8.2 calories per minute; walking, 5.2 calories per minute; and repose, 1.3 calories per minute.

Energy values in excess of those used for physical activities are stored in the body in the form of fat.

KINDS OF FOOD	AMOUNT	FOOD ENERGY (Calories)	PROTEIN (Grams)	FAT (Grams)	CARBOHYDRATES (Grams)
BEVERAGES, MILK, FATS					
Beer	12 oz.	150	1	0	14
Butter or margarine (¼ lb.)	½ cup	815	1	92	T
Butter or margarine	1 pat	25	T	4	T
Buttermilk	1 cup	100	8	2	12
Club soda (unsweetened)	12 oz.	0	0	0	0
Cocoa	1 cup	245	10	12	27
Cola beverages	12 oz.	145	0	0	37
Cream, half-and-half	1 tbsp.	20	T	2	1
Cream, sour	1 tbsp.	25	T	3	1
Fats, vegetable	1 tbsp.	110	0	13	0
Gin, rum, vodka, whisky	1½ oz.	110	0	0	T
Ginger ale	12 oz.	115	0	0	29
Lard	1 tbsp.	115	0	13	0
Malted milk	1 cup	235	11	10	27
Milk, skim	1 cup	85	8	T	12
Milk, whole	1 cup	150	8	8	11
Oils, salad or cooking	1 tbsp.	120	0	14	0
Root beer	12 oz.	150	0	0	39
Soda, fruit-flavored	12 oz.	170	0	0	45
Wine, table	3½ oz.	85	T	0	4
BREADS, CEREALS, DESSERTS, PASTAS, SNACKS					
Bagel (egg)	1	165	6	2	28
Biscuit	1	105	2	5	13
Bread:					
Raisin	1 slice	65	2	1	13
Rye	1 slice	60	2	T	13
White	1 slice	70	2	1	13
Whole-wheat	1 slice	60	3	1	12
Breakfast cereals:					
Bran flakes	1 cup	105	4	1	28
Corn flakes, plain	1 cup	95	2	T	21
Oatmeal	1 cup	130	5	2	23
Puffed rice	1 cup	60	1	T	13
Puffed wheat	1 cup	55	2	T	12
Shredded wheat	1 piece	90	2	1	20
Brownie with nuts	1	95	1	6	10
Cakes (pieces):					
Angel food	1	135	3	T	32
Cupcake (iced)	1	130	2	5	21
Devil's food (iced)	1	235	3	8	40
Fruitcake	1	55	1	2	9
Gingerbread	1	175	2	4	32
Sponge	1	195	5	4	36
White (iced)	1	250	3	8	45
Candy:					
Caramel	1 oz.	115	1	3	22
Chocolate—milk	1 oz.	145	2	9	16
Chocolate—nuts	1 oz.	160	5	12	11
Fudge, plain	1 oz.	115	1	3	21
Gumdrops	1 oz.	100	T	T	25
Marshmallows	1 oz.	90	1	T	23
Mints, uncoated	1 oz.	105	T	1	25
Chocolate, baking	1 oz.	145	3	15	8
Chocolate, semisweet	1 oz.	145	1	10	16
Chocolate topping	1 oz.	125	2	5	20
Corn muffin	1	125	3	4	19
Crackers, graham	4	110	2	2	20
Crackers, saltine	4	50	1	1	8
Custard, baked	1 cup	305	14	15	29
Danish pastry (4¼" diam.)	1	275	5	15	30
Doughnut	1	205	3	11	16
Fig bar	1	50	1	1	11
Gelatin dessert	1 cup	140	4	0	34
Honey	1 tbsp.	65	T	0	17
Ice cream	1 cup	270	5	14	32
Ice milk	1 cup	185	5	6	29
Jams and preserves	1 tbsp.	55	T	T	14
Macaroni, plain	1 cup	190	7	1	39
Macaroni w/cheese	1 cup	430	17	22	40
Muffin	1	120	3	4	17
Noodles	1 cup	200	7	2	37
Pancake (4" diam.)	1	50	2	2	9
Pies (⅐ wedges of 9" pie.):					
Apple	1	345	3	15	51
Lemon meringue	1	305	4	12	45
Mince	1	365	3	16	56
Pecan	1	495	6	27	61
Pizza, cheese (⅛ piece)	1	145	6	4	22
Popcorn, plain	1 cup	25	1	T	5
Popcorn, buttered	1 cup	40	1	2	5
Popcorn, caramel	1 cup	135	2	1	30
Popsicle	1	70	0	0	18
Pretzel, thin twisted	1	25	1	T	5
Pudding, chocolate	1 cup	385	8	12	67
Pudding, tapioca	1 cup	220	8	8	28
Roll, frankfurter	1	120	3	2	21
Sherbet	1 cup	260	2	2	59
Spaghetti, plain	1 cup	155	5	1	32
Spaghetti, tomato & cheese	1 cup	260	9	9	37
Sugar, white granular	1 tbsp.	45	0	0	12
Syrup	1 tbsp.	60	0	0	15
Waffle (7" diam.)	1	205	7	8	27
Whipped cream	1 tbsp.	10	T	1	T
FRUITS AND FRUIT JUICES					
Apple, raw (2¾ in. dia.)	1	80	T	1	20
Apple juice	1 cup	120	T	T	30
Applesauce, sweetened	1 cup	230	T	T	61
Apricots, raw	3	55	1	T	14
Apricots, canned in syrup	1 cup	220	2	T	57
Apricots, dried, uncooked	1 cup	340	7	1	86
Avocado, raw	1	370	5	37	13
Banana, raw	1	100	1	T	26
Blackberries, raw	1 cup	85	2	1	19
Blueberries, raw	1 cup	90	1	1	22
Cantaloupe, raw	½	80	2	T	20
Cherries, canned	1 cup	105	2	1	26
Cranberry juice, canned	1 cup	165	T	1	42
Cranberry sauce, sweet	1 cup	405	T	1	104
Dates, pitted	1 cup	490	4	1	130
Fruit cocktail, canned	1 cup	195	1	T	50
Grapefruit, raw	½	50	1	T	13
Grapefruit, canned	1 cup	180	2	T	45
Grapefruit juice	1 cup	95	1	T	23

KINDS OF FOOD	AMOUNT	FOOD ENERGY (Calories)	PROTEIN (Grams)	FAT (Grams)	CARBOHYDRATES (Grams)
Grape juice, bottled	1 cup	165	T	T	42
Grapes, raw	1 cup	70	1	1	16
Lemon, raw	1	20	1	T	6
Lemonade	1 cup	105	T	T	28
Limeade	1 cup	100	T	T	27
Orange, raw	1	65	1	T	16
Orange juice	1 cup	110	2	T	26
Peach, raw	1	40	1	T	10
Peaches, canned in syrup	1 cup	200	T	T	51
Pear, raw	1	100	1	1	25
Pears, canned in syrup	1 cup	195	T	T	50
Pineapple, raw, diced	1 cup	80	1	T	21
Pineapple, canned in syrup	1 cup	190	1	T	49
Pineapple juice	1 cup	140	1	T	34
Plum, raw	1	30	T	T	8
Prunes, cooked	1 cup	255	2	1	67
Prune juice	1 cup	195	1	T	49
Raisins (½ oz. package)	1 pkg.	40	T	T	11
Raspberries, red, raw	1 cup	70	1	2	17
Rhubarb, cooked with sugar	1 cup	380	1	T	97
Strawberries, raw	1 cup	55	1	1	13
Watermelon, wedge 4"x 8"	1	110	2	1	27
MEAT, CHEESE, EGGS, POULTRY, FISH					
Bacon (slices)	2	85	4	8	T
Beef, dried or chipped	2½ oz.	145	24	4	T
Beef, hamburger	3 oz.	235	20	17	0
Beef, roast (lean only)	3 oz.	210	25	12	0
Beef, steak, broiled	3 oz.	220	24	13	0
Beef potpie (4¼" diam.)	1	515	21	30	39
Bologna (slices)	2	170	6	16	1
Cheese:					
American	1 oz.	105	6	9	T
American spread	1 oz.	82	5	6	2
Blue or Roquefort	1 oz.	105	6	8	1
Cheddar	1 oz.	115	7	9	1
Cottage	1 cup	235	28	10	6
Cream	1 oz.	100	2	10	1
Parmesan	1 oz.	130	12	9	1
Yogurt	1 cup	140	8	7	11
Chicken, broiled	3 oz.	115	20	3	0
Chicken, fried	3 oz.	215	26	10	4
Chicken potpie (9" diam.)	⅓	545	23	31	42
Chili con carne w/beans	1 cup	340	19	16	31
Corned beef (canned)	3 oz.	185	22	10	0
Egg, scrambled in fat	1	95	6	7	1
Egg, whole (boiled)	1	80	6	6	T
Fish and seafood:					
Clams, raw	3 oz.	65	11	1	2
Fish sticks	3 oz.	150	15	9	6
Haddock, fried	3 oz.	140	17	5	5
Lobster, canned	3 oz.	80	16	1	T
Oysters, raw	1 cup	160	20	4	8
Salmon, canned	3 oz.	120	17	5	0
Sardines, canned	3 oz.	175	20	9	0
Tuna, canned	3 oz.	170	25	7	0
Ham, baked	3 oz.	185	25	8	0
Hot dog (frankfurter)	2 oz.	170	7	16	1
Lamb, chop (broiled)	3.1 oz.	360	18	32	0
Lamb, leg (roasted)	3 oz.	235	22	16	0
Liver, beef (fried)	3 oz.	195	22	9	5
Luncheon ham (canned)	slice	175	9	15	1
Pork, chop	2.7 oz.	305	19	25	0
Pork, roast	3 oz.	310	21	24	0
Pork, sausage links	2	120	4	12	T
Salami	3 oz.	450	20	40	T
Veal, cutlet	3 oz.	185	23	9	0
Veal, roast	3 oz.	230	23	14	0

KINDS OF FOOD	AMOUNT	FOOD ENERGY (Calories)	PROTEIN (Grams)	FAT (Grams)	CARBOHYDRATES (Grams)
VEGETABLES AND NUTS					
Almonds, shelled, chopped	1 cup	775	24	70	25
Asparagus	1 cup	30	3	T	5
Beans, green	1 cup	30	2	T	7
Beans, lima	1 cup	260	16	1	49
Beans, navy	1 cup	210	14	1	38
Beans and pork (canned)	1 cup	310	16	7	48
Beets	1 cup	55	2	T	12
Broccoli	1 cup	40	5	T	7
Brussels sprouts	1 cup	55	6	1	10
Cabbage, cooked	1 cup	30	2	T	6
Cabbage, raw	1 cup	15	1	T	4
Carrot, raw (7" long)	1	30	1	T	7
Carrots, cooked	1 cup	50	1	T	11
Cashew nuts	1 cup	785	24	64	41
Cauliflower, cooked	1 cup	31	3	T	6
Celery, diced, raw	1 cup	20	1	T	5
Coconut, grated	1 cup	275	3	28	8
Collards	1 cup	65	7	1	10
Corn, canned (whole kernel)	1 cup	175	5	1	43
Corn, sweet	1 ear	70	2	1	16
Cucumber, peeled	1	20	1	T	5
Lettuce, iceberg (head)	1	70	5	T	16
Mushrooms, raw	1 cup	20	2	T	3
Onion, cooked	1 cup	60	3	T	14
Onion, raw (2½" diam.)	1	40	2	T	10
Parsnips	1 cup	100	2	1	23
Peanut butter	1 tbsp.	95	4	8	3
Peanuts, roasted	1 cup	840	38	72	27
Peas, green, canned	1 cup	150	8	1	29
Pecan halves	1 cup	810	11	84	17
Pepper, green, raw	1 pod	15	1	T	4
Pickle, sweet	1	20	T	T	5
Potato, baked	1	145	4	T	33
Potato, boiled	1	105	3	T	23
Potato, french-fry pieces	10	135	2	7	18
Potato, mashed	1 cup	135	4	2	27
Potato chips	10	115	1	8	10
Radishes, raw	10	10	T	T	2
Rice, cooked	1 cup	225	4	T	50
Sauerkraut, canned	1 cup	40	2	T	9
Spinach	1 cup	40	5	T	6
Sweet potato, baked	1	160	2	1	37
Tomato, raw (3" diam.)	1	40	2	T	9
Tomato catsup	1 tbsp.	15	T	T	4
Tomato juice	1 cup	45	2	T	10
Tomatoes, canned	1 cup	50	2	T	10
Turnip greens	1 cup	30	3	T	5
Turnips, diced	1 cup	35	1	T	8
Walnuts, black	1 cup	785	26	74	19
SALAD DRESSINGS, SAUCES, AND SOUPS					
Barbecue sauce	1 cup	230	4	17	20
Bean with pork soup	1 cup	170	8	6	22
Beef broth	1 cup	30	5	0	3
Bouillon cube	1	5	1	T	T
Cream of chicken soup	1 cup	180	7	10	15
Cream of mushroom soup	1 cup	215	7	14	16
Cream of tomato soup	1 cup	175	7	7	23
Salad dressings:					
Blue cheese	1 tbsp.	75	1	8	1
French	1 tbsp.	65	T	6	3
Mayonnaise	1 tbsp.	100	T	11	T
Thousand Island	1 tbsp.	80	T	8	2
Tartar sauce	1 tbsp.	75	T	8	1
Tomato soup	1 cup	90	2	3	16
Vegetarian soup	1 cup	80	2	2	13
White sauce	1 cup	405	10	31	22

FOOD IS THE SOURCE OF HEALTH

Source: U.S. Departments of Agriculture and Health and Human Services; *Food Is More Than Just Something To Eat*

In this land of plenty, millions of Americans aren't eating wisely.

The problem is not that Americans haven't enough to eat, but that they eat too many of the wrong things or too little of the right.

Food is what you eat; nutrition is how your body uses food. And if you aren't eating foods to meet your bodily needs, you may be suffering from poor nutrition. Some of the damages caused by severe malnutrition may be irreversible.

FOOD IS THE BASIS OF LIFE

Food is the source of health and well-being, gives you the energy you need for everyday living, affects your weight and height and even your strength to a great extent.

In other words, everything in life begins with food, and there is much to the saying "You are what you eat."

Food contains protein, carbohydrates, fats, vitamins, minerals, and water. All of these are nutrients; that is, they nourish the body.

The important thing to remember is that no single food does everything and all foods have something to offer. A variety of different types of food will provide all the nutrients most of us need.

PROTEIN

After water and possibly fat, protein is the most plentiful substance in the body. The substances, called enzymes, which control the processes that keep the body working are made of protein.

Protein is also part of the hemoglobin molecule in red blood cells that carries oxygen into the system.

The antibodies in the bloodstream that fight off disease and infection are also protein.

Another important use of protein in the body is for building the muscle tissue that holds the bone structure together and provides the strength to move and work. *Most Americans get more than enough protein.*

Where is protein found? Meat, poultry, fish, milk, cheese, and eggs provide good quantities of it. Bread and cereal are also important sources.

And such vegetables as soybeans, chickpeas, dry beans, and peanuts are also good sources of protein. You do not have to load up on meat, poultry, or eggs to get enough protein in your diet.

Combining cereal or vegetable foods with a little milk, cheese, or other animal protein can provide good protein in your diet.

For example, eat cereal with milk, rice with fish, spaghetti with meatballs, or simply drink a glass of milk during a meal. All these combinations provide the high-quality protein the body needs.

FATS

Fats provide energy and add flavor and variety to foods. They make meals more satisfying.

Fats carry vitamins A, D, E, and K and are essential parts of the structure of the cells that make up the body's tissues.

Our body fat protects vital organs by providing a cushion around them.

Fats are plentiful in butter, margarine, shortening, salad oils, cream, most cheeses, mayonnaise, salad dressings, nuts, and bacon.

CARBOHYDRATES

Carbohydrates are starches and sugars found in cereal grains, fruits, vegetables, and sugar added to foods for sweetening.

Carbohydrates are the major source of energy in the diet. Wheat, oats, corn, and rice—and the foods made from them, such as bread, spaghetti, macaroni, noodles, or grits—provide starch along with other important nutrients. So do potatoes, sweet potatoes, and vegetables such as peas, dry beans, peanuts, and soybeans.

Most of the other vegetables contain smaller amounts of carbohydrates.

Carbohydrates in vegetables are usually in the form of starch; in fruits they occur as sugar. Candies, jams, molasses, and syrups are primarily sugar.

WATER

Water is a vitally important nutrient. Water stands next to air in importance to life. You can get along for days, even weeks, without food but you can live only a few days without water.

Water is necessary for all the processes of digestion.

Nutrients are dissolved in water so they may pass through the intestinal wall and into the bloodstream for use throughout the body.

Water carries waste out of the body and also helps to regulate body temperature.

The body's most obvious source of water is the water a person drinks, but some is produced by the body's burning of food for energy. Coffee and tea are mostly water, and so are fruit juices and milk.

Soup is a source of water, and so are many fruits and vegetables. Even meat can be up to 80% water.

MINERALS

The most abundant mineral in the body is calcium and, except for iron, it is the most likely to be inadequate in the diets of many age groups.

From the age of 9, the diets of girls and women may lack as much as 25% to 30% of the calcium they need.

Almost all calcium, and most phosphorus, which works closely with calcium in the body, is in bones and teeth.

The other minerals play a vital role in tissue and body fluids. Soft tissue, or muscle, especially has a high phosphorus content. Calcium is required for blood to clot and for the heart to function normally. The nervous system does not work properly when calcium levels in the blood are below normal.

People who buy from the milk counter are stocking up on calcium supplies.

In the U.S. we rely on milk as a basic source of calcium. Two cups of milk, or an equivalent amount of cheese or other dairy products except butter, go a long way toward supplying all the calcium needed for the day.

But milk is not the only source. Dark-green leafy vegetables like collards, mustard greens, or turnip greens provide some calcium, and salmon and sardines supply useful amounts of it if the very tiny bones are eaten.

IRON

Iron is another essential mineral. Women of childbearing age require more iron than men do.

The diets of infants and pregnant women may need special attention to see that they contain the iron needed.

Unfortunately, only a few foods provide iron in very useful amounts. However, liver, heart, kidney, and most lean meats are generously supplied with it. So are shellfish, particularly oysters.

Whole-grain and enriched breads and cereals can provide 20% to 25% or more of the daily iron need.

Dark-green leafy vegetables are also sources of iron.

IODINE

The most important fact about iodine is that a deficiency of it can cause goiter—a swelling of the thyroid gland. The most practical ways to be sure of getting enough iodine are to use iodized salt regularly and to add seafood to the diet whenever possible.

OTHER ESSENTIAL ELEMENTS

Calcium, iron, and iodine are not the only minerals you need. Most of the others—zinc, copper, sodium, potassium, magnesium, and phosphorus—are widely available in so many foods that a little variety in selecting groceries takes care of them easily. Magnesium, for example, is abundant in nuts, whole-grain products, dry beans, and dark-green vegetables.

Phosphorus shows up in the same foods that supply you with protein and calcium, although leafy vegetables contain little phosphorus.

FLUORINE

Fluorine—an element that helps protect teeth from decay—is not so readily found in food. Many metropolitan areas add minute amounts of fluorine to local sources of drinking water.

VITAMINS

Scientists know of a dozen or more vitamins that you must have to enjoy good health. Ordinarily, you can get them from a well-chosen assortment of everyday foods.

A few of these vitamins are of great importance, and you should know what foods provide them.

VITAMIN A

Vitamin A plays a very important role in eye function, and in keeping the skin and mucous membranes resistant to infection.

Although vitamin A occurs only in foods of animal origin, the deep-yellow and dark-green vegetables and fruits supply a material—carotene—that your body can turn into vitamin A.

Vegetables and fruits can easily supply all the vitamin A you need. Such items as collards, turnip greens, kale, carrots, squash, and sweet potatoes can more than take care of daily needs; yellow peaches, apricots, cantaloupe, and papayas also help.

Many people, however, do not regularly eat these foods.

Liver is an excellent source of vitamin A. A 2-ounce serving of cooked beef liver provides more than 30,000 international units of the vitamin. That amounts to six times more vitamin A than you would need during the day. Kidney is also an excellent source of vitamin A.

There are plenty of other sources of vitamin A. Whole milk is a source, but skim milk doesn't have any vitamin A unless it is fortified—that is, vitamin A has been added to it.

Cheese made from whole milk, and margarine enriched with vitamin A, both supply this vitamin.

THE B VITAMINS

Three of the best-known vitamins—riboflavin, thiamin, and niacin—release the

FOOD IS THE SOURCE OF HEALTH *(continued)*

energy in food. They also have a role in the nervous system, keep the digestive system working calmly, and help maintain healthy skin.

Vitamin B_2 (riboflavin) is easy to find and extremely important to your diet. It is plentifully supplied by meats, milk, whole-grain or enriched breads, and cereals.

Organ meats (liver, kidney, etc.) also supply this vitamin.

A lack of thiamin (vitamin B_1) causes beriberi. Fortunately, this disease is now almost nonexistent in the U.S., although it is still detected in some alcoholics.

Thiamin is abundant in only a few foods. Lean pork is one. Dry beans and peas, some organ meats, and some nuts supply some thiamin.

Whole-grain and enriched cereals and breads are also dependable sources of the vitamin.

Niacin can be found in whole-grain and enriched cereals, meat and meat products, and peas and beans.

Other B vitamins such as B_6, B_{12}, and folacin are needed to maintain normal hemoglobin, the substance in blood that carries oxygen to the tissues. The signs of B_{12} deficiency include soreness of the mouth and tongue, numbness and tingling in the hands and legs, anemia, and loss of coordination.

Folacin is available in many foods but in small quantities.

VITAMIN C

Vitamin C, ascorbic acid, is not completely understood, but it is considered important in helping to maintain the cementing material that holds body cells together.

The citrus-fruit juice you may have for breakfast can give you more than half of the vitamin C needed for the day.

In fact, unless good foods are consciously avoided, the rest of the fruits and vegetables eaten during the day will help to provide the vitamin C required.

Potatoes and sweet potatoes provide helpful amounts of vitamin C, and so do tomatoes and peppers. In addition, green vegetables such as broccoli, turnip greens, raw cabbage, and collards make a contribution of vitamin C.

VITAMIN D

Although few foods contain vitamin D, it is readily available in milk fortified with it. Sunlight enables the body to produce vitamin D if it shines directly on the skin.

Vitamin D is important in building strong bones and teeth and is needed throughout the growth period.

Without vitamin D the body cannot absorb the calcium supplied by food. For this reason milk is often fortified with vitamin D.

Adults rarely need more vitamin D than they get in food and from the sun. However, infants and young children sometimes do not get enough.

A disease called rickets results from a lack of vitamin D. Children who suffer from this disease have absorbed too little calcium. Their bodies cannot form strong and rigid bones, and consequently they may have enlarged joints, bowed legs, knock-knees, or beaded ribs.

On the other hand, too much vitamin D can be dangerous. This causes a calcium overload in the blood and tissues. Infants given too much vitamin D may develop calcium deposits in the kidneys and end up with permanent kidney damage.

VITAMIN E

Vitamin E is known to be essential, but its exact role in the body is not fully understood by scientists.

Vitamin E is abundant in vegetable oils and margarine and is contained in such foods as wheat germ and lettuce.

A diet usually does not lack in vitamin E if it regularly includes fruits, vegetables, vegetable oil, milk, meat, and eggs.

VITAMIN K

Vitamin K is essential for the manufacture of a substance that helps blood to clot. Vitamin K is widely distributed in a variety of foods such as the green and leafy vegetables, tomatoes, cauliflower, egg yolks, soybean oil, and any kind of liver.

NUTRIENTS AND ENERGY

Almost all foods provide energy—some more than others.

This energy is measured in calories. Foods that are rich in fats, starches, or sugars contain large amounts of calories—or energy.

Fat is the most concentrated source of energy. Ounce for ounce, it provides more than twice as much energy as protein or the carbohydrates.

Foods that contain a lot of water, like watermelon and cucumbers, have few calories because water, which makes up most of their weight, provides no calories and therefore no energy.

When you eat a diet that furnishes more energy—or calories—than you need, the excess supply is stored in the body as fat. And when you continue to overeat you become overweight or fat.

When you eat less calories than the body uses, you lose weight.

HOW TO STRETCH YOUR FOOD DOLLAR

You can save a great deal of money on food if you shop carefully and cautiously.

Here are some general rules for feeding your family at less cost.

1. Learn the facts about basic nutrition. Then you will know how much protein your family needs each day and what foods provide it. You will also understand how to meet the daily minimum requirements of vitamins and minerals. See pages 398–402.

2. Plan the week's menu ahead of time. If you shop only once or twice a week instead of every day, you will spend less. Impulse buying of exotic foods will be kept to a minimum.

3. Shop around for the best prices. Special sale prices in one store can be attractive enough to make you overlook the fact that the prices of staples, bread, and milk are higher than those in another store.

4. Watch for specials and sales. Read supermarket advertisements in the newspapers on Wednesday and Thursday. These advertisements offer bargains from 6% to 34% below regular prices. It often pays to buy in quantity if the items will keep.

5. Privately labeled foods in supermarket chains usually cost less. They are often as good as well-known brands.

6. Learn how to store foods properly. Waste through spoilage can be a constant drain on your food budget. For example, use frozen foods as quickly as possible, and do not let them thaw before putting them in your freezer. Remove the store wrappings from meat and store it in a covered dish. If you freeze meat, wrap it *tightly* in foil or other material to prevent freezer burn.

7. Save on meat costs. Remember that all meat has about the same nutritional value. Lamb chops, T-bone steak, and veal cost more because they are tender and may have superior flavor.

But there are some meats with a high initial cost that, because they have little waste, are good buys—for example, canned ham and round steak. Chicken is one of the best buys in the market.

Most seafood has risen in price. Substitute cheese and egg dishes once or twice a week. Dry beans and peas are also rich in protein.

8. Stretch food by using leftovers. Think in terms of double-duty foods, especially meats. Steaks and chops are usually good for one meal only. On the other hand, leftovers from roasts, chicken, turkey, and ham can be made into a wide variety of dishes.

You can grind leftover meats for hash and casseroles, and cut up leftover poultry, meats, and vegetables for pies, stews, salads, or soups. The stripped carcass of a roasted chicken or turkey and the bones from a beef roast or smoked ham can be boiled to make a rich soup stock.

9. Do not avoid unfamiliar foods, especially meats, that are on sale, just because you don't know how to cook them. Consult a reputable cookbook that tells you how to prepare such cuts as lamb's breast, beef and lamb kidneys, tripe, and the like.

10. Be aware of the high cost of convenience foods. These include TV dinners, frozen pasta and Chinese dishes, and frozen vegetables prepared with butter sauce and other garnishes. A package of frozen green beans with mushrooms may cost from 11 to 15 cents more than one of plain green beans.

11. Buying staples in large quantities is usually economical if you have sufficient storage space. Sugar, flour, cereals, rice, potatoes, and canned foods are often better bargains in large quantities. Buying milk in a two-quart container costs less than two separate containers. Do not overlook the various brands of powdered milk, which offer substantial savings.

12. If you live in or near a large city, discuss the idea of a cooperative food-buying plan with your friends and neighbors. A dozen or more families can band together to purchase food supplies wholesale from city markets and meat warehouses at savings up to 40%. In order to do this you must have a central place, such as a garage or basement, in which to store the items. The plan also requires some bookkeeping as well as purchasing and distributing work.

TOO MUCH SALT CAN KILL

The average American eats from 2 to $2\frac{1}{2}$ teaspoons of salt each day—or about $8\frac{1}{2}$ pounds a year, according to the Food and Drug Administration (FDA). Only about one-third comes from sprinkling salt on your food, about one-third occurs naturally in the food you eat, and about one-third comes as flavoring in processed foods in your diet.

However, the National Research Council of the National Academy of Sciences estimates that an "adequate and safe intake" should be only about one-fourth of the amount normally consumed.

Too much salt in the diet can be especially dangerous to the 10% to 30% of persons who have inherited a tendency to develop high blood pressure, according to studies sponsored by the FDA. High blood pressure often leads to stroke, heart disease, and kidney failure.

PLANTING AND GROWING GARDEN ANNUALS

Source: U.S. Department of Agriculture

Most garden annuals, plants that live only one year, should be planted outdoors only after the last frost of spring.

To find the approximate date of the last frost in your area, see the table *Freeze Dates and Growing Season for Gardeners* on pages 406–409.

PLANT	WHEN TO PLANT SEEDS	EXPOSURE	GERMINA-TION TIME (days)	PLANT SPACING (inches)	REMARKS
Ageratum	After last frost	Semishade or full sun	5	10 to 12	Pinch tips to encourage branching; remove dead flowers.
Balsam	After last frost	Sun	10	12 to 14	
Calendula	Early spring or late fall	Shade or sun	10	8 to 10	
Calliopsis	After last frost	Shade or sun	8	10 to 14	
China aster	After last frost	Shade or sun	8	10 to 12	Start early in cold frame; resow for prolonged blooming.
Cockscomb	After last frost	Shade or sun	10	10 to 12	
Coleus	Sow indoors any time; outdoors after last frost	Sun or partial shade	10	10 to 12	
Cornflower	Early spring	Partial shade	5	12 to 14	
Cosmos	After last frost	Sun	5	10 to 12	
Dahlia	After last frost	Sun	5	12 to 14	For best blooms, sow several weeks before other annuals.
Forget-me-not	Spring or summer; shade in summer	Partial shade	10	10 to 12	
Four-o'clock	After last frost	Sun	5	12 to 14	Store roots; plant next year.
Globe amaranth	Early spring	Sun	15	10 to 12	
Impatiens	Indoors any time; outdoors after last frost	Partial or deep shade	15	10 to 12	
Larkspur	South late fall; North early spring	Sun	20	6 to 8	Hard to transplant; grow in peat pots.
Lupine	Early spring or late fall	Sun	20	6 to 8	
Marigold	After last frost	Sun	5	10 to 14	High fertility delays bloom.
Morning glory	After last frost	Sun	5	24 to 36	Reseeds itself.
Nasturtium	After last frost	Sun	8	8 to 12	For best flowers, grow in soil of low fertility.
Pansy	Spring or summer; shade in summer	Sun or shade	10	6 to 8	Does best in cool season.
Petunia	Early spring indoors	Sun	10	12 to 14	Transplant outdoors early summer; keep cool.
Pink	Early spring through summer; shade in summer	Sun or shade	5	8 to 12	Start early in spring indoors; keep cool; remove dead flowers.
Poppy	Early spring through summer; shade in summer	Sun	10	6 to 10	Difficult to transplant; start in peat pots; make successive plantings.
Portulaca	After last frost or in late fall	Sun	10	10 to 12	
Salpiglossis	Early spring	Sun	15	10 to 12	Needs supports; avoid cold.
Scabiosa	Spring or summer; shade in summer	Sun	10	12 to 14	Remove old flowers.
Scarlet sage	Spring or summer; shade in summer	Sun	15	8 to 12	
Snapdragon	Spring or late fall	Sun	15	6 to 10	Start cool; pinch tips to encourage branching.
Spider plant	Early spring, spring, or fall	Sun	10	12 to 14	Reseeds freely; pinch to keep plant short; water and fertilize freely.
Stock	After last frost	Sun	5	6 to 10	
Strawflower	Early spring	Sun	5	10 to 12	
Summer cypress	Early spring	Sun	15	18 to 24	
Sunflower	After last frost	Sun	5	12 to 14	
Sweet alyssum	Early spring	Sun	5	10 to 12	Damps off easily; sow in hills; do not thin.
Sweetpea	Early spring or late summer through late fall	Sun	15	6 to 8	Select heat-resistant types.
Verbena	After last frost	Sun	20	18 to 24	Pinch to encourage branching.
Vinca	After last frost	Sun	15	10 to 12	Avoid overwatering.
Zinnia	After last frost	Sun	5	8 to 12	Thin after plants begin to bloom; remove poor-flowering plants.

PLANTING AND GROWING VEGETABLES
Source: U.S. Department of Agriculture

Home-grown vegetables picked at the peak of their maturity have a tasty quality seldom found in those bought in a store.

Vegetable gardening requires labor and time. But vegetables grown at home can save on grocery bills as well as provide an enjoyable hobby.

Be cautious about how large a garden you plant the first time. A small well-kept garden will give you more enjoyment than a large neglected one.

Even though you live in a one-room apartment, you can have a vegetable garden in containers on a windowsill or balcony.

If you use plastic containers, allow for drainage by boring several small holes in the side of the container near the bottom. Put about half an inch of coarse gravel in the bottom of the con-

tainer before filling it with soil.

The inexperienced gardener should choose only a few crops to plant the first year.

When you buy seeds for your garden, check to make sure they are stamped with this year's date. Old seed germinates poorly.

You can get a jump on the growing season by planting your seeds indoors, and then transplanting the plants to your garden when the weather is warmer.

The vegetables suggested in the table below all can be grown in a minigarden. Vegetables such as corn and potatoes take a great deal of space in order to provide a worthwhile harvest.

The approximate date of the last spring frost in your area can be found in the table *Freeze Dates and Growing Season for Gardeners* on pages 406–409.

VEGETABLE	PLANTING			GROWING	COMMENTS
	Weeks before frost-free date	Depth of seeds	Space between plants	Days from seed to harvest	
Beets	2 to 4 weeks	½ in.	2 to 3 in.	50 to 60 days	Tolerate partial shade; thin plants when 6 to 8 inches high.
Cabbage	4 to 6 weeks	½ in.	12 to 18 in.	65 to 120 days	Tolerates partial shade; can also be set out for a fall crop.
Carrots	2 to 4 weeks	½ in.	2 to 3 in.	65 to 80 days	Tolerate partial shade; for several harvests make plantings at 3-week intervals until 3 months before fall freezing date.
Chives	4 to 6 weeks	½ in.	2 to 3 in.	60 to 70 days	Grow in partial shade; bulbs should be divided occasionally so they do not get too thick.
Cucumbers	1 week after frost-free date	½ in.	18 in.	70 to 80 days	Need full sunlight and hot weather; start seeds indoors 3 weeks before time to set out.
Eggplant	See comments	½ in.	18 in.	100 to 140 days	Start seeds indoors 8 to 9 weeks before planting outdoors; set out on frost-free date in warm soil; needs full sunlight; cover plants during cool weather.
Leaf lettuce	4 to 6 weeks	¼ in.	4 to 6 in.	30 to 35 days	Tolerates partial shade and temperatures as low as 28° F.; make several later plantings for summer lettuce.
Mustard greens	2 to 4 weeks	¼ in.	4 to 5 in.	35 to 40 days	Make plantings at 10-day intervals for successive crops; tolerate partial shade.
Onions	4 to 6 weeks	1 to 1½ in.	2 to 3 in.	100 to 120 days	Green onions grow in partial shade; mature bulbs need full sun; onions need lots of water.
Parsley	4 to 6 weeks	¼ in.	6 to 8 in.	80 to 85 days	Does well in partial shade; start seeds indoors, soaking them overnight before planting; keep soil moist to help seeds germinate.
Peppers	1 week after frost-free date	½ in.	14 to 18 in.	110 to 120 days	Require full sunlight and hot weather; start seeds indoors 5 to 6 weeks before outdoor planting.
Radishes	2 to 4 weeks	½ in.	1 in.	22 to 35 days	Do well in partial shade; cannot withstand heat; make several plantings at 1-week intervals.
Summer squash	See comments	1 to 2 in.	18 in.	50 to 60 days	Plant on frost-free date; does best in full sunlight; plant bush types.
Tomatoes	See comments	½ in.	14 to 18 in.	55 to 100 days	Start seeds 5 to 7 weeks before transplanting on frost-free date; require full sunlight and warm weather.
Turnips	4 to 6 weeks	½ in.	3 to 4 in.	30 to 80 days	Tolerate partial shade; thin when plants are large enough to use for greens, leaving others to mature as vegetables.

FREEZE DATES AND GROWING SEASON FOR GARDENERS

Gardeners and farmers need to know the approximate date they can expect the last freezing day in the spring so they can schedule when to set out plants susceptible to frost. The length of the growing season—the time until the first freezing day in the fall—helps determine what kinds of flowers or vegetables can be grown in a certain climate.

Information in the following table comes from the *Annual Summary of Climatological Data*, National Oceanic and Atmospheric Administration.

LOCATION	LAST SPRING FREEZE	GROWING SEASON	FIRST FALL FREEZE
ALABAMA			
Athens	March 25	27 weeks	Oct. 3
Birmingham	March 23	33 weeks	Nov. 8
Gadsden	March 22	33 weeks	Nov. 12
Haleyville	April 9	25 weeks	Oct. 3
Huntsville	March 30	31 weeks	Oct. 31
Jasper	April 10	25 weeks	Oct. 3
Mobile	Feb. 27	39 weeks	Dec. 1
Montgomery	Feb. 28	37 weeks	Nov. 13
Ozark	Feb. 27	37 weeks	Nov. 13
Pittsview	April 10	25 weeks	Oct. 5
Selma	Feb. 27	37 weeks	Nov. 13
Tuscaloosa	April 10	25 weeks	Oct. 3
ALASKA			
Adak	May 31	20 weeks	Oct. 24
Anchorage	May 15	18 weeks	Sept. 16
Fairbanks	May 21	14 weeks	Aug. 30
Juneau	April 22	26 weeks	Oct. 21
Ketchikan	March 31	32 weeks	Nov. 12
Kodiak	May 22	19 weeks	Oct. 2
Seward	April 26	22 weeks	Sept. 29
Sitka	May 25	18 weeks	Oct. 3
Valdez	May 26	15 weeks	Sept. 12
Wrangell	April 23	23 weeks	Oct. 4
ARIZONA			
Bisbee	April 16	24 weeks	Oct. 31
Flagstaff	June 9	17 weeks	Sept. 16
Mesa	Feb. 9	44 weeks	Dec. 15
Nogales	May 21	19 weeks	Oct. 31
Phoenix	Jan. 3	49 weeks	Dec. 15
Prescott	May 21	19 weeks	Oct. 30
Scottsdale	Feb. 21	41 weeks	Dec. 10
Tombstone	March 10	37 weeks	Nov. 29
Tucson	April 4	33 weeks	Nov. 24
Winslow	April 22	27 weeks	Oct. 25
ARKANSAS			
Arkadelphia	April 9	31 weeks	Nov. 13
El Dorado	March 24	34 weeks	Nov. 14
Fayetteville	April 17	26 weeks	Oct. 16
Fort Smith	April 9	31 weeks	Nov. 14
Helena	April 6	32 weeks	Nov. 15
Hot Springs	March 26	33 weeks	Nov. 15
Jonesboro	March 25	30 weeks	Oct. 22
Little Rock	April 6	33 weeks	Nov. 15
Mammoth Spring	April 17	26 weeks	Oct. 16
Pine Bluff	March 24	34 weeks	Nov. 15
Texarkana	March 24	34 weeks	Nov. 15
CALIFORNIA			
Bakersfield	Feb. 7	46 weeks	Dec. 23
Barstow	April 10	33 weeks	Nov. 24
Death Valley	Jan. 5	51 weeks	none
El Centro	Feb. 6	44 weeks	Dec. 11
Eureka	Feb. 23	43 weeks	Dec. 23
Fairmont	April 19	31 weeks	Nov. 23
Fresno	Feb. 23	40 weeks	Dec. 1
Los Angeles	none	52 weeks	none
Modesto	Feb. 7	46 weeks	Dec. 23
Oakland	none	52 weeks	none
Palmdale	May 19	24 weeks	Oct. 31

LOCATION	LAST SPRING FREEZE	GROWING SEASON	FIRST FALL FREEZE
CALIFORNIA *(continued)*			
Paradise	March 3	42 weeks	Dec. 22
Red Bluff	Feb. 22	40 weeks	Nov. 30
Sacramento	Feb. 8	46 weeks	Dec. 24
San Bernardino	Jan. 3	51 weeks	Dec. 26
San Diego	none	52 weeks	none
San Francisco	Jan. 8	50 weeks	Dec. 25
San Jose	Jan. 9	46 weeks	Nov. 28
San Rafael	none	51 weeks	Nov. 30
Santa Rosa	March 9	37 weeks	Nov. 26
Stockton	Feb. 9	42 weeks	Nov. 28
Woodland	March 9	37 weeks	Nov. 23
COLORADO			
Aspen	June 8	12 weeks	Sept. 3
Boulder	April 30	19 weeks	Sept. 12
Burlington	April 22	28 weeks	Nov. 2
Colorado Springs	May 8	21 weeks	Oct. 4
Del Norte	June 3	17 weeks	Sept. 28
Denver	April 16	29 weeks	Oct. 30
Durango	June 9	15 weeks	Sept. 23
Grand Junction	April 15	29 weeks	Nov. 5
Greeley	April 16	24 weeks	Sept. 28
Lakewood	June 8	15 weeks	Sept. 12
Manassa	June 10	12 weeks	Sept. 3
Pueblo	April 22	27 weeks	Oct. 31
CONNECTICUT			
Bridgeport	April 10	24 weeks	Oct. 18
Danbury	May 8	20 weeks	Sept. 24
Hartford	April 22	24 weeks	Oct. 15
Middletown	May 8	20 weeks	Sept. 24
New Haven	April 10	24 weeks	Oct. 19
Norfolk	May 8	20 weeks	Sept. 24
Stamford	May 8	20 weeks	Sept. 24
Storrs	May 2	22 weeks	Oct. 4
Westbrook	May 9	21 weeks	Oct. 3
DELAWARE			
Bridgeville	April 20	24 weeks	Oct. 4
Dover	April 7	26 weeks	Oct. 3
Georgetown	May 8	26 weeks	Oct. 4
Middletown	April 20	24 weeks	Oct. 3
Milford	May 8	25 weeks	Oct. 3
Wilmington	April 7	26 weeks	Oct. 3
DIST. OF COLUMBIA			
Washington	May 8	20 weeks	Sept. 24
FLORIDA			
Fort Lauderdale	none	52 weeks	none
Fort Myers	none	52 weeks	none
Gainesville	Feb. 27	40 weeks	Dec. 2
Jacksonville	Feb. 27	39 weeks	Nov. 14
Key West	none	52 weeks	none
Miami	none	52 weeks	none
Orlando	Feb. 26	51 weeks	none
St. Augustine	Feb. 27	42 weeks	Dec. 18
St. Petersburg	none	52 weeks	none
Tallahassee	Feb. 28	38 weeks	Nov. 25
Tampa	Feb. 27	51 weeks	none
Tavernier	none	52 weeks	none
Titusville	Feb. 26	51 weeks	none

LOCATION	LAST SPRING FREEZE	GROWING SEASON	FIRST FALL FREEZE
GEORGIA			
Albany	March 1	37 weeks	Nov. 13
Athens	April 2	31 weeks	Nov. 7
Atlanta	March 24	33 weeks	Nov. 12
Augusta	March 16	34 weeks	Nov. 12
Brunswick	Feb. 28	40 weeks	Dec. 4
Cartersville	April 25	23 weeks	Oct. 3
Columbus	Feb. 28	37 weeks	Nov. 15
Gainesville	April 7	28 weeks	Oct. 22
Macon	March 15	35 weeks	Nov. 16
Moultrie	Feb. 28	37 weeks	Nov. 13
Rome	April 10	30 weeks	Oct. 3
Savannah	Feb. 26	39 weeks	Nov. 26
Valdosta	Feb. 28	37 weeks	Nov. 13
HAWAII			
Honolulu	none	52 weeks	none
Kailua	none	52 weeks	none
IDAHO			
Boise	May 6	20 weeks	Oct. 12
Idaho Falls	May 31	15 weeks	Sept. 13
Lewiston	April 13	28 weeks	Oct. 6
Oakley	June 8	18 weeks	Oct. 13
Pocatello	May 16	17 weeks	Sept. 13
Potlatch	June 9	9 weeks	Aug. 13
Twin Falls	May 16	20 weeks	Oct. 5
ILLINOIS			
Chicago	April 29	21 weeks	Oct. 12
Decatur	April 24	23 weeks	Oct. 2
Joliet	May 7	20 weeks	Sept. 23
Marion	April 18	24 weeks	Oct. 3
Moline	April 21	25 weeks	Oct. 14
Mount Vernon	April 17	24 weeks	Oct. 3
Olney	April 17	24 weeks	Oct. 3
Peoria	April 16	29 weeks	Oct. 21
Quincy	April 9	25 weeks	Oct. 2
Rockford	May 2	22 weeks	Oct. 9
Springfield	April 9	25 weeks	Oct. 2
Urbana	April 24	23 weeks	Oct. 2
INDIANA			
Bloomington	April 10	25 weeks	Oct. 3
Columbus	May 8	21 weeks	Oct. 2
Crawfordsville	May 8	21 weeks	Oct. 2
Evansville	April 7	28 weeks	Oct. 23
Fort Wayne	April 26	25 weeks	Oct. 17
Greencastle	May 7	21 weeks	Oct. 2
Hobart	May 10	19 weeks	Sept. 23
Indianapolis	April 23	25 weeks	Oct. 22
New Castle	May 8	20 weeks	Sept. 23
Scottsburg	May 7	21 weeks	Oct. 2
South Bend	May 2	24 weeks	Sept. 18
IOWA			
Cedar Rapids	May 6	20 weeks	Sept. 22
Davenport	April 24	23 weeks	Oct. 2
Des Moines	April 30	27 weeks	Oct. 10
Mason City	May 6	17 weeks	Sept. 3
Oskaloosa	April 24	22 weeks	Sept. 22
Pocahontas	May 6	20 weeks	Sept. 22
Sioux City	April 16	23 weeks	Sept. 22
Waterloo	May 6	22 weeks	Oct. 3
KANSAS			
Atchison	April 8	30 weeks	Nov. 6
Concordia	April 17	27 weeks	Oct. 21
Dodge City	April 16	26 weeks	Oct. 15
Fort Scott	April 5	31 weeks	Nov. 6
Goodland	May 3	23 weeks	Oct. 11
Healy	April 16	20 weeks	Sept. 3
Hill City	April 16	26 weeks	Sept. 13
Lawrence	April 5	31 weeks	Nov. 6
Lincoln	April 16	26 weeks	Oct. 15
Mankato	April 16	26 weeks	Oct. 15

LOCATION	LAST SPRING FREEZE	GROWING SEASON	FIRST FALL FREEZE
KANSAS (continued)			
Topeka	April 15	24 weeks	Oct. 1
Wichita	April 15	29 weeks	Nov. 6
KENTUCKY			
Ashland	May 8	20 weeks	Sept. 23
Danville	April 10	25 weeks	Oct. 3
Frankfort	May 8	26 weeks	Oct. 3
Lexington	April 25	23 weeks	Oct. 2
Louisville	April 9	28 weeks	Oct. 21
Middlesboro	May 7	26 weeks	Oct. 3
Owensboro	April 9	25 weeks	Oct. 3
Somerset	April 25	23 weeks	Oct. 3
LOUISIANA			
Alexandria	Feb. 27	40 weeks	Dec. 1
Bastrop	March 24	37 weeks	Nov. 15
Baton Rouge	Feb. 22	39 weeks	Nov. 22
Lafayette	Feb. 26	40 weeks	Dec. 1
Lake Charles	Feb. 22	39 weeks	Nov. 26
Monroe	Feb. 26	37 weeks	Nov. 14
Natchitoches	Feb. 26	37 weeks	Nov. 15
New Orleans	Feb. 27	39 weeks	Nov. 27
Shreveport	Feb. 26	37 weeks	Nov. 15
MAINE			
Augusta	May 5	20 weeks	Sept. 24
Bangor	May 6	20 weeks	Sept. 25
Bar Harbor	May 5	24 weeks	Oct. 19
Caribou	May 18	18 weeks	Sept. 22
Houlton	May 29	16 weeks	Sept. 19
Lewiston	May 2	23 weeks	Oct. 14
Portland	May 12	12 weeks	Sept. 27
MARYLAND			
Annapolis	March 26	28 weeks	Oct. 5
Baltimore	April 15	27 weeks	Oct. 21
Bittinger	May 8	20 weeks	Sept. 23
Boonsboro	April 20	27 weeks	Sept. 24
La Plata	May 8	21 weeks	Oct. 3
Salisbury	April 11	25 weeks	Oct. 4
MASSACHUSETTS			
Amherst	May 8	20 weeks	Sept. 24
Boston	April 8	30 weeks	Nov. 7
Chester	May 26	15 weeks	Sept. 5
Hyannis	May 2	24 weeks	Oct. 19
Milton	April 26	25 weeks	Oct. 21
Provincetown	April 20	25 weeks	Oct. 14
Springfield	April 26	23 weeks	Oct. 4
Stockbridge	May 21	18 weeks	Sept. 24
Woods Hole	April 25	30 weeks	Nov. 22
Worcester	April 26	24 weeks	Oct. 15
MICHIGAN			
Alpena	May 12	20 weeks	Oct. 4
Bad Axe	May 8	21 weeks	Oct. 2
Detroit	April 23	26 weeks	Oct. 21
Escanaba	May 7	20 weeks	Sept. 22
Grand Rapids	April 25	24 weeks	Oct. 12
Lansing	May 7	22 weeks	Oct. 8
Marquette	May 2	25 weeks	Oct. 26
Midland	May 8	20 weeks	Sept. 22
Muskegon	May 10	24 weeks	Oct. 2
Sault Ste. Marie	May 18	19 weeks	Sept. 29
Traverse City	May 10	19 weeks	Sept. 23
MINNESOTA			
Albert Lea	May 13	19 weeks	Sept. 21
Baudette	May 25	17 weeks	Sept. 21
Duluth	May 22	18 weeks	Sept. 24
Fergus Falls	May 15	16 weeks	Sept. 3
Rochester	May 8	20 weeks	Sept. 28
St. Cloud	May 25	20 weeks	Sept. 30
St. Paul	April 29	24 weeks	Oct. 13

FREEZE DATES AND GROWING SEASON FOR GARDENERS (continued)

LOCATION	LAST SPRING FREEZE	GROWING SEASON	FIRST FALL FREEZE
MINNESOTA (continued)			
Stillwater	May 23	17 weeks	Sept. 22
Tyler	May 7	20 weeks	Sept. 22
MISSISSIPPI			
Aberdeen	March 22	34 weeks	Nov. 15
Biloxi	Feb. 27	35 weeks	Nov. 28
Greenville	March 24	34 weeks	Nov. 15
Grenada	April 7	32 weeks	Nov. 15
Hattiesburg	Feb. 28	37 weeks	Nov. 13
Jackson	March 18	34 weeks	Nov. 8
McComb	March 22	34 weeks	Nov. 13
Meridian	March 19	34 weeks	Nov. 7
Tupelo	April 10	25 weeks	Oct. 3
MISSOURI			
Butler	April 17	29 weeks	Nov. 6
Cape Girardeau	April 9	25 weeks	Oct. 3
Columbia	April 9	28 weeks	Oct. 24
Dexter	April 9	31 weeks	Nov. 14
Festus	April 24	22 weeks	Sept. 23
Jefferson City	April 24	23 weeks	Oct. 2
Joplin	March 25	32 weeks	Nov. 6
Kansas City	April 5	31 weeks	Nov. 6
Poplar Bluff	April 10	28 weeks	Oct. 21
St. Joseph	April 13	28 weeks	Oct. 22
St. Louis	April 15	28 weeks	Oct. 20
Springfield	April 9	29 weeks	Oct. 25
MONTANA			
Bigfork	May 17	17 weeks	Sept. 13
Billings	May 16	19 weeks	Sept. 27
Butte	June 10	12 weeks	Sept. 2
Goldbutte	May 23	14 weeks	Sept. 1
Great Falls	May 16	19 weeks	Sept. 29
Havre	May 9	20 weeks	Sept. 23
Helena	May 12	19 weeks	Sept. 23
Miles City	April 25	22 weeks	Oct. 5
Missoula	May 15	19 weeks	Sept. 13
Shonkin	June 1	14 weeks	Sept. 2
NEBRASKA			
Dalton	May 22	15 weeks	Sept. 3
Grand Island	May 1	23 weeks	Oct. 11
Imperial	April 16	24 weeks	Sept. 30
Lincoln	April 23	23 weeks	Oct. 1
North Platte	May 12	16 weeks	Sept. 3
Omaha	April 16	29 weeks	Oct. 20
Scottsbluff	May 12	16 weeks	Sept. 3
NEVADA			
Carson City	June 8	14 weeks	Sept. 12
Eureka	June 8	10 weeks	Aug. 20
Las Vegas	March 4	39 weeks	Nov. 30
NEW HAMPSHIRE			
Bethlehem	May 21	18 weeks	Sept. 24
Concord	May 17	18 weeks	Sept. 24
Hanover	May 5	20 weeks	Sept. 24
Lebanon	May 20	18 weeks	Sept. 24
Monroe	May 21	18 weeks	Sept. 24
Woodstock	May 20	18 weeks	Sept. 24
NEW JERSEY			
Atlantic City	April 10	27 weeks	Oct. 19
Jersey City	April 10	27 weeks	Oct. 19
Moorestown	May 8	21 weeks	Oct. 3
Newark	April 7	29 weeks	Nov. 2
Sandy Hook	April 10	32 weeks	Nov. 23
Trenton	April 10	27 weeks	Oct. 19
NEW MEXICO			
Alamogordo	April 5	30 weeks	Nov. 4
Albuquerque	April 5	30 weeks	Oct. 31
Carlsbad	March 25	32 weeks	Nov. 5
Gallup	June 10	16 weeks	Sept. 28
Mescalero	May 22	21 weeks	Oct. 15
San Mateo	May 21	23 weeks	Sept. 27
Santa Fe	April 27	27 weeks	Oct. 30
Taos	June 9	16 weeks	Sept. 27
NEW YORK			
Albany	April 27	23 weeks	Oct. 13
Buffalo	May 8	21 weeks	Oct. 3
Cooperstown	May 20	18 weeks	Sept. 23
Glens Falls	May 5	20 weeks	Sept. 23
New York City	April 10	27 weeks	Oct. 19
Plattsburgh	May 5	20 weeks	Sept. 24
Rochester	April 25	25 weeks	Oct. 20
Scarsdale	May 8	22 weeks	Oct. 8
Syracuse	April 28	24 weeks	Oct. 16
Utica	May 5	20 weeks	Sept. 24
NORTH CAROLINA			
Asheville	April 12	28 weeks	Oct. 24
Boone	May 7	21 weeks	Oct. 3
Charlotte	April 2	31 weeks	Nov. 4
Greensboro	April 15	29 weeks	Nov. 1
Greenville	March 27	27 weeks	Oct. 4
Hatteras	March 15	39 weeks	Dec. 10
Lenoir	April 7	21 weeks	Oct. 3
Raleigh	April 5	30 weeks	Nov. 1
Wilmington	March 17	35 weeks	Nov. 16
Winston-Salem	April 11	25 weeks	Oct. 3
NORTH DAKOTA			
Bismarck	May 11	19 weeks	Sept. 22
Fargo	May 12	19 weeks	Sept. 26
Grand Forks	May 15	16 weeks	Sept. 1
Minot	May 17	18 weeks	Sept. 21
Sheyenne	May 15	16 weeks	Sept. 1
Washburn	May 24	22 weeks	Sept. 28
OHIO			
Akron	April 30	24 weeks	Oct. 22
Cadiz	May 7	21 weeks	Oct. 1
Carpenter	May 7	20 weeks	Sept. 23
Cincinnati	April 10	28 weeks	Oct. 25
Cleveland	May 7	21 weeks	Oct. 3
Columbus	April 16	27 weeks	Oct. 31
Dayton	April 19	28 weeks	Oct. 26
Kenton	May 7	20 weeks	Sept. 23
Mansfield	May 9	22 weeks	Oct. 6
Oberlin	May 10	19 weeks	Sept. 23
Toledo	April 27	23 weeks	Sept. 24
Youngstown	May 8	21 weeks	Oct. 3
Zanesville	May 7	20 weeks	Sept. 23
OKLAHOMA			
Ada	April 5	32 weeks	Nov. 7
Beaver	April 17	26 weeks	Oct. 15
Chattanooga	April 5	32 weeks	Nov. 15
Clinton	April 4	32 weeks	Nov. 12
McAlester	April 5	32 weeks	Nov. 14
Meeker	April 6	32 weeks	Nov. 14
Oklahoma City	April 1	32 weeks	Nov. 7
Ponca City	April 5	31 weeks	Nov. 6
Tulsa	March 30	31 weeks	Nov. 1
Tuskahoma	April 9	27 weeks	Oct. 16
OREGON			
Astoria	April 13	36 weeks	Dec. 22

LOCATION	LAST SPRING FREEZE	GROWING SEASON	FIRST FALL FREEZE
OREGON (continued)			
Baker	June 8	14 weeks	Sept. 13
Beulah	May 30	17 weeks	Sept. 27
Eugene	April 9	29 weeks	Oct. 31
Medford	April 30	24 weeks	Oct. 17
Pendleton	April 17	25 weeks	Oct. 24
Portland	March 18	36 weeks	Nov. 28
Salem	April 14	26 weeks	Oct. 28
PENNSYLVANIA			
Allentown	April 23	25 weeks	Oct. 17
Altoona	May 11	19 weeks	Sept. 23
Erie	April 20	27 weeks	Nov. 1
Harrisburg	April 15	27 weeks	Oct. 24
Philadelphia	April 11	27 weeks	Oct. 19
Pittsburgh	April 10	25 weeks	Oct. 4
Scranton	May 5	20 weeks	Sept. 23
Williamsport	April 29	24 weeks	Oct. 14
RHODE ISLAND			
Block Island	April 26	25 weeks	Oct. 21
Kingston	May 9	21 weeks	Oct. 1
Newport	April 26	25 weeks	Oct. 19
Providence	April 14	28 weeks	Oct. 26
SOUTH CAROLINA			
Charleston	Feb. 19	42 weeks	Dec. 10
Columbia	March 30	31 weeks	Nov. 3
Greenville	March 25	32 weeks	Nov. 6
Ridgeland	April 10	25 weeks	Oct. 4
Sumter	March 18	29 weeks	Oct. 4
SOUTH DAKOTA			
Aberdeen	May 31	19 weeks	Sept. 15
Deadwood	June 1	13 weeks	Sept. 2
Dupree	May 24	18 weeks	Sept. 28
Huron	May 6	20 weeks	Sept. 29
Pierre	May 15	19 weeks	Sept. 28
Rapid City	May 23	18 weeks	Sept. 28
Sioux Falls	May 6	22 weeks	Oct. 3
TENNESSEE			
Bristol	April 20	26 weeks	Oct. 15
Chattanooga	April 3	32 weeks	Nov. 9
Cleveland	April 25	26 weeks	Oct. 21
Jackson	April 9	31 weeks	Nov. 14
Knoxville	March 22	34 weeks	Nov. 15
Memphis	April 3	30 weeks	Oct. 31
Nashville	April 9	31 weeks	Nov. 14
Waverly	April 25	23 weeks	Oct. 2
TEXAS			
Abilene	April 5	33 weeks	Nov. 25
Amarillo	April 16	29 weeks	Oct. 30
Austin	March 3	39 weeks	Nov. 28
Corpus Christi	None	52 weeks	None
Dallas	March 16	36 weeks	Nov. 21
Del Rio	Feb. 12	43 weeks	Dec. 9
El Paso	March 11	35 weeks	Nov. 13
Houston	Feb. 5	44 weeks	Dec. 11
San Angelo	March 24	33 weeks	Nov. 13
San Antonio	Feb. 26	39 weeks	Nov. 26
Texarkana	March 25	34 weeks	Nov. 15
Victoria	Feb. 25	41 weeks	Dec. 5
Waco	March 24	36 weeks	Nov. 29
UTAH			
Bonanza	June 10	13 weeks	Sept. 12
Cedar City	June 8	16 weeks	Sept. 28
Emery	June 10	13 weeks	Sept. 12
Ogden	May 20	20 weeks	Oct. 6
Milford	May 21	18 weeks	Sept. 26

LOCATION	LAST SPRING FREEZE	GROWING SEASON	FIRST FALL FREEZE
UTAH (continued)			
Park Valley	June 9	14 weeks	Sept. 13
Saint George	March 6	38 weeks	Nov. 24
Salt Lake City	April 28	27 weeks	Nov. 5
VERMONT			
Burlington	May 10	21 weeks	Oct. 3
Montpelier	May 5	20 weeks	Sept. 24
Newport	May 20	18 weeks	Sept. 24
Rutland	May 7	20 weeks	Sept. 24
Woodstock	May 21	18 weeks	Sept. 23
VIRGINIA			
Appomattox	April 11	25 weeks	Oct. 3
Elkwood	May 8	20 weeks	Sept. 24
Lexington	May 7	21 weeks	Oct. 3
Lynchburg	April 11	25 weeks	Oct. 3
Norfolk	March 22	34 weeks	Nov. 21
Richmond	April 11	31 weeks	Oct. 18
Roanoke	April 15	27 weeks	Oct. 22
Winchester	May 8	20 weeks	Sept. 24
Wytheville	May 8	20 weeks	Sept. 24
WASHINGTON			
Aberdeen	April 13	36 weeks	Dec. 22
Cougar	April 8	37 weeks	Dec. 23
Olympia	April 14	25 weeks	Oct. 6
Pullman	May 16	19 weeks	Sept. 27
Spokane	May 16	20 weeks	Oct. 5
Tacoma	March 8	38 weeks	Nov. 29
Vancouver	April 13	29 weeks	Oct. 5
Walla Walla	April 21	24 weeks	Oct. 9
Winthrop	May 20	17 weeks	Sept. 13
Yakima	May 13	22 weeks	Oct. 1
WEST VIRGINIA			
Beckley	May 7	20 weeks	Sept. 24
Bluefield	April 10	25 weeks	Oct. 2
Charleston	May 7	21 weeks	Oct. 2
Clarksburg	May 8	20 weeks	Sept. 24
Elkins	May 10	23 weeks	Oct. 5
Franklin	May 8	20 weeks	Sept. 23
Lewisburg	May 8	20 weeks	Sept. 24
Martinsburg	May 8	20 weeks	Sept. 24
Morgantown	May 7	20 weeks	Sept. 24
Parkersburg	April 10	25 weeks	Oct. 3
WISCONSIN			
Antigo	May 26	14 weeks	Sept. 1
Beloit	May 7	20 weeks	Sept. 22
Cumberland	May 13	19 weeks	Sept. 22
Green Bay	April 10	23 weeks	Sept. 21
LaCrosse	April 25	25 weeks	Oct. 16
Madison	April 25	25 weeks	Oct. 16
Milwaukee	May 10	19 weeks	Sept. 22
Platteville	May 7	20 weeks	Sept. 22
Stevens Point	May 13	19 weeks	Sept. 22
Superior	May 26	17 weeks	Sept. 22
West Bend	May 10	19 weeks	Sept. 22
WYOMING			
Buffalo	May 16	17 weeks	Sept. 13
Casper	May 22	18 weeks	Sept. 28
Cheyenne	May 18	19 weeks	Sept. 27
Clark	June 1	13 weeks	Sept. 2
Dillinger	June 11	12 weeks	Sept. 4
Grass Creek	June 1	11 weeks	Aug. 18
Lander	May 20	18 weeks	Sept. 23
Laramie	June 9	12 weeks	Sept. 2
Morrisey	May 14	17 weeks	Sept. 13
Sheridan	May 21	17 weeks	Sept. 18
Wamsutter	June 8	12 weeks	Sept. 3

CALENDAR OF TRADITIONAL RETAIL SALES IN STORES

Source: Citibank

MONTH	ITEMS ON SALE
January	Storewide clearances; beds; cars; Christmas cards; clothing and accessories; cosmetics; decorating accessories; decorations (Christmas); diamonds; fabrics; floor coverings; furniture; furs; infant needs; linens; lingerie; luggage; major appliances (end of month); notions; radios; stationery; television sets; tires; wrappings.
February ...	Storewide sales on Lincoln's and Washington's birthdays; cars; decorating accessories; fabrics; floor coverings; furniture; furs; major appliances; menswear; women's coats; women's stockings.
March	China and glassware; housewares.
April	Storewide sales after Easter; children's clothing; diamonds; fabrics; fashion clearances; lingerie; sleepwear; women's coats.
May	Storewide sales on Memorial Day; clothing for men, women, and children; decorating accessories; diamonds; housewares; infant needs; linens; luggage.
June	Floor coverings; furniture and beds; lingerie; men's clothing; sleepwear; stockings; summer sportswear (mid-month).
July	Fabrics; furniture and beds; garden equipment and garden furniture (end of month); jewelry; linens; major appliances (end of month); storm windows; summer fashion clearances (men's, women's, and children's); tires.
August	Cars; furniture and beds; furs; garden equipment and garden furniture; infant needs; linens; major appliances; rugs; stationery; women's accessories.
September .	Labor Day sales on tires and special items; cars (end of model year).
October	Storewide sales on Columbus Day; cars (old models); children's clothing; infant needs; women's coats.
November ..	Storewide sales on Election Day and Veterans Day; furs; women's coats.
December ..	After-Christmas sales on cards, decorations, and wrappings; infant needs; women's coats.

WEDDING ANNIVERSARY GIFTS

ANNIVERSARY	GIFTS	ANNIVERSARY	GIFTS
First	Paper, plastics, clocks	Sixteenth	Silver hollowware
Second	Cotton, china	Seventeenth	Furniture
Third	Leather, crystal, glass	Eighteenth	Porcelain
Fourth	Fruit, flowers, silk, appliances	Nineteenth	Bronze
Fifth	Wood, silverware	Twentieth	China, platinum, furniture
Sixth	Iron, candy, sugar, wood	Twenty-fifth	Silver
Seventh	Wood, copper, brass, desk sets	Thirtieth	Pearl, diamond
Eighth	Bronze, pottery, appliances, linen	Thirty-fifth	Coral, jade
Ninth	Leather, willow, pottery, glass	Fortieth	Ruby, garnet
Tenth	Tin, aluminum, diamond jewelry	Forty-fifth	Sapphire, tourmaline
Eleventh	Steel, fashion jewelry	Fiftieth	Gold
Twelfth	Silk, linen, pearl, colored gems	Fifty-fifth	Emerald, turquoise
Thirteenth	Lace, textiles, furs	Sixtieth	Diamond
Fourteenth	Gold jewelry, ivory, agate	Seventy-fifth	Diamond, gold
Fifteenth	Crystal, glass, watches		

BIRTHSTONES AND FLOWERS

MONTH	BIRTHSTONE AND MEANING	FLOWER	MONTH	BIRTHSTONE AND MEANING	FLOWER
January	Garnet—constancy, fidelity	Carnation or Snowdrop	July	Ruby—contentment	Larkspur or Water Lily
February	Amethyst—sincerity	Violet or Primrose	August	Peridot or Sardonyx—felicity	Gladiolus or Poppy
March	Aquamarine or Bloodstone—courage, truthfulness	Jonquil or Violet	September	Sapphire—love, wisdom	Morning Glory or Aster
April	Diamond—innocence	Daisy or Sweet Pea	October	Opal or Tourmaline—hope	Calendula or Cosmos
May	Emerald—happiness, success	Hawthorn or Lily of the Valley	November	Topaz—fidelity	Chrysanthemum
June	Pearl, Alexandrite, or Moonstone—health	Rose or Honeysuckle	December	Turquoise or Zircon—prosperity, success	Narcissus, Holly, or Poinsettia

HOW TO REMOVE COMMON STAINS

Knowing how to remove stains from fabrics can save dollars. Act quickly. Do not permit fresh stains to dry and become set. Because there are so many washable synthetic fibers on the market, it is wise to save the garment tags on which washing or dry-cleaning instructions are given. There are four principal types of stain removers:

1. Absorbents include cornstarch, cornmeal, chalk, fuller's earth, and paper towels. Use them to blot grease and liquids from fabrics.

2. Washing agents include detergents, soaps, borax, washing soda, and ammonia. Detergents (dry or liquid) remove most nongreasy and some greasy stains. Borax, washing soda, and ammonia loosen dirt and grease from fabrics. Mild soap is often safer than detergents on delicate materials.

3. Chemical solvents such as acetone, rubbing alcohol, and turpentine remove many nongreasy stains. Dry-cleaning solutions and "spot lifters" are effective in removing grease stains from both washables and dry-clean-only fabrics, but be certain to follow directions on the label.

4. Bleaches, to be used only on washables, include hydrogen peroxide, liquid or dry chlorine bleach, and dry oxygen bleach. Chlorine bleach is safe only for cottons and linens. It will damage other fabrics. Oxygen bleach is less effective than chlorine, but it is safe for most washables.

Many stains can be removed at home by following these simple rules:

Blood. While stain is fresh, sponge or soak with cold water (*never* warm or hot) until stain is light brown. Wash in warm suds. Soak stubborn stains in a weak solution of bleach, and then relaunder.

Candle wax. Scrape off excess and press stain between white blotters with a hot iron. Rub spot with lard or turpentine and wash.

Chewing gum. Rub with a piece of ice until gum hardens and can be lifted off. Then sponge with dry-cleaning fluid.

Chocolate or cocoa. Soak in cool water. Rub on detergent. Wash in hot suds with bleach. Treat any remaining stain with a weak solution of bleach or hydrogen peroxide. Then relaunder in hot suds.

Coffee and tea. Pour boiling water through fabric. Then wash in hot suds with bleach.

Egg. Scrape off excess. Soak fabric in cool water with bleach, then wash in warm suds.

Fruits and berries. Sponge peach, pear, cherry, and plum stains at once with cool water and rub with glycerine. After 2 hours apply a few drops of vinegar, then launder.

Grass and foliage. Scrub with hot water and suds. If needed, use a mild bleach. Then wash promptly in warm suds.

Grease, oil, tar, butter. Apply dry-cleaning fluid. Rub on detergent. Launder. Dry. Soak in weak bleach solution. Relaunder.

Ice cream. Sponge with cool water to remove sugar and protein, then with warm suds to remove grease.

Lipstick. Soften with glycerine, then wash in hot suds.

Mildew. Soak in suds and hang out with stain exposed to sunlight. If spots persist, rub with lemon juice and salt, then bleach in the sun.

Paint. If oil-based paint use lots of hot suds for fresh stains. For stains that have set, apply turpentine, kerosene, or lard, and then wash in hot suds. Water-emulsion paint that is still wet usually comes out in hot suds.

Pet stains. When these occur on rugs or upholstery, sponge with cold water. Make a solution of one-fourth cup of white vinegar to a quart of water, and sponge again. Allow the solution to work for 15 minutes. Then wash the stain with cool detergent suds and rinse.

Rust. Place the stained portion over a pot of boiling water and pour lemon juice on the fabric. Rinse and then launder.

Wine. Once a wine stain has set, it is very hard to remove. Cover wet stains generously with salt, which will absorb the color. Then launder in warm suds.

BIRTH DATES FOR ASTROLOGY'S SIGNS OF THE ZODIAC

BIRTH DATES	SIGN NAME	SYMBOL	ASTROLOGICAL PERSONALITY TRAITS
Mar. 21–Apr. 19	Aries, or Ram	♈	Active, dynamic, charming, diplomatic, restless
Apr. 20–May 20	Taurus, or Bull	♉	Amusing, honest, affectionate, methodical
May 21–June 20	Gemini, or Twins	♊	Intellectual, magnetic, changeable, sensitive
June 21–July 22	Cancer, or Crab	♋	Managerial, overly serious, artistic, extroverted
July 23–Aug. 22	Leo, or Lion	♌	Generous, sympathetic, imaginative, impulsive
Aug. 23–Sept. 22	Virgo, or Virgin	♍	Independent, kind, sincere, reliable, emotional
Sept. 23–Oct. 22	Libra, or Scales	♎	Practical, poised, attractive, loyal, quick-tempered
Oct. 23–Nov. 21	Scorpio, or Scorpion	♏	Inventive, intuitive, dynamic, obstinate, selfish
Nov. 22–Dec. 21	Sagittarius, or Archer	♐	Trustworthy, outgoing, moody, prideful, bright
Dec. 22–Jan. 19	Capricorn, or Goat	♑	Calm, pleasant, serious, mild-mannered, reliable
Jan. 20–Feb. 18	Aquarius, or Water Bearer	♒	Changeable, indolent, expressive, altruistic
Feb. 19–Mar. 20	Pisces, or Fishes	♓	Faithful, perceptive, reserved, imaginative, jealous

STATE MARRIAGE LAWS

STATE	RELATIVES ONE CANNOT MARRY [1]	MINIMUM AGE WITH PARENT CONSENT [2]		BLOOD TEST REQUIRED	COMMON-LAW MARRIAGE RECOGNIZED	WAIT BETWEEN APPLICATION AND LICENSE	TIME LICENSE IS VALID
		Male	Female				
Alabama	AB	14	14	Yes	Yes	None	30 days
Alaska	—	16	16	Yes	No	3 days	90 days
Arizona	F	16	16	No	No	None	30 days
Arkansas	F	17	16	No	No	None	60 days
California	—	—[3]	—[3]	Yes	No	None	90 days
Colorado	—	16	16	Yes	Yes	None	30 days
Connecticut	—	16	16	Yes	No	4 days	65 days
Delaware	F	18	16	No	No	None	30 days
Florida	—	16	16	Yes	No [6]	3 days	30 days
Georgia	—	16	16	Yes	Yes	3 days	30 days
Hawaii	—	16	16	Yes	No	None [19]	30 days
Idaho	F	16	16	Yes	Yes	None	30 days
Illinois	F	16	16	Yes	No [7]	None	60 days
Indiana	FH	17	17	Yes	No [8]	3 days	60 days
Iowa	ABEFIJ	16	16	Yes	Yes	3 days	20 days
Kansas	F	—[3]	—[3]	No	Yes[17]	3 days	NSP [21]
Kentucky	FH	—[3]	—[3]	No	No	None	30 days
Louisiana	F	18	16	Yes	No	None	30 days
Maine	—	16	16	Yes	No	3 days	60 days
Maryland	ABEIJKM	16	16	No	No	2 days	6 months
Massachusetts	ABEIL	18[4]	18[4]	Yes	No	3 days	60 days
Michigan	ABEFIJKL	18	16	No	No [9]	3 days	33 days
Minnesota	F	16	18	No	No [10]	5 days	6 months
Mississippi	ABCEFJL	—[3]	—[3]	Yes	No [11]	3 days	NSP [21]
Missouri	F	15	15	No	No [12]	3 days	30 days
Montana	F	16	16	Yes	Yes	None	180 days
Nebraska	F	17	17	Yes	No [13]	2 days	NSP [21]
Nevada	FH	16	16	No	No	None	NSP [21]
New Hampshire	ABEFIJKM	14	13	No	No	3 days	90 days
New Jersey	—	16	16	Yes	No [14]	3 days	30 days
New Mexico	—	16	16	Yes	No	None	NSP [21]
New York	—	16	16	No	No [18]	None	60 days
North Carolina	O	16	16	Yes [5]	No	None	NSP [21]
North Dakota	F	16	16	No	No	None	60 days
Ohio	FH	18	16	No	Yes	5 days	60 days
Oklahoma	FAB	16	16	Yes	Yes	None [20]	30 days
Oregon	F	17	17	No	No	3 days	30 days
Pennsylvania	—	16	16	Yes	Yes	3 days	60 days
Rhode Island	BCIJLMQ	18	16	Yes	Yes	None	3 months
South Carolina	ABEIJKM	16	14	No	Yes	1 day	NSP [21]
South Dakota	ABF	16	16	No	No [15]	None	20 days
Tennessee	ABCN	16	16	Yes	No	None [20]	30 days
Texas	AB	14	14	No	Yes	None	NSP[21]
Utah	F	14	14	No	No	None	30 days
Vermont	—	16	16	Yes	No	None	60 days
Virginia	—	16	16	No	No	None	60 days
Washington	FH	17	17	Yes	No	3 days	60 days
West Virginia	FO	16	16	Yes	No	3 days	60 days
Wisconsin	GH	16	16	No	No [16]	5 days	30 days
Wyoming	F	16	16	Yes	No	None	NSP [21]
Dist. of Columbia	ABEIJKLM	16	16	Yes	Yes	3 days	NSP [21]

[1] In every state it is illegal for a man to marry his sister, half sister, mother, daughter, granddaughter, grandmother, great-grandmother, aunt, or niece. Many states also prohibit other marriages as indicated by these capital letters: A stepparent; B stepchild; C stepgrandchild; D Half niece or half nephew; E son-in-law or daughter-in-law; F first cousin; G first cousin, except female 55 or older; H first cousin once removed; I father-in-law or mother-in-law; J spouse of grandchild; K spouse of grandparent; L stepgrandparent; M spouse's grandparent or grandchild; N great-uncle, great-aunt, grandnephew, or grandniece; O double first cousin; P grandnephew or grandniece; Q marriages between Jews permitted by their religion are recognized; R any relative by adoption; S spouse's niece, spouse's grandchild, brother or sister by adoption. [2] Without parental consent, minimum age for marriage is 18, with these exceptions: Mississippi, 17 for men, 15 for women; Nebraska, 19. [3] No minimum age with parental consent and court order. [4] Marriage below 18 must have court approval and parental consent. [5] Physical exam also required. [6] Unless before 1968. [7] Unless before June 30, 1905. [8] Unless before 1958. [9] Unless before 1957. [10] Unless before April 26, 1941. [11] Unless before April 5, 1956. [12] Unless before March 31, 1921. [13] Unless before 1923. [14] Unless before Dec. 1, 1939. [15] Unless before July 1, 1959. [16] Unless before 1917. [17] But both parties guilty of misdemeanor. [18] Unless before April 29, 1933. [19] Except 3-day wait if one party under 18. [20] Except 3 days if either is under 18. [21] No statutory provision.

MARRIAGES AND DIVORCES

Source: U.S. Public Health Service

The divorce rate in the United States decreased slightly in 1984 to 4.9 per 1,000 population compared with 5.0 in 1983. The divorce rate has more than doubled since the 1960s, increasing from 2.2 per 1,000 in 1962.

The number of marriages increased in 1984 to 2,487,000 from 2,444,000 in 1983.

The marriage rate remained steady in 1984 at 10.5 per 1,000 population. The total number of marriages exceeded divorces by 1,332,000.

STATE	MARRIAGES			DIVORCES		
	1984 [1]	1983	1970	1984 [1]	1983	1970
UNITED STATES	2,487,000	2,440,000	2,158,802	1,155,000	1,179,000	708,000
Alabama	47,487	48,923	46,959	25,483	25,739	15,109
Alaska	6,519	6,852	3,390	3,904	3,878	1,695
Arizona	31,506	30,322	18,508	19,796	20,891	12,714
Arkansas	31,427	30,393	23,307	15,553	15,786	9,310
California	226,560	224,891	172,388	N.A.	129,131	112,942
Colorado	34,630	36,031	24,988	18,413	19,738	10,400
Connecticut	25,080	26,333	24,929	11,226	9,868	5,812
Delaware	5,463	5,555	4,254	2,908	3,060	1,732
Florida	124,088	119,532	69,249	75,342	71,295	37,208
Georgia	75,817	71,552	63,896	34,084	32,448	18,649
Hawaii	14,891	14,121	10,599	4,756	4,574	2,589
Idaho	12,518	13,390	10,915	6,033	6,240	3,612
Illinois	102,504	103,519	115,478	48,914	50,514	36,450
Indiana	52,705	53,445	55,202	N.A.	40,333 [2]	15,153
Iowa	26,960	26,747	24,648	10,406	10,653	7,188
Kansas	24,795	25,836	22,421	12,915	12,431	8,785
Kentucky	44,006	39,713	36,269	17,369	17,144	10,664
Louisiana	41,295	45,710	35,416	N.A.	13,229 [2]	5,065
Maine	12,430	12,584	10,975	5,864	5,920	3,853
Maryland	46,815	47,182	52,237	15,817	15,957	9,252
Massachusetts	53,198	43,587	47,403	16,957	17,670	10,994
Michigan	89,391	70,735	89,694	42,112	39,733	29,993
Minnesota	36,873	36,553	31,280	14,696	14,501	8,290
Mississippi	26,158	26,416	26,328	12,524	14,020	8,211
Missouri	54,148	53,487	50,149	25,038	26,749	17,852
Montana	7,677	8,061	6,919	4,407	4,650	3,047
Nebraska	13,341	13,512	15,666	6,487	6,323	3,712
Nevada	107,422	122,329	97,605	12,487	11,404	9,138
New Hampshire	11,363	11,084	10,006	4,808	4,634	2,433
New Jersey	62,429	60,752	56,625	28,469	26,593	10,834
New Mexico	15,171	16,728	12,422	9,205	9,063	4,375
New York	176,654	156,440	161,246	61,075	64,480	26,404
North Carolina	52,123	51,991	48,291	29,125	30,285	13,702
North Dakota	5,806	5,966	5,340	2,258	2,326	985
Ohio	98,708	99,991	90,056	53,492	53,999	39,302
Oklahoma	38,612	44,043	39,004	24,002	23,752	16,842
Oregon	22,594	23,337	17,302	15,463	16,548	9,583
Pennsylvania	92,596	91,438	94,516	40,581	40,369	22,622
Rhode Island	7,942	8,040	7,531	3,640	3,532	1,687
South Carolina	55,882	53,572	57,887	13,753	13,685	5,829
South Dakota	8,035	7,970	11,034	2,506	2,550	1,357
Tennessee	55,205	56,827	45,361	30,684	30,740	16,623
Texas	207,631	194,962	139,491	98,074	96,988	51,530
Utah	17,579	18,346	11,692	8,134	8,467	3,912
Vermont	5,375	5,513	4,524	2,173	2,529	1,028
Virginia	65,976	61,784	51,964	24,837	25,519	11,879
Washington	44,730	46,247	41,313	27,313	27,268	17,887
West Virginia	15,456	15,988	15,948	9,491	10,125	5,584
Wisconsin	41,104	40,795	34,415	16,552	17,123	8,930
Wyoming	5,723	6,200	4,495	3,700	3,983	1,797
District of Columbia	5,488	5,436	7,267	2,874	2,731	2,268

[1] Provisional 1984 data. [2] Final 1978 data. N.A. = Not available.

HOW TO RID YOUR HOME OF HOUSEHOLD PESTS

Despite modern building methods and pesticide techniques, certain insects and rodents are still household problems.

There are only two ways in which they can be controlled: systematic and thorough housekeeping and the use of the proper pesticide at the right time.

Housekeepers are concerned chiefly with *insecticides* to control insects and *rodenticides* to kill rats and mice.

Insecticides come in the form of surface sprays, dusts, liquids, and pastes for crawling insects and space sprays or aerosols for flying insects.

Rodenticides are usually small poisoned pellets put out to be eaten by both rats and mice.

Below is a list of 10 insects and rodents that can be eliminated in the home with pesticides. Termite infestation is such a complex problem that it should be referred to an expert exterminator.

Ants. If you can find the ant nest by following the insects' line of march, treat it with a liquid or spray insecticide containing diazinon, malathion, carbaryl, baygon, or dursban.

Apply the substance to surfaces on which the ants crawl, and treat cracks or openings they may be using to enter the room or house.

Bedbugs. Spray the bed slats, springs, and frame. Cover the mattress completely with spray, but do not soak it.

Products used on mattresses should not contain more than 1% malathion.

Clothes Moths and Carpet Beetles. Preventive measures should be taken against clothes moths before storing woolens. Have the garments dry-cleaned. Place paradichlorobenzene crystals or naphthalene flakes or balls in the garment bags or other containers before sealing. It is best to store furs at a commercial storage company.

To get rid of carpet beetles, vacuum rugs, upholstered furniture, draperies, and the surrounding floors. Spray rugs and other woolen or mohair fabrics with a stainless insecticide containing methoxychlor, cython, or diazinon.

Cockroaches. Preparations containing diazinon, malathion, ronnel, dursban, or ficam will control all types of cockroaches, although some may have developed resistance to certain compounds. Apply the insecticide to places where cockroaches hide and breed—under kitchen sinks, in cracks around or beneath cupboards, places where pipes pass along a wall, behind loose baseboards or moldings, and on the undersides of tables and chairs. Powered insecticide may

be applied after spraying. Severe infestations should be handled by an exterminator.

Cockroaches seek warmth, moisture, and food. They hide during the day in sheltered, dark places in the home, and come out at night to forage. They feed on garbage as well as human food.

Cockroaches may transmit some diseases caused by food-poisoning organisms, and they may also damage fabrics and books.

Fleas. These insects bite humans as well as dogs and cats. The first method for keeping fleas from infesting the home is to shampoo your pet, then apply a spray, dip, or powder containing organophosphates, carbamates, or pyrethrins.

Thoroughly vacuum carpets, floors, and upholstered furniture.

Use a carbaryl flea powder to treat lint-collecting areas and on rugs where the pet rests. Consult labels of insecticide-bearing flea collars.

House Flies. You can help keep your home free of flies by installing tight-fitting screens in windows and doors.

Because flies breed in decaying organic matter, promptly dispose of garbage, pet droppings, and the like. If flies have invaded your home in large numbers, use a household or aerosol spray especially prepared for flying insects.

Mice and Rats. The first steps in keeping out these rodents are to seal holes in walls, floors, and foundations and to make certain that food is not left where they can get to it. If you have only a few mice, place snap traps along walls and holes. Bait the traps with peanut butter, bacon, cheese, or soft candy. A pet cat is often a deterrent to mice.

Rats are a more serious problem, as they ruin property, carry disease, and bite when cornered. Poisoned bait is the best weapon against them, although traps will get rid of some of them. If rats are a neighborhood problem, community action must be taken and pest-control operators called in.

Mosquitoes. Check for larvae (wigglers) in any potential breeding areas such as filled vases, rain barrels, fish tanks, and the like. Screens will help keep out adult mosquitoes. They may be exterminated with a spray designed to kill flying insects.

Pantry Pests. Some types of insect larvae, popularly called "weevils," may infest dry food products such as cornmeal, flour, and cereals. Before buying such foods, examine the packages for tears or cracks. Keep your pantry shelves clean of spilled food particles, and store dry foods in metal or glass containers having tight-fitting lids.

HIGHLIGHTS: 1985

See separate *Focus* articles on aspects of international relations including the change in Soviet leadership (page 13), U.S. policy in Central America (page 15), and the Arab terrorist hijacking of a TWA airliner (page 19). For many other developments in international relations in 1985, see the chronology of world events on pages 8–26 and articles on specific nations from Afghanistan to Zimbabwe on pages 484–686.

U.S.–SOVIET RELATIONS

World tensions relaxed somewhat in 1985 as relations improved between the world's two superpowers—the United States and the Soviet Union.

Negotiations resumed on March 12, 1985, between the U.S. and the Soviet Union on efforts to write a new treaty to reduce or limit nuclear arms. The Soviet Union had broken off the talks in 1983 in a show of anger over the deployment in Europe of new U.S. Pershing II and cruise missiles.

Although details of the U.S.-Soviet arms talks in Geneva, Switzerland, were shrouded in secrecy, Soviet leaders publicly declared that the negotiations could not succeed as long as President Reagan continued to go forward with the "Star Wars" plan for an elaborate defensive system against enemy nuclear missiles.

U.S. Secretary of State George P. Shultz detailed U.S. objectives in the arms talks in a speech in Austin, Tex., on March 28. He said in part:

"Our fundamental goal is to defend our freedom and that of our allies and to reduce the risk of war, especially nuclear war....

"We are prepared to be flexible, however about ways to achieve our objectives. We will meet the Soviet Union halfway in finding a mutually acceptable approach....

"The Geneva talks will be of unprecedented complexity. We must be careful not to permit our revulsion against war to lower our guard. We must not let our hopes, noble as they are, blind us to the daunting realities of the arms control process. But there are favorable factors at work. America is recovering its economic vitality, its military strength, and its self-confidence. We stand firm with our staunch allies. If we in the West are patient and united, combining resolution with flexibility, then we have good prospects of success. We can attain the goal we all share: reducing the danger of war and building a constructive and secure relationship with the Soviet Union in the nuclear age."

Both the United States and the Soviet Union continued to jockey in an effort to win the support of world public opinion. On July 29 the U.S. and the Soviet Union made public new proposals on the underground testing of nuclear weapons. The U.S. invited the Soviet Union to send observers to U.S. test explosions in Nevada. The Soviet Union announced it was placing a moratorium on the testing of nuclear weapons for the rest of 1985 and invited the U.S. to do likewise. Each rejected the offer made by the other.

Of most significance in the improvement of U.S.-Soviet relations was an agreement reached in July that President Reagan would meet with Soviet leader Mikhail S. Gorbachev for two days in Geneva on Nov. 19–20, 1985.

White House officials stressed that the Reagan-Gorbachev summit was largely a get-acquainted meeting and was not expected to achieve any immediate major agreements. Instead, they said, the President mainly hoped that he and the Soviet leader could agree on "an agenda for the future" that could provide a framework to solve such major problems as arms control.

In mid-June the United States and the Soviet Union reached agreement on a treaty to resume the exchange of agricultural information that had been broken off after the Soviet invasion of Afghanistan in 1979. The treaty provides for exchange of 15 American and 15 Soviet farmers to learn about farming methods.

MIDEAST PEACE EFFORTS

In February Jordan's King Hussein announced that he had reached an agreement with Yasir Arafat, leader of the Palestine Liberation Organization (PLO), that could lead to negotiations on a Mideast peace agreement at an international conference. The PLO would join the Jordanian delegation to such a conference. However, the executive committee of the PLO later said the agreement had to be amended to provide for the establishment of an independent Palestinian state.

In mid-August U.S. Assistant Secretary of State Richard W. Murphy went to the Mid-

UNITED STATES AID TO OTHER NATIONS

Source: National Advisory Council on International Monetary and Financial Policies

The United States has provided other nations with more than $311 billion in grants and loans for military, economic, and technical aid since the end of World War II.

Over $123 billion of this foreign aid has been in the form of loans, some $60 billion of which have been repaid. The figures in this table are for July 1, 1945, to Jan. 1, 1984.

NATION	GRANTS BY U.S.	LOANS BY U.S.	LOANS STILL OWED TO U.S.[1]	NATION	GRANTS BY U.S.	LOANS BY U.S.	LOANS STILL OWED TO U.S.[1]
Afghanistan	$ 396,000,000	$ 183,000,000	$ 124,000,000	Korea, South	$10,895,000,000	$6,683,000,000	$3,977,000,000
Albania	20,000,000	—	—	Kuwait	—	50,000,000	—
Algeria	192,000,000	1,051,000,000	791,000,000	Laos	2,558,000,000	—	—
Angola	22,000,000	99,000,000	64,000,000	Lebanon	223,000,000	264,000,000	128,000,000
Argentina	109,000,000	1,418,000,000	338,000,000	Lesotho	159,000,000	—	—
Australia	13,000,000	1,392,000,000	316,000,000	Liberia	357,000,000	342,000,000	173,000,000
Austria	1,205,000,000	222,000,000	63,000,000	Libya	224,000,000	7,000,000	**
Bahamas	**	59,000,000	2,000,000	Madagascar	38,000,000	26,000,000	23,000,000
Bangladesh	1,002,000,000	1,180,000,000	929,000,000	Malawi	40,000,000	33,000,000	33,000,000
Belgium	1,850,000,000	413,000,000	77,000,000	Malaysia	75,000,000	241,000,000	38,000,000
Benin	31,000,000	23,000,000	23,000,000	Mali	180,000,000	6,000,000	6,000,000
Bolivia	563,000,000	553,000,000	367,000,000	Malta	79,000,000	6,000,000	5,000,000
Botswana	121,000,000	24,000,000	23,000,000	Mauritania	112,000,000	6,000,000	5,000,000
Brazil	984,000,000	5,225,000,000	2,222,000,000	Mauritius	23,000,000	15,000,000	14,000,000
Britain	4,939,000,000	6,256,000,000	1,854,000,000	Mexico	232,000,000	4,020,000,000	1,521,000,000
Burkina Faso	236,000,000	1,000,000	**	Morocco	657,000,000	1,217,000,000	719,000,000
Burma	190,000,000	61,000,000	26,000,000	Nepal	315,000,000	4,000,000	3,000,000
Cambodia	1,999,000,000	289,000,000	210,000,000	Netherlands	2,178,000,000	600,000,000	−59,000,000
Cameroon	99,000,000	133,000,000	92,000,000	New Zealand	5,000,000	234,000,000	53,000,000
Canada	13,000,000	1,143,000,000	572,000,000	Nicaragua	165,000,000	321,000,000	259,000,000
Central Africa	17,000,000	10,000,000	7,000,000	Niger	165,000,000	10,000,000	9,000,000
Chad	103,000,000	—	—	Nigeria	277,000,000	210,000,000	160,000,000
Chile	465,000,000	2,236,000,000	538,000,000	Norway	1,182,000,000	558,000,000	64,000,000
Colombia	473,000,000	1,704,000,000	950,000,000	Oman	4,000,000	85,000,000	66,000,000
Congo	18,000,000	9,000,000	8,000,000	Pakistan	3,042,000,000	4,286,000,000	3,266,000,000
Costa Rica	194,000,000	386,000,000	299,000,000	Panama	237,000,000	378,000,000	199,000,000
Cuba	21,000,000	40,000,000	36,000,000	Paraguay	131,000,000	103,000,000	46,000,000
Cyprus	155,000,000	30,000,000	4,000,000	Peru	564,000,000	1,423,000,000	411,000,000
Czechoslov.	186,000,000	16,000,000	3,000,000	Philippines	2,509,000,000	1,740,000,000	826,000,000
Denmark	888,000,000	208,000,000	55,000,000	Poland	525,000,000	2,439,000,000	973,000,000
Dominican R.	375,000,000	649,000,000	424,000,000	Portugal	765,000,000	1,490,000,000	537,000,000
Ecuador	248,000,000	316,000,000	117,000,000	Romania	11,000,000	485,000,000	120,000,000
Egypt	2,756,000,000	8,551,000,000	7,861,000,000	Saudi Arabia	69,000,000	280,000,000	−13,000,000
El Salvador	554,000,000	442,000,000	386,000,000	Senegal	263,000,000	56,000,000	36,000,000
Ethiopia	516,000,000	201,000,000	117,000,000	Sierra Leone	86,000,000	56,000,000	36,000,000
Finland	4,000,000	276,000,000	65,000,000	Singapore	3,000,000	291,000,000	182,000,000
France	8,835,000,000	2,515,000,000	−194,000,000	Somalia	289,000,000	152,000,000	144,000,000
Gabon	12,000,000	32,000,000	8,000,000	Soviet Union	465,000,000	1,012,000,000	217,000,000
Germany, E.	17,000,000	—	—	Spain	1,530,000,000	2,858,000,000	1,373,000,000
Germany, W.	4,860,000,000	524,000,000	−991,000,000	Sri Lanka	181,000,000	462,000,000	393,000,000
Ghana	180,000,000	344,000,000	194,000,000	Sudan	498,000,000	408,000,000	331,000,000
Greece	4,150,000,000	1,882,000,000	697,000,000	Suriname	5,000,000	7,000,000	**
Guatemala	354,000,000	237,000,000	160,000,000	Swaziland	40,000,000	10,000,000	10,000,000
Guinea	80,000,000	135,000,000	95,000,000	Sweden	87,000,000	87,000,000	24,000,000
Guyana	40,000,000	90,000,000	75,000,000	Switzerland	**	101,000,000	23,000,000
Haiti	307,000,000	133,000,000	101,000,000	Syria	85,000,000	281,000,000	246,000,000
Honduras	242,000,000	341,000,000	277,000,000	Taiwan	4,860,000,000	2,728,000,000	1,664,000,000
Hungary	17,000,000	44,000,000	6,000,000	Tanzania	252,000,000	134,000,000	122,000,000
Iceland	36,000,000	69,000,000	14,000,000	Thailand	2,140,000,000	630,000,000	349,000,000
India	5,946,000,000	7,769,000,000	3,591,000,000	Togo	66,000,000	7,000,000	3,000,000
Indonesia	907,000,000	3,505,000,000	2,413,000,000	Trinidad–Tob.	35,000,000	241,000,000	175,000,000
Iran	1,371,000,000	1,905,000,000	87,000,000	Tunisia	556,000,000	891,000,000	637,000,000
Iraq	81,000,000	57,000,000	30	Turkey	6,380,000,000	4,915,000,000	3,509,000,000
Ireland	18,000,000	245,000,000	71,000,000	Uganda	66,000,000	15,000,000	10,000,000
Israel	13,751,000,000	11,756,000,000	9,360,000,000	Uruguay	102,000,000	174,000,000	98,000,000
Italy	5,457,000,000	1,710,000,000	367,000,000	Venezuela	88,000,000	829,000,000	224,000,000
Ivory Coast	29,000,000	131,000,000	85,000,000	Vietnam	23,592,000,000	560,000,000	102,000,000
Jamaica	87,000,000	485,000,000	393,000,000	Yugoslavia	1,804,000,000	1,945,000,000	914,000,000
Japan	4,388,000,000	3,477,000,000	−251,000,000	Zaire	374,000,000	1,186,000,000	866,000,000
Jordan	1,657,000,000	1,179,000,000	836,000,000	Zambia	31,000,000	268,000,000	206,000,000
Kenya	294,000,000	288,000,000	211,000,000	Zimbabwe	115,000,000	28,000,000	28,000,000

[1] A negative credit indicates an excess of principal payments over new credits utilized. ** Less than $500,000.

INTERNATIONAL RELATIONS 419

HIGHLIGHTS: 1985 (continued)

east in an effort to get Israeli leaders to meet directly with King Hussein to work out details of a peace plan. However, King Hussein insisted that negotiations should take place at an international conference that would include representatives of both the PLO and Israel. On the other hand, Israel continued to reject any discussions that would include members of the PLO until that organization officially recognizes Israel's right to exist.

SOUTH AFRICAN APARTHEID

Pressure mounted in the United States and other Western nations in an effort to force the South African government to end its apartheid policies that restrict the rights of blacks and keep a white minority in control of the country. Demonstrators called for economic sanctions against South Africa and an end to investments in South African businesses.

In the worst outbreak of violence in the history of South Africa more than 600 people were killed in riots and clashes between blacks and police in the year since South Africa adopted a new constitution that excluded blacks from the government.

On July 21 South African President P. W. Botha imposed a state of emergency that gave police almost unlimited powers in dealing with black unrest. Hundreds of black leaders were arrested.

In protest against the state of emergency, the government of France recalled its ambassador from South Africa on July 24 and announced it had imposed economic sanctions against any new investments in South Africa.

The U.S. House of Representatives on Aug. 1 approved 380–48 on Aug. 1 a bill imposing limited economic sanctions on South Africa. However, the measure awaited a vote in the Senate after the congressional summer recess.

President Botha in a speech in Durban on Aug. 15 declared his government would negotiate with black leaders but never would give in to outside pressures to be "forced into a position of doing what we don't want to do."

EUROPEAN COMMON MARKET EXPANDS

Spain and Portugal signed a treaty on June 12 admitting them on Jan. 1, 1986, to the European Economic Community (commonly called the European Common Market). With inclusion of the two, membership expands to 12 nations.

The organization began functioning on Jan. 1, 1958, with six members: Belgium, France, West Germany, Italy, Luxembourg, and Netherlands. In 1973 Britain, Denmark,

and Ireland became members. In 1981 Greece became the 10th member.

Founders of the European Economic Community had hoped that it would lead to a "United States of Europe" through political and economic integration of the member nations.

The organization has developed a complex set of agricultural price subsidies, but has failed to integrate Western Europe because the governments of the member nations have sought to protect their own national interests.

At a summit conference of European heads of state in Milan, Italy, in June 1985, the European Community members voted 7–3 to hold a meeting aimed at amending the organization's charter treaty to provide more unity. Britain, Denmark, and Greece voted against holding such a meeting. Britain's Prime Minister Margaret Thatcher said she saw little possibility that the members would give up their individual power to veto actions of the organization.

UN POPULATION AWARD

The United Nations Population Award for 1985 was presented to the International Planned Parenthood Federation of national family planning associations in 121 countries.

The award, presented annually by the Secretary General of the UN, includes a gold medal, citation, and $25,000. Financed by a trust fund established by voluntary contributions from member states of the UN, the award seeks to promote "the solution of population questions."

Previous recipients of the award have been: 1983—Prime Minister Indira Gandhi of India and China's Qian Xinzhong, minister in charge of the state family planning commission; 1984—Carmen Miro of Panama, former director of the Latin American Demographic Center, and Sheldon Segal of the United States, director of the population division of the Rockefeller Foundation.

UNESCO CUTS BUDGET

The United Nations Educational, Scientific, and Cultural Organization (UNESCO) executive board met for six weeks in 1985 in an effort to find ways to cut the organization's $363 million 2-year budget. The reductions were necessary because the United States, which withdrew from the organization in December 1984, had provided 25% of its

The U.S., Britain, and tions have ch

NET U.S. FOREIGN ASSISTANCE SINCE 1945[1]

Source: National Advisory Council on International Monetary and Financial Policies

REGION/COUNTRY	1945–83	1983	1982	1981	1980	1979	1978
WORLD TOTAL	$234,997	$10,025	$10,902	$9,407	$10,210	$7,322	$7,131
WESTERN EUROPE	57,249	660	507	511	1,141	462	824
Austria	1,214	**	8	12	14	-5	-5
Belgium/Luxembourg	1,913	-17	-15	-11	52	-7	-7
Britain	6,258	-119	-208	-125	178	-123	-142
Cyprus	159	**	-2	-1	17	14	24
Denmark	920	-13	-4	2	14	-3	-10
Finland	76	19	-6	17	9	-3	-9
France	8,389	6	-5	34	-31	-49	-45
Germany, West	3,690	-6	-9	-13	-15	-15	-15
Greece	4,757	19	-29	-47	-32	43	163
Iceland	49	-1	-1	-1	-5	-5	-2
Ireland	89	-7	8	44	**	-5	-9
Italy	5,722	-25	-28	122	184	-17	-9
Malta	84	—	—	—	—	—	10
Netherlands	2,060	-20	-26	-33	-27	-29	-25
Norway	1,216	-12	-26	-36	-52	-44	-46
Portugal	1,296	55	**	-93	-88	110	503
Spain	2,793	97	16	73	176	145	160
Sweden	111	-5	-4	-1	5	-3	1
Switzerland	23	-14	-17	-14	-9	-6	-9
Turkey	9,864	491	695	394	571	374	183
Yugoslavia	2,845	19	-31	12	22	-25	39
EASTERN EUROPE	2,781	13	44	174	-285	206	424
Albania	20	—	—	—	—	—	—
Czechoslovakia	189	-2	**	—	—	—	—
Germany, East	17	—	—	—	—	—	—
Hungary	23	-2	-4	3	-4	8	5
Poland	1,757	33	76	236	-243	129	343
Romania	130	5	-16	-49	-23	76	45
Soviet Union	644	-21	-11	-17	-14	-7	32
AFRICA	23,940	3,232	3,515	2,637	2,581	1,642	1,244
Algeria	982	-83	**	172	125	150	113
Angola	85	-9	35	45	8	1	**
Benin	54	2	4	4	2	4	4
Botswana	144	16	19	20	16	11	13
Burkina Faso	236	25	27	40	31	24	21
Burundi	47	7	8	9	5	3	4
Cameroon	191	3	14	52	25	14	3
Cape Verde	56	10	12	8	6	4	7
Central Africa	24	6	1	2	2	1	**
Chad	103	22	6	2	6	12	13
Congo	25	2	9	**	2	1	1
Djibouti	16	4	3	3	4	1	1
Egypt	10,748	2,050	2,337	1,398	1,470	890	620
Ethiopia	628	2	**	3	20	13	11
Gabon	20	-2	1	-5	-4	**	**
Gambia	37	6	6	6	4	2	1
Ghana	378	6	6	19	16	21	9
Guinea	185	2	1	17	7	4	10
Guinea-Bissau	27	3	4	8	2	1	6
Ivory Coast	114	-3	-5	9	27	1	5
Kenya	505	79	53	87	50	28	21
Lesotho	159	25	26	32	20	11	7
Liberia	530	68	73	76	30	9	10
Libya	224	—	—	—	—	—	**
Madagascar	61	10	14	10	**	2	4
Malawi	73	7	4	5	4	4	4
Mali	186	16	15	18	25	16	16
Mauritania	117	21	13	21	17	6	5
Mauritius	37	3	7	5	4	3	**
Morocco	1,376	111	56	52	40	32	55
Mozambique	103	11	5	17	17	24	10
Niger	174	18	22	12	10	17	10
Nigeria	437	80	-5	7	-3	-3	-6
Rwanda	68	9	11	11	8	5	4
Senegal	299	48	34	37	38	32	23
Sierra Leone	122	10	8	6	9	5	9
	433	88	74	70	70	22	14

(add 000,000); a negative amount indicates an excess of grants returned over

REGION/COUNTRY	1945–83	1983	1982	1981	1980	1979	1978
South Africa	−92	**	**	**	**	**	**
Sudan	830	211	262	104	73	25	12
Swaziland	50	11	7	7	11	3	2
Tanzania	374	19	27	31	30	24	15
Togo	69	7	7	5	7	7	2
Tunisia	1,195	124	118	25	50	11	31
Uganda	77	4	2	10	15	**	**
Zaire	1,264	44	85	65	149	101	62
Zambia	262	25	15	29	42	40	35
Zimbabwe	143	62	27	28	26	—	—
WESTERN HEMISPHERE	18,247	621	1,763	546	597	371	316
Argentina	452	26	31	−25	−30	−29	−8
Barbados	17	8	1	1	1	**	1
Belize	15	6	1	**	**	**	**
Bolivia	931	45	31	19	30	39	63
Brazil	3,347	35	−138	−83	−29	−17	−36
Canada	581	97	91	47	95	−9	−8
Chile	1,027	−55	−52	−86	−68	−186	−32
Colombia	1,439	83	−7	−4	7	−6	8
Costa Rica	493	203	46	11	3	8	7
Cuba	57	—	—	—	—	—	—
Dominican Rep.	799	37	74	23	30	60	−3
Ecuador	366	10	−4	−1	6	7	17
El Salvador	940	323	239	127	49	10	11
Guatemala	514	27	21	18	15	18	16
Guyana	115	2	5	7	3	3	4
Haiti	408	38	45	40	37	29	29
Honduras	518	110	85	46	21	29	17
Jamaica	480	114	106	58	12	19	19
Mexico	1,753	−610	1,084	160	180	103	17
Neth. Antilles	25	1	20	3	−1	**	—
Nicaragua	424	3	6	15	78	30	26
Panama	436	20	16	4	13	5	7
Paraguay	177	3	2	**	**	3	3
Peru	977	51	−1	−10	−1	93	71
Trinidad-Tobago	209	−19	11	51	89	29	−2
Uruguay	212	−5	10	−4	−2	−4	−3
Venezuela	309	6	−1	40	18	12	−3
ASIA	115,323	4,279	3,567	4,090	4,729	3,669	3,452
Afghanistan	523	−2	−1	−5	4	38	12
Bangladesh	1,931	218	203	130	175	161	168
Burma	220	3	6	**	**	**	2
Cambodia	2,208	2	7	23	44	5	**
China	23	9	12	1	1	—	—
Hong Kong	118	−9	11	32	10	−5	−3
India	9,963	47	89	215	168	95	81
Indonesia	3,537	256	19	19	156	233	190
Iran	1,443	−306	—	**	**	−158	−170
Iraq	110	30	−1	−1	−1	−1	−1
Israel	23,148	2,660	2,181	2,439	2,961	2,185	1,814
Japan	4,042	−16	−84	68	−50	−69	46
Jordan	2,492	68	182	271	223	162	137
Korea, South	14,846	450	476	300	240	265	704
Laos	2,558	**	**	**	**	2	2
Lebanon	351	57	−2	30	20	9	14
Malaysia	174	61	−5	−17	−10	−18	6
Nepal	319	26	21	19	17	8	6
Oman	69	3	22	30	13	**	**
Pakistan	6,390	343	158	94	66	18	45
Philippines	3,331	235	52	66	57	162	130
Saudi Arabia	55	−2	−1	6	4	−2	−4
Singapore	185	−34	−15	−14	25	93	39
Sri Lanka	576	59	49	32	55	39	41
Syria	334	25	27	17	23	80	19
Taiwan	6,513	−43	34	191	403	168	53
Thailand	2,474	61	49	36	44	135	38
Yemen, North	206	37	30	26	16	10	8
OCEANIA	1,994	194	211	211	107	95	65
Australia	309	75	37	81	**	−29	−36
Fiji	22	1	2	8	2	1	1
New Zealand	58	−15	−19	−18	−4	−3	−1
Trust Territory of the Pacific Islands	1,573	130	188	133	108	125	100

[1] All figures in millions of U.S. dollars (add 000,000); a negative amount indicates an excess of grants returned over grants used. ** Less than $500,000.

HISTORY OF THE UNITED NATIONS

1941 (June 12) Inter-Allied Declaration signed in London by all nations then at war with Germany to work for "a world in which, relieved of the menace of aggression, all may enjoy economic and social security."

1941 (Aug. 14) Atlantic Charter issued by U.S. President Franklin D. Roosevelt and British Prime Minister Winston Churchill detailing eight points to "base their hopes for a better future for the world."

1942 (Jan. 1) Declaration by United Nations signed by 26 nations in Washington approving basic points of Atlantic Charter; first official use of name "United Nations."

1943 (Oct. 30) Moscow Declaration on General Security signed by Britain, China, Soviet Union, and United States, recognizing "the necessity of establishing at the earliest practicable date a general international organization, based on the principle of sovereign equality."

1944 (Aug. 21) Dumbarton Oaks Conference in Washington, D.C., at which for three months representatives of 39 nations discuss proposals for establishing United Nations organization, agreeing on Security Council as executive branch of UN.

1945 (June 26) UN Charter approved by delegates of 50 nations at international conference in San Francisco.

1945 (Oct. 16) Food and Agriculture Organization of United Nations established to improve consumption, production, and distribution of food throughout world.

1945 (Oct. 24) UN Charter goes into effect upon ratification by majority of nations, including Britain, China, France, Soviet Union, and United States. Day celebrated annually as United Nations Day.

1946 (Jan. 10) UN General Assembly begins first meeting in London with delegates of 51 nations as members. Trygve Lie of Norway is elected first secretary-general of UN.

1946 (June 25) International Bank for Reconstruction and Development begins operations to assist nations by government loans.

1946 (Nov. 4) UNESCO, United Nations Educational, Scientific, and Cultural Organization, formed to promote international cooperation in solving such problems as illiteracy.

1946 (Dec. 14) Gift of $8,500,000 from U.S. millionaire John D. Rockefeller Jr. accepted by UN to buy 18 acres in New York City as site of permanent headquarters.

1947 (April 4) International Civil Aviation Organization established to develop international standards and regulations for civil aviation.

1948 (April 7) World Health Organization established to promote world health.

1948 (Sept. 17) UN peace negotiator Count Folke Bernadotte of Sweden assassinated in Jerusalem while trying to arrange truce in fighting between Arabs and Israelis.

1948 (Dec. 10) Universal Declaration of Human Rights adopted by UN General Assembly.

1949 (Jan. 1) Cease-fire between India and Pakistan obtained by UN to end two years of fighting over control of Kashmir.

1949 (Feb.–July) Cease-fire agreements arranged between Israel and Arab states by UN negotiator Ralph J. Bunche.

1949 (Dec. 27) Netherlands grants independence to Indonesia after conference arranged by UN to settle fighting.

1950 (March 23) World Meteorological Organization established to promote international reporting and observation of weather.

1950 (June 27) UN Security Council calls for member nations to send troops to aid South Korea, which had been attacked by communist North Korea. Soviet Union was boycotting meetings of Security Council at this time and so could not veto measure. Troops of U.S. and 15 other nations dispatched to aid South Korea.

1953 (July 27) UN signs truce with North Korea, ending over three years of fighting.

1956 (Nov. 7) UN obtains cease-fire in Suez Canal fighting between Egypt and Israeli-British-French forces; sends UN Emergency Force to supervise truce.

1957 (July 29) International Atomic Energy Agency created to promote peaceful uses of atomic energy.

1961 (Sept. 13) UN troops begin fighting in Congo (now Zaire) to restore order in civil war.

1961 (Sept. 18) UN Secretary-General Dag Hammarskjold killed in air crash in Africa while on Congo peace mission.

1961 (Nov. 3) U Thant of Burma elected as UN's third secretary-general to succeed Dag Hammarskjold.

1964 (March 4) UN peacekeeping force sent to Cyprus to prevent fighting between Turkish and Greek forces.

1966 (Dec. 16) UN Security Council asks member nations to stop trading with Rhodesia because of its policies against blacks.

1967 (June 10) UN negotiates truce in Six-Day Israeli-Arab War.

1971 (Oct. 25) Communist China admitted to UN and nationalist China expelled by 76–35 vote of General Assembly.

1971 (Dec. 13) UN General Assembly votes 79 to 7 with 36 abstentions for Israel to restore to Arab countries territories acquired by force.

1972 Kurt Waldheim appointed UN secretary-general on resignation of U Thant.

1973 (Oct. 22) Cease-fire in 17-day-old Middle East War ordered by UN Security Council.

1973 (Oct. 25) UN peacekeeping force sent to Middle East to prevent further fighting between Arab nations and Israel.

1974 Special session of UN General Assembly establishes emergency relief fund for poor nations of world.

1975 International Women's Year declared by UN to promote women's equality.

1977 (Nov. 4) Mandatory embargo on military supply shipments to South Africa ordered by UN; first such action against UN member.

1978 UN 6,100-man peacekeeping force stationed in southern Lebanon: Bring withdrawal of Israeli troops that invaded in March.

1984 UN membership reaches 159 with admission of Brunei.

1985 For 1985 events, see pages 7–26.

HISTORY OF THE MIDDLE EAST

The strategic importance of the Middle East, linking the continents of Europe, Asia, and Africa, has caused the region to be the scene of bloody wars since the dawn of history.

3200–2800 B.C. Egyptians in Africa and Sumerians in Mesopotamia (Iraq) separately invent writing.

3000–539 B.C. Egypt contends with Sumeria, Babylonia, and Assyria for control of Middle East.

539–333 B.C. Persia (Iran) conquers Assyria and Egypt, establishing Persian rule of region.

333–30 B.C. Alexander the Great of Macedonia conquers Persia and Egypt; Greek rulers govern region.

30 B.C.–A.D. 260 Rome conquers and rules Middle East.

260–637 Wars between Persia and Roman Empire (later Byzantine Empire) for control of region.

637–1055 Arabs conquer and rule Middle East.

1055 Turks conquer Middle East; region ruled as part of Ottoman Empire until World War I.

1859–69 Suez Canal constructed, linking Mediterranean Sea with Red Sea and Indian Ocean.

1878 Britain takes control of Cyprus.

1882 British troops occupy Egypt to protect British interests in Suez Canal.

1896 Zionist movement founded by Theodor Herzl, calling for Jewish state in former homeland of Palestine.

1897–1914 About 50,000 Jews migrate to Palestine to escape persecution in Europe.

1901 Iranian oil fields discovered.

1902–25 Ibn Saud conquers most of Arabia; proclaims himself king of Hejaz and Nejd in 1927; changes country's name to Saudi Arabia in 1932.

1914 Egypt declared protectorate by Britain.

1916–18 Lawrence of Arabia, British Col. T.E. Lawrence, leads Arabs seeking independence in attacks on Turks.

1917 Balfour Declaration by Britain promises help in establishing "national home" for Jews in Palestine without violating rights of Arab majority.

1918 Turkey defeated by British troops with aid of Arabs in World War I, dismembering Ottoman Empire.

1920 Britain given mandate over Palestine by League of Nations.

1920 France given mandate over Syria and Lebanon by League of Nations.

1921 Arab emirate of Transjordan (later Jordan) founded under British control.

1921 Arab kingdom of Iraq established under British control, with Faisal I as king.

1921 Arabs in Palestine riot, protesting increased Jewish immigration; Britain issues proposed Palestine constitution, but Arabs refuse to take part in elections.

1922 (Feb. 28) Britain formally ends protectorate over Egypt, but British troops remain.

1922–23 Turkey's sultanate abolished; republic proclaimed by Kemal Ataturk, president (1923–38).

1926 Lebanon republic founded under French control.

1929 Arabs attack and kill Jews in Jerusalem, Palestine, in dispute over use of Wailing Wall.

1930 Iraq granted independence by Britain.

1933–45 Tens of thousands of Jews migrate to Palestine to escape Nazi Holocaust in which 6 million European Jews were killed.

1935 Saudi Arabia's major oil fields discovered.

1935 Persia's name changed to Iran by Reza Shah Pahlevi, army officer who deposed previous shah in 1925.

1937 British commission recommends partition of Palestine between Arabs and Jews.

1939 (May 23) British parliament approves plan to create independent Palestine state within 10 years with safeguards to protect rights of Jewish minority; Jewish immigration to Palestine to be banned after 1944.

1941 Syria and Lebanon granted independence by Free French leaders after fall of France early in World War II.

1945 Arab League created by Egypt, Iraq, Jordan, Lebanon, Saudi Arabia, Syria, and Yemen to coordinate Arab interests.

1945–48 Thousands of displaced European Jews immigrate to Palestine despite efforts of British to stop them.

1946 British and French troops withdraw from Syria.

1946 (April 25) Kingdom of Transjordan (later Jordan) becomes independent, but British officers control army.

1947 (Oct. 26) British troops withdraw from Iraq.

1947 (Nov. 29) UN General Assembly votes to partition Palestine into Arab and Jewish states; Arabs reject plan.

1948 (May 14) Israel declares its independence as a Jewish state simultaneously with Britain ending its mandate.

1948–49 First Arab-Israeli War: All of Israel's Arab neighbors attack and attempt to destroy new nation, but Israel with help of arms from U.S. is able to drive back Arab forces.

1949 About 1 million Palestinian Arab refugees who had fled from Israel settle in camps in Arab nations, creating major problem in succeeding decades.

1956 (June 13) British withdraw troops from Egypt after 74 years of occupation.

1956 (July 26) Egypt nationalizes Suez Canal, seizing it from British and French owners.

1956 (Oct. 29–Nov. 6) Second Arab-Israeli War: with support of Britain and France, Israel attacks Egypt.

1956 (Nov. 15) UN peace-keeping force sent to Suez Canal.

1957 (March 1) Israel withdraws from Egyptian territory.

1958 (July 15) U.S. Marines land in Lebanon, carrying out "Eisenhower Doctrine" to prevent communist takeover of government; troops withdrawn in November.

1958–61 Syria and Egypt unite to form United Arab Republic, finally dissolved by Syria.

1960 Britain grants independence to Cyprus.

1964 UN sends peace-keeping force to Cyprus to prevent outbreak of war between Greece and Turkey over island.

1964 Palestine Liberation Organization founded by Arab nations to conduct terrorist raids on Israel.

1967 (May 18) Egypt demands and obtains immediate withdrawal of UN forces from its borders with Israel.

1967 (June 5–10) Third Arab-Israeli War: Israel attacks Egypt, Syria, and Jordan; captures all of Jerusalem and Jordanian land west of Jordan River, all of Egypt's Sinai Peninsula, and Syria's Golan Heights.

1973 (Oct. 6–24) Fourth Arab-Israeli War: Egypt and Syria, supported with military supplies from Soviet Union, attack Israel; Israel fights back, aided by arms from U.S., driving across Suez Canal into Egypt and pushing beyond Golan Heights into Syria.

1974 Truce agreements negotiated with Egypt and Syria by U.S. Secretary of State Henry Kissinger.

1974 Turkish troops invade Cyprus after Greek-led revolt overthrows island's government.

1975–76 Civil War in Lebanon with leftist Muslims and Palestinian Arabs fighting against rightist Christians; ends after Syria sends in army to impose peace.

1977 (Nov. 19–21) Egypt's President Sadat visits Israel in effort to achieve lasting peace agreement.

1979 (Jan. 16) Muslim revolt overthrows Shah of Iran, making country Islamic republic.

1979 (March 26) Peace treaty signed by Egypt and Israel: Goes into effect April 25; other Arab countries angered, breaking relations with Egypt; Israel withdraws from Egypt's Sinai region on April 25, 1982.

1979 (Dec. 27) Soviet troops invade Afghanistan; set up puppet communist government.

1981 (Dec. 14) Israel annexes Syria's Golan Heights, seized in 1967 war.

1982 (June 6) Israeli troops invade Lebanon; capture Beirut; expel PLO; withdraw to southern Lebanon in 1983.

1983 (Oct. 23) 241 U.S. Marines and 56 French troops killed by terrorist suicide bombers in Beirut, Lebanon.

1984 U.S., France and Britian withdraw peace-keeping troops from Lebanon in face of terrorist attacks.

1985 For 1985 events, see pages 8–26.

UNITED NATIONS HEADQUARTERS

The present site of the United Nations headquarters is an 18-acre tract along the East River in midtown Manhattan. Purchased with an $8.5 million gift from John D. Rockefeller Jr., the site is now international territory.

The UN's address is United Nations, NY 10017.

In November 1947 the world body approved a design submitted by an international consulting board under the direction of Wallace K. Harrison, an American architect.

The United States loaned the organization $65 million, and construction began in September 1948. Total cost was $73 million.

The General Assembly met at "United Nations, New York" for the first time in October 1952. (Interim business had been conducted from temporary quarters at Hunter College in New York City and at Lake Success, N.Y.)

The present headquarters comprise three interconnected buildings and a library, surrounded by plazas, gardens, and lawns.

The Secretariat building is a 30-story rectangular column, sheathed in glass and marble. The Secretariat building contains offices and working space for the headquarters staff.

The General Assembly building faces a landscaped plaza to the north. It is a sloping, doubly concave structure, topped by a shallow dome.

The General Assembly Hall, in which representatives of all the member nations convene in formal session at least once a year, is 165 feet long, 115 feet wide, and three stories high. Seats for delegates and alternates are arranged in curved rows on the floor, facing the officials' podium, and flanked by seats for advisers and observers. In the rear are places for alternate delegates, representatives' guests, and the press. Public galleries overlook the hall.

Translation and press booths line the walls of the General Assembly Hall. All 2,098 seats are equipped with earphones, enabling participants and spectators to listen to proceedings in any of the UN's five official languages: Chinese, English, French, Spanish, and Russian.

The UN buildings and grounds are decorated by works of art donated by various nations.

Buildings are open to the public from 9 A.M. to 5:30 P.M. daily, except Christmas and New Year's Day. An international staff of guides conducts tours of the headquarters between 9:00 A.M. and 4:45 P.M. daily. About one million persons take the tours each year.

UNITED STATES AMBASSADOR TO THE UNITED NATIONS

Vernon A. Walters, *Ambassador Extraordinary and Plenipotentiary*, Permanent Representative to the United Nations

MEMBERSHIP IN PRINCIPAL UNITED NATIONS BODIES: 1985

SECURITY COUNCIL

Fifteen members: Five (indicated by *) are designated in the Charter as permanent. Ten are elected by the General Assembly for 2-year terms, ending December 31 of the year indicated.

Australia (1986)	China *	France *	Soviet Union *	Trinidad-	Ukraine (1985)
Britain *	Denmark (1986)	India (1985)	Thailand (1986)	Tobago (1986)	United States *
Burkinafaso (1985)	Egypt (1985)	Peru (1985)			

ECONOMIC AND SOCIAL COUNCIL

The General Assembly elects 54 members for 3-year terms, ending Dec. 31 of year indicated.

Algeria (1985)	Costa Rica (1986)	India (1987)	Papua New Guinea (1986)	Suriname (1985)
Argentina (1986)	Djibouti (1985)	Indonesia (1986)	Poland (1986)	Sweden (1986)
Bangladesh (1987)	Ecuador (1985)	Japan (1987)	Romania (1987)	Thailand (1985)
Botswana (1985)	Finland (1986)	Lebanon (1985)	Rwanda (1986)	Turkey (1987)
Brazil (1987)	France (1987)	Luxembourg (1985)	Saudi Arabia (1985)	Uganda (1986)
Britain (1986)	Germany, East (1985)	Malaysia (1985)	Senegal (1987)	United States (1985)
Bulgaria (1985)	Germany, West (1987)	Mexico (1985)	Sierra Leone (1985)	Venezuela (1987)
Canada (1986)	Guinea (1987)	Morocco (1985)	Somalia (1986)	Yugoslavia (1986)
China (1986)	Guyana (1986)	Netherlands (1985)	Soviet Union (1986)	Zaire (1986)
Colombia (1987)	Haiti (1987)	New Zealand (1985)	Spain (1987)	Zimbabwe (1987)
Congo (1985)	Iceland (1987)	Nigeria (1987)	Sri Lanka (1986)	

INTERNATIONAL COURT OF JUSTICE (WORLD COURT)

Fifteen members, elected by the General Assembly and the Security Council to 9-year terms ending February 5 of the year indicated.

Taslim O. Elias, Nigeria, President	1994	Nagendra Singh, India	1991
Manfred Lachs, Poland	1994	José María Ruda, Argentina	1991
Shigeru Oda, Japan	1994	Robert Y. Jennings, Britain	1991
Steven M. Schwebel, United States	1988	Guy Ladreit de Lacharrière, France	1991
Roberto Ago, Italy	1988	Keba Mbaye, Senegal	1991
Abdullah Ali El-Erian, Egypt	1988	Jens Evensen, Norway	1994
José Sette Câmara, Brazil	1988	Ni Zengyu, China	1994
Platon Morozov, Soviet Union	1988		

THE 159 MEMBERS OF THE UNITED NATIONS

When the UN charter went into effect on Oct. 24, 1945, there were 51 members. Among them were Belorussia and Ukraine, two of the 15 states or republics of the Soviet Union.

New members of the UN must first be passed on by the UN Security Council, and therefore may be vetoed by any of the five permanent members. Membership then must be approved by a vote of the UN General Assembly.

Some nations are *not* members of the UN, such as: Andorra, Bophuthatswana, Ciskei, North Korea, South Korea, Liechtenstein, Monaco, Namibia, Nauru, San Marino, Switzerland, Taiwan, Tonga, Transkei, and Tuvalu.

MEMBER	SINCE	MEMBER	SINCE	MEMBER	SINCE
Afghanistan	1946 (Nov. 19)	Gabon	1960 (Sept. 20)	Oman	1971 (Oct. 7)
Albania	1955 (Dec. 14)	Gambia	1965 (Sept. 21)	Pakistan	1947 (Sept. 30)
Algeria	1962 (Oct. 8)	Germany, East	1973 (Sept. 18)	Panama	1945 (Nov. 13)
Angola	1976 (Dec. 1)	Germany, West	1973 (Sept. 18)	Papua New Guinea	1975 (Oct. 10)
Antigua	1981 (Nov. 11)	Ghana	1957 (March 8)	Paraguay	1945 (Oct. 24)
Argentina	1945 (Oct. 24)	Greece	1945 (Oct. 25)	Peru	1945 (Oct. 31)
Australia	1945 (Nov. 1)	Grenada	1974 (Sept. 17)	Philippines	1945 (Oct. 24)
Austria	1955 (Dec. 14)	Guatemala	1945 (Nov. 21)	Poland	1945 (Oct. 24)
Bahamas	1973 (Sept. 18)	Guinea	1958 (Dec. 12)	Portugal	1955 (Dec. 14)
Bahrain	1971 (Sept. 21)	Guinea-Bissau	1974 (Sept. 17)	Qatar	1971 (Sept. 21)
Bangladesh	1974 (Sept. 17)	Guyana	1966 (Sept. 20)	Romania	1955 (Dec. 14)
Barbados	1966 (Dec. 9)	Haiti	1945 (Oct. 24)	Rwanda	1962 (Sept. 18)
Belgium	1945 (Dec. 27)	Honduras	1945 (Dec. 17)	St. Christopher	1983 (Sept. 23)
Belize	1981 (Sept. 25)	Hungary	1955 (Dec. 14)	St. Lucia	1979 (Sept. 18)
Belorussia	1945 (Oct. 24)	Iceland	1946 (Nov. 19)	St. Vincent	1980 (Sept. 16)
Benin	1960 (Sept. 20)	India	1945 (Oct. 30)	São Tomé and Príncipe	1975 (Sept. 16)
Bhutan	1971 (Sept. 21)	Indonesia	1950 (Sept. 28)	Saudi Arabia	1945 (Oct. 24)
Bolivia	1945 (Nov. 14)	Iran	1945 (Oct. 24)	Senegal	1960 (Sept. 28)
Botswana	1966 (Oct. 17)	Iraq	1945 (Dec. 21)	Seychelles	1976 (Sept. 28)
Brazil	1945 (Oct. 24)	Ireland	1955 (Dec. 14)	Sierra Leone	1961 (Sept. 27)
Britain	1945 (Oct. 24)	Israel	1949 (May 11)	Singapore	1965 (Sept. 21)
Brunei	1984 (Sept. 21)	Italy	1955 (Dec. 14)	Solomons	1978 (Sept. 19)
Bulgaria	1955 (Dec. 14)	Ivory Coast	1960 (Sept. 20)	Somalia	1960 (Sept. 20)
Burkinafaso	1960 (Sept. 20)	Jamaica	1962 (Sept. 18)	South Africa	1945 (Nov. 7)
Burma	1948 (April 19)	Japan	1956 (Dec. 18)	Soviet Union	1945 (Oct. 24)
Burundi	1962 (Sept. 18)	Jordan	1955 (Dec. 14)	Spain	1955 (Dec. 14)
Cambodia	1955 (Dec. 14)	Kenya	1963 (Dec. 16)	Sri Lanka	1955 (Dec. 14)
Cameroon	1960 (Sept. 20)	Kuwait	1963 (May 14)	Sudan	1956 (Nov. 12)
Canada	1945 (Nov. 9)	Laos	1955 (Dec. 14)	Suriname	1975 (Dec. 4)
Cape Verde	1975 (Sept. 16)	Lebanon	1945 (Oct. 24)	Swaziland	1968 (Sept. 24)
Central Africa	1960 (Sept. 20)	Lesotho	1966 (Oct. 17)	Sweden	1946 (Nov. 19)
Chad	1960 (Sept. 20)	Liberia	1945 (Nov. 2)	Syria	1945 (Oct. 24)
Chile	1945 (Oct. 24)	Libya	1955 (Dec. 14)	Tanzania	1961 (Dec. 14)
China	1945 (Oct. 24)	Luxembourg	1945 (Oct. 24)	Thailand	1946 (Dec. 16)
Colombia	1945 (Nov. 5)	Madagascar	1960 (Sept. 20)	Togo	1960 (Sept. 20)
Comoros	1975 (Nov. 12)	Malawi	1964 (Dec. 1)	Trinidad-Tobago	1962 (Sept. 18)
Congo	1960 (Sept. 20)	Malaysia	1957 (Sept. 17)	Tunisia	1956 (Nov. 12)
Costa Rica	1945 (Nov. 2)	Maldives	1965 (Sept. 21)	Turkey	1945 (Oct. 24)
Cuba	1945 (Oct. 24)	Mali	1960 (Sept. 28)	Uganda	1962 (Oct. 25)
Cyprus	1960 (Sept. 20)	Malta	1964 (Dec. 1)	Ukraine	1945 (Oct. 24)
Czechoslovakia	1945 (Oct. 24)	Mauritania	1961 (Oct. 27)	United Arab Emirates	1971 (Dec. 9)
Denmark	1945 (Oct. 24)	Mauritius	1968 (April 24)	United States	1945 (Oct. 24)
Djibouti	1977 (Sept. 20)	Mexico	1945 (Nov. 7)	Uruguay	1945 (Dec. 18)
Dominica	1978 (Dec. 18)	Mongolia	1961 (Oct. 27)	Vanuatu	1981 (Sept. 15)
Dominican Republic	1945 (Oct. 24)	Morocco	1956 (Nov. 12)	Venezuela	1945 (Nov. 15)
Ecuador	1945 (Dec. 21)	Mozambique	1975 (Sept. 16)	Vietnam	1977 (Sept. 20)
Egypt	1945 (Oct. 24)	Nepal	1955 (Dec. 14)	Western Samoa	1976 (Dec. 15)
El Salvador	1945 (Oct. 24)	Netherlands	1945 (Dec. 10)	Yemen, North	1947 (Sept. 30)
Equatorial Guinea	1968 (Nov. 12)	New Zealand	1945 (Oct. 24)	Yemen, South	1967 (Dec. 14)
Ethiopia	1945 (Nov. 13)	Nicaragua	1945 (Oct. 24)	Yugoslavia	1945 (Oct. 24)
Fiji	1970 (Oct. 13)	Niger	1960 (Sept. 20)	Zaire	1960 (Sept. 20)
Finland	1955 (Dec. 14)	Nigeria	1960 (Oct. 7)	Zambia	1964 (Dec. 1)
France	1945 (Oct. 24)	Norway	1945 (Nov. 27)	Zimbabwe	1980 (Aug. 25)

UN SECRETARIES-GENERAL

The secretary-general is the UN's chief administrative officer. Since its beginning in 1945 the United Nations has had five secretaries-general: **Trygve Lie** (1896–1968) of Norway served from Feb. 1, 1946, until he resigned in September 1952 during his second term in office.
Dag Hammarskjöld (1905–61) of Sweden, named in April 1953, was serving a second term when he died in a plane crash while on a UN mission in the Congo on Sept. 18, 1961.

U Thant (1909–74) of Burma was appointed in 1962 and resigned in 1972.

Kurt Waldheim (1918–) of Austria served from 1972 to 1981.

Javier Pérez de Cuellar (1920–) of Peru took office on Jan. 1, 1982.

PRINCIPAL ORGANS OF THE UNITED NATIONS

GENERAL ASSEMBLY

The General Assembly is the main delibera-tive organ of the United Nations. Including representatives from all UN member nations, it discusses and makes recommendations on matters within the scope of the organiza-ion's Charter. It also approves the UN bud-get and apportions expenses among the mem-bers. A president, elected at the beginning of each session, presides.

The General Assembly convenes annually on the third Tuesday in September. Each member nation has one vote and is permitted to send up to 5 representatives to each ses-sion. On ordinary matters, decisions are car-ried by a simple majority of members present and voting; on more important matters, by a two-thirds majority.

The General Assembly works through 7 main committees: Political and Security; Special Political Committee; Economic and Financial; Social, Humanitarian, and Cultur-al; Trusteeship; Administrative and Budget-ary; and Legal.

SECURITY COUNCIL

The UN Security Council has primary re-sponsibility for maintaining peace and securi-ty. The Council has 5 permanent members—Britain, China, France, the Soviet Union, and the United States—and 10 nonpermanent members elected to 2-year terms by the Gen-eral Assembly. The Security Council is orga-nized to function continuously. Each member has one vote. Decisions on procedural mat-ters are carried by a majority of 9 members. However, on important matters, the 9 affirm-ative votes must include concurrence of the 5 permanent members. This is known as the "veto" privilege. Abstention does not consti-tute a veto.

The Security Council is empowered to in-vestigate any situation that might lead to friction between two or more countries. All UN members are pledged to carry out its de-cisions, as well as to make available to the Council assistance and facilities—including armed forces—for maintenance of interna-tional peace. A country that is a member of the United Nations, but not of the Security Council, may participate in its discussions when that nation's interests are specially af-fected. Nonmembers can be invited to partic-ipate in Security Council discussions of dis-putes to which they are parties. A member that is a party to a dispute may not vote.

The Disarmament Commission includes all UN member nations. It prepares proposals for regulation, limitation, and reduction of armed forces and armaments; for elimination of all weapons adaptable to mass destruction; and for international control of atomic energy to ensure its use for peaceful purposes.

The Military Staff Committee is composed of the chiefs of staff of the 5 permanent members—Britain, China, France, the Soviet Union, and the United States—or their rep-resentatives. It advises and assists the Securi-ty Council on such questions as the Coun-cil's military requirements for the mainte-nance of peace, the strategic direction of armed forces placed at its disposal, and the regulation of armaments.

ECONOMIC AND SOCIAL COUNCIL

The UN Economic and Social Council exam-ines and makes recommendations on interna-tional economic, social, cultural, educational, and health issues. The Council comprises 54 members, 18 of whom are elected each year to 3-year terms by the General Assembly. It is aided by separate regional commissions for Europe, Asia and the Far East, Latin Ameri-ca, and Africa.

TRUSTEESHIP COUNCIL

The UN Trusteeship Council is the principal organ assisting the General Assembly in su-pervision and administration of trust territo-ries. It comprises member nations adminis-tering trust territories, permanent members of the Security Council not administering trust territories, and as many other members (elected to 3-year terms by the General As-sembly) as are required to provide an equal number of administering and nonadminister-ing members.

Originally, 11 territories were placed un-der the trusteeship system; 10 have become independent or joined other independent states. The one still under UN trusteeship is the Trust Territory of the Pacific Islands (Micronesia), under U.S. administration.

INTERNATIONAL COURT OF JUSTICE

The International Court of Justice, or *World Court*, is the judicial organ of the UN. It sits at The Hague, in the Netherlands. Fifteen judges are elected to 9-year terms by the General Assembly and the Security Council, voting in-dependently. Every UN member has automatic access to the Court and is pledged to comply with its decisions. The Court has jurisdiction over all cases specifically referred to it, and over all matters specially provided for in the Charter or in treaties and conventions in force. The Court renders legal opinions on matters re-ferred to it by the General Assembly, Security Council, and specialized agencies authorized by the General Assembly.

UN SPECIALIZED AGENCIES AND AUTONOMOUS BODIES

Food and Agriculture Organization of the United Nations (FAO)
Headquarters: Rome, Italy
Established Oct. 16, 1945, to promote development of agriculture and good nutrition

General Agreement on Tariffs and Trade (GATT)
Headquarters: Geneva, Switzerland
Established Jan. 1, 1948, to provide international trade and tariff standards

Intergovernmental Maritime Consultative Organization (IMCO)
Headquarters: London, England
Established March 17, 1958, to promote international cooperation in maritime navigation

International Atomic Energy Agency (IAEA)
Headquarters: Vienna, Austria
Established July 29, 1957, to promote development of nuclear power for peaceful purposes

International Bank for Reconstruction and Development (World Bank)
Headquarters: Washington, D.C.
Established Dec. 27, 1945, to assist reconstruction and development of member states

International Civil Aviation Organization (ICAO)
Headquarters: Montreal, Quebec
Established April 4, 1947, to study international civil aviation problems and set standards

International Development Association (IDA)
Headquarters: Washington, D.C.
Established Sept. 24, 1960, for the purpose of making loans to less-developed countries

International Finance Corporation (IFC)
Headquarters: Washington, D.C.
Established July 20, 1956, to further economic development by encouraging private enterprise

International Fund for Agricultural Development (IFAD)
Headquarters: Rome, Italy.
Established Dec. 29, 1977, to help developing countries obtain investments to aid agricultural production

International Labor Organization (ILO)
Headquarters: Geneva, Switzerland
Established April 11, 1919, for the purpose of improving labor conditions and living standards through international action

International Monetary Fund (IMF)
Headquarters: Washington, D.C.
Established Dec. 27, 1945, for the purpose of promoting international monetary cooperation

International Telecommunication Union (ITU)
Headquarters: Geneva, Switzerland
Founded at Paris May 17, 1865, to establish international regulations for telegraph, telephone, and radio services

United Nations Capital Development Fund (UNCDF)
Headquarters: New York City.
Established Dec. 13, 1966, to provide grants and loans to developing countries

United Nations Children's Fund (UNICEF)
Headquarters: United Nations, N.Y.
Established Dec. 11, 1946, to aid the world's children by helping solve problems of health, hunger, and education

United Nations Conference on Trade and Development (UNCTAD)
Headquarters: Geneva, Switzerland
Established Dec. 30, 1964, to encourage economic growth in countries dependent on international trade

United Nations Development Program (UNDP)
Headquarters: Geneva, Switzerland
Established Nov. 22, 1966, to assist economic growth of developing nations

United Nations Disaster Relief Office (UNDRO)
Headquarters: Geneva, Switzerland
Established Dec. 14, 1971, to help coordinate aid in disaster areas

United Nations Educational, Scientific, and Cultural Organization (UNESCO)
Headquarters: Paris, France
Established Nov. 4, 1946, for the purpose of promoting international collaboration in education, science, and culture

United Nations Environment Program (UNEP)
Headquarters: Nairobi, Kenya
Established Dec. 15, 1972, as an outgrowth of the Stockholm Conference on the Human Environment, to identify major international environmental problems, monitoring the environment through the "Earthwatch" system

United Nations Fund for Population Activities (UNFPA)
Headquarters: United Nations, N.Y.
Established July 1967, to study and assist in population and family-planning problems

United Nations Industrial Development Organization (UNIDO)
Headquarters: Vienna, Austria
Established Nov. 17, 1966, to promote industrial growth in developing countries

United Nations Institute for Training and Research (UNITAR)
Headquarters: United Nations, N.Y.
Established Dec. 11, 1963, to carry out research and training programs to help developing nations

United Nations Office of High Commissioner for Refugees (UNHCR)
Headquarters: Geneva, Switzerland
Established Dec. 3, 1949, to protect the rights of refugees in foreign countries

United Nations Relief and Works Agency for Palestine Refugees in the Near East (UNRWA)
Headquarters: Vienna, Austria, and Amman, Jordan
Established Dec. 8, 1949, to aid refugees from Arab-Israeli War of 1948

United Nations Research Institute for Social Development (UNRISD)
Headquarters: Geneva, Switzerland
Established July 1, 1964, to research social problems related to economic growth

United Nations University (UNU)
Headquarters: Tokyo, Japan
Established Dec. 11, 1972, to provide a worldwide network of institutions of higher education

Universal Postal Union (UPU)
Headquarters: Bern, Switzerland
Established July 1, 1875, to promote cooperation in international postal services

World Food Council (WFC)
Headquarters: Rome, Italy
Established Dec. 17, 1974, on recommendation of World Food Conference to coordinate international efforts to feed hungry persons and to assist agricultural development of poor nations

World Health Organization (WHO)
Headquarters: Geneva, Switzerland
Established April 7, 1948, to promote world health through advisory and technical services

World Intellectual Property Organization (WIPO)
Headquarters: Geneva, Switzerland
Established April 26, 1970; affiliated with UN in 1974; promotes the protection of such intellectual properties as rights to literary, artistic, and scientific works

World Meteorological Organization (WMO)
Headquarters: Geneva, Switzerland
Established April 4, 1951, to promote international cooperation in weather observation

INTERNATIONAL ORGANIZATIONS AND ALLIANCES

Agency for the Prohibition of Nuclear Weapons in Latin America (OPANAL)
Headquarters: Mexico City. Established Sept. 2, 1969, to prevent introduction of nuclear weapons in Latin America. *Members:* Bahamas, Barbados, Bolivia, Brazil, Chile, Colombia, Costa Rica, Dominican Republic, Ecuador, El Salvador, Grenada, Guatemala, Haiti, Honduras, Jamaica, Mexico, Nicaragua, Panama, Paraguay, Peru, Suriname, Trinidad-Tobago, Uruguay, Venezuela.

Andean Pact
Established Oct. 16, 1969, to end trade barriers among member nations and create a common market. *Members:* Bolivia, Colombia, Ecuador, Peru, Venezuela.

ANZUS Pact
Defense alliance established April 29, 1952. *Members:* Australia, New Zealand, U.S.

Arab League
Established March 22, 1945; headquarters in Tunis, Tunisia; fosters cooperation among Arab nations. *Members:* Algeria, Bahrain, Djibouti, Egypt (suspended), Iraq, Jordan, Kuwait, Lebanon, Libya, Mauritania, Morocco, Oman, Palestinians (PLO), Qatar, Saudi Arabia, Somalia, Sudan, Syria, Tunisia, United Arab Emirates, North Yemen, South Yemen.

Association of Southeast Asian Nations (ASEAN)
Established Aug. 9, 1967, to stimulate economic growth of region. *Members:* Brunei, Indonesia, Malaysia, Philippines, Singapore, Thailand.

Caribbean Community and Common Market (CARICOM)
Established Aug. 1, 1973, to coordinate economic and foreign policies. *Members:* Antigua, Bahamas, Barbados, Belize, Dominica, Grenada, Guyana, Jamaica, Montserrat, St. Kitts-Nevis, St. Lucia, St. Vincent, Trinidad-Tobago.

Central African Customs and Economic Union (UDEAC)
Established Jan. 1, 1966, to aid economic, social, technical, and cultural development of members. *Members:* Cameroon, Central Africa, Congo, Gabon.

Central American Common Market (CACM)
Established June 3, 1961, to form a common market. *Headquarters:* Guatemala City. *Members:* Costa Rica, El Salvador, Guatemala, and Nicaragua.

Colombo Plan
Headquarters: Colombo, Sri Lanka. Established July 1, 1951, to aid development of members: Afghanistan, Australia, Bangladesh, Bhutan, Britain, Burma, Cambodia, Canada, Fiji, India, Indonesia, Iran, Japan, South Korea, Laos, Malaysia, Maldives, Nepal, New Zealand, Pakistan, Papua New Guinea, Philippines, Singapore, Sri Lanka, Thailand, United States, Vietnam.

Conference on Security and Cooperation in Europe (CSCE—Helsinki Pact)
Formed in 1975 by signing of Helsinki Agreement to cooperate in economics, peacekeeping, and promotion of human rights. *Members:* Austria, Belgium, Britain, Bulgaria, Canada, Cyprus, Czechoslovakia, Denmark, East Germany, Finland, France, Greece, Hungary, Iceland, Ireland, Italy, Liechtenstein, Luxembourg, Malta, Monaco, Netherlands, Norway, Poland, Portugal, Romania, San Marino, Soviet Union, Spain, Sweden, Swit- zerland, Turkey, United States, Vatican, West Germany, Yugoslavia.

Council for Mutual Economic Assistance (COMECON)
An economic organization of communist-bloc nations, founded Jan. 25, 1949, with headquarters in Moscow. *Members:* Bulgaria, Cuba, Czechoslovakia, East Germany, Hungary, Mongolia, Poland, Romania, Soviet Union, Vietnam. *Associate Member,* Yugoslavia.

Council of Europe
Headquarters: Strasbourg, France. Established Aug. 3, 1949, to promote unity, economic progress, and social progress among members. *Members:* Austria, Belgium, Britain, Cyprus, Denmark, France, West Germany, Greece, Iceland, Ireland, Italy, Liechtenstein, Luxembourg, Malta, Netherlands, Norway, Portugal, Spain, Sweden, Switzerland, Turkey.

Economic Community of West African States (ECOWAS)
Established by treaty signed May 28, 1975, at Lagos, Nigeria, to provide economic cooperation among members: Benin, Cape Verde, Gambia, Ghana, Guinea, Guinea-Bissau, Ivory Coast, Liberia, Mali, Mauritania, Niger, Nigeria, Senegal, Sierra Leone, Togo, Upper Volta.

European Economic Community (EEC)
European Common Market, established Jan. 1, 1958; also includes European Coal and Steel Community (ECSC), European Atomic Energy Community (EURATOM), and European Parliament. *Members:* Belgium, Britain, Denmark, France, West Germany, Greece, Italy, Ireland, Luxembourg, Netherlands, Portugal, Spain.

European Free Trade Association (EFTA)
Established May 3, 1960, for free trade among members. *Members:* Austria, Iceland, Norway, Sweden, Switzerland. *Associate member:* Finland.

Gulf Cooperation Council
Established May 26, 1981, to strengthen security and stability in the Persian Gulf oil-producing area. *Members:* Bahrain, Kuwait, Oman, Qatar, Saudi Arabia, United Arab Emirates.

Latin American Free Trade Association (LAFTA)
Founded June 2, 1961, with headquarters in Montevideo. *Members:* Argentina, Bolivia, Brazil, Chile, Colombia, Ecuador, Mexico, Paraguay, Peru, Uruguay, and Venezuela.

Nordic Council
Established Feb. 12, 1953, as an interparliamentary union to promote cooperation of Scandinavian nations in nonmilitary matters. *Members:* Denmark, Finland, Iceland, Norway, Sweden.

North Atlantic Treaty Organization (NATO)
Defense alliance, established Sept. 17, 1949. *Headquarters:* Brussels. *Members:* Belgium, Britain, Canada, Denmark, France, West Germany, Greece, Iceland, Italy, Luxembourg, Netherlands, Norway, Portugal, Spain, Turkey, United States.

Organization for Economic Cooperation and Development (OECD)
Established Sept. 30, 1961, to promote economic cooperation among members: Australia, Austria, Belgium, Britain, Canada, Denmark, Finland, France, West Germany, Greece, Iceland, Ireland, Italy, Japan, Luxembourg, Netherlands, New Zealand, Norway, Portugal, Spain, Sweden, Switzerland, Turkey, United States, Yugoslavia.

Organization of African Unity (OAU)
Established May 25, 1963, OAU promotes the unity and development of members: Algeria, Angola, Benin, Botswana, Burundi, Cameroon, Cape Verde, Central Africa, Chad, Comoros, Congo, Djibouti, Egypt, Equatorial Guinea, Ethiopia, Gabon, Gambia, Ghana, Guinea, Guinea-Bissau, Ivory Coast, Kenya, Lesotho, Liberia, Libya, Madagascar, Malawi, Mali, Mauritania, Mauritius, Morocco, Mozambique, Niger, Nigeria, Rwanda, São Tomé and Príncipe, Senegal, Seychelles, Sierra Leone, Somalia, Sudan, Swaziland, Tanzania, Togo, Tunisia, Uganda, Upper Volta, Zaire, Zambia, Zimbabwe.

Organization of American States (OAS)
Headquarters: Washington, D.C. Formerly the Pan American Union, the OAS was organized Dec. 31, 1951, for defense and cooperation. *Members:* Antigua, Argentina, Barbados, Bolivia, Brazil, Chile, Colombia, Costa Rica, Cuba, Dominica, Dominican Republic, Ecuador, El Salvador, Grenada, Guatemala, Haiti, Honduras, Jamaica, Mexico, Nicaragua, Panama, Paraguay, Peru, St. Christopher and Nevis, St. Lucia, St. Vincent, Suriname, Trinidad-Tobago, United States, Uruguay, Venezuela.

Organization of Eastern Caribbean States (OECS)
Established June 18, 1981. Headquarters: Castries, St. Lucia. *Members:* Antigua, Dominica, Grenada, Monserrat, St. Kitts, St. Lucia, St. Vincent.

Organization of Petroleum Exporting Countries (OPEC)
Established Nov. 14, 1960, to control production and pricing of crude oil. *Members:* Algeria, Ecuador, Gabon, Indonesia, Iran, Iraq, Kuwait, Libya, Nigeria, Qatar, Saudi Arabia, United Arab Emirates, Venezuela.

South Pacific Forum
Headquarters: Suva, Fiji. Established August 1971 to promote economic and political cooperation. *Members:* Australia, Cook Islands, Fiji, Kiribati, Nauru, New Zealand, Niue, Papua New Guinea, Solomon Islands, Tonga, Tuvalu, Vanuatu, Western Samoa.

Southern African Development Coordination Conference
Established April 1, 1980, to promote regional economic cooperation and reduce dependence on South Africa. *Members:* Angola, Botswana, Lesotho, Malawi, Mozambique, Swaziland, Tanzania, Zambia, Zimbabwe.

Warsaw Treaty Organization
Headquarters: Moscow. Military alliance of communist states, established June 5, 1955. *Members:* Bulgaria, Czechoslovakia, East Germany, Hungary, Poland, Romania, Soviet Union.

NEW WORDS

The American language is growing at a rapid rate as dozens of new words come into use each year. These words come from a wide variety of fields including science, technology, politics, economics, and education. Each specialized group coins new words, and some of these spread quickly, especially when they are picked up by newspapers and the television and radio media. Others may become popular only in one city or geographic region.

Words new in 1984 and in recent years are listed below:

acid fog—fog laden with sulfuric acid droplets released by industrial or oil-refining operations

advertorial—advertising insert similar in appearance and content to the regular content of a magazine or newspaper

AIDS—*a*cquired *i*mmune *d*eficiency *s*yndrome, fatal disorder of body's immune system thought to be transmitted mainly by sexual contact or contaminated blood for transfusions

airhead—dumb person

air-pocket stock—stock that falls sharply on bad news

algeny—upgrading of existing organisms and design of wholly new ones with intent of perfecting their performance (term coined by Joshua Lederberg, Nobel laureate in physics)

alibi store—carnival game in which operator encourages customer by pretending to give advice on how to win

anomalons—subatomic particles whose function is anomalous or unknown

apple green—very hard bullet coated with tough light-green plastic capable of penetrating bullet-proof vest

arctophile—person who loves teddy bears

aspartame—sweetener many times sweeter than sugar; made from two amino acids, L-aspartic acid and L-phenylalanine, found in protein-bearing foods such as bananas and beans

Atari Democrat—young liberal member of Democratic Party that seeks to use computers and other high technology to solve political problems

baby bonds—bonds sold in denominations of less than $1,000

beam weapon—futuristic weapon that uses beam of energy or particles to destroy target

block modeling—computer programming technique that evaluates how persons relate to each other in group situation, especially as employees within corporation

Bo Dereks—U.S. Treasury bonds that mature in the year 2010; such bonds also are known as "tens"

Bone Valley—five-county area in central Florida where phosphate is mined and turned into fertilizer

boomed—failed something

boomerang divorce—divorce after which couple continue living together

boss—slang adjective meaning something is very good

break dancing—acrobatic dancing that developed in slum areas as an alternative competition to street gang fights

breakers—persons who do break dancing

candy store problem—problem that seems to have wide variety of solutions that are equally attractive

celebrity rot—decline in aging entertainer's ability to perform as well as in younger years

CETI—Communication with Extraterrestrial Intelligence; efforts to establish communication with civilizations elsewhere in the universe

chill out—relax

co-generation—production of power by combined combustion of fuels, offering higher efficiency than conventional methods by recycling exhaust fumes and excess steam

compusex—sexy conversations carried on via computer terminal

computer literacy—ability to understand terminology and use of computers

condop—building in which residential tenants form one cooperative unit and commercial tenants another unit

copycat syndrome—irrational tendency to commit antisocial or criminal act in imitation of others who have done so

corporate raider—person or corporation seeking to take control of a corporation against the wishes of the management of the corporation being taken over

coyote—person who charges aliens exorbitant sums to smuggle them into United States

designer drugs—dangerous illegal drugs created in underground chemical laboratories for sale to addicts

directed-energy weapon—weapon that uses beam of energy or particles to destroy target

dirty questions book—notebook of information prepared for officials testifying before a congressional committee in order to answer anticipated difficult questions

downscale—to reduce from a larger or more expensive scale

dry painting—see *powder coating*

electronic cottage—concept of enabling workers to perform services at home linked to employer by electronic communication equipment

exit poll—poll taken by asking voters how they cast their ballots; used in forecasting how election will turn out

fair-bank—practice by operator of carnival game in letting customer win often enough to keep him playing

feet people—refugees traveling overland on foot, as from war-torn countries in Central America

NEW WORDS *(continued)*

flat game—carnival game that consumer has no chance of winning

flexible benefits—program by which employees of company may select wage and fringe benefits to suit special needs

Flexibook—book with strong pliable cover combining durability of hardcover with economy of paperback

flip-over pill—defensive strategy by a corporation against an unfriendly takeover by providing that its shareholders can buy shares of the merged corporation at a large discount

footprint—area of major destruction produced by nuclear weapon

fugitive air emission—pollutant inadvertently released into atmosphere

G'ed—carnival term for game that is rigged so consumer cannot win

gaff—hidden device used by carnival worker to rig game against consumer

garn—unit of measure of space sickness; named by astronauts for Sen. Jake Garn (R-Utah) who suffered space sickness during flight in space shuttle in 1985

gender gap—real or supposed difference in attitude or character between men and women

ghetto blaster—loud portable radio carried by user in public places, such as on beaches and in parks

giveback—in labor-management affairs, return by workers of benefits or contractual arrangements in exchange for job security or other consideration

glam—glamour

glitz—showy, glittery

greenmail—form of corporate blackmail in which company buys stock at inflated price to avoid being taken over by a corporate raider

green vote—voters concerned with environmental issues, considered as bloc

greeny—slang for environmentalist or conservationist

GRF—growth hormone *r*eleasing *f*actor, substance in brain vital in controlling release of hormone responsible for growth in humans and animals

hacker—one who explores resources of home computer for fun or profit

haircut—trimming down the costs of a project without damaging its main purpose

hand glide—balancing on one hand and spinning in break dancing

heavy beads—the most expensive items included in the Defense Department's annual budget

heavy-metal—rock music with especially strong beat and highly amplified sound

heptathlete—athlete who takes part in heptathlon

heptathlon—athletic event that includes running, jumping, and shot put

hip hop—synonym for break dancing

heavy breather—popular romantic fiction, especially in paperback or magazine

impact player—in football, offensive back capable of changing course of game by running, pass catching, or kick returning

incognoscenti—persons who lack knowledge about a specific area of knowledge

infill—construction of building on vacant lot in mainly built-up area

James Bond—U.S. Treasury bond due in the year 2007

jock couture—athletic apparel, such as warmup suits and sweatshirts, considered as fashion

joint—carnival workers' term for a carnival booth

junk bonds—securities that receive low ratings from credit evaluating agencies

junk financing—means of raising capital for takeover of a corporation by issuing securities bearing high rates of interest

King Tut—moving arms and head from one side to the other in break dancing

KISS—Keep It Simple, Stupid

knowledge engineering—study of how human decisions are made; used in developing computer programs that can help make decisions

locking—robot-like movements used in break dancing

loose cannon—person or something that is out of control

lurker—person who looks in on but does not take part in other people's conversations carried on computer networks

microscape—artistic rendering of high-technology object using camera aided by microscope

mips—computer term meaning millions of instructions per second

misery index—combined rate of inflation and unemployment at any given time

mouse-milking—using too much effort to achieve a small result

mule—person employed by criminals to smuggle illegal narcotics into a country

noodge—Yiddish word for person who is a pest

nothing-burger—something that is totally useless

nouvelle cuisine—type of French cooking using unusual combinations of ingredients; servings are decorative and in small quantities

on a roll—everything is happening for the best; from dice gambling in which player makes series of lucky rolls of dice

oncogene—type of gene found in all cells capable of turning normal cell into cancerous one

Orthotron—physical-therapy device that concentrates on rehabilitation of muscles around joint after injury to knee, ankle, or shoulder

outro—part of radio or television broadcast in which announcer or commentator signs off

PET—acronym for *p*ositron *e*mission *t*omography, technique for scanning brain to study disorders by injecting solution carrying radioactive isotope in bloodstream to show areas of greatest activity

photino—undetected atomic particle believed by some physicists to be a more massive counterpart of a photon

Planck scale—in theoretical physics, a scale as much smaller than the nucleus of a hydrogen atom as an atom is smaller than the solar system

plasma furnace—furnace that shoots super-heated gas into raw materials to produce iron and steel

plaster—a cheap carnival prize

pobiz—readings by poets of their own works; from *show biz*

poison pill—defense by a corporation from being taken over by an outsider, such as a rule allowing its stockholders the right to buy shares at a

special price if an unfriendly bidder tries to take control

powder coating—paint applied as powder by spray gun to appliance, electrical equipment, or other objects; spraying gives each particle electrical charge for even deposit and exact thickness; also called *dry painting*

refusenik—Soviet Jew whose request for exit visa is denied by government

requirements creep—new performance requirements added to a weapons system after it has been contracted with lesser requirements

ruppie—young Republican professionals

safety net—government benefits that help protect persons from disastrous consequences of poverty, aging, or medical problems

satietin—protein in human blood that sends message to brain that hunger has been satisfied

SETI—Search for Extraterrestrial Intelligence; efforts to make contact with other civilizations in the universe

shadow matter—in theroretical physics, matter that responds only to the force of gravity

shadow world—in theoretical physics, a star or planet that would be invisible because it would be made up entirely of shadow matter

shark repellent—rules adopted by a corporation's board of directors to ward off unwanted takeovers or mergers

slepton—undetected atomic particle believed by some physicists to be a more massive counterpart of a lepton

sliver—in real estate, tall narrow building looming over adjacent structures

slum—a cheap carnival prize

Skycam—computer-controlled robot TV camera that can fly over stadiums to take aerial views of sports events or entertainment productions

soliton—ultrashort pulse of light; used in communicating through glass fibers

speedball—mixture of two dangerous drugs, such as combination of cocaine and heroin

squeal rule—proposed legislation that would require government-sponsored clinic offering birth-control prescriptions to persons under 18 to inform parents of action taken

squamous—scaly

squark—undetected atomic particle believed by some physicists to be a more massive counterpart of a quark

Star Wars weapons—military defense system against nuclear missiles in space

Steel Valley—area of industrial suburbs southeast of Pittsburgh, Pa., along Monongahela River, with high concentration of steel mills

stolport—small airport built especially for STOLs (short takeoff and landing aircraft)

structural unemployment—loss of employment due to changes in job requirements and character of labor force

Sunday School—carnival term for honest game of chance

superstring theory—in physics, concept that the basic materials that make up all matter are tiny strings

supersymmetry—concept in physics that each atomic particle has an undetected counterpart that has greater mass

taxspeak—vocabulary of special terms and abbreviations used by tax accountants in discussing federal income tax information

teeny bidder—stock broker term for traders who buy and sell on changes in price of $\frac{1}{16}$ of a point

teletext—system that enables TV viewer to choose pages of text to be displayed on TV screen

terradiddle—little white lie

tevatron—atom smasher capable of speeding electrons to energy level of 1,000 billion electron volts, or TeV

three-hump camel—weapons system designed to meet objectives by air force, army, and navy

time-shifting—use of a video recorder to tape TV programs so they can be viewed at a later time

transdermal medication—procedure for administering medicine through skin: patch with microscopic membrane applied to skin allows measured release of medicine for circulation in bloodstream

transposon—gene or group of genes capable of moving from one cell to another and transferring genetic instructions; thought to be responsible for transmittal of diseases

ultralight—very light, open-sided, single-seat aircraft made of metal tubing, wire, and fabric and powered by small engine

underground economy—economic activity by persons whose incomes from services, sales, or trading are unreported

unfolding house—prefabricated house assembled and folded at factory for delivery and setting up at buyer's lot

upscale—to increase in scale, making something larger or more expensive

urban amenity zone—area in city designed to attract private enterprise by provision of improved housing, transportation, and shopping facilities

vaporware—new computer software or hardware announced by a developer that has not yet been produced for consumers

variable rate mortgage—mortgage with interest rate that can be adjusted in relation to changing economic conditions

videotex—two-way system of communication between customer and outside service source, using telephone to make requests and television to receive responses

violent peace—phrase describing international relations in 1980s that are not outright war but are not entirely peaceful

wacko—weird or eccentric person

white knight—friendly corporation that steps in to save another corporation from being taken over by a hostile bidder

wicked—slang superlative, such as "That sports car is wicked expensive."

wimp—slang for obnoxious or ineffectual person

windmill—rolling on shoulders and scissor kicking legs in air while break dancing

window—time period favorable for a specific event to take place

yellow snow—yellowish dustlike particles from acid-bearing paper in library books

yumpie—young upwardly mobile professional

yuppie—young urban professional person

zero-discount note—corporate note selling at discount and paying full amount at maturity but offering no interest payments

HOW TO WRITE A REPORT

Preparing a report is a time-consuming, mentally taxing task. It can also be absorbing and rewarding. Involved are eight essential steps.

1. Choose and analyze a subject. Select a subject in which you are interested. It is difficult to write effectively unless you are concerned with your material.

Choose a subject about which sufficient information is available to you in the form of printed materials or from experts who can be reached.

Select a subject about which you can arrive at a conclusion or a set of conclusions. An effective report is a group of facts that *prove* or *disprove* a specific statement, theory, or idea about a particular subject.

2. Make a careful investigation. In gathering material for a report, start by reading a good résumé of the subject. Most often you should start with an encyclopedia article. If your topic is not covered in a general or special-subject encyclopedia, you may find the needed summary in a magazine article or in a chapter from a book.

Find the books that can help you. Begin your search in the card catalog of your library for books mentioned in the bibliography following the résumé article you have read.

Search for recently written material. Examine recent issues of the *Reader's Guide to Periodical Literature*. You can then compare what is listed there with entries in the *International Index to Periodicals* and *Bulletin of the Public Affairs Information Service* (P.A.I.S.). In addition, you might consult entries in the *Art Index, Agricultural Index, Education Index, Applied Science and Technology Index,* and *Business Periodical Index.*

If necessary, write or telephone people who can provide information.

3. Take notes on your findings. Take notes on 3-by-5-inch cards, which can be easily shuffled into place according to the subject outline. Place no more than one note on a card; *never* use both sides of the card.

Each book or other source used should be entered on a separate card *in full bibliographical detail*, giving full name of the author, title, place of publication, publisher, and date.

You will then have two files of cards: (1) a master file that will include *all* bibliographical details on each book or article used, and (2) a file containing notes taken for the body of your paper.

Notes must be *legible* to avoid misinterpretation later, and must be *full* so that repeated trips to the library to verify them will not be necessary.

Distinguish between fact and opinion in the notes made. They all should be worded so that there will be no confusion later as to what *you* wrote or thought and what the *author* meant.

4. Prepare an outline. No one can write an effective report without some sort of outline.

An outline need not be detailed or elaborate. Only a few minutes may be needed to prepare a rough "sketch" outline that may pay big dividends.

You will probably make a number of tentative outlines as your work proceeds. When you are ready to state conclusions and have some idea of the framework of the entire structure, you can rearrange your notes under the outline headings.

5. Write a first draft. Prepare a first draft as a working copy. You can then make changes in sequence, strengthen your beginning, eliminate overlapping details, or make your discussion more effective.

Write in a clear, straightforward manner. A research paper need not be stiff, overly formal, or pedantic. It can be enlivened by touches of humor.

You must avoid *plagiarism*. You must *not* copy the words written by someone else unless you put them in quotation marks and name their source. Unless the idea and the phrasing are your own, refer the reader in a footnote to the source for your statement.

6. Add footnotes or explanatory comments. The purpose of a footnote is to name the authority for some fact or to develop some point referred to in the body of a paper.

7. Prepare a bibliography. In a report a bibliography is an alphabetical, sometimes classified, list containing the names of all works quoted from or generally used in preparation. The bibliography should be placed at the end of the report on a separate page.

Unless instructed otherwise, arrange items in the bibliography alphabetically by last names of the authors. List titles by the same author alphabetically. Citing the publisher's name is optional, but the place and date of publication are usually given.

8. Revise and proofread with care. The final version of a report must be carefully prepared. It should be as nearly letter-perfect as possible. To make sure of this, read slowly through the text to correct spelling and punctuation. Larger errors involving revision or addition may necessitate redoing a page.

Check your footnotes and bibliography.

If time permits, lay the paper aside for at least one day. Then reread it with fresh eyes. You may be surprised at how many errors and lapses you discover.

HOW TO PREPARE A SPEECH

So you were asked to speak at the next club meeting. And you were so flattered that you accepted. But now the time is rapidly approaching when you must make your appearance, and you haven't yet prepared your speech. Worried? Here are some tips that can help you overcome your stage fright.

1. Choose a topic to interest your audience. Who are the people you are speaking to? What are their interests? Write out what you believe is a fair profile of your audience. What is their average age? Will there be more men than women, or vice versa? What are their occupations? What common bond or interest brings them together as a group? Once you know your audience you should be ready to make a list of topics that might interest them.

2. Make sure your topic fits the occasion. What is the purpose of the meeting? If it is a Little League dinner celebrating the end of the season, you certainly shouldn't give a speech on *How to Pot Geraniums*, even if you happen to be the world's greatest authority on that subject.

3. Try to make your topic timely. If the meeting is a week before Christmas, you shouldn't try to speak on the events leading up to the Declaration of Independence. Think ahead to what events are going to take place at the time of the meeting or soon after. What can you talk about that will relate to those events?

4. Make sure your topic fits the time allowed. How long is your speech supposed to be? If you have only been allowed five minutes, don't choose such a broad topic that it can't possibly be discussed thoroughly within that period. For example, *The History of Space Exploration* would require much more than five minutes. So reduce your topic to *Man's First Walk on the Moon* to fit the time allowed.

5. Stimulate your audience to action. After the audience has heard your speech, what do you want them to do? If you want them to stop littering the streets with waste paper, then you must make them want to use the litter baskets. Even if you are giving a purely informative speech, such as *The History of the Bill of Rights*, you should try to get your audience to go out and read more about the subject because of the interest you have evoked by your speech. So in planning your topic, consider what you are going to ask your audience to do about it.

6. Be specific with your topic. Avoid a generalized topic, narrowing it to a specific aspect of the subject. For example, *Baseball* is too broad a subject for a good speech. Instead, talk on a specific aspect of baseball, such as *Four Ways to Hit More Home Runs* or *How One Boy Learned What Team Spirit Means.*

7. Choose a topic you are interested in. Avoid choosing a topic that you yourself find uninteresting. Otherwise, how can you possibly excite your audience about it?

8. Prepare your speech in three parts. Your speech should be divided into three main parts: (1) the introductory remarks, (2) the main body of the speech, and (3) the conclusion.

As you gather materials for your speech and make notes, arrange them into these three parts.

9. Wake up the audience at the outset. The introductory remarks, the first part of your speech, must catch the attention of the audience and make them want to listen to you. You may want to ask a question: "How many of you ever hit a home run?" or "Which one of you threw this gum wrapper on the floor?" Or you may wish to open with a startling statement: "Look down the row you are sitting in. At least one of the people you see will die of a heart attack within the next two years."

10. Avoid jokes unless you are a practiced storyteller. If you have tried telling jokes to your family and friends, and have received only weak smiles in return, avoid trying to open your speech with a joke.

If you are determined to use a joke, practice it on strangers. If they don't laugh, discard it.

11. Limit the main points you want to make. As you prepare the main body of your speech, limit yourself to making only two, three, or four main points. Organize your speech so that it will be clear to the audience exactly what are the main points you are trying to get across. Many speakers ramble on from one topic to another, and at the end the members of the audience ask each other, "What was he trying to say?"

12. Use specific examples. Back up each point with at least one specific example.

13. Avoid technical vocabulary. Although you are an authority on your subject, your audience is not. Make sure that the vocabulary you use is simplified so your audience can understand you. If you have to use a technical term, define it for the audience.

14. Conclude with a climax. The conclusion should be the best part of the speech and the part the audience remembers longest. You should summarize your main points and make your audience want to act on what you have said.

PUNCTUATE IT RIGHT!

Too much punctuation may be as confusing as too little. If a sentence is so complicated that no amount of punctuation seems adequate, the writer should reorganize it.

PERIOD (.)

The period is used at the end of sentences, after an indirect question, and after a polite request resembling a question. It is also the end mark for initials and certain abbreviations.

Here are examples of sentences that end with a period.

Declarative: *Mrs. Morris placed the book on the table.*

Imperative: *Do it today. Sit down.*

Indirect Question: *The members of the committee asked when the meeting would take place.*

Polite Request: *Will you open the door for me, please.*

QUESTION MARK (?)

The question mark signifies that the sentence asks a question: *What time is it? Am I late?*

Sometimes a sentence consists of several questions, each of which should end with a question mark. However, the separate questions within the sentence do not begin with a capital, since they are part of the sentence: *Who will attend the conference? the president? the vice president? the secretary?*

EXCLAMATION POINT (!)

The exclamation point at the end of a statement denotes strong emotion or a sense of urgency. Often this may be a phrase or even a single word: *What a show! Hurrah! Please hurry!*

An interjection such as *Oh!* or *Ah!* at the beginning of a sentence is usually followed by a comma, and the sentence is ended with an exclamation point: *Oh, what a day this has been!*

COMMA (,)

Here are examples of sentence structure that call for the comma:

Series: The comma separates various elements in a series—either words, phrases, or clauses—when there are at least three units: *The dog jumped up, barked ferociously, bared his teeth, and took off after the rabbit.*

Style adopted by some newspapers, magazines, and publishing firms does not require the comma before the conjunction in a series, as in: *The flag is red, white and blue.*

When *et cetera,* or its abbreviation *etc.,* ends a series it should be preceded by a comma. A comma should also follow *etc.* when it

is not the last word in a sentence: *She stopped off to get some fruit, vegetables, etc., on the way home.*

Introductory Elements: When the main clause of the sentence comes first, there is no need for a comma in the sentence: *Take along a few magazines when you visit him.*

An introductory phrase containing a verb usually should be followed by a comma: *After making the survey, the committee published its report.*

If the introductory phrase is very short or does not contain a verb, it need not be followed by a comma unless the phrase is parenthetical or explanatory: *After much debate the meeting was adjourned.* But: *On the contrary, I believe the President was absolutely right.*

A comma sets off an introductory *yes* or *no*: *No, we shall not be ready on time.*

A parenthetical expression (word, phrase, or clause) that can be omitted without drastically changing the meaning of the sentence should be set off by commas: *The king, who was ill, was not present.*

Quotations: Use the comma before direct quotations, unless they are very long—usually a paragraph or more. In such cases a colon should be used: *She asked, "Is the train on time?"*

Appositives: A comma or commas should set off an identifying or explanatory word or phrase (called an *appositive*) which helps to make the meaning of the sentence clearer: *Mr. Jones, our grocer, traveled last summer to Canada, his native country.*

Contrasting Expressions: Use a comma to separate contrasting expressions—word, phrase, or clause: *We shall leave today, not tomorrow.*

Parallel Adjectives: Commas should separate parallel adjectives: *The tall, thin, scowling man made a poor impression.*

Conjunctions: The comma should be used before a conjunction (*but, and, or,* etc.) that connects two independent clauses: *John played shortstop, and he filled in a few times when the regular catcher was hurt.*

If the clauses are short and uncomplicated the comma may be omitted: *We were drenched but Mother didn't scold us.*

When two verbs have the same subject, the connecting conjunction is not usually preceded by a comma: *It snowed all morning but stopped at noon.*

Numbers and Dates: Use the comma with numbers in the thousands: *1,792 new cars.* Omit the comma in a date using only month and year: *April 1970.* But do use commas with the day of the month: *April 2, 1970.*

SEMICOLON (;)

The semicolon separates two independent clauses when the conjunction is omitted: *We are enclosing an envelope for your convenience; it requires no postage.*

Compound Sentences: The semicolon separates members of a compound sentence when the clauses are connected by such words as *however, nevertheless, consequently,* thus: *The team was undefeated; however, three games ended in ties.*

When part of a compound sentence contains a comma, the semicolon must be used to separate the members: *If nominated, he will run; but his chances seem rather slim.*

Series: Phrases or clauses in a series are separated by the semicolon when one or more contain a comma: *Our profits for the three years were unusually high: 1974, $2,345,000; 1975, $2,070,400; 1976, $2,545,000.*

COLON (:)

The colon generally indicates that a list, example, or strong assertion will follow: *Johnny had three jobs to do: clean the garage, mow the lawn, and sweep the back porch.*

The colon is also used after the salutation of a formal letter (*Dear Sir:*); between elements of a biblical citation (*Exodus 16:1-4*); after the name of the speaker in a play (*Hamlet: To be, or not to be: that is the question*); and to separate hours and minutes when time is expressed in figures (*We shall be there at 3:30* P.M.).

APOSTROPHE (')

The apostrophe commonly forms the possessive of nouns and pronouns. (However, personal pronouns such as *mine, yours, theirs* do not take the apostrophe.) With words ending in an *s,* use *'s* with one-syllable words, but use only an apostrophe with words of two or more syllables unless the *s* is not sounded: *James's, Adams', Arkansas's.*

Be careful not to use an apostrophe in the plurals of proper nouns where no possessive is intended: *We are going to see the Smiths and the Jeffersons* (not *Smith's* or *Smiths', Jefferson's* or *Jeffersons'*).

Contractions: An apostrophe is also used to show that one or more letters have been omitted from a word, or that numerals have been omitted from a number: *it's*—it is; *can't*—cannot; '29—1929.

QUOTATION MARKS (" ") (' ')

Double quotation marks (" ") are required at the beginning and end of a word or words spoken in direct discourse: *Roy said, "I'm reading a good book."*

If a direct quotation is interrupted by one or more words, double quotation marks are placed around the quoted matter only, and not around the interrupting words: *"Hurry along," said the coach, "or the game will not start on time."*

Double quotation marks set off words or phrases the writer does not wish to claim as his or her own: *Let my opponent produce his "incontrovertible evidence."*

Single quotation marks (' ') enclose a quotation within a quotation: *Jack remarked, "I believe that Patrick Henry said, 'Give me liberty or give me death.'"*

Enclose in double quotation marks the titles of essays, magazine articles, lectures, term papers, and book chapters.

HYPHEN (-)

Use the hyphen for end-of-line word divisions and in compound words.

Words may be divided at the end of a line *only* between syllables. (If in doubt as to how to divide a word, check your dictionary.) Never divide one-syllable words.

Compound Words: When two or more words precede a noun and form a single idea modifying the noun, they should be hyphenated: *He spoke in a matter-of-fact tone.*

Prefixes: Hyphens are sometimes used to separate prefixes from words where the meaning might otherwise be distorted: *The upholsterer re-covered the chair. Mr. Aiken recovered his stolen property.*

The hyphen is generally used when words are compounded with the prefix *self: self-satisfied; self-sufficient.*

The hyphen is also used to separate a prefix from a proper noun: *anti-American.*

Numbers: Hyphens are used in all numbers from *twenty-one* to *ninety-nine,* and in fractions: *one-half, three-quarters.*

DASH (—)

A word of caution against confusing the hyphen (-) and the dash (—). The hyphen connects. The dash often separates. The dash may be used in place of the comma and parentheses in handling appositive and parenthetical expressions. It is also used to mark intentional repetition and interruption: *Exercise every day—I mean every day.*

PARENTHESES [()]

Parentheses marks are used to enclose words that give additional information but have little, if any, direct connection with the main thought expressed. They should be used sparingly: *If we win the contest (and I feel certain we shall), we shall compete in the finals.*

Parentheses are widely used to enclose references to statements, authors, and so forth: *We are using the book Effective Business English* (Jones and Smith).

FORMS OF ADDRESS

Many people either may meet or have the occasion to write letters to persons of importance—high government officials, congressmen, judges, officers of the armed services, clergymen, physicians, and college professors. There are certain proper forms of address that should be used.

PRESIDENT OF THE UNITED STATES

Address Business: The President
 The White House
 Washington, D.C. 20500
 Social: The President
 and Mrs. . . .
 The White House
 Washington, D.C. 20500

Salutation Formal: Sir:
 Informal: My Dear Mr. President:

Closing Formal: I have honor to remain,
 Most respectfully yours,
 Informal: Very respectfully yours,
 In conversation: Mr. President *or* Sir

CHIEF JUSTICE OF THE UNITED STATES

Address Business: The Chief Justice
 The Supreme Court
 Washington, D.C. 20543
 Social: The Chief Justice
 and Mrs. . . .
 Home address

Salutation Formal: Sir:
 Informal: My Dear Mr. Chief Justice:

Closing Formal: Very truly yours,
 Informal: Sincerely yours, *or*
 Faithfully yours,
 In conversation: Mr. Chief Justice *or* Sir

ASSOCIATE JUSTICE OF THE SUPREME COURT

Address Business: Mr. Justice . . .
 The Supreme Court
 Washington, D.C. 20543
 Social: Mr. Justice . . .
 and Mrs. . . .
 Home address

Salutation Formal: Sir:
 Informal: My Dear Mr. Justice . . . :

Closing Formal: Very truly yours,
 Informal: Sincerely yours,
 In conversation: Mr. Justice *or* Mr.
 Justice . . . *or* Sir

CABINET OFFICER

Address Business: The Honorable . . .
 The Secretary of the
 Treasury *or* The
 Attorney General
 Washington, D.C.
 Social: The Honorable . . .
 The Secretary of the Treasury *or* The Attorney
 General and Mrs. . . .
 Home address

Salutation Formal: Sir: *or* Dear Sir:
 Informal: My Dear Mr. Secretary:
 or My Dear Mr. Attorney General:

Closing Formal: Very truly yours,
 Informal: Sincerely yours,
 In conversation: Mr. Secretary *or*
 Mr. Attorney General *or* . . . Sir.

UNITED STATES SENATOR

Address Business: The Honorable . . .
 United States Senate
 Washington, D.C. 20510
 Social: The Honorable . . .
 and Mrs. . . .
 Home address

Salutation Formal: Sir: *or* Madam:
 Informal: My Dear Senator . . . :

Closing Formal: Very truly yours,
 Informal: Sincerely yours,
 In conversation: Senator *or* Senator . . .
 or Sir *or* Madam

UNITED STATES REPRESENTATIVE

Address Business: The Honorable . . .
 United States House of
 Representatives
 Washington, D.C. 20515
 Social: The Honorable . . .
 and Mrs. . . .
 Home address
 or (for a woman member)
 Mr. and Mrs. . . .

Salutation Formal: Sir: *or* Madam:
 Informal: My Dear Mr. (or
 Mrs.) . . . :

Closing Formal: Very truly yours,
 Informal: Sincerely yours,
 In conversation: Mr. . . . *or* Mrs. . . . *or*
 Sir *or* Madam

STATE SENATORS AND REPRESENTATIVES

Address like U.S. senators and representatives.

AMBASSADOR OF THE UNITED STATES

Address Business: The Honorable . . .
 The Ambassador of the
 United States
 American Embassy
 Address
 Social: The Honorable . . .
 and Mrs. . . .
 Home address
 or (for a woman ambassador) Mr. and Mrs. . . .

Salutation Formal: Sir: *or* Madam:
 Informal: My Dear Mr. (*or* My Dear
 Madam) Ambassador:

Closing Formal: Very truly yours,
 Informal: Sincerely yours,
 In conversation: My Dear Mr. (*or* Madam)
 Ambassador *or* Sir (*or* Madam)

CONSUL OF THE UNITED STATES

Address Business: Mr. . . .
 American Consul
 Address
 Social: Mr. and Mrs. . . .
 Home Address

Salutation Formal: Sir: *or* My Dear Sir:
 Informal: Dear Mr.
 In conversation: Mr. . . .
Title of Introduction: Mr.

AMBASSADOR OF A FOREIGN COUNTRY

Address Business: His Excellency, . . .
The Ambassador of . . .
Washington, D.C.
Social: His Excellency,
The Ambassador of . . .
Home address
Salutation Formal: Excellency:
Informal: My Dear Mr.
Ambassador:
Closing Formal: Very truly yours,
Informal: Sincerely yours,
In conversation: Mr. Ambassador *or*
Excellency *or* Sir

GOVERNOR OF A STATE

Address Business: The Honorable . . .
Governor of . . .
(capital city, state)
Social: The Honorable . . .
and Mrs. . . .
Home address
Salutation Formal: Sir:
Informal: Dear Governor . . . :
Closing Formal: Very truly yours,
In conversation: Governor . . . *or* Sir

MAYOR

Address Business: His (*or* Her) Honor the
Mayor
City Hall
Address
Social: His Honor the Mayor
and Mrs. *or* (*for woman
mayor*) Mr. and Mrs.
Home address
Salutation Formal: Sir: *or* Madam:
Informal: Dear Mayor . . . :
Closing Formal: Very truly yours,
In conversation: Mr. (*or* Madam) Mayor

JUDGE

Address Business: The Honorable . . .
Justice Appellate
Division
Supreme Court of the
State of . . .
Address
Social: The Honorable . . .
and Mrs. . . .
Home address
Salutation Formal: Sir: *or* Madam:
Informal: Dear Judge . . .
Closing Formal: Very truly yours,
In conversation: Mr. (*or* Madam) Justice

PROTESTANT CLERGYMAN

Address Business: The Reverend . . . *or* (if
he holds the degree) The
Reverend . . . , D.D.
Social: The Reverend . . . and
Mrs. . . .
Home address
Salutation Formal: Sir: *or* My Dear Sir:
Informal: Dear Mr. (*or* Dr.) . . . :
Closing Formal: Sincerely yours, *or*
Faithfully yours,
In conversation: Mr. (*or* Dr.) . . . (*never*
Reverend . . .)

RABBI

Address Business: Rabbi . . . *or* (if he
holds the degree)
Dr. . . . , D.D.
Address of his synagogue
Social: Rabbi (*or* Dr.) and
Mrs. . . .
Home address
Salutation Formal: Dear Sir:
Informal: Dear Rabbi (*or* Dr.) . . .
Closing Formal: Sincerely yours,
Informal: Sincerely yours,
In conversation: Rabbi (*or* Dr.)

CATHOLIC PRIEST

Address Business: The Reverend . . . (and
the initials of his order,
if needed)
Address of his church
Salutation Formal: Reverend Father:
Informal: Dear Father . . . :
Closing Formal: I remain, Reverend
Father, yours faithfully,
Informal: Faithfully yours,
In conversation: Father *or* Father . . .
or Your Reverence

OFFICERS OF THE ARMED SERVICES

(Commander or higher in the Navy; captain or
higher in the Air Force, Army, and Marines)
Address Business: Admiral . . . , USN *or*
Colonel . . . , USMC
or General . . . , USA
or USAF (plus any title)
Address of base, ship, or
government department
Social: Admiral (*or* Colonel *or*
General) and Mrs. . . .
Home address
Salutation Formal: Sir:
Informal: My Dear Admiral
(*or* Colonel
or General) . . . :
Closing Formal: Very truly yours,
Informal: Sincerely yours,

PHYSICIAN

Address Business: . . . , M.D.
Office address
Social: Dr. and Mrs. . . .
Home address
Salutation Formal: Dear Sir:
Informal: Dear Dr. . . . :
Closing Formal: Very truly yours,
Informal: Sincerely yours,

COLLEGE (OR UNIVERSITY) PROFESSOR

Address Business: Professor *or* (if he
holds the Ph.D. degree)
Dr. *or* Mr. . . .
Office address
Social: Professor (*or* Dr. *or*
Mr.) and Mrs. . . .
Salutation Formal: Dear Sir:
Informal: Dear Professor (*or* Dr.
or Mr.) . . .
Closing Formal: Very truly yours,
Informal: Sincerely yours,
In conversation: Professor (*or* Dr.) . . .
(within the college);
Mr. . . . (elsewhere)

SPELL IT RIGHT!

Here are five tips to better spelling:

1. Keep a list of your spelling errors and study them.

2. Learn to spell the most commonly misspelled words. (See opposite page.)

3. Use newly acquired words and make them a part of your oral and written vocabulary.

4. When in doubt as to the correct spelling of a word, consult your dictionary.

5. Study the following rules. These will help you overcome many of the most common spelling pitfalls.

Which is it: -ant or -ent? -ance or -ence? If you know that a word ends in *-ant,* related words will always end in *-ance* and *-ancy.* And if a word ends in *-ent,* related words will end in *-ence* and *-ency.*

Here are 8 representative *-ant, -ance, -ancy* words: *acceptance, assistant, attendant, insurance, maintenance, relevancy, resistant, tolerant.* In the *-ent, -ence, -ency* group the following 12 words are troublesome to many people: *apparent, coincident, conference, confident, consistency, correspondent, dependent, existence, occurrence, persistent, reference, superintendent.*

Which is it: -cede, -ceed, or **sede?** There is only one word that ends in *-sede: supersede.* Only three words end in *-ceed: proceed* (but *procedure*), *exceed, succeed.* All other words with this phonetic sound end in *-cede: precede, recede, secede.*

Which is it: ie or ei? After *c,* when the sound is long *e,* the *e* usually precedes the *i* (ei): *ceiling, deceive, receipt, receive.*

After most other letters, the *i* precedes the *e* (ie): *achieve, believe, grief, lien, siege, thief.*

When the sound is not long *e,* and especially if the sound is long *a,* the *e* precedes the *i* (ei): *sleigh, veil, weigh.*

Which is it: -ary or -ery? Because the word endings *-ary* and *-ery* sound alike, they can cause spelling problems. However, one fact will solve most of the problems. More than 300 words end in *-ary;* only a few words end in *-ery.* If you learn these few you will conquer the difficulty: *artillery, bakery, brewery, celery, cemetery, confectionery, distillery, dysentery, millinery, monastery, refinery, stationery* (writing paper).

Which is it: -ar, -er, or **-or?** Here are two tips on *-ar, -er,* and *-or* words. First, the ending *-ar* is not common. All you need do is to learn a few common *-ar* words such as *beggar, cedar, collar, dollar, liar, registrar, scholar,* and *similar.*

The more confusing endings are *-er* and *-or.* So here's a second tip: For simple, common words *-er* is usually the right ending.

The Latin *-or* goes with advanced words.

In American English *-re* is not a common ending. Learn the correct spelling of these six *-re* words: *acre, lucre, macabre, massacre, mediocre, ogre.*

Which is it: -al, -el, or **-le?** No good rule has ever been devised to help you decide whether a word ends in *-al, -el,* or *-le.* Pronunciation will not help you either, because all three sound alike when spoken.

You must try to memorize the spelling of words with these endings. When in doubt, consult your dictionary.

Which is it: -able or -ible? Two points about *-able* and *-ible* simplify the decision as to which spelling is correct:

1. *-able* is the basic form. Many more words end in *-able* than in *-ible.*

2. An *a* for an *a* and an *i* for an *i:* If the adjective is closely related to a noun that ends in *-ation,* the adjective is almost certain to end in *-able.* If a related noun ends in *-ion* instead of *-ation,* the adjective is pretty sure to end in *-ible.*

Which is it: c or ck? If a word ends in a *c,* you must add a *k* before a suffix beginning with *e, i,* or *y* to keep the *c* hard: *frolic* becomes *frolicking; mimic* becomes *mimicking; panic* becomes *panicking; picnic* becomes *picnicking* and *picnicker; traffic* becomes *trafficking* and *trafficker.*

The final -e rule: A final silent *e* is usually dropped before a suffix beginning with a vowel (like *-able, -ion, -ing*): *blam(e)able, confus(e)ion, hop(e)ing.* But a final silent *e* is retained before a consonant: *blameworthy, hopeless.*

Which is it: -efy or -ify? The ending *-ify* is much more common than *-efy.* In fact, words ending in *-efy* may be considered exceptions. Here are some *-efy* words (the exceptions): *liquefy, putrefy, rarefy, stupefy.*

Which is it: -ise, -ize, or **-yze?** The usual suffix is *-ize,* and *-yze* and *-ise* are rather rare exceptions. Only two common words end in *-yze: analyze* and *paralyze.* Only about 30 common words end in *-ise: advertise, comprise, despise, exercise,* among them.

Which is it: -ly or -ally ? When the original ends in *-ic,* the adverb-making suffix sometimes is *-ally* instead of *-ly,* as in *artistically* and *fantastically.* One common word ending in *-ic* that is made into an adverb by adding only *-ly* is *public;* the adverb is *publicly.*

When is a final y changed to i ? If a word ends in *y* preceded by a consonant (any letter other than *a, e, i, o, u*), change the *y* to an *i* when you add a suffix. Here are some examples: *ally* becomes *allies* and *allied; city* becomes *cities; duty* becomes *duties* and *dutiful.*

SPELLING DEMONS

SIXTH GRADE SPELLING DEMONS

Here are some of the words most frequently misspelled by sixth-graders. Many adults still misspell some of them. Check yourself to see if you need to relearn any of these words.

accommodate	athletics	challenge	February	Halloween	separate
across	balloon	coming	forth	minute	similar
already	bicycle	deceive	fourth	missile	sincerely
arithmetic	business	describe	good night	niece	surprise
athlete	ceiling	description	grammar	really	writing

HIGH SCHOOL SPELLING DEMONS

Here are some of the words taken from school and job-placement tests most frequently misspelled by high school seniors and graduates. How many of them do you find troublesome?

absence	conscious	dispensable	guidance	occasion	receive
absurd	convenient	embarrass	humorous	occurred	recommend
accidentally	correspondence	environment	immediately	omitted	repetition
advertisement	criticize	escape	independent	opportunity	restaurant
all right	definite	exaggerate	irresistible	parallel	rhythm
amateur	dependent	existence	laboratory	performance	schedule
attendance	descend	experience	lightning	permanent	success
believe	desperate	fascinate	losing	prejudice	tragedy
committee	develop	foreign	necessary	privilege	villain
condemn	difference	government	neighbor	professor	weird

CIVIL SERVICE WORDS

Since many people who take Civil Service exams are high school graduates, the words most frequently misspelled are much the same as those on high school lists. Civil Service spelling tests also show 24 more demons related to government and office work.

accident	enforcement	monetary	simplified
auxiliary	expedient	municipal	society
career	federal	personnel (vs. personal)	supervisor
clerical	filing (vs. filling)	president	technical
county (vs. country)	legality	responsibility	tendency
comptroller	mechanism	salary	yield

COLLEGE WORDS

This list contains words most often misspelled by students who have had two years of college. Demons from the high school list above are not repeated although many of those words continue to be misspelled by college and university students.

achieve	competition	desirable	exercise	noticeable	pronunciation
aggravate	conscientious	despair	grievance	occurrence	responsibility
appearance	convenience	dining	knowledge	permissible	superintendent
argument	council	disappear	maintenance	precede	supersede
athlete	definitely	enforcement	marriage	procedure	usage
cemetery	descend	exceed	mischievous	proceed	wholly

ADULT SPELLING DEMONS

Many business executives and professionals with college degrees still have spelling problems. Here are some words they misspell most often, not repeating demons from the above lists.

accessible	assistant	coolly	incidentally	irritable	perseverance
acquainted	burglar	drunkenness	insistent	license	recognize
analyze	campaign	envelope	intercede	mortgage	seize

HOW DO THE EXPERTS DO?

Editors, writers, and English teachers are especially good spellers. The following list consists of 60 everyday words most often misspelled by such experts. How many can you spell correctly?

abscess	chrysanthemum	fission	inoculate	phlegm	sacrilegious
accelerator	connoisseur	fricassee	liquefy	picnicking	sheriff
aggressor	demagogue	fuselage	millennium	poliomyelitis	sieve
allotted	desiccate	gaiety	millionaire	prairie	subpoena
annihilate	dilapidated	gynecologist	miscellaneous	prescription	tariff
assassin	discriminate	harebrained	moccasin	propeller	tonsillitis
besiege	dissipate	hippopotamus	paraffin	questionnaire	tyranny
broccoli	ecstasy	hypocrisy	paralyze	raspberry	vacillate
catalyst	effervescent	immaculate	penitentiary	requiem	vengeance
category	exhilarate	innocuous	perspiration	rhinoceros	zephyr

WAYS TO BUILD YOUR VOCABULARY

Building a large vocabulary—understanding and using a wide variety of words—is important for success in almost any field. To build such a vocabulary sometimes requires bone-hard work.

Each person has three vocabularies.

First, there is an *active,* or *speaking,* vocabulary—the words we use every day in speaking.

Second, there is our *writing* vocabulary. It contains some words we do not use in speech.

Third, each person has a *recognition,* or *reading,* vocabulary, the largest of the three. Through this recognition vocabulary we can understand speakers and read books, magazines, and newspapers.

Consistent effort is needed to move words from our recognition to our active vocabulary.

Here are seven commonsense, time-tested suggestions for building your vocabulary:

1. Make friends with your dictionary. The most important element in vocabulary growth is the *will* to learn new words and to learn how to use them.

All reading and listening should lead straight to a good dictionary. You should actually *study* each word you look up. It requires only a moment to learn the spelling, pronunciation, or one meaning of a word. But hasty examination will prevent your mastering the word and adding it to your active vocabulary.

Equip yourself with a large dictionary that contains 100,000 words or more. It is unwise to buy a "cheap" dictionary when an excellent one can be purchased for only a few dollars more.

2. Learn a few basic word elements. Numerous word elements rarely appear independently but do form parts of longer words. Such elements, known as "combining forms," may be illustrated by "graph," as in *photograph, lithography, telegraph, phonograph, geography;* and "micro," as in *microphone, microscope, microcosm,* and *microfilm.*

3. Learn the meanings of common prefixes. A prefix is a letter of the alphabet (or a group of letters) put before a word to add to or qualify meaning. Understanding the meaning (or meanings) of constantly appearing prefixes, such as *anti-, post-,* and *pre-,* will build your vocabulary by making large numbers of words instantly recognizable and usable

4. Learn the meaning of common suffixes. A suffix is an element that is placed after a word or word root to make a term of different meaning or use, such as *-ful, -less, -ly,* or *-some.*

5. Make a study of synonyms. A synonym is a word having the same meaning, or nearly the same meaning, as another. A study of synonyms for the word "old" might add these words, among others, to your vocabulary: *aged, immemorial, ancient, aboriginal, hoary, antique, elderly, patriarchal, passé, venerable, antediluvian,* and *antiquated.*

6. Make a study of antonyms. An antonym is a word that is opposite in meaning to another word: *small* and *little* are antonyms of "large"; *happy* is an antonym of "sad."

Learning the opposite, or negative, of one or more of the meanings of another word will not be so valuable as studying synonyms, but the effort is worthwhile. Seeking antonyms for the verb *praise* may add these words, among others, to your vocabulary: *abuse, blame, censure, condemn, deprecate, disparage, impugn, inveigh against, lampoon, stigmatize, vilify.* The word *join,* for example, has such opposites as *cleave, disconnect, sever, separate,* and *sunder.*

These opposite meanings are not all-inclusive: A word may be an antonym of another only in a limited meaning. For example, one antonym of *man* (*woman*) concerns sex; another (*child*), age; another (*animal*), biology; another (*God*), religion. Like synonyms, antonyms must be selected carefully and used with exactness.

7. Use your vocabulary. How to use words exactly and emphatically is the most important phase of the problem of vocabulary building. It is indeed necessary to increase your vocabulary and not use words incorrectly. But the mere size of your vocabulary is not always a test of speaking or writing ability. Nor does it follow that if you stick to the principles of correct usage you will write effectively. Much dull and feeble speech and writing is correct, but correctness alone is a negative virtue. Using words clearly, exactly, strongly—that is most important and most difficult to do.

Who is the best conversationalist you know? What are the characteristics of his or her language? If you reply honestly, you will probably select a person whose speech seems *forceful* or *vivid* to you, someone who talks clearly, someone whose conversation is *smooth, logical, precise, animated.* Few will select a person whose talk is merely *correct.* Rarely will any comment be made on the niceties of conventional grammar, on violations of established usage, on subject-verb agreement, or on the right case of pronouns. True, the person you choose may use correct English—more often than not he or she will—but your remarks will not be "He uses correct English" nearly so often as "He's interesting to listen to."

Medicine and Health

HIGHLIGHTS: 1985

AIDS CONTINUES TO INCREASE

The Centers for Disease Control in Atlanta, Ga., reported that the number of cases of the fatal disease AIDS (acquired immune deficiency syndrome) continues to increase and can be expected to more than double in 1986.

By mid-1985 more than 10,000 cases of AIDS had been reported since the disease was discovered in 1981, with 50% of the cases being diagnosed within the past 10 months. Some 75% of the patients have died who were diagnosed as having AIDS before January 1983.

New cases of AIDS averaged more than 140 per week in 1985. Only two states, Idaho and Montana, have reported no cases of AIDS. In the first 29 weeks of 1985, New York led other states with 1,295 new AIDS cases, followed by California with 1,012 and Florida with 261.

The Centers for Disease Control said that 93% of AIDS patients are homosexual or bisexual men. About 2% of the total are believed to have acquired AIDS through blood transfusions. However, tests of blood donated to blood banks were begun in 1985 and are expected to reduce the number of AIDS cases caused by blood transfusions.

Scientists working to solve the problem of AIDS reported that victims may carry the virus of the disease for five years or more before displaying symptoms of the disease.

In June the *Journal of the American Medical Association* declared that the only way to bring AIDS under control is for people to change their lifestyle and "stop copulating indiscriminately."

Until a technological method of prevention and treatment can be developed," the *Journal* said, "it will be necessary to contain this virus by changing the lifestyle of many people—by no means all of them homosexual men."

ROBOT-ASSISTED SURGERY

Neurosurgeons made the first use of a robot in human brain surgery in 1985. Experimental operations were conducted using a robotic arm developed by Dr. Yik San Kwoh, director of research of the radiology department of Long Beach (Calif.) Memorial Medical Center.

Doctors said that because of the robot's accuracy its use eliminates the need for general anesthesia in a brain operation, enabling a patient to go home the next day after surgery instead of remaining hospitalized for a week or more.

In one operation described by doctors, the robot was used to obtain a section of a brain tumor deep inside the patient's brain. The robot was attached to the patient's skull by three pins, then the location of the tumor was fed into the robot by computer. Because the robot knew exactly where to find the tumor it could drill a much smaller hole in the skull than a surgeon ordinarily would require for such an operation. The robot successfully retrieved a sample of the tumor, which proved to be malignant.

Before using the robot on human patients, surgeons practiced having it drill into watermelons in which tiny metal targets had been inserted to be found by the robot.

LIVER CANCER BREAKTHROUGH

A medical scientist at Johns Hopkins University reported on Aug. 13 the "first effective treatment" for liver cancer—a disease that usually has resulted in death within six months after being detected.

Dr. Stanley E. Order, professor of radiation oncology, said that the new treatment uses radio labeled antibodies that seek and destroy cancer cells in the liver.

He said the treatment had been used at Johns Hopkins and at the University of California medical school in San Francisco on 104 patients whose liver cancer tumors could not be removed by surgery. He said the treatment completely eradicated the disease in 7 patients and had reduced the size of tumors in 50 (48%) of the patients.

STERILIZATION GROWS IN POPULARITY

Sterilization has replaced birth-control pills as the most widely used form of contraception for married women, according to data released in July by the National Center for Health Statistics.

The data showed that while 7% of married women had had sterilization operations in 1965, the percentage had grown to 26% of married women in 1982. During the same period the use of birth control pills by married women dropped from 24% in 1965 to 20% in 1982.

The government agency said that the num-

ber of married men who had been sterilized rose from 5% in 1965 to 15% in 1982.

NEW HYPERTENSION DRUG

The Squibb Corporation received approval in July by the Food and Drug Administration (FDA) for its Capoten drug to be used in treating patients at all levels of hypertension.

Capotene previously had been used only for cases of severe high blood pressure and congestive heart failure. The drug is of a type called an ACE inhibitor. It prevents the body from producing a chemical called angotensin II, which constricts blood vessels. The drug is said to have fewer side effects than the diuretics and beta-blockers that previously have been used to treat patients with mild to moderate hypertension.

BEWARE OF ICE

Medical researchers at the University of Texas warned travelers to beware of ice in a report issued in June.

The researchers, Herbert L. DuPont, D. Lunn Dickens, and Philip C. Johnson, studied how well bacteria survive in an ice cube.

They found that weeks of freezing still does not kill about 10% of the bacteria in an ice cube, leaving enough bacteria to cause a severe case of dysentery in an unwary traveler.

The researchers further tested the ice with various liquids. They found that straight 80-proof scotch or 86-proof tequila killed most of the remaining bacteria in an impure ice cube. However, scotch diluted with soda only "slightly inhibited" the bacteria from the ice. And cola or soda had no effect on bacteria from the melting ice.

TREATING TRAVELERS' DIARRHEA

A conference of more than 250 experts was held at the National Institutes of Health in 1985 to consider the problems of treating and preventing travelers' diarrhea that afflicts nearly 3 million Americans traveling abroad each year.

The conference recommended that travelers take prudent dietary preventive measures as reflected in the statement, "Boil it, cook it, peel it, or forget it."

The recommendations for treatment of the disease were:

1. Take fluids such as fruit juices or caffeine-free soft drinks and salted crackers to maintain fluid and electrolyte balance. Alcohol and dairy products should be avoided.

2. For rapid relief of symptoms, antimotility drugs such as diphenoxylate (Lomotil) or loperamide (Imodium) may be taken. Alternatively, bismuth salicylate (Pepto Bismol) may be used.

3. If the symptoms continue, a short course of antimicrobial agents may be of benefit. These should be obtained in advance of travel to avoid buying potentially dangerous over-the-counter drugs abroad. Recommended antimicrobial drugs are trimethoprim/sulfamethoxazole, trimethoprim alone, or doxycycline.

4. Medical attention is recommended if the symptoms persist or grow worse with fever and blood or mucus in stools.

SMALLPOX REVIEW

The World Health Organization (WHO) reported in 1985 that the world has remained free of smallpox for five years.

In the period from 1979 to 1984 the organization investigated 179 cases of suspected smallpox, none of which proved to be valid.

Smallpox vaccine no longer is available to civilians in the United States other than for laboratory workers who may be exposed to the smallpox virus. Since 1982 International Health Regulations have not included smallpox vaccination and international travelers no longer are required to receive vaccination for the disease. However, U.S. military personnel continue to be routinely vaccinated for smallpox.

ABORTION RATE INCREASES

New data released in July 1985 by the National Center for Health Statistics showed that the ratio of abortions to live births is increasing in the 1980s.

The latest statistics were from data provided by 12 states in 1979-1981: Colorado, Kansas, Missouri, Montana, New York, Oregon, Rhode Island, South Carolina, Tennessee, Utah, Vermont, and Virginia.

The 12 states reported a total of 299,407 induced abortions in 1981, an increase of 1% from the 295,932 in 1980. The ratio of abortions to live births was 391, an increase of 0.7% since 1980.

The abortion rate for the entire 1979–81 period for the 12 states was 24.8 abortions per 1,000 women aged 15–44 years.

In the 12 states in 1981 the largest percentage of induced abortions—38%—were to women 25 years of age and older. Nearly as many (35%) were to women aged 20–24. More than one-fourth (28%) were to women under the age of 20. Girls 14 years of age and younger accounted for 0.9% of the abortions—a total of 2,673 for that age group. Unmarried women accounted for 77% of the abortions.

The rate of abortions was more than twice as high for black as for white women, 50.8 abortions per 1,000 for black women com-

pared to 20.6 per 1,000 for white women.

RISING HEALTH CARE COSTS

The Health Care Financing Administration of the Department of Health and Human Services reported that an estimated $355 billion was spent on health care in the United States in 1983, an increase of 10.3% from 1982. The amount spent on health care amounted to 10.8% of the gross national product (GNP).

Health expenditures amounted to $1,459 per person in 1983, some $122 more than in 1982.

Federal, state, and local governments picked up 42% of the costs of health care, or $149 billion. The federal government paid the largest share—$103 billion.

Outlays for Medicare and Medicaid benefits totaled $91 billion, or 29% of total personal health care costs.

Private health insurers, government, private charities, and industry financed 73% of the $313 billion spent for personal health care, accounting for 92% of hospital care services, 72% of physicians' services, and 44% of other costs.

Hospital care, costing $147 billion, amounted to 41% of the total health expenditures in 1983, an increase of 9.1% from 1982.

The amount spent for the services of physicians rose 11.7% to $69 billion, or 19% of total health care spending.

PARKINSON'S DISEASE RESEARCH

New research in 1985 brought hope for the eventual relief of the half million persons afflicted with Parkinson's disease, which causes severe trembling and muscular weakness.

Dr. Roy A. E. Bakay, a neurosurgeon, was successful in eliminating most of the symptoms of Parkinson's disease from two monkeys that had the disease.

His accomplishment was achieved by implanting brain cells from monkey fetuses in the brains of the diseased monkeys.

Bakay said it took about two months for the implanted fetus cells to restore the dopamine level in the diseased monkeys' brains and alleviate their symptoms.

He said that it likely would be several years before such a procedure could be tested on a human patient.

PDQ CANCER EXPERTISE

The National Cancer Institute (NCI) initiated a computerized database for physicians in 1985 that is expected to save thousands of lives each year from cancer.

Called PDQ (Physician Data Query), the service will provide physicians with the latest and best treatments for their cancer patients.

Dr. Vincent T. DeVita Jr., director of the NCI, said of the new service:

"Now any physician who has a word processor or computer with a telephone hookup, can find the best available treatment options for a cancer type, can identify other physicians who treat a specific cancer, or can locate the nearest treatment research study that is accepting patients with a particular type of cancer."

A board of 72 cancer experts from throughout the United States keeps the medical information in PDQ current and accurate.

Physicians can obtain information on subscribing to PDQ by phoning 1-800-468-0908.

DIABETES RESEARCHER WINS $100,000

The Wolf Foundation of Israel awarded its annual $100,000 prize for medicine to Donald F. Steiner, a University of Chicago biochemist, for his discoveries about insulin that aided treatment of diabetes.

FOUR SCIENTISTS WIN HAMMER AWARD

The third annual $100,000 Hammer Prize for cancer research was divided among four scientists in 1985.

Half of the award, $50,000, went to Dr. Robert Gallo, chief of the laboratory of tumor cell biology of the National Cancer Institute. The other half was divided among three Japanese scientists; Yorio Hinuma of the Institute for Virus Research at Kyoto University; Isao Miyoshi of the Kochi Medical School; and Kiyoshi Takatsuki of Kumamoto University.

The four were cited for establishing that adult T-cell leukemia is caused by a virus.

$100,000 MEDICAL RESEARCH AWARD

The $100,000 Lita Annenberg Hazen Award for excellence in clinical research was presented to Dr. Yuet Wai Kan of the University of California at San Francisco.

He was presented the prize for his work in detecting the genetic factors responsible for sickle cell anemia and the blood disease thalassemia. He also was cited as the first scientist to develop an artificial gene to counteract a mutation that causes disease.

RIGHT TO DIE POLL

A survey conducted by Research and Forecasts Inc. reported that in a poll of 1,007 persons, some 60% believed that a terminally ill patient should have the right to choose death over continued treatment even if a doctor does not agree. Only 7% said a patient never should be given the choice of death or continued treatment.

444 MEDICINE AND HEALTH

RISING HEALTH COSTS IN THE U.S.: 1935–1990

Source: Health Care Financing Administration, Dept. of Health and Human Services, by fiscal years

YEAR	TOTAL SPENT	AV. SPENT PER PERSON	HOSPITAL CARE	PHYSICIANS' SERVICES	DENTISTS' SERVICES	MEDICINES AND SUPPLIES
1935	$ 3,600,000,000	$ 29.49	$ 700,000,000	$ 1,000,000,000	$ 500,000,000	$ 600,000,000
1940	$ 3,978,000,000	$ 29.62	$ 1,011,000,000	$ 973,000,000	$ 419,000,000	$ 637,000,000
1950	$ 12,662,000,000	$ 81.86	$ 3,851,000,000	$ 2,747,000,000	$ 961,000,000	$ 1,726,000,000
1960	$ 26,895,000,000	$ 146.30	$ 9,062,000,000	$ 5,684,000,000	$ 1,977,000,000	$ 3,657,000,000
1965	$ 41,749,000,000	$ 210.98	$ 13,878,000,000	$ 8,473,000,000	$ 2,809,000,000	$ 5,180,000,000
1970	$ 74,663,000,000	$ 357.90	$ 27,756,000,000	$ 14,340,000,000	$ 4,750,000,000	$ 7,996,000,000
1971	$ 83,284,000,000	$ 394.23	$ 30,817,000,000	$ 15,918,000,000	$ 5,068,000,000	$ 8,579,000,000
1972	$ 93,493,000,000	$ 437.77	$ 34,938,000,000	$ 17,162,000,000	$ 5,625,000,000	$ 9,335,000,000
1973	$103,161,000,000	$ 478.34	$ 38,681,000,000	$ 19,075,000,000	$ 6,531,000,000	$10,056,000,000
1974	$116,379,000,000	$ 534.63	$ 44,780,000,000	$ 21,245,000,000	$ 7,366,000,000	$10,999,000,000
1975	$132,720,000,000	$ 603.57	$ 52,106,000,000	$ 24,932,000,000	$ 8,237,000,000	$11,940,000,000
1976	$149,655,000,000	$ 674.14	$ 59,888,000,000	$ 27,565,000,000	$ 9,448,000,000	$13,022,000,000
1977	$169,248,000,000	$ 754.81	$ 67,761,000,000	$ 31,852,000,000	$10,535,000,000	$14,066,000,000
1978	$189,325,000,000	$ 835.57	$ 75,700,000,000	$ 35,807,000,000	$11,779,000,000	$15,413,000,000
1979	$214,612,000,000	$ 936.92	$ 85,665,000,000	$ 40,692,000,000	$13,502,000,000	$17,186,000,000
1980	$249,000,000,000	$1,075.00	$100,400,000,000	$ 46,800,000,000	$15,400,000,000	$19,300,000,000
1981	$286,600,000,000	$1,225.00	$118,000,000,000	$ 54,800,000,000	$17,300,000,000	$21,400,000,000
1982	$322,400,000,000	$1,365.00	$135,500,000,000	$ 61,800,000,000	$19,500,000,000	$22,400,000,000
1983	$355,400,000,000	$1,459.00	$147,200,000,000	$ 69,000,000,000	$21,800,000,000	$23,700,000,000
1984*	$392,700,000,000	$1,632.00	$165,700,000,000	$ 76,100,000,000	$23,700,000,000	$26,700,000,000
1985*	$419,500,000,000	$1,693.00	$170,600,000,000	$ 83,900,000,000	$27,300,000,000	$28,100,000,000
1990*	$660,100,000,000	$2,551.00	$277,400,000,000	$129,100,000,000	$40,500,000,000	$42,400,000,000

* Estimates

DANGEROUS DISEASES IN THE UNITED STATES

Source: U.S. Centers for Disease Control

	1970 Cases	1970 Rate [1]	1975 Cases	1975 Rate [1]	1980 Cases	1980 Rate [1]	1982 Cases	1982 Rate [1]	1983 Cases	1983 Rate [1]
Amebiasis	2,888	1.42	2,775	1.30	5,271	2.38	7,304	3.23	6,658	2.95
Anthrax	2	0.00	2	0.00	1	0.00	—	0.00	—	0.00
Aseptic meningitis	6,480	3.18	4,475	2.10	8,028	3.61	9,680	4.18	12,696	5.49
Botulism	12	0.01	20	0.01	89	0.04	97	0.04	133	0.06
Brucellosis (undulant fever)	213	0.10	310	0.15	183	0.08	173	0.07	200	0.09
Chickenpox[3]	—	—	154,248	72.38	190,894	96.69	167,423	94.37	177,462	99.65
Diphtheria	435	0.21	307	0.14	3	0.00	2	0.00	5	0.00
Encephalitis, primary [2]	1,580	0.78	4,064	1.91	1,362	0.60	1,464	0.63	1,761	0.75
Encephalitis, postinfectious	370	0.18	237	0.11	40	0.02	36	0.02	34	0.01
Hepatitis A	56,797	27.87	35,855	16.82	29,087	12.84	23,403	10.11	21,532	9.20
Hepatitis B	8,310	4.08	13,121	6.16	19,015	8.39	22,177	9.58	24,318	10.39
Hepatitis, unspecified	—	—	7,158	3.36	11,894	5.25	8,564	3.70	7,149	3.09
Leprosy	129	0.06	162	0.08	223	0.10	250	0.11	259	0.11
Leptospirosis	47	0.02	93	0.04	85	0.04	100	0.04	61	0.03
Malaria	3,051	1.50	373	0.18	2,062	0.91	1,056	0.46	813	0.35
Measles (rubeola)	47,351	23.23	24,374	11.44	13,506	5.96	1,714	0.74	1,497	0.64
Meningococcal infections	2,505	1.23	1,478	0.69	2,840	1.25	3,056	1.32	2,736	1.17
Mumps	104,953	55.55	59,647	27.99	8,576	3.86	5,270	2.46	3,355	1.55
Pertussis (whooping cough)	4,249	2.08	1,738	0.82	1,730	0.76	1,895	0.82	2,463	1.05
Poliomyelitis, total	33	0.02	8	0.00	9	0.00	8	0.00	15	0.01
Paralytic	31	0.02	8	0.00	8	0.00	8	0.00	15	0.01
Psittacosis	35	0.02	49	0.02	124	0.05	152	0.07	142	0.06
Rabies in man	2	0.00	2	0.00	—	0.00	—	0.00	2	0.00
Rheumatic fever, acute [3]	3,227	2.45	2,854	2.01	432	0.30	137	0.09	88	0.06
Rubella (German measles)	56,552	27.75	16,652	7.81	3,904	1.72	2,325	1.00	970	0.41
Rubella, congenital [4]	77	0.04	30	0.01	50	0.01	7	0.00	22	0.01
Salmonellosis	22,096	10.84	22,612	10.61	33,715	14.88	40,936	17.68	44,250	18.91
Shigellosis (dysentery)	13,845	6.79	16,584	7.78	19,041	8.41	18,129	7.83	19,719	8.43
Tetanus	148	0.07	102	0.05	95	0.04	88	0.04	91	0.04
Trichinosis	109	0.05	252	0.12	131	0.06	115	0.05	45	0.02
Tuberculosis [5]	37,137	18.22	33,989	15.95	27,749	12.25	25,520	11.02	23,846	10.19
Tularemia	172	0.08	129	0.06	234	0.10	275	0.12	310	0.13
Typhoid fever	346	0.17	375	0.18	510	0.23	425	0.18	507	0.22
Typhus fever, flea-borne	27	0.01	41	0.02	81	0.04	58	0.03	62	0.03
Typhus fever, tick-borne	380	0.19	844	0.40	1,163	0.52	976	0.42	1,126	0.48
Venereal diseases										
Syphilis	91,382	45.30	80,356	37.70	68,832	30.39	75,579	32.88	74,637	32.13
Gonorrhea	600,072	297.47	999,937	469.19	1,004,029	443.27	960,633	417.91	900,435	387.64

[1] Rate per 100,000 population. [2] Includes indeterminate category. [3] Not all states reporting. [4] Rate per 1,000 live births. [5] Data prior to 1974 not comparable to later data.

MAJOR CONTAGIOUS DISEASES

DISEASE	CAUSE	INCU-BATION	SYMPTOMS	DURATION	DANGERS	PREVENTION
Chicken pox or varicella	Virus; contact with infected person; breathing infectious droplets	10 to 20 days	Fever; loss of appetite; red itchy rash; pus forms crusts	About 2 weeks	Scratching rash can cause infection and scars	None; having chicken pox causes future immunity
Common cold	Viruses; contact with infected person; breathing infectious droplets	18 to 48 hours	Stuffy or runny nose; headache; sore throat; coughing	Several days to several weeks	Can weaken resistance to other diseases	None; improve general physical condition by drinking orange juice and taking vitamins
Diphtheria	Bacillus; contact with infected person	2 to 5 days	Like cold; high fever; gray membrane in throat	Several weeks	Can be fatal without medical treatment	Immunization; begin at age 2 months
Flu or influenza	Viruses; contact with infected person; breathing infectious germs	1 to 4 days	Fever; chills; aches and pains; weakness	Few days to few weeks	Can lead to fatal pneumonia	Immunization against certain strains of viruses
Measles or rubeola	Virus; contact with infected person	2 to 3 weeks	Fever as high as 106°; pink rash	Several weeks	Weakens resistance to diseases	Immunization; begin at age 1 year
Mono, mono-nucleosis, or glandular fever	Virus; direct contact with infected person, such as kissing	Few days to few weeks	Fever; fatigue; headache; swollen glands in neck	Usually 3 to 6 weeks	Can lead to hepatitis	None
Mumps or parotitis	Virus; contact with saliva of infected person	2 to 3 weeks	Painful swelling of face and neck; fever up to 104°	Usually 2 to 3 weeks	Can lead to other serious diseases	Immunization; especially important for men; begin at age 1 year
Pinworms or seatworms	Parasitic worm; contact with worm eggs	Few days	Itching around rectum; mild stomach pain	Not limited	Go to doctor for treatment	None; eggs are not killed by disinfectants and stay alive in dust
Pneumonia	Bacteria; viruses; foreign matter in lungs	Variable	Chills; chest pain; hard dry cough	Several weeks	Cause of many deaths	None; especially dangerous to pre-school children and elderly persons
Polio, polio-myelitis, or infantile paralysis	Virus; not known how it spreads	Few days to few weeks	Fever; head-ache; vomiting; drowsiness; stiff neck and back	No known cure	Can cause death or paralysis	Immunization; important for persons of all ages; begin at age 2 months
Rubella, German measles, or three-day measles	Virus; contact with victim	2 to 3 weeks	Mild fever; sore throat; rash	Few days	In pregnant woman causes birth defects in baby	Immunization; important for women before pregnancy; begin at age 1 year
Scarlet fever or scarlatina	Streptococcus bacteria	2 to 5 days	Vomiting; headache; fever; bright red rash; very red tongue	Several weeks	Can lead to kidney disease	None; having scarlet fever usually causes future immunity
Smallpox	Virus; breathing infectious droplets; contact with victim's belongings	10 to 14 days	Fever; headache; nausea; red pus-filled spots	Several weeks	Causes death or leaves deep scars	Vaccination; very important for all persons
Tetanus or lockjaw	Bacteria invade body through wounds	Few days to few weeks	Muscle spasms; locking of jaw muscles	Variable	Causes death unless treated	Immunization; germs live in dust, so any dirt in wound can cause disease
Tuberculosis, TB, or consumption	Bacteria in air, in dust, in unpas-teurized milk	Variable	Persistent cough; fatigue; loss of weight	Several years	Causes death unless treated	None; do not drink unpasteurized milk; keep away from persons who have tuberculosis
Whooping cough or pertussis	Bacteria; very contagious	1 to 2 weeks	Like heavy cold; vomiting; deep cough	Several weeks	Causes death unless treated	Immunization; especially important for infants

HEART AND BLOOD VESSEL DISEASE: NO. 1 KILLER

Source: American Heart Association; U.S. Department of Health and Human Services

Nearly 1,000,000 Americans die each year of heart and blood vessel diseases—over twice as many as die of cancer and over 20 times as many as are killed in automobile accidents. An estimated 63.3 million Americans have various forms of heart and blood vessel disease, and the economic cost of cardiovascular disease amounts to about $78.6 billion annually.

CORONARY HEART DISEASE

Coronary heart disease is the most frequent and dangerous form of heart disease among adults, afflicting about 4.7 million. It causes nearly 62% of heart-disease deaths in persons between the ages of 45 and 64. Coronary heart disease usually develops as a result of the buildup of cholesterol and other fatty substances in the arteries that supply the heart with blood.

WATCH YOUR BLOOD PRESSURE!

The most prevalent cause of heart and blood vessel diseases is high blood pressure, also called *hypertension.*

Nearly 58 million Americans have high blood pressure, which can lead to hardening of the arteries (arteriosclerosis), coronary heart attacks, and stroke.

High blood pressure usually can be brought under control once it has been diagnosed. But often by the time it has been discovered, damage already has been done to the heart and to the arteries.

Consequently it is very important for persons of all ages to have their blood pressure checked regularly by a doctor.

Normal blood pressure for adults is below 140/90. The first number is the *systolic* pressure, when the heart is contracting. The second number is the *diastolic* pressure, when the heart is relaxed and filling. Systolic pressures over 140 and diastolic pressures over 90 often require treatment.

TREATMENT OF HIGH BLOOD PRESSURE

High blood pressure cannot be cured. However, it can be brought under control, so that it may not cause damage to the heart and other body systems. Therefore, the person who has high blood pressure often must continue treatment for the disease for the rest of his life.

The usual treatment for mild cases of high blood pressure is a change of diet to reduce the amount of sodium taken into the body. Because table salt is the commonest source of sodium in food, the diet usually calls for eating salt-free foods.

For severe cases of high blood pressure a doctor usually prescribes antihypertensive drugs. A wide range of drugs can be used to bring down the blood pressure. Often a doctor and patient have to work together for some time to find which of these medications can control the patient's blood pressure with the fewest undesirable side effects.

PREVENTING HIGH BLOOD PRESSURE

Although doctors do not know the causes of high blood pressure in about 90% of cases, they do know that over-weight people and cigarette smokers have a tendency to develop the disease. Emotions and worry also can cause blood pressure to rise, so regular relaxation and adequate sleep and rest are desirable for all persons.

STROKE

Over 156,000 Americans die each year as a result of a *stroke,* a medical emergency occurring when the brain receives an insufficient supply of blood. Most major strokes result from *cerebral thrombosis,* a blood clot formed in a major artery; *cerebral hemorrhage,* when an artery in the brain ruptures; or *cerebral embolism,* when a clot forms in another part of the body, then moves to clog an artery that supplies the brain.

RHEUMATIC HEART DISEASE

In children, when a streptococcal sore throat is not properly treated, rheumatic fever may result, damaging the heart. Nearly 2 million adult Americans have rheumatic heart disease.

The heart disease that results from rheumatic fever causes about 6,700 deaths a year, usually after the age of 25. This highlights the importance of taking your child to a doctor when he develops a bad sore throat, so that it can be correctly treated to avoid rheumatic fever.

CONGENITAL HEART DEFECTS

About 25,000 American babies each year are born with a heart defect, the leading cause of heart-disease deaths among infants. Over 6,000 people, primarily babies and older children, die each year from these congenital heart defects. Many of the defects can be corrected by surgery if detected early enough.

PULMONARY HEART DISEASES

These are heart diseases of the right ventricle of the heart, which pumps all of the blood through the vessels of the lungs. These diseases may develop as a result of chronic bronchitis or emphysema.

FIRST AID FOR EMERGENCIES

BASIC MEASURES, INCLUDING BURNS

Do NOT move an injured person, especially if the injuries have been caused by a fall, crash, or other violence. *Only* move an injured person to save him from further danger.

Act fast if the victim is in danger of dying of bleeding, suffocation, burns, or shock. If breathing stops, a person may die within three minutes.

Keep the victim lying quietly. Keep him warm with blankets, but do not overheat him.

If the victim has vomited—and there is no danger of the neck being broken—turn his body and head to one side to prevent choking.

Call a doctor. Ask what steps to take until the doctor can get there.

Examine the person gently. Do NOT pull clothing away from burns.

Do NOT wash third-degree burns. Cover them immediately with sterile dressing. (Third-degree burns are those destroying tissue in the deepest layer of the skin.)

Always expect shock and be ready to treat shock (see advice in second column).

Reassure the victim while keeping yourself calm.

Do NOT give liquids to an unconscious or semiconscious person. Fluids may enter his windpipe and cause suffocation.

Do NOT try to awaken an unconscious person by slapping, shaking, or shouting.

Do NOT give alcohol to a badly injured person.

USE PRESSURE TO STOP BLEEDING

Stop the bleeding by direct pressure on or around the wound. If the wound is very wide, you may have to press directly *in* the wound to stop the bleeding.

Apply constant pressure. Do NOT release the pressure every few seconds to see if the bleeding has stopped.

Raise wounded arms or legs, if there are no other complicating injuries. Raising the injured limb as high as possible causes less blood to flow into it.

If bleeding does not stop from pressure, an artery or vein may be cut. Apply pressure on arteries to cut off the flow of blood from the heart to the wound:

For a hand wound, press your thumbs hard on the inside of the wrist.

For an arm wound, press your fingers on the inside of the arm just below the armpit.

For a leg wound, press the heel of the palm of your hand against the inside of the leg just below the groin.

For a face wound, press your fingers under the side of the jaw.

For a scalp wound, press against the side of the head just in front of the ear.

For a neck or head wound, press on the neck just below and forward of the ear.

A tourniquet may be used to stop bleeding from a severe arm or leg wound when other measures have failed. Place the tourniquet just above the wound. If the wound is in or just below a joint area, place the tourniquet immediately above the joint. Make sure the tourniquet is at least 2" wide. Tighten it *only enough* to stop the bleeding. The tourniquet should NOT be loosened except on advice of a physician. Note time it was applied and attach note to patient.

MOUTH-TO-MOUTH RESUSCITATION

Remove any obstruction to breathing from inside the victim's mouth, such as food, gum, or mud.

Place victim on back with mouth up.

Pull victim's jaw open and forward, and continue to hold it this way throughout resuscitation.

Pinch victim's nose closed.

Blow into the victim's mouth. Then remove your mouth and listen for an outward rush of air from the victim. If there is none, again check the victim's mouth for obstructions.

Continue blowing into the victim's mouth. *For an adult,* blow 12 deep breaths each minute. *For a child,* blow 20 shallow breaths each minute.

CLOSED-CHEST HEART MASSAGE

Start massage IMMEDIATELY after the heart stops.

Place one hand on top of the other on victim's chest at bottom of breastbone.

Apply pressure with heel of bottom hand, pushing downward about 2 inches.

Repeat the pressure 60 times a minute.

HOW TO HELP A POISON VICTIM

Dilute the poison by having the victim drink water or milk. The first minute may be the most critical.

Induce vomiting, if the victim is conscious, by placing a finger down the victim's throat.

Do NOT induce vomiting if the victim is unconscious or if the victim has swallowed acid, ammonia, cleaning fluid, drain cleaner, lye, or a petroleum product, such as gasoline.

Call a doctor *after* you have diluted the poison. Otherwise the victim may die while you are phoning.

Save the poison container and remaining poison. Take both with you when you take the victim to a hospital or to a doctor.

EMERGENCY TREATMENT FOR SHOCK

When a person goes into shock, he becomes pale and his skin feels cold and clammy. He breathes rapidly.

Raise the victim's feet higher than his head, unless he has a head injury.

Keep the victim warm with blankets, but too much heat can be harmful.

Give the victim a nonalcoholic drink containing sugar or salt, if the victim is fully conscious.

Do NOT give any liquid if the victim is unconscious or has a possible abdominal injury.

Talk reassuringly to the victim and hold his hand.

HOW TO HELP A CHOKING VICTIM

Stand behind the person. Hug the person by wrapping your arms around his waist. Let his head and upper body hang forward.

Clench one of your hands as a fist. Grasp the wrist of that hand with your other hand, so the fist is against the victim's stomach, just below the ribs and above the navel.

With all your strength, pull your fist into the victim's stomach with a quick upward jerk. Repeat until the food is forced out of the victim's throat.

GROWTH OF THE AMERICAN LIFE SPAN

Source: U.S. Public Health Service

YEAR	LIFE SPAN (in yrs.)	YEAR	LIFE SPAN (in yrs.)	YEAR	LIFE SPAN (in yrs.)	YEAR	LIFE SPAN (in yrs.)	YEAR	LIFE SPAN (in yrs.)	YEAR	LIFE SPAN (in yrs.)
1900	47.3	1935	61.7	1960	69.7	1966	70.1	1972	71.1	1978	73.3
1910	50.0	1940	62.9	1961	70.2	1967	70.5	1973	71.3	1979	73.8
1915	54.5	1945	65.9	1962	70.0	1968	70.2	1974	71.9	1980	73.6
1920	54.1	1950	68.2	1963	69.6	1969	70.4	1975	72.5	1981	74.2
1925	59.0	1955	69.6	1964	70.2	1970	70.9	1976	72.8	1982	74.5
1930	59.7	1958	69.6	1965	70.2	1971	71.1	1977	73.2	1983[1]	74.7

[1] Provisional.

LIFE EXPECTANCY BY AGE, SEX, AND RACE

Source: U.S. Public Health Service; 1983 estimates.

AGE	TOTAL POPULATION			AVERAGE YEARS OF LIFE REMAINING WHITE POPULATION			OTHER POPULATION		
	Both Sexes	Male	Female	Both Sexes	Male	Female	Both Sexes	Male	Female
Under 1 year	74.7	71.0	78.3	75.2	71.6	78.8	71.3	67.1	75.3
1– 5 years	74.5	70.9	78.0	74.9	71.4	78.4	71.5	67.4	75.4
5–10 years	70.6	67.0	74.2	71.1	67.6	74.6	67.6	63.6	71.6
10–15 years	65.7	62.1	69.2	66.2	62.6	69.6	62.7	58.7	66.7
15–20 years	60.8	57.3	64.3	61.3	57.7	64.7	57.8	53.8	61.8
20–25 years	56.1	52.6	59.5	56.5	53.1	59.9	53.1	49.1	56.9
25–30 years	51.3	48.0	54.6	51.8	48.5	55.0	48.4	44.5	52.1
30–35 years	46.6	43.4	49.8	47.1	43.8	50.2	43.8	40.1	47.3
35–40 years	41.9	38.7	45.0	42.3	39.2	45.3	39.2	35.7	42.6
40–45 years	37.3	34.1	40.2	37.6	34.5	40.5	34.8	31.3	38.0
45–50 years	32.7	29.7	35.5	33.0	30.0	35.8	30.5	27.2	33.5
50–55 years	28.3	25.4	31.0	28.6	25.6	31.3	26.4	23.4	29.2
55–60 years	24.2	21.4	26.7	24.4	21.6	26.9	22.7	19.9	25.2
60–65 years	20.3	17.8	22.6	20.5	17.9	22.8	19.3	16.8	21.5
65–70 years	16.8	14.5	18.8	16.9	14.5	18.9	16.3	14.1	18.2
70–75 years	13.6	11.5	15.2	13.6	11.5	15.2	13.5	11.6	15.0
75–80 years	10.7	9.0	11.9	10.7	9.0	11.9	11.0	9.5	12.2
80–85 years	8.2	6.9	9.0	8.2	6.9	9.0	8.7	7.5	9.5
85 or older	6.1	5.1	6.6	6.1	5.1	6.6	6.6	5.7	7.2

LEADING CAUSES OF DEATH AMONG AMERICANS

Source: U.S. Public Health Service

CAUSE OF DEATH	NUMBER OF DEATHS 1983	1970	DEATH RATE PER 100,000 1983	1970	CAUSE OF DEATH	NUMBER OF DEATHS 1983	1970	DEATH RATE PER 100,000 1983	1970
Heart & artery diseases	822,920	800,818	351.3	394.2	Ill-defined conditions ..	29,780	25,781	12.7	12.7
Sudden heart attack	287,520	357,241	122.9	175.8	Cirrhosis of the liver ..	27,840	31,399	11.9	15.5
Atherosclerosis	25,940	31,682	11.1	15.6	Infant mortality	18,970	43,205	8.1	21.3
Rheumatic fever....	6,730	14,889	2.9	7.3	Injuries in birth.....	5,300	22,801	2.3	11.2
Hypertensive heart .	21,240	14,991	9.1	7.3	Other infant diseases	13,670	20,404	5.8	10.0
Hypertension	7,720	8,273	3.3	4.1	Nephritis and nephrosis	18,440	8,877	7.9	4.4
Cancer	440,620	330,730	188.3	162.8	Blood poisoning	13,350	3,535	5.7	1.7
Lungs	120,660	69,517	51.6	34.2	Emphysema	13,250	16,824	5.7	8.3
Digestive organs ..	112,910	94,703	48.3	46.6	Congenital defects ..	12,780	22,721	5.5	11.2
Genital organs	47,880	41,190	20.5	20.3	Benign tumors	6,450	4,828	2.8	2.4
Breast	38,540	29,917	16.5	14.7	Peptic ulcer..........	6,340	8,607	2.7	4.2
Urinary organs	18,310	15,514	7.8	7.6	Hernia and intestinal obstructions	5,150	7,235	2.2	3.6
Leukemia..........	16,920	14,492	7.2	7.1	Anemias.............	3,640	3,427	1.6	1.7
Mouth and pharynx .	7,890	7,612	3.4	3.7	Bronchitis	3,480	7,156	1.5	3.5
Other cancer.......	77,500	57,785	33.1	28.4	Asthma	3,440	2,322	1.5	1.1
Stroke	156,380	207,166	66.8	101.9	Gallstones	3,170	3,973	1.4	2.0
Cerebral thrombosis	26,180	57,845	11.2	28.5	Nutritional deficiencies	2,420	2,470	1.0	1.2
Cerebral hemorrhage	19,380	41,379	8.3	20.4	Tuberculosis	1,910	5,217	0.8	2.6
Other cerebrovascular diseases.........	110,830	107,942	47.4	53.1	Kidney infections	1,890	8,190	0.8	4.0
Accidents	91,290	114,638	39.0	56.4	Influenza	1,370	3,707	0.6	1.8
Motor vehicle	43,700	54,633	18.7	26.9	Meningitis	1,320	1,701	0.6	0.8
All other accidents..	47,580	60,006	20.3	29.5	Hepatitis, infectious ..	840	1,014	0.4	0.7
Pneumonia	52,220	59,032	22.3	29.0	Appendicitis	580	1,397	0.2	0.7
Violent deaths	48,380	40,328	20.6	19.9	Prostate disease	540	2,168	0.2	0.5
Suicides	29,080	23,480	12.4	11.6	Intestinal infection	370	2,567	0.2	1.3
Homicides..........	19,300	16,848	8.2	8.3	Complications of pregnancy	290	803	0.1	0.4
Diabetes	35,530	38,324	15.2	18.9					

U.S. BIRTHS AND DEATHS

Source: U.S. Public Health Service

The U.S. birthrate rose to 15.7 births per 1,000 people in 1984, compared with 15.5 in 1983. An estimated 3,697,000 live births occurred during the year. The death rate rose to 9.1 deaths per 1,000 population. Altogether some 1,650,000 persons were added to the population in 1984 by natural increase—the difference between the number of births and the number of deaths.

AREA	BIRTHS			DEATHS		
	1984[1]	1983	1970	1984[1]	1983	1970
UNITED STATES	3,697,000	3,614,000	3,731,386	2,047,000	2,010,000	1,921,031
New England	168,430	170,078	200,048	119,326	112,956	115,567
Maine	16,513	16,323	17,750	10,796	11,242	11,053
New Hampshire	12,656	13,973	13,188	7,749	7,771	7,356
Vermont	7,419	7,671	8,354	4,455	4,908	4,449
Massachusetts	79,386	78,670	94,618	59,104	54,275	57,258
Rhode Island	13,219	13,061	15,648	9,589	9,487	9,492
Connecticut	39,237	40,380	50,490	27,633	25,273	25,939
Middle Atlantic	505,017	504,234	630,460	357,567	358,460	383,205
New York	251,062	249,618	317,714	168,852	170,464	188,020
New Jersey	94,044	95,406	120,242	66,511	66,404	68,183
Pennsylvania	159,911	159,210	192,504	122,204	121,592	126,996
East North Central	622,585	622,662	754,174	359,072	361,892	376,814
Ohio	159,939	160,330	199,696	96,937	98,234	100,453
Indiana	79,134	82,169	99,306	47,195	48,268	48,556
Illinois	175,907	175,679	205,472	98,151	99,964	110,680
Michigan	134,517	131,873	171,922	75,515	74,302	76,334
Wisconsin	73,088	72,611	77,778	41,274	41,124	40,791
West North Central	277,090	277,143	284,170	160,979	160,296	164,232
Minnesota	65,788	64,698	68,456	33,525	34,099	33,888
Iowa	42,611	43,783	48,290	26,093	27,169	29,387
Missouri	78,517	76,739	80,902	52,332	50,419	51,851
North Dakota	12,738	13,200	10,902	5,897	5,880	5,613
South Dakota	12,383	12,409	11,690	6,417	6,545	6,566
Nebraska	26,483	26,816	25,726	14,973	14,819	15,039
Kansas	38,570	39,498	38,204	21,742	21,365	21,888
South Atlantic	573,718	563,299	574,244	351,942	346,713	289,916
Delaware	9,487	9,538	10,502	5,098	5,071	4,916
Maryland	58,790	57,857	68,864	34,875	34,524	32,832
District of Columbia	19,123	18,592	15,230	8,302	8,349	8,851
Virginia	79,342	77,448	86,424	43,899	43,226	39,015
West Virginia	25,059	26,911	30,964	19,114	19,210	20,063
North Carolina	86,705	84,655	98,184	51,496	50,602	44,737
South Carolina	48,215	48,513	52,160	25,340	25,300	22,780
Georgia	91,761	91,090	96,880	47,303	45,988	41,819
Florida	155,236	148,695	115,036	116,515	114,443	74,903
East South Central	223,670	224,701	248,310	139,034	133,715	128,478
Kentucky	51,964	55,252	60,212	33,449	33,590	33,277
Tennessee	70,407	67,739	72,182	45,570	42,148	38,157
Alabama	58,604	57,685	66,832	37,551	34,855	33,743
Mississippi	42,695	44,025	49,084	22,464	23,122	23,301
West South Central	476,252	455,369	385,792	208,816	202,390	175,207
Arkansas	33,440	33,630	35,492	23,478	23,093	20,664
Louisiana	83,195	80,610	74,374	36,549	35,755	33,445
Oklahoma	53,425	54,085	44,890	29,258	28,414	26,763
Texas	306,192	287,044	231,036	119,531	115,128	94,335
Mountain	230,474	234,856	171,554	88,021	85,508	66,343
Montana	13,846	13,794	12,622	6,644	6,697	6,602
Idaho	17,072	18,540	14,486	6,649	6,951	6,155
Wyoming	9,026	9,515	6,502	3,000	2,990	2,937
Colorado	54,471	55,159	41,570	20,941	19,978	17,433
New Mexico	26,285	30,186	22,098	9,806	9,927	7,434
Arizona	54,821	52,659	37,672	24,384	23,183	14,865
Utah	39,677	40,752	27,032	9,295	8,834	7,061
Nevada	15,276	14,251	9,572	7,302	6,948	3,856
Pacific	599,121	549,194	482,634	261,830	248,189	221,269
Washington	73,605	63,729	60,748	35,212	31,039	29,954
Oregon	39,536	41,045	35,166	23,229	21,579	19,516
California	455,075	413,915	362,756	195,430	187,938	166,338
Alaska	12,247	11,500	7,528	1,993	1,921	1,438
Hawaii	18,658	19,005	16,436	5,966	5,712	4,023

[1] Provisional 1984 data. [2] Per 1,000 population.

ALCOHOLISM—NO. 1 DRUG PROBLEM

Source: National Institute on Alcohol Abuse and Alcoholism

What is the No. 1 dangerous drug problem in the United States? Heroin addiction? Wrong.

Alcohol is the drug that dwarfs all others in its grip on many Americans, in the toll of agony, in illness, in economic loss, in disrupted families, and in neglected children.

Alcohol is believed to be a major factor in causing heart disease, birth defects leading to mental retardation, and cancer.

Alcohol is a mood-altering drug that consumed in moderate amounts can produce euphoria. But alcohol also depresses the central nervous system, so that the initial "lift" wears off as intoxication deepens. Large amounts of alcohol over a long period of time produce anxiety.

Like other dangerous drugs, alcohol may induce psychological and physical dependence. This dependence, an illness, is called *alcoholism*.

DANGERS OF ALCOHOLISM

Some 78 million Americans drink alcoholic beverages. Experts estimate that about 14 million of this group are alcoholics or problem drinkers, including 3.3 million youths aged 14 to 17. About one-fourth of alcoholics are women.

The vast majority of people who are alcoholics are in their mid-30s, with good jobs, homes, and families.

■ Alcoholism costs Americans about $116 billion a year in lost work, medical expenses, auto accidents; and other problems.

■ As many as 95,000 deaths a year can be blamed on drinking.

■ An alcoholic is 2 to 6 times more likely to die of disease, accident, or violence than the average person.

■ 93% of high school seniors have tried alcohol.

WARNING SIGNS OF ALCOHOLISM

Not all alcoholics follow the same course, so not all of the signs listed below will necessarily be seen in every case. Still, if someone you know shows more than a very few of them, he or she may have, or be close to developing, a serious problem:

■ Relying heavily and often on alcohol to relax around other people.
■ Looking forward to occasions for drinking.
■ Getting drunk without planning to.
■ Trying to control drinking by changing brands or types of alcoholic beverage, or making pledges.
■ Sneaking drinks and lying about drinking.
■ Being arrested on alcohol-related charges.
■ Hiding bottles.
■ Drinking in the morning.
■ Drinking at work.
■ Having blackouts.
■ Neglecting proper eating habits.
■ Experiencing tremors, hallucinations, or convulsions when withdrawn from alcohol.

■ 26% of the admissions to state and county mental institutions are persons with alcohol-related problems.
■ Between 30% and 40% of delinquent children come from alcoholic homes.
■ Drivers and pedestrians who drink cause more than 17,800 traffic deaths in the United States each year.
■ 24% of alcoholics die in accidents, falls, fires, and suicides.
■ 33% of those who take their own lives are alcoholics—a suicide rate 58 times higher than for the rest of the population.

FREE INFORMATION

The National Clearinghouse for Alcohol Information, Box 2345, Rockville, Md. 20852, supplies answers to specific questions on alcoholism.

HOW TO HELP AN ALCOHOLIC

If a friend or relative drinks too much, here are some ways to help:

1. Avoid moral judgment. Do not attempt to punish, threaten, preach, or act like a martyr.
2. Try to remain calm and honest in talking with the person about his or her behavior.
3. Do not try to shield the person from the consequences by covering up or making excuses for his or her behavior.
4. Do not hide or dump bottles, or try to shelter the problem drinker from situations where alcohol is served.
5. Let him or her know that you are reading about and learning more about alcoholism.
6. Do not argue with an alcoholic while he or she is drunk.
7. Get expert advice. Consult a specialist—usually called "intervention counselor"—on specific problems and strategies.
8. Organize a team. The more people, the better, including family members and employers, to make the arguments for treatment more persuasive.
9. Explain the nature of alcoholism as an illness to children in the alcoholic's family.
10. Do not drink with the problem drinker.
11. Refuse to ride with the alcoholic person if he or she insists on driving while drunk.
12. Do not, above all, accept personal guilt for the alcoholic person's behavior.
13. Be patient and live one day at a time. Recovery from alcoholism does not occur overnight. Try to accept setbacks and relapses with calm and understanding.
14. Help guide the alcoholic to obtain a specific treatment program.

CANCER FACTS THAT CAN SAVE YOUR LIFE

Source: American Cancer Society

Cancer will eventually strike approximately 30% of all Americans now living, according to present rates—about 71 million persons, affecting about 3 of every 4 families.

During the year about 910,000 Americans will be diagnosed as having cancer. About 462,000 will die, at a rate of over 1,266 a day. Some 340,000 Americans, or 3 out of 8 patients who get cancer this year, will be alive 5 years after diagnosis, but about 160,000 will die in 1985 who might have been saved by earlier diagnosis and prompt treatment.

BREAST CANCER

Breast cancer is the leading cause of cancer deaths in women today. About 119,000 cases of breast cancer will occur during the year, and over 38,700 will die.

If breast cancer is detected before it has spread to other parts of the body, the victim has a 96% chance of surviving 5 or more years. But if it has already spread, the patient's chance of recovery drops to 70%.

Every woman should follow a monthly program of breast self-examination. If you do not understand this self-examination procedure, go to your physician or to a health clinic at once and have it explained to you. Then follow up by carrying out your own monthly examination.

If you feel a lump or thickening of the tissue in one of your breasts, do not delay going to a physician.

LUNG CANCER

Lung cancer is the leading cause of cancer deaths in men today, and is expected to surpass breast cancer as the number one cancer killer of women before long. An estimated 126,000 Americans will die of lung cancer during the year. Unlike breast cancer, lung cancer is not easy to detect in its early stages. As a result, only 13% of lung cancer patients live five or more years after diagnosis.

If you have a nagging cough or hoarseness, see your doctor before it is too late.

But the best way to avoid lung cancer is prevention. Medical researchers believe that most lung cancer is caused by smoking.

COLON–RECTUM CANCER

About 59,900 people will die this year from colon-rectum cancer. Many of these deaths could have been prevented if the cancer had been detected earlier.

The best way to save your life from this cancer is by an annual medical examination that includes a proctoscopic examination of the rectum every 3 to 5 years after age 50.

FREE PHONE INFORMATION

For toll-free phone information about cancer, from the National Cancer Institute, dial 1-800-4-CANCER (1-800-422-6237).

An annual at-home detection test, the stool blood slide test, is recommended after 50.

ORAL CANCER

Cancer of the mouth and throat strikes about 29,000 Americans each year, and about 40% overall survive five years after diagnosis.

If you have a mouth sore that does not heal quickly or have difficulty in swallowing, see a physician with no further delay.

SKIN CANCER

About 7,400 Americans die each year from skin cancer. Medical researchers stress that most cases of skin cancer can be prevented if you will resist overexposure to the sun.

Examine your skin regularly. If you have a skin sore that does not heal quickly, or if a mole or wart begins to increase in size, report it to your physician immediately.

UTERINE CANCER

Some 52,000 American women each year are diagnosed with uterine cancer, and 9,700 die.

The increasing awareness by women of the need for regular pelvic examinations by a physician and the use of the Pap test for detection of uterine cancer have caused deaths from this type of cancer to decline by 70% in the past 40 years.

If you are a woman, help save your life by having an annual pelvic examination and a Pap test at least every three years.

LEUKEMIA

Cancer of the blood-forming tissues strikes about 25,000 Americans each year, and over 17,000 die of the disease each year.

Acute leukemia mainly strikes children and is usually treated with chemotherapy. Chronic leukemia mainly affects adults, who treated by drugs can lead nearly normal lives for many years.

CANCER'S 7 WARNING SIGNALS

If you detect one of these signals, see your doctor.

- Change in bowel or bladder habits
- A sore that does not heal
- Unusual bleeding or discharge
- Thickening or lump in breast or elsewhere
- Indigestion or difficulty in swallowing
- Obvious change in wart or mole
- Nagging cough or hoarseness

452 MEDICINE AND HEALTH

DRUGS COMMONLY ABUSED AND MISUSED

Sources: U.S. Bureau of Narcotics and Dangerous Drugs and National Institute on Drug Abuse

How can you guard your children from drug abuse and misuse? Learn more about drugs.

Even before your son or daughter goes to school, you should teach that *any* drug is harmful if misused. You should make sure your child understands that, even when the doctor gives a prescription, harm may result if more than the prescribed amount is taken.

DRUG NAME	SLANG OR TRADE NAMES	HOW USED	EFFECTS AND SYMPTOMS	DANGERS
Amphetamines, other stimulants	Pep pills, eye-openers, lid poppers, uppers, wake-ups, truck drivers, dexies, browns, bennies, cartwheels, greenies, footballs, jolly beans	Swallowed, sometimes injected	Talkativeness, hyperactivity, bright shiny eyes, dilated pupils, irritability, loss of appetite, restlessness, increased sweating	Death from overdose, psychological dependence, psychosis
Barbiturates, sleeping pills, other depressants	Barbs, blues, seccy, seggy, phennies, red devils, reds and blues, tooies, nimbles, double trouble, yellow jackets, blue devils, blue birds, nimby, goofballs, candy, peanuts	Swallowed, sometimes injected	Drowsiness, sluggishness, faulty judgment, slurred speech, irrational behavior, constricted eye pupils, increased sweating, excessive laughter, confusion, depression, poor coordination	Death from overdose, (especially if taken with alcohol), death from withdrawal, convulsions, physical dependence
Cocaine	Coke, happy dust, joy powder, snow, the leaf, bernies, Bernice, C, gold dust, heaven dust, star dust, white girl	Sniffed, injected	Hallucinations, dilated eye pupils, tremors, euphoria, talkativeness, anxiety, loss of appetite, irritability, restlessness, hyperactivity	Death from overdose, convulsions, psychological dependence, paranoia
Codeine	Schoolboy	Swallowed, injected	Drowsiness, constricted eye pupils, slurred speech; on withdrawal—anxiety, tremors, nausea, cramps, diarrhea	Death from overdose, physical dependence, psychological dependence
DMT, Dimethyl-tryptamine	Businessman's special, 45-minute psychosis	Smoked, injected	Hallucinations, irrational behavior, rambling speech, dilated eye pupils, euphoria	Psychological dependence
Heroin	Horse, junk, skag, snow, stuff, big Harry, H, hard stuff, white stuff, joy powder, the thing	Injected, sniffed	Drowsiness, anxiety, constricted eye pupils, loss of appetite, constipation	Death from overdose, convulsions, physical dependence
Hydromorphone	Lords, Dilaudid	Swallowed, injected	Euphoria, constricted eye pupils, slurred speech	Death from overdose, physical dependence
LSD, Lysergic Acid Diethylamide	Acid, cubes, sugar, sugar lump, Big D, the chief, royal blue, blue acid, pearly gates	Swallowed, injected	Hallucinations, tremors, euphoria, increased sweating, dilated eye pupils, rambling speech, distortion of space and time	Psychosis, possible chromosome damage, psychological dependence
Marijuana, hashish, hash oil	Pot, grass, reefers, roach, bone, hay, hemp, tea, Acapulco gold, love weed, joint, muggles, pod, straw, Texas tea, hash, boo, red, Mary Jane, stick	Smoked, swallowed	Hallucinations, talkativeness, irritability and restlessness, inflamed eyes, increased appetite, reduced motivation, impulsive behavior	Psychological dependence
Meperidine	Demerol, Dolantol, Isonipecaine, Pethidine	Swallowed, injected	Drowsiness, anxiety, euphoria, constricted eye pupils, loss of appetite, poor reflexes	Death from overdose, physical dependence
Methadone	Dolophine, dolls, dollies, amidone	Injected, swallowed	Impaired coordination, loss of appetite, euphoria, anxiety	Death from overdose, physical dependence
Methamphetamine	Speed, meth, Methedrine, splash, crystal bombita, Doe	Swallowed, injected	Abnormal alertness, loss of appetite, aggressiveness, depression, distortion of time and space	Death from overdose, psychosis, paranoia, psychological dependence
Methaqualone	Quaalude, Rorer, Sopor, Parest, Optimil, Somnafac	Swallowed	Drunken euphoria, loss of coordination, convulsions during withdrawal	Death from overdose, physical dependence
Morphine	Morph, dreamer, melter, monkey, Miss Emma, tab	Injected	Sleepiness, poor coordination, loss of appetite, hallucinations	Physical dependence
Peyote, Psilocybin	Mesc, mescal beans, mushrooms, cactus	Swallowed	Hallucinations, irrational behavior, nausea, rambling speech, hyperactivity	Psychotic reactions, psychological dependence
Phencyclidine	PCP, Angeldust	Swallowed, smoked with marijuana, snorted	Estrangement from surroundings, hallucinations, bizarre behavior	Death from overdose, schizophrenia, memory problems

QUESTIONS AND ANSWERS ABOUT DRUG ABUSE

MARIJUANA

What are the effects of smoking a marijuana cigarette? The psychological effects include illusions and distortions of hearing, vision, and the sense of time. The feeling from smoking marijuana often is one of a passive euphoria, or "high," and sometimes the person may tend to withdraw into himself.

How long do the effects of marijuana last? A few inhalations of strong marijuana can intoxicate a person for several hours.

Does the heavy use of marijuana affect a young person's personality development? Heavy, chronic marijuana use has been associated with the *amotivational syndrome,* a loss of desire to work and to compete.

Is marijuana an addicting drug? Chronic users become psychologically dependent upon the drug, according to researchers.

Is there anything in marijuana that leads to other drugs? Marijuana users are more likely to experiment with other types of drugs than those who have never used it. However, nothing in marijuana itself produces a need to use other drugs.

HALLUCINOGENS

What are hallucinogens? Also called *psychedelics* and *psychotomimetics,* they are drugs capable of provoking alterations of sensation. LSD is one of the most potent and a widely studied of the hallucinogens.

What is LSD? LSD (lysergic acid diethylamide) is derived from lysergic acid, which comes from ergot, a fungus growth on rye. One ounce of LSD is enough to provide 300,000 average doses, each of which is a tiny speck whose effect lasts from 8 to 12 hours.

Is LSD an addicting drug? Although a person may use LSD habitually, the user does not experience physical withdrawal symptoms if it is suddenly discontinued.

What are the effects of LSD? LSD basically causes changes in sensation. Hallucinations can occur, and the sense of time and of self is altered. Emotional variations may range from bliss to sheer horror. In the parlance of the LSD user a "good trip" consists of pleasant imagery and feelings. In a "bad trip" or "bummer," perceived images arouse dread and horror.

Is LSD dangerous? Clinical reports on the illicit use of LSD have warned of the following dangers: (1) *Panic*—the user may grow frightened because he cannot "turn off" the drug's action. (2) *Flashbacks*—a flashback is a recurrence of some of the features of the LSD state days or months after the last dose, causing the user to believe he is losing his mind. (3) *Accidental death*—because LSD users may feel invulnerable, some have walked into traffic or jumped from high windows.

Does LSD cause mental problems? There is no doubt that it can bring about acute and sometimes long-lasting mental problems in susceptible persons.

NARCOTICS

What is a narcotic? A narcotic or analgesic is a drug that relieves pain and induces sleep.

Which narcotics are abused? Heroin accounts for about 90% of the illegal opiates in use. Paregoric and cough medicines containing codeine are also abused.

What are the effects of heroin? When sniffed, injected under the skin ("skin popping"), or shot directly into a vein, heroin causes a dreamlike state of great well-being. As tolerance to the drug develops, however, the physically dependent person cannot reach the same "high" as easily, requiring more and more heroin.

What are withdrawal symptoms like? Some 12 to 16 hours after the last injection, the addict gets chills, muscle aches and jerks, and severe abdominal discomfort. Frightful hallucinations may develop.

Why is heroin addiction dangerous? Users may contract hepatitis from dirty needles. An overdose, resulting in death, occurs when a user has lost or has never developed tolerance to strong heroin. If the addict should obtain such a dose, death may occur minutes after injection.

What are the social problems in addiction? The life of the addict is centered around obtaining money to buy heroin. The user may steal from family members, commit burglaries and muggings, and deal in heroin. Female addicts often turn to prostitution.

STIMULANTS

What are stimulants? Stimulants are drugs, usually amphetamines, that increase alertness. They are used in medicine to relieve depression. A powerful stimulant contained in coca leaves is cocaine, or coke. The use of cocaine causes insomnia and loss of appetite. An overdose of cocaine causes convulsions and death.

What is amphetamine abuse? When amphetamines are taken in large quantities, an ecstatic "high" occurs that may last a few hours. The user talks a lot, is restless and anxious, and has little desire for food and sleep. In a heavy user, withdrawal causes lethargy, fatigue, and sometimes depression.

SEDATIVES OR SLEEPING PILLS

What are sedative drugs? Sedative drugs are used in medicine to reduce tension and anxiety, to treat certain psychosomatic disorders, and to induce sleep.

Are sedatives addicting? Yes. Tolerance to large doses of barbiturates develops, and sudden withdrawal can cause severe convulsions.

Why are large amounts of sedatives dangerous? Accidental deaths are not uncommon, because a person who takes sleeping pills regularly may repeat the prescribed dosage several times without realizing it. The consumption of just a few sleeping pills with an alcoholic drink can cause sudden death.

PIONEERS IN MEDICINE

The symbol (N) indicates scientist was awarded Nobel Prize: see pages 73–75. For deaths in 1985, see pages 981–986.

Alfred Adler (1870–1937), Austrian psychiatrist: founded first child psychology clinic (1920).

Fred H. Albee (1876–1945), American orthopedic surgeon: made first practical bone grafts.

Karl Ernest von Baer (1792–1876), German biologist: founded science of embryology.

Sir Frederick G. Banting (1891–1941), Canadian physician: with C. H. Best, discovered insulin (1921) for treatment of diabetes. (N)

Christiaan N. Barnard (1922–), South African surgeon: performed first successful human heart transplant (1967).

George Wells Beadle (1903–), American geneticist: discovered that genes control chemical processes in living cells. (N)

William Beaumont (1785–1853), American physician: made first experiments on live patient to understand digestive process (published 1833).

Emil von Behring (1854–1917), German physiologist: discovered diphtheria and tetanus antitoxins (1890). (N)

Martinus Willem Beijerinck (1851–1931), Dutch botanist: discovered and named the *virus* (1895).

Hans Berger (1873–1941), German neuropsychiatrist: developed first electroencephalograph (1929) to measure brain waves.

Albert C. T. Billroth (1829–94), German surgeon: discovered bacteria cause infections in wounds.

Elizabeth Blackwell (1821–1910), first American woman physician: founded women's medical college in New York (1857).

Alfred Blalock (1899–1964), American surgeon: with Helen Taussig, developed corrective heart surgery for "blue babies" (1944).

Konrad Emil Bloch (1912–), German-American biochemist: discovered how living cells make cholesterol. (N)

Richard Bright (1789–1858), British physician: defined nephritis or Bright's disease (1827).

Robert Brown (1773–1858), British physician: discovered nucleus in living cells (1831).

Sir David Bruce (1855–1931), British surgeon: isolated germs causing Malta fever and sleeping sickness.

Albert Léon Calmette (1863–1933), French bacteriologist: co-discoverer of BCG vaccine, introduced in 1921 for prevention of tuberculosis.

Alexis Carrel (1873–1944), French surgeon: first kept tissues alive outside the body. (N)

Ferdinand J. Cohn (1828–98), German biologist: first to prove bacteria are plants.

Carl Ferdinand Cori (1896–1984) and his wife **Gerty Theresa Radnitz Cori** (1896–1957), Czech-American physiologists: discovered how enzymes change starch into sugar. (N)

Francis H. C. Crick (1916–), British biologist and physicist: helped develop radar in World War II; co-discoverer (1953) of structure of DNA, basic substance in genes responsible for heredity. (N)

George Washington Crile (1864–1943), American surgeon: contributed to surgical treatment of high blood pressure, nerve-block anesthesia, and blood transfusion.

Harvey Cushing (1869–1939), American surgeon: developed brain surgery techniques.

Michael Ellis De Bakey (1908–), American surgeon: developed artificial heart; first person to surgically repair weakened blood vessels.

George F. Dick (1881–1967), American physician: with his wife, Gladys Dick, isolated germ causing scarlet fever (1923).

Carl Djerassi (1923–), Austrian-American chemist: developed first practical birth-control pills (1954).

Edward Adelbert Doisy (1893–), American chemist: discovered vitamin K, isolated female sex hormone. (N)

Gerhard Domagk (1895–1964), German physician: discovered first sulfa drug (1932). (N)

Charles Richard Drew (1904–50), American black surgeon: developed blood and plasma banks (1940).

Paul Ehrlich (1854–1915), German bacteriologist: developed blood count (1897), chemotherapy to kill germs with drugs (1904), and Salvarsan drug for treatment of syphilis (1909). (N)

Christiaan Eijkman (1858–1930), Dutch physician: discovered rice hulls contain substance that prevents the disease beriberi (1900), leading others to discover vitamins.

Willem Einthoven (1860–1927), Dutch physiologist: developed electrocardiograph (1903). (N)

John Franklin Enders (1897–), American bacteriologist: developed measles vaccine (1963). (N)

Carlos Juan Finlay (1833–1915), Cuban physician: identified mosquito that carries yellow fever (1900).

Sir Alexander Fleming (1881–1955), British bacteriologist: discovered penicillin (1928). (N)

Sigmund Freud (1856–1939), Austrian psychiatrist: founded psychoanalysis; devised new theory about mental disorders.

Casimir Funk (1884–1967), Polish biochemist: discovered and named vitamins (1912).

Galen (c.130–200), Greek-Roman physician: systematized medical knowledge of his time.

Joseph Goldberger (1874–1929), Hungarian-American physician: discovered cure for pellagra (1915).

Camillo Golgi (1844–1926), Italian physician: developed way of staining tissues with silver nitrate for microscopic study (1873). (N)

Camille Guérin (1872–1961), French bacteriologist: co-discoverer of BCG vaccine, introduced in 1921 for prevention of tuberculosis.

Samuel F. C. Hahnemann (1755–1843), German physician: founded homeopathic medicine.

Stephen Hales (1677–1761), British physiologist: first to measure blood pressure (1705).

Bernard Naftali Halpern (1904–78), French physician: discovered antihistamine drugs.

William Harvey (1578–1657), English physician: discovered circulation of blood (1628).

Sir Walter Norman Haworth (1883–1950), British chemist: first to make vitamin C. (N)

Hermann L. F. von Helmholtz (1821–94), German physiologist: invented ophthalmoscope (1846), measured nerve impulses.

Philip Showalter Hench (1896–1965), American physician: co-discoverer of use of ACTH for treatment of rheumatic diseases. (N)

Hippocrates (c.460–377 B.C.), Greek physician

and the "father of medicine": first to base medical treatment on scientific observation.

Chevalier Jackson (1865–1958), American surgeon: developed lighted esophagoscope.

Edward Jenner (1749–1823), British physician: developed vaccination against smallpox (1796).

Carl Gustav Jung (1875–1961), Swiss psychiatrist: founded analytical psychology.

Paul Karrer (1889–1971), Swiss chemist: did valuable research on vitamins A, E, K, and the carotenes. (N)

Edward Calvin Kendall (1886–1972), American biochemist: discovered thyroxine, hormone of thyroid gland (1914); discovered cortisone (1936), used to treat arthritis and other diseases. (N)

Shibasaburo Kitasato (1852–1931), Japanese bacteriologist: isolated tetanus germ (1889) and bubonic plague bacillus (1894).

Edwin Klebs (1834–1913), German-American bacteriologist: discovered pneumonia bacillus (1875) and, with Friedrich Löffler, diphtheria bacillus (1884).

Robert Koch (1843–1910), German physician: established science of bacteriology; discovered microorganisms causing anthrax (1876), tuberculosis (1882), and cholera (1884). (N)

Emil Theodor Kocher (1841–1917), Swiss surgeon: performed first goiter operation to remove enlarged thyroid gland (1878). (N)

Arthur Kornberg (1918–), American biochemist: co-discoverer of synthetic nucleic acids, key substance in heredity; developed nucleic acid that reproduces itself (1967). (N)

Hans Adolf Krebs (1900–81), German biochemist: discovered citric-acid cycle in sugar metabolism (1953), called Krebs cycle. (N)

Richard Kuhn (1900–67), German chemist: discovered vitamin B$_2$, riboflavin. (N)

René Théophile Hyacinthe Laënnec (1781–1826), French physician: invented stethoscope (1816).

Karl Landsteiner (1868–1943), Austrian-American physician: discovered main blood types (1900), polio virus (1908); with A. S. Wiener, discovered Rh blood factor (1940). (N)

Charles L. A. Laveran (1845–1922), French physician: discovered parasite causing malaria (1880). (N)

Anton van Leeuwenhoek (1632–1723), Dutch biologist: perfected single-lens microscope; first to describe bacteria, protozoa, and blood cells.

Sir Joseph Lister (1827–1912), British surgeon: introduced antisepsis in surgery (1865).

Friedrich Löffler (1852–1915), German bacteriologist: with Edwin Klebs, discovered diphtheria bacillus (1884); with Paul Frosch, discovered virus causing hoof-and-mouth disease in cattle (1897).

Crawford Williamson Long (1815–78), American physician: first to use ether as anesthetic in surgery (1842).

Feodor Lynen (1911–79), German chemist: helped discover how body uses and makes cholesterol and fatty acids. (N)

John James Rickard Macleod (1876–1935), British physiologist: co-discoverer of insulin (1921). (N)

Marcello Malpighi (1628–94), Italian physician: discovered capillary blood vessels.

Sir Patrick Manson (1844–1922), British physician: discovered parasite causing elephantiasis (1877); called "father of tropical medicine."

William Worral Mayo (1819–1911) and sons, **William James Mayo** (1861–1939) and **Charles Horace Mayo** (1865–1939), American surgeons: founded Mayo Clinic in Rochester, Minn. (1889).

Elmer Verner McCollum (1879–1967), American biochemist: invented alphabet system of naming vitamins (1915).

Ephraim McDowell (1771–1830), American surgeon: performed first successful removal of tumor from ovary (1809).

Sir Peter Brian Medawar (1915–), British zoologist: proved organs and tissues transplantable between unrelated animals (1953). (N)

Charles Frederick Menninger (1862–1953) and sons, **Karl Augustus Menninger** (1893–) and **William Claire Menninger** (1899–1966), American psychiatrists: founded Menninger Clinic in Topeka, Kan. (1919).

Franz Mesmer (1734–1815), Austrian physician: pioneered hypnotism in medicine (1778).

Elie Metchnikoff (1845–1916), Russian biologist: developed theory that white blood cells attack disease germs. (N)

George Minot (1885–1950), American physician: discovered liver-extract treatment for pernicious anemia (1926). (N)

Egas Moniz (1874–1955), Portuguese neurologist: developed prefrontal lobotomy as surgical treatment of severe mental illness. (N)

Thomas Hunt Morgan (1866–1945), American biologist: advanced knowledge of heredity by discovering that genes transmit inherited characteristics (1926). (N)

Giovanni Battista Morgagni (1682–1771), Italian physician: pioneered use of autopsies to study causes of diseases.

William T. G. Morton (1819–68), American dentist: first to use ether as anesthetic in dentistry (1846).

Florence Nightingale (1820–1910), British nurse: founder of nursing as profession.

Hideyo Noguchi (1876–1928), Japanese bacteriologist: developed skin test for diagnosis of syphilis; discovered parasite of yellow fever.

Sir William Osler (1849–1919), Canadian physician: developed method of teaching new doctors as interns in hospital wards.

George Nicholas Papanicolaou (1883–1962), American physician: devised "Pap" smear test for cancer detection.

Philippus Aureolus Paracelsus (1493–1541), Swiss physician: introduced use of specific chemicals as treatment for specific illnesses.

Ambroise Paré (1510–90), French surgeon: introduced use of artificial limbs.

Louis Pasteur (1822–95), French bacteriologist: first to prove bacteria cause disease; developed pasteurization to kill bacteria with heat (1864); developed vaccine for rabies (1885).

Ivan Petrovich Pavlov (1849–1936), Russian physiologist: proved nerves control flow of digestive juices; pioneered in study of conditioned reflexes. (N)

Walter Reed (1851–1902), U.S. Army surgeon: helped discover cause of yellow fever.

Tadeus Reichstein (1897–), Swiss chemist: discovered how to make ascorbic acid, vitamin C (1933); isolated cortisone (1936). (N)

PIONEERS IN MEDICINE (continued)

Howard Taylor Ricketts (1871–1910), American pathologist: identified microorganisms (named *rickettsia* after his death) that cause Rocky Mountain spotted fever and typhus.

Sir Ronald Ross (1857–1932), British physician: proved *Anopheles* mosquito carries malaria (1898).

Benjamin Rush (1745–1813), American physician and signer of Declaration of Independence: established first free U.S. medical clinic at Philadelphia (1786).

Albert Sabin (1906–), Russian-American bacteriologist: developed oral polio vaccine (1957).

Jonas Salk (1914–), American physician: developed first successful vaccine for polio (1953).

Frederick Sanger (1918–), British chemist: helped determine structure of insulin. (N)

Béla Schick (1877–1967), Hungarian-American pediatrician: devised test for susceptibility to diphtheria (1913).

Theodor Schwann (1810–82), German physiologist and histologist: discovered that cell is fundamental unit of life (1839).

Ignaz Philipp Semmelweiss (1818–65), Hungarian physician: pioneered use of antiseptic methods in childbirth (1860).

Sir James Young Simpson (1811–70), British physician: first to use chloroform as anesthetic in childbirth (1847).

Lazzaro Spallanzani (1729–99), Italian biologist: proved bacteria float in air and heating kills bacteria.

Wendell M. Stanley (1904–71), American biochemist: proved viruses are solid particles that contain protein (1935). (N)

Andrew Taylor Still (1828–1917), American founder of osteopathic medicine: organized osteopathic college, Kirksville, Mo., in 1892.

James Batcheller Sumner (1887–1955), American biochemist: first to isolate pure crystals of an enzyme (1926). (N)

Albert Szent–Gyorgyi (1893–), Hungarian-American biochemist: discovered actin, a muscle protein. (N)

Helen Taussig (1898–), American pediatrician: with A. Blalock, developed corrective heart surgery for "blue babies" (1944).

Max Theiler (1899–1972), South African physician: discovered vaccine against yellow fever (1937). (N)

Andreas Vesalius (1514–64), Flemish physician: wrote first comprehensive textbook on human anatomy (1543).

Rudolf Virchow (1821–1902), German physician: pioneered scientific study of diseases, or *pathology* (1850s).

Selman A. Waksman (1888–1973), U.S. microbiologist: discovered streptomycin (1943). (N)

August von Wassermann (1866–1925), German physiologist and bacteriologist: developed blood test for diagnosing syphilis (1906).

James Dewey Watson (1928–), American biochemist: co-discoverer of molecular structure of DNA (1953). (N)

Maurice H. F. Wilkins (1916–), British biophysicist: first to explain structure of deoxyribonucleic acid (DNA). (N)

Daniel Hale Williams (1856–1931), American black physician: first surgeon to repair pericardium, sac around the heart (1893).

Alexandre E. J. Yersin (1863–1943), Swiss-French bacteriologist: independently discovered bubonic plague bacillus (1894).

MAJOR ADVANCES IN MEDICINE AND DRUGS

Year	Advance	Year	Advance	Year	Advance
1628	Blood circulation described	1909	Salvarsan, for syphilis	1943	Streptomycin, a broad-spectrum antibiotic
1676	Bacteria and blood cells discovered	1912	Phenobarbital, sedative	1943	ACTH, a pituitary hormone
1707	Pulse rate measured	1913	Niacin, antipellagra vitamin	1945	Methadone, a synthetic narcotic for control of drug addiction
1733	Blood pressure measured	1913	Vitamin A		
1794	Therapeutic oxygen inhalation	1914	Blood storage developed	1946	Iodine[131], for exophthalmic goiter and diagnosis of thyroid disorders
1796	Smallpox vaccine	1920	Cod liver oil (vitamin D)		
1820	Quinine, for malaria	1921	Insulin, a pancreatic hormone, to control diabetes mellitus	1948	Aureomycin, antibiotic
1839	Iodine, as antiseptic			1948	Vitamin B$_{12}$, for pernicious anemia
1842	Ether, as surgical anesthetic	1921	BCG tuberculosis vaccine	1950	First successful human organ transplant operation with kidney
1844	Nitrous oxide, anesthetic	1923	Scarlet-fever germ isolated		
1847	Chloroform, anesthetic	1926	Gene theory of heredity	1952	Isoniazid, a synthetic chemical effective against tuberculosis
1864	Pasteurization developed	1926	Thiamine, a vitamin		
1865	Phenol (carbolic acid), for surgical asepsis	1926	Liver extract, for anemia	1953	Salk polio vaccine
		1927	Ephedrine, a stimulant and nasal decongestant	1953	DNA structure discovered
1869	Chloral hydrate, sedative			1954	Reserpine, a tranquilizer obtained from rauwolfia
1876	Anthrax bacteria discovered	1928	Vitamin C (ascorbic acid) isolated		
1878	First operation to remove goiter	1929	Cyclopropane, an anesthetic	1954	Enovid, first birth-control pill
1882	Tuberculosis bacteria discovered	1932	Curare (arrow poison) alkaloids, for tetanus and spastic disorders	1957	Growth (pituitary) hormone, for dwarfism
1884	Cholera bacteria discovered				
1884	Cocaine, as local anesthetic	1933	Whooping-cough vaccine	1957	Sabin oral polio vaccine
1885	Rabies immunization	1935	Sulfa drugs proved effective	1963	Measles vaccine
1890	Diphtheria antitoxin	1935	Amphetamine, a stimulant	1967	First successful human heart transplant operation
1890	Tetanus antitoxin	1935	Blood bank developed		
1894	Thyroid extract, for goiter	1936	Cortisone discovered	1968	First synthesis of an enzyme
1895	Viruses discovered	1937	Yellow-fever vaccine	1969	Rubella vaccine
1895	X rays discovered	1937	Antihistamines, to control allergic reactions and motion sickness	1970	L-Dopa, for Parkinsonism; first gene synthesized
1897	Blood count developed				
1898	Radium discovered	1937	Heparin, an anticoagulant	1977	Ara-A, first antivirus drug, proved effective
1899	Aspirin, an analgesic	1940	Rh blood factor		
1900	Blood types discovered	1941	Penicillin, first antibiotic, proved effective	1978	Pneumonia vaccine
1903	Barbitol (veronal), barbiturate			1981	First vaccine produced by gene-splicing
1904	Chemotherapy first used	1941	Fluorides, for prevention of dental caries		

MEDICAL TERMS AND WHAT THEY MEAN

abasia—inability to walk from lack of muscular coordination; caused by damage to brain or nervous system

abdomen—region of body below chest and above pelvis; muscular wall of diaphragm separates abdominal cavity from chest; abdomen contains digestive, excretory, and sex organs

abortion—induced or natural loss or destruction of fertilized ovum or fetus before birth

abrasion—skin scrape with bleeding; can become infected unless cleaned and treated

abscess—area of infection in which pus forms, usually caused by bacteria

acetanilid—drug used to reduce fever and pain

Achilles tendon—thick tendon at back of ankle connecting calf muscles in leg to heel bone

acidosis—condition caused by lack of alkali in blood; symptoms include weakness, drowsiness

acne—pimples and blackheads caused by skin pores becoming blocked; may come from improper diet or lack of cleanliness

acromegaly—abnormal enlargement of hands, feet, or features of face; results from excess of growth hormones

ACTH—hormone produced by pituitary gland; has been used to relieve pain in treatment of various diseases

addiction—craving for certain foods or drugs, such as alcohol or habit-forming narcotics

Addison's disease—debilitating disease that causes weakness, darkening of skin, low blood pressure; results from insufficient hormone production by cortex of adrenal glands

adenoids—glandular tissue at upper part of throat, behind nose; excessive growth or infection of adenoids causes breathing difficulty

adrenalin—hormone secreted by adrenal glands; stimulates heart to beat faster, increasing blood pressure, and enabling muscles to work faster and harder

agoraphobia—fear of large open spaces

allergen—allergy-producing substance

allergy—unusual reaction of body to substances normally having no adverse effect on most other persons

allopathy—medical treatment to create effects opposed to those of specific disease

alopecia—loss of hair, usually hereditary

amblyopia—dimness of vision; may be hereditary or caused by improper diet or excessive use of tobacco or alcohol

amnesia—temporary or permanent loss of memory

analgesic—medicine that relieves pain; aspirin is one of commonest analgesics

androgen—male sex hormone that determines such characteristics as deep voice and beard

anemia—blood disorder with reduced hemoglobin or red cells; symptoms: paleness, constant tiredness

aneurysm—abnormal weakening of artery wall, forming pulsating blood-filled sac; rupture of weakened artery wall can cause death

angina pectoris—pain in chest, shoulder, neck, or left arm, generally caused by *arteriosclerosis*

anodontia—failure of teeth to grow in; may be hereditary or glandular malfunction

anorexia nervosa—disorder marked by intentional starvation and severe weight loss; typically involves eating binges followed by self-induced vomiting; mainly affects young women with abnormal fear of obesity

antacid—remedy for upset stomach; baking soda is common antacid

antibiotic—medicine produced by microorganisms, such as molds; antibiotics prevent growth and reproduction of certain disease germs; common antibiotics include penicillin, streptomycin, Aureomycin, Chloromycetin

antibody—natural substance in body that protects against disease or infection

anticoagulant—substance that slows clotting of blood; example: heparin

antidote—remedy to counteract poison

antigen—substance that stimulates production of *antibodies* when it enters body; examples: bacteria, pollen, viruses

antihistamine—medicine used to counteract symptoms of hay fever, allergies, and common cold; may cause drowsiness

antitoxin—type of *antibody*, acts against poison (toxin) that enters body; antitoxins produced in the blood of animals used to treat such diseases as *tetanus*

anxiety—in psychiatry, irrational worry or fear in absence of obvious danger

aphasia—loss or impairment of ability to speak, write, or understand others; caused by brain damage, often after *stroke*

aphonia—loss of voice or ability to speak louder than whisper; may be caused by excessive use of voice, brain damage, or cancer of larynx (voice box)

aphrodisiac—substance supposed to stimulate sexual powers

apoplexy—stroke caused by blockage of blood vessel in brain by blood clot

appendicitis—inflammation and swelling of appendix; if not surgically removed, it may rupture and cause death; symptom: pain around navel, spreading to lower right of abdomen

arteriosclerosis—hardening of arteries; caused by accumulation of calcium and cholesterol on artery walls; brings about clots in blood that may cause stroke in brain or heart attack

artery—vessel carrying blood from heart to parts of body

arthritis—disease affecting joints and supporting tissues; causes swelling, pain; can cripple hands, arms, and legs

asepsis—absence of germs, achieved by use of germ-killing antiseptics and sterilization

asphyxia—suffocation from lack of oxygen

asthma—chronic disease of bronchial tubes; causes breathing difficulty

atherosclerosis—accumulation of fatty deposits on artery walls, causing arteriosclerosis

athlete's foot—contagious infection of foot; caused by fungus in wet, warm places

autism—brain disorder that causes problems in communication, learning, and social behavior

bacitracin—antibiotic used as treatment for skin infections

bedsore—ulcer of skin caused by lying in bed in same position for long time

benign—not harmful in itself and likely not to

458 MEDICINE AND HEALTH

MEDICAL TERMS *(continued)*

recur after being removed, as a tumor

biopsy—removal of bit of tissue from living body for microscopic examination; used in diagnosing such diseases as *cancer* and *cirrhosis*

blood poisoning—presence in bloodstream of bacteria from infection; symptoms include weakness, chills, fever; fatal if not treated

blood pressure—force of blood against artery walls; normal blood pressure for adults aged 18 to 45 is 120/80; first number is *systolic* pressure caused by heart contracting; second number is *diastolic* pressure when heart relaxes; high blood pressure can cause stroke or heart attack

blood types—four main types of blood: O, A, B, and AB based on substances found in red blood cells and *plasma*; before *transfusions*, blood types must be determined for correct matching; *Rh factor* also important in classifying blood; only O-type can be given to anyone

body temperature—normal heat of body; averages 98.6° F. (37°C.); temperature over 100° F. (37.8°C.) in adult indicates fever

boil—pus-filled infection on skin caused by bacteria; never open boil yourself because pus can get into bloodstream, causing *blood poisoning*

botulism—bacterial infection from improperly canned, bottled, or preserved food

bronchitis—inflammation of respiratory passages; caused by viral infection, smoking, air pollution

bubonic plague—acute contagious disease usually transmitted to people by fleas of rats; in past has caused widespread epidemics, killing millions of persons; symptoms appear suddenly: chills, fever, vomiting, delerium

bursitis—painful inflammation at joint caused by irritation of bursa (liquid-filled sac at joint)

cancer—group of diseases characterized by abnormal cell growth, crowding out healthy tissue and interfering with vital function of affected organs; malignant tumors develop

carcinogen—cancer-causing substance

carcinoma—cancer that originates in skin or mucous membranes

cardiac—pertaining to heart

caries—bacterial decay of tooth or bone

cataract—clouded condition in lens of eye, resulting in blurred vision; can be corrected by surgery

cauterize—to destroy abnormal or infected tissue by applying hot iron, laser beam, or other means

cerebral hemorrhage—bleeding inside brain from ruptured blood vessel; symptoms: headache, nausea, unconsciousness, paralysis

cerebral palsy—disorders caused by damage to brain before, during, or after birth

chemotherapy—use of chemicals and drugs to treat or to prevent disease

chicken pox—contagious disease; symptoms: fever, eruptions on skin; lasts about two weeks

cholera—acute epidemic disease; spread by polluted water, contaminated food, insects; symptoms: vomiting, diarrhea

cholesterol—substance in fats and oils, main material of *gallstones*; contributes to hardening of arteries; high cholesterol diet may help cause heart disease

chorea—involuntary twitching, once called "St. Vitus's dance"; often associated with *rheumatic fever*

chromosome—part of every plant or animal cell; carries genes determining physical characteristics of specific plant or animal

chronic—lasting long time without rapid change for better or worse

cirrhosis—chronic disease of liver; often associated with alcoholism

claustrophobia—fear of confined space

coagulant—substance that speeds up clotting of blood

congenital—existing at birth

conjunctivitis—inflammation of conjunctiva (mucous membrane covering eyeball and inner part of eyelids); also called pinkeye

contraception—prevention of pregnancy by use of methods of birth control

coronary thrombosis—blocking of artery supplying blood to heart muscles; common cause of heart attacks

cystic fibrosis—incurable hereditary disease of childhood; sweat glands and mucus-secreting glands do not function properly, involving lungs and pancreas

cystitis—bladder infection or inflammation

cystoscope—hollow tube with lights and mirrors used to examine interior of bladder

depilatory—agent for removing unwanted hair

diabetes—noncontagious disease in which pancreas does not produce enough insulin or body does not use insulin properly; symptoms: thirst, excessive urination

edema—excessive water and salt in tissues, causing swelling

electrocardiograph—instrument that records electrical current produced by action of heart muscle; resulting electrocardiogram (EKG) shows wave pattern traced on paper; used to diagnose heart ailments

electroencephalograph—instrument that records electrical impulses in brain (brain waves); resulting electroencephalogram (EEG) used in diagnosing brain disorders

embolism—blocking of blood vessel by loose blood clot, air bubble, or other material; can cause *stroke*

emphysema—incurable respiratory disorder; air sacs in lungs lose elasticity, causing impaired breathing, heart strain; contributing factors: smoking, air pollution

encephalitis—acute inflammation of brain; commonly known as "sleeping sickness" because main symptom is sleepiness; caused by virus carried by mosquitoes and ticks

endocarditis—inflammation of heart lining

enteritis—inflammation of intestine

epilepsy—chronic disorder of nervous system; causes periodic convulsions and unconsciousness; caused by brain injury or brain infection

erysipelas—also called "St. Anthony's fire"; skin disease; symptoms: hot red patches on skin, fever, headache, nausea

estrogens—female hormones responsible for regulating female sex functions

fluoridation—addition of fluoride salts to drinking water to reduce tooth decay

food poisoning—acute illness caused by eating contaminated food; symptoms: pain in abdomen, vomiting, diarrhea

frostbite—injury to skin, ears, nose, toes, or fingers from cold; body tissues freeze without pain when exposed to cold; may cause *gangrene*; any pressure on frozen toes or fingers may cause permanent injury; do not massage frozen parts; professional treatment necessary

gallstone—solid rocklike mass that forms in gallbladder; can cause inflammation of gallbladder; symptoms: pain in upper abdomen, fever, vomiting, tiredness; treated by surgery

gamma globulin—protein in blood *plasma*; contains numerous kinds of *antibodies*; used as serum to produce immunity for diseases such as measles

gangrene—death of body tissues in part of body; may be caused by infection or frostbite; severe cases require surgery

gastritis—inflammation of stomach lining

German measles—also called rubella; contagious virus infection; symptoms: swollen lymph glands, 3-day rash; if contracted during early pregnancy, can cause miscarriage or birth defects; vaccine available

gingivitis—inflammation of gums around teeth; symptom: bleeding gums; can lead to *pyorrhea*

glaucoma—disorder of eyes marked by increased pressure within eyeballs; symptoms: pain in eyes, blurred vision, appearance of halos around electric lights

gonorrhea—highly contagious bacterial infection; usually transmitted during sexual intercourse; readily cured in early stages by professional treatment

gout—high level of uric acid in tissues and joints, causing sharp pain

hallucination—vivid perception of something not present in reality

hallucinogen—substance that produces *hallucinations*; includes such drugs as marijuana, mescaline, LSD

hematoma—swelling under skin, caused by ruptured blood vessel

hemophilia—hereditary disorder affecting males; blood clots too slowly to prevent excessive bleeding from minor injuries

hemorrhage—heavy bleeding from blood vessel

hemorrhoids—enlarged veins in region of anus, usually painful; also known as "piles"

hepatic—pertaining to liver

hepatitis—inflammation of liver; usually caused by virus; contagious; symptoms: loss of appetite, fever, pain in upper right abdomen

hernia—abnormal protrusion of organ through tissue wall surrounding it; corrected by surgery

herpes—viral infection of genital skin from sexual contact with infected person

hyperglycemia—condition caused by too much sugar in blood; symptom of diabetes

hypertension—high blood pressure

hypochondria—excessive concern with one's health; person exaggerates trivial symptoms or suffers imaginary ailments; type of *neurosis*

hypoglycemia—deficiency of glucose in blood; may be caused by insulin injection

hysterectomy—removal by surgery of uterus, and in some cases ovaries, Fallopian tubes, and cervix

immunization—procedure for protection against disease; introduces or induces production of antibodies, usually by inoculation; natural immunity may be developed to specific disease after contracting it and recovering

interferon—protein substance produced in body cells of humans and other mammals that stops growth of viral infections in uninfected cells; subject of research as possible drug to use in treating or preventing cancer

intrauterine device (IUD)—contraceptive device inserted into uterus; common types include spirals or loops of flexible plastic

leukemia—type of cancer affecting blood-forming tissues; produces abnormally large number of white blood cells; symptoms: fever, loss of appetite

lumbago—pain in lumbar region of lower back; may be due to *arthritis*

malignant—likely to grow or spread, as a tumor

mastectomy—surgical removal of breast tissue, usually to treat breast cancer

measles—also called rubeola; acute virus disease, sometimes followed by complications; vaccine should be given at age 1 year

meningitis—contagious disease causing inflammation of membrane covering brain and lung; symptoms: headache, vomiting, fever, spasms pulling head back; in infants, spots on skin

metabolism—total of processes by which food, water, and oxygen are converted into living tissue, energy, and waste

metastasis—transfer of disease from one part of body to another by germs or by abnormal cells transported in blood or lymph

mononucleosis—contagious disease producing abnormally large number of monocytes (type of white blood cell); sometimes called "kissing disease" because of way it can be transmitted; symptoms: chills, fever, sore throat, tiredness

multiple sclerosis—progressive disease forming hardened patches on nerve sheaths in brain and spinal cord, preventing nerves from responding normally; symptoms: unsteady balance, jerky movements of arms and legs, stiff muscles

mumps—acute contagious disease, usually of childhood; causes swelling of salivary glands; vaccine available

muscular dystrophy—hereditary disease causing muscles to weaken and deteriorate; mostly affects boys

nephritis—inflammation of kidneys

neuralgia—severe pain along a nerve in the face, mouth, or throat

neuritis—inflammation of nerve causing pain in any part of body

neurology—study or treatment of disorders of nervous system

neurosis—emotional disturbance produced by unresolved and unconscious conflicts; often accompanied by *anxiety* and depression

nyctophobia—fear of darkness

oral contraception—method of birth control by taking pills containing sex hormones

osteo—pertaining to bones

ovulation—release of egg cell from ovary

pacemaker—nerve and muscle cells in heart that establish and regulate heart rhythm; when natural pacemaker does not function properly, artificial pacemaker may be implanted to stimulate heart with small electrical impulses

palsy—type of paralysis and disorder marked by

MEDICAL TERMS *(continued)*

constant trembling of parts of body; injury or disorder of nervous system impairs ability to control voluntary muscles

Pap test—quick, painless test to detect some types of cancer, especially of cervix; women over 30 should have Pap test annually

paranoia—mental disorder characterized by delusions of persecution or power

Parkinsonism—chronic, slowly progressive disorder that affects part of brain controlling voluntary movement; also known as Parkinson's disease

phlebitis—inflammation of vein forming blood clot, commonly in leg

phobia—extreme fear, usually so overpowering as to prevent person from functioning normally

phobophobia—fear of fear

physical therapy—treatment of injury, disability, or physical defect by massage, heat, exercise, or other external means

placebo—harmless substance given to humor patient; used in research as control to check effectiveness of drug

plasma—liquid part of blood; used rather than whole blood for some transfusions; can be used in transfusing persons of any *blood type*

platelets—part of blood that causes blood to clot; person with deficiency of platelets may bleed excessively from minor injuries

pleurisy—inflammation of pleura (double membrane that covers each lung and lines chest cavity)

pneumonia—acute infection of lungs; tiny air sacs become filled with fluid; breathing impaired

polyp—growth in mucous membrane, as in nasal passage, vocal cord, or alimentary tract

postpartum—postnatal; occurring after delivery of baby

prosthesis—artificial substitute for part of body, ranging from denture to artificial leg

psoriasis—skin disease marked by red patches

psychiatry—study, diagnosis, and treatment of mental illness and personality disorders

psychoanalysis—technique developed by Sigmund Freud to bring back repressed memories and understand unconscious impulses

psychology—science of study of mind, especially concerned with behavior

psychosis—severe mental disorder, often involving disintegration of personality

psychosomatic—denoting disorders, such as ulcers and migraine headaches, that may be completely or partly due to emotional causes

psychotherapy—treatment of emotional and mental disorders largely through discussion of them

pyorrhea alveolaris—disease forming pus at roots of teeth; tissue of gums shrinks; teeth become loose, causing loss of teeth

rabies—disease usually transmitted by bite of animal; symptoms: muscle spasms, convulsions, periodic rage and calm, spasms of throat when attempting to drink; death follows within 2 to 3 days after appearance of symptoms

renal—pertaining to kidneys

Rh factor—inherited substance in red blood cells; if present, as in most persons, blood is Rh positive; if absent, blood is Rh negative; person with Rh negative blood never should receive transfusion of Rh positive blood

rheumatic fever—bacterial disease of children and young adults; usually follows untreated streptococcus infections; symptoms: fever, swollen joints, nosebleed; may cause heart damage

ringworm—fungus infection of skin

rubella—German measles

schizophrenia—serious mental disorder characterized by delusions, retreat from reality, and possible deterioration of personality

sciatica—severe pain in sciatic nerve, affecting buttocks, thigh, leg, and foot

shock—signs and symptoms associated with failure or collapse of circulatory system; may follow extensive surgery, severe injury, or heavy bleeding; requires emergency medical treatment

silicosis—chronic disease of lungs from long exposure to mines or silica (sand and stone) products

sphygmomanometer—instrument used to measure blood pressure

streptococcus—type of bacteria that causes scarlet fever and strep throat

stroke—damage to brain from blocked or ruptured artery; symptoms: unconsciousness, paralysis of one side of body; high blood pressure and hardening of arteries are underlying causes

syphilis—contagious bacterial disease transmitted in sexual intercourse; can cause brain disease, blindness, heart disease; treated with penicillin

tendinitis—painful inflammation of tendon, commonly in shoulder

thrombosis—blocking of blood vessel by blood clot; can cause gangrene, stroke, or heart attack

toxic shock syndrome—systemic bacterial infection associated with prolonged use of menstrual pads or diaphragm

toxin—poisonous substance produced by germs, chemicals, and some plants and animals

trachoma—highly contagious virus disease of eyelids; can lead to blindness if untreated; widespread in tropical areas

transfusion—injection of blood or blood parts into person's circulatory system

trauma—injury caused to organ by blow or wound; in *psychiatry*, grave emotional shock that may have lasting effect on personality

trichinosis—disease caused by eating undercooked pork; parasitic roundworms invade blood and body organs; symptoms: fever, nausea, vomiting, diarrhea, abdominal pain

tuberculosis—chronic communicable disease; attacks lungs and other body parts

tumor—abnormal tissue growth on or in body; may be *benign* or *malignant*

ulcer—inflamed open sore on skin or on mucous membrane lining stomach, small intestine, or other body cavity

uremia—toxic condition of blood caused by wastes normally removed by kidneys and excreted in urine

vaccine—preparation containing bacteria or viruses treated to give immunity against specific diseases

venereal disease—infection transmitted mainly by sexual intercourse, such as *syphilis* and *gonorrhea*

Wassermann test—method of determining presence of syphilis

zoophobia—fear of animals

National Defense

HIGHLIGHTS: 1985

NEW DEFENSE LINE

President Reagan and Canadian Prime Minister Brian Mulroney signed an agreement in March to develop a new $1.3 billion radar system to detect enemy aircraft. The new chain of radar stations would replace the outmoded Distant Early Warning System built in northern Canada after World War II. Canada agreed to pay 40% of the cost of the new radar system.

SUCCESSFUL ANTIMISSILE TEST

Air Force scientists conducted a spectacular test on June 21 that took them a step forward toward the development of the "Star Wars" defense system against enemy nuclear missiles.

In the test, the Air Force Optical Station on Maui, Hawaii, succeeded in aiming a laser beam that struck and locked onto an 8-inch target mirror on the shuttle *Discovery* while it sped through space at 17,000 mph some 220 miles above the surface of the Earth.

A 22-cent commemorative stamp honoring America's World War I veterans was issued August 26 in Milwaukee, Wisc., during the Veterans of World War I annual convention. The design is based on Harvey Dunn's drawing, "The Battle of the Marne."

The shuttle was traveling much faster than would an enemy nuclear missile.

Astronauts on the shuttle sent back TV

JOINT CHIEFS OF STAFF

The Joint Chiefs of Staff of the U.S. armed forces was established in the Defense Department in 1947. The position of Chairman of the Joint Chiefs of Staff was created in 1949.

CHAIRMAN

Adm. William J. Crowe Jr., USN (Oct. 1985–Current)
Gen. John W. Vessey Jr., USA (July 1, 1982–Oct. 1985)
Gen. David C. Jones, USAF (June 1978–June 1982)
Gen. George S. Brown, USAF (July 1974–June 1978)
Adm. Thomas H. Moorer, USN (July 1970–July 1974)
Gen. Earle G. Wheeler, USA (July 1964–July 1970)
Gen. Maxwell D. Taylor, USA (Oct. 1962–July 1964)
Gen. Lyman L. Lemnitzer, USA (Oct. 1960–Sept. 1962)
Gen. Nathan F. Twining, USAF (Aug. 1957–Sept. 1960)
Adm. Arthur W. Radford, USN (Aug. 1953–Aug. 1957)
Gen. of the Army Omar N. Bradley, USA (Aug. 1949–Aug. 1953)

CHIEF OF STAFF, UNITED STATES ARMY

Gen. John A. Wickham Jr. (June 1983–Current)
Gen. Edward Charles Meyer (June 1979–June 1983)
Gen. Bernard W. Rogers (Sept. 1976–June 1979)
Gen. Frederick C. Weyand (Oct. 1974–Sept. 1976)
Gen. Creighton W. Abrams (Oct. 1972–Sept. 1974)
Gen. William C. Westmoreland (July 1968–June 1972)
Gen. Harold K. Johnson (July 1964–July 1968)
Gen. Earle G. Wheeler (Oct. 1962–July 1964)
Gen. George H. Decker (Sept. 1960–Sept. 1962)
Gen. Lyman L. Lemnitzer (July 1959–Sept. 1960)
Gen. Maxwell D. Taylor (June 1955–June 1959)
Gen. Matthew B. Ridgway (Aug. 1953–June 1955)
Gen. J. Lawton Collins (Aug. 1949–Aug. 1953)
Gen. Omar N. Bradley (Feb. 1948–Aug. 1949)
Gen. of the Army Dwight D. Eisenhower (Nov. 1945–Feb. 1948)

CHIEF OF NAVAL OPERATIONS

Adm. James D. Watkins (July 1, 1982–Current)
Adm. Thomas B. Hayward (July 1978–June 1982)
Adm. James J. Holloway III (June 1974–June 1978)

Adm. Elmo R. Zumwalt Jr. (July 1970–June 1974)
Adm. Thomas H. Moorer (Aug. 1967–June 1970)
Adm. David L. McDonald (Aug. 1963–Aug. 1967)
Adm. George W. Anderson (Aug. 1961–July 1963)
Adm. Arleigh A. Burke (Aug. 1955–Aug. 1961)
Adm. Robert B. Carney (Aug. 1953–Aug. 1955)
Adm. William M. Fechteler (Aug. 1951–Aug. 1953)
Adm. Forrest P. Sherman (Nov. 1949–July 1951)
Adm. Louis E. Denfield (Dec. 1947–Nov. 1949)
Fleet Adm. Chester W. Nimitz (Dec. 1945–Dec. 1947)

CHIEF OF STAFF, UNITED STATES AIR FORCE

Gen. Charles A. Gabriel (July 1, 1982–Current)
Gen. Lew Allen Jr. (July 1978–June 1982)
Gen. David C. Jones (July 1974–June 1978)
Gen. George S. Brown (July 1973–July 1974)
Gen. John D. Ryan (Aug. 1969–July 1973)
Gen. John P. McConnell (Feb. 1965–Aug. 1969)
Gen. Curtis E. LeMay (June 1961–Jan. 1965)
Gen. Thomas D. White (July 1957–June 1961)
Gen. Nathan F. Twining (June 1953–June 1957)
Gen. Hoyt S. Vandenberg (April 1948–June 1953)
Gen. Carl Spaatz (Sept. 1947–April 1948)

COMMANDANT OF THE MARINE CORPS

Gen. Paul X. Kelley (July 1983–Current)
Gen. Robert H. Barrow (July 1979–June 1983)
Gen. Louis H. Wilson Jr. (July 1975–July 1979)
Gen. R.E. Cushman Jr. (Jan. 1972–July 1975)
Gen. Leonard F. Chapman Jr. (Jan. 1968–Dec. 1971)
Gen. Wallace M. Greene Jr. (Jan. 1964–Dec. 1967)
Gen. David M. Shoup (Jan. 1960–Dec. 1963)
Gen. Randolph McC. Pate (Jan. 1956–Dec. 1959)
Gen. Lemuel C. Shepherd (Jan. 1952–Dec. 1955)

HIGHLIGHTS: 1985 *(continued)*

pictures showing the blue green beam of light from the laser as it searched for and found its target. The laser beam was only about the width of a pencil when it left the Earth, but it spread out to a width of about 30 feet at the altitude of the shuttle.

As used in an antimissile defense system, a more powerful laser would be used to destroy an enemy missile while it still was speeding through space toward its target.

The Defense Department announced in June that 15 universities and laboratories had been selected to carry out research for the antimissile defense system. They included: Air Force Geophysics Laboratory, Cambridge, Mass., University of Kansas, Lawrence, Kan.; John Hopkins University Applied Physics Laboratory, Baltimore, Md.; University of Maryland, College Park, Md.; Utah State University, Logan, Utah; University of California at Los Angeles; University

of Michigan, Ann Arbor, Mich.; University of Iowa, Iowa City, Iowa; Massachusetts Institute of Technology, Cambridge, Mass.; Vanderbilt University, Nashville, Tenn.; Naval Research Laboratory, Washington, D.C.; University of Arizona, Tucson, Ariz.; Stanford University, Palo Alto, Calif.; University of California at Berkeley, Calif.; and New York University, New York City.

PACKARD TO STUDY DEFENSE BUYING

Throughout 1985 allegations of waste, fraud, and abuse by the nation's defense contractors made headlines. The news reports highlighted the purchase of $7,622 coffee makers, $600 toilet seats, $659 ashtrays for Navy planes, and the government paying $11,750 for the sponsorship by the Boeing Co. of a paper airplane contest. In addition prominent defense contractors were fined for fraud and waste in carrying out Defense Department contracts.

ARMED FORCES MONTHLY BASIC PAY SCALES[1]

COMMISSIONED OFFICERS' PAY GRADES

YEARS	0–1[2]	0–2[2]	0–3[2]	0–4	0–5	0–6	0–7	0–8	0–9	0–10
0–2	$1,188.60	$1,369.20	$1,570.20	$1,689.60	$2,004.60	$2,506.20	$3,381.60	$4,069.50	$4,493.10	$5,069.40
2+	1,237.50	1,495.20	1,755.30	2,057.40	2,354.10	2,753.70	3,611.40	4,191.30	4,610.70	5,247.90
3+	1,495.20	1,796.10	1,876.50	2,194.80	2,516.40	2,934.00	3,611.40	4,290.90	4,708.80	5,247.90
4+	1,495.20	1,856.70	2,076.30	2,194.80	2,516.40	2,934.00	3,611.40	4,290.90	4,708.80	5,247.90
6+	1,495.20	1,895.70	2,175.60	2,235.30	2,516.40	2,934.00	3,773.10	4,290.90	4,708.80	5,247.90
8+	1,495.20	1,895.70	2,254.20	2,334.30	2,516.40	2,934.00	3,773.10	4,610.70	4,828.50	5,449.20
10+	1,495.20	1,895.70	2,375.70	2,493.30	2,592.90	2,934.00	3,992.10	4,610.70	4,828.50	5,449.20
12+	1,495.20	1,895.70	2,493.30	2,633.70	2,732.10	2,934.00	3,992.10	4,828.50	5,029.50	5,724.90
14+	1,495.20	1,895.70	2,554.80	2,753.70	2,915.10	3,033.60	4,191.30	4,828.50	5,029.50	5,724.90
16+	1,495.20	1,895.70	2,554.80	2,874.60	3,133.20	3,513.30	4,610.70	5,029.50	5,449.20	5,724.90
18+	1,495.20	1,895.70	2,554.80	2,954.10	3,313.20	3,693.00	4,927.50	5,247.90	5,449.20	5,724.90
20+	1,495.20	1,895.70	2,554.80	2,954.10	3,413.40	3,773.10	4,927.50	5,449.20	5,724.90	5,724.90
22+	1,495.20	1,895.70	2,554.80	2,954.10	3,532.50	3,992.10	4,927.50	5,667.60	5,724.90	5,724.90
26+	1,495.20	1,895.70	2,554.80	2,954.10	3,532.50	4,329.60	4,927.50	5,667.60	5,724.90	5,724.90

WARRANT OFFICERS' PAY GRADES

YEARS	W–1	W–2	W–3	W–4	YEARS	W–1	W–2	W–3	W–4
0–2	$1,061.10	$1,273.50	$1,453.80	$1,599.60	12+	$1,557.30	$1,696.80	$1,895.70	$2,136.00
2+	1,216.50	1,377.60	1,577.10	1,716.00	14+	1,616.10	1,755.30	1,955.70	2,235.30
3+	1,216.50	1,377.60	1,577.10	1,716.00	16+	1,675.80	1,816.80	2,014.20	2,313.90
4+	1,317.90	1,417.80	1,597.20	1,755.30	18+	1,734.30	1,876.50	2,076.30	2,375.70
6+	1,377.60	1,495.20	1,616.10	1,835.10	20+	1,796.10	1,935.90	2,157.00	2,452.50
8+	1,436.70	1,577.10	1,734.30	1,916.10	22+	1,796.10	2,014.20	2,235.30	2,534.70
10+	1,495.20	1,636.80	1,835.10	1,996.50	26+	1,796.10	2,014.20	2,313.90	2,732.10

ENLISTED PAY GRADES

YEARS	E-1	E-2	E-3	E-4	E-5	E-6	E-7	E-8	E-9
0–2	$620.40	$695.40	$723.00	$767.40	$822.60	$937.20	$1,089.60	—	—
2+	620.40	695.40	762.30	810.30	895.50	1,021.80	1,176.00	—	—
3+	620.40	695.40	793.20	857.70	938.70	1,064.40	1,219.80	—	—
4+	620.40	695.40	824.70	924.60	979.80	1,109.70	1,262.40	—	—
6+	620.40	695.40	824.70	960.90	1,044.00	1,150.80	1,305.60	—	—
8+	620.40	695.40	824.70	960.90	1,086.30	1,192.80	1,347.00	$1,560.60	—
10+	620.40	695.40	824.70	960.90	1,129.80	1,236.60	1,390.20	1,605.00	$1,860.60
12+	620.40	695.40	824.70	960.90	1,171.20	1,300.20	1,433.40	1,647.00	1,902.90
14+	620.40	695.40	824.70	960.90	1,192.80	1,341.00	1,498.20	1,690.20	1,945.80
16+	620.40	695.40	824.70	960.90	1,192.80	1,384.20	1,540.80	1,734.60	1,990.50
18+	620.40	695.40	824.70	960.90	1,192.80	1,405.20	1,584.00	1,774.80	2,034.90
20+	620.40	695.40	824.70	960.90	1,192.80	1,405.20	1,604.70	1,818.30	2,074.50
22+	620.40	695.40	824.70	960.90	1,192.80	1,405.20	1,712.40	1,925.10	2,183.70
26+	620.40	695.40	824.70	960.90	1,192.80	1,405.20	1,925.10	2,139.90	2,395.80

[1] Pay scale effective Jan. 1, 1985. Pay for an enlisted E-1 with less than 4 months service is $573.60 per month. Basic allowance for quarters ranges from $133.50 per month for an enlisted E-1 with no dependents and less than 4 months service to $660.90 per month for an officer with dependents in grade 0-10. [2] Officers in the first 3 pay grades who have had 4 years of enlisted service receive some additional pay.

In an effort to find ways to produce defense materials at lower costs, the President announced on June 17 the appointment of David Packard, the co-founder of the computer manufacturer Hewlett-Packard who was Deputy Secretary of Defense in 1969-71, to head a bipartisan commission to investigate the problems and recommend solutions.

NAVY EXPANSION

A major part of the Reagan administration's buildup of military power has been expansion of the U.S. Navy's fleet of warships. When President Reagan came to the White House, the Navy had 479 ships. By 1985 the Navy had expanded the fleet to 542, and in the 1990s the size of the fleet is planned to increase to 600.

The Navy's expansion will bring prosperity to many many port cities, adding thousands of civilian jobs to provide services for the ships and their crews.

The Navy announced in June the selection of San Francisco as the home port for the refurbished battleship U.S.S. Missouri, while other units of the expanded West Coast fleet will be stationed at Long Beach, Calif.; Hunters Point, Calif.; and Pearl Harbor, Hawaii.

In July the Navy assigned the refitted battleship U.S.S. Wisconsin to Corpus Christi, Texas, as its home port. Other warships of the enlarged Gulf Coast-Caribbean fleet will be stationed at Houston and Galveston, Texas; New Orleans, La.; Lake Charles, La.; Mobile, Ala.; Pensacola, Fla.; Key West, Fla.; Pascagoula, Miss.; and Gulfport, Miss.

U.S. MILITARY FORCES ACTIVE STRENGTH

Source: U.S. Department of Defense

MILITARY PERSONNEL	1970	1975	1980	1983	1984	1985
Army	1,322,548	784,333	774,607	774,723	781,147	780,648
Navy	692,660	539,100	527,296	554,885	567,355	568,781
Marine Corps	259,737	195,951	187,647	192,429	195,897	198,241
Air Force	791,349	612,751	559,282	593,253	598,859	603,898
Totals	3,066,294	2,132,136	2,048,832	2,115,290	2,143,258	2,151,568

U.S. AIR FORCE ACTIVE AIRCRAFT

Source: U.S. Department of Defense

	1960	1970	1975	1980	1982	1983	1984	1985
U.S. Air Force total	15,312	11,245	7,239	7,034	7,119	7,194	7,231	7,250
Bomber, strategic	2,193	570	498	414	391	338	327	327
Tanker	1,230	663	657	529	542	546	550	560
Fighter/Attack/Interceptor	3,922	3,404	2,299	2,769	2,900	2,997	3,005	3,063
Reconnaissance/Electronic Warfare	685	1,017	494	354	363	385	427	424
Cargo/Transport	2,549	1,854	927	836	825	827	844	847
Search and Rescue (Fixed Wing)	129	87	44	35	36	35	36	36
Helicopter (including Rescue)	372	457	269	230	227	236	240	239
Trainer	3,914	2,625	1,861	1,678	1,642	1,624	1,614	1,603
Utility/Observation	316	568	189	189	193	206	188	203
Support of allied nations	—	948	243	—	—	—	—	—
Air National Guard	2,269	1,900	1,647	1,560	1,647	1,703	1,682	1,680
Air Force Reserve	770	420	448	474	447	458	456	464
Total active Air Force aircraft	18,712	14,725	9,577	9,069	9,213	9,355	9,369	9,394

U.S. NAVY AND MARINE CORPS STRENGTH

Source: U.S. Department of Defense

	1968	1972	1976	1980	1984	1985 *	1986 *
TOTAL U.S. FLEET	957	645	484	479	523	542	555
Strategic Forces	51	50	50	48	41	43	44
FBM Submarines (SSBN)	41	41	41	40	35	37	38
Support (AS, TAK)	10	9	9	8	6	6	6
Battle Forces	756	520	367	384	425	433	439
Carriers (CV, CVN, CVS)	23	17	13	13	13	13	13
Battleships (BB)	1	—	—	—	2	2	3
Cruisers (CG, CAG, CGN, CA, CC)	34	28	26	26	29	30	32
Destroyers (DD, DDR, DDG)	221	131	69	80	68	68	68
Frigates (FF, FFG)	50	66	64	71	94	99	97
Submarines (SS, SSN, SSG, SSGN)	105	94	74	79	98	100	99
Patrol Combatants	6	16	8	3	6	6	6
Amphibious Warfare Ships	157	77	62	63	59	59	60
Mine Warfare	84	31	3	3	3	3	7
Mobile Logistics Ships	75	60	48	46	53	53	54
Support Forces	100	69	63	41	45	52	54
Mobilization Forces	50	6	4	6	12	14	18
Auxiliaries and Sealift	59	19	14	15	96	118	132
Mobilization Forces, secondary	39	49	57	44	24	20	21
U.S. Navy Aircraft, operating	7,103	5,658	4,931	4,436	4,439	5,032	5,147
Marine Corps Divisions	4	3	3	3	3	3	3

* Planned strength.

WORLDWIDE U.S. MILITARY STRENGTH: 1984

Source: U.S. Department of Defense; date for Sept. 30, 1984.

REGION/COUNTRY	TOTAL	ARMY	NAVY	MARINE CORPS	AIR FORCE
U.S. TERRITORY	1,627,427	516,914	474,739	166,487	469,287
Continental U.S.	1,318,968	468,328	270,163	149,107	431,370
Alaska	20,662	8,098	1,586	212	10,766
Hawaii	47,648	19,222	12,960	8,703	6,763
Guam	9,175	37	4,715	377	4,046
Johnston Atoll	140	133	0	0	7
Puerto Rico	3,877	474	3,181	178	44
Trust Territory of Pacific	102	59	30	0	13
Transients	58,362	20,552	13,629	7,910	16,271
Afloat	168,462	0	168,462	0	0
WESTERN AND SOUTHERN EUROPE	351,683	222,028	37,329	3,148	89,178
Belgium*	2,484	1,354	121	30	979
Britain	28,823	213	2,291	348	25,971
Denmark*	58	8	18	10	22
France*	73	15	11	36	11
Germany, West	253,722	213,276	341	93	40,012
Greece*	3,711	523	470	13	2,705
Greenland*	329	0	0	0	329
Iceland*	3,117	2	1,839	106	1,170
Italy*	14,809	4,359	4,790	257	5,403
Netherlands*	2,823	835	15	10	1,963
Norway*	226	43	42	17	124
Portugal*	1,705	64	396	10	1,235
Spain*	9,436	20	4,012	214	5,190
Switzerland	44	20	0	21	3
Turkey*	5,449	1,278	101	18	4,052
Afloat	24,782	0	22,875	1,907	0
EAST ASIA AND PACIFIC	121,299	32,028	29,326	24,286	35,659
Australia	746	9	434	10	293
Hong Kong	42	11	15	11	5
Indonesia	47	11	14	11	11
Japan (including Okinawa)	45,761	2,646	7,504	20,643	14,968
New Zealand	68	4	48	5	11
Philippines	15,319	45	5,332	665	9,277
Korea, South	40,785	29,221	373	133	11,058
Thailand	105	55	9	14	27
Afloat	18,338	0	15,578	2,760	0
AFRICA AND SOUTH ASIA	16,997	1,371	14,684	530	412
Bahrain	98	4	93	0	1
British Indian Ocean Territory	1,253	0	1,239	0	14
Egypt	1,048	913	26	25	84
India	32	5	3	19	5
Israel	77	23	9	26	19
Jordan	29	16	0	8	5
Kenya	39	9	2	19	9
Morocco	54	17	4	18	15
Pakistan	34	7	2	18	7
Saudi Arabia	537	249	63	20	205
Afloat	13,353	0	13,223	130	0
WESTERN HEMISPHERE	20,094	7,672	8,341	1,675	2,406
Antigua	77	2	74	0	1
Bahamas	45	1	21	7	16
Bermuda	1,493	0	1,404	89	0
Brazil	48	12	7	22	7
Canada	542	17	395	9	121
Colombia	33	12	2	13	6
Cuba (Guantanamo)	2,347	0	1,889	456	2
El Salvador	51	25	0	23	3
Grenada	165	159	0	6	0
Honduras	846	747	2	88	9
Mexico	32	11	3	12	6
Panama	9,354	6,620	391	156	2,187
Venezuela	37	5	6	8	18
Afloat	4,787	0	4,124	663	0
ANTARCTICA	65	0	65	0	0
EASTERN EUROPE	179	67	5	88	19
Germany, East	48	42	0	6	0
Soviet Union	51	8	4	33	6
TOTAL FOREIGN COUNTRIES	510,730	263,266	89,899	29,727	127,838
TOTAL WORLDWIDE	2,138,157	780,180	564,638	196,214	597,125

1 Countries shown are those where over 30 U.S. military personnel are stationed.

WORLD MILITARY EXPENDITURES AND SIZE OF ARMED FORCES

Source: U.S. Arms Control and Disarmament Agency, data for 1983, except otherwise footnoted.

NATIONS	MILITARY EXPENDITURES	ARMED FORCES	NATIONS	MILITARY EXPENDITURES	ARMED FORCES
WORLD TOTAL	$811,900,000,000	28,355,000	Korea, South	$4,717,000,000	602,000
Afghanistan	198,000,000[1]	75,000[2]	Kuwait	1,173,000,000[1]	13,000
Albania	188,000,000[3]	42,000	Laos	50,000,000[6]	46,000
Algeria	1,334,000,000[1]	130,000	Lebanon	437,000,000	25,000
Angola	155,800,000[1]	54,000	Liberia	27,000,000	5,000
Argentina	1,523,000,000	175,000	Libya	4,223,000,000[1]	68,000
Australia	4,637,000,000	73,000	Luxembourg	44,000,000	1,000
Austria	937,000,000	50,000	Madagascar	61,000,000[1]	29,000
Bahrain	168,000,000	2,000	Malawi	23,000,000[1]	6,000
Bangladesh	290,000,000	81,000	Malaysia	1,432,000,000[1]	105,000
Barbados	8,000,000[4]	1,000	Mali..............	30,000,000	11,000
Belgium	2,911,000,000	109,000	Malta.............	15,000,000[1]	1,000
Benin	20,000,000	7,000	Mauritania	40,000,000[1]	16,000
Bolivia	100,000,000[4]	27,000	Mauritius	2,000,000	1,000
Botswana	26,000,000	3,000	Mexico	872,000,000[1]	131,000
Brazil	1,769,000,000[1]	460,000	Morocco	1,318,000,000	135,000
Britain	27,444,000,000	333,000	Mozambique	172,000,000[4]	32,000
Bulgaria	4,282,000,000[1]	177,000	Nepal	27,000,000[1]	25,000
Burkina Faso	33,000,000	9,000	Netherlands	4,673,000,000	104,000
Burma............	209,000,000[1]	210,000	New Zealand	519,000,000	13,000
Burundi	41,000,000[1]	7,000	Nicaragua	272,000,000[1]	46,000
Cambodia	67,000,000[5]	20,000	Niger	12,000,000[1]	5,000
Cameroon	160,000,000	15,000	Nigeria	1,723,000,000	222,000
Canada	6,439,000,000	81,000	Norway	1,844,000,000	41,000
Cape Verde	13,000,000[3]	4,000	Oman	1,944,000,000	20,000
Central Africa	13,000,000	4,000	Pakistan	1,984,000,000[1]	584,000
Chad	6,000,000	4,000	Panama	60,000,000[1]	11,000
Chile	1,021,000,000	126,000	Papua New Guinea .	30,000,000	3,000
China	34,500,000,000[1]	4,100,000	Paraguay	89,000,000[1]	16,000
Colombia	456,000,000	70,000	Peru	1,065,000,000[1]	167,000
Congo	79,000,000	11,000	Philippines	771,000,000[1]	157,000
Costa Rica	17,000,000[1]	4,000	Poland	12,282,000,000[1]	430,000
Cuba	1,306,000,000	250,000	Portugal	814,000,000	93,000
Cyprus	83,000,000[1]	10,000	Qatar	604,000,000[2]	6,000
Czechoslovakia	7,157,000,000[1]	214,000	Romania	5,159,000,000	244,000
Denmark	1,482,000,000	30,000	Rwanda	21,000,000[1]	5,000
Dominican Republic	122,000,000[1]	23,000	Saudi Arabia	27,192,000,000	55,000
Ecuador	184,000,000[1]	39,000	Senegal	60,000,000[1]	18,000
Egypt	2,679,000,000[1]	447,000	Sierra Leone	11,000,000	6,000
El Salvador	150,000,000[1]	28,000	Singapore.........	955,000,000[1]	60,000
Ethiopia	381,000,000[1,4]	199,000	Somalia	114,000,000	48,000
Fiji	14,000,000[4]	2,000	South Africa	3,132,000,000[1]	77,000
Finland	785,000,000[1]	40,000	Soviet Union	258,000,000,000	4,400,000
France	23,793,000,000	578,000	Spain	4,070,000,000	340,000
Gabon	79,000,000	7,000	Sri Lanka	76,000,000	19,000
Germany, East	9,806,000,000[1]	240,000	Sudan	180,000,000[1]	86,000
Germany, West	23,565,000,000	496,000	Swaziland.........	18,000,000[1]	3,000
Ghana...........	213,000,000[4]	8,000	Sweden	3,332,000,000	68,000
Greece	2,526,000,000	177,000	Switzerland	1,961,000,000[1]	28,000
Guatemala	209,000,000[1]	19,000	Syria	2,138,000,000[1]	222,000
Guinea	51,000,000[1]	52,000	Taiwan	3,925,000,000[1]	454,000
Guinea–Bissau	9,000,000[4]	9,000	Tanzania	122,000,000[1]	43,000
Guyana	23,000,000[1]	7,000	Thailand	1,539,000,000	250,000
Haiti	24,000,000	8,000	Togo	17,000,000	6,000
Honduras	47,000,000[6]	14,000	Trinidad–Tobago ..	232,000,000[1]	2,000
Hungary	3,134,000,000[1]	105,000	Tunisia	256,000,000[1]	28,000
India	6,546,000,000[1]	1,120,000	Turkey	2,840,000,000	824,000
Indonesia	2,649,000,000[1]	280,000	Uganda	61,000,000	13,000
Iran	5,520,000,000[1]	470,000	United Arab Emirates	1,867,000,000	49,000
Iraq	11,900,000,000[1]	500,000	UNITED STATES ...	217,154,000,000	2,222,000
Ireland	303,000,000[1]	18,000	Uruguay	283,000,000	30,000
Israel............	6,229,000,000[1]	180,000	Venezuela	920,000,000	56,000
Italy.............	9,609,000,000	498,000	Vietnam	N.A.	1,200,000
Ivory Coast	85,000,000[1]	14,000	Yemen, North	599,000,000	22,000
Jamaica	37,000,000	3,000	Yemen, South	179,000,000	25,000
Japan	11,500,000,000	241,000	Yugoslavia	2,309,000,000	259,000
Jordan	645,000,000[1]	68,000	Zaire	82,000,000[1]	42,000
Kenya	138,000,000	18,000	Zambia	461,000,000[1,2]	16,000
Korea, North	3,600,000,000[1]	784,000	Zimbabwe	403,000,000[1]	46,000

[1] Estimated. [2] 1980. [3] 1981. [4] 1982. [5] 1975. [6] 1979. N.A.=Not Available.

U.S. ARMED FORCES IN MAJOR CONFLICTS

Source: U.S. Department of Defense

The military services of the U.S. have taken part in nine major wars in which nearly 650,000 American military personnel were killed in action.

More American men and women served in the armed services in World War II than in any other war—over 16 million. More were killed or wounded in that war than in any other—more than 1 million.

The Continental Army was first formed by order of the Continental Congress on June 15, 1775, with George Washington as commander in chief. A Continental Navy

was formed by the Continental Congress on Dec. 22, 1775, with the appointment of Esek Hopkins as its commander. Various congressional committees and boards maintained civilian control over the armed forces during the early part of the Revolutionary War.

The first secretary of war, Maj. Gen. Benjamin Lincoln, was appointed by Congress on Oct. 30, 1781.

The Department of Defense, created by Congress in 1949, provides civilian administration of the armed services. The secretary of defense is a cabinet-level officer.

WARS	BRANCH OF SERVICE	NUMBER SERVING	MILITARY CASUALTIES Total	Deaths in Action	Other Deaths	Nonfatal Wounds
Revolutionary War	Total	184,000 to 250,000	10,623	4,435	—	6,188
1775–1783	Army	—	10,048	4,044	—	6,004
	Navy	—	456	342	—	114
	Marines	—	119	49	—	70
War of 1812	Total	286,730	6,765	2,260	—	4,505
1812–1815	Army	—	5,950	1,950	—	4,000
	Navy	—	704	265	—	439
	Marines	—	111	45	—	66
Mexican War	Total	78,718	17,435	1,733	11,550	4,152
1846–1848	Army	—	17,373	1,721	11,550	4,102
	Navy	—	4	1	—	3
	Marines	—	58	11	—	47
Civil War	Union Forces	2,213,363	646,392	140,414	224,097	281,881
1861–1865	Army	2,128,948	639,568	138,154	221,374	280,040
	Navy	84,415	6,233	2,112	2,411	1,710
	Marines		591	148	312	131
	Confederate Forces [1]	600,000 to 1,500,000	159,821 to 164,821 +	74,524	85,297 to 90,297	—
Spanish-American War	Total	306,760	4,108	385	2,061	1,662
1898	Army	280,564	4,024	369	2,061	1,594
	Navy	22,875	57	10	—	47
	Marines	3,321	27	6	—	21
World War I	Total	4,734,991	320,518	53,402	63,114	204,002
1917–1918	Army	4,057,101	300,041	50,510	55,868	193,663
	Navy	599,051	8,106	431	6,856	819
	Marines	78,839	12,371	2,461	390	9,520
World War II	Total	16,112,566	1,076,245	291,557	113,842	670,846
1941–1945	Army	11,260,000	884,135	234,874	83,400	565,861
	Navy	4,183,466	100,392	36,950	25,664	37,778
	Marines	669,100	91,718	19,733	4,778	67,207
Korean War	Total	5,720,000	157,530	33,629	20,617	103,284
1950–1953	Army	2,834,000	114,729	27,704	9,429	77,596
	Navy	1,177,000	6,077	458	4,043	1,576
	Marines	424,000	29,272	4,267	1,261	23,744
	Air Force	1,285,000	7,452	1,200	5,884	368
Vietnam War	Total	8,744,000	211,005	47,321	10,700	153,303
1961–1973	Army	4,368,000	134,921	30,899	7,271	96,802
	Navy [2]	1,842,000	6,694	1,611	915	4,178
	Marines	794,000	66,141	13,073	1,748	51,392
	Air Force	1,740,000	3,249	1,738	766	931

[1] Other deaths include 26,000 to 31,000 Confederates who died in Union prisons. [2] Includes small number of Coast Guard casualties.

Nations of the World

LARGEST NATIONS IN POPULATION

RANK	NATION	POPULATION[1]	LOCATION	RANK	NATION	POPULATION[1]	LOCATION
1	China	1,053,610,000	Asia	46	Iraq	15,825,000	Asia
2	India	770,064,000	Asia	47	Malaysia	15,793,000	Southeast Asia
3	Soviet Union	277,996,000	Europe-Asia	48	Australia	15,765,000	South Pacific
4	United States	239,855,000	North America	49	Uganda	15,559,000	Africa
5	Indonesia	175,075,000	Southeast Asia	50	Czechoslovakia	15,536,000	Europe
6	Brazil	137,610,000	South America	51	Afghanistan	15,000,000	Asia
7	Japan	120,977,000	Asia	52	Mozambique	14,546,000	Africa
8	Pakistan	100,429,000	Asia	53	Netherlands	14,524,000	Europe
9	Bangladesh	100,206,000	Asia	54	Ghana	13,711,000	Africa
10	Nigeria	93,324,000	Africa	55	Chile	12,305,000	South America
11	Mexico	80,490,000	North America	56	Saudi Arabia	11,667,000	Asia
12	Germany, West	61,385,000	Europe	57	Hungary	10,676,000	Europe
13	Vietnam	60,338,000	Southeast Asia	58	Syria	10,422,000	Asia
14	Philippines	57,458,000	Southeast Asia	59	Ivory Coast	10,287,000	Africa
15	Italy	57,255,000	Europe	60	Madagascar	10,150,000	Indian Ocean
16	Britain	56,050,000	Europe	61	Cuba	10,143,000	Caribbean
17	France	55,202,000	Europe	62	Greece	10,120,000	Europe
18	Thailand	53,396,000	Southeast Asia	63	Portugal	10,105,000	Europe
19	Egypt	50,055,000	Africa	64	Cameroon	10,016,000	Africa
20	Turkey	49,686,000	Europe-Turkey	65	Belgium	9,887,000	Europe
21	Iran	45,901,000	Asia	66	Ecuador	9,663,000	South America
22	Korea, South	42,949,000	Asia	67	Bulgaria	9,010,000	Europe
23	Spain	38,709,000	Europe	68	Angola	8,959,000	Africa
24	Poland	37,386,000	Europe	69	Sweden	8,339,000	Europe
25	Burma	37,290,000	Southeast Asia	70	Zimbabwe	8,315,000	Africa
26	Ethiopia	33,680,000	Africa	71	Guatemala	8,249,000	Central America
27	Zaire	33,467,000	Africa	72	Mali	8,009,000	Africa
28	Argentina	31,008,000	South America	73	Austria	7,590,000	Europe
29	Colombia	28,350,000	South America	74	Tunisia	7,362,000	North Africa
30	South Africa	26,674,000	Africa	75	Burkina Faso	6,960,000	Africa
31	Canada	25,600,000	North America	76	Senegal	6,902,000	Africa
32	Yugoslavia	23,321,000	Europe	77	Malawi	6,857,000	Africa
33	Morocco	22,893,000	North Africa	78	Zambia	6,788,000	Africa
34	Romania	22,853,000	Europe	79	Bolivia	6,744,000	South America
35	Algeria	22,078,000	North Africa	80	Switzerland	6,596,000	Europe
36	Tanzania	22,054,000	Africa	81	Yemen, North	6,565,000	Asia
37	Sudan	21,677,000	Africa	82	Dominican Republic	6,390,000	Caribbean
38	Kenya	20,777,000	Africa	83	Rwanda	6,305,000	Africa
39	Korea, North	20,312,000	Asia	84	Cambodia	6,303,000	SE Asia
40	Peru	20,166,000	South America	85	Somalia	6,027,000	Africa
41	Venezuela	19,617,000	South America	86	Haiti	6,000,000	Caribbean
42	Taiwan	19,607,000	Asia	87	Niger	5,874,000	Africa
43	Nepal	17,205,000	Asia	88	El Salvador	5,857,000	Central America
44	Germany, East	16,720,000	Europe	89	Guinea	5,467,000	Africa
45	Sri Lanka	16,042,000	Indian Ocean	90	Denmark	5,110,000	Europe

SMALLEST NATIONS IN POPULATION

RANK	NATION	POPULATION[1]	LOCATION	RANK	NATION	POPULATION[1]	LOCATION
178	Vatican City	730	Europe	160	St. Lucia	121,000	Caribbean
177	Nauru	8,100	South Pacific	159	Vanuatu	135,300	South Pacific
176	Tuvalu	8,200	South Pacific	158	St. Vincent	146,500	Caribbean
175	Belau	14,000	South Pacific	157	Belize	165,600	Central America
174	San Marino	23,600	Europe	156	Western Samoa	168,300	South Pacific
173	Liechtenstein	27,700	Europe	155	Maldives	181,000	Indian Ocean
172	Monaco	28,500	Europe	154	Brunei	231,000	Southeast Asia
171	Marshalls	36,000	South Pacific	153	Bahamas	232,000	Caribbean
170	St. Christopher and Nevis	44,000	Caribbean	152	Iceland	240,000	North Atlantic
169	Andorra	48,700	Europe	151	Barbados	254,500	Caribbean
168	Kiribati	62,500	South Pacific	150	Solomons	284,400	South Pacific
167	Seychelles	65,800	Indian Ocean	149	Qatar	290,000	Asia
166	Dominica	74,000	Caribbean	148	Equatorial Guinea	310,000	Africa
165	Antigua	80,800	Caribbean	147	Djibouti	330,000	Africa
164	Micronesia	85,000	South Pacific	146	Malta	353,000	Mediterranean
163	São Tomé-Príncipe	96,200	South Atlantic	145	Cape Verde	362,000	Africa
162	Tonga	108,700	South Pacific	144	Luxembourg	366,700	Europe
161	Grenada	115,000	Caribbean	143	Suriname	386,000	South America

[1] Jan. 1, 1986, population estimates.

SMALLEST NATIONS IN POPULATION *(continued)*

RANK	NATION	POPULATION[1]	LOCATION	RANK	NATION	POPULATION[1]	LOCATION
142	Venda	417,400	Africa	116	Yemen, South	2,329,800	Asia
141	Bahrain	434,000	Asia	115	Costa Rica	2,525,000	Central America
140	Comoros	458,000	Indian Ocean	114	Singapore	2,578,000	SE Asia
139	Swaziland	651,500	Africa	113	Central Africa	2,630,000	Africa
138	Cyprus	675,000	Mediterranean	112	Lebanon	2,640,000	Asia
137	Ciskei	691,200	Africa	111	Jamaica	2,689,000	Caribbean
136	Fiji	708,000	South Pacific	110	Jordan	2,844,000	Asia
135	Gambia	738,300	Africa	109	Togo	2,996,000	Africa
134	Guyana	845,000	South America	108	Albania	3,000,000	Europe
133	Guinea-Bissau	934,000	Africa	107	Transkei	3,008,500	Africa
132	Mauritius	1,031,000	Indian Ocean	106	Uruguay	3,028,000	South America
131	Oman	1,056,000	Asia	105	New Zealand	3,292,000	South Pacific
130	Botswana	1,111,000	Africa	104	Paraguay	3,366,000	South America
129	Trinidad-Tobago	1,225,000	Caribbean	103	Nicaragua	3,391,000	Central America
128	Gabon	1,256,000	Africa	102	Papua New Guinea	3,495,000	South Pacific
127	United Arab Emirates	1,390,000	Asia	101	Ireland	3,640,000	Europe
126	Bhutan	1,464,000	Asia	100	Libya	3,721,000	North Africa
125	Lesotho	1,536,000	Africa	99	Laos	3,862,000	SE Asia
124	Namibia	1,600,000	Africa	98	Sierra Leone	3,949,000	Africa
123	Bophuthatswana	1,653,000	Africa	97	Benin	3,967,000	Africa
122	Cougo	1,852,000	Africa	96	Norway	4,170,000	Europe
121	Kuwait	1,925,000	Asia	95	Israel	4,318,000	Asia
120	Mongolia	1,938,000	Asia	94	Honduras	4,700,000	Central America
119	Mauritania	1,939,000	Africa	93	Burundi	4,727,000	Africa
118	Liberia	2,226,000	Africa	92	Finland	4,901,000	Europe
117	Panama	2,257,000	Central America	91	Chad	5,037,000	Africa

LARGEST NATIONS IN AREA

RANK	NATION	AREA (sq. mi.)	LOCATION	RANK	NATION	AREA (sq. mi.)	LOCATION
1	Soviet Union	8,649,538	Europe-Asia	26	Bolivia	424,165	South America
2	Canada	3,849,670	North America	27	Mauritania	397,955	Africa
3	China	3,692,950	Asia	28	Egypt	386,900	Africa
4	United States	3,618,770	North America	29	Tanzania	364,900	Africa
5	Brazil	3,286,488	South America	30	Nigeria	356,669	Africa
6	Australia	2,967,909	South Pacific	31	Venezuela	352,145	South America
7	India	1,269,346	Asia	32	Namibia	318,261	Africa
8	Argentina	1,068,301	South America	33	Pakistan	310,404	Asia
9	Sudan	967,500	Africa	34	Mozambique	309,496	Africa
10	Algeria	919,595	North Africa	35	Turkey	301,382	Europe-Asia
11	Zaire	905,568	Africa	36	Chile	292,258	South America
12	Saudi Arabia	830,000	Asia	37	Zambia	290,586	Africa
13	Indonesia	782,662	Southeast Asia	38	Morocco	275,117	Africa
14	Mexico	761,605	North America	39	Burma	261,218	Asia
15	Libya	679,362	Africa	40	Afghanistan	250,000	Asia
16	Iran	636,296	Asia	41	Somalia	246,201	Africa
17	Mongolia	604,250	Asia	42	Central Africa	240,535	Africa
18	Peru	496,225	South America	43	Botswana	231,805	Africa
19	Chad	495,755	Africa	44	Madagascar	226,658	Indian Ocean
20	Niger	489,191	Africa	45	Kenya	224,961	Africa
21	Angola	481,354	Africa	46	France	211,208	Europe
22	Mali	478,767	Africa	47	Thailand	198,457	Southeast Asia
23	Ethiopia	471,778	Africa	48	Spain	194,897	Europe
24	Colombia	439,737	South America	49	Cameroon	183,569	Africa
25	South Africa	434,674	Africa	50	Papua New Guinea	178,260	South Pacific

SMALLEST NATIONS IN AREA

RANK	NATION	AREA (sq. mi.)	LOCATION	RANK	NATION	AREA (sq. mi.)	LOCATION
178	Vatican City	0.17	Europe	165	Seychelles	171	Indian Ocean
177	Monaco	0.58	Europe	164	Antigua	171	Caribbean
176	Nauru	8	South Pacific	163	Andorra	175	Europe
175	Tuvalu	10	South Pacific	162	Belau	191	South Pacific
174	San Marino	23.6	Europe	161	Singapore	224	Asia
173	Liechetenstein	61	Europe	160	St. Lucia	238	Caribbean
172	Marshalls	70	South Pacific	159	Bahrain	258	Asia
171	St. Christopher and Nevis	101	Caribbean	158	Tonga	270	South Pacific
170	Maldives	115	Indian Ocean	157	Micronesia	271	South Pacific
169	Malta	122	Mediterranean	156	Kiribati	278	South Pacific
168	Grenada	133	Caribbean	155	Dominica	290	Caribbean
167	St. Vincent	150	Caribbean	154	São-Tomé Príncipe	372	South Atlantic
166	Barbados	166	Caribbean	153	Comoros	694	Indian Ocean

[1] Jan. 1, 1986, population estimates.

SMALLEST NATIONS IN AREA *(continued)*

RANK	NATION	AREA (sq. mi.)	LOCATION	RANK	NATION	AREA (sq. mi.)	LOCATION
152	Mauritius	790	Indian Ocean	140	Gambia	4,361	Africa
151	Luxembourg......	998	Europe	139	Bahamas........	5,380	Caribbean
150	Western Samoa ...	1,097	South Pacific	138	Vanuatu	5,700	South Pacific
149	Cape Verde.......	1,557	Africa	137	Swaziland	6,704	Africa
148	Trinidad-Tobago ..	1,981	Caribbean	136	Kuwait..........	6,880	Asia
147	Brunei	2,226	Southeast Asia	135	Fiji	7,056	South Pacific
146	Venda	2,510	Africa	134	El Salvador	8,124	Central America
145	Ciskei	3,205	Africa	133	Djibouti	8,494	Africa
144	Cyprus	3,572	Mediterranean	132	Belize...........	8,867	Central America
143	Lebanon	4,015	Asia	131	Rwanda	10,169	Africa
142	Jamaica	4,244	Caribbean	130	Haiti............	10,714	Caribbean
141	Qatar...........	4,247	Asia	129	Israel	10,715	Asia

POPULATIONS[1] OF CONTINENTS

Africa	570,500,000	Asia	3,152,600,000
North America....................	405,100,000	Europe	492,900,000
South America...................	275,200,000	Australia and Oceania	24,000,000

178 NATIONS OF THE WORLD: LOCATION, AREA, POPULATION, CAPITALS

NATION	LOCATION	AREA In Sq. Mi.	Rank	POPULATION[1] Total	Rank	Per Sq. Mi.	CAPITAL
WORLD	—	57,506,000	—	4,885,000,000	—	84.9	New York (UN)
Afghanistan	Asia	250,000	40	15,000,000	51	60.0	Kabul
Albania	Europe	11,100	126	3,000,000	108	270.3	Tiranë
Algeria.............	North Africa	919,595	10	22,078,000	35	24.0	Algiers
Andorra............	Europe	175	163	48,700	169	278.3	Andorra la Vella
Angola.............	Africa	481,354	21	8,959,000	68	18.6	Luanda
Antigua............	Caribbean	171	164	80,800	165	472.5	St. John's
Argentina	South America	1,068,301	8	31,008,000	28	29.0	Buenos Aires
Australia	South Pacific	2,967,909	6	15,765,000	48	5.3	Canberra
Austria	Europe	32,374	106	7,590,000	73	234.4	Vienna
Bahamas...........	Caribbean	5,380	139	232,000	153	43.1	Nassau
Bahrain	Asia	258	159	434,000	141	1,682.2	Manama
Bangladesh	Asia	55,598	87	100,206,000	9	1,802.3	Dhaka
Barbados	Caribbean	166	166	254,500	151	1,533.1	Bridgetown
Belau	South Pacific	191	162	14,000	175	73.3	Koror
Belgium............	Europe	11,781	123	9,887,000	65	839.2	Brussels
Belize.............	Central America	8,867	132	165,600	157	18.7	Belmopan
Benin	Africa	43,484	95	3,967,000	97	91.2	Porto Novo
Bhutan	Asia	18,147	115	1,464,000	126	80.7	Thimphu
Bolivia	South America	424,165	26	6,744,000	79	15.9	La Paz; Sucre
Bophuthatswana	Africa	17,010	116	1,653,500	123	97.2	Mmabatho
Botswana	Africa	231,805	43	1,111,000	130	4.8	Gaborone
Brazil.............	South America	3,286,488	5	137,610,000	6	41.8	Brasilia
Britain	Europe	94,515	73	56,050,000	16	593.0	London
Brunei	SE Asia	2,226	147	231,000	154	103.8	Bandar Seri Begawan
Bulgaria	Europe	42,823	98	9,010,000	67	210.4	Sofia
Burkina Faso	Africa	105,869	67	6,960,000	75	65.7	Ouagadougou
Burma	Asia	261,218	39	37,290,000	25	142.8	Rangoon
Burundi	Africa	10,747	128	4,727,000	93	439.8	Bujumbura
Cambodia	SE Asia	69,898	83	6,303,000	84	90.2	Phnom Penh
Cameroon	Africa	183,569	49	10,016,000	64	54.6	Yaoundé
Canada	North America	3,849,670	2	25,600,000	31	6.6	Ottawa
Cape Verde.........	Africa	1,557	149	362,000	145	232.5	Praia
Central Africa	Africa	240,535	42	2,630,000	113	10.9	Bangui
Chad	Africa	495,755	19	5,037,000	91	10.2	N'Djaména
Chile	South America	292,258	36	12,305,000	55	40.2	Santiago
China	Asia	3,692,950	3	1,053,610,000	1	285.3	Peking
Ciskei	Africa	3,205	145	691,200	137	215.7	Bisho
Colombia	South America	439,737	24	28,350,000	29	64.5	Bogotá
Comoros	Indian Ocean	694	153	458,000	140	659.9	Moroni
Congo	Africa	132,047	56	1,852,000	122	14.0	Brazzaville
Costa Rica	Central America	19,575	113	2,525,000	115	129.0	San José
Cuba	Caribbean	44,218	94	10,143,000	61	229.4	Havana
Cyprus	Mediterranean	3,572	144	675,000	138	189.0	Nicosia
Czechoslovakia	Europe	49,371	91	15,536,000	50	314.7	Prague

[1] Jan. 1, 1986, population estimates.

LOCATION, AREA, POPULATION, CAPITALS (continued)

NATION	LOCATION	AREA In Sq. Mi.	Rank	POPULATION[1] Total	Rank	Per Sq. Mi.	CAPITAL
Denmark	Europe	16,629	117	5,110,000	90	307.2	Copenhagen
Djibouti	Africa	8,494	133	330,000	147	38.9	Djibouti
Dominica	Caribbean	290	155	74,000	166	255.2	Roseau
Dominican Republic	Caribbean	18,816	114	6,390,000	82	339.6	Santo Domingo
Ecuador	South America	109,484	66	9,663,000	66	88.3	Quito
Egypt	Africa	386,900	28	50,055,000	19	129.4	Cairo
El Salvador	Central America	8,124	134	5,857,000	88	721.0	San Salvador
Equatorial Guinea	Africa	10,831	127	310,000	148	28.6	Malabo
Ethiopia	Africa	471,778	23	33,680,000	26	71.4	Addis Ababa
Fiji	South Pacific	7,056	135	708,000	136	100.3	Suva
Finland	Europe	130,120	57	4,901,000	92	37.7	Helsinki
France	Europe	211,208	46	55,202,000	17	261.4	Paris
Gabon	Africa	103,347	69	1,256,000	128	12.2	Libreville
Gambia	Africa	4,361	140	738,300	135	169.3	Banjul
Germany, East	Europe	41,768	100	16,720,000	44	400.3	East Berlin
Germany, West	Europe	95,976	71	61,385,000	12	639.6	Bonn
Ghana	Africa	92,100	74	13,711,000	54	148.8	Accra
Greece	Europe	50,944	89	10,120,000	62	198.6	Athens
Grenada	Caribbean	133	168	115,000	161	864.7	St. George's
Guatemala	Central America	42,042	99	8,249,000	71	196.2	Guatemala City
Guinea	Africa	94,926	72	5,467,000	89	57.6	Conakry
Guinea–Bissau	Africa	13,948	121	934,000	133	66.9	Bissau
Guyana	South America	83,000	78	845,000	134	10.2	Georgetown
Haiti	Caribbean	10,714	130	6,000,000	86	560.0	Port-au-Prince
Honduras	Central America	43,277	96	4,700,000	94	108.6	Tegucigalpa
Hungary	Europe	35,919	104	10,676,000	57	297.2	Budapest
Iceland	North Atlantic	39,768	101	240,000	152	6.0	Reykjavík
India	Asia	1,269,346	7	770,064,000	2	606.6	New Delhi
Indonesia	SE Asia	782,662	13	175,075,000	5	223.7	Jakarta
Iran	Asia	636,296	16	45,901,000	21	72.1	Teheran
Iraq	Asia	167,925	52	15,825,000	46	94.2	Baghdad
Ireland	Europe	27,136	110	3,640,000	101	134.1	Dublin
Israel	Asia	10,715	129	4,318,000	95	403.0	Jerusalem
Italy	Europe	116,304	64	57,255,000	15	492.3	Rome
Ivory Coast	Africa	124,504	62	10,287,000	59	82.6	Yamoussoukro
Jamaica	Caribbean	4,244	142	2,689,000	111	633.6	Kingston
Japan	Asia	145,809	55	120,977,000	7	829.7	Tokyo
Jordan	Asia	37,738	103	2,844,000	110	75.4	Amman
Kenya	Africa	224,961	45	20,777,000	38	92.4	Nairobi
Kiribati	South Pacific	278	156	62,500	168	224.8	Bairiki, Tarawa
Korea, North	Asia	46,540	92	20,312,000	39	436.4	Pyongyang
Korea, South	Asia	38,025	102	42,949,000	22	1,129.5	Seoul
Kuwait	Asia	6,880	136	1,925,000	121	279.8	Kuwait
Laos	SE Asia	91,429	76	3,862,000	99	42.2	Vientiane
Lebanon	Asia	4,015	143	2,640,000	112	657.5	Beirut
Lesotho	Africa	11,720	124	1,536,000	125	131.1	Maseru
Liberia	Africa	43,000	97	2,226,000	118	51.8	Monrovia
Libya	North Africa	679,362	15	3,721,000	100	5.5	Tripoli
Liechtenstein	Europe	61	173	27,700	173	454.1	Vaduz
Luxembourg	Europe	998	151	366,700	144	367.4	Luxembourg-Ville
Madagascar	Indian Ocean	226,658	44	10,150,000	60	44.8	Antananarivo
Malawi	Africa	45,747	93	6,857,000	77	149.9	Lilongwe
Malaysia	SE Asia	127,317	59	15,793,000	47	124.0	Kuala Lumpur
Maldives	Indian Ocean	115	170	181,000	155	1,573.9	Male
Mali	Africa	478,767	22	8,009,000	72	16.7	Bamako
Malta	Mediterranean	122	169	353,000	146	2,893.4	Valletta
Marshalls	South Pacific	70	172	36,000	171	514.3	Majuro
Mauritania	Africa	397,955	27	1,939,000	119	4.9	Nouakchott
Mauritius	Indian Ocean	790	152	1,031,000	132	1,305.1	Port-Louis
Mexico	North America	761,605	14	80,490,000	11	105.7	Mexico City
Micronesia	South Pacific	271	157	85,000	164	313.7	Kolonia
Monaco	Europe	0.58	177	28,500	172	49,137.9	Monaco-Ville
Mongolia	Asia	604,250	17	1,938,000	120	3.2	Ulaanbaatar
Morocco	North Africa	275,117	38	22,893,000	33	83.2	Rabat
Mozambique	Africa	309,496	34	14,546,000	52	47.0	Maputo
Namibia	Africa	318,261	32	1,600,000	124	5.0	Windhoek
Nauru	South Pacific	8	176	8,100	177	1,012.5	Yaren
Nepal	Asia	54,362	88	17,205,000	43	316.5	Kathmandu
Netherlands	Europe	15,770	120	14,524,000	53	921.0	Amsterdam; The Hague

[1] Jan. 1, 1986, population estimates.

LOCATION, AREA, POPULATION, CAPITALS *(continued)*

NATION	LOCATION	AREA In Sq. Mi.	Rank	POPULATION[1] Total	Rank	Per Sq. Mi.	CAPITAL
New Zealand	South Pacific	103,736	68	3,292,000	105	31.7	Wellington
Nicaragua	Central America	50,193	90	3,391,000	103	67.6	Managua
Niger	Africa	489,191	20	5,874,000	87	12.0	Niamey
Nigeria	Africa	356,669	30	93,324,000	10	261.7	Abuja
Norway	Europe	125,182	61	4,170,000	96	33.3	Oslo
Oman	Asia	82,030	79	1,056,000	131	12.9	Muscat
Pakistan	Asia	310,404	33	100,429,000	8	323.5	Islamabad
Panama	Central America	29,762	108	2,257,000	117	75.8	Panama City
Papua New Guinea	South Pacific	178,260	50	3,495,000	102	19.6	Port Moresby
Paraguay	South America	157,048	53	3,366,000	104	21.4	Asunción
Peru	South America	496,225	18	20,166,000	40	40.6	Lima
Philippines	SE Asia	115,830	65	57,458,000	14	496.1	Manila
Poland	Europe	120,725	63	37,386,000	24	309.7	Warsaw
Portugal	Europe	35,553	105	10,105,000	63	284.2	Lisbon
Qatar	Asia	4,247	141	290,000	149	68.3	Doha
Romania	Europe	91,699	75	22,853,000	34	249.2	Bucharest
Rwanda	Africa	10,169	131	6,305,000	83	620.0	Kigali
St. Christopher and Nevis	Caribbean	101	171	44,000	170	435.6	Basseterre
St. Lucia	Caribbean	238	160	121,000	160	508.4	Castries
St. Vincent	Caribbean	150	167	146,500	158	976.7	Kingstown
San Marino	Europe	23.6	174	23,600	174	1,000.0	San Marino
São Tomé–Príncipe	South Atlantic	372	154	96,200	163	258.6	São Tomé
Saudi Arabia	Asia	830,000	12	11,667,000	56	14.1	Riyadh
Senegal	Africa	75,750	80	6,902,000	76	91.1	Dakar
Seychelles	Indian Ocean	171	165	65,800	167	384.7	Port Victoria
Sierra Leone	Africa	27,699	109	3,949,000	98	142.6	Freetown
Singapore	SE Asia	224	161	2,578,000	114	11,508.9	Singapore
Solomons	South Pacific	11,500	125	284,400	150	24.7	Honiara
Somalia	Africa	246,201	41	6,027,000	85	24.5	Mogadishu
South Africa	Africa	434,674	25	26,674,000	30	61.3	Cape Town; Pretoria
Soviet Union	Europe–Asia	8,649,538	1	277,996,000	3	32.1	Moscow
Spain	Europe	194,897	48	38,709,000	23	198.6	Madrid
Sri Lanka	Indian Ocean	25,332	111	16,042,000	45	625.5	Colombo
Sudan	Africa	967,500	9	21,677,000	37	22.4	Khartoum
Suriname	South America	63,037	86	386,000	143	6.1	Paramaribo
Swaziland	Africa	6,704	137	651,500	139	97.2	Mbabane; Lobamba
Sweden	Europe	173,732	51	8,339,000	69	48.0	Stockholm
Switzerland	Europe	15,941	119	6,596,000	80	413.8	Bern
Syria	Asia	71,498	82	10,422,000	58	145.8	Damascus
Taiwan	Asia	13,892	122	19,607,000	42	1,411.4	Taipei
Tanzania	Africa	364,900	29	22,054,000	36	60.4	Dodoma; Dar es Salaam
Thailand	SE Asia	198,457	47	53,396,000	18	269.1	Bangkok
Togo	Africa	21,925	112	2,996,000	109	136.6	Lomé
Tonga	South Pacific	270	158	108,700	162	402.6	Nukualofa
Transkei	Africa	16,070	118	3,008,500	107	187.2	Umtata
Trinidad–Tobago	Caribbean	1,981	148	1,225,000	129	618.4	Port-of-Spain
Tunisia	North Africa	63,170	85	7,362,000	74	116.5	Tunis
Turkey	Europe–Asia	301,382	35	49,686,000	20	164.9	Ankara
Tuvalu	South Pacific	10	175	8,200	176	820.0	Fongafale
Uganda	Africa	91,134	77	15,559,000	49	170.7	Kampala
United Arab Emirates	Asia	32,278	107	1,390,000	127	43.1	Abu Dhabi
UNITED STATES	North America	3,618,770	4	239,855,000	4	66.3	Washington, D.C.
Uruguay	South America	68,037	84	3,028,000	106	44.5	Montevideo
Vanuatu	South Pacific	5,700	138	135,300	159	23.7	Port Vila
Vatican City	Europe	0.17	178	730	178	4,294.1	—
Venda	Africa	2,510	146	417,400	142	166.3	Thohoyandou
Venezuela	South America	352,145	31	19,617,000	41	55.7	Caracas
Vietnam	SE Asia	127,242	60	60,388,000	13	474.6	Hanoi
Western Samoa	South Pacific	1,097	150	168,300	156	153.4	Apia
Yemen, North	Asia	75,290	81	6,565,000	81	87.2	Sana
Yemen, South	Asia	128,560	58	2,329,800	116	18.1	Aden
Yugoslavia	Europe	98,766	70	23,321,000	32	236.1	Belgrade
Zaire	Africa	905,568	11	33,467,000	27	36.9	Kinshasa
Zambia	Africa	290,586	37	6,788,000	78	23.4	Lusaka
Zimbabwe	Africa	150,804	54	8,315,000	70	55.1	Harare

[1] Jan. 1, 1986, population estimates.

VITAL STATISTICS, EDUCATION, COMMUNICATIONS

NATION	VITAL STATISTICS					COMMUNICATIONS				
	Birth Rate[1]	Death Rate[1]	Infant Deaths[2]	Life Expectancy Men/Women	Urban Pop.	Literacy Rate[3]	Phones[1]	Radio Sets[1]	TV Sets[1]	News-papers[4]
WORLD	29.0	11.0	98.0	55.0	83.6%	—	191	6	0.7	4
Afghanistan	45.2	21.1	184.6	40.0/41.0	14.5%	12%	3	75	1.9	54
Albania	33.3	8.1	86.8	64.9/67.0	33.8%	75%	5	168	39	22
Algeria	47.4	14.2	125.3	54.4/56.3	52.0%	35%	25	219	113	250
Andorra	17.4	4.6	—	—	37.0%	100%	435	—	—	—
Angola	47.6	23.1	160.4	39.5/42.6	16.6%	15%	5	18	—	17
Antigua	16.5	5.6	31.5	60.5/64.3	33.8%	88%	92	225	207	80
Argentina	25.2	8.9	40.8	65.2/71.4	80.4%	85%	103	838	176	154
Australia	15.3	7.3	11.0	70.8/77.8	86.0%	98.5%	526	770	383	336
Austria	12.0	12.2	13.9	68.9/76.1	51.9%	98%	398	352	282	351
Bahamas	21.6	4.7	31.9	64.0/69.3	57.9%	93%	344	475	—	118
Bahrain	34.4	6.3	35.5	64.1/68.1	78.1%	40%	210	342	257	21
Bangladesh	46.8	18.7	132.0	45.8/46.6	10.1%	24%	1	8	0.5	5
Barbados	17.0	8.5	25.1	62.7/67.4	3.7%	90%	219	524	200	85
Belau	21.1	4.3	46.4	—	63.6%	45%	86	—	—	—
Belgium	12.7	11.6	11.2	68.6/75.1	94.6%	97%	468	452	293	228
Belize	38.7	5.3	33.7	45.0/49.0	59.0%	80%	43	449	—	41
Benin	48.8	19.1	109.6	44.3/47.5	13.9%	20%	3	58	0.1	0.3
Bhutan	42.7	20.6	—	44.0/42.5	4.1%	5%	1	9	—	—
Bolivia	46.6	18.0	77.3	46.5/50.9	41.7%	62%	26	92	18	39
Bophuthatswana	43.0	14.0	100.0	55.7/62.7	12.1%	—	—	—	—	—
Botswana	50.7	17.5	—	46.7/50.0	16.1%	32%	11	82	—	21
Brazil	33.3	9.1	24.2	57.6/61.1	63.5%	83%	63	295	126	45
Britain	13.3	11.8	12.0	70.0/76.2	77.7%	99%	497	931	394	410
Brunei	27.8	3.6	20.0	61.9/62.1	—	95%	141	164	122	—
Bulgaria	14.3	10.7	19.9	68.7/73.9	62.1%	—	—	314	196	234
Burkina Faso	47.8	22.1	182.0	32.1/31.1	3.7%	7%	1	16	1	0.2
Burma	38.6	14.3	97.5	51.0/54.1	20.0%	75%	4	21	—	10
Burundi	42.0	20.4	150.0	40.0/43.0	2.2%	15%	1	34	—	0.3
Cambodia	30.9	29.4	127.0	29.0/31.4	10.3%	48%	1	14	4.2	10
Cameroon	42.3	19.4	137.2	44.4/47.6	28.0%	50%	2	91	—	3
Canada	15.5	7.1	10.9	70.2/77.5	75.5%	98%	671	1,104	466	241
Cape Verde	27.6	9.4	104.9	58.3/62.0	19.7%	37%	6	129	—	—
Central Africa	44.3	22.5	190.0	33.0/36.0	26.6%	20%	2	36	—	0.3
Chad	44.1	24.1	160.0	29.0/35.0	18.4%	15%	1	23	—	0.4
Chile	21.5	6.8	14.7	61.3/67.6	81.1%	90%	50	297	112	87
China	21.3	7.4	55.0	66.0/68.6	25.5%	75%	—	16	3.4	8
Ciskei	—	—	—	—	—	—	—	—	—	—
Colombia	32.1	8.2	39.5	60.0/64.5	59.5%	81%	60	114	76	48
Comoros	47.3	18.6	96.9	44.4/47.6	20.3%	20%	3	114	—	—
Congo	44.6	19.0	180.0	44.4/47.6	29.7%	50%	10	61	2.2	1
Costa Rica	29.2	4.2	24.2	66.3/70.5	43.8%	90%	104	82	73	70
Cuba	14.7	5.6	19.3	68.5/71.8	60.3%	96%	33	263	114	91
Cyprus	19.6	9.1	17.2	71.9/74.9	42.2%	86%	179	483	161	108
Czechoslovakia	16.2	12.1	16.6	67.1/74.1	66.7%	99%	206	291	256	304
Denmark	11.2	10.9	8.8	71.3/77.4	82.6%	99%	636	377	358	367
Djibouti	42.0	7.6	—	—	—	—	12	138	32	307
Dominica	21.4	5.3	19.6	57.0/59.2	—	80%	56	426	—	88
Dominican Republic	36.7	9.0	37.2	57.2/58.6	39.8%	68%	29	41	57	42
Ecuador	41.6	10.4	70.9	59.5/61.8	43.1%	81%	33	279	49	49
Egypt	41.0	11.0	73.5	51.6/53.8	44.2%	44%	12	132	32	79
El Salvador	39.2	7.4	53.0	56.6/60.4	40.1%	63%	16	340	62	51
Equatorial Guinea	42.3	19.4	53.2	44.4/47.6	35.1%	20%	5	253	2.8	4
Ethiopia	49.8	25.2	84.2	37.5/40.6	13.6%	15%	3	7	0.8	2
Fiji	28.6	4.2	9.9	69.5/73.1	37.2%	80%	73	485	—	87
Finland	13.1	9.4	7.7	68.8/77.2	59.7%	99%	496	525	316	480
France	14.8	10.1	10.0	69.9/78.0	73.0%	99%	459	337	292	205
Gabon	31.2	21.3	229.0	25.0/45.0	32.0%	40%	12	176	16	—
Gambia	47.5	22.9	165.0	39.4/42.6	18.2%	15%	5	109	—	21
Germany, East	14.6	14.2	12.1	68.8/74.7	76.2%	99%	189	376	309	517
Germany, West	10.0	11.5	13.5	69.0/75.6	38.4%	99%	463	370	337	423
Ghana	48.4	17.2	156.0	46.7/50.0	31.4%	30%	6	106	4.4	42
Greece	15.9	8.7	18.7	70.1/73.6	64.8%	95%	289	307	147	107
Grenada	24.5	6.8	15.4	60.1/65.6	14.8%	—	54	303	—	31
Guatemala	41.8	7.1	65.9	53.7/55.5	36.8%	47%	16	40	19	39
Guinea	46.1	20.7	216.0	41.9/45.1	11.2%	20%	2	25	—	4
Guinea–Bissau	40.0	23.0	47.1	39.4/42.6	18.1%	5%	5	36	—	11

[1] Per 1,000 population. [2] Per 1,000 live births. [3] Percent of population over age 15 who can read and write.
[4] Daily newspaper circulation per 1,000 population.

NATION	VITAL STATISTICS					COMMUNICATIONS				
	Birth Rate [1]	Death Rate [1]	Infant Deaths [2]	Life Expectancy Men/Women	Urban Pop.	Literacy Rate [3]	Phones [1]	Radio Sets [1]	TV Sets [1]	News-papers [4]
Guyana	28.3	7.3	45.9	59.0/63.0	29.6%	86%	33	358	—	77
Haiti	41.8	15.7	120.9	49.1/52.2	27.5%	23%	7	21	3	7
Honduras	47.1	11.8	95.4	59.9/55.5	31.4%	60%	10	49	14	63
Hungary	13.9	13.6	23.1	66.7/73.6	53.1%	97%	118	243	249	242
Iceland	19.8	6.6	5.4	73.4/79.3	87.4%	99%	475	579	270	557
India	16.8	5.1	122.0	67.3/75.0	21.9%	36%	4	24	1.0	20
Indonesia	33.2	14.1	134.0	47.5	18.2%	60%	2	40	2.3	18
Iran	42.5	11.5	108.1	57.6/57.4	48.8%	50%	32	63	54	15
Iraq	47.0	13.0	30.6	53.6/56.7	63.7%	40%	26	157	47	22
Ireland	21.9	9.7	11.2	68.8/73.5	52.2%	98%	187	371	223	229
Israel	24.1	6.7	14.1	71.5/75.0	87.9%	88%	313	212	153	208
Italy	11.2	9.7	14.3	69.7/75.9	48.0%	95%	337	240	231	97
Ivory Coast	47.5	18.2	138.0	44.4/47.6	32.4%	22%	12	120	51	7
Jamaica	26.7	5.8	16.2	62.7/66.6	37.1%	82%	60	332	77	59
Japan	13.7	6.2	7.4	73.5/78.9	75.9%	99%	494	777	245	569
Jordan	46.9	10.5	14.9	52.6/52.0	59.8%	70%	22	174	53	29
Kenya	53.8	14.4	51.4	46.9/51.2	9.9%	40%	12	35	3.9	10
Kiribati	21.9	6.5	48.9	56.9/59.0	29.7%	90%	12	198	—	—
Korea, North	32.5	8.3		60.5/64.6	14.7%	85%	—	40	—	20
Korea, South	25.3	8.1	5.0	62.7/69.1	57.3%	90%	90	151	48	197
Kuwait	41.5	4.8	39.1	66.4/71.5	22.1%	60%	153	409	425	159
Laos	44.1	20.3	123.0	42.1/45.0	14.7%	28%	2	83	—	3
Lebanon	30.1	8.7	13.6	63.2/67.1	60.1%	86%	112	648	194	92
Lesotho	36.7	14.5	114.4	49.2/51.4	1.0%	55%	3	23	—	1
Liberia	49.8	20.9	159.2	45.8/44.0	27.6%	18%	5	•177	11	6
Libya	47.4	12.7	130.0	53.8/57.0	29.8%	35%	20	46	56	26
Liechtenstein	14.3	6.7	10.8	—	28.6%	100%	770	481	231	477
Luxembourg	11.6	11.5	11.5	66.8/72.8	67.9%	98%	548	512	245	358
Madagascar	46.0	25.0	102.0	37.5/38.3	14.1%	53%	5	135	1	9
Malawi	48.5	25.1	130.0	40.9/44.2	8.5%	25%	3	43	—	5
Malaysia	30.0	5.7	26.7	67.1/72.7	28.8%	48%	44	150	64	87
Maldives	44.4	13.9	120.0	—	11.3%	36%	5	28	—	—
Mali	49.4	22.2	120.0	40.6/43.8	16.8%	9%	7	14	—	0.5
Malta	15.4	9.1	15.5	69.4/73.4	94.3%	87%	262	433	230	195
Marshalls	35.2	3.0	24.2							
Mauritania	50.2	22.3	187.0	40.6/43.8	22.8%	17%	1	69	—	0.2
Mauritius	26.4	7.2	33.0	60.7/65.3	43.0%	60%	40	196	73	79
Mexico	38.3	7.8	59.8	62.8/68.0	66.0%	74%	75	288	108	85
Micronesia	28.6	4.4	28.0				16			
Monaco	20.6	21.1	1.9	—	100.0%	99%	1,607	360	680	432
Mongolia	37.1	8.3	59.1	60.5/64.6	51.0%	95%	25	92	3.1	69
Morocco	45.4	13.6	149.0	53.8/57.0	40.6%	28%	11	108	39	21
Mozambique	44.8	19.0	19.1	44.4/47.6	7.0%	20%	43	25	0.1	4
Namibia	43.5	15.1	125.3	50.0/52.5	—		57	—	—	—
Nauru	19.8	4.5	19.0	44.0	—	99%	220	463	—	—
Nepal	43.7	20.7	169.0	44.0/42.5	4.0%	20%	2	18	—	3
Netherlands	12.8	8.1	8.7	72.4/78.9	88.1%	99%	509	308	293	325
New Zealand	16.9	8.2	12.6	69.0/75.5	83.0%	98%	568	888	278	345
Nicaragua	46.6	12.2	101.7	51.2/54.6	53.1%	87%	22	262	40	69
Niger	51.4	22.4	200.0	40.6/43.8	8.2%	8%	1	39	0.1	1
Nigeria	49.8	17.8	180.0	37.2/36.7	22.8%	30%	2	74	6	9
Norway	12.5	10.0	8.8	72.3/78.7	43.7%	99%	453	327	288	456
Oman	48.9	18.6	138.0	46.2/48.4	5.3%	50%	14	—	—	—
Pakistan	36.0	12.0	124.0	53.7/48.8	25.5%	24%	4	66	9	14
Panama	31.4	6.0	21.3	64.3/67.5	51.2%	82%	99	152	117	79
Papua New Guinea	42.5	15.7	159.0	50.5/50.0	12.6%	32%	16	52	—	6
Paraguay	36.7	7.6	38.6	61.9/66.4	39.6%	74%	18	63	19	39
Peru	38.6	11.6	70.3	52.6/55.5	67.4%	50%	28	145	49	51
Philippines	36.2	8.6	56.8	59.1/62.4	31.8%	83%	11	45	21	18
Poland	19.5	9.8	21.2	67.3/75.0	57.7%	98%	95	240	216	237
Portugal	16.3	9.4	26.0	65.1/72.9	26.4%	70%	138	160	122	54
Qatar	29.9	9.4	138.0	54.8/58.3	72.8%	25%	261	476	302	33
Romania	18.6	9.9	31.6	67.4/72.1	48.6%	98%	51	145	163	181
Rwanda	51.0	22.0	127.0	44.3/47.5	3.5%	25%	1	32	—	0.1
St. Christopher-Nevis	24.4	10.7	49.5	58.0/62.0	—	89%	—	299	63	22
St. Lucia	31.5	7.2	33.0	55.1/58.5	—	80%	71	752	16	35
St. Vincent	35.1	7.1	38.1	58.5/59.7	—	80%	46	300	7	—
San Marino	10.3	7.8	13.8	—/—	74.4%	97%	257	381	41	65
São Tomé-Príncipe	41.9	9.6	49.7	33.8	20.5%	10%	10	247	—	—

[1] Per 1,000 population. [2] Per 1,000 live births. [3] Percent of population over age 15 who can read and write.
[4] Daily newspaper circulation per 1,000 population.

VITAL STATISTICS, EDUCATION, COMMUNICATIONS (continued)

NATION	VITAL STATISTICS					COMMUNICATIONS				
	Birth Rate [1]	Death Rate [1]	Infant Deaths [2]	Life Expectancy Men/Women	Urban Pop.	Literacy Rate [3]	Phones [1]	Radio Sets [1]	TV Sets [1]	News-papers [4]
Saudi Arabia	45.9	14.4	152.0	51.5/54.6	14.0%	25%	53	37	38	11
Senegal	47.8	22.1	92.9	40.6/43.8	31.7%	10%	8	54	0.4	5
Seychelles	27.6	7.0	26.6	64.6/71.1	26.1%	60%	111	317	—	56
Sierra Leone	45.5	19.2	136.3	44.3/47.5	13.9%	15%	5	22	6	10
Singapore	17.3	5.2	13.2	65.1/70.0	100.0%	84.2%	291	179	212	249
Solomons	36.1	13.0	52.4	—	9.1%	60%	11	68	—	—
Somalia	46.2	19.9	177.0	40.9/44.1	20.2%	10%	2	23	—	1
South Africa	37.9	10.3	117.0	58.9/61.7	47.9%	75%	121	96	69	66
Soviet Union	18.3	10.3	39.0	70.0	62.3%	99.8%	89	473	303	251
Spain	15.1	7.7	11.1	70.4/76.2	64.2%	97%	310	258	253	128
Sri Lanka	28.5	6.6	37.1	68.0	22.4%	85%	6	47	—	42
Sudan	45.8	18.4	93.6	45.5/47.5	20.4%	20%	3	74	6	1
Suriname	28.0	7.9	30.4	62.5/66.7	37.8%	80%	61	394	105	74
Swaziland	47.5	19.1	149.0	44.3/47.5	7.9%	35%	22	151	0.9	15
Sweden	11.7	11.0	6.7	72.5/78.7	82.7%	99%	796	390	374	526
Switzerland	11.6	9.3	8.5	70.3/76.2	54.6%	99%	725	355	312	395
Syria	46.4	8.9	57.0	64.0	47.9%	70%	25	224	45	12
Taiwan	26.0	5.0	11.0	72.1	77.0%	90%	177	103	79	99
Tanzania	46.3	15.8	103.0	52.0	13.3%	66%	6	28	0.3	10
Thailand	32.3	8.9	16.6	53.6/58.7	13.2%	82%	11	128	17	21
Togo	47.8	18.9	127.0	31.6/38.5	15.2%	18%	3	208	0.6	3
Tonga	13.0	1.9	20.5	—	21.8%	95%	23	211	—	—
Transkei	—	—	—	55.7/62.7	7.1%	—	6	—	—	—
Trinidad-Tobago	25.7	6.5	26.4	64.1/68.1	49.4%	95%	70	263	133	171
Tunisia	36.0	11.1	125.0	57.4/58.4	40.1%	62%	30	141	48	44
Turkey	39.6	14.6	153.0	53.7	44.6%	62%	42	97	70	41
Tuvalu	22.3	6.5	48.9	56.9/59.0	29.7%	49%	0.5	0.5	—	—
Uganda	44.7	14.4	160.0	50.8/54.3	7.1%	25%	3	19	5	2
United Arab Emirates	30.5	7.3	138.0	59.6/63.5	57.0%	25%	200	316	—	8
UNITED STATES	15.8	8.7	12.6	69.5/77.2	73.5%	99%	837	2,040	635	282
Uruguay	18.6	10.6	37.4	65.5/71.6	83.0%	94%	99	566	126	267
Vanuatu	45.0	20.0	—	—	23.1%	20%	25	170	—	—
Vatican City	0.0	11.4	0.0	—	100.0%	100%	—	—	—	250
Venda	—	—	—	—	—	—	—	—	—	—
Venezuela	36.9	6.1	33.1	65.0/69.7	76.1%	78%	85	407	127	176
Vietnam	40.1	14.3	42.8	51.1/54.3	24.2%	78%	1	121	26	5
Western Samoa	36.9	6.7	40.0	60.8/65.2	21.3%	90%	37	329	13	1
Yemen	48.6	24.1	22.7	40.4/42.2	5.8%	15%	1	18	0.2	10
Yemen, South	47.6	20.9	22.7	43.0/45.1	33.3%	25%	6	54	18	1
Yugoslavia	17.0	9.0	32.8	65.4/70.2	38.6%	85%	96	209	189	103
Zaire	46.2	18.7	117.0	44.4/47.6	30.3%	40%	1	101	0.3	9
Zambia	49.2	17.2	140.0	46.7/50.0	40.4%	54%	11	22	11	19
Zimbabwe	47.3	13.6	122.0	51.8/55.3	19.6%	30%	30	39	10	16

[1] Per 1,000 population. [2] Per 1,000 live births. [3] Percent of population over age 15 who can read and write.
[4] Daily newspaper circulation per 1,000 population.

NATIONS OF THE WORLD: MONEY, ECONOMY, TRANSPORTATION

NATION	MONETARY UNIT	Value [1]	ECONOMIC INDICATORS Gross Domestic Product Annual [1]	Per Capita [1]	Cost of Living	Electric Power [2]	TRANSPORTATION Highways [3]	Rail-roads [4]
Afghanistan	afghani	2 ¢	$3,400,000,000	$ 230	— [5]	49	2,846	9.6
Albania	lek	14 ¢	2,150,000,000	820	—	1,611	1,287	277
Algeria	dinar	20 ¢	40,000,000,000	1,951	258 [9]	440	45,070	3,908
Andorra........	Fr. franc ...	11 ¢	—	—	—	3,800	96	0
	Sp. peseta ..	⅔ ¢						
Angola	kwanza	3 ¢	3,900,000,000	591	—	210	8,577	3,189
Antigua	E.C. dollar ..	37 ¢	124,500,000	1,640	333 [5]	780	240	78
Argentina	austral	$1.25	53,000,000,000	1,800	3,600 [9]	1,260	47,550	39,738
Australia	dollar	70 ¢	153,545,000,000	10,087	128 [9]	6,662	243,750	42,855
Austria	schilling	4½ ¢	64,700,000,000	8,580	148 [8]	5,525	21,812	6,497
Bahamas........	dollar	$1.00	1,083,000,000	5,756	139 [9]	3,500	1,350	—
Bahrain	dinar	$2.65	4,000,000,000	10,000	125 [9]	13,786	93	—
Bangladesh	taka........	4 ¢	12,050,000,000	126	357 [10]	27	4,076	4,085
Barbados	dollar	50 ¢	955,000,000	3,799	478 [5]	1,315	1,450	—
Belau	dollar	$1.00	—	—	—	—	—	—

[1] In $U.S. [2] Kilowatt hours per capita. [3] Paved kilometers. [4] Total kilometers. [5] 100 = 1970 prices.
[6] 100 = 1972 prices. [7] 100 = 1979 prices. [8] 100 = 1976 prices. [9] 100 = 1980 prices. [10] 100 = 1974 prices.

NATION	MONETARY UNIT	Value [1]	ECONOMIC INDICATORS Gross Domestic Product Annual [1]	Per Capita [1]	Cost of Living	Electric Power [2]	Highways [3]	Railroads [4]
Belgium.........	franc	1½ ¢	$ 83,227,000,000	$ 8,317	131 [12]	5,160	49,280	4,130
Belize..........	dollar......	50 ¢	176,000,000	1,000	—	310	340	—
Benin..........	CFA franc ..	⅕ ¢	1,061,050,000	310	128 [13]	2	705	579
Bhutan.........	ngultrum...	11 ¢	131,000,000	109	—	7	418	—
Bolivia	peso.......	⅕ ¢	7,011,000,000	1,083	—	306	1,400	3,651
Bophuthatswana	S. Af. rand ..	60 ¢	15,168,000	110	—	—	—	—
Botswana	pula	58 ¢	963,200,000	1,000	120 [13]	450	1,105	726
Brazil..........	cruzeiro....	⅟₅₀ ¢	212,100,000,000	1,618	—	1,140	83,965	24,600
Britain.........	pound	$1.24	390,336,000,000	6,916	335 [14]	4,900	339,483	17,664
Brunei	dollar......	50 ¢	4,000,000,000	18,244	—	1,646	1,090	13
Bulgaria	lev	$1.04	63,840,000,000	7,105	—	4,304	4,291	4,341
Burkina Faso ...	CFA franc ..	⅕ ¢	1,079,000,000	170	127 [5]	20	967	1,689
Burma	kyat	11 ¢	5,900,000,000	180	275 [5]	55	3,200	4,353
Burundi........	franc	1 ¢	963,000,000	257	367 [5]	.05	300	—
Cambodia......	riel	25 ¢	500,000,000	50	—	19	2,622	612
Cameroon......	CFA franc ..	⅕ ¢	6,873,000,000	763	243 [5]	180	2,682	1,173
Canada	dollar......	73 ¢	323,700,000,000	12,800	130 [12]	15,900	189,800	67,067
Cape Verde.....	escudo	1 ¢	112,000,000	363	—	30	—	—
Central Africa ..	CFA franc ..	⅕ ¢	616,600,000	235	198 [6]	30	285	—
Chad	CFA franc ..	⅕ ¢	500,000,000	110	—	15	242	—
Chile	peso.......	½ ¢	23,600,000,000	2,178	—	1,070	9,365	8,293
China..........	yuan.......	35 ¢	274,900,000,000	257	106 [13]	300	262,000	52,500
Ciskei	S. Af. rand ..	60 ¢	—	60	—	—	800	—
Colombia	peso.......	1 ¢	37,578,000,000	1,358	295 [7]	825	9,160	3,436
Comoros	CFA franc ..	⅕ ¢	92,400,000	240	—	10	295	—
Congo	CFA franc ..	⅕ ¢	2,042,000,000	1,200	132 [13]	85	555	800
Costa Rica	colón	2 ½ ¢	2,977,500,000	1,243	353 [13]	835	2,425	790
Cuba	peso.......	$1.16	14,900,000,000	1,534	—	1,015	9,000	14,725
Cyprus	pound	$1.58	2,181,856,500	4,000	125 [13]	1,700	4,580	—
Czechoslovakia .	koruna	8 ¢	147,100,000,000	9,550	113 [5]	4,993	60,300	13,131
Denmark.......	krone	9 ¢	62,200,000,000	12,175	140 [13]	4,175	64,551	5,758
Djibouti	franc .. :...	½ ¢	116,000,000	400	—	725	279	97
Dominica.......	E.C. dollar..	37 ¢	67,000,000	910	160 [6]	200	360	—
Dominican Rep..	peso.......	30 ¢	7,600,000,000	1,400	137 [7]	515	5,800	1,600
Ecuador	sucre	1½ ¢	12,947,000,000	1,431	379 [8]	350	11,925	1,121
Egypt..........	pound	$1.42	26,800,000,000	686	—	531	12,300	4,857
El Salvador	colón	40 ¢	3,873,000,000	778	—	260	1,500	602
Eq. Guinea	ekuele	⅓ ¢	75,000,000	250	—	100	331	—
Ethiopia........	birr........	48 ¢	4,405,000,000	131	—	25	3,650	1,089
Fiji	dollar......	85 ¢	1,850,000,000	1,852	—	537	390	644
Finland	markka	16 ¢	53,790,000,000	10,970	149 [13]	8,500	31,000	6,071
France.........	franc	10 ¢	1,023,000,000	18,618	149 [13]	5,200	803,000	36,500
Gabon	CFA franc ..	⅕ ¢	3,364,000,000	2,613	344 [9]	890	459	970
Gambia	dalasi	25 ¢	240,000,000	370	333 [5]	65	431	—
Germany, East..	mark	33 ¢	165,600,000,000	9,903	—	6,273	47,475	14,248
Germany, West .	mark	33 ¢	555,000,000,000	9,100	118 [13]	6,000	169,568	32,555
Ghana	cedi	2 ¢	10,500,000,000	760	868 [6]	280	6,084	985
Greece.........	drachma ...	⅜ ¢	38,600,000,000	3,959	438 [8]	2,840	16,090	2,476
Grenada	E.C. dollar..	37 ¢	119,000,000	870	100 [13]	239	600	—
Guatemala	quetzal	$1.00	9,900,000,000	1,185	185 [8]	235	1,740	909
Guinea.........	syli	4 ¢	1,520,000,000	305	—	95	4,780	1,610
Guinea–Bissau..	peso.......	1 ¢	177,000,000	198	—	40	418	—
Guyana	dollar......	24 ¢	419,000,000	457	—	600	550	110
Haiti	gourde	20 ¢	1,810,000,000	300	—	51	600	88
Honduras	lempira	50 ¢	2,968,000,000	660	172 [7]	195	1,700	751
Hungary	forint	2 ¢	65,200,000,000	6,900	—	2,437	25,000	7,864
Iceland	króna	2 ⅓ ¢	2,205,700,000	9,100	—	15,450	166	—
India	rupee......	8 ¢	178,300,000,000	241	591 [15]	180	514,250	60,693
Indonesia	rupiah	⅟₁₀ ¢	90,000,000,000	566	—	95	26,583	6,964
Iran	rial	1 ¢	66,500,000,000	1,621	—	580	19,000	4,601
Iraq	dinar	$3.21	30,000,000,000	2,150	—	742	6,490	1,700
Ireland.........	pound	$1.02	16,491,000,000	4,678	—	3,115	87,422	2,675
Israel	shekel	⅟₁₀₀ ¢	24,000,000,000	5,928	—	3,705	4,459	767
Italy	lira	⅟₂₀ ¢	347,000,000,000	5,314	—	3,220	260,500	20,085
Ivory Coast	CFA franc ..	⅕ ¢	6,953,000,000	747	—	245	3,461	657
Jamaica........	dollar......	18 ¢	3,258,000,000	1,590	—	871	12,600	370
Japan	yen........	½ ¢	1,235,378,000,000	10,300	112 [13]	4,435	474,434	29,711
Jordan	dinar	$2.48	4,100,000,000	1,653	122 [13]	467	4,837	817
Kenya	shilling.....	6 ¢	5,684,700,000	309	245 [6]	100	6,425	2,040

[1] In U.S. dollars. [2] Kilowatt hours per capita. [3] Paved kilometers. [4] Total kilometers. [5] 100 = 1970 prices. [6] 100 = 1977 prices. [7] 100 = 1978 prices. [8] 100 = 1975 prices. [9] 100 = 1972 prices. [10] 100 = 1973 prices. [11] 100 = 1979 prices. [12] 100 = 1981 prices. [13] 100 = 1980 prices. [14] 100 = 1974 prices. [15] 100 = 1960 prices.

MONEY, ECONOMY, TRANSPORTATION *(continued)*

NATION	MONETARY UNIT	Value[1]	ECONOMIC INDICATORS Gross Domestic Product Annual[1]	Per Capita[1]	Cost of Living	Electric Power[2]	TRANSPORTATION Highways[3]	Railroads[4]
Kiribati	Austr. dollar	70¢	$ 36,000,000	$ 630	—	102	483	—
Korea, North	won	$1.06	16,200,000,000	786	—	1,800	304	4,535
Korea, South	won	1/10¢	79,662,000,000	1,963	137[15]	1,024	9,290	—
Kuwait	dinar	$3.30	21,609,000,000	14,400	138[13]	6,687	2,255	—
Laos	kip	3¢	320,000,000	90	—	223	1,300	—
Lebanon	pound	6¢	4,100,000,000	1,169	—	827	6,270	378
Lesotho	maloti	52¢	569,000,000	424	—	36	320	1.6
Liberia	U.S. dollar	$1.00	716,000,000	348	—	1,140	804	499
Libya	dinar	$3.37	26,500,000,000	7,600	—	1,805	10,800	—
Liechtenstein	Swiss franc	38¢	292,000,000	14,000	—	2,110	131	19
Luxembourg	Belg. franc	1½¢	4,111,000,000	11,200	—	2,550	4,981	592
Madagascar	franc	1/5¢	3,005,700,000	295	476[11]	75	4,694	884
Malawi	kwacha	65¢	1,246,000,000	200	—	70	1,940	754
Malaysia	ringgit	40¢	30,429,000,000	2,070	120[15]	592	15,900	1,678
Maldives	rufiya	14¢	74,000,000	462	—	57	0	0
Mali	franc	1/5¢	1,000,000,000	138	—	20	1,670	642
Malta	pound	$2.07	1,248,000,000	3,824	185[6]	1,380	1,179	—
Marshalls	dollar	$1.00	—	—	—	—	—	—
Mauritania	ouguiya	1⅓¢	598,790,000	330	—	100	1,350	650
Mauritius	rupee	6¢	1,071,000,000	925	—	415	1,636	—
Mexico	peso	1/20¢	115,970,000,000	1,546	1,092[13]	825	65,000	20,680
Micronesia	dollar	$1.00	—	—	—	—	—	—
Monaco	French franc	10¢	—	—	—	—	—	1.6
Mongolia	tugrik	31¢	1,200,000,000	380	—	1,110	700	1,585
Morocco	dirham	10¢	13,046,000,000	570	—	284	24,700	1,756
Mozambique	metical	2¢	2,050,000,000	159	—	880	4,593	3,436
Namibia	S. Af. rand	52¢	1,712,000,000	1,695	—	845	4,079	2,340
Nauru	Austr. dollar	70¢	155,400,000	21,400	—	3,333	21	0
Nepal	rupee	6¢	2,342,000,000	145	263[11]	24	1,751	63
Netherlands	guilder	29¢	137,947,000,000	9,580	122[15]	4,100	92,525	3,016
New Zealand	NZ dollar	46¢	21,430,000,000	7,916	—	9.2	46,716	4,716
Nicaragua	córdoba	10¢	3,094,000,000	938	445[10]	490	1,655	344
Niger	CFA franc	1/5¢	1,997,100,000	350	—	20	3,001	0
Nigeria	naira	$1.13	58,450,000,000	623	545[8]	80	30,019	3,505
Norway	krone	11¢	60,600,000,000	14,630	162[12]	22,470	17,699	4,257
Oman	rial	$2.90	7,950,000,000	7,530	118[13]	1,762	2,200	0
Pakistan	rupee	6¢	30,875,000,000	336	442[5]	180	40,000	9,967
Panama	balboa	$1.00	4,400,000,000	2,070	113[15]	1,020	2,715	278
Papua New Guin.	kina	98¢	2,286,200,000	650	—	400	640	0
Paraguay	guarani	½¢	2,446,000,000	684	142[16]	400	1,530	970
Peru	inti	17¢	15,984,000,000	868	1,320[12]	640	6,030	1,876
Phillipines	peso	5¢	33,853,000,000	652	271[13]	368	27,800	474
Poland	zloty	1¢	186,800,000,000	5,160	—	3,048	67,537	27,158
Portugal	escudo	½¢	19,366,000,000	1,925	536[9]	1,410	49,537	3,602
Qatar	riyal	27¢	7,900,000,000	27,790	—	12,385	490	0
Romania	lei	6¢	104,800,000,000	4,238	—	2,825	29,228	11,110
Rwanda	franc	1¢	1,630,000,000	285	128[15]	30	460	0
St. Christopher-Nevis	EC dollar	37¢	41,600,000	920	—	670	125	58
St. Lucia	EC dollar	37¢	121,500,000	980	—	460	500	0
St. Vincent	EC dollar	37¢	69,200,000	540	—	155	300	0
San Marino	It. lira	1/200¢	—	—	—	—	104	0
São Tomé-Prínc.	dobra	2¢	30,000,000	300	—	170	—	0
Saudi Arabia	riyal	28¢	121,100,000,000	12,615	111[12]	4,241	22,000	575
Senegal	CFA franc	1/5¢	2,480,000,000	400	—	180	3,461	1,033
Seychelles	rupee	14¢	128,000,000	1,330	—	2,460	145	0
Sierra Leone	leone	17¢	1,241,000,000	350	—	60	1,225	84
Singapore	dollar	45¢	16,316,000,000	6,520	133[13]	3,179	2,006	38
Solomons	dollar	72¢	110,000,000	460	—	117	241	0
Somalia	shilling	3¢	1,875,000,000	375	217[10]	16	2,335	—
South Africa	rand	52¢	73,212,000,000	2,515	319[5]	3,840	80,296	35,434
Soviet Union	ruble	$1.39	1,843,000,000,000	6,731	—	146	402,000	143,000
Spain	peseta	½¢	155,910,000,000	4,050	305[6]	3,840	63,042	16,282
Sri Lanka	rupee	4¢	5,633,560,000	355	155[15]	130	24,300	1,496
Sudan	pound	40¢	8,009,000,000	360	—	70	1,576	5,516
Suriname	guilder	56¢	1,080,000,000	3,042	—	3,370	2,210	166
Swaziland	emilangeni	52¢	425,000,000	840	—	200	510	292
Sweden	krona	11¢	90,666,000,000	10,900	134[15]	12,665	51,899	12,518

[1] In U.S. dollars. [2] Kilowatt hours per capita. [3] Paved kilometers. [4] Total kilometers. [5] 100 = 1970 prices. [6] 100 = 1974 prices. [7] 100 = 1971 prices. [8] 100 = 1975 prices. [9] 100 = 1976 prices. [10] 100 = 1977 prices. [11] 100 = 1972 prices. [12] 100 = 1979 prices. [13] 100 = 1978 prices. [14] 100 = 1981 prices [15] 100 = 1980 prices. [16] 100 = 1982 prices.

MONEY, ECONOMY, TRANSPORTATION (continued)

NATION	MONETARY UNIT	Value [1]	ECONOMY INDICATORS Gross Domestic Product Annual [1]	Per Capita [1]	Cost of Living	Electric Power [2]	TRANSPORTATION Highways [3]	Railroads [4]
Switzerland	franc	38 ¢	$ 96,551,724,000	$15,243	114 [6]	8,165	62,145	5,157
Syria	pound	25 ¢	16,750,000,000	1,700	—	522	12,051	1,543
Taiwan.........	NT dollar ...	2 ½ ¢	58,870,000,000	3,112	—	2,216	12,900	4,591
Tanzania.......	shilling	6 ¢	4,470,800,000	240	—	75	3,588	3,555
Thailand.......	baht	3 ½ ¢	39,237,000,000	793	188 [7]	355	16,244	3,800
Togo	CFA franc	⅓ ¢	723,500,000	257	—	25	1,320	442
Tonga	dollar	93 ¢	50,000,000	520	—	78	198	0
Transkei ..	S. Af. rand ..	52 ¢	180,000,000	90	—	—	788	209
Trinidad–Tobago	dollar	42 ¢	7,316,000,000	6,651	—	1,650	3,980	0
Tunisia	dinar	$1.17	8,206,000,000	805	183 [7]	449	9,970	2,089
Turkey	lira	⅛ ¢	51,266,000,000	1,084	7,656 [9]	549	36,670	8,193
Tuvalu	Austr. dollar	70 ¢	4,000,000	570	—	333	8	0
Uganda	shilling	⅕ ¢	4,800,000,000	300	—	70	1,934	1,216
United Arab Emir.	dirham	27 ¢	30,963,000,000	25,885	—	8,985	885	0
UNITED STATES	dollar	$1.00	3,304,800,000,000	14,170	263 [5]	10,455	3,241,510	270,312
Uruguay	peso	1 ¢	5,393,000,000	1,817	—	1,680	6,700	2,795
Vanuatu	vatu.........	1 ¢	—	—	—	163	240	0
Vatican City	It. lira	1/20 ¢	—	—	—	—	—	0
Venda	S. Af. rand ..	52 ¢	—	—	—	—	—	—
Venezuela......	bolívar	13 ¢	64,416,000,000	4,045	329 [10]	2,000	22,780	173
Vietnam	dong	10 ¢	10,700,000,000	189	—	77	5,471	2,816
Western Samoa .	tala	44 ¢	130,000,000	770	—	282	375	0
Yemen, North...	rial	15 ¢	5,220,000,000	614	—	62	1,775	0
Yemen, South ..	dinar	$2.90	792,000,000	430	—	191	1,700	0
Yugoslavia	dinar	½ ¢	48,300,000,000	2,080	—	2,506	59,500	9,393
Zaire	zaïre	2 ¢	3,400,000,000	570	—	150	2,350	5,254
Zambia	kwacha	43 ¢	3,406,000,000	546	279 [11]	1,735	5,596	1,204
Zimbabwe	dollar	65 ¢	5,649,000,000	694	934 [12]	895	12,243	3,394

[1] In U.S. dollars. [2] Kilowatt hours per capita. [3] Paved kilometers. [4] Total kilometers. [5] 100 = 1970 prices.
[6] 100 = 1973 prices. [7] 100 = 1977 prices. [8] 100 = 1980 prices. [9] 100 = 1963 prices. [10] 100 = 1968 prices.
[11] 100 = 1975 prices. [12] 100 = 1965 prices.

SELECTED DEPENDENCIES, TERRITORIES, COLONIES, AND POSSESSIONS

NAME	CONTROLLED BY	LOCATION	AREA (sq. mi.)	POPULATION [1] Total	Per sq. mi.	CAPITAL
Andamans–Nicobars ..	India	Bay of Bengal	3,203	219,714	68.6	Port Blair
Anguilla	Britain	Caribbean	35	6,800	194.3	The Valley
Azores	Portugal	Atlantic Ocean	902	263,000	291.6	Ponta Delgada
Balearic Islands	Spain	Mediterranean	1,936	663,630	342.8	Palma
Bermuda	Britain	North Atlantic	20	58,600	2,930.0	Hamilton
Canary Islands	Spain	Atlantic Ocean	2,808	1,353,680	482.1	Las Palmas, Santa Cruz
Cayman Islands	Britain	Caribbean	100	20,000	200.0	George Town
Channel Islands	Britain	English Channel	75	150,000	2,000.0	St. Peter Port, St. Helier
Christmas Island	Australia	South Pacific	52	3,485	67.0	Flying Fish Cove
Cook Islands	New Zealand	South Pacific	90	17,000	188.9	Avarua
Corsica	France	Mediterranean	3,367	204,232	60.7	Ajaccio, Bastia
Faeroe Islands	Denmark	North Atlantic	540	45,000	83.3	Tórshavn
Falkland Islands.......	Britain	South Atlantic	4,700	2,000	0.42	Stanley
Galápagos Islands.....	Ecuador	Pacific	3,028	6,000	2.0	Baquerizo Moreno
Gibraltar.............	Britain	Europe	2.3	30,000	13,043.5	Gibraltar
Greenland	Denmark	North Atlantic	840,000	53,000	0.06	Godthaab (Nuuk)
Guadeloupe	France	Caribbean	687	335,000	487.6	Basse-Terre
Guiana, French	France	South America	35,135	81,000	2.3	Cayenne
Hong Kong	Britain	SE Asia	403	5,516,000	13,687.3	Victoria
Macau	Portugal	SE Asia	6.2	316,000	50,967.7	Macau
Madeira	Portugal	Atlantic Ocean	307	272,000	886.0	Funchal
Mahore	France	Indian Ocean	144	56,000	388.9	Dzaoudzi
Man, Isle of	Britain	Irish Sea	227	69,000	304.0	Douglas
Martinique	France	Caribbean	425	330,000	776.5	Fort-de-France
Montserrat	Britain	Caribbean	38	13,000	342.1	Plymouth
Netherlands Antilles	Netherlands	Caribbean	371	250,000	673.8	Willemstad, Curaçao
New Caledonia	France	South Pacific	7,374	149,000	20.2	Nouméa
Polynesia, French	France	South Pacific	1,544	161,000	104.0	Papeete, Tahiti
Réunion	France	Indian Ocean	970	550,000	567.0	Saint-Denis
Saint Pierre–Miquelon .	France	North Atlantic	93	6,100	65.6	St. John's
Samoa, American	U.S.	South Pacific	77	35,400	459.7	Pago Pago
Sardinia	Italy	Mediterranean	9,301	1,700,000	182.8	Cagliari
Sicily	Italy	Mediterranean	9,926	5,100,000	513.8	Palermo
Turks and Caicos......	Britain	Caribbean	166	8,300	50.0	Cockburn Town
Virgin Islands, British ..	Britain	Caribbean	59	12,600	213.6	Road Town
Wallis and Futuna	France	South Pacific	106	12,100	114.2	Matu Utu

[1] Jan. 1, 1986, population estimates.

NORTH AMERICA

SOUTH AMERICA

EUROPE

MILES 0 100 200 300 400 500

REYKJAVIK ICELAND

NORWEGIAN SEA

FAEROE IS. (DEN.)

Trondheim

NORWAY SWEDEN FINLAND HELSINKI

Leningrad

SHETLAND IS. Bergen OSLO STOCKHOLM

ORKNEY IS. NORTH SEA Talling

HEBRIDES

MOSCOW

SCOTLAND Goteborg Riga

Glasgow Edinburgh DENMARK

NORTHERN IRELAND Belfast GREAT BRITAIN (UNITED KINGDOM) COPENHAGEN Malmo Vilnius

IRELAND DUBLIN Liverpool SOVIET UNION (U.S.S.R.)

Limerick Manchester NETHER- Hamburg WARSAW Kiev

Cork WALES Birmingham LANDS Amsterdam BERLIN Lodz

Cardiff ENGLAND EAST POLAND

LONDON BELGIUM GERMANY Dresden Krakow

ENGLISH CHANNEL BRUSSELS BONN Leipzig

CHANNEL IS. LUXEMBOURG PRAGUE Odessa

PARIS WEST CZECHOSLOVAKIA

Nantes Strasbourg GERMANY

FRANCE Munich VIENNA BUDAPEST ROMANIA

BERNE LIECHTENSTEIN AUSTRIA HUNGARY

BAY OF BISCAY Lyon SWITZ. Trieste BUCHAREST

Bordeaux Milan Venice BLACK SEA

Marseille Florence BELGRADE BULGARIA

Porto Nice MONACO YUGOSLAVIA SOFIA

LISBON PYRENEES ANDORRA SAN MARINO ITALY Istanbul

SPAIN CORSICA ROME ALBANIA TURKEY

MADRID Barcelona TIRANA

Valencia SARDINIA Naples GREECE

Seville BALEARIC IS. TYRRHENIAN SEA IONIAN SEA ATHENS

GIBRALTAR (Brit.) MEDITERRANEAN SICILY MALTA CRETE

ATLANTIC OCEAN

PORTUGAL

BALTIC SEA

GULF OF BOTHNIA

ADRIATIC SEA

AEGEAN SEA

SEA

A F R I C A

AFRICA

ASIA

AUSTRALIA AND OCEANIA

MILES
0 100 200 300 400 500

AFGHANISTAN

Official Name: Democratic Republic of Afghanistan.
Area: 250,000 square miles (647,497 sq. km.).
Population: 15,000,000.
Chief Cities: Kabul, capital, 1,127,417; Kandahar, 198,161; Herat, 155,858.
Government: Soviet-controlled communist state.
President: Babrak Karmal (since 1979).
Prime Minister: Ali Kishtmand (since 1981).
Flag: Black, red, and green stripes; emblem has star above rising sun and open book.
Languages: Pushtu (50%), Persian or Dari (35%), Turkic (11%).
Ethnic Groups: Pushtuns (50%), Tajiks (25%), Uzbeks (9%), Hazaras (9%).
Religion: Sunni Muslim (87%), Shia Muslim (12%), other (1%).
Leading Industries: Agriculture (sheep, goats, fruits, wheat, cotton, nuts, vegetables); mining (natural gas, copper, iron); manufacturing (fur and leather products, carpets, textiles, food processing).
Foreign Trade: *Major exports*—fruits and nuts, natural gas, karakul skins, raw cotton, carpets, wool; *major imports*—petroleum products, sugar, tea, machinery, textiles.
Places of Interest: Kabul museum and bazaar; Khyber Pass; ancient ruins of Balkh; Blue Mosque at Mazar-i-Sharif; Paghman summer resort; largest Buddha statue in world (180 ft. high) in Valley of the Gods at Bamian; temples of Herat.

AFGHANISTAN TODAY

A landlocked country of southwest Asia, Afghanistan was torn by civil war in 1980–83 as Muslim guerrillas fought against Soviet troops supporting the puppet communist national government.

One of the world's poor nations, Afghanistan has difficulty raising enough food to meet the needs of its population. The mountainous terrain prevents most land from being farmed. Most farmers have just enough land to raise crops for their families. Only about 1 person in 27 goes to school, and no more than 1 in 10 can read and write. Most live and dress as they have for hundreds of years.

The country has substantial mineral resources of coal, gas, and petroleum, but these have been mined only to a limited degree.

The Soviet Union lies to the north, China to the northeast, Pakistan to the east and south, and Iran to the west.

EARLY HISTORY

In ancient times the region was called *Bactria.* It was the home of the two-humped Bactrian camel, still used as a beast of burden in Afghanistan.

Persian rulers of Bactria were overthrown by Alexander the Great in the 300s B.C. Then the country was overrun by a series of overlords, including Greeks, Turks, and Arabs.

The invading Mongol hordes of Genghis Khan in the 1200s and Tamerlane in the 1300s were followed by the Mogul emperors of India.

Afghanistan achieved independence under the leadership of Ahmad Shah Durrani, who became shah (king) in 1747.

British efforts to control India and central Asia led to the First Afghan War (1832–42). Afghan resistance caused the British to withdraw temporarily.

British fear of expanding Russian influence in central Asia brought on the Second Afghan War (1878–79), won by Britain. Abdur Rahman became king in 1881, agreeing to let Britain manage foreign affairs.

Amanullah Shah, grandson of Abdur Rahman, brought about the Third Afghan War (1919), in which Afghanistan won independence.

Amanullah's cousin, Sardar Mohammad Nadir Shah, became king in 1929. He was assassinated in 1933 and was succeeded by his son Mohammad Zahir Shah.

On July 17, 1973, while King Mohammad Zahir was visiting Italy, his brother-in-law Prime Minister Mohammad Daoud overthrew the government. Daoud proclaimed a republic with himself as president and prime minister.

The opening of the Trans-Asia Highway across Afghanistan from Istanbul to Calcutta in the mid-1970s brought auto tourists from Europe.

COMMUNIST STATE

Using Soviet-built tanks and fighter planes, Afghan troops led by Col. Abdul Qader, deputy commander of the air force, overthrew the government on April 27, 1978. President Daoud and 30 members of his family were executed.

The rebels established a communist government under domination of the pro-Soviet People's Democratic Party (PDP). The rebels released from prison the head of the PDP, 61-year-old novelist Noor Mohammad Taraki, and made him president. Moscow poured in millions of dollars of aid to Taraki's government and sent in "military advisers." Muslim tribesmen rebelled against the communist central government.

In a bloody palace coup on Sept. 14, 1979, U.S.-educated Prime Minister Hafizullah Amin took over the government, making himself president. Former President Taraki and many of his supporters were killed during the takeover.

The Soviet Union invaded Afghanistan with about 85,000 troops beginning on Christmas 1979. Amin was executed on Dec. 27 and was replaced by Babrak Karmal, an Afghan communist in exile under Soviet protection.

U.S. President Carter led Western powers in denouncing the Soviet action. On Jan. 4, 1980, he reduced U.S. grain sales to the Soviet Union and led a boycott of Moscow's Olympic Games.

Fighting spread throughout the country in 1980–85 as Muslims opposed the Soviet occupation. An estimated 2.8 million Afghans fled to neighboring Pakistan and Iran. Although Soviet troops managed to control the main cities and highways, Muslim guerrillas dominated the countryside. An estimated million Afghans died in the fighting and in executions by the Soviet regime.

An explosion in a Soviet-built 1.7-mile-long highway tunnel in Salang Pass in the Hindu Kush mountains on Nov. 3, 1982, was reported to have killed about 1,100 person, including several hundred Soviet troops.

The UN General Assembly for the fourth year in a row appealed to the Soviet Union in 1983, to withdraw its troops from Afghanistan.

Covert U.S. military aid to the Afghan rebels was said to have been stepped up to the level of about $50 million a year in 1983. U.S. intelligence sources said casualties among Soviet forces had reached 15,000 in 1983.

U.S. Secretary of State George Shultz traveled to Pakistan in July 1983 for consultations concerning Pakistan's negotiations with the Soviet Union to obtain the withdrawal of Soviet troops from Afghanistan. Shultz visited Afghan refugee camps near the Khyber Pass, telling them, "Fellow fighters for freedom, we are with you!"

Abdul Rasool Sayaf, an Afghan guerrilla leader, claimed that in fighting in July 1983 northwest of Kabul the rebels killed 1,500 Soviet and government troops, destroyed 40 tanks, and shot down three Soviet planes.

Western diplomats reported that more than 100 were killed in Herat in August 1983 in a clash between rival communist factions.

In September 1983 guerrillas took control of the roads in the eastern province of Paktia, cutting off food and water supplies for Soviet and government troops in the town of Urgun.

Thousands of Soviet troops and guerrillas died in fighting in 1984 and 1985.

The UN Human Rights Commission reported in 1985 that Soviet Troops have repeatedly massacred hundreds of Afghan villagers, including women and children.

Seven Afghan rebel groups announced in May 1985 that they had formed a united front called the Islamic Alliance of Afghan Mujahedeen (Islamic warriors) to step up their war against the Soviet occupation of their country.

ALBANIA

Official Name: People's Socialist Republic of Albania.
Area: 11,100 square miles (28,748 sq. km.).
Population: 3,000,000.
Capital: Tirana (Tiranë), 169,300.
Government: One-party communist state.
Heads of Government: Ramiz Alia, First Secretary of Albanian Workers Party (AWP) (since 1985) and President of the Presidium (since 1982); Adil Carcani, Prime Minister (since 1982).
Legislature: *National Assembly*, 250 members.
Flag: Red field with centered black two-headed eagle topped by gold-edged red star.
Language: Albanian (Gheg and Tosk dialects).
Main Ethnic Group: Albanians (96%).
Religions: Abolished in 1967, but Albanians are believed to be 70% Muslim and 30% Christian.
Leading Industries: Agriculture (corn, wheat, goats, sheep, cattle, cotton, sugar beets, tobacco, vegetables); mining (chrome, copper, nickel, petroleum, bitumen); manufacturing (food processing, textiles, chemicals, metalwork).

Foreign Trade: *Major exports*—metal ores, petroleum, bitumen, tobacco; *major imports*—machinery, iron and steel, coke, sugar, wheat, processed food.
Places of Interest: 15th century Mesi Bridge near Shkodër; various mosques; old quarter and Venetian clock tower in Tirana.

ALBANIA TODAY

About the size of Maryland, Albania is the poorest nation of Europe. Fearful of foreign domination, Albania's communist dictatorship has largely isolated the country. The U. S. has had no diplomatic relations with Albania since 1939.

Two-thirds of the Albanian people live on state-owned farms or in small villages, making their living by raising crops or livestock. Few Albanians had any education before World War II, but the government reports that today 3 out of 4 Albanians can read and write. The government closed 2,169 churches and mosques in 1967, proclaiming Albania "the first atheist state in the world." Since then the government has carried on an active campaign against all religions.

The Adriatic Sea lies to the west, Yugoslavia to the northeast, and Greece to the southeast.

EARLY HISTORY

Once part of the kingdom of Illyria and then of the Roman and Byzantine empires, Albania was later invaded by Slavic tribes and was absorbed in the 800s by Bulgaria.

The country became a target of Ottoman Turkish expansion in the late 1300s. The Turks controlled Albania from 1478 (when they completed its conquest) until 1912 (when the Albanians won independence).

Italian, Greek, French, and Serbo-Montenegrin forces occupied the land during World War I. The Albanians eventually expelled all foreign troops and also successfully resisted Yugoslav and Greek encroachments.

Ahmed Zogu emerged from Albania's internal political struggle to seize power in 1925. At first he proclaimed a republic with himself as president, but in 1928 he made himself King Zog I. He ruled as a dictator until the spring of 1939, when Italy invaded and annexed the country.

A COMMUNIST NATION

Following Italy's World War II surrender in 1943, German troops replaced the Italians. The Nazis withdrew at the end of 1944, leaving Albania to the communist-led National Liberation Front headed by Enver Hoxha. He set up a communist state in 1946.

With over 750,000 Albanians living in neighboring Yugoslavia, fear of that country has been a constant factor in Albania.

When Stalin expelled Yugoslavia from the Cominform in 1948, Albania sided with Moscow. After Stalin's death in 1953, Hoxha continued to follow a hard "Stalinist" line.

SPLIT WITH MOSCOW

When communist China split with the Soviet Union over ideology in 1960, Albania sided with China. The Soviets broke diplomatic relations with Albania in 1961 and then cut off all military

ALBANIA (continued)

and economic aid. The vacuum was filled by China, which provided hundreds of industrial and military experts and financed industrial projects.

Albania played a conspicuous role in the expulsion of nationalist China (Taiwan) from the United Nations in 1971.

Albania isolated itself from its neighbors from 1946 until 1971, when diplomatic relations were finally resumed with Greece and Yugoslavia.

An attempted coup in 1973 brought a purge of hundreds of officials.

The government said 15 senior army officers were executed in 1975 for plotting with China to end Albania's sovereignty.

A new constitution in 1976 made it illegal to accept loans or aid from capitalist nations.

Albania lost its last powerful friend when China on July 13, 1978, cut off aid to the Balkan nation after having supplied about $5 billion over the past 24 years. Chinese technicians withdrew from Albania, and Albanian students left China. The break came after Albania sided with Vietnam in that country's dispute with China.

Mehemet Shehu, 68, who had been prime minister since 1954, was officially reported to have killed himself on Dec. 17, 1981. But Western officials believed he was killed in a dispute with Hoxha.

Hoxha declared Shehu had been unmasked as a foreign agent. He then purged most other top officials in 1982, naming Ramiz Alia to replace Haxhi Leshi, who had been the country's president for 29 years.

The government said it had "liquidated" an armed invasion on Sept. 25, 1982. Leka I, son of King Zog, claimed credit for the invasion.

The 76-year-old Hoxha died on April 11, 1985.

President Alia, who succeeded Hoxha as head of the nation's communist party, indicated Alabania would continue its policy of isolation.

ALGERIA

Official Name: Democratic and Popular Republic of Algeria.
Area: 919,595 square miles (2,381,741 sq. km.).
Population: 22,078,000.
Chief Cities: Alger (Algiers), capital, 903,530; Ouahran (Oran), 327,493; Constantine, 243,558; Annaba (Bône), 152,006.
Largest Metropolitan Area: Algiers, 943,142.
Government: Socialist military junta.
President: Chadli Benjedid (since 1979).
Prime Minister: Abdelhamid Brahimi (since 1984).
Legislature: *National Assembly,* 261 members.
U.S. Ambassador to Algeria: L. Craig Johnstone.
Algerian Ambassador to U.S.: Mohamed Sahnoun.
Languages: Arabic (80%), Berber (18%), French (1%), other (1%).
Flag: Green and white bar, with centered red crescent enclosing red star.
Principal Ethnic Group: Arabic-Berber (98%).
State Religion: Islam (99%).

Leading Industries: Mining (petroleum, gas, iron ore, phosphates, lead, zinc, mercury); agriculture (wheat, barley, oats, wine grapes, citrus fruits, olives, vegetables, figs, dates, tobacco, livestock); manufacturing (oil refining, chemicals, iron and steel, fertilizers, textiles, transportation equipment); tourism.
Foreign Trade: *Major exports*—crude petroleum, wine, citrus fruits; *major imports*—grain, food, manufactured goods, machinery.
Places of Interest: Sahara Desert; Atlas Mountains. *In Algiers:* Court of the Great Mosque; the Casbah; government buildings. *In Constantine:* Perregaux Bridge; Muslim College.

ALGERIA TODAY

Although Algeria ranks as the world's 10th- largest country in area, 34 other nations have larger populations. This disparity between population and area exists because the sandy wastelands of the Sahara Desert cover seven-eighths of Algeria. The country imports about 60% of its food.

Most Algerians live on the narrow strip of fertile land along the Mediterranean coast between Morocco to the west and Tunisia to the east. The majority farm crops or raise livestock. Only about 1 in 4 can read and write. Over half of the people are under the age of 20 with a life expectancy of 53 years.

Few Algerians live in the Sahara, but large petroleum and natural-gas deposits found there have made Algeria one of the world's important producers of oil and natural gas. The country has 6% to 7% of the world's reserves of oil and gas. Revenues from oil and gas pay for much of Algeria's industrial development.

EARLY HISTORY

The Phoenician colony of Carthage in nearby Tunisia controlled the Algerian coast from about 800 to 146 B.C.

After crushing Carthage, Rome governed the coastal areas and parts of the interior.

Islam was introduced by Arab invaders in the 600s A.D. Berber Muslim rulers united Algeria with Morocco and Spain.

A Turkish pirate, Barbarossa, helped Algeria expel Spanish invaders in the 1500s. He then declared himself sultan. Thus Algeria came under the rule of the Ottoman Empire.

In the 1700s and 1800s Algeria fought wars with the U.S. as a Barbary Coast pirate state.

FRENCH RULE

France invaded Algeria in 1830. Northern Algeria was made an integral part of France in 1848.

Fierce Berber resistance delayed French control of the Sahara region for many years.

On Nov. 1, 1954, the National Liberation Front (FLN) began a war for independence. Thousands died as a 500,000-man French army tried to put down the revolt. The war ended with a cease-fire on March 18, 1962.

INDEPENDENCE

France granted independence to Algeria on July 3, 1962. A power struggle among FLN leaders was resolved when Ahmed Ben Bella gained control in August 1962. A new constitution was approved in 1963, and Ben Bella was elected Algeria's first president.

On June 19, 1965, a military coup led by Col. Houari Boumediene overthrew Ben Bella, and he was imprisoned for 15 years. All political parties except the FLN were outlawed. Boumediene implemented a socialist program.

Algeria joined with other Arab nations in halting oil shipments to the United States and other nations in the energy crisis of 1973–74.

Diplomatic relations with the United States, broken in 1967 as a result of the third Arab-Israeli war, were resumed on Nov. 12, 1974.

Algeria broke relations with Morocco and Mauretania in 1976 when those countries took possession of Spain's former colony, the Spanish Sahara. Algerian troops aided guerrillas seeking independence for the region.

Algerians voted on Nov. 19, 1976, ratifying a new constitution. All persons 18 or over could vote, with women allowed to cast ballots for the first time.

Algerians took a major step toward democracy on Feb. 24, 1977, when for the first time in 14 years they elected a 261-member parliament.

The 46-year-old Boumediene died on Dec. 27, 1978. The FLN chose as his successor 49-year-old Col. Chadli Benjedid, who was formally elected president on Feb. 7, 1979, in a national election in which he was the only candidate.

A severe earthquake destroyed the town of Al Asnam on Oct. 10, 1980, killing about 2,950 persons and leaving 300,000 homeless.

Algerian diplomats played a major role in negotiations that brought the release in 1981 of 52 American hostages held prisoner for over a year in Iran.

Algeria's 5-year plan for 1980–84 stressed expansion of private enterprise and decreased reliance on government-owned industries.

ANDORRA TODAY

Located high in the Pyrenees Mountains between Spain and France, Andorra is a 700-year-old nation with a land area smaller than the city of Chicago. Isolated from the wars and political turmoil of Europe, the people of Andorra lead peaceful lives. Winters in Andorra are cold with much snow, while summer weather is usually mild.

Over 7 million tourists visit Andorra each year to buy products cheaply and to enjoy winter skiing. Andorra has over 250 hotels and restaurants. Smuggling of goods between Spain and France is a thriving industry because Andorra is a free port. Thus, manufactured goods cost less there than in Spain or France.

The land is rugged and mountainous. Little of it can be farmed for crops. Most of the farmers, therefore, raise sheep or cattle.

HISTORY

Tradition says that Charlemagne granted the Andorrans a charter for their support after driving the Muslim Moors from Andorra in the 800s. The bishop of Urgel and the count of Foix were established as co-princes of Andorra in 1278. The rights of the latter passed to the kings, and later the presidents, of France.

Women first won the right to vote in 1970.

An influx of foreign residents in the 1960s and 1970s gave foreigners about a 2 to 1 majority over native-born Andorrans.

With prosperity brought by the booming tourist industry in the 1970s and 1980s, Andorrans debate whether they should liberalize their constitution, which limits the vote to heads of families. For the first time, a woman won election to Andorra's parliament in October 1984.

ANDORRA

ANGOLA

Official Name: Principality of Andorra.
Area: 175 square miles (453 sq. km.).
Population: 48,700.
Capital: Andorra la Vella, 19,764.
Government: Parliamentary principality.
Chiefs of State: President of France and bishop of Urgel (Spain).
Legislature: *General Council of the Valleys,* 24 *members.*
Flag: Blue, yellow, and red bars, with coat of arms in yellow bar.
Languages: Catalan (official), Spanish, French.
Principal Ethnic Group: Catalan.
Official Religion: Roman Catholicism (99%).
Leading Industries: Tourism; agriculture (sheep, cattle, oats, barley, tobacco); manufacturing (electricity, cigarettes, handicrafts, matches, postage stamps, anisette, footwear); mining (iron ore, lead).
Places of Interest: Pyrenees Mountains; Engolasters Lake; Valira River; Les Escaldes thermal springs; Our Lady of Meritxell shrine and government building at Andorra la Vella.

Official Name: People's Republic of Angola.
Area: 481,354 square miles (1,246,700 sq. km.).
Population: 8,959,000.
Capital: Luanda, 475,328.
Government: Communist state.
President: José Eduardo dos Santos (since 1979).
Flag: Red stripe over black stripe; yellow symbol represents socialism, industry, and agriculture.
Languages: Portuguese, Bantu.
Ethnic Groups: Ovimbundu (33%), Bakongo (25%), Kimbundu (25%), Chokwe (8%), Portuguese and Cunhama (9%).
Religions: Animism, Roman Catholicism, Protestant.
Leading Industries: Mining (diamonds, iron ore, petroleum); agriculture (coffee, cotton, sisal, corn, livestock); manufacturing (chemicals, tobacco products, food processing).
Foreign Trade: *Major exports*—coffee, petroleum, diamonds, iron ore; *major imports*—food, raw materials, consumer goods.
Places of Interest: Government buildings in Luanda; Matala Dam on the Cunene River.

QUICK QUIZ: Who was Vice President in President Truman's administration? See page 392.

ANGOLA (continued)
ANGOLA TODAY

Almost twice as large as Texas, Angola was the last major European colony in Africa to gain independence, after nearly five centuries of Portuguese domination.

Aided by the Soviet Union and Cuba, communists won control of the country in a civil war in 1975–76. However, some 30,000 Cuban troops based in Angola continue to battle anticommunist guerrillas in southern Angola.

A small part of Angola, called Cabinda, lies north of the Congo (Zaire) River, separated from Angola proper by a strip of land that is Zaire's only outlet to the Atlantic Ocean. Cabinda has major oil reserves.

The U.S. does not officially recognize the communist government of Angola. But U.S. oil companies aid the development of the nation's petroleum resources.

Although the country has rich mineral resources of diamonds, iron ore, and petroleum, most of the people are uneducated Bantu tribesmen. Many Angolans work on huge coffee plantations that provide the country's second major export after minerals.

Northern Angola is forested and has hot tropical temperatures from November to April. Southern Angola is a dry semidesert.

HISTORY

Portuguese explorer Diogo Cão landed at the mouth of the Congo River in 1483, establishing Portugal's control of Angola. The Dutch occupied Angola's ports briefly from 1641 to 1648. From the 1500s to the 1800s Portugal shipped an estimated 3 million slaves from Angola to Brazil.

Guerrilla warfare began in Angola in 1961 as the black majority sought independence. For more than 13 years 50,000 Portuguese soldiers fought the guerrillas. In 1974 Portugal's revolutionary government promised Angola independence.

Civil war raged throughout 1975 as rival political groups battled for control of Angola. With independence on Nov. 11, 1975, Portuguese troops withdrew. The U.S. Congress in 1976 forbade sending military aid to the anticommunists.

By mid-February 1976, the Marxist Popular Movement for the Liberation of Angola (MPLA) led by Agostinho Neto won control, aided by Soviet weapons and Cuban troops. South Africa, which had intervened on the side of the anticommunists, withdrew its troops on March 27, 1976.

President Neto died of cancer in Moscow on Sept. 10, 1979. The ruling Marxist party chose as his successor Soviet-educated Deputy Prime Minister José Eduardo dos Santos, 37.

The government executed by firing squad in August 1980 more than 20 persons accused as anticommunist guerrillas. In retaliation the guerrillas bombed government petroleum facilities at the port of Lobito.

In 1981–83 South African troops supported by planes and tanks drove deep into southern Angola to destroy Namibian guerrilla bases. South Africa reported killing hundreds of guerrillas and Angolan troops, including Soviet military advisers.

Jonas Savimbi, leader of the rebel Union for the Total Independence of Angola (UNITA), which is supplied by South Africa, controls much of the southern third of the country.

The U.S. mediated a truce agreement between Angola and South Africa in 1984. South Africa began withdrawing its troops to a 25-mile-wide corridor in southern Angola on Jan. 31. Angola agreed not to allow guerrillas to use the region for attacks on South African forces in neighboring Namibia. On Feb. 16 a joint Angola-South African commission was set up to supervise the truce.

Meanwhile, UNITA rebels stepped up fighting throughout Angola in 1984 in an effort to overthrow the communist government.

ANTIGUA

Official Name: Antigua and Barbuda.
Area: 171 square miles (442 sq. km.).
Islands: Antigua (108 sq. mi.), Barbuda (62 sq. mi.), Redona (1 sq. mi.).
Population: 80,800.
Capital: St. John's, 21,814.
Government: Parliamentary democracy.
Prime Minister: Vere Cornwall Bird (since 1976).
Parliament: House of Representatives, 17 members.
U.S. Ambassador to Antigua: Milan Bish.
Antiguan Ambassador to U.S. Edmund Hawkins Lake.
Flag: Yellow sun rising against black sky and over blue water; red triangles at lower corners; white triangle in bottom center.
Language: English.
Principal Ethnic Group: Blacks of African descent.
Main Religion: Christianity, majority Anglican.
Leading Industries: Tourism, agriculture (cotton, vegetables, fruits, livestock), fishing, manufacturing (rum distilling, clothing, food processing).
Foreign Trade: *Major exports*—clothing, rum, lobsters; *major imports*—food, fuel, machinery.
Places of Interest: Beaches; in St. John's, cathedral from 1683, government buildings, shops; Shirley Heights and Nelson's Dockyard at English Harbor.

ANTIGUA TODAY

One of the 20 smallest nations in population and area, Antigua includes three islands and several islets in the Caribbean Sea. The main islands are Antigua, Barbuda, and Redonda.

The year-round warm climate and sandy beaches attract many northern visitors, making tourism the leading money-producing industry.

The main agricultural crop for export is cotton, but the islanders grow many vegetables and fruits for local consumption. Fishing also is an important food source, as well as providing some export income.

Although most Antiguans are poor, almost all can read and write because education is compulsory through the elementary grades. About two-thirds of the people are under the age of 25.

The U.S. maintains military facilities in Antigua under a lease that provides about 5% of the country's national budget.

HISTORY

Discovered by Christopher Columbus in 1493, Antigua was named after the Church of Santa Maria de la Antigua in Seville, Spain.

The Spanish and French made early unsuccessful attempts to settle the islands, being driven off by the fierce Carib Indians. But British settlers led by Sir Thomas Warner succeeded in establishing a colony in 1632 that remained part of the British empire for the next three centuries.

Until slavery was abolished in 1834, many African slaves were imported to work on sugar plantations, which throughout most of the colonial period made up the leading industry.

From 1871 to 1956 Antigua was governed as part of the Federation of the Leeward Islands. As a separate colony it was joined to the British Federation of the West Indies from 1958 to 1962.

Britain gave Antigua complete control of its internal affairs in 1967 with status as an associated state in the British Commonwealth of Nations.

The country's two main political parties are the Antigua Labour Party (ALP) and the Progressive Labour Movement (PLM).

The PLM under Prime Minister George Walter governed until losing an election in 1976 to the ALP, whose leader, Vere Cornwall Bird, became prime minister.

Bird led his ALP party to another election victory on April 24, 1980, winning 13 of the 17 seats in the House of Representatives.

INDEPENDENCE

Britain granted Antigua its independence on Nov. 1, 1981. The 71-year-old Bird became the independent nation's first prime minister.

The government spent more than $1,000,000 for its independence celebration. It lifted a 15% sales tax on paint, encouraging merchants in St. John's to repaint shops and offices in a rainbow of colors. A new parliament building and a new airport terminal were dedicated as part of the festivities. Britain's Princess Margaret represented the crown during the ceremonial lowering of the British Union Jack and the raising of Antigua's new flag.

The first election since independence was held on April 17, 1984. Bird's Labor Party won 16 of 17 seats in the national assembly, assuring him of another 5-year term as the nation's prime minister.

ARGENTINA

Official Name: Republic of Argentina.
Area: 1,068,301 square miles (2,766,889 sq. km.).
Population: 31,008,000.
Chief Cities: Buenos Aires, capital, 2,908,001; Córdoba, 968,664; Rosario, 875,623; La Plata, 454,884; Mar del Plata, 407,024; Tucumán, 392,751.
Largest Metropolitan Area: Buenos Aires, 9,927,404.
Government: Democratic republic.

President: Raúl Alfonsín (since 1983).
Congress: *Chamber of Deputies,* 254 members; *Senate,* 46 members.
U.S. Ambassador to Argentina: Frank V. Ortiz Jr.
Argentinian Ambassador to U.S.: Lucio Garcia del Solar.
Flag: Blue, white, and blue stripes; golden sun in white stripe has 32 rays.
Official Language: Spanish.
Main Ethnic Group: Spanish ancestry.
Official Religion: Roman Catholicism (94%).
Leading Industries: Manufacturing (steel, food processing, textiles, chemicals, vehicles, machinery, petroleum refining); agriculture (cattle, sheep, hogs, corn, wheat, cotton, citrus fruits, rye, alfalfa); mining (petroleum, gas, coal, iron ore, salt, uranium).
Foreign Trade: *Major exports*—meat, corn, wheat, hides and skins, wool, Quebracho extract, linseed; *major imports*—nonelectric machinery, iron, steel, motor vehicles, paper and paperboard.
Places of Interest: Iguassú Falls; Nahuel Huapi National Park; Lake Traful; Mar del Plata beach resort; colonial buildings in La Plata; Mendoza; Córdoba; Salta. *In Buenos Aires:* Paleimo Park; Casa Rosada (Government House); National Historical Museum; cathedral.

ARGENTINA TODAY

The world's eighth-largest country in area, Argentina has many natural resources. Its people enjoy high standards of living and education.

The nation's economy suffered a severe decline in the 1980s after Argentina lost the Falkland Islands war with Britain.

Argentina shares with Chile the majestic mountain peaks of the Andes range. Mt. Aconcagua, near the Chilean border, is the highest peak in the Western Hemisphere. In the east are the fertile plains of the Pampa, home of the Argentine cowboy, the gaucho. To the northeast lie subtropical deltas, dense forests, and grassy savannas. In the north are dry lowlands. South of the Pampa lies uninhabited Patagonia.

EARLY HISTORY

The Spanish navigator Juan Díaz de Solís discovered Argentina in 1516.

In 1810 revolutionists seeking independence from Spain overthrew the viceroyalty and set up a governing junta in Buenos Aires. Other Argentine provinces joined, led by Gen. José de San Martín, and in 1816 declared independence.

PERONISM

An army colonel, Juan Perón, became Argentina's president in 1946 and ruled dictatorially for a decade, welding a coalition between the army and labor unions.

In 1955 anti-Peronists overthrew Perón. He fled and later settled in Spain.

A series of provisional, military-dominated governments then succeeded each other.

The 77-year-old Perón returned from exile in 1973 and was elected president. His third wife, Isabel Martínez de Perón, became vice president.

Upon Perón's death on July 1, 1974, his 43-year-old widow succeeded him as president, becoming the first woman to head a national government in the Western Hemisphere.

Commanders of the armed forces overthrew

QUICK QUIZ: How many U.S. Presidents did not complete their full elected term? See page 392.

ARGENTINA *(continued)*

and imprisoned Mrs. Perón in a bloodless coup on March 24, 1976. Martial law was proclaimed and the nation's congress was dismissed. Mrs. Perón was inprisoned until July 1981, when she was allowed to fly to exile in Spain.

MILITARY RULE

The commander in chief of the army, Lt. Gen. Rafael Videla, was sworn in as Argentina's 39th president on March 29, 1976.

The military junta arrested some 6,000 to 30,000 persons in 1976–79 in an effort to end terrorist activities. About 9,000 disappeared, never to be seen again. In 1983 the military government announced that all were dead.

The United States reduced military aid to Argentina in 1977 because of the military regime's violation of human rights.

To reinstitute "civilian" government, President Videla on Aug. 1, 1978, resigned from the army. However, he remained responsible to the military junta of heads of the armed forces.

The junta chose Gen. Roberto Eduardo Viola, 56, retired commander of the armed forces, to replace Videla in 1981.

The military junta stepped up activities against opponents in 1981. Dozens of human-rights activists were arrested, although the winner of the 1980 Nobel Peace Prize, human-rights leader Adolfo Pérez Esquivel, was not jailed.

Inflation of consumer prices began to run out of control in 1981. The peso fell in value, while the nation's annual foreign-trade deficit mounted.

After Viola became ill in November, the junta replaced him as president on Dec. 22, 1981, with Gen. Leopoldo Galtieri, 55, commander of the army.

In an attempt to divert the people from criticism of the government, the military junta on April 2, 1982, made a surprise invasion of Britain's Falkland Islands colony, which Argentinians call the Malvinas. After a short but fierce war, Argentine troops surrendered on June 14. President Galtieri was forced to resign three days later. He was replaced by Maj. Gen. Reynaldo Bignone.

In the months following Argentina's defeat, inflation soared. As the nation teetered on the edge of bankruptcy, the military permitted the first free elections in 10 years on Oct. 30, 1983.

Raúl Alfonsín, 56, a former congressman who had repeatedly denounced the military junta, won the presidency in a surprise victory, capturing 52% of the vote. His moderate, middle-class Radical Civic Union gave the Peronist Party its first defeat in a national election in four decades, winning a majority of seats in the lower house of the new Congress. Alfonsín took office as president on Dec. 10, 1983.

With inflation climbing at a rate of more than 600% in 1984–85, Alfonsín struggled to impose austerity measures and pay interest on the nation's huge $48 billion debt to foreign banks.

Alfonsín emphasized his civilian control over the armed forces by firing and replacing four top generals in July 1984.

A public trial began on April 22, 1985, of nine high-ranking military officers on charges of murder, torture, and kidnapping. The defendants included former presidents Videla, Viola, and Galtieri.

AUSTRALIA

Official Name: Commonwealth of Australia.
Area: 2,967,909 square miles (7,686,848 sq. km.).
Population: 15,765,000.
Chief Metropolitan Areas: Canberra, capital, 246,100; Sydney, 3,280,900; Melbourne, 2,803,600; Brisbane, 1,086,500; Adelaide, 952,700; Perth, 918,000; Newcastle, 402,300; Wollongong, 231,000; Hobart, 170,900; Gold Coast, 164,100; Geelong, 142,100.
Government: Federal parliamentary state.
Prime Minister: Robert Hawke (since 1983).
Chief of State: Queen Elizabeth II.
Parliament: *Senate,* 76 members; *House of Representatives,* 128 members.
U.S. Ambassador to Australia: Robert Dean Nesen.
Australian Ambassador to U.S.: Sir Robert Cotton.
Flag: Blue field with red, white, and blue Union Jack in upper left and large white seven-pointed star below; five smaller white stars on right represent Southern Cross.
Official Language: English.
Principal Ethnic Group: British descent.
Main Religions: Anglicanism (38%), Roman Catholicism (23%), Methodism (11%), Presbyterianism (10%).
Leading Industries: Manufacturing (steel, aluminum, vehicles, textiles, machines); agriculture (cattle, sheep, hogs, wheat, oats, fruits, vegetables); mining (bauxite, iron ore, coal, tin, copper, zinc, lead, gold, uranium); fishing.
Foreign Trade: *Major exports*—coal, wool, petroleum, wheat, meat, sugar, metal ores; *major imports*—machinery, transport equipment, electrical machinery, textiles, drugs and chemicals.
Places of Interest: Great Barrier Reef off Queensland coast; Botany Bay; Blue Mountains, with Jenolan Caves; Mount Kosciusko National Park; Parliament House and St. Paul's Cathedral in Melbourne; St. James' Church, Opera House, and Australian Museum in Sydney; Canberra; Shepparton resort in Victoria; Ballarat, reconstructed village of 1850s; 12,000-year-old rock paintings in Queensland.

AUSTRALIA TODAY

The only nation to cover an entire continent, Australia is the world's sixth-largest country. It is a federation of six states.

The land is rich in natural resources, and the people, mostly of British descent, enjoy one of the highest standards of living in the world. Most Australians live along the east coast.

STATES AND MAINLAND TERRITORIES

	Area[1]	Population[2]	Capital
New South Wales ..	309,499	5,216,070	Sydney
Queensland	666,875	2,405,340	Brisbane
South Australia	379,924	1,291,290	Adelaide
Tasmania	26,178	422,112	Hobart
Victoria	87,877	3,841,710	Melbourne
Western Australia ..	975,101	1,284,000	Perth
Capital Territory ...	927	230,035	Canberra
Northern Territory .	519,771	136,752	Darwin

[1] In square miles. [2] Jan. 1984 estimate.

However, Australia is sparsely settled in relation to its size. Nearly as large as the United States, it has only about one-fifteenth as many people. Government encouragement of immigration has helped double the population in the past four decades.

Transportation is a major problem because there are few highways or railroads. Air travel is the only way to reach many parts of the interior.

Bordering the narrow eastern coastal plain is the Great Dividing Range, which extends from Queensland to the south of New South Wales. The highest peak, Mt. Kosciusko in New South Wales, is only 7,310 feet. Much of the interior is barren desert. Major rivers include the Murray and its tributary, the Darling. Northern Australia has a tropical climate.

DISCOVERY AND COLONIZATION

Aborigines were the continent's only inhabitants when Capt. James Cook took formal possession of the east coast for Britain in 1770.

The first European settlement was a British penal colony established in 1788 at Port Jackson (the port of Sydney).

Many of the early settlers were convicts or soldiers. As the number of free settlers increased, the practice of transporting convicts from Britain was curtailed and finally was discontinued altogether in 1868.

Gold strikes in the colonies of Victoria and New South Wales in 1851 brought thousands of new settlers. By 1859 six colonies, including the island of Tasmania, had been organized.

FORMATION OF THE COMMONWEALTH

A constitution drafted in 1897–98 was approved by the colonists and the British parliament. The Commonwealth of Australia came into being in

PRIME MINISTERS OF AUSTRALIA

1901–03	Edmund Barton	Protectionist
1903–04	Alfred Deakin	Protectionist
1904	John C. Watson	Labor
1904–05	George H. Reid	Free trade
1905–08	Alfred Deakin	Protectionist
1908–09	Andrew Fisher	Labor
1909–10	Alfred Deakin	Fusion
1910–13	Andrew Fisher	Labor
1913–14	Joseph Cook	Liberal
1914–15	Andrew Fisher	Labor
1915–17	William M. Hughes	Labor
1917–23	William M. Hughes	Nationalist
1923–29	Stanley M. Bruce	Nationalist
1929–32	James Scullin	Labor
1932–39	Joseph A. Lyons	United
1939	Earle Page	Country
1939–41	Robert G. Menzies	United
1941	Arthur Fadden	Country
1941–45	John Curtin	Labor
1945	Francis M. Forde	Labor
1945–49	Ben Chifley	Labor
1949–66	Robert G. Menzies	Liberal
1966–67	Harold E. Holt	Liberal
1967–68	John McEwen	Country
1968–71	John G. Gorton	Liberal
1971–72	William McMahon	Liberal
1972–75	Edward Gough Whitlam	Labor
1975–83	Malcolm Fraser	Liberal
1983–	Robert Hawke	Labor

1901. The parliament of the federal government met in Melbourne until moved to Canberra in 1927. Australian soldiers fought with distinction on the side of the Allies in both world wars.

EXPANDING INDUSTRIAL NATION

Australia began the century as an agricultural country but by the end of World War II had become an industrial one.

A surprise victory by the Labor Party in a national election in December 1972 ended 23 years of coalition rule. The head of the Labor Party, Edward Gough Whitlam, became prime minister and immediately launched a series of liberal reforms in domestic and foreign policies.

In a general election on May 18, 1974, Prime Minister Whitlam's Labor Party won a 5-vote majority in the House of Representatives. In the Senate, Labor tied with the Liberal-Country coalition, each receiving 29 seats.

In October-November 1975 a coalition of the Liberal and National Country parties forced a governmental crisis by blocking appropriations in the Senate because Whitlam refused to call new national elections. On Nov. 11 Governor-General Sir John Kerr removed Prime Minister Whitlam from office and appointed opposition leader Malcolm Fraser to succeed him as head of a coalition cabinet. In national elections on Dec. 13, 1975, Fraser's coalition parties won majorities in both houses of parliament.

Parliament in August 1977 passed legislation outlawing strikes by public employees and giving the government the right to dismiss strikers.

In August 1977 Prime Minister Fraser lifted a ban on mining and exporting uranium imposed by the Labor government in 1972. Australian uranium deposits, valued at about $150 billion, account for 20% of the known reserves of noncommunist nations.

Fraser called early parliamentary elections on Dec. 10, 1977, in which his conservative coalition surprised political forecasters by winning a larger majority than in the 1975 election.

A large-scale diamond rush developed in northwestern Australia after the discovery in July 1978 of major deposits of the valuable gems. Some 20 mining companies quickly staked claims.

Labor unrest grew in Australia in 1979 as a result of government efforts to prevent unauthorized strikes. When the government arrested 10 union leaders for failing to obtain police permits before addressing meetings, 200 unions called a 24-hour general strike on June 21, 1979, that shut down most industry.

Prime Minister Fraser's government reacted strongly in 1980 against the Soviet Union's invasion of Afghanistan, substantially increasing spending on national defense.

Fraser's conservative coalition won parliamentary elections on Oct. 18, 1980.

Australia experienced an economic boom in 1981 with unemployment falling to 5.1%. Increased exports of coal, petroleum, and other mining products led a greater growth rate than in any other major industrial nation.

A gold rush developed after a prospector in 1980 discovered north of Melbourne a 60-pound

QUICK QUIZ: Austria regained independence how many years after World War II? See page 293.

gold nugget that sold for $1 million.

A severe drought struck Australia in 1982–83, cutting farm production and causing food prices to soar. The government provided economic assistance to hard-hit farmers. The drought was broken by heavy rains in May and June 1983.

The Labor Party regained control of the government in an election on March 5, 1983, winning a majority of 25 seats in the lower house of parliament. Labor leader Robert Hawke, 52, replaced Fraser as prime minister.

Faced with recession, an unemployment rate of more than 10%, and an inflation rate of more than 11%, the government devalued the Australian dollar by 10% immediately after the election.

Hawke's government approved plans in July 1983 for a $300 million communications satellite system. The first of three satellites would be launched by the U.S. space shuttle in July 1985.

Australia's economy improved in 1984 as the rate of inflation fell and the gross national product began to grow at an annual rate of about 6%.

In a parliamentary election on Dec. 1, 1984, Hawke's Labor Party won a reduced majority as small parties calling for nuclear disarmament took votes away from the governing party.

AUSTRALIAN DEPENDENCIES

AUSTRALIAN CAPITAL TERRITORY
Area: 927 square miles (2,400 sq. km.).
Capital: Canberra, 246,100.
The Capital Territory is bordered on all sides by New South Wales. The land was transferred to the commonwealth for the seat of government in 1911. Residents are represented in parliament by one elected member. The federal minister for the interior supervises general administration.

NORTHERN TERRITORY
Area: 519,771 square miles (1,346,200 sq. km.).
Population: 136,752.
Capital: Darwin, 61,412.
The Northern Territory is largely a tableland that rises to a maximum elevation of 1,200 feet from the 1,040-mile-long coastline. There are large areas of fine pasturelands, especially in the north and northeast, but much of the interior is desert, especially in the west.

Products include manganese, gold, sorghum, beef, and pearl shell.

South Australia formally transferred the territory to the federal government in 1911.

In an election on Aug. 13, 1977, voters gave a majority of seats in the new 19-member legislative assembly to the Liberal-Country Party, which had promised to win statehood for the territory.

AUSTRALIAN ANTARCTIC TERRITORY
Area: 2,360,000 square miles (6,112,372 sq. km.).
Australia claimed the area in 1936.

CHRISTMAS ISLAND
Area: 52 square miles (135 sq. km.).
Population: 3,485.
Christmas Island is in the Indian Ocean, 220 miles south of Java Head. Sovereignty was transferred to Australia from Singapore in 1958. About 60% of its people are Chinese. The island's only economic activity is phosphate extraction and export.

COCOS (KEELING) ISLANDS
Area: 5.4 square miles (14 sq. km.).
Population: 300.
Capital: Bantam.
The territory, two atolls comprising 27 small coral islands, lies in the Indian Ocean, about 1,400 miles south of Sri Lanka. The Cocos Islands were discovered in 1609 by Capt. William Keeling. The islands were given to the Clunies-Ross family by Queen Victoria in 1886. Australia reached agreement in 1978 to purchase the islands for $7.2 million from the Clunies-Ross family. The islanders voted on April 6, 1984, to become part of Australia, rejecting independence.

HEARD AND McDONALD ISLANDS
Area: 142 square miles (368 sq. km.).
The islands, in the Indian Ocean about 2,500 miles southwest of Perth, were transferred to Australia by Britain in 1947. The territory is governed under the laws of the Australian Capital Territory and is uninhabited.

LORD HOWE ISLAND
Area: 7 square miles (17 sq. km.).
Population: 300.
Lord Howe Island, the most southerly island known to have coral reefs, is situated in the Tasman Sea, 436 miles northeast of Sydney. It was discovered in 1788. It is a dependency of New South Wales.

MACQUARIE ISLAND
Macquarie, about 1,000 miles southeast of Hobart, has been a dependency of Tasmania since the 1800s. It is uninhabited except for a federal government weather and research base.

NORFOLK ISLAND
Area: 15 square miles (40 sq. km.).
Population: 1,800.
Capital: Kingston.
Norfolk Island, situated in the Tasman Sea, 1,035 miles northeast of Sydney, was discovered by Capt. James Cook in 1774. The island was settled in 1856 by 194 descendants of the *Bounty* mutineers from Pitcairn Island. Their descendants make up about one-fourth of the population.

The scenic beauty and climate attract many visitors, making tourism a major industry.

AUSTRIA

Official Name: Republic of Austria.
Area: 32,374 square miles (83,849 sq. km.).
Population: 7,590,000.
Largest Cities: Wien (Vienna), capital, 1,515,666; Graz, 243,405; Linz, 197,962; Salzburg, 138,213; Innsbruck, 116,100.
Government: Federal republic.
Chancellor: Fred Sinowatz (since 1983).
President: Rudolf Kirchschläger (since 1974).

Legislature: *Bundesrat,* 58 members; *Nationalrat,* 183 members.

U.S. Ambassador to Austria: Helene von Damm.

Austrian Ambassador to U.S.: Thomas Klestil.

Flag: Red, white, and red stripes, with coat of arms in center.

Official Language: German.

Main Ethnic Group: German descent (98%).

Religions: Roman Catholic (90%), Protestant (6%).

Leading Industries: Manufacturing (steel, chemicals, machinery, consumer products); agriculture (livestock, dairy products, barley, oats, corn, sugar beets, potatoes); tourism; mining (magnesite, graphite, iron ore, lignite).

Foreign Trade: *Major exports*—iron and steel, machinery, yarn and fabrics, lumber; *major imports*—automobiles, coal, petroleum products.

Places of Interest: Danube River; Vienna Woods; Mozart's birthplace at Salzburg and the Salzburg Music Festival; Tyrol; Innsbruck old quarters; Graz; Brenner Pass in the Alps between Austria and Italy. *In Vienna:* Schönbrunn Palace; St. Stephen's Cathedral; State Opera House; Spanish Riding School; UN City.

AUSTRIA TODAY

Austria's major problem is its location between the communist powers of eastern Europe and the West. Defeated as an ally of Germany in World Wars I and II, Austria today is about the size of the state of Maine—only a remnant of an empire that once dominated central Europe. Austria endeavors to maintain its neutrality by constitutional law. It takes part in no military alliances and has no foreign military bases. However, Austria maintains a modern army and requires all men to have a minimum of eight months of military training.

Other than fearing the consequences of a war between East and West, the Austrians are contented and prosperous. Most live in cities, working in business and industry.

Each month several hundred refugees from Soviet-bloc countries seek asylum in Austria.

Many tourists visit Austria each year for winter sports in the snow-covered Alps, to attend music festivals, to go to art museums, or to view the scenic attractions along the beautiful Danube River.

EARLY HISTORY

From prehistoric times Austria has been a crossroads of Europe. Rome conquered the territory between 16 and 9 B.C. From the end of the Roman Empire until 803, when it became part of Charlemagne's empire, it was overrun by Germanic tribes. In the 900s Austria was added to the Holy Roman Empire.

By 1273 the Austrian lands had come under the control of the House of Hapsburg, which ruled until 1918. With one brief interruption, the Hapsburgs were rulers of the Holy Roman Empire from 1438 until 1806, when it was dissolved by Napoleon.

By the end of the 1400s the Hapsburg territories ranged from the plains north of the Danube to the Adriatic. They formed a multinational empire with the German-speaking lands (in substance, the future Austrian republic) in the center. To the north, east, and south were Czech, Hungarian, Italian, Polish, Ruthenian, Romanian, Slovak, and southern Slav territories.

The cultural development of present-day Austria was strongly influenced both by its German ethnic, social, and political composition and by ties to Slavic and Romance peoples and to the Magyars (Hungarians).

An Austrian empire was officially established in 1804. By 1815 Austria became the leading power in the German confederation and in the Holy Alliance. Austria's skillful foreign minister, Prince Klemens von Metternich, acted as chief arbiter of Europe. Revolutions in Hungary, Bohemia, and Vienna brought an end to the Age of Metternich in 1848.

Hungary forced Emperor Franz Josef I to accord it equal rights in a dual monarchy, forming the Austro-Hungarian Empire in 1867.

The assassination on June 28, 1914, of Archduke Franz Ferdinand, the emperor's nephew and heir, triggered World War I. Defeat of Austria and Germany by the Allies ended the Austro-Hungarian Empire in 1918. Austria became a republic.

FEDERAL REPUBLIC OF AUSTRIA

In the 1920s Austria suffered economic collapse and social and political unrest. Austrian Nazis assassinated Chancellor Engelbert Dollfuss in 1934 but failed in an attempted coup. In March 1938 Adolf Hitler annexed Austria to Germany.

After World War II Austria was divided into four occupation zones. The Soviet Union refused for more than a decade to end the occupation. Austria was finally reestablished as an independent republic on Oct. 25, 1955. On the following day the Austrian parliament adopted a constitutional law proclaiming permanent neutrality.

After parliamentary elections in March 1970, Chancellor Bruno Kreisky formed Austria's first socialist government since World War II.

Upon the death in 1974 of Franz Jonas, who had been president since 1965, Rudolf Kirchschläger, a socialist, was elected president. He was reelected in 1980. Kreisky's Socialist Party won a parliamentary majority in national elections on Oct. 5, 1975.

In a national referendum on Nov. 5, 1978, voters turned down use of atomic power.

Kreisky led his Socialist Party to victory in national parliamentary elections on May 6, 1979, increasing its majority to 96 seats in the lower house.

In Vienna the city's first subway system began operating in 1981. The $1 billion subway project had been under construction since 1969.

The government permitted 90-year-old former Empress Zita to return for a visit in May 1982 after 64 years of exile. However, she continued to refuse to give up her claim to the Austrian throne.

In a national election on April 24, 1983, the Socialist Party lost its majority control of parliament. Fred Sinowatz, 54, who had been the 72-year-old Kreisky's first deputy, became chancellor, heading a coalition cabinet of socialists and members of the conservative Freedom Party.

The government increased taxes in 1984 in an effort to reduce the nation's growing foreign debt of about $7 billion.

QUICK QUIZ: Who was Vice President during Grant's second term? See page 391.

BAHAMAS

Official Name: Commonwealth of The Bahamas.
Area: 5,380 square miles (13,935 sq. km.).
Population: 232,000.
Capital: Nassau, 3,233 (metropolitan area, 101,503).
Government: Parliamentary state.
Prime Minister: Lynden O. Pindling (since 1968).
Legislature: *House of Assembly,* 43 members; *Senate,* 16 members.
U.S. Ambassador to Bahamas: Lev E. Dobriansky.
Bahamian Ambassador to U.S.: Reginald L. Wood.
Flag: Black triangle and three stripes, with aquamarine stripes at top and bottom and gold band in middle.
Language: English.
Main Ethnic Group: Black (85%).
Chief Religions: Anglicanism, Roman Catholicism, Methodism, Baptist.
Leading Industries: Tourism; banking; fishing; petroleum refining; agriculture (fruits, vegetables); cement; salt; chemicals.
Foreign Trade: *Major exports*—petroleum products, tomatoes, salt, rum, seafood, cement, pulpwood; *major imports*—food, manufactured products.
Places of Interest: San Salvador (Watling) Island, believed to have been Christopher Columbus' first landing place in New World; Exuma Cays National Land and Sea Park, 176-square-mile preserve for sea life; gambling casinos at Freeport on Grand Bahama Island; resort hotels; swimming beaches. *In Nassau:* Fort Fincastle, the Bahamian Museum, Fort Charlotte, Seafloor Aquarium.

BAHAMAS TODAY

An island country off the east coast of Florida, the Bahamas attract about 2 million American tourists each year. Money spent by the tourists represents over three-fourths of the Bahamas' income.

Since 1955 gambling has been legalized in the Freeport area of Grand Bahama Island, only a few minutes flight from Florida. Many gambling casinos and resort hotels have been built.

The islands' second major industry is banking. Because of the nation's low taxation, many foreign corporations had established headquarters there. But in 1976 the government imposed taxes on corporations that were not 60% Bahamian owned. As a result many corporations moved to other tax havens.

The government seeks to diversify the islands' economy by encouraging new industries and better utilization of the natural resources.

A large oil refinery completed in the late 1960s at Freeport caused a 70% increase in the value of the nation's exports and made petroleum products the Bahamas' leading export commodity. In addition, the Freeport area has seen the development of cement, pharmaceutical, and light manufacturing plants.

Before the development of the tourist industry and oil refining, the islands depended largely on fishing and agriculture.

The more than 700 islands that make up the Bahamas extend over about 90,000 square miles.

They lie in a band 500 miles long and 200 miles wide, starting about 50 miles east of Florida.

Only about 40 of the largest islands are inhabited. Most of the rest are little more than small sandy or rocky beaches.

The largest, Andros Island, lies about midway between Florida and Cuba. The capital, Nassau, is on New Providence Island. The closest large island to the United States is Grand Bahama Island whose largest city is Freeport. Other major islands include Acklins, Cat, Eleuthera, Great Abaco, Great Exuma, Great Inagua, Little Abaco, and San Salvador.

DISCOVERY AND COLONIZATION

The Bahamas were the first land discovered by Christopher Columbus in the New World in 1492 when he landed on San Salvador (or Watling) Island. Although Columbus claimed the islands for Spain, the Spaniards made no effort to colonize them.

British colonists began developing the islands after Charles I granted the Bahamas to Sir Robert Heath in 1626.

The Bahamas became a crown colony of Britain in 1717.

The first royal governor, Capt. Woodes Rogers, devoted his efforts to rooting out the pirates. The motto of the islands, part of the Great Seal of the Bahamas, became *Expulsis Piratis Restituta Commercia,* or "Pirates Expelled, Commerce Restored."

During the American Revolution, the islands were the scene of one of the first operations of the new U.S. Continental Navy, when its first commander, Esek Hopkins, led a raid in 1776. U.S. Marines landed and carried off cannon and gunpowder. Many British Loyalists fled from the United States to settle in the Bahamas.

In the 1920s American bootleggers used the Bahamas as a smuggling base as did drug smugglers in the 1960s–1980s.

The Bahamas were granted complete internal self-government in 1964.

The islands were governed until 1967 by the white-dominated United Bahamian Party.

Widespread government scandals involving payoffs for gambling licenses in the late 1960s led to victory in the election of 1967 by the black-led Progressive Liberal Party (PLP). PLP leader Lynden O. Pindling became prime minister. Pindling's PLP again won election in 1972.

INDEPENDENCE

The Bahamas received full independence from Britain on July 10, 1973, retaining their status as a member of the Commonwealth of Nations. Pindling continued in office as the sovereign nation's first prime minister. On Aug. 1, 1973, the first Bahamian took office as governor-general—Sir Milo Butler.

In August 1975 the government banned fishing for lobsters in the Bahama Banks to the south and east of the islands. The action hurt the Florida fishing industry.

In the first national election since independence, on July 19, 1977, Pindling's PLP party won a landslide victory, taking 30 of the seats in the 38-member assembly.

In the 1970s–1980s the islands became the main

transshipment point for illegal drugs being smuggled into the United States. Smugglers hide their boats by day among the islands' thousands of cays and then run their cargoes overnight to the coast of Florida. With only a handful of police boats to search among the hundreds of islands, the government has expressed helplessness in trying to halt the smuggling.

An influx of about 25,000 illegal immigrants from Haiti in the 1970s–1980s strained the nation's economy.

In a general election on June 10, 1982, Pindling's PLP party won another five-year term in office, capturing 32 assembly seats to 11 for the opposition Free National Movement (FNM).

Pindling denied a report broadcast in the U.S. by NBC in September 1983 that charged the prime minister and members of his cabinet received as much as $100,000 a month in bribes paid by drug smugglers. A royal commission of inquiry in 1984 revealed evidence that Pindling spent over $3 million more than he earned in the period 1977 to 1983.

BAHRAIN

Official Name: State of Bahrain.
Area: 258 square miles (668 sq. km.).
Population: 434,000.
Capital: Manama, 88,785.
Government: Arab emirate.
Chief of State: Emir Isa bin Salman Al Khalifa (reigned since 1961).
Prime Minister: Khalifa bin Salman Al Khalifa (appointed in 1970).
U.S. Ambassador to Bahrain: Donald Charles Leidel.
Bahrainian Ambassador to U.S.: Ghazi Muhammad al Gosaibi.
Flag: Red flag with broad white serrated band in hoist.
Languages: Arabic (official), Persian, English.
Main Ethnic Group: Arab (80%).
Religion: Islam.
Leading Industries: Petroleum mining and refining; aluminum refining; construction; ship repairs; fishing; agriculture (dates, vegetables, livestock).
Foreign Trade: *Major export*—petroleum products; *major imports*—consumer goods, automobiles, machinery, food, oil-industry equipment.
Places of Interest: Ancient burial mounds in uplands; oil refineries; royal residences.

BAHRAIN TODAY

Bahrain is an island nation in the Persian Gulf, important as an oil-refining and trading center. Its 33 islets halfway down the gulf, off Saudi Arabia, form an archipelago 30 miles long and 10 miles wide. Bahrain enjoys a temperate climate and splendid offshore fishing.

About 70% of Bahrain's biennial government budget of over $1.7 billion derives from oil income. The government uses the revenues to provide free education and health services, to subsidize housing, and to develop industries.

Bahrain collects no customs duties on goods passing through the country, promoting use of port facilities by export-import companies.

HISTORY

From the mid-1500s Bahrain was occupied successively by the Portuguese, Persians, and Omanese. In 1783 it was taken over by the Atabi Arabs from the mainland, founders of the present ruling dynasty. In 1820 the sheik signed a general treaty of peace with Britain. Bahrain became a British protectorate in 1861.

Oil deposits were discovered in 1932, the first in the Arabian peninsula. One of the largest oil refineries in the Middle East, with a capacity of 200,000 barrels a day, was built at Sitrah. More than half the oil refined comes by pipeline from Saudi Arabia.

Iran abandoned its long-standing claim to Bahrain in 1970, paving the way for the termination of the British protectorate.

To help diversify the nation's economy, an international consortium in 1971 completed the largest aluminum smelter in the Middle East.

Emir Al Khalifa declared the country independent on Aug. 15, 1971, and proclaimed the nation's first constitution in 1973. Leftists won control of the 30-member national assembly. Then the emir ended the nation's experiment with democracy on Aug. 26, 1975, dissolving the assembly.

Since 1974 Bahrain has enjoyed a construction boom, especially in housing and new hotels. To hold inflation down, the government began in 1977 to subsidize the cost of food.

Bahrain's banking industry flourished in the 1970s–80s as some 40 international banks transferred operations from Lebanon after that country was devastated by civil war. Bahrain levies no taxes on the banks.

Bahrain did not renew the U.S. Navy's lease on port facilities when it expired in June 1977, ending the stigma of being an Arab country with a U.S. military base. However, arrangements were made to continue to service the U.S. Middle Eastern fleet.

In May 1982, 73 radical Muslims were convicted of attempting to overthrow the royal government in December 1981. Evidence indicated the plot had been backed by the revolutionary government of Iran, which claims Bahrain as part of its territory.

The emir of Bahrain visited President-Reagan in Washington, D.C., in July 1983 for discussions on ways to achieve peace in the Middle East.

Bahrain's weather service reported on Aug. 11, 1983, that for the first time in 81 years rain had fallen on the island during the month of August.

The U.S. in September 1983 agreed to sell $180 million worth of jet fighter planes to Bahrain for delivery in 1986. The planes would be the nucleus of the island nation's first air force.

Linking Bahrain to the Saudi Arabian mainland for the first time, a $1 billion 15-mile highway causeway was built in the 1980s. Saudi Arabia financed the construction.

QUICK QUIZ: When was Adlai E. Stevenson U.S. Vice President? See page 391.

BANGLADESH

Official Name: People's Republic of Bangladesh.
Area: 55,598 square miles (143,998 sq. km.).
Population: 100,206,000.
Chief Metropolitan Areas: Dhaka, capital, 2,064,743; Chittagong, 1,388,476; Khulna, 623,184; Rajshahi, 171,600.
Government: Martial law.
President: Lt. Gen. H.M. Ershad (since 1982).
Prime Minister: Ataur Rahman Khan (since 1984).
U.S. Ambassador to Bangladesh: Howard B. Schaffer.
Bangladesh Ambassador to United States: A.Z.M. Obaidullah Khan.
Flag: Off-centered brilliant orange circle on field of brilliant bottle green.
Languages: Bengali (official), English.
Main Ethnic Group: Bengali (98%).
Chief Religions: Islam (85%), Hinduism (14%).
Leading Industries: Agriculture (rice, jute, cattle, sugarcane, tobacco, cotton, tea); food processing; jute processing; manufacturing (rope, textiles, chemicals, paper); fishing.
Foreign Trade: *Major exports*—jute, clothing, animal hides, leather, fish, tea; *major imports*—food, coal, machines, vehicles, textiles.
Places of Interest: Bay of Bengal; Chittagong; Cox's Bazaar beach resort. *In Dhaka:* Lal Bagh fort; tomb of Bibi Peri; Bara Katra caravansary; Husaini Dalan monument; Tejgaon Church; Shrine of Ba Yazid.

BANGLADESH TODAY

The eighth-largest country in the world in population, Bangladesh also is one of the most poverty-stricken. Although Bangladesh covers an area only about the size of Wisconsin, it has about as many people as live in all the states west of the Mississippi River. And four or more babies are born every minute—about 6,000 a day. However, 2 of every 5 babies die within their first month.

With so many people to feed and so little land on which to grow food, the Bangladeshis constantly verge on starvation even when the rice harvest is good. Most Bangladeshis cannot read and write.

Food shortages and poor sanitation contribute to continual epidemics of cholera and other diseases. Cyclones and tidal waves from the Bay of Bengal have repeatedly flooded low-lying areas, killing tens of thousands of persons.

Jute, a fiber used in making burlap bags, is Bangladesh's most important export.

EARLY HISTORY

Located in the northeastern corner of India at the mouth of the Ganges River, Bangladesh was known for many years as East Bengal. In the 1200s Turkish Muslims conquered the area, converting the population to Islam. In the 1500s it became part of the Mogul empire. In the 1700s and 1800s the region became part of Britain's colonial empire in India.

When the British gave up colonial rule of India in 1947, the subcontinent was divided into Muslim Pakistan and Hindu India. East Bengal became East Pakistan, although separated from West Pakistan by 1,000 miles of Indian territory.

In November 1970 about 300,000 Bengalis drowned in a massive tidal wave during a cyclone.

Sheik Mujibur (Mujib) Rahman led his Awami Party to victory in the East Pakistan parliamentary elections of December 1970, giving strong support to a Bengali separatist movement. When the Pakistan government refused to let the new parliament meet in March, the Bengalis began a civil disobedience demonstration.

Gen. Agha Yahya Khan, president of Pakistan, led his army in a bloody repression of East Bengal on March 25, 1971. Mujib was arrested and tried for treason. The Bengalis fought back in a civil war that produced thousands of casualties plus nearly 9 million refugees who fled to India. In support of Bangladesh independence, India entered the war on Dec. 3, 1971, and in 13 days defeated Pakistan.

INDEPENDENCE

Bangladesh became an independent nation on Dec. 16, 1971. Released from prison in January 1972, Mujib returned to become Bangladesh's first prime minister. Indian troops withdrew in March 1972.

In March 1973, in the first national election, Mujib's Awami League party won all but a handful of the 315 seats in the national parliament.

Mujib became president with dictatorial powers on Jan. 26, 1975, a day after parliament had amended the constitution to enable him to do so. A month later, on Feb. 24, Mujib decreed Bangladesh a one-party state.

On Aug. 15, 1975, Mujib and members of his family were slain by rebelling army officers. Khandaker Moshtaque Ahmed, the commerce minister, seized power, becoming the nation's president. However, on Nov. 5, 1975, he was overthrown in another coup and imprisoned.

Maj. Gen. Ziaur (Zia) Rahman, commander of the army, took control of the government in November 1975, invoking martial law. The former chief justice of the supreme court, Abu Sadat Mohammed Sayem, was named president.

On April 21, 1977, Zia proclaimed himself president.

Over 230 persons were killed on Oct. 2, 1977, in an unsuccessful coup by lower-echelon army and air force officers. Subsequently, the government convicted more than 400 persons of taking part in the rebellion, and 92 were sentenced to death. On Oct. 14 President Zia banned the three main political parties for inciting violence.

The government ended restrictions on political activities in April 1978 in preparation for the nation's first presidential election on June 3. Zia won the election by a majority of nearly 4 to 1.

In the first parliamentary election in six years, on Feb. 18, 1979, President Zia's Bangladesh National Party (BNP) won two-thirds of the elective seats. Seven weeks later, on April 7, Zia ended martial law, restoring civilian rule.

President Zia was slain on May 30, 1981, in an attempted coup. The coup leader, Maj. Gen. Mohammas Abdul Manzoor, and two of his aides were killed by loyal troops.

Vice President Abdus Sattar, 75, became acting president. He was elected president in a national vote on Nov. 15, 1981, with a 3 to 1 lead over his major opponent

Army commander Lt. Gen. Hussain Mohammed Ershad, 52, seized control of the government on March 24, 1982. He suspended the constitution and imposed martial law. In December 1983 Ershad proclaimed himself as president.

Relations with India deteriorated in 1984 after that country began building a $500 million barbed-wire fence along the 1,000-mile boundary between the two to prevent Bangladeshis from illegally immigrating to India. India estimated that about 40,000 Bangladeshis had illegally moved to India in 1982.

President Ershad tightened martial law on March 1, 1985, banning all political activity and placing leaders of political parties under house arrest. Then a national referendum was held on March 21 in which his policies received overwhelming endorsement by the voters.

A step toward restoring democracy was taken on May 16 and 20, 1985, when elections for local officials were held in 460 rural districts.

A hurricane roared out of the Bay of Bengal on May 25, 1985, devastating lowland areas at the delta of the Ganges river. The storm killed an estimated 10,000 or more persons and left about 275,000 homeless.

BARBADOS

Official Name: Barbados.
Area: 166 square miles (431 sq. km.).
Population: 254,500.
Capital: Bridgetown, 100,000 (metropolitan area).
Government: Parliamentary democracy.
Prime Minister: Bernard St. John (since 1985).
Chief of State: Queen Elizabeth II.
Legislature: *Senate,* 21 members; *House of Assembly,* 27 members.
U.S. Ambassador to Barbados: Thomas H. Anderson Jr.
Barbadian Ambassador to U.S.: Peter Douglas Laurie.
Flag: Blue, gold, and blue bars, with black trident in gold bar.
Official Language: English.
Main Ethnic Groups: Blacks (80%), mixed (15%).
Principal Religion: Anglicanism (70%).
Leading Industries: Tourism; agriculture (sugarcane, corn, yams, fruits); sugar refining; manufacturing (rum, molasses, soap); fishing.
Foreign Trade: *Major exports*—raw sugar, seafood, molasses, rum; *major imports*—petroleum, meat, dairy products, automobiles, steel.
Places of Interest: Deep-sea fishing ports and marinas; beach resorts; Andromeda Gardens at Bathsheba; Welchman Hall Gully gardens; sugar farms; old plantation homes. *In Bridgetown:* St. Michael's Anglican Cathedral; Sam Lord's Castle.

BARBADOS TODAY

A prosperous Caribbean island nation with a stable democratic government, Barbados has an economy based on tourism and sugar.

Barbados is the most densely populated island

in the West Indies. But a determined family-planning program has succeeded in reducing the population growth rate to less than 1%.

The island has many resort hotels for tourists attracted to Barbados by the year-round warm weather and the hundreds of miles of swimming beaches.

Barbados lies on the eastern edge of the Lesser Antilles, with its eastern coast facing the Atlantic Ocean and its western coast on the Caribbean Sea. The generally flat land rises to a central high point of 1,104 feet at Mt. Hillaby.

HISTORY

Barbados was claimed for England by Capt. John Powell in 1625 and was settled in 1627. Its parliament, founded in 1639, is the third oldest in the Americas (after Bermuda's and Virginia's).

The slaves who were imported to work the extensive sugar plantations were freed in 1834. However, the plantation owners retained political control of the island.

Political control by whites was broken only after universal suffrage was achieved in 1951, largely as a result of the efforts of a black attorney, Sir Grantley Adams.

The country has two major political parties. Adams' Barbados Labour Party (BLP) headed the government from 1954 to 1961 and since 1976. The Democratic Labour Party (DLP) led by Errol Barrow won majority control of parliament in 1961–76.

Barbados received independence from Britain on Nov. 30, 1966. Barrow became the independent nation's first prime minister. His DLP party won national elections in 1966 and 1971.

In an election upset, the BLP party won a majority in the national assembly on Sept. 2, 1976. BLP leader J.M.G. (Tom) Adams, son of Sir Grantley Adams, became prime minister.

Adams led his party to another victory in a national election on June 18, 1981, winning 17 of the 27 seats in the House of Assembly.

Bernard St. John became prime minister on March 11, 1985, after Adams died unexpectedly of a heart attack.

BELAU

Official Name: Republic of Belau.
Area: 190.66 square miles (494 sq. km.)
Population: 14,000.
Capital: Koror, 7,685.
Government: Self-governing republic.
President: Alfonso Oiterong (since 1985).
Legislature: 38 members.
Flag: Light blue field with yellow disk in middle representing the Moon.
Languages: Micronesian dialects, English.
Main Religion: Christian.
Chief Ethnic Group: Micronesian.
Leading Industries: Fishing; agriculture (coconut

QUICK QUIZ: Who was the first labor-union leader to become President? See page 384.

BELAU *(continued)*
palms, fruits, vegetables, poultry, hogs).
Foreign Trade: *Major export*—copra; *major imports*—consumer goods.

A poor island nation in the western Pacific Ocean, Belau includes 350 islands with a land area about the size of New Orleans but with only a fortieth as many people as that city.

The main islands are Babeldaob (Babelthuap), 153.2 sq. mi.; Peleliu (Beleliou), 4.5 sq. mi.; Koror, 3.6 sq. mi.; and Angaur, 3.3 sq. mi.

The economy depends largely on U.S. aid for imported consumer goods. But most Belauans live on the abundance of fish, fruits, and vegetables.

Rain forests cover much of Babeldaob.

The first European to visit was the Spanish explorer Ruy López de Villalobos in 1543.

Germany bought the islands from Spain in 1899, but lost them to Japan in World War I.

In World War II, U.S. Marines landed on Peleliu and Angaur in September 1944, capturing them after heavy fighting. After the war Belau became part of the UN Trust Territory of the Pacific Islands.

Moving toward self-government, Belauans voted on July 12, 1978, to separate from Micronesia. After several attempts, a constitution was approved in a referendum on July 9, 1980.

Haruo I. Remeliik was elected on Nov. 4, 1980, the first president of Belau. He was re-elected to a second 4-year term in 1984.

Belau became self-governing when the constitution went into effect on Jan. 1, 1981.

The U.S. and Belau signed a compact of free association on Aug. 26, 1982, giving the U.S. national defense rights in the islands for 50 years in return for $1 billion in aid during the period.

In a plebiscite on Feb. 10, 1983, about 60% of Belau's 7,000 voters approved autonomy under the compact with the U.S. However, a constitutional amendment to permit transit and storage of nuclear weapons by the U.S. did not receive a required 75% voter approval.

To resolve the issue, the U.S. and Belau signed a new treaty on July 1, 1983, that would permit U.S. nuclear ships to enter Belau's waters but would prohibit storage, testing, or disposal of nuclear armaments.

Belau's voters approved the compact of free association with the U.S. 4,209 to 2,013 in a referendum on Sept. 4, 1984.

President Remeliik was assassinated on June 30, 1985. Four relatives and associates of his chief political rival were arrested and charged with the slaying.

Vice President Alfonso Oiterong became president, pending new elections.

BELGIUM

Official Name: Kingdom of Belgium.
Area: 11,781 square miles (30,513 sq. km.).
Population: 9,887,000.
Chief Cities: Bruxelles (Brussels), capital, 785,969;

Ghent, 239,959; Charleroi, 218,944; Liège, 216,604; Antwerp, 190,652; Bruges, 118,212.
Largest Metropolitan Area: Brussels, 1,000,221.
Government: Constitutional monarchy.
Prime Minister: Wilfried Martens (since 1981).
King: Baudouin (since 1951).
Parliament: *Senate,* 181 members; *Chamber of Representatives,* 212 members.
U.S. Ambassador to Belgium: Geoffrey Swaebe.
Belgian Ambassador to U.S.: Raoul Shoumaker.
Flag: Bars of black, yellow, and red.
Official Languages: Flemish (Dutch) and French.
Chief Ethnic Groups: Flemish (Dutch-speaking; 56%), Walloon (French-speaking; 32%).
Main Religion: Roman Catholicism (75%).
Leading Industries: Manufacturing (steel, textiles, machinery, chemicals); agriculture (wheat, oats, rye, barley, cattle, poultry, horses, sugar beets, vegetables); mining (coal, zinc, lead, copper).
Foreign Trade: *Major exports*—iron and steel, transport equipment, textile yarn and fabrics, cut diamonds, glassware, chemical products, nonferrous metals; *major imports*—motor vehicles, copper, wool, machinery, iron ore, cotton, wheat, petroleum products.
Places of Interest: Ardennes Forest; Meuse Valley; cathedrals, palaces, and museums in Brussels; cathedral and Rubens' house in Antwerp; Bruges city canals; Mons churches; Ypres war memorials; Ghent; Liège; Ostend seaside resort; Industrial Exhibition Halls and Palace of Fine Arts at Charleroi; Grottoes of Han at Han-sur-Lesse; Namur resort.

BELGIUM TODAY

A small industrial nation in western Europe, Belgium is a little larger than the state of Maryland. Because of its location between France and Germany, Belgium historically has been a battleground for its more powerful neighbors.

Belgium's highly industrialized economy prospered after the establishment of the European Common Market in 1958. But because the country has few natural resources, Belgium suffered economically from the skyrocketing prices of petroleum in the 1970s–80s.

A parliamentary democracy whose king is a figurehead, Belgium has had difficulty in achieving internal political harmony. The root of the nation's domestic problems lies in the country's division into three language regions, each having its own goals. The Dutch-speaking Flemish people live in Flanders, the northern part of the country along the border with the Netherlands. French-speaking Walloons live in the southern Ardennes region along the border with France. Brussels, in the central plain between the two, is a bilingual political battleground.

Because of the conflicting regional and language-group interests, the people of Belgium divide their votes among six or more political parties none of which is able to win a majority of seats in the parliament. As a result, coalition governments representing two or more parties join forces to run Belgium's government. When the parties to the coalition disagree, the government falls.

EARLY HISTORY

The country was part of the Roman province of *Belgica* and later part of Charlemagne's empire. Under Burgundian rule since the mid-1300s, Belgium became a hereditary possession of the Germanic Hapsburg dynasty by marriage in 1477.

Hapsburg King Felipe II of Spain gained con-

trol of Belgium in 1555 when his father, Karl V, divided his kingdom. In 1568 the Low Countries (modern Belgium, the Netherlands, and Luxembourg) revolted against King Felipe. The northern provinces won their independence, but Belgium was reconquered by Spain.

France took Belgium in 1797 and held it until Napoleon's final defeat at the Battle of Waterloo, fought in Belgium in 1815.

The victorious powers of the Napoleonic wars again united Belgium with the Netherlands and Luxembourg under Dutch King Willem I to form a buffer state against France.

INDEPENDENCE

When the Belgians revolted in 1830, England and France imposed an armistice, dissolved the unitary kingdom, and guaranteed Belgium's independence and neutrality.

The new state chose Leopold of Saxe-Coburg as its king in 1831. Upon his death in 1865 he was succeeded by his son Leopold II, whose encouragement of rapid industrialization and colonial acquisition brought prosperity. He established the African Congo as a private colony, but it was transferred to the state in 1908.

Albert I, nephew of Leopold II, succeeded to the throne in 1909.

Disregarding Belgium's neutrality, Germany invaded Belgium in 1914, crossing it to attack France. In protest Britain immediately declared war on Germany. King Albert's small army was quickly overpowered by the Germans.

After World War I Belgium ended its status of guaranteed neutrality and entered into a defensive alliance with France. King Albert died in 1934 and was succeeded by Leopold III.

With the resurgence of Germany under Hitler, Belgium withdrew from alliance with France in 1936 and declared a policy of independent neutrality. When the Germans invaded Belgium in 1940, King Leopold, as chief of his country's army, resisted for 18 days. He then surrendered and refused to accompany his government to London. The cabinet declared the surrender illegal.

Leopold's unpopularity caused a long political crisis after the liberation of Belgium in 1944. Leopold finally gave up the throne to his son Baudouin, who became king on July 17, 1951.

Belgium gave up its colonial empire, granting independence to the Congo (now Zaire) in 1960.

A government crisis was brought about by the resignation of Prime Minister Gaston Eyskens in November 1972. It ended in January 1973 with the formation of a coalition government under Prime Minister Edmond Leburton, the first socialist to head the government since 1958.

Leburton's coalition government collapsed early in 1974. In elections in March the moderate Social Christians won the largest bloc, 72 seats, in the Chamber of Deputies. Their leader, Dutch-speaking Leo Tindemans, became premier.

In a national election on April 17, 1977, the Social Christians won the largest number of seats, 80, in the 212-member chamber of deputies.

Tindemans began a new term as prime minister in June 1977, forming a coalition government of four parties.

Paul vanden Boeynants, leader of the French-speaking members of the Social Christian Party, became prime minister on Oct. 20, 1978, after Tindemans resigned when parliament turned down his regionalization plan to settle the country's language conflict. Boeynants previously served as prime minister in 1966-68.

A new parliamentary election was held on Dec. 17, 1978. Boeyants resigned the following day, declaring the election had decided nothing, although his Social Christian Party had gained 2 seats, increasing its plurality to 82.

After months of negotiations, Wilfried Martens, leader of the Flemish Social Christians, became prime minister on April 3, 1979.

BELGIUM IN THE 1980s

The parliament approved legislation on Aug. 5, 1980, granting partial autonomy to Dutch-speaking Flanders and French-speaking Wallonia. Each region was given the power to elect its own assembly to control local matters.

Faced with a worsening economic situation, Prime Minister Martens announced plans in March 1981 to suspend the indexing of wages to inflation. In the subsequent uproar by labor unions, he was forced to resign.

Mark Eyskens, finance minister in Martens' cabinet, became prime minister on April 6, 1981, heading a new coalition of Socialists and Christian Democrats. In parliamentary elections on Nov. 8, 1981, Christian Democrats and Socialists tied with 61 seats each.

Wilfried Martens again became prime minister on Dec. 17, 1981, after putting together a right-center cabinet from a four-party coalition.

The government arrested an official of the foreign ministry in August 1983 for selling documents revealing Western technology secrets to the Soviet Union. Six Soviet and Romanian diplomats were expelled. An electronics company in Brussels had provided the cover for the spy ring.

The nation's 800,000 government employes went on strike for two weeks in September 1983, shutting down all public services in protest against the government's refusal to grant them wage increases.

Despite massive demonstrations by nuclear armament protesters, Prime Minister Martens won parliamentary approval in a 116-93 vote on March 20, 1985, for deployment of U.S. cruise missiles in Belgium.

In an effort to reduce Belgium's 14% unemployment rate, the government began in 1985 to pay jobless immigrants a bonus of about $5,000 to return to their home countries.

BELIZE

Official Name: Belize.
Area: 8,867 square miles (22,965 sq. km.).

QUICK QUIZ: When did South Africa become an independent republic? See page 294.

BELIZE *(continued)*

Population: 165,600.
Chief Cities: Belmopan, capital, 3,000; Belize, 39,050.
Government: Parliamentary democracy.
Prime Minister: Manuel Esquivel (since 1984).
Belize Ambassador to U.S.: Henry Edney Conrad Cain.
U.S. Ambassador to Belize: Malcom R. Barnebey.
Flag: Blue field with red stripes at top and bottom; coat of arms in center.
Parliament: *National Assembly,* 28 members; *Senate,* 8 members.
Languages: English (official), Spanish, Mayan.
Chief Ethnic Groups: Black (51%), mestizo (22%), Indian (19%), other (8%).
Main Religion: Christianity, majority Roman Catholic.
Leading Industries: Agriculture (sugarcane, citrus fruits, bananas, livestock), fishing, manufacturing (sugar refining, clothing, cigarettes).
Foreign Trade: *Major exports*—sugar, molasses, bananas, clothing, citrus fruits, lobsters; *major imports*—food, fuel, consumer goods, vehicles, machinery.
Places of Interest: Ancient Mayan ruins of Xunantunich and Altun Ha; government buildings in planned city, Belmopan; Carib Indian village of Hopkins; Mayan Indian village of San Jose.

BELIZE TODAY

Somewhat larger than Massachusetts, Belize is a poor English-speaking Central American country, once known as British Honduras.

Agriculture has been the mainstay of the country's economy with sugar and molasses, made from sugarcane, its chief export. However, because much of the country's fertile cropland remains undeveloped, Belize must import about 25% its food needs.

The country pins its hope for the future on tourism and on geologic surveys that indicate large petroleum reserves lying beneath its soil.

A spectacular barrier reef lies along the east coast that faces the Caribbean Sea. Rainfall ranges from 69 to 156 inches a year.

Mexico is to the north and Guatemala to the west and south.

HISTORY

The Mayan Indian civilization flourished in what is now Belize for many centuries, leaving behind the ruins of great temples.

The first European settlers were shipwrecked British seamen, who founded the town of Belize in 1638.

Britain defeated a Spanish attack on the colony in 1798, but it was not formally named as the colony of British Honduras until 1840.

Britain gave the colony complete control of its internal affairs in 1964. George C. Price, leader of the People's United Party (PUP), became the chief minister. He remained in power in the following decades as his party won each successive election through 1979.

For many years neighboring Guatemala claimed Belize as rightfully its territory. In 1975 and 1977 British troops were sent to the colony to protect it from threatened Guatemalan invasions.

Britain granted Belize independence on Sept. 21, 1981. Price became the first prime minister of the sovereign nation.

Neighboring Guatemala refused to give Belize diplomatic recognition, and in 1982–83 renewed its territorial claims.

The government opened its doors to refugees from El Salvador and Haiti in 1983, offering 50-acre plots of land to each family along with financial aid to help them become farmers.

The first national election since independence was held on Dec. 14, 1984. The conservative United Democratic Party won control of parliament and its leader, Manuel Esquivel, 44, became prime minister.

BENIN

Official Name: People's Republic of Benin.
Area: 43,484 square miles (112,622 sq. km.).
Population: 3,967,000.
Chief Cities: Porto Novo, official capital, 144,000; Cotonou, political capital, 383,250.
Government: One-party communist state.
President and Premier: Mathieu Kerekou (seized power in 1972).
Benin Ambassador to U.S.: Guy-Landry Hazoume.
U.S. Ambassador to Benin: George E. Moose.
Parliament: *Revolutionary National Assembly,* 365 members.
Flag: Green field with red star in upper hoist corner.
Official Language: French.
Ethnic Groups: Fons or Dahomey (50%), Samba, Baroba, Chabe.
Religions: Animism (65%), Roman Catholicism (15%), Islam (13%).
Leading Industries: Agriculture (corn, rice, manioc, beans, palm products, peanuts, yams, cotton, kapok, tobacco, cashew nuts); manufacturing and processing (cotton ginning, palm-kernel oil, textiles, beer, soap, cement).
Foreign Trade: *Major exports*—palm products, raw cotton, peanuts; *major imports*—fabrics, motor vehicles, petroleum products, iron and steel.
Places of Interest: Pendjari Game Preserve; national park of the "W"; Cotonou floating fishing village; Porto Novo Ethnographic Museum; Abomey historical museum; Temple of the Serpents in Ouidah.

BENIN TODAY

A small, densely populated West African nation, Benin (formerly called Dahomey) is a poverty-stricken communist one-party state.

About the size of Tennessee, Benin is largely dependent on agriculture for its economy. Cotton and palm-kernel oil account for about three-fourths of the country's exports.

What little manufacturing and processing industry Benin has is concerned mostly with the ginning of cotton and the production of palm products. The government opened the nation's largest single industrial plant in 1975, a textile mill employing 2,000.

About 9 out of every 10 Beninese farm for their living. Few can read and write.

Most of the country's foreign trade passes through the port of Cotonou, Benin's largest city, which lies on the 75-mile-long coastline. Most government operations are located in Cotonou, the unofficial political capital.

Long beaches, a tradition of hospitality to visitors, and unspoiled wildlife reserves provide

the potential for a tourist industry.

Togo lies to the west, with Burkina Faso and Niger to the north, and Nigeria to the east.

EARLY HISTORY AND FRENCH RULE

Benin's earliest known settlers, the Adja, established a kingdom near the coast before the 1100s. The kingdom of Benin grew to control the interior region in the 1300s to 1400s. Both Benin and the adjacent kingdom of Dahomey were subject to the larger empire of Oyo. At annual festivals the kings sacrificed hundreds of their subjects to tribal gods.

In 1485 Portuguese traders reached the area. Dahomey and Benin soon became centers of the African slave trade.

In 1822 King Gezo of Dahomey, leading an army of female warriors, ended Oyo supremacy.

French influence began in 1851. After several attacks by tribesmen on French coastal trading posts between 1889 and 1891, France established a protectorate. In 1904 Dahomey became a territory of French West Africa.

The people of Dahomey were given French citizenship in 1946 and the opportunity to take part in local assemblies. In 1958 Dahomey received a large measure of self-government.

INDEPENDENCE

The country was granted independence on Aug. 1, 1960. Hubert Maga (from the north), the first president, was deposed in October 1963 by Col. Christophe Soglo, a southerner. In December 1967 Soglo was deposed in a bloodless coup led by Lt. Col. Alphonse Alley. His regime was overthrown by the army in December 1969.

Maga again became president in May 1970 and was peacefully succeeded in May 1972 by Justin Ahomadegbé Tometin. On Oct. 26, 1972, an army coup overthrew the government, and Mathieu Kerekou was installed as president and premier.

A severe drought in 1972–74 set back the nation's already poor economy.

In November 1974 Kerekou proclaimed that the country would thenceforth be a Marxist-Leninist state. The government then nationalized banks, insurance companies, and manufacturing and processing plants.

Kerekou renamed the country the *People's Republic of Benin* on Nov. 30, 1975.

An armed force landed by transport plane at Cotonou on Jan. 16, 1977, and then escaped after an unsuccessful attempt to overthrow Kerekou. The Beninese leader blamed "French imperialists" aided by Morocco, Gabon, Togo, Ivory Coast, and Senegal.

The UN Security Council, after an investigation and lengthy debate, condemned the raid but avoided naming those responsible.

To provide a broader base for his Marxist-Leninist government, Kerekou established a one-party Revolutionary National Assembly that began meeting in February 1980.

When Nigeria expelled illegal aliens in 1983, tens of thousands of the refugees settled in Benin, adding a new burden to the nation's stagnant economy.

BHUTAN

Official Name: Kingdom of Bhutan.
Area: 18,147 square miles (47,000 sq. km.).
Population: 1,464,000.
Capital: Thimphu, 8,922.
Government: Constitutional monarchy.
King: Jigme Singye Wangchuk (reigned since 1972).
Legislature: *National Assembly (Tsongdu),* not more than 150 members.
Flag: Yellow triangle above orange one, divided diagonally; white dragon in center.
Official Language: Druk-ke.
Religions: Buddhism (75%), Hinduism (25%).
Ethnic Groups: Bhotia (60%), Nepalese (25%), Lepcha and Santal (15%).
Leading Industries: Agriculture (rice, corn, wheat, barley, yaks, fruits); forestry; handicrafts; mining (dolomite, coal).
Foreign Trade: *Major exports*—postage stamps, rice, dolomite, handicrafts, fruits; *major imports*—kerosene, sugar, textiles.
Places of Interest: Royal residences in Punakka and Thimphu; fortified town of Wangdu Phodrang; 16th century bridge over Sankosh River; Buddhist monasteries.

Bhutan, a small country in the eastern Himalayan hill area, is bordered on the north by the Tibet region of China and on the south by India.

The terrain varies from the icy 24,000-foot peaks of the Himalaya to the steamy jungles of the southern lowland. Between these extremes lie eight fertile valleys.

Most Bhutanese farm or raise yaks. Few know how to read and write. They produce enough food to support themselves without importing food products.

The country's major source of revenue for foreign trade is money received from about 1,500 tourists yearly. India provides about $10 million a year in aid.

Bhutan's early history is obscure. About 1630 a refugee Dukpa Lama from Tibet became the first Dharma Raja, with both spiritual and temporal powers. In the following centuries Bhutan was beset by internal rivalry among powerful penlops (governors).

After a war in 1865 the British annexed part of southern Bhutan and in 1910 assumed control of Bhutan's foreign relations.

A hereditary monarchy was established in 1907. A government council selected Sir Ugyen Wangchuk as the country's first maharaja. He was succeeded in 1927 by his son, and in 1952 by his grandson Jigme Dorji Wangchuk.

India in 1949 returned part of the lands previously annexed by Britain.

Jigme Singye Wangchuck, 16, succeeded to the throne upon the death of his father in 1972. The new king, the fourth of his line, was crowned at Thimphu on June 2, 1974.

QUICK QUIZ: Who won the third largest vote in the 1976 U.S. presidential election? See page 383.

BOLIVIA

Official Name: Republic of Bolivia.
Area: 424,165 square miles (1,098,581 sq. km.).
Population: 6,744,000.
Chief Cities: La Paz, administrative capital, 635,283; Sucre, legal capital, 63,625; Santa Cruz, 254,682; Cochabamba, 204,684; Oruro, 124,213.
Government: Democracy.
President: Victor Paz Estenssoro (since 1985).
U.S. Ambassador to Bolivia: Edward Morgan Rowell.
Bolivian Ambassador to U.S.: Mariano Baptista Gumucio.
Flag: Stripes of red, gold, and green, with coat of arms on center stripe.
Official Languages: Spanish, Quechua, Aymará.
Ethnic Groups: Indian (65%), Cholo (mixed Indian-European descent, 25%), Spanish descent (10%).
Official Religion: Roman Catholicism (95%).
Leading Industries: Agriculture (potatoes, corn, sugarcane, cassava, cotton, barley, rice, wheat, coffee, bananas, llamas, alpacas); mining (tin, petroleum, natural gas, lead, zinc, copper, tungsten, bismuth, antimony, gold, sulfur, silver, iron ore); manufacturing (textiles, handicrafts, food processing).
Foreign Trade: *Major exports*—tin, antimony, tungsten, zinc, silver, lead, oil, natural gas; *major imports*—flour, motor vehicles.
Places of Interest: Lake Titicaca; Chacaltaya ski resort; San Francisco Church and Tiwanaci ancient ruins in La Paz.

BOLIVIA TODAY

A landlocked South American country, Bolivia has extensive natural resources. However, Bolivians have benefited little from them because of two disastrous wars and many revolutions.

Over half the people are Indians, who live in thatched mud huts and raise just enough food to feed their families. Corn and potatoes are the staples. Few Indians have gone to school, and most cannot read and write. Many work in the country's tin mines and oil fields.

The country is one of the main sources of cocaine in the international narcotics traffic.

Bolivia is divided into three regions. Two bleak Andean ranges that flank a high plateau (Altiplano) stretch along the Chilean border in the west. The valleys (Yungas) scar the eastern slopes of the Andes. The tropical plains (Llanos and Chaco) are in the east.

EARLY HISTORY

Pre-Inca ruins, such as those at Tiahuanaco, indicate the existence of an early Indian civilization in Bolivia. About 1200 the country came under the rule of the Incas. The Spanish conquest of the Inca empire brought the subjugation of the Bolivian region by 1538.

Called Upper Peru under Spanish rule, Bolivia was one of the first colonies to rebel. Its War of Independence lasted from 1809 to 1825.

Bolivia became an independent republic on Aug. 6, 1825. It was named for its liberator, Gen. Simón Bolívar.

In 1879 Chile seized Bolivia's only access to the ocean, the mineral-rich Atacama Desert.

From 1932 to 1935 Bolivia fought the bloody Chaco War with Paraguay, losing much land and suffering a humiliating defeat.

The Movement of the National Revolution (MNR), which seized power in 1952, gave equality to the Indian masses, began land reforms, and nationalized big foreign mining companies.

MILITARY RULE

Gen. Alfredo Ovando Candia overthrew the civilian government and assumed the presidency on Sept. 26, 1969. Ovando was forced to resign on Oct. 6, 1970. Gen. Juan José Torres, a leftist, became president. Col. Hugo Banzer Suárez overthrew Torres in August 1971.

Bolivia held its first presidential election in a dozen years on July 9, 1978, but fraud was so prevalent that a court annulled the results.

Air Force Gen. Juan Pereda Asbún seized power on July 21, 1978, deposing Banzer. Four months later, on Nov. 24, 1978, Army Gen. David Padilla Arancibia ousted Pereda.

Bolivia made a new effort to return to democracy with a national election held on July 1, 1979. None of the eight presidential candidates received a majority. Congress decided on Aug. 6, 1979, to give the presidency on an interim basis to Walter Guevara Arze, 68, a former foreign minister.

Conservative Col. Alberto Natusch Busch overthrew Guevara on Nov. 1, 1979. When the people of La Paz demonstrated against him, Natusch's troops and planes fired into the crowds, killing about 60 persons.

Natusch agreed to step down on Nov. 16, and the president of Congress, Lydia Gueiler Tejada, 51, was chosen as interim president.

In a national election on June 29, 1980, Hernán Siles Zuazo, a leftist who had been president in 1956–60, won a plurality in the race for president.

Army commander Gen. Luis García Metza Tejada overthrew the government on July 17, 1980, to prevent Siles Zuazo from taking office. He launched a campaign of terror against opponents, arresting and killing hundreds. The U.S. cut off all military and economic aid.

The U.S. continued to withhold aid in 1981 on evidence that President García Metza and other high military officers were receiving millions of dollars in payoffs from the country's $1.5 billion illegal traffic in cocaine.

On Aug. 4, 1981, Gen. García Metza resigned. A month later the junta named a new president, Gen. Celso Torrelio Villa. The junta replaced him on July 21, 1982, with Gen. Guido Vildoso Caldeson

DEMOCRACY RESTORED

With inflation running at an annual rate of 150%, President Vildoso on Sept. 14, 1982, decreed stiff austerity measures that increased prices and held down wages. Labor unions immediately called a general strike, declaring workers would not return to their jobs until Vildoso resigned. On Sept. 27 the military junta gave in to the unions, ordering the nation's congress to reconvene.

Congress voted 113–29 to restore the presidency to 69-year-old Siles Zuazo, recalling him

from exile in Peru.

After being sworn into office on Oct. 10, 1982, President Siles Zuazo immediately fired the commanders of the armed forces, naming as commander in chief Gen. Alfredo Villaroel Barja, a moderate who had formerly served as defense minister.

The president also appointed two communists as members of his cabinet.

In February 1983 the government expelled to France Nazi war criminal Klaus Barbie, whom France had sought to extradite since 1972.

The worst drought in the nation's history in 1983 destroyed most of the crops of subsistence farmers, bringing great hardship. The nearly bankrupt government struggled to import millions of dollars of food to prevent mass starvation.

President Siles Zuazo was kidnapped from his bedroom on June 30, 1984, and held prisoner for 10 hours in an unsuccessful attempted coup. Two former cabinet ministers and about 100 other persons were arrested and charged with rebellion.

The nation's economy went from bad to worse in 1984-85 with inflation soaring to a level of about 40,000% annually. Hundreds of strikes shut down services, factories, and mines as workers demanded raises.

In a presidential election on July 14, 1985, none of the 18 candidates won a majority of the vote. Although former dictator Gen. Hugo Banzer won the largest number of votes, Congress voted to give the office to Victor Paz Estenssoro, who had come in second.

Paz Estenssoro, 77, a conservative who had been president in 1952 to 1964, was sworn in again as president on Aug. 6, 1985.

BOPHUTHATSWANA

Official Name: Republic of Bophuthatswana.
Area: 17,010 square miles (44,055 sq. km.).
Population: 1,653,500.
Leading Cities: Mmabatho, capital, 5,000; GaRankuwa, 72,518; Mabopane, 64,854; Mafikeng, 10,000.
Government: Republic.
President: Chief Lucas M. Mangope (since 1977).
National Assembly: 96 members (48 elected).
Flag: Dark blue background divided by diagonal orange bar; leopard's head in white circle in upper hoist corner.
Official Languages: Tswana, English, Afrikaans.
Chief Ethnic Group: Tswana (Western Sotho of Bantus).
Main Religion: Animism.
Leading Industries: Tourism, agriculture (wheat, corn, peanuts, vegetables, alfalfa, cotton, cattle, sheep, goats); manufacturing (food processing, pottery, furniture, textiles, plastics); mining (platinum, asbestos, iron ore, chrome, vanadium, diamonds).
Foreign Trade: *Major exports*—asbestos, chrome, diamonds, iron ore, manganese, platinum; *major imports*—consumer goods, food.
Places of Interest: *In Mmabatho:* government buildings; Sun City, casino-resort complex.

Although declared an independent nation by South Africa, Bophuthatswana has failed to gain recognition as sovereign by any other country.

Given its freedom as part of South Africa's apartheid policy of separating the races, Bophuthatswana is made up of six areas separated by land that remains part of South Africa. Two regions lie along the border of Botswana.

Bophuthatswana is a major source of platinum for Western industrial countries.

Much of the nation's income derives from South African tourists who flock to Bophuthatswana's casino-resort Sun City.

The Bantu-speaking Sotho tribes, from which the Tswana are descended, migrated to southern Africa in the 900s to 1600s. In the 1820s and 1830s life in the region was disrupted by invasions of tribes driven from the coastal areas by European colonists.

Bophuthatswana was granted independence on Dec. 6, 1977, by South Africa, which at the same time deprived the 1 million Tswana of South African citizenship. Chief Lucas M. Mangope became Bophuthatswana's first president.

A new capital, Mmabatho, was built in 1977, just outside the South African city of Mafeking.

South Africa on Sept. 19, 1980, transferred the city of Mafeking to Bophuthatswana, which changed the name to Mafikeng.

BOTSWANA

Official Name: Republic of Botswana.
Area: 231,805 square miles (600,372 sq. km.).
Population: 1,111,000.
Capital: Gaborone, 59,700.
Government: Parliamentary democracy.
President: Quett Masire (since 1980).
Legislature: *National Assembly*, 36 members.
U.S. Ambassador to Botswana: Theodore C. Maino.
Botswana Ambassador to U.S.: Serara Tsholofelo Ketlogetswe.
Flag: Wide light-blue bands separated from a central black band by narrow white stripes.
Languages: English (official), Bantu (Tswana).
Main Ethnic Group: Tswana (98%).
Religion: Animism (85%).
Leading Industries: Agriculture (cattle, corn, sorghum); mining (diamonds, copper, nickel, manganese, coal); tourism; food processing.
Foreign Trade: *Major exports*—meat, hides, diamonds, copper, nickel, manganese; *major imports*—grains, fuels, motor vehicles, textiles, clothing.
Places of Interest: Kalahari Desert; Okavango swamps; Makarikari salt pans; game and bird sanctuaries; Gaborone gambling casino; Stone Age rock paintings on cliffs of Tsodilo Hills.

QUICK QUIZ: Who was Britain's king in 1830-37? See page 295.

BOTSWANA *(continued)*

The southern African country of Botswana is one of the few nations on the continent that has maintained a multiparty democracy since attaining independence. However, Botswana remains economically dependent on South Africa.

With about the same area and climate as Texas, Botswana has specialized for many years in cattle raising. Most of the people follow a tribal way of life that has changed little in hundreds of years.

Tourists from Zimbabwe and South Africa visit Botswana to gamble at the casino in Gaborone and to hunt, fish, bird-watch, and photograph at the parks in the Okavango delta region, the Chobe game park, and the Khutse game reserve.

Most of Botswana's exports and imports pass through South Africa and parts of Bophuthatswana, which lie to the south. Zambia and Zimbabwe border Botswana on the northeast. Namibia is to the west and north.

The Kalahari Desert covers much of the south. The Okavango River forms an extensive swamp in the northwest.

Under Khama the Great and other chiefs, the Bechuana (Tswana) people sought British protection against the Transvaal Boers in the 1880s. Britain established the Bechuanaland Protectorate in 1885. In 1909–55 it was threatened by incorporation into South Africa.

In 1948 the country was thrown into turmoil when Oxford-educated Seretse Khama, heir to the throne of the leading Bamandwato tribe, married a white English girl, Ruth Williams. He was forced by the British to live in exile. When he renounced his claim to the chieftainship, he was allowed to return to Bechuanaland in 1956.

Organizing the Bechuanaland Democratic Party, Khama helped lead his people to self-government.

In the first general election, in 1965, his party won an overwhelming majority, and Khama became chief minister.

The nation achieved full independence on Sept. 30, 1966, and was renamed Botswana. Sir Seretse Khama was elected by the national assembly as the first president of the new republic. He was reelected in 1969, 1974, and 1979 when his Botswana Democratic Party (BDP) again won parliamentary elections.

The discovery of substantial mineral deposits in Botswana in the 1970s stimulated its impoverished economy. British and American interests developed a diamond mine at Orapa. A large copper-nickel mine began production at Selbi-Pikwe in 1975. The country's GNP grew at an annual rate of about 20%.

Upon the death of Sir Seretse Khama in 1980, he was succeeded as president by Dr. Quett Masire, who had served as vice president.

Drought destroyed about 75% of the nation's crops in 1981–82. President Masire appealed for international aid to prevent starvation.

On Sept. 8, 1984, in the first general election since Masire became president, his Democratic Party retained control of the national assembly but lost several seats to the opposition Botswana National Front.

South African troops invaded Botswana on June 14, 1985, in a raid on headquarters of a black guerrilla group in Gaborone, killing 16 persons.

BRAZIL

Official Name: Federative Republic of Brazil.
Area: 3,286,488 square miles (8,511,965 sq. km.).
Population: 137,610,000.
Largest Cities: Brasília, capital, 411,305; São Paulo, 7,033,529; Rio de Janeiro, 5,093,232; Belo Horizonte, 1,442,483; Salvador, 1,496,276; Recife, 1,184,215; Pôrto Alegre, 1,108,883; Curitiba, 843,733; Belém, 758,117; Fortaleza, 648,815; Manaus, 613,068.
Government: Multi-party democracy.
President: José Sarney (since 1985).
National Congress: *Senate,* 67 members; *Chamber of Deputies,* 479 members.
U.S. Ambassador to Brazil: Diego C. Asencio.
Brazilian Ambassador to U.S.: Sergio Correa Affonso da Costa.
Flag: Green field with centered yellow diamond enclosing blue globe with 22 stars (five of which form Southern Cross) and motto "Ordem e Progresso."
Main Ethnic Groups: European descent (62%), mixed European-Indian-black (26%).
Official Language: Portuguese.
Main Religion: Roman Catholicism (93%).
Leading Industries: Agriculture (cattle, coffee, corn, rice, sugarcane, rubber, cocoa, soybeans); manufacturing (steel, automobiles, plastics, paper, alcohol, chemicals, machinery, consumer goods); mining (iron ore, manganese, gold, uranium, diamonds, coal, petroleum, bauxite, nickel); construction.
Foreign Trade: *Major exports*—industrial products, cocoa, coffee, soybeans, sugar, iron ore, manganese; *major imports*—petroleum, wheat, machinery.
Places of Interest: Brasília; Rio de Janeiro; Christ of Corcovado statue; Amazon River; Iguassú Falls; Portuguese colonial sites at Salvador; Ouro Preto, Congonhas, Sabara—the "Cities of Gold"; Ipiranga Museum and Monument at São Paulo; St. John del Rey gold mine; Copacabana and Santos beach resorts; scenic highway between São Paulo and Santos.

BRAZIL TODAY

The world's fifth-largest country in area, Brazil also is the seventh largest in population.

After 20 years of military rule in which constitutional civil rights were stifled, Brazil restored political democracy in 1985 under a civilian president.

During the period of military rule, Brazil made tremendous strides in the industrialization of its economy. No longer reliant entirely on agricultural products such as coffee for its export income, more than half of the nation's foreign exchange comes from industrial products.

The military rulers also left behind a huge foreign debt of about $100 billion, accumulated in financing industrial projects. Payments on the debt weigh down the economy. Inflation has run wild at a rate of 10% or more each month during the 1980s. Wages and the prices of most products are indexed to inflation. Millions of Brazilians live in poverty in squalid city slums and in rural areas.

Almost as large as the United States, but with half as many people, Brazil has huge undeveloped areas in the interior along the Amazon River. The Amazon basin accounts for 60% of Brazil's area but contains only 8% of its population. The government has made a concerted effort to open up and settle the western region. One of the keys to this program has been the construction of a $100 million 3,500-mile Trans-Amazon Highway, begun in 1970. The highway created boom towns along its route, just as the coming of the railroads once brought boom towns in the western U.S. Settlers are given interest-free loans to start farms.

The same spirit of lawlessness and treatment of Indians that marked the American West is prevalent on the new Brazilian frontier. Indians wearing war paint have attacked settlers and highway construction crews invading their territory. In turn the Indians often have been mistreated and killed with little provocation. Only about 100,000 Indians survive of the 1 to 5 million who once lived in Brazil.

GEOGRAPHY

Occupying almost half the South American continent, Brazil is bordered on the north by French Guiana, Suriname, Guyana, Venezuela, and Colombia. Peru and Bolivia lie to the west. Paraguay and Argentina are to the southwest and Uruguay to the south.

A tropical climate prevails in the Amazon River basin in the north. Over half the country's area consists of highlands between 650 and 3,000 feet above sea level, where the climate is temperate. Brazil's major waterways are the Amazon, the second-longest river in the world, the Paraná, and the São Francisco.

PORTUGUESE DISCOVERY AND COLONIZATION

In 1500 Pedro Alvares Cabral, a Portuguese admiral, claimed the region for his country. In 1532 Martim Afonso de Sousa founded the first colony at São Vicente and introduced sugarcane cultivation. When Brazil became the major source of sugar in the 17th century, many Negro slaves were imported.

Between 1693 and 1700 mineral wealth was discovered in central Brazil, and the region flourished for a century as a major world supplier of gold and diamonds. By 1763 Rio de Janeiro had replaced Salvador as the colony's capital. In 1808, after Napoleon's capture of Lisbon, Portugal's royal family fled to Brazil. Rio became the seat of the Portuguese empire.

BRAZILIAN EMPIRE

King João VI returned to Portugal in 1821, leaving his son, Dom Pedro, as regent. In 1822, acceding to widespread demands for liberty, Dom Pedro became Pedro I, emperor of an independent Brazil. His popularity diminished, and in 1831 he abdicated in favor of his son Pedro de Alcântara (Pedro II), who governed until 1889. The progressive rule of Pedro II laid the foundation of modern Brazil.

Foreign demand for rubber stimulated the growth of such cities as Belém and Manaus.

The abolition of slavery in 1888 fanned rebellion as the owners of plantations supported the republican movement.

REPUBLIC OF BRAZIL

In 1889 a bloodless revolt established the United States of Brazil, with Manuel Deodoro da Fonseca as first president.

By 1914 Brazil had gained political stability and international recognition. The country's rubber monopoly ended, however, with the development of plantations in Southeast Asia.

In 1930 a revolution brought Getúlio Vargas to the presidency. His regime degenerated into a dictatorship and was overthrown in 1945. Vargas became president again in 1950, this time by popular vote, but he committed suicide in 1954.

Juscelino Kubitschek, elected president in 1955, initiated heavy construction programs and industrial expansion. He created a new capital, Brasília, in the country's wilderness to encourage development of the interior.

Jânio Quadros, elected president in 1960 by the largest plurality vote in Brazil's history, failed to stem an economic crisis. He resigned after seven months. João Goulart, the vice president, took over in 1961. His 30-month regime was marked by strikes, riots, and inflation.

MILITARY RULE

A military uprising forced Goulart into exile in 1964. Marshal Humberto de Alencar Castello Branco became interim president. In 1966 Marshal Artur da Costa e Silva became president.

President Costa e Silva arrested opposition political leaders. He dissolved the national assembly, suspended constitutional rights, imposed strict censorship, and seized total power on Dec. 13, 1968. He suffered a stroke and died in December 1969.

Military leaders named Gen. Emilio Garrastazú Médici to the presidency on Oct. 7, 1969. He set up ambitious economic and social goals. Prosperity made him popular.

Gen. Ernesto Geisel was sworn in as president on March 15, 1974, having been chosen to succeed Médici by the military leadership.

Work got under way in 1976 on the world's biggest hydroelectric project—the Itaipu Dam on the Paraná River. The $15 billion project will have a capacity of 12,600 megawatts, doubling the nation's electricity production, when completed by the end of the 1980s.

The military government's emphasis on industrialization caused the nation's gross national product to increase fivefold during the 1970s—from about $40 billion to $236 billion by 1980.

Because the U.S. State Department criticized human-rights practices in Brazil, the government in March 1977 canceled its 25-year-old military assistance treaty with the U.S. and rejected $50 million in American military aid for 1978.

In 1977 President Geisel extended his own term of office by an additional year to six years and made it possible for a simple majority in congress to approve a constitutional amendment instead of the previous two-thirds majority.

Despite the opposition of Roman Catholic

QUICK QUIZ: Which First Lady previously was a professional dancer? See page 382.

BRAZIL *(continued)*

leaders, the Brazilian congress passed legislation in 1977 legalizing divorce in what is the world's largest Roman Catholic country.

President Carter visited Brazil on March 29–30, 1978, receiving a rather cool reception from the nation's military leaders who still resented criticisms by the U.S. government about their restrictions on human rights for Brazilians.

However, during the next several months the government relaxed several of its limitations on human rights. For the first time in a decade, unions were allowed to strike against private employers. In June the government ended its prepublication censorship of newspapers.

Gen. João Baptista de Figueiredo, chief of the national intelligence service, was elected president by a special 592-member electoral college in 1978. He took office on March 15, 1979, pledging to return the country to full civilian control.

The government announced plans in 1979 to reduce dependency on imported petroleum by investing $5 billion through 1985 to produce alcohol fuel from sugarcane and other farm crops. Plans called for auto manufacturers to produce nearly 2 million cars to use 100% alcohol as fuel, while other automobiles would use a gasohol mixture including 20% alcohol.

President Figueiredo signed an amnesty on Aug. 28, 1979, that permitted an estimated 5,000 political exiles to return to Brazil in the following months. The government announced it had freed its last political prisoner on Oct. 8, 1980.

The nation's first nuclear electric-power reactor began operation in 1981 with a capacity of 625 megawatts. A second reactor nearly twice as large is scheduled for completion in 1987.

Brazil and the Soviet Union signed a 5-year $6 billion trade pact on July 15, 1981.

The discovery of gold at Serra Pelada in northern Brazil in 1978 brought a gold rush of thousands of prospectors to that region. In 1981–82 mines in the area produced $180 million in gold. A miner in July 1982 found a 7.5-kilogram nugget worth $100,000.

Development progressed in the 1980s on what is believed to be the world's largest mineral deposit, discovered in 1968 at Carajas in northern Brazil. It contains an estimated 18 billion tons of high-grade iron ore as well as large amounts of copper, managanese, nickel, and copper. Government plans call for investment of $61 billion in development of the Carajas project.

RESTORING DEMOCRACY

The first major step toward a return to democracy was taken on Nov. 15, 1982, with the first secret-ballot election of state and local officials since 1962. Government-backed candidates won a majority of the offices, with the opposition divided among four main parties.

Early in 1984 millions of Brazilians took part in demonstrations calling for direct election of a civilian president. However, the military regime insisted that Figueiredo's civilian successor as president be elected indirectly by an electoral college of 686 members, consisting of the members of the national congress and representatives of state legislatures and municipalities.

Political conventions were held during the summer of 1984 and a political campaign was waged for the remainder of the year.

The electoral college on Jan. 15, 1985, chose as president 75-year-old Tancredo Neves, head of the Brazilian Democratic Movement Party, which had opposed military rule for two decades. However, Neves became critically ill and died before he could take office.

José Sarney, who had been chosen as vice president, was sworn in as Brazil's interim president on March 15, 1985. After Neves's death, Sarney was formally installed as president on April 22.

Sarney's fledgling democratic government faced severe economic problems in trying to control the nation's raging inflation which has caused prices to more than double each year.

BRITAIN

Official Name: United Kingdom of Great Britain and Northern Ireland.

Area: 94,515 square miles (244,794 sq. km.).

Population: 56,050,000.

Largest Cities: London, capital, 6,696,008; Manchester, 449,168; Birmingham, 920,389; Leeds, 448,528; Glasgow, 767,456; Liverpool, 510,306; Sheffield, 477,142; Edinburgh, 446,361.

Government: Constitutional monarchy.

Prime Minister: Margaret Thatcher (since 1979).

Queen: Elizabeth II (since 1952).

Parliament: *House of Lords,* 1,173 members; *House of Commons,* 650 members.

U.S. Ambassador to Britain: Charles H. Price 2d.

British Ambassador to U.S.: Sir Oliver Wright.

Flag: The Union Jack, combination of red-on-white crosses of England's St. George and Ireland's St. Patrick, with white-on-blue cross of Scotland's St. Andrew.

Main Religions: Anglicanism (66%), Roman Catholicism (9%), Presbyterianism (2%).

Languages: English (official), Gaelic, Irish, Welsh.

Leading Industries: Manufacturing (steel, machinery, cement, paper, electricity, motor vehicles, chemicals, aluminum, textiles, consumer goods); agriculture (sheep, cattle, dairy products, poultry, barley, potatoes, sugar beets, wheat, oats, fruits, vegetables); mining (coal, iron ore, natural gas, tin, petroleum); tourism; fishing.

Foreign Trade: *Major exports*—machinery, motor vehicles, metals and metal products, chemicals and drugs, textiles; *major imports*—food products, raw materials and fuels, machinery, motor vehicles, petroleum.

Places of Interest: *England*—Windsor Castle; Hampton Court; Shakespeare country around Stratford; Brighton; Lake District; Stonehenge; Devon and Cornwall; Oxford and Cambridge university towns; cathedral towns; Bath; York, reconstructed Viking village of Jorvik. *In London*—Westminster Abbey; Tower of London; Buckingham Palace; British Museum; Museum of London. *Wales*—Tintern Abbey; Caernarvon Castle. *Scotland*—Edinburgh; Scottish Highlands; the Trossachs. *Northern Ireland*—Giant's Causeway; County Fermanagh.

BRITAIN TODAY

An island kingdom that once was the most powerful nation in the world, Britain faces many serious economic problems. With the loss of the bulk of its worldwide empire in the past three decades, Britain today is a nation only half as large as its ancient rival France.

Britain is a union of England, Scotland, Wales, and Northern Ireland. A scattering of islands and small territories around the world still are British colonies and dependencies. But most of Britain's former colonies have been granted complete independence. Many, such as Australia and Canada, retain ties through membership in the British Commonwealth of Nations.

Britain was the birthplace of the Industrial Revolution in the mid-1700s and became the world's first industrial nation. But with the loss of the captive markets of its major colonies, Britain has been unable to compete successfully in today's free-for-all foreign trade. As recently as 1958 Britain ranked second only to the United States in world trade, but today it stands fifth in the value of its exports behind the U.S., West Germany, Japan, and France.

The British people also have seen a decline in their standard of living. The per capita gross domestic product has fallen to about half that of the United States. Because Britain must import much of the food its people eat and many of the raw materials its factories process, the nation has been hard hit by worldwide inflation. The average Briton has to pay taxes equal to about a third of his income.

The idea that many problems might be solved by membership in the European Common Market, accomplished in 1973, has proved illusory. However, a bright hope for Britain's future developed in the 1970s–1980s as offshore oil discoveries promised petroleum self-sufficiency.

EARLY HISTORY

A people called the Iberians are thought to have inhabited Britain during the Stone Age. Sometime before the 500s B.C. Celtic tribes from northern Europe began a centuries-long series of invasions. Troops under Julius Caesar landed in Britain in 55 B.C. By A.D. 142 Rome held all the land to the River Clyde, where Hadrian's Wall was put up to keep out the Picts of Scotland. The Romans introduced Christianity.

As their empire declined, the Romans withdrew their legions, and Germanic invaders from northern Europe—Angles, Saxons, and Jutes—took their place in Britain. Driving the Britons west to Wales and Cornwall, they formed the kingdoms of Kent, Essex, Wessex, Sussex, East Anglia, Mercia, and Northumbria in the south and east between 500 and 800.

Late in the 700s Danish Vikings began to harass the Anglo-Saxon kingdoms. In the 860s the Danes invaded the island. By 1016 Canute, a Dane, was king of England, and Anglo-Saxon rule was over, except for a brief period under Edward the Confessor.

MIDDLE AGES

In 1066 a Norman duke, William the Conqueror, led the last successful invasion of Britain. He became William I (1066–87) of England when his Norman troops beat a force of Anglo-Saxons under Harold at Hastings. William imposed a feudal system.

The first Plantagenet ruler, Henry II (1154–89), began the conquest of Ireland.

Feudal nobles forced King John (1199–1216) to approve the Magna Carta in 1215, the first step toward the parliamentary system.

Edward I (1272–1307), who completed the conquest of Wales in 1282, enlarged parliament, increasing its powers. In 1296 he conquered Scotland, but the defeat of his son Edward II (1307–27) at Bannockburn by Robert the Bruce in 1314 restored Scottish independence, which England recognized by treaty in 1328. Long-standing English claims to French territory and commercial rivalry with France precipitated the Hundred Years War (1338–1453). In 1346 Edward III (1327–77) invaded Normandy. He crushed the French at Crécy in 1346. Ten years later his son Edward, the Black Prince, won a second victory for England at Poitiers.

The war continued under Henry IV (1399–1413), Britain's first ruler of the Lancastrian line. Henry V (1413–22) routed the French at Agincourt (1415) and was acknowledged heir to the throne of France. After Henry's death the French rallied under Joan of Arc. The French victory at Orléans was the first of a series which, in time, left England only the port of Calais.

At the end of the Hundred Years War the rival families of York and Lancaster began a bloody struggle for the English throne: the Wars of the Roses (1455–85). Henry Tudor, a Lancastrian, ended the wars by defeating Richard III (1483–85) of York at Bosworth Field in 1485, and founded the Tudor dynasty as Henry VII (1485–1509).

REFORMATION

Henry VIII (1509–47) broke with the pope when denied the right to divorce the first of his six wives. He then claimed supreme authority over the Catholic Church in England. Under Henry, the Church of England emerged as Anglican Protestant. His eldest daughter, Mary (1553–58), restored Catholicism as the state religion, but supremacy of the Protestant Church of England was permanently reestablished by another of Henry's daughters, Elizabeth I (1558–1603).

BUILDING A COLONIAL EMPIRE

Elizabeth's reign was one of the glories of English history. The defeat of the Spanish Armada in 1588 made England a major naval power. The previous year Mary Stuart, Queen of Scots, a Catholic rival for the throne, had been executed. Men of daring such as Sir Walter Raleigh and Sir Francis Drake staked out an overseas empire. Men of genius such as William Shakespeare and Francis Bacon brought a flowering of English arts and science.

Elizabeth was succeeded by James VI of Scotland, the Protestant son of Mary Stuart. Ruling over Scotland and England as James I (1603–25), he established the first English colonies in North

BRITAIN *(continued)*
America at Jamestown and Plymouth.

COMMONWEALTH AND RESTORATION

Conflict with parliament arose from James' belief in the divine right of kings. His son Charles I (1625–49) aggravated the conflict. Civil war broke out in 1642 between his supporters and the Puritan partisans of parliament. Oliver Cromwell led the Puritans to victory, and King Charles was captured and beheaded in 1649.

England, now a commonwealth, was governed by parliamentary committee until 1653, when Cromwell dismissed parliament and ruled as Lord Protector, or dictator.

In 1660, two years after Cromwell's death, the monarchy was restored with the popular reign of Charles II (1660–85), a Stuart. The austere Puritan social code was replaced by a renewed sense of freedom. Political and religious strife returned when Charles was succeeded by his brother James II (1685–88), who reasserted the discredited divine right of kings and plotted to restore Roman Catholicism. James was deposed in 1688, without bloodshed, in the "Glorious Revolution." His Protestant daughter Mary and her husband, William of Orange, the ruler of Holland, were invited to govern England. The rule of William III (1689–1702) and Mary II (1689–94) ushered in a period of political stability. The Bill of Rights was passed and political parties were established.

CREATING THE UNITED KINGDOM

Under Queen Anne (1702–14), last of the Protestant Stuarts, the Act of Union (1707) created the United Kingdom of Great Britain by uniting Scotland with England and Wales.

Anne's death brought her German cousin George I (1714–27), the first of the Hanover line, to the throne. Like him, his son and successor George II (1727–60) spoke little English. The parliament became more powerful than the king. Under George II Britain added to its empire, chiefly at the expense of Bourbon France, emerging from the Seven Years War (1756–63) in possession of India and of North America from the Atlantic coastline to the Mississippi River.

King George III (1760–1820) dismissed William Pitt the Elder, the prime minister responsible for Britain's colonial successes. He then attempted to impose his own views on parliament. In the American Revolution (1775–83) all the North American colonies except Canada were lost. Following the defeat of Napoleon (1815) by an army under the command of the Duke of Wellington, Britain acquired new colonies in the Mediterranean, the Caribbean, Africa, and Asia.

INDUSTRIAL REVOLUTION

The Industrial Revolution, which began in the mid-1700s, gave Britain the world's first industrial economy. But the factory system brought many abuses to workers.

The first of a series of reforms, in 1832, extended the right to vote to the middle classes and made parliament more truly representative. In the following year child-labor and factory-inspection laws were passed, and slavery was abolished in the colonies. Repeal of the Corn Laws in 1846 was intended to lower the price of grain

for ordinary consumers. Prime Minister Benjamin Disraeli's Reform Bill of 1867 extended voting privileges to many factory laborers. Prime Minister William Gladstone's Reform Bill of 1884 established universal male suffrage.

Many of these reforms occurred during the long reign of Queen Victoria (1837–1901), which also witnessed the transfer of India from rule by the British East India Company to the British crown (1859) and the annexation of South Africa after the Boer War (1899–1902). The globe-girdling British Empire, rich, stable, and prosperous, was at the peak of its power.

WORLD WARS I AND II

Britain allied itself with its traditional enemy, France, in 1904. Ten years later Britain and France fought World War I against the empires of Germany and Austria-Hungary. Under Prime Minister David Lloyd George, Britain emerged victorious. To its empire were added former German colonies in Africa and the Middle East.

World War I marked the end of British expansion. Ireland's rebellion (1916–21) brought division of the island into the Irish Free State and Northern Ireland.

Britain granted independence in 1931 to Australia, Canada, Ireland, New Zealand, and South Africa, which became the first members of the British Commonwealth of Nations.

In 1936 Edward VIII abdicated to marry an American divorcée, a marriage disapproved of by the Church of England and the cabinet. His brother became king as George VI.

Hoping to avoid another war, Neville Chamberlain's government adopted a policy of appeasement toward Nazi Germany. But when Hitler's troops invaded Poland in 1939, Britain immediately declared war on Germany.

During World War II the British people rallied under the inspired leadership of Prime Minister Winston Churchill, holding out against intensive air attacks by Nazi bombers.

SOCIALIST BRITAIN

In July 1945 the socialist Labour Party, led by Clement Attlee, won an overwhelming electoral victory. In the next six years the Labour Party nationalized such basic industries as coal mines, steel mills, the railways, and the Bank of England. An extensive social-welfare program included socialized medicine.

The Labour government in 1947 granted independence within the Commonwealth to India and Pakistan, heralding the end of Britain's empire. In the following decades most of Britain's remaining colonies received independence.

Churchill returned to power in 1951–55.

King George VI died in 1952. His daughter became Queen Elizabeth II.

The Labour Party won elections in 1964, making Harold Wilson prime minister. Conservatives led by Edward Heath won control in June 1970.

Britain joined the European Economic Community (the Common Market) on Jan. 1, 1973.

Britain was hard hit by the Arab oil embargo that began in October 1973. A parliamentary election called for Feb. 28, 1974, resulted in neither the Conservative nor Labour Party receiving a majority, although Labour won a

plurality. Wilson again became prime minister.

Prime Minister Wilson called new parliamentary elections on Oct. 10, 1974, in which his Labour Party won a firm majority in the House of Commons for the next five years.

Because many Britons blamed the slumping economy on membership in the European Common Market, the Labour government held an unprecedented national referendum on the issue on June 5, 1975, in which 67.2% of the people supported continued British participation.

On March 16, 1976, Wilson announced his retirement. Foreign Minister James Callaghan was sworn in as prime minister on April 5.

Reflecting Britain's declining prestige, the value of the pound dropped as low as $1.57 late in October 1976—35% lower than its value of $2.40 in 1975.

Racial tensions caused by an influx of some 2 million black and Asian immigrants in the 1960s and 1970s brought race riots in 1977.

FIRST WOMAN PRIME MINISTER

The nation's continuing inflation and a wave of strikes for large wage increases brought increasing disenchantment with Callaghan's government. On March 28, 1979, he became the first prime minister in 55 years to be forced out of office by a parliamentary no-confidence vote.

In a national election on May 3, 1979, the Conservative Party won a landslide victory with a 43-seat majority in the House of Commons. Conservative leader Margaret Thatcher, 53, became Britain's first woman prime minister, promising to move the nation away from socialism.

The Conservatives cut government spending in 1979 by about $9 billion, reduced government controls on business, and announced plans for income tax cuts and restrictions on labor unions.

Increasing production of petroleum from the North Sea enabled Britain to reduce its imports of foreign oil in the 1980s.

For the first time in 10 years the nation achieved a favorable balance of trade in 1981.

The pomp and ceremony of the wedding of Prince Charles, the heir to the throne, on July 29, 1981, helped heal the nation's tensions. On June 21, 1982, he and Princess Diana had their first child, Prince William, who became second in line for the throne.

Britons were shocked in 1982 by two incidents concerning the royal family. On July 9 an intruder exposed lax security at Buckingham Palace by climbing a drainpipe, entering the queen's bedroom, sitting on her bed, and carrying on a conversation with her for about 10 minutes before being carted off to jail. In October Prince Andrew, 22, third in line to the throne, was revealed to be holidaying with actress Kathleen (Koo) Stark, who had appeared nude in movies.

When Argentine troops seized the British colony of the Falkland Islands on April 2, 1982, Britons rallied behind the government's determination to recapture the lost possession. A British fleet and troops dispatched to the islands engaged in a short, hard-fought war, forcing the Argentinians to surrender on June 14.

Prime Minister Thatcher, whose popularity

NATIONS OF THE WORLD 509

BRITISH COMMONWEALTH OF NATIONS

The Commonwealth of Nations is an association of countries and dependencies that formerly were part of the British Empire. Independent members voluntarily maintain trade and military ties.

INDEPENDENT MEMBERS

Antigua	Gambia	Nauru	Sri Lanka
Australia	Ghana	New Zealand	Swaziland
Bahamas	Grenada	Nigeria	Tanzania
Bangladesh	Guyana	Papua	Tonga
Barbados	India	New Guinea	Trinidad-
Belize	Jamaica	Saint Christopher	Tobago
Botswana	Kenya	and Nevis	Tuvalu
Britain	Kiribati	Saint Lucia	Uganda
Brunei	Lesotho	Saint Vincent	Vanuatu
Canada	Malawi	Seychelles	Vanuatu
Cyprus	Malaysia	Sierra Leone	Western Samoa
Dominica	Malta	Singapore	Zambia
Fiji	Mauritius	Solomons	Zimbabwe

BRITISH COLONIES AND DEPENDENCIES

Anguilla	Gibraltar
Bermuda	Hong Kong
British Antarctic Territory	Isle of Man
British Indian Ocean Territory	Montserrat
British Virgin Islands	Pitcairn Islands
Cayman Islands	Saint Helena
Channel Islands	Turks and Caicos
Falkland Islands	

soared as a result of the victory in the Falkland War, stuck resolutely to economic austerity. When railroad engineers struck for two weeks in 1982 demanding a higher wage increase than the 3% offered by the government, Mrs. Thatcher ended the walkout by threatening to fire all 24,000 strikers. Wage-increase limits of 3% for public employees were ordered for 1983.

In a national election on June 9, 1983, Prime Minister Thatcher's Conservative Party won the largest landslide victory since the Labour Party defeated Winston Churchill in 1945. She became the first prime minister since 1900 to win two consecutive elections with margins large enough to ensure a full 5-year term. The conservatives

PRIME MINISTERS OF BRITAIN

1902-05	Arthur J. Balfour	Conservative
1905-08	Henry Campbell-Bannerman	Liberal
1908-16	Herbert H. Asquith	Liberal
1916-22	David Lloyd George	Liberal
1922-23	Andrew Bonar Law	Conservative
1923-24	Stanley Baldwin	Conservative
1924	J. Ramsay MacDonald	Labour
1924-29	Stanley Baldwin	Conservative
1929-35	J. Ramsay MacDonald	Labour
1935-37	Stanley Baldwin	Conservative
1937-40	Neville Chamberlain	Conservative
1940-45	Winston Churchill	Conservative
1945-51	Clement R. Attlee	Labour
1951-55	Winston Churchill	Conservative
1955-57	Anthony Eden	Conservative
1957-63	Harold Macmillan	Conservative
1963-64	Alexander Douglas-Home	Conservative
1964-70	Harold Wilson	Labour
1970-74	Edward Heath	Conservative
1974-76	Harold Wilson	Labour
1976-79	James Callaghan	Labour
1979-	Margaret Thatcher	Conservative

QUICK QUIZ: Who was the first person appointed as U.S. Vice President? See page 381.

BRITAIN *(continued)*

took 397 seats in parliament, the Labour Party 209, and minor parties 44.

Britain broke diplomatic relations with Libya in April 1984 after gunfire from the Libyan embassy in London killed a British policewoman and Libya refused to turn the gunman over to authorities.

The opposition Labor Party voted in October 1984 to call for dismantling all British nuclear arms and expelling all U.S. atomic weapons.

Prime Minister Thatcher and the entire British cabinet narrowly escaped death on Oct. 12, 1984, when a bomb planted by Irish terrorists demolished much of a hotel in which they were staying during a Conservative Party conference in Brighton, England. The blast killed 4 persons and injured 32.

The strong-willed Prime Minister Thatcher won a major victory over labor unions in 1985. About 100,000 coal miners had gone on strike against government-owned mines on March 6, 1984, demanding that the government reopen several mines that had been closed for economic reasons. In the past, coal mining strikes had forced other British prime ministers out of office. But Mrs. Thatcher refused to negotiate with the union. After nearly a year, the strikers gave up and returned to work on March 5, 1985.

The British economy slowly improved in 1984-85. Inflation fell to an annual rate of about 5% and the gross national product made gains. However, unemployment remained at about 13%.

THE FOUR COUNTRIES OF THE UNITED KINGDOM

ENGLAND

Area: 50,331 square miles (130,357 sq. km.).
Population: 47,572,240.
Capital: London, 6,696,008.
Members in House of Commons: 516.

England is the largest of the four countries of the United Kingdom. It covers the southeastern three-fifths of the island of Great Britain. Its explorers and colonists spread the English language to all parts of the world and made London the capital of a worldwide empire. The history of England is detailed on preceding pages.

WALES

Area: 8,016 square miles (20,761 sq. km.).
Population: 2,900,000.
Capital: Cardiff, 273,856.
Members in House of Commons: 36.

Wales is the third largest of the four countries of the United Kingdom.

Wales has huge reserves of coal that helped make Britain a leading industrial power.

When the Germanic Angles and Saxons conquered England in the 400s, the original Britons escaped to Wales, the mountainous western part of the island of Great Britain. They preserved the independence of Wales until William the Conqueror proclaimed himself Lord of Wales in 1071.

English King Edward I claimed control of Wales in 1284. He started naming the heir to the English throne the Prince of Wales in 1301.

In 1536 Henry VIII of England united the two countries, giving the Welsh seats in the English parliament and making English the coun-

try's official language. In 1976 the Welsh language was returned to equal status with English in the schools. Bilingual road signs replaced English-only signs.

Nationalist demands for home rule suffered a setback on March 1, 1979, when voters rejected a plan for limited self-government.

SCOTLAND

Area: 30,410 square miles (78,762 sq. km.).
Population: 5,400,000.
Capital: Edinburgh, 446,361.
Largest Metropolitan Area: Glasgow, 1,727,625.
Members in House of Commons: 71.

Scotland is the second largest of the four countries of the United Kingdom. A mountainous country, Scotland covers the northern third of the island of Great Britain.

When the Roman general Agricola conquered Scotland in A.D. 80, he called the country *Caledonia* and the people *Picts*, meaning painted, because they painted their bodies. In the 500s a Celtic tribe from Ireland, called the *Scots*, invaded and conquered Scotland.

In succeeding centuries English kings endeavored to make Scotland part of England, but the Scots resisted. In 1603 the Scottish king James VI inherited the English throne upon the death of Queen Elizabeth I. He became James I of England but ruled Scotland as a separate country.

During the reign of Queen Anne, the Scottish parliament voted in 1707 to unite with England and Wales to form the United Kingdom.

The discovery of oil and gas fields offshore from eastern Scotland in 1973–74 brought an economic boom. It also stimulated demands by Scottish nationalists for home rule and for Scotland to be given a major share of the oil revenues.

But a plan for home rule was defeated in a referendum on March 1, 1979, when fewer than 40% of Scotland's registered voters cast ballots in favor of the measure.

NORTHERN IRELAND

Area: 5,463 square miles (14,148 sq. km.).
Population: 1,600,000.
Capital: Belfast, 345,800.
Members in House of Commons: 17.

The smallest of the four countries of the United Kingdom, Northern Ireland is the northeastern tip of the island of Ireland. About two-thirds of the people are Protestants and one-third Roman Catholics.

Because of Irish revolts against attempted English domination, England's King James I in 1603 forced Irish Roman Catholics in Northern Ireland to give up their land to English and Scottish Protestants whose descendants still constitute a majority in Northern Ireland.

In 1801 the British parliament united all of Ireland with the United Kingdom. After a revolt in Ireland during World War I, Britain separated Northern Ireland from the rest of Ireland in 1920. The Protestant majority of Northern Ireland chose to remain part of the United Kingdom.

Seeking to unite all of Ireland, the outlawed Irish Republican Army (IRA) has carried on a campaign of assassinations and bombings against the Northern Ireland Protestants and British soldiers stationed in the country since 1969. Protestant extremists have retaliated.

On May 1, 1975, voters elected 78 members to a convention given the task of devising a government acceptable to both Protestants and Catholics. But the convention disbanded on March 3, 1976, after 10 months of futile efforts to write a new constitution. Britain announced it would continue direct rule of Northern Ireland.

On Aug. 27, 1979, the IRA shocked the world by assassinating the senior statesman of the royal family, Earl Mountbatten of Burma, 79.

Ten imprisoned IRA dissidents died in 1981 in a hunger strike in which they had tried to win status as political prisoners.

Under British guidance a new 78-member assembly was elected on Oct. 20, 1982, but the assembly was boycotted by Catholics.

In the 16-year period 1969–85 terrorists killed over 2,400 persons.

BRITISH DEPENDENCIES
ANGUILLA

Area: 35 square miles (91 sq. km.).
Population: 6,800.
Capital: The Valley.

One of the northernmost Caribbean islands, Anguilla lies about 160 miles east of Puerto Rico and about 60 miles north of St. Kitts. Fishing is the main industry.

The island first became a British colony about 1650. After being ruled from St. Kitts for two centuries, Anguillans revolted on May 30, 1967, demanding self-government. Two years later the islanders declared independence and announced the severing of all ties with Britain. British paratroops and London police invaded the island on March 19, 1969, and put down the revolt.

On Feb. 10, 1976, Britain granted Anguilla a constitution as a separate self-governing dependency. The People's Progressive Party led by Ronald Webster won 6 of the 7 seats in the national assembly elected on March 15, 1976.

When Webster lost a confidence vote in the assembly in 1977, the British governor-general named Emile Gumbs as chief minister.

Webster regained power as chief minister in 1980 when his Anguilla United Movement won 6 of the 7 elective seats in the legislative assembly. His party won another general election in 1981.

Gumbs again became chief minister after defeating Webster's party in an election on March 9, 1984.

BERMUDA

Area: 20 square miles (53 sq. km.).
Population: 58,600.
Capital: Hamilton, 2,060.

Situated in the Atlantic Ocean some 580 miles east of Cape Hatteras, N.C., Bermuda consists of 150 coral islands, 20 inhabited.

Discovered in 1503 by the Spaniard Juan de Bermúdez, the islands were settled in 1612 by a group of Englishmen who had been shipwrecked while on their way to Virginia. The crown acquired the islands from a chartered company in 1684. Bermuda has the oldest British colonial legislature in the world. The crown-appointed governor is assisted by a 9-member executive council, an appointed legislative council of 11 members, and a 40-member house of assembly.

In 1968 Bermuda was granted internal autonomy. The governing, mainly white, United Bermuda Party (UBP) won control in parliamentary elections.

Rioting broke out in December 1977, and British troops were flown in to restore order.

Led by Premier John David Gibbons, the UNP retained control of the government in an election on Dec. 9, 1980. Gibbons resigned on Jan. 15, 1982. He was succeeded as premier and head of the UNP by John W. Swan, 46.

BRITISH ANTARCTIC TERRITORY

Area: 2,025 square miles (5,245 sq. km.), excluding Graham Land,

The British Antarctic Territory was formed in 1962 to include the South Shetland Islands (1,785 square miles), the South Orkney Islands (240 square miles), and Graham Land (the British territory on Palmer Peninsula, Antarctica, 473,000 square miles).

BRITISH INDIAN OCEAN TERRITORY

Area: 30 square miles (78 sq. km.).
Population: 2,000.

Situated in the Indian Ocean about 700 miles south of India, the territory consists only of the Chagos Archipelago, or Oil Islands. The three main inhabited islands are Diego Garcia, Peros Banhos, and Salomon. The people fish and raise coconuts for a living. The U.S. Navy built a major base on Diego Garcia in the 1970s.

From 1965 to 1976 the territory included the Aldabra Islands, Desroches Island, and the Farquhar Group, all of which were transferred to the administration of Seychelles in 1976.

BRITISH VIRGIN ISLANDS

Area: 59 square miles (153 sq. km.).
Population: 12,600.
Capital: Road Town, 2,260.

The British Virgin Islands consist of 36 islands and islets in the Caribbean east of Puerto Rico. Almost all the people are of African descent. Britain obtained the islands in 1666.

About 90% of the people live on the largest island, Tortola.

The climate is subtropical with winter temperatures ranging from 67° to 82°F.

Livestock raising, farming, fishing, and tourism all contribute to the economy.

CAYMAN ISLANDS

Area: 100 square miles (259 sq. km.).
Population: 20,000.
Capital: Georgetown, 3,975.

The Cayman Islands consist of Grand Cayman, the principal island, Little Cayman, and Cayman Brac. They lie in the Caribbean Sea some 200 miles northwest of Jamaica. About a third of the people are European, a fifth black, and the rest of mixed races. Tourism is the chief industry.

Noted for their underwater beauty, the islands are visited by about 20,000 scuba divers each year.

Although discovered by Columbus in 1503, the islands were never settled by the Spanish. Spain ceded the islands to Britain in the Treaty of Madrid in 1670. They were colonized by British from Jamaica and were its dependency until

QUICK QUIZ: Who was the last Archaemenid shah of Persia? See page 297.

BRITISH DEPENDENCIES *(continued)*
1959. In 1962 they became a separate colony.

CHANNEL ISLANDS
Area: 75 square miles (194 sq. km.).
Population: 150,000.
Capitals: St. Helier, Jersey, 25,698; St. Peter Port, Guernsey, 16,800.

Lying in the English Channel near the French coast, the main Channel Islands are Jersey, Guernsey, Alderney, and Sark.

The islands were acquired by the Duke of Normandy in the 900s and became part of Britain after the Norman Conquest (1066). In World War II they were occupied by Germany.

The islands ship large quantities of vegetables, fruits, and flowers to the English market. Jersey and Guernsey cattle are raised.

FALKLAND ISLANDS
Area: 4,700 square miles (12,173 sq. km.).
Population: 2,000.
Capital: Stanley, 1,079.

Situated in the South Atlantic some 480 miles northeast of Cape Horn, the Falklands crown colony has two principal islands, East Falkland and West Falkland. They are mostly hilly moorlands with a cool, rainy, and windy climate. The people are Christians of British stock.

An English navigator, John Davis, sighted the islands in 1592, but the first settlement was made by the French in 1764 on East Falkland. The British settled West Falkland in 1765, but both colonies were later abandoned. In 1820 Argentina colonized East Falkland. The British recaptured it in 1832–33. South Georgia, a whaling settlement 800 miles to the east, and the South Sandwich Islands are part of the colony. The main industry is sheep farming.

Argentina, which calls the islands the *Malvinas,* invaded and captured the colony on April 2, 1982. After a short but bloody war, Britain recaptured the islands, forcing Argentine troops to surrender on June 14.

Britain completed construction in 1985 of a $342 million airport to accommodate jet airliners.

GIBRALTAR
Area: 2.3 square miles (6 sq. km.).
Population: 30,000.
Capital: Gibraltar.

The Rock of Gibraltar, towering 1,400 feet high, is a peninsula jutting into the Mediterranean from Spain's southwest coast.

The Moors settled Gibraltar in 711, naming it Jebel-al-Tarik (Mount of Tarik). The Spanish took it in 1309, lost it again to the Moors, and regained it in 1462. The English won possession in 1704 and have maintained it since, although besieged many times by the Spanish and French. Spain renewed its claim after World War II.

In a referendum on Sept. 10, 1967, the people of Gibraltar voted overwhelmingly to keep their special ties with Britain.

In 1969 the border was sealed by the Spanish government. Britain and Spain reached agreement on April 10, 1980, to reopen the border. Later, Spain refused to honor the agreement.

However, on Feb. 5, 1985, Spain ended the 15-year blockade.

HONG KONG
Area: 403 square miles (1,045 sq. km.).
Population: 5,516,000.
Chief Cities: Victoria, capital, 633,138; New Kowloon, 1,478,581; Kowloon, 716,272.

Hong Kong lies on the China coast, 91 miles southeast of Canton. It includes Hong Kong Island (29 square miles), the mainland peninsula of Kowloon (3.5 square miles), the New Territories (369.5 square miles) between Kowloon and China, and over 230 offshore islets. The climate is subtropical.

Hong Kong harbor is one of the world's busiest. Victoria, the administrative capital, rises sharply from the waterfront and extends halfway up Victoria Peak. Kowloon and New Kowloon are crowded commercial and industrial centers.

More than 98% of the people are of Chinese descent. English and Chinese are both official languages.

China ceded Hong Kong Island to Britain in 1842 following British occupation during the Opium War. Kowloon became part of the colony in 1860. China leased the New Territories to Britain in 1898 for 99 years.

The colony's location, its deep, sheltered harbor, abundant labor supply, and free-port economy have made it an important center of trade, commerce, and industry. The largest industry is textile manufacturing. Much food, raw material, and water come from communist China. The colony is also an international banking center.

In the 1970s and 1980s Hong Kong had one of the most rapidly growing economies in the world.

Britain and China reached agreement on Sept. 26, 1984, on a plan under which Hong Kong would retain its capitalist economy and a large degree of political autonomy for at least 50 years after it reverts to rule by China upon the expiration of Britain's lease on June 30, 1997. Under China's administration, Hong Kong will become a special administrative zone, retaining its own currency and its status as a free port.

ISLE OF MAN
Area: 221 square miles (572 sq. km.).
Population: 69,000.
Capital: Douglas, 19,944.

The Isle of Man lies in the north Irish Sea midway between Britain and Northern Ireland.

Inhabited since Neolithic times, Man was ruled by the Vikings until about 800, by the Norwegians until 1266, and by the Scots until the 1300s, when it passed to the earls of Salisbury and Derby. It came under the direct administration of the British crown in 1765.

Tourism, dairying, fishing, quarrying, and agriculture support the economy.

MONTSERRAT
Area: 38 square miles (98 sq. km.).
Population: 13,000.
Capital: Plymouth, 1,267.

Montserrat was discovered in the Caribbean by Christopher Columbus in 1493 and named after a monastery in Spain. First settlers were English and Irish colonists from the nearby island of St. Kitts in 1632. The French disputed British control of the island, holding it briefly in 1782–83.

Montserrat became self-governing in 1960.

Tourism, construction, and agriculture are the main industries. Cotton is the main export.

PITCAIRN ISLANDS

Area: 18.5 square miles (48 sq. km.).
Population: 54.
Capital: Adamstown.

Pitcairn is a volcanic, mountainous Pacific island about 1,200 miles southeast of Tahiti. Its area is 1.75 sq. mi., but the colony also includes three uninhabited islands: Henderson (12 sq. mi.), Ducie (2.5 sq. mi.), and Oeno (2 sq. mi.).

Pitcairn was discovered by the British in 1767 and settled in 1790 by mutineers off H.M.S. *Bounty* and some Tahitian women.

SAINT HELENA

Area: 47 square miles (122 sq. km.).
Population: 5,000.
Capital: Jamestown, 1,475.

A mountainous island in the South Atlantic Ocean about 1,200 miles west of Africa, St. Helena was discovered by the Portuguese in 1502 and claimed by the Dutch in 1633. The British East India Company took the island in 1659. The Dutch unsuccessfully attempted to regain it in 1673. Napoleon I was exiled on the island from 1815 to 1821. In 1834 it became a crown colony.

Ascension Island (34 sq. mi. [88 sq. km.]; population: 1,146), about 700 miles northwest of St. Helena, was annexed in 1922.

Tristano da Cunha (40 sq. mi. [104 sq. km.]; population: 292) and the uninhabited islands of Gough, Nightingale, and Inaccessible became dependencies of St. Helena in 1938. The four islands lie about 1,500 miles southwest of St. Helena. Tristan da Cunha was evacuated after a volcanic eruption in 1961, but its people returned in 1963.

TURKS AND CAICOS ISLANDS

Area: 166 square miles (430 sq. km.).
Population: 8,300.
Capital: Cockburn Town, Grand Turk, 2,287.

The Turks and Caicos lie east of Cuba. The only regularly inhabited of the eight Turk Islands are Grand Turk and Salt Cay. South and North Caicos are the most important of the Caicos group. The population is mostly black.

Though discovered by Juan Ponce de León in 1512, the islands were uninhabited until Bermudians arrived to gather salt in 1678. Administered as part of Jamaica until 1962, the islands are ; dministered by a crown-appointed governor and a partly elected state council. Lobster and conch are the main exports. Britain promised independence whenever the islanders want it.

To encourage tourism, the government completed construction of a new $7 million airport in 1983.

BRUNEI

Official Name: Brunei Darussalam.
Area: 2,226 square miles (5,765 sq. km.).
Population: 231,000.

Capital: Bandar Seri Begawan, 36,987.
Government: Monarchy.
Head of Government: Sultan Sir Hassanal Bolkiah (since 1968).
Legislative Council: 21 members (10 elected).
U.S. Ambassador to Brunei: Barrington King.
Ambassador to U.S.: Pengiran Haji Idriss.
Flag: White and black diagonal stripes on yellow field; state arms in center.
Languages: Malay (official), English.
Main Ethnic Groups: Malay (65%), Chinese (25%).
Official Religion: Islam.
Leading Industries: Petroleum mining; agriculture (rubber, rice, coconuts, fruits, vegetables, livestock); fishing; forestry.
Foreign Trade: *Major exports*—petroleum, rubber, natural gas; *major imports*—machinery, transportation equipment, food, beverages, tobacco, chemicals, drugs.
Places of Interest: Kampong Ayer, water village, where about 20,000 people live in houses built on stilts over the Brunei River; sultan's palace and markets in Bandar Seri Begawan.

Somewhat larger than Delaware, Brunei lies on the northwest South China Sea coast of the island of Borneo. The country is made up of two heavily forested parks that are bordered by and separated from each other by Malaysia's state of Sarawak.

Brunei is one of the richest countries of the world, receiving most of its income from the export of oil. Its foreign reserves of $14 billion equal about two-thirds of those of the United States.

Although many of the people still live in waterside houses built on stilts, most have a color TV set in the living room. Many live as subsistence farmers or fishermen.

Ruled as an absolute monarchy by a sultan, the government spends a high percentage of its income on armaments to equip its small army. The government provides free health care, inexpensive housing, and interest-free loans for cars and TV sets. And there is no income tax.

Once a powerful state controlling Borneo and other islands, the sultan of Brunei lost all but the present territory in the mid-1800s.

Brunei became a protectorate of Britain by a treaty in 1888 under which Britain took control of the nation's defense and foreign affairs.

The discovery of petroleum deposits in 1929 laid the basis for the nation's later prosperity.

Japan occupied Brunei during World War II.

When the nation of Malaysia was formed in 1963 by consolidating British colonies in the region, Brunei refused to join.

Sir Omar Ali Saifuddin, was sultan from 1950 to 1967. His son, Hassanal Bolkiah, was crowned as Brunei's 29th sultan on Aug. 1, 1968.

Britain granted Brunei its independence on Jan. 1, 1984. The official celebration took place on Feb. 23, 1984, at a new $50 million stadium in the capital city. After the ceremonies, 4,000 invited guests banqueted in the sultan's gold-domed palace, built in 1980-84 at a cost of about $300 million. The palace, whose 1,788 rooms cover 16 acres, is the world's largest residential palace.

When Brunei took its place as the 159th member of the UN on Sept. 21, 1984, the sultan celebrated with gifts of $1 million to UNICEF and $500,000 to New York City for meals for the elderly.

QUICK QUIZ: Who was king of Spain in 1808-13? See page 299.

BULGARIA

Official Name: People's Republic of Bulgaria.
Area: 42,823 square miles (110,912 sq. km.).
Population: 9,010,000.
Chief Cities: Sofia, capital, 1,052,433; Plovdiv, 346,219; Varna, 288,803; Ruse, 171,688; Bourgas, 167,203.
Government: Communist state.
Head of Government: First Secretary of the Communist Party, Todor Zhivkov (since 1954).
Prime Minister: Grisha Filipov (since 1981).
Legislature: *National Assembly,* 400 members.
U.S. Ambassador to Bulgaria: Melvin Levitsky.
Bulgarian Ambassador to U.S.: Stoyan I. Zhulev.
Flag: Stripes of white, green, and red, with national coat of arms in top left-hand corner.
Main Language: Bulgarian.
Ethnic Groups: Bulgarian (85%), Turk (9%).
Principal Religion: Eastern Orthodox.
Leading Industries: Manufacturing (machinery, food and tobacco processing, metals, leather goods, lumber, textiles, chemicals, fertilizers); agriculture (livestock, wheat, grapes, roses, tobacco, barley, tomatoes, mushrooms, sugar beets).
Foreign Trade: *Major exports*—food, tobacco, metals, textiles, machinery, rose oil, wine, leather; *major imports*—grain, clothing, oil, gas, steel, wood.
Places of Interest: Shipka Pass; Kazanluk, in Valley of Roses; Varna Black Sea resort; Old Plovdiv; Rila Monastery; Veliko Turnovo. *In Sofia:* Alexander Nevsky Memorial Church; Boyana Church; Georgi Dimitrov mausoleum; Park of Liberty; museums.

BULGARIA TODAY

Bulgaria is a communist nation on the Black Sea northeast of Greece. A mountainous country about the size of Tennessee, Bulgaria has changed from an agricultural to an industrial nation in the decades since World War II. The major industries are food processing and the production of chemicals and machinery.

However, about a third of the Bulgarians still depend on farming for their living. A leading tobacco-grower, Bulgaria makes many of the cigarettes smoked in the Soviet Union.

Western police officials have accused the Bulgarian government of being deeply involved in the smuggling of drugs, arms, and tobacco to western Europe, using the revenues to finance terrorist activities.

The Balkan Mountains cross Bulgaria from east to west between the Danubian tableland in the north and the Thracian Plain in the south. The Danube flows along Bulgaria's northern boundary, and the Maritsa River drains the Thracian Plain region.

EARLY HISTORY

Bulgaria, part of ancient Thrace and Moesia, was settled by Slavic tribes in the 500s A.D. The Bulgars, a Turkic-speaking people, crossed the Danube, conquered the Slavs, and, led by Khan Asparukh, founded the first Bulgarian empire in 681.

Under the leadership of Krum (802?–814), the Bulgars expanded and consolidated their empire. Krum's forces captured Sofia and killed the Byzantine emperor Nicephorus I. Under Boris I the Bulgars adopted Christianity (865). The first Bulgarian empire fell in 1018, when it was annexed by the Byzantine empire. The second empire, founded in 1186, lasted until the Ottoman Turks subdued the Bulgars in 1396.

TURKISH RULE

For nearly 500 years the Turks held Bulgaria. A revolt in 1876 was savagely put down by the Turks in the "Bulgarian Massacres." Russia intervened, defeated the Turks, and created an expanded, pro-Russian Bulgaria.

Other European powers, particularly Britain and Austria-Hungary, feared Russian penetration into the Balkans. At their insistence Russia was forced to accept a treaty revision at the Congress of Berlin (1878). Northern Bulgaria was made a principality under Ottoman control. Alexander of Battenberg was its first prince.

Eastern Rumelia, south of the Balkan Mountains, was annexed by Bulgaria in 1885. His successor, Prince Ferdinand of Saxe-Coburg-Gotha, came to power in 1887.

INDEPENDENT KINGDOM

In 1908 Ferdinand proclaimed full independence and assumed the title of czar.

Bulgaria sided with Germany in World War I. In 1918 Ferdinand abdicated in favor of his son Boris III. Bulgaria lost much territory as the result of the peace treaty.

Bulgaria backed the Axis powers in World War II. Boris died in 1943. His 6-year-old son was named King Simeon II.

COMMUNIST RULE

Soviet troops seized the country in 1944. A Soviet-supervised election overthrew the monarchy, and Simeon II went into exile. A communist state was organized in 1945 under the leadership of Prime Minister Georgi Dimitrov.

After Dimitrov's death in 1949, his brother-in-law Vulko Chervenkov became dictator. In 1954 he gave up his position as head of the Communist Party to Todor Zhivkov.

To encourage foreign investment the government in 1980 began permitting foreign companies to own up to 90% of joint ventures.

The nation celebrated its 1300th anniversary in 1981 with a series of cultural events.

In an effort to reduce the high cost of imported fuel, the government pressed ahead in the 1980s to build more nuclear power plants.

The government established in 1982 what it called the New Economic Mechanism (NEM) in which each enterprise must not pay more in wages and salaries than its revenues after expenses.

A diplomatic crisis developed between Bulgaria and Italy in 1982 after Italian police arrested a Bulgarian official suspected of directing the attempt to assassinate Pope John Paul II in 1981.

Bulgaria protested the arrest in New York on Sept. 23, 1983, of Bulgarian official Penyu Kostadinov on charges of nuclear espionage.

In an effort to create what it calls a "single-nationality state," the government in 1984–85 forced nearly 1 million Bulgarians of Turkish descent to adopt Slavic names. The government also halted Turkish-language newspapers and radio broadcasts. The program caused clashes between Turkish ethnics and Bulgarian authorities that resulted in several hundred deaths.

BURKINA FASO

Official Name: Burkina Faso.
Area: 105,869 square miles (274,200 sq. km.).
Population: 6,960,000.
Capital: Ouagadougou, 200,000.
Government: Military junta.
Head of State: Capt. Thomas Sankara (since 1983).
U.S. Ambassador to Burkina Faso: Leonard Neher.
Ambassador to U.S.: Doulaye Corentin Ki.
Flag: Red and green with gold star.
Official Language: French.
Main Ethnic Groups: Mossi (67%), Bobo (15%).
Principal Religion: Animism.
Leading Industries: Agriculture (cattle, poultry, millet, sorghum, corn, cotton, sugar, peanuts, fruits, vegetables); fishing; forestry and lumbering; manufacturing (electricity, bicycles, food processing, textiles, plastics, soap); mining (manganese).
Foreign Trade: *Major exports*—livestock, meat, peanuts, cotton; *major imports*—petroleum products, textiles, clothing, machinery.
Places of Interest: Spiked mosque at Bobo Dioulasso; Ouagadougou.

BURKINA FASO TODAY

About the size of Colorado, Burkina Faso (formerly Upper Volta) is one of the world's 10 poorest countries, depending on aid from France and other countries.

Like other African nations bordering the Sahara Desert, Burkina Faso has suffered from drought since 1970 that has reduced its average annual rainfall to about 10 inches.

The people depend on international relief organizations to provide food. But relief supplies often are late because they must be trucked hundreds of miles over dirt roads from the coastal ports of Togo and Ivory Coast.

Most of the people consider themselves lucky if they can get enough food to keep from starving. Only about 1 person in 10 can read and write. Most live by farming or herding cattle.

A landlocked country, Burkina Faso covers a plateau 650 to 1,000 feet high. The main rivers are the Black, White, and Red Volta rivers.

Much of the fertile land in the valleys remains fallow because people fear the river-blindness disease carried by black flies along the rivers.

Mali lies to the northwest, Niger to the northeast, and Ivory Coast, Ghana, Togo, and Benin to the south.

HISTORY OF BURKINA FASO

By the 1300s the Mossi people of the area were raiding the wealthy trading cities on the Niger River and beyond. They organized the state of Ouagadougou, Yatenga, and Fada-n-Gurma. They later founded the Dagomba state.

The French claimed the region in 1896. At first it was included in the Ivory Coast colony. In 1919 it was detached. In 1933 the territory was divided among the Ivory Coast, Niger, and French Sudan colonies.

France granted independence to the Republic of Upper Volta on Aug. 5, 1960. Maurice Yaméogo was elected president.

In January 1966, Lt. Col. Aboubakar Sangoulé Lamizana seized power.

New elections held in 1970 were won by the Democratic Union. Its leader, Gerard Kango Ouedraogo, was named premier in February 1971.

On Feb. 8, 1974, Lamizana, with the help of the army, threw out Ouedraogo.

Lamizana restored multiparty democracy in 1978. In parliamentary elections on April 30, 1978, Ouedraogo's Democratic Union won a majority of 28 seats in the national assembly. In a presidential election in May Lamizana defeated Macaire Ouedraogo, a banker, by a margin of 56% to 44% for a 5-year term.

Pope John Paul II visited the country on May 10, 1980, as part of a 6-nation African tour. He appealed to the world for more aid to help the poor country.

After striking unions paralyzed the country for several months, Col. Saye Zerbo, a former foreign minister, led a coup that overthrew the government on Nov. 25, 1980. He headed a military junta that banned all political activity.

Maj. Jean-Baptist Ouedraogo made himself president in a military revolt on Nov. 7, 1982.

Supplied with arms by Libya, Marxist Capt. Thomas Sankara, 35, overthrew Ouedraogo on Aug. 5, 1983, in a coup in which 13 persons were killed. Sankara had been dismissed as prime minister and jailed by Ouedraogo three months earlier.

After military officers unsuccessfully attempted to overthrow Sankara on May 22, 1984, seven persons were found guilty in a secret court-martial and were executed by firing squad.

On the first anniversary of his rule, in August 1984, Sankara changed the name of the country from Upper Volta to Burkina Faso, meaning "land of incorruptible men." He declared that the name change was only one symbol of the revolution he was leading against corruption and ignorance. He appointed three women as members of his governing cabinet as a demonstration of women's liberation.

In an amnesty decree, Sankara freed former President Yaméogo and 10 former cabinet ministers who had been under house arrest.

In addition to food relief to overcome the nation's crop shortages, Sankara expressed hope in 1985 that the United States, France, and other nations would undertake major development projects to improve Burkina Faso's faltering economy.

QUICK QUIZ: When did Constantine I rule the Roman Empire? See page 300–1.

BURMA

Official Name: Socialist Republic of the Union of Burma.

Area: 261,218 square miles (676,552 sq. km.).

Population: 37,290,000.

Chief Cities: Rangoon, capital, 2,276,000; Mandalay, 458,000; Karbe, 253,600; Moulmein, 188,000.

Government: One-party republic.

Head of Government: Gen. U Ne Win, Chairman of Burmese Socialist Program Party (since 1962).

President: U San Yu (since 1981).

Prime Minister: U Maung Maung Kha (since 1977).

Legislature: *National Assembly,* 475 members.

U.S. Ambassador to Burma: Daniel A. O'Donohue.

Burmese Ambassador to U.S.: U Maung Maung Gyi.

Flag: Red field with blue rectangle in upper hoist corner containing gear wheel and rice encircled by 14 white stars representing Burma's states.

Languages: Burmese (official), English.

Main Ethnic Groups: Burman (65%), Shan (11%), Karen (7%), Kachin (6%), Chin (2%).

Religion: Buddhism (85%).

Leading Industries: Agriculture (rice, tobacco, sugarcane, rubber, jute, peanuts); forestry and lumber; mining (petroleum, natural gas, lead, zinc, tungsten, nickel); manufacturing (food processing, textiles, construction materials).

Foreign Trade: *Major exports*—rice, teak, jute, rubber; *major imports*—textile yarn and fabrics, nonelectric machinery, vehicles, chemicals.

Places of Interest: Inle Lake; Sagaing Hills. *In Rangoon:* Shwedagon and Sule pagodas; national museum. *In Pegu:* Shwemaudaw Pagoda and 181-foot-long Shwethalyaung (Reclining Buddha). *In Pagan:* Over 2,500 monuments in ancient royal capital.

BURMA TODAY

About the size of Texas, Burma is a Southeast Asian nation that for nearly two decades rejected most contact with the outside world. An isolationist socialist-military regime allowed the country's once prosperous economy to stagnate.

Nearly all of its people are poor with an average income of less than $180 per year. Only about 7 in 10 can read and write.

Burma was relatively unaffected by the soaring oil prices of the 1970s because it is nearly self-sufficient in petroleum. However, inflation was fueled by a thriving black market in consumer goods smuggled in from Thailand to avoid the government's ban on luxury imports.

The country has fertile plains and delta in the south and central area. Uplands form a protective arc of hills across the northern frontiers with Bangladesh, India, China, Laos, and Thailand.

BRITISH RULE

Conflict between the British and the Burmese for influence over states bordering Burma brought about an Anglo-Burmese war (1824–26), as a result of which the British gained control of part of lower Burma. A second Anglo-Burmese war in 1852 and a third in 1885 ended Burma's independence. Grafted onto India as a province, Burma was governed from New Delhi.

Under British rule Burma became the world's largest exporter of rice—"the rice bowl of Asia."

In 1937 Burma was separated from India.

In 1942 the Japanese, aided by Burmese nationalists, expelled the British from most of Burma. British rule was restored in 1946.

INDEPENDENCE

The independent Union of Burma was formed on Jan. 4, 1948. U Nu was named premier. He led the country for most of its first 10 years.

In the late 1950s U Nu's party split into rival groups. Fearing the outbreak of civil war, U Nu asked the head of the armed forces, Gen. U Ne Win, to take charge of the government temporarily in 1958. When U Nu's party won the parliamentary election in 1960, Ne Win stepped aside and U Nu again became premier.

When civil war threatened in 1962, Ne Win again took over the government and established a socialist military dictatorship. U Nu was imprisoned, and then exiled from 1966 to 1980.

Under Ne Win the government took over ownership of most businesses and industries. Foreign private investment and aid were rejected.

A new constitution was adopted on Jan. 4, 1974, creating a one-party state under Ne Win's Burmese Socialist Program Party (BSPP).

Sporadic fighting has gone on along Burma's borders for more than three decades. In northeast Burma communist rebels hold an estimated 7,000 square miles along the Chinese border. Altogether some 20 different ethnic groups carry on warfare against the government.

The government on Sept. 1, 1976, ended martial law that had been imposed in 1974. About 1,600 persons were ordered released from prison, and sentences were reduced for 3,300 others.

Prime Minister U Sein Win resigned on March 29, 1977, after he and other cabinet members were criticized for failure to follow the nation's economic plan.

U Sein Win was replaced as prime minister by 57-year-old U Maung Maung Kha.

A bumper rice crop in 1978–79 stimulated a spurt in growth in Burma's economy, permitting the export of about 700,000 tons of rice.

Ne Win's regime became disenchanted with communist domination of the third-world movement and announced its official withdrawal in 1979. Subsequently a more friendly relationship developed with Western nations. U.S. economic aid to Burma resumed in 1980.

A 475-member parliament was chosen in a one-party election on Oct. 4, 1981.

Citing illness, the 70-year-old Ne Win resigned as president and was succeeded on Nov. 9, 1981, by U San Yu, 63, a retired general. However, Ne Win remained in charge of the government as chairman of the BSPP party.

Burma broke relations on Nov. 4, 1983, with North Korea, which it accused of a terrorist bombing on Oct. 9 at Rangoon that killed 17 visiting South Korean officials and 4 Burmese.

The nation's gross national product grew at a rate of about 7% a year in the 1980s as the government focused on improving agriculture, forestry, and mining.

BURUNDI

Official Name: Republic of Burundi.
Area: 10,747 square miles (27,834 sq. km.).
Population: 4,727,000.
Capital: Bujumbura, 78,810.
Government: One-party dictatorship.
President: Jean-Baptiste Bagaza (since 1976).
U.S. Ambassador to Burundi: James R. Bullington.
Burundi Ambassador to U.S.: Simon Sabimbona.
Flag: White diagonal cross, with red quarters on top and bottom and green quarters to left and right; centered white circle bears three red stars edged in green.
Official Languages: Kirundi, French.
Ethnic Groups: Hutu (85%), Tutsi (14%), Twa (1%).
Religions: Roman Catholicism (50%), animism (40%), Protestantism (10%).
Leading Industries: Agriculture (coffee, cotton, tea, peanuts, cattle); food processing; fishing; mining.
Foreign Trade: *Major exports*—coffee, cotton, tea, hides; *major imports*—clothing, textiles, motor vehicles, flour, petroleum products.
Places of Interest: Lake Tanganyika; Ruvuvu River, source of Nile; Bujumbura.

BURUNDI TODAY

About the size of Maryland in area and population, Burundi is one of the poorest countries of Africa. It has few natural resources. Even its soil is mostly eroded and unfertile. Coffee accounts for about 90% of Burundi's exports.

Most people lead primitive tribal lives, raising beans, corn, and yams, or fishing in Lake Tanganyika. Few can read or write.

The country has few villages or towns. Most Burundians live with members of their own extended families in rural compounds called *rugos*.

A land of grassy plains, forests, and rocky hills, Burundi has a hot equatorial climate in its lowlands. But its upland regions have cool nights with an occasional frost. The White Nile River has its southernmost source in Burundi.

Landlocked Burundi has no railroads and less than 200 miles of paved roads. Rwanda lies to the north, Tanzania to the east and south, and Zaire to the west. Burundi's border with Zaire runs down the middle of Lake Tanganyika.

HISTORY

Tall Watutsi (Tutsi) warriors dominated the shorter Bahutu (Hutu) for centuries under an absolute monarch call the *mwami*.

Burundi was absorbed by German East Africa in 1898. Then it was mandated to Belgium after World War I as part of Ruanda-Urundi.

On July 1, 1962, Urundi was granted independence as a monarchy, renamed Burundi.

Mwami (king) Mwambutsa IV was deposed on July 8, 1966, by his son, who became Ntare V. Prime Minister Michel Micombero overthrew

Ntare V on Nov. 28, 1966, and proclaimed Burundi a republic. Micombero, a Tutsi, named himself president. He ruled as dictator by decree.

The Hutu majority revolted in April 1972 and May 1973. An estimated 150,000 Hutu and tens of thousands of Tutsi died in the fighting.

The Minority Rights Group (MRG), a British organization, accused Micombero's government in 1976 of having systematically killed all Hutus who had more than a high school education.

Lt. Col. Jean-Baptiste Bagaza led a military coup on Nov. 1, 1976, that overthrew Micombero. A Belgian-educated political scientist, Bagaza said he would try to end tribal strife.

President Bagaza established "civilian government" in 1980, making the Central Committee of Burundi's sole political party the main legislative body to approve his decrees and dissolving his military junta of army officers.

CAMBODIA

Official Name: Democratic Kampuchea.
Area: 69,898 square miles (181,035 sq. km.).
Population: 6,303,000.
Capital: Phnom Penh, 150,000.
Government: One-party communist state, supported by Vietnamese troops.
President: Heng Samrin (since 1979).
Prime Minister: Hun Sen (since 1985).
Flag: Red field with Angkor Wat pagoda in yellow.
Official Language: Khmer.
Main Ethnic Groups: Khmer (85%), Chinese (6%).
Religion: Buddhism (85%).
Leading Industries: Agriculture (rubber, rice, corn); fishing; forest products.
Foreign Trade: *major export*—rubber; *major imports*—food, fuel, machinery.
Places of Interest: Angkor Wat ruins and other ornamental monuments, temples, and palaces covering over 60 square miles, located at Siemreap. *In Phnom Penh:* national museum; royal palace; Silver Pagoda; floating villages on Mekong River.

CAMBODIA TODAY

A devastated country of Southeast Asia, Cambodia was ruined in the 1970s–1980s by wars and by the repressive measures of its communist leaders. Millions of Cambodians—half the population—died or fled to neighboring countries.

The communist government is a puppet of Vietnam, kept in power with an occupation army of about 180,000 Vietnamese troops. Opponents of the regime have waged guerrilla warfare since 1979, supported by China and other nations.

Most Cambodians are farmers. Before the disasters of the 1970s–1980s, the country exported large amounts of rice, corn, and rubber.

Mountains along the border with Thailand rise sharply from the Gulf of Thailand coast, drop to a plains region, and ascend again in the

QUICK QUIZ: Who did President Nixon fire on Oct. 30, 1973? See page 380.

CAMBODIA *(continued)*

north. Much of the best land for rice farming lies in the central basin along the Mekong River and around Tonle Sap (Great Lake).

About the size of Oklahoma, Cambodia lies south of Thailand. Laos is to the northeast. Vietnam lies to the east and south.

EARLY HISTORY

About A.D. 100 the Kingdom of Funan was established in southern Cambodia. Three centuries later an Indian Brahman took control of Funan. Indian influences shaped the country's customs, alphabet, and legal code.

The Khmer Empire was established in northern Cambodia in 802. It conquered Funan and most of Southeast Asia. A vast complex of shrines and temples was built at its capital, Angkor.

After disintegration of the Khmer Empire in the 1400s, Cambodia was dominated alternately by the Thais and the Vietnamese. In the 1700s Thailand annexed three of Cambodia's provinces.

France established a protectorate over Cambodia in 1863. It later became part of French Indochina.

Anti-French sentiment spread during World War II, when Vichy France bowed to Japan's demands for Cambodian bases. King Norodom Sihanouk, who had become monarch in 1941 at the age of 18, cooperated with Japan.

France granted Cambodia independence under King Sihanouk within the French Union on Nov. 9, 1953. Sihanouk abdicated in favor of his parents in 1955. He then became premier. Cambodia left the French Union in 1955, declaring its complete independence. In 1960 Prince Sihanouk was installed as chief of state.

Beginning in 1963, Sihanouk permitted North Vietnamese and Vietcong troops to build up military bases along Cambodia's border. The communists armed the Khmer Rouge, Cambodia's Communist Party, and staged border raids into South Vietnam. The U.S. Air Force at President Nixon's direction secretly began bombing communist forces in Cambodia in 1969.

In March 1970 Cambodian Premier Lon Nol overthrew Sihanouk, who fled to communist China. On April 30 the U.S. and South Vietnam sent 20,000 troops into Cambodia to destroy communist bases. American troops were withdrawn on June 29, but South Vietnamese forces remained and the U.S. continued bombing communist forces in Cambodia.

On Oct. 9, 1970, Lon Nol proclaimed the nation a republic named the *Khmer Republic*. In elections on June 4, 1972, Lon Nol became the nation's first elected president.

President Nixon announced on March 27, 1973, that U.S. planes would continue to bomb communist troops in Cambodia until the communists agreed to a cease-fire. But the U.S. Congress passed legislation that ended all U.S. military action in Indochina on Aug. 15, 1973.

The communists closed Phnom Penh's major supply route, the Mekong River, in February 1975. The U.S. then initiated an airlift to supply government forces fighting around the capital. Communist troops pressed their offensive on Phnom Penh, and on April 1 President Lon Nol fled from Cambodia, leaving the government in the hands of Premier Long Boret. On April 12 the U.S. ambassador and his staff flew out of Phnom Penh, and the U.S. airlift ended.

COMMUNIST AND VIETNAMESE RULE

Refusing attempts by Premier Long Boret to negotiate a cease-fire, Khmer Rouge troops captured Phnom Penh on April 16, 1975, ending the war. Communist firing squads executed Long Boret and other officials and generals of the former government.

Hundreds of thousands died when communists forced city dwellers to march into the countryside and work as farm laborers.

The Khmer Rouge announced on April 25, 1975, that Prince Norodom Sihanouk would be chief of state for life. But Sihanouk resigned on April 2, 1976, and went into seclusion. Khieu Samphan then took the title of president, but the government was controlled by Pol Pot as secretary-general of the Cambodian Communist Party.

The communists changed the country's official name to *Democratic Kampuchea*. However, the government was the reverse of "democratic." Thousands of opponents were tortured and executed, some for nothing more than criticizing the quantity or quality of their food rations. Few foreigners were allowed to remain in the country.

In April 1978 President Carter denounced Cambodia as "the worst violator of human rights in the world today." Officials estimated that about 2.5 million Cambodians had been killed by the Pol Pot government.

Vietnam launched a full-scale invasion of Cambodia on Dec. 25, 1978, and two weeks later captured Phnom Penh on Jan. 7, 1979.

Pol Pot and members of his government fled to the jungles, carrying on guerrilla warfare.

Soviet-supported Vietnam set up a new government with Heng Samrin as president.

Prince Sihanouk escaped from Cambodia in January 1979, appearing at a special meeting of the UN Security Council, where he denounced the Vietnamese invasion.

International agencies mounted a huge relief effort in 1979–80 to prevent Cambodians from starving because continued fighting prevented the growing of rice. The U.S. provided over $150 million in food and aid for relief.

About 500,000 Cambodian refugees fled to Thailand in 1978–80.

Khieu Samphan, prime minister of the Pol Pot government, called Western news correspondents to his jungle headquarters in August 1980 to announce that the Khmer Rouge had decided to reject communism as a philosophy.

In an agreement signed in Kuala Lumpur, Malaysia, on June 22, 1982, Prince Sihanouk became president of a Cambodian government-in-exile, bringing together three major groups opposing the Vietnamese-backed regime of Heng Samrin. Most posts in the Sihanouk government went to leaders of the former Pol Pot regime. The U.S., China, and anticommunist nations of Asia supported the Sihanouk government, while the Soviet Union backed the Vietnam puppet regime.

Heavy fighting concentrated along the border of Thailand in 1985—the seventh year of combat between Vietnamese occupation forces and Cambodian guerrillas.

CAMEROON

Official Name: United Republic of Cameroon.
Area: 183,569 square miles (475,442 sq. km.).
Population: 10,016,000.
Chief Cities: Yaoundé, capital, 291,071; Douala, 395,813; Nkongsamba, 100,000.
Government: One-party republic.
President: Paul Biya (since 1982).
Prime Minister: Bello Bouba Maigari (since 1982).
National Assembly: 120 members.
U.S. Ambassador to Cameroon: Myles Frechette.
Cameroonian Ambassador to U.S.: Paul Pondi.
Flag: Tricolor of green, red, and yellow bars, with yellow star centered on red bar.
Official Languages: French and English.
Main Ethnic Group: Over 200 Bantu tribes.
Religions: Animism (40%), Islam (25%), Roman Catholicism (20%).
Leading Industries: Mining (petroleum); agriculture (cocoa, coffee, cotton, bananas, cattle, rice, sugarcane, palm oil); forestry; manufacturing (food processing, aluminum, textiles, jute bags, soap).
Foreign Trade: *Major exports*—petroleum, cocoa, coffee, cotton, wood, prawns, aluminum; *major imports*—machinery, textiles, transport equipment, consumer goods, alumina, chemicals.
Places of Interest: Bamiléké Plateau; Waza Forest and wildlife preserve; Bamoun country; beaches.

CAMEROON TODAY

Cameroon is a prosperous West African oil-exporting country that is making progress in its efforts to leap from primitive to modern times.

Somewhat larger than California, Cameroon has not experienced the political unrest that has set back many of its neighbors.

While establishing extensive preserves to protect its wildlife, Cameroon has moved ahead to improve agricultural production.

About four-fifths of the Cameroonians live in the French-speaking eastern part of the country. Altogether there are over 200 tribes that speak 24 different African languages.

The people are poor, and the majority still follow a primitive tribal culture. But Cameroon boasts that a higher proportion of its children are in school or have graduated from school than in any other African nation.

By encouraging foreign investment, Cameroon has been able to build hydroelectric power plants and railroads to develop its large deposits of bauxite, thus becoming the largest aluminum-producing nation in Africa. Cameroon also is one of the world's important producers of cocoa.

Southern Cameroon rises eastward from the coastal plains to a densely wooded plateau about 1,000 feet high. In the central interior region is the Adamaoua Plateau, 2,500 to 4,500 feet above sea level. The principal rivers are the Benoué and the Sanaga.

Mount Cameroon, the highest point in the country, rises to 13,350 feet on the Atlantic coastline northeast of Douala.

Nigeria lies to the north. Chad and Central Africa are to the east. Congo, Gabon, and Equatorial Guinea are to the south.

HISTORY

The Portuguese visited the area in the 1400s but made no permanent settlements. From the 1500s to the 1800s the Cameroon coast was a regular source of supply for the slave trade of Spain, Britain, and the Netherlands.

Germany established a protectorate in 1884. British and French armies invaded the German protectorate in 1914. After World War I the western part of Cameroon was turned over to Britain. The remainder, about four-fifths of the total territory, was ceded to France.

During World War II French Cameroon was seized by the Free French.

The French and British Cameroons became United Nations trusteeships in 1946. The Cameroonians were granted limited self-government by the administering European powers.

The French Cameroon assembly voted for full independence in 1957. France and the UN concurred, and the Republic of Cameroon became independent on Jan. 1, 1960.

Plebiscites were held in British Cameroons in 1961. The northern region chose to unite with Nigeria. The southern region elected to join with Cameroon. The northern region of British Cameroons became part of Nigeria on June 1, 1961.

The southern region, newly named West Cameroon, joined East Cameroon, formerly French Cameroon, on Oct. 1, 1961, forming the new Federal Republic of Cameroon. West Cameroon and East Cameroon each had its own parliament.

Ahmadou Ahidjo was chosen as first president of the nation in 1961, serving for the next 21 years. Ahidjo consolidated all political parties into one party, the National Cameroonian Union (UNC), in 1966.

In a referendum on May 20, 1972, the people approved Ahidjo's proposal to change Cameroon from a federal to a unitary state.

The Trans-Cameroon Railway was completed in 1974, linking Douala and Ngaoundere.

Offshore oil wells began production in 1977, and by 1981 were pumping about 100,000 barrels a day. An oil refinery built in 1975–81 made the nation self-sufficient in petroleum products. Huge natural-gas reserves held promise of increased prosperity in the future. The government receives 60% of the revenues from oil and gas produced by foreign companies.

Paul Biya, 49, who had been prime minister, was sworn in as president on Nov. 6, 1982, following the resignation of President Ahidjo.

A mutiny by the president's guards was put down by loyal army troops on April 8, 1984, with 500 to 1,000 persons killed in the fighting. In following weeks, scores of persons were said to have been executed as plotters against the government.

The nation's fifth 5-year development plan for 1981–86 calls for the expenditure of $7.6 billion to improve agriculture and industry while further utilizing Cameroon's natural resources.

QUICK QUIZ: Who established France's claim to North America in 1524? See page 301.

CANADA

Official Name: Canada.
Area: 3,849,670 square miles (9,970,610 sq. km.).
Population: 25,600,000.
Chief Cities: Ottawa, capital, 295,163; Montreal, 980,354; Toronto, 599,217; Calgary, 592,743; Winnipeg, 564,473; North York, 559,521; Edmonton, 532,246; Scarborough, 443,353.
Largest Metropolitan Areas: Toronto, 2,998,947; Montreal, 2,828,349; Vancouver, 1,268,183; Ottawa, 717,978; Edmonton, 657,057; Winnipeg, 584,842.
Government: Federal parliamentary state.
Prime Minister: Brian Mulroney (since 1984).
Chief of State: Queen Elizabeth II, represented by Governor-General Jeanne Sauvé (since 1984).
Parliament: *Senate,* 102 members (appointed); *House of Commons,* 282 members (elected to 5-year terms).
U.S. Ambassador to Canada: Paul Robinson.
Canadian Ambassador to U.S.: Allan E. Gotlieb.
Flag: Red maple leaf on white field, with red bars at each side.
Official Languages: English and French.
Ethnic Backgrounds: British (44%); French (30%); native Indian and Eskimo (1%); other (25%).
Main Religions: Roman Catholicism (46%), United Church of Canada (18%), Anglicanism (12%).
Leading Industries: Manufacturing (steel, paper, electricity, aluminum, food processing, vehicles); mining (petroleum, copper, zinc, iron, lead, natural gas, asbestos, nickel, salt); agriculture (cattle, hogs, poultry, dairy products, wheat, barley, potatoes, corn, rapeseed, tobacco); forestry; fishing; tourism.
Foreign Trade: *Major exports*—manufactured goods, newsprint, wood, wood pulp, wheat, natural gas; *major imports*—motor vehicles and parts, chemical products, tools, machinery, aircraft, petroleum, communications equipment.
Places of Interest: Banff National Park, Alta.; Barkerville (gold-rush town), B.C.; Bell Homestead, Brantford, Ont.; Calgary Stampede, Alta.; Citadel, Quebec City, Que.; CN Tower, Toronto, Ont.; Fort Macleod Mounted Police Museum, Alta.; Fortress of Louisbourg, N.S.; Gaspé Peninsula, Que.; Man and His World exhibition, Montreal, Que.; L'Anse aux Meadows (Viking site), Nfld.; Niagara Falls, Ont.; parliament buildings, Ottawa, Ont.; parks, Vancouver, B.C.; Royal Botanical Gardens, Hamilton, Ont.; Acadian Museum and Province House, Charlottetown, Prince Edward Island; Citadel, Halifax, N.S.

CANADA TODAY

The second-largest nation in the world in land area, Canada is rich in natural resources. But Canada, like Australia, is underpopulated. Only 7% of the land is under cultivation, and only about 27% of its area is used for production of lumber or paper. The difficulties in transporting oil to the east coast from its large but dwindling western reserves explain Canada's unique position as both a leading oil exporter and an increasingly dependent oil importer.

One of Canada's major problems has been in maintaining its identity as a nation in relation to the more powerful United States, which lies to the south and is Canada's best foreign-trade customer. U.S. investments are important to Canada's economy. Investment proposals by foreign companies are subject to screening under the Foreign Investment Review Act (1973) to assure that they benefit Canada.

Another major problem is the division of the nation into two language groups: French-speaking, mainly in Quebec, and English-speaking, throughout most of the rest of Canada.

GEOGRAPHY

Canada is a federation of 10 provinces and two territories.

Most of the country's population is concentrated in the southeastern region in Ontario and Quebec near the Great Lakes and the St. Lawrence River.

To the east of this region is the Atlantic coastal area of New Brunswick, Newfoundland, Nova Scotia, and Prince Edward Island.

The Canadian Shield, a vast, U-shaped, rocky expanse, surrounds Hudson Bay. Thousands of lakes are scattered over this area. To the north are the Hudson Bay lowlands. Farther north is Canada's Arctic Archipelago, which includes Baffin, Victoria, and Ellesmere islands.

Canada's interior plains stretch to the west of the Shield.

The far west is mountainous. Major mountain systems are the Canadian Rockies, the Cascades, and the Coast Mountains. Vancouver Island and the Queen Charlotte Islands lie in the Pacific Ocean near the west coast.

Canada has more lakes than any other country in the world. Among the largest are Great Bear Lake, Great Slave Lake, and Lake Winnipeg. Major rivers include the St. Lawrence, Yukon, Fraser, Columbia, Mackenzie, Peace, and Slave. The southeast and far west have generally temperate climates with mild winters and warm summers. Seasonal variations are more extreme in the

CANADA'S PROVINCES AND TERRITORIES

NAME	AREA			POPULATION		ADMISSION		CAPITAL
	Sq. Mi.	Sq. Km.	Rank	Number	Rank	Date	Rank	
Alberta	255,287	661,190	5	2,476,910	4	1905 (Sept. 1)	8	Edmonton
British Columbia	365,947	947,800	4	2,903,420	3	1871 (July 20)	6	Victoria
Manitoba	250,947	649,950	7	1,028,900	5	1870 (July 15)	5	Winnipeg
New Brunswick	28,355	73,440	10	707,256	8	1867 (July 1)	1	Fredericton
Newfoundland	156,649	405,720	9	573,570	9	1949 (Mar. 31)	10	St. John's
Nova Scotia	21,425	55,490	11	858,439	7	1867 (July 1)	1	Halifax
Ontario	412,581	1,068,580	3	8,827,250	1	1867 (July 1)	1	Toronto
Prince Edward Island	2,185	5,660	12	124,735	10	1873 (July 1)	7	Charlottetown
Quebec	594,860	1,540,680	2	6,538,750	2	1867 (July 1)	1	Quebec
Saskatchewan	251,866	652,330	6	993,550	6	1905 (Sept. 1)	8	Regina
Northwest Territories	1,322,910	3,426,320	1	47,415	11	—	—	Yellowknife
Yukon Territory	186,661	483,450	8	23,878	12	—	—	Whitehorse

CANADA

CANADA *(continued)*

interior plains, where summers are dry and hot and winters are cold. To the north, summers are short and winters are long and very cold. The northernmost Canada has an Arctic climate. Rainfall ranges from 2.40 in. (6.1 cm.) a year at Eureka in the Arctic to 115.39 in. (293.1 cm.) at Estevan Point, British Columbia.

DISCOVERY AND COLONIZATION

The Vikings explored the coast of Newfoundland about A.D. 1000, but their colonies did not survive. In 1497 Canada was claimed for England by John Cabot, an Italian-born explorer in the service of Henry VII. In 1524 Giovanni da Verrazano explored the coast, and in 1534 Jacques Cartier erected a cross at Gaspé and claimed the land for the king of France.

The first permanent settlement was established by the Frenchmen Samuel de Champlain and the Sieur de Monts at Port Royal in Nova Scotia (1605). They founded Quebec in 1608.

In 1610–11 Henry Hudson explored Hudson Bay and James Bay.

The struggle between the British and French became intense after Britain established its first settlement in Nova Scotia in 1623. Port Royal and Quebec were captured by Sir David Kirke in 1628 and 1629, respectively, but were returned to the French in 1632. The French gradually pushed westward in search of furs, following such explorers as Nicolet, La Salle, Brulé, Joliet, and Marquette. The French settlement in Acadia was captured by an expedition from New England in 1654 but was restored to the French in 1655.

The French and Indian Wars with Britain in the early 1700s culminated in the defeat of the French on the Plains of Abraham and the surrender of Quebec in 1759. New France was ceded to the British by the Treaty of Paris in 1763.

BRITISH RULE

The Quebec Act of 1774 provided for preservation of the French-Canadian language, religion, and culture. During and after the American Revolution, Canada became a haven for Americans loyal to England.

The Constitutional Act of 1791 created a division between Upper Canada (later Ontario) and Lower Canada (later Quebec), making a total of six colonial units with Nova Scotia, New Brunswick (separated from Nova Scotia in 1784), Newfoundland and Ile St. Jean (renamed Prince Edward Island in 1798).

Westward expansion brought settlement of Manitoba in 1812 on land obtained from the Hudson's Bay Company. Many battles of the War of 1812 between Britain and the U.S. were fought in Canada. Grain and timber began to replace fur and fish in importance.

Rebellions in Upper and Lower Canada led to Lord Durham's report (1839) that set forth the principles of responsible cabinet government. Upper and Lower Canada were reunited in 1841.

DOMINION OF CANADA

Following conferences at Charlottetown and Quebec, the British North America Act of 1867 created the Dominion of Canada with the four provinces of Quebec, Ontario, Nova Scotia, and New Brunswick.

The Hudson's Bay Company territories in the Northwest were surrendered to Canada in 1869. The province of Manitoba was established in 1870, British Columbia in 1871, Prince Edward Island in 1873, Alberta and Saskatchewan in 1905, and Newfoundland in 1949.

Canada entered the 20th century with a population of more than 5 million. Participation on the side of Britain in World War I led to strong nationalism.

CANADA AS A WORLD POWER

The Statute of Westminster in 1931 established the political equality of Canada with Britain in the Commonwealth of Nations. Thereafter Canada moved quickly to develop an autonomous role in the world. Canada declared war on Germany on Sept. 10, 1939, a week after Britain.

Since World War II Canada has taken a leading part in world affairs as a "middle power." It has played a significant role in the UN.

Pierre Elliott Trudeau, a French-Canadian lawyer who had been minister of justice, succeeded Pearson in 1968. Trudeau called for elections on June 25, 1968. The decisive Liberal victory gave Canada its first majority government since 1962.

The 1970s recession was slower in hitting Canada than other industrial nations partly because of its oil export income.

Following the lead of Britain earlier in the month, Canadians turned conservative at parliamentary elections held on May 22, 1979. The Progressive Conservative Party won a plurality of 137 members in the 282-seat House of Commons, enabling Conservative 39-year-old Joe Clark to become prime minister on June 4.

Less than six months after attaining office, Clark was defeated in a vote of confidence in the House of Commons on Dec. 13, 1979.

CANADA IN THE 1980s

Trudeau led his Liberal Party to victory in a national election on Feb. 18, 1980, winning a clear majority of 146 seats to the Conservatives' 103 in

PRIME MINISTERS OF CANADA

Years	Name	Party
1867–1873	Sir John A. Macdonald	Conservative
1873–1878	Alexander Mackenzie	Liberal
1878–1891	Sir John A. Macdonald	Conservative
1891–1892	Sir John J. C. Abbott	Conservative
1892–1894	Sir John S. D. Thompson	Conservative
1894–1896	Sir Mackenzie Bowell	Conservative
1896	Sir Charles Tupper	Conservative
1896–1911	Sir Wilfrid Laurier	Liberal
1911–1917	Sir Robert L. Borden	Conservative
1917–1920	Sir Robert L. Borden	Unionist
1920–1921	Arthur Meighen	Unionist
1921–1926	W. L. Mackenzie King	Liberal
1926	Arthur Meighen	Conservative
1926–1930	W. L. Mackenzie King	Liberal
1930–1935	Richard B. Bennett	Conservative
1935–1948	W. L. Mackenzie King	Liberal
1948–1957	Louis S. St. Laurent	Liberal
1957–1963	John G. Diefenbaker	Prog. Cons.
1963–1968	Lester B. Pearson	Liberal
1968–1979	Pierre E. Trudeau	Liberal
1979–1980	Joe Clark	Prog. Cons.
1980–1984	Pierre E. Trudeau	Liberal
1984	John N. Turner	Liberal
1984–	Brian Mulroney	Prog. Cons.

the House of Commons and regaining the office of prime minister.

Efforts by Quebec's premier René Lévesque to win sovereignty for his French-speaking province were defeated in a referendum on May 20, 1980.

Determined that Canada should have its own constitution containing a bill of rights, Trudeau called a conference of provincial prime ministers and on Nov. 5, 1981, won the approval of 9 out of 10 for the new constitution. Quebec's prime minister opposed a provision that guaranteed English-speaking Canadians a right to education in that language in French-speaking Quebec.

The new Canadian constitution, embodying a bill of rights and severing the power of the British parliament to amend the constitution, was approved 246–24 by Canada's house of commons on Dec. 2, 1981. The following week it was passed by the senate. In March 1982 the British parliament gave the document its formal approval. Then on April 17, 1982, Queen Elizabeth II formally proclaimed the Canadian constitution.

Canada's recession-ridden economy deteriorated in 1982–83. Unemployment soared to a rate of more than 12%.

Jeanne Sauvé, 62, became Canada's first woman governor-general on May 14, 1984. She previously had been the first woman speaker of Canada's House of Commons.

Prime Minister Trudeau, 64, announced on Feb. 29, 1984, that he had decided to resign after heading the government for more than 15 years. The governing Liberal Party chose former finance minister John Turner, 55, as his successor. Turner was sworn in as prime minister on June 30, and almost immediately called general elections.

Brian Mulroney, 45, led the Progressive Conservative Party to its largest landslide victory in history in parliamentary elections on Sept. 4, 1984, winning a clear majority of 211 seats.

Mulroney, sworn in as prime minister on Sept. 17, 1984, promised during the election campaign to revitalize Canada's economy with a $4.3 billion government spending program through 1986.

In the first visit of a pope to Canada, Pope John Paul II made a 12-day coast-to-coast tour in September 1984.

Queen Elizabeth II and Prince Philip visited Canada on Sept. 24 to Oct. 7, 1984, taking part in the 200th anniversary celebration of the settlement in Canada of British loyalists who fled north during the American Revolution.

Improved U.S.–Canadian relations were demonstrated on March 17, 1985, when President Reagan and Prime Minister Mulroney met in Quebec to sign several agreements, including one for development of a $1.3 billion radar system to protect North America from enemy bombers.

The nation's Charter of Rights and Freedoms, section 15 of the constitution, went into effect on April 17, 1985, forbidding discrimination by sex, race, color, ethnic origin, religion, or disability. The effective date of the charter had been delayed for three years to give local governments time to change conflicting laws.

A world's fair called Expo 86 was scheduled to open in Vancouver on May 2, 1986, marking the city's centennial anniversary.

CAPE VERDE

Official Name: Republic of Cape Verde.
Area: 1,750 square miles (4,352 sq. km.).
Population: 362,000.
Capital: Praia, 20,000.
Government: One-party state.
President: Aristedes Pereira (since 1975).
Prime Minister: Pedro Pires (since 1975).
National Assembly: 56 members.
U.S. Ambassador to Cape Verde: John M. Yates.
Ambassador to U.S.: Jose Luis Fernandes Lopes.
Flag: Red vertical bar at hoist with black star flanked by two green cornstalks and yellow seashell; two horizontal stripes, yellow over green.
Languages: Portuguese (official), Crioulo.
Main Ethnic Groups: Creole (mulatto—71%), black (28%).
Principal Religions: Roman Catholicism (65%), animism (30%).
Leading Industries: Agriculture (coffee, bananas, corn, vegetables, sugarcane, beans, potatoes, peanuts, fruits); fishing; shipping; tourism; food processing.
Foreign trade: *Major exports*—tuna, lobsters, bananas, coffee, salt, peanuts; *major imports*—petroleum, consumer goods, corn, rice, sugar.
Places of Interest: White sand beaches; 9,281-foot Pico volcano and Chã das Caldeiras, black sand lake on Fogo; ruins of first European settlement on São Tiago; 15th century capital city of Ribeira Grande on Santo Antão, ancient fortress, tiled cathedral, Gothic tombs.

CAPE VERDE TODAY

Ranking among the smallest of the world's nations in area and population, Cape Verde faces a bleak future because of its lack of resources.

Lying about 400 miles off the coast of West Africa, the nation's main islands are São Tiago (383 sq. mi.), Santa Antão (301), Boa Vista (239), Fogo (184), São Nicolau (132), Maio (104), and Sal (83).

Most Cape Verdeans make their living by herding livestock or farming. But years of drought from 1968 to 1985 severely hurt agriculture. As a result about 40,000 Cape Verdeans migrated to Portugal to find work. Money they send home to their families helps pay for imports.

Tourism promises to become an important industry because of the white sand beaches, year-round mild climate, and absence of cloudy or rainy weather. Some islands have recorded no rainfall in more than 11 years.

HISTORY

Portuguese explorer Diogo Gomes discovered the uninhabited islands in 1460. The islands soon became an important provisioning stop for ships sailing around Africa and to Brazil. Portuguese trade in slaves from Guinea was controlled from the islands for hundreds of years. The wealthy capital city of Ribeira Grande on Santo Antão was often attacked by pirates.

QUICK QUIZ: How many persons were executed as witches in Salem, Mass., in 1692? See page 301.

CAPE VERDE *(continued)*

Severe droughts repeatedly caused many deaths: 20,000 in 1900–03, 25,000 in 1920–22, 20,000 in 1940–43, and 3,000 in 1946–48.

After more than five centuries of Portuguese rule the islands were granted independence on July 5, 1975.

Aristedes Pereira, leader of the nation's only political party, the African Party for the Independence of Guinea-Bissau and Cape Verde (PIAGC), became Cape Verde's first president.

CENTRAL AFRICA

Official Name: Central African Republic.
Area: 240,535 square miles (622,984 sq. km.).
Population: 2,630,000.
Chief Cities: Bangui, capital, 187,000.
Government: Military junta.
Head of State: Gen. André Kolingba (since 1981).
U.S. Ambassador to Central Africa: Edmund DeJarnette.
Ambassador to U.S.: Christian Lingama-Toleque.
Flag: Blue, white, green, and yellow stripes crossed by vertical red bar; gold star in upper hoist corner.
Languages: French (official), Sangho.
Ethnic Groups: Banda (29%), Baya (28%), Mandia (24%), Ubangi (14%), Sara (5%).
Religions: Protestantism (40%), Roman Catholicism (28%), animism (24%), Islam (8%).
Leading Industries: Agriculture (cattle, cotton, coffee, bananas, rubber, mangoes, manioc); mining (diamonds, uranium); manufacturing (textiles, food processing); forestry and lumbering.
Foreign Trade: *Major exports*—diamonds, cotton, coffee, wood; *major imports*—textile and leather machinery, textiles.
Places of Interest: Game reserves in north; Bangui.

CENTRAL AFRICA TODAY

Although nearly as large as Texas, Central Africa is a poor, landlocked country that has few resources. Nine out of ten of the people raise crops and livestock, mostly to feed their families. The country's only two important cash crops are coffee and cotton.

Large tropical forests provide the potential for a substantial lumber industry, but the lack of good transportation facilities makes the export of large amounts of lumber difficult.

The country's best hope for improving its economic situation seems to lie in the development of its mining industry. Gem and industrial diamonds account for over half the value of the country's exports. In the 1970s the French Atomic Energy Commission cooperated in the development of mining and refining facilities to work a large deposit of uranium found in the eastern part of the country. France is the nation's main trading partner.

The nation stretches north to Chad, east to the Sudan, south to Congo and Zaire, and west to Cameroon. The terrain is chiefly rolling plateau, becoming tropical forest in the south and hilly savanna in the north.

From October to June the weather is dry and hot; temperatures exceed 110 ° F. in the daytime and range from 55 ° to 70 ° F. at night. From June through September temperatures range from 75 ° to 110 ° F. Tornadoes and floods are frequent.

HISTORY

In 1889 the French established an outpost at Bangui. In 1894 the area between the Ubangi and Shari rivers was made a French territory. It was united with Chad in 1905 to form the Ubangi-Shari-Chad Colony. In 1910 the colony became part of French Equatorial Africa. Chad was detached from Ubangi-Shari in 1920.

The first representative assembly was created in 1945. A year later Ubangi-Shari received representation in the French parliament.

As the Central African Republic, the country was proclaimed autonomous within the French Community in 1958. Its first president, Barthelemy Boganda, was killed in a plane crash in 1959.

The nation won full independence on Aug. 13, 1960. David Dacko, Boganda's nephew and leader of the African Social Evolution Party (MESAN), was elected president in 1960 and 1964. He outlawed opposition parties.

Col. Jean-Bédel Bokassa ousted Dacko by a military coup on Jan. 1, 1966. He dissolved the national assembly and abolished the constitution. Suspected political opponents were jailed without trial, tortured, and often beaten to death. He also was said to practice cannibalism.

Bokassa renamed the country the *Central African Empire* on Dec. 4, 1976, and crowned himself as Emperor Bokassa I in a ceremony at the Bangui sports stadium.

When schoolboys demonstrated against a government decree ordering them to buy uniforms from a shop partly owned by one of Bokassa's three wives, Bokassa ordered them arrested and about 100 were killed on April 18–19, 1979. Despite Bokassa's denials of involvement, an international investigative team reported that the emperor personally killed 39 of the students. In reaction to the incident, the U.S. cut off $2.5 million annual foreign aid.

Former President Dacko, 49, who had acted as an adviser to Bokassa, overthrew the emperor on Sept. 20, 1979, reestablishing a republic with himself as president. The coup was accomplished with the aid of French troops. Bokassa was in Libya at the time of the coup and remained abroad.

In an election on March 15, 1981, Dacko announced he had defeated other candidates by winning 50.23% of the vote. .

Gen. André Kolingba, chief of staff of the army, seized power on Sept. 1, 1981, making himself head of state. He established a 22-man military junta to govern the country with himself as chairman. Political parties and the constitution were suspended.

Ange Patasse, a cabinet minister under Emperor Bokassa, tried to oust Kolingba on March 3, 1982. Loyalist troops put down the coup, and Patasse took refuge in the French embassy.

The 1980–1985 five-year plan of the Central African government provided for a $12 million rehabilitation of the national road network, which includes only 177 miles of paved highways.

CHAD

Official Name: Republic of Chad.
Area: 495,755 square miles (1,284,000 sq. km.).
Population: 5,037,000.
Capital: N'Djaména, 179,000.
Government: Rule by decree.
President: Hissen Habré (since 1982).
U.S. Ambassador to Chad: Jay P. Moffat.
Chad Ambassador to U.S.: Mahamat Ali Adoum.
Flag: Blue, yellow, red bars.
Languages: French (official), Arabic, Sara.
Ethnic Groups: Arab, Bantu, Sudanese.
Religions: Animism (50%), Islam (45%), Roman Catholicism (5%).
Leading Industries: Agriculture (cotton, cattle, millet, sorghum, rice, sweet potatoes); mining (natron); manufacturing (textiles, food processing).
Foreign Trade: *Major exports*—cotton, cattle; *major imports*—petroleum products, machinery, motor vehicles.
Places of Interest: Lake Chad; Sahara Desert.

CHAD TODAY

Chad is almost as large as the combined area of California, Arizona, New Mexico, and Nevada, but more than half the country is covered by the wasteland of the Sahara Desert.

One of the world's poorest countries, Chad has been made even poorer by many years of civil war and severe drought.

The nation's economy is almost entirely dependent upon agriculture and foreign aid. Most of the people of the northern part of the country are Muslim nomads who tend flocks of sheep, goats, and cattle. The people of southern Chad are mostly black farmers who grow grain crops.

Animosity between the Arabs of northern Chad and the blacks of southern Chad has existed for hundreds of years. The Arabs call southern Chad *Dar al-Abib*, meaning "Territory of Slaves," because it was the region where the Arabs frequently captured blacks for slaves.

The northern Sahara region of Chad is a dry barren land relieved only by occasional oases. Chad's central area is semidesert with some tropical trees and grazing land.

Lake Chad, on the western border, is a broad body of water surrounded by huge marshes.

Landlocked Chad is bordered by Libya on the north, Sudan to the east, Central Africa to the south, Cameroon and Nigeria to the southwest, and Niger to the west.

HISTORY

In the 700s A.D. peoples from the upper Nile built walled city-states on the eastern shores of Lake Chad. Saharan Berbers forged these states into a centralized kingdom called *Kanem*, which later was absorbed into the empire of Bornu in what is now Nigeria.

British explorers first entered the area in 1822.

The French pushed northward into Chad in the 1890s, killing Rabeh, a military adventurer who had devastated the Muslim states (1892-98).

The French created the Military Territory of Chad in 1900. Chad was united in 1906 with Ubangi-Shari (now Central Africa). In 1910 it became a part of French Equatorial Africa.

Chad was detached from Ubangi-Shari in 1920. It became an autonomous state in 1958.

Chad won independence on Aug. 11, 1960, remaining within the French Community. François Tombalbaye, became president.

A civil war began in 1965 between Muslim northerners and Christian-led blacks of the south.

In June 1973 Tombalbaye imprisoned Gen. Félix Malloum, commander of the army. The army attacked the presidential palace on April 13, 1975, killing Tombalbaye. Malloum became ruler.

The government agreed to a cease-fire on Jan. 22, 1978, with Arab rebel leader Hissen Habré. On Aug. 29, 1978, the ruling military junta was dissolved. Malloum became president and Habré became prime minister.

Civil war broke out anew in February 1979 between troops of Malloum and Habré. French paratroops flew into N'Djaména to rescue about 4,000 westerners from the fighting. Malloum resigned on March 23, 1979, and flew to exile.

A new government was formed on Aug. 21, 1979, with Muslim guerrilla leader Goukouni Oueddei as president.

New fighting began on March 22, 1980, between troops of Goukouni and Habré. In May 1980 France withdrew its last 1,100 troops. An estimated 100,000 Chadians fled to neighboring countries.

Libya intervened in the civil war in 1980 on the side of President Goukouni, invading Chad with about 4,000 troops. The Libyans won control of the capital, N'Djaména on Dec. 15.

Habré and his supporters retreated to eastern Chad, where they continued guerrilla warfare in 1981-82, supported by Sudan and Egypt.

On Jan. 6, 1981, Libyan leader Col. Mu'ammar al-Qadhafi announced that Libya and Chad would be merged as one nation. However, responding to pressure from other African nations, Libya withdrew its army in November 1981. It was replaced by a peacekeeping force of the Organization for African Unity (OAU).

On June 7, 1982, rebel forces of Habré captured the capital without opposition by OAU forces. President Goukouni fled. Habré consolidated his rule over most of the country, being sworn in as president on Oct. 21, 1983.

The civil war resumed with new intensity in the spring of 1983 in northern Chad. Backed by Libyan troops, forces of former President Goukouni captured much of northeastern Chad by July. To counter Libya, the U.S. airlifted military supplies and advisers to aid Habre. France sent about 2,500 troops and 10 fighter planes. And Zaire provided about 2,700 troops. The civil war quieted to a stalemate by September.

France and Libya announced on Sept. 17, 1984, an agreement to withdraw all their troops. France withdrew its troops in November, but those of Libya remained in northern Chad.

QUICK QUIZ: What was "Lady Bird" Johnson's full name? See page 378.

CHILE

Official Name: Republic of Chile.
Area: 292,258 square miles (756,945 sq. km.).
Population: 12,305,000.
Chief Cities: Santiago, capital, 4,039,287; Viña del Mar, 290,014; Valparaíso, 266,577; Concepción, 206,107; Talcahuano, 208,941; Antofagasta, 166,964.
Government: Military dictatorship.
President: Gen. Augusto Pinochet Ugarte (seized power in 1973).
U.S. Ambassador to Chile: Harry George Barnes Jr.
Chilean Ambassador to U.S.: Hernan Felipe Errazuriz.
Flag: Stripes of white and red; union is blue square with five-pointed white star.
Language: Spanish.
Principal Ethnic Group: Mestizo (mixed Spanish- Indian ancestry).
Main Religions: Roman Catholicism (official, 67%), Protestantism (9%).
Leading Industries: Mining (copper, iron ore, sodium nitrate, coal); manufacturing (steel, textiles, food processing, consumer goods); agriculture (wheat, sugar beets, livestock, potatoes, corn, beans).
Foreign Trade: *Major exports*—copper, iron ore, nitrates, coal; *major imports*—electrical machinery, chemical products, cereals, crude petroleum.
Places of Interest: Chilean lake country; Valparaíso; Indian ruins of Antofagasta province; Villarrica mountain area; Viña del Mar beach resort. *In Santiago:* Santa Lucia and San Cristóbal hills; presidential palace, cathedral; historical museum and national library; Forestal and President Balmaceda parks.

CHILE TODAY

A long narrow country, Chile stretches 2,650 miles along the western coast of South America. It averages only 110 miles in width and is 221 miles across at its widest point.

For many years Chile was one of the few Latin American countries where the government was regularly chosen by constitutional free elections and human rights were respected. But today Chile is ruled by a military dictatorship that has suspended all civil liberties. The change came in September 1973 when the armed forces overthrew the country's elected Marxist president because they feared he was leading Chile to become a satellite of the Soviet Union.

Although rich in natural resources and one of the world's leading producers of copper, Chile has lagged in developing improved farming methods and manufacturing industries. As a result it must import much of its food and consumer products.

Chileans are better educated and have a higher standard of living than their neighbors in Peru and Bolivia. About three-fourths of the people live in cities.

A land of dramatic contrasts, Chile is hemmed in by natural frontiers of desert, mountains, and ocean. Its white deserts in the north, especially the Atacama Desert, are among the driest regions in the world. They are rich in nitrate, copper, and other mineral deposits. In the east are the immense Andes Mountains. Mt. Aconcagua, in Argentina near the Chilean border, is 22,834 feet high—the loftiest peak in the Western Hemisphere. The Andes decrease in height as they run south to Chile's beautiful lake country. About 30 rivers drain into the Pacific from the Andes. To the west, a lower coastal range runs along the ocean.

A fertile central valley, about 600 miles long and 45 miles wide, is the center of Chile's agriculture and industry and the home of 90% of the population. Chile has many earthquakes.

EARLY HISTORY

Led by Pedro de Valdivia, the Spanish conquistadores founded Santiago in 1541 and later established other settlements in the central region. During Chile's colonial period, which was marked by savage Indian wars and internal dissension, the country was essentially a neglected land of pioneers.

On Sept. 18, 1810, Chile declared its independence from Spain. A 7-year war followed in which Chilean patriots led by Bernardo O'Higgins won the country's freedom.

The constitution of 1833, chiefly the work of Diego Portales, paved the way for parliamentary government. It lasted until 1925 with few amendments. The years 1841 to 1961 were marked by political reform and material progress.

Chile won the "War of the Pacific" against Bolivia and Peru in 1884, acquiring the northern desert regions with their mineral wealth.

In 1920, when employment and political unrest had brought Chile to the verge of revolution, Arturo Alessandri was elected president with the support of the working and middle classes. He was ousted by a military coup in 1924, but was recalled in 1925. Alessandri introduced labor reforms and a new constitution. Conservative opposition led to his second ouster in 1925 and to the 6-year military dictatorship of Col. Carlos Ibáñez, which in turn collapsed in 1931.

Constitutional government was restored with Alessandri again elected to the presidency in 1932.

In 1938 a "Popular Front" of Democrats, Radicals, Socialists, and Communists carried Pedro Aguirre Cerda into the presidency. Various coalitions of the center and left parties held power to the end of the decade.

Chile established traditions of constitutional democracy with the successive elections to the presidency of Juan Antonio Ríos in 1942, of Gabriel Gonzáles Videla in 1946, of former dictator Carlos Ibáñez in 1952, of Jorge Alessandri in 1958, and of Eduardo Frei in 1964.

MARXIST REGIME

In a presidential election in September 1970, Salvador Allende Gossens, head of Chile's Socialist Party, was the candidate of a leftist Popular Unity (UP) coalition that included the Communists. He won by a narrow plurality, with 36.3% of the vote in a three-way race. Congress confirmed his election after amending the constitution to guarantee continued democratic government. Allende was the first avowed Marxist to be freely elected as president of a nation.

Former U.S. President Richard Nixon revealed in 1976 that he had ordered the CIA to try to prevent Allende from becoming Chile's president. The CIA was unsuccessful in attempts to foment a military coup.

President Allende established diplomatic relations with communist states. He expropriated many banks, vital industries, and farm estates. His government nationalized foreign-owned businesses, among them properties of four U.S. corporations—Anaconda, Kennecott, Cerro, and ITT.

Chile's economic situation worsened as wage increases led to increased demands for consumer goods, while curbs on profits and declining productivity reduced total output.

MILITARY DICTATORSHIP

On Sept. 11, 1973, military forces led by the commander of the army, Gen. Augusto Pinochet Ugarte, surrounded and bombarded the presidential palace. Allende died during the coup.

The country was placed under strict military rule. Some 2,500 or more of Allende's followers were summarily executed. Many were imprisoned in military camps without trial—estimates of those jailed ranged from 10,000 to more than 80,000. The UN and the World Council of Churches helped more than 6,000 foreign refugees leave the country. About 30,000 Chileans were exiled.

In 1975 the U.S. Congress cut off military aid to Chile because of human-rights violations.

Shifting to a free-market economy in 1975, the government reduced tariffs and sold off to private enterprise 400 state-owned businesses. An economic boom resulted.

Relations between the U.S. and Chile worsened in 1978–79 when the U.S. formally demanded the extradition of Gen. Juan Manuel Contreras Sepulveda, former head of the secret police, and two of his associates on charges of plotting and carrying out the assassination in Washington D.C., in 1976 of Orlando Letelier, a critic of the Pinochet government. Chile's supreme court refused U.S. requests for extradition on Oct. 1, 1979.

Although strikes had been outlawed since 1973, the government announced new decrees in July 1979 banning labor unions from any activity that affected the public interest.

A national referendum on Sept. 12, 1980, approved a new constitution to continue Pinochet in power until 1989.

The U.S. sought to restore better relations with Chile in 1981. On Feb. 20, U.S. President Reagan revoked economic sanctions that had been imposed by President Carter in 1979.

Although the government's free economy had brought inflation under control, reducing it from a rate of 600% in 1978 to 10% in 1981, Chile was hit hard in 1982–83 by falling copper prices and the world recession. Unemployment rose to 25%, and many businesses went bankrupt.

President Pinochet on Sept. 11, 1982, declared that he would call a congressional election in 1990 and a free presidential election in 1997.

A rising tide of protest in 1983-84 called for a return to democracy. Beginning in May 1983, opponents organized monthly antigovernment demonstrations. Dozens of demonstrators were killed and hundreds were arrested when police and soldiers broke up these protests. In an effort to appease opponents, the government permitted about 2,000 political exiles to return.

The nation's five leading political parties formed a coalition Democratic Alliance that urged Pinochet's resignation.

After labor unions called a general strike on Oct. 30, 1984, to protest the continuation of military rule, Pinochet declared a state of siege. Police arrested thousands of the regime's opponents.

A severe earthquake on March 3, 1985, centered on the port city of San Antonio and nearby towns, killing 146 persons, injuring about 2,000, and leaving 200,000 homeless.

Pinochet lifted the state of siege on June 17, 1985, ending censorship, but retaining a nightly curfew.

CHILE'S DEPENDENCIES

EASTER ISLAND

Area: 63 square miles (163 sq. km.).
Population: 2,000.
Capital: Hanga Roa.
Easter Island (or Rapa Nui) is a volcanic island in the South Pacific about 2,350 miles west of Chile. It is famed for its hieroglyphics and large stone heads carved from volcanic stone.

The people of Easter Island are of Polynesian origin and raise yams, taro roots, bananas, potatoes, and sugarcane. The island is governed by Valparaíso province.

JUAN FERNANDEZ

Area: 57 square miles (148 sq. km.).
Population: 615.
The Juan Fernández group includes two major islands: Robinson Crusoe (36 sq. mi.) and Alexander Selkirk (21 sq. mi.). They are the largest of several volcanic islands in the group, which is located about 400 miles west of Valparaíso. Lobster fishing is the main industry.

The islands are believed to have been discovered by a Spanish explorer, possibly before 1572. The English author Daniel Defoe is believed to have based his story *Robinson Crusoe* on the four-years that the Scottish castaway Alexander Selkirk spent on Más Atierra (the original name of Robinson Crusoe Island).

CHILEAN ANTARCTIC TERRITORY

Area: 482,625 square miles (1,249,993 sq. km.).
Population: 200.
Chile claimed the Palmer Peninsula section of Antarctica in 1940 and has established four bases there. Parts of the territory also are claimed by Britain and Argentina.

DIEGO RAMIREZ ISLANDS

This group of uninhabited islands is situated 60 miles southwest of Cape Horn.

SALAY GOMEZ ISLAND, SAN AMBROSIO ISLAND, AND SAN FELIX ISLAND

These islands are small, uninhabited Pacific Ocean possessions of Chile.

CHINA

Official Name: People's Republic of China.
Area: 3,692,950 square miles (9,564,701 sq. km.).
Population: 1,053,610,000.
Chief Metropolitan Areas: Peking (Beijing), capital, 7,570,000; Shanghai, 10,820,000; Tientsin (Tianjin), 4,280,000; Shenyang, 2,411,000; Wuhan, 2,146,000; Chungking (Chongqing), 2,121,000; Canton (Guangzhou), 1,840,000; Harbin, 1,552,000; Dairen-Port Arthur (Dalian-Lushun), 1,508,000; Nanking (Nanjing), 1,419,000; Sian (Xian), 1,310,000; Tsingtao (Qingdao), 1,121,000; Chengtu (Chengdu), 1,107,000; Taiyuan, 1,020,000.
Government: One-party communist state.
Heads of Government: Deng Xiaoping, Chairman of the Communist Party's advisory commission (since 1977); Hu Yaobang, secretary-general of the Communist Party (since 1981); Zhao Ziyang, prime minister (since 1980); Li Xiannian, state president (since 1983).
Legislature: *National People's Congress,* 3,221 members.
U.S. Ambassador to China: Arthur W. Hummel Jr.
Chinese Ambassador to U.S.: Han Xu.
Flag: Red field, with gold star in upper hoist corner; four smaller gold stars form arc on right.
Official Language: Chinese
Main Ethnic Group: Han Chinese (94%).
Religions: Confucianism, Buddhism, and Taoism.
Leading Industries: Agriculture (rice, cotton, sugarcane, sugar beets, jute and hemp, livestock, tobacco, vegetables, corn, tea, wheat, potatoes, soybeans); fishing; manufacturing (steel, machinery, fertilizer, vehicles, chemicals, textiles); mining (coal, petroleum, natural gas, iron ore, other minerals).
Foreign Trade: *Major exports*—petroleum, agricultural products, iron and steel, textiles, tin, consumer products; *major imports*—machinery, grain.
Places of Interest: Great Wall of China; waterfalls in the Kweichow Mountains; Gobi Desert; Shanghai; Hangchow. *In Peking:* former Imperial Palace; Temple of Heaven complex; Summer Palace; city gate.

CHINA TODAY

China has the largest population of any country in the world—about five times that of the United States. Even so, it is not as crowded as other large countries of Asia, such as Bangladesh and India, because it has the third-largest area after the Soviet Union and Canada.

To hold down population growth, the government penalizes parents who have more than one child.

Many of China's problems stem from trying to change in only a few decades from a largely agricultural country into a modern industrial nation. Its problems have been similar to those of the Soviet Union in the 1920s and 1930s.

To speed industrialization, the communist government since 1980 has encouraged the development of more than 2.6 million privately-owned small businesses.

The nation's science and technology have enabled it to build and test atomic and hydrogen bombs and launch space satellites and intercon-tinental ballistic missiles.

About one-fifth of China, mainly in the east, is a region of lowlands. The rest consists of great plateaus, plains, and massive mountains. The diverse regions range from areas of tropical abundance to barren deserts, and from dense evergreen forests to depleted woodlands.

The principal mountain systems are the Altai in the northwest, the Himalaya in the southwest, the Tien Shan range in the far west, and the Kunlun range in the east.

The country's chief waterways include the Yangtze River, over 3,600 miles long, in central China; the Yellow River, the chief waterway of northern China; the Amur, on the northeastern border; and the Min, Si, and headwaters of the Mekong and Red rivers in the south.

EARLY HISTORY

The story of the Hsia, traditionally China's first dynasty, is largely legendary. The recording of history began only during the subsequent Shang dynasty (about 1766–1123 B.C.).

The Chou dynasty (about 1122–256 B.C.), ruled during a classical era that produced the philosophers Confucius and Lao-tzu.

The Ch'in dynasty (221–207 B.C.) gave China its name and its first emperor, ended feudalism, and centralized the government. Roads, canals, and much of the Great Wall were constructed.

The Han dynasty (202 B.C.–A.D. 220) was noted for its artistry and territorial expansion.

CHINA'S PROVINCES AND REGIONS

NAME[1]	AREA		POPULATION[3]
	Sq. Mi.	Sq. Km.	
Anhwei (Anhui)	54,016	139,900	49,665,724
Chekiang (Zhejiang)	39,305	101,800	38,884,603
Fukien (Fujian)	47,529	123,100	25,931,106
Heilungkiang (Heilongjiang) . . .	178,997	463,600	32,665,546
Honan (Henan)	64,479	167,000	74,422,739
Hopei (Hebei)	78,263	202,700	53,005,875
Hunan (Hunan)	81,275	210,500	54,008,851
Hupeh (Hubei)	72,394	187,500	47,084,150
Inner Mongolia[2] (Nei Monggol) . . .	454,635	1,177,500	18,510,000
Kansu (Gansu)	141,506	366,500	19,569,261
Kiangsi (Jiangxi) . . .	63,630	164,800	33,184,827
Kiangsu (Jiangsu) . .	39,460	102,200	60,521,114
Kirin (Jilin)	72,200	187,000	22,560,053
Kwangsi-Chuang[2] (Guangxi Zhuang)	85,097	220,400	36,420,960
Kwangtung (Guangdong)	89,344	231,400	59,299,220
Kweichow (Guizhou)	67,182	174,000	28,552,997
Liaoning (Liaoning)	57,915	150,000	35,721,693
Ningsia Hui[2] (Ningxia Hui) . . .	25,637	66,400	3,895,578
Shansi (Shanxi)	60,657	157,100	25,291,389
Shantung (Shandong)	59,189	153,300	74,419,054
Shensi (Shaanxi) . . .	75,600	195,800	28,904,423
Sinkiang-Uighur[2] (Xinjiang Uygur) .	635,833	1,646,800	13,081,681
Szechwan (Sichuan)	219,692	569,000	99,713,310
Tibet[2] (Xizang)	471,662	1,221,600	1,892,393
Tsinghai (Qinghai) . .	278,380	721,000	3,895,706
Yunnan (Yunnan) . .	168,418	436,200	32,553,817

[1] Pinyin spellings in parentheses. [2] Autonomous region. [3] 1982 census.

RULING DYNASTIES OF CHINA

c.2200–1766 B.C. Legendary Hsia dynasty: Stone Age civilization; used painted, then black, pottery.

c.1766–1123 B.C. Shang (or Yin) dynasty: Bronze Age civilization; writing developed.

c.1122–256 B.C. Chou dynasty: Advanced feudal society.

221–207 B.C. Ch'in dynasty: First emperors with centralized government; Great Wall built.

202 B.C.–A.D. 220 Han dynasty: Science and arts flourished; paper invented.

220–589 Six dynasties: China divided among local feudal rulers; invasions by Huns and Turks.

589–618 Sui dynasty: Empire reunited; Buddhism flourished; poetry and sculpture outstanding.

618–907 T'ang dynasty: Printing on paper and mechanical clocks invented.

907–959 Five dynasties: Anarchy prevailed.

960–1279 Sung dynasty: Advanced civilization; magnetic compass invented; gunpowder used in warfare.

1260–1368 Yuan dynasty of Mongol rulers, founded by Kublai Khan; extensive public works; advancements in science and arts; novel developed in literature.

1368–1644 Ming dynasty: Mongols driven out of China; many cultural achievements.

1644–1912 Manchu (or Ch'ing) dynasty: European colonial incursions, ended with establishment of republic.

Under the Sung dynasty (960–1279) many innovations occurred, including gunpowder for military use, printing, the magnetic compass, and a new literary form, the novel.

The Mongols, under Genghis Khan, invaded and by 1215 had taken northern China. Genghis' grandson Kublai Khan founded the Yuan dynasty and completed the conquest of the Sung.

The Mongols were ousted in 1368 by the founders of the Ming dynasty.

European penetration began in 1557 when the Portuguese established a colony at Macao.

MANCHU DYNASTY

The Manchus, meanwhile, were advancing from the north. They took Peking in 1644. Their dynasty, the Ch'ing, ruled until 1911.

China's vast riches increasingly lured European and American traders. China forbade the import of opium, but foreign traders smuggled in huge quantities of the narcotic. This precipitated the first Opium War (1839–42). China was forced to open five ports to British trade and to cede Hong Kong.

In the second Opium War (1856–60), the British and French joined forces. Ports were opened from the Yangtze north to Manchuria.

The U.S. sought equal trading rights, calling in 1900 for an Open Door policy to give all nations the right to trade in Chinese ports. The Boxer Rebellion of 1900 marked a desperate popular attempt to eliminate foreign domination.

NATIONALIST CHINA

A revolution in 1911 led by Dr. Sun Yat-sen forced the abdication of the boy emperor Hsüant'ung (P'u-i) on Feb. 12, 1912. Sun was named provisional president of the new Republic of China, but soon resigned. His successor's dictatorial rule brought another revolt led by Sun in 1913. It failed and Sun was exiled.

Sun created the Kuomintang (Nationalist) Party, returning to China in 1917. Civil war began. Sun died in 1925, but the Kuomintang army went on under Chiang Kai-shek to defeat the central and northern warlords. In 1928 his government received foreign recognition. Chiang continued to fight the communists, forcing them into the 6,000-mile Long March to the northwest, where they settled in Shensi province in 1935.

Japan invaded Manchuria in 1931, setting up a puppet state called *Manchukuo* with China's former emperor P'u-i as the figurehead ruler.

Japan launched full-scale war on China in 1937. World War II brought Allied aid to China.

COMMUNIST RULE BY MAO

After World War II Chiang received U.S. support and supplies, but by 1949 communists had won control of the mainland. Chiang and his supporters fled to the island of Taiwan.

The *People's Republic of China* was declared by the communists on Oct. 1, 1949, under leadership of Mao Tse-tung (Mao Zedong) as chairman of the Communist Party and Chou En-lai (Zhou Enlai) as prime minister. Agriculture was collectivized and industry was nationalized.

In 1950 China intervened in the Korean War on the side of the North Koreans. Also in 1950 China conquered Tibet. In 1962 an undeclared border war was waged with India.

In 1960 China split with the Soviet Union in a continuing controversy over ideology.

China became a nuclear power with its first explosion of an atomic bomb in 1964. It exploded its first hydrogen bomb in 1967.

Influenced by his wife Jiang Qing, Mao launched the Great Proletarian Cultural Revolution in 1966 to purge her opponents from power.

The chief target of the revolution was the Communist Party establishment led by Liu Shao-chi, who had been chairman of the party since 1959. China veered toward anarchy as millions of zealous pro-Mao Red Guard students seized power in provincial capitals.

By the end of 1968 the Cultural Revolution appeared to be over, with the expulsion of Liu Shao-chi from the party in October.

China's seat in the United Nations from 1949 to 1971 was held by Taiwan (Chiang's Republic of China). Admission of mainland China was repeatedly voted down, because of U.S. opposition. But in 1971 the U.S. reversed its position. Then the UN General Assembly voted to admit the Peking government and to expel Taiwan.

A weeklong visit by President Nixon to China in February 1972 demonstrated easing relations.

Climaxing a 6-day visit to Peking on Sept. 29, 1972, Japan's Premier Kakuei Tanaka agreed to establish diplomatic relations with China.

In mid-February 1973, U.S. Secretary of State Henry Kissinger visited Peking where he had cordial talks with Chairman Mao and Premier Chou that resulted in an exchange of diplomats below the rank of ambassador.

China launched a New Cultural Revolution under the leadership of Chairman Mao in February 1974. The new campaign was directed at "reactionaries" who clung to the beliefs of the ancient philosopher Confucius.

QUICK QUIZ: What President started the Interstate Highway System? See page 376.

CHINA (continued)

Communists supported by China conquered Cambodia, South Vietnam, and Laos in 1975, turning those Southeast Asian countries into communist states.

In September 1975 China established diplomatic relations with the European Common Market.

U.S. President Gerald Ford and First Lady Betty Ford visited China on Dec. 2–5, 1975, meeting with Chairman Mao and other leaders.

The 77-year-old Prime Minister Chou En-lai died on Jan. 8, 1976. He was succeeded by Hua Guofeng. Chou's chosen successor, Deputy Prime Minister Deng Xiaoping, was fired. In April 1976 riots broke out in Peking and other cities in support of Deng.

Major earthquakes in July 1976 caused severe damage to the industrial region of Tientsin and Tangshan. Some 242,000 persons were killed.

CHINA UNDER HUA AND DENG

After ruling China for nearly 27 years, 82-year-old Mao died on Sept. 9, 1976. More than 750,000 Chinese attended a memorial for Mao on Sept. 18, which was presided over by his successor, Hua Guofeng, who became chairman of the Communist Party as well as prime minister.

Mao's widow, Jiang Qing, and three other members of the Communist Party's politburo were arrested in October 1976. They were branded as a radical "Gang of Four" who were trying to take over China. In following months there were reports that over a million of their followers were arrested and over 7,000 killed.

The 74-year-old Deng was restored as deputy prime minister in July 1977, and it soon became clear he had taken charge of running the government. His previous downfall was officially blamed on the discredited "Gang of Four."

Well known as a pragmatist, Deng told the Chinese Communist Party's 11th congress in August 1977: "The minimum requirement for a communist is to be an honest person. There must be less empty talk and more hard work."

Hundreds of thousands of persons who had been purged during Mao's "cultural revolutions" were restored to official positions.

China signed a $20 billion trade pact with Japan on Feb. 16, 1978. This was followed on Aug. 12 with the signing of a treaty of peace and friendship with Japan. Ratification on Oct. 23, 1978, brought a formal end to four decades of war between China and Japan.

China actively began encouraging Western tourists to visit the country in 1978, ending its reclusiveness of three decades.

China and the U.S. established formal diplomatic relations on Jan. 1, 1979, as the U.S. ended diplomatic ties with the Taiwan government. In late January and early February 1979, Deng made a 9-day visit to the U.S., the first by a Chinese communist leader. He and President Carter signed agreements to strengthen relations.

On July 7, 1979, China and the U.S. signed a comprehensive trade agreement giving China most-favored-nation trade status. The pact was approved by the U.S. Congress on Jan. 24, 1980. Within a year the U.S. became China's second most important trading partner, after Japan.

Angered by what it regarded as the mistreatment of ethnic Chinese by the Vietnamese government and by Vietnam's overthrow of the pro-Chinese government of Cambodia, China "punished" its neighbor to the south with a large-scale four-week border war from Feb. 17 to March 15, 1979.

CHINA IN THE 1980s

Mao's chosen successor, Hua Guofeng, was ousted in 1980-81 as Deng took full power at the head of the Communist Party.

Zhao Ziyang, 61, was appointed prime minister on Sept. 7, 1980. Zhao promised to carry on the economic reforms initiated by Deng.

A meeting of the National People's Congress in September 1980 ratified the changes in leadership. It approved an amendment to the constitution abolishing the right of people to air dissenting views in critical wall posters. The congress also ratified a law designed to reduce the birthrate by raising the minimum age for marriage to 22 for men and 20 for women. The Communist Party called on its 38 million members to have no more than one child per family.

The U.S. and China signed new agreements on Sept. 17, 1980, paving the way for scheduled airline service and mutual use of each other's ports by merchant ships.

Drought and floods cut China's food production in 1980, causing it to sign a 4-year agreement with the U.S. on Oct. 22, 1980, to buy 6 to 8 million tons of grain annually.

Mao's widow, Jiang Qing, and nine of her associates in the "Gang of Four" were brought to trial in televised proceedings that began on Nov. 20, 1980, and concluded with their sentencing more than two months later on Jan. 25, 1981. They were found guilty of persecuting more than 725,000 persons, of whom nearly 35,000 died, during the Cultural Revolution. The 67-year-old Jiang Qing was given a suspended death sentence, later commuted to life imprisonment.

Deng made his supreme position clear in 1981 at a meeting of the Communist Party's Central Committee. Mao's self-chosen successor, Hua, was demoted and replaced as chairman by a protégé of Deng—Hu Yaobang. At the same time Deng took control of the armed forces, making himself chairman of the party's military commission, a post previously held by Hua.

China began construction in 1982 of its first full-scale nuclear power plant near Shanghai.

After spending some 33 years in prison, more than 4,000 Chinese nationalists were freed in a government amnesty announced in March 1982.

Strained relations between the U.S. and China eased with agreement on a joint communiqué issued on Aug. 17, 1982, in which the U.S. pledged to limit sales of arms to Taiwan, and China agreed to use peaceful means in seeking political reunification of the island with mainland China.

The 12th Communist Party Congress held in September 1982 reaffirmed 78-year-old Deng Xiaoping's leadership, electing him chairman of a newly created advisory commission. It endorsed his plans to quadruple China's industrial production by the year 2000. To further discredit Mao, his handpicked successor Hua was ousted as a member of the politburo.

A new constitution was adopted on Dec. 4,

1982. It stresses the importance of human rights, but denies workers the right to strike. To reduce population growth, the constitution requires all married couples to practice birth control.

The government began a program in 1982 of dismantling Mao's system of communal farms. Instead, township governments were established in rural areas and the land was leased to individual farm families.

China and the Soviet Union conducted talks in 1983 and 1984 on the resumption of normal relations. However, China demanded the Soviet Union end its occupation of Afghanistan and stop supporting Vietnamese occupation of Cambodia.

New economic reforms were introduced in February 1983. Shops and factories no longer were required to turn over all profits to the government. Instead, taxes on businesses were established, permitting remaining profits to be used by managers for investment or for employee benefits.

The government harshly cracked down on career criminals in 1983–84. In sports stadiums before cheering crowds, public executions were conducted of hundreds of murderers and other criminals.

The U.S. in June 1983 relaxed its ban on the sale of high-technology equipment to China.

Improving relations with the U.S. were signaled when Prime Minister Zhao made a 9-day tour of the U.S. in January, including a meeting with President Reagan in Washington. Zhao declared: "China has opened its door and will never close it again." President Reagan reciprocated with a 6-day visit to China in April.

Relations also eased with the Soviet Union as China signed an agreement with that nation on Feb. 10, 1984, to increase trade to about $1.2 billion each year from a previous level of about $800 million.

In June Zhao made an 18-day tour of Western European nations.

In celebrating the 35th anniversary of communist rule of China on Oct. 1, 1984, China for the first time publicly revealed its intercontinental ballistic missiles in a military parade in Peking.

The Communist Party's Central Committee announced on Oct. 20, 1984, the adoption of sweeping economic reforms that abandoned Soviet-style centralized control: Millions of state-owned businesses would be freed from government planning to compete with each other. Prices would be set by supply and demand instead of being subsidized. Managers of enterprises would set wages and be free to hire and fire employees. Some state-owned businesses would be leased to individuals or groups to operate.

The 80-year-old Deng Xiaoping took steps in 1985 to ensure that his reform program would be carried on "into the next century." He ordered 1,000 younger executives to be promoted to positions in which they would be prepared to take over leadership of the party and the government. Some 900,000 aged officials were retired from office and over 1 million more were slated for retirement in 1986.

The government announced in 1985 that China's 4.2 million-man army was to be reduced by 1 million soldiers and that 47,000 officers were being retired.

CISKEI

Official Name: Ciskei.
Area: 3,205 square miles (8,300 sq. km.).
Population: 691,200.
Capital: Bisho.
Government: One-party state.
Head of State: Chief Lennox L. Sebe (since 1973).
Parliament: National Assembly, 22 members.
Flag: A crane, symbol of courage and energy, centered on white diagonal stripe; blue triangles in upper left and lower right corners.
Language: Xhosa.
Principal Ethnic Group: Ciskei Xhosa.
Main Religions: Christianity, animism.
Leading Industries: Agriculture (cattle, sheep, corn, tea, coffee, nuts), fishing, forestry.
Foreign Trade: *Major exports*—livestock, meat, wool, hides; *major imports*—food, fuel.

About two-thirds the size of Connecticut, Ciskei is the fourth of South Africa's black homelands to be granted "independence." As with its sister states, none of the world's nations except South Africa recognizes its sovereignty.

Although larger than about a fourth of the world's independent nations both in area and population, Ciskei is poorer than most because it has no known valuable resources.

Most of the people live by subsistence farming. But large quantities of food must be imported. About two-thirds of the income of the people comes from money sent home by Ciskei's men who work in other parts of South Africa.

Ciskei borders the Indian Ocean on South Africa's southeastern coast. Lying west of the Great Kei River, it is adjacent to another "independent" black homeland, Transkei, whose people speak the same Xhosa language. Two South African towns are just outside Ciskei's border—East London and King William's Town.

Granted partial self-government in 1971, Ciskei held its first general election in February 1973. The Ciskeian National Independence Party, led by Chief Lennox L. Sebe, won every seat in the national assembly, soundly defeating the Ciskeian National Party, led by Chief J. Mabandla. Mabandla's party had favored merging Ciskei with neighboring Transkei.

Ciskei was declared a self-governing territory on Aug. 1, 1973.

Chief Sebe placed his brother, Gen. Charles Sebe, in charge of security police and stifled all opposition.

In a referendum held on Dec. 4, 1980, 97% of the people of Ciskei voted in favor of independence. A year later, on Dec. 4, 1981, South Africa granted Ciskei its "sovereignty" with Chief Sebe as head of the government.

On July 19, 1983, Chief Sebe jailed his powerful brother and many of his associates on charges of corruption.

QUICK QUIZ: Which U.S. President was a Pulitzer Prize winning author? See page 377.

COLOMBIA

Official Name: Republic of Colombia.
Area: 439,737 square miles (1,138,914 sq. km.).
Population: 28,350,000.
Largest Cities: Bogotá, capital, 2,836,361; Medellín, 1,112,390; Cali, 967,908; Barranquilla, 690,471; Cartagena, 309,428; Bucaramanga, 315,565.
Government: Democracy.
President: Belisario Betancur (since 1982).
Parliament: *Senate,* 114 members; *House of Representatives,* 199 members.
U.S. Ambassador to Colombia: Charles A. Gillespie Jr.
Colombian Ambassador to U.S.: Rodrigo Lloreda.
Flag: Tricolor with wide yellow stripe atop narrower blue and red stripes.
Official Language: Spanish.
Main Ethnic Groups: Mestizo (mixed Indian-Spanish, 58%), European descent (20%), mulatto (14%).
Principal Religion: Roman Catholicism (95%).
Leading Industries: Agriculture (corn, rice, cassava, sugar, coffee, cattle, bananas, tobacco, cotton, wheat, potatoes); mining (oil, natural gas, gold, silver, platinum, emeralds, coal, iron, nickel); manufacturing (textiles, steel, chemicals).
Foreign Trade: *Major exports*—coffee, petroleum, coal, bananas, cotton, beef, sugar; *major imports*—machinery, motor vehicles, consumer goods.
Places of Interest: Island of San Andrés; Zipaquira underground Salt Mine Cathedral; Guatavita Lake; San Agustín Archaeological Park. *In Bogotá:* Plaza Bolívar; Gold Museum; national museum; Museum of July 20th, 1810; colonial buildings; planetarium; museum of modern art.

COLOMBIA TODAY

Colombia is a South American nation larger than Texas and California combined. With a wealth of natural resources, Colombia is an important petroleum producer and contains 60% of South America's coal reserves. It is second only to Brazil in coffee production.

Colombia also is one of the main sources of marijuana and cocaine smuggled into the U.S.

Colombia is one of the few South American nations governed by freely elected civilians.

Most Colombians are poor. Many farm workers, eke out a subsistence for their families by growing corn and beans.

An intensive family-planning program reduced the population growth rate from 3.2% in 1965 to 2.1% by the 1980s.

Government-owned oil refineries and hydroelectric plants have been developed to speed industrialization. The government welcomes foreign investors and protects their interests.

Colombia has coastlines on the Caribbean to the north and the Pacific to the west. Called the "Gateway to South America," the country is bordered on the northwest by Panama, on the northeast by Venezuela, on the southeast by Brazil, and on the south by Peru and Ecuador.

Three ranges of the Andes Mountains cross Colombia, roughly paralleling the Pacific coast.

The Magdalena and Cauca rivers converge in the north and empty into the Caribbean.

SPANISH COLONIZATION

Spanish explorers who came to Colombia in 1499 found some gold and jewels. The Colimas Indians of the Cauca Valley were especially noted for their works of gold. Over 15,000 gold objects of pre-Spanish art are preserved today in Bogotá's Gold Museum.

Permanent colonization on the isthmus began after 1514. The region—including portions of present-day Panama, Venezuela, Ecuador, and most of Colombia—was called New Granada, a Spanish colony for three centuries.

INDEPENDENCE

The colonists began their struggle for independence from Spain on July 20, 1810. In 1819 Simón Bolívar became president of the republic of Gran Colombia. By 1830 Venezuela and Ecuador had declared themselves separate states. The remaining territory became the republic of New Granada, which assumed its present name, Colombia, in 1866.

Two political parties developed: Conservatives, favoring centralized government and close ties with the church, and Liberals, advocating a loose federal government and separation of church and state. Their rivalry caused nearly a hundred civil wars by 1899, when the War of a Thousand Days took 100,000 lives.

In 1903 Colombia refused to ratify the leasing of territory to the U.S. to build a canal, and Panama declared itself independent.

An undeclared civil war, called *La Violencia,* between Conservatives and Liberals in 1948–57 resulted in an estimated 300,000 deaths.

Constitutional amendments adopted in 1957 established a unique system that required the presidency to alternate between the Liberal and Conservative parties until 1974.

RETURN TO TWO-PARTY DEMOCRACY

In the first major two-party national election in more than two decades, on April 21, 1974, Alfonso López Michelsen, the Liberal Party candidate, was elected president. His term was marred by widespread political corruption.

In a closely contested election on June 4, 1978, Liberal candidate Julio César Turbay Ayala defeated Conservative Belisario Betancur, 2,506,228 to 2,358,644, to win a 4-year term as president.

Guerrillas of the Movement of April 19 (M-19) took the embassy of the Dominican Republic on Feb. 27, holding hostage 58 persons, including ambassadors of the U.S. and 13 other countries. Colombian troops besieged the embassy for two months until April 27 when the guerrillas were allowed to fly to Cuba.

In congressional elections on March 14, 1982, the governing Liberal Party won majorities in both houses of congress.

However, a split in the Liberal Party enabled Betancur, 59, to defeat former President Alfonso Lopez in a presidential election on May 30, 1982, with 3.2 million votes to 2.8 million, ending eight years of Liberal Party government. Betancur pledged to end the state of siege in effect for more than three decades to fight the guerrillas, and less than a month later the government did so.

Sworn in as Colombia's 73d president on Aug. 7, 1982, Betancur offered amnesty to guerrillas. He faced major problems with inflation at a rate of about 30% and unemployment nearing 10%.

Although hundreds of guerrillas accepted the amnesty and put down their arms, fighting, killing, and kidnapping continued in 1983.

A major earthquake nearly destroyed the provincial capital Popayan on March 31, 1983, killing 157 persons and making 70,000 homeless.

When the nation's justice minister was assassinated on April 30, 1984, apparently by criminals engaged in the illegal narcotics trade, the government intensified its war on drug smugglers.

Occidental Petroleum Corp. announced in August 1984 that it had discovered major oil deposits in Colombia that could produce an additional 100,000 barrels of oil per day by 1986.

The government signed truce agreements with three left-wing guerrilla groups in 1984, hopeful that the pacts would end the violence that had wracked the country since the 1940s.

To further the nation's industrial development, the government undertook a massive expansion of the electric power system with construction of 23 new plants to provide 14,000 megawatts of power by 1996.

COMOROS

Official Name: Federal and Islamic Republic of the Comoros.
Area: 694 square miles (1,797 sq. km.).
Population: 458,000.
Capital: Moroni, Grande Comore, 12,000.
Government: Political-military directorate.
President: Ahmed Abdallah (since 1978).
Prime Minister: Ali Mroudjae (since 1981).
Parliament: Federal Assembly, 39 elected members.
U.S. Ambassador to Comoros: Robert B. Keating.
Comoros Ambassador to U.S.: Ali Mlahaili.
Flag: Green field with white crescent and four white stars in center.
Languages: Arabic and Swahili.
Main Ethnic Group: Antalaotra (mixed Arab-Malay-African ancestry).
Principal Religion: Islam.
Leading Industries: Agriculture (coconuts, coffee, sisal, vanilla, cocoa, sugarcane, cassava, sweet potatoes, vegetables, mangoes, bananas, goats, cattle); fishing; manufacturing (food processing, soap, lumber).
Foreign Trade: *Major exports*—copra, vanilla, spices, cocoa; *major imports*—food, consumer goods.
Places of Interest: Kartala volcano (7,746 feet) on Grande Comore; swimming beaches; fishing villages.

COMOROS TODAY

Lying between the east coast of Africa and the island of Madagascar, Comoros is one of the smallest and poorest nations in the world.

The main islands of Comoros are: Grande Comore, 443 sq. mi.; Anjouan, 164 sq. mi.; and Moheli, 81 sq. mi. The Comoros island Mahore (Mayotte) remains a French dependency.

The Comoro islanders make their living mainly by farming and fishing. Many work on the large plantations that produce vanilla, coffee, coconuts, sisal, cocoa, spices, and plants from which are made essential oils used in perfumes. Families grow their own food on small farms that provide sweet potatoes, cassava, fruits, and vegetables. However, much food has to be imported.

Few people can read and write, and only 3 of every 10 children attend school.

The islands have a hot climate the year round. The dry season, from May to October, has temperatures that fall to about 70 ° F. in the evening. In the wet season, from November to April, the temperature rarely falls below 80 ° F.

There are many tropical storms. Reservoirs catch water during the rainy season, but deep wells must be sunk to supplement the supply of drinking water in the dry season.

The mountainous islands are of volcanic origin. The highest volcano is 7,746-foot Kartala on Grande Comore.

HISTORY

The islands became part of the East African empire of the sultan of Oman in the 800s. They appeared on Portuguese sailing charts by 1527.

France acquired rights to Mahore from the local chiefs, making it a colony in 1843. A protectorate was extended over all the Comoros in 1886.

On July 25, 1912, France made all the Comoros a colony. From 1914 they were administered from Madagascar.

France gave the Comoros the status of an overseas territory on Jan. 1, 1947. Local self-government developed with a 30-member assembly.

The islands were granted complete internal self-government in 1960. In a referendum on Dec. 22, 1974, 95% of the people voted for immediate independence.

The Comoros national assembly declared independence from France on July 6, 1975, and elected Ahmed Abdallah as president.

The residents of Mahore appealed to France to preserve their colonial status. When French troops withdrew from most of the Comoros in July, some remained on Mahore as a sign of continued French protection.

On Aug. 3, 1975, President Abdallah was overthrown in a bloodless coup led by Ali Soilih, head of the National United Front. He nationalized all French-owned property and tried to create a Chinese Maoist state. His youthful followers persecuted conservatives and attempted to stamp out the Islamic religion. France terminated its annual $18.5 million aid.

The people of Mahore voted almost unanimously on Feb. 8, 1976, to remain a dependency of France. See page 553.

A military coup on May 13, 1978, overthrew Soilih. He was killed while trying to escape.

Former president Abdallah was restored to power, winning election as president without opposition on Oct. 22, 1978. He was reelected to another 6-year term on Sept. 30, 1984.

QUICK QUIZ: When did the battle between the *Bonhomme Richard* and the *Serapis* take place? See page 302.

CONGO

Official Name: People's Republic of the Congo.
Area: 132,047 square miles (342,000 sq. km.).
Population: 1,852,000.
Largest Metropolitan Areas: Brazzaville, capital, 136,200; Pointe-Noire, 115,000.
Government: Marxist military junta.
President: Denis Sassou-Nguessou (since 1979).
Prime Minister: Ange Edouard Poungui (since 1984).
U.S. Ambassador to Congo: Alan Lukens.
Congo Ambassador to U.S.: Nicolas Mondjo.
Flag: Red field with green wreath, yellow star, hammer, and hoe in upper corner.
Languages: French (official), Lingala, Kikongo.
Main Ethnic Groups: Bakongo (45%), Bateke (20%), M'Bochi (10%).
Religions: Animism (48%); Roman Catholicism (47%); Islam (5%).
Leading Industries: Agriculture (corn, bananas, cassava, rice, peanuts, goats, poultry, palm nuts, sugarcane, tobacco, coffee, cocoa); forestry and lumbering; manufacturing (cement, textiles, food processing, tobacco products, soap, sugar, palm oil); mining (petroleum, diamonds, potash).
Foreign Trade: *Major exports*—Petroleum, wood, diamonds, sugar, palm nuts, coffee, cocoa, peanuts, tobacco; *major imports*—machinery, vehicles.
Places of Interest: Mayombé Mountains; rain forest; Bateke Plateau; Brazzaville.

CONGO TODAY

Ruled by a Marxist military junta, Congo is a hot, prosperous African country that straddles the equator. It is about the size of New Mexico both in area and population. Thick tropical forests cover much of the country. Income from offshore oil fields provides about 70% of the government's income. Congo's Atlantic coast port of Pointe-Noire is a major shipping center.

The majority of Congolese make their living by subsistence agriculture. But about 4 out of 10 people live in cities and towns, employed in businesses and services. As a result a higher percentage of the people can read and write and have a somewhat better standard of living than those in many other black countries of Africa.

A narrow, treeless coastal plain is bordered by the Mayombé Mountains, which run parallel to the coastline. To the north is a grassy plateau region, and to the east the Niari River valley.

The Congo (Zaire) and Ubangi rivers form the eastern border with Zaire. Gabon and Cameroon lie to the east and Central Africa to the north.

EARLY HISTORY

A large Congo empire reached the peak of its power during the 1500s. In the preceding century the Portuguese were the first European explorers of the coastal areas of the Congo, discovering the mouth of the Congo River in 1484.

Beginning in the 1600s French traders, interested in slaves and ivory, began to establish trading centers. By 1785 at least a hundred French ships a year visited the region.

Exploration of the interior was undertaken by the French beginning in the 1870s. The Congress of Berlin in 1885 recognized French claims to the area.

The colony was first called *French Congo* and was later renamed *Middle Congo*. In 1910 Middle Congo, Gabon, and Ubangi-Shari were combined as French Equatorial Africa. By 1956 Middle Congo had gained local autonomy, and in 1958 the colony's voters approved making it the autonomous *Congo Republic*.

INDEPENDENCE

On Aug. 15, 1960, the Congo Republic became fully independent. Fulbert Youlou was elected first president, with the support of all parties. On Aug. 13–15, 1963, Youlou was toppled by a revolt. In December 1963 a new constitution was approved. Alphonse Massamba-Débat was elected to a 5-year term as president.

On Aug. 3, 1968, four days after President Massamba-Débat had dissolved the national assembly, the army seized power. Massamba-Débat was forced to resign on Sept. 5.

Maj. Marien Ngouabi, head of the army, declared himself president on Jan. 1, 1969.

Ngouabi proclaimed a new constitution on Jan. 3, 1970, establishing a one-party Marxist communist state. The official name of the Congo was changed to the *People's Republic of the Congo*. A Marxist Congolese Labor Party (CLP) was created with Ngouabi as its leader.

An offshore oil field began production in 1972, contributing to an improvement in the economy. However, the fields were expected to be depleted by the late 1980s.

Ngouabi was slain on March 18, 1977, by assassins who escaped. Four days later the Roman Catholic archbishop of Brazzaville, Emile Cardinal Biayenda, was murdered in reprisal by members of Ngouabi's family.

The ruling military junta executed former President Massamba-Débat on March 25, 1977, after announcing that he had confessed to plotting Ngouabi's assassination. Sixteen other persons also were executed for complicity.

Col. Joachim Yhombi Opango, 38, was made president on April 13, 1977, by the military junta. Two days later he abolished the national assembly and made the military junta supreme.

Diplomatic relations between Congo and the United States were restored on June 7, 1977, after a 12-year break that had begun in 1965.

The Marxist military junta announced on Feb. 8, 1979, that Col. Denis Sassou-Nguessou had become head of state, replacing President Opango, who was imprisoned on charges of treason. The new leader previously had been minister of defense.

Congo experienced an economic boom in the 1980s with increased revenues from oil production. President Sassou-Nguessou encouraged U.S. oil companies and other foreign investors to aid in promoting "Marxist-capitalism."

The nation's $1.69 billion 5-year plan for 1982–86 emphasized road building and industrial development. With such new industries as paper pulp factories, the government aims to sustain growth and prosperity after oil reserves are depleted in the 1990s.

COSTA RICA

Official Name: Republic of Costa Rica.
Area: 19,575 square miles (50,700 sq. km.).
Population: 2,525,000.
Chief Cities: San José, capital, 236,747.
Largest Metropolitan Area: San José, 395,401.
Government: Democratic republic.
President: Luis Alberto Monge (since 1982).
Parliament: *Legislative Assembly,* 57 members.
U.S. Ambassador to Costa Rica: Lewis A. Tambs.
Costa Rican Ambassador to U.S.: Claudio Antonio Volio.
Flag: Stripes top to bottom of blue, white, red, white, blue; national crest in white oval on red stripe.
Official Language: Spanish.
Ethnic Groups: Spanish descent and mestizo (97%), black (2%), Indian (1%).
Official Religion: Roman Catholicism (97%).
Leading Industries: Agriculture (coffee, bananas, cattle, cocoa, maize, pineapples, sugarcane, tobacco, rice, potatoes); food processing; manufacturing (textiles, clothing, footwear, cigarettes, furniture, construction materials); mining (gold, salt).
Foreign Trade: *Major exports*—coffee, bananas, beef, sugar, cocoa; *major imports*—paper products, machinery, iron and steel, pharmaceuticals, petroleum, chemicals, food, manufactured goods.
Places of Interest: Irazú Volcano; Arenal and Poas volcanoes; Osa Peninsula, national biological preserve; basalt balls near Palmar Monte; Valley of Orosi; Puntarenas. *In San José:* Canvillo Park; national museum; national palace; national theater.

COSTA RICA TODAY

About the size of West Virginia in area and population, Costa Rica has a more stable democratic government than other Central American countries.

In the early 1980s the economy floundered with high unemployment and inflation. Bananas and coffee remained the most important products, but other agricultural and manufacturing products account for more than 40% of the exports.

The development of bauxite mining and the manufacture of aluminum as well as an expanding tourist industry provide the best opportunities for future economic growth.

Costa Rica's traditional foreign policy has been one of nonintervention in the affairs of neighboring Central American countries. The country has been an active participant in the Organization of American States (OAS).

Many Americans retire to Costa Rica because the government collects no tax on the income of retirees and allows them to import automobiles and household goods duty free.

Costa Rica lies entirely within the tropical zone, but its climate, flora, and living conditions are tempered by the altitude.

The capital, San José, is located in a fertile central valley.

Most Costa Ricans live at altitudes of 3,000 to 4,000 feet. At these heights the climate is springlike throughout the year.

Costa Rica has several active volcanoes, two of which, Irazú, 11,260 ft., and Arenal, 5,092 ft., erupted in the 1960s.

Nicaragua lies to the north; Panama to the east.

HISTORY

The country was discovered and probably named by Columbus during his voyage of 1502. Spain ignored its small colony because of the scarcity of minerals, and the province grew slowly.

Costa Rica, along with the rest of Central America, declared independence from Spain without violence on Sept. 15, 1821. In 1824 it became a state in the Federal Republic of Central America. When that government failed in 1838, Costa Rica resumed independence.

An invasion led by the American military adventurer William Walker was put down in 1856 by a united Costa Rican people.

The 1890s saw the arrival of the great fruit companies and the construction of a railroad from the Caribbean to the city of San José.

Since independence Costa Rica has only been ruled by dictators during three periods.

Gen. Tomás Guardia seized power in 1870 and ruled by dictatorial means for a dozen years until his death in 1882.

A second military rule, established by Gen. Federico Tinoco in 1917, was overthrown by a popular revolt in 1919 that restored democratic government.

In 1948 the national assembly declared invalid the presidential election of Otilio Ulate. Col. José Figuéres Ferrer, a supporter of Ulate, led a revolt and temporarily seized power. He then turned over the presidency to Ulate in 1949.

Figuéres himself was chosen president in the 1953 election, serving until 1958. Figuéres staged an impressive political comeback in the February 1970 presidential election.

Daniel Oduber Quirós, candidate of the ruling National Liberation Party (PLN), was elected president on Feb. 3, 1974, with 42.5% of the popular vote.

Rodrigo Carazo Odio, leader of the opposition Unity Party, won a 4-year term as president in a national election on Feb. 5, 1978. He defeated the governing PLN candidate Luis Alberto Monge with 51% to 43% of the vote.

In 1979 the government permitted Nicaragua's Sandinista rebels to use Costa Rican border areas as bases in their successful civil war that overthrew Nicaragua's Somoza dictatorship. In addition Costa Rica provided camps for an estimated 100,000 Nicaraguan refugees.

Falling coffee prices in 1981–82 brought the worst economic crisis since the Great Depression. In 1981 the government defaulted on payments of its foreign debt of $3.2 billion.

Luis Alberto Monge, 56, a social democrat and former labor organizer, took office as president on May 8, 1982, after his National Liberation Party soundly defeated the governing Unity Party in national elections in February. He immediately imposed austerity measures to reduce imports and attempt to revive the economy.

QUICK QUIZ: What was President Eisenhower's campaign slogan? See page 375.

CUBA

Official Name: Republic of Cuba.
Area: 44,218 square miles (114,524 sq. km.).
Population: 10,143,000.
Chief Cities: Havana (La Habana), capital, 1,924,886; Santiago de Cuba, 345,289; Camagüey, 345,235; Holguín, 186,013; Guantánamo, 167,405; Santa Clara, 171,914; Cienfuegos, 102,426.
Largest Metropolitan Area: Havana, 1,861,442.
Government: One-party communist state.
President: Fidel Castro Ruz (since 1959).
Legislature: *Council of Ministers*, 23 members.
U.S. Diplomatic Representative to Cuba: Lyle Franklin Lane.
Cuban Diplomatic Representative to U.S.: Ramón Sánchez Parodi.
Flag: Alternate blue and white stripes; red triangle at hoist bears five-pointed white star.
Official Language: Spanish.
Ethnic Groups: Spanish descent (75%), mixed (13%), black (12%).
Main Religion: Roman Catholicism (85%).
Leading Industries: Agriculture (sugarcane, tobacco, bananas, pineapples, citrus fruits, cattle, rice, cotton, coffee, cocoa, vegetables); fishing; manufacturing (sugar refining, textiles, rum, tobacco products, oil refining, cement, machine parts); mining (nickel, iron, chromite, copper, manganese, clay, petroleum).
Foreign Trade: *Major exports*—sugar, inorganic chemicals, tobacco, nickel; *major imports*—crude petroleum, wheat, tractors, cotton fabrics, nonelectrical machinery.
Places of Interest: Morro Castle fortress in Havana Harbor; Guantánamo U.S. Naval Base; Bay of Pigs; Isle of Pines (Isle of Youth); Santa Maria Beach; Hanabanilla Mountain and Lake Resort.

CUBA TODAY

The communist government of this Caribbean island has survived for more than two decades largely because of billions of dollars of aid each year from the Soviet Union. It has alienated the governments of many South and Central American nations by supporting revolutionary terrorists and guerrillas. Thousands of Cuban troops have been sent to Africa to help communists control Ethiopia and Angola.

U.S. officials have accused Cuba of aiding the smuggling of drugs into the U.S. to pay for subversive activities in Latin America.

All power rests with President Fidel Castro. Radio and television speeches and mass meetings have replaced parliamentary deliberations. Political opponents are subject to summary trial by a revolutionary tribunal.

The Castro regime has made sweeping economic changes aimed at increasing Cuba's production and replacing capitalism with a controlled communist economy. All land, industries, and businesses have been placed under state control.

The largest island in the Caribbean Sea, Cuba lies 90 miles south of Key West, Fla. Jamaica is about 100 miles to the southeast. Windward Passage separates Cuba's eastern tip from Haiti.

The island is about 745 miles long and 60 miles wide. Its nearly 2,500-mile-long coast has many bays, inlets, coral reefs, and marshes.

There are three mountainous regions. The rugged Sierra Maestra in the easternmost province, Oriente, rise to 6,542 feet. The lower Sierra de los Organos are in the west. The Sierra de Trinidad stand in central Cuba. Tropical forests cover the mountains.

Several small islands lie off the coast. The largest is the Isle of Pines, renamed the Isle of Youth by Castro in 1978. The island is said to be the setting of Robert Louis Stevenson's *Treasure Island.*

Cuba's largest river, the Cauto, winds across the southeastern corner of the island.

The climate of Cuba remains hot throughout the year with an average of 70° F. in the winter and 81° F. in the summer. About 54 inches of rain fall annually.

SPANISH RULE

Discovered by Columbus on his first voyage to America in 1492, Cuba remained under Spanish rule until 1898. During the early colonial period Havana served as the last port visited by ships carrying treasure back to Spain.

In 1762 the British captured Havana. Their occupation lasted only a year.

In 1868 Carlos Manuel de Céspedes and other patriots issued a proclamation calling for revolt against Spain. The civil conflict lasted 10 years before being crushed.

Patriot and writer José Marti formed the Cuban Revolutionary Party while in exile in the United States. His call to arms in 1895 sparked a new civil war. He was killed in battle the same year, but the revolt continued.

INDEPENDENCE

After the U.S. battleship *Maine* was blown up in Havana harbor in 1898, the United States declared war on Spain. Spain was defeated by U.S. forces in the Spanish-American War, and Cuba became independent. Cuba's constitution was adopted in 1901. The island remained under U.S. occupation until 1902, when Tomás Estrada Palma became the republic's first president.

Cuba was ostensibly free, but the U.S. government had insisted that it ratify the Platt Amendment, giving the United States the right to intervene in Cuban affairs. In addition, U.S. companies owned or controlled about half of Cuba's economic resources.

In a 1903 treaty, Cuba gave the U.S. perpetual rights to a naval base at Guantánamo Bay.

In 1906 President Estrada Palma, unable to suppress a revolt by the opposition Liberal Party, called in U.S. troops. A U.S. military governor took over for the next two years and four months. U.S. Marines also intervened briefly in 1912 and 1917. Beginning in 1920 a U.S. supervisor was imposed on the Cuban government for several years.

The Platt Amendment was abrogated by President Franklin D. Roosevelt in 1934.

With the post-World War I economic decline, Cuba fell victim to increasing unemployment and poverty. President Gerardo Machado y Morales, inaugurated in 1925, established dictatorial rule.

He was ousted in 1933 by the democratic opposition, which in turn fell victim in 1934 to a coup led by Fulgencio Batista y Zaldívar, then an army sergeant. Batista ruled through puppet presidents until 1940, when he proclaimed a new constitution and was elected president. He was supported by the communists, to whom he gave control of the trade-union movement. His candidate lost the 1944 election. In 1952 Batista again seized power through an army coup. In 1953 a raid on an army barracks by rebels led by Fidel Castro resulted in about 100 deaths. Castro was captured, but he was released from prison in 1955 under a general amnesty and left Cuba.

COMMUNIST TAKEOVER OF CUBA

In December 1956 Castro launched an uprising. The rebellion spread. On Jan. 1, 1959, Batista fled the country. Once in power, Castro failed to implement his promise to restore the democratic constitution. He made Cuba a police state, arresting thousands of opponents. Many Cubans fled to the United States. U.S.-owned property, valued at about $1.8 billion, was seized and nationalized in 1960.

The United States retaliated by halting purchases of Cuban sugar and beginning a trade boycott. On Jan. 3, 1961, the United States broke diplomatic relations.

On April 17, 1961, an invasion force of Cuban exiles, trained and equipped by the American CIA, landed at the Bay of Pigs with the intention of launching a rebellion against the Castro government. The invaders were quickly overwhelmed, and many were captured.

Castro announced on May 1, 1961, that Cuba would become a one-party communist state.

At the urging of the United States, the Organization of American States (OAS) voted in January 1962 by a slim majority to exclude Cuba from further participation in OAS activities.

The U.S. and the Soviet Union came close to war in 1962 when the Soviets secretly began to install atomic missiles on Cuban soil. Faced with a naval blockade of Cuba ordered by President Kennedy in October 1962, the Soviets removed their missiles.

Because of Cuba's support of a communist guerrilla movement in Venezuela, the OAS voted on July 26, 1964, to brand Cuba an aggressor, to break all diplomatic ties, and to suspend all trade except for food and medical supplies.

The United States and Cuba on Feb. 15, 1973, signed an agreement to prevent the hijacking of planes and boats between the two countries. Between 1961 and 1973 some 85 airplanes had been hijacked in the U. S. and flown to Cuba.

The U.S. joined 15 Latin American nations on July 29, 1975, in voting to end the OAS sanctions against Cuba.

In the first nationwide vote since the revolution, 5.5 million Cubans went to the polls on Feb. 15, 1976, to give 97.7% approval to a new constitution formalizing Communist Party rule.

Castro said in 1977 that he had released all but 2,000 to 3,000 of the more than 15,000 political prisoners arrested in the early years of his regime.

The United States took several major steps toward restoration of normal relations with Cuba in 1977. In March restrictions were lifted on the spending of U.S. dollars by Americans in Cuba, and American tourists again began visiting the island on Caribbean cruises. On Sept. 1, 1977, Cuba and the United States exchanged diplomatic representatives, calling them "counselors" rather than ambassadors.

There were repeated angry exchanges between Castro and U.S. President Carter over the use of Cuban troops in Africa. On May 13 Carter said U.S.-Cuban relations could not improve so long as Cuba disregarded human rights by holding thousands of political prisoners.

In August 1978 Cuba agreed to release 480 Cuban-Americans who had been prevented for 17 years from emigrating to the U.S.

Revelation in August 1979 that a brigade of 3,000 Soviet troops had been stationed in Cuba since 1962 brought U.S. protests.

Castro sought to enhance his leadership among developing nations by hosting a meeting of heads of state of about 60 countries in Cuba in 1979.

CUBA IN THE 1980s

Disease struck Cuba's two most important export crops, sugar and tobacco, in 1980, causing an economic slump. In the first wage increase in 15 years, agricultural workers had their monthly pay raised to $115 on July 1, 1980.

To help relieve the bad economic conditions in 1980, Castro allowed about 126,000 persons, including criminals released from prison, to leave the country and go to the U.S. by boat.

The Cuban economy suffered in 1982 from a drop in world sugar prices to record lows. As a result, Castro's government was unable to meet payments on about $1.3 billion in foreign debts.

Demanding that Cuba stop supplying arms to the leftist government of Nicaragua and to guerrillas fighting in El Salvador, the U.S. tightened the economic screws by barring tourist and business travel to Cuba after May 15, 1982. This action cut off Cuba's main source of American currency.

U.S. relations with Cuba worsened in 1983 after U.S. troops landed on Grenada, defeating Cuban troops that supported the communist government of that island nation and ousting Cuban and Soviet diplomats.

As a gesture of good will during a visit by the American civil rights leader Rev. Jesse Jackson, Castro on June 17, 1984, ordered the release of 48 American and Cuban prisoners and let them fly to exile in the U.S.

In the first major agreement in seven years, the United States and Cuba reached an accord on Dec. 14, 1984, for the return to Cuba of 2,746 mental patients and criminals who were among the 126,000 Cubans encouraged to go to the U.S. in 1980. The agreement also provided for the release of several hundred Cuban political prisoners to the U.S. and the admission to the U.S. of about 20,000 Cuban immigrants each year.

Castro suspended the 1984 immigration agreement in May 1985 when the U.S. began broadcasting Voice of America news to Cuba over a powerful radio station called Radio Marti.

QUICK QUIZ: When did the U.S. Bill of Rights amendments become effective? See page 303.

CYPRUS

Official Name: Republic of Cyprus.
Area: 3,572 square miles (9,251 sq. km.).
Population: 675,000.
Capital: Nicosia, 161,000.
Government: Republic.
President: Spyros Achilles Kyprianou (since 1977).
Legislature: *House of Representatives,* 50 members.
U.S. Ambassador to Cyprus: Raymond C. Ewing.
Cyprus Ambassador to U.S.: Andreas J. Jacovides.
Flag: White field with outline map of Cyprus in gold above crossed green olive branches.
Languages: Greek, Turkish, English.
Chief Ethnic Groups: Greek (80%), Turkish (18%).
Main Religions: Greek Orthodox (80%), Islam (18%).
Leading Industries: Agriculture (grapes, wheat, barley, citrus fruits, potatoes, vegetables); tourism; mining (asbestos, copper, iron, chromium); food processing (wine, olive oil); manufacturing (textiles, shoes, furniture).
Foreign Trade: *Major exports*—minerals, fruits, vegetables, nuts, wine, cheese, clothing; *major imports*—machinery, textiles, motor vehicles, petroleum products, medicines, food, consumer goods.
Places of Interest: National museum, Nicosia; Kourion museum and sanctuary, Episkopi; medieval castle, Kolossi; Temple of Aphrodite, Kouklia; archaeological sites at Larnaca, Episcopi, Paphos, Politico, and Kakopetria; Mt. Olympus; Tomb of St. Lazarus, Larnaca; beach resorts.

CYPRUS TODAY

Cyprus is a prosperous, sunny island in the Mediterranean about 44 miles south of Turkey and 64 miles west of Syria. Although Cyprus is about the size of Puerto Rico, it has only one-fifth as large a population.

The island has been divided into two separate states since 1974. Greek Cypriots rule 64% of the island as the government officially recognized by the U.S. and Britain. The northern 36% of the island is governed by Turkish Cypriots.

More than half the people make their living as farmers. Grapes, olives, oranges, lemons, and grapefruit are among the important products.

Over 500,000 tourists each year enjoy the warm climate and pleasant swimming beaches.

EARLY HISTORY

Cyprus was inhabited as long ago as 6000 B.C. By 2200 B.C. it was the major source of the ancient world's copper. About 1500 B.C. Greeks began to colonize the island. For centuries Cyprus was ruled variously by Egyptians, Assyrians, Persians, Greeks, Romans, and Byzantines. Christianity was brought by the Apostles Paul and Mark. King Richard I of England took the island from its Byzantine rulers in 1191. It was annexed by Venice in 1489 and fell under Ottoman Turkish rule in 1571.

The Congress of Berlin in 1878 placed Cyprus under Britain, which annexed the island in 1914 and made it a crown colony in 1925.

The Greek Cypriot movement for *enosis* (union with Greece) was resisted by the Turkish Cypriots and the British. It flared in violence in 1931 and again in 1954. In 1955 a Greek ex-army officer, Col. George Grivas, launched a terrorist campaign for enosis. The campaign intensified in 1956, when the British deported Greek Orthodox Archbishop Makarios III.

INDEPENDENCE AND CIVIL WAR

Britain granted independence to Cyprus on Aug. 16, 1960, with Archbishop Makarios as president.

In 1963 an attempt by Makarios to give the Greek Cypriots control of the government precipitated civil war. A UN peacekeeping force arrived in 1964 to keep Greeks and Turks apart.

Makarios began a third 5-year term as president on Feb. 8, 1973, after elections were canceled because no opposition candidate had registered. Grivas, leader of the forces calling for union with Greece, had ordered his followers to boycott the elections, as had the Turkish Cypriots.

The Cyprus national guard led by Greek army officers on July 15, 1974, overthrew Makarios, who escaped capture and fled to Malta. Five days later some 40,000 Turkish troops invaded Cyprus to protect Turkish Cypriots.

Amid fears of war between Greece and Turkey, the UN ordered a cease-fire on July 22, 1974. Fighting continued sporadically. About 180,000 Greeks had been driven from their homes.

On Dec. 7, 1974, President Makarios returned from his temporary exile and resumed control.

Antagonism between Greece and Turkey over Cyprus continued in 1975–76 to threaten disruption of the NATO military alliance. Greek Cypriots blamed the U.S. for the Turkish invasion.

Turkey proclaimed the Turkish-held northern part of Cyprus an autonomous state on Feb. 13, 1975. Rauf Denktash became its acting president. Denktash won the first presidential election held by the Turkish state on June 20, 1976.

Archbishop Makarios in 1976 rejected Turkish proposals for a federation of the separate Greek and Turkish states. He died on Aug. 3, 1977, and was succeeded as president by Spyros Kyprianou.

After about 1,500 Turkish troops were withdrawn from the island in May 1979, UN Secretary-General Kurt Waldheim succeeded in getting the nation's Greek and Turkish leaders to meet for discussions about settlement of their differences. But no results were achieved.

In a parliamentary election on May 24, 1981, communists won the largest number of votes, 32.8%. The pro-Western Democratic Rally received 31.9%. But the balance of power continued to be held by the centrist Democratic Party of President Kyprianou that won only 20%.

In alliance with the communist AKEL Party, Kyprianou won election to a five-year term as president on Feb. 13, 1983, with 56.54% of the vote.

Turkish Cypriots declared the northern part of the island an independent republic on Nov. 15, 1983. The UN Security Council adopted a resolution calling the act "legally invalid."

The UN developed a plan to create a federal government for Cyprus with autonomous Greek and Turkish states, but this plan was rejected in January 1985 by President Kyprianou.

CZECHOSLOVAKIA

Official Name: Czechoslovak Socialist Republic.
Area: 49,371 square miles (127,869 sq. km.).
Population: 15,536,000.
Chief Cities: Praha (Prague), capital, 1,183,724; Bratislava, 391,620; Brno, 376,627; Ostrava, 323,365.
Government: Communist state.
Heads of Government: Gustav Husák, president (since 1975) and first secretary of the Czechoslovak Communist Party (since 1969); premier, Lubomír Strougal (since 1970).
Federal Assembly: *Chamber of the Nations, 75 Czechs and 75 Slovaks; Chamber of the People,* 200 members.
U.S. Ambassador to Czechoslovakia: William H. Luers.
Czechoslovakian Ambassador to U.S.: Stanislav Suja.
Flag: White over red stripe with blue triangle at hoist.
Official Languages: Czech and Slovak.
Chief Ethnic Groups: Czech (65%), Slovak (30%).
Main Religions: Roman Catholicism (77%), Protestantism (20%).
Leading Industries: Manufacturing (steel, coke, iron, cement, fertilizers, textiles, chemicals, vehicles, weapons); agriculture (potatoes, sugar beets, wheat, barley, oats, rye, corn, cattle, dairy products, hogs, sheep); mining (coal, iron ore, uranium, mercury, antimony, magnesium).
Foreign Trade: *Major exports*—motor vehicles, iron and steel, footwear, metalworking machinery, railway vehicles, coal; *major imports*—metal scrap, crude petroleum, agricultural machinery, cotton, motor vehicles.
Places of Interest: High Tatras Mountains; Carlsbad and Marienbad resorts; Primate's Castle in Bratislava; Spílberk Castle in Brno; Capuchin Monastery; Košice; 'Olomouc. *In Prague:* Hradčany Castle; Charles Bridge; St. Vitus Cathedral; Old Town Square.

CZECHOSLOVAKIA TODAY

Czechoslovakia is a communist industrial nation about the size of the state of New York.

The nation is one of the most prosperous communist countries. The people enjoy a comparatively high standard of living, but their civil rights are severely restricted.

Many of the country's problems stem from rivalry by its two major ethnic groups: a Czech majority and a Slovak minority.

Struggles between the Czechs and Slovaks contributed to political instability that enabled communists to take over after World War II.

Efforts by Czech leaders to liberalize the communist state in 1968 were smashed by an invasion of tanks and troops of the Soviet Union and its eastern European satellites.

One of the world's 10 leading steelmaking nations, Czechoslovakia supplies the Soviet Union and other communist nations with such products as machinery, chemicals, and textiles. However, about half the people are farmers.

GEOGRAPHY

Landlocked in central Europe, Czechoslovakia is bordered on the north by Poland, on the east by the Soviet Union, and on the south by Hungary and Austria. West Germany lies to the southwest, and East Germany to the northwest.

The Carpathian Mountains and the Sudeten range form a natural boundary in the north, as do the Erzgebirge (Ore Mountains) in the northwest and the Bohemian Forest in the west. From these northern heights the country slopes to an area of hills, lowlands, and plains.

The country's three main regions are Bohemia in the west, central Moravia, and eastern Slovakia.

The Moravian Gate cuts across the country from north to south, a natural line of travel along the Oder and Morava rivers. Other principal rivers are the Danube, the Elbe, and the Moldau (Vltava).

EARLY HISTORY

The first known settlers of the Czech lands of Bohemia and Moravia were Celts, followed by Germanic tribes about 100 B.C. Slovak settlers from the east displaced both the Celtic and Germanic peoples by the 400s A.D., and Slavs spread into Slovakia by the 500s. Christianity was introduced by the 800s.

The kingdom of Bohemia emerged under "Good King Wenceslas" in the 900s, but was soon absorbed into the Holy Roman Empire. The Thirty Years War (1618–48) began between the Catholic Hapsburg emperor and the Protestant Czech nobility.

As part of the Austrian Empire for 300 years until 1918, the country was superficially Germanized, with Czech used only as the language of the peasants. Between 1848 and 1914 the refusal of the Germans, particularly in Bohemia, to grant the Czechs equality contributed to the collapse of the Austro-Hungarian Empire in World War I.

FIRST CZECHOSLOVAK REPUBLIC

On Oct. 28, 1918, the first Czechoslovak Republic came into being. It included formerly Austrian Bohemia and Moravia, which were mainly Czech, and formerly Hungarian Slovakia. Ruthenia, which was mainly Ukrainian, was added in 1919. Tomáš G. Masaryk became the first president. Eduard Beneš succeeded him in 1935.

The first Czechoslovak Republic enjoyed the benefits of a liberal, democratic constitution, internationally respected leadership, and economic advantages because most of Austria-Hungary's industries were in territory incorporated into Czechoslovakia. However, ethnic-group differences resulted in serious problems.

The large German minority living in the Sudeten border districts of Bohemia demanded union with Hitler's Germany. In September 1938, the Munich Pact, signed by Czechoslovakia's allies Britain and France, awarded the Sudetenland to Germany.

In March 1939 Hitler occupied the rest of Bohemia as well as Moravia.

Beneš established a Czech government-in-exile in London during World War II.

QUICK QUIZ: What President made the first coast-to-coast TV broadcast? See page 374.

COMMUNIST CZECHOSLOVAKIA

After Germany's defeat in 1945, Beneš returned to Prague and resumed the presidency of Czechoslovakia. In the 1946 elections the communists emerged as the strongest among many minority parties. Klement Gottwald, the communist leader, headed a coalition cabinet.

A Moscow-directed coup in February 1948 and the threat of Soviet invasion forced the democratic Prague government to surrender all power to the communist minority. Beneš resigned in June 1948. Gottwald became president.

The Soviet subjection of Czechoslovakia shocked the free world and is often regarded as the start of the Cold War. The event led to the formation of the Western NATO military alliance, which was soon matched by the Warsaw Pact of communist countries.

For the next two decades Czech life was marked by political purges, rigid censorship, concentration camps, and suppression of freedoms.

In the late 1950s purge trials took the lives of many Czech leaders. Czechoslovakia's economy and living standards declined steadily.

Gottwald was succeeded as president in 1953 by Antonín Zapotocký. In 1957 Communist Party head Antonín Novotny took over the presidency.

PERIOD OF LIBERALIZATION

During the first half of 1968 old-guard Stalinists were replaced in the Czech government by younger, more moderate men. Antonín Novotny was deposed as secretary of the Communist Party and replaced by Alexander Dubček. Ludvík Svoboda became president. A new cabinet pledged liberal political and economic reforms.

The press, radio, theater, and all other media became increasingly outspoken, subjecting the past history of the regime to criticism.

In mid-July 1968 Dubček refused demands by Moscow and the Warsaw Pact nations that the new leaders of Czechoslovakia slow the pace of liberalization.

SOVIET INVASION

On Aug. 21, 1968, Soviet, East German, Polish, Hungarian, and Bulgarian troops, led by Soviet tanks and planes, suddenly invaded and occupied Czechoslovakia.

In mid-April 1969 Dubček was ousted as party secretary and succeeded by Gustav Husák.

As a warning to other communist states, the Kremlin announced the "Brezhnev doctrine," asserting the right of the Soviet Union to intervene forcibly in any "socialist" country it considered menaced from within or without.

Political purge trials continued to 1973. Supporters of the liberal Dubček were charged with antigovernment activities. The trials all ended with convictions and prison terms.

The first direct word from Dubček on the results of his ouster came in a letter smuggled into Italy in 1974 in which he described himself as "dishonored and defenseless."

When Dubček wrote a letter of complaint about being harassed by the secret police in 1975, he was denounced as a traitor by Husák, who said Dubček could leave Czechoslovakia if he did not like living there.

COMMUNIST CONSOLIDATION

Soviet communist leader Leonid I. Brezhnev visited Prague in February 1973 during the country's celebration of the 25th anniversary of communist rule. He declared that the situation in Czechoslovakia had "returned to normal" and that the role of the Communist Party had been "consolidated." As part of the celebration, President Svoboda declared an amnesty for the 50,000 persons who fled the country after the 1968 invasion. But few took the opportunity to return.

Through agreement with the Vatican, the first Roman Catholic bishops in 25 years were appointed in Czechoslovakia in 1973.

The Czechoslovakian federal assembly ratified a treaty with West Germany in July 1974, normalizing relations between the two nations for the first time since World War II.

When Svoboda became too ill to continue in office, Husák took over the title of president in 1975 while retaining his position as head of the Communist Party.

Early in January 1977 a group of Czech intellectuals calling themselves "Charter 77" issued a manifesto declaring that their nation's government was violating the human-rights covenants of the 1975 Helsinki agreement by depriving the people of freedom of speech, freedom of religion, and many other civil rights. The statement was signed by 242 prominent writers, artists, scientists, and others.

On Jan. 26, 1977, the U.S. State Department officially charged Czechoslovakia with violating the Helsinki pact by arresting and harassing human-rights activists.

The government in October 1977 tried and convicted three of the signers of Charter 77 and a fourth dissident for "antistate activities." Two were sent to jail for terms of 3 and $3\frac{1}{2}$ years. The other two received suspended sentences.

The communist government moved to collectivize in 1978 the remaining privately owned farms, which had continued to provide about half the nation's fruits and vegetables.

When Brezhnev visited Czechoslovakia on May 30, 1978, police arrested many persons suspected of being human-rights activists.

On Aug. 21, 1978, on the 10th anniversary of Soviet occupation, a few students gathered at the statue of St. Wenceslas in Prague. Riot police in armored trucks stood ready, but no large-scale demonstrations developed.

Reflecting worldwide inflation, the government raised prices in July 1979 by 50% to 100%.

Six Czech human-rights activists, including the playwright Vaclav Havel, were tried and convicted of subversion on Oct. 22–23, 1979. The six were given jail terms up to 5 years.

Apprehension about the actions of the Solidarity movement in neighboring Poland caused a new government crackdown in 1981 with arrests of dozens of Czech human-rights activists. Many were exiled.

The U.S., Britain, and France returned to Czechoslovakia in 1982 some 18.4 metric tons of gold that had been seized by the Nazis in World War II and then captured by the Allies. The gold was returned after the Czech government agreed to pay compensation for property nationalized after the communists took power.

DENMARK

EUROPE

Official Name: Kingdom of Denmark.
Area: 16,629 square miles (43,069 sq. km.).
Population: 5,110,000.
Chief Cities: Kobenhaven (Copenhagen), capital, 646,959; Arhus, 246,111; Odense, 167,911; Alborg, 154,605; Frederiksberg, 101,899.
Largest Metropolitan Area: Copenhagen, 1,379,473.
Government: Constitutional monarchy.
Prime Minister: Poul Schluter (since 1982).
Queen: Margrethe II (since 1972).
Legislature: Folketing, 179 members.
U.S. Ambassador to Denmark: Terence A. Todman.
Danish Ambassador to U.S.: Egil Jørgenson.
Flag: White Latin cross on red field.
Official Language: Danish.
Principal Ethnic Group: Danes (98%).
Official Religion: Evangelical Lutheranism (97%).
Leading Industries: Manufacturing (electronic equipment, machinery, furniture, engines, chemicals, food processing, ships); tourism; agriculture (dairy products, hogs, poultry, cattle, barley, rye, potatoes, oats, wheat); fishing; mining (iron ore).
Foreign Trade: *Major exports*—manufactured goods, bacon, butter; *major imports*—machinery, motor vehicles, steel, petroleum.
Places of Interest: Silkeborg lakes; Kronborg (Hamlet's) Castle at Elsinore; Hans Christian Andersen's House at Odense; Egeskov Castle at Funen; Old Town Museum at Arhus; ancient town of Ribe; Ebeltoft. *In Copenhagen:* Little Mermaid statue; Christiansborg Palace; zoo; Tivoli amusement park.

DENMARK TODAY

Once the homeland of a Viking empire that stretched from England to Russia, Denmark today is a small industrial country in Europe. It ranks as one of the 10 leading fishing nations.

The Danes enjoy a high standard of living and have strong democratic traditions. More than half the people make their living from service industries, many in the tourist industry.

The government provides free medical care and extensive social-welfare benefits, supporting the programs with high taxation.

Denmark has many political parties reflecting a variety of political views. Usually no one party can command majority support.

The homeland of Denmark is slightly smaller than the combined areas of Vermont and New Hampshire, but the island of Greenland, an integral part of Denmark since 1953, is bigger than Alaska and Texas combined.

The country's only land connection with the European continent is its 42-mile southern boundary with West Germany.

On the north Denmark faces the Skagerrak. On the east are the Kattegat, the Sound, and the Baltic Sea. The North Sea lies to the west.

Denmark consists of the peninsula of Jutland and 483 neighboring islands, of which 97 are in-

habited. The five largest islands are Fyn (Funen), Lolland, Bornholm, Falster, and Zealand (Sjaelland), where Copenhagen is located.

The countryside is predominantly rolling flatlands. The climate is moderate.

EARLY HISTORY

In the Viking Age (about A.D. 790–1030) Danish Vikings raided France and invaded England. Harold Bluetooth became a Christian in 960. He fell in battle (985) against his son Sweyn Forkbeard. Sweyn held parts of Norway and all of England. His son Canute the Great ruled over a huge northern empire that included England.

In 1397 Norway and Sweden joined Denmark in the Union of Kalmar under Danish Queen Margrethe I, who reigned from 1387 to 1412. A Swedish revolt in 1523 ended the union, but Norway remained united with Denmark until 1814. The Lutheran creed was adopted in 1536. In 1660 Frederik III established royal absolutism.

In the Napoleonic wars, Frederik VI allied with the French. By the Treaty of Kiel (1814) Denmark had to give up Norway to Sweden.

CONSTITUTIONAL MONARCHY

Under Frederik VII (1848–63) liberal trends brought domestic reforms. Absolutism was abolished. A liberal constitution was adopted in 1849.

An uprising in the duchies of Schleswig and Holstein led to two wars with Prussia in 1848–49 and 1864. At the conclusion of the last war, Denmark had to cede the duchies.

Denmark was neutral during World War I, but the nation's economy was disrupted by the Allied blockade. A plebiscite was held in 1920 in the northern parts of Schleswig, and the mainly Danish-speaking areas were returned to Denmark.

Nazi Germany invaded Denmark and occupied the country in 1940–45.

POSTWAR DENMARK

After World War II Denmark joined the United Nations, NATO, and the inter-Scandinavian Nordic Council.

King Frederik IX died on Jan. 14, 1972. His eldest daughter was crowned the next day as Queen Margrethe II, the first woman to sit on the throne of Denmark in over five centuries.

Denmark's entry into the European Common Market on Jan 1, 1973, opened new opportunities for the expansion of the economy.

After parliamentary elections in December 1973, Poul Hartling, leader of the Liberal Party, became prime minister.

In an election on Jan. 9, 1975, the Social Democrats won and Anker Jorgensen became prime minister.

In a national referendum on Sept. 19, 1978, Danes approved a constitutional amendment lowering the voting age to 18.

Denmark suffered in the 1970s and early 1980s from inflation, a growing foreign-trade deficit, and unemployment. The government's social programs caused a rising national debt.

Although unable to win a majority in parliamentary elections in 1977, 1979, and 1981, Jorgensen continued as prime minister, forming mi-

QUICK QUIZ: When did Illinois become a U.S. state? See page 303.

DENMARK (continued)

nority coalition cabinets. However, when parliament rejected his proposals for tough economic measures to bring inflation under control, he left office, resigning on Sept. 2, 1982.

Poul Schluter, 53, Denmark's first conservative prime minister in 81 years, was sworn in on Sept. 10, 1982, heading a coalition government.

Schluter's austerity program was narrowly approved by parliament on Oct. 16, 1982. It froze wages, ended pay raises linked to inflation, and cut social welfare and unemployment benefits.

In an election on Jan. 10, 1984, Prime Minister Schluter's Conservative Party increased its number of seats in parliament but failed to obtain a majority.

With members of the governing coalition abstaining, Denmark's parliament voted on May 10, 1984, to halt payments for NATO's deployment of new U.S. nuclear missiles in Western Europe.

When strikes demanding wage increases by hundreds of thousands of workers nearly shut the nation down, parliament passed emergency laws on March 30, 1985, ending the strikes and granting raises of 2% in 1985 and 1.5% in 1986.

DENMARK'S OVERSEAS AREAS

GREENLAND (Kâlatdlit-Numât)

Area: 840,000 square miles (2,175,600 sq. km.).
Population: 53,000.
Capital: Godthaab (Nuuk), 3,585.
Languages: Greenlandic (official) and Danish.
Greenland, the world's largest island (1,660 miles long, with a maximum width of 650 miles), is considered part of North America.

The ice cap that covers 84% of the island has an average thickness of nearly 5,000 feet, but may be over 14,000 feet thick in some areas.

Most Greenlanders are of mixed Eskimo and European ancestry.

The main industry is fishing.

Greenland was first colonized about A.D. 981 by Eric the Red. The early colonists died out in the 1400s when the climate turned colder. Modern colonization by Europeans was begun in 1721 by Hans Egede, a Norwegian missionary. Greenland became a possession of Denmark in 1380.

An offer to buy Greenland by U.S. Secretary of State James F. Byrnes in 1946 was rejected by Denmark. The U.S. maintains two air bases and several early-warning radar stations in Greenland.

Denmark granted self-government on May 1, 1979. Greenlandic (Eskimo) replaced Danish as the official language. Denmark retained control of foreign relations and continued to provide about $250 million in annual aid.

In a referendum on Feb. 23, 1982, Greenlanders voted 52% to 46% to withdraw from the European Common Market in order to be able to charge other nations for fishing rights.

FAEROE ISLANDS

Area: 540 square miles (1,399 sq. km.).
Population: 45,000.
Capital: Tórshavn, 10,726.
The Faeroe Islands lie in the Atlantic between Scotland's Shetland Islands and Iceland.

Seventeen of the 19 islands are inhabited. The capital, Tórshavn, is located on Streymoy, the largest island. The main industry of the Faeroes

is fishing. The principal language is Faeroese.

Celts were the earliest known inhabitants, but in the 700s Norsemen settled the islands.

With Norway the Faeroes came under the Danish crown in 1380. The islands obtained home rule in 1948. The popularly elected parliament (the Lagting) meets in Tórshavn. Two Faeroese representatives sit in the Danish parliament.

DJIBOUTI

Official Name: Republic of Djibouti.
Area: 8,494 square miles (22,000 sq. km.).
Population: 330,000.
Capital: Djibouti, 62,000.
Government: One-party republic.
President: Hassan Gouled Aptidon (since 1977).
Legislature: Assembly, 65 deputies.
U.S. Ambassador to Djibouti: Alvin P. Adams Jr.
Djiboutian Ambassador to U.S.: Salah Hadji Farah Dirir.
Flag: Light green stripe over light blue with red star on white triangle.
Languages: Arabic (official), Somali, Afar, French.
Main Ethnic Groups: Issa (Somali; 45%), Afar (45%).
Religion: Islam.
Leading Industries: Service (port facilities, transportation, ship repairs); commerce; agriculture (cattle, sheep, goats, donkeys, dates); mining (salt); processing (hides, skins); handicrafts.
Foreign Trade (excluding transit shipments to and from Ethiopia): Major exports—hides, skins, cattle; major imports—food, textiles, consumer goods.
Places of Interest: Free-port shops in Djibouti; beach resorts; Lake Assal (512 feet below sea level).

DJIBOUTI TODAY

A little larger than Massachusetts, Djibouti is an East African country that was known as French Somaliland and later as Afars and Issas (the names of its two main tribes). It owes its existence as a nation largely to its location at the southern entrance to the Red Sea, making it an important stopping place for vessels traveling through the Suez Canal.

Most Djiboutians live in and around Djibouti, the port city and capital. They work mainly in the extensive shipping trade. The bulk of Ethiopia's exports and imports flow through the port.

Many Djiboutians are dependent on khat, a narcotic leaf that is a mild stimulant when chewed while still fresh. About 10 tons a day of khat are imported from Ethiopia. The drug is legal, so the government collects about $15 million a year in import duties.

Most of the country's land away from the coast is barren and desolate with little or no vegetation other than thorn bushes. Only about 10% of the land can provide pasture for livestock. Nomadic tribesmen lead poverty-stricken lives tending herds of goats, sheep, camels, and cattle.

Mountains near the northern coast of the Gulf of Tadjoura rise to a height of 5,426 feet.

The country has a hot climate with little rainfall. Temperatures average above 90° F. from May to October, often soaring above 110° F.

HISTORY OF DJIBOUTI

In early times Muslim Arabs and Persians established trading posts on the Gulf of Tadjoura. Camel caravans from Ethiopia brought gems, ostrich feathers, coffee, and slaves that were carried by ship to the Arab and Persian empires. The local people converted to Islam and were ruled by Muslim sultans.

The French purchased from the local sultan an anchorage at Obock on the north coast of the Gulf of Tadjoura in 1862.

When the British claimed what is now northern Somalia in the 1880s, the French took possession of the area around the Gulf of Tadjoura, naming the colony French Somaliland in 1888.

Leonce Lagarde, the first governor of French Somaliland, began construction of Djibouti in 1888. The city quickly became a thriving seaport and was made the capital in 1892.

Completion of a 486-mile railroad between Djibouti and Addis Ababa on June 7, 1917, brought the area increased prosperity.

In World War II the colony was administered by the pro-Nazi Vichy government of France from 1940 to 1942. But an allied blockade of Djibouti forced the colony to come over to the side of the Free French.

In a referendum in September 1958 the people voted by a narrow margin to remain the overseas territory of French Somaliland with representation in France's parliament.

The name of the territory was changed on July 5, 1967, to the *French Territory of Afars and Issas.*

The pro-French political party of the Afars won control of the territory's government in elections in 1963, 1968, and 1973 with their leader, Ali Aref Bourhan, as president.

The French government announced on Dec. 31, 1975, that it planned to grant Afars and Issas independence but would maintain troops in the country to protect French interests.

The people of the territory voted on May 8, 1977, in favor of independence. At the same time they elected a national assembly from a single list of 65 candidates that had previously been agreed to by the four main political parties.

Djibouti was granted its independence by France on June 27, 1977. Hassan Gouled Aptidon, leader of the Issas majority in the legislature, was chosen by his fellow representatives as the nation's first president.

Gouled declared the new nation would remain neutral in the undeclared war between its larger neighbors, Somalia and Ethiopia, both of which promised to respect Djibouti's independence.

About 30,000 refugees from the Somali-Ethiopian war and drought in 1979–80 increased hardship in poverty-stricken Djibouti.

Gouled was reelected president in June 1981, winning 84% of the vote as the sole candidate.

In October 1981 the national assembly voted to make Gouled's Popular Assembly for Progress the nation's only legal political party.

DOMINICA

Official Name: Commonwealth of Dominica.
Area: 290 square miles (751 sq. km.).
Population: 74,000.
Capital: Roseau, 16,000.
Government: Parliamentary republic.
Prime Minister: Eugenia Charles (since 1980).
President: Jenner Armour (since 1979).
Legislature: *House of Assembly,* 21 members.
U.S. Ambassador to Dominica: Milan D. Bish.
Ambassador to U.S.: Franklin Baron.
Flag: Dark green field with parrot on red disk in center; tricolor cross of yellow, white, and black bars.
Languages: English (official), French patois.
Chief Ethnic Group: Black
Principal Religion: Roman Catholicism.
Leading Industries: Agriculture (bananas, citrus fruits, coconuts, cocoa); manufacturing (soap, food processing, floor mats); mining (pumice); tourism.
Foreign Trade: *Major exports*—bananas, citrus fruits, coconuts, cocoa; *major imports*—food, tobacco, clothing, machinery, petroleum.
Places of Interest: Black volcanic sand beach; scenic mountain rivers; tropical forests; hot mineral springs; Carib Indian reserve.

The Caribbean island of Dominica lies between the French islands of Guadeloupe to the north and Martinique to the south. Tourism and raising bananas and citrus fruits are the main industries.

Sparsely populated compared with most other Caribbean islands, mountainous Dominica has preserved much of its natural tropical beauty. The island is about 20 miles long and 16 miles wide. The highest point is Morne Diablotins (4,747 ft.).

The island was discovered on Nov. 3, 1493, by Christopher Columbus. Settlement began with French colonists in 1632. Dominica was taken by Britain in 1759, recaptured by France in 1778, and restored to Britain in 1783. It became self-governing on March 1, 1967.

Britain granted Dominica independence on Nov. 3, 1978, with Patrick R. John as the first prime minister. He was forced to resign after one person was killed and eight were wounded on May 29, 1979, when soldiers fired into a crowd demonstrating against restrictive labor legislation he had proposed.

Two hurricanes struck the island in 1979, leaving thousands homeless.

In the first national election since independence, on July 21, 1980, the Dominica Freedom Party won 17 of the 21 seats in parliament. Its leader, Eugenia Charles, 61, became prime minister—the first woman head of government in the Caribbean. In one of her first acts, she disbanded the nation's 99-man army.

Prime Minister Charles, 66, led her party to victory in a national election in July 1985, winning a second 5-year term.

DOMINICAN REPUBLIC

Official Name: Dominican Republic.
Area: 18,816 square miles (48,734 sq. km.).
Population: 6,390,000.
Chief Cities: Santo Domingo, the capital, 673,470; Santiago de los Caballeros, 155,000.
Largest Metropolitan Area: Santo Domingo, 817,645.
Government: Republic.
President: Salvador Jorge Blanco (since 1982).
National Congress: *Senate,* 27 members; *Chamber of Deputies,* 91 members.
U.S. Ambassador to Dom. Rep.: Lowell C. Kilday.
Dominican Republic Ambassador to U.S.: Carlos Despradel.
Flag: White cross bearing national coat of arms; two red and two blue quarters.
Languages: Spanish (official), French, English.
Ethnic Groups: Mulatto (73%), Spanish descent (16%), black (11%).
Official Religion: Roman Catholicism (97%).
Leading Industries: Agriculture (sugarcane, tobacco, vegetables, coffee, cocoa, bananas, rice, corn, cattle, poultry); food processing (sugar, molasses, rum); tourism; manufacturing (textiles, cement, bottles, paper, matches, tobacco products); mining (bauxite, gold, silver, iron ore, salt, gypsum).
Foreign Trade: *Major exports*—sugar, gold, silver, nickel, coffee, cacao, bauxite, tobacco, *major imports*—petroleum, iron and steel, machinery, chemical and pharmaceutical products, foodstuffs.
Places of Interest: *In Santo Domingo:* Basilica Santa Maria la Menor, with the Columbus Tomb and Cross; Alcázar de Colón, built by Columbus' son; viceregal museum; Tower of Homage; national capitol; Plaza de la Cultura.

DOMINICAN REPUBLIC TODAY

The Dominican Republic is a Caribbean island nation about twice the size of New Hampshire.

About 200,000 American visitors a year come to enjoy the nation's beaches and resorts.

Dominicans have a much lower standard of living than the people of nearby Puerto Rico. Most are farm workers. About a third of the people cannot read and write. Many Dominicans live close to starvation the year round.

Dependent on oil imports for its energy needs, the nation suffered in the 1970s and 1980s from high inflation and unemployment.

The Dominican Republic covers the eastern two-thirds of the island of Hispaniola. It has a 193-mile border on the west with Haiti. The Mona Passage separates it from Puerto Rico.

The climate is mildly tropical and humid. Temperatures range from 72° to 83° F., but the winters are colder in the mountain areas.

EARLY HISTORY

Columbus discovered the island in 1492, claimed it for Spain, and named it Las Española (Hispaniola). Santo Domingo, founded in 1496, was the first permanent European settlement in the Western Hemisphere.

In 1697 Spain was forced by the Treaty of Ryswick to cede to France the western third of the island now known as Haiti. France acquired the rest of Hispaniola in 1795.

With British aid the Dominicans revolted against French rule in 1809, proclaiming the first Dominican Republic. The 1814 Treaty of Paris returned the country to Spanish rule.

In 1822 it was overrun and annexed by Haiti.

INDEPENDENCE

Led by Juan Pablo Duarte, the Dominicans rebelled, drove out the Haitians, and once again proclaimed a republic on Feb. 27, 1844.

In 1870 the Dominicans approved a treaty that would have annexed the republic to the United States, but the U.S. Senate refused to ratify it.

In 1904 several foreign powers threatened to intervene to collect their debts. To forestall such a move, the U.S. in 1905 took over the administration of Dominican customs. In 1916 the U.S. occupied the republic and established a military government that ruled until 1924. The U.S. retained customs control until 1941.

From 1930 the Dominican Republic was governed by dictator Gen. Rafael Leonidas Trujillo Molina, until his assassination in 1961.

Joaquín Balaguer, a conservative, who had been appointed by Trujillo, continued to rule.

At the nation's first free elections in four decades, on Dec. 20, 1962, leftist Juan Bosch of the Dominican Revolutionary Party (PR) won the presidency. He took office in February 1963 but was overthrown seven months later by a military coup. A junta took control.

In 1965 civil war broke out as left-wing forces tried to restore Bosch to power. Fearing a communist takeover, U.S. President Johnson sent in 28,000 U.S. Marines in April. About 3,000 Dominicans were killed before the revolt was put down. U.S. troops were withdrawn in 1966.

Balaguer defeated Bosch in a presidential election in 1966. He was reelected in 1970 and 1974.

Antonio Guzmán Fernandez of the leftist Dominican Revolutionary Party defeated Balaguer in a presidential election on May 16, 1978.

The country was devastated on Aug. 31, 1979, by hurricane David that killed 1,380 persons, injured 4,000, and left 200,000 without homes.

DEVELOPMENTS IN THE 1980s

In an election of May 16, 1982, Salvador Jorge Blanco, 56, of the governing Dominican Revolutionary Party, defeated 13 other presidential candidates with a plurality of 46.7%.

President Guzmán, 71, who had not been a candidate in the election, killed himself on July 3, 1982, apparently because he learned that aides had betrayed him with extensive corruption.

President Jorge Blanco in his inaugural address on Aug. 16, 1982, described the nation as "financially bankrupt," outlining a program of increased taxes and reduced government spending to bring under control unemployment (30%) and inflation (12%).

When the government announced price increases on food and imports in April 1984 to raise money to pay foreign debts, widespread rioting broke out and some 55 persons were killed as police quelled the demonstrations.

ECUADOR

Official Name: Republic of Ecuador.
Area: 109,484 square miles (283,561 sq. km.).
Population: 9,663,000.
Chief Cities: Quito, capital, 880,971; Guayaquil, 1,278,908; Cuenca, 150,987.
Government: Democratic republic.
President: León Febres Cordero (since 1984).
Congress: 71 members.
Ambassador to U.S.: Mario Ribadeneira.
U.S. Ambassador to Ecuador: Fernando E. Rondon.
Flag: Yellow, blue, and red stripes, with national coat of arms at center.
Languages: Spanish (official), Quechua, Jivaro.
Ethnic Groups: Mestizo (55%), Indian (25%), black (10%), Spanish descent (10%).
Official Religion: Roman Catholicism (95%).
Leading Industries: Agriculture (bananas, cocoa, coffee, sugarcane, cattle, dairying); mining (petroleum, gold, copper, sulfur, natural gas); manufacturing (textiles, cement, lumber, tobacco products, sugar); fishing.
Foreign Trade: *Major exports*—petroleum, bananas, coffee, cocoa, sugar, seafood; *major imports*—machinery, vehicles, paper, textiles, consumer goods.
Places of Interest: Andes Mountains; Panecillo; Cotopaxi Volcano; Equatorial Monument; Valley of Chillos; Guayas River; Galápagos Islands; Playas beach resort; Guayaquil; Quito.

ECUADOR TODAY

About the size of Nevada, Ecuador is an oil-exporting nation. Petroleum provides about two-thirds of its foreign-exchange income. However, most Ecuadoreans remain poor.

Ecuador is so named because the equator passes through the country. Colombia lies to the north and Peru to the south.

The Pacific coast region is a rich agricultural belt in which most of Ecuador's export crops are grown. Two parallel ranges of the Andes run north-south in mid-country.

About three-fourths of Ecuador is covered by forests. Climate varies with the region. Most of the northern coast is a wet, tropical forest. The southern coastal area, including Guayaquil, is cooled by the Peru Current.

HISTORY

The small tribes of Indians who first inhabited Ecuador were conquered near the end of the 1400s by Incas from the south. The Incas ruled until the Spanish conquest in 1534.

Ecuador won independence from Spain on May 24, 1822. It then became part of Simón Bolívar's Gran Colombia. When that confederation was dissolved in 1830, Ecuador became a separate, independent nation. The country's first and second presidents were conservative Juan José Flores and liberal Vicente Rocafuerte.

From 1830 to 1948 Ecuador had 62 presidents, dictators, and juntas.

More stable government began in 1948 with the election of Galo Plaza Lasso, the first freely elected president to serve his full term. He was followed in 1952 by liberal José María Velasco Ibarra. A conservative, Camilo Ponce Enríquez, was elected in 1956. In 1960 Velasco, running as an independent, was reelected, but he was forced into exile in 1961 by a leftist coup. Vice President Carlos Julio Arosemena Monroy held the presidency until ousted by a military junta in July 1963.

A constitutional assembly elected in 1966 chose a provisional president, Otto Arosemena Gómez. In June 1968 Velasco was again elected. He assumed dictatorial powers in June 1970. On Feb. 15, 1972, he was overthrown by a military junta, and Gen. Guillermo Rodríguez Lara assumed the presidency.

Ecuador became an oil-exporting nation with completion in August 1972 of a pipeline from oil fields in the Amazon basin across the Andes mountains to the Pacific coast.

The government took over 25% of the production of U.S.-owned oil companies in 1974.

A military junta headed by Vice Adm. Alfredo Poveda Burbano deposed Rodríguez in 1976.

Under pressure from the U.S. to restore democracy, the military junta took steps to establish civilian rule. On Jan. 15, 1978, voters approved a new constitution that gave illiterates the vote.

Jaime Roldós Aquilera, 38, won a runoff presidential election on April 29, 1979, with 68% of the popular vote. Democratic civilian rule was restored on Aug. 10, 1979, when the military junta turned the government over to Roldós.

President Roldós, his wife, his defense minister, and six others were killed in a plane crash on May 24, 1981. He was succeeded by 41-year-old Vice President Osvaldo Hurtado Larrea, head of the moderate Popular Democracy Party.

Torrential rains in the winter of 1982–83 brought the worst flooding in 50 years, causing 30 deaths and $400 million in damage.

In a presidential run-off election on May 6, 1984, self-made millionaire businessman León Febres Cordero, 53, of the conservative National Reconstruction Front, won a surprise victory over the leftist Social Democratic Party candidate, Rodrigo Boja Cevallos.

Taking office as president on Aug. 10, 1984, Febres Cordero promised to expand the nation's stagnant economy by reducing government interference in business.

GALAPAGOS ISLANDS

Area: 3,028 square miles (7,842 sq. km.).
Population: 6,000.
Capital: Baquerizo Moreno.

This Ecuadorian territory—60 volcanic islands in the Pacific about 650 miles west of Ecuador—was declared a national park in 1936 to protect its unique wildlife.

The British scientist Charles Darwin studied the animal life of the islands in 1835 as he was developing his theory of evolution.

The Galápagos tortoises, with a life span of over 200 years, are believed to be the world's longest-living animals.

QUICK QUIZ: When did Congress first meet in Washington, D.C.? See page 303.

EGYPT

Official Name: Arab Republic of Egypt.

Area: 386,900 square miles (1,002,066 sq. km.).

Population: 50,055,000.

Chief Cities: Cairo, capital, 5,074,016; Alexandria, 2,317,705; Giza, 1,246,713; Shubra El-Khema, 393,700; El-Mahalla El-Kubra, 292,853; Tanta, 284,636; Port Said, 262,760; Mansura, 257,866.

Government: Strong-president parliamentary republic.

President: Hosni Mubarak (since 1981).

Prime Minister: Kamal Hassan Ali (since 1984).

Legislature: *National Assembly*, 458 members.

U.S. Ambassador to Egypt: Nicholas A. Veliotes.

Egyptian Ambassador to U.S.: El Sayed Abdel Raouf el Reedy.

Flag: Red, white, and black stripes, with gold hawk emblem in white stripe.

Languages: Arabic (official), English.

Ethnic Groups: Egyptian, Copt, Bedouin, Nubian.

Main Religions: Islam (85%), Coptic Christian (15%).

Leading Industries: Agriculture (cotton, rice, corn, wheat, barley, beans, sugarcane, poultry, cattle); manufacturing (textiles, chemicals, steel, machinery, electrical equipment, food processing); tourism; mining (iron ore, petroleum, uranium, phosphate).

Foreign Trade: *Major exports*—petroleum, cotton, textiles; *major imports*—machinery, wheat, transport equipment, iron and steel, tea.

Places of Interest: Pyramids and Sphinx at Giza; Nile River; Abu Simbel temples; Aswan Dam; Alexandria; Luxor and Karnak temples, Valley of the Kings, Queen Hatshepsut Temple, and Memmon Colossi at Luxor. *In Cairo:* Citadel; Mohammed Ali Mosque; Coptic churches.

EGYPT TODAY

Egypt is the largest and most powerful of the Arab countries of the Middle East. Petroleum is its major export, but it has limited oil reserves. With few other natural resources than its soil and electric power generated by the Nile River, Egypt relies on other nations for aid in developing its industries. The U.S. provides over $2 billion in military and economic aid annually.

Most Egyptians live a hand-to-mouth existence as farmers and livestock herdsmen. Only 4 of 10 Egyptians can read and write.

The government's major problems involve trying to control population growth and to expand food production. Antiquated farming methods prevent Egypt from growing enough food to feed its people.

Four wars with Israel in 1948–73 cost Egypt the lives of 100,000 soldiers and left it with huge foreign debts.

The northward-flowing Nile River divides eastern and western Egypt. The vast, rainless Sahara covers most of Egypt.

Lower Egypt in the north includes the Nile Delta, 8,500 square miles of rich cropland.

The productive portion of Upper Egypt in the south consists of a narrow strip of irrigated land about 20 miles wide that follows the course of the Nile River from Cairo to the Sudan.

Libya lies to the west, Sudan to the south, and Israel to the east.

EARLY HISTORY

The earliest Egyptian dynasty united the kingdoms of Upper and Lower Egypt about 3200 B.C. The great pyramids were built as tombs for kings about 2650–2500 B.C.

Egypt fell under Persian control in 525 B.C. Greek rule by the Macedonians under Alexander the Great and the Ptolemy dynasty followed. Then came Roman rule. The present culture of Egypt was basically set by the Muslim conquest of A.D. 640 that brought the Islamic religion.

After the breakup of the Abbasid empire in the 800s, Egypt was ruled by local caliphs and sultans.

The Ottoman Turks conquered Egypt in 1517 and held it for nearly 300 years.

Napoleon invaded Egypt in 1798. After French withdrawal, a soldier named Mohammed Ali seized power. Under his rule Egypt remained part of the Ottoman Empire.

France and Britain exerted increasing influence on Egyptian affairs after completion of the Suez Canal in 1869. A nationalist revolt in 1882 caused Britain to send troops to protect British interests. Britain made Egypt a protectorate in 1914.

INDEPENDENT MONARCHY

In 1922 Britain granted Egypt its independence under the former sultan as King Fuad I. However, Britain kept troops in Egypt to protect the Suez Canal.

Upon Fuad's death in 1936, his son Faruk succeeded him.

In World War II Egypt was a crucial base for the Allies in North Africa.

Egypt took the major part in the Arab-Israeli war of 1948. The defeat of Egyptian forces and corruption brought decline in royal prestige. In 1952 Faruk was exiled after a military coup.

ARAB REPUBLIC OF EGYPT

Egypt became a republic on June 18, 1953. Gen. Mohammed Naguib was the first president.

Col. Gamal Abdel Nasser ousted Naguib in November 1954, making himself dictator.

Nasser had his greatest success in the second Arab-Israeli War in 1956 when he turned a military defeat at the hands of Britain, France, and Israel into a political victory—retaining control of the Suez Canal, which he had seized.

In 1958 Nasser established a federation with Syria called the United Arab Republic (U.A.R.). The federation collapsed in 1961.

Israel attacked Egypt on June 5, 1967, in the third Arab-Israeli War, capturing the Sinai Peninsula.

During the next three years, Egypt rebuilt its armed forces with Soviet assistance.

Anwar al-Sadat became president after Nasser died of a heart attack on Sept. 28, 1970.

Relations with the Soviet Union became strained. In mid-1972 President Sadat ordered the withdrawal of Soviet military personnel.

Egypt and Syria attacked Israel in October 1973 in a fourth war that lasted 18 days. Israel counterattacked, making new territorial gains.

U.S.-Egyptian diplomatic relations, broken in 1967, resumed in 1974.

In March 1976 Sadat abrogated the 1971 treaty of friendship with the Soviet Union.

The development of new oil fields enabled Egypt to become an oil-exporting nation in 1977.

In a dramatic reversal of policy, Sadat initiated a drive to achieve peace in the Mideast by visiting Israel in November 1977. After months of negotiation, Sadat and Israeli Prime Minister Menachem Begin signed a peace treaty on March 26, 1979. Eighteen Arab League countries denounced the treaty, ordering an economic boycott of Egypt and breaking diplomatic relations with Sadat's government. Egyptians voted 99% approval of the treaty on April 19, 1979.

EGYPT IN THE 1980s

Egyptian voters in 1980 approved constitutional amendments Sadat had proposed. Among the amendments, Islamic law was made the basis for legislation and a multiparty political system was institutionalized.

The government announced in 1980 the discovery of the largest uranium deposit in the Middle East. Plans were made to develop three mines to exploit the deposits.

In February 1980 Egypt and Israel established formal diplomatic relations for the first time.

A $140 million tunnel under the Suez Canal was completed in 1980, connecting Cairo by highway to Israel and Jordan.

Throughout the first eight months of 1981 Egypt experienced a growing wave of riots and protests led by fanatic Muslims and Christian Copts. On Sept. 3, Sadat cracked down, arresting more than 1,500 radicals.

Charging that the Soviet Union had been inciting "sedition and conflicts among Egyptians" as part of a "hostile plot," Sadat on Sept. 15, 1981, expelled the Soviet ambassador, his staff, and over a thousand Soviet technicians.

Less than a month later, Sadat was assassinated on Oct. 6, 1981, while reviewing a military parade near Cairo. Five radical Muslims convicted of the crime were executed on April 15, 1982. Another 17 received prison terms.

Hosni Mubarak, former head of the air force chosen by Sadat as his vice president, succeeded to the presidency. He declared he would carry on Sadat's policies to seek peace in the Mideast.

In accordance with the 1979 peace treaty, Egypt reoccupied its Sinai region after withdrawal of Israelis on April 25, 1982.

In a multi-party parliamentary election on May 27, 1984, Mubarak's National Democratic Party received 87.2% of the vote. The major opposition party, the conservative New Wafd Party, won 12.7% of the vote and 57 seats in the 458-member national assembly.

Mubarak moved Egypt in 1984 toward a wider role in international affairs as diplomatic relations were resumed with Jordan and the Soviet Union.

Egypt accused Libya of trying to disrupt traffic on the Suez Canal by laying mines in the Red Sea that damaged many ships in 1984.

Mubarak tried to persuade the U.S. and Israel in 1985 to start new negotiations for peace in the Middle East that would involve the Palestine Liberation Organization (PLO).

EL SALVADOR

Official Name: Republic of El Salvador.
Area: 8,124 square miles (21,041 sq. km.).
Population: 5,857,000.
Capital: San Salvador, 335,930.
Government: Multi-party democracy.
President: José Napoleón Duarte (since 1984).
National Assembly: 60 members.
U.S. Ambassador to El Salvador: Edwin G. Corr.
El Salvador Ambassador to U.S.: Pablo Mauricio Alvergue.
Flag: Blue, white, and blue stripes, with nation's coat of arms in center.
Official Language: Spanish.
Main Ethnic Groups: Mestizo (89%), Indian (10%).
Religion: Roman Catholicism (98%).
Leading Industries: Agriculture (coffee, cotton, corn, millet, sugarcane, henequen, beans, cattle, sheep, goats); mining (gold, silver); food processing; manufacturing (textiles, steel, cement, consumer goods); fishing (shrimp).
Foreign Trade: *Major exports*—coffee, cotton, sugar, shrimp, textiles; *major imports*—crude petroleum, iron and steel, fertilizers, medicines, paper.
Places of Interest: San Salvador; Izalco Volcano; El Tazumal ruins at Chalchuapa; Santa Ana Cathedral; Ilopango and Coatepeque lakes.

EL SALVADOR TODAY

About the size of Massachusetts, El Salvador is the most densely populated country in Central America. Coffee accounts for over half the country's exports.

El Salvador has been wracked by civil war since the 1970s, with thousands killed each year. More are killed in assassinations and massacres than in military fighting. Leftist guerrillas seeking to overthrow the government are supported by the pro-Soviet regime in Nicaragua. Trying to prevent a communist takeover, the U.S. provides substantial military and economic aid to El Salvador.

The majority of people work as farm laborers, barely earning food and shelter. Only about half of all Salvadorans can read and write.

Most of the people live in the central plateau between volcanic mountain ranges.

EARLY HISTORY

Before the Spanish conquest, El Salvador, called *Cuscatlán* (Land of Jewels), was the home of the Aztec-related Pipil Indians and probably an Aztec colony. Spanish conquistador Pedro de Alvarado conquered El Salvador in 1525.

Subsequently, Spain neglected the area in favor of wealthier territories.

San Salvador declared independence from Spain on Sept. 22, 1821, becoming part of the United Provinces of Central America.

The country became separately independent in 1838. Since then its history has been beset by internal strife and military dictatorship.

QUICK QUIZ: Which U.S. President was a graduate of Stanford University? See page 370.

EL SALVADOR *(continued)*

In the 1950s and 1960s some 300,000 Salvadorans migrated to sparsely populated neighboring Honduras in search of jobs and land. On July 14, 1969, El Salvador's army invaded Honduras. A cease-fire was arranged after five days, but the war took at least 1,000 lives and left bitter feelings on both sides. Troops of El Salvador and Honduras again clashed along their jungle frontier in July 1976.

The National Conciliation Party (PCN), controlled by the armed forces, governed from 1961.

Gen. Carlos Humberto Romero became president in 1977.

Junior military officers overthrew Romero in a bloodless coup on Oct. 15, 1979. A military-civilian junta took control.

EL SALVADOR IN THE 1980s

Under U.S. pressure to end dominance of the nation by wealthy families, the junta in 1980 announced a land-reform program and nationalization of banks and financial institutions.

The nation's leading spokesman for human rights, Roman Catholic Archbishop Oscar Arnulfo Romero, was slain by rightist terrorists while conducting mass on March 24, 1980. About 30 persons were killed when battling broke out at his funeral.

The junta appointed José Napoléon Duarte as president on Dec. 13, 1980—the first civilian head of government in 49 years.

On evidence that Cuba and Nicaragua were supplying arms to leftist guerrillas, the U.S. on Jan. 16, 1981, resumed sale of arms to El Salvador that had been suspended for three years. In mid-1981, 55 U.S. military trainers were sent to aid El Salvador, but with orders not to engage in combat.

In a free election supervised by international observers on March 28, 1982, voters chose members of a new constituent assembly. Ultrarightist Roberto d'Aubuisson became president of the constituent assembly. The assembly chose Alvaro Alfredo Magaṭa, an economist, as the nation's provisional president.

The constituent assembly in May 1982 suspended the government's land-reform program.

The civil war continued to rage in 1983–85, with the number of deaths estimated at over 50,000 since 1979.

In an effort to intimidate Nicaragua from continuing aid to the guerrillas, the U.S. carried out massive military exercises in 1983.

A government peace mission met with rebel leaders in Colombia in 1983, trying to get them to cease fighting and take part in elections.

In a presidential run-off election on May 6, 1984, Duarte, candidate of the moderate Christian Democrats, won 54% of the vote to defeat d'Aubuisson, candidate of the rightist Nationalist Republican Alliance. Duarte was sworn-in on June 1 as the nation's first freely elected president.

Seeking to end the nation's civil war, Duarte met with rebel leaders at La Palma, El Salvador, on Oct. 15, 1984, where the two sides agreed to form a joint commission to formulate a truce.

Duarte's position was strengthened when his party won majority control of the national assembly in an election on March 31, 1985.

EQUATORIAL GUINEA

Official Name: Republic of Equatorial Guinea.
Area: 10,831 square miles (28,051 sq. km.).
Population: 310,000.
Capital: Malabo, 37,237.
Government: Military dictatorship.
President: Col. Teodoro Obiang Nguema (since 1979).
National Assembly: 60 members.
U.S. Ambassador: Hume A. Horan.
Equatorial Guinean Ambassador to U.S.: Florencio Maye Ela.
Flag: Green, white, and red stripes, with blue triangle at hoist; coat of arms centered in white stripe.
Languages: Spanish (official), tribal dialects.
Chief Ethnic Group: Fang (75%).
Main Religion: Roman Catholicism (60%).
Leading Industries: Agriculture (cocoa, coffee, bananas, oil palms, sisal, cattle, vegetables, fruits); forestry and lumbering; food processing.
Foreign Trade: *Major exports*—cocoa, coffee, wood; *major imports*—food, tobacco, textiles.
Places of Interest: Swimming beaches; tropical islets; art exhibits at Spanish-Guinean Cultural Center in Malabo; art museum in Bata.

Somewhat smaller than Maryland, Equatorial Guinea has two widely separated provinces:

(1) The western Africa mainland area of Río Muni (10,046 sq. mi.) is a forested region with about three-fourths of the population.

(2) The island of Bioko (formerly Fernando Po) (785 sq. mi.) lies about 20 miles off the coast of Cameroon. It also controls the smaller island of Pagalu (formerly Annobíon), over 200 miles to the southwest.

The farms and plantations of the offshore island of Bioko grow cocoa. Exports of coffee and okume wood, used in the production of plywood, come from Río Muni.

Bioko, discovered by the Portuguese in 1471, was ceded to Spain in 1778. Río Muni was awarded to Spain by the Treaty of Berlin (1885).

The two areas were joined as the colony of Spanish Guinea.

On Oct. 12, 1968, Equatorial Guinea became independent with Francisco Macias Nguema as its first president. He established a one-party dictatorship. In 1976 he Africanized his name by changing it to *Masie* and dropped "Francisco."

During Masie's 11-year reign about one-third of the population, some 100,000, fled to exile, and an estimated 40,000 were tortured and killed.

Col. Teodoro Obiang Nguema, 33, a nephew of the dictator, overthrew Masie on Aug. 3, 1979. The former ruler was captured, tried for genocide, and executed with 6 aides on Sept. 29, 1979.

The U.S., which had broken diplomatic relations in 1976, resumed friendly relations in 1980.

Voters approved a new constitution on Aug. 15, 1982, to keep President Obiang in office until 1989. A one-party legislative assembly was elected on Aug. 28, 1983.

ETHIOPIA

Official Name: Ethiopia.
Area: 471,778 square miles (1,221,900 sq. km.).
Population: 33,680,000.
Chief Cities: Addis Ababa, capital, 1,408,068; Asmara (Āsmera), 468,047.
Government: Communist one-party state.
Dictator: Mengistu Haile Mariam (since 1977).
Flag: Green, yellow, and red stripes.
Languages: Amharic (official), Gallinya, Tigrinya, Arabic.
Main Ethnic Groups: Galla (40%), Amhara (25%), Tigre (12%), Sidama (9%), Somali (2%).
Leading Religions: Islam (40%), Ethiopian Orthodox Christian (35%), animism (20%).
Leading Industries: Agriculture (coffee, cotton, cattle, grains, fruits, vegetables, sugarcane); manufacturing (processing farm products, textiles, cement); mining (gold, platinum).
Foreign Trade: *Major exports*—coffee, cereal, oilseeds, hides and skins; *major imports*—petroleum products, vehicles, machinery, steel, textiles.
Places of Interest: Addis Ababa; Gondar fortress city; Lake Tana; Blue Nile Falls; Lalībela churches carved out of solid rock; ruins at Axum (Āksum); Asmara; Harar; Āwash Game Reserve; beach resorts.

ETHIOPIA TODAY

Ethiopia is a large but poor communist-ruled African country. Almost twice as large as Texas, Ethiopia has the third-largest African population after Nigeria and Egypt. Coffee accounts for more than half the nation's exports.

About 6,000 Soviet and 12,000 Cuban troops aid the government in fighting rebels.

Ethiopians are divided among more than 40 different tribes. Most are farmers or cattle-raising herdsmen who lead primitive lives unaffected by modern technology. They have a life expectancy of only 40 years.

Ethiopia is a land of geographical contrasts. Snow-capped Ras Dashan, the highest mountain, rises to 15,158 feet. The Great Rift Valley slices through the plateau region that makes up about two-thirds of the land. Lake Tana is the headwater of the Blue Nile River.

The Red Sea lies to the north, Djibouti and Somalia to the east, Kenya to the south, and Sudan to the west.

EARLY HISTORY

Menelik, the legendary first son of Solomon and the Queen of Sheba, is said to have founded the Ethiopian empire about 1000 B.C. Semitic tribes from Arabia arrived in the 900s to 600s B.C. Christianity was introduced in the 300s A.D.

About A.D. 1260 a new Ethiopian dynasty came to power that allegedly returned the throne to the line of Solomon. By 1855 authority was centralized under Emperor Theodore II.

Menelik II became emperor of Ethiopia in 1889. Italy's army invaded the country in 1895 but was defeated the next year at Aduwa.

Ras Tafari Makonnen, a favorite grandnephew of Menelik II, had Menelik's daughter Judith crowned empress in 1916 with himself as regent.

On the death of the empress in 1930, Ras Tafari became emperor as Haile Selassie I.

In 1935 the Italians invaded and conquered the country, forcing the emperor to flee to Britain in 1936. With British help in World War II, Haile Selassie regained his throne in 1941.

Ethiopia obtained its Red Sea coastline in 1952 when Eritrea, with UN approval, federated with Ethiopia. Eritrea became a province in 1962, but at the same time Eritrean nationalists began a civil war for independence.

A drought in the Tigre and Wallo regions caused about 200,000 Ethiopians to die of starvation in 1973–74.

COMMUNIST ETHIOPIA

On June 29, 1974, Ethiopian troops seized control of the government, declaring a "war on feudalism." They arrested 200 former cabinet members and advisers to the emperor.

The army deposed Haile Selassie on Sept. 12, 1974, ending his 58 years of rule. He died a prisoner in 1975. The junta officially abolished the Ethiopian monarchy on March 21, 1975.

A 120-man military committee known as the *Dergue* took power, headed by Lt. Gen. Aman Michael Andom. General Aman, an Eritrean, was himself arrested and killed by the junta on Nov. 24, 1974. On the same day 59 nobles and former officials were executed, including two former premiers. Leadership of the junta was taken over by Gen. Teferi Bante as chairman.

Chief of state Gen. Teferi Bante was too slow on the draw on Feb. 3, 1977, when a shoot-out developed at a meeting of the military junta. When the smoke cleared, Teferi and 10 other junta members were dead. Lt. Col. Mengistu Haile Mariam emerged as dictator.

A reign of terror inspired by Mengistu swept Ethiopia in 1977–78. An estimated 5,000 persons were killed.

Ethiopia expelled 300 U.S. officials in April 1977 and closed U.S. aid agencies. Western news correspondents also were expelled.

Full-scale war developed with Somalia in 1977 as Somalis sought to take the southeastern Ogaden region from Ethiopia. On Sept. 14, 1977, the Somalis captured the Ethiopian city of Jijiga, about 100 miles from the Somali border.

But in 1978, with some $1 billion in Soviet arms flown in by airlift, with about 16,000 Cuban troops, and with a Soviet general and 1,500 Soviet "military advisers," the Ethiopians succeeded in driving the Somalis back and recapturing Jijiga on March 5. Fighting with Somali guerrillas in the Ogaden continued intermittently in 1979–85.

In the northeast, an estimated 100,000 Ethiopian troops launched a counteroffensive in May 1978 against Eritrean rebels supplied by Arab nations. On July 27 Ethiopia broke the 10-month siege by the rebels of the major city of Asmara. In August the Ethiopian government

ETHIOPIA (continued)
announced that 33,000 of its troops had been killed or wounded fighting the Eritreans.

The government reported nine assassination attempts on the life of Mengistu in 1978. Many members of the ruling military junta were executed.

Mengistu flew to Moscow in 1978, where on Nov. 20 he signed a 20-year treaty of friendship with the Soviet Union.

The U.S. recalled its ambassador in 1980 at the request of the Mengistu government.

Amnesty International estimated in 1981 that from 10,000 to 40,000 political prisoners remained in Ethiopia's jails.

At the urging of the Soviet Union, Mengistu formed a Communist Workers Party in 1984, appointing the members of the military junta to the party's politburo.

Ethiopia had one of the worst droughts in its history in 1982-85. An estimated 9 million persons faced starvation. The United States and other nations sent more than $700 million in government and private aid including medicine and thousands of tons of grain.

The 23-year-old civil war in Eritrea continued in 1985.

FIJI

Official Name: Dominion of Fiji.
Area: 7,056 square miles (18,274 sq. km.).
Population: 708,000.
Capital: Suva, 63,628.
Government: Parliamentary democracy.
Prime Minister: Ratu Sir Kamisese K.T. Mara (since 1970).
Governor-General: Ratu Sir George Cakobau (since 1973).
Parliament: *Senate*, 22 members; *House of Representatives*, 52 members.
U.S. Ambassador to Fiji: Carl E. Dillery.
Fijian Ambassador to U.S.: Ratu Jone Filipe Radrodro.
Flag: Azure blue with Fiji shield centered on right; Union Jack in upper hoist quarter.
Languages: English (official), Fijian, Hindustani.
Main Ethnic Groups: Indian (50%), Fijian (45%).
Religions: Christianity (41%), Hinduism (35%), Islam (12%).
Leading Industries: Agriculture (sugarcane, coconuts, rice, bananas, cocoa, tobacco, fruits, vegetables, poultry); mining (gold); tourism; food processing; forestry and lumbering; fishing; manufacturing (cement, consumer goods).
Foreign Trade: *Major exports*—sugar, coconut products, gold; *major imports*—machinery, manufactured goods, foodstuffs.
Places of Interest: Beach resorts; native villages; volcanic islands. *In Suva:* Fiji Museum, Botanical Gardens; University of the South Pacific.

FIJI TODAY

The South Pacific nation of Fiji has many economic problems that stem from poor roads, lack of cheap electric power, the difficulties of farmers

obtaining land, and the lack of technicians and managers for industry. Asian Indians make up a majority of the population.

Fiji's economy depends on four principal industries—sugar, copra, gold mining, and tourism.

Sugarcane, the main crop, is almost entirely raised by Asian Indian farmers, descendants of plantation laborers imported in the 1870s.

Industrial development and tourism are becoming increasingly important. Many new hotels have been built. Fiji is an important port of call for cruise ships. More than 130,000 tourists visit each year.

The native Fijians, a mixture of Melanesians and Polynesians, own about 83% of the land, which is held in trust for them by a government agency. The protective land-tenure system has limited development. Asian Indians can lease the land only for periods of 10 years at a time.

About 100 of Fiji's 844 islands are inhabited. The two main islands are Viti Levu (4,011 sq. mi.) and Vanua Levu (2,137 sq. mi.). Suva, the capital, is located on Viti Levu.

Most of Fiji's larger islands are mountainous and volcanic, with rugged, craggy interiors. Mount Victoria, on Viti Levu, is the highest mountain (about 4,300 feet). Fertile river deltas thick with mangroves intersect the coastal plains. Most of the smaller islands are of limestone and coral, their cliffs rising steeply to flat tops with little vegetation. The climate is warm and humid. A 300-mile arc of coral, the Great Sea Reef, protects the western archipelago.

EARLY HISTORY

Discovered by the Dutch explorer Abel Tasman in 1643, the Fiji islands were visited by British Capt. James Cook in 1774. Later, trading vessels came for sandalwood.

For many years the region was known as the "Cannibal Islands" because of the reputation of the Fijians as fearsome man-eaters.

Tribal wars for island supremacy were climaxed in 1855 by the victory of the chief of Bau, with the help of neighboring Tonga.

Fiji remained under Tonga's domination for the next 20 years.

Attempts at confederation failed, and tribal chiefs asked the British to intervene. From 1874 British governors administered the islands.

Local government was introduced in 1876.

INDEPENDENCE

Britain granted Fiji independence on Oct. 10, 1970—the 96th anniversary of the cession of the islands to Queen Victoria. Ratu Sir Kamisese K.T. Mara became the first prime minister.

The country's two main political parties are the Alliance Party, which has governed since 1967, and the opposition National Federation Party (NFP), made up largely of Asian Indians.

Fiji sent half of its army, 500 men, to Lebanon in 1978 as part of the UN peace-keeping force in that country.

Mara's governing Alliance Party again won a general election in July 1982, but with a majority reduced to 28 seats in the lower house.

One of the few nations without broadcast TV, the government began in 1982 to provide community centers with equipment to show videotaped programs.

FINLAND

EUROPE

Official Name: Republic of Finland.
Area: 130,120 square miles (337,009 sq. km.).
Population: 4,901,000.
Chief Cities: Helsinki, capital, 483,044; Tampere, 166,628; Turku, 163,603; Espoo, 139,377.
Largest Metropolitan Area: Helsinki, 905,766.
Government: Multiparty parliamentary democracy.
President: Mauno Koivisto (since 1982).
Prime Minister: Kalevi Sorsa (since 1982).
Parliament: 200 members.
U.S. Ambassador to Finland: Keith Foote Nyborg.
Finnish Ambassador to U.S.: Richard Bertil Muller.
Flag: Light blue cross on a white field.
Official Languages: Finnish, Swedish.
Ethnic Groups: Finnish (94%), Swedish (6%).
Main Religions: Lutheran (97%), Russian Orthodox (1%).
Leading Industries: Manufacturing (paper, furniture, machinery, electrical products, vehicles, chemicals, textiles, ships, ceramics, furs); forestry and lumbering; agriculture (dairy products, poultry, cattle, wheat, rye, potatoes); mining (copper, zinc, iron).
Foreign Trade: *Major exports*—paper, wood, machinery, ships, chemicals, furs; *major imports*—petroleum, machinery, electronics, food, aircraft.
Places of Interest: *In Helsinki:* Temple Square underground church, Mannerheim's house, cathedral, Finlandia Hall, Suomenlinna island fortress. *In Järvenpää:* Jean Sibelius' house. *In Vuokatti:* Kainuu Nature and Play Park. Savonlinna Opera Festival in July; inland waterway cruises; Lapland.

FINLAND TODAY

Somewhat smaller than Montana, Finland lies northwest of the Soviet Union. After having fought three wars with its huge neighbor in this century, Finland today walks a tightrope of neutrality to preserve its democratic freedom.

Finland is one of the world's leading producers of newsprint. Like most industrialized nations of the West, Finland has struggled in the 1970–80s to cope with the problems of inflation.

About one-third its hardworking people live in cities, making their living from manufacturing and service industries. The others live in small towns or on farms. The people enjoy a much higher standard of living than that of the neighboring Soviet Union. Finland has no illiteracy.

The U.S. maintains an exchange program with Finland financed in part from a trust fund established in 1976 from Finland's final repayment of its post-World War I debt to the U.S.

GEOGRAPHY AND CLIMATE

More than 60,000 lakes dot Finland's forested landscape. Northern Finland above the Arctic Circle forms part of Lapland. It has many low mountains. In the central and southern regions the land is mainly low-lying and undulating.

July temperatures in Helsinki rarely go above 75° F. In February, winter temperatures range from 12° F. to –30° F.

Norway lies to the north, Sweden and the Gulf of Bothnia to the west, the Gulf of Finland and the Baltic Sea to the south, and the Soviet Union to the east.

EARLY HISTORY

The Finns' ancestors came into the land from the south through Estonia and Russia about 2,000 years ago.

By the 700s the Finns had taken the country from the Lapps.

From the 1100s Sweden controlled the region. In 1809 Czar Alexander I joined Finland to the Russian Empire as an autonomous grand duchy. In 1863 the Finnish legislature met for the first time since the Russian annexation.

INDEPENDENCE

During Russia's communist revolution the Finns declared their independence on Dec. 6, 1917. After a war of independence Finland adopted a republican constitution on July 17, 1919.

The Soviet Union invaded Finland in 1939–40. The Finns put up stiff resistance, but were forced to cede one-tenth of their land.

Finland began a second war with the Soviet Union in June 1941. The Soviets mounted a fierce offensive in 1944 that made Finland accept an armistice in September. The boundaries and peace terms of 1940 were reestablished, and Finland was forced to pay huge war reparations.

A friendship treaty with the Soviet Union in 1948 accepted the principle of Finnish neutrality, but provided for Soviet military assistance if Finland is attacked.

Under the leadership of Presidents J. K. Paasikivi (1944–56) and Urho Kekkonen (1956–81), Finland pursued a policy of cooperation with the Soviet Union as well as friendship with the West.

Parliament in 1973 approved an agreement for free trade in industrial products with the Common Market nations. In 1974 free-trade agreements also were made with Bulgaria and Hungary.

In parliamentary elections on March 18–19, 1979, voters shifted to the right as the largest party, the Social Democrats, lost 2 seats for a total of 52. The Conservative Party gained 12 seats for a total of 47, making it the second strongest. The remaining 101 seats were split among smaller parties. Women candidates won 26% of the seats.

Social Democrat Mauno Koivisto, president of the Bank of Finland, became prime minister on May 26, 1979, heading a left-center cabinet.

Prime Minister Koivisto became acting president on Sept. 11, 1981, when 81-year-old President Kekkonen became ill. The 57-year-old Kovisto easily won a presidential election in 1982.

Kalevi Sorsa, 51, also a Social Democrat, succeeded Kovisto as prime minister.

Sorsa's centrist coalition government increased its parliamentary majority in a national election on March 20–21, 1983.

QUICK QUIZ: What was the name of the 1928 pact that outlawed war? See page 370.

FRANCE

Official Name: French Republic.
Area: 211,208 square miles (547,026 sq. km.).
Population: 55,202,000.
Chief Cities: Paris, capital, 2,317,227; Marseille, 914,356; Lyon, 462,841; Toulouse, 383,176; Nice, 346,620; Nantes, 263,689; Strasbourg, 257,303; Bordeaux, 226,281; Saint-Étienne, 221,775.
Largest Metropolitan Area: Paris, 8,612,531.
Government: Presidential-parliamentary democracy.
President: François Mitterrand (since 1981).
Prime Minister: Laurent Fabius (since 1984).
Parliament: *Senate,* 283 members; *National Assembly,* 491 members.
U.S. Ambassador to France: Arthur A. Hartman.
French Ambassador to U.S.: Emmanuel Jacquin de la Margerie.
Flag: Tricolor of blue, white, and red bars.
Official Language: French.
Main Religions: Roman Catholicism (90%), Islam (4%), Protestantism (2%), Judaism (1%).
Leading Industries: Manufacturing (steel, paper, electricity, aluminum, cement, automobiles, aircraft, chemicals, textiles, perfume, furniture); food processing; tourism; construction; agriculture (cattle, sheep, dairy products, poultry, hogs, sugar beets, corn, wheat, oats, barley, potatoes, grapes, fruits, vegetables); mining (iron ore, bauxite, uranium, salt, coal, natural gas, petroleum); fishing.
Foreign Trade: *Major exports*—automobiles, iron and steel, alcoholic beverages, petroleum products, clothing; *major imports*—crude petroleum, fruits, office machines, chemicals, copper.
Places of Interest: Angoulême; Avignon; Bourges; Brittany peninsula; Carcassonne; Chartres; the château country (Loire Valley); Clermont-Ferrand; Colmar; Dijon; Grasse; Grenoble; Nîmes; Pau; Rheims; the Riviera; Rouen; Strasbourg; Vienne. *In Paris:* Nôtre-Dame, Ste. Chapelle, the Madeleine, Tuileries gardens, the Louvre, Arc de Triomphe, Montmartre, Sorbonne, Luxembourg Palace and Gardens, Hôtel des Invalides, Opéra, Panthéon, Eiffel Tower. *Near Paris:* Fontainebleau, Versailles.

FRANCE TODAY

About a third larger than California, France has more land than any other nation in western Europe. However, France ranks fourth in population after West Germany, Italy, and Britain.

France is a leading producer of bauxite, cement, electric power, steel, and uranium.

For hundreds of years France fought wars with Germany, Britain, Austria, and Italy to establish itself as a world power. With the rise of the United States and the Soviet Union as superpowers, France has had difficulty reconciling itself to a secondary role in world politics.

To enhance its status and military independence, France developed its own atomic weapons. Like China, France test-explodes them in the atmosphere in defiance of world opinion.

Although France granted independence in the past quarter of a century to most of its former colonies, many of these new nations continued as members of the French Community. This organization preserves use of the French franc as its money and establishes economic and military links. France also maintains control over a scattering of its former colonial possessions as overseas departments and territories.

France is a highly industrialized nation. But about half its people continue to live on farms or in rural villages. With a long tradition of democracy and freedom, the people take a vigorous part in their government.

GEOGRAPHY AND CLIMATE

France is bordered on the north by Belgium, Luxembourg, and West Germany; on the east by Switzerland and Italy; and on the south by Monaco, Spain, and Andorra.

The land is varied and rich. In the southwest the Pyrenees rise along the Spanish border. In the east are the rugged peaks of the Alps and the Jura Mountains, and the wooded mountains of the Vosges range and the Ardennes plateau.

Four major river systems water the country. The Seine rises in the Plateau de Langres and flows northwest through the Paris Basin to the English Channel. The Loire, flowing from the Massif Central, courses westward to the Atlantic. The Garonne runs northwest from the Pyrenees to the Atlantic estuary of the Gironde. The Rhone-Saône system flows from the Alps into the Mediterranean. The Rhine River runs along the Franco-German frontier.

The country has four distinct climatic regions. The dry Mediterranean south has hot summers and mild winters. The central and eastern uplands are moist and seasonally varied. The oceanic west and northwest have cool temperatures and considerable rainfall. The mountainous regions in the southwest and southeast have cold winters, often with heavy snowstorms.

EARLY HISTORY

France was a crossroads of migrant agricultural peoples for hundreds of years. Conquering Celtic invaders brought a degree of order among the quarreling inhabitants, imposed their language to some extent, and gave the area the name *Gaul.*

Greek settlers began colonizing southern France about 600 B.C.

Roman armies in the 100s B.C. conquered part of Gaul. Julius Caesar subjugated the rest of the region in 58–44 B.C. A Latin tongue took root, and a network of military roads brought some degree of unity. Christianity was introduced.

When the Roman Empire weakened after the 200s A.D., a northern tribe, the Salian Franks, subdued much of the country.

After making an alliance with the Roman Catholic Church, Clovis, a leader of the Franks, extended Frankish rule and Christianity by force of arms in the 400s. Clovis founded the Merovingian dynasty.

MIDDLE AGES

Beset by Muslim invaders moving up from Spain, the Frank leader Charles Martel defeated the Arab cavalry at the Battle of Tours in 732, preventing a Muslim conquest of France.

Charlemagne was Charles Martel's grandson.

A militant imperialist and ally of the church, he was crowned emperor of the Western Roman Empire on Christmas Day in the year 800. Under Charlemagne, France was only part of a vast Frankish domain.

Following Charlemagne's death the empire fell apart from Viking invasions and regional revolts.

In 987 a fresh beginning was made with the election to the throne of Hugh Capet, duke of Francia. The Capetians, as the new ruling group was known, allied themselves with the church and the growing urban classes to extend their rule slowly over all of France.

For more than 300 years the Capetians wore down the feudal forces in France. They disciplined the bishops, created the beginnings of a central administrative system, crusaded against infidels and heretics, and warded off the English. Their line ended in 1328.

In the Hundred Years War (1337–1453) with England, France was devastated. At the Battle of Orléans on May 7, 1429, Joan of Arc inspired the French army to rout the English, leading to ultimate French victory.

KINGDOM OF FRANCE

In the late 1550s the Reformation swept through France, pitting Catholic against Protestant. Civil war followed.

A strong central government with a high degree of religious tolerance was now considered necessary to save the nation. A Protestant, the Bourbon Prince Henri of Navarre, took the throne. Embracing Catholicism himself and granting religious freedom to the Protestants (Huguenots) in the Edict of Nantes (1598), he became the most popular king France ever had. Although the wealthy urban classes enjoyed power, France was still a feudal monarchy.

The assassination of Henri in 1610 left the royal government open to challenges from both nobles and bourgeoisie. In this struggle Henri's successors were supported by two great statesmen, Cardinals Richelieu and Mazarin, who were enemies of the nobles, of Protestantism, and of urban democratic tendencies. Guiding France through the perils of the Thirty Years War (1618–48), the cardinals put down internal revolt (the Fronde of 1648–53), continued the colonial expansion begun in the previous century, and helped project the Bourbon house in the person of Louis XIV (1643–1715) to the peak of France's power.

Louis XIV and his lieutenants held the nobility in check, helped industry expand, and systematically eliminated old provincial, municipal, and religious liberties. Royal control was absolute.

Warlike and authoritarian, Louis made France the greatest of Europe's powers, but he also brought the country to economic ruin.

The reign of Louis XV was marked by opposition at home, the loss of empire abroad (Canada fell to England in 1763), and a dazzling display of art and literature. This was the great age of the Enlightenment, and France was the intellectual capital of Europe.

FRENCH REVOLUTION

The French state, however, was insolvent, and the farmers suffered from landlords seeking higher revenues in an expanding economy. The monarchy was finally bankrupted, in part through involvement in the American Revolution.

The bourgeois creditors of the state refused to advance more credit unless they got social and political concessions from the crown.

The aristocracy was determined to reverse the trend toward absolute monarchy and to regain its former authority.

The common people of rural France waited for some royal action that would ease their lot.

Nobles and bourgeois joined forces to compel Louis XVI to summon the States-General, which had not met since 1614. Then the struggle for power became more complex.

The middle-class representatives of the common people challenged the aristocracy in 1789. They rallied the king temporarily to their side. Within months, following riots against crown and nobility, they seized control of the state.

The revolutionary government overturned the social and political structure of France, launched the egalitarian creed throughout Europe, and reduced the church to a department of state. Finally the revolutionaries executed the king, who had turned against them and had hoped to be rescued by other European monarchs.

The strains of war and resultant unrest at home precipitated a bloody reign of terror that set the stage for the rise of Napoleon.

NAPOLEONIC ERA

By 1799, after a decade of domestic turmoil, the epochal French Revolution ended in military dictatorship. Young, brilliant, ambitious Gen. Napoleon Bonaparte seized total power.

Napoleon crowned himself emperor of the French in 1804. At home he squashed political conflict and restricted the powers of the church.

France reached its height of power as Napoleon won victory after victory until he controlled most of Europe.

After Napoleon's disastrous defeat in Russia in 1812, his conquests were stripped away by the victory of an allied coalition in 1814.

Napoleon returned from exile in 1815 to rally France again, but was routed at Waterloo.

The former emperor was imprisoned on St. Helena, where he died in 1821.

RESTORATION OF MONARCHY

The unpopular Bourbons were restored under Louis XVIII in 1814 by allied arms, but the old order never returned.

In 1830 Charles X was driven out by the revolt of the middle and lower classes in the cities.

His successor, Louis Philippe, was ousted in the 1848 revolution.

SECOND REPUBLIC AND NAPOLEON III

The Second Republic, founded in 1848, was undermined by clashes between the new French factions. The republic then was eliminated by its elected president, Louis Napoleon Bonaparte.

Like his uncle, France's new ruler established a dictatorship to end political quarrels and to preserve the social order. Proclaimed Emperor

QUICK QUIZ: When was Alaska purchased from Russia? See page 304.

FRANCE (continued)

Napoleon III in 1852, he presided until 1870.

The regime enriched the industrial and commercial classes but won no loyalty from them.

Napoleon III expanded the empire in Southeast Asia but was unsuccessful in Mexico. He helped bring about the unification of Italy but was defeated in a war with Germany (Prussia).

THIRD REPUBLIC AND WORLD WARS I AND II

Out of defeat by Germany (1870–71) another republic was born. It accepted severe peace terms, mastered the revolt of the Paris commune, and by 1875 had all but banished the ghost of monarchy.

The Third Republic had a conservative parliamentary government. It expanded the school system and extended its empire in Africa and Asia. It made an ally of Russia in 1894 and of Britain in 1904.

Like much of armed and divided Europe, France took up arms in 1914 hoping to win security. It also hoped to recover Alsace-Lorraine, surrendered to Germany in 1871.

France emerged victorious but exhausted from World War I.

France reacted to Hitler's invasion of Poland by declaring war on Germany in 1939. It suffered swift and total defeat in 1940. World War I hero Marshal Henri Philippe Pétain established a government in southern France at Vichy that collaborated with the Nazis.

A Free French movement led by Gen. Charles de Gaulle from abroad condemned the government at Vichy, won over the loyalty of much of the empire, and fought on the side of the Allies. After liberation, France was ruled by de Gaulle until he resigned in 1946.

FOURTH REPUBLIC

For 12 years the unstable Fourth Republic struggled to modernize the economy and cope with nationalist movements in the crumbling empire, while French prestige sank in the world.

The regime collapsed in 1958 when faced with a French army rebellion in Algeria.

To avoid civil war, Paris called de Gaulle from retirement. The nation gave him a mandate to rule and to prepare a new constitution.

FIFTH REPUBLIC

General de Gaulle in September 1958 established a Fifth Republic with himself as a strong president. He governed by decree when necessary.

Driving forcefully toward the leadership of western Europe, de Gaulle granted independence to Algeria. He prevented Britain from joining the European Common Market. And in 1968 he withdrew French military forces from NATO as a protest against U.S. foreign policy.

The regime concentrated on foreign affairs and building atomic weapons while social and economic problems continued to await solution.

In May 1968 a student revolt and a nationwide general strike brought the republic close to anarchy. De Gaulle, however, appealed for law and order, promising reforms. His government received an overwhelming endorsement in general elections on June 23, 1968.

In April 1969, however, de Gaulle resigned after a proposed constitutional reform was defeated in a nationwide referendum.

Georges Pompidou was elected president in 1969 to succeed de Gaulle. Pompidou reversed de Gaulle's policy of opposing Britain's entry into the European Common Market. On July 5, 1972, he named Pierre Messmer, as prime minister.

The French government caused a storm of world criticism by test-exploding atomic weapons at Mururoa Atoll in the South Pacific Ocean in the summers of 1973 and 1974. The International Court of Justice, acting on complaints by Australia and New Zealand, ordered France to cancel the tests. The French government, however, proceeded with the explosions.

The death of President Pompidou on April 2, 1974, brought new national elections.

FRANCE UNDER GISCARD d'ESTAING

Valéry Giscard d'Estaing, a conservative who had served as minister of finance, won the presidency in the runoff election on May 19, 1974.

President Giscard d'Estaing appointed Jacques Chirac, Pompidou's former minister of the interior, as premier on May 27, 1974.

Giscard d'Estaing quickly established himself as more liberal than his Gaullist predecessors. He added a woman to the cabinet, lowered to 18 the age for voting and attaining full legal rights of an adult, and increased the minimum wage for workers. Unemployed workers were guaranteed a year's pay.

Raymond Barre, an economist, became prime minister on Aug. 25, 1976, after Chirac resigned.

President Giscard D'Estaing's center-right coalition won a resounding victory in the national assembly elections on March 19, 1978.

France was particularly hard hit by soaring fuel prices in the 1970s. To help reduce dependency on imported fuel, the government ordered a speed-up in the construction and planning of nuclear power plants.

The government announced on June 26, 1980, the successful test of a neutron bomb, a type of atomic bomb designed to kill enemy soldiers while limiting damage to surrounding structures.

FRANCE TURNS TO SOCIALISM

In the first round of a presidential election held on April 26, 1981, President Giscard d'Estaing won a plurality of 28% of the vote against the nine other candidates. But a close second was socialist candidate François Mitterrand with 26%.

Mitterrand's victory in the May 10, 1981, run-off election with 55% of the vote caused panic selling of stocks by investors in the French financial markets. After his inauguration on May 21, 1981, he appointed Pierre Mauroy as prime minister. In elections in June 1981, the socialists won a majority in parliament. The first leftist cabinet for France since 1958 included four communists.

The first major legislation adopted by the socialist parliament on July 15, 1981, was a plan to decentralize the nation's government by restoring power to elected local governments, eliminating the veto powers of appointed regional and departmental prefects.

The death penalty was abolished by parliament in September 1981, bringing to an end the work of the guillotine.

Faced with unemployment that had risen to more than 2 million (10% of the work force), the government, on Feb. 1, 1982, reduced the work-week to 39 hours from 40 and increased vacation time to 5 weeks. The socialists promised to cut the workweek to 35 hours by 1985.

Beginning on Feb. 13, 1982, the socialist government began nationalizing about 30% of the nation's industry, including 39 banks, 5 industrial groups, 2 steel companies, 2 financial holding concerns, and companies in the armaments and aerospace industries. The government paid some $8 billion in bonds to stockholders of the companies.

France suffered a huge trade deficit in 1982, causing the value of the French franc to fall to a low of $0.14—compared with $0.24 in 1980. To preserve the franc's value, the government obtained a $4 billion loan from an international group of banks on Oct. 27, 1982.

With inflation running at a rate of about 14%, the government on June 12, 1982, froze wages and prices, a move opposed by labor unions. Faced with a wave of strikes, the freeze was lifted on Nov. 1. However, severe restrictions were placed on wage and price increases.

By mid-1983 public-opinion polls showed that more than half the people were dissatisfied with Mitterrand's government. Unemployment stood at about 9% of the work force and inflation continued at a high rate. Industries nationalized by the socialists had lost $2.5 billion in two years.

President Mitterrand on July 17, 1984, appointed a new prime minister, Laurent Fabius, 37, who had been minister of industry. Communists refused to accept any seats in the new cabinet. Fabius promised tax cuts and reduced government spending.

CORSICA

Area: 3,367 square miles (8,722 sq. km.).
Population: 204,232.
Cities: Ajaccio, capital, 40,834; Bastia, 49,375.
Called *Corse* in French, the mountainous Mediterranean island of Corsica is nearly three times as large as the state of Rhode Island. It lies about 100 miles southeast of France.

Corsica is separated from the Italian island of Sardinia by an 8-mile-wide strait. It is best known as the birthplace of Napoleon I.

Most of the people make their living farming and raising livestock. Great herds of sheep graze on the mountain slopes, providing the island's two most profitable products, wool and cheese.

Prehistoric people lived on the island at least as early as 2000 B.C., leaving large stone monuments.

Greeks from Phocaea, in what is now Turkey, established a colony on Corsica about 560 B.C. These invaders were followed by Carthaginians, Romans, Vandals, and Arabs. The Italian cities of Pisa and Genoa drove out the Arabs in the 1000s A.D. and then fought each other for control of the island for several centuries.

France invaded and conquered Corsica in 1768, and the following year Napoleon was born there. British forces landed on the island in the 1790s and during the Napoleonic wars. But Corsica was restored to France in 1815.

France granted Corsica limited autonomy in

THE FRENCH COMMUNITY

Independent nations that once were part of the French colonial empire and present dependencies of France are bound together by economic and military agreements, although not by a formal international organization.

INDEPENDENT MEMBERS

Central Africa	Djibouti	Gabon
Chad	France	Senegal

OVERSEAS DEPARTMENTS OF FRANCE

French Guiana	Martinique	Réunion	St. Pierre and
Guadeloupe	Mahore		Miquelon

OVERSEAS TERRITORIES OF FRANCE

French Polynesia	New Caledonia
French Southern and	Wallis and Futuna
Antarctic Territories	Islands

ASSOCIATES BY SPECIAL AGREEMENTS

Algeria	Ivory Coast	Niger
Benin	Mali	Togo
Cameroon	Mauritania	Upper Volta

1982. In the first election for a 61-member regional assembly on Aug. 8, 1982, no party won a majority. A moderate leftist, Prosper Alfonsi, was elected first president of the assembly.

Nationalists seeking complete independence continued terrorist bombing attacks in 1982–85.

FRANCE'S DEPENDENCIES

FRENCH GUIANA (GUYANE)

Area: 35,135 square miles (91,000 sq. km.).
Population: 81,000.
Capital: Cayenne, 33,288.
Located on the northern coast of South America, French Guiana is bordered on the north by the Atlantic Ocean, on the east and south by Brazil, and on the west by Suriname.

Most French Guianese are blacks. About 7 in 10 are literate in the French language.

Guiana's farmers raise cattle, bananas, pineapples, sugarcane, fruits, and vegetables. Gold is mined, but large deposits of bauxite have not been developed.

France began to colonize Guiana in 1635 but did not establish firm control until 1677. For nearly a century (1852–1947) French convicts were sent to Guiana's penal colony, Devil's Island. The territory's borders were settled in 1854. It became an overseas department of France in 1946 with representation in France's parliament.

In the 1960s France built its main space-research center at the former prison camp at Kourou. In 1975 the French government began investing $160 million to develop paper manufacturing to utilize the area's forests.

FRENCH POLYNESIA

Area: 1,544 square miles (4,000 sq. km.).
Population: 161,000.
Capital: Papeete, Tahiti, 25,342.
The nearly 130 islands of French Polynesia are scattered over a vast area of the South Pacific.

For administrative purposes, the islands have been divided into five groups: the *Windward Islands,* including Tahiti and Moorea; the *Lee-*

QUICK QUIZ: Which President campaigned with the slogan "He kept us out of war"? See page 368.

FRENCH DEPENDENCIES (continued)

ward Islands, including Raiatea and Bora-Bora (the Windward and Leeward islands make up the Society Islands); the Tuamotu and Gambier Islands; the Austral Islands; and the Marquesas Islands.

Most of the people are French-speaking Christian Polynesians.

Exports include copra, vanilla, coffee, and phosphates.

Tourism is an important revenue source.

The Society Islands were discovered and claimed for England in 1767, but French claims were established a year later. In 1842 France declared a protectorate, and in 1880 the islands became a French colony.

The Tuamotu Islands were discovered by Spain in 1606. They became a French protectorate in 1844 and were annexed in 1881.

The Gambier Islands, discovered by the British in 1797, were annexed by France in 1881.

The Austral Islands came under French control in 1880.

The southern Marquesas were discovered by Spain in 1595, and the northern Marquesas were sighted by an American in 1791. In 1842 French sovereignty over the Marquesas was recognized by local chieftains.

The islands of French Polynesia were grouped into a single colony in 1903. They became an overseas territory of France in 1946.

France's nuclear-testing center, on Mururoa (720 miles southeast of Tahiti), began operating in 1966, when France exploded its first atomic bomb. In 1968 France's first hydrogen bomb was detonated near Mururoa.

GUADELOUPE AND DEPENDENCIES

Area: 687 square miles (1,779 sq. km.).
Population: 335,000.
Capital: Basse-Terre, 20,000.
Largest City: Point-à-Pitre, 70,000.

Guadeloupe is located in the Leeward Islands of the Lesser Antilles in the eastern Caribbean Sea. It consists of two islands, Basse-Terre and Grande-Terre, separated by a narrow channel, the Rivière Salée. Volcanic Basse-Terre lies to the west, while the flat island of Grande-Terre is to the east.

Most of the French-speaking inhabitants of Guadeloupe are of black or mixed descent.

The economy is based on tourism and farming. The main crops are sugarcane, bananas, and pineapples.

Guadeloupe's dependencies include the islands of Marie Galante, Les Saintes, Désirade, and St. Barthélemy. About two-thirds of the island of St. Martin, located about 110 miles northeast of Guadeloupe, is administered by Guadeloupe. The other third is the Dutch St. Maarten.

Columbus discovered Guadeloupe in 1493, and France founded the first permanent colony in 1635. Except for British occupation in the 1700s and during the Napoleonic wars, Guadeloupe remained French. It became an overseas department of France in 1946.

The people enjoy the same social-welfare benefits as the people of France, including family allowances and medical aid.

Guadeloupe has become a popular winter resort for Americans and Canadians. Its climate is warm the year round with mean temperatures of 74°F. in January and 87°F. in August.

More than 72,000 persons evacuated the southern half of the island of Basse-Terre before the 4,813-foot La Soufrière volcano exploded on Aug. 30, 1976, throwing out lava and rocks.

Separatist terrorists seeking independence carried out a series of bombings in 1981-85.

MAHORE

Area: 144 square miles (375 sq. km.).
Population: 56,000.
Capital: Dzaoudzi.

The island of Mahore (formerly Mayotte) lies in the Mozambique Channel off the coast of Africa about midway between Madagascar and Mozambique. It is the southernmost of the Comoro Islands and the only one whose people chose to remain a French dependency when the Comoros declared their independence.

The majority of the people earn their living by farming or fishing. Their most important export products are essential oils, used in perfume making, and spices. The economy depends on subsidies from France to import food and necessities.

France obtained the right from the local chiefs to use Mahore as a military base in 1840-41. Mahore was made a French colony in 1843. French settlers began cultivating sugarcane plantations on the island. By 1912 France had taken over all the Comoros as a colony administered from Madagascar. The islands became an overseas territory of France in 1958 and were granted internal self-government in 1960.

When the other Comoros declared their independence in July 1975, the people of Mahore refused to go along and repelled an attempted invasion by the new Comoros government. On Feb. 8, 1976, Mahore voted 99% in favor of remaining a French dependency. In a vote on April 11, 1976, the islanders chose by an 80% majority to become an overseas department of France.

MARTINIQUE

Area: 425 square miles (1,100 sq. km.).
Population: 330,000.
Capital: Fort-de-France, 97,814.

Martinique is situated in the Windward Islands of the Lesser Antilles in the eastern Caribbean Sea. The island's terrain is mountainous, and the highest peak is volcanic Mt. Pelée (4,583 feet).

The people are French-speaking and mostly of black or mixed descent. Sugar, pineapples, bananas, and rum are the main products.

Famed for the beauty of its forested mountains and sandy beaches, Martinique has been called the *Pearl of the Antilles*. The island has a thriving tourist industry, as many visitors come to enjoy the warm climate that averages from 76° to 81°F. the year round.

Columbus discovered Martinique in 1502. France settled the island in 1635. Britain occupied the island in 1762-63 and 1794-1815.

An eruption of Mt. Pelée on May 8, 1902, destroyed the city of St. Pierre, killing about 40,000 persons.

Martinique became an overseas department of France in 1946. It is represented in the French parliament by two senators and three deputies.

NEW CALEDONIA

Area: 7,374 square miles (19,103 sq. km.).
Population: 149,000.
Capital: Nouméa, 56,078.

New Caledonia is a territory of France that includes several island groups in the South Pacific. The island of New Caledonia itself has an area of 6,530 square miles.

Main dependencies of New Caledonia include: the *Loyalty Islands* (area 756 sq. mi.), a chain of islands that lie about 78 miles to the east; the *Chesterfield Islands,* uninhabited coral islets about 400 miles to the northwest; the *Isle of Pines,* about 30 miles to the southeast.

Located about 750 miles east of Australia, the island is mountainous and covered with lush vegetation. Nearly half the people are Melanesian. About 40% are European, mostly French.

Mining is the most important industry. New Caledonia has large reserves of nickel, iron, manganese, and chrome.

The French explorer Louis Antoine de Bougainville sailed near New Caledonia in 1768. Capt. James Cook gave the island its name, landing there on Sept. 4, 1774. The island was annexed by France in 1853 and was used as a penal colony from 1864 to 1894. Following occupation by U.S. forces in World War II, the island became an overseas territory of France in 1946.

A French-appointed governor is assisted by a council of government chosen by the popularly elected territorial assembly.

The government declared a state of emergency and flew in 1,000 additional troops in 1985 after violence escalated into riots and gun battles between Melanesians seeking independence and French settlers who prefer French territorial status.

RÉUNION

Area: 970 square miles (2,512 sq. km.).
Population: 550,000.
Capital: Saint-Denis, 115,687.

Réunion is located in the Indian Ocean about 450 miles east of the island of Madagascar. The island has one active and nine inactive volcanoes. The people are descendants of French settlers, blacks, Malays, Indochinese, and Malabar Indians.

The island has a prosperous economy based largely on growing sugarcane. All children attend school, and most people read and write French. About 25% of the people are of French descent. Portuguese explorers visited Réunion in the 1500s. The island was claimed for France in 1638 and settled in 1665. Until 1793 Réunion was called Bourbon Island. In 1946 it became an overseas department of France.

SAINT PIERRE AND MIQUELON

Area: 93 square miles (242 sq. km.).
Population: 6,100.
Capital: St. John's, 5,416.

Saint Pierre and Miquelon lie in the Atlantic Ocean about 15 miles southwest of Newfoundland. There are two main islands—Saint Pierre (10 sq. mi.) and Miquelon (83 sq. mi.). The southern part of Miquelon sometimes is considered to be a separate island called Lauglade.

Most of the people are descendants of early Basque and French settlers and are Roman Catholics. Fishing is the main industry. The soil is so rocky and the climate so cold that no food crops can be grown.

The Portuguese explorer Faguendez visited Saint Pierre and Miquelon in 1520. The islands were claimed for France in 1535 by Jacques Cartier. The first French settlement was founded in 1604. The islands were ceded to Britain in 1713, restored to France in 1763, retaken by Britain from 1778 to 1783 and during the Napoleonic wars, and finally returned to the French in 1816. In 1935 the islands were granted local autonomy. They were made a department of France in 1976.

SOUTHERN AND ANTARCTIC TERRITORIES

Area: 1,138,616 square miles (439,622 sq. km.).
Population: 180.
Capital: Port aux Français, Kerguélen.

The French Southern and Antarctic Territories consists of two archipelagos, two islands, and an area on the Antarctic continent.

Kerguélen Archipelago, a large subantarctic island and 300 smaller islands in the South Indian Ocean, was discovered by Yves Joseph de Kerguélen-Trémarec in 1772. Research stations, a hospital, and a military camp are located there.

Crozet Archipelago, 5 large and 15 small islands in the South Indian Ocean about 800 miles west of Kerguélen, was also discovered in 1772. A meteorological station was built there in 1964.

Saint Paul is a tiny, uninhabited island in the Indian Ocean northeast of Kerguélen.

New Amsterdam Island, located about 50 miles north of Saint Paul, has research stations and a hospital.

Terre Adélie, situated on the Antarctic continent, was discovered on Jan. 19, 1840, by Dumont d'Urville. Nearby Commonwealth Bay is said to be the windiest place in the world, with wind speeds reaching 200 mph.

WALLIS AND FUTUNA

Area: 106 square miles (274 sq. km.).
Population: 12,100.
Capital: Mata Utu, Uvéa, 6,000.

Wallis and Futuna are two small groups of Pacific islands located about 250 miles west of Samoa. The Wallis Islands consist of Uvéa and about 20 smaller islands. The islands of Futuna and Alofi make up the Hoorn (or Horne) Islands, located about 125 miles west of the Wallis Islands. Most of the population is Polynesian, and the main economic activities are copra production and fishing.

Dutch navigators discovered the Hoorn Islands in 1617. The Wallis Islands were sighted in 1767 by the English explorer Samuel Wallis. France established a protectorate over the islands in 1887–88.

In 1961 Wallis and Futuna became an overseas territory of France. The islands are governed by a French administrator with the assistance of a territorial council consisting of the kings of each of the three main islands and three appointed members.

QUICK QUIZ: Which U.S. President was assassinated in 1881? See page 305.

GABON

Official Name: Gabonese Republic.
Area: 103,347 square miles (267,667 sq. km.).
Population: 1,256,000.
Capital: Libreville, 57,000.
Government: One-party state.
President: Omar Bongo (since 1967).
Premier: Léon Mebiame (since 1975).
National Assembly: 47 members.
U.S. Ambassador to Gabon: Larry C. Williamson.
Ambassador to U.S.: Abdoulaye Mocktar-Mbingt.
Flag: Stripes of green (top), yellow (middle), and blue
(bottom).
Official Language: French.
Chief Ethnic Groups: Fang (32%), Eshira (19%),
Adouma (12%), Okande (5%).
Religions: Christianity (46%), animism, Islam.
Leading Industries: Mining (petroleum, manganese,
uranium, iron ore, lead, zinc, copper, diamonds);
forestry and lumbering; agriculture (cocoa, coffee,
vegetables, fruits); construction; fishing.
Foreign Trade: *Major exports*—petroleum, wood, man-
ganese, uranium; *major imports*—petroleum prod-
ucts, iron and steel, trucks, agricultural machinery,
clothing.
Places of Interest: Dense hardwood forests; Crystal
Mountains; Mt. Iboundji; Libreville; Lambaréné, site
of Dr. Albert Schweitzer's hospital; national parks.

GABON TODAY

Gabon, about the size of Colorado, is a prosper-
ous oil-exporting country of West Africa.

Rich in natural resources, Gabon is one of the
world's leading producers of uranium, with
about 1,000 tons exported to France each year.

Gabon also has large deposits of petroleum,
manganese, and iron ore. Oil accounts for about
three-fourths of its export income. Its forests
support a thriving lumber industry, and its riv-
ers provide substantial hydroelectric potential.

The government has offered encouragement to
foreign investors to develop the natural re-
sources, and has worked hard to improve port
and transportation facilities.

Its people have a higher per capita income
than any other African nation. The nation's
prosperity nearly eliminated unemployment. But
most of the people do not have enough educa-
tion to handle high-paying jobs in industry. Only
about 1 person in 5 can read and write.

Disease and malnutrition give the Gabonese
one of the lowest life expectancies in the world,
with the average man dying by the age of 25.

An equatorial country in western Africa, Gabon
has a hot and humid climate. Much of the land is
covered by dense tropical rain forests. The coun-
try's major waterway is the Ougooé River.

During the rainy season, from February to June,
more than 100 inches of rain fall in Libreville. The
heavy rains make jungle roads impassable, so the
country relies on aircraft for interior travel.

The coastal lowlands extend 20 to 125 miles

into the interior and adjoin a 60-mile-wide belt
of rocky cliffs.

Equatorial Guinea and Cameroon lie to the
north, and Congo to the east and south.

EARLY HISTORY

Portuguese exploration began about 1470, fol-
lowed by the British, Dutch, Spanish, and French
during the centuries of slave trading.

In 1839 French explorer Edouard Bouet-Wil-
laumez signed a treaty of peace with "King"
Denis of Gabon. Denis, a notorious African
slave trader, turned over part of northern Gabon
to France in return for protection.

The capital, Libreville (place of liberation),
was founded in 1849 when the French captured
a slave ship and released its captives at the
mouth of the Como River. Control by France
gradually expanded, and the colony of Gabon was
established in 1885. Gabon became one of the four
territories of French Equatorial Africa in 1910.

Dr. Albert Schweitzer established the first
hospital in the region in 1913 at Lambaréné.

Gabon was granted internal self-government
in 1957. Leon M'ba became chief minister.

INDEPENDENCE

Gabon was proclaimed fully independent on Aug.
17, 1960. Leon M'ba was elected president.

M'ba was reelected in March 1967, but died
in office that November. Vice President Albert-
Bernard Bongo became president.

Bongo declared Gabon a one-party state in
March 1968, dissolving the powerful Gabonese
Democratic bloc and creating a new party, the
Gabonese Democratic Party (PDG). He was re-
elected president in 1973 without opposition.

Gabon became a full member of the Organiza-
tion of Petroleum Exporting Countries (OPEC)
in 1975. Symbolizing his nation's closer relations
with the Arab oil producers, President Bongo
changed his French given name of Albert-Ber-
nard to the Arabic name *Omar*.

Work began in 1975 on the 600-mile Trans-
Gabon Railway from Libreville to the interior
cities of Mékambo and Franceville. The first
115-mile section of the railroad opened to regu-
lar traffic in 1979.

Bongo expelled 10,000 Benin workers from
Gabon by airlift in July 1978. The action came
after Benin's ruler Mathieu Kerekou accused
Gabon of attempting to overthrow him.

As host to a 1977 conference of the Organiza-
tion of African Unity (OAU), Gabon borrowed
more than $2 billion to prepare for the meeting.
As a result, the government had to use nearly
half its revenues in 1979–80 in paying off inter-
est and part of the debt.

However, new oil finds in 1979 indicated pe-
troleum production could be increased in the
1980s with consequent growth in the economy.

Gabon's 1984-88 development plan calls for
spending $200 to $280 million per year on ex-
pansion of the Trans-Gabon Railway. Extending
the line to interior cities will enable expansion of
uranium and iron mining. The development plan
also provides for construction of a new $100
million minerals shipping port at Owendo near
Libreville to handle 3 to 4 million tons of man-
ganese ore annually.

GAMBIA

Official Name: Republic of The Gambia.
Area: 4,361 square miles (11,295 sq. km.).
Population: 738,300.
Capital: Banjul, 49,181.
Government: Presidential-parliamentary democracy.
President: Sir Dawda Kairaba Jawara (since 1970).
House of Representatives: 37 members.
U.S. Ambassador to Gambia: Robert T. Hennemeyer.
Ambassador to U.S.: Lamin Abdou Mbye.
Flag: Red, blue, and green stripes from top to bottom, separated by narrow white stripes.
Official Language: English.
Chief Ethnic Groups: Mandingo (40%), Fula (13%), Wolof (12%), Serahuli (7%), Jola (7%).
Leading Religions: Islam (85%), animism, Christianity.
Leading Industries: Agriculture (peanuts, cattle, rice, palm kernels, bees, vegetables, fruits); fishing; tourism; food processing; handicrafts.
Foreign Trade: *Major exports*—peanuts, palm kernels, hides, fish, beeswax; *major imports*—textiles, food, machinery, hardware, consumer goods.
Places of Interest: Flora and fauna along the Gambia River; Banjul; beaches.

GAMBIA TODAY

Africa's smallest independent country, Gambia is a shining example of two-party democracy amid the many dictatorships of the continent.

With a smaller area than the state of Connecticut, Gambia averages only about 20 miles in width but is about 200 miles long from east to west. It is surrounded by Senegal, except for an Atlantic shoreline of about 50 miles.

Unlike most of the small nations of Africa that quickly eradicated signs of colonialism upon attaining independence, Gambia remains proud of its British colonial heritage. Many Britons continue to work in the government offices. And the capital, Banjul, retains the appearance of a British city of the Victorian age.

The Gambia River, which extends the length of the country, provides excellent transportation. However, Gambia has few natural resources.

Most Gambians are poor tribesmen. Some are nomads who raise cattle. Many are farmers who raise just enough food to feed their families. Only about 12 persons in 100 can read and write, and only about 20,000 children go to school.

Peanuts, the only sizable cash crop, provide 95% of Gambia's exports.

The government uses much of its limited resources to promote tourism. About 50,000 visitors each year, mostly from Europe.

The village of Juffure attracts an unusual number of foreign visitors as the ancestral home of Kunta Kinte of the book *Roots* written by American author Alex Haley. President Jawara declared Juffure a national monument. The village has changed little since Kunta Kinte was stolen by slave traders in 1767.

Because Gambia has relatively low import duties and low prices compared with Senegal, a substantial amount of smuggling takes place between the two countries.

The country is generally low-lying and flat, with elevations ranging from sea level to 120 feet. Temperatures vary from a low of 60° F. in winter to a high of 110° F. in summer. The country averages 11 hours of sunshine every day from November to May. Rainfall averages 30 to 55 inches a year, largely in June to September.

EARLY HISTORY

The Gambia River was discovered in 1456 by Portuguese explorers. It was then part of the kingdom of Mali. Portugal controlled the region until the late 1500s.

Britain and France fought for the territory and the moderately profitable slave trade until the 1800s.

After 1815 France controlled Saint-Louis and Gorée islands.

The British established the first permanent settlement at Bathurst (now Banjul) in 1816. Gambia was administered through a governor-general in Sierra Leone in 1821–43 and 1866–88. It was a separate colony between 1843 and 1866 and returned to crown-colony status in 1888. The country's present boundaries were established by agreement with France in 1889.

Sir Dawda K. Jawara was elected prime minister in 1962. Under his leadership Gambia was granted full internal self-government in 1963.

INDEPENDENCE

Gambia received independence from Britain on Feb. 18, 1965.

The nation became a republic within the British Commonwealth of Nations with a new constitution promulgated on April 24, 1970. It took the official name *Republic of the Gambia*. Jawara became the nation's first president.

One of the few African countries with a multiparty political system, Gambia held its first national elections in March 1972. Jawara was elected to a 5-year term as president. His People's Progressive Party (PPP) won 28 seats in the house of representatives, and the opposition United Party won 3 seats. Four representatives are appointed by the tribal chiefs.

While President Jawara was attending the wedding of Britain's Prince Charles in London, a communist-led rebellion attempted to overthrow the government on July 30, 1981.

At Jawara's request, Senegal sent troops that defeated the rebels and freed 135 hostages, including the president's senior wife. About 500 persons were killed in a week of fighting.

Gambia joined with Senegal in a confederation called *Senegambia* that became effective on Feb. 1, 1982.

Each nation retained its sovereignty but agreed to develop joint policies for defense, foreign affairs, finance, and customs.

The 58-year-old Jawara was reelected to his third five-year term as president on May 5, 1982.

QUICK QUIZ: Which U.S. President was a former governor of the Philippines? See page 366.

GERMANY, EAST

Official Name: German Democratic Republic.
Area: 41,768 square miles (108,178 sq. km.).
Population: 16,720,000.
Chief Cities: East Berlin, capital, 1,157,557; Leipzig, 561,867; Dresden, 516,604; Karl-Marx-Stadt, 317,696; Magdeburg, 289,292; Halle, 232,396.
Government: One-party communist state.
Heads of Government: First Secretary of Communist Party, Erich Honecker (since 1971); Premier, Willi Stoph (appointed in 1973).
Legislature: *Volkskammer,* 500 members.
U.S. Ambassador to East Germany: Herbert Stuart Okun.
East German Ambassador to U.S.: Gerhard Herder.
Flag: Black, red, and gold stripes, with centered coat of arms.
Official Language: German.
Principal Ethnic Group: German (99.8%).
Main Religions: Protestantism (59%), Roman Catholicism (8%).
Leading Industries: Manufacturing (steel, chemicals, textiles, cement, machinery, electronic computers, consumer products); agriculture (dairy products, cattle, poultry, potatoes, sugar beets, wheat, rye, barley, oats); construction; mining (lignite, potash, coal, iron ore, copper, uranium, cobalt).
Foreign Trade: *Major exports*—machinery, coal briquettes, chemicals; *major imports*—coal, crude petroleum, coke, machinery, wheat, iron ore.
Places of Interest: East Berlin's Brandenburg Gate; Dresden's Frauenkirche; Jena's Goethe monument; Leipzig. *In Potsdam:* state buildings; Karl-Marx-Stadt.

EAST GERMANY TODAY

The communist leaders of East Germany look enviously at the booming industrial production of neighboring West Germany, while the people look equally enviously at the freedom and higher standard of living across the border. Although forbidden to watch TV broadcasts from West Germany, most East Germans do so in the privacy of their homes.

A repressive communist police state, East Germany guards its borders with barbed wire and machine guns to prevent its people from escaping to the West. Even so several thousand each year do escape, although dozens are killed by guards and land mines. Thousands of people who unsuccessfully try to escape are imprisoned.

From year to year, the government allows varying numbers of East Germans to leave each year for ransom payments by the West German government.

The government owns and controls all industrial and agricultural facilities. It emphasizes heavy industry at the expense of consumer goods.

GEOGRAPHY AND CLIMATE

The sandy Baltic coast in the north has hills and lakes. The central region has fertile plains as well as the Harz Mountains. The Thuringian Forest range dominates the southern region. In the southeast the Erzgebirge range forms a natural frontier with Czechoslovakia. The principal rivers are the Elbe, Saale, Havel, and Spree.

Winter temperatures average at freezing or below, while summer temperatures rise to an average of about 64 ° F.

West Germany lies to the west and south, Poland and Czechoslovakia are to the east, and the Baltic Sea is to the north.

COMMUNIST STATE

East Germany and East Berlin came under Soviet occupation at the end of World War II. For the earlier history of Germany see article *Germany, West,* on the following pages.

The Soviet Union turned its occupied zone into the *German Democratic Republic (GDR)* on Oct. 7, 1949. This followed the creation of the Federal Republic of Germany (West Germany) three weeks earlier by the Allies.

As head of the Communist Party, Walter Ulbricht dominated the GDR from its formation.

The Western powers refused to recognize the new government of East Germany, but all Soviet-bloc countries extended recognition immediately.

Soviet troops effectively crushed an anticommunist revolt in East Germany in June 1953.

Between 1949 and 1961 some 3.5 million East Germans escaped to West Germany.

In August 1961 the East German government constructed a wall of barbed wire and concrete around the western sector of Berlin to stop the flow of East Germans into West Berlin.

DEVELOPMENTS IN 1970s–1980s

Erich Honecker succeeded Ulbricht as communist ruler in 1971.

After long negotiations, East and West Germany began to relax relations in 1972. A treaty establishing diplomatic relations between the two states was signed on Dec. 21, 1972. Ratification by the parliaments of both states was completed in six months, and the pact went into effect on June 21, 1973.

The new understanding opened the door to UN membership for both Germanys in September 1973, and brought about diplomatic recognition by the U.S. and other Western nations.

Amnesty International reported in October 1977 that from 100,000 to 200,000 East Germans had asked permission to emigrate but had been refused. The report said thousands of them had been jailed as political prisoners.

New restrictive laws went into effect Aug. 1, 1979, providing long jail terms for anyone taking part in an antigovernment demonstration or for passing on any information damaging to the government to "foreign organizations." Security was further tightened in 1981–82.

The government marked the 20th anniversary of the building of the Berlin Wall with a huge military parade on Aug. 13, 1981, at which Honecker declared it had "saved peace in Europe." An estimated 185,000 East Germans escaped over the wall in those two decades.

The government allowed 40,000 persons to move to West Germany in 1984—the largest number of legal immigrants permitted since construction of the Berlin Wall.

NATIONS OF THE WORLD

GERMANY, WEST

Official Name: Federal Republic of Germany.
Area: 95,976 square miles (248,577 sq. km.).
Population: 61,385,000.
Chief Cities: Bonn, capital, 291,464; West Berlin, 1,888,669; Hamburg, 1,637,132; Munich, 1,291,828; Cologne (Köln), 971,403; Essen, 643,640; Frankfurt am Main, 625,352; Dortmund, 605,418; Düsseldorf, 588,808; Stuttgart, 583,001.
Government: Parliamentary democracy.
Chancellor: Helmut Kohl (since 1982).
President: Richard von Weizsaecker (since 1984).
Legislature: *Bundesrat,* 41 members; *Bundestag,* 498 members.
U.S. Ambassador to W. Germany: Richard R. Burt.
West German Ambassador to U.S.: Gunther van Well.
Flag: Black, red, and gold stripes.
Language: German.
Principal Ethnic Group: German (99%).
Leading Religions: Protestantism (47%), Roman Catholicism (45%).
Leading Industries: Manufacturing (steel, cement, paper, aluminum, electricity, machinery, motor vehicles, chemicals, textiles); agriculture (dairy products, cattle, hogs, poultry, potatoes, sugar beets, rye, wheat, oats, barley, vegetables, fruits); mining (coal, lignite, zinc, natural gas, gold, salt, petroleum); construction.
Foreign Trade: *Major exports*—automobiles, organic chemicals, plastics, scientific instruments; *major imports*—crude petroleum, fresh fruits, foodstuffs, copper, petroleum products, clothing, automobiles.
Places of Interest: The Alps; Black Forest; Harz Mountains; Weser Hills; Rhine and Danube rivers; Heidelberg; Bremen; Bayreuth; Berchtesgaden; Goethe's house and museum in Frankfurt; Germanic National Museum in Nuremberg; Hamburg botanical gardens and flower park; Cologne Cathedral; Charlemagne's throne in Aachen; Passau medieval town. *In Berlin:* Wall between West and East Berlin; Grünewald Hunting Lodge; Kaiser Wilhelm Memorial Church; Hansa Quarter; Dahlem Museum.

WEST GERMANY TODAY

West Germany is smaller than Oregon, but it has risen from destruction and defeat in World War II to become the leading industrial nation of western Europe. The main competitor of the U.S. and Japan in world trade, West Germany ranks among the world's leading producers of steel, cement, aluminum, electricity, coal-lignite, gold, paper, natural gas, and zinc.

West Germany has the largest population of any country of western Europe. It is also the most crowded of the major European nations because of land lost by World War II. As a result West Germany depends heavily on imports to feed its population.

Although ruled for hundreds of years by kings, emperors, and dictators, the West German people in the generations since World War II have developed a stable, democratic government that has become a beacon of freedom for refugees from communist eastern Europe. Ancient enmities with France and Britain have been healed.

West Germany today plays an important role in cooperative international organizations, such as NATO, the European Common Market, and the United Nations.

GEOGRAPHY AND CLIMATE

Wide lowlands extend from the Netherlands to East Germany in the north.

The upland regions of the central German mountains stretch from the Rhine to the East German border.

The wide valley and gorge of the Rhine cross the southeastern part of West Germany.

Mountains and plateaus range across southern Germany, with the Black Forest in the west, the Bavarian Forest in the east, and the Bavarian Alps in the far south.

The Rhine River, whose two main tributaries are the Mosel and the Main, empties into the North Sea. To the east are the Ems, Weser, and Elbe rivers, all with important ports on their estuaries. To the south the Danube flows eastward for about 400 miles.

Lake Constance, lying on the Swiss and Austrian borders, is the largest lake.

The average temperature ranges from below 21° F. in the mountains during the winter to about 68° F. in the valleys during the summer. Rain, falling throughout the year, varies from 20 to 78 inches, depending on the region and altitude. Snow may reach a depth of 6 feet in some areas during January and February.

West Germany is bordered on the north by Denmark; on the east by East Germany and Czechoslovakia; on the south by Austria and Switzerland; and on the west by France, Luxembourg, Belgium, and the Netherlands.

EARLY HISTORY

The Teutons and the Cimbri are thought to be among the earliest Germanic tribes. Roman records report their defeat by the general Marius in 102–101 B.C. Germanic tribes that included the Alemanni, Burgundians, Franks, Lombards, Ostrogoths, and Visigoths advanced south as the Roman Empire weakened and collapsed.

Charlemagne, the Germanic leader of the Franks who was crowned Roman emperor in A.D. 800, extended his sovereignty over most of Germany.

MIDDLE AGES

Powerful feudal princes divided Germany at a time when it was being invaded by Slavs, Norsemen, and Magyars.

Otto I, Saxon king of the Germans, created the Holy Roman Empire. He was crowned its first emperor in Rome in 962. However, rivalry among the feudal states in Germany and the struggle for supremacy between the emperors and the popes rendered the empire a loose and ineffective federation with little central authority.

The empire was strengthened under the Hohenstaufens, who subdued many of the large duchies. In 1180 Friedrich I Barbarossa dismembered Sax

GERMANY, WEST *(continued)*

ony, the last remaining great duchy.

His grandson Friedrich II was king of Sicily. He also became king of the Germans (1212) and emperor of the Holy Roman Empire (1220–1250). Friedrich II ruled from Sicily, paying little attention to German problems. By the end of his reign the French monarchy and Italian city-states had begun their ascendancy.

REFORMATION

The weakness of the Holy Roman Empire became particularly evident when Germany found itself the center of the Reformation, the religious schism initiated by Martin Luther in 1517.

The Roman Catholic German emperor could not enforce his own religious policies or halt the conversion to Protestantism of many nobles.

The empire was torn by the Thirty Years War (1618–48). The Treaty of Westphalia in 1648 elevated the territorial sovereignty of the states above that of the empire.

PRUSSIA AND AUSTRIA COMPETE

Prussia grew into the only German state that could challenge Austria. When Friedrich the Great defeated Austria in 1740, Prussia joined the ranks of the great European powers.

Napoleon's rise to power in Europe brought an end to the Holy Roman Empire.

At the Congress of Vienna (1814–15) the German states were reduced in number, and a national structure was formed through the German Confederation, with Prussia and Austria as the dominant states. Austria, however, gained control of the confederation.

In 1848 liberal revolutions in Germany failed to unify the nation. The Prussian monarchy tried its own scheme of unification, but in 1850 Austria checked Prussian ambitions by threatening war.

GERMAN EMPIRE

In 1862 Prime Minister Otto von Bismarck of Prussia resolved to eliminate Austrian influence over Germany.

Bismarck achieved his goal with victory over Austria in the Austro-Prussian War (1866). Prussia went on to win the Franco-Prussian War of 1870–71 and was able to unify Germany under Emperor Wilhelm I in 1871. Bismarck became Germany's first chancellor.

From 1871 to 1914 the German Empire expanded rapidly. Its economy flourished. The acquisition of colonies and construction of a navy enhanced its power and prestige.

In 1888 Wilhelm II became emperor and two years later dismissed Bismarck as chancellor.

The rulers of Germany and Austria seized upon the assassination of the heir to the Austrian throne in 1914 as an opportune occasion to defeat or at least to divide their enemies.

Europe was thus plunged into World War I, which ended with Germany's defeat.

WEIMAR REPUBLIC

With the German defeat the Weimar Republic replaced the empire. At its inception the republic was saddled with the humiliating Treaty of Versailles (1919). Germany lost its overseas possessions and had to pay heavy reparations.

In the late 1920s the worldwide depression hit the German economy particularly hard, causing massive unemployment and social chaos.

HITLER'S NAZI GERMANY

By 1932 Adolf Hitler's National Socialist (Nazi) Party was the largest in the Reichstag. He became chancellor in January 1933. Within the year Hitler assumed dictatorial powers.

Hitler launched a campaign to eliminate all Jews from Germany. The official policy of anti-Semitism culminated during World War II in the "final solution"—the extermination of an estimated 6 million Jews in death camps.

In violation of the Versailles Treaty, Hitler remilitarized the Rhineland in 1936, annexed Austria in March 1938, and seized the Sudetenland of Czechoslovakia in September 1938.

In March 1939 Germany took over the rest of Czechoslovakia and demanded Danzig and the Polish Corridor that separated most of Germany from East Prussia.

World War II began when Germany invaded Poland on Sept. 1, 1939. The Nazis enjoyed spectacular successes up to 1941, but beginning with the invasion of Russia in that year, the tide turned. The war ended in May 1945 with Germany's unconditional surrender after Hitler's suicide.

ALLIED OCCUPATION

At conferences in Yalta and Potsdam the U.S., Britain, France, and the Soviet Union decided to divide Germany into four occupation zones, with Berlin under four-power control.

The Soviet Union, however, embarked on its own policy, and efforts to govern Germany through the Allied Control Commission collapsed.

In 1948–49 East Germany cut off land access to Berlin from West Germany. The U.S., Britain, and France organized an airlift to supply Berlin. As a result, the East Germans restored land access.

On Sept. 21, 1949, the democratic *Federal Republic of Germany* was granted self-government. It was created out of the U.S., British, and French zones of Germany. Theodor Heuss was elected president, and the Bundestag chose Konrad Adenauer as chancellor.

INDEPENDENCE FOR WEST GERMANY

West Germany was granted full independence on May 5, 1955, by the U.S., Britain, and France. The United States gave West Germany over $5 billion in aid to rebuild its industries and become a bulwark against the Soviet Union.

Under Adenauer the country achieved economic recovery and political stability.

Adenauer's foreign policy was built on cooperation with the United States, support of NATO, and reconciliation with France. In 1955 West Germany was allowed to rearm under supervision of NATO members. It established diplomatic relations with the Soviet Union. Efforts to reunite East and West Germany were defeated by Cold War tensions.

In 1961 East Germany built the Berlin Wall between the east and west sectors of Berlin to try to prevent East Germans from escaping.

Adenauer retired in 1963. Ludwig Erhard, who as economics minister had been largely responsible for Germany's "economic miracle," became

chancellor. Erhard was succeeded in 1966 by Kurt Georg Kiesinger, who governed until 1969 with a coalition of Christian Democrats and Social Democrats.

The Allies gave up their last occupation rights in May 1968.

OSTPOLITIK OF CHANCELLOR BRANDT

Following the parliamentary elections on Sept. 28, 1969, a coalition of Social Democrats and Free Democrats was formed under Chancellor Willy Brandt, who had been foreign minister in the Kiesinger cabinet.

The German political scene under Brandt was dominated by his *Ostpolitik*, a drive to normalize relations with the communist bloc, including East Germany. *Ostpolitik* led to treaties with the Soviet Union and Poland in 1970 that recognized the inviolability of postwar borders. The Bundestag ratified the treaties on May 17–19, 1972.

The first formal treaty between West and East Germany was ratified and went into effect Oct. 17, 1972, enabling more West Germans to visit East Germany. Brandt then went on to win a November election with his coalition parties receiving over 54% of the popular vote.

A week after Brandt's reelection, he signed a treaty with East Germany establishing diplomatic relations. The treaty went into effect on June 21, 1973. The two Germanys then were admitted to the UN in September 1973.

REGIME OF CHANCELLOR SCHMIDT

Chancellor Brandt resigned suddenly on May 6, accepting complete responsibility for "negligence" in having employed a communist East German spy as an assistant. Brandt designated 55-year-old Helmut Schmidt, his finance minister, as West Germany's fifth chancellor.

Chancellor Schmidt's coalition of the Social Democratic Party (SPD) and Free Democratic Party (FDP) won a close election over the Christian Democratic Party (CDU) on Oct. 3, 1976.

Terrorists of the left, attempting to bring anarchy to West Germany, stepped up their attacks in 1977. On Sept. 5 the terrorists kidnapped and later killed one of the nation's leading industrialists, Hanns-Martin Schleyer. Four of the gang hijacked a Lufthansa Boeing 737 airliner at Majorca on Oct. 13, 1977. The terrorists took the airliner on a 6,000-mile four-day flight to Somalia, killed the pilot en route, and threatened to kill the remaining passengers and crew. Schmidt's government won widespread acclaim when a 60-man West German commando unit made a daring raid on the hijacked airliner at Mogadishu, Somalia, on Oct. 18, 1977, freeing the 86 hostages while killing three of the hijackers.

Schmidt and Soviet Leader Leonid I. Brezhnev signed on May 6, 1978, a 25-year economic cooperation agreement.

Karl Carstens, 64, speaker of the Bundestag and a former member of the Nazi Party, was elected as the nation's by an electoral assembly on May 23, 1979.

Parliament in 1979 lifted the statute of limitations that would have prevented the continued prosecution in the 1980s of former Nazis.

CHANCELLORS OF WEST GERMANY

1949–63	Konrad Adenauer.....	Christian Democrat
1963–66	Ludwig Erhard	Christian Democrat
1966–69	Kurt Georg Kiesinger..	Christian Democrat
1969–74	Willy Brandt	Social Democrat
1974–82	Helmut Schmidt	Social Democrat
1982–	Helmut Kohl	Christian Democrat

West Germany and East Germany continued to strengthen ties in 1980 with agreement on a $282 million pact to improve road, rail, and waterway links between the two nations.

In a national election on Oct. 5, 1980, Chancellor Schmidt's coalition strengthened its majority control of the lower house of parliament, winning 53.5% of the vote and gaining 16 seats. He had been opposed by the conservative governor of Bavaria, Franz Josef Strauss.

The growth of West Germany's economy ground almost to a halt in 1981 as the country's balance-of-trade deficit soared to $15 billion.

CHRISTIAN DEMOCRATS REGAIN POWER

With the nation hurting from the worldwide recession, squabbling on economic issues developed among the members of Schmidt's coalition. The Free Democratic Party decided to switch its support from Schmidt. On Oct. 1, 1982, the Bundestag voted 256 to 235 to oust Schmidt.

Helmut Kohl, 52, head of the conservative Christian Democrats, became chancellor. In presenting his program to the Bundestag on Oct. 13, 1982, he said he planned to revive the nation from its "worst economic crisis" by cutting social-welfare benefits, encouraging private investment, and restricting immigration. He said he planned to strengthen relations with the U.S. Kohl promised a national election in March 1983.

Unemployment rose to a peak of more than 10% early in 1983. As the recession eased, unemployment remained at 9.6% in 1985.

The main issue in a parliamentary election on March 6, 1983, was whether the government should approve the stationing of new U.S. missiles in West Germany. Kohl's pro-American conservative coalition won an increased majority, while the socialists who opposed deployment of the missiles suffered their worst defeat in more than 20 years.

The federal assembly on May 23, 1984, elected Richard von Weizsaecker, 64, as the nation's 6th president, a largely ceremonial post. Weizsaecker, a Christian Democrat, formerly served as mayor of West Berlin.

As part of the observance of the 40th anniversary of Germany's surrender in World War II, President Reagan accepted an invitation by Chancellor Kohl to visit a German military cemetery at Bitburg on May 5, 1985. Although President Reagan described the occasion as a symbol of reconciliation between Americans and Germans, he was severely criticized by Jewish groups who believed the visit could be interpreted as forgiveness for the Nazi extermination of Jews.

Kohn's government was shaken by a major spy scandal that developed in August 1985 when a high ranking official in charge of catching communist spies defected to East Germany.

QUICK QUIZ: Which U.S. President had served on the U.S. Civil Service Commission? See page 364.

GHANA

Official Name: Republic of Ghana.
Area: 92,100 square miles (238,537 sq. km.).
Population: 13,711,000.
Chief Cities: Accra, capital, 564,194; Kumasi, 260,286; Sekondi-Takoradi, 91,874.
Largest Metropolitan Area: Accra, 738,498.
Government: Leftist military-civilian junta.
Head of Government: Jerry J. Rawlings (since 1981).
U.S. Ambassador to Ghana: Robert E. Fritts.
Ghanian Ambassador to U.S.: Eric Kwamena Otoo.
Flag: Red, gold, and green stripes, with black star in gold stripe.
Languages: English (official), Akan, Ewe, Ga, Hausa.
Main Ethnic Group: Black.
Religions: Animism (45%), Christianity (43%), Islam (12%).
Leading Industries: Agriculture (cocoa, coffee, palm kernels, corn, rice, peanuts, rabbits, tobacco, rubber, cassava, sweet potatoes, tomatoes, cotton, vegetables, fruits); forestry and lumbering; mining (gold, diamonds, manganese, bauxite); manufacturing (electricity, aluminum, steel, tires, vehicle assembly, oil refining); fishing (tuna).
Foreign Trade: *Major exports*—cocoa, aluminum, petroleum, tuna, wood, gold, diamonds, manganese; *major imports*—auto parts, automobiles, food, medicines, textile machinery.
Places of Interest: Cape Coast Castle; Boti Waterfall; Elmina resort; national museum, Accra; Kumasi Cultural Center; Bolgatanga market; Mole Game Reserve at Damongo; Aburi Botanical Garden; Paga crocodile pond; Dawhenya irrigation project.

GHANA TODAY

About the size of Illinois and Indiana combined, Ghana is the world's leading grower of cacao beans, from which cocoa and chocolate are made.

Most Ghanaians are poor. Only about 1 in 4 can read and write.

In the west a forested belt extends north from the coast into the hilly Ashanti region.

The climate is hot and humid in the south, and warm and humid in the north. A rainy season lasts from May to September.

Burkina Faso lies to the north, Togo to the east, and Ivory Coast to the west.

EARLY HISTORY

The ancient Ghana empire flourished from the 300s to the 1000s.

The Portuguese came in 1470, developing gold mining and slave trading. The first British trading visit to the area was by Thomas Windham in 1553.

After Britain declared the slave trade illegal in 1807, all Europeans except the British withdrew.

From 1826 to 1900 the British fought a long series of campaigns against the Ashantis of the interior. The coastal region was annexed by Britain as the Gold Coast Colony in 1874.

The Gold Coast became one of the most politically advanced African colonies. Blacks were admitted into the government in 1942.

The Convention People's Party (CPP), founded by Kwame Nkrumah, won legislative elections in 1951, and for the first time the black majority had power.

INDEPENDENCE

On March 6, 1957, Ghana (as the Gold Coast was renamed) became the first black African colony granted independence by Britain.

In 1960 Ghana became a republic. Nkrumah, a communist, was elected president. He then established a one-party dictatorship.

In 1966 while in Peking, Nkrumah was deposed by a military coup. A military junta headed by Gen. A.A. Afrifa ruled until 1969.

Ghana's first free general elections since 1956 were held Aug. 29, 1969. The Progress Party of Kofi Busia, leader of the opposition to Nkrumah, won a majority of seats in the national assembly.

On Jan. 13, 1972, a military coup, led by Col. Ignatius Kutu Acheampong, overthrew Busia.

Lt. Gen. Fred W.K. Akuffo seized power in a bloodless coup on July 5, 1978.

Petroleum was discovered in commercial amounts in 1978.

Flight Lt. Jerry J. Rawlings, 31, led a coup that overthrew the government on June 4, 1979. Declaring a "moral revolution," Rawlings arrested dozens of officials on charges of corruption. Eight were executed, including three former heads of state, Akuffo, Acheampong, and Afrifa.

After a new constitution similar to that of the U.S. was drawn up, Rawlings ordered the first multiparty elections since 1969. Ghanaians elected a national assembly and chose as president Dr. Hilla Limann, 52, an economist.

The nation's economy declined in 1980–81 because of crop failures. President Limann appealed in 1981 to foreign governments for aid.

Rawlings overthrew Limann's government on Dec. 31, 1981, declaring it had brought Ghana "total economic ruin." He suspended the constitution and appointed a seven-man leftist military-civilian council to help him rule. Several hundred persons were killed in the uprising. Limann and more than 200 former officials were imprisoned. Many Ghanaians fled to neighboring countries.

An admirer of Libyan strong man Col. Mu'ammar al-Qadhafi, Rawlings reestablished diplomatic relations with Libya that had been broken by Limann in 1980. Libya sent financial aid and food to Rawlings' government. Soviet-bloc nations also promised economic help. Rawlings froze prices in an effort to bring under control inflation that had been running at an annual rate of 116%.

In 1983, Rawlings abolished the entire judicial system, setting up 5–member "people's tribunals" to hear charges and mete out "swift justice."

Ghana's economy suffered when Nigeria expelled 500,000 poverty-stricken Ghanians in 1983. Loans from the World Bank and the International Monetary Fund helped the country begin a modest economic recovery in 1984–85. But a new blow came in May 1985 when Nigeria forced another 300,000 to return to Ghana. To help finance their repatriation, Ghana's government forced the returning Ghanians to pay import taxes on their goods or have them confiscated and auctioned.

GREECE

Official Name: Hellenic Republic.
Area: 50,944 square miles (131,944 sq. km.).
Population: 10,120,000.
Chief Cities: Athinai (Athens), capital, 867,023; Thessaloniki (Salonika), 345,799; Piraiéus (Piraeus), 187,362; Péristéri, 118,413.
Largest Metropolitan Area: Athens, 2,101,103.
Government: Parliamentary democracy.
Prime Minister: Andreas Papandreou (since 1981).
President: Christos Sartzetakis (since 1985).
Parliament: 300 members.
Greek Ambassador to U.S.: George D. Papoulias.
U.S. Ambassador to Greece: Monteagle Stearns.
Flag: White cross on blue field in upper hoist corner; blue and white stripes.
Language: Greek.
Chief Ethnic Group: Greek (97%).
Main Religion: Greek Orthodox (98%).
Leading Industries: Manufacturing (textiles, chemicals, steel, tobacco products, aluminum, consumer products); agriculture (tobacco, cotton, wheat, raisins, currants, olives, grapes, fruits, vegetables); shipping; tourism; mining (petroleum, bauxite, iron, zinc, lead, lignite, chrome, nickel).
Foreign Trade: *Major exports*—tobacco, currants, raisins, grapes; *major imports*—machinery, transport equipment, iron and steel, crude petroleum.
Places of Interest: Mount Olympus; Pindus Mountains; islands of Corfu, Rhodes, Cyclades, Mykonos, and Crete—Minoan ruins; Temple of Apollo in Corinth; Delphi ruins; Temple of Poseidon in Sounion. *In Athens:* Parthenon, Acropolis, and Acropolis Museum; temples of Nike, Theseus, Zeus.

GREECE TODAY

Although ancient Greece was the birthplace of democracy, modern Greece has experienced only a few brief periods of democratic government. Civilian government, civil rights, and political democracy were restored only in the 1970s.

The U.S. maintains four military bases in Greece.

The people of Greece have one of the lowest standards of living in western Europe. About 4 out of 10 are farmers, barely making a living for their families. But most people are educated. Only about 1 in 10 cannot read and write.

Greece has lacked basic mineral and energy resources to become a leading industrial nation. Manufacturing provides only about one-fifth of the national income. As a result, Greece has a huge annual trade deficit with the cost of imports three times that of exports. Petroleum from deposits in the Aegean Sea fill only about one-fifth of Greece's requirements.

The tourism and shipping industries provide a major share of the money Greece uses to import needed petroleum and manufactured products.

Hundreds of thousands of visitors each year are attracted by the Acropolis, the Parthenon, and other ruins of ancient Greece. Others come to Greece to enjoy the blue skies and warm beaches of the Greek isles.

Greece is a mountainous and heavily wooded country. The Pindus range, running north and south, is the most important. Mount Olympus, home of the gods in Greek mythology, is the highest peak (9,551 feet). Valleys and plains lie between the mountains.

The main rivers are in the north and have their origins in other countries. None is navigable. Southern Greece includes the Peloponnesian peninsula and some 437 offshore islands, the largest of which is Crete.

Greece, the southernmost country of the Balkan peninsula, is bordered on the north by Albania, Yugoslavia, and Bulgaria; on the east by Turkey and the Aegean Sea; on the south by the Mediterranean Sea; and on the west by the Ionian Sea.

EARLY HISTORY

Neolithic man lived in Greece at least as early as 4000 B.C. Beginning about 2000 B.C., successive waves of Greek-speaking Achaeans, an Indo-European people, migrated into the area, supplanting the existing cultures.

By 1100 B.C. two major civilizations had flourished and vanished. The Minoan civilization was centered on the island of Crete and later influenced the mainland from the south. The Mycenaean civilization, generally less advanced than the Minoan, was on the mainland.

ANCIENT GREEK EMPIRE

Greek city-states began to develop about 1000 B.C. They were sufficiently well established by 800 B.C. to become the source of democracy and of colonization efforts. By 600 B.C. colonies founded from the city-states were located on islands in the Ionian, Aegean, and Mediterranean seas, in Asia Minor, on the African coast, and as far west as France and Spain.

Ancient Greek civilization reached its zenith in the 400s B.C., when Athens was the center of a vast overseas empire.

After the death of Alexander the Great in 323 B.C., Greek power disintegrated. By 146 B.C. Greece had become a province of the new Mediterranean power, the Roman Empire.

BYZANTINE AND TURKISH RULE

After Roman Emperor Constantine moved the capital of the empire in A.D. 330 to Constantinople (now Istanbul, Turkey), the Grecian influence was strongly felt.

While Rome languished under barbarian control, Constantinople and Greece were the centers of a thriving Byzantine Greek civilization.

In the Fourth Crusade, Constantinople was sacked by crusaders en route to the Holy Land (1204). The Greeks won it back in 1261.

Constantinople fell to the Turks in 1453. Greece then became a Turkish province in 1460.

INDEPENDENT MONARCHY

After almost four centuries of subjugation by the Turks, a war of independence was begun by the Greeks on March 25, 1821. Supported by Britain,

QUICK QUIZ: Which U.S. President was paralyzed by a stroke? See page 306.

GREECE (continued)

France, and Russia, the revolt was ultimately successful, and in July 1832 the sultan recognized the independence of Greece.

Prince Otto of Bavaria was made king of Greece in 1833. He was overthrown in 1862 and was succeeded by Prince William George of Denmark, who became George I.

Greece unsuccessfully attempted to enlarge its territory in the Greco-Turkish war of 1897.

In the early 1900s the Greeks fought with neighboring Slavs and Turks in an effort to reclaim national territory. In the two Balkan wars (1912 and 1913), Greece obtained Epirus, parts of Thrace and Macedonia, and Crete.

Greece fought on the side of the Allies in World War I and was rewarded with territory from Bulgaria and Turkey.

The people voted for a monarchy in 1920 and for a republic in 1924. King George II, who was dethroned in 1924, returned in 1935 following a plebiscite. On Aug. 4, 1936, he accepted Gen. Ioannis Metaxas as dictator.

Metaxas headed the resistance when Italy invaded Greece in 1940. Greece was occupied by Italy and Germany in 1941–44.

After World War II, five years of civil war ensued between the government and communist guerrillas. U.S. aid under the Truman Doctrine helped bring final defeat of the communists in 1949. About 120,000 Greeks were killed in the fighting.

King George II died in 1947 and was succeeded by his brother Paul I. Upon Paul's death in 1964, his son Constantine II came to the throne.

MILITARY RULE

A military coup took place on April 21, 1967. A military junta took control, naming Col. George Papadopoulos as premier and defense minister.

On Dec. 13, 1967, King Constantine unsuccessfully attempted a countercoup. In its aftermath, he and the royal family fled to Rome.

Papadopoulos deposed the exiled king on June 1, 1973. He decreed Greece a republic and took the title of president.

On Nov. 25, 1973, military leaders overthrew Papadopoulos. Brig. Gen. Dimitrios Ioannides seized control.

The military junta supported the overthrow of the government of Archbishop Makarios on Cyprus in July 1974. When Turkey invaded Cyprus and threatened war if Greece intervened, the military junta collapsed.

DEMOCRATIC REPUBLIC

Constantine Karamanlis, a conservative former premier in 1955–63 who had been living in France, was called home and sworn in as premier on July 24, 1974. Premier Karamanlis ordered a general amnesty for political prisoners. He restored freedom of the press and freedom of speech.

Anti-American demonstrations broke out in August 1974 as Greeks blamed the U.S. for failing to prevent Turkey's invasion of Cyprus. Karamanlis withdrew Greece from the NATO alliance.

The first free parliamentary elections in 10 years were held on Nov. 17, 1974. Karamanlis' New Democracy Party won a sweeping victory, capturing more than two-thirds of the 300 seats.

In a referendum held on Dec. 8, 1974, voters overwhelmingly rejected a return to monarchy.

A new constitution was adopted in June 1975, establishing a parliamentary republic. Parliament elected Constantine Tsatsos, 76, as president.

After a month-long trial former President Papadopoulos and two other leaders of the 1967 coup were sentenced to death for treason on Aug. 23, 1975. But the Greek cabinet commuted the sentences to life imprisonment.

To overcome dependence on imported oil, the government announced plans in 1978 to build 18 new hydroelectric generating plants, 10 new lignite-fired generators, and one 600-megawatt nuclear power plant.

Having led Greece back to democracy, the 73-year-old Karamanlis decided in 1980 to turn leadership of his party over to younger men and accepted parliamentary election to the less demanding post as the nation's president. Foreign minister George John Rallis, 62, was chosen on May 8 to succeed Karamanlis as prime minister.

Turkey agreed to Greece's readmission to NATO on Oct. 20, 1980.

Greece joined the European Community (Common Market) on Jan. 1, 1981.

In a landslide victory in elections on Oct. 18, 1981, socialists won a majority of 174 of parliament's 300 seats to 113 for Prime Minister Rallis' New Democracy Party.

Socialist Andreas Papandreou, 62, a former American economics professor who gave up U.S. citizenship to enter Greek politics, became prime minister on Oct. 21, 1981.

Because Greece's economy declined in 1981–83 as a result of the worldwide recession, the socialist government postponed plans for nationalization of industries. Instead, it concentrated on social reforms, passing laws in 1982 that legalized civil marriage and ended criminal prosecution of adultery. Other laws were drawn to separate the government from the Greek Orthodox Church, to expropriate hundreds of thousands of acres of church land, to permit divorce without church sanction, to break the communist hold on labor unions, and to emancipate women.

Elected on a platform calling for Greece's withdrawal from NATO and the closing of U.S. military bases in Greece, Papandreou reversed himself by agreeing in 1983 to permit the U.S. bases to continue to operate at least until 1988. At the same time the U.S. promised Greece about $500 million in annual military aid.

However, Papandreou broke ranks with other Western leaders in 1983 by refusing to condemn the Soviet Union for shooting down a South Korean airliner and by campaigning for postponement of the deployment of new U.S. missiles in Europe.

President Karamanlis resigned on March 10, 1985, refusing to accept constitutional amendments proposed by Papandreou to further restrict presidential powers. A new president, supported by Papandreou, 56-year-old judge Christos Sartzetakis, was elected three weeks later by parliament. Parliament then approved the amendments limiting presidential powers.

In parliamentary elections on June 2, 1985, Papandreou's Socialist Party won a 161-seat majority. The conservative New Democracy Party captured 125 seats.

GRENADA

Official Name: State of Grenada.
Area: 133 square miles (344 sq. km.).
Population: 115,000.
Capital: St. George's, 7,303.
Government: Parliamentary democracy.
Prime Minister: Herbert A. Blaize (since 1984).
Parliament: 15 members.
Flag: Red border with yellow stars above and below green and yellow triangles; red circle with yellow star in center; nutmeg on green triangle.
Official Language: English.
Main Ethnic Group: Black.
Principal Religions: Roman Catholic, Anglican.
Leading Industries: Tourism; agriculture (nutmegs, cocoa, bananas, fruits, vegetables, sugarcane, cotton, spices); fishing; food processing.
Foreign Trade: *Major exports*—nutmegs, cocoa beans, mace, bananas; *major imports*—petroleum, food, consumer goods.
Places of Interest: *In St. George's: Fort George, government buildings, shops; Sauteurs; Grenville; island of Carricou; beaches.*

GRENADA TODAY

A Caribbean island nation, Grenada is one of the smallest nations in the world.

Part of the Windward Islands chain, the mountainous island of Grenada lies less than 100 miles off the coast of Venezuela. The country also includes part of the small Grenadines islands to the north.

The source of much of the world's nutmeg, the island displays a nutmeg on its national flag.

HISTORY

Settled by French colonists in the 1600s, Grenada became a British possession in 1763.

Grenada was granted self-government in 1967. Prime Minister Eric M. Gairy's United Labor Party won elections in 1967 and 1972.

The nation achieved full independence within the British Commonwealth of Nations on Feb. 7, 1974, with Gairy continuing as prime minister.

A coup in which two persons were killed overthrew Gairy's dictatorial rule on March 13, 1979, while Gairy was visiting the U.S.

The head of the Marxist New Jewel Movement, Maurice Bishop, 33, whose father was killed by Gairy's secret police in 1974, became prime minister. Bishop suspended the constitution and set up a governing 14-member Marxist revolutionary council.

On Oct. 15, 1979, Bishop's government shut down the only opposition newspaper.

Bishop was slain on Oct. 19, 1983, by his Marxist associates in a coup that began six days earlier.

The U.S. landed troops on Oct. 25, 1983, defeating a Cuban military garrison and arresting the coup leaders. In the fighting, 45 Grenadians, 24 Cubans, and 18 American servicemen were killed.

An international airport, begun in 1980 by Cuba, was completed in 1984 with about $19 million in funds from the U.S.

In the first election in eight years, on Dec. 3, 1984, the centerist New National Party won 14 of the 15 seats in parliament. Its leader, Herbert A. Blaize, 66, became prime minister.

GUATEMALA

Official Name: Republic of Guatemala.
Area: 42,042 square miles (108,889 sq. km.).
Population: 8,249,000.
Capital: Guatemala City, 793,336.
Government: Martial-law dictatorship.
President: Gen. Oscar Mejia Victores (since 1983).
U.S. Ambassador to Guatemala: Alberto M. Piedra.
Guatemalan Ambassador to U.S.: Eduardo Palomo.
Flag: Blue, white, and blue bars, with national coat of arms in center.
Languages: Spanish (official), Maya.
Main Ethnic Groups: Maya-Quiché Indians (55%), mestizo (42%).
Religion: Roman Catholicism (92%).
Leading Industries: Agriculture (coffee, cotton, bananas, sugarcane, cattle, corn, rice, beans, wheat, spices, tobacco); manufacturing (tobacco products, chemicals, textiles, plastics, tires, chemicals, consumer goods); food processing; construction; mining (nickel, petroleum); fishing (shrimp).
Foreign Trade: *Major exports*—coffee, cotton, bananas, sugar, beef, wood, chicle; *major imports*—iron and steel, textiles, pharmaceuticals, vehicles, petroleum, food, consumer goods.
Places of Interest: National palace at Guatemala City; Mayan ruins at Tikal, Uaxactum, Piedras Negras, Zaculeu; Spanish ruins at Antigua Guatemala.

GUATEMALA TODAY

About the size of Tennessee, Guatemala is a poor Central American nation dominated by its generals. Thousands of persons are killed or disappear each year in a civil war between the government and rebel guerrillas.

The U.S. is Guatemala's main trading partner, buying about a fourth of its exports.

Guatemala's economy depends largely on agriculture. Coffee makes up about half the country's exports, followed in importance by cotton, bananas, and sugar.

Most Guatemalans are poor farmers.

The country has a 50-mile coastline on the Caribbean and a 200-mile coast on the Pacific. The land ranges from a coastal plain to mountainous areas.

There are 30 volcanoes, 8 of which are active.

Mexico lies to the west and north. Belize is to the northeast. Honduras lies to the east and El Salvador to the southeast.

EARLY HISTORY OF GUATEMALA

Guatemala was part of the territory occupied originally by the Mayas, whose influence and power began to decline in the 1100s.

From 1524 to 1821 Central America from Yucatán to Panama was ruled by the Spanish.

By the mid-1700s Antigua, the capital, was one of the great cities of the New World, comparable to Mexico City and Lima. Severe earthquakes in 1773 destroyed the city, and the capital was moved to Guatemala City.

INDEPENDENCE

Guatemala declared its independence from Spain on Sept. 15, 1821. It was briefly annexed by Mexico, and then was a member of the Central American Federation until 1838. Since then it has been ruled largely by military dictators.

An earthquake on Feb. 4, 1976, destroyed much of the capital city and scores of other towns. Some 22,934 persons were killed.

Petroleum in commercial quantities was discovered in 1976, but reserves are limited.

The U.S. cut off military aid in 1977 because of the government's human-rights violations.

The nation's congress chose Gen. Romeo Lucas García as president in 1978.

Amnesty International in 1981 accused President Lucas of directing a campaign of torture and murder that killed 3,000 in 1980.

In a presidential election on March 7, 1982, the ruling party's candidate, Gen. Angel Anibal Guevara, was declared the winner.

Before Guevara could take office, Gen. Efrain Rios Montt, a born-again Christian, overthrew the government on March 23, 1982.

In October 1982 Amnesty International reported that Gen. Rios Montt's forces had "massacred more than 2,600 Indians and peasants".

Gen. Oscar Mejia Victores, 53, the minister of defense, overthrew Montt on Aug. 8, 1983.

Some 1.7 million Guatemalans voted on July 1, 1984, to elect an 88-member assembly to write a new democratic constitution.

Gen. Mejia announced on Feb. 22, 1985, that national elections would be held on Oct. 24, 1985, and that the military junta would turn control of the government over to elected civilians on Jan. 14, 1986.

GUINEA

Official Name: Republic of Guinea.
Area: 94,926 square miles (245,857 sq. km.).
Population: 5,467,000.
Capital: Conakry, 197,267.
Government: Military junta.
President: Col. Lansana Conté (since 1984).
U.S. Ambassador to Guinea: James D. Rosenthal.
Guinean Ambassador to U.S.: Tolo Beavogui.
Flag: Red, yellow, and green bars.
Languages: French (official), Fulani, Malinké, Susu.
Principal Religion: Islam.

Main Ethnic Groups: Fulani (Hamitic; 28%), Malinké (17%), Susu (9%).
Leading Industries: Agriculture (rice, palm kernels, tea, bananas, coffee, yams, pineapples, peanuts, manioc, millet, corn, vegetables, fruits, livestock); mining (bauxite, diamonds, gold, iron); manufacturing (bauxite refining); fishing.
Foreign Trade: *Major exports*—alumina, pineapples, bananas, palm kernels, coffee; *major imports*—machinery, metals, food, transport equipment.
Places of Interest: Mount Nimba National Reserve; national museum in Conakry.

GUINEA TODAY

About the size of Oregon, Guinea is one of Africa's poorest countries. Most of the people live in thatched mud huts in tribal villages, growing enough food to feed their families and little else. Few adults can read or write.

However, Guinea has large deposits of bauxite, iron, gold, and diamonds, as well as the potential for hydroelectric development.

The coastal plain ascends to a mountainous region called Futa Jallon. Interior Guinea is a rolling plain, partly woodland and partly grassy savanna, averaging about 1,000 feet in height.

The climate is humid and tropical. Temperatures range from 60° to 100° F. Annual rainfall has measured 168 inches at Conakry.

Guinea is bordered on the north by Guinea-Bissau, Senegal, and Mali; on the east by Mali and Ivory Coast; and on the south by Liberia and Sierra Leone.

HISTORY

The empires of Ghana and the Malinkés dominated Guinea in medieval times.

Portuguese explorers and slave traders came to the Guinea coast in the 1400s. The Treaty of Paris of 1814 secured French rights in Guinea. In 1849 a French protectorate was established.

Guinea declared itself independent on Oct. 2, 1958, with Ahmed Sékou Touré as its first president. Touré, a Marxist, turned to the Soviet Union and communist China for help.

Guinea's export revenues rose nearly 800% from 1972 to 1976 as two large bauxite mining developments began production.

The International League for Human Rights appealed to the UN in 1977 to intervene in Guinea to halt what it called a "reign of terror" by Touré. The organization said thousands of Guineans were imprisoned and tortured and 2 million fled to other countries.

Touré visited President Carter in Washington, D.C., in 1979 and President Reagan in 1982 seeking increases in U.S. economic aid.

Touré, 62, who had ruled Guinea for 26 years, died in the U.S. on March 26, 1984, during an emergency heart operation.

A week later, Col. Lansana Conté, 39, led a coup on April 2, 1984, overthrowing the Marxist government. He promised to restore free enterprise, liberty, and democracy.

Russian-trained Col. Diara Traore, who had briefly served as Conté's prime minister, unsuccessfully attempted to overthrow the government on July 4, 1985. He and 18 others were arrested after the coup attempt in which 18 persons were killed and several hundred wounded.

GUINEA–BISSAU

GUYANA

Official Name: Republic of Guinea-Bissau.
Area: 13,948 square miles (36,125 sq. km.).
Population: 934,000.
Capital: Bissau, 60,000.
Government: Military junta.
Head of Government: João Bernardo Veira (since 1980).
U.S. Ambassador to Guinea-Bissau: Wesley W. Egan Jr.
Ambassador to U.S.: Inacio Semedo Jr.
Flag: Red vertical bar at hoist with black star; two horizontal stripes, yellow above green.
Languages: Portuguese, Fulani, Malinké, Felup, Papel, Balanta, Mandyako.
Main Ethnic Group: Bantu (97%).
Principal Religions: Animism (66%), Islam (30%).
Leading Industries: Agriculture (rice, millet, palm kernels, peanuts, cattle); fishing; forestry.
Foreign Trade: *Major exports*—peanuts, palm kernels, fish, wood, shrimp; *major imports*—petroleum products, food, consumer goods.
Places of Interest: Bissau; islands of the Bijagos archipelago; Boloma, capital until 1948.

About the size of Massachusetts and Connecticut combined, Guinea-Bissau was the first of Portugal's African colonies to win independence.

One of the poorest countries of Africa, Guinea-Bissau has an economy that depends on farming, fishing, livestock raising, and lumbering. It spends four times more for imports than it receives from exports. Most Guinea-Bissauans live in tribes whose way of life has changed little in thousands of years.

A tropical country with a hot humid climate. Guinea-Bissau has an Atlantic coastline indented by many rivers. Many people live in the offshore islands of the Bijagos archipelago. Senegal is to the north and Guinea to the south.

The Portuguese explorer Nuno Tristão first visited the area in 1446. The region became a center for the Portuguese slave trade.

Called Portuguese Guinea for over 500 years of Portuguese rule, the area was made an overseas province in 1951. An independence movement began in 1959 with guerrilla warfare that raged for the next 15 years.

The African Independence Party (PAIGC) declared independence on Sept. 24, 1973, with Luis Cabral as president. Portugal recognized Guinea-Bissau's independence on Sept. 10, 1974.

Brig. Gen. João Bernardo Veira overthrew and imprisoned Cabral in 1980, accusing him of directing the murder of hundreds of opponents.

In May 1981 Veira ended the government monopoly on rice, permitting small merchants to resume buying and selling the food staple.

The government sought assistance from wealthier countries in the 1980s to develop rice farming to become self-sufficient in food production. Mineral exploration was begun seeking bauxite and petroleum deposits.

Official Name: Cooperative Republic of Guyana.
Area: 83,000 square miles (214,969 sq. km.).
Population: 845,000.
Capital: Georgetown, 72,049.
Government: Marxist socialist republic.
President: Desmond Hoyte (since 1985).
National Assembly: 53 members.
U.S. Ambassador to Guyana: Clint Lauderdale.
Guyanese Ambassador to U.S.: Cedric Hilburn Grant.
Flag: Green field with black-edged red triangle superimposed on white-edged yellow triangle.
Languages: English (official), East Indian dialects.
Main Ethnic Groups: East Indian (55%), black (35%).
Principal Religions: Christianity (57%), Hinduism (33%), Islam (9%).
Leading Industries: Mining (bauxite, petroleum, gold, diamonds); agriculture (rice, sugarcane, palm kernels, coffee, fruits, vegetables); food processing; fishing; forestry and lumbering.
Foreign Trade: *Major exports*—sugar, bauxite, alumina, rice, gold, diamonds, shrimp; *major imports*—machinery, petroleum, textiles, motor vehicles, wheat.
Places of Interest: Kaieteur Waterfall; St. George's Cathedral and Guyana Museum in Georgetown; Bartica area; Rupununi savanna country.

Guyana is the only South American country with a British cultural background. The Marxist socialist government operates most industry, including the profitable bauxite mines.

About the size of Idaho, the country is largely covered by a thick, uninhabited tropical forest. Most Guyanese live in the narrow plain along the Atlantic coast.

By 1620 the Dutch had partially settled the country. The three colonies of Berbice, Demerara, and Essequibo were ceded to Britain in 1814 and united as British Guiana in 1831. Britain granted independence on May 26, 1966.

In 1964 elections Forbes Burnham of the People's National Congress became prime minister. He was reelected in 1968 and 1973.

Guyana became a republic on Feb. 23, 1970.

World attention focused on Guyana in 1978 when members of an American religious cult murdered a visiting U.S. congressman on Nov. 18. The cult's founder, the Rev. Jim Jones, and over 900 followers committed mass suicide.

Burnham became president on Oct. 6, 1980, under a new constitution that gave the office strengthened powers as chief executive.

Burnham was declared winner of a presidental election on Dec. 15, 1980. However, international observers reported that the election was conducted with "massive and blatant fraud."

Petroleum was discovered in April 1982 in the region near the border with Brazil.

Desmond Hoyte, who had been prime minister since 1984, became president on Aug. 6, 1985, after Burnham died while undergoing surgery.

HAITI

Official Name: Republic of Haiti.
Area: 10,714 square miles (27,750 sq. km.).
Population: 6,000,000.
Capital: Port-au-Prince, 862,900.
Government: Dictatorship.
President: Jean-Claude Duvalier (since 1971).
National Assembly: 59 members.
U.S. Ambassador to Haiti: Clayton E. McManaway Jr.
Haitian Ambassador to U.S.: Adrien Raymond.
Flag: Black and red bars; centered white rectangle contains emblems of war around palm tree.
Languages: French (official), Creole.
Ethnic Groups: Black (95%), Mulatto (5%).
Religions: Roman Catholicism (official; 80%), voodooism.
Leading Industries: Agriculture (coffee, sisal, sugar cane, rice, cocoa, poultry, vegetables, fruits); food processing; mining (copper, bauxite); tourism; manufacturing (textiles, soap, cement, assembly plants); fishing.
Foreign Trade: *Major exports*—coffee, sugar, sisal, mangos; *major imports*—cotton textiles, foodstuffs, petroleum, machinery.
Places of Interest: Sans Souci Palace ruins and King Henri Christophe fortress La Citadelle; Toussaint L'Ouverture Monument in Cap-Haïtien; national museum in Port-au-Prince; vacation resorts at Pétionville and Kenscoff.

HAITI TODAY

About the size of Maryland, Haiti is a poor, over-populated Caribbean nation. It has been ruled as a police state by the Duvalier family for nearly three decades.

Only about 1 in 5 Haitians can read and write. Some farm only to raise their own food. Others work on coffee or sugar plantations. About half the people are unemployed.

About two-thirds of the government's national budget comes from foreign loans and aid by the U.S. and other nations. The U.S. has provided over $300 million in aid in the past three decades.

Development of the island's resources has been hampered by corruption and by the lack of highways. About two-thirds of the country is too mountainous to be farmed.

During the Duvalier regimes an estimated 300,000 to 400,000 Haitians have made their way to new homes in the U.S.

Haiti occupies the western third of the island of Hispaniola, which it shares with the Dominican Republic to the east.

EARLY HISTORY

The island of Hispaniola was discovered for Spain by Christopher Columbus in 1492.

Having killed most of the Arawak natives by 1533, the Spanish settled mainly on the eastern side of the island in the vicinity of Santo Domingo. The western area became a base for French and English pirates.

By the Treaty of Ryswick (1697) Spain ceded the western region, now Haiti, to France. French settlers imported many slaves.

The French Revolution, which began in 1789, sparked black slave rebellions in which most of the white colonists were killed or fled.

In 1792 French troops were sent to crush the revolt but were defeated by a self-educated, freed slave, Pierre-Dominique Toussaint L'Ouverture. Agreeing in 1799 to govern for France, Toussaint occupied Santo Domingo in the eastern part of the island, abolished slavery, and gave the island a constitution. In 1802, however, France's new ruler, Napoleon Bonaparte, sent troops to restore French authority. Toussaint, captured by treachery, died in a French prison.

INDEPENDENT KINGDOM

The French troops were decimated by disease and by clashes with blacks led by Jean-Jacques Dessalines. The army withdrew in 1803, and in 1804 Dessalines declared Haiti's independence. Dessalines ruled as a despot under the title of Emperor Jacques I until his assassination in 1806.

The country then divided, with the north ruled autocratically by Henri Christophe, a black who proclaimed himself King Henri I. A republic in the south and west was governed by a mulatto, Alexandre Pétion, until his death in 1818. His successor, was Jean Pierre Boyer. Following the suicide of King Henri in 1820, the entire island was united in 1822 when Boyer's forces conquered Santo Domingo. A year after Boyer's ouster in 1843, Santo Domingo gained independence as the Dominican Republic. From 1843 to 1915, Haiti was ruled by 22 dictators.

HAITI IN THE 1900s

In 1905 the U.S. took Haiti's customs into receivership, and 10 years later the U.S. seized full control. The U.S. withdrew its troops in 1934, but retained financial control until 1947.

François "Papa Doc" Duvalier became dictator after being elected president in 1957. His regime, faced by economic decline and political unrest, became repressive, with all opposition held in check by secret-police terror. The economy of Haiti stagnated.

Duvalier died on April 21, 1971, and was succeeded by his 19-year-old son, Jean-Claude "Baby Doc" Duvalier, as president for life.

The Duvalier fortune, acquired during more than two decades of rule, is unofficially estimated at over $400 million.

Duvalier cracked down on opponents in 1979, launching a new wave of arrests. Political opponents were given long jail terms.

About 30,000 Haitians fled to the United States in 1980 and were granted political asylum.

U.S. President Reagan on Sept. 29, 1981, ordered the Coast Guard to intercept and turn back to Haiti boats carrying illegal immigrants bound for the United States.

The island's tourism industry was badly hurt in the 1980s when U.S. health authorities named Haitians as one of the high risk groups affected by the fatal disease AIDS.

Amnesty International charged in March 1985 that Duvalier's secret police repeatedly arrest and torture political opponents, journalists, and labor union leaders.

HONDURAS

Official Name: Republic of Honduras.

Area: 43,277 square miles (112,088 sq. km.).

Population: 4,700,000.

Chief Cities: Tegucigalpa, capital, 444,230; San Pedro Sula, 276,826.

Government: Democratic republic.

President: Roberto Suazo Córdova (since 1982).

Congress: 78 members.

U.S. Ambassador to Honduras: John A. Ferch.

Honduran Ambassador to U.S.: Juan Agurcia Ewing.

Flag: Stripes of blue, white, and blue, with five blue stars in center.

Official Language: Spanish.

Main Ethnic Groups: Mestizo (90%), African (5%), Indian (4%).

Main Religion: Roman Catholicism (90%).

Leading Industries: Agriculture (bananas, coffee, cattle, corn, beans, rice, sugarcane, tobacco, vegetables, fruits); forestry and lumbering; manufacturing (textiles, detergents, cement, paper, chemicals, food products, clothing); mining (gold, silver, copper, lead, zinc).

Foreign Trade: *Major exports*—bananas, coffee, meat, sugar, lumber, seafood, silver, tobacco; *major imports*—petroleum products, paper and paperboard, textile yarn and fabrics, electrical machinery.

Places of Interest: Tegucigalpa; Mayan ruins at Copán; Comayagua and Trujillo ancient cities; Bay Islands; Yojoa Lake; San Fernando Castle at Omoa; La Ceiba, Puerto Cortés, Tela beaches.

HONDURAS TODAY

About the size of Tennessee, Honduras is a poor Central American country. Banana- and coffee-growing are its most important industries.

About two-thirds of the people are impoverished farm workers. Over half cannot read or write.

Development of the country has been hampered because there are few roads and highways. Much of the eastern part of Honduras can only be reached by airplanes or coastal boats.

Narrow lowlands along the Gulf of Fonseca and the Caribbean coast fringe this mountainous land, whose northern peaks exceed 7,500 feet.

The climate varies from wet and tropical on the coastal plains to dry and cool in the highlands. The capital, Tegucigalpa (elevation 3,500 feet), has a continual springlike climate. The wet season is May to November.

Rainfall averages 100 inches annually on the northern coast and 30 inches in the south.

Nicaragua lies to the south, El Salvador to the southwest, and Guatemala to the west.

HISTORY

A center of Mayan civilization before A.D. 900, Honduras was discovered by Columbus in 1502 on his fourth voyage to the New World.

Attracted by exaggerated tales of gold and silver in Honduras, rival Spanish factions from

Mexico, Guatemala, and Panama struggled for control. Invaders included Hernán Cortés, who in 1524 made a historic march from Mexico to impose his rule on the region. In 1538 Honduras became a part of Guatemala.

On Sept. 15, 1821, Honduras and the other Central American provinces declared their independence from Spain. They were annexed by Mexico, but broke away within a year.

From 1823 to 1838 Honduras joined its neighbors in the United Provinces of Central America.

Honduras declared its independence as a republic on Nov. 5, 1838.

U.S. Marines were sent to the country several times between 1912 and 1925 to preserve order.

On Dec. 4, 1972, Gen. Oswaldo López Arellano, who had ruled as dictator in 1963–71, overthrew the government and made himself president.

Hurricane Fifi devastated Honduras with 110-mph winds and tidal waves on Sept. 18–19, 1974, killing 2,000 persons and destroying property and banana crops worth $500 million.

In March 1975 army officers forced President López to give up command of the armed forces to Col. Juan Melgar Castro.

Early in April 1975 the U.S. Securities and Exchange Commission (SEC) accused a U.S. firm, United Brands, of concealing from its stockholders the payment of a $1.25 million bribe to an unnamed "high" Honduran official to reduce banana export taxes. When López refused to cooperate with investigators, the junta deposed him, making Colonel Melgar president on April 22. Melgar ruled as dictator by decree.

The new government promised to expropriate 1.5 million acres of land for distribution to 120,000 landless farm families.

In 1975 tens of thousands of peasants demonstrated, urging a speed-up in land reforms. Soldiers killed about 15 peasants to halt a mass march on the capital. Gunfights broke out between landowners and peasants.

Gen. Policarpo Paz García, commander of the armed forces, and two other generals overthrew Melgar on Aug. 7, 1978. Fulfilling a promise to restore civilian government, Paz García called an election on April 20, 1980, for a 71-member assembly that wrote a new constitution.

After 18 years of military rule, Hondurans elected a civilian government on Nov. 29, 1981. The right-of-center Liberal Party won the presidency and a majority in the congress.

Roberto Suazo Córdova, 55, a physician, was sworn in as president on Jan. 27, 1982. He faced severe problems. The country was nearing economic collapse with declining export income.

Honduras became a refuge in the 1980s for tens of thousands of Nicaraguans, Salvadorans, and Guatemalans fleeing civil wars.

Fearing an invasion by troops of the leftist government of Nicaragua, Honduras beefed up its armed forces in 1982–84 with U.S. assistance. About 8,000 Nicaraguan rebel guerrillas called *Contras* are based in Honduras.

Political candidates began campaigning early in 1985 for a presidential election scheduled for November.

QUICK QUIZ: Which President installed the first electric lights in the White House? See page 362.

HUNGARY

Official Name: Hungarian People's Republic.
Area: 35,929 square miles (93,030 sq. km.).
Population: 10,676,000.
Chief Cities: Budapest, capital, 2,062,195; Miskolc, 209,828; Debrecen, 195,021; Szeged, 172,787.
Government: One-party communist state.
Heads of Government: Janós Kádár, first secretary, Hungarian Socialist Workers Party (since 1956); Gyorgy Lazar, prime minister (since 1975); president of the presidential council, Pál Losonczi (took office in 1967).
National Assembly: 387 members.
U.S. Ambassador to Hungary: Nicolas Salgo.
Hungarian Ambassador to U.S.: Vencel Hazi.
Flag: Red, white, and green tricolor.
Official Language: Hungarian.
Main Ethnic Group: Magyar (96%).
Religions: Roman Catholicism (67%), Protestantism (25%), Unitarianism, Judaism (8%).
Leading Industries: Manufacturing (steel, cement, textiles, chemicals, machinery, transportation equipment); agriculture (corn, wheat, sugar beets, potatoes, fruits, vegetables, livestock); mining (bauxite, coal, natural gas); tourism.
Foreign Trade: *Major exports*—transport equipment, machinery, bauxite, wheat, corn, meat, steel; *major imports*—petroleum, coke, textile fibers.
Places of Interest: Visegrad fortress on the Danube Bend; Lake Balaton; Eger fortress; Esztergom Palace and Cathedral; Tihanyi and Pannonhalma abbeys; Heviz thermal spa; Hortebagy Horse Show. *In Budapest:* The Citadel; Matthias Church; opera house.

HUNGARY TODAY

About the size of Indiana, Hungary is a communist country in eastern Europe.

Hungarians enjoy a higher standard of living than the people of neighboring communist nations because of an innovative economic system that enables managers and workers to make profits. Small businesses and small farms are operated privately for a profit. The government encourages foreign investments in joint ventures. Foreign trade accounts for more than half of Hungary's gross national product.

The Danube River forms over one-third the length of the northern border with Czechoslovakia, and then veers south through Budapest and into Yugoslavia. Plains lie to the east and west of the Danube. The Tisza is Hungary's second most important river.

The uplands in the northeast occupy about one-third of the land area. The highest mountain is Kekes (3,300 feet). Lake Balaton, in west central Hungary, is the country's largest lake.

Hungary has hot summers (average July temperature 71° F.) and cold winters (average January temperature 31° F.). Rainfall averages 25 inches a year. Summer droughts are frequent.

Austria lies to the west, Czechoslovakia to the north, the Soviet Union to the northeast, Romania to the east, and Yugoslavia to the south.

EARLY HISTORY

Hungary was founded in the 800s A.D. by Arpád, a semilegendary chief of the Magyars.

In 1001 Hungary was unified under István (Stephen) I. For Christianizing his people, he was canonized as St. István in 1087.

Nobles forced András II to sign in 1222 the Golden Bull, the "Magna Carta of Hungary."

The country fell into anarchy after András III died in 1301.

Mátáyas Hollos (Matthias Corvinus), elected king in 1458, restored Hungary to an era of glory.

By 1526 Hungary fell under Turkish domination. But at the end of the 1600s the Austrian Hapsburg armies expelled the Turks and took control of Hungary. Resistance against Austria was led by Francis II Rákoczy, one of Hungary's national heroes, but by 1711 he had been defeated.

A rebellion exploded in 1848 led by Louis Kossuth, who declared Hungary an independent republic in 1849. With Russian assistance, Austria put down the revolt.

Following Austria's defeat by the Prussians in 1866, Hungarian nationalism was recognized by creation of the Austro-Hungarian dual empire.

INDEPENDENCE

Hungary declared itself an independent republic on Nov. 16, 1918. In March 1919 the communist dictator Béla Kun took over the government. Romanian troops intervened, and Kun fled. In November a new government was established with Adm. Nicholas Horthy as regent and head of state. His authoritarian regime lasted 25 years.

During World War II German troops occupied the country and in 1944 arrested Horthy. Soviet troops took Hungary in February 1945.

Hungary's last free election, held in November 1945, gave anticommunists a majority. A Hungarian republic was proclaimed in 1946 with Zoltan Tildy as president.

COMMUNIST RULE

Tildy was ousted in 1948 by a Soviet-assisted communist coup. A Soviet-style *Hungarian People's Republic* came into being on Aug. 20, 1949.

After Stalin's death in 1953 Premier Imre Nagy relaxed controls, but two years later he and his cabinet were ousted for "anti-Marxism."

In October 1956 a revolt erupted in Budapest. Imre Nagy again became premier. He announced that free multiparty elections would be held. Two days later Soviet troops intervened. Communist rule was forcibly restored under János Kádár.

Thousands of Hungarians fled as refugees to other countries. Nagy was executed.

For a dozen years Hungary remained one of the most repressive communist police states. But most freedom of expression was restored by the 1980s.

In 1968 Hungary and the United States formally resumed full diplomatic relations.

Kádár's government introduced the New Economic Mechanism (NEM) in 1968, which allows profits at various levels.

Hungary received most-favored nation trade status with the U.S. in 1978.

Hungary took a major step toward capitalism

with a law that went into effect on Jan. 1, 1982, permitting the establishment of privately owned profit-making firms with up to 30 employees. Many government-owned small businesses, such as restaurants, were leased to private managers.

In the freest elections since the communists took power, Hungarians voted for a new parliament on June 8, 1985, with a choice of two candidates for each seat. In all, 25 independents who were not sponsored by the communists won office.

ICELAND

Official Name: Republic of Iceland.
Area: 39,768 square miles (103,000 sq. km.).
Population: 240,000.
Capital: Reykjaví, 83,766.
Government: Parliamentary republic.
President: Vigdís Finnbogadóttir (since 1980).
Prime Minister: Steingrimur Hermannsson (since 1983).
Parliament *(Althing)*: Upper House, 20 members; Lower House, 40 members.
U.S. Ambassador to Iceland: Nicholas Rowe.
Icelandic Ambassador to U.S.: Hans G. Andersen.
Flag: White-bordered red cross on blue field.
Official Language: Icelandic.
Principal Ethnic Group: Norwegian descent (99%).
Official Religion: Evangelical Lutheranism.
Leading Industries: Fishing and fish processing; manufacturing (electricity, metal products, clothing, furniture, fertilizer, cement); construction; agriculture (cattle, sheep, hay, vegetables); mining (diatomite).
Foreign Trade: *Major exports*—frozen fish, salted fish, herring meal fodder, herring oil, aluminum; *major imports*—ships and boats, petroleum products, aircraft, cord nets and netting.
Places of Interest: National Park at Thingvellir (Parliament Plains); Surtsey Island; Golden Fall; Great Geyser; Myvatn; Mt. Hekla. *In Reykjaví:* hot spring reservoirs that heat city; Lutheran Cathedral.

ICELAND TODAY

About the size of Kentucky, Iceland is an island in the North Atlantic. It lies just south of the Arctic Circle, 200 miles southeast of Greenland.

The sparsely settled island has few mineral resources. Fishing has been developed as Iceland's most profitable industry. The island's hydroelectric potential has been tapped to create an aluminum manufacturing industry. The geothermal energy of hot springs and volcanoes is used to heat homes as well as greenhouses where vegetables are raised. The U.S. maintains a large NATO air base at Keflavík.

The people have achieved a high standard of living, but depend on imports of oil and manufactured goods.

Iceland has many active volcanoes. The highest peak, Hvannadalshnúkur, rises 6,952 feet. Huge glaciers cover much of the interior. But the Gulf Stream provides a relatively mild coastal climate.

EARLY HISTORY

Norse settlers colonized the island about A.D. 870. The *Althing*, established in 930, is the oldest active parliament in the world.

Iceland came under Norwegian control in 1262 and became part of the Danish-Norwegian state in 1381.

Jón Sigurdsson, an Icelandic statesman, helped win a constitution and limited home rule in 1874. With the 1918 Act of Union, the country obtained full self-government under the Danish crown.

INDEPENDENCE

On June 17, 1944, while Denmark was occupied by Germany, Iceland declared its independence. Under the terms of a 1951 agreement, the U.S. is responsible for the island's defense.

Asgeir Asgeirsson was president from 1952 to 1968. He was succeeded by Kristján Eldjárn, president from 1968 to 1980.

A major issue in 1974 national elections was continued U.S. operation of the NATO air base at Keflavík, opposed by leftists and supported by conservatives. The leftist parties lost their majority in parliament. Geir Hallgrimsson became prime minister with a conservative coalition that rescinded leftist plans to close the U.S. base.

Iceland on Oct. 15, 1975, banned foreign fishing within 200 miles of its coastline. The resulting "cod war" with Britain was settled in 1977 when all British trawlers were excluded from Iceland's 200-mile zone pending agreement with the European Common Market.

A strike for higher pay by 12,000 government employees in October 1977 isolated Iceland for about two weeks. The walkout cut off flights in and out of the country.

In a national election on June 25, 1978, socialists and communists made substantial gains at the expense of the governing conservative-center coalition, causing Prime Minister Hallgrimsson to resign.

Olafur Johannesson, of the centrist Progressive Party, became prime minister after forming a coalition cabinet on Aug. 31, 1978.

Unable to reduce the nation's 55% inflation rate, Johannesson's coalition government collapsed and new elections were held on Dec. 2–3, 1979. Results were inconclusive.

Gunnar Thoroddsen, 69, of the Independence Party, became prime minister on Feb. 8, 1980.

Iceland became the first European country to elect a woman as ceremonial head of state on June 29, 1980, when voters chose Vigdis Finnbogadottir, 50, as the nation's president. She was reelected to another 4-year term in 1984.

A national election on April 23, 1983, divided the national legislature's seats among six parties. Steingrimur Hermannsson, 54, head of the Progressive Party became prime minister in coalition with the Independence Party.

The government announced in 1985 that all ships carrying nuclear arms were banned from its territorial waters.

QUICK QUIZ: When was the first atomic-powered submarine launched? See page 307.

INDIA

Official name: Republic of India.
Area: 1,269,346 square miles (3,287,590 sq. km.).
Population: 770,064,000.
Capital: New Delhi, 271,990.
Largest Metropolitan Areas: Calcutta, 9,165,650; Bombay, 8,227,332; Delhi, 5,713,581; Madras, 4,276,635; Bangalore, 2,913,537; Hyderabad, 2,528,198; Ahmedabad, 2,515,195; Kanpur, 1,688,242; Poona, 1,685,300; Nagpur, 1,297,977; Lucknow, 1,006,538; Jaipur, 1,004,669.
Government: Parliamentary republic.
President: Zail Singh (since 1982).
Prime Minister: Rajiv Gandhi (since 1984).
U.S. Ambassador to India: Harry G. Barnes Jr.
Indian Ambassador to U.S.: Kayatyani Shankar Bajpai.
Parliament: *Rajya Sabha* (Council of States), 240 members; *Lok Sabha* (House of the People), 545 members.
Flag: Deep saffron, white, and green stripes, with centered 24-spoke Wheel of Asoka in blue.
Official Languages: Hindi, English, Assamese, Bengali, Gujarati, Kannada, Kashmiri, Malayallam, Marathi, Oriya, Punjabi, Sanskrit, Tamil, Telegu, Urdu.
Main Ethnic Groups: Aryan in the north (72%), Dravidian in the south (25%).
Chief Religions: Hinduism (84%), Islam (10%).
Leading Industries: Agriculture (sugarcane, pepper, tea, peanuts, rice, jute, bananas, tobacco, cotton, wheat, vegetables, cattle); manufacturing (steel, machinery, cement, motor vehicles, sugar refining, textiles, jute products, handicrafts); construction; tourism; mining (petroleum, iron ore, coal, chrome, thorium, nickel, copper, lead, zinc, bauxite, natural gas, manganese).
Foreign Trade: *Major exports*—jute, tea, iron ore, leather, cotton; *major imports*—wheat, fertilizer, chemicals, machinery, steel, petroleum.
Places of Interest: Taj Mahal in Agra; Ganges River; Khajuraho temples; Ajanta and Ellora temple caves; Red Fort and Qutb Minar tombs and mosques in Delhi; Amber Palace in Jaipur; ancient temples in Madras; Srinagar in the Vale of Kashmir; Dal Lake.

INDIA TODAY

India is the second most heavily populated country in the world, next to China. Although India has less than one-third the area of the U.S., it has about three times as many people. And the population increases at the rate of 25 babies born each minute—over 13 million a year.

India's people are among the poorest in the world. Many nearly starve year after year. Almost half the people earn less than $7.50 a month. Only 1 person in 4 can read and write.

Rich in natural resources, India ranks among the world's leading nations in production of coal, electricity, forestry products, iron, and natural rubber.

In the north the Himalaya mountains—rising to the highest elevations in the world—serve as a barrier between India and China. The area's three great rivers—Indus, Ganges, and Brahmaputra—start in the Himalaya.

The lowlands of India stretch eastward for 2,000 miles from the Indus River delta to the delta of the Ganges and the Brahmaputra. Centered in the peninsula, the Deccan Plateau is surrounded by hills and mountains. Beyond the Eastern Ghat mountain range are the plains of the Coromandel Coast on the Bay of Bengal.

The coasts and the Ganges delta are hot and humid. In the far west are the semiarid steppes and the barren Thar Desert, while in the north the climate changes from near tropical to arctic as the land rises in the Himalaya.

EARLY HISTORY

About 3000 B.C. civilization developed in the Indus Valley. About 1500 B.C. Aryans invaded the country and absorbed this civilization. The following 2,000 years saw Hinduism and the caste system come into being. The first important Aryan kingdom, Magadha, during the reign of Bimbisara (542–490 B.C.), heard the teachings of Jainism and Buddhism from the mouths of their founders.

Alexander the Great invaded in 327–325 B.C., but his armies were overcome by Chandragupta, who founded the Maurya empire.

Asoka (273–236 B.C.) unified northern India and established Buddhism as the state religion.

The Gupta dynasty reached its height under Samudragupta (about A.D. 340–380).

In the 1000s the Muslim Mahmud of Ghanzi invaded India and extended his empire to the Ganges and the deserts of Rajputana.

The greatest Mogul emperor, Akbar (reigned 1556–1605), extended his rule from northern India well into the Deccan. His policy of religious toleration was not continued by his successors.

European colonization of India began with the arrival of Vasco da Gama in 1498.

By the mid-1800s Britain had won control of most of India. British domination and rising internal strife led to the Sepoy Mutiny of 1857, a rebellion by native troops. In 1877 Queen Victoria was crowned empress of India.

After World War I the nationalist movement came under the sway of Mohandas K. (Mahatma) Gandhi. He organized a series of passive-resistance campaigns.

INDEPENDENCE

Britain partitioned the peninsula in 1947 into Hindu India and Muslim Pakistan. On Aug. 15, India was granted independence. Jawaharlal Nehru became India's first prime minister.

Partition led to religious riots, killings, and a crisscrossing migration of millions of people. Gandhi attempted to stop the religious violence, but on Jan. 30, 1948, he was assassinated.

India fought Pakistan for control of Kashmir in 1948–49 and again in 1965.

On Jan. 26, 1950, India became a parliamentary republic in the British Commonwealth.

Chinese troops invaded Kashmir and northeastern India on Oct. 20, 1962. After stiff Indian resistance, the Chinese withdrew a month later.

Nehru died in 1964, and Lal Bahadur Shastri succeeded him as prime minister.

When Shastri died suddenly, Mrs. Indira Gandhi, Nehru's daughter, was chosen prime

minister on Jan. 19, 1966, and won general elections in 1967 and 1971.

DEVELOPMENTS IN THE 1970s

A flood of 9 million Bengali refugees poured into India after the outbreak of civil war in east Pakistan (now Bangladesh) in March 1971. In support of the rebels, India invaded the province on Dec. 3. Pakistan surrendered 13 days later.

India, on May 18, 1974, became the first of the world's underdeveloped nations to explode an atomic device.

In 1975 India annexed the independent nation of Sikkim, making it India's 22d state.

When a court ruled that Mrs. Gandhi was guilty of violating election laws, she declared a state of emergency on June 26, 1975, suspended civil liberties, and imposed censorship. Mrs. Gandhi had 28,836 political opponents arrested and jailed "to save India from anarchy."

In 1976 India resumed full diplomatic relations with China for the first time since 1961, and with Pakistan for the first time since 1971.

In an effort to reduce the population growth rate, the government in 1976 raised the minimum age for marriage to 21 for men and 18 for women and launched a vigorous sterilization program.

Mrs. Gandhi put through constitutional amendments, in December 1976, that gave her dictatorial powers. But a month later she called a general election.

Mrs. Gandhi and her Congress Party were overwhelmingly defeated in the election held on March 16–20, 1977. The opposition Janata Party captured a majority in parliament.

Morarji Ranchhodji Desai, 81, leader of the Janata Party became prime minister. He had been imprisoned for 18 months by Mrs. Gandhi during her emergency rule, after having served as her deputy prime minister in 1967–69.

Desai freed the remaining 17,000 political prisoners and restored human rights.

Desai, who had criticized Mrs. Gandhi as being pro-Soviet, declared India would observe "true nonalignment" in international affairs.

Neelam Sanjiva Reddy, 64, was chosen unanimously as president of India in July 1977.

Mrs. Gandhi began efforts to make a political comeback after being ousted from the Congress Party on Jan. 3, 1978. She set up her own political party and won election to parliament in November 1978. But in December 1978 she was ousted from parliament and jailed for one week for having harassed officials in 1975.

Because of a split in his Janata Party, the 83-year-old Desai resigned as prime minister on July 15, 1979. He was succeeded by his deputy prime minister, Charan Singh, 77.

PRIME MINISTERS OF INDIA

1947–64	Jawaharlal Nehru	Congress
1964–66	Lal Bahadur Shastri	Congress
1966–77	Indira Gandhi	Congress
1977–79	Morarji Desai	Janata
1979–80	Charan Singh	Janata-Secular
1980–84	Indira Gandhi	Congress (I)
1984–	Rajiv Gandhi	Congress (I)

INDIA'S 22 STATES

STATE	AREA (sq. mi.)	CAPITAL
Andhra Pradesh	106,855	Hyderabad
Assam	30,318	Shillong
Bihar	67,134	Patna
Gujarat	75,670	Ahmadabad
Haryana	17,074	Chandigarh
Himachal Pradesh	21,495	Simla
Jammu and Kashmir *..	85,806	Srinagar
Karnataka	74,044	Bangalore
Kerala	15,005	Trivandrum
Madhya Pradesh	170,982	Bhopal
Maharashtra	118,828	Bombay
Manipur	8,632	Imphal
Meghalaya	8,683	Shillong
Nagaland	6,381	Kohima
Orissa	60,171	Bhubaneswar
Punjab	19,445	Chandigarh
Rajasthan.............	132,130	Jaipur
Sikkim	2,744	Gangtok
Tamil Nadu	50,220	Madras
Tripura	4,045	Agartala
Uttar Pradesh	133,674	Lucknow
West Bengal	33,920	Calcutta

* Disputed by Pakistan.

INDIA IN THE 1980s

Indira Gandhi's new Congress (I) Party won a landslide victory in elections in January 1980, capturing four-fifths of the seats in parliament. The 62-year-old Mrs. Gandhi resumed office as prime minister on Jan. 14, 1980.

Strengthening her socialist government's control over business, Mrs. Gandhi nationalized six of India's largest banks by decree in April 1980.

India put a space satellite into orbit on July 18, 1980, the sixth nation to do so.

The government contracted with the Soviet Union in May 1980 for $1.6 billion in weapons.

At Prime Minister Gandhi's urging parliament adopted a law in September 1981 that gave the government sweeping powers to arrest without warrant strikers in essential services, such as transportation and communications.

Zail Singh, 67, a Sikh, was elected in 1982 as the nation's 7th president.

Sikhs demanding autonomy for their home state Punjab attacked India's parliament building on Oct. 11, 1982, killing 5 persons.

India's hopes of becoming self-sufficient in petroleum by the 1990s were buoyed in 1982–83 as production from its offshore Bombay High oil field reached 21.1 million metric tons. Plans call for nearly doubling the amount of petroleum produced by 1990.

An estimated 5,000 persons were killed and 250,000 made homeless in massacres and fighting between Hindus and Muslims in February and March 1983 in the state of Assam.

Prime Minister Gandhi dismissed the state government of Punjab on Oct. 6, 1983, instituting direct rule from New Delhi to end strife between Hindus and Sikhs.

Sikh fanatics seeking independence for a Sikh nation to be called *Khalistan* launched a series of terrorist incidents in Punjab in April and May 1984 in which more than 200 persons were killed.

QUICK QUIZ: Which U.S. President was nicknamed "the Gentleman Boss"? See page 360.

INDIA (continued)

To halt the violence, Indian troops stormed a Sikh stronghold at the Golden Temple in Amritsar on June 5–6, 1984. About 600 to 1,000 persons were killed, including the radical Sikh leader Jarnail Singh Bhindranwale. Hundreds of Sikhs were jailed. About 5,000 Sikhs in the Indian army mutinied, but were put down by loyalist troops.

Prime Minister Gandhi's followers in August 1984 ousted from office one of her leading opponents, the popular chief minister of Andhra Pradesh state, N. T. Rama Rao, a former movie star. After hundreds of thousands of his followers demonstrated against the action, Rama Rao won reinstatement to his office in September.

Mrs. Gandhi was assassinated on Oct. 31, 1984, by two Sikhs who were members of her personal bodyguard. Days of disorder followed in which grieving Hindus pillaged Sikh neighborhoods, killing thousands of Sikhs before troops restored order.

Rajiv Gandhi, 40, Mrs. Gandhi's son, was sworn in as prime minister after her death.

The world's worst industrial accident took place on Dec. 3, 1984, at Bhopal when poisonous gas leaked from a chemical plant of the Union Carbide Corp., killing over 2,000 persons and injuring about 200,000.

Prime Minister Rajiv Gandhi's Congress (I) Party won in a landslide in a national election in late December 1984. His supporters captured a record 400 of the 508 contested parliamentary seats, more than the previous record of 357 achieved by Nehru in 1957.

The 40-year-old prime minister promised to move India's development forward at a faster rate, cutting taxes, reducing government regulation of business and industry, and rooting out corruption in government.

In an election of state legislatures in March 1985, the Congress (I) Party again won a majority of seats, but received only about 57% of the votes compared with 80% in the national election three months earlier.

Demonstrating his independent course in foreign relations, Prime Minister Gandhi visited both the Soviet Union and the United States in 1985. Prior to Gandhi's June 1985 visit to the U.S., the FBI arrested five Sikhs charged with plotting to assassinate him.

The nation's seventh 5-year plan for 1985–1990 emphasizes expansion in the areas of agriculture, electric power, and petroleum mining.

INDIA'S TERRITORIES

In addition to those below, India also administers the cities of Chandigarth and Delhi as territories.

ANDAMAN AND NICOBAR ISLANDS

With an area of 3,203 sq. mi., the islands lie in the Bay of Bengal. Port Blair, the capital is 780 miles southeast of Calcutta. The Andamans include 5 large islands designated the Great Andamans, an island to the south called Little Andaman, and more than 200 islets. The Nicobars, 75 miles to the south, consist of 19 islands, 12 inhabited.

The Negrito people of the Andamans lead a tribal life in the interior—hunting, fishing, and avoiding contact with civilization. Most of the Andaman islanders are Indians, with some Burmese Karennis. The Nicobarese are of Mongoloid stock.

The Andamans were first settled as a penal colony by the British in 1858. In World War II the Japanese occupied them in 1942. Britain settled the Nicobars in 1869.

ARUNACHAL PRADESH

The mountainous 32,270 sq. mi. region on the border with China and Burma formerly was known as the North East Frontier Agency.

Most of the people are Mongol tribesmen.

The northern boundary with the Tibet region of China, called the McMahon Line, was established by Britain in 1914. China invaded the North East Frontier Agency briefly in 1962.

The region was renamed and made a union territory of India on Jan. 21, 1972.

DADRA AND NAGAR HAVELI

These 190 sq. mi. former colonies of Portugal lie north of Bombay, India. More than a third of the region is covered with teak forests.

Portugal obtained the region in 1780. In 1954 Indian nationalists invaded. It was made a union territory of India on Aug. 11, 1961.

GOA, DAMAN, AND DIU

The 1,472 sq. mi. territory encompasses what once was Portuguese India. It includes three widely separated former Portuguese colonies on India's west coast: Goa, Daman, and Diu.

Goa was captured in March 1510 by Afonso de Albuquerque and became the capital of Portugal's empire in Asia. The Portuguese acquired Damão (now Daman) in 1531 and Diu in 1534.

On Dec. 18, 1961, Indian troops invaded and captured all three colonies. The colonies were made a union territory of India in March 1962.

In 1974–75 many Roman Catholics traveled to Goa for an exposition in which the body of missionary St. Francis Xavier was displayed in a glass coffin in the Se Cathedral. The fact that his body has not decomposed since his death in 1522 is regarded as a miracle by Catholics.

LAKSHADWEEP

With an area of 12.4 sq. mi., the 27 islands in the territory lie in the Arabian Sea 200 miles west of Kerala. They include the Laccadives and Amindivis. The largest is Minicoy.

MIZORAM

The 8,142 sq. mi. Mizoram territory borders on Bangladesh and Burma. During British rule of India efforts were made to stamp out headhunting among the Lushai tribes that live in the evergreen forests covering Mizoram's hills.

Until it was made a union territory on Jan. 21, 1972, Mizoram was known as the Mizo Hills district of Assam.

PONDICHERRY

The 185 sq. mi. Pondicherry administers four widely separated former French colonies in India. Pondicherry itself lies on India's east coast, south of the city of Madras. The district of Karikal is a coastal enclave 90 miles south of Pondicherry. The district of Yanam lies about 400 miles to the north of Pondicherry. Mahé, the fourth district, stands on India's west coast, a few miles north of the city of Calicut.

Settled by the French in 1674, Pondicherry was ceded to India on May 28, 1956. It was made a union territory on Aug. 16, 1962.

INDONESIA

Official Name: Republic of Indonesia.
Area: 788,662 square miles (2,027,087 sq. km.)
Population: 175,075,000.
Chief Cities: Jakarta, capital, 6,503,449; Surabaja, 2,027,913; Bandung, 1,462,637; Semarang, 1,026,671; Medan, 1,378,955; Palembang, 787,187.
Government: Military-controlled republic.
President: General Suharto (took office in 1967).
Parliament: *People's Representation Council,* 460 members.
U.S. Ambassador to Indonesia: John H. Holdridge.
Indonesian Ambassador to U.S.: A. Hasnan Habib.
Flag: Red stripe above white stripe.
Languages: Indonesian (official), English.
Ethnic Groups: Malay (95%), Chinese, Papuan, Arab.
Leading Religions: Islam (90%), Christianity (4%), Hinduism (3%), Buddhism (1%).
Leading Industries: Agriculture (rice, corn, sugarcane, tea, coffee, rubber, tobacco, cassava, coconuts, peanuts, spices, vegetables, fruits); manufacturing (textiles, assembly of motor vehicles, food processing, cement, consumer goods); mining (petroleum, tin, bauxite, coal, natural gas, copper, diamonds, gold, silver, sulfur, nickel, manganese); fishing; forestry and lumbering.
Foreign Trade: *Major exports*—crude petroleum and products, rubber, coffee, tin, spices, wood products; *major imports*—rice, cotton, machinery, flour, consumer goods.
Places of Interest: Botanical gardens of Bogor; Puncak resort area; Tangkubanperahu Volcano; Borobudur Temple on Java; Bali; Sumatra; Beautiful Indonesia in Miniature, near Jakarta.

INDONESIA TODAY

Indonesia includes 13,677 islands between the mainland of Southeast Asia and Australia. The islands stretch 3,300 miles from east to west—nearly as far as from New York to Paris.

Once known as the *East Indies,* Indonesia has the fifth-largest population in the world, after China, India, the Soviet Union, and the United States. Indonesia's islands cover an area about five times larger than that of California. However, its people cannot raise enough farm products to feed themselves. So Indonesia is one of the largest importers of rice.

The government imposes censorship on news and is believed to hold many political prisoners.

Transportation is one of the country's major problems. Boats and planes must be used for travel between islands. The larger islands are mountainous and heavily forested with relatively few paved roads.

Indonesia has many natural resources. It is one of the world's leading nations in the production of natural rubber, petroleum, and tin. However, Indonesia's industrial production remains underdeveloped. Its gross national product is only about one-twentieth that of Japan.

Indonesians are among the poorest people in the world. Less than half can read and write. About two-thirds do not get enough to eat daily. About one-fourth of the workers are unemployed.

With annual revenues of more than $13 billion from oil exports, Indonesia has pressed forward to make greater use of the islands' natural resources. New highways have been built, port facilities have been improved, and many electric-power projects have been constructed.

The islands of Indonesia have many mountains and volcanoes. The highest, Jaya in Irian Jaya (western New Guinea), rises to 16,500 feet. Mt. Kerinci on Sumatra is 12,467 feet high.

Indonesia straddles the equator, so the coastal lowland areas have a hot, tropical climate the year round. The interior upland regions of the larger islands enjoy a cooler climate.

EARLY HISTORY

Migrants from the Asian mainland populated Indonesia between 2500 and 1000 B.C.

In the precolonial period Indian cultural influence was dominant. The great Shrivijaya maritime empire, with its capital in southern Sumatra, was a renowned center of Buddhist learning. About A.D. 800 the Sailendra dynasty built the great Buddhist temple Borobudur in central Java.

From the 1100s, Arab traders spread the Islamic religion. In the 1300s Hinduism was ascendant in the powerful, Java-based Majapahit empire.

Western dominance began in 1511 when the Portuguese landed at Malacca, on the Malayan peninsula, "in search of Christians and spices."

NETHERLANDS EAST INDIES

By 1623 the Netherlands East India Company was able to establish a monopoly. The Dutch government revoked the company's charter in 1790 and assumed full administration of the islands 10 years later.

Independence movements began in the early 1900s. The first successful mass organization was Sarakat Islam (Islamic Association). Immediately after World War I the organization's Marxist faction founded the Indonesian Communist Party. Tension mounted between the communist and noncommunist branches. In 1921 the communists were expelled from the Islamic Association.

The Indonesian Nationalist Party was formed in 1927 by Sukarno and Mohamad Hatta. The Dutch exiled Sukarno and other nationalist leaders to remote island outposts.

Japanese occupation of the islands during World War II further stimulated the nationalist movement.

INDEPENDENCE

With Japan's defeat, Sukarno and Hatta declared the independence of the Republic of Indonesia on Aug. 17, 1945. For the next four years the Indonesians battled to keep the Dutch from resuming colonial rule.

The UN succeeded in getting both sides to end the conflict. Sukarno was elected president on Dec. 16, 1949. Eleven days later, on Dec. 27, the Netherlands formally recognized Indonesia's

QUICK QUIZ: When did astronaut John H. Glenn Jr. first orbit the Earth? See page 308.

INDONESIA *(continued)*
independence.

The first elections to the nation's parliament, held in 1955, sharpened party cleavages and indicated strength for the Communist Party.

Tensions developed between President Sukarno and Vice President Hatta, due partly to Sukarno's tolerance of the communists and his antagonism to the Muslim Masjumi Party, favored by Hatta. In 1956 the vice president resigned.

Sukarno became dictator, declaring martial law in 1957.

In 1960 diplomatic relations with the Netherlands were severed, and Indonesian troops began infiltration of Netherlands New Guinea (Irian Jaya). The Netherlands turned the region over to the United Nations in 1962. The UN placed the territory under Indonesia's jurisdiction in May 1963.

Sukarno strongly opposed the formation of Malaysia in 1963, and openly waged war against that nation.

After the failure of an attempted communist coup on Oct. 1, 1965, anticommunist rioting swept the country with 100,000 to 400,000 persons killed.

Lt. Gen. Suharto emerged as the strong man of a new regime. He ordered the army to eliminate all traces of the Communist Party. An estimated 500,000 persons were jailed.

In March 1967 the national assembly formally revoked Sukarno's governing authority and appointed Suharto as acting president. In March 1968 Suharto was elected to a 5-year term as president by the assembly. Sukarno was arrested in 1969 and died in June 1970.

DEVELOPMENTS IN THE 1970s–1980s

In 1971 elections Suharto's Golkar Party won 73% of the seats in parliament.

The People's Consultative Assembly, a 960-member presidential electoral body, unanimously reelected President Suharto to a second 5-year term on March 22, 1973.

In August 1975 a civil war broke out in the Portuguese colony on the island of Timor, the western half of which already was part of Indonesia. Indonesian troops intervened in the fighting. Indonesia formally incorporated the former Portuguese colony on July 17, 1976, making it the nation's 27th province, Loro Sae. However, guerrilla fighting against Indonesian troops continued into the 1980s.

Indonesia in 1976 became the fourth nation to own its own space satellite communications system. The satellites link 40 earth stations.

The U.S. Securities and Exchange Commission (SEC) charged in February 1977 that dozens of U.S. corporations had been shaken down for $1.11 million by the former head of Indonesia's government oil company. In April 1977 the official, Gen. Ibnu Sutowo, was arrested.

The first national election in six years was held on May 2, 1977. However, the government censored the topics that could be discussed, preventing corruption from becoming an issue. The ruling Golkar Party won 62% of the vote.

A national assembly reelected Suharto to a third 5-year term as president on March 22, 1978.

In October 1977 Amnesty International reported that Indonesia still was holding about 100,000

INDONESIA'S 27 PROVINCES (by island groups)

	AREA (sq. mi.)	CAPITAL
Borneo (Kalimantan) ..	208,286	
Central Kalimantan ..	—	Palangkaraya
East Kalimantan.....	—	Samarinda
South Kalimantan ...	—	Banjarmasin
West Kalimantan	—	Pontianak
Celebes (Sulawesi) ...	69,255	
Central Sulawesi ...	—	Palu
North Sulawesi......	—	Manado
South Sulawesi......	—	Ujungpandang
Southeast Sulawesi ..	—	Kendari
Java (Jawa)	48,763	
Central Jawa........	—	Semarang
East Jawa	—	Surabaja
Jakarta	—	Jakarta
Yogyakarta	—	Yogyakarta
West Jawa	—	Bandung
Lesser Sunda Islands (Nusa Tenggara) .	36,179	
Bali.................	—	Denpasar
East Nusa Tenggara .	—	Kupang, Timor
West Nusa Tenggara.	—	Mataram, Lombok
Loro Sae (East Timor)	—	Dili
Moluccas (Maluku) ...	28,766	Ambon
Sumatra (Sumatera) ..	165,000	
Aceh................	—	Banda Aceh
Bengkulu............	—	Bengkulu
Jambi..............	—	Jambi
Lampung...........	—	Tandjungkarang-Telukbetung
North Sumatera	—	Medan
Riau	—	Pekanbaru
South Sumatera	—	Palembang
West Sumatera	—	Padang
West New Guinea (Irian Jaya)	151,789	Jayapura

political prisoners, disputing a claim by the Indonesian government that only 30,000 remained in prison. From December 1977 through 1979 the government released 31,226 political prisoners.

Opposition to President Suharto's military government was aired in 1980 with publication of charges that he and other high officials enriched themselves with multimillion dollar kickbacks.

Galunggung volcano on Java began erupting on April 5, 1982. About 30,000 villagers were forced to abandon their homes as subsequent eruptions turned the region around the volcano into a wasteland. About 30 persons died.

A drought in the summer of 1982 hurt rice production, causing food shortages.

President Suharto visited the U.S. in October 1982, conferring with President Reagan.

Suharto was elected by the national assembly to a fourth 5-year term in March 1983.

Falling oil prices hurt Indonesia's economy in 1982–85, causing the government to cut back planned public-works projects.

Human rights organizations reported that 3,000 to 4,000 criminals had been killed in 1983-84 by death squads believed to be off-duty policemen.

Indonesia's fourth 5-year plan for 1984-1989 calls for moving 750,000 poor farm families from Java and other islands to Irian Jaya, the Indonesian half of the island of New Guinea. A government official described the program as one to "bring Irian Jaya from the Stone Age to the 20th century."

IRAN

Official Name: Islamic Republic of Iran.
Area: 636,296 square miles (1,648,000 sq. km.).
Population: 45,901,000.
Chief Cities: Teheran, capital, 4,530,223; Esfahan, 661,510; Mashdad, 667,770; Tabriz, 597,976.
Government: Islamic dictatorship.
Head of State: Ayatollah Ruhollah Khomeini (since 1979).
President: Hojatolislam Ali Khamenei (since 1981).
Prime Minister: Mir Hussein Moussavi (since 1981).
Parliament: *Majlis,* 270 members.
Flag: Stripes of green (*top*), white, and red; word "Allah" in red on white center stripe.
Main Languages: Iranian, Kurdish, Arabic, Turkic, English, French.
Chief Ethnic Groups: Iranian, Turk, Kurd, Arab, Armenian.
Main Religion: Islam (98%).
Leading Industries: Mining (petroleum, natural gas, coal, salt, chromite, lead, copper, iron ore); agriculture (sheep, cattle, goats, wheat, sugar beets, barley, rice, cotton, tea, tobacco); manufacturing (oil refining, steel, electrical equipment, cement, textiles, sugar, flour, furniture, building materials); fishing.
Foreign Trade: *Major exports*—petroleum, carpets and rugs, cotton textiles; *major imports*—machinery, iron and steel, pharmaceuticals and medicinal products, wheat.
Places of Interest: Elburz Mountains; Caspian shore resorts; gold-domed mosque in shrine city of Meshed; Mt. Damavaud; ruins of Persepolis and royal tombs; Sepah Mosque and Golestan Palace Museum in Teheran; Shiraz; Esfahan.

IRAN TODAY

About five times the size of California, Iran is an oil-rich nation in the Middle East wracked by revolution and war. It is ruled by radical-conservative Islamic religious leaders who use torture and execution against opponents.

The majority of people are very poor. Only about 1 in 4 can read and write.

Most of Iran is a plateau averaging 4,000 feet above sea level. The Elburz and Zagros mountains cover extensive areas. Large sections of the interior are desert. Rainfall is generally meager.

Iran is bordered on the north by the Soviet Union. Afghanistan and Pakistan lie to the east, and Iraq and Turkey to the west.

EARLY HISTORY

The early inhabitants of present-day Iran, the Elamites, developed a high degree of civilization by about 3100 B.C. Two Aryan tribes, the Medes and the Persians, settled in the area about 900 B.C. The Medes ruled what is now western Iran.

The powerful Persian ruler Cyrus (559–530 B.C.) brought the Medes under his control. He then conquered Babylonia, founding the Persian Empire that eventually encompassed Egypt and eastern Greece. Persian power was crushed in 331 B.C. by Alexander the Great. Alexander's empire crumbled after his death, and his successors battled for supremacy. Most of Persia went to Seleucus I, the Greek ruler of Syria who had been one of Alexander's generals. The Seleucid dynasty tried to follow the Persian pattern of government, but its hold was weak. Parthian rule succeeded the Seleucids. The Sassanian dynasty overthrew the Parthians in A.D. 224.

Arabs invaded Persia and crushed the Sassanian dynasty about 651. Islam became the dominant religion. Turkish invasions and settlement followed in the 900s. The land later fell to the Mongol invaders, Genghis Khan in the 1200s and Tamerlane in the 1300s.

Native Iranian rule was restored by the Safavid rulers (1502–1736). The dynasty reached its peak during the regime of Shah Abbas I (1587–1629).

A Turkish general, Nadir Shah, ruled in 1736–47, raiding and looting India.

The Zand dynasty (1750–94) restored order before being overthrown by Aga Mohammed Khan, whose Kajar dynasty lasted until 1925. Persia's borders shrank steadily. Land was lost to the Afghans, and in 1813 and 1828 Caucasian territories were taken over by Russia, which exploited the oil deposits.

In 1906 the shah approved formation of a parliament, or Majlis, and the constitution it enacted. In 1907 an Anglo-Russian pact divided Persia into spheres of influence, but the treaty was annulled after World War I.

MODERN EMPIRE OF IRAN

In 1921 a coup directed by army officer Reza Khan resulted in a military dictatorship. Four years later Reza Khan deposed the shah and adopted the title Reza Shah Pahlevi.

He undertook reforms in all aspects of Persian life, and in 1935 officially changed the country's name to Iran. In 1935 Teheran University was opened. In 1937 women were unveiled. In 1938 the first railroad was built.

The shah's friendly relations with Germany, however, led to the occupation of Iran by British and Russian troops in 1941. The shah abdicated in favor of his son, Mohammed Reza Pahlevi.

In 1945 the Soviets, who had occupied northern Iran, refused to evacuate their troops. But promised U.S. aid under the Truman Doctrine led to the withdrawal of the Soviet troops.

When militant nationalist Mohammed Mossadegh, leader of the extremist National Front, became premier in 1951, he promptly seized control of the Anglo-Iranian Oil Company. The British retaliated with a blockade.

With aid by the U.S., royalists overthrew Mossadegh in 1953, and the shah regained absolute power.

The shah announced on March 16, 1973, the nationalization of the oil industry.

The shah decreed Iran a one-party state on March 2, 1975, establishing the National Resurrection Party. The shah's secret police imprisoned, tortured, and killed his opponents.

Riots in Iran grew in intensity throughout 1978,

QUICK QUIZ: In which U.S. election did the loser in the popular vote become President? See page 358.

IRAN *(continued)*

organized by Muslim extremists who objected to the shah's efforts to modernize Iran.

After the U.S. advised him not to call out his army against the rebels, the shah flew to exile on Jan. 16, 1979. He died in Egypt in 1980.

FANATIC ISLAMIC STATE

The uprising against the shah had been directed from abroad by Ayatollah Ruhollah Khomeini, a Muslim religious leader who had been exiled by the shah 15 years earlier. Khomeini returned to Iran on Feb. 1, 1979. The shah's prime minister resigned on Feb. 11 and fled to exile. Terror swept Iran as Khomeini's militia arrested and executed hundreds of former officials and military officers. On March 30–31, 1979, a national referendum approved establishment of an Islamic republic.

Relations between the U.S. and Iran reached a crisis after President Carter permitted the exiled shah to enter the U.S. in 1979 for medical treatment. Iranian terrorists seized the U.S. embassy in Teheran on Nov. 4, 1979, holding over 50 Americans hostage. The Iranian government refused to negotiate release of the hostages, and a U.S. attempt to free them by military force failed in April 1980. The U.S. broke diplomatic relations with Iran on April 7, 1980. With the help of Algerian diplomats, the U.S. hostages were finally freed on Jan. 20, 1981.

Abol Hasan Bani-Sadr was elected as Iran's first president on Jan. 25, 1980.

Border clashes between Iran and Iraq escalated into a full-scale war on Sept. 22, 1980, with each inflicting severe damage to the other.

On June 21, 1981, Khomeini dismissed President Bani-Sadr, who fled into exile, replacing him with Mohammed Ali Rajai as president.

President Rajai and his prime minister were assassinated on Aug. 30, 1981.

Khomeini chose as the new president Hojatolislam Ali Khamenei, who was formally elected on Oct. 2, 1981.

Sadegh Ghotbzadeh, 46, Iran's foreign minister during the U.S. hostage crisis, was executed on Sept. 15, 1982, for trying to overthrow Khomeini.

Iranian exiles reported in 1984 that Khomeini's government had executed 10,231 persons in 1981-84 and imprisoned 100,000 political opponents.

The U.S. blamed Iran for supporting terrorists that bombed U.S. installations in Beirut, Lebanon, in 1983-84. In retaliation, the U.S. banned the export of any war materials to Iran.

U.S. Secretary of State George P. Shultz warned Iran in February 1985 that it runs the risk of military retaliation if any American hostages held by Khomeini's followers in Lebanon were killed.

Iranian President Khamenei escaped assassination on March 15, 1985, when a man exploded a bomb, killing himself and five other persons during a religious service.

A sister of President Khamenei fled to Iraq as a refugee in May 1985.

The stalemated Iraq-Iran war entered its sixth year in 1985. Khomeini declared that Iran would cut off all oil shipments in the Persian Gulf if Iraq attacked its oil fields. The U.S. warned Iran that it would use military force to keep the strategic waterway open.

IRAQ

Official Name: Republic of Iraq.
Area: 167,925 square miles (434,924 sq. km.).
Population: 15,825,000.
Chief Cities: Baghdad, capital, 1,490,759; Basra, 310,950; Mosul, 264,146; Kirkuk, 175,303; Najaf, 134,027; Hilla, 84,704.
Largest Metropolitan Area: Baghdad, 1,657,424.
Government: One-party socialist-military state.
President: Saddam Hussein (since 1979).
Legislature: *National Assembly,* 250 members.
Iraq Ambassador to U.S.: Nizar Hamdoon.
U.S. Ambassador to Iraq: David George Newton.
Flag: Red, white, and black stripes, with three green stars in center stripe.
Languages: Arabic (official), Kurdish.
Main Ethnic Groups: Arab (75%), Kurd (20%).
Chief Religion: Islam (95%).
Leading Industries: Mining (petroleum); agriculture (sheep, dates, wheat, barley, rice, cotton, cattle, goats, camels); food processing; manufacturing (textiles, cement, leather products).
Foreign Trade: *Major exports*—petroleum, dates, cement, wool; *major imports*—motor vehicles, sugar, textiles.
Places of Interest: Ruins of Babylon, Hanging Gardens, throne room of "writing on the wall," Lion of Babylon; Agarguf ruins; Arch of Ctesiphon. *In Baghdad:* Iraq Museum; mosques; tomb of Sitt Zubaidah.

IRAQ TODAY

A little larger than California, Iraq ranks among the leading oil-producing nations of the world, but its petroleum facilities were damaged in a war with Iran in 1980–83.

Most of the people are poor, and only about 4 out of 10 can read and write. The majority are farmers or nomadic herdsmen.

The leftist military government runs the country as a police state. Iraq broke diplomatic relations with the United States in 1967 because of U.S. aid to Israel in the Arab-Israeli war in June of that year. But the U.S. maintains a diplomatic mission at the Belgian embassy, and U.S. companies carry on foreign trade with Iraq.

The Tigris and Euphrates rivers flow across Iraq from northwest to southeast. They join to form the Shatt Al Arab that empties into the Persian Gulf.

The northern climate is temperate, but the plains suffer heat and strong northeasterly winds during the summer. Temperatures may reach 120° F. between May and October. Winters are damp, with average temperatures of 50° F.

ANCIENT MESOPOTAMIA

Archaeological excavations have established that cultures existed in this region, once known as Mesopotamia, for more than 10,000 years.

The written history of the area began about 4000 B.C. when the Sumerians established city-

states in southern Mesopotamia. In the 2300s B.C. Sumer was absorbed into a huge empire ruled by Sargon, king of Akkad. The area later became part of the Assyrian and Babylonian empires.

Arabs overran Mesopotamia in the 600s A.D. Baghdad was made the capital of the Abbasid caliphate in 762. The fifth caliph, Harun-al-Rashid, figured in the stories of *the Thousand and One Nights.*

Mongol conquerors devastated the country in 1258 and again in 1401. Baghdad was captured in 1534 by the Ottoman Turks, and Mesopotamia stayed under Turkish control until World War I.

KINGDOM OF IRAQ

During World War I, Britain, with the help of Hussein, the sharif of Mecca, gained control of the country, known since 1918 as Iraq.

The League of Nations in 1920 made Iraq a mandated territory under British administration. Britain arranged for Faisal I, the son of Hussein, to become king of Iraq. In 1932 the League of Nations mandate was ended, and Iraq joined the League as an independent nation.

Upon Faisal's death in 1933, he was succeeded by his son Ghazi, who was killed in an auto accident in 1939. The throne was inherited by Ghazi's three-year-old son Faisal II.

A pro-Axis government, briefly in power in 1941, collapsed under British military pressure.

Led by pro-Western statesman Nuri es-Said, Iraq in 1955 joined Turkey, Iran, Pakistan, and Britain in the Baghdad Pact defense treaty.

REPUBLIC OF IRAQ

On July 14, 1958, Gen. Abdul Karim Kassem overthrew the regime. He killed Nuri es-Said and young King Faisal II, establishing the Republic of Iraq. Kassem withdrew Iraq from the Baghdad Pact in 1959.

A military coup on Feb. 8, 1963, overthrew Kassem. He and many Iraqi communists were executed. The Arab Socialist Baath Party took control with Abdul Salam Arif as president. Iraq became a one-party military-socialist state.

In April 1966 Abdul Salam Arif died in a helicopter crash. He was succeeded as president by his elder brother, Abdul Rahman Arif.

President Arif, who was held responsible for Iraq's defeat in the 1967 war with Israel, was ousted by a bloodless military coup on July 17, 1968. The leader of the coup, former premier Ahmed Hassan al-Bakr, took over as president and formed a new government.

DEVELOPMENTS IN THE 1970s

Iraq joined other Arab nations in the October 1973 war against Israel and cut off oil shipments to the U.S. for several months.

Angered at not being given independence, the Kurdish minority in the Zagros Mountains began a rebellion in March 1974, receiving military support from Iran.

In an agreement with Iraq on March 5, 1975, Iran stopped supplying the Kurdish rebels, after which the revolt collapsed.

Iraq completed nationalizing its entire oil industry in December 1975.

The International League for Human Rights reported to the UN in 1977 that the Iraqi government was systematically destroying the Kurds. Refugees said thousands of Kurds were pressed into forced labor, clearing a strip 20 kilometers (12.4 miles) wide along the border facing Iran and Turkey.

Iraq's relations with the Soviet Union noticeably cooled after exposure in 1978 of a communist plot to overthrow the government. The government, which had been dependent on Soviet weapons for two decades, began buying arms from France and other Western nations.

The government began a $36 million project in 1978 to excavate and restore the ancient city of Babylon, which stands about 55 miles south of Baghdad. Archaeologists estimated the project would not be completed before the 1990s.

After 11 years as president, the 68-year-old Bakr resigned on July 16, 1979. He was succeeded by Gen. Saddam Hussein, 42.

Within two weeks of taking over as president, Hussein arrested scores of officials, charging them with plotting to overthrow him. A firing squad executed 21 of the plotters on Aug. 8, 1979, including five members of the Revolutionary Command Council. A special court also sentenced 33 others to prison for the coup attempt.

In the first national election in 20 years, on June 20, 1980, voters chose the 250 members of a new parliament from among 800 candidates approved by the country's only political party, the Arab Baath Socialist Party.

WAR WITH IRAN

Ayatollah Khomeini, ruler of neighboring Iran, called in 1980 for the overthrow of Hussein by the Shiite Muslims, who make up the majority of Iraq's population.

In retaliation, Hussein launched a full-scale war with Iran beginning on Sept. 22, 1980, as Iraq claimed control of the Shatt Al Arab waterway that previously had been shared with Iran.

Israeli warplanes bombed a nuclear reactor near Baghdad on June 7, 1981, claiming Iraq intended to use it to produce atomic bombs.

After initially invading Iran in 1980, Iraq withdrew its troops in June 1982. In turn, Iran invaded Iraq in July 1982.

When Iraq threatened in 1983 to use French Exocet missiles to destroy Iranian oil facilities, Iran warned it would retaliate by cutting off all shipping in the Persian Gulf.

Iraq's economy suffered in 1983 as Saudi Arabia and other Arab supporters cut aid in half.

To protect its oil deliveries from Iranian attacks in the Persian Gulf, Iraq contracted in 1984 for two pipelines at a cost of about $1.5 billion. One 540-mile pipeline would run through Jordan to the Gulf of Aqaba. The other 400-mile pipeline would go through Saudi Arabia to the Red Sea port of Yanbu. The pipelines, capable of carrying about 1.5 million barrels of oil per day, were scheduled for completion in 1986.

The U.S. and Iraq resumed diplomatic relations in November 1984 that had been broken in 1967.

As Iraq's war with Iran entered its sixth year in 1985, observers estimated that as many as 250,000 persons had died in the fighting.

QUICK QUIZ: When did Hurricane Agnes rake the U.S. East Coast? See page 308.

IRELAND

Official Name: Ireland (*Eire* in Gaelic).
Area: 27,136 square miles (70,283 sq. km.).
Population: 3,640,000.
Chief Cities: Dublin, capital, 525,360; Cork, 136,269.
Largest Metropolitan Area: Dublin, 650,153.
Government: Parliamentary republic.
Prime Minister: Garret FitzGerald (since 1982).
President: Patrick Hillery (since 1976).
Parliament: Seanad Eireann (Senate), 60 members; Dáil Eireann (House), 166 members.
U.S. Ambassador to Ireland: Margaret M. Heckler.
Irish Ambassador to U.S.: Tadhg O'Sullivan.
Flag: Green, white, and orange bars.
Official Languages: Irish (Gaelic) and English.
Leading Ethnic Group: Irish.
Main Religions: Roman Catholicism (94%), Anglicanism (4%).
Leading Industries: Manufacturing (electronics, brewing, distilling, food processing, textiles, paper, machinery, chemicals, vehicle assembly); agriculture (sheep, cattle, horses, hay, potatoes, turnips, sugar beets, barley, wheat, oats, rye); fishing; tourism.
Foreign Trade: Major exports—machinery, textiles, chemicals, meat, dairy products; major imports—machinery, iron and steel, textiles, petroleum.
Places of Interest: Blarney Castle near Cork; Great Rock of Cashel; Killarney lakes; River Shannon; Galway castles; Limerick; Waterford; Kennedy family home and memorial park at Dunganstown. In Dublin: Castle; St. Patrick's Cathedral; Daniel O'Connell Monument; Phoenix Park; Abbey Theatre.

IRELAND TODAY

Somewhat larger than the state of West Virginia, the Republic of Ireland covers five-sixths of the island of Ireland.

Ireland shares the island with Northern Ireland, which is part of Britain's United Kingdom.

The island of Ireland is separated from the island of Great Britain by the narrow Irish Sea.

Although industrialization proceeded rapidly in the 1960s–80s, about half the people live on farms or in small villages. Because it must import more than it can export, Ireland depends on income from tourism to make up the difference.

Coastal highlands and a central plain give a saucer shape to the island.

Mild winds from Europe and warm, damp air from the Gulf Stream combine to give the country a temperate climate.

Temperatures average 40° F. in the winter and 60° F. in the summer.

EARLY HISTORY

Prehistoric people lived in Ireland as early as 6000 B.C. They were conquered by Celtic tribes from Britain and Europe about 400 B.C.

St. Patrick brought Christianity in A.D. 432.

In the 700s to 1000s Norse Vikings established seaports in Ireland.

King Henry II of England forced Irish nobles to recognize his overlordship in 1171.

To stem rising rebellion after the Reformation in the 1500s, Britain gave confiscated Irish lands to pro-British Irish and English Protestants. In the 1700s Irish Catholics lost all legal rights.

In 1801 the Act of Union created the United Kingdom of Great Britain and Ireland.

In the 1840s the country was devastated by a great potato famine. A million Irish died in five years, and 1.6 million emigrated.

Sinn Fein, the political arm of the secret Irish Republican Army (IRA), instigated the 1916 Easter Rebellion in Dublin. In the 1919 general elections Sinn Fein won enough seats to set up its own parliament (Dáil Eireann) in Dublin, while the IRA waged guerrilla warfare against Britain.

The Irish Free State was established in 1922 as a British dominion.

Eamon De Valera led Sinn Fein extremists in a fight for full independence. In 1937 a new constitution changed the country's name to *Eire*. De Valera was named prime minister.

INDEPENDENT REPUBLIC OF IRELAND

John A. Costello, head of the Fine Gael Party, became prime minister in 1948. On April 18, 1949, he declared Ireland an independent republic.

De Valera, of the Fianna Fáil Party, returned to power as prime minister in 1951–54 and 1957–59. He then served as president in 1959–73.

In parliamentary elections on Feb. 28, 1973, a coalition of the Fine Gael and smaller Labor Party won a narrow victory. Liam Cosgrave of the Fine Gael became prime minister.

Cosgrave acknowledged officially for the first time in March 1974 that Northern Ireland was part of Britain's United Kingdom.

The Fianna Fail Party won a surprise victory in a national election on June 16, 1977, taking 84 seats in the 148-member Dáil Eireann. John Lynch, head of Fianna Fail, became prime minister in July. He had promised tax cuts and called for the British to leave Northern Ireland.

Charles J. Haughey, 54, succeeded Lynch as prime minister and head of Fianna Fail on Dec. 11, 1979.

In an election on June 11, 1981, none of the parties won a majority.

Garret FitzGerald, head of the Fine Gael Party, became prime minister on June 30, 1981, with the aid of minor parties.

Haughey again became prime minister after his party won a narrow victory in a general election on Feb. 18, 1982. However, the economy grew worse with unemployment rising to 12% and inflation to 20%.

After a national election on Nov. 24, 1982, FitzGerald again became prime minister, heading a coalition government with the small Labor Party. He established an austerity budget for 1983 that cut government spending and raised taxes.

The discovery of oil off Ireland's southeast coast, announced on Aug. 2, 1983, spurred hopes that the country, which spends $1 billion each year on oil imports, might become self-sufficient in oil by the 1990s.

As Ireland's economy continued to slide, unemployment rose to a rate of about 17% in 1984–85—the highest in Western Europe.

See also *Northern Ireland*, page 510.

ISRAEL

Official Name: State of Israel.
Area: 10,715 sq. mi. (27,752 sq. km.).
Population: 4,318,000.
Chief Cities: Jerusalem, capital, 398,200; Tel Aviv-Yafo (Jaffa), 336,300; Haifa, 229,300; Ramat Gan, 120,400; Bat Yam, 130,100; Holon, 128,400.
Largest Metropolitan Area: Tel Aviv-Yafo, 1,260,200.
Government: Parliamentary republic.
Prime Minister: Shimon Peres (since 1984).
President: Chaim Herzog (since 1983).
Parliament: *Knesset,* 120 members.
U.S. Ambassador to Israel: Thomas R. Pickering.
Israeli Ambassador to U.S.: Meir Rosenne.
Flag: White field bearing blue Star of David between two blue stripes.
Languages: Hebrew, Arabic, English.
Main Ethnic Groups: Jewish (85%), Arab (15%).
Leading Religions: Judaism (official–85%), Islam, Christianity.
Leading Industries: Manufacturing (food processing, textiles, clothing, aircraft, chemicals, metal products, vehicle assembly, machinery, cut diamonds, cement); agriculture (poultry, dairy products, citrus fruits, grapes, wheat, sugar beets, cotton, olives, figs, vegetables); mining (potash, petroleum, phosphates, bromine, natural gas); construction.
Foreign Trade: *Major exports*—diamonds, citrus fruits, textile yarn and thread, potassic fertilizers; *major imports*—diamonds, crude petroleum, ships and boats, meat, corn.
Places of Interest: Many Old and New Testament sites; ruins of Masada on Dead Sea; Mt. Carmel in Haifa; Nazareth; Bethlehem; Capernaum; Sodom; King Solomon's copper mines. *In Jerusalem:* Wailing Wall; Dome of the Rock; Church of the Holy Sepulchre.

ISRAEL TODAY

About the size of New Jersey, Israel is a small Middle Eastern nation on the east coast of the Mediterranean Sea. It is the only nation in the world in which Judaism is the official religion. Most of the people are or descend from Jewish immigrants to their biblical homeland.

Surrounded by Arab nations that wanted to destroy the Jewish state, Israel fought four wars for its existence since declaring its independence in 1948. The nation remained continually on the alert against attack from its neighbors, spending two-thirds of its national budget for military preparedness.

The nation has few natural resources, and much of the land is desert. However, with hard work and over $2 billion annual aid from the U.S., Israel has developed an industrial economy.

Israeli pioneers have reclaimed large desert areas for farming and citrus-fruit orchards.

Israel's people enjoy a much higher standard of living than Arabs in neighboring countries. Most Israelis live in cities and make their living from manufacturing or service industries.

The northern part of the country is hilly, with valleys and plains. South of this region is a narrow coastal plain. In the south is the Negev Desert.

The climate ranges from moderate in the northern part of the country to very hot in the desert. Rain falls from September to May.

Lebanon lies to the north, Syria to the northeast, Jordan to the east, and Egypt to the southwest.

EARLY HISTORY

About 1000 B.C. scattered Hebrew tribes in Israel (then called Canaan) banded together under King Saul to fight invading Philistines.

Political unity was achieved under King David, who established the capital at Jerusalem. His son and successor, Solomon, built the Temple and made Jerusalem the cultural and religious capital of Israel about 961–922 B.C.

After Solomon's death the kingdom split into two quarrelsome parts, Judah and Israel. Both soon fell to Assyrian conquerors, who enslaved about 27,000 Israelites in 722 B.C.

In Judah the Assyrians were followed by Egyptians and Babylonians, who exiled the ruling class of Judah in 587–582 B.C. Although the exiles were soon allowed to return, the area was repeatedly overrun by conquerors—Persians, Greeks, Seleucids, Romans, Byzantines, Arabs, Crusaders, and Turks. In 1516 the region became part of the Ottoman Empire.

In the 1890s Zionism, an international movement, was founded by Theodor Herzl to restore Palestine to the Jews. Many European Jews left their homes to settle in Palestine.

In World War I the region fell into British hands. Anxious for Jewish help, England in 1917 issued the Balfour Declaration, promising a national home for the Jews.

As Jews fled to Israel in the 1930s and 1940s to escape Nazi German persecution, an Arab rebellion caused Britain to limit Zionist immigration during and after World War II.

INDEPENDENCE AND ARAB WARS

In 1947 the United Nations agreed to divide Palestine into two independent states, one Jewish and one Arab, with Jerusalem serving as an international or neutral zone.

The plan was accepted by the Jews. On May 14, 1948, they proclaimed Israel's independence when the British withdrew.

On the same day Egypt, Iraq, Jordan, Lebanon, Syria, and Saudi Arabia attacked Israel. U.S. aid helped preserve Israel's independence. Cease-fires were concluded in 1949.

In 1956 an Egyptian-Syrian-Jordanian military alliance threatened Israel with hostile encirclement. At the same time Egypt's expropriation of the Suez Canal alienated Britain and France.

Israel attacked Egypt on Oct. 29, 1956. Two days later an Anglo-French attack knocked out the Egyptian air force. Israeli forces quickly overran Egypt's Sinai region.

Combined pressure from the U.S. and the Soviet Union in the UN caused Israel's eventual withdrawal. A UN emergency force was stationed along the Egyptian-Israeli border.

QUICK QUIZ: Which U.S. President changed his name twice? See page 357.

ISRAEL (continued)

Israeli armed forces launched air and land strikes on Egypt, Jordan, and Syria on June 5, 1967.

In six days Israeli forces captured Jerusalem, the Sinai peninsula, the West Bank of the Jordan, the Gaza strip, and Golan Heights of Syria. A cease-fire began on June 11, 1967.

About 2 million Arabs displaced from their homes by the Arab-Israeli wars lived in refugee camps in Arab countries. In 1964 the militant Palestine Liberation Organization (PLO) was formed by the refugees to create an armed force that would compel Israel to give up land for an independent Arab Palestine. In the years that followed, the PLO carried out terrorist attacks on Israel, and Israelis retaliated with raids on PLO installations in Lebanon and elsewhere.

Egypt and Syria launched a fourth war on Israel on two fronts on Oct. 6, 1973, during Yom Kippur. Other Arab nations soon joined the war.

After heavy fighting, Israeli troops were advancing in Syria and Egypt when the UN Security Council ordered a cease-fire on October 22. Three days later the UN sent a peacekeeping force to the Middle East to prevent further fighting.

The war resulted in a worldwide fuel crisis when Arab oil-producing nations cut off oil shipments for six months to the United States, Japan, and other nations that had aided Israel.

PEACE WITH EGYPT

In a parliamentary election on May 17, 1977, the right-wing Likud Party won an upset victory, capturing a plurality of 41 seats to Labor's 34.

Menachem Begin, 63, leader of the Likud Party, became prime minister on June 21, 1977. Considered one of Israel's founding fathers, Begin had headed the guerrilla army called Irgun Zvai Leumi that in the 1940s killed many British soldiers in an effort to drive Britain out of Palestine.

Events took a dramatic turn on Nov. 19–21, 1977, when Egyptian President Sadat flew to Israel to address the Israeli parliament at the invitation of Prime Minister Begin, breaking the 30-year deadlock in which Arab leaders had refused to meet face to face with Israeli officials.

Begin returned Sadat's visit in December 1977, becoming the first Israeli prime minister to travel to Egypt. Formal peace negotiations began in January 1978.

Fears of a new Mideast war rose in March 1978 when Israel invaded southern Lebanon to destroy Palestinian terrorists. After the UN sent a 4,000-man peacekeeping force to the area, Israeli troops withdrew from Lebanon by June.

Culminating more than a year of negotiations spearheaded by U.S. President Carter, Israel and Egypt signed a peace treaty in Washington, D.C., on March 26, 1979. Upon ratification, the treaty became effective on April 25, 1979.

Israel began withdrawing from Egypt's Sinai peninsula on May 25, 1979, turning over the town of El Arish to Egyptian control. The first Israeli ships were allowed to sail through Egypt's Suez Canal on May 29.

ISRAEL IN THE 1980s

Israel continued steps toward absorbing former Jordanian territories on the West Bank of the Jordan River, establishing new settlements there in

ISRAEL'S PRIME MINISTERS

1948–53	David Ben-Gurion	Mapai Workers' Party
1953–55	Moshe Sharrett	Mapai Workers' Party
1955–63	David Ben-Gurion	Mapai Workers' Party
1963–69	Levi Eshkol	Mapai Workers' Party
1969–74	Golda Meir	Labor Party
1974–77	Yitzhak Rabin	Labor Party
1977	Shimon Peres*	Labor Party
1977–83	Menachem Begin	Likud Party
1983–84	Yitzhak Shamir	Herut Party
1984–	Shimon Peres	Labor Party

*Acting prime minister.

disregard of protests from Arab nations, the UN, and the U.S. Israel and Egypt restored formal diplomatic relations on Feb. 26, 1980.

The Israeli parliament on July 30, 1980, formally made the Arab eastern part of Jerusalem part of the nation's capital.

Israel warplanes on June 7, 1981, destroyed a nuclear plant in Iraq, claiming it was going to be used to produce atomic weapons.

Israel's parliament on Dec. 14, 1981, formally annexed the Golan Heights area taken from Syria in 1967.

However, Israel made good on its peace treaty obligations by returning the Sinai region to Egypt on April 25, 1982, even though Israeli troops had to forcibly eject thousands of Israeli settlers from the area. An 11-nation 3,000-man military force, about half from the U.S., took up peacekeeping positions along the new Sinai border. The U.S. also completed two new $1.1-billion air bases for Israel in the Negev desert to compensate for facilities given up in the Sinai.

Israeli troops invaded Lebanon on June 6, 1982, to end use of that country as a PLO military base. In fierce battles, Israel quickly defeated the PLO and the Syrian occupation army. The world was horrified in September 1982 by the massacre of more than 700 Palestinians in Israeli-occupied Beirut. Defense Minister Ariel Sharon and three generals were forced to resign. Israel withdrew its troops to southern Lebanon on Sept. 3, 1983, and completely evacuated Lebanon in June 1985.

Chaim Herzog, 64, of the Labor Party began a 5-year term as the nation's president on May 5, 1983, after being elected by parliament to the largely ceremonial office.

The ailing 70-year-old Begin resigned on Sept. 15, 1983. Yitzhak Shamir, 68, foreign minister under Begin, became prime minister.

In a parliamentary election on July 23, 1984, the 120 seats were divided among 15 political parties. Neither major party won a majority, Labor taking 44 seats and the Likud bloc 41.

After seven weeks of political negotiations, the rival parties agreed on a compromise: Shimon Peres, head of the Labor Party, would serve as prime minister for 25 months with Shamir, head of the Likud bloc, as deputy prime minister. For the next 25 months the two leaders would reverse offices. Peres was sworn in as prime minister on Sept. 14, 1984.

The U.S. and Israel signed a trade pact on April 22, 1985, that will end all tariffs between the two nations by 1996.

Israel freed 1,150 Arab guerrillas on May 20, 1985, in exchange for three Israeli soldiers held prisoner by Muslims in Lebanon.

ITALY

Official Name: Italian Republic.
Area: 116,304 square miles (301,225 sq. km).
Population: 57,255,000.
Chief Cities: Roma (Rome), capital, 2,914,042; Milano (Milan), 1,666,354; Napoli (Naples), 1,221,295; Torino (Turin), 1,151,974; Genova (Genoa), 778,559.
Government: Parliamentary republic.
Prime Minister: Bettino Craxi (since 1983).
President: Francesco Cossiga (since 1985).
Parliament: *Senate,* 322 members; *Chamber of Deputies,* 630 members.
U.S. Ambassador to Italy: Maxwell M. Rabb.
Italian Ambassador to U.S.: Rinaldo Petrignani.
Flag: Green, white, and red bars.
Official Language: Italian.
Main Ethnic Group: Italian.
Major Religion: Roman Catholicism (99%).
Leading Industries: Manufacturing (steel, automobiles, chemicals, electricity, office machines, electronic equipment, appliances, machinery, clothing, shoes, publishing); food processing; tourism; agriculture (sheep, goats, cattle, wheat, potatoes, corn, rice, grapes, olives, barley, oats, tobacco, fruits, vegetables); mining (natural gas, petroleum, mercury, sulfur, marble, asbestos, bauxite).
Foreign Trade: *Major exports*—automobiles, petroleum products, clothing, shoes, office machines, citrus fruits, vegetables; *major imports*—petroleum, machinery, food, scrap iron and steel, coal, cotton.
Places of Interest: Renaissance art galleries in Florence; Isle of Capri; St. Mark's Square in Venice; La Scala opera house in Milan; Adriatic coast resorts; Dolomite winter-sports at Trentino; Naples; Genoa; Sicily; Sardinia. *In Rome:* St. Peter's Basilica; Vatican; Sistine Chapel; Colosseum; Pantheon.

ITALY TODAY

About the size of Florida and Georgia combined, Italy has few natural resources. Lack of such mineral resources as iron ore, coal, and petroleum has handicapped Italy's industrial growth. However, it is among the world's leading producers of cement, electricity, natural gas, and steel.

Almost a third of Italy is mountainous and unable to be farmed. This along with backward farming methods combine to limit food production, making Italy dependent on imports to feed its people.

Italy's government lacks stability because no party has a majority of seats in the parliament. The conservative Christian Democrats control only a few more seats than the Communist Party.

In the 1970s–1980s leftist and rightist terrorist groups defied government authority with thousands of kidnappings, bombings, and killings.

Only the Po River valley, the coastal plains, and lowland relieve the mountainous landscape of Italy. Alpine ranges in the north include the Maritime, Graian, Pennine, Bergamasque, Dolomites, and Carnic mountains. Below them lies the great fertile basin of the Po Valley, Italy's agricultural and industrial core.

From the valley's lower limits rise the rugged Apennine chain. It runs down the length of the peninsula and leaps the Strait of Messina to cover much of northern Sicily.

Southern Italy and Sicily are in the midst of an earthquake belt that has given rise to Europe's three best-known active volcanoes; Vesuvius (4,190 feet), Etna (10,958 feet), and Stromboli (3,308 feet).

Italy's largest and most famous lakes—Maggiore, Como, and Garda—are all located in the Alps. The country's most important rivers are the Po and the Adige in the north, and the Arno and the Tiber in the central region.

EARLY HISTORY

The earliest known settlers—Latins, Sabines, Umbrians, and Ligurians—took over large areas in the northern part of the peninsula. They were displaced in the 800s B.C. by the Etruscans. Greeks and Phoenicians began their expansion into Sicily and the southern part of the peninsula about the 700s B.C.

Rome, the home of the Latins, lay between the Etruscan and Greek settlements. The Roman republic annexed the Etruscan kingdom in the 400s B.C. and united most of Italy by 270 B.C.

The Punic Wars (264–146 B.C.) between Rome and Carthage ended with Carthage destroyed and Rome the dominant power in the Mediterranean region. During the next century the Romans expanded into Gaul (France) and Britain.

ROMAN EMPIRE

In 27 B.C. Rome became an empire with Augustus as its first emperor. Early in the 300s A.D. Emperor Constantine accepted Christianity, and churches spread throughout Italy and all of the Roman Empire. At the same time, Constantine moved the imperial capital to Constantinople (now Istanbul).

Rome subsequently declined, and fell in 476 to German tribes.

The Ostrogoths and Lombards occupied the peninsula in the 500s, but in 774 their kingdom was absorbed by the Frankish empire headed by Charlemagne. During the 900s the powerful German king Otto I extended his rule into the Italian peninsula. In 962 he was crowned emperor of the Holy Roman Empire by the pope.

ITALIAN CITY-STATES

From the 900s to the 1300s the Italian city-states, the popes, and the Holy Roman emperors vied for power. Towns were divided and most noble families backed one of the two opposition parties: the papal Guelphs and the imperial Ghibellines. After the 1200s the Italian cities of Venice, Bologna, and Florence emerged as autonomous centers of political power and of learning. By the 1500s the Italian Renaissance had breathed new life into European art and learning.

Invasions by France, Spain, and Austria during the 1500s and 1600s divided the Italian states and brought most of them under foreign rule. In the early 1800s Austria became the dominant power in

QUICK QUIZ: Which U.S. Vice President resigned after conviction for income-tax evasion? See page 309.

ITALY (continued)

the Italian peninsula. Sporadic attempts to drive out the Austrians were effectively checked. Failing to achieve their goals in the revolutions of 1848 and 1849, nationalist leaders such as Giuseppe Garibaldi and Giuseppe Mazzini turned for help to Piedmont, the only Italian state to gain a liberal constitution, and to its able prime minister, Count Camillo Cavour. With the aid of France, Piedmont drove out the Austrians in 1859.

INDEPENDENT KINGDOM AND FASCIST RULE

Cavour succeeded in uniting most of the Italian states in the Kingdom of Italy, proclaimed on March 17, 1861, under the rule of Victor Emmanuel II of Savoy. The entire Italian peninsula was unified by 1870 with Rome as the capital.

Although at first neutral in World War I, promises of territories and concessions induced Italy to enter the war on the Allied side.

Fascist leader Benito Mussolini seized control in 1923. His dictatorship soon controlled all aspects of Italian life. Mussolini set out to assert Italy's power by the conquest of Ethiopia in 1935–36 and by annexing Albania in 1939.

Italy entered World War II on the side of Germany on June 11, 1940. Italian defeats aroused popular discontent with the fascist regime. In July 1943 King Victor Emmanuel III ordered Mussolini's arrest. The new government concluded an armistice with the Allies, who had already begun to invade Sicily. But German forces took control of northern and central Italy. The Allies entered Rome on June 4, 1944. Mussolini was executed by Italian partisans in April 1945.

A formal peace treaty was signed between Italy and the Allies on Feb. 10, 1947.

ITALIAN REPUBLIC

A popular referendum on June 2, 1946, ended Italy's monarchy. The Italian Republic officially came into being on Jan. 1, 1948. Alcide de Gasperi of the Christian Democratic Party headed Italy's government in 1945–53.

Italy and Yugoslavia agreed on a draft treaty on Oct. 1, 1975, bringing final settlement of their 30-year Trieste dispute. The treaty formally gave the area south of Trieste to Yugoslavia.

The wave of terror by which the anarchist Red Brigades sought to disrupt Italy reached a peak in 1978 with the kidnapping and murder of former Prime Minister Aldo Moro.

Giovanni Leone, who had served as Italy's president since 1971, resigned on June 15, 1978, after newspaper charges of tax fraud in relation to $1.6 million in bribes allegedly paid by the U.S. Lockheed corporation to Italian officials.

Socialist Alessandro Pertini, 81, who was jailed for 11 years by Mussolini, was chosen president by a special electoral assembly on July 8, 1978.

New parliamentary elections were held June 3–4, 1979. Christian Democrats retained their plurality in the 630-seat lower house, losing only 1 seat and holding 262.

ITALY IN THE 1980s

In one of the worst terrorist incidents neofascists killed 84 persons in the bombing of the railway station in Bologna on Aug. 2, 1980.

ITALY'S PRIME MINISTERS SINCE 1945

1945–53	Alcide de Gasperi	1968–70	Mariano Rumor
1953–54	Giuseppe Pella	1970–72	Emilio Colombo
1954–55	Mario Scelba	1972–73	Giulio Andreotti
1955–57	Antonio Segni	1973–74	Mariano Rumor
1957–58	Adone Zoli	1974–76	Aldo Moro
1958–59	Amintore Fanfani	1976–79	Giulio Andreotti
1959–60	Antonio Segni	1979–80	Francesco Cossiga
1960–63	Amintore Fanfani	1980–81	Arnaldo Forlani
1963–64	Giovanni Leone	1981–82	Giovanni Spadolini
1964–68	Aldo Moro	1982–83	Amintore Fanfani
1968	Giovanni Leone	1983–	Bettino Craxi

After 13 years of work and an expenditure of about $375 million, a 9-mile subway line was opened in Rome in Feb. 16, 1980, designed to serve commuters from southeastern suburbs.

Prime Minister Francesco Cossiga survived a vote of confidence in July 1980 after he had been accused of aiding the son of a fellow legislator to escape from arrest as a terrorist. But on Sept. 27 he was defeated and forced to resign when he lost by one vote on an austerity program that had sought to raise taxes.

Arnaldo Forlani, president of the Christian Democratic Party, was invited by President Pertini on Oct. 2, 1980, to become prime minister.

A major earthquake struck southern Italy on Nov. 23–24, 1980, destroying 133 towns and villages, killing more than 3,000 persons.

Revelation in 1981 that many high government officials belonged to an illegal secret Masonic lodge engaged in criminal activities caused Prime Minister Forlani to resign on May 26.

After a month-long government crisis, Giovanni Spadolini, 56, head of the small Republican Party, became prime minister with a coalition cabinet on June 28, 1981. He was the first non-Christian Democrat to hold the office since Italy became a republic.

Spadolini announced a rigorous economic program, calling for $8 billion cuts in spending for social programs and aid to local governments.

Italy's Marxist Red Brigade terrorists kidnapped U.S. Brig. Gen. James L. Dozier on Dec. 17, 1981, in Verona. Forty-two days later he was rescued unhurt by police who stormed a Red Bridgade hideaway in Padua on Jan. 28, 1982. Seventeen of the kidnappers were sentenced to jail terms of 2 to 27 years.

Spadolini resigned in November 1982 when he lost the support of socialists in parliament.

Christian Democrat Amintore Fanfani, 74, who had headed the government in the 1950s–1960s, became prime minister in December 1982.

In a general election on June 26–27, the nation's leading political party, the Christian Democrats, suffered a crushing defeat as its share of parliamentary votes fell from 38.3% to 32.9%. The communist share fell slightly to 29.9, while socialists made substantial gains, rising from 9.8% to 11.4%.

Bettino Craxi, 49, became Italy's first socialist prime minister on Aug. 4, 1983, heading a five-party coalition cabinet that included the Christian Democrats. Craxi sought to cut government spending in an effort to improve Italy's economy, which in 1983 had 10% unemployment and an inflation rate of nearly 16%.

Italian police cracked down on the Mafia in

October 1984, arresting hundreds of criminals after a Mafia leader revealed inner workings of the crime organization to investigators.

After 18 years of negotiations, Italy and the Vatican ratified a concordat on June 3, 1985, that ended the status of Roman Catholicism as Italy's official religion while continuing to recognize Vatican City as a sovereign state.

Fráncesco Cossiga, 56, a Christian Democrat, was elected to a 7-year term as Italy's president by a special electoral assembly on June 24, 1985.

ITALY'S SEMIAUTONOMOUS ISLANDS

SARDINIA

Area: 9,194 square miles (23,812 sq. km.)
Population: 1,700,000.
Capital: Cagliari, 236,931.

About the size of New Hampshire, Sardinia is the second-largest island in the Mediterranean after Sicily. It lies about 100 miles west of Italy. It is separated only by a narrow strait from the French island of Corsica to the north.

Thousands of stone monuments built by prehistoric Stone Age people dot the countryside.

In about the 800s B.C. Phoenicians established trading colonies on the coast. They were followed by Carthaginians, Romans, Vandals, and the Greek Byzantine Empire.

In the 1000s A.D. Arab rulers of Spain took control of the island. The Italian city-states of Pisa and Genoa contended for mastery of the island in the 1100s and 1200s. In the 1300s it passed to rule by Spain. In 1718 it was awarded to the rulers of Savoy in northern Italy, who became kings of Sardinia until 1861, when they became rulers of Italy. In 1948 Sardinia was granted semiautonomous status.

SICILY

Area: 9,817 square miles (25,426 sq. km.).
Population: 5,100,000.
Chief Cities: Palermo, capital, 662,567; Catania, 398,642; Messina, 261,332; Siracusa (Syracuse), 118,025.

The largest island in the Mediterranean Sea, Sicily has been a stepping-stone between Italy and Africa throughout its history.

The island lies southwest of the toe of Italy's boot, separated from the mainland by the 2- to 10-mile-wide Strait of Messina.

Peoples called the Sicani and Siculi lived on the island in prehistoric times. Greeks began colonies in the 700s B.C., making Syracuse a major center. Carthage won control in the 300s B.C.

The Romans took Sicily in 211 B.C., making it their first overseas province. It fell to the Byzantine Empire in A.D. 535. Arabs from Africa conquered Sicily in the 800s. Normans under Roger I captured Sicily in the 1000s. It came under the rule of German kings in the 1100s and was the seat of the Holy Roman Empire under Frederick II in 1215–1250. French, Spanish, Austrian, and Italian rulers contended for Sicily for the next 600 years.

In 1861 Sicily became part of the new Kingdom of Italy. The island was granted semiautonomous status on May 15, 1946.

IVORY COAST

Official Name: Republic of the Ivory Coast.
Area: 124,504 square miles (322,463 sq. km.).
Population: 10,287,000.
Capital: Yamoussoukro.
Largest City: Abidjan, 282,000.
Government: One-party republic.
President: Félix Houphouët-Boigny (since 1960).
National Assembly: 147 members.
U.S. Ambassador to Ivory Coast: Robert H. Miller.
Ivory Coast Ambassador to U.S.: Rene Anamy.
Flag: Tricolor of orange, white, and green bars.
Languages: French (official), Baoulé, Dioula, Mandingo, Mande.
Main Ethnic Group: Black.
Religions: Animism (64%), Islam (24%), Christianity (12%).
Leading Industries: Agriculture (coffee, cocoa, cotton, bananas, pineapples, coconuts, rubber, sugar); forestry and lumbering; food processing; tourism; manufacturing (textiles, shoes, consumer products); mining (petroleum, diamonds, iron ore).
Foreign Trade: *Major exports*—cocoa, coffee, petroleum, wood, palm oil, cotton, pineapples, sugar; *major imports*—cotton fabrics, automobiles, tractors.
Places of Interest: Abidjan plateau; Ebrié lagoon; Banco National Park; Grand Bassam; Dabou; Bingerville; Bouaké; beach resorts.

IVORY COAST TODAY

A little larger than New Mexico, the Ivory Coast is a West African country with many natural resources. Ivorians enjoy a standard of living somewhat higher than those of their neighbors.

Benefiting from a stable government since becoming independent in 1960, Ivory Coast has used foreign aid and loans to diversify its agriculture so that coffee, cocoa, and wood each provide a major share of export income.

The country's valuable resources include petroleum, iron ore, and timber.

From the coast the land slopes gradually to a height of about 1,400 feet in the north. The narrow 340-mile coastline—flat and sandy in the east—becomes more indented and rocky in the west. Beyond the coast is a vast forest region occupying nearly one-third of the country. In the northwest mountain ranges reach 5,000 feet.

The coastal region has a tropical climate with year-round temperatures of 73° to 80° F. Annual rainfall of 80 to 120 inches falls mostly from mid-May to mid-July.

Liberia and Guinea lie to the west, Mali and BurkinaFaso to the north, and Ghana to the east.

EARLY HISTORY

Before its organization as a French colony, the area that is now the Ivory Coast had no political or cultural unity. Several traditional kingdoms existed in parts of the country, while in others politi-

QUICK QUIZ: Who was the first former U.S. President elected to the U.S. Senate? See page 356.

IVORY COAST *(continued)*

cal organization rarely exceeded the village level.

French explorers reached the region in 1483, beginning the lucrative ivory trade from which the area later derived its name.

French missionaries, landing at Assinie in 1687, were the first white settlers. The settlement was soon abandoned, however, and the Ivory Coast remained relatively free of European influence until the 1800s, thus avoiding being drawn into the slave trade.

French interest was reasserted in 1842 with the establishment of a protectorate over the coastal area. Thereafter, mostly as a result of private initiative, French influence was carried to the interior.

In 1893 the territory was declared a colony. Treaties with local chieftains strengthened France's hold, but major military action was necessary to establish effective control.

Complete French control of the Ivory Coast was finally achieved in 1917.

The French began to develop the country in the 1920s. Yet the colonial administration, based on government by decree, was little changed until the creation of the French Union in 1946. At that time some political rights were extended to native Africans.

Over the next 10 years the Parti Démocratique de Côte d'Ivoire (PDCI), under the leadership of Félix Houphouët-Boigny, emerged as the dominant political force. Most of its opposition had been eliminated by 1956, the year internal autonomy was granted.

INDEPENDENCE

The Ivory Coast became an autonomous state within the French Community in 1958. Two years later, on Aug. 7, 1960, it proclaimed its independence as a republic.

Houphouët-Boigny became president after winning 98% of the votes in an election in November 1960. He was reelected in 1965, 1970, 1975, and 1980.

Since independence the economic development of the nation has proceeded rapidly, spurred in large part by the unusually liberal terms offered to foreign investors. The government of Ivory Coast has maintained strong ties with France, the U.S., and West Germany.

In 1972 Ivory Coast was among seven French-speaking states that set up a West African Economic Community (CEAO) to promote trade among its members.

France's President Giscard d'Estaing visited in 1978, praising the country for having "proved it is possible to escape from the curse of underdevelopment in the framework of a free economy."

Production of petroleum began in 1980 from fields discovered in 1978–80. By 1983 Ivory Coast became an oil-exporting nation.

In a step toward democracy, Ivory Coast held its first national assembly election with a choice of candidates in November 1980.

The government announced in March 1983 that the nation's capital would be moved from Abidjan to the inland city Yamoussoukro, the birthplace of President Houphouët-Boigny.

Drought and falling cocoa and coffee prices hurt the nation's economy in 1982–85.

JAMAICA

Official Name: Jamaica.
Area: 4,244 square miles (10,991 sq. km.).
Populaton: 2,689,000.
Capital: Kingston, 111,879.
Government: Parliamentary democracy.
Prime Minister: Edward P. G. Seaga (since 1980).
Chief of State: Governor-general Florizel Glasspole (appointed in 1973).
Parliament: *Senate,* 21 members; *House of Representatives,* 60 members.
U.S. Ambassador to Jamaica: William A. Hewitt.
Jamaican Ambassador to U.S.: Keith Johnson.
Flag: Gold cross with green field in top and bottom quarters; black to left and right.
Official Language: English.
Main Ethnic Groups: Black (76%), mulatto (15%).
Leading Religions: Anglicanism (20%), Baptist (19%), Church of God (12%), Roman Catholicism (7%).
Leading Industries: Agriculture (sugarcane, bananas, cattle, hogs, poultry, cocoa, coconuts, fruits, vegetables); mining (bauxite, gypsum); tourism; manufacturing and processing (alumina, rum, molasses, cement, chemicals, petroleum products, consumer products); fishing.
Foreign Trade: *Major exports*—alumina, bauxite, sugar, bananas; *major imports*—crude petroleum, automobiles.
Places of Interest: Kingston; Port Royal; Montego Bay; Ocho Rios resort; Negril Beach; Port Antonio; Royal Botanical Gardens at Hope.

JAMAICA TODAY

About the size of Connecticut, Jamaica is the world's second-largest producer of bauxite (aluminum ore).

The mining of bauxite, the processing of alumina, sugar, and tourism support the economy of the British Commonwealth nation.

Sugar and other agricultural products for many years provided the bulk of the island's income, but today farm products account for less than a fifth of Jamaica's exports. The decreasing importance of agriculture brought many families to the cities, causing serious unemployment.

The island of Jamaica lies in the Caribbean, about 90 miles south of Cuba. A limestone-based plateau, its average elevation is about 1,500 feet. Alluvial coastal deposits surround a mountainous interior dominated in the east by the Blue Mountains, which rise to 7,402 feet.

EARLY HISTORY

Jamaica was discovered by Columbus in 1494. It was settled 15 years later by Spaniards, who introduced the cultivation of sugarcane. The native Arawaks, unaccustomed to hard labor, soon died out. Then the Spaniards imported Africans to work the plantations.

At war with Spain, England captured Jamaica in 1655. The Spaniards left after freeing their slaves, who took to the hills and harassed the settlers. The former slaves, called Maroons, were

finally granted land and freedom in 1739.

The island became a base for pirates, who grew rich plundering Spanish galleons. Port Royal, the capital, acquired a reputation for wickedness.

The English imported African slaves to raise sugarcane. Slavery was abolished in 1838.

Jamaica became a crown colony in 1866. It was granted full internal autonomy in 1953.

In 1958 Jamaica joined with several other British Caribbean possessions in a West Indian Federation. Three years later Jamaica withdrew.

INDEPENDENCE

On Aug. 6, 1962, Jamaica was granted full independence, with Sir Alexander Bustamante, a labor leader, as the first prime minister. Hugh Shearer became prime minister in 1967.

The ruling Jamaica Labour Party lost in general elections on Feb. 29, 1972, to the People's National Party. The PNP leader, Michael Manley, a socialist, became the prime minister. His government acquired majority control of the island's sugar industry in 1974 and its bauxite mines in 1975.

Manley, an admirer of Cuba's Fidel Castro, said he hoped to preside over "the most peaceful and constitutional revolution in history."

The government began a land-reform program that from 1973 to 1975 allocated land to 11,000 small farmers and farm cooperatives.

Thousands of unemployed persons were hired by the government at $26 a week to clean streets and improve the island's appearance in what was called the Crash Work Program. A national minimum wage of $20 for a 40-hour week was adopted in 1975.

Despite claims by the opposition that Prime Minister Manley would soon turn Jamaica into "another Cuba," his PLP party won a landslide victory in an election on Dec. 15, 1976, taking 48 of the 60 seats in the house of representatives.

The island's economy declined year after year during the late 1970s with 1 worker in 3 unemployed by the 1980s while prices rose at an annual rate of more than 30%. The U.S. and other Western nations reduced economic aid as Manley's government leaned closer to communism.

In a bitter 9-month election campaign in 1980 some 450 persons were killed.

The pro-Western Jamaica Labor Party (JLP) won a surprise landslide victory on Oct. 30, 1980, capturing 51 of the 60 seats in parliament's lower house. Its leader, Edward P. G. Seaga, 50, was sworn in as prime minister on Nov. 1.

As one of his first acts as prime minister, Seaga expelled Cuba's ambassador. He then broke diplomatic relations on Oct. 29, 1981.

Seaga promised to restore Jamaica's economy in the 1980s by revitalizing the tourist industry while turning from socialism to free enterprise. For the first time in eight years, the gross national product rose in 1981 and the unemployment rate declined. Improvement continued in 1982–84.

Riding a wave of popularity, Seaga's party won all 60 seats in parliament in an election on Dec. 15, 1983.

Riots and street violence in 1984–85 severely hurt the islands tourist industry.

JAPAN

Official Name: Japan.
Area: 145,809 square miles (377,644 sq. km.).
Population: 120,977,000.
Chief Cities: Tokyo, capital, 8,334,860; Yokohama, 2,806,523; Osaka, 2,635,211; Nagoya, 2,089,163; Kyoto, 1,477,028; Kobe, 1,375,006; Sapporo, 1,433,355; Kitakyushu, 1,065,032; Fukuoka, 1,104,483; Kawasaki, 1,045,244.
Largest Metropolitan Area: Tokyo, 11,634,428.
Government: Constitutional monarchy.
Prime Minister: Yasuhiro Nakasone (since 1982).
Emperor: Hirohito (since 1926).
Diet: *House of Councillors,* 252 members; *House of Representatives,* 511 members.
U.S. Ambassador to Japan: Michael J. Mansfield.
Japanese Ambassador to U.S.: Nobuo Matsunaga.
Flag: Red sun on white field.
Official Language: Japanese.
Principal Ethnic Group: Japanese.
Main Religions: Shintoism and Buddhism.
Leading Industries: Manufacturing (shipbuilding, textiles, aluminum, electricity, electrical and electronic equipment, steel, cement, paper, consumer goods); shipping; agriculture (rice, barley, tea, poultry, wheat, soybeans, sweet potatoes, sugar beets, vegetables, fruits); fishing; forestry; mining (coal, manganese, zinc, copper, lead, sulfur); tourism.
Foreign Trade: *Major exports*—ships and boats, electrical and electronic products, steel, synthetic fabrics, automobiles; *major imports*—crude petroleum, wood, iron ore, cotton.
Places of Interest: Mt. Fuji; Fuji-Hakone-Izu National Park; Nikko National Park and resort; Lake Chuzenji; Island of Hokkaido; Kyoto; Osaka; Kobe; Nagoya; Hiroshima; Nagasaki; Tanegashima Island space center. *In Tokyo:* Tokyo Tower atop Kasumigaseki Building; Imperial Palace; Hibiya and Meiji parks; Shiba Zojo-ji Temple; Great Buddha at Kamakura.

JAPAN TODAY

Although smaller than Montana, Japan is the third most important industrial nation in the world after the United States and the Soviet Union. It is the major competitor of the United States in world trade. Because Japan lacks the three most important minerals needed for industrialization—iron, petroleum, and coking coal, it must import raw materials from other countries.

Japan also lacks sufficient hydroelectric potential to power its industries and light its cities, so it has become a leading developer of atomic electric generating plants. It plans to decrease dependence on foreign oil imports to 50% of en-

AREA OF JAPAN'S MAIN ISLANDS

	SQ. MI.	SQ. KM.	LARGEST CITY
Honshu	87,805	227,414	Tokyo
Hokkaido	30,144	78,073	Sapporo
Kyushu	14,114	36,555	Kitakyushu
Shikoku	7,049	18,257	Matsuyama

QUICK QUIZ: What were the names of President Lincoln's four sons? See page 355.

JAPAN (continued)
ergy needs by the 1990s.

Japan is so mountainous that only 19% of its land is suitable for farming. By use of up-to-date scientific methods Japanese farmers attain the world's highest crop yields per acre, but even so the country must import about 35% of its food.

About three-fourths of the Japanese people live in and around the cities. Consequently Japan has many problems of urban pollution and urban transit. Most Japanese are well educated. Their standard of living is at about the same level as that of Americans.

Stretching in a 1,500-mile arc from north to south are four main islands: Hokkaido, Honshu, Shikoku, and Kyushu; and nearly 3,000 smaller islands, mostly tiny islets. Japan has 192 volcanoes, 40 of them still active. Dormant Mt. Fuji (12,388 feet) is the tallest.

EARLY HISTORY

Japanese myths say Jimmu Tenno, descendant of the sun goddess and ancestor of the present emperor, founded the empire about 660 B.C.

Anthropologists believe Chinese colonists about 200 B.C. brought China's ideographic script as well as its philosophy, literature, arts, and sciences to Japan. Buddhism was officially introduced in the 500s A.D.

Under the empress Suiko (593–628) a constitution and an official calendar were adopted.

In the 1100s power fell into the hands of the Minamoto, whose leader, Yoritomo, set up a military government in 1192 at Kamakura. For 700 years military governors, called *shoguns,* ruled Japan in the emperor's name.

China's Mongol ruler Kublai Khan twice launched invasions of Japan in 1274 and 1281, but each time the Mongols were driven off.

Portuguese navigators, arriving in 1542, were the first Europeans seen in Japan. They brought with them the first firearms. In 1549 St. Francis Xavier introduced Christianity.

By 1601 Ieyasu Tokugawa, a warrior, had unified Japan. He was appointed shogun in 1603 and established the Tokugawa shogunate that ruled until 1868. Ieyasu's center of government was Edo, the present Tokyo. After Ieyasu's death in 1616 a policy of national isolation was adopted. Christians were executed. Society became ossified under the ruling lords into four classes: *samurai* (warriors), merchants, artisans, and peasants. For the next two centuries Japan remained isolated from the world, permitting only the Dutch to conduct foreign trade.

JAPAN'S GROWTH AS A MILITARY POWER

U.S. Commodore Matthew C. Perry forced Japan to open its ports to trade with a treaty concluded on March 3, 1854. The first Japanese ambassador arrived in Washington in 1860.

Ruling power was restored to the emperor in 1868, and the capital was moved from Kyoto to Tokyo. This development was known as the Meiji Restoration. Feudalism was abolished. In 1889 the emperor granted a new constitution, establishing a bicameral parliament.

Japan took Formosa (now Taiwan) and the Pescadores from China in the Sino-Japanese War of 1894–95. After forming an alliance with Britain

JAPAN'S PRIME MINISTERS SINCE 1945

1945–46	Kijuro Shidehara	Nonpartisan
1946–47	Shigeru Yoshida	Coalition
1947–48	Tetsu Katayama	Socialist
1948	Hitoshi Ashida	Democratic
1948–54	Shigeru Yoshida	Democratic-Liberal
1954–56	Ichiro Hatoyama	Democratic
1956–57	Tanzan Ishibashi	Liberal Democratic
1957–60	Nobusuke Kishi	Liberal Democratic
1960–64	Hayato Ikeda	Liberal Democratic
1964–72	Eisaku Sato	Liberal Democratic
1972–74	Kakuei Tanaka	Liberal Democratic
1974–76	Takeo Miki	Liberal Democratic
1976–78	Takeo Fukuda	Liberal Democratic
1978–80	Masayoshi Ohira	Liberal Democratic
1980–82	Zenko Suzuki	Liberal Democratic
1982–	Yasuhiro Nakasone	Liberal Democratic

in 1902, Japan defeated Russia in the Russo-Japanese War of 1904–05. It gained the Liaotung peninsula in Manchuria and half of Sakhalin Island. Korea was annexed in 1910.

As a reward for supporting the Allies in World War I, Japan received a mandate over the northern Pacific islands formerly held by Germany. At the Washington Naval Conference of 1922, Japan was recognized as the third-leading naval power.

Universal manhood suffrage was introduced in 1925. Hirohito became emperor in 1926.

Japan's military leaders invaded and occupied China's province of Manchuria in 1931, and they ended Japan's parliamentary government in 1932.

Beginning in 1937 Japan waged an undeclared war with China. Japan signed a military alliance in 1939 with Nazi Germany and Fascist Italy. The defeat of France by Germany in 1940 enabled Japan to gain a foothold in Indochina.

JAPAN'S DEFEAT IN WORLD WAR II

In an attempt to halt Japanese aggression in Asia, the U.S. began to reduce its shipments of oil and steel to Japan. On Dec. 7, 1941, Japan launched a surprise attack on Pearl Harbor, Hawaii, nearly wiping out the entire U.S. fleet. The U.S. immediately declared war.

After 1944 Japan's losses grew swiftly and steadily, culminating in the atomic bombing of Hiroshima and Nagasaki by the U.S. on Aug. 6 and 9, 1945. Japan capitulated on Aug. 14, 1945, and the formal surrender was signed on September 2. The country was occupied by U.S. forces. A new constitution, adopted in 1946, established a parliamentary government.

A Japanese peace treaty was signed in San Francisco on Sept. 8, 1951, by Japan and 48 other nations, including the U.S. Japan signed a bilateral security treaty with the U.S. the same day.

JAPAN'S RECOVERY AS A WORLD POWER

Japan regained full independence on April 28, 1952. The United States returned the Bonin Islands and Iwo Jima to Japan in 1968 and the Ryukyu Islands in May 1972, while retaining military installations on Okinawa. Ending an era of conflict that had begun in 1937, Japan and China reestablished diplomatic relations in 1972.

The U.S. and Japan reached agreement in September 1977 enabling Japan to open the Tokai Mura atomic fuel reprocessing plant north of Tokyo to produce fuel for atomic power.

A dispute within the ruling party over economic policies resulted in Masayoshi Ohira, 68, replacing Takeo Fukuda as prime minister on Dec. 7, 1978.

In a parliamentary election on Oct. 7, 1979, the governing Liberal Democratic Party lost ground after Prime Minister Ohira called for higher taxes during the campaign. The party won 249 seats, 1 less than in 1976. It retained its governing majority in the lower house by a slim 2 votes.

Japan's economy slowed in 1979, registering a trade deficit of more than $9 billion in 1979, largely because of rising prices of oil imports.

JAPAN IN THE 1980s

On May 16, 1980, Ohira's government was defeated by a no-confidence vote, 243–187, the first such loss by a Japanese prime minister in 27 years. After scheduling national elections, the 70-year-old Ohira died of a heart attack on June 12, 1980, at the height of the political campaign.

The governing Liberal Democratic Party in the election on June 22, 1980, strengthened its leadership with clear majorities in both the lower and upper houses of parliament.

Zenko Suzuki, a former cabinet minister, became prime minister on July 17, 1980. He said Japan should build its armed forces without relying entirely on the U.S.-Japanese military alliance.

Yasuhiro Nakasone, 64, became prime minister on Nov. 26, 1982, after winning a mail-in vote by more than a million members of the Liberal Democratic Party. He said he would endeavor to improve trade relations with the U.S.

Prime Minister Nakasone won endorsement by voters in an election on June 26, 1983, as his Liberal Democratic Party increased its majority in the upper house of parliament.

In a sensational trial in 1983 Kakuei Tanaka, widely regarded as Japan's behind-the-scenes political boss, was convicted and sentenced to four years in prison for taking $2.1 million in bribes to arrange airline purchases of Lockheed aircraft while he was prime minister in 1972–74.

In an effort to ease strained economic relations with the U.S., the government announced that it would begin reducing tariffs on 1,268 categories of products in 1984, three years earlier than previously planned.

President Reagan visited Japan on Nov. 9-12, 1983.

In an election on Dec. 18, 1983, Nakosone's conservative party lost its majority in parliament, winning only 250 seats. However, he retained office as prime minister by forming a coalition with a small conservative party and several independent members.

Japan's foreign trade surplus shot up from $31 billion in 1983 to $44 billion in 1984, largely at the expense of a growing U.S. trade deficit. This caused the U.S. Congress in 1985 to threaten to impose protective tariffs or other measures to reduce imports from Japan. To ward off such actions, Prime Minister Nakasone appealed directly to the Japanese people on April 9, 1985, asking them to buy more foreign goods. At the same time he promised to ease Japanese trade barriers to make it easier to import products from the U.S. and other countries.

JORDAN

Official Name: Hashemite Kingdom of Jordan.
Area: 37,738 square miles (97,740 sq. km.).
Population: 2,740,000.
Chief Cities: Amman, capital, 623,925; Zarqa, 216,065; Irbid, 113,048.
Government: Absolute monarchy.
King: Hussein (reigned since 1952).
Prime Minister: Zaid Rifai (since 1985).
Parliament: *Senate,* 30 members; *House of Representatives,* 60 members.
U.S. Ambassador to Jordan: Paul H. Boeker.
Jordanian Ambassador to U.S.: Mohammed Kamal.
Flag: Black, white, and green stripes, with seven-pointed white star in red triangle on left.
Languages: Arabic (official), Circassian.
Main Ethnic Group: Arab (95%).
Religions: Islam (95%), Christianity (5%).
Leading Industries: Agriculture (wheat, barley, figs, olives, grapes, tobacco, sheep, goats, poultry, fruits, vegetables); mining (phosphate); manufacturing (cement, textiles, chemicals, petroleum refining, food processing); tourism.
Foreign Trade: *Major exports*—phosphates, tomatoes; *major imports*—motor vehicles, crude petroleum, sugar, rice, textiles, machinery, weapons, consumer goods.
Places of Interest: Citadel Hill and Roman theater in Amman; Petra, city of red rock; Greco-Roman ruins at Jerash; Crusader architecture at Kerak; Aqaba seaport; Azraq National Park; Wadi Rum Valley; forts and palaces.

JORDAN TODAY

A little larger than Indiana, Jordan lacks the petroleum resources that have vitalized the economies of other formerly poor Arab nations.

However, Jordan has received over $2 billion in economic aid from the U.S. since World War II. The Arab nation has used this aid in developing its agriculture and the mining of its phosphate deposits. Irrigation projects have opened new farmland.

About half of the people are Arab refugees made homeless by the Arab-Israeli wars.

EARLY HISTORY

Jordan includes the biblical lands of Gilead, Ammon, Bashan, Edom, and Moab. The later Nabataean kingdom was annexed to the Roman Empire in A.D. 106. Arabs conquered the land in the 600s. After the Crusades it fell to the Mamelukes of Egypt, then in the 1500s to the Ottoman Turks. It remained part of their empire until British armies took the area in 1917–18.

Called Transjordan, the region became a British mandate in 1920. The British placed Abdullah ibn Hussein on the throne as emir in 1921.

Britain ended its mandate and on May 25, 1946, recognized Abdullah as king of independent Transjordan (renamed Jordan in 1950).

QUICK QUIZ: When did the U.S. population reach 220 million? See page 309.

JORDAN (continued)

In 1948 Jordan joined the Arab states in attacking the newly independent state of Israel. Jordan's British-led troops captured Jerusalem on May 15, 1948. After concluding an armistice with Israel in 1949, Abdullah annexed the Palestine area west of the Jordan River.

Abdullah was assassinated in 1951 and was succeeded by his son Talal, who was in turn deposed by parliament in 1952 because of mental illness. Talal's son Hussein became king in 1952 and was formally crowned on May 2, 1953.

Because Britain sided with Israel in the second Arab-Israeli war, in 1956, Jordan ordered Britain to remove its troops that had remained stationed in the country since 1946.

In the third Arab-Israeli war, in 1967, Israel defeated Jordan, capturing Arab Jerusalem and all of Jordan's territory west of the Jordan River.

After that war Palestine Arab guerrillas in Jordan continued attacks on Israel until King Hussein agreed to a new Arab-Israeli cease-fire on Aug. 7, 1970. This prompted the guerrillas to focus attention on their cause with a series of dramatic skyjackings. The Jordanian army persuaded Hussein to attack the Palestinians. A brief civil war erupted.

JORDAN IN THE 1970s-1980s

Although Jordan did not directly attack Israel in the fourth Arab-Israeli war, in October 1973, it sent troops to assist Syria.

In 1975 King Hussein, bowing to a decision by other Arab nations, gave up his claims to the west bank of the Jordan to the Palestine Liberation Organization (PLO), which hopes to establish an Arab Palestine state. Hussein's action brought him aid from oil-rich Arab nations.

King Hussein in February 1976 convened the nation's parliament. It adopted a constitutional amendment enabling the king to postpone indefinitely any new parliamentary election.

King Hussein denied reports published in American newspapers in February 1977 that he had received millions of dollars in payments from the CIA over the past 20 years.

Hussein met with PLO leader Yasir Arafat in March 1977 for the first time since the Jordanian army fought the Palestinians in 1970. The two discussed plans for a future Palestinian state on the west bank of the Jordan River.

On June 15, 1978, Hussein, 42, married Elizabeth Halaby, 26, an American.

Hussein refused invitations to join peace negotiations in 1978–80 between Israel and Egypt.

In the Iraq-Iran war in 1980–84 Jordan supported Iraq. Jordan's port of Aqaba on the Red Sea became the main base for ships of the Soviet Union and other nations that brought war supplies to Iraq.

Jordan's parliament met for the first time in nine years on Jan. 9, 1984, approving an amendment to the constitution to permit elections to fill vacancies. Two months later, on March 12, Jordanians voted for the first time in 17 years to fill eight parliamentary seats. Women were allowed to vote for the first time in the nation's history.

King Hussein took the lead in 1985 in promoting a Middle East peace conference to be attended by Jordan, Israel, and the PLO.

KENYA

Official Name: Republic of Kenya.
Area: 224,961 square miles (582,646 sq. km.).
Population: 20,777,000.
Chief Metropolitan Areas: Nairobi, capital, 818,000; Mombasa, 391,000.
Government: One-party republic.
President: Daniel arap Moi (since 1978).
National Assembly: 170 members.
U.S. Ambassador to Kenya: Gerald Thomas.
Kenyan Ambassador to U.S.: Wafula Wabuge.
Flag: Black, red, and green bands separated by white stripes; red, black, and white shield over crossed white spears in center.
Languages: English and Swahili (official), Arabic.
Main Ethnic Groups: Kikuyu (20%), Luo (15%), Baluhya (13%), Kamba (11%), Kisii (6%), Meru (5%).
Religions: Animism (38%), Protestantism (37%), Roman Catholicism (22%), Islam (3%).
Leading Industries: Agriculture (coffee, tea, cattle, sugar cane, dairy products, poultry, pyrethrum [flower used in insecticides], sisal, corn, fruits, vegetables); tourism; manufacturing (processing farm products, oil refining, consumer goods); forestry and lumbering; mining (copper).
Foreign Trade: *Major exports*—coffee, tea, sugar, sisal; *major imports*—crude petroleum, motor vehicles, agricultural machinery.
Places of Interest: Rift Valley; Treetops Hotel, west of Mt. Kenya; national museum in Nairobi; Nairobi, Tsavo, Aberdare, Lake Nakuru national parks; Masai Mara, Amboseli, and Samburu game reserves.

KENYA TODAY

About as large as Arizona and New Mexico combined, Kenya has few important natural resources. Although the country's economy depends largely on agriculture, only about 12% of the land can be farmed and about 6% used for grazing livestock. Kenya's major exports are coffee and tea.

About three-fourths of the people depend on agriculture for a living. Only about 1 Kenyan in 5 can read and write, and many children never attend school.

Because Kenya must import all the petroleum it needs for energy, the nation was hard hit by soaring oil prices of the 1970s–1980s. About one-third of its income from foreign trade goes to the purchase of petroleum, severely limiting the amount of money that can be used in development projects to broaden the base of the economy.

The single most important contribution to cash income is tourism, which brings more than 300,000 visitors each year. The nation's leading tourist attractions are the national park sanctuaries for lions, elephants, leopards, cheetahs, giraffes, zebras, gazelles, and other wild animals.

The country is noted for its topographic variety. The low-lying coast rises gently to a dry coastal plain that gives way to a high plateau in the southwest (10,000 feet above sea level at some

points). Most of the people and economic activity are located in the plateau area. Mt. Kenya, a perpetually snow-clad 17,058-foot peak, stands in the semidesert northern region.

The Great Rift Valley includes Lake Turkana (formerly Rudolf), the country's largest lake.

EARLY HISTORY

Throughout the Middle Ages Kenya attracted Indian Ocean trade.

In 1498 Portuguese explorers arrived and established trading posts, but they were driven out by the Arabs in 1729. From 1740 Arabs ruled the Kenyan coast from Zanzibar.

In 1887 the British East Africa Company leased the Kenyan coast from the sultan of Zanzibar. Kenya became a British protectorate in 1895. It was organized as a crown colony in 1920.

Jomo Kenyatta, as secretary of an association of the Kikuyu tribe, began campaigning in 1928 for land reform and political rights for Africans. When his campaign was ignored, Kenyatta organized a group called the Mau Mau that began a rebellion in 1952.

During the next eight years over 12,000 persons died in the fighting. The British jailed Kenyatta from 1954 to 1961.

Britain agreed in 1960 to grant self-government to the black majority. Although Kenyatta's party, the Kenyan African National Union (KANU), won an election in February 1961, its members refused to take office until Kenyatta was released from confinement in August. KANU won another election in May 1963.

INDEPENDENCE

Kenya was granted independence by Britain on Dec. 12, 1963, with Kenyatta as prime minister. Exactly one year later Kenya became a republic in the British Commonwealth of Nations with Kenyatta taking office as president.

In the spring of 1966 Ogingo Odinga, the nation's vice president, broke with Kenyatta and formed an opposition party, the Kenya People's Union (KPU).

Odinga was put under house arrest on Oct. 27, 1969, following an antigovernment demonstration by the KPU. Three days later the KPU was banned, leaving KANU the only legal political party in Kenya. On Nov. 11, 1969, Kenyatta was reelected to a second term.

The Kenyan government began a campaign to Africanize the country in March 1968. In the next six years thousands of Asian shopkeepers and businessmen were forced to leave Kenya.

The nation was hard hit by drought in 1974. Some 250,000 cattle—90% of the herds of the Masai tribes—were reported to have died.

Although Kenya is a one-party state, voters chose between rival KANU candidates in the 1974 parliamentary election. The voters defeated four of Kenyatta's cabinet ministers.

In July 1976 President Idi Amin of neighboring Uganda threatened to bomb Kenya. His threats came because Kenya had allowed Israel's planes to land for refueling after the daring July 4 raid on Uganda to rescue hostages held by Arab hijackers. Kenya called on its nationals to leave Uganda as war threatened. However, friendly relations were reestablished in August.

Because Kenyatta was in his eighties, concern rose in the 1970s as to what would happen to the nation when he died.

When politicians attempted to hold public meetings on the subject of a successor for Kenyatta they were warned by the attorney general in October 1976 that it was a crime punishable by death even to imagine his death.

Tanzania closed its border with Kenya on Feb. 3, 1977, in a dispute over the shutting down of an airline that had been jointly operated by Kenya, Tanzania, and Uganda. Kenyan officials said it was an effort to prevent the people of socialist Tanzania from coming to Kenya to see the economic growth possible under free enterprise.

In an effort to preserve Kenya's wildlife, which attracts thousands of tourists each year, the government announced on May 19, 1977, a ban on the killing of elephants, rhinoceroses, leopards, zebras, and other wild animals. The move was applauded by conservationists but was deplored by Kenya's 300 or more professional hunters, who were told to convert hunting trips for tourists into photographic safaris.

Kenyatta died in his sleep on Aug. 22, 1978. He was believed to be about 89, but had no record of his birth. Hundreds of thousands of Kenyans lined the route of his funeral procession.

Daniel arap Moi, 54, who had served as vice president under Kenyatta, succeeded to the presidency without opposition. He was formally inaugurated as president on Oct. 14, 1978. He was elected to 5-year terms in 1979 and 1983.

A former school headmaster, President Moi made one of his first decrees the abolition of school fees. He also ordered free milk served at schools and promised to increase the number of teachers and other school personnel by 10%.

To emphasize his belief in human rights, President Moi on Dec. 12, 1978, released all 16 political prisoners of the Kenyatta regime.

Kenya and the U.S. reached agreement on June 27, 1980, for American ships, planes, and troops to use Kenya's ports and bases in return for increased economic and military aid.

Kenya officially became a one-party state on June 9, 1982, when parliament unanimously approved the ruling Kenya African National Union (KANU) as the only legal party.

An attempt to overthrow the government was put down by police on Aug. 1, 1982, with 145 persons killed and several hundred wounded. The nation's 2,100-man air force was disbanded and its members jailed for taking part in the rebellion. Universities also were closed because of student support for the rebellion.

Drought in 1981-84 caused severe food shortages. The U.S. provided more than $15 million in grain and other food in 1984.

Kenya's fifth 5-year plan for 1984–88 provided major investments to increase the income levels of small farmers and provide greater employment opportunities in the cities. One of the major projects continued the resettlement of farmers on unused or mismanaged land to increase the country's agricultural output.

QUICK QUIZ: Which U.S. President had the first cooking stove in the White House? See page 352.

KIRIBATI

Official Name: Republic of Kiribati.
Area: 278 square miles (720 sq. km.).
Population: 62,500.
Capital: Bairiki, Tarawa, 17,921.
Government: Democratic republic.
President: Ieremia Tabai (since 1979).
National Assembly: 35 members.
U.S. Ambassador to Kiribati: Carl E. Dillery.
Kiribati Ambassador to U.S.: Atanraoi Baiteke.
Flag: Bird flying over rising gold sun in red sky; white and blue wavy stripes.
Languages: English and Gilbertese.
Main Ethnic Group: Micronesians.
Major Religion: Christianity.
Leading Industries: Agriculture (coconuts, breadfruit, pandanus, bananas, pawpaws); fishing (tuna, shrimp); handicrafts.
Foreign Trade: *Major exports*—copra from coconuts, shrimp, handicrafts, postage stamps; *major imports*—food, fuel, clothing, lumber, consumer goods.
Places of Interest: Island villages, beaches.

KIRIBATI TODAY

Formerly known as the British colony of the Gilbert Islands, Kiribati includes 33 islands scattered across about 2 million square miles of the central and south Pacific Ocean.

The islands stretch about 3,000 miles from Ocean Island (Banaba) in the west to the southern Line Islands in the east.

The islands have almost no natural resources. Even the sandy soil is of poor quality for growing crops. The national economy is largely dependent on aid from Britain.

HISTORY

The first Europeans to sight the islands were Spanish navigators in the 1500s and 1600s.

The first European settlers in 1837 were deserters from whaling ships. From the 1850s to the 1870s trading ships visited the islands, kidnapping islanders to work as laborers on plantations elsewhere in the South Pacific.

Christianity was brought to the islands with the arrival in 1857 of American missionaries.

In 1892 a British protectorate was declared for the Gilberts and the neighboring Ellice Islands (now Tuvalu). In 1916 Britain made the Gilbert and Ellice Islands a colony.

The islands were occupied by Japan in World War II, but they were recovered by the Allies in a fierce battle on Tarawa on Nov. 20–23, 1943, in which 4,690 Japanese troops and 1,087 U.S. Marines were killed.

Britain granted independence to Kiribati on July 12, 1979. Ieremia (Jeremiah) Tabai, 29, was chosen in 1979 as Kiribati's first president.

In a treaty with the U.S. signed in September 1979, Kiribati received sovereignty over 14 islands in the Phoenix and Line groups, including Canton and Enderbury islands.

KOREA, NORTH

Official Name: Democratic People's Republic of Korea.
Area: 46,540 square miles (120,538, sq. km.).
Population: 20,312,000.
Chief Cities: Pyongyang, the capital, 653,100; Chongjin, 184,300; Hungnam, 143,600; Kaesong, 139,900.
Government: One-party communist state.
President: Kim Il Sung (ruler since 1948).
Prime Minister: Kang Song-San (since 1984).
Supreme People's Assembly: 541 members.
Flag: Large red center stripe bordered by thin white stripes and wider blue stripes; white circle enclosing red 5-pointed star on center stripe near hoist.
Language: Korean.
Main Ethnic Group: Korean.
Major Religions: Confucianism, Buddhism.
Leading Industries: Manufacturing (machines, electricity, chemicals, steel, textiles, cement, petroleum refining, aluminum); agriculture (rice, corn, vegetables); mining (coal, iron ore, graphite, petroleum, lead, nickel, tungsten, zinc).
Foreign Trade: *Major exports*—food products, minerals; *major imports*—oil, wheat, machines.
Places of Interest: Diamond Mountains; Buddhist monasteries; Mt. Kwanmo; Pyongyang.

NORTH KOREA TODAY

About the size of Mississippi, North Korea is a communist police state.

With economic and technical assistance from the Soviet Union and China, the country has developed heavy industry to produce machinery. It is among the world's leading nations in mining coal, lead, and zinc.

About half the people work and live on collective farms. The most important crop is rice.

The Korean peninsula is mountainous. The highest peak is Mt. Paektu (9,003 feet).

COMMUNIST RULE

Korea's history (see Korea, South) is regionally inseparable until 1945. With the Japanese defeat at the end of World War II, the 38th parallel was established as an administrative convenience, not as a political dividing line. Americans accepted the surrender of Japanese forces in the south, and Soviet forces did the same in the north.

The Soviet Union set up the communist government of North Korea on Sept. 9, 1948. Kim Il Sung, a guerrilla in Manchuria before he fled to the Soviet Union in 1941, was made head of the government.

On June 25, 1950, the North Korean army invaded South Korea. The U.S. and 15 other United Nations members sent military forces to aid South Korea. Communist China entered the conflict in support of North Korea. A cease-fire agreement was reached in July 1953, and Korea was again divided at the 38th parallel.

On Jan. 23, 1968, the North Koreans captured the USS *Pueblo* and imprisoned the crew for nearly a year before releasing them.

A new constitution was adopted in December

1972, establishing the office of president. Kim Il Sung, who had ruled for 24 years as premier, became president.

In 1974–79 South Koreans discovered that North Korea had made extensive new preparations for war, digging highway-wide tunnels under defenses at the 38th parallel.

North Korea established a 200-mile economic sea limit on Aug. 1, 1977, banning Japanese fishermen from an area extending all the way to Japan itself.

At the same time it forbade all foreign military craft from coming closer than 50 miles of its coast without permission.

A recession and failure to meet economic goals by its heavy industry forced North Korea to default in 1977 on its estimated $2 billion in foreign debts, causing Japan, Switzerland, Sweden and other creditors to cut off further loans.

To ensure that his 39-year-old son Kim Jong Il would succeed him as ruler, 68-year-old President Kim Il Sung in 1980 named his son to the influential post of secretary of the country's Communist Party.

Relations between the two Koreas improved in 1984. When floods in South Korea in September 1984 killed 190 persons and left 200,000 homeless, North Korea sent ships and truck convoys to South Korea, bringing more than 100 tons of relief supplies, including rice, textiles, and cement. In October 1984 the two Koreas reestablished a direct telephone hot line that had been broken by North Korea in 1976.

KOREA, SOUTH

Official Name: Republic of Korea.
Area: 38,025 square miles (98,484 sq. km.).
Population: 42,949,000.
Chief Cities: Seoul, capital, 8,364,379; Pusan, 3,159,766; Taegu, 1,604,934; Inchon, 1,803,906.
Government: Martial law.
President: Chun Doo Hwan (since 1980).
Prime Minister: Lho Shin-yong (since 1985).
National Assembly: 276 members.
U.S. Ambassador to South Korea: Richard L. Walker.
South Korean Ambassador to U.S.: Byong Hion Lew.
Flag: White field with circular emblem divided in half by curved line (red top and blue bottom); black bar design in each corner.
Language: Korean.
Principal Ethnic Group: Korean.
Religions: Confucianism, Shamanism, Christianity, Buddhism, Chodokyo.
Leading Industries: Agriculture (rice, wheat, barley, beans, cotton, livestock, poultry); manufacturing (steel, textiles, cement, electricity, plastics, clothing, plywood, electronics, chemicals); fishing; forestry and lumbering; mining (coal, iron ore, tungsten, graphite).
Foreign Trade: *Major exports*—plywood, raw silk,

cotton fabrics, electronics, iron and steel; *major imports*—transport equipment, rice, raw cotton, wheat, crude petroleum, textile machinery.
Places of Interest: Restored ancient capital, Kyongju; Cheju Island. *In Seoul:* National museum in Duksoo Palace; Changduk Palace and Secret Garden; Kyungbok Palace; Pagoda Park; Kings' Tomb.

SOUTH KOREA TODAY

About the size of Indiana, South Korea is a small Asian country that won its independence from Japan after World War II. In the 1950s the U.S. and the United Nations helped South Korea preserve its independence during the Korean War, in which communist North Korea and China attempted to overrun the country.

South Korea had one of the most rapidly expanding economies in the world in the 1960s–80s. Its gross national product grew from $2.27 billion in 1962 to an estimated $80 billion in 1984. However, most of the people are poor.

Although South Korea is a constitutional republic, the country has been ruled since it was created by dictators.

The U.S. maintains armed forces in South Korea to protect it from attack by North Korea.

The mountainous peninsula has many harbors along the west coast. Summers are hot and humid. Winters are cold and dry.

EARLY HISTORY

According to Korean legend, Tangun founded Korean civilization about 4,300 years ago. Korea's recorded history began in the 1100s B.C. when a Chinese prince, Ki-tze, founded a colony at Pyongyang. Chinese influence remained until about 100 B.C., when three warring tribes (Silla, Koguryo, and Paekche) came to power.

Silla kings with their capital at Kyongju united the country in A.D. 668. A new kingdom, Koryo, ruled the Korean peninsula in 935–1392. In the 1200s the Mongols conquered the land. In 1637 Korea fell to the Manchu rulers of China. Because of its isolation, Korea became known as the Hermit Kingdom.

In 1876 Korea was forced by Japan to open its ports to outside trade. Six years later Korea signed a commercial treaty with the U.S. In 1895 Japan won a war against the Chinese in Korea. Russia tried to acquire Korea but was defeated by Japan in 1905.

In 1910 Japan formally annexed Korea as a colony. The Koreans opposed Japanese rule. In 1919 a government-in-exile was formed in Shanghai under Syngman Rhee.

In 1945, near the end of World War II, Soviet troops entered the northern part of Korea. A month later, American forces landed in the south. The U.S. and Soviet Union agreed on a purely administrative dividing line across Korea—the 38th parallel.

INDEPENDENT SOUTH KOREA

On Aug. 15, 1948, a separate pro-Western government was established for South Korea. Syngman Rhee became president.

U.S. troops were withdrawn by June 1949.

On June 25, 1950, the North Korean army in-

QUICK QUIZ: Which was the fist state to ratify the U.S. Constitution? See page 312.

KOREA, SOUTH *(continued)*

vaded South Korea. The U.S. and UN came to the support of South Korea, and 16 member nations sent troops. Communist China entered the war on the side of North Korea in 1951. A ceasefire was achieved in July 1953. Korea remained divided at the 38th parallel.

President Rhee served from 1948 to 1960, when charges of election-rigging led to his resignation and subsequent exile. New elections were held, but on May 16, 1961, the government was ousted by a military junta headed by Gen. Park Chung Hee.

In 1972 Park imposed martial law on South Korea. In 1975 he made it a crime for anyone to criticize the government to foreigners.

In a parliamentary election on Dec. 12, 1978, the opposition New Democratic Party (NDP) won 34% of the vote to 32% by President Park's Democratic Republican Party (DRP). However, Park's control of parliament was augmented by the appointment of 77 additional members.

For the first time in almost six years, South Korean and North Korean officials met in 1979 at Panmunjom in a series of sessions to discuss possible reunification of Korea.

U.S. President Carter visited South Korea from June 29 to July 1, 1979. After returning to the United States, he announced on July 20 that withdrawal of the remaining 32,000 U.S. combat troops in South Korea would be postponed.

President Park was assassinated on Oct. 26, 1979, by Kim Jae Kyu, head of the Korean central intelligence agency, who was arrested and executed. Martial law was imposed throughout the nation under army chief of staff Gen. Chung Seung Hwa. Prime Minister Choi Kyu Han became president. Younger military officers overthrew Gen. Chung on Dec. 12, 1979.

Maj. Gen. Chun Doo Hwan emerged as the new military strong man. In the following months tens of thousands of opponents to the regime were imprisoned without trial. Former presidential candidate Kim Dae Jung, the most prominent spokesman for democracy, was arrested, tried by a military court, and was sentenced to death. However, he later was freed and allowed to visit the U.S. for medical treatment. He returned home in 1985.

Chun made himself president in September 1980. He was sworn in to a seven-year term on March 3, 1981. In carefully controlled parliamentary elections on March 25, 1981, President Chun's party easily won a substantial majority.

The Soviet Union on Sept. 1, 1983, shot down a South Korean airliner that had strayed over its territory, killing all 269 aboard.

A bomb explosion in Rangoon, Burma, on Oct. 9, 1983, killed 17 South Korean officials, including four cabinet ministers. North Korean terrorists were blamed for the slayings.

President Reagan visited South Korea on Nov. 12–14, 1983, reaffirming U.S. friendship.

In 1984-85 President Chun relaxed controls on students and opposition political parties.

South Korea's economy continued to boom in 1983-85 with an annual growth rate of about 9%, one of the highest in the world.

In a parliamentary election on Feb. 12, 1985, President Chun's political party won a majority with 148 seats to 68 for the opposition party of Kim Dae Jung.

In a meeting in Washington with President Reagan in April 1985, President Chun reiterated that at the end of his term in 1988 he would turn the government over to an elected civilian.

KUWAIT

Official Name: State of Kuwait.
Area: 6,880 square miles (17,818 sq. km.).
Population: 1,925,000.
Chief Cities: Kuwait, capital, 700,000; Hawalli, 130,565; Salmiyyah, 113,943.
Government: Monarchy (emirate).
Emir: Sheik Jabir al-Ahmad al-Sabah (since 1977).
Prime Minister and Crown Prince: Sheik Saad al-Abdullah Al-Sabah (since 1977).
National Assembly: 66 members (50 elected).
U.S. Ambassador to Kuwait: C. E. Quainton.
Kuwaiti Ambassador to U.S.: Saud Nasir al-Sabah.
Flag: Green, white, and red stripes, with black trapezoid at flagstaff.
Languages: Arabic (official), Persian, English.
Main Ethnic Group: Arab (85%).
Religion: Islam (99%).
Leading Industries: Mining (petroleum, natural gas); construction; manufacturing and processing (electricity, desalinization of seawater, oil refining, ammonia, fertilizer, cement, consumer products); shipping; fishing; agriculture (sheep, goats, wheat, dates, vegetables).
Foreign Trade: *Major export*—petroleum; *major imports*—food, oil refinery equipment, automobiles, trucks, machinery, consumer goods.
Places of Interest: Oil wells; modern city of Kuwait; royal residences; seaport at Mina al-Ahmad.

KUWAIT TODAY

About the size of New Jersey, Kuwait is one of the most prosperous countries in the world. The Middle East's third-largest producer of oil, Kuwait has about one-quarter of the world's oil reserves. Its people pay no taxes.

Kuwait has given and loaned billions of dollars to poorer Arab states, has invested billions in the United States and other industrial countries, and has purchased planes and other equipment for Arab states opposing Israel.

The government also has used its oil wealth to give free medical services, education, a 124-acre amusement park, and other benefits to everyone in Kuwait. Local telephone service is also free, and almost every family owns at least one car and one TV set.

The government holds down food costs by subsidizing food imports.

Abundant natural gas provides energy for Kuwait's expanding industries. The nation's capital is a thriving modern city on Kuwait Bay.

EARLY HISTORY

Kuwait was founded about 1740 by Arab nomads who migrated from northern Arabia to the Persian

Gulf coast. Sabah Abu Abdullah founded an emirate there in 1756. Under his successors, Kuwait's population grew to several thousand.

The British came to Kuwait's aid when it was threatened in the first half of the 1800s by the Wahabi of Arabia, a puritanical Muslim sect that waged holy war against all other forms of Islam.

In 1897 the emir of Kuwait, fearful that the Turks would take over his territory, asked the British for protection. An agreement in 1899 made Kuwait a quasi-protectorate of Britain.

In 1919 Saudi Arabia invaded Kuwait but was repelled with the help of the British. The Saudis placed a land blockade on Kuwait that lasted 20 years, although in 1922 the two governments established the Neutral Zone in which they shared sovereignty until 1966.

With the discovery of oil in Kuwait in 1938, and its development after 1945, Iraq decided in 1952 to renew an ancient claim to Kuwait. This was promptly rejected by the British.

INDEPENDENCE

By mutual consent the British protectorate was revoked on June 19, 1961, and Kuwait became a fully independent nation.

Kuwait and Saudi Arabia signed an agreement on Dec. 18, 1969, dividing a previous 2,000-square-mile Neutral Zone between them and establishing a new boundary.

Iraqi troops invaded Kuwait on March 20, 1973, near the Persian Gulf, claiming the boundary between the countries had never been settled. After Saudi Arabia sent more than 15,000 troops to assist Kuwait, Iraq withdrew.

In 1975 the government bought complete control of the oil and gas industry from the U.S. and other foreign owners.

Sheik Jabir al-Ahmad al-Sabah became emir on Dec. 31, 1977.

A new conservative national assembly was elected on Feb. 23, 1981. About 90% of the 42,000 registered voters went to the polls. Only male Kuwaitis over 21 were eligible to vote.

Parliament rejected a proposal in January 1982 that would have given women the right to vote. But later in the month, as hundreds of women demonstrated in the streets, the legislators legalized abortion, making Kuwait the first Persian Gulf Arab state to do so.

Because of Kuwaiti support of Iraq in the Iraq-Iran war, terrorists exploded bombs on Dec. 12, 1983, at seven targets including the airport, government buildings, and the U.S. and French embassies, killing 6 persons and injuring 80. A Kuwati court in March 1984 found 25 members of a pro-Iranian terrorist organization guilty of the crime. Six were sentenced to death.

The U.S. refused to sell its most advanced anti-aircraft missile, the Stinger, to Kuwait in June 1984 for fear it might fall into the hands of terrorists. So Kuwait's defense minister went to Moscow the following month where he negotiated an agreement to buy Soviet anti-aircraft weapons.

Voters expressed dissatisfaction with government economic policies by defeating half the incumbents in a parliamentary election on Feb. 20, 1985.

LAOS

Official Name: Lao People's Democratic Republic.
Area: 91,429 square miles (236,800 sq. km.).
Population: 3,862,000.
Chief Cities: Vientiane, capital, 132,253; Luang Prabang, 42,000.
Government: Communist one-party state.
President: Prince Souphanouvong (since 1975).
Prime Minister: Kaysone Phomvihan (since 1975).
Flag: Narrow red stripes top and bottom; wide blue stripe in middle with large white circle.
Languages: Lao (official), French.
Main Ethnic Group: Lao.
Religions: Buddhism and animism.
Leading Industries: Agriculture (rice, coffee, tea, cattle, fruits, vegetables, corn, cotton, tobacco); mining (tin, iron ore); fishing; manufacturing (textiles, handicrafts); forestry and lumbering.
Foreign Trade: *Major exports*—tin, teak, coffee; *major imports*—rice and other foods, petroleum, transport equipment, consumer goods.
Places of Interest: Annamite Cordillera; former royal palace, wats (temples) and pagodas. *In Vientiane:* Shrine of That Luang; Luang Prabang.

LAOS TODAY

Somewhat smaller than Oregon, Laos is a mountainous Southeast Asian country ruled by communists. The government relies heavily on foreign aid from the Soviet Union and Vietnam.

One of the poorest and most underdeveloped nations of the world, Laos must import food and other goods its people need to survive.

Most Laotians are poverty-stricken rice farmers. Few can read or write.

Over 80% of the country is rugged jungle terrain. The flatlands are mostly in the valleys of the Mekong River and its tributaries.

EARLY HISTORY

First settled in the 1100s by refugee Thai tribes from China, Laotian territory was the seat of the Buddhist kingdom of Lan Xang, founded in 1353 by King Fa Ngum. In 1707 the kingdom split into two regions: Luang Prabang in the north and Vientiane in the south.

France made Laos a protectorate in 1893.

Japanese forces invaded Laos in 1941. Just before Japan's World War II surrender in September 1945, King Sisavang Vong of Luang Prabang proclaimed himself king of all Laos. On Oct. 12, 1945, nationalists of the Free Laos movement declared the country independent. French troops reoccupied Laos in May 1946.

Laos became an associated state in the French Union on July 19, 1949. France granted Laos full independence on Oct. 22, 1953.

A communist movement, the Pathet Lao, was created by Prince Souphanouvong in 1950. Three years later Vietnamese communists invaded Laos

QUICK QUIZ: When was direct election of U.S. Senators adopted? See page 318.

LAOS (continued)

to assist the Pathet Lao. The conference at Geneva in 1954 that ended the Indochina War brought a cease-fire to Laos.

In 1957 Laos' premier, Prince Souvanna Phouma, and his half-brother, Prince Souphanouvong, formed a coalition government. Sri Savang Vatthanna became king on Nov. 4, 1959, after the death of his father, King Sisavang Vong.

Civil war with the communist Pathet Lao again broke out in 1960. The U.S. supported government troops.

On Feb. 8, 1971, South Vietnam forces, with U.S. air support, drove into Laos to cut the Ho Chi Minh Trail, a road used by North Vietnam.

The Laotian government signed a cease-fire agreement with the Pathet Lao, ending 10 years of war at noon on Feb. 22, 1973.

COMMUNIST TAKE-OVER OF LAOS

After North Vietnam conquered South Vietnam, the Pathet Lao on Dec. 3, 1975, forced King Sri Savang Vatthanna to abdicate. Prince Souphanouvong became the first president of Laos. The new premier was Kaysone Phomvihan, secretary-general of the Laotian Communist Party.

The government arrested hundreds of former political leaders in April 1976 in what was called a "cultural revolution."

A severe drought in 1977 caused an estimated 60% loss in the rice crop. The government appealed to other countries to send food.

As an ally of Vietnam and the Soviet Union, Laos sent troops to aid Vietnam in its 1979 conquest of Cambodia.

Thousands of Laotians fled from the country to neighboring Thailand in 1979–85, adding to the estimated 200,000 Laotian refugees who had left the country in 1975–78 to escape the repression of the communist regime.

LEBANON

Official Name: Republic of Lebanon.
Area: 4,015 square miles (10,400 sq. km.).
Population: 2,640,000.
Chief Cities: Beirut (Bayrūt), capital, 474,870; Tripoli, 127,611.
Largest Metropolitan Area: Beirut, 938,940.
Government: Parliamentary republic.
President: Amin Gemayel (since 1982).
Prime Minister: Rashid Karami (since 1984).
Chamber of Deputies: 99 members.
U.S. Ambassador to Lebanon: Reginald Bartholomew.
Lebanese Ambassador to U.S.: Abdallah Bouhabib.
Flag: Red, white, and red stripes, with green cedar tree in white stripe.
Languages: Arabic (official), French, English, Armenian.
Principal Ethnic Groups: Arab (94%), Armenian (6%).
Religions: Christianity (50%), Islam (50%).
Leading Industries: Trade and banking; manufacturing (oil refining, textiles, food processing, cement, tobacco

products); agriculture (sheep, poultry, fruits, vegetables, grapes, figs, wheat, cotton); tourism.
Foreign Trade: *Major exports*—apples, pears, quinces, eggs, dried beans, wool; *major imports*—animals, automobiles, wheat, beans, gasoline.
Places of Interest: Baalbeck temple; ruins at Anjar and Byblos; Tyre excavations; Beit-Eddine Palace; Castle of the Sea at Saida (Sidon); Jeita Grotto; Beirut Museum; Tripoli citadel.

LEBANON TODAY

Smaller than Connecticut, Lebanon is a Middle Eastern Arab nation torn by fighting among Christian rightists, Muslim leftists, and troops of Syria and Israel. The battles wrecked the nation's cities and destroyed Lebanon's previously prosperous economy.

With a population almost evenly divided between Christians and Muslims, Lebanon before the civil war had achieved political stability by traditionally choosing a Christian as president and a Muslim as prime minister. Unlike the people in other Arab countries, most Lebanese could read and write and took an active part in elective politics.

The Lebanon Mountains dominate the country's landscape. To the west is a narrow coastal plain where the largest cities are located.

The Mediterranean coast has a mild climate the year round. But the mountain regions have heavy snows that attract skiing enthusiasts.

EARLY HISTORY

In ancient times the Phoenicians, who lived in what is now Lebanon, spread civilization throughout the Mediterranean as seafaring traders and colonizers. The Phoenician city-state of Tyre reached its peak of prosperity about 1000 B.C.

Persians, Assyrians, Babylonians, Egyptians, and Greeks under Alexander the Great fought in turn for the area. In time it came under Roman rule along with Syria. A Christian sect, the Maronites, settled in Lebanon, making it mainly Christian.

After centuries of warfare and invasion, the Middle East was unified under the Ottoman Empire in the 1500s. Egyptian occupation in 1832 increased tension between the Christian Maronites and the Islamic Druses. Fearing annihilation, the Maronites appealed for help.

European powers in 1864 forced the Turks to agree to a pro-Christian government for the province of Mount Lebanon that was created.

After World War I France received a mandate over Lebanon. It became a republic in 1926.

Lebanon declared its independence on Nov. 26, 1941, but France refused to recognize Lebanon's sovereignty until Nov. 27, 1943. French troops withdrew in December 1946.

During the Arab-Israeli wars of 1948–1973, many Palestinian refugees settled in Lebanon. The Palestine Liberation Organization (PLO) made Lebanon a base for attacks on Israel.

CIVIL WAR

A civil war began on April 13, 1975, among rightist Christians, leftist Muslims, and PLO guerrillas. With the acquiescence of the U.S. and Israel, 30,000 Syrian troops intervened in April 1976. The Syrian army took control of Beirut on Nov. 15, 1976, putting an end to the heaviest fighting

that had killed about 60,000.

Israeli troops invaded southern Lebanon on March 14, 1978, destroying PLO strongholds, but withdrew in June after a UN peacekeeping force arrived in the area.

Israel invaded Lebanon on June 6, 1982, and quickly defeated PLO and Syrian forces, capturing Beirut. In August 1982 U.S. Marines and troops of Italy and France supervised the evacuation of 14,000 PLO guerrillas from Beirut.

With Israeli troops holding southern Lebanon and Syrian forces occupying the northern and eastern parts, parliament on Aug. 23, 1982, elected a new president, Bashir Gemayel, 34, leader of the rightist Christian militia. Before he could take office, the president-elect and 25 others were slain in a bomb explosion on Sept. 14, 1982. The Phalangists took revenge with a massacre of over 700 Palestinians in Beirut on Sept. 16–18.

A week later parliament elected Gemayel's brother, Amin Gemayel, 40, as the nation's president. He took office on Sept. 23, 1982.

At the request of Gemayel's government on Sept. 24, 1982, the U.S., Italy, France, and Britain brought in troops to establish an international peacekeeping force in Beirut.

Terrorists bombed the U.S. embassy in Beirut on April 18, 1983, killing 17 Americans.

Israel unilaterally pulled back its troops on Sept. 4, 1983, to the Awwali River in southern Lebanon. Lebanese government troops sought to establish control over areas abandoned by the Israelis. But they met stiff resistance from PLO and Muslim militiamen. To support the Lebanese army, the U.S. began on Sept. 17 to use its warships to bombard guerrillas.

On Oct. 23, 1983, terrorists almost simultaneously bombed headquarters of the U.S. and French peacekeeping forces, killing 241 U.S. marines and sailors and 58 French troops..

Early in 1984, the U.S., Italy, and France ordered their peacekeeping troops to leave Lebanon, completing the evacuation in March.

Former Prime Minister Rashid Karami, 62, a pro-Syrian Muslim, was appointed prime minister on April 26, 1984, as head of a national unity government representing all major political and religious groups. Karami set as goals the end of all fighting and the removal of Israeli forces from southern Lebanon.

A pull-back of opposing Lebanese guerrilla forces was accomplished in July and August 1984, creating buffers patrolled by the Lebanese army.

On Sept. 20, 1984, terrorists car-bombed the U.S. embassy annex in Beirut, killing 14 persons, including two Americans.

Some of the heaviest fighting in the civil war between Christians and Muslims broke out in April-May 1985 in Beirut, killing scores of persons and demolishing many buildings.

Israel completed its withdrawal of troops from southern Lebanon in June 1985.

Muslim terrorists hijacked a TWA airliner, forcing it to land in Beirut in June 1985. They killed one American passenger and held 40 others prisoner demanding the release of 766 Muslim terrorists held prisoner by Israel. See page 19.

LESOTHO

Official Name: Kingdom of Lesotho.
Area: 11,720 square miles (30,355 sq. km.).
Population: 1,536,000.
Capital: Maseru, 75,000.
Government: Dictatorship.
Prime Minister: Leabua Jonathan (since 1965).
King: Motlotlehi Moshoeshoe II (since 1966).
Parliament: *National Assembly*, 60; *Senate*, 33.
U.S. Ambassador to Lesotho: S.L. Abbott.
Lesotho Ambassador to U.S.: 'M'alineo N. Tau.
Flag: Parallel bars of green and red at hoist, with white conical Basuto hat on blue field.
Official Languages: English and Sesotho.
Ethnic Groups: Sotho (85%), Nguini (15%).
Religions: Christianity (70%), animism (30%).
Leading Industries: Agriculture (corn, wheat, sorghum, peas, beans, sheep, cattle); mining (diamonds); manufacturing (carpets, candles, fertilizer, pottery, jewelry).
Foreign Trade: *Major exports*—wool, cattle, mohair, diamonds; *major imports*—food, machinery, vehicles, consumer goods.
Places of Interest: Drakensberg Mountains; bushmen cave and cliff paintings in Cave Sandstone area; Sehlabathebe National Park.

A little larger than the state of Maryland, Lesotho has few known natural resources. About a fourth of the country's men travel to South Africa for several months each year to earn cash by working in the mines. Otherwise most of the people live in tribal villages, farming for a living. Heavily dependent on foreign aid, Lesotho imports food and goods worth 12 times its exports.

Lesotho is a rugged, mile-high plateau country nestled amid the 11,000-foot peaks of the Drakensberg Mountains. Only about 10% of the land can be farmed. Temperatures average 45° F. in July and 70° F. in January.

Formerly called *Basutoland*, Lesotho is landlocked by South Africa on three sides and by Transkei to the south.

The Basotho nation came into being in 1818 under the leadership of Moshesh I. In 1867 the Basotho requested British protection against Boer advances from South Africa, and in 1868 Britain annexed Basutoland. Internal self-government was introduced in 1959.

Independence was granted on Oct. 4, 1966, with Leabua Jonathan as prime minister.

The country's first election since independence was held on Jan. 31, 1970. Jonathan declared the results invalid and suspended the constitution.

Jonathan ruled as dictator by decree. In April 1973 he established an appointed national assembly. Opponents tried to overthrow Jonathan's rule in January 1975. A court found 18 persons guilty of treason in the coup attempt.

South African troops raided Lesotho in 1982 and 1983 to kill guerrillas.

QUICK QUIZ: When was Lancaster, Pa., the capital of the U.S.? See page 319.

LIBERIA

Official Name: Republic of Liberia.
Area: 43,000 square miles (111,369 sq. km.).
Population: 2,226,000.
Capital: Monrovia, 96,226.
Government: Transitional.
President: Samuel Kanyon Doe (since 1980).
National Assembly: 57 members.
U.S. Ambassador to Liberia: Edward J. Perkins.
Liberian Ambassador to U.S.: George T. Washington.
Flag: Alternating stripes of red and white, with blue square containing white star in upper hoist corner.
Religions: Animism (75%), Islam (15%), Christianity (10%).
Main Ethnic Group: Black.
Languages: English (official), many tribal languages.
Leading Industries: Agriculture (rice, cassava, coffee, sugarcane, tobacco, cocoa, rubber, palm kernels, citrus fruits, vegetables); mining (iron ore, diamonds, gold); shipping; manufacturing (soap, plastics, paint, paper products, textiles, building materials, fertilizer, tobacco products); forestry and lumbering; tourism.
Foreign Trade: *Major exports*—iron ore, rubber, diamonds, lumber, coffee; *major imports*—machinery, transport equipment, manufactured goods.
Places of Interest: Atlantic coast beaches and resorts; Providence Island; Monrovia; Lake Piso; Bong mine; Totota Zoo; LAMCO mining site.

LIBERIA TODAY

About the size of Ohio, Liberia is one of the world's 10 leading producers of iron ore and natural rubber. Most Liberians lead a tribal life in the country's tropical forests.

The government is heavily dependent on aid from the U.S. and Israel.

One of Liberia's most pressing problems as it seeks to become an industrial nation is to improve and expand its educational system to provide skilled workers and technicians and managers. Only about 1 in 4 Liberians can read and write. The majority of the people speak tribal dialects.

A large merchant fleet sails under the Liberian flag—over 2,000 ships. Most are owned by Americans and other foreigners who register the ships in Liberia to avoid strict control.

Liberia lies on the west coast of Africa. Guinea is to the north, Ivory Coast to the east, and Sierra Leone to the northwest.

LIBERIA'S HISTORY

The colony of Liberia was founded for liberated American slaves in 1822 by the National Colonization Society, a white abolitionist group whose agents governed the area until 1847.

The Republic of Liberia was established on July 26, 1847, becoming the first black African colony to gain independence.

Beginning in 1926, Liberia encouraged American companies to develop rubber plantations that became a mainstay of the economy.

Huge iron-ore deposits were discovered in 1955

at Mt. Nimba on the border with Guinea. Shipments from the mines began in 1963. Iron ore accounts for over half of the nation's exports.

From 1877 to 1980 the True Whigs governed as the country's only political party. William V. S. Tubman, was president of Liberia from 1943 until his death on July 23, 1971. He was succeeded by William R. Tolbert Jr.

Master Sgt. Samuel K. Doe, 28, led a coup on April 12, 1980, in which President Tolbert and 27 others were killed. Doe made himself president, forming a 17-member military junta called the People's Redemption Council (PRC) to run the government under martial law. On April 22 the new rulers publicly executed 13 of the leading officials of Tolbert's government.

Doe had five members of his junta executed by firing squad on Aug. 14, 1981, accusing them of plotting his overthrow.

President Doe declared in 1982 that he would return the nation to civilian rule in 1985. He visited the White House in August 1982 to demonstrate his friendship for the United States.

In a referendum on July 3, 1984, a new constitution was adopted. Three weeks later President Doe converted his 22-member military council into a national assembly by adding 35 civilians. He lifted a 4-year ban on political activity on July 26, 1984.

In August 1984 Doe jailed 10 political leaders on charges they were plotting his overthrow. But on Oct. 10, 1984, he freed them.

President Doe escaped assassination on April 1, 1985, when his jeep was machine-gunned. A week later a firing squad executed Lt. Col. Moses Flanzamaton, deputy commander of the presidential guard, on charges of having organized the assassination attempt.

LIBYA

Official Name: Socialist People's Libyan Arab Jamahiriya.
Area: 679,362 square miles (1,759,540 sq. km.).
Population: 3,721,000.
Chief Cities: Tripoli, capital, 213,506; Benghazi, 137,295.
Government: Socialist military dictatorship.
Head of State: Col. Mu'ammar al-Qadhafi (since 1969).
Flag: Green field.
Languages: Arabic (official), Berber.
Main Ethnic Groups: Arab and Berber.
Official Religion: Islam (97%).
Leading Industries: Mining (petroleum); agriculture (cattle, sheep, goats, peanuts, olives, grapes, dates, barley, wheat); construction; manufacturing (petroleum products, textiles, tobacco products).
Foreign Trade: *Major exports*—petroleum, hides and skins, peanuts; *major imports*—machinery, clothing, automobiles, wheat flour.
Places of Interest: Marble arch of Marcus Aurelius in Tripoli; 2d century amphitheater at Sabratha; ancient city of Leptis; Cyrene archaeological site.

Over twice as large as Texas, Libya is largely covered by the hot, nearly uninhabited Sahara Desert. Most Libyans live along the 1,100-mile Mediterranean coast. Yet oil fields in the Sahara make Libya a leading oil-producing nation.

The socialist military dictator who rules Libya gives the people little voice in their government.

The government uses much of its oil riches to finance terrorism and to purchase jet fighter planes and other military equipment.

Egypt and Sudan lie to the east, Tunisia and Algeria to the west, and Niger and Chad to the south.

Beginning about 630 B.C. Greeks colonized northeastern Libya, called Cyrenaica. About the same time Phoenicians colonized northwestern Libya, or Tripolitania, which became part of the state of Carthage. In the 1st century B.C. both became part of the Roman Empire.

In A.D. 642–643 Libya was conquered by Arabs, who converted the local Berber peoples to Islam.

Libya became part of the Ottoman Turkish Empire in 1551. Ottoman rule ended when Italy invaded Libya in 1911, making it a colony.

The Muslim leader Mohammed Idris fought Italian rule from 1916 until British troops captured Libya during World War II in October 1942. The country remained under British administration as a UN trust until 1951.

Libya became independent on Dec. 24, 1951, with Idris as king.

The discovery of oil in 1959 brought wealth.

The 79-year-old King Idris was overthrown on Sept. 1, 1969, in a bloodless military coup led by Col. Mu'ammar al-Qadhafi.

Libya nationalized foreign-owned oil companies in 1973–74 and joined the Arab oil embargo of countries that had befriended Israel in the Arab-Israeli war in 1973.

A Libyan mob attacked and burned the U.S. embassy in Tripoli on Dec. 2, 1979. Four months later, in May 1980, the U.S. withdrew all diplomats but did not break diplomatic relations.

The Libyan government paid $220,000 to the U.S. President Carter's brother Billy in 1980 in an effort to influence U.S. government policies.

Accusing Libya of international terrorism, the U.S. on May 6, 1981, ordered Libya's diplomats in Washington to leave the country.

Two Libyan fighter planes were shot down by U.S. Navy jets on Aug. 19, 1981, when they attacked the American planes off Libya's coast.

The U.S. revealed in 1981 that Qadhafi had hired assassins to kill President Reagan. The 2,500 Americans working in Libya were asked to leave the country.

On March 10, 1982, the U.S. banned oil imports from and high-technology exports to Libya.

Britain broke diplomatic relations with Libya in April 1984 after Libya refused to give up a gunman who shot and killed a British policewoman by firing from Libya's London embassy.

Opponents made an unsuccessful attempt to assassinate Qadhafi with an attack on his home in Tripoli on May 8, 1984. Some 60 persons were killed in the fighting. Seven persons were executed for taking part in the plot and several hundred were imprisoned.

LIECHTENSTEIN

Official Name: Principality of Liechtenstein.
Area: 61 square miles (157 sq. km.).
Population: 27,700.
Capital: Vaduz, 4,980.
Government: Constitutional monarchy.
Prime Minister: Hans Brunhart (since 1978).
Monarch: Franz Josef II (since 1938).
Chief of State: Crown Prince Hans Adam (since 1984).
Legislature: *Diet,* 15 members.
Flag: Blue and red, with gold crown in blue stripe.
Language: German.
Principal Ethnic Group: German.
Religion: Roman Catholicism (92%).
Leading Industries: Manufacturing (precision instruments, textiles, ceramics, pharmaceuticals, false teeth, food processing); banking; tourism; agriculture (cattle, dairy products, grapes, corn, potatoes, wheat, vegetables).
Foreign Trade: *Major exports*—textiles, pottery, instruments, pharmaceuticals, postage stamps; *major imports*—food, manufactured goods.
Place of Interest: Mt. Naafkopf; medieval village of Vaduz and the prince's 700-year-old castle; ski resort at Malbun.

Liechtenstein is the most highly industrialized country in the world, with only 3% of the people dependent on farming for their living. Its prosperous people enjoy a high standard of living.

Because of low taxes, about 50,000 foreign businesses have headquarters in Liechtenstein.

Thousands of tourists visit each year.

The sale of postage stamps provides a large share of the government's annual budget.

Covering an area smaller than Cleveland, Ohio, Liechtenstein is bordered by Austria on the east and Switzerland on the north, south, and west. Warm winds protect the country from temperature extremes. Summers are cool and winters are cold with much snow.

The barony of Schellenberg and the county of Vaduz, founded in 814, were bought by Johann Adam von Liechtenstein in 1699 and 1712. The Holy Roman emperor joined the two areas to create the principality of Liechtenstein in 1719.

Following French and Russian invasions during the Napoleonic wars, Liechtenstein joined the German Confederation in 1815. Ties with Austria developed, leading to withdrawal from the confederation in 1866. It remained neutral in both World War I and World War II.

Since 1924 Switzerland has administered the principality's defense, foreign affairs, and customs.

In elections in 1978 and 1982, the Patriotic Union Party won control of parliament.

In a national referendum on July 1, 1984, male voters approved giving women the right to vote.

After 46 years of rule, 78-year-old Prince Franz Josef II on Aug. 26, 1984, turned over executive duties to his son Crown Prince Hans Adam.

QUICK QUIZ: Which U.S. President was nicknamed "Old Rough and Ready"? See page 351.

LUXEMBOURG

Official Name: Grand Duchy of Luxembourg.
Area: 998 square miles (2,586 sq. km.).
Population: 366,700.
Capital: Luxembourg-Ville, 79,600.
Government: Constitutional grand duchy.
Prime Minister: Jacques Santer (since 1984).
Chief of State: Grand Duke Jean (since 1964).
Legislature: *Council of State,* 21 members; *Chamber of Deputies,* 59 members.
U.S. Ambassador to Luxembourg: John E. Dolibois.
Luxembourgian Ambassador to U.S.: Paul Peters.
Flag: Red, white, and light blue stripes.
Languages: French, German, Luxembourgish.
Principal Ethnic Group: Gallo-Germanic.
Religion: Roman Catholicism (97%).
Leading Industries: Manufacturing (steel, machinery, rubber, chemicals, wine, fertilizer); mining (iron ore); trade and banking; agriculture (grapes, poultry, hogs, cattle, dairy products, sheep, oats, potatoes, wheat, vegetables).
Foreign Trade: *Major exports*—iron and steel; *major imports*—coal, petroleum.
Places of Interest: Grand ducal palace; national museum; Cathedral of Notre Dame; Citadel of St. Espirit; Quirinus rock chapel; Chervaux and Vianden castles.

Somewhat smaller than Rhode Island, Luxembourg is one of the world's 20 most important steel-producing nations.

Luxembourg has the highest per capita usage of electricity among industrialized nations—50% greater than that of the United States.

Lowlands rise gradually from the Luxembourg-Lorraine iron-mining basin in the southwest to the Ardennes Plateau in the north.

Belgium lies to the west, France to the south, and West Germany to the east.

Luxembourg began as a feudal domain in A.D. 963. In 1308 the count of Luxembourg became Holy Roman Emperor Henry VII, and in 1354 Luxembourg was raised to a duchy.

After 1443 it was governed by the rulers of the Netherlands. Luxembourg was granted autonomy in 1839, but Dutch kings continued to rule.

In 1867 the Treaty of London declared Luxembourg an independent, neutral state. It became a parliamentary democracy under a constitution adopted in 1868. At the death of Dutch King Willem III in 1890, the grand duchy went to Duke Adolf of Nassau.

Luxembourg was occupied by German troops in both world wars.

Grand Duke Jean became the country's ruler on Nov. 12, 1964, when his mother, Grand Duchess Charlotte, abdicated.

In a national parliamentary election on June 17, 1984, the Christian Social Party won a plurality of seats. Jacques Santer became prime minister, forming a coalition cabinet.

Grand Duke Jean visited President Reagan in Washington in November 1984.

MADAGASCAR

Official Name: Democratic Republic of Madagascar.
Area: 226,658 square miles (587,041 sq. km.).
Population: 10,150,000.
Capital: Antananarivo (Tananarive), 347,466.
Government: One-party Marxist socialist state.
President: Didier Ratsiraka (since 1975).
Prime Minister: Desire Rakotoarijaona (since 1977).
Parliament: *National People's Assembly,* 137 members.
U.S. Ambassador: Robert B. Keating.
Ambassador to U.S.: Leon Maxime Rajaobelina.
Flag: White bar; stripes of red over green.
Official Languages: Malagasy and French.
Main Ethnic Group: Merina (Malayo-Polynesian descent).
Religions: Christianity (40%), animism, Islam.
Leading Industries: Agriculture (coffee, cotton, cloves, vanilla, tobacco, rice, sugar, sisal, cattle); mining (chromite, graphite, mica); food processing; manufacturing (leather products, textiles, paper, consumer goods, tobacco products); fishing.
Foreign Trade: *Major exports*—chromite, graphite, coffee, vanilla, cloves, meat, sugar, sisal; *major imports*—machinery, electrical equipment, chemicals, rice, textiles, trucks, petroleum.
Places of Interest: Antananarivo marketplaces.

MADAGASCAR TODAY

Although nearly as large as Texas, Madagascar is an underdeveloped island nation with few known natural resources.

The country's Marxist socialist government rules through a one-party parliamentary system. Banks, insurance companies, mines, and shipping have been nationalized.

Once an exporter of rice, the nation has become a rice importer as its economy has declined.

The former French colony depends heavily on economic aid from France.

Most of the people are poor farmers. Only 4 in 10 persons can read and write.

Madagascar, the world's fourth-largest island, lies in the Indian Ocean about 250 miles east of the African coast of Mozambique. Its west coast is deeply indented and bordered by a gradually rising plain leading to a central plateau. The highest mountain, 9,450-foot Mt. Tsaratanana, stands in the north.

EARLY HISTORY

Immigration to Madagascar from the southwest Pacific began before the Christian era and continued until the 1400s. These immigrants, later known as Merinas, settled mainly in the central highlands. The coastal regions were colonized by immigrants from Africa and Arabia. In the 1500s and 1600s the Merina kingdom became the strongest on the island and later imposed its rule over most of Madagascar.

In the 1800s King Radama I (reigned 1810–28) allowed English and French missionaries to open churches and schools, and they devised a

written form of the Malagasy language.

French efforts to take Madagascar were opposed by the Merina rulers in the wars of 1883–85 and 1895–96. Madagascar became a French colony in 1896. The monarchy was abolished and the last queen was exiled.

In 1947 an armed uprising broke out. Between 60,000 and 90,000 people were killed before it was crushed by French troops in 1947.

Madagascar was granted self-government as the autonomous Malagasy Republic within the French Community on Oct. 14, 1958.

INDEPENDENCE

Madagascar attained full independence on June 26, 1960. Philibert Tsiranana, head of the dominant Social Democratic Party, became president. He was reelected president in 1965 and 1972. During his administration French settlers continued to dominate the economy.

After a week of student riots and a general strike, President Tsiranana turned over his powers to the army chief, Maj. Gen. Gabriel Ramanantsoa, on May 18, 1972.

At a national referendum in October 1972 the voters approved extending military rule for five years, ousting Tsiranana from the government.

On Feb. 5, 1975, Lt. Col. Richard Ratsimandrava became the new military government leader. Six days later, on Feb. 11, Ratsimandrava was assassinated in an ambush in Antananarivo.

On Feb. 13–14, 1975, government troops stormed military police barracks and socialist headquarters, killing 21 persons and arresting 297, including former President Tsiranana.

About two-thirds of the 140,000 French settlers fled from Madagascar in 1975, leaving the nation short of managers and technicians.

The new government forced the United States and France to close military bases.

Didier Ratsiraka, a former naval officer, who had served as foreign minister since 1972, was chosen president and head of the 19-member military junta on June 15, 1975.

At a referendum on Dec. 21, 1975, the people approved a new constitution written by Ratsiraka and elected him to a 7-year term as president.

In an election on June 30, 1977, the 137 members of the national assembly were elected to 5-year terms. All were selected by the single political party, the National Front for the Defense of the Malagasy Socialist Revolution.

After riots in which up to 1,000 Comoros immigrants were killed in northwestern Madagascar, the Comoros government in 1977 undertook to repatriate the remaining 25,000 or more Comorians living in Madagascar.

Three persons were killed and 150 were arrested in two days of riots on May 29–30, 1978, by students protesting lowered educational standards. Additional riots occurred in 1981–84.

Because of the declining economy, the government was unable to meet interest payments on its foreign debt of $1 billion in 1982, and foreign commercial banks refused to make further loans until austerity plans were instituted.

Ratsiraka won a 7-year term as president in an election on Nov. 7, 1982, receiving 80% of the vote.

MALAWI

Official Name: Republic of Malawi.
Area: 45,747 square miles (118,484 sq. km.).
Population: 6,857,000.
Chief Cities: Lilongwe, capital, 130,000; Balantyre-Limbe, 219,000.
Government: One-party republic.
President: Hastings Kamuzu Banda (since 1966).
National Assembly: 107 members.
U.S. Ambassador to Malawi: Weston Adams.
Malawi Ambassador to U.S.: Nelson T. Mizere.
Flag: Black, red, and green stripes, with red rising sun on black stripe.
Official Languages: Chichewa and English.
Main Ethnic Groups: Chewa, Nyanja.
Religions: Animism (67%), Christianity, Islam.
Leading Industries: Agriculture (cotton, peanuts, coffee, tea, tobacco, maize, cattle, sorghum, sugar, millet); fishing; food processing; construction.
Foreign Trade: *Major exports*—sugar, tobacco, tea, peanuts, cotton; *major imports*—machinery, consumer products, motor vehicles, petroleum.
Places of Interest: Lake Malawi; Mlanje Mountains; Great Rift Valley; public gardens at Lilongwe; Blantyre-Limbe tea estates.

MALAWI TODAY

About the size of Pennsylvania, Malawi has few resources other than farm and grazing land. Lake Malawi (formerly Lake Nyasa) covers about 20% of the country's area, and much of the rest is too mountainous to be farmed.

Most of the people live in tribal villages, seldom seeing any money from one year to the next. They live by fishing and farming. Only about 1 in 7 persons can read and write.

Long and narrow, Malawi is a landlocked country in southeast Africa. Lake Malawi extends along the eastern border with Tanzania and Mozambique. Zambia is to the west.

Lake Malawi drains south into the Shire River. The steep cliffs of the Rift Valley rise to the west.

EARLY HISTORY

For several centuries Lake Malawi attracted Bantu tribes from the northwest. The Malawi kingdom was established in the region in the 1300s. By the 1600s the Malawi people had fallen under dominance of the Yao tribes, who sold the Malawi as slaves to Arab traders.

The Scottish missionary-explorer David Livingstone became the first European to reach Lake Malawi, on Sept. 16, 1859. He and Scottish missionaries who followed him fought the Arab slave trade.

Britain established a protectorate in 1891, calling the area *Nyasaland.*

Resentful of mistreatment by British plantation owners, Malawi tribesmen led by John Chilembwe staged an unsuccessful uprising in 1915.

QUICK QUIZ: Which U.S. President was nicknamed the "Napoleon of the Stump"? See page 350.

MALAWI (continued)

In 1953 Nyasaland was forced by the British into federation with North and South Rhodesia.

The Nyasaland African Congress (NAC), founded in 1944, opposed the federation. The NAC gained strength in 1958 when its leaders recalled Dr. Hastings Kamuzu Banda from 40 years of study abroad.

The British, faced with rising protests, outlawed the NAC in 1959 and imprisoned Banda and 1,200 of his followers. Other followers, however, built up the Malawi Congress Party (MCP). The British released Banda in 1960.

In elections in August 1961 Banda won control of the territorial government. The federation was dissolved on Dec. 31, 1963.

INDEPENDENCE

Under Banda's leadership, Nyasaland became the independent state of Malawi within the British Commonwealth of Nations on July 6, 1964. A coup in 1964 proved unsuccessful, and Banda was able to resolve dissension within his party.

Malawi became a republic on July 6, 1966, with Banda as its first president.

Since 1967 a program of persecution has been carried on against the Jehovah's Witnesses sect, whose members refuse to salute the Malawi flag. The government banned the group and placed about 30,000 in prison camps. In December 1975 officials of the sect protested their members were being beaten, tortured, and raped.

In 1970 Banda was acclaimed president for life by a convention of the Malawi Congress Party, the only authorized political party in the country.

In ruling his country Banda brooks no opposition. When one of his cabinet ministers, Aleke Banda, mentioned himself as a possible successor to the president in an article published in Zambia, he was dismissed in March 1973 from both the cabinet and the party.

Malawi passed a law in 1974 banning miniskirts, with a penalty of six months in prison for any woman baring her knees.

The government moved its capital in 1975 from Zomba to the new centrally located city of Lilongwe to encourage opening up the interior of the country. The capital was developed at a cost of more than $250 million by a profit-making corporation. Lilongwe's extensive public gardens employ 2,000 workers.

Some $68 million was budgeted by the government in 1976 for expenditure on agricultural development and hydroelectric power projects. Wages and prices were controlled by the government in an effort to reduce inflation.

The former head of the secret police, Martin Gwede, and the former head of the MCP party, Albert Andrew Muwalo Nqumayo, were convicted of treason on Feb. 14, 1977, and sentenced to death for plotting to overthrow President Banda.

On July 4, 1977, Banda released most of the remaining 2,000 political prisoners he had jailed.

The first general election in 17 years was held on June 29, 1978. Although all candidates were members of the MCP party, several contested for 47 of the 87 seats in the national assembly. A national election was held on June 29, 1983, for an expanded 107-member parliament. Candidates were not permitted to campaign before the election.

MALAYSIA

Official Name: Malaysia.
Area: 127,317 square miles (329,749 sq. km.).
Population: 15,793,000.
Chief Cities: Kuala Lumpur, capital, 451,977; George Town, 269,603; Ipoh, 247,953; Johore Bahru, 136,234; Klang, 113,611.
Government: Constitutional monarchy.
Prime Minister: Datuk Seri Mahathir Mohamad (since 1981).
King: Sultan Mahmood Iskander of Jahore (since 1984).
Parliament: Senate (Dewan Negara), 58 members; House of Representatives (Dewan Ra'ayat), 154.
U.S. Ambassador to Malaysia: Thomas P. Shoesmith.
Malaysian Ambassador to U.S.: Dato' Lew Sip Hon.
Flag: Red and white stripes with blue field containing gold crescent and 14-pointed gold star.
Languages: Malay and English (both official), Chinese, Tamil.
Main Ethnic Groups: Malay (44%), Chinese (36%), Indian and Pakistani (10%).
Religions: Islam, Buddhism, Christianity, Hinduism.
Leading Industries: Agriculture (rubber, rice, palm kernels, tea, peppers, coconuts); mining (tin, petroleum, iron ore, natural gas, bauxite); forestry and lumbering; manufacturing (steel, automobiles, electronics, petroleum products, rubber products, palm oil, chemicals, textiles); fishing; tourism.
Foreign Trade: Major exports—petroleum, rubber, lumber, palm oil, tin, iron ore; major imports—machinery, rice, textiles.
Places of Interest: Batu Cave; Cameron Highlands; Malaysia National Park. In Kuala Lumpur: National museum; national mosque; houses on stilts.

MALAYSIA TODAY

Although about the size of New Mexico, Malaysia has over 10 times as many people.

The nation has two parts separated by 400 miles of the South China Sea. West Malaysia lies on a peninsula in Southeast Asia just south of Thailand. East Malaysia covers the northern coast of the island of Borneo.

Malaysia is an oil-exporting nation and the world's leading producer of tin and natural rubber.

Because Malaysia has abundant natural resources, it has a stronger economy and more industry than most other nations of Southeast Asia. But about 1 in 3 Malaysians are poor farm workers who cannot read and write.

Malaysia's king is elected for a 5-year term by the sultans of nine states of Malaysia.

About 80% of West Malaysia is covered by mountains and tropical forests. Most of the people live along the more than 1,200 miles of coast.

The East Malaysian states of Sarawak and Sabah lie on the island of Borneo. The nation's highest mountain, Mt. Kinabalu (13,455 feet), stands in Sabah.

The climate along the coasts is hot, but it becomes cool in the hills and mountains of the interior. Annual rainfall averages 100 inches.

EARLY HISTORY

Portuguese traders first arrived on the Malay peninsula in 1511.

In 1786 the British East India Company leased the island of Penang.

By the early 1900s Britain controlled all the Malay states as colonies or protectorates.

In 1946 the Union of Malaya was formed, uniting Penang and Malacca with the nine Malay states. The union became the Federation of Malaya in 1948.

Communist insurrections erupted in 1948. The guerrilla terrorism in the countryside finally was brought under control in 1959.

INDEPENDENT MALAYSIA

The Federation of Malaya was granted independence by Britain on Aug. 31, 1957, with Tunku Abdul Rahman as prime minister.

Malaysia became an independent constitutional monarchy on Sept. 16, 1963. It incorporated the former Federation of Malaya and the former British colonies of Singapore, Sarawak, and North Borneo (Sabah).

Singapore was expelled and given its separate independence in 1965.

The worst racial rioting in Malaysia's history broke out May 13, 1969, in Kuala Lumpur between Malays and Chinese.

Tun Abdul Razak became prime minister upon Rahman's retirement in September 1970.

Offshore oil strikes made in 1973 went into production in 1975, boosting the economy.

Razak died of leukemia on Jan. 14, 1976. He was succeeded as prime minister on the following day by his brother-in-law Datuk Hussein Onn.

Prime Minister Datuk Hussein's National Front coalition won a comfortable two-thirds majority in parliamentary elections held in 1978.

MALAYSIA IN THE 1980s

Datuk Seri Mahathir Mohamad succeeded Hussein as prime minister in 1981. His party retained control in parliamentary elections in 1982.

The prospering economy, which grew at an average rate of 8% a year in the 1970s, slowed somewhat in the 1980s, but still outperformed that of most other nations with a growth rate of 5% in 1982–84.

The number of Malaysians living at the poverty level declined from 49.3% in 1970 to 29.2% in 1980. The government plans to reduce this to 16.7% in 1990 and eliminate poverty altogether by 2000.

Sultan Mahmood Iskandar of Johore, 52, took the oath of office on April 26, 1984, for a 5-year term as Malaysia's eighth king. He had been elected to the office in a secret ballot in February by the sultans of the nation's nine states. The new king, who wears a gun belt with pistols on each hip, was convicted of a slaying in 1977, but was pardoned by his father who was then sultan.

An $18.6 billion 5-year plan for 1981–85 emphasized private investment in the development of heavy industry, including a liquid natural-gas plant and a project to make the nation self-sufficient in producing fertilizer.

MALDIVES

Official Name: Republic of Maldives.
Area: 115 square miles (298 sq. km.).
Population: 181,000.
Capital: Malé, 29,522.
Government: Republic ruled by decree.
President: Maumoon Abdul Gayoom (since 1978).
Legislature: *Majlis,* 48 members.
U.S. Ambassador to Maldives: John Hathaway Reed.
Maldivian Ambassador to U.S.: Abdul Sattar.
Flag: Red field with green panel containing white crescent.
Languages: Divehi (official), Arabic.
Ethnic Groups: Sinhalese, Arab, Dravidian.
Official Religion: Sunni Islam.
Leading Industries: Fishing; agriculture (coconuts, corn, millet, pumpkins, sweet potatoes, fruits); tourism; shipping; handicrafts, rope making..
Foreign Trade: *Major exports*—fish, rope, copra, ambergris, lace, shells, handicrafts; *major imports*—grain, drugs, textiles, consumer goods.
Places of Interest: Plants and animals of the various islands; Malé; beach resorts.

One of the 10 smallest and poorest nations in the world, the Maldives have a land area smaller than the city of Philadelphia. Only a few Maldivians can read and write.

The 2,000 or more Maldive islands string out over 550 miles of the Indian Ocean. The largest has an area of about 5 square miles. About 215 are inhabited. The climate is hot and humid.

Almost all the men of the Maldives fish for a living. Dried fish is the country's main export, with Sri Lanka the main customer. Rice, the main staple of the islanders, must be imported.

About 50,000 tourists visit the islands each year. A tourist who breaks the law is subject to punishment by banishment to an uninhabited isle with no food other than what he can catch from the sea or pick from coconut palms.

The islands were ruled as a sultanate by members of the Didi clan from about 1100 until 1968. Arab traders visited in 1153, converting the people to Islam. In the 1600s the Maldives came under the protection of Sri Lanka (Ceylon), then under Dutch rule.

The Maldives became a protectorate of Britain in December 1887.

The Maldives were granted full independence on July 26, 1965. The nation was a constitutional monarchy until Nov. 11, 1968, when Sultan Mohammed Farid Didi I was deposed. A republic was proclaimed under President Amir Ibrahim Nasir, the sultan's prime minister in 1956–68.

President Nasir suspended the constitution and imposed rule by decree on March 6, 1975. Nasir resigned because of illness in 1978.

Without opposition Maumoon Abdul Gayoom was elected president by the national legislature in 1978 and 1983.

QUICK QUIZ: Which U.S. President of Congress defected to the British in 1780? See page 319.

MALI

Official Name: Republic of Mali.
Area: 478,767 square miles (1,240,000 sq. km.).
Population: 8,009,000.
Capital: Bamako, 404,022.
Government: One-party state.
President: Col. Moussa Traoré (since 1968).
National Assembly: 137 deputies.
U.S. Ambassador to Mali: Robert J. Ryan.
Mali Ambassador to U.S.: Lassana Keita.
Flag: Bars of green, yellow, and red.
Languages: French (official), Bambra.
Ethnic Groups: Mande (50%), Peul (17%), Voltaic (12%), Songhai (6%), Tuareg and Moors (5%).
Main Religion: Islam (90%).
Leading Industries: Agriculture (cattle, cotton, rice, peanuts, sorghum, millet, goats, sheep); fishing; mining (gold); manufacturing (textiles, cigarettes, matches, baskets, food processing).
Foreign Trade: *Major exports*—cotton, peanuts, fish, livestock; *major imports*—textiles, food, machinery, motor vehicles, petroleum products.
Places of Interest: Cliff-dwelling Dogon tribes near Sangha; Bamako; Timbuktu; Lake Débo.

MALI TODAY

A little larger than the combined areas of Texas and California, Mali is one of the most poverty-stricken nations in the world.

Ironically, the country counts among its mineral resources bauxite, uranium, iron ore, copper, manganese, phosphate, and gold. Currently only gold is mined, and that in small quantities, because the primitive transportation system of the landlocked country cannot handle large ore shipments.

The military government hopes to find foreign investors willing to develop the minerals and the necessary transportation and communications facilities.

Meanwhile, most of the people farm crops or herd livestock, barely raising enough food to feed their families.

The northern half of Mali is covered by the Sahara Desert. To the south is semidesert, and in the far southwest are savanna lands. The country generally has a hot climate with little rainfall.

Mali is bordered by Senegal, Mauritania, Algeria, Niger, Burkina Faso, Ivory Coast, and Guinea. The greater part of the country spreads north, east, and west of the great bend of the Niger River, while a rather small area lies south of the Niger.

EARLY HISTORY

For many years Mali was part of the empire of Ghana.

As Islam expanded in the western Sahara, Almoravid Berbers from Mauritania launched a *jihad,* or holy war, against peoples to the south. In 1076 Abu Bakr overthrew Ghana. Although in 1087 the Soninke leaders of Ghana recovered their independence for a century, their great empire had been disrupted.

In the 1000s the small Malinke state of Kangaba, south of Ghana, also embraced Islam and began to annex nearby kingdoms. The emperor Sundiata Keita conquered Ghana in 1235 and established the Muslim empire of Mali.

Under the leadership of Mansa Musa (1307–32), Mali reached its peak as a center of Muslim trade and learning. The empire disintegrated after his death.

The Songhai controlled the next great Islamic empire, with its center at Gao, until 1591, when the Moroccans defeated the Songhai at Tondibi and became the new rulers.

French troops conquered the region in 1881 to 1898. It became known as the territory of *French Soudan* in the colony of French West Africa, which was established in 1904.

INDEPENDENT REPUBLIC OF MALI

The French Soudan was granted self-government in 1958 as a member state in the French Community.

In 1959 the colony, renamed the *Sudanese Republic,* joined Senegal in the Mali Federation, which became independent on June 20, 1960. The federation dissolved on Aug. 20, 1960.

The former French Soudan proclaimed itself the *Republic of Mali* on Sept. 22, 1960, and withdrew from the French Community.

Modibo Keita, head of the Sudanese Union Party, became Mali's first president. Keita socialized Mali's economy, and formed close ties with the Soviet Union and communist China. These moves had a disastrous effect on Mali's economy and caused a split in the Sudanese Union Party among pro-Soviet, pro-Chinese, and pro-French factions. In 1967 Keita tried to appease the pro-French faction by reestablishing economic ties with France.

Keita took steps to strengthen his power in late 1967 and 1968. He dissolved the national assembly and began ruling by decree.

Mali's army, fearing the growing role of Keita's Chinese-trained militia, overthrew and imprisoned Keita on Nov. 19, 1968.

Lt. Moussa Traoré became president, and Capt. Yoro Diakité was named premier. Following an attempt to reinstate Keita on Aug. 13, 1969, Traoré assumed the premiership. For attempting a coup in 1971, Diakité was sentenced to life imprisonment in 1972.

Six years of drought from 1969 to 1974 killed up to 100,000 people and about three-fourths of the cattle in the nation. Many of the 700,000 Tuareg nomads of northern Mali migrated to other countries.

President Traoré invoked emergency powers in 1977 after demonstrations in May at the funeral of former President Keita, who died after being imprisoned since the 1968 coup.

Traoré arrested several cabinet members in February 1978, charging them with treason and fraud of more than $1.2 million in distribution of grain to drought victims.

One-party elections were held in 1979 and 1982 for 137-member national assembly.

Drought in 1984–85 caused food shortages affecting about 2 million of Mali's people.

MALTA

Official Name: Republic of Malta.
Area: 122 square miles (316 sq. km.).
Population: 353,000.
Cities: Valletta, capital, 14,020; Sliema, 22,000.
Government: Parliamentary republic.
Prime Minister: Carmelo Mifsud Bonnici (since 1984).
President: Agatha Barbara (since 1982).
House of Representatives: 65 members.
U.S. Ambassador to Malta: James M. Rentschler.
Maltese Ambassador to U.S.: Leslie Agius.
Flag: White and red bars, with George Cross in silver on white bar.
Languages: Maltese, English.
Official Religion: Roman Catholicism (99%).
Ethnic Groups: Arab, Italian, English.
Leading Industries: Shipbuilding and ship repairs; tourism; agriculture (poultry, dairy products, flowers, vegetables, fruits); manufacturing (textiles, yarn, clothing, electronic equipment, food processing).
Foreign Trade: *Major exports*—cotton yarn, textiles, cut flowers, ships and boats, wine; *major imports*—food, petroleum, automobiles, consumer products.
Places of Interest: Valletta; Hypogeum underground Neolithic temple at Paola; cave of Ghar Dalam; Blue Grotto at Zurrieq; cathedral museum at Mdina.

With a land area about as large as Kansas City, Mo., the island nation of Malta has only one major resource—its strategic location. It lies at the geographic center of the Mediterranean Sea, about 60 miles south of Sicily.

The socialist government depends on foreign aid to develop industries in an effort to become a "nonaligned" neutral nation.

The government also seeks to expand tourism to exploit Malta's year-round sunny climate and many historic monuments and buildings.

Malta includes two main islands, Malta and Gozo, and the small island of Comino.

Malta's strategic position has attracted successive waves of invaders. Phoenicians, Greeks, Carthaginians, Romans, Byzantines, and Arabs occupied the islands. In 1090 Malta was seized by the Normans.

In 1530 the Holy Roman emperor Charles V awarded Malta to the Knights of St. John of Jerusalem, who beat off repeated Turkish attacks.

Napoleon seized control in 1798. The Maltese rose against the French and, with the help of Britain, evicted them two years later.

In 1814 Malta became a British colony.

Maltese courage while under siege during World War II was rewarded in 1942, when the George Cross was bestowed on Malta itself—the first time an entire people had been so honored.

Malta became independent on Sept. 21, 1964. The country was governed from 1964 to 1971 by the conservative Nationalist Party, led by Prime Minister Giorgio Borg Olivier.

In a national election held in June 1971, the Malta Labor Party won by a narrow margin. Its leader, Dom Mintoff, became prime minister.

Malta's house of representatives declared the nation an independent republic in the British Commonwealth of Nations on Dec. 13, 1974. The constitution was amended to restrict political activities of the Roman Catholic Church.

Mintoff's socialist policies narrowly received voter approval in an election on Sept. 18, 1976, when the Labor Party won a majority of 34 seats in the 65-member House of Representatives.

For nearly two centuries Malta's economy had been dependent on jobs and money provided by British military bases located there. But the socialist government refused to renew leases on the bases. On April 1, 1979, the British military presence in Malta ended after 179 years.

Libya promised aid to Malta to make up for the loss of income from Britain.

After receiving aid from Libya for several years, Malta expelled Libyan advisers in August 1980 in a dispute over rights to offshore oil.

Malta and Italy signed an agreement on Sept. 15, 1980, under which Italy promised to protect Malta's neutrality.

Mintoff's government established diplomatic relations with the Soviet Union in 1981 and agreed to allow the Soviets to use the former British naval base as an oil-storage depot for their ships.

In an election on Dec. 12, 1981, Mintoff's socialist Labor Party narrowly kept control of the house of representatives by 34 seats to 31, even though the opposition Nationalist Party won a majority of votes, 114,132 to 109,990. Nationalist members boycotted sessions of the new house until March 29, 1983, charging that gerrymandering of election districts had robbed them of victory.

Agatha Barbara, 59, former minister of education, was chosen by the house of representatives on Feb. 16, 1982, as the nation's president, the first woman to hold the ceremonial office.

Mintoff pushed through legislation on June 29, 1983, permitting the government to confiscate property of the Roman Catholic Church, the largest landowner in Malta.

Mintoff ordered Roman Catholic schools to provide free education to their students or face confiscation by the government in July 1984. Church officials, who said they could not afford to operate their 72 schools without tuition payments, closed the schools in protest.

After 13 years as prime minister, Mintoff, 68, resigned on Dec. 22, 1984.

Carmelo Mifsud Bonnici, 51, Mintoff's handpicked successor, became prime minister.

MARSHALLS

Official Name: Republic of the Marshall Islands.
Area: 69.84 square miles (181 sq. km.).
Population: 36,000.

QUICK QUIZ: Who was the first U.S. Vice President to become President upon death of his predecessor? See page 349.

MARSHALLS *(continued)*
Capital: Majuro, 11,898.
Government: Self-governing republic.
President: Amata Kabua (since 1979).
Legislature: *Nitijela,* 33 members.
Flag: Blue field with white star in upper hoist corner; diagonal widening stripes, red over white.
Languages: Marshallese, English.
Main Religion: Christian.
Chief Ethnic Group: Micronesian.
Leading Industries: Fishing; agriculture (coconut palms, fruits, vegetables, poultry, hogs).
Foreign Trade: *major export*—copra; *major imports*—food, consumer goods.

One of the 10 smallest countries in the world both in population and land area, the Marshalls include 34 atolls and 1,225 islands. The land area and population are about equal to those of the city of Palm Springs, Calif.

Major atolls include Kwajalein, 6 sq. mi.; Alinglapalap, 5.7 sq. mi.; Arno, 5 sq. mi.; Jaluit, 4.4 sq. mi.; Majuro, 3.5 sq. mi.; Enewetak, 2.5 sq. mi.; Namu, 2.4 sq. mi.; and Bikini, 2.3 sq. mi.

The Marshalls' economy depends heavily on U.S. payments for use of a $1 billion military base on Kwajelein atoll to test and recover missiles fired 4,200 miles from California.

The Marshalls lie about 2,000 miles southwest of Hawaii. Micronesia is to the west and Kiribati is to the south.

The first European to visit the islands was Spanish explorer Alvaro de Saavedra in the 1520s. British sea captain John Marshall came to the islands in 1788, giving them his name.

Germany established a protectorate in 1886 and bought the islands from Spain in 1899.

During World War I Japanese forces occupied the Marshalls. In 1920 Japan was given a League of Nations mandate over the islands.

In World War II, the U.S. captured the Marshalls in February 1944, killing about 8,000 Japanese troops with a loss of about 300 Americans.

In 1947 the Marshalls became part of the U.S. Trust Territory of the Pacific Islands.

From 1946 to 1958 the U.S. tested 64 nuclear weapons at Bikini and Enewetak atolls, after relocating residents of those islands.

The Marshalls became self-governing in 1979. A constitution was approved in a referendum on March 1, and the 33 members of the first constitutional legislature, the Nitijela, were elected on April 10.

The legislature chose Amata Kabua, 50, a tribal chief, as the nation's first president.

President Kabua signed an agreement with the U.S. on Oct. 20, 1982, granting the U.S. military rights to Kwajalein atoll for 30 years in return for economic aid of about $750 million.

Hundreds of Marshall islanders filed court suits in 1981–83 totaling over $4 billion for damages from American nuclear tests in the 1940s to 1960s.

The U.S. agreed on June 25, 1983, to pay residents of the islands $183.7 million over a 15-year period to compensate for the nuclear tests.

In a referendum on Sept. 7, 1983, the Marshall islanders approved by a margin of 4 to 1 the compact of free association with the U.S. The agreement must be ratified by the U.S. Congress and by the United Nations.

MAURITANIA

Official Name: Islamic Republic of Mauritania.
Area: 397,955 square miles (1,030,700 sq. km.).
Population: 1,939,000.
Capital: Nouakchott, 134,986.
Government: Military junta.
President: Col. Maaouniya Ould Sidi Ahmed Taya (since 1984).
U.S. Ambassador to Mauritania: Robert L. Pugh.
Mauritanian Ambassador to U.S.: Abdellah Ould Daddah.
Flag: Gold star and crescent on green field.
Languages: French (official), Arabic.
Ethnic Groups: Arab-Berber (35%), black (65%).
Religion: Islam.
Leading Industries: Agriculture (cattle, sheep, goats, horses, millet, dates, gum arabic, vegetables, fruits); mining (iron ore, copper, gold, salt); fishing.
Foreign Trade: *Major exports*—iron ore, copper, livestock, gum arabic, fish, salt, dates; *major imports*—food, vehicles, petroleum, machinery, textiles.
Places of Interest: Kédia d'Idjit Mountains; iron mines; Nouakchott; Port-Etienne.

MAURITANIA TODAY

Larger than Texas and California combined, Mauritania depends on the export of iron ore and copper for most of the cash income that has enabled it to obtain a few benefits of modern civilization. European companies share profits from the mining operations with the government.

Most Mauritanians live as they have for hundreds of years—the Arabs and Berbers as nomadic herdsmen and the black tribesmen as subsistence farmers and livestock raisers. Few can read and write, and only about 10% of the children attend school.

Most of the country is desert. The Senegal River on the southern border is the only waterway. Mauritania's climate is mostly hot and dry.

MAURITANIA'S HISTORY

In Roman times *Mauretania* was the name of a vast kingdom that included western Algeria, Morocco, and part of what is now Mauritania.

In the 1000s A.D. Berber invasions into the present-day Mauritania area pushed the black African inhabitants southward. The area became the base for holy wars in which the Muslims conquered Morocco, Algeria, Spain, and Ghana.

The French began invading Mauritania in 1904. Mauritania became part of French West Africa in 1920 and was administered from Saint-Louis along with Senegal.

In 1958 it became the self-governing Islamic Republic of Mauritania within the French Community.

Mauritania was granted full independence on Nov. 28, 1960, under President Mokhtar Ould Daddah, who previously had been prime minister. He was reelected to 5-year terms as president in 1966, 1971, and 1976.

Six years of drought and famine brought the nation to the verge of disaster in 1974.

In November 1974 the government nationalized the iron-mining industry.

Mauritania joined with Morocco in 1976 in partitioning the former Spanish Sahara. Mauritanian troops clashed with those of the Algerian-backed Polisario guerrillas who sought independence for the Western Sahara.

Army Chief of Staff Lt. Col. Mustapha Ould Salek overthrew and imprisoned President Daddah and his cabinet on July 9, 1978.

Prime Minister Ahmed Ould Bousseif and 11 other persons were killed in a plane crash in the Atlantic Ocean off Senegal on May 27, 1979. A week later on June 3, President Salek resigned and was replaced by Lt. Col. Mohammed Mahmoud Ould Luly. Lt. Col. Mohammed Khouna Ould Haidala was appointed prime minister.

A peace agreement was signed with the Polisario guerrillas on Aug. 5, 1979, in which Mauritania gave up its claims to the Western Sahara region.

Haidala overthrew Luly on Jan. 4, 1980, making himself president.

Although the military junta outlawed slavery in a decree of July 1980, the Anti-Slavery Society of London estimated in 1981 that about 100,000 black Mauritanians remained in slavery to Muslim Moors.

Col. Maaouniya Ould Sidi Ahmed Taya, head of the army, overthrew Haidalla on Dec. 12, 1984, and placed him under house arrest.

MAURITIUS

Official Name: Mauritius.
Area: 790 square miles (2,045 sq. km.).
Population: 1,031,000.
Capital: Port-Louis, 146,844.
Government: Parliamentary democracy.
Prime Minister: Aneerood Jugnauth (since 1982).
Legislative Assembly: 70 members.
Ambassador to U.S.: Chitmansing Jesseransing.
U.S. Ambassador to Mauritius: George Andrews.
Flag: Red, blue, yellow, and green stripes.
Languages: English (official), Creole, Hindi, Urdu, French.
Main Ethnic Groups: Asian Indian descent (67%), Creole (28%), Chinese descent (3%).
Chief Religions: Hinduism (47%), Christianity (34%), Islam (16%).
Leading Industries: Agriculture (sugarcane, rice, tea, tobacco, aloe, potatoes, onions, vegetables, fruits, livestock, poultry); manufacturing (textiles); food processing; fishing.
Foreign Trade: *Major exports*—sugar, molasses, tea; textiles; *major imports*—rice, wheat, cotton fabrics, petroleum products, fertilizers, machinery, consumer goods.
Places of Interest: Pamplemousses Garden; Nicolière Reservoir; Plaine Champagne; Black River gorges; Grand Bassin Lake; Morne Brabant; Mahebourg Naval Museum; Blue Bay Beach; Belle Mare.

MAURITIUS TODAY

About two-thirds the size of Rhode Island, Mauritius has no important mineral deposits. The economy depends almost entirely on sugar, which accounts for more than 90% of its exports. Tea and molasses are also exported. Tourism is being developed as a source of foreign exchange.

Mauritius was the home of the flightless dodo bird until it became extinct in the 1600s.

An island of volcanic origin, Mauritius lies in the Indian Ocean about 500 miles east of Madagascar. The island of Mauritius itself has an area of 720 square miles. The nation also includes several smaller islands, including Rodriguez (42 sq. mi.), Agalega, and Cargados Carajos. On Mauritius a plain rises toward a central plateau of about 2,200 feet before dropping to the southern and western coasts.

HISTORY OF MAURITIUS

Although Mauritius was probably visited by Arabs, Malays, and Portuguese, the first colonists were the Dutch in 1589. They named the island after their ruler, Prince Maurice of Nassau. A Dutch settlement, established in 1638, was abandoned in 1710.

The French claimed the island in 1713, but it was taken by the British in 1810. It was formally ceded to Britain by the Treaty of Paris in 1814. The island was administered jointly with Seychelles until 1903.

In 1965 the British detached the island of Diego Garcia from Mauritius control and leased it to the U.S. as a military base for intercontinental bombers. The 1,200 residents of the island were relocated to other islands.

Parliamentary elections in 1967 were won by a coalition that included the island's Labor Party and parties representing Muslims and Hindus.

Mauritius was granted full independence as a parliamentary state within the British Commonwealth of Nations on March 12, 1968. Sir Seewoosagur Ramgoolam, who had headed the colonial government since 1947 as leader of the Labor Party, became prime minister.

As president of the Organization of African Unity (OAU), Prime Minister Ramgoolam helped lead the drive for black majority rule in South Africa, even though South Africa is one of Mauritius' main trading partners.

In a national election on Dec. 20, 1976, the Marxist Militant Mauritian Movement (MMM) party won 34 seats in the 70-member national assembly, but the other parties joined in a coalition that kept Ramgoolam as prime minister.

The Marxist MMM in a landslide election victory on June 12, 1982, ended 35 years of governing by the pro-Western 81-year-old Ramgoolam. The new prime minister, Aneerood Jugnauth, 52, formed a leftist coalition cabinet that included the MMM.

When the MMM withdrew from the cabinet coalition, Jugnauth called new elections on Aug. 21, 1983. He formed a new socialist party and arranged a coalition with two minor parties. Jugnauth's coalition decisively defeated the MMM to win a majority of 41 seats to the MMM's 19.

QUICK QUIZ: When did the U.S. buy Florida from Spain? See page 321.

MEXICO

Official Name: United Mexican States.
Area: 761,605 square miles (1,972,547 sq. km.).
Population: 80,490,000.
Chief Cities: Mexico City, capital, 9,191,295; Netzahualcoyotl, 2,331,151; Guadalajara, 1,906,145; Monterrey, 1,064,629; Puebla de Zaragoza, 710,833; Juárez, 625,040; León, 624,816; Tijuana, 566,344; Acapulco, 462,144; Chihuahua, 385,953; Mexicali, 348,528.
Largest Metropolitan Area: Mexico City, 14,750,182.
Government: Federal republic.
President: Miguel de la Madrid Hurtado (since 1982).
National Congress: *Senate,* 64 members; *Chamber of Deputies,* 400 members.
U.S. Ambassador to Mexico: John Gavin.
Mexican Ambassador to U.S.: Jorge Espinosa de los Reyes.
Flag: Green, white, and red bars; coat of arms in white bar—brown eagle on cactus devouring green serpent (representing Aztec legend), encircled by laurel wreath.
Official Language: Spanish.
Main Ethnic Groups: Mestizo (mixed Spanish-Indian descent), (60%), American Indian (30%).
Religion: Roman Catholicism (97%).
Leading Industries: Trade and services; manufacturing (steel, petroleum products, cement, automobiles, fertilizers, textiles, paper, aluminum, electricity); tourism; agriculture (sugarcane, coffee, cattle, cotton, wheat, rice, maize, fruits, vegetables); mining (petroleum, natural gas, coal, iron ore, copper, manganese, zinc, lead); fishing; construction.
Foreign Trade: *Major exports*—petroleum, cotton, sugar, coffee, shrimp, zinc, lead, copper; *major imports*—food, machinery, consumer goods.
Places of Interest: Mayan archaeological ruins on Yucatán peninsula; Aztec ruins and pyramids near Mexico City; Popocatepetl, Parícutin, Ixtaccíhuatl and Citlaltépetl volcanoes; Sierra Madre mountains; luxury tourist resorts at Acapulco, Manzanillo, Cozumel; Guadalajara; Oaxaca. *In and near Mexico City:* Cathedral of Zócalo; University of Mexico; national palace; Chapultepec Park; Xochimilco floating gardens; National Museum of Anthropology; Museum of Modern Art.

MEXICO TODAY

With huge oil reserves and one of the most stable governments in Latin America, Mexico has hopes of becoming a major industrial nation.

Because one-third of the people still depend on agriculture for their living, Mexico has been a leader in the "green revolution" that encourages farmers to use more productive seed, hybrids, and fertilizers. The government has spent millions of dollars on irrigation projects to reclaim unproductive land. However, many Mexicans still live at a subsistence level. About 1 in 3 cannot read and write.

In an effort to encourage decentralization of manufacturing, the government gives tax reductions to industries locating in rural areas.

Mexico is about one-fourth the size of the U.S., which lies to the north. Guatemala and Belize lie to the south.

The land is dominated by a high central plateau running north and south, enclosed by the mountain ranges of the Sierra Madre. The longest river is the Rio Grande.

Climate ranges from subtropical in the coastal zones to extreme cold in the mountains.

EARLY HISTORY

Indian civilizations developed in Mexico more than 2,000 years ago.

The Maya Indians in the Yucatán peninsula mastered the arts of construction and stonecarving, built cities, developed a calendar, and studied astronomy. The Nahuatl culture, established much later in the central plains, included the Toltecs and the Aztecs.

Mexico came under Spanish rule after conquistador Hernán Cortés landed at Veracruz in 1519 and conquered the highly civilized Aztecs.

INDEPENDENCE

A drive for independence began on Sept. 16, 1810, led by Miguel Hidalgo, a Mexican priest. Independence from Spain was finally achieved in 1821 under the leadership of Agustín de Iturbide and Vicente Guerrero. Iturbide became emperor in 1822, but was deposed in 1823.

Gen. Antonio López de Santa Anna ruled in the 1830s and 1840s. The territory of Texas seceded in 1836 and joined the U.S. in 1844.

After the Mexican War (1846–48), Mexico was forced to cede half its territory to the U.S.

STATES OF MEXICO

NAME	AREA (sq. mi.)	CAPITAL	NAME	AREA (sq. mi.)	CAPITAL
Aguascalientes	2,158	Aguascalientes	Morelos	1,908	Cuernavaca
Baja California Norte	27,071	Mexicali	Nayarit	10,665	Tepic
Baja California Sur	28,447	La Paz	Nuevo León	24,925	Monterrey
Campeche	21,666	Campeche	Oaxaca	36,820	Oaxaca
Chiapas	28,528	Tuxtla	Puebla	13,096	Puebla
Chihuahua	95,401	Chihuahua	Querétaro	4,544	Querétaro
Coahuila	58,522	Saltillo	Quintana Roo	16,228	Chetumal
Colima	2,106	Colima	San Luis Potosí	24,266	San Luis Potosí
Durango	46,196	Durango	Sinaloa	22,429	Culiacán
Federal District	579	Mexico City	Sonora	71,403	Hermosillo
Guanajuato	11,810	Guanajuato	Tabasco	9,522	Villahermosa
Guerrero	24,631	Chilpancingo	Tamaulipas	30,822	Ciudad Victoria
Hidalgo	8,103	Pachuca	Tlaxcala	1,511	Tlaxcala
Jalisco	30,941	Guadalajara	Veracruz	28,114	Jalapa
México	8,286	Toluca	Yucatán	16,749	Mérida
Michoacán	23,114	Morelia	Zacatecas	28,973	Zacatecas

In 1861, during a period of internal disorder, French troops captured the capital and crowned Austrian Archduke Maximilian as emperor.

After the French withdrew, the forces of Benito Juárez regained control, and in 1867 Maximilian was executed. Mexico again became a republic.

Gen. Porfirio Díaz seized power in 1876 and ruled as dictator. He was overthrown in 1911 by a liberal revolt led by Francisco Madero.

Liberal factions disputed, and leaders such as Francisco Villa and Emiliano Zapata rose and fell. A violent anticlerical movement persecuted the Roman Catholic Church.

A reform constitution was adopted in 1917. A succession of leaders attempted to bring stability to the political and governmental structure. Most notable of the leaders were Alvaro Obregón and Plutarco Elías Calles.

From 1934 to 1940 the liberal regime of Lázaro Cárdenas instituted widespread reforms.

In 1938 Mexico became the first noncommunist country to nationalize its petroleum industry, taking over all foreign-owned oil companies. Pemex, a government corporation, was established to manage the petroleum holdings.

PRESIDENTS AND RULERS OF MEXICO

YEARS	NAME	PARTY
1821–22	Agustín de Iturbide, president	
1822–23	Agustín de Iturbide, emperor	
1824–28	Gen. Guadalupe Victoria	
1828–29	Vicente Guerrero	C
1829–32	Gen. Anastasio Bustamante	C
1833–36	Gen. Antonio López de Santa Anna	C
1837–41	Gen. Anastasio Bustamante	C
1841–44	Gen. Antonio López de Santa Anna	C
1844–46	José Joaquín Herrera	M
1846	Mariano Paredes	C
1846–47	Gen. Antonio López de Santa Anna	C
1848–51	José Joaquín Herrera	M
1851–53	Mariano Arista	M
1853–55	Gen. Antonio López de Santa Anna	C
1855	Juan Álvarez	L
1855–58	Ignacio Comonfort	L
1858–72	Benito Juárez	L
1864–67	Maximilian, emperor	
1872–76	Sebastián Lerdo de Tejada	L
1876–80	Gen. Porfirio Díaz	L
1880–84	Manuel González	L
1884–1911	Gen. Porfirio Díaz, dictator	
1911–13	Francisco Madero	L
1913–14	Gen. Victoriano Huerta, dictator	
1914–20	Venustiano Carranza	L
1920–24	Álvaro Obregón	L
1924–28	Plutarco Elías Calles	L
1929	Emilio Portes Gil	PNR
1929–32	Pascual Órtiz Rubio	PNR
1932–34	Abelardo Rodríguez	PNR
1934–40	Lázaro Cárdenas	PNR
1940–46	Gen. Manuel Ávila Camacho	PRM
1946–52	Miquel Alemán Valdéz	PRI
1952–58	Adolfo Ruiz Corines	PRI
1958–64	Adolfo López Mateos	PRI
1964–70	Gustavo Díaz Ordaz	PRI
1970–76	Luis Echeverrá Álvarez	PRI
1976–82	José López Portillo	PRI
1982–	Miguel de la Madrid Hurtado	PRI

C = Conservative; M = Moderate; L = Liberal; PNR = National Revolutionary Party; PRM = Party of the Mexican Revolution; PRI = Institutional Revolutionary Party.

Mexican affairs since 1940 have been marked by political stability with the dominance of the Institutional Revolutionary Party (PRI) during the presidency of Gen. Manuel Avila Camacho (1940–46) and his successors.

Mexico became an oil exporter after major oil finds in the 1970s–1980s.

José López Portillo, 55, who had served as minister of finance, was elected president on July 4, 1976, as the PRI candidate.

President López Portillo declared on Sept. 1, 1979, that Mexico's energy needs were secure for 60 years with proven reserves of oil and natural gas at the equivalent of nearly 46 billion barrels and potential reserves of 200 billion barrels.

In 1982 Mexico became the United States' second-largest supplier of foreign oil at a rate of more than 530,000 barrels a day.

A decline in oil prices and the worldwide recession drove Mexico into a severe economic crisis in 1982. The peso was devaluated twice, reducing its value in U.S. dollars to one-third that at the beginning of 1982.

President López Portillo nationalized the Mexico's banks on Sept. 1, 1982, and at the same time imposed restrictions to prevent pesos from being converted into U.S. dollars. He ordered Mexicans owning an estimated $23 billion in property in the U.S. to sell it immediately and return the money to Mexico. Some $5 billion in American bank accounts in Mexico was converted to pesos.

To aid Mexico in the payment of its debts, the U.S. government in 1982 paid $1 billion in advance on orders for petroleum and granted credits of $1 billion to buy U.S. farm products.

Miguel de la Madrid Hurtado, 47, became president on Dec. 1, 1982, having won election on July 4 as candidate of the ruling party.

De la Madrid adopted austerity economic policies in 1983 that brought some reduction from 1982's annual inflation rate of 100%. Mexico's workers were forced to accept a reduced standard of living as the government allowed wage increases of only 25% in January and 15.6% in July.

Devaluation of the peso brought an influx of bargain-hunting American tourists in 1983–85. Tourist dollars and oil exports gave Mexico a foreign exchange surplus, enabling the government to reschedule payments on its $95 billion foreign debt.

A severe earthquake struck Mexico on Sept. 19, 1985, and was followed with heavy aftershocks. As many as 10,000 persons died as tall buildings toppled in Mexico City. Damage was estimated at $5 billion.

MICRONESIA

Official Name: Federated States of Micronesia.
Area: 270.79 square miles (701 sq. km.)
Population: 85,000.
Capital: Kolonia, Ponape, 5,550.
Government: Self-governing republic.

QUICK QUIZ: What percent of the area of the U.S. is owned by the federal government? See page 321.

President: Tosiwo Nakayama (since 1979).
Congress: 14 members.
Flag: Medium blue field with four white stars arranged in circle in center.
Languages: Micronesian dialects, English.
Chief Ethnic Group: Micronesian.
Main Religion: Christian.
Leading Industries: Fishing; agriculture (coconut palms, fruits, vegetables, poultry, hogs); mining (bauxite, phosphates).
Foreign Trade: *Major exports*—copra, bauxite, phosphates; *major imports*—food, consumer goods.
Places of Interest: Sunken Japanese warships in Truk lagoon; "Venice" ruins of ancient civilization on Ponape.

MICRONESIA TODAY

Although Micronesia covers a vast area of the central Pacific Ocean, its land area is only about as large as the city of Columbus, Ohio.

Micronesia includes some 607 islands and islets. Among its largest islands and atolls are Ponape, 129 sq. mi.; Kosrae, 42.3 sq. mi.; Yap, 38.7 sq. mi.; Truk, 38.6 sq. mi.; and Ulithi, 1.8 sq. mi.

The government is a federation of four states: Yap, Ponape, Kosrae, and Truk.

Many Micronesians lead a traditional way of life, living on tropical fruits, vegetables, and fish. However, the islanders are dependent on aid from the U.S. for modern consumer goods.

The Marshalls lie to the northeast. Guam and the Marianas are to the north. Palau (Belau) is to the southwest.

HISTORY

The islands are believed to have been settled by peoples from Asia about 4,000 years ago. A prehistoric civilization developed on Ponape with cities built on canals like those of Venice.

Spain claimed the islands in the 1500s as part of its Pacific empire, but did not colonize them. Named Carolina after Spain's King Charles II, the group became known for many centuries as the Caroline Islands.

The expanding German empire bought the islands from Spain in 1899, but lost them to Japan during World War I.

Truk and Yap served as important Japanese military bases in World War II. Neutralizing Truk and Yap by air bombardment, the U.S. captured Ulithi atoll on Sept. 23, 1944, and made it a major naval supply base. After the war, the islands became part of the U.S. Trust Territory of the Pacific Islands.

In a referendum on a constitution for the Federated States of Micronesia on July 12, 1978, the Marshalls and Palau voted to separate.

Micronesia became self-governing on May 10, 1979, with the swearing-in of the 14 members of the unicameral legislature. Having been chosen by the legislature, Tosiwo Nakayama of Truk took office as president on May 15.

The U.S. and Micronesia signed a compact of free association on Oct. 1, 1982, in which American aid and grants of about $1 billion over 15 years were promised in return for military rights in specific islands.

In a referendum on June 21, 1983, Micronesian voters approved the compact by 79% to 21%. It must be ratified by the U.S. Congress and the United Nations before it becomes effective.

MONACO

Official Name: Principality of Monaco.
Area: 0.58 square miles (1.49 sq. km.).
Population: 28,500.
Capital: Monaco-Ville, 27,063.
Government: Constitutional principality.
Chief of State: Prince Rainier III (since 1949).
Head of Government: Minister of State Jean Herly (since 1981).
National Council: 18 members.
Flag: Red stripe over white stripe.
Main Ethnic Groups: French (58%), Italian (17%), Monegasque (15%).
Languages: French (official), English, Italian, Monegasque.
Official Religion: Roman Catholicism (95%).
Leading Industries: Tourism and gambling, chemicals, food products, plastics, instruments.
Places of Interest: Royal palace; oceanographic museum; garden; Monte Carlo Casino.

MONACO TODAY

Less than half as large as New York City's Central Park, Monaco is the second-smallest nation in the world after Vatican City. It is surrounded by France except for its coast on the Mediterranean Sea. Tourists provide more than half of Monaco's income, much from the Monte Carlo gambling casino founded in 1863.

Because Monaco has no income tax and no direct corporation tax, many wealthy persons and foreign corporations locate there.

Rocky cliffs overhang sandy beaches of the Riviera coast. Two peninsulas enclose an excellent harbor. Winters are mild, and summer temperatures are moderated by sea breezes.

HISTORY

Monaco was probably settled by Phoenicians. In 1215 the Genoese built a fortified castle on the site of present-day Monaco. In 1297 control passed to the Grimaldi family of Genoa. Monaco was a Spanish protectorate from 1524 to 1641, a French protectorate from 1641 to 1793, and part of France from 1793 to 1814. Following Napoleon's defeat, the Treaty of Vienna (1815) established Monaco as a protectorate of Sardinia. In 1861 France assumed the protectorate.

The last absolute monarch, Prince Albert, reigned from 1889 to 1922. He provided the first constitution in 1911 and signed a treaty in 1918 establishing French protection of Monaco.

Louis II ruled from 1922 until 1949, when he was followed by his grandson Prince Rainier III.

In 1956 Prince Rainier married American movie star Grace Kelly, who died on Sept. 14, 1982, after an auto accident.

Prince Rainier in 1962 announced a new constitution giving women the right to vote.

In a national election on Jan. 15, 1978, the National and Democratic Union (UND) won all 18 seats in the National Council.

MONGOLIA

Official Name: Mongolian People's Republic.
Area: 604,250 square miles (1,565,000 sq. km.).
Population: 1,938,000.
Capital: Ulaanbaatar, 435,400.
Government: One-party communist state.
Chief of State: Dzhambiin Batmunkh, chairman, Presidium of Great People's Khural, and first secretary of Communist Party (since 1984).
Legislature: *People's Great Khural,* 354 members.
Flag: Red, blue, and red bars, with national "soyombo" emblem in gold below five-pointed gold star.
Official Language: Mongolian.
Main Ethnic Groups: Mongolian (90%), Turk (7%).
Religion: Buddhism.
Leading Industries: Agriculture (cattle, horses, sheep, goats, camels, dairy products, wheat, hay, potatoes, vegetables); manufacturing (processing agricultural products); mining (coal, petroleum, copper, molybdenum, gold, fluorspar).
Foreign Trade: *Major exports*—livestock, butter, wool and hair, hides, furs; *major imports*—machinery, petroleum, cloth, building materials.
Places of Interest: Khangai Mountains; Erdeni-Dzuu monastery, ruins of ancient Mongol capital. *In Ulaanbaatar:* government buildings, opera house.

MONGOLIA TODAY

Over twice as large as Texas but with fewer people than live in the Houston metropolitan area, Mongolia is a sparsely populated communist country. Landlocked between the Soviet Union to the north and China to the east, west, and south, Mongolia itself with the Soviet Union. Its 1,500-mile border with China's Inner Mongolia is heavily fortified.

Mongolia is a large plateau, with an average elevation of 3,000 to 4,000 feet. In the southeast is the vast Gobi Desert. The climate is generally dry, with cold winters and hot summers.

Forests in the northern mountains, hills, and highland steppes give way gradually to lower steppe grasslands, semidesert country, and barren desert. The principal rivers are the Selenga, Orkhon, and Kerulen.

HISTORY OF MONGOLIA

In the 1200s Genghis Khan established the Mongolian Empire, with its capital at Karakorum. After 1368 Mongolia fell under the rule of China.

The revolution in China in 1911 led to Mongolia's autonomy. Russian-supported Mongolian communists took over the government in July 1921. The Jebtsun Damba Khutukhtu remained as titular leader until his death in 1924, when the *Mongolian People's Republic* was established. Khorloin Choybalsan became head of the communist government. Yumjaagiyn Tsedenbal succeeded Choybalsan in 1952.

The government ended private ownership of livestock in 1958, establishing collectivized herds.

Mongolia and the Soviet Union agreed to a joint project in 1973 to exploit huge copper and molybdenum deposits northwest of Ulaanbaatar.

Mongolia in 1983 ordered about 8,000 Chinese living in the country either to work on state farms or be expelled.

Dzhambiin Batmunkh, 56, prime minister since 1974, took over as Mongolia's ruler in August 1984 from the ailing 67-year-old Tsedenbal.

Mongolia's seventh 5-year plan for 1981-85 emphasized development of mining to exploit coal reserves and other mineral resources.

MOROCCO

Official Name: Kingdom of Morocco.
Area: 275,117 square miles (712,550 sq. km.).
Population: 22,893,000.
Chief Cities: Rabat, capital, 435,510; Casablanca, 1,371,330; Marrakech, 330,400; Fez, 321,460; Meknès, 244,520, Tangier (Tanger) 185,850.
Largest Metropolitan Area: Casablanca, 1,753,400.
Government: Constitutional monarchy.
King: Hassan II (reigned since 1961).
Prime Minister: Muhammad Karim Lamrani (since 1983).
Parliament: 264 members.
U.S. Ambassador to Morocco: Thomas A. Nassif.
Moroccan Ambassador to U.S.: Maati Jorio.
Flag: Red field with green five-pointed star.
Languages: Arabic (official), Berber dialects, French, Spanish.
Main Ethnic Groups: Arab, Berber, black.
Official Religion: Islam (98%).
Leading Industries: Agriculture (poultry, goats, cattle, citrus fruits, olives, raisins, barley, wheat, corn, potatoes, grapes, vegetables); forestry and lumbering; mining (phosphates, manganese, cobalt, iron ore, lead, zinc, petroleum); fishing; tourism; manufacturing (food processing, textiles, leather, cement, wine, paint).
Foreign Trade: *Major exports*—phosphates, fruits, tomatoes, preserved fish, manganese; *major imports*—machinery, fuels, food, consumer goods.
Places of Interest: Tombs of the Merinides princes and 1,000-year-old university in Fez; Bahia Palace and tombs of the Saadians in Marrakech; the Casbah in Tangier; Mohammed V Mausoleum in Rabat; Casablanca.

MOROCCO TODAY

Almost as large as Texas, Morocco has a wide variety of mineral resources, but only phosphates and manganese are mined and exported in large quantities. These two minerals account for over half of the country's exports. Otherwise, Morocco depends on tourism and agriculture as the mainstays of its economy. Government planning calls for improved tourist facilities, new irrigation projects, and training of more skilled workers.

The country prospered in the 1970s-80s be

QUICK QUIZ: Which U.S. President was once a waiter in a tavern? See page 347.

MOROCCO *(continued)*

cause of high demand and high prices for phosphates for fertilizer.

But most Moroccans are poor, and only 1 in 4 can read and write. Many still wear the traditional costume of a long hooded robe called a *djellaba* and pointed slippers called *babouche.* Many of the women wear veils.

Algeria lies to the east, the Mediterranean Sea to the north, the Atlantic Ocean to the west, and Mauritania to the south.

Two small Spanish overseas provinces are in Morocco: Ceuta, on the northernmost tip, and Melilla, on the northeastern coast.

The northern coastal plain along the Mediterranean Sea includes the Rif Mountains, rising to 7,000 feet above sea level.

The Atlas Mountains, with peaks as high as 13,600 feet, extend in three parallel ranges from the Atlantic coast in the southwest to Algeria and the Mediterranean Sea in the northeast.

In the south and east semiarid steppes stretch into the Sahara Desert.

Rain (about 40 inches annually) and mountain snow make northwestern Morocco the best-watered country of North Africa.

The U.S. and Morocco have had a treaty of peace and friendship since 1787—the longest unbroken treaty relationship in American history.

HISTORY OF MOROCCO

Phoenician settlements existed at Melilla, Tangier, and Larache from 1100 B.C. The Romans formed northeast Morocco into the province of Mauritania Tingitana.

Arab conquest in the 600s A.D. introduced the religion of Islam. From 1064 to 1269 two great dynasties, the Almoravides and the Almohades, united Morocco and, at times, ruled all North Africa and most of Spain.

In the early 1500s Spain and Portugal took nearly all of Morocco's ports.

From the mid-1880s France, Spain, Britain, Italy, and Germany competed for influence in Morocco. In 1912 Morocco signed the Treaty of Fez, becoming a French protectorate, with Spain administering some areas.

Abdelkrim al-Khattabi, a Rif Berber chief, led a war of resistance from 1921 to 1926.

After World War II Sultan Sidi Mohammed led a nationalist movement.

Morocco was granted independence by France on March 2, 1956, with Sidi Mohammed as King Mohammed V. In 1961 he was succeeded by his son King Hassan II.

The 579-square-mile Spanish colony of Ifni on the Atlantic coast was ceded to Morocco by Spain in 1969.

A new constitution, proposed by the king and reducing his absolute power, was confirmed by a popular referendum in March 1972.

An attempt to shoot down a plane carrying the king failed in 1972. The head of the plot, Gen. Mohammed Oufkir, killed himself.

In April 1974 Morocco nationalized foreign-owned oil companies. That same year, Hassan began a campaign to force Spain to give up its overseas provinces of Ceuta and Melilla and Spanish Sahara to Morocco.

King Hassan organized a march of 350,000 unarmed Moroccans into the phosphate-rich Spanish Sahara on Nov. 6, 1975, but withdrew at the urging of the UN Security Council.

Spain withdrew its troops from the Western Sahara, formally turning it over to Morocco and Mauritania on Feb. 26, 1976. On the following day the Saharan nationalists, called the Polisario Front, declared independence as the *Sahara Arab Democratic Republic.*

Morocco and Mauritania broke relations with Algeria on March 7, 1976. They agreed on April 14, 1976, to partition the 102,703-square-mile area. Morocco annexed the northern two-thirds and Mauritania the southern third.

On June 3, 1977, in the first freely contested national election in 14 years, independent candidates supporting King Hassan won a majority of seats in the 264-member parliament.

The U.S. gave up its last military base on Sept. 30, 1978, turning over to the Moroccan government its communications facilities at Kenitra.

After Mauritania signed a peace agreement with the Polisario guerrillas and withdrew its claims to the Western Sahara in August 1979, Morocco announced it had taken over the southern part of the region, making it the nation's 37th province. Fighting continued in 1979–85 with the Polisario guerrillas.

The U.S. and Morocco signed an agreement on May 27, 1982, giving American planes the right to use the nation's air bases in an emergency. U.S. military aid to Morocco was increased.

King Hassan announced on Aug. 14, 1984, that he had signed a treaty of "union" with Libya. Under the agreement Libya withdrew its support for the Polisario guerrillas in the Western Sahara. Hassan gave assurances that the treaty would not affect Morocco's friendship with the U.S.

Morocco's 5-year plan for 1981–85 placed emphasis on energy production with $766 million to develop the nation's huge oil shale reserves and construct the first of several electric power stations fueled by oil shale.

MOZAMBIQUE

Official Name: People's Republic of Mozambique.
Area: 302,330 square miles (783,030 sq. km.).
Population: 14,546,000.
Cities: Maputo, capital, 383,775; Beria, 115,000.
Government: One-party communist state.
President: Samora Machel (since 1975).
Legislature: *People's Assembly,* 210 members.
U.S. Ambassador to Mozambique: Peter Jon de Vos.
Mozambican Ambassador to U.S.: Valeriano Inocencio de Araujo Ferrao.
Flag: Five unequal stripes: green (top), white, black, white, and yellow; red triangle at hoist with yellow star with book, hoe, and rifle representing motto, "Study, Produce, Struggle."
Languages: Portuguese (official), tribal.
Main Ethnic Group: Black.
Religions: Animism (65%), Christianity (22%), Islam (11%).

Leading Industries: Agriculture (cashew nuts, cotton, sugarcane, sisal, tea, corn, sweet potatoes, peanuts, millet, manioc, palm kernels, fruits, vegetables); manufacturing (processing agricultural products, glass, paint, automobile assembly, cement, furniture); mining (coal, iron, tantalite, fluorite).

Foreign Trade: *Major exports*—cashews, cotton, sugar, tea, copra; *major imports*—machinery, textiles, vehicles, petroleum, steel.

Places of Interest: Maputo; Cabora Bassa dam on Zambesi River.

Almost twice as large as California, Mozambique is a communist-ruled African nation.

The former Portuguese colony has substantial mineral resources, but the development of mining has been hindered by poor transportation.

Most of the people are poor African tribesmen. About 1 in 10 can read and write.

Although the government opposes South Africa's racial policies, it depends for most of its foreign exchange on revenues from transshipment of South African exports and money sent home by 60,000 Mozambican workers in South Africa.

The lowland climate is hot, with a rainy season from November to March.

Vasco da Gama visited Mozambique en route to India in 1498. Portuguese trading posts were established in the 1500s. At the end of World War I part of German East Africa was added to the colony. In 1952 the colony was made part of Portugal as an overseas province.

African nationalists began waging guerrilla war in 1964. Some 70,000 Portuguese troops fought against the guerrillas for a decade.

After a military coup overthrew the government of Portugal, Mozambique was granted a provisional government on Sept. 20, 1974.

The 3,600-megawatt capacity Cabora Bassa hydroelectric dam on the Zambesi River was completed on Dec. 5, 1974.

Full independence was achieved on June 25, 1975, with Marxist socialist, Samora Machel, 41, becoming the country's first president.

The first national election was held on Dec. 4, 1977, in which voters ratified the choice of the Frelimo Party of 210 members of the legislature.

South African commandos raided Maputo in 1981 and 1983, destroying the headquarters of anti-South African guerrillas.

Government officials reported in November 1983 that 700,000 or more persons were starving because of a prolonged drought. The U.S. sent 83,000 tons of grain in 1983–84.

Anti communist guerrillas stepped up attacks in 1982–85 to disrupt the economy.

Mozambique and South Africa signed a nonaggression pact called the Nkomati Accord on March 16, 1984, seeking an end to a decade of border fighting. Each nation pledged not to support guerrillas fighting against the other nor to let its territory be used as a guerrilla base.

The U.S. in June 1984 lifted its 7-year-old ban on providing economic aid to Mozambique.

South Africa announced on Oct. 3, 1984, that it had negotiated a cease-fire agreement between Mozambique's government and the rebels under which South African troops entered Mozambique to monitor a truce.

NAMIBIA

Area: 318,261 square miles (824,292 sq. km.).
Population: 1,600,000.
Capital: Windhoek, 61,369.
Government: Internal self-rule.
Legislature: 62 members.
Flag: Prior to independence, flag of South Africa with horizontal orange, white, and blue stripes; in center of white band are miniature reproductions of British Union Jack and flags of Orange Free State and Transvaal Republic.
Main Languages: Afrikaans, English, German.
Ethnic groups: Black (88%), white (12%).
Principal Religion: Lutheran.
Leading Industries: Agriculture (corn, millet, sorghum, livestock); mining (diamonds, copper, lead, zinc, uranium); manufacturing (food processing, textiles, clothing, ore smelting); fishing.
Foreign Trade: *Major exports*—diamonds, copper, lead, zinc, uranium, fish, cattle, karakul fur pelts; *major imports*—construction materials, fertilizer, grain, food, consumer goods.
Places of Interest: Game reserve at Etosha; karakul sheep ranches; Walvis Bay; government buildings in Windhoek; prehistoric cave paintings.

NAMIBIA TODAY

About as large as Texas and Louisiana combined, Namibia has been a center of international controversy and guerrilla warfare for two decades as the United Nations has sought to free the region from control by South Africa.

Most Namibians live as members of tribal groups that follow ancient customs. Few can read and write.

Walvis Bay on the Atlantic coast is the country's main port. Nearly 1,500 miles of rail lines connect the port to mining and ranching areas.

As one of the world's leading diamond-mining countries, Namibia depends on diamond exports for nearly a third of its gross national product. Another third comes from the wages of Namibians who work in South Africa.

The climate is hot and dry with annual rainfall averaging only 2 inches along the coast and increasing to 22 inches inland. Walvis Bay has an average temperature of 74 °F. in its warmest month, February, and 57° F. during August.

Namibia is bordered on the north by Angola and Zambia, on the east by Botswana, and on the southeast and south by South Africa.

EARLY HISTORY

The earliest people to live in Namibia are believed to have been the Bushmen. Beautifully colored paintings dating from prehistoric Stone Age times decorate many caves in Namibia.

Although the coastal region was explored by the Portuguese in the late 1400s, the inhospitable desert climate and warlike tribes discour-

NAMIBIA *(continued)*

aged exploration of the interior until the 1800s.

Britain annexed Walvis Bay in 1878 and incorporated it as part of the Cape of Good Hope Colony in 1884.

A German merchant, F.A.W. Lüderitz, purchased much of the coastal area from Hottentot tribes in the early 1800s. He placed the region, then known as *South West Africa,* under protection of the German empire in 1884. Diamonds were discovered on the southwest coast in 1908.

During World War I, South African troops invaded the region, forcing the Germans to surrender in July 1915.

South Africa remained in control of the country, receiving a League of Nations mandate for South West Africa on Dec. 17, 1920.

UNITED NATIONS–SOUTH AFRICAN DISPUTE

After World War II and the demise of the League of Nations, South Africa proposed to the United Nations in 1946 a plan to annex South West Africa. The UN rejected this proposal, insisting that South Africa submit to a trusteeship for the region.

The UN General Assembly adopted a resolution on Oct. 27, 1966, stating that South Africa had forfeited its mandatory rights. Two years later the General Assembly resolved that South West Africa would thenceforth be known as Namibia. South Africa refused to accept either resolution. In 1971 the World Court handed down an advisory opinion that South Africa had no jurisdiction over South West Africa and should withdraw its administration.

Black nationalists of the Ovambo tribes formed the South West Africa Peoples Organization (SWAPO), which has fought guerrilla warfare for the independence of Namibia since 1966. SWAPO is recognized by the UN as the authoritative representative of the Namibian people.

A constitutional conference with delegates from all ethnic groups in Namibia met in Windhoek in 1975–77 to draft a plan for a government.

On Jan. 31, 1976, the UN Security Council unanimously approved a resolution calling for UN-supervised elections in Namibia.

The UN General Assembly approved a resolution in December 1976 endorsing an "armed struggle" by blacks to win independence.

Namibians voted on Dec. 4–8, 1978, in the first multi-racial elections to choose members of an assembly to draw up a constitution. Boycotted by several political parties including SWAPO, the election was won by the South African-backed Democratic Turnhalle Alliance (DTA) that captured 41 of the 50 seats.

In May 1979 the assembly was converted into a 65-man national legislature with the appointment of 15 additional delegates. In 1983 South Africa dissolved the assembly and resumed direct rule.

South Africa restored internal self-rule to Namibia on June 17, 1985. However, the new multi-racial 62-seat legislature was forbidden from making "any law altering the international status of the territory."

Throughout 1979–85 discussions were held between South African leaders and representatives of the UN in an effort to reach agreement on independence for Namibia.

NAURU

Official Name: Republic of Nauru.
Area: 8 square miles (21 sq. km.).
Population: 8,100.
Capital: Yaren.
Government: Parliamentary republic.
President: Hammer DeRoburt (since 1978).
Parliament: 18 members.
U.S. Ambassador to Nauru: Robert Dean Nesen.
Nauruan Ambassador to U.S.: T. W. Star.
Flag: Blue field halved by horizontal gold stripe, white star at lower hoist corner.
Languages: English and Nauruan.
Main Ethnic Groups: Nauruan (50%), Gilbert and Ellice islanders (27%), Chinese (16%).
Religion: Christianity.
Leading Industry: Mining (phosphates).
Foreign Trade: *Major export*—phosphates; *major imports*—food, water, consumer goods.
Places of Interest: Phosphate mines.

NAURU TODAY

The world's smallest republic, Nauru covers an area smaller than that of Sioux Falls, S.D. The island nation lies in the Pacific Ocean 2,200 miles northeast of Sydney, Australia.

The people of Nauru have one of the highest per capita incomes in the world.

Deposits of guano left by millions of migrating birds left the island rich in phosphate used to make fertilizer.

The people pay no taxes. The government subsidizes all imports, making food available at a nominal cost. Everyone can read and write.

To ensure Nauru's continued prosperity when the phosphate deposits run out, a substantial fund estimated at $400 million has been established to cover long-term investments and development.

A coral reef surrounds the island and fringes a sandy beach. Beyond the island's narrow coastal belt, a coral cliff rises 100 feet above sea level.

HISTORY OF NAURU

The first European to discover Nauru was British sea captain John Fearn in 1798.

In 1888 the island was annexed by Germany, and in 1914 it was occupied by Australia.

After World War I Nauru became a mandate under Australian administration.

Japanese forces occupied Nauru in 1942–45.

In 1947 Australia placed Nauru under the UN trusteeship system.

The nation became independent on Jan. 31, 1968. Hammer DeRoburt, head chief since 1956, was chosen as its first president.

The phosphate mines were nationalized in 1970 with $20 million paid to the British owners.

Britain's Queen Elizabeth visited Nauru on Oct. 21, 1982, the first time a British monarch ever had come to the smallest member of the British Commonwealth of Nations.

NEPAL

Official Name: Kingdom of Nepal.
Area: 54,362 square miles (140,797 sq. km.).
Population: 17,205,000.
Chief Cities: Kathmandu, capital, 150,402.
Government: Constitutional monarchy.
King: Birendra Bir Bikram Shah Dev (since 1972).
Prime Minister: Lokandra Chand (since 1983).
Parliament: *National Panchayat,* 135 members.
U.S. Ambassador to Nepal: Leon Jerome Weil.
Nepalese Ambassador to U.S.: Bhekh Bahadur Thapa.
Flag: Red bordered in blue with white moon in upper triangle and white sun below.
Languages: Nepali (official), Newari, 11 others.
Ethnic Groups: Brahman, Chetris, Gurung, Magyar, Tamang, Newar, Bhotia, Rais, Limbu, Sherpa.
Official Religion: Hinduism (90%).
Leading Industries: Agriculture (cattle, rice, corn, millet, wheat, tea, barley, opium poppies, jute, pepper, tobacco); tourism; forestry and lumbering; food processing; mining (copper, iron, mica, zinc, cobalt); manufacturing (burlap bags, textiles).
Foreign Trade: *Major exports*—farm products, timber; *major imports*—clothing, food, consumer goods.
Places of Interest: Durbar Square, Temple of Teleja, and other temples in Kathmandu; Swayambhunath Buddha; Tiger Tops resort in King Mahendra National Park; Mount Everest National Park; Langtang National Park.

About the size of Arkansas, Nepal is one of the least developed and most isolated nations.

Most Nepalese are poor farmers who cannot read and write. Their average life is 42 years.

The Himalaya mountains on the northern border with China include Mt. Everest, the world's highest peak (29,028 feet).

At Kathmandu the average temperature is 86° F. in May and 35° F. in December.

The Shah dynasty of Gurkha has ruled Nepal since the 1700s. Wars with Tibet and China (1791–92) and with British India (1814–16) set its present boundaries. The Gurkha rulers were reduced to figureheads in 1847 by the Ranas, who governed as hereditary prime ministers.

In 1951 a rebellion led to the overthrow of the Rana regime. King Tribhuvan became an absolute monarch. He was followed in 1955 by King Mahendra, who died in 1972. Mahendra was succeeded by his son Birendra.

In a national referendum on May 2, 1980, a majority voted to retain a partyless governmental system rather than adopt multiparty democracy.

In a national election in 1981 a new 135-member parliament was chosen. Prime Minister Surya Bahadur Thapa, who had served since 1972, continued as head of the government.

A no-confidence vote of 108–17 in parliament forced Thapa to resign on July 11, 1983. Lokandra Chand, 49, former speaker of parliament, succeeded him as prime minister on the following day.

NETHERLANDS

Official Name: Kingdom of the Netherlands.
Area: 15,770 square miles (40,844 sq. km.).
Population: 14,524,000.
Chief Cities: Amsterdam, capital, 706,526; The Hague ('s Gravenhage), seat of government, 455,513; Rotterdam, 572,248; Utrecht, 235,377.
Largest Metropolitan Area: Rotterdam, 1,024,749.
Government: Parliamentary democracy.
Queen: Beatrix (since 1980).
Prime Minister: Ruud Lubbers (since 1982).
Legislature: *First Chamber,* 75 members; *Second Chamber,* 150 members.
U.S. Ambassador to Netherlands: L. Paul Brenner III.
Netherlands Ambassador to U.S.: Richard H. Fein.
Flag: Red, white, and blue stripes.
Official Language: Dutch.
Main Ethnic Group: Dutch (of Germanic origin).
Chief Religions: Protestantism (41%), Roman Catholicism (40%).
Leading Industries: Trade and services; manufacturing (steel, chemicals, food processing, textiles, clothing, printing, furniture, diamond cutting, leather products, electricity, ceramics); agriculture (cattle, hogs, sheep, poultry, wheat, sugar beets, potatoes, oats, flowers, vegetables); mining (natural gas, petroleum); fishing; shipping; tourism.
Foreign Trade: *Major exports*—food, machinery, chemicals, textiles, petroleum products, consumer goods, flower bulbs; *major imports*—automobiles, corn, coal, lumber, petroleum, metal ores.
Places of Interest: The Hague; Soestdijk Royal Palace near Baarn; villages around Lake Ijssel; cheese centers of Gouda and Edam; Utrecht; Rotterdam. *In Amsterdam:* Anne Frank House; botanical gardens; Artis Zoological Gardens; Rembrandt's home; Rijks Museum; monuments.

NETHERLANDS TODAY

About twice the size of New Jersey, the Netherlands is a prosperous European nation that continues to increase its area by building dikes and pumping out seawater to reclaim land covered by the Zuider Zee.

For many years the Netherlands controlled a colonial empire that stretched around the world. But today that empire has dwindled to one overseas province, the Netherlands Antilles in the Caribbean Sea (see page 618).

With a long tradition of democratic government, the Netherlands has been a leading proponent of unifying Europe. It has urged its larger neighbors to give up their nationalism and accept a democratic European parliament.

The Netherlands' most important resource is natural gas. Its Groningen natural-gas field is one of the largest energy sources in Europe, and makes the country the third most important producer of natural gas in the world.

The land is generally low and flat, with the exception of a few rolling hills along the south-

QUICK QUIZ: Henry Clay was Secretary of State under which U.S. President? See page 345.

NETHERLANDS *(continued)*
eastern border. At least 25% of the country's area lies below sea level and must be protected by dikes. Irrigation is provided by an extensive system of canals.

The climate is moderate, with few extremes. Summer temperatures rarely exceed 75° F., but winters are damp and cold.

Dutch flowers, particularly tulips and hyacinths, are world renowned.

The Netherlands is bordered on the east by West Germany and on the south by Belgium.

EARLY HISTORY

The Batavi, the Frisii, and other Germanic and Celtic tribes first settled the marshy Rhine and Meuse delta areas of the Low Countries. Julius Caesar conquered the region about 55 B.C. The Romans developed the canals and dikes.

The area became part of Charlemagne's empire in the 700s.

Following collapse of the empire, principalities in Holland and Utrecht and the cities of Amsterdam, Haarlem, and Groningen rose to importance during the Middle Ages.

The dukes of Burgundy extended control over the area in the 1300s and 1400s. In 1515 Karl V of the House of Hapsburg inherited the Burgundian lands. He abdicated in 1555 in favor of his son King Felipe II of Spain. Felipe's suppression of religious, political, and economic freedoms was met with fierce resistance.

INDEPENDENT NETHERLANDS REPUBLIC

In 1568 the Netherlands' 80-year war of liberation broke out. It was led by Willem the Silent, prince of Orange. Under his leadership the seven northern provinces united in 1581 as the *Republic of the United Netherlands.* They continued the fight even after the southern provinces gave in to Spanish rule. The struggle was not resolved until the Treaty of Westphalia (1648), ending the Thirty Years War, recognized the Netherlands Republic as independent from Spain.

By the end of the 1600s the Netherlands had become the world's greatest maritime and commercial power, with colonies in Asia and the Americas. During the 1700s colonial rivalry with England, France, and Spain resulted in the loss of colonies and a decline in power. The Netherlands aided the American colonists with loans in the Revolutionary War (1775–83).

In 1795 French troops invaded and founded the Republic of Batavia, which in 1806 became the Napoleonic Kingdom of Holland.

KINGDOM OF THE NETHERLANDS

After Napoleon's defeat in 1815, the Congress of Vienna restored the nation's independence as the *Kingdom of the United Netherlands,* comprising the Netherlands and what is now Belgium, under Willem I of the House of Orange.

During the reign of Willem I (1813–40) the country again became a maritime and commercial power. In 1830 the Belgians revolted and formed a separate kingdom.

Reforms under Willem II (1840–48) and Willem III (1849–90) led to internal prosperity.

The Netherlands remained neutral until World War II, when the country was overrun by German

troops. After enduring ruthless suppression by the Nazis, the country was liberated in 1945.

Queen Wilhelmina, after 58 years of rule, abdicated in 1948 to her daughter Juliana.

After four years of periodic fighting and negotiations, Indonesia was granted independence in 1949. The Dutch were forced to give up Netherlands New Guinea to Indonesia in 1962.

Thousands of persons immigrated to the Netherlands from Surinam in 1974–75 before that former South American colony was granted its independence on Nov. 25, 1975.

The government began construction in 1976 on a $1.5 billion, 5.6-mile dam across the Eastern Scheldt estuary. To be completed by 1985, the dam will have openings to admit small ships and to preserve marine ecology.

In the late 1970s the economy developed what was called the "Dutch disease." Income from the nation's huge gas reserves was spent to expand social welfare benefits instead of developing industry. Dutch products became uncompetitive and unemployment rose.

In a national election on May 25, 1977, Prime Minister Joop den Uyl's socialist Labor Party won a plurality of 53 seats. The Christian Democrats won 49 and the Liberals 28.

After months of haggling, a new center-right coalition government was formed on Dec. 19, 1977, with Andreas A.M. van Agt, head of the Christian Democratic Party, as prime minister. He served as prime minister until 1982.

NETHERLANDS IN THE 1980s

Having reigned since 1948, the 71-year-old Juliana abdicated on April 30, 1980. Her 42-year-old daughter Beatrix became queen.

In national elections on May 26, 1981, no party won a parliamentary majority, but conservative Christian Democrats achieved a plurality of 48 seats. The Labor Party was second with 44.

Queen Beatrix visited the U.S. in April 1982 to celebrate 200 years of close friendship between the U.S. and the Netherlands, which helped finance the American Revolution.

In a general election on Sept. 8, 1982, the socialist Labor Party opposed the deployment of 48 U.S. cruise missiles in the Netherlands and demanded that the government provide jobs for the nation's 550,000 unemployed. The conservative Christian Democratic Party favored the deployment of the missiles and called for cuts in welfare and unemployment benefits to curb government spending.

The Labor Party gained a plurality of 47 seats in the lower house of parliament, the conservative Christian Democrats held onto 45, and the Liberals were third with 36. While politicians maneuvered to establish a majority coalition, van Agt, 51, resigned on Oct. 13, 1982.

Ruud Lubbers, 43, a millionaire economist and new head of the conservative Christian Democrats, became the youngest prime minister in the nation's history on Nov. 5, 1982, forming a coalition cabinet with the Liberal Party. He promised heavy cuts in government spending.

The Dutch parliament voted 79-71 on June 14, 1984, to delay deployment of U.S. cruise missiles in the Netherlands until 1988. NATO had planned to base 48 of the missiles in the Netherlands by 1986.

NETHERLANDS ANTILLES

Area: 371 square miles (961 sq. km.).
Population: 250,000.
Capital: Willemstad, Curaçao, 149,091.
Main Islands: Curaçao (173 sq. mi.), Bonaire (95 sq. mi.), Aruba (69 sq. mi.), St. Maarten (southern half of St. Martin, 17 sq. mi.), St. Eustatius (21 sq. mi.), Saba (5 sq. mi.).

The last remnant of the Dutch empire, these Caribbean islands divide into two groups. The Windward Islands (Curaçao, Aruba, and Bonaire) lie about 15 to 40 miles off the northwestern coast of Venezuela. The Leeward Islands (St. Maarten [part of St. Martin Island, shared with Guadeloupe], Saba, and St. Eustatius) are about 220 miles east of Puerto Rico.

The Windward Islands are volcanic-based, partly coral, semiarid, and covered with desert-like vegetation. The smaller Leeward Islands are hilly and fertile. The Antilles' temperature ranges between 77° and 87° F.

About 85% of the people are mestizo, a mixture of black, Indian, Spanish, and Dutch ancestry. Most are Christians. The people speak Dutch (official), Papiamento, and English.

Aruba and Curaçao, with some of the world's largest oil refineries, have a prosperous economy based largely on the petroleum industry.

The Antilles' year-round warm climate and unique blend of Dutch, African, and Spanish cultures draw large numbers of tourists, providing a major source of revenue.

Aruba is noted for its many miles of fine swimming beaches and Curaçao for its shops filled with imported goods. Washington National Park on Bonaire is a bird sanctuary with many flamingos. Scuba divers enjoy exploring the coral reefs off Bonaire.

After oil refining and tourism, the mining of phosphates provides the largest share of the islands' income. The Netherlands Antilles has one of the higher per capita incomes in the Caribbean.

Curaçao, the largest island in the Antilles, was discovered in 1499 by the explorers Alonso de Ojeda and Amerigo Vespucci.

Along with Aruba and Bonaire, Curaçao was captured by the Dutch in 1634, and Peter Stuyvesant became Curaçao's first governor. Britain occupied Curaçao during the Napoleonic wars, but it was restored to the Netherlands in 1816.

Curaçao was the center of the Dutch slave trade in the Caribbean area until the government freed slaves in 1863.

The Netherlands Antilles became a coequal part of the Kingdom of the Netherlands in December 1954. The Netherlands Antilles is divided into four territories: Aruba, Bonaire, Curaçao, and the Windward Islands. Each has its own elected council that governs local affairs.

A 21-member unicameral legislature enacts laws for the entire Netherlands Antilles.

Racial rioting in 1969 severly hurt the islands' tourism industry, which did not recover until the late 1970's.

The Dutch government agreed in 1983 to grant Aruba separate status on Jan. 1, 1986, and full independence in 1996.

NEW ZEALAND

Official Name: Dominion of New Zealand.
Area: 103,736 square miles (268,675 sq. km.).
Population: 3,292,000.
Chief Cities: Wellington, capital, 135,688; Christchurch, 164,680; Auckland, 145,000; Manukau, 159,362.
Largest Metropolitan Areas: Auckland, 321,004.
Government: Parliamentary democracy.
Prime Minister: David Lange (since 1984).
Chief of State: Queen Elizabeth II, represented by Governor-General Sir David Beattie.
House of Representatives: 95 members.
U.S. Ambassador to New Zealand: H. Monroe Browne.
Ambassador to U.S.: Sir Wallace Rowling.
Flag: Blue field with British Union Jack at upper hoist corner; four red stars outlined in white represent Southern Cross constellation.
Languages: English (official), Maori.
Ethnic Groups: European (92%), Maori (8%).
Main Religions: Anglicanism (34%), Presbyterianism (22%), Roman Catholicism (15%), Methodism (7%).
Leading Industries: Trade and services; manufacturing (food processing, machinery, clothing, furniture, cement, fertilizers); agriculture (sheep, cattle, dairy products, wheat, barley, oats, corn, fruits, vegetables); forestry and lumbering; fishing; mining (gold, coal, petroleum, natural gas); tourism.
Foreign Trade: *Major exports*—wool, lamb and mutton, butter; *major imports*—automobiles, petroleum and petroleum products, cotton fabrics, agricultural machinery.
Places of Interest: Tongariro and Egmont national parks; Franz Josef and Fox glaciers; Milford Sound fjords; Hanmer (thermal) Springs resort; Glowworm Grotto at Waitomo; Mt. Cook ski resort.

NEW ZEALAND TODAY

About the size of Colorado, New Zealand is a mountainous island nation some 1,200 miles southeast of Australia. Most of its people are of British descent, and they preserve British traditions. New Zealand also administers several island dependencies (see next page).

Despite expansion of the nation's manufacturing industry, agricultural products account for 95% of New Zealand's exports.

New Zealand has one of the most comprehensive social-welfare programs of any nation, including old-age pensions, free hospital care for everyone, and compensation for all accidents, no matter what their cause.

Most New Zealanders take a summer vacation from mid-December to mid-January.

The nation includes two principal islands, North Island (44,035 sq. mi.) and South Island (58,305 sq. mi.), separated by Cook Strait. Other islands are Steward Island, off the southern tip of South Island, and the Chatham Islands, about 500 miles east of South Island.

QUICK QUIZ: When was the U.S. flag changed to have 15 stripes? See page 323.

NEW ZEALAND *(continued)*

The Southern Alps run the length of South Island and contain several glaciers. The highest of these mountains is 12,349-foot Mt. Cook.

The majority of people live in the narrow coastlands in the eastern part of North Island. This island has many active volcanoes, including 9,175-foot Mt. Ruapehu.

The climate ranges from year-round warm temperatures at the northern tip of North Island to cold winters in August on South Island.

EARLY HISTORY

The race of Polynesians called Maoris came to New Zealand from Southeast Asia at least as early as 1350. When the Dutch explorer Abel J. Tasman discovered the islands in 1642, the unfriendly Maoris prevented him from landing. In 1769 Capt. James Cook of England visited the islands, and in the 1790s several small English whaling settlements were established.

In 1840 the New Zealand Company organized the first large migration to the islands and established a settlement at Wellington. In that year the Maoris granted sovereignty over New Zealand to the British crown. In 1845–48 and 1860–70 Maori uprisings were suppressed by military force.

A major stimulus to New Zealand's settlement was the discovery of gold on South Island in 1861. Development of an export trade in butter and meat, primarily to Britain, was accelerated by refrigerated ships after 1882.

Parliamentary democracy was well established by 1890. New Zealand became a self-governing dominion on Sept. 26, 1907.

INDEPENDENT NEW ZEALAND

In 1947 New Zealand was the last dominion to ratify the 1931 Statute of Westminster, granting independence to members of the British Commonwealth.

The Labor Party governed New Zealand in 1935–49, 1957–60, and 1972–75.

New Zealand placed new restrictions on immigration in 1974 to limit newcomers to 12,000 to 15,000 persons a year.

Discovery of a large offshore gas field in 1975 promised to reduce New Zealand's dependency on imported oil in the 1980s.

In elections on Nov. 29, 1975, the conservative National Party which previously had governed in 1960–72, defeated Labour. Its leader, Robert D. Muldoon, became prime minister.

Muldoon's party won a national election on Nov. 25, 1978, but with a reduced majority.

The government expelled the Soviet Union's ambassador on Jan. 25, 1980, on charges of contributing a large sum of money to the New Zealand Communist Party.

A national election on Nov. 28, 1981, further reduced Muldoon's party to 47 seats.

An anti-American bill sponsored by the Labour Party to ban nuclear weapons from New Zealand was defeated by Muldoon by a single vote on April 29, 1982, just three weeks before the visit of a U.S. nuclear submarine.

In an effort to reduce the 15% inflation rate in 1982, the government froze wages and prices. To combat unemployment, income taxes were cut drastically for middle-income taxpayers.

The Labor Party won a general election on July 14, 1984, taking 55 seats in the 95-member parliament. Labor's leader, David Lange, 41, became prime minister.

During the election campaign, Lange had declared that he would forbid U.S. nuclear-powered or nuclear-armed ships from using New Zealand's ports.

When the U.S. refused to tell Lange whether or not one of its destroyers carried nuclear arms, he announced on Feb. 4, 1985, that the ship would not be allowed to visit New Zealand. The U.S. retaliated by cancelling planned joint military exercises with New Zealand and halted the sharing of intelligence data.

NEW ZEALAND DEPENDENCIES

COOK ISLANDS

Area: 90 square miles (234 sq. km.).
Population: 17,000.
Capital: Avarua, on Rarotonga.

The Cook Islands in the South Pacific divide into two groups.

The seven Northern Group islands are low-lying, sparsely populated, scattered coral atolls.

The fertile islands in the Lower Group are more heavily populated. Rarotonga, the largest Cook island, is volcanic. Citrus fruits and juices, copra, and tomatoes are the leading exports.

Some of the islands were discovered in 1773 by Capt. James Cook, others by John Williams 50 years later. They became a British protectorate in 1888 and were annexed to New Zealand in 1901. The islands' constitution, adopted in 1965, provides for full internal self-government in association with New Zealand.

A monthly ship and a weekly airplane carry passengers, freight, and mail between New Zealand and Rarotonga. A $22 million jet airport was completed at Rarotonga in 1974.

NIUE

Area: 100 square miles (259 sq. km.).
Population: 3,300.
Capital: Tufukla.

Niue, part of the Cook group but separately administered since 1903, lies in the Pacific 580 miles northwest of Rarotonga. The people are Polynesian and speak Samoan. Niue became self-governing in 1974 with a prime minister and a 14-member elected assembly. The soil is fertile.

ROSS DEPENDENCY

Area: 160,000 square miles (414,398 sq. km.).

This region includes the Antarctic continent between longitude 160° E. and 150° W. and the islands south of latitude 60° S. New Zealand took jurisdiction in 1923. The region includes a whaling center and a research station.

TOKELAU

Area: 4 square miles (10 sq. km.).
Population: 1,600.

The islands, consisting of three atolls, lie about 300 miles north of Western Samoa and are administered from there. Once part of the Gilbert and Ellice Islands colony, they became a New Zealand territory in 1925. The people are Polynesian. Copra is the islands' principal export.

NICARAGUA

Area: 50,193 square miles (130,000 sq. km.).
Population: 3,391,000.
Capital: Managua, 608,020.
Government: Marxist socialist.
President: Daniel Ortega Saavedra (since 1984).
Ambassador to U.S.: Carlos Tunnermann Bernheim.
U.S. Ambassador: Harry E. Bergold, Jr.
Flag: Blue, white, and blue stripes, with coat of arms on white stripe.
Languages: Spanish (official), English, Indian dialects.
Ethnic Groups: Mestizo (70%), European descent (17%), black (9%), Indian (4%).
Religion: Roman Catholicism (95%).
Leading Industries: Trade and services; agriculture (coffee, cotton, sugarcane, cattle, bananas, corn, tobacco, rice, beans, fruits, vegetables); mining (gold, silver, gypsum); fishing; manufacturing (food processing, textiles, clothing, footwear, tobacco products).
Foreign Trade: *Major exports*—cotton, meat, coffee, sugar, sesame, cottonseed; *major imports*—insecticides, motor vehicles, pharmaceuticals, iron and steel, petroleum, machinery.
Places of Interest: Lake Nicaragua; Mt. Momotombo and other volcanoes; earthquake ruins and rebuilding in Managua; Granada; León Cathedral; Pacific beach resorts; Great Corn Island in the Caribbean.

NICARAGUA TODAY

About the size of Iowa, Nicaragua is a poverty-stricken Central American country torn by civil war and natural disasters.

Although the nation has substantial natural resources and hydroelectric potential, these have remained largely undeveloped.

More than half of Nicaragua's fertile land remains covered by tropical forests.

Most of the people are poor. Only about half can read and write.

The nation's population, principal cities, and major industries are largely concentrated in a narrow, fertile, volcanic belt between Lakes Nicaragua and Managua and the Pacific Ocean.

The climate is warm and humid, with an average annual temperature of 81° F.

Honduras lies to the north and Costa Rica to the south.

EARLY HISTORY

Discovered by Christopher Columbus in 1502, Nicaragua was explored in 1522 and 1523 by the Spanish conquistadores Gil González Dávila and Francisco Hernández de Córdoba. The latter founded Granada and León.

Nicaragua was ruled by the captaincy-general of Guatemala until it declared independence from Spain on Sept. 15, 1821. Nicaragua belonged to the United Provinces of Central America from 1823 until it became an independent republic in 1838.

William Walker, an American military adventurer, led an expeditionary army to Nicaragua making himself president in 1856. He was expelled in 1857 and was executed in 1860 in Honduras.

Internal chaos led to the stationing of U.S. Marines in Nicaragua in 1912–25 and 1927–33.

In the 1920s and early 1930s the U.S. occupation was fought by guerrillas led by Augusto César Sandino, who was assassinated in 1934.

Gen. Anastasio Somoza seized the presidency in 1936. He ruled as dictator until his assassination in 1956. Two sons continued his dictatorship: Luis Somoza, president in 1956–63, and Anastasio Somoza Debayle, president in 1967–79.

A revolutionary movement called the Sandinistas (after the guerrilla martyr Sandino) fought the Somozas from 1962. But the Somozas merely became more powerful, amassing a fortune estimated at $900 million.

On Aug. 22, 1978, guerrillas led by Edén Pastora Gómez, known as "Commander Zero," stormed the national palace in Managua. They held the congress hostage two days until Somoza paid $500,000 ransom and freed 83 political prisoners.

The Sandinistas began a major offensive from Costa Rica on May 29, 1979, that carried them to victory. Somoza fled into exile on July 17. A 5-member Sandinista military junta took control of the government on July 20.

The civil war was estimated to have cost 50,000 lives and $1.3 billion in property damage.

The Marxist Socialist junta expropriated the property of Somoza and his associates, which included about 30% of Nicaragua's farmland, and distributed it to landless peasants directly or as cooperatives. About 5,000 of Somoza's supporters were jailed and many were executed.

NICARAGUA IN THE 1980s

The Reagan administration suspended economic aid to Nicaragua in January 1981 because of evidence the junta was aiding left-wing rebels fighting in El Salvador. The U.S. CIA began training and arming guerrilla groups that mounted border attacks from Honduras.

When conservative businessmen complained in October 1981 that the junta was turning the nation into a communist state, the government threw opposition leaders in prison and shut down opposition newspapers.

The former Sandinista leader Pastora announced on April 15, 1982, that because of the procommunist slant of the ruling junta he would lead a new guerrilla movement to overthrow it. He was wounded on May 30, 1984, by a terrorist bomb that killed four other persons at a news conference he was conducting.

In October 1983 the government offered to sign non-aggression treaties with the U.S. that would end Nicaraguan aid to guerrillas in El Salvador if the U.S. would agree to end military training of forces in Honduras and El Salvador.

The government began in January 1984 to increase the size of its 50,000-man army by drafting all young men from 17 to 22, the first military draft in the nation's history.

After the World Court ordered the U.S. in

QUICK QUIZ: Which U.S. President had served as a lieutenant in the Revolutionary War? See page 344.

NICARAGUA *(continued)*

May 1984 to stop helping rebels mine Nicaraguan ports, the U.S. Congress cut off aid to the anti-Sandinista guerrillas.

Daniel Ortega Saavedra, head of the ruling junta, became president after a Nov. 4, 1984, election that was boycotted by moderates.

Ortega called up all military reserves and placed the nation in a "state of alert" on Nov. 12, 1984, claiming a U.S. invasion was imminent.

President Ortega visited the Soviet Union and seven other communist nations in April and May 1985, appealing for more aid.

Declaring that Nicaragua's government was a threat to U.S. security, President Reagan ordered an embargo on U.S. trade with Nicaragua beginning May 7, 1985. The U.S. previously had been Nicaragua's main trading partner, buying about $58 million in exports and selling over $100 million in imports to Nicaragua.

NIGER

Official Name: Republic of Niger.
Area: 489,191 square miles (1,267,000 sq. km.).
Population: 5,874,000.
Capital: Niamey, 130,299.
Government: Military junta.
Chief of State and Head of Government: Lt. Col. Seyni Kountché (seized power in 1974).
Supreme Military Council: 12 members.
U.S. Ambassador to Niger: William R. Casey Jr.
Niger Ambassador to U.S.: Joseph Diatta.
Flag: Orange, white, and green stripes, with centered orange disk—the sun.
Languages: French (official), Hausa, Djerma.
Main Ethnic Groups: Hausa (50%), Djerma (23%), Fulani (15%), Tuareg (10%).
Chief Religion: Islam (85%).
Leading Industries: Mining (uranium, tin, coal, iron, phosphate); agriculture (peanuts, cotton, cattle, sorghum).
Foreign Trade: *Major exports*—uranium, peanuts, cotton, meat, hides; *major imports*—petroleum, machinery, food, consumer goods.
Places of Interest: Lake Chad; native villages.

NIGER TODAY

Although larger than Texas and California combined, Niger is a poor, landlocked African nation. The northern four-fifths of Niger is covered by the wasteland of the Sahara Desert. The climate is hot, dry, and dusty.

Most of the people are desert nomads or farmers who raise only enough food to support their families. Only about 1 in 20 can read and write. Children under 15 make up almost half the population.

Formerly a French colony, Niger maintains close relationship with France, which is its main trading partner.

High-grade uranium ore is the nation's main export. Niger also has large deposits of iron ore

and phosphates, but exploitation of these important minerals is handicapped by the nation's poor transportation system. There is no railroad to the nearest port—1,000 miles away on the Atlantic coast. And there are few hard-surfaced roads for use by trucks. Consequently, much freight has to be flown in and out of the country.

Niger encourages development of the country's resources by foreign investors.

Niger's main political problems result from internal antagonisms—between Arab-Berber nomads and black farmers, between Djerma-Songhai and Hausa ethnic groups, and between traditional conservatives and Western-educated young radicals.

The most fertile cropland is in the southwestern part of Niger in the 300-mile-long valley of the Niger River.

Algeria and Libya lie to the north, Chad to the east, Nigeria and Benin to the south, and Mali and BurkinaFaso to the west.

HISTORY OF NIGER

From the 600s until the late 1800s, portions of Niger successively belonged to the Songhai, Hausa, and Fulani empires. In the 1600s Tuareg tribes formed confederations in the north.

European explorers who first reached Niger in the 1800s found a state of chronic warfare and anarchy. French penetration began in the 1890s with the establishment of military posts along the Niger River. Through conquest and treaties with local sultans and Britain, most of the country's present boundaries were set by 1914.

In 1922 Niger became a French colony under civil administration in the French West Africa federation. Niger became autonomous in 1958.

France granted Niger full independence on Aug. 3, 1960. Hamani Diori was elected president in 1960 and was reelected in 1965 and 1970. He banned political parties other than his own Parti Progressiste Nigérien (PPN).

Uranium was discovered in 1955 and began to be mined in 1971, stimulating the nation's economy.

On April 15, 1974, Lt. Col. Seyni Kountché, chief of staff of Niger's 2,500-man army, overthrew Diori.

In August 1975 Kountché arrested his chief aide, Vice President Sani Souna Sido, on charges of plotting against him.

Oil and phosphate deposits were discovered in 1975, but their extent remained to be determined.

In February 1976 the government made an emergency appeal to other nations for 200,000 tons of food to save 1.2 million of its people from starving because of drought.

Loyal troops put down an attempt to overthrow Kountché's government on March 15, 1976. The leader of the revolt, Capt. Sidi Mohamed, and nine others were sentenced to death.

To reduce petroleum imports, Niger put into operation in 1981 a combined coal mine and 18-megawatt coal-fired electric power plant to supply electricity to uranium mines and towns in the north-central region.

Although climbing uranium-ore exports made the gross national product of Niger grow at an annual rate of 10% during the late 1970s, falling uranium prices caused the nation's economy to stagnate in the 1980s.

NIGERIA

Official Name: Federal Republic of Nigeria.
Area: 356,669 square miles (923,768 sq. km.).
Population: 93,324,000.
Chief Cities: Abuja, capital, 50,000; Lagos, 1,060,848; Ibadan, 847,000; Ogbomosho, 432,000; Kano, 399,000.
Largest Metropolitan Area: Lagos, 1,476,837.
Government: Military dictatorship.
Head of Government: Maj. Gen. Ibrahim Babangida (since 1985).
U.S. Ambassador to Nigeria: Thomas W.M. Smith.
Nigeria's Ambassador to U.S.: Ignatius C. Olisemeka.
Flag: Bars of green, white, and green.
Languages: English (official), tribal dialects.
Chief Ethnic Groups: Hausa (21%), Yoruba (20%), Ibo (17%), Fulani (8%).
Main Religions: Islam (47%), Christianity (34%), animism (19%).
Leading Industries: Mining (petroleum, natural gas, tin, coal, iron ore); agriculture (peanuts, cattle, cotton, palm kernels, cocoa, rubber, bananas, corn, yams, rice, fruits, vegetables); manufacturing (food processing, cement, petroleum products, textiles, tobacco products, consumer goods).
Foreign Trade: *Major exports*—crude petroleum, cacao, peanuts and oil, tin, palm nuts and oil, rubber, cotton; *major imports*—food, iron and steel, textiles, automobiles.
Places of Interest: Museum of Nigerian antiquities in Lagos; Muslim city of Kano; Ibadan; Benin.

NIGERIA TODAY

Nigeria is the world's richest, most heavily populated, black nation. A federation of 19 states, it is somewhat larger than Texas and Oklahoma combined. It is one of the world's 10 leading producers of petroleum, forestry products, natural rubber, and tin.

Using its oil wealth to build needed facilities of all kinds, the government has placed emphasis on improving the educational system to reduce illiteracy and enable more Nigerians to find jobs as skilled workers and managers. Additional money was spent in building and improving roads to open up interior regions.

The government also has invested large sums to create a "green revolution" to improve the country's agriculture. However, most Nigerians continue to live as subsistence farmers.

Nigeria has about 250 tribes, each with its own language. Three groups are dominant: Hausa-Fulani in the north, Yoruba in the west, and Ibo in the east.

Benin lies to the west, Niger to the north, Lake Chad to the northeast, and Cameroon to the east.

EARLY HISTORY OF NIGERIA

Nigeria's earliest known culture, Nok, flourished in 500 B.C. Later, migrants from the northeast founded the Yoruba and Edo kingdoms of Oyo and Benin and the spiritual center of Ife.

Sub-Saharan states were founded in the 600s to 700s A.D. by the Zaghawa nomads, thought to be of Berber origin. These states were the forerunners of the Kanem empire established in the 700s. Islamic traditions of the Kanem empire were diffused through the seven Hausa city-states on the savanna fringes of the Sahara.

In the 1400s and 1500s the Portuguese and then the British engaged in slave trading on the Atlantic coast. The Hausa city-states were conquered in the early 1800s in the Islamic crusade of the Fulani warrior Usman dan Fodio.

Slavery ended after 1861 when Britain annexed Lagos as a colony.

In 1883 the Niger Coast Protectorate was declared, and in 1885 the Berlin Conference recognized Britain's claim to southern Nigeria. British troops captured the Muslim stronghold at Kano in 1903. The British created the unified colony and protectorate of Nigeria in 1914.

A nationalist movement after World War I received strong support from Ibo leaders. In 1954 Nigeria became a federation of three autonomous regions, later increased to four.

INDEPENDENCE

Nigeria was granted full independence on Oct. 1, 1960, with a constitution providing for a federal parliamentary democracy.

Through 1965 an uneasy political balance was maintained by a coalition in the federal government between the northern Hausa-Fulani and the eastern Ibo. The Yoruba of the west formed the opposition.

On Jan. 15, 1966, the Nigerian national government was ousted by a military coup attributed to young Ibo officers. The federal prime minister, Sir Abubakr Tafawa Balewa, and the premiers of the western and northern regions were among those murdered. Army Chief of Staff Maj. Gen. Johnson Aguiyi-Ironsi, an Ibo, became chief of state.

Ironsi dissolved the federation and established a unitary republic in May 1966, triggering anti-Ibo riots in the north.

A new military coup on July 29, 1966, killed Ironsi and brought to power Lt. Col. Yakubu Gowon, a northern Christian from a non-Hausa minority group. Some 30,000 Ibo were massacred, and over 1 million were driven from the north.

On May 30, 1967, the young Ibo leader Col. Odumegwu Ojukwu proclaimed the independence of the Republic of Biafra (the 29,484-square-mile former Eastern Region). Biafra's secession was resisted by federal troops who invaded Biafra on July 6, 1967. In the next 30 months tens of thousands died in battles and of starvation. On Jan. 15, 1970, Biafran leaders surrendered.

NIGERIA IN THE 1970s

Nigeria took over thousands of foreign-owned businesses in March 1974, as the government forbade foreign ownership of most businesses.

Brig. Gen. Murtala Muhammed ousted Gowon in a bloodless coup on July 29, 1975.

On Feb. 13, 1976, Gen. Muhammed was killed in an unsuccessful coup.

Lt. Gen. Olusegun Obasanjo, commander of

NIGERIA *(continued)*

the army, succeeded Muhammed as head of state.

Thirty-seven persons were executed in 1976 for implication in Muhammed's assassination.

The first nationwide elections in over 11 years were held on Aug. 31, 1977, to choose members for an assembly to write a new constitution.

U.S. President Carter toured Nigeria on March 31–April 3, 1978—the first visit by an American chief executive.

The military government nationalized British petroleum interests in Nigeria on July 31, 1979.

In a series of elections in July and August 1979, Nigerians elected a president, members of a national congress, 19 state governors, and state legislators. Alhaji Shehu Shagari, 54, winner of the presidential election, took office on Oct. 1, 1979.

NIGERIA IN THE 1980s

In 1980 President Shagari visited the United States to appeal for aid in improving Nigeria's farm production to achieve food self-sufficiency.

Some 5,000 to 7,000 were killed in northern Nigeria in December 1980 in battles between the army and a fanatic Muslim sect.

The government in 1982 began moving its departments from Lagos to the new capital city Abuja built at a cost of $3 billion.

Nigeria's booming economy slackened in the 1980s as the worldwide oil glut reduced petroleum exports. The lower oil revenues forced the government to cut back on many of its projects.

Because of worsening economic conditions, the government in January and February 1983 expelled about 1.2 million illegal aliens who had come to Nigeria from Ghana and other West African countries. The exodus was one of the largest forced migrations in modern history.

In elections from Aug. 6 to Sept. 3, 1983, Shagari won reelection to a second four-year term.

Maj. Gen. Mohammed Buhari, 41, overthrew the civilian government in a bloodless coup on Dec. 31, 1983, becoming Nigeria's seventh leader since independence. He said he took the action to save the country from economic collapse.

The coup came only two days after Shagari had announced a government budget reflecting a 50% drop in Nigeria's oil revenues since 1981.

The military government imposed strict controls on the press in April 1984, forbidding criticism of the government.

More than 500 former government officials, including President Shagari, were jailed awaiting trials by military tribunals on charges of stealing millions of dollars from the government.

The Nigerian secret police in July 1984 were caught by British police in an unsuccessful attempt to kidnap from London one of Shagari's former cabinet ministers wanted for corruption.

Nigeria broke with other members of OPEC in October 1984, reducing the price of its petroleum by $2 a barrel.

As the economy continued to decline in 1985, the government ordered the second mass expulsion of aliens in two years. It gave 700,000 aliens from neighboring countries three weeks to pack their belongings and leave by May 10, 1985.

Maj. Gen. Ibrahim Babangida, 43, overthrew Buhari in a bloodless coup on Aug. 27, 1985.

NORWAY

Official Name: Kingdom of Norway.
Area: 125,182 square miles (324,219 sq. km.).
Population: 4,170,000.
Chief Cities: Oslo, capital, 451,204; Bergen, 207,609; Trondheim, 134,833.
Largest Metropolitan Area: Oslo, 642,954.
Government: Constitutional monarchy.
Prime Minister: Kaare Willoch (since 1981).
King: Olav V (reigned since 1957).
Legislature: *Storting,* 155 members.
U.S. Ambassador to Norway: Robert D. Stuart.
Norwegian Ambassador to U.S.: Kjell Eliassen.
Flag: Blue Latin cross bordered in white on red field.
Language: Norwegian (Bokmal and Nynorsk dialects).
Principal Ethnic Group: Norwegian.
State Religion: Lutheranism (96%).
Leading Industries: Manufacturing (aluminum, paper, chemicals, ships, furniture); trade and shipping; services; construction; mining (petroleum, natural gas, iron ore, lead, zinc, copper, molybdenum); agriculture (cattle, sheep, goats, dairy products, barley, potatoes, fruits, vegetables); fishing; forestry and lumbering.
Foreign Trade: *Major exports*—petroleum, gas, manufactured goods, shipping services, aluminum, fish, paper, pulp; *major imports*—machinery, ships, food.
Places of Interest: North Cape and "land of the midnight sun"; fjord country; old Bergen; Nidaros Cathedral at Trondheim; Stavanger Cathedral; Mai- haugen museum at Lillehammer. *In Oslo:* Akershus Castle; Vigeland sculptures, Frogner Park; museums.

NORWAY TODAY

Somewhat larger than New Mexico, Norway is an important industrial and trading nation of northern Europe. Production from huge offshore deposits of oil and gas has brought Norway increased prosperity.

Since the time of the Vikings, Norwegians have been seafarers. Norway has the world's third-largest merchant fleet, and, until surpassed by oil exports, income from shipping was Norway's largest source of foreign exchange.

Norway has experienced tremendous economic expansion, especially in mining, shipbuilding, and manufacturing industries. Growth has enabled mining and manufacturing to surpass in importance the country's traditional industries of agriculture, forestry, and fishing, bringing the Norwegian people a high standard of living.

Wealth from its offshore oil and gas fields has enabled Norway to cut income taxes, while at the same time increasing social benefits. The government placed restrictions on the production of petroleum and gas to ensure a steady income for many years into the future.

To protect its well-paid labor force from an influx of cheap labor, Norway severely limits most immigration.

Norway occupies the western and northernmost part of the Scandinavian peninsula. Sweden lies to the east and south. Finland and the Soviet

Union are to the northeast.

About one-third of the country lies within the Arctic Circle. The terrain is mountainous, and the 1,700-mile coastline is deeply marked with fjords, bays, and inlets.

The warming waters of the Gulf Stream keep Norway's climate comparatively mild. The far north is the land of the midnight sun with continuous daylight from mid-May to the last of July. From late November to the end of January the sun does not rise above the horizon.

EARLY HISTORY

Hunters and fishermen lived in Norway at least 8,000 years ago. Fortified settlements began to be built about A.D. 400.

The Viking Age in which Norwegian seafarers raided and plundered along the coasts of Europe began about 900. Much of Norway was united for the first time in 900–940 by King Harold Fairhair (Harold I). Christianity was introduced by Olav I (995–1000). Olav II was killed by a peasant army in 1030, and Norway then passed under the rule of Canute the Great of England and Denmark.

In the 1200's Haakon IV acquired Iceland, Greenland, the Faeroe Islands, the Shetlands, and the Orkneys.

The royal male line died out with Haakon V in 1319, so Norway entered into union with Sweden under Magnus V. Queen Margrethe I of Denmark united the three Scandinavian kingdoms in the Union of Kalmar (1397), which lasted until Sweden broke away in 1523. Union between Norway and Denmark continued until 1814, when Denmark ceded Norway to Sweden.

INDEPENDENT KINGDOM OF NORWAY

On June 7, 1905, the Norwegian parliament declared the union with Sweden dissolved. Norway became an independent kingdom under Haakon VII, a Danish prince.

Norway was neutral in World War I and sought neutrality in World War II. However, Germany invaded in April 1940, occupying the country until 1945. A puppet government was established under Vidkun Quisling, whose name became a synonym for traitor.

Olav V became king in 1957 upon the death of Haakon VII.

Odvar Nordli, head of the Labor Party, became prime minister on Jan. 12, 1976.

Norway set a 200-mile fishing and economic zone along its coast on Jan. 1, 1977, closing much of the North Sea to foreign fishermen.

The government agreed in September 1980 to stockpile large amounts of military equipment and arms for use by U.S. Marines who would be flown in by airlift in the event of a war with the Soviet Union, but continued not to permit NATO troops to be stationed in Norway.

Nordli was succeeded in 1981 by the nation's first woman prime minister, Gro Harlem Brundtage, 41, a physician.

In a national election on Sept. 13–14, 1981, voters ousted the socialist Labor Party.

Economist Kaare Willoch, head of the Conservative Party, became prime minister on Oct. 13, 1981, leading the nation's first right-wing

government in 12 years. He promised to cut taxes and reduce social-welfare spending.

Dependent on oil exports for 25% of its foreign exchange, Norway's economy stagnated in 1981–85 because of lower petroleum prices.

In Norway's biggest spy scandal in history, a leftist Labor Party former deputy foreign minister, Arne Treholt, 41, was arrested on Jan. 20, 1984, on charges of spying for the Soviet Union and Iraq for 10 years. A week later the government expelled five Soviet diplomats for espionage and told the Soviet Union it could not replace them. Treholt was sentenced to 20 years in prison after a trial in 1985.

NORWEGIAN OVERSEAS AREAS

SVALBARD

Area: 23,957 square miles (62,004 sq. km.).
Population: 3,700.

Svalbard, some 400 miles north of Norway, is a barren archipelago with an Arctic climate and rich coal deposits. West Spitsbergen is the largest island. The islands first were found by Norwegians in the 1100s. The Dutch rediscovered them in 1596. From the 1600s rival claims were made by the Dutch, British, and Norwegians. Svalbard became part of Norway in 1925.

JAN MAYEN: Island (144 sq. mi.) 300 miles north of Iceland; annexed in 1929.

BOUVET ISLAND: Uninhabited South Atlantic island (23 sq. mi.); became a dependency in 1930.

PETER I ISLAND: Uninhabited Antarctic island (96 sq. mi.); became a dependency in 1933.

QUEEN MAUD LAND: Part of Antarctic continent; claimed by Norway in 1939.

OMAN

Official Name: Sultanate of Oman.
Area: 82,030 square miles (212,457 sq. km.).
Population: 1,056,000.
Cities: Muscat, capital, 10,000; Matrah, 70,000.
Government: Absolute monarchy.
Sultan: Qaboos Bin Said (reigned since 1970).
U.S. Ambassador to Oman: George C. Montgomery.
Omani Ambassador to U.S.: Ali Salim Bader Al-Hinai.
Flag: Red bar with crossed white swords next to staff; white, red, and green stripes.
Official Language: Arabic.
Chief Ethnic Groups: Arab, Iranian, Baluchi.
Main Religion: Islam.
Leading Industries: Mining (petroleum, copper); construction; agriculture (dates, livestock, pomegranates, coconuts, grains, fruits, vegetables); oil refining; fishing; food processing.
Foreign Trade: *Major exports*—petroleum, dates, pomegranates, limes, fish, hides; *major imports*—food, cotton goods, rice, coffee, tea, motor vehicles, construction materials.
Places of Interest: Royal palace; ancient forts.

QUICK QUIZ: Which former First Lady was voted an honorary seat in Congress? See page 343.

OMAN TODAY

About the size of Kansas, Oman is an oil-rich Arab sultanate on the Arabian Sea.

Oman has used much of its oil income of more than $2 billion a year to educate its children, to provide free outdoor color television sets for each community, to build a lavish new palace for the sultan, and to equip its army. Airports, highways, and sewerage systems have been constructed.

Because about three-fourths of the people depend on farming for their living, the government stimulated agriculture by importing new breeds of livestock and constructing model farms.

The country generally has a hot desert climate, averaging between 69° and 90° F. Average annual rainfall is less than 4 inches in Muscat.

HISTORY

Oman was an important farming and trading area with many towns and villages and an elaborate irrigation system in the 2000s B.C.

In the 600s A.D. Saudi Arabian traders spread Muslim influence to the Persian Gulf.

In the 1500s the Portuguese conquered the region now called Oman, using Muscat as a base to control Persian Gulf trade. Arabs ejected the Portuguese in 1650.

In 1696–98 Oman drove the Portuguese out of bases in East Africa, captured Mombassa in Kenya, and won control of Zanzibar.

The present Said dynasty came to power in Muscat and Oman in 1741. British influence was established with a treaty of friendship in 1798.

In the early 1800s Oman was the most powerful state in Arabia, controlling much of East Africa. But after the ruler died in 1856, his sons divided the empire in 1861.

Zanzibar continued to pay tribute to the sultans until its independence in 1964.

Oman had become a poor country before oil began to be produced in 1967.

In July 1970 the sultan's son, Qaboos Bin Said, overthrew his father. The new sultan changed the name of the country from Muscat and Oman to Oman. He began using the oil income for progressive economic and social reforms.

The sultan took majority control of the oil industry on Jan. 1, 1974.

After a dozen years of fighting in southern Oman, the government announced in January 1976 that rebel leaders had surrendered. The civil war had begun in 1964 as rebels sought independence for the Dhofar area. The rebels were supplied with Chinese and Soviet arms from Southern Yemen.

Britain closed its military base at Masira, Oman, on March 31, 1977, its last military outpost in the Middle East.

The U.S. on June 5, 1980, announced an agreement with Oman for use of ports and air bases by American military forces.

The country's $21.3 billion 5-year plan for 1981–85 placed emphasis on the development of companies to oversee expansion of production from agriculture and fisheries. The nation's first oil refinery began production in 1982.

Unlike other Arab nations, Oman increased oil production in the 1980s to keep its economy growing.

PAKISTAN

Official Name: Islamic Republic of Pakistan.
Area: 310,404 square miles (803,943 sq. km.).
Population: 100,429,000.
Chief Cities: Islamabad, capital, 77,318; Karachi, 3,498,634; Lahore, 2,165,372; Shah Faisalabad (formerly Lyallpur), 822,263; Hyderabad, 628,310; Rawalpindi, 615,392.
Government: Military dictatorship.
President: Gen. Mohammad Zia ul-Haq (since 1978).
Prime Minister: Mohammed Khan Junejo (since 1985).
National Assembly: 237 members.
U.S. Ambassador to Pakistan: Ronald I. Spiers.
Pakistani Ambassador to U.S.: Ejaz Azim.
Flag: Green field with white crescent and star; white bar along hoist.
Chief Ethnic Groups: Punjabi (65%), Sindhi (11%), Pathan (8%).
Principal Languages: Urdu (official), English, Punjabi.
Main Religion: Islam (97%).
Leading Industries: Agriculture (wheat, cattle, sugarcane, rice, cotton, barley, corn, tobacco); manufacturing (textiles, chemicals, steel, electricity); mining (natural gas, petroleum, coal); fishing.
Foreign Trade: *Major exports*—cotton, rice, textiles; *major imports*—machinery, raw materials.
Places of Interest: Modern capital of Islamabad; Karachi museum; Shalimar Gardens, fort and Badshahi Mosque in Lahore; Peshawar museum and bazaars; Mohenjo-Daro excavations; Taxila ruins near Rawalpindi; Khyber Pass near Peshawar; Kaghan Valley; Tarbela Dam.

PAKISTAN TODAY

About as large as Texas and Louisiana combined, Pakistan has the ninth-largest population among the nations of the world.

The country is burdened by more than 2.8 million refugees from Afghanistan.

Unlike most developing countries, Pakistan is self-sufficient in raising wheat to meet the food needs of its people. Most Pakistanis are poor farm workers who earn less than $300 per year. Less than 1 in 5 can read and write.

The government owns most large basic manufacturing industries, as well as transportation, banking, and insurance.

The country's major export is its workers for construction projects in other countries. They send home over $2 billion each year.

Because Pakistan is an Islamic state, the oil-rich Arab nations of the Middle East have invested hundreds of millions of dollars to help develop its industrialization program. In addition, large amounts of aid have been provided by the United States, China, and other nations.

Pakistan rises from the deserts of Sind in the south and Baluchistan in the west to the forested hills in the north, and then to the soaring Himalayas. The Indus River waters much of the eastern and central region.

The climate is hot and dry near the coast of

the Arabian Sea, but is cool and temperate in the northeastern uplands.

Iran lies to the west, Afghanistan to the north, China to the northeast, and India to the east.

EARLY HISTORY

In the 700s the Islamic faith was introduced by Arab traders. In the 900s Muslim warriors swept into the subcontinent and conquered most of Pakistan. Muslim rule lasted 1,000 years, reaching its peak under the Mogul empire in the 1500s.

Portuguese traders arrived in the 1400s. By the 1800s the British East India Company had become the dominant power, with the last Mogul emperor deposed in 1859.

Under the leadership of Mohammed Ali Jinnah and Liaquat Ali Khan, the Muslim League began demanding in 1940 a separate state composed of areas where Muslims were in the majority.

INDEPENDENCE

In 1947 Britain agreed to the formation of separate Hindu and Islamic states. Pakistan came into being as an independent dominion within the British Commonwealth of Nations on Aug. 14, 1947, with Liaquat Ali Khan as prime minister and with Mohammed Ali Jinnah as governor-general. Islamic Pakistan consisted of two provinces, East and West Pakistan, separated from each other by 1,000 miles of Indian territory.

Muslim-Hindu disputes intensified after independence. States with Hindu majorities but Muslim rulers were forcibly joined to India. Kashmir, a state with a majority of Muslim residents but ruled by a Hindu minority, became the chief point of contention, and fighting over control of Kashmir broke out between Pakistan and India in 1948. The UN negotiated a cease-fire the following year, but tension remained high. Pakistani-Indian fighting resumed in September 1965. A peace accord was signed early in 1966.

Elsewhere, Pakistan faced economic and political difficulties. Following the death of Mohammed Ali Jinnah in 1948 and the assassination of Liaquat Ali Khan in 1951, the precarious control of the new government gradually disintegrated.

A new constitution went into effect on March 23, 1956, making the nation the *Islamic Republic of Pakistan*. Maj. Gen. Iskander Mirza became the first president.

By 1958 the East Pakistan provincial legislature was in turmoil. In West Pakistan the khan of Kalat moved toward secession. On Oct. 7, 1958, the commander in chief of the army, Gen. Mohammed Ayub Khan, took over the government.

Violent antigovernment riots erupted in late 1968 and early 1969.

On March 25, 1969, President Ayub resigned and turned the government over to Gen. Agha Mohammed Yahya Khan, commander in chief of the armed forces.

WAR WITH INDIA AND BANGLADESH

In general elections in March 1971 the nationalist Awami League, led by Sheik Mujibur (Mujib) Rahman, won nearly all of East Pakistan's seats, giving it a majority in the national assembly.

When President Yahya postponed convoca-

tion of the assembly, revolt swept East Pakistan. The league proclaimed the province an independent nation called *Bangladesh*. Pakistan outlawed the league and imprisoned Mujib.

The Pakistani army attempted to crush the rebellion in East Pakistan. About 9 million Bengali refugees flooded into India.

India, which sided with the rebels, began an armed invasion of Pakistan on Dec. 3, 1971. Pakistani forces surrendered on Dec. 16.

RULE BY BHUTTO IN THE 1970s

The defeated military junta in Pakistan collapsed. Zulfikar Ali Bhutto, head of the National Party, was sworn in as provisional president in late December 1971. Bhutto released Mujib, who returned to Bangladesh.

In January 1972 Pakistan withdrew from the Commonwealth of Nations because Britain had established diplomatic relations with Bangladesh.

On April 12, 1973, President Bhutto signed into law a new constitution that provided for a president and a prime minister elected by the national assembly. Bhutto gave up the presidency to become prime minister.

Bhutto's socialist government completed the nationalization of basic industries in 1974.

The government also began a program in 1974 of giving 1,350 square feet of free land to each homeless rural family.

Bhutto in August 1974 announced restoration of basic civil rights that had been suspended since 1970. But six months later, on Feb. 10, 1975, he banned the main opposition political party, the National Awami Party (NAP).

The United States ended a 10-year arms embargo against Pakistan on Feb. 23, 1975.

After six years of construction the world's second-largest dam, the $1.3 billion Tarbela Dam on the Indus River, was completed in 1976.

The government announced plans in 1976 to construct 24 nuclear power plants by 1996.

After a parliamentary election on March 7, 1977, Bhutto announced that his Pakistan People's Party had won a landslide victory, taking 133 of the 200 elective seats. Opponents declared the election had been stolen by fraud.

MILITARY RULE BY PRESIDENT ZIA

Gen. Mohammad Zia ul-Haq, 53, chief of staff of the army, seized control of the government on July 5, 1977, jailing Bhutto and his closest aides. Zia imposed martial law but freed the press, radio, and TV of censorship. He established severe Islamic punishments, including amputations of hands and public whipping, for such crimes as theft and annoying women.

Bhutto was convicted of murder in 1978. He was hanged on April 4, 1979.

When President Fazal Elahi Chaudry completed his elected 5-year term, Zia took over the presidency on Sept. 16, 1978, while retaining his titles as chief martial-law administrator and armed forces commander.

After the CIA confirmed in 1979 that Pakistan was building a secret plant to manufacture enriched uranium that could be used to make atomic weapons, the U.S. cut off economic and

QUICK QUIZ: Who established the first American settlement in Texas? See page 326.

PAKISTAN (continued)

military aid of about $40 million a year. Zia denied Pakistan planned to build atomic weapons and appealed for restoration of U.S. aid, but he said Pakistan might explode a research device.

Relations between Pakistan and the Soviet Union worsened in 1979–80 when Zia permitted millions of Afghan tribesmen to take refuge and use Pakistan as a base for guerrilla raids against Afghanistan's communist government and troops of its Soviet ally. The influx of Afghan refugees added to Pakistan's difficult economic and social problems.

After scheduling a national election for November 1979, Zia canceled it on Oct. 16, 1979.

Mobs of Pakistani Muslims, inflamed by anti-American statements by Iran's Ayatollah Khomeini, attacked and burned the U.S. embassy in Islamabad on Nov. 21, 1979, killing two Americans and two Pakistani employees.

After Soviet troops invaded Afghanistan to control its communist government, the U.S. in January 1980 offered $400 million in military aid to bolster Pakistan's defenses. However, President Zia rejected the offer as "peanuts," explaining that substantially more aid was necessary. He also indicated he feared the U.S. would attach strings to the aid to try to halt Pakistan's effort to develop an atomic bomb.

In the face of the threat posed by Soviet troops on Pakistan's border with Afghanistan, the U.S. reached agreement with President Zia on Sept. 15, 1981, to provide $3.2 billion in military and economic aid over a five-year period.

The nation's first blast furnace began producing pig iron in 1981, part of a $2.5 billion steel mill being built with Soviet help. When completed in 1985 it will be able to produce 1.1 million tons of steel annually. Imported iron ore and coal are carried from ships to the mill by a 28-mile-long conveyor belt.

China and Pakistan formally opened on Aug. 27, 1982, the 468-mile Karakoram highway link from Xinjiang, China, across the Himalayas and through Kashmir.

President Zia decreed on Sept. 28, 1982, that anyone sheltering terrorists would be publicly executed.

Pakistan and India moved to improve relations with the first meeting in a decade between the leaders of the two countries that have fought each other in three wars in the past four decades. President Zia and India's Prime Minister Gandhi conferred in New Delhi on Nov. 1, 1982.

Pakistan was torn by riots throughout 1983 as opponents led demonstrations against Zia's martial law government. In discussions with political leaders Zia promised national elections in 1985.

Pakistan had a prosperous economy in 1982–84 with an annual growth of about 6% in the gross national product.

In the first general election in eight years, Pakistanis elected a new national assembly on Feb. 25, 1985. Seven of President Zia's cabinet ministers were defeated.

The nation's sixth 5-year plan for 1983–1988 devotes $8.6 billion to overcome energy shortages by installing new electric power generators and by increasing natural gas and oil production.

PANAMA

Official Name: Republic of Panama.
Area: 29,762 square miles (77,083 sq. km.).
Population: 2,257,000.
Capital: Panama City, 386,393.
Government: Republic.
President: Eric Arturo Delvalle (since 1985).
Parliament: *Legislative Council,* 57 members; *National Assembly,* 505 members.
U.S. Ambassador to Panama: Everett E. Briggs.
Ambassador to U.S.: Gabriel de la Guardia.
Flag: Quarters of blue, red, and white, with blue and red stars on the two white portions.
Official Language: Spanish.
Main Ethnic Groups: Mestizo (70%), black (13%), European descent (10%), Indian (6%).
Official Religion: Roman Catholicism (93%).
Leading Industries: Agriculture (rice, bananas, corn, cocoa, abaca, tobacco, coffee, palm kernels, livestock); fishing; trade and services; manufacturing (food processing, oil refining, tobacco products, textiles, soap, cement); forestry and lumbering; mining (gold).
Foreign Trade: *Major exports*—bananas, refined petroleum, shrimp, cocoa; *major imports*—crude petroleum, motor vehicles, foodstuffs.
Places of Interest: Panama Canal; Panama City; El Valle; Darién; Contadora, Taboga, San Blas islands; Pacific coast beaches; Piñas Bay; Portobelo ruins near Colón.

PANAMA TODAY

Almost as large as South Carolina, Panama numbers among its resources large copper deposits, rich farmland, and the Panama Canal. About half the people are farmers. Most of the rest make a living directly or indirectly from the canal.

For many years U.S. control of the Panama Canal had been a major point of contention between the U.S. and Panama. Panamanians felt that their country did not receive a fair share of the profits from operation of the canal and that Panama should have sovereignty over the Panama Canal Zone. In 1979 the U.S. gave up sovereignty over the canal zone.

Panama lies between the Caribbean and the Pacific on the isthmus linking North and South America.

There are lowlands on both coasts of Panama. The eastern portion of the country is covered by rain forest. Colombia is to the east and Costa Rica to the west.

EARLY HISTORY

Panama's history has been shaped by its strategic location between two oceans. The Spanish explorer Rodrigo de Bastidas visited eastern Panama in 1501, and Columbus claimed the area for Spain in the following year. In 1513 Vasco Núñez de Balboa became the first European to cross the narrow isthmus to reach the Pacific. Occupied by Spaniards, Panama served as the route for shipping Inca treasures to Spain in the 1500s and

1600s. Spanish rule was overthrown in 1821, and Panama became a province of Colombia.

The California gold rush in 1849 revived interest in Panama's geographical importance as a route from the Atlantic to the Pacific. The Panama Railroad (completed in 1855) carried goldrush traffic across the isthmus.

French attempts during the 1880s to build a canal were unsuccessful because 20,000 workers died of yellow fever.

The U.S. bought the canal rights from France, but Colombia demanded more money.

INDEPENDENCE AND THE PANAMA CANAL

On Nov. 3, 1903, Panamanians revolted and declared independence from Colombia. President Theodore Roosevelt immediately sent U.S. Marines to protect the new government. On Nov. 18, 1903, the U.S. and Panama signed the Hay–Bunau-Varilla Treaty giving the U.S. control of the 10-mile-wide Panama Canal Zone for a payment of $10 million plus $250,000 a year.

U.S. Col. William C. Gorgas in 1904–13 wiped out the mosquitoes in Panama that caused yellow fever and malaria.

Construction of the canal began in 1907 under Col. George W. Goethals. On Aug. 15, 1914, the first ship went through the canal from the Atlantic to the Pacific. Officially opened on July 12, 1920, the canal cost about $350 million.

Brig. Gen. Omar Torrijos Herrera, commander of the national guard, seized control of the government on Oct. 11, 1968.

After 13 years of negotiations, the U.S. agreed in 1977 to treaties returning control of the canal to Panama. Ratification by the U.S. Senate was completed on April 18, 1978.

In October 1978 Torrijos stepped down as chief of state after the National Assembly elected his choice as president, Aristedes Royo.

The U.S. on Oct. 1, 1979, formally returned to Panama sovereignty over the 553-square-mile Panama Canal Zone that had been governed by the U.S. since 1904. All U.S. control over the canal will end at noon on Dec. 31, 1999.

Gen. Torrijos was killed in the crash of a military plane in western Panama on July 31, 1981.

The first oil pipeline across the Isthmus of Panama, completed at a cost of $300 million, began pumping in 1982. It enables tankers too large to go through the canal to pump oil from the Pacific to the Atlantic.

President Royo was ousted on July 30, 1982, by national guard commander Gen. Rubén Darío Paredes. Ricardo de la Espriella, who had been vice president, succeeded Royo as president.

President de la Espriella was forced by the military to resign on Feb. 13, 1984. He was succeeded by Vice President Jorge Illueca.

Panama held its first presidential election in 16 years on May 6, 1984. Nicolas Ardito Baletta, 45, an economist who was backed by the military, was declared winner by the thin margin of 1,713 votes out of nearly 600,000 cast.

President Ardito Barletta was ousted on Sept. 28, 1985, by military commander Gen. Manuel A. Noriega. Eric Arturo Delvalle, 48, who had been vice president, was sworn in as president.

PAPUA NEW GUINEA

Official Name: Papua New Guinea.
Area: 178,260 square miles (461,691 sq. km.).
Population: 3,495,000.
Capital: Port Moresby, 116,952.
Government: Parliamentary state.
Prime Minister: Michael Somare (since 1982).
Parliament: *House of Assembly,* 109 members.
U.S. Ambassador: Paul F. Gardner.
PNG Ambassador to U.S.: Renagi Lohia.
Flag: Five-star constellation on lower black triangle; gold bird of paradise on upper red triangle.
Languages: English, Pidgin English, Motu, more than 700 tribal dialects.
Ethnic Groups: Melanesians, Asians, Australians..
Religions: Christianity, tribal religions.
Leading Industries: Mining (copper, gold); agriculture (cocoa, copra, rubber, tea, fruits, vegetables); forestry and lumbering; fishing; food processing.
Foreign Trade: *Major exports*—copper, gold, plywood, lumber, seafood, cocoa, rubber, tea; *major imports*—machinery, vehicles, food.
Places of Interest: Port Moresby government buildings; thatched-roof tribal villages; copper mines on island of Bougainville; Rabaul on island of New Britain; towns of Mt. Hagan, Lae, Goroka, Aitape, Wewak, Popondetta, Madang, Kerema, and Daru on mainland New Guinea.

PAPUA NEW GUINEA TODAY

Larger than California, Papua New Guinea is an island nation just north of Australia. Most of the mountainous country is covered by tropical rain forests with few roads. The extent of the country's mineral resources is unknown, but copper and gold are mined for export. Only a small portion of the nation's land is farmed.

Communication among the people is a major difficulty. More than 700 tribal dialects are spoken, with one tribe being unable to understand another. Many of the people speak Pidgin English. Few can read and write. Most people live in tribal villages leading the same primitive life as their ancestors. Wars between tribes are frequent.

The country depends heavily on over $200 million annual aid from Australia.

The country covers the eastern half of New Guinea. Its largest offshore islands are New Britain (14,600 sq. mi.), Bougainville (3,880 sq. mi.), and New Ireland (3,340 sq. mi.). The western half of New Guinea is the Indonesian province of Irian Jaya.

The coastal plain is 50 to 150 miles wide. Inland mountains tower to 14,500 feet.

The climate is hot along the coasts, with cooler temperatures in the uplands. There is much rain.

EARLY HISTORY

The people of Papua New Guinea are believed to have come to the islands from the Asian main-

QUICK QUIZ: Who sponsored the exploration of Lewis and Clarke? See page 342.

PAPUA NEW GUINEA *(continued)*

land thousands of years ago.

The first European known to have visited New Guinea was the Portuguese governor of the Molucca Islands, Jorge de Meneses, in 1526.

In 1884 Britain made southeastern New Guinea a protectorate, and Germany claimed northeastern New Guinea and the offshore islands.

Southeastern New Guinea became Australia's Territory of Papua on Sept. 1, 1906. With the defeat of Germany in World War I, the League of Nations transferred administration of northeastern New Guinea and the offshore islands to Australia in 1920.

During World War II the Japanese captured northern New Guinea, but Port Moresby became an important Allied military base. The U.S. and Australia recaptured all New Guinea by 1944.

In 1949 Australia united northeastern and southeastern New Guinea under a single administration called *Papua New Guinea.*

Papua New Guinea's first house of assembly convened in 1964.

After national elections in 1972 a coalition government was formed with Michael Somare of the Pangu Party as chief minister. Australia granted complete self-government on Dec. 1, 1973.

Nationalists on the copper-rich island of Bougainville declared their independence from Papua New Guinea on Sept. 1, 1975, naming their government the Republic of the Northern Solomons. But the rebellion was put down.

INDEPENDENCE

Australia gave Papua New Guinea complete independence on Sept. 16 1975, with Somare as the nation's first prime minister.

Papua New Guinea reached agreement with the European Economic Community (EEC) in March 1977, allowing it to export products to the EEC without having to pay tariffs.

The first national election since independence was held June 18 to July 9, 1977. Prime Minister Somare's coalition parties won a majority of 60 seats in the 109-member parliament.

Increasing unemployment and a soaring crime rate brought criticism of Somare's administration. On March 11, 1980, he lost a vote of confidence 57 to 49. He was succeeded as prime minister by Sir Julius Chan, 43, head of the opposition People's Progress Party.

A $13 million American tuna boat was confiscated in February 1982 because it violated the country's 200-mile offshore economic zone.

Eight political parties and 1,126 candidates competed for 109 parliamentary seats in a 3-week election that began on June 5, 1982. The process takes so long because of the difficulty of collecting ballots from remote areas.

Former Prime Minister Somare, 47, was returned to office on Aug. 3, 1982. His Pangu Party won a plurality of 41 seats and he was supported by smaller parties to form a majority coalition. Chan's People's Progress Party won only 10 seats with almost half his cabinet members defeated.

Somare cut the government budget in 1983, firing 10% of government workers.

The OK Tedi gold and copper mine, built at a cost of $1 billion, began producing over $500,000 in gold per day in May 1984.

PARAGUAY

Official Name: Republic of Paraguay.
Area: 157,048 square miles (406,752 sq. km.).
Population: 3,366,000.
Capital: Asunción, 463,735 (met. area, 601,645).
Government: Republic under dictatorship.
President: Gen. Alfredo Stroessner (since 1954).
Legislature: *Senate,* 30 members; *Chamber of Deputies,* 60 members.
U.S. Ambassador to Paraguay: Arthur H. Davis Jr.
Ambassador to U.S.: Marcos Martinez Mendieta.
Flag: Red, white, and blue stripes; national coat of arms in center.
Official Languages: Spanish, Guaraní.
Main Ethnic Group: Mestizo (95%).
Official Religion: Roman Catholicism (97%).
Leading Industries: Agriculture (cotton, soybeans, livestock, tobacco; wheat, corn, manioc, sweet potatoes, beans, rice, sugarcane, fruits; lumbering and forestry; food processing; manufacturing (electricity, oil refining, cement, consumer goods).
Foreign Trade: *Major exports*—cotton, meat, timber, oilseed, tobacco, quebracho extract, hides; *major imports*—machinery, food, steel, consumer goods.
Places of Interest: Guairá Falls; Port President Stroessner; San Bernardino and El Tirol tourist resorts; Jesuit missions in south. *In Asunción:* Cathedral; Pantheon of the Heroes; botanical garden.

PARAGUAY TODAY

About the size of California, Paraguay is a landlocked South American country.

The nation has no mineral resources to aid in building a modern economy.

Most Paraguayans are farm and ranch workers. Most raise only enough food for their families. In the past two decades about a million persons migrated to Argentina to escape poverty and political repression.

Throughout most of its history the nation has been ruled by a succession of dictators, so that the people have grown used to lack of political freedom. Two major wars in the 1870s and 1930s contributed to the nation's poverty.

The country's only paved highway links the capital, Asunción, with Brazil. Most villages and towns have dirt streets and no sidewalks.

The Paraguay and Alto Paraná rivers are important waterways. To the west of the Paraguay River lies the arid, sparsely settled region of the Chaco Boreal.

Argentina lies to the south and west, Brazil to the northeast, and Bolivia to the northwest.

EARLY HISTORY

Spanish conquistadores came to Paraguay in 1524, establishing Asunción in 1537 and intermarrying with the docile Guaraní Indians. In the 1500s and 1600s Jesuit missionaries instituted a written form of the Guaraní language, still used by most Paraguayans today.

In 1721 a successful revolt led by José de Antequera enabled him to rule an independent Pa-

raguay for about 10 years.

Paraguay declared independence from Spain on May 14, 1811. The first of three strong dictators who shaped the nation took power in 1814—José Gaspar Rodríguez Francia, who ruled until his death in 1840. Then came Carlos Antonio López (1842–62) and López's son, Francisco Solano López (1862–70).

In 1865 López plunged his country into the War of the Triple Alliance against Brazil, Argentina, and Uruguay. At the war's end in 1870 Paraguay had lost 55,000 square miles of territory and over 500,000 people.

In 1932 a territorial dispute led to a 3-year Chaco War with Bolivia. Paraguay won, although at a cost of some 40,000 men.

Higinio Morínigo established a dictatorship in 1940, but resigned in 1948. From 1949 to 1954 the country was ruled by Federico Chavez.

STROESSNER'S DICTATORSHIP

In 1954 Gen. Alfredo Stroessner, commander of the army, made himself dictator.

In March 1973 the British Anti-Slavery Society urged the UN Human Rights Commission to take action to prevent the extermination of the Ache Indians in Paraguay, charging that most men of the tribe had been slain and the women and children sold into slavery.

Paraguay and Brazil signed an agreement on April 26, 1973, to build a $3 billion dam and hydroelectric project at Itaipu on the Paraná River between the two countries. Two other major hydroelectric projects were undertaken jointly with Argentina, the Yacyreta Dam and the Corpus Project, costing about $7 billion.

In apparent response to U.S. President Jimmy Carter's call for human rights, the government in January 1977 freed three communists who had been jailed for 19 years. In February the government also released 11 women political prisoners and their 17 children. However, human-rights organizations said that about 350 political prisoners remained in Paraguay's jails.

Opposition political parties boycotted an election on Feb. 6, 1977, for a constituent assembly, so supporters of Stroessner won all 120 seats. The assembly met on March 7–11 to amend the constitution to enable the president to be elected to office more than twice.

Stroessner won his sixth 5-year term as president in an election on Feb. 12, 1978, receiving 86% of the vote against candidates of the Liberal and Liberal-Radical parties.

President Stroessner in 1979 provided a haven in Paraguay for deposed Nicaraguan dictator Anastasio Somoza Debayle, who had been refused admission by other nations. However, Somoza was assassinated in Asunción on Sept. 17, 1980. Stroessner's government broke diplomatic relations with Nicaragua a few days later, charging its government with complicity in the slaying.

The 70-year-old Stroessner won election in 1983 to his seventh 5-year term as president.

The Itaipu Dam, the world's largest hydroelectric project, began producing electricity in 1983.

The nation plunged into a recession with high inflation in 1982-85.

PERU

Official Name: Republic of Peru.
Area: 496,225 square miles (1,285,216 sq. km.).
Population: 20,166,000.
Chief Cities: Lima, capital, 3,968,972; Arequipa, 447,431, Callao, 441,374; Trujillo, 354,557.
Largest Metropolitan Area: Lima, 4,600,891.
Government: Multiparty democracy.
President: Alan Garcia Perez (since 1985).
Prime Minister: Sandro Mariategui (since 1984).
Congress: *Chamber of Deputies,* 180 members; *Senate,* 60 members.
U.S. Ambassador to Peru: David C. Jordan.
Peruvian Ambassador to U.S.: Luis Marchand.
Flag: Red, white, and red bars, with coat of arms centered on white bar.
Official Languages: Spanish, Quechua.
Ethnic Groups: Indian (46%), mestizo (43%), European descent (11%).
Official Religion: Roman Catholicism.
Leading Industries: Agriculture (sugarcane, cotton, rice, wheat, coffee, potatoes, livestock, fruits, vegetables); mining (petroleum, iron ore, copper, gold, silver, lead, zinc, tungsten, manganese, coal); fishing; food processing; manufacturing (textiles, cement, leather products, plastics, chemicals).
Foreign Trade: *Major exports*—petroleum, copper, sugar, iron ore, silver, cotton, zinc, coffee, lead; *major imports*—machinery, food, trucks, chemicals.
Places of Interest: Inca ruins Machu Picchu and Cuzco; prehistoric ruins of Chavín de Huantar near Huarás; Lake Titicaca; El Misti Volcano. *In Lima:* Cathedral and tomb of Pizarro; Court of the Inquisition; Plaza de Armas; Torre Tagle Palace. *In Arequipa:* Cathedral; Lucioni Gardens.

PERU TODAY

Almost twice as large as Texas, Peru is a South American country experiencing the restoration of democracy after years of military rule.

Richer in natural resources than most other nations of its size, Peru is among the world's leading nations in fishing and the mining of lead and zinc. But its people have remained poor.

The Andes Mountains split the country in two. A narrow coastal desert, from 10 to 100 miles wide, extends about 1,400 miles along the Pacific coast. The temperate slopes of the Andes make up Peru's most populous region.

About half of Peru lies east of the Andes—a sparsely populated lowland area of rain forests.

Ecuador and Colombia lie on the north, Brazil and Bolivia on the east, and Chile on the south.

HISTORY OF PERU

As early as 300 B.C. the Nazca people of Peru drew on the ground hundreds of huge pictures, such as a hummingbird with a 900-foot wing-span.

The Nazca and other early cultures were absorbed by the Inca Empire in the 1400s A.D. The Incas, with their capital at Cuzco, con-

QUICK QUIZ: What was Billy the Kid's real name? See page 327.

PERU *(continued)*

trolled territory from Ecuador to Chile.

Drawn by the Inca treasure, Francisco Pizarro conquered the empire in 1533. Lima, established in 1535, was for three centuries the seat of Spanish control over all Hispanic South America except Venezuela. In the 1780s Inca leader Túpac Amaru led an unsuccessful revolt against Spain.

Peru's independence was declared on July 28, 1821, by Gen. José de San Martín. Venezuela's liberator Simón Bolívar led Peru's armies in battling Spain's troops to final victory in 1826.

Peru suffered a costly defeat by Chile in the War of the Pacific in 1879–83, losing its southern provinces of Tacna, Arica, and Tarapacá. Later, in 1929, Tacna was restored to Peru.

Fernando Belaúnde Terry of the Popular Action Party was elected president in 1963.

A military coup on Oct. 3, 1968, overthrew Belaúnde, who was exiled to Argentina.

Gen. Juan Velasco Alvarado, army chief of staff, became president, heading a socialist military junta that nationalized privately owned property. About 17 million acres of land were distributed to 300,000 peasants. But the socialist policies drove the nation to the verge of bankruptcy.

Gen. Francisco Morales Bermúdez, a moderate, was named premier by Velasco on Feb. 1, 1975. Seven months later, on Aug. 29, 1975, Morales overthrew Velasco, making himself president. He dropped Marxists from the government and began turning a number of nationalized industries back to private ownership.

In the first free election in 15 years, Peruvians in 1978 elected a 100-member assembly that drafted a new constitution.

DEMOCRACY RESTORED

In a national election on May 18, 1980, former President Belaúnde, 68, regained the office with a 5-year term, receiving 45% of the popular vote. His Popular Action Party also won control of the Congress. The military turned the government over to Belaúnde and the new Congress on Peru's Independence Day, July 28, 1980.

Belaúnde's government received help from international loan agencies to finance a 5-year development plan for 1981-85 to develop agriculture, transportation, and public services.

Although Peru's economy grew at a higher rate than most other South American countries in 1980–82, lower prices for oil, copper, and silver cut government revenues. About half of Peru's workers were unemployed or underemployed in 1982–83, and inflation continued at a rate of 50%.

The Peruvian economy slid into depression in 1983 with the gross national product falling by 25% as drought in the south hurt farm production and floods in the north caused $1 billion destruction, wiping out highways and whole villages.

In July 1984 President Belaunde ordered the armed forces to undertake an all-out offensive to destroy Maoist guerrillas who since 1980 have killed thousands of persons.

Alan Garcia Perez, 35, of the centerist American Popular Revolutionary Alliance (APRA), won a presidential election on April 14, 1985, with 48% of the popular vote. He took office on July 28, 1985. Garcia's party also won majority control of both houses of congress.

PHILIPPINES

Official name: Republic of the Philippines.
Area: 115,830 square miles (300,000 sq. km.).
Population: 57,458,000.
Chief Cities: Manila, capital, 1,630,485; Davao, 515,520; Cebu, 490,281; Iloilo, 244,827; Zamboanga, 240,066.
Government: Republic under rule by decree.
President: Ferdinand Marcos (since 1965).
Prime Minister: Cesar Virata (since 1981).
National Assembly: 200 members.
U.S. Ambassador to Philippines: Stephen Warren Bosworth.
Philippine Ambassador to U.S.: Benjamin T. Romualdez.
Flag: Blue and red stripes bordered by white triangle containing yellow stars and sun.
Official Languages: Filipino, English, Spanish.
Main Ethnic Group: Malayo-Polynesian (90%).
Religions: Roman Catholicism (83%), Protestantism (9%), Islam (5%), animism (3%).
Leading Industries: Agriculture (rice, abaca, coconuts, sugarcane, corn, tobacco, livestock, fruits, vegetables); food processing; manufacturing (tobacco products, textiles, clothing, automobiles, oil refining); forestry and lumbering; fishing; mining (gold, silver, copper, iron, chromite, nickel).
Foreign Trade: *Major exports*—coconut products, sugar, wood, abaca; *major imports*—food, petroleum, consumer goods.
Places of Interest: Nayong Filipino (Philippine village) and Malacanang Palace in Manila; Tagaytay Ridge overlooking Lake Taal; Pagsanjan Falls; Corregidor Island; Banawe rice terraces at Ifugao; Mayon Volcano at Legaspi; Baguio; Cebu City.

PHILIPPINES TODAY

Once called "the show window of democracy in Asia," the Philippines today is ruled as a dictatorship by Ferdinand Marcos. However, political groups may speak out against the government.

The country is among the world's leading producers of copper, gold, and natural rubber. Agriculture employs over half of the nation's workers and provides about a third of the national income. But most Filipinos are very poor.

The U.S. maintains military air and naval bases in the Philippines.

The Philippines include 7,107 islands, stretching some 1,100 miles from within 150 miles of Taiwan to less than 15 miles of Borneo.

From May to November, typhoons are a hazard. Temperatures range from hot jungles and rain forests to cool pine-clad highlands.

EARLY HISTORY

In prehistoric times the Philippines were settled by peoples who came from the islands of Indonesia and the Malay peninsula. In the 1200s the islands became part of the Indo-Malay empires. The missionary zeal of Islam swept the region in the 1300s.

Ferdinand Magellan claimed the islands for

Spain in 1521. He was slain during his stay, but one of his vessels went on to become the first to circle the earth. The islands were named the Philippines in honor of Philip (Felipe) II of Spain. In 1564 Miguel López de Legaspi arrived with soldiers instructed to Christianize the islands. In 20 years he was able to establish control over the major inhabited areas except for Muslim Mindanao and Sulu. The colony was placed under the administration of the viceroy of Mexico.

Growing Filipino nationalism, inspired by the writings of José Rizal, caused an unsuccessful revolt in 1896. Although Rizal was executed by the Spanish authorities, the rebellion continued under the leadership of Emilio Aguinaldo. The Filipino rebels declared independence in 1898.

AMERICAN RULE

After Adm. George Dewey destroyed the Spanish fleet in Manila Bay on May 1, 1898, the U.S. paid Spain $20 million for the Philippines. When U.S. rule was established, Aguinaldo angrily began fighting the U.S. troops. The battles went on for two years until Aguinaldo was captured. William Howard Taft, later President, became the first U.S. governor in 1901.

Beginning in 1907 representatives to the national legislature were elected. In 1935 the Tydings-McDuffie Act gave the islands commonwealth status with self-government.

On Dec. 8, 1941, Japan launched a surprise attack and within a month occupied Manila. Gen. Douglas MacArthur, commanding some 90,000 American and Filipino troops, was forced to retreat to Luzon. He withdrew to Australia, but U.S. troops, commanded by Gen. Jonathan Wainwright, held out on Bataan, and then on the island of Corregidor, until May 6, 1942.

On Oct. 20, 1944, a U.S. invasion force, under MacArthur's command, landed on the central Philippine island of Leyte. By July 5, 1945, the Philippines had been recaptured.

INDEPENDENCE

The United States granted the Philippines independence on July 4, 1946. The presidents of the new republic in succession were Manuel Roxas (1946–48), Elpidio Quirino (1948–53), Ramón Magsaysay (1953–57), Carlos P. Garcia (1957–61), and Diosado Macapagal (1961–65).

Ferdinand Marcos was elected president in 1965 and reelected in 1969. Claiming communist subversion threatened the Philippines, Marcos declared

MAIN ISLANDS OF THE PHILIPPINES

NAME	AREA (sq. mi.)	LARGEST CITY
Luzon	47,765	Manila
Mindanao	38,344	Davao
Palawan	5,751	Puerto Princesa
Negros	5,278	Bacolod
Samar	5,185	Calbayog
Panay	4,748	Iloilo
Mindoro	3,955	Pinamalayan
Leyte	3,090	Tacloban
Cebu	1,965	Cebu
Bohol	1,590	Tagbilaran
Masbate	1,563	Masbate
Catanduanes	583	Virac

martial law on Sept. 21, 1972, arresting opposition leaders and newsmen.

A revolt by Muslims in the southern Philippines began in 1972, and fighting continued into the 1980s.

The government signed a 5-year $500 million agreement with the U.S. on Jan. 7, 1979, that assured continued U.S. use of air and naval bases.

After 7½ years in solitary confinement under sentence of death, the man who had been expected to become president if national elections had been held in 1973, Benigno S. Aquino Jr., was permitted to leave prison to fly to the U.S. on May 8, 1980, to undergo a heart operation.

Marcos ended martial law on Jan. 17, 1981, but retained his right to legislate by decree.

A referendum, branded a fraud by opponents, approved constitutional amendments in April 1981 to permit Marcos to serve another term.

Marcos won reelection on June 16, 1981, with 86% of the votes in a poll in which nonvoters were threatened with imprisonment.

Under the revised constitution, Marcos appointed his finance minister, Cesar Virata, as prime minister on July 3, 1981.

Marcos fired all 14 judges on the nation's supreme court on May 10, 1982, after they were exposed in a scandal for raising the bar exam score for the son of one of the judges. But five days later he reappointed 12 of them.

For the first time in 16 years, Marcos and his wife visited Washington, D.C., on Sept. 16, 1982, where they were warmly received by President Reagan. Opponents of Marcos in the Philippines denounced Reagan for praising Marcos for "great progress" in the area of human rights.

The military killed a Roman Catholic priest in 1982 for having joined guerrillas opposed to the government and put bounties on the heads of several others.

Marcos' chief political opponent, Benigno S. Aquino Jr., was assassinated at the Manila airport on Aug. 21, 1983, as he returned from three years of exile in the U.S.

Although Marcos denied complicity in the slaying, the incident touched off widespread demonstrations against the government. President Reagan cancelled a planned November 1983 visit to the Philippines because of the turbulence.

In one of the freest elections in many years, voters chose new members of the national assembly on May 14, 1984. Candidates opposing the government won a third of the seats.

The worst storm in 15 years to hit the Philippines, typhoon Ike, swept across seven major islands on Sept. 2–3, 1984, killing at least 1,363 persons and leaving over 1 million homeless. Over 500 more were killed when typhoon Agnes hit Panay Island on Nov. 5, 1984.

An investigative commission appointed by Marcos reported on Oct. 24, 1984, that Acquino was assassinated in a military conspiracy that involved three generals, including armed forces chief of staff Gen. Fabian C. Ver, a cousin of the president.

Communist guerrillas stepped up attacks in the southern islands in 1985 with more than a thousand people killed in incidents during the first half of the year.

QUICK QUIZ: Who served as Vice President under President Jefferson? See page 341.

POLAND

Official Name: Polish People's Republic.
Area: 120,725 square miles (312,677 sq. km.).
Population: 37,386,000.
Chief Cities: Warszawa (Warsaw), capital, 1,602,784; Lódz, 841,666; Kraków, 718,107; Wroclaw, 617,459; Poznan, 555,973; Gdansk, 456,198; Szczecin, 388,391; Katowice, 361,590; Bydgoszecz, 350,128.
Government: Communist state.
Head of Government: Prime Minister and First Secretary of the Central Committee of the Communist Party, Gen. Wojciech Jaruzelski (since 1981).
Legislature: *Sejm,* 460 members.
U.S. Ambassador to Poland: Francis J. Meehan.
Polish Ambassador to U.S.: Romuald Spasowski.
Flag: White stripe over red stripe.
Official Language: Polish.
Principal Ethnic Group: Polish (98%).
Religion: Roman Catholicism (95%).
Leading Industries: Manufacturing (steel, electricity, cement, chemicals, ships, vehicles, machinery, textiles, paper); mining (coal, lignite, zinc, lead, natural gas, copper, sulfur); agriculture (wheat, sugar beets, potatoes, oats, barley, corn, livestock, fruits, vegetables); construction; trade and services.
Foreign Trade: *Major exports*—coal, lignite, coke, railway rolling stock, ships, cement; *major imports*—iron ore, petroleum and petroleum products, fertilizers, wheat, food.
Places of Interest: Masurian and Augustow Lake district; Baltic Sea resorts; Sudetan and Tatra Mountains; Malbork Castle near Gdansk; Kraków. *In Warsaw:* Palace of Culture and Science; Kampinos Forest National Park; Old Town; Wilanow Palace; birthplace of Chopin.

POLAND TODAY

About the size of New Mexico, Poland has ample mineral resources as well as rich farmland. It is one of the world's 10 leading producers of cement, coal, copper, electricity, steel, and zinc. But more Poles make their living from farming than from any other industry.

As with other communist nations, the standard of living of the people is substantially below that of the industrial nations of western Europe.

The communists rule Poland as a police state. However, the people are allowed greater religious freedom than in most other communist states. A person can be a member of both the Communist Party and the Roman Catholic Church.

Poland also is the only communist country in Europe where farmers still own as much as 85% of the land.

The Soviet Union maintains large armed forces in Poland.

The land is generally low and flat, about nine-tenths of it lying below 1,000 feet.

Temperatures range from an average of 60° F. in summer to below 30° F. in winter.

The principal rivers are the Vistula, Oder, Bug, and Warta.

The Soviet Union lies to the east, Czechoslovakia to the south, East Germany to the west, and the Baltic Sea to the north.

EARLY HISTORY

Slavic tribes in Poland were united during the 800s A.D. by the Piast dynasty. In 966 Duke Mieszko I adopted Christianity. His son, Boleslaw the Brave, became king in 1025.

A new dynasty was established in 1386 by a Lithuanian grand duke, Jagiello, who became King Wladyslaw II of Poland. The Polish-Lithuanian empire extended from the Baltic to the Black Sea. The Jagiellonian dynasty ended without heir in 1572. The throne became elective.

In 1772 Russia, Prussia, and Austria seized about one-third of Poland's territory in the *first partition*. In the *second partition* in 1793 Russia acquired Lithuania and the Ukraine from Poland while Prussia took about 22,000 square miles of western Poland. The patriot Thaddeus Kosciusko, who had served in the Continental Army during the American Revolution, led an unsuccessful Polish uprising in 1794. His defeat by the Russians led to the *third partition* in 1795–96, in which the remainder of Poland was divided among Russia, Prussia, and Austria.

After World War I a Polish republic was formed in 1918. Józef Pilsudski became the first president. The noted pianist Jan Paderewski served as prime minister. Pilsudski ruled as dictator from 1926 until his death in 1935.

In 1939 a Soviet-German pact opened the way for a new partition of Poland. The Germans attacked the country on Sept. 1, 1939, beginning World War II. Less than three weeks later the Soviets invaded from the east. The Germans murdered 6 million Poles, half of them Jews. The Russians executed 15,000 Polish army officers and deported 1.7 million Poles.

After World War II the Soviet Union annexed 70,000 square miles of Poland, but gave the new Poland 40,000 square miles of former German East Prussia, Pomerania, and Silesia.

COMMUNIST RULE

The 1945 Yalta agreement by the Allies pledged free elections in Poland. But under Soviet military occupation communists won control in national elections in 1947. Wladyslaw Gomulka headed the communist puppet government.

On December 12, 1970, strikes and riots erupted at Gdansk (formerly Danzig), Szczecin (Stettin), and other cities, in protest against food price increases. Police and troops crushed the disorders, with heavy casualties. Gomulka was replaced by Edward Gierek on Dec. 20, 1970.

On Oct. 16, 1978, Karol Cardinal Wojtyla was elevated to pope as John Paul II—the first Polish pope. He visited Poland in 1979 and 1983, drawing huge crowds as he called on communist leaders to grant greater freedom.

Widespread labor unrest flared in the weeks that followed a government order on July 1, 1980, raising meat prices 40% to 60%. The climax came during Aug. 13–31, when 17,000 workers seized a Gdansk shipyard and were supported by strikers in other cities. Under leadership of 37-year-old Lech Walesa, the strikers won written agreement from the government to permit the organization of independent labor unions.

Stanislaw Kania, 53, a former head of the secret police, replaced Gierek on Sept. 6, 1980.

The Polish government on Nov. 9, 1980, approved the charter of Walesa's Solidarity union as the first free labor union officially recognized in a communist nation.

With Soviet approval, 58-year-old Gen. Wojciech Jaruzelski ousted Kania on Oct. 18, 1981.

Solidarity leaders at a meeting in Gdansk on Dec. 12, 1981, were secretly taped while discussing a possible ouster of the communist government. Gen. Jaruzelski cracked down on Dec. 13, declaring martial law. Walesa and thousands of other Solidarity activists were imprisoned. Tens of thousands of Poles fled as refugees. The U.S. imposed economic sanctions on the Polish and Soviet governments as a protest.

Jaruzelski controlled Poland as a rigid police state in 1982. Strikes and demonstrations called by underground Solidarity leaders were broken up by the police and the army. The Polish Communist Party ousted 50,000 of its members.

Poland's parliament on Oct. 8, 1982, banned Solidarity, replacing it with government-controlled trade unions. U.S. President Reagan reacted the next day by announcing suspension of Poland's most-favored-nation trade agreement.

In an agreement between Jaruzelski and the Roman Catholic Church, Archbishop Josef Glemp discouraged Poles from taking part in a general strike called by underground Solidarity leaders for Nov. 10, 1982.

Solidarity leader Lech Walesa was released from imprisonment on Nov. 13, 1982, and allowed to return to his home in Gdansk.

The government officially ended martial law on July 22, 1983, but adopted new laws to enforce restrictions on human rights.

Riot police quelled demonstrations in many cities on Aug. 31, 1983, as workers marked the third anniversary of the founding of Solidarity.

Walesa was awarded the Nobel Peace Prize in 1983 for his work with the Solidarity union. The government press declared the award was part of an anti-Polish campaign by Western powers. Walesa donated the $190,000 award to a fund to aid individual Polish farmers.

To mark the 40th anniversary of Soviet defeat of German troops in Poland, the Polish parliament on July 21, 1984, granted amnesty to 652 political prisoners and 35,000 criminals. Those released during the next few weeks included all the imprisoned leaders of the Solidarity labor movement.

In response to the release of the political prisoners, the U.S. government announced on Aug. 3, 1984, the lifting of some economic sanctions. President Reagan said remaining sanctions would be removed one by one as Poland's government restored more human rights.

The slaying of an outspoken pro-Solidarity priest in October 1984, brought new demonstrations and protests. Four secret polic officers were arrested for the slaying. After a trial they were sentenced to jail terms of up to 25 years.

The government increased the pressure on dissidents in 1985. Three Solidarity activists were sentenced to prison in June 1985 for planning a strike that did not take place.

PORTUGAL

Official Name: Republic of Portugal.
Area: 35,553 square miles (92,082 sq. km.).
Population: 10,105,000.
Chief Cities: Lisboa (Lisbon), capital, 812,400; Pôrto, 329,100.
Largest Metropolitan Area: Lisbon, 1,611,887.
Government: Multiparty democratic republic.
President: Gen. António Ramalho Eanes (since 1976).
Prime Minister: See page 26.
Assembly of the Republic: 250 deputies.
U.S. Ambassador to Portugal: Henry A. Holmes.
Portuguese Ambassador to U.S.: Leonardo Charles de Zaffiri Duarte Mathias.
Flag: Green and red bars with national coat of arms.
Official Language: Portuguese.
Principal Ethnic Group: Portuguese.
Religion: Roman Catholicism (97%).
Leading Industries: Trade and services; manufacturing (textiles, cork products, cement, petroleum refining, steel, wine, food processing; agriculture (wheat, potatoes, maize, rye, oats, olives, livestock, fruits, vegetables); forestry and lumbering; mining (coal, pyrites, copper, tungsten); fishing.
Foreign Trade: *Major exports*—wine, cork, fish, tomato paste, textiles; *major imports*—diamonds, automobiles, petroleum products, peanuts, plastics, textile machinery, sugar.
Places of Interest: Bucaco mountain and forest; Praja de Rocha beach resort; Nazaré fishing village; Azores and Madeira islands; Fatima sanctuary; Queluz; Coimbra; Pôrto. *In Lisbon:* Moorish fortress and palace; Jerónimos monastery; Monument to Christ.

PORTUGAL TODAY

Somewhat smaller than Indiana, Portugal is a poor European nation struggling to achieve a stable political democracy after half a century of fascist dictatorship.

Lying between the Atlantic on the west and Spain on the east, Portugal occupies about one-sixth of the Iberian peninsula.

Extensive plains extend from the Tagus River south to Cape Saint Vincent, Europe's southwestern tip. Portugal's highest point is the 6,532-foot Serra da Estréla, northeast of Lisbon.

Important rivers include the Douro, Tagus, Minho, and Guadiana, all originating in Spain.

The weather varies with cool summers and cold winters in the north, and a warm Mediterranean climate in the south.

EARLY HISTORY

Ancient Phoenicians, Carthaginians, and Greeks all established colonies on the coast. In 27 B.C. the Romans made the region a province called *Lusitania.* After the Romans, Visigoths controlled the region until they were defeated in 711 by the Moors.

In 1143 Portugal became an independent nation under King Afonso Henriques.

Portugal's era of glory began with the reign of

QUICK QUIZ: Which U.S. Vice President became a Confederate general? See page 327.

PORTUGAL *(continued)*

João I (1385–1433). His son, Henry the Navigator, encouraged exploration that brought Portugal a huge overseas colonial empire.

From 1580 to 1640 Spain ruled Portugal. Independence was reestablished in 1640 when the Portuguese revolted and made João VI king.

Napoleon's forces invaded Portugal in 1807, and the royal family fled to Brazil. King João VI returned to Portugal in 1820.

THE PORTUGUESE REPUBLIC

The monarchy was overthrown in 1910, and a republic was established. Portugal was ruled as a fascist dictatorship by António de Oliveira Salazar in 1928–68 and by Marcello Caetano in 1968–74.

On April 25, 1974, Gen. António de Spinola, a leftist, overthrew Caetano. The military junta replaced Spinola as president on Sept. 30, 1974, with Gen. Francisco da Costa Gomes.

The junta let voters go to the polls on April 25, 1975, in the first free election since 1926, choosing an assembly to draw up a constitution.

The Marxist revolutionary government in 1975 nationalized most industries and expropriated large landholdings. It also ended Portugal's 500-year-old African colonial empire.

Under a new democratic constitution, a national assembly was elected on April 25, 1976, with socialists led by Mário Soares winning a plurality of 106 of the 263 seats. Army Chief of Staff Gen. António Ramalho Eanes, 41, was elected president on June 27, 1976. Soares became prime minister.

Many persons were injured in riots in farming areas after parliament adopted a law on Aug. 11, 1977, that small farms seized in the 1975 revolution should be returned to their owners.

Soares' coalition cabinet disintegrated in 1978. A politically independent industrialist, Alfredo Nobre da Costa, served 17 days as prime minister. President Eanes then appointed as prime minister a law professor, Carlos da Mota Pinto, 42, whose government lasted only to June 6, 1979.

President Eanes then appointed as the nation's first woman prime minister, Maria de Lurdes Pintassilgo, 49, a moderate leftist.

Portuguese voters moved toward the right in parliamentary elections held on Dec. 2, 1979, and on Oct. 5, 1980. The conservative Democratic Alliance of Francisco Sá Carneiro, who became prime minister on Jan. 3, 1980, won majorities in both elections, with 128 seats and then with 134.

Sá Carneiro was killed in a plane crash on Dec. 4, 1980. Minister of State Francisco Pinto Balsemão was named as prime minister.

In a presidential election on Dec. 7, 1980, President Eanes won reelection to another 4-year term, receiving about 57% of the vote.

In a national election on April 25, 1983, the socialists won a plurality of 101 parliamentary seats, followed by the centrist social democrats with 75, and the communists with 41. Soares again became prime minister in June 1983, after forming a coalition with the social democrats.

In an effort to help the sagging economy, Soares adopted a tough austerity program in 1983, ending government subsidies that had held down food and energy prices.

The U.S. and Portugal signed an agreement on Dec. 12, 1983, extending American use of an air base in the Azores to 1991. The U.S. agreed to increase aid to Portugal to $145 million per year.

Soares resigned after his coalition collapsed in June 1985.

Antonio de Almeida Santos, the new leader of the Socialist Party, was expected to become prime minister after parliamentary elections on Oct. 6, 1985. See page 26.

Portugal won admission to the European Common Market on Jan. 1, 1986, broadening its opportunities for foreign trade.

PORTUGUESE OVERSEAS AREAS

AZORES

Area: 902 square miles (2,336 sq. km.).
Population: 263,000.
Capital: Ponta Delgada, 69,930.

Lying in the Atlantic Ocean about 750 miles west of Europe, the Azores include nine main islands and several small ones. Most people make their living as fishermen and farmers. Main exports include canned fish, pineapples, butter, and cheese.

The Azores were discovered in 1427–31 by the Portuguese explorer Diogo de Sevilla. Settled by Portuguese and Flemish colonists, the Azores became an important stop for ships during the exploration of the Americas.

The U.S. maintains an air base on Terceira Island. Portugal and the U.S. signed a treaty on Dec. 12, 1983, providing for continued U.S. use of the air base until 1991.

On April 30, 1976, Portugal granted the Azores internal self-government with an elected assembly. Nationalists continued to demonstrate in 1977–80, calling for complete independence.

MACAU (formerly MACAO)

Area: 6.2 square miles (16 sq. km.).
Population: 316,000.
Capital: Macau City, 241,413.

Macau, at the mouth of mainland China's Pearl River, is about 40 miles from Hong Kong.

The colony consists of Macau City on Macau peninsula, and two smaller islands—Taipa and Coloane. About 99% of the people are Chinese.

Portugal colonized Macau in 1557 and paid rent to China until 1949. When Portugal began freeing its colonies in 1975, China indicated it preferred Macau's status to remain unchanged.

Macau's main income is from gambling casinos patronized by Chinese from Hong Kong, where gambling is banned.

MADEIRA

Area: 307 square miles (795 sq. km.).
Population: 272,000.
Capital: Funchal, 105,791.

Situated in the Atlantic Ocean about 600 miles southwest of Portugal, the group includes two main islands, Madeira and Pôrto Santo, and several uninhabited smaller islands.

Thousands of tourists go to Madeira each year to enjoy the beaches and tropical scenery.

The Portuguese explorer João Gonçalves Zarco first sighted the islands in 1418. Portuguese settlers colonized Madeira, importing slaves to work the plantations. On April 30, 1976, Portugal granted Madeira autonomy with an elected assembly for internal self-government.

QATAR

Official Name: State of Qatar.
Area: 4,247 square miles (11,000 sq. km.).
Population: 290,000.
Capital: Doha, 100,000.
Government: Absolute monarchy.
Emir: Khalifa bin Hamad al-Thani (since 1972).
U.S. Ambassador to Qatar: Charles F. Dunbar.
Ambassador to U.S.: Abdelkader Braik al-Ameri.
Flag: Maroon field; white serrated band at hoist.
Official Language: Arabic.
Main Ethnic Groups: Qatari (45%), Pakistani (35%).
Religion: Islam (98%).
Leading Industries: Mining (petroleum, natural gas); construction; manufacturing (electricity, cement, oil refining, steel); agriculture (livestock, vegetables, fruits); fishing.
Foreign Trade: *Major exports*—petroleum, gas, steel, chemicals; *major imports*—food, consumer goods.
Places of Interest: Royal residence; oil refineries.

About the size of Massachusetts, Qatar is an oil-rich Arab country that is largely a hot, sandy desert. Most of the people live in and around the capital city of Doha.

New industries have been developed with oil revenues, including an electric power plant, a desalting plant to supply drinking water from the sea, and improved harbor facilities.

Qatar's population more than doubled in the 1970s as thousands of Pakistanis and other foreigners came to work on development projects.

The desert land has sparse vegetation, although vegetables, grain, and fruits are grown.

Qatar is a peninsula jutting into the Persian Gulf. Saudi Arabia and the United Arab Emirates border it on the south.

For many years Qatar was dominated by the rulers of Bahrain. In 1868 Britain undertook negotiations to end Bahrain's rule. But in 1872 the Ottoman Turks absorbed Qatar.

With the collapse of the Turkish empire in World War I, Britain in 1916 made Qatar a protectorate.

Oil was discovered in Qatar in 1940. Commercial production began in 1949.

Qatar declared its independence on Sept. 1, 1971. A treaty of friendship replaced the "special treaty" relationship with Britain.

Emir Ahmed bin Ali al-Thani ruled from 1960 to 1972. He was deposed in a bloodless coup on Feb. 22, 1972, by his cousin Sheik Khalifa bin Hamad al-Thani.

The ruler uses a substantial part of the nation's oil and gas income to develop social services, free housing for Qataris, and heavy industry, including a $300 million steel plant completed in 1978 and a $500 million petrochemical industry that began production in 1980. A new 50,000 barrel per day refinery began operations in 1984.

Qatar's economy suffered in 1982-85 with declining oil prices and restrictions on petroleum production imposed by OPEC.

ROMANIA

Official Name: Socialist Republic of Romania.
Area: 91,699 square miles (237,500 sq. km.).
Population: 22,853,000.
Chief Cities: Bucureşti (Bucharest), capital, 1,979,076; Braşov, 334,136; Constanţa, 306,879; Timisora, 301,612; Cluj-Napoca, 300,677.
Government: Communist state.
President: Nicolae Ceausescu (since 1974).
Prime Minister: Constantin Dascalescu (since 1982).
Grand National Assembly: 369 members.
U.S. Ambassador to Romania: David B. Funderburk.
Romanian Ambassador to U.S.: Nicolae Gavrilescu.
Flag: Blue, yellow, and red vertical bars, with national emblem in center.
Official Language: Romanian.
Main Ethnic Groups: Romanian (89%), Magyars (8%), German (2%).
Leading Religions: Eastern Orthodox (80%), Roman Catholic (9%).
Leading Industries: Manufacturing (steel, electricity, cement, chemicals, ships, motor vehicles, machinery, furniture, paper, textiles, shoes); mining (oil, coal, natural gas, iron, salt, copper, lead, gold, silver, uranium); agriculture (livestock, poultry, dairying, grain, sugar beets, vegetables, fruits); construction; lumbering; fishing.
Foreign Trade: *Major exports*—machinery, petroleum products, chemicals, consumer goods, furniture, textiles, shoes, food products; *major imports*—petroleum, iron ore, machinery, chemicals.
Places of Interest: Danube delta; Black Sea beach resorts; monasteries in northern Moldavia; Mt. Retezat; over 120 spas throughout country; ruins of the ancient Greek cities of Histria, Tomis, and Callatis; wine tasting at the Murfatlar Winery. *In Bucharest:* Old Court, Patriarchate, History Museum, Liberty Park, Herastrau Park, museums and art galleries.

ROMANIA TODAY

One of the least industrialized communist countries of eastern Europe, Romania depends heavily on agriculture, which long has made it one of the leading wheat- and corn-growing nations. Once a major oil-exporting country, it now imports about 40% of its petroleum needs.

Under leadership of Nicolae Ceausescu since 1965, Romania is one of the most repressive communist police states.

Romania is economically dependent on the Soviet Union as its main trading partner. However, it sometimes criticizes Soviet foreign policy

Government economic planning has placed emphasis on the development of heavy industry. Neglect of modernizing agriculture production resulted in food shortages in the 1980s.

About the size of Oregon, Romania is a land

QUICK QUIZ: Who was the first black American to win a Nobel Prize? See page 328.

ROMANIA *(continued)*

of great geographical contrasts. The Carpathian Mountains surround the central plateau of Transylvania. Beyond are three major plateaus: Moldavia to the east, Wallachia to the south, and Dobruja on the Black Sea coast between Bulgaria and the Soviet Union.

The Soviet Union lies to the north and northeast, Bulgaria to the south, and Hungary and Yugoslavia to the west.

EARLY HISTORY

The Roman province of Dacia included most of present-day Romania in the 100s A.D. After Rome withdrew in 271, the area was overrun successively by Goths, Huns, Avars, Slavs, and Mongols.

In the 1000s Hungary took control of Transylvania, ruling it until the early 1900s.

The states of Wallachia and Moldavia were founded in the 1300s.

Prince Vlad Tepes of Wallachia, said to be the original for the fictional vampire Count Dracula, fought off Turkish invaders until he was killed when they finally conquered Wallachia in 1476. The Turks then took Moldavia in 1504.

In 1859 Moldavia and Wallachia united under Prince Alexander John Cuza, with the principality taking the name *Romania* in 1862. Cuza was cast aside in 1866 in favor of Prince Karl of the house of Hohenzollern-Sigmaringen.

Romania declared independence on May 9, 1877. Prince Karl became King Carol I in 1881.

After fighting on the side of the Allies in World War I, Romania acquired Transylvania and the Banat from Hungary, Bukovina from Austria, and Bessarabia from Russia.

In June 1940 Hungary seized Transylvania, the Soviet Union annexed the northern part of Romania called Bessarabia, and Bulgaria took Dobruja in the southeast.

During World War II, Marshal Ion Antonescu ousted King Carol II in September 1940, placing his young son Michael on the throne with the help of the Iron Guard—a fascist military organization. Romania joined the Axis Powers. On Aug. 23, 1944, Antonescu was overthrown by a coalition of anti-fascists, and Romania switched to the Allied side.

COMMUNIST RULE

After the Soviet advance into the country in 1944–45, a communist-led coalition headed by Petri Groza came to power. In 1947 King Michael was forced to abdicate. Romania was declared a communist republic.

A peace treaty in 1947 restored Transylvania to Romania, but gave Bessarabia to the Soviet Union and part of Dobruja to Bulgaria.

Romania remained an obedient Soviet satellite until 1962, when the Soviet Union attempted unsuccessfully to persuade it to abandon its plan for industrialization and become an agricultural reserve for the Soviet bloc. Since then Romanian leaders Gheorghe Gheorgiu-Dej (1961–65) and Nicolae Ceausescu (since 1965) have pursued a somewhat more independent course.

While the Soviet bloc supported the Arab countries during the June 1967 Arab-Israeli war, Romania refused to condemn Israel as the aggressor and did not break relations with it.

The Ceausescu regime supported the liberalization program in Czechoslovakia, refusing to join in Warsaw Pact military action against the Dubček government in Czechoslovakia in 1968.

Although the Soviet Union broke off trade agreements with the U.S. in a dispute over freedom of immigration, Romania negotiated a new trade agreement with the U.S. on April 2, 1975, and eased immigration restrictions.

Ceausescu appointed his brother-in-law, Ilie Verdet, 54, as prime minister on March 30, 1979.

Increased energy usage and declining petroleum production caused Romania to become a net importer of petroleum in 1976. The government announced plans to build six nuclear power plants and turn to other energy sources to achieve energy self-sufficiency by 1990.

ROMANIA IN THE 1980s

Increasing food shortages caused the government to decree on Oct. 17, 1981, rationing of grain products and banning their use as livestock feed. Then on Feb. 9, 1982, the government hiked food prices by 35% while raising wages only 16%.

In an attempt to divert blame for the country's declining economy from himself, Ceausescu fired Prime Minister Verdet and a dozen other high officials in May 1982, accusing them of inefficiency and corruption. Constantin Dascalescu was named the new prime minister.

The largest construction project in Romanian history, a 40-mile canal from the Danube River to the Black Sea, was inaugurated on May 26, 1984, by President Ceausescu. The canal, built over 8 years at a cost of nearly $2 billion, will cut 250 miles off travel on the waterway.

Romania showed its independence in international relations in 1984 by taking part in the summer Olympics in Los Angeles despite a boycott by the Soviet Union and its other allies.

RWANDA

Official Name: Republic of Rwanda.
Area: 10,169 square miles (26,338 sq. km.).
Population: 6,305,000.
Capital: Kigali, 54,403.
Government: One-party dictatorship.
President: Juvenal Habyarimana (since 1973).
U.S. Ambassador to Rwanda: John Blane.
Rwandan Ambassador to U.S.: Simon Insoner.
Flag: Bars of red, yellow, and green, with black *R* in center.
Official Languages: French and Kinyarwanda.
Main Ethnic Groups: Hutu (89%), Tutsi (10%).
Religions: Christianity (60%), Islam, animism.
Leading Industries: Agriculture (coffee, cattle, pyrethrum, tea, beans, corn); manufacturing (light consumer goods); mining (tin, wolfram).
Foreign Trade: *Major exports*—coffee, tin, tea; *major imports*—textiles, oil and gasoline, food, machinery.
Places of Interest: Kigali; Gisenyi; Butare Museum; Akagera and Virungas national parks; Rusumo Falls; Gabiro guesthouse at Kibungo.

RWANDA TODAY

About the size of Vermont, Rwanda is one of the poorest countries in the world. Most Rwandans live as they have for centuries, growing enough food and raising enough cattle to subsist, but not enough to afford more than a primitive existence. Only about 10% can read and write. The average Rwandan lives only to age 44.

Only a few Europeans live in Rwanda, and most of those who do supervise the tin and wolfram mines—the country's only substantial industry other than agriculture.

Violence between the Hutu and the Tutsi has continued sporadically since independence. The Tutsi government of neighboring Burundi has accused the Hutu government of Rwanda of massacring Tutsi tribesmen. In turn the Rwanda government has accused Burundi of harboring Tutsi guerrillas.

Rwanda's exports and imports travel by truck along a 1,000-mile road through Uganda to the port of Mombasa, Kenya.

The land is mountainous, with elevations ranging from 4,800 feet at Lake Kivu in the west to 14,787-foot Mt. Karisimbi in the northwest. In the east are a hilly plateau and lakes. The climate is tropical.

Uganda lies to the north, Tanzania to the east, Burundi to the south, and Zaire to the west.

EARLY HISTORY

The kingdom of Rwanda can be traced back to the 1500s. Led by a royal clan from Ethiopia, waves of Tutsi conquered the local Hutu tribes.

In 1899 Rwanda was incorporated as a colony into German East Africa.

After World War I the League of Nations mandated Rwanda and its neighbor Burundi to Belgium as the territory of Rwanda-Urundi.

After World War II, Rwanda-Urundi became a UN trust territory administered by Belgium.

In November 1959 an uprising by the Hutu against the Tutsi brought the massacre of thousands of Tutsi and the flight of thousands of others to neighboring Burundi and to Uganda. The Tutsi king was overthrown and a republic was proclaimed in 1961.

INDEPENDENCE

Belgium granted self-government to Rwanda on Jan. 1, 1962, with Gregoire Kayibanda, head of the Parmehutu Party, as president.

Rwanda received independence on July 1, 1962. Kayibanda was reelected in 1965 and 1969.

In a bloodless coup on July 5, 1973, Defense Minister Maj. Gen. Juvenal Habyarimana overthrew Kayibanda.

Habyarimana dissolved the national assembly and ruled by decree. He made his National Revolutionary Movement for Development (MRND) the only political party in 1975. Habyarimana was elected without opposition to a 5-year term as president on Dec. 17, 1978.

Rwanda appealed for international help in 1982 when Uganda uprooted about 25,000 Rwandan immigrants, burning their homes and stealing their cattle. Thousands fled back to Rwanda, pleading for food and shelter.

ST. CHRISTOPHER AND NEVIS

Official Name: St. Christopher and Nevis.
Area: 101 square miles (262 sq. km.)
Population: 44,000.
Capital: Basseterre, 15,000.
Government: Multiparty parliamentary democracy.
Prime Minister: Kennedy Simmonds (since 1980).
National Assembly: 11 members.
U.S. Ambassador: Milan D. Bish.
Ambassador to U.S.: William V. Herbert.
Flag: Two white stars on black diagonal stripe bordered by thin yellow stripes; green triangle in upper hoist corner and red triangle at bottom.
Main Language: English.
Largest Ethnic Group: Blacks.
Chief Religion: Anglican.
Leading Industries: Agriculture (sugarcane, cotton, vegetables, fruits, livestock); tourism; manufacturing (sugar refining, brewing, electronic equipment, textiles, furniture); fishing.
Foreign Trade: *Major exports*—sugar, cotton; *major imports*—food, consumer products, petroleum.
Places of Interest: Mount Misery; Brimstone Hill fort; beach resorts.

One of the smallest countries, St. Christopher and Nevis lies in the Caribbean Sea, southeast of Puerto Rico. Usually called St. Kitts, the country consists of two volcanic islands: St. Christopher (65 sq. mi.) and Nevis (36 sq. mi.)

About a third of the people make their living from agriculture. Sugar, grown largely on St. Christopher, accounts for about two-thirds of the exports. The main crop on the island of Nevis is cotton.

Christopher Columbus landed on Saint Christopher during his second voyage in 1493, and the island was named for his patron saint.

In 1623 Sir Thomas Warner established on St. Christopher the first British colony in the Caribbean. French colonists also arrived on the island in 1624. British colonists landed on Nevis in 1629. Britain and France disputed possession until 1783 when France gave up its claim.

St. Christopher, Nevis, and the island of Anguilla became a self-governing associated state of Britain on Feb. 27, 1967. But three months later Anguilla withdrew from the state.

In an election in February 1980, the Labor Party, which had dominated the state's politics since the 1960s, won only four seats. Dr. Kennedy Simmonds, leader of the People's Action Movement, became prime minister after forming a coalition with the Nevis Reform Party.

Britain granted the nation full independence on Sept. 19, 1983. Four days later it joined the United Nations.

After abolishing personal income taxes, Simmonds called the first election since independence on June 21, 1984. His coalition won an increased majority with 9 of the 11 parliamentary seats.

QUICK QUIZ: Who was the first printer in what now is the United States? See page 329.

SAINT LUCIA

Official Name: State of St. Lucia.
Area: 238 square miles (616 sq. km.).
Population: 121,000.
Capital: Castries, 45,000.
Government: Multiparty parliamentary democracy.
Prime Minister: John Compton (since 1982).
House of Assembly: 17 members.
U.S. Ambassador to St. Lucia: Milan D. Bish.
Ambassador to U.S.: Joseph Edsal Edmunds.
Flag: Blue field with white, black, and yellow triangle in center.
Main Languages: English (official); French patois widely spoken.
Ethnic Groups: Black (97%), white (3%).
Principal Religion: Roman Catholicism.
Leading Industries: Agriculture (bananas, coconuts, cocoa, citrus fruits, spices); fishing; forestry; manufacturing (rum, food processing, clothing, electricity, fertilizer, batteries); tourism.
Foreign Trade: *Major exports*—bananas, coconut products, coconuts, fruits and vegetables, spices; *major imports*—flour, meat, fish, sugar, milk, alcoholic beverages, metals, lumber, fuel oil, clothing, shoes, machinery, automobiles.
Places of Interest: Fort Rodney on Pigeon Island; Morne Fortune (Lucky Hill) battlefield; beach resorts; Piton volcanoes near Soufrière.

ST. LUCIA TODAY

A volcanic Caribbean island about one-twelfth the size of Puerto Rico, St. Lucia lies closer to South America than to the United States. Its nearest neighbors are the French island of Martinique to the north, St. Vincent to the south, and Barbados to the east.

Most of the people are descendants of African slaves.

Although English is generally understood, most of the people speak a French patois.

Most of the islanders make their living from tourism or from agriculture.

About one-third of the population live in the capital city of Castries.

The agricultural land largely is divided into small family farms of less than 5 acres.

More than 10,000 families raise bananas, which account for about 80% of the island's exports.

Coconuts provide the second most important export crop.

Income from tourism amounts to almost as much as receipts from exports. Over 100,000 tourists visit St. Lucia each year, about half of whom are passengers on cruise ships.

Tropical rain forests cover the steep slopes of the island's volcanoes. The highest peak is 3,117-foot Mt. Gimie. Twin volcanoes called the Pitons rise sharply from the sea near Soufrière on the southwest coast.

The island has a year-round tropical climate with an average temperature of 80° F. (26° C.).

Annual rainfall of 60 to 138 inches comes mainly from May to August.

EARLY HISTORY

The earliest inhabitants of St. Lucia were the Arawak Indians from South America. They later were driven out by the fierce Carib Indians.

English colonists who tried to settle the island in 1605 and 1638 were killed or driven off by the Carib Indians.

French colonists subjugated the Carib Indians in 1660.

During the next 150 years the French and English battled for possession of the island.

In 1778 some 1,300 British troops repulsed an attack by 5,000 French soldiers.

In May 1781 French Adm. Comte de Grasse unsuccessfully attacked the island with a fleet of 25 warships. However, St. Lucia was given to France in the 1783 peace treaty.

Britain took the island again in April 1796 with an assault by 12,000 troops under command of Lt. Gen. Sir Ralph Abercrombie with most of the fighting taking place on Morne Fortune (Lucky Hill) near Castries. But France again won possession in a peace treaty.

The final battle for St. Lucia took place in June 1803, during the Napoleonic wars, when British troops again stormed ashore and defeated French defenders.

In the 1814 Treaty of Paris, France ceded the island to Britain.

Britain ended slavery on St. Lucia in 1834, compensating owners for freeing 13,291 slaves, who made up 80% of the island's population.

St. Lucia was administered as a separate British colony until 1838, when it was annexed to the British Windward Islands Colony.

St. Lucia received its own British governor in 1959 as part of the short-lived Federation of the West Indies.

Britain granted St. Lucia self-government on May 3, 1967. The government was controlled for 15 years by the conservative United Workers Party (UWP), which won national elections in 1964, 1968, and 1974. UWP leader John Compton served as chief minister.

INDEPENDENT NATION

Compton conducted lengthy negotiations with Britain that gained independence for St. Lucia on Feb. 22, 1979. The new nation remained part of the British Commonwealth of Nations.

The leftist St. Lucia Labour Party (SLP), campaigning for closer relations with communist nations, won a national election on July 2, 1979, capturing 12 of the 17 seats in the House of Assembly. Allan Louisy, 62, head of the SLP became prime minister.

A split in the SLP caused Louisy to be replaced as prime minister by Winston Cenac in 1981. Strikes opposing Cenac's policies forced him to resign on Jan. 16, 1982. He was succeeded by Michael Pilgrim.

John Compton again became prime minister after his pro-Western United Workers Party (UWP) won 14 of the 17 seats in the national assembly in an election on May 3, 1982.

Compton appealed to the U.S. and Britain for additional aid to help revive the ailing economy.

SAINT VINCENT

Official Name: St. Vincent and the Grenadines.
Area: 150 square miles (388 sq. km.)
Population: 146,500.
Capital: Kingstown, 23,645.
Government: Multiparty parliamentary democracy.
Prime Minister: James Mitchell (since 1984).
House of Assembly: 13 members.
Flag: Vertical stripes of blue, yellow, and green; green coat of arms on yellow stripe.
U.S. Ambassador to St. Vincent: Milan D. Bish.
Ambassador to U.S.: Hudson K. Tannis.
Language: English.
Main Ethnic Group: Black.
Chief Religions: Methodism, Anglicanism, Roman Catholicism.
Leading Industries: Agriculture (bananas, sweet potatoes, arrowroot, coconuts, nutmegs, peanuts, mace, cocoa, food crops); tourism; manufacturing and processing (starch, coconut oil, cigarettes, rum distilling, furniture, flour, clothing); fishing; forestry.
Foreign Trade: *Major exports*—bananas, sweet potatoes, arrowroot, coconut oil, nutmegs, peanuts; *major imports*—food, textiles, cement, lumber, petroleum products, fertilizer, automobiles.
Places of Interest: Soufrière volcano; beach resorts; in Layou, prehistoric Carib Indian altar; in Kingstown, botanic garden.

ST. VINCENT TODAY

One of the chain of Windward Islands in the eastern Caribbean Sea, St. Vincent has an area about the size of Carson City, Nev. But its population is over four times that of Carson City.

The nation also includes hundreds of islets called the Grenadines that stretch to the south.

Most Vincentians earn their living from agriculture or from industries that process farm products. About half the farmland is divided among huge plantations and the rest among small farms of 10 acres or less.

The island's fastest-growing industry is tourism. About 20,000 visitors come to St. Vincent annually to enjoy the black sand beaches, the tropical scenery, and the climate.

Although many of the people are poor, most can read and write because of the excellent school system.

The island's tallest volcano, 4,048-foot Soufrière, erupts periodically. Its eruption in 1902 killed about 2,000 persons. The volcano came to life in April 1979, sending smoke thousands of feet into the air. Some 20,000 persons were evacuated from the northern part of the island around the volcano.

St. Vincent often experiences water shortages during the dry season from January to May. In the rest of the year, annual rainfall varies from 60 inches on the coast to 150 inches in the mountains of the interior.

Temperatures seldom rise to more than 90° F. in daytime and may fall to 64° F. at night.

St. Vincent lies 21 miles south of St. Lucia and about 100 miles west of Barbados.

HISTORY

The earliest known inhabitants were the Arawak Indians, who later were killed or driven out by the warlike Carib Indians.

Christopher Columbus landed on St. Vincent on Jan. 22, 1498.

The Carib Indians remained in control of the island throughout most of the 1700s, although a few French colonists, established settlements.

British forces captured the island from the French in 1762. It was retaken by the French in 1779 during the American Revolution, but was restored to Britain by treaty in 1783.

In 1795–96 the British deported most of the Carib Indians to the island of Rattan in the Bay of Honduras.

From 1958 to 1962 St. Vincent was part of the Federation of the West Indies.

The island received the status of an associated state in the British Commonwealth of Nations on Oct. 27, 1969, with complete control of its own domestic affairs.

In a general election on Dec. 9, 1974, the conservative St. Vincent Labor Party (SVLP) won control of the House of Assembly with SLVP leader Robert Milton Cato as prime minister.

INDEPENDENCE

St. Vincent was granted independence by Britain, on Oct. 27, 1979, with Cato as prime minister. Britain promised $23 million in aid.

In the first national election since independence, held on Dec. 5, 1979, Cato's party won 11 of the national assembly's 13 seats.

Leftist rebels on Union Island tried to secede from St. Vincent, but were subdued in a battle with police on Dec. 8, 1979, in which one was killed and 19 arrested.

James Mitchell became prime minister after his New Democratic Party won control of the national assembly in an election on July 25, 1984.

SAN MARINO

Official Name: Most Serene Republic of San Marino.
Area: 23.6 square miles (61 sq. km.).
Population: 23,600.
Capital: San Marino, 2,658.
Government: Communist-governed republic.
Chiefs of State: Co-regents chosen for 6-month terms; 11-man Congress of State (cabinet).
Legislature: *Grand and General Council,* 60 members.
Flag: White stripe over blue stripe with national coat of arms in center.
Language: Italian.
Main Ethnic Group: Sanmarinese.

QUICK QUIZ: When did the last Ice Age end? See page 283.

SAN MARINO *(continued)*

Principal Religion: Roman Catholicism.
Leading Industries: Tourism; agriculture (wheat, grapes, vegetables, livestock); manufacturing (wine, textiles, leather products, ceramics).
Foreign Trade: *Major exports*—wine, textiles, ceramics, postage stamps; *major imports*—manufactured goods.
Places of Interest: Mt. Titano; Rocca medieval fortress; San Marino Cathedral; Pinacoteca di Stato Museum; Palazzo dei Valloni.

SAN MARINO TODAY

With an area only as large as Newark, N.J., San Marino is surrounded by the mountains of northeast Italy. It has two main industries—farming and tourism.

The government has two main sources of income: (1) the sale of postage stamps and (2) an annual subsidy paid by Italy.

More tourists usually visit each day in the summer than the country's entire population.

The capital city, also called San Marino, lies on the slopes of 2,425-foot Mt. Titano, about 65 miles east of Florence, Italy.

HISTORY

According to legend, San Marino was founded in the 300s by Marinus, a Christian stonecutter from Dalmatia fleeing religious persecution. The independence of San Marino was recognized in 1631 by Pope Urban VIII.

Since 1862 San Marino and Italy have had treaties regulating customs and common interests. San Marino declared war on Germany in World War I but tried to remain neutral in World War II. A coalition of communists and socialists governed from 1945 to 1957. Women received the right to vote in 1960.

The neutrality of San Marino was confirmed in a new agreement with Italy in 1971.

In parliamentary elections on May 28, 1978, leftist parties gained seats. Although the conservative Christian Democrats retained their plurality with 26 seats, they were unable to form a coalition cabinet with the socialists after the election.

In the first papal visit in the republic's more than 1,600-year history, Pope John Paul II visited the tiny country on Aug. 29, 1982.

In general elections in 1980 and 1983 the leftist coalition retained control of the government.

The city of San Marino, Calif., raised $50,000 in 1984 to pay the expenses of bringing the nation of San Marino's team to the Olympics.

SÃO TOMÉ AND PRÍNCIPE

Official Name: Democratic Republic of São Tomé and Príncipe.
Area: 372 square miles (964 sq. km.).
Population: 96,200.
Capital: São Tomé, 5,714.
Government: One-party socialist state.
President: Manuel Pinto da Costa (since 1975).

Prime Minister: Miguel Trovoada (since 1975).
Ambassador to U.S.: Joaquim R. Branco.
U.S. Ambassador to: Larry C. Williamson.
Flag: Stripes of green, yellow, and green with red triangle at hoist; two black stars on center yellow stripe.
Language: Portuguese.
Main Ethnic Groups: Black (90%), mixed Portuguese black ancestry (7%).
Religions: Roman Catholicism, animism.
Leading Industries: Agriculture (coffee, cocoa, coconuts, palm kernels, vegetables, fruits); fishing; turtle shell products; food processing; tourism.
Foreign Trade: *Major exports*—coffee, cocoa; *major imports*—food, consumer goods.
Places of Interest: Swimming beaches; medieval plays and festivals on religious feast days; saltwater fishing; coffee plantations; volcanic craters.

SÃO TOMÉ AND PRÍNCIPE TODAY

Only one-third the size of Rhode Island, the island country of São Tomé and Príncipe lies in the Gulf of Guinea, about 125 miles off the west coast of Africa. The largest island is São Tomé (330 sq. mi.). Príncipe (42 sq. mi.) lies about 93 miles to the northeast.

Most of the people are descendants of African slaves. They make their living by farming and fishing. The main exports are coffee and cocoa.

São Tomé has 10 volcanic peaks. The highest, Pico de São Tomé, rises to 6,640 feet. Rain forests cover the mountain slopes, harboring 60 types of tropical birds.

Beaches, saltwater fishing, and a mild climate that averages 62.6° F. attract tourists.

HISTORY

São Tomé was discovered by Portuguese explorers João de Santarém and Pedro Escobar on Dec. 21, 1470. Príncipe was sighted almost a month later, on Jan. 17, 1471. Neither island was inhabited.

In the late 1400s Portugal sent convicts and exiled Jews to the islands. Sugar plantations were founded, worked by slaves from Africa. São Tomé became a major slave trading port for transshipment of African slaves to the Americas. Coffee was introduced in 1800 and cocoa in 1822.

Prosperity declined after 1909 when Britain and Germany boycotted cocoa from the islands because plantation laborers continued to be treated as slaves by their Portuguese masters.

The islands were made an overseas province of Portugal in 1951.

Full independence was granted by Portugal on July 12, 1975, with Manuel Pinto da Costa as the first president. Most of the islands' 4,000 Portuguese residents returned to Portugal.

Under a constitution that became effective on Dec. 12, 1975, the socialist Movement for the Liberation of São Tomé and Príncipe (MLSTP) was designated as the only political party. The president was given absolute power to choose or dismiss a prime minister and cabinet officers.

The country depends on foreign aid and loans to make up annual trade deficits as the import costs outweigh revenues from exports. The main trading partners are Portugal and Netherlands.

The government's economic plans for the 1980s call for diversification of agriculture to end the country's dependence on food imports.

SAUDI ARABIA

Official Name: Kingdom of Saudi Arabia.
Area: 830,000 square miles (2,149,690 sq. km.).
Population: 11,667,000.
Chief Cities: Riyadh, capital, 666,840; Jidda, 561,104; Mecca, 366,801; Taif, 204,857; Medina, 198,186.
Government: Absolute monarchy.
King and Prime Minister: Fahd ibn Abdul-Aziz (since 1982).
First Deputy Prime Minister: Crown Prince Abdullah ibn Abdul-Aziz (since 1982).
U.S. Ambassador to Saudi Arabia: Walter L. Cutler.
Ambassador to U.S.: Prince Bandar Bin Sultan.
Flag: Green, with inscription "There is no god but Allah and Mohammed is His messenger" in white Arabic characters above white sword.
Official Language: Arabic.
Principal Ethnic Group: Arab (99%).
State Religion: Islam (99%).
Leading Industries: Mining (petroleum, copper, gold, silver); construction; agriculture (livestock, dates, wheat, corn, alfalfa, grapes, rice, coffee, fruits, vegetables); manufacturing (oil refining, cement, steel).
Foreign Trade: *Major export*—petroleum; *major imports*—vehicles, machinery, iron and steel.
Places of Interest: Kaaba, Islam's most sacred shrine, in Mecca; mosques and palaces; Asir Kingdom National Park.

SAUDI ARABIA TODAY

About one-fourth the size of the United States, Saudi Arabia is a desert kingdom populated by nomadic Arab tribes. But huge deposits of petroleum have changed Saudi Arabia in a few decades from a poor nation to one of the world's richest with an annual oil income of about $100 billion. It is a major source of U.S. oil imports.

The government has used much of the oil revenues to build highways and other public works. Thousands of new schools have been opened. Much money also has been given or loaned to poor Arab countries. Two new cities, each planned for a population of 250,000, have been built—Yanbu on the Red Sea and Jubail on the Persian Gulf.

Occupying most of the Arabian peninsula, Saudi Arabia stretches from the Persian Gulf in the east to the Red Sea and the Gulf of Aqaba in the west. Qatar and the United Arab Emirates lie to the east. To the north are Jordan, Iraq, and Kuwait. To the south are Oman, South Yemen, and North Yemen.

Most of Saudi Arabia is desert. In the west is a fertile coastal plain 10 to 40 miles wide, giving way to steep mountains that rise to over 8,000 feet in the southwest. The Nejd plateau slopes eastward and is bordered by the desert areas of Nefud in the north, Dahna and Nefud Dahi in the east, and Rab al Khali in the south. In the deserts, temperatures range from 70° to 130° F.

EARLY HISTORY

Historians believe Arabia was the original home of the Semitic peoples of the Middle East.

Mohammed founded the religion of Islam at Mecca and Medina about A.D. 622–632. The Muslim armies of the caliph Omar conquered most of the Middle East by 644. The Arab empire extended from Spain and North Africa to the subcontinent of India from the 700s to 1000s. Baghdad, the capital of the Arab empire, fell to the Seljuk Turks in 1055.

From the 1500s Arabia was part of the Ottoman Turkish empire.

In the 1700s Mohammed ibn Saud, the Arab ruler of Nejd, gathered a Bedouin army to gain control of Arabia. His son and successor Abdullah I was defeated by Egypt's Mohammed Ali in 1815–16.

In 1902 young Abdul Aziz ibn Saud regained control of Nejd. By 1925 he had annexed the Kingdom of Hejaz. Britain endorsed independence of his dominions in 1927.

KINGDOM OF SAUDI ARABIA

Saudi Arabia was proclaimed a unified kingdom in 1932 under King Abdul Aziz ibn Saud. Huge oil deposits were discovered in 1935.

In 1945 Saudi Arabia joined the United Nations and the Arab League, ending its isolation.

Ibn Saud was succeeded by his son Saud in 1953. But King Saud was deposed in 1964 to be followed by his younger brother Faisal.

Saudi Arabia did not join directly in the Arab-Israeli war of October 1973, but led in the 1973–74 oil embargo of the U.S. and other nations friendly to Israel.

In June 1974 the government took 60% control of foreign-owned oil companies.

King Faisal was assassinated by a nephew on March 25, 1975, and was succeeded by his half-brother Khalid Abdul-Aziz.

The discovery of new offshore oil fields in the Persian Gulf in 1975 pushed the nation's known oil reserves to about 180 billion barrels, enough to last 60 years at the present rate of production.

Saudi Arabia's royal family was shaken when several hundred rebels seized Islam's holiest shrine, the Grand Mosque, in Mecca on Nov. 20, 1979, and their leader proclaimed himself the savior of Islam. Saudi troops besieged the mosque for two weeks before forcing the rebels to surrender. About 220 persons died in the fighting, including 120 soldiers. On Jan. 9, 1980, 63 of the captured rebels were beheaded in public executions.

With the outbreak of war between Iraq and Iran in 1980, Saudi Arabia stepped up oil production to stabilize the world supply available to oil-importing nations.

Despite opposition from Israel, the U.S. agreed in 1981 to sell Saudi Arabia $8.5 billion of arms, including its most sophisticated Advanced Warning and Control System (AWACS) aircraft.

King Fahd ibn Abdul-Aziz, 60, succeeded to the throne on June 13, 1982, after the death of his half-brother, King Khalid. Friendly to the U.S., King Fahd became known as a modernist in previous government service, being credited with opening education to Saudi Arabian women.

QUICK QUIZ: What city did the Elamites build? See page 283.

SENEGAL

Official Name: Republic of Senegal.
Area: 75,750 square miles (196,192 sq. km.).
Population: 6,902,000.
Capital: Dakar, 798,792.
Government: Multiparty socialist republic.
President: Abdou Diouf (since 1981).
National Assembly: 120 members.
U.S. Ambassador to Senegal: Lannon Walker.
Senegalese Ambassador to U.S.: Falilou Kane.
Flag: Bars of green, gold, and red, with centered green star.
Languages: French (official), English, tribal dialects.
Main Ethnic Groups: Wolof (36%), Peuhl (18%), Serere (17%), Toucouleur (9%), Diola (9%), Mandingo (7%).
Religions: Islam (80%), animism, Christianity.
Leading Industries: Agriculture (peanuts, millet, sorghum, cotton, sugarcane, rice, livestock, vegetables, fruits); fishing; mining (phosphates); food processing; tourism; forestry.
Foreign Trade: *Major exports*—peanuts and peanut oil, phosphates, fish; *major imports*—food, consumer goods, machinery, transport equipment.
Places of Interest: Gorée Island; Niokolo-Koba national park. *In Dakar:* Native markets; French Institute of Black Africa.

SENEGAL TODAY

About the size of South Dakota, Senegal is one of the few multiparty democracies in Africa. Because Dakar was for half a century the capital of French colonies in West Africa, Senegal is more industrially developed than most other West African countries. However, its economy depends heavily on aid from France. Peanuts account for about one-fourth of Senegal's exports and seafood makes up another fourth.

Severe droughts in the 1980s caused a decline in the economy.

Most of Senegal consists of hot, dry savanna with light, low-fertility soil. Some parts of the north are semidesert. The south is forested and rises to a height of 1,315 feet. Chief rivers include the Gambia and the Senegal.

Located on the west coast of Africa's bulge into the Atlantic Ocean, Senegal lies south of Mauritania. Mali is to the east. Guinea and Guinea-Bissau are to the south. Senegal surrounds the small country of Gambia, except for that nation's outlet to the Atlantic.

The capital, Dakar, lies on Cape Verde, the westernmost part of the African continent.

EARLY HISTORY

Stone Age artifacts indicate that Senegal has been populated for thousands of years.

The name *Senegal* came from the Zenaga Berbers of Mauritania who invaded the region in the 100s, converting the Toucouleur people of the region to Islam. By the mid-1400s Portuguese explorers reached the area. They were followed by Dutch, French, and British traders.

FRENCH RULE

After the Napoleonic wars Britain recognized French claims to the area north of the Gambia River.

The French first built a fort at Dakar in 1857. French designs on the interior were long blocked by the Toucouleur empire of El Hadj Omar, which did not fall to French conquest until 1893, although by 1861 the French had absorbed western Senegal.

France agreed to give Britain control of the Gambia River in a treaty in 1889, resulting in the present-day nation of Gambia.

In 1902 Dakar became the administrative center for French West Africa.

Remaining loyal to the Vichy regime in World War II, Senegal repulsed an attempt by the Free French to take Dakar in 1940.

After the war, Senegalese leaders worked for a viable French Union, but when Guinea defected from the union in 1958, Senegal became an autonomous member of the French Community.

In 1959 the country joined with the Sudanese Republic to form the Mali Federation.

INDEPENDENCE

On Aug. 20, 1960, Senegal declared itself independent, with Léopold Sédar Senghor as the first president. It was admitted to the UN that year.

An attempt to overthrow Senghor in 1962 resulted in the imprisonment of Premier Mamadou Dia until 1974.

Throughout the 1960s and early 1970s Senghor and his ruling party forbade political opposition while winning reelection to 5-year terms in 1963, 1968, and 1973.

In February 1976 Senegal extended its territorial limits 150 miles to sea and forbade foreign fishing within 200 miles of its coast.

The constitution was amended in 1976 to allow opposition parties to exist in addition to Senghor's ruling Socialist Party.

In the nation's first multiparty election on Feb. 26, 1978, Senghor won 82% of the vote and his Socialist Party took 83 of the 100 seats in the national assembly. The opposition Democratic Party won the other 17 seats.

The 74-year-old Senghor turned the presidency over to his chosen successor, Abdou Diouf, on Jan. 1, 1981. Diouf, 45, had served as the nation's prime minister since 1970.

Work began in 1981 on a $2 billion irrigation project on the Senegal River financed by loans from Arab oil-exporting nations. The project is planned to develop a million acres of new farmland in Senegal, Mali, and Mauritania.

When communists tried to overthrow the government of neighboring Gambia in August 1981, Senegal put down the rebellion.

On Feb. 1, 1982, Senegal and Gambia formed the confederation of *Senegambia* to link their economies, national security forces, and foreign policy. But each nation retained its sovereignty.

In a free election on Feb. 27, 1983, President Diouf easily defeated four other presidential candidates, winning with about 85% of the vote. His Socialist Party captured 109 seats in the national assembly.

SEYCHELLES

Official Name: Republic of Seychelles.
Area: 171 square miles (444 sq. km.).
Population: 65,800.
Capital: Port Victoria, 23,012.
Government: One-party socialist state.
President: France Albert René (since 1977).
Legislative Assembly: 23 members.
U.S. Ambassador to Seychelles: Walter C. Wallace.
Seychelles Ambassador to U.S.: Giovinella Gonthier.
Flag: Red stripe at top, wavy white band in middle, and green stripe at bottom.
Languages: English and French (official), Creole.
Main Ethnic Group: Creole (mixed French and black descent; 94%).
Principal Religion: Roman Catholicism.
Leading Industries: Agriculture (coconuts, cinnamon, vanilla, fruits, vegetables); tourism; fishing.
Foreign Trade: *Major exports*—cinnamon, coconuts; *major imports*—machinery, vehicles, food.
Places of Interest: Vallée de Mai on Praslin Island; tourist resorts; beaches; Bird Island bird sanctuary.

Seychelles is a small nation of 92 islands off the east coast of Africa. The largest islands are Mahé (55 sq. mi.) and Praslin (17 sq. mi.).

Tourism is the main industry with thousands of visitors attracted each year by the Seychelles' tropical beauty and many swimming beaches.

Other than caring for tourists, most Seychellois make their living by farming and fishing.

The climate seldom varies from a temperature of 75 °to 85 ° F. on the coast. Mountains rise to a height of 2,993 feet on Mahé. Rainfall ranges from 70 to 135 inches a year.

Arab ships visited in the 1100s. French settlers brought African slaves in the 1770s.

The British captured the islands in 1810, and the French formally gave them up in the Treaty of Paris of 1814. The islands were administered as part of the British colony of Mauritius until 1903, when they were made a separate crown colony. Islanders were first given the opportunity to vote in 1948. A U.S. space-tracking station was established on Mahé in 1963.

The conservative Seychelles Democratic Party (SDP) won elections in 1970 and 1974 with SDP leader James R. Mancham as chief minister.

Britain granted Seychelles independence on June 29, 1976, with Mancham as president.

Sixty armed rebels overthrew Mancham's government on June 5, 1977. For president they chose France Albert René, head of the Seychelles People's United Party (SPUP).

René established a one-party Marxist socialist state. However, he continued to lease land to the U.S. for the space-tracking station.

Attempted coups were put down by René's forces in November 1979, November 1981, and August 1982.

A new 23-member national assembly was chosen on May 7, 1983, in a one-party election.

SIERRA LEONE

Official Name: Republic of Sierra Leone.
Area: 27,699 square miles (71,740 sq. km.).
Population: 3,949,000.
Capital: Freetown 214,443.
Government: One-party republic.
President: Siaka Stevens (since 1971).
House of Representatives: 104 members.
U.S. Ambassador to Sierra Leone: Arthur W. Lewis.
Sierra Leone Ambassador to U.S.: Dauda Sulaiman Kamara.
Flag: Stripes of green (top), white, and blue.
Languages: English (official), Krio (Pidgin English), tribal dialects.
Ethnic Groups: Mende (30%), Temne (30%), others (40%).
Religions: Animism (66%), Islam (28%), Christianity (6%).
Leading Industries: Mining (diamonds, iron, bauxite, rutile); agriculture (rice, peanuts, coffee, palm kernels, cocoa, cassava, ginger, livestock); fishing; forestry and lumbering; food processing; tourism.
Foreign Trade: *Major exports*—diamonds, iron ore, palm kernels; *major imports*—cotton fabrics, petroleum products, mining machinery, rice.
Places of Interest: Mountainous area of the Sierra Leone peninsula; Freetown; swimming beaches.

SIERRA LEONE TODAY

Although Sierra Leone has large deposits of diamonds, bauxite, and other minerals, it is a poor country. About three-fourths of the Sierra Leonians are farmers, but they do not raise even enough of their basic crop, rice, to feed everyone.

Britain is Sierra Leone's largest customer, purchasing more than half the nation's exports.

About the size of South Carolina, wet, mountainous Sierra Leone is bordered by Guinea in the north and by Liberia in the southeast.

The peninsula in the extreme west is a hilly area. The remainder of western Sierra Leone consists of a coastal plain. Farther inland the land rises abruptly to a low plateau. Freetown, the capital, has one of the world's largest harbors.

HISTORY

The area was named *Serra Lyoa* (later corrupted to Sierra Leone)—meaning "Lion Mountains"—in the 1400s by Portuguese seamen.

In 1787 British abolitionists, in a plan to return former English and American slaves to Africa, sent a small expedition to Sierra Leone. They were driven away by the local tribal chief, but other expeditions followed. By 1792 nearly all of England's destitute blacks had been transported to Sierra Leone. They were joined by captured Maroons from Jamaica and by former

QUICK QUIZ: What king founded the Mali Empire? See page 285.

SIERRA LEONE *(continued)*

slaves from other British colonies.

In 1808 the British took over the colony for use as a naval base.

During the next 60 years Sierra Leone received thousands of liberated slaves.

The British expanded inland from Freetown, and in 1896 the interior was declared a protectorate. The two areas later were merged.

Sierra Leone was granted independence on April 21, 1961, remaining in the British Commonwealth of Nations.

The results of the March 17, 1967, elections gave a slight edge to the All People's Congress, led by Siaka Stevens, over the ruling Sierra Leone People's Party, led by Prime Minister Albert Margai. But army officers staged a coup, installing a military government.

A group of noncommissioned army officers ousted the military regime in 1968. Siaka Stevens was sworn in as prime minister.

In April 1971 Stevens declared Sierra Leone a republic, becoming its president.

Stevens' APC party won general elections in 1973, after the opposition party boycotted the election because of police intimidation.

On May 6, 1977, President Stevens' APC again won a general election as opposition parties charged murder and police brutality had prevented them from fully participating. He declared the country a one-party state in 1978.

Stevens hosted the organization of African Unity (OAU) conference in June 1980.

Protesting high food prices caused by a 200% inflation rate, labor unions conducted a six-week general strike in 1981.

The first election for the one-party parliament was held on May 1, 1982.

SINGAPORE

Official Name: Republic of Singapore.
Area: 224 square miles (581 sq. km.).
Population: 2,578,000.
Capital: Singapore, 2,471,800.
Government: Parliamentary state.
Prime Minister: Lee Kuan Yew (appointed in 1959).
Legislative Assembly: 79 members.
U.S. Ambassador to Singapore: J. Stapleton Roy.
Singapore Ambassador to United States: Tommy T.B. Koh.
Flag: Red and white stripes, with white crescent and five white stars on red stripe.
Languages: Malay, Chinese, English, and Tamil.
Main Ethnic Groups: Chinese (74%), Malay (14%), Indian and Pakistani (8%).
Religions: Buddhism, Islam, Hinduism, Christianity.
Foreign Trade: *Major exports*—petroleum products, arms, rubber; *major imports*—petroleum products, rubber, crude petroleum.
Places of Interest: St. Andrew's Cathedral; Muslim Holy Sultan Mosque; Fort Canning Hill garrison; national museum; botanical gardens; various Chinese temples; Van Cleef Aquarium; House of Jade.

SINGAPORE TODAY

Singapore is a prosperous island nation with an area about the same as that of Chicago but with only about three-fourths as large a population. Its people have the highest standard of living in the Orient after Japan.

Most of the main island of Singapore is a sprawling city. Little land is available for farming, so most food is imported, as are fuel and raw materials. To reduce population growth, extra taxes are levied on couples who have more than two children. Stiff license fees on automobiles and taxicabs entering the downtown area have reduced traffic congestion.

Public opposition to the government's suppressive measures against political opponents has been blunted by Singapore's remarkable prosperity and low unemployment rate. As a regional center for banking, finance, and technology, the island nation attracts ever-larger foreign investment.

The nation's economy depends on processing, packing, and transshipping to world markets the basic products of Southeast Asia. It also distributes within the region manufactured goods from the world's industrial nations.

Singapore's oil-refinery complex, the third largest in the world, provides about one-fourth of the nation's manufacturing income. Oil-rig construction became a growth industry.

Malaysia and the United States are Singapore's major trading partners.

Singapore lies between the southern tip of Southeast Asia's Malay peninsula and Indonesia's island of Sumatra. The weather is usually hot and humid with much rain.

EARLY HISTORY

The earliest known colonizers of Singapore were Sumatrans in the 1000s.

In the 1700s Singapore became part of the Dutch colony of Johore.

In 1819 Sir Thomas Stamford Raffles, an agent of the British East India Company, set up a trading station at Singapore. Five years later the British bought the island from the Dutch. Singapore was made a part of the Straits Settlements, with Malacca and Penang in 1826. The island became a British crown colony in 1867.

Singapore was an important British naval base before World War II. In 1941 Japanese forces seized the city after a fierce battle. It was retaken, without fighting, in 1945. In 1946 Singapore was made a separate crown colony. It became a self-governing state in 1959.

In 1963 Singapore joined the Federation of Malaysia, but tensions grew between Singapore's local Chinese leaders and the Malaysians.

INDEPENDENCE

On Aug. 9, 1965, it withdrew from Malaysia and became the independent *Republic of Singapore*.

In 1971 Prime Minister Lee Kuan Yew, charging that communists were fomenting racial rioting, restricted freedom of the press.

In a war on crime, the government requires mandatory death sentences for criminals convicted of armed robbery and other crimes of violence. In 1976 the death penalty was extended to anyone found in possession of 15 grams of heroin or 30 grams of morphine.

In 1977 the government launched a new drive against its critics, imprisoning and fining newsmen and others who spoke out against Lee.

Prime Minister Lee's party won its seventh general election in 25 years on Dec. 22, 1984, taking 77 of the 79 parliamentary seats.

Singapore's economy grew at an annual average rate of 9.4% in the 1970s. The rate rose to more than 10% in the early 1980s, slowed to 6% in 1982–83, and then resumed the 10% growth rate in 1984.

In 1984 the government initiated a plan designed to improve the intelligence level of the population. Mothers with college degrees were offered incentives to have more children. Mothers with little or no education were offered about two years salary if they agreed to be sterilized so they could have no more children.

SOLOMONS

Official Name: Solomon Islands.
Area: 11,500 square miles (29,785 sq. km.).
Population: 284,400.
Capital: Honiara, 14,942.
Government: Parliamentary democracy.
Prime Minister: Solomon Mamaloni (since 1981).
Legislative Assembly: 38 members.
U.S. Ambassador to Solomons: Paul F. Gardner.
Solomons Ambassador to U.S.: Francis J. Saemala.
Flag: Blue and green triangles divided by diagonal yellow stripe; five white stars in upper hoist corner.
Languages: English (official), Pidgin English, tribal dialects.
Main Ethnic Groups: Melanesians (93%), Polynesians (4%), Micronesians (2%), others (1%).
Leading Industries: Agriculture (coconuts and oil palms, rice, cocoa, yams, taro, cassava, vegetables, peanuts, cattle), processing (copra and palm oil), forestry (lumber), fishing, mining (gold, bauxite, copper, nickel).
Foreign Trade: *Major exports*—fish, timber, copra, cocoa, seashells, gold; *major imports*—petroleum, manufactured goods.
Places of Interest: Swimming beaches, tropical forests, shell-money manufacturing on Malaita, palm plantations, Mt. Popomanaseu on Guadalcanal.

SOLOMONS TODAY

A South Pacific nation of six large islands and many smaller ones, the Solomons lie about 1,800 miles southwest of Hawaii and some 1,100 miles northeast of Australia. The island chain extends about 900 miles in a southeasterly direction from Papua New Guinea's island of Bougainville.

Although the thatch-roofed shops of the small capital city of Honiara on Guadalcanal boast air conditioning and a plentiful supply of Japanese-made products, most of the dark-skinned Melanesian people of the Solomons follow much the same way of life their ancestors did hundreds of years ago. However, all have given up the practice of cannibalism that persisted into the early 1900s.

Most people live by raising their own fruits and vegetables and by fishing.

Dense tropical rain forests cover the mountainous islands, erasing the scars of the furious World War II battles fought between Americans and Japanese. The highest mountain, Mt. Popomanaseu, rises 7,647 feet on Guadalcanal. That 2,500-square-mile island also has extensive palm plantations and beef cattle ranches.

Altogether the Solomons have a land area somewhat larger than the state of Maryland, but stretch out over an ocean area larger than Texas. The main islands include Guadalcanal, Malaita, San Cristóbal, New Georgia, Santa Isabel, and Choiseul. Airlines provide service among the islands and to Australia and Fiji.

The nation's Shortland Islands lie just east of Bougainville, about 340 miles northwest of Honiara. The northernmost island is the coral atoll of Ontong Java, about 290 miles north of Honiara. The most southeasterly islet is Fataka in the Santa Cruz group, about 650 miles southeast of Honiara.

HISTORY OF THE SOLOMONS

Melanesians settled the islands centuries ago, possibly from Malaysia in Southeast Asia.

The first European to find the islands was the Spaniard Alvaro de Mendaña in 1568. He gave them their name because he believed they contained the lost gold mines of King Solomon. His beliefs were not completely without foundation, because in this century gold mining has become the islands' fifth-ranking export industry.

In the 1800s British sea captains began enslaving the islanders, taking them to Fiji and to Australia as plantation workers.

Britain established a protectorate over the main islands in 1893. In 1898–99 the Santa Cruz Islands to the southeast were added to the protectorate. In 1900 the Shortland Islands to the northwest, Ontong Java to the north, and other islands were transferred to British control by Germany in exchange for what is now Western Samoa.

The Solomons were the scene of heavy fighting in World War II. The Japanese captured the islands in May–July 1942. The U.S. began its counteroffensive in the South Pacific with the landing of Marines on Guadalcanal on Aug. 8, 1942. Fighting in the Solomons continued until late 1943 when the Japanese finally were driven out after about 20,000 had been killed.

Britain granted the Solomons independence on July 7, 1978. Highly dependent on aid from Britain, the Solomons remained part of the British Commonwealth of Nations. Peter Kenilorea became the first prime minister.

In the nation's first election since independence in 1980, Prime Minister Kenilorea's United Party won 14 seats, the People's Alliance Party took 8, the National Democratic Party won 2, and independent candidates captured the remaining 14 parliamentary seats.

Solomon Mamaloni, head of the People's Alliance Party, was chosen prime minister in a 20–17 vote by the legislative assembly in August 1981 because of dissatisfaction with Kenilorea's administration.

QUICK QUIZ: Who conquered Greece in 338 B.C.? See page 284.

SOMALIA

Official Name: Somali Democratic Republic.
Area: 246,201 square miles (637,657 sq. km.).
Population: 6,027,000.
Capital: Mogadishu, 230,000.
Government: One-party socialist state.
President: Maj. Gen. Mohammed Siad Barre (since 1969).
Parliament: People's Assembly, 171 members.
U.S. Ambassador to Somalia: Peter Scott Bridges.
Somali Ambassador to U.S.: Mohamud Haji Nur.
Flag: Light blue field with centered white star.
Languages: Somali, Arabic.
Main Ethnic Group: Somali (mixture of Arab, Persian, and Cushitic descent).
State Religion: Islam.
Leading Industries: Agriculture (cattle, sheep, goats, camels, bananas, sorghum, corn, beans, peanuts, sugarcane, cotton); fishing; food processing; manufacturing (leather products, textiles); mining (tin).
Foreign Trade: *Major exports*—livestock, bananas, hides and skins; *major imports*—food, rice, cotton, fabrics, petroleum products, machinery, transport equipment, paper products, tea.
Places of Interest: Lac Badana National Park; Gedka-Dabley, Benadir, and Lower Juba wildlife reserves; Dallo forests; Indian Ocean resorts; Bajuni Islands.

SOMALIA TODAY

Although almost as large as Texas, Somalia is one of the world's 25 poorest countries. Most Somalis live as nomadic herdsmen, raising camels, cattle, goats, and sheep.

The country has some deposits of iron and other minerals, but there is little mining and almost no manufacturing.

Somalia's economy worsened with the influx in 1978–81 of more than a million refugees from revolution and war in Ethiopia. The UN, U.S., and international organizations sent food and economic aid while searching for some long-range solution to the massive refugee problem.

The greater part of the country is covered by the vast Ogaden plateau, mountain-bordered in the north but sloping in the south to a lowland area crossed by the Webi Shabeelle and Jubba rivers.

Kenya and Ethiopia lie to the west, and Djibouti to the northwest.

EARLY HISTORY

Somali tribes have occupied the region for more than 2,000 years. From the 900s to 1400s it was part of the Zenj empire, which was overthrown by the Portuguese in the 1500s.

In the 1600s Muscat and Oman gained control of the coastal towns. In the 1800s their authority passed to the sultan of Zanzibar.

A British protectorate was established in the north between 1884 and 1886, and an Italian protectorate in the south in 1889. British rule was reinstated by Mohammed Ibn Abdullah Hassan, until his defeat in 1920.

From 1934 to 1936 Italian Somalia was a staging area for the Italian conquest of Ethiopia. During World War II Italian troops briefly occupied British Somaliland. Italian Somalia was returned to Italian control in 1950 under a 10-year UN trusteeship. In 1954 part of British Somaliland was transferred to Ethiopia.

INDEPENDENCE

British Somaliland and Italian Somalia joined on July 1, 1960, to form independent Somalia.

Large numbers of Somalis live in Ethiopia, Kenya, and adjacent areas. Pressures for a Greater Somalia have been, and remain, a source of conflict with neighbors.

Aden Abdulla Osman was president of Somalia from 1960 to 1967, when he was defeated by Abdirashid Ali Shermarke. President Shermarke was assassinated on Oct. 15, 1969.

On Oct. 21, 1969, a leftist military junta led by Maj. Gen. Mohammed Siad Barre seized power.

In 1970 the country was renamed the *Somali Democratic Republic.* All foreign banks and oil companies were nationalized. The army was equipped and trained by Soviet advisers.

The first Somali written language was introduced by the government in 1972.

The U.S. government reported in 1975 that the Soviet Union had installed atomic guided-missile facilities in Somalia. The Soviet activities were cited as a major reason for the building of a U.S. Navy base on the island of Diego Garcia in the Indian Ocean.

In June 1976 the Socialist Revolutionary Party was organized as the nation's only political party. The following month the party's 7-man central committee was made Somalia's ruling body under President Mohammed Siad Barre.

In mid-1977 Somali guerrillas began a major drive to capture the Ogaden region of Ethiopia. When the Soviet Union and Cuba aided Ethiopia, Somalia on Nov. 13, 1977, canceled its treaty of friendship with the Soviet Union and broke relations with Cuba.

An Ethiopian offensive in March 1978 forced Somali troops to withdraw from Ethiopia's northern Ogaden region. But guerrilla fighting continued into the 1980s.

The first election since Barre seized power was held on Dec. 30, 1979, with members of the national People's Assembly and local district assemblies approved from a single slate of candidates.

The U.S. and Somalia signed an agreement on Aug. 22, 1980, permitting the U.S. to use military bases in Somalia in return for economic and military aid.

Drought and floods compounded the nation's economic problems in 1981–85.

The Somali government reported in July 1983 that it had driven back Ethiopian forces that had pushed three miles inside the border. Additional border fighting was reported in December 1984 and January 1985.

A cholera epidemic at an Ethiopian refugee camp killed over 1,500 persons in April 1985.

Under auspices of the World Bank, a group of industrial nations agreed to provide Somalia with $1.3 billion in aid for a new three-year plan for 1984–86. More than half the money was to be spent in rebuilding the agricultural industry.

SOUTH AFRICA

Official Name: Republic of South Africa.
Area: 434,674 square miles (1,125,800 sq. km.).
Population: 26,674,000.
Chief Metropolitan Areas: Cape Town, legislative capital, 1,490,935; Pretoria, administrative capital, 739,043; Bloemfontein, judicial capital, 198,343; Johannesburg, 1,726,073; Durban, 960,792; East Rand, 848,396; Port Elizabeth, 585,399.
Government: Minority controlled republic.
President: Pieter Willem Botha (since 1984).
Parliament: House of Assembly (white), 178 members; House of Representatives for Coloreds, 85 members; House of Delegates for Indians, 45 members.
U.S. Ambassador to South Africa: Herman W. Nickel.
South African Ambassador to U.S.: Herbert Beukes.
Flag: Orange, white, and blue stripes; in center, replicas of Union Jack, old flag of Orange Free State, and old Transvaal Vierkleur (four-color).
Languages: Afrikaans, English (both official), many black languages.
Ethnic Groups: Black (70%), white (17%), "colored" (mixed-race) (10%), Indian (Asian descent) (3%).
Main Religions: Christianity (73%), animism (13%), Hinduism (2%), Islam (1%).
Leading Industries: Trade and services; manufacturing (steel, chemicals, automobiles, textiles, metal products, machinery, consumer products); mining (diamonds, gold, coal, iron, copper, uranium, many others); agriculture (corn, sheep, dairy products, cattle, wheat, sugarcane, tobacco, fruits, vegetables); fishing.
Foreign Trade: *Major exports*—gold, metal products, food, diamonds, wool; *major imports*—automobiles, petroleum, machinery, manufactured goods.
Places of Interest: Kruger National Park; Cape Point; Kirstenbosch National Botanical Gardens; garden route tour from Cape Town to Durban; Oudtshoorn caves; Johannesburg gold mines; Kimberley diamond mine; Indian market and beaches at Durban; Zululand game reserves; Sudwala caves and adjoining Dinosaur Park.

SOUTH AFRICA TODAY

Rich in natural resources, white-ruled South Africa leads the world in gold mining and produces about a third of the world's diamonds. It also has large amounts of iron, coal, copper, tin, and uranium. It lacks only natural petroleum, but has undertaken large scale production of petroleum from coal.

South Africa's farmlands produce ample amounts of wheat and other food crops, with some left over for export.

Most of the world opposes South Africa's racial segregation policies, which include barring blacks from voting in national elections.

About three times the size of California, South Africa is bordered on the northwest by Namibia (South West Africa), on the north by Botswana and Zimbabwe Rhodesia, and on the northeast by Mozambique and Swaziland. The eastern part of South Africa surrounds Lesotho,

Transkei, Bophuthatswana, Ciskei, and Venda.

Most of South Africa is a plateau, with an average height of 4,000 feet. In the east the land rises steeply from fertile coastal lowlands to the Drakensberg Mountains.

In the east central and northern regions are the prairie-like veld. Cape Agulhas is the continent's southern tip.

The Orange River rises in the Drakensberg Mountains and with its tributary, the Vaal, flows westward into the Atlantic. The Limpopo River rises in the Witwatersrand in the Transvaal.

APARTHEID (SEPARATE RACIAL DEVELOPMENT)

Less than 1 person in 5 in South Africa is white. Yet whites control the government and all aspects of life by the policy of racial segregation called *apartheid*. To enforce the policy, parliament passed restrictive racial laws in the 1950s and 1960s. Some restrictions in sports and other areas were lifted in the 1970s, including removal in 1979 of the ban on black labor unions.

Police can arrest and imprison people without a court order and hold them indefinitely without letting them communicate with lawyers, families, or friends. Or they can be "banned" to their homes and denied rights of free speech. The security police are protected from court restraints, but may be prosecuted for excesses.

About two-thirds of the blacks live on tribal reserves that cover about 13% of the country's land area. Millions of blacks have been forcibly moved from white areas to nine *homelands*: Bophuthatswana, Ciskei, Gazankulu, KwaZulu, Lebowa, Qwaqwa, Swazi, Transkei, and Venda. South Africa granted sovereignty to Transkei in 1976, to Bophuthatswana in 1977, to Venda in 1979, and to Ciskei in 1981.

Other nations have refused to recognize the sovereignty of the South Africa homelands because they view the homelands program as part of the nation's apartheid policy of racial segregation. The program requires blacks who are members of tribes that have independent homelands to give up their South African citizenship, even though they live in South Africa. Thus, by the time all the homelands are "independent" most blacks would no longer be citizens of South Africa, so the whites then would be the majority of South African citizens.

Wholly dependent on South Africa for their economic existence, the homelands are "landlocked islands" surrounded by South Africa.

Migrant blacks who take jobs in the cities of South Africa are forbidden to bring their wives and children with them. They and permanent black resident families live in "locations" set aside on the outskirts of cities or towns. Asians and those of mixed ancestry are similarly restricted to specific living areas. Education is segregated, except in some private schools.

Most professional and supervisory jobs are held by whites. Blacks do most unskilled and semiskilled labor on farms, in mines, in manufacturing plants, and in public service.

EARLY HISTORY

Hottentots, Bushmen, and other Africans lived in

QUICK QUIZ: Who established the Kingdom of the Franks? See page 285.

SOUTH AFRICA *(continued)*

southern Africa for thousands of years, but little is known of their history other than the cave paintings they drew.

Portuguese explorer Bartolomeu Dias in 1488 became the first European to reach the Cape of Good Hope. The first permanent European settlement was made at Cape Town in 1652 by the Dutch East India Company. The Dutch were soon joined by French and German settlers. These early arrivals came to be known as *Boers*.

BRITISH RULE

Through the Napoleonic wars, Britain gained formal possession of the Cape Colony in 1814.

Because of dissatisfaction with British rule and the abolition of slavery in 1833, many Boers migrated to the interior in the Great Trek of 1835–48.

The Boers then founded the Transvaal, Natal, and the Orange Free State territories. Their migration led to war with the Zulus and other Bantu tribesmen. The Boers defeated the Zulus in 1838 at the Battle of Blood River.

Britain annexed Natal in 1843. After discovery of gold and diamonds, it annexed part of the Orange Free State in 1871 and the South Africa Republic (Transvaal) in 1877.

Boer resentment of British encroachment erupted in 1899 into the Boer War, or South African War, which the British won in 1902.

Britain formed the Union of South Africa on May 31, 1910, joining Cape Colony, Natal, the Orange River Colony (Orange Free State), and the Transvaal. The Union of South Africa gained sovereignty in 1934.

Apartheid became official policy under Prime Minister Dr. Daniel Malan, whose party won the 1948 elections.

REPUBLIC OF SOUTH AFRICA

On May 31, 1961, the country became the independent *Republic of South Africa*. Six months later it withdrew from the British Commonwealth of Nations, reacting to criticism of its racial policies.

With the growing number of independent black African nations, pressures mounted in the U.S. and UN against South African apartheid. The U.S. ended the sale of all military equipment to South Africa on Dec. 31, 1963.

South Africa continued its rigid policy of apartheid under Prime Minister Hendrik F. Verwoerd, who was assassinated in 1966, and under his successor, Balthazar Johannes Vorster.

In November 1974 the UN General Assembly suspended South Africa's voting privileges in the international organization.

A wave of protest riots and strikes by black students began on June 16, 1976, in Soweto, a black suburb of Johannesburg. Over 500 were killed and nearly 4,000 injured.

The UN Security Council on Nov. 4, 1977, unanimously ordered a worldwide mandatory embargo on the shipment of military supplies to South Africa—the first such action ever taken by the UN against a member nation.

In December 1977 the UN General Assembly adopted by huge majorities resolutions calling on the UN Security Council to embargo oil shipments to South Africa and to cut off foreign investment in South African enterprises.

President Nicolaas Diederichs, 75, died on Aug. 21, 1978. A month later Vorster resigned as prime minister and was elected president by the electoral college of parliament.

Pieter Willem Botha, 62, formerly defense minister under Vorster, was chosen as prime minister on Sept. 28, 1978, by the ruling National Party.

Vorster resigned as president in June 1979 and was succeeded by Marais Viljoen, 63.

As the price of gasoline rose to $2.43 a gallon in 1979, the government rushed construction of several plants to convert coal into oil. The plants were expected to provide from one-third to one-half of the country's oil needs by the late 1980s.

A flash of light detected by a U.S. satellite off the southern coast of South Africa on Sept. 22, 1979, was interpreted by some nuclear scientists as evidence South Africa had tested an atomic bomb. However, the government denied doing so.

In 1980 South Africa experienced the worst wave of racial violence since 1976. In June guerrillas bombed two of the country's new coal-to-oil conversion plants and an oil refinery. Later in the same month police fired on black demonstrators in Cape Town.

In an all-white parliamentary election on April 29, 1981, Prime Minister Botha's National Party won all but 35 of the 165 elected seats, seven less than in the previous election.

In 1982–84 the worst drought in the nation's history reduced grain harvests by about 50%, devastating the economy in the black homelands.

South Africa took steps in 1984 to end nearly a decade of hostilities with neighboring Angola and Mozambique. South Africa and Angola signed an agreement on Feb. 16 ending South Africa's occupation of southern Angola. A month later, South Africa and neighboring Mozambique signed a nonagression pact on March 16, 1984. Both Angola and Mozambique agreed to stop supporting guerrillas opposing the South African government.

A new constitution went into effect on Sept. 3, 1984, providing a three-house parliament—one for whites, one for Asians, and one for mixed-blood "coloreds." Blacks continued to be excluded from representation and from voting. The constitution, which had been approved nearly 2 to 1 in a referendum in 1973, also strengthened the powers of the nation's president.

Botha was elected president on Sept. 5, 1984, by an electoral college made up of members of the three houses of parliament.

More than 260 persons were killed in racial violence in 1984–1985 as blacks protested the new constitution and other apartheid policies. In the worst incident in 25 years, police opened fire on black demonstrators near the manufacturing center of Uitenhage on March 21, 1985, killing 20. The government declared a state of emergency on July 20, arresting scores of activists in an effort to end the violence.

More than three decades of wrangling between the UN and South Africa over the status of Namibia (South West Africa) continued in the 1980s as South West Africa refused to give up control of the former German colony. See pages 615–616.

SOVIET UNION

Official Name: Union of Soviet Socialist Republics.
Area: 8,649,538 square miles (22,402,200 sq. km.).
Population: 277,996,000.
Chief Cities: Moskva (Moscow), capital, 8,302,000; Leningrad, 4,722,000; Kiev, 2,297,000; Tashkent, 1,902,-000; Baku, 1,616,000; Kharkov, 1,503,000; Gorki, 1,373,000; Novosibirsk, 1,357,000; Minsk, 1,370,000; Kuibyshev, 1,243,000; Sverdlovsk, 1,252,000; Dnepropetrovsk, 1,114,000; Tbilisi, 1,110,000; Erevan, 1,076,-000; Chelyabinsk, 1,066,000; Donetsk, 1,047,000.
Government: Communist one-party state.
Head of the Soviet government: Mikhail S. Gorbachev, general secretary of the Communist Party (since 1985).
President: Andrei A. Gromyko (since 1985).
Prime Minister: Nikolai A. Tikhonov (since 1980).
Supreme Soviet: *Soviet of the Union,* 750 members; *Soviet of Nationalities,* 750 members.
U.S. Ambassador to Soviet Union: Arthur A. Hartman.
Soviet Ambassador to U.S.: Anatoliy F. Dobrynin.
Flag: Red field with gold hammer and sickle below gold-bordered star in upper hoist corner.
Major Languages: Russian (official), Slavic (76%), Altaic (8%), other (16%).
Main Ethnic Groups: Russian (52%), Ukrainian (16%), Uzbek (5%), Belorussian (4%).
Religions: Atheism (official), Russian Orthodoxy (18%).
Leading Industries: Manufacturing (steel, cement, paper, electricity, vehicles, electronics, armaments); agriculture (wheat, livestock, corn, rye, oats, potatoes, fruits, vegetables); mining (petroleum, natural gas, coal, lignite, iron ore, diamonds, bauxite, copper, lead, zinc, salt); forestry and lumbering; fishing.
Foreign Trade: *Major exports*—equipment for industrial plants, petroleum; *major imports*—machinery, clothing, ships, raw sugar, metal ores, wheat.
Places of Interest: Lake Baikal; Black Sea resorts; Caucasus area; the Crimea; Baltic Sea area; Kiev. *In Moscow:* The Kremlin, containing Nikolai Palace (now home of Supreme Soviet), Kremlin Theater, belfry of Ivan the Terrible, Cathedral of the Archangel Michael, Patriarch's Palace; Lenin Mausoleum; St. Basil's Cathedral. *In Leningrad:* Hermitage Museum (former Winter Palace).

SOVIET UNION TODAY

As one of the world's two great superpowers, the Soviet Union competes with the United States for world leadership.

Stretching from eastern Europe across the continent of Asia, the Soviet Union has nearly two-and-a-half times the area of the U.S. and a population about 18% larger.

The Soviet Union has a communist form of government with one-party domination of political activities and state ownership of economic activities.

The government suppresses such civil rights as freedom of speech and freedom of the press. Refus-

ing to work is a crime punishable by imprisonment.

Since World War II the Soviet Union and the U.S. have engaged in a costly arms race in which each nation has built atomic intercontinental missiles capable of destroying the other.

SOVIET GOVERNMENT

Though the constitution of the Soviet government is patterned somewhat after those of Western democracies, there are no checks and balances and little real separation of powers.

The country is ruled by the Communist Party's Politburo, whose 14 members are also the chief officials of the government and of the party.

In theory, the highest legislative body is the bicameral Supreme Soviet, elected by universal suffrage from single lists of Communist Party-approved candidates. It meets twice yearly but functions as a rubber stamp. A 38-member presidium acts as a council to the president.

The Communist Party controls all levels of government and practically every phase of Soviet life. It is the only political party in the country—its power guaranteed by the constitution. Membership in the party is about 14.5 million, or 9% of the adult population.

The party's highest organ, theoretically, is its congress, which normally meets every four years to formalize broad policies of the Politburo. The congress elects a central committee to act for it between sessions.

GEOGRAPHY

The world's largest country, the Soviet Union covers nearly one-sixth of the earth's land area.

The Soviet Union extends through 11 time zones, varying widely in terrain and climate.

Its Ural Mountains are considered the dividing line between Europe and Asia. The Carpathian Mountains fringe the Soviet Union in the west. The Caucasus Mountains lie between the Black and Caspian seas. The Pamir, Tien Shan, Altai, and other ranges rise along the southern border.

The Soviet Union includes 15 Soviet states. The largest is Russia (Russian Soviet Federated Socialist Republic), with 70% of the total land area and more than half the people. Second most populous is the Ukraine (Ukrainian Soviet Socialist Republic), with 20% of the people.

STATES OF THE SOVIET UNION

NAME	AREA (sq. mi.)	CAPITAL
Armenia	11,506	Yerevan
Azerbaijan	33,436	Baku
Belorussia	80,155	Minsk
Estonia	17,413	Tallinn
Georgia	26,911	Tbilisi
Kazakhstan	1,048,306	Alma-Ata
Kirghizstan	76,641	Frunze
Latvia	24,595	Riga
Lithuania	25,174	Vilnius
Moldavia	13,012	Kishinev
Russia	6,592,850	Moscow
Tadzhikistan	55,251	Dushanbe
Turkmenistan	188,456	Ashkhabad
Ukraine	233,090	Kiev
Uzbekistan	173,592	Tashkent

QUICK QUIZ: When was Timbuktu founded? See page 285.

EARLY HISTORY OF RUSSIA

Rurik, an almost legendary Swede, is generally credited with founding the Russian state when he led his Varangian tribe into Novgorod in the year 862. Rurik's dynasty later ruled the duchy of Moscow and eventually all of Russia.

Saint Vladimir (Vladimir I, reigned 980–1015), initially a pagan, became the first Christian ruler of Kiev. Through his victories over Lithuanians, Bulgars, and the Greeks in the Crimea, he is considered the founder of the powerful Kievan state. Under Yaroslav the Wise in the 1000s, Kiev reached a peak of prosperity and culture. In 1240 Kiev fell to the Mongols, who, under Batu Khan, created an empire called the Golden Horde that ruled most of what is now the eastern and southern Soviet Union.

Northern Russia fell under domination of Moscow. Its power was solidified by Dmitri Donskoi. Under Ivan III (1462–1505), who drove out the Mongols, and Vasily III (1505–33), many principalities were brought under Russian control.

CZARIST RUSSIA

Ivan IV, known as "Ivan the Terrible," was the first ruler crowned czar (caesar) of all Russia (1547).

The nobleman Mikhail Romanov was elected czar (1613), founding the last Russian dynasty. Peter the Great (1689–1725) opened Russia to Westernization. Ekaterina II (Catherine the Great; 1762–96) made Russia a leading power.

Under Aleksandr I (1801–25) more lands were added to the empire. With Napoleon's defeat on Russian soil (1812), Aleksandr became one of Europe's most powerful rulers.

The spread of liberal ideas among many of the aristocrats and educated bourgeois led to the abortive Decembrist Conspiracy (1825), an attempt to block the accession of Nikolai I.

After Britain and France defeated Russia in the Crimean War (1854–56), Czar Aleksandr II (1855–81) inaugurated a series of reforms. He freed the serfs, modernized the courts, and established provincial, county, and town self-government on a modest scale. He also extended the Russian empire in the Far East. He was assassinated in 1881 by a terrorist group.

Aleksandr III (1881–94) repudiated his father's policies and instituted a period of severe repression, especially against the Jews. He was followed by Nikolai II (1894–1917), the last czar. During Nikolai's administration, Russia was defeated in the Russo-Japanese War (1904–05). Popular discontent in 1905 forced Nikolai to accept a constitution, establishing a representative parliament, the Duma.

In World War I a poorly prepared Russia joined the Allies against the Central Powers. Russian armies suffered massive setbacks.

RUSSIAN REVOLUTION

Revolution erupted in February 1917, when troops refused to fire upon crowds milling in the streets of St. Petersburg (Leningrad) as part of a general strike. The czar abdicated, and a moderate provisional government took over, headed successively by Prince Georgi Lvov and Aleksandr Kerensky.

In November 1917 the Bolsheviks (communists), led by Vladimir Lenin and Leon Trotsky, seized power. The royal family was executed. Lenin had founded the Bolshevik Party in 1903. Although the communists represented only a small minority of the population, Lenin ruled as a dictator until his death in 1924. His government successfully fought off attempts to overthrow it during a civil war (1918–20). The Communist International (Comintern), founded in 1919, attempted to undermine western governments.

STALIN'S RULE

After Lenin's death, Joseph Stalin, general secretary of the Central Committee of the Communist Party since 1922, won a bitter power struggle against Leon Trotsky (murdered in Mexico, 1940). Stalin created a brutal police state. He pushed the nation into rapid industrialization, forcibly collectivized agriculture, and expanded the secret police, censorship, forced labor, and concentration camps. In "blood purges" in the late 1930s he executed tens of thousands, mostly without trials, including surviving founding fathers of the Soviet state and a majority of the military leadership. Stalin also systematically imprisoned hundreds of thousands of people.

The Soviet Union received diplomatic recognition by a number of European governments in 1924 and by the United States in 1933. It became a member of the League of Nations in 1934.

In 1939 the Soviet Union signed a nonagression pact with Nazi Germany that preceded World War II. The Soviet Union absorbed Latvia, Lithuania, Estonia (political conquests still not recognized by the United States and many other nations), and later the eastern half of Poland. Also in 1939 Russia attacked Finland, eventually taking a large part of its eastern territory.

In 1941 Hitler launched a surprise attack on Russia, inflicting civilian and military losses of 20 million lives and driving the Soviet Union to join the Allied side. With U.S. lend-lease aid, Soviet armies drove back the Germans.

Following Allied victory, the Soviet Union imposed communist governments in eastern European countries occupied by the Red Army. By mid-1948 Poland, Czechoslovakia, Hungary, Romania, Bulgaria, East Germany, Yugoslavia, and Albania were Soviet satellites.

COLD WAR

With the breakup of the wartime alliance, mutual hostility (the Cold War) came to characterize Soviet relations with the West.

The Soviet Union's test explosion of its first atomic bomb in 1949, using secrets stolen from Britain and the U.S., brought fears that an attack on noncommunist countries might be launched without warning.

The formation of the NATO military alliance by the U.S., Canada, and western European nations in 1950 was countered by Moscow with the Warsaw Pact alliance of its satellites.

After Stalin's death in 1953, Georgi M. Malenkov became chairman of the Council of Ministers, but in 1955 he was replaced by Nikolai Bulganin. In October 1956 Soviet troops crushed a popular revolt in Hungary.

By 1956 Nikita S. Khrushchev, Communist Par-

SOVIET UNION

SOVIET UNION *(continued)*

ty first secretary, emerged as the most powerful figure in the Soviet Union. In 1963 he agreed to a limited nuclear test-ban treaty with the U.S.

The Chinese communists rejected destalinization and the "peaceful coexistence" formula. Sino-Soviet differences produced a schism that divided the communist movement throughout the world.

The Soviet Union and the United States came close to war in 1962 when Khrushchev installed atomic missiles in Cuba that could be used to attack the U.S. However, war was averted after President Kennedy imposed a naval blockade on Cuba, forcing Khrushchev to withdraw the missiles.

RULE BY LEONID BREZHNEV

In 1964 Khrushchev was abruptly removed from office, to be succeeded by Leonid Brezhnev as Communist Party first secretary and Alexei Kosygin as premier.

In August 1968 the Soviet Union and its Warsaw Pact allies (except Romania) invaded Czechoslovakia and crushed a more liberal communist government under Alexander Dub-ček. Moscow announced the "Brezhnev Doctrine," proclaiming the Soviet Union's right to intervene in any "socialist" country.

As part of his "détente" policies to ease tensions with communist regimes, President Nixon held a summit meeting with Brezhnev in Moscow on May 22–30, 1972, where they signed two agreements limiting production of nuclear weapons, as formulated during four years of SALT (Strategic Arms Limitation Talks) negotiations.

In June 1973 Brezhnev made a 9-day visit to the U.S. for a meeting with President Nixon hailed as the official end to the Cold War.

When Nobel Prize-winner Aleksandr I. Solzhenitsyn published a book, *The Gulag Archipelago, 1918–1956,* exposing the horrors of Soviet secret labor-prisons, he was arrested and exiled in 1974.

The Soviet Union began construction of a second Trans-Siberian railroad in 1974. A work force of 100,000 was employed in building the 2,000-mile line, completed in the late 1980s.

The Soviet government on Jan. 10, 1975, canceled its 1972 trade agreement with the U.S. because of requirements by the U.S. Congress that the Soviet Union relax its restrictive emigration.

In May 1977 the 70-year-old Brezhnev ousted 74-year-old Nikolai V. Podgorny from the presidency. He then took the title of president, becoming the first Soviet ruler to hold titles as both head of the party and chief of state.

A new "hot line" communication system using space satellites to carry messages between the White House and the Kremlin went into service on Jan. 16, 1978. It replaced a land cable "hot line" that had been installed in 1963.

In 1979 the Soviet government eased restrictions on the emigration of Jews, permitting a record 51,000 to leave the country and bringing to about 240,000 the number allowed to leave during the 1970s. But in the 1980s Jewish emigration was reduced to a trickle.

Seven years of negotiations between the U.S. and the Soviet Union for a new pact limiting strategic arms resulted in a SALT II treaty signed by Brezhnev and President Carter on June 18, 1979. But deteriorating relations with the U.S. prevent-

ed U.S. Senate ratification of the treaty.

The Soviet Union invaded Afghanistan in December 1979, setting up a puppet government loyal to Moscow. Soviet troops remained bogged down in Afghanistan in 1981–85 in their effort to suppress anticommunist guerrillas.

On Jan. 4, 1980, U.S. President Carter denounced the Soviet actions in Afghanistan, cut grain sales to the Soviet Union, and suspended the sale of high-technology equipment such as computers. He also organized a partial boycott of summer Olympic Games in Moscow.

On Jan. 22, 1980, Andrei D. Sakharov, Nobel Prize-winning father of the Soviet hydrogen bomb, was arrested and exiled without trial to the city of Gorki for having criticized the Soviet invasion of Afghanistan.

Nikolai A. Tikhonov, 75, was appointed prime minister on Oct. 23, 1980, succeeding Kosygin.

After the Soviet Union pressured its puppet government in Poland to crackdown on that country's Solidarity labor union in December 1981, President Reagan imposed new trade sanctions on both the Soviet Union and Poland.

NEW LEADERS

After the death of the 75-year-old Brezhnev on Nov. 10, 1982, the new head of the Communist Party was Yuri V. Andropov, 68, former head of the KGB, the Soviet secret police and spy network.

U.S. President Reagan and other world leaders denounced the Soviet Union after a Soviet fighter plane shot down a South Korean airliner that had strayed over Soviet territory on Sept. 1, 1983, killing all 269 persons aboard.

When the U.S. began deployment of new medium-range missiles in Europe in November 1983, the Soviet Union broke off all talks with the U.S. on reduction of armaments.

During Andropov's regime a widespread purge was undertaken in which thousands of party officials were replaced.

Seriously ill from a kidney ailment that kept him from official duties for six months, the 69-year-old Andropov died on Feb. 9, 1984.

Konstantin U. Chernenko, 72, the oldest man to become leader of the Soviet Union, was chosen as general secretary of the Communist Party on Feb. 13, 1984. Two months later, on April 11, he was named president of the Soviet Union.

In retribution for the U.S.-led boycott in 1980 of Olympic Games held in Moscow, the Soviet Union and other communist-bloc countries boycotted the 1984 Olympics in Los Angeles.

A series of explosions at the Severomorsk naval base on May 13, 1984, reportedly killed 200 persons and destroyed hundreds of missiles used by the nation's nuclear submarines.

The ailing Chernenko died on March 10, 1985, and was immediately succeeded by 54-year-old Mikhail S. Gorbachev, who apparently had been in charge of the Soviet government during Chernenko's illness. See page 13.

The United States and the Soviet Union resumed negotiations on ways to reduce nuclear armaments on March 12, 1985.

Andrei A. Gromyko, 75, who had been Soviet foreign minister for 28 years, was chosen as the largely figurehead president of the Soviet Union on July 2, 1985.

SPAN

Official Name: Spanish State.
Area: 194,897 square miles (504,782 sq. km.).
Population: 38,709,000.
Chief Cities: Madrid, capital, 3,188,297; Barcelona, 1,754,900; Valencia, 751,734; Seville, 653,833; Zaragoza, 590,750; Bilbao, 433,030; Málaga, 503,251.
Government: Parliamentary monarchy.
King: Juan Carlos I (since 1975).
Prime Minister: Felipe González Márquez (since 1982).
Legislature *(Cortes): Congress of Deputies,* 350 members; *Senate,* 248 members.
U.S. Ambassador to Spain: Thomas O. Enders.
Spanish Ambassador to U.S.: Gabriel Manueco de Lecea.
Flag: Wide yellow stripe in center with narrow red stripes at top and bottom.
Official Language: Castilian Spanish.
Ethnic Groups: Spanish-Castilian, Basque, Catalan, Galician, Andalusian.
Main Religion: Roman Catholicism.
Leading Industries: Trade and services; manufacturing (steel, ships, automobiles, textiles, cement, paper, cork products, consumer goods); agriculture (livestock, wheat, sugar beets, potatoes, barley, olives, grapes, fruits, vegetables); tourism; mining (lead, coal, iron, petroleum, uranium); forestry and lumbering; fishing.
Foreign Trade: *Major exports*—Shoes, textiles, automobiles, citrus fruits, olive oil, wine; *major imports*—crude petroleum, corn, soybeans, meat.
Places of Interest: *In Madrid:* Prado Museum, royal palace, nearby El Escorial palace and monastery. *In Toledo:* cathedral, Sto. Tomé Church. *In Barcelona:* Sagrada Familia Church, Gothic Quarter, cathedral. *In Seville:* Giralda tower and cathedral, Alcázar palaces. *In Granada:* Alhambra Moorish palace-citadel. *In Cordoba:* Great Mosque; Costa del Sol resort area. *In Segovia:* Roman aqueduct.

SPAIN TODAY

Larger than California both in area and population, Spain is the fifth most important industrial nation of western Europe. It is among the leading producers of cement, fish, and uranium.

Although Spain has experienced substantial economic growth with the aid of large loans and grants from the U.S., it has a per capita income about half that of West Germany.

The U.S. maintains three air bases and a naval base in Spain.

Over 30 million tourists visit Spain each year because of its mild climate and many historical and cultural attractions.

The rugged Pyrenees mountains and the republic of Andorra on the north separate Spain from France. Portugal lies to the west. Gibraltar stands at the southern tip of Spain.

The nation is divided into 17 autonomous regions, which each elect their own local parliaments.

Spain has six mountain ranges, grazing lands, a vast central plateau, plains, and rocky coast-lines. The most important rivers are the Ebro, Douro, Tagus, Guadalquivir, and Guadiana.

EARLY HISTORY

In the 800s B.C. Phoenician traders settled on the southwest coast. Carthaginians colonized the Mediterranean east coast and the Balearic Islands, where Greeks also planted colonies.

In the 200s B.C. the Carthaginians conquered most of Iberia but subsequently were defeated by the Romans. Christianity was established in the 200s and 300s A.D. Then hordes of Germanic tribes began sweeping into the peninsula in 409.

In the 700s Spain was conquered by Muslim Berbers (Moors). Under Abd-ar-Rahman III (891–961) Muslim Spain reached its apex.

The Moors lost their last stronghold (Granada) in 1492, when it fell to the forces of Fernando V and Isabel I, rulers of Castile and Aragon. In that same year Columbus made his first voyage of discovery to America.

Spain's "golden century" was the 1500s, under rule by the Hapsburg dynasty. The country acquired a huge overseas empire. Spain ruled the seas and had the strongest military force in Europe. But incessant wars with England, the Netherlands, and France squandered Spain's resources.

Napoleon forced King Carlos IV to abdicate in 1808 and installed Joseph Bonaparte as king. By 1814 British forces under the Duke of Wellington succeeded in driving out the French. Colonial rebellions and the Spanish-American War (1898) brought an end to most of Spain's overseas empire.

A military dictatorship led by Primo de Rivera took power in 1923 under the Bourbon king Alfonso XIII. De Rivera was ousted in 1930.

CIVIL WAR AND FRANCISCO FRANCO

A republican victory at the polls in 1931 brought an end to the monarchy. A Popular Front (republicans, socialists, communists, and syndicalists) won elections in February 1936.

Gen. Francisco Franco began a revolt on July 18, 1936, taking command of the Spanish army in Morocco. He led an invasion of Spain and began three years of devastating civil war.

The defending Loyalists (republicans) were backed by the Popular Front, the Basques, and the Catalans. Franco received substantial aid from Nazi Germany and Fascist Italy. The Loyalists were aided by the Soviet Union. By 1939 Franco defeated the republican forces.

Spain was ruled as a harsh dictatorship by Franco for 36 years in 1939–75. He headed the only legal political party, the National Movement.

During World War II Spain favored the Axis Powers but remained technically neutral.

Franco announced in 1969 that Prince Juan Carlos de Borbón y Borbón would be his successor and heir to the Spanish throne.

CONSTITUTIONAL MONARCHY RESTORED

Juan Carlos was proclaimed king on Nov. 22, 1975, two days after Franco's death. He dedicated himself to restore political liberties.

Spain gave up its last large overseas colony on

QUICK QUIZ: What ended the War of the Roses? See page 286.

SPAIN *(continued)*

Feb. 26, 1976, turning over the 102,703-square-mile Spanish Sahara on the west coast of Africa to Morocco and Mauritania.

The parliament lifted Franco's ban on political parties in June 1976.

King Juan Carlos I dismissed Franco's last prime minister, Carlos Arias Navarro, on July 2, 1976, replacing him with Adolfo Suárez Gonzáles, head of the National Movement Party.

In 1977 Spain restored diplomatic relations with the Soviet Union for the first time since 1939.

The first free national election since the Spanish civil war was held on June 15, 1977, to elect a new two-house parliament to replace the unicameral *Cortes* of the Franco years. A coalition of center-right parties led by Prime Minister Suárez won the election.

A national referendum on Dec. 6, 1978, approved by a vote of 87.7% a new democratic constitution to replace the dictatorial "Fundamental Laws" of Generalissimo Franco. King Juan Carlos signed the constitution on Dec. 27, 1978, making Spain a parliamentary democracy with guarantees of human rights and free enterprise. It also removed the official status of Roman Catholicism, previously the state religion.

In the first election under the new constitution on March 1, 1979, Prime Minister Suárez's centrist party, the Union of the Democratic Center (UCD), won control of parliament.

SPAIN IN THE 1980s

Prime Minister Suárez resigned on Jan. 29, 1981. He was succeeded by Deputy Prime Minister Leopoldo Calvo Sotelo, a former industrialist.

Rightist army and national police officers attempted a coup on Feb. 23, 1981, as civil guards seized the parliament building, holding the members hostage. However, King Juan Carlos saved Spain's fledgling democracy by going on TV to denounce the rebels and to order the army to support the government. Three leaders of the revolt later were sentenced to 30 years in prison.

The Franco government's ban on divorce was lifted when parliament adopted a divorce law on June 22, 1981.

Ending its political and military isolation from the rest of western Europe, Spain formally joined the NATO military alliance on May 30, 1982.

Recession slowed Spain's industrial growth in 1981–83, bringing both unemployment and inflation to a rate of 15%. Farmers in southern Spain suffered the worst drought in a century.

Felipe González Márquez, 40, led his Socialist Party to an overwhelming victory in the election on Oct. 28, 1982. The socialists took a clear majority of 201 members in the 350-seat congress of deputies.

González, who had promised no sweeping changes, became prime minister on Dec. 2, 1982, forming the first socialist cabinet since the Spanish Civil War of 1936–39.

González' government seized control of Spain's largest multibillion-dollar corporation, Rumasa, on Feb. 24, 1983, and five months later indicted its chairman for fraudulent bookkeeping.

The socialists consolidated their position in local elections on May 8, 1983, winning most city and regional posts with about 42% of the votes.

Prime Minister González visited the U.S. in June 1983 for talks with President Reagan.

King Juan Carlos and Queen Sofia toured the Soviet Union on May 10–16, 1984, in the first such visit by a Spanish head of state.

Spain ended its 16-year blockade of the British colony of Gibraltar on Feb. 5, 1985, and began negotiations with Britain in an effort to restore Gibraltar to Spain.

Foreign ministers of the European Common Market nations agreed in 1985 to permit Spain and Portugal to join the organization on Jan. 1, 1986, increasing its membership to 12. Spanish leaders predicted that membership would expand the nation's economy.

SPANISH OVERSEAS AREAS

BALEARIC ISLANDS

Area: 1,936 square miles (5,014 sq. km.).
Population: 663,630.
Capital: Palma, 267,081.

The Balearic Islands *(Islas Baleares)* lie in the Mediterranean Sea off the east coast of Spain. The largest islands are Majorca *(Mallorca)*, 1,400 sq. mi.; Minorca *(Menorca)*, 266 sq. mi.; Ibiza *(Iviza)*, 209 sq. mi.; and Formentera, 32 sq. mi. The year-round warm climate makes the islands a popular tourist resort area.

Many Stone Age monuments built by prehistoric people dot the countryside of Majorca and Minorca. The islands were colonized by Phoenicians and Carthaginians. Fought over for centuries by contending powers, the islands came under the rule of Spanish kings in the 1200s. Limited local autonomy was granted on June 30, 1978.

CANARY ISLANDS

Area: 2,808 square miles (7,273 sq. km.).
Population: 1,353,680.
Capitals: Las Palmas de Gran Canaria, 328,187; Santa Cruz de Tenerife, 157,791.

The 13 Canary Islands lie off the northwest coast of Morocco in the Atlantic Ocean. The largest islands are Tenerife, 795 sq. mi.; Fuerteventura, 668 sq. mi.; and Grand Canary, 592 sq. mi. The islands have many mountains and volcanoes, the highest of which is snow-capped 12,198-foot Pico de Teide on Tenerife.

The warm subtropical climate of the Canaries attracts over a million tourists each year.

The islands received their name from the Latin word for dog, *canis*, because of the fierce dogs found there. Songbirds called canaries were first discovered in these islands by ancient Phoenician traders. The French explorer Jean de Béthencourt conquered the islands in 1402–04, making himself king. Spain gained sovereignty over the Canaries in 1479. The islands were divided into two provinces by Spain on Sept. 21, 1927.

CEUTA AND MELILLA

Area: 12 square miles (31 sq. km.).
Population: 176,211.

These two city enclaves stand on the Mediterranean coast of Morocco. Both are governed as parts of Spain. Ceuta was built on the site of a Phoenician colony and may have been the location of one of the ancient Pillars of Hercules. It was seized from the Arabs by Portugal in 1415 and passed into Spanish hands in 1580. Melilla has been Spanish since 1496. Morocco pressed claims for the cities in the 1970s–1980s.

SRI LANKA

Official Name: Democratic Socialist Republic of Sri Lanka.
Area: 25,332 square miles (65,610 sq. km.).
Population: 16,042,000.
Chief Cities: Colombo, capital, 585,776; Dehiwala–Mt. Lavinia, 174,385; Moratuwa, 136,610.
Government: Presidential-parliamentary democracy.
President: Junius Richard Jayewardene (since 1978).
Prime Minister: Ranasinghe Premadasa (since 1978).
Legislature: *National State Assembly,* 169 members.
U.S. Ambassador to Sri Lanka: John Hathaway Reed.
Sri Lanka Ambassador to U.S.: H.E. Ernest Corea.
Flag: Yellow border around maroon rectangle with bo leaves in each corner; yellow sword-carrying lion in center; green and orange bars at hoist.
Languages: Sinhalese (official), English, Tamil.
Main Ethnic Groups: Sinhalese (72%), Tamil (20%), Moors (7%), others (1%).
Principal Religions: Buddhism (67%), Hinduism (17%), Christianity (8%), Islam (7%).
Leading Industries: Agriculture (tea, rubber, coconuts, rice, cocoa, corn, spices, fruits, vegetables); forestry and lumbering; fishing; manufacturing (cement, textiles); mining (gems, salt, graphite).
Foreign Trade: *Major exports*—tea, rubber, coconut products; *major imports*—wheat, rice, food, fertilizer, machinery, textiles, petroleum products, sugar, flour, transportation equipment.
Places of Interest: Gal Oya Valley, Wilpattu, Ruhunu national parks; ruins at Anuradhapura and Polonnaruwa; Fortress in the Sky at Sigiriya; Buddhist Temple of the Tooth at Kandy; Bentota, Ambalangoda, Mt. Lavinia beach resorts. *In Colombo: Pettah (Old Town); Colombo Museum; Victoria Park.*

SRI LANKA TODAY

An island-nation about the size of West Virginia, Sri Lanka lies in the Indian Ocean only 18 miles off India's southern coast. Unlike many other developing nations, Sri Lanka has maintained a democratic government since gaining independence in 1948. Although the majority of people are poor, 9 out of 10 can read and write.

Sri Lanka has few natural resources. Because much of the land is used to raise tea, rubber, and coconuts for export, Sri Lanka does not grow enough food to feed its people.

Hostility between the island's two major ethnic groups, the Buddhist Sinhalese majority and the Hindu Tamil minority, repeatedly flares in violent riots and massacres.

The island's highest point is Pidurutalagala (8,281 feet), but most of Sri Lanka has elevations of 1,000 feet or less.

EARLY HISTORY

Formerly called *Ceylon,* Sri Lanka was settled in the 500s B.C. by Sinhalese from northern India, conquering the ancient Veddas. In 483 B.C. Vijaya, an Indian prince, established the first Sinhalese kingdom, with the capital at Anuradhapura. Buddhism was introduced in the 200s B.C.

Rajaraja I, ruler of the Tamil kingdom of Chola in southern India, extended his domain to Ceylon in the 1000s A.D. Polonnaruwa became the capital of Chola.

During the "Golden Age of Lanka" in the mid-1100s, the Sinhalese under King Prakrama Bahu I ruled the whole island.

The first Western conquerors were Portuguese, who began to introduce Christianity in 1505. They were followed by the Dutch in the 1600s. In 1796 the British took over. Britain conquered the last free Ceylonese kingdom, Kandy, in 1815.

In 1931 Ceylon became the first Asian country to extend voting rights to women.

INDEPENDENCE

On Feb. 4, 1948, Ceylon became independent as a British dominion. Don Stephen Senanayake, the first prime minister, was succeeded in 1952 by his son Dudley. In elections that year his United National Party (UNP) retained power.

The Sri Lanka Freedom Party (SLEP) won the 1956 elections. S.W.R.D. Bandaranaike, who became prime minister, was assassinated in 1959.

New elections held in 1960 made Bandaranaike's widow, Sirimavo Bandaranaike, the world's first woman prime minister.

From 1965 to 1970 Senanayake returned as prime minister of a pro-Western government.

Mrs. Bandaranaike again became prime minister in 1970, forming a leftist coalition government.

On May 22, 1972, the nation became a republic within the British Commonwealth of Nations.

J.R. Jayewardene, a 70-year-old Buddhist nicknamed "Yankee Dick" because of his pro-Western capitalist views, became prime minister in 1977. His UNP party had overwhelmingly defeated Mrs. Bandaranaike's leftist SLEP party in parliamentary elections on July 21.

Parliament amended the constitution in October 1977 to establish a strong presidential-parliamentary system similar to that of France. Jayewardene became president on Feb. 3, 1978. A new constitution was proclaimed on Sept. 7, 1978, strengthening the presidency.

The government began construction in March 1980 of the huge Victoria Reservoir on the Mahaweli River in the north-central part of the island. The hydroelectric project, which will help relieve the nation's dependence on imported petroleum, was financed in large part by about $250 million in aid from Britain.

The success of Jaywardene's private enterprise policies brought prosperity as the gross national product soared 25% from 1980 to 1981.

The 76-year old President Jayewardene was rewarded with a full six-year term in the nation's first presidential election on Oct. 20, 1982, receiving about 53% of the vote.

In the 1980s violence escalated between the Buddhist Sinhalese majority and the Hindu Tamils who sought establishment of an independent Tamil nation in northern Sri Lanka. Ambushes and massacres occurred almost daily, killing an estimated 2,500 persons in 1984 and hundreds more in the early months of 1985.

QUICK QUIZ: Where were muskets developed? See page 287.

SUDAN

Official Name: Democratic Republic of the Sudan.
Area: 967,500 square miles (2,505,813 sq. km.).
Population: 21,677,000.
Chief Cities: Khartoum, capital, 561,000; Omdurman, 454,000; Khartoum North, 249,000; Port Sudan, 205,000; Medani, 153,000.
Government: Military dictatorship.
Head of Government: Gen. Abdel Rahman Siwar el-Dahab (seized power in 1985).
Prime Minister: Dr. Al-Gazouly Dafallah (since 1985).
U.S. Ambassador to Sudan: Hume A. Horan.
Sudanese Ambassador to U.S.: Omer Salih Eissa.
Flag: Green triangle; red, white, and black stripes.
Official Language: Arabic.
Main Ethnic Groups: Arab (70%), black (23%).
Principal Religions: Islam (70%), animism (25%), Christianity (5%).
Leading Industries: Agriculture (livestock, cotton, sorghum, wheat, sesame, peanuts, castor beans, fruits, vegetables); food processing; mining (petroleum); manufacturing (textiles, handicrafts).
Foreign Trade: *Major exports*—cotton, sesame, peanuts; *major imports*—fertilizers, sugar, wheat, flour, machinery, petroleum, chemicals.
Places of Interest: Archaeological ruins along Nile; Nubian Desert; Dindar National Park.

SUDAN TODAY

About one-fourth the size of the United States, Sudan is the largest country in Africa. But it also is one of the 25 poorest countries. Although its major resource is soil, Sudan must import much of the food its people need.

New strains were put on the economy in 1978–85 as over 1.5 million refugees fled to Sudan from wars, revolutions and drought in Chad, Ethiopia, Uganda, and Zaire.

The nation has foreign debts of about $8 billion dollars and spends about $1 billion more on imports than it receives each year for exports.

Most Sudanese live by subsistence farming or by herding livestock. Only about 1 person in 10 can read and write.

The Nile River flows north through the Sudan plain. A rain forest in the south gives way to savanna grasslands in the central region and to a desert in the north.

Egypt lies to the north; the Red Sea and Ethiopia to the east; Kenya, Uganda, and Zaire to the south; and Central Africa, Chad, and Libya to the west.

EARLY HISTORY

Ancient Egypt established outposts in the Sudan from which developed the kingdom of Kush. In A.D. 350 Kush was destroyed by the Aksumites from Ethiopia. In the 500s Christian missionaries established states that coexisted with Muslim-Arab Egypt for over 600 years. By the 1300s Arabs had taken over Christian Nubia and settled in the Sudan, where they introduced Islam.

In 1820–21 troops of the Ottoman viceroy of Egypt, Mohammed Ali, imposed Turko-Egyptian rule over northern Sudan. Southern Sudan was conquered by Egypt in 1863–79.

The Sudanese revolted, under the leadership of Mohammed Ahmed, the Mahdi. His forces massacred a British army led by Gen. Charles Gordon at Khartoum on Jan. 26, 1885, and drove out the Egyptians. British Gen. Herbert Kitchener invaded the Sudan in 1898, ending Mahdist rule. From 1899 to 1956 Britain and Egypt controlled Sudan.

INDEPENDENCE

On Jan. 1, 1956, Sudan gained independence from Britain and Egypt as a republic. Two years later army officers seized control.

A popular revolution in 1964 reestablished civilian rule. The assembly elected in 1965 was controlled by Mohammed Ahmed Mahgoub.

In May 1969 the Mahgoub regime was ousted in a military coup. Maj. Gen. Gaafar Muhammed Nimeiri became president.

In October 1971 Nimeiri was elected president in a national referendum. He then dissolved the military revolutionary council and announced creation of a new political party, the Sudanese Socialist Union (SSU).

An uprising by blacks in the south against government Arabization policies raged from 1955 until a cease-fire was achieved in 1972. The civil war cost perhaps 500,000 lives.

In May 1977 Sudan expelled Soviet military advisers and turned to the U.S. for aid.

The first major oil find in Sudan was made in July 1979 at Abu Jabra by the American Chevron company, bringing in a 500-barrel-a-day well.

The government announced on March 16, 1981, it had thwarted the 15th attempted coup since Nimeiri took power. A general and several other military officers were arrested for the plot.

On March 22, 1981, Sudan broke ranks with other Arab nations to restore diplomatic relations with Egypt that had been severed in 1979.

Believing that the leader of Libya was involved in plotting to overthrow him, Nimeiri expelled all Libyan diplomats from Sudan on June 25, 1981.

Nimeiri was reelected without opposition to a third six-year term as president in April 1983.

Under an Islamic penal code adopted in September 1983, thieves are punished by having a hand chopped off. All alcoholic drinks are prohibited.

When moderate Muslims distributed pamphlets calling for a modern interpretation of Islamic law, including equality for women, their leader, 76-year-old Mahmoud Mohammed Taha was arrested. He was publicly hanged on Jan. 18, 1985.

As Sudan's economy deteriorated in 1985, the United States and other nations cut off economic aid in March in an effort to make Sudan adopt reforms to pay its foreign debts. When the government increased food and gasoline prices late in March, the action touched off riots and protest strikes in Khartoum.

Gen. Abdel Rahman Siwar el-Dahab, commander of the army, overthrew the government on April 6, 1985, while Nimeiri was in the United States seeking restoration of economic aid.

SURINAME

Official Name: Republic of Suriname.
Area: 63,037 square miles (163,265 sq. km.).
Population: 386,000.
Capital: Paramaribo, 150,000.
Government: Socialist-military state.
Head of Military Junta: Lt. Col. Desire Bouterse (since 1981).
Prime Minister: Wim Edenhout (since 1984).
U.S. Ambassador: Robert E. Barbour.
Suriname's Ambassador to U.S.: Donald A. McLeod.
Flag: Stripes of green, white, red, white, and green with yellow star centered on red stripe.
Languages: Dutch (official), English, Sranang Tongo.
Main Ethnic Groups: Asian Indian descent (37%), Creole (mixed black-European descent) (31%), Javanese descent (13%), Bush Negro (8%).
Principal Religions: Hinduism (26%), Islam (26%), Roman Catholicism (21%), Protestantism (18%).
Leading Industries: Mining (bauxite); agriculture (rice, bananas, coconuts, fruits, vegetables); manufacturing (aluminum, electricity, food processing, clothing); forestry and lumbering; fishing.
Foreign Trade: *Major exports*—bauxite, aluminum, alumina; *major imports*—food, machinery, petroleum, steel, cotton, grain, consumer goods.
Places of Interest: *In Paramaribo:* colonial buildings, oriental bazaars; swimming beaches; jungle villages; sport fishing and hunting; river canoeing.

SURINAME TODAY

Somewhat larger than the state of Georgia, Suriname is the smallest and newest of South America's independent nations.

The former Dutch colony's most important resource is bauxite, the ore from which aluminum is made. The country's rivers produce electricity to power aluminum-making plants.

Farms grow ample quantities of rice, the people's major food staple.

Most of Suriname's farms are along the northern coast at the mouths of the Suriname, Saramacca, Coppername, and Nickerie rivers. The center of the country is heavily forested. The southern three-fourths of the land is a hilly, largely uninhabited area that rises to 4,120 feet in the Wilhelmina Mountains.

The country has a hot tropical climate that averages 79° F. the year round. There are two rainy seasons—from November to February and from March through July.

Suriname lies on the northeast coast of South America. Guyana is to the west, Brazil to the south, and French Guiana to the east.

EARLY HISTORY

The first European settlement was established in 1651 by Lord Willoughby of England. He encouraged experienced colonists to emigrate from other settlements in the Americas. Among them were Portuguese Jews from Brazil, who built the first synagogue in the Western Hemisphere in 1665.

After the English captured New York from the Dutch, the Treaty of Breda was signed in 1667 by which the Dutch received Suriname in exchange for giving up claims to New York.

During the 1700s and early 1800s the colony, known as *Dutch Guiana*, changed hands several times but ended in possession of the Dutch by the Vienna treaty of 1815.

INDEPENDENCE

The Netherlands granted Suriname independence on Nov. 25, 1975.

On Nov. 1, 1977, Prime Minister Henck Arron's National Party Combination (NPK) won the first parliamentary election since independence.

An army coup overthrew Arron on Feb. 25, 1980. The military made Henk Chin A Sen, a civilian, prime minister.

In a second military coup, on Aug. 13, 1980, the sergeants who had headed the junta were arrested. The new junta named Chin A Sen as president.

Lt. Col. Desire Bouterse, head of the military junta, ousted Chin A Sen on Feb. 5, 1982.

Bouterse approved a new constitution on March 25, 1982, proclaiming Suriname a socialist state.

Fifteen prominent Surinamers were arrested by the military on Sunday morning Dec. 8, 1982, charged with plotting the overthrow of the military government. All were slain later in the day "while trying to escape."

Outraged by the incident, the Netherlands and the U.S. suspended economic aid to Suriname.

Faced with a growing government deficit because of lack of foreign aid, Bouterse's government announced tax increases to take effect Jan. 1, 1984. This triggered a four-week strike by 4,000 bauxite workers that forced Bouterse to cancel the tax increases.

A new prime minister, Wim Edenhout, took office in February 1984 with promises by Bouterse that some civil rights would be restored.

SWAZILAND

Official Name: Kingdom of Swaziland.
Area: 6,704 square miles (17,363 sq. km.).
Population: 651,500.
Capital: (administrative) Mbabane, 23,109; (traditional) Lobamba.
Government: Absolute monarchy.
Regent: Queen Mother Ntombi (since 1983).
Prime Minister: Prince Bhekimpi Dlamini (since 1983).
Crown Prince: Makhosetive (since 1983).
Parliament: 50 members.
U.S. Ambassador to Swaziland: Robert H. Phinny.
Swazi Ambassador to U.S.: Peter Helemisi Mtetwa.
Flag: Stripes of blue, yellow, red, yellow, and blue, with black and white Swazi shield of Emasotsha regiment.
Languages: siSwati and English (both official), Zulu.
Main Ethnic Groups: Swazi, Zulu.

QUICK QUIZ: What was the War of the Spanish Succession called in America? See page 288.

SWAZILAND *(continued)*

Religions: Christianity (60%), animism (40%).

Leading Industries: Agriculture (cattle, goats, poultry, sugarcane, rice, citrus fruits, cotton, maize, sorghum, tobacco, pineapples); forestry and lumbering; mining (iron, coal, asbestos); manufacturing (food processing, chemicals, machinery, consumer goods); tourism.

Foreign Trade: *Major exports*—iron ore, sugar, wood products, asbestos, coal, canned fruits; *major imports*—food, clothing, vehicles, machinery, petroleum.

Places of Interest: Mountain scenery in the west; hot springs at Mbabane; game preserves.

SWAZILAND TODAY

Once dependent on subsistence farming for its economy, Swaziland has become one of the most prosperous small nations of Africa. British and South African investors helped develop iron mines, sugar refineries, a pulp paper mill, and sugar, pineapple, and orange plantations. An east-west railroad also was built across the country to carry exports to the port of Maputo, Mozambique.

Called "the Switzerland of Africa," Swaziland attracts tourists each year to its gambling casinos, hotels, golf courses, and game preserves.

Despite efforts to develop a diversified economy, about three-fourths of Swaziland's people live by raising cattle and corn. Only about 1 Swazi in 3 can read and write.

Average temperatures range from 60 degrees F. in the mountainous west to 72 degrees F. in the subtropical lowlands in the east.

Somewhat larger than Connecticut, Swaziland is bordered on the north, west, and south by South Africa and on the east by Mozambique.

HISTORY

The Swazi settled in northern Zululand about 1750. They had their first formal relations with Britain in the 1840s when they sought help against the Zulus. Mineral rights were granted to the Europeans by the Swazi, and in 1894 South Africa assumed responsibility for the protection and administration of the country.

After the Boer War, Swaziland was administered by the British governor of the Transvaal. In 1907 a British resident commissioner was appointed. Sobhuza II became king in 1921.

Political parties were formed in the 1960s that demanded independence from British rule. In 1964 the first election was held in which the Swazi could vote. The king's political party, Imbokodvo, won all 24 seats in the national assembly.

Swaziland became independent on Sept. 6, 1968. King Sobhuza II in 1973 scrapped the constitution prepared by the British and took over absolute power. He outlawed political parties and political meetings.

The 83-year-old King Sobhuza died on Aug. 21, 1982, a year after celebrating the diamond jubilee of his rule. He was believed to have had as many as 100 wives and about 600 children. The king's senior wife, Dzewile, became regent.

The royal council of elders, called the Liqoqo, announced in August 1983 that 15-year-old Prince Makhosetive had been chosen to succeed as king when he reaches his majority. His mother, Queen Ntombi, replaced Queen Dzeliwe as regent, with the title Indlovukazi, or Great She-Elephant.

SWEDEN

Official Name: Kingdom of Sweden.

Area: 173,732 square miles (449,964 sq. km.).

Population: 8,339,000.

Chief Cities: Stockholm, capital, 647,219; Göteborg, 431,273; Malmö, 233,803; Uppsala, 146,192; Norrkoping, 119,238; Västerås, 117,487; Örebro, 116,969; Linköping, 112,600; Jönköping, 107,561.

Largest Metropolitan Area: Stockholm, 1,386,980.

Government: Parliamentary monarchy.

Prime Minister: Olaf Palme (since 1982).

King: Karl XVI Gustaf (since 1973).

Legislature: *Riksdag*, 349 members.

U.S. Ambassador to Sweden: Franklin S. Forsberg.

Swedish Ambassador to U.S.: Count Wilhelm Wachtmeister.

Flag: Light blue field with yellow cross.

Official Language: Swedish.

Main Ethnic Group: Swedes.

State Religion: Evangelical Lutheranism (95%).

Leading Industries: Trade and services; manufacturing (paper, electricity, steel, metal products, machinery, automobiles, aircraft, consumer goods); mining (iron, coal, copper, lead, zinc, manganese); agriculture (dairy products, cattle, hay, sugar beets, barley, oats, wheat, potatoes, fruits, vegetables); forestry; lumbering; fishing.

Foreign Trade: *Major exports*—machinery and transport equipment, manufactured goods, paper, wood pulp, wood, iron ore; *major imports*—machinery and transport equipment, manufactured goods, fuels.

Places of Interest: "Land of the Midnight Sun"—Lapland; Gotland Island; Lake Siljan; "The Crystal Land"—glassworks near Kalmar; Göta Canal; New Älvsborg Fortress in Göteborg. *In Stockholm:* Drottningholm Palace; Royal Warship Wasa Museum.

SWEDEN TODAY

About twice as large as Minnesota, Sweden has a higher standard of living than the United States and the world's longest life expectancy.

Sweden has one of the most extensive social-welfare programs in the world, paid with taxes that absorb about 70% of the national income.

The south has a temperate climate with about a two-month winter and four-month summer. The long, cold winter in the north lasts more than seven months.

Norway lies to the west and Finland to the northeast. Sweden's largest islands are Gotland and Oland in the Baltic Sea.

EARLY HISTORY

Tacitus, the Roman historian, first mentioned the Swedes (Suiones) about A.D. 100. In the 800s their semilegendary chieftain Rurik is said to have founded Russia. By the 900s Swedish influence extended south to the Black Sea. Warfare against Norsemen and Danes went on for centuries. In 1397 all the Scandinavian crowns were united under Queen Margrethe I of Denmark.

Sweden became an independent kingdom in 1523, when the Swedes elected Gustaf I as ruler. By

the time of its involvement in the Thirty Years War (1618–48), Sweden, under Gustaf II Adolf (1611–32), was the foremost Protestant power.

Sweden became a constitutional monarchy under Queen Ulrika Eleonora (1718–20).

Sweden warred with Napoleon I and lost Finland to Russia (1809). Napoleon's brilliant marshal Jean Baptiste Jules Bernadotte was elected by the *Riksdag* to succeed the childless Karl XIII. Bernadotte ascended the throne in 1818 as Karl XIV, founding the present Swedish dynasty.

The last war in Swedish history was fought in 1814, when Bernadotte enforced the Treaty of Kiel's award of Norway to Sweden. Norway remained in union with Sweden until 1905.

With neutrality as its foreign policy, Sweden kept out of both world wars.

The Social Democratic Party was dominant in 1932–76, except for a short period in 1936.

A coalition of opposition parties defeated the socialists after 44 years of rule in national elections on Sept. 19, 1976. Thorbjorn Falldin, head of the Center Party, became prime minister. Liberal leader Ola Ullsten became prime minister on Oct. 13, 1978, after Falldin's coalition collapsed.

After a national election in 1979, Falldin again became prime minister in October.

SWEDEN IN THE 1980s

In Sweden's first nationwide strike-lockout in 70 years, about 1 million workers were idled for 10 days on May 2–11, 1980. The dispute was settled with a 7% wage increase.

A nationwide referendum on March 23, 1980, decided 3 to 2 favor of an ambitious program to double the number of Sweden's nuclear electric generating plants to reduce oil imports.

By a 1-vote margin parliament adopted on Sept. 6, 1980, the highest value-added tax (sales tax) in Europe—a record 23.46%.

Socialist Olof Palme, 55, who previously had served as prime minister in 1969–76, was restored to the office on Oct. 7, 1982, two weeks after his Social Democratic Party won control of parliament in a general election.

A day after taking office, Palme ordered an economic austerity program, devaluing the krona 16% and establishing a general price freeze. He told the nation that taxes also had to be increased to meet the rising expenses of government.

After counting 40 violations of Swedish territorial waters in a year by what were believed to be Soviet submarines, the government recalled its ambassador to Moscow in protest in April 1983. Orders were issued to the Swedish navy to attack such intruders without warning.

Over 75,000 persons paraded through Stockholm on Oct. 5, 1983, in the largest political demonstration in the nation's history. They protested heavier taxes on business to be used to purchase stock in the businesses by labor unions. However, the government adopted the measures in December 1983.

In an effort to halt inflation, running at a rate of about 9%, the government in April 1984 froze prices and corporate dividend increases.

For results of September 1985 parliamentary election, see page 24.

SWITZERLAND

Official Name: Swiss Confederation.
Area: 15,941 square miles (41,288 sq. km.).
Population: 6,596,000.
Chief Cities: Bern, capital, 147,300; Zurich, 371,600; Basel, 183,000; Geneva, 147,300; Lausanne, 127,700.
Largest Metropolitan Area: Zurich, 709,300.
Government: Federal republic of 23 cantons.
Executive: *Federal Council,* 7 members elected by Federal Assembly. President chosen annually.
Federal Assembly: *Council of States,* 46 members; *National Council,* 200 members.
U.S. Ambassador to Switzerland: Faith Ryan Whittlesey.
Swiss Ambassador to U.S.: Klaus Jacobi.
Flag: White cross on red field.
Languages: German (65%), French (18%), Italian (12%), Romansch (1%), other (4%).
Main Religions: Roman Catholicism (49.4%), Protestantism (47.8%).
Leading Industries: Manufacturing (machinery, electrical equipment, watches, precision instruments, chocolate, cheese, chemicals, textiles, electricity, consumer products); tourism; banking, trade, and services; agriculture (dairy products, cattle, goats, hogs, sheep, sugar beets, grains, potatoes, grapes, fruits, vegetables); forestry and lumbering; mining (salt, building stone).
Foreign Trade: *Major exports*—watches, instruments, cheese, chocolate, textile machinery, organic chemicals, medical supplies, metalworking machine tools; *major imports*—iron and steel, automobiles, petroleum, clothing.
Places of Interest: Swiss National Park; Alps; Lake Lucerne; Interlaken, Gstaad, St. Moritz resorts; Rhone Valley. *In Zurich:* Grossmünster Cathedral; churches. *In Geneva:* Ariana Park, UN headquarters in Europe. *In Basel:* Art museum; 11th century cathedral. *In Bern:* Clock tower; the Bear Pit; town hall, Gothic cathedral and rose gardens. *In Lucerne:* Lion Monument; Wagner's home, Tribschen.

SWITZERLAND TODAY

About twice the size of New Jersey, Switzerland has enjoyed peace and neutrality for more than a century and a half. It is a leading center for banking and finance and a favorite meeting place for diplomats. Its people enjoy one of the world's highest standards of living.

About half the country's income comes from manufacturing. Most of the rest comes from service industries, particularly those accommodating the many tourists who visit Switzerland each year to enjoy the mountain scenery or take part in winter sports.

Lacking coal and oil to power an industrialized economy, the Swiss use their mountain rivers to provide electric power for factories.

Only about a fourth of the land can be used for crops, so much food must be imported.

In a $3 billion civil-defense program begun in 1962, underground nuclear shelters will be pro-

QUICK QUIZ: When did the Holy Roman Empire end? See page 289.

SWITZERLAND *(continued)*

vided for the entire population by the year 2000.

Swiss citizens have more of a voice in their laws than those of other countries, voting in national referendums up to four times each year to approve or reject proposed laws. A petition with only 50,000 signatures can force a referendum.

Switzerland is bordered on the north by West Germany, on the east by Austria and Liechtenstein, on the south by Italy, and on the west by France.

Two mountain systems cover most of the country—the Alps in the south and the Jura in the west and northwest. In the central Alps rise the Rhine, the Rhone, and the Ticino rivers. The highest peak is 15,203-foot Monte Rosa.

HISTORY

The Helvetians, who lived in the northern foothills of the Alps, were conquered by the Romans in 58 B.C. After A.D. 401, the area was dominated by a succession of rival neighbors.

In the 800s the area was part of the Empire of Charlemagne. As the Carolingian Empire fell into decay, the Hapsburg, Zähringer, and Savoy dynasties made encroachments.

In 1291 a defensive league against the Hapsburgs was formed by the cantons of Unterwalden, Uri, and Schwyz (from which the country takes its name). This marks the beginning of the *Swiss Confederation,* the nation's present official name.

By 1513 the confederation had grown to 13 largely autonomous cantons. The Treaty of Westphalia, which in 1648 ended the Thirty Years War, recognized Swiss independence.

In 1798 French revolutionary forces invaded Switzerland and formed the Helvetic Republic. Napoleon's Act of Mediation in 1803 restored the old confederation, but under French dominance.

NEUTRAL SWITZERLAND

In 1815 the Treaty of Paris and the Congress of Vienna guaranteed Switzerland's neutrality.

Switzerland's 23 cantons are governed today under a constitution adopted in 1874.

Since 1959 a coalition of four major parties has controlled the government.

In February 1971, Swiss women for the first time won the right to vote in federal elections.

In a national referendum on March 1, 1980, Swiss voters rejected by about 4 to 1 a proposal to sever ties between government and religion. The proposal would have ended the practice of supporting religious sects with government taxes.

By a 3–2 margin, Swiss voters on June 14, 1981, approved a constitutional amendment guaranteeing equal rights to women.

The Swiss government scheduled a referendum on joining the UN for the mid-1980's.

The government closed the Soviet Union's Novosti news agency in Bern on April 29, 1983, and expelled its bureau chief, charging the Soviets with infiltrating antinuclear peace groups.

In national elections on Oct. 23, 1983, the four-party governing coalition retained power. Communists lost two of their three seats.

Swiss voters in May 1984 turned down 3–1 a proposal to end the secrecy of Swiss bank accounts.

Pope John Paul II made a six-day tour of Switzerland in June—the first papal visit in more than 500 years.

SYRIA

Official Name: Syrian Arab Republic.
Area: 71,498 square miles (185,180 sq. km.).
Population: 10,422,000.
Chief Cities: Damascus, capital, 1,251,028; Aleppo, 976,727; Homs, 354,508; Lattakia, 196,791; Hama, 176,640.
Government: Republic.
President: Hafiz al-Assad (since 1971).
Prime Minister: Abdul Rauf al-Kasm (since 1980).
Legislature: *People's Council,* 173 members.
U.S. Ambassador to Syria: William L. Eagleton Jr.
Syrian Ambassador to U.S.: Dr. Rafic Jouejati.
Flag: Red, white, and black stripes, with two green stars in center stripe.
Languages: Arabic (official), Armenian, Kurdish, French, English.
Ethnic Groups: Arab (90%), Kurd, Armenian, Turkmen, Circassian.
Main Religions: Islam (86%), Christianity (13%).
Leading Industries: Agriculture (livestock, cotton, wheat, barley, sugar beets, fruits, vegetables); mining (petroleum, phosphates); construction; manufacturing (textiles, cement, ceramics, food processing, oil refining, electricity); trade and services; tourism.
Foreign Trade: *Major exports*—cotton, barley, wool, wheat; *major imports*—iron and steel, machinery, petroleum products, weapons.
Places of Interest: Palmyra monuments; Krak des Chevaliers (Crusaders Castle) in Homs district; Aleppo; waterwheels at Hama. *In Damascus:* Omayyad Mosque; Azem Palace; Hamidieh Bazaar; biblical street called Straight.

SYRIA TODAY

A militant Arab state, Syria has taken part in five wars with its neighbor Israel. Its leaders refuse to negotiate peace until Israel gives back all territory it won in those wars.

Syria's socialist government has nationalized most industry and expropriated and redistributed most large landholdings. The country is dependent on more than $1 billion a year in aid from wealthy Arab oil countries. It also is supplied with arms by the Soviet Union.

Western Syria consists of a narrow Mediterranean coastal plain and the Alawite and Anti-Lebanon mountains and plateau. A fertile region in the north gives way to a central steppe area and a desert region in the south. The main rivers are the Euphrates, Khabur, and Barada.

Somewhat larger than North Dakota, Syria lies at the eastern end of the Mediterranean Sea. Turkey is on the north, Iraq on the east and southeast, Jordan on the south, Israel on the southwest, and Lebanon on the west.

EARLY HISTORY

Ancient Syria was the home of the Amorites, Canaanites, Phoenicians, and Hebrews. It was conquered by several waves of foreign invaders— Aramaeans, Assyrians, Babylonians, and Persians. Syria was unified after its conquest by Alexander

the Great in 332 B.C. It passed to the Romans in 63 B.C. and to the Byzantines in A.D. 395.

In the 600s Syria fell to the Arabs, who introduced the Arabic language and culture. From 661 to 750, under the Damascus caliphate of the Omayyads, Syria controlled a vast Islamic domain.

From 1516 to World War I Syria was part of the Ottoman Turkish Empire.

From 1920 to 1946 France controlled Syria as a League of Nations mandate.

INDEPENDENCE

Syria gained independence as a republic on April 17, 1946.

From 1958 to 1961 Syria was part of the United Arab Republic (Egypt and Syria) under the presidency of Egypt's President Nasser.

Syrian troops participated in four Arab-Israeli wars (1948, 1956, 1967, 1973).

A military coup in February 1968 installed Nureddin al-Attassi as head of state. His regime received substantial military equipment from the Soviet Union. In November 1970, however, he was ousted by rightist military officers, who made Hafiz al-Assad president in 1971.

In 1972 Syria nationalized all properties of the Western-owned Iraq Petroleum Company.

Syria joined Egypt in attacking Israel in October 1973. After the UN-ordered cease-fire on October 24, artillery duels and border clashes between Syria and Israel continued into 1974. Finally, on May 31, 1974, Syria signed a U.S.-negotiated pact with Israel for mutual withdrawal of their armed forces.

In 1974 the U.S. and Syria resumed diplomatic relations, broken since 1967.

Syria sent troops and tanks into Lebanon on May 31, 1976 to police that country's warring factions.

Syria and Iraq broke diplomatic relations in August 1980 after Iraq expelled Syrian diplomats for stocking their Baghdad embassy with arms. When war broke out between Iraq and Iran later in the year, Syria aided Iran.

On Oct. 8, 1980, Syria and the Soviet Union signed a 20-year military and economic treaty.

Muslim fanatics seeking to overthrow Assad waged a campaign of terrorism in 1978–82.

When the radical Muslim Brotherhood began a revolt in the city of Hama in February 1982, government troops stormed the city. An estimated 6,000 persons were killed. Bulldozers were used to level entire neighborhoods.

The Syrian army in Lebanon lost huge amounts of Soviet-supplied arms to the Israelis who invaded that country in 1982.

Syria refused requests by Lebanon in 1983 that it withdraw its troops.

The Soviet Union in 1983 sent 5,000 troops to aid Syria with SS21 missiles capable of devastating Israel's cities.

Syria was regarded as having won a major victory when U.S. and other members of an international peacekeeping force withdrew from Lebanon in 1984, leaving Syria's army as the major force in that strife-torn country.

President Assad, 54, won a third 7-year term in an election in February 1985 in which he was the only candidate.

QUICK QUIZ: When did the Suez Canal open? See page 290.

TAIWAN

Official Name: Republic of China.
Area: 12,456 square miles (32,260 sq. km.).
Population: 19,607,000.
Chief Cities: Taipei, capital, 1,769,568; Kaohsiung, 1,000,000; Taichung, 575,000; Tainan, 550,000.
Government: One-party parliamentary republic.
President: Chiang Ching-kuo (took office in 1978).
Prime Minister: Yu Kuo-hwa (since 1984).
Legislature: National Assembly, 1,064 members.
Flag: Red field bearing blue rectangle, upper left, that contains 12-pointed white sun.
Languages: Chinese (Peking dialect; official), English, Japanese, Hokkien, Hakka.
Ethnic Groups: Han Chinese, 98% (Taiwanese 80%, mainlanders 18%), aborigines (2%).
Religions: Confucianism, Taoism, Buddhism, Christianity.
Leading Industries: Manufacturing (electronics, textiles, chemicals, fertilizer, cement, glass, plastics, aircraft); agriculture (poultry, hogs, rice, sugarcane, tea, fruits, vegetables); forestry and lumbering; tourism; fishing; mining (coal, natural gas, sulfur).
Foreign Trade: *Major exports*—textiles, electronic equipment, plywood, canned food; *major imports*—machinery, iron and steel, raw cotton, soybeans, motor vehicles, wheat, petroleum.
Places of Interest: Sun-Moon Lake; Fo Kuang Mountain temple; Taroko Gorge. *In Taipei:* national palace museum; botanical gardens; temples; Grass Mountain resort area; 75th Buddha, near Changhua. *In Tainan:* forts and temples.

TAIWAN TODAY

About twice the size of Hawaii, Taiwan has achieved a strong and prosperous economy in the more than three decades since the government of nationalist China retreated to the island. Its people enjoy one of the highest standards of living in the Far East.

With a variety of major public works and industrial projects under way, the government hopes to move from the status of a developing nation to that of a developed nation. Projects include improved port facilities, railroad and highway construction, airport development, and the building of a steel mill, shipyards, and petrochemical plants.

Tourism is a major industry with about 1.5 million visitors each year.

While Taiwan's economy has grown, its influence in world politics has diminished because of the insistence of its leaders that it represents the legal government of mainland China. As a result many nations, including the U.S., officially have broken diplomatic relations with Taiwan, and it has lost its seat in the UN. But most of these nations continue to trade with Taiwan. The U.S. sells more than half a billion dollars of arms to Taiwan each year.

The authoritarian government controls communication with strict censorship and prevents

TAIWAN *(continued)*

expression of political opposition.

Taiwan (formerly called *Formosa*) is an island about 100 miles from the China mainland. It measures some 240 miles north to south, and 85 miles at its greatest width.

The Pescadores (Penghu Islands), an island group belonging to Taiwan, lie about 25 miles from the southwest coast. Matsu and Quemoy (Kinmen), two small island groups controlled by Taiwan, are just off the mainland coast.

Mountains cover about two-thirds of Taiwan. Their eastern slope is rugged and sparsely settled, while the western slope is fertile and has one of the world's greatest population densities. The highest mountain, Yü Shan, rises to 13,110 feet.

The U.S. government has emphasized that it does not intend to build up Taiwan's armies for an invasion of communist-governed mainland China.

HISTORY OF TAIWAN

Chinese immigration to Taiwan began as early as the T'ang dynasty (618–907). In 1628 Dutch forces defeated Spaniards for control of Taiwan. After the Manchu conquest of the island in 1683, Taiwan was administered as part of China. In 1895 it was ceded to Japan following the Sino-Japanese War. Uprisings continued for decades.

After World War II, Japan surrendered Taiwan to China in 1945. Later, Japan renounced all claims to Taiwan in 1951.

In 1949 the advancing communist forces of Mao Tse-tung forced President Chiang Kai-shek's nationalist government to flee from the mainland to Taiwan. Communist China's plans to invade the island were blocked in 1950 when President Harry S. Truman sent the U.S. Seventh Fleet to patrol Taiwan Strait.

The U.S. signed an agreement in 1955 to defend Taiwan and the Pescadores from any attack by Communist China.

In October 1971 the UN General Assembly with U.S. support voted for Red China's admission but, despite U.S. objections, expelled Taiwan. President Nixon declared that U.S.-Taiwan alliances would be maintained.

In 1972, at the age of 85, Chiang Kai-shek turned over the running of the government to his eldest son, Chiang Ching-kuo, as premier.

After Chiang Kai-shek died in 1975, Premier Chiang became head of the ruling Nationalist Party (Kuomintang). The 65-year-old Chiang was elected president without opposition by the national assembly on March 21, 1978. Two months later he was sworn into the office that had been held by his father for three decades. He was reelected to a second 6-year term on March 21, 1984.

To extend diplomatic recognition to China, the U.S. ended formal relations with Taiwan on Jan. 1, 1979. President Carter also abrogated the 1955 mutual defense pact with Taiwan, effective Dec. 31, 1979. However, the U.S. continued to maintain unofficial diplomatic relations.

In an effort to strengthen relations with China, President Reagan agreed on Aug. 17, 1982, to "gradually reduce" U.S. arms sales to Taiwan in return for China's assurance that it would not use military force to take Taiwan.

TANZANIA

Official Name: United Republic of Tanzania.
Area: 364,900 square miles (945,087 sq. km.).
Population: 22,054,000.
Capital: Official capital, Dodoma, 60,000; actual capital, Dar es Salaam, 757,346.
Government: One-party socialist republic.
President: Julius Kambarage Nyerere (since 1961).
Prime Minister: Salim Ahmed Salim (since 1984).
Legislature: *National Assembly* (mainland), 219 members; House of Representatives (Zanzibar), 40 members.
U.S. Ambassador to Tanzania: John W. Shirley.
Tanzanian Ambassador to U.S.: Asterius M. Hyera.
Flag: Green triangle (upper left) and blue triangle (lower right) separated by diagonal gold-bordered black stripe.
Languages: Swahili (official), English.
Main Ethnic Group: Black.
Principal Religions: Islam (35%), Christianity (35%); animism (30%).
Leading Industries: Agriculture (livestock, cotton, coffee, sisal, cloves, coconuts, tea, tobacco, cashews, sugarcane); mining (diamonds, gold, tin, gemstones); manufacturing (food processing, oil refining, textiles, cement, consumer goods); tourism.
Foreign Trade: *Major exports*—cotton, coffee, sisal, diamonds, cloves; *major imports*—corn, machinery, transport equipment, steel, crude petroleum.
Places of Interest: Mt. Kilimanjaro; Ngorongoro Crater; nine national parks; five game preserves; Olduvai Gorge; Amboni Caves; Pemba and Mafia islands; Dar es Salaam; former sultan's palace, Zanzibar.

TANZANIA TODAY

Although more than twice as large as California, Tanzania is one of the poorest African nations. It is a federation of a mainland area formerly called Tanganyika and the island of Zanzibar.

Tanzania is one of the world's leading diamond-mining nations. But its economy is largely based on agriculture.

Most Tanzanians scratch out a bare living, raising corn, beans, and cassava. About two-thirds can read and write.

Mainland Tanzania is largely an infertile plateau, 1,000 to 4,000 feet high, bisected from north to south by the Great Rift Valley. On the more fertile margins of the plateau are Lakes Victoria, Tanganyika, and Malawi. Mt. Kilimanjaro (19,340 feet), the highest mountain in Africa, is in the northeast.

Tanzania is bordered on the south by Zambia, Malawi, and Mozambique; on the west by Rwanda, Burundi, and Zaire; and on the north by Kenya and Uganda.

EARLY HISTORY OF TANZANIA

Archaeological discoveries at Olduvai Gorge indicate that manlike creatures lived in the area 3 million years ago. Ancient Greek mariners called the coast *Azania*.

Zanzibar and various coastal cities, especially

Kilwa, were colonized from the Persian Gulf area, probably in the 700s. A series of autonomous Muslim city-states flourished with a Swahili language and culture.

In the 1500s the Portuguese destroyed the Muslim city-states and then controlled the coast until ousted by Arabs from Oman in the 1700s.

European colonization led to establishment in 1890 of a British protectorate in Zanzibar and to German colonization of Tanganyika, as the mainland area was called. German control ended after World War I when Britain took over Tanganyika under a League of Nations mandate.

INDEPENDENCE

The Tanganyika African National Union (TANU), headed by Julius Nyerere, led Tanganyika to independence on Dec. 9, 1961. Zanzibar became independent in December 1963.

On April 26, 1964, Tanganyika and Zanzibar united with Nyerere as president. The new country was named the *United Republic of Tanzania* in October 1964.

The socialist government nationalized clove plantations in Zanzibar in 1964 and took over many major companies in 1967 and 1968.

Nyerere was unopposed in reelections in 1970, 1975, and 1980.

With massive economic and technical aid from China, a 1,162-mile railroad was built in 1970–76 from Dar es Salaam to Kapiri Mposhi, Zambia.

Centrally located Dodoma has been named the official capital, but few government offices have been transferred there from Dar es Salaam pending completion of a $550 million construction program by 1985.

President Nyerere reported that by mid-1975 over 9 million Tanzanians had been moved into more than 6,900 socialist collective villages. The government in 1976 moved thousands of unemployed from Dar es Salaam to the countryside.

President Nyerere uses the Swahili word *ujamaa,* meaning "familyhood," to describe the village socialism he fosters. He explains that familyhood calls for sharing.

Full-scale war began in 1978 after Ugandan President Idi Amin announced on Nov. 1 that his troops had annexed 710 square miles of Tanzanian territory. Tanzania fought back, invaded Uganda, and drove Amin into exile, capturing Uganda's capital on April 11, 1979. Victorious Tanzanian troops began withdrawing from Uganda in July 1979. Tanzania's economy suffered because of the estimated $500 million cost of the war.

Zanzibar was granted autonomy in 1979 with a separate constitution. In the first Zanzibar election since 1964, its people chose a 40-member House of Representatives on Jan. 7, 1980, from among 80 candidates nominated by the only political party, Chama Cha Mapinduzi (CCM). Ali Hassan Mwinyi was elected president of Zanzibar on April 19, 1984.

Hard hit by drought in 1980–84, Tanzania appealed for aid to prevent starvation. The U.S. and other nations responded with grain shipments.

President Nyerere announced that he would retire from office at the end of 1985.

QUICK QUIZ: When was the Boxer War in China? See page 291.

THAILAND

Official Name: Kingdom of Thailand.
Area: 198,457 square miles (514,000 sq. km.).
Population: 53,396,000.
Chief Cities: Bangkok, capital, 3,077,361; Thonburi, 627,989.
Government: Monarchy controlled by military.
King: Phumiphon Adunyadet (reigned since 1950).
Prime Minister: Prem Tinsulanonda (since 1980).
Parliament: *House of Representatives,* 324 elected members; *Senate,* 225 appointed members.
U.S. Ambassador to Thailand: William Andreas Brown.
Thailand Ambassador to U.S.: Kasem S. Kasemsri.
Flag: From top to bottom, five stripes: red, white, blue (double width), white, and red.
Official Language: Thai.
Main Ethnic Groups: Thai (75%), Chinese (14%).
Principal Religions: Buddhism (96%), Islam (4%).
Leading Industries: Agriculture (rice, corn, sugarcane, rubber, cotton, livestock, poultry); mining (tin, gems, tungsten); forestry and lumbering; fishing; manufacturing (food processing, cement, paper).
Foreign Trade: *Major exports*—rice, corn, rubber, tin, tapioca products, kenaf; *major imports*—machinery, textiles, petroleum.
Places of Interest: Chiangmai; Ayutthaya palaces and temples; Lop Buri ruins; old city of Nakhon Pathom. *In Bangkok:* Grand Palace; Emerald Buddha Temple; Temple of Dawn; rose garden; floating market.

THAILAND TODAY

Larger than California, Thailand is a noncommunist country in Southeast Asia. The word *Thai* means "free," and the Thais, unlike their neighbors, have maintained independence from both European colonialism and communist expansion.

Thailand is one of the world's leading producers of natural rubber and tin. The Thai government has done little to foster the development of industry or manufacturing. The economy depends on rice farming and U.S. aid.

The country has four main regions. The north is a forest highland area. A series of mountain ranges in the northwest rise to more than 8,500 feet in Inthanon Peak. The central plains are a fertile lowland with silt accumulations from the Chao Phraya River, which flows into the Gulf of Siam. The most fertile region is the Bangkok Delta, known as the rice basket or heartland of the country. To the northeast rises a dry upland area, ending at the Mekong River on the border with Laos. Peninsular Thailand, reaching to Malaysia, is a mountainous ridge.

Laos lies to the east, Cambodia and Malaysia to the south, and Burma to the west.

EARLY HISTORY OF THAILAND

Archaeological discoveries indicate that an early civilization developed in the 4000s B.C. in Thailand. By 3600 B.C. it had become the first culture in history to use bronze.

THAILAND *(continued)*

But the ancestors of the present-day Thai people, who lived in what is now China's Yunnan province, only began migrating to the region about 1,000 years ago. They established a kingdom at Sukhothai in the 1200s.

The Thai capital was moved in the 1300s to Ayutthaya on the Chao Phraya River north of present-day Bangkok.

In 1782 the Chakkri dynasty was established with its capital at Bangkok. That dynasty has continued to reign to the present time.

Modernization began under the enlightened rule of King Mongkut (Rama IV, 1851–68) and his son Chulalongkorn (Rama V, 1868–1910), who abolished slavery. The Western powers acquired extensive extraterritorial privileges, which they retained until 1937.

CONSTITUTIONAL MONARCHY

In 1932 a coup by young radicals forced King Prajadipok (Rama VII, 1925–35), to give up his absolute powers and accept a constitution.

During World War II Japan occupied Thailand. After the war King Phumiphon Adunyadet (Rama IX) became ruler in 1946 while still a student in Switzerland. He returned to Thailand in 1950.

A military coup brought Field Marshal Sarit Thanarat to power in 1957. Upon Sarit's death in 1963, Lt. Gen. Thanom Kittikachorn became premier.

During the Vietnam War, the U.S. built some 93 military installations including a dozen air bases from which B-52s bombed communist forces in Cambodia, Laos, and Vietnam. Some 48,000 U.S. servicemen were stationed in Thailand. Subsidized with $50 million a year by the U.S., Thailand sent 11,000 troops to fight in Vietnam from 1968 to 1972.

In October 1973, college students led mobs that overthrew Thanom. A democratic constitution was adopted on Oct. 7, 1974. Free national elections were held on Jan. 26, 1975.

Kukrit Pramoj became premier on March 13, 1975. He immediately called on the U.S. to withdraw its remaining military personnel.

After communists took over Cambodia, Laos, and South Vietnam in 1975, hundreds of thousands of refugees fled to Thailand.

In elections on April 4, 1976, Kukrit Pramoj lost his seat in parliament. His 71-year-old brother Seni Pramoj became prime minister.

A right-wing military junta led by Defense Minister Adm. Sa-ngad Chaloryu seized power on Oct. 6, 1976.

The junta chose a civilian judge, Thanin Kraivichien, as prime minister on Oct. 8, 1976.

Gen. Kriangsak Chamanand led a bloodless coup on Oct. 20, 1977, that overthrew Prime Minister Thanin. Kriangsak became prime minister on Nov. 11, 1977.

A new constitution adopted in December 1978 ensured continued control by the military.

In the first national election under the new constitution on April 22, 1979, the Social Action Party of former prime minister Kukrit Pramoj won the largest number of elected seats in parliament. However, Prime Minister Kriangsak remained in power.

THAILAND IN THE 1980s

Soaring oil prices brought antigovernment demonstrations in Bangkok in 1980, causing Kriangsak to resign as prime minister on Feb. 29.

Gen. Prem Tinsulanonda, 59, succeeded Kriangsak.

In what became known as the "April Fool's coup," army generals seized control of Bangkok on April 1–3, 1981, in an attempt to overthrow Prime Minister Prem. However, the royal family fled from the capital with Prem and broadcast appeals in his behalf. The rebel officers then surrendered and later were pardoned.

Thousands of industrial workers were dismissed from their jobs when the government established a $2.75 per hour minimum wage on Oct. 1, 1981.

A 265-mile undersea pipeline was completed in 1981, bringing to the mainland natural gas from large deposits discovered in the Gulf of Thailand.

In a parliamentary election on April 18, 1983, none of the 15 political parties won a majority. Prem remained prime minister, heading a coalition cabinet.

The government reported in 1983 that it was helping care for over 350,000 refugees from Cambodia, Laos, and Vietnam. An appeal was issued to Western nations to let more of the refugees immigrate from Thailand.

Since Vietnamese troops invaded Cambodia in 1978, border fighting has repeatedly broken out between Thai forces and Vietnamese units that have pursued Cambodian guerrillas seeking refuge in Thailand.

The nation's five-year plan for 1981–86 calls for the development of iron and steel mills and other heavy industry fueled by natural gas.

TOGO

Official Name: Republic of Togo.
Area: 21,925 square miles (56,785 sq. km.).
Population: 2,996,000.
Capital: Lomé, 148,156.
Government: One-party dictatorship.
President: Gen. Gnassingbe Eyadema (since 1967).
U.S. Ambassador to Togo: Owen W. Roberts.
Togo Ambassador to U.S.: Ellom-Kodjo Schuppius.
Parliament: General Assembly.
Flag: Green and yellow stripes, with white star centered in red square at upper hoist corner.
Languages: French (official), tribal dialects.
Main Ethnic Groups: Hamitic and Bantu tribes.
Religions: Animism (60%), Christianity (20%), Islam (20%).
Leading Industries: Agriculture (cocoa, coffee, palm kernels, corn, peanuts, cotton, manioc, millet, sorghum, livestock, fruits, vegetables); mining (phosphates); manufacturing (textiles, food processing, construction materials); fishing.
Foreign Trade: *Major exports*—phosphates, cocoa, coffee, palm nuts, cotton, peanuts, fish, manioc flour and starch; *major imports*—manufactured goods,

machinery, transport equipment, food, cotton fabrics, tobacco.

Places of Interest: Togo Mountains; native villages; Lomé.

TOGO TODAY

Togo is a hot tropical country of West Africa, about the size of West Virginia. Its most important resource, other than its farmland, is a huge deposit of phosphates. Otherwise the country's economy depends mostly on subsistence farming and fishing.

To balance the annual budget, the government counts on foreign aid each year.

The people are poor. Most struggle for their existence by raising food on plots of land owned in common by several families. Some work on large plantations that grow coffee for export. Few children go to school. The hard life of the people of Togo results in one of the lowest life-expectancy rates in the world, with the average Togolese living only to the age of 40.

The government has endeavored to diversify the economy with the construction of roads, hotels, and industrial plants.

Togo is a narrow country about 75 miles wide and 360 long. Burkina Faso lies on the north, Dahomey on the east, and Ghana on the west.

Because of coastal sandbars and lagoons, there is no good harbor. Inland the terrain is hilly and mountainous.

HISTORY OF TOGO

As a nation Togo has little precolonial history. The colony of Togoland, created by Germany in 1885, consisted of today's Togo in the east and part of present-day Ghana in the west.

In 1922 the League of Nations divided Togoland into French and British mandates, with Togo going to the French.

The United Nations assumed trusteeship of the territory in 1946. In a 1956 plebiscite the Togolese voted 3 to 1 for autonomy, and in April 1960 Togo became an independent state.

Sylvanus Olympio, a man of great ability, was president of Togo until his assassination in the military coup of 1963. His successor was Nicolas Grunitzky, appointed by the military.

In January 1967 Grunitzky was ousted by Gen. Gnassingbe Eyadema, who became president on April 14.

To get a larger share of the profits from the mining of phosphate, the government nationalized the phosphate industry on Feb. 4, 1975.

The government began an active campaign in 1976–77 to obtain the 11,200-square-mile area of the former colony of British Togoland, which was absorbed by Ghana in 1957.

As head of the only political party, the Togolese People's Rally, Eyadema was reelected to a 7-year term on Dec. 30, 1979. A one-party general assembly also was elected.

In 1980 Amnesty International protested Eyadema's imprisonment without trial of opponents.

To lure more tourists, Togo in May 1981 became the first African country to eliminate visa requirements for U.S. and Canadian visitors.

Falling commodity prices caused severe governmental finance problems in the 1980s.

QUICK QUIZ: When did Mussolini become dictator of Italy? See page 292.

TONGA

Official Name: Kingdom of Tonga.
Area: 270 square miles (699 sq. km.).
Population: 108,700.
Capital: Nuku'alofa, 18,312.
Government: Constitutional monarchy.
King: Taufa'ahau Tupou IV (reigned since 1965).
Prime Minister: Prince Tu'ipelehake (since 1965).
Legislative Assembly: 23 members.
Tonga Ambassador to U.S.: Sonatana Tu'a Taumoepeau-Tupou.
U.S. Ambassador to Tonga: Carl E. Dillery.
Flag: Red field with red cross on white square in upper hoist corner.
Language: Tongan (official), English.
Main Ethnic Group: Tongan (98%).
Religions: Methodism (60%), Mormonism (20%), other Christian denominations (20%).
Leading Industries: Agriculture (bananas, coconuts, fruits, vegetables); fishing; food processing.
Foreign Trade: *Major exports*—bananas, coconut products; *major imports*— textiles, food, timber, steel.
Places of Interest: Royal palace and chapel; terraced tombs; blow holes; sacred flying foxes; Nuku'alofa; five undersea marine national parks; national parks and game preserves on the islands of Eua and Pelehake.

The South Pacific island kingdom of Tonga has a land area about equal to the city of Dallas, Texas, but only about one-eighth as many people. Two-thirds of Tonga's people live on the largest island, Tongatapu, which covers about 99 square miles.

The government owns all the land. But each man, upon reaching the age of 16, is entitled to rent an *api* of 8.25 acres for farming and a village plot of 0.375 acre on which to build a house. Most Tongans live by raising tropical fruits and vegetables and catching fish to feed their families.

An archipelago of 150 islands and islets, Tonga lies east of Fiji and south of Western Samoa. The islands stretch across about 500 miles of ocean from north to south.

Tonga's hereditary monarchs date at least from the 1000s A.D. In the 1200s the power of the Tonga monarchy extended as far as Hawaii.

One of the islands was discovered by the Dutch in 1616, and others by Capt. James Cook in 1773 and 1777. Cook called them the Friendly Islands because of their good-natured inhabitants.

The famous mutiny aboard the British ship *Bounty* took place in 1789 in waters off Tonga.

British missionaries arrived in 1797.

The present dynasty was founded by the Christian king George Tupou I in 1845.

A British protectorate was proclaimed in 1900.

On June 4, 1970, Tonga was granted independence with membership in the British Commonwealth of Nations.

A hurricane and tidal wave on March 3, 1982, destroyed many villages, killing six persons, and leaving thousands homeless.

TRANSKEI

TRINIDAD-TOBAGO

Official Name: Republic of Transkei.
Area: 16,070 square miles (41,620 sq. km).
Population: 3,008,500.
Capital: Umtata, 30,000.
Government: Parliamentary republic.
Prime Minister: Chief George Matanzima (since 1979).
President: Chief Kaiser Matanzima (since 1979).
Flag: Stripes of red (top), white, and green (bottom).
National Assembly: *The Bunga,* 150 members (75 tribal chiefs and 75 elected members).
Chief Languages: Xhosa (official), English, Afrikaans, Sesotho.
Principal Ethnic Group: Xhosa-speaking Bantus.
Main Religions: Methodist (60%), animism (40%).
Leading Industries: Agriculture (cattle, sheep, corn, tea, coffee, nuts); manufacturing (electricity, food processing, textiles); fishing; forestry; tourism.
Foreign Trade: *Major exports*—livestock, meat products, wool, hides; *major imports*—petroleum products, consumer goods, vehicles, machinery.
Places of Interest: Wild Coast nature area between Kei and Umtamvuna rivers; Magwa Falls; beaches; Execution Rock between Umtata and Port St. Johns; weaving factories in Umtata.

A poor south African nation about twice the size of New Jersey, Transkei is completely dependent on South Africa. It has a 168-mile coastline on the Indian Ocean, with a harbor at Port St. Johns.

The small capital city of Umtata boasts a twin-tower 14-story government building. But most of the people live in tribal villages.

Cattle and corn are the main products. When in need of cash money, the men go to South Africa to work in the mines. Polygamy is legal.

The climate is mild. Winters are cool and dry with an occasional frost. Summers are warm to hot with about 25 inches of rain.

South Africa borders Transkei on the west and the northeast. Lesotho lies to the north.

Britain annexed the region in 1872–94.

South Africa gave Transkei independence as a republic on Oct. 26, 1976. Chief Kaiser Matanzima, head of the Transkei National Independence Party, became the first prime minister.

With Transkei's independence, 1.5 million Xhosa tribesmen living outside Transkei automatically lost their South African citizenship and became citizens of Transkei. Other nations refused to grant Transkei diplomatic recognition, claiming it was a puppet of South Africa.

Chief Botha Sigcau, the country's president since 1976, died on Dec. 1, 1978. Chief Kaiser Matanzima gave up the office of prime minister in February 1979 to accept election as president. He appointed his brother, George Matanzima, as prime minister.

In an effort to demonstrate Transkei's sovereignty, Chief Matanzima broke diplomatic relations with South Africa on April 10, 1978. Relations were restored on Feb. 7, 1980.

Official Name: Republic of Trinidad and Tobago.
Area: 1,981 square miles (5,130 sq. km.).
Population: 1,225,000.
Capital: Port of Spain, 11,032.
Government: Parliamentary republic.
Prime Minister: George M. Chambers (since 1981).
President: Sir Ellis Clarke (since 1976).
Parliament: *Senate,* 31 appointed members; *House of Representatives,* 36 elected members.
U.S. Ambassador to Trinidad-Tobago: Sheldon J. Krys.
Trinidad-Tobago Ambassador to U.S.: James O'Neil-Lewis.
Flag: Red field crossed diagonally by white-bordered black stripe.
Languages: English (official), Spanish.
Main Ethnic Groups: Black (41%), Asian Indian (50%).
Principal Religions: Roman Catholicism (32%), Protestantism (15%), Hinduism (24%), Islam (6%).
Leading Industries: Mining (petroleum, natural gas); manufacturing (oil refining, chemicals, textiles, cement, food processing); agriculture (sugarcane, cocoa, coconuts, fruits, vegetables); tourism; fishing.
Foreign Trade: Major exports—petroleum, sugar, cocoa, natural asphalt, chemicals; major imports—steel, food, chemicals, machinery, vehicles.
Places of Interest: *On Trinidad:* The Saddle; Caroni Bird Sanctuary; Maracas Bay; Pitch Lake; Port of Spain. *On Tobago:* Bird of Paradise Sanctuary; Man O'War Bay; Pigeon Point; Coral Sea Gardens; Turtle Beach.

TRINIDAD-TOBAGO TODAY

The mining and refining of petroleum are the largest industries of Trinidad-Tobago. Oil products make up about 85% of the country's exports. Huge natural gas reserves promise a source of power for developing industry.

Other important industries are the raising of sugarcane and the refining of sugar. Many islanders work in the cane fields.

The revenues from oil and sugar provide the islanders with one of the highest per capita incomes in the Caribbean. However, unemployment stands at about 15%.

The warm climate, ocean beaches, and mountain scenery of Trinidad and Tobago make the islands a popular winter vacation spot for tourists from the United States. Calypso, the steel band, and limbo all originated in Trinidad. These are featured in the colorful celebrations and carnival leading up to Ash Wednesday each year. Tourists enjoy seeing the bird of paradise and scarlet ibis in bird sanctuaries.

The islands of Trinidad and Tobago lie about 20 miles apart in the Caribbean Sea off Venezuela's northeast coast.

Trinidad, the largest island, has an area of 1,864 square miles. It has three mountain ranges, which run roughly east to west. Mountains in the northern range rise to 3,085 feet. Small streams flow to the sea through gently roll-

ing flatlands between the mountains.

Tobago (116 sq. mi.) is generally more rugged than Trinidad. It has a central volcanic core that ascends to 1,890 feet.

Daily high temperatures average 92°F. throughout the year.

EARLY HISTORY

The islands were discovered by Columbus in 1498, bringing them under Spanish rule.

During the 1600s and 1700s cocoa and sugar plantations were established with slave labor imported from Africa. In 1783 the Spanish government offered free land grants that attracted many non-Spanish settlers, especially French.

Trinidad was captured by the British in 1797 during a war with France. It was officially ceded to Britain in 1802, when it became a crown colony. Tobago was acquired by Britain in 1814 and was made a crown colony in 1877. Trinidad and Tobago were joined as a single colony in 1889.

Slaves on Trinidad were emancipated in 1833. To replace these plantation workers, the British brought in 150,000 Hindus and Muslims from India between 1845 and 1917.

INDEPENDENCE

Under the leadership of Dr. Eric Williams, the islands won independence on Aug. 31, 1962. Williams became the nation's first prime minister.

Black-power demonstrations marked by arson and looting shook the country in the first months of 1970. They reached a climax in a mutiny staged by half of the 800-man army. The government suppressed the rebellion in three days.

Offshore oil and gas fields discovered in 1972-75 brought Trinidad-Tobago sudden wealth as it joined the rolls of the oil-exporting nations. The oil revenues made it possible for the government to cut personal income taxes, to increase welfare benefits, and to subsidize food prices.

Trinidad-Tobago became a republic within the British Commonwealth on Aug. 1, 1976. Sir Ellis Clarke, who had served as governor-general, was chosen as the first president.

Prime Minister Williams' PNM party won its fifth 5-year term in national elections in 1976.

The main political party, the People's Nationalist Movement (PNM), draws its strength primarily from blacks, who make up 41% of the population. The chief opposition is the leftist United Labor Front (ULF).

After the death of the 69-year-old Williams on March 29, 1981, George M. Chambers succeeded him as prime minister.

Chambers led the PNM party to victory in a parliamentary election on Nov. 9, 1981, winning 26 of the 36 seats in the lower house.

Pope John Paul II visited Trinidad on Feb. 5, 1985, as the last stop in a tour of Latin American nations.

When Texaco Inc. announced plans to close its large oil refinery on Trinidad's east coast because of falling oil prices, the government agreed in April 1985 to purchase the installation for $189.2 million to save jobs for 3,000 workers.

TUNISIA

Official Name: Republic of Tunisia.
Area: 63,170 square miles (163,610 sq. km.).
Population: 7,362,000.
Chief Cities: Tunis, capital, 468,997; Bizerte, 95,023; Sousse, 82,666; Sfax, 79,595.
Government: Republic.
President: Habib Bourguiba (since 1957).
Prime Minister: Muhammed Mzali (since 1980).
Legislature: *National Assembly,* 136 members.
U.S. Ambassador to Tunisia: Peter Sebastian.
Tunisian Ambassador to U.S.: Habib Ben Yahia.
Flag: Red field with white circle containing red crescent and star.
Languages: Arabic (official), French.
Main Ethnic Group: Arab-Berber (98%).
Official Religion: Islam.
Leading Industries: Agriculture (olives, grapes, wheat, fruits, vegetables); manufacturing (oil refining), chemicals, textiles, wine, electricity, cement, consumer products); mining (petroleum, natural gas, phosphates, iron, zinc, lead); tourism; fishing.
Foreign Trade: *Major exports*—crude oil, olive oil, phosphates, citrus fruits, iron, wine, lead; *major imports*—wheat, motor vehicles, textile yarn and thread, vegetable oils, sulfur, wood.
Places of Interest: Roman ruins; beach resorts; Djerba Island; ancient city of Kairouan; fortified city of Monastir; Bardo Museum and Belvédère Park in Tunis; site of ancient Carthage; national parks.

TUNISIA TODAY

Helped by about $1 billion in aid from the United States since World War II, Tunisia has developed a diversified economy that is no longer solely dependent on agriculture.

While its richer North African neighbors Algeria and Libya have turned to state-controlled socialism, Tunisia has relied on private enterprise to develop its economy. Tourism has become the main industry.

However, not enough new industries have been developed to provide jobs for the many Tunisians who leave their farms each year to seek a better life in the cities. Many young people educated in Tunisia's colleges and universities must go to Europe to obtain well-paying jobs.

Most of the people are poor. About half earn a living as farmers. Only about 4 of 10 Tunisians can read and write.

Somewhat larger than the state of Georgia, Tunisia lies on the Mediterranean coast of Africa between Algeria in the west and Libya in the southeast.

The east-west Atlas mountain range divides Tunisia into two main regions. North of the mountains is the relatively well-watered, fertile Tell zone with groves of olive trees and pastures for livestock. To the south are a semiarid plain and plateau that extend into the Sahara Desert.

The majority of people live in the coastal

QUICK QUIZ: On what date did the Philippines win independence? See page 293.

670 NATIONS OF THE WORLD

TUNISIA *(continued)*

plain bordering the Mediterranean Sea. Nomadic tribes live in the southern region.

EARLY HISTORY OF TUNISIA

Tunisia was the center of ancient Carthage and later, from the 100s B.C., of a Roman province.

Tunisia was occupied by the Vandals in the 400s A.D. and recovered by the Byzantine Empire in the 500s. The country was finally conquered by the Arabs in the 600s.

During the Middle Ages it was the center from which Arab power and Islam spread south and west and also north across the Mediterranean. In 1535 Carthage was captured by the Holy Roman Emperor Karl V. The ruling dynasty turned for help to the Turks, who expelled the Spaniards in 1574 and made Tunisia a Turkish province.

Britain, France, and Italy assumed financial control of Tunisia in 1869. Tunisia became a French protectorate in 1883.

After the fall of France in World War II, Tunisia remained loyal to the Vichy government. The country became a central theater of the war in North Africa.

Habib Bourguiba, leader of the Neo-Destour Party, led the struggle for independence from France in the 1940s and 1950s.

INDEPENDENCE

On March 20, 1956, France granted Tunisia independence as a monarchy.

Tunisia's constituent assembly abolished the monarchy on July 25, 1957, establishing a republic with Habib Bourguiba as president. He won election without opposition in 1959, 1964, and 1969. The national assembly elected Bourguiba president for life in 1974.

Floods struck Tunisia in March 1973, leaving 53,000 homeless and 119 dead or missing.

To clarify the line of succession, Bourguiba changed the constitution in 1973. It provides that on his death he will be succeeded as head of the government by the prime minister. Then a presidential election will be held within 45 days.

Guerrillas crossed into Tunisia from Algeria on Jan. 27, 1980, attacking the mining city of Gafsa. Forty-five persons were killed and over 100 injured before most of the guerrillas were captured. The Tunisian government claimed Libya had trained the guerrillas and had planned to invade Tunisia to support the attackers. Thirteen of the captured guerrillas were hanged on April 17, 1980, and others were sentenced to prison. Tunisia expelled Libya's ambassador and recalled its own ambassador.

Bourguiba named former education minister Muhammed Mzali, 54, as prime minister on April 23, 1980, replacing ailing 69-year-old Hedi Nouira, who had held the office since 1970.

In the first multiparty election in 25 years of independence, Tunisians chose members of a new national assembly on Nov. 1, 1981. Bourguiba's party won a majority.

Tunisia and Libya restored friendly relations on Feb. 28, 1982, with the signing of a reconciliation agreement providing for cooperation in foreign relations and economic affairs.

Two women were appointed to the nation's cabinet for the first time in 1983.

TURKEY

Official Name: Republic of Turkey.
Area: 301,382 square miles (780,576 sq. km.).
Population: 49,686,000.
Chief Cities: Ankara, capital, 1,877,755; Istanbul, 2,772,708; Izmir, 757,854; Adana, 574,515; Bursa, 445,113; Gaziantep, 374,290; Eskisehir, 309,431.
Largest Metropolitan Area: Istanbul, 2,909,455.
Government: Republic with strong president.
President: Gen. Kenan Evren (since 1982).
Prime Minister: Turgut Ozal (since 1983).
National Assembly: 400 elected members.
U.S. Ambassador to Turkey: Robert Strausz-Hupe.
Turkish Ambassador to U.S.: Sukru Elekdag.
Flag: White star and crescent on red field.
Languages: Turkish (official), Kurdish.
Main Ethnic Groups: Turk (85%), Kurd (12%).
Religion: Islam (98%).
Leading Industries: Manufacturing (steel, textiles, electricity, tobacco products, food processing, consumer products); agriculture (wheat, barley, corn, cotton, sugar beets, livestock, tobacco, fruits, vegetables); mining (coal, lignite, iron, petroleum); services; fishing.
Foreign Trade: *Major exports*—cotton, tobacco; *major imports*—petroleum, motor vehicles, machinery.
Places of Interest: Bosporus bridge; Black Sea and Mediterranean resorts; Göreme Valley; ruins of Troy; ancient city of Sardis; Temple of Diana at Ephesus; tomb of Antiochus I on Mt. Nimrud; Ankara; Izmir. *In Istanbul:* Topkapi Palace; Grand Bazaar; St. Sofia; the Blue Sofia; the Blue Mosque.

TURKEY TODAY

Larger than Texas, Turkey was for 1,600 years the seat of empires that dominated southeastern Europe and the Middle East. Today Turkey's largest city, Istanbul (once called Constantinople), stands on the southeastern tip of Europe, but 97% of Turkey lies in Asia.

The country's strategic position on the Soviet Union's southwestern frontier makes Turkey a key member of the NATO military alliance. The U.S. uses 12 military bases in Turkey.

Turkey is a developing country striving to become an industrial nation. The people of Turkey are poorer than those of neighboring countries. About half cannot read or write. Hundreds of thousands of Turkish workers have gone to West Germany and other European nations to find work. The money they send home to their families has been an important part of the foreign exchange used in developing new industries in Turkey. In addition the U.S. has given and loaned Turkey about $8 billion in economic and military assistance in the past three decades.

Lacking most important industrial natural resources, Turkey pins hopes for the future on developing oil wells in the adjacent Aegean Sea in areas disputed with Greece.

Turkey controls the only outlet for Soviet ships from the Black Sea to the Mediterranean Sea, including the Bosporus, the Sea of Marmara,

and the Dardanelles. Completion of the huge Bosporus bridge across the strait in 1973 linked European and Asian Turkey by highway.

Greece lies to the west, Bulgaria to the north, the Soviet Union to the northeast, Syria and Iraq to the south, and Iran to the east.

EARLY HISTORY

In about 600 B.C. Greeks founded the city of Byzantium (now Istanbul) on hills strategically commanding the Bosporus. Roman legions captured Byzantium in A.D. 196.

In A.D. 330 the Christian emperor Constantine moved his capital from Rome to Byzantium, renamed Constantinople. The Byzantine Empire ruled eastern Europe and the Middle East for more than 1,000 years.

In 1453 the Turks, led by Ottoman Sultan Mohammed II, ended the Byzantine Empire with the capture of Constantinople. Islam supplanted Christianity. The Ottoman Empire dominated the Middle East until the early 1900s.

Turkey entered World War I on the German side. After Turkey's surrender in 1918, Sultan Mohammed VI, last of the Ottoman rulers, accepted the Treaty of Sèvres (1920), which reduced the empire to a minor state.

REPUBLIC OF TURKEY

A Turkish national resistance movement, led by Mustafa Kemal (later called Kemal Ataturk), rejected the Sèvres settlement. Ataturk declared the sultan deposed in 1922 and repulsed a Greek offensive in the west.

A republic, with Kemal Ataturk as president, was proclaimed in 1923. The Treaty of Lausanne (1923) established the present Turkish boundaries. The next year Ataturk introduced a new constitution that set up a national legislative assembly. Ataturk abolished Islam as the state religion, replaced Islamic law with European law. He moved the capital to Ankara.

Former Premier Ismet Inonu became president after Ataturk's death in 1938. Turkey did not declare war on Germany and Japan until 1945. Ataturk's successors remained in power until 1950, when Celal Bayar, leader of the Democratic Party, won the presidency. He appointed Adnan Menderes as premier.

In May 1960 an army revolt overthrew the elected government. Menderes was sentenced to death and hanged in 1961. In the same year a new constitution was adopted restoring parliamentary democracy.

Gen. Cemal Gursel, head of a faction favoring strict adherence to the principles of Ataturk, won the presidency in 1961. Gursel died in 1966. Gen. Cevdet Sunay succeeded him.

TURBULENT 1970s–1980s

In 1973 parliament elected Adm. Fahri Koruturk to a 7-year term as president.

Throughout the 1970s neither of the country's leading political parties was able to hold a clear majority in parliament.

Conservative Suleyman Demirel, head of the Justice Party, and Bulent Ecevit, leader of the socialist Republican People's Party (RPU), alter-nated in serving as prime minister.

The Greek-led overthrow of the Cyprus government in July 1974 caused Turkey to invade the island with 40,000 troops.

The U.S. cut off arms shipments to Turkey on Feb. 5, 1975, because Turkey had used NATO arms in its invasion of Cyprus. In retaliation, Turkey took over U.S. military bases.

In a national parliamentary election on June 5, 1977, the socialist RPU won the largest number of seats, 213, but not a clear majority. RPU leader Ecevit again became prime minister, but after 10 days in office he was defeated in a confidence vote, 229 to 217. He regained the office in 1978.

Threatening to change the East-West balance of power in the Middle East unless the U.S. ended its arms ban on Turkey, Ecevit visited Moscow and signed pacts on June 23, 1978, that pledged nonaggression and expanded trade with the Soviet Union. The U.S. Congress repealed its ban on arms sales to Turkey in September 1978. The Turkish government agreed in October to let the U.S. reopen four military bases.

Lacking petroleum resources of its own, Turkey was especially hard hit by soaring oil prices in the 1970s–1980s. The country's economy reached a state of crisis in 1979 with inflation at a rate of 70% and some 25% of its workers unemployed.

The U.S. and Turkey signed a 5-year agreement on March 29, 1980, providing continued use by the U.S. of 12 military bases. In return, the U.S. promised $2.5 billion in economic and military aid to Turkey over the period of the agreement.

After his conservative party won all five seats at stake in parliamentary by-elections, Demirel became prime minister on Nov. 12, 1979.

Violence between terrorists of the left and right increased during the first 9 months of 1980 with some 2,000 persons killed.

Promising to end the violence, Gen. Kenan Evren, chief of the armed forces, led a bloodless coup on Sept. 12, 1980. All political activity was banned until 1983. Demirel, Ecevit, and other political leaders were repeatedly arrested and jailed for short periods.

Evren became chief of state as head of a military junta called the National Security Council. The junta appointed a retired admiral, Bulent Ulusu, as prime minister. In all, some 56,000 persons were arrested in the following weeks.

Gen. Evren assured the U.S. and other NATO allies of continued cooperation. He said democratic government would be restored by 1984.

The 65-year-old Evren became president for a 7-year term after voters on Nov. 7, 1982, approved a new constitution that formalized the military rule in effect since 1980. The constitution gave the president wide powers.

Three political parties competed in an election on Nov. 6, 1983, to choose the 400 members of a new national assembly. The conservative Motherland Party won a 212-seat majority. Its leader, Turgut Ozal, 56, an electronic engineer, became prime minister on Dec. 12, 1983.

The government's five-year plan for 1985-89 calls for increased exports and preparation for full membership in the European Common Market.

QUICK QUIZ: Who was the first man to orbit the Earth in space? See page 294.

TUVALU

Official Name: Tuvalu.
Area: 10 square miles (26 sq. km.).
Population: 8,200.
Capital: Fongafale on Funafuti, 826.
Government: Parliamentary state.
Prime Minister: Tomasi Puapua (since 1982).
Chief of State: Queen Elizabeth II of Britain.
Tuvalu Ambassador to U.S.: Ionatana Ionatana.
U.S. Ambassador to Tuvalu: Carl E. Dillery.
Parliament: 12 members.
Flag: British blue ensign with nine yellow stars representing the nation's islands.
Languages: Tuvaluan, English.
Main Ethnic Group: Tuvaluans of Polynesian descent.
Principal Religion: Christianity, largely Protestant.
Leading Industries: Agriculture (coconuts, pulaka or taro, pandanus fruit, bananas, pawpaws); fishing.
Foreign Trade: *Major export*—copra from coconuts; *major imports*—food, fuel.
Places of Interest: villages; beaches.

One of the smallest of the world's nations, Tuvalu encompasses nine tropical islands in the South Pacific, about 600 miles north of Fiji. The group formerly was the Ellice Islands.

The Tuvaluans lead a simple existence, living in thatched huts on a diet of tropical fruits, vegetables, and fish. The only export is copra from coconuts, which provides money to import additional food, fuel, and manufactured goods. Islanders receive an elementary education.

The islands are scattered over an area of about half a million square miles of ocean. Stretching about 450 miles from northwest to southeast. The nine islands are: Nanumea, Nanumanga, Niutao, Nui, Vaitupu, Nukufetau, Funafuti, Nukulaelae, and Niulakita.

All the islands are coral atolls, rising no more than 15 feet above sea level.

HISTORY

In prehistoric times, Polynesians from Samoa settled the islands.

The first European explorer to visit was the Spanish navigator Alvaro de Mendaña, who discovered Nui in 1568 and Niulakita in 1595.

In the mid-1800's "blackbirders" raided the islands, carrying off as slaves all but about 3,000 of an estimated population of 20,000.

In 1892 Britain established a protectorate over Tuvalu, then called the Ellice Islands, governing them from the Gilbert Islands, which lie to the northwest. Britain created the Gilbert and Ellice Islands colony in 1916. During World War II the islands were occupied by Japanese troops in 1942–43, until driven out by U.S. forces.

The islanders voted in 1974 to separate from the Gilberts, becoming the separate territory of Tuvalu on Jan. 1, 1976. Britain granted Tuvalu complete independence on Oct. 1, 1978.

Queen Elizabeth II of Britain visited Tuvalu in October 1982.

UGANDA

Official Name: Republic of Uganda.
Area: 91,134 square miles (236,036 sq. km.).
Population: 15,559,000.
Capital: Kampala, 330,700.
Government: Military rule.
Head of government: Lt. Gen. Tito Okello (since 1985).
Prime Minister: Paulo Muwanga (since 1985).
Ambassador to U.S.: John Wycliffe Lwamafa.
U.S. Ambassador to Uganda: Allen Clayton Davis.
Flag: Black, yellow, and red stripes, with crested crane on white circle in center.
Languages: English (official), Luganda, Swahili.
Main Ethnic Group: Black.
Religions: Christianity (50%), animism (35%), Islam (15%).
Leading Industries: Agriculture (coffee, cotton, tea, tobacco, peanuts, livestock, fruits, vegetables); manufacturing (food, copper smelting, textiles, cement, shoes, fertilizer); mining (copper, tin).
Foreign Trade: *Major exports*—coffee, cotton, copper, tea; *major imports*—petroleum products, machinery, cotton fabrics, vehicles.
Places of Interest: Lake Victoria; "Mountains of the Moon" in the Ruwenzori Range; Queen Elizabeth and Kidepo Valley national parks; Kabalega Falls; wildlife preserves; Kampala.

Somewhat smaller than Oregon, Uganda is a poor African country struggling to regain stability after a decade of repressive dictatorship and war.

Dependent largely on agriculture, forestry, and fishing to support its economy, Uganda has few mineral resources other than copper and tin. Only about 1 out of 5 Ugandans can read and write.

Although the equator runs through the southern part of the country, the high altitude gives Uganda a moderate climate.

The Ruwenzori Mountains are in the west with Mt. Margherita rising to 16,763 feet on the Zaire border. Lake Victoria is in the southeast.

Kenya lies to the east, Sudan to the north, Zaire to the west, and Tanzania and Rwanda to the south.

Powerful kingdoms began to develop in the lakes area south of the Nile during the 1400s or early 1500s. Bunyoro was the most powerful of the southern kingdoms until the 1800s. Then a succession of able rulers made Buganda the leading kingdom. The first visitors were Arab and Swahili ivory and slave traders.

Britain and Germany agreed in 1890 that Britain should control the region. In 1894 Britain established a protectorate over Buganda that was later extended to the rest of Uganda.

Uganda gained its independence on Oct. 9, 1962, remaining a member of the British Commonwealth of Nations. In 1963 King Mutesa of Buganda became Uganda's first president with Milton Obote as prime minister.

In February 1966 Obote suspended the constitution, and the king fled to Britain. Obote then

made himself president.

On Jan. 25, 1971, while Obote was abroad, Gen. Idi Amin seized power.

The human-rights organization Amnesty International reported that during Amin's first six years in office he had been responsible for killing as many as 300,000 persons.

In 1972 Amin expelled about 60,000 British Asians, seizing their businesses and property.

The United States, Britain, Canada, and other countries cut off financial aid and technical assistance in 1973. The U.S. closed its embassy in Uganda in November 1973.

Amin began a war with neighboring Tanzania in 1978, announcing on Nov. 1 that his troops had annexed 710 square miles of Tanzania.

Determined to destroy the Ugandan dictator, Tanzania resisted the invasion and then counterattacked, routing Amin's forces and capturing Uganda's capital, Kampala, on April 11, 1979. Amin escaped into exile.

In a national election on Dec. 10–11, 1980, former President Milton Obote's Ugandan People's Congress won a majority of the 126 elective seats in the national assembly. Obote was sworn in as president on Dec. 15 and a few days later appointed Otema Alimadi as prime minister.

Throughout 1981–85 Uganda was torn by antigovernment guerrilla terrorists and retaliatory summary executions and massacres of suspected guerrillas by government troops.

Lt. Gen. Tito Okello, 71, led a military coup on July 27, 1985, that overthrew the government. Obote fled to Kenya.

UNITED ARAB EMIRATES

Official Name: United Arab Emirates.
Area: 32,278 square miles (83,600 sq. km.).
Population: 1,390,000.
Largest Cities: Abu Dhabi, capital, 242,975; Dubai, 265,702; Sharjah, 125,149; Ap-Ain, 101,663.
Government: Confederation of monarchies.
President: Sheik Zayid bin Sultan al Nuhayan, ruler of Abu Dhabi (since 1971).
Prime Minister and Vice President: Sheik Rashid bin Said al Maktum, ruler of Dubai (since 1979).
Legislature: *National Assembly,* 40 members.
U.S. Ambassador to United Arab Emirates: George Quincey Lumsden.
United Arab Emirates Ambassador to U.S.: Ahmad Salem Al-Mokarrab.
Flag: Red bar at hoist; stripes of green, white, and black.
Languages: Arabic (official), Persian, English.
Main Ethnic Group: Arab (72%).
Principal Religion: Islam (90%).
Leading Industries: Mining (petroleum, natural gas); manufacturing (petroleum refining, gas liquefaction, aluminum, chemicals, fertilizer, cement, plastics); agriculture (dates, sheep, goats, tobacco, fruits).
Foreign Trade: *Major exports*—petroleum, natural gas; *major imports*—manufactured goods, machinery, vehicles, construction materials.
Places of Interest: Oil refineries; royal residences; national zoo at Al Ain; beaches.

UNITED ARAB EMIRATES TODAY

About the size of the state of Maine, the country is mostly a desert with temperatures of 120°F. in the shade. Until oil began to be produced in 1962, the sheikdoms were very poor. But in the 1980s oil income soared over $20 billion a year.

The government receives 60% of all oil produced. Much of the income is spent for welfare projects, port improvements, water de- salinization, oil refineries, and industrial plants. Free education, health care, and phone service are provided by the government. There are no income taxes. Foreign immigrants make up about 85% of the population.

The United Arab Emirates (UAE) is a confederation of seven Arab sheikdoms on the Persian Gulf. The sheikdoms are: Abu Dhabi, Dubai, Sharjah, Ajman, Ras al-Khaimah, Umm al-Qaiwain, and Fujairah.

Saudi Arabia and Qatar lie to the west. Oman is to the east.

EARLY HISTORY

The coastal area was ruled by Portugal in the 1500s to 1600s and then by Iran. The Iranians were expelled in 1783 by an Arab tribe.

Known as the *Trucial States,* the Persian Gulf sheikdoms subsequently were called the Pirate Coast, a base of operation for over 800 Arab pirate ships as well as European marauders.

From 1806 onward, the Persian Gulf states gradually came under British protection. Piracy was brought to an end in 1853 when sheiks signed the Perpetual Maritime Truce, which was arranged and supervised by Britain.

Between 1880 and 1916 the sheiks of the Persian Gulf states concluded protective treaties with Britain. Economic development began after oil was discovered in Abu Dhabi in 1958.

After Britain announced in 1967 that it would withdraw its military forces from the Persian Gulf area by the end of 1971, the sheikdoms set up a provisional government.

On Dec. 2, 1971, six of the sheikdoms proclaimed themselves the independent United Arab Emirates with Sheik Zayid of Abu Dhabi as president. A seventh sheikdom joined the union on Feb. 1, 1972.

The country also has large natural-gas deposits, and in 1974–75 huge plants were built on Das Island to liquefy 3 million tons of gas a year for shipment to Japan.

In December 1976 Sheik Zayid was elected to a second 5-year term as president by the rulers of the other emirates. They also greeted to turn over to his control the military forces.

In the 1970s and 1980s the government spent huge sums to build industries to support the country when its oil reserves are exhausted. A port with berths for 66 large ships was built at Jebel Ali, in Dubai, along with a steel fabrication unit, power plant and associated desalination units, an aluminum smelter, and a liquid petroleum facility.

QUICK QUIZ: Who governed China in 1928-1949? See page 295.

URUGUAY

Official Name: Oriental Republic of Uruguay.
Area: 68,037 square miles (176,215 sq. km.).
Population: 3,028,000.
Capital: Montevideo, 1,173,254.
Government: Multi-party democracy.
President: Julio Maria Sanguinetti (since 1985).
Parliament: Lower house, 99 deputies; upper house, 30 senators.
U.S. Ambassador to Uruguay: Thomas Aranda Jr.
Ambassador to U.S.: Walter Ravenna.
Flag: Blue stripes on white field, with golden sun in upper hoist corner.
Language: Spanish.
Ethnic Groups: European descent (85%), mestizo (10%), mulatto and black (5%).
Principal Religions: Roman Catholicism (66%), Protestantism (2%), Judaism (2%).
Leading Industries: Agriculture (cattle, sheep, hogs, rice, wheat, corn, fruits, vegetables); manufacturing (food processing, electricity, leather products, glass, ceramics, furniture, clothing); forestry and lumbering; tourism; fishing; construction.
Foreign Trade: *Major exports*—meat, wool, leather, fish, rice, shoes, glass, ceramics, cement; *major imports*—petroleum, machinery, motor vehicles and aircraft, chemicals, iron and steel.
Places of Interest: Santa Teresa National Park; beach resorts; Pan de Azúcar (Sugar Loaf peak); Castle of Piria; Lobos Island. *In Montevideo:* Plaza Independencia; town hall (*cabildo*); legislative palace.

URUGUAY TODAY

About the size of Missouri, Uruguay is a small South American country with few natural resources. Uruguay's economy depends primarily upon tourism, banking, and livestock raising.

Because Uruguay is poor in natural mineral resources, it has lagged in the development of manufacturing. The government owns and operates basic industries.

Austerity in spending and reduced taxes on imports have held inflation to a lower rate than in neighboring countries.

Brazil lies to the northeast and Argentina to the west.

EARLY HISTORY OF URUGUAY

Spaniards explored the Río de la Plata as early as 1515, but permanent settlement did not occur until 1624. Uruguay's native Charrúa Indians, who strenuously resisted Spanish occupation, were killed off or absorbed by the 1830s. Portuguese from Brazil fortified the present site of Montevideo in 1717, but the Spaniards later drove them off, and Uruguay became part of the Spanish viceroyalty centered in Argentina. Montevideo was permanently settled in 1726.

A war of independence, led by José Gervasio Artigas, began in 1810. Portuguese forces captured Montevideo in 1820, and for five years Uruguay was part of Brazil.

INDEPENDENCE

In 1825 the "Thirty-three Immortals," led by Juan Antonio Lavalleja, declared Uruguay's independence. On Aug. 25, 1828, Uruguay was established as an independent buffer state between Brazil and Argentina. A constitution was adopted in 1830. Fructuoso Rivera became president.

The following decades were marked by internal strife, disputes with Brazil and Argentina, and violent changes of government.

José Batlle y Ordóñez, a liberal, served two terms as president (1903–07, 1911–15). He launched social, economic, and political reforms.

From 1952 to 1966 Uruguay was governed by a council. In November 1966 the people elected as president Oscar Daniel Gestido of the liberal Colorado Party. He died in 1967 and was succeeded by Vice President Jorge Pacheco Areco.

Strikes and unrest brought periods of limited martial law in 1968 and 1969. Terrorist activities included abductions of foreign diplomats by leftist urban guerrillas called *Tupamaros*.

URUGUAY IN THE 1970s–1980s

In 1971 conservative Juan M. Bordaberry was elected president after a 79-day recount.

The army, air force, and navy rebelled in February 1973, demanding an important voice in running the country. In June 1973 Bordaberry ended 40 years of democratic government in Uruguay. All political activities were banned.

Military leaders ousted Bordaberry on June 12, 1976. A 45-member council in July 1976 elected 72-year-old Aparicio Méndez as president.

When President Méndez took office on Sept. 1, 1976, he immediately banned the political rights of all Uruguayans who had held office in the past 10 years. Only officeholders in the existing government were exempted.

In March 1977 the government said it would reject all U.S. aid because of American criticism.

The $1 billion Salto Grande Dam on the Uruguay River, constructed by Argentina and Uruguay in 1974–81, stimulated industrial development with its hydroelectric 1.8 billion kilowatt capacity.

Permitted to vote for the first time in 7 years on Nov. 30, 1980, Uruguayans turned down, 58% to 42%, a new constitution that would have given the military continuing control.

The junta appointed former army commander in chief Gen. Gregorio Alvarez to succeed Méndez as president on Sept. 1, 1981.

The three main political parties were permitted to resume activities in 1982.

The military announced an agreement on Aug. 3, 1984, with opposing political parties, providing for restoration of democracy.

In a general election on Nov. 25, 1984, voters elected members of a new parliament, a national president, 19 mayors, and hundreds of provincial council members.

The elected president, Julio Maria Sanguinetti, 49, of the centerist Colorado Party, was sworn in on March 1, 1985.

Sanguinetti immediately signed decrees revoking repressive dictates of the military government. An amnesty approved by parliament freed the remainder of 7,000 political prisoners who had been jailed by the military.

VANUATU

Official Name: Republic of Vanuatu.
Area: 5,700 square miles (14,763 sq. km.).
Population: 135,300.
Capital: Vila, Efate, 3,072.
Government: Democratic parliamentary republic.
President: George Sokomanu (since 1980).
Prime Minister: Rev. Walter Lini (since 1980).
Representative Assembly: 39 members.
Flag: Emblem of crossed mele leaves surrounded by yellow hog tusk on black triangle at hoist; red upper panel and green lower panel separated by thin black and yellow stripes.
Languages: English and French (official), Bislama (New Hebrides pidgin), Melanesian languages.
Chief Ethnic Group: Melanesian (92%).
Main Religions: Christianity, animism.
Leading Industries: Agriculture (coconuts, cocoa, coffee, cattle, taros, yams); fishing; food processing; mining (manganese); tourism; handicrafts.
Foreign Trade: *Major exports*—copra, fish, manganese, meat; *major imports*—food, petroleum, machinery; consumer goods.
Places of Interest: Swimming beaches; tropical rain forests; villages; volcanoes.

VANUATU TODAY

The first nation to win independence in the 1980s, Vanuatu had been jointly ruled by Britain and France for 74 years as the condominium of New Hebrides.

A group of more than 70 islands and islets in the southwest Pacific Ocean, Vanuatu has an area nearly as large as Hawaii. The main islands are Espiritu Santo, Malekula, Efate, Erromango, Tanna, Ambrym, Pentecost, Maevo, Aoba, and Aneityum. The island chain stretches about 500 miles from the Torres Islands in the north to Aneityum in the south.

Vanuatu lies about 1,000 miles northeast of Australia, 600 miles west of Fiji, and 250 miles northeast of New Caledonia.

The larger islands are covered by thick rain forests. Active volcanoes stand on several islands, including Ambrym and Tanna. The highest peak, Tabwemasana, on Espiritu Santo Island, is 6,160 feet high.

Most Vanuatuans are dark-skinned Melanesians, whose ancestors were cannibals less than a century ago. Most make their living from agriculture or fishing. Only about 1 person in 10 can read and write.

Because the value of imports are three times that of exports, Vanuatu depends heavily on economic aid from Britain and France.

Tourism is a growing industry. Some 40,000 cruise-ship passengers visit each year. Several hotels are located at Vila on Efate Island and at Luganville on Espiritu Santo. Commercial airlines provide two flights a week to and from Australia.

The climate is generally hot, humid, and rainy. Annual rainfall averages 91 inches.

EARLY HISTORY

The Portuguese explorer Pedro Fernándes de Queirós discovered the islands in 1606, naming the main one Australia del Espiritu Santo. British explorer Capt. James Cook gave the islands the name New Hebrides in 1774.

During the early 1800s French and British missionaries, planters, and traders settled in the islands. The native Melanesians suffered depredations by "blackbirder" ships that shanghaied them to work as laborers on plantations in Fiji.

Britain and France agreed in 1887 to jointly administer the islands.

ANGLO-FRENCH CONDOMINIUM

The government of the New Hebrides was established as an Anglo-French condominium by the London Convention of Oct. 20, 1906. This agreement was replaced by the Anglo-French Protocol of Aug. 6, 1914, which was ratified in 1922.

The islands were placed under joint administration of British and French commissioners.

During World War II the U.S. constructed a huge air and naval base at Esperitu Santo that was used as a staging facility for the invasions of Japanese-held Guadalcanal, Tarawa, and other islands in the south Pacific. The U.S. built 17 airstrips and many miles of roads on the islands.

From 1957 to 1975 an appointed advisory council, including the French and British resident commissioners, controlled local government.

The advisory council was replaced in 1976 with a 42-member representative assembly, including 29 elected members.

The first general election, in November 1975, was won by the Vanu aku Party (VAP), which captured 21 seats. However, disagreements among the political parties, which represent French, British, and local interests, delayed formation of a unified government until Dec. 22, 1978.

Parliamentary elections in November 1979 were won by the VAP, whose leader, Rev. Walter Lini, an Anglican priest, became chief minister.

INDEPENDENCE

France and Britain granted Vanuatu independence as a republic on July 30, 1980, with Lini as the sovereign nation's first prime minister. George Sokomanu, who had served as Lini's deputy chief minister, was chosen as Vanuatu's first president by vote of a special electoral college.

One of the first acts of the new government was to ask a force of 200 British and French troops to temporarily remain in occupation of the island of Espiritu Santo, where rebels armed with bows and arrows threatened to secede from Vanuatu as the separate nation of Vemarana.

The French and British troops were replaced in mid-August by 150 soldiers loaned by Papua New Guinea. On Aug. 31, 1980, they captured rebel Jimmy Stevens and about 70 of his followers, ending the rebellion. Stevens was sentenced to 14 years in prison.

In the first election since independence in November 1983, Prime Minister Lini's party won a 13-seat majority in the assembly.

QUICK QUIZ: Who was the first Capetian king of France? See page 296.

VATICAN CITY

Official Name: State of the Vatican City.
Area: 0.17 sq. mi. (109 acres) (0.44 sq. km.).
Population: 730.
Government: Ecclesiastical state.
Pope: John Paul II (since 1978).
U.S. Ambassador to Vatican City: William A. Wilson.
Vatican Ambassador to U.S.: Archbishop Pio Laghi.
Flag: Yellow and white bars; crossed keys of St. Peter under papal tiara on white bar.
Languages: Latin (official), Italian.
Official Religion: Roman Catholicism (100%).
Places of Interest: St. Peter's Basilica; Vatican museums, including the Sistine Chapel.

VATICAN CITY TODAY

The world's smallest sovereign nation, Vatican City lies entirely within the Italian city of Rome. It occupies a small triangle on the west bank of the Tiber River. Vatican City also has jurisdiction over several churches and palaces in Rome and nearby Castel Gandolfo.

The government is an absolute monarchy with all powers vested in the pope of the Roman Catholic Church. He in turn delegates most of these powers, including diplomatic relations with other nations, to a secretary of state that he appoints. The government is often called merely the *Vatican.* The pope's court is known as the *Holy See.*

The government's security force consists of 75 Swiss guards. The official radio station is Radio Vatican. The official newspaper is *l'Osservatore Romano.* The state has its own postal and telephone systems. Most citizens are Vatican employees, who can buy tax-free food and goods.

Through the pope, the Vatican affects the lives of more than half a billion Roman Catholics throughout the world.

HISTORY

For many centuries after the fall of the Roman Empire, popes ruled Rome and central Italy, which were called the *Papal States.* With the unification of Italy in 1861, most of the Papal States except Rome were added to the new kingdom of Italy. In 1870 the Italian king took Rome from the pope, annexing it to Italy and making it his capital. Then, for more than half a century, Pope Pius IX and his successors refused to acknowledge Italy's sovereignty and regarded themselves as prisoners in Vatican City.

Treaties called the Lateran Accords signed on Feb. 11, 1929, by Italy and the Vatican established the independence and sovereignty of Vatican City. The accords were brought up to date with revisions in 1976–77 and in 1984, ending Roman Catholicism's status as the official religion of Italy and reducing the pope's authority over education and marriage in Italy.

Britain and the Vatican resumed full diplomatic relations in 1982 some 450 years after they were broken by Britain's King Henry VIII in 1532.

The U.S. established full diplomatic relations on Jan. 10, 1984, after 116 years of unofficial ties.

See also the list of popes on page 713.

VENDA

Official Name: Republic of Venda.
Area: 2,510 square miles (6,500 sq. km.).
Population: 417,400.
Capital: Thohoyandou.
Government: Parliamentary republic.
Prime Minister: Chief Patrick Mphephu (since 1973).
Flag: Blue stripe at hoist; green, yellow and brown horizontal stripes; brown Von yellow stripe.
Parliament: Legislative Assembly, 84 members (42 elected and 42 tribal chiefs).
Chief Languages: Venda (official), English, Afrikaans.
Principal Ethnic Group: Venda-speaking Bantus.
Main Religions: Christianity, animism.
Leading Industries: Agriculture (cattle, sheep, corn); personal services; forestry; mining (graphite).
Foreign Trade: *Major exports*—agricultural products; *major imports*—petroleum products, consumer goods, vehicles, machinery.

One of the black homelands established by South Africa as part of its apartheid policy of separation of the races, Venda is a small country about the size of Delaware.

Granted independence by South Africa, Venda has been unable to gain recognition for its sovereignty from other nations.

Most of the people live on the food they raise, seldom seeing any money except what they receive from relatives working in South Africa.

The country is divided into two parts, both surrounded by South Africa. Although Venda lies close to the southern border of Zimbabwe, a South African defense zone separates Venda from Zimbabwe. South Africa's Kruger Game Park lies between Venda and Mozambique to the east.

Chief Patrick Mphephu became chief minister of Venda when it was granted internal self-government in 1973. In elections that year his Venda National Party won only 5 of the 18 elective seats in the legislative assembly, but he was made chief minister by the vote of tribal chiefs.

In a new election in 1978, Mphephu retained power, again with the vote of the nonelected chiefs, even though his party won only 11 of the 42 elective seats in the new legislature.

When the Venda Independence Party of Baldwin Mudau challenged his leadership in 1978, Mphephu ordered the arrest of about 50 of its members. The Independence Party had won 31 of the elective seats in the legislature.

South Africa granted Venda independence on Sept. 13, 1979, while continuing to provide about $35 million annual aid to support its economy. The UN Security Council denounced Venda's independence as a "totally invalid" effort "to perpetuate" South African apartheid.

VENEZUELA

Official Name: Republic of Venezuela.
Area: 352,145 square miles (912,050 sq. km.).
Population: 19,617,000.
Chief Cities: Caracas, capital, 1,662,627; Maracaibo, 901,000; Valencia, 506,000; Barquisimeto, 489,000; Maracay, 344,000; Barcelona–Puerto La Cruz, 275,000; San Cristóbal, 272,000; Ciudad Guayana, 206,000; Cabimas, 178,000.
Largest Metropolitan Area: Caracas, 2,944,000.
Government: Republic.
President: Jaime Lusinchi (since 1984).
Congress: *Senate,* 49 members; *Chamber of Deputies,* 200 members.
U.S. Ambassador to Venezuela: George W. Landau.
Venezuelan Ambassador to U.S.: Marcial Perez Chiriboga.
Flag: Yellow, blue, and red stripes, with seven white stars in semicircle in center; national coat of arms in upper hoist corner.
Official Language: Spanish.
Ethnic Groups: Mestizo (70%), mulatto (13%), European descent (10%), black (5%), Indian (2%).
Religions: Roman Catholicism (96%), Protestantism (2%), Judaism (0.1%).
Leading Industries: Manufacturing (steel, motor vehicles, ships, oil refining, chemicals, food processing, textiles, cement); mining (petroleum, iron, diamonds, manganese); services; agriculture (livestock, coffee, cocoa, corn, rice, sugar, tobacco, cotton, fruits, vegetables); tourism; forestry and lumbering.
Foreign Trade: *Major exports*—petroleum and petroleum products, iron ore, coffee, cocoa; *major imports*—machinery, steel, automobiles, wheat.
Places of Interest: Angel Falls; Mt. Avila; Margarita Island; Lake Maracaibo; Bavarian village of Colonía Tovar; beach resorts; home of Simón Bolívar in Caracas; Spanish colonial buildings in Merida.

VENEZUELA TODAY

Larger than California, Oregon, and Washington combined, Venezuela is the most prosperous country in South America.

Venezuela is a leading oil-exporting nation. It also is one of the world's 10 most important producers of iron ore. Oil and iron ore account for about 98% of the value of the country's annual exports, although these industries employ only about 2% of Venezuela's workers. A fifth of the people are farmers.

Caracas, the capital, resembles Los Angeles or Miami with many skyscrapers and freeways.

The government's vigorous support of education has nearly wiped out illiteracy.

Venezuela has a 1,750-mile coastline on the Caribbean Sea. Its beaches and resorts attract many tourists. Colombia lies to the west, Brazil to the south, and Guyana to the east.

EARLY HISTORY

Columbus discovered the Orinoco River in 1498.

PRESIDENTS SINCE 1958

1958–1964	Rómulo Betancourt	Democratic Action
1964–1969	Raúl Leoni	Democratic Action
1969–1974	Rafael Caldera	Christian Social
1974–1979	Carlos Andrés Pérez	Democratic Action
1979–1984	Luis Herrera Campíns	Christian Social
1984–	Jaime Lusinchi	Democratic Action

German adventurers followed, but organization of the country was undertaken by Spain. Caracas was founded in 1567.

In 1811 Francisco de Miranda led a revolt against Spanish leaders. Independence was declared on July 5, 1811. Simón Bolívar completed the struggle for independence in 1821. Bolívar's dream of a Greater Colombia to include Venezuela was realized briefly, but after his death in 1830 Venezuela became independent. Dictator followed dictator in succeeding decades.

A revolution in 1945 brought to power a liberal democratic government headed by Rómulo Betancourt. In 1947 Rómulo Gallegos won a free presidential election but was ousted by a military coup in 1948. Marcos Pérez Jiménez became president and dictator in 1953.

DECADES OF DEMOCRACY

After the overthrow of Pérez Jiménez in 1958, Rómulo Betancourt of the Democratic Action Party was elected president. During his administration a new constitution was adopted limiting the presidency to one 5-year term.

Betancourt began a land-reform program that redistributed millions of acres of land to more than 100,000 small farmers.

After Venezuela broke relations with Cuba in 1961, Cuban-supported communist guerrillas tried to overthrow Betancourt.

Rafael Caldera of the Christian Social Party won the 1968 presidential election. At his inauguration in March 1969 a milestone was achieved as he became the first president in Venezuelan history to peacefully take over the government from an opposition party.

On Jan. 1, 1975, the government nationalized U.S.-owned iron mines, and on Jan. 1, 1976, nationalized the petroleum industry, paying the foreign owners with government bonds.

Work began in 1977 on a new $2 billion subway system for Caracas. It opened on Jan. 2, 1983.

Luis Herrera Campíns became president on March 12, 1979. As candidate of the Christian Social Party, he had won an upset victory in a national election on Dec. 3, 1978, that ousted the governing Democratic Action Party from office. President Herrera criticized the outgoing regime for having run up an $11 billion national debt.

Jaime Lusinchi, 59, leader of the opposition Democratic Action Party, won the presidential election by a wide margin on Dec. 4, 1983, defeating former President Rafael Caldera, 67, candidate of the governing Social Christian Party.

After taking office on Feb. 2, 1984, President Lusinchi announced a comprehensive program to revive the nation's stagnant economy and deal with a mounting $35 billion foreign debt, which more than tripled during President Herrea's administration.

VIETNAM

Official Name: Socialist Republic of Vietnam.
Area: 127,242 square miles (329,556 sq. km.).
Population: 60,388,000.
Chief Cities: Hanoi, capital, 414,620; Ho Chi Minh City (Saigon), 1,825,297; Danang, 492,194; Nhatrang, 216,227; Quinhon, 213,757; Hué, 209,043; Haiphong, 182,490.
Government: One-party communist state.
Government Leaders: Le Duan, secretary-general of the Communist Party (since 1960); prime minister, Pham Van Dong (since 1955); Truong Chinh (since 1981), head of state council.
Legislature: *National Assembly,* 496 members.
Flag: Gold star centered on red field.
Languages: Vietnamese (official), French, Chinese.
Main Ethnic Groups: Kinh (87%), Chinese (6%).
Principal Religions: Buddhism (70%), Roman Catholicism (10%).
Leading Industries: Agriculture (rice, poultry, rubber, tea, livestock, coffee, tobacco, sugarcane, corn, manioc, fruits, vegetables); manufacturing (food processing, textiles, cement, fertilizer, consumer products); fishing; forestry and lumbering; mining (coal, phosphates, iron, bauxite, gold, petroleum, chrome, zinc, tungsten).
Foreign Trade: *Major exports*—coal, rubber; *major imports*—food, petroleum, machinery, vehicles.
Places of Interest: Hanoi, government buildings; Ho Chi Minh City (Saigon), gardens, zoos, museums.

VIETNAM TODAY

Although somewhat smaller than Montana, Vietnam has the third-largest population of any communist nation after China and the Soviet Union.

Wars from the 1940s to 1970s devastated many of Vietnam's cities, towns, and villages, leaving behind countless problems.

In the 1980s the Soviet Union provided about $1 billion annual aid in exchange for use of former U.S. military bases in Vietnam.

About half of Vietnamese adults cannot read and write. In the area of health, diseases that have been eliminated in more developed countries kill from one-third to one-half of Vietnamese babies before they reach the age of six.

The nation's economy depends largely on agriculture, but cannot supply enough food for the people. Most Vietnamese earn their living as rice farmers. However, Vietnam has the potential for substantial industrial development with ample mineral resources that include coal and iron ore.

Vietnam is a long, narrow country that extends for about 1,000 miles from north to south. Northern Vietnam is hilly and mountainous while southern Vietnam is the low, flat delta of the Mekong River. Tropical forests cover much of the country.

The country has a year-round warm and wet tropical climate. Mountain regions are cool from about October to March. Heavy rains fall from May to September.

China lies to the north. Laos and Cambodia are to the west. The Gulf of Tonkin and the South China Sea are to the east.

EARLY HISTORY

Vietnamese legend attributes the founding of the nation more than 4,000 years ago to King Hung.

China's Han dynasty conquered Vietnam in 111 B.C. For more than 1,000 years China ruled northern Vietnam. A revolt by the Vietnamese threw off Chinese rule in A.D. 939.

Meanwhile, in southern Vietnam a kingdom called Champa had been founded by an Indonesian people. Champa carried on trade with India for many centuries and was influenced by Hindu art and religion.

Vietnam's emperor Le Thanh-Ton conquered Champa in 1471, unifying the region. But by the early 1600s Vietnam again had become divided with the kingdoms of Tonkin in the north and Cochin China in the south.

European traders began visiting the region in the 1500s.

FRENCH CONTROL

In the late 1700s French military officers helped Prince Nguyen Anh of Cochin China win control of the entire country. In 1802 he established himself as Emperor Gia-Long with his capital at Hué. His descendants continued to rule for the next century and a half.

By the mid-1800s French missionaries had converted about 2 million Vietnamese to Roman Catholicism. Fearing the foreign influence of the Christians, the government began a campaign of persecution, killing many of them.

France's Emperor Napoleon III demanded in 1858 that Vietnamese Emperor Tu-Duc stop the persecution of Christians. Then France, in 1859, began its conquest of the country, first capturing Saigon with the aid of Spain.

France made southern Vietnam (Cochin China) a colony in 1867. After much fighting, France established a protectorate over all of Vietnam on June 6, 1884.

By 1893 France also had won control of Cambodia and Laos. It then incorporated these countries with Vietnam into the Indochinese Union, headed by a French governor-general. Vietnam was divided into three parts: Tonkin in the north, Annam in the center, and Cochin China in the south.

During the next half century Indochina became France's most prosperous colony. Hanoi became the capital of French Indochina.

In the 1930s Vietnamese aspirations for independence were spurred by the Indochinese Communist Party founded by Ho Chi Minh, who had been educated in France.

After the defeat of France by Germany in World War II, the Vichy French colonial administration gave Japan complete control of Indochina. Ho Chi Minh organized Vietnamese patriots into the Vietminh movement, which carried out guerrilla attacks on the Japanese.

INDOCHINA WAR

When Japan surrendered to the U.S. in World War II in August 1945, the Vietminh seized control of Hanoi and forced Emperor Bao Dai to abdicate. Ho Chi Minh declared Vietnam an in-

dependent republic on Sept. 2, 1945.

France tried to reassert its control of Vietnam, establishing a separate regime in Cochin China (southern Vietnam) in June 1946. Fighting soon began between the French troops and the Vietminh. The Indochina War dragged on for eight years, ending with French defeat in 1954 and a peace settlement at Geneva.

The nation was divided at the 17th parallel into North Vietnam (capital at Hanoi) and South Vietnam (capital at Saigon). The settlement provided that elections should be held in 1956 to vote on reuniting the country. However, the U.S. and South Vietnam refused to sign the Geneva agreement and repudiated a unification referendum. The U.S. signed a defense treaty with South Vietnam in 1954.

VIETNAM WAR

In South Vietnam, Emperor Bao Dai was ousted in October 1955 by his prime minister, Ngo Dinh Diem, who declared the nation a republic with himself as its first president. Communists began guerrilla warfare against South Vietnam.

The U.S. sent constantly increasing supplies and military advisers to South Vietnam.

In the belief Diem was incapable of winning the war, the U.S. government encouraged a coup in 1963 in which Diem was assassinated.

After attacks by North Vietnamese patrol craft on U.S. destroyers in the Gulf of Tonkin in 1964, the U.S. Congress gave President Lyndon Johnson authority to use any means to prevent further aggression by North Vietnam.

U.S. troops began combat operations in Vietnam in 1965. Within four years more than 500,000 U.S. servicemen were fighting against North Vietnamese troops and guerrillas.

Meanwhile, Nguyen Van Thieu had been elected president of South Vietnam in 1967.

Ho Chi Minh, the leader of North Vietnam, died in September 1969. He was succeeded as president by Ton Duc Thang, who died in 1980.

Antiwar sentiment in the U.S. caused President Richard Nixon to begin withdrawing U.S. forces from Vietnam in 1969. A cease-fire agreement became effective on Jan. 28, 1973. All U.S. forces left by March 29, 1973.

Over 57,000 Americans died in the war.

North Vietnam launched a new offensive in March 1975. South Vietnam's defenses quickly collapsed. The war ended on April 30, 1975, with South Vietnam's unconditional surrender.

UNIFIED COMMUNIST VIETNAM

The communists quickly moved to unify Vietnam. Hanoi became the capital for the entire country. Saigon was renamed Ho Chi Minh City. An estimated 65,000 political prisoners were executed in addition to thousands who died in labor camps and prisons.

On July 2, 1976, the national assembly approved unification and elected North Vietnam leaders as heads of the new state.

American and Vietnamese diplomats met in Paris on Nov. 12, 1976, for the first talks since

HIGHLIGHTS OF THE INDOCHINA AND VIETNAM WARS: 1945–1975

1945 (Sept. 2) Independence of Democratic Republic of Vietnam proclaimed by communist Ho Chi Minh.

1946 (March 6) France recognizes Ho's government, granting internal self-rule to Vietnam.

1946 (June 1) After disputes with Ho, France declares southern Vietnam independent, calling it Cochin China.

1946 (Dec. 19) War begins with surprise attack by troops of Ho Chi Minh launched on French military bases.

1954 (May 7) French army surrenders fortress of Dien Bien Phu after 55-day siege by North Vietnamese.

1954 (July 21) Truce signed, ending 8-year Indochina War; nation divided into North and South Vietnam.

1954 (Aug. 11) Peace agreement signed in Geneva, Switzerland, providing referendum in 1956 to decide government of unified Vietnam. United States and South Vietnam refuse to sign agreement.

1954 (Sept. 8) Southeast Asia Collective Defense Treaty signed by U.S. and seven other nations pledging joint action to protect South Vietnam and other nations in area.

1964 (Aug. 2–4) U.S. destroyers in Gulf of Tonkin attacked by North Vietnamese torpedo boat.

1964 (Aug. 5) Retaliatory bombing of North Vietnam by U.S. planes ordered by President Johnson.

1964 (Aug. 7) Congress votes Gulf of Tonkin Resolution, giving President authority "to prevent further aggression."

1965 (June 28) First U.S. combat operations on ground authorized by President Johnson.

1968 (Jan. 30) Tet offensive, biggest communist attack of war begun, directed at Saigon.

1968 (March 16) My Lai massacre of 100 to 400 Vietnamese civilians by U.S. troops led by Lt. William L. Calley Jr.

1968 (May 13) Peace talks begin in Paris between U.S. and North Vietnam as war rages.

1969 (March) U.S. troops fighting in Vietnam reach peak level of 541,500.

1969 (June 8) President Nixon announces U.S. will begin to withdraw troops.

1969 (Nov. 15) About 300,000 antiwar demonstrators march on Washington.

1970 (April 30–June 30) U.S. troops enter Cambodia to destroy North Vietnamese supply bases.

1972 (April 2) North Vietnamese troops invade South Vietnam in major new offensive.

1972 (May 8) Mining of North Vietnam's ports and bombing of supply routes to China ordered by Nixon.

1972 (August) Last U.S. combat troops leave Vietnam.

1972 (Oct. 26) Peace Negotiator Henry Kissinger reports U.S. and North Vietnam are in substantial agreement on 9-point plan; expresses belief "peace is at hand."

1972 (Dec. 13) U.S. suspends Kissinger-Tho talks, claiming North Vietnamese have changed their position on previously agreed-upon points.

1972 (Dec. 18) President Nixon orders heaviest bombing of war on North Vietnam; 28 U.S. planes lost in 13 days.

1973 (Jan. 27) Truce agreements formally signed in Paris by U.S., North Vietnam, South Vietnam, and Vietcong.

1973 (Jan. 28) Cease-fire begins in Vietnam at 8 A.M.

1973 (March 29) Last U.S. military personnel leave.

1973 (April 1) Last of 590 U.S. prisoners of war released.

1975 (March 10) North Vietnamese troops begin offensive on provincial capital of Ban Me Thuot.

1975 (March 16) South Vietnam orders withdrawal of troops from northern and central provinces; withdrawal quickly turns into headlong retreat.

1975 (April 21) South Vietnam's President Nguyen Van Thieu resigns and flees to safety in Taiwan a few days later.

1975 (April 29) U.S. ambassador and 1,000 Americans evacuate Saigon by helicopter as communist troops attack city's outskirts.

1975 (April 30) Unconditional surrender of South Vietnam announced by President Duong Van Minh.

QUICK QUIZ: Who was the last king of Italy? See page 298.

VIETNAM *(continued)*

the end of the Vietnam War. The meetings, which continued intermittently into 1977, sought to settle problem issues and lead to the establishment of regular diplomatic relations.

Letters made public in 1977 showed that President Nixon secretly had promised North Vietnam $4.75 billion in postwar aid when the communists agreed to a cease-fire in 1973.

The U.S. Congress passed legislation in July 1977 forbidding the expenditure of funds for aid to Vietnam.

In September 1977 Vietnam was admitted to membership in the United Nations after the U.S. withdrew its objections.

Relations worsened between the U.S. and Vietnam in February 1978 when the U.S. government expelled Vietnam's UN representative Dinh Ba Thi for participation in espionage in the U.S. with an American and a Vietnamese refugee.

The Vietnamese government announced in March 1978 that it was banning all private business and confiscating the property of capitalists.

The government announced in May 1978 that it had resettled some 1.3 million persons from cities into previously uninhabited forest areas.

Vietnam signed an alliance with the Soviet Union on Nov. 3, 1978, which the Chinese denounced as directed against them.

Soviet-equipped Vietnamese troops launched an offensive on Dec. 25, 1978, against the Chinese-supported regime of Pol Pot in Cambodia. In a lightning drive the Vietnamese army captured the Cambodian capital Phnom Penh on Jan. 7, 1979, and set up a new government allied with Vietnam. However, Pol Pot's forces took to the jungles and fought a guerrilla war against the 200,000 Vietnamese troops in Cambodia.

Vowing that Vietnam needed to be "punished," China invaded northern Vietnam on Feb. 17, 1979, with about 200,000 troops. In a hard-fought four-week war, the Chinese destroyed Vietnamese cities and towns within about 40 miles of the Chinese border. China said it had inflicted about 50,000 casualties on the Vietnamese while suffering 20,000.

In 1978–79 hundreds of thousands of refugees left Vietnam, becoming known as "boat people" because of the leaky boats in which they escaped. Evidence mounted that Vietnam was extorting millions of dollars from the refugees to allow them to leave. After protests by neighboring countries about the burden of caring for them, an international conference of 65 nations was called in Geneva, Switzerland, in July 1979. At the conference, the Vietnamese government promised to try to stem the flow of refugees.

The U.S. government in 1981–84 refused to consider establishing diplomatic relations until the Vietnamese government accounts for the fate of some 2,490 American military personnel missing since the end of the Vietnam War.

The government announced in October 1983 the resettlement of 97,000 city dwellers on state-run rubber and coffee plantations.

In 1984 and 1985 a series of border clashes took place between Vietnamese and Chinese troops. Chinese leaders claimed Vietnam was preparing to invade China to distract its people from criticism of the government for Vietnam's faltering economy.

WESTERN SAMOA

Official Name: Western Samoa.
Area: 1,097 square miles (2,842 sq. km.).
Population: 168,300.
Capital: Apia, 32,616.
Government: Parliamentary democracy.
Chief of State: Malietoa Tanumafili II (since 1963).
Prime Minister: Tofilau Eti (since 1982).
Legislature: *Legislative Assembly*, 47 members.
U.S. Ambassador: W. Monroe Browne.
Western Samoan Ambassador to U.S.: Iulia Toma.
Flag: Red field with blue rectangle in upper hoist corner; five white stars represent Southern Cross.
Official Languages: Samoan and English.
Main Ethnic Group: Samoan (89%).
Religions: Congregationalism (50%), Methodism (20%), Roman Catholicism (20%).
Leading Industries: Agriculture (bananas, coconuts, cocoa, poultry, fruits, vegetables); fishing; forestry and lumbering; manufacturing (food processing, handicrafts); tourism.
Foreign Trade: *Major exports*—copra, cocoa, bananas; *major imports*—food, manufactured goods.
Places of Interest: Home of Robert Louis Stevenson; Mt. Vaea on Upolu Island.

About the size of Rhode Island, the Pacific islands of Western Samoa have an economy that depends mostly on agriculture and fishing.

The nation's major exports are bananas, copra, and cocoa. Tourism also brings cash.

The Samoans live in tribal villages, following social customs that have survived for many centuries. There are no political parties. Most Samoans are Christians.

Halfway between Honolulu and Sydney, Western Samoa has two principal islands (Savai'i and Upolu) and seven small islands. About 113 inches of rain falls from October to March.

The first Europeans to sight the islands were the Dutch in 1772. English missionaries arrived in 1830, in the midst of a long struggle among the native chiefs that ended in 1889 when Samoa was declared neutral and independent. Malietoa Laupepa was recognized as king.

In 1900 Eastern Samoa was annexed by the U.S. and Western Samoa by Germany.

From 1919 to 1962 New Zealand administered Western Samoa.

The country was granted independence by New Zealand on Jan. 1, 1962. Malietoa Tanumafili II became chief of state in 1963. Western Samoa became a member of the British Commonwealth of Nations in 1970 and the UN in 1976.

A modern airport and a highway were completed in the mid-1970s.

A strike by some 4,000 government employees for higher wages that began on April 6, 1981, cut off all but emergency services for 90 days.

In a general election on Feb. 23, 1985, Prime Minister Tofilau Eti's Human Rights Protection Party won two-thirds of the seats in the national assembly.

YEMEN, NORTH

Official Name: Yemen Arab Republic.
Area: 75,290 square miles (195,000 sq. km.).
Population: 6,565,000.
Chief Cities: Sana, capital, 140,339; Taiz, 40,000; Hodeida, 40,000.
Government: Military-controlled republic.
President: Lt. Col. Ali Abdullah Saleh (since 1978).
Prime Minister: Abdul Aziz Abd al-Ghani (since 1983).
Constituent People's Assembly: 99 members.
U.S. Ambassador to North Yemen: William A. Rugh.
Yemen Ambassador to U.S.: Mohsin Ahmed Alaini. –
Flag: Red, white, and black stripes, green star.
Language: Arabic.
Main Ethnic Group: Arab.
Official Religion: Islam.
Leading Industries: Agriculture (wheat, sorghum, coffee, cattle, sheep, qat, cotton, fruits); manufacturing (handicrafts, textiles, cement, cigarettes, nails, shoes).
Foreign Trade: *Major exports*—qat, coffee, cotton; *major imports*—food, machinery, vehicles.
Places of Interest: Dhafar antiquities; Throne of Belgis and ruins of Marib Dam at Marib; Al-Janad Mosque; Salah Palace in Taiz.

North Yemen is about the size of South Dakota. Its government, which fosters private enterprise, remains in a state of cold war with its Marxist neighbor South Yemen.

The country has a cooler climate, more rain, and greater possibilities for agriculture development than other areas of the Arabian peninsula.

In North Yemen's interior, mountains rise to a height of more than 12,000 feet. Hills and mountainsides have been terraced by the farmers.

Most of the people are poor. Over a million Yemeni men work in Saudi Arabia, sending home about $2 billion to their families each year Saudi Arabia lies to the north, South Yemen to the south, and the Red Sea to the west.

HISTORY _

North Yemen contained the biblical kingdom of Sheba. The area was ruled by the Himyarites from 115 B.C. to A.D. 525. Yemenis claim to have built the first skyscraper 2,000 years ago, the 20-story Palace of Ghamdan at Sana.

About 885 the Zaidi founded the Rassid dynasty of imams (rulers). Two successive periods of Egyptian control began in the 1200s. In 1517 the Turks occupied the region. After Turkey's defeat in World War I, Yemen was ruled by the Hamid al-Din dynasty of imams.

In 1962 Imam Ahmed's death and the succession of his son Muhammad Badr were followed by a republican revolution led by Col. Abdullah al-Sallal and supported by Egyptian troops. The Yemen Arab Republic was established on Sept. 26, 1962. Republican control soon was established in the coastal Tihama area, while royalist Imani forces held the highlands.

Egypt, the Soviet Union, and communist China supported the republicans in the ensuing civil war, while Saudi Arabia backed the royalists.

Republican forces broke a siege of Sana by royalist troops in 1968. The 8-year civil war came to an end in 1970 with agreement to include royalist leaders in future cabinets.

Col. Ibrahim al-Hamdi, deputy commander of the army, overthrew the government in a bloodless coup on June 13, 1974.

President Hamdi and his brother Lt. Col. Abdullah al-Hamdi were assassinated on Oct. 11, 1977. Lt. Col. Ahmed Hussein al-Ghashmi, Hamdi's second in command, took control.

President Ghashmi was assassinated on June 24, 1978, by a bomb carried by a South Yemen envoy, who also was killed. He was succeeded by 36-year-old Lt. Col. Ali Abdullah Saleh.

Nine high-ranking army officers were reported killed in another unsuccessful coup on Oct. 15, 1978. Twenty-one persons, including a former cabinet minister, were executed for the plot.

Soviet-supplied South Yemen troops invaded North Yemen on Feb. 23, 1979. Reacting to this attempted communist expansion in the Middle East, the U.S. announced on March 9 it was rushing $390 million in arms to North Yemen to aid its army. On March 16 the two nations agreed to a truce, and South Yemen withdrew its troops.

An earthquake destroyed many villages on Dec. 13, 1982, killing more than 2,000 persons.

President Saleh announced that the first major oil discoveries in North Yemen had been made in 1984. He said the nation would begin to export oil by 1987.

YEMEN, SOUTH

Official Name: People's Democratic Republic of Yemen.
Area: 128,560 square miles (332,968 sq. km.).
Population: 2,329,800.
Capital: Aden, 271,590.
Government: One-party Marxist state.
Chief of State and Prime Minister: Ali Nasir Muhammad al-Hasani (since 1980).
People's Supreme Assembly: 111 members.
Flag: Red, white, and black stripes with light blue triangle containing red star at hoist.
Languages: Arabic (official), English.
Main Ethnic Group: Arab (90%).
Religion: Islam.
Leading Industries: Agriculture (cotton, livestock, coffee, sorghum, sesame, millet, tobacco, fruits); oil refining; manufacturing (soap, cigarettes, handicrafts); fishing; mining (salt).
Foreign Trade: *Major exports*—petroleum products, cotton, cottonseed, salt, hides and skins, coffee; *major imports*—food, building materials, automobiles, machinery, manufactured goods, crude oil.
Places of Interest: Ancient ruined cities; Socotra Island; biblical valley of Hadhramant at Shibam.

QUICK QUIZ: Who was the first king of Saudi Arabia? See page 299.

SOUTH YEMEN TODAY

South Yemen is the only Arab Marxist nation. About the size of Nevada, it is a desert country at the southern end of the Arabian peninsula. The main industry is the refining of petroleum at the port city and capital of Aden.

Most of the people are poor farmers or nomadic livestock herders. Only about 1 person in 10 can read and write. With few natural resources, the country depends on foreign aid largely from communist nations.

South Yemen has a hot dry climate. Summer temperatures soar above 130° F.

Extending the length of the Arabian Sea coast is a low, rugged plain. The interior contains a series of increasingly higher ridges that merge into a rugged highland plateau fragmented by a series of deep, dry valleys (wadis).

EARLY HISTORY

South Yemen was included in the Minaean, Sabaean, and Himyarite kingdoms of Arabia that flourished from about 1200 to 50 B.C.

The spread of Judaism and Christianity to southern Yemen in the 500s A.D. brought about religious rivalry. Abyssinian and Persian occupation followed.

By 885 the highland areas of southern Yemen belonged to the Islamic rulers of Yemen. The coastal area recognized the Baghdad caliphate, and was later ruled by Egyptians and Turks.

The British captured Aden in 1839, making it part of the British Empire for more than a century. Aden increased in importance after the opening of the Suez Canal in 1869.

In 1962 Aden joined the British-sponsored Federation of South Arabia to protect itself from Yemeni republicans who had deposed the imam.

INDEPENDENCE

In September 1967, as British troops withdrew from all parts of the country except Aden, the National Liberation Front (NLF) took charge. In November fierce street battles broke out in Aden, and Britain decided to withdraw its military forces.

South Yemen became independent on Nov. 30, 1967. The moderate government of President Qahtan al-Shaabi resigned on June 22, 1969, and was replaced by a Marxist regime.

South Yemen broke diplomatic relations with the United States on Oct. 24, 1969.

On June 26, 1978, President Salim Rubayya Ali of South Yemen was overthrown and executed by his Marxist colleagues. Ali Nasir Muhammad al-Hasani, who had been prime minister since 1972, succeeded to the presidency.

Six months later, on Dec. 28, 1978, Abd al-Fattah Ismail, secretary-general of the Marxist National Front, took over the presidency.

An invasion of North Yemen in a 3-week war from Feb. 23 to March 16, 1979, ended with a truce negotiated by other Arab countries.

South Yemen signed a 20-year friendship pact with the Soviet Union in October 1979.

On April 21, 1980, Prime Minister Hasani overthrew Ismail, taking over as chief of state. Seeking better international relations, he went to Saudi Arabia in June 1980 for the first official visit since South Yemen's independence.

YUGOSLAVIA

Official Name: Socialist Federal Republic of Yugoslavia.
Area: 98,766 square miles (255,804 sq. km.).
Population: 23,321,000.
Chief Cities: Beograd (Belgrade), capital, 746,105; Zagreb, 566,224; Skoplje, 312,980; Sarajevo, 243,980; Ljubljana, 173,853.
Largest Metropolitan Area: Belgrade, 774,744.
Government: One-party communist republic.
President: Chosen annually from among 8-member presidency committee.
Prime Minister: Milka Planinc (since 1982).
Legislature: Assembly—Federal Council, 220 delegates; Council of the Republics and Provinces, 58 delegates.
U.S. Ambassador to Yugoslavia: John D. Scanlan.
Yugoslavian Ambassador to U.S.: Mico Rakic.
Flag: Red star outlined in gold, centered on stripes of blue, white, and red.
Languages: Serbo-Croatian, Slovenian, Macedonian, Hungarian, Albanian.
Main Ethnic Groups: Serb (40%), Croat (22%), Slovene and Bosnian (8%), Macedonian (6%), Albanian (6%), Montenegrin and Hungarian (2%), Turk (1%).
Principal Religions: Eastern Orthodox (41%), Roman Catholicism (32%), Islam (12%).
Leading Industries: Agriculture (wheat, potatoes, corn, barley, tobacco, sugar beets, fruits, vegetables, livestock); manufacturing (steel, cement, chemicals, food processing, fertilizer, textiles); mining (bauxite, lignite, zinc, lead, petroleum, natural gas, iron, coal, copper, gold); forestry and lumbering; tourism.
Foreign Trade: Major exports—timber, nonferrous metals, livestock and meat, machinery, metal products; major imports—machinery, metal products, chemicals, textiles, petroleum.
Places of Interest: Mountain and coastal resorts; Roman, Byzantine, Serbian, and Turkish antiquities at Skoplje; Plitvice lakes; Postoina caves; Dubrovnik; Split; Opatija; Ljubljana; Zagreb. In Belgrade: national museum; Museum of Modern Art; Kalemegdan citadel (now a museum).

YUGOSLAVIA TODAY

About the size of Wyoming, Yugoslavia is a communist nation in southeastern Europe. It is among the world's leading producers of bauxite, lead, and lignite.

The country's main problem in international relations has been to maintain independence from the Soviet Union and play a leading role among the nonaligned nations of the world.

About two-thirds of the people speak the Serbo-Croatian language.

The two largest ethnic groups, the Serbs and Croatians, have feuded with each other for hundreds of years.

The remaining third of the population includes large minority groups of Slovenes, Macedonians, Albanians, Bosnian Muslims, Montenegrins, Hungarians, and Turks.

In an effort to give these various ethnic groups local self-government, Yugoslavia is divided into

six republics and two autonomous provinces within Serbia (Kosovo and Vojvodina).

Croatian nationalists, many living in exile, continue to work for independence of a Croatian state, sometimes carrying out bombings and airplane hijackings to call attention to their cause.

Although Yugoslavia has made progress toward industrialization through use of its wealth of natural resources, almost three-fourths of the people still live on farms and in villages. However, Yugoslavs enjoy more consumer goods then most other communist nations of Europe.

The nation's official name is the *Socialist Federal Republic of Yugoslavia.*

The Danube River and its tributaries drain Yugoslavia's fertile lowland area in the north and northeast. Yugoslavia's coastline along the Adriatic Sea is about 1,000 miles long. About two-thirds of the country is covered by mountain ranges that run northwest to southeast a few miles inland from the Adriatic coast. The climate is similar to that of the U.S. east coast.

Yugoslavia is bounded on the north by Italy, Austria, and Hungary; on the east by Romania and Bulgaria; and on the south by Greece and Albania.

EARLY HISTORY

The various parts of Yugoslavia had never been united under one government before 1918:

Serbia was under Turkish domination from 1371 to 1878. After the Balkan Wars of 1912–13, Serbia became independent and acquired Macedonia, an ancient kingdom that had been under Turkish control.

Montenegro, under Turkish rule for centuries, became independent in 1878.

Slovenia, passing to Austrian Hapsburg rule in 1335, was under their domination until 1918.

Croatia was part of Hungary from the 1000s and then was ruled by Austria-Hungary from 1867. It became part of Serbia after World War I.

Bosnia and Herzegovina became Turkish possessions in the 1500s and were annexed by Austria in 1908.

The 1914 assassination by Serbian nationalists in Sarajevo, Bosnia, of Austria's Archduke Franz Ferdinand led to World War I. The collapse of the Austro-Hungarian and Turkish empires opened the way for unification of the Balkan Slavs.

King Peter I of Serbia became the ruler of the new Kingdom of the Serbs, Croats, and Slovenes in 1918, but his son Alexander ruled as regent until Peter's death in 1921.

King Alexander declared himself absolute ruler in 1929 and changed the kingdom's name to Yugoslavia. In 1934 Alexander was assassinated. His heir, Peter II, succeeded under the regency of Prince Paul.

Yugoslavia attempted to remain neutral in World War II, but Germany invaded the country on April 6, 1941, and defeated its army in two weeks. King Peter II fled to London.

Several resistance movements emerged. The most important were the royalist Chetniks, led by a Serb general, Draja Mikhailovich, and the pro-Soviet partisans led by the Croat communist Josip Broz Tito. Both guerrilla armies fought

REPUBLICS OF YUGOSLAVIA

REPUBLIC	CAPITAL	AREA
Bosnia and Herzegovina	Sarajevo	19,741 sq. mi.
Croatia	Zagreb	21,829 sq. mi.
Macedonia	Skoplje	9,928 sq. mi.
Montenegro	Titograd	5,333 sq. mi.
Serbia	Belgrade	34,116 sq. mi.
Slovenia	Ljubljana	7,819 sq. mi.

against the Germans and each other.

By 1944 Britain and the U.S. switched support to Tito, who also received military aid from the Soviet Union.

COMMUNIST RULE

A leftist coalition headed by Tito declared a republic on Nov. 29, 1945. Tito became president. Mikhailovich was captured, tried as a war criminal, and executed on July 17, 1946.

Although the Communist Party ruled the country, it resisted Soviet efforts to penetrate and control Yugoslavia. Matters came to a head in January 1948 when the recently created Communist Information Bureau (Cominform), dominated by Moscow, expelled Yugoslavia, charging it with "revisionism." This break forced Tito to draw closer to the West.

After the death of Stalin in 1953, however, diplomatic and trade relations with the Soviet Union were resumed. A dramatic visit to Yugoslavia by Soviet leader Nikita Khrushchev in 1955 restored cooperative relations.

A meeting between President Tito and Chancellor Willy Brandt of West Germany in 1973 worked out differences between the two nations regarding reparations Yugoslavia claimed for damages during World War II.

To combat low productivity, the government for the first time in 1975 gave the managers of communist businesses the right to fire workers who fail to meet production goals.

In January 1976 the U.S. resumed selling arms to Yugoslavia. American military aid had been suspended since 1961.

At a meeting between Soviet leader Leonid Brezhnev and Tito in Yugoslavia in November 1976, the Yugoslav president turned down Soviet requests for closer military cooperation.

After a protracted illness, Tito died on May 4, 1980, three days short of his 88th birthday.

In March and April 1981 riots in the southern region of Kosovo left 9 dead and about 200 injured. The agitation was fomented by Albanian nationalists seeking unification of the region with Albania.

Milka Planinc, 58, was elected by parliament as prime minister on May 16, 1982, becoming the first woman to head the nation's government. She formerly had been leader of the Communist Party in Croatia.

Prime Minister Planinc was faced with difficult economic problems in meeting $5.3 billion in annual payments on the nation's $21 billion foreign debt.

The government announced that recession and 58% inflation had caused a 10% decline in the nation's standard of living in the 1980's.

QUICK QUIZ: Who ruled Spain in 1516–1556? See page 299.

ZAIRE

Official Name: Republic of Zaire.
Area: 905,568 square miles (2,345,409 sq. km.).
Population: 33,467,000.
Chief Cities: Kinshasa, capital, 2,242,297; Kananga, 376,770; Luluabourg, 506,033; Lubumbashi, 480,875; Mbuji-Mayi, 283,279; Kisangani, 297,888.
Government: One-party dictatorship.
President: Mobutu Sese Seko (seized power in 1965).
Prime Minister: Joseph Nsigna (since 1981).
Legislature: *National Assembly,* 420 members.
U.S. Ambassador to Zaire: Brandon H. Grove Jr.
Zairian Ambassador to U.S.: Kasongo Mutuale.
Flag: Green field with yellow circle in center showing arm carrying torch.
Languages: French (official), tribal dialects.
Main Ethnic Group: Bantu (80%).
Religions: Animism (50%), Christianity (50%).
Leading Industries: Agriculture (coffee, cocoa, tea, rubber, palm kernels, cotton, sugarcane, livestock, fruits, vegetables); mining (copper, petroleum, zinc, tin, cobalt, diamonds, gold); forestry and lumbering; manufacturing (food processing, textiles, clothing, cement, consumer goods).
Foreign Trade: *Major exports*—copper, diamonds, cobalt, coffee, tin, palm oil; *major imports*—food, motor vehicles, cotton fabrics, petroleum products.
Places of Interest: Boyoma Falls, Point Kalina, Cristal Mountains—all on Zaire River. *In Kinshasa:* Botanical and zoological gardens; Museum of Native Life; St. Anne's Cathedral; Pioneers and Stanley monuments.

ZAIRE TODAY

About one-fourth the size of the United States, Zaire is rich in natural resources. The country's economy has suffered because of low copper prices since the mid-1970s.

Zaire is the world's largest producer of cobalt and industrial diamonds and the sixth most important copper-mining country. It ranks eighth in tin-ore mining and ninth in natural rubber. Offshore oil wells began production in 1975. In addition its rivers provide potential for hydroelectric power. Hopeful of becoming the leading industrial nation of Africa, the government has sought loans and investments from both communist and noncommunist nations.

As with most other African countries, a problem equal to the lack of capital is the scarcity of educated skilled workers. Most of the people belong to the more than 200 Bantu tribes that live in the tropical forests or on the upland plains. Few can read and write. The tribesmen support themselves with primitive subsistence farming that has changed little in hundreds of years. But Zaire also must import much food.

The third-largest nation in Africa, Zaire derives its name from the Zaire (Congo) River, whose course lies within the country's borders. Except for a narrow corridor on the northern bank of the Zaire River, the country is landlocked.

Much of the central Zaire River basin area, comprising nearly half the country, is densely forested. The land in the higher regions to the north and south is savanna or bush country. Southeast of the central plateau the elevation gradually rises to 6,000 feet, and to the east mountain ranges reach a height of 16,763 feet at the crest of Margherita Peak.

In the lower western and central regions the climate is tropically hot and humid. The climate in the higher eastern elevations is more temperate. South of the equator rains are heavy and frequent from fall to late spring. North of the equator the season of heaviest rainfall is from April to November.

Congo lies to the west; Central Africa and Sudan to the north; Uganda, Rwanda, Burundi, and Tanzania to the east; and Zambia and Angola to the south.

EARLY HISTORY

Pygmies or Bushmen probably first occupied the Zaire basin. They were later displaced by migrants (mostly Bantu), who settled the area in the 600s and 700s and established kingdoms. The kingdom of Kongo (Congo) gave its name to the river and to the French and Belgian colonial territories carved from the basin.

Henry Stanley of Britain explored the Congo River in 1877. His reports sparked the interest of King Leopold II of Belgium, who in 1878 formed a company to exploit the region.

The Congress of Berlin in 1885 recognized Leopold's claims, and he became absolute monarch of the Congo Free State.

International protests over reported abuse of the Congolese population forced Leopold to cede his private state to Belgium. It became the colony of Belgian Congo in 1908.

INDEPENDENCE

Belgium granted the country independence on June 30, 1960. Parliament chose Joseph Kasavubu as president and Patrice Lumumba as premier. Almost immediately the country was swept by disorders. Belgian troops intervened to protect Belgian nationals. The gravest challenge was the secession of the richest province, Katanga, led by Moše Tshombe.

When rivalry between Kasavubu and Lumumba crippled the government, Col. Joseph-Désiré Mobutu (now Mobutu Sese Seko), head of the army, supported Kasavubu. Lumumba was jailed but escaped, and then was murdered.

In January 1963 the central government, with UN military aid, took over Katanga province.

Tshombe was invited in 1964 to return from exile to become premier. Fighting intensified in Katanga. In October 1965 Kasavubu replaced Tshombe as premier with Evariste Kimba.

Mobutu, now a general, proclaimed himself president and assumed total power on Nov. 24, 1965. Kimba and other opponents were hanged.

In 1973–74 Zaire confiscated stores and plantations owned by foreigners, and in January 1975 nationalized all industries, building trades, and distribution services.

On March 8, 1977, Katangan rebels invaded Zaire's eastern province of Shaba from Angola. They were defeated in May after Morocco sent 1,500 troops to aid Zaire.

In May 1978 Katangan rebels again invaded Zaire from Angola. Capturing the copper-mining town of Kolwezi, they massacred about 200 whites. French and Belgian paratroops drove out the invaders.

The human rights organization Amnesty International issued a report on May 20, 1980, accusing Mobutu's regime of executing and starving to death hundreds of political prisoners.

The longest and most powerful electric power line in the world was constructed in 1974–81 from the Inga Dam in western Zaire across 1,100 miles of jungle to the copper-mining center of Kolwezi.

Prime Minister Nguza Karl-i-Bond fled to exile in Europe where he resigned on April 16, 1981. He accused Mobutu of taking more than $150 million in government funds for personal use.

Low world-market prices for copper, Zaire's main export product, have crippled the nation's economy since the mid-1970s.

Unable to meet payments on its debts of about $6 billion, the government was forced by its foreign creditors to adopt stringent financial measures. The International Monetary Fund on June 22, 1981, granted Zaire a 3-year credit of $1.2 billion.

Israel and Zaire reached agreement in January 1983 on a 5-year military pact to strengthen Zaire's defenses.

Mobutu was reelected without opposition in July 1984 to a third seven-year term.

ZAMBIA

Official Name: Republic of Zambia.
Area: 290,586 square miles (752,614 sq. km.).
Population: 6,788,000.
Chief Cities: Lusaka, capital, 641,000; Kitwe, 341,000; Ndola, 323,000; Chingola, 192,000.
Government: One-party republic.
President: Kenneth D. Kaunda (took office in 1964).
Prime Minister: Nalumino Mundia (since 1981).
Legislature: *National Assembly*, 136 members.
U.S. Ambassador to Zambia: Paul Julian Hare.
Zambian Ambassador to U.S.: Putteho Muketoi Ngonda.
Flag: Green field with red, black, and orange bars on right surmounted by eagle.
Languages: English (official), tribal languages, including Bemba, Tnga, Nyanja.
Main Ethnic Group: Black (99%).
Religions: Animism (70%), Christianity (30%).
Leading Industries: Agriculture (corn, tobacco, peanuts, cotton, livestock, fruits, vegetables); mining (copper, cobalt, zinc, lead, coal); manufacturing (textiles, food processing, tobacco products).
Foreign Trade: *Major exports*—copper, lead, zinc, cobalt; *major imports*—machinery, vehicles.
Places of Interest: Victoria Falls; Lake Tanganyika; Zambezi River; Luangwa Valley and Kafue national parks; Lusaka; Maramba Cultural Center and national museum in Livingstone.

ZAMBIA TODAY

Somewhat larger than Texas, Zambia has an abundance of natural resources. It is one of the world's largest producers of copper. It is also an important source of cobalt, zinc, and lead.

The Zambian government obtained a majority interest in previously foreign-owned mining industries in 1970, agreeing to compensate the owners out of future earnings. Since then, the government has financed large-scale agricultural and industrial development projects.

Although Zambia's per capita national income is twice that of many of Africa's black nations, most Zambians still are poor farmers who barely raise enough food to live. Only about half the people can read and write.

Most of the country is a plateau of flat, wooded grassland broken by scrub-covered hills and by valleys of the Zambezi and Luangwa rivers.

Landlocked Zambia is surrounded by Zaire, Tanzania, Malawi, Mozambique, Zimbabwe (Rhodesia), Botswana, Namibia, and Angola.

HISTORY

In the 1400s Bantu tribesmen moved into the area from the north.

In the early 1800s Nguni-speaking Africans and Swahili-speaking slave traders arrived.

Explorer David Livingstone first saw Victoria Falls in 1855.

British developer Cecil Rhodes in 1888 obtained mineral rights. The region became known as *Northern Rhodesia*. The British South African Company, developing the copper resources, governed the territory.

In 1924 Northern Rhodesia became a British protectorate. In 1953 Britain founded the Federation of Rhodesia and Nyasaland, transferring control to white-ruled Southern Rhodesia (now Zimbabwe). The federation was dissolved in 1963. Northern Rhodesia then proceeded toward independence under African majority rule.

Zambia, as the new republic was named, became independent within the British Commonwealth of Nations on Oct. 24, 1964. Kenneth Kaunda was elected as Zambia's first president.

A new constitution adopted in 1973 made Kaunda's United National Independence Party (UNIP) the nation's only political party.

On July 1, 1975, President Kaunda decreed the nationalization of privately owned land, movie theaters, private hospitals, and newspapers.

Completion of the 1,162-mile TanZam Railway in 1976, linking Zambia's copper mines with the Tanzanian port of Dar es Salaam, promised increased economic growth.

Faced with a worsening economy, Zambia lifted its trade embargo on neighboring Zimbabwe on Oct. 6, 1978, in order to use its rail lines for trade with Mozambique and South Africa.

Strikes by miners at government-owned copper mines in 1981 prompted Kaunda to arrest four top union leaders in July. The union leaders likened themselves to those of Poland's Solidarity movement in opposing the government's adherence to a one-party socialist state.

Kaunda won reelection as president without opposition on Oct. 27, 1983.

QUICK QUIZ: When did Nero rule in Rome? See page 300.

ZIMBABWE

Official Name: Republic of Zimbabwe.
Area: 150,804 square miles (390,580 sq. km.).
Population: 8,315,000.
Chief Cities: Harare (Salisbury), capital, 656,000; Bulawayo, 414,000, Chitungwiza, 173,000.
Government: Parliamentary democracy.
Prime Minister: Robert Mugabe (since 1980).
President: Rev. Canaan Banana (since 1980).
Parliament: *House of Assembly,* 100 members (80 black, 20 white); *Senate,* 40 members.
U.S. Ambassador to Zimbabwe: David C. Miller, Jr.
Zimbabwe Ambassador to U.S.: Edmund Richard Mashoko Garwe.
Flag: Zimbabwe bird on red star in white triangle at hoist; stripes, top to bottom, of green, gold, red, black, red, gold, and green.
Languages: English (official), Shona, Ndebele.
Main Ethnic Groups: Blacks (96%), European descent (4%).
Religions: Animism, Anglicanism, Presbyterianism, Roman Catholicism.
Leading Industries: Agriculture (corn, tobacco, sugarcane, cotton, wheat, tea, millet, sorghum, livestock, vegetables, fruits); mining (coal, chrome, asbestos, gold, copper); manufacturing (electricity, clothing, chemicals, steel, vehicles, petroleum products).
Foreign Trade: *Major exports*—maize, tobacco, asbestos, copper, clothing, meat; *major imports*—textiles, fertilizers, automobiles, petroleum, tobacco.
Places of Interest: Victoria Falls; Wankie National Park; Inyanga and Vumba mountains; Mana pools; Harare (Salisbury); Bulawayo; Zimbabwe ruins.

ZIMBABWE TODAY

Formerly called Rhodesia, Zimbabwe won international recognition as an independent nation in 1980. After 15 years in which a white minority resisted world pressure and guerrilla warfare to retain control of the government, a peaceful transition to black majority rule was achieved.

The new black government pledged itself to protect the rights of whites, who have enjoyed a standard of living comparable to that of Americans. At the same time it sought massive international aid to improve the lot of blacks, most of whom live as tribal subsistence farmers. Fewer than 1 black in 3 can read and write.

One of the leading gold-mining countries, Zimbabwe lies between the Limpopo and Zambezi rivers. Mt. Inyangani, on the eastern border, rises to 8,514 feet. Zambia is on the north, Mozambique on the east, South Africa on the south, and Botswana on the west.

EARLY HISTORY

The name Zimbabwe comes from the stone ruins of a city built by a black civilization in the 1000s to 1400s.

In the 1890s the British South Africa Company of Cecil Rhodes acquired the area.

In 1923 the British government took over the region, calling the colony Southern Rhodesia.

Britain refused independence to Southern Rhodesia in 1964 unless representative government was assured for the black majority.

In the 1965 elections the Rhodesia Front, representing white nationalism, won an overwhelming victory, retaining in office Ian Smith, who had been prime minister since 1964.

INDEPENDENCE

On Nov. 11, 1965, Southern Rhodesia declared independence from Britain. Britain and other nations refused to grant diplomatic recognition because the all-white government restricted the rights of blacks. The United Nations in 1966 called for a trade embargo on Rhodesia. The U.S. joined in the trade boycott.

All ties between Britain and Rhodesia were severed on March 2, 1970, when the government proclaimed itself the *Republic of Rhodesia.*

Black guerrillas fought government troops and civilians from 1965 to 1979.

On March 3, 1978, the Rhodesian government signed an agreement with leaders of the United African National Council (UANC) providing for a transitional government leading to black majority rule. The head of the UANC, American-educated Methodist Bishop Abel Muzorewa, joined Smith's government.

In a national election on April 17–21, 1979, 1.7 million blacks voted for the first time, giving 51 parliamentary seats to Muzorewa's UANC party. On May 29, 1979, Muzorewa became the nation's first black prime minister.

Under the leadership of Lord Carrington, Britain's foreign minister, Muzorewa and guerrilla leaders signed a peace agreement on Dec. 21, 1979, after a conference in London. A cease-fire went into effect on Dec. 28, 1979.

In an election on Feb. 27–29, the Zanu-Patriotic Front party of former guerrilla leader Robert Mugabe won control of parliament with 57 of the 80 seats reserved for blacks.

Britain formally recognized independence for the Republic of Zimbabwe on April 18, 1980, with Mugabe, a Marxist socialist, as prime minister. Mugabe formed a coalition government that included Joshua Nkomo, a former guerrilla leader who was Mugabe's main rival.

Despite Mugabe's assurances of protection, whites continued to leave the country, over 100,000 emigrating in 1980–84.

To display opposition to South Africa's apartheid policy, Zimbabwe broke diplomatic relations on Sept. 3, 1980. But because of economic dependence on South Africa, trade relations continued.

On Feb. 17, 1982, Mugabe dismissed Nkomo from his cabinet, accusing him of plotting to overthrow the government. Later, Mugabe announced that he planned to convert Zimbabwe into a one-party state and to eliminate private enterprise. After Nkomo's ouster from the cabinet, the nation experienced increasing violence between Mugabe's armed forces and Nkomo's followers. Several foreign tourists were kidnapped and killed.

Former prime minister Bishop Abel Muzorewa was imprisoned on Oct. 31, 1983, on charges of "clandestine" activities after he returned from a visit to Israel. He was freed Sept. 4, 1984.

Mugabe's party won a decisive victory in parliamentary elections in July 1985.

Newspapers and Magazines

HIGHLIGHTS: 1985

TIME WINS SHARON LIBEL SUIT

A six-member jury ruled on Jan. 24, 1985, that Time magazine did not libel former Israeli Defense Minister Ariel Sharon. He had sued the weekly news magazine for $50 million in damages because of an article that said secret Israeli documents blamed him for encouraging a massacre of hundreds of Palestinian refugees in Beirut in September 1982 by Christian Lebanese militiamen.

The trial began in New York City on Nov. 13, 1984.

The 56-year-old Israeli politician and former general brought the suit in federal court based on an article headlined "Verdict on the Massacre" in the magazine's issue of Feb. 21, 1983.

Sharon, who currently is Israel's minister of industry and commerce, took the stand to testify on his own behalf as the first witness in the trial. He denied he had discussed with the Christian militia any plans for them to revenge themselves for the assassination of their leader, Bashir Gemayel, who had been elected President of Lebanon.

In early January 1985 the Israeli government reported to the federal judge trying the case that the secret document referred to in the Time magazine article contained no evidence that Sharon had discussed revenge with the Christian militia.

To win his case Sharon had to prove that the article was (1) defamatory, (2) false, and (3) published with reckless disregard for the truth. The jury announced on Jan. 16 that it had decided the article was defamatory. Two days later the jury announced a decision that the article was false. Finally on Jan. 24, after 11 days of deliberation, the jury announced that Sharon had been unable to prove that Time magazine published the article with "actual malice."

Although Sharon received no damages, the jury scored Time with a statement declaring the magazine had been negligent and careless in its reporting.

WESTMORELAND DROPS CBS LIBEL SUIT

Gen. William C. Westmoreland, commanding general of U.S. forces in the Vietnam War in 1964-68, dropped his $120 million libel suit against CBS on Feb. 18, 1985, after four months of testimony and only days before a jury was to begin considering a verdict.

At issue was a CBS documentary program, "The Uncounted Enemy: A Vietnam Deception," that was broadcast on TV on Jan. 23, 1982.

Westmoreland filed suit on Sept. 13, 1982, charging that CBS had defamed him by accusing him of deceiving President Lyndon Johnson and the Joint Chiefs of Staff by understating the true strength of enemy forces in Vietnam. The suit also sought damages from George Crile, producer of the documentary; Mike Wallace, the narrator of the program; and Samuel A. Adams, a former CIA analyst who was a consultant for the show.

The trial began on Oct. 9, 1984, with selection of a jury.

In November, the 70-year-old retired general took the witness stand for nine days of testimony, denying that he had done anything improper.

As the trial entered its 17th week in February, Westmoreland's former chief of intelligence, Maj. Gen. Joseph A. McChristian took the stand to testify that in May 1967 he had shown Westmoreland a cable that he planned to send to Washington showing a major increase in enemy strength. "He asked to hold it up based on political considerations," McChristian testified.

In the 18th week of the trial, on Feb. 12, Col. Gains B. Hawkins, who had been in charge of determining enemy strength under Westmoreland, testified as CBS's 16th witness concerning the charges made by CBS that Westmoreland had set a ceiling of 300,000 on reports of enemy forces. He said that Westmoreland had told him that "higher figures were politically unacceptable."

Suddenly, on Feb. 18, Westmoreland decided to drop the suit in return for a joint statement with CBS that declared:

"CBS respects General Westmoreland's

U.S. DAILY NEWSPAPERS

Source: *American Newspaper Publishers Association*

YEAR	NO.	CIRCULATION	YEAR	NO.	CIRCULATION
1945	1,749	48,384,188	1975	1,756	60,655,431
1950	1,772	53,829,000	1976	1,762	60,977,011
1955	1,760	56,147,000	1977	1,753	61,495,140
1960	1,763	58,882,000	1978	1,576	61,989,997
1965	1,751	60,358,000	1979	1,763	62,223,040
1969	1,758	62,060,000	1980	1,746	62,201,840
1970	1,748	62,108,000	1981	1,730	61,432,434
1971	1,749	61,743,141	1982	1,711	62,487,177
1972	1,761	62,510,242	1983	1,701	62,644,603
1973	1,774	63,147,280	1984	1,688	63,081,740
1974	1,768	61,877,197			

HIGHLIGHTS: 1985 *(continued)*

long and faithful service to his country and never intended to assert, and does not believe, that General Westmoreland was unpatriotic or disloyal in performing his duties as he saw them.

"General Westmoreland respects the long and distinguished journalistic tradition of CBS and the rights of journalists to examine the complex issues of Vietnam and to present perspectives contrary to his own."

The foreman of the jury was quoted by news reporters as telling them that if the case had continued, "It probably would have been a verdict in favor of CBS."

However, Westmoreland called the statement by CBS an "apology" and declared, "I consider that I won."

Each side paid its own court costs, which together were estimated to have been $7 million to $9 million.

BANKRUPT UPI TURNS PROFITABLE

United Press International (UPI), the nation's No. 2 news service, on April 28, 1985, filed under Chapter 11 of the bankruptcy

U.S. DAILY NEWSPAPER CIRCULATION LEADERS: 1984

Source: American Newspaper Publishers Association

NEWSPAPER	CIRCULATION	NEWSPAPER	CIRCULATION
New York (NY) *Wall Street Journal* (m)	1,959,873	Tampa (FL) *Tribune* (all day)	208,798
New York (NY) *Daily News* (m)	1,346,840	Columbus (OH) *Dispatch* (e)	206,207
Washington (DC) *USA Today* (m)	1,247,324	Baltimore (MD) *Sun* (m)	192,067
Los Angeles (CA) *Times* (m)	1,046,965	Seattle (WA) *Post-Intelligencer* (m)	191,825
New York (NY) *Times* (m)	934,616	Cincinnati (OH) *Enquirer* (m)	189,840
New York (NY) *Post* (all day)	930,026	Charlotte (NC) *Observer* (m)	185,876
Chicago (IL) *Tribune* (all day)	776,348	Milwaukee (WI) *Sentinel* (m)	183,621
Washington (DC) *Post* (m)	728,857	Atlanta (GA) *Journal* (e)	183,287
Detroit (MI) *News* (all day)	656,367	Louisville (KY) *Courier-Journal* (m)	174,399
Chicago (IL) *Sun-Times* (m)	649,891	Pittsburgh (PA) *Post-Gazette* (m)	173,838
Detroit (MI) *Free Press* (m)	647,130	San Antonio (TX) *Express-News* (all day)	169,884
Long Island (NY) *Newsday* (e)	539,065	Birmingham (AL) *News* (e)	165,212
San Francisco (CA) *Chronicle* (m)	535,796	Toledo (OH) *Blade* (e)	163,881
Philadelphia (PA) *Inquirer* (m)	525,569	Akron (OH) *Beacon Journal* (e)	163,597
Boston (MA) *Globe* (m)	520,081	Jacksonville (FL) *Times-Union* (m)	160,989
Cleveland (OH) *Plain Dealer* (m)	482,564	Austin (TX) *American-Statesman* (all day)	160,526
Houston (TX) *Chronicle* (all day)	441,557	Baltimore (MD) *Evening Sun* (e)	155,607
Miami (FL) *Herald* (m)	435,418	Hackensack (NJ) *Record* (e)	150,885
Newark (NJ) *Star-Ledger* (m)	434,117	San Francisco (CA) *Examiner* (e)	148,700
Minneapolis (MN) *Star and Tribune* (m)	373,145	Oakland (CA) *Tribune* (m)	148,088
Dallas (TX) *Morning News* (m)	360,347	Los Angeles (CA) *Daily News* (m)	144,023
Boston (MA) *Herald* (m)	343,581	Norfolk (VA) *Virginian-Pilot* (m)	141,714
Houston (TX) *Post* (m)	326,556	Boston (MA) *Christian Science Monitor* (m)	141,247
Denver (CO) *Rocky Mountain News* (m)	317,638	San Antonio (TX) *Light* (all day)	140,141
Buffalo (NY) *News* (all day)	315,111	Richmond (VA) *Times-Dispatch* (m)	136,598
Milwaukee (WI) *Journal* (e)	303,127	Fresno (CA) *Bee* (m)	135,832
Philadelphia (PA) *Daily News* (e)	295,747	Grand Rapids (MI) *Press* (e)	134,406
Portland (OR) *Oregonian* (all day)	290,228	Louisville (KY) *Times* (e)	134,343
Orange County-Santa Ana (CA) *Register* (all day)	284,951	Tulsa (OK) *World* (m)	132,789
Phoenix (AZ) *Republic* (m)	283,550	Indianapolis (IN) *News* (e)	132,308
Kansas City (MO) *Times* (m)	281,974	Raleigh (NC) *News & Observer* (m)	131,760
New Orleans (LA) *Times-Picayune/States-Item* (all day)	276,556	Rochester (NY) *Democrat & Chronicle* (m)	131,140
Dallas (TX) *Times Herald* (all day)	270,622	Cincinnati (OH) *Post* (e)	129,697
St. Petersburg (FL) *Times* (m)	267,266	Fort Worth (TX) *Star-Telegram* (e)	129,632
St. Louis (MO) *Post-Dispatch* (m)	264,721	Allentown (PA) *Morning Call* (m)	129,469
San Jose (CA) *Mercury-News* (all day)	246,226	Providence (RI) *Bulletin* (e)	127,553
Pittsburgh (PA) *Press* (e)	243,865	Little Rock (AR) *Gazette* (m)	126,922
Oklahoma City (OK) *Oklahoman* (m)	236,470	Asbury Park (NJ) *Press* (e)	125,659
Des Moines (IA) *Register* (m)	234,927	Nashville (TN) *Tennessean* (m)	123,454
Indianapolis (IN) *Star* (m)	234,554	Wichita (KS) *Eagle-Beacon* (m)	123,074
Denver (CO) *Post* (m)	234,303	San Diego (CA) *Tribune* (e)	121,008
Kansas City (MO) *Star* (e)	233,691	Columbus (OH) *Citizen-Journal* (m)	119,850
Los Angeles (CA) *Herald Examiner* (m)	233,193	Omaha (NE) *World-Herald* (m)	119,790
Memphis (TN) *Commercial Appeal* (m)	230,666	Fort Worth (TX) *Star-Telegram* (m)	117,172
Orlando (FL) *Sentinel* (all day)	227,932	Riverside (CA) *Press-Enterprise* (m)	115,795
Atlanta (GA) *Constitution* (m)	227,755	Dayton (OH) *Daily News* (e)	114,100
Seattle (WA) *Times* (e)	222,916	Richmond (VA) *News-Leader* (e)	113,466
San Diego (CA) *Union* (m)	221,650	Long Beach (CA) *Press-Telegram* (m)	112,738
Sacramento (CA) *Bee* (m)	221,407	Honolulu (HI) *Star-Bulletin* (e)	110,788
Hartford (CT) *Courant* (m)	219,387		
St. Louis (MO) *Globe-Democrat* (m)	210,712		

m = morning e = evening

laws for protection from creditors owed about $40 million. But two months later, the company was able to report to the bankruptcy court that it made an operating profit of $439,000 on revenues of $8.6 million in May.

The company's improved financial picture was due to severe austerity measures. In September 1984 Wire Service Guild members at UPI agreed to a 25% pay cut for three months. In June UPI asked employees to accept a 10% pay cut for one year along with reduced health care benefits, and a longer work week.

UPI has about 800 newspaper clients and 3,800 radio and TV stations. In news bureaus throughout the world it has about 2,000 employees.

GANNETT BUYS PUBLICATIONS

The Gannett Co., ranking as the biggest newspaper publisher in the United States with an average daily circulation of over 4 million by its 85 dailies, announced two major purchases in February.

Directors of the Des Moines (Iowa) Register and Tribune agreed to an offer of $200 million from Gannett. As well as the highly respected Iowa newspaper, the sale included the Jackson (Tenn.) Sun and weekly newspapers in Indianola and Independence, Iowa.

Gannett also bought the Family Weekly Sunday newspaper supplement for $42.5 million from CBS Inc. Family Weekly has a weekly circulation of about 13 million. Gannett reportedly planned to change the publication's name to USA Weekend and adopt a format similar to that of the company's national daily USA Today.

TIME INC. EXPANDS

Time Inc. purchased Southern Progress Corp. for $480 million, acquiring three new magazines: Southern Living, Progressive Farmer, and Creative Ideas for Living.

Time executives also announced that one new magazine would be launched in 1985, Picture Week, which would feature "pictures you might not ordinarily see." Dick Stolley, who has been managing editor of Life magazine, was named editor of Picture Week.

The Company deferred other new magazine projects that had included Flash, a women's magazine; Then and Now, a nostalgia magazine; Leisure, a travel and leisure magazine; and Investment Week, a personal finance magazine.

U.S. MAGAZINE CIRCULATION LEADERS: 1984

Source: Magazine Publishers Association

MAGAZINE	CIRCULATION	MAGAZINE	CIRCULATION	MAGAZINE	CIRCULATION
Reader's Digest	17,866,798	Seventeen	1,744,435	US	952,625
TV Guide	17,115,233	Ebony	1,705,455	Travel & Leisure	941,246
Modern Maturity	10,770,668	Parents	1,694,236	Scouting	936,272
NRTA/AARP News		Popular Mechanics	1,640,503	Sport	932,546
Bulletins	10,431,921	Elks Magazine	1,624,033	Weekly World News	917,307
National Geographic	10,392,548	Mechanix Illustrated	1,582,147	Popular Photography	905,171
Better Homes &		1,001 Home Ideas	1,546,479	Farm Journal	904,708
Gardens	8,058,839	True Story	1,542,478	Workbench	881,833
Family Circle	6,920,333	Adventure Road	1,531,010	Car & Driver	881,285
Woman's Day	6,517,684	Outdoor Life	1,514,660	House Beautiful	867,736
McCall's	6,311,011	Motorland	1,509,337	Hot Rod	865,609
Good Housekeeping	5,184,559	Money	1,505,964	Nation's Business	865,590
Ladies Home Journal	5,058,538	American Hunter	1,464,993	Rolling Stone	860,991
Time	4,619,777	American Rifleman	1,457,148	Business Week (World	
National Enquirer	4,512,689	Life	1,445,124	Wide)	857,600
Playboy	4,217,324	Boys' Life	1,410,415	Mother Earth News	857,010
Guideposts	4,133,566	Sunset	1,387,855	Weight Watchers	
Redbook	4,009,584	Changing Times	1,383,513	Magazine	852,275
Penthouse	3,771,404	Organic Gardening	1,378,628	Psychology Today	850,845
Star	3,213,728	Woman's World	1,346,159	Omni	842,282
Newsweek	3,012,746	Country Living	1,319,823	Jet	842,172
People Weekly	2,840,775	Bon Appetit	1,300,887	Soap Opera Digest	840,732
Cosmopolitan	2,826,282	Discovery	1,264,710	Michigan Living	815,235
Prevention	2,821,501	Dial	1,256,676	Signature	812,547
Sports Illustrated	2,637,751	Golf Digest	1,225,397	Junior Scholastic	792,626
The American Legion	2,503,017	Vogue	1,218,742	Young Miss	786,314
Glamour	2,288,988	Mademoiselle	1,211,080	Golf	778,798
Southern Living	2,253,569	Family Handyman	1,204,148	Motor Trend	778,171
Smithsonian	2,135,953	Self	1,066,181	American Health	750,113
U.S. News & World		Health	1,022,064	Road & Track	741,430
Report	2,071,241	Consumers Digest	1,021,229	Harper's Bazaar	737,430
Field & Stream	2,002,883	New Woman	1,014,244	Creative Ideas for	
V.F.W. Magazine	1,942,265	'Teen	1,011,482	Living	732,127
Popular Science	1,803,994	Discover	977,526	Modern Photography	727,389
The Workbasket	1,762,060	National Examiner	967,448		
Globe	1,750,819	Yankee	959,827		

NEWSPAPER AND MAGAZINE AWARDS: 1985

In addition to awards listed below, see the Pulitzer Prizes on pages 76–83.

GEORGE POLK AWARDS

The George Polk Awards, sponsored by Long Island University (New York) to honor the memory of a CBS correspondent killed in Greece in 1948, included:

Foreign reporting: Mark Fineman, *Philadelphia Inquirer,* for coverage of events in India.

National reporting: Robert Parry, *Associated Press,* for articles about CIA manuals advising Nicaraguan rebels on "neutralizing" government officials.

Magazine reporting: John Vinocur, *New York Times Magazine,* for article about Paraguay.

Local reporting: Ellen Whitford, *Norfolk Virginian-Pilot,* for expose of clinic performing false abortions on women who were not pregnant.

News photography: Ozier Muhammad, *Newsday (Long Island, N.Y.),* for photo of starving Ethiopian Child.

Environmental reporting: Tom Harris and Jim Morris, *Sacramento* (Calif.) *Bee,* articles about toxic waste disposal at U.S. millitary bases.

Medical reporting: William R. Ritz and John Aloysius Farrell, *Denver Post,* for articles on defective anesthesia machines.

Special interest reporting: Lois R. Ember, *Chemical and Engineering News,* for study ₐof U.S. government reports about germ warfare.

National television reporting: Alex Kotlowitz, Kwame Holman, and Susan Ades, *MacNeil/Lehrer Newshour,* report on abortion opponents.

Foreign television reporting: Michael Buerk, *British Broadcasting Co.,* and Mohammed Amin, *VisNews,* for first photos of Ethiopian famine victims.

Special award: *Amnesty International,* for annual report on human-rights violations.

Career award: Red Barber for his career as a sportscaster.

OVERSEAS PRESS CLUB AWARDS

The annual awards presented by the Overseas Press Club for distinguished reporting and interpretation of foreign affairs included:

Hal Boyle Award for best daily newspaper or wire service reporting from abroad: Jeff Sommer, *Newsday,* for coverage of events in India.

Bob Considine Award for best daily newspaper or wire service interpretation of foreign affairs: Drew Middleton, *New York Times,* for "Return to Normandy."

Robert Capa Gold Medal for best photographic reporting from abroad requiring exceptional courage and enterprise: Jim Nachtwey, *Black Star for Time* magazine, for photos of El Salvador.

Best photographic reporting from abroad for magazines and books: David Burnett, *Contact Press Images* for *Time* magazine, for photos of Jamaica, D-Day Plus, and Ethiopian famine.

Best photographic reporting from abroad for newspapers and wire services: Larry Price, *Philadelphia Inquirer,* for photos of Nigeria, Angola, and El Salvador.

Ben Grauer Award for best radio spot news reporting from abroad: Cameron Swayze and Philip Till, *NBC Radio News,* for Beirut coverage.

Lowell Thomas Award for best radio interpretation of foreign affairs: Alan Berlow, *National Public Radio,* for "Hotel Intrigue."

Best TV spot news reporting from abroad: Mohammed Amin, *Visnews,* for "Ethiopian Famine."

Edward R. Murrow Award for best TV interpretation or documentary on foreign affairs: Garrick Utley and Bryant Gumbel, *NBC TV,* for "The New Gold War."

Ed Cunningham Award for best magazine reporting from abroad: Scott Sullivan, *Newsweek,* for "The Decline of Europe."

Hallie & Whit Burnett Award for best magazine story on foreign affairs: V.S Nsipaul, *Harper's,* for "Grenada: In Island Betrayed."

Best cartoon on foreign affairs: Don Wright, *Miami News.*

Best business news reporting from abroad for magazines and books: Peter Koenig, *Institutional Investor,* for "Anatomy of a Eurobond Scandal."

Best economics news reporting from abroad for magazines and books: John Pearson, Carla Anne Robbins, and Sarah Bartlett, *Business Week,* for "Will Mexico Make It."

Best economics news reporting from abroad for newspapers and wire services: William Montalbano, Juan DeOnis, and Juan Vasquez, *Los Angeles Times,* for "Mexican Economy."

Madeline Dane Ross Award for international reporting in any medium which demonstrates a concern for humanity: Stan Grossfeld and Colin Nickerson, *Boston Globe,* for "Ethiopia: Famine and Flight."

NATIONAL MAGAZINE AWARDS

Sponsored by the American Society of Magazine Editors and administered by the Columbia University Graduate School of Journalism:

Public Service: *The Washingtonian* for "Where Have All the Warriors Gone?" by Nick Kotz, Nancy B. Nathan, and Cathryn Donohoe.

Design: *Forbes* magazine.

Fiction: *Playboy* for "The Trail of Your Blood on the Snow" by Gabriel Garcia Marquez; "Forky" by Andre Dubus 3d, and "Julius Caesar and the Werewolf" by John Gardner.

Reporting: *Texas Monthly* for "The Man in the Black Hat" by Paul Burka.

Essays and criticism: *Boston* magazine for Howard Carr's "incisive and elegant recreation of the character and spirit of Boston's changing political scene."

Single-topic issue: *American Heritage* for "A Medical Picture of the United States."

Service to the individual: *The Washingtonian* for "How to Save Your Life" about a teen-ager's auto accident.

General excellence: (under 100,000 circulation) *Manhattan, inc.;* (100,000 to 400,000 circulation) *American Heritage;* (400,000 to 1 million circulation) *American Health;* (over 1 million circulation) *Time.*

People in the News

HIGHLIGHTS: 1985

STATESMEN, POLITICIANS, OTHERS

The nation's highest honor to a civilian, the Congressional Gold Medal of Achievement, was presented by **President Reagan** on April 19 to author and theologian **Elie Wiesel**, who survived the Nazi death camps of Auschwitz and Buchenwald.

The **Rev. Jesse Jackson** visited **Pope John Paul II** in Rome on Jan. 3 and urged the pope to visit South Africa to denounce apartheid.... The U.S. granted asylum to Soviet atomic physicist **Vladimirovich Kulikov**, 51, on Jan. 4, after he defected to the U.S. in Chicago where he had been working under an exchange program.

Sen. Edward Kennedy (D-Mass.) made an 8-day trip to South Africa in January to investigate that country's racial policies.... Publisher **Malcolm Forbes** set a record for the purchase price of a photograph when he paid $104,500 at a Sotheby auction in New York for an autographed 1864 photo of **Abraham Lincoln** and his youngest son, **Todd**.

A mountain in Yosemite National Park was renamed for famed photographer **Ansel Adams**, who died in 1984, according to an announcement in March by the National Park Service.

Artist **Yaacov Agan** used 490 gallons of paint in more than 50 colors to complete in March his painting *Hommage a Mondrian* that covers the 100,000 square foot surface of a 145-foot-tall West Hollywood, Calif., apartment building.... Women's fashion designer **Albert Nipon**, 57, was sentenced in May to three years in prison after pleading quilty to evading the payment of more than $800,000 in income taxes.... **Robert B. Sutton**, an Oklahoma oilman who is said to be one of the wealthiest persons in the world, was convicted on Feb. 14 by a federal jury of bribery and conspiracy. He already had been sentenced to three years in prison on another charge stemming from a Department of Energy investigation.

In his first extensive interview since being defeated in the 1984 presidential election, former Vice President **Walter Mondale** gave his opinion of **President Reagan**: "I think history will say that this President was enormously popular—and lucky."

Britain's **Prince Charles** and **Princess Diana** announced plans to visit Washington, D.C.,

U.S. Postal Service

The U.S. Postal Service issued this new Love stamp on April 17 in Hollywood in a ceremony with cast members of TV's "Love Boat." The design of the stamp was unveiled at a New Year's Eve celebration in Washington, D.C., when a large replica was lowered from the clock tower at the Old Post Office, which has been renamed the Nancy Hanks Center for Performing Arts. The stamp was designed by Corita Kent of Boston, Mass, using six colors.

on Nov. 8-12, 1985, to have dinner at the White House and to visit an exhibit of British paintings at the national Gallery.

When **Frederick Koch**, 54, of Guilford, Vt., became angry at the way people pronounced his last name, he legally changed his name to **Coke-Is-It** in November 1984. After the Coca-Cola Co. filed objections to his new name as a violation of their trade mark, he reached an out-of-court settlement with the soft drink corporation in March that lets him continue to use his new name as long as it is not for commercial purposes.

Authors **Erskine Caldwell**, 81, and **Norman Mailer**, 61, were elected to the prestigious 50-member American Academy of Arts and Letters to fill the places left vacant by the deaths of **Lillian Hellman** and **Tennessee Williams**.

Former head of the Environmental Protection Agency's toxic-waste cleanup program **Rita M. Lavelle**, 37, entered prison in California on April 19 to begin serving a six-month sentence for perjury and obstructing a congressional investigation.

Paul Thayer, 65, former deputy secretary of defense, and Dallas stockbroker **Billy Bob Harris** were sentenced on May 8 to four years in prison and fines of $5,000 each for obstructing justice in an investigation of insider stock trading.

To bring more dignity to his courtroom, Judge **Richard Feder** in Miami, Fla., in June ordered lawyers to wear black robes while trying cases in his court.

When **Millard Harmon**, 59, a retired educator from Delmar, N.Y., flew his private plane from Helsinki, Finland, to Moscow in June on what he called a "friendship flight," he was locked up in a hotel throughout his three-day visit because he had failed to bring with him a Soviet visa.

Gov. George C. Wallace of Alabama, who in 1963 defied efforts of the federal government to end racial segregation in schools, testified in a federal court suit in Birmingham, Ala., on July 2 that "I am not for segregation now and I haven't been for a long, long time."

The Hollywood Bachelorettes Association in July named the "10 Most Exciting Bachelors" of 1985: New York City Mayor **Ed Koch**; tennis star **John McEnroe**; basketball star **Kareem Abdul-Jabbar**, owner of the Los Angeles Lakers and Los Angeles Kings **Dr. Jerry Buss**, actors **James Caan, Lee Majors, Warren Beatty, Eddie Murphy**, and **Matthew Broderick**; and **Robin Leach**, host of TV's *Lifestyles of the Rich and Famous.*

AMONG THE YOUNG

Peter Leppik, a 15-year-old Minneapolis, Minn., computer hacker who broke into a bank's computer, but who was not prosecuted when he promised not to do it again, was asked by police in January to help them crack the computer code of a man they suspected of child abuse. Police had been trying to read the computer code for a month before asking the boy's help. It took the young hacker only 45 minutes to solve the problem for the grateful police.

Bobby Smith, 13, was reunited with his parents in January in Providence, R.I., 21 months after he disappeared from his home in Long Beach, Calif. Rhode Island police found him living with a man who was charged with abducting and abusing the boy. Bobby advised other children, "Watch out for people when you are walking to school every day."

When a 2-ton truck fell on **Charles Bowen** while he was working under it, his 4-year-old son **Brandon Bowen** jacked up the truck, pulled his father out, and then got a neighbor to phone for an ambulance. . . .While at his job delivering newspapers in Detroit on Feb. 24, **Collin Boatright**, 14, saw a man drag an 11-year-old girl into an abandoned building. After yelling at a neighbor to call the police, he ran into the building and held the girl's attacker at bay with a club until police arrived to arrest the man.

When an intruder put a knife to the throat of **Mrs. Jacquelyn Roland** in Shawnee, Okla., her 6-year-old son **Jimmy Roland** picked up a rifle and said: "Turn my mommy loose or I'm gonna shoot you." The intruder fled. "It wasn't loaded," the boy told police, "but I knew he wouldn't know that."

LIFE AMONG THE ENTERTAINERS

Actor **Paul Newman** gave $250,000 to the Catholic Relief Services on Jan. 3 to help Ethiopian famine victims. The money represented profits from "Newman's Own" popcorn, salad oil, and spaghetti sauce business that he operates with partner **A.E. Hotchner**. During 1984 they gave all the $1.9 million profits of the food business to charities.

Actress **Elizabeth Taylor**, 52, announced on Feb. 4 that she had broken her engagement with New Yorker **Dennis Stein**, who had been planning to become her 7th husband.

"The Night of 100 Stars II," a benefit for the Actors Fund held at Radio City Music Hall on Feb. 17, actually had 308 stars and near stars present including such luminaries as **Jimmy Stewart, Joan Collins, Ginger Rogers, Michael Caine, Donny Osmond, Cab Calloway, Lloyd Bridges, Leonard Bernstein, Placido Domingo, Brooke Shields, Robert Wagner, Joe DiMaggio, Christopher Reeve, Jane Powell, Matt Dillon, Raquel Welch, Dinah Shore, Sugar Ray Robinson, Alexander Godunov, Tony Randall, Carol Channing**, and **Howard Cosell**. The six-hour show, presented before an audience of 5,700 who paid from $50 to $1,000 for seats, was reported to have raised about $1 million for the benefit of retired actors. ABC TV broadcast an edited version of the show in March.

Superstar **Michael Jackson** flew to London in March to take part in the unveiling of a figure of himself in Madame Tussaud's wax museum. . . . Actress **Jody Foster**, 22, graduated from Yale University on May 24 with a B.A. in English literature.

Dan Haggerty, 41, who starred in the TV series "The Life and Times of Grizzly Adams," was sentenced on April 4 to spend 90

days in prison and serve three years probation for selling cocaine to undercover police. . . . Actor **Stacy Keach**, 44, who plays detective Mike Hammer on TV, was released from prison in Britain on June 7 after serving six months of a nine-month sentence for smuggling cocaine.

Singer-songwriter **Stevie Wonder** was awarded a special citation on May 13 by the UN General Assembly's Special Committee Against Apartheid because of his out-spoken criticism of South African apartheid.

A New York court on May 22 ordered actor Tony Curtis to repay publisher Doubleday & Co. a $50,000 advance he had received in 1977 for writing a novel. The publisher claimed the manuscript submitted by Curtis could not be edited. . . . Singer **Frank Sinatra**, 69, received an honorary doctorate of engineering from Stevens Institute of Technology in Hoboken, N.J., on May 23, despite protests by a group of students that singing and engineering had little in common and that the degree-giving should not be based on the singer having been born in Hoboken.

Rock singing star **Bruce Springsteen**, 35, married actress **Julianne Phillips**, 25, in Lake Oswego, Ore., on May 13. . . . Former Beatle **Paul McCartney** was sued for $8.6 million in a breach of contract suit filed in New York in February by survivors of the famous singing group—**George Harrison, Ringo Starr**, and the widow of **John Lennon, Yoko Ono**.

TV personality **Cristina Ferrare**, 34, obtained a divorce from former automaker **John De Lorean** in April and less than two weeks later married ABC TV executive **Anthony Thomopoulos**. However, on July 3 a New Jersey judge ruled that her California divorce was invalid and that she was still married to De Lorean.

Actress **Lynne Frederick**, 29, widow of actor **Peter Sellers**, was awarded $1 million by a British court on May 24 in her suit against United Artists for damages she said had been done to Sellers reputation by release of the film "Trail of the Pink Panther" in 1982.

A Los Angeles court on June 18 refused to issue an injunction requested by actress **Donna Reed** to prevent the TV series "Dallas" from replacing her with actress **Barbara Bel Geddes** in the role of Miss Ellie.

Residents of Alton, Ill., raised $60,000 for a life-size statue of the town's most famous son—**Robert Wadlow**, the tallest man in history with a height of 8 feet 11.1 inches. He toured with a circus before dying at age 22 in 1940.

Playboy magazine founder **Hugh Hefner**, 59, suffered a stroke in March, but a spokesman reported he had fully recovered within a few weeks. . . . Fashion model **Christie Brinkley**, 31, and singer-songwriter **Billy Joel**, 35, were married on March 23 aboard a yacht in New York Harbor.

Princess Yasmin Aga Khan, daughter of film star **Rita Hayworth** and the late **Prince Aga Khan**, married Greek shipping heir **Basil Embiricos** in a civil ceremony in New York City on May 15.

Actor **Yul Brynner** retired on June 30 from *The King and I* after playing the lead role 4,625 times over a period of 34 years.

WINNERS

President Reagan awarded the Presidential Medal of Freedom to 13 famous persons in White House ceremonies on May 23. Those chosen for the award were **Mother Teresa**, the Nobel Prize-winning nun; **Jacques-Yves Cousteau**, the undersea explorer; **Jerome Holland**, first black to serve on the board of the New York Stock Exchange; **Sidney Hook**, 82-year-old philosopher and educator; **Jeane J. Kirkpatrick**, former U.S. chief delegate to the UN; **S. Dillion Ripley**, 71, former director of the Smithsonian Institution; **Frank Sinatra**, singer and actor; **James Stewart**, 77, movie star; **Gen. Albert Coady Wedemeyer**, 87, a World War II hero; **Gen. Charles Yeager**, 61, first man to fly faster than sound; the late **Count Basie**, jazz pianst; the late **Frank Reynolds**, journalist and TV news anchorman; and the late **George Low**, former administrator of the National Aeronautics and Space Administration. Only 214 persons have been awarded the medal since it was created by President Kennedy in 1963, as the American version of France's Legion of Honor or Britain's knighthood.

The winner of the $183,500 Templeton Prize for Progress in Religion was announced in February, going to 89-year-old **Sir Alistair Hardy**, a British marine biologist who sought to reconcile Charles Darwin's theory of evolution with traditional religion. However, he died on May 23 in Oxford, England, just two days before he was to be formally presented the prize.

Balu Natarajan, 13, of Bolingbrook, Ill., won $1,000 and the title of champion speller by beating out 167 other contestants in the 58th National Spelling Bee in Washington, D.C., on June 6. The word he spelled to win the championship was *milieu* (meaning *environment*). The only other contestants to reach Round 13 in the competition were **Tanya Solomon** of Kansas City, Mo., who was defeated by *syllepsis* (a grammar form), and **Kate Lingley** of Dover-Foxcroft, Maine, who missed on *farrago* (a mixture).

Theresa Knecht Dozier, 32, a high school

history teacher in Columbia, S.C., was named on April 4 as 1985 National Teacher of the Year. Born in Vietnam to a Vietnamese woman and a German member of the French Foreign Legion, she ended up in an orphanage where she was found by an American army adviser and his wife in 1954, adopted by them, and brought to the United States.

Dale Morris, 19, won the first prize of $1,400 at the 23d annual National Oldtime Fiddlers' Contest in Fort Worth, Tex., in June.

James Brady, 44, the presidential press secretary who was severely wounded during the attempted assassination of **President Reagan** in 1981, was honored on Jan. 21 by receiving USA Today's first Unity Award as representing "the spirit and courage of the United States."

Jerry Parr, 54, the Secret Service agent credited with saving the President's life during the assassination attempt, retired in February after 22 years of service. **President Reagan** gave him a pair of presidential cuff links in a special White House ceremony.

The U.S. Energy Department's $200,000 Enrico Fermi Award was shared by American Physicist **Robert Wilson** and French scientist **Georges Venndryes**... Canadian ambassador **Kenneth Taylor,** who helped six Americans escape from Iran during the 1979 hostage crisis, became the first non-American to receive the Harry S. Truman Good Neighbor Award on May 8.

The Carnegie Hero Fund Commission in April awarded the Carnegie Medal for Heroism and $2,500 to each of 15 Americans and Canadians: **Jerry W. Ashcraft,** 35, of Pine Bluff, Ark., a train engineer who pushed three boys out of the path of a moving train on May 20, 1984; **Thomas Lee Chasen,** 33, of Fredericksburg, Va., a railway ticket clerk who tried to rescue a man from being run over by a train on July 22, 1984; **Raimie Finn,** 12, who died while trying unsuccessfully to help another student escape from a school bus stalled on a railroad track in Port St. Lucie, Fla., on Sept. 27, 1984; **Robert D. Hesse,** 59, of Pinellas Park, Fla., and **Matthew Pinelli,** 32, of St. Petersburg, Fla., who saved two persons from a tidal current in the ocean off Madeira Beach, Fla., on Sept. 16, 1984; **Rene M. Jalbert,** sergeant-at-arms of the Quebec legislature who talked a gunman into surrendering in May 1984; **Dennis J. Meyers,** 32, of Leipsic, Ohio, a truck driver who pulled an unconscious man from a burning truck at Benton, Ill., on Jan. 13, 1984; **Harold F. Perry,** 36, of Bluff City, Tenn., who saved two persons from the Holston River on Aug. 27, 1983; **Kelly Elwood Sluss,** 49, who was killed while rescuing a girl drowning in the Gulf of Mexico at Dunedin, Fla., on June 25, 1984; **John W. Walker,** 62, of Fort Lauderdale, Fla., who saved an 8-year-old boy whose head was held in the jaws of a savage dog by beating the animal with a board on Oct. 24, 1984; **Charles T. Walt,** 47, of Reedsville, Wis., who saved two men who had been overcome by methane gas in an underground manure pit on June 13, 1984; **Jeffrey R. Weiser,** 29, of Davis, Calif., and **Thomas J. Norsworthy,** 18, of Orange, Calif., who saved three persons from a burning automobile in Devore, Calif., on Sept. 3, 1982; **Claude Ray Williams,** 18, who was killed while trying to save a man who had fallen through the ice on a pond in San Marcos, Texas, on Jan. 1, 1984; and **Victor Zabbo,** 23, of Antioch, Calif., who saved two persons from drowning in the American River on Jan. 31, 1984. Earlier, in February, the Carnegie Hero Fund Commission had awarded $2,500 and a medal to 15 other Americans and Canadians, including **Peter P. Bobetich Jr.,** 35, of Baden, Pa., who saved two women from a burning apartment in Aliquippa, Pa., on Aug. 2, 1984; **Joseph W. Gardner,** 36, and **Orval Herbert Roulston,** 44, of Douglas Lake, B.C., who saved an injured man from freezing on Dec. 7, 1982; **Robert J. Henderson,** 42, of Opa-Locka, Fla., who saved the life of a fellow worker who had been stabbed on March 29, 1984; **Wallace L. Jensen,** 51, of Oberlin, Kan., who saved a 2-year-old girl from a burning car; **Timothy M. McKeown,** 13, of Millersburg, Pa., who saved a child from drowning on June 21, 1984; **Michael R. Santino,** 32, of Soap Lake, Wash., who saved a man from a burning house on July 30, 1984; **Kent A. Self,** 20, of Addyston, Ohio, and **Konstantinos Tallman,** of Cincinnati, who saved a policeman who was being stabbed on Dec. 6, 1983; **Kevin J. Stone,** 19, of Norfolk, Neb., who saved an injured man from the Platte River on June 10, 1984; **Michael A. Gigliotti,** 57, of Haverhill, Mass., and **Joseph G. Gallo,** 61, of New York City, who died trying to save a drowning woman at Salisbury Beach, Mass., on Aug. 18, 1984; **Robert B. Granaas,** 24, of Trenton, Mich., who died while unsuccessfully trying to rescue a fellow worker who had suffocated while cleaning a gasoline storage tank in Detroit on Oct. 10, 1983; **David Kasti,** 17, of Southgate, Mich., who drowned while trying to save his two sisters from drowning in Lake Michigan; and **Joseph W. Manford,** 27, of Boonsboro, Md., who died while trying to save a woman from drowning at Hagerstown, Md., on July 14, 1984.

Vincent J. Zito, 35, of Paterson, N.J., received an award of $3,000, heading a list of

66 heroic firemen chosen for their accomplishments by Firehouse magazine in February. He had rescued two persons in a hotel fire on Oct. 18, 1984. Firefighter **Guy Warren** of Brooklyn, N.Y., was awarded the second prize of $2,000. Three Winners of $1,000 firefighting awards were **James P. O'Donnell** of Chicago, **Robert R. Lichtenberg** of Baltimore, and **Dennis L. Baker** of Dayton, Ohio.

Robert W. Allington, 49, of Nebraska was honored in May by the Small Business Administration as "National Small Business Person of the Year." Confined to a wheelchair since his teens by a crippling case of polio, he built his Instrumentation Specialties Co. into a $20 million per year business.

The winners of the 44th annual Westinghouse Science Talent Search were announced on March 4. The top ten, who shared scholarships of $74,500, were in order: **Alan J. Hu,** 17, of La Jolla, Calif., computer science; **Anna A. Penn,** 17, of Chicago, viruses; **Michael Friedman,** 17, of New York City, numbers theory; **Michael S. Graziano,** 17, of Buffalo, N.Y., psychology; **John S. Kuo,** of New York City, genetics; **Anthony M. Ciabarra,** 17, of Wyncote, Pa., biochemistry; **Mark Kantrowitz,** 17, of Brookline, Mass., mathematics; **Michael W. Gesner,** 17, of Avon, Mass., rockets; **Audrey Zelicof,** 16, of New York City, mathematics; and **Allan M. Goldstein,** 17, of Wyncote, Pa., biochemistry.

The U.S. Jaycees in February honored four men as Outstanding Young Farmers: **Abbott W. Lee,** 34, of Chatsworth, N.J., who grows berries; **Peter A. Nygaard Jr.,** 33, of Williston, N.D., a wheat farmer; **W. Bruce Nelson,** 34, of Farmington, Wash., a lentil farmer; and **Dale W. Hermreck,** 35, of Williamsburg, Kan., who operates a corn and cattle farm.

The Horatio Alger Association of Distinguished Americans on May 10 presented 1985 Horatio Alger Awards to 10 persons who "exemplify the merits of America's free-enterprise system." They included: **Norman Brinker,** chairman of Chili's Restaurants, Dallas, Texas; **John C. Crean,** chairman of Fleetwood Enterprises Inc., a manufacturer of mobile homes; **Mario M. Cuomo,** governor of New York; **Leonard L. Farber,** of Pompano Beach, Fla., chairman of Leonard L. Farber Inc.; **Henry A. Johnson,** president of the mail-order firm Spiegel Inc.; **Dr. Rodrique Mortel,** chairman of the department of obstetrics and gynecology at Pennsylvania State University College of Medicine; **Allen E. Paulson,** chairman of Gulfstream Aerospace Corp.; **Jack D. Sparks,** chairman of Whirlpool Corp., a manufacturer of appliances; **Fred C. Trump,** chairman of the Trump Organization in New York City; and **Hicks B. Waldron,** chairman of Avon Products Inc., a cosmetics company.

Fortune magazine added six executives to its U.S. Business Hall of Fame in April: **Reginald Harold Jones,** 67, former chief executive of General Electric Co.; **Arnold Orville Beckman,** 84, founder of Beckman Instruments Inc.; **William F. Laporte,** 71, former chief executive of American Home Products Corp.; **Alden James Laborde,** 69, founder of Ocean Drilling & Exploration Co.; the late **Henry Morrison Flagler,** Standard Oil Co. executive and Florida developer; and the late **George Jacob Mecherie,** founder of State Farm Mutual Automobile Insurance Co.

THE GOLDEN YEARS

Former **President Richard Nixon** observed his 72nd birthday on Jan. 9 while laid up at his home in Saddle River, N.J., with a severe case of shingles.... Actor **Cary Grant,** 81, when asked in San Francisco on Jan. 29 how he stayed so trim and youthful, answered: "I've never done a damn thing, especially exercise. The best exercise I know of is making love."

W. Averell Harriman, 94, who was U.S. ambassador to Moscow during World War II, was honored by the Soviet Union in May with award of its Order of the Patriotic War, First Degree.

Actor **Buddy Ebsen,** 77, returned to New York City in May from a Hawaiian honeymoon with his third wife, **Dorothy Knott,** to be the honored guest at a meeting of the Barnaby Jones Luncheon Club, a group of about 400 elderly businessmen who are fans of the actor's TV detective series "Barnaby Jones."

Underwater explorer **Jacques-Yves Cousteau** celebrated his 75th birthday in June with a party aboard his vessel Calypso in the Potomac River in Virginia. Among the guests at the celebration were **Ben Vereen, David Brinkley, Stefanie Powers,** and **John Denver.**

Alfred M. Butts, 85, of Stanfordville, N.Y., who invented the game Scrabble in 1931, introduced his newest word game, called Alfred's Other Game, at the International Toy Fair in New York in February.

Edward L. Bernays, 93, of Cambridge, Mass., called the "Father of Public Relations" since writing Crystalizing Public Opinion in 1923, still works for his clients 12 hours a day in addition to campaigning against mandatory retirement rules and laws. **Shigechiyo Izumi,** said to be the world's oldest man, celebrated his 120th birthday on June 29 on the Japanese island Tokunoshima.

Gladys Burr, 78, was awarded $235,000 compensation in July by a federal judge in Hartford, Conn., because she had been illegally detained in a state institution for the mentally retarded for 42 years.

WOMEN IN THE NEWS

Jihan Sadat, 49, widow of Egyptian President Anwar Sadat, began commuting by air in January to fill two jobs: as a visiting professor at the University of South Carolina campus in Columbia, S.C., and as a distinguished professor in residence at the American University in Washington, D.C.

Bantam Books paid a reported $1 million in January for rights to the memoirs of former Democratic vice-presidential candidate **Geraldine Ferraro.** She and her daughters **Laura,** 22, and **Donna,** 18, split $750,000 for taking part in a Diet Pepsi TV commercial aired in February. Her husband, **John Zaccaro,** 51, was sentenced on Feb. 20, to 150 hours of community service after pleading guilty to taking part in a real estate fraud.

Mrs. **Patricia Frustaci,** 30, an English teacher in Riverside, Calif., set a U.S. record on May 21 when she gave birth to septuplets—six of the tiny premature babies were born alive and one was dead. Only three survived their first month of life, **Patricia Ann, Stephen Earl,** and **Richard Charles.** Their father, **Sam Frustaci,** 32, is a salesman.

Marie Lee McBroom, 59, of Jersey City, N.J., was freed in February after a Nigerian military court acquitted her of exporting oil illegally. She had faced a possible death penalty if found guilty.

Ann Landers, syndicated advice columnist, reported in January that a poll of 90,000 women readers showed that 70% preferred affectionate hugging and cuddling to sexual intercourse.

Tina Marie Machado had her crown as Miss Hawaii USA taken from her a week after she won it in February. Beauty pageant officials said she was too old at age 25. They gave the crown to 18-year-old **Toni Meimomi Costa.** . . . Only four days after **Rhonda Niles,** 19, won the title of Miss New Hampshire USA in February, she was arrested at Plymouth State College for possession of clothing stolen from a dress shop. After she gave up her crown, the store owner dropped the charges.

ABC TV commentator **Barbara Walters** announced in June that she was planning an autumn wedding with **Merv Adelson,** chairman of Lorimar Inc., which produces the TV series "Dallas," "Knots Landing," and "Falcon Crest."

The official painting of former First Lady **Rosalynn Carter** by artist **George Augusta** was unveiled in the White House on March 4 between the portraits of **Jacqueline Kennedy** and **Betty Ford.** . . . Former **President Jimmy Carter** was presented the World Methodist Peace Award in March for his efforts as a negotiator for peace and arms control, for his championing of human rights, and for his work as a carpenter to build houses for the poor. . . . **Amy Carter,** 17, daughter of the former President, was arrested and booked by police in Washington, D.C., on April 8, for taking part in an antiapartheid protest at the South African embassy.

Good Housekeeping magazine's list of the richest women in the United States was headed by **Margaret Hunt Hill** and **Caroline Hunt Schoellkopf,** daughters of oil magnate H.L. Hunt. Each is said to have a fortune of more than $1 billion.

Natalya Solzhenitsyn, wife of exiled Soviet author **Aleksandr Solzhenitsyn,** took the oath of U.S. citizenship at Rutland, Vt., on June 24. Her reclusive husband, who also had applied for American citizenship, failed to show up for the ceremony.

When CBS TV's **Phyllis George** completed her stint on the "CBS Morning News" on June 25 she was greeted by a surprise party thrown by co-workers to celebrate her 36th birthday.

Penny E. Harrington, 42, became police chief of Portland, Ore., on Jan. 24—the first woman to head the police force of a major city. . . . U.S. Secretary of Health and Human Services **Margaret M. Heckler,** 53, was divorced from her husband **John M. Heckler,** 57, on Feb. 13 after 31 years of marriage.

Joanna Carson, estranged wife of TV host **Johnny Carson,** had her request refused by a Los Angeles judge on Feb. 8 that her $44,600 monthly support from the entertainer be increased by an additional $6,000 monthly. . . . **Dawn Steel,** 38, was promoted on April 15 to president of Paramount Pictures production, making her the only woman to hold such a high post at a major movie company.

Brigitte Gerney, 49, was walking at her lunch hour on May 30 in New York City when a 35-ton construction crane toppled onto her, pinning her for six hours and partially severing her legs. Doctors used microsurgery to repair her legs and expressed hope that she might regain their use.

Christine Craft, 40, former Kansas City TV anchor newscaster, lost the $325,000 a jury had awarded her when a federal appeals court on June 28 reversed the lower court in her suit charging KMBC-TV officials demoted her because she would not change her appearance.

Postal Service

The U.S. Postal Service issued this $10.75 stamp on April 29 in San Francisco for use on items weighing up to 2 pounds that are sent via Express Mail Next Day Service. Express Mail promises delivery on time or postage is refunded upon application by the mailer. Insurance coverage is included in the postage.

U.S. Postal Service

HIGHLIGHTS: 1985

NEW POSTMASTER GENERAL

Paul N. Carlin of California became the 66th U.S. Postmaster General on Jan. 1, 1985, succeeding William F. Bolger. Carlin joined the Postal Service in 1969. The next year he received the Benjamin Franklin Award, the Postal Service's highest management honor, for his leadership in developing the Postal Reorganization Act that became effective in 1971.

NEW HIGHER POSTAL RATES

New U.S. postage rates went into effect at 12:01 A.M. on Feb. 17. The higher rates added 2 cents to the cost of mailing an ordinary first class letter, increasing it to 22 cents for the first ounce and 17 cents for each additional ounce to 12 ounces. The rate added 1 cent to the postage needed for a postal card, raising it to 14 cents. Most other postal rates also rose, including the cost for letters and packages mailed to other countries. For details of the new rates, see pages 699-702.

The Postal Service cautioned consumers that they could save money by remembering that on heavier letters they should add 17 cents for each additional ounce instead of the 22 cents required for the first ounce.

The postal rate increase was the fifth since 1971 when Congress converted the old Post Office Department into a corporation called the U.S. Postal Service and began phasing out taxpayer subsidies for postal services. At that time the rate for a first class stamp was 8 cents. The price was increased to 10 cents in 1974, to 13 cents in 1975, to 15 cents in 1978, and to 20 cents in 1981.

CRACKDOWN ON STAMP LAUNDERERS

Postal inspectors in 1985 intensified their efforts to stop the proliferating crime of stamp laundering—the washing of used stamps to remove their cancellation marks and their sale for reuse on mail.

At the same time they issued warnings of prosecution to persons guilty of the crime of reusing postage stamps that the Postal Service has failed to cancel.

Postal inspectors said that some criminals had been arrested who were making as much as $50,000 a year by gathering used postage stamps from trash barrels, soaking them in a solution of laundry bleach, and then selling them at a discount for reuse.

On July 12, 1985, Alvin Gould, 82, was convicted of selling laundered stamps in Cin-

cinnati, Ohio. He was fined $5,000, ordered to pay $47,000 in restitution to the federal government, and given a suspended prison sentence. Authorities confiscated four truckloads of used and laundered stamps from Gould's office.

The Postal Service said that its mail-handling machines fail to cancel from 300 million to 900 million envelopes each year, but that soaking those uncancelled stamps off envelopes and using them is as much of a crime as laundering cancelled stamps for reuse.

TIPS ON USING THE POSTAL SERVICE

The U.S. Postal Service tries to meet your needs as a sender and receiver of mail by providing a variety of services. Some services and regulations that may be unfamiliar to you are described below.

MINIMUM AND MAXIMUM SIZES

The Postal Service will not handle cards or letters less than $3\frac{1}{2}$ inches high and 5 inches long unless they are more than $\frac{1}{4}$ inch thick. Cards less than seven-thousandths of an inch thick also are prohibited.

Cards or letters more than 6 inches high or $11\frac{1}{2}$ inches wide are subject to a surcharge, as letter mail of odd shapes in which the length is more than 1.3 times the height or less than 2.5 times the height.

EXPRESS MAIL

If you send a letter or package up to 70 pounds by Express Mail, the U.S. Postal Service *guarantees* to return your money if it is not delivered within the time stated.

The Express Mail customer can choose one of four delivery options: (1) custom designed service, (2) next-day service, (3) same-day airport service, and (4) international service.

FORWARDING MAIL TO A NEW ADDRESS

If you move to a new address, you can obtain a "Change of Address Kit" from your local post office.

The kit contains change of address cards for you to send to magazines, charge accounts, and friends. There is also a change of address form with which to notify your local post office as to when you plan to move and your new address. Postal workers will forward mail to your new address for one year.

ADDRESS CORRECTION SERVICE

If one of your friends or correspondents moves and neglects to notify you of the new address, the Postal Service may be able to help you obtain the new address.

Mail a letter to your friend at the old address, and mark on the envelope "Address Correction Requested."

If your friend has notified the post office of his new address, the post office will then forward your letter to the new address and return to you a form containing your friend's new address with a charge of 25¢.

If the post office cannot determine the new address of your friend, it will merely return your letter at no charge.

PACKAGING FOR SECURE DELIVERY

The way you package a parcel sent by mail can affect the condition in which the contents arrive at their destination.

Packages containing breakable items should be marked "Fragile" above the address and below the postage. Those containing food that can spoil should be marked "Perishable." Before sealing the carton, place a list of the contents, your address, and the address of the person to whom it is being sent *inside* the package.

Wrap your package in paper at least as strong as that used for large grocery bags.

Use tape to seal all openings in the wrapping, including those at each end.

Reinforce the package by using nylon filament tape instead of twine, running it completely around the length and the width of the parcel.

ZIP CODES

If you put the correct ZIP Code on the address of all mail that you send, the post office can deliver it more quickly. The ZIP Codes for many cities and towns are listed on pages 112–135.

Here is how ZIP Code works. The first digit of every five-digit ZIP Code designates a national area, from "0" in the Northeast states to "9" in the Western states.

The first three digits together stand for one of 552 large cities or sectional centers. The last two digits designate a delivery area or post office within the sectional center.

In the nine-digit ZIP Code the last four digits indicate the exact block or building. It is voluntary, and called "ZIP PLUS 4."

The *National Zip Code and Post Office Directory* lists the names of all the post offices and the five-digit codes for every postal delivery zone in the United States.

You can use the directory at your local post office or buy it there for $9; or (if you turn in the front cover of a prior issue) for $8. You also can obtain a copy of the directory by sending $9 to:

Superintendent of Documents
Government Printing Office
Washington, D.C. 20420

U.S. POSTAL RATES AND FEES

DOMESTIC MAIL	RATE
Express Mail (overnight delivery):	
up to 2 lbs.	$10.75
over 2 lbs. to 5 lbs.	$12.85
up to 70 lbs.	consult postmaster
First Class (air):	
1st ounce	22¢
2d to 12th ounces	17¢ per ounce
Over 12 ounces	See Priority Mail table on page 700
Postal and postcards	14¢
Double postcards	14¢ each half
Business reply letters:	
with advance deposit	7¢
without advance deposit . .	23¢
Second Class (newspapers, periodicals):	
Mailed singly by public	Same as 3d or 4th class rates
Bulk rates:	
In county per pound	5.8¢
In county per piece	3.3¢ to 1.5¢
Outside county	Consult postmaster
Third Class:	
Mailed singly	22¢ up to 1 ounce
(circulars, books, catalogs,	each added
merchandise, etc.,	oz. to 4 ozs. 17¢;
weighing less than one	up to 1 lb. $1.38
lb. each)	
Bulk rates	Consult postmaster
Fourth Class:	
Parcel Post	See table on page 700
Books, records, and	
computer software	
rates	Consult postmaster
Library rate:	
1st pound	40¢
2d to 7th pounds	14¢ per pound
Over 7 pounds :	8¢ per pound
Special Delivery (fee in addition to postage):	
1st class	$2.95 to $4.00
2d, 3d, and 4th class	$3.10 to $4.50
Money Orders (for safe transmission of money):	
Amount $0.01 to $700	75¢ to $1.00
Special Handling (fee in addition to postage; 3d and 4th class only):	$1.10 for first 10 lbs. $1.60 over 10 lbs.
Restricted delivery (not available for mail insured for $25 or less):	Additional $1.25 fee
Special Services:	
Certificate of mailing	45¢
Insurance (in addition to postage):	
Liability up to $25	$0.50
Liability up to $50	$1.10
Liability up to $100	$1.40
Liability up to $150	$1.80
Liability up to $200	$2.10
Liability up to $300	$3.00
Liability up to $400	$3.70
Liability up to $500	$4.40

DOMESTIC MAIL *(continued)*	RATE
Registered Mail (in addition to postage) (If covered by postal Insurance):	
Value $0.01 to $100	$3.60
Value $100.01 to $500	$3.90
Value $500.01 to $1,000	$4.25
Value over $1,000	Consult postmaster
Return Receipts for certified, registered, or insured (not available for mail insured for $25 or less):	
Requested at time of mailing:	
Showing to whom and date delivered	Additional 70¢ fee
Also showing address where delivered	Additional 90¢ fee
Requested after mailing to show to whom and date delivered	Additional $4.50 fee
C.O.D. Mail	Consult postmaster
INTERNATIONAL MAIL	RATE
Mail to Canada or Mexico:	
Air Mail—1 ounce	22¢
Air Mail—2d to 12th ounce	18¢ per ounce
Air Mail—over 12 ounces (Max. weight 4 lbs.)	$2.84 up to 1 lb. 54¢ per each additional 8 oz.
Postal and postcards (air)	14¢
Small packets or printed matter (air mail):	
up to 1 oz.	22¢
each additional ounce up to 12 oz.	18¢ per oz.
up to 1 lb.	$2.84
each additional 8 oz. up to 5 lb.	54¢
up to 5 lb.	$7.16
up to 11 lb.	$13.64
Mexico only, up to 22 lbs. . . .	$25.52
Mail to Other Countries:	
Air letters: (To Central America, Colombia, Venezuela, Caribbean islands, Bahamas, Bermuda, and St. Pierre and Miquelon)	39¢ per ½ oz. up to 2 oz.; 33¢ for each additional ½ oz. up to 32 oz., then 33¢ for each additional oz. to 4 lb.
Air letters: (To all other countries)	44¢ per ½ oz. up to 2 oz.; 39¢ each additional ½ oz. up to 2 lb.; then 39¢ each additional oz. up to 4 lb.
Aerogrammes (folded as envelope and sent by air) . . .	36¢ each
Postal and postcards—surface	25¢
Postal and postcards—airmail .	33¢
Letters (surface):	
up to 1 oz.	37¢
each additonal oz. to 8 oz.	20¢
up to 1 lb.	$3.40
up to 2 lbs.	$5.92
up to 3 lbs.	$7.76
up to 4 lbs. (max.)	$9.60
Small packets of merchandise or samples, 2 lbs. maximum—surface:	
up to 1 oz.	29¢
each added oz. to 4 ozs.	18¢
each added 2 ozs. to 32 ozs. .	19¢

700 POSTAL SERVICE

U.S. FOURTH CLASS (PARCEL POST)

Weight in pounds up to	Zone Local	Up to 150 miles 1-2	150–300 miles 3	300–600 miles 4	600–1,000 miles 5	1,000–1,400 miles 6	1,400–1,800 miles 7	Over 1,800 miles 8
2	$1.35	$1.41	$1.51	$1.66	$1.89	$2.13	$2.25	$2.30
3	1.41	1.49	1.65	1.87	2.21	2.58	2.99	3.87
4	1.47	1.57	1.78	2.08	2.54	3.03	3.57	4.74
5	1.52	1.65	1.92	2.29	2.86	3.47	4.16	5.62
6	1.58	1.74	2.05	2.50	3.18	3.92	4.74	6.49
7	1.63	1.82	2.19	2.71	3.51	4.37	5.32	7.36
8	1.69	1.90	2.32	2.92	3.83	4.82	5.91	8.25
9	1.75	1.99	2.46	3.13	4.15	5.26	6.49	9.12
10	1.80	2.07	2.59	3.34	4.48	5.71	7.07	10.00
11	1.85	2.13	2.70	3.49	4.71	6.03	7.49	10.62
12	1.90	2.20	2.79	3.65	4.94	6.34	7.89	11.23
13	1.94	2.26	2.89	3.79	5.15	6.63	8.27	11.78
14	1.98	2.32	2.98	3.92	5.35	6.90	8.62	12.30
15	2.02	2.37	3.06	4.04	5.54	7.15	8.94	12.79
16	2.06	2.42	3.14	4.16	5.71	7.39	9.25	13.24
17	2.10	2.48	3.22	4.27	5.88	7.61	9.54	13.67
18	2.14	2.52	3.29	4.38	6.03	7.83	9.81	14.08
19	2.18	2.57	3.36	4.48	6.18	8.03	10.07	14.46
20	2.21	2.62	3.43	4.58	6.33	8.22	10.32	14.83
21	2.25	2.67	3.49	4.67	6.47	8.41	10.56	15.18
22	2.28	2.71	3.56	4.76	6.60	8.59	10.79	15.51
23	2.32	2.75	3.62	4.85	6.73	8.76	11.01	15.83
24	2.35	2.80	3.68	4.94	6.85	8.92	11.22	16.14
25	2.39	2.84	3.74	5.02	6.97	9.08	11.42	16.43
26	2.42	2.88	3.80	5.10	7.08	9.23	11.61	16.72
27	2.45	2.92	3.85	5.18	7.20	9.38	11.80	16.99
28	2.48	2.96	3.91	5.25	7.30	9.52	11.98	17.26
29	2.52	3.00	3.96	5.33	7.41	9.66	12.16	17.52
30	2.55	3.04	4.01	5.40	7.51	9.80	12.33	17.77
31	2.58	3.08	4.07	5.47	7.61	9.93	12.50	18.01
32	2.61	3.12	4.12	5.54	7.71	10.06	12.66	18.24
33	2.64	3.15	4.17	5.61	7.81	10.19	12.82	18.47
34	2.67	3.19	4.22	5.68	7.90	10.31	12.97	18.70
35	2.70	3.23	4.26	5.74	7.99	10.43	13.12	18.91
36	2.73	3.26	4.31	5.81	8.08	10.54	13.27	19.12
37	2.76	3.30	4.36	5.87	8.17	10.66	13.41	19.33
38	2.79	3.33	4.41	5.93	8.25	10.77	13.55	19.53
39	2.82	3.37	4.45	5.99	8.34	10.88	13.69	19.73
40	2.85	3.40	4.50	6.05	8.42	10.98	13.83	19.92
41	2.88	3.44	4.54	6.11	8.50	11.09	13.96	20.11
42	2.91	3.47	4.58	6.17	8.58	11.19	14.09	20.29
43	2.94	3.50	4.63	6.23	8.66	11.29	14.21	20.47
44	2.97	3.54	4.67	6.28	8.74	11.39	14.34	20.65
45	3.00	3.57	4.71	6.34	8.81	11.49	14.46	20.82
46	3.02	3.61	4.76	6.39	8.89	11.59	14.58	20.99
47	3.05	3.64	4.80	6.45	8.96	11.68	14.69	21.16
48	3.08	3.67	4.84	6.50	9.03	11.77	14.81	21.32
49	3.11	3.70	4.88	6.55	9.10	11.86	14.92	21.48
50	3.14	3.74	4.92	6.61	9.17	11.95	15.03	21.64
51	3.17	3.77	4.96	6.66	9.24	12.04	15.14	21.80
52	3.19	3.80	5.00	6.71	9.31	12.13	15.25	21.95
53	3.22	3.83	5.04	6.76	9.38	12.22	15.36	22.10
54	3.25	3.86	5.08	6.81	9.45	12.30	15.46	22.25
55	3.28	3.89	5.12	6.86	9.51	12.39	15.57	22.39
56	3.30	3.93	5.16	6.91	9.58	12.47	15.67	22.54
57	3.33	3.96	5.20	6.96	9.64	12.55	15.77	22.68
58	3.36	3.99	5.23	7.01	9.71	12.63	15.87	22.82
59	3.39	4.02	5.27	7.06	9.77	12.71	15.97	22.95
60	3.41	4.05	5.31	7.10	9.83	12.79	16.06	23.09
61	3.44	4.08	5.35	7.15	9.90	12.87	16.16	23.22
62	3.47	4.11	5.38	7.20	9.96	12.94	16.25	23.35
63	3.50	4.14	5.42	7.24	10.02	13.02	16.35	23.48
64	3.52	4.17	5.46	7.29	10.08	13.10	16.44	23.61
65	3.55	4.20	5.49	7.33	10.14	13.17	16.53	23.74
66	3.58	4.23	5.53	7.38	10.19	13.24	16.62	23.86
68	3.63	4.29	5.60	7.47	10.31	13.39	16.80	24.11
70	3.68	4.35	5.67	7.56	10.43	13.53	16.97	24.35

U.S. PRIORITY MAIL (over 12 oz.)

Weight in pounds up to	Local (Local 1-2-3)	300–600 miles 4	600–1,000 miles 5	1,000–1,400 miles 6	1,400–1,800 miles 7	Over 1,800 miles 8
2	$2.40	$2.40	$2.40	$2.40	$2.40	$2.40
3	2.74	3.16	3.45	3.74	3.96	4.32
4	3.18	3.75	4.13	4.53	4.92	5.33
5	3.61	4.32	4.86	5.27	5.81	6.37
6	4.15	5.08	5.71	6.31	6.91	7.66
7	4.58	5.66	6.39	7.09	7.80	8.67
8	5.00	6.23	7.07	7.87	8.68	9.68
9	5.43	6.81	7.76	8.66	9.57	10.69
10	5.85	7.39	8.44	9.44	10.45	11.70
11	6.27	7.97	9.12	10.22	11.33	12.71
12	6.70	8.55	9.81	11.01	12.22	13.72
13	7.12	9.12	10.49	11.79	13.10	14.73
14	7.55	9.70	11.17	12.57	13.99	15.74
15	7.97	10.28	11.86	13.36	14.87	16.75
16	8.39	10.86	12.54	14.14	15.75	17.75
17	8.82	11.44	13.22	14.92	16.64	18.76
18	9.24	12.01	13.90	15.70	17.52	19.77
19	9.67	12.59	14.59	16.49	18.41	20.78
20	10.09	13.17	15.27	17.27	19.29	21.79
21	10.51	13.75	15.95	18.05	20.17	22.80
22	10.94	14.33	16.64	18.84	21.06	23.81
23	11.36	14.90	17.32	19.62	21.94	24.82
24	11.79	15.48	18.00	20.40	22.83	25.83
25	12.21	16.06	18.69	21.19	23.71	26.84
26	12.63	16.64	19.37	21.97	24.59	27.84
27	13.06	17.22	20.05	22.75	25.48	28.85
28	13.48	17.79	20.73	23.53	26.36	29.86
29	13.91	18.37	21.42	24.32	27.25	30.87
30	14.33	18.95	22.10	25.10	28.13	31.88
31	14.75	19.53	22.78	25.88	29.01	32.89
32	15.18	20.11	23.47	26.67	29.90	33.90
33	15.60	20.68	24.15	27.45	30.78	34.91
34	16.03	21.26	24.83	28.23	31.67	35.92
35	16.45	21.84	25.52	29.02	32.55	36.93
36	16.87	22.42	26.20	29.80	33.43	37.93
37	17.30	23.00	26.88	30.58	34.32	38.94
38	17.72	23.57	27.56	31.36	35.20	39.95
39	18.15	24.15	28.25	32.15	36.09	40.96
40	18.57	24.73	28.93	32.93	36.97	41.97
41	18.99	25.31	29.61	33.71	37.85	42.98
42	19.42	25.89	30.30	34.50	38.74	43.99
43	19.84	26.46	30.98	35.28	39.62	45.00
44	20.27	27.04	31.66	36.06	40.51	46.01
45	20.69	27.62	32.35	36.85	41.39	47.02
46	21.11	28.20	33.03	37.63	42.27	48.02
47	21.54	28.78	33.71	38.41	43.16	49.03
48	21.96	29.35	34.39	39.19	44.04	50.04
49	22.39	29.93	35.08	39.98	44.93	51.05
50	22.81	30.51	35.76	40.76	45.81	52.06
51	23.23	31.09	36.44	41.54	46.69	53.07
52	23.66	31.67	37.13	42.33	47.58	54.08
53	24.08	32.24	37.81	43.11	48.46	55.09
54	24.51	32.82	38.49	43.89	49.35	56.10
55	24.93	33.40	39.18	44.68	50.23	57.11
56	25.35	33.98	39.86	45.46	51.11	58.11
57	25.78	34.56	40.54	47.24	52.00	59.12
58	26.20	35.13	41.22	47.02	52.88	60.13
59	26.63	35.71	41.91	47.81	53.77	61.14
60	27.05	36.29	42.59	48.59	54.65	62.15
61	27.47	36.87	43.27	49.37	55.53	63.16
62	27.90	37.45	43.96	50.16	56.42	64.17
63	28.32	38.02	44.64	50.94	57.30	65.18
64	28.75	38.60	45.32	51.72	58.19	66.19
65	29.17	39.18	46.01	52.51	59.07	67.20
66	29.59	39.76	46.69	53.29	59.95	68.20
68	30.44	40.91	48.05	54.85	61.72	70.22
70	31.29	42.07	49.42	56.42	63.49	72.24

POSTAL SERVICE ADDRESS ABBREVIATIONS

STATES AND TERRITORIES

Alabama AL	Georgia GA	Maryland MD	New Mexico NM	South Dakota SD
Alaska AK	Guam GU	Massachusetts .. MA	New York NY	Tennessee TN
Arizona AZ	Hawaii HI	Michigan MI	North Carolina .. NC	Texas TX
Arkansas AR	Idaho ID	Minnesota MN	North Dakota ND	Utah UT
California CA	Illinois IL	Mississippi MS	Ohio OH	Vermont VT
Canal Zone CZ	Indiana IN	Missouri MO	Oklahoma OK	Virginia VA
Colorado CO	Iowa IA	Montana MT	Oregon OR	Virgin Islands ... VI
Connecticut CT	Kansas KS	Nebraska NE	Pennsylvania PA	Washington WA
Delaware DE	Kentucky KY	Nevada NV	Puerto Rico PR	West Virginia WV
District of Columbia DC	Louisiana LA	New Hampshire .. NH	Rhode Island RI	Wisconsin WI
Florida FL	Maine ME	New Jersey NJ	South Carolina ... SC	Wyoming WY

OTHER POSTAL SERVICE ADDRESS ABBREVIATIONS

Academy ... ACAD	Central CTL	Fort FT	Junction JCT	Parkway PKY	Spring SPG
Airport ARPRT	Church CHR	Fountain FTN	Lake LK	Place PL	Square SQ
Alley ALY	Circle CIR	Freeway FWY	Lane LN	Plaza PLZ	State ST
Annex ANX	City CY	Gateway ... GTWY	Light LGT	Point PT	Station STA
Avenue AVE	College CLG	Great GR	Little LTL	Prairie PR	Street ST
Bayou BYU	Court CT	Grove GRV	Lower LWR	Ridge RDG	Terrace TER
Beach BCH	Creek CRK	Harbor HBR	Manor MNR	River RIV	Tower TWR
Boulevard .. BLVD	Crossing ... XING	Heights HTS	Meadows .. MDWS	Road RD	Trail TRL
Bluff BLF	Drive DR	High HI	Memorial ... MEM	Rural R	Trailer TRLR
Branch BR	East E	Highway ... HWY	Middle MDL	Saint ST	Turnpike TPKE
Bridge BRG	Estates EST	Hill HL	Mission MSN	Sainte ST	Upper UPR
Brook BRK	Expressway .EXPY	Hospital HOSP	Mount MT	San SN	Union UN
Camp CP	Extension EXT	House HSE	Mountain ... MTN	Santa SN	University .. UNIV
Cape CPE	Ferry FRY	Institute INST	National ... NAT	School SCH	Valley VLY
Causeway . CWSY	Field FLD	Island IS	North N	Seminary . SMNRY	Village VLG
Center CTR	Forest FRST	Isle IS	Park PK	South S	West W

AIR PARCEL POST RATES FROM THE U.S. TO OTHER COUNTRIES

Air parcel post service is available to most countries of the world. Insured parcels must be sealed. To most countries the greatest length of a package allowed is $3\frac{1}{2}$ feet, and the greatest length and girth combined is 6 feet. To some countries, parcels may measure 4 feet in length if not more than 16 inches in girth. Consult your local post office.

Country	First 4 oz.	Added 4 oz.[1]	Max. insurance	Max. weight in lbs.	Country	First 4 oz.	Added 4 oz.[1]	Max. insurance	Max. weight in lbs.
Afghanistan	$7.05	$1.35	No	22	Cameroon	$7.05	$1.35	No	22
Albania	6.00	1.10	No	22	Canada [3]	—	—	$ 400	35
Algeria	7.05	1.35	No	44	Canary Islands	6.00	1.10	$ 210	22
Andorra	4.95	0.90	$ 420	44	Cape Verde	7.05	1.35	$ 21	22
Angola	8.10	1.60	No	22	Central Africa	8.10	1.60	No	44
Antigua	3.90	0.65	$ 100	22	Chad	7.05	1.35	No	44
Argentina	7.05	1.35	$ 210	44	Chile	7.05	1.35	No	22
Aruba	3.90	0.65	$ 210	44	China [2]	7.05	1.35	$ 420	44
Australia	7.05	1.35	$ 426	44	Colombia	4.95	0.90	$ 210	44
Austria	4.95	0.90	$ 420	44	Comoros	8.10	1.60	No	44
Azores	6.00	1.10	$ 420	22	Congo	7.05	1.35	No	44
Bahamas	3.90	0.65	$ 126	22	Corsica	8.10	1.60	$ 420	44
Bahrain	7.05	1.35	$ 100	22	Costa Rica	3.90	0.65	No	44
Balearic Islands	6.00	1.10	$ 210	22	Curacao	3.90	0.65	$ 210	44
Bangladesh	8.10	1.60	$ 200	22	Cyprus	7.05	1.35	$ 420	44
Barbados	4.95	0.90	$ 100	22	Czechoslovakia	6.00	1.10	$ 200	44
Belgium	7.05	1.35	$ 210	44	Denmark	6.00	1.10	$ 420	44
Belize	3.90	0.65	No	22	Djibouti	8.10	1.60	$ 420	44
Benin	7.05	1.35	No	44	Dominica	3.90	0.65	$ 100	22
Bermuda	3.90	0.65	No	33	Dominican Republic ..	3.90	0.65	No	44
Bolivia	4.95	0.90	No	44	Ecuador	4.95	0.90	No	44
Botswana	8.10	1.60	No	22	Egypt	6.00	1.10	$ 210	44
Brazil	7.05	1.35	No	44	El Salvador	3.90	0.65	No	44
Britain	6.00	1.10	$1,200	44	Equatorial Guinea	7.05	1.35	No	44
Brunei	7.05	1.35	No	22	Ethiopia	7.05	1.35	$ 210	44
Bulgaria	7.05	1.35	No	22	Faeroe Islands	6.00	1.10	$ 210	44
Burkina Faso........	6.00	1.10	No	44	Falkland Islands	7.05	1.35	No	22
Burma	7.05	1.35	No	22	Fiji	4.95	0.90	$ 126	22
Burundi	8.10	1.60	No	22	Finland	7.05	1.35	$ 420	44

[1] Additional 4 ounces or fraction up to 5 pounds. [2] Mail must be addressed to the "People's Republic of China." [3] First 1 lb. 8 oz. $3.38, then $0.54 for each added 8 oz. up to 5 lb., then $1.08 per lb. up to 66 lbs.

AIR PARCEL POST RATES TO OTHER COUNTRIES (continued)

Country	First 4 oz.	Added 4 oz.[1]	Max. insur- ance	Max. weight in lbs.	Country	First 4 oz.	Added 4 oz.[1]	Max. insur- ance	Max. weight in lbs.
France	$7.05	$1.35	$ 420	44	Nicaragua	$4.95	$0.90	$ 210	44
French Guiana	6.00	1.10	No	44	Niger	7.05	1.35	No	44
French Polynesia	7.05	1.35	$ 420	44	Nigeria	6.00	1.10	No	22
Gabon	7.05	1.35	No	44	Norway	7.05	1.35	$ 420	44
Gambia	4.95	0.90	No	22	Oman	7.05	1.35	$ 100	22
Germany, East	6.00	1.10	$ 210	22	Pakistan	7.05	1.35	$ 210	22
Germany, West	6.00	1.10	$ 420	44	Panama	3.90	0.65	No	44
Ghana	7.05	1.35	$ 80	22	Papua New Guinea	7.05	1.35	$ 105	22
Gibraltar	7.05	1.35	$ 50	22	Paraguay	6.00	1.10	No	44
Greece	6.00	1.10	$ 210	44	Peru	4.95	0.90	No	44
Greenland	7.05	1.35	$ 420	44	Philippines	7.05	1.35	$ 210	44
Grenada	4.95	0.90	$ 100	22	Pitcairn Islands	4.95	0.90	No	22
Guadeloupe	3.90	0.65	No	44	Poland	6.00	1.10	No	44
Guatemala	3.90	0.65	$ 100	44	Portugal	6.00	1.10	$ 420	22
Guinea	4.95	0.90	No	44	Qatar	6.00	1.10	$ 100	22
Guinea–Bissau	4.95	0.90	$ 210	22	Réunion	8.10	1.60	No	44
Guyana	4.95	0.90	$ 210	22	Romania	6.00	1.10	No	22
Haiti	3.90	0.65	No	44	Rwanda	7.05	1.35	No	22
Honduras	4.95	0.90	No	22	St. Christopher	3.90	0.65	$ 100	22
Hong Kong	6.00	1.10	$ 420	22	St. Helena	6.00	1.10	No	22
Hungary	6.00	1.10	$ 420	44	St. Lucia	3.90	0.65	$ 100	22
Iceland	7.05	1.35	$ 210	44	St. Pierre & Miquelon	3.90	0.65	No	44
India	7.05	1.35	$ 210	22	St. Vincent	3.90	0.65	$ 100	22
Indonesia	8.10	1.60	No	22	San Marino	6.00	1.10	$ 120	44
Iran	7.05	1.35	$ 210	44	Santa Cruz Islands	6.00	1.10	No	44
Iraq	7.05	1.35	No	44	Sao Tome & Principe	7.05	1.35	No	22
Ireland	6.00	1.10	$1,000	22	Saudi Arabia	7.05	1.35	No	22
Israel	6.00	1.10	No	33	Senegal	7.05	1.35	No	44
Italy	6.00	1.10	$ 210	44	Seychelles	8.10	1.60	No	22
Ivory Coast	7.05	1.35	No	44	Sierra Leone	7.05	1.35	No	22
Jamaica	3.90	0.65	No	22	Singapore	7.05	1.35	$ 100	22
Japan	8.10	1.60	$ 420	22	Solomons	6.00	1.10	No	22
Jordan	6.00	1.10	No	22	Somalia	7.05	1.35	No	22
Kenya	7.05	1.35	No	22	South Africa	7.05	1.35	No	22
Kiribati	4.95	0.90	No	44	Soviet Union	8.10	1.60	$ 210	22
Korea, South	6.00	1.10	$ 210	22	Spain	6.00	1.10	$ 210	22
Kuwait	6.00	1.10	$ 210	44	Sri Lanka	7.05	1.35	$ 210	22
Laos	8.10	1.60	No	22	Sudan	7.05	1.35	No	22
Lebanon	6.00	1.10	No	11	Suriname	4.95	0.90	$ 100	44
Lesotho	8.10	1.60	No	22	Swaziland	7.05	1.35	No	22
Liberia	6.00	1.10	$ 105	22	Sweden	7.05	1.35	$ 420	44
Libya	6.00	1.10	No	44	Switzerland	4.95	0.90	$ 420	44
Liechtenstein	4.95	0.90	$ 420	44	Syria	6.00	1.10	$ 210	44
Luxembourg	4.95	0.90	$ 210	44	Taiwan	6.00	1.10	$ 210	44
Macau	6.00	1.10	$ 126	22	Tanzania	8.10	1.60	No	22
Madagascar	8.10	1.60	No	44	Thailand	7.05	1.35	$ 126	22
Madeira Islands	4.95	0.90	$ 420	22	Togo	7.05	1.35	No	44
Malawi	7.05	1.35	No	22	Tonga	4.95	0.90	No	22
Malaysia	7.05	1.35	$ 105	22	Trinidad–Tobago	4.95	0.90	$ 153	22
Maldives	8.10	1.60	No	22	Tristan da Cunha	8.10	1.60	No	22
Mali	6.00	1.10	No	44	Tunisia	6.00	1.10	No	44
Malta	6.00	1.10	No	22	Turkey	6.00	1.10	$ 210	44
Martinique	3.90	0.65	No	44	Turks and Caicos Is.	3.90	0.65	No	22
Mauritania	7.05	1.35	No	44	Tuvalu	4.95	0.90	No	22
Mauritius	8.10	1.60	No	22	Uganda	7.05	1.35	No	22
Mexico	3.90	0.65	No	44	United Arab Emirates	7.05	1.35	$ 100	22
Monaco	7.05	1.35	$ 420	44	Uruguay	4.95	0.90	No	44
Montserrat	3.90	0.65	$ 100	44	Vanuatu	4.95	0.90	No	44
Morocco	6.00	1.10	No	44	Vatican City	6.00	1.10	No	44
Mozambique	8.10	1.60	No	22	Venezuela	4.95	0.90	No	44
Namibia	7.05	1.35	No	22	Wallis and Futuna	7.05	1.35	$ 420	44
Nauru	6.00	1.10	$ 210	22	Western Samoa	4.95	0.90	$ 210	22
Nepal	7.05	1.35	No	22	Yemen, North	7.05	1.35	No	44
Netherlands	6.00	1.10	$ 420	44	Yemen, South	7.05	1.35	No	22
Netherlands Antilles	3.90	0.65	$ 210	44	Yugoslavia	6.00	1.10	$ 210	44
Nevis	3.90	0.65	$ 100	22	Zaire	7.05	1.35	No	44
New Calendonia	7.05	1.35	$ 420	44	Zambia	8.10	1.60	No	22
New Zealand	7.05	1.35	$ 210	22	Zimbabwe	8.10	1.60	No	22

[1] Additional 4 ounces or fraction up to 5 pounds.

Religion

HIGHLIGHTS: 1985

SANCTUARY MOVEMENT

The federal government on Jan. 14 indicted 16 members of the sanctuary movement on 71 counts of transporting and concealing illegal aliens. Subsequently two of those indicted pleaded guilty to misdemeanor counts. The government also dropped charges against two nuns who had been indicted. The remaining 12 included the pastor of a Tuscon, Ariz., Presbyterian church, two Roman Catholic priests, a nun, and eight church workers. Their trial was set to start in Phoenix on Sept. 17.

Jack Elder, 41, a leader of the sanctuary movement who ran a shelter for refugees in San Benito, Texas, was convicted in Houston in February of conspiracy for helping illegal aliens enter the U.S. He began serving a 150-day prison sentence in April.

The sanctuary movement claims to have 180 churches as members, providing haven for Central American refugees who have fled from political violence. The U.S. Immigration and Naturalization Service claims that the refugees are illegal aliens seeking only an economic advantage by living in the U.S.

The convention of the Presbyterian Church (U.S.A.) on June 14 approved a contribution of $100,000 to the defense fund for indicted members of the sanctuary movement.

The Rev. Emilio Castro, secretary general of the World Council of Churches, on June 14 presented a check for $20,000 to Thomas E. Ambrogi, coordinator of the National Sanctuary Defense Fund. Castro announced that the interdenominational group would raise $150,000 for the defense fund.

BAPTIST FUNDAMENTALISTS WIN

The nation's largest Protestant denomination, the 14.1-million-member Southern Baptists, held their largest ever annual national convention in Dallas, Texas, in June. More than 47,000 delegates attended the 128th annual gathering, almost twice as many as the previous record 22,872 that attended the church's 1978 convention in Atlanta.

The large turnout came as fundamentalists, who believe the Bible should be interpreted literally, sought to retain control of the denomination as they have since 1979 in the face of a challenge by moderates who believe individual Baptists have the right to interpret the Bible according to their own conscience.

Moderates had hoped to defeat fundamentalist TV evangelist Rev. Charles F. Stanley, 52, pastor of Atlanta's First Baptist Church, who was seeking a second one-year term as the body's national president. Stanley, who was supported by evangelist Billy Graham, won by a vote of 24,453 to 19,795 over the Rev. W. Winfred Moore, 65, pastor of the First Baptist Church of Amarillo, Texas. Then, in a gesture of conciliation, the convention elected Moore as the body's first vice president.

PRESBYTERIANS SUPPORT LIBERALS

At the 197th general assembly of the Presbyterian Church (U.S.A.) held in June in Indianapolis, Ind., liberals beat back efforts by conservatives to change the church's official position on abortion.

A majority of the 676 delegates refused to support Pro-Life resolutions denouncing abortion under all circumstances but approved a statement that abortion should not be used as a method of birth control.

The unification of the Presbyterian's Northern and Southern branches in 1983 made the church the sixth largest Protestant denomination in the United States. It has 3.1 million members.

COURT ORDERS MINIMUM WAGES

The Supreme Court ruled unanimously in April that businesses run by religious groups must pay their workers federal minimum wages or equivalent benefits.

The ruling came in a case brought against the Tony and Susan Alamo Foundation, a controversial evangelical group based in Alma, Ark., which has distributed anti-Catholic literature.

The organization raises money by operating some 30 businesses from grocery stores to hog farms, but it has paid no wages to about 300 workers whom it claims are volunteers.

The court ruled that complying with the federal minimum wage laws in running its businesses would not intrude on the religious practices of the foundation.

BRAZILIAN PRIEST SILENCED

Pope John Paul II on April 26 ordered Fran-

HIGHLIGHTS: 1985 *(continued)*

ciscan priest Leonardo Boff, 45, of Brazil to maintain "a period of obsequious silence," the strongest penalty against a Roman Catholic theologian issued by the Vatican in recent times.

Boff has been a leading exponent of what has been called "liberation theology"—a philosophy that has used church teaching to support social activism. It has been denounced by the pope as embracing the Marxist concept of armed class struggle.

FIRST CONSERVATIVE WOMAN RABBI

Amy Eilberg, 30, on June 12, 1985, became the first woman ordained a rabbi in the 100-year history of Judaism's Conservative movement. The more liberal Reform movement of Judaism ordained its first female rabbi 13 years earlier in 1972. Orthodox Judaism continues to bar women as rabbis.

MILITANT MINISTER DEFROCKED

A synod of the Lutheran Church in America held at Greenville, Pa., voted 499 to 33 on June 7 to strip the Rev. D. Douglas Roth, 33, of his ministry. Roth and a supporter rushed to the speaker's platform where he charged church leaders with "corruption." Order was restored after police arrested him and forced him to leave. He later was released on bond.

In 1984 Roth refused an order from Bishop Kenneth R. May that he give up his church in Clairton, Pa. He was arrested on Nov. 13, found guilty of contempt of court, and served 112 days in jail. Roth's wife and six of his followers were arrested and jailed on Jan. 4 for barricading themselves inside the disputed Clairton church.

Roth had been condemned by the church for his activities in which he and his followers held demonstrations at churches and corporations attempting to force them into actions to reduce unemployment in the depressed steel-making industry. Churches in the area have been attacked by local unions for "harboring" businessmen whose decisions brought unemployment.

The Lutheran Church in America has 2.9 million members, the largest of four U.S. Lutheran denominations.

ARCHBISHOP JAILED

Roman Catholic Archbishop John Roach, 63, of St. Paul-Minneapolis was sentenced to 30 days in jail and a $445 fine on March 25 after pleading guilty to a charge of drunk driving. The judge stayed 28 days of the sentence, ordering him to enter a drug treatment program. Roach already had spent 10 hours in jail after his arrest. Archbishop Roach made a public apology for his conduct and said his jail sentence would provide "a pretty rich prayer time."

POPE CALLS SPECIAL SYNOD

Pope John Paul II announced on Jan. 25 that a special assembly of Roman Catholic bishops would be convened in Rome from Nov. 25 to Dec. 8, 1985, to examine the results of the Second Vatican Council held in 1962-1965 that made many changes in church practices.

28 NEW CARDINALS

Pope John Paul II consecreted 28 new cardinals of the Roman Catholic Church in an outdoor ceremony in Rome on May 25. Those elevated to cardinal were:

Archbishop Francis Arinze of Nigeria.

Archbishop Giacomo Biffi of Bologna, Italy.

Archbishop Rosalio Jose Castillo Lara of Venezuela.

Archbishop Luigi Dadaglio of Italy.

Archbishop Albert Decourtray of France.

Archbishop Andrzej Maria Dekur of Poland.

Archbishop Juan Francisco Fresno Larrain of Chile.

Archbishop Edouard Gagnon of Canada.

Archbishop Henryk Roman Gulbinowicz of Poland.

Archbishop Jean-Jerome Hamer of Belgium.

Archbishop Antonio Innocenti of Italy.

Archbishop Bernard Law of Boston.

Archbishop Simon Lourdusamy of India.

Archbishop Myroslav Ivan Lubachivsky of the Ukraine.

Archbishop Augustin Mayer of West Germany.

Archbishop Miguel Obando y Bravo of Nicaragua.

Archbishop John J. O'Connor of New York.

Rev. Pietro Pavan of Italy.

Archbishop Silvano Piovanelli of Florence, Italy.

Archbishop Paul Poupard of France.

Archbishop Paulos Tzadua of Ethiopia.

Archbishop Alfons Stickler of Austria.

Archbishop Adrianus Simonis of Netherlands.

Archbishop Angel Suquia Goiocoechea of Madrid, Spain.

Archbishop Jozef Tomko of Czechoslovakia.

Archbishop Louis-Albert Vachon of Quebec.

Archbishop Ricardo Vidal of the Philippines.

Archbishop Friedrich Wetter of West Germany.

MAJOR WORLD RELIGIONS

	Christianity		Buddhism		Judaism	
	Islam		Confucianism and Taoism		Hinduism	

Shinto

Primitive Religions or unpopulated regions

This map gives a general idea of the areas where the world's major religions have exerted their strongest direct influence. Not shown are North and South America, where the Christian religion has been predominant.

Throughout history man has turned to religion to find meaning for life and to explain the unknown.

Man's awareness of God, or of some supernatural power or powers, has impelled belief in a sacred, transcendent order that deals with human experience in the world or beyond it.

The nine largest world religions are: Buddhism, Christianity, Confucianism, Hinduism, Islam, Judaism, Shinto, Sikhism, and Taoism.

BUDDHISM

Adherents Worldwide: About 245 million, chiefly in Southeast Asia, Sri Lanka, Korea, China, Japan, and Tibet.
Adherents in U.S.: About 100,000.
Chief Scripture: The Pali Canon.
Dates from: The time of Prince Siddhartha Gautama, the Buddha (about 2,500 years ago).

Buddhism teaches that the way beyond sorrow and suffering is a middle path between striving and spiritual contemplation. Its ethical system is based upon compassion and elimination of self-interest. Its theology accepts the rebirth of persons through the transmigration of souls.

An object of Buddhist life is to achieve nirvana, blissful detachment from the world, through which the cycle of rebirth stops.

Early Buddhism was close to Hinduism, but eventually split into several branches. The main branches include: Mahayana Buddhism, which stresses salvation and contemplation; and Hinayana, which preserves the monastic tradition of the early believers. Zen Buddhism is a Japanese type of Mahayana. The Lamaism of Tibet is a combination of Buddhism and the primitive beliefs of the region.

Buddhism has long ceased to be an important influence on the Indian subcontinent, the area where it originated. About A.D. 1000 many areas in southern Asia that were formerly Buddhist fell to the influence of Islam.

Buddhist precepts have influenced some Western philosophers, most notably Arthur Schopenhauer (1788–1860).

The Buddhist Churches of America were incorporated under that name in 1942.

MAJOR WORLD RELIGIONS (continued)

CHRISTIANITY

Adherents Worldwide: About 1 billion (including 565 million Roman Catholics, 324 million Protestants, and 92 million Eastern Orthodox).
Church Members in U.S.: About 140 million.
Chief Scripture: The Bible (the Old Testament and the New Testament).
Dates from: The time of Jesus Christ (about 2,000 years ago).
Major Holidays: Christmas (Dec. 25), the Epiphany (Jan. 6), All Saints' Day (Nov. 1); Ash Wednesday, Palm Sunday, Good Friday, Easter Sunday, Ascension Day, and Pentecost; dates vary annually.

A continuation of the Judaic tradition, Christianity began with Jesus of Nazareth, who lived from about 5 B.C. to A.D. 30.

The Christian article of faith is that Jesus was the Son of God, that He came to save the world and was crucified, that He was resurrected and will come again on the world's last day to judge mankind.

The primary commandments of Jesus were to believe in God and love Him, and to love thy neighbor as thyself.

The foundation of Christianity is the New Testament, which recounts the life and teachings of Jesus Christ, and the works of his early followers, notably St. Paul.

The largest Christian body is the Roman Catholic Church, centralized under the authority of the pope, the bishop of Rome.

The Protestant churches are the products of the Reformation of the 1500s. The term "Protestant" derives from the *protestatio* issued in 1529 by the Lutheran rulers in the Holy Roman Empire against the repressive Diet of Speyer. It became the name for all who argued against the papal claim of universal supremacy.

The third great Christian group is the Eastern Orthodox, arising mainly from the ancient political split of the Roman Empire into East and West. The patriarch of Constantinople (in Istanbul) is first in honor among all the Orthodox leaders, and most of the churches consider him the spiritual leader of Eastern Orthodoxy. Over 3.8 million Americans belong to various branches of Eastern Orthodoxy.

CONFUCIANISM

Adherents Worldwide: About 275 million, mainly in China and Taiwan.
Chief Scripture: The Analects.
Dates from: The time of Confucius (about 2,500 years ago).

Confucianism is primarily a body of ethics, and can be considered an institutional religion only in that it requires sacrifices to the gods and ancestors. However, Confucianism does not restrict itself to any formalized theology.

Confucians generally conduct their lives according to five cardinal virtues: kindness, righteousness, decorous behavior, wisdom, and uprightness. Confucius taught that the chief ethic was benevolence, and one of his prime precepts was "Treat inferiors with propriety."

The basis of Confucianism derives from the Analects of Confucius and the writings of Mencius, a sage of the 4th century B.C. Confucius was the foremost philosopher of China.

With the overthrow of China's monarchy in 1911–12, Confucianism waned. In the 1970s the communist government of China launched a campaign to wipe out Confucianism.

HINDUISM

Adherents: Over 500 million live in India or in Indian communities in other lands.
Chief Scriptures: The Veda, a huge body of sacred texts, including the Upanishads (Secret Doctrines), Bhagavad-Gita (Song of the Blessed One), and many other writings.
Dates from: Prehistoric times, although the earliest writings date from about 1000 B.C.

The religion of the majority of people of India, Hinduism holds that divinity, or *ātman*, is contained in all beings.

Hinduism interprets God as embodying many different personalities, representing all aspects of reality. Among the most important of these deities are: *Siva*, a god both of creation and destruction, usually represented as a dancing figure with an extra pair of arms; *Brahma*, a creator; *Vishnu*, a sleeping figure who dreams of the universe, thereby keeping it in existence; *Kali*, goddess of death, sickness, and chaos; and *Krishna*, god of love.

The religion, which developed gradually over 5,000 years, has not given birth to any widely held ethical system. Although some sects exist, the great majority of Hindus are not sectarians.

Being a Hindu is contingent upon having membership in an Indian caste. A Hindu believes that his caste, or social position, is determined by his actions, or *Karma*, in his present life. If he leads a good life, he will be reborn into a superior caste. However, if his soul achieves perfection, he will be saved from continual rebirth and death.

About 1000 B.C., at the same time that the earliest of the Vedas were being recorded, the caste system began to become important in the Hindu social structure. The Brahman caste became the high priests of Hinduism about 800 B.C., a position that they hold to the present time.

Since India won independence in 1947, the government has tried to end the caste system. Most of today's Hindus worship according to the Puranic creed, a theological school that stabilized about A.D. 1500.

ISLAM

Adherents Worldwide: About 700 million.
Adherents in U.S.: About 2 million.
Chief Scripture: The Koran.
Dates from: The time of Mohammed (about 1,400 years ago).
Major Holidays: Eid-al-Fitr (after fasting month of Ramadan) and Eid-al-Azha (feast of sacrifice on last day of Hajj).

Islam, an Arabic word meaning "submission to Allah (God)," is based on the revelations of Allah to Mohammed, who was born in Mecca (now in Saudi Arabia) and who lived from about A.D. 570 to 632. Among Muslims, Mohammed is believed to have been a descendant of Abraham, the founder of Judaism.

Mohammed received the revelations of Allah

compiled in the Koran, and provided explanations of Koranic teachings in the Sunna.

The main Islamic article of faith is a simple one: "There is no god but God (Allah), and Mohammed is His messenger." In addition, the followers of Islam have other major articles of faith: recitation of five daily prayers; observance of Ramadan (a monthlong period of fasting and self-examination); giving of alms (zakat); and, if possible, a pilgrimage to Mecca, the birthplace of Mohammed. The most important religious service is held at midday each Friday.

Islam divides into four interpretations: Hanafi, Shafai, Hanbali, and Maliki.

In the century after the death of Mohammed, Arab Muslim armies conquered the Middle East, North Africa, Spain, and southern France.

Although Muslim influence was prevented from spreading farther into Europe after Charles Martel's Christian military victory at Tours in 732, Islam continued its eastern growth. It served as a unifying force among the many Arab tribes.

Islam's missionary organization, the Ahmadiyya movement, was founded in 1889 by Hazrat Ahmad (1835–1908). It brought Islam to the U.S. in 1920. Today a majority of persons in 57 nations are Muslims.

JUDAISM

Adherents Worldwide: About 15 million.
Adherents in U.S.: About 5.7 million.
Chief Scriptures: The Torah (Old Testament) and the Talmud.
Dates from: The time of Abraham (about 1800 B.C.).
Major Holidays: Pesach (Passover), Shavuot (Pentecost), Sukkot (Tabernacles), Rosh Hashanah (New Year), Yom Kippur (Day of Atonement), Hanukkah (Festival of Lights); dates vary annually.

Judaism recognizes one God, sometimes called *Elohim* or *Jehovah.*

The basic prayer of Judaism, called the Shema, begins: "Hear, O Israel, the Lord our God, the Lord is one."

The Jewish Sabbath is from sunset Friday to sunset Saturday.

Beginning with the patriarch Abraham, the Jews have had many great leaders and prophets, including Moses, who freed his people from Egyptian bondage in the 1200s B.C. and received the Ten Commandments and the Torah as a constitution for a new nation.

The ancient city of Jerusalem once was, and again is, central to Judaism. However, in ancient times Jerusalem was repeatedly destroyed and rebuilt. About A.D. 135 the Romans put down a Jewish revolt and forced the Jews to leave the Holy Land in what is called the *Diaspora.*

For many centuries Jews were persecuted by Christians in the belief they were responsible for the death of Jesus Christ. About 6 million Jews were slaughtered by Germans and others during World War II.

The Zionist movement for a Jewish homeland, which began in the 1800s, bore fruit in 1948, when the Jewish state of Israel was created in Palestine.

In the United States and in much of Europe, Jewish congregations are classified as Orthodox, Conservative, or Reform, depending on their degree of adherence to ancient religious customs and dietary laws.

SHINTO

Adherents Worldwide: About 63 million, all of whom are Japanese.
Chief Scripture: None.
Dates from: Antiquity; originated with the beginnings of the Japanese culture.

Shinto is a set of rituals and customs involving pilgrimages, festivals, and worship of a great host of gods. It is a folk religion, limited strictly to the Japanese people, and thus without any universal prophetic message. The word *shin-to* means "way of the gods."

The highest deity is the sun goddess, known as the Ruler of Heaven.

Gods are worshiped through the sacrifice of rice and rice wine (sake).

Shinto did not evolve an ethical system of its own, but gradually borrowed ethical principles from Buddhism and Confucianism.

From about the 500s A.D., the emperor of Japan was considered the chief Shinto priest and had the immortal status of a deity. In the 1800s a state form of Shinto was organized in coordination with Japan's newly awakened imperialism. This militaristic form of Shinto disappeared after World War II, when Emperor Hirohito disavowed his divinity. Many of today's Shinto sects stress world peace and brotherhood.

SIKHISM

Adherents Worldwide: About 8 million.
Chief Scripture: Granth Sahib.
Dates from: About A.D. 1500.

Most of the people who follow the religion of Sikhism live in the state of Punjab in northwestern India. The religion combines the beliefs of Islam and Hinduism.

Sikhism was founded by Guru Nanak (1469–1539). He taught that there was a single God, rejecting the many deities of Hinduism and the worship of idols. He attempted to eliminate the caste system of Hinduism, uniting his followers into one class.

The sacred writings of Sikhism began to be compiled by Guru Arjan (1563–1606), who also built the Sikhs' sacred city of Amritsar.

TAOISM

Adherents Worldwide: About 30 million.
Chief Scripture: Tao-te ching.
Dates from: About 2,600 years ago, founded by Lao-tzu.

Tao in Chinese means "path," and the basis of early Taoism is the allowance of the affairs of men to take the path of nature. The religion stresses quietism, contemplation, and the elimination of all striving and strong passions.

After the 500s A.D., Taoism took on aspects of Confucianism and Buddhism. Taoist monasteries were established throughout China.

Taoism developed beliefs concerning an afterlife, which included a heaven and hell, as well as a cosmology that divided all reality into male and female principles, or *yang* and *yin.* In its later development, Taoism became concerned with magic and also provided the basis for many secret societies.

PATRON SAINTS

Since the early days of Christianity certain saints and angels have been regarded as patrons of specific occupations, groups, localities, and nations.

SUPPLIANTS	SAINTS
Accountants	St. Matthew
Actors	St. Genesius
Advertisers	St. Bernardine of Siena
Altar boys	St. John Berchmans
Anesthetists	St. René Goupil
Archers	St. Sebastian
Architects	St. Thomas, apostle; St. Barbara
Art	St. Catherine of Bologna
Artists	St. Luke
Astronomers	St. Dominic
Athletes	St. Sebastian
Authors	St. Francis de Sales
Aviators	Our Lady of Loreto; St. Thérèse of Lisieux; St. Joseph of Cupertino
Bakers	St. Elizabeth of Hungary; St. Nicholas
Bankers	St. Matthew
Barbers	Sts. Cosmas and Damian; St. Louis
Barren women	St. Anthony of Padua; St. Felicitas
Beggars	St. Alexius
Blacksmiths	St. Dunstan
Blind	St. Odilia; St. Raphael
Bookkeepers	St. Matthew
Booksellers	St. John of God
Boy Scouts	St. George
Brewers	St. Augustine of Hippo; St. Luke; St. Nicholas of Myra
Bricklayers	St. Stephen
Brides	St. Nicholas of Myra
Builders	St. Vincent Ferrer
Butchers	St. Anthony of Egypt; St. Hadrian; St. Luke
Cabinetmakers	St. Anne
Canada	St. Joseph; St. Anne
Cancer patients	St. Peregrine
Carpenters	St. Joseph
Children	St. Nicholas of Myra
China	St. Joseph
Choir boys	St. Dominic Savio
Comedians	St. Vitus
Confessors	St. Alphonsus Liguori; St. John Nepomucene
Cooks	St. Lawrence; St. Martha
Dairy workers	St. Brigid
Deaf	St. Francis de Sales
Denmark	St. Ansgar; St. Canute
Dentists	St. Apollonia
Desperate	St. Jude
Dying	St. Joseph; St. Barbara
Ecology	St. Francis of Assisi
Editors	St. John Bosco
Emigrants	St. Frances Xavier Cabrini
Engineers	St. Ferdinand III
England	St. George
Ethiopia	St. Frumentius
Eye Sufferers	St. Lucy
Falsely accused	St. Raymund Nonnatus
Farmers	St. George; St. Isidore
Firemen	St. Florian
Fishermen	St. Andrew
Florists	St. Dorothy; St. Thérèse of Lisieux

SUPPLIANTS	SAINTS
France	St. Joan of Arc; St. Thérèse; Our Lady of Assumption
Funeral dirs.	St. Dismas; St. Joseph of Arimathea
Gardeners	St. Dorothy; St. Adelard; St. Tryphon; St. Fiacre; St. Phocas
Germany	St. Boniface; St. Michael
Glassworkers	St. Luke
Gravediggers	St. Anthony, abbot
Greece	St. Nicholas; St. Andrew
Grocers	St. Michael
Headaches	St. Teresa of Avila
Heart Patients	St. John of God
Hopeless	St. Jude
Housewives	St. Anne
Hunters	St. Hubert; St. Eustachius
India	Our Lady of Ass'pt'n
Infantrymen	St. Maurice
Innkeepers	St. Amand
Invalids	St. Roch
Ireland	St. Patrick; St. Brigid; St. Columba
Italy	St. Francis of Assisi; St. Catherine of Siena
Japan	St. Peter Baptist
Jewelers	St. Eligius
Journalists	St. Francis de Sales
Jurists	St. Catherine of Alexandria; St. John Capistran
Laborers	St. Isidore; St. James; St. John Bosco
Lawyers	St. Ivo; St. Genesius; St. Thomas More
Librarians	St. Jerome
Maids	St. Zita
Mentally ill	St. Dympna
Merchants	St. Francis of Assisi; St. Nicholas of Myra
Messengers	St. Gabriel
Metal workers	St. Eligius
Mexico	Our Lady of Guad'l'pe
Miners	St. Barbara
Mothers	St. Monica
Motorcyclists	Our Lady of Grace
Motorists	St. Christopher; St. Frances of Rome
Mountaineers	St. Bernard, Menthon
Musicians	St. Gregory the Great; St. Cecilia; St. Dunstan
Norway	St. Olaf
Nurses	St. Camillus de Lellis; St. John of God; St. Agatha; St. Alexius; St. Raphael
Orators	St. John Chrysostom
Orphans	St. Jerome Aemilian
Painters	St. Luke
Paratroopers	St. Michael
Pawnbrokers	St. Nicholas
Pharmacists	Sts. Cosmas and Damian; St. James the Greater
Philosophers	St. Justin; St. Catherine of Alexandria
Physicians	St. Pantaleon; Sts. Cosmas and Damian; St. Luke, St. Raphael

SUPPLIANTS	SAINTS
Pilgrims	St. Alexius; St. James
Plasterers	St. Bartholomew
Poets	St. David; St. Cecilia
Poison sufferers	St. Benedict
Poland	St. Casimir; St. Stanislaus of Kracow; Our Lady of Czestochowa
Policemen	St. Michael
Poor	St. Lawrence; St. Anthony of Padua
Possessed	St. Bruno; St. Denis
Postal workers	St. Gabriel
Preg. mothers	St. Margaret; St. Raymund Nonnatus; St. Gerard Majella
Priests	St. Jean-Baptiste Vianney
Printers	St. John of God; St. Augustine of Hippo; St. Genesius
Prisoners	St. Dismas; St. Barbara; St. Joseph Cafasso
Public relations	St. Bernardino, Siena
Radio workers	St. Gabriel
Rheumatics	St. James the Greater
Sailors	St. Cuthbert; St. Brendan; St. Eulalia; St. Christopher; St. Peter Gonzales; St. Erasmus
Scholars	St. Brigid
Scientists	St. Albert
Scotland	St. Andrew; St. Columba
Sculptors	St. Claude
Searchers for lost articles	St. Anthony of Padua
Secretaries	St. Genesius
Servants	St. Martha; St. Zita
Shoemakers	Sts. Crispin and Crispinian
Sick	St. Michael; St. John of God; St. Camillus de Lellis
Singers	St. Gregory; St. Cecilia
Skaters	St. Lidwina
Skiers	St. Bernard
Social workers	St. Louise de Marillac
Soldiers	St. Hadrian; St. George; St. Ignatius; St. Sebastian; St. Martin of Tours; St. Joan of Arc
Spain	St. James; St. Teresa
Stenographers	St. Genesius; St. Cassian
Students	St. Thomas Aquinas; St. Catherine of Alexandria
Sweden	St. Bridget; St. Eric
Tailors	St. Homobonus
Tax collectors	St. Matthew
Taxi drivers	St. Fiacre
Teachers	St. Gregory the Great; St. Catherine of Alexandria; St. John Baptist de la Salle
TV workers	St. Gabriel
Throat sufferers	St. Blaise
Travelers	St. Christopher; St. Anthony of Padua; St. Nicholas of Myra; St. Raphael
United States	Immaculate Concept.
Wales	St. David
Women in labor	St. Anne
Young girls	St. Agnes

U.S. RELIGIOUS DENOMINATIONS

Church membership in the United States increased in 1984 to 140,816,385 from a total of 139,603,059, according to the National Council of Churches of Christ.

Some 60.1% of the U.S. population belonged to an organized religion in 1984, and there were 338,244 churches.

Adventist: Advent Christian Church: Organized, 1860; address, P.O. Box 23152, Charlotte, NC 28212; churches, 364; membership, 29,838.

Adventist: Seventh-day Adventists: Organized, 1863; address, 6840 Eastern Ave. N.W., Washington, DC 20012; churches, 3,907; membership, 623,563.

Baha'i Faith: Founded in Iraq, 1863; address, National Spiritual Assembly, 536 Sheridan Rd., Wilmette, IL 60091; assemblies, 1,700.

Baptist: American Baptist Association: Organized, 1905; address, 4605 N. State Line Ave., Texarkana, TX 75501; churches, 1,641; membership, 225,000.

Baptist: American Baptist Churches in the U.S.A.: Organized, 1907; address, Valley Forge, PA 19481; churches, 5,851; membership, 1,637,099.

Baptist: Baptist General Conference: Organized, 1879; address, 2002 S. Arlington Heights Rd., Arlington Heights, IL 60005; churches, 732; membership, 129,912.

Baptist: Baptist Missionary Association of America: Organized, 1950; address, 721 Main St., Little Rock, AR 72201; churches, 1,411; membership, 234,142.

Baptist: Conservative Baptist Association of America: Organized, 1947; address, 25 W. 560 Geneva Rd., Box 66, Wheaton, IL 60187; churches, 1,140; membership, 225,000.

Baptist: Free Will Baptists: Organized, 1727;

Roman Catholicism remained the largest single religion in the U.S. Its 52,286,043 members in 1984 represented an increase of 197,269 since 1983.

Because of space limitations, only U.S. religious denominations reporting more than 20,000 members are listed in the following table.

address, 1134 Murfreesboro Rd., Nashville, TN 37217; churches, 2,480; membership, 226,422.

Baptist: General Association of Regular Baptist Churches: Organized, 1932; address, 1300 N. Meacham Rd., Schaumberg, IL 60195; churches, 1,571; membership, 300,839.

Baptist: General Baptists, General Association of: Founded in England, 1607; address, 100 Stinson Drive, Poplar Bluff, MO 63901; churches, 870; membership, 75,028.

Baptist: National Baptist Convention of America: Organized, 1880; address, 2823 N. Houston, Fort Worth, TX 76106; churches, 11,398; membership, 2,668,799.

Baptist: National Baptist Convention, United States of America, Inc.: Organized, 1880; address, 915 Sprain St., Baton Rouge, LA 70802; churches, 26,000; membership, 5,500,000.

Baptist: National Primitive Baptist Convention, Inc.: Organized, 1907; address, P.O. Box 2355, Tallahassee, FL 32301; churches, 606; membership, 250,000.

Baptist: North American Baptist Conference: 1 S. 210 Summit Ave., Oakbrook Terrace, IL 60181; churches, 260; membership, 43,286.

Baptist: Primitive Baptists: Address, S. Second St., Thornton, AR 71766; churches, 1,000; membership, 72,000.

Baptist: Progressive National Baptist Convention, Inc.: Organized, 1961; address, 601 50th

50 LARGEST U.S. RELIGIOUS DENOMINATIONS

Source: Yearbook of American and Canadian Churches 1985.

DENOMINATION	MEMBERSHIP	DENOMINATION	MEMBERSHIP
Roman Catholic Church	52,286,043	Seventh-Day Adventists	623,563
Southern Baptist Convention	14,178,051	Progressive National Baptist Convention, Inc.	521,692
United Methodist Church	9,405,164	Church of the Nazarene	507,574
Judaism	5,728,075	Church of God (Cleveland, Tenn.)	493,904
National Baptist Convention, U.S.A., Inc.	5,500,000	United Pentecostal Church, International	465,000
Church of God in Christ	3,709,661	Armenian Church of America (Orthodox)	450,000
Church of Jesus Christ of Latter-Day Saints	3,602,000	Salvation Army	428,046
Presbyterian Church (U.S.A.)	3,122,213	Wisconsin Evangelical Lutheran Synod	414,199
Lutheran Church in America	2,925,008	Armenian Apostolic Church of America	350,000
Episcopal Church	2,794,690	Reformed Church in America	344,520
National Baptist Convention of America	2,668,799	General Assn. of Regular Baptist Churches	300,839
Lutheran Church—Missouri Synod	2,630,947	Polish National Catholic Church of America	282,411
American Lutheran Church	2,343,412	Antiochian Orthodox Christian Archdiocese	280,000
African Methodist Episcopal Church	2,210,000	National Primitive Baptist Convention, Inc.	250,000
Islam	2,000,000	Baptist Missionary Assn. of America	234,142
Greek Orthodox Archdiocese	1,950,000	Free Will Baptists	226,422
Assemblies of God	1,992,754	American Baptist Association	225,000
United Church of Christ	1,701,513	Conservative Baptist Association of America	225,000
American Baptist Churches in the U.S.A.	1,637,099	Christian and Missionary Alliance	215,857
Churches of Christ	1,600,000	Christian Reformed Church in North	
Christian Church (Disciples of Christ)	1,145,918	America	213,659
African Methodist Episcopal Zion Church	1,134,179	Church of God in Christ, Int.	200,000
Christian Church and Churches of Christ	1,043,642	Reorganized Church of Jesus Christ of	
Orthodox Church in America (Russian)	1,000,000	Latter Day Saints	192,830
Christian Methodist Episcopal Church	718,922	Church of God (Anderson, Ind.)	182,190
Jehovah's Witnesses	649,697	International Council of Community Churches	173,500

U.S. RELIGIOUS DENOMINATIONS *(continued)*
St., N.E., Washington, DC 20019; churches, 655; membership, 521,692.

Baptist: Southern Baptist Convention: Formed, 1845; address, 901 Commerce, Nashville, TN 37203; churches, 34,464; membership, 14,178,051.

Baptist: United Free Will Baptist Church: Organized, 1870; address, 1101 University St., Kinston, NC 28501; churches, 836; membership, 100,000.

Bible Way Church of Our Lord Jesus Christ World Wide, Inc.: Established, 1957; address, 1100 New Jersey Ave., N.W., Washington, DC 20001; churches, 350; membership, 30,000.

Brethren: Church of the Brethren: Founded in Germany, 1708; address, 1451 Dundee Ave., Elgin, IL 60120; churches, 1,067; membership, 164,680.

Brethren: Fellowship of Grace Brethren Churches: Separated from Church of the Brethren in 1882; address, Box 544, Winona Lake, IN 46590; churches, 284; membership, 42,023.

Brethren in Christ Church: Founded, 1778; address, P.O. Box 245, Upland, CA 91785; churches, 172; membership, 15,058.

Buddhist Churches of America: Founded, 1899; 1710 Octavia St., San Francisco, CA 94109; churches, 100; membership, 700,000.

Christadelphians: Organized, 1844; address, 1002 Webster Lane, Des Plaines, IL 60016; churches, 850; membership, 15,800.

Christian and Missionary Alliance: Organized, 1887; address, 350 N. Highland Ave., Nyack, NY 10960; churches, 1,532; membership; 215,857.

Christian Church (Disciples of Christ): Organized, 1832; address, Box 1986, 222 S. Downey Ave., Indianapolis, IN 46206; churches, 4,608; membership, 1,145,918.

Christian Churches and Churches of Christ: Founded, early 1800s; address, Box 39456, Cincinnati, OH 45239; churches, 5,502; membership, 1,043,642.

Christian Congregation, Inc.: Organized, 1887; address, 804 W. Hemlock St., LaFollette, TN 37766; churches, 1,429; members 101,351.

Christian Reformed Church in North America: Organized 1857; address 2850 Kalamazoo Ave. S.E., Grand Rapids, MI 49560; churches, 639; members, 213,659.

Christian Science: Church of Christ, Scientist: Founded, 1879; address, Christian Science Center, Boston, MA 02115; branches, 3,000.

Church of God: Organized, about 1880; address, Box 2420, Anderson, IN 46018; churches, 2,286; membership, 182,190.

Church of God: General Conference of Churches of God: Organized, 1825; address, Room 200, 900 S. Arlington Ave., Harrisburg, PA 17109; churches, 352; membership, 34,424.

Church of the Nazarene: Organized, 1908; address, 6401 The Paseo, Kansas City, MO 64131; churches, 4,931; membership, 507,574.

Churches of Christ: No general organization higher than local congregation; churches, 13,056; membership, 1,600,000.

Community Churches, International Council of: Organized, 1950; 900 Ridge Rd., Homewood, IL 60430; churches, 250; membership, 173,500.

Congregational Christian Churches, National Association of: Organized, 1955; address, P.O. Box 1620, Oak Creek, WI 53154; churches, 457; membership, 105,865.

Congregational Christian Conference, Conservative: Founded, 1948; address, 7582 Currell Blvd., Ste. 108, St. Paul, MN 55125; churches, 148; membership, 26,765.

Eastern Orthodox: Albanian Orthodox Archdiocese in America: Established, 1908; address, 529 E. Broadway, S. Boston, MA 02127; churches, 16; membership, 40,000.

Eastern Orthodox: American Carpatho-Russian Orthodox Greek Catholic Church: Organized, 1938; address, Johnstown, PA 15906; churches, 70; membership, 100,000.

Eastern Orthodox: Antiochian Orthodox Christian Archdiocese of All North America: Established, 1975; address, 358 Mountain Rd., Englewood, NJ 07631; churches, 120; membership, 280,000.

Eastern Orthodox: Armenian Apostolic Church of America: Established, 1887; address, 138 E. 39th St., New York, NY 10016; churches, 33; membership, 350,000.

Eastern Orthodox: Armenian Church of America, Diocese of the: Established, 1889; address, 630 Second Ave., New York, NY 10016; churches, 66; membership, 450,000.

Eastern Orthodox: Bulgarian Eastern Orthodox Church: Founded, 1907; address, 550 A W. 50th St., New York, NY 10019; churches, 13; membership, 86,000.

Eastern Orthodox: Coptic Orthodox Church: Founded, ancient Egypt; address, 427 West Side Ave., Jersey City, NJ 07304; churches, 29; membership, 100,000.

Eastern Orthodox: Greek Orthodox Archdiocese of North and South America: Founded, 1864; address, 8–10 East 79th St., New York, NY 10021; churches, 535; membership, 1,950,000.

Eastern Orthodox: Holy Apostolic and Catholic Church of the East (Assyrian): Founded, 37 A.D.; address, 7444 N. Kildare, Skokie, IL 60076; churches, 13; membership, 35,000.

Eastern Orthodox: Orthodox Church in America (formerly Russian Orthodox Greek Catholic Church of America): Established, 1792; address, P.O. Box 675, Syosset, NY 11791; churches, 440; membership, 1,000,000.

Eastern Orthodox: Romanian Orthodox Episcopate of America: Organized, 1929; address, 2522 Grey Tower Rd., Jackson, MI 49201; churches, 35; membership, 41,000.

Eastern Orthodox: Russian Orthodox Church in the U.S.A., Patriarchal Parishes of the: Address, 15 E. 97th St., New York, NY 10029; churches, 41; membership, 51,500.

Eastern Orthodox: Russian Orthodox Church Outside Russia: Organized, 1920; address, 75 E. 93d St., New York, NY 10028; churches, 81; membership, 55,000.

Eastern Orthodox: Serbian Eastern Orthodox Church in the U.S.A. and Canada: Organized, 1921; address, P.O. Box 519, Libertyville, IL 60048; churches, 78; membership, 97,123.

Eastern Orthodox: Syrian Orthodox Church of Antioch: Organized, 1957; address, 49 Kipp Ave., Lodi, NJ 07644; churches, 13; membership, 30,000.

Eastern Orthodox: Ukrainian Orthodox Church

in the U.S.A.: Organized, 1919; address, P.O. Box 495, South Bound Brook, NJ 08880; churches, 107; membership, 87,745.

Eastern Orthodox: Ukrainian Orthodox Church in America (Ecumenical Patriarchate): Organized, 1928; address, 90–34 139th St., Jamaica, NY 11435; churches, 28; membership, 25,000.

Episcopal Church: Became autonomous from the Anglican Church of England in 1789; address, 815 Second Avenue, New York, NY 10017; churches, 7,387; membership, 2,794,690.

Evangelical Congregational Church: Formed, 1928; 100 W. Park Ave., Myerstown, PA 17067; churches, 160; membership, 38,432.

Evangelical Covenant Church: Organized, 1885; address, 5101 N. Francisco Ave., Chicago, IL 60625; churches, 554; membership, 82,943.

Evangelical Free Church of America: Organized, 1880s; address, 1515 E. 66th St., Minneapolis, MN 55423; churches, 900; membership, 146,000.

Evangelistic: Missionary Church: Formed by merger of United Missionary Church and Missionary Church Association, 1969; address, 3901 S. Wayne Ave., Fort Wayne, IN 46807; churches, 290; membership, 26,055.

Free Christian Zion Church of Christ: Organized, 1905; address, 1315 Hutchinson Street, Nashville, AR 71852; churches, 742; membership, 22,260.

Independent Fundamental Churches of America: Organized, 1930; address, 1860 Mannheim Rd., Box 7250, Westchester, IL 60153; churches, 1,019; membership, 120,446.

Islam: Address, Islamic Center, 2551 Massachusetts Ave., N.W., Washington, DC 20008.

Jehovah's Witnesses: Organized, 1870s; 25 Columbia Heights, Brooklyn, NY 11201; congregations, 7,921; membership, 649,697.

Judaism: First congregation in America, 1654; total membership, 5,728,075.

Judaism (Conservative): United Synagogue of America: Address, 155 Fifth Ave., New York, NY 10010; congregations, 800.

Judaism (Orthodox): Union of Orthodox Jewish Congregations of America: Address, 45 W. 36th St., New York, NY 10018; congregations, 3,000.

Judaism (Reform): Union of American Hebrew Congregations: Address, 838 Fifth Ave., New York, NY 10021; congregations, 700.

Lutheran: American Lutheran Church: Organized, 1960; address, 422 S. 5th St., Minneapolis, MN 55415; churches, 4,905; membership, 2,343,412.

Lutheran: Evangelical Lutheran Churches, Association of: Organized, 1976; address, 12015 Manchester Rd., Ste. 80LL, St. Louis, MO 63131; churches, 272; membership, 110,934.

Lutheran: Evangelical Lutheran Synod: Organized, 1853; address, Bethany Lutheran College, Mankato, MN 56001; churches, 111; membership, 20,556.

Lutheran Church in America: Organized, 1962; address, 231 Madison Ave., New York, NY 10016; churches, 5,815; membership, 2,925,008.

Lutheran Church—Missouri Synod: Organized, 1847; address, 1333 S. Kirkwood Rd., St. Louis, MO 63122; churches, 5,829; membership, 2,630,947.

Lutheran: Wisconsin Evangelical Lutheran Syn-od: Organized, 1850; address, 2929 North Mayfair Rd., Wauwatosa, WI 53222; churches, 1,193; membership, 414,199.

Mennonite: General Conference of Mennonite Brethren Churches: Established in America, 1874; address, Hillsboro, KS 67063; churches, 124; membership, 17,065.

Mennonite: Old Order Amish Church: address, Raber's Bookstore, Baltic, OH 43804; churches, no general organization.

Mennonite Church: Established in America, 1683; address, 528 E. Madison St., Lombard, IL 60148; churches, 1,201; membership, 110,294.

Mennonite Church, The General Conference: Organized, 1860; address, 722 Main Street, Newton, KS 67114; churches, 213; membership, 37,000.

Methodist: African Methodist Episcopal Church: Founded, 1787; address, P.O. Box 2140, Jacksonville, FL 32203; churches, 6,200; membership, 2,210,000.

Methodist: African Methodist Episcopal Zion Church: Founded, 1796; address, 1200 Windermere Dr., Pittsburgh, PA 15218; churches, 6,023; membership, 1,134,179.

Methodist: Christian Methodist Episcopal Church: Organized, 1870; address, P.O. Box 655, Memphis, TN 38101; churches, 2,340; membership, 718,922.

Methodist: Free Methodist Church of North America: Organized, 1860; address, 901 College Ave., Winona Lake, IN 46590; churches, 1,012; membership, 70,657.

Methodist: Reformed Zion Union Apostolic Church: Organized, 1869; address, 416 South Hill Ave., South Hill, VA 23970; churches, 50; membership, 16,000.

Methodist: United Methodist Church: Formed, 1968; address, 168 Mt. Vernon St. Newtonville, MA 02160; churches, 38,181; membership, 9,405,164.

Metropolitan Community Churches, Universal Fellowship of: Founded, 1968; address, 5300 Santa Monica Blvd., #304, Los Angeles, CA 90029; churches, 200; membership, 33,500.

Moravian Church in America: Established, 1735; address, P.O. Box 1245, 69 W. Church St., Bethlehem, PA 18018; churches, 154; membership, 54,621.

Mormon: Church of Jesus Christ of Latter-Day Saints: Organized, 1830; address, 50 East North Temple St., Salt Lake City, UT 84150; churches, 8,017; membership, 3,602,000.

New Apostolic Church of North America: Established, 1863; address, 3753 N. Troy St., Chicago, IL 60618; churches, 432; membership, 31,623.

Old Roman Catholic Church, North American: Established in America, 1916; address, 4200 N. Kedvale Ave., Chicago, IL 60641; churches, 130; membership, 62,383.

Pentecostal: Apostolic Overcoming Holy Church of God: Organized, 1920; address, 1120 N. 24th St., Birmingham, AL 35234; churches, 300; membership, 75,000.

Pentecostal: Assemblies of God: Founded, 1914; address, 1445 Boonville Avenue, Springfield, MO 65802; churches, 10,386; membership, 1,992,754.

Pentecostal: Church of God: Organized, 1903; 2504 Arrow Wood Dr., S.E., Huntsville, AL

U.S. RELIGIOUS DENOMINATIONS *(continued)*
35803; churches, 2,035; membership, 75,890.
Pentecostal: Church of God (Cleveland, Tenn.):
Organized, 1886; address, Keith St. at 25th
N.W., Cleveland, TN 37311; churches, 5,410;
membership, 493,904.
Pentecostal: Church of God in Christ: Orga-
nized, 1895; address, 939 Mason St., Memphis,
TN 38126; churches, 9,982; membership,
3,709,661.
**Pentecostal: Church of God in Christ, Interna-
tional:** Organized, 1969; address, 170 Adelphi
St., Brooklyn, NY 11025; churches, 300; mem-
bership, 200,000.
Pentecostal: Church of God of Prophecy: Orga-
nized, 1903; Bible Pl., Cleveland, TN 37311;
churches, 2,040; membership, 74,384.
**Pentecostal: Church of Our Lord Jesus Christ
of the Apostolic Faith, Inc.:** Organized, 1919;
address, 2081 Adam Clayton Powell, Jr. Blvd.,
New York, NY 10027; churches, 155; member-
ship, 45,000.
**Pentecostal: Full Gospel Fellowship of Churches
and Ministers, Int'l.:** Founded, 1962; address,
1545 W. Mockingbird Lane, Ste. 1012, Lock
Box 209, Dallas, TX 75235; churches, 401;
membership, 65,000.
**Pentecostal: International Church of the Four-
square Gospel:** Organized, 1927; address, Angelus
Temple, 1100 Glendale Boulevard, Los Angeles,
CA 90026; churches, 113; membership, 164,688.
**Pentecostal: Open Bible Standard Churches,
Inc.:** Formed, 1935; address, 2020 Bell Ave.,
Des Moines, IA 50315; churches, 290; member-
ship, 46,351.
**Pentecostal: The (Original) Church of God,
Inc.:** Organized, 1886; address, P.O. Box 3086,
Chattanooga, TN 37404; churches, 70; member-
ship, 20,000.
Pentecostal Church of God, Inc.: Organized,
1919; address, Messenger Plaza, 602 Main St.,
Joplin, MO 64802; churches, 1,120; member-
ship, 89,559.
Pentecostal Holiness Church, Int'l.: Organized,
about 1895; address, P.O. Box 12609, Oklahoma
City, OK 73157; churches, 1,143; membership,
108,229.
**Pentecostal: United Holy Church of America,
Inc.:** Organized, 1886; address, P.O. Box 19846,
Philadelphia, PA 19143; churches, 470; member-
ship, 28,980.
**Pentecostal: United Pentecostal Church Interna-
tional:** Formed, 1945; address, 8855 Dunn Rd.,
Hazelwood, MO 63042; churches, 3,300; mem-
bership, 465,000.
Plymouth Brethren: Organized, 1820s; address,
P.O. Box 294, Wheaton, IL 60187; churches,
1,100; membership, 98,000.
Polish National Catholic Church of America:
Organized, 1897; address, 529 E. Locust St.,
Scranton, PA 18505; churches, 162; member-
ship, 282,411.
**Presbyterian: Associate Reformed Presbyterian
Church (General Synod):** Reorganized, 1935;
address, 1 Cleveland St., Greenville, SC 29601;
churches, 170; membership, 35,934.
Presbyterian Church (U.S.A.): Established,
1706; merger, 1983; addresses: 475 Riverside
Dr., N.Y., NY 10115, 341 Ponce de Leon Ave.
N.E., Atlanta, GA 30365; churches, 11,596;

membership, 3,122,213.
Presbyterian Church in America: Established,
1973; address, P.O. Box 1428, Decatur, GA
30031; churches, 825; membership, 155,988.
Presbyterian: Cumberland Presbyterian Church:
Organized, 1810; address, 1978 Union Ave.,
Memphis, TN 38104; churches, 878; member-
ship, 99,887.
Presbyterian: Orthodox Presbyterian Church:
Organized, 1936; address, 7401 Old York Rd.,
Philadelphia, PA 19126; churches, 166; member-
ship, 17,304.
**Presbyterian: Second Cumberland Presbyterian
Church in U.S.:** Organized, 1869; address, 226
Church St.; Huntsville, AL 35801; churches,
121; membership, 30,000.
Quaker: Evangelical Friends Alliance: Formed,
1965; address, 29 N. Garland Ave., Colorado
Spgs., CO 80909; churches, 217; membership,
24,095.
Quaker: Friends General Conference: Orga-
nized, 1900; address, 1520-B Race St., Philadel-
phia, PA 19102; churches, 233; membership,
26,184.
Quaker: Friends United Meeting: Organized,
1965; address, 101 Quaker Hill Dr., Richmond,
IN 47374; churches, 534; membership, 58,371.
Reformed Church in America: Established 1628
as the Reformed Protestant Dutch Church; ad-
dress, 475 Riverside Dr., New York, NY 10115;
churches, 920; membership, 344,520.
**Reorganized Church of Jesus Christ of Latter
Day Saints:** Reorganized, 1860; address, The
Auditorium, P.O. Box 1059, Independence, MO
64051; churches, 1,059; membership, 192,830.
Roman Catholic Church: Established in Mary-
land, 1634; address, 1312 Massachusetts Ave.
N.W., Washington, DC 20005; parishes,
churches, and missions, 24,260; membership,
52,286,043.
Salvation Army: Established, 1880; address, 799
Bloomfield Ave., Verona, NJ 07044; churches,
1,061; membership, 428,046.
Scientology, Church of: Founded, 1950; address,
5930 Franklin Ave., Los Angeles, CA 90028;
churches, 47.
**Triumph the Church and Kingdom of God in
Christ (International):** Founded, 1902; address,
Rt. 4, Box 77056, Birmingham, AL 35228;
churches, 475; membership, 54,307.
Unitarian Universalist Association: Universalists
organized, 1793; Unitarians organized, 1825;
merger, 1961; address, 25 Beacon Street, Boston,
MA 02108; churches, 945; membership, 169,168.
United Brethren in Christ: Founded, 1800; ad-
dress, 302 Lake St., Huntington, IN 46750;
churches, 256; membership, 26,869.
United Church of Christ: Union, 1957, of the
Evangelical and Reformed Church and the Con-
gregational Christian Churches; 105 Madison
Ave., New York, NY 10016; churches, 6,427;
membership, 1,701,513.
Volunteers of America: Founded, 1896; address,
3939 North Causeway Boulevard, Ste. 202, Me-
tairie, LA 70002; churches, 607; membership,
36,634.
Wesleyan Church: Union, 1968, of the Pilgrim
Holiness Church and Wesleyan Methodist
Church; address, P.O. Box 2000, Marion, IN
46953; churches, 1,722; membership, 107,672.

ROMAN CATHOLIC POPES

POPE	REIGN	POPE	REIGN	POPE	REIGN	POPE	REIGN
St. Peter	d.67	St. Boniface IV	608–15	Benedict V[2]	964–66	Innocent VI	1352–62
St. Linus	67–76	St. Deusdedit or Adeodatus I	615–18	John XIII	965–72	Urban V	1362–70
St. Cletus or Anacletus	76–88	Boniface V	619–25	Benedict VI	973–74	Gregory XI	1370–78
St. Clement I	88–97	Honorius I	625–38	Benedict VII	974–83	Urban VI	1378–89
St. Evaristus	97–105	Severinus	640	John XIV	983–84	Boniface IX	1389–1404
St. Alexander I	105–15	John IV	640–42	John XV	985–96	Innocent VII	1404–06
St. Sixtus I	115–25	Theodore I	642–49	Gregory V	996–99	Gregory XII	1406–15
St. Telesphorus	125–36	St. Martin I	649–55	Sylvester II	999–1003	Martin V	1417–31
St. Hyginus	136–40	St. Eugene I	654–57	John XVII	1003	Benedict XIV	1425–30
St. Pius I	140–55	St. Vitalian	657–72	John XVIII	1004–09	Eugene IV	1431–47
St. Anicetus	155–66	Adeodatus II	672–76	Sergius IV	1009–12	Nicholas V	1447–55
St. Soter	166–75	Donus	676–78	Benedict VIII	1012–24	Callistus III	1455–58
St. Eleutherius	175–89	St. Agatho	678–81	John XIX	1024–32	Pius II	1458–64
St. Victor I	189–99	St. Leo II	682–83	Benedict IX[3]	1032–44, 1045, 1047–48	Paul II	1464–71
St. Zephyrinus	199(?)–217	St. Benedict II	684–85	Sylvester III[3]	1045	Sixtus IV	1471–84
St. Callistus I	217–22	John V	685–86	Gregory VI[3]	1045–46	Innocent VIII	1484–92
St. Urban I	222–30	Conon	686–87	Clement II[3]	1046–47	Alexander VI	1492–1503
St. Pontian	230–35	St. Sergius I	687–701	Damasus II	1048	Pius III	1503
St. Anterus	235–36	John VI	701–05	St. Leo IX	1049–54	Julius II	1503–13
St. Fabian	236–50	John VII	705–07	Victor II	1055–57	Leo X	1513–21
St. Cornelius	251–53	Sisinnius	708	Stephen IX (X)	1057–58	Adrian VI	1522–23
St. Lucius I	253–54	Constantine	708–15	Nicholas II	1059–61	Clement VII	1523–34
St. Stephen I	254–57	St. Gregory II	715–31	Alexander II	1061–73	Paul III	1534–49
St. Sixtus II	257–58	St. Gregory III	731–41	St. Gregory VII	1073–85	Julius III	1550–55
St. Dionysius	259–68	St. Zacharias	741–52	Victor III	1086–87	Marcellus II	1555
St. Felix I	269–74	Stephen II	752	Urban II	1088–99	Paul IV	1555–59
St. Eutychian	275–83	Stephen II (III)	752–57	Paschal II	1099–1118	Pius IV	1559–65
St. Caius	283–96	St. Paul I	757–67	Gelasius II	1118–19	St. Pius V	1566–72
St. Marcellinus	296–304	Stephen III (IV)	768–72	Callistus II	1119–24	Gregory XIII	1572–85
St. Marcellus I	308–09	Adrian I	772–95	Honorius II	1124–30	Sixtus V	1585–90
St. Eusebius	309 or 310	St. Leo III	795–816	Innocent II	1130–43	Urban VII	1590
St. Miltiades	311–14	Stephen IV (V)	816–17	Victor IV	1138	Gregory XIV	1590–91
St. Sylvester I	314–35	St. Paschal	817–24	Celestine II	143–44	Innocent IX	1591
St. Marcus	336	Eugene II	824–27	Lucius II	1144–45	Clement VIII	1592–1605
St. Julius I	337–52	Valentine	827	Eugene III	1145–53	Leo XI	1605
Liberius	352–66	Gregory IV	827–44	Anastasius IV	1153–54	Paul V	1605–21
St. Damasus I	366–84	Sergius II	844–47	Adrian IV	1154–59	Gregory XV	1621–23
St. Siricius	384–99	St. Leo IV	847–55	Alexander III	1159–81	Urban VIII	1623–44
St. Anastasius I	399–401	Benedict III	855–58	Lucius III	1181–85	Innocent X	1644–55
St. Innocent I	401–17	St. Nicholas I	858–67	Urban III	1185–87	Alexander VII	1655–67
St. Zosimus	417–18	Adrian II	867–72	Gregory VIII	1187	Clement IX	1667–69
St. Boniface I	418–22	John VIII	872–82	Clement III	1187–91	Clement X	1670–76
St. Celestine I	422–32	Marinus I	882–84	Celestine III	1191–98	Innocent XI	1676–89
St. Sixtus III	432–40	St. Adrian III	884–85	Innocent III	1198–1216	Alexander VIII	1689–91
St. Leo I	440–61	Stephen V (VI)	885–91	Honorius III	1216–27	Innocent XII	1691–1700
St. Hilarius	461–68	Formosus	891–96	Gregory IX	1227–41	Clement XI	1700–21
St. Simplicius	468–83	Boniface VI	896	Celestine IV	1241	Innocent XIII	1721–24
St. Felix III (II)[1]	483–92	Stephen VI (VII)	896–97	Innocent IV	1243–54	Benedict XIII	1724–30
St. Gelasius I	492–96	Romanus	897	Alexander IV	1254–61	Clement XII	1730–40
Anastasius II	496–98	Theodore II	897	Urban IV	1261–64	Benedict XIV	1740–58
St. Symmachus	498–514	John IX	898–900	Clement IV	1265–68	Clement XIII	1758–69
St. Hormisdas	514–23	Benedict IV	900–03	Gregory X	1271–76	Clement XIV	1769–74
St. John I	523–26	Leo V	903	Innocent V	1276	Pius VI	1775–99
St. Felix IV (III)	526–30	Sergius III	904–11	Adrian V	1276	Pius VII	1800–23
Boniface II	530–32	Anastasius III	911–13	John XXI	1276–77	Leo XII	1823–29
John II	533–35	Lando	913–14	Nicholas III	1277–80	Pius VIII	1829–30
St. Agapetus I	535–36	John X	914–28	Martin IV	1281–85	Gregory XVI	1831–46
St. Silverius	536–37	Leo VI	928	Honorius IV	1285–87	Pius IX	1846–78
Vigilius	537(?)–55	Stephen VII (VIII)	928–31	Nicholas IV	1288–92	Leo XIII	1878–1903
Pelagius I	556–61	John XI	931–35	St. Celestine V	1294	St. Pius X	1903–14
John III	561–74	Leo VII	936–39	Boniface VIII	1294–1303	Benedict XV	1914–22
Benedict I	575–79	Stephen VIII (IX)	939–42	Benedict XI	1303–04	Pius XI	1922–39
Pelagius II	579–90	Marinus II	942–46	Clement V	1305–14	Pius XII	1939–58
St. Gregory I	590–604	Agapetus II	946–55	John XXII	1316–34	John XXIII	1958–63
Sabinianus	604–06	John XII[2]	955–64	Benedict XII	1334–42	Paul VI	1963–78
Boniface III	607	Leo VIII[2]	963–65	Clement VI	1342–52	John Paul I	1978
						John Paul II	1978–

[1] The presence of antipopes (not listed here) sometimes places question on a pope's number. In all such cases, the alternate number is cited on this list in parentheses. [2] John XII was deposed in 963 by a church council. If this deposition was invalid, Leo was an antipope. If the deposition was valid, Leo was the legitimate pope and Benedict an antipope. [3] Benedict IX was deposed on three different occasions (in 1044, 1046, and 1048). If the depositions were illegitimate, Sylvester III, Gregory VI, and Clement II were antipopes.

THEOLOGIANS AND PHILOSOPHERS

Peter Abelard (1079–1142), French philosopher and theologian who used a dialectic method in an effort to support Christian dogma. He is best known for his tragic romance with Héloïse, an abbess, and their exchange of love letters.

Aristotle (384–322 B.C.), Greek philosopher whose writings have greatly influenced Western thought. His philosophy became dominant in the 13th century when it was largely adopted by the Christian scholastic philosophers.

Asoka (died 232 B.C.), Indian emperor who galvanized growth of Buddhism in Asia by making it India's state religion and by sending Buddhist missionaries to distant countries. Asoka thus transformed Buddhism from a local religion to a faith of world importance.

Averroës (1126–98), Islamic Spanish philosopher whose studies and interpretations of Aristotle's thought exerted considerable influence on European philosophy and Christian theology, including that of Thomas Aquinas.

Karl Barth (1886–1968), Swiss Protestant theologian whose views stress the importance of Christian revelation and tend to favor the theology of the prescientific age.

Henri Bergson (1859–1941), French philosopher of Jewish origin but inclined toward Christian mysticism, who stressed the importance of intuition in the perception of reality.

George Berkeley (1685–1753), Anglo-Irish clergyman and philosopher who saw an ordered coherence in the world as proof of God's existence. He spent three years in America attempting to establish a college to train missionaries to convert the Indians.

Bernard of Clairvaux (1090–1153), French abbot whose mystical teachings exerted a powerful influence on Christianity throughout western Europe.

John Biddle (1615–62), English theologian who founded Unitarianism, a Christian denomination that affirms the existence of God but denies the Holy Trinity.

Jakob Böhme or **Boehme** (1575–1624), German theosophist and mystic whose writings were concerned with the necessity of evil because of the dualism of the divine nature of God. One of his works was declared heretical.

Dietrich Bonhoeffer (1906–45), German theologian and Lutheran pastor who advocated a secularized reinterpretation of Christianity. His anti-Hitler sentiments resulted in his execution by the Nazis.

Martin Buber (1878–1965), Jewish mystical philosopher who was influenced by the Christian existentialism of Kierkegaard. In turn, Buber exerted influence on modern Christian thought in the form of a highly personalized ("I-Thou") approach to God and the world.

Buddha (Siddhartha Gautama; c. 563–483 B.C.), Indian nobleman who founded Buddhism, one of the major Asian religions. He renounced sensual pleasures and advocated total spiritual detachment from the world.

Rudolf Karl Bultmann (1884–1976), German Protestant existentialist theologian and scholar who attempted to distinguish between what he interpreted as the mythical and the historical elements in the New Testament.

John Calvin (1509–64), French theologian who was one of the most important figures of the Reformation. His doctrines are central to the Presbyterian and Reformed churches.

Chuang-tse (369?–275? B.C.), Chinese Taoist philosopher whose writings are among the most important in Taoist literature.

Clement of Alexandria (150?–215?), Greek Christian theologian who was possibly the first to attempt to reconcile Platonistic and Stoic thought with Christian belief and ethics.

Confucius (c. 551–479? B.C.), Chinese philosopher whose ethical precepts, the *Analects*, set forth standards of personal behavior with a view toward social harmony in an ideal state.

Thomas Cranmer (1489–1556), English churchman who was archbishop of Canterbury and a supporter of Henry VIII against Rome. He contributed to the preparation of the Book of Common Prayer.

René Descartes (1596–1650), French philosopher and scientist whose method of achieving certitude began with the assertion of self (*cogito ergo sum*) and proceeded to attempt a rational proof of God's existence.

Jonathan Edwards (1703–58), American theologian whose preaching, based largely on the thought of Calvin, Berkeley, and Locke, exerted a powerful influence on colonial America.

Ralph Waldo Emerson (1803–82), American essayist, poet, and philosopher whose belief in a mystical unity of nature (transcendentalism) has been an important influence in American thought.

Gamaliel II (1st century A.D.), Jewish teacher and an innovator of Jewish prayers and rituals in the wake of the upheaval following the Roman destruction of Jerusalem. He was a grandson of Gamaliel, cited in the New Testament (Acts 5:33–39).

Georg Wilhelm Friedrich Hegel (1770–1831), German idealist philosopher whose dialectical interpretation of history influenced such diverse thinkers as Marx, Kierkegaard, and Dewey.

Martin Heidegger (1889–1976), German philosopher whose writing, an extension of the phenomenological school of Edmund Husserl, interprets "being" as the continual, elusive process of "becoming." His major work, *Being and Time* (1927), has influenced existentialism.

Theodor Herzl (1860–1904), Hungarian Jewish religious leader, considered the father of modern Zionism. Primarily a writer, his best-known work is the pamphlet *Der Judenstaat* (The Jewish State). He convened the first Zionist Congress at Basel, Switzerland, in 1897.

Hillel (1st century B.C.), Jewish scholar and one of the leading figures in the compilation of Talmudic law. He laid the foundation of a systematic legal interpretation of Hebrew writings. Although born in Babylonia, he went to Palestine, the center of Judaism, at age 40 and was elected leader of the Sanhedrin.

Richard Hooker (1554?–1600), English theologian whose writings constitute a major influence on Anglican theological concepts and ecclesiastical organization.

John Huss or Jan Hus (1369?–1415), Bohemian religious reformer whose denunciation of abuses of the Catholic hierarchy ultimately led to his martyrdom. He is considered a forerunner of the Protestant Reformation and is regarded as a Czech national hero.

William Ralph Inge (1860–1954), English theologian who was influential as a teacher at Cambridge and Oxford universities. His writings explore the mystical aspects of Christianity.

Jesus Christ (c. 5 B.C.–A.D. 30), founder of Christianity. The books of the New Testament tell about his life on earth, his teachings, the miracles that he performed, and his trial, crucifixion, and resurrection. His disciples and followers spread Christianity throughout the Roman Empire.

Immanuel Kant (1724–1804), German philosopher who ranks among the greatest figures in the history of Western thought. His *Critique of Pure Reason* (1781) denies that God's existence can be verified by rational proofs.

Sören Kierkegaard (1813–55), Danish philosopher whose belief in the superiority of subjective over objective truth led him to conclude that adherence to Christian belief is of less value than the acting out of a Christian life. He is considered the father of existentialism.

John Knox (1513?–72), Scottish religious leader who founded Scottish Presbyterianism. He was closely associated with John Calvin.

Lao-tzu (604–531 B.C.), Chinese philosopher who is considered the founder of the Taoist religion. His only known writing is a treatise on the origins of the universe, entitled *Tao Teh King*.

Hugh Latimer (1485?–1555), English bishop whose staunch faithfulness to Protestantism led to his martyrdom by Queen Mary I.

John Locke (1632–1704), English philosopher who believed that all ideas originate from sensory perception. This set the foundation for the empirical school of philosophy. His belief in man's tendency toward social good influenced modern democratic thought.

Martin Luther (1483–1546), German leader of the Protestant Reformation whose rebellion against abuses of the Roman Catholic Church marked a major turning point in Europe's social and religious history. Founder of the Lutheran Church, his teachings have been a major influence on all of Protestantism.

Maimonides (Moses ben Maimon; 1135–1204), Jewish philosopher and physician who organized Jewish oral law into concepts that were understandable to the layman. His most important work is *Moreh Nevukhim* (Guide for the Perplexed).

Jacques Maritain (1882–1973), French Catholic philosopher who attempted to reconcile Aquinas' teachings with contemporary thought.

Cotton Mather (1663–1728), American Puritan clergyman who exercised great influence through his preaching and writings in colonial New England. He was among the chief investigators of suspected witchcraft in Salem, Mass.

Increase Mather (1639–1723), American clergyman and a leading advocate of Puritan theocracy. He was the father of Cotton Mather.

Philipp Melanchthon (1497–1560), German theologian and humanist who was an associate of Martin Luther and an important voice in the Reformation.

Mencius or Meng-tse (372–289 B.C.), Chinese religious reformer and sage who influenced a resurgence of Confucian thought during his lifetime, and who was later venerated in Confucian temples.

Moses Mendelssohn (1729–86), German Jewish philosopher who espoused reforms of Jewish ritual law, thus pioneering a faith adaptable to modern needs.

Mohammed (570?–632), Arab prophet of the religion of Islam. Incorporating Jewish and Christian beliefs with his own distinctive theology, he is believed by his Muslim followers to be the last great prophet of the Jewish and Christian traditions and successor to Jesus. He wrote the Koran as the revelations of Allah (God).

John Courtney Murray (1904–67), American Catholic theologian and scholar who was a leader in the liberal Catholic movement.

Nestorius (died after 451), Middle Eastern theologian who founded the Nestorian Church, an early Christian heretical sect.

John Henry Newman (1801–90), English Roman Catholic cardinal and a leader of the Oxford Movement, a major reorganizational effort within the Anglican Church. His decision to become a Roman Catholic stirred controversy within England's church circles; he justified his action in *Apologia pro Vita Sua*.

Helmut Richard Niebuhr (1894–1962), American Protestant theologian who attempted to reconcile Christian doctrine with the dominant ideas of the 20th century.

Reinhold Niebuhr (1892–1971), American Protestant theologian who wrote extensively on the social aspects of modern Christian life.

Friedrich Wilhelm Nietzsche (1844–1900), German moral philosopher who viewed his contemporary Christian civilization as decadent and looked forward to an era when a new breed of men would revivify the civilization.

Matthew Parker (1504–75), English religious leader who, as archbishop of Canterbury, led the Anglican Church in a middle course between Roman Catholicism and Protestantism.

Blaise Pascal (1623–62), French religious thinker and scientist who stressed that faith was the ultimate bridge between man and God.

Philo Judaeus (20? B.C.–A.D. 50?), Jewish Alexandrian philosopher whose teachings regarding God's perfection and total transcendence over man had a marked influence on early Christian writings. His thought amounts to a fusion of Platonic philosophy with the doctrines of Hebrew scriptures.

Plato (427?–347? B.C.), Greek philosopher and disciple of Socrates. Plato's writings have had immense influence on the religious and secular thought of Western civilization.

Plotinus (205–270), Alexandrian philosopher of the Neoplatonist school whose thought influenced early Christian doctrine.

Nicholas Ridley (1500?–55), English church reformer who took part in compiling the Book of Common Prayer. A staunch adherent of Anglicanism, he was martyred, along with Hugh Latimer, by Queen Mary I.

THEOLOGIANS AND PHILOSOPHERS *(continued)*

Saint Thomas Aquinas (1225–74), Italian theologian and philosopher who ranks as the most influential figure in medieval philosophy. He formulated the official Roman Catholic philosophy, most explicitly in *Summa Theologica*.

Saint Augustine (354–430), Latin bishop and doctor of the Christian church, considered by many to be the founder of a formalized Christian theology. His books include the *Confessions*, a spiritual autobiography; and *City of God*, a defense of Christian beliefs.

Saint Thomas à Becket (1118?–70), archbishop of Canterbury. A defender of church rights against lay power, he quarreled with Henry II and was murdered in Canterbury Cathedral by the king's knights.

Saint Francis of Assisi (1182–1226), Italian friar and preacher who founded the Franciscan order in 1209. His monastic rule demanded poverty, and the members of his order lived by begging. According to legend he experienced the miracle of the stigmata in 1224.

Saint John of the Cross (San Juan de la Cruz; 1542–91), Spanish mystic and poet. With St. Theresa of Ávila he founded the Discalced Carmelites. His works include three great mystical poems: *The Dark Night of the Soul, The Flame of Divine Love*, and *The Spiritual Canticle*.

Saint Ignatius Loyola (1491–1556), Spanish Catholic founder of the Jesuit order.

Saint John Nepomucene Neuman (1811–60), first American man canonized by Roman Catholic Church (1977). Born in Bohemia (now Czechoslovakia), he came to U.S. in 1836. He was vicar of the Redemptionists order, 1847–52, and then served as bishop of Philadelphia, 1852–60, expanding parochial school enrollment from 500 to 9,000.

Saint Patrick (389?–461?), patron saint of Ireland who converted the Irish people to Christianity and established churches.

Saint Paul (died A.D. 67?), an organizer of the Christian church. Jewish by birth, he tried to stamp out the Christian movement in Jerusalem, but he was converted on the way to Damascus. He made several missionary journeys and founded churches to which he sent letters (the Pauline epistles of the New Testament).

Saint Peter (died A.D. 67?), one of Jesus' disciples, helped organize the early Christian church. He is regarded as the first pope by the Roman Catholic Church.

Saint Elizabeth Ann Seton (1774–1821), first person born in U.S. canonized a saint by Roman Catholic Church (1975). Founded Sisters of Charity in 1809. Pioneered parochial education and charitable institutions in U.S.

Saint Theresa of Ávila (1515–82), Spanish Roman Catholic nun of the Carmelite order. Both a vigorous administrator and author of religious tracts, she exerted great influence on the 16th century Catholic Reformation.

Girolamo Savonarola (1452–98), Italian Catholic reformer and religious leader of Florence whose attacks against the papacy ultimately led to his execution.

Friedrich Daniel Ernst Schleiermacher (1768–1834), German theologian who claimed that religion and philosophy do not contradict

each other, but that religion should be purged of metaphysical overtones.

Arthur Schopenhauer (1788–1860), German philosopher whose writings utilized the philosophy of Kant and showed influences of Buddhism in negation of the individual will. His major work is *The World as Will and Representation* (1818).

Albert Schweitzer (1875–1965), Alsatian theologian and medical missionary who established a hospital for African natives in Lambaréné, Gabon. His ethical principle, Reverence for Life, requires a respect for all living creatures.

Joseph Smith (1805–44), American religious leader who founded the Church of Jesus Christ of the Latter-day Saints (Mormons), published the *Book of Mormon* in 1830.

Baruch Spinoza (1632–77), Dutch Jewish rationalist philosopher. He believed God to be identical with nature and thus conceived of man as an extension, or attribute, of divinity.

Emanuel Swedenborg (1688–1772), Swedish theologian and scientist who wrote extensively on physiology before writing religious tracts. His religious thinking became most widely known after his death.

Jeremy Taylor (1613–67), Anglican bishop and religious writer whose finely styled prose was widely popular in the 1600s.

William Temple (1881–1944), archbishop of Canterbury considered the leading influence in forming the British Council of Churches and the World Council of Churches.

Thomas à Kempis (1379?–1471), German monk and devotional writer. He probably wrote *The Imitation of Christ*, still widely read.

Paul Johannes Tillich (1886–1965), German-American existentialist theologian who incorporated psychology into his theological system.

William Tyndale (1494?–1536), English Protestant martyr whose scriptural translations later formed the basis of the King James Bible.

Vardhamana (called **Mahavira**; 500s B.C.), Indian prophet. He founded Jainist religion in reaction against certain Hindu beliefs and practices. Jainism emphasizes man's need to transcend all of his passions.

John Wesley (1703–91), English Anglican minister who founded the Methodist Church. In 1784 he ordained the first American Methodist bishops.

William of Ockham (1285?–1347), English scholastic philosopher who drew a sharp distinction between the realms of philosophy and theology to avoid purported contradictions.

John Wyclif or **Wycliffe** (1330?–84), English ecclesiastical reformer and forerunner of the Reformation. He insisted on the supremacy of scripture over the authority of the church.

Brigham Young (1801–77), American Mormon preacher who led his sect in its migration west.

Zoroaster or **Zarathustra** (628?–551? B.C.), ancient Persian religious teacher and prophet. He founded Zoroastrianism, which disappeared only with rise of Islam in 600s A.D. Zoroastrianism introduced the idea of an ultimate resurrection of the dead.

Huldreich Zwingli (1484–1531), Swiss religious leader who was major figure behind Protestant Reformation in Switzerland.

Science and Invention

HIGHLIGHTS: 1985

In addition to the 1985 developments in science and invention included in this section, see also the separate sections *Awards, Climate and Weather, Computers, Earth, Ecology and Environment, Energy and Resources, Medicine and Health,* and *Space and Astronomy.*

BIOLOGISTS VS. ECOLOGISTS

Molecular biologists met with ecologists in a conference in Philadelphia on June 10 to 13 in an effort to reach agreement on how genetically engineered organisms might be tested for use in agriculture.

The conference, titled "Engineered Organisms in the environment: Scientific Issues," was sponsored by the American Society for Microbiology. It focused on four proposed genetic engineering projects that the biologists wish to field test and which the ecologists fear may unloose new and uncontrollable organisms into the environment. The meeting was unable to reach agreement.

NATIONAL TECHNOLOGY AWARDS

In a ceremony at the White House on Feb. 19, President Reagan presented the first National Technology Medals to 14 persons.

"The story of American technology is long and proud," the President said. "It might be said to have begun with a blacksmith at his bellows, hammering out fine tools, and the Yankee craftsman using simple wood planes, saws, and mallets to fashion the fastest sailing ships on the ocean. And then came the railroad men, driving spikes across our country.

"And today the story continues with the workers who built the computer in a child's room; the engineers who designed the communications satellite that silently rotates with the Earth, shining in the sunlight against the blackness of space; and the men and women of skill and determination who helped to put American footprints on the Moon."

Those who received the medals were:

Steven P. Jobs and Stephen G. Wozniak of Apple Computer, Inc., for launching the personal computer revolution.

Joseph F. Sutter of Boeing Co., for developing several generations of jet aircraft including the Boeing 747.

Bob O. Evans, Frederick P. Brooks Jr., and Erich Bloch for development of the IBM Series 360 computer that ushered in the era of business use of computers in 1964.

Allen E. Puckett and Harold A. Rosen of Hughes Aircraft Co., for development of geostationary satellites.

Marvin M. Johnson of Phillips Petroleum Co., for a landmark refinery process.

John T. Parsons and Frank L. Stulen of John T. Parsons Co., for development of computer-controlled machine tools.

Ralph Landau, formerly with Halson S.D. Group, Inc., for development of petrochemical processes.

Ian Ross and William O. Baker of Bell Laboratories, Inc., for contributions to communications.

SCIENCE MEDAL AWARDED TO 19

President Reagan presented 19 National Medals of Science in a ceremony at the White House on Feb. 27.

"There's no nation on earth that can match our scientific capability, our standard of living, and our national security," the President told the scientists. "We stand on the verge of more advances than mankind has ever known."

Those who received the medal were:

Howard L. Bachrach of the U.S. Department of Agriculture's Plum Island, N.Y., Animal Disease Center, for research in molecular virology.

Paul Berg of Stanford University, for probing the mechanisms of genes.

Margaret Burbridge of the University of California at San Diego, for leadership in observational astronomy.

Maurice Goldharber of Brookhaven National Laboratory, for contributions to nuclear physics.

Herman H. Goldstine, executive officer of the American Philosophical Society in Philadelphia, for fundamental contributions to the development of the digital computer, computer programming, and numerical analysis.

William R. Hewlett, vice chairman of the Hewlett-Packard Co., for accomplishments in developing and manufacturing electronic instruments.

Roald Hoffmann of Cornell University, for creative applications of theory to organic and inorganic chemistry.

Helmut E. Landsberg of the University of Maryland, for contributions to the advancement of knowledge of climatology.

Walter H. Munk of the University of Cali-

HIGHLIGHTS: 1985 (continued)

fornia at San Diego, for contributions to geophysics and physical oceanography.

George C. Pimentel of the University of California at Berkeley, for discoveries using infrared spectroscopy to study chemical bonding and molecular dynamics.

Frederick Reines of the University of California at Irvine, for his discovery of the subatomic particle the free neutrino and his reports on its properties and interactions.

Wendell L. Roelofs of Cornell University, for his contributions to basic and applied biology of insects.

Bruno B. Rossi of the Massachusetts Institute of Technology, for research into the nature and origin of cosmic rays.

Berta Scharrer of Albert Einstein College of Medicine, for contributions to the establishment of the concept of neurosecretion.

J. Robert Schrieffer of the University of California at Santa Barbara, for insight into cooperative effects in solids and solid surfaces.

Isadore M. Singer of the Massachusetts Institute of Technology, for developments in differential geometry and its use in analysis.

Richard N. Zare of Stanford University, for contributions to molecular spectroscopy, photochemistry, and chemical reaction dynamics.

Posthumously to George M. Low, late president of Rensselaer Polytechnic Institute, for contributions to manned space flight.

Posthumously to John G. Trump of the Massachusetts Institute of Technology, for introducing new machines and methods for application of ionizing radiation to medicine.

BIGGEST NON-NUCLEAR EXPLOSION

What was believed to be the largest blast using chemical explosives rather than an atomic bomb was set off on June 27, 1985, at White Sands Missile Range in New Mexico. The explosion, conducted by U.S. military scientists in an operation called "Minor Scale," simulated the effects of a tactical nuclear weapon that might be used in battle. Such tests using conventional explosives have been conducted since the United States and the Soviet Union agreed in 1983 to ban testing nuclear weapons in the atmosphere.

The test explosion of 4,880 tons of high explosives had about two-thirds of the power of the bomb dropped on Hiroshima in 1945. The largest previous test used 660 tons of explosives.

The blast shattered windows in buildings 10 miles from the site, but details of the effects of explosion on ground-level targets were a military secret.

ATOMIC WAR ANTENNA

One of the fears of atomic war is that the electromagnetic pulse given off by a nuclear explosion would cause a surge of energy that would destroy sensitive communications devices, possibly blacking out electronic communications.

As protection against such a possibility, three engineers of the Rockwell International Corp. invented a radio antenna that would not be ruined by such a surge of energy. The three, Theodore A. Dumas, Maarten Vet, and Samuel Buchmeyer, who work at Rockwell's Collins Communications Systems in Richardson, Texas, were granted a patent on the device in March.

ENGINEERING RESEARCH CENTERS

The National Science Foundation announced the selection of six universities to receive grants for the establishment of engineering research centers to speed the flow of new information to be applied by industry.

Columbia University in New York will receive $20 million over five years to study the development of a telecommunications network integrating the transmission of data, graphics, voice, and video.

The Massachusetts Institute of Technology also will get about $20 million for a center to study new ways of processing and purifying complex biological materials.

Purdue University in West Lafayette, Ind., will receive $17 million for a center to develop robotic manufacturing systems.

The University of Maryland will receive $16 million for a center to study problems of data gathering from arrays of sensors.

The University of California at Santa Barbara will get $14 million over five years to establish a center to improve the automation of manufacturing semiconductor chips.

Some $7.5 million was awarded to the University of Delaware to design new composite materials and develop automated ways to manufacture them.

SCIENTISTS AND INVENTORS

Scientists who have won Nobel Prizes are indicated below by (N). Their prize-winning achievements are listed on pages 68–75. Members of the National Inventors Hall of Fame are indicated below by (I). For deaths of scientists and inventors in 1985, see pages 981–986.

Jean Louis Agassiz (1807–73), Swiss-American biologist and geologist: proved glaciers once covered much of the Earth.

Howard Hathaway Aiken (1900–73), American mathematician: designed world's first large-scale digital computer, the Mark I, for International

Business Machines Corp. (1944).

Ernst Frederik Werner Alexanderson (1878–1975), Swedish-American inventor: in 1906 built high frequency alternator that made possible radio transmission of voices and music; transmitted first facsimile message across Atlantic Ocean in 1924; demonstrated in 1927 first home reception of television, using perforated scanning disk. (I)

Andrew Alford (born 1904), American inventor: developed antennas for radio navigation systems. (I)

Luis Walter Alvarez (born 1911), American physicist: invented radar ground-controlled landing approach system for aircraft, receiving patent in 1949 for radio distance and direction indicator; built first large linear accelerator at University of California in 1946; won Nobel Prize in Physics in 1968 for discoveries of subatomic particles. (N) (I)

André Marie Ampère (1775–1836), French physicist and mathematician: developed laws of electromagnetism, using electric currents; *ampere*, unit to measure flow of electric current, named after him.

Carl D. Anderson (1905–), American physicist: discovered *positron*, or anti-electron, a unit of matter (1932) and with Seth H. Neddermeyer was co-discoverer of the *meson* particle (1937). (N)

Sir Edward Victor Appleton (1892–1965), British physicist: discovered Appleton layer of free electrons in ionosphere that bounces radio waves back to Earth, leading to development of radar. (N)

Archimedes (287–212 B.C.), Greek mathematician and engineer: father of experimental science; discovered laws of lever, pulley, displacement, and buoyancy; invented catapult and Archimedean screw, a kind of pump.

Aristarchus (200s B.C.) Greek astronomer: first to say Earth revolves around Sun, but theory disregarded for hundreds of years.

Aristotle (384–322 B.C.) Greek philosopher: father of objective science; developed syllogism in logic; made first scientific study of biology.

Sir Richard Arkwright (1732–92), British inventor: developed water-powered spinning machine (1769), starting Industrial Revolution.

Edwin Howard Armstrong (1890–1954), American electrical engineer: invented hetrodyne circuit to amplify weak radio waves in 1918; invented FM (frequency modulation) radio, eliminating static (1933). (I)

Francis W. Aston (1877–1945), British physicist: invented mass spectrograph (1919). (N)

Amedeo Avogadro (1776–1856), Italian physicist: developed Avogadro's law of gases (1811); differentiated molecules and atoms; provided basis for determining correct atomic weights.

Roger Bacon (1214?–94), English philosopher and scientist: pioneered in controlled experiments and observation of phenomena; introduced gunpowder formula to Europe (1242).

Leo Hendrik Baekeland (1863–1944), Belgian-American chemist: invented Bakelite, first artificial resin plastic (1909). (I)

Adolf von Baeyer (1835–1917), German chemist: developed synthetic dyes. (N)

John Bardeen (1908–), American physicist: co-inventor of transistor (1947); also developed theories of super-conductivity and theory to explain properties of semiconductors. (N) (I)

Nikolai G. Basov (1922–), Russian physicist: developed masers (1955), using molecular energy to amplify radio waves. (N)

Antoine Henri Becquerel (1852–1908), French physicist: co-discoverer with Curies of natural radioactivity. (N)

Alexander Graham Bell (1847–1922), American scientist: invented telephone (1875–76). (I)

Karl Benz (1844–1929), German engineer: invented first gasoline-powered automobile (1885).

Friedrich Bergius (1884–1949), German chemist: converted coal dust to oil. (N)

Jöns Jakob Berzelius (1779–1848), Swedish chemist: developed system still used to write chemical symbols and formulas; discovered elements selenium (1817), silicon (1823), thorium (1828); co-discovered cerium (1803).

Sir Henry Bessemer (1813–98), British inventor: developed Bessemer process for converting pig iron into steel (1856).

Alfred Binet (1857–1911), French psychologist: developed first standard test for intelligence in 1905, leading to intelligence quotient (I.Q.) as measure of intelligence.

Clarence Birdseye (1886–1956), American inventor: invented fast-frozen food processing (1925) and dehydrated food processing (1949).

Harold Stephen Black (born 1898), American engineer: in 1927 invented negative feedback as means of eliminating distortion in amplifying telephone messages. (I)

Max Bodenstein (1871–1942), German chemist: first described chain reactions (1916) in chemical processes.

Niels Bohr (1885–1962), Danish physicist: described atom as miniature solar system with electrons in orbits around nucleus (1913). (N)

William Cranch Bond (1789–1859) and his son **George Phillips Bond** (1825–65), American astronomers: took first photograph of star (1850); discovered dark ring of Saturn and Saturn's eighth moon.

Max Born (1882–1970), German physicist: pioneered research in quantum mechanics. (N)

Carl Bosch (1874–1940), German chemist: developed commercial process using Friedrich Bergius' discovery to convert coal into oil. (N)

Johann Friedrich Böttger (1682–1719), German chemist: first European to discover how to make porcelain (1708).

Nathaniel Bowditch (1773–1838), American astronomer and mathematician: wrote *The American Practical Navigator* (1799).

Seth Boyden (1788–1870), American inventor: developed patent-leather process (1819).

Robert Boyle (1627–91), Irish alchemist and chemist: proved air, earth, fire, and water were not elements as alchemists had believed; developed Boyle's law of gases.

James Bradley (1693–1762), English astronomer: discovered aberration of light.

Sir William Henry Bragg (1862–1942) and his son **Sir William Lawrence Bragg** (1890–1971), British physicists: developed X-ray spectrometer to explore atomic structures. (N)

Tycho Brahe (1546–1601), Danish astronomer: proved changes occur in stars with discovery of new star (1572); proved comets originate in

SCIENTISTS AND INVENTORS *(continued)*
outer space (1577).

Jacques Edwin Brandenberger (1872–1954), Swiss chemist: invented cellophane (1908).

Walter Houser Brattain (1902–), American physicist: co-inventor with John Bardeen and William Shockley of transistor (1947). (N) (I)

John Moses Browning (1855–1926), American inventor: designed Browning machine gun (1890) and Browning automatic rifle (1917).

Robert Wilhelm Bunsen (1811–99), German chemist: developed electrolytic cell to produce magnesium (1852), Bunsen burner (1855).

William Burroughs (1855–98), American inventor: first reliable adding machine (1889).

William Meriam Burton (1865–1954), American chemist: in 1913 invented chemical process to double yield of gasoline from crude oil. (I)

Vannevar Bush (1890–1974), American electrical engineer: invented first analog computer, called differential analyzer, in 1930, used in World War II to aim antiaircraft guns.

Melvin Calvin (1911–), American chemist: discovered how plants make food by photosynthesis. (N)

Marvin Camras (born 1916), American engineer: received patent in 1944 for magnetic recording device, which led to tape recorders; also invented many devices used in stereo sound, motion picture sound, and video recorders. (I)

Georg Cantor (1845–1918), German mathematician: developed theory of sets (1870s).

Chester F. Carlson (1906–68), American physicist: invented xerography method of electrostatic dry printing in 1937–38. (I)

Wallace H. Carothers (1896–1937), American chemist: developed nylon (1935). (I)

Willis Haviland Carrier (1876–1950), American engineer: designed first air-conditioner in 1902, receiving patent in 1906; founded Carrier Corporation in 1915 to manufacture air-conditioners. (I)

Rachel Carson (1907–64), American biologist: her book *Silent Spring* warned of dangers to wildlife by misuse of insecticides.

Edmund Cartwright (1743–1823), English clergyman and inventor: invented first successful steam-powered loom to weave cloth (1786).

George Washington Carver (1859?–1943), American botanist and chemist: invented hundreds of products made from peanuts, sweet potatoes, pecans, and other farm crops.

Henry Cavendish (1731–1810), English physicist and chemist: discovered hydrogen (1766); demonstrated water is compound of oxygen and hydrogen.

Sir James Chadwick (1891–1974), British physicist: discovered neutron (1932). (N)

Owen Chamberlain (1920–), American physicist: co-discoverer of antiproton (1955). (N)

Hilaire Chardonnet (1839–1924), French chemist: invented rayon (1884).

Rudolf J. E. Clausius (1822–88), German physicist: discovered thermodynamics laws (1850).

Sir John Douglas Cockcroft (1897–1967), British physicist: with Ernest T. S. Walton, first to split atoms by bombardment with protons. (N)

Samuel Colt (1814–62), American inventor: developed first successful revolver (1835).

Arthur Holly Compton (1892–1962), American physicist: helped prove quantum theory with discovery of Compton effect in which X rays act as atomic particles; helped develop atomic bomb. (N)

Sir William Congreve (1772–1828), British inventor: developed military rockets (1808), used by British Army against Napoleon and against Americans in War of 1812.

William D. Coolidge (1873–1975), American chemist: invented ductile tungsten, the filament material used in incandescent lamps, and developed an efficient X-ray tube in 1913. (I)

Peter Cooper (1791–1883), American inventor: built *Tom Thumb*, first U.S. steam locomotive used on commercial railroad (1830).

Nicolaus Copernicus (1473–1543), Polish astronomer: revolutionized astronomy by demonstrating that Earth moves around Sun instead of being the stationary center of universe.

Frederick Gardener Cottrell (1877–1948), American chemist: invented first electrical precipitator to reduce pollution from industrial smokestacks (1910).

Bernard Courtois (1777–1838), French chemist: discovered element iodine (1811).

Jacques-Yves Cousteau (1910–), French inventor: developed Aqua-Lung (1943) for skin divers to breathe underwater.

Sir William Crookes (1832–1919), British chemist: discovered element thallium (1861); invented a cathode-ray tube, the radiometer, and the spinthariscope.

Pierre Curie (1859–1906) and his wife **Marie Sklodowska Curie** (1867–1934), French chemists and physicists: discovered radioactive elements radium and polonium (1898). (N)

John Dalton (1766–1844), English chemist: developed atomic theory (1803); made first table of atomic weights.

Charles Robert Darwin (1809–82), British naturalist: wrote *On the Origin of Species* (1859), his theory of evolution.

Leonardo da Vinci (1452–1519), Italian artist and scientist: drew sketches and plans for many devices invented hundreds of years later, including helicopter, machine gun, parachute.

Sir Humphry Davy (1778–1829), English chemist: discovered elements potassium and sodium (1807); invented electric arc (1808); discovered elements barium, calcium, and magnesium (1808); invented miner's safety lamp (1815).

Louis Victor de Broglie (1892–), French physicist: developed wave mechanics (1923).

Lee De Forest (1873–1961), American inventor: developed triode vacuum tube (1906), making possible long-distance radio and TV. (I)

Willem de Sitter (1872–1934), Dutch astronomer: first proposed theory of expanding universe (1917).

John Deere (1804–86), American inventor: invented first steel plow (1837).

Arthur Jeffrey Dempster (1886–1950), American physicist: discovered uranium 235 (in 1935), basic material used in atomic bombs.

René Descartes (1596–1650), French philosopher and mathematician: developed analytical geometry (1637).

Rudolf Diesel (1858–1913), German physicist: demonstrated at Augsburg, France, on Aug. 10, 1893, first successful pressure-ignited internal

combustion engine, commonly called the diesel engine. (I)

Joseph Dixon (1799–1869), American inventor: made lead pencils from graphite (1827).

Carl Djerassi (born 1923), Austrian-American chemist: invented first practical birth control pills in 1954. (I)

Amos E. Dolbear (1837–1910), American physicist and inventor: invented "talking machine" (1864), 12 years before Bell patented telephone; produced first radio waves (1882).

Herbert Henry Dow (1866–1930), American chemist: received more than 90 patents for inventions, best known for developments in halogen chemistry, particularly the production of bromine and chlorine; founded Dow Chemical Company in 1897. (I)

Charles Stark Draper (born 1901), American inventor: developed gyroscopic devices used to stabilize antiaircraft gunsights and bombsights; also invented devices used for navigation in aircraft and spacecraft. (I)

Charles E. Duryea (1861–1938) and **J. Frank Duryea** (1869–1967), brothers, American inventors: built first successful gasoline-powered automobile in U.S. (1893).

James Buchanan Eads (1820–87), American engineer: developed armored warships (1862).

George Eastman (1854–1932), American inventor: invented photographic roll film in 1884; developed first Kodak camera using roll film (1888); began mass-producing cameras at $1 each (1900). (I)

Sir Arthur Stanley Eddington (1882–1944), British astronomer: discovered relationship between mass and brightness in stars; discovered deflection of light by Sun's gravitational field (1919).

Harold Eugene Edgerton (1903–). American electrical engineer: invented photographic electronic flash equipment (1931).

Thomas Alva Edison (1847–1931), American inventor: among his 1,093 inventions were phonograph (1877), electric light (1879), stencil duplicating process for mimeograph machines (1887), and motion-picture projector (1889). (I)

Albert Einstein (1879–1955), German-American physicist: developed theory of relativity (1905) and unified field theory (1929); his theories made possible development of atomic bombs and atomic energy.

John Ericsson (1803–89), Swedish-American engineer: invented first successful propeller with blades for use on ships (1837).

Euclid (c.300 B.C.), Greek mathematician: compiled first geometry textbook.

Oliver Evans (1755–1819), American inventor: built first steam-powered land vehicle in U.S. (1805).

Gabriel Daniel Fahrenheit (1686–1736), German physicist: developed scale of temperatures.

Thaddeus Fairbanks (1796–1886), American inventor: platform weighing scale (1831).

Michael Faraday (1791–1867), English chemist and physicist: discovered electromagnetic induction (1831), leading to development of electric generators and motors; formulated laws of electrolysis.

Philo Taylor Farnsworth (1906–71), American inventor: patented image dissector (1928), electronic device basic to television; patented first all-electronic television system in 1930. (I)

Pierre de Fermat (1601–65), French mathematician: introduced theory of mathematical probability and modern theory of numbers.

Enrico Fermi (1901–54), Italian-American physicist: split the atom in nuclear fission (1934); produced first atomic chain reaction (1942); helped develop atomic bomb. (N)

Cyrus West Field (1819–92), American businessman: laid first successful telegraph cable across Atlantic (1858); laid new cable in 1866.

John Fitch (1743–98), American inventor: built first successful steamboat (1787).

Henry Ford (1863–1947), American inventor and businessman: introduced moving assembly line to produce "Model T" Fords (1913). (I)

Jay Wright Forrester (born 1918), American engineer: developed electric and hydraulic servomechanisms for gun mounts and radar in World War II; in 1951 invented random-access magnetic-core storage as standard memory device used in digital computers. (I)

Jean B. L. Foucault (1819–68), French physicist: proved light travels more slowly in water (1850); used pendulum to prove rotation of Earth (1851); built first gyroscope (1852).

Benjamin Franklin (1706–90), American statesman and scientist: proved lightning is electricity (1752); invented lightning rod (1752) and bifocal glasses (1780).

R. Buckminster Fuller (1895–1983), American inventor: designed Dymaxion prefabricated metal home in 1927; invented geodesic dome of triangular elements in 1960s.

Robert Fulton (1765–1815), American artist and inventor: built *Clermont*, first commercially successful steamboat in U.S. (1807).

Galileo Galilei (1564–1642), Italian physicist and astronomer: discovered law of pendulum (1584), law of falling bodies (1589), four moons of Jupiter (1610); proved Copernican theory of astronomy.

Richard Jordan Gatling (1818–1903), American inventor: developed first practical machine gun in U.S. (1862).

Karl Friedrich Gauss (1777–1855), German mathematician: helped develop modern number theory and laws of electromagnetism.

Joseph Louis Gay-Lussac (1778–1850), French chemist and physicist: made discoveries about gases; co-discovered element boron (1808),

Hans Geiger (1882–1947), German physicist: invented Geiger counter (1908).

Josiah Willard Gibbs (1839–1903), American mathematician and physicist: founder of physical chemistry and thermodynamics; member American Hall of Fame.

Donald Arthur Glaser (1926–), American physicist: invented bubble chamber (1953), device used to study subatomic particles. (N)

Carlos Glidden (1834–77), American co-inventor of typewriter (1867).

Robert Hutchings Goddard (1882–1945), American physicist: developed theory of rocket propulsion in 1912; built first successful liquid-fueled rocket (1926), making space travel possible. (I)

Charles Goodyear (1800–60), American inven-

SCIENTISTS AND INVENTORS (continued)·

tor: discovery of vulcanization process (1839) initiated rubber industry. (I)

John Gorrie (1803–55), American physician: invented first ice-making machine (1851).

Gordon Gould (1920–), American physicist: invented first practical ruby laser (1957).

Thomas Graham (1805–69), Scottish chemist: pioneer in physical chemistry; stated how gases mix in Graham's law of diffusion (1833).

Otto von Guericke (1602–86), German scientist: invented 34-foot-high water barometer; invented air pump (1650).

Johann Gutenberg (1395?–1468?), German inventor: invented metal type molding of letters, making mass printing possible (c. 1455).

Fritz Haber (1868–1934), German chemist: developed process for making synthetic ammonia (1913) for fertilizers and explosives. (N)

Otto Hahn (1879–1968), German chemist: codiscoverer of element protactinium (1917); with Fritz Strassman, split nucleus of uranium atom (1938). (N)

George Ellery Hale (1868–1938), American astronomer: invented spectroheliograph (1889) for photographing Sun; founded three major observatories, Yerkes (1895), Mt. Wilson (1904), and Mt. Palomar (1928).

Charles Martin Hall (1863–1914), American chemist: discovered how to make aluminum from bauxite (1886), working independently of **Paul Héroult** (1863–1914), French chemist who discovered same process in same year.

Edmund Halley (1656–1742), English astronomer: developed star catalog for Southern Hemisphere; correctly forecast return of Halley's comet in 1910.

James Hargreaves (1722?–78), English inventor: developed first spinning jenny to spin many threads at same time (1770).

Werner Heisenberg (1901–76), German physicist: founded study of subatomic particles (1927). (N)

Hermann L. F. von Helmholtz (1821–94), German physicist: developed law of conservation of energy; invented ophthalmoscope (1851).

Sir William Herschel (1738–1822), British astronomer: first person to discover a planet since prehistoric times when he sighted Uranus in 1781; discovered infrared radiation (1800).

Heinrich Rudolf Hertz (1857–94), German physicist: discovered electromagnetic waves (1887), making possible radio and TV.

Georg von Hevesy (1885–1966), Hungarian chemist: co-discoverer of hafnium (1923). (N)

James Hillier (born 1915), American inventor: developed electron microscope in 1937 that magnified 7,000 times. (I)

Hipparchus (100s B.C.), Greek astronomer: made first catalog of stars; discovered changes of equinoxes.

John Philip Holland (1840–1914), Irish-American inventor: built first practical submarine for U.S. Navy (1898).

Elias Howe (1819–67), American inventor: built first practical sewing machine (1846).

Edwin Powell Hubble (1889–1953), American astronomer: in 1929 discovered theory that universe is expanding—became known as the Big Bang theory.

James Hutton (1726–97), Scottish geologist: founded modern geology with theory that rocks were formed by lava from volcanoes (1785).

Christian Huygens (1629–95), Dutch scientist: developed telescope lens (1655) with which he discovered Saturn's ring and one of Saturn's moons; discovered wave theory of light; invented micrometer to measure small objects; invented pendulum clock (1673).

Joseph M. Jacquard (1752–1834), French inventor: invented automatic pattern loom (1801–04).

Karl Guthe Jansky (1905–50), American engineer: discovered radio waves from outer space (1932), leading to radio astronomy.

Thomas Jefferson (1743–1826), American President and inventor: among his many inventions were swivel chair and dumbwaiter.

Charles Francis Jenkins (1867–1934), American inventor: developed phantascope (1891–94), first successful motion-picture projector.

J. Hans Jensen (1906–), German physicist: discovered nuclear shell structure of atomic nuclei. (N)

Frédéric Joliot (1900–58) and his wife **Irène Joliot-Curie** (1897–1956), French physicists: produced isotopes by high-energy bombardment of elements (1934). (N)

James Prescott Joule (1818–89), English physicist: determined relationship between heat and mechanical energy (conservation of energy).

Lord Kelvin (William Thomson; 1824–1907), British physicist: invented Kelvin temperature scale for use with gas thermometers, with absolute zero equal to −273 ° C.

Johannes Kepler (1571–1630), German astronomer and mathematician: wrote laws of motion of the planets.

Donald William Kerst (1911–), American physicist: developed betatron (1940), an atomic accelerator.

Charles Franklin Kettering (1876–1958), American inventor: invented automobile self-starter (1911) and other auto improvements; altogether patented 140 inventions. (I).

Jack St. Clair Kilby (born 1923), American inventor: in 1958–59 invented miniaturized monolithic integrated circuits used in such electronic devices as calculators and computers (I)

Willem Johan Kolf (born 1911), Dutch-American medical doctor and inventor: pioneered in development of artificial kidney in 1943, of oxygenator in 1956, and received patent for artificial heart in 1972. (I)

Chevalier de Lamarck (1744–1829), French naturalist: founder of invertebrate paleontology; concluded plants and animals change to adapt to their environments; made first efforts to scientifically forecast weather.

Edwin Herbert Land (1909–), American inventor: invented polarized plastic sheets (1928); invented polarized light filters to eliminate glare (1934); developed polaroid camera that takes and prints pictures in a few seconds (1947); invented self-developing color film (1963). (I)

Marquis de Laplace (1749–1827), French astronomer and mathematician: described origin of solar system from a nebula (1796).

Antoine Laurent Lavoisier (1743–94), French chemist: gave first scientific explanation of fire as union of material with oxygen (1777); proved

law of conservation of matter; wrote first modern textbook of chemistry (1789).

Ernest Orlando Lawrence (1901–58), American physicist: invented cyclotron (1930) and bevatron (1954), atomic particle accelerators; produced first man-made mesons (1948). (N)

Nicolas Leblanc (1742–1806), French physician: discovered process for making soda from common salt (1790).

Gottfried Wilhelm von Leibniz (1646–1716), German mathematician: developed theories of differential and integral calculus; invented an early type of calculating or adding machine.

Jean Joseph Etienne Lenoir (1822–1900), French inventor: invented first internal-combustion engine, using illuminating gas as fuel (1860); built vehicle using his engine (1863).

Willard Frank Libby (1908–80), American chemist: discovered carbon 14 (radiocarbon) in 1947; developed method of using it to date prehistoric plant and animal fossils. (N)

Carolus Linnaeus (1707–78), Swedish botanist: established present-day scientific method of naming and classifying plants and animals.

Hendrick Antoon Lorentz (1853–1928), Dutch physicist: developed electron theory. (N)

Sir Bernard Lovell (1913–), British astronomer: built first completely directional radio telescope, at Jodrell Bank, England.

Archibald M. Low (1888–1956), British physicist: demonstrated principles of television (1914); invented radio control systems for torpedoes and rockets.

Percival Lowell (1855–1916), American astronomer: predicted discovery of Pluto (1905).

Theodore Harold Maiman (born 1927), American physicist: developed and demonstrated first operable optical ruby laser in 1960. (I)

Guglielmo Marconi (1874–1937), Italian electrical engineer: invented first practical radio system (1895); sent first transatlantic radio signal (1901). (N) (I)

Sir Hiram Stevens Maxim (1840–1916), British-American inventor: invented first completely automatic machine gun (1889).

James Clerk Maxwell (1831–79), British mathematician and physicist: developed mathematical descriptions of electricity and magnetism; predicted (1864) electromagnetic waves.

Julius Robert von Mayer (1814–78), German physician and physicist: independently discovered law of conservation of energy (1842).

Maria Goeppert Mayer (1906–72), German-American physicist: independently developed theory of structure of atomic nuclei. (N)

Cyrus Hall McCormick (1809–84), American inventor: invented reaping machine to harvest wheat (1831); founded in 1847 farm machinery company than became International Harvester Company. (I).

Lise Meitner (1878–1968), Austrian physicist: co-discoverer of element protactinium (1917); mathematically determined energy released by nuclear fission, helping lead to atomic bomb.

Gregor Johann Mendel (1822–84), Austrian monk and botanist: developed theory of heredity and founded science of genetics.

Dmitri Ivanovich Mendeleev (1834–1907), Russian chemist: developed periodic table of elements, predicting elements not yet discovered.

Ottmar Mergenthaler (1854–99), German-American inventor: invented Linotype typesetting machine (1883).

Charles Messier (1730–1817), French astronomer: made first star catalog of northern sky (1784).

Julius Lothar Meyer (1830–95), German chemist: demonstrated relationship of atomic weights to properties of elements (1869).

Albert Abraham Michelson (1852–1931), German-American physicist: with Edward W. Morley, disproved that substance called ether fills vacuums (1887); invented interferometer (1880); made first accurate measurements of diameter of a star (1920) and speed of light (1926). (N)

Robert Andrews Millikan (1868–1953), American physicist: measured electric charge of electron and intensity of cosmic rays. (N)

Samuel Finley Breese Morse (1791–1872), American artist and inventor: invented electric telegraph (1832–37), successfully demonstrated by sending message "What hath God wrought!" between Baltimore and Washington, D.C., on May 24, 1844. (I)

Paul Mueller (1899–1965), Swiss chemist: discovered power of DDT insecticide (1939). (N)

Walther Hermann Nernst (1864–1941), German chemist: developed third law of thermodynamics. (N)

Simon Newcomb (1835–1909), American astronomer: computed new, more accurate, tables of orbits of Moon and planets.

Thomas Newcomen (1663–1729), English inventor: with Thomas Savery, built first piston steam engine (c.1712).

Sir Isaac Newton (1642–1727), English scientist and mathematician: described basic laws of gravity and motion (1687); invented calculus, new branch of mathematics (independently of Leibniz); invented reflecting telescope.

Joseph Nicéphore Niepce (1765–1833), French scientist: made first crude photograph (1826), using process called *heliography.*

Alfred Otto Carl Nier (1911–), American physicist: separated from uranium the isotope U-235, basic atomic material (1940).

Alfred Bernhard Nobel (1833–96), Swedish chemist: invented dynamite (1867); established Nobel prizes to encourage peace and progress.

Robert N. Noyce (1927–), American physicist: developed electronic integrated circuit on silicon chip, making possible development of microcomputers and hand-held calculators; co-founder in 1968 of Intel Corporation. (I)

Hans Christian Oersted (1777–1851), Danish physicist: discovered magnetic field surrounds any wire carrying electricity (1819); made first aluminum (1825).

Ransom Eli Olds (1864–1950), American inventor: first to use assembly line to mass-produce automobiles (1901).

J. Robert Oppenheimer (1904–67), American physicist: directed construction of first atomic bombs (1943–45).

Elisha Graves Otis (1811–61), American inventor: invented safety elevator (1852), steam plow (1857), bake oven (1858).

Nikolaus August Otto (1832–1891), German engineer: in 1876 built first practical four-stroke

SCIENTISTS AND INVENTORS *(continued)*
internal combustion engine. (I)

Blaise Pascal (1623–62), French mathematician and scientist: formulated Pascal's law, explaining pressures of liquid; invented theory of probability; invented adding machine (1642).

Louis Pasteur (1822–1895), French chemist: founded science of microbiology; developed theory that germs cause disease in 1857; invented pasteurization process to kill germs with heat in 1864; invented vaccine for rabies in 1885. (I)

Linus Carl Pauling (1901–), American chemist: built accurate models of molecules; led scientists in trying to ban atomic testing. (N)

Karl Pearson (1857–1936), British mathematician: founded science of statistics; developed chi-square test in 1900 to provide standard measure of theory compared to fact.

Sir William Henry Perkin (1838–1907), British chemist: made synthetic aniline dye (1856).

Auguste Piccard (1884–1962), Swiss physicist: invented stratosphere balloon to ascend to high altitudes (1931); invented bathyscaph to descend to depths of ocean (1953).

Max Planck (1858–1947), German physicist: revolutionized physics with quantum theory of energy (1901). (N)

Charles J. Plank (born 1915), American chemist: with Edward Rosinski invented first commercially useful zeolite catalyst used by petroleum industry for catalytic cracking. (I)

Roy J. Plunkett, American chemist: in 1941 received patent for his invention of Teflon (terafluorethylene polymers), used in coating pans to prevent burned food from sticking; patented in 1941. (I)

Joseph Priestley (1733–1804), British clergyman and chemist: discovered hydrochloric acid (1772), laughing gas (1772), sulfur dioxide (1774), oxygen (1774).

Alexander M. Prokhorov (1916–), Russian physicist: with Nikolai Basov, discovered masers (1955), a means of amplifying radio waves with molecular energy.

Ptolemy (100s A.D.), Greek astronomer and geographer: his theory of Earth being motionless at center of universe was accepted for 1,500 years; his miscalculation of size of Earth led Columbus to believe he had reached Asia when he discovered Americas.

Michael Idvorsky Pupin (1858–1935), Hungarian-American physicist: invented 34 devices to improve telephone, telegraph, and radio.

Pythagoras (500s B.C.), Greek philosopher and mathematician: believed Earth was round and had motions, but his ideas were discounted for hundreds of years.

Isidor Isaac Rabi (1898–), Austrian-American physicist: supervised U.S. development of radar (1940–45); developed data on magnetic properties of atomic nuclei. (N)

Sir William Ramsay (1852–1916), British chemist: co-discoverer of elements argon (1894), helium (1895), and krypton, neon, xenon (all 1898). (N)

Ira Remsen (1846–1927), American physician and chemist: founded *American Chemical Journal* (1879), first scientific journal in U.S.

David Rittenhouse (1732–96), American astronomer: accurately measured Earth's distance

from Sun (1769); built accurate model of solar system (1770).

James Ritty (1836–1918), American inventor: invented first practical cash register (1879).

Wilhelm Conrad Roentgen (1845–1923), German physicist: discovered X rays (1895). (N)

Edward J. Rosinski (born 1921), American chemist: co-inventor with Charles J. Plank of zeolite catalyst used industrially in cracking petroleum. (I)

Henry Augustus Rowland (1848–1901), American physicist: determined value of *ohm*, unit for measuring resistance to electric current.

Bertrand Arthur William Russell (1872–1970), English mathematician and philosopher: coauthor of *Principia Mathematica*, landmark in symbolic logic.

Ernest Rutherford (1871–1937), British physicist: called father of nuclear physics; stated theory of atomic transmutation (1902); described nuclear structure of atom (1911); produced protons by bombarding nitrogen atoms with alpha particles (1919). (N)

Andrei Dmitriyevich Sakharov (1921–): Soviet physicist: developed first hydrogen bomb for Soviet Union in 1950s; became outspoken critic of communist restrictions on human rights. (N)

Lewis H. Sarett (born 1917), American chemist: developed first synthetic cortisone in 1944. (I)

Carl Wilhelm Scheele (1742–86), German-Swedish chemist: discovered oxygen (1774), chlorine (1774), and molybdenum (1778).

Erwin Schrödinger (1887–1961), Austrian physicist: provided mathematical basis for quantum theory with Schrödinger equation. (N)

Glenn Theodore Seaborg (1912–), American chemist: co-discoverer of six elements—plutonium (1940), curium (1944), americium (1945), berkelium (1949), californium (1950), mendelevium (1955); chairman, U.S. Atomic Energy Commission (1961–71).

Alois Senefelder (1771–1834), German inventor: invented lithography (1798).

Harlow Shapley (1885–1972), American astronomer: developed new information about Milky Way.

William Shockley (1910–), American physicist: co-discoverer of transistor (1947). (N) (I)

Christopher Latham Sholes (1819–90), American inventor: co-invented typewriter (1867–68).

George H. Shull (1874–1954), American botanist: in 1904–09 discovered how to improve food crops by breeding pure strains of hybrid corn.

Sir Charles William Siemens (1823–83), German-British inventor: invented furnace (1856) that led to open-hearth steelmaking process.

Igor I. Sikorsky (1889–1972), Russian-American aircraft designer: designed and built first four-engine plane (1913) and first successful single-rotor helicopter (1939).

Isaac Merrit Singer (1811–75), American inventor: invented improvements on early sewing machines to make them practical (1851).

Frederick Soddy (1877–1956), British chemist: coined term *isotopes* for atoms of same element that have different weights. (N)

Elmer Ambrose Sperry (1860–1930), American inventor: invented gyrocompass (1911), leading to automatic pilots for aircraft.

SCIENTISTS AND INVENTORS *(continued)*

Hermann Staudinger (1881–1965), German chemist: his exploration of giant molecules led to development of many plastics. (N)

Charles Proteus Steinmetz (1865–1923), German-American mathematician and engineer: solved problems of using alternating current in generating and transmitting electricity, making possible longdistance electric power transmission system used in the United States. (I)

George R. Stibitz (born 1904), American inventor: recognized as "father of the modern digital computer" for some 34 patented inventions; at Bell Labs, he constructed a two-digit binary adder in 1937, a full-scale calculator for complex arithmetic in 1938–39, and more sophisticated digital computers in the 1940s (I)

George Stephenson (1781–1848), British inventor: built one of first practical locomotives, *Puffing Billy* (1814); his locomotive *The Rocket* (1829) reached speed of 30 mph.

Fritz Strassmann (1902–), German chemist: co-discoverer of method of splitting uranium atom (1938).

Theodor Svedberg (1884–1971), Swedish chemist: invented ultracentrifuge. (N)

Richard L. M. Synge (1914–), British biochemist: invented partition chromatography, method of analyzing tiny samples. (N)

Leo Szilard (1898–1964), Hungarian-American physicist: helped develop nuclear reactor (1942).

Edward Teller (1908–), American physicist: developed hydrogen bomb (1952).

Nikola Tesla (1856–1943), Slavic-American electrical engineer: invented some 700 devices, including alternating-current electric motor (1888). (I)

Thales (c.640–c.546 B.C.), Greek philosopher: pioneered scientific method of observation; used geometry to predict eclipse of Sun.

Sir Joseph John Thomson (1856–1940), British physicist: discovered electron (1897). (N)

Max Tishler (born 1906), American chemist: invented more than 100 chemicals, vitamins, and hormones, including riboflavin. (I)

Clyde William Tombaugh (1906–), American astronomer: discovered planet Pluto (1930).

Evangelista Torricelli (1608–47), Italian mathematician and physicist: invented mercury barometer (1643).

Charles Hard Townes (1915–), American physicist: invented maser (microwave amplication by stimulated emission of radiation), first demonstrated in December 1953. (N) (I)

John Tyndall (1820–93), British scientist: discovered Tyndall effect in scattering of light passing through small particles; described effects of *Penicillium* mold slowing growth of bacteria (1876) half a century before its value in medicine was recognized.

Harold Clayton Urey (1893–1981), American chemist: discovered heavy hydrogen (1932), used in development of atomic energy. (N)

Jacobus Henricus Van't Hoff (1852–1911), Dutch chemist: pioneered in stereochemistry, study of internal molecular structure. (N)

Alessandro Volta (1745–1827), Italian physicist: invented electric battery (1800); electromagnetic unit, *volt*, named after him.

Wernher Von Braun (1912–77), German-American rocket engineer: developed V-2 guided missile rocket for Germany in World War II; developed Jupiter and Saturn rockets for U.S. space program.

Theodore von Kármán (1881–1963), Hungarian-American aeronautical engineer whose aerodynamic designs led to supersonic flight.

John Von Neumann (1903–57), Hungarian-American mathematician: wrote *The Mathematical Foundations of Quantum Mechanics* (1944); helped develop high-speed electronic computers.

Ernest T. S. Walton (1903–), British physicist: co-developer of first nuclear accelerators (1932). (N)

Sir Robert Alexander Watson-Watt (1892–1973), British electronics engineer and inventor: invented practical radar (1935).

James Watt (1736–1819), Scottish engineer: made steam engines practical with invention of separate condenser (1769); invented steam radiators for heating (1784).

Carl Auer Welsbach (1858–1929), Austrian chemist: discovered elements neodymium and praseodymium (1885); invented mantle used in gas lighting before invention of electric lights.

George Westinghouse (1846–1914), American inventor: invented railroad air brake (1868).

Sir Charles Wheatstone (1802–75), British physicist and inventor: independently invented electric telegraph (1837).

Alfred North Whitehead (1861–1947), British mathematician and philosopher: coauthor of *Principia Mathematica.*

Eli Whitney (1765–1825), American inventor: invented cotton gin to remove seeds from cotton (1793); introduced use of interchangeable parts, enabling mass production of guns (1798). (I)

Sir Frank Whittle (1907–), British inventor: invented turbojet engine for airplanes (1930).

Norbert Wiener (1894–1964), American mathematician: devised mathematical theory of cybernetics (1948); helped develop high-speed electronic computers.

Eugene Paul Wigner (1902–), Hungarian-American physicist: made many contributions to development of atomic energy. (N)

Charles T. R. Wilson (1869–1959), British physicist: invented Wilson cloud chamber (1912), device to make visible tracks of high-speed atomic particles. (N)

Friedrich Wöhler (1800–82), German chemist: first to synthesize organic compounds from inorganic material (1828).

Jethro Wood (1774–1834), American inventor: invented cast-iron plow (1819).

Wilbur Wright (1867–1912) and his brother **Orville Wright** (1871–1948), American inventors: invented and flew first successful airplane (1903). (I)

Hideki Yukawa (1907–81), Japanese physicist: developed theory showing existence of meson (1935), discovered next year. (N)

Richard Zsigmondy (1865–1929), Austrian chemist: invented ultramicroscope, aiding in research in colloid chemistry. (N)

Vladimir Kosma Zworykin (1889–1982), Russian-American physicist and electronics engineer: invented iconoscope TV camera tube (1923) and kinescope TV picture tube (1929); perfected electron microscope (1939). (I)

GREAT INVENTIONS

The origins of many great inventions are shrouded in the distant past. The inventors of writing, the wheel, and fire making will forever remain anonymous. And subsequent development of innovations such as the abacus, the windmill, gunpowder, the cannon, and the concrete arch must be attributed to countries or civilizations rather than to any particular individual or group of individuals.

Abacus: Uncertain; possibly by Babylonians as long ago as 3,500 years. In various forms it was known and used by ancient Chinese, Hindus, Egyptians, and Greeks
Adding machine (first commercially successful): William Burroughs, United States (1888)
Adding machine (simple): Blaise Pascal, France (1642)
Addressograph: J. S. Duncan, United States (1893)
Air brake, Westinghouse: George Westinghouse, U.S. (1868)
Air conditioning: Willis H. Carrier, United States (1902)
Air pump: Otto von Guericke, Germany (1654)
Airplane (first successful heavier-than-air): Orville and Wilbur Wright, United States (1903)
Airship (nonrigid): Henri Giffard, France (1852)
Aluminum (processing): Charles M. Hall, United States (1886); Paul Héroult, France (1886)
Atomic bomb: International team of scientists, U.S. (1945)
Atomic pile (self-sustaining nuclear chain reaction): Enrico Fermi and staff, United States (1942)
Automatic pilot (airplane): William Green, U.S. (1929)
Automobile: Karl Benz, Germany (1885)
Bakelite (plastic): Leo H. Baekeland, United States (1909)
Balloon (hot air): Jacques and Joseph Montgolfier, France (1783)
Barbed wire: Joseph F. Glidden, United States (1873)
Barometer: Evangelista Torricelli, Italy (1643)
Bessemer steel process: Henry Bessemer, England (1856)
Bicycle: Baron Karl Drais von Sauerbronn, Germany (1816–18)
Bifocal lens: Benjamin Franklin, United States (1780)
Bottle-making machine (automatic): M. J. Owens, U.S. (1898)
Braille printing: Louis Braille, France (1829)
Bridge, suspension (chain): James Finley, U.S. (1800)
Bridge, suspension (wire cable): John A. Roebling, U.S. (1845)
Bunsen burner: Robert Wilhelm von Bunsen, Germany (1855)
Camera (camera obscura): Europe (early 1500s)
Camera (photographic): Joseph Niepce, France (1826)
Camera (Kodak): George Eastman, United States (1888)
Canning (food): Nicolas Appert, France (1809)
Cannon (iron): Germans, Germany (c.1320)
Car (steam-driven): Nicolas Cugnot, France (c.1769)
Carburetor: Gottlieb Daimler, Germany (1892)
Carpet sweeper: M. R. Bissell, United States (1876)
Cash register: James Ritty, United States (1879)
Cathode-ray tube: Sir William Crookes, Britain (1878)
Cellophane: Jacques E. Brandenberger, Switzerland (1908)
Celluloid: Alexander Parkes, Britain (1855)
Cement: Joseph Aspdin, England (1824)
Chronometer: John Harrison, England (1759)
Clock (mechanical): I-Hsing and Liang Ling-Tsan, China (725)
Clock (pendulum): Christiaan Huygens, Netherlands (1656)
Compass (mariner's): Arabs (800s)
Computer (analog): Vannevar Bush, United States (1930)
Computer (digital): Howard Aiken, United States (1944)
Cotton gin: Eli Whitney, United States (1793)
Cream separator: Carl Gustaf de Laval, Sweden (1878)
Cyclotron: Ernest O. Lawrence, United States (1930)
Cylinder lock: Linus Yale, United States (1860)
Daguerreotype: Louis J. M. Daguerre, France (1839)
Diesel engine: Rudolf Diesel, Germany (1892)
Disc brake: Frederick W. Lanchester, Britain (1902)
Dynamite: Alfred B. Nobel, Sweden (1867)
Electric fan: Schuyler S. Wheeler, United States (1886)
Electric flat iron: H. W. Seeley, United States (1882)
Electric generator (disk): Michael Faraday, England (1831)
Electric generator (coil): Hippolyte Pixii, France (1832)
Electric motor (A.C.): Nikola Tesla, United States (1888)
Electric motor (D.C.): Zenobe Gramme, Belgium (1873)

Electric power generating plant (commercial): Thomas A. Edison, United States (1882)
Electrocardiograph: Willem Einthoven, Netherlands (1903)
Electroencephalograph: Hans Berger, Germany (1929)
Electromagnet: Joseph Henry, United States; William Sturgeon, England (1824)
Electroplating: George and Henry Elkington, Britain (1840)
Elevator (safety): Elisha G. Otis, United States (1852)
Engraving (half-tone process): Frederick E. Ives, U.S. (1878)
Flush toilet: Joseph Brahmah, Britain (1778)
Frequency modulation (FM): Edwin H. Armstrong, U.S. (1933)
Frozen food (retail): Clarence Birdseye, U.S. (1917–29)
Gas lighting: William Murdock, Scotland (1792)
Gasoline (antiknock tetraethyl lead): Thomas Midgley, United States (1921)
Geiger counter: Hans Geiger, Germany (1908)
Glider: Sir George Cayley, England (1804)
Gunpowder: Chinese, China (800s)
Gyrocompass: Elmer A. Sperry, United States (1911)
Gyroscope: G. C. Bohnenberger, Germany (1810)
Helicopter: Igor Sikorsky, United States (1939)
Holography: Dennis Gabor, England (1948)
Hydroplane: Glenn H. Curtiss, United States (1911)
Ice-making machine: John Gorrie, United States (1851)
Internal-combustion engine (first workable): Jean Joseph E. Lenoir, France (1860)
Internal-combustion engine (high-speed): Gottlieb Daimler, Germany (1885); Karl Benz, Germany (1885)
Jet aircraft engine: Sir Frank Whittle, England (1930)
Jet airplane: Ernst Heinkel Co., Germany (1939).
Kaleidoscope: Sir David Brewster, Britain (1817)
Kerosene (coal oil): Abraham Gesner, Canada (1852)
Knitting machine: William Lee, England (1589)
Lamp (arc): Humphry Davy, England (1809)
Lamp (arc, commercial): Paul Jablochkov, Russia (1876)
Lamp (carbon-filament electric): Joseph W. Swan, England (1850)
Lamp (incandescent carbon-filament electric): Thomas A. Edison, United States (1879)
Lamp (incandescent drawn tungsten-filament electric): William D. Coolidge, United States (1910)
Lamp (miner's safety): Humphry Davy, England (1815)
Lamp (neon): Georges Claude, France (1915)
Lamp (oil with glass chimney): Aimé Argand, Switzerland (1784)
Laser: Gordon Gould, United States (1957)
Lathe: Greeks, Greece (c.1500 b.c.)
Lever: Archimedes, Greece (200s b.c.)
Lightning rod: Benjamin Franklin, Pennsylvania (1752)
Linoleum: Frederick Walton, England (1860)
Lithography: Aloys Senefelder, Bohemia (1798)
Lock (cylinder): Linus Yale Jr., United States (1861)
Locomotive (steam): Richard Trevithick, Wales (1804)
Locomotive (electric): Werner von Siemens, Germany (1879)
Loom (power): Edmund Cartwright, England (1786)
Machine gun: Richard J. Gatling, United States (1862)
Mass spectrograph: F. Aston, Britain (1919)
Match (book): Joshua Pusey, United States (1892)
Match (friction): John Walker, England (1827)
Match (safety): Gustave E. Pasch, Sweden (1844)
Microcomputer (silicon chip): Michael J. Cochrane, Gary W. Boone, U.S. (1971)
Micrometer: William Gascoigne, Britain (1636)
Microphone: Alexander Graham Bell, United States (1875–76)
Microscope (compound): Hans and Zacharias Janssen, Netherlands (1590)

Microscope (electron): Ernst Ruska, Germany (1933)
Microscope (field ion): Erwin W. Mueller, U.S. (1936)
Microwave oven: Percy L. Spencer, United States (1945)
Milking machine: Anna Baldwin, U.S. (1878)
Motion pictures (camera): Thomas A. Edison, U.S. (1891)
Motion picture (peep show): Thomas A. Edison, U.S. (1894)
Motion picture (projected): Auguste Marie Louis Nicolas Lumière and Louis Jean Lumière, France (1895)
Motor scooter: Greville Bradshaw, England (1919)
Motorcycle: Gottlieb Daimler, Germany (1885)
Music synthesizer: Robert A. Moog, U.S. (1967)
Nylon: Wallace H. Carothers, United States (1935)
Oil well (modern): Edwin Drake, United States (1859)
Outboard engine: Ole Evinrude, United States (1909)
Parachute: André-Jacques Garnerin, France (1797)
Parking meter: Carlton C. Magee, United States (1935)
Patent leather: Seth Boyden, United States (1819)
Pen (ball-point): John Loud, United States (1888)
Pen (fountain): Lewis Waterman, United States (1884)
Pen (lever-fill): W. A. Sheaffer, United States (1913)
Phonograph (cylinder): Thomas A. Edison, U.S. (1877)
Phonograph (disk): Emile Berliner, United States (1890–94)
Photoelectric cell: G. R. Carey, United States (1875)
Photoengraving: William Fox Talbot, England (1852)
Photography (color): Gabriel Lippmann, France (1891)
Photography (on celluloid film): Rev. Hannibal W. Goodwin, United States (1887)
Photography (on transparent paper strip film): George Eastman, United States (1884)
Photography (on metal): Joseph Niepce, France (1826)
Photography (on paper): William Fox Talbot, England (1839)
Pipeline (oil): Samuel van Syckel, United States (1865)
Plastic (celluloid): John W. Hyatt, United States (1869)
Plow (steel): John Deere, United States (1837)
Polaroid Land camera: Edwin Land, United States (1947)
Porcelain: Chinese, China (700s A.D.)
Potter's wheel: Asia Minor (c.6500 B.C.)
Printing (movable type): Pi Sheng, China (c. 1045); Johann Gutenberg, Germany (c. 1454)
Printing (offset): Ira Rubel, United States (1905)
Printing (rotary): Richard Hoe, United States (1846)
Radar: Albert H. Taylor and Leo C. Young, United States (1922)
Radio (wireless): Guglielmo Marconi, Italy (1895)
Radio (transatlantic): Guglielmo Marconi, Italy (1901)
Radio (voice): Valdemar Poulsen, Denmark (1904)
Radio (automobile): William P. Lear, U.S. (1926)
Radio tube diode: John A. Fleming, England (1904)
Radio tube triode: Lee De Forest, United States (1906)
Railroad (steam): George Stephenson, England (1825)
Railway car coupling: Eli H. Jannery, United States (1868)
Railway sleeping coach: George M. Pullman, U.S. (1859)
Raincoat (waterproof): Charles Macintosh, Scotland (1819)
Rayon: Hilaire Chardonnet, France (1884)
Razor (electric): Col. Jacob Schick, United States (1931)
Razor (safety): King C. Gillette, United States (1895)
Reaping machine: Cyrus H. McCormick, United States (1831)
Record (long playing): Peter Goldmark, United States (1948)
Recording (magnetic tape): J. A. O'Neill, United States (1927)
Recording (magnetic wire): Valdemar Poulsen, Denmark (1898)
Revolver: Samuel Colt, United States (1835)
Rifle (automatic): John Moses Browning, United States (1917)
Rifle (repeating): O. F. Winchester, United States (1860)
Rocket (liquid-fuel): Robert H. Goddard, U.S.; Hermann Oberth, Germany; Konstantin S. Tsiolkovsky, Soviet Union (1920s)
Rocket (military): Sir William Congreve, Britain (1808)
Rubber (latex foam): Dunlop Rubber Co., England (1928)
Rubber (vulcanized): Charles Goodyear, United States (1839)
Rubber tire (pneumatic): John B. Dunlop, Britain (1888)
Rubber tire (solid): Thomas Hancock, England (1846)
Rudder (ship): Vikings (1100s)
Safety pin: Walter Hunt, United States (1849)
Screw propeller: John Ericsson, United States (1837)
Self-starter (internal-combustion engine): Charles F. Kettering, United States (1911)

Sewing machine: Barthélemy Thimonnier, France (1841); Elias Howe, U.S. (1846)
Sewing machine (foot-operated): Isaac Singer, U.S. (1851)
Sewing machine (electric): Singer Sewing Machine Co., United States (1889)
Sextant: John Hadley, England; Thomas Godfrey, U.S. (1730)
Ship (seagoing): Egyptians or Phoenicians (2500 B.C.)
Ship (steam): J. C. Périer, France (1775)
Ship (steam, commercial): Robert Fulton, U.S. (1807)
Ship (turbine): Sir Charles Parsons, Britain (1894)
Slot machine: Charles Fey, U.S. (1895)
Spectacles (curved glass): Salvino D'Armato, Italy (1285)
Spectroscope: Joseph von Fraunhofer, Germany (1814)
Spinning frame: Sir Richard Arkwright, England (1769)
Spinning jenny: James Hargreaves, England (1770)
Spinning mule: Samuel Crompton, England (1779)
Stainless steel: Harry Brearley, England (1913)
Steam engine (no moving parts): Thomas Savery, England (1698)
Steam engine (piston): Thomas Newcomen, England (c.1712)
Steam engine (condenser): James Watt, Scotland (1769)
Steam shovel: William S. Otis, U.S. (1838)
Steel production: Henry Bessemer, England (1856)
Stethoscope: René Laënnec, France (1816)
Stirrups (metal): China (500s A.D.)
Stove (coal): Jordan L. Mott, United States (1833)
Stove (Franklin): Benjamin Franklin, United States (1740)
Stove (gas): Robert W. Bunsen, Germany (1855)
Stove (electric): W. S. Hadaway, United States (1896)
Submarine: David Bushnell, United States (1776)
Submarine (nuclear-powered, Nautilus): Government scientists, United States (1955)
Tank (armored): Sir Ernest Swinton, England (1914)
Telegraph (electric): Samuel F. B. Morse, U.S. (1832–37)
Telegraph (visual semaphore): Claude Chappe, France (1793)
Telephone: Alexander Graham Bell, United States (1875–76)
Telescope (simple): Hans Lippershey, Netherlands (1608)
Telescope (refracting): Galileo Galilei, Italy (1609)
Telescope (reflecting): Isaac Newton, England (1668)
Telescope (radio): Karl Jansky, United States (1931)
Television (electronic): Vladimir K. Zworykin, United States (1923)
Television (mechanical): John L. Baird, Scotland (1926)
Thermometer: Galileo Galilei, Italy (1593)
Thermometer (improved): Gabriel D. Fahrenheit, Germany (1714)
Thermos bottle: Sir James Dewar, Britain (1892)
Torpedo (self-propelled): Robert Whitehead, Scotland (1866)
Tractor (steam): Nicolas Cugnot, France (1769)
Tractor (track-type): Benjamin Holt, United States (1906)
Tram (railed): Mine rail tracks, Alsace (1550)
Transformer: Otto Bláthy, Hungary (1884)
Transistor: John Bardeen, William Shockley, and Walter Brattain, United States (1947)
Tungsten filament: Irving Langmuir, United States (1915)
Typesetting machine (Linotype): Ottmar Mergenthaler, United States (1884)
Typesetting machine (Monotype): Tolbert Lanston, United States (1885)
Typewriter: Christopher L. Sholes, Carlos Glidden, U.S. (1867)
Vacuum cleaner: I. W. McGaffey, United States (1869)
Vacuum tube (triode): Lee De Forest, United States (1906)
Washing machine (manual): Hamilton E. Smith, U.S. (1858)
Washing machine (electric): Alva J. Fisher, U.S. (1907)
Watch (mainspring): Peter Henlein, Germany (c.1500)
Watch (self-winding): Louis Recordon, Britain (1780)
Welder (electric): Elihu Thomson, United States (1877)
Wheel (solid): Sumerians (c.3300 B.C.)
Wheel (spoked): Egypt (c.1900 B.C.)
Windmill: Iran (corn-grinding mills; c.600 A.D.)
Xerography: Chester Carlson, United States (1937–48)
X ray: Wilhelm Roentgen, Germany (1895)
Zipper: Whitcomb L. Judson, United States (1891)
Zipper (meshed-tooth): Gideon Sundback, United States (1913)

HOW TO PROTECT YOUR INVENTION

What Can Be Patented? If you have invented something that you wish to patent, it would have to meet the statutory standard that it be "any new and useful process, machine, manufacture, or composition of matter, or any new and useful improvements thereof." This includes practically everything made by man and the processes for making them.

Patents may also be granted on new life forms, on any distinct and new variety of plant, other than a tuber-propagated plant, which is asexually reproduced, or any new, original, and ornamental design for an article of manufacture.

What Cannot Be Patented? A patent may *not* be granted on a useless invention, on a method of doing business, on mere printed matter, or on a device or machine that will not operate. Furthermore, even if your invention is novel or new, a patent may not be obtained if your invention would have been obvious to a person having ordinary skill in the same area at the time of your invention. And a patent may not be obtained if the invention was in public use or on sale in the U.S. for more than one year prior to the filing of your patent application, or the invention has been patented or described in a printed publication anywhere in the world more than a year before your U.S. patent application is filed. Finally, you may not receive a patent for an invention useful only in applying nuclear material for military purposes.

Applying for a Patent. If your invention appears worthy of a patent, the law gives you the privilege of preparing your own application. But since the law is complicated, you would be wise to consult an expert—a registered patent attorney or agent.

Your application will include a claim or claims describing the scope of your invention.

Patentability (novelty and unobviousness) is judged by the claims.

After a patent is granted, questions of patent validity and infringement are determined by a court on the basis of the claims.

Obviously you cannot know that your invention is unique unless you have done some research. The Patent and Trademark Office has a Public Search Room at its offices (2021 Jefferson Davis Highway, Arlington, Va.). Here you can conduct your own search, or employ a patent attorney to do so.

Once the search is done and it appears that your invention may be unique and patentable, your attorney will prepare a final draft of your application. The original should be signed by you and sent to the Commissioner of Patents and Trademarks, Washington, D.C. 20231. There is a basic filing fee of $150 for the small inventor and $300 for a large corporation. Small additional amounts are charged if claims exceed a certain number.

Patent Rights. If you are to receive a utility patent, there is a basic $250 fee for the small inventor and $500 for a large corporation.

After payment, you will receive your patent, which gives you "the right to exclude others from making, using, or selling" the invention for a period of 17 years from the date of the patent. Payment of periodic maintenance fees is required to assure a full 17-year term. Information from your patent will also be published in the Patent and Trademark Office's *Official Gazette.*

The entire process, from application to grant, currently averages 24 months.

Patent Laws. Your right to be granted a patent—the exclusive privilege to control something that you have invented and to share in any compensation that your invention brings—is derived from Article I, Section 8, of the United States Constitution. The first U.S. patent law was passed by Congress in 1790. In 1836 the patent laws were revised, the office of Commissioner of Patents was established, and Patent No. 1, the first numbered patent, was issued to Sen. John Ruggles of Maine on July 13, 1836. The Patent and Trademark Office was transferred to the Interior Department in 1849 and to the Commerce Department in 1925.

Trademarks and Service Marks. A trademark is a word, name, symbol, or device used to indicate the source of goods being sold. It distinguishes these goods from other similar goods.

Trademark rights may be used to prevent others from using a confusingly similar mark. But trademark rights do NOT prevent others from making the same kind of goods or selling similar goods using a nonconfusing mark.

A *service mark* is similar to a trademark but is used in the sale or advertising of services rather than goods.

Trademarks or service marks used in interstate or foreign commerce may be registered in the Patent and Trademark Office.

You can obtain more information about trademarks by writing to Commissioner of Patents and Trademarks, Washington, D.C. 20231.

WHAT IS A COPYRIGHT?

A copyright protects an author or artist from having others make copies of his work without permission.

Plays, articles, books, musical compositions, pictures, computer programs, and forms of art can be protected by copyright.

A copyright protects the *form* of the expression, rather than the subject matter. For example, you might copyright your written description of how an automobile works. This copyright would prevent others from copying *your* description without your permission. But it would NOT prevent others from writing their own descriptions of how an automobile works.

Under a revised copyright law effective on Jan. 1, 1978, works copyrighted on or after that date are protected for the life of the author and for 50 years after the author's death.

Copyrights are registered in the Copyright Office in the Library of Congress.

You can obtain more information about copyrights or copyright forms by writing to Register of Copyrights, Library of Congress, Washington, D.C. 20559, or by phoning (202)287-9100.

TEMPERATURE CONVERSION TABLE *

Source: Ever Ready Thermometer Company

The numbers in boldface type in the center columns—the key to the table—refer to the temperature in either Celsius (formerly centigrade) or Fahrenheit degrees. Thus, for example, +30 in the center column, if chosen to represent 30° Fahrenheit, will convert to −1.1° Celsius, the figure found to the left of the column. If, on the other hand, it is made to represent 30° Celsius, it will convert to 86.0° Fahrenheit, the figure to the right of the column.

For degrees of temperature not included in this table, the following formulas provide the necessary conversion:

$$F° = (C° \times 1.8) + 32 \text{ or } C° = (F° - 32) \times 5 \div 9$$

DEGREES C.	DEGREES	DEGREES F.		DEGREES C.	DEGREES	DEGREES F.		DEGREES C.	DEGREES	DEGREES F.
−34.4	−30	−22.0		−9.4	+15	+59.0		+15.6	+60	+140.0
−33.9	−29	−20.2		−8.9	+16	+60.8		+16.1	+61	+141.8
−33.3	−28	−18.4		−8.3	+17	+62.6		+16.7	+62	+143.6
−32.8	−27	−16.6		−7.8	+18	+64.4		+17.2	+63	+145.4
−32.2	−26	−14.8		−7.2	+19	+66.2		+17.8	+64	+147.2
−31.7	−25	−13.0		−6.7	+20	+68.0		+18.3	+65	+149.0
−31.1	−24	−11.2		−6.1	+21	+69.8		+18.9	+66	+150.8
−30.6	−23	−9.4		−5.5	+22	+71.6		+19.4	+67	+152.6
−30.0	−22	−7.6		−5.0	+23	+73.4		+20.0	+68	+154.4
−29.4	−21	−5.8		−4.4	+24	+75.2		+20.6	+69	+156.2
−28.9	−20	−4.0		−3.9	+25	+77.0		+21.1	+70	+158.0
−28.3	−19	−2.2		−3.3	+26	+78.8		+21.7	+71	+159.8
−27.8	−18	−0.4		−2.8	+27	+80.6		+22.2	+72	+161.6
−27.2	−17	+1.4		−2.2	+28	+82.4		+22.8	+73	+163.4
−26.7	−16	+3.2		−1.7	+29	+84.2		+23.3	+74	+165.2
−26.1	−15	+5.0		−1.1	+30	+86.0		+23.9	+75	+167.0
−25.6	−14	+6.8		−0.6	+31	+87.8		+24.4	+76	+168.8
−25.0	−13	+8.6		0.0	+32	+89.6		+25.0	+77	+170.6
−24.4	−12	+10.4		+0.6	+33	+91.4		+25.6	+78	+172.4
−23.9	−11	+12.2		+1.1	+34	+93.2		+26.1	+79	+174.2
−23.3	−10	+14.0		+1.7	+35	+95.0		+26.7	+80	+176.0
−22.8	−9	+15.8		+2.2	+36	+96.8		+27.2	+81	+177.8
−22.2	−8	+17.6		+2.8	+37	+98.6		+27.8	+82	+179.6
−21.7	−7	+19.4		+3.3	+38	+100.4		+28.3	+83	+181.4
−21.1	−6	+21.2		+3.9	+39	+102.2		+28.9	+84	+183.2
−20.6	−5	+23.0		+4.4	+40	+104.0		+29.4	+85	+185.0
−20.0	−4	+24.8		+5.0	+41	+105.8		+30.0	+86	+186.8
−19.4	−3	+26.6		+5.5	+42	+107.6		+30.6	+87	+188.6
−18.9	−2	+28.4		+6.1	+43	+109.4		+31.1	+88	+190.4
−18.3	−1	+30.2		+6.7	+44	+111.2		+31.7	+89	+192.2
−17.8	0	+32.0		+7.2	+45	+113.0		+32.2	+90	+194.0
−17.2	+1	+33.8		+7.8	+46	+114.8		+32.8	+91	+195.8
−16.7	+2	+35.6		+8.3	+47	+116.6		+33.3	+92	+197.6
−16.1	+3	+37.4		+8.9	+48	+118.4		+33.9	+93	+199.4
−15.6	+4	+39.2		+9.4	+49	+120.2		+34.4	+94	+201.2
−15.0	+5	+41.0		+10.0	+50	+122.0		+35.0	+95	+203.0
−14.4	+6	+42.8		+10.6	+51	+123.8		+35.6	+96	+204.8
−13.9	+7	+44.6		+11.1	+52	+125.6		+36.1	+97	+206.6
−13.3	+8	+46.4		+11.7	+53	+127.4		+36.7	+98	+208.4
−12.8	+9	+48.2		+12.2	+54	+129.2		+37.2	+99	+210.2
−12.2	+10	+50.0		+12.8	+55	+131.0		+37.8	+100	+212.0
−11.7	+11	+51.8		+13.3	+56	+132.8		+38.3	+101	+213.8
−11.1	+12	+53.6		+13.9	+57	+134.6		+38.9	+102	+215.6
−10.6	+13	+55.4		+14.4	+58	+136.4		+39.4	+103	+217.4
−10.0	+14	+57.2		+15.0	+59	+138.2		+40.0	+104	+219.2

* Absolute zero is −273.15° C. or −459.67° F.

KELVIN SCALE

The British physicist Lord Kelvin (1824–1907) devised a temperature scale based on thermodynamic laws. Known also as the absolute scale, Kelvin's system became a fundamental temperature scale used in scientific measurement. Absolute temperatures are used in formulas derived from the laws governing the behavior of gases, which expand and contract in volume at high and low temperatures. According to the kinetic molecular theory, absolute zero is the point at which the molecules of substances have no heat energy. Absolute zero, −273.15° on the Celsius scale, is 0° Kelvin. Thus degrees Kelvin are equivalent to degrees of Celsius plus 273.15. The freezing point of water (0° Celsius and 32° Fahrenheit) is 273.15° Kelvin. The conversion formulas are: K° = C° + 273.15 or K° = (F° − 32) × (5 ÷ 9) + 273.15

THE CHEMICAL ELEMENTS

At one time a chemical element could be defined as a substance that could not be broken down into two or more different kinds of matter. But in the late 1930s and early 1940s, scientists found that atoms of elements could be broken apart into subatomic particles. Ever since, scientists have had to qualify their definition of an element as a substance that cannot be broken down into anything else *by ordinary chemical means.*

The ancients and medieval alchemists are usually credited with the discovery of 12 elements, including gold, silver, tin, carbon, sulfur, iron, copper, zinc, arsenic, mercury, lead, and bismuth.

The concept of an "element" was not really developed until about 200 years ago. In 1789 the French scientist Antoine Lavoisier proposed a definition of an "element" and listed 23 of what scientists now regard as true chemical elements.

Alessandro Volta's discoveries concerning electric current (about 1800) led to Sir Humphry Davy's discovery of 6 new elements in the early 1800s.

In the 1860s and 1870s almost 30 new elements were discovered because of the new technique of spectroscopy and the arrangement of known elements into a periodic table with elements grouped according to their atomic numbers and atomic weights. Finally, the advent of atom smashers led to the discovery of more than a dozen elements with atomic numbers above uranium.

The atomic number of an element tells the number of protons (positively charged particles) it contains in its nucleus.

SYMBOL, NAME, AND ATOMIC NUMBER			ATOMIC WEIGHT[1]	DATE OF DISCOVERY AND DISCOVERER	
H	Hydrogen	1	1.00797	1766	H. Cavendish, Britain
He	Helium	2	4.0026	1868	In the sun: P. Janssen, France
				1895	On the earth: W. Ramsay, Britain; N. Langlet and P. T. Cleve, Sweden
Li	Lithium	3	6.939	1817	J. A. Arfvedson, Sweden
Be	Beryllium	4	9.01218	1798	L. N. Vauquelin, France
B	Boron	5	10.811	1808	H. Davy, Britain; J. L. Gay–Lussac and L. J. Thénard, France
C	Carbon	6	12.01115	—	Ancient
N	Nitrogen	7	14.0067	1772	D. Rutherford, Britain
O	Oxygen	8	15.9994	1774	J. Priestley, Britain
F	Fluorine	9	18.9984	1886	H. Moissan, France
Ne	Neon	10	20.179	1898	W. Ramsay and M. W. Travers, Britain
Na	Sodium	11	22.98977	1807	H. Davy, Britain
Mg	Magnesium	12	24.312	1808	H. Davy, Britain
Al	Aluminum	13	26.98154	1825	H. C. Oersted, Denmark
Si	Silicon	14	28.86	1823	J. J. Berzelius, Sweden
P	Phosphorus	15	30.97376	1669	H. Brand, Germany
S	Sulfur	16	32.064	—	Ancient
Cl	Chlorine	17	35.453	1774	K. W. Scheele, Sweden
A	Argon	18	39.948	1894	W. Ramsay and J. Rayleigh, Britain
K	Potassium	19	39.102	1807	H. Davy, Britain
Ca	Calcium	20	40.08	1808	H. Davy, Britain
Sc	Scandium	21	44.9559	1879	L. F. Nilson, Sweden
Ti	Titanium	22	47.90	1791	W. Gregor, Britain
V	Vanadium	23	50.9414	1830	N. G. Sefstrдom, Sweden
Cr	Chromium	24	51.996	1797	L. N. Vauquelin, France
Mn	Manganese	25	54.938	1774	K. W. Scheele and J. G. Gahn, Sweden
Fe	Iron	26	55.847	—	Ancient
Co	Cobalt	27	58.9332	1735	G. Brandt, Sweden
Ni	Nickel	28	58.70	1751	A. F. Cronstedt, Sweden
Cu	Copper	29	63.546	—	Ancient
Zn	Zinc	30	65.37	1746	A. Marggraf, Germany
Ga	Gallium	31	69.72	1875	L. de Boisbaudran, France
Ge	Germanium	32	72.59	1886	C. A. Winkler, Germany
As	Arsenic	33	74.9216	—	Medieval
Se	Selenium	34	78.96	1817	J. J. Berzelius, Sweden
Br	Bromine	35	79.904	1826	A. J. Balard, France
Kr	Krypton	36	83.80	1898	W. Ramsay and M. W. Travers, Britain
Rb	Rubidium	37	85.4678	1861	R. W. Bunsen and G. R. Kirchhoff, Germany
Sr	Strontium	38	87.62	1790	A. Crawford, Scotland
Y	Yttrium	39	88.905	1794	J. Gadolin, Finland
Zr	Zirconium	40	91.22	1789	M. H. Klaproth, Germany
Nb	Niobium	41	92.9064	1801	C. Hatchett, Britain
Mo	Molybdenum	42	95.94	1778	K. W. Scheele, Sweden
Tc	Technetium	43	97 [2]	1937	E. Segre and C. Perrier, Italy
Ru	Ruthenium	44	101.07	1844	K. Klaus, Estonia

SYMBOL, NAME, AND ATOMIC NUMBER			ATOMIC WEIGHT[1]	DATE OF DISCOVERY AND DISCOVERER	
Rh	Rhodium	45	102.9055	1803	W. H. Wollaston, Britain
Pd	Palladium	46	106.4	1803	W. H. Wollaston, Britain
Ag	Silver	47	107.868	—	Ancient
Cd	Cadmium	48	112.40	1817	F. Stromeyer, Germany
In	Indium	49	114.82	1863	F. Reich and H. T. Richter, Germany
Sn	Tin	50	118.69	—	Ancient
Sb	Antimony	51	121.75	—	Ancient
Te	Tellurium	52	127.60	1782	M. von Reichenstein, Austria
I	Iodine	53	126.9044	1811	B. Courtois, France
Xe	Xenon	54	131.30	1898	W. Ramsay and M. W. Travers, Britain
Cs	Cesium	55	132.9054	1860	R. Bunsen and G. R. Kirchhoff, Germany
Ba	Barium	56	137.34	1808	H. Davy, Britain
La	Lanthanum	57	138.9055	1839	C. G. Mosander, Sweden
Ce	Cerium	58	140.12	1803	J. J. Berzelius and W. von Hisinger, Sweden; M. H. Klaproth, Germany
Pr	Praseodymium	59	140.9077	1885	C. A. von Welsbach, Austria
Nd	Neodymium	60	144.24	1885	C. A. von Welsbach, Austria
Pm	Promethium	61	145[2]	1945	J. A. Marinsky, L. E. Glendenin, and C. D. Coryell, U.S.
Sm	Samarium	62	150.35	1879	L. de Boisbaudran, France
Eu	Europium	63	151.96	1896	E. A. Demarcay, France
Gd	Gadolinium	64	157.25	1880	J. C. de Marignac, Switzerland
Tb	Terbium	65	158.9254	1843	C. G. Mosander, Sweden
Dy	Dysprosium	66	162.50	1886	L. de Boisbaudran, France
Ho	Holmium	67	164.9304	1878	J. L. Soret, Switzerland
Er	Erbium	68	167.26	1843	C. G. Mosander, Sweden
Tm	Thulium	69	168.9342	1879	P. T. Cleve, Sweden
Yb	Ytterbium	70	173.04	1878	J. de Marignac, Switzerland
Lu	Lutetium	71	174.97	1907	G. Urbain, France
Hf	Hafnium	72	178.49	1923	G. von Hevesy, Sweden; D. Coster, Netherlands
Ta	Tantalum	73	180.9479	1802	A. G. Ekeberg, Sweden
W	Tungsten	74	183.85	1783	J. J. d'Elhuyar and D. F. d'Elhuyar, Spain
Re	Rhenium	75	186.207	1925	W. Noddack and I. E. Tacke, Germany
Os	Osmium	76	190.2	1804	S. Tennant, Britain
Ir	Iridium	77	192.22	1804	S. Tennant, Britain
Pt	Platinum	78	195.09	1735	A. De Ulloa, Spain
Au	Gold	79	196.9665	—	Ancient
Hg	Mercury	80	200.59	—	Ancient
Tl	Thallium	81	204.37	1861	W. Crookes, Britain
Pb	Lead	82	207.19	—	Ancient
Bi	Bismuth	83	208.9804	—	Medieval
Po	Polonium	84	210[2]	1898	M. Curie and P. Curie, France
At	Astatine	85	210[2]	1940	E. G. Segre, D. R. Corson, and K. R. MacKenzie, U.S.
Rn	Radon	86	222[2]	1900	F. E. Dorn, Germany
Fr	Francium	87	223[2]	1939	M. Perey, France
Ra	Radium	88	226[2]	1898	M. Curie and P. Curie, France
Ac	Actinium	89	227[2]	1899	A. L. Debierne, France
Th	Thorium	90	232.0381	1828	J. J. Berzelius, Sweden
Pa	Protactinium	91	231.0359	1917	O. Hahn and L. Meitner, Germany; J. Cranston and F. Soddy, Britain
U	Uranium	92	238.029	1789	M. H. Klaproth, Germany
Np	Neptunium	93	237[2]	1940	E. McMillan and P. Abelson, U.S.
Pu	Plutonium	94	244[2]	1940	G. T. Seaborg, E. M. McMillan, A. C. Wahl, and J. W. Kennedy, U.S.
Am	Americium	95	243[2]	1945	G. T. Seaborg, R. A. James, S. G. Thompson, and A. Ghiorso, U.S.
Cm	Curium	96	247[2]	1944	G. T. Seaborg, R. A. James and A. Ghiorso, U.S.
Bk	Berkelium	97	247[2]	1949	S. G. Thompson, A. Ghiorso and G. T. Seaborg, U.S.
Cf	Californium	98	251[2]	1950	S. G. Thompson, K. Street Jr., A. Ghiorso, and G. T. Seaborg, U.S.
E	Einsteinium	99	254[2]	1952	A. Ghiorso et al., U.S.
Fm	Fermium	100	257[2]	1953	A. Ghiorso et al., U.S.
Mv	Mendelevium	101	258[2]	1955	A. Ghiorso, B. Harvey, G. Choppin, S. G. Thompson, G. T. Seaborg, U.S.
No	Nobelium	102	255[2]	1958	A. Ghiorso, T. Sikkeland, J. Walton, and G. T. Seaborg, U.S.
Lr	Lawrencium	103	260[2]	1961	A. Ghiorso, A. E. Larsh, R. M. Latimer, and T. Sikkeland, U.S.
Rf	Kurchatovium / Rutherfordium	104	A257[2]	1964 / 1969	G. N. Flerov et al., U.S.S.R. / A. Ghiorso et al., U.S. } Soviet claim disputed by U.S.
Ha	Bohrium / Hahnium	105	A261[2]	1968 / 1970	G. N. Flerov et al., U.S.S.R. / A. Ghiorso et al., U.S. } Soviet claim disputed by U.S.
	Unnamed	106	263[2]	1974 / 1974	G. N. Flerov et al., U.S.S.R. / G. T. Seaborg, A. Ghiorso, et al., U.S. } Soviet claim disputed by U.S.
	Unnamed	107	—	1981	Peter Ambruster, Gottfried Munzenberg, West Germany
	Unnamed	108	—	1984	Peter Ambruster, Gottfried Munzenberg, West Germany
	Unnamed	109	—	1982	Peter Ambruster, Gottfried Munzenberg, West Germany

[1] The standard for chemical atomic weights (adopted in 1961) is that of carbon—12.011. [2] Most stable known isotope.

MATHEMATICAL TABLES

NAMES OF LARGE NUMBERS

NAME	EQUIVALENT	Number of Zeros	Power of 10	NAME	EQUIVALENT	Number of Zeros	Power of 10
million	1,000 thousands	6	10^6	duodecillion	1,000 undecillions	39	10^{39}
billion	1,000 millions	9	10^9	tredecillion	1,000 duodecillions	42	10^{42}
trillion	1,000 billions	12	10^{12}	quattuordecillion	1,000 tredecillions	45	10^{45}
quadrillion	1,000 trillions	15	10^{15}	quindecillion	1,000 quattuordecillions	48	10^{48}
quintillion	1,000 quadrillions	18	10^{18}	sexdecillion	1,000 quindecillions	51	10^{51}
sextillion	1,000 quintillions	21	10^{21}	septendecillion	1,000 sexdecillions	54	10^{54}
septillion	1,000 sextillions	24	10^{24}	octodecillion	1,000 septendecillions	57	10^{57}
octillion	1,000 septillions	27	10^{27}	novemdecillion	1,000 octodecillions	60	10^{60}
nonillion	1,000 octillions	30	10^{30}	vigintillion	1,000 novemdecillions	63	10^{63}
decillion	1,000 nonillions	33	10^{33}	googol	——	100	10^{100}
undecillion	1,000 decillions	36	10^{36}				

ROMAN NUMERALS

I	1	V	5	IX	9	XIII	13	XVII	17	XXX	30	LXX	70	D 500
II	2	VI	6	X	10	XIV	14	XVIII	18	XL	40	LXXX	80	M 1,000
III	3	VII	7	XI	11	XV	15	XIX	19	L	50	XC	90	$\bar{V}$ 5,000
IV	4	VIII	8	XII	12	XVI	16	XX	20	LX	60	C	100	$\bar{X}$ 10,000

DECIMAL EQUIVALENTS OF FRACTIONS

.015625 = 1/64	.171875 = 11/64	.350000 = 7/20	.531250 = 17/32	.687500 = 11/16	.857143 = 6/7	
.031250 = 1/32	.187500 = 3/16	.359375 = 23/64	.546875 = 35/64	.700000 = 7/10	.859375 = 55/64	
.046875 = 3/64	.200000 = 1/5	.375000 = 3/8	.550000 = 11/20	.703125 = 45/64	.875000 = 7/8	
.050000 = 1/20	.203125 = 13/64	.390625 = 25/64	.555555 = 5/9	.714286 = 5/7	.888889 = 8/9	
.062500 = 1/16	.218750 = 7/32	.400000 = 2/5	.562500 = 9/16	.718750 = 23/32	.890625 = 57/64	
.078125 = 5/64	.222222 = 2/9	.406250 = 13/32	.571429 = 4/7	.734375 = 47/64	.900000 = 9/10	
.083333 = 1/12	.234375 = 15/64	.416667 = 5/12	.578125 = 37/64	.750000 = 3/4	.906250 = 29/32	
.093750 = 3/32	.250000 = 1/4	.421875 = 27/64	.583333 = 7/12	.765625 = 49/64	.916667 = 11/12	
.100000 = 1/10	.265625 = 17/64	.428571 = 3/7	.593750 = 19/32	.777778 = 7/9	.921875 = 59/64	
.109375 = 7/64	.281250 = 9/32	.437500 = 7/16	.600000 = 3/5	.781250 = 25/32	.950000 = 19/20	
.111111 = 1/9	.285714 = 2/7	.444444 = 4/9	.609375 = 39/64	.796875 = 51/64	.953125 = 61/64	
.125000 = 1/8	.296875 = 19/64	.450000 = 9/20	.625000 = 5/8	.800000 = 4/5	.968750 = 31/32	
.140625 = 9/64	.300000 = 3/10	.453125 = 29/64	.640625 = 41/64	.812500 = 13/16	.984375 = 63/64	
.142857 = 1/7	.312500 = 5/16	.468750 = 15/32	.650000 = 13/20	.828125 = 53/64		
.150000 = 3/20	.328125 = 21/64	.484375 = 31/64	.656250 = 21/32	.833333 = 5/6		
.156250 = 5/32	.333333 = 1/3	.500000 = 1/2	.666667 = 2/3	.843750 = 27/32		
.166667 = 1/6	.343750 = 11/32	.515625 = 33/64	.671875 = 43/64	.850000 = 17/20		

COMMON AREA FORMULAS

FIGURE	FORMULA	MEANING OF LETTERS
Rectangle	$A = ab$	a = base, b = height
Square	$A = a^2$	a = one side
Triangle	$A = \dfrac{ab}{2}$	a = base, b = height
Parallelogram	$A = ab$	a = base, b = height
Regular pentagon	$A = 1.720a^2$	a = one side
Regular hexagon	$A = 2.598a^2$	a = one side
Regular octagon	$A = 4.828a^2$	a = one side
Circle	$A = \pi r^2$	$\pi = 3.1416$, r = radius

COMMON VOLUME FORMULAS

FIGURE	FORMULA	MEANING OF LETTERS
Cube	$V = a^3$	a = one side
Pyramid	$V = \dfrac{ah}{3}$	a = area of base, h = height
Cylinder	$V = \pi r^2 h$	$\pi = 3.1416$, h = height, r = radius of base
Cone	$V = \dfrac{\pi r^2 h}{3}$	$\pi = 3.1416$, r = radius of base, h = height
Sphere	$V = \dfrac{4\pi r^3}{3}$	$\pi = 3.1416$, r = radius

MULTIPLES OF PI

No.	Value	No.	Value
1π	3.1416	$\dfrac{1}{\pi}$	0.3183
2π	6.2832	$1/2\pi$	1.5708
3π	9.4248	$1/3\pi$	1.0472
4π	12.5664	$1/4\pi$	0.7854
5π	15.7080	$1/5\pi$	0.6283
6π	18.8496	$1/6\pi$	0.5236
7π	21.9912	$1/7\pi$	0.4488
8π	25.1328	$1/8\pi$	0.3927
9π	28.2744	$1/9\pi$	0.3491
π^2	9.8696	$\sqrt{\pi}$	1.7725

GEOMETRY OF REGULAR POLYGONS

No. of Sides	Name of Polygon	If length of side = 1, then: Area =	Radius of Circum-scribed Circle =	Radius of Inscribed Circle =	If Radius of Circum-scribed Circle = 1, then Side =
3	triangle	0.433013	0.5773	0.2887	1.7321
4	square	1.000000	0.7071	0.5000	1.4142
5	pentagon	1.720477	0.8506	0.6882	1.1756
6	hexagon	2.598076	1.0000	0.8660	1.0000
7	heptagon	3.633912	1.1524	1.0383	0.8677
8	octagon	4.828427	1.3066	1.2071	0.7653
9	nonagon	6.181824	1.4619	1.3737	0.6840
10	decagon	7.694209	1.6180	1.5388	0.6180

POWERS OF 10

10^1 = 10	
10^2 = 100	
10^3 = 1,000	
10^4 = 10,000	
10^5 = 100,000	
10^6 = 1,000,000	
10^7 = 10,000,000	
10^{-1} = 0.1	
10^{-2} = 0.01	
10^{-3} = 0.001	
10^{-4} = 0.0001	
10^{-5} = 0.00001	
10^{-6} = 0.000001	
10^{-7} = 0.0000001	

LENGTH AND DISTANCE: U.S. MEASURES (AND METRIC EQUIVALENTS)

1 mil = 0.001 inch = 0.0254 millimeter
1 inch (in.) = 25.4 millimeters = 2.54 centimeters
1 foot (ft.) = 12 inches = ⅓ yard = 0.00018939 mile
 = 30.48 centimeters =0.3048 meter
1 yard (yd.) = 3 feet = 36 inches = 0.9144 meter
1 rod (rd.) = 16½ feet = 5½ yards = 5.0292 meters

1 furlong (fur.) = ⅛ mile = 40 rods = 220 yards
 = 660 feet = 201.168 meters
1 statute mile (mi.) = 8 furlongs = 320 rods
 = 1,760 yards = 5,280 feet = 1.609344 kilometers
 = 0.86897624 nautical mile
1 league (land) = 3 statute miles = 4.8280 kilometers

NAUTICAL MEASURES OF LENGTH AND DISTANCE

1 span = 9 inches = 22.86 centimeters
1 fathom (fm.) = 8 spans = 72 inches = 6 feet
 = 1.8288 meters
1 cable = 120 fathoms = 240 yards = 720 feet
 = 219.4560 meters
1 league (nautical) = 3 nautical miles
 = 5,556 meters = 3.452338 statute miles

1 nautical mile (or international mile) (mi.)
 = 2,025.37182852 yards = 6,076.11548556 feet
 = 1,852 meters = 1.852 kilometers
 = 1.150779448 statute miles
 = 1' (minute) latitude
1 ° (degree) latitude
 = 60 nautical miles

SURVEYOR'S (or GUNTER'S) CHAIN MEASURES

1 link (li.) = 7.92 inches = 0.201168 meter
1 chain (ch.) = 100 links = 66 feet = 20.1168 meters
1 furlong (fur.) = 10 chains = 40 rods = 660 feet
 = 201.168 meters
1 statute mile = 80 chains = 8 furlongs = 5,280 feet
 = 1.609344 kilometers

ENGINEER'S CHAIN MEASURES

1 link (li.) = 1 foot
 = 0.3048 meter
1 chain (ch.) = 100 links
 = 100 feet = 30.48 meters
1 statute mile = 52.8 chains = 5,280 feet
 = 1.609344 kilometers

AREA: U.S. MEASURES (AND METRIC EQUIVALENTS)

1 square inch (sq. in.) = 6.45160 square centimeters
 = 0.00694444 square foot
1 square foot (sq. ft.) = 144 square inches
 = 929.0304 square centimeters
1 square yard (sq. yd.) = 1,296 square inches
 = 9 square feet = 0.83612736 square meter

1 square rod (sq. rd.) = 30¼ square yards
 = 272¼ square feet = 25.29285264 square meters
1 acre (A.) = 160 square rods = 4,840 square yards
 = 43,560 square feet = 0.40468564224 hectare
1 square mile (sq. mi.) = 640 acres = 27,878,400 sq. ft.
 = 2.589988110336 square kilometers

SURVEYOR'S MEASURES OF LAND AREA

1 square link (sq. li.) = 62.7264 square inches
 = 404.68564 square centimeters
1 square pole (sq. p.) = 625 square links
 = 30¼ square yards = 25.29285264 square meters
1 square chain (sq. ch.) = 16 square poles
 = 484 square yards = 404.68564224 square meters

1 acre (A.) = 10 square chains = 4,840 square yards
 = 43,560 square feet = 0.40468564324 hectare
1 section (sec.) = 640 acres = 1 square mile
 = 2.589988110336 square kilometers
1 township (tp.) = 36 sections = 36 square miles
 = 93.23957 square kilometers

WEIGHT OR MASS: U.S. MEASURES (AND METRIC EQUIVALENTS)

AVOIRDUPOIS UNITS OF WEIGHT

Everyday weights are measured in avoirdupois units in the United States. When necessary to distinguish these units from other measuring units, such as fluid ounces or troy ounces, use the abbreviation **avdp.**

1 grain (gr.) = 0.00228571 ounce = 0.00208333 troy ounce
 = 64.79891 milligrams = 0.00017361 troy pound
1 dram (dr.) = 27¹¹⁄₃₂ grains = 27.34375 grains
 = 1.7718449 grams
1 ounce (oz.) = 16 drams = 437½ grains
 = 0.9114583 troy ounce = 0.9114583 apothecaries' ounce
 = 0.0625 pound = 0.07595486 troy pound
 = 28.349523125 grams

1 pound (lb.) = 16 ounces = 256 drams = 7,000 grains
 = 1.215278 troy pound = 1.215278 apothecaries' lbs.
 = 453.59237 grams = 0.45359237 kilogram
1 hundredweight (cwt.) = 100 pounds = 0.05 ton
 = 45.359237 kilograms
1 ton (designated as **short** ton or **net** ton)
 = 2,000 pounds = 0.8928571 long ton (or gross ton)
 = 907.18474 kilograms = 0.90718474 metric ton

BRITISH UNITS OF AVOIRDUPOIS WEIGHT

1 stone = 14 pounds = 6.35029318 kilograms
1 hundredweight = 112 pounds = 50.80234544 kilograms

1 ton (designated as **long** ton or **gross** ton)
 = 2,240 pounds = 1.12 short tons = 1,016.0469088 kilograms

TROY UNITS OF WEIGHT

Gems and precious metals are measured using troy weight.

1 grain = 0.0022857 avdp. ounce = 64.79891 milligrams
1 carat = 3.086 grains = 0.00705 avdp. ounce
 = 200 milligrams = 0.2 gram
1 assay ton (AT) = 29,166⅔ milligrams (same as number of troy ounces in short ton)
1 pennyweight (dwt.) = 24 grains = T0.05485715 avdp. ounce
 = 1.55517384 grams

1 ounce = 480 grains = 20 pennyweights
 = 1.097143 avdp. ounces = 31.1034768 grams
1 pound = 5,760 grains = 240 pennyweights
 = 12 troy ounces = 0.8228571 avdp. pound
 = 13.16571 avdp. ounces = 373.2417216 grams
 = 0.3732417216 kilogram
1 short ton = 2,000 avdp. pounds = 29,166⅔ troy ounces

APOTHECARIES' UNITS OF WEIGHT

1 grain = 0.0022857 avdp. ounce = 64.79891 milligrams
1 scruple = 20 grains = 0.04571429167 avdp. ounce
 = 1.29584782 grams
1 dram =60 grains = 3 scruples = 0.137142875 avdp. ounce
 = 3.8879346 grams

1 ounce = 480 grains = 24 scruples = 8 drams
 = 1.097143 avdp. ounces = 31.1034768 grams
1 pound = 5,760 grains = 288 scruples = 96 drams
 = 12 apothecaries' ounces = 13.16571 avdp. ounces
 = 373.2417216 grams = 0.3732417216 kilogram

VOLUME AND CAPACITY: U.S. MEASURES (AND METRIC EQUIVALENTS)

1 cubic inch (cu. in.) = 16.387064 cubic centimeters
 = 0.5541126 fluid ounce = 0.016387064 liter
1 cubic foot = 1,728 cubic inches = 957.5065 fluid ounces
 = 0.028316846592 cubic meter = 29.92208 fluid quarts
 = 7.480519 U.S. gallons = 28.316846592 liters
 = 6.228822724 British imperial gallons

1 cubic yard (cu. yd.) = 46,656 cubic inches
 = 27 cubic feet
 = 0.764554857984 cubic meter
 = 201.9740 U.S. gallons
 = 168.1782135 British imperial gallons
 = 764.554857984 liters

MEASURES OF VOLUME-MASS

1 cubic foot of seawater = 64 pounds
1 cubic foot of fresh water = 62.428 pounds at 39.2° F.
1 cubic foot of ice = 56 pounds
1 measurement ton = 40 cubic feet = 1 freight ton

1 displacement ton = 35 cubic feet of seawater
 = 1 long ton
1 register ton = 100 cubic feet
 = 2.8316846592 cubic meters

HOUSEHOLD MEASURES OF LIQUID CAPACITY

1 teaspoon = 1/3 tablespoon = 1/6 fluid ounce = 80 drops
 = 4.928921667 milliliters
1 tablespoon = 3 teaspoons = 1/2 fluid ounce = 240 drops
 = 14.786765 milliliters
1 fluid ounce (fl. oz.) = 2 tablespoons = 6 teaspoons
 = 29.57353 milliliters = 1.8046875 cubic inches
1 gill (gi.) = 1/2 cup = 4 fluid ounces = 7.21875 cubic inches
 = 118.29411825 milliliters = 1,920 minims
1 cup = 16 tablespoons = 8 fluid ounces
 = 14.4375 cubic inches = 236.58824 milliliters
1 pint (pt.) = 2 cups = 4 gills = 16 fluid ounces
 = 28.875 cubic inches = 0.473176473 liter
1 quart (qt.) = 2 pints = 4 cups = 32 fluid ounces
 = 57.75 cubic inches = 0.832672482 British quart
 = 0.946352946 liter = 0.03342014 cubic foot

1 British imperial quart = 1.20095 U.S. quarts
 = 69.355 cubic inches = 1.1365248824 liters
1 gallon (gal.) = 4 quarts = 8 pints = 16 cups
 = 128 fluid ounces = 231 cubic inches
 = 3,785.411784 milliliters
 = 0.832672482 British imperial gallon
 = 3.785411784 liters
1 British imperial gallon = 1.20095 U.S. gallons
 = 160 British fluid ounces = 277.42 cubic inches
 = 4.546099295 liters
1 barrel (liquids) = 31.5 U.S. gallons = 4.21 cubic feet
 = 119.2404712 liters
1 barrel (petroleum) = 42 U.S. gallons
 = 0.1589872949 cubic meter = 5.6145852 cubic feet
 = 158.9872949 liters

APOTHECARIES' MEASURES OF LIQUID CAPACITY

1 minim (or drop) (min.) = 1/60 fluid dram
 = 1/480 fluid ounce = 0.0020833 fluid ounce
 = 0.0037597656 cubic inch = 0.06161152 milliliter
1 British fluid drachm = 0.961 U.S. fluid dram
 = 0.216734 cubic inch = 3.55164 milliliters
1 fluid dram (fl. dr.) = 60 minims = 1/8 fluid ounce
 = 0.125 fluid ounce = 0.225585937 cubic inch
 = 3.69669125 cubic centimeters = 3.69669125 milliliters
1 British fluid ounce = 0.961 U.S. fluid ounce
 = 1.733875 cubic inches = 28.41312 milliliters
1 fluid ounce (fl. oz.) = 8 fluid drams = 1/16 fluid pint
 = 1.8046875 cubic inches = 29.57353 cubic
centimeters
 = 29.57353 milliliters = 1.041 British fluid ounces

1 pint = 128 fluid drams = 16 fluid ounces = 7,680 minims
 = 28.875 cubic inches = 473.176473 cubic centimeters
 = 473.176473 milliliters
 = 0.473176473 liter
1 quart = 2 pints = 32 fluid ounces = 256 fluid drams
 = 57.75 cubic inches = 946.352946 cubic centimeters
 = 0.946352946 liter
 = 0.832672482 British quart
1 gallon = 4 quarts = 8 pints = 128 fluid ounces
 = 231 cubic inches
 = 3,785.411784 cubic centimeters
 = 3.785411784 liters
 = 0.832672482 British gallon

CUSTOMARY DRY MEASURES OF CAPACITY

1 pint = 33.6003125 cubic inches
 = 550.61047 cubic centimeters = 0.55061047 liters
1 quart = 2 pints = 67.200625 cubic inches
 = 1,101.22094 cubic centimeters
 = 1.10122094 liters = 0.969 British dry quart
1 British imperial dry quart = 1.032 U.S. dry quarts
 = 69.355 cubic inches = 1.1365 liters
1 peck (pk.) = 8 quarts = 16 pints = 0.25 bushel
 = 537.605 cubic inches = 8,809.7675 cubic centimeters
 = 8.8097675 liters
1 bushel (bu.), U.S. struck measure = 4 pecks = 32 dry quarts
 = 64 dry pints = 2,150.42 cubic inches = 35.23907 liters

1 British imperial bushel = 1.032 U.S. struck measure bushels
 = 2,219.36 cubic inches = 36.368735 liters
1 bushel, U.S. heaped measure = 1¼ struck measure
 bushels = 1.278 struck measure bushels
 = 2,747.715 cubic inches = 45.035527 liters
1 barrel (bbl.), **cranberries** = 5,286 cubic inches
 = 86^45/64 dry quarts = 2.709 struck measure bushels
1 barrel (bbl.), **standard** (other fruits and vegetables and
 dry commodities) = 7,056 cubic inches = 105 dry quarts
 = 3.281 struck measure bushels
 = 0.115627 cubic meter

LENGTH: METRIC MEASURES AND EQUIVALENTS

1 nanometer (nm.) = 0.00000003937008 inch
1 micron (m.) = 1,000 nanometers = 0.00003937008 inch
1 millimeter (mm.) = 0.03937008 inch
1 centimeter (cm.) = 10 millimeters = 0.3937008 inch
1 decimeter (dm.) = 100 millimeters = 10 centimeters
 = 3.937008 inches
1 meter (m.) = 1,000 millimeters = 100 centimeters
 = 10 decimeters = 39.37008 inches = 3.280840 feet
 = 1.093613 yards = 0.54680665 fathom
 = 0.00062137 statute mile = 0.00053996 nautical mile

1 decameter (dam.) = 10 meters
 = 32.80840 feet = 10.93613 yards
 = 393.7008 inches = 0.0062137 mile
1 hectometer (hm.) = 10 decameters = 100 meters
 = 328.0840 feet
 = 109.3613 yards
1 kilometer (km.) = 1,000 meters = 100 decameters
 = 10 hectometers = 3,280.83990 feet = 1,093.61330 yards
 = 0.621371192 statute mile
 = 0.53995680 nautical mile

AREA: METRIC MEASURES AND EQUIVALENTS

1 **square millimeter** (mm.²) = 0.0015500031 square inch
1 **square centimeter** (cm.²) = 100 square millimeters
= 0.15500031 square inch = 0.001076391 square foot
1 **square decimeter** (dm.²) = 100 square centimeters
= 15.500031 square inches = 0.1076391 square foot
1 **square meter** (m.²) = 1,000,000 square millimeters
= 10,000 square centimeters = 100 square decimeters
= 10.76391045 square feet = 1.19599005 square yards

1 **are** (a.) = 100 square meters = 119.599005 square yards
= 0.02471053815 acre
1 **hectare** (ha.) = 10,000 square meters = 100 ares
= 2.471053815 acres
1 **square kilometer** (km.²) = 1,000,000 square meters
= 100 hectares = 247.1053815 acres
= 0.38610216 square statute mile
= 0.29155335 square nautical mile

VOLUME: METRIC MEASURES AND EQUIVALENTS

1 **cubic millimeter** (mm.³) = 0.001 cubic centimeter
= 0.00006102374 cubic inch
1 **cubic centimeter** (cm.³) = 1,000 cubic millimeters
= 0.06102374 cubic inch = 0.00026417205 U.S. gallon
1 **cubic decimeter** (dm.³) = 1,000 cubic centimeters = 1 liter
= 61.02374 cubic inches = 0.03531467 cubic foot
1 **stere** (s) = 1 cubic meter

1 **cubic meter** (m.³) = 1,000,000 cubic centimeters
= 1,000 cubic decimeters = 35.31467 cubic feet
= 1.30795059 cubic yards = 264.17205 U.S. gallons
1 **cubic decameter** (dam.³) = 1,000 cubic meters
= 1,307.9506 cubic yards
1 **cubic hectometer** (hm.³) = 1,000 cubic decameters
= 1,307,950.6 cubic yards

CAPACITY: METRIC MEASURES AND EQUIVALENTS

1 **milliliter** (ml.) = 0.001 liter = 0.03381402 fluid ounce
= 16.23073 minims = 0.06102374 cubic inch
1 **centiliter** (cl.) = 10 milliliters = 0.01 liter
= 0.3381402 fluid ounce = 0.6102374 cubic inch
1 **deciliter** (dl.) = 100 milliliters = 10 centiliters
= 3.381402 fluid ounces = 6.102374 cubic inches
1 **liter** (l.) = 1,000 milliliters = 10 deciliters
= 33.81402 fluid ounces = 1 cubic decimeter
= 61.02374 cubic inches = 1.056688 fluid quarts
= 0.26417205 U.S. gallon = 0.90808298 dry quart

1 **decaliter** (dal.) = 10 liters
= 2.6417205 U.S. gallons
1 **hectoliter** (hl.) = 100 liters
= 10 decaliters
= 26.417205 U.S. gallons
= 2.837759 U.S. bushels
= 3.531467 cubic feet
1 **kiloliter** (kl.) = 1,000 liters = 10 hectoliters
= 35.31467 cubic feet
= 264.17205 U.S. gallons

WEIGHT: METRIC MEASURES AND EQUIVALENTS

1 **microgram** (μg.) = 0.000001 gram
= 0.00001543236 grain
1 **milligram** (mg.) = 1,000 micrograms = 0.001 gram
= 0.01543236 grain
1 **centigram** (cg.) = 10 milligrams = 0.01 gram
= 0.1543236 grain = 0.003527396 avdp. ounce
1 **decigram** (dg.) = 10 centigrams = 0.1 gram
= 1.543236 grains = 0.03527396 avdp. ounce
1 **gram** (g.) = 1,000 milligrams = 10 decigrams
= 15.43236 grains = 0.03527396 avdp. ounce
1 **decagram** (dag.) = 10 grams = 0.3527396 avdp. ounce

1 **hectogram** (hg.) = 100 grams = 10 decagrams
= 3.527396 avdp. ounces
1 **kilogram** (kg.) = 1,000 grams = 10 hectograms
= 35.27396 avdp. ounces = 32.15075 troy ounces
= 2.204623 avdp. pounds
= 2.679229 troy pounds
1 **quintal** (q.) = 100 kilograms = 220.4623 avdp. pounds
1 **metric ton** (M.T.) = 1,000 kilograms
= 2,204.623 advp. pounds
= 1.1023113 short tons
= 0.9842065 long ton

HOW TO CONVERT UNITS OF MEASURE BY MULTIPLICATION

U.S. MEASURE	MULTIPLY BY	TO GET METRIC	METRIC MEASURE	MULTIPLY BY	TO GET U.S.
LENGTH AND DISTANCE					
inches	× 25.4	= millimeters	millimeters	× 0.03937008	= inches
inches	× 2.54	= centimeters	centimeters	× 0.3937008	= inches
feet	× 0.3048	= meters	meters	× 3.280840	= feet
yards	× 0.9144	= meters	meters	× 1.093613	= yards
miles	× 1.609344	= kilometers	kilometers	× 0.62137	= miles
AREA OR SURFACE					
square inches	× 6.4516	= square centimeters	square centimeters	× 0.1550031	= square inches
square feet	× 0.09290304	= square meters	square meters	× 10.76391	= square feet
square yards	× 0.83612736	= square meters	square meters	× 1.195990	= square yards
acres	× 0.40468564224	= hectares	hectares	× 2.47105	= acres
square miles	× 2.58998811	= square kilometers	square kilometers	× 0.386102	= square miles
VOLUME					
cubic inches	× 16.387064	= cubic centimeters	cubic centimeters	× 0.06102374	= cubic inches
cubic feet	× 0.028316846592	= cubic meters	cubic meters	× 35.31467	= cubic feet
cubic yards	× 0.764554857984	= cubic meters	cubic meters	× 1.3079506	= cubic yards
CAPACITY					
fluid ounces	× 29.57353	= milliliters	milliliters	× 0.03381402	= fluid ounces
liquid pint	× 0.473176473	= liters	liters	× 2.113376	= liquid pints
liquid quart	× 0.946352946	= liters	liters	× 1.056688	= liquid quarts
gallons	× 3.785411784	= liters	liters	× 0.26417205	= gallons
bushels	× 35.23907	= liters	liters	× 0.02837759	= bushels
WEIGHT					
grains	× 0.06479891	= grams	grams	× 15.43236	= grains
ounces avdp.	× 28.349523125	= grams	grams	× 0.03527396	= ounces avdp.
pounds avdp.	× 0.45359237	= kilograms	kilograms	× 2.204623	= pounds avdp.
tons	× 0.90718474	= metric tons	metric tons	× 1.1023113	= tons

TIME MEASUREMENTS

1 **microsecond** = 0.000001 second 1 **second** = 1,000,000 microseconds = 0.016667 minute = 0.00027778 hour = 0.0000115 day = 15″ longitude 1 **minute** = 60 seconds = 0.0166667 hour = 0.00069444 day = 15′ longitude 1 **hour** = 3,600 seconds = 60 minutes = 15° longitude = 0.04166667 day 1 **day** = 24 hours = 1,440 minutes = 86,400 seconds = 360° longitude 1 **mean solar day** (1 rotation of Earth with respect to Sun) = 24 hours, 3 minutes, 56.55536 seconds = 1.00273791 rotations with respect to vernal equinox = 1.0027378118868 rotations of Earth with respect to stars	1 **sidereal month** = 27.321661 days = 27 days, 7 hours, 43 minutes, 11.5 seconds 1 **synodical month** = 29.530588 days = 29 days, 12 hours, 44 minutes, 2.8 seconds 1 **calendar year** = 31,536,000 seconds = 525,600 minutes = 8,760 hours = 365 days 1 **solar year** = 31,556,925.975 seconds = 525,948.766 minutes = 8,765.8128 hours = 365 days, 5 hours, 48 minutes, 46 seconds 1 **light-year** = 5,880,000,000,000 statute miles = 9,460,000,000,000 kilometers = 5,110,000,000,000 nautical miles

SPEED: U.S. AND METRIC MEASURES

1 **foot per minute** = 0.01666667 foot per second = 0.00508 meter per second 1 **yard per minute** = 3 feet per minute = 0.05 foot per second = 0.03409091 statute mile per hour = 0.02962419 knot = 0.01524 meter per second 1 **statute mile per hour** = 88 feet per minute = 29.333 yards per minute = 1.466667 feet per second = 1.609344 kilometers per hour = 0.86897624 knot = 0.44704 meter per second 1 **knot** = 101.26859143 feet per minute = 6,076.11548556 feet per hour = 33.75619714 yards per minute = 1.852 kilometers per hour = 1.68780986 feet per second = 1.15077945 statute miles per hour = 0.51444444 meter per second 1 **meter per second** = 196.85039340 feet per minute = 65.6167978 yards per minute = 3.6 kilometers per hour = 3.28083990 feet per second = 2.23693632 statute miles per hour = 1.94384449 knots	1 **kilometer per hour** = 0.53995680 knot = 0.62137119 statute mile per hour **Speed of light** (in vacuum) = 186,282 statute miles per second = 161,875 nautical miles per second = 299,792,458 meters per second = 983.570 feet per microsecond **Speed of light** (in air) = 186,230 statute miles per second = 299,708 kilometers per second = 161,829 nautical miles per second = 983.294 feet per second **Speed of sound** (in air at 60°F. at sea level) = 1,116.99 feet per second = 761.59 statute miles per hour = 661.80 knots = 340.46 meters per second **Speed of sound** (in salt water at 60°F.) = 4,945.37 feet per second = 3,371.85 statute miles per hour = 2,930.05 knots = 1,507.35 meters per second

SPECIAL UNITS OF MEASUREMENT

Ampere: Unit of electric current. A potential difference of 1 volt across a resistance of 1 ohm produces a current of 1 ampere.

Bale: Bale of cotton weighs 500 pounds gross or 480 pounds net.

Board Foot: Volume of 1-inch-thick, 1-foot-square board, rough sawn.

BTU: British thermal unit, equal to 252 calories; amount of heat needed to increase temperature of 1 pound of pure water by 1°F.

Calorie: Amount of heat needed to increase the temperature of 1 gram of pure water by 1°C.

Carat: Used to indicate purity of gold alloys, on a scale of 24: 14 carats means 14 parts gold to 10 parts alloy.

Cord: Equals 128 cubic feet of firewood (4 ft. × 4 ft. × 8 ft.).

Decibel: Unit of relative loudness in acoustics.

Hand: Unit used in measuring height of horses; equals 4 inches.

Hertz: Modern unit in electronics, equivalent to and replacing the former "cycles per second"; abbreviated as *hz.*

Horsepower: Standard theoretical unit of the time rate of work or power. It is equal to the work done in lifting 550 pounds 1 foot in 1 second; equals 745.7 watts.

Joule: Unit of energy measurement equal to 0.24 calorie or 10 million ergs.

Kilowatt-hour: Equal to consumption of 1,000 watts of power over a period of 1 hour.

Ohm: Unit of electrical resistance. A circuit in which a potential difference of 1 volt produces a current of 1 ampere has a resistance of 1 ohm.

Pi (π)**:** Ratio (3.14159 . . .) of the circumference of circle to its total diameter.

Pica: In typography, equals 12 points; about 1/6 inch; 0.166044 inch; 4.2175176 millimeters.

Point: In typography, about 1/72 inch; 0.013837 inch; 0.3514598 millimeter.

Quire: Either 24 or 25 sheets of paper of uniform size and quality; equal to 1/20 of a ream.

Ream: Twenty quires or 480 uniform sheets of paper, except newsprint or book paper (equal to 500 sheets), or a "perfect ream" of 516.

Roentgen: Dosage unit of radiation exposure produced by X rays and gamma rays, alpha, beta, and neutron; it applies to biological effects only.

Talent: Ancient unit of coin and weight equal to about 3,600 shekels as a weight, and about 3,000 shekels as silver or gold revenue. Hebrew gold *shekel* probably weighed about 252 grains troy, or slightly over 1/2 ounce.

Volt: Unit of electromotive force, or potential difference; potential difference of 1 volt across a resistance of 1 ohm produces a current of 1 ampere.

Watt: Power expended by current of 1 ampere across potential difference of 1 volt equals 1 watt.

Social Welfare

HIGHLIGHTS: 1985

Nearly half of all American households (47%) receive government aid, according to a new study by the U.S. Bureau of the Census.

The survey showed that a total of 22,497,000 households (26.7%) had no income in 1984 from wages, salary, or self-employment.

The Census Bureau reported that 37% of the nation's 84,002,000 non-farm households receive benefits that are not based on proving their financial need—such aid as Social Security or Medicare. Some 19% of households receive benefits based on their financial need—such as food stamps or veterans' pensions. About 9% of households receive both kinds of benefits.

Social Security or railroad retirement benefits accounted for the most widely used government aid, going to 23,508,000 households—28%.

Some 20,550,000 households receive Medi-care benefits and 7,553,000 households get Medicaid benefits.

Food stamps go to 6,292,000 households and 2,963,000 households receive Supplemental Security Income.

Aid to Families with Dependent Children and other cash assistance goes to 3,823,000 households.

In other categories of government benefits, 3,688,000 households use free or reduced-price school meals, 3,668,000 households live in public or subsidized rental housing, 3,326,000 receive veterans' compensation or pensions, 2,512,000 get state and local government employee pensions, 2,293,000 households receive government assistance in paying energy bills, 1,671,000 households receive federal government employee pensions, 1,283,000 households collect U.S. military pensions, and 1,247,000 get aid from the Special Supplemental Food Program for Women, Infants, and Children.

SOCIAL WELFARE EXPENDITURES

Source: Social Security Bulletin, data for fiscal years

Federal, state, and local governments spent $592.6 billion on social welfare in 1982, a rise of $42.1 billion, or 7.6%, over the previous year.

Combined federal, state, and local government expenditures for social-welfare programs are shown in millions of dollars (add 000,000).

	1950	1960	1965	1970	1975	1980	1982
TOTAL	$23,508.4	$52,293.3	$77,175.3	$145,855.7	$290,047.3	$493,354.5	$592,550.7
Social insurance	4,946.6	19,306.7	28,122.8	54,691.2	$23,013.1	$229,552.3	300,740.9
Social security and Medicare	784.1	11,032.3	16,997.5	36,835.4	78,429.9	152,110.4	204,567.8
Railroad retirement	306.4	934.7	1,128.1	1,609.9	3,085.1	4,768.7	5,766.4
Public employee retirement	817.9	2,569.9	4,528.5	8,658.7	20,118.6	39,490.2	50,090.8
Unemployment benefits	2,190.1	2,829.6	3,002.6	3,819.5	13,835.9	18,326.4	21,355.5
State temporary disability	72.1	347.9	483.5	717.7	990.0	1,379.1	1,688.3
Workers' compensation	625.1	1,308.5	1,859.4	2,950.4	6,479.1	13,253.4	16,911.1
Public aid	2,496.2	4,101.1	6,283.4	16,487.7	41,326.4	72,385.1	80,785.5
Public assistance	2,490.2	4,041.7	5,874.9	14,433.5	27,378.5	45,474.0	53,388.1
Supplemental security income	—	—	—	—	6,091.6	8,226.5	9,753.0
Food stamps	—	—	—	576.9	4,693.9	9,083.3	10,761.0
Health and medical programs	2,063.5	4,463.8	6,246.4	9,906.8	17,707.5	28,118.8	32,892.0
Hospital and medical care	1,222.3	2,853.3	3,452.3	5,313.4	9,407.0	12,202.8	14,968.0
Maternal and child health	29.8	141.3	227.3	431.4	545.5	798.0	888.0
Medical research	69.2	448.9	1,165.2	1,635.4	2,646.0	5,218.0	5,270.0
School health	30.6	101.0	142.2	246.6	321.0	569.0	709.0
Other public health	350.8	401.2	671.0	1,348.0	2,919.0	6,848.0	8,452.0
Veterans' programs	6,865.7	5,479.2	6,031.0	9,078.0	17,018.8	21,465.5	24,708.1
Pensions and compensation	2,092.1	3,402.7	4,141.4	5,393.8	7,578.5	11,306.0	13,301.6
Health and medical	748.0	954.0	1,228.7	1,784.0	3,516.8	6,203.9	7,825.8
Education	2,691.6	490.6	40.9	1,018.5	4,433.8	2,400.7	1,816.3
Life insurance	475.7	494.1	434.3	502.3	566.0	664.5	747.0
Education	6,674.1	17,626.2	28,107.9	50,845.5	80,863.2	170,587.6	133,874.1
Elementary and secondary	5,596.2	15,109.0	22,357.7	38,632.3	59,774.6	86,773.0	97,419.5
Higher	914.7	2,190.7	4,826.4	9,907.1	16,384.2	26,090.7	28,153.8
Vocational and adult	160.8	298.0	853.9	2,144.4	4,441.3	7,375.2	7,997.3
Housing	14.6	176.8	318.1	701.2	3,171.7	7,209.1	7,954.2
Other social welfare	447.7	1,139.4	2,065.7	4,145.2	6,946.6	14,036.1	11,596.0
Vocational rehabilitation	30.0	96.3	210.5	703.8	1,036.4	1,125.1	1,233.7
Institutional care	145.5	420.5	789.5	201.7	296.1	482.4	594.4
Child nutrition	160.2	398.7	617.4	896.0	2,517.6	5,289.3	4,045.4
Child welfare	104.9	211.5	354.3	585.3	597.0	800.0	800.0

YOUR SOCIAL SECURITY BENEFITS
Source: Social Security Administration

For most Americans, Social Security provides a partial replacement of income when family earnings drop or stop because of retirement, disability, or death.

The average monthly benefit paid to a retired worker with no dependents in January 1985 was $450, and that for a couple, both of whom were receiving benefits, was $780. The maximum benefit for a single worker retiring at 65 in 1985 was $717.

In addition, Social Security's Medicare program helps pay hospital and medical bills for most persons 65 and over and for some younger disabled persons.

Almost every American is covered by Social Security. Today about 1 of every 6 Americans receives a monthly Social Security benefit check.

You must include in gross income for federal income tax purposes up to half of your Social Security benefits if your income, including tax-exempt interest and half your benefits, exceeds $25,000 a year if single and $32,000 if married and filing jointly.

The government will deposit your benefits directly in your bank account if you wish.

The money collected in Social Security taxes is maintained in separate trust funds by the U.S. Treasury. The funds can be used only for payment of Social Security benefits and expenses or for investment at interest in federal securities.

SOCIAL SECURITY NUMBER AND RECORD

You should have a Social Security card that contains your number, your name, and your signature. *You keep this same Social Security identification number all your life.*

If you do not have a Social Security number, you should apply for one at once at any local Social Security office.

You must have a Social Security number when you obtain a job. You also need a Social Security number for such purposes as identification on tax forms or in case you ever have to apply for public assistance.

Make sure your employer has your correct Social Security number. If your employer does not use your correct number, you may not receive credit under Social Security.

Once you have a Social Security number, the Social Security Administration will maintain a separate earnings record in your name for the rest of your life. This record keeps track of the credits you accumulate toward Social Security benefits. Information in your Social Security earnings record is confidential and only can be disclosed under limited circumstances.

All wage earners and persons who are self-employed should check on their Social Security earnings record *every three years.* To do so, you should obtain a "Request for Statement of Earnings" form from any local Social Security office. After you mail it in, the Social Security Administration will report what earnings have been credited.

Before you or your family can get monthly cash Social Security benefits, you or your spouse (or one of your parents, if you are a child) must have credit for a certain amount of work under Social Security, depending on your age and the type of benefit.

GROWTH OF SOCIAL SECURITY
Source: Social Security Administration, data for fiscal years

YEAR	PENSION PAYMENT EXPENDITURES			BENEFICIARIES		AVERAGE MONTHLY BENEFITS			
	Total	Retirement & Survivors	Disability	Retirement & Survivors	Disability	Retired Worker	Retired Couple	Widow or Widower	Disabled Worker
1940	$ 23,500,000	$ 15,805,000	—	222,488	—	$ 22.60	$ 34.73	$ 20.28	—
1945	247,800,000	239,834,000	—	1,288,107	—	24.19	37.01	20.19	—
1950	928,400,000	727,266,000	—	3,477,243	—	43.86	67.46	36.54	—
1955	4,855,300,000	4,333,147,000	—	7,960,616	—	61.90	94.97	48.69	—
1960	11,080,500,000	10,269,709,000	$ 528,304,000	14,157,138	687,451	74.04	112.76	57.68	$ 89.31
1965	18,093,700,000	15,225,894,000	1,392,190,000	19,127,716	1,739,051	83.92	127.55	73.75	97.76
1969	26,459,600,000	23,732,010,000	2,443,437,000	22,826,514	2,487,548	100.40	152.28	87.27	112.74
1970	31,569,600,000	26,266,928,000	2,778,118,000	23,563,634	2,664,995	118.10	179.29	101.71	131.29
1971	36,865,100,000	31,101,018,000	3,381,448,000	24,361,500	2,930,008	132.17	200.52	113.17	146.52
1972	41,275,200,000	34,540,813,000	4,045,895,000	25,204,542	3,271,486	162.35	246.44	137.66	179.00
1973	51,130,500,000	42,169,744,000	5,161,840,000	26,309,163	3,558,982	166.40	251.18	156.35	183.00
1974	58,194,100,000	47,848,838,000	6,158,569,000	26,941,483	3,911,334	188.20	283.96	176.03	205.70
1975	66,585,700,000	54,838,818,000	7,629,796,000	25,732,311	4,352,200	207.18	312.37	192.33	225.89
1976	75,332,100,000	62,140,449,000	9,222,211,000	28,399,725	4,623,827	224.86	338.99	207.13	245.17
1977	84,263,800,000	71,270,519,000	11,135,237,000	29,228,350	4,854,206	242.98	366.05	221.95	265.19
1978	92,530,700,000	78,524,090,000	12,213,895,000	29,718,195	4,868,576	263.19	439.00	238.84	288.25
1979	103,967,300,000	87,591,968,000	13,428,454,000	30,347,848	4,777,218	294.27	442.63	266.87	322.03
1980	120,117,557,000	104,560,850,000	15,437,473,000	30,843,914	4,682,172	341.41	513.36	311.16	370.74
1981	136,266,778,000	119,413,467,000	16,853,311,000	31,474,000	4,456,000	385.97	580.72	346.08	413.15
1982	152,054,034,000	134,654,629,000	17,399,405,000	31,867,000	3,973,000	419.25	631.74	375.28	440.60
1983	165,564,275,000	148,024,189,000	17,540,086,000	32,272,000	3,813,000	440.77	666.43	393.03	456.20
1984	173,556,929,000	155,824,605,000	17,732,324,000	32,657,000	3,822,000	460.57	696.95	412.87	470.67

SOCIAL SECURITY TAXES

If you are employed, your employer deducts Social Security taxes from your paycheck and matches them. The self-employed pay taxes at the combined employer-employee rate, partially offset by an income-tax credit, and by a tax deduction after 1989.

RETIREMENT BENEFITS

If you have enough work credits you can retire with benefits as early as the age of 62, but if you do so you will receive for the rest of your life only 80% of the monthly benefits to which you would be entitled if you waited until you were 65 to retire. The age at which you may receive full benefits will increase gradually, beginning in the year 2000, to 66 in 2009 and to 67 in 2027.

The size of the monthly benefits you will collect when you retire at age 65 depends on your covered earnings under Social Security over a period of years.

A retired worker 65 to 69 could earn up to $7,320 in 1985 without losing any Social Security benefits. Workers under age 65 could earn up to $5,400. For every $2 earned above that amount the retiree loses $1 of benefits. Beginning in 1990, benefits for persons who reach the normal retirement age will be reduced $1 for each $3 of excess earnings.

A person who is 70 may earn any amount without losing benefits, starting with the month in which he or she is 70.

There is a special rule that generally applies only in the first year of retirement: Even though earnings may exceed the annual exempt amount, a benefit can be paid for any *month* a person performs little or no work. More information on this can be obtained at any Social Security office.

A worker who delays retirement past 65 will have his or her benefits increased. For persons who reached age 62 before 1979, the credit is 1% for each year (or $\frac{1}{12}$ of 1% for each month) in which he or she does not collect benefits from 65 to 70.

For persons who reach 62 after 1978 and before 1987 the credit is 3% for each year ($\frac{1}{4}$% for each month).

The credit will gradually increase, reaching 8% a year ($\frac{2}{3}$ of 1% for each month) for persons who reach 62 after 2004.

Your Social Security retirement benefits generally will be automatically increased each December if the Consumer Price Index rises by 3% or more over a specified measuring period.

If you plan to retire in the next few years and wish to estimate your retirement income, consult officials at your local Social Security office and they will assist you.

DISABILITY BENEFITS

If you have enough work credits and become disabled by accident or illness so that your physical or mental condition prevents you from working, Social Security provides monthly cash benefits designed to replace, in part, the covered earnings you have lost because of your disability. The disability must have lasted or be expected to last at least a year, or be expected to be fatal.

Your checks can start for the sixth full month of your disability.

You will receive checks monthly as long as you are disabled and continue to be unable to work.

The amount of the monthly benefit for disability depends on the worker's age and covered earnings under Social Security.

A Social Security recipient's unmarried child 18 or older who becomes severely disabled before reaching 22 can receive monthly checks as long as the disability continues.

SOCIAL SECURITY TAXES[1]

YEARS	MAXIMUM TAXABLE WAGE	EMPLOYEE TAXES[2] Rate	EMPLOYEE TAXES[2] Maximum Tax	SELF-EMPLOYED TAX Rate	SELF-EMPLOYED TAX Maximum Tax	YEARS	MAXIMUM TAXABLE WAGE	EMPLOYEE TAXES[2] Rate	EMPLOYEE TAXES[2] Maximum Tax	SELF-EMPLOYED TAX[3] Rate	SELF-EMPLOYED TAX[3] Maximum Tax
1937–49	$3,000	1.00%	$ 30.00	—	—	1973	10,800	5.85%	$ 631.80	8.00%	$ 864.00
1950	3,000	1.50%	45.00	—	—	1974	13,200	5.85%	772.20	7.90%	1,042.80
1951–53	3,600	1.50%	54.00	2.25%	$ 81.00	1975	14,100	5.85%	824.85	7.90%	1,113.90
1954	3,600	2.00%	72.00	3.00%	108.00	1976	15,300	5.85%	895.05	7.90%	1,208.70
1955–56	4,200	2.00%	84.00	3.00%	126.00	1977	16,500	5.85%	965.25	7.90%	1,303.50
1957–58	4,200	2.25%	94.50	3.375%	141.75	1978	17,700	6.05%	1,070.85	8.10%	1,433.70
1959	4,800	2.50%	120.00	3.75%	180.00	1979	22,900	6.13%	1,403.77	8.10%	1,854.90
1960–61	4,800	3.00%	144.00	4.50%	216.00	1980	25,900	6.13%	1,587.67	8.10%	2,097.90
1962	4,800	3.125%	150.00	4.70%	225.60	1981	29,700	6.65%	1,975.05	9.30%	2,762.10
1963–65	4,800	3.625%	174.00	5.40%	259.20	1982	32,400	6.70%	2,170.80	9.35%	3,029.40
1966	6,600	4.20%	277.20	6.15%	405.90	1983	35,700	6.70%	2,391.90	9.35%	3,337.95
1967	6,600	4.40%	290.40	6.40%	422.40	1984	37,800	7.00%	2,646.00	11.30%	4,271.40
1968	7,800	4.40%	343.20	6.40%	499.20	1985	39,600	7.05%	2,791.80	11.80%	4,672.80
1969–70	7,800	4.80%	374.40	6.90%	538.20	1986	N.A.	7.15%	N.A.	12.30%	N.A.
1971	$7,800	5.20%	405.60	7.50%	585.00	1987	N.A.	7.15%	N.A.	12.30%	N.A.
1972	9,000	5.20%	468.00	7.50%	675.00	1988	N.A.	7.51%	N.A.	13.02%	N.A.

[1] Source: Social Security Administration [2] Payroll taxes deducted from wages are equally matched by employers.
[3] Special tax credits in 1984-89 reduce effective tax rates. N.A.=not available.

And the disabled worker's spouse, divorced spouse, or unmarried children up to 19 may be eligible for benefits.

Total monthly benefits to the family of a disabled worker who first becomes entitled to disability benefits after June 1980 are limited to the *lower* of 85% of the worker's average earnings before becoming disabled or 150% of the worker's disability benefit.

SURVIVORS' BENEFITS

Somewhat like life insurance, Social Security provides monthly benefits for the family of a worker who dies.

A lump-sum funeral expense payment of $255 can be made to certain relatives.

Family members of a deceased worker who are eligible for monthly cash benefits include:

1. Unmarried children under 18 (or up to 19 if full-time students).
2. Unmarried son or daughter 18 or over who was severely disabled before 22 and continues to be disabled.
3. Widow or widower 60 or older.
4. Widow or widower under 60, or surviving divorced spouse, if caring for worker's child under 16 (or disabled) who is getting a benefit based on the deceased worker's earnings.
5. Widow or widower 50 or older who becomes disabled not later than seven years after worker's death, or within seven years after ceasing to receive checks for care of deceased worker's children.
6. Dependent parents 62 or older.
7. Unmarried divorced spouse 60 or older (50 if disabled), if marriage to insured worker lasted 10 years before divorce.
8. Grandchildren, under certain conditions.

The monthly payments to these survivors may range from 50% to 100% of the amount the worker would receive at 65 as retirement benefits.

APPLYING FOR SOCIAL SECURITY BENEFITS

Before you or your family can get any Social Security checks, you must apply for them at a Social Security office. When you apply, you should have with you:

1. **Social Security number:** Your own Social Security card or a record of your number. If your claim is on another person's record, you will need that person's Social Security number.
2. **Proof of your age:** A birth certificate or a baptismal certificate that records birth date.
3. **Your marriage certificate,** if applying for spouse's benefits, or widow's or widower's benefits.
4. **Your children's birth certificates,** if applying for children's benefits.
5. **Your Form W-2 for the previous year,** or copies of your last two federal income tax returns if you are self-employed.
6. **Proof of your dependence for support** on the insured worker, if you are applying for benefits as a dependent parent.

If you do not have these proofs, do not delay applying. When you apply, a Social Security official will tell you about alternate means of proof that you can obtain.

RIGHT OF APPEAL

If you believe that a decision made on your claim is not correct, you may ask the Social Security Administration to reconsider it. Employees of any Social Security office will explain how you may appeal and will help you get your claim reconsidered or request a hearing.

FOOD STAMPS

The Food Stamp Program helps low-income people buy more food.

Food stamps are available to all low-income persons who qualify, *not* just those receiving public assistance or social security benefits.

Unemployed families and working families with low incomes also may qualify.

To find out whether or not you are eligible for food stamps, inquire at your local food stamp or welfare office. Eligibility depends on your household's income and assets and whether it contains elderly or disabled persons.

Households whose gross incomes are more than 130% of the poverty level and do not have an elderly or disabled member are ineligible for food stamps.

Food stamps can be used at any approved supermarket or grocery store for the purchase of most food items.

FOOD STAMP PROGRAM
Source: U.S. Department of Agriculture

YEAR	NUMBER OF PARTICIPANTS	TOTAL BENEFITS	AV. MONTHLY BENEFITS PER PERSON
1962	143,000	$ 13,153,000	$ 7.67
1965	425,000	32,505,000	6.38
1967	1,447,000	105,550,000	6.08
1970	4,340,000	549,664,000	10.55
1971	9,368,000	1,522,749,000	13.55
1972	11,109,000	1,797,286,000	13.48
1973	12,166,000	2,131,405,000	14.60
1974	12,862,000	2,718,296,000	17.61
1975	17,064,000	4,385,501,000	21.42
1976	18,549,000	5,326,505,000	23.93
1977	17,077,000	5,066,950,000	24.73
1978	16,001,000	5,139,216,000	26.77
1979	17,653,000	6,480,189,000	30.59
1980	21,071,000	8,685,379,000	34.35
1981	22,431,000	10,629,913,000	39.49
1982[1]	22,133,000	10,408,682,000	39.19
1983[2]	21,630,000	11,155,071,000	42.99
1984[2]	20,870,000	10,710,623,000	42.77

[1] Puerto Rico included. [2] Puerto Rico excluded.

MEDICARE AND MEDICAID

Medicare includes separate hospital insurance and medical insurance programs administered by the Health Care Financing Administration of the Department of Health and Human Services.

Medicaid, on the other hand, is a health assistance program for about 23 million low-income people, especially for those receiving welfare or Supplementary Security Income.

MEDICARE HOSPITAL INSURANCE

Persons 65 and older eligible for social security or rail retirement benefits automatically receive free Medicare hospital insurance. Others 65 and older can purchase hospital insurance by paying a monthly premium of $174.

Younger persons can receive Medicare if they have been entitled for 24 months to disability benefits under social security, somewhat longer under railroad retirement, or if they need continuing hemodialysis treatment for kidney disease.

Anyone 65 or over, or anyone under 65 entitled to Medicare hospital insurance, may enroll for medical insurance.

A person who is not already receiving social security benefits should check with the local social security office about Medicare 3 months before the 65th birthday.

The Medicare hospital insurance provides:
Hospitalization: Coverage of up to 90 days of hospital benefits in a period of time called a "benefit period." A benefit period begins when you enter the hospital and ends when you have been out of a hospital or skilled nursing facility for 60 days in a row.

The patient pays the first $400 of costs during the first 60 days of inpatient hospital care, and then pays $100 for each day of hospitalization from 61 to 90 days.

If all 90 days are used up, a "lifetime reserve" can be drawn on for up to 60 more days of benefits. During these additional days, the Medicare beneficiary pays $200 a day of the hospital expenses.

After each "benefit period," the 90 days of hospital benefits are renewed but "lifetime

reserve" days are not renewable.

Subject to those limitations, hospital insurance covers (1) the cost of a semiprivate room (two to four patients to a room), a private room only if medically necessary (if the patient elects a private room, he pays the difference); (2) board; (3) hospital services except private-duty nursing; (4) the services of interns or residents in approved teaching programs; and (5) drugs and medical supplies used by the patient in the hospital.

The same coverage extends to hospitalization in tuberculosis or psychiatric institutions. There is a lifetime limit of 190 days of coverage for treatment in a psychiatric hospital.
Skilled Nursing Facility: Up to 100 days if medically necessary, in a skilled nursing facility after at least 3 days of hospitalization.

The patient pays $50 for each day in excess of 20 days, up to the limit of 100 days. Subject to that limitation, insurance covers cost of a semiprivate room, board, general nursing (but not private-duty nursing), prescribed drugs, and therapy by employees of the skilled nursing facility.
Home Health Services: All covered home visits by nurses or therapists of an approved home health agency when recommended by an attending physician.
Hospices: Terminal Medicare patients can elect care in certified hospices.

MEDICARE MEDICAL INSURANCE

A person who enrolls when first eligible pays $15.50 a month for coverage by Medicare medical insurance. The person also pays the first $75 of covered medical expenses each year. Medicare then pays 80% of approved charges for covered services received for the rest of the year. The medical insurance covers physicians' and surgeons' services and medical and health services such as diagnostic tests, surgical dressings, certain ambulance services, hospital outpatient charges, and home health services.

Payments for home health services are 100% of reasonable costs.

MEDICARE AND MEDICAID: 1970–1984

Source: Health Care Financing Administration

YEAR	MEDICARE PAYMENTS			NUMBER OF MEDICARE BILLS PAID		MEDICAID
	Total	Hospital	Medical	Hospital	Medical	Expenditures
1970	$ 7,099,000,000	$ 5,124,000,000	$1,975,000,000	7,512,000	39,695,000	$ 4,516,000,000
1975	15,588,000,000	11,315,000,000	4,273,000,000	10,318,000	83,106,000	12,086,000,000
1976	18,420,000,000	13,340,000,000	5,080,000,000	11,170,000	87,116,000	13,977,000,000
1977	21,774,000,000	15,737,000,000	6,038,000,000	11,758,000	111,723,000	16,239,000,000
1978	24,934,000,000	17,682,000,000	7,252,000,000	12,285,000	112,659,000	17,992,000,000
1979	29,231,000,000	20,623,000,000	8,708,000,000	12,831,000	142,726,000	20,472,000,000
1980	35,700,000,000	25,064,000,000	10,635,000,000	13,832,000	154,388,000	23,311,000,000
1981	43,455,000,000	30,342,000,000	13,113,000,000	14,829,000	169,540,000	27,204,000,000
1982	51,086,000,000	35,631,000,000	15,455,000,000	16,638,000	187,700,000	29,399,000,000
1983	57,443,000,000	39,337,000,000	18,106,000,000	17,174,000	195,642,000	32,391,000,000
1984	62,918,000,000	43,257,000,000	19,661,000,000	16,750,000	204,693,000	34,244,199,694

VETERANS' BENEFITS

Source: Veterans Administration

Almost 100 million Americans are potentially eligible for veterans' benefits and services, including 30 million living veterans, their 66 million family members, and 4 million survivors of deceased veterans.

The federal government spends more than $27 billion yearly for veterans' benefits.

To find out about your own eligibility for specific veterans' benefits, contact your local Veterans Administration (VA) office. Consult your telephone directory for the number to call. Toll-free special telephone service is available for calls to the VA.

Veterans with dishonorable discharges are *not* eligible for benefits described here.

HOSPITALIZATION

Veterans with service-connected disabilities have priority for treatment at Veterans Administration hospitals.

However, if beds are available, needed hospitalization is provided to (1) any war veteran who is 65 or older, or (2) any younger veteran who cannot pay the cost of hospitalization.

AUTOMOBILES FOR THE DISABLED

The VA will pay up to $5,000 toward the purchase of a car plus the cost of adaptive equipment for a veteran whose service-connected disability resulted in loss of use of one or both hands or feet or severe permanent impairment of vision in both eyes.

CLOTHING ALLOWANCE

An annual clothing allowance of $349 can be paid to any veteran entitled to receive compensation for a service-connected disability who wears or uses a prosthetic or orthopedic appliance that tends to wear out clothing.

PENSIONS AND DISABILITY COMPENSATION

The VA has two basic programs providing monthly cash benefits to veterans and their survivors.

Disability Compensation. Veterans with service-connected disabilities receive monthly payments ranging from $66 to $3,697, depending on the extent of their disability. Additional allowances are paid for dependents if the veteran's disability is 30% or more.

Veterans' Pensions. Needy war veterans 65 or older (or younger war veterans totally disabled by nonservice injury or illness) are eligible for monthly pension payments.

The size of the pension depends on the amount of the veteran's additional yearly income. Eligible veterans are guaranteed an annual income level of $5,709 if they are single. Those with one dependent receive a pension to bring their income level to $7,478, and this is increased by $968 for each additional dependent.

Death Benefits. Dependents of a veteran who dies of service-connected injuries or illness are eligible for substantial benefits. Lesser amounts are payable to needy dependents of veterans who die of other causes.

MEDICAL AND DENTAL TREATMENT

Veterans can receive free medical and dental treatment for service-connected disabilities.

Medical aid also covers the purchase of needed prosthetic appliances and aids for the blind, including a trained guide dog.

All veterans who have not been dishonorably discharged can receive treatment for alcohol and drug dependency.

EDUCATIONAL BENEFITS

Veterans with service between Feb. 1, 1955, and Dec. 31, 1976, can receive up to 45 months of GI Bill payments for attending school or on-the-job training. Eligibility expires Dec. 31, 1989, or 10 years after last discharge, whichever occurs first.

A single veteran with a full-time course of study receives $342 per month.

On-the-job payments for a single trainee start at $274 for the first 6 months.

VETERANS' BENEFITS: 1940–1986

Source: U.S. Veterans Administration

YEAR	Compensation & Pensions	Education & Readjustment Benefits	Medical Care & Administrative Expenses
1940	$ 429,153,465	—	$ 94,456,620
1945	771,796,517	—	159,559,021
1950	2,223,092,285	$2,792,589,648	901,988,427
1955	2,681,726,077	707,946,023	869,576,297
1960	3,367,449,929	514,175,433	1,086,674,142
1965	4,107,721,052	49,392,151	1,358,410,178
1967	4,494,130,947	297,601,153	1,518,644,942
1968	4,611,180,643	461,506,628	1,620,046,513
1969	4,939,409,724	678,903,395	1,735,043,428
1970	5,357,407,811	1,018,861,723	2,007,783,909
1971	5,839,390,281	1,631,738,617	2,256,979,848
1972	6,167,996,446	1,935,797,731	2,650,982,373
1973	6,568,081,137	2,696,239,516	2,966,237,960
1974	6,734,790,004	3,268,556,875	3,290,194,883
1975	7,551,176,877	4,529,227,472	3,919,256,993
1976	8,242,088,546	5,543,354,200	4,446,765,605
1977	9,038,809,712	3,891,448,932	5,072,993,821
1978	9,630,682,830	3,336,618,918	5,683,811,346
1979	10,540,135,154	2,800,897,985	6,205,941,745
1980	11,256,935,680	2,383,912,481	6,646,752,559
1981	12,491,391,279	2,332,820,985	7,199,253,633
1982	13,361,476,722	2,001,298,853	8,008,923,888
1983	13,880,930,659	1,673,731,254	8,003,013,000
1984	13,944,962,795	1,403,093,349	8,547,146,000
1985*	14,232,939,000	1,235,126,000	9,149,691,000
1986*	N.A.	N.A.	9,355,459,000

* Estimates. N.A. = Not Available.

A separate voluntary contributory program is available for veterans who entered active duty on or after Jan. 1, 1977.

Another educational program is available for veterans who began service between July 1, 1985, and June 30, 1988.

The children and spouse of a veteran who died or was totally and permanently service-disabled also are eligible for educational benefits. Eligibility for children extends until they are 26 years old. Eligibility for a spouse extends for 10 years from the time the veteran became totally disabled or died.

About 6.7 million Vietnam-era veterans—almost 72%—have participated.

Only 50.5% of World War II veterans took advantage of the GI Bill.

LOANS FOR HOMES

Veterans, service personnel on active duty, and certain unmarried surviving spouses of veterans may apply for home loans guaranteed or insured by the VA. The VA guarantee may be 60% of the loan amount or $27,500, whichever is less, for conventionally built homes. The maximum guarantee for manufactured or mobile homes is 50% or $20,000, whichever is less.

There is no time limit on using this loan privilege. Such loans often can be arranged with no down payment by the borrower. Veterans also have preferences for FHA insured loans.

Since 1944 the VA has guaranteed or insured over 11.8 million loans with a value of more than $236 billion.

GRANTS FOR "SPECIALLY ADAPTED" HOMES

Certain disabled veterans, who are generally confined to a wheelchair, may be entitled to a grant of up to $35,500 to construct a new house or to remodel an existing house to meet their needs. Others may receive smaller grants for adaptation of living quarters.

In addition the VA provides up to $40,000 mortgage life insurance on such a home.

GI INSURANCE

Up to $10,000 of Service-Disabled Veterans Insurance (S-DVI) can be issued to veterans separated on or after April 25, 1951, with a service-connected disability. Application must be made within one year of notice granting such a disability.

Dividends are paid on government life insurance policies prefixed with the letters K, V, RS, W, J, JR, and JS. On all but K, dividends may purchase paid-up insurance additions.

Most VA policies waive premiums if the insured becomes totally disabled for 6 or more consecutive months prior to the 65th birthday. Some policies have riders providing income in cases of total disability.

VA programs include Servicemen's Group Life Insurance (SGLI), Veterans Group Life Insurance (VGLI), and Veterans Mortgage Life Insurance (VMLI).

SGLI provides up to $35,000 group life insurance to active-duty service personnel, ready reservists, and retired reservists. Upon separation from active duty veterans may convert their SGLI to VGLI.

VGLI provides up to $35,000 group life insurance for a 5-year term. At the end of the term, VGLI may be converted to an individual policy with a participating commercial insurance company.

VMLI provides up to $40,000 of mortgage life insurance protection to disabled veterans with specially adapted housing.

BURIAL BENEFITS

The VA will pay up to $150 toward the burial plot of war veterans or certain peace-time veterans. If the eligible veteran was receiving pension or compensation funds at death, up to $300 is payable toward funeral expenses.

When a veteran dies, his or her family usually is also eligible for a $255 lump-sum death payment from Social Security.

An American flag to drape the casket of a veteran can be obtained from a local VA office or from most local post offices. After the funeral, the flag is given to the next of kin.

A headstone or a small allowance for its purchase will be supplied for the burial place of a deceased veteran.

Burial space will be provided for a deceased veteran in a national cemetery as well as for the veteran's spouse, minor children, and, under special conditions, adult unmarried children. Special restrictions apply to burial in Arlington National Cemetery.

When a member of the armed forces dies on active duty and the body is not recovered, the family may obtain a headstone or marker for placement in a private cemetery or in the memorial section of a national cemetery.

REEMPLOYMENT AND UNEMPLOYMENT

Veterans with 5 years or less of military service have their job rights protected in their previous employment and acquire seniority for the time in military service. The veteran must apply for reemployment within 90 days after discharge. Veterans seeking a job can apply for unemployment benefits from the state immediately upon discharge.

Eligible disabled veterans can receive 4 years or more of vocational rehabilitation training to help them find employment. The VA will pay for tuition, books, fees, and a subsistence allowance.

UNEMPLOYMENT INSURANCE

If you have lost your job through no fault of your own, you may be eligible to receive weekly unemployment insurance payments while looking for new employment.

You should apply for the benefits at your local state employment office.

FEDERAL–STATE UNEMPLOYMENT INSURANCE

About 87.6 million workers in the United States are covered by federal-state unemployment insurance.

The federal and state governments collect payroll taxes from employers at a rate of 3.5% of up to the first $7,000 of each worker's wages to pay the benefits.

In a few states employees also pay a small tax to the unemployment fund.

Because each state has its own laws regarding unemployment insurance, the benefits vary from state to state. Depending on how much you previously were earning, your benefits may range from a low of $5 weekly in some states to a high of $196 a week in another. The average amount received is about $125 a week.

Regular benefits end after 26 to 36 weeks of unemployment.

INELIGIBILITY

You cannot collect unemployment insurance if you voluntarily quit your last job or if you were fired because of misconduct. Most states also will not pay unemployment benefits to workers who are unemployed because of a labor dispute.

While collecting unemployment benefits, you lose your eligibility if you refuse to take a suitable job that is offered you.

If you believe you are being unfairly denied unemployment benefits, each state has a procedure by which you can appeal the decision to a review tribunal.

OTHER UNEMPLOYMENT COMPENSATION

The federal government funds separate unemployment compensation plans for federal civilian employees and for military personnel who cannot find jobs after they have been discharged. And the federal government also administers a separate unemployment insurance program for railroad workers.

Some corporations and labor unions also have programs that pay an unemployed worker extra benefits over those received from the regular state plan.

HISTORY

The first state unemployment insurance law was adopted by Wisconsin in 1932.

When the federal government enacted the Social Security Act of 1935, it instituted the present system of unemployment insurance in which the federal government collects payroll taxes and makes money available to states whose unemployment compensation laws meet federal standards.

FEDERAL–STATE UNEMPLOYMENT INSURANCE: 1940–1984

Source: U.S. Department of Labor

Year	Average Weekly Benefit	Average Weekly Beneficiaries	Total Benefits Paid	Number of First Payments	Weeks Compensated	Claimants Exhausting Benefits	Funds Available for Benefits at End of Year
1940	$ 10.56	982,392	$ 518,700,000	5,220,073	51,084,375	2,596,128	$ 1,817,108,000
1945	18.77	464,996	445,866,000	2,861,190	24,179,769	254,271	6,914,009,000
1950	20.76	1,304,991	1,373,114,000	5,211,883	67,859,529	1,853,336	6,972,295,000
1955	25.04	1,099,466	1,350,268,000	4,507,894	56,099,729	1,272,232	8,263,850,000
1960	32.87	1,640,429	2,726,656,000	6,753,387	85,630,399	1,603,372	6,643,257,000
1965	37.19	1,131,025	2,166,004,000	4,813,229	58,813,298	1,085,977	8,357,350,000
1967	41.25	1,017,356	2,092,338,000	4,628,083	52,902,523	867,403	10,778,138,000
1968	43.43	935,930	2,031,617,000	4,197,699	48,668,357	848,179	11,717,246,000
1969	46.17	922,503	2,127,877,000	4,213,803	47,948,702	811,532	12,637,508,000
1970	50.34	1,516,500	3,848,467,000	6,401,782	78,857,992	1,295,319	11,895,901,000
1971	54.02	1,813,700	4,957,026,000	6,540,358	94,312,380	2,006,700	9,703,424,000
1972	56.76	1,562,706	4,470,969,000	5,703,866	81,260,712	1,809,450	9,422,799,000
1973	59.00	1,369,669	4,007,562,000	5,328,998	71,222,809	1,495,092	10,933,767,000
1974	64.25	1,880,833	5,974,922,000	7,729,590	97,803,299	1,926,147	10,593,936,000
1975	70.23	3,371,246	11,754,684,646	11,160,042	175,304,812	4,195,023	4,522,933,588
1976	75.16	2,450,476	8,974,546,269	8,560,107	127,424,765	3,270,042	3,361,647,042
1977	78.79	2,188,672	8,357,160,144	7,985,099	113,244,354	2,850,136	4,387,301,806
1978	83.67	1,946,073	8,214,290,495	7,580,045	101,195,817	2,032,776	9,307,267,000
1979	89.67	2,036,552	9,263,468,406	8,077,727	106,307,994	2,044,131	12,459,909,222
1980	98.87	2,739,773	14,485,642,608	10,002,397	149,130,050	3,076,957	11,463,586,659
1981	106.48	2,605,617	14,113,804,758	9,399,675	136,013,195	2,990,817	12,017,254,000
1982	119.34	3,559,459	20,404,462,000	11,648,448	185,387,401	4,174,709	7,984,273,000
1983	123.55	2,990,878	18,649,613,332	8,909,505	155,525,663	4,180,911	7,569,343,807
1984	123.22	2,148,943	13,363,499	7,767,707	112,174,808	2,614,813	11,697,056,888

WORKERS' COMPENSATION

State workers' compensation laws cover about 86 of every 100 civilian workers, providing cash benefits and medical payments to workers and their survivors for work-related deaths, injuries, and illnesses.

Each state has its own workers' compensation laws, so benefits vary considerably from state to state. Employers are held responsible for work-related injuries and occupational diseases regardless of fault. Employers are required to purchase insurance with private insurance companies, pay premiums into a state insurance fund, or qualify as self-insurers.

Cash benefits to the worker and his or her family may be paid in weekly payments or a lump-sum settlement. In addition, hospital and other medical expenses are paid. Generally the weekly benefits amount to two-thirds of the worker's average weekly wages, ranging from $126 to $1,114 per week.

A disabled worker or survivor can collect workers' compensation payments in addition to those provided by federal social security, although a social security offset exists that is based on the worker's average weekly wage.

You can find out more about your coverage by talking to your employer or writing to your state compensation agency.

You or your family will not automatically

WORKERS' COMPENSATION
Source: Social Security Administration

YEAR	TOTAL BENEFITS	CASH BENEFITS	MEDICAL
1940	$ 256,000,000	$ 161,000,000	$ 95,000,000
1945	408,000,000	283,000,000	125,000,000
1950	615,000,000	415,000,000	200,000,000
1955	916,000,000	591,000,000	325,000,000
1960	1,295,000,000	860,000,000	435,000,000
1965	1,814,000,000	1,214,000,000	600,000,000
1966	2,000,000,000	1,320,000,000	680,000,000
1967	2,189,000,000	1,439,000,000	750,000,000
1968	2,376,000,000	1,546,000,000	830,000,000
1969	2,634,000,000	1,714,000,000	920,000,000
1970	3,031,000,000	1,981,000,000	1,050,000,000
1971	3,563,000,000	2,433,000,000	1,130,000,000
1972	4,061,000,000	2,811,000,000	1,250,000,000
1973	5,103,000,000	3,623,000,000	1,480,000,000
1974	5,781,000,000	4,021,000,000	1,760,000,000
1975	6,598,000,000	4,568,000,000	2,030,000,000
1976	7,584,000,000	5,204,000,000	2,380,000,000
1977	8,630,000,000	5,950,000,000	2,680,000,000
1978	9,793,000,000	6,813,000,000	2,980,000,000
1979	12,027,000,000	8,507,000,000	3,520,000,000
1980	13,562,000,000	9,632,000,000	3,930,000,000
1981	15,016,000,000	10,596,000,000	4,420,000,000
1982	16,263,000,000	11,403,000,000	4,860,000,000
1983	17,533,000,000	12,183,000,000	5,350,000,000

receive these benefits if you are injured or are killed at work. You or your family must file a claim for the benefits with your employer or the appropriate state agency.

PENSION AND RETIREMENT BENEFIT PLANS

Because social security payments amount to only a fraction of the annual amount earned before retirement, most retired persons must supplement their social security benefits with additional income if they are to maintain their accustomed standard of living.

Most commonly such supplemental income, often with benefits larger than those of social security, comes from pension and retirement benefit plans.

Pension plans may be provided to their employees by federal, state, or local governments, by private businesses, or by the individuals themselves.

The first pensions by the U.S. government were established for disabled veterans of the American Revolution in legislation by Congress in 1792. The first local government pensions were established by New York City in 1859 for its police. The first pension plan by a U.S. business came in 1875 by the American Express Company. Columbia University adopted the first American college pension plan for professors in 1892. The following year Chicago established the first pension plan for public school teachers. Pensions for federal Civil Service employees were first adopted by Congress in 1920.

Private pension and retirement plans are regulated by the federal government under the Employee Retirement Income Security Act (ERISA) of 1974. These plans are administered by the Office of Pension and Welfare Benefit Programs of the U.S. Department of Labor and the Internal Revenue Service.

ERISA also established the Pension Benefit Guaranty Corporation, which insures certain types of private pension plans.

The Retirement Equity Act of 1984 amends ERISA to broaden coverage for workers, especially women, who leave jobs to raise a family and then return to work. It also guarantees pension rights for homemakers whose wage-earner husbands die before retirement, and requires spousal consent if the participant waives an early retirement annuity. In addition, maternity and paternity leave is permitted without a break in service, and longer absences from the job, up to 5 years, are allowed. Previously, such breaks led to loss of pension benefits.

Over 65 million workers participate in 775,000 private pension plans in the United States whose assets are valued at over $900 billion.

PUBLIC ASSISTANCE—SSI AND AFDC

The federal government pays monthly checks to persons in financial need who are 65 or older or who are blind or disabled.

The Supplemental Security Income (SSI) program began in 1974, replacing earlier federal-state public assistance programs for the aged, blind, and disabled.

The federal government also pays a major share of the welfare benefits to needy families with children under the state-administered program called Aid to Families with Dependent Children (AFDC).

MONTHLY INCOME FLOOR

The SSI program, administered by the Social Security Administration, establishes a basic nationwide monthly payment standard for persons in financial need who are 65 or over, or blind, or disabled.

This basic monthly payment standard automatically rises to keep pace with the cost of living. Such an automatic increase of 3.5% went into effect on Dec. 31, 1984, raising the SSI monthly payment to $325 for individuals and $488 for couples.

Monthly checks sent by the federal government make up the difference between a person's low income and the basic payment standard. Benefits for eligible recipients are higher in some states because those states add to the federal payments.

INELIGIBILITY

Supplemental Security Income payments may be suspended, reduced, or terminated in any of the following circumstances:
1. An increase in income or resources.
2. Confinement in a public institution.
3. Refusal to accept or undergo treatment for drug addiction or alcoholism.
4. Absence from the U.S. for 30 or more consecutive days.
5. Refusal to accept vocational rehabilitation services without good cause.
6. Loss of U.S. citizenship or of permission to live in the U.S.
7. Failure to apply for or obtain benefits under other programs that may be payable to the recipient.
8. Termination of blindness or disability.
9. Death of a person getting SSI payments.

A recipient must be given written notice of any proposed change in his payments and has 60 days to appeal the action.

WELFARE—AFDC

The nation's largest cash-assistance welfare program—Aid to Families with Dependent Children (AFDC)—was not included in the SSI program. It is operated by the states with federal help. In this program about 10.4 million needy parents and children receive about $13 billion in support payments each year.

Because most of the persons receiving this assistance are families deserted by fathers, the government has made an effort to find the missing fathers, getting them to provide $4.72 billion in 1976–83.

The average monthly AFDC payment in 1983 was $305 per family.

GROWTH OF PUBLIC ASSISTANCE, AFDC, AND SSI

Source: Social Security Administration

YEAR	FEDERALLY ADMINISTERED PAYMENTS					RECIPIENTS OF BENEFITS			
	Total [1]	Old-age	Blind	Disabled	AFDC [2]	Old-age	Blind	Disabled	AFDC [2]
1940	$1,020,115,000	$472,778,000	$21,735,000	—	$ 133,770,000	2,070,000	73,400	—	1,222,000
1945	990,700,000	725,683,000	26,515,000	—	149,667,000	2,056,000	71,500	—	943,000
1950	2,372,200,000	1,453,917,000	52,567,000	$ 8,042,000	551,653,000	2,786,000	97,500	69,000	2,233,000
1955	2,525,600,000	1,487,991,000	67,804,000	134,630,000	617,841,000	2,538,000	104,100	241,000	2,192,000
1960	3,276,700,000	1,626,021,000	86,080,000	236,402,000	1,000,784,000	2,305,000	106,900	369,000	3,073,000
1965	4,025,900,000	1,594,183,000	77,308,000	416,765,000	1,660,186,000	2,087,000	85,100	557,000	4,396,000
1968	5,672,143,000	1,673,191,000	87,828,000	655,792,000	2,849,298,000	2,027,000	80,700	702,000	6,086,000
1969	6,866,956,000	1,746,714,000	91,300,000	786,757,000	3,563,427,000	2,074,000	80,600	803,000	7,313,000
1970	8,864,400,000	1,866,087,000	97,496,000	975,504,000	4,852,964,000	2,082,000	81,000	935,000	9,659,000
1971	10,814,400,000	1,919,693,000	100,691,000	1,185,314,000	6,203,528,000	2,024,000	80,300	1,068,000	10,653,000
1972	11,066,700,000	1,893,982,000	104,736,000	1,392,896,000	6,909,260,000	1,934,000	79,800	1,168,000	11,065,000
1973	11,397,200,000	1,749,324,000	102,978,000	1,566,140,000	7,212,035,000	1,820,000	77,900	1,275,000	10,815,000
1974	14,059,500,000	2,414,034,000	125,791,000	2,556,988,000	7,916,563,000	2,285,909	74,616	1,635,539	11,006,000
1975	16,312,600,000	2,516,515,000	132,155,000	3,335,028,000	9,210,995,000	2,307,105	74,489	1,932,681	11,383,000
1976	17,496,900,000	2,472,571,000	134,060,000	3,345,778,000	10,140,543,000	2,147,697	76,366	2,011,876	11,184,000
1977	18,221,100,000	2,363,887,000	142,138,000	3,628,060,000	10,603,820,000	2,050,921	77,362	2,109,409	10,761,000
1978	18,575,700,000	2,342,080,000	148,027,000	3,881,531,000	10,730,415,000	1,967,900	77,135	2,171,890	11,050,270
1979	19,198,436,000	2,420,720,000	162,444,000	4,285,559,000	10,658,500,000	1,871,716	77,250	2,200,609	10,210,000
1980	21,463,955,000	2,781,228,000	200,616,000	5,357,412,000	12,031,000,000	1,807,776	78,401	2,255,840	10,674,000
1981	21,660,034,000	2,697,680,000	202,119,000	5,456,897,000	13,066,600,000	1,678,090	78,570	2,262,215	11,079,000
1982	21,827,685,000	2,698,708,000	212,691,000	5,794,097,000	12,877,905,000	1,548,741	77,356	2,231,493	10,358,000
1983	N.A.	2,679,283,000	224,713,000	6,229,847,000	N.A.	1,515,400	78,960	2,307,137	N.A.
1984	N.A.	2,832,660,000	244,049,000	6,996,397,000	N.A.	1,530,287	80,524	2,418,522	N.A.

[1] Total includes general assistance federal payments. The total also includes state payments under the Supplemental Security Income program after 1973. [2] Aid to Families with Dependent Children. N.A.=not available.

Space and Astronomy

Artist's concept of the $1.2 billion Hubble Space Telescope that is scheduled to be launched into orbit above the Earth in 1986. The 42-foot long telescope with its 94.5-inch mirror will be able to look at objects 50 times fainter and seven times farther away than any ground-based optical telescope. Named after American astronomer Edwin P. Hubble (1889–1953), the telescope will record what it sees with a TV-type system of much higher sensitivity than photographic film.

NASA

HIGHLIGHTS: 1985

VISIT BY HALLEY'S COMET

Halley's comet, whose orbit brings it into view about every 76 years, makes its closest approach to Earth on April 6, 1986.

The period when the comet will be brightest for viewing will be from April 9 to April 17, while the Moon is dark. But, unfortunately for observers in the northern hemisphere, the head of the comet will be below the southern horizon and only part of its tail is likely to be visible low in the southern sky.

The best views of the comet will be from Australia, South America, Africa, and the South Pacific.

The comet will not be nearly as bright as during its last appearance in 1910. At that time its head shone as brilliantly as the brightest star and its tail was a streak across nearly one-third of the sky. But its approach to the Earth in 1910 was about three times closer than in 1986 when its nearest distance

will be about 37 million miles—farther away than even the planet Venus.

In July 1985 the European Space Agency launched a spacecraft called *Giotto* to take a close-up look at the comet and to fly through its tail. The Soviet Union also sent two spacecraft, *Vega 1* and *Vega 2*, to gather information about the comet.

SPACE SHUTTLE SCHEDULE

The National Aeronautics and Space Administration (NASA) plans 15 space shuttle flights in 1986 and 17 in 1987.

Highlights for 1986 will include:

March—the first space shuttle launch from Vandenberg Air Force Base, Calif.
May—first use by the shuttle of the liquid-hydrogen-powered Centaur upper stage rocket for the deployment of the Ulysses (International Solar Polar) spacecraft.
Later in May—the launching of the Galileo spacecraft to explore the planet Jupiter and its moons.
August—the flight of the Hubble Space Telescope.

SPACELAB MISSION

In the 17th successful mission of the space shuttle program on April 29 to May 6, 1985, the *Challenger* carried the 12-ton European Spacelab on its first operational flight. The reusable $1 billion Spacelab was built by a consortium of 10 nations.

Five scientists worked in the Spacelab to conduct 15 kinds of experiments. A cargo of two monkeys and 24 laboratory rats also went along so that the scientists could observe the effect of weightlessness on animals.

Among the main scientific successes of the Spacelab mission were:

An experiment called Atmos identified over 40 chemicals in the upper atmosphere, providing data that can be used in controlling air pollution.

The *Challenger* flew through the aurora, or northern lights, giving scientists an opportunity to measure the bands of electrified particles that cause lights in the sky.

Experiments on the handling of fluids and other materials.

Altogether the scientists said they obtained 3 million photographs and the equivalent of 10 million pages of data.

SKY-WATCHER'S CALENDAR: 1985-1986

Source: *Astronomical Phenomena,* U.S. Naval Observatory

This calendar lists various astronomical phenomena that will occur in 1985-86.

Evening and Morning Stars. The planets in the western sky shortly after sunset are *evening stars,* and those seen in the eastern sky shortly before sunrise are *morning stars.*

Occultation. When the Moon passes between the Earth and one of the planets or bright stars, this phenomenon is called *occultation.* The occultation of Venus by a crescent moon is depicted on the flags of many Islamic countries.

Meteor Showers. Meteors, or shooting stars, are visible on almost any night of the year, but at certain times the Earth encounters large numbers of meteors all moving together along the same orbit.

These groups of meteors are named for the constellations from which they seem to radiate.

Meteors are pieces of rock or metal traveling in orbit around the Sun. Scientists estimate that about 1,000 tons of meteorites fall on the Earth every day.

Comets are bodies traveling around the Sun in greatly elongated orbits. Most comets can only be seen with telescopes, but from time to time a comet develops a tail of gas or dust that reflects the light from the Sun.

Conjunction of Planets. The orbits of the planets work out so that from time to time the planets appear to pass quite close to each other or to the Sun.

NOVEMBER 1985

11 (6:00 A.M. EST) Venus 0.8° north of Moon.
12 Total Eclipse of Sun: Visible only in Antarctica and southern tip of South America.
13 (11:00 P.M. EST) Mercury 0.5° north of Moon.
16–17 Leonid meteor shower at maximum: About 10 meteors per hour seem to radiate from constellation Leo; major showers occur at about 33-year intervals with next major display expected in 1999.
27 (7:42 A.M. EST) Full Moon.

DECEMBER 1985

8 (5:00 A.M. EST) Mars 0.01° south of Moon.
10–31 Saturn seen as morning star.
13–14 Geminid meteor shower at maximum: About 55 per hour seem to radiate from constellation Gemini.
21 Winter solstice: Winter begins at 5:08 P.M. EST.
21–22 Ursid meteor shower at maximum: About 10 per hour seem to radiate from vicinity of North Star.
27 (2:30 A.M. EST) Full Moon.

JANUARY 1986

1–Feb. 5 Jupiter seen as evening star.
1–May 28 Saturn seen as morning star.
1–July 10 Mars seen as morning star.
2–3 Quadrantid meteor shower at maximum About 110 meteors per hour visible, seeming to radiate from handle of Big Dipper.
5 (8 P.M. EST) Mars 1° .7 North of Moon.
24 Comet Ashbrook-Jackson makes closest approach to Sun in its 7.5-year orbit.
25 (7:31 P.M. EST) Full Moon.
26 Comet Boethin makes closest approach to Sun in its 11.2-year orbit.

FEBRUARY 1986

3 (7 A.M. EST) Mars 3° North of Moon.
3 (8 P.M. EST) Saturn 5° North of Moon.
4 (5 P.M. EST) Uranus 4° North of Moon.
9 Halley's Comet makes closest approach to Sun in its 76-year orbit.
9 (10 P.M. EST) Saturn 7° North of Antares.
18 (7 P.M. EST) Mars in conjunction with Saturn: Mars 1° .3 South of Saturn.
24 (10:02 A.M. EST) Full Moon.

MARCH 1986

2–Oct. 31 Venus seen as evening star.
3 (3 A.M. EST) Saturn 5° North of Moon.
4 (midnight EST) Uranus 4° North of Moon.
4 (10 P.M. EST) Neptune 6° North of Moon.
4–Sept. 10 Jupiter seen as morning star.
13 (4 A.M. EST) Mars 0° .3 North of Uranus.
14 Comet Holmes makes its closest approach to Sun in its 7.1–year orbit.
20 Spring equinox: Spring begins at 5:03 p.m. EST.
20 Comet Wirtanen makes closest approach to Sun in its 5.5–year orbit.
25 (10:02 P.M. EST) Full Moon.
31 (10 P.M. EST) Mars 5° North of Moon.

APRIL 1986

1 (4 A.M. EST) Neptune 6° North of Moon.
5 (9 P.M. EST) Jupiter 3° North of Moon.
5 Comet Kojima makes closest approach to Sun in its 7.9-year orbit.
8 (5 P.M. EST) Mars 1° .4 South of Neptune.
9 Partial Eclipse of the Sun: Visible only in Australia, Antarctica, and South Pacific.
10 (9 P.M. EST) Venus 1° .3 South of Moon.
11 Halley's Comet makes closest approach to Earth.
21–22 Lyrid meteor shower at maximum: About 20 to 30 per hour seem to radiate from constellation Lyra.
24 (7:46 P.M. EST) Full Moon.
24 Total Eclipse of the Moon: Visible in western half of North America; midpoint of eclipse is at 7:12 a.m. EST.
27 (2:00 A.M. EST) Daylight-saving time begins: Set clocks ahead 1 hour.
29 (2 A.M. EDT) Mars 4° North of Moon.

PRINCE AND SENATOR IN SPACE

A prince and a U.S. senator rode along on space shuttle flights in 1985.

In April Sen. Jake Garn (R-Utah) was one of a 7-person crew on a voyage of the *Discovery*. The 52-year-old Garn chairs the Senate subcommittee that oversees NASA.

Prince Sultan Salman ibn Abdel Aziz al-Saud, 28, a nephew of the king of Saudi Arabia, made a flight aboard *Discovery* in June. He observed at first hand as the shuttle crew launched *Arabsat 1-B*, a powerful communications satellite sponsored by 21 Arab countries and the Palestine Liberation Organization (PLO).

TEACHER TO FLY IN SPACE

Sharon Christa McAuliffe, 36, a high school social studies teacher in Concord, N.H., was chosen by NASA in July to become the first ordinary American citizen to fly in space. She was picked from more than 11,000 applications received after President Reagan announced in August 1984 that a teacher should be the first such passenger aboard a NASA space shuttle flight.

Mrs. McAuliffe, who is a mother of two young children, had undergone two weeks of intensive medical and psychological testing by NASA scientists before being chosen from a group of 10 finalists.

She will fly aboard the space shuttle *Challenger* in its mission scheduled to blast off on Jan. 22, 1986, after she completes four months of special NASA training at the Johnson Space Center in Houston, Texas.

Mrs. McAuliffe said she plans to keep a diary of her experiences and will share them with others in a series of talks to educational groups across the nation after the flight.

SKY-WATCHER'S CALENDAR: *(Continued)*

MAY 1986
3 (11 P.M. EDT) Vesta 0°.9 South of Moon.
3–4 Eta Aquarids shower at maximum: About 20 per hour seem to radiate from constellation Aquarius.
17 Comet Spitaler makes its closest approach to Sun in its 6.5-year orbit.
23 (4:45 P.M. EDT) Full Moon.
24 (1 A.M. EDT) Saturn 5° North of Moon.
24 (4 A.M. EDT) Antares 1°.2 South of Moon.
24 (11 P.M. EDT) Uranus 4° North of Moon.
25 (8 P.M. EDT) Neptune 6° North of Moon.
26 (11 P.M. EDT) Mars 3° North of Moon.
27 Comet Shajn-Schaldach makes its closest approach to Sun in its 7.5-year orbit.
28–Nov. 17 Saturn seen as evening star.
31 (4 A.M. EDT) Jupiter 2° North of Moon.

JUNE 1986
9 (2 A.M. EDT) Mercury 3° South of Moon.
16 Lyrid meteor shower at maximum: About 8 per hour seem to radiate from constellation Lyra.
21 Summer solstice: Summer begins at 12:30 p.m. EDT.
21 (11:42 P.M. EDT) Full Moon.
25 Comet Whipple makes its closest approach to sun in its 8.5-year orbit.

JULY 1986
10 (9 P.M. EDT) Venus 1°.1 North of Regulus.
10–Dec. 31 Mars seen as evening star.
16 (7 A.M. EDT) Mars closest approach to Earth.
18 (midnight EDT) Occultation of Antares: 1°.0 South of Moon.
21 (6:40 A.M. EDT) Full Moon.
25 (2 A.M. EDT) Jupiter 1°.5 North of Moon.
27–28 Delta Aquarids meteor shower at maximum: About 35 per hour seem to radiate from constellation Aquarius.

AUGUST 1986
4 (2 A.M. EDT) Mercury 8° South of Moon.
12 Perseid meteor shower at maximum: About 70 per hour seem to radiate from constellation Perseus.
13 (10 P.M. EDT) Saturn 5° North of Moon.
14 (11 P.M. EDT) Uranus 4° North of Moon.
15 (11 P.M. EDT) Neptune 6° North of Moon.
19 (2:54 P.M. EDT) Full Moon.

SEPTEMBER 1986
10 (5 A.M. EDT) Saturn 5° North of Moon.
10–Dec. 31 Jupiter seen as evening star.
11 (5 A.M. EDT) Uranus 4° North of Moon.
12 (4 A.M. EDT) Neptune 6° North of Moon.
13 (6 A.M. EDT) Occultation of Mars: Mars 0°.9 North of Moon.

18 (1:34 A.M. EDT) Full Moon.
23 Autumn equinox: Autumn begins at 3:59 a.m. EDT.
29 (4 A.M. EDT) Mercury 1°.5 North of Spica.

OCTOBER 1986
1 (6 A.M. EDT) Venus at greatest brilliancy.
1 Comet Wild 1 makes its closest approach to Sun in its 13.3-year orbit.
3 Annular total Eclipse of the Sun: Visible over most of North America; total eclipse begins at 2:57 p.m. EDT and ends at 3:15 p.m. EDT.
5 (3 A.M. EDT) Occultation of Mercury: Mercury 0°.4 South of Moon.
6 (6 A.M. EDT) Venus 4° South of Moon.
7 (7 P.M. EDT) Occultation of Antares: Antares 0°.6 South of Moon.
17 (3:22 P.M. EDT) Full Moon.
17 Total Eclipse of the Moon: Not visible in the United States
20–21 Orionid meteor shower at maximum: About 30 per hour seem to radiate from constellation Orion.
26 (2:00 A.M. EDT) Daylight-saving time ends: Set clocks back 1 hour.

NOVEMBER 1986
4 (2 A.M. EST) Saturn 6° North of Moon.
4 (2 A.M. EST) Occultation of Antares: Antares 0°.6 South of Moon.
4 (8 P.M. EST) Uranus 4° North of Moon.
5 (5 P.M. EST) Neptune 6° North of Moon.
8 (7 P.M. EST) Mars 3° North of Moon.
12– Dec. 31 Venus seen as morning star.
16 (7:12 A.M. EST) Full Moon.
16–17 Leonid meteor shower at maximum: About 10 per hour seem to radiate from constellation Leo.
29 (6 A.M. EST) Venus 2° North of Moon.
30 (4 A.M. EST) Mercury 5° North of Moon.

DECEMBER 1986
3 (3 A.M. EST) Neptune 6° North of Moon.
7 (11 P.M. EST) Jupiter 1°.8 North of Moon.
11 Venus seen at greatest brilliance.
13–14 Geminid meteor shower at maximum: about 55 per hour seem to radiate from constellation Gemini.
15 (8 P.M. EST) Mercury 5° North of Antares.
16 (2:04 A.M. EST) Full Moon.
19 (2 A.M. EST) Mars 0°.5 North of Jupiter.
21 Winter solstice: Winter begins at 11:02 p.m. EST.
21–22 Ursid meteor shower at maximum: About 10 per hour seem to radiate from vicinity of North Star.
22–31 Saturn seen as morning star.
27 (8 P.M. EST) Venus 7° North of Moon.
29 (midnight EST) Occulation of Antares: Antares 0°.6 South of Moon.

COLLISIONS FORMED PLANETS

Dr. George W. Wetherill, director of the department of terrestrial magnetism, reported in *Science* in May that immense collisions with other planet-like objects may have formed the Earth, Venus, Mercury, and Mars.

He said his research, including a computer simulation of the events, shows that once there were as many as 500 objects about the size of the Moon in close orbit around the sun. As these objects collided with each other over a period of about 100 million years, they melted each other and gradually formed larger and larger planets.

PLANET OR BROWN STAR?

Astronomers debated in 1985 what to call an object found orbiting a distant star. Some said it is the first planet discovered outside our own solar system. Others believed it should be called a brown dwarf star.

The object, which is somewhat smaller than the planet Jupiter, has been named Van Biesbroeck 8B after the star Van Biesbroeck 8 that it orbits.

It was discovered by a team of astronomers headed by Donald McCarthy Jr. of the University of Arizona. The object was located using infrared telescopes that measure the heat given off by distant objects.

Astronomers who described the object as a planet did so largely because of its size. Those who preferred calling it a brown dwarf star did so because the object is much hotter than any of the planets of our solar system.

ECLIPSES OF PLUTO

The first observed eclipse of the planet Pluto by its moon Charon was made by Dr. Edward Tedesco of NASA's Jet Propulsion Laboratory on Jan. 16, 1985. Additional eclipses were observed in February by astronomers at the University of Texas and the University of Hawaii.

The observations were the first visual evidence of the existence of Charon.

Such eclipses occur only for a 5-year span every 124 years as the planet takes nearly 248 years to make a single orbit around the sun.

QUALIFICATIONS FOR ASTRONAUTS

NASA announced in 1985 that it now will accept applications from would-be astronauts at any time, and that selections for new astronauts would be made each spring.

To qualify as a pilot-astronaut, the minimum requirements are: (1) a bachelor's degree from an accredited institution in engineering, physical science, biological science, or mathematics; (2) 1,000 hours pilot-in-command time in jet aircraft; (3) ability to pass a NASA Class I flight physical; and (4) height between 64 and 76 inches.

To qualify as a mission specialist astronaut, minimum qualifications are: (1) A bachelor's degree from an accredited institution in engineering, physical science, biological science, or mathematics; (2) degree must be supplemented by three years of related professional experience or an advanced degree; (3) ability to pass a NASA Class II flight physical; and (4) height between 60 and 76 inches.

FACTS ABOUT THE MOON

More has been learned about the Moon than any other of the Earth's neighbors in space because of the Apollo program that enabled men to walk on the Moon and bring back hundreds of pounds of rocks. Following are some of the important facts we now know about the Moon.

Age of the Moon: Over 4.6 billion years. Moon rocks brought back by the astronauts have been dated as old as 4.6 billion years.

Composition of the Moon: The content of rocks on the Moon is much different from that of the Earth. The Moon has only an estimated 8.5% iron, while the Earth is about 36% iron. The Moon has proportionately three times as much uranium as the Earth, but only about one-third the Earth's percentage of gold and only about half the proportion of potassium.

Diameter of the Moon: 2,160 miles, about the distance from San Francisco to Chicago.

Circumference of the Moon: 6,785 miles, about the distance from Chicago to Athens, Greece.

Surface area: 14,650,000 square miles, about four times the area of the United States.

Mass: 81,000 trillion tons.

Gravity: One-sixth that of the Earth. A man who weighs 180 pounds on Earth weighs only 30 pounds when on the surface of the Moon.

Sidereal month (period of Moon's revolution around Earth in relation to the stars): 27 days, 7 hours, 43 minutes, 11.5 seconds.

Synodic month (period of Moon's revolution around Earth in relation to Sun): 29 days, 12 hours, and 44 minutes.

Average speed traveling around the Earth: 2,287 miles an hour.

Distance from the Earth: *Closest,* 221,456 miles; *farthest,* 252,711 miles, *mean distance,* 238,875 miles.

Length of a day on the Moon: 14 Earth days.

Distance traveled in orbit each year: 1,500,000 miles.

Temperature at noon on the Moon: 243 ° F., hot enough to boil water.

Temperature at midnight on the Moon: –297 ° F., cold enough to freeze carbon dioxide into dry ice.

Escape velocity from the Moon: 1.5 miles per second, or about 5,400 miles an hour.

CALENDAR OF PHASES OF THE MOON: 1985-1986

Source: *Astronomical Phenomena*, U.S. Naval Observatory; all times are Eastern Standard Time (EST)

NEW MOON		FIRST QUARTER		FULL MOON		LAST QUARTER	
Day	Time	Day	Time	Day	Time	Day	Time
Nov. 12, 1985	9:20 A.M.	Nov. 19, 1985	4:04 A.M.	Nov. 27, 1985	7:42 A.M.	Dec. 5, 1985	4:01 A.M.
Dec. 11, 1985	7:54 P.M.	Dec. 18, 1985	8:58 P.M.	Dec. 27, 1985	2:30 A.M.	Jan. 3, 1986	2:47 P.M.
Jan. 10, 1986	7:22 A.M.	Jan. 17, 1986	5:13 P.M.	Jan. 25, 1986	7:31 P.M.	Feb. 1, 1986	11:41 P.M.
Feb. 8, 1986	7:55 P.M.	Feb. 16, 1986	2:55 P.M.	Feb. 24, 1986	10:02 A.M.	Mar. 3, 1986	7:17 A.M.
Mar. 10, 1986	9:52 A.M.	Mar. 18, 1986	11:39 A.M.	Mar. 25, 1986	10:02 P.M.	Apr. 1, 1986	2:30 P.M.
Apr. 9, 1986	1:08 A.M.	Apr. 17, 1986	5:35 A.M.	Apr. 24, 1986	7:46 A.M.	May 2, 1986	10:22 P.M.
May 8, 1986	5:10 P.M.	May 16, 1986	8:00 P.M.	May 23, 1986	3:45 P.M.	May 30, 1986	7:55 A.M.
Jun. 7, 1986	9:00 A.M.	Jun. 15, 1985	7:00 A.M.	Jun. 21, 1986	10:42 P.M.	Jun. 28, 1986	7:53 P.M.
Jul. 6, 1986	11:55 P.M.	Jul. 14, 1986	3:10 P.M.	Jul. 21, 1986	5:40 A.M.	Jul. 28, 1986	10:34 A.M.
Aug. 5, 1986	1:36 P.M.	Aug. 12, 1986	9:21 P.M.	Aug. 19, 1986	1:54 P.M.	Aug. 27, 1986	3:38 A.M.
Sep. 4, 1986	2:10 A.M.	Sep. 11, 1986	2:41 A.M.	Sep. 18, 1986	12:34 A.M.	Sep. 25, 1986	10:17 P.M.
Oct. 3, 1986	1:55 P.M.	Oct. 10, 1986	8:28 A.M.	Oct. 17, 1986	2:22 P.M.	Oct. 25, 1986	5:26 P.M.
Nov. 2, 1986	1:02 A.M.	Nov. 8, 1986	4:11 P.M.	Nov. 16, 1986	7:12 A.M.	Nov. 24, 1986	11:50 A.M.
Dec. 1, 1986	11.43 A.M.	Dec. 8, 1986	3:01 A.M.	Dec. 16, 1986	2:04 A.M.	Dec. 24, 1986	4:17 A.M.
Dec. 30, 1986	10:10 P.M.						

PHASES OF THE MOON

The Moon shines only by reflected light. Its phases, or apparent changes in shape, result from the varying part of the sunlit hemisphere of the Moon visible to observers on Earth. Its lighted portion varies in shape because of the relative positions of the Moon, the Sun, and the Earth.

At New Moon, when the Moon is on the line between the Sun and the Earth, eclipses of the Sun by the Moon may occur if the Moon is properly positioned.

The Moon moves on in its orbit of the Earth from west to east. It passes through its waxing Crescent phase into First Quarter when it is at Half Moon.

Through the waxing Gibbous phase, it comes then to Full Moon, on the opposite side of the Earth from the Sun, when the Earth's shadow may be cast across the Moon in lunar eclipses.

The Moon moves on through waning Gibbous into Last Quarter. It then passes through the waning Crescent phase into New Moon again.

Occasionally the unlit portion of the Moon facing the Earth glows in "earthshine" (sunlight reflected from the Earth to the Moon and back again). Certain parts of the Moon, such as the bright crater Aristarchus, are especially reflective.

The worst storms have been found to be significantly related to lunar phases. Such storms seem more likely to occur, in the long run, from 1 to 3 days after New Moon and from 3 to 5 days after Full Moon. Similar relationships between storms and the phases of the Moon have been reported in many parts of the world.

The magnetic disturbances that sometimes disrupt radio communications, and the beginning of hurricanes in the Caribbean, have been found to be similarly related to lunar positions. The way in which these effects are produced is still a mystery.

SUNRISE AND SUNSET CALENDAR: 1985-1986

Tables on the following pages enable you to find the times for sunrise and sunset. Suggestions for using the tables follow.

CONVERTING TIME TO A.M. AND P.M.

The times used in the table are based on a 24-hour clock. The time 0 00 is midnight and 12 00 is noon. The times from 0 01 to 11 59 are morning or A.M., and the times from 12 01 to 23 59 are afternoon and evening or P.M.

To convert the times shown to those commonly used with a 12-hour clock, subtract 12 hours from all times from 13 00 to 23 59. Thus 14 12 would be the same as 2:12 P.M., or 20 23 would be 8:23 P.M.

LATITUDE AND LONGITUDE

To use the table to find the time of sunrise or sunset, you need to know the latitude and longitude of the place where you live.

The latitude and longitude of more than 300 cities are listed on pages 136–138. Use the latitude and longitude of your nearest city listed.

The table shows the time of events in northern latitudes—those north of the equator. For your convenience a state or city is named in each of the latitude columns. Thus 20 ° N. latitude passes

through the state of Hawaii; New Orleans is close to the line of 30 ° N. latitude; and so on.

CONVERT MEAN TIME TO REAL TIME

The times given in the table are for local *mean* time. This is the time on the standard time meridian that passes through your time zone. The standard time meridians (longitude) are Atlantic 60 °, Eastern 75 °, Central 90 °, Mountain 105 °, Pacific 120 °, and Alaska-Hawaii 150 °.

To convert mean time to real local time, find out the longitude of the place where you live. For each degree of longitude that your home is east of the standard time meridian, subtract 4 minutes from the mean time shown in the table. For each degree of longitude west, add 4 minutes.

For example, if you live at 78 ° longitude, you are 3 ° west of the Eastern Standard Time meridian (78 ° – 75 ° = 3 ° west). Therefore, add 12 minutes to the times shown (3 ° × 4 min. = 12 min.). Thus, for the place where you live a mean time 7 07 shown in the table actually should be changed to 7 19 (7 07 + 0 12 = 7 19).

INTERPOLATING TIME FOR YOUR LATITUDE

Because the times in the table are given for specif-

SUNRISE AND SUNSET (*continued*)

ic degrees of latitude and it is unlikely that your home lies exactly on one of these parallels, it is necessary also to correct the times by interpolating for your own latitude.

Suppose, for example, that your home has a latitude of 38°. This falls between the 35° and 40° columns shown in the table. The difference between 35° and 40° is 5° (40° − 35° = 5°),

and the difference between 35° and 38° is 3° (38° − 35° = 3°). To correct the times for your latitude, you would have to subtract 3/5 of the difference between the times shown for 35° and 40°. For example, in the sunrise table for May 6, the difference in time between 35° and 40° is 10 minutes (5 05 − 4 55 = 10 min.). Three-fifths of 10 minutes is 6 minutes (10 × 3/5 = 6). So you would subtract 6 minutes from the time shown for

SUNRISE AND SUNSET: 1985-1986
Source: U.S. Naval Observatory.

	TIME OF SUNRISE						TIME OF SUNSET					
DATE 1985	20° N. Latitude (Hawaii) h m	30° N. Latitude (New Orleans) h m	35° N. Latitude (Albuquerque) h m	40° N. Latitude (Philadelphia) h m	48° N. Latitude (Seattle) h m	60° N. Latitude (Alaska) h m	20° N. Latitude (Hawaii) h m	30° N. Latitude (New Orleans) h m	35° N. Latitude (Albuquerque) h m	40° N. Latitude (Philadelphia) h m	48° N. Latitude (Seattle) h m	60° N. Latitude (Alaska) h m
Nov. 2	6 02	6 15	6 22	6 30	6 46	7 24	17 25	17 12	17 05	16 57	16 40	16 02
Nov. 6	6 04	6 18	6 26	6 35	6 52	7 35	17 23	17 09	17 01	16 52	16 34	15 52
Nov. 10 ...	6 06	6 21	6 29	6 39	6 59	7 45	17 22	17 07	16 58	16 48	16 29	15 42
Nov. 14 ...	6 08	6 24	6 33	6 44	7 05	7 55	17 21	17 04	16 55	16 45	16 24	15 33
Nov. 18 ...	6 11	6 27	6 37	6 48	7 11	8 05	17 20	17 03	16 53	16 42	16 19	15 24
Nov. 22 ...	6 13	6 31	6 41	6 53	7 16	8 15	17 19	17 01	16 51	16 39	16 15	15 17
Nov. 26 ...	6 15	6 34	6 45	6 57	7 22	8 24	17 19	17 00	16 49	16 37	16 12	15 10
Nov. 30 ...	6 18	6 37	6 49	7 01	7 27	8 33	17 19	17 00	16 49	16 36	16 10	15 04
Dec. 4	6 20	6 40	6 52	7 05	7 32	8 41	17 20	17 00	16 48	16 35	16 08	14 59
Dec. 8	6 23	6 43	6 55	7 09	7 37	8 48	17 21	17 00	16 48	16 35	16 07	14 56
Dec. 12 ...	6 25	6 46	6 58	7 12	7 41	8 54	17 22	17 01	16 49	16 35	16 07	14 54
Dec. 16 ...	6 28	6 49	7 01	7 15	7 44	8 58	17 24	17 02	16 50	16 36	16 07	14 53
Dec. 20 ...	6 30	6 51	7 04	7 18	7 46	9 01	17 25	17 04	16 52	16 37	16 09	14 54
Dec. 24 ...	6 32	6 53	7 06	7 20	7 48	9 03	17 27	17 06	16 54	16 40	16 11	14 56
Dec. 28 ...	6 34	6 55	7 07	7 21	7 50	9 04	17 30	17 09	16 56	16 42	16 14	15 00
1986												
Jan. 2 ...	6 35	6 56	7 08	7 22	7 50	9 02	17 33	17 12	17 00	16 46	16 18	15 06
Jan. 6 ...	6 37	6 57	7 09	7 22	7 49	8 59	17 35	17 15	17 03	16 50	16 22	15 13
Jan. 10 ...	6 37	6 57	7 09	7 22	7 48	8 55	17 38	17 18	17 07	16 54	16 27	15 20
Jan. 14 ...	6 38	6 57	7 08	7 21	7 46	8 50	17 40	17 21	17 10	16 58	16 33	15 29
Jan. 18 ...	6 38	6 56	7 07	7 19	7 43	8 43	17 43	17 25	17 14	17 02	16 38	15 38
Jan. 22 ...	6 38	6 55	7 05	7 17	7 40	8 36	17 46	17 28	17 18	17 07	16 44	15 48
Jan. 26 ...	6 37	6 54	7 03	7 14	7 36	8 28	17 48	17 32	17 22	17 12	16 50	15 58
Jan. 30 ...	6 36	6 52	7 01	7 11	7 31	8 19	17 51	17 35	17 26	17 16	16 56	16 08
Feb. 3 ...	6 35	6 49	6 58	7 07	7 26	8 10	17 53	17 39	17 30	17 21	17 03	16 19
Feb. 7 ...	6 33	6 47	6 54	7 03	7 20	8 00	17 55	17 42	17 34	17 26	17 09	16 29
Feb. 11 ...	6 32	6 44	6 51	6 58	7 14	7 50	17 57	17 45	17 38	17 31	17 16	16 40
Feb. 15 ...	6 29	6 40	6 46	6 53	7 07	7 39	17 59	57 48	17 42	17 35	17 22	16 50
Feb. 19 ...	6 27	6 37	6 42	6 48	7 00	7 28	18 01	17 52	17 46	17 40	17 28	17 01
Feb. 23 ...	6 24	6 33	6 37	6 43	6 53	7 17	18 03	17 55	17 50	17 45	17 35	17 11
Feb. 27 ...	6 22	6 29	6 33	6 37	6 46	7 05	18 04	17 57	17 54	17 49	17 41	17 21
Mar. 3 ...	6 19	6 24	6 27	6 31	6 38	6 54	18 06	18 00	17 57	17 54	17 47	17 32
Mar. 7 ...	6 15	6 20	6 22	6 25	6 30	6 42	18 07	18 03	18 01	17 58	17 53	17 42
Mar. 11 ...	6 12	6 15	6 17	6 19	6 22	6 30	18 08	18 06	18 04	18 02	17 59	17 52
Mar. 15 ...	6 09	6 10	6 11	6 12	6 14	6 18	18 10	18 08	18 07	18 06	18 05	18 01
Mar. 19 ...	6 05	6 06	6 06	6 06	6 06	6 06	18 11	18 11	18 11	18 11	18 11	18 11
Mar. 23 ...	6 02	6 01	6 00	5 59	5 58	5 54	18 12	18 13	18 14	18 15	18 17	18 21
Mar. 27 ...	5 58	5 56	5 54	5 53	5 49	5 42	18 13	18 15	18 17	18 19	18 22	18 31
Mar. 31 ...	5 55	5 51	5 49	5 46	5 41	5 29	18 14	18 18	18 20	18 23	18 28	18 41
Apr. 4 ...	5 51	5 46	5 43	5 40	5 33	5 17	18 15	18 20	18 23	18 27	18 34	18 50
Apr. 8 ...	5 48	5 42	5 38	5 34	5 25	5 05	18 16	18 23	18 27	18 31	18 40	19 00
Apr. 12 ...	5 45	5 37	5 33	5 27	5 17	4 53	18 17	18 25	18 30	18 35	18 45	19 10
Apr. 16 ...	5 42	5 33	5 27	5 21	5 10	4 42	18 18	18 28	18 33	18 39	18 51	19 20
Apr. 20 ...	5 39	5 28	5 22	5 15	5 02	4 30	18 20	18 30	18 36	18 43	18 57	19 30
Apr. 24 ...	5 36	5 24	5 17	5 10	4 55	4 18	18 21	18 33	18 39	18 47	19 03	19 40
Apr. 28 ...	5 33	5 20	5 13	5 04	4 48	4 07	18 22	18 35	18 43	18 51	19 08	19 50
May 2 ...	5 30	5 17	5 09	4 59	4 41	3 56	18 24	18 38	18 46	18 55	19 14	19 59
May 6 ...	5 28	5 13	5 05	4 55	4 35	3 46	18 25	18 40	18 49	18 59	19 20	20 09
May 10 ...	5 26	5 10	5 01	4 50	4 29	3 35	18 27	18 43	18 52	19 03	19 25	20 19
May 14 ...	5 24	5 07	4 58	4 46	4 23	3 25	18 28	18 46	18 56	19 07	19 30	20 29
May 18 ...	5 23	5 05	4 55	4 42	4 18	3 16	18 30	18 48	18 59	19 11	19 35	20 38
May 22 ...	5 22	5 03	4 52	4 39	4 14	3 08	18 32	18 51	19 02	19 14	19 40	20 47
May 26 ...	5 21	5 01	4 50	4 37	4 10	3 00	18 33	18 53	19 04	19 18	19 45	20 56
May 30 ...	5 20	5 00	4 48	4 34	4 06	2 53	18 35	18 55	19 07	19 21	19 49	21 03

35° to obtain the local mean time for the place where you live (5 05 – 6 min.= 4 59). Note: If the time at the higher latitude is *later* (instead of earlier), you would *add* the difference (rather than subtract).

STANDARD AND DAYLIGHT TIMES

The times given in the sunrise and sunset table are for the local standard time zone where you live. During those periods of the year in which you use daylight time, add 1 hour to the time shown in a table to change it to daylight time.

CALCULATING SUNRISE AND SUNSET

Using the suggestions above, correct the times shown in the sunrise and sunset table:
(1) Interpolate them for your latitude.
(2) Convert them from mean time to real time (based on your longitude).
(3) If you are using daylight time, add 1 hour.

DATE 1986	\[TIME OF SUNRISE\] 20° N. Latitude (Hawaii)	30° N. Latitude (New Orleans)	35° N. Latitude (Albuquerque)	40° N. Latitude (Philadelphia)	48° N. Latitude (Seattle)	60° N. Latitude (Alaska)	\[TIME OF SUNSET\] 20° N. Latitude (Hawaii)	30° N. Latitude (New Orleans)	35° N. Latitude (Albuquerque)	40° N. Latitude (Philadelphia)	48° N. Latitude (Seattle)	60° N. Latitude (Alaska)
	h m	h m	h m	h m	h m	h m	h m	h m	h m	h m	h m	h m
June 3...	5 20	4 59	4 47	4 33	4 04	2 47	18 36	18 57	19 10	19 24	19 53	21 10
June 7...	5 20	4 58	4 46	4 31	4 02	2 42	18 38	18 59	19 12	19 26	19 56	21 16
June 11...	5 20	4 58	4 45	4 31	4 00	2 38	18 39	19 01	19 14	19 29	19 59	21 21
June 15...	5 20	4 58	4 45	4 30	4 00	2 36	18 40	19 02	19 15	19 30	20 01	21 25
June 19...	5 21	4 59	4 46	4 31	4 00	2 35	18 42	19 04	19 17	19 32	20 03	21 27
June 23...	5 22	5 00	4 47	4 32	4 01	2 36	18 42	19 04	19 17	19 33	20 03	21 28
June 27...	5 23	5 01	4 48	4 33	4 02	2 38	18 43	19 05	19 18	19 33	20 04	21 27
July 1...	5 24	5 02	4 49	4 35	4 04	2 42	18 43	19 05	19 18	19 33	20 03	21 25
July 5...	5 25	5 04	4 51	4 37	4 07	2 46	18 44	19 05	19 18	19 32	20 02	21 22
July 9...	5 27	5 06	4 53	4 39	4 10	2 52	18 43	19 04	19 17	19 31	20 00	21 17
July 13...	5 28	5 08	4 56	4 42	4 14	2 59	18 43	19 03	19 15	19 29	19 57	21 11
July 17...	5 30	5 10	4 58	4 45	4 18	3 07	18 42	19 02	19 14	19 27	19 54	21 04
July 21...	5 31	5 12	5 01	4 48	4 22	3 15	18 41	19 00	19 11	19 24	19 50	20 56
July 25...	5 33	5 14	5 04	4 52	4 27	3 24	18 40	18 58	19 09	19 21	19 45	20 48
July 29...	5 34	5 17	5 07	4 55	4 32	3 33	18 38	18 56	19 06	19 17	19 40	20 39
Aug. 2...	5 36	5 19	5 10	4 59	4 37	3 42	18 37	18 53	19 02	19 13	19 35	20 29
Aug. 6...	5 37	5 22	5 13	5 03	4 42	3 52	18 35	18 50	18 58	19 09	19 29	20 19
Aug. 10...	5 38	5 24	5 16	5 06	4 47	4 01	18 32	18 46	18 54	19 04	19 22	20 08
Aug. 14...	5 40	5 26	5 19	5 10	4 53	4 11	18 30	18 42	18 50	18 59	19 16	19 57
Aug. 18...	5 41	5 29	5 22	5 14	4 58	4 20	18 27	18 38	18 45	18 53	19 09	19 46
Aug. 22...	5 42	5 31	5 25	5 18	5 04	4 30	18 24	18 34	18 40	18 47	19 01	19 34
Aug. 26...	5 43	5 34	5 28	5 22	5 09	4 40	18 21	18 30	18 35	18 41	18 54	19 22
Aug. 30...	5 44	5 36	5 31	5 25	5 15	4 49	18 17	18 25	18 30	18 35	18 46	19 11
Sept. 3...	5 45	5 38	5 34	5 29	5 20	4 59	18 14	18 21	18 24	18 29	18 38	18 59
Sept. 7...	5 46	5 40	5 37	5 33	5 26	5 08	18 10	18 16	18 19	18 23	18 30	18 47
Sept. 11...	5 46	5 42	5 40	5 37	5 31	5 17	18 07	18 11	18 13	18 16	18 22	18 34
Sept. 15...	5 47	5 44	5 43	5 40	5 36	5 27	18 03	18 06	18 08	18 09	18 13	18 22
Sept. 19...	5 48	5 46	5 45	5 44	5 42	5 36	17 59	18 01	18 02	18 03	18 05	18 10
Sept. 23...	5 49	5 49	5 48	5 48	5 47	5 46	17 56	17 56	17 56	17 56	17 57	17 58
Sept. 27...	5 50	5 51	5 51	5 52	5 53	5 55	17 52	17 51	17 50	17 50	17 48	17 46
Oct. 1...	5 51	5 53	5 54	5 56	5 59	6 05	17 48	17 46	17 45	17 43	17 40	17 34
Oct. 5...	5 52	5 55	5 57	6 00	6 04	6 14	17 45	17 41	17 39	17 37	17 32	17 22
Oct. 9...	5 53	5 58	6 01	6 04	6 10	6 24	17 42	17 36	17 34	17 30	17 24	17 10
Oct. 13...	5 54	6 00	6 04	6 08	6 16	6 34	17 38	17 32	17 28	17 24	17 16	16 58
Oct. 17...	5 55	6 03	6 07	6 12	6 22	6 43	17 35	17 28	17 23	17 18	17 08	16 46
Oct. 21...	5 57	6 06	6 11	6 16	6 28	6 53	17 32	17 23	17 18	17 12	17 01	16 35
Oct. 25...	5 58	6 08	6 14	6 21	6 34	7 03	17 30	17 19	17 14	17 07	16 54	16 24
Oct. 29...	6 00	6 11	6 18	6 25	6 40	7 14	17 27	17 16	17 09	17 02	16 47	16 13
Nov. 2...	6 02	6 14	6 22	6 30	6 46	7 24	17 25	17 12	17 05	16 57	16 41	16 02
Nov. 6...	6 04	6 17	6 25	6 34	6 52	7 34	17 23	17 09	17 02	16 52	16 35	15 52
Nov. 10...	6 06	6 21	6 29	6 39	6 58	7 44	17 22	17 07	16 58	16 48	16 29	15 43
Nov. 14...	6 08	6 24	6 33	6 44	7 04	7 55	17 21	17 05	16 55	16 45	16 24	15 33
Nov. 18...	6 10	6 27	6 37	6 48	7 10	8 05	17 20	17 03	16 53	16 42	16 20	15 25
Nov. 22...	6 13	6 31	6 41	6 53	7 16	8 14	17 19	17 01	16 51	16 39	16 16	15 17
Nov. 26...	6 15	6 34	6 45	6 57	7 22	8 24	17 19	17 00	16 50	16 37	16 12	15 10
Nov. 30...	6 18	6 37	6 48	7 01	7 27	8 32	17 19	17 00	16 49	16 36	16 10	15 04
Dec. 4...	6 20	6 40	6 52	7 05	7 32	8 40	17 20	17 00	16 48	16 35	16 08	15 00
Dec. 8...	6 23	6 43	6 55	7 09	7 36	8 47	17 21	17 00	16 48	16 35	16 07	14 56
Dec. 12...	6 25	6 46	6 58	7 12	7 40	8 53	17 22	17 01	16 49	16 35	16 07	14 54
Dec. 16...	6 28	6 49	7 01	7 15	7 44	8 58	17 23	17 02	16 50	16 36	16 07	14 53
Dec. 20...	6 30	6 51	7 03	7 18	7 46	9 01	17 25	17 04	16 52	16 37	16 09	14 54
Dec. 24...	6 32	6 53	7 05	7 20	7 48	9 03	17 27	17 06	16 54	16 39	16 11	14 54
Dec. 28...	6 34	6 55	7 07	7 21	7 50	9 04	17 29	17 08	16 56	16 42	16 14	14 59

(FURTHER THAN NEPTUNE, JUNE 13, 1983)

SATURN

JUPITER

URANUS

NEPTUNE

SUN

PIONEER 10 (FURTHER THAN PLUTO, APRIL 25, 1983)

PLUTO

The spacecraft *Pioneer 10* became the first man-made object to leave the solar system on June 13, 1983. The spacecraft took more than 11 years since its launch on March 2, 1972, to travel 2.8 million miles to the outer limit. Scientists said they believe *Pioneer 10* will continue speeding through space for billions of years—long after mankind and the Earth itself have ceased to exist. They saw little chance it would strike another object.

EXPLORING THE SOLAR SYSTEM

The solar system includes the Sun and all the celestial objects that orbit it—planets, asteroids, meteors, comets, dust, gas, and man-made satellites. The nine planets in order of distance from the Sun are Mercury, Venus, Earth, Mars, Jupiter, Saturn, Uranus, Neptune, and Pluto.

Since the advent of the Space Age, space probes have been sent to the Sun and the planets, greatly expanding knowledge about man's neighbors in space.

THE SUN

One of the many stars in the Milky Way galaxy, the Sun has a surface temperature

FACTS ABOUT THE SUN

Distance from Earth: Closest, 91.4 million miles; farthest, 94.5 million miles; average, 92.9 million miles.

Diameter: About 864,000 miles, or more than 109 times the width of Earth.

Source of life on Earth: All life on Earth depends on heat and light from the Sun. Sunlight travels at the speed of light, reaching Earth about 8 minutes and 20 seconds after being radiated from the Sun.

Speed: The Sun travels around the center of the Milky Way at about 150 miles per second, taking 225 million years to make one orbit around the galaxy.

Rotation: The Sun revolves on its axis from west to east, like Earth. It makes a complete revolution in about 30 days. Because the Sun is a ball of gases, its equator rotates faster than its polar regions.

Age: About 4.6 billion years. This means that in the lifetime of the Sun, it has only revolved around the center of the Milky Way galaxy 20 times. Thus, if we consider that one revolution is the equivalent of one year in the Sun's life, the Sun would be only 20 years old.

of about 11,000 ° F. The main form of energy radiating from this sphere of seething gas is light. Other radiations include gamma rays, X rays, infrared rays, cosmic rays, and radio waves. The Sun also sprays out what is known as the *solar wind,* a continuous flow of charged particles, protons and electrons.

The Sun is essentially a huge ball of hydrogen. In its interior, where temperatures approach 25,000,000 ° F., this element is converted into helium, releasing immense quantities of energy.

The Sun has polar caps, as have Earth and Mars. However, with a temperature of about 1,800,000 ° F., the caps are not frozen ice.

The atmosphere of the Sun consists of several layers of gases. The layer next to the surface, about 10,000 miles thick, is called the *chromosphere.* Enveloping this layer are the inner and outer *coronas.* You can see the corona during a total solar eclipse.

A giant ring of microscopic dust that is 600,000 miles wide encircles the Sun at a distance of 900,000 miles from the surface.

A ring of gas and dust also is believed to encircle the entire solar system at a distance of 9.3 billion miles from the Sun.

Sunspots are dark, turbulent regions often seen within larger, brighter areas known as *flocculi* on the surface of the Sun. The presence of a sunspot is frequently accompanied by a surge of energy called a *solar flare.* They often disrupt radio communications.

MERCURY

Mercury is the planet nearest the Sun. It is also the smallest and fastest.

Because Mercury orbits between Earth and the Sun, it is seen in phases like those of the Moon. Its eccentric orbit makes it appear largest when in the crescent phases and much smaller when it is full. It has many craters, like those of the Moon and Mars.

A very hot planet, Mercury has an atmosphere made up largely of the gas helium.

VENUS

Venus is the planet closest to Earth. After the Sun and Moon, it is the brightest object in our view.

The diameter of Venus is only about 400 miles less than that of the Earth.

Venus revolves about the Sun in a nearly circular orbit at a distance of 67,200,000 miles. When Venus is closest to Earth, it is about 26,000,000 miles away.

The U.S. and the Soviet Union have sent

NATURAL SATELLITES OF THE PLANETS

PLANETS AND SATELLITES [1]	AVERAGE DISTANCE FROM PLANET (in miles)	DIAMETER (in miles)	PERIOD OF REVOLUTION AROUND PLANET days hrs. mins.			APPARENT MAGNITUDE	DISCOVERER AND DATE
EARTH							
Moon	238,866	2,057.6	27	7	43	-12.7	—
MARS							
Phobos	5,825	5	0	57	39	11.5	Asaph Hall, 1877
Deimos	14,580	3	1	6	18	12.5	Asaph Hall, 1877
JUPITER							
XVI Metis	79,500	25	0	7	4	—	Stephen P. Synnott, 1980
XV Adresta	79,500	19–25	0	7	8	—	Voyager 1, 1979
V Amalthea	112,779	149	0	11	57	13.0	Edward Barnard, 1892
XIV Thebe	137,000	43–50	0	16	16	—	Stephen P. Synnott, 1980
I Io	262,219	2,256	1	18	28	5.5	Galileo, 1610
II Europa	417,189	1,942	3	13	14	5.8	Galileo, 1610
III Ganymede	665,489	3,278	7	3	43	5.1	Galileo, 1610
IV Callisto.......	1,170,663	2,994	16	16	32	6.3	Galileo. 1610
XIII Leda	6,893,492	4	239	—	—	20.0	Charles Kowal, 1974
VI Himalia	7,137,691	106	251	—	—	14.0	Charles Perrine, 1904
VII Elara	7,299,247	50	260	—	—	18.0	Charles Perrine, 1905
X Lysithea	7,370,084	9	264	—	—	19.0	Seth Nicholson, 1938
XII Ananke (R)...	13,204,137	3.7–17	631	—	—	19.0	Seth Nicholson, 1951
XI Carme (R) ...	14,005,706	5–25	692	—	—	19.0	Seth Nicholson, 1938
VIII Pasiphae (R) .	14,608,436	5–28.5	739	—	—	18.5	P.J. Melotte, 1908
IX Sinope (R)	14,707,856	3.7–22	758	—	—	19.0	Seth Nicholson, 1914
SATURN [2]							
XIV 1980 S27 ..	85,540	19	0	14	20	—	Voyager 1, 1980
XIII 1980 S26 ...	86,590	136	0	14	43	—	Voyager 1, 1980
XV Atlas	88,050	120	0	14	20	—	Voyager 1, 1980
XI 1980 S3	94,089	55x25	0	14	43	—	Pioneer 11, 1980
X 1980 S1	94,120	60x55	0	15	5	—	Voyager 1, 1980
I Mimas	115,300	242	0	22	37	12.1	Sir William Herschel, 1789
II Enceladus	147,900	310	1	8	53	11.8	Sir William Herschel, 1789
III Tethys	183,100	652	1	21	18	10.3	Giovanni Cassini, 1684
XVII 1980 S25 ..	183,100	19–25	1	21	18	—	Univ. of Arizona, 1980
XVI 1980 S13 ..	183,100	19–25	1	21	18	—	French astronomers, 1980
XII 1980 S6	234,920	100	2	17	44	—	Voyager 1, 1980
IV Dione	234,600	696	2	17	44	10.4	Giovanni Cassini, 1684
V Rhea	327,600	951	4	12	25	9.8	Giovanni Cassini, 1672
VI Titan	759,100	3,194	15	23	20	8.4	Christian Huygens, 1655
VII Hyperion.....	921,100	180	21	7	40	14.2	G.P. & W.C. Bond, 1848
VIII Iapetus......	2,212,100	895	79	22	6	11.0	Giovanni Cassini, 1671
IX Phoebe (R) ...	8,047,000	136	550	10	50	16.5	William Pickering, 1898
URANUS							
V Miranda	80,700	124	1	9	56	16.9	Gerard Kuiper, 1948
I Ariel	119,100	826	2	12	29	14.0	William Lassell, 1851
II Umbriel	165,900	690	4	3	28	15.0	William Lassell, 1851
III Titania	272,100	994	8	16	56	13.8	Sir William Herschel, 1787
IV Oberon.......	363,900	1,013	13	11	7	14.0	Sir William Herschel, 1787
NEPTUNE							
Triton (R)	219,500	1,988	5	21	3	13.6	William Lassell, 1846
Nereid	3,461,000	200?	359	10	—	19.7	Gerard Kuiper, 1949
PLUTO							
Charon	11,800	1,250	6	9	17	17.0	James W. Christy, 1978

[1] An (R) following a satellite's name indicates it revolves retrograde to planet's rotation. [2] Four to six additional small moons of Saturn were discovered in 1982.

EXPLORING THE SOLAR SYSTEM *(continued)*

many unmanned spaceships to explore the planet, whose surface is obscured from view by a heavy cloud layer. Using radar to penetrate the clouds, the spaceships have discovered that the surface is much more rugged than that of Earth, with higher mountains and deeper canyons.

Incapable of supporting life as known on Earth, Venus has a surface temperature of 869 ° F. that seems to be evenly distributed in all regions. Huge thunderstorms apparently rage continually.

Although the clouds have winds of 100 to 200 mph, winds at the surface of the planet were measured at only 10 mph.

Sulfur gases in the planet's atmosphere seem to burn and glow continuously from the intense heat, turning the sky orange.

MARS

Mars is half again as far from the Sun as is Earth, and thus is colder. Its summer noon temperature reaches only about 80 ° F. at its equator.

The planet takes 1.88 years to orbit the Sun, so its seasons are about twice as long as those on Earth. It is inclined 24 ° to its orbit, nearly the same as is Earth.

A day on Mars is just slightly longer than Earth's—24 hours and 37 minutes. The planet, which is 4,218 miles in diameter, has about 11% of Earth's mass and is of lower density—an object of 100 pounds on Earth would weigh a mere 38 pounds on Mars.

Circling Mars are two small satellites, Phobos (*fear*) and Deimos (*panic*). Deimos orbits Mars once a day, but Phobos makes almost three daily revolutions.

Two U.S. *Viking* spacecraft landed on Mars in 1976, sending back the first photos and data from the surface of the planet.

The *Viking I* lander reported in July 1976 that the Martian atmosphere is composed of 95% carbon dioxide, 2% to 3% nitrogen, 1% to 2% argon-40, and 0.3% oxygen.

The planet's low atmospheric pressure prevents water from remaining on the surface, except as ice in the northern polar region.

There are regions of quite different geological character on Mars: vast valleys and "stream" channels, towering mountains, and some densely cratered Moon-like areas. The 1972 photo map of Mars, produced from *Mariner 9* data, revealed such remarkable features as Nix Olympica, a volcanic mountain 300 miles wide and $10\frac{1}{2}$ miles high. The photos also showed channels apparently once cut by rivers of water on the planet's surface.

Mars is best seen when opposite the Sun in the sky. Because of the motion of Mars and Earth about the Sun, this point at "opposition" occurs every two years and two months.

ASTEROIDS

About 20,000 to 30,000 asteroids, or minor planets, circle the Sun, mostly in orbits that lie between those of Mars and Jupiter. The first and largest asteroid, Ceres, was discovered on Jan. 1, 1801, by Italian astronomer Giuseppe Piazzi.

All the asteroids are smaller than the Moon. Diameters of the larger asteroids include: Ceres, 600 miles; Pallas, 350 miles; Vesta, 310 miles; Hygeia, 240 miles; Interamnia, 200 miles; and Davida, 170 miles.

Some scientists believe that asteroids and comets are pieces of a large planet that exploded about 6 million years ago.

JUPITER

The largest planet, Jupiter has a volume that would engulf 1,347 Earths. Its mass is twice that of the rest of the planets combined.

Scientists believe there is a possibility that some forms of life exist in Jupiter's atmosphere, which has zones of water vapor at temperatures comparable to those on Earth.

Jupiter rotates once in somewhat less than 10 hours. Because of this rapid rotation—fastest of all the planets—Jupiter is oblate, its poles are flattened, and its equator bulges. Jupiter has 16 moons. Ganymede, the larg-

PLANETS OF OUR SOLAR SYSTEM

PLANET	DIAMETER (in miles)	MASS (Earth = 1)	DENSITY (water = 1)	GRAVITY (Earth = 1)	ESCAPE VELOCITY (in miles per sec.)	INCLI-NATION OF AXIS	ALBEDO OR REFLEC-TIVITY	SPEED IN SOLAR ORBIT (in miles per sec.)
MERCURY	3,100	0.056	5.13	0.36	2.6	unknown	0.056	29.8
VENUS	7,519	0.815	5.26	0.87	6.4	6°	0.76	21.8
EARTH	7,926	1.00	5.52	1.00	7.0	23°27'	0.36	18.5
MARS	4,218	0.108	3.94	0.38	3.1	24°	0.16	15.0
JUPITER	88,732	317.9	1.33	2.61	37.9	3°1'	0.73	8.1
SATURN	74,316	95.2	0.69	0.90	23.0	26°7'	0.76	6.0
URANUS	29,200	14.6	1.56	1.07	13.7	97°9'	0.93	4.2
NEPTUNE	27,700	17.3	2.27	1.41	15.5	28°8'	0.84	3.4
PLUTO	1,900	0.06 ?	4.00 ?	0.3 ?	unknown	unknown	0.14 ?	3.0

PLANETARY EXPLORATION BY U.S. SPACECRAFT

PLANET	DISTANCE [1]	SPACECRAFT	ENCOUNTER
Venus	26,000,000	Mariner 2	Flyby: Dec. 14, 1962; returns surface temperature measurements
		Mariner 5	Flyby: Oct. 19, 1967; closes within 2,480 miles of planet
		Mariner 10	Flybys: March 29, 1974; Sept. 21, 1974; March 16, 1975
		Pioneer Venus 1	Eight-month orbiting of planet, beginning Dec. 5, 1978
		Pioneer Venus 2	Five probes sent into Venus' atmosphere on Dec. 9, 1978
Mars	35,000,000	Mariner 4	Flyby: July 14, 1965; sends first close photos from 6,118 miles
		Mariner 6	Flyby: July 31, 1969
		Mariner 7	Flyby: Aug. 5, 1969
		Mariner 9	Orbited Mars from Nov. 13, 1971, to Oct. 27, 1972
		Viking 1	Lander 1 touched down on planet's surface on July 20, 1976; sends first photos from surface of Mars
		Viking 2	Lander 2 touched down on Sept. 3, 1976; analysis of soil samples failed to prove or disprove existence of microbial life
Mercury	48,000,000	Mariner 10	Flybys: March 29, 1974; Sept. 21, 1974; March 16, 1975
Jupiter	366,000,000	Pioneer 10	Flyby: Dec. 4, 1973
		Pioneer 11	Flyby: Dec. 5, 1974
		Voyager 1	Flyby: March 5, 1979; discovered ring around planet and 3 new moons
		Voyager 2	Flyby: July 9, 1979
		Galileo	Planned probe in 1989
Saturn	743,000,000	Pioneer 11	Flyby: Sept. 1, 1979; discovered new 11th moon and new rings
		Voyager 1	Flyby: Nov. 12, 1980; discovered new moons and many rings
		Voyager 2	Flyby: Aug. 25, 1981
Uranus	1,606,000,000	Voyager 2	Flyby: scheduled Jan. 24, 1986

[1] Minimum distance from Earth in miles.

est, is bigger than Mercury.

Approaching Jupiter from space, an observer would see a huge yellowish globe striped with multicolored dark and light bands—all in a kind of mottled motion that reveals a turbulent cloud layer.

The planet also is surrounded by a thin ring of rock and dust particles.

The smooth surface of the planet is a gigantic sea of compressed hydrogen and helium. Jupiter has a central rocky core surrounded by liquid metallic hydrogen at a temperature of 54,000° F., about six times the heat of the surface of the Sun. Because of its internal heat, Jupiter gives off more heat than it receives from the Sun.

Clouds of methane, ammonia, water, and other compounds float in bands around the planet, whipped along by winds of 200 mph.

Hydrogen makes up more than 76% of Jupiter's mass. Helium is about 22%.

Photos sent back by space probes indicate Jupiter's Great Red Spot—an oval about 30,000 miles long and 7,000 miles wide—is a huge hurricane-like storm.

SATURN

Over 700,000,000 miles from Earth, Saturn is yellowish overall and has atmospheric bands across its face. It is girdled by many glittering rings in the plane of its equator. These rings extend about 286,000 miles from the planet.

Most experts think the rings are probably bits of ice-covered rock, between dust and gravel in size—or perhaps chunks of water ice itself. The rings are incredibly thin for their span and are so tenuous that stars can be seen through them. Their thickness is at most a few thousand feet.

Saturn, second-largest planet in the solar system, is so gaseous that it is also the least dense. If there were a celestial sea of water to dunk it in, it would float.

PERIOD OF ROTATION				PERIOD OF REVOLUTION (in Earth days)	UNIT SOLAR RADIATION AVAILABLE (Earth=1)	AVERAGE DISTANCE FROM SUN (in million miles)	MINIMUM DISTANCE FROM EARTH (in million miles)	AVERAGE TRAVEL TIME FROM EARTH	PLANET
days	hrs.	min.	sec.						
58.65	—	—	—	88 days	6.7	36.0	48	115 days	MERCURY
243.10	—	—	—	116.8 days	1.9	67.2	26	146 days	VENUS
—	23	56	4	365.26 days	1.00	92.9	—	—	EARTH
—	24	37	23	687 days	0.43	141.5	35	237 days	MARS
—	9	55	33	11.86 years	0.04	483.4	366	2.6 years	JUPITER
—	10	39	26	29.46 years	0.01	886.0	743	5.6 years	SATURN
—	12	18	—	84.01 years	0.0031	1,782.0	1,606	15 years	URANUS
—	18	12	—	164.8 years	0.001	2,792.0	2,678	30 years	NEPTUNE
6.387	—	—	—	247.7 years	0.0006	3,675.0	2,650	30 years	PLUTO

EXPLORING THE SOLAR SYSTEM (continued)

The planet has possibly as many as 23 moons. The largest of these moons—Titan, with a diameter of 3,194 miles—has an atmosphere, largely of nitrogen. Its surface is concealed by clouds. Its surface temperature is believed to be about −288° F.

URANUS

The pale green planet Uranus orbits 1.79 billion miles from the Sun. About 29,200 miles in diameter, Uranus has its axis inclined 8° from the orbital plane. An observer living at one of the poles would see a "midnight Sun" for about 42 years and live in darkness the next 42 years.

Uranus has nine rings encircling it, like those of Saturn but smaller.

Uranus has 5 moons. Like the other giant planets, it is rich in light elements, especially hydrogen and helium. But it is denser than Jupiter and Saturn.

NEPTUNE

The bluish green hue of Neptune, a near twin of Uranus, stems from the methane in its atmosphere. Astronomers discovered two faint rings around the planet in 1982. It has two moons. One, Triton, is remarkably similar to Earth's moon. At 2.8 billion miles from the Sun, a spacecraft orbiting Neptune would chill to −370° F. if it were not heated. Since Neptune's discovery in 1846, it has made less than three-quarters of one revolution of the Sun.

PLUTO

At 3.7 billion miles from the Sun, Pluto is cold and dark. Its diameter is only about one-third that of the Earth. Pluto is made up of frozen methane and water.

Its orbit about the Sun departs by 17° from the plane of the other planets' orbits.

Charon, a moon circling around Pluto, was discovered on June 22, 1978, by U.S. astronomer James W. Christy.

HIGHLIGHTS OF SPACE EXPLORATION

The Space Age was inaugurated by the Soviet Union on Oct. 4, 1957, when it launched *Sputnik I*, the first man-made satellite to orbit Earth.

Four months later, on Jan. 31, 1958, the United States launched *Explorer I* as part of the first U.S. satellite program, Project Vanguard, initiated as part of the 1957–58 International Geophysical Year (IGY). *Vanguard I*, the project's second satellite, launched March 17, 1958, was the first with solar-powered batteries.

The U.S. space program had begun on Nov. 7, 1957, when President Eisenhower created a Scientific Advisory Committee, headed by Massachusetts Institute of Technology president, Dr. James R. Killian. In March 1958 the Killian Committee recommended creation of a civilian space agency. Congress passed the National Aeronautics and Space Act of 1958.

Two months later, on October 1, the National Aeronautics and Space Administration (NASA) was born. Its nucleus was the National Advisory Committee for Aeronautics (NACA), which for 43 years had been active in U.S. aeronautical research.

President John F. Kennedy said in a historic address to Congress on May 25, 1961:

"I believe that this Nation should commit itself to achieving the goal, before this decade is out, of landing a man on the Moon and returning him safely to Earth."

This goal was achieved with man's first walk on the Moon in July 1969.

The NASA program has been marred by only one major tragedy. On Jan. 27, 1967, a fire erupted inside an *Apollo* spacecraft during ground testing, resulting in the death of three astronauts—Lt. Col. Virgil I. Grissom, USAF; Lt. Col. Edward H. White II, USAF; and Lt. Comdr. Roger B. Chaffee, USN.

1957 (Oct. 4) First man-made satellite: *Sputnik I* orbited by Soviet Union.

1958 (Jan. 31) First U.S. satellite successfully launched: *Explorer I* remains in orbit until March 31, 1970, circling Earth 58,408 times and traveling 2.67 billion miles.

1958 (Oct. 11) First NASA launch: *Pioneer I* reaches altitude of 70,717 miles. The 84-pound spacecraft had a life of only 43 hours.

1959 (Feb. 17) First weather satellite: *Vanguard II* is first satellite to send weather information back to Earth.

1959 (Aug. 2) First TV photo of Earth from space: Transmitted by Explorer 6 as it orbits Earth.

1959 (Sept. 12) First space probe to strike Moon: *Luna 2* launched by Soviet Union.

1959 (Oct. 4) First photos of far side of Moon: Soviet Unions *Luna 3* spacecraft accomplishes feat.

1960 (March 11) Interplanetary radiation measured: *Pioneer 5* launched to measure interstellar radiation en route to Venus.

1960 (April 1) First meteorological satellite: *Tiros I* begins series of 10 consecutive successful research missions, providing 22,952 cloud-cover photos.

1960 (Aug. 12) First passive communications satellite: 100-foot balloon, *Echo I*, inflated in orbit.

1961 (April 12) First manned orbital flight: Soviet Union sends Yuri A. Gagarin on 1 hr. 48-min. flight aboard *Vostok I* for one orbit around Earth.

1961 (May 5) First American in space: Astronaut Alan B. Shepard Jr. takes 14.8-min. suborbital flight aboard *Freedom 7*.

1961 (July 21) Second U.S. suborbital flight: Astronaut Virgil I. Grissom makes 15-min., 118-mile-high, 303-mile-long flight in *Liberty Bell 7*.

1961 (Aug. 6–7) First long-duration orbital flight: Soviet Union launches Gherman S. Titov into space aboard *Vostok II*; flight takes 25 hrs. 18 min.; includes 17.5 orbits.

1962 (Feb. 20) First American in orbit: Astronaut John H.

Glenn Jr. in *Friendship 7 (Mercury-Atlas 6)* flies 81,000 miles, orbiting Earth 3 times in 4 hrs. 55 min.

1962 (April 23) First U.S. probe to strike Moon: *Ranger IV* fails to televise pictures to Earth.

1962 (March 7) First scientific observatory spacecraft: *OSO 1* placed in orbit with 13 experiments to study Sun.

1962 (April 26) First international satellite: *Ariel-1* carries British experiments.

1962 (May 24) Second U.S. manned orbital flight: Astronaut M. Scott Carpenter pilots *Aurora 7* in 3 orbits of Earth; overshoots landing area by 250 miles.

1962 (July 10) First privately financed satellite: *Telstar I* carries out series of communication transmission tests, including TV, telephone, data, and photo facsimile.

1962 (Aug. 11) Third Soviet manned orbital flight: *Vostok III* carries cosmonaut Andrian G. Nikolayev on 64 orbits around Earth.

1962 (Aug. 12) Fourth Soviet manned orbital flight: *Vostok IV* carries cosmonaut Pavel R. Popovich on 48 orbits; comes within 3 miles of *Vostok III* on first orbit.

1962 (Oct. 3) Third U.S. manned orbital flight: Astronaut Walter M. Schirra Jr. makes nearly 6 orbits, traveling 160,000 miles in 9 hrs. 13 min. in *Sigma 7.*

1963 (May 15–16) Final flight of Mercury Project: Astronaut Gordon Cooper in *Faith 7* orbits Earth 22 times in 34 hrs. 20 min.

1963 (June 14) Fifth Soviet manned orbital flight: *Vostok V* carries cosmonaut Valery F. Bykovsky on 81 Earth orbits.

1963 (June 16) First woman in space: Valentina V. Tereshkova pilots Soviet craft, *Vostok VI,* on 48 Earth orbits.

1963 (July 26) First satellite communication between U.S. and Africa: *Syncom 2* communications satellite placed in stationary orbit over Brazil.

1964 (Jan. 25) First joint U.S.-Soviet Union space experiment: *Echo 2* passive communications satellite orbited.

1964 (July 20) First successful electric rocket engine tested in space: Used aboard U.S. *Sert I* spacecraft.

1964 (July 28–31) Spacecraft photographs Moon: *Ranger 7* sends back 4,316 clear photos before crashing into lunar surface.

1964 (Sept. 5) Orbiting Geophysical Observatory program: *OGO 1* placed in orbit for space experiments.

1964 (Oct. 12) First 3-man orbital flight: Soviet cosmonauts Konstantin Feoktistov, Vladimir Komarov, and Boris Yegorov fly 16 orbits in *Voshkod I.*

1964 (Nov. 28) First close photos of Mars: *Mariner 4* launched on 228-day, 325-million-mile flight to Mars, sending back first close photos of planet.

1965 (March 18) First space walk: Aleksei A. Leonov leaves *Voshkod II* spacecraft for 10 minutes; fellow cosmonaut Pavel I. Belyayev also aboard Soviet craft in 17 orbits.

1965 (March 23) First maneuvering of manned spacecraft in orbit: Second phase of U.S. manned space program begun with 3-orbit flight of *Gemini 3* by astronauts Virgil I. (Gus) Grissom and John W. Young.

1965 (April 6) First commercial communications satellite: *Early Bird (Intelsat 1)* placed in synchronous equatorial orbit over Atlantic Ocean.

1965 (June 3–7) First U.S. space walk: *Gemini 4* orbits Earth 62 times with astronauts James A. McDivitt and Edward H. White; White leaves spaceship for first U.S. walk in space.

1965 (Aug. 21–29) Third Gemini flight: Astronauts L. Gordon Cooper and Charles Conrad Jr. make 120 orbits around Earth during 8-day mission in Gemini 5.

1965 (Dec. 4–18) Fourth Gemini flight: 14-day endurance mission flown by astronauts Frank Borman and James A. Lovell Jr. in *Gemini 7,* making 206 Earth orbits.

1965 (Dec. 15) First rendezvous by spacecraft: *Gemini 6,* piloted by astronauts Walter Schirra Jr. and Thomas P. Stafford, rendezvous within 6 feet of *Gemini 7* in orbit.

1966 (Feb. 3) Weather satellite system inaugurated: U.S. Weather Bureau's satellite information system becomes operational with launch of 305-pound *ESSA-1.*

1966 (March 16–17) First space docking experiment:

Performed by astronauts Neil Armstrong and David R. Scott in *Gemini 8* with Gemini unmanned target vehicle.

1966 (April 3) First spacecraft orbits Moon: Soviet *Luna 10* was launched on March 31.

1966 (May 30–June 2) First U.S. unmanned space landing on Moon: Spacecraft *Surveyor I* makes soft landing on Moon's Ocean of Storms; sends back 11,327 photos.

1966 (June 3–6) Longest spacewalk: Astronauts Thomas P. Stafford and Eugene A. Cernan launched on 3-day flight aboard *Gemini 9;* Cernan performs longest spacewalk to date—more than 2 hours.

1966 (July 18–21) First successful docking of spacecraft: *Gemini 10,* piloted by astronauts John W. Young and Michael Collins, overtakes and docks with Gemini vehicle.

1966 (Aug. 10) First U.S. spacecraft orbits Moon: Unmanned *Lunar Orbiter 1* takes first photos of Earth as seen from vicinity of Moon.

1966 (Nov. 11–15) Final Gemini mission: Astronauts James A. Lovell Jr. and Edwin A. Aldrin Jr. in *Gemini 12* successfully docked with target vehicle in Earth orbit; Aldrin performed two walks in space.

1967 (Jan. 27) Disaster in Apollo flight experiment: Three astronauts training as crew for first Apollo mission killed when fire sweeps through vehicle during ground test.

1967 (April 23) Soviet cosmonaut killed: Vladimir M. Komarov killed as *Soyuz I* crashes after reentry.

1967 (Aug. 1) Mapping of Moon completed by spacecraft: U.S. *Lunar Orbiter 5* launched, completing mapping mission preparatory to manned Apollo flights to Moon.

1967 (Sept. 7–9) First successful U.S. biological research spacecraft: *Biosatellite 2* carries radiation and general biological experiments into orbit around Earth.

1967 (Sept. 8–11) Spacecraft explores possible landing sites for Apollo mission: *Surveyor 5* lands on Moon, takes photos of potential landing areas and begins chemical analysis of Moon's surface.

1967 (Nov. 9) First Apollo unmanned flight test: *Saturn V* 3-stage launch vehicle sent aloft and brought back to Earth at lunar-return velocity.

1968 (Jan. 7–10) Laser beam from Earth received on Moon: Unmanned *Surveyor 7* receives light signal from Earth while returning TV pictures of Moon's surface and performing digging experiments.

1968 (July 4) Astonomy research craft launched: *Radio Astronomy Explorer Satellite* provides data on new elements and distant regions of universe.

1968 (Oct. 11–22) First manned Apollo flight: Mission lasts 10 days and 20 hours orbiting Earth with *Apollo 7* manned by astronauts Walter M. Schirra Jr., Donn F. Eisele, and R. Walter Cunningham; crew seen by home TV viewers in first telecast from space.

1968 (Oct. 26–30) First Soviet manned rendezvous: Cosmonaut Georgi T. Beregovoi pilots *Soyuz 3* to rendezvous with unmanned *Soyuz 2.*

1968 (Dec. 21–27) First manned Moon-orbiting mission: Astronauts Frank Borman, James A. Lovell, and William Anders in *Apollo 8* orbit Moon 10 times.

1969 (Jan. 14) Soviet docking in space: Cosmonaut Vladimir A. Shatalov pilots *Soyuz 4* to docking with *Soyuz 5.*

1969 (March 3–13) First manned flight of Lunar Module: Astronauts James A. McDivitt, David R. Scott, and Russell L. Schweickart pilot *Apollo 9;* first manned flight of lunar hardware in Earth orbit tests human reactions to space and weightlessness.

1969 (May 18–26) Second manned Moon-orbiting mission: *Apollo 10,* crewed by astronauts Eugene A. Cernan, John W. Young, and Thomas P. Stafford, circles Moon 31 times; *Lunar Module* (LM) flown to within 47,000 feet of Moon's surface; first live color TV pictures sent from space.

1969 (July 20) First astronauts land on Moon: Launched on July 16, *Apollo 11* manned by astronauts Neil A. Armstrong, Edwin E. Aldrin Jr. and Michael Collins; Armstrong and Aldrin become first men to walk on Moon; President Nixon congratulates astronauts in first telephone call to Moon; astronauts remain on Moon for more than 21 hours;

return to Earth on July 24.

1969 (Oct. 11–18) Three Soviet spacecraft orbit simultaneously: *Soyuz 6, Soyuz 7,* and *Soyuz 8* launched a day apart to perform experiments in welding metals and tests for building orbiting space laboratory.

1969 (Nov. 14–24) Second Moon-landing flight: *Apollo 12* flown by astronauts Charles Conrad Jr., Richard E. Gordon Jr., and Alan L. Bean; Conrad and Bean stay on Moon for 32 hours.

1970 (April 13) Accident in space aborts Moon flight: *Apollo 13* launched on April 11, manned by astronauts James A. Lovell, John L. Swigert Jr., and Fred W. Haise Jr. Rupture of oxygen tank forces crew to take emergency action, returning to Earth on April 17.

1970 (Dec. 12) First American spacecraft launched with foreign crew: *Explorer 42* launched into equatorial orbit from San Marco platform off coast of Kenya by Italian crew.

1971 (Jan. 31–Feb. 9) Third successful lunar landing mission: *Apollo 14* manned by astronauts Alan B. Shepard Jr., Stuart A. Roosa, and Edgar D. Mitchell; Shepard and Mitchell stay on Moon for over 33 hours.

1971 (April 22–24) Soviet spacecraft links up with orbiting space station: Cosmonauts Vladimir A. Shatalov, Aleksei S. Yeliseyev, and Nikolai Rukavishnikov, aboard *Soyuz 10,* link up with orbiting space station, *Salyut,* for 5½ hours.

1971 (June 6–30) Soviet cosmonauts die after link-up with *Salyut I* space station: Cosmonauts Georgi T. Dobrovolsky, Vladislav N. Volkov, and Viktor I. Patsayev aboard *Soyuz 11,* docked with space station and orbited with *Salyut* for 23 days; crew died during reentry from failure of pressurization.

1971 (July 26–Aug. 7) Fourth lunar landing mission: *Apollo 15* flown by astronauts David R. Scott, James B. Irwin, and Alfred M. Worden; Scott and Irwin became first to use *Lunar Roving Vehicle* (LRV) to travel over 17 miles exploring Moon's surface.

1971 (Nov. 13) First close photos of Mars' moons: *Mariner 9,* launched May 30, in Mars' orbit, takes first close photos of moons Deimos and Phobos and of Mars dust storm.

1972 (March 2) *Pioneer 10* launched to explore distant planets: Unmanned spacecraft is first powered completely by nuclear energy; after photographing Jupiter and Saturn, it left the solar system on June 13, 1983.

1972 (April 16–27) *Apollo 16* mission to Moon: Fifth lunar landing flight manned by astronauts John W. Young, Thomas K. Mattingly II, and Charles M. Duke Jr.; Young and Duke remained on Moon for 71 hours.

1972 (Dec. 7–19) Final Apollo flight to Moon: *Apollo 17* flown by astronauts Eugene A. Cernan, Ronald B. Evans, and Harrison H. Schmidt; Cernan and Schmidt stay on Moon more than 3 days.

1973 (April 6) *Pioneer 11* sent to explore planets: Flyby of Jupiter occurs on Dec. 5, 1974; flyby of Saturn on Sept. 1, 1979, discovers new 11th moon and rings.

1973 (May 14) *Skylab* becomes first U.S. space station: Orbits 268.7 miles above Earth.

1973 (May 25–June 22) First manned *Skylab* expedition: Astronauts Charles Conrad Jr., Joseph P. Kerwin, and Paul J. Weitz, aboard *Skylab 2,* rendezvous with *Skylab 1,* repair it, and conduct experiments during 28-day mission.

1973 (July 28–Sept. 25) Second manned *Skylab* expedition: Astronauts Alan L. Bean, Jack R. Lousma, and Owen K. Garriott, launched aboard *Skylab 3,* spend over 59 days in space.

1973 (Sept. 27–29) First Soviet manned flight after 2-year hiatus: Cosmonauts Vasily G. Lazarev and Oleg K. Makharov pilot *Soyuz 12* on 2-day test flight.

1973 (Nov. 3) First probe to fly past two planets: *Mariner 10* sends photos and data from Venus on Feb. 5, 1974, and photos and data from Mercury on March 29 and Sept. 21, 1974, and March 16, 1975.

1973 (Nov. 16) to 1974 (Feb. 8) Final *Skylab* mission: Astronauts Gerald Carr, Edward Gibson, and William Pogue remain in space more than 84 days, after launch aboard *Skylab 4.*

1973 (Dec. 18–26) Soviet cosmonauts grow nutritive protein samples: Tests done by Pyotr Klimuk and Valentin Lebedev aboard *Soyuz 13.*

1974 (July 3–19) *Soyuz 14* launched: Cosmonauts spend two weeks on board space sation *Salyut 3.*

1975 (Jan. 11–Feb. 9) Soviets set endurance record: Cosmonauts Aleksei Gubarev and Georgi Grechko remain 30 days aboard *Salyut 4* space station, after launch in spaceship *Soyuz 17.*

1975 (July 17) First international rendezvous and docking in space: U.S astronauts Thomas P. Stafford, Vance D. Brand, and Donald K. Slayton dock their *Apollo* spacecraft with Soviet *Soyuz 19,* manned by cosmonauts Aleksei Leonov and Valeri Kubasov; crews exchange visits.

1975 (Aug. 20) First U.S. attempt to softland spacecraft on other planet: *Viking 1* reaches Mars July 20, 1976, and begins relaying first analysis of surface material on another planet.

1975 (Sept. 9) *Viking 2* launched: Sister ship to *Viking 1* lands on Mars on Sept. 3, 1976.

1976 (July 6–Aug. 24) Soviet *Soyuz 21* launched: Cosmonauts Boris Volynov and Vitaly Zholobov spend 50 days aboard *Salyut 5* space station, launched June 22.

1977 (Aug. 12) Orbiting astronomical observatory launched: *HEAO-1* maps X-rays and gamma rays.

1977 (Aug. 20) *Voyager 2* launched to study distant planets: Flyby of Jupiter occurs July 9, 1979; on flyby of Saturn Aug. 25, 1981, sends back more than 18,000 photos; scheduled to encounter Uranus in January 1986 and Neptune in August 1989.

1977 (Sept. 5) *Voyager 1* sets off to investigate Jupiter and Saturn: Jupiter flyby March 5, 1979, discovers ring around planet and 3 new moons; Saturn flyby on Nov. 12, 1980, discovers additional new moons and rings.

1978 (May 20) *Pioneer-Venus 1* to study Venus: Begins orbiting planet Dec. 5, 1978.

1978 (June 26) First ocean-monitoring satellite: U.S. SEASAT-1 launched.

1978 (Aug. 8) Multiprobe spacecraft to study Venus: *Pioneer-Venus 2* sent into Venus' atmosphere on Dec. 9, 1978.

1979 (July 11) *Skylab* falls out of orbit: 77-ton spacecraft, launched May 14, 1973, scatters debris over desert area of Western Australia.

1980 (April 9–Oct. 11) Soviets set new endurance record: Cosmonauts Leonid Popov and Valery Ryumin spend 185 days aboard the *Salyut 6* space station and the spaceships *Soyuz 35* and *Soyuz 37.*

1981 (April 12–14) Reusable space shuttle *Columbia:* Makes first successful flight, orbiting Earth 36.5 times; manned by astronauts John W. Young and R. L. Crippen.

1981 (Nov. 12–14) Second space shuttle flight: Astronauts Joe H. Engle and Richard H. Truly pilot *Columbia* for 36.5 orbits.

1982 (March 22–30) Third space shuttle flight: Astronauts Jack Lousma and Gordon A. Fullerton pilot *Columbia* for 129 orbits.

1982 (April 19) Soviets launch new *Salyut 7* space station: replaces *Salyut 6,* which burns on reentry July 30.

1982 (May 13–Dec. 10) Soviets set new endurance record: Cosmonauts Lt. Col. Anatoly Berezovnoy and Valentin Lebedov spend record 211 days in space, living aboard *Salyut 7* orbiting space station.

1982 (June 24–July 2) French astronaut visits *Salyut 7:* Col. Jean-Loup Chrétien becomes first noncommunist to fly in Soviet spacecraft.

1982 (June 27–July 4) Final *Columbia* test flight: Astronauts Thomas K. Mattingly II and Henry W. Harstfield Jr. pilot shuttle for 112 orbits in fourth and final test flight.

1982 (Nov. 11–16) Space shuttle *Columbia* completes first operational flight: 4-man crew launches satellites.

1983 (June 18–24) First U.S. woman in space: Astronaut Sally K. Ride travels as member of crew of space shuttle *Challenger.*

1985 For space events of the year, see pages 8–26 and 747–749.

DISTANCES OF THE STARS

We live some 93 million miles from the nearest star, our Sun.

Light from the Sun takes over 8 minutes to reach Earth, even though it travels at some 186,282 miles a second.

Other distances in our solar system are so immense that the Astronomical Unit (AU) is used to measure them—one AU is the average Earth-Sun distance.

The AU is too small, however, to measure the distances to stars other than our Sun. Instead, the light-year unit is used. A light-year is the distance light travels in a year—about 6 *trillion* miles.

Thus the next nearest star to Earth—a double one named Rigil Centaurus (Alpha Centauri A) and a companion—is 4.3 light-years distant, as shown below.

The table shows some other stars known to be located within a distance of 17 light-years. Also indicated are the spectral types of these stars and their luminosity, or brightness.

Beyond these "nearby" stars lie other stars in our galaxy, the Milky Way. Containing billions of stars, the Milky Way is a great disk about 100,000 light-years in diameter.

The nearest galaxies to the Earth are the Magellanic Clouds, at a distance of about 170,000 light-years.

STAR	SPECTRAL TYPE	DISTANCE IN LIGHT-YEARS	BRIGHTNESS (Sun = 1.0)	STAR	SPECTRAL TYPE	DISTANCE IN LIGHT-YEARS	BRIGHTNESS (Sun = 1.0)
Sun.............	G2	—	1.0	BD-12° 4523....	M5	13.1	0.0013
Alpha Cen A*....	G2	4.3	1.3	van Maanen's ...	white dwarf F	13.9	0.00017
Barnard's*......	M5	5.9	0.00044	Wolf 424 A*....	M6	14.1	0.0014
Wolf 359	M6	7.6	0.00002	CD-37° 15492...	M3	14.5	0.0058
Lalande 21185*.	M2	8.1	0.0052	Groombridge 1618.........	M0	15.0	0.040
Sirius A*.......	A1	8.6	23.0	CD-46° 11540....	M4	15.1	0.0030
Luyten 726-8A*.	M6	8.9	0.00006	CD-49° 13515....	M3	15.2	0.0058
Ross 154	M5	9.4	0.0004	CD-44° 11909....	M5	15.3	0.00063
Ross 248	M6	10.3	0.00011	Luyten 1159-16 .	M7	15.4	0.00023
Epsilon Eri.....	K2	10.7	0.30	Lalande 25372 ..	M3.5	15.7	0.0076
Luyten 789-6....	M6	10.8	0.00012	AOe 17415-6*...	M3.5	15.7	0.0044
Ross 128	M5	10.8	0.00033	CC 658.........	white dwarf	15.8	0.0008
61 Cygni A*.....	K5	11.2	0.083	Ross 780	M5	15.8	0.0016
Epsilon Ind.....	K5	11.2	0.13	Omicron² Eri A*.	K0	15.9	0.33
Procyon A*......	F5	11.4	7.6	BD + 20° 2465*	M4.5	16.1	0.0036
Sigma 2398 A*..	M3.5	11.5	0.0028	Altair	A7	16.6	10.0
Groombridge 34A*	M1	11.6	0.0058	70 Oph. A*.....	K1	16.7	0.44
Lacaille 9352 ...	M2	11.7	0.012	AC + 79° 3888 .	M4	16.8	0.0009
Tau Ceti........	G8	11.9	0.44	BD + 43° 4305*	M5	16.9	0.0021
BD + 5° 1668 ..	M4	12.2	0.0014	Stein 2051A* ...	M5	17.0	0.0008
Lacaille 8760 ...	M1	12.5	0.025				
Kapteyn's	M0	12.7	0.0040				
Kruger 60 A* ...	M4	12.8	0.0017				
Ross 614 A*	M5	13.1	0.0004				

* These stars are binary or larger multiples—that is, they have one or more smaller stars associated with them.

STAR COLORS AND TEMPERATURES

The floods of radiation given off by stars range the whole electromagnetic spectrum from gamma rays and X rays through light and heat to radio waves.

These radiations come from nuclear-fusion reactions maintained by the great pressures and temperatures deep within the stars. The calculated temperature of the center of the Sun is about 25,000,000°F. At such extremes, hydrogen atoms will fuse into helium atoms with a loss in total mass and the release of tremendous quantities of energy.

Stars vary greatly in color and temperature as well as in size. Astronomers analyze the radiations from stars with many instruments, including the spectroscope, which divides light into a color spectrum. The spectra of stars indicate their temperatures. The standard spectral classification of stars is given in the capital letters in the following table, with the color and approximate surface temperatures of stars in these classes.

The stars that fall into intermediate positions are indicated by a range of numbers from 0 to 9 with each letter. Our Sun, for example, has the spectral classification of G2 and a surface temperature of about 10,440°F.

SPECTRAL CLASSIFICATION	COLOR SCALE	STAR SURFACE TEMPERATURE (° Fahrenheit)
O...............	Blue..........	63,000
B...............	Bluish........	45,000
A...............	White	19,800
F...............	Yellowish	13,500
G Dwarf	Yellow........	10,440
G Giant	Yellow........	9,540
K Dwarf	Orange	8,820
K Giant.........	Orange	7,200
M Dwarf........	Orange-red ...	6,120
M Giant	Orange-red ...	5,400
S...............	Red..........	4,680
N...............	Red	4,680
R...............	Red	4,140

THE CONSTELLATIONS

When you look up on a clear night at the stars, many of them appear to be clustered in groups called constellations.

Ancient observers gave 48 constellations names suggested by the patterns of their stars.

Usually the stars forming these apparent groups are entirely unrelated and are located at greatly varying distances, although all the stars visible to the naked eye are in our own Milky Way galaxy.

Modern astronomers recognize 88 constellations, including most of the ancient ones.

Strict boundaries for the constellations were established by the International Astronomical Union in 1928.

The constellation boundaries are used as reference areas for locating, naming, and classifying the stars, and for roughly fixing the positions of comets, meteors, and other celestial bodies viewed in the sky.

The table names the constellations. Those marked with an asterisk (*) are not visible from midnorthern latitudes.

LATIN NAME	ENGLISH	LATIN NAME	ENGLISH	LATIN NAME	ENGLISH
Andromeda	Chained Maiden	Boötes	Herdsman	Carina *	Keel
Antila	Air Pump	Caelum	Chisel	Cassiopeia	Lady in Chair
Apus *	Bird of Paradise	Camelopardalis	Giraffe	Centaurus *	Centaur
Aquarius	Water Bearer	Cancer	Crab	Cepheus	King
Aquila	Eagle	Canes Venatici	Hunting Dogs	Cetus	Whale
Ara *	Altar	Canis Major	Great Dog	Chamaeleon *	Chameleon
Aries	Ram	Canis Minor	Small Dog	Circinus *	Compasses
Auriga	Charioteer	Capricornus	Sea Goat	Columba	Dove

NORTHERN SKY

LATIN NAME	ENGLISH	LATIN NAME	ENGLISH	LATIN NAME	ENGLISH
Coma Berenices ...	Berenice's Hair	Leo Minor	Small Lion	Pyxis.............	Compass
Corona Australis ..	Southern Crown	Lepus	Hare	Reticulum *.......	Net
Corona Borealis ...	Northern Crown	Libra.............	Scales	Sagitta	Arrow
Corvus	Crow	Lupus *	Wolf	Sagittarius	Archer
Crater	Cup	Lynx	Lynx	Scorpius	Scorpion
Crux *	(Southern) Cross	Lyra	Lyre	Sculptor	Sculptor
Cygnus	Swan	Mensa *	Table (Mountain)	Scutum	Shield
Delphinus	Dolphin	Microscopium.....	Microscope	Serpens	Serpent
Dorado *	Swordfish	Monoceros	Unicorn	Sextans	Sextant
Draco	Dragon	Musca *	Fly	Taurus	Bull
Equuleus	Little Horse	Norma *..........	Square	Telescopium *	Telescope
Eridanus	River Eridanus	Octans *	Octant	Triangulum	Triangle
Fornax	Furnace	Ophiuchus........	Serpent Bearer	Triangulum Australe*	Southern Triangle
Gemini	Twins	Orion	Hunter	Tucana *	Toucan
Grus *	Crane	Pavo *	Peacock	Ursa Major	Great Bear
Hercules	Hercules	Pegasus	Pegasus	Ursa Minor	Small Bear
Horologium *	Clock	Perseus	Champion	Vela *	Sails
Hydra............	Sea Serpent	Phoenix *........	Phoenix	Virgo	Virgin
Hydrus *	Water Snake	Pictor *	Painter's (Easel)	Volans *	Flying Fish
Indus *	Indian	Pisces	Fishes	Vulpecula	Fox
Lacerta	Lizard	Piscis Austrinus ...	Southern Fish		
Leo	Lion	Puppis	Poop (Stern)		

ASTRONOMICAL TELESCOPES

A *refractor* telescope uses a lens to collect light from a distant object and bring it to a focus. A *reflector* telescope uses a concave mirror for the same purpose.

Because lenses fail to bring all colors to the same focus, most large astronomical telescopes built in the past 50 years are reflectors.

Today, visual observations are rarely made with astronomical telescopes, for photographs can record objects much fainter than the eye can see. Large telescopes thus are used as cameras or to collect light for analysis in other ways.

Radio telescopes are used to study radio waves coming from celestial objects.

LARGE REFRACTING TELESCOPES
Source: U. S. Naval Observatory

DIAMETER OF LENS	OBSERVATORY AND LOCATION	YEAR
40.0 in. (1.02 m.)	Yerkes Observatory, Williams Bay, Wisconsin	1897
36.0 in. (0.91 m.)	Lick Observatory, Mt. Hamilton, California	1888
32.7 in. (0.83 m.)	Paris Observatory, Meudon, France	1889
32.0 in. (0.81 m.)	Astrophysical Observatory, Potsdam, East Germany	1899
30.0 in. (0.76 m.)	Allegheny Observatory, Pittsburgh, Pennsylvania	1914
29.1 in. (0.74 m.)	Nice Observatory at Mont Gros, Nice, France	1886

LARGE RADIO AND RADAR TELESCOPES
Source: U.S. National Radio Astronomy Observatory

SIZE	OBSERVATORY	YEAR
27 x 82 ft., 23 mi. (36 km.)[1]	National Radio Astronomy Observatory, Socorro, N.M.	1980
16,000 ft. (4.9 km.)[1]	Mullard Observatory, Cambridge, England	1972
2.05 mi. (3.3 km.)[1] interferometer.	Clark Lake Radio Obs., Borrego Springs, Calif.	1975
1.86 mi. (3 km.)[2]	CSIRO, Culgoora, Australia	1967
1.86 mi. (3 km.)[1]	Netherlands Foundation for Radio Astronomy, Westerbork, Neth.	1973
1.44 mi. (2.3 km.)[1] interferometer.	U. of Tokyo Observatory, Nobeyama, Japan	1970
1,890 ft. (576 m.)[3]	Special Astrophysical Obs., Zelenchukskaya, USSR	1976
1,837 ft. (560 m.)[1]	U. of Tokyo Observatory, Nobeyama, Japan	1983
1,000 ft. (305 m.)[3]	Arecibo Obs., Puerto Rico	1974[5]
1,000 ft. (305 m.)[3]	Radio Astronomy Station, Nançay, France	1964
328 ft. (100 m.)[3]	Max Planck Institute, Effelsberg, West Germany	1970
300 ft. (91.4 m.)[3]	National Radio Astronomy Obs., Green Bank, W. Va.	1963
250 ft. (76.2 m.)[3]	Nuffield Laboratories, Jodrell Bank, England	1971[5]
210 ft. (64 m.)[3]	NASA, Goldstone, California.	1966

LARGE REFLECTING TELESCOPES
Source: U.S. Naval Observatory

DIAMETER OF MIRROR	OBSERVATORY AND LOCATION	YEAR
236 in. (6 m.)	Special Astrophysical Obs., Zelenchukskaya, USSR	1976
200 in. (5.08 m.)	Hale Observatory, Palomar Mountain, California	1948
175 in. (4.5 m.) (6 x 72 in. mirrors)	Multiple Mirror Telescope, Mt. Hopkins, Arizona	1979
166 in. (4.22 m.)	William Herschel Telescope, La Palma, Canary Islands	UC
158 in. (4 m.)	Kitt Peak National Observatory, Tucson, Arizona	1973
158 in. (4 m.)	Cerro Tololo Inter-American Observatory, Chile	1974
153 in. (3.9 m.)	Anglo-Australian Telescope, Siding Spring, Australia	1975
150 in. (3.8 m.)[6]	British Infrared Telescope, Mauna Kea, Hawaii	1978
144 in. (3.66 m.)	Canada-France-Hawaii Telescope, Mauna Kea, Hawaii	1979
141 in. (3.57 m.)	European Southern Observatory, La Silla, Chile	1976
138 in. (3.5 m.)	Max Planck Inst. for Astronomy, Calar Alto, Spain	1984
126 in. (3.20 m.)[6]	NASA-U. of Hawaii, Telescope, Mauna Kea, Hawaii	1979
120 in. (3.05 m.)	Lick Observatory, Mt. Hamilton, California	1959
107 in. (2.72 m.)	McDonald Observatory, Fort Davis, Texas	1968
102 in. (2.59 m.)	Crimean Astrophysical Obs., Simferopol, USSR	1960
100 in. (2.54 m.)	Hale Observatory, Mt. Wilson, California	1917
100 in. (2.54 m.)	Carnegie Southern Station, Las Campanas, Chile	1976
100 in. (2.54 m.)	Nordic Telescope, La Palma, Canary Islands	UC

[1] Baseline interferometer. [2] Diameter, radioheliograph. [3] Diameter, single antenna for centimeter wavelengths and longer. [4] Diameter, single antennas for millimeter wavelengths. [5] Upgraded. [6] Infrared telescope. UC=under construction.

BRIGHTEST STARS

STARS	GREEK LETTER AND CONSTELLATION	APPARENT MAGNITUDE	ABSOLUTE MAGNITUDE	DISTANCE IN LIGHT-YEARS
Sun	Sun	−26.73	4.84	—
Sirius	Alpha Canis Majoris	−1.42	1.45	8.7
Canopus	Alpha Carinae	−0.72	−3.10	98
Rigil Kentaurus	Alpha Centauri A	−0.01	4.39	4.3
Arcturus	Alpha Boötis	−0.06	−0.3	36
Vega	Alpha Lyrae	0.04	0.5	26.5
Capella	Alpha Aurigae	0.05	−0.6	45
Rigel	Beta Orionis	0.14	−7.1	900
Procyon	Alpha Canis Minoris	0.37	2.7	11.3
Betelgeuse	Alpha Orionis	0.41	−5.6	520

Sports and Games

A 22-cent stamp commemorating the Winter Special Olympics was issued March 25 in Park City, Utah, during the opening of the 1985 International Winter Special Olympic Games. The first special olympics competition for the mentally retarded was sponsored by the Chicago Park District and the Joseph P. Kennedy Jr. Foundation in 1968.

U. S. Postal Service

PEOPLE IN SPORTS

AUTOMOBILE RACING

Driver **Bill Elliott,** 29, won $1 million—the biggest single bonus prize in the history of auto racing—on Sept. 1, 1985, by capturing first place in the Southern 500 Grand National stock car race at Darlington, S.C. The prize had been offered by the R.J. Reynolds Tobacco Company to any driver that won three of the "Big Four" stock car races. In winning 10 races in 20 starts, Eliott lost only one of the "Big Four" races—the World 600 in May.

Dale Earnhardt at a speed of 167.702 mph set an unofficial world record for stock cars on a 1.5-mile track during practice for The Winston in April. The previous record 166.067 mph had been set by Tim Richmond in October 1984.

At the 16th annual National Hot Rod Association (NHRA) Motorcraft Gatornationals in Gainesville, Fla., in March, **Kenny Bernstein** of Dallas set an NHRA record with a quarter-mile time of 5.64 seconds.

The old record of 5.66 seconds had been set by **John Lombardo** of Saugus, Calif.

A.J. Foyt and his partner **Bob Wolleck** won the Sebring 12-hour endurance race in Florida in March with a record average speed of 113.98 mph, covering a total of 1,365.66 miles in their Porsche 962.

Four drivers were named to the Indianapolis 500 Hall of Fame in May: **Joe Boyer,** co-winner of the race in 1924 with a record speed of 98.23 mph; **Floyd Roberts,** who won the 500 in 1938, setting a speed record of 117.2; **Parnelli Jones,** who set an Indy 500 speed record of 143.137 mph while winning in 1963; and **Henry Banks,** who was national driving champion in 1950.

BASEBALL

Von Hayes of the Philadelphia Phillies on June 11 became the first player in major league history to hit two home runs in the first inning, helping win a game against the New York Mets by a score of 26 to 7 ... **Jim**

SPORTS AND GAMES: CONTENTS

PEOPLE IN SPORTS *(continued)*

Abbott, 17, who was born without a right hand, compiled a 10-3 record with four no-hitters as pitcher for Flint (Mich.) Central High School. He accepted a baseball scholarship to the University of Michigan in June, having turned down a bid to turn pro that was offered by the Toronto Blue Jays.

Former all-star player **Willie Stargell,** who helped lead the Pittsburgh Pirates to two world championships, was hired in June as the Pirates' first-base coach. ... **Earl Weaver,** who spent two years as a TV sports analyst after retiring as manager of the Balti-more Orioles, replaced **Joe Altobelli** as the Orioles' manager in June. ... **Billy Gardner,** 57, was dismissed as manager of the Minnesota Twins on June 21 and replaced by **Ray Miller,** 40, who has been pitching coach of the Baltimore Orioles.

Baseball Commissioner **Peter Ueberroth** on May 7 ordered more than 4,000 pro baseball personnel except for major league players to undergo tests for drugs in an effort to stamp out the use of drugs by persons involved in baseball. The baseball players union refused to undergo the tests on grounds it was an invasion of privacy. Since 1980

ATHLETE OF THE YEAR (Associated Press)

YEAR	MALE ATHLETE	SPORT	YEAR	FEMALE ATHLETE	SPORT
1931	Pepper Martin	Baseball	1931	Helene Madison	Swimming
1932	Gene Sarazen	Golf	1932	Babe Didrikson	Track
1933	Carl Hubbell	Baseball	1933	Helen Jacobs	Tennis
1934	Dizzy Dean	Baseball	1934	Virginia Van Wie	Golf
1935	Joe Louis	Boxing	1935	Helen Wills Moody	Tennis
1936	Jesse Owens	Track	1936	Helen Stephens	Track
1937	Don Budge	Tennis	1937	Katherine Rawls	Swimming
1938	Don Budge	Tennis	1938	Patty Berg	Golf
1939	Nile Kinnick	Football	1939	Alice Marble	Tennis
1940	Tommy Harmon	Football	1940	Alice Marble	Tennis
1941	Joe DiMaggio	Baseball	1941	Betty Hicks Newell	Golf
1942	Frank Sinkwich	Football	1942	Gloria Callen	Swimming
1943	Gunder Haegg	Track	1943	Patty Berg	Golf
1944	Byron Nelson	Golf	1944	Ann Curtis	Swimming
1945	Byron Nelson	Golf	1945	Babe Didrikson Zaharias	Golf
1946	Glenn Davis	Football	1946	Babe Didrikson Zaharias	Golf
1947	Johnny Lujack	Football	1947	Babe Didrikson Zaharias	Golf
1948	Lou Boudreau	Baseball	1948	Fanny Blankers-Koen	Track
1949	Leon Hart	Football	1949	Marlene Bauer	Golf
1950	Jim Konstanty	Baseball	1950	Babe Didrikson Zaharias	Golf
1951	Dick Kazmaier	Football	1951	Maureen Connolly	Tennis
1952	Bob Mathias	Track and Football	1952	Maureen Connolly	Tennis
1953	Ben Hogan	Golf	1953	Maureen Connolly	Tennis
1954	Willie Mays	Baseball	1954	Babe Didrikson Zaharias	Golf
1955	Hopalong Cassady	Football	1955	Patty Berg	Golf
1956	Mickey Mantle	Baseball	1956	Pat McCormick	Diving
1957	Ted Williams	Baseball	1957	Althea Gibson	Tennis
1958	Herb Elliott	Track	1958	Althea Gibson	Tennis
1959	Ingemar Johansson	Boxing	1959	Maria Bueno	Tennis
1960	Rafer Johnson	Decathlon	1960	Wilma Rudolph	Track
1961	Roger Maris	Baseball	1961	Wilma Rudolph	Track
1962	Maury Wills	Baseball	1962	Dawn Fraser	Swimming
1963	Sandy Koufax	Baseball	1963	Mickey Wright	Golf
1964	Don Schollander	Swimming	1964	Mickey Wright	Golf
1965	Sandy Koufax	Baseball	1965	Kathy Whitworth	Golf
1966	Frank Robinson	Baseball	1966	Kathy Whitworth	Golf
1967	Carl Yastrzemski	Baseball	1967	Billie Jean King	Tennis
1968	Denny McLain	Baseball	1968	Peggy Fleming	Ice Skating
1969	Tom Seaver	Baseball	1969	Debbie Meyer	Swimming
1970	George Blanda	Football	1970	Chi Cheng	Track
1971	Lee Trevino	Golf	1971	Evonne Goolagong	Tennis
1972	Mark Spitz	Swimming	1972	Olga Korbut	Gymnastics
1973	O.J. Simpson	Football	1973	Billie Jean King	Tennis
1974	Muhammad Ali	Boxing	1974	Chris Evert	Tennis
1975	Fred Lynn	Baseball	1975	Chris Evert	Tennis
1976	Bruce Jenner	Track	1976	Nadia Comaneci	Gymnastics
1977	Steve Cauthen	Horse Racing	1977	Chris Evert	Tennis
1978	Ron Guidry	Baseball	1978	Nancy Lopez	Golf
1979	Willie Stargell	Baseball	1979	Tracy Austin	Tennis
1980	U.S. Olympic Team	Hockey	1980	Chris Evert	Tennis
1981	John McEnroe	Tennis	1981	Tracy Austin	Tennis
1982	Wayne Gretzky	Hockey	1982	Mary Decker	Track
1983	Carl Lewis	Track	1983	Martina Navratilova	Tennis
1984	Carl Lewis	Track	1984	Mary Lou Retton	Gymnastics

some 25 major league players have admitted use of illegal drugs, many being convicted of possession or sale of narcotics. In September seven players testified at a trial in Pittsburgh they had bought and used drugs from a man convicted as a drug dealer. . . . Two-time Cy Young award winner **Denny McLain,** 41, was sentenced on April 25 to 23 years in prison for racketeering, extortion, and possession of cocaine.

A group of baseball fans including 63 men and two women had the time of their lives in May at the Baseball Fantasies Fulfilled camp in Florida. Each paid $2,995 for a week of baseball training camp workouts, mingling with such former baseball greats as **Mickey Mantle, Willie Mays, Ernie Banks, Monte Irvin,** and **Bob Feller.** Climax came with a game they played against the former major leaguers in St. Petersburg, losing 13 to 12.

Marty Burke, a senior at Huffman High School in Birmingham, Ala., set a national schoolboy record in May by hitting three grand slam homers to help win a 26 to 8 victory over rival Woodlawn High School. . . . **Kirk McCaskill,** 24, set a baseball record when he made his debut as a pitcher with the Los Angeles Angels on May 1 as the first professional hockey player to become a major league baseball player, having previously played with the Winnipeg Jets.

BASKETBALL

Don Nelson, coach of the Milwaukee Bucks, was chosen coach of the year of the National Basketball Association by sports writers and broadcasters. . . . **Matt Guokas,** 41, assistant coach of the Philadelphia 76ers, was named in June to move up to replace **Billy Cunningham** as coach of the NBA team. . . . When **Jim Lynam** was fired in March as coach of the San Diego Clippers, his assistant coach, **Don Chaney,** was named as his replacement. . . . **John Kuester,** coach at Boston University, was named in May to replace **Gerry Gimmelstob** as coach at George Washington University.

Bruce Morris, a 6-foot-4 senior guard for Marshall University in Huntington, W. Va., claimed a record with a 92-foot 5$\frac{1}{4}$-inch field goal with one second left in the first half of a game with Appalachian State on Feb. 7, 1985. Marshall won 93-82.

The Basketball Hall of Fame at Springfield, Mass., inducted its first three women members in July: **Margaret Wade,** 72, former coach of Delta State University; **Bertha Teague,** 84, who coached at Byng High School in Ada, Okla.; and the late **Senda Barenson Abbott,** who helped develop the official rules for women's basketball in 1892.

BICYCLING

Joop Zoetemelk, 38, won the men's professional world cycling championship on Sept. 1 at Giavera del Montello, Italy, completing the 265.5 kilometers in 6 hours 26 minutes and 38 seconds. **Greg LeMond,** 24, of Reno, Nev., came in second, only 3 seconds behind the winner.

To attend his 45th reunion at Lafayette College, **Cliff Hoehne,** 66, made the 1,000-

JAMES E. SULLIVAN MEMORIAL TROPHY (Amateur Athletic Union)

Year	Name	Sport	Year	Name	Sport
1930	Bobby Jones	Golf	1958	Glenn Davis	Track (Sprinter)
1931	Bernard Berlinger	All-around	1959	Parry O'Brien	Track (Shot Put)
1932	James Bausch	All-around	1960	Rafer Johnson	Track (Decathlon)
1933	Glenn Cunningham	Track	1961	Wilma Rudolph	Track (Sprinter)
1934	Bill Bonthron	Track	1962	Jim Beatty	Track
1935	Lawson Little	Golf	1963	John Pennel	Track (Pole Vaulter)
1936	Glenn Morris	Track (Decathlon)	1964	Don Schollander	Swimming
1937	Don Budge	Tennis	1965	Bill Bradley	Basketball
1938	Don Lash	Track	1966	Jim Ryun	Track (Mile Runner)
1939	Joe Burk	Rowing	1967	Randy Matson	Track (Shot Put)
1940	Greg Rice	Track	1968	Debbie Meyer	Swimming
1941	Les MacMitchell	Track	1969	Bill Toomey	Track (Decathlon)
1942	Cornelius Warmerdam	Track (Pole Vaulter)	1970	John Kinsella	Swimming
1943	Gil Dodds	Track	1971	Mark Spitz	Swimming
1944	Ann Curtis	Swimming	1972	Frank Shorter	Track (Distance Runner)
1945	Doc Blanchard	Football	1973	Bill Walton	Basketball
1946	Arnold Tucker	Football	1974	Rick Wohlhuter	Track
1947	Jack Kelly Jr.	Rowing	1975	Tim Shaw	Swimming
1948	Bob Mathias	Track (Decathlon)	1976	Bruce Jenner	Track
1949	Dick Button	Figure Skating	1977	John Naber	Swimming
1950	Fred Wilt	Track	1978	Tracy Caulkins	Swimming
1951	Bob Richards	Track (Pole Vaulter)	1979	Kurt Thomas	Gymnastics
1952	Horace Ashenfelter	Track (Distance Runner)	1980	Eric Heiden	Speed skating
1953	Sammy Lee	Diving	1981	Carl Lewis	Track
1954	Mal Whitfield	Track (Runner)	1982	Mary Decker	Track
1955	Harrison Dillard	Track (Sprinter)	1983	Carl Lewis	Track
1956	Pat McCormick	Diving	1984	Greg Louganis	Diving
1957	Bobby Joe Morrow	Track (Sprinter)			

mile trip from his home in Memphis, Tenn., to Easton, Pa., by bicycle in June, averaging 75 to 85 miles a day.

BOXING

Matthew Saad Muhammad, former World Boxing Council lightheavyweight champion who earned more than $1 million during his career, filed for bankruptcy in Philadelphia in June, unable to pay $240,000 in back income taxes. . . . **Jake LaMotta,** 63, former world middleweight champion, was married for the sixth time in Las Vegas, Nev., on April 14. It was the second marriage for the bride, **Theresa Miller,** 41. **Sugar Ray Robinson,** who won the middleweight championship from LaMotta, served as best man.

Livingston Bramble, lightweight champion of the World Boxing Association, was fined $15,000 by the Nevada Athletic Commission in April for the use of an illegal stimulant before he defeated Ray "Boom Boom" Mancini in a match in Reno in February.

FOOTBALL

Former Ohio State football coach **Woody Hayes,** 72, suffered a stroke in May during a trip to Canada. . . . **Carl Garret,** a former pro running back who was rookie of the year with the New England Patriots in 1969, was sentenced to nine years in prison after being found guilty in June of molesting a 12-year-old girl in Denton, Texas.

Carl Butler, who played as a running back for Michigan State, had been signed by the Atlanta Falcons, but was sent home in May after a physical examination revealed that he had a glass eye that the Falcons did not know about.

Offensive guard **Bob Kuechenberg,** 37, announced his retirement in May, the last member of the unbeaten 1972 Miami Dolphins to do so. . . . **Darryl Stingley,** 33, former New England Patriot wide receiver who received a spinal injury in a game in 1978 that has confined him to a wheelchair, was awarded an honorary degree in May by Springfield College for his work with the disabled.

GOLF

Because **Sam Randolph,** 21, had a sore back, he asked chiropractor **Richard Gueci** to accompany him and massage his back between holes as he won the final match of the United States Amateur golf championship at West Orange, N.J., on Sept. 1.

GOODWILL GAMES

TV, yachting, and baseball mogul **Ted Turner** announced in June that he had reached agreement with the Soviet Union to hold "Goodwill Games" between Soviet and American athletes in non-Olympic Game years with his TV network having exclusive rights to coverage of the competition.

GYMNASTICS

Olympic champion **Mary Lou Retton,** 17, told the *Baltimore Sun* in an interview in May that she does not plan to take part in the 1988 Olympics in South Korea except possibly as a TV commentator.

HOCKEY

Harry Neale was fired in May as coach and general manager of the Vancouver Canucks. He was replaced as general manager by his former assistant **Jack Gordon** and as coach by **Tom Watt,** former coach of the Winnipeg Jets.

Ted Sator, 35, formerly assistant coach of the Philadelphia Flyers, was named head coach of the New York Rangers on June 19, replacing **Herb Brooks,** who had been fired in January.

PARAPLEGIC TREK

Michael King, 26, a paraplegic, arrived in Washington, D.C., in August after a 4-month 5,605-mile trek in a wheelchair from Fairbanks, Alaska. The trip by the University of Pennsylvania graduate student helped raise $30,000 for rehabilitation centers. He averaged 40 to 45 miles a day during the trip.

PING-PONG

Jiang Jialiang of China won the men's single championship and **Cao Yanhua** of China won the women's singles championship in April at the 38th World Table Tennis Championships in Goteborg, Sweden.

ROWING

Princeton's varsity crew, under the guidance of coach **Larry Gluckman,** defeated the University of Pennsylvania and Columbia University in April to win the Child's Cup Regatta, the oldest cup competition in American collegiate rowing. The Child's Cup was first placed in competition in 1872. Princeton's winning time was 5 minutes 53.9 seconds for the 2,000-meter course. The Princeton team went on to win the 83rd Intercollegiate Rowing Association Championship at Syracuse, N.Y., on June 2.

In their 131st race since 1854 on England's Thames River, an Oxford University crew defeated Cambridge University on April 6 for the 10th time in a row. However, Cambridge still leads the series 68-62. One race in 1877 was a dead heat.

SQUASH

Jahangir Khan, 21, of Pakistan, won the British Open squash tournament in London for the fourth time in a row on April 23 and then flew to New York City where he won the North American Squash Open tournament for the second time on April 28.

Iceboat 1880s
USA
14

A 14-cent stamp featuring an 1880s iceboat was issued on March 23 in Rochester, N.Y., for use in mailing postcards. Iceboating in the Great Lakes region and the Northeast states is the fastest of all winter sports. Many of the boats can skim over the ice at speeds of more than 100 mph.

U.S. Postal Service

RUNNING

Jeff Keith, 22, of Fairfield, Conn., who lost his right leg to cancer while still a child, completed a coast-to-coast run when he jumped into the Pacific Ocean at Marina Del Rey, Calif., on Feb. 18. He began the run more than eight months earlier on June 4, 1984, at Faneuil Hall in Boston. Keith averaged about 16 miles of running each day. He said the feat proved "that I'm not physically handicapped—I was physicially challenged." **Michael McGee,** director of athletics at the University of Southern California, awarded Keith a full tuition scholarship for graduate study at the University of Southern California.

Runner's World magazine in its May issue estimated the 1984 earnings of top runners as $783,000 for **Carl Lewis,** $617,000 for **Edwin Moses,** $520,000 for **Bill Rodgers,** $402,000 for **Joan Benoit,** $360,000 for **Alberto Salazar,** and $355,000 for **Mary Decker.**

Geoff Smith, 31, of Britain won the Boston Marathon on April 15 for the second year in a row. His time was 2 hours 14 minutes 5 seconds for the 26-mile-385-yard course.

Lisa Larsen Weidenbach, 23, of Battle Creek, Mich., won the women's division of the Boston race with a time of 2 hours 34 minutes 6 seconds.

Marie Evangelista, 33, was disqualified as winner of the Pittsburgh Marathon in May after it was learned that she rode a city bus over part of the course.

SKATING

Dianne Holum, coach of the U.S. speed skating teams in the 1980 and 1984 Olympics, was dismissed in May and replaced by her assistant, **Mike Crowe.**

TENNIS

Arthur Ashe, 41, who was forced to give up tennis competition after heart surgery in 1979, became the first black elected to the Tennis Hall of Fame.

Star players **John McEnroe** and **Jimmy Conners** announced in May that they would not play on the U.S. Davis Cup team after the U.S. Tennis Association adopted a code of conduct for Davis Cup directed against their behavior exhibited in the Davis Cup finals with Sweden in 1984.

AUTOMOBILE RACING

WINNERS OF THE INDIANAPOLIS 500

YEAR	WINNER	CAR	AVG. SPEED	YEAR	WINNER	CAR	AVG. SPEED
1911	Ray Harroun ..	Marmon	74.590	1950	Johnny Parsons	Wynn's Special	124.002 [3]
1912	Joe Dawson ...	National	78.720	1951	Lee Wallard	Balanger Special.....	126.244
1913	Jules Goux	Peugeot	75.930	1952	Troy Ruttman .	Agajanian Special ...	128.922
1914	Rene Thomas .	Delage	82.470	1953	Bill Vukovich ..	Fuel Injection Special .	128,740
1915	Ralph De Palma	Mercedes	89.840	1954	Bill Vukovich ..	Fuel Injection Special .	130.840
1916	Dario Resta ...	Peugeot	84.000 [1]	1955	Bob Sweikert ..	John Zink Special	128.209
1919	Howard Wilcox	Peugeot	88.050	1956	Pat Flaherty ...	John Zink Special ...	128.490
1920	Gaston Chevrolet	Monroe	88.620	1957	Sam Hanks ...	Belond Exhaust Spcl..	135.601
1921	Tommy Milton .	Frontenac.........	89.620	1958	Jimmy Bryan ..	Belond AP Special ...	133.791
1922	Jim Murphy ...	Murphy Special	94.480	1959	Rodger Ward ..	Leader Card 500.....	135.857
1923	Tommy Milton .	H.C.S. Special	90.950	1960	Jim Rathman ..	Ken-Paul Special.....	138.767
1924	L. L. Corum,			1961	A. J. Foyt	Bowes Seal Special...	139.130
	Joe Boyer...	Duesenberg Special ..	98.230	1962	Rodger Ward ..	Leader Card 500	140.293
1925	Peter De Paolo	Duesenberg Special ..	101.130	1963	Parnelli Jones .	Agajanian-Willard Spcl.	143.137
1926	Frank Lockhart	Miller Special........	95.904 [2]	1964	A. J. Foyt	S.T.W. Offenhauser .	147.350
1927	George			1965	Jim Clark	Lotus-Ford	150.686
	Souders	Duesenberg	97.545	1966	Graham Hill ...	Lotus-Ford	144.317
1928	Louis Meyer ...	Miller Special........	99.482	1967	A. J. Foyt	Coyote Ford	151.207
1929	Ray Keech	Simplex Special	97.585	1968	Bobby Unser ...	Eagle-Offenhauser ...	152.882
1930	Billy Arnold ...	Hartz-Miller	100.448	1969	Mario Andretti ..	Hawk-Ford	156.867
1931	Louis			1970	Al Unser	Lola-Ford	155.749
	Schneider...	Bowes Special	96.629	1971	Al Unser	P.J. Colt-Ford	157.735
1932	Fred Frame ...	Miller Special........	104.144	1972	Mark Donohue	McLaren-Offenhauser	162.962
1933	Louis Meyer ...	Miller Special........	104.162	1973	Gordon Johncock	McLaren-Offenhauser	158.589 [4]
1934	Bill Cummings .	Miller Special........	104.863	1974	Johnny		
1935	Kelly Petillo ...	Gilmore Special......	106.240		Rutherford ..	McLaren-Offenhauser	158.589
1936	Louis Meyer ...	Ring Free Special	109.069	1975	Bobby Unser ...	Eagle-Offenhauser ...	149.213 [5]
1937	Wilbur Shaw ..	Shaw-Gilmore Spcl. ..	113.580	1976	J. Rutherford..	McLaren-Offenhauser	148.725 [6]
1938	Floyd Roberts .	Burd Piston Reg. Special	117.200	1977	A. J. Foyt	Coyote Foyt	161.331
				1978	Al Unser	Lola-Cosworth	161.363
1939	Wilbur Shaw ..	Boyle Special	115.035	1979	Rick Mears....	Penske-Cosworth	158.899
1940	Wilbur Shaw ..	Boyle Special	114.277	1980	J. Rutherford..	Chaparral-Cosworth..	142.862
1941	Mauri Rose, Floyd Davis .	Noc-Out Hose Clamp Special	115.117	1981	Bobby Unser ...	Penske-Cosworth	139.084
				1982	Gordon Johncock	Wildcat-Cosworth	162.026
1946	George Robson	Thorne Eng. Special ..	114.820	1983	Tom Sneva....	March-Cosworth	162.117
1947	Mauri Rose ...	Blue Crown Special ..	116.338	1984	Rick Mears....	March-Cosworth	163.612*
1948	Mauri Rose ...	Blue Crown Special ..	119.814	1985	Danny Sullivan	March-Cosworth	152.982
1949	Bill Holland ...	Blue Crown Special ..	121.327				

* Track record. [1] 300 miles. [2] 400 miles. [3] 345 miles. [4] 332.5 miles. [5] 435 miles. [6] 255 miles.

U.S. AUTO CLUB NATIONAL CHAMPIONS (Indy-type cars)

1910	Ray Harroun	1928–29	Louis Meyer	1951	Tony Bettenhausen	1969	Mario Andretti
1911	Ralph Mulford	1930	Billy Arnold	1952	Chuck Stevenson	1970	Al Unser
1912	Ralph De Palma	1931	Louis Schneider	1953	Sam Hanks	1971	Joe Leonard
1913	Earl Cooper	1932	Bob Carey	1954	Jimmy Bryan	1972	Joe Leonard
1914	Ralph De Palma	1933	Louis Meyer	1955	Bob Sweikert	1973	Roger McCluskey
1915	Earl Cooper	1934	Bill Cummings	1956	Jimmy Bryan	1974	Bobby Unser
1916	Dario Resta	1935	Kelly Petillo	1957	Jimmy Bryan	1975	A. J. Foyt
1917	Earl Cooper	1936	Mauri Rose	1958	Tony Bettenhausen	1976	Gordon Johncock
1918	Ralph Mulford	1937	Wilbur Shaw	1959	Rodger Ward	1977	Tom Sneva
1919	Howard Wilcox	1938	Floyd Roberts	1960	A. J. Foyt	1978	Tom Sneva
1920	Gaston Chevrolet	1939	Wilbur Shaw	1961	A. J. Foyt	1979	A. J. Foyt
1921	Tommy Milton	1940	Rex Mays	1962	Rodger Ward	1980	Johnny Rutherford
1922	James Murphy	1941	Rex Mays	1963	A. J. Foyt	1981	George Snider
1923	Eddie Hearne	1946	Ted Horn	1964	A. J. Foyt	1982	George Snider
1924	James Murphy	1947	Ted Horn	1965	Mario Andretti	1983	Tom Sneva
1925	Peter De Paolo	1948	Ted Horn	1966	Mario Andretti	1984	Rick Mears
1926	Harry Hartz	1949	Johnnie Parsons	1967	A. J. Foyt		
1927	Peter De Paolo	1950	Henry Banks	1968	Bobby Unser		

GRAND PRIX WORLD CHAMPIONS (Formula 1 cars)

1950	Giuseppe Farina, Italy	1962	Graham Hill, Britain	1974	Emerson Fittipaldi, Brazil
1951	Juan M. Fangio, Argentina	1963	Jim Clark, Britain	1975	Niki Lauda, Austria
1952	Alberto Ascari, Italy	1964	John Surtees, Britain	1976	James Hunt, Britain
1953	Alberto Ascari, Italy	1965	Jim Clark, Britain	1977	Niki Lauda, Austria
1954	Juan M. Fangio, Argentina	1966	Jack Brabham, Australia	1978	Mario Andretti, United States
1955	Juan M. Fangio, Argentina	1967	Denis Hulme, New Zealand	1979	Jody Scheckter, South Africa
1956	Juan M. Fangio, Argentina	1968	Graham Hill, Britain	1980	Alan Jones, Australia
1957	Juan M. Fangio, Argentina	1969	Jackie Stewart, Britain	1981	Nelson Piquet, Brazil
1958	Mike Hawthorn, Britain	1970	Jochen Rindt, Austria	1982	Keke Rosberg, Finland
1959	Jack Brabham, Australia	1971	Jackie Stewart, Britain	1983	Nelson Piquet, Brazil
1960	Jack Brabham, Australia	1972	Emerson Fittipaldi, Brazil	1984	Niki Lauda, Austria
1961	Phil Hill, United States	1973	Jackie Stewart, Britain	1985	Alain Prost, France

SPORTS CAR CLUB OF AMERICA (SCCA) CAN-AM CHALLENGE

YEAR	SERIES WINNER	CAR	YEAR	SERIES WINNER	CAR
1966	John Surtees	Lola-Chevrolet	1975–76	Not Held	
1967	Bruce McLaren	McLaren M6A-Chevrolet	1977	Patrick Tambay	Lola T-333CS-Chevy
1968	Denis Hulme	McLaren M8A-Chevrolet	1978	Alan Jones	Lola T-333CS-Chevy
1969	Bruce McLaren	McLaren M8B-Chevrolet	1979	Jacky Ickx	Lola T-333CS-Chevy
1970	Denis Hulme	McLaren M8D-Chevrolet	1980	Patrick Tambay	Lola T-530-Chevy
1971	Peter Revson	McLaren M8F-Chevrolet	1981	Geoff Brabham	V.D.S.-001
1972	George Follmer	Porsche 917/10-Porsche (T)	1982	Al Unser Jr.	Galles GR3
1973	Mark Donohue	Porsche 917/30-Porsche (T)	1983	Jacques Villeneuve	Frissbee & Galles GR3
1974	Jackie Oliver	Shadow DN4-Dodge	1984	Michael Roe	V.D.S.-004

WINSTON CUP GRAND NATIONAL CHAMPIONS OF NASCAR (National Association for Stock Car Auto Racing)

YEAR	CHAMPION	CAR	YEAR	CHAMPION	CAR	YEAR	CHAMPION	CAR
1949	Red Byron	Oldsmobile	1961	Ned Jarrett	Chevrolet	1973	Benny Parsons	Chevrolet
1950	Bill Rexford	Oldsmobile	1962	Joe Weatherly	Pontiac-Merc.	1974	Richard Petty	Dodge
1951	Herb Thomas	Plymouth-Hudson	1963	Joe Weatherly	Pontiac-Merc.	1975	Richard Petty	Dodge
1952	Tim Flock	Hudson	1964	Richard Petty	Plymouth	1976	Cale Yarborough	Chev./Olds.
1953	Herb Thomas	Hudson	1965	Ned Jarrett	Ford	1977	Cale Yarborough	Chev./Olds.
1954	Lee Petty	Chrysler	1966	David Pearson	Dodge	1978	Cale Yarborough	Chev./Olds.
1955	Tim Flock	Chrysler	1967	Richard Petty	Plymouth	1979	Richard Petty	Olds./Chev.
1956	Buck Baker	Chrysler-Dodge	1968	David Pearson	Ford	1980	Dale Earnhardt	Chevrolet
1957	Buck Baker	Chevrolet	1969	David Pearson	Ford	1981	Darrell Waltrip	Buick
1958	Lee Petty	Olds./Plym.	1970	Bobby Isaac	Dodge	1982	Darrell Waltrip	Buick
1959	Lee Petty	Olds./Plym.	1971	Richard Petty	Plym./Dodge	1983	Bobby Allison	Buick
1960	Rex White	Chevrolet	1972	Richard Petty	Plym./Dodge	1984	Terry Labonte	Chevrolet

DAYTONA 500 (Stock Cars)

YEAR	WINNER	CAR	SPEED (mph)	YEAR	WINNER	CAR	SPEED (mph)
1959	Lee Petty	Oldsmobile	135.521	1973	Richard Petty	Dodge	157.205
1960	Junior Johnson	Chevrolet	124.740	1974	Richard Petty	Dodge	140.894
1961	Marvin Panch	Pontiac	149.601	1975	Benny Parsons	Chevrolet	153.649
1962	Fireball Roberts	Pontiac	152.529	1976	David Pearson	Mercury	152.181
1963	Tiny Lund	Ford	151.566	1977	Cale Yarborough	Chevrolet	153.218
1964	Richard Petty	Plymouth	154.334	1978	Bobby Allison	Ford	159.730
1965[1]	Fred Lorenzen	Ford	141.539	1979	Richard Petty	Oldsmobile	143.997
1966[2]	Richard Petty	Plymouth	160.627	1980	Buddy Baker	Oldsmobile	177.602
1967	Mario Andretti	Ford	146.926	1981	Richard Petty	Buick	169.651
1968	Cale Yarborough	Mercury	143.251	1982	Bobby Allison	Buick	153.991
1969	Lee Roy Yarborough	Ford	157.950	1983	Cale Yarborough	Pontiac	155.979
1970	Pete Hamilton	Plymouth	149.601	1984	Cale Yarborough	Chevrolet	150.994
1971	Richard Petty	Plymouth	144.462	1985	Bill Elliott	Ford	172.265
1972	A. J. Foyt	Mercury	161.550				

[1] 332.5 miles (rain). [2] 495 miles (rain).

WORLD SPEED RECORDS (One Mile)

YEAR	DRIVER	CAR	SPEED (mph)	YEAR	DRIVER	CAR	SPEED (mph)
Gasoline-engine cars				**Gasoline-engine cars**			
1898	Chasseloup Laubat	Jeantaud	39.24	1935	Sir Malcolm Campbell	Bluebird Special	301.13
1904	Henry Ford	Ford	91.37	1939	John R. Cobb	Railton	368.90
1910	Barney Oldfield	Benz	131.72	1947	John R. Cobb	Railton-Mobil	394.19
1919	Ralph De Palma	Packard	149.88	1964	Donald Campbell	Bluebird	403.10
1920	Tommy Milton	Duesenberg	155.05	1965	Bob Summers	Goldenrod	409.23
1927	H. O. D. Seagrave	Sunbeam	203.79	**Jet- or rocket-powered cars**			
1928	Ray Keech	White Triplex	207.55	1963	Craig Breedlove	Spirit of America	407.45
1929	H. O. D. Seagrave	Irving Napier	231.45	1964	Art Arfons	Green Monster	536.71
1931	Sir Malcolm Campbell	Napier-Campbell	246.09	1965	Craig Breedlove	Spirit of America	600.60
1932	Sir Malcolm Campbell	Napier-Campbell	253.96	1970	Gary Gabelich	Blue Flame	622.41
1933	Sir Malcolm Campbell	Napier-Campbell	272.11	1983	Richard Noble	Thrust 2	633.468

BASEBALL

1985 FINAL STANDINGS—MAJOR LEAGUE BASEBALL

NATIONAL LEAGUE

EASTERN DIVISION	WON	LOST	PCT.	G.B.[1]	WESTERN DIVISION	WON	LOST	PCT.	G.B.[1]
St. Louis Cardinals .	101	61	.623	—	Los Angeles Dodgers	95	67	.586	—
New York Mets	98	64	.605	3	Cincinnati Reds. . . .	89	72	.553	5½
Montreal Expos	84	77	.522	16½	Houston Astros	83	79	.512	12
Chicago Cubs	77	84	.478	23½	San Diego Padres . .	83	79	.512	12
Philadelphia Phillies	75	87	.463	26	Atlanta Braves	66	96	.407	29
Pittsburgh Pirates .	57	104	.354	43½	San Francisco Giants	62	100	.383	33

AMERICAN LEAGUE

EASTERN DIVISION	WON	LOST	PCT.	G.B.[1]	WESTERN DIVISION	WON	LOST	PCT.	G.B.[1]
Toronto Blue Jays .	99	62	.615	—	Kansas City Royals .	91	71	.562	—
New York Yankees . .	97	64	.602	2	California Angels . . .	90	72	.556	1
Detroit Tigers	84	77	.522	15	Chicago White Sox .	85	77	.525	6
Baltimore Orioles . .	83	78	.516	16	Minnesota Twins . . .	77	85	.475	14
Boston Red Sox . .	81	81	.500	18½	Oakland Athletics . .	77	85	.475	14
Milwaukee Brewers .	71	90	.441	28	Seattle Mariners . . .	74	88	.457	17
Cleveland Indians . .	60	102	.370	39½	Texas Rangers	62	99	.385	28½

[1] Games behind.

WORLD SERIES CHAMPIONS

YEAR	WINNERS	LOSERS	GAMES	YEAR	WINNERS	LOSERS	GAMES
1903[1]	Boston (A)	Pittsburgh	5–3	1945	Detroit (A)	Chicago (N)	4–3
1904	Not played		—	1946	St. Louis (N)	Boston (A)	4–3
1905	New York (N)	Philadelphia (A)	4–1	1947	New York (A)	Brooklyn (N)	4–3
1906	Chicago (A)	Chicago (N)	4–2	1948	Cleveland (A)	Boston (N)	4–2
1907[2]	Chicago (N)	Detroit (A)	4–0	1949	New York (A)	Brooklyn (N)	4–1
1908	Chicago (N)	Detroit (A)	4–1	1950	New York (A)	Philadelphia (N)	4–0
1909	Pittsburgh (N)	Detroit (A)	4–3	1951	New York (A)	New York (N)	4–2
1910	Philadelphia (A)	Chicago (N)	4–1	1952	New York (A)	Brooklyn (N)	4–3
1911	Philadelphia (A)	New York (N)	4–2	1953	New York (A)	Brooklyn (N)	4–2
1912[2]	Boston (A)	New York (N)	4–3	1954	New York (N)	Cleveland (A)	4–0
1913	Philadelphia (A)	New York (N)	4–1	1955	Brooklyn (N)	New York (A)	4–3
1914	Boston (N)	Philadelphia (A)	4–0	1956	New York (A)	Brooklyn (N)	4–3
1915	Boston (A)	Philadelphia (N)	4–1	1957	Milwaukee (N)	New York (A)	4–3
1916	Boston (A)	Brooklyn (N)	4–1	1958	New York (A)	Milwaukee (N)	4–3
1917	Chicago (A)	New York (N)	4–2	1959	Los Angeles (N)	Chicago (A)	4–2
1918	Boston (A)	Chicago (N)	4–2	1960	Pittsburgh (N)	New York (A)	4–3
1919[1]	Cincinnati (N)	Chicago (A)	5–3	1961	New York (A)	Cincinnati (N)	4–1
1920[1]	Cleveland (A)	Brooklyn (N)	5–2	1962	New York (A)	San Francisco (N)	4–3
1921[1]	New York (N)	New York (A)	5–3	1963	Los Angeles (N)	New York (A)	4–0
1922[2]	New York (N)	New York (A)	4–0	1964	St. Louis (N)	New York (A)	4–3
1923	New York (A)	New York (N)	4–2	1965	Los Angeles (N)	Minnesota (A)	4–3
1924	Washington (A)	New York (N)	4–3	1966	Baltimore (A)	Los Angeles (N)	4–0
1925	Pittsburgh (N)	Washington (A)	4–3	1967	St. Louis (N)	Boston (A)	4–3
1926	St. Louis (N)	New York (A)	4–3	1968	Detroit (A)	St. Louis (N)	4–3
1927	New York (A)	Pittsburgh (N)	4–0	1969	N.Y. Mets (N)	Baltimore (A)	4–1
1928	New York (A)	St. Louis (N)	4–0	1970	Baltimore (A)	Cincinnati (N)	4–1
1929	Philadelphia (A)	Chicago (N)	4–1	1971	Pittsburgh (N)	Baltimore (A)	4–3
1930	Philadelphia (A)	St. Louis (N)	4–2	1972	Oakland (A)	Cincinnati (N)	4–3
1931	St. Louis (N)	Philadelphia (A)	4–3	1973	Oakland (A)	N.Y. Mets (N)	4–3
1932	New York (A)	Chicago (N)	4–0	1974	Oakland (A)	Los Angeles (N)	4–1
1933	New York (N)	Washington (A)	4–1	1975	Cincinnati (N)	Boston (A)	4–3
1934	St. Louis (N)	Detroit (A)	4–3	1976	Cincinnati (N)	New York (A)	4–0
1935	Detroit (A)	Chicago (N)	4–2	1977	New York (A)	Los Angeles (N)	4–2
1936	New York (A)	New York (N)	4–2	1978	New York (A)	Los Angeles (N)	4–2
1937	New York (A)	New York (N)	4–1	1979	Pittsburgh (N)	Baltimore (A)	4–3
1938	New York (A)	Chicago (N)	4–0	1980	Philadelphia (N)	Kansas City (A)	4–2
1939	New York (A)	Cincinnati (N)	4–0	1981	Los Angeles (N)	New York (A)	4–2
1940	Cincinnati (N)	Detroit (A)	4–3	1982	St. Louis (N)	Milwaukee (A)	4–3
1941	New York (A)	Brooklyn (N)	4–1	1983	Baltimore (A)	Philadelphia (N)	4–1
1942	St. Louis (N)	New York (A)	4–1	1984	Detroit (A)	San Diego (N)	4–1
1943	New York (A)	St. Louis (N)	4–1	1985	*	*	*
1944	St. Louis (N)	St. Louis (A)	4–2				

[1] A nine-game World Series was scheduled. [2] One tie game played. *See page 26.

SELECTED WORLD SERIES BASEBALL RECORDS[1]

TEAM RECORDS:

World championships won	New York Yankees (AL)—22; St. Louis Cardinals (NL)—8
Played in most World Series	New York Yankees (AL)—33 times from 1921 through 1981
Games won	New York Yankees (AL)—109
Played in most World Series, National League .	Giants, New York/San Francisco (NL)—15 times from 1905 through 1962 (14 times representing New York and once San Francisco)
Hits by one team, one game	New York Giants (NL) and St. Louis Cardinals (NL), tie—20. The Giants made 20 hits against the Yankees in the Oct. 7, 1921, World Series game; the Cardinals did the same against the Boston Red Sox in the Oct. 10, 1946, series game
Batting average, highest	New York Yankees (AL)—.338 in the seven-game series against the Pittsburgh Pirates in 1960
Batting average, lowest, one series	Los Angeles Dodgers (NL)—.142 against Baltimore pitchers in 1966
Runs batted in, one series	New York Yankees (AL)—54 runs in seven games in 1960
Runs, one series	New York Yankees (AL)—55 in seven-game series against Pittsburgh Pirates (NL) in 1960
Home runs, one series	New York Yankee batters (AL)—12 home runs in seven games against the Brooklyn Dodgers in 1956
Home runs, one game	New York Yankee batters (AL)—5 home runs against St. Louis Cardinal pitching in a game played Oct. 9, 1928
Doubles, one series	St. Louis Cardinals (NL)—19 doubles against the Boston Red Sox in 1946; the Philadelphia Athletics (AL) also scored 19 series doubles against the Chicago Cubs in 1910
Bases on balls received, one series	New York Yankee batters (AL)—38 times against Brooklyn Dodger pitching in seven games in 1947
Strike outs, one series	Oakland A's batters (AL)—62 times against New York Mets pitching in seven games in 1973
Double plays, one series	Brooklyn Dodgers (NL)—12, in a seven-game series against the New York Yankees in 1955
Triple plays, one series	Cleveland Indians (AL)—1. The only World Series triple play was an unassisted one made by Cleveland 2d baseman Billy Wambsganss in the 1920 series against Brooklyn
Fielding record, one series	New York Yankees (AL)—1.000 (no errors) in the 1937 World Series against the New York Giants; Baltimore Orioles (AL)—1.000 (no errors) in the 1966 World Series against Los Angeles

INDIVIDUAL RECORDS:

Home runs, one game	Babe Ruth, New York Yankees (AL)—3 home runs on Oct. 6, 1926, and again on Oct. 9, 1928; Reggie Jackson, New York Yankees (AL)—3 consecutive home runs on Oct. 18, 1977
Home runs in single World Series	Reggie Jackson, New York Yankees (AL)—5 against Los Angeles Dodgers (NL) in 1977
Home runs in World Series, lifetime	Mickey Mantle, New York Yankees (AL)—18
Batting average, lifetime, 20 or more games ...	Lou Brock, St. Louis (NL)—.391, in three World Series: 1964, 1967, 1968 (21 games, 87 at-bats, 34 hits)
Hits, lifetime	Yogi Berra, New York Yankees (AL)—71, between 1947 and 1963
Hits, game	Paul Molitor, Milwaukee Brewers (AL)—5 on Oct. 12, 1982
Batting average in single World Series by regular starting player	Babe Ruth, New York Yankees (AL)—.625, in the 1928 series against the St. Louis Cardinals (four games)
Game-winning home runs, one series	Casey Stengel, New York Giants (NL)—won two games with home runs in 1923 series; Rudy York of Boston Red Sox (AL) also won two games with home runs in 1946 series
Game-winning home runs, lifetime	Hank Greenberg, Detroit Tigers (AL)—won three series games with home runs: in 1935 against Chicago Cubs; in 1940 against Cincinnati Reds; and in 1945 against Chicago Cubs
Runs batted in, one game	Bobby Richardson, New York Yankees (AL)—6 on Oct. 8, 1960, against the Pittsburgh Pirates (NL)
Runs, in one series	Reggie Jackson, N.Y. Yankees (AL)—10 in 1977
Runs, lifetime	Mickey Mantle, N.Y. Yankees (AL)—42 in 12 series, 65 games (1951–64)
Errors, one game	Willie Davis, Los Angeles Dodgers (NL)—three errors, all in the same inning against the Baltimore Orioles on Oct. 6, 1966
Played in most World Series	Yogi Berra, New York Yankees (AL)—14 times from 1947 to 1963
Played on most championship teams	Yogi Berra, New York Yankees (AL)—10 times
Pitching no-hitter, one game	Don Larsen, New York Yankees (AL)—won a perfect no-hitter against the Brooklyn Dodgers, Oct. 8, 1956. He faced the minimum 27 batters, threw 97 pitches, and allowed no base runners
Pitcher with most World Series wins, lifetime ..	Whitey Ford, New York Yankees (AL)—10, between 1950 and 1964
Pitcher with most strikeouts, one game	Bob Gibson, St. Louis Cardinals (NL)—17, against the Detroit Tigers in the first game of the 1968 World Series
Pitching consecutive scoreless innings	Whitey Ford, New York Yankees (AL)—33 $\frac{2}{3}$ innings, during the 1960, 1961, and 1962 series

[1] Does not include 1985 season.

MAJOR LEAGUE BASEBALL PARKS

TEAM	STADIUM	SEATING CAPACITY	DISTANCE FROM HOME PLATE (in feet)		
			Right Field	Center Field	Left Field
NATIONAL LEAGUE					
Atlanta Braves	Atlanta Stadium	53,046	330	402	330
Chicago Cubs	Wrigley Field	37,242	355	400	353
Cincinnati Reds	Riverfront Stadium............	52,392	330	404	330
Houston Astros	The Astrodome	45,000	340	406	340
Los Angeles Dodgers	Dodger Stadium	56,000	330	400	330
Montreal Expos	Olympic Stadium	59,149	325	404	325
New York Mets	Shea Stadium	55,601	338	410	338
Philadelphia Phillies	Veterans Stadium.............	66,507	330	408	330
Pittsburgh Pirates ..	Three Rivers Stadium	58,365	335	400	335
St. Louis Cardinals..	Busch Memorial Stadium	50,222	330	414	330
San Diego Padres ..	Jack Murphy Stadium	58,671	330	405	330
San Francisco Giants	Candlestick Park	58,000	335	400	335
AMERICAN LEAGUE					
Baltimore Orioles...	Memorial Stadium	53,196	309	405	309
Boston Red Sox	Fenway Park	33,583	302	390	315
California Angels ...	Anaheim Stadium	67,335	370	404	370
Chicago White Sox..	Comiskey Park	44,432	341	401	341
Cleveland Indians...	Cleveland Stadium	74,208	320	400	320
Detroit Tigers	Tiger Stadium	52,687	325	440	340
Kansas City Royals .	Royals Stadium	40,635	330	410	330
Milwaukee Brewers .	County Stadium	53,192	362	402	362
Minnesota Twins ...	Hubert H. Humphrey Metrodome	55,122	367	408	385
New York Yankees ..	Yankee Stadium	57,545	353	417	387
Oakland Athletics ..	Oakland Coliseum	50,219	330	397	330
Seattle Mariners....	The Kingdome.................	59,438	316	410	316
Texas Rangers	Arlington Stadium	43,508	330	380	330
Toronto Blue Jays ..	Exhibition Stadium	43,737	330	400	330

TEAM-BY-TEAM VICTORIES: 1985

To determine a team's regular-season wins read horizontally. To determine a team's regular-season losses read down the proper column. For 1985 postseason playoff results, see page 777.

NATIONAL LEAGUE

EASTERN DIVISION	St.L.	N.Y.	Mtl.	Chi.	Phi.	Pitt.	L.A.	Cin.	Hou.	S.D.	Atl.	S.F.	TOTAL WINS
St. Louis	–	10	7	14	10	15	5	7	6	8	9	10	101
New York	8	–	9	14	11	10	5	8	8	7	10	8	98
Montreal..........	11	9	–	11	8	9	5	4	6	5	9	7	84
Chicago	4	4	7	–	13	13	5	5	5	8	7	6	77
Philadelphia.......	8	7	10	5	–	11	8	5	8	5	2	6	75
Pittsburgh........	3	8	8	5	7	–	4	3	6	4	6	3	57
WESTERN DIVISION													
Los Angeles	7	7	7	7	4	8	–	11	12	8	13	11	95
Cincinnati........	5	4	8	6	7	9	7	–	11	9	11	12	89
Houston	6	4	6	7	4	6	6	7	–	12	10	15	83
San Diego.........	4	5	7	4	7	8	10	9	6	–	11	12	83
Atlanta	3	2	3	5	10	6	5	7	8	7	–	10	66
San Francisco	2	4	5	6	6	9	7	6	3	6	8	–	62
TOTAL LOSSES ...	61	64	77	84	87	104	67	72	79	79	96	100	–

AMERICAN LEAGUE

EASTERN DIVISION	Tor.	N.Y.	Det.	Bal.	Bos.	Mil.	Cle.	K.C.	Cal.	Chi.	Min.	Oak.	Sea.	Tex.	TOTAL WINS
Toronto	–	7	7	8	4	9	9	5	7	9	8	7	10	9	99
New York	6	–	3	12	8	6	7	7	9	6	9	7	9	8	97
Detroit	6	9	–	7	7	9	8	5	4	6	3	8	5	7	84
Baltimore	4	1	6	–	5	9	8	6	7	8	6	7	6	10	83
Boston	9	5	6	8	–	5	8	5	5	4	7	8	6	5	81
Milwaukee	4	7	4	4	8	–	6	4	3	7	9	3	4	8	71
Cleveland	4	6	5	5	5	7	–	2	4	2	4	3	6	7	60
WESTERN DIVISION															
Kansas City	7	5	7	6	7	8	10	–	9	8	7	8	3	6	91
California	5	3	8	5	7	9	8	4	–	8	9	6	9	9	90
Chicago	3	6	6	4	8	5	10	5	5	–	6	8	9	10	85
Minnesota	4	3	9	6	5	3	8	6	4	7	–	8	6	8	77
Oakland	5	5	4	5	4	9	9	5	7	5	5	–	8	6	77
Seattle	2	5	3	7	6	6	8	6	10	4	4	7	–	6	74
Texas	3	4	5	2	7	3	5	7	4	3	5	7	7	–	62
TOTAL LOSSES ...	62	64	77	78	81	90	102	71	72	77	85	85	88	99	–

1985 LEADING BASEBALL BATTERS[1]

NATIONAL LEAGUE
(Close of regular season)

PLAYER—CLUB	PCT.	AB	R	H	HR	RBI
McGee, St. Louis	.353	612	114	216	10	82
Guerrero, Los Angeles ..	.320	487	99	156	33	87
Raines, Montreal	.320	575	115	184	11	41
Gwynn, San Diego	.317	622	90	197	6	46
Parker, Cincinnati	.312	635	88	198	34	125
Hernandez, New York ...	.309	593	87	183	10	91
Moreland, Chicago......	.307	587	74	180	14	106
Sandberg, Chicago	.305	609	113	186	26	83
Herr, St. Louis	.302	596	97	180	8	110
Murphy, Atlanta	.300	616	118	185	37	111

AMERICAN LEAGUE
(Close of regular season)

PLAYER—CLUB	PCT.	AB	R	H	HR	RBI
Boggs, Boston	.368	653	107	240	8	78
Brett, Kansas City	.335	550	108	184	30	112
Mattingly, New York	.324	652	107	211	35	145
Henderson, New York ...	.314	547	146	172	24	72
Butler, Cleveland	.311	591	106	184	5	50
Baines, Chicago	.309	640	86	198	22	113
Bradley, Seattle	.300	641	100	192	26	88
Buckner, Boston	.299	673	89	201	16	110
Molitor, Milwaukee	.297	576	93	171	10	48
Murray, Baltimore	.297	583	111	173	31	124

[1] Based on 3.1 plate appearances for each game player's team played in 1985 season.

1985 LEADING BASEBALL PITCHERS[1]

NATIONAL LEAGUE

PITCHER—CLUB	ERA	W	L	IP	H	BB	SO
Gooden, New York...	1.53	24	4	276.2	198	69	268
Tudor, St. Louis ...	1.93	21	8	275.0	209	49	169
Hershiser, Los Angeles	2.03	19	3	239.2	179	68	157
Reuschel, Pittsburgh	2.27	14	8	194.0	153	52	138
Welch, Los Angeles	2.31	14	4	167.1	141	35	96
Valenzuela, Los Angeles	2.45	17	10	272.1	211	101	208
Fernandez, New York	2.80	9	9	170.1	108	80	180
Cox, St. Louis	2.88	18	9	241.0	226	64	131
Darling, New York .	2.90	16	6	248.0	214	114	167
Smith, Montreal ...	2.91	18	5	222.1	193	41	127

AMERICAN LEAGUE

PITCHER—CLUB	ERA	W	L	IP	H	BB	SO
Stieb, Toronto	2.48	14	13	265.0	206	96	167
Leibrandt, Kansas City	2.69	17	9	237.2	223	68	108
Saberhagen, Kansas City	2.87	20	6	235.1	211	38	158
Key, Toronto	3.00	14	6	212.2	188	50	85
Blyleven, Minnesota	3.16	17	16	293.2	264	75	206
Seaver, Chicago ...	3.17	16	11	238.2	223	69	134
Guidry, New York ..	3.27	22	6	259.0	243	42	143
Hough, Texas	3.31	14	16	250.1	198	83	141
Morris, Detroit	3.33	16	11	257.0	212	110	191
Petry, Detroit.......	3.36	15	13	238.2	190	81	109

[1] 162 or more innings pitched; 1985 season.

1985 TEAM BATTING—MAJOR LEAGUE BASEBALL REGULAR SEASON

NATIONAL LEAGUE

TEAM	AVG.	AB	R	H	HR	RBI
St. Louis	.264	5,467	747	1,446	87	687
Houston	.261	5,582	706	1,457	121	666
Los Angeles ...	.261	5,502	682	1,424	129	632
New York	.257	5,549	695	1,425	134	651
San Diego.....	.255	5,507	650	1,405	109	611
Cincinnati	.255	5,431	677	1,385	114	634
Chicago	.254	5,492	686	1,397	150	640
Montreal......	.247	5,429	633	1,342	118	593
Pittsburgh	.247	5,435	568	1,340	80	535
Atlanta	.246	5,526	632	1,359	126	598
Philadelphia...	.245	5,477	667	1,343	141	628
San Francisco .	.233	5,420	556	1,263	115	517

AMERICAN LEAGUE

TEAM	AVG.	AB	R	H	HR	RBI
Boston	.282	5,720	800	1,615	162	760
Toronto	.269	5,508	759	1,482	158	715
New York	.267	5,458	839	1,458	176	793
Cleveland	.265	5,527	729	1,465	116	689
Oakland	.264	5,581	757	1,475	155	691
Minnesota	.264	5,509	705	1,453	141	678
Milwaukee	.263	5,568	690	1,467	101	636
Baltimore	.263	5,517	818	1,451	214	773
Seattle	.255	5,521	719	1,410	171	686
Texas	.253	5,361	617	1,359	129	578
Detroit	.253	5,575	729	1,413	202	703
Chicago	.253	5,470	736	1,386	146	695
Kansas City ...	.252	5,500	687	1,384	154	657
California	.251	5,442	732	1,364	153	685

PENNANT WINNERS—MAJOR LEAGUE BASEBALL

NATIONAL LEAGUE

YEAR	CLUB	W	L	PCT.	MANAGER
1901	Pittsburgh	90	49	.647	Fred Clarke
1902	Pittsburgh	103	36	.741	Fred Clarke
1903	Pittsburgh	91	49	.650	Fred Clarke
1904	New York	106	47	.693	John McGraw
1905	New York	105	48	.686	John McGraw
1906	Chicago	116	36	.763	Frank Chance
1907	Chicago	107	45	.704	Frank Chance
1908	Chicago	99	55	.643	Frank Chance
1909	Pittsburgh	110	42	.724	Fred Clarke
1910	Chicago	104	50	.675	Frank Chance
1911	New York	99	54	.647	John McGraw
1912	New York	103	48	.682	John McGraw
1913	New York	101	51	.664	John McGraw
1914	Boston	94	59	.614	G. Stallings

AMERICAN LEAGUE

YEAR	CLUB	W	L	PCT.	MANAGER
1901	Chicago	83	53	.610	Clark Griffith
1902	Philadelphia	83	53	.610	Connie Mack
1903	Boston	91	47	.659	James Collins
1904	Boston	95	59	.617	James Collins
1905	Philadelphia	92	56	.622	Connie Mack
1906	Chicago	93	58	.616	Fielder Jones
1907	Detroit	92	58	.613	Hugh Jennings
1908	Detroit	90	63	.588	Hugh Jennings
1909	Detroit	98	54	.645	Hugh Jennings
1910	Philadelphia	102	48	.680	Connie Mack
1911	Philadelphia	101	50	.669	Connie Mack
1912	Boston	105	47	.691	Jake Stahl
1913	Philadelphia	96	57	.627	Connie Mack
1914	Philadelphia	99	53	.651	Connie Mack

PENNANT WINNERS (continued)

NATIONAL LEAGUE					AMERICAN LEAGUE						
YEAR	CLUB	W	L	PCT.	MANAGER	YEAR	CLUB	W	L	PCT.	MANAGER
1915	Philadelphia	90	62	.592	Pat Moran	1915	Boston	101	50	.669	W. Carrigan
1916	Brooklyn	94	60	.610	W. Robinson	1916	Boston	91	63	.591	W. Carrigan
1917	New York	98	56	.636	John McGraw	1917	Chicago	100	54	.649	C. Rowland
1918	Chicago	84	45	.651	F. Mitchell	1918	Boston	75	51	.595	Ed Barrow
1919	Cincinnati	96	44	.686	Pat Moran	1919	Chicago	88	52	.629	Kid Gleason
1920	Brooklyn	93	61	.604	W. Robinson	1920	Cleveland	98	56	.636	Tris Speaker
1921	New York	94	59	.614	John McGraw	1921	New York	98	55	.641	M. Huggins
1922	New York	93	61	.604	John McGraw	1922	New York	94	60	.610	M. Huggins
1923	New York	95	58	.621	John McGraw	1923	New York	98	54	.645	M. Huggins
1924	New York	93	60	.608	John McGraw	1924	Washington	92	62	.597	Bucky Harris
1925	Pittsburgh	95	58	.621	W. McKechnie	1925	Washington	96	55	.636	Bucky Harris
1926	St. Louis	89	65	.578	Roger Hornsby	1926	New York	91	63	.591	M. Huggins
1927	Pittsburgh	94	60	.610	Donie Bush	1927	New York	110	44	.714	M. Huggins
1928	St. Louis	95	59	.617	W. McKechnie	1928	New York	101	53	.656	M. Huggins
1929	Chicago	98	54	.645	Joe McCarthy	1929	Philadelphia	104	46	.693	Connie Mack
1930	St. Louis	92	62	.597	Gabby Street	1930	Philadelphia	102	52	.662	Connie Mack
1931	St. Louis	101	53	.656	Gabby Street	1931	Philadelphia	107	45	.704	Connie Mack
1932	Chicago	90	64	.584	C. Grimm	1932	New York	107	47	.695	Joe McCarthy
1933	New York	91	61	.599	Bill Terry	1933	Washington	99	53	.651	Joe Cronin
1934	St. Louis	95	58	.621	Frank Frisch	1934	Detroit	101	53	.656	G. Cochrane
1935	Chicago	100	54	.649	C. Grimm	1935	Detroit	93	58	.616	G. Cochrane
1936	New York	92	62	.597	Bill Terry	1936	New York	102	51	.667	Joe McCarthy
1937	New York	95	57	.625	Bill Terry	1937	New York	102	52	.662	Joe McCarthy
1938	Chicago	89	63	.586	C. Hartnett	1938	New York	99	53	.651	Joe McCarthy
1939	Cincinnati	97	57	.630	W. McKechnie	1939	New York	106	45	.702	Joe McCarthy
1940	Cincinnati	100	53	.654	W. McKechnie	1940	Detroit	90	64	.584	D. Baker
1941	Brooklyn	100	54	.649	Leo Durocher	1941	New York	101	53	.656	Joe McCarthy
1942	St. Louis	106	48	.688	W. Southworth	1942	New York	103	51	.669	Joe McCarthy
1943	St. Louis	105	49	.682	W. Southworth	1943	New York	98	56	.636	Joe McCarthy
1944	St. Louis	105	49	.682	W. Southworth	1944	St. Louis	89	65	.578	Luke Sewell
1945	Chicago	98	56	.636	C. Grimm	1945	Detroit	88	65	.575	Steve O'Neill
1946	St. Louis	98	58	.628	Eddie Dyer	1946	Boston	104	50	.675	Joe Cronin
1947	Brooklyn	94	60	.610	Barney Shotton	1947	New York	97	57	.630	Bucky Harris
1948	Boston	91	62	.595	W. Southworth	1948	Cleveland	97	58	.626	Lou Boudreau
1949	Brooklyn	97	57	.630	Barney Shotton	1949	New York	97	57	.630	Casey Stengel
1950	Philadelphia	91	63	.591	Eddie Sawyer	1950	New York	98	56	.636	Casey Stengel
1951	New York	98	59	.624	Leo Durocher	1951	New York	98	56	.636	Casey Stengel
1952	Brooklyn	96	57	.627	Chuck Dressen	1952	New York	95	59	.617	Casey Stengel
1953	Brooklyn	105	49	.682	Chuck Dressen	1953	New York	99	52	.656	Casey Stengel
1954	New York	97	57	.630	Leo Durocher	1954	Cleveland	111	43	.721	Al Lopez
1955	Brooklyn	98	55	.641	Walt Alston	1955	New York	96	58	.623	Casey Stengel
1956	Brooklyn	93	61	.604	Walt Alston	1956	New York	97	57	.630	Casey Stengel
1957	Milwaukee	95	59	.617	Fred Haney	1957	New York	98	56	.636	Casey Stengel
1958	Milwaukee	92	62	.597	Fred Haney	1958	New York	92	62	.597	Casey Stengel
1959	Los Angeles	88	68	.564	Walt Alston	1959	Chicago	94	60	.610	Al Lopez
1960	Pittsburgh	95	59	.617	Danny Murtaugh	1960	New York	97	57	.630	Casey Stengel
1961	Cincinnati	93	61	.604	Fred Hutchinson	1961	New York	109	53	.673	Ralph Houk
1962	San Fran.	103	62	.624	Alvin Dark	1962	New York	96	66	.593	Ralph Houk
1963	Los Angeles	99	63	.611	Walt Alston	1963	New York	104	57	.646	Ralph Houk
1964	St. Louis	93	69	.574	Johnny Keane	1964	New York	99	63	.611	Yogi Berra
1965	Los Angeles	97	65	.599	Walt Alston	1965	Minnesota	102	60	.630	Sam Mele
1966	Los Angeles	95	67	.586	Walt Alston	1966	Baltimore	97	63	.606	Hank Bauer
1967	St. Louis	101	60	.627	A. Schoendienst	1967	Boston	92	70	.568	Dick Williams
1968	St. Louis	97	65	.599	A. Schoendienst	1968	Detroit	103	59	.636	M. Smith
1969	N.Y. Mets	100	62	.617	Gil Hodges	1969	Baltimore	109	53	.673	Earl Weaver
1970	Cincinnati	102	60	.630	Sparky Anderson	1970	Baltimore	108	54	.667	Earl Weaver
1971	Pittsburgh	97	65	.599	Danny Murtaugh	1971	Baltimore	101	57	.639	Earl Weaver
1972	Cincinnati	95	59	.617	Sparky Anderson	1972	Oakland	93	62	.600	Dick Williams
1973	N.Y. Mets	82	79	.509	Yogi Berra	1973	Oakland	94	68	.580	Dick Williams
1974	Los Angeles	102	60	.630	Walt Alston	1974	Oakland	90	72	.556	Alvin Dark
1975	Cincinnati	108	54	.667	Sparky Anderson	1975	Boston	95	65	.594	Darrell Johnson
1976	Cincinnati	102	60	.630	Sparky Anderson	1976	New York	97	62	.610	Billy Martin
1977	Los Angeles	98	64	.605	Tommy Lasorda	1977	New York	100	62	.617	Billy Martin
1978	Los Angeles	95	67	.586	Tommy Lasorda	1978	New York	100	63	.613	Bob Lemon
1979	Pittsburgh	98	64	.605	Chuck Tanner	1979	Baltimore	102	57	.642	Earl Weaver
1980	Philadelphia	91	71	.562	Dallas Green	1980	Kansas City	97	65	.599	Jim Frey
1981	Los Angeles	63	47	.573	Tommy Lasorda	1981	New York	59	48	.551	Bob Lemon
1982	St. Louis	92	70	.568	Whitey Herzog	1982	Milwaukee	95	67	.586	Harvey Kuenn
1983	Philadelphia	90	72	.556	Paul Owens	1983	Baltimore	98	64	.605	Joe Altobelli
1984	San Diego	92	70	.596	Dick Williams	1984	Detroit	104	58	.642	Sparky Anderson
1985	St. Louis	101	61	.623	Whitey Herzog	1985	Kansas City	91	71	.562	Dick Howser

ALL-STAR BASEBALL GAME RESULTS: 1933–1985

YEAR	WINNING LEAGUE	SCORE	YEAR	WINNING LEAGUE	SCORE	YEAR	WINNING LEAGUE	SCORE	YEAR	WINNING LEAGUE	SCORE
1933	American	4–2	1948	American	5–2	1961	National	5–4	1974	National	7–2
1934	American	9–7	1949	American	11–7		Tie game	1–1	1975	National	6–3
1935	American	4–1	1950	National	4–3	1962	National	3–1	1976	National	7–1
1936	National	4–3	1951	National	8–3		American	9–4	1977	National	7–5
1937	American	8–3	1952	National	3–2	1963	National	5–3	1978	National	7–3
1938	National	4–1	1953	National	5–1	1964	National	7–4	1979	National	7–6
1939	American	3–1	1954	American	11–9	1965	National	6–5	1980	National	4–2
1940	National	4–0	1955	National	6–5	1966	National	2–1	1981	National	5–4
1941	American	7–5	1956	National	7–3	1967	National	2–1	1982	National	4–1
1942	American	3–1	1957	American	6–5	1968	National	1–0	1983	American	13–3
1943	American	5–3	1958	American	4–3	1969	National	9–3	1984	National	3–1
1944	National	7–1	1959	National	5–4	1970	National	5–4	1985	National	6–1
1945	No game			American	5–3	1971	American	6–4			
1946	American	12–0	1960	National	5–3	1972	National	4–3			
1947	American	2–1		National	6–0	1973	National	7–1			

POSTSEASON BASEBALL PLAYOFFS

NATIONAL LEAGUE

1969	New York defeated Atlanta, 3 games to 0
1970	Cincinnati defeated Pittsburgh, 3 games to 0
1971	Pittsburgh defeated San Francisco, 3 games to 1
1972	Cincinnati defeated Pittsburgh, 3 games to 2
1973	New York defeated Cincinnati, 3 games to 2
1974	Los Angeles defeated Pittsburgh, 3 games to 1
1975	Cincinnati defeated Pittsburgh, 3 games to 0
1976	Cincinnati defeated Philadelphia, 3 games to 0
1977	Los Angeles defeated Philadelphia, 3 games to 1
1978	Los Angeles defeated Philadelphia, 3 games to 1
1979	Pittsburgh defeated Cincinnati, 3 games to 0
1980	Philadelphia defeated Houston, 3 games to 2
1981	Los Angeles defeated Montreal, 3 games to 2
1982	St. Louis defeated Atlanta, 3 games to 0
1983	Philadelphia defeated Los Angeles, 3 games to 1
1984	San Diego defeated the Chicago Cubs, 3 games to 2
1985	St. Louis defeated Los Angeles, 4 games to 2

AMERICAN LEAGUE

1969	Baltimore defeated Minnesota, 3 games to 0
1970	Baltimore defeated Minnesota, 3 games to 0
1971	Baltimore defeated Oakland, 3 games to 0
1972	Oakland defeated Detroit, 3 games to 2
1973	Oakland defeated Baltimore, 3 games to 2
1974	Oakland defeated Baltimore, 3 games to 1
1975	Boston defeated Oakland, 3 games to 0
1976	New York defeated Kansas City, 3 games to 2
1977	New York defeated Kansas City, 3 games to 2
1978	New York defeated Kansas City, 3 games to 1
1979	Baltimore defeated California, 3 games to 1
1980	Kansas City defeated New York, 3 games to 0
1981	New York defeated Oakland, 3 games to 0
1982	Milwaukee defeated California, 3 games to 2
1983	Baltimore defeated Chicago, 3 games to 1
1984	Detroit defeated Kansas City, 3 games to 0
1985	Kansas City defeated Toronto, 4 games to 3

INDIVIDUAL MAJOR LEAGUE PITCHING RECORDS

PITCHING	AMERICAN LEAGUE	NATIONAL LEAGUE
Games pitched, career	899—Sparky Lyle, Boston, N.Y., Texas, Chicago, Phil. (NL) (1967–82)[1]	1,070—J. Hoyt Wilhelm (1952–69)[1]
Games pitched, league	807—Sparky Lyle, Boston, N.Y., Texas, Chicago, (1967–82)	846—Elroy Face, Pittsburgh, Montreal (1953–69)
Games pitched, season	90—Mike Marshall, Minn. (1979)	106—Mike Marshall, L.A. (1974)
Games started, career	666—Walter Johnson, Wash. (1907–27)	665—Warren Spahn (1942–65)
Games started, season	51—Jack Chesbro, N.Y. (1904)	48—Joe McGinnity, N.Y. (1903)
Games completed, career	531—Walter Johnson, Wash. (1907–27)	437—Grover Alexander (1911–29)
Games completed, season	48—Jack Chesbro, N.Y. (1904)	45—Victor Willis, Boston (1902)
Earned run average, career (2,000 or more innings)	2.37—Walter Johnson, Wash. (1907–1927)	2.33—James L. Vaughn, Chicago (1913–21)
Earned run average, season	1.01—Hubert Leonard, Boston (1914)	1.12—Bob Gibson, St. Louis (1968)
Games won, career	416—Walter Johnson, Wash. (1907–27)	373—Grover Alexander, Christy Mathewson, N.Y., Cin. (1900–16)
Games won, season	41—Jack Chesbro, N.Y. (1904)	37—Christy Mathewson (1908)
Games won, consecutive	17—John Allen, Cleveland (1936–37); Dave McNally, Baltimore (1968–69)	24—Carl Hubbell, New York (1936–37)
Shutout games, career	113—Walter Johnson, Wash. (1907–27)	90—Grover Alexander (1911–29)
Shutout games, season	13—John Coombs, Philadelphia (1910)	16—Grover Alexander (1916)
Shutout innings, consecutive	56—Walter Johnson, Wash. (1913)	58—Don Drysdale, Los Angeles (1968)
No-hit games, career	4—Nolan Ryan, California, 1973 (2), 1974 (1), 1975 (1)[2]	4—Sandy Koufax, Los Angeles (1962–65)
Strikeouts, 9-inning game	19—Nolan Ryan, Calif. (1974)	19—Steve Carlton, St. Louis (1969); Tom Seaver, New York (1970)
Strikeouts, season	383—Nolan Ryan, California (1973)	382—Sandy Koufax, Los Angeles (1965)
Strikeouts, career	3,508—Walter Johnson, Wash. (1907–27)	4,083—Nolan Ryan (1966–85)[1]
Won-lost percentage, season, 16 or more decisions	.938—John Allen, Cleveland (1937), won 15, lost 1	.947—ElRoy Face, Pittsburgh (1959), won 18, lost 1

[1] Career total includes play in both leagues. [2] Fifth no-hitter for Houston (NL), Sept. 26, 1981.

INDIVIDUAL MAJOR LEAGUE BATTING RECORDS

BATTING	AMERICAN LEAGUE	NATIONAL LEAGUE
Games, career	3,308—Carl Yastrzemski, Boston (1961–83)	3,371—Pete Rose (1963-84)
Games, consecutive, runs scored	18—Red Rolfe, New York (Aug. 9-25, 1939)	17—Ted Kluszewski, Cincinnati (Aug. 27-Sept. 13, 1954)
Batting average, years leading league	12—Ty Cobb, Detroit (1907–15, 1917–19)	8—Honus Wagner, Pittsburgh (1900, 1903–04, 1906–09, 1911)
Batting average, career	.367—Ty Cobb, Detroit (1905–26), Philadelphia (1927–28)	.359—Rogers Hornsby, St. Louis, N.Y., Boston, Chicago (1915–32)
Batting average, season	.422—Napoleon Lajoie, Phila. (1901)	.424—Rogers Hornsby, St. Louis (1924)
Games, consecutive	2,130—Lou Gehrig, New York (1925–39)	1,207—Steve Garvey, San Diego (1975–83)
Runs scored, career	2,244—Ty Cobb, Detroit, Phil. (1905–28)	2,174—Hank Aaron (1954–76) *
Runs scored, season...........	177—Babe Ruth, New York (1921)	158—Chuck Klein, Philadelphia (1930)
Runs scored, one game	6—John Pesky, Boston, (May 8, 1946)	6—Mel Ott, New York (April 30, 1944); Frank Torre, Milwaukee (Sept. 2, 1957)
Runs batted in, career	2,209—Babe Ruth, Boston (1914–19), New York (1920–34), Boston (NL) (1935) *	2,297—Hank Aaron, (1954-76) Milw. (NL), Atlanta (NL), Milw. (AL) *
Runs batted in, season	184—Lou Gehrig, New York (1931)	190—Hack Wilson, Chicago (1930)
Runs batted in, game	11—Tony Lazzeri, New York (1936)	12—Jim Bottomley, St. Louis (1924)
Hits, career	4,191—Ty Cobb, Detroit, Philadelphia	4,204—Pete Rose, Cincinnati, Philadelphia (1963–85)
Hits, season	257—George Sisler, St. Louis (1920)	254—Frank O'Doul, Philadelphia (1929); Bill Terry, New York (1930)
Games with 1 or more hits in season	133—Al Simmons, Philadelphia (1925)	135—Chuck Klein, Philadelphia (1930)
Games batted safely, consecutive	56—Joe DiMaggio, New York (1941)	44—Pete Rose, Cincinnati (1978)
Total bases, season	457—Babe Ruth, New York (1921)	450—Rogers Hornsby, St. Louis (1922)
Long hits (doubles, triples, home runs) career	1,356—Babe Ruth, Boston, New York, Boston (NL) (1914–35) *	1,477—Hank Aaron (1954–76), Milw. (NL), Atlanta (NL), Milw. (AL)) *
Long hits, season	119—Babe Ruth (1921)	107—Chuck Klein, Philadelphia (1930)
Slugging average, career	.690—Babe Ruth (1914–35) *	.578—Rogers Hornsby (1915–32)
Two base hits, career	793—Tris Speaker (1907–28)	726—Pete Rose (1963-84)
Three base hits, league	297—Ty Cobb (1905–28)	252—Honus Wagner (1897–1917)
Home runs, career	714—Babe Ruth (1914–35) *	755—Hank Aaron (1954–76), Milw. (NL), Atlanta (NL), Milw. (AL) *
Home runs, season (162 games, Maris; 154 games, Ruth)	61—Roger Maris, N.Y. (1961) 60—Babe Ruth, N.Y. (1927)	56—Hack Wilson, Chicago (1930) 54—Ralph Kiner, Pittsburgh (1949)
Home runs, game	4—Lou Gehrig, New York (1932)	4—Chuck Klein, Philadelphia (1936)
Home runs, grand slam, career	23—Lou Gehrig, New York (1925–39)	18—Willie McCovey (1959–80), San Fran., San Diego, Oakland, San Fran.
Home runs, grand slam, season .	5—Jim Gentile, Baltimore (1961)	5—Ernie Banks, Chicago (1955)
Strikeouts, career	2,511—Reggie Jackson, K.C., Oakland, Baltimore, N.Y., Calif. (1967–85)	1,936—Willie Stargell (1962–82), Pittsburgh
Games, no strikeouts, consecutive	115—Joe Sewell, Cleveland (1929)	77—Lloyd Waner, Pittsburgh, Boston, Cincinnati (1941)
Stolen bases, career	892—Ty Cobb, Detroit, Philadelphia (1905–28)	938—Lou Brock, Chicago, St. Louis, (1961–79)
Stolen bases, season	130—Rickey Henderson, Oakland (1982)	118—Lou Brock, St. Louis (1974)
Stolen bases, game...........	6—Eddie Collins, Philadelphia (1912)	5—Dennis McGann, N.Y. (1904)
Stealing home, career	35—Ty Cobb, Detroit, Philadelphia (1905–28)	27—George Burns (1911–25), N.Y., Cincinnati, Philadelphia
Stealing home, season	7—Rod Carew, Minnesota (1969)	7—Pete Reiser, Brooklyn (1946)

* Career total includes play in both leagues.

BATTING CHAMPIONS

NATIONAL LEAGUE

YEAR	BATTER AND CLUB	AVG.
1901	Jesse Burkett, St. Louis	.382
1902	Ginger Beaumont, Pittsburgh	.357
1903	Honus Wagner, Pittsburgh	.355
1904	Honus Wagner, Pittsburgh	.349
1905	Cy Seymour, Cincinnati	.377
1906	Honus Wagner, Pittsburgh	.339
1907	Honus Wagner, Pittsburgh	.350
1908	Honus Wagner, Pittsburgh	.354
1909	Honus Wagner, Pittsburgh	.339
1910	Sherry Magee, Philadelphia	.331
1911	Honus Wgner, Pittsburgh	.334
1912	Heinie Zimmerman, Chicago	.372
1913	Jake Daubert, Brooklyn	.350
1914	Jake Daubert, Brooklyn	.329
1915	Larry Doyle, New York	.320
1916	Hal Chase, Cincinnati	.339
1917	Edd Roush, Cincinnati	.341

AMERICAN LEAGUE

YEAR	BATTER AND CLUB	AVG.
1901	Napoleon Lajoie, Philadelphia	.422
1902	Ed Delahanty, Washington	.376
1903	Napoleon Lajoie, Cleveland.............	.355
1904	Napoleon Lajoie, Cleveland	.381
1905	Elmer Flick, Cleveland	.306
1906	George Stone, St. Louis	.358
1907	Ty Cobb, Detroit	.350
1908	Ty Cobb, Detroit	.324
1909	Ty Cobb, Detroit	.377
1910	Ty Cobb, Detroit	.385
1911	Ty Cobb, Detroit	.420
1912	Ty Cobb, Detroit	.410
1913	Ty Cobb, Detroit	.390
1914	Ty Cobb, Detroit	.368
1915	Ty Cobb, Detroit	.369
1916	Tris Speaker, Cleveland	.386
1917	Ty Cobb, Detroit	.383

BATTING CHAMPIONS (continued)

NATIONAL LEAGUE			AMERICAN LEAGUE		
YEAR	BATTER AND CLUB	AVG.	YEAR	BATTER AND CLUB	AVG.
1918	Zack Wheat, Brooklyn	.335	1918	Ty Cobb, Detroit	.382
1919	Edd Roush, Cincinnati	.321	1919	Ty Cobb, Detroit	.384
1920	Rogers Hornsby, St. Louis	.370	1920	George Sister, St. Louis	.407
1921	Rogers Hornsby, St. Louis	.397	1921	Harry Heilmann, Detroit	.394
1922	Rogers Hornsby, St. Louis	.401	1922	George Sisler, St. Louis	.420
1923	Rogers Hornsby, St. Louis	.384	1923	Harry Heilmann, Detroit	.403
1924	Rogers Hornsby, St. Louis	.424	1924	Babe Ruth, New York	.378
1925	Rogers Hornsby, St. Louis	.403	1925	Harry Heilmann, Detroit	.393
1926	Gene Hargrave, Cincinnati	.353	1926	Heinie Manush, Detroit	.378
1927	Paul Waner, Pittsburgh	.380	1927	Harry Heilmann, Detroit	.398
1928	Rogers Hornsby, Boston	.387	1928	Goose Goslin, Washington	.379
1929	Lefty O'Doul, Philadelphia	.398	1929	Lew Fonseca, Cleveland	.369
1930	Bill Terry, New York	.401	1930	Al Simmons, Philadelphia	.381
1931	Chick Hafey, St. Louis	.349 [1]	1931	Al Simmons, Philadelphia	.390
1932	Lefty O'Doul, Brooklyn	.368	1932	Dale Alexander, Detroit–Boston	.367
1933	Chuck Klein, Philadelphia	.368	1933	Jimmy Foxx, Philadelphia	.356
1934	Paul Waner, Pittsburgh	.362	1934	Lou Gehrig, New York	.363
1935	Arky Vaughan, Pittsburgh	.385	1935	Buddy Myer, Washington	.349
1936	Paul Waner, Pittsburgh	.373	1936	Luke Appling, Chicago	.388
1937	Joe Medwick, St. Louis	.374	1937	Charley Gehringer, Detroit	.371
1938	Ernie Lombardi, Cincinnati	.342	1938	Jimmy Foxx, Boston	.349
1939	Johnny Mize, St. Louis	.349	1939	Joe DiMaggio, New York	.381
1940	Debs Garms, Pittsburgh	.355	1940	Joe DiMaggio, New York	.352
1941	Pete Reiser, Brooklyn	.343	1941	Ted Williams, Boston	.406
1942	Ernie Lombardi, Boston	.330	1942	Ted Williams, Boston	.356
1943	Stan Musial, St. Louis	.357	1943	Luke Appling, Chicago	.328
1944	Dixie Walker, Brooklyn	.357	1944	Lou Boudreau, Cleveland	.327
1945	Phil Cavarretta, Chicago	.355	1945	George Sternweiss, New York	.309
1946	Stan Musial, St. Louis	.365	1946	Mickey Vernon, Washington	.353
1947	Harry Walker, St. Louis–Philadelphia	.363	1947	Ted Williams, Boston	.343
1948	Stan Musial, St. Louis	.376	1948	Ted Williams, Boston	.369
1949	Jackie Robinson, Brooklyn	.342	1949	George Kell, Detroit	.343 [2]
1950	Stan Musial, St. Louis	.346	1950	Billy Goodman, Boston	.354
1951	Stan Musial, St. Louis	.355	1951	Ferris Fain, Philadelphia	.344
1952	Stan Musial, St. Louis	.336	1952	Ferris Fain, Philadelphia	.327
1953	Carl Furillo, Brooklyn	.344	1953	Mickey Vernon, Washington	.337
1954	Willie Mays, New York	.345	1954	Bobby Avila, Cleveland	.341
1955	Richie Ashburn, Philadelphia	.338	1955	Al Kaline, Detroit	.340
1956	Hank Aaron, Milwaukee	.328	1956	Mickey Mantle, New York	.353
1957	Stan Musial, St. Louis	.351	1957	Ted Williams, Boston	.388
1958	Richie Ashburn, Philadelphia	.350	1958	Ted Williams, Boston	.328
1959	Hank Aaron, Milwaukee	.355	1959	Harvey Kuenn, Detroit	.353
1960	Dick Groat, Pittsburgh	.325	1960	Pete Runnels, Boston	.320
1961	Roberto Clemente, Pittsburgh	.351	1961	Norm Cash, Detroit	.361
1962	Tommy Davis, Los Angeles	.346	1962	Pete Runnels, Boston	.326
1963	Tommy Davis, Los Angeles	.326	1963	Carl Yastrzemski, Boston	.321
1964	Roberto Clemente, Pittsburgh	.339	1964	Tony Oliva, Minnesota	.323
1965	Roberto Clemente, Pittsburgh	.329	1965	Tony Oliva, Minnesota	.321
1966	Matty Alou, Pittsburgh	.342	1966	Frank Robinson, Baltimore	.316
1967	Roberto Clemente, Pittsburgh	.357	1967	Carl Yastrzemski, Boston	.326
1968	Pete Rose, Cincinnati	.335	1968	Carl Yastrzemski, Boston	.301
1969	Pete Rose, Cincinnati	.348	1969	Rod Carew, Minnesota	.332
1970	Rico Carty, Atlanta	.366	1970	Alex Johnson, California	.329
1971	Joe Torre, St. Louis	.363	1971	Tony Oliva, Minnesota	.337
1972	Billy Williams, Chicago	.333	1972	Rod Carew, Minnesota	.318
1973	Pete Rose, Cincinnati	.338	1973	Rod Carew, Minnesota	.350
1974	Ralph Garr, Atlanta	.353	1974	Rod Carew, Minnesota	.364
1975	Bill Madlock, Chicago	.354	1975	Rod Carew, Minnesota	.359
1976	Bill Madlock, Chicago	.339	1976	George Brett, Kansas City	.333
1977	Dave Parker, Pittsburgh	.338	1977	Rod Carew, Minnesota	.388
1978	Dave Parker, Pittsburgh	.334	1978	Rod Carew, Minnesota	.333
1979	Keith Hernandez, St Louis	.344	1979	Fred Lynn, Boston	.333
1980	Bill Buckner, Chicago	.324	1980	George Brett, Kansas City	.390
1981	Bill Madlock, Pittsburgh	.341	1981	Carney Lansford, Boston	.336
1982	Al Oliver, Montreal	.331	1982	Willie Wilson, Kansas City	.332
1983	Bill Madlock, Pittsburgh	.323	1983	Wade Boggs, Boston	.361
1984	Tony Gwynn, San Diego	.351	1984	Don Mattingly, New York	.343
1985	Willie McGee, St. Louis	.353	1985	Wade Boggs, Boston	.368

[1] In 1931 Hafey compiled an average of .3489. Bill Terry of New York was second with .3486, and Jim Bottomley of St. Louis was third with .3482. [2] In 1949 Kell compiled .3429. Ted Williams of Boston was second with .3427.

RUNS-BATTED-IN LEADERS — MAJOR LEAGUE BASEBALL

NATIONAL LEAGUE

YEAR	PLAYER AND TEAM	RBIs
1911	Frank Schulte, Chicago	121
1912	Heinie Zimmerman, Chicago	106
1913	Cliff Cravath, Philadelphia	129
1914	Sherwood Magee, Philadelphia	101
1915	Cliff Cravath, Philadelphia	118
1916	Hal Chase, Cincinnati	84
1917	Heinie Zimmerman, New York	100
1918	Fred Merkle, Chicago	71
1919	Henry (Hi) Myers, Brooklyn	72
1920	George Kelly, New York	94
	Rogers Hornsby, St. Louis	94
1921	Rogers Hornsby, St. Louis	126
1922	Rogers Hornsby, St. Louis	152
1923	Irish Meusel, New York	125
1924	George Kelly, New York	136
1925	Rogers Hornsby, St. Louis	143
1926	Jim Bottomley, St. Louis	120
1927	Paul Waner, Pittsburgh	131
1928	Jim Bottomley, St. Louis	136
1929	Hack Wilson, Chicago	159
1930	Hack Wilson, Chicago	190
1931	Chuck Klein, Philadelphia	121
1932	Frank Hurst, Philadelphia	143
1933	Chuck Klein, Philadelphia	120
1934	Mel Ott, New York	135
1935	Wally Berger, Boston	130
1936	Joe Medwick, St. Louis	138
1937	Joe Medwick, St. Louis	154
1938	Joe Medwick, St. Louis	122
1939	Frank McCormick, Cincinnati	128
1940	Johnny Mize, St. Louis	137
1941	Dolph Camilli, Brooklyn	120
1942	Johnny Mize, New York	110
1943	Bill Nicholson, Chicago	128
1944	Bill Nicholson, Chicago	122
1945	Dixie Walker, Brooklyn	124
1946	Enos Slaughter, St. Louis	130
1947	Johnny Mize, New York	138
1948	Stan Musial, St. Louis	131
1949	Ralph Kiner, Pittsburgh	127
1950	Del Ennis, Philadelphia	126
1951	Monte Irvin, New York	121
1952	Hank Sauer, Chicago	121
1953	Roy Campanella, Brooklyn	142
1954	Ted Kluszewski, Cincinnati	141
1955	Duke Snider, Brooklyn	136
1956	Stan Musial, St. Louis	109
1957	Hank Aaron, Milwaukee	132
1958	Ernie Banks, Chicago	129
1959	Ernie Banks, Chicago	143
1960	Hank Aaron, Milwaukee	126
1961	Orlando Cepeda, San Francisco	142
1962	Tommy Davis, Los Angeles	153
1963	Hank Aaron, Milwaukee	130
1964	Ken Boyer, St. Louis	119
1965	Deron Johnson, Cincinnati	130
1966	Hank Aaron, Atlanta	121
1967	Orlando Cepeda, St. Louis	111
1968	Willie McCovey, San Francisco	105
1969	Willie McCovey, San Francisco	126
1970	Johnny Bench, Cincinnati	148
1971	Joe Torre, St. Louis	137
1972	Johnny Bench, Cincinnati	125
1973	Willie Stargell, Pittsburgh	119
1974	Johnny Bench, Cincinnati	129

AMERICAN LEAGUE

YEAR	PLAYER AND TEAM	RBIs
1911	Ty Cobb, Detroit	144
1912	Frank Baker, Philadelphia	133
1913	Frank Baker, Philadelphia	126
1914	Sam Crawford, Detroit	112
1915	Sam Crawford, Detroit	116
1916	Wally Pipp, New York	99
1917	Robert Veach, Detroit	115
1918	George Burns, Philadelphia	74
1918	Robert Veach, Detroit	74
1919	Babe Ruth, Boston	112
1920	Babe Ruth, New York	137
1921	Babe Ruth, New York	170
1922	Ken Williams, St. Louis	155
1923	Tris Speaker, Cleveland	130
	Babe Ruth, New York	130
1924	Goose Goslin, Washington	129
1925	Bob Meusel, New York	138
1926	Babe Ruth, New York	145
1927	Lou Gehrig, New York	175
1928	Babe Ruth, New York	142
	Lou Gehrig, New York	142
1929	Al Simmons, Philadelphia	157
1930	Lou Gehrig, New York	174
1931	Lou Gehrig, New York	184
1932	Jimmy Foxx, Philadelphia	169
1933	Jimmy Foxx, Philadelphia	163
1934	Lou Gehrig, New York	165
1935	Hank Greenberg, Detroit	170
1936	Hal Trosky, Cleveland	162
1937	Hank Greenberg, Detroit	183
1938	Jimmy Foxx, Boston	175
1939	Ted Williams, Boston	145
1940	Hank Greenberg, Detroit	150
1941	Joe DiMaggio, New York	125
1942	Ted Williams, Boston	137
1943	Rudy York, Detroit	118
1944	Vern Stephens, St. Louis	109
1945	Nick Etten, New York	111
1946	Hank Greenberg, Detroit	127
1947	Ted Williams, Boston	114
1948	Joe DiMaggio, New York	155
1949	Ted Williams, Boston	159
	Vern Stephens, Boston	159
1950	Vern Stephens, Boston	144
	Walt Dropo, Boston	144
1951	Gus Zernial, Chicago-Philadelphia	129
1952	Al Rosen, Cleveland	105
1953	Al Rosen, Cleveland	145
1954	Larry Doby, Cleveland	126
1955	Ike Boone, Detroit	116
	Jackie Jensen, Boston	116
1956	Mickey Mantle, New York	130
1957	Roy Sievers, Washington	114
1958	Jackie Jensen, Boston	122
1959	Jackie Jensen, Boston	112
1960	Roger Maris, New York	112
1961	Roger Maris, New York	142
1962	Harmon Killebrew, Minnesota	126
1963	Dick Stuart, Boston	118
1964	Brooks Robinson, Baltimore	118
1965	Rocky Colavito, Cleveland	108
1966	Frank Robinson, Baltimore	122
1967	Carl Yastrzemski, Boston	121
1968	Ken Harrelson, Boston	109
1969	Harmon Killebrew, Minnesota	140
1970	Frank Howard, Washington	126
1971	Harmon Killebrew, Minnesota	119
1972	Dick Allen, Chicago	113
1973	Reggie Jackson, Oakland	117
1974	Jeff Burroughs, Texas	118

RUNS-BATTED-IN LEADERS *(continued)*

NATIONAL LEAGUE

YEAR	PLAYER AND TEAM	RBIs
1975	Greg Luzinski, Philadelphia	120
1976	George Foster, Cincinnati	121
1977	George Foster, Cincinnati	149
1978	George Foster, Cincinnati	120
1979	Dave Winfield, San Diego	118
1980	Mike Schmidt, Philadelphia	121
1981	Mike Schmidt, Philadelphia	91
1982	Al Oliver, Montreal	109
	Dale Murphy, Atlanta	109
1983	Dale Murphy, Atlanta	121
1984	Gary Carter, Montreal	106
	Mike Schmidt, Philadelphia	106
1985	Dave Parker, Cincinnati	125

AMERICAN LEAGUE

YEAR	PLAYER AND TEAM	RBIs
1975	George Scott, Milwaukee	109
1976	Lee May, Baltimore	109
1977	Larry Hisle, Minnesota	119
1978	Jim Rice, Boston	139
1979	Don Baylor, California	139
1980	Cecil Cooper, Milwaukee	122
1981	Eddie Murray, Baltimore	78
1982	Hal McRae, Kansas City	133
1983	Cecil Cooper, Milwaukee	126
	Jim Rice, Boston	126
1984	Tony Armas, Boston	123
1985	Don Mattingly, New York	145

STAR BASEBALL HITTERS OF THE PAST

PLAYER AND TEAM(S)	YEARS	GAMES	AT BAT	RUNS	HITS	BAT. AV.
Ty Cobb, Detroit, Philadelphia (AL)	1905–28	3,033	11,429	2,244	4,191	.367
Rogers Hornsby, St. Louis, N.Y., Boston, Chicago (NL)	1915–32	2,259	8,173	1,579	2,930	.359
Tris Speaker, Bost., Clev., Wash., Phil. (AL)	1907–28	2,789	10,208	1,881	3,515	.344
Ted Williams, Boston (AL)	1939–60	2,292	7,706	1,798	2,654	.344
Babe Ruth, Boston, New York (AL), Boston (NL)	1914–35	2,503	8,399	2,174	2,873	.342
Harry Heilmann, Detroit (AL), Cincinnati (NL)	1914–32	2,146	7,787	1,291	2,660	.342
Bill Terry, New York (NL)	1923–36	1,721	6,428	1,120	2,193	.341
Lou Gehrig, New York (AL)	1923–39	2,164	8,001	1,888	2,721	.340
George Sisler, mainly with St. Louis (AL)	1915–30	2,055	8,267	1,284	2,812	.340
Napoleon Lajoie, mainly with Philadelphia (AL)	1896–1916	2,475	9,589	1,503	3,251	.339
Eddie Collins, Philadelphia, Chicago (AL)	1906–30	2,826	9,952	1,818	3,313	.333
Paul Waner, Pitt., Brooklyn, Boston (NL), N.Y. (AL)	1926–45	2,549	9,459	1,626	3,152	.333
Stan Musial, St. Louis (NL)	1941–63	3,026	10,972	1,949	3,630	.331
Jimmy Foxx, Phil., Boston (AL), Chicago, Phil, (NL)	1925–45	2,317	8,134	1,751	2,646	.325
Joe DiMaggio, New York (AL)	1936–51	1,736	6,821	1,390	2,214	.325
Joe Medwick, St. Louis, Brooklyn, N.Y., Boston (NL)	1932–48	1,984	7,635	1,198	2,471	.324
Charley Gehringer, Detroit (AL)	1924–42	2,323	8,858	1,773	2,838	.321
Chuck Klein, Philadelphia, Chicago, Pittsburgh (NL)	1928–44	1,753	6,486	1,168	2,076	.320
Frank Frisch, New York, St. Louis (NL)	1919–37	2,311	9,112	1,532	2,880	.316
Hank Aaron, Milw. (NL), Atlanta (NL), Milw. (AL)	1954–76	3,298	12,364	2,174	3,771	.305
Willie Mays, N.Y. (NL), San. Fran. (NL), N.Y. (NL)	1951–73	2,992	10,881	2,062	3,283	.302
Mickey Mantle, New York (AL)	1951–68	2,401	8,102	1,677	2,415	.298

LEADING HOME RUN HITTERS—LIFETIME TOTALS

PLAYER	HR	PLAYER	HR	PLAYER	HR	PLAYER	HR
Hank Aaron	755	Ernie Banks	512	Dave Kingman *	407	Graig Nettles *	368
Babe Ruth	714	Eddie Matthews	512	Al Kaline	399	Joe DiMaggio	361
Willie Mays	660	Mel Ott	511	Johnny Bench	389	Johnny Mize	359
Frank Robinson	586	Lou Gehrig	493	Frank Howard	382	Yogi Berra	358
Harmon Killebrew	573	Stan Musial	475	Orlando Cepeda	379	Lee May	354
Mickey Mantle	536	Willie Stargell	475	Norm Cash	377	Dick Allen	351
Jimmy Foxx	534	Mike Schmidt *	458	Tony Perez *	377	Ron Santo	342
Reggie Jackson *	530	Carl Yastrzemski	452	Rocky Colavito	374		
Ted Williams	521	Billy Williams	426	Gil Hodges	370		
Willie McCovey	521	Duke Snider	407	Ralph Kiner	369		

* Active player in 1985 season.

HOME RUN CHAMPIONS—MAJOR LEAGUE BASEBALL

NATIONAL LEAGUE

YEAR	PLAYER AND CLUB	HOME RUNS
1919	Cliff Cravath, Philadelphia	12
1920	Fred Williams, Philadelphia	15
1921	George Kelly, New York	23
1922	Rogers Hornsby, St. Louis	42
1923	Fred Williams, Philadelphia	41
1924	Jacques Fournier, Brooklyn	27
1925	Rogers Hornsby, St. Louis	39
1926	Hack Wilson, Chicago	21
1927	Hack Wilson, Chicago	30
	Fred Williams, Philadelphia	30
1928	Hack Wilson, Chicago	31
	Jim Bottomley, St. Louis	31
1929	Chuck Klein, Philadelphia	43

AMERICAN LEAGUE

YEAR	PLAYER AND CLUB	HOME RUNS
1919	Babe Ruth, Boston	29
1920	Babe Ruth, New York	54
1921	Babe Ruth, New York	59
1922	Kenneth R. Williams, St. Louis	39
1923	Babe Ruth, New York	41
1924	Babe Ruth, New York	46
1925	Bob Meusel, New York	33
1926	Babe Ruth, New York	47
1927	Babe Ruth, New York	60
1928	Babe Ruth, New York	54
1929	Babe Ruth, New York	46

HOME RUN CHAMPIONS (continued)

NATIONAL LEAGUE			AMERICAN LEAGUE		
YEAR	PLAYER AND CLUB	HOME RUNS	YEAR	PLAYER AND CLUB	HOME RUNS
1929	Chuck Klein, Philadelphia	43	1929	Babe Ruth, New York	46
1930	Hack Wilson, Chicago	56	1930	Babe Ruth, New York	49
1931	Chuck Klein, Philadelphia	31	1931	Babe Ruth, New York	46
				Lou Gehrig, New York	46
1932	Chuck Klein, Philadelphia	38	1932	Jimmy Foxx, Philadelphia	58
	Mel Ott, New York	38			
1933	Chuck Klein, Philadelphia	28	1933	Jimmy Foxx, Philadelphia	48
1934	Mel Ott, New York	35	1934	Lou Gehrig, New York	49
	Rip Collins, St. Louis	35			
1935	Wally Berger, Boston	34	1935	Jimmy Foxx, Philadelphia	36
				Hank Greenberg, Detroit	36
1936	Mel Ott, New York	33	1936	Lou Gehrig, New York	49
1937	Mel Ott, New York	31	1937	Joe DiMaggio, New York	46
	Joe Medwick, St. Louis	31			
1938	Mel Ott, New York	36	1938	Hank Greenberg, Detroit	58
1939	Johnny Mize, St. Louis	28	1939	Jimmy Foxx, Boston	35
1940	Johnny Mize, St. Louis	43	1940	Hank Greenberg, Detroit	41
1941	Dolph Camilli, Brooklyn	34	1941	Ted Williams, Boston	37
1942	Mel Ott, New York	30	1942	Ted Williams, Boston	36
1943	Bill Nicholson, Chicago	29	1943	Rudy York, Detroit	34
1944	Bill Nicholson, Chicago	33	1944	Nick Etten, New York	22
1945	Tommy Holmes, Boston	28	1945	Vern Stephens, St. Louis	24
1946	Ralph Kiner, Pittsburgh	23	1946	Hank Greenberg, Detroit	44
1947	Ralph Kiner, Pittsburgh	51	1947	Ted Williams, Boston	32
	Johnny Mize, New York	51			
1948	Ralph Kiner, Pittsburgh	40	1948	Joe DiMaggio, New York	39
	Johnny Mize, New York	40			
1949	Ralph Kiner, Pittsburgh	54	1949	Ted Williams, Boston	43
1950	Ralph Kiner, Pittsburgh	47	1950	Al Rosen, Cleveland	37
1951	Ralph Kiner, Pittsburgh	42	1951	Gus Zernial, Chicago–Phil.	33
1952	R. Kiner, Pitt.; H. Sauer, Chi.	37	1952	Larry Doby, Cleveland	32
1953	Eddie Mathews, Milwaukee	47	1953	Al Rosen, Cleveland	43
1954	Ted Kluszewski, Cincinnati	49	1954	Larry Doby, Cleveland	32
1955	Willie Mays, New York	51	1955	Mickey Mantle, New York	37
1956	Duke Snider, Brooklyn	43	1956	Mickey Mantle, New York	52
1957	Hank Aaron, Milwaukee	44	1957	Roy Sievers, Washington	42
1958	Ernie Banks, Chicago	47	1958	Mickey Mantle, New York	42
1959	Eddie Mathews, Milwaukee	46	1959	Harmon Killebrew, Washington	42
				Rocky Colavito, Cleveland	42
1960	Ernie Banks, Chicago	41	1960	Mickey Mantle, New York	40
1961	Orlando Cepeda, San Francisco	46	1961	Roger Maris, New York	61
1962	Willie Mays, San Francisco	49	1962	Harmon Killebrew, Minnesota	48
1963	Hank Aaron, Milwaukee	44	1963	Harmon Killebrew, Minnesota	45
	Willie McCovey, San Francisco	44			
1964	Willie Mays, San Francisco	47	1964	Harmon Killebrew, Minnesota	49
1965	Willie Mays, San Francisco	52	1965	Tony Conigliaro, Boston	32
1966	Hank Aaron, Atlanta	44	1966	Frank Robinson, Baltimore	49
1967	Hank Aaron, Atlanta	39	1967	Carl Yastrzemski, Boston	44
				Harmon Killebrew, Minnesota	44
1968	Willie McCovey, San Francisco	36	1968	Frank Howard, Washington	44
1969	Willie McCovey, San Francisco	45	1969	Harmon Killebrew, Minnesota	49
1970	Johnny Bench, Cincinnati	45	1970	Frank Howard, Washington	44
1971	Willie Stargell, Pittsburgh	48	1971	Bill Melton, Chicago	33
1972	Johnny Bench, Cincinnati	40	1972	Dick Allen, Chicago	37
1973	Willie Stargell, Pittsburgh	44	1973	Reggie Jackson, Oakland	32
1974	Mike Schmidt, Philadelphia	36	1974	Dick Allen, Chicago	32
1975	Mike Schmidt, Philadelphia	38	1975	Reggie Jackson, Oakland	36
				George Scott, Milwaukee	36
1976	Mike Schmidt, Philadelphia	38	1976	Graig Nettles, New York	32
1977	George Foster, Cincinnati	52	1977	Jim Rice, Boston	39
1978	George Foster, Cincinnati	40	1978	Jim Rice, Boston	46
1979	Dave Kingman, Chicago	48	1979	Gorman Thomas, Milwaukee	45
1980	Mike Schmidt, Philadelphia	48	1980	Ben Oglivie, Milwaukee	41
				Reggie Jackson, New York	41
1981	Mike Schmidt, Philadelphia	31	1981	Four-way tie[1]	22
1982	Dave Kingman, N.Y. Mets	37	1982	Reggie Jackson, California	39
				Gorman Thomas, Milwaukee	39
1983	Mike Schmidt, Philadelphia	40	1983	Jim Rice, Boston	39
1984	Mike Schmidt, Philadelphia	36	1984	Tony Armas, Boston	43
	Dale Murphy, Atlanta	36			
1985	Dale Murphy, Atlanta	37	1985	Darrell Evans, Detroit	40

[1] Tony Armas, Oakland; Eddie Murray, Baltimore; Dwight Evans, Boston; Bobby Grich, California.

PITCHERS WITH LOWEST EARNED RUN AVERAGE (ERA)[1]

	NATIONAL LEAGUE			AMERICAN LEAGUE		
YEAR	PITCHER AND CLUB	INNINGS	ERA	PITCHER AND CLUB	INNINGS	ERA
1942	Mort Cooper, St. Louis	279	1.77	Ted Lyons, Chicago	180	2.10
1943	Howie Pollet, St. Louis	118	1.75	Spud Chandler, New York	253	1.64
1944	Ed Heusser, Cincinnati	193	2.38	Paul (Dizzy) Trout, Detroit	352	2.12
1945	Hank Borowy, Chicago	122	2.14	Hal Newhouser, Detroit	313	1.81
1946	Howie Pollet, St. Louis	266	2.10	Hal Newhouser, Detroit	293	1.94
1947	Warren Spahn, Boston	290	2.33	Spud Chandler, New York	128	2.46
1948	Harry Brecheen, St. Louis	233	2.24	Gene Bearden, Cleveland	230	2.43
1949	Dave Koslo, New York	212	2.50	Mel Parnell, Boston	295	2.78
1950	Jim Hearn, St. Louis—New York	134	2.49	Early Wynn, Cleveland	214	3.20
1951	Chet Nichols, Boston	156	2.88	Saul Rogovin, Detroit—Chicago	217	2.78
1952	Hoyt Wilhelm, New York	159	2.43	Allie Reynolds, New York	244	2.07
1953	Warren Spahn, Milwaukee	266	2.10	Eddie Lopat, New York	178	2.43
1954	John Antonelli, New York	259	2.29	Mike Garcia, Cleveland	259	2.64
1955	Bob Friend, Pittsburgh	200	2.84	Billy Pierce, Chicago	206	1.97
1956	Lew Burdette, Milwaukee	256	2.71	Whitey Ford, New York	226	2.47
1957	John Podres, Brooklyn	196	2.66	Bobby Shantz, New York	173	2.45
1958	Stu Miller, San Francisco	182	2.47	Whitey Ford, New York	219	2.01
1959	Sam Jones, San Francisco	271	2.82	Hoyt Wilhelm, Baltimore	226	2.19
1960	Mike McCormick, San Francisco	253	2.70	Frank Baumann, Chicago	185	2.68
1961	Warren Spahn, Milwaukee	263	3.01	Dick Donovan, Washington	169	2.40
1962	Sandy Koufax, Los Angeles	184	2.54	Hank Aguirre, Detroit	216	2.21
1963	Sandy Koufax, Los Angeles	311	1.88	Gary Peters, Chicago	243	2.33
1964	Sandy Koufax, Los Angeles	223	1.74	Dean Chance, Los Angeles	278	1.65
1965	Sandy Koufax, Los Angeles	336	2.04	Sam McDowell, Cleveland	274	2.17
1966	Sandy Koufax, Los Angeles	323	1.73	Gary Peters, Chicago	204	2.03
1967	Phil Niekro, Atlanta	207	1.96	Joe Horlen, Chicago	258	2.06
1968	Bob Gibson, St. Louis	304	1.12	Luis Tiant, Cleveland	258	1.60
1969	Juan Marichal, San Francisco	299	2.10	Dick Bosman, Washington	193	2.19
1970	Tom Seaver, New York	291	2.81	Diego Segui, Oakland	162	2.56
1971	Tom Seaver, New York	286	1.76	Vida Blue, Oakland	312	1.82
1972	Steve Carlton, Philadelphia	346	1.98	Luis Tiant, Boston	179	1.91
1973	Tom Seaver, New York	290	2.07	Jim Palmer, Baltimore	296	2.40
1974	Buzz Capra, Atlanta	217	2.28	Jim (Catfish) Hunter, Oakland	318	2.49
1975	Randy Jones, San Diego	285	2.24	Jim Palmer, Baltimore	323	2.09
1976	John Denny, St. Louis	207	2.52	Mark Fidrych, Detroit	250⅓	2.34
1977	John Candelaria, Pittsburgh	231	2.34	Frank Tanana, California	241	2.54
1978	Craig Swan, New York	207	2.43	Ron Guidry, New York	274	1.74
1979	James Richard, Houston	292	2.71	Ron Guidry, New York	236	2.78
1980	Don Sutton, Los Angeles	212	2.21	Rudy May, New York	175	2.47
1981 [2]	Nolan Ryan, Houston	149	1.69	Steve McCatty, Oakland	186	2.32
1982	Stephen Rogers, Montreal	277	2.40	Rick Sutcliffe, Cleveland	216	2.96
1983	Atlee Hammaker, San Francisco	172	2.25	Rick Honeycutt, Texas	174	2.42
1984	Alejandro Pena, Los Angeles	199	2.48	Mike Boddicker, Baltimore	261	2.79
1985	Dwight (Dr.K) Gooden, New York	276.2	1.53	Dave Steib, Toronto	265	2.48

PITCHERS WITH HIGHEST WON-LOST PERCENTAGES [3]

	NATIONAL LEAGUE	GAMES		PCT.	AMERICAN LEAGUE	GAMES		PCT.
YEAR	PITCHER AND CLUB	Won	Lost		PITCHER AND CLUB	Won	Lost	
1901	Jack Chesbro, Pittsburgh	21	9	.700	Cy Young, Boston	31	10	.756
1902	Jack Chesbro, Pittsburgh	27	6	.818	George (Rube) Waddell, Philadelphia	24	7	.774
1903	Sam Leever, Pittsburgh	25	7	.781	Earl Moore, Cleveland	22	7	.759
1904	Joe (Iron Man) McGinnity, New York	35	8	.814	Jack Chesbro, New York	41	13	.759
1905	Christy Mathewson, New York	32	8	.800	Andrew Coakley, Philadelphia	20	8	.714
1906	Big Ed Reulbach, Chicago	19	4	.826	Eddie Plank, Philadelphia	19	6	.760
1907	Big Ed Reulbach, Chicago	17	4	.810	Wild Bill Donovan, Detroit	25	4	.862
1908	Big Ed Reulbach, Chicago	24	7	.774	Ed Walsh, Chicago	40	15	.727
1909	Christy Mathewson, New York (tie)	25	6	.806	George Mullin, Detroit	29	8	.784
	Howie Camnitz, Pittsburgh (tie)	25	6	.806				
1910	Leonard (King) Cole, Chicago	20	4	.833	Charles (Chief) Bender, Philadelphia	23	5	.821
1911	Richard (Rube) Marquard, New York	24	7	.774	Charles (Chief) Bender, Philadelphia	17	5	.773
1912	Claude Hendrix, Pittsburgh	24	9	.727	Smokey Joe Wood, Boston	34	5	.872
1913	Bert Humphries, Chicago	16	4	.800	Walter Johnson, Washington	36	7	.837
1914	Seattle Bill James, Boston	26	7	.788	Charles (Chief) Bender, Philadelphia	17	3	.850
1915	Grover Alexander, Philadelphia	31	10	.756	Babe Ruth, Boston	18	6	.750
1916	Salida Tom Hughes, Boston	16	3	.842	Edward (Knuckles) Cicotte, Chicago	15	7	.682
1917	Ferdinand Schupp, New York	21	7	.750	Ewell (Reb) Russell, Chicago	15	5	.750
1918	Claude Hendrix, Chicago	20	7	.741	Sad Sam Jones, Boston	16	5	.762
1919	Walter (Dutch) Ruether, Cincinnati	19	6	.760	Edward (Knuckles) Cicotte, Chicago	29	7	.806
1920	Burleigh Grimes, Brooklyn	23	11	.676	James (Sarge) Babgy, Cleveland	31	12	.721

[1] Before 1951 must have pitched 10 complete games; 1951-61, at least 154 innings; since 1962, at least 162 innings. [2] Strike shortened season. [3] Must have had 15 won-lost decisions.

PITCHERS WITH HIGHEST WON-LOST PERCENTAGES (continued)

YEAR	NATIONAL LEAGUE PITCHER AND CLUB	GAMES Won	Lost	PCT.	AMERICAN LEAGUE PITCHER AND CLUB	GAMES Won	Lost	PCT.
1921	Spittin' Bill Doak, St. Louis	15	6	.714	Carl Mays, New York	27	9	.750
1922	Pete Donohue, Cincinnati	18	9	.667	Bullet Joe Bush, New York	26	7	.788
1923	Dolf Luque, Cincinnati	27	8	.771	Herb Pennock, New York	19	6	.760
1924	Emil Yde, Pittsburgh..........	16	3	.842	Walter Johnson, Washington	23	7	.767
1925	Wee Willie Sherdel, St. Louis	15	6	.714	Stanley Coveleski, Washington	20	5	.800
1926	Ray Kremer, Pittsburgh	20	6	.769	George (The Bull) Uhle, Cleveland ...	27	11	.711
1927	Lawrence Benton, Boston-N.Y. ...	17	7	.708	Waite Hoyte, New York	22	7	.759
1928	Lawrence Benton, New York	25	9	.806	Alvin (General) Crowder, St. Louis ...	21	5	.808
1929	Charlie Root, Chicago	19	6	.760	Robert (Lefty) Grove, Philadelphia ..	20	6	.769
1930	Fat Freddie Fitzsimmons, New York	19	7	.731	Robert (Lefty) Grove, Philadelphia ..	28	5	.848
1931	Duke Derringer, St. Louis	18	8	.692	Robert (Lefty) Grove, Philadelphia ...	31	4	.886
1932	Lon Warneke, Chicago	22	6	.786	John Allen, New York...............	17	4	.810
1933	Bud Tinning, Chicago	13	6	.684	Robert (Lefty) Grove, Philadelphia ..	24	8	.750
1934	Jerome (Dizzy) Dean, St. Louis..	30	7	.811	Vernon (Lefty) Gomez, New York	26	5	.839
1935	Big Bill Lee, Chicago	20	6	.769	Eldon (Submarine) Auker, Detroit....	18	7	.720
1936	Carl Hubbell, New York	26	6	.813	Bump Hadley, New York	14	4	.778
1937	Carl Hubbell, New York	22	8	.733	John Allen, Cleveland	15	1	.938
1938	Big Bill Lee, Chicago	22	9	.710	Robert (Lefty) Grove, Boston	14	4	.778
1939	Duke Derringer, Cincinnati	25	7	.781	Richard (Swampy) Donald, New York.	13	3	.813
1940	Fat Freddie Fitzsimmons, Brooklyn	16	2	.889	Schoolboy Rowe, Detroit............	16	3	.842
1941	Elmer Riddle, Cincinnati	19	4	.826	Vernon (Lefty) Gomez, New York	15	5	.750
1942	Spud Krist, St. Louis	13	3	.813	Ernest (Tiny) Bonham, New York	21	5	.808
1943	Clyde (Hardrock) Shoun, Cinn...	14	5	.737	Spud Chandler, New York...........	20	4	.833
1944	Ted Wilks, St. Louis	17	4	.810	Tex Hughson, Boston...............	18	5	.783
1945	Harry (The Cat) Brecheen, St. Louis	15	4	.789	Bob Muncrief, St. Louis	13	4	.765
1946	Schoolboy Rowe, Philadelphia ..	11	4	.733	Dave Ferriss, Boston	25	6	.806
1947	Larry Jansen, New York.........	21	5	.808	Spec Shea, New York	14	5	.737
1948	Rip Sewell, Pittsburgh	13	3	.813	Jack Kramer, Boston	18	5	.783
1949	Ralph Branca, Brooklyn	13	5	.722	Ellis Kinder, Boston	23	6	.793
1950	Sal Maglie, New York	18	4	.818	Vic Raschi, New York	21	8	.724
1951	Elwin (Preacher) Roe, Brooklyn .	22	3	.880	Bob Feller, Cleveland (tie).........	22	8	.733
					Morrie Martin, Philadelphia (tie)	11	4	.733
1952	Hoyt Wilhelm, New York	15	3	.833	Bobby Shantz, Philadelphia	24	7	.774
1953	Carl Erskine, Brooklyn	20	6	.769	Eddie Lopat, New York	16	4	.800
1954	John Antonelli, New York (tie) ..	21	7	.750	Sandy Consuegra, Chicago	16	3	.842
	Hoyt Wilhelm, New York (tie) ...	12	4	.750				
1955	Don Newcombe, Brooklyn	20	5	.800	Tommy Byrne, New York	16	5	.762
1956	Don Newcombe, Brooklyn	27	7	.794	Whitey Ford, New York	19	6	.760
1957	Bob Buhl, Milwaukee	18	7	.720	Dick Donovan, Chicago (tie)	16	6	.727
					Tom Sturdivant, New York (tie)	16	6	.727
1958	Warren Spahn, Milwaukee (tie)..	22	11	.667	Bob Turley, New York	21	7	.750
	Lew Burdette, Milwaukee (tie) ..	20	10	.667				
1959	Elroy Face, Pittsburgh	18	1	.947	Bob Shaw, Chicago	18	6	.750
1960	Lindy McDaniel, St. Louis	12	4	.750	Jim Coates, New York	13	3	.813
1961	Johnny Podres, Los Angeles	18	5	.783	Whitey Ford, New York	25	4	.862
1962	Bob Purkey, Cincinnati.........	23	5	.821	D.C. Wickersham, Kansas City	11	4	.733
1963	Ron Perranoski, Los Angeles ...	16	3	.842	Whitey Ford, New York	24	7	.774
1964	Sandy Koufax, Los Angeles	19	5	.792	Wally Bunker, Baltimore	19	5	.792
1965	Sandy Koufax, Los Angeles	26	8	.765	Jim Grant, Minnesota	21	7	.750
1966	P.R. Regan, Los Angeles	14	1	.933	Dave Boswell, Minnesota	12	5	.706
1967	Nelson Briles, St. Louis	14	5	.737	J.R. Santiago, Boston	12	4	.750
1968	Steve Blass, Pittsburgh	18	6	.750	Dennis McLain, Detroit	31	6	.838
1969	Bob Moose, Pittsburgh	14	3	.824	Jim Palmer, Baltimore	16	4	.800
1970	Wayne Simpson, Cincinnati	14	3	.824	Miguel Cuellar, Baltimore	24	8	.750
1971	Tug McGraw, New York	11	4	.733	Dave McNally, Baltimore	21	5	.808
1972	Gary Nolan, Cincinnati	15	5	.750	Jim Hunter, Oakland	21	7	.750
1973	George Stone, New York	12	3	.800	Roger Moret, Boston	13	2	.867
1974	Tommy John, Los Angeles......	13	3	.813	Bill Champion, Milwaukee	11	4	.733
1975	Al Hrabosky, St. Louis	13	3	.813	Roger Moret, Boston	14	3	.824
1976	Richard Rhoden, Los Angeles ...	12	3	.800	Bill Campbell, Minnesota	17	5	.773
1977	John Candelaria, Pittsburgh	20	5	.800	Don Gullett, New York	14	4	.778
1978	Gaylord Perry, San Diego	21	6	.778	Ron Guidry, New York	25	3	.893
1979	James Bibby, Pittsburgh	12	4	.750	Ron Davis, New York	14	2	.875
1980	James Bibby, Pittsburgh	19	6	.760	Steve Stone, Baltimore	25	7	.781
1981[1]	Tom Seaver, Cincinnati	14	2	.875	Pete Vuckovich, Milwaukee	14	4	.778
1982	Phil Niekro, Atlanta............	17	4	.810	Jim Palmer, Baltimore (tie)	15	5	.750
					Pete Vuckovich, Milwaukee (tie)	18	6	.750
1983	John Denny, Philadelphia	19	6	.760	Richard Dotson, Chicago	22	7	.759
1984	Rick Sutcliffe, Chicago	16	1	.941	Doyle Alexander, Toronto	17	6	.739
1985	Orel Hershiser, Los Angeles	19	3	.864	Ron Guidry, New York	22	6	.786

[1] Strike shortened season.

STAR BASEBALL PITCHERS OF THE PAST

PITCHERS	CAREER	YEARS	G	IP	W	L	PCT	H	R	ER	SO	BB	ERA
Grover Cleveland Alexander .	1911–1930	20	696	5,189	373	208	.642	4,868	1,851	—	2,198	951	2.56
Charles (Chief) Bender	1903–1925	16	459	3,026	212	128	.624	2,653	989	—	1,720	705	2.46
Mordecai (Three-finger) Brown	1903–1916	14	481	3,168	239	130	.631	2,707	863	—	1,381	674	2.03
Jack Chesbro	1899–1909	11	392	2,886	198	127	.609	2,602	1,202	—	1,276	674	2.68
John Clarkson	1882–1894	12	517	4,514	327	176	.650	4,384	—	—	2,013	1,192	
Stan Coveleski	1912–1928	14	450	3,083	216	142	.603	3,055	1,244	N.A.	981	802	2.87
Jerome (Dizzy) Dean	1930–1947	12	317	1,966	150	83	.644	1,921	776	663	1,155	458	3.04
Urban (Red) Faber	1914–1933	20	669	4,087	254	212	.545	4,104	1,794	1,420	1,471	1,213	3.15
Bob Feller	1936–1956	18	570	3,828	266	162	.621	3,271	1,557	1,384	2,581	1,764	3.25
Whitey Ford	1950–1967	16	498	3,171	236	106	.690	2,766	1,107	967	1,956	1,086	2.74
James (Pud) Galvin	1879–1892	14	675	5,959	361	309	.539	6,334	—	—	1,786	744	
Vernon (Lefty) Gomez	1930–1943	14	368	2,503	189	102	.649	2,290	1,091	929	1,468	1,095	3.34
Clark Griffith	1891–1914	21	416	3,370	240	140	.632	3,372	—	—	962	800	
Burleigh Grimes	1916–1934	19	615	4,178	270	212	.560	4,406	2,043	1,636	1,512	1,295	3.52
Robert (Lefty) Grove	1925–1941	17	616	3,940	300	141	.680	3,849	1,594	1,339	2,266	1,187	3.06
Jesse J. (Pop) Haines	1918–1937	19	555	3,207	210	158	.571	3,460	1,556	1,298	981	871	3.64
Waite Hoyt	1918–1938	21	674	3,762	237	182	.566	4,037	1,781	1,500	1,206	1,003	3.59
Carl Hubbell	1928–1943	16	535	3,591	253	154	.622	3,461	1,380	1,188	1,677	725	2.98
Walter Johnson	1907–1927	21	802	5,924	416	279	.599	4,920	1,902	N.A.	3,508	1,353	2.17
Tim Keefe	1880–1893	14	599	5,050	344	225	.605	4,452	—	—	2,542	1,225	
Sandy Koufax	1955–1966	12	397	2,325	165	87	.655	1,754	806	713	2,396	817	2.76
Bob Lemon	1941–1958	18	460	2,849	207	128	.618	2,559	1,185	1,024	1,277	1,251	3.23
Ted Lyons	1923–1946	21	594	4,162	260	230	.531	4,489	2,056	1,696	1,073	1,121	3.67
Richard (Rube) Marquard...	1908–1925	18	536	3,307	201	177	.532	3,233	1,443	—	1,593	858	3.08
Christy Mathewson	1900–1916	17	635	4,781	373	188	.655	4,203	1,613	—	2,505	837	2.13
Joe McGinnity	1899–1908	10	467	3,455	247	145	.630	3,236	1,442	—	1,058	803	2.66
Charles (Kid) Nichols.......	1890–1906	15	582	5,067	360	202	.641	4,854	—	—	1,866	1,245	2.95
Herb Pennock	1912–1934	22	617	3,558	240	162	.597	3,900	1,693	1,403	1,227	916	3.55
Eddie Plank	1901–1917	17	623	4,503	326	192	.629	3,898	1,470	—	2,257	1,042	2.34
Charles (Hoss) Radbourne .	1880–1891	12	517	4,543	308	191	.617	4,500	2,300	—	1,746	856	
Eppa Rixey	1912–1933	21	692	4,494	266	251	.515	4,633	1,986	1,572	1,350	1,082	3.15
Robin Roberts	1948–1966	19	676	4,689	286	245	.539	4,582	1,962	1,774	2,357	902	3.40
Charles (Red) Ruffing ...	1924–1947	22	624	4,342	273	225	.548	4,294	2,117	1,833	1,987	1,541	3.80
Warren Spahn	1942–1965	21	750	5,246	363	245	.597	4,830	2,016	1,798	2,583	1,434	3.08
Arthur (Dazzy) Vance	1915–1935	16	442	2,967	197	140	.585	2,809	1,246	1,066	2,045	840	3.24
George (Rube) Waddell	1897–1910	13	407	2,958	191	142	.574	2,480	1,104	—	2,310	771	2.16
Ed Walsh	1904–1917	14	431	2,968	195	126	.607	2,335	877	—	1,731	620	1.82
Mickey Welch	1880–1892	13	565	4,783	308	209	.596	4,648	2,548	—	1,841	1,305	—
Early Wynn	1939–1963	23	691	4,566	300	244	.551	4,291	2,037	1,796	2,334	1,775	3.54
Denton T. (Cy) Young	1890–1911	22	906	7,377	511	313	.620	7,078	3,168	—	2,819	1,209	2.63

BASEBALL HALL OF FAME

The National Baseball Hall of Fame and Museum was dedicated on June 12, 1939, at Cooperstown, N.Y., where legend holds that Abner Doubleday invented baseball a hundred years earlier. The Hall of Fame had its origin in 1936 when baseball writers chose five players as the greatest to that time: Ty Cobb, Babe Ruth, Christy Mathewson, Honus Wagner, and Walter Johnson.

Since 1939 a committee of veteran members of the Baseball Writers Association of America an- nually has chosen additional players to be honored in the Hall of Fame. To be eligible, a player must have begun his career 30 years before the date of selection and must have ended his career five years before being chosen. In addition, a special Veterans Committee annually selects out- standing players from the earlier days of baseball, and another special committee has chosen black players from the years when blacks were not per- mitted to play on major league baseball teams.

PITCHERS	CAREER	Won	Lost
Grover Alexander	1911–1930	373	208
Charles (Chief) Bender	1903–1925	212	128
Mordecai (Three-finger) Brown	1903–1916	239	130
Jack Chesbro	1899–1909	199	128
John Clarkson	1882–1894	328	175
Stan Coveleski	1912–1925	216	142
W. A. Cummings	1872–1877	146	92
Jerome (Dizzy) Dean	1930–1947	150	83
Don Drysdale	1956–1969	209	166
Urban (Red) Faber	1914–1933	253	211
Bob Feller	1936–1956	266	162
Edward (Whitey) Ford	1950–1967	236	106
James (Pud) Galvin	1876–1892	365	309
Bob Gibson	1959–1975	251	174
Vernon (Lefty) Gomez	1930–1942	189	95
Clark Griffith	1891–1914	237	140
Burleigh Grimes	1916–1934	270	212
Robert (Lefty) Grove	1925–1941	300	141

PITCHERS	CAREER	Won	Lost
Jesse J. (Pop) Haines	1920–1937	210	158
Waite Hoyte	1919–1938	237	182
Carl Hubbell	1928–1943	253	154
Walter Johnson	1907–1927	416	279
Addie Joss	1902–1910	159	96
Tim Keefe	1880–1893	346	225
Sandy Koufax	1955–1966	165	87
Bob Lemon	1946–1958	207	128
Ted Lyons	1923–1946	260	230
Juan Marichal	1960–1975	243	142
Richard (Rube) Marquard...	1908–1925	201	177
Christy Mathewson	1900–1916	373	188
Joe McGinnity	1899–1908	247	145
Charles (Kid) Nichols	1890–1906	360	202
Leroy (Satchel) Paige.......	1948–1952	28	31
Herb Pennock	1912–1934	241	163
Eddie Plank	1901–1917	325	190
Charles (Hoss) Radbourne ..	1880–1891	308	191

BASEBALL HALL OF FAME *(continued)*

PITCHERS (continued)	CAREER	Won	Lost
Eppa Rixey	1912–1933	266	251
Robin Roberts	1948–1966	286	245
Charles (Red) Ruffing	1924–1947	273	225
Amos Rusie	1889–1901	243	160
Warren Spahn	1940–1967	363	245
A. G. Spalding	1871–1877	252	68
Arthur (Dazzy) Vance	1915–1935	197	140
George (Rube) Waddell	1897–1910	193	140
Ed Walsh	1904–1917	195	126
John Ward	1878–1894	158	102
Mickey Welch	1880–1892	309	211
Hoyt Wilhelm	1952–1972	143	122
Early Wynn	1939–1963	300	244
Denton T. (Cy) Young	1890–1911	511	315

CATCHERS	CAREER	AVERAGE
Lawrence (Yogi) Berra	1946–1965	.285
Roger Bresnahan	1897–1915	.279
Roy Campanella	1948–1957	.276
Gordon (Mickey) Cochrane	1925–1937	.320
Bill Dickey	1928–1946	.313
William (Buck) Ewing	1880–1897	.311
Richard (Rick) Ferrell	1929–1947	.281
Charles (Gabby) Hartnett	1922–1941	.297
Mike Kelly	1878–1893	.315
Connie Mack	1886–1896	.249
Wilbert Robinson	1886–1902	.280
Ray Schalk	1912–1929	.253

FIRST BASEMEN	CAREER	AVERAGE
Adrian (Cap) Anson	1876–1897	.339
Jake Beckley	1888–1907	.309
Sunny Jim Bottomley	1922–1935	.310
Dennis (Dan) Brouthers	1879–1896	.348
Frank Chance	1898–1914	.297
Charles Comiskey	1882–1894	.269
Roger Connor	1880–1897	.317
Jimmy Foxx	1925–1945	.325
Henry (Lou) Gehrig	1923–1939	.340
Henry (Hank) Greenberg	1933–1947	.313
George Kelly	1915–1932	.297
Harmon Killebrew	1954–1975	.256
Buck Leonard	1930–1944	(Negro leag.)
Johnny Mize	1936–1953	.312
George Sisler	1915–1930	.340
Bill Terry	1923–1936	.341

SECOND BASEMEN	CAREER	AVERAGE
Eddie Collins	1906–1930	.333
Johnny Evers	1902–1919	.270
Frank Frisch	1919–1937	.316
Charley Gehringer	1924–1942	.321
Billy Herman	1931–1947	.304
Rogers Hornsby	1915–1937	.359
Napoleon Lajoie	1896–1916	.339
Jackie Robinson	1947–1956	.311

THIRD BASEMEN	CAREER	AVERAGE
Frank (Home Run) Baker	1908–1922	.307
Jimmy Collins	1895–1908	.294
William (Judy) Johnson	1918–1938	.340
George Kell	1943–1957	.306
Eddie Mathews	1952–1968	.271
John McGraw	1891–1906	.334
Brooks Robinson	1955–1977	.267
Harold (Pie) Traynor	1920–1937	.320

SHORTSTOPS	CAREER	AVERAGE
Luis Aparicio	1956–1973	.262
Luke Appling	1930–1950	.310
Dave Bancroft	1915–1929	.279
Ernie Banks	1953–1971	.274
Lou Boudreau	1938–1952	.295
Joe Cronin	1926–1945	.302
Travis Jackson	1922–1937	.291
Hugh Jennings	1891–1918	.314

	CAREER	AVERAGE
Walter (Rabbit) Maranville	1912–1935	.258
Harold (Pee Wee) Reese	1941–1958	.269
Joe Sewell	1920–1933	.312
Joe Tinker	1902–1916	.264
Arky Vaughan	1932–1948	.318
John (Honus) Wagner	1897–1917	.329
Roderick (Bobby) Wallace	1894–1918	.267
George Wright	1876–1882	.251

OUTFIELDERS	CAREER	AVERAGE
Henry Aaron	1954–1976	.305
Earl Averill	1929–1941	.318
James (Cool Papa) Bell	1921–1950	(Negro leag.)
Lou Brock	1961–1979	.293
Jesse Burkett	1890–1905	.342
Max Carey	1910–1929	.285
Oscar Charleston	1915–1944	(Negro leag.)
Fred Clarke	1894–1915	.315
Roberto Clemente	1955–1972	.317
Ty Cobb	1905–1928	.367
Earl B. Combs	1924–1935	.325
Sam Crawford	1899–1917	.309
Hazen (Kiki) Cuyler	1921–1938	.321
Ed Delahanty	1888–1903	.346
Martin Dihigo	1923–1950	.320
Joe DiMaggio	1936–1951	.325
Hugh Duffy	1888–1906	.330
Elmer Flick	1898–1910	.315
Josh Gibson	1929–1946	(Negro leag.)
Leon (Goose) Goslin	1921–1938	.316
Billy Hamilton	1888–1901	.344
Harry Heilmann	1914–1932	.342
Harry Hooper	1909–1925	.281
Monte Irvin	1930s–40s	(Negro leag.)
Al Kaline	1953–1974	.297
Willie Keeler	1892–1910	.345
Joe Kelley	1892–1910	.321
Ralph Kiner	1946–1955	.279
Chuck Klein	1928–1944	.320
Fred Lindstrom	1924–1936	.311
John Henry Lloyd	1905–1931	.362
Mickey Mantle	1951–1968	.298
Henry (Heinie) Manush	1923–1939	.330
Willie Mays	1951–1973	.302
Thomas McCarthy	1884–1896	.294
Joe Medwick	1932–1948	.324
Stan Musial	1941–1963	.331
James O'Rourke	1876–1894	.315
Mel Ott	1926–1947	.304
Edgar (Sam) Rice	1915–1934	.322
Frank Robinson	1956–1976	.294
Edd Roush	1913–1931	.323
George (Babe) Ruth	1914–1935	.342
Al Simmons	1924–1944	.334
Enos Slaughter	1938–1959	.300
Duke Snider	1947–1964	.295
Tris Speaker	1907–1928	.344
Sam Thompson	1885–1898	.336
Lloyd Waner	1927–1945	.316
Paul Waner	1926–1945	.333
Zack Wheat	1909–1927	.317
Ted Williams	1939–1960	.344
Lewis R. (Hack) Wilson	1923–1934	.319
Ross Youngs	1917–1926	.322

OTHERS ELECTED FOR MERITORIOUS SERVICE

Walter Alston, manager, Brooklyn, Los Angeles (1954–76)
Edward G. Barrow, American League executive
Morgan G. Bulkeley, first National League president
Alexander J. Cartwright, organized first baseball club
Henry Chadwick, wrote first baseball rule book
Albert B. (Happy) Chandler, baseball commissioner, 1946–51
Charles A. Comiskey, player, manager, and executive
John (Jocko) Conlan, National League umpire (1941–65)
Tom Connolly, American League umpire for 52 years
Billy Evans, umpire and later general manager of Cleveland Indians and Boston Red Sox

BASEBALL HALL OF FAME (continued)
MERITORIOUS SERVICE (continued)

Andrew (Rube) Foster, founder of Negro National League
Ford C. Frick, National League president (1934–51) and baseball commissioner (1951–65)
Warren Giles, president of the National League (1951–69)
Will Harridge, president of the American League (1931–58)
Bucky Harris, player and manager (1919–47)
Cal Hubbard, American League umpire (1936–52)
Miller Huggins, managed N.Y. Yankees to six pennants
Ban Johnson, first American League president
Bill Klem, National League umpire for 46 years
Kenesaw M. Landis, baseball's first commissioner

Al Lopez, catcher 1928–47; manager, Cleveland Indians 1951–57, Chicago White Sox 1957–65, 1968–69
Leland MacPhail, manager, Cincinnati, Brooklyn, N.Y. Yankees (1933–47); introduced night games (1935)
Joe McCarthy, managed N.Y. Yankees to nine pennants and won seven World Series
Bill McKechnie, managed three different clubs to pennants
Branch Rickey, executive of three National League clubs
Casey Stengel, manager N.Y. Yankees and N.Y. Mets
George Weiss, general manager of N.Y. Yankees and Mets
Harry Wright, National League manager for 30 years
Tom Yawkey, owner of Boston Red Sox (1933–76)

CY YOUNG AWARD (Top Major League Pitchers)

The Cy Young Award for the best pitcher of the year is chosen by vote of members of the Baseball Writers Association. Since 1967 the award has gone to the best pitcher in each major baseball league.

1956	Don Newcombe, Brooklyn (NL)	1962	Don Drysdale, Los Angeles (NL)
1957	Warren Spahn, Milwaukee (NL)	1963	Sandy Koufax, Los Angeles (NL)
1958	Bob Turley, New York (AL)	1964	Dean Chance, Los Angeles (AL)
1959	Early Wynn, Chicago (AL)	1965	Sandy Koufax, Los Angeles (NL)
1960	Vernon Law, Pittsburgh (NL)	1966	Sandy Koufax, Los Angeles (NL)
1961	Whitey Ford, New York (AL)		

NATIONAL LEAGUE		AMERICAN LEAGUE	
1967	Mike McCormick, San Francisco	1967	Jim Lonborg, Boston
1968	Bob Gibson, St. Louis	1968	Dennis McLain, Detroit
1969	Tom Seaver, New York	1969	Miguel Cuellar, Baltimore (tie) Dennis McLain, Detroit
1970	Bob Gibson, St. Louis	1970	Jim Perry, Minnesota
1971	Ferguson Jenkins, Chicago	1971	Vida Blue, Oakland
1972	Steve Carlton, Philadelphia	1972	Gaylord Perry, Cleveland
1973	Tom Seaver, New York	1973	Jim Palmer, Baltimore
1974	Mike Marshall, Los Angeles	1974	Jim (Catfish) Hunter, Oakland
1975	Tom Seaver, New York	1975	Jim Palmer, Baltimore
1976	Randy Jones, San Diego	1976	Jim Palmer, Baltimore
1977	Steve Carlton, Philadelphia	1977	Sparky Lyle, New York
1978	Gaylord Perry, San Diego	1978	Ron Guidry, New York
1979	Bruce Sutter, Chicago	1979	Mike Flanagan, Baltimore
1980	Steve Carlton, Philadelphia	1980	Steve Stone, Baltimore
1981	Fernando Valenzuela, Los Angeles	1981	Rollie Fingers, Milwaukee
1982	Steve Carlton, Philadelphia	1982	Pete Vuckovich, Milwaukee
1983	John Denny, Philadelphia	1983	LaMarr Hoyt, Chicago
1984	Rick Sutcliffe, Chicago	1984	Willie Hernandez, Detroit

BASEBALL MOST VALUABLE PLAYER AWARDS

NATIONAL LEAGUE			AMERICAN LEAGUE		
YEAR	PLAYER	CLUB	YEAR	PLAYER	CLUB
1931	Frank Frisch, second baseman	St. Louis	1931	Robert (Lefty) Grove, pitcher	Philadelphia
1932	Chuck Klein, outfielder	Philadelphia	1932	Jimmy Foxx, first baseman	Philadelphia
1933	Carl Hubbell, pitcher	New York	1933	Jimmy Foxx, first baseman	Philadelphia
1934	Jerome (Dizzy) Dean, pitcher	St. Louis	1934	Gordon (Mickey) Cochrane, catcher	Detroit
1935	Charles (Gabby) Hartnett, catcher	Chicago	1935	Hank Greenberg, first baseman	Detroit
1936	Carl Hubbell, pitcher	New York	1936	Lou Gehrig, first baseman	New York
1937	Joe Medwick, outfielder	St. Louis	1937	Charley Gehringer, second baseman	Detroit
1938	Ernie Lombardi, catcher	Cincinnati	1938	Jimmy Foxx, first baseman	Philadelphia
1939	William H. Walters, pitcher	Cincinnati	1939	Joe DiMaggio, outfielder	New York
1940	Frank McCormick, first baseman	Cincinnati	1940	Hank Greenberg, outfielder	Detroit
1941	Adolph Camilli, first baseman	Brooklyn	1941	Joe DiMaggio, outfielder	New York
1942	Morton Cooper, pitcher	St. Louis	1942	Joe Gordon, second baseman	New York
1943	Stan Musial, outfielder	St. Louis	1943	Spurgeon Chandler, pitcher	New York
1944	Martin Marion, shortstop	St. Louis	1944	Harold Newhouser, pitcher	Detroit
1945	Phil Cavarretta, first baseman	Chicago	1945	Harold Newhouser, pitcher	Detroit
1946	Stan Musial, outfielder	St. Louis	1946	Ted Williams, outfielder	Boston
1947	Bob Elliott, third baseman	Boston	1947	Joe DiMaggio, outfielder	New York
1948	Stan Musial, outfielder	St. Louis	1948	Lou Boudreau, shortstop	Cleveland
1949	Jackie Robinson, second baseman	Brooklyn	1949	Ted Williams, outfielder	Boston
1950	Jim Konstanty, pitcher	Philadelphia	1950	Phil Rizzuto, shortstop	New York
1951	Roy Campanella, catcher	Brooklyn	1951	Yogi Berra, catcher	New York
1952	Hank Sauer, outfielder	Chicago	1952	Bobby Shantz, pitcher	Philadelphia
1953	Roy Campanella, catcher	Brooklyn	1953	Al Rosen, third baseman	Cleveland
1954	Willie Mays, outfielder	New York	1954	Yogi Berra, catcher	New York
1955	Roy Campanella, catcher	Brooklyn	1955	Yogi Berra, catcher	New York
1956	Don Newcombe, pitcher	Brooklyn	1956	Mickey Mantle, outfielder	New York
1957	Hank Aaron, outfielder	Milwaukee	1957	Mickey Mantle, outfielder	New York
1958	Ernie Banks, shortstop	Chicago	1958	Jackie Jensen, outfielder	Boston
1959	Ernie Banks, shortstop	Chicago	1959	Nellie Fox, second baseman	Chicago

MOST VALUABLE PLAYERS (continued)

NATIONAL LEAGUE			AMERICAN LEAGUE		
YEAR	PLAYER	CLUB	YEAR	PLAYER	CLUB
1960	Dick Groat, shortstop	Pittsburgh	1960	Roger Maris, outfielder	New York
1961	Frank Robinson, outfielder	Cincinnati	1961	Roger Maris, outfielder	New York
1962	Maury Wills, shortstop	Los Angeles	1962	Mickey Mantle, outfielder	New York
1963	Sandy Koufax, pitcher	Los Angeles	1963	Elston Howard, catcher	New York
1964	Ken Boyer, third baseman	St. Louis	1964	Brooks Robinson, third baseman	Baltimore
1965	Willie Mays, outfielder	San Francisco	1965	Zoilo Versalles, shortstop	Minnesota
1966	Roberto Clemente, outfielder	Pittsburgh	1966	Frank Robinson, outfielder	Baltimore
1967	Orlando Cepeda, first baseman	St. Louis	1967	Carl Yastrzemski, outfielder	Boston
1968	Bob Gibson, pitcher	St. Louis	1968	Dennis McLain, pitcher	Detroit
1969	Willie McCovey, first baseman	San Francisco	1969	Harmon Killebrew, infielder	Minnesota
1970	Johnny Bench, catcher	Cincinnati	1970	Boog Powell, first baseman	Baltimore
1971	Joe Torre, third baseman	St. Louis	1971	Vida Blue, pitcher	Oakland
1972	Johnny Bench, catcher	Cincinnati	1972	Dick Allen, first baseman	Chicago
1973	Pete Rose, outfielder	Cincinnati	1973	Reggie Jackson, outfielder	Oakland
1974	Steve Garvey, first baseman	Los Angeles	1974	Jeff Burroughs, outfielder	Texas
1975	Joe Morgan, second baseman	Cincinnati	1975	Fred Lynn, outfielder	Boston
1976	Joe Morgan, second baseman	Cincinnati	1976	Thurman Munson, catcher	New York
1977	George Foster, outfielder	Cincinnati	1977	Rod Carew, first baseman	Minnesota
1978	Dave Parker, outfielder	Pittsburgh	1978	Jim Rice, outfielder	Boston
1979	Willie Stargell, first baseman	Pittsburgh	1979	Don Baylor, outfielder	California
	Keith Hernandez, first baseman	St. Louis			
1980	Mike Schmidt, third baseman	Philadelphia	1980	George Brett, third baseman	Kansas City
1981	Mike Schmidt, third baseman	Philadelphia	1981	Rollie Fingers, pitcher	Milwaukee
1982	Dale Murphy, outfielder	Atlanta	1982	Robin Yount, shortstop	Milwaukee
1983	Dale Murphy, outfielder	Atlanta	1983	Cal Ripken Jr., shortstop	Baltimore
1984	Ryne Sandberg, second baseman,	Chicago	1984	Willie Hernandez, pitcher	Detroit

BASEBALL ROOKIE OF THE YEAR AWARDS

Before 1949 the Baseball Writers' Association chose only one Rookie of the Year from both the American League and the National League. The award in 1947 went to Jackie Robinson, first baseman for the Broklyn Dodgers (NL), and in 1948 it went to Alvin Dark, shortstop for Boston (NL).

NATIONAL LEAGUE			AMERICAN LEAGUE		
YEAR	PLAYER AND POSITION	CLUB	YEAR	PLAYER AND POSITION	CLUB
1949	Don Newcombe, pitcher	Brooklyn	1949	Roy Sievers, outfielder	St. Louis
1950	Samuel Jethroe, outfielder	Boston	1950	Walt Dropo, first baseman	Boston
1951	Willie Mays, outfielder	New York	1951	Gilbert McDougald, third baseman	New York
1952	Joseph Black, pitcher	Brooklyn	1952	Harry Byrd, pitcher	Philadelphia
1953	James Gilliam, second baseman	Brooklyn	1953	Harvey Kuenn, shortstop	Detroit
1954	Wallace Moon, outfielder	St. Louis	1954	Robert Grim, pitcher	New York
1955	Bill Virdon, outfielder	St. Louis	1955	Herb Score, pitcher	Cleveland
1956	Frank Robinson, outfielder	Cincinnati	1956	Luis Aparicio, shortstop	Chicago
1957	John Sanford, pitcher	Philadelphia	1957	Tony Kubek, infielder	New York
1958	Orlando Cepeda, first baseman	San Francisco	1958	Albie Pearson, outfielder	Washington
1959	Willie McCovey, first baseman	San Francisco	1959	Bob Allison, outfielder	Washington
1960	Frank Howard, outfielder	Los Angeles	1960	Ron Hansen, shortstop	Baltimore
1961	Billy Williams, outfielder	Chicago	1961	Don Schwall, pitcher	Boston
1962	Ken Hubbs, second baseman	Chicago	1962	Tom Tresh, outfielder-shortstop	New York
1963	Pete Rose, second baseman	Cincinnati	1963	Gary Peters, pitcher	Chicago
1964	Dick Allen, third baseman	Philadelphia	1964	Tony Oliva, outfielder	Minnesota
1965	Jim Lefebvre, second baseman	Los Angeles	1965	Curt Blefary, outfielder	Baltimore
1966	Tommy Helms, third baseman	Cincinnati	1966	Tommie Agee, outfielder	Chicago
1967	Tom Seaver, pitcher	New York	1967	Rod Carew, second baseman	Minnesota
1968	Johnny Bench, catcher	Cincinnati	1968	Stan Bahnsen, pitcher	New York
1969	Ted Sizemore, second baseman	Los Angeles	1969	Lou Piniella, outfielder	Kansas City
1970	Carl Morton, pitcher	Montreal	1970	Thurman Munson, catcher	New York
1971	Earl Williams, catcher	Atlanta	1971	Chris Chambliss, first baseman	Cleveland
1972	Jon Matlack, pitcher	New York	1972	Carlton Fisk, catcher	Boston
1973	Gary Matthews, outfielder	San Francisco	1973	Al Bumbry, outfielder	Baltimore
1974	Bake McBride, outfielder	St. Louis	1974	Mike Hargrove, first baseman	Texas
1975	John Montefusco, pitcher	San Francisco	1975	Fred Lynn, outfielder	Boston
1976	Pat Zachry, pitcher	Cincinnati	1976	Mark Fidrych, pitcher	Detroit
	Butch Metzger, pitcher	San Diego	1977	Eddie Murray, DH, outfielder	Baltimore
1977	Andre Dawson, outfielder	Montreal	1978	Lou Whitaker, second baseman	Detroit
1978	Bob Horner, third baseman	Atlanta	1979	Alfredo Griffin, shortstop	Toronto
1979	Rick Sutcliffe, pitcher	Los Angeles		John Castino, third baseman	Minnesota
1980	Steve Howe, pitcher	Los Angeles	1980	Joe Charboneau, outfielder	Cleveland
1981	Fernando Valenzuela, pitcher	Los Angeles	1981	Dave Righetti, pitcher	New York
1982	Steve Sax, second baseman	Los Angeles	1982	Cal Ripken Jr., shortstop	Baltimore
1983	Darryl Strawberry, outfielder	New York	1983	Ron Kittle, outfielder	Chicago
1984	Dwight Gooden, pitcher	New York	1984	Alvin Davis, first baseman	Seattle

BASKETBALL

COLLEGE BASKETBALL

NCAA CHAMPIONSHIP TOURNAMENT

YEAR	CHAMPION	COACH	SCORE	RUNNER-UP	HOST OR SITE
1939	Oregon	Howard Hobson	46–33	Ohio State	Evanston, Ill.
1940	Indiana	Branch McCracken	60–42	Kansas	Kansas City, Mo.
1941	Wisconsin	Harold Foster	39–34	Washington State	Kansas City, Mo.
1942	Stanford	Everett Dean	53–38	Dartmouth	Kansas City, Mo.
1943	Wyoming	Everett Shelton	46–34	Georgetown	New York City
1944	Utah	Vadal Peterson	42–40[1]	Dartmouth	New York City
1945	Oklahoma State	Henry Iba	49–45	New York U.	New York City
1946	Oklahoma State	Henry Iba	43–40	North Carolina	New York City
1947	Holy Cross	Alvin Julian	58–47	Oklahoma	New York City
1948	Kentucky	Adolph Rupp	58–42	Baylor	New York City
1949	Kentucky	Adolph Rupp	46–36	Oklahoma State	Seattle, Wash.
1950	City College N.Y.	Nat Holman	71–68	Bradley	New York City
1951	Kentucky	Adolph Rupp	68–58	Kansas City	Minneapolis, Minn.
1952	Kansas	Forrest Allen	80–63	St. John's	Seattle, Wash.
1953	Indiana	Branch McCracken	69–68	Kansas	Kansas City, Mo.
1954	La Salle	Kenneth Loeffler	92–76	Bradley	Kansas City, Mo.
1955	San Francisco	Phil Woolpert	77–63	La Salle	Kansas City, Mo.
1956	San Francisco	Phil Woolpert	83–71	Iowa	Evanston, Ill.
1957	North Carolina	Frank McGuire	54–53[2]	Kansas	Kansas City, Mo.
1958	Kentucky	Adolph Rupp	84–72	Seattle	Louisville, Ky.
1959	California	Pete Newell	71–70	West Virginia	Louisville, Ky.
1960	Ohio State	Fred Taylor	75–55	California	San Francisco, Calif.
1961	Cincinnati	Edward Jucker	70–65[1]	Ohio State	Kansas City, Mo.
1962	Cincinnati	Edward Jucker	71–59	Ohio State	Louisville, Ky.
1963	Loyola (Ill.)	George Ireland	60–58[1]	Cincinnati	Louisville, Ky.
1964	UCLA	John Wooden	98–83	Duke	Kansas City, Mo.
1965	UCLA	John Wooden	91–80	Michigan	Portland, Oregon
1966	Texas Western	Don Haskins	72–65	Kentucky	College Park, Md.
1967	UCLA	John Wooden	79–64	Dayton	Louisville, Ky.
1968	UCLA	John Wooden	78–55	North Carolina	Los Angeles, Calif.
1969	UCLA	John Wooden	92–72	Purdue	Louisville, Ky.
1970	UCLA	John Wooden	80–69	Jacksonville	College Park, Md.
1971	UCLA	John Wooden	68–62	Vacated	Houston, Texas
1972	UCLA	John Wooden	81–76	Florida State	Los Angeles, Calif.
1973	UCLA	John Wooden	87–66	Memphis State	St. Louis, Mo.
1974	North Carolina State	Norm Sloan	76–64	Marquette	Greensboro, N.C.
1975	UCLA	John Wooden	92–85	Kentucky	San Diego, Calif.
1976	Indiana	Bob Knight	86–68	Michigan	Philadelphia, Pa.
1977	Marquette	Al McGuire	67–59	North Carolina	Atlanta, Georgia
1978	Kentucky	Joe Hall	94–88	Duke	St. Louis, Mo.
1979	Michigan State	Jud Heathcote	75–64	Indiana State	Salt Lake City, Utah
1980	Louisville	Denny Crum	59–54	Vacated	Indianapolis, Ind.
1981	Indiana	Bob Knight	63–50	North Carolina	Philadelphia, Pa.
1982	North Carolina	Dean Smith	63–62	Georgetown	New Orleans, La.
1983	North Carolina State	Jim Valvano	54–52	Houston	Albuquerque, N.M.
1984	Georgetown	John Thompson	84–75	Houston	Seattle, Wash.
1985	Villanova	Rollie Massimino	66–64	Georgetown	Lexington, Ky.

[1]Overtime. [2]Three overtimes.

NCAA OUTSTANDING PLAYER AWARD

1940 Marvin Huffman, Indiana	1956 Hal Lear, Temple	1972 Bill Walton, UCLA
1941 John Kotz, Wisconsin	1957 Wilt Chamberlain, Kansas	1973 Bill Walton, UCLA
1942 Howard Dallmar, Stanford	1958 Elgin Baylor, Seattle	1974 David Thompson, North Carolina State
1943 Ken Sailors, Wyoming	1959 Jerry West, West Virginia	1975 Rick Washington, UCLA
1944 Arnold Ferrin, Utah	1960 Jerry Lucas, Ohio State	1976 Kent Benson, Indiana
1945 Bob Kurland, Oklahoma State	1961 Jerry Lucas, Ohio State	1977 Butch Lee, Marquette
1946 Bob Kurland, Oklahoma State	1962 Paul Hogue, Cincinnati	1978 Jack Givens, Kentucky
1947 George Kaftan, Holy Cross	1963 Art Heyman, Duke	1979 Earvin Johnson, Michigan State
1948 Alex Groza, Kentucky	1964 Walt Hazzard, UCLA	1980 Darrell Griffith, Louisville
1949 Alex Groza, Kentucky	1965 Bill Bradley, Princeton	1981 Isiah Thomas, Indiana
1950 Irwin Dambrot, City College N.Y.	1966 Jerry Chambers, Utah	1982 James Worthy, North Carolina
1951 None chosen	1967 Lew Alcindor, UCLA	1983 Akeem Olajuwon, Houston
1952 Clyde Lovellette, Kansas	1968 Lew Alcindor, UCLA	1984 Patrick Ewing, Georgetown
1953 B. H. Born, Kansas	1969 Lew Alcindor, UCLA	1985 Ed Pinckney, Villanova
1954 Tom Gola, La Salle	1970 Sidney Wicks, UCLA	
1955 Bill Russell, San Francisco	1971 vacated	

NATIONAL INVITATION TOURNAMENT

YEAR	CHAMPION	COACH	YEAR	CHAMPION	COACH
1938	Temple	Jim Usilton	1962	Dayton	Tom Blackburn
1939	Long Island U.	Clair Bee	1963	Providence College	Joe Mullaney
1940	Colorado	Forest Cox	1964	Bradley	Chuck Orsborn
1941	Long Island U.	Clair Bee	1965	St. John's (N.Y.)	Joe Lapchick
1942	West Virginia	Byke Raese	1966	Brigham Young	Stanley Watts
1943	St. John's	Joe Lapchick	1967	Southern Illinois	Jack Hartman
1944	St. John's	Joe Lapchick	1968	Dayton	Don Donoker
1945	DePaul	Raymond Meyer	1969	Temple	Harry Litwack
1946	Kentucky	Adolph Rupp	1970	Marquette	Al McGuire
1947	Utah	Vadal Peterson	1971	North Carolina	Dean Smith
1948	St. Louis	Edward Hickey	1972	Maryland	Lefty Driesell
1949	San Francisco	Pete Newell	1973	Virginia Tech	Don DeVoe
1950	City College (N.Y.)	Nat Holman	1974	Purdue	Fred Schaus
1951	Brigham Young	Stanley Watts	1975	Princeton	Pete Carril
1952	La Salle	Kenneth Loeffler	1976	Kentucky	Joe Hall
1953	Seton Hall	John Russell	1977	St. Bonaventure (N.Y.)	Jim Satalin
1954	Holy Cross	Lester Sheary	1978	Texas	Abe Lemons
1955	Duquesne	Donald Moore	1979	Indiana	Bobby Knight
1956	Louisville	Bernard Hickman	1980	Virginia	Terry Holland
1957	Bradley	Chuck Orsborn	1981	Tulsa	Nolan Richardson
1958	Xavier of Ohio	James McCafferty	1982	Bradley	Dick Versace
1959	St. John's (N.Y.)	Joe Lapchick	1983	Fresno State	Boyd Grant
1960	Bradley	Chuck Orsborn	1984	Michigan	Bill Frieder
1961	Providence College	Joe Mullaney	1985	UCLA	Walt Hazzard

COLLEGE SCORING CHAMPIONS[1]

YEAR	PLAYER, SCHOOL	G[2]	PTS	AVG
1951	Bill Mlkvy, Temple	25	731	29.2
1952	Clyde Lovellette, Kansas	28	795	28.4
1953	Frank Selvy, Furman	25	738	29.5
1954	Frank Selvy, Furman	29	1209	41.7
1955	Darrell Floyd, Furman	25	897	35.9
1956	Darrell Floyd, Furman	28	946	33.8
1957	Grady Wallace, South Carolina	29	906	31.2
1958	Oscar Robertson, Cincinnati	28	984	35.1
1959	Oscar Robertson, Cincinnati	30	978	32.6
1960	Oscar Robertson, Cincinnati	30	1011	33.7
1961	Frank Burgess, Gonzaga	26	842	32.4
1962	Billy McGill, Utah	26	1009	38.8
1963	Nick Werkman, Seton Hall	22	650	29.5
1964	Howard Komives, Bowling Green	23	844	36.7
1965	Rick Barry, Miami (Fla.)	26	973	37.4
1966	Dave Schellhase, Purdue	24	781	32.5
1967	Jim Walker, Providence	28	851	30.4
1968	Pete Maravich, Louisiana State	26	1138	43.8
1969	Pete Maravich, Louisiana State	26	1148	44.2
1970	Pete Maravich, Louisiana State	31	1381	44.5
1971	Johnny Neumann, Mississippi	23	923	40.1
1972	Dwight Lamar, SW Louisiana	29	1054	36.3
1973	William Averitt, Pepperdine	25	848	33.9
1974	Larry Fogle, Canisius	25	835	33.4
1975	Bob McCurdy, Richmond	26	855	32.9
1976	Marshall Rodgers, Pan American	25	919	36.8
1977	Freeman Williams, Portland State	26	1010	38.8
1978	Freeman Williams, Portland State	27	969	35.9
1979	Lawrence Butler, Idaho State	27	812	30.1
1980	Tony Murphy, Southern-Baton Rouge	29	932	32.1
1981	Z. Frederick, South Carolina	27	781	28.9
1982	H. Kelly, Texas Southern	29	862	29.7
1983	H. Kelly, Texas Southern	29	835	28.8
1984	J. Jakubick, Akron	27	814	30.1
1985	Xavier McDaniel, Wichita St.	30	822	27.4
	Alfrederick Hughes, Loyola	30	822	27.4

COLLEGE REBOUND CHAMPIONS[1,3]

YEAR	PLAYER, SCHOOL	G[2]	No.	Avg.
1951	Ernie Beck, Pennsylvania	27	556	20.6
1952	Bill Hannon, Army	17	355	20.9
1953	Ed Conlin, Fordham	26	612	23.5
1954	Art Quimby, Connecticut	26	588	22.6
1955	Charlie Slack, Marshall	21	538	25.6
1956	Joe Holup, George Washington	26	604	.256
1957	Elgin Baylor, Seattle	25	508	.235
1958	Alex Ellis, Niagara	25	536	.262
1959	Leroy Wright, Pacific	26	652	.238
1960	Leroy Wright, Pacific	17	380	.234
1961	Jerry Lucas, Ohio State	27	470	.198
1962	Jerry Lucas, Ohio State	28	499	.211
1963	Paul Silas, Creighton	27	557	20.6
1964	Bob Pelkington, Xavier	26	567	21.8
1965	Toby Kimball, Connecticut	23	483	21.0
1966	Jim Ware, Oklahoma City	29	607	20.9
1967	Dick Cunningham, Murray State	22	479	21.8
1968	Neal Walk, Florida	25	494	19.8
1969	Spencer Haywood, Detroit	22	472	21.5
1970	Artis Gilmore, Jacksonville	28	621	22.2
1971	Artis Gilmore, Jacksonville	26	603	23.2
1972	Kermit Washington, American	23	455	19.8
1973	Kermit Washington, American	22	439	20.0
1974	Marvin Barnes, Providence	32	597	18.7
1975	John Irving, Hofstra	21	323	15.4
1976	Sam Pellom, Buffalo	26	420	16.2
1977	Glenn Mosley, Seton Hall	29	473	16.3
1978	Ken Williams, North Texas State	28	411	14.7
1979	Monti Davis, Tennessee State	26	421	16.2
1980	Larry Smith, Alcorn State	26	392	15.1
1981	D. Watson, Mississippi Valley	27	379	14.0
1982	L. Thompson, Texas	27	365	13.5
1983	Xavier McDaniel, Wichita State	28	403	14.4
1984	Akeem Alajuwon, Houston	32	441	13.8
1985	Xavier McDaniel, Wichita State	30	449	15.0

[1] Regular season. [2] Games. [3] From 1956 through 1962, championship determined in highest individual recoveries out of total by both teams in all games.

COLLEGE TEAM SCORING LEADERS: 1984–1985

	TOP OFFENSIVE TEAMS	GAMES	POINTS FOR	AVERAGE		TOP DEFENSIVE TEAMS	GAMES	POINTS AGAINST	AVERAGE
1948	Rhode Island	23	1,755	76.3	1948	Oklahoma State	31	1,006	32.5
1949	Rhode Island	22	1,575	71.6	1949	Oklahoma State	28	985	35.2
1950	Villanova	29	2,111	72.8	1950	Oklahoma State	27	1,059	39.2
1951	Cincinnati	22	1,694	77.0	1951	Texas A&M	29	1,275	44.0
1952	Kentucky	32	2,635	82.3	1952	Oklahoma State	27	1,228	45.5
1953	Furman	27	2,435	90.2	1953	Oklahoma State	30	1,614	53.8
1954	Furman	29	2,658	91.7	1954	Oklahoma State	29	1,539	53.1
1955	Furman	27	2,572	95.3	1955	San Francisco	29	1,511	52.1
1956	Morehead State	29	2,782	95.9	1956	San Francisco	29	1,514	52.2
1957	Connecticut	25	2,183	87.3	1957	Oklahoma State	26	1,420	54.6
1958	Marshall	24	2,113	88.0	1958	San Francisco	27	1,363	50.5
1959	Miami (Fla.)	25	2,190	87.6	1959	California	29	1,480	51.0
1960	Ohio State	28	2,532	90.4	1960	California	30	1,486	49.5
1961	St. Bonaventure	28	2,479	88.5	1961	Santa Clara	27	1,314	48.7
1962	Loyola (Ill.)	27	2,436	90.2	1962	Santa Clara	25	1,302	52.1
1963	Loyola (Ill.)	31	2,847	91.8	1963	Cincinnati	28	1,480	52.9
1964	Detroit	25	2,402	96.1	1964	San Jose State	24	1,307	54.5
1965	Miami (Fla.)	26	2,558	98.4	1965	Tennessee	25	1,391	55.6
1966	Syracuse	28	2,773	99.0	1966	Oregon State	28	1,527	54.5
1967	Oklahoma City	26	2,496	96.0	1967	Tennessee	28	1,511	54.0
1968	Houston	33	3,226	97.8	1968	Army	25	1,448	57.9
1969	Purdue	28	2,605	93.0	1969	Army	28	1,498	53.5
1970	Jacksonville	28	2,809	100.3	1970	Army	28	1,515	54.1
1971	Jacksonville	26	2,598	99.9	1971	Fairleigh Dickinson	23	1,236	53.7
1972	Oral Roberts	28	2,943	105.1	1972	Minnesota	25	1,451	58.0
1973	Oral Roberts	27	2,626	97.3	1973	Texas-El Paso	26	1,460	56.2
1974	Maryland-Eastern Shore	29	2,831	97.6	1974	Texas-El Paso	25	1,413	56.5
1975	South Alabama	26	2,412	92.8	1975	Texas-El Paso	26	1,491	57.3
1976	Nevada-Las Vegas	31	3,426	110.5	1976	Princeton	27	1,427	52.9
1977	Nevada-Las Vegas	32	3,426	107.1	1977	Princeton	26	1,343	51.7
1978	New Mexico	28	2,731	97.5	1978	Fresno State	27	1,417	52.5
1979	Nevada-Las Vegas	29	2,700	93.1	1979	Princeton	26	1,452	55.8
1980	Alcorn State	30	2,729	92.0	1980	St. Peters	31	1,563	50.4
1981	California-Irvine	27	2,332	86.4	1981	Fresno State	29	1,470	50.7
1982	Long Island U.	30	2,605	86.8	1982	Fresno State	30	1,472	47.1
1983	Boston College	32	2,697	84.3	1983	Princeton	29	1,507	52.0
1984	Tulsa	31	2,816	90.8	1984	Princeton	28	1,403	50.1
1985	Oklahoma	33	3,010	91.2	1985	Fresno State	29	1,567	54.0

COLLEGE BASKETBALL CONFERENCE CHAMPIONS: 1984–1985

CONFERENCE	REGULAR SEASON TITLE	WON-LOST	WON CONFERENCE TOURNAMENT	WON-LOST
Atlantic Coast	North Carolina	24-8	Georgia Tech	24-7
Atlantic 10	West Virginia	20-8	Temple	24-5
Big East	St. John's	27-3	Georgetown	30-2
Big Eight	Oklahoma	28-5	Oklahoma	28-5
Big Sky	Nevada-Reno	21-9	Nevada-Reno	21-9
Big Ten	Michigan	25-3		
East Coast	Bucknell	19-10	Lehigh	12-18
ECAC South	Navy	25-5	Navy	25-5
Ivy League	Pennsylvania	13-13		
Mid-American	Ohio University	22-7	Ohio University	22-7
Metro Conference	Mississippi St. U.	27-3	Mississippi St. U.	27-3
Mid-Continent	Cleveland State	21-8	Eastern Illinois	20-10
Mid-Eastern	North Carolina A&T	19-9	North Carolina A&T	19-9
Midwestern City	Loyola (Ill.)	25-5	Loyola (Ill.)	25-5
Missouri Valley	Tulsa	23-7	Wichita State	18-12
Ohio Valley	Tennessee Tech	19-8	Mid. Tennessee	17-13
Pacific Coast	Nevada-Las Vegas	27-3	Nevada-Las Vegas	27-3
Pacific Ten	Washington	22-9		
Southeastern	Louisiana State U.	19-9	Auburn	20-11
Southern	Tennessee-Chattanooga	22-7	Marshall	21-12
Southland	Louisiana Tech	27-2	Louisiana Tech	27-2
Southwest	Texas Tech	23-7	Texas Tech	23-7
Southwestern	Alcorn State	23-6	South. U.	19-10
Sun Belt	Virginia Com. U.	25-5	Virginia Com. U.	25-5
West Coast	Pepperdine	23-8		
Western Athletic	Utah Tech.-Provo	21-9	South Dakota State	23-7

PROFESSIONAL BASKETBALL

NATIONAL BASKETBALL ASSOCIATION CHAMPIONS:

Year	Eastern Conference	Won	Lost	Pct.	Western Conference	Won	Lost	Pct.	PLAYOFF CHAMPIONSHIP Winner
	REGULAR SEASON								
1947	Washington	49	11	.817	Chicago	39	22	.639	Philadelphia over Chicago (4-1)
1948	Philadelphia	27	21	.563	St. Louis	29	19	.604	Baltimore over Philadelphia (4-2)
1949	Washington	38	22	.633	Rochester	45	15	.750	Minneapolis over Washington (4-2)
1950	Syracuse	51	13	.797	Indianapolis	39	25	.609	Minneapolis over Syracuse (4-2)
	Minneapolis (Central)	51	17	.750					
1951	Philadelphia	40	26	.606	Minneapolis	44	24	.647	Rochester over New York (4-3)
1952	Syracuse	40	26	.606	Rochester	41	25	.621	Minneapolis over New York (4-3)
1953	New York	47	23	.671	Minneapolis	48	22	.686	Minneapolis over New York (4-1)
1954	New York	44	28	.611	Minneapolis	46	26	.639	Minneapolis over Syracuse (4-3)
1955	Syracuse	43	29	.597	Fort Wayne	43	29	.597	Syracuse over Fort Wayne (4-3)
1956	Philadelphia	45	27	.625	Fort Wayne	37	35	.514	Philadelphia over Fort Wayne (4-1)
1957	Boston	44	28	.611	St. Louis	34	38	.472	Boston over St. Louis (4-3)
1958	Boston	49	23	.681	St. Louis	41	31	.569	St. Louis over Boston (4-2)
1959	Boston	52	20	.722	St. Louis	49	23	.681	Boston over Minneapolis (4-0)
1960	Boston	59	16	.787	St. Louis	46	29	.613	Boston over St. Louis (4-3)
1961	Boston	57	22	.722	St. Louis	51	28	.646	Boston over St. Louis (4-1)
1962	Boston	60	20	.750	Los Angeles	54	26	.675	Boston over Los Angeles (4-3)
1963	Boston	58	22	.725	Los Angeles	53	27	.663	Boston over Los Angeles (4-2)
1964	Boston	59	21	.738	San Francisco	48	32	.600	Boston over San Francisco (4-1)
1965	Boston	62	18	.775	Los Angeles	49	31	.613	Boston over Los Angeles (4-1)
1966	Philadelphia	55	25	.688	Los Angeles	45	35	.563	Boston over Los Angeles (4-3)
1967	Philadelphia	68	13	.840	San Francisco	44	37	.543	Philadelphia over San Francisco (4-2)
1968	Philadelphia	62	20	.756	St. Louis	56	26	.683	Boston over Los Angeles (4-2)
1969	Baltimore...........	57	25	.695	Los Angeles	55	27	.671	Boston over Los Angeles (4-3)
1970	New York	60	22	.732	Atlanta	48	34	.585	New York over Los Angeles (4-3)
1971*	New York (Atlantic) ..	52	30	.634	Milwaukee (Midwest).	66	16	.805	Milwaukee over Baltimore (4-0)
	Baltimore (Central) ..	42	40	.512	Los Angeles (Pacific).	48	34	.585	
1972	Boston (Atlantic)	56	26	.683	Los Angeles (Pacific).	69	13	.841	Los Angeles over New York (4-1)
	Baltimore (Central) ..	38	44	.463	Milwaukee (Midwest).	63	19	.768	
1973	Boston (Atlantic)	68	14	.829	Milwaukee (Midwest).	60	22	.732	New York over Los Angeles (4-1)
	Baltimore (Central) ..	52	30	.634	Los Angeles (Pacific).	60	22	.732	
1974	Boston (Atlantic)	56	26	.683	Milwaukee (Midwest).	59	23	.720	Boston over Milwaukee (4-3)
	Washington (Central)	47	35	.573	Los Angeles (Pacific).	47	35	.573	
1975	Boston (Atlantic)	60	22	.732	Chicago (Midwest) ...	47	35	.573	Golden St. over Washington (4-0)
	Washington (Central)	60	22	.732	Golden State (Pacific)	48	34	.585	
1976	Boston (Atlantic)	54	28	.659	Milwaukee (Midwest).	38	44	.463	Boston over Phoenix (4-2)
	Cleveland (Central) ..	49	33	.598	Golden State (Pacific)	59	23	.720	
1977	Philadelphia (Atlantic)	50	32	.610	Denver (Midwest)....	50	32	.610	Portland over Philadelphia (4-2)
	Houston (Central) ...	49	33	.598	Los Angeles (Pacific).	53	29	.646	
1978	Philadelphia (Atlantic)	55	27	.671	Denver (Midwest)....	48	34	.585	Washington over Seattle (4-3)
	San Antonio (Central)	52	30	.634	Portland (Pacific)	58	24	.707	
1979	Washington (Atlantic)	54	28	.659	Kansas City (Midwest)	48	34	.585	Seattle over Washington (4-1)
	San Antonio (Central)	48	34	.585	Seattle (Pacific)	52	30	.634	
1980	Boston (Atlantic)	61	21	.744	Milwaukee (Midwest).	49	33	.598	Los Angeles over Philadelphia (4-2)
	Atlanta (Central)	50	32	.610	Los Angeles (Pacific).	60	22	.732	
1981	Boston (Atlantic)	62	20	.756	San Antonio (Midwest)	52	30	.634	Boston over Houston (4-2)
	Milwaukee (Central) .	60	22	.732	Phoenix (Pacific)	57	25	.695	
1982	Boston (Atlantic)	63	19	.768	San Antonio (Midwest)	48	34	.585	Los Angeles over Philadelphia (4-2)
	Milwaukee (Central) .	55	27	.671	Los Angeles (Pacific).	57	25	.695	
1983	Philadelphia (Atlantic)	65	17	.793	San Antonio (Midwest)	53	29	.646	Philadelphia over Los Angeles (4-0)
	Milwaukee (Central) .	51	31	.622	Los Angeles (Pacific).	58	24	.707	
1984	Boston (Atlantic)	62	20	.756	Utah (Midwest)	45	37	.549	Boston over Los Angeles (4-3)
	Milwaukee (Central) .	50	32	.610	Los Angeles (Pacific).	54	28	.659	
1985	Boston (Atlantic)	63	19	.768	Denver (Midwest)....	52	30	.634	Los Angeles over Boston (4-2)
	Milwaukee (Central) .	59	23	.720	Los Angeles (Pacific).	62	20	.756	

* In 1970-71 the NBA reorganized into four conferences: Atlantic, Central, Midwest, and Pacific.

NATIONAL BASKETBALL ASSOCIATION SCORING LEADERS

SEASON	PLAYER AND TEAM	G[1]	FG[2]	FT[3]	TP[4]	AVG[5]
1946–47	Joe Fulks, Philadelphia Warriors	60	475	439	1,389	23.2
1947–48	Max Zaslofsky, Chicago Stags	48	373	261	1,007	21.0
1948–49	George Mikan, Minneapolis Lakers	60	583	532	1,698	28.3
1949–50	George Mikan, Minneapolis Lakers	68	649	567	1,865	27.4
1950–51	George Mikan, Minneapolis Lakers	68	678	576	1,932	28.4
1951–52	Paul Arizin, Philadelphia Warriors	66	548	578	1,674	25.4
1952–53	Neil Johnston, Philadelphia Warriors	70	504	556	1,564	22.3
1953–54	Neil Johnston, Philadelphia Warriors	72	591	577	1,759	24.4
1954–55	Neil Johnston, Philadelphia Warriors	72	521	589	1,631	22.7
1955–56	Bob Pettit, St. Louis Hawks	72	646	557	1,849	25.7
1956–57	Paul Arizin, Philadelphia Warriors	71	613	591	1,817	25.6
1957–58	George Yardley, Detroit Pistons	72	673	655	2,001	27.8
1958–59	Bob Pettit, St. Louis Hawks	72	719	667	2,105	29.2
1959–60	Wilt Chamberlain, Philadelphia Warriors	72	1,065	577	2,707	37.6
1960–61	Wilt Chamberlain, Philadelphia Warriors	79	1,251	531	3,033	38.4
1961–62	Wilt Chamberlain, Philadelphia Warriors	80	1,597	835	4,029	50.4
1962–63	Wilt Chamberlain, San Francisco Warriors	80	1,463	660	3,586	44.8
1963–64	Wilt Chamberlain, San Francisco Warriors	80	1,204	540	2,948	36.5
1964–65	Wilt Chamberlain, Philadelphia 76ers	73	1,063	408	2,534	34.7
1965–66	Wilt Chamberlain, Philadelphia 76ers	79	1,074	501	2,649	33.5
1966–67	Rick Barry, San Francisco Warriors	78	1,011	753	2,775	35.6
1967–68	Dave Bing, Detroit Pistons	79	835	472	2,142	27.1
1968–69	Elvin Hayes, San Diego Rockets	82	930	467	2,327	28.4
1969–70	Jerry West, Los Angeles Lakers	74	831	647	2,309	31.2
1970–71	Lew Alcindor (Kareem Abdul-Jabbar), Milwaukee Bucks	82	1,063	470	2,596	31.7
1971–72	Kareem Abdul-Jabbar, Milwaukee Bucks	81	1,159	504	2,822	34.8
1972–73	Nate Archibald, Kansas City–Omaha Kings	82	1,028	603	2,719	34.0
1973–74	Bob McAdoo, Buffalo Braves	74	901	459	2,261	30.6
1974–75	Bob McAdoo, Buffalo Braves	82	1,095	641	2,831	34.5
1975–76	Bob McAdoo, Buffalo Braves	78	934	559	2,427	31.1
1976–77	Pete Maravich, New Orleans Jazz	73	886	501	2,273	31.1
1977–78	George Gervin, San Antonio Spurs	82	864	504	2,232	27.2
1978–79	George Gervin, San Antonio Spurs	80	947	471	2,365	29.6
1979–80	George Gervin, San Antonio Spurs	78	1,024	505	2,585	33.1
1980–81	Adrian Dantley, Utah Jazz	80	909	632	2,452	30.7
1981–82	George Gervin, San Antonio	79	993	555	2,551	32.3
1982–83	Alex English, Denver Nuggets	82	959	406	2,326	28.4
1983–84	Adrian Dantley, Utah Jazz	79	802	813	2,418	30.6
1984–85	Bernard King, New York Knicks	55	691	426	1,809	32.9

[1] Games. [2] Field Goals. [3] Free Throws. [4] Total Points. [5] Average per Game.

NATIONAL BASKETBALL ASSOCIATION INDIVIDUAL AWARDS

MOST VALUABLE PLAYER (PODOLOFF CUP) AND ROOKIE OF THE YEAR (GOTTLIEB TROPHY)

YEAR	MVP	ROOKIE OF THE YEAR	YEAR	MVP	ROOKIE OF THE YEAR
1956	Bob Pettit, St. Louis	Maurice Stokes, Rochester	1971	Abdul-Jabbar, Milw.	Dave Cowens, Boston; Geoff Petrie, Portland (tie)
1957	Bob Cousy, Boston	Tom Heinsohn, Boston	1972	Abdul-Jabbar, Milw.	Sidney Wicks, Portland
1958	Bill Russell, Boston	Woody Sauldsberry, Phil.	1973	Dave Cowens, Boston	Bob McAdoo, Buffalo
1959	Bob Pettit, St. Louis	Elgin Baylor, Minn.	1974	Abdul-Jabbar, Milw.	Ernie DiGregorio, Buffalo
1960	Wilt Chamberlain, Phil.	Wilt Chamberlain, Phil.	1975	Bob McAdoo, Buffalo	Keith Wilkes, Golden State
1961	Bill Russell, Boston	Oscar Robertson, Cinn.	1976	Abdul-Jabbar, L.A.	Alvan Adams, Phoenix
1962	Bill Russell, Boston	Walt Bellamy, Chicago	1977	Abdul-Jabbar, L.A.	Adrian Dantley, Buffalo
1963	Bill Russell, Boston	Terry Dischinger, Chicago	1978	Bill Walton, Portland	Walter Davis, Phoenix
1964	Oscar Robertson, Cinn.	Jerry Lucas, Cinn.	1979	Moses Malone, Houston	Phil Ford, Kansas City
1965	Bill Russell, Boston	Willis Reed, New York	1980	Abdul-Jabbar, L.A.	Larry Bird, Boston
1966	Wilt Chamberlain, Phil.	Rick Barry, San Francisco	1981	Julius Erving, Phil.	Darrell Griffith, Utah
1967	Wilt Chamberlain, Phil.	Dave Bing, Detroit	1982	Moses Malone, Houston	Isiah Thomas, Detroit
1968	Wilt Chamberlain, Phil.	Earl Monroe, Baltimore	1983	Moses Malone, Phil.	Terry Cummings, San Diego
1969	Wes Unseld, Baltimore	Wes Unseld, Baltimore	1984	Larry Bird, Boston	Ralph Sampson, Houston
1970	Willis Reed, N.Y.	Abdul-Jabbar, Milw.	1985	Larry Bird, Boston	Michael Jordan, Chicago

NBA LEADERS IN REBOUNDS: 1951–1985

YEAR	PLAYER AND TEAM	GAMES	NUMBER	AVG.	YEAR	PLAYER AND TEAM	GAMES	NUMBER	AVG.
1951	Dolph Schayers, Syracuse	66	1,080	16.4	1968	Wilt Chamberlain, Phil.	82	1,952	23.8
1952	Larry Foust, Fort Wayne	66	880	13.3	1969	Wilt Chamberlain, Phil.	81	1,712	21.1
	Mel Hutchins, Milwaukee	66	880	13.3	1970	Elvin Hayes, San Diego	82	1,386	16.9
1953	George Milsan, Minneapolis	70	1,007	14.4	1971	Wilt Chamberlain, Phil.	82	1,493	18.2
1954	Harry Gallatin, New York	72	1,098	15.3	1972	Wilt Chamberlain, L.A.	82	1,572	19.2
1955	Neil Johnson, Philadelphia	72	1,085	15.1	1973	Wilt Chamberlain, L.A.	82	1,526	18.6
1956	Bob Pettit, St. Louis .	72	1,164	16.2	1974	Elvin Hayes, Washington	81	1,463	18.1
1957	Maurice Stokes, Rochester	72	1,256	17.4	1975	Wes Unseld, Washington	73	1,077	14.8
1958	Bill Russell, Boston .	69	1,564	22.7	1976	K. Abdul-Jabbar, Los Angeles	82	1,383	16.9
1959	Bill Russell, Boston . .	70	1,612	23.0	1977	Bill Walton, Portland	65	934	14.4
1960	Wilt Chamberlain, Phil.	72	1,941	27.0	1978	Len Robinson, New Orleans	82	1,288	15.7
1961	Wilt Chamberlain, Phil.	79	2,149	27.2	1979	Moses Malone, Houston	82	1,444	17.6
1962	Wilt Chamberlain, Phil.	80	2,052	25.7	1980	Swen Nater, San Diego	81	1,216	15.0
1963	Wilt Chamberlain, Phil.	80	1,946	24.3	1981	Moses Malone, Houston	80	1,180	14.8
1964	Bill Russell, Boston . .	78	1,930	24.7	1982	Moses Malone, Houston	81	1,188	14.7
1965	Bill Russell, Boston . .	78	1,878	24.1	1983	Moses Malone, Houston	78	1,194	15.3
1966	Wilt Chamberlain, Phil.	79	1,943	24.6	1984	Moses Malone, Philadelphia	71	950	13.4
1967	Wilt Chamberlain, Phil.	81	1,957	24.2	1985	Moses Malone, Philadelphia	79	1,031	13.1

NBA LEADERS IN ASSISTS: 1947–1985

YEAR	PLAYER AND TEAM	GAMES	NUMBER	AVG.	YEAR	PLAYER AND TEAM	GAMES	NUMBER	AVG.
1947	Ernie Calverley, Providence	59	202	3.4	1967	Guy Rodgers, Chicago	81	908	11.2
1948	Howie Dallmar, Philadelphia	48	120	2.5	1968	Wilt Chamberlain, Phil.	82	702	8.6
1949	Bob Davies, Rochester	60	321	5.4	1969	Oscar Robertson, Cincinnati	79	772	9.8
1950	Dick McGuire, New York	68	386	5.7	1970	Lenny Wilkens, Seattle	75	683	9.1
1951	Andy Phillip, Philadelphia	66	414	6.3	1971	Norm Van Lier, Cincinnati	82	832	10.1
1952	Andy Phillip, Philadelphia	66	539	8.2	1972	Jerry West, Los Angeles	77	747	9.7
1953	Bob Cousy, Boston . .	71	547	7.7	1973	Nate Archibald, K. C.–Omaha	80	910	11.4
1954	Bob Cousy, Boston . .	72	518	7.2	1974	Ernie DiGregorio, Buffalo	81	663	8.2
1955	Bob Cousy, Boston . .	71	557	7.8	1975	Kevin Porter, Washington	81	650	8.0
1956	Bob Cousy, Boston . .	72	642	8.9	1976	Don Watts, Seattle . .	82	661	8.1
1957	Bob Cousy, Boston . .	64	478	7.5	1977	Don Buse, Indiana . . .	81	685	8.5
1958	Bob Cousy, Boston . .	65	463	7.1	1978	Kevin Porter, Detroit–N.J.	82	837	10.2
1959	Bob Cousy, Boston . .	65	557	8.6	1979	Kevin Porter, Detroit	82	1,099	13.4
1960	Bob Cousy, Boston . .	75	715	9.5	1980	Michael Richardson, N.Y.	82	832	10.1
1961	Oscar Robertson, Cincinnati	71	690	9.7	1981	Kevin Porter, Washington	81	734	9.1
1962	Oscar Robertson, Cincinnati	79	899	11.4	1982	Johnny Moore, San Antonio	79	762	9.6
1963	Guy Rodgers, San Francisco	79	825	10.4	1983	Magic Johnson, Los Angeles	79	829	10.5
1964	Oscar Robertson, Cincinnati	79	868	11.0	1984	Magic Johnson, Los Angeles	67	875	13.1
1965	Oscar Robertson, Cincinnati	75	861	11.5	1985	Isiah Thomas, Detroit	81	1,123	13.9
1966	Oscar Robertson, Cincinnati	76	847	11.1					

FIRST PLAYER CHOSEN NBA DRAFT: 1966–1985

YEAR	PLAYER, COLLEGE, PRO TEAM	YEAR	PLAYER, COLLEGE, PRO TEAM
1966	Dave Bing, Syracuse, by Detroit Pistons	1976	John Lucas, Maryland, by Houston Rockets
1967	Jimmy Walker, Providence, by Detroit Pistons	1977	Kent Benson, Indiana, by Milwaukee Bucks
1968	Elvin Hayes, Houston, by Houston Rockets	1978	Mychal Thompson, Minnesota, by Portland Trail Blazers
1969	Kareem Abdul-Jabbar, UCLA, by Milwaukee Bucks	1979	Earvin Johnson, Michigan State, by Los Angeles Lakers
1970	Bob Lanier, St. Bonaventure, by Detroit Pistons	1980	Joe Barry Carroll, Purdue, by Golden State Warriors
1971	Austin Carr, Notre Dame, by Cleveland Cavaliers	1981	Mark Aguirre, DePaul, by Dallas Mavericks
1972	LaRue Martin, Loyola, by Portland Trail Blazers	1982	James Worthy, North Carolina, by Los Angeles Lakers
1973	Doug Collins, Illinois State, by Philadelphia 76ers	1983	Ralph Sampson, Virginia, by Houston Rockets
1974	Bill Walton, UCLA, by Portland Trail Blazers	1984	Akeem Olajuwon, Houston, by Houston Rockets
1975	David Thompson, North Carolina State, by Atlanta Hawks	1985	Patrick Erwing, Georgetown, by New York Knicks

NBA ALL-STAR GAMES: 1951–1985

1951	East 111, West 94	1963	East 115, West 108	1975	East 108, West 102
1952	East 108, West 91	1964	East 111, West 107	1976	East 123, West 109
1953	West 79, East 75	1965	East 124, West 123	1977	West 125, East 124
1954	East 98, West 93, OT	1966	East 137, West 94	1978	East 133, West 125
1955	East 100, West 91	1967	West 135, East 120	1979	West 134, East 129
1956	West 108, East 94	1968	East 144, West 124	1980	East 144, West 136, OT
1957	East 109, West 97	1969	East 123, West 112	1981	East 123, West 120
1958	East 130, West 118	1970	East 142, West 135	1982	East 120, West 118
1959	West 124, East 108	1971	West 108, West 107	1983	East 132, West 123
1960	East 125, West 115	1972	West 112, East 110	1984	East 154, West 145, OT
1961	West 153, East 131	1973	East 104, West 84	1985	West 140, East 129
1962	West 150, East 130	1974	West 134, East 123		

OT = overtime.

BICYCLING

UNITED STATES BICYCLING CHAMPIONS

Source: U.S. Cycling Federation and *Cycle USA*

SENIOR MEN BICYCLING CHAMPIONS

	ROAD	SPRINT	4,000-METER PURSUIT	POINTS RACE	1,000 METERS
1977	Wayne Stetina	Les Barczewski	Paul Deem	Nelson Saldana	Jerry Ash
1978	Dale Stetina	Les Barczewski	Dave Grylls	Ron Skarin	Jerry Ash
1979	Steve Wood	Les Barczewski	Dave Grylls	Gus Pipenhagen	Jerry Ash
1980	Dale Stetina	Mark Gorski	Leonard Nitz	Scott Hembree	Brent Emery
1981	Tom Broznowski	Les Barczewski	Leonard Nitz	John Beckman	Brent Emery
1982	Greg Demgen	Mark Gorski	Leonard Nitz	John Beckman	Leonard Nitz
1983	Thurlow Rogers	Mark Gorski	Leonard Nitz	Brent Emery	Mark Whitehead
1984	Matt Eaton	Nelson Vails	Steve Hegg	Mark Whitehead	Leonard Nitz
1985	Wayne Stetina	Mark Gorski	Carl Sundquist	Pat McDonough	Rory O'Reilly

SENIOR WOMEN BICYCLING CHAMPIONS / JUNIOR MEN BICYCLING CHAMPIONS

	ROAD	SPRINT	3,000-METER PURSUIT	ROAD	TRACK
1977	Connie Carpenter	Sue Novara	Connie Carpenter	Greg LeMond	Chris Springer
1978	Barbara Hintzen	Sue Novara	Mary Jane Reoch	Jeff Bradley	Eric Baltes
1979	Connie Carpenter	Sue Novara	Connie Carpenter	Greg LeMond	Mark Whitehead
1980	Beth Heiden	Sue Novara	Elizabeth Davis	Sterling McBride	John Butler
1981	Connie Carpenter	Sheila Young	Rebecca Twigg	Mike Jensen	Russ Dalbey
1982	Sue Novara-Reber	Connie Paraskevin	Rebecca Twigg	Roy Knickman	Dave Lettieri
1983	Rebecca Twigg	Connie Paraskevin	Cindy Olavarri	Roy Knickman	Roy Knickman
1984	Rebecca Daughton	Rebecca Twigg	Rebecca Twigg	Fred Boos	Paul Swift
1985	Rebecca Daughton	Connie Paraskevin	Betsy Davis	Paul Orwicz	Steve Ziegler

BOWLING

U.S. MEN'S OPEN CHAMPIONSHIP (Bowling Proprietors Association of America)

1959	Billy Welu	1965-66	Dick Weber	1971	Mike Limongello	1976	Paul Moser	1981	Marshall Holman
1960	Harry Smith	1967	Les Schissler	1972	Don Johnson	1977	Johnny Petraglia	1982	Dave Husted
1961	Bill Tucker	1968	Jim Stefanich	1973	Mike McGrath	1978	Nelson Burton Jr.	1983	Gary Dickinson
1962-63	Dick Weber	1969	Billy Hardwick	1974	Larry Laub	1979	Joe Berardi	1984	Mark Roth
1964	Bob Strampe	1970	Bobby Cooper	1975	Steve Neff	1980	Steve Martin	1985	Marshall Holman

Note: the above table columns are (Year, Name) repeated five times:

Year	Name	Year	Name	Year	Name	Year	Name	Year	Name
1959	Billy Welu	1965-66	Dick Weber	1971	Mike Limongello	1976	Paul Moser	1981	Marshall Holman
1960	Harry Smith	1967	Les Schissler	1972	Don Johnson	1977	Johnny Petraglia	1982	Dave Husted
1961	Bill Tucker	1968	Jim Stefanich	1973	Mike McGrath	1978	Nelson Burton Jr.	1983	Gary Dickinson
1962-63	Dick Weber	1969	Billy Hardwick	1974	Larry Laub	1979	Joe Berardi	1984	Mark Roth
1964	Bob Strampe	1970	Bobby Cooper	1975	Steve Neff	1980	Steve Martin	1985	Marshall Holman

U.S. WOMEN'S OPEN CHAMPIONSHIP (Bowling Proprietors Association of America)

Year	Name	Year	Name	Year	Name	Year	Name	Year	Name
1963	Marion Ladewig	1968-69	D. Fothergill	1974	Pat Costello	1979	Diana Silva	1984	Karen Ellingsworth
1964	La Verne Carter	1970	Mary Baker	1975	Paula Sperber	1980	Pat Costello	1985	Pat Mercatanti
1965	Ann Slattery	1971	Paula Sperber	1976	Patty Costello	1981	Donna Adamek		
1966	Joy Abel	1972	Lorrie Koch	1977	Betty Morris	1982	Shinobu Saitoh		
1967	Gloria Bouvia	1973	Millie Martorella	1978	Donna Adamek	1983	Dana Miller		

AMERICAN BOWLING CONGRESS ALL-EVENTS CHAMPIONSHIP

Year	Name	Year	Name	Year	Name	Year	Name	Year	Name
1961	Luke Karan	1966	John Wilcox	1971	Al Cohn	1976	Jim Lindquist	1981	Rod Toft
1962	Billy Young	1967	Gary Lewis	1972	Mac Lowry	1977	Bud Debenham	1982	Rich Wonders
1963	Bus Oswalt	1968	Vince Mazzanti	1973	Ron Woolet	1978	Chris Cobus	1983	Tony Cariello
1964	Les Zikes	1969	Edward Jackson	1974	Bob Hart	1979	Bob Busacchi	1984	Bob Goike
1965	Tom Hathaway	1970	Mike Berlin	1975	Bobby Meadows	1980	Steve Fehr	1985	Barry Asher

WOMEN'S INTERNATIONAL BOWLING CONGRESS ALL-EVENTS CHAMPIONSHIP

Year	Name	Year	Name	Year	Name	Year	Name	Year	Name
1952	Virginia Turner	1959	Pat McBride	1966	Kate Helbig	1973	Toni Calvary	1980	Cheryl Robinson
1953	Doris Knechtges	1960	Judy Roberts	1967	Carol Miller	1974	Judy Soutar	1981	Virginia Norton
1954	Anne Johnson	1961	Evelyn Teal	1968	Susie Reichley	1975	Virginia Park	1982	Aleta Rzepecki
1955	Marion Ladewig	1962	Flossie Argent	1969	Helen Duval	1976	Betty Morris	1983	Virginia Norton
1956	Doris Knechtges	1963	Helen Shablis	1970	D. Fothergill	1977	Akiko Yamaga	1984	Shinobu Saitoh
1957	Anita Cantaline	1964	Jean Havlish	1971	Lorrie Koch	1978	Annese Kelly	1985	Aleta Sill
1958	Mae Ploegman	1965	D. Zimmerman	1972	Millie Martorella	1979	Betty Morris		

AMERICAN BOWLING CONGRESS MASTERS CHAMPIONSHIP

Year	Name	Year	Name	Year	Name	Year	Name	Year	Name
1955	Buzz Fazio	1961	Don Carter	1968	Pete Tountas	1974	Paul Colwell	1980	Neil Burton
1956	Dick Hoover	1962	Bill Golembiewski	1969	Jim Chestney	1975	Ed Ressler	1981	Randy Lightfoot
1957	Dick Hoover	1963	Harry Smith	1970	Don Glover	1976	Nelson Burton Jr.	1982	Joe Berardi
1958	Tom Hennessey	1964-65	Billy Welu	1971	Jim Godman	1977	Earl Anthony	1983	Mike Lastowski
1959	Ray Bluth	1966	Bob Strampe	1972	Bill Beach	1978	Frank Ellenburg	1984	Earl Anthony
1960	Bill Golembiewski	1967	Lou Scalia	1973	Dave Soutar	1979	Doug Myers	1985	Steve Wunderlich

AMERICAN BOWLING CONGRESS SINGLES CHAMPIONSHIP

Year	Name	Year	Name	Year	Name	Year	Name	Year	Name
1967	Frank Perry	1971	Al Cohn	1975	Jim Setser	1979	Rick Peters	1983	Ricky Kendrick
1968	Wayne Kowalski	1972	Bill Pointer	1976	Mike Putzer	1980	Mike Eaton	1984	Bob Antczak
1969	Greg Campbell	1973	Ed Thompson	1977	Frank Gadaleto	1981	Rob Vital		Neal Young
1970	Jake Yoder	1974	Gene Krause	1978	Rich Mersek	1982	Bruce Bohm	1985	Glenn Harbison

PROFESSIONAL BOWLERS ASSOCIATION FIRESTONE TOURNAMENT OF CHAMPIONS

Year	Name	Year	Name	Year	Name	Year	Name	Year	Name
1967	Jim Stefanich	1971	John Petraglia	1975	Dave Davis	1979	George Pappas	1983	Joe Berardi
1968	Dave Davis	1972	Mike Durbin	1976	Marshall Holman	1980	Wayne Webb	1984	Mike Durbin
1969	Jim Godman	1973	Jim Godman	1977	Mike Berlin	1981	Steve Cook	1985	Mark Williams
1970	Don Johnson	1974	Earl Anthony	1978	Earl Anthony	1982	Mike Durbin		

BOXING

PROFESSIONAL BOXING CHAMPIONS BY CLASSES: 1985

Source: *The Ring Magazine*

The table below, prepared by the editors of *The Ring Magazine*, indicates with an * their choice of the fighter in a division who most deserves the title of "world champion."

Source for historical data is the *Ring Record Book*, edited by Herbert G. Goldman and published by The Ring Record Book, Inc., 130 West 37th Street, New York, N.Y. 10018.

WORLD BOXING ASSOCIATION (WBA)	WORLD BOXING COUNCIL (WBC)	INTERNATIONAL BOXING FED. (IBF)
HEAVYWEIGHT (over 195 pounds)		
Tony Tubbs, U.S.	Pinklon Thomas, U.S.	*Michael Spinks, U.S.
CRUISERWEIGHT or JUNIOR HEAVYWEIGHT (176-195 pounds)		
Dwight Braxton (U.S.)	Bernard Benton (U.S.)	Lee Roy Murphy, U.S.
LIGHT HEAVYWEIGHT (161-175 pounds)		
*Michael Spinks, U.S.	*Michael Spinks, U.S.	*Michael Spinks, U.S.
MIDDLEWEIGHT (155-160 pounds)		
*Marvin Hagler, U.S.	*Marvin Hagler, U.S.	*Marvin Hagler, U.S.
JUNIOR MIDDLEWEIGHT or SUPER WELTERWEIGHT (148-154 pounds)		
Mike McCallum, Jamaica	*Thomas Hearns, U.S.	Carlos Santos, Puerto Rico
WELTERWEIGHT (141-147 pounds)		
Donald Curry, U.S.	Milton McCrory, U.S.	Donald Curry, U.S.
JUNIOR WELTERWEIGHT or SUPER LIGHTWEIGHT (136-140 pounds)		
Ubaldo Sacco, Argentina	Lonnie Smith, U.S.	Aaron Pryor, U.S.
LIGHTWEIGHT (131-135 pounds)		
Livingstone Bramble, Virgin Islands	Hector Camacho, U.S.	Jimmy Paul, U.S.
JUNIOR LIGHTWEIGHT or SUPER FEATHERWEIGHT (127-130 pounds)		
*Wilfredo Gomez, Puerto Rico	Julio Cesar Chavez, Mexico	Barry Michael, Australia
FEATHERWEIGHT (123-126 pounds)		
*Barry McGuigan, Ireland	Azumah Nelson, Ghana	Min-Keun Oh, South Korea
JUNIOR FEATHERWEIGHT or SUPER BANTAMWEIGHT (119-122 pounds)		
Victor Callejas, Puerto Rico	Lupe Pintor, Mexico	Ji-Won Kim, Korea
BANTAMWEIGHT (116-118 pounds)		
*Richie Sandoval, U.S.	Miguel Lora, Colombia	Jeff Fenech, Australia
JUNIOR BANTAMWEIGHT or SUPER FLYWEIGHT (113-115 pounds)		
Kaosai Galaxy, Thailand	Jiro Watanabe, Japan	Elly Pical, Indonesia
FLYWEIGHT (109-112 pounds)		
Vacant	*Sot Chitalada, Thailand	Soon-Chung Kwon, South Korea
JUNIOR FLYWEIGHT or LIGHT FLYWEIGHT (under 109 pounds)		
Joey Olivo, U.S.	Jung-Koo Chang, South Korea	Dodie Penalosa, Philippines

HEAVYWEIGHT BOXING CHAMPIONS (over 175 pounds)

Source: *The Ring Magazine*

CHAMPION	REIGN	CHAMPION	REIGN	CHAMPION	REIGN
John L. Sullivan	1882–92	Jack Sharkey	1932–33	Sonny Liston	1962–64
James J. Corbett	1892–97	Primo Carnera	1933–34	Cassius Clay (M. Ali)	1964–70
Bob Fitzsimmons	1897–99	Max Baer	1934–35	Joe Frazier	1970–73
James J. Jeffries	1899–1905	Jim Braddock	1935–37	George Foreman	1973–74
Marvin Hart	1905–06	Joe Louis	1937–49	Muhammad Ali	1974–78
Tommy Burns	1906–08	Ezzard Charles	1949–51	Leon Spinks	1978
Jack Johnson	1908–15	Jersey Joe Walcott	1951–52	Muhammad Ali	1978–79
Jess Willard	1915–19	Rocky Marciano	1952–56	Larry Holmes	1980–85
Jack Dempsey	1919–26	Floyd Patterson	1956–59	Michael Spinks	1985–
Gene Tunney	1926–28	Ingemar Johansson	1959–60		
Max Schmeling	1930–32	Floyd Patterson	1960–62		

LIGHT HEAVYWEIGHT BOXING CHAMPIONS (Up to 175 pounds)

Source: *The Ring Magazine*

CHAMPION	REIGN	CHAMPION	REIGN	CHAMPION	REIGN
Jack Root	1903	Mike McTigue	1927	Joey Maxim	1950–52
George Gardner	1903	Tommy Loughran	1927–29	Archie Moore	1952–62
Bob Fitzsimmons	1903–05	Jimmy Slattery	1930	Harold Johnson	1962–63
"Philadelphia" Jack O'Brien	1905–07	Maxie Rosenbloom	1930–34	Willie Pastrano	1963–65
Jack Dillon	1914–16	Bob Olin	1934–35	Jose Torres	1965–66
Battling Levinsky	1916–20	John Henry Lewis	1935–38	Dick Tiger	1966–68
Georges Carpentier	1920–22	Melio Bettina	1939	Bob Foster	1968–74
Battling Siki	1922–23	Billy Conn	1939–40	Vacant	1974–83
Mike McTigue	1923–25	Anton Christoforidis	1941	Michael Spinks	1983–85
Paul Berlenbach	1925–26	Gus Lesnevich	1941–48		
Jack Delaney	1926–27	Freddie Mills	1948–50		

MIDDLEWEIGHT BOXING CHAMPIONS (Up to 160 pounds)*

CHAMPION	REIGN	CHAMPION	REIGN	CHAMPION	REIGN
Jack Dempsey ("The Nonpareil") ...	1884–91	Marcel Thil	1932–37	Carmen Basilio	1957–58
Bob Fitzsimmons	1891–97	Fred Apostoli	1937–39	Sugar Ray Robinson....	1958–60
Charles (Kid) McCoy ...	1897–98	Ceferino Garcia	1939–40	Paul Pender	1960–62
Tommy Ryan	1898–1907	Ken Overlin	1940–41	Dick Tiger	1962–63
Stanley Ketchel	1908	Billy Soose	1941	Joey Giardello	1963–65
Billy Papke	1908	Tony Zale	1941–47	Dick Tiger	1965–66
Stanley Ketchel	1908–10	Rocky Graziano........	1947–48	Emile Griffith..........	1966–67
Frank Klaus	1913	Tony Zale	1948	Nino Benvenuti	1967
George Chip	1913–14	Marcel Cerdan	1948–49	Emile Griffith..........	1967–68
Al McCoy	1914–17	Jake LaMotta..........	1949–51	Nino Benvenuti	1968–70
Mike O'Dowd	1917–20	Sugar Ray Robinson....	1951	Carlos Monzon	1970–77
Johnny Wilson.........	1920–23	Randy Turpin	1951	Rodrigo Valdez	1977–78
Harry Greb	1923–26	Sugar Ray Robinson....	1951–52	Hugo Corro	1978–79
Tiger Flowers.........	1926	Bobo Olson	1953–55	Vito Antuofermo	1979–80
Mickey Walker........	1926–31	Sugar Ray Robinson....	1955–57	Alan Minter	1980
Gorilla Jones	1931–32	Gene Fullmer..........	1957	Marvin Hagler	1980–
		Sugar Ray Robinson....	1957		

WELTERWEIGHT BOXING CHAMPIONS (Up to 147 pounds)*

CHAMPION	REIGN	CHAMPION	REIGN	CHAMPION	REIGN
Mysterious Billy Smith..	1892–94	Joe Dundee	1927–29	Johnny Saxton	1956
Tommy Ryan	1894–98	Jackie Fields	1929–30	Carmen Basilio	1956–57
Mysterious Billy Smith..	1898–1900	Young Jack Thompson .	1930	Virgil Akins	1958
Rube Ferns	1900	Tommy Freeman	1930–31	Don Jordan	1958–60
Matty Matthews	1900–01	Young Jack Thompson .	1931	Benny (Kid) Paret	1960–61
Rube Ferns	1901	Lou Brouillard	1931–32	Emile Griffith	1961
Joe Walcott	1901–04	Jackie Fields	1932–33	Benny (Kid) Paret	1961–62
Dixie Kid	1904–05	Young Corbett 3d	1933	Emile Griffith	1962–63
Joe Gans	1906	Jimmy McLarnin	1933–34	Luis Rodriguez	1963
Honey Mellody	1906–07	Barney Ross	1934	Emile Griffith	1963–66
Mike (Twin) Sullivan....	1907–08	Jimmy McLarnin	1934–35	Curtis Cokes	1966–69
Jimmy Gardner........	1908–09	Barney Ross	1935–38	Jose Napoles	1969–70
Jimmy Clabby	1910-11	Henry Armstrong	1938–40	Billy Backus	1970–71
Waldemar Holberg	1914	Fritzie Zivic	1940–41	Jose Napoles	1971–75
Tom McCormick	1914	Freddie Cochrane	1941–46	John H. Stracey	1975–76
Matt Wells	1914–15	Marty Servo	1946	Carlos Palomino	1976–79
Mike Glover	1915	Sugar Ray Robinson ...	1946–51	Wilfred Benitez	1979
Jack Britton	1915	Johnny Bratton	1951	Sugar Ray Leonard.....	1979–80
Ted (Kid) Lewis........	1915–19	Kid Gavilan	1951–54	Roberto Duran	1980
Jack Britton...........	1919–22	Johnny Saxton	1954–55	Sugar Ray Leonard.....	1980–82
Mickey Walker........	1922–26	Tony DeMarco........	1955		
Peter Latzo	1926–27	Carmen Basilio	1955–56		

LIGHTWEIGHT BOXING CHAMPIONS (Up to 135 pounds)*

CHAMPION	REIGN	CHAMPION	REIGN	CHAMPION	REIGN
George (Kid) Lavigne ...	1896–99	Al Singer	1930	Jimmy Carter	1954–55
Frank Erne...........	1899–1902	Tony Canzoneri........	1930–33	Wallace (Bud) Smith ...	1955–56
Joe Gans	1902–04	Barney Ross	1933–35	Joe Brown	1956–62
Jimmy Britt	1904–05	Tony Canzoneri........	1935–36	Carlos Ortiz	1962–65
Battling Nelson	1905–06	Lou Ambers	1936–38	Ismael Laguna........	1965
Joe Gans	1906–09	Henry Armstrong	1938–39	Carlos Ortiz	1965–68
Battling Nelson	1909–10	Lou Ambers	1939–40	Teo Cruz	1968–69
Ad Wolgast	1910–12	Lew Jenkins	1940–41	Mando Ramos	1969–70
Willie Ritchie	1912–14	Sammy Angott	1941–42	Ismael Laguna........	1970
Freddie Welsh	1914–17	Ike Williams	1947–51	Ken Buchanan	1970–72
Benny Leonard	1917–24	Jimmy Carter	1951–52	Roberto Duran	1972–79
Jimmy Goodrich	1925	Lauro Salas	1952	Alexis Arguello	1981–83
Rocky Kansas	1925–26	Jimmy Carter	1952–54		
Sammy Mandell	1926–30	Paddy DeMarco	1954		

FEATHERWEIGHT BOXING CHAMPIONS (Up to 126 pounds)*

CHAMPION	REIGN	CHAMPION	REIGN	CHAMPION	REIGN
Torpedo Billy Murphy ..	1890	Abe Attell.............	1903	Tony Canzoneri	1928
Young Griffo	1890–92	Tommy Sullivan	1904–05	Andre Routis	1928–29
George Dixon	1892–97	Abe Attell	1906–12	Battling Battalino	1929–32
Solly Smith	1897–98	Johnny Kilbane	1912–23	Tommy Paul	1932–33
Dave Sullivan.........	1898	Eugene Criqui	1923	Freddie Miller	1933–36
George Dixon	1898–1900	Johnny Dundee	1923–25	Petey Sarron	1936–37
Terry McGovern	1900–01	Louis (Kid) Kaplan	1926–27	Henry Armstrong	1937–38
Young Corbett........	1901–03	Benny Bass	1927–28	Joey Archibald	1938–40

*Source: *The Ring Magazine*

FEATHERWEIGHT BOXING CHAMPIONS (continued)

CHAMPION	REIGN	CHAMPION	REIGN	CHAMPION	REIGN
Harry Jeffra	1940–41	Davey Moore	1959–63	Eder Jofre	1973–74
Joey Archibald	1941	Sugar Ramos	1963–64	Alexis Arguello	1974–77
Chalky Wright	1941–42	Vicente Saldivar	1964–67	Danny Lopez	1978–80
Willie Pep	1942–48	Johnny Famechon	1969–70	Salvador Sanchez	1980–82
Sandy Saddler	1948–49	Vicente Saldivar	1970	Eusebio Pedroza	1982–85
Willie Pep	1949–50	Kuniaki Shibata	1970–72	Barry McGuigan	1985–
Sandy Saddler	1950–57	Clemente Sanchez	1972		
Kid Bassey	1957–59	Jose Legra	1972–73		

BANTAMWEIGHT BOXING CHAMPIONS (Up to 118 pounds)*

Source: The Ring Magazine

CHAMPION	REIGN	CHAMPION	REIGN	CHAMPION	REIGN
Billy Plimmer	1829–95	Charley Rosenberg	1925–27	Eder Jofre	1961–65
Pedlar Palmer	1895–99	Bud Taylor	1927–28	Masahiko Harada	1965–68
Terry McGovern	1899–1900	Al Brown	1929–35	Lionel Rose	1968–69
Harry Forbes	1901–03	Baltazar Sangchili	1935–36	Ruben Olivares	1969–70
Frankie Neil	1903–04	Tony Marino	1936	Jesus Castillo	1970–71
Joe Bowker	1904–05	Sixto Escobar	1936–47	Ruben Olivares	1971–72
Jimmy Walsh	1905–06	Harry Jeffra	1937–38	Rafael Herrera	1972
Owen Moran	1907–08	Sixto Escobar	1938–40	Enrique Pinder	1972–73
Monte Attell	1909–10	Georgie Pace	1940	Romeo Anaya	1973
Frankie Conley	1910–11	Lou Salica	1940–42	Arnold Taylor	1973–74
Johnny Coulon	1911–14	Manuel Ortiz	1942–47	Soo Hwan Hong	1974–75
Kid Williams	1914–17	Harold Dade	1947	Alfonso Zamora	1975–77
Pete Herman	1917–20	Manuel Ortiz	1947–50	Jorge Lujan	1977–80
Joe Lynch	1920–21	Vic Toweel	1950–52	Julian Solis	1980
Pete Herman	1921	Jimmy Carruthers	1952–54	Jeff Chandler	1980–84
Johnny Buff	1921–22	Robert Cohen	1954–56	Richie Sandoval	1984–
Joe Lynch	1922–24	Mario D'Agata	1956–57		
Abe Goldstein	1924	Alphonse Halimi	1957–59		
Eddie Martin	1924–25	Jose Becerra	1959–60		

FLYWEIGHT BOXING CHAMPIONS (Up to 112 pounds)*

Source: The Ring Magazine

CHAMPION	REIGN	CHAMPION	REIGN	CHAMPION	REIGN
Sid Smith	1913	Vacant	1941–42	Chartchai Chionoi	1970
Bill Ladbury	1913–14	Jackie Paterson	1943–47	Erbito Salavarria	1970–73
Percy Jones	1914	Rinty Monaghan	1948–50	Venice Borkorsor	1973
Joe Symonds	1914–16	Dado Marino	1950–52	Miguel Canto	1975–79
Jimmy Wilde	1916–23	Yoshio Shirai	1952–54	Chan-Hee Park	1979–80
Pancho Villa	1923–25	Pascual Perez	1954–60	Shoji Oguma	1980–81
Fidel La Barba	1925–27	Pone Kingpetch	1960–62	Antonio Avelar	1981–82
Frenchy Belanger	1927–28	Masahiko Harado	1962–63	Prudencio Cardona	1982
Frankie Genaro	1928–31	Pone Kingpetch	1963	Freddie Castillo	1982
Spider Pladner	1929	Hiroyuki Ebihara	1963–64	Eleoncio Mercedes	1982–83
Frankie Genaro	1929–31	Pone Kingpetch	1964–65	Charlie Magri	1983
Victor Perez	1931–32	Salvatore Burruni	1965–66	Frank Cedeño	1983–84
Jackie Brown	1932–35	Walter McGowan	1966	Koji Kobayashi	1984
Benny Lynch	1935–38	Chartchai Chionoi	1966–69	Gabriel Bernal	1984
Peter Kane	1938–41	Efren Torres	1969–70	Sot Chitalada	1984–

UNITED STATES AMATEUR BOXING CHAMPIONS

Source: U.S.A. Amateur Boxing Federation, Inc.

106 POUNDS

1981	Jesse Benavides, Corpus Christi, Texas	1983	Paul Gonzales, Los Angeles, Calif.
1982	Mario Lesperance, Vallejo, Calif.	1984	James Harris, Washington, D.C.

112 POUNDS

1981	Fred Perkins, U.S. Army	1983	Steve McCrory, Detroit, Mich.
1982	Steve McCrory, Detroit, Mich.	1984	Bernard Price, Muncie, Ind.

119 POUNDS

1981	Richard Savage, West Monroe, La.	1983	Jesse Benavides, Corpus Christi, Tex.
1982	Floyd Favors, Capitol Heights, Md.	1984	Eugene Speed, Palmer Park, Md.

125 POUNDS

1981	Guadalupe Suarez, Corpus Christi, Texas	1983	Andrew Minsker, Milaukie, Ore.
1982	Orlando Johnson, Chicago, Ill.	1984	Lyndon Walker, Washington, D.C.

132 POUNDS

1981	Joe Manley, U.S. Army	1983	Clifford Gray, Boynton Beach, Fla.
1982	Pernell Whitaker, Norfolk, Va.	1984	Victor Levine, Kokomo, Ind.

139 POUNDS

1981	James Mitchell, U.S. Army	1983	Zachary Padilla, Azusa, Calif.
1982	Henry Hughes, Cleveland, Ohio	1984	Elvis Yero, Miami Beach, Fla.

U.S. AMATEUR BOXING CHAMPIONS (continued)

147 POUNDS

1981	Darryl Tobinson, Houston, Texas	1983	Mark Breland, New York City, N.Y.
1982	Mark Breland, New York City	1984	Daryl Lattimore, Washington, D.C.

156 POUNDS

1981	James Rayford, U.S. Navy	1983	Frank Tate, Detroit, Mich.
1982	Dennis Milton, New York City	1984	Kevin Bryant, New York City

165 POUNDS

1981	Michael Grogan, Atlanta, Ga.	1983	Michael Grogan, Atlanta, Ga.
1982	Michael Grogan, Atlanta, Ga.	1984	Percy Harris, Baltimore, Md.

178 POUNDS

1981	Alex DeLucia, Portland, Ore.	1983	Ricky Womack, Detroit, Mich.
1982	Bennie Heard, Augusta, Georgia	1984	Loren Ross, Fort Hood, Texas

HEAVYWEIGHT—201 POUNDS

1981	Mark Mahone, U.S. Navy	1983	Henry Mulligan, Hockessin, Del.
1982	Elmer Martin, U.S. Navy	1984	Michael Bent, New York City

SUPER HEAVYWEIGHT—201+ POUNDS

1981	Tyrell Biggs, Philadelphia, Pa.	1983	Tyrell Biggs, Philadelphia, Pa.
1982	Tyrell Biggs, Philadelphia, Pa.	1984	Nathanial Fitch, Fort Bragg, N.C.

BOXING TERMS

bandages—protective wrappings on boxer's hands

bare-knuckle—fight in which boxers do not wear protective boxing gloves

bell—signal at beginning and end of each round

block—use of gloves, arms, or elbows to absorb force of opponent's blows

blow—hard punch delivered to opponent's head or body

bout—boxing match between two fighters

break—to end a clinch, either voluntarily or when ordered to do so by referee

catch—use of open glove to block a punch

clinch—holding or hugging opponent to prevent blows from being struck

canvas—floor of ring in which boxing match takes place

counter punch—one made immediately after one by opponent in effort to catch opponent with guard down

cross—counter punch in which fighter's arm crosses over that of opponent

decision—award of fight based on points scored by judges or upon disqualification of one of fighters

down—when any part of boxer's body (except his feet) touches floor of ring

duck—avoiding blow to head by dropping head below opponent's punch

feint—motion made in effort to mislead opponent about when and where blow is to be struck

glass jaw—jaw of fighter who can be knocked out easily by blow to jaw

gloves—padded leather gloves worn by boxer; weight of glove for pro bout is 8 ounces; amateur bouts use gloves with more padding that may weigh up to 12 ounces

handler—attendant who assists boxer

heel—to push inside of boxing glove against opponent's face

hook—blow delivered from side with bent arm

infighting—boxing in which opponents stand close to each other

jab—light punch to head or body

knockdown—fighter falls to canvas as result of blow by opponent

knockout—fighter is knocked unconscious or is floored and unable to return to corner within 10 seconds

KO—knockout

lead—boxer presses fight against opponent

mouse—swelling under fighter's eye

mouthpiece—rubber device worn in fighter's mouth to protect his teeth

one-two punch—two punches delivered in quick succession; usually left jab followed by straight right

parry—deflection of opponent's blow

punch—blow delivered to opponent

punch drunk—fighter made groggy by blows he has received

rabbit punch—illegal blow to back of opponent's neck

reach—measurement of distance from tips of fingers of one hand to other when arms are outstretched at sides of body

ring—area from 18 to 24 square feet in which boxing match takes place; is ringed by ropes attached to padded posts in corners

roadwork—running or walking during training to improve fighter's endurance

round—period of 3 minutes in pro fights or 2 minutes in amateur bouts in which boxers fight each other; they rest in their corners for 1 minute between rounds; pro fights may have up to 15 rounds; amateur bouts are 3 rounds long

roundhouse—widely swung punch to head

shadow boxing—fighting an imaginary opponent

sparring partner—opponent of boxer in training bout

technical knockout—when referee halts fight in belief one fighter cannot or should not continue bout

thumb—illegally hitting opponent in eye with thumb of glove

TKO—technical knockout

toe-to-toe—when boxers throw punches while close to each other

uppercut—bent arm blow brought up from the waist or below

weigh-in—official weighing of boxers prior to match

CHESS

WORLD CHESS CHAMPIONS

YEARS	CHAMPION	COUNTRY	YEARS	CHAMPION	COUNTRY
1851–58	Adolph Anderssen	Germany	1948–57	Mikhail Botvinnik	Soviet Union
1858–62	Paul C. Morphy	United States	1957–58	Vassily Smyssky	Soviet Union
1862–66	Adolph Anderssen	Germany	1958–60	Mikhail Botvinnik	Soviet Union
1866–94	Wilhelm Steinitz	Austria, U.S.	1960–61	Mikhail Tal	Soviet Union
1894–1921	Emanuel Lasker	Germany	1961–63	Mikhail Botvinnik	Soviet Union
1921–27	José R. Capablanca	Cuba	1963–69	Tigran Petrosian	Soviet Union
1927–35	Alexander A. Alekhine	France	1969–72	Boris Spassky	Soviet Union
1935–37	Max Euwe	Netherlands	1972–75	Bobby Fischer	United States
1937–46	Alexander A. Alekhine	France	1975–	Anatoly Karpov	Soviet Union

FENCING

NATIONAL COLLEGIATE ATHLETIC ASSOCIATION FENCING CHAMPIONSHIPS

TEAM CHAMPIONSHIPS

1941	North Western	1954	Columbia;	1962	Navy	1971	New York U.;	1979	Wayne State
1942	Ohio State		New York U.	1963	Columbia		Columbia	1980	Wayne State
1947	New York U.	1955	Columbia	1964	Princeton	1972	Detroit	1981	Pennsylvania
1948	City College N.Y.	1956	Illinois	1965	Columbia	1973	New York U.	1982	Wayne State
1949	Army; Rutgers	1957	New York U.	1966	New York U.	1974	New York U.	1983	Wayne State
1950	Navy	1958	Illinois	1967	New York U.	1975	Wayne State	1984	Wayne State
1951	Columbia	1959	Navy	1968	Columbia	1976	New York U.	1985	Wayne State
1952	Columbia	1960	New York U.	1969	Pennsylvania	1977	Notre Dame		
1953	Pennsylvania	1961	New York U.	1970	New York U.	1978	Notre Dame		

FOIL CHAMPIONS

1941	Edward McNamara, Northwestern	1960	Gene Glazer, New York U.	1975	Greg Benko, Wayne State
1942	Byron Kreiger, Wayne State	1961	Herbert Cohen, New York U.	1976	Greg Benko, Wayne State
1947	Abraham Balk, New York U.	1962	Herbert Cohen, New York U.	1977	Pat Gerard, Notre Dame
1948	Albert Axelrod, City College, N.Y.	1963	Jay Lustig, Columbia	1978	Ernest Simon, Wayne State
1949	Ralph Tedeschi, Rutgers	1964	Bill Hicks, Princeton	1979	Andy Bonk, Wayne State
1950	Robert Nielsen, Columbia	1965	Joe Nalven, Columbia	1980	Ernie Simon, Wayne State
1951	Robert Nielson, Columbia	1966	Al Davis, New York U.	1981	Ernie Simon, Wayne State
1952	Harold Goldsmith, City College, N.Y.	1967	Mike Gaylor, New York U.	1982	Alexander Flom, George Mason
1953	Ed Nober, Brooklyn College	1968	Gerard Esponda, San Francisco	1983	Paul Schmidt, Princeton
1954	Robert Goldman, Pennsylvania	1969	Norman Braslow, Pennsylvania	1984	Charles Higgs-Coulthard, Notre Dame
1955	Herman Velasco, Illinois	1970	Walter Krause, New York U.		
1956	Ralph DeMarco, Columbia	1971	Tyrone Simmons, Detroit	1985	Stephan Chauvel, Wayne State
1957	Bruce Davis, Wayne State	1972	Tyrone Simmons, Detroit		
1958	Bruce Davis, Wayne State	1973	Brooke Makler, Pennsylvania		
1959	Joe Paletta, Navy	1974	Greg Benko, Wayne State		

SABER CHAMPIONS

1941	William Meyer, Dartmouth	1959	Al Morales, Navy	1973	Peter Westbrook, New York U.
1942	Andre Deladrier, St. John's	1960	Mike Desaro, New York U.	1974	Steve Danosi, Wayne State
1947	Oscar Parsons, Temple	1961	Israel Colon, New York U.	1975	Yuri Rabinovich, Wayne State
1948	James Day, Navy	1962	Barton Nisonson, Columbia	1976	Brian Smith, Columbia
1949	Alex Treves, Rutgers	1963	Bela Szentivanyi, Wayne State	1977	Mike Sullivan, Notre Dame
1950	Alex Treves, Rutgers	1964	Craig Bell, Illinois	1978	Mike Sullivan, Notre Dame
1951	Chambless Johnston, Princeton	1965	Howard Goodman, New York U.	1979	Yuri Rabinovich, Wayne State
1952	Frank Zimolzak, Navy	1966	Paul Apostol, New York U.	1980	Paul Friedberg, Pennsylvania
1953	Robert Parmacek, Pennsylvania	1967	Todd Makler, Pennsylvania	1981	Paul Friedberg, Pennsylvania
1954	Steve Sobel, Columbia	1968	Todd Makler, Pennsylvania	1982	Neil Hick, Wayne State
1955	Barry Pariser, Columbia	1969	Antony Kestler, Columbia	1983	John Friedberg, North Carolina
1956	Gerald Kaufman, Columbia	1970	Bruce Soriano, Columbia	1984	Michael Lofton, N.Y.U.
1957	Bernie Balaban, New York U.	1971	Bruce Soriano, Columbia	1985	Michael Lofton, N.Y.U.
1958	Art Schankin, Illinois	1972	Bruce Soriano, Columbia		

ÉPÉE CHAMPIONS

1941	G. H. Boland, Illinois	1959	Roland Wommack, Navy	1973	Risto Hurme, New York U.
1942	Ben Burtt, Ohio State	1960	Gil Eisner, New York U.	1974	Risto Hurme, New York U.
1947	Abraham Balk, New York U.	1961	Jerry Halpern, New York U.	1975	Risto Hurme, New York U.
1948	William Bryan, Navy	1962	Thane Hawkins, Navy	1976	Randy Eggleton, Pennsylvania
1949	Richard C. Bowman, Army	1963	Larry Crum, Navy	1977	Hans Wieselgren, New York U.
1950	Thomas Stuart, Navy	1964	Paul Pesthy, Rutgers	1978	Bjorne Vaggo, Notre Dame
1951	Daniel Chafetz, Columbia	1965	Paul Pesthy, Rutgers	1979	Carlo Songini, Cleveland State
1952	James Wallner, New York U.	1966	Bernhardt Hermann, Iowa	1980	Gil Pezza, Wayne State
1953	Jack Tori, Pennsylvania	1967	George Masin, New York U.	1981	Gil Pezza, Wayne State
1954	Henry Kolowrat, Princeton	1968	Don Sieja, Cornell	1982	Peter Schifrin, San Jose State
1955	Donald Tadrawski, Notre Dame	1969	James Wetzler, Pennsylvania	1983	Ola Harstrom, Notre Dame
1956	Kinmont Hoitsma, Princeton	1970	John Nadas, Case Western Reserve	1984	Ettore Bianchi, Wayne State
1957	James Margolis, Columbia	1971	George Szunyogh, New York U.	1985	Ettore Bianchi, Wayne State
1958	Roland Wommack, Navy	1972	Ernesto Fernandez, Pennsylvania		

FISHING

WORLD FISHING RECORDS

Source: *International Game Fish Association*

SPECIES	WEIGHT[1]	LENGTH[2]	GIRTH[2]	PLACE CAUGHT	DATE	ANGLER
Albacore, S	88– 2	50.00	37.00	Canary Islands	Nov. 19, 1977	Siegfried Dickemann
Amberjack, greater, S	155–10	73.00	40.00	Bermuda	June 24, 1981	Joseph Dawson
Amberjack, Pacific, S	104– 0	57.75	42.00	Mexico	July 4, 1984	R. W. Cresswell
Barracuda, great, S	83– 0	72.25	29.00	Nigeria	Jan. 13, 1952	K. J. W. Hackett
Barracuda, Mexican, S	15– 4	46.50	15.25	Mexico	Oct. 7, 1984	Tony A. Pena
Barracuda, slender, S	14–10	45.50	13.00	Australia	June 16, 1984	Virginia T. Pena
Barramundi, F	59–12	—	—	Australia	April 7, 1983	Andrew Davern
Bass, barred sand, S	8– 4	24.75	18.00	California	March 14, 1981	Richard L. Marsell
Bass, black sea, S	9– 0	25.00	17.00	New York	Oct. 10, 1983	Salvatore Vicari
Bass, European, S	11–15	—	—	France	July 25, 1983	Bernard Peron
Bass, giant sea, S	563– 8	89.00	72.00	California	Aug. 20, 1968	J. D. McAdam, Jr.
Bass, largemouth, F	22– 4	—	—	Georgia	June 2, 1932	George W. Perry
Bass, peacock, F	26– 8	26.00	8.00	Colombia	Jan. 26, 1982	Rod Neubert, D.V.M.
Bass, redeye, F	8– 3	23.00	16.50	Georgia	Oct. 23, 1977	David A. Hubbard
Bass, rock, F	3– 0	13.50	10.75	Ontario	Aug. 1, 1974	Peter Gulgin
Bass, smallmouth, F	11–15	—	—	Kentucky	July 9, 1955	David L. Hayes
Bass, spotted, F	8–15	25.50	18.50	Alabama	March 18, 1978	Philip C. Terry, Jr.
Bass, spotted, F	9– 0	22.50	19.50	California	Feb. 5, 1984	Jeffery L. Mathews
Bass, striped, S	78– 8	53.00	34.50	New Jersey	Sept. 21, 1982	Albert R. McReynolds
Bass, striped (landlocked), F	59–12	56.00	33.50	Arizona	May 26, 1977	Frank W. Smith
Bass, suwannee, F	3–14	15.75	15.13	Florida	March 2, 1985	Ronnie Everett
Bass, white, F	5– 9	20.75	17.00	Texas	March 31, 1977	David S. Cordill
Bass, whiterock, F	20– 6	31.10	—	Georgia	May 28, 1978	Danny Wood
Bass, yellow, F	2– 4	16.25	12.75	Indiana	March 27, 1977	Donald L. Stalker
Blackjack, S	20–15	—	—	Costa Rica	Feb. 15, 1985	C. M. Barrantes R.
Bluefish, , S	31–12	47.00	23.00	North Carolina	Jan. 30, 1972	James M. Hussey
Bluegill, F	4–12	—	—	Alabama	April 9, 1950	T. S. Hudson
Bocaccio, S	15–12	30.75	22.00	California	Jan. 20, 1985	Mike Baron
Bonefish, S	19– 0	39.75	17.00	South Africa	May 26, 1962	Brian W. Batchelor
Bonito, Atlantic, S	18– 4	33.07	20.08	Azores	July 8, 1984	D. Gama Higgs
Bonito, Pacific, S	23– 8	—	—	Seychelles	Feb. 19, 1975	Anne Cochain
Bowfin, F	21– 8	36.00	21.50	South Carolina	Jan. 29, 1980	Robert L. Harmon
Bream, bronze, F	13– 3	25.59	27.17	Sweden	May 11, 1984	Luis Kilian Rasmussen
Buffalo, bigmouth, F	70– 5	48.50	38.00	Louisiana	April 21, 1980	Delbert Sisk
Buffalo, black, F	55– 0	45.00	30.00	Tennessee	May 3, 1984	Edward H. McLain
Buffalo, smallmouth, F	68– 8	43.50	36.00	Arkansas	May 16, 1984	Jerry L. Dolezal
Bullhead, black, F	8– 0	24.00	17.75	New York	Aug. 1, 1951	Kani Evans
Bullhead, brown, F	5– 8	19.00	13.00	Georgia	May 22, 1975	Jimmy Andrews
Bullhead, yellow, F	4– 4	17.25	14.50	Arizona	May 11, 1984	Emily Williams
Burbot, F	18– 4	38.00	20.00	Michigan	Jan. 31, 1980	Thomas Courtemanche
Cabezon, S	9–11	25.50	18.50	British Columbia	Aug. 16, 1983	Doug Olander
Carp, F	57–13	38.00	—	Washington, DC	June 19, 1983	David Nikolow
Catfish, blue, F	97– 0	57.00	37.00	South Dakota	Sept. 16, 1959	Edward B. Elliott
Catfish, channel, F	58– 0	47.25	29.18	South Carolina	July 7, 1964	W. B. Whaley
Catfish, flathead, F	91– 4	52.00	—	Texas	March 28, 1982	Mike Rogers
Catfish, gafftopsail, S	6–15	21.00	7.00	Florida	Feb. 19, 1984	Nick Smicklas
Catfish, tiger, F	36– 8	43.00	24.50	Guyana	Dec. 4, 1981	William T. Miller
Catfish, white, F	17– 7	34.00	20.25	California	Nov. 15, 1981	Chuck Idell
Char, Arctic, F	32– 9	40.50	25.25	Canada	July 30, 1981	Jeffery L. Ward
Cobia, S	110– 5	63.00	34.00	Kenya	Sept. 8, 1964	Eric Tinworth
Cod, Atlantic, S	98–12	63.00	41.00	New Hampshire	June 8, 1969	Alphonse J. Bielevich
Cod, Pacific, S	30– 0	39.50	28.00	Alaska	July 7, 1984	Donald R. Vaughn
Coger, S	102– 8	95.50	26.50	England	July 18, 1983	Raymond Ewart Street
Corvina, orangemouth, S	14–14	35.50	18.75	California	Aug. 17, 1984	Bert Bjurman
Crappie, black, F	4– 8	19.25	17.25	Virginia	March 1, 1981	L. Carl Herring, Jr.
Crappie, white, F	5– 3	21.00	19.00	Mississippi	July 31, 1957	Fred L. Bright
Cusk, S	24– 9	—	—	Norway	April 16, 1983	Odd Hjelmeland
Dentex, S	14– 1	27.55	19.29	Italy	July 29, 1982	Gianni de Marpillero
Dolly Varden, F	7– 8	33.25	16.25	Alaska	Sept. 22, 1984	Louie K. Brunner
Dolphin, S	87– 0	81.50	28.00	Costa Rica	Sept. 25, 1976	Manuel Salazar
Dorado, F	51– 5	37.40	19.69	Argentina	Sept. 27, 1984	Armando Giudice
Drum, black, S	113– 1	53.25	43.50	Delaware	Sept. 15, 1975	Gerald M. Townsend
Drum, freshwater, F	54– 8	31.50	29.00	Tennessee	April 20, 1972	Benney E. Hull
Drum, red, S	94– 2	57.00	38.00	North Carolina	Nov. 7, 1984	David G. Deuel
Eel, African mottled, S	36– 1	69.29	17.72	South Africa	June 10, 1984	Ferdie Van Nooten
Flounder, southern, S	20– 9	33.00	28.00	Florida	Dec. 23, 1983	Larenza W. Mungin

S=saltwater species. F=freshwater species. [1] In pounds and ounces. [2] Inches.

WORLD FISHING RECORDS *(continued)*

SPECIES	WEIGHT[1]	LENGTH[2]	GIRTH[2]	PLACE CAUGHT	DATE	ANGLER
Flounder, summer, S	22– 7	35.00	34.00	New York	Sept. 15, 1975	Charles Nappi
Gar, alligator, F	279– 0	93.00	—	Texas	Dec. 2, 1951	Bill Valverde
Gar, Florida, F	21– 3	53.00	17.25	Florida	June 3, 1981	Jeff Sabol
Gar, longnose, F	50– 5	72.25	22.25	Texas	July 30, 1954	Townsend Miller
Gar, shortnose, F	4– 9	34.60	10.00	Minnesota	July 22, 1984	M. "Dewy" Ocel
Gar, spotted, F	7– 6	35.50	12.50	Alabama	Aug. 14, 1984	Linda Baker
Goldeye, F	1–10	13.60	5.00	Canada	Aug. 26, 1984	Andrew Gillich
Grayling, Arctic, F	5–15	29.88	15.18	Canada	Aug. 16, 1967	Jeanne P. Branson
Grouper, dusky, S	11–10	78.00	53.00	Senegal	Jan. 30, 1984	Michel Calendini
Grouper, red, S	15– 4	29.00	23.00	Florida	Dec. 21, 1984	Kenneth E. Roy
Grouper, white, S	15– 1	78.00	53.00	Senegal	Jan. 24, 1984	Michel Calendini
Haddock, S	8–12	—	—	Norway	July 17, 1983	Olaf Hjelmeland
Halibut, Atlantic, S	250– 0	81.60	66.00	Massachusetts	July 3, 1981	Louis P. Sirard
Halibut, California, S	45– 0	45.00	33.00	California	June 19, 1982	Jack C. Meserve
Halibut, Pacific, S	350– 0	93.00	75.00	Alaska	June 30, 1982	Vern S. Foster
Herring, skipjack, S	1–12	15.25	9.75	Ohio	Dec. 5, 1984	J. Donald Conover
Herring, skipjack, S	3–12	18.50	13.00	Tennessee	Feb. 14, 1982	Paul D. Goddard
Hind, red, S	1–15	16.25	12.00	Florida	Oct. 1, 1984	Patrick Flynn
Houndfish, S	5– 3	38.00	8.50	Bahamas	April 5, 1984	Todd Patton
Huchen, F	70–12	56.69	33.46	Austria	Jan. 1, 1980	Martin F.P. Esterl
Inconnu, F	38– 2	39.50	20.00	Alaska	Sept. 12, 1982	Mark L. Feldman
Jack, almaco, S	21– 3	36.00	22.50	Florida	Aug. 13, 1983	William T. Porter
Jack, cottonmouth, S	2– 7	15.50	6.25	Florida	July 18, 1984	Jane M. Huntsinger
Jack, crevalle, S	54– 7	51.20	32.70	Gabon	Jan. 15, 1982	Thomas F. Gibson, Jr.
Jack, horse-eye, S	24– 8	38.50	25.00	Florida	Dec. 20, 1982	Tito Schnau
Jack, horse-eye, S	22–15	33.75	11.75	Ecuador	Nov. 19, 1983	Emilio Kronfle
Jack, yellow, S	13– 4	28.00	20.00	Florida	July 12, 1980	William J. Hillgardner
Jewfish, S	680– 0	85.50	66.00	Florida	May 20, 1961	Lynn Joyner
Kahawai, S	6– 2	—	—	New Zealand	Dec. 29, 1984	Larry E. Dyer
Kawakawa, S	26– 0	39.50	22.75	Australia	Jan. 26, 1980	Wally Elfring
Kokanee, F	6– 9	24.50	14.50	Idaho	June 9, 1975	Jerry Verge
Ling, S	21– 0	47.24	18.11	England	June 18, 1980	Roland Hansson
Lingcod, S	46– 0	46.00	—	British Columbia	Aug. 31, 1983	Betty I. Moore
Mackerel, cero, S	15– 8	36.00	16.00	Florida	Nov. 3, 1984	Jerrold J. Weinstock
Mackerel, frigate, S	2– 6	16.00	10.25	California	Sept. 13, 1983	John Chuckta, II
Mackerel, king, S	90– 0	71.00	30.00	Florida	Feb. 16, 1976	Norton I. Thomton
Mackerel, Pacific sierra, S	12– 0	35.00	15.00	Ecuador	Aug. 17, 1984	Gerald L. Cunningham
Mackerel, serra Spanish, S	12–12	33.86	15.35	Venezuela	Oct. 4, 1984	Gustavo A. Nava
Mackerel, Spanish, S	12– 0	35.00	14.50	Florida	Nov. 17, 1984	John F. Colligan
Mackerel, spotted, S	11– 7	—	—	Australia	April 7, 1983	David J. Payne
Mahseer, F	95– 0	53.00	40.00	India	March 26, 1984	Robert Howitt
Margate, S	9– 4	23.00	18.50	Florida	April 10, 1984	Robert George Carl
Marlin, black, S	1,560– 0	174.00	81.00	Peru	Aug. 4, 1953	Alfred C. Glassell, Jr.
Marlin, blue (Atlantic), S	1,282– 0	176.00	76.50	Virgin Islands	Aug. 6, 1977	Larry Martin
Marlin, blue (Pacific), S	1,376– 0	193.00	82.00	Hawaii	May 31, 1982	Jay Wm. deBeaubien
Marlin, striped, S	455– 4	127.00	52.00	New Zealand	March 8, 1982	Bruce Jenkinson
Marlin, white, S	181–14	107.50	37.40	Brazil	Dec. 8, 1979	Evandro Luiz Coser
Meagre, S	95– 2	—	—	Portugal	Feb. 24, 1983	M.L. Nicolau do Carmo
Moi threadfin, S	6– 0	25.50	14.75	Hawaii	Nov. 2, 1983	Jack N. Gushiken
Mullet, thin lipped, S	5– 4	20.50	12.50	England	June 14, 1984	Raymond John White
Muskellunge, F	69–15	64.50	31.75	New York	Sept. 22, 1957	Arthur Lawton
Muskellunge, tiger, F	51– 3	—	—	Wis./Mich.	July 16, 1919	John A. Knobla
Needlefish, Mexican, S	12–10	54.50	11.75	Panama	Aug. 19, 1979	Robert L. Spaulding
Payara, S	31– 8	—	—	Colombia	March 11, 1982	K. E. von Sneidern
Perch, white, F	4–12	19.50	13.00	Maine	June 4, 1949	Mrs. Earl Small
Perch, yellow, F	4– 3	—	—	New Jersey	May, 1865	Dr. C.C. Abbot
Permit, S	51– 8	42.25	35.00	Florida	April 28, 1978	William M. Kenney
Pickerel, chain, F	9– 6	31.00	14.00	Georgia	Feb. 17, 1961	Baxley McQuaig, Jr.
Pickerel, redfin, F	1– 8	15.50	8.75	South Carolina	Aug. 6, 1984	Al Johnson
Pike, Northern, F	46– 2	—	—	New York	Sept. 15, 1940	Peter Dubuc
Pollack, S	26– 0	41.73	23.62	France	Aug. 30, 1981	Loïk Le Chat
Pollock, S	46– 7	50.50	30.00	New Jersey	May 26, 1975	John Tomes Holton
Pompano, African, S	49– 0	—	—	Florida	Feb. 4, 1977	Lawrence Hofman
Pompano, Florida, S	8– 1	18.75	18.00	Florida	March 19, 1984	Chester E. Dietrick
Queenfish (Leatherskin), S	13– 0	33.50	20.00	Australia	June 16, 1984	Tony A. Pena

S=saltwater species. F=freshwater species. [1] In pounds and ounces. [2] In inches.

WORLD FISHING RECORDS *(continued)*

SPECIES	WEIGHT[1]	LENGTH[2]	GIRTH[2]	PLACE CAUGHT	DATE	ANGLER
Ray, painted (small-eyed), S .	9–12	31.00	46.00	England	Oct. 2, 1983	Brian S. Taylor
Ray, spiny butterfly, S	132– 4	49.21	76.77	Mauritania	May 5, 1984	Robin Michel
Redfish (Ocean perch),S	5–13	—	—	Greenland	Aug. 18, 1982	Peter W. Kogebohn
Redhorse, golden, F	2– 0	15.50	9.50	Pennsylvania	April 9, 1984	Richard E. Faler, Jr.
Redhorse, shorthead, F	4–12	20.50	12.25	Indiana	May 18, 1984	William A. Merrick
Redhorse, silver, F	9–11	27.00	16.00	Manitoba	May 22, 1982	John D. Richards
Roach, S	4– 1	16.90	—	England	June 16, 1975	R.G. Jones
Rockfish, black, S	9–11	26.00	20.00	Washington	May 6, 1984	Randy Harris
Rockfish, vermilion, S	7– 0	23.25	18.00	British Columbia	Aug. 18, 1983	Doug Olander
Rockfish, yelloweye, S	18– 4	29.75	24.75	Washington	July 3, 1983	Doug Olander
Roosterfish, S	114– 0	64.00	33.00	Mexico	June 1, 1960	Abe Sackheim
Runner, blue, S	5– 0	19.50	14.00	Florida	Dec. 24, 1983	Thomas C. Buffham
Runner, rainbow, S	33–10	55.25	22.50	Mexico	March 14, 1976	Ralph A. Mikkelsen
Sailfish, Atlantic, S	128– 1	106.00	34.00	Angola	March 27, 1974	Harm Steyn
Sailfish, Pacific, S	221– 0	129.00	—	Ecuador	Feb. 12, 1947	C.W. Stewart
Salmon, Atlantic, F/S	79– 2	—	—	Norway	1928	Henrik Henriksen
Salmon, chinook, F/S	93– 0	50.00	39.00	Alaska	June 24, 1977	Howard C. Rider
Salmon, chum, F/S	27– 3	39.38	24.50	Alaska	June 11, 1977	Robert A. Jahnke
Salmon, coho, F/S	31– 0	—	—	British Columbia	Oct. 11, 1947	Mrs. Lee Hallberg
Salmon, pink, F/S	12– 9	30.00	22.00	Alaska	Aug. 17, 1974	Steven Alan Lee
Salmon, sockeye, F/S	12– 8	30.00	18.25	Alaska	June 23, 1983	Mike Boswell
Sauger, F	8–12	28.00	15.00	North Dakota	Oct. 6, 1971	Mike Fischer
Scamp, S	6– 6	23.50	15.50	Florida	Dec. 21, 1984	Kenneth E. Roy
Scup, S	1– 0	10.50	9.75	Massachusetts	Sept. 25, 1983	Adam Kolek
Seabass, Japanese Suzuki, S	17–13	—	—	Japan	Dec. 16, 1983	Tsutom Kinura
Seabass, white, S .	83–12	65.50	34.00	Mexico	March 31, 1953	L.C. Baumgardner
Seatrout, spotted, S	16– 0	32.50	21.75	Virginia	May 28, 1977	William Katko
Shad, American, F	11– 1	24.75	20.50	New Jersey	May 5, 1984	Charles J. Mower
Shark, blue, S	437– 0	143.00	53.00	Australia	Oct. 2, 1976	Peter Hyde
Shark, bull, S	486– 0	—	—	Florida	April 10, 1978	Pete Peacock
Shark, dusky, S	764– 0	117.00	72.00	Florida	May 28, 1982	Warren Girle
Shark, Greenland, S	952– 6	—	—	Norway	May 19, 1984	Eirik Nielsen
Shark, hammerhead, S	991– 0	176.00	76.00	Florida	May 30, 1982	Allen Ogle
Shark, mako, S	1,080– 0	136.00	81.00	New York	Aug. 26, 1979	James L. Melanson
Shark, porbeagle, S	465– 0	111.00	56.00	England	July 23, 1976	Jorge Potier
Shark, reef white-tip, S	40– 4	48.00	24.00	Panama	Aug. 8, 1979	Jack Kamerman
Shark, sand tiger, S	318– 0	99.00	57.00	North Carolina	May 25, 1979	Dave Wolfe
Shark, spinner, S .	89– 4	58.50	31.00	Panama	Aug. 22, 1979	Richard Vrablik
Shark, spiny dogfish, S	8– 0	32.75	13.25	Massachusetts	Aug. 26, 1977	David E. Singer
Shark, thresher, S	802– 0	192.12	64.96	New Zealand	Feb. 8, 1981	Dianne North
Shark, tiger, S	1,780– 0	166.50	103.00	S. Carolina	June 14, 1964	Walter Maxwell
Shark, white, S	2,664– 0	202.00	114.00	Australia	April 21, 1959	Alfred Dean
Sheepshead, S	21– 4	25.00	27.00	Louisiana	April 16, 1982	Wayne Desselle
Skate, S	144– 0	50.00	117.00	Scotland	Nov. 16, 1984	Brian J. Swinbanks
Skate, thorny, S	9– 5	—	—	Norway	Oct. 10, 1982	Knut Hedlund
Skipjack, black, S	20– 5	31.00	22.50	Mexico	Oct. 14, 1983	Roger Torriero
Smooth hound, Starry, S	10– 8	38.00	14.00	England	July 18, 1984	Sylvia M. Steed
Snapper, barred pargo, S	10–14	24.00	20.00	Mexico	Oct. 10, 1984	Linda S. Niles
Snapper, cubera, S	121– 8	55.00	45.00	Louisiana	July 5, 1982	Mike Hebert
Snapper, dog, S .	22–10	36.25	24.00	Mexico	Jan. 14, 1984	Tony A. Pena
Snapper, yellowtail, S	5– 1	20.00	14.00	Bermuda	Sept. 28, 1980	Andrew Down
Snook, S	53–10	48.50	36.00	Costa Rica	Oct. 18, 1978	Gilbert Ponzi
Snook, fat, S	6–14	22.75	6.67	Florida	March 17, 1984	Heidi Benham
Snook, Pacific black, S	14–10	34.00	17.50	Mexico	Feb. 27, 1984	Tony A. Pena
Spearfish, S	90–13	93.30	10.60	Portugal	June 2, 1980	Joseph Larkin
Splake, F	16–12	—	—	Colorado	Sept. 14, 1973	Del Canty
Spurdog, S	10– 4	35.25	16.13	Scotland	Nov. 20, 1984	Duncan Swinbanks
Steenbras, red, F .	115– 1	50.79	42.91	Transkei	Aug. 19, 1984	Dr. Brian Hulley
Sturgeon, S	468– 0	102.00	60.00	California	July 9, 1983	Joey Pallotta, III
Sucker, longnose, F	5– 8	22.50	12.25	Michigan	Feb. 19, 1983	Ben Knoll
Sucker, spotted, F	2–11	17.00	10.50	Georgia	March 6, 1985	J. Paul Diprima, Jr.
Sucker, white, F .	6– 8	21.50	14.25	Minnesota	April 20, 1984	Joel M. Anderson
Sunfish, green, F .	2– 2	14.75	14.00	Missouri	June 18, 1971	Paul M. Dilley
Sunfish, pumpkinseed, F	1– 2	10.00	5.50	Virginia	April 7, 1984	Paul Kendrick
Sunfish, redbreast, F	1–12	10.75	13.75	Florida	May 29, 1984	Alvin Buchanan
Sunfish, redear, F	4– 8	—	—	Virginia	June 19, 1970	Maurice E. Ball
Swordfish, S	1,182– 0	179.25	78.00	Chile	May 7, 1953	L. Marron
Tanguigue, S	99– 0	—	—	South Africa	March 14, 1982	Michael John Wilkinson

S=saltwater species. F=freshwater species. [1] In pounds and ounces. [2] In inches.

WORLD FISHING RECORDS (continued)

SPECIES	WEIGHT[1]	LENGTH[2]	GIRTH[2]	PLACE CAUGHT	DATE	ANGLER
Tarpon, S........	283– 0	86.25	—	Venezuela	March 19, 1956	M. Salazar
Tautog, S.........	21– 8	32.25	23.75	Virginia............	Aug. 4, 1984	Tommy Wood
Tench, F..........	9–11	24.80	19.69	Sweden............	June 1, 1984	Dan Dellerfjord
Tigerfish, F	61–11	—	—	Zambia............	Feb. 4, 1984	Don Hunter
Tilapia, F	4– 5	18.00	15.75	Arizona............	Sept. 17, 1984	John Burton Adkins
Tolstolob, F......	35– 4	41.34	29.53	Austria............	Nov. 10, 1983	Josef Windholz
Tope, S	71–10	63.09	27.55	South Africa	July 10, 1982	William F. DeWet
Trevally, bigeye, S	15– 0	31.50	26.00	Panama	Jan. 18, 1984	Sally S. Timms
Trevally, bluefin (Omilu), S	20– 7	30.50	24.25	Panama	Aug. 13, 1979	Stewart M. Cox
Trevally, giant, S .	137– 9	57.00	44.50	Hawaii.............	July 13, 1983	Roy K. Gushiken
Trevally, golden, S	10–13	23.50	20.00	Hawaii.............	April 2, 1982	Charles S.H. Lee
Trevally, thicklip, S	5–10	20.00	8.00	Kiribati	Aug. 12, 1982	Derek Dunn Rankin
Triggerfish, gray, S	4– 0	17.25	19.25	Texas	Oct. 26, 1984	Louis A. Kusey, III
Tripletail, S	31– 4	—	—	Florida	Nov. 11, 1978	Michael K. Stephan
Trout, Apache, F ..	1– 8	14.50	8.25	Arizona	Oct. 19, 1984	Burton R. Leed
Trout, brook, F ...	14– 8	—	—	Ontario	July 1916	Dr. W.J. Cook
Trout, brown, F...	35–15	38.90	26.80	Argentina	Dec. 16, 1952	Eugenio Cavaglia
Trout, bull, F	32– 0	40.50	29.75	Idaho.............	Oct. 27, 1949	N.L. Higgins
Trout, cutthroat, F	41– 0	—	—	Nevada	Dec. 1925	John Skimmerhorn
Trout, golden, F ..	11– 0	28.00	16.00	Wyoming	Aug. 5, 1948	Chas S. Reed
Trout, lake, F	65– 0	52.00	—	Canada	Aug. 8, 1970	Larry Daunis
Trout, ohrid, F ...	9– 2	28.80	16.25	Wyoming	Nov. 27, 1984	Kent Erickson
Trout, rainbow[3], F	42– 2	43.00	23.50	Alaska............	June 22, 1970	David Robert White
Trout, tiger, F	20–13	33.75	21.68	Wisconsin	Aug. 12, 1978	Pete M. Friedland
Tuna, bigeye (Atlantic), S.....	375– 8	91.00	61.00	Maryland	Aug. 26, 1977	Cecil Browne
Tuna, bigeye (Pacific), S	435– 0	93.00	63.50	Peru	April 17, 1957	Dr. Russel V.A. Lee
Tuna, blackfin, S .	42– 0	42.50	29.50	Bermuda	June 2, 1978	Alan J. Card
Tuna, bluefin, S ..	1,496– 0	128.50	99.00	Nova Scotia	Oct. 26, 1979	Ken Fraser
Tuna, dogtooth, S	288–12	97.63	26.77	South Korea........	Oct. 6, 1982	Boo-Il Oh
Tuna, longtail, S ..	79– 2	57.08	33.85	Australia	April 12, 1982	Tim Simpson
Tuna, skipjack, S .	41–12	41.00	27.00	Mauritius	March 13, 1982	Bruno de Ravel
Tuna, southern bluefin, S......	348– 5	85.82	56.69	New Zealand	Jan. 16, 1981	Rex Wood
Tuna, yellowfin, S.	388–12	91.25	62.25	Mexico	April 1, 1977	Curt Wiesenhutter
Tunny, little, S ...	27– 0	39.00	22.00	Florida	April 20, 1976	William E. Allison
Vimma (Zahrte), F	2– 0	—	—	Sweden............	May 24, 1984	Hakan Brugard
Wahoo, S	149– 0	79.75	37.50	Bahamas	June 15, 1962	John Pirovano
Walleye, F	25– 0	41.00	29.00	Tennessee	April 1, 1960	Mabry Harper
Warmouth, F	2– 2	11.88	13.18	S. Carolina	May 19, 1973	Willie Singletary
Weakfish, S	19– 2	37.00	22.00	New York	Oct. 11, 1984	Dennis Roger Rooney
Weakfish, S	19– 0	34.50	22.50	Virginia	May 19, 1983	Philip W. Halstead
Weaver, greater, S	3–11	19.29	11.42	Canary Islands	March 31, 1984	Arild J. Danielsen
Whitefish, broad, F	5– 1	22.83	13.78	Sweden............	April 16, 1984	Dan Dellerfjord
Whitefish, lake, F .	14– 6	31.00	19.50	Ontario	May 21, 1984	Dennis M. Laycock
Whitefish, mountain, F	5– 2	21.00	13.50	Washington	Nov. 30, 1983	Steven W. Becken
Whitefish, river, F	11– 2	27.40	18.31	Sweden............	Dec. 9, 1984	Jorgen Larsson
Whitefish, round, F	6– 0	23.50	14.00	Manitoba	June 14, 1984	Allan J. Ristori
Wolffish, Atlantic, S	47– 4	51.00	34.00	Massachusetts	May 16, 1984	Harry Heckrote
Wolffish, northern, S	37– 7	—	—	Greenland	Aug. 19, 1982	Jens Ploug Hansen
Wolffish, spotted, S	51– 7	—	—	Greenland	Aug. 20, 1982	Jens Ploug Hansen
Wrasse, Ballan, S	4– 5	18.75	13.50	England	July 3, 1984	Raymond John White
Yellowtail, Asian, S	40– 5	41.30	25.50	Japan	Oct. 23, 1982	Masahiko Kuwata
Yellowtail, California, S	71–15	58.75	32.00	Mexico	June 24, 1979	Michael Carpenter
Yellowtail, southern, S	114–10	61.50	39.00	New Zealand	Feb. 5, 1984	Mike Godfrey
Zander, F........	19–13	37.40	19.29	Austria	July 15, 1983	Dr. Rudolf Wehrl

S=saltwater species. F=freshwater species. [1] In pounds and ounces. [2] In inches. [3] Also known as Steelhead or Kamloops.

AMERICAN CASTING ASSOCIATION RECORDS

Men: All Distance [1]...	Chris Korich	1984	5,211 ft.	Women: All Accuracy [2]	B. Mac Sporran	1984	569 pts.
Men: All Accuracy [2] .	Steve Rajeff	1984	595 pts.	Women: Accuracy Plugs [4]	B. Mac Sporran	1985	286 pts.
Men: Distance Plugs [3]	Chris Korich	1983	3,347 ft.	Women: Accuracy Flies [4]	B. Mac Sporran	1984	286 pts.
Men: Distance Flies [3] .	Steve Rajeff	1984	1,985 ft.	Intm.: All Accuracy [2] .	Matt Rickerd	1984	570 pts.
Men: Accuracy Plugs [4]	Steve Rajeff	1977	297 pts.	Intm.: Accuracy Plugs [4]	Don Lanser	1970	284 pts.
Men: Accuracy Flies [4]	Tim Rajeff	1981	300 pts.	Intm.: Accuracy Flies [4]	Luke Brugnara	1978	298 pts.

[1] Total of 12 casts. [2] Of possible 600 points. [3] Total of 6 casts. [4] Of possible 300 points.

FOOTBALL—PROFESSIONAL FOOTBALL

SUPER BOWL GAMES: 1967–1985

1967	Super Bowl I The Coliseum, Los Angeles, Calif.					
	Green Bay (NFL)	7	7	14	7	35
	Kansas City (AFL)	0	10	0	0	10
1968	Super Bowl II Orange Bowl Stadium, Miami, Fla.					
	Green Bay (NFL)	3	13	10	7	33
	Oakland (AFL)	0	7	0	7	14
1969	Super Bowl III Orange Bowl Stadium, Miami, Fla.					
	New York (AFL)	0	7	6	3	16
	Baltimore (NFL)	0	0	0	7	7
1970	Super Bowl IV Tulane Stadium, New Orleans, La.					
	Kansas City (AFL)	3	13	7	0	23
	Minnesota (NFL)	0	0	7	0	7
1971	Super Bowl V Orange Bowl Stadium, Miami, Fla.					
	Baltimore (AFC)	0	6	0	10	16
	Dallas (NFC)	3	10	0	0	13
1972	Super Bowl VI Tulane Stadium, New Orleans, La.					
	Dallas (NFC)	3	7	7	7	24
	Miami (AFC)	0	3	0	0	3
1973	Super Bowl VII The Coliseum, Los Angeles, Calif.					
	Miami (AFC)	7	7	0	0	14
	Washington (NFC)	0	0	0	7	7
1974	Super Bowl VIII Rice Stadium, Houston, Texas					
	Miami (AFC)	14	3	7	0	24
	Minnesota (NFC)	0	0	0	7	7
1975	Super Bowl IX Tulane Stadium, New Orleans, La.					
	Pittsburgh (AFC)	0	2	7	7	16
	Minnesota (NFC)	0	0	0	6	6
1976	Super Bowl X Orange Bowl Stadium, Miami, Fla.					
	Pittsburgh (AFC)	7	0	0	14	21
	Dallas (NFC)	7	3	0	7	17
1977	Super Bowl XI Rose Bowl, Pasadena, Calif.					
	Oakland (AFC)	0	16	3	13	32
	Minnesota (NFC)	0	0	7	7	14
1978	Super Bowl XII La. Superdome, New Orleans, La.					
	Dallas (NFC)	10	3	7	7	27
	Denver (AFC)	0	0	10	0	10
1979	Super Bowl XIII Orange Bowl, Miami, Fla.					
	Pittsburgh (AFC)	7	14	0	14	35
	Dallas (NFC)	7	7	3	14	31
1980	Super Bowl XIV Rose Bowl, Pasadena, Calif.					
	Pittsburgh (AFC)	3	7	7	14	31
	Los Angeles (NFC)	7	6	6	0	19
1981	Super Bowl XV La. Superdome, New Orleans, La.					
	Oakland (AFC)	14	0	10	3	27
	Philadelphia (NFC)	0	3	0	7	10
1982	Super Bowl XVI Pontiac Superdome, Pontiac, Mich.					
	San Francisco (NFC)	7	13	0	6	26
	Cincinnati (AFC)	0	0	7	14	21
1983	Super Bowl XVII Rose Bowl, Pasadena, Calif.					
	Washington (NFC)	0	10	3	14	27
	Miami (AFC)	7	10	0	0	17
1984	Super Bowl XVIII Tampa, Fla.					
	Los Angeles (AFC)	7	14	14	3	38
	Washington (NFC)	0	3	6	0	9
1985	Super Bowl XIX Stanford U. Stadium, Palo Alto, CA					
	San Francisco (NFC)	7	21	10	0	38
	Miami (AFC)	10	6	0	0	16

SUPER BOWL INDIVIDUAL RECORDS

Games, coach: 6, Don Shula, Baltimore, 1969, Miami, 1972, 1973, 1974, 1983, 1985

Winning games, coach: 4, Chuck Noll, Pittsburgh, 1975, 1976, 1979, 1980

Points, career: 24, Franco Harris, Pittsburgh, 4 touchdowns

Points, game: 18, Roger Craig, San Francisco vs. Miami, 1985 (3-td)

Touchdowns, career: 4, Franco Harris, Pittsburgh

Field goals, game: 4, Don Chandler, Green Bay vs. Oakland, 1968; Ray Wersching, San Francisco vs. Cincinnati, 1982

Field goal, longest: 48 yards, Jan Stenerud, Kansas City vs. Minnesota, 1970

Rushing, yards gained, career: 354, Franco Harris, Pittsburgh, 4 games

Rushing, yards gained, game: 191, Marcus Allen, Los Angeles Raiders vs. Washington, 1984

Total yards gained, career: 468, Franco Harris, Pittsburgh, 4 games

Total yards gained, game: 209, Marcus Allen, Los Angeles Raiders vs. Washington, 1984

Rushing, longest run from scrimmage: 74 yards, Marcus Allen, Los Angeles Raiders vs. Washington, 1984

Passes completed, career: 61, Roger Staubach, Dallas, 4 games

Passes completed, game: 29, Dan Marino, Miami vs. San Francisco, 1985

Passing, yards gained, career: 932, Terry Bradshaw, Pittsburgh, 4 games

Passing, yards gained, game: 331, Joe Montana, San Francisco vs. Miami, 1985

Pass completion, longest: 80 yards, Jim Plunkett to Kenny King, Oakland vs. Philadelphia, 1981

Touchdown passes, career: 9, Terry Bradshaw, Pittsburgh, 4 games

Pass receptions, game: 11, Dan Ross, Cincinnati vs. San Francisco, 1982

Pass receptions, yards gained, career: 364, Lynn Swann, Pittsburgh, 4 games

Pass receptions, yards gained, game: 161, Lynn Swann, Pittsburgh vs. Dallas, 1976

Pass interceptions, game: 3, Rod Martin, Oakland vs. Philadelphia, 1981

Pass interceptions, yards gained, game: 75, Willie Brown, Oakland vs. Minnesota, 1977

Punts, game: 9, Ron Widby, Dallas vs. Baltimore, 1971

Punt, longest: 61 yards, Jerrel Wilson, Kansas City vs. Green Bay, 1967

Punt return, longest: 34 yards, Darrell Green, Washington vs. Los Angeles Raiders, 1984

Kickoff returns, career: 8, Larry Anderson, Pittsburgh, 2 games

Kickoff returns, yards gained, career: 283 yards, Fulton Walker, Miami, 2 games

Kickoff returns, yards gained, game: 190 yards, Fulton Walker, Miami vs. Washington, 1983

Kickoff return, longest: 98 yards, Fulton Walker, Miami vs. Washington, 1983

SUPER BOWL TEAM RECORDS

Games won: 4, Pittsburgh, 1975, 1976, 1979, 1980

Games lost: 4, Minnesota, 1970, 1974, 1975, 1977

Points, game: 38, Los Angeles Raiders vs. Washington, 1984

Touchdowns, game: 5, Green Bay vs. Kansas City, 1967; Pittsburgh vs. Dallas, 1979; Los Angeles Raiders vs. Washington, 1984; San Francisco vs. Miami, 1985

First downs, game: 31, San Francisco vs. Miami, 1985

Yards gained, game: 537, San Francisco vs. Miami, 1985

Passes completed, game: 29, Miami vs. San Francisco, 1985

Passing, yards gained, game: 326, San Francisco vs. Miami, 1985

NATIONAL FOOTBALL LEAGUE CONFERENCE CHAMPIONS

YEAR	EASTERN CONFERENCE	W	L	T	YEAR	WESTERN CONFERENCE	W	L	T
1940	Washington Redskins	9	2	0	1940	Chicago Bears	8	3	0
1941	New York Giants	8	3	0	1941	Chicago Bears	10	1	1
1942	Washington Redskins	10	1	1	1942	Chicago Bears	11	0	0
1943	Washington Redskins	6	3	1	1943	Chicago Bears	8	1	1
1944	New York Giants	8	1	1	1944	Green Bay Packers	8	2	0
1945	Washington Redskins	8	2	0	1945	Cleveland Rams	9	1	0
1946	New York Giants	7	3	1	1946	Chicago Bears	8	2	1
1947	Philadelphia Eagles	8	4	0	1947	Chicago Cardinals	9	3	0
1948	Philadelphia Eagles	9	2	1	1948	Chicago Cardinals	11	1	0
1949	Philadelphia Eagles	11	1	0	1949	Los Angeles Rams	8	2	2
1950	Cleveland Browns	10	2	0	1950	Los Angeles Rams	9	3	0
1951	Cleveland Browns	11	1	0	1951	Los Angeles Rams	8	4	0
1952	Cleveland Browns	8	4	0	1952	Detroit Lions	9	3	0
1953	Cleveland Browns	11	1	0	1953	Detroit Lions	10	2	0
1954	Cleveland Browns	9	3	0	1954	Detroit Lions	9	2	1
1955	Cleveland Browns	9	2	1	1955	Los Angeles Rams	8	3	1
1956	New York Giants	8	3	1	1956	Chicago Bears	9	2	1
1957	Cleveland Browns	9	2	1	1957	Detroit Lions	8	4	0
1958	New York Giants	9	3	0	1958	Baltimore Colts	9	3	0
1959	New York Giants	10	2	0	1959	Baltimore Colts	9	3	0
1960	Philadelphia Eagles	10	2	0	1960	Green Bay Packers	8	4	0
1961	New York Giants	10	3	1	1961	Green Bay Packers	11	3	0
1962	New York Giants	12	2	0	1962	Green Bay Packers	13	1	0
1963	New York Giants	11	3	0	1963	Chicago Bears	11	1	2
1964	Cleveland Browns	10	3	1	1964	Baltimore Colts	12	2	0
1965	Cleveland Browns	11	3	0	1965	Green Bay Packers	10	3	1
1966	Dallas Cowboys	10	3	1	1966	Green Bay Packers	12	2	0
1967	Dallas Cowboys	9	5	0	1967	Green Bay Packers	9	4	1
1968	Cleveland Browns	10	4	0	1968	Baltimore Colts	13	1	0
1969	Cleveland Browns	10	3	1	1969	Minnesota Vikings	12	2	0
	AMERICAN CONFERENCE [1]					NATIONAL CONFERENCE [1]			
1970	Baltimore Colts	11	2	1	1970	Dallas Cowboys	10	4	0
1971	Miami Dolphins	10	3	1	1971	Dallas Cowboys	11	3	0
1972	Miami Dolphins	14	0	0	1972	Washington Redskins	11	3	0
1973	Miami Dolphins	12	2	0	1973	Minnesota Vikings	12	2	0
1974	Pittsburgh Steelers	10	3	1	1974	Minnesota Vikings	10	4	0
1975	Pittsburgh Steelers	12	2	0	1975	Dallas Cowboys	10	4	0
1976	Oakland Raiders	13	1	0	1976	Minnesota Vikings	11	2	1
1977	Denver Broncos	12	2	0	1977	Dallas Cowboys	12	2	0
1978	Pittsburgh Steelers	14	2	0	1978	Dallas Cowboys	12	4	0
1979	Pittsburgh Steelers	12	4	0	1979	Los Angeles Rams	9	7	0
1980	Oakland Raiders	11	5	0	1980	Philadelphia Eagles	12	4	0
1981	Cincinnati Bengals	12	4	0	1981	San Francisco 49ers	13	3	0
1982	Miami Dolphins	7	2	0	1982	Washington Redskins	8	1	0
1983	Los Angeles Raiders	12	4	0	1983	Washington Redskins	14	2	0
1984	Miami Dolphins	14	2	0	1984	San Francisco 49ers	15	1	0

[1] NFL reorganization in 1970 (records exclude playoff games).

DIVISIONAL CHAMPIONSHIP PLAYOFF GAMES

	AMERICAN FOOTBALL CONFERENCE				NATIONAL FOOTBALL CONFERENCE			
Season	Winner	Loser	Score	Site	Winner	Loser	Score	Site
1964	Buffalo	San Diego	20–7	Buffalo	Cleveland	Baltimore	27–10	Cleveland
1965	Buffalo	San Diego	23–0	San Diego	Green Bay	Cleveland	23–12	Green Bay
1966	Kansas City	Buffalo	31–7	Buffalo	Green Bay	Dallas	34–27	Dallas
1967	Oakland	Houston	40–7	Oakland	Green Bay	Dallas	21–17	Green Bay
1968	N.Y. Jets	Oakland	27–23	New York	Baltimore	Cleveland	34–0	Cleveland
1969	Kansas City	Oakland	17–7	Oakland	Minnesota	Cleveland	27–7	Minnesota
1970	Baltimore	Oakland	21–17	Baltimore	Dallas	San Francisco	17–10	San Francisco
1971	Miami	Baltimore	21–0	Miami	Dallas	San Francisco	14–3	Dallas
1972	Miami	Pittsburgh	21–17	Pittsburgh	Washington	Dallas	26–3	Washington
1973	Miami	Oakland	27–10	Miami	Minnesota	Dallas	27–10	Dallas
1974	Pittsburgh	Oakland	24–13	Oakland	Minnesota	Los Angeles	14–10	Minnesota
1975	Pittsburgh	Oakland	16–10	Pittsburgh	Dallas	Los Angeles	37–7	Los Angeles
1976	Oakland	Pittsburgh	24–7	Oakland	Minnesota	Los Angeles	24–13	Minnesota
1977	Denver	Oakland	20–17	Denver	Dallas	Minnesota	23–6	Dallas
1978	Pittsburgh	Houston	34–5	Pittsburgh	Dallas	Los Angeles	28–0	Los Angeles
1979	Pittsburgh	Houston	27–13	Pittsburgh	Los Angeles	Tampa Bay	9–0	Tampa Bay
1980	Oakland	San Diego	34–27	San Diego	Philadelphia	Dallas	20–7	Philadelphia
1981	Cincinnati	San Diego	27–7	Cincinnati	San Francisco	Dallas	28–27	San Francisco
1982	Miami	N.Y. Jets	14–0	Miami	Washington	Dallas	31–17	Washington
1983	L.A. Raiders	Seattle	30–14	Los Angeles	Washington	San Francisco	24–21	Washington
1984	Miami	Pittsburgh	45–28	Miami	San Francisco	Chicago	23–0	San Francisco

STARS OF THE NATIONAL FOOTBALL LEAGUE

LEADING PASSERS

Year	Player	A[1]	C[2]	YG[3]	Year	Player	A[1]	C[2]	YG[3]
1949	Sammy Baugh, Washington .	255	145	1,903	1967	Sonny Jurgensen, Washington	508	288	3,747
1950	Norm Van Brocklin, L.A.	233	127	2,061	1968	Earl Morrall, Baltimore	317	182	2,909
1951	Bob Waterfield, L.A.	176	88	1,556	1969	Sonny Jurgensen, Washington	442	274	3,102
1952	Norm Van Brocklin, L.A.	205	113	1,736	1970	John Brodie, San Francisco .	378	223	2,941
1953	Otto Graham, Cleveland	258	167	2,722	1971	Bob Griese, Miami	263	145	2,089
1954	Norm Van Brocklin, L.A.	260	139	2,637	1972	Norm Snead, N.Y. Giants ...	325	196	2,307
1955	Otto Graham, Cleveland	185	98	1,721	1973	Roger Staubach, Dallas	286	179	2,428
1956	Ed Brown, Chicago Bears ...	168	96	1,667	1974	Ken Anderson, Cincinnati ...	328	213	2,667
1957	Tom O'Connell, Cleveland ...	110	63	1,229	1975	Ken Anderson, Cincinnati ...	377	228	3,169
1958	Eddie LeBaron, Washington .	145	79	1,365	1976	Ken Stabler, Oakland	291	194	2,737
1959	Charley Conerly, New York ..	194	113	1,706	1977	Bob Griese, Miami	307	180	2,252
1960	Milt Plum, Cleveland	250	151	2,297	1978	Roger Staubach, Dallas	413	231	3,190
1961	Milt Plum, Cleveland	302	177	2,416	1979	Roger Staubach, Dallas	461	267	3,586
1962	Bart Starr, Green Bay	285	178	2,438	1980	Brian Sipe, Cleveland	554	337	4,132
1963	Y.A. Tittle, New York	367	221	3,145	1981	Ken Anderson, Cincinnati ...	479	300	3,754
1964	Bart Starr, Green Bay	272	163	2,144	1982	Dan Fouts, San Diego	330	204	2,889[5]
1965	Rudy Bukich, Chicago Bears	312	176	2,641	1983	Steve Bartkowski, Atlanta ...	432	274	3,167
1966	Bart Starr, Green Bay	251	156	2,257	1984	Dan Marino, Miami	564	362	5,084

LEADING PASS RECEIVERS

Year	Player	PASSES RECEIVED	Year	Player	PASSES RECEIVED
1949	Tom Fears, Los Angeles	77	1966	Charles Taylor, Washington	72
1950	Tom Fears, Los Angeles	84	1967	Charles Taylor, Washington	70
1951	Elroy Hirsch, Los Angeles	66	1968	Clifton McNeil, San Francisco	71
1952	Mac Speedie, Cleveland	62	1969	Dan Abramowicz, New Orleans	73
1953	Pete Pihos, Philadelphia	63	1970	Dick Gordon, Chicago	71
1954	Pete Pihos, Philadelphia (tie).....	60	1971	Fred Biletnikoff, Oakland	61
	Billy Wilson, San Francisco (tie)....	60	1972	Harold Jackson, Philadelphia	62
1955	Pete Pihos, Philadelphia	62	1973	Harold Carmichael, Philadelphia	67
1956	Billy Wilson, San Francisco	60	1974	Lydell Mitchell, Baltimore	72
1957	Billy Wilson, San Francisco	52	1975	Chuck Foreman, Minnesota	73
1958	Ray Berry, Baltimore (tie)	56	1976	MacArthur Lane, Kansas City	66
	Pete Retzlaff, Philadelphia (tie)	56	1977	Lydell Mitchell, Baltimore	71
1959	Ray Berry, Baltimore	66	1978	Rickey Young, Minnesota	88
1960	Ray Berry, Baltimore	74	1979	Joe Washington, Baltimore	82
1961	Jim Phillips, Los Angeles	78	1980	Kellen Winslow, San Diego	89
1962	Bobby Mitchell, Washington	72	1981	Kellen Winslow, San Diego	88
1963	Bobby Joe Conrad, St. Louis	73	1982	Kellen Winslow, San Diego	54[5]
1964	Johnny Morris, Chicago Bears	93	1983	Todd Christensen, L.A. Raiders	92
1965	Dave Parks, San Francisco	80	1984	Art Monk, Washington	106

RUSHING LEADERS

Year	Player	YARDS GAINED	Year	Player	YARDS GAINED
1949	Steve Van Buren, Philadelphia	1,146	1967	Leroy Kelly, Cleveland	1,205
1950	Marion Motley, Cleveland	810	1968	Leroy Kelly, Cleveland	1,239
1951	Eddie Price, New York	971	1969	Gale Sayers, Chicago	1,032
1952	Dan Towler, Los Angeles	894	1970	Larry Brown, Washington	1,125
1953	Joe Perry, San Francisco...........	1,018	1971	Floyd Little, Denver	1,133
1954	Joe Perry, San Francisco...........	1,049	1972	O.J. Simpson, Buffalo	1,251
1955	Alan Ameche, Baltimore	961	1973	O.J. Simpson, Buffalo	2,003[4]
1956	Rick Casares, Chicago Bears	1,126	1974	Otis Armstrong, Denver	1,407
1957	Jim Brown, Cleveland	942	1975	O.J. Simpson, Buffalo	1,817
1958	Jim Brown, Cleveland	1,527	1976	O.J. Simpson, Buffalo	1,503
1959	Jim Brown, Cleveland	1,329	1977	Walter Payton, Chicago	1,852
1960	Jim Brown, Cleveland	1,257	1978	Earl Campbell, Houston	1,450
1961	Jim Brown, Cleveland	1,408	1979	Earl Campbell, Houston	1,697
1962	Jim Taylor, Green Bay	1,474	1980	Earl Campbell, Houston	1,934
1963	Jim Brown, Cleveland	1,863	1981	George Rogers, New Orleans	1,674
1964	Jim Brown, Cleveland	1,446	1982	Freeman McNeil, N.Y. Jets	786[5]
1965	Jim Brown, Cleveland	1,544	1983	Eric Dickerson, Los Angeles Rams ..	1,808
1966	Gale Sayers, Chicago Bears	1,231	1984	Eric Dickerson, Los Angeles Rams ..	2,105

SCORING LEADERS

Year	Player	POINTS	Year	Player	POINTS
1946	Ted Fritsch, Green Bay	100	1956	Bobby Layne, Detroit	99
1947	Pat Harder, Chicago Cardinals......	102	1957	Sam Baker, Washington	77
1948	Pat Harder, Chicago Cardinals......	110		Lou Groza, Cleveland.............	77
1949	Pat Harder, Chi., Gene Roberts, N.Y. .	102	1958	Jimmy Brown, Cleveland	108
1950	Doak Walker, Detroit	128	1959	Paul Hornung, Green Bay	94
1951	Elroy Hirsch, Los Angeles	102	1960	Paul Hornung, Green Bay	176[4]
1952	Gordon Soltau, San Francisco	94	1961	Paul Hornung, Green Bay	146
1953	Gordon Soltau, San Francisco	114	1962	Jim Taylor, Green Bay	114
1954	Bob Walston, Philadelphia	114	1963	Don Chandler, New York	106
1955	Doak Walker, Detroit	96	1964	Lenny Moore, Baltimore	128

[1] Attempts. [2] Completions. [3] Yards gained. [4] Record. [5] Season reduced to 9 games due to strike.

SCORING LEADERS (continued)

YEAR		POINTS	YEAR		POINTS
1965	Gale Sayers, Chicago	132	1975	O.J. Simpson, Buffalo	138
1966	Bruce Gossett, Los Angeles	120	1976	Toni Linhart, Baltimore	109
1967	Jim Bakken, St. Louis	132	1977	Errol Mann, Oakland	99
1968	Leroy Kelly, Cleveland	113	1978	Frank Corral, Los Angeles	118
1969	Fred Cox, Minnesota	117	1979	John Smith, New England	115
1970	Fred Cox, Minnesota	120	1980	John Smith, New England	129
1971	Garo Yepremian, Miami	121	1981	Ed Murray, Detroit	121
1972	Chester Marcol, Green Bay	125	1982	Marcus Allen, Los Angeles	84[1]
1973	David Ray, Los Angeles	130	1983	Mark Mosely, Washington	161
1974	Chester Marcol, Green Bay	94	1984	Ray Wersching, San Francisco	131

[1] Season reduced to 9 games due to strike.

NO. 1 NFL DRAFT CHOICES: 1964–1985

YEAR	CLUB	PLAYER	POSITION	SCHOOL
1955	Baltimore Colts	George Shaw	Quarterback	Oregon
1956	Pittsburgh Steelers	Gary Glick	Defensive Back	Colorado A&M
1957	Green Bay Packers	Paul Horning	Halfback	Notre Dame
1958	Chicago Cardinals	King Hill	Quarterback	Rice
1959	Green Bay Packers	Randy Duncan	Quarterback	Iowa
1960	Los Angeles Rams	Billy Cannon	Running Back	Louisiana State
1961	Minnesota Vikings (NFL)	Tommy Mason	Running Back	Tulane
1961	Buffalo Bills (AFL)	Ken Rice	Guard	Auburn
1962	Washington Redskins (NFL)	Ernie Davis	Running Back	Syracuse
1962	Oakland Raiders (AFL)	Roman Gabriel	Quarterback	North Carolina State
1963	Los Angeles Rams (NFL)	Terry Baker	Quarterback	Oregon State
1963	Kansas City Chiefs (AFL)	Buck Buchanan	Defensive Tackle	Grambling
1964	Boston (AFL)	Jack Concannon	Quarterback	Boston College
1964	San Francisco 49ers (NFL)	Dave Parks	End	Texas Tech
1965	Houston Oilers (AFL)	Lawrence Elkins	End	Baylor
1965	New York Giants (NFL)	Tucker Frederickson	Running Back	Auburn
1966	Miami Dolphins (AFL)	Jim Grabowski	Running Back	Illinois
1966	Atlanta Falcons (NFL)	Tommy Nobis	Line Backer	Texas
1967	Baltimore Colts	Bubba Smith	Tackle	Michigan State
1968	Minnesota Vikings	Ron Yary	Tackle	Southern California
1969	Buffalo Bills	O.J. Simpson	Running Back	Southern California
1970	Pittsburgh Steelers	Terry Bradshaw	Quarterback	Louisiana Tech
1971	New England Patriots	Jim Plunkett	Quarterback	Stanford
1972	Buffalo Bills	Walt Patulski	Defensive End	Notre Dame
1973	Houston Oilers	John Matuszak	Defensive End	Tampa
1974	Dallas Cowboys	Ed Jones	Defensive End	Tennessee State
1975	Atlanta Falcons	Steve Bartkowski	Quarterback	California
1976	Tampa Bay Buccaneers	Le Roy Selmon	Defensive End	Oklahoma
1977	Tampa Bay Buccaneers	Ricky Bell	Running Back	Southern California
1978	Houston Oilers	Earl Campbell	Running Back	Texas
1979	Buffalo Bills	Tom Cousineau	Line Backer	Ohio State
1980	Detroit Lions	Billy Sims	Running Back	Oklahoma
1981	New Orleans Saints	George Rogers	Running Back	South Carolina
1982	New England Patriots	Kenneth Sims	Defensive Tackle	Texas
1983	Baltimore Colts	John Elway	Quarterback	Stanford
1984	New England Patriots	Irving Fryar	Wide Receiver	Nebraska
1985	Buffalo Bills	Bruce Smith	Defensive End	Virginia Tech

NATIONAL FOOTBALL LEAGUE STADIUMS

NATIONAL CONFERENCE

TEAM	STADIUM	SEATING
Atlanta Falcons	Atlanta Stadium	60,748
Chicago Bears	Soldier Field	65,790
Dallas Cowboys	Texas Stadium	63,749
Detroit Lions	Pontiac Silverdome	80,638
Green Bay Packers	Lambeau Field &	56,926
	Milwaukee Co. Stadium	55,976
Los Angeles Rams	Anaheim Stadium	69,007
Minnesota Vikings	Hubert H. Humphrey Metrodome	62,212
New Orleans Saints	Louisiana Superdome	71,272
New York Giants	Giants Stadium, N.J.	76,891
Philadelphia Eagles	Veterans Stadium	71,640
St. Louis Cardinals	Busch Memorial Stadium	51,392
San Francisco 49ers	Candlestick Park	61,413
Tampa Bay Buccaneers	Tampa Stadium	74,270
Washington Redskins	Robert F. Kennedy Stadium	55,431

AMERICAN CONFERENCE

TEAM	STADIUM	SEATING
Buffalo Bills	Rich Stadium	80,290
Cincinnati Bengals	Riverfront Stadium	59,754
Cleveland Browns	Cleveland Stadium	80,098
Denver Broncos	Denver Mile High Stadium	75,100
Houston Oilers	Astrodome	50,496
Indianapolis Colts	Hoosier Dome	60,127
Kansas City Chiefs	Arrowhead Stadium	78,067
Los Angeles Raiders	Los Angeles Memorial Coliseum	92,516
Miami Dolphins	Orange Bowl	75,206
New England Patriots	Sullivan Stadium, Foxboro, Mass.	60,890
New York Jets	Giants Stadium, N.J.	76,891
Pittsburgh Steelers	Three Rivers Stadium	59,000
San Diego Chargers	San Diego Jack Murphy Stadium	60,100
Seattle Seahawks	Kingdome	64,984

NATIONAL PROFESSIONAL FOOTBALL HALL OF FAME

Herb Adderley, def. back: Green Bay (1961–69), Dallas (1970–72)

Lance Alworth, wide receiver: San Diego (1962–70)

Doug Atkins, end: Cleveland, Chicago, New Orleans (1953–69)

Morris (Red) Badgro, end: N.Y. Yankees, N.Y. Giants, Brooklyn Dodgers (1927–36)

Cliff Battles, halfback: Boston, Washington (1932–37)

Sammy Baugh, quarterback: Washington (1937–52)

Chuck Bednarik, center: Philadelphia (1949–62)

Bert Bell, NFL commissioner (1949–59)

Bobby Bell, linebacker: Kansas City (1963–74)

Raymond Berry, end: Balt. (1955–67)

Charles W. Bidwill, owner: Chicago Cardinals (1933–47)

George Blanda, quarterback, place-kicker: Chi., Hou., Oak. (1949–76)

Jim Brown, fullback: Cleve. (1957–65)

Paul Brown, coach: Cleveland (1946–52), Cincinnati (1968–69)

Roosevelt Brown, tackle: New York Giants (1953–65)

Willie Brown, cornerback: Denver, Oakland (1963–78)

Dick Butkus, linebacker: Chi. (1965–73)

Tony Canadeo, halfback: Green Bay (1940–52)

Joe Carr, NFL pres. (1921–38)

Guy Chamberlin, end, coach: Canton, Cleveland, Frankford, Chicago (1919–28)

Jack Christiansen, defensive back: Detroit (1951–58)

Dutch Clark, quarterback: Portsmouth, Detroit (1931–38)

George Connor, tackle, linebacker: Chicago Bears (1948–55)

Jimmy Conzelman, quarterback, coach, executive: Decatur, Rock Island, Milwaukee, Detroit, Providence, Chicago (1920–48)

Willie Davis, defensive end: Cleveland, Green Bay (1958–69)

Art Donovan, defensive tackle: Baltimore, N.Y., Dallas (1950–61)

Paddy Driscoll, quarterback, coach: Decatur, Chicago Cardinals, Chicago Bears (1920–57)

Bill Dudley, halfback: Pittsburgh, Detroit, Washington (1942–53)

Turk Edwards, tackle, Boston, Washington (1942–53)

Weeb Ewbank, coach: Baltimore (1954–62), N.Y. Jets (1963–73)

Tom Fears, end: L.A. (1948–56)

Ray Flaherty, coach: (1926–49)

Len Ford, end: Los Angeles, Cleveland (1948–58)

Danny Fortmann, M.D., guard: Chicago, N.Y. Yankees (1936–43)

Frank Gatski, center: Cleveland Browns, Detroit Lions (1946–57)

Bill George, linebacker: Chicago Bears, Los Angeles (1952–66)

Frank Gifford, halfback: New York Giants (1952–60, 1962–64)

Sid Gillman, coach: Los Angeles, San Diego, Houston (1955–74)

Otto Graham, quarterback: Cleveland (1946–55)

Red Grange, halfback: Chicago Bears, N.Y. Yankees (1925–34)

Forrest Gregg, tackle: Green Bay, Dallas (1956, 1958–71)

Lou Groza, tackle, kicker: Cleveland (1946–59, 1961–67)

Joe Guyon, halfback: Canton, Cleveland, Oorang Indians, Rock Island,

K.C., N.Y. (1918–27)

George Halas, end, coach, owner: Chicago Bears (1920–67)

Ed Healey, tackle: Rock Island, Chicago Bears (1920–27)

Mel Hein, center: New York Giants (1931–45)

Pete (Fats) Henry, tackle: Canton, Akron, New York, Pottsville, Pittsburgh (1920–30)

Arnie Herber, quarterback: Green Bay, New York (1930–45)

Bill Hewitt, end: Chicago, Philadelphia, Pittsburgh (1932–39, 1943)

Clarke Hinkle, fullback: Green Bay (1932–41)

Elroy (Crazylegs) Hirsch, end, halfback: Chicago Rockets, Los Angeles (1946–57)

Cal Hubbard, tackle, end: N.Y., Green Bay, Pittsburgh (1927–36)

Sam Huff, linebacker: N.Y. Giants, Washington (1956–68)

Lamar Hunt, first president of the AFL (1960)

Don Hutson, end: G.B. (1935–45)

David (Deacon) Jones, def. end: L.A., San Diego, Wash. (1961–74)

Sonny Jurgenson, quarterback: Philadelphia, Washington (1957–74)

Walter Kiesling, guard, coach: Duluth, Pottsville, Boston, Chicago Bears, Green Bay, Pittsburgh (1926–56)

Frank (Bruiser) Kinard, tackle: Brooklyn, N.Y. (1938–47)

Curly Lambeau, coach: Green Bay Packers (1919–49), Chicago Cardinals (1950–51), Washington Redskins (1952–53)

Dick (Night Train) Lane, defensive back: Los Angeles, Chicago Cardinals, Detroit (1952–65)

Yale Lary, defensive back, punter: Detroit (1952–53, 1956–64)

Dante Lavelli, end: Cleveland (1946–56)

Bobby Layne, quarterback: Chicago Bears, New York, Detroit, Pittsburgh (1948–62)

Alphonse (Tuffy) Leemans, fullback: N.Y. Giants (1937–43)

Bob Lilly, def. tackle: Dallas (1961–74)

Vince Lombardi, coach: Green Bay, Washington (1958–69)

Sid Luckman, quarterback: Chicago Bears (1939–50)

Roy (Link) Lyman, tackle: Canton, Cleveland, Frankford, Chicago Bears (1922–34)

Tim Mara, owner: New York Giants (1925–59)

Gino Marchetti, defensive end: Dallas, Baltimore (1953–66)

George Preston Marshall, owner: Boston Braves (1932), Boston Redskins (1933–36), Washington Redskins (1937–69)

Ollie Matson, halfback: Chi. Cardinals, L.A., Detroit, Phil. (1952–66)

George McAfee, halfback: Chicago Bears (1940–41, 1945–50)

Mike McCormack, offensive tackle: N.Y. Yanks, Cleveland (1951–62)

Hugh McElhenny, halfback: San Francisco (1952–60)

John Blood McNally, halfback: Milwaukee, Duluth, Pottsville, Green Bay, Pittsburgh (1925–39)

Mike Michalske, guard: New York, Green Bay (1927–37)

Wayne Millner, end: Boston, Washington (1936–41, 1945)

Bobby Mitchell, wide receiver: Cleveland, Washington (1958–68)

Ron Mix, tackle: San Diego (1960–69),

Oakland (1971)

Lenny Moore, running back: Baltimore (1956–67)

Marion Motley, fullback: Cleveland, Pittsburgh (1946–55)

George Musso, guard: Chi. (1933–44)

Bronko Nagurski, fullback: Chicago Bears (1930–37, 1943)

Joe Namath, quarterback: N.Y. Jets, L.A. Rams (1965–77)

Earle (Greasy) Neale, coach: Philadelphia (1941–50)

Ernie Nevers, fullback: Duluth, Chicago Cardinals (1926–37)

Ray Nitschke, linebacker: Green Bay Packers (1958–72)

Leo Nomellini, defensive tackle: San Francisco (1953–63)

Merlin Olsen, tackle: L.A. (1962–76)

Jim Otto, center: Oak. (1960–74)

Steve Owen, tackle: K.C.(1924–25), N.Y. Giants (1926–30); coach, N.Y. Giants (1931–53)

Ace Parker, quarterback: Brooklyn Dodgers, Boston Yanks, New York Yankees (1937–46)

Jim Parker, guard, tackle: Baltimore (1957–67)

Joe Perry, fullback: San Francisco, Baltimore (1948–62)

Pete Pihos, end: Phil. (1947–55)

Hugh (Shorty) Ray, NFL official (1938–56)

Daniel F. Reeves, owner: Los Angeles Rams (1946–71)

Jim Ringo, center: Green Bay, Philadelphia (1953–67)

Andy Robustelli, end: Los Angeles, New York Giants (1951–64)

Art Rooney, owner: Pittsburgh Pirates (1933–40), Pittsburgh Steelers (1941–42, 1949–77)

Pete Rozelle, Football commissioner (1960–85)

Gale Sayers, running back: Chicago Bears (1965–71)

Joe Schmidt, linebacker: Detroit (1953–65)

O. J. Simpson, running back: Buffalo Bills, S.F. 49ers (1969–79)

Bart Starr, quarterback: Green Bay (1956–71)

Roger Staubach quarterback: Dallas Cowboys (1969–79)

Ernie Stautner, defensive tackle: Pittsburgh (1950–63)

Ken Strong, halfback, place-kicker: Staten Island, New York (1929–39, 1944–47)

Joe Stydahar, tackle: Chicago Bears (1936–42, 1945–46)

Charley Taylor, wide receiver: Washington (1964–77)

Jim Taylor, fullback: Green Bay, New Orleans (1958–67)

Jim Thorpe, halfback: Canton, Oorang Indians, Cleveland, Toledo, Rock Island, New York (1915–26, 1929)

Y. A. Tittle, quarterback: Baltimore, San Francisco, New York Giants (1948–64)

George Trafton, center: Decatur, Chi. Staleys, Chi. Bears (1920–32)

Charley Trippi, halfback: Chicago Cardinals (1947–55)

Emlen Tunnell, safety: New York, Green Bay (1948–61)

Clyde (Bulldog) Turner, center: Chicago Bears (1940–52)

Johnny Unitas, quarterback: Baltimore (1956–72), San Diego (1973)

Norm Van Brocklin, quarterback: Los Angeles, Phila. (1949–60)

HALL OF FAME *(continued)*

Steve Van Buren, halfback: Philadelphia (1944–52)

Paul Warfield, wide receiver: Cleveland, Miami, WFL (1964–77)

Bob Waterfield, quarterback: Cleveland, Los Angeles (1945–52)

Arnie Weinmeister, defensive tackle: N.Y. Yanks, N.Y. Giants (1948–53)

Bill Willis, guard: Cleve. (1946–53)

Larry Wilson, defensive back: St. Louis Cardinals (1960–72)

Alex Wojciechowicz, center: Detroit, Philadelphia (1938–50)

PRO FOOTBALL INDIVIDUAL ALL-TIME RECORDS

The records listed on this page do not include statistics from the 1985 season, because those figures were incomplete when the *Reader's Digest Almanac* went to press.

Seasons, active player: 26, George Blanda (1949–75)

Points, lifetime: 2,002, George Blanda (1949–75), Chicago Bears, Baltimore, Oakland

Points, season: 176, Paul Hornung, Green Bay, (1960)—15 touchdowns, 41 points after touchdown, 15 field goals

Points, one game: 40, Ernie Nevers for Chicago Cardinals against Chicago Bears, Nov. 28, 1929—6 touchdowns and 4 points after touchdown

Touchdowns, season: 24, John Riggins, Washington Redskins (1983) 24 rushing

Touchdowns, game: 6, Ernie Nevers, Chicago Cardinals against Chicago Bears, Nov. 28, 1929

Field goals, lifetime: 358, Jan Stenerud (1967–84), Kansas City, Green Bay, Minnesota

Field goals, season: 35, Ali Haji-Sheikh, N.Y. Giants, 1983

Field goals, one game: 7, Jim Bakken for St. Louis against Pittsburgh, Sept. 24, 1967

Field goal, longest: 63 yards, Tom Dempsey for New Orleans against Detroit, Nov. 8, 1970

Field goals, highest completion percentage, season: 95.24, Mark Moseley, Washington (1982)

Rushing—most seasons leading league: 8, Jim Brown, Cleveland (1957–61) and (1963–65)

Rushing—most yards gained lifetime: 13,309, Walter Payton, Chicago Bears (1975–84)

Rushing—most yards gained, season: 2,105, Eric Dickerson, Los Angeles Rams (1984)

Rushing—most yards gained, game: 275, Walter Payton for Chicago against Minnesota, Nov. 20, 1977

Run, longest from scrimmage: 99 yards for touchdown, by Tony Dorsett for Dallas Cowboys against Minnesota Vikings, Jan. 3, 1983.

Touchdowns rushing, lifetime: 106, Jim Brown, Cleveland (1957–65)

Touchdowns rushing, season: 24, John Riggins, Washington (1983)

Touchdowns rushing, game: 6, Ernie Nevers, Chicago Cardinals against Chicago Bears, Nov. 28, 1929

Passes completed, lifetime: 3,686, Fran Tarkenton, N.Y. Giants (1967–71), Minnesota (1961–66; 1972–78), 6,467 attempts

Passes completed, season: 362, Dan Marino, Miami Dolphins (1984)

Passes completed, game: 42, Richard Todd for New York Jets against San Francisco 49ers, Sept. 21, 1980, 59 attempts

Passes, most consecutive completed: 20, Ken Anderson, Cincinnati vs. Houston, Jan. 1, 1983

Passing, most yards gained, career: 47,003, Fran Tarkenton, (1967–78), Minnesota, N.Y. Giants

Passing, most yards gained, season: 5,084, Dan Marino, Miami Dolphins (1984)

Touchdown passes, lifetime: 342, Fran Tarkenton, N.Y. (1967–71), Minnesota (1961–66; 1972–78)

Touchdown passes, season: 48, Dan Marino, Miami Dolphins (1984)

Touchdown passes, game: 7, Sid Luckman for Chicago Bears against New York, Nov. 14, 1943.

Pass receptions, lifetime: 657, Charlie Joiner, (1969–84), Houston, Cincinnati, San Diego

Pass receptions, season: 106, Art Monk, Washington Redskins (1984)

Pass receptions, game: 18, Tom Fears for Los Angeles against Green Bay, Dec. 3, 1950.

Pass interception return, longest: 102 yards for touchdown, Bob Smith, Detroit against Chicago Bears, Nov. 24, 1949

Punt, longest: 98 yards by Steve O'Neal for New York Jets against Denver, Sept. 21, 1969

Punting, highest average, lifetime: 45.1 yards, Sammy Baugh, Washington (1937–52)

Punting, highest average, season: 51.4 yards, Sammy Baugh, Washington (1940)

Punting, highest average, game (at least 4 punts): 61.75, Bob Cifers, Detroit against Chicago Bears, Nov. 24, 1946

Kickoff return, longest: 106 yards for a touchdown, by Al Carmichael for Green Bay against Chicago, Oct. 7, 1956.

NFL TOP 10 PASSERS—LIFETIME [1]

PLAYER	YEARS	ATTEMPTS	COMPLETIONS		YARDS	TOUCHDOWNS		INTERCEPTIONS		AVERAGE GAIN	RATING[2]
			Total	Pct.		Total	Pct.	Total	Pct.		
Joe Montana	6	2,077	1,324	63.7	15,609	106	5.1	54	2.6	7.52	92.7
Roger Staubach . . .	11	2,958	1,685	57.0	22,700	153	5.2	109	3.7	7.67	83.4
Danny White.	9	1,943	1,155	59.4	14,754	109	5.6	90	4.6	7.59	82.7
Sonny Jurgensen . .	18	4,262	2,433	57.1	32,224	255	6.0	189	4.4	7.56	82.6
Len Dawson	19	3,741	2,136	57.1	28,711	239	6.4	183	4.9	7.67	82.6
Ken Anderson	14	4,420	2,627	59.4	32,497	194	4.4	158	3.6	7.35	82.0
Dan Fouts	12	4,380	2,585	59.0	33,854	201	4.6	185	4.2	7.73	81.2
Bart Starr	16	3,149	1,808	57.4	24,718	152	4.8	138	4.4	7.85	80.5
Fran Tarkenton . . .	18	6,467	3,686	57.0	47,003	342	5.3	266	4.1	7.27	80.4
Joe Theismann . . .	11	3,301	1,877	56.9	23,432	152	4.6	122	3.7	7.10	79.0

NFL TOP 10 RUSHERS—LIFETIME [1]

PLAYER	YEARS	ATTEMPTS	YARDS	AVERAGE GAIN	LONGEST RUN	TOUCHDOWNS
Walter Payton	10	3,047	13,309	4.4	76	89
Jim Brown	9	2,359	12,312	5.2	80	106
Franco Harris.	13	2,949	12,120	4.1	75	91
O.J. Simpson	11	2,404	11,236	4.7	94	61
John Riggins	13	2,740	10,675	3.9	66	96
Tony Dorsett	8	2,136	9,525	4.5	99	59
Earl Campbell	7	2,029	8,764	4.3	81	73
Jim Taylor	10	1,941	8,597	4.4	84	83
Joe Perry	14	1,737	8,378	4.8	78	53
Larry Csonka	11	1,891	8,081	4.3	54	64

[1] Does not include 1985. [2] Rating points awarded for percent of completions, TDs, interceptions, and average gain.

NFL TOP PASS RECEIVERS [1]

PLAYER	YEARS	NUMBER	YARDS	AVERAGE	LONGEST	TOUCHDOWNS
Charlie Joiner	16	657	10,774	16.4	87	56
Charley Taylor	13	649	9,110	14.0	88	79
Don Maynard	15	633	11,834	18.7	87	88
Raymond Berry ...	13	631	9,275	14.7	70	68
Harold Carmichael	14	590	8,985	15.2	85	79
Fred Biletnikoff ...	14	589	8,974	15.2	82	76
Harold Jackson ...	16	579	10,372	17.9	79	76
Lionel Taylor	10	567	7,195	12.7	80	45
Steve Largent.....	9	545	8,772	16.1	74	60
Lance Alworth	11	542	10,266	18.9	85	85

NFL TOP INTERCEPTORS [1]

PLAYER	YEARS	NUMBER	YARDS	AVERAGE	LONGEST	TOUCHDOWNS
Paul Krause	16	81	1,185	14.6	81	3
Emlen Tunnell	14	79	1,282	16.2	55	4
Dick (Night Train) Lane	14	68	1,207	17.8	80	5
Ken Riley.........	15	65	596	9.2	66	5
Dick LeBeau	13	62	762	12.3	70	3
Emmitt Thomas...	13	58	937	16.2	73	5
Bobby Boyd	9	57	994	17.4	74	4
Johnny Robinson..	12	57	741	13.0	57	1
Mel Blount	14	57	736	12.9	52	2
Lem Barney	11	56	1,077	19.2	71	7
Pat Fischer	17	56	941	16.8	69	4

NFL TOP PUNTERS [1,2]

PLAYER	YEARS	NUMBER	YARDS	AVERAGE	LONGEST	BLOCKED
Sammy Baugh	16	338	15,245	45.1	85	9
Tommy Davis	11	511	22,833	44.7	82	2
Yale Lary.........	11	503	22,279	44.3	74	4
Horace Gillom	7	385	16,872	43.8	80	5
Jerry Norton	11	358	15,671	43.8	78	2
Don Chandler.....	12	660	28,678	43.5	90	4
Jerrel Wilson	16	1,072	46,139	43.0	72	12
Norm Van Brocklin	12	523	22,413	42.9	72	3
Ray Guy	12	870	37,246	42.8	74	3
Danny Villanueva..	8	488	20,862	42.8	68	2

NFL TOP PUNT RETURNERS [1,3]

PLAYER	YEARS	NUMBER	YARDS	AVERAGE	LONGEST	TOUCHDOWNS
George McAfee ...	8	112	1,431	12.8	74	2
Jack Christiansen .	8	85	1,084	12.8	89	8
Claude Gibson	5	110	1,381	12.6	85	3
Billy Johnson	10	240	2,954	12.3	87	6
Bill Dudley	9	124	1,515	12.2	96	3
Dana McLemore ..	3	83	1,008	12.1	93	3
Rick Upchurch	9	248	3,008	12.1	92	8
Mack Herron	3	84	982	11.7	66	0
Bill Thompson	13	157	1,814	11.6	60	0
Rodger Bird	3	94	1,063	11.3	78	0

NFL TOP KICKOFF RETURNERS [1,3]

PLAYER	YEARS	NUMBER	YARDS	AVERAGE	LONGEST	TOUCHDOWNS
Gale Sayers	7	91	2,781	30.6	103	6
Lynn Chandnois....	7	92	2,720	29.6	93	3
Abe Woodson.....	9	193	5,538	28.7	105	5
Claude (Buddy) Young	6	90	2,514	27.9	104	2
Travis Williams ...	5	102	2,801	27.5	105	6
Joe Arenas	7	139	3,798	27.3	96	1
Clarence Davis....	8	79	2,140	27.1	76	0
Steve Van Buren ..	8	76	2,030	26.7	98	3
Lenny Lyles	12	81	2,161	26.7	103	3
Eugene (Mercury) Morris	8	111	2,947	26.5	105	3

[1] Does not include 1985 season. [2] 300 or more punts. [3] 75 or more returns.

COLLEGE FOOTBALL

MAJOR BOWL GAMES

ROSE BOWL (at Pasadena, Calif.) (played in January)

1902	Michigan 49, Stanford 0	1937	Pittsburgh 21, Washington 0	1962	Minnesota 21, UCLA 3
1916	Washington State 14, Brown 0	1938	California 13, Alabama 0	1963	So. Calif. 42, Wisconsin 37
1917	Oregon 14, Pennsylvania 0	1939	Southern California 7, Duke 3	1964	Illinois 17, Washington 7
1918	Mare Island Marines 19, Camp	1940	So. Calif. 14, Tennessee 0	1965	Michigan 34, Oregon State 7
	Lewis (Army) 7	1941	Stanford 21, Nebraska 13	1966	UCLA 14, Michigan State 12
1919	Great Lakes (Navy) 17, Mare	1942	Oregon State 20, Duke 16	1967	Purdue 14, So. Calif. 13
	Island Marines 0	1943	Georgia 9, UCLA 0	1968	So. Calif. 14, Indiana 3
1920	Harvard 7, Oregon 6	1944	So. Calif. 29, Wash. 0	1969	Ohio State 27, So. Calif. 16
1921	California 28, Ohio State 0	1945	So. Calif. 25, Tenn. 0	1970	So. Calif. 10, Michigan 3
1922	Washington and Jefferson 0,	1946	Alabama 34, So. Calif. 14	1971	Stanford 27, Ohio State 17
	California 0	1947	Illinois 45, UCLA 14	1972	Stanford 13, Michigan 12
1923	So. Calif. 14, Penn State 3	1948	Michigan 49, So. Calif. 0	1973	So. Calif. 42, Ohio State 17
1924	Navy 14, Washington 14	1949	Northwestern 20, California 14	1974	Ohio State 42, So. Calif. 21
1925	Notre Dame 27, Stanford 10	1950	Ohio State 17, California 14	1975	So. Calif. 18, Ohio State 17
1926	Alabama 20, Washington 19	1951	Michigan 14, California 6	1976	UCLA 23, Ohio State 10
1927	Alabama 7, Stanford 7	1952	Illinois 40, Stanford 7	1977	So. Calif. 14, Michigan 6
1928	Stanford 7, Pittsburgh 6	1953	So. Calif. 7, Wisconsin 0	1978	Washington 27, Michigan 20
1929	Georgia Tech. 8, California 7	1954	Michigan State 28, UCLA 20	1979	So. Calif. 17, Michigan 10
1930	So. Calif. 47, Pittsburgh 14	1955	Ohio State 20, So. Calif. 7	1980	So. Calif. 17, Ohio State 16
1931	Alabama 24, Washington State 0	1956	Michigan State 17, UCLA 14	1981	Michigan 23, Washington 6
1932	So. Calif. 21, Tulane 12	1957	Iowa 35, Oregon State 19	1982	Washington 28, Iowa 0
1933	So. Calif. 35, Pittsburgh 0	1958	Ohio State 10, Oregon 7	1983	UCLA 24, Michigan 14
1934	Columbia 7, Stanford 0	1959	Iowa 38, California 12	1984	UCLA 45, Illinois 9
1935	Alabama 29, Stanford 13	1960	Washington 44, Wisconsin 8	1985	So. Calif. 20, Ohio State 17
1936	Stanford 7, SMU 0	1961	Washington 17, Minnesota 7		

ORANGE BOWL (at Miami, Fla.) (played in January)

1935	Bucknell 26, Miami (Fla.) 0	1952	Georgia Tech 17, Baylor 14	1970	Penn State 10, Missouri 3
1936	Catholic University 20,	1953	Alabama 61, Syracuse 6	1971	Nebraska 17, LSU 12
	Mississippi 19	1954	Oklahoma 7, Maryland 0	1972	Nebraska 38, Alabama 6
1937	Duquesne 13, Miss. State 12	1955	Duke 36, Nebraska 7	1973	Nebraska 40, Notre Dame 6
1938	Alabama Poly 6, Michigan State 0	1956	Oklahoma 20, Maryland 6	1974	Penn State 16, LSU 9
1939	Tennessee 17, Oklahoma 0	1957	Colorado 27, Clemson 21	1975	Notre Dame 13, Alabama 11
1940	Georgia Tech 21, Missouri 7	1958	Oklahoma 48, Duke 21	1976	Oklahoma 14, Michigan 6
1941	Miss. State 14, Georgetown 7	1959	Oklahoma 21, Syracuse 6	1977	Ohio State 27, Colorado 10
1942	Georgia 40, Texas Christian 26	1960	Georgia 14, Missouri 0	1978	Arkansas 31, Oklahoma 6
1943	Alabama 37, Boston College 21	1961	Missouri 21, Navy 14	1979	Oklahoma 31, Nebraska 24
1944	LSU 19, Texas A & M 14	1962	LSU 25, Colorado 7	1980	Oklahoma 24, Fla. State 7
1945	Tulsa 26, Georgia Tech 12	1963	Alabama 17, Oklahoma 0	1981	Oklahoma 18, Florida State 17
1946	Miami (Fla.) 13, Holy Cross 6	1964	Nebraska 13, Auburn 7	1982	Clemson 22, Nebraska 15
1947	Rice 8, Tennessee 0	1965	Texas 21, Alabama 17	1983	Nebraska 21, La. State 20
1948	Georgia Tech 20, Kansas 14	1966	Alabama 39, Nebraska 28	1984	Miami 31, Nebraska 30
1949	Texas 41, Georgia 28	1967	Florida 27, Georgia Tech 12	1985	Washington 28, Okla. 17
1950	Santa Clara 21, Kentucky 13	1968	Oklahoma 26, Tennessee 24		
1951	Clemson 15, Miami 14	1969	Penn State 15, Kansas 14		

SUGAR BOWL (at New Orleans, La.) (played in January)

1935	Tulane 20, Temple 14	1951	Kentucky 13, Oklahoma 7	1969	Arkansas 16, Georgia Tech 2
1936	Texas Christian 3, La. State 2	1952	Maryland 28, Tennessee 13	1970	Mississippi 27, Arkansas 22
1937	Santa Clara 21, La. State 14	1953	Georgia Tech 24, Mississippi 7	1971	Tennessee 34, Air Force 13
1938	Santa Clara 6, Louisiana State 0	1954	Georgia Tech 42, West Virginia 19	1972	Oklahoma 40, Auburn 22
1939	Texas Christian 15,	1955	Navy 21, Mississippi 0	1973	Oklahoma 14, Penn State 0
	Carnegie Tech 7	1956	Georgia Tech 7, Pittsburgh 0	1974	Notre Dame 24, Alabama 23
1940	Texas A&M 14, Tulane 13	1957	Baylor 13, Tennessee 7	1975	Nebraska 13, Florida 10
1941	Boston College 19, Tennessee 13	1958	Mississippi 39, Texas 7	1976	Alabama 13, Penn State 6
1942	Fordham 2, Missouri 0	1959	Louisiana State 7, Clemson 0	1977	Pittsburgh 27, Georgia 3
1943	Tennessee 14, Tulsa 7	1960	Mississippi 21, LSU 0	1978	Alabama 35, Ohio State 6
1944	Georgia Tech 20, Tulsa 18	1961	Mississippi 14, Rice 6	1979	Alabama 14, Penn State 7
1945	Duke 29, Alabama 26	1962	Alabama 10, Arkansas 3	1980	Alabama 24, Arkansas 9
1946	Oklahoma A & M 33,	1963	Mississippi 17, Arkansas 13	1981	Georgia 17, Notre Dame 10
	St. Mary's (Calif.) 13	1964	Alabama 12, Mississippi 7	1982	Pittsburgh 24, Georgia 20
1947	Georgia 20, North Carolina 10	1965	La. State 13, Syracuse 10	1983	Penn St. 27, Georgia 23
1948	Texas 27, Alabama 7	1966	Missouri 20, Florida 18	1984	Auburn 9, Michigan 7
1949	Oklahoma 14, North Carolina 6	1967	Alabama 34, Nebraska 7	1985	Nebraska 28, La. State 10
1950	Oklahoma 35, Louisiana State 0	1968	LSU 20, Wyoming 13		

COTTON BOWL (at Dallas) (played in January)

1937	Texas Christian 16, Marquette 6	1940	Clemson 6, Boston College 3	1943	Texas 14, Georgia Tech 7
1938	Rice 28, Colorado 14	1941	Texas A & M 13, Fordham 12	1944	Randolph Field 7, Texas 7
1939	St. Mary's 20, Texas Tech 13	1942	Alabama 29, Texas A & M 21	1945	Oklahoma A & M 34, TCU 0

COTTON BOWL (continued)

1946	Texas 40, Missouri 27	1960	Syracuse 23, Texas 14	1974	Nebraska 19, Texas 3
1947	Louisiana State 0, Arkansas 0	1961	Duke 7, Arkansas 6	1975	Penn State 41, Baylor 20
1948	So. Methodist 13, Penn State 13	1962	Texas 12, Mississippi 7	1976	Arkansas 31, Georgia 10
1949	So. Methodist 21, Oregon 13	1963	Louisiana State 13, Texas 0	1977	Houston 30, Maryland 21
1950	Rice 27, North Carolina 13	1964	Texas 28, Navy 6	1978	Notre Dame 38, Texas 10
1951	Tennessee 20, Texas 14	1965	Arkansas 10, Nebraska 7	1979	Notre Dame 35, Houston 34
1952	Kentucky 20, Texas Christian 7	1966	Louisiana State 14, Arkansas 7	1980	Houston 17, Nebraska 14
1953	Texas 16, Tennessee 0	1967	Georgia 24, So. Methodist 9	1981	Alabama 30, Baylor 2
1954	Rice 28, Alabama 6	1968	Texas A & M 20, Alabama 16	1982	Texas 14, Alabama 12
1955	Georgia Tech 14, Arkansas 6	1969	Texas 36, Tennessee 13	1983	SMU 7, Pittsburgh 3
1956	Miss. 14, Texas Christian 13	1970	Texas 21, Notre Dame 17	1984	Georgia 10, Texas 9
1957	Texas Christian 28, Syracuse 27	1971	Notre Dame 24, Texas 11	1985	Boston Col 45, Houston 28
1958	Navy 20, Rice 7	1972	Penn State 30, Texas 6		
1959	Air Force 0, Texas Christian 0	1973	Texas 17, Alabama 13		

SUN BOWL (at El Paso, Texas)*

1936	Hardin-Simmons 14, N.M. State 14	1953	Col. Pacific 26, Miss. Southern 7	1970	Nebraska 45, Georgia 6
1937	Hardin-Simmons 34, Tex.-El Paso 6	1954	U. Tex. El Paso 37, Miss. South. 14	1971	Georgia Tech 17, Texas Tech 9
1938	West Virginia 7, Texas Tech 6	1955	U. Texas El Paso 47, Florida St. 20	1972	LSU 33, Iowa State 15
1939	Utah 26, New Mexico 0	1956	Wyoming 21, Texas Tech 14	1973	North Carolina 32, Texas Tech 28
1940	Catholic U. 0, Arizona St. 0	1957	Geo. Wash. 13, U. Texas El Paso 0	1974	Missouri 34, Auburn 17
1941	Western Reserve 26, Arizona St. 13	1958	Louisville 34, Drake 20	1975	Mississippi St. 26, N. Carolina 24
1942	Tulsa 6, Texas Tech 0	1959	Wyoming 14, Hardin-Simmons 6	1976	Pittsburgh 33, Kansas 19
1943	2d Air Force 13, Hardin-Simmons 7	1960	New Mexico St. 28, N.M. State 8	1977	Oklahoma 44, Wyoming 7
1944	Southwest. (Tex.) 7, N. Mexico 0	1961	New Mexico St. 20, Utah State 13	1978	Stanford 24, Louisiana State 14
1945	Southwest. (Tex.) 35, U. of Mex. 0	1962	Villanova 17, Wichita 9	1979	Texas 42, Maryland 0
1946	New Mexico 34, Denver 24	1963	West Texas St. 15, Ohio U. 14	1980	Washington 14, Texas 7
1947	Cincinnati 38, Virginia Tech 6	1964	Oregon 21, So. Methodist 14	1981	Nebraska 31, Mississippi State 17
1948	Miami (O.) 13, Texas El Paso 12	1965	Georgia 7, Texas Tech 0	1982	Oklahoma 40, Houston 14
1949	West Virginia 21, Texas Mines 12	1966	U. Texas El Paso 13, TCU 12	1983	N. Carolina 26, Texas 10
1950	U. Tex. El Paso 33, Georgetown 20	1967	Wyoming 28, Florida St. 20	1984	Alabama 28, SMU 7
1951	West Texas St. 14, Cincinnati 13	1968	U. Texas El Paso 14, Mississippi 7	1985	Maryland 28, Tenn. 27
1952	Texas Tech 25, Col. Pacific 14	1969	Auburn 34, Arizona 10		

GATOR BOWL (at Jacksonville, Fla.) (played in December)

1945	Wake Forest 26, S. Carolina 14	1959	Arkansas 14, Georgia Tech 7	1973	Texas Tech 28, Tennessee 19
1946	Oklahoma 34, N.C. State 13	1960	Florida 13, Baylor 12	1974	Auburn 27, Texas 3
1947	Maryland 20, Georgia 20	1961	Penn State 30, Georgia Tech 15	1975	Maryland 13, Florida 0
1948	Clemson 24, Missouri 23	1962	Florida 17, Penn State 7	1976	Notre Dame 20, Penn State 9
1949	Maryland 20, Missouri 7	1963	North Carolina 35, Air Force 0	1977	Pittsburgh 34, Clemson 3
1950	Wyoming 20, Washington & Lee 7	1964	Florida State 36, Oklahoma 19	1978	Clemson 17, Ohio State 15
1951	Miami (Fla.) 14, Clemson 0	1965	Georgia Tech 31, Texas Tech 21	1979	No. Carolina 17, Michigan 15
1952	Florida 14, Tulsa 13	1966	Tennessee 18, Syracuse 12	1980	Pittsburgh 37, South Carolina 9
1953	Texas Tech 35, Auburn 13	1967	Penn State 17, Fla. State 17	1981	North Carolina 31, Arkansas 27
1954	Auburn 33, Baylor 13	1968	Missouri 35, Alabama 10	1982	Florida St. 31, W. Va. 12
1955	Vanderbilt 25, Auburn 13	1969	Florida 14, Tennessee 13	1983	Florida 14, Iowa 6
1956	Georgia Tech 21, Pittsburgh 14	1970	Auburn 35, Mississippi 28	1984	Okla. St. 21, S. Carolina 14
1957	Tennessee 3, Texas A & M 0	1971	Georgia 7, North Carolina 3		
1958	Mississippi 7, Florida 3	1972	Auburn 24, Colorado 3		

ASTRO-BLUEBONNET BOWL (at Houston, Texas) (played in December)

1959	Clemson 23, TCU 7	1968	SMU 28, Oklahoma 27	1977	So. Calif. 47, Texas A & M 28
1960	Texas 3, Alabama 3	1969	Houston 36, Auburn 7	1978	Stanford 25, Georgia 22
1961	Kansas 33, Rice 7	1970	Oklahoma 24, Alabama 24	1979	Purdue 27, Tennessee 22
1962	Missouri 14, Georgia Tech 10	1971	Colorado 29, Houston 17	1980	North Carolina 16, Texas 7
1963	Baylor 14, LSU 7	1972	Tennessee 24, Louisiana St. 17	1981	Michigan 33, UCLA 14
1964	Tulsa 14, Mississippi 7	1973	Houston 47, Tulane 7	1982	Arkansas 28, Florida 24
1965	Tennessee 27, Tulsa 6	1974	Houston 31, N. Carolina State 31	1983	Oklahoma State 24, Baylor 14
1966	Texas 19, Mississippi 0	1975	Texas 38, Colorado 21	1984	West Va. 31, TCU 14
1967	Colorado 31, Miami (Fla.) 21	1976	Nebraska 27, Texas Tech 24		

LIBERTY BOWL (at Memphis, Tenn.) (played in December)

1959	Penn State 7, Alabama 0	1968	Mississippi 34, Va. Tech 17	1977	Nebraska 21, North Carolina 17
1960	Penn State 41, Oregon 12	1969	Colorado 47, Alabama 33	1978	Missouri 20, LSU 15
1961	Syracuse 15, Miami 14	1970	Tulane 17, Colorado 3	1979	Penn State 9, Tulane 6
1962	Oregon State 6, Villanova 0	1971	Tennessee 14, Arkansas 13	1980	Purdue 28, Missouri 25
1963	Miss. State 16, N.C. State 12	1972	Georgia Tech 31, Iowa State 30	1981	Ohio State 31, Navy 28
1964	Utah 32, West Virginia 6	1973	No. Carolina St. 31, Kansas 18	1982	Alabama 21, Illinois 15
1965	Mississippi 13, Auburn 7	1974	Tennessee 7, Maryland 3	1983	Notre Dame 19, Boston C. 18
1966	Miami (Fla.) 14, Va. Tech 7	1975	So. Calif. 20, Texas A & M 0	1984	Auburn 21, Arkansas 15
1967	N.C. State 14, Georgia 7	1976	Alabama 36, UCLA 6		

* Games for 1959–80 played in December of previous year.

PEACH BOWL (at Atlanta, Georgia) (played in December)

1968	LSU 31, Florida State 27	1974	Texas Tech 6, Vanderbilt 6	1980[1]	Miami (Fla.) 20, Virginia 10
1969	West Virginia 14, South Carolina 3	1975	West Virginia 13, N.C. State 10	1981	W. Virginia 26, Florida 6
1970	Arizona State 48, N. Carolina 26	1976	Kentucky 21, N. Carolina 0	1982	Iowa 28, Tennessee 22
1971	Mississippi 41, Georgia Tech 18	1977	N.C. State 24, Iowa State 14	1983	Florida St. 28, N.C. 3
1972	North Carolina St. 49, West Va. 13	1978	Purdue 41, Georgia Tech 21	1984	Virginia 27, Purdue 24
1973	Georgia 17, Maryland 16	1979	Baylor 24, Clemson 18		

FIESTA BOWL (at Tempe, Arizona) (played in December)

1971	Arizona State 45, Florida State 38	1976	Oklahoma 41, Wyoming 7	1981[1]	Penn St. 26, So. California 10
1972	Arizona State 49, Missouri 35	1977	Penn State 42, Arizona State 30	1982[1]	Ariz. St. 32, Oklahoma 21
1973	Arizona State 28, Pittsburgh 7	1978	UCLA 10, Arkansas 10	1983[1]	Ohio St. 28, Pittsburgh 23
1974	Okla. State 16, Brigham Young 6	1979	Pittsburgh 16, Arizona 10	1984[1]	UCLA 39, Miami 37
1975	Arizona State 17, Nebraska 14	1980	Penn State 31, Ohio State 19		

HALL OF FAME CLASSIC (at Birmingham, Alabama) (played in December)

1977	Maryland 17, Minnesota 7	1980	Arkansas 34, Tulane 15	1983	West Virginia 20, Kentucky 16
1978	Texas A&M 28, Iowa State 12	1981	Mississippi St. 10, Kansas 0	1984	Kentucky 20, Wisconsin 19
1979	Missouri 24, South Carolina 14	1982	Air Force 36, Vanderbilt 28		

INDEPENDENCE BOWL (at Shreveport, Louisiana) (played in December)

1976	McNeese State 20, Tulsa 16	1979	Syracuse 31, McNeese St. 7	1982	Wisconsin 14, Kansas St. 3
1977	Louisiana Tech 24, Louisville 14	1980	S. Mississippi 16, McNeese St. 14	1983	Air Force 9, Mississippi 3
1978	East Carolina 35, La. Tech 13	1981	Texas A&M 33, Oklahoma St. 16	1984	Air Force 23, Virginia Tech 7

HOLIDAY BOWL (at San Diego, California) (played in December)

1978	Navy 23, Brigham Young 16	1981	Brigham Young 38, Washington St. 36	1984	Brigham Young 24, Michigan 17
1979	Indiana 38, Brigham Young 37	1982	Ohio State 47, Brigham Young 17		
1980	Brigham Young 46, SMU 45	1983	Brigham Young 21, Missouri 17		

COLLEGE FOOTBALL NATIONAL CHAMPIONSHIP TEAMS

Various groups have picked the annual college football team champion since 1924. The Associated Press started polling sportswriters in 1936 to determine the team winner. In 1950 United Press International began to poll football coaches. The NCAA recognizes both polls.

1925	Dartmouth	1943	Notre Dame	1959	Syracuse	1974	Oklahoma (AP)
1926	Stanford	1944	Army	1960	Minnesota		So. Calif. (UPI)
1927	Illinois	1945	Army	1961	Alabama	1975	Oklahoma
1928	So. California	1946	Notre Dame	1962	So. California	1976	Pittsburgh
1929	Notre Dame	1947	Notre Dame	1963	Texas	1977	Notre Dame
1930	Notre Dame	1948	Michigan	1964	Alabama	1978	Alabama (AP)
1931	So. California	1949	Notre Dame	1965	Alabama		So. Calif. (UPI)
1932	Michigan	1950	Oklahoma	1966	Notre Dame	1979	Alabama
1933	Michigan	1951	Tennessee	1967	So. California	1980	Georgia
1934	Minnesota	1952	Michigan State	1968	So. Calif. (AP)	1981	Clemson
1935	Southern Methodist	1953	Maryland		Ohio State (UPI)	1982	Penn State
1936	Minnesota	1954	Ohio State (AP);	1969	Texas	1983	Miami
1937	Pittsburgh		UCLA (UPI)	1970	Nebraska (AP)	1984	Brigham Young
1938	Texas Christian	1955	Oklahoma		Texas (UPI)		
1939	Texas A & M	1956	Oklahoma	1971	Nebraska		
1940	Minnesota	1957	Auburn (AP)	1972	So. California		
1941	Minnesota		Ohio State (UPI)	1973	Notre Dame		
1942	Ohio State	1958	Louisiana State				

COLLEGE FOOTBALL CONFERENCE CHAMPIONS

ATLANTIC COAST CONFERENCE CHAMPIONS

1953	Duke	1961	Duke	1969	South Carolina	1977	North Carolina
1954	Duke	1962	Duke	1970	Wake Forest	1978	Clemson
1955*	Maryland—Duke	1963	North Carolina State	1971	North Carolina	1979	North Carolina State
1956	Clemson	1964	North Carolina State	1972	North Carolina	1980	North Carolina
1957	North Carolina State	1965	Duke	1973	North Carolina State	1981	Clemson
1958	Clemson	1966	Clemson	1974	Maryland	1982	Clemson
1959	Clemson	1967	Clemson	1975	Maryland	1983	Maryland
1960	Duke	1968	North Carolina State	1976	Maryland	1984	Maryland

IVY LEAGUE CHAMPIONS

1956	Yale	1964	Princeton	1970	Dartmouth	1978	Dartmouth
1957	Princeton	1965	Dartmouth	1971*	Cornell—Dartmouth	1979	Yale
1958	Dartmouth	1966*	Dartmouth—Harvard	1972	Dartmouth	1980	Yale
1959	Pennsylvania		—Princeton	1973	Dartmouth	1981*	Yale—Dartmouth
1960	Yale	1967	Yale	1974*	Harvard—Yale	1982*	Harvard—
1961*	Columbia—Harvard	1968*	Harvard—Yale	1975	Harvard		Dartmouth—Penn
1962	Dartmouth	1969*	Dartmouth—	1976*	Yale—Brown	1983*	Harvard—Penn
1963*	Dartmouth—Princeton		Princeton—Yale	1977	Yale	1984	Penn

[1] Played in January of next year. * Tie.

BIG EIGHT CONFERENCE CHAMPIONS

1935 Nebraska	1948 Oklahoma	1961 Colorado	1974 Oklahoma
1936 Nebraska	1949 Oklahoma	1962 Oklahoma	1975* Oklahoma—Nebraska
1937 Nebraska	1950 Oklahoma	1963 Nebraska	1976* Oklahoma—Colorado
1938 Oklahoma	1951 Oklahoma	1964 Nebraska	—Oklahoma State
1939 Missouri	1952 Oklahoma	1965 Nebraska	1977 Oklahoma
1940 Nebraska	1953 Oklahoma	1966 Nebraska	1978* Oklahoma—Nebraska
1941 Missouri	1954 Oklahoma	1967 Oklahoma	1979 Oklahoma
1942 Missouri	1955 Oklahoma	1968 Kansas	1980 Oklahoma
1943 Oklahoma	1956 Oklahoma	1969* Missouri—Nebraska	1981 Nebraska
1944 Oklahoma	1957 Oklahoma	1970 Nebraska	1982 Nebraska
1945 Missouri	1958 Oklahoma	1971 Nebraska	1983 Nebraska
1946* Oklahoma—Kansas	1959 Oklahoma	1972 Oklahoma	1984* Nebraska-Okla.
1947* Oklahoma—Kansas	1960 Missouri	1973 Oklahoma	

BIG TEN CHAMPIONS

1935* Minnesota—Ohio State	1948 Michigan	1961 Ohio State	1973* Ohio State—Michigan
1936 Northwestern	1949* Ohio State—Michigan	1962 Wisconsin	1974* Ohio State—Michigan
1937 Minnesota	1950 Michigan	1963 Illinois	1975 Ohio State
1938 Minnesota	1951 Illinois	1964 Michigan	1976* Michigan—Ohio State
1939 Ohio State	1952* Wisconsin—Purdue	1965 Michigan State	1977* Michigan—Ohio State
1940 Minnesota	1953* Illinois—Mich. State	1966 Michigan State	1978* Michigan—
1941 Minnesota	1954 Ohio State	1967* Indiana—Purdue—	Michigan State
1942 Ohio State	1955 Ohio State	Minnesota	1979 Ohio State
1943* Michigan—Purdue	1956 Iowa	1968 Ohio State	1980 Michigan
1944 Ohio State	1957 Ohio State	1969* Michigan—Ohio State	1981* Iowa—Ohio State
1945 Indiana	1958 Iowa	1970 Ohio State	1982 Michigan
1946 Illinois	1959 Wisconsin	1971 Michigan	1983 Illinois
1947 Michigan	1960* Minnesota—Iowa	1972* Ohio State—Michigan	1984 Ohio State

MISSOURI VALLEY CONFERENCE CHAMPIONS

1935* Tulsa—Washington	1948 Oklahoma A & M	1961 Wichita	1973 North Texas
1936 Creighton	1949 Detroit	1962 Tulsa	1974 Tulsa
1937 Tulsa	1950 Tulsa	1963* Cincinnati—Wichita	1975 Tulsa
1938 Tulsa	1951 Tulsa	1964 Cincinnati	1976* Tulsa—New Mexico St.
1939 Washington	1952 Houston	1965 Tulsa	1977 West Texas State
1940 Tulsa	1953* Okla. A&M—Detroit	1966* North Texas—Tulsa	1978 New Mexico State
1941 Tulsa	1954 Wichita	1967 North Texas	1979 West Texas State
1942 Tulsa	1955* Detroit—Wichita	1968 Memphis State	1980 Tulsa
1943 Tulsa	1956 Houston	1969 Memphis State	1981* Drake—Tulsa
1944 Oklahoma A & M	1957 Houston	1970 Louisville	1982 Tulsa
1945 Oklahoma A & M	1958 North Texas	1971 North Texas	1983 Tulsa
1946 Tulsa	1959* North Texas—Houston	1972* Louisville—West	1984 Tulsa
1947 Tulsa	1960 Wichita	Texas—Drake	

PACIFIC COAST ATHLETIC CONFERENCE CHAMPIONS

1969 San Diego State	1973 San Diego State	1977 Fresno State	1981 San Jose State
1970 Long Beach State	1974 San Diego State	1978* Utah St.—San Jose St.	1982 Fresno State
1971 Long Beach State	1975 San Jose State	1979 San Jose State	1983 Calif. St., Fullerton
1972 San Diego State	1976 San Diego State	1980 Long Beach State	1984 Calif. St., Fullerton

PACIFIC TEN CHAMPIONS

1934 Stanford	1946 UCLA	1960 Washington	1972 Southern California
1935* California—	1947 Southern California	1961 UCLA	1973 Southern California
Stanford—UCLA	1948* Oregon—California	1962 Southern California	1974 Southern California
1936* Washington—So. Cal.	1949 California	1963 Washington	1975* California—UCLA
1937 California	1950 California	1964* Oregon State—	1976 Southern California
1938* California—So. Cal.	1951 Stanford	Southern California	1977 Washington
1939 Southern California	1952 Southern California	1965 UCLA	1978 Southern California
1940 Stanford	1953-55 UCLA	1966 Southern California	1979 Southern California
1941 Oregon State	1956 Oregon State	1967 Southern California	1980 Washington
1942 UCLA	1957* Oregon State—Oregon	1968 Southern California	1981 Washington
1943 Southern California	1958 California	1969 Southern California	1982 UCLA
1944 Southern California	1959* Washington—Southern	1970 Stanford	1983 UCLA
1945 Southern California	California—UCLA	1971 Stanford	1984 Southern California

WESTERN ATHLETIC CONFERENCE CHAMPIONS

1962 New Mexico	1968 Wyoming	1975 Arizona State	1981 Brigham Young
1963 New Mexico	1969 Arizona State	1976* Brigham Young—Wyo.	1982 Brigham Young
1964* New Mexico—	1970 Arizona State	1977* Brigham Young—	1983 Brigham Young
Utah—Arizona	1971 Arizona State	Arizona State	1984 Brigham Young
1965 Brigham Young	1972 Arizona State	1978 Brigham Young	
1966 Wyoming	1973* Arizona—Arizona State	1979 Brigham Young	
1967 Wyoming	1974 Brigham Young	1980 Brigham Young	

* Tie.

SOUTHEASTERN CONFERENCE CHAMPIONS

1933	Alabama	1946*	Georgia—Tennessee	1959	Georgia	1972	Alabama
1934	Tulane	1947	Mississippi	1960	Mississippi	1973	Alabama
1935	LSU	1948	Georgia	1961*	Alabama—LSU	1974	Alabama
1936	LSU	1949	Tulane	1962	Mississippi	1975	Alabama
1937	Alabama	1950	Kentucky	1963	Mississippi	1976	Georgia
1938	Tennessee	1951*	Georgia Tech—Tenn.	1964	Alabama	1977*	Alabama—Kentucky
1939*	Tennessee—Ga. Tech.	1952	Georgia Tech	1965	Alabama	1978	Alabama
1940	Tennessee	1953	Alabama	1966*	Georgia—Alabama	1979	Alabama
1941	Mississippi State	1954	Mississippi	1967	Tennessee	1980	Georgia
1942	Georgia	1955	Mississippi	1968	Georgia	1981*	Georgia—Alabama
1943	Georgia Tech	1956	Tennessee	1969	Tennessee	1982	Georgia
1944	Georgia Tech	1957	Auburn	1970	LSU	1983	Auburn
1945	Alabama	1958	LSU	1971	Alabama	1984	Florida

SOUTHERN CONFERENCE CHAMPIONS

1933	Duke	1947	William & Mary	1961	Citadel	1972	East Carolina
1934	Washington & Lee	1948	Clemson	1962	VMI	1973	East Carolina
1935	Duke	1949	North Carolina	1963	Virginia Tech	1974	VMI
1936	Duke	1950	Washington & Lee	1964	West Virginia	1975	Richmond
1937	Maryland	1951*	Maryland—VMI	1965	West Virginia	1976	East Carolina
1938	Duke	1952	Duke	1966*	William & Mary—	1977*	Tenn.–Chat.—VMI
1939	Duke	1953	West Virginia		East Carolina	1978*	Tenn.–Chat.—Furman
1940	Clemson	1954	West Virginia	1967	West Virginia	1979	Tennessee–Chat.
1941	Duke	1955	West Virginia	1968	Richmond	1980	Furman
1942	William & Mary	1956	West Virginia	1969*	Davidson—	1981	Furman
1943	Duke	1957	VMI		Richmond	1982	Furman
1944	Duke	1958	West Virginia	1970	William & Mary	1983	Furman
1945	Duke	1959	VMI	1971	Richmond	1984	Tenn.–Chat.
1946	North Carolina	1960	VMI	1972	East Carolina		

SOUTHWEST CONFERENCE CHAMPIONS

1935	SMU	1948	SMU	1961*	Texas—Arkansas	1974	Baylor
1936	Arkansas	1949	Rice	1962	Texas	1975*	Texas A & M—
1937	Rice	1950	Texas	1963	Texas		Arkansas—Texas
1938	TCU	1951	TCU	1964	Arkansas	1976*	Houston—Texas Tech
1939	Texas A & M	1952	Texas	1965	Arkansas	1977	Texas
1940	Texas A & M—SMU	1953*	Rice—Texas	1966	SMU	1978	Houston
1941	Texas A & M	1954	Arkansas	1967	Texas A & M	1979*	Arkansas—Houston
1942	Texas	1955	Texas	1968	Texas	1980	Baylor
1943	Texas	1956	Texas A & M	1969	Texas	1981	SMU
1944	TCU	1957	Rice	1970	Texas	1982	SMU
1945	Texas	1958	TCU	1971	Texas	1983	Texas
1946*	Arkansas—Rice	1959*	Texas—TCU—Ark.	1972	Texas	1984	SMU
1947	SMU	1960	Arkansas	1973	Texas		

* Tie.

WON-LOST SEASON RECORDS OF MAJOR COLLEGE FOOTBALL TEAMS: 1984

TEAM	W	L	T	TEAM	W	L	T	TEAM	W	L	T
Air Force	7	4	0	Kentucky	8	3	0	Rutgers	7	3	0
Alabama	5	6	0	Louisiana State	8	2	1	San Jose State	6	5	0
Arizona	7	4	0	Maryland	9	3	0	South Carolina	10	1	0
Arizona State	5	6	0	Memphis State	5	5	1	Southern Cal	8	3	0
Arkansas	7	3	1	Miami, Fla	8	4	0	Southern Methodist	9	2	0
Army	7	3	1	Michigan	6	5	0	Stanford	5	6	0
Auburn	8	4	0	Michigan State	6	5	0	Syracuse	6	5	0
Baylor	6	5	0	Minnesota	4	7	0	Temple	6	5	0
Boston College	9	2	0	Mississippi	4	6	1	Tennessee	7	3	1
Bowling Green	8	3	0	Mississippi State	4	7	0	Texas	7	3	1
Brigham Young	12	0	0	Navy	4	6	1	Texas A&M	6	5	0
Central Michigan	8	2	1	Nebraska	9	2	0	Texas Christian	8	3	0
Clemson	7	4	0	Nevada-Las Vegas	10	2	0	Toledo	8	2	1
Florida	9	1	1	North Carolina	5	5	1	Tulane	3	8	0
Florida State	7	3	1	Notre Dame	7	4	0	UCLA	8	3	0
Fullerton State	11	1	0	Ohio State	9	2	0	Utah	6	5	1
Georgia	7	4	0	Oklahoma	9	1	1	Vanderbilt	5	6	0
Georgia Tech	6	4	1	Oklahoma State	9	2	0	Virginia	7	2	2
Hawaii	7	4	0	Oregon	6	5	0	Virginia Tech	8	3	0
Houston	7	4	0	Penn State	6	5	0	Wake Forest	6	5	0
Illinois	7	4	0	Pittsburgh	3	7	1	Washington	10	1	0
Iowa	7	4	1	Purdue	7	4	0	West Virginia	7	4	0
Kansas	5	6	0	Rhode Island	10	2	0	Wisconsin	7	3	1

MAJOR COLLEGE FOOTBALL RECORDS

INDIVIDUAL RECORDS

Touchdowns scored in one game: 7 by Arnold Boykin, Mississippi versus Mississippi State, Dec. 1, 1951; 11* by Philip King, Princeton versus Columbia, Nov. 4, 1890; 11 by Jefferson Fletcher, Harvard versus Exeter, Nov. 3, 1886; 11 by Henry Beecher, Yale versus Wesleyan, Oct. 30, 1886.

Touchdowns scored in one season: 29 by Lydell Mitchell, Penn State, in 1971; 38* by Mayes McLain, Haskell, in 1926.

Touchdowns scored in a career: 59 by Glenn Davis, Army, 1943–46; 59 by Tony Dorsett, Pittsburgh, in 1973–76; 72* by Willie Heston, Michigan, 1901–04; 66 by Henry Beecher, Yale, 1885–87.

Points scored in one game: 43 by Jim Brown, Syracuse versus Colgate, Nov. 17, 1956 (6 TDs, 7 PATs); 64* by Bernard Trafford, Harvard versus Wesleyan, Nov. 3, 1891 (7 TDs, 4 points each; 18 PATs, 2 points each).

Points scored in a season: 174 by Lydell Mitchell, Penn State, 1971 (29 TDs); 270* by Bernard Trafford, Harvard, 1891 (24 TDs, 4 points each; 77 PATs, 2 points each; 4 FGs, 5 points each).

Points scored in a career: 356 by Tony Dorsett, Pittsburgh, 1973–76; 730* by Knowlton Ames, Princeton, 1886–89 (62 TDs, 4 points each; 176 PATs, 2 points each; 6 FGs, 5 points each).

Yards gained in one game: 599 by Virgil Carter, Brigham Young versus U. Texas–El Paso, Nov. 5, 1966 (86 rushing, 513 passing).

Yards gained in a season: 4,627 by Jim McMahon, Brigham Young, 1979 (56 rushing, 4,571 passing).

Yards gained in a career: 11,317 by Doug Flutie, Boston College (1981–84).

Yards gained by rushing in one game: 356 by Eddie Lee Ivery, Georgia Tech versus Air Force, Nov. 11, 1978; 362* by Jim Thorpe, Carlisle versus Pennsylvania, Nov. 16, 1912 (29 rushes).

Yards gained by rushing in one season: 2,342 by Marcus Allen, Southern California, 1981 (403 rushes); 2,148 by Mike Rozier, Nebraska, 1983 (275 rushes).

Yards gained by rushing in a career: 6,082 by Tony Dorsett, Pittsburgh, 1973–76; 5,598 by Charles White, Southern California, 1977–79; 5,259 by Herschel Walker, Georgia, 1980–82.

Passes completed in one game: 45 by Sandy Schwab, Northwestern against Michigan, Oct. 23, 1982; 44 by Jim McMahon, Brigham Young, against Colorado State, Nov. 7, 1981.

Passes completed in one season: 306 by Steve Young, Brigham Young, 1983 (attempted 429).

Passes completed in a career: 820 by Ben Bennett, Duke, 1980–83 (attempted 1,375).

Passes, consecutive completed: 22 by Steve Young, Brigham Young, (last 8 versus Utah State, Oct. 30, 1982; first 14 versus Wyoming, Nov. 6, 1982).

Passes, highest percentage completed in one game (minimum 20 completed): 92.6% by Rick Neuheisel, UCLA vs. Washington, Oct. 29, 1983 (25 of 27).

Passes, highest percentage completed in a season (minimum 150 attempts): 71.3% by Steve Young, Brigham Young, 1983 (306 of 429).

Passes, highest percentage completed in a career (minimum 400 attempts): 65.2% by Steve Young, Brigham Young, 1981–83 (592 of 908).

Passing yards gained in one game: 621 by Dave Wilson, Illinois, against Ohio State, Nov. 8, 1980.

Passing yards gained in one season: 4,571 by Jim McMahon, Brigham Young, 1980.

Passing yards gained in career: 10,579 by Doug Flutie, Boston College (1981-84).

Touchdown passes in one game: 9 by Dennis Shaw, San Diego State versus New Mexico State, Nov. 15, 1969.

Touchdown passes in a season: 47 by Jim McMahon, Brigham Young, 1980.

Touchdown passes in a career: 84 by Jim McMahon, Brigham Young, 1977–78, 1980–81.

Passes caught in one game: 22 by Jay Miller, Brigham Young versus New Mexico, Nov. 3, 1973 (263 yards).

Touchdown passes caught in one game: 6 by Tim Delaney, San Diego State versus New Mexico State, Nov. 15, 1969.

Field goals in one game: 6 by Charley Gogolak, Princeton versus Rutgers, Sept. 25, 1965 (attempted 6); 7* by Edward Robertson, Purdue versus Rose Poly, Oct. 27, 1900 (attempted 12).

Field goals, season: 28, Paul Woodside, West Virginia, 1982.

Points by kicker, game: 23 by Bobby Raymond, Florida vs. Florida State, Dec. 3, 1983.

Points by kicker, season: 112 by Luis Zendejas, Arizona St., 1983.

Field goal, longest made: 67 yards by Russell Erxleben, Texas versus Rice, Oct. 1, 1977.

Points kicked after touchdown in one game: 13 by Terry Leiweke, Houston versus Tulsa, Nov. 23, 1968 (attempted 14). 23* by Arlo Davis, Oklahoma versus Kingfisher, Sept. 29, 1917 (attempted 26).

TEAM RECORDS

Touchdowns in one game: 15 by Wyoming versus Colorado State College, Nov. 5, 1949 (9 rushing, 6 passing). 32* by Georgia Tech versus Cumberland, Oct. 7, 1916.

Touchdowns in one season: 89 by Nebraska in 1983. 144* by Harvard in 1886 (4 points each).

Points scored in one game: 103 by Wyoming versus Colorado State (0), Nov. 5, 1949. 222* by Georgia Tech versus Cumberland (0), Oct. 7, 1916.

Points scored in one season: 624 by Nebraska, 1983.

Yards gained in one game: 883 by Nebraska versus New Mexico State, Sept. 18, 1982. 1,261* by Michigan versus Buffalo, Oct. 26, 1901.

Yards gained rushing in one game: 758 by Oklahoma versus Colorado, Oct. 4, 1980. 1,261* by Michigan versus Buffalo, Oct. 26, 1901 (76 rushes).

Passes completed in one game: 47 by Wake Forest versus Maryland, Oct. 17, 1981.

Touchdown passes in one game: 10 by San Diego State versus New Mexico State, Nov. 15, 1969.

First downs in one game: 43 by Nebraska versus New Mexico State, Sept. 18, 1982 (28 by rushing, 15 passing).

Points kicked after touchdown in one game: 13 by Wyoming versus Northern Colo., Nov. 5, 1949.

Yards gained by passes in one game: 698 by Tulsa versus Idaho State, Oct. 7, 1967 (completed 39 of 62).

Yards on punt returns in one game: 319 by Texas A & M versus North Texas State, Sept. 21, 1946 (10 returns).

Yards on kickoff returns in one game: 295 by Cincinnati versus Memphis State, Oct. 30, 1971.

Average points per game in a season: 56.0 by Army in 1949 (504 points in 9 games).

Fumbles lost in a game: 10 by Wichita State versus Florida State, Sept. 20, 1969.

* Pre-1937 records: There was no general clearinghouse for national records until the NCAA took over the task in 1937. Touchdowns—TDs; points after touchdown—PATs; field goals—FGs.

UNDEFEATED, UNTIED MAJOR TEAMS: 1913–1984

YEAR	COLLEGE	WINS [1]	YEAR	COLLEGE	WINS [1]	YEAR	COLLEGE	WINS [1]
1913	Auburn	8	1929	Notre Dame	9	1953	Maryland	10 L
	Chicago	7		Pittsburgh	9 L	1954	Ohio State	9 W
	Harvard	9		Purdue	8		Oklahoma	10
	Michigan St.	7		Tulane	9		UCLA	9
	Nebraska	8		Utah	7	1955	Maryland	10 L
	Notre Dame	7	1930	Alabama	9 W		Oklahoma	10 W
	Washington	7		Notre Dame	10	1956	Oklahoma	10
1914	Army	9		Utah	8		Tennessee	10 L
	Illinois	7		Washington State	9 L		Wyoming	10
	Tennessee	9	1931	Tulane	11 L	1957	Arizona State	10
	Texas	8	1932	Colgate	9		Auburn	10
	Wash. & Lee	9		Michigan	8	1958	LSU	10 W
1915	Colorado State	7		Southern Cal	9 W	1959	Syracuse	10 W
	Columbia	5	1933	Princeton	9	1960	New Mexico State	10 W
	Cornell	9	1934	Alabama	9		Yale	9
	Nebraska	8		Minnesota	8	1961	Alabama	10 W
	Oklahoma	10	1935	Minnesota	8		Rutgers	9
	Pittsburgh	8		Princeton	9	1962	Dartmouth	9
	Washington	7		SMU	12 L		Mississippi	9 W
	Washington State	6 W	1936	(None)			Southern Cal	10 W
1916	Army	9	1937	Alabama	9 L	1963	Texas	10 W
	Ohio State	7		Colorado	8 L	1964	Alabama	10 L
	Pittsburgh	8		Santa Clara	8 W		Arkansas	10 W
	Tulsa	10	1938	Duke	9 L		Princeton	9
1917	Denver	9		Georgetown	8	1965	Arkansas	10 L
	Georgia Tech	9		Oklahoma	10 L		Dartmouth	9
	Pittsburgh	9		Tennessee	10 W		Michigan State	10 L
	Texas A&M	8		TCU	10 W		Nebraska	10 L
	Washington State	6		Texas Tech	10 L	1966	Alabama	10 W
1918	Michigan	5	1939	Cornell	8	1967	Wyoming	10 L
	Oklahoma	6		Tennessee	10 L	1968	Ohio State	9 W
	Texas	9		Texas A&M	10 W		Ohio U.	10 L
	Virginia Tech	7	1940	Boston College	10 W		Penn State	10 W
	Washington, Mo.	6		Lafayette	9	1969	Penn State	10 W
1919	Notre Dame	9		Minnesota	8		San Diego State	10 W
	Texas A&M	10		Stanford	9 W		Texas	10 W
1920	Boston College	8		Tennessee	10 L		Toledo	10 W
	California	8 W	1941	Duke	9 L	1970	Arizona State	10 W
	Notre Dame	9		Duquesne	8		Dartmouth	9
	Ohio State	7 L		Minnesota	8		Ohio State	9 L
	Southern Cal	6	1942	Tulsa	10 L		Texas	10 L
	Texas	9	1943	Purdue	9		Toledo	11 W
	VMI	9	1944	Army	9	1971	Alabama	11 L
1921	California	9 T		Ohio State	9		Michigan	11 L
	Cornell	8	1945	Alabama	9 W		Nebraska	12 W
	Iowa	7		Army	9		Toledo	11 W
1922	California	9		Oklahoma State	8	1972	Southern Cal	11 W
	Cornell	8	1946	Georgia	10 W	1973	Alabama	11 L
	Drake	7		Hardin-Simmons	10 W		Miami (O.)	10 W
	Iowa	7		UCLA	10 L		Notre Dame	10 W
	Princeton	8	1947	Michigan	9 W		Penn State	11 W
	Tulsa	7		Notre Dame	9	1974	Alabama	11 L
1923	Colorado	9		Penn State	9 T		Oklahoma	11
	Cornell	8	1948	California	10 L	1975	Arizona State	11 W
	Illinois	8		Clemson	10 W		Arkansas State	11
	Michigan	8		Michigan	9		Ohio State	11 L
	SMU	9	1949	Army	9	1976	Maryland	11 L
	Yale	8		California	10 L		Pittsburgh	11 W
1924	Notre Dame	9 W		Notre Dame	10		Rutgers	11
1925	Alabama	9 W		Oklahoma	10 W	1977	Texas	11 L
	Dartmouth	8	1950	Oklahoma	10 L	1978	Penn State	11 L
1926	Alabama	9 T		Princeton	9	1979	Alabama	11 W
	Stanford	10 T		Wyoming	9 L		Ohio State	11 L
	Utah	7	1951	Maryland	9 W		Florida State	11 L
1927	(None)			Michigan State	9		Brigham Young	11 L
1928	Boston College	9		Princeton	9	1980	Georgia	11 W
	Detroit	9		San Francisco	9	1981	Clemson	11 W
	Georgia Tech	9 W	1952	Tennessee	10 L	1982	Georgia	11 L
				Georgia Tech	11 W	1983	Nebraska	12 L
				Michigan State	9		Texas	11 L
						1984	Brigham Young	12 W

[1] Regular season games only. Subsequent bowl win=W, loss=L, tie=T.

COLLEGE RUSHING CHAMPIONS

YEAR	PLAYER, TEAM	GAMES	PLAYS	YARDS [1]
1954	Art Luppino, Arizona	10	179	1,359
1955	Art Luppino, Arizona	10	209	1,313
1956	Jim Crawford, Wyoming	10	200	1,104
1957	Leon Burton, Arizona State	10	117	1,126
1958	Dick Bass, Pacific	10	205	1,361
1959	Pervis Atkins, New Mexico State	10	130	971
1960	Bob Gaiters, New Mexico State	10	197	1,338
1961	Jim Pilot, New Mexico State	10	191	1,278
1962	Jim Pilot, New Mexico State	10	208	1,247
1963	Dave Casinelli, Memphis State	10	219	1,016
1964	Brian Piccolo, Wake Forest	10	252	1,044
1965	Mike Garrett, So. California	10	267	1,440
1966	Ray McDonald, Idaho	10	259	1,329
1967	O. J. Simpson, So. California	9	266	1,415
1968	O. J. Simpson, So. California	10	355	1,709
1969	Steve Owens, Oklahoma	10	358*	1,523
1970	Ed Marinaro, Cornell	9	285	158.3
1971	Ed Marinaro, Cornell	9	356	209.0
1972	Pete VanValkenburg, Brig. Young	10	232	138.6
1973	Mark Kellar, Northern Illinois	11	291	156.3
1974	Louie Giammona, Utah State	10	329	153.4
1975	Ricky Bell, So. California	11	357	170.5
1976	Tony Dorsett, Pittsburgh	11	338	177.1
1977	Earl Campbell, Texas	11	267	158.5
1978	Billy Sims, Oklahoma	11	231	160.2
1979	Charles White, So. California	10	293	180.3
1980	George Rogers, So. Carolina	11	297	161.9
1981	Marcus Allen, So. California	11	403	212.9*
1982	Ernest Anderson, Oklahoma St.	11	353	170.6
1983	Mike Rozier, Nebraska	12	275	179.0
1984	Keith Byars, Ohio State	11	313	150.5

COLLEGE SCORING CHAMPIONS

YEAR	PLAYER, TEAM	GAMES	TD	XPT.	FG	PTS. [2]
1954	Art Luppino, Arizona	10	24	22	0	166
1955	Jim Swink, TCU	10	20	5	0	125
1956	Clendon Thomas, Oklahoma	10	18	0	0	108
1957	Leon Burton, Arizona State	10	16	0	0	96
1958	Dick Bass, Pacific	10	18	8	0	116
1959	Pervis Atkins, N.M. State	10	17	5	0	107
1960	Bob Gaiters, N.M. State	10	23	7	0	145
1961	Jim Pilot, New Mexico State	10	21	12	0	138
1962	Jerry Logan, W. Texas State	10	13	32	0	110
1963	Cosmo Iacavazzi, Princeton	9	14	0	0	84
	Dave Casinelli, Memph. State	10	14	0	0	84
1964	Brian Piccolo, Wake Forest	10	17	9	0	111
1965	Howard Twilley, Tulsa	10	16	31	0	127
1966	Ken Hebert, Houston	10	11	41	2	113
1967	Leroy Keyes, Purdue	10	19	0	0	114
1968	Jim O'Brien, Cincinnati	10	12	31	13	142
1969	Steve Owens, Oklahoma	10	23	0	0	138
1970	Brian Bream, Air Force	10	20	0	0	12.0
	Gary Kosins, Dayton	9	18	0	0	12.0
1971	Ed Marinaro, Cornell	9	24	4	0	16.4
1972	Harold Henson, Ohio State	10	20	0	0	12.0
1973	Jim Jennings, Rutgers	11	21	2	0	11.6
1974	Bill Marek, Wisconsin	9	19	0	0	12.7
1975	Pete Johnson, Ohio State	11	25	0	0	13.6
1976	Tony Dorsett, Pittsburgh	11	22	2	0	12.2
1977	Earl Campbell, Texas	11	19	0	0	10.4
1978	Billy Sims, Oklahoma	11	20	0	0	10.9
1979	Billy Sims, Oklahoma	11	22	0	0	12.0
1980	Sammy Windner, So. Miss.	11	20	0	0	10.9
1981	Marcus Allen, So. California	11	23	0	0	12.5
1982	Greg Allen, Florida State	11	20	0	0	12.0
1983	Mike Rozier, Nebraska	12	29	0	0	14.5
1984	Keith Byars, Ohio State	11	24	0	0	13.1

* Record. [1] Beginning in 1970, ranked on per-game (instead of total) yards. [2] Beginning in 1970, ranked on per-game (instead of total) points. Source: National Collegiate Sports Services.

COLLEGE FOOTBALL PASSING CHAMPIONS [1]

YEAR	PLAYER, TEAM	GAMES	ATT.	CMP.	CMP. AVG.	CMP. PCT.	INT.	YDS.	YDS./ ATT.	TD	RATING POINTS
1954	Paul Larson, California	–	195	125	–	.641	8	1,537	7.88	10	–
1955	George Welsh, Navy	–	150	94	–	.627	6	1,319	8.79	8	–
1956	John Brodie, Stanford	–	240	139	–	.579	14	1,633	6.80	12	–
1957	Ken Ford, Hardin-Simmons	–	205	115	–	.561	11	1,254	6.12	14	–
1958	Buddy Humphrey, Baylor	–	195	112	–	.574	8	1,316	6.75	7	–
1959	Dick Norman, Stanford	–	263	152	–	.578	12	1,963	7.46	11	–
1960	Harold Stephens, Hardin-Simmons	–	256	145	–	.566	14	1,254	4.90	3	–
1961	Chon Gallegos, San Jose State	–	197	117	–	.594	13	1,480	7.51	14	–
1962	Don Trull, Baylor	–	229	125	–	.546	12	1,627	7.10	11	–
1963	Don Trull, Baylor	–	308	174	–	.565	12	2,157	7.00	12	–
1964	Jerry Rhome, Tulsa	10	326	224	22.4	.687	4	2,870	8.80	32	172.6
1965	Bill Anderson, Tulsa	10	509	296	29.6	.582	14	3,464	6.81	30	–
1966	John Eckman, Wichita State	–	458	195	–	.426	34	2,339	5.11	7	–
1967	Terry Stone, New Mexico	–	336	160	–	.476	19	1,946	5.79	9	–
1968	Chuck Hixson, Southern Methodist	10	468	265	26.5	.566	23	3,103	6.63	21	–
1969	John Reaves, Florida	–	396	222	–	.561	19	2,896	7.31	24	–
1970	Sonny Sixkiller, Washington	10	362	186	18.6	.514	22	2,303	6.36	15	–
1971	Brian Sipe, San Diego State	11	369	196	17.8	.531	21	2,532	6.86	17	–
1972	Don Strock, Virginia Tech	11	427	228	20.7	.534	27	3,243	7.59	16	–
1973	Jesse Freitas, San Diego State	11	347	227	20.6	.654	17	2,993	8.63	21	–
1974	Steve Bartkowski, California	11	325	182	16.5	.560	7	2,580	7.94	12	–
1975	Craig Penrose, San Diego State	11	349	198	18.0	.567	24	2,660	7.62	15	–
1976	Tommy Cramer, Rice	11	501	269	24.5	.537	19	3,317	6.62	21	–
1977	Guy Benjamin, Stanford	10	330	208	20.8	.630	15	2,521	7.64	19	–
1978	Steve Dils, Stanford	11	391	247	22.5	.632	15	2,943	7.53	22	–
1979	Turk Schonert, Stanford	11	221	148	13.5	.670	6	1,922	8.70	19	163.0
1980	Jim McMahon, Brigham Young	12	445	284	23.7	.638	18	4,571	10.27	47	176.9
1981	Jim McMahon, Brigham Young	10	423	272	27.2	.643	7	3,555	8.40	30	155.0
1982	Tom Ramsey, UCLA	11	311	191	17.4	.614	10	2,824	9.08	21	153.5
1983	Steve Young, Brigham Young	11	429	306	27.8	.713	10	3,902	9.10	33	168.5
1984	Doug Flutie, Boston College	11	386	232	21.1	.601	11	3,454	8.95	27	152.9

[1] Minimum of 15 attempts per game. In 1954–69 ranked on total completions. In 1970–78 based on average per game completions. Since 1979 based on points for passing efficiency.

HEISMAN MEMORIAL TROPHY WINNERS

The John W. Heisman Memorial Trophy is awarded annually to the nation's leading college football player. It was originated in 1935 by the Downtown Athletic Club of New York.

YEAR	PLAYER	POSITION	TEAM	YEAR	PLAYER	POSITION	TEAM
1935	Jay Berwanger ..	Back	Chicago	1960	Joe Bellino	Back	Navy
1936	Larry Kelley	End	Yale	1961	Ernie Davis	Back	Syracuse
1937	Clint Frank......	Quarterback	Yale	1962	Terry Baker	Back	Oregon State
1938	Davey O'Brien ..	Quarterback	TCU	1963	Roger Staubach ..	Quarterback	Navy
1939	Nile Kinnick	Back	Iowa	1964	John Huarte	Quarterback	Notre Dame
1940	Tom Harmon	Back	Michigan	1965	Mike Garrett	Back	So. California
1941	Bruce Smith	Back	Minnesota	1966	Steve Spurrier ...	Quarterback	Florida
1942	Frank Sinkwich ..	Back	Georgia	1967	Gary Beban	Quarterback	UCLA
1943	Angelo Bertelli...	Quarterback	Notre Dame	1968	O. J. Simpson ...	Tailback	So. California
1944	Les Horvath	Quarterback	Ohio State	1969	Steve Owens	Back	Oklahoma
1945	Felix Blanchard ..	Back	Army	1970	Jim Plunkett	Quarterback	Stanford
1946	Glenn Davis	Back	Army	1971	Pat Sullivan	Quarterback	Auburn
1947	Johnny Lujack ...	Quarterback	Notre Dame	1972	Johnny Rodgers ..	Back	Nebraska
1948	Doak Walker	Back	So. Methodist	1973	John Cappelletti .	Tailback	Penn State
1949	Leon Hart.......	End	Notre Dame	1974	Archie Griffin ...	Tailback	Ohio State
1950	Vic Janowicz	Back	Ohio State	1975	Archie Griffin ...	Tailback	Ohio State
1951	Dick Kazmaier ...	Back	Princeton	1976	Tony Dorsett	Tailback	Pittsburgh
1952	Billy Vessels.....	Back	Oklahoma	1977	Earl Campbell ...	Back	Texas
1953	Johnny Lattner ..	Back	Notre Dame	1978	Billy Sims	Tailback	Oklahoma
1954	Alan Ameche	Back	Wisconsin	1979	Charles White ...	Running Back	So. California
1955	Howard Cassady .	Back	Ohio State	1980	George Rogers ...	Running Back	So. Carolina
1956	Paul Hornung ...	Quarterback	Notre Dame	1981	Marcus Allen	Running Back	So. California
1957	John Crow	Back	Texas A&M	1982	Herschel Walker .	Running Back	Georgia
1958	Pete Dawkins ...	Back	Army	1983	Mike Rozier	Running Back	Nebraska
1959	Billy Cannon	Back	Louisiana State	1984	Doug Flutie	Quarterback	Boston College

OUTLAND TROPHY

The Outland Trophy, awarded by the Football Writers of America since 1946, honors the outstanding college football interior lineman each year.

YEAR	PLAYER	POSITION	TEAM	YEAR	PLAYER	POSITION	TEAM
1946	George Connor ..	Tackle	Notre Dame	1966	Loyd Phillips	Tackle	Arkansas
1947	Joe Steffy.......	Guard	Army	1967	Ron Yary	Tackle	So. Calif.
1948	Bill Fischer	Guard	Notre Dame	1968	Bill Stanfill	Tackle	Georgia
1949	Ed Bagdon	Guard	Michigan	1969	Mike Reid	Def. tackle	Penn State
1950	Bob Gain	Tackle	Kentucky	1970	Jim Stillwagon ...	Linebacker	Ohio State
1951	Jim Weatherall ..	Tackle	Oklahoma	1971	Larry Jacobson ..	Def. tackle	Nebraska
1952	Dick Modzelewski .	Tackle	Maryland	1972	Rich Glover	Middle guard	Nebraska
1953	J.D. Roberts.....	Guard	Oklahoma	1973	John Hicks......	Guard	Ohio State
1954	Bill Brooks	Guard	Arkansas	1974	Randy White	Defensive end	Maryland
1955	Calvin Jones	Guard	Iowa	1975	Leroy Selmon ...	Def. tackle	Oklahoma
1956	Jim Parker	Guard	Ohio State	1976	Ross Browner ...	Defensive end	Notre Dame
1957	Alex Karras	Tackle	Iowa	1977	Brad Shearer....	Def. tackle	Texas
1958	Zeke Smith	Guard	Auburn	1978	Greg Roberts....	Guard	Oklahoma
1959	Mike McGee.....	Tackle	Duke	1979	Jim Ritcher.....	Center	N.C. State
1960	Tom Brown	Guard	Minnesota	1980	Mark May......	Offens. Tackle	Pittsburgh
1961	Merlin Olsen	Tackle	Utah State	1981	Dave Rimington .	Center	Nebraska
1962	Bobby Bell	Tackle	Minnesota	1982	Dave Rimington .	Center	Nebraska
1963	Scott Appleton ..	Tackle	Texas	1983	Dean Steinkuhler .	Guard	Nebraska
1964	Steve Delong	Tackle	Tennessee	1984	Bruce Smith	Def. lineman	Va. Tech
1965	Tommy Nobis ...	Guard	Texas				

ALL-AMERICA COLLEGE FOOTBALL TEAM: 1984

FOOTBALL WRITERS ASSOCIATION OF AMERICA

OFFENSIVE TEAM	POSITIONS	DEFENSIVE TEAM	POSITIONS
Jerry Rice, Mississippi Valley	Wide Receiver	Tony Castillas, Oklahoma............	Lineman
David Williams, Illinois	Wide Receiver	Tony DeGrate, Texas.................	Lineman
Mark Traynowicz, Nebraska	Center	Ron Holmes, Washington	Lineman
Lornas Brown, Florida...............	Lineman	Bruce Smith, Virginia Tech	Lineman
Bill Fralic, Pittsburgh	Lineman	Duane Bickett, Southern Cal..........	Linebacker
Jim Lachey, Ohio State	Lineman	Jack Del Rio, Southern Cal.	Linebacker
Carlton Walker, Utah................	Lineman	James Seawright, South Carolina	Linebacker
Doug Flutie, Boston College	Quarterback	Bret Clark, Nebraska	Back
Keith Byars, Ohio State.............	Running Back	David Fulcher, Arizona State	Back
Kenneth Davis, Texas Christian	Running Back	Jerry Gray, Texas..................	Back
Reuben Mayes, Washington State.....	Running Back	Richard Johnson, Wisconsin	Back
Kevin Butler, Georgia	Placekicker	Ricky Anderson, Vanderbilt	Punter

GOLF

U.S. PROFESSIONAL GOLF ASSOCIATION CHAMPIONS

Year	Champion	Year	Champion	Year	Champion	Year	Champion
1916	Jim Barnes	1935	Johnny Revolta	1949	Sam Snead	1962	Gary Player
1917–18	No play	1936–37	Denny Shute	1950	Chandler Harper	1963	Jack Nicklaus
1919	Jim Barnes	1938	Paul Runyan	1951	Sam Snead	1964	Bobby Nichols
1920	Jock Hutchison	1939	Henry Picard	1952	Jim Turnesa	1965	Dave Marr
1921	Walter Hagen	1940	Byron Nelson	1953	Walter Burkemo	1966	Al Geiberger
1922–23	Gene Sarazen	1941	Victor Ghezzi	1954	Chick Harbert	1967	Don January
1924–27	Walter Hagen	1942	Sam Snead	1955	Doug Ford	1968	Julius Boros
1928–29	Leo Diegel	1943	No play	1956	Jack Burke	1969	Ray Floyd
1930	Tommy Armour	1944	Bob Hamilton	1957	Lionel Hebert	1970	Dave Stockton
1931	Tom Creavy	1945	Byron Nelson	1958	Dow Finsterwald	1971	Jack Nicklaus
1932	Olin Dutra	1946	Ben Hogan	1959	Bob Rosburg	1972	Gary Player
1933	Gene Sarazen	1947	Jim Ferrier	1960	Jay Hebert	1973	Jack Nicklaus
1934	Paul Runyan	1948	Ben Hogan	1961	Jerry Barber	1974	Lee Trevino

Year	Champion
1975	Jack Nicklaus
1976	Dave Stockton
1977	Lanny Wadkins
1978	John Mahaffey
1979	David Graham
1980	Jack Nicklaus
1981	Larry Nelson
1982	Ray Floyd
1983	Hal Sutton
1984	Lee Trevino
1985	Hubert Green

U.S. WOMEN'S OPEN GOLF CHAMPIONS

Year	Champion	Year	Champion	Year	Champion	Year	Champion
1946	Patty Berg	1955	Fay Crocker	1965	Carol Mann	1976	JoAnne Carner [1]
1947	Betty Jameson	1956	Kathy Cornelius [1]	1966	Sandra Spuzich	1977–78	Hollis Stacy
1948	Babe Didrikson Zaharias	1957	Betsy Rawls	1967	Catherine Lacoste [2]	1979	Jerilyn Britz
1949	Louise Suggs	1958–59	Mickey Wright	1968	Susie Maxwell Berning	1980	Amy Alcott
1950	Babe Didrikson Zaharias	1960	Betsy Rawls	1969–70	Donna Caponi	1981	Pat Bradley
1951	Betsy Rawls	1961	Mickey Wright	1971	JoAnne Carner	1982	Janet Alex
1952	Louise Suggs	1962	Murie Lindstrom	1972–73	Susie M. Berning	1983	Jan Stephenson
1953	Betsy Rawls [1]	1963	Mary Mills	1974	Sandra Haynie	1984	Hollis Stacy
1954	Babe Didrikson Zaharias	1964	Mickey Wright [1]	1975	Sandra Palmer	1985	Kathy Baker

MASTERS GOLF CHAMPIONS

Year	Champion	Year	Champion	Year	Champion	Year	Champion
1934	Horton Smith	1949	Sam Snead	1961	Gary Player	1974	Gary Player
1935	Gene Sarazen	1950	Jimmy Demaret	1962	Arnold Palmer	1975	Jack Nicklaus
1936	Horton Smith	1951	Ben Hogan	1963	Jack Nicklaus	1976	Ray Floyd
1937	Byron Nelson	1952	Sam Snead	1964	Arnold Palmer	1977	Tom Watson
1938	Henry Picard	1953	Ben Hogan	1965–66	Jack Nicklaus	1978	Gary Player
1939	Ralph Guldahl	1954	Sam Snead	1967	Gay Brewer	1979	Fuzzy Zoeller [1]
1940	Jimmy Demaret	1955	Cary Middlecoff	1968	Bob Goalby	1980	Seve Ballesteros
1941	Craig Wood	1956	Jack Burke	1969	George Archer	1981	Tom Watson
1942	Byron Nelson	1957	Doug Ford	1970	Billy Casper	1982	Craig Stadler[1]
1946	Herman Keiser	1958	Arnold Palmer	1971	Charles Coody	1983	Seve Ballesteros
1947	Jimmy Demaret	1959	Art Wall Jr.	1972	Jack Nicklaus	1984	Ben Crenshaw
1948	Claude Harmon	1960	Arnold Palmer	1973	Tommy Aaron	1985	Bernhard Langer

PGA TOUR LEADING MONEY WINNERS

Year	Winner	Amount	Year	Winner	Amount	Year	Winner	Amount
1940	Ben Hogan	$ 10,655	1956	Ted Kroll	$ 72,836	1971	Jack Nicklaus	$244,491
1941	Ben Hogan	18,358	1957	Dick Mayer	65,835	1972	Jack Nicklaus	320,542
1942	Ben Hogan	13,143	1958	Arnold Palmer	42,407	1973	Jack Nicklaus	308,362
1944	Byron Nelson	37,968	1959	Art Wall Jr.	53,168	1974	Johnny Miller	353,201
1945	Byron Nelson	63,336	1960	Arnold Palmer	75,263	1975	Jack Nicklaus	323,149
1946	Ben Hogan	42,556	1961	Gary Player	64,540	1976	Jack Nicklaus	266,438
1947	Jimmy Demaret	27,937	1962	Arnold Palmer	81,448	1977	Tom Watson	310,653
1948	Ben Hogan	32,112	1963	Arnold Palmer	128,230	1978	Tom Watson	362,429
1949	Sam Snead	31,594	1964	Jack Nicklaus	113,285	1979	Tom Watson	462,636
1950	Sam Snead	35,759	1965	Jack Nicklaus	140,752	1980	Tom Watson	530,808
1951	Lloyd Mangrum	26,089	1966	Billy Casper	121,945	1981	Tom Kite	375,699
1952	Julius Boros	37,033	1967	Jack Nicklaus	188,988	1982	Craig Stadler	446,462
1953	Lew Worsham	34,002	1968	Billy Casper	205,169	1983	Hal Sutton	426,668
1954	Bob Toski	65,820	1969	Frank Beard	175,224	1984	Tom Watson	476,260
1955	Julius Boros	65,122	1970	Lee Trevino	150,037	1985	Curtis Strange	542,321

LPGA TOUR LEADING MONEY WINNERS

Year	Winner	Amount	Year	Winner	Amount	Year	Winner	Amount
1953	Louise Suggs	$ 19,816	1964	Mickey Wright	$29,800	1975	Sandra Palmer	$ 94,805
1954	Patty Berg	16,011	1965	Kathy Whitworth	28,658	1976	Judy Rankin	150,734
1955	Patty Berg	16,492	1966	Kathy Whitworth	33,518	1977	Judy Rankin	122,890
1956	Marlene Hagge	20,235	1967	Kathy Whitworth	32,938	1978	Nancy Lopez	189,813
1957	Patty Berg	16,272	1968	Kathy Whitworth	48,380	1979	Nancy Lopez	215,987
1958	Beverly Hanson	12,640	1969	Carol Mann	49,153	1980	Beth Daniel	231,000
1959	Betsy Rawls	26,774	1970	Kathy Whitworth	30,235	1981	Beth Daniel	206,978
1960	Louise Suggs	16,892	1971	Kathy Whitworth	41,182	1982	JoAnne Carner	310,399
1961	Mickey Wright	22,236	1972	Kathy Whitworth	65,064	1983	JoAnne Carner	291,404
1962	Mickey Wright	21,641	1973	Kathy Whitworth	82,864	1984	Betsy King	266,771
1963	Mickey Wright	31,270	1974	JoAnne Carner	87,094	1985	Nancy Lopez	400,222

[1] Won in playoff. [2] Amateur golfer.

U.S. OPEN GOLF CHAMPIONS

YEAR	CHAMPION	SCORE [1]	YEAR	CHAMPION	SCORE [1]	YEAR	CHAMPION	SCORE [1]
1895	Horace Rawlins ..	173	1925	Willie Macfarlane	291*	1957	Dick Mayer......	282*
1896	James Foulis	152	1926	Bobby Jones [2]...	293	1958	Tommy Bolt	283
1897	Joe Lloyd	162	1927	Tommy Armour .	301*	1959	Billy Casper	282
1898	Fred Herd	328	1928	Johnny Farrell ...	294*	1960	Arnold Palmer ...	280
1899	Willie Smith	315	1929	Bobby Jones [2]...	294*	1961	Gene Littler	281
1900	Harry Vardon	313	1930	Bobby Jones [2]...	287	1962	Jack Nicklaus ...	283*
1901	Willie Anderson..	331*	1931	Billie Burke	292*	1963	Julius Boros.....	293*
1902	L. Auchterlonie ..	307	1932	Gene Sarazen ...	286	1964	Ken Venturi	278
1903	Willie Anderson..	307*	1933	Johnny Goodman[2]	287	1965	Gary Player	282*
1904	Willie Anderson..	303	1934	Olin Dutra	293	1966	Billy Casper	278*
1905	Willie Anderson..	314	1935	Sam Parks Jr. ...	299	1967	Jack Nicklaus ...	275
1906	Alex Smith	295	1936	Tony Manero	282	1968	Lee Trevino	275
1907	Alex Ross	302	1937	Ralph Guldahl ...	281	1969	Orville Moody ...	281
1908	Fred McLeod	322*	1938	Ralph Guldahl ...	284	1970	Tony Jacklin	281
1909	George Sargent..	290	1939	Byron Nelson ...	284*	1971	Lee Trevino	280*
1910	Alex Smith	298*	1940	Lawson Little	287*	1972	Jack Nicklaus ...	290
1911	John McDermott.	307*	1941	Craig Wood	284	1973	Johnny Miller....	279
1912	John McDermott.	294	1942–45	No match		1974	Hale Irwin.......	287
1913	Francis Ouimet [2]	304	1946	Lloyd Mangrum..	284*	1975	Lou Graham.....	287*
1914	Walter Hagen ...	290	1947	Lew Worsham ...	282*	1976	Jerry Pate	277
1915	J. D. Travers [2]...	297	1948	Ben Hogan	276	1977	Hubert Green ...	278
1916	Chick Evans Jr. [2]	286	1949	Cary Middlecoff .	286	1978	Andrew North ...	285
1917–18	No match		1950	Ben Hogan	287*	1979	Hale Irwin.......	284
1919	Walter Hagen ...	301*	1951	Ben Hogan	287	1980	Jack Nicklaus ...	272
1920	Edward Ray	295	1952	Julius Boros.....	281	1981	David Graham ...	273
1921	Jim Barnes	289	1953	Ben Hogan	283	1982	Tom Watson	282
1922	Gene Sarazen ...	288	1954	Ed Furgol	284	1983	Larry Nelson	280
1923	Bobby Jones [2]...	296*	1955	Jack Fleck	287*	1984	Fuzzy Zoeller....	276*
1924	Cyril Walker	297	1956	Cary Middlecoff .	281	1985	Andy North	279

* Tie for first place, playoff determined champion. [1] For 72 holes except for 1895-97 when 36 holes were played. [2] Amateur.

BRITISH OPEN GOLF CHAMPIONS

1860	Willie Park Sr.	1888	Jack Burns	1909	J. H. Taylor	1934	Henry Cotton	1963	Bob Charles
1861–62	Tom Morris Sr.	1889	Willie Park Jr.	1910	James Braid	1935	Alf Perry	1964	Tony Lema *
1863	Willie Park Sr.	1890	John Ball	1911	Harry Vardon	1936	Alf Padgham	1965	Peter Thomson
1864	Tom Morris Sr.	1891	Hugh Kirkaldy	1912	Ted Ray	1937	Henry Cotton	1966	Jack Nicklaus *
1865	A. L. Strath	1892	H. H. Hilton	1913	J. H. Taylor	1938	R.A.Whitecombe	1967	R. de Vicenzo
1866	Willie Park Sr.	1893	W. Auchterlonie	1914	Harry Vardon	1939	Richard Burton	1968	Gary Player
1867	Tom Morris Sr.	1894	J. H. Taylor	1915–19	No Play	1940–45	No play	1969	Tony Jacklin
1868–70	Tom Morris Jr.	1895	J. H. Taylor	1920	George Duncan	1946	Sam Snead *	1970	Jack Nicklaus *
1871	No play	1896	Harry Vardon	1921	Jock Hutchison *	1947	Fred Daly	1971–72	Lee Trevino *
1872	Tom Morris Jr.	1897	H. H. Hilton	1922	Walter Hagen *	1948	Henry Cotton	1973	Tom Weiskopf *
1873	Tom Kidd	1898	Harry Vardon	1923	Arthur Havers	1949	Bobby Locke	1974	Gary Player
1874	Mungo Park	1899	Harry Vardon	1924	Walter Hagen *	1950	Bobby Locke	1975	Tom Watson *
1875	Willie Park Sr.	1900	J. H. Taylor	1925	Jim Barnes *	1951	Max Faulkner	1976	Johnny Miller *
1876	Bob Martin	1901	James Braid	1926	Bobby Jones *	1952	Bobby Locke	1977	Tom Watson *
1877–79	Jamie Anderson	1902	Alex Herd	1927	Bobby Jones *	1953	Ben Hogan *	1978	Jack Nicklaus *
1880–82	Bob Ferguson	1903	Harry Vardon	1928	Walter Hagen *	1954–56	Peter Thomson	1979	S. Ballesteros
1883	W. L. Fernie	1904	Jack White	1929	Walter Hagen *	1957	Bobby Locke	1980	Tom Watson *
1884	Jack Simpson	1905	James Braid	1930	Bobby Jones *	1958	Peter Thomson	1981	Bill Rogers *
1885	Bob Martin	1906	James Braid	1931	Tommy Armour *	1959	Gary Player	1982–83	Tom Watson *
1886	D. L. Brown	1907	Arnaud Massy	1932	Gene Sarazen *	1960	Kel Nagle	1984	S. Ballesteros
1887	Willie Park Jr.	1908	James Braid	1933	Denny Shute *	1961–62	Arnold Palmer *	1985	Sandy Lyle

* American.

RYDER CUP INTERNATIONAL PROFESSIONAL GOLF MATCH

1927	United States 9½, Britain 2½	1961	United States 14½, Britain 9½
1929	Britain 7, United States 5	1963	United States 23, Britain 9
1931	United States 9, Britain 3	1965	United States 19½, Britain 12½
1933	Britain 6½, United States 5½	1967	United States 23½, Britain 8½
1935	United States 9, Britain 3	1969	United States 16, Britain 16 (tie)
1937	United States 8, Britain 4	1971	United States 18½, Britain 13½
1939–45	No matches	1973	United States 18, Britain 13
1947	United States 11, Britain 1	1975	United States 21, Britain 11
1949	United States 7, Britain 5	1977	United States 12½, Britain 7½
1951	United States 9½, Britain 2½	1979	United States 17, Britain 11
1953	United States 6½, Britain 5½	1981	United States 18½, Britain 9½
1955	United States 8, Britain 4	1983	United States 14½, Britain 13½
1957	Britain 7½, United States 4½	1985	Britain 16½, United States 11½
1959	United States 8½, Britain 3½		

UNITED STATES AMATEUR GOLF CHAMPIONS: MEN

Robert T. "Bobby" Jones Jr., generally regarded as America's greatest amateur golfer, won the USGA amateur championship a record five times in 1924, 1925, 1927, 1928, and 1930.

1895 C. MacDonald	1916 Chick Evans, Jr.	1934 Lawson Little	1953 Gene Littler	1969 Steve Melnyk
1896–98 H. Whigham	1917–18 No play	1935 Lawson Little	1954 Arnold Palmer	1970 Lanny Wadkins
1899 H. Harriman	1919 Davidson Herron	1936 John Fischer	1955 Harvie Ward	1971 Gary Cowan
1900–01 Walter Travis	1920 Chick Evans, Jr.	1937 John Goodman	1956 Harvie Ward	1972 Vinny Giles
1902 Louis James	1921 Jesse Guilford	1938 Willie Turnesa	1957 Hillman Robbins	1973 Craig Stadler
1903 Walter Travis	1922 Jess Sweetser	1939 Bud Ward	1958 Charles Coe	1974 Jerry Pate
1904–05 Chandler Egan	1923 Max Marston	1940 Dick Chapman	1959 Jack Nicklaus	1975 Fred Ridley
1906 Eben Byers	1924 Bobby Jones	1941 Bud Ward	1960 Deane Beman	1976 Bill Sander
1907 Jerry Travers	1925 Bobby Jones	1942–45 No play	1961 Jack Nicklaus	1977 John Faught
1908 Jerry Travers	1926 George Von Elm	1946 Ted Bishop	1962 Labron Harris Jr.	1978 John Cook
1909 Robert Gardner	1927–28 Bobby Jones	1947 Skee Riegel	1963 Deane Beman	1979 Mark O'Meara
1910 William Fownes Jr.	1929 Harrison Johnston	1948 Willie Turnesa	1964 Bill Campbell	1980 Hal Sutton
1911 Harold Hilton	1930 Bobby Jones	1949 Charles Coe	1965 Robert Murphy Jr.	1981 Nathaniel Crosby
1912–13 Jerry Travers	1931 Francis Ouimet	1950 Sam Urzetta	1966 Gary Cowan	1982–83 Jay Sigel
1914 Francis Ouimet	1932 Ross Somerville	1951 Billy Maxwell	1967 Bob Dickson	1984 Scott Verplank
1915 Robert Gardner	1933 George Dunlap, Jr.	1952 Jack Westland	1968 Bruce Fleisher	1985 Sam Randolph

NATIONAL COLLEGIATE ATHLETIC ASSOCIATION GOLF CHAMPIONS

1897 Louis Bayard Jr., Princeton	1928 Maurice McCarthy, Georgetown	1957 Rex Baxter Jr., Houston
1898 James Reid Jr., Yale	1929 Tom Aycock, Yale	1958 Phil Rodgers, Houston
James Curtis, Harvard	1930–31 George Dunlap Jr., Princeton	1959–60 Dick Crawford, Houston
1899 Percy Pyne, Princeton	1932 J. W. Fischer, Michigan	1961 Jack Nicklaus, Ohio State
1901 H. Lindsley, Harvard	1933 Walter Emery, Oklahoma	1962 Kermit Zarley, Houston
1902 Charles Hitchcock Jr., Yale	1934 Charles Yates, Georgia Tech	1963 R. H. Sikes, Arkansas
1903 F. O. Reinhart, Princeton	1935 Ed White, Texas	1964 Terry Small, San Jose State
1904 A. L. White, Harvard	1936 Charles Kocsis, Michigan	1965 Marty Fleckman, Houston
1905 Robert Abbott, Yale	1937 Fred Haas Jr., Louisiana State	1966 Bob Murphy, Florida
1906 W. E. Clow Jr., Yale	1938 John Burke, Georgetown	1967 Hale Irwin, Colorado
1907 Ellis Knowles, Yale	1939 Vincent D'Antoni, Tulane	1968 Grier Jones, Oklahoma State
1908 H. H. Wilder, Harvard	1940 Dixon Brooke, Virginia	1969 Bob Clark, Los Angeles State
1909 Albert Seckel, Princeton	1941 Earl Stewart, Louisiana State	1970 John Mahaffey, Houston
1910 Robert Hunter, Yale	1942 Frank Tatum Jr., Stanford	1971 Ben Crenshaw, Texas
1911 George Stanley, Yale	1943 Wallace Ulrich, Carleton	1972 Ben Crenshaw, Texas
1912 F. C. Davison, Harvard	1944 Louis Lick, Minnesota	Tom Kite, Texas
1913 Nathaniel Wheeler, Yale	1945 John Lorms, Ohio State	1973 Ben Crenshaw, Texas
1914 Edward Allis, Harvard	1946 George Hamer, Georgia	1974 Curtis Strange, Wake Forest
1915 Francis Blossom, Yale	1947 Dave Barclay, Michigan	1975 Jay Haas, Wake Forest
1916 J. W. Hubbell, Harvard	1948 Bob Harris, San Jose State	1976–77 Scott Simpson, USC
1917–18 No play	1949 Harvie Ward, North Carolina	1978 David Edwards, Oklahoma State
1919 A. L. Walker Jr., Columbia	1950 Fred Wampler, Purdue	1979 Gary Hallberg, Wake Forest
1920 Jess Sweetser, Yale	1951 Tom Nieporte, Ohio State	1980 Jay Don Blake, Utah State
1921 Simpson Dean, Princeton	1952 Jim Vickers, Oklahoma	1981 Ron Commans, So. California
1922 Pollack Boyd, Dartmouth	1953 Earl Moeller, Oklahoma State	1982 Billy Brown, Houston
1923–24 Dexter Cummings, Yale	1954 Hillman Robbins, Memphis State	1983 Jim Carter, Arizona State
1925–26 Fred Lamprecht, Yale	1955 Joe Campbell, Purdue	1984 John Inman, North Carolina
1927 Watts Gunn, Georgia Tech	1956 Rick Jones, Ohio State	1985 Clark Burroughs, Ohio State

BRITISH AMATEUR GOLF CHAMPIONS

The oldest golf tournament for amateurs is the British Amateur Tournament, played since 1885. It has been won 18 times by American amateur golfers, most recently in 1979.

1885 A. F. MacFie	1903 R. Maxwell	1925 Robert Harris	1948 Frank Stranahan*	1966 Bobby Cole
1886 H. G. Hutchinson	1904 W. J. Travis	1926 Jess Sweetser*	1949 Sam McCready	1967 Bob Dickson*
1987 H. G. Hutchinson	1905 A. G. Barry	1927 W. Tweddell	1950 Frank Stranahan*	1968–70 Mike Bonallack
1888 John Ball	1906 James Robb	1928 T. P. Perkins	1951 Dick Chapman*	1971 Steve Melnyk*
1889 J. E. Laidlay	1907 John Ball	1929 Cyril Tolley	1952 Harvie Ward*	1972 Trevor Homer
1890 John Ball	1908 E. A. Lassen	1930 Bobby Jones*	1953 Joseph Carr	1973 Dick Siderowf*
1891 J. E. Laidlay	1909 R. Maxwell	1931 E. Martin Smith	1954 Doug Bachli	1974 Trevor Homer
1892 John Ball	1910 John Ball	1932 J. De Forest	1955 Joseph Conrad*	1975 Marvin M. Giles
1893 P. L. Anderson	1911 H. H. Hilton	1933 Michael Scott	1956 John Beharrell	1976 Dick Siderowf*
1894 John Ball	1912 John Ball	1934 Lawson Little*	1957 Reid Jack	1977–78 Peter McEvoy
1895 L. M. B. Melville	1913 H. H. Hilton	1935 Lawson Little*	1958 Joseph Carr	1979 Jay Sigel*
1896 F. G. Tait	1914 J. L. C. Jenkins	1936 H. Thompson	1959 Deane Beman*	1980 David Evans
1897 A. J. T. Allan	1915–19 No play	1937 Robert Sweeny Jr.	1960 Joseph Carr	1981 Phillipe Ploujoux
1898 F. G. Tait	1920 Cyril J. Tolley	1938 C. R. Yates*	1961 Michael Bonallack	1982 Martin Thompson
1899 John Ball	1921 W. I. Hunter	1939 Alex Kyle	1962 Richard Davies*	1983 Philip Parkins
1900 H. H. Hilton	1922 E. W. Holderness	1940–45 No play	1963 Michael Lunt	1984 Jose Maria Olazabal
1901 H. H. Hilton	1923 R. Wethered	1946 James Bruen	1964 Gordon Clark	1985 Garth McGimpsey
1902 C. Hutchings	1924 E. W. Holderness	1947 Willie Turnesa*	1965 Mike Bonallack	

* United States golfer.

U.S. AMATEUR GOLF CHAMPIONS: WOMEN

The United States Golf Association (USGA) held its first amateur women's championship in 1895. Glenna Collett Vare won the championship six times between 1922 and 1935.

1895	Mrs. C. S. Brown	1921	Marion Hollins	1948	Grace Lenczyk	1967	Lou Dill
1896–98	Beatrix Hoyt	1922	Glenna Collett	1949	Dorothy Porter	1968	JoAnne Carner
1899	Ruth Underhill	1923	Edith Cummings	1950	Beverly Hanson	1969	Catherine Lacoste
1900	Frances Griscom	1924	Dorothy Campbell Hurd	1951	Dorothy Kirby	1970	Martha Wilkinson
1901–02	Genevieve Hecker	1925	Glenna Collett	1952	Jacqueline Pung	1971	Laura Baugh
1903	Bessie Anthony	1926	Helen Stetson	1953	Mary Lena Faulk	1972	Mary Budke
1904	Georgiana Bishop	1927	Miriam Burns Horn	1954	Barbara Romack	1973	Carol Semple
1905	Pauline Mackay	1928–30	Glenna Collett	1955	Patricia Lesser	1974	Cynthia Rill
1906	Harriot Curtis	1931	Helen Hicks	1956	Marlene Stewart	1975	Beth Daniel
1907	Margaret Curtis	1932–34	Virginia Van Wie	1957	JoAnne Gunderson	1976	Donna Horton
1908	Kate Harley	1935	Glenna Collett Vare	1958	Anne Quast	1977	Beth Daniel
1909–10	Dorothy Campbell	1936	Pamela Barton	1959	Barbara McIntire	1978	Cathy Sherk
1911–12	Margaret Curtis	1937	Mrs. J. A. Page Jr.	1960	JoAnne Gunderson	1979	Carolyn Hill
1913	Gladys Ravenscroft	1938	Patty Berg	1961	Anne Quast Decker	1980	Juli Simpson Inkster
1914	Mrs. H. A. Jackson	1939–40	Betty Jameson	1962	JoAnne Gunderson	1981	Juli Simpson Inkster
1915	Mrs. C. H. Vanderbeck	1941	Mrs. Frank Newell	1963	Anne Quast Welts	1982	Juli Simpson Inkster
1916	Alexa Stirling	1942–45	No play	1964	Barbara McIntire	1983	Joanne Pacillo
1917–18	No play	1946	Babe Zaharias	1965	Jean Ashley	1984	Deb Richard
1919–20	Alexa Stirling	1947	Louise Suggs	1966	JoAnne Carner	1985	Michiko Hattori

CURTIS CUP INTERNATIONAL WOMEN'S GOLF TEAM MATCH

The United States has dominated this series of matches between women amateur golf teams representing the U.S. and Britain. The matches are played every two years in even years.

1932	United States 5½, Britain 3½	1956	Britain 5, United States 4	1972	United States 10, Britain 8
1934	United States 6½, Britain 2½	1958*	Britain 4½, United States 4½	1974	United States 13, Britain 5
1936*	United States 4½, Britain 4½	1960	United States 6½, Britain 2½	1976	United States 11½, Britain 8½
1938	United States 5½, Britain 3½	1962	United States 8, Britain 1	1978	United States 12, Britain 6
1948	United States 6½, Britain 2½	1964	United States 10½, Britain 7½	1980	United States 13, Britain 5
1950	United States 7½, Britain 1½	1966	United States 13, Britain 5	1982	United States 14½, Britain 3½
1952	Britain 5, United States 4	1968	United States 10½, Britain 7½	1984	United States 9½, Britain 8½
1954	United States 6, Britain 3	1970	United States 11½, Britain 6½		

* Tie.

WALKER CUP INTERNATIONAL MEN'S GOLF TEAM MATCH

The oldest international amateur golf team match, the Walker Cup competition is played between teams representing the United States and Britain. The cup was presented by G. Herbert Walker, former president of the United States Golf Association, and the first competition was held in 1922. Since 1924 the match has taken place every two years.

1922	United States 8; Britain 4	National Golf Links of America, Southampton, N.Y.
1923	United States 6; Britain 5; one match halved	St. Andrews, Scotland
1924	United States 9; Britain 3	Garden City Golf Club, Garden City, N.Y.
1926	United States 6; Britain 5; one match halved	St. Andrews, Scotland
1928	United States 11; Britain 1	Chicago Golf Club, Wheaton, Ill.
1930	United States 10; Britain 2	Royal St. George's Golf Club, Sandwich, England
1932	United States 8; Britain 1; three matches halved	The Country Club, Brookline, Mass.
1934	United States 9; Britain 2; one match halved	St. Andrews, Scotland
1936	United States 9; Britain 0; three matches halved	Pine Valley Golf Club, Clementon, N.J.
1938	Britain 7; United States 4; one match halved	St. Andrews, Scotland
1940–45	No competition because of World War II	
1947	United States 8; Britain 4	St. Andrews, Scotland
1949	United States 10; Britain 2	Winged Foot Golf Club, Mamaroneck, N.Y.
1951	United States 6; Britain 3; three matches halved	Birkdale Golf Club, Southport, England
1953	United States 9; Britain 3	Kittansett Club, Marion, Mass.
1955	United States 10; Britain 2	St. Andrews, Scotland
1957	United States 8; Britain 3; one match halved	Minikahda Club, Minneapolis, Minn.
1959	United States 9; Britain 3	Muirfield, Scotland
1961	United States 11; Britain 1	Seattle Golf Club, Seattle, Wash.
1963	United States 12; Britain 8; four matches halved	Turnberry, Scotland
1965	United States 11; Britain 11	Baltimore Country Club, Baltimore, Md.
1967	United States 13; Britain 7	Royal St. George's Golf Club, Sandwich, England
1969	United States 10; Britain 8	Milwaukee Country Club, Milwaukee, Wis.
1971	Britain 13; United States 11	St. Andrews, Scotland
1973	United States 14; Britain 10	The Country Club, Brookline, Mass.
1975	United States 15½; Britain 8½	St. Andrews, Scotland
1977	United States 16; Britain 8	Shinnecock Hills Golf Club, Southampton, N.Y.
1979	United States 15½; Britain 8½	Muirfield, Scotland
1981	United States 15; Britain 9	Pebble Beach, Calif.
1983	United States 13½; Britain 10½	Royal Liverpool Club, Hoylake, England
1985	United States 13; Britain 11	Pine Valley Golf Club, Pine Valley, N.J.

GYMNASTICS

NATIONAL COLLEGIATE ATHLETIC ASSOCIATION GYMNASTIC CHAMPIONS

NCAA TEAM CHAMPIONS: MEN

1976	Penn State	1979	Nebraska	1984	UCLA
1977	Indiana St.—Oklahoma	1980-83	Nebraska	1985	Ohio State
1978	Oklahoma				

NCAA INDIVIDUAL CHAMPIONS (ALL-AROUND): MEN

1976	Peter Kormann, S. Conn.	1979	Kurt Thomas, Indiana St.	1984	Mitch Gaylord, UCLA
1977	Kurt Thomas, Indiana St.	1980–81	Jim Hartung, Nebraska	1985	Wes Suter, Nebraska
1978	Bart Conner, Oklahoma	1982–83	Peter Vidmar, UCLA		

FLOOR EXERCISE: MEN

1976	Bob Robbins, Colorado State	1980	Steve Elliott, Nebraska	1983	David Branch, Arizona State
1977	Ron Gallimore, Louisiana State	1981	James Yuhashi, Oregon		Don Hinton, Arizona State
1978	Curtis Austin, Iowa State	1982	Steve Elliott, Nebraska		Scott Johnson, Nebraska
1979	Mike Wilson, Oklahoma		Jim Mikus, Nebraska	1984	Kevin Eckburg, Northern Illinois
	Bart Conner, Oklahoma			1985	Wes Suter, Nebraska

POMMEL HORSE (SIDE HORSE): MEN

1976	Ted Marcy, Stanford	1980	David Stoldt, Illinois	1983	Doug Kieso, Northern Illinois
1977	Chuck Walter, New Mexico	1981	Steve Jennings, New Mexico	1984	Tim Daggett, UCLA
1978–79	Mike Burke, N. Illinois	1982	Peter Vidmar, UCLA	1985	Tony Pineda, UCLA

RINGS: MEN

1976	Doug Wood, Iowa State	1980	Jim Hartung, Nebraska	1983	Alex Schwartz, UCLA
1977	Doug Wood, Iowa State	1981	Jim Hartung, Nebraska	1984	Tim Daggett, UCLA
1978	Scott McEldowney, Oregon	1982	Jim Hartung, Nebraska	1985	Mark Diab, Iowa State
1979	Kirk Mango, N. Illinois		Alex Schwartz, UCLA		

VAULT: MEN

1976	Sam Shaw, Fullerton State	1979	Leslie Moore, Oklahoma	1983	Chris Riegel, Nebraska
1977	Steve Wejmar, Washington	1980–81	Ron Galimore, Iowa State	1984	Chris Riegel, Nebraska
1978	Ron Galimore, Louisiana St.	1982	Randall Wickstrom, California	1985	Derrick Cornelius, Cortland State

PARALLEL BARS: MEN

1976	Gene Whelan, Penn State	1980	Philip Cahoy, Nebraska	1984	Tim Daggett, UCLA
1977	Kurt Thomas, Indiana State	1981	Philip Cahoy, Nebraska	1985	Dan Hayden, Arizona State
1978	John Corritore, Michigan	1982	Philip Cahoy, Nebraska		Noah Riskin, Ohio State
1979	Kurt Thomas, Indiana St.	1983	Scott Johnson, Nebraska		Seth Riskin, Ohio State

HORIZONTAL BAR: MEN

1976	Tom Beach, California	1980	Philip Cahoy, Nebraska	1984	Charles Lakes, Illinois
1977	John Hart, UCLA	1981	Philip Cahoy, Nebraska	1985	Dan Hayden, Arizona State
1978	Mel Cooley, Washington	1982	Bill Paul, California		Wes Suter, Nebraska
1979	Kurt Thomas, Indiana St.	1983	Scott Johnson, Nebraska		

NCAA TEAM CHAMPIONS: WOMEN

1982	Utah	1984	Utah	
1983	Utah	1985	Utah	

NCAA INDIVIDUAL CHAMPIONS (ALL-AROUND): WOMEN

1982	Sue Stednitz, Utah	1984	Megan McC. Marsden, Utah	
1983	Megan McCunniff, Utah	1985	Penny Hauschild, Alabama	

VAULT: WOMEN

1982	Elaine Alfano, Utah	1984	Megan McC. Marsden, Utah	
1983	Elaine Alfano, Utah	1985	Elaine Alfano, Utah	

UNEVEN PARALLEL BARS: WOMEN

1982	Lisa Shirk, Pittsburgh	1984	Jackie Brummer, Arizona State	
1983	Jeri Cameron, Arizona State	1985	Penny Hauschild, Alabama	

BALANCE BEAM: WOMEN

1982	Sue Stednitz, Utah	1984	Heidi Anderson, Oregon State	
1983	Julie Goewey, Fullerton State	1985	Lisa Zeis, Arizona State	

FLOOR EXERCISE: WOMEN

1982	Mary Ayotte-Law, Oregon State	1984	Maria Anz, Florida	
1983	Kim Neal, Arizona State	1985	Lisa Mitzel, Utah	

HOCKEY

NATIONAL HOCKEY LEAGUE FINAL STANDINGS: 1984–85

TEAM	WON	LOST	TIED	GOALS	POINTS
PRINCE OF WALES CONFERENCE					
Adams Division					
Montreal	41	27	12	309	94
Quebec	41	30	9	323	91
Buffalo.......	38	28	14	290	90
Boston	36	34	10	303	82
Hartford	30	41	9	268	69
Patrick Division					
Philadelphia ..	53	20	7	348	113
Washington ...	46	25	9	322	101
NY Islanders ..	40	34	6	345	86
NY Rangers...	26	44	10	295	62
New Jersey ...	22	48	10	264	54
Pittsburgh	24	51	5	276	53

TEAM	WON	LOST	TIED	GOALS	POINTS
CLARENCE CAMPBELL CONFERENCE					
Norris Division					
St. Louis	37	31	12	299	86
Chicago	38	35	7	309	83
Detroit	27	41	12	313	66
Minnesota	25	43	12	268	62
Toronto	20	52	8	253	48
Smythe Division					
Edmonton	49	20	11	401	109
Winnipeg	43	27	10	358	96
Calgary	41	27	12	363	94
Los Angeles...	34	32	14	339	82
Vancouver	25	46	9	284	59

NHL STANLEY CUP PLAYOFFS: 1985

Championship Series:
Edmonton Oilers won finals and Stanley Cup, defeating Philadelphia Flyers, 4 games to 1.

Conference Finals:
Philadelphia defeated Quebec, 4 games to 2.
Edmonton defeated Chicago, 4 games to 2.

Division Finals:
Philadelphia defeated New York Islanders, 4 games to 1.
Quebec defeated Montreal, 4 games to 3.
Edmonton defeated Winnipeg, 4 games to 0.
Chicago defeated Minnesota, 4 games to 2.

STANLEY CUP NHL CHAMPIONS

Year	Champion	Year	Champion	Year	Champion	Year	Champion
1893	Montreal A.A.A.	1915	Vancouver Millionaires	1938	Chi. Black Hawks	1962	Toronto Maple Leafs
1894	Montreal A.A.A.			1939	Boston Bruins	1963	Toronto Maple Leafs
1895	Montreal Victorias	1916	Montreal Canadiens	1940	New York Rangers	1964	Toronto Maple Leafs
1896	Winnipeg Victorias,	1917	Seattle Met.	1941	Boston Bruins	1965	Montreal Canadiens
	Montreal Victorias	1918	Toronto Arenas	1942	Toronto Maple Leafs	1966	Montreal Canadiens
1897	Montreal Victorias	1919	No decision	1943	Detroit Red Wings	1967	Toronto Maple Leafs
1898	Montreal Victorias	1920	Ottawa Senators	1944	Montreal Canadiens	1968	Montreal Canadiens
1899	Montreal Shamrocks	1921	Ottawa Senators	1945	Toronto Maple Leafs	1969	Montreal Canadiens
1900	Montreal Shamrocks	1922	Toronto St. Pats	1946	Montreal Canadiens	1970	Boston Bruins
1901	Winnipeg Victorias	1923	Ottawa Senators	1947	Toronto Maple Leafs	1971	Montreal Canadiens
1902	Montreal A.A.A.	1924	Montreal Canadiens	1948	Toronto Maple Leafs	1972	Boston Bruins
1903	Ottawa Silver Seven	1925	Victoria Cougars	1949	Toronto Maple Leafs	1973	Montreal Canadiens
1904	Ottawa Silver Seven	1926	Montreal Maroons	1950	Detroit Red Wings	1974	Philadelphia Flyers
1905	Ottawa Silver Seven	1927	Ottawa Senators	1951	Toronto Maple Leafs	1975	Philadelphia Flyers
1906	Montreal Wanderers	1928	New York Rangers	1952	Detroit Red Wings	1976	Montreal Canadiens
1907	Kenora Thistles,	1929	Boston Bruins	1953	Montreal Canadiens	1978	Montreal Canadiens
	Mont. Wanderers	1930	Montreal Canadiens	1954	Detroit Red Wings	1979	Montreal Canadiens
1908	Montreal Wanderers	1931	Montreal Canadiens	1955	Detroit Red Wings	1980	New York Islanders
1909	Ottawa Senators	1932	Toronto Maple Leafs	1956	Montreal Canadiens	1981	New York Islanders
1910	Montreal Wanderers	1933	New York Rangers	1957	Montreal Canadiens	1982	New York Islanders
1911	Ottawa Senators	1934	Chi. Black Hawks	1958	Montreal Canadiens	1983	New York Islanders
1912	Quebec Bulldogs	1935	Montreal Maroons	1959	Montreal Canadiens	1984	Edmonton Oilers
1913	Quebec Bulldogs	1936	Detroit Red Wings	1960	Montreal Canadiens	1985	Edmonton Oilers
1914	Toronto Blueshirts	1937	Detroit Red Wings	1961	Chi. Black Hawks		

NATIONAL HOCKEY LEAGUE LEADING SCORERS: 1984–1985

PLAYER	TEAM	GAMES	GOALS	ASSISTS	POINTS
Wayne Gretzky	Edmonton	80	73	135	208
Jari Kurri	Edmonton	73	71	64	135
Dale Hawerchuk	Winnipeg	80	53	77	130
Marcel Dionne	Los Angeles	80	46	80	126
Paul Coffey	Edmonton	80	37	84	121
Mike Bossy	NY Islanders	76	58	59	117
John Ogrodnick	Detroit	79	55	50	105
Denis Savard	Chicago	79	38	67	105
Bernie Federko	St. Louis	76	30	73	103
Mike Gartner	Washington	80	50	52	102
Brent Sutter	NY Islanders	72	42	60	102
Paul Maclean	Winnipeg	79	41	60	101
Bernie Nicholls	Los Angeles	80	46	54	100
Mario Lemieux	Pittsburgh	73	43	57	100
John Tonelli	NY Islanders	80	42	58	100
Peter Stastny	Quebec	75	32	68	100

NATIONAL HOCKEY LEAGUE TROPHY WINNERS

ART ROSS TROPHY (Leading scorer in regular season)

Year	Winner	Year	Winner	Year	Winner
1917–18	Joe Malone, Montreal	1940–41	Bill Cowley, Boston	1963–64	Stan Mikita, Chicago
1918–19	Newsy Lalonde, Montreal	1941–42	Bryan Hextall, NY Rangers	1964–65	Stan Mikita, Chicago
1919–20	Joe Malone, Quebec	1942–43	Boug Bentley, Chicago	1965–66	Bobby Hull, Chicago
1920–21	Newsy lalonde, Montreal	1943–44	Herbie Cain, Boston	1966–67	Stan Mikita, Chicago
1921–22	Punch Broadbent, Ottawa Senators	1944–45	Elmer Lach, Montreal	1967–68	Stan Mikita, Chicago
1922–23	Babe Dye, Toronto	1945–46	Max Bentley, Chicago	1968–69	Phil Esposito, Boston
1923–24	Cy Denneny, Ottawa Senators	1946–47	Max Bentley, Chicago	1969–70	Bobby Orr, Boston
1924–25	Babe Dye, Toronto	1947–48	Elmer Lach, Montreal	1970–71	Phil Esposito, Boston
1925–26	Nels Stewart, Montreal Maroons	1948–49	Roy Conacher, Chicago	1971–72	Phil Esposito, Boston
1926–27	Bill Cook, NY Rangers	1949–50	Ted Lindsay, Detroit	1972–73	Phil Esposito, Boston
1927–28	Howie Morenz, Montreal	1950–51	Gordie Howe, Detroit	1973–74	Phil Esposito, Boston
1928–29	Ace Bailey, Toronto	1951–52	Gordie Howe, Detroit	1974–75	Bobby Orr, Boston
1929–30	Cooney Weiland, Boston	1952–53	Gordie Howe, Detroit	1975–76	Guy Lafleur, Montreal
1930–31	Howie Morenz, Montreal	1953–54	Gordie Howe, Detroit	1976–77	Guy Lafleur, Montreal
1931–32	Harvey Jackson, Toronto	1954–55	Bernie Geoffrion, Montreal	1977–78	Guy Lafleur, Montreal
1932–33	Bill Cook, NY Rangers	1955–56	Jean Beliveau, Montreal	1978–79	Bryan Trottier, N.Y. Islanders
1933–34	Charlie Conacher, Toronto	1956–57	Gordie Howe, Detroit	1979–80	Marcel Dionne, L.A. Kings
1934–35	Charlie Conacher, Toronto	1957–58	Dickie Moore, Montreal	1980–81	Wayne Gretzky, Edmonton
1935–36	Dave Schriner, NY Americans	1958–59	Dickie Moore, Montreal	1981–82	Wayne Gretzky, Edmonton
1936–37	Dave Schriner, NY Americans	1959–60	Bobby Hull, Chicago	1982–83	Wayne Gretzky, Edmonton
1937–38	Gordie Drillon, Toronto	1960–61	Bernie Geoffrion, Montreal	1983–84	Wayne Gretzky, Edmonton
1938–39	Toe Blake, Montreal	1961–62	Bobby Hull, Chicago	1984–85	Wayne Gretzky, Edmonton
1939–40	Milt Schmidt, Boston	1962–63	Gordie Howe, Detroit		

HART MEMORIAL TROPHY (Most valuable player)

Year	Winner	Year	Winner	Year	Winner
1923–24	Frank Nighbor, Ottawa Senators	1944–45	Elmer Lach, Montreal	1965–66	Bobby Hull, Chicago
1924–25	Billy Burch, Hamilton	1945–46	Max Bentley, Chicago	1966–67	Stan Mikita, Chicago
1925–26	Nels Stewart, Montreal Maroons	1946–47	Maurice Richard, Montreal	1967–68	Stan Mitika, Chicago
1926–27	Herb Gardiner, Montreal	1947–48	Herbert O'Connor, New York	1968–69	Phil Esposito, Boston
1927–28	Howie Morenz, Montreal	1948–49	Sid Abel, Detroit	1969–70	Bobby Orr, Boston
1928–29	Roy Worters, N.Y. Americans	1949–50	Chuck Rayner, New York	1970–71	Bobby Orr, Boston
1929–30	Nels Stewart, Montreal Maroons	1950–51	Milt Schmidt, Boston	1971–72	Bobby Orr, Boston
1930–31	Howie Morenz, Montreal	1951–52	Gordie Howe, Detroit	1972–73	Bobby Clarke, Philadelphia
1931–32	Howie Morenz, Montreal	1952–53	Gordie Howe, Detroit	1973–74	Phil Esposito, Boston
1932–33	Eddie Shore, Boston	1953–54	Al Rollins, Chicago	1974–75	Bobby Clarke, Philadelphia
1933–34	Aurel Joliat, Montreal	1954–55	Ted Kennedy, Detroit	1975–76	Bobby Clarke, Philadelphia
1934–35	Eddie Shore, Boston	1955–56	Jean Beliveau, Montreal	1976–77	Guy Lafleur, Montreal
1935–36	Eddie Shore, Boston	1956–57	Gordie Howe, Detroit	1977–78	Guy Lafleur, Montreal
1936–37	Babe Siebert, Montreal	1957–58	Gordie Howe, Detroit	1978–79	Bryan Trottier, N.Y. Islanders
1937–38	Eddie Shore, Boston	1958–59	Andy Bathgate, New York	1979–80	Wayne Gretzky, Edmonton
1938–39	Toe Blake, Montreal	1959–60	Gordie Howe, Detroit	1980–81	Wayne Gretzky, Edmonton
1939–40	Ebbie Goodfellow, Detroit	1960–61	Bernie Geoffrion, Montreal	1981–82	Wayne Gretzky, Edmonton
1940–41	Bill Cowley, Boston	1961–62	Jacques Plante, Montreal	1982–83	Wayne Gretzky, Edmonton
1941–42	Tom Anderson, N.Y. Americans	1962–63	Gordie Howe, Detroit	1983–84	Wayne Gretzky, Edmonton
1942–43	Bill Cowley, Boston	1963–64	Jean Beliveau, Montreal	1984–85	Wayne Gretzky, Edmonton
1943–44	Babe Pratt, Toronto	1964–65	Bobby Hull, Chicago		

VEZINA TROPHY (Best goalkeeper record)

Year	Winner	Year	Winner	Year	Winner
1926–27	George Hainsworth, Montreal	1949–50	Bill Durnan, Montreal		Glenn Hall, St. Louis
1927–28	George Hainsworth, Montreal	1950–51	Al Rollins, Toronto	1969–70	Tony Esposito, Chicago
1928–29	George Hainsworth, Montreal	1951–52	Terry Sawchuk, Detroit	1970–71	Ed Giacomin and
1929–30	Tiny Thompson, Boston	1952–53	Terry Sawchuk, Detroit		Gilles Villemure, New York
1930–31	Roy Worters, NY Americans	1953–54	Harry Lumley, Toronto	1971–72	Tony Esposito and
1931–32	Chuck Gardiner, Chicago	1954–55	Terry Sawchuk, Detroit		Gary Smith, Chicago
1932–33	Tiny Thompson, Boston	1955–56	Jacques Plante, Montreal	1972–73	Ken Dryden, Montreal
1933–34	Chuck Gardiner, Chicago	1956–57	Jacques Plante, Montreal	1973–74	Tony Esposito, Chicago, and
1934–35	Lorne Chabot, Chicago	1957–58	Jacques Plante, Montreal		Bernie Parent, Philadelphia
1935–36	Tiny Thompson, Boston	1958–59	Jacques Plante, Montreal	1974–75	Bernie Parent, Philadelphia
1936–37	Normie Smith, Detroit	1959–60	Jacques Plante, Montreal	1975–76	Ken Dryden, Montreal
1937–38	Tiny Thompson, Boston	1960–61	Johnny Bower, Toronto	1976–79	Ken Dryden, Montreal, and
1938–39	Frank Brimsek, Boston	1961–62	Jacques Plante, Montreal		Michel Larocque, Montreal
1939–40	Dave Kerr, NY Rangers	1962–63	Glenn Hall, Chicago	1979–80	Bob Suave and
1940–41	Turk Broda, Toronto	1963–64	Charlie Hodge, Montreal		Don Edwards, Buffalo
1941–42	Frank Brimsek, Boston	1964–65	Johnny Bower, Toronto	1980–81	Richard Sevigny, Denis Herron,
1942–43	Johnny Mowers, Detroit		Terry Sawchuk, Toronto		Michel Larocque, Montreal
1943–44	Bill Durnan, Montreal	1965–66	Lorne Worsley, Montreal	1981–82	Bill Smith, N.Y. Islanders
1944–45	Bill Durnan, Montreal		Charlie Hodge, Montreal	1982–83	Pete Peeters, Boston
1945–46	Bill Durnan, Montreal	1966–67	Denis De Jordy and	1983–84	Tom Barrasso, Buffalo
1946–47	Bill Durnan, Montreal		Glenn Hall, Chicago	1984–85	Pelle Lindbergh, Philadelphia
1947–48	Turk Troda, Toronto	1967–68	L. Worsley, R. Vachon, Mont.		
1948–49	Bill Durnan, Montreal	1968–69	Jacques Plante and		

NHL TROPHY WINNERS (continued)

CALDER MEMORIAL TROPHY (Rookie of the year)

Year	Winner	Year	Winner	Year	Winner
1932–33	Carl Voss, Detroit	1950–51	Terry Sawchuk, Detroit	1968–69	Danny Grant, Minnesota
1933–34	Russ Binko, Montreal Maroons	1951–52	Bernie Geoffrion, Montreal	1969–70	Tony Esposito, Chicago
1934–35	Dave Schriner, N.Y. Americans	1952–53	Lorne Worsley, N.Y. Rangers	1970–71	Gil Perreault, Buffalo
1935–36	Mike Karakas, Chicago	1953–54	Camille Henry, N.Y. Rangers	1971–72	Ken Dryden, Montreal
1936–37	Syl Apps, Toronto	1954–55	Ed Litzenberger, Chicago	1972–73	Steve Vickers, New York
1937–38	Cully Dahlstrom, Chicago	1955–56	Glenn Hall, Detroit	1973–74	Denis Potvin, N.Y. Islanders
1938–39	Frank Brimsek, Boston	1956–57	Larry Regan, Boston	1974–75	Eric Vail, Atlanta
1939–40	Kilby MacDonald, N.Y. Rangers	1957–58	Frank Mahovlich, Toronto	1975–76	Bryan Trottier, N.Y. Islanders
1940–41	Johnny Quilty, Montreal	1958–59	Ralph Backstrom, Montreal	1976–77	Willi Plett, Atlanta
1941–42	Grant Warwick, N.Y. Rangers	1959–60	Bill Hay, Chicago	1977–78	Mike Bossy, N.Y. Islanders
1942–43	Gaye Stewart, Toronto	1960–61	Dave Keon, Toronto	1978–79	Bobby Smith, Minnesota
1943–44	Gus Bodnar, Toronto	1961–62	Bobby Rousseau, Montreal	1979–80	Ray Bourque, Montreal
1944–45	Frank McCool, Toronto	1962–63	Kent Douglas, Toronto	1980–81	Peter Stastny, Quebec
1945–46	Edgar Laprade, N.Y. Rangers	1963–64	Jacques Laperriere, Montreal	1981–82	Dale Hawerchuk, Chicago
1946–47	Howie Meeker, Toronto	1964–65	Roger Crozier, Detroit	1982–83	Steve Larmer, Chicago
1947–48	Jim McFadden, Detroit	1965–66	Brit Selby, Toronto	1983–84	Tom Barrasso, Buffalo
1948–49	Pentti Lund, N.Y. Rangers	1966–67	Bobby Orr, Boston	1984–85	Mario Lemieux, Pittsburgh
1949–50	Jack Gelineau, Boston	1967–68	Derek Sanderson, Boston		

LADY BYNG MEMORIAL TROPHY (For skillful and sportsmanlike play)

Year	Winner	Year	Winner	Year	Winner
1924–25	Frank Nighbor, Ottawa Senators	1945–46	Toe Blake, Montreal	1966–67	Stan Mikita, Chicago
1925–26	Frank Nighbor, Ottawa Senators	1946–47	Bobby Bauer, Boston	1967–68	Stan Mikita, Chicago
1926–27	Billy Burch, N.Y. Americans	1947–48	Buddy O'Connor, N.Y. Rangers	1968–69	Alex Delvecchio, Detroit
1927–28	Frank Boucher, N.Y. Rangers	1948–49	Bill Quackenbush, Detroit	1969–70	Phil Goyette, St. Louis
1928–29	Frank Boucher, N.Y. Rangers	1949–50	Edgar Laprade, N.Y. Rangers	1970–71	Johnny Bucyk, Boston
1929–30	Frank Boucher, N.Y. Rangers	1950–51	Red Kelly, Detroit	1971–72	Jean Ratelle, New York
1930–31	Frank Boucher, N.Y. Rangers	1951–52	Sid Smith, Toronto	1972–73	Gil Perreault, Buffalo
1931–32	Joe Primeau, Toronto	1952–53	Red Kelly, Detroit	1973–74	Johnny Bucyk, Boston
1932–33	Frank Boucher, N.Y. Rangers	1953–54	Red Kelly, Detroit	1974–75	Marcel Dionne, Detroit
1933–34	Frank Boucher, N.Y. Rangers	1954–55	Sid Smith, Toronto	1975–76	Jean Ratelle, Boston
1934–35	Frank Boucher, N.Y. Rangers	1955–56	Earl Reibel, Detroit	1976–77	Marcel Dionne, Los Angeles
1935–36	Doc Romnes, Chicago	1956–57	Andy Hebenton, New York	1977–78	Butch Goring, Los Angeles
1936–37	Marty Barry, Detroit	1957–58	Camille Henry, New York	1978–79	Bob MacMillan, Atlanta
1937–38	Gordie Drillon, Toronto	1958–59	Alex Delvecchio, Detroit	1979–80	Wayne Gretzky, Edmonton
1938–39	Clint Smith, N.Y. Rangers	1959–60	Don McKenney, Boston	1980–81	Rick Kehoe, Pittsburgh
1939–40	Bobby Bauer, Boston	1960–61	Red Kelly, Toronto	1981–82	Rick Middleton, Boston
1940–41	Bobby Bauer, Boston	1961–62	Dave Keon, Toronto	1982–83	Mike Bossy, N.Y. Islanders
1941–42	Syl Apps, Toronto	1962–63	Dave Keon, Toronto	1983–84	Mike Bossy, N.Y. Islanders
1942–43	Max Bentley, Chicago	1963–64	Ken Wharram, Chicago	1984–85	Jari Kurri, Edmonton
1943–44	Clint Smith Chicago	1964–65	Bobby Hull, Chicago		
1944–45	Bill Mosienko, Chicago	1965–66	Alex Delvecchio, Detroit		

JAMES NORRIS MEMORIAL TROPHY (Outstanding defenseman)

Year	Winner	Year	Winner	Year	Winner
1953–54	Red Kelly, Detroit	1964–65	Pierre Pilote, Chicago	1975–76	Denis Potvin, N.Y. Islanders
1954–55	Doug Harvey, Montreal	1965–66	J. Laperriere, Montreal	1976–77	Larry Robinson, Montreal
1955–56	Doug Harvey, Montreal	1966–67	Harry Howell, New York	1977–78	Denis Potvin, N.Y. Islanders
1956–57	Doug Harvey, Montreal	1967–68	Bobby Orr, Boston	1978–79	Denis Potvin, N.Y. Islanders
1957–58	Doug Harvey, Montreal	1968–69	Bobby Orr, Boston	1979–80	Larry Robinson, Montreal
1958–59	Tom Johnson, Montreal	1969–70	Bobby Orr, Boston	1980–81	Randy Carlyle, Pittsburgh
1959–60	Doug Harvey, Montreal	1970–71	Bobby Orr, Boston	1981–82	Doug Wilson, Chicago
1960–61	Doug Harvey, Montreal	1971–72	Bobby Orr, Boston	1982–83	Rod Langway, Washington
1961–62	Doug Harvey, N.Y. Rangers	1972–73	Bobby Orr, Boston	1983–84	Rod Langway, Washington
1962–63	Pierre Pilote, Chicago	1973–74	Bobby Orr, Boston	1984–85	Paul Coffey, Edmonton
1963–64	Pierre Pilote, Chicago	1974–75	Bobby Orr, Boston		

CONN SMYTHE TROPHY (Most valuable player in the Stanley Cup playoffs)

Year	Winner	Year	Winner	Year	Winner
1964–65	Jean Beliveau, Montreal	1971–72	Bobby Orr, Boston	1978–79	Bob Gainey, Montreal
1965–66	Roger Crozier, Detroit	1972–73	Yvan Cournoyer, Montreal	1979–80	Bryan Trottier, N.Y. Islanders
1966–67	Dave Keon, Toronto	1973–74	Bernie Parent, Philadelphia	1980–81	Butch Goring, N.Y. Islanders
1967–68	Glenn Hall, St. Louis	1974–75	Bernie Parent, Philadelphia	1981–82	Mike Bossy, N.Y. Islanders
1968–69	Serge Savard, Montreal	1975–76	Reggie Leach, Philadelphia	1982–83	Billy Smith, N.Y. Islanders
1969–70	Bobby Orr, Boston	1976–77	Guy Lafleur, Montreal	1983–84	Mark Messier, Edmonton
1970–71	Ken Dryden, Montreal	1977–78	Larry Robinson, Montreal	1984–85	Wayne Gretzky, Edmonton

NATIONAL HOCKEY LEAGUE PRINCE OF WALES TROPHY WINNERS

Year	Team	Year	Team	Year	Team	Year	Team
1924–25	Montreal Canadiens	1933–34	Detroit Red Wings	1942–43	Detroit Red Wings	1951–52	Detroit Red Wings
1925–26	Montreal Maroons	1934–35	Boston Bruins	1943–44	Montreal Canadiens	1952–53	Detroit Red Wings
1926–27	Ottawa Senators	1935–36	Detroit Red Wings	1944–45	Montreal Canadiens	1953–54	Detroit Red Wings
1927–28	Boston Bruins	1936–37	Detroit Red Wings	1945–46	Montreal Canadiens	1954–55	Detroit Red Wings
1928–29	Boston Bruins	1937–38	Boston Bruins	1946–47	Montreal Canadiens	1955–56	Montreal Canadiens
1929–30	Boston Bruins	1938–39	Boston Bruins	1947–48	Toronto Maple Leafs	1956–57	Detroit Red Wings
1930–31	Boston Bruins	1939–40	Boston Bruins	1948–49	Detroit Red Wings	1957–58	Montreal Canadiens
1931–32	New York Rangers	1940–41	Boston Bruins	1949–50	Detroit Red Wings	1958–59	Montreal Canadiens
1932–33	Boston Bruins	1941–42	New York Rangers	1950–51	Detroit Red Wings	1959–60	Montreal Canadiens

PRINCE OF WALES TROPHY WINNERS *(continued)*

1960–61	Montreal Canadiens	1967–68	Montreal Canadiens	1974–75	Buffalo Sabres	1981–82	New York Islanders
1961–62	Montreal Canadiens	1968–69	Montreal Canadiens	1975–76	Montreal Canadiens	1982–83	New York Islanders
1962–63	Toronto Maple Leafs	1969–70	Chicago Black Hawks	1976–77	Montreal Canadiens	1983–84	New York Islanders
1963–64	Montreal Canadiens	1970–71	Boston Bruins	1977–78	Montreal Canadiens	1984–85	Philadelphia Flyers
1964–65	Detroit Red Wings	1971–72	Boston Bruins	1978–79	Montreal Canadiens		
1965–66	Montreal Canadiens	1972–73	Montreal Canadiens	1979–80	Buffalo Sabres		
1966–67	Chicago Black Hawks	1973–74	Boston Bruins	1980–81	Montreal Canadiens		

NATIONAL HOCKEY LEAGUE CLARENCE S. CAMPBELL BOWL WINNERS

1967–68	Philadelphia Flyers	1973–74	Philadelphia Flyers	1979–80	Philadelphia Flyers
1968–69	St. Louis Blues	1974–75	Philadelphia Flyers	1980–81	New York Islanders
1969–70	St. Louis Blues	1975–76	Philadelphia Flyers	1981–82	Vancouver Canucks
1970–71	Chicago Black Hawks	1976–77	Philadelphia Flyers	1982–83	Edmonton Oilers
1971–72	Chicago Black Hawks	1977–78	New York Islanders	1983–84	Edmonton Oilers
1972–73	Chicago Black Hawks	1978–79	New York Islanders	1984–85	Edmonton Oilers

NATIONAL HOCKEY LEAGUE ALL-STAR GAMES

1947	All-Stars 4, Toronto 3	1964	All-Stars 3, Toronto 2	1978	Prince of Wales Conf. 3, C.S. Campbell Conf. 2
1948	All-Stars 3, Toronto 1	1965	All-Stars 5, Montreal 2		
1949	All-Stars 3, Toronto 1	*1967	Montreal 3, All-Stars 0	1979	Soviet National Stars 2, NHL All-Stars 1
1950	Detroit 7, All-Stars 1	1968	Toronto 4, All-Stars 3		
1951	1st Team 2, 2d Team 2	1969	East 3, West 3	1980	Prince of Wales Conf. 6, C.S. Campbell Conf. 3
1952	1st Team 1, 2d Team 1	1970	East 4, West 1		
1953	All-Stars 3, Montreal 1	1971	West 2, East 1	1981	C.S. Campbell Conf. 4, Prince of Wales Conf. 1
1954	All-Stars 2, Detroit 2	1972	East 3, West 2		
1955	Detroit 3, All-Stars 1	1973	East 5, West 4	1982	Prince of Wales Conf. 4, C.S. Campbell Conf. 2
1956	All-Stars 1, Montreal 1	1974	West 6, East 4		
1957	All-Stars 5, Montreal 3	1975	Prince of Wales Conf. 7, C.S. Campbell Conf. 1	1983	C.S. Campbell Conf. 9, Prince of Wales Conf. 3
1958	Montreal 6, All-Stars 3				
1959	Montreal 6, All-Stars 1	1976	Prince of Wales Conf. 7, C.S. Campbell Conf. 5	1984	Prince of Wales Conf. 7, C.S. Campbell Conf. 6
1960	All-Stars 2, Montreal 1				
1961	All-Stars 3, Chicago 1	1977	Prince of Wales Conf. 4, C.S. Campbell Conf. 3	1985	Prince of Wales Conf. 6, C.S. Campbell Conf. 4
1962	Toronto 4, All-Stars 1				
1963	All-Stars 3, Toronto 3				

* Game shifted to midseason.

SELECTED NATIONAL HOCKEY LEAGUE RECORDS

TEAM RECORDS

Most scoring points, one season	1,182—Edmonton Oilers, 1983–84 (80 games)
Most wins, one season	60—Montreal Canadiens, 1976–77
Longest undefeated streak	35 games—Philadelphia Flyers, Oct. 14, 1979–Jan. 6, 1980 (25 wins, 10 ties)
Most goals, one season	446—Edmonton Oilers, 1983–84
Most goals, both teams, one game . . .	21—Jan. 10, 1920: Montreal Canadiens defeated Toronto St. Patricks, 14–7
Most average goals per game	5.575—Edmonton Oilers, 1982–83

INDIVIDUAL RECORDS

Most seasons .	26—Gordie Howe, Detroit Red Wings, 1946–47 through 1970–71; Hartford Whalers, 1979–80
Most games .	1,767—Gordie Howe, Detroit Red Wings, 1946–71, Hartford Whalers, 1979–80
Most goals .	801—Gordie Howe, Detroit Red Wings, 1946–71, Hartford Whalers, 1979–80
Most assists .	1,049—Gordie Howe, Detroit Red Wings, 1946–71, Hartford Whalers, 1979–80
Most 50-or-more goal seasons	8—Mike Bossy, N.Y. Islanders, in 8 seasons.
Most goals, one season	92—Wayne Gretzky, Edmonton Oilers, 1981–82
Most penalty minutes, one season . . .	472—Dave Schultz, Philadelphia Flyers, 1974–75
Longest consecutive point-scoring streak .	51 games—Wayne Gretzky, Edmonton Oilers, 1983–84
Most goals, one game	7—Joe Malone, Quebec Bulldogs, Jan. 31, 1920, against Toronto St. Patricks
Most points, one game	10—Darryl Sittler, Toronto Maple Leafs, Feb. 7, 1976, against Boston; 6 goals, 4 assists

NATIONAL COLLEGIATE ATHLETIC ASSOCIATION HOCKEY CHAMPIONSHIPS

1962	Michigan Tech over Clarkson, 7–1	1975	Michigan Tech over Minnesota, 6–1
1963	North Dakota over Denver, 6–5	1976	Minnesota over Michigan Tech, 6–4
1964	Michigan over Denver, 6–3	1977	Wisconsin over Michigan, 6–5
1965	Michigan Tech over Boston College, 8–2	1978	Boston U. over Boston College, 5–3
1966	Michigan State over Clarkson, 6–1	1979	Minnesota over North Dakota, 4–3
1967	Cornell over Boston U., 4–1	1980	North Dakota over Northern Michigan, 5–2
1968	Denver over North Dakota, 4–0	1981	Wisconsin over Minnesota, 6–3
1969	Denver over Cornell, 4–3	1982	North Dakota over Wisconsin, 5–2
1970	Cornell over Clarkson, 6–4	1983	Wisconsin over Harvard, 6–2
1971	Boston U. over Minnesota, 4–2	1984	Bowling Green over Minnesota-Duluth, 5–4
1972	Boston U. over Cornell, 4–0	1985	Rensselear Polytechnic Institute over Providence, 2–1
1973	Wisconsin over Denver, 4–2		
1974	Minnesota over Michigan Tech, 4–2		

HORSE RACING

LEADING MONEY-WINNING RACEHORSES

Source: Thoroughbred Racing Association of North America

YEAR	HORSE	AGE (in years)	STARTS	WINS	SECONDS	THIRDS	AMOUNT WON	YEAR	HORSE	AGE (in years)	STARTS	WINS	SECONDS	THIRDS	AMOUNT WON
1920	Man o' War	3	11	11	0	0	$166,140	1953	Native Dancer	3	10	9	1	0	$513,425
1921	Morvich	2	11	11	0	0	115,234	1954	Determine	3	15	10	3	2	328,700
1922	Pillory	3	7	4	1	1	96,654	1955	Nashua	3	12	10	1	1	752,550
1923	Zev	3	14	12	1	0	272,008	1956	Needles	3	8	4	2	0	440,850
1924	Sarazen	3	12	8	1	1	95,640	1957	Round Table	3	22	15	1	3	600,383
1925	Pompey	2	10	7	2	0	121,630	1958	Round Table	4	20	14	4	0	662,780
1926	Crusader	3	15	9	4	0	166,033	1959	Sword Dancer	3	13	8	4	0	537,004
1927	Anita Peabody	2	7	6	0	1	111,905	1960	Bally Ache	3	15	10	3	1	455,045
1928	High Strung	2	6	5	0	0	153,590	1961	Carry Back	3	16	9	1	3	565,349
1929	Blue Larkspur	3	6	4	1	0	153,450	1962	Never Bend	2	10	7	1	2	402,969
1930	Gallant Fox	3	10	9	1	0	308,275	1963	Candy Spots	3	12	7	2	1	604,481
1931	Top Flight	2	7	7	0	0	219,000	1964	Gun Bow	4	16	8	4	2	580,100
1932	Gusto	3	16	4	3	2	145,940	1965	Buckpasser	2	11	9	1	0	568,096
1933	Singing Wood	2	9	3	2	2	88,050	1966	Buckpasser	3	14	13	1	0	669,078
1934	Cavalcade	3	7	6	1	0	111,235	1967	Damascus	3	16	12	3	1	817,944
1935	Omaha	3	9	6	1	2	142,255	1968	Forward Pass	3	13	7	2	0	546,674
1936	Granville	3	11	7	3	0	110,295	1969	Arts and Letters	3	14	8	5	1	555,604
1937	Seabiscuit	4	15	11	2	2	168,580	1970	Personality	3	18	8	2	1	444,049
1938	Stagehand	3	15	8	2	3	189,710	1971	Riva Ridge	2	9	7	0	0	503,263
1939	Challedon	3	15	9	2	3	184,535	1972	Droll Roll	4	8	4	1	2	471,633
1940	Bimelech	3	7	4	2	1	110,005	1973	Secretariat	3	21	16	3	1	860,404
1941	Whirlaway	3	20	13	5	2	272,386	1974	Chris Evert	3	7	4	1	2	551,063
1942	Shut Out	3	12	8	2	0	238,872	1975	Foolish Pleasure	3	11	5	4	1	716,278
1943	Count Fleet	3	6	6	0	0	174,055	1976	Forego	6	8	6	1	1	491,701
1944	Pavot	2	8	8	0	0	179,040	1977	Seattle Slew	3	7	6	0	0	641,370
1945	Busher	3	13	10	2	1	273,735	1978	Affirmed	3	11	8	2	0	901,541
1946	Assault	3	15	8	2	3	424,195	1979	Spectacular Bid	3	12	10	1	1	1,279,333
1947	Armed	6	17	11	4	1	376,325	1980	Temperence Hill	3	17	8	3	1	1,130,452
1948	Citation	3	20	19	1	0	709,470	1981	John Henry	6	10	8	0	0	1,798,030
1949	Ponder	3	21	9	5	2	321,825	1982	Perrault	5	8	4	1	2	1,197,400
1950	Noor	5	12	7	4	1	346,940	1983	All Along	4	7	4	1	1	2,138,963
1951	Counterpoint	3	15	7	2	2	250,525	1984	Slew O'Gold	4	6	5	1	0	2,627,944
1952	Crafty Admiral	4	16	9	4	1	277,225								

THOROUGHBRED HORSE OF THE YEAR (ECLIPSE AWARD)

YEAR	HORSE	YEAR	HORSE	YEAR	HORSE	YEAR	HORSE
1936	Granville	1949	Capot	1962	Kelso	1975	Forego
1937	War Admiral	1950	Hill Prince	1963	Kelso	1976	Forego
1938	Seabiscuit	1951	Counterpoint	1964	Kelso	1977	Seattle Slew
1939	Challedon	1952	Native Dancer	1965	Moccasin	1978	Affirmed
1940	Challedon	1953	Tom Fool	1966	Buckpasser	1979	Affirmed
1941	Whirlaway	1954	Native Dancer	1967	Damascus	1980	Spectacular Bid
1942	Whirlaway	1955	Nashua	1968	Dr. Fager	1981	John Henry
1943	Count Fleet	1956	Swaps	1969	Arts and Letters	1982	Conquistador Cielo
1944	Twilight Tear	1957	Dedicate	1970	Personality	1983	All Along
1945	Busher	1958	Round Table	1971	Ack Ack	1984	John Henry
1946	Assault	1959	Sword Dancer	1972	Secretariat		
1947	Armed	1960	Kelso	1973	Secretariat		
1948	Citation	1961	Kelso	1974	Forego		

THOROUGHBRED HORSE RACING'S TRIPLE CROWN

The Triple Crown of Thoroughbred horse racing in the United States consists of winning three races for 3-year-olds: the Kentucky Derby, the Preakness Stakes, and the Belmont Stakes.

Only 11 horses have won the Triple Crown: Sir Barton in 1919, Gallant Fox in 1930, Omaha in 1935, War Admiral in 1937, Whirlaway in 1941, Count Fleet in 1943, Assault in 1946, Citation in 1948, Secretariat in 1973, Seattle Slew in 1977, and Affirmed in 1978.

KENTUCKY DERBY

The Kentucky Derby is the oldest continually run horse race in the U.S. The 1¼-mile race for 3-year-old horses is run annually at Churchill Downs in Louisville, Ky., on the first Saturday in May. From 1875 through 1895 the race was 1½ miles. Two jockeys have won five times: Eddie Arcaro in 1938, 1941, 1945, 1948, and 1952; and Bill Hartack in 1957, 1960, 1962, 1964, and 1969.

YEAR	WINNER	PURSE	JOCKEY	TIME	YEAR	WINNER	PURSE	JOCKEY	TIME
1875	Aristides	$2,850	Oliver Lewis	2:37¾	1878	Day Star	$4,050	J. Carter	2:37¼
1876	Vagrant	2,950	Bobby Swim	2:38¼	1879	Lord Murphy	3,550	C. Shaver	2:37
1877	Baden Baden	3,300	Billy Walker	2:38	1880	Fonso	3,800	George Lewis	2:37½

KENTUCKY DERBY (continued)

YEAR	WINNER	PURSE	JOCKEY	TIME	YEAR	WINNER	PURSE	JOCKEY	TIME
1881	Hindoo	$4,410	Jimmy McLaughlin	2:40	1934	Cavalcade	$28,175	Mack Garner	2:04
1882	Apollo	4,560	Babe Hurd	2:40 1/4	1935	Omaha	39,525	Willie Saunders	2:05
1883	Leonatus	3,760	Billy Donohue	2:43	1936	Bold Venture	37,725	Ira Hanford	2:03 3/5
1884	Buchanan	3,990	Isaac Murphy	2:40 1/4	1937	War Admiral	52,050	Charles Kurtsinger	2:03 1/5
1885	Joe Cotton	4,630	Erskine Henderson	2:37 1/5	1938	Lawrin	47,050	Eddie Arcaro	2:04 4/5
1886	Ben Ali	4,890	P. Duffy	2:36 1/2	1939	Johnstown	46,350	James Stout	2:03 2/5
1887	Montrose	4,200	Isaac Lewis	2:39 1/4	1940	Gallahadion	60,150	Carroll Bierman	2:05
1888	Macbeth II	4,740	G. Covington	2:38 1/4	1941	Whirlaway	61,275	Eddie Arcaro	2:01 2/5
1889	Spokane	4,970	Thomas Kiley	2:34 1/2	1942	Shut Out	64,225	Wayne D. Wright	2:04 2/5
1890	Riley	5,460	Isaac Murphy	2:45	1943	Count Fleet	60,725	Johnny Longden	2:04
1891	Kingman	4,680	Isaac Murphy	2:52 1/2	1944	Pensive	64,675	Con McCreary	2:04 1/5
1892	Azra	4,230	Alonzo Clayton	2:41 1/2	1945	Hoop Jr.	64,850	Eddie Arcaro	2:07
1893	Lookout	4,090	E. Kunze	2:39 1/4	1946	Assault	96,400	Warren Mehrtens	2:06 3/5
1894	Chant	4,020	Frank Goodale	2:41	1947	Jet Pilot	92,160	Eric Guerin	2:06 4/5
1895	Halma	2,970	James Perkins	2:37 1/2	1948	Citation	83,400	Eddie Arcaro	2:05 2/5
1896	Ben Brush	4,850	Willie Simms	2:07 3/4	1949	Ponder	91,600	Steve Brooks	2:04 1/5
1897	Typhoon II	4,850	Buttons Garner	2:12 1/2	1950	Middleground	92,650	Willie Boland	2:01 3/5
1898	Plaudit	4,850	Willie Simms	2:09	1951	Count Turf	98,050	Conn McCreary	2:02 3/5
1899	Manuel	4,850	Fred Taral	2:12	1952	Hill Gail	96,300	Eddie Arcaro	2:01 3/5
1900	Lt. Gibson	4,850	Jimmy Boland	2:06 1/4	1953	Dark Star	90,050	Henry Moreno	2:02
1901	His Eminence	4,850	Jimmy Winkfield	2:07 3/4	1954	Determine	102,050	Ray York	2:03
1902	Alan-a-Dale	4,850	Jimmy Winkfield	2:08 3/4	1955	Swaps	108,400	Willie Shoemaker	2:01 4/5
1903	Judge Himes	4,850	Hal Booker	2:09	1956	Needles	123,450	Dave Erb	2:03 3/5
1904	Elwood	4,850	Frankie Prior	2:08 1/2	1957	Iron Liege	109,550	Bill Hartack	2:02 1/5
1905	Agile	4,850	Jack Martin	2:10 3/4	1958	Tim Tam	116,400	Ismael Valenzuela	2:05
1906	Sir Huron	4,850	Roscoe Troxler	2:08 4/5	1959	Tomy Lee	119,650	Willie Shoemaker	2:02 1/5
1907	Pink Star	4,850	Andy Minder	2:12 3/5	1960	Venetian Way	114,850	Bill Hartack	2:02 2/5
1908	Stone Street	4,850	Arthur Pickens	2:15 1/5	1961	Carry Back	120,500	John Sellers	2:04
1909	Wintergreen	4,850	Vince Powers	2:08 1/5	1962	Decidedly	119,650	Bill Hartack	2:00 2/5
1910	Donau	4,850	Robert Herbert	2:06 2/5	1963	Chateaugay	108,900	Braulio Baeza	2:01 4/5
1911	Meridian	4,850	George Archibald	2:05	1964	Northern Dancer	114,300	Bill Hartack	2:00
1912	Worth	4,850	Carroll Shilling	2:09 2/5	1965	Lucky Debonair	112,000	Willie Shoemaker	2:01 1/5
1913	Donerail	5,475	Roscoe Goose	2:04 4/5	1966	Kauai King	120,500	Don Brumfield	2:02
1914	Old Rosebud	9,125	John McCabe	2:03 2/5	1967	Proud Clarion	119,700	Bobby Ussery	2:00 3/5
1915	Regret	11,450	Joe Notter	2:05 2/5	1968	Dancer's Image	122,600	Ismael Valenzuela	2:02 1/5
1916	George Smith	9,750	Johnny Loftus	2:04	1969	Majestic Prince	155,700	Bill Hartack	2:01 4/5
1917	Omar Khayyam	16,600	Charles Borel	2:04 3/5	1970	Dust Commander	128,000	Mike Manganello	2:03 2/5
1918	Exterminator	14,700	Willie Knap	2:10 4/5	1971	Canonero II	125,000	Gustavo Avila	2:03 1/5
1919	Sir Barton	20,825	Johnny Loftus	2:09 4/5	1972	Riva Ridge	140,300	Ron Turcotte	2:01 4/5
1920	Paul Jones	30,375	Ted Rice	2:09	1973	Secretariat	155,050	Ron Turcotte	1:59 2/5
1921	Behave Yourself	38,450	Charles Thompson	2:04 1/5	1974	Cannonade	274,000	Angel Cordero Jr.	2:04
1922	Morvich	46,775	Albert Johnson	2:04 3/5	1975	Foolish Pleasure	209,600	Jacinto Vasquez	2:02
1923	Zev	53,600	Earl Sande	2:05 2/5	1976	Bold Forbes	165,200	Angel Cordero Jr.	2:01 3/5
1924	Black Gold	52,775	John D. Mooney	2:05 1/5	1977	Seattle Slew	214,700	Jean Cruguet	2:02 1/5
1925	Flying Ebony	52,950	Earl Sande	2:07 3/5	1978	Affirmed	186,900	Steve Cauthen	2:01 1/5
1926	Bubbling Over	50,075	Albert Johnson	2:03 4/5	1979	Spectacular Bid	324,900	Ron Franklin	2:02 2/5
1927	Whiskery	51,000	Linus McAtee	2:06	1980	Genuine Risk	339,300	Jacinto Vasquez	2:02
1928	Reigh Count	55,375	Chick Lang	2:10 2/5	1981	Pleasant Colony	317,200	Jorge Velasquez	2:02
1929	Clyde Van Dusen	53,950	Linus McAtee	2:10 4/5	1982	Gato del Sol	428,850	Eddie Delahoussaye	2:02 2/5
1930	Gallant Fox	50,725	Earl Sande	2:07 3/5	1983	Sunny's Halo	426,000	Eddie Delahoussaye	2:02 1/5
1931	Twenty Grand	48,725	Charles Kurtsinger	2:01 4/5	1984	Swale	537,400	Laffit Pincay Jr.	2:02 2/5
1932	Burgoo King	52,350	Eugene James	2:05 1/5	1985	Spend A Buck	406,800	Angel Cordero Jr.	2:00 1/5
1933	Brokers Tip	48,925	Don Meade	2:06 4/5					

PREAKNESS STAKES (at Pimlico, Baltimore, Md., 1 3/16 miles for 3-year-olds)

YEAR	WINNER	PURSE	JOCKEY	TIME	YEAR	WINNER	PURSE	JOCKEY	TIME
1930	Gallant Fox	$51,925	Earl Sande	2:00 3/5	1945	Polynesian	$66,170	Wayne D. Wright	1:58 4/5
1931	Mate	48,225	G. Ellis	1:59	1946	Assault	96,620	Warren Mehrtens	2:01 1/5
1932	Burgoo King	50,375	E. James	1:59 4/5	1947	Faultless	96,005	D. Dodson	1:59
1933	Head Play	26,850	Charles Kurtsinger	2:02	1948	Citation	91,870	Eddie Arcaro	2:02 2/5
1934	High Quest	25,175	R. Jones	1:58 1/5	1949	Capot	79,985	T. Atkinson	1:56
1935	Omaha	25,325	Willie Saunders	1:58 2/5	1950	Hill Prince	56,115	Eddie Arcaro	1:59 1/5
1936	Bold Venture	27,325	G. Woolf	1:59	1951	Bold	83,110	Eddie Arcaro	1:56 2/5
1937	War Admiral	45,600	Charles Kurtsinger	1:58 2/5	1952	Blue Man	86,135	Conn McCreary	1:57 2/5
1938	Dauber	51,875	M. Peters	1:59 4/5	1953	Native Dancer	65,200	Eric Guerin	1:57 4/5
1939	Challedon	53,710	G. Seabo	1:59 4/5	1954	Hasty Road	91,600	J. Adams	1:57 2/5
1940	Bimelech	53,230	F.A. Smith	1:58 3/5	1955	Nashua	67,550	Eddie Arcaro	1:54 3/5
1941	Whirlaway	49,365	Eddie Arcaro	1:58 4/5	1956	Fabius	84,250	Bill Hartack	1:58 2/5
1942	Alsab	58,175	B. James	1:57	1957	Bold Ruler	62,250	Eddie Arcaro	1:56 1/5
1943	Count Fleet	43,190	Johnny Longden	1:57 2/5	1958	Tim Tam	97,900	Ismael Valenzuela	1:57 1/5
1944	Pensive	60,075	Conn McCreary	1:59 1/5	1959	Royal Orbit	136,200	W. Harmatz	1:57

PREAKNESS STAKES (continued)

YEAR	WINNER	PURSE	JOCKEY	TIME	YEAR	WINNER	PURSE	JOCKEY	TIME
1960	Bally Ache	$121,000	Bobby Ussery	1:57 3/5	1973	Secretariat	$129,900	Ron Turcotte	1:54 2/5
1961	Carry Back	126,200	John Sellers	1:57 3/5	1974	Little Current	156,500	Miguel Rivera	1:54 3/5
1962	Greek Money	135,800	J. L. Rotz	1:56 1/5	1975	Master Derby	158,100	Darrel McHargue	1:56 2/5
1963	Candy Spots	127,500	Willie Shoemaker	1:56 1/5	1976	Elocutionist	129,700	John Lively	1:55
1964	Northern Dancer	124,200	Bill Hartack	1:56 4/5	1977	Seattle Slew	138,600	Jean Cruguet	1:54 2/5
1965	Tom Rolfe	128,100	Ron Turcotte	1:56 1/5	1978	Affirmed	136,200	Steve Cauthen	1:54 2/5
1966	Kauai King	129,000	Don Brumfield	1:55 2/5	1979	Spectacular Bid	295,300	Ron Franklin	1:54 1/5
1967	Damascus	141,500	Willie Shoemaker	1:55 1/5	1980	Codex	250,600	Angel Cordero Jr.	1:54 1/5
1968	Forward Pass	142,700	Ismael Valenzuela	1:56 4/5	1981	Pleasant Colony	200,800	Jorge Velasquez	1:54 1/5
1969	Majestic Prince	129,500	Bill Hartack	1:55 3/5	1982	Aloma's Ruler	209,900	Jack Kaenel	1:55 2/5
1970	Personality	150,000	E. Belmonte	1:56 1/5	1983	Deputed Testamony	253,700	Donald A. Miller Jr.	1:55 2/5
1971	Canonero II	137,400	Gustavo Avila	1:54	1984	Gate Dancer	243,600	Angel Cordero Jr.	1:53 3/5
1972	Bee Bee Bee	135,300	E. Nelson	1:55 3/5	1985	Tank's Prospect	423,200	Pat Day	1:53 2/5

BELMONT STAKES (at Belmont Park, L.I., N.Y., 1½ miles for 3-year-olds)

YEAR	WINNER	PURSE	JOCKEY	TIME	YEAR	WINNER	PURSE	JOCKEY	TIME
1928	Vito	$63,430	C. Kummer	2:33 1/5	1957	Gallant Man	$ 77,300	Willie Shoemaker	2:26 3/5
1929	Blue Larkspur	59,650	M. Garner	2:32 4/5	1958	Cavan	73,430	P. Anderson	2:30 1/5
1930	Gallant Fox	66,040	Earl Sande	2:31 3/5	1959	Sword Dancer	93,525	Willie Shoemaker	2:28 2/5
1931	Twenty Grand	58,770	C. Kurtsinger	2:29 3/5	1960	Celtic Ash	96,785	Bill Hartack	2:29 3/5
1932	Fairengo	55,120	T. Malley	2:32 4/5	1961	Sherluck	104,900	Braulio Baeza	2:29 1/5
1933	Hurryoff	49,490	M. Garner	2:32 3/5	1962	Jaipur	109,500	Willie Shoemaker	2:28 4/5
1934	Peace Chance	43,410	W.D. Wright	2:29 1/5	1963	Chateaugay	101,700	Braulio Baeza	2:30 1/5
1935	Omaha	35,480	Willie Saunders	2:30 3/5	1964	Quadrangle	110,850	Manuel Ycaza	2:28 2/5
1936	Granville	29,800	Willie Saunders	2:30 3/5	1965	Hail to All	104,150	John Sellers	2:28 2/5
1937	War Admiral	38,020	Charles Kurtsinger	2:28 3/5	1966	Amberoid	117,700	Willie Boland	2:29 3/5
1938	Pasteurized	34,530	James Stout	2:29 3/5	1967	Damascus	104,950	Willie Shoemaker	2:28 4/5
1939	Johnstown	37,020	James Stout	2:29 3/5	1968	Stage Door Johnny	117,700	H. Gustines	2:27 1/5
1940	Bimelech	35,030	F.A. Smith	2:29 3/5	1969	Arts and Letters	104,050	Braulio Baeza	2:28 4/5
1941	Whirlaway	39,770	Eddie Arcaro	2:31	1970	High Echelon	125,000	J. L. Rotz	2:34
1942	Shut Out	44,520	Eddie Arcaro	2:29 1/5	1971	Pass Catcher	125,000	W. Blum	2:30 3/5
1943	Count Fleet	35,340	Johnny Longden	2:28 1/5	1972	Riva Ridge	93,540	Ron Turcotte	2:28
1944	Bounding Home	55,000	G.L. Smith	2:32 1/5	1973	Secretariat	90,120	Ron Turcotte	2:24
1945	Pavot	52,675	Eddie Arcaro	2:30 1/5	1974	Little Current	52,564	Miguel Rivera	2:29 1/5
1946	Assault	75,400	Warren Mehrtens	2:30 4/5	1975	Avatar	116,160	Willie Shoemaker	2:28 1/5
1947	Phalanx	78,900	R.Donoso	2:29 2/5	1976	Bold Forbes	117,000	Angel Cordero Jr.	2:29
1948	Citation	77,700	Eddie Arcaro	2:28 1/5	1977	Seattle Slew	109,080	Jean Cruguet	2:29 3/5
1949	Capot	60,900	T. Atkinson	2:30 1/5	1978	Affirmed	110,580	Steve Cauthen	2:26 4/5
1950	Middleground	61,350	Willie Boland	2:28 3/5	1979	Coastal	269,000	Ruben Hernandez	2:28 3/5
1951	Counterpoint	82,000	D. Gorman	2:29	1980	Temperence Hill	293,700	Eddie Maple	2:29 4/5
1952	One Count	82,400	Eddie Arcaro	2:30 1/5	1981	Summing	170,580	George Martens	2:29
1953	Native Dancer	82,500	Eric Guerin	2:28 3/5	1982	Conquistador Cielo	159,720	Laffit Pincay Jr.	2:28 1/5
1954	High Gun	89,000	Eric Guerin	2:30 4/5	1983	Caveat	215,100	Laffit Pincay Jr.	2:27 4/5
1955	Nashua	83,700	Eddie Arcaro	2:29	1984	Swale	516,700	Laffit Pincay Jr.	2:27 1/5
1956	Needles	83,600	Dave Erb	2:29 4/5	1985	Creme Fraiche	307,740	Eddie Maple	2:27

THOROUGHBRED RACING WORLD RECORDS

Source: The American Racing Manual (Daily Racing Form)

DISTANCE	TIME	HORSE	AGE	WEIGHT	TRACK OR PLACE	DATE
¼ mile	0:20 4/5	Big Racket	4	114	Hipodromo, Mexico City	1945 (Feb. 5)
2 ½ furlongs	0:26 4/5	Tie Score	5	115	Hipodromo, Mexico City	1946 (Feb. 5)
⅜ mile	0:33 1/5	Atoka	6	105	Butte, Mont.	1906 (Sept. 7)
3 ½ furlongs	0:38 1/5	Steel Penny Back	2	115	Northlands Park, Edmonton, Can.	1984 (June 14)
½ mile	0:44 2/5	Western Romance	3	116	Stampede Park, Alta, Canada	1980 (Apr. 19)
4 ½ furlongs	0:50 2/5	Kathryn's Doll	2	111	Turf Paradise, Phoenix, Ariz.	1967 (April 9)
⅝ mile	0:55 1/5	Chinook Pass	3	113	Longacres, Wash.	1982 (Sept. 17)
5 ½ furlongs	1:01 3/5	Zip Pocket	3	129	Turf Paradise, Phoenix, Ariz.	1967 (Nov. 19)
5 ¾ furlongs	1:07 1/5	Last Freeby	4	116	Timonium, Md.	1974 (July 20)
¾ mile [1]	1:06 1/5	Gelding [2]	3	123	Brighton, England [3]	1929 (Aug. 6)
¾ mile	1:07 1/5	Grey Papa	6	116	Longacres, Seattle, Wash.	1972 (Sept. 4)
6 ½ furlongs	1:13 4/5	Best Hitter	4	114	Longacres, Seattle, Wash.	1973 (Aug. 4)
⅞ mile	1:19 2/5	Rich Cream	5	115	Hollywood Park, Inglewood, Calif.	1980 (May 16)
1 mile	1:32 1/5	Dr. Fager	4	134	Arlington Heights, Ill.	1968 (Aug. 24)
1 mile, 40 yards	1:38 2/5	Impecunious	3	126	Salem Depot, N.H.	1973 (Sept. 3)
1 mile, 70 yards [1]	1:37 1/5	Aborigine	6	119	Penn National, Pa.	1978 (Aug. 20)
1 1/16 miles	1:38	Told	4	123	Penn National, Pa.	1980 (Sept. 14)
1 ⅛ miles [1]	1:45 2/5	Tentam	4	118	Saratoga Springs, N.Y.	1973 (Aug. 10)
1 ⅛ miles	1:45 2/5	Secretariat	3	124	Belmont Park, Elmont, N.Y.	1973 (Sept. 15)
1 3/16 miles	1:51 1/5	Toonerville	N.A.	N.A.	Hialeah, Hialeah, Fla.	1976 (Feb. 7)
1 ¼ miles [1]	1:57 2/5	Double Discount	4	116	Santa Anita Park, Arcadia, Calif.	1977 (Oct. 6)
1 5/16 miles	2:07	Roberto	3	122	York, England	1972 (Aug. 15)

THOROUGHBRED RACING WORLD RECORDS *(continued)*

DISTANCE	TIME	HORSE	AGE	WEIGHT	TRACK OR PLACE	DATE
1 ¾ miles [1]	2:11	Cougar II	6	126	Hollywood Park, Inglewood, Calif.	1972 (April 29)
1 ½ miles	2:23	John Henry	5	126	Santa Anita, Arcadia, Calif.	1980 (March 16)
1 ⁹⁄₁₆ miles	2:37 ⅗	Lone Wolf	5	115	Keeneland, Lexington, Ky.	1961 (Oct. 31)
1 ⅝ miles [1]	2:37 ⅘	Red Reality	6	113	Saratoga Springs, N.Y.	1972 (Aug. 23)
1 ⅝ miles [1]	2:37 ⅘	Malwak	5	110	Saratoga Springs, N.Y.	1973 (Aug. 22)
1 mi., 5 ½ furlongs	2:51 ⅜	Distribute	9	109	River Downs, Cincinnati, Ohio	1940 (Sept. 7)
1 ¾ miles [2]	2:50 ⅘	Swartz Pete	6	N.A.	Auckland, New Zealand	1966 (Jan. 1)
1 ⅞ miles [1]	3:11 ⅘	El Moro	8	116	Delaware Park, Wilmington, Del.	1963 (July 22)
2 miles [1]	3:15	Polazel	3	N.A.	Salisbury, England	1924 (July 8)
2 miles, 40 yards	3:29 ⅖	Winning Mark	4	107	Thistledown, Cleveland, Ohio	1940 (July 20)
2 miles, 70 yards	3:30 ⅖	Sun n Shine	4	113	Hawthorne, Cicero, Ill.	1974 (Oct. 19)
2 ¹⁄₁₆ miles	3:29 ⅜	Midafternoon	4	126	Jamaica, L.I., N.Y.	1956 (Nov. 15)
2 ¹⁄₁₆ miles [1]	3:35	Centurion	5	119	Newbury, England	1923 (Sept. 29)
2 ³⁄₁₆ miles	3:51 ⅛	Santiago	5	112	Narragansett Park, Pawtucket, R.I.	1941 (Sept. 24)
2 ¼ miles [1]	3:37 ⅖	Dakota	4	116	Lingfield, England	1927 (May 27)
2 ⅜ miles	4:15	Wiki Jack	4	97	Tijuana, Mexico	1925 (Feb. 8)
2 ½ miles	4:14 ⅗	Miss Grillo	6	118	Pimlico, Baltimore, Md.	1948 (Nov. 12)
2 ⅝ miles [4]	4:51 ⅖	Worthman	4	101	Tijuana, Mexico	1925 (Feb. 22)
2 ¾ miles	4:48 ⅘	Shot Put	4	126	Washington Park, Homewood, Ill.	1940 (Aug. 14)
2 ⅞ miles [5]	5:23	Bosh	5	100	Tijuana, Mexico	1925 (March 8)
3 miles	5:15	Farragut	5	113	Agua Caliente, Mexico	1941 (March 9)
3 ⅜ miles	6:13	Winning Mark	4	104	Washington Park, Homewood, Ill.	1940 (Aug. 21)
4 miles	7:10 ⅘	Sotemia	5	119	Churchill Downs, Louisville, Ky.	1912 (Oct. 7)

[1] Turf. [2] By Blink-Broken Tendril. [3] Downhill course. [4] Track heavy. [5] Track sloppy. [6] N.A.=Not available.

HARNESS RACING'S TRIPLE CROWN FOR 3-YEAR-OLDS

Source: The United States Trotting Association

HAMBLETONIAN [1]

YEAR	PURSE	WINNER	DRIVER	TIME	YEAR	PURSE	WINNER	DRIVER	TIME
1951	$ 95,263	Mainliner	Guy Crippen	2:02 ⅗	1969	$124,910	Lindy's Pride	Howard Beissinger	1:57 ⅗
1952	87,638	Sharp Note	Bion Shively	2:02 ¾	1970	143,620	Timothy T	John Simpson Jr.	1:58 ⅗
1953	117,118	Helicopter	Harry Harvey	2:01 ⅗	1971	129,770	Speedy Crown	Howard Beissinger	1:57 ⅗
1954	106,831	Newport Dream	Del Cameron	2:02 ⅘	1972	119,090	Super Bowl	Stanley Dancer	1:56 ⅖
1955	86,863	Scott Frost	Joe O'Brien	2:00 ⅗	1973	144,710	Flirth	Ralph Baldwin	1:57 ¼
1956	100,604	The Intruder	Ned Bower	2:01 ⅖	1974	160,150	Christopher T	Billy Haughton	1:58 ⅗
1957	111,126	Hickory Smoke	John Simpson	2:00 ⅕	1975	232,192	Bonefish	Stanley Dancer	1:59
1958	106,719	Emily's Pride	Flave Nipe	1:59 ⅘	1976	263,524	Steve Lobell	Billy Haughton	1:56 ⅖
1959	125,283	Diller Hanover	Frank Ervin	2:01 ⅕	1977	284,131	Green Speed	Billy Haughton	1:55 ⅗
1960	147,481	Blaze Hanover	Joe O'Brien	1:59 ⅗	1978	241,280	Speedy Somolli	Howard Beissinger	1:55
1961	131,573	Harlan Dean	James Arthur	1:58 ⅖	1979	300,000	Legend Hanover	George Sholty	1:56 ⅕
1962	116,612	A. C.'s Viking	Sanders Russell	1:59 ⅗	1980	300,000	Burgomeister	Wm. Haughton	1:56 ⅗
1963	115,549	Speedy Scot	Ralph Baldwin	1:57 ⅗	1981	837,000	Shiaway St. Pat	Ray Remmer	2:01 ⅕
1964	115,281	Ayres	John Simpson	1:56 ⅘	1982	875,000	Speed Bowl	Tom Haughton	1:57
1965	122,245	Egyptian Candor	Del Cameron	2:03 ⅘	1983	1,080,000	Duenna	Stanley Dancer	1:57 ⅖
1966	122,540	Kerry Way	Frank Ervin	1:58 ⅘	1984	1,219,000	Historic Freight	Ben Webster	1:57 ⅗
1967	122,650	Speedy Streak	Del Cameron	2:00	1985	1,272,000	Prakas	Bill O'Donnell	1:55 ⅕
1968	116,190	Nevele Pride	Stanley Dancer	1:59 ⅖					

[1] At Du Quoin, Ill., until 1981 when moved to East Rutherford, N. J.

KENTUCKY FUTURITY (at Lexington, Ky.)

YEAR	PURSE	WINNER	DRIVER	TIME	YEAR	PURSE	WINNER	DRIVER	TIME
1951	$ 66,659	Ford Hanover	John Simpson	2:01 ⅖	1969	$ 64,757	Lindy's Pride	Howard Beissinger	1:59
1952	66,231	Sharp Note	Bion Shively	2:00	1970	76,351	Timothy T	Joe Simpson Jr	1:59 ⅘
1953	67,485	Kimberly Kid	Thomas Berry	2:00 ⅗	1971	63,415	Savoir	James Arthur	1:58 ⅕
1954	63,121	Harlan	Del Miller	2:01	1972	56,210	Super Bowl	Stanley Dancer	1:59
1955	62,702	Scott Frost	Joe O'Brien	2:00 ⅗	1973	64,174	Arnie Almahurst	Joe O'Brien	1:59 ⅕
1956	53,731	Nimble Colby	Ralph Baldwin	2:02	1974	100,000	Waymaker	John Simpson Jr.	1:58 ⅖
1957	50,460	Cassin Hanover	Fred Egan	2:02 ⅕	1975	100,000	Noble Rouge	William Herman	1:59 ⅗
1958	53,330	Emily's Pride	Flave Nipe	1:59 ⅕	1976	100,000	Quick Pay	Peter Haughton	1:59
1959	53,810	Diller Hanover	Ralph Baldwin	2:01 ⅕	1977	100,000	Texas	Billy Herman	1:57 ⅗
1960	64,040	Elaine Rodney	Clint Hodgins	1:58 ⅗	1978	100,000	Doublemint	Peter Haughton	1:58 ⅗
1961	59,330	Duke Rodney	Eddie Wheeler	1:58 ⅕	1979	100,000	Classical Way	John Simpson Jr.	1:57 ⅘
1962	55,230	Safe Mission	Joe O'Brien	1:59 ⅕	1980	100,000	Final Score	Tom Haughton	1:58
1963	61,128	Speedy Scot	Ralph Baldwin	1:57 ⅕	1981	124,311	Filet of Sole	John Simpson Jr.	1:57 ⅗
1964	57,096	Ayres	John Simpson	1:58 ⅕	1982	116,200	Jazz Cosmos	Mickey McNichol	1:57
1965	65,133	Armbro Flight	Joe O'Brien	1:59 ⅗	1983	150,000	Power Seat	William O'Donnell	1:54 ⅘
1966	61,460	Governor Armbro	Joe O'Brien	2:00 ⅖	1984	168,010	Fancy Crown	William O'Donnell	1:55 ⅘
1967	58,642	Speed Model	Art Hult	1:59 ⅕	1985	185,500	Flak Bait	Ben Webster	1:59 ⅗
1968	57,000	Nevele Pride	Stanley Dancer	1:57					

YONKERS TROT (at Yonkers, N.Y.—1 1/16-mile race before 1963, now 1 mile)

YEAR	PURSE	WINNER	DRIVER	TIME	YEAR	PURSE	WINNER	DRIVER	TIME
1958	$ 56,157	Spunky Hanover	Howard Camper	2:13⅕	1972	$ 94,097	Super Bowl …	Stanley Dancer	2:02
1959	56,397	John A. Hanover	Stanley Dancer	2:11	1973	93,242	Tamerlane	Charles Clark .	2:04⅘
1960	74,265	Duke of Decatur	Del Miller ……	2:13¾	1974	125,822	Spitfire Hanover	Del Miller ……	2:05⅗
1961	100,330	Duke Rodney …	Eddie Wheeler .	2:10⅗	1975	200,000	Surefire Hanover	Stanley Dancer	2:03
1962	105,422	A. C.'s Viking ..	Sanders Russell	2:10⅖	1976	202,004	Steve Lobell …	Billy Haughton	2:01⅘
1963	135,127	Speedy Scot …	Ralph Baldwin ..	2:03⅘	1977	239,000	Green Speed ..	Billy Haughton	1:59
1964	116,691	Ayres ………	John Simpson .	2:01⅗	1978	233,594	Speedy Somolli	Howard Beissinger	1:59⅗
1965	122,236	Noble Victory .	Stanley Dancer	2:02	1979	237,765	Chiola Hanover	James Allen …	2:04⅖
1966	123,375	Polaris ………	George Sholty .	2:06	1980	263,540	Nevele Impulse	Dick Macomber	2:03⅗
1967	150,000	Pomp ………	Harry Pownall .	2:04⅘	1981	279,700	Ma Bandy ……	Carl Allen ……	2:02⅕
1968	150,000	Nevele Pride ..	Stanley Dancer	2:03⅖	1982	415,160	Mystic Park …	Frank O'Mara .	2:02⅗
1969	100,000	Lindy's Pride ..	Howard Beissinger	2:03⅖	1983	486,150	Joie De Vie ….	William Gilmour	2:00⅗
1970	106,770	Victory Star …	Vernon Dancer	2:03	1984	431,780	Baltic Speed ..	Jan Nordin ….	2:01⅖
1971	110,795	Quick Pride …	Stanley Dancer	2:02⅖	1985	440,840	Master Willie ..	Jan Nordin ….	1:59⅗

PACING'S TRIPLE CROWN

LITTLE BROWN JUG (at Delaware, Ohio—1 mile)

Source: United States Trotting Association.

YEAR	PURSE	WINNER	DRIVER	TIME	YEAR	PURSE	WINNER	DRIVER	TIME
1952	$60,463	Meadow Rice	Wayne Smart..	2:01⅗	1969	$109,731	Laverne Hanover	William Haughton	2:00⅗
1953	54,972	Keystoner……	Frank Ervin …	2:02⅖	1970	100,110	Most Happy Fella	Stanley Dancer	1:57⅕
1954	69,332	Adios Harry …	Morris MacDonald	2:01⅖	1971	102,964	Nansemond …	Herve Filion …	1:57⅕
1955	66,608	Quick Chief …	Billy Haughton	2:00	1972	104,916	Strike Out ….	Keith Waples ..	1:56⅗
1956	52,666	Noble Adios …	John Simpson .	2:00⅘	1973	120,000	Melvin's Woe ..	Joe O'Brien …	1:57⅗
1957	73,528	Torpid………	John Simpson .	2:00⅘	1974	132,630	Armbro Omaha	William Haughton	1:57⅗
1958	65,252	Shadow Wave .	Joe O'Brien …	2:01	1975	147,813	Seatrain ……	Ben Webster ..	1:56⅘
1959	76,582	Adios Butler…	Clint Hodgins ..	1:59⅖	1976	153,799	Keystone Ore..	Stanley Dancer	1:56⅘
1960	66,510	Bullet Hanover	John Simpson .	1:58⅗	1977	170,000	Governor Skipper	John Chapman	1:56⅕
1961	70,069	Henry T. Adios	Stanley Dancer	1:58⅗	1978	186,760	Happy Escort ..	Bill Popfinger ..	1:57⅖
1962	75,038	Lehigh Hanover	Stanley Dancer	1:58⅖	1979	226,455	Hot Hitter ….	Herve Filion …	1:55⅗
1963	68,294	Overtrick ……	John Patterson	1:57⅕	1980	207,361	Niatross ……	Clint Galbraith..	1:54⅘
1964	66,590	Vicar Hanover .	William Haughton	2:00⅘	1981	243,779	Fan Hanover ..	Glen Garnsey ..	1:56⅗
1965	70,000	Bret Hanover ..	Frank Ervin …	1:57	1982	328,900	Merger ……	John Campbell	1:56⅗
1966	74,616	Romeo Hanover	George Sholty .	1:59⅗	1983	358,800	Ralph Hanover	Ron Waples ..	1:55⅗
1967	84,778	Best of All ….	Jim Hackett …	1:59⅕	1984	366,717	Colt Fortysix ..	Chris Boring ..	1:55
1968	104,226	Rum Customer	William Haughton	1:59⅗	1985	350,730	Nihilator ……	Bill O'Donnell .	1:52⅕

CANE PACE (at Yonkers, N.Y.—1 mile)

YEAR	PURSE	WINNER	DRIVER	TIME	YEAR	PURSE	WINNER	DRIVER	TIME
1959	$ 64,457	Adios Butler…	Clint Hodgins .	2:09	1973	$101,242	Smog ………	Vernon Dancer	1:58⅘
1960	65,245	Countess Adios	Del Miller ….	2:08	1974	121,822	Boyden Hanover	William Herman	1:59⅕
1961	110,950	Cold Front …	Clint Hodgins .	2:08⅗	1975	200,000	Nero ………	Joe O'Brien …	1:58⅘
1962	117,542	Ranger Knight .	Clint Hodgins .	2:13⅕	1976	200,000	Keystone Ore..	Stanley Dancer	1:57⅕
1963	163,187	Meadow Skipper	Earle Avery …	1:58⅘	1977	286,500	Jade Princess	Jack Kopas …	1:59
1964	123,191	Race Time …	George Sholty .	2:01⅘	1978	307,594	Armbro Tiger ..	Herve Filion …	1:59⅕
1965	125,236	Bret Hanover ..	Frank Ervin …	2:01	1979	336,420	Happy Motoring	Wm. Popfinger	1:57⅗
1966	126,915	Romeo Hanover	William Myer ..	1:59⅘	1980	321,365	Niatross ……	Clint Galbraith.	1:57⅗
1967	150,000	Meadow Paige	William Haughton	2:03	1981	373,850	Wildwood Jeb .	James Marohn	1:58⅕
1968	150,000	Rum Customer	William Haughton	1:59⅘	1982	307,980	Cam Fella ….	Pat Crowe …	1:57⅗
1969	100,000	Kat Byrd ……	Eldon Harner ..	2:02⅕	1983	559,230	Ralph Hanover	Ron Waples ..	1:57
1970	102,770	Most Happy Fella	Stanley Dancer	1:58⅗	1984	600,000	On the Road A.	Wm. Gilmoor ..	1:56⅘
1971	106,795	Albatross ……	Stanley Dancer	2:00	1985	600,000	Chairman of	John Campbell	1:55⅕
1972	107,097	Hilarious Way ..	John Simpson Jr.	2:02⅖			the board ……		

MESSENGER STAKE (at Westbury, L.I., N.Y.—1 mile)

YEAR	PURSE	WINNER	DRIVER	TIME	YEAR	PURSE	WINNER	DRIVER	TIME
1959	$110,994	Adios Butler…	Clint Hodgins .	2:00⅕	1973	$122,732	Valiant Bret …	Lucien Fontaine	2:00⅗
1960	142,786	Countess Adios	Del Miller ….	2:02⅕	1974	151,044	Armbro Omaha	William Haughton	1:59⅗
1961	145,377	Adios Don ….	Howard Camper	2:02⅖	1975	154,223	Bret's Champ .	William Haughton	1:59⅕
1962	169,430	Thor Hanover .	John Simpson .	2:01⅕	1976	161,290	Windshield Wiper	William Haughton	2:00
1963	146,324	Overtrick ……	John Patterson	2:00⅘	1977	159,155	Governor Skipper	John Chapman	1:59⅕
1964	150,960	Race Time …	Ralph Baldwin .	2:01⅖	1978	167,862	Abercrombie ..	Glen Garnsey .	1:58⅖
1965	151,252	Bret Hanover ..	Frank Ervin …	2:02	1979	180,225	Hot Hitter ….	Henri Filion …	1:59⅖
1966	169,885	Romeo Hanover	George Sholty .	2:01	1980	173,522	Niatross ……	Clint Galbraith.	1:59⅗
1967	178,064	Romulus Hanover	William Haughton	1:59¹⁄₁₀	1981	224,954	Seahawk Hanover	Ben Webster ..	1:58
1968	189,018	Rum Customer	William Haughton	2:01⅘	1982	259,000	Cam Fella ….	Pat Crowe …	1:59
1969	182,976	Bye Bye Sam ..	Stanley Dancer	2:02⅗	1983	379,004	Ralph Hanover	Ron Waples ..	1:57
1970	123,450	Most Happy Fella	Stanley Dancer	2:00⅗	1984	379,343	Troublemaker .	Bill O'Donnell .	1:57⅗
1971	114,977	Albatross ……	Stanley Dancer	2:00⅖	1985	483,560	Pershing Square	Bill O'Donnell .	1:55⅗
1972	154,733	Silent Majority	William Haughton	2:01⅘					

HARNESS HORSE RACING RECORDS AND CHAMPIONS

Source: United States Trotting Association

WORLD HARNESS RACE ONE-MILE RECORDS

HORSE	SEX	DRIVER	YEAR	TRACK	TIME
Trotting—Mile Track					
Cornstalk	Horse	Howard Beissinger	1984	Springfield, IL	1:53 4/5
Fancy Crown	Mare	William O'Donnell	1984	Springfield, IL	1:53 4/5
Iris De Vandel	Gelding	Ron Turcotte	1983	E. Rutherford, N.J.	1:55 2/5
Pacing—Mile Track					
Colt Fortysix	Horse	Chris Boring	1984	Springfield, IL	1:50 3/5
Don't Dally	Mare	John Campbell	1984	Du Quoin, IL	1:51 3/5
Hobo's Willy	Gelding	John Campbell	1984	E. Rutherford, N.J.	1:53
Trotting—Five-eighths-mile Track					
Lindy's Crown	Horse	Howard Beissinger	1980	Wilmington, DE	1:57 1/5
Keystone Sister	Mare	Del Miller	1981	Meadow Lands, PA	1:58
Bobbo	Gelding	Norman Jones	1984	Montreal, Quebec	1:57 3/5
Pacing—Five-eighths-mile Track					
It's Fritz	Horse	Marty Allen	1983	Meadow Lands, PA	1:52 1/5
Naughty But Nice	Mare	William Fahy	1984	Meadow Lands, PA	1:54
Ambro Breton	Gelding	Howard Parker	1984	Laurel, MD	1:54 1/5
Trotting—Half-mile Track					
Nevele Pride	Horse	Stanley Dancer	1969	Saratoga Springs, N.Y.	1:56 4/5
Fancy Crown	Mare	William O'Donnel	1984	Delaware, Ohio	1:57 1/5
Bobbo	Gelding	Norman Jones	1984	Yonkers, NY	1:58 2/5
Pacing—Half-mile Track					
It's Fritz	Horse	Marty Allen	1983	Louisville, Ky.	1:53 3/5
Legal Notice	Horse	John Hayes, Jr.	1984	Delaware, Ohio	1:53 3/5
Naughty But Nice	Mare	Tom Haughton	1984	Delaware, Ohio	1:55 2/5
Majestic Charger	Gelding	William O'Donnell	1984	Freehold, N.J.	1:55 4/5
Happy Seven	Gelding	Robert Myers	1984	Ft. Washington, MD	1:55 4/5

HARNESS HORSE OF THE YEAR

YEAR	HORSE	GAIT	YEAR	HORSE	GAIT	YEAR	HORSE	GAIT
1949	Good Time	pacer	1959	Bye Bye Byrd	pacer	1974	Delmonica Hanover	trotter
1950	Proximity	trotter	1960–61	Adios Butler	pacer	1975	Savoir	trotter
1951	Pronto Don	trotter	1962	Su Mac Lad	trotter	1976	Keystone Ore	pacer
1952	Good Time	pacer	1963	Speedy Scot	trotter	1977	Green Speed	trotter
1953	Hi-Lo's Forbes	pacer	1964–66	Bret Hanover	pacer	1978	Abercrombie	pacer
1954	Stenographer	trotter	1967–69	Nevele Pride	trotter	1979–80	Niatross	pacer
1955–56	Scott Frost	trotter	1970	Fresh Yankee	trotter	1981	Fan Hanover	pacer
1957	Torpid	pacer	1971–72	Albatross	pacer	1982-83	Cam Fella	pacer
1958	Emily's Pride	trotter	1973	Sir Dalrae	pacer	1984	Fancy Crown	trotter

QUARTER HORSE RACING

Source: American Quarter Horse Association

WORLD RECORDS

DIST.	HORSE	AGE	WT.	DATE	TIME	DIST.	HORSE	AGE	WT.	DATE	TIME
220 yds.	Junior Meyers	4	120	8/10/69	0:11.62	440 yds.	Truckle Feature	3	120	8/26/73	0:21.02
250 yds.	Junior Meyers	6	121	5/16/71	0:13.00	550 yds.	Sissys Bug	3	119	7/29/84	0:26.41
300 yds.	Sissy Sails	3	120	2/16/85	0:15.17	660 yds.	Deckum Larum	5	122	7/23/85	0:33.51
330 yds.	Miss Top Flame	3	125	7/23/67	0:16.42	770 yds.	Mr. Brick Man	5	121	8/09/80	0:40.03
350 yds.	Mr. Summer Jet	4	120	7/21/85	0:17.21	870 yds.	Savannah One Time	12	122	8/17/85	0:44.30
400 yds.	Bold Love	3	120	3/28/80	0:19.18						

ALL AMERICAN FUTURITY, RUIDOSO DOWNS, N.M., 2-YEAR-OLD QUARTER HORSES [1]

YEAR	WINNER	TIME	PURSE	OWNER	TRAINER	JOCKEY
1970	Rocket Wrangler	0:20.09	$ 670,000	J. R. Adams	Charles Cascio	Jerry Nicodemus
1971	Mr. Kid Charge	0:19.65	$ 753,910	Will F. Whitehead	James Chapman	Johnny Cox
1972	Possumjet	0:20.04	$1,035,900	Jack M. Byers	Jack Byers	Pete Herrera
1973	Timeto Thinkrich	0:21.58	$1,030,000	Frank Vessels	Jerry Fisher	John Watson
1974	Easy Date	0:21.60	$1,030,000	Walter Merrick	James McArthur	Don Knight
1975	Bugs Alive in 75	0:21.98	$1,030,000	Ralph W. Shebester	J. B. Montgomery	Jerry Burgess
1976	Real Wind	0:21.70	$1,030,000	J.D. & E. Kitchens	T. A. Walker	Gary Sumpter
1977	Hot Idea	0:21.76	$ 766,000	Jackson/Bruce	G. Tefertiller	Terry Lipham
1978	Moon Lark	0:21.85	$1,000,000	Jas/Paul/Sam Howard	Jack Brooks	Jackie Martin
1979	Pie in the Sky	0:21.76	$1,000,000	Dan & Jolene Urschel	Leo Wood	Danny Cardoza
1980	Higheasterjet	0:22.15	$1,000,000	Jerry Highsmith	Johnie Goodman	Billy Hunt
1981	Special Effort	0:21.69	$1,000,000	Dan & Jolene Urschel	Johnie Goodman	Billy Hunt
1982	Mr. Master Bug	0:22.20	$2,000,000	Marvin L. Barnes	Jack Brooks	Jacky Martin
1983	On A High	0:22.04	$2,000,000	J. Rheudasl, P. Carter, B.F. Phillips Jr.	Dwayne Gilbreath	Steve Harris
1984	Eastex	0:21.42	$2,000,000	H. & M. Hall	James McArthur	Bruce Pilkenton
1985	Mr. Trucka Jet	0:21.41	$2,000,000	Miami Cattle Co.	C. Wade Navarre	Jacky Martin

[1] Previously 400 yards, the All American Futurity was changed to 440 yards in 1973.

OLYMPIC GAMES

WINTER OLYMPIC GAMES FINAL MEDAL STANDINGS: 1984

NATION	GOLD	SILVER	BRONZE	TOTAL	NATION	GOLD	SILVER	BRONZE	TOTAL
Soviet Union ...	6	10	9	25	West Germany .	2	1	1	4
East Germany ..	9	9	6	24	France	0	1	2	3
Finland	4	3	6	13	Italy	2	0	0	2
Norway	3	2	4	9	Liechtenstein ..	0	0	2	2
United States ..	4	4	0	8	Britain	1	0	0	1
Sweden	4	2	2	8	Japan	0	1	0	1
Czechoslovakia	0	2	4	6	Yugoslavia	0	1	0	1
Switzerland	2	2	1	5	Austria	0	0	1	1
Canada	2	1	1	4					

SUMMER OLYMPIC GAMES FINAL MEDAL STANDINGS: 1984

NATION	GOLD	SILVER	BRONZE	TOTAL	NATION	GOLD	SILVER	BRONZE	TOTAL
United States ..	83	61	30	174	Jamaica	0	1	2	3
West Germany .	17	19	23	59	Norway	0	1	2	3
Romania	20	16	17	53	Turkey	0	0	3	3
Canada	10	18	16	44	Venezuela	0	0	3	3
Britain	5	10	22	37	Morocco	2	0	0	2
China	15	8	9	32	Kenya	1	0	1	2
Italy	14	6	12	32	Greece	0	1	1	2
Japan	10	8	14	32	Nigeria	0	1	1	2
France	5	7	15	27	Puerto Rico	0	1	1	2
Australia	4	8	12	24	Algeria	0	0	2	2
South Korea ...	6	6	7	19	Pakistan	1	0	0	1
Sweden	2	11	6	19	Colombia	0	1	0	1
Yugoslavia	7	4	7	18	Egypt	0	1	0	1
Netherlands ...	5	2	6	13	Ireland	0	1	0	1
Finland	4	3	6	13	Ivory Coast	0	1	0	1
New Zealand ...	8	1	2	11	Peru	0	1	0	1
Brazil	1	5	2	8	Syria	0	1	0	1
Switzerland	0	4	4	8	Thailand	0	1	0	1
Mexico	2	3	1	6	Cameroon	0	0	1	1
Denmark	0	3	3	6	Dom. Republic .	0	0	1	1
Spain	1	2	2	5	Iceland	0	0	1	1
Belgium	1	1	2	4	Taiwan	0	0	1	1
Austria	1	1	1	3	Zambia	0	0	1	1
Portugal	1	0	2	3					

WINTER OLYMPIC GAMES FINAL MEDAL STANDINGS: 1980

NATION	GOLD	SILVER	BRONZE	TOTAL	NATION	GOLD	SILVER	BRONZE	TOTAL
East Germany ..	9	7	7	23	Sweden	3	0	1	4
Soviet Union ...	10	6	6	22	Italy	0	2	0	2
United States ..	6	4	2	12	Canada	0	1	1	2
Norway	1	3	6	10	Britain	1	0	0	1
Finland	1	5	3	9	Hungary	0	1	0	1
Austria	3	2	2	7	Japan	0	1	0	1
West Germany .	0	2	3	5	Bulgaria	0	0	1	1
Switzerland	1	1	3	5	Czechoslovakia	0	0	1	1
Liechtenstein ..	2	2	1	5	France	0	0	1	1
Netherlands ...	1	2	1	4					

SUMMER OLYMPIC GAMES FINAL MEDAL STANDINGS: 1980

NATION	GOLD	SILVER	BRONZE	TOTAL	NATION	GOLD	SILVER	BRONZE	TOTAL
Soviet Union ...	80	70	47	197	North Korea ...	0	3	2	5
East Germany ..	47	36	43	126	Brazil	2	0	2	4
Bulgaria	8	16	16	40	Ethiopia	2	0	2	4
Hungary	7	10	15	32	Mongolia	0	2	2	4
Poland	3	14	14	31	Netherlands ...	0	1	3	4
Romania	6	6	13	25	Mexico	0	1	3	4
Britain	5	7	9	21	Greece	1	0	2	3
Cuba	8	7	5	20	Jamaica	0	0	3	3
Italy	8	3	4	15	Switzerland	2	0	0	2
France	6	5	3	14	Tanzania	0	2	0	2
Czechoslovakia	2	2	9	13	Ireland	0	1	1	2
Sweden	3	3	6	12	Belgium	1	0	0	1
Australia	2	2	5	9	India	1	0	0	1
Yugoslavia	2	3	4	9	Zambabwe	1	0	0	1
Finland	3	1	4	8	Venezuela	0	1	0	1
Spain	1	3	2	6	Uganda	0	1	0	1
Denmark	2	1	2	5	Lebanon	0	0	1	1
Austria	1	3	1	5	Guyana	0	0	1	1

SUMMER OLYMPIC GAMES: 1896–1988

	YEAR	PLACE	NATIONS	EVENTS	LEADING WINNERS OF GOLD MEDAL CHAMPIONSHIPS		
					First	Second	Third
I	1896	Athens, Greece	10	42	United States (11)	Greece (8)	Germany (3½)
II	1900	Paris, France	20	60	France (28)	United States (22)	Britain (14)
III	1904	St. Louis, Mo.	10	67	United States (78)	Cuba (5) [2] Germany (5) [2]	
—[1]	1906	Athens, Greece	21	75	France (14)	United States (12)	Greece (8) [2] Britain (8) [2]
IV	1908	London, England	22	104	Britain (56)	United States (22)	Sweden (8)
V	1912	Stockholm, Sweden	28	106	United States (25)	Sweden (23½)	Britain (10)
VI	1916	Berlin, Germany	—	—	Canceled because of World War I		
VII	1920	Antwerp, Belgium	29	154	United States (41)	Sweden (19)	Finland (15)
VIII	1924	Paris, France	44	137	United States (45)	Finland (14)	France (13)
IX	1928	Amsterdam, Neth.	46	120	United States (22)	Germany (9½)	Italy (7) [2] Switzerland (7) [2]
X	1932	Los Angeles, Calif.	37	124	United States (41)	Italy (12)	France (10)
XI	1936	Berlin, Germany	49	142	Germany (33)	United States (24)	Hungary (10)
XII	1940	Helsinki, Finland	—	—	Canceled because of World War II		
XIII	1944	Unawarded	—	—	Canceled because of World War II		
XIV	1948	London, England	59	138	United States (38)	Sweden (17)	Hungary (10)
XV	1952	Helsinki, Finland	69	149	United States (40)	Soviet Union (22)	Hungary (16)
XVI	1956	Melbourne, Australia	67	145	Soviet Union (37) [4]	United States (32)	Australia (13)
XVII	1960	Rome, Italy	84	150	Soviet Union (43)	United States (34)	Italy (13)
XVIII	1964	Tokyo, Japan	94	162	United States (36)	Soviet Union (30)	Japan (16)
XIX	1968	Mexico City, Mexico	109	172	United States (45)	Soviet Union (28)	France (10) [2] Japan (10) [2]
XX	1972	Munich, W. Germany	112	195	Soviet Union (50)	United States (33)	East Germany (20)
XXI	1976	Montreal, Canada	89	198	Soviet Union (47)	East Germany (40)	United States (34)
XXII	1980	Moscow, Soviet Union	81	203	Soviet Union (80)	East Germany (47)	Bulgaria (8)
XXIII	1984	Los Angeles, Calif.	139	226	United States (83)	Romania (20)	West Germany (17)
XXIV	1988	Seoul, South Korea	—	—	—	—	—

WINTER OLYMPICS: 1924–1988

	YEAR	PLACE	NATIONS	EVENTS	LEADING WINNERS OF GOLD MEDAL CHAMPIONSHIPS		
					First	Second	Third
I	1924	Chamonix, France	16	16	Norway (4)	Finland (3)	Austria (2)
II	1928	St. Moritz, Switzerland	25	15	Norway (5½)	United States (2) [2] Sweden (2) [2]	—
III	1932	Lake Placid, N.Y.	17	19	United States (6)	Norway (3)	France (1) [2] Sweden (1) [2] Finland (1) [2] Canada (1) [2] Austria (1) [2]
IV	1936	Garmisch-Partenkirchen, Germany	28	21	Norway (7)	United States (3)	Sweden (2)
V	1948	St. Moritz, Switzerland	28	24	Sweden (4) [2] Norway (4) [2]	—	United States (3) [2] Switzerland (3) [2]
VI	1952	Oslo, Norway	30	23	Norway (7)	United States (4)	Finland (3) [2] Germany (3) [2]
VII	1956	Cortina, Italy	32	24	Soviet Union (6)	Austria (4)	Finland (3)
VIII	1960	Squaw Valley, Calif.	30	27	Soviet Union (6)	Germany (4)	United States (3) [2] Sweden (3) [2] Norway (3) [2]
IX	1964	Innsbruck, Austria	36	34	Soviet Union (11)	Austria (4) [2]	Germany (3) [2] France (3) [2] Finland (3) [2] Sweden (3) [2] Norway (3) [2]
X	1968	Grenoble, France	37	35	Norway (6)	Soviet Union (5)	France (4) [2] Italy (4) [2]
XI	1972	Sapporo, Japan	35	35	Soviet Union (8)	Switzerland (4) [2] Netherlands (4) [2] East Germany (4) [2]	
XII	1976	Innsbruck, Austria	37	35	Soviet Union (13)	East Germany (7)	United States (3) [2] Norway (3) [2]
XIII	1980	Lake Placid, N.Y.	38	39	Soviet Union (10)	East Germany (9)	United States (6)
XIV	1984	Sarajevo, Yugoslavia	49	39	Soviet Union (25)	E. Germany (24)	Finland (13)
XV	1988	Calgary, Canada	—	—	—	—	—

[1] Unofficial Olympics. [2] Tie. [3] Equestrian events held in Stockholm, Sweden. [4] Includes full credit for ties.

SUMMER OLYMPIC WINNERS AND RECORDS

ARCHERY: MEN

		POINTS
1972	John Williams, United States	2,528
1976*	Darrell Pace, United States	2,571
1980	T. Poikolainen, Finland	2,455
1984	Darrel Pace, United States	2,616

ARCHERY: WOMEN

		POINTS
1972	Doreen Wilber, United States	2,424
1976*	Luann Ryon, United States	2,499
1980	K. Losaberidze, USSR	2,491
1984	Hyang-Soon Seo, South Korea	2,568

BASKETBALL: MEN

1936	United States	1956	United States	1968	United States	1980	Yugoslavia
1948	United States	1960	United States	1972	Soviet Union	1984	United States
1952	United States	1964	United States	1976	United States		

BASKETBALL: WOMEN

1976	Soviet Union	1980	Soviet Union	1984	United States

BOXING: LIGHT FLYWEIGHT

1968	Francisco Rodriguez, Venezuela	1976	Jorge Hernandez, Cuba	1984	Paul Gonzales, U.S.A.
1972	Gyoergy Gedeo, Hungary	1980	Shamil Sabyrov, USSR		

BOXING: FLYWEIGHT

1904	G. Finnegan, U.S.A.	1932	I. Enekes, Hungary	1956	T. Spinks, Britain	1972	G. Kostadinov, Bulgaria
1920	F. De Genaro, U.S.A.	1936	W. Kaiser, Germany	1960	G. Torck, Hungary	1976	Leo Randolph, U.S.A.
1924	F. La Barba, U.S.A.	1948	P. Perez, Argentina	1964	F. Atzori, Italy	1980	Petar Lessov, Bulgaria
1928	A. Kocsis, Hungary	1952	N. Brooks, U.S.A.	1968	R. Delgado, Mexico	1984	Steve McCrory, U.S.A.

BOXING: BANTAMWEIGHT

1904	O. L. Kirk, U.S.A.	1932	H. Gwynne, Canada	1960	O. Grigoryev, USSR	1980	Juan Hernandez, Cuba
1908	A. Thomas, Britain	1936	U. Sergo, Italy	1964	T. Sakurai, Japan	1984	M. Stecca, Italy
1920	C. Walker, S. Africa	1948	T. Csik, Hungary	1968	V. Sokolov, USSR		
1924	W. Smith, S. Africa	1952	P. Hamalainen, Finland	1972	O. Martinez, Cuba		
1928	V. Tamagnini, Italy	1956	W. Behrendt, W. Ger.	1976	Gu Yong Jo, N. Korea		

BOXING: FEATHERWEIGHT

1904	O. L. Kirk, U.S.A.	1932	C. Robledo, Argentina	1960	F. Musso, Italy	1980	Rudi Fink, E. Germany
1908	R. K. Gunn, Britain	1936	O. Casanovas, Argentina	1964	S. Stepashkin, USSR	1984	M. Taylor, U.S.A.
1920	P. Fritsch, France	1948	E. Formenti, Italy	1968	A. Roldan, Mexico		
1924	J. Fields, U.S.A.	1952	J. Zachara, Czech.	1972	B. Kousnetsov, USSR		
1928	L. Van Klaveren, Neth.	1956	V. Sefronov, USSR	1976	A. Herrara, Cuba		

BOXING: LIGHTWEIGHT

1904	H. J. Spanger, U.S.A.	1932	L. Stevens, S. Africa	1960	K. Pazdzier, Poland	1980	Angel Herrera, Cuba
1908	F. Grace, Britain	1936	I. Harangi, Hungary	1964	J. Grudzien, Poland	1984	P. Whitaker, U.S.A.
1920	S. Mosberg, U.S.A.	1948	G. Dreyer, S. Africa	1968	R. Harris, U.S.A.		
1924	H. Nielsen, Denmark	1952	A. Bolognesi, Italy	1972	J. Szczepanski, Poland		
1928	C. Orlandi, Italy	1956	R. McTaggart, Britain	1976	Howard Davis, U.S.A.		

BOXING: LIGHT WELTERWEIGHT

1952	C. Adkins, U.S.A.	1964	J. Kulei, Poland	1976	Ray Leonard, U.S.A.
1956	V. Engoibarian, USSR	1968	J. Kulei, Poland	1980	Patrizio Oliva, Italy
1960	B. Nemecek, Czech.	1972	R. Seales, U.S.A.	1984	J. Page, U.S.A.

BOXING: WELTERWEIGHT

1904	A. Yong, U.S.A.	1932	E. Flynn, U.S.A.	1956	N. Linca, Romania	1972	E. Correa, Cuba
1920	T. Schneider, Canada	1936	S. Suvio, Finland	1960	G. Benvenuti, Italy	1976	J. Bachfeld, E. Germany
1924	J. Delarge, Belgium	1948	J. Torma, Czech.	1964	M. Kasprzyk, Poland	1980	A. Aldama, Cuba
1928	E. Morgan, N. Zealand	1952	Z. Chychia, Poland	1968	M. Wolke, E. Germany	1984	Mark Breland, U.S.A.

BOXING: LIGHT MIDDLEWEIGHT

1952	L. Papp, Hungary	1964	M. Kasprzyk, Poland	1976	J. Rybicki, Poland
1956	L. Papp, Hungary	1968	B. Lagutin, USSR	1980	A. Martinez, Cuba
1960	W. McClure, U.S.A.	1972	D. Kottysch, W. Ger.	1984	F. Tate, U.S.A.

BOXING: MIDDLEWEIGHT

1904	C. Mayer, U.S.A.	1932	C. Barth, U.S.A.	1960	E. Crook, U.S.A.	1980	Jose Gomez, Cuba
1908	J. Douglas, Britain	1936	J. Despeaux, France	1964	V. Popenchenko, USSR	1984	J.-S. Shin, S. Korea
1920	H. Mallin, Britain	1948	L. Papp, Hungary	1968	C. Finnegan, Britain		
1924	H. Mallin, Britain	1952	Floyd Patterson, U.S.A.	1972	V. Lemechev, USSR		
1928	P. Toscani, Italy	1956	G. Chatkov, USSR	1976	Mike Spinks, U.S.A.		

BOXING: LIGHT HEAVYWEIGHT

1920	E. Eagan, U.S.A.	1936	R. Michelot, France	1960	Cassius Clay, U.S.A.	1976	Leon Spinks, U.S.A.
1924	H. Mitchell, Britain	1948	G. Hunter, S. Africa	1964	C. Pinto, Italy	1980	S. Kacar, Yugoslavia
1928	V. Avendano, Argentina	1952	Norvel Lee, U.S.A.	1968	D. Pozdniak, USSR	1984	A. Josipovic,
1932	D. Carstens, S. Africa	1956	James Boyd, U.S.A.	1972	M. Parlov, Yugoslavia		Yugoslavia

* Olympic record.

BOXING: HEAVYWEIGHT

1904	S. Berger, U.S.A.	1932	S. Lovell, Argentina	1960	F. De Piccoli, Italy	1980	T. Stevenson, Cuba
1908	A. Oldham, Britain	1936	H. Runge, Germany	1964	Joe Frazier, U.S.A.	1984	H. Tillman, U.S.A.
1920	R. Rawson, Britain	1948	R. Iglesias, Argentina	1968	George Foreman, U.S.A.		
1924	O. von Porat, Norway	1952	E. Sanders, U.S.A.	1972	T. Stevenson, Cuba		
1928	R. Jurado, Argentina	1956	P. Rademacher, U.S.A.	1976	T. Stevenson, Cuba		

BOXING: SUPER HEAVYWEIGHT

1984	Tyrell Biggs, U.S.A.

CANOEING: KAYAK SINGLES—WOMEN: 500 METERS

1948	K. Hoff, Denmark	2:31.9	1964	L. Khvedosiuk, USSR	2:12.87	1980*	B. Fischer, E. Germany	1:57.96
1952	S. Saimo, Finland	2:18.4	1968	L. Pinaeva, USSR	2:11.09	1984	A. Andersson, Sweden	1:58.72
1956	E. Dementieva, USSR	2:18.9	1972	Y. Ryabchinskaya, USSR	2:03.17			
1960	A. Seredina, USSR	2:08.08	1976	C. Zirzow, E. Germany	2:01.05			

CANOEING: KAYAK PAIRS—WOMEN: 500 METERS

1960	USSR: M. Shubina, A. Seredina	1:54.76	1976	USSR: Popova, Kreft	1:51.15	
1964	W. Germany: R. Esser, A. Zimmerman	1:56.95	1980*	E. Germany: Bischof, Genauss	1:43.88	
1968	W. Germany: A. Zimmermann, R. Esser	1:56.44	1984	Sweden: Andersson, Olsson	1:45.25	
1972	USSR: L. Pinaeva, E. Kuryshko	1:53.50				

CANOEING: KAYAK PAIRS—MEN: 500 METERS

1976	E. Germany: Mattern, Olbricht	1:35.87	1984	New Zealand: Ferguson, MacDonald	1:34.21
1980*	Soviet Union: Parfenovich, Chukhrai	1:32.38			

CANOEING: KAYAK SINGLES—MEN: 1,000 METERS

1936	G. Hradetzky, Austria	4:22.9	1960	E. Hansen, Denmark	3:53.0	1976	R. Helm, E. Germany	3:48.20
1948	G. Fredriksson, Sweden	4:33.2	1964	R. Peterson, Sweden	3:57.13	1980	R. Helm, E. Germany	3:48.77
1952	G. Fredriksson, Sweden	4:07.9	1968	M. Hesz, Hungary	4:02.63	1984	A. Thompson, N. Zea.	3:45.73
1956	G. Fredriksson, Sweden	4:12.8	1972*	A. Shaparenko, USSR	3:48.06			

CANOEING: CANOE SINGLES—MEN: 1,000 METERS

1936	F. Amyot, Canada	5:32.1	1960	J. Parti, Hungary	4:33.9	1976	M. Ljubek, Yugoslavia	4:09.51
1948	J. Holocek, Czech	5:42.0	1964	J. Eschert, W. Germany	4:35.14	1980	L. Lubenov, Romania	4:12.38
1952	J. Holocek, Czech	4:56.3	1968	T. Tatai, Hungary	4:36.14	1984	U. Eicke, W. Germany	4:06.32
1956	L. Rottman, Romania	5:05.3	1972*	I. Patzaichin, Romania	4:08.94			

CANOEING: KAYAK PAIRS—MEN: 1,000 METERS

1936	Austria: A. Kainz, A. Dorfner	4:03.8	1968	USSR: A. Shaparenko, V. Morozov	3:37.54
1948	Sweden: H. Berglund, L. Klingstroem	4:07.3	1972	USSR: N. Gorbachev, V. Kratassyuk	3:31.23
1952	Finland: K. Wires, Y. Hietanen	3:51.1	1976	USSR: Nagorny, Romanovsky	3:29.01
1956	W. Germany: M. Scheuer, M. Miltenberger	3:49.6	1980	USSR: V. Parfenovich, S. Chukhrai	3:26.72
1960	Sweden: G. Fredriksson, S. Sjodelius	3:34.73	1984*	Canada: H. Fisher, A. Moris	3:24.22
1964	Sweden: S. Sjodelius, G. Utterberg	3:28.54			

CANOEING: CANOE DOUBLES—MEN: 1,000 METERS

1936	Czechoslovakia: V. Syrovatka, J. Brzak	4:50.1	1968	Romania: I. Potzaichin, S. Covaliov	4:07.18
1948	Czechoslovakia: J. Brzak, B. Kudrna	5:07.1	1972	USSR: V. Chessyunas, Y. Lobanov	3:52.60
1952	Denmark: B. Rasch, F. Haunstoft	4:38.3	1976	USSR: S. Petrenko, A. Vinogradov	3:52.76
1956	Romania: A. Dumitru, S. Ismailciuc	4:47.4	1980	Romania: I. Potzaichin, T. Simionov	3:47.65
1960	USSR: L. Geyshter, S. Makarenko	4:17.9	1984*	Romania: I. Potzaichin, T. Simionov	3:40.60
1964	USSR: A. Khimich, S. Oschepkov	4:04.65			

CANOEING: KAYAK FOURS—MEN: 1,000 METERS

1960	W. Germany	7:39.43	1968	Norway	3:14.38	1976	USSR	3:06.69	1984* N. Zealand 3:02.81
1964	USSR	3:14.67	1972	USSR	3:14.02	1980	E. Germany	3:13.76	

CANOEING: KAYAK FOURS—WOMEN: 500 METERS

1984	Romania	1:38.34

CANOEING: MEN: 500 METERS

KAYAK: SINGLES		CANOE: SINGLES		CANOE: DOUBLES	
1972	Siegbert Horn, E. Germany	1972	Reinhard Eiben, E. Germany	1972	E. Germany: W. Hofmann, R. Amend
1976	V. Diba, Romania	1976	A. Rogov, USSR	1976	USSR: Petrenko, Vinogradov
1980	V. Parfenovich, USSR	1980	S. Postrekhin, USSR	1980	Hungary: Foltan, Vaskuti
1984	I. Ferguson, N. Zealand	1984	Larry Cain, Canada	1984	Yugoslavia: Ljubek, Nisovic

CYCLING: ROAD RACE—INDIVIDUAL

1896	A. Konstantinidis, Greece	1928	H. Hansen, Denmark	1956	E. Baldini, Italy	1976	B. Johansson, Sweden
1906	Vast, Bardonneau (tie), France	1932	A. Pavesi, Italy	1960	V. Kapitonov, USSR	1980	S. Sukhoruchenkov,
1912	R. Lewis, S. Africa	1936	R. Charpentier, France	1964	M. Zanin, Italy		USSR
1920	H. Stenquist, Sweden	1948	J. Bayaert, France	1968	P. Vianelli, Italy	1984	Alexi Grewal, U.S.A.
1924	A. Blanchonnet, France	1952	A. Noyelle, Belgium	1972	H. Kuiper, Neth.		

*
Olympic record.

SUMMER OLYMPIC WINNERS AND RECORDS (continued)

CYCLING: ROAD RACE—TEAM: 100 KILOMETERS

1912	Sweden	1928	Denmark	1948	Belgium	1960	Italy	1972	USSR	1984	Italy
1920	France	1932	Italy	1952	Belgium	1964	Netherlands	1976	USSR		
1924	France	1936	France	1956	France	1968	Netherlands	1980	USSR		

CYCLING: INDIVIDUAL TIME TRIAL—1,000 METERS

1928	W. Falck-Hansen, Denmark	1:14.2	1956	L. Faggin, Italy	1:09.8	1976	K.J.Gruenke, E.Germany	1:05.927
1932	E. Gray, Australia	1:13.0	1960	S. Gaiardoni, Italy	1:07.27	1980*	L. Thoms	1:02.955
1936	A. van Vliet, Netherlands	1:12.0	1964	P. Sercu, Belgium	1:09.59	1984	Fredy Schmidtke, W.	
1948	J. Dupont, France	1:13.5	1968	P. Trentin, France	1:03.91		Germany	1:06.104
1952	Mockridge, Australia	1:11.1	1972	N. Fredborg, Denmark	1:06.44			

CYCLING: INDIVIDUAL PURSUIT—4,000 METERS

1964	J. Daller, Czechoslovakia	5:04.7	1976	G. Braun, W. Germany	4:47.61
1968	D. Rebillard, France	4:41.71	1980*	R. Dill-Bundi, Switzerland	4:35.66
1972	K. Knudsen, Norway	4:45.74	1984	Steve Hegg, U.S.A.	4:39.35

CYCLING: TEAM PURSUIT—4,000 METERS

1920	Italy 5:20.0	1932	Italy ..4:53.0	1952	Italy 4:46.1	1964	W.Germany 4:35.6	1976	W.Germany 4:21.06
1924	Italy 5:15.0	1936	France 4:45.0	1956	Italy 4:37.4	1968	Denmark ..4:22.44	1980*	USSR ...4:15.70
1928	Italy 5:01.8	1948	France 4:57.8	1960	Italy 4:30.9	1972	W.Germany 4:22.14	1984	Australia ..4:25.99

CYCLING: SCRATCH SPRINT (Time for final 200 meters in seconds)

1924	L. Michard, France	12.8	1952	E. Sacchi, Italy	12.0	1976	A. Tkac, Czechoslovakia	—[1]
1928	R. Beaufrand, France	13.2	1956	M. Rousseau, France	11.4	1980	L. Hesslich, E. Germany	—[1]
1932	J. van Edmond, Netherlands	13.2	1964	G. Pettenella, Italy	13.6	1984	Mark Gorski, U.S.A.	10.49
1936	T. Merkens, Germany	11.8	1968*	D. Morelon, France	10.68			
1948	M. Ghella, Italy	12.0	1972	D. Morelon, France	—[1]			

CYCLING: ROAD RACE—WOMEN: 79.2 KILOMETERS

1984*	Connie Carpenter, U.S.A.	2:11.14

CYCLING: POINTS RACE—MEN

1984	Roger Ilegems, Belgium

CYCLING: TANDEM—2,000 METERS

1908	France	1928	Netherlands	1948	Italy	1960	Italy	1972	USSR
1920	Britain	1932	France	1952	Australia	1964	Italy		
1924	France	1936	Germany	1956	Australia	1968	France		

EQUESTRIAN: INDIVIDUAL—THREE-DAY EVENT

1912	A. Nordlander, Sweden	1948	B. Chevallier, France	1972	R. Meade, Britian
1920	Helmer Morner, Sweden	1952	H. von Blixen-Finecke, Sweden	1976	E. Coffin, U.S.A.
1924	A. van der Voort van Zijp, Neth.	1956	P. Kastenman, Sweden	1980	F.E. Roman, Italy
1928	F.P. de Mortanges, Netherlands	1960	L. Morgan, Australia	1984	Mark Todd, New Zealand
1932	F. P. de Mortanges, Netherlands	1964	M. Checcoli, Italy		
1936	L. Stubbendorff, Germany	1968	J. Guyon, France		

EQUESTRIAN: INDIVIDUAL—DRESSAGE

1912	C. Bonde, Sweden	1948	H. Moser, Switzerland	1972	L. Linsenhoff, W. Germany
1920	J. Lundblad, Sweden	1952	H. St. Cyr, Sweden	1976	C. Stueckelberger, Switzerland
1924	E. Linder, Sweden	1956	H. St. Cyr, Sweden	1980	E. Theurer, Austria
1928	C. von Langen, Germany	1960	S. Filatov, USSR	1984	R. Klimke, W. Germany
1932	R. Lesage, France	1964	H. Chammartin, Switzerland		
1936	H. Pollary, Germany	1968	I. Kizimov, USSR		

EQUESTRIAN: INDIVIDUAL—GRAND PRIX JUMPING

1912	J. Cariou, France	1948	H. Mariles Cortes, Mexico	1972	G. Mancinelli, Italy
1920	T. Lequio, Italy	1952	P. d'Oriola, France	1976	A. Schockemoehle, W. Germany
1924	A. Gemuseus, Switzerland	1956	H. Winkler, W. Germany	1980	J. Kowalczyk, Poland
1928	F. Ventura, Czechoslovakia	1960	R. d'Inzeo, Italy	1984	Joe Fargis, U.S.A.
1932	T. Nishi, Japan	1964	P. d'Oriola, France		
1936	K. Hasse, Germany	1968	W.C. Steinkraus, U.S.A.		

EQUESTRIAN: TEAM—THREE-DAY EVENT

1912	Sweden	1928	Netherlands	1948	U.S.A.	1960	Australia	1972	Britain	1984	U.S.A.
1920	Sweden	1932	U.S.A.	1952	Sweden	1964	Italy	1976	U.S.A.		
1924	Netherlands	1936	Germany	1956	Britain	1968	Britain	1980	USSR		

EQUESTRIAN: TEAM—DRESSAGE

1928	Germany	1948	France	1964	W. Germany	1976	W. Germany
1932	France	1952	Sweden	1968	W. Germany	1980	USSR
1936	Germany	1956	Sweden	1972	USSR	1984	W. Germany

EQUESTRIAN: TEAM—GRAND PRIX JUMPING

1912	Sweden	1928	Spain	1952	Britain	1964	W. Germany	1976	France
1920	Sweden	1936	Germany	1956	W. Germany	1968	Canada	1980	USSR
1924	Sweden	1948	Mexico	1960	W. Germany	1972	W. Germany	1984	U.S.A.

* Olympic record. [1] Time not available.

FENCING: FOILS—MEN: INDIVIDUAL

1896	E. Gravelotte, France	1924	R. Ducret, France	1952	C. d'Oriola, France	1972	W. Woyda, Poland
1900	C. Coste, France	1928	L. Gauldin, France	1956	C. d'Oriola, France	1976	F. dal Zotto, Italy
1904	R. Fonst, Cuba	1932	G. Marzi, Italy	1960	V. Zhdanovich, USSR	1980	V. Smirnov, USSR
1912	N. Nadi, Italy	1936	G. Gaudini, Italy	1964	E. Franke, Poland	1984	M. Numa, Italy
1920	N. Nadi, Italy	1948	J. Buhan, France	1968	I. Drima, Romania		

FENCING: FOILS—WOMEN: INDIVIDUAL

1924	E. Osiier, Denmark	1952	I. Camber, Italy	1972	Ragno Lonzi, Italy
1928	H. Mayer, Germany	1956	G. Sheen, Britain	1976	I. Schwarczenberger, Hungary
1932	E. Preis, Austria	1960	A. Schmid, W. Germany	1980	P. Trinquet, France
1936	I. Elek, Hungary	1964	I. Rejto, Hungary	1984	Luan Jujie, China
1948	I. Elek, Hungary	1968	E. Novikova, USSR		

FENCING: FOILS—MEN: TEAM

1904	Cuba	1928	Italy	1948	France	1960	USSR	1972	Poland	1984	Italy
1920	Italy	1932	France	1952	France	1964	USSR	1976	W. Germany		
1924	France	1936	Italy	1956	Italy	1968	France	1980	France		

FENCING: FOILS—WOMEN: TEAM

1960	USSR	1968	USSR	1972	USSR	1976	USSR	1980	France	1984	W. Germany
1964	Hungary										

FENCING: ÉPÉE—MEN: INDIVIDUAL

1900	R. Fonst, Cuba	1928	C. Cornaggia-Medici, Italy	1968	G. Kulcsar, Hungary
1904	R. Fonst, Cuba	1936	F. Riccardi, Italy	1972	C. Fenyvesi, Hungary
1908	G. Alibert, France	1948	L. Cantone, Italy	1976	A. Pusch, W. Germany
1912	P. Anspach, Belgium	1952	E. Mangiarotti, Italy	1980	J. Harmenberg, Sweden
1920	A. Massard, France	1956	C. Pavesi, Italy	1984	P. Boisse, France
1924	C. Delporte, Belgium	1960	G. Delfino, Italy		
1928	L. Gaudin, France	1964	G. Kriss, USSR		

FENCING: ÉPÉE—MEN: TEAM

1908	France	1924	France	1936	Italy	1956	Italy	1968	Hungary	1980	France
1912	Belgium	1928	Italy	1948	France	1960	Italy	1972	Hungary	1984	W. Germany
1920	Italy	1932	France	1952	Italy	1964	Hungary	1976	Sweden		

FENCING: SABRE—MEN: INDIVIDUAL

1896	J. Georgiadis, Greece	1932	G. Piller, Hungary	1972	V. Sidiak, USSR
1900	G. de la Falaise, France	1936	E. Kabos, Hungary	1976	V. Krovopuskov, USSR
1904	M. Diaz, Cuba	1948	A. Gerevich, Hungary	1980	V. Krovopuskov, USSR
1908	J. Fuchs, Hungary	1952	P. Kovacs, Hungary	1984	J.F. Lamour, France
1912	J. Fuchs, Hungary	1956	R. Karpati, Hungary		
1920	N. Nadi, Italy	1960	R. Karpati, Hungary		
1924	S. Posta, Hungary	1964	T. Pezsa, Hungary		
1928	O. Tersztyanszky, Hungary	1968	J. Pawlowski, Poland		

FENCING: SABRE—MEN: TEAM

1904	Cuba	1920	Italy	1932	Hungary	1952	Hungary	1964	USSR	1976	USSR
1908	Hungary	1924	Italy	1936	Hungary	1956	Hungary	1968	USSR	1980	USSR
1912	Hungary	1928	Hungary	1948	Hungary	1960	Hungary	1972	Italy	1984	Italy

FIELD HOCKEY—MEN

1908	Britain	1928	India	1948	India	1956	India	1964	India	1972	W. Germany	1980	India
1920	Britain	1936	India	1952	India	1960	Pakistan	1968	Pakistan	1976	New Zealand	1984	Pakistan

FIELD HOCKEY—WOMEN

1980	Zimbabwe	1984	Netherlands

GYMNASTICS: ALL-AROUND—MEN: TEAM

1896	Germany	1920	Italy	1936	Germany	1960	Japan	1976	Japan
1904	U.S.A.	1924	Italy	1948	Finland	1964	Japan	1980	USSR
1908	Sweden	1928	Switzerland	1952	USSR	1968	Japan	1984	U.S.A.
1912	Italy	1932	Italy	1956	USSR	1972	Japan		

GYMNASTICS: ALL-AROUND—WOMEN: TEAM

1928	Netherlands	1948	Czech.	1956	USSR	1964	USSR	1972	USSR	1980	USSR
1936	Germany	1952	USSR	1960	USSR	1968	USSR	1976	USSR	1984	Romania

GYMNASTICS: ALL-AROUND—MEN: INDIVIDUAL

1900	S. Sandras, France	1932	R. Neri, Italy	1968	S. Kato, Japan
1904	A. Heida, U.S.A.	1936	A. Schwarzmann, Germany	1972	S. Kato, Japan
1908	A. Braglia, Italy	1948	V. Huhtanen, Finland	1976	N. Andrianov, USSR
1912	A. Braglia, Italy	1952	V. Chukarin, USSR	1980	A. Dityatin, USSR
1920	G. Zampori, Italy	1956	V. Chukarin, USSR	1984	Koji Gushiken, Japan
1924	L. Stukelj, Yugoslavia	1960	B. Shakhlin, USSR		
1928	G. Miez, Switzerland	1964	Y. Endo, Japan		

SUMMER OLYMPIC WINNERS AND RECORDS (continued)

GYMNASTICS: ALL-AROUND—WOMEN: INDIVIDUAL

1952	M. Gorokhovskaja, USSR	1964	V. Caslavska, Czech.	1976	N. Comaneci, Romania
1956	L. Latynina, USSR	1968	V. Caslavska, Czech.	1980	Y. Davydova, USSR
1960	L. Latynina, USSR	1972	L. Turischeva, USSR	1984	Mary Lou Retton, U.S.A.

GYMNASTICS: VAULT—MEN

1896	K. Schumann, Germany	1948	P. Aaltonen, Finland	1964	H. Yamashita, Japan
1904	(tie) A. Heida, G. Eyser, U.S.A.	1952	V. Chukarin, USSR	1968	M. Voronin, USSR
1924	F. Kriz, U.S.A.	1956	(tie) H. Bantz, W. Germany;	1972	K. Koeste, E. Germany
1928	E. Mack, Switzerland		V. Mouratov, USSR	1976	N. Andrianov, USSR
1932	S. Guglielmetti, Italy	1960	(tie) B. Shakhlin, USSR;	1980	N. Andrianov, USSR
1936	K. Schwarzmann, Germany		T. Ono, Japan	1984	Lou Yun, China

GYMNASTICS: VAULT—WOMEN

1952	Y. Kalinthouk, USSR	1964	V. Caslavska, Czech.	1976	N. Kim, USSR
1956	L. Latynina, USSR	1968	V. Caslavska, Czech.	1980	N. Shaposhnikova, USSR
1960	M. Nikolaeva, USSR	1972	K. Janz, E. Germany	1984	E. Szabo, Romania

GYMNASTICS: PARALLEL BARS—MEN

1896	A. Flatow, Germany	1932	R. Neri, Italy	1956	V. Chukarin, USSR	1972	S. Kato, Japan
1904	G. Eyser, U.S.A.	1936	K. Frey, Germany	1960	B. Shakhlin, USSR	1976	S. Kato, Japan
1924	A. Guttinger, Switz.	1948	M. Reusch, Switz.	1964	Y. Endo, Japan	1980	A. Tkachyov, USSR
1928	L. Vacha, Czech.	1952	H. Eugster, Switz.	1968	A. Nakayama, Japan	1984	Bart Conner, U.S.A.

GYMNASTICS: UNEVEN BARS—WOMEN

1952	M. Korondi, Hungary	1964	P. Astakhova, USSR	1976	N. Comaneci, Romania	1984	(tie) J. McNamara, U.S.A.
1956	A. Keleti, Hungary	1968	V. Caslavska, Czech.	1980	M. Gnauck, E. Germany		Yanhong Ma, China
1960	P. Astakhova, USSR	1972	K. Janz, E. Germany				

GYMANASTICS: FLOOR EXERCISES—MEN

1956	V. Mouratov, USSR	1964	F. Menichelli, Italy	1972	N. Andrianov, USSR	1980	R. Bruckner, E. Germany
1960	N. Aihara, Japan	1968	S. Kato, Japan	1976	N. Andrianov, USSR	1984	Li Ning, China

GYMNASTICS: FLOOR EXERCISES—WOMEN

1952	A. Keleti, Hungary	1964	L. Latynina, USSR	1976	N. Kim, USSR
1956	(tie) A. Keleti, Hungary	1968	(tie) V. Caslavska, Czech.;	1980	(tie) N. Kim, USSR,
	L. Latynina, USSR		L. Petrik, USSR		N. Comaneci, Romania
1960	L. Latynina, USSR	1972	Olga Korbut, USSR	1984	E. Szabo, Romania

GYMNASTICS: BALANCE BEAM—WOMEN

1952	N. Botcharova, USSR	1964	V. Caslavska, Czech.	1976	N. Comaneci, Romania	1984	(tie) S. Pauca, Romania
1956	A. Keleti, Hungary	1968	N. Kutchinskava, USSR	1980	N. Comaneci, Romania		E. Szabo, Romania
1960	E. Bosakova, Czech.	1972	Olga Korbut, USSR				

GYMNASTICS: POMMEL HORSE—MEN

1896	L. Zutter, Switzerland	1952	V. Chukarin, USSR	1980	Z. Magyar, Hungary
1904	A. Heida, U.S.A.	1956	B. Shakhlin, USSR	1984	(tie) Li Ning, China
1924	J. Wilhelm, Switzerland	1960	(tie) E. Ekman, Finland;		Peter Vidmar, U.S.A.
1928	H. Hanggi, Switzerland		B. Shakhlin, USSR		
1932	I. Pelle, Hungary	1964	M. Cerar, Yugoslavia		
1936	K. Frey, Germany	1968	M. Voronin, USSR		
1948	(tie) P. Aaltonen, V. Houtanen,	1972	V. Klimenko, USSR		
	I. Savolainen, Finland	1976	Z. Magyar, Hungary		

GYMNASTICS: RHYTHMIC—WOMEN

1984	Lori Fung, Canada

GYMNASTICS: RINGS—MEN

1896	J. Mitropoulos, Greece	1936	A. Hudec, Czech.	1964	T. Hayata, Japan	1984	(tie) Koji Gushiken,
1904	H. Glass, U.S.A.	1948	K. Frei, Switz.	1968	A. Nakayama, Japan		Japan;
1924	F. Martino, Italy	1952	G. Chaguinian, USSR	1972	A. Nakayama, Japan		Li Ning, China
1928	L. Stukelj, Yugoslavia	1956	A. Azarian, USSR	1976	N. Andrainov, USSR		
1932	G. Gulack, U.S.A.	1960	A. Azarian, USSR	1980	A. Dityatin, USSR		

GYMNASTICS: HORIZONTAL BAR—MEN

1896	H. Weingaertner, Ger.	1932	D. Bixler, U.S.A.	1960	T. Ono, Japan	1976	M. Tsukahara, Japan
1904	(tie) A. Heida, E. Hennig,	1936	A. Saarvala, Finland	1964	B. Shakhlin, USSR	1980	S. Deltchev, Bulgaria
1904	U.S.A.	1948	J. Stalder, Switz.	1968	(tie) M. Voronin, USSR;	1984	S. Morisue, Japan
1924	L. Stukelj, Yugoslavia	1952	J. Gunthard, Switz.		A. Nakayama, Japan		
1928	G. Miez, Switzerland	1956	T. Ono, Japan	1972	M. Tsukahara, Japan		

HANDBALL: TEAM (MEN)

1972	Yugoslavia	1980	E. Germany
1976	USSR	1984	Yugoslavia

HANDBALL: TEAM (WOMEN)

1980	USSR	1984	Yugoslavia

JUDO

EXTRA LIGHTWEIGHT		HALF LIGHTWEIGHT		LIGHTWEIGHT		HALF MIDDLEWEIGHT	
1980	T. Rey, France	1980	N. Solodukin, USSR	1964	T. Nakatani, Japan	1972	T. Nomura, Japan
1984	S. Hosokawa, Japan	1984	Y. Matsuoka, Japan	1972	T. Kawaguchi, Japan	1976	V. Nevzorov, USSR
				1976	H. Rodriguez, Cuba	1980	S. Khabareli, USSR
				1980	E. Gamba, Italy	1984	F. Weineke, W. Germany
				1984	B. K. Ahn, S. Korea		

JUDO

MIDDLEWEIGHT	HALF HEAVYWEIGHT	HEAVYWEIGHT	OPEN
1964 I. Okano, Japan	1972 S. Chochoshvily, USSR	1964 I. Inokuma, Japan	1964 A. Geesink, Neth.
1972 S. Sekine, Japan	1976 K. Ninomiya, Japan	1972 W. Ruska, Neth.	1972 W. Ruska, Neth.
1976 I. Sonada, Japan	1980 R. Van de Walle,	1976 S. Novikov, USSR	1976 H. Uemura, Japan
1980 J. Roethlisberger,	Belgium	1980 A. Parisi, France;	1980 D. Lorenz, E. Germany
Switzerland;	1984 H. Zoo Ha, S. Korea	1984 H. Saito, Japan	1984 Y. Yamashita, Japan
1984 P. Seisenbacher,			
Austria			

MODERN PENTATHLON: WOMEN—INDIVIDUAL

1964 I. Press, USSR	1972 Mary Peters, Britain	1980 O. Tkachenko, USSR	
1968 I. Becker, W. Germany	1976 Sigurn Siegl, E. Germany	1984 D. Masala, Italy	

MODERN PENTATHLON: INDIVIDUAL

1912 Jim Thorpe, U.S.A.	1932 J. Oxenstierna, Sweden	1960 F. Nemeth, Hungary	1980 A. Starostin, USSR
G. Lilliehood, Sweden	1936 G. Handrick, Germany	1964 F. Torok, Hungary	
1920 J. Dyrssen, Sweden	1948 W. Grut, Sweden	1968 B. Ferm, Sweden	
1924 Bo Lindman, Sweden	1952 L. Hall, Sweden	1972 A. Balczo, Hungary	
1928 S. Thofelt, Sweden	1956 L. Hall, Sweden	1976 J. Pyciak-Peciak, Poland	

MODERN PENTATHLON: TEAM

1952 Hungary	1960 Hungary	1968 Hungary	1976 Britain	1984 Italy
1956 USSR	1964 USSR	1972 USSR	1980 USSR	

ROWING: SINGLE SCULLS—MEN

1900 H. Pearce, Australia	1928 H. Pearce, Australia	1956 V. Ivanov, USSR	1976 P. Karppinen, Finland
1908 H. Blackstaffe, Britain	1932 H. Pearce, Australia	1960 V. Ivanov, USSR	1980 P. Karppinen, Finland
1912 W. Kinnear, Britain	1936 G. Schafer, Germany	1964 V. Ivanov, USSR	1984 P. Karppinen, Finland
1920 John Kelly, U.S.A.	1948 M. Wood, Australia	1968 J. Wienese, Neth.	
1924 J. Beresford, Britain	1952 Y. Chukalov, USSR	1972 Y. Malishev, USSR	

ROWING: DOUBLE SCULLS—MEN

1920 U.S.A.	1932 Britain	1952 Argentina	1964 USSR	1976 Norway
1924 U.S.A.	1936 Germany	1956 USSR	1968 USSR	1980 E. Germany
1928 U.S.A.	1948 Britain	1960 Czechoslovakia	1972 USSR	1984 U.S.A.

ROWING: QUADRUPLE SCULLS—MEN

1984 West Germany	

ROWING: PAIRS WITHOUT COXSWAIN—MEN

1908 Britain	1932 Britain	1956 U.S.A.	1968 E. Germany	1980 E. Germany
1920 Italy	1936 Germany	1960 USSR	1972 E. Germany	1984 Romania
1924 Netherlands	1948 Britain	1964 Canada	1976 E. Germany	
1928 Germany	1952 U.S.A.			

ROWING: PAIRS WITH COXSWAIN—MEN

1900 Netherlands	1932 U.S.A.	1952 France	1964 U.S.A.	1976 E. Germany
1924 Switzerland	1936 Germany	1956 U.S.A.	1968 Italy	1980 E. Germany
1928 Switzerland	1948 Denmark	1960 W. Germany	1972 E. Germany	1984 Italy

ROWING: FOURS WITHOUT COXSWAIN—MEN

1908 Britain	1932 Britain	1952 Yugoslavia	1964 Denmark	1976 E. Germany
1924 Britain	1936 Germany	1956 Canada	1968 E. Germany	1980 E. Germany
1928 Britain	1948 Italy	1960 U.S.A	1972 W. Germany	1984 New Zealand

ROWING: FOURS WITH COXSWAIN—MEN

1912 Germany	1932 Germany	1956 Italy	1972 W. Germany	
1920 Switzerland	1936 Germany	1960 W. Germany	1976 USSR	
1924 Switzerland	1948 U.S.A.	1964 W. Germany	1980 E. Germany	
1928 Italy	1952 Czechoslovakia	1968 New Zealand	1984 Britain	

ROWING: EIGHTS WITH COXSWAIN—MEN

1900 U.S.A.	1920 U.S.A.	1932 U.S.A.	1952 U.S.A.	1964 U.S.A.	1976 E. Germany
1908 Britain	1924 U.S.A.	1936 U.S.A.	1956 U.S.A.	1968 W. Germany	1980 E. Germany
1912 Britain	1928 U.S.A.	1948 U.S.A.	1960 W. Germany	1972 New Zealand	1984 Canada

ROWING: WOMEN

SINGLE SCULLS		DOUBLE SCULLS		PAIRS WITHOUT COXSWAIN	
1976 E. Germany	1984 Romania	1976 Bulgaria	1984 Romania	1976 Bulgaria	1984 Romania
1980 Romania		1980 USSR		1980 E. Germany	

FOURS WITH COXSWAIN		EIGHTS WITH COXSWAIN		QUADRUPLE SCULLS WITH COXSWAIN	
1976 E. Germany	1984 Romania	1976 E. Germany	1984 U.S.A.	1976 E. Germany	1984 Romania
1980 E. Germany		1980 E. Germany		1980 E. Germany	

SHOOTING: MEN TRAPSHOOTING

1908 W.H. Ewing, Canada72	1956 G. Rossini, Italy195	1976 D. Haldeman, U.S.A.190	
1912 James Graham, U.S.A.96	1960 I. Dumitrescu, Romania ...192	1980 L. Giovannetti, Italy198	
1920 Mark Arie, U.S.A.95	1964 E. Mattarelli, Italy198	1984 L. Giovannetti, Italy192	
1924 G. Halasy, Hungary98	1968 J. Brathwaite, Britain198		
1952 G. Genereux, Canada192	1972 * A. Scalzone, Italy199		

SHOOTING: MEN PISTOL—RAPID FIRE: 25 METERS

1936 C. van Oyen, Germany36	1960 W. McMillan, U.S.A.587	1976 * N. Klaar, E. Germany597	
1948 K. Takacs, Hungary580	1964 P. Linnosvuop, Finland ...592	1980 C. Ion596	
1952 K. Takacs, Hungary579	1968 J. Zapedski, Poland593	1984 Taskeo Kamachi, Japan....	
1956 S. Petrescu, Romania587	1972 J. Zapedzki, Poland595		

SUMMER OLYMPIC WINNERS AND RECORDS *(continued)*

SHOOTING: MEN PISTOL—FREE: 50 METERS

Year	Winner	Score	Year	Winner	Score	Year	Winner	Score
1936	T. Ullmann, Sweden	539	1960	A. Gustchin, USSR	560	1976	V. Potteck, E. Germany	573
1948	C.E. Vasquez, Peru	545	1964	V. Markkanen, Finland	560	1980	A. Melemtev, USSR	581
1952	Huelet Benner, U.S.A.	553	1968	G. Kosykh, USSR	562	1984	Xu Haifeng, China	566
1956	P. Linnosvuoo, Finland	556	1972	R. Skanaker, Sweden	567			

SHOOTING: MEN SMALL-BORE RIFLE—PRONE: 50 METERS

Year	Winner	Score	Year	Winner	Score	Year	Winner	Score
1960	P. Kohnke, W. Germany	590	1972 *	Ho Jun Li, North Korea	599	1980	K. Varga, Hungary, H. Heilfort, E. Germany	599
1964	L. Hammerl, Hungary	597	1976	K. Smiezek, W. Germany	599			
1968	Jan Kurka, Czech.	598				1984	Edward Etzell, U.S.A.	599

SHOOTING: MEN SMALL-BORE RIFLE—3-POSITION

Year	Winner	Score	Year	Winner	Score	Year	Winner	Score
1960	V. Shamburkin, USSR	1,149	1972	John Writer, U.S.A.	1,166	1984	Malcolm Cooper, Britain	1,173
1964	Lones Wigger, U.S.A.	1,164	1976	K. Smiezek, W. Germany	599			
1968	B. Klingner, W. Ger.	1,157	1980 *	V. Vlasov, USSR	1,173			

SHOOTING: MEN SKEET SHOOTING

Year	Winner	Score	Year	Winner	Score
1968 *	Evgeny Petrov, USSR	198	1980	H. Rasmussen, Den.	196
1972	Konrad Wirnhier, W. Germany	195	1984	Matthew Dryke, U.S.A.	198
1976 *	J. Panacek, Czech.	198			

SHOOTING: MOVING TARGET

Year	Winner	Score
1972	Lakov Zhelezniak, USSR	569
1976	A. Gazov, USSR	579
1980 *	I. Sokolov, USSR	589
1984	Li Yuwei, China	587

SHOOTING: WOMEN: SMALL BORE RIFLE

Year	Winner	Score
1984	Wu Xiaoxuan, China	581

SHOOTING: WOMEN: SPORTS RIFLE

Year	Winner	Score
1984	Linda Thom, Canada	585

SHOOTING: WOMEN: AIR RIFLE

Year	Winner	Score
1984	Pat Spurgin, U.S.A.	393

SHOOTING: MEN: AIR RIFLE

Year	Winner	Score
1984	Phillippe Heberle, France	589

SOCCER

Year	Winner	Year	Winner	Year	Winner	Year	Winner	Year	Winner	Year	Winner
1900	Britain	1912	Britain	1928	Uruguay	1952	Hungary	1964	Hungary	1976	E. Germany
1904	Canada	1920	Belgium	1936	Italy	1956	USSR	1968	Hungary	1980	Czech.
1908	Britain	1924	Uruguay	1948	Sweden	1958	Yugoslavia	1972	Poland	1984	France

SWIMMING: 100-METER FREESTYLE—MEN

Year	Winner	Time	Year	Winner	Time	Year	Winner	Time
1896	A. Hajos, Hungary	1:22.2	1928	John Weissmuller, U.S.A.	0:58.6	1964	D. Schollander, U.S.A.	0:53.40
1900	Jarvis, Britain	1:16.0	1932	Y. Miyazaki, Japan	0:58.2	1968	M. Wenden, Australia	0:52.22
1904	†de Halmay, Hungary	1:02.8	1936	Ferenc Csik, Hungary	0:57.6	1972	Mark Spitz, U.S.A.	0:51.22
1908	Charles Daniels, U.S.A.	1:05.6	1948	Walter Ris, U.S.A.	0:57.3	1976	J. Montgomery, U.S.A.	0:49.99
1912	Duke Kahanamoku, U.S.A.	1:03.4	1952	Clarke Scholes, U.S.A.	0:57.4	1980	J. Woithe, E. Germany	0:50.40
1920	Duke Kahanamoku, U.S.A.	1:01.4	1956	Jon Henricks, Australia	0:55.4	1984 *	Rowdy Gaines, U.S.A.	0:49.80
1924	John Weissmuller, U.S.A.	0:59.0	1960	J. Devitt, Australia	0:55.2			

SWIMMING: 100-METER FREESTYLE—WOMEN

Year	Winner	Time	Year	Winner	Time	Year	Winner	Time
1912	F. Durack, Australia	1:22.2	1948	Greta Andersen, Denmark	1:06.3	1972	Sandra Neilson, U.S.A.	0:58.59
1920	Ethelda Bleibtrey, U.S.A.	1:13.6	1952	Katalin Szoke, Hungary	1:06.8	1976	K. Ender, E. Germany	0:55.65
1924	Ethel Lackie, U.S.A.	1:12.4	1956	Dawn Fraser, Australia	1:02.0	1980 *	B. Krause, E. Germany	0:54.79
1928	Albina Osipowich, U.S.A.	1:11.0	1960	Dawn Fraser, Australia	1:01.2	1984	Carrie Steinseifer, U.S.A., and Nancy Hogshead, U.S.A.	0:55.92
1932	Helene Madison, U.S.A.	1:06.8	1964	Dawn Fraser, Australia	0:59.50			
1936	H. Mastenbroek, Neth.	1:05.9	1968	Margo Jan Henne, U.S.A.	1:00.00			

SWIMMING: 400-METER FREESTYLE—MEN

Year	Winner	Time	Year	Winner	Time	Year	Winner	Time
1908	Henry Taylor, Britain	5:35.8	1936	Jack Medica, U.S.A.	4:44.5	1968	Michael Burton, U.S.A.	4:09.00
1912	G. Hodgson, Canada	5:24.4	1948	William Smith, U.S.A.	4:41.0	1972	B. Cooper, Australia	4:00.27
1920	Norman Ross, U.S.A.	5:26.8	1952	Jean Boiteux, France	4:30.7	1976	B. Goodell, U.S.A.	3:51.93
1924	John Weissmuller, U.S.A.	5:04.2	1956	Murray Rose, Australia	4:27.3	1980	V. Salnikov, USSR	3:51.31
1928	A. Zorilla, Argentina	5:01.6	1960	Murray Rose, Australia	4:18.3	1984 *	George DiCarlo, U.S.A.	3:51.23
1932	Clarence Crabbe, U.S.A.	4:48.4	1964	Don Schollander, U.S.A.	4:12.2			

SWIMMING: 400-METER FREESTYLE—WOMEN

Year	Winner	Time	Year	Winner	Time	Year	Winner	Time
1924	Martha Norelius, U.S.A.	6:02.2	1952	V. Gyenge, Hungary	5:12.1	1972	Shane Gould, Australia	4:19.04
1928	Martha Norelius, U.S.A.	5:26.4	1956	L. Crapp, Australia	4:54.6	1976	Petra Thuemer, E. Ger.	4:09.89
1932	Helene Madison, U.S.A.	5:28.5	1960	C. von Saltza, U.S.A.	4:50.6	1980	Ines Diers, E. Germany	4:08.76
1936	H. Mastenbroek, Neth.	5:26.4	1964	Ginny Duenkel, U.S.A.	4:43.3	1984 *	Tiffany Cohen, U.S.A.	4:07.10
1948	Ann Curtis, U.S.A.	5:17.8	1968	Deborah Meyer, U.S.A.	4:31.8			

SWIMMING: 100-METER BACKSTROKE—MEN

Year	Winner	Time	Year	Winner	Time	Year	Winner	Time
1908	Arno Bieberstein, Germany	1:24.6	1936	Adolf Kiefer, U.S.A.	1:05.9	1968	R. Matthes, E. Germany	0:58.7
1912	Harry Hebner, U.S.A.	1:21.2	1948	Allen Stack, U.S.A.	1:06.4	1972	R. Matthes, E. Germany	0:56.58
1920	Warren Kealoha, U.S.A.	1:15.2	1952	Y. Oyakawa, U.S.A.	1:05.4	1976 *	J. Naber, U.S.A.	0:55.49
1924	Warren Kealoha, U.S.A.	1:13.2	1956	D. Thiele, Australia	1:02.2	1980	B. Baron, Sweden	0:56.53
1928	George Kojac, U.S.A.	1:08.2	1960	D. Thiele, Australia	1:01.9	1984	Rick Carey, U.S.A.	0:55.79
1932	M. Kiyokawa, Japan	1:08.6	1964	Event not held				

SWIMMING: 100-METER BACKSTROKE—WOMEN

Year	Winner	Time	Year	Winner	Time	Year	Winner	Time
1924	Sybil Bauer, U.S.A.	1:23.2	1952	J. Harrison, S. Africa	1:14.3	1972	Melissa Belote, U.S.A.	1:05.78
1928	Marie Braun, Netherlands	1:22.0	1956	J. Grinham, Britain	1:12.9	1976	U. Richter, E. Germany	1:01.83
1932	Eleanor Holm, U.S.A.	1:19.4	1960	Lynn Burke, U.S.A.	1:09.3	1980 *	R. Reinisch, E. Germany	1:00.86
1936	Dina Senff, Netherlands	1:18.9	1964	Cathy Ferguson, U.S.A.	1:07.7	1984	Theresa Andrews, U.S.A.	1:02.55
1948	Karen Harup, Denmark	1:14.4	1968	Kaye Hall, U.S.A.	1:06.2			

* Olympic record.

SWIMMING: 200-METER BREASTSTROKE—MEN

1908	F. Holman, Britain 3:09.2	1936	T. Hamuro, Japan 2:41.5	1968	F. Munoz, Mexico 2:28.7
1912	W. Bathe, Germany 3:01.8	1948	Joseph Verduer, U.S.A. . 2:39.3	1972	John Hencken, U.S.A. .. 2:21.55
1920	H. Malmroth, Sweden .. 3:04.4	1952	J. Davis, Australia 2:34.4	1976	D. Wilkie, Britain 2:15.11
1924	Robert Skelton, U.S.A... 2:56.6	1956	M. Furukawa, Japan 2:34.7	1980	R. Zulpa, USSR 2:15.85
1928	Y. Tsuruta, Japan...... 2:48.8	1960	W. Mulliken, U.S.A. 2:37.4	1984*	Victor Davis, Canada.. 2:13.34
1932	Y. Tsuruta, Japan...... 2:45.4	1964	Ian O'Brian, Australia .. 2:27.8		

SWIMMING: 200-METER BREASTSTROKE—WOMEN

1924	Lucy Morton, Britain ... 3:33.2	1956	U. Happe, W. Germany . 2:53.1	1976	M. Koshevaia, USSR .. 2:33.35
1928	Hilde Schrader, Germany 3:12.6	1960	A. Lonsbrough, Britain.... 2:49.5	1980	L. Kachushite, USSR .. 2:29.54
1932	C. Dennis, Australia 3:06.3	1964	G. Prozumenschikova,	1984	Anne Ottenbrite, Canada 2:30.38
1936	H. Maehata, Japan 3:03.6		USSR 2:46.4		
1948	Nel Vliet, Netherlands .. 2:57.2	1968	Sharon Wichman, U.S.A.. 2:44.4		
1952	Eva Szekely, Hungary .. 2:51.7	1972	B. Whitfield, Australia.... 2:41.71		

SWIMMING: 100-METER BUTTERFLY STROKE—MEN

1968	D. Russell, U.S.A. 0:55.9	1976	M. Vogel, U.S.A......... 54.35	1984*	Michael Gross, W. Germany 53.08
1972	M. Spitz, U.S.A. 0:54.27	1980	P. Arvidsson, Sweden ... 54.92		

SWIMMING: 100-METER BUTTERFLY STROKE—WOMEN

1956	Shelley Mann, U.S.A. ... 1:11.0	1968	L. McClements, Australia 1:05.5	1980	C. Metschuck 1:00.42
1960	Carolyn Schuler, U.S.A. . 1:09.5	1972	M. Aoki, Japan 1:03.34	1984*	Mary T. Meagher, U.S.A. 0:59.26
1964	Sharon Stouder, U.S.A.. 1:04.7	1976	K. Ender, E. Germany . 1:00.13		

SWIMMING: 400-METER INDIVIDUAL MEDLEY—MEN

1964	Dick Roth, U.S.A. 4:45.4	1972	G. Larsson, Sweden ... 4:31.98	1980	A. Sidorenko, USSR ... 4:22.89
1968	Charles Hickcox, U.S.A. 4:48.4	1976	R. Strachan, U.S.A. ... 4:23.68	1984*	Alex Baumann, Canada 4:17.41

SWIMMING: 400-METER INDIVIDUAL MEDLEY—WOMEN

1964	Donna de Varona, U.S.A. 5:18.7	1972	G. Neall, Australia 5:02.97	1980*	P. Schneider, E. Germany 4:36.29
1968	Claudia Kolb, U.S.A. ... 5:08.5	1976	U. Tauber, E. Germany 4:42.77	1984	Tracy Caulkins, U.S.A. 4:39.24

SWIMMING: 400-METER FREESTYLE RELAY—WOMEN

1912	Britain 5:52.8	1932	U.S.A....... 4:38.0	1956	Australia 4:17.1	1972	U.S.A. 3:55.19
1920	U.S.A. 5:11.6	1936	Netherlands . 4:36.0	1960	U.S.A. 4:08.9	1976	U.S.A. 3:44.82
1924	U.S.A........ 4:58.8	1948	U.S.A........ 4:29.2	1964	U.S.A. 4:03.8	1980*	E. Germany . 3:42.71
1928	U.S.A........ 4:47.6	1952	Hungary 4:24.4	1968	U.S.A. 4:02.5	1984	U.S.A. 3:43.43

SWIMMING: 400-METER FREESTYLE RELAY—MEN

1984*	U.S.A.....................................3:19.03

SWIMMING: 400-METER MEDLEY RELAY—MEN

1960	U.S.A. 4:05.4	1968	U.S.A. 3:54.9	1976	U.S.A. 3:42.22	1984*	U.S.A. 3:39.30
1964	U.S.A. 3:58.4	1972	U.S.A. 3:48.16	1980	Australia ... 3:45.70		

SWIMMING: 400-METER MEDLEY RELAY—WOMEN

1960	U.S.A. 4:41.1	1968	U.S.A. 4:28.3	1976	E. Germany . 4:07.95	1984	U.S.A. 4:08.34
1964	U.S.A. 4:33.9	1972	U.S.A. 4:20.75	1980*	E. Germany . 4:06.67		

SWIMMING: 200-METER BACKSTROKE—MEN

1964	Jed Graef, Australia ... 2:10.3	1972	R. Matthes, E. Germany 2:02.82	1980	S. Wladar, Hungary ... 2:01.93
1968	R. Matthes, E. Germany 2:09.6	1976	J. Naber, U.S.A. 1:59.19	1984*	Rick Carey, U.S.A. 2:00.23

SWIMMING: 200-METER BACKSTROKE—WOMEN

1968	L. Watson, U.S.A. 2:24.8	1972	U. Richter, E. Germany 2:13.43	1984	Jolanda De Rover,
1972	M. Belote, U.S.A. 2:19.19	1980*	R. Reinisch, E. Germany 2:11.77		Netherlands 2:12.35

SWIMMING: 200-METER BUTTERFLY STROKE—MEN

1956	William Yorzyk, U.S.A. .. 2:19.3	1968	Carl Robie, U.S.A. 2:08.7	1980	S. Fesenko, USSR 1:59.76
1960	Michael Troy, U.S.A. .. 2:12.8	1972	Mark Spitz, U.S.A. 2:00.70	1984*	Jon Sieben, Australia . 1:57.04
1964	Kevin Berry, Australia .. 2:06.6	1976*	M. Bruner, U.S.A....... 1:59.23		

SWIMMING: 200-METER BUTTERFLY STROKE—WOMEN

1968	A. Kok, Netherlands .. 2:24.7	1976	A. Pollack, E. Germany 2:11.43	1984*	Mary Meagher, U.S.A. . 2:06.90
1972	K. Moe, U.S.A........ 2:15.57	1980	I. Geissler, E. Germany 2:10.44		

SWIMMING: 100-METER BREASTSTROKE—MEN

1968	D. McKenzie, U.S.A.... 1:07.7	1976	J. Hencken, U.S.A. 1:03.11	1984*	Steve Lundquist, U.S.A. 1:01.65
1972	N. Taguchi, Japan 1:04.94	1980	D. Goodhew, Britain .. 1:03.34		

SWIMMING: 100-METER BREASTSTROKE—WOMEN

1968	D. Bjedov, Yugoslavia .. 1:15.8	1976	H. Anke, E. Germany .. 1:11.16	1984*	Petra Van Staveren, Neth. 1:09.88
1972	Catherine Carr, U.S.A.. 1:13.58	1980	U. Geweniger, E. Germany 1:10.22		

SWIMMING: 200-METER FREESTYLE—MEN

1968	Mike Wenden, Australia . 1:55.2	1976	B. Furness, U.S.A. 1:50.29	1984*	Michael Gross, W. Germany 1:47.44
1972	Mark Spitz, U.S.A. 1:52.78	1980	S. Kopliakov, USSR ... 1:49.81		

SWIMMING: 200-METER FREESTYLE—WOMEN

1968	Deborah Meyer, U.S.A. . 2:10.5	1976	K. Ender, E. Germany . 1:59.26	1984	Mary Wayte, U.S.A. ... 1:59.23
1972	Shane Gould, Australia 2:03.56	1980*	B. Krause, E. Germany 1:58.33		

SWIMMING: 200-METER INDIVIDUAL MEDLEY—MEN

1968	Charles Hickok, U.S.A. 2:12.0	1972	Gunnar Larsson, Sweden 2:07.17	1984*	Alex Bauman, Canada 2:01.42

* Olympic record.

SUMMER OLYMPIC WINNERS AND RECORDS *(continued)*

SWIMMING: 200-METER INDIVIDUAL MEDLEY—WOMEN

1968	Claudia Kolb, U.S.A. 2:24.7	1972	Shane Gould, Australia 2:23.07	1984*	Tracy Caulkins, U.S.A. 2:12.64

SWIMMING: 800-METER FREESTYLE—WOMEN

1968	D. Meyer, U.S.A. 9:24.0	1976	P. Thuemer, E. Germany 8:37.14	1984*	Tiffany Cohen, U.S.A. . 8:24.95
1972	K. Rothhammer, U.S.A. 8:53.68	1980	M. Ford, Australia 8:28.90		

SWIMMING: 800-METER FREESTYLE RELAY—MEN

1908	Britain 10:55.6	1936	Japan 8:51.5	1964	U.S.A. 7:52.1	1984*	U.S.A. 7:15.69
1912	Australia ... 10:11.6	1936	Japan 8:51.5	1964	U.S.A. 7:52.1		
1920	U.S.A. 10:04.4	1948	U.S.A. 8:46.0	1968	U.S.A. 7:52.3		
1924	U.S.A. 9:53.4	1952	U.S.A. 8:31.1	1972	U.S.A. 7:35.78		
1928	U.S.A. 9:36.2	1956	Australia ... 8:23.6	1976	U.S.A. 7:23.22		
1908		1960	U.S.A. 8:10.2	1980	USSR 7:23.50		

SWIMMING: 1,500—METER FREESTYLE—MEN

1908	H. Taylor, Britain .. 22:48.4	1936	N. Terada, Japan ... 19:13.7	1968	Michael Burton, U.S.A. 16:38.9
1912	G. Hodgson, Canada .. 22:00.0	1948	James McLane, U.S.A. 19:18.5	1972	Michael Burton, U.S.A. 15:52.58
1920	Norman Ross, U.S.A.. 22:23.2	1952	Ford Konno, U.S.A. .. 18:30.0	1976	B. Goodell, U.S.A. ... 15:02.40
1924	A. Charlton, Australia . 20:06.6	1956	M. Rose, Australia ... 17:58.9	1980*	V. Salnikov, USSR ... 14:58.27
1928	Arne Borg, Sweden .. 19:51.8	1960	J. Konrads, Australia .. 17:19.6	1984	Mike O'Brien, U.S.A. . 15:05.20
1932	K. Kitamura, Japan ... 19:12.4	1964	R. Windle, Australia ... 17:01.7		

SWIMMING: 3-METER SPRINGBOARD DIVING—MEN

1908	A. Zurner, Germany	1932	M. Galitzen, U.S.A.	1960	G. Tobian, U.S.A.	1980	A. Portnov, USSR
1912	P. Gunther, Germany	1936	R. Degener, U.S.A.	1964	K. Sitzberger, U.S.A.	1984	G. Louganis, U.S.A.
1920	L. Keuhn, U.S.A.	1948	B. Harlan, U.S.A.	1968	B. Wrightson, U.S.A.		
1924	A. White, U.S.A.	1952	D. Browning, U.S.A.	1972	V. Vasin, USSR		
1928	P. Desjardins, U.S.A.	1956	R. Clotworthy, U.S.A.	1976	P. Boggs, U.S.A.		

SWIMMING: 3-METER SPRINGBOARD DIVING—WOMEN

1920	A. Riggin, U.S.A.	1936	M. Gestring, U.S.A.	1960	I. Kramer, W. Germany	1976	J. Chandler, U.S.A.
1924	E. Becker, U.S.A.	1948	V. Draves, U.S.A.	1964	I. Engel-Kramer, W. Germany	1980	I. Kalinina, USSR
1928	H. Meany, U.S.A.	1952	P. McCormick, U.S.A.	1968	S. Gossick, U.S.A.	1984	S. Bernier, Canada
1932	G. Coleman, U.S.A.	1956	P. McCormick, U.S.A.	1972	M. King, U.S.A.		

SWIMMING: 10-METER PLATFORM DIVING—MEN

1904	G.E. Sheldon, U.S.A.	1928	F. Desjardins, U.S.A.	1956	J. Capilla, Mexico	1976	K. Di Biasi, Italy
1908	H. Johansson, Sweden	1932	Harold Smith, U.S.A.	1960	R. Webster, U.S.A.	1980	F. Hoffmann,
1912	E. Adlerz, Sweden	1936	M. Wayne, U.S.A.	1964	R. Webster, U.S.A.		E. Germany
1920	Clarence Pinkston, U.S.A.	1948	Samuel Lee, U.S.A.	1968	K. Di Biasi, Italy	1984	G. Louganis, U.S.A.
1924	Albert White, U.S.A.	1952	Samuel Lee, U.S.A.	1972	K. Di Biasi, Italy		

SWIMMING: 10-METER PLATFORM DIVING—WOMEN

1912	G. Johansson, Sweden	1948	Victoria Draves, U.S.A.	1972	Ulrika Knape, Sweden
1920	S. Fryland-Clausen, Denmark	1952	Patricia McCormick, U.S.A.	1976	E. Vaytsekhovskaia, USSR
1924	Caroline Smith, U.S.A.	1956	Patricia McCormick, U.S.A.	1980	M. Jaschke, E. Germany
1928	Elizabeth Pinkston, U.S.A.	1960	Ingrid Kramer, W. Germany	1984	Zhou Jihong, China
1932	Dorothy Poynton, U.S.A.	1964	Lesley Bush, U.S.A.		
1936	D. Poynton-Hill, U.S.A.	1968	M. Duchkova, Czechoslovakia		

SWIMMING: SYNCHRONIZED: DUET—WOMEN

1984	United States

SWIMMING: SYNCHRONIZED: SOLO—WOMEN

1984	Tracie Ruiz, U.S.A.

TRACK AND FIELD: 100-METER DASH—MEN

1896	Thomas Burke, U.S.A. .. 0:12.0	1928	P. Williams, Canada 0:10.8	1964	Bob Hayes, U.S.A. 0:10.0
1900	Francis Jarvis, U.S.A. .. 0:10.8	1932	Eddie Tolan, U.S.A. 0:10.3	1968*	James Hines, U.S.A. 0:09.9
1904	Archie Hahn, U.S.A. 0:11.0	1936	Jesse Owens, U.S.A. 0:10.3	1972	Valery Borzov, USSR .. 0:10.14
1908	R. Walker, S. Africa 0:10.8	1948	H. Dillard, U.S.A. 0:10.3	1976	Hasley Crawford,
1912	Ralph Craig, U.S.A. 0:10.8	1952	L. Remigino, U.S.A. 0:10.4		Trinidad-Tobago 0:10.06
1920	C. Paddock, U.S.A. 0:10.8	1956	Bobby Morrow, U.S.A. .. 0:10.5	1980	Allan Wells, Britain .. 0:10.25
1924	H. Abrahams, Britain ... 0:10.6	1960	Armin Hary, W. Germany 0:10.2	1984	Carl Lewis, U.S.A. 0:09.99

TRACK AND FIELD: 100-METER DASH—WOMEN

1928	Elizabeth Robinson, U.S.A. 0:12.2	1956	B. Cuthbert, Australia . 0:11.5	1976	A. Richter, W. Germany 0:11.08
1932	S. Walasiewicz, Poland .. 0:11.9	1960	Wilma Rudolph, U.S.A. .. 0:11.0	1980	L. Kondratyeva, USSR . 0:11.06
1936	Helen Stephens, U.S.A. . 0:11.5	1964	Wyomia Tyus, U.S.A. .. 0:11.4	1984*	E. Ashford, U.S.A. 0:10.97
1948	F. Blankers-Koen, Neth. 0:11.9	1968	Wyomia Tyus, U.S.A. .. 0:11.0		
1952	M. Jackson, Australia .. 0:11.5	1972	R. Stecher, E. Germany 0:11.07		

TRACK AND FIELD: 200-METER DASH—MEN

1900	W.B. Tewksbury, U.S.A. 0:22.2	1932	Eddie Tolan, U.S.A. 0:21.2	1968	Tommie Smith, U.S.A. .. 0:19.83
1904	Archie Hahn, U.S.A. 0:21.6	1936	Jesse Owens, U.S.A. ... 0:20.7	1972	Valery Borzov, USSR .. 0:20.00
1908	R. Kerr, Canada 0:22.6	1948	Mel Patton, U.S.A. 0:21.1	1976	D. Quarrie, Jamaica .. 0:20.23
1912	Ralph Craig, U.S.A. 0:21.7	1952	A. Stanfield, U.S.A...... 0:20.7	1980	Pietro Mennea, Italy .. 0:20.19
1920	Allan Woodring, U.S.A. 0:22.0	1956	Bobby Morrow, U.S.A. .. 0:20.6	1984	Carl Lewis, U.S.A. 0:19.80
1924	Jackson Scholz, U.S.A. . 0:21.6	1960	Livio Berruti, Italy 0:20.5		
1928	P. Williams, Canada 0:21.8	1964	Henry Carr, U.S.A. 0:20.3		

* Olympic record.

TRACK AND FIELD: 200-METER DASH—WOMEN

1948 F. Blankers-Koen, Netherlands 0:24.4	1960 Wilma Rudolph, U.S.A. . 0:24.0	1976 B. Eckert, E. Germany . 0:22.37
	1964 Edith McGuire, U.S.A. .. 0:23.0	1980 B. Wockel, E. Germany 0.22.03
1952 M. Jackson, Australia .. 0:23.7	1968 I. Kirszenstein, Poland.. 0:22.5	1984* V. Brisco-Hooks, U.S.A. 0:21.81
1956 Betty Cuthbert, Australia 0:23.4	1972 R. Stecher, E. Germany . 0:22.4	

TRACK AND FIELD: 400-METER RACE—MEN

1896 Thomas Burke, U.S.A... 0:54.2	1928 Ray Barbuti, U.S.A. 0:47.8	1964 Mike Larrabee, U.S.A. . 0:45.1
1900 Maxey Long, U.S.A. ... 0:49.4	1932 William Carr. U.S.A. ... 0:46.2	1968* Lee Evans, U.S.A..... 0:43.8
1904 Harry Hillman, U.S.A. . 0:49.2	1936 Archie Williams, U.S.A. . 0:46.5	1972 Vincent Matthews, U.S.A. 0:44.66
1908 W. Halswelle, Britain .. 0:50.0	1948 Arthur Wint, Jamaica .. 0:46.2	1976 A. Juantorena, Cuba .. 0:44.26
1912 Charles Reidpath, U.S.A. 0:48.2	1952 G. Rhoden, Jamaica.... 0:45.9	1980 V. Markin, USSR..... 0:44.60
1920 Bevil Rudd, S. Africa ... 0:49.6	1956 Charles Jenkins, U.S.A.. 0:46.7	1984 Alonzo Babers, U.S.A. 0:44.27
1924 Eric Liddell, Britain ... 0:47.6	1960 Otis Davis, U.S.A....... 0:44.9	

TRACK AND FIELD: 400-METER RACE—WOMEN

1964 Betty Cuthbert, Australia 0:52.0	1972 M. Zehrt, E. Germany . 0:51.08	1980 Marita Koch, E. Germany 0:48.88
1968 C. Besson, France 0:52.0	1976 Irena Szcwinska, Poland 0:49.29	1984* V. Brisco-Hooks, U.S.A. 0:48.83

TRACK AND FIELD: 800-METER RACE—MEN

1896 E. Flack, Australia 2:11.0	1928 Douglas Lowe, Britain .. 1:51.8	1964 P. Snell, New Zealand . 1:45.1
1900 A. Tysoe, Britain...... 2:01.4	1932 T. Hampson, Britain .. 1:49.8	1968 R. Doubell, Australia .. 1:44.3
1904 James Lightbody, U.S.A. 1:56.0	1936 John Woodruff, U.S.A... 1:52.9	1972 David Wottle, U.S.A. .. 1:45.9
1908 Melvin Sheppard, U.S.A. 1.52.8	1948 Mal Whitfield, U.S.A. ... 1:49.2	1976 A. Juantorena, Cuba .. 1:43.50
1912 James Meredith, U.S.A. 1:51.9	1952 Mal Whitfield, U.S.A. ... 1:49.2	1980 Steve Ovett, Britain ... 1:45.40
1920 Albert Hill, Britain 1.53.4	1956 Thomas Courtney, U.S.A. 1:47.7	1984* J. Cruz, Brazil........ 1:43.00
1924 Douglas Lowe, Britain .. 1:52.4	1960 P. Snell, New Zealand .. 1:46.3	

TRACK AND FIELD: 800-METER RACE—WOMEN

1928 L. Radke-Batschauer, Germany 2:16.8	1964 Ann Packer, Britain ... 2:01.1	1976 Tatiana Kazankina, USSR 1:54.94
	1968 M. Manning U.S.A. 2:00.9	1980* N. Olizarenko, USSR .. 1:53.50
1960 L. Shevcova, USSR.... 2:04.3	1972 H. Falck, W. Germany . 1:58.6	1984 D. Melinte, Romania .. 1:57.60

TRACK AND FIELD: 1,500-METER RACE—MEN

1896 E. Flack, Australia 4:33.2	1928 Harri Larva, Finland ... 3:53.2	1964 P. Snell, N. Zealand .. 3:38.1
1900 E. Bennett, Britain 4:06.2	1932 Luigi Beccali, Italy 3:51.2	1968* K. Keino, Kenya 3:34.9
1904 James Lightbody, U.S.A. 4:05.4	1936 Jack Lovelock, N. Zealand 3:47.8	1972 P. Vasala, Finland 3:36.3
1908 Melvin Sheppard, U.S.A. 4:03.4	1948 H. Ericksson, Sweden .. 3:49.8	1976 John Walker, N. Zealand 3:39.17
1912 A. Jackson, Britain..... 3:56.8	1952 J. Barthel, Luxembourg. 3:45.2	1980 Sebastian Coe, Britain 3:38.4
1920 Albert Hill, Britain 4:01.8	1956 Ron Delany, Ireland ... 3:41.2	1984* Sebastian Coe, Britain 3.32.53
1924 Paavo Nurmi, Finland .. 3:53.6	1960 H. Elliott, Australia..... 3:35.6	

TRACK AND FIELD: 1,500-METER RACE—WOMEN

1972 Ludmila Bragina, USSR 4:01.4	1980* Tatiana Kazankina, USSR 3:56.6	
1976 Tatiana Kazankina, USSR 4:05.48	1984 Gabriella Dorio, Italy 4:03.25	

TRACK AND FIELD: 3,000-METER RACE—WOMEN

1984* Maricica Puica, Romania 8:35.96

TRACK AND FIELD: 5,000-METER RACE—MEN

1912 H. Kolehmainen, Finland 14:36.6	1948 G. Reiff, Belgium 14:17.6	1972 L. Viren, Finland 13:26.4
1920 J. Guillemot, France .. 14:55.6	1952 E. Zatopek, Czech..... 14:06.6	1976 Brendan Foster, Britain 13:20.3
1924 Paavo Nurmi, Finland . 14:31.2	1956 Vladimir Kuts, USSR ... 13:39.6	1980 M. Yifter, Ethiopia ... 13:21.0
1928 Villie Ritola, Finland ... 14:38.0	1960 M. Halberg, N. Zealand 13:43.4	1984* Said Aouita, Morocco 13:05.59
1932 L. Lehtinen, Finland ... 14:30.0	1964 Bob Schul, U.S.A...... 13:48.8	
1936 G. Hockert, Finland ... 14:22.2	1968 M. Gammoudi, Tunisia 14:05.0	

TRACK AND FIELD: 10,000-METER RACE—MEN

1912 H. Kolehmainen, Finland 31:20.8	1948 Emil Zatopek, Czech .. 29:59.6	1972* L. Viren, Finland 27:38.4
1920 Paavo Nurmi, Finland . 31:45.8	1952 Emil Zatopek, Czech .. 29:17.0	1976 L. Viren, Finland 27:40.38
1924 Villie Ritola, Finland ... 30:23.2	1956 Vladimir Kuts, USSR .. 28:45.6	1980 M. Yifter, Ethiopia ... 27:42.70
1928 Paavo Nurmi, Finland . 30:18.8	1960 P. Bolotnikov, USSR .. 28:32.2	1984 Albert Cova, Italy 27:47.54
1932 J. Kusocinski, Poland . 30:11.4	1964 Billy Mills, U.S.A...... 28:24.4	
1936 I. Salminen, Finland ... 30:15.4	1968 N. Temu, Kenya 29:27.4	

TRACK AND FIELD: MARATHON—MEN

1896 S. Loues, Greece 2:58:50.0	1928 A.B. El Ouafi, France 2:32:57.0	1964 A. Bikila, Ethiopia .. 2:12:11.2
1900 M. Theato, France... 2:59:45.0	1932 J. Zabala, Argentina . 2:31:36.0	1968 M. Wolde, Ethiopia .. 2:20:26.4
1904 Thomas Hicks, U.S.A. 3:28:53.0	1936 K. Son, Japan 2:29:19.2	1972 Frank Shorter, U.S.A. 2:12:19.8
1908 John Hayes, U.S.A... 2:55:18.4	1948 D. Cabrera, Argentina 2:34:51.6	1976 W. Cierpinski, E. Ger. 2:09:55.0
1912 K. McArthur, S. Africa 2:36:54.8	1952 E. Zatopek, Czech... 2:23:03.2	1980 W. Cierpinski, E. Ger. 2:11:03.0
1920 H. Kolehmainen, Finland 2:32:35.8	1956 A. Mimoun, France .. 2:25:00.0	1984* Carlos Lopes, Portugal 2:09:21.0
1924 A. Stenroos, Finland . 2:41:22.6	1960 A. Bikila, Ethiopia .. 2:15:16.2	

TRACK AND FIELD: 400-METER HURDLES—MEN

1900 W.B. Tewksbury, U.S.A. 0:57.6	1932 Robert Tisdall, Ireland.. 0:51.8	1964 Rex Cawley, U.S.A... 0:49.6
1904 Harry Hillman, U.S.A. . 0:53.0	1936 Glenn Hardin, U.S.A. ... 0:52.4	1968 David Hemery, Britain. 0:48.1
1908 Charles Bacon, U.S.A. . 0:55.0	1948 Roy Cochran, U.S.A. ... 0:51.1	1972 J. Akii-bua, Uganda .. 0:47.82
1920 Frank Loomis, U.S.A... 0:54.0	1952 Charles Moore, U.S.A... 0:50.8	1976* Edwin Moses, U.S.A.. 0:47.64
1924 Morgan Taylor, U.S.A. . 0:52.6	1956 Glenn Davis, U.S.A..... 0:50.1	1980 Volker Beck, E. Ger. . 0:48.70
1928 Lord David Burgley, Britain 0:53.4	1960 Glenn Davis, U.S.A..... 0:49.3	1984 Edwin Moses, U.S.A.. 0:47.75

* Olympic record.

SUMMER OLYMPIC WINNERS AND RECORDS *(continued)*

TRACK AND FIELD: MARATHON—WOMEN

1984*	Joan Benoit, U.S.A.	2:24:52.0

TRACK AND FIELD: 110-METER HURDLES—MEN

Year	Name	Time	Year	Name	Time	Year	Name	Time
1896	Thomas Curtis, U.S.A.	0:17.6	1928	S. Atkinson, S. Africa	0:14.8	1964	Hayes Jones, U.S.A.	0:13.6
1900	Alvin Kraenzlein, U.S.A.	0:15.4	1932	George Saling, U.S.A.	0:14.6	1968	W. Davenport, U.S.A.	0:13.3
1904	Frederick Schule, U.S.A.	0:16.0	1936	Forrest Towns, U.S.A.	0:14.2	1972	Rodney Milburn, U.S.A.	0:13.24
1908	Forrest Smithson, U.S.A.	0:15.0	1948	William Porter, U.S.A.	0:13.9	1976	Guy Drut, France	0:13.30
1912	Frederick Kelly, U.S.A.	0:15.1	1952	H. Dillard, U.S.A.	0:13.7	1980	T. Munkelt, E. Germany	0:13.39
1920	E. Thomson, Canada	0:14.8	1956	Lee Calhoun, U.S.A.	0:13.5	1984*	Roger Kingdom, U.S.A.	0:13.20
1924	Daniel Kinsey, U.S.A.	0:15.0	1960	Lee Calhoun, U.S.A.	0:13.8			

TRACK AND FIELD: 100-METER HURDLES—WOMEN

Year	Name	Time	Year	Name	Time
1972	Annelie Ehrhardt, E. Germany	0:12.59	1980*	V. Komisova, USSR	0:12.56
1976	J. Schaller, E. Germany	0:12.77	1984	Benita Fitzgerald-Brown, U.S.A.	0:12.84

TRACK AND FIELD: 400-METER HURDLES—WOMEN

1984*	Nawal El Moutawakel, Morocco	0:54.61

TRACK AND FIELD: 3,000-METER STEEPLECHASE—MEN

Year	Name	Time	Year	Name	Time	Year	Name	Time
1920	P. Hodges, Britain	10:00.4	1948	T. Sjostrand, Sweden	9:04.6	1968	Amos Biwott, Kenya	8:51.0
1924	V. Ritola, Finland	9:33.6	1952	H. Ashenfelter, U.S.A.	8:45.4	1972	K. Keino, Kenya	8:23.6
1928	T. Loukola, Finland	9:21.8	1956	Chris Brasher, Britain	8:41.2	1976*	A. Garderud, Sweden	8:08.02
1932	V. Iso-Hollo, Finland	10:33.4	1960	Z. Krzyszkowiak, Poland	8:34.2	1980	B. Malinowski, Poland	8:09.70
1936	V. Iso-Hollo, Finland	9:03.8	1964	Gaston Roelants, Belgium	8:30.8	1984	J. Korir, Kenya	8:11.80

TRACK AND FIELD: 400-METER RELAY—MEN

Year		Time	Year		Time	Year		Time	Year		Time
1912	Britain	0:42.4	1932	U.S.A.	0:40.0	1956	U.S.A.	0:39.5	1972	U.S.A.	0:38.19
1920	U.S.A.	0:42.2	1936	U.S.A.	0:40.0	1960	W. Germany	0:39.5	1976	U.S.A.	0:38.33
1924	U.S.A.	0:41.0	1948	U.S.A.	0:40.3	1964	U.S.A.	0:39.0	1980	USSR	0:38.26
1928	U.S.A.	0:41.0	1952	U.S.A.	0:40.1	1968	U.S.A.	0:38.2	1984*	U.S.A.	0:37.83

TRACK AND FIELD: 400-METER RELAY—WOMEN

Year		Time	Year		Time	Year		Time	Year		Time
1928	Canada	0:48.4	1952	U.S.A.	0:45.9	1968	U.S.A.	0:42.8	1984	U.S.A.	0:41.65
1932	U.S.A.	0:47.0	1956	Australia	0:44.5	1972	W. Germany	0:42.81			
1936	U.S.A.	0:46.9	1960	U.S.A.	0:44.5	1976	E. Germany	0:42.55			
1948	Netherlands	0:47.5	1964	Poland	0:43.6	1980*	E. Germany	0:41.60			

TRACK AND FIELD: 1,600-METER RELAY—MEN

Year		Time	Year		Time	Year		Time	Year		Time
1908	U.S.A.	3:29.4	1932	U.S.A.	3:08.2	1960	U.S.A.	3:02.2	1980	USSR	3:01.1
1912	U.S.A.	3:16.6	1936	Britain	3:09.0	1964	U.S.A.	3:00.7	1984	U.S.A.	2:57.91
1920	Britain	3:22.2	1948	U.S.A.	3:10.4	1968*	U.S.A.	2:56.1			
1924	U.S.A.	3:16.0	1952	Jamaica	3:03.9	1972	Kenya	2:59.8			
1928	U.S.A.	3:14.2	1956	U.S.A.	3:04.8	1976	U.S.A.	2:59.52			

TRACK AND FIELD: 1,600-METER RELAY—WOMEN

Year		Time	Year		Time	Year		Time	Year		Time
1972	E. Germany	3:23.0	1976	E. Germany	3:19.23	1980	USSR	3:20.2	1984*	U.S.A.	3:18.29

TRACK AND FIELD: 20-KILOMETER WALK—MEN

Year	Name	Time	Year	Name	Time
1956	L. Spirine, USSR	1:31:27.0	1972	P. Frenkel, E. Germany	1:26:42.4
1960	V. Golubnichy, USSR	1:34:07.2	1976	D. Bautista, Mexico	1:24:40.6
1964	Ken Matthews, U.S.A.	1:29:34.0	1980	M. Damilano, Italy	1:23:35.5
1968	L. Golubnichy, USSR	1:33:58.4	1984*	Ernesto Canto, Mexico	1:23:12.36

TRACK AND FIELD: 50-KILOMETER WALK—MEN

Year	Name	Time	Year	Name	Time	Year	Name	Time
1932	T. Green, Britain	4:50:10.0	1956	N. Read, N. Zealand	4:30:42.8	1972	B. Kannenberg, W. Ger.	3:56:11.6
1936	H. Whitlock, Britain	4:30:41.4	1960	D. Thompson, Britain	4:25:30.0	1980	H. Gauder, E. Germany	3:49:24.0
1948	J. Ljunggren, Sweden	4:41:52.0	1964	A. Pamich, Italy	4:11:12.4	1984*	Raul Gonzales, Mexico	3:47:26.0
1952	G. Dordoni, Italy	4:28:07.8	1968	C. Hohne, E. Germany	4:20:13.6			

TRACK AND FIELD: 1,500-METER WHEELCHAIR—MEN

1984*	Paul Van Winkel, Belgium	3:58.50

TRACK AND FIELD: 800-METER WHEELCHAIR—WOMEN

1984*	Sharon Hedrick, U.S.A.	2:15.73

TRACK AND FIELD: HIGH JUMP—MEN

Year	Name	Height	Year	Name	Height	Year	Name	Height
1896	Ellery Clark, U.S.A.	5' 11¼"	1928	R.W. King, U.S.A.	6' 4⅜"	1964	V. Brumel, USSR	7' 1⅘"
1900	Irving Baxter, U.S.A.	6' 2⅘"	1932	D. McNaughton, Can.	6' 5⅝"	1968	Dick Fosbury, U.S.A.	7' 4¼"
1904	Samuel Jones, U.S.A.	5' 11"	1936	C. Johnson, U.S.A.	6' 7¹⁵⁄₁₆"	1972	Yuri Tarmak, USSR	7' 3¾"
1908	Harry Porter, U.S.A.	6' 2¾"	1948	J. Winter, Australia	6' 6"	1976	J. Wszola, Poland	7' 4½"
1912	Almer Richards, U.S.A.	6' 4"	1952	Walter Davis, U.S.A.	6' 8¼"	1980*	G. Wessig, E. Germany	7' 9"
1920	R. Landon, U.S.A.	6' 4¼"	1956	Charles Dumas, U.S.A.	6' 11¼"	1984	D. Mogenburg, W. Germany	7' 8½"
1924	Harold Osborn, U.S.A.	6' 5¹⁵⁄₁₆"	1960	R. Shavlakadze, USSR	7' 1"			

* Olympic record.

TRACK AND FIELD: HIGH JUMP—WOMEN

1928 E. Catherwood, Canada . 5'3"	1956 M. McDaniel, U.S.A. 5'9¼"	1976 R. Ackermann, W. Germany 6' 3¾"
1932 Jean Shiley, U.S.A. 5'5¼"	1960 I. Balas, Romania 6' ¼"	1980 S. Simeoni, Italy 6' 5½"
1936 I. Csak, Hungary 5'3"	1964 I. Balas, Romania 6' 2⅜"	1984*U. Meyfarth, W. Germany 6' 7½"
1948 Alice Coachman, U.S.A. . 5' 6⅛"	1968 M. Rezkova, Czech. 5'11¾"	
1952 E. Brand, S. Africa 5' 5¾"	1972 U. Meyfarth, W. Germany 6' 3¼"	

TRACK AND FIELD: LONG JUMP—MEN

1896 Ellery Clark, U.S.A. 20'10"	1928 Edward Hamm, U.S.A. ... 25' 4¾"	1964 L. Davies, Britain 26' 5⁷⁄₁₀"
1900 A. Kraenzlein, U.S.A. ... 23' 6⅞"	1932 Edward Gordon, U.S.A. .. 25' ¾"	1968*Bob Beamon, U.S.A. ... 29' 2½"
1904 Myer Prinstein, U.S.A. .. 24' 1⅜"	1936 Jesse Owens, U.S.A. ... 26' 5⅜"	1972 Randy Williams, U.S.A. .. 27' ½"
1908 Frank Irons, U.S.A. 24' 6½"	1948 Willie Steele, U.S.A. ... 25' 8"	1976 Arnie Robinson, U.S.A. . 27' 4½"
1912 A. Gutterson, U.S.A. 24' 11¼"	1952 Jerome Biffle, U.S.A. ... 24' 10"	1980 L. Dombroski,
1920 W. Pettersson Sweden .. 23' 5½"	1956 Gregory Bell, U.S.A. ... 25' 8¼"	E. Germany 28' ¼"
1924 DeHart Hubbard, U.S.A.. 24' 5⅛"	1960 Ralph Boston, U.S.A..... 26' 7¾"	1984. Carl Lewis, U.S.A. 28' ¼"

TRACK AND FIELD: LONG JUMP—WOMEN

1948 O. Gyarmati, Hungary ... 18' 8¼"	1964 Mary Rand, Britain 22' 2⅛"	1980* T. Kolpakova, USSR 23' 2"
1952 Y. Williams, New Zealand 20' 5¾"	1968 V. Viscopoleanu, Rom. .. 22' 4½"	1984 A. Stanciu, Romania ... 22' 10"
1956 E. Krzesinska, Poland ... 20' 9¾"	1972 Rosendahl, W. Germany . 22' 3"	
1960 V. Krepkina, USSR 20' 10¾"	1976 A. Voigt, E. Germany 22' 2½"	

TRACK AND FIELD: DISCUS THROW—MEN

1896 R. Garrett, U.S.A. 95' 7½"	1928 C. Houser, U.S.A. 155' 2⅝"	1964 A. Oerter, U.S.A. 200' 1½"
1900 R. Bauer, Hungary 118' 2⁷⁄₈"	1932 J. Anderson, U.S.A. ... 162' 4⅞"	1968 A. Oerter, U.S.A. 212' 6½"
1904 M. Sheridan, U.S.A. ... 128' 10½"	1936 K. Carpenter, U.S.A. ... 165' 7½"	1972 L. Danek, Czech. 211' 3"
1908 M. Sheridan, U.S.A. ... 134' 2"	1948 A. Consolini, Italy 173' 2"	1976*Mac Wilkens, U.S.A..... 221' 5.4"
1912 A. Taipale, Finland 145' ⁹⁄₁₆"	1952 Sim Iness, U.S.A. 180' 6½"	1980 V. Rasshchupkin, USSR . 218' 7"
1920 E. Niklander, Finland ... 146' 7"	1956 A. Oerter, U.S.A. 184' 10½"	1984 R. Danneberg, W. Germany 218' 6"
1924 C. Houser, U.S.A. 151' 5¼"	1960 A. Oerter, U.S.A. 194' 2"	

TRACK AND FIELD: DISCUS THROW—WOMEN

1928 Konopacka, Poland 129' 11⅞"	1952 N. Romaschkova,	1968 L. Manoliu, Romania 191' 2½"
1932 L. Copeland, U.S.A. 132' 2"	USSR 168' 8½"	1972 Faina Melnik, USSR 218' 7"
1936 Mauermayer, Germany .. 156' 3³⁄₁₆"	1956 O. Fikotova, Czech. ... 176' 1½"	1976 E. Schlaak, E. Germany . 226' 4½"
1948 M. Ostermeyer,	1960 N. Ponomareva, USSR .. 180' 8¼"	1980*E. Jahl, E. Germany 229' 6½"
France 137' 6½"	1964 Tamara Press, USSR ... 187' 10¾"	1984 R. Stalman, Netherlands 214' 5"

TRACK AND FIELD: SHOT PUT—MEN

1896 R. Garrett, U.S.A. 36' 9¾"	1928 John Kuck, U.S.A. 52' 11⁄₁₆"	1964 Dallas Long, U.S.A. ... 66' 8⅔"
1900 R. Sheldon, U.S.A. 46' 3⅛"	1932 Leo Sexton, U.S.A. 52' 6³⁄₁₆"	1968 R. Matson, U.S.A. 67' 4¾"
1904 Ralph Rose, U.S.A. 48' 7"	1936 H. Woellke, Germany ... 53' 1¾"	1972 W. Komar, Poland 69' 6"
1908 Ralph Rose, U.S.A. 46' 7½"	1948 W. Thompson, U.S.A. .. 56' 2"	1976 U. Beyer, E. Germany .. 69' ¾"
1912 P. McDonald, U.S.A. 50' 4"	1952 P. O'Brien Jr., U.S.A. .. 57' 1½"	1980*V. Kiselyov, USSR 70' ½"
1920 V. Porhola, Finland 48' 7⅛"	1956 P. O'Brien Jr., U.S.A. .. 60' 11"	1984 A. Andrei, Italy 69' 9"
1924 C. Houser, U.S.A. 49' 2½"	1960 W. Nieder, U.S.A. 64' 6¾"	

TRACK AND FIELD: SHOT PUT—WOMEN

1948 M. Ostermeyer, France . . 45' 1½"	1964 Tamara Press, USSR ... 59' 6⅛"	1980*I. Slupianek, E. Germany . 73' 6¼"
1952 G. Zybina, USSR 50' 1½"	1968 M. Gummel, E. Ger. 64' 4"	1984 Claudia Loch, West Germany
1956 T. Tishkyevich, USSR ... 54' 5"	1972 N. Chizova, USSR 69' 0"	
1960 Tamara Press, USSR ... 56' 9⅞"	1976 I. Christova, Bulgaria .. 69' 5"	

TRACK AND FIELD: JAVELIN THROW—MEN

1908 E. Lemming, Sweden ... 179' 10½"	1948 T. Rautavaara,	1972 W. Wolfermann,
1912 E. Lemming, Sweden ... 198' 11¼"	Finland 228' 10½"	W. Germany 296' 10"
1920 Jonni Myrra, Finland ... 215' 9¾"	1952 Cy Young, U.S.A. 242' ¾"	1976*M. Nemeth, Hungary 310' 4"
1924 Jonni Myrra, Finland ... 206' 6¾"	1956 E. Danielson, Norway .. 281' 2¼"	1980 D. Kula, USSR 299' 2"
1928 E. Lundquist, Sweden .. 218' 6⅛"	1960 V. Tsibulenko, USSR ... 277' 8⅜"	1984 A. Haerkoenen, Finland . 284' 8"
1932 M. Jarvinen, Finland 238' 7"	1964 P. Nevala, Finland 271' 2½"	
1936 G. Stock, Germany 235' 8⁵⁄₁₆"	1968 Jan Lusis, USSR 295' 7¼"	

TRACK AND FIELD: JAVELIN THROW—WOMEN

1932 Mildred Didrikson, U.S.A. 143' 4"	1956 I. Janzeme, USSR 176' 8"	1972 R. Fuchs, E. Germany .. 209' 7"
1936 T. Fleischer, Germany .. 148' 2¾"	1960 E. Ozolina, USSR 183' 8"	1976 R. Fuchs, E. Germany .. 216' 4"
1948 H. Baume, Austria 149' 6"	1964 M. Penes, Romania 198' 7½"	1980 M. Colon, Cuba 224' 5"
1952 D. Zatopkova, Czech. .. 165' 7"	1968 A. Nemeth, Hungary ... 198' ½"	1984* T. Sanderson, Britain .. 228' 2"

TRACK AND FIELD: POLE VAULT—MEN

1896 W. Hoyt, U.S.A. 10' 9¾"	1924 L. Barnes, U.S.A. 12' 11½"	1960 D. Bragg, U.S.A. 15' 5⅛"
1900 I. Baxter, U.S.A. 10' 9⅞"	1928 S. Carr, U.S.A. 13' 9⅜"	1964 F. Hansen, U.S.A. 16' 8¾"
1904 C. Dvorak, U.S.A. 11' 6"	1932 Wm Miller, U.S.A. 14' 1⅞"	1968 B. Seagren, U.S.A. 17' 8½"
1908 (tie) A. Gilbert;	1936 E. Meadows, U.S.A. ... 14' 3¼"	1972 W. Nordwig, E. Germany 18' ½"
E. Cook Jr., U.S.A. 12' 2"	1948 G. Smith, U.S.A. 14' 1¼"	1976 T. Slusarski, Poland ... 18' ½"
1912 H. Babcock, U.S.A. 12' 11½"	1952 B. Richards, U.S.A. 14' 11¼"	1980*W. Kozakiewicz, Poland 18' 11½"
1920 F. Foss, U.S.A. 12' 5⁹⁄₁₆"	1956 B. Richards, U.S.A. 14' 11½"	1984 P. Quinon, France 18' 10¼"

* Olympic record.

SUMMER OLYMPIC WINNERS AND RECORDS (continued)

TRACK AND FIELD: TRIPLE JUMP—MEN

Year	Winner	Result		Year	Winner	Result
1896	James Connolly, U.S.A.	45'		1948	A. Ahman, Sweden	50' 6¼"
1900	Myer Prinstein, U.S.A.	47' 4¼"		1952	A. Ferreira da Silva, Brazil	53' 2½"
1904	Myer Prinstein, U.S.A.	47'		1956	A. Ferreira da Silva, Brazil	53' 7½"
1908	T. Ahearne, Britain	48' 11¼"		1960	J. Schmidt, Poland	55' 1⅝"
1912	G. Lindblom, Sweden	48' 5⅛"		1964	J. Schmidt, Poland	55' 3¾"
1920	V. Tuulos, Finland	47' 7⁷⁄₁₆"		1968*	V. Saneev, USSR	57' ¾"
1924	A. Winter, Australia	50' 11⅛"		1972	V. Saneev, USSR	56' 11"
1928	M. Oda, Japan	49' 10¹³⁄₁₆"		1976	V. Saneev, USSR	56' 8¾"
1932	C. Nambu, Japan	51' 7"		1980	J. Uudmae, USSR	56' 11⅛"
1936	N. Tajima, Japan	52' 5⅞"		1984	Al Joyner, U.S.A.	56' 7½"

TRACK AND FIELD: HAMMER THROW—MEN

Year	Winner	Result		Year	Winner	Result
1900	John Flanagan, U.S.A.	167' 4"		1952	J. Csermak, Hungary	197' 11¾"
1904	John Flanagan, U.S.A.	168' 1"		1956	H. Connolly, U.S.A.	207' 3½"
1908	John Flanagan, U.S.A.	170' 4¼"		1960	V. Rudenkov, USSR	220' 1⅝"
1912	M. McGrath, U.S.A.	179' 7⅛"		1964	R. Klim, USSR	228' 9⅔"
1920	Patrick Ryan, U.S.A.	173' 5⅝"		1968	G. Zsivotzky, Hungary	240' 8"
1924	F. Tootell, U.S.A.	174' 10¼"		1972	A. Bondarchuk, USSR	248' 8"
1928	P. O'Callaghan, Ireland	168' 7½"		1976	J. Sedych, USSR	254' 4"
1932	P. O'Callaghan, Ireland	176' 11⅝"		1980*	Y. Sedykh, USSR	268' 4½"
1936	Karl Hein, Germany	185' 4¼"		1984	Juha Tiainen, Finland	256' 2"
1948	I. Nemeth, Hungary	183' 11½"				

TRACK AND FIELD: DECATHLON—MEN

Year	Winner		Year	Winner		Year	Winner		Year	Winner
1912	J. Thorpe, U.S.A.		1932	J. Bausch, U.S.A.		1956	M. Campbell, U.S.A.		1972	N. Avilov, USSR
1920	H. Lovland, Norway		1936	G. Morris, U.S.A.		1960	R. Johnson, U.S.A.		1976	B. Jenner, U.S.A.
1924	H. Osborn, U.S.A.		1948	B. Mathias, U.S.A.		1964	W. Holdorf, W. Germany		1980	D. Thompson, Britain
1928	P. Yrjola, Finland		1952	B. Mathias, U.S.A.		1968	B. Toomey, U.S.A.		1984	D. Thompson, Britain

TRACK AND FIELD: HEPTATHLON—WOMEN

Year	Winner	Result
1984	Glynnis Nunn, Australia	6,390

VOLLEYBALL—MEN

Year	Winner		Year	Winner		Year	Winner		Year	Winner
1964	USSR		1972	Japan		1980	USSR			
1968	USSR		1976	Poland		1984	U.S.A.			

VOLLEYBALL—WOMEN

Year	Winner		Year	Winner		Year	Winner
1964	Japan		1972	USSR		1980	USSR
1968	USSR		1976	Japan		1984	China

WATER POLO—MEN

Year	Winner		Year	Winner		Year	Winner		Year	Winner		Year	Winner		Year	Winner		Year	Winner
1900	Britain		1912	Britain		1928	Germany		1948	Italy		1960	Italy		1972	USSR		1984	Yugoslavia
1904	U.S.A.		1920	Britain		1932	Hungary		1952	Hungary		1964	Hungary		1976	Hungary			
1908	Britain		1924	France		1936	Hungary		1956	Hungary		1968	Yugoslavia		1980	USSR			

WEIGHTLIFTING: FLYWEIGHT (114.5 lbs.)

Year	Winner	Result		Year	Winner	Result
1972	Z. Smalcerz, Poland	745 lbs.		1980*	K. Osmanoliev, USSR	540 lbs.
1976	A. Voronin, USSR	534.5 lbs.		1984	Guogiang Zeng, China	535 lbs.

WEIGHTLIFTING: BANTAMWEIGHT (123 lbs.)

Year	Winner	Result		Year	Winner	Result		Year	Winner	Result
1948	Joe DePietro, U.S.A.	677		1964	A. Vakhonin, USSR	788.1		1980	D. Nunez, Cuba	606.2
1952	Ivan Udovov, USSR	694		1968	M.N. Seresht, Iran	808.5		1984	Wu Shude, China	589.5
1956	Charles Vinci, U.S.A.	754.5		1972	Imre Foldi, Hungary	833				
1960	Charles Vinci, U.S.A.	760		1976	N. Nourikian, Bulgaria	578.5				

WEIGHTLIFTING: FEATHERWEIGHT (132 lbs.)

Year	Winner	Result		Year	Winner	Result		Year	Winner	Result
1920	L. de Haes, Belgium	485		1948	M. Fayad, Egypt	733		1968	Y. Miyake, Japan	863.5
1924	P. Gabetti, Italy	887		1952	R. Chimishyan, USSR	743.5		1972	N. Nourikian, Bulgaria	888
1928	F. Andrysek, Austria	633		1956	Isaac Berger, U.S.A.	776.75		1976	N. Kolesnikov, USSR	628
1932	R. Suvigny, France	633		1960	Y. Minaev, USSR	821		1980	V. Mazin, USSR	639
1936	A. Teriazzo, U.S.A.	688		1964	Y. Miyake, Japan	876.3		1984	Chen Weiqiang, China	622.5

WEIGHTLIFTING: LIGHTWEIGHT (149 lbs.)

Year	Winner	Result		Year	Winner	Result		Year	Winner	Result
1920	A. Neyland, Estonia	567		1948	I. Shams, Egypt	793		1972	M. Kirzhinov, USSR	1,014
1924	E. Decottignies, France	970		1952	Tommy Kono, U.S.A.	798.75		1976	Z. Kaczmarek, Poland	677.5
1928	(tie) D. Helbig, Germany;			1956	Igor Rybak, USSR	837		1980	Y. Roussev, Bulgaria	755
	H. Haas, Austria	710		1960	V. Bushuev, USSR	876		1984	Yao Jingyuan, China	705
1932	R. Duverger, France	716		1964	W. Baszanowski, Poland	953.5				
1936	M. Mesbah, Egypt	755		1968	W. Baszanowski, Poland	962.5				

WEIGHTLIFTING: MIDDLEWEIGHT (165 lbs.)

Year	Winner	Result		Year	Winner	Result		Year	Winner	Result
1920	B. Gance, France	540		1948	Frank Spellman, U.S.A.	859		1968	V. Kurentsov, USSR	1,045
1924	C. Galimberti, Italy	1,085		1952	Peter George, U.S.A.	881.5		1972	Y. Bikov, Bulgaria	1,069.23
1928	F. Roger, France	738		1956	F. Bogdanovskii, USSR	925.5		1976	Y. Mitkov, Bulgaria	738.5
1932	R. Ismayr, Germany	760		1960	A. Kurynov, USSR	964.25		1980	A. Zlatev, Bulgaria	792
1936	K. El Touni, Egypt	854		1964	H. Zdrazila, Czech.	981		1984	K.-H. Radschinsky, W. Germany	771

WEIGHTLIFTING: LIGHT HEAVYWEIGHT (181.5 lbs.)

Year	Winner	Result		Year	Winner	Result		Year	Winner	Result
1920	E. Cadine, France	639		1948	S. Stanczyk, U.S.A.	920.00		1968	B. Selitsky, USSR	1,067.00
1924	C. Rigoulot, France	1,107		1952	T. Lomakin, USSR	920.25		1972	L. Jenssen, Norway	1,118.00
1928	S. Nosseir, Egypt	782		1956	Tommy Kono, U.S.A.	986.25		1976	V. Shary, USSR	803.00
1932	L. Hostin, France	804		1960	I. Palinski, Poland	975.25		1980	Y. Vardanyan, USSR	882
1936	L. Hostin, France	821		1964	R. Plyukfeider, USSR	1,047.20		1984	P. Becheru, Romania	782

* Olympic record.

WEIGHTLIFTING: MIDDLE HEAVYWEIGHT (198 lbs.)

1952	N. Schemansky, U.S.A. 980.75	1964	V. Golovanov, USSR .1,074.70	1976	D. Rigert, USSR 841.50
1956	A. Vorobiev, USSR . . .1,019.25	1968	K. Kangasniemi, Finland 1,138.50	1980	P. Baczako, Hungary .. 832.2
1960	A. Vorobiev, USSR . . .1,041.25	1972	A. Nikolov, Bulgaria..1,157.00	1984*	Nicu Vlad, Romania ... 865.0

WEIGHTLIFTING: 1st HEAVYWEIGHT (220 lbs.)

1980	O. Zaremba, Czechoslovakia870.8	1984	R. Milser, W. Germany848.75

WEIGHTLIFTING: 2d HEAVYWEIGHT (Up to 242 lbs.)

1920	F. Bottini, Italy 595	1948	John Davis, U.S.A. ... 997.00	1964	L. Zhabotinsky, USSR 1,259.50
1924	G. Tonani, Italy1,140	1952	John Davis, U.S.A. ...1,013.75	1972	Yan Talts, USSR.....1,278.00
1928	J. Strassberger, Germany 821	1956	Paul Anderson, U.S.A.1,102.00	1976	V. Khristov, Bulgaria.... 880
1932	J. Skobia, Czechoslovakia 837	1960	Y. Vlasov, USSR1,184.25	1980	L. Taranenko, USSR .. 931.4
1936	J. Manger, Germany 903	1968	L. Zhabotinsky, USSR 1,262.10	1984	N. Oberburger, Italy... 860

WEIGHTLIFTING: SUPER HEAVYWEIGHT (Over 242 lbs.)

1972	V. Alexeev, USSR 1,411	1976	V. Alexeev, USSR 968	1980	S. Rakhmanov, USSR 970	1984	D. Lukim, Australia 909

WRESTLING: FREESTYLE—PAPERWEIGHT (105.5 lbs.)

1972	Roman Dmitriev, USSR	1976	K. Issaev, USSR	1980	C. Pollio, Italy	1984	Bobby Weaver, U.S.A.

WRESTLING: FREESTYLE—FLYWEIGHT (114.5 lbs.)

1948	L.Viitala, Finland	1960	A. Bilek, Turkey	1972	K. Kato, Japan	1980	A. Beloglazov, USSR
1952	H. Gemici, Turkey	1964	Y. Yoshida, Japan	1976	Y. Takada, Japan	1984	S. Trstena, Yugoslavia
1956	M. Tzalkalmanidze, USSR	1968	S. Nakata, Japan				

WRESTLING: FREESTYLE—BANTAMWEIGHT (125.5 lbs.)

1904	G. Mehnert, U.S.A.	1932	Robert Pearce, U.S.A.	1956	M. Dagistanli, Turkey	1972	H. Yanagida, Japan
1908	G. Mehnert, U.S.A.	1936	O. Zombori, Hungary	1960	Terrence McCann, U.S.A.	1976	V. Umin, USSR
1924	K. Pihlajamaki, Finland	1948	N. Akar, Turkey	1964	Y. Uetake, Japan	1980	S. Beloglazov, USSR
1928	K. Makinen, Finland	1952	S. Ishii, Japan	1968	Y. Uetake, Japan	1984	H. Tomiyama, Japan

WRESTLING: FREESTYLE—FEATHERWEIGHT (136.5 lbs.)

1908	George Dole, U.S.A.	1932	H. Pihlajamaki, Finland	1956	S. Sasahara, Japan	1972	Z. Abdulbekov, USSR
1920	Charles Ackerly, U.S.A.	1936	K. Pihlajamaki, Finland	1960	M. Dagistanli, Turkey	1976	Yang Jung Mo, S. Korea
1924	Robin Reed, U.S.A.	1948	G. Bilge, Turkey	1964	O. Watanabe, Japan	1980	M. Abushev, USSR
1928	Allie Morrison, U.S.A.	1952	B. Sit, Turkey	1968	M. Kaneko, Japan	1984	Randy Lewis, U.S.A.

WRESTLING: FREESTYLE—LIGHTWEIGHT (149.5 lbs.)

1908	G. de Relwyskow, Britain	1932	C. Pacome, France	1960	Shelby Wilson, U.S.A.	1980	S. Absaidov, USSR
1920	K. Antilla, Finland	1936	K. Karpati, Hungary	1964	E. Dimov, Bulgaria	1984	In-Tak Yoo, S. Korea
1924	Russell Vis, U.S.A.	1948	C. Atik, Turkey	1968	A. Movahed, Iran		
1928	O. Kapp, Estonia	1952	O. Anderberg, Sweden	1972	Dan Gable, U.S.A.		
		1956	E. Habibi, Iran	1976	P. Pinegin, USSR		

WRESTLING: FREESTYLE—WELTERWEIGHT (163 lbs.)

1924	H. Gehri, Switzerland	1948	Y. Dogu, Turkey	1964	I. Ogan, Turkey	1980	V. Raitchev, Bulgaria
1928	A. Haavisto, Finland	1952	William Smith, U.S.A.	1968	M. Atalay, Turkey	1984	Dave Schultz, U.S.A.
1932	Jack Van Bebber, U.S.A.	1956	M. Ikeda, Japan	1972	Wayne Wells, U.S.A.		
1936	Frank Lewis, U.S.A.	1960	D. Blubaugh, U.S.A.	1976	I. Date, Japan		

WRESTLING: FREESTYLE—MIDDLEWEIGHT (180 lbs.)

1908	S. Bacon, Britain	1932	I. Johansson, Sweden	1960	H. Gungor, Turkey	1980	I. Abilov, Bulgaria
1920	E. Leino, Finland	1936	E. Poilve, France	1964	P. Gardjev, Bulgaria	1984	Mark Schultz, U.S.A.
1924	F. Haggmann, Switzerland	1948	Glen Brand, U.S.A.	1968	B. Gurevitch, USSR		
		1952	D. Cimakuridze, USSR	1972	L. Tediashvili, USSR		
1928	E. Kyburz, Switzerland	1956	N. Nikolov, Bulgaria	1976	J. Peterson, U.S.A.		

WRESTLING: FREESTYLE—LIGHT HEAVYWEIGHT (198 lbs.)

1920	A. Larsson, Sweden	1936	K. Fridell, Sweden	1960	I. Atli, Turkey	1976	L. Tediashvili, USSR
1924	John Spellman, U.S.A.	1948	Henry Wittenberg, U.S.A.	1964	A. Medved, USSR	1980	S. Oganesyan, USSR
1928	T. Sjostedt, Sweden	1952	W. Palm, Sweden	1968	A. Ayuk, Turkey	1984	Ed Banach, U.S.A.
1932	Peter Mehringer, U.S.A.	1956	G. Takhti, Iran	1972	Ben Peterson, U.S.A.		

WRESTLING: FREESTYLE—HEAVYWEIGHT (220 lbs.)

1908	G.C. O'Kelly, Britain	1936	K. Palusalu, Estonia	1960	W. Dietrich, W. Germany	1972	Ivan Yarygin, USSR
1920	R. Roth, Switzerland	1948	G. Bobis, Hungary			1976	Ivan Yarygin, USSR
1924	Harry Steele, U.S.A.	1952	A. Mekokishvili, USSR	1964	A. Ivanitsky, USSR	1980	Ilya Mate, USSR
1928	J. Richthoff, Sweden	1956	H. Kaplan, Turkey	1968	A. Medved, USSR	1984	Lou Banach, U.S.A.
1932	J. Richthoff, Sweden						

WRESTLING: FREESTYLE—SUPER HEAVYWEIGHT (Over 220 lbs.)

1972	Aleksandr Medved, USSR	1976	Soslan Andiev, USSR	1980	S. Andiev, USSR	1984	B. Baumgartner, U.S.A.

WRESTLING: GRECO-ROMAN—PAPERWEIGHT (105.5 lbs.)

1972	G. Berceanu, Romania	1976	A. Shumakov, USSR	1980	Z. Ushkempirov, USSR	1984	V. Maenza, Italy

SUMMER OLYMPIC WINNERS AND RECORDS (continued)

WRESTLING: GRECO-ROMAN—FLYWEIGHT (114.5 lbs.)

1948 P. Lombardi, Italy	**1964** T. Hanahara, Japan	**1980** V. Blagidze, USSR
1952 B. Gourevitch, USSR	**1968** P. Kirov, Bulgaria	**1984** Atsuji Miyahara, Japan
1956 N. Soloviev, USSR	**1972** P. Kirov, Bulgaria	
1960 D. Pirvulescu, Romania	**1976** V. Konstantinov, USSR	

WRESTLING: GRECO-ROMAN—BANTAMWEIGHT (125.5 lbs.)

1924 E. Putsep, Estonia	**1948** K. Pettersen, Sweden	**1964** M. Ichiguchi, Japan	**1980** S. Serikov, USSR
1928 K. Leucht, Germany	**1952** I. Hodos, Hungary	**1968** J. Varga, Hungary	**1984** P. Passarelli, W. Germany
1932 J. Brendel, Germany	**1956** K. Vyropaev, USSR	**1972** R. Kazakov, USSR	
1936 M. Lorinc, Hungary	**1960** O. Karavaev, USSR	**1976** P. Ukkola, Finland	

WRESTLING: GRECO—ROMAN—FEATHERWEIGHT (136.5 lbs.)

1912 K. Koskelo, Finland	**1932** G. Gozzo, Italy	**1956** R. Makinen, Finland	**1972** G. Markov, Bulgaria
1920 O. Friman, Finland	**1936** Y. Erkan, Turkey	**1960** M. Sille, Turkey	**1976** K. Lipien, Poland
1924 K. Anttila, Finland	**1948** M. Oktav, Turkey	**1964** I. Polyak, Hungary	**1980** S. Migiakis, Greece
1928 V. Vali, Estonia	**1952** Y. Punkin, USSR	**1968** R. Rurua, USSR	**1984** Weon Kee Kim, S. Korea

WRESTLING: GRECO-ROMAN—LIGHTWEIGHT (149.5 lbs.)

1908 E. Porro, Italy	**1932** E. Malmberg, Sweden	**1960** A. Kordidze, USSR	**1980** S. Rusu, Romania
1912 E. Vare, Finland	**1936** L. Koskela, Finland	**1964** K. Ayvaz, Turkey	**1984** V. Lisjak, Yugoslavia
1920 E. Vare, Finland	**1948** K. Freij, Sweden	**1968** M. Mumemura, Japan	
1924 O. Friman, Finland	**1952** C. Safin, USSR	**1972** S. Khisamutdinov, USSR	
1928 L. Keresztes, Hungary	**1956** K. Lehtonen, Finland	**1976** S. Nalbandian, USSR	

WRESTLING: GRECO-ROMAN—WELTERWEIGHT (163 lbs.)

1932 I. Johansson, Sweden	**1952** M. Szilvasi, Hungary	**1964** A. Kolesov, USSR	**1976** A. Bykov, USSR
1936 R. Svedberg, Sweden	**1956** M. Bayrak, Turkey	**1968** R. Vesper, E. Germany	**1980** F. Kocsis, Hungary
1948 G. Andersson, Sweden	**1960** M. Bayrak, Turkey	**1972** V. Macha, Czechoslovakia	**1984** Jouko Salomaki, Finland

WRESTLING: GRECO-ROMAN—MIDDLEWEIGHT (180 lbs.)

1908 F. Martenson, Sweden	**1936** I. Johansson, Sweden	**1968** L. Metz, E. Germany
1912 C. Johansson, Sweden	**1948** A. Gronberg, Sweden	**1972** C. Hegedus, Hungary
1920 C. Westergren, Sweden	**1952** A. Gronberg, Sweden	**1976** M. Petkovic, Yugoslavia
1924 E. Vesterland, Finland	**1956** G. Kartosa, USSR	**1980** G. Korban, USSR
1928 V. Kokkinen, Finland	**1960** D. Dobrev, Bulgaria	**1984** I. Dracia, Romania
1932 V. Kokkinen, Finland	**1964** B. Simic, Yugoslavia	

WRESTLING: GRECO-ROMAN—LIGHT HEAVYWEIGHT (198 lbs.)

1908 V. Weckmann, Finland	**1932** R. Svensson, Sweden	**1964** B. Alexandrov, Bulgaria
1912 (tie) A. Ahlgren, Sweden	**1936** A. Cadier, Sweden	**1968** B. Radev, Bulgaria
I. Boling, Finland	**1948** K. Nilsson, Sweden	**1972** V. Rezantsev, USSR
1920 C. Johansson, Sweden	**1952** K. Grondhal, Finland	**1976** V. Rezantsev, USSR
1924 C. Westergren, Sweden	**1956** V. Nikolaev, USSR	**1980** N. Nottny, Hungary
1928 I. Moustafa, Egypt	**1960** Tevik Kis, Turkey	**1984** Steven Fraser, U.S.A.

WRESTLING: GRECO-ROMAN—HEAVYWEIGHT (220 lbs.)

1896 K. Schumann, Germany	**1928** R. Svensson, Sweden	**1956** A. Parfenov, USSR	**1976** N. Bolboshin, USSR
1908 R. Weisz, Hungary	**1932** C. Westergren, Sweden	**1960** I. Bogdan, USSR	**1980** G. Raikov, Bulgaria
1912 Y. Saarela, Finland	**1936** K. Palusalu, Estonia	**1964** I. Kozma, Hungary	**1984** V. Andrei, Romania
1920 A. Lindfors, Finland	**1948** A. Kirecci, Turkey	**1968** I. Kozma, Hungary	
1924 H. Degiane, France	**1952** J. Kotkas, USSR	**1972** N. Martinescu, Romania	

WRESTLING: GRECO-ROMAN—SUPER HEAVYWEIGHT (Over 220 lbs.)

1972 Anatoly Roshin, USSR	**1976** A. Kolchinsky, USSR	**1980** A. Kolchinsky, USSR	**1984** Jeff Blatnick, U.S.A.

YACHTING: FINN CLASS

1952 Denmark	**1960** Denmark	**1968** USSR	**1976** East Germany	**1984** New Zealand
1956 Denmark	**1964** West Germany	**1972** France	**1980** Finland	

YACHTING: FLYING DUTCHMAN CLASS

1960 Norway	**1968** Britain	**1976** W. Germany	**1980** Spain	**1984** U.S.A.
1964 New Zealand	**1972** Britain			

YACHTING: TEMPEST CLASS YACHTING: SOLING CLASS YACHTING: TORNADO CLASS YACHTING: 470 CLASS

1972 USSR	**1972** U.S.A.	**1976** Britain	**1976** West Germany
1976 Sweden	**1976** Denmark	**1980** Brazil	**1980** Brazil
	1980 Denmark	**1984** New Zealand	**1984** Spain
	1984 USA		

YACHTING: STAR CLASS

1932 U.S.A.	**1948** U.S.A.	**1956** U.S.A.	**1964** Bahamas	**1972** Australia	**1984** U.S.A.
1936 Germany	**1952** Italy	**1960** USSR	**1968** U.S.A.	**1980** USSR	

YACHTING: WIND GLIDER

1984 S. van den Berg, Netherlands

YACHTING: DRAGON CLASS

1948 Norway	**1956** Sweden	**1964** Denmark	**1968** U.S.A.	**1972** Australia
1952 Norway	**1960** Greece			

WINTER OLYMPIC WINNERS AND RECORDS

BIATHLON—10 km

1980	Frank Ullrich, E. Germany	0:32:10.69	1984 Eirik Kvalfoss, Norway ... 30:53.8

BIATHLON—20 km

1960	Klas Lestander, Sweden	1:33:21.6	1976 Nikolai Kruglov, USSR ... 1:14:12.26
1964	Vladimir Melanin, USSR	1:20:26.8	1980* Anatoli Aljabiev, USSR ... 1:08:16.31
1968	Magnar Solberg, Norway	1:13:45.9	1984 Peter Angerer, W. Germany ... 1:11:52.7
1972	Magnar Solberg, Norway	1:15:55.50	

BIATHLON RELAY

1968	USSR	2:13.02	1976 USSR	1:57:55.67	1984 USSR	1:38:51.7
1972	USSR	1:51.44	1980* USSR	1:34:03.27		

BOBSLED: 2-MAN BOB (winning driver)

1932	U.S.A., Hubert Stevens	8:14.74	1968 Italy, Eugenio Monti ... 4:41.54
1936	U.S.A., Ivan Brown	5:29.29	1972 W. Germany, Wolfgang Zimmerer ... 4:47.07
1948	Switzerland, F. Endrich	5:29.2	1976 E. Germany, Meinhard Nehmer ... 3:40.43
1952	W. Germany, Andreas Ostler	5:24.54	1980 Switzerland, Erich Schaerer ... 4:09.36
1956	Italy, Dalla Costa	5:30.14	1984* E. Germany, Wolfgang Hoppe ... 3:25.56
1964	Britain, Antony Nash	4:21.90	

BOBSLED: 4-MAN BOB (winning driver)

1924	Switzerland, Edward Scherrer	5:45.54	1964 Canada, Victor Emery ... 4:14.46
1928	U.S.A., William Fiske	3:20.5	1968* Italy, Eugenio Monti ... 2:17.39
1932	U.S.A., William Fiske	7:53.68	1972 Switzerland, Jean Wicki ... 4:43.07
1936	Switzerland, Perre Musy	5:19.85	1976 E. Germany, Meinhard Nehmer ... 3:44.42
1948	U.S.A., Edward Rimkus	5:20.1	1980 E. Germany, Meinhard Nehmer ... 3:59.92
1952	W. Germany, Andreas Ostler	5:07.84	1984 E. Germany, Wolfgang Hoppe ... 3:20.22
1956	Switzerland, Franz Kapus	5:10.44	

ICE HOCKEY

1920	Canada	1932	Canada	1952	Canada	1964	USSR	1976	USSR
1924	Canada	1936	Britain	1956	USSR	1968	USSR	1980	U.S.A.
1928	Canada	1948	Canada	1960	U.S.A.	1972	USSR	1984	USSR

SKATING: FIGURE SKATING—MEN

1908	Ulrich Salchow, Sweden	1948	Richard Button, U.S.A.	1972	Ondrej Nepela, Czechoslovakia
1920	Gillis Grafstrom, Sweden	1952	Richard Button, U.S.A.	1976	John Curry, Britain
1924	Gillis Grafstrom, Sweden	1956	H.A. Jenkins, U.S.A.	1980	Robin Cousins, Britain
1928	Gillis Grafstrom, Sweden	1960	David Jenkins, U.S.A.	1984	Scott Hamilton, U.S.A.
1932	Karl Schafer, Austria	1964	Manfred Schnelldorfer, W. Ger.		
1936	Karl Schafer, Austria	1968	Wolfgang Schwarz, Austria		

SKATING: FIGURE SKATING—WOMEN

1908	Madge Syers, Britain	1948	Barbara Ann Scott, Canada	1972	Beatrix Schuba, Austria
1920	Magda Julin-Mauroy, Sweden	1952	Jeanette Altwegg, Britain	1976	Dorothy Hamill, U.S.A.
1924	Heima von Szabo-Planck, Austria	1956	Tenley Albright, U.S.A.	1980	Anett Poetzsch, E. Germany
1928	Sonja Henie, Norway	1960	Carol Heiss, U.S.A.	1984	Katarina Witt, E. Germany
1932	Sonja Henie, Norway	1964	Sjoukje Dijkstra, Netherlands		
1936	Sonja Henie, Norway	1968	Peggy Fleming, U.S.A.		

SKATING: FIGURE SKATING—PAIRS

1908	Germany: Anna Hubler, Heinrich Burger	1960	Canada: Barbara Wagner, Robert Paul
1920	Finland: Ludovika and Walter Jakobsson	1964	USSR: Ludmila Beloussova, Oleg Protopopov
1924	Austria: Helene Engelmann, Alfred Berger	1968	USSR: Ludmila Beloussova, Oleg Protopopov
1928	France: Andrée Joly, Pierre Brunet	1972	USSR: Irina Rodnina, Aleksei Ulanov
1932	France: Andrée and Pierre Brunet	1976	USSR: Irina Rodnina, Aleksandr Zaitsev
1936	Germany: Maxie Heber, Ernest Baier	1980	USSR: Irina Rodnina, Aleksandr Zaitsev
1952	W. Germany: Ria and Paul Falk	1984	USSR: Elena Valova, Oleg Vasilev
1956	Austria: Elizabeth Schwarz, Kurt Oppelt		

SKATING: ICE DANCING

1976	USSR: Ludmila Pakhoma, Aleksandr Gorshkov	1984	Britain: Jane Torvill, Christopher Dean
1980	USSR: Natalia Linichuk, Gennadi Karponosov		

SKATING: SPEED SKATING—MEN: 500 METERS

1924	C. Jewtraw, U.S.A. ... 0:44.0	1948	F. Helgesen, Norway ... 0:43.1	1968	E. Keller, W. Germany . 0:40.30
1928	C. Thunberg, Finland, and B. Evensen, Norway (tie) 0:43.4	1952	K. Henry, U.S.A. ... 0:43.2	1972	E. Keller, W. Germany . 0:39.40
		1956	E. Grishin, USSR ... 0:40.2	1976	E. Kulikov, USSR ... 0:39.17
1932	J. Shea, U.S.A. ... 0:43.4	1960	E. Grishin, USSR ... 0:40.2	1980*	E. Heiden, U.S.A. ... 0:38.03
1936	I. Ballangrud, Norway . 0:43.4	1964	R. McDermott, U.S.A. ... 0:40.1	1984	S. Fokichev, USSR ... 0:38.19

SKATING: SPEED SKATING—WOMEN: 500 METERS

1932	Jean Wilson, Canada.. 0:58.0	1968	Ludmila Titova, USSR. 0:46.1	1980	Karin Enke, E. Germany 0:41.78
1960	Helga Haase, W. Germany 0:45.9	1972	Anne Henning, U.S.A. . 0:43.3	1984*	C. Rothenburger, E. Germany 0:41.02
1964	Lidia Skoblikova, USSR 0:45.0	1976	Sheila Young, U.S.A. ... 0:42.76		

* Olympic record.

WINTER OLYMPIC WINNERS AND RECORDS (continued)

SKATING: SPEED SKATING—MEN: 1,000 METERS

Year	Winner	Time	Year	Winner	Time	Year	Winner	Time
1976	P. Mueller, U.S.A.	1:19.32	1980*	E. Heiden, U.S.A.	1:15.18	1984	G. Boucher, Canada	1:15.80

SKATING: SPEED SKATING—WOMEN: 1,000 METERS

Year	Winner	Time	Year	Winner	Time
1932	Elizabeth Du Bois, U.S.A.	2:04.0	1972	Monika Pflug, W. Germany	1:31.40
1960	Kara Guseva, USSR	1:34.1	1976	Tatiana Averina, USSR	1:28.43
1964	Lidia Skoblikova, USSR	1:33.2	1980	Natalia Petruseva, USSR	1:24.10
1968	Carolina Geijssen, Netherlands	1:32.60	1984*	K. Enke, E. Germany	1:21.61

SKATING: SPEED SKATING—MEN: 1,500 METERS

Year	Winner	Time	Year	Winner	Time
1924	Clas Thunberg, Finland	2:20.8	1960	E. Roadaas, Norway, E. Grishin, USSR (tie)	2:10.4
1928	Clas Thunberg, Finland	2:21.1	1964	Ants Antson, USSR	2:10.3
1932	John A. Shea, U.S.A.	2:57.5	1968	Cornelis Verkerk, Netherlands	2:03.4
1936	Charles Mathisen, Norway	2:19.2	1972	Ard Schenk, Netherlands	2:02.96
1948	Sverre Farstad, Norway	2:17.6	1976	Jan-Egil Storholt, Norway	1:59.38
1952	Hjalmar Anderson, Norway	2:20.4	1980*	Eric Heiden, U.S.A.	1:55.44
1956	Evgeniy Grishin and Y. Mikhailov, USSR (tie)	2:08.6	1984	Gaetan Boucher, Canada	1:58.36

SKATING: SPEED SKATING—WOMEN: 1,500 METERS

Year	Winner	Time	Year	Winner	Time	Year	Winner	Time
1932	K. Klein, U.S.A.	3:06.0	1968	K. Mustonen, Finland	2:22.40	1980	A. Borckink, Netherlands	2:10.95
1960	L. Skoblikova, USSR	2:52.2	1972	D. Holum, U.S.A.	2:20.80	1984*	K. Enke, E. Germany	2:03.42
1964	L. Skoblikova, USSR	2:22.6	1976	G. Stepanskaya, USSR	2:16.58			

SKATING: SPEED SKATING—MEN: 5,000 METERS

Year	Winner	Time	Year	Winner	Time	Year	Winner	Time
1924	C. Thunberg, Finland	8:39.0	1952	H. Anderson, Norway	8:10.6	1972	A. Schenk, Netherlands	7:23.60
1928	I. Ballangrud, Norway	8:50.5	1956	B. Shilkov, USSR	7:48.70	1976	S. Stenson, Norway	7:24.48
1932	I. Jaffee, U.S.A.	9:40.8	1960	V. Kosichkin, USSR	7:51.30	1980*	E. Heiden, U.S.A.	7:02.29
1936	I. Ballangrud, Norway	8:19.6	1964	K. Johannesen, Norway	7:38.40	1984	T. Gustafson, Sweden	7:12.28
1948	R. Liaklev, Norway	8:29.4	1968	F. Anton Maier, Norway	7:22.40			

SKATING: SPEED SKATING—WOMEN: 3,000 METERS

Year	Winner	Time	Year	Winner	Time	Year	Winner	Time
1960	L. Skoblikova, USSR	5:14.3	1972	S. Kaiser-Baas, Netherlands	4:52.14	1984*	A. Schone, E. Germany	4:24.79
1964	L. Skoblikova, USSR	5:14.9	1976	T. Averina, USSR	4:45.19			
1968	J. Schut, Netherlands	4:56.2	1980	B. Jensen, Norway	4:32.13			

SKATING: SPEED SKATING—MEN: 10,000 METERS

Year	Winner	Time	Year	Winner	Time
1924	Julien Skutnabb, Finland	18:04.8	1960	Knut Johannesen, Norway	15:46.6
1928	No decision because of thawing ice		1964	Jonny Nilsson, Sweden	15:50.1
1932	Irving Jaffee, U.S.A.	19:13.6	1968	Johnny Hoeglin, Sweden	15:23.6
1936	Ivar Ballangrud, Norway	17:24.3	1972	Ard Schenk, Netherlands	15:01.35
1948	Ake Seyffarth, Norway	17:26.3	1976	Piet Kleine, Netherlands	14:50.59
1952	Hjalmar Anderson, Norway	16:45.8	1980*	Eric Heiden, U.S.A.	14:28.13
1956	Sigvard Ericsson, Sweden	16:35.9	1984	Igor Malkov, USSR	14:39.90

SKIING: ALPINE—MEN: DOWNHILL

Year	Winner	Time	Year	Winner	Time	Year	Winner	Time
1948	Henry Oreiller, France	2:55.0	1964	Egon Zimmermann, Austria	2:18.16	1980*	Leonhard Stock, Austria	1:45.50
1952	Zeno Colo, Italy	2:30.8	1968	Jean-Claude Killy, France	1:59.85	1984	Bill Johnson, U.S.A.	1:45.59
1956	Anton Sailer, Austria	2:52.2	1972	Bernhard Russi, Switzerland	1:51.43			
1960	Jean Vuarnet, France	2:06.0	1976	Franz Klammer, Austria	1:45.73			

SKIING: ALPINE—WOMEN: DOWNHILL

Year	Winner	Time	Year	Winner	Time
1948	Hedi Schlunegger, Switzerland	2:28.3	1968	Olga Pall, Austria	1:40.8
1952	Trude Jochum-Beiser, Austria	1:47.1	1972	Marie Theres Nadig, Switzerland	1:36.68
1956	Madeleine Berthod, Switzerland	1:40.7	1976	Rosi Mittermaier, W. Germany	1:46.16
1960	Heidi Biebl, W. Germany	1:37.6	1980	Annemarie Moser, Austria	1:37.52
1964	Christi Haas, Austria	1:55.3	1984*	Michela Figini, Switzerland	1:13.36

SKIING: ALPINE—MEN: GIANT SLALOM

Year	Winner	Time	Year	Winner	Time	Year	Winner	Time
1952	Stein Eriksen, Norway	2:25.0	1964*	F. Bonlieu, France	1:46.7	1976	H. Hemmii, Switzerland	3:26.97
1956	A. Sailer, Austria	3:00.1	1968	J. Killy, France	3:29.28	1980	I. Stenmark, Sweden	2:40.74
1960	R. Staub, Switzerland	1:48.3	1972	G. Thoeni, Italy	3:09.62	1984	M. Julen, Switzerland	2:41.18

SKIING: ALPINE—WOMEN: GIANT SLALOM

Year	Winner	Time	Year	Winner	Time
1952	Andrea Mead Lawrence, U.S.A.	2:06.8	1972	Marie Theres Nadig, Switzerland	1:29.90
1956	Ossi Reichert, W. Germany	1:56.5	1976*	Kathy Kreiner, Canada	1:29.13
1960	Yvonne Ruegg, Switzerland	1:39.9	1980	Hanni Wenzel, Liechtenstein	2:41.66
1964	Marielle Goitschel, France	1:52.2	1984	Debbie Armstrong, U.S.A.	2:20.98
1968	Nancy Greene, Canada	1:51.97			

SKIING: ALPINE—MEN: SLALOM

Year	Winner	Time	Year	Winner	Time	Year	Winner	Time
1948	E. Reinhalter, Switzerland	2:10.3	1964	J. Stiegler, Austria	2:11.13	1976	P. Gros, Italy	2:03.29
1952	O. Schneider, Austria	2:00.0	1968	J. Killy, France	1:39.73	1980	I. Stenmark, Sweden	1:44.26
1956[1]	A. Sailer, Austria	—	1972*	F. Fernandez Ochoa, Spain	1:09.27	1984	Phil Mahre, U.S.A.	1:39.41
1960	E. Hinterseer, Austria	2:08.9						

* Olympic record. [1] Scored in points instead of time.

SKIING: ALPINE—WOMEN: SLALOM

1948	Gretchen Fraser, U.S.A.	1:57.2	1968	Marielle Goitschel, France	1:25.86
1952	Andrea Mead Lawrence, U.S.A.	2:10.6	1972	Barbara Cochran, U.S.A.	1:31.24
1956[1]	Renee Colliard, Switzerland	—	1976	Rosi Mittermaier, W. Germany	1:30.54
1960	Anne Heggtveigt, Canada	1:49.6	1980*	Hanni Wenzel, Liechtenstein	1:25.09
1964	Christine Goitschel, France	1:29.8	1984	Paoletta Magoni, Italy	1:36.47

SKIING: NORDIC—WOMEN: 5 KILOMETERS

1964	C. Boyarskikh, USSR	17:50.5	1972	G. Koulacova, USSR	17:00.50	1980*	R. Smetanina, USSR	15:06.92
1968	T. Gustafsson, Sweden	16:45.2	1976	H. Takalo, Finland	15:48.69	1984	M. Hamaelainen, Finland	17:04.00

SKIING: NORDIC—WOMEN: 10 KILOMETERS

1952	L. Wideman, Finland	41:40.0	1964	C. Boyarskikh, USSR	40:24.3	1976*	R. Smetanina, USSR	30:13.41
1956	L. Kazyreva, USSR	38:11.0	1968	T. Gustafsson, Sweden	36:46.5	1980	B. Petzold, E. Germany	30:31.54
1960	M. Gusacova, USSR	39:46.6	1972	G. Koulacova, USSR	34:17.8	1984	M. Hamaelainen, Finland	31:44.20

SKIING: NORDIC—WOMEN: 20 KILOMETERS

1984	M. Hamaelainen, Finland	1:01:45.0

SKIING: NORDIC—WOMEN: 20–KILOMETER RELAY[2]

1956	Finland	1:09:01.0	1964	USSR	59:20.2	1972*	USSR	48:46.10	1980	E. Ger.	1:02:11.10
1960	Sweden	1:04:21.4	1968	Norway	57:30.00	1976	USSR	1:07:49.75	1984	Norway	1:06:49.70

SKIING: NORDIC—MEN: 15 KILOMETERS

1956	Hallgier Brenden, Norway	49:39.0	1972	Sven-Ake Lundback, Sweden	45:28.20
1960	Hakon Brusveen, Norway	51:55.5	1976	N. Bashukov, USSR	43:58.47
1964	Eero Maentyranta, Finland	50:54.1	1980	Thomas Wassberg, Sweden	41:57.63
1968	Harald Groenningen, Norway	47:54.20	1984*	G. Svan, Sweden	41:25.60

SKIING: NORDIC—MEN: 30 KILOMETERS

1956	V. Hakulinen, Finland	1:44:06.0	1968	F. Nones, Italy	1:35:39.20	1980*	N. Zimjatov, USSR	1:27:02.80
1960	S. Jernberg, Sweden	1:51:03.9	1972	V. Vedenin, USSR	1:36:31.10	1984	N. Zimjatov, USSR	1:28:56.30
1964	E. Maentyranta, Finland	1:30:50.7	1976	S. Saveliev, USSR	1:30:29.38			

SKIING: NORDIC—MEN: 50 KILOMETERS

1924	T. Haug, Norway	3:44:32.0	1952	V. Hakulinen, Finland	3:33:33.0	1972	P. Tyldum, Norway	2:43:14.75
1928	P. Hedlund, Sweden	4:52:03.0	1956	S. Jernberg, Sweden	2:50:27.0	1976	I. Formo, Norway	2:37:30.05
1932	V. Saarinen, Finland	4:28:00.0	1960	K. Hamalainen, Finland	2:59:06.3	1980	N. Zimjatov, USSR	2:27:24.50
1936	E. Viklund, Sweden	3:30:11.0	1964	S. Jernberg, Sweden	2:43:52.6	1984*	T. Wassberg, Sweden	2:15:58.80
1948	N. Karlsson, Sweden	3:47:48.0	1968	O. Ellefsaeter, Norway	2:28:45.8			

SKIING: NORDIC—MEN: 40–KILOMETER RELAY

1936	Finland	2:41:33.0	1956	USSR	2:15:30.0	1968	Norway	2:08:33.50	1980	USSR	1:57:03.46
1948	Sweden	2:32:08.0	1960	Finland	2:18:45.6	1972	USSR	2:04:47.90	1984*	Sweden	1:55:06.3
1952	Finland	2:20:16.0	1964	Sweden	2:18:34.6	1976	Finland	2:07:59.72			

SKIING: NORDIC—MEN: COMBINED CROSS COUNTRY AND JUMPING[1]

1924	Thorlief Haug, Norway	453.800	1960	Georg Thoma, W. Germany	457.952
1928	Johan Grottumsbraaten, Norway	427.800	1964	Tormod Knutsen, Norway	469.280
1932	Johan Grottumsbraaten, Norway	446.200	1968	Franz Keller, W. Germany	449.040
1936	Oddbjorn Hagen, Norway	430.300	1972	Ulrich Wehling, E. Germany	413.340
1948	Heikki Hasu, Finland	448.800	1976	Ulrich Wehling, E. Germany	423.390
1952	Simon Slattvik, Norway	451.621	1980	Ulrich Wehling, E. Germany	432.200
1956	Sverre Stenersen, Norway	455.000	1984	T. Sandberg, Norway	422.595

SKIING: NORDIC—MEN: 90–METER SKI JUMPING

1924	J. Thams, Norway	227.5	1952	A. Bergmann, Norway	226.0	1972	W. Fortuna, Poland	219.9
1928*	A. Andersen, Norway	330.5	1956	A. Hyvarinen, Finland	227.0	1976	K. Schnabl, Austria	234.8
1932	B. Ruud, Norway	228.0	1960	H. Recknagel, W. Germany	227.2	1980	J. Tormanen, Finland	271.0
1936	B. Ruud, Norway	232.0	1964	T. Engan, Norway	230.7	1984	M. Nykänen, Finland	231.2
1948	P. Hugsted, Norway	228.1	1968	V. Beloussov, USSR	231.3			

SKIING: NORDIC—MEN: 70–METER SKI JUMPING

1964	Veikko Kankkonen, Finland	229.9	1976	Hans-Georg Aschenbach, E. Germany	252.0
1968	Jiri Raska, Czechoslovakia	216.5	1980	Anton Innauer, Austria	266.3
1972	Yukio Kasaya, Japan	244.2	1984	J. Weissflog, E. Germany	215.2

TOBOGGAN (LUGE)—MEN: SINGLES

1964	Thomas Koehler, W. Germany	3:26.77	1976	Detlef Guenther, E. Germany	3:27.688
1968*	Manfred Schmid, Austria	2:52.48	1980	Bernhard Glass, E. Germany	2:54.796
1972	Wolfgang Scheidel, E. Germany	3:27.580	1984	Paul Hildgartner, Italy	3:04.258

TOBOGGAN (LUGE)—WOMEN: SINGLES

1964	O. Enderlein, W. Germany	3:26.77	1972	A. Muller, E. Germany	2:59.180	1980	V. Zozulia, USSR	2:36.537
1968*	E. Lechner, Italy	2:28.66	1976	M. Schumann, E. Germany	2:50.621	1984	S. Martin, E. Germany	2:46.570

TOBOGGAN (LUGE)—MEN: DOUBLES

1964	Austria: Josef Feistmantl, Manfred Stengl	1:41.62	1976	E. Germany: Hans Rinn, Norbert Hahn	1:25.604
1968	E. Germany: Klaus Bonsack, Thomas Koehler	1:35.85	1980*	E. Germany: Hans Rinn, Norbert Hahn	1:19.331
1972	tie: Italy and E. Germany	1:28.35	1984	W. Germany: Stangassiner, Wembacher	1:23.620

* Olympic record. [1] Scored in points instead of time. [2] Event was 15 km. in 1956-72.

RODEOS

Source: The Rodeo Cowboys Association

ALL-AROUND RODEO COWBOY CHAMPIONS

1966	Larry Mahan	$40,358	1973	Larry Mahan	$ 64,447	1979	Tom Ferguson	$117,222
1967	Larry Mahan	$51,996	1974	Tom Ferguson	$ 66,929	1980	Paul Tierney	$105,568
1968	Larry Mahan	$49,129	1975	Leo Camarillo	$ 50,300	1981	Jimmie Cooper	$105,862
1969	Larry Mahan	$57,726		Tom Ferguson	$ 50,300	1982	Chris Lybbert	$123,709
1970	Larry Mahan	$41,493	1976	Tom Ferguson	$ 96,913	1983	Roy Cooper	$153,391
1971	Phil Lyne	$49,245	1977	Tom Ferguson	$ 76,730	1984	Dee Pickett	$122,618
1972	Phil Lyne	$60,852	1978	Tom Ferguson	$131,233			

SHOOTING

U.S. NATIONAL RIFLE AND PISTOL CHAMPIONSHIPS

Source: National Rifle Association of America

Pistol

1974	Hershel L. Anderson, U.S. Army	1978	Charles E. McCowan, U.S. Army	1982	Bonnie D. Harmon, U.S. Army
1975	Bonnie D. Harmon, U.S. Army	1979	Darius R. Young, U.S. Army Reserve	1983	Roger H. Willis, U.S. Army
1976	Bonnie D. Harmon, U.S. Army	1980	J. Pascarella, National Guard	1984	James R.I. Laguana, U.S. Army
1977	Hershel L. Anderson, U.S. Army	1981	J. Pascarella, National Guard	1985	Max J. Barrington, Bellingham, Wa.

High Power Rifle

1974	Jack P. Sicola	1978	Carl R. Bernosky, Gordon, Pa.	1982	Middleton W. Tompkins, Long Beach, Calif.
1975	Garry L. Anderson	1979	Carl R. Bernosky, Gordon, Pa.	1983	Patrick M. McCann, Staunton, Ill.
1976	Garry L. Anderson	1980	Carl R. Bernosky, Gordon, Pa.	1984	Patrick M. McCann, Staunton, Ill.
1977	Carl R. Bernosky, Gordon, Pa.	1981	David Boyd, Triangle, Va.	1985	David Tubb, Canadian, Tex.

Smallbore Rifle—3-Position

1974	Lones W. Wigger Jr., U.S. Army	1978	Lones W. Wigger Jr., U.S. Army	1982	Lones W. Wigger Jr., U.S. Army
1975	Robert A. Gustin, U.S. Army Reserve	1979	Lones W. Wigger Jr., U.S. Army	1983	Lones W. Wigger Jr., U.S. Army
1976	Lones W. Wigger Jr., U.S. Army	1980	Lones W. Wigger Jr., U.S. Army	1984	Lones W. Wigger Jr., U.S. Army
1977	Lones W. Wigger Jr., U.S. Army	1981	Lones W. Wigger Jr., U.S. Army	1985	Carl R. Bernosky, Gordon, Pa.

Smallbore Rifle—Prone

1974	Presley W. Kendall, U.S. Army	1978	Mary E. Stidworthy, National Guard	1982	P. Kendall, Carlisle, Ky.
1975	Lones W. Wigger Jr., U.S. Army	1979	David P. Weaver, Oil City, Pa.	1983	David P. Weaver, Oil City, Pa.
1976	David P. Weaver, Oil City, Pa.	1980	E. Vande Zande, U.S. Army	1984	Ronald O. West, Zanesville, Ohio
1977	Mary E. Stidworthy, National Guard	1981	Mary E. Stidworthy, Prescott, Ariz.	1985	Lones W. Wigger Jr., U.S. Army

NATIONAL SKEET SHOOTING ASSOCIATION CHAMPIONS

Source: *Skeet Shooting Review*

Overall Champions

1974	Robert Paxton, San Antonio, Texas	1978	Dave Starrett, New Boston, Ohio	1982	R. Boss, Grand Island, N.Y.
1975	Robert Paxton, San Antonio, Texas	1979	Wayne Mayes, Hixon, Tenn.	1983	Phil Murray, San Antonio, Texas
1976	Martin F. Woods, Dallas, Texas	1980	T. Bender, San Antonio, Texas	1984	Bob Uknalis, Pennsylvania
1977	Gary Randall, Orlando, Fla.	1981	John Shima, San Antonio, Texas	1985	Charlie Martin, New Mexico

Women Champions

1974	Karla Roberts, Brigeton, Mo.	1978	Conni Place, Pompano Beach, Fla.	1982	Sheri Confer, Royal Oak, Mich.
1975	Jackie Ramsey, Dallas, Texas	1979	D. Burriesci, Sunnyvale, Calif.	1983	Lori Desatoff, Pomona, Calif.
1976	Valerie Johnson, San Antonio, Texas	1980	C. Confer, Warren, Mich.	1984	Louise Terry, New York
1977	Conni Place, Pompano Beach, Fla.	1981	S. Petrovich, Roselle, N.J.	1985	Jodie Robertson, Colorado

.410-Gauge Champions

1974	Kenny Barnes, Bakersfield, Calif.	1978	Walt Badorek, Klamath Falls, Ore.	1982	Mike Wooten, Chattanooga, Tenn.
1975	Alger Mullins, New York	1979	D. Brunkhorst, Oak Harbor, Ohio	1983	Donnie Parks, Winston Salem, N.C.
1976	Charles Parks, Homeworth, Ohio	1980	Wayne Mayes, Hixon, Tenn.	1984	Dave Starrett, Ohio
1977	A. Chris Brown, La Grange, Ga.	1981	Wayne Mayes, Cleveland, Tenn.	1985	Wayne Mayes, Cleveland, Tenn.

12-Gauge Champions

1974	Tito Killian, San Antonio, Texas	1978	Chip Youngblood, Ft. Lauderdale, Fla.	1982	John Shima, Oak Park, Ill.
1975	Ken Barnes, Bakersfield, Calif.	1979	Wayne Mayes, Hixon, Tenn.	1983	Wayne Mayes, Cleveland, Tenn.
1976	Martin F. Woods, Dallas, Texas	1980	Tito Killian, San Antonio, Texas	1984	Wayne Mayes, Cleveland, Tenn.
1977	Murray Jackson, Conway, S.C.	1981	John Shima, San Antonio, Texas	1985	Alan Clark, California

20-Gauge Champions

1974	Terry Nichols, Shelton, Conn.	1978	John Dail, Anderson, S.C.	1982	Wayne Mayes, Cleveland, Tenn.
1975	Doug Burdett, Ontario, Canada	1979	A.T. Oliver, Madill, Okla.	1983	Tal Sprinkles, Round Rock, Texas
1976	Tito Killian, San Antonio, Texas	1980	B. Evans, Burnet, Texas	1984	Alan Clark, California
1977	Wayne Mayes, Hixon, Tenn.	1981	John Shima, San Antonio, Texas	1985	Wayne Mayes, Cleveland, Tenn.

28-Gauge Champions

1974	Dennis Thomas, Scottsdale, Ariz.	1978	John Dail, Anderson, S.C.	1982	Don Kaufman, Garland, Texas
1975	Martin Wood, Dallas, Texas	1979	G. Sanderson, Ottawa, Ont.	1983	Bill Rodgers, Montreal, Canada
1976	Ricky Pope, San Antonio, Texas	1980	G. Desatoff, Hacienda Heights, Canada	1984	Tal Sprinkles, Round Rock, Texas
1977	John Shima, San Antonio, Texas	1981	Dave Starrett, New Boston, Ohio	1985	Charlie Martin, New Mexico

SKATING

WORLD SPEED SKATING RECORDS

500 METERS: MEN
Evgeny Kulikov, USSR, March 27, 19810:36.91
1,000 METERS: MEN
Pavel Pegov, USSR, March 25, 19831:12.58
1,500 METERS: MEN
Eric Heiden, U.S., Jan. 19, 19801:54.79
3,000 METERS: MEN
Eric Heiden, U.S., March 2, 19784:07.01
5,000 METERS: MEN
Viktor Shasherin, Soviet Union, March 23, 1984 ...6:49.15
10,000 METERS: MEN
Thomas Gustafson, Sweden, Jan. 31, 198214:23.59

500 METERS: WOMEN
Christa Rothenburger, E. Germany, Mar. 27, 1981 .0:40.18
1,000 METERS: WOMEN
Natalya Petruseva, USSR, Mar. 27, 19801:20.21
1,500 METERS: WOMEN
Karin Enke, E. Germany, Feb. 9, 19842:03.42
3,000 METERS: WOMEN
Andrea Schone, E. Germany, March 23, 19844:20.91
5,000 METERS: WOMEN
Andrea Schone, East Germany, Feb. 10, 1985.....7:32.82

WORLD SPEED SKATING CHAMPIONS

MEN

1977 Eric Heiden, United States	1980 Hilbert van der Duim, Netherlands	1983 Rolf Falk-Larssen, Norway
1978 Eric Heiden, United States	1981 Armund Sjoebrend, Norway	1984 Rolf Falk-Larssen, Norway
1979 Eric Heiden, United States	1982 Hilbert van der Duim, Netherlands	1985 Hein Vergeer, Netherlands

WOMEN

1979 Beth Heiden, United States	1982 Natalia Petruseva, Soviet Union	1985 Andrea Schone, East Germany
1980 Natalia Petruseva, Soviet Union	1983 Andrea Schone, East Germany	
1981 Natalia Petruseva, Soviet Union	1984 Karin Enke, East Germany	

WORLD FIGURE SKATING CHAMPIONS

MEN

1951 Richard Button, U.S.	1963 Don McPherson, Canada	1975 Sergei Volkov, Soviet Union
1952 Richard Button, U.S.	1964 M. Schnelldorfer, West Germany	1976 John Curry, Britain
1953 Hayes Jenkins, U.S.	1965 Alain Calmat, France	1977 Vladimir Kovalev, Soviet Union
1954 Hayes Jenkins, U.S.	1966 Emmerich Danzer, Austria	1978 Charles Tickner, U.S.
1955 Hayes Jenkins, U.S.	1967 Emmerich Danzer, Austria	1979 Vladimir Kovalev, Soviet Union
1956 Hayes Jenkins, U.S.	1968 Emmerich Danzer, Austria	1980 Jan Hoffman, East Germany
1957 Dave Jenkins, U.S.	1969 Tim Wood, U.S.	1981 Scott Hamilton, U.S.
1958 Dave Jenkins, U.S.	1970 Tim Wood, U.S.	1982 Scott Hamilton, U.S.
1959 Dave Jenkins, U.S.	1971 Ondrej Nepela, Czechoslovakia	1983 Scott Hamilton, U.S.
1960 Alain Giletti, France	1972 Ondrej Nepela, Czechoslovakia	1984 Scott Hamilton, U.S.
1961 None	1973 Ondrej Nepela, Czechoslovakia	1985 Aleksander Fadeev, Soviet Union
1962 Don Jackson, Canada	1974 Jan Hoffman, East Germany	

WOMEN

1951 Jeannette Altwegg, Britain	1963 Sjoukje Dijkstra, Netherlands	1975 Dianne DeLeeuw, Netherlands
1952 Jacqueline du Bief, France	1964 Sjoukje Dijkstra, Netherlands	1976 Dorothy Hamill, U.S.
1953 Tenley Albright, U.S.	1965 Petra Burka, Canada	1977 Linda Fratianne, U.S.
1954 Gundi Busch, West Germany	1966 Peggy Fleming, U.S.	1978 Anett Poetzsch, East Germany
1955 Tenley Albright, U.S.	1967 Peggy Fleming, U.S.	1979 Linda Fratianne, U.S.
1956 Carol Heiss, U.S.	1968 Peggy Fleming, U.S.	1980 Anett Poetzsch, East Germany
1957 Carol Heiss, U.S.	1969 Gabriele Seyfert, East Germany	1981 Denise Biellmann, Switzerland
1958 Carol Heiss, U.S.	1970 Gabriele Seyfert, East Germany	1982 Elaine Zayak, U.S.
1959 Carol Heiss, U.S.	1971 Beatrix Schuba, Austria	1983 Rosalynn Sumners, U.S.
1960 Carol Heiss, U.S.	1972 Beatrix Schuba, Austria	1984 Katerina Witt, East Germany
1961 None	1973 Karen Magnussen, Canada	1985 Katerina Witt, East Germany
1962 Sjoukje Dijkstra, Netherlands	1974 Christine Errath, East Germany	

PAIRS

1978 Irina Rodnina and Aleksander Zaitsev, Soviet Union	1982 Sabine Baess and Tassilo Thierbach, East Germany
1979 Tai Babilonia and Randy Gardner, United States	1983 Elena Valova and Oleg Vasiliev, Soviet Union
1980 Marina Chersekova and Sergei Shahrai, Soviet Union	1984 Barbara Underhill and Paul Martini, Britain
1981 Irina Vorobieva and Igor Lisovsky, Soviet Union	1985 Elena Valova and Oleg Vasiliev, Soviet Union

ICE DANCING

1978 Natalia Linichuk and Gennadij Karponosov, Soviet Union	1982 Jayne Torvill and Christopher Dean, Britain
1979 Natalia Linichuk and Gennadij Karponosov, Soviet Union	1983 Jayne Torvill and Christopher Dean, Britain
1980 Natalia Linichuk and Gennadij Karponosov, Soviet Union	1984 Jayne Torvill and Christopher Dean, Britain
1981 Jayne Torvill and Christopher Dean, Britain	1985 Natalia Bestemianova and Andrei Bukin, Soviet Union

UNITED STATES FIGURE SKATING CHAMPIONS

MEN

1951	Richard Button	1960	Dave Jenkins	1969	Tim Wood	1978	Charles Tickner
1952	Richard Button	1961	Bradley Lord	1970	Tim Wood	1979	Charles Tickner
1953	Hayes Jenkins	1962	Monty Hoyt	1971	John Petkvich	1980	Charles Tickner
1954	Hayes Jenkins	1963	Tommy Litz	1972	Ken Shelley	1981	Scott Hamilton
1955	Hayes Jenkins	1964	Scott Allen	1973	Gordon McKellen Jr.	1982	Scott Hamilton
1956	Hayes Jenkins	1965	Gary Visconti	1974	Gordon McKellen Jr.	1983	Scott Hamilton
1957	Dave Jenkins	1966	Tim Wood	1975	Gordon McKellen Jr.	1984	Scott Hamilton
1958	Dave Jenkins	1967	Gary Visconti	1976	Terry Kubicka	1985	Brian Boitano
1959	Dave Jenkins	1968	Tim Wood	1977	Charles Tickner		

WOMEN

1952	Tenley Albright	1961	Laurence Owen	1970	Janet Lynn	1979	Linda Fratianne
1953	Tenley Albright	1962	Barbara Pursley	1971	Janet Lynn	1980	Linda Fratianne
1954	Tenley Albright	1963	Lorraine Hanlon	1972	Janet Lynn	1981	Elaine Zayak
1955	Tenley Albright	1964	Peggy Fleming	1973	Janet Lynn	1982	Rosalynn Sumners
1956	Tenley Albright	1965	Peggy Fleming	1974	Dorothy Hamill	1983	Rosalynn Sumners
1957	Carol Heiss	1966	Peggy Fleming	1975	Dorothy Hamill	1984	Rosalynn Sumners
1958	Carol Heiss	1967	Peggy Fleming	1976	Dorothy Hamill	1985	Tiffany Chin
1959	Carol Heiss	1968	Peggy Fleming	1977	Linda Fratianne		
1960	Carol Heiss	1969	Janet Lynn	1978	Linda Fratianne		

PAIRS

1980	Tai Babilonia and Randy Gardner	1983	Kitty and Peter Carruthers
1981	Tai Babilonia and Randy Gardner	1984	Kitty and Peter Carruthers
1982	Tai Babilonia and Randy Gardner	1985	Jill Watson and Peter Oppegard

ICE DANCING

1981	Judy Blumberg and Michael Seibert	1984	Judy Blumberg and Michael Seibert
1982	Judy Blumberg and Michael Seibert	1985	Judy Blumberg and Michael Seibert
1983	Judy Blumberg and Michael Seibert		

SKIING

WORLD CUP SKIING CHAMPIONS

MEN

1967	Jean Claude Killy, France	1974	Piero Gros, Italy	1981	Phil Mahre, United States
1968	Jean Claude Killy, France	1975	Gustavo Thoeni, Italy	1982	Phil Mahre, United States
1969	Karl Schranz, Austria	1976	Ingemar Stenmark, Sweden	1983	Phil Mahre, United States
1970	Karl Schranz, Austria	1977	Ingemar Stenmark, Sweden	1984	Pirmin Zurbriggen, Switzerland
1971	Gustavo Thoeni, Italy	1978	Ingemar Stenmark, Sweden	1985	Marc Girardelli, Luxembourg
1972	Gustavo Thoeni, Italy	1979	Peter Luescher, Switzerland		
1973	Gustavo Thoeni, Italy	1980	Andreas Wenzel, Liechtenstein		

WOMEN

1967	Nancy Greene, Canada	1974	Annemarie Proell, Austria	1981	Marie Theres Nadig, Switzerland
1968	Nancy Greene, Canada	1975	Annemarie Proell, Austria	1982	Erika Hess, Switzerland
1969	Gertrud Gabl, Austria	1976	Rosi Mittermaier, West Germany	1983	Tamara McKinney, United States
1970	Michele Jacot, France	1977	Lisa-Marie Morerod, Switzerland	1984	Erika Hess, Switzerland
1971	Annemarie Proell, Austria	1978	Hanni Wenzel, Liechtenstein	1985	Michela Figini, Switzerland
1972	Annemarie Proell, Austria	1979	Annemarie Proell Moser, Austria		
1973	Annemarie Proell, Austria	1980	Hanni Wenzel, Liechtenstein		

NATIONAL COLLEGIATE ATHLETIC ASSOCIATION SKIING CHAMPIONSHIPS

TEAM CHAMPIONSHIPS

YEAR	CHAMPION	RUNNER-UP	YEAR	CHAMPION	RUNNER-UP
1954	Denver	Seattle	1971	Denver	Colorado
1955	Denver	Dartmouth	1972	Colorado	Denver
1956	Denver	Middlebury	1973	Colorado	Wyoming
1957	Denver	Colorado	1974	Colorado	Wyoming
1958	Dartmouth	Denver	1975	Colorado	Vermont
1959	Colorado	Denver	1976	Colorado	
1960	Colorado	Denver		Dartmouth	
1961	Denver	Middlebury	1977	Colorado	Wyoming
1962	Denver	Colorado	1978	Colorado	Wyoming
1963	Denver	Colorado	1979	Colorado	Utah
1964	Denver	Dartmouth	1980	Vermont	Utah
1965	Denver	Utah	1981	Utah	Vermont
1966	Denver	Western Colo.	1982	Colorado	Vermont
1967	Denver	Wyoming	1983	Utah	Vermont
1968	Wyoming	Denver	1984	Utah	Vermont
1969	Denver	Dartmouth	1985	Wyoming	Utah
1970	Denver	Dartmouth			

NCAA MEN'S CROSS COUNTRY CHAMPIONS

1954 Marvin Crawford, Denver	1964 Eddie Demers, Western	1975 Steiner Hybersen, Wyoming
1955 Larry Damon, Vermont	Colorado	1976 Stan Dunklee, Vermont
1956 Erik Berggren, Idaho	1965 Mike Elliott, Fort Lewis	1977 Helge Aamodt, Colorado
1957 Mack Miller, Western Colorado	1966 Mike Elliott, Fort Lewis	1978 Sigurd Kjerpeseth, Colorado
1958 Clarence Servold, Denver	1967 Ned Gillette, Dartmouth	1979 Svein Ame Olsen, Utah
1959 Clarence Servold, Denver	1968 Clark Matis, Colorado	1980 Pal Sjulstad, Vermont
1960 John Denhahl, Colorado	1969 Clark Matis, Colorado	1981 Bernt Lund, Utah
1961 Charles Akers, Maine	1970 Ole Hansen, Denver	1982 Egil Nilsen, Colorado
1962 James Page, Dartmouth	1971 Ole Hansen, Denver	1983 Rune Helland, Wyoming
1963 Eddie Demers, Western	1972 Stale Engen, Wyoming	1984 John Aalberg, Utah
Colorado	1973 Steiner Hybersen, Wyoming	1985 John Aalberg, Utah
	1974 Steiner Hybersen, Wyoming	

NCAA WOMEN'S CROSS COUNTRY CHAMPIONS

1983 Beth Heiden, Vermont	1984 Heidi Sorensen, New Mexico	1985 Kristen Petty, Colorado

NCAA MEN'S CROSS COUNTRY RELAY

1981 Vermont	1983 Vermont	1985 Vermont
1982 Colorado	1984 Utah	

NCAA WOMEN'S CROSS COUNTRY RELAY

1983 New Mexico	1984 Vermont	1985 Wyoming

NCAA MEN'S SLALOM CHAMPIONS

1954 John L'Orange, Denver	1965 Rick Chaffee, Denver	1976 Mike Meleski, Wyoming
1955 Chiharu Igaya, Dartmouth	1966 Bill Marolt, Colorado	1977 Stephen Hienzsch, Colorado
1956 Chiharu Igaya, Dartmouth	1967 Rick Chaffee, Denver	1978 Dan Brelsford, Montana
1957 Chiharu Igaya, Dartmouth	1968 Dennis McCoy, Denver	1979 Per Nicholaysen, Utah
1958 Robert Gebhardt, Dartmouth	1969 Paul Rachetto, Denver	1980 Bret Williams, No. Michigan
1959 Marvin Melville, Utah	1970 Mike Porcarelli, Colorado	1981 Scott Hoffman, Utah
1960 Rudy Ruana, Montana	1971 Otto Tschudi, Denver	1982 Tiger Shaw, Dartmouth
1961 Buddy Werner, Colorado	1972 Mike Porcarelli, Colorado	1983 Niklas Scherrer, Colorado
1962 Jim Gaddis, Utah	1973 Peik Christensen, Denver	1984 James Marceau, Colorado
1963 James Heuga, Colorado	1974 Bill Shaw, Boise State	1985 Jeff Durtschi, Utah
1964 John Clough, Middlebury	1975 Peik Christensen, Denver	

NCAA WOMEN'S SLALOM CHAMPIONS

1983 Asa Svedmark, Wyoming	1984 Bente Dahlum, Utah	1985 Ann Melander, Wyoming

NCAA MEN'S GIANT SLALOM CHAMPIONS

1976 Dave Cleveland, Dartmouth	1980 John Teague, Vermont	1984 Andrew Shaw, Vermont
1977 Stephen Hienzsch, Colorado	1981 Tor Melander, Vermont	1985 Tom Foote, Dartmouth
1978 Dale Merrill, Wyoming	1982 Seth Bayer, Colorado	
1979 Chris Mikell, Vermont	1983 Tor Melander, Vermont	

NCAA WOMEN'S GIANT SLALOM CHAMPIONS

1983 Kathy Kreiner, Utah	1984 Bente Dahlum, Utah	1985 Ann Melander, Wyoming

NCAA MEN'S DOWNHILL[1] CHAMPIONS

1954 Pat Myers, Nevada-Reno	1962 Mike Baar, Denver	1968 Barney Peet, Fort Lewis
1955 Chiharu Igaya, Dartmouth	1963 Dave Gorusch, Western Colorado	1969 Mike Lafferty, Colorado
1956 Walt Taulbee, Washington	Bill Marolt, Colorado	1970 Otto Tschudi, Denver
1957 Ralph Miller, Dartmouth	Buddy Werner, Colorado	1971 Otto Tschudi, Denver
1958 Gary Vaughn, Norwich	1964 John Clough, Middlebury	1972 Otto Tschudi, Denver
1959 Marvin Melville, Utah	1965 Bill Marolt, Colorado	1973 Bob Cochran, Vermont
1960 Dave Butts, Colorado	1966 Terje Overland, Denver	1974 Larry Kennison, Wyoming
1961 Gordon Eaton, Middlebury	1967 Dennis McCoy, Denver	1975 Mark Ford, Colorado

NCAA MEN'S SKI JUMPING[1] CHAMPIONS

1954 Willis Olson, Denver	1963 Tom Nord, Washington	1972 Odd Hammernes, Denver
1955 Willis Olson, Denver	1964 Frithjof Prydz, Utah	1973 Vidar Nilsgard, Colorado
1956 Willis Olson, Denver	Erik Jansen, Denver	1974 Didrik Ellefsen, Colorado
1957 Alf Vincelette, Denver	1965 Erik Jansen, Denver	1975 Didrik Ellefsen, Colorado
1958 Oddvar Ronnestead, Denver	1966 Frithjof Prydz, Utah	1976 Kip Sundgaard, Utah
1959 Dave Butts, Colorado	1967 Bjorn Loken, Utah	1977 Ron Steele, Utah
1960 Dag Helgestad, Washington	1968 Peter Robes, Wyoming	1978 Tom Holmen Jensen, Colorado
State	1969 Odd Hammernes, Denver	Kare Herje, Vermont
1961 Cris Selback, Denver	1970 Jay Rand, Colorado	1979 Roger Holden, Vermont
1962 Oyvind Floystad, Denver	1971 Vidar Nilsgard, Colorado	1980 Jorn Stromberg, Wyoming

NCAA MEN'S SKIMEISTER[1] CHAMPIONS

1954 Marvin Crawford, Denver	1962 James Page, Dartmouth	1968 Eric Piene, Wyoming
1955 Les Streeter, Middlebury	1963 James Page, Dartmouth	1969 Ed Damon, Dartmouth
1956 John Cross, Denver	1964 Jennings Cress, Denver	1970 John Kendall, New Hampshire
1957 Ralph Miller, Dartmouth	1965 Loris Werner, Western	1971 John Kendall, New Hampshire
1958 Dave Harwood, Dartmouth	Colorado	1972 Kim Kendall, New Hampshire
1959 Dave Butts, Colorado	1966 Loris Werner, Western	1973 Kim Kendall, New Hampshire
1960 John Denhahl, Colorado	Colorado	
1961 Art Bookstrom, Dartmouth	1967 Matz Jenssen, Utah	

[1] Discontinued event.

SOCCER

WORLD CUP

The World Cup soccer championship is played every four years, although the cycle was broken between 1938 and 1950 because of World War II. The 1986 games will be held in Mexico.

YEAR	CHAMPIONSHIP FINAL	HOST	YEAR	CHAMPIONSHIP FINAL	HOST
1934	Italy 2, Czechoslovakia 1	Italy	1966	England 4, West Germany 2	England
1938	Italy 4, Hungary 2	France	1970	Brazil 4, Italy 1	Mexico
1950	Uruguay 2, Brazil 1	Brazil	1974	West Germany 2, Netherlands 1	West Germany
1954	West Germany 3, Hungary 2	Switzerland	1978	Argentina 3, Netherlands 1	Argentina
1958	Brazil 5, Sweden 2	Sweden	1982	Italy 3, West Germany 1	Spain
1962	Brazil 3, Czechoslovakia 1	Chile	1986		Mexico

MAJOR INDOOR SOCCER LEAGUE (MISL)

CHAMPIONSHIP

The San Diego Sockers defeated the Baltimore Blast 4 games to 1 in the championship playoff series in May 1985.

Baltimore was the MISL champion in 1984. San Diego won the North American Soccer League (NASL) indoor title in 1984.

MISL FINAL STANDINGS REGULAR SEASON 1984-1985

EASTERN DIVISION	WON	LOST	PCT.	WESTERN DIVISION	WON	LOST	PCT.
Baltimore Blast	32	15	.667	San Diego Sockers	37	11	.771
Chicago Sting	28	20	.583	Las Vegas Americans...	30	18	.625
Cleveland Force	27	21	.563	Los Angeles Lazers	24	24	.500
Minnesota Strikers	24	24	.500	Kansas City Comets	22	26	.458
St. Louis Steamers	24	24	.500	Wichita Wings	21	26	.447
Pittsburgh Spirit	19	29	.396	Tacoma Stars	17	31	.354
New York Cosmos[1]	11	22	.333	Dallas Sidekicks	12	36	.250

[1] New York Cosmos suspended play in mid-season 1985.

NATIONAL COLLEGIATE ATHLETIC ASSOCIATION MEN'S SOCCER CHAMPIONS

YEAR	CHAMPION	COACH	SCORE	RUNNER-UP	SITE OR HOST
1959	St. Louis	Bob Guelker	5-2	Bridgeport	Connecticut
1960	St. Louis	Bob Guelker	3-2	Maryland	Brooklyn
1961	West Chester	Mel Lorback	2-0	St. Louis	St. Louis
1962	St. Louis	Bob Guelker	4-3	Maryland	St. Louis
1963	St. Louis	Bob Guelker	3-0	Navy	Rutgers
1964	Navy	F.H. Warner	1-0	Michigan State	Brown
1965	St. Louis	Bob Guelker	1-0	Michigan State	St. Louis
1966	San Francisco	Steve Negoesco	5-2	Long Island	California
1967	Michigan State St. Louis	Gene Kenney Harry Keough	0-0	(Game called due to inclement weather)	St. Louis
1968	Maryland Michigan State	Doyle Royal Gene Kenney	2-2(2 ot)		Ga. Tech-Emory
1969	St. Louis	Harry Keough	4-0	San Francisco	San Jose State
1970	St. Louis	Harry Keough	1-0	UCLA	SIU-Edwardsville
1971	Vacated		3-2	St. Louis	Miami, Fla.
1972	St. Louis	Harry Keough	4-2	UCLA	Miami, Fla.
1973	St. Louis	Harry Keough	2-1(ot)	UCLA	Miami, Fla.
1974	Howard	Lincoln Phillips	2-1(ot)	St. Louis	St. Louis
1975	San Francisco	Steve Negoesco	4-0	SIU-Edwardsville	SIU-Edwardsville
1976	San Francisco	Steve Negoesco	1-0	Indiana	Pennsylvania
1977	Hartwick	Jim Lennox	2-1	San Francisco	California
1978	Vacated		2-0	Indiana	Tampa, Fla.
1979	SIU-Edwardsville	Bob Guelker	3-2	Clemson	Tampa, Fla.
1980	San Francisco	Steve Negoesco	4-3(ot)	Indiana	Tampa, Fla.
1981	Connecticut	Joe Morrone	2-1(ot)	Alabama A&M	Stanford
1982	Indiana	Jerry Yeagley	2-1(8 ot)	Duke	Ft. Lauderdale Fla.
1983	Indiana	Jerry Yeagley	1-0(ot)	Columbia	Ft. Lauderdale Fla.
1984	Clemson	I.M. Ibrahim	2-1	Indiana	Seattle Kingdome

ot=overtime

NORTH AMERICAN SOCCER LEAGUE CHAMPIONS[1]

1968	Atlanta Chiefs	1972	New York Cosmos	1976	Toronto Metros	1981	Chicago Sting
1969	Kansas City Spurs	1973	Philadelphia Atoms	1977-78	New York Cosmos	1982	New York Cosmos
1970	Rochester Lancers	1974	Los Angeles Aztecs	1979	Vancouver Whitecaps	1983	Tulsa Roughnecks
1971	Dallas Tornado	1975	Tampa Bay Rowdies	1980	New York Cosmos	1984	Chicago Sting

[1] North American Soccer League suspended operations in 1985.

SWIMMING

WORLD SWIMMING RECORDS

Source: United States Swimming

MEN'S RECORDS

EVENTS	TIME	SWIMMER AND NATION	DATE	SITE
100-Meter Freestyle	0:48.95	Matt Biondi, United States	8-6-85	Mission Viejo, Calif.
200-Meter Freestyle	1:47.44	Michael Gross, West Germany	7-29-84	Los Angeles, California
400-Meter Freestyle	3:47.80	Michael Gross, West Germany	6-27-85	Remscheid, West Germany
800-Meter Freestyle	7:52.33	Vladimir Salnikov, Soviet Union	7-14-83	Los Angeles, California
1,500-Meter Freestyle	14:54.76	Vladimir Salnikov, Soviet Union	2-22-83	Moscow, Soviet Union
100-Meter Backstroke	0:55.19	Rick Carey, U.S.	8-21-83	Caracas, Venezuela
200-Meter Backstroke	1:58.14	Igor Polyanski, Soviet Union	3-21-85	Erfurt, East Germany
100-Meter Breaststroke	1:01.65	Steve Lundquist, U.S.	7-29-84	Los Angeles, California
200-Meter Breaststroke	2:13.34	Victor Davis, Canada	8-2-84	Los Angeles, California
100-Meter Butterfly	0:53.08	Michael Gross, West Germany	7-30-84	Los Angeles, California
200-Meter Butterfly	1:56.65	Michael Gross, West Germany	8-10-85	Sofia, Bulgaria
200-Meter Individual Medley	2:01.42	Alex Baumann, Canada	8-4-84	Los Angeles, California
400-Meter Individual Medley	4:17.41	Alex Baumann, Canada	7-30-84	Los Angeles, California
400-Meter Freestyle Relay	3:17.08	United States team	8-17-85	Tokyo, Japan
800-Meter Freestyle Relay	7:15.69	United States team	7-30-84	Los Angeles, California
400-Meter Medley Relay	3:38.28	United States team	8-18-85	Tokyo, Japan

WOMEN'S RECORDS

EVENTS	TIME	SWIMMER AND NATION	DATE	SITE
100-Meter Freestyle	0:54.79	Barbara Krause, East Germany	7-21-80	Moscow, Soviet Union
200-Meter Freestyle	1:57.75	Kristin Otto, East Germany	5-23-84	Magdeburg, E. Germany
400-Meter Freestyle	4:06.28	Tracey Wickham, Australia	8-24-78	Berlin, W. Germany
800-Meter Freestyle	8:24.62	Tracey Wickham, Australia	8-5-78	Edmonton, Canada
1,500-Meter Freestyle	16:04.49	Kim Linehan, U.S.	8-19-79	Fort Lauderdale, Fla.
100-Meter Breaststroke	1:08.29	Sylvia Gerasch, East Germany	8-23-84	Moscow, Soviet Union
200-Meter Breaststroke	2:28.33	Silke Hoerner, East Germany	6-5-85	Leipzig, East Germany
100-Meter Butterfly	0:57.93	Mary Meagher, U.S.	8-16-81	Brown Deer, Wis.
200-Meter Butterfly	2:05.96	Mary Meagher, U.S.	8-13-81	Brown Deer, Wis.
100-Meter Backstroke	1:00.59	Ina Kleber, East Germany	8-24-84	Moscow, Soviet Union
200-Meter Backstroke	2:09.91	Cornelia Sirch, East Germany	8-7-82	Guayaquil, Ecuador
200-Meter Individual Medley	2:11.73	Ute Geweniger, East Germany	7-4-81	Berlin, East Germany
400-Meter Individual Medley	4:36.10	Petra Schneider, East Germany	8-1-82	Guayaquil, Ecuador
400-Meter Freestyle Relay	3:42.41	East German team	8-21-84	Moscow, Soviet Union
400-Meter Medley Relay	4:03.69	East German team	8-24-84	Moscow, Soviet Union
800-Meter Freestyle Relay	8:02.27	East German team	8-22-83	Rome, Italy

NATIONAL COLLEGIATE ATHLETIC ASSOCIATION SWIMMING CHAMPIONS

NCAA TEAM CHAMPIONSHIP: WOMEN

1982 Florida	1983 Stanford	1984 Texas	1985 Texas

50–YARD FREESTYLE: WOMEN

1982 Diane Johnson, Arizona .. 23.16	1984 Krissie Bush, Stanford 22.98	1985 Conny Van Bentum, California 23.18
1983 Tammy Thomas, Kansas .. 22.17		

100–YARD FREESTYLE: WOMEN

1982 Amy Caulkins, Florida 49.37	1984 Agneta Erikson, Texas 49.63	1985 Mary Wayte, Florida 49.70
1983 Tammy Thomas, Kansas .. 48.40		

200–YARD FREESTYLE: WOMEN

1982 Marybeth Linzmeir, Stanford 1:45.82	1984 Marybeth Linzmeir, Stanford 1:45.47	1985 Susan Habernigg, So. California 1:45.73
1983 Sue Habernigg, So. California 1:46.35		

500–YARD FREESTYLE: WOMEN

1982 Marybeth Linzmeir, Stanford 4:41.61	1984 Marybeth Linzmeir, Stanford 4:38.91	1985 Tiffany Cohen, Texas ... 4:37.90
1983 Marybeth Linzmeir, Stanford 4:39.95		

1,650–YARD FREESTYLE: WOMEN

1982 Marybeth Linzmeir, Stanford 16:02.94	1984 Marybeth Linzmeir, Stanford 16:02.38	1985 Tiffany Cohen, Texas .. 15:53.85
1983 Marybeth Linzmeir, Stanford 16:03.76		

100–YARD BACKSTROKE: WOMEN

1982 Sue Walsh, North Carolina 54.81	1984 Sue Walsh, North Carolina 55.32	1985 Deborah Risen, Texas 55.44
1983 Sue Walsh, North Carolina 55.62		

200–YARD BACKSTROKE: WOMEN

1982 Sue Walsh, North Carolina 1:59.47	1984 Sue Walsh, North Carolina 1:59.84	1985 Tori Trees, Texas 1:59.11
1983 Sue Walsh, North Carolina 1:59.05		

100–YARD BREASTSTROKE: WOMEN

1982 Kathy Treible, Florida ... 1:02.44	1984 Tracy Caulkins, Florida . 1:01.37	1985 Tracey McFarlane, Texas 1:02.50
1983 Jeanne Childs, Hawaii .. 1:02.69		

200–YARD BREASTSTROKE: WOMEN

1982 Kathy Treible, Florida ... 2:14.20	1984 Susan Rapp, Stanford ... 2:12.84	1985 Kim Rhodenbaugh, Texas 2:14.92
1983 Jeanne Childs, Hawaii .. 2:13.35		

NCAA SWIMMING AND DIVING CHAMPIONS (continued)

100–YARD BUTTERFLY: WOMEN
1982 Tracy Caulkins, Florida ... 53.91	1984 Joan Pennington, Texas .. 53.70	1985 Mary T. Meagher, California 53.50
1983 Jill Sterkel, Texas 53.54		

200–YARD BUTTERFLY: WOMEN
1982 Tracy Caulkins, Florida . 1:57.23	1984 Tracy Caulkins, Florida . 1:55.55	1985 Mary T. Meagher, California 1:55.13
1983 Mary T. Meagher, California 1:56.71		

200–YARD INDIVIDUAL MEDLEY: WOMEN
1982 Tracy Caulkins, Florida . 2:00.77	1984 Tracy Caulkins, Florida . 1:57.06	1985 Kim Rhodenbaugh, Texas 2:01.93
1983 Tracy Caulkins, Florida . 2:00.34		

400–YARD INDIVIDUAL MEDLEY: WOMEN
1982 Tracy Caulkins, Florida . 4:12.64	1984 Tracy Caulkins, Florida . 4:08.38	1985 Mary Wayte, Florida 4:13.27
1983 Tracy Caulkins, Florida . 4:15.24		

200–YARD MEDLEY RELAY: WOMEN
1982 Florida 1:42.10	1984 Stanford 1:42.81	1985 Texas 1:42.21
1983 Stanford 1:43.03		

400–YARD MEDLEY RELAY: WOMEN
1982 Florida 3:40.99	1984 Texas 3:41.80	1985 Texas 3:42.98
1983 Florida 3:43.00		

200–YARD FREESTYLE RELAY: WOMEN
1982 Stanford 1:32.07	1984 Texas 1:31.95	1985 Texas 1:32.06
1983 Stanford 1:31.67		

400–YARD FREESTYLE RELAY: WOMEN
1982 Stanford 3:20.98	1984 Florida 3:18.52	1985 Florida 3:21.72
1983 Texas 3:21.34		

800–YARD FREESTYLE RELAY: WOMEN
1982 Stanford 7:16.10	1984 Florida 7:06.98	1985 Florida 7:11.88
1983 Stanford 7:16.50		

ONE–METER DIVING: WOMEN
1982 Megan Neyer, Florida	1984 Megan Neyer, Florida	1985 Wendy Lucero, Southern Illinois
1983 Megan Neyer, Florida		

THREE–METER DIVING: WOMEN
1982 Megan Neyer, Florida	1984 Megan Neyer, Florida	1985 Robin Ford, Arkansas
1983 Megan Neyer, Florida		

NCAA TEAM CHAMPIONS: MEN
1953	Yale	1962	Ohio State	1978	Tennessee	1983	Florida
1954–56	Ohio State	1963–66	USC	1979	California	1984	Florida
1957–59	Michigan	1967	Stanford	1980	California	1985	Stanford
1960	USC	1968–73	Indiana	1981	Texas		
1961	Michigan	1974–77	USC	1982	UCLA		

50–YARD FREESTYLE: MEN
1971 David Edgar, Tenn. 0:20.930	1976 Joe Bottom, USC...... 0:20.081	1981 K. Kirchner, Texas..... 0:19.660
1972 David Edgar, Tenn. 0:20.300	1977 Joe Bottom, USC...... 0:19.750	1982 Robin Leamy, UCLA ... 0:19.850
1973 John Trembley, Tenn. . 0:20.337	1978 Andy Coan, Tennessee. 0:20.290	1983 P. Ang, Houston 0:19.700
1974 John Trembley, Tenn. . 0:20.230	1979 Ambrose Gaines, Auburn 0:19.990	1984 Tom Jager, UCLA 0:19.550
1975 Joe Bottom, USC...... 0:20.118	1980 Andy Coan, Tennessee. 0:19.920	1985 Tom Jager, UCLA 0:19.240

100–YARD FREESTYLE: MEN
1971 David Edgar, Tenn. 0:44.690	1976 James Montgomery, Ind. 0:44.400	1981 Ambrose Gaines, Auburn 0:42.380
1972 David Edgar, Tenn. 0:45.003	1977 David Fairbank, Stanford 0:43.680	1982 Robin Leamy, UCLA ... 0:43.590
1973 John Trembley, Tenn. . 0:45.090	1978 Andy Coan, Tennessee. 0:44.100	1983 Tom Jager, UCLA 0:43.060
1974 Joe Bottom, USC...... 0:45.067	1979 Andy Coan, Tennessee. 0:43.420	1984 Tom Jager, UCLA 0:42.850
1975 Jonty Skinner, Alabama 0:43.927	1980 Ambrose Gaines, Auburn 0:43.360	1985 Matt Biondi, Calif 0:41.870

200–YARD FREESTYLE: MEN
1971 James McConia, So. Cal. 1:39.625	1976 James Montgomery, Ind. 1:36.530	1981 Ambrose Gaines, Auburn 1:33.910
1972 Jerry Heidenreich, So. Meth. 1:38.357	1977 Bruce Furniss, USC.... 1:36.160	1982 P. Holmhertz, Calif. ... 1:36.460
1973 James McConica, USC . 1:39.600	1978 Bruce Furniss, USC.... 1:37.020	1983 M. Orn, Ariz. State 1:36.020
1974 James Montgomery, Ind. 1:39.188	1979 Andy Coan, Tennessee. 1:35.620	1984 Mike Heath, Florida ... 1:35.210
1975 G. McDonnell, UCLA ... 1:38.042	1980 Ambrose Gaines, Auburn 1:34.570	1985 Matt Biondi, Calif...... 1:33.220

500–YARD FREESTYLE: MEN
1971 John Kinsella, Indiana . 4:27.390	1976 Tim Shaw, Long Beach St. 4:19.053	1981 Doug Towne, Arizona .. 4:16.540
1972 John Kinsella, Indiana . 4:24.496	1977 Tim Shaw, Long Beach St. 4:17.390	1982 A. Astbury, Arizona St.. 4:18.150
1973 John Kinselle, Indiana . 4:37.290	1978 Brian Goodell, UCLA ... 4:18.050	1983 G. DiCarlo, Arizona 4:16.930
1974 John Naber, USC...... 4:26.855	1979 Brian Goodell, UCLA ... 4:16.430	1984 G. DiCarlo, Arizona 4:15.360
1975 John Naber, USC...... 4:20.450	1980 Brian Goodell, UCLA... 4:17.810	1985 Mike O'Brien, So. Calif. 4:13.060

NCAA SWIMMING AND DIVING CHAMPIONS (continued)

1,650–YARD FREESTYLE: MEN

1974 Jack Tingley, USC.... 15:29.287	1978 Brian Goodell, UCLA . 14:55.530	1982 A. Borgstrom, Alabama 15:02.240
1975 M. Bruner, Stanford .. 15:16.540	1979 Brian Goodell, UCLA . 14:54.130	1983 T. Corbisiero, Columbia 14:46.290
1976 Tim Shaw, Long Beach St. 15:06.760	1980 Brian Goodell, UCLA . 14:54.070	1984 Jeff Kostoff, Stanford 14:38.220
1977 Keith Converse, Alabama 14:57.300	1981 Rafael Escalas, UCLA. 14:53.900	1985 Mike O'Brien, So. Cal. 14:41.430

100–YARD BACKSTROKE: MEN

1974 John Naber, USC.... 0:50.516	1978 Robert Jackson, Long Bch. 0:49.880	1982 Clay Britt, Texas 0:49.090
1975 John Naber, USC...... 0:49.947	1979 Carlos Berrocal, Alabama 0:49.710	1983 Rick Carey, Texas 0:48.250
1976 John Naber, USC...... 0:49.940	1980 Clay Britt, Texas 0:49.520	1984 Rick Carey, Texas 0:48.630
1977 John Naber, USC...... 0:49.360	1981 Clay Britt, Texas 0:49.080	1985 Tom Jager, UCLA 0:48.210

200–YARD BACKSTROKE: MEN

1974 John Naber, USC 1:48.950	1978 Pete Rocca, California . 1:47.480	1982 Rick Carey, Texas 1:46.010
1975 John Naber, USC 1:46.827	1979 Pete Rocca, California . 1:45.530	1983 Rick Carey, Texas 1:45.210
1976 John Naber, USC...... 1:46.960	1980 James Fowler, USC.... 1:47.760	1984 Rick Carey, Texas 1:44.820
1977 John Naber, USC...... 1:46.090	1981 Wade Flemons, Stanford 1:46.300	1985 Sean Murphy, Stanford 1:46.290

100–YARD BREASTSTROKE: MEN

1974 David Wilkie, Miami ... 0:56.720	1978 Scott Spann, Auburn .. 0:56.620	1982 Steve Lundquist, SMU . 0:53.090
1975 John Hencken, Stanford 0:55.596	1979 Graham Smith, California 0:54.910	1983 Steve Lundquist, SMU . 0:52.480
1976 John Hencken, Stanford 0:56.040	1980 Steve Lundquist, SMU . 0:53.590	1984 John Moffet, Stanford . 0:54.380
1977 Graham Smith, California 0:55.100	1981 Steve Lundquist, SMU . 0:52.930	1985 John Moffet, Stanford . 0:53.620

200–YARD BREASTSTROKE: MEN

1974 John Hencken, Stanford 2:01.748	1978 Graham Smith, California 2:02.240	1982 Steve Lundquist, SMU . 1:56.840
1975 John Hencken, Stanford 2:00.839	1979 Graham Smith, California 2:00.370	1983 Glenn Mills, Alabama . 1:58.330
1976 David Wilkie, Miami ... 2:00.740	1980 William Barrett, UCLA . 1:58.430	1984 John Moffet, Stanford . 1:57.990
1977 Graham Smith, California 2:00.050	1981 Steve Lundquist, SMU . 1:55.010	1985 John Moffet, Stanford . 1:55.960

100–YARD BUTTERFLY: MEN

1974 John Trembley, Tenn. . 0:48.718	1978 Greg Jagenburg, Long Bch. 0:48.770	1982 Matt Gribble, Miami (Fla.) 0:47.350
1975 Jeff Rolan, Utah 0:48.953	1979 Par Arvidsson, California 0:47.760	1983 Matt Gribble, Miami (Fla.) 0:47.260
1976 Matt Vogel, Tennessee . 0:48.950	1980 Par Arvidsson, California 0:47.360	1984 P. Morales, Stanford... 0:47.020
1977 Joe Bottom, USC...... 0:47.770	1981 Scott Spann, Texas 0:47.220	1985 P. Morales, Stanford... 0:46.520

200–YARD BUTTERFLY: MEN

1974 Robin Backhaus, Wash. 1:47.040	1978 Greg Jagenburg, Long Bch. 1:46.010	1982 Craig Beardsley, Florida 1:44.100
1975 Robin Backhaus, Wash. 1:47.168	1979 Par Arvidsson, California 1:45.530	1983 Ricardo Prado, SMU ... 1:44.960
1976 Steve Gregg, N.C. St. . 1:47.000	1980 Par Arvidsson, California 1:44.430	1984 P. Morales, Stanford... 1:44.330
1977 Mike Bruner, Stanford . 1:45.270	1981 Craig Beardsley, Florida 1:44.150	1985 P. Morales, Stanford... 1:42.850

200–YARD INDIVIDUAL MEDLEY: MEN

1974 Steve Furniss, USC 1:51.522	1978 Scott Spann, Auburn .. 1:49.300	1982 William Barrett, UCLA . 1:45.000
1975 Fredrick Tyler, Indiana . 1:50.628	1979 Graham Smith, California 1:48.440	1983 Steve Lundquist, SMU . 1:45.540
1976 Leroy Engstrand, Tenn. 1:50.129	1980 William Barrett, UCLA . 1:46.250	1984 Ricardo Prado, SMU ... 1:47.950
1977 Scott Spann, Auburn .. 1:48.260	1981 William Barrett, UCLA . 1:45.010	1985 P. Morales, Stanford... 1:46.080

400–YARD INDIVIDUAL MEDLEY: MEN

1974 Steve Furniss, USC 3:57.800	1978 Brian Goodell, UCLA... 3:53.610	1982 Jeff Float, USC 3:49.000
1975 Leroy Engstrand, Tenn. 3:57.801	1979 Brian Goodell, UCLA... 3:50.800	1983 Ricardo Prado, SMU ... 3:48.190
1976 Rodney Strachan, USC. 3:55.640	1980 Brian Goodell, UCLA... 3:31.380	1984 Ricardo Prado, SMU ... 3:46.860
1977 Rodney Strachan, USC. 3:54.760	1981 J. Vassallo, Miami (Fla.) 3:48.160	1985 Jeff Kostoff, Stanford . 3:47.110

400–YARD FREESTYLE RELAY: MEN

1970 USC 3:03.910	1974 Indiana 3:00.359	1978 Tennessee .. 2:55.280	1982 UCLA 2:53.150
1971 USC 3:02.380	1975 Indiana 2:58.421	1979 Tennessee .. 2:54.740	1983 Florida 2:54.060
1972 Tennessee .. 3:01.118	1976 USC 2:57.540	1980 Auburn..... 2:55.160	1984 UCLA 2:54.110
1973 Tennessee . 3:00.363	1977 USC 2:55.280	1981 Texas 2:54.840	1985 California .. 2:53.150

800–YARD FREESTYLE RELAY: MEN

1974 Indiana 6:40.321	1978 Auburn 6:31.930	1982 California 6:28.940
1975 Indiana 6:36.293	1979 Florida 6:28.010	1983 Florida 6:25.290
1976 USC 6:33.130	1980 Auburn 6:28.070	1984 Florida.............. 6:21.290
1977 USC 6:28.010	1981 Florida 6:27.020	1985 California 6:24.400

400–YARD MEDLEY RELAY: MEN

1974 Tennessee 3:22.788	1978 California 3:18.260	1982 Texas 3:14.240
1975 USC 3:19.221	1979 California 3:15.220	1983 SMU 3:12.630
1976 USC 3:20.020	1980 Texas............... 3:14.590	1984 Texas............... 3:13.350
1977 Indiana 3:17.140	1981 Texas............... 3:12.930	1985 Stanford 3:10.920

ONE–METER DIVING: MEN

1974 Tim Moore, Ohio St..... 494.25	1978 Wayne Chester, Alabama 485.10	1982 Robert Bollinger, Indiana 554.95
1975 Tim Moore, Ohio St.... 502.71	1979 Greg Louganis, Miami (Fla.) 513.75	1983 Matt Scoggin, Texas ... 557.25
1976 James Kennedy, Tenn. .. 514.29	1980 Greg Louganis, Miami (Fla.) 557.20	1984 Matt Scoggin, Texas 528.85
1977 Matthew Chelich, Mich... 503.13	1981 Randal Ableman, Iowa ... 509.30	1985 Ron Meyer, Arkansas.... 548.10

THREE–METER DIVING: MEN

1974 Rick McAllister, Air Force 526.41	1978 Christopher Snode, Florida 543.18	1982 Ron Merriott, Michigan .. 600.30
1975 Tim Moore, Ohio St. 590.61	1979 Matthew Chelich, Michigan 527.85	1983 M. Bradshaw, Ohio State 575.45
1976 Brian Bungum, Indiana .. 542.19	1980 Greg Louganis, Miami (Fla.) 608.10	1984 Kent Ferguson, Michigan 560.85
1977 Brian Bungum, Indiana .. 542.40	1981 Robert Bollinger, Indiana 540.70	1985 Ron Meyer, Arkansas.... 606.70

864 SPORTS AND GAMES (TENNIS)

TENNIS

U.S. OPEN TENNIS CHAMPIONS

U.S. MEN'S SINGLES CHAMPIONS

1881 Richard D. Sears (U.S.)	1916 R. Norris Williams II (U.S.)	1951 Frank Sedgman (Australia)
1882 Richard D. Sears (U.S.)	1917 R. Lindley Murray (U.S.)	1952 Frank Sedgman (Australia)
1883 Richard D. Sears (U.S.)	1918 R. Lindley Murray (U.S.)	1953 Tony Trabert (U.S.)
1884 Richard D. Sears (U.S.)	1919 William M. Johnston (U.S.)	1954 Vic Seixas (U.S.)
1885 Richard D. Sears (U.S.)	1920 Bill Tilden (U.S.)	1955 Tony Trabert (U.S.)
1886 Richard D. Sears (U.S.)	1921 Bill Tilden (U.S.)	1956 Ken Rosewall (Australia)
1887 Richard D. Sears (U.S.)	1922 Bill Tilden (U.S.)	1957 Mal Anderson (Australia)
1888 Henry W. Slocum (U.S.)	1923 Bill Tilden (U.S.)	1958 Ashley Cooper (Australia)
1889 Henry W. Slocum (U.S.)	1924 Bill Tilden (U.S.)	1959 Neale Fraser (Australia)
1890 Oliver S. Campbell (U.S.)	1925 Bill Tilden (U.S.)	1960 Neale Fraser (Australia)
1891 Oliver S. Campbell (U.S.)	1926 Rene Lacoste (France)	1961 Roy Emerson (Australia)
1892 Oliver S. Campbell (U.S.)	1927 Rene Lacoste (France)	1962 Rod Laver (Australia)
1893 Robert D. Wrenn (U.S.)	1928 Henri Cochet (France)	1963 Rafael Osuna (Mexico)
1894 Robert D. Wrenn (U.S.)	1929 Henri Cochet (France)	1964 Roy Emerson (Australia)
1895 Fred H. Hovey (U.S.)	1930 John Doeg (U.S.)	1965 Manuel Santana (Spain)
1896 Robert D. Wrenn (U.S.)	1931 Ellsworth Vines (U.S.)	1966 Fred Stolle (Australia)
1897 Robert D. Wrenn (U.S.)	1932 Ellsworth Vines (U.S.)	1967 John Newcombe (Australia)
1898 Malcolm Whitman (U.S.)	1933 Fred Perry (England)	1968 Arthur Ashe (U.S.)
1899 Malcolm Whitman (U.S.)	1934 Fred Perry (England)	1969 Rod Laver (Australia)
1900 Malcolm Whitman (U.S.)	1935 Wilmer Allison (U.S.)	1970 Ken Rosewall (Australia)
1901 William A. Larned (U.S.)	1936 Fred Perry (England)	1971 Stan Smith (U.S.)
1902 William A. Larned (U.S.)	1937 Don Budge (U.S.)	1972 Ilie Nastase (Romania)
1903 Hugh L. Doherty (England)	1938 Don Budge (U.S.)	1973 John Newcombe (Australia)
1904 Holcombe Ward (U.S.)	1939 Bobby Riggs (U.S.)	1974 Jimmy Connors (U.S.)
1905 Beals C. Wright (U.S.)	1940 Don McNeill (U.S.)	1975 Manuel Orantes (Spain)
1906 William J. Clothier (U.S.)	1941 Bobby Riggs (U.S.)	1976 Jimmy Connors (U.S.)
1907 William A. Larned (U.S.)	1942 Ted Schroeder (U.S.)	1977 Guillermo Vilas (Argentina)
1908 William A. Larned (U.S.)	1943 Joe Hunt (U.S.)	1978 Jimmy Connors (U.S.)
1909 William A. Larned (U.S.)	1944 Frank Parker (U.S.)	1979 John McEnroe (U.S.)
1910 William A. Larned (U.S.)	1945 Frank Parker (U.S.)	1980 John McEnroe (U.S.)
1911 William A. Larned (U.S.)	1946 Jack Kramer (U.S.)	1981 John McEnroe (U.S.)
1912 Maurice E. McLaughlin (U.S.)	1947 Jack Kramer (U.S.)	1982 Jimmy Connors (U.S.)
1913 Maurice E. McLaughlin (U.S.)	1948 Pancho Gonzales (U.S.)	1983 Jimmy Connors (U.S.)
1914 R. Norris Williams (U.S.)	1949 Pancho Gonzales (U.S.)	1984 John McEnroe (U.S.)
1915 William M. Johnston (U.S.)	1950 Art Larsen (U.S.)	1985 Ivan Lendl (Czech.)

U.S. WOMEN'S SINGLES CHAMPIONS

1887 Ellen F. Hansell (U.S.)	1920 Molla Bjurstedt Mallory (U.S.)	1953 Maureen Connolly (U.S.)
1888 Bertha L. Townsend (U.S.)	1921 Molla Bjurstedt Mallory (U.S.)	1954 Doris Hart (U.S.)
1889 Bertha L. Townsend (U.S.)	1922 Molla Bjurstedt Mallory (U.S.)	1955 Doris Hart (U.S.)
1890 Ellen C. Roosevelt (U.S.)	1923 Helen Wills (U.S.)	1956 Shirley Fry (U.S.)
1891 Mabel E. Cahill (U.S.)	1924 Helen Wills (U.S.)	1957 Althea Gibson (U.S.)
1892 Mabel E. Cahill (U.S.)	1925 Helen Wills (U.S.)	1958 Althea Gibson (U.S.)
1893 Aline M. Terry (U.S.)	1926 Molla Bjurstedt Mallory (U.S.)	1959 Maria Bueno (Brazil)
1894 Helen R. Helwig (U.S.)	1927 Helen Wills (U.S.)	1960 Darlene Hard (U.S.)
1895 Juliette P. Atkinson (U.S.)	1928 Helen Wills (U.S.)	1961 Darlene Hard (U.S.)
1896 Elisabeth H. Moore (U.S.)	1929 Helen Wills (U.S.)	1962 Margaret Smith (Australia)
1897 Juliette P. Atkinson (U.S.)	1930 Betty Nuthall (England)	1963 Maria Bueno (Brazil)
1898 Juliette P. Atkinson (U.S.)	1931 Helen Wills Moody (U.S.)	1964 Maria Bueno (Brazil)
1899 Marion Jones (U.S.)	1932 Helen Hull Jacobs (U.S.)	1965 Margaret Smith (Australia)
1900 Myrtle McAteer (U.S.)	1933 Helen Hull Jacobs (U.S.)	1966 Maria Bueno (Brazil)
1901 Elisabeth H. Moore (U.S.)	1934 Helen Hull Jacobs (U.S.)	1967 Billie Jean King (U.S.)
1902 Marion Jones (U.S.)	1935 Helen Hull Jacobs (U.S.)	1968 Virginia Wade (England)
1903 Elisabeth H. Moore (U.S.)	1936 Alice Marble (U.S.)	1969 Margaret S. Court (Australia)
1904 May G. Sutton (U.S.)	1937 Anita Lizana (Chile)	1970 Margaret S. Court (Australia)
1905 Elisabeth H. Moore (U.S.)	1938 Alice Marble (U.S.)	1971 Billie Jean King (U.S.)
1906 Helen Homans (U.S.)	1939 Alice Marble (U.S.)	1972 Billie Jean King (U.S.)
1907 Evelyn Sears (U.S.)	1940 Alice Marble (U.S.)	1973 Margaret S. Court (Australia)
1908 Maud Bargar-Wallach (U.S.)	1941 Sarah Palfrey Cooke (U.S.)	1974 Billie Jean King (U.S.)
1909 Hazel V. Hotchkiss (U.S.)	1942 Pauline Betz (U.S.)	1975 Chris Evert (U.S.)
1910 Hazel V. Hotchkiss (U.S.)	1943 Pauline Betz (U.S.)	1976 Chris Evert (U.S.)
1911 Hazel V. Hotchkiss (U.S.)	1944 Pauline Betz (U.S.)	1977 Chris Evert (U.S.)
1912 Mary K. Browne (U.S.)	1945 Sarah Palfrey Cooke (U.S.)	1978 Chris Evert (U.S.)
1913 Mary K. Browne (U.S.)	1946 Pauline Betz (U.S.)	1979 Tracy Austin (U.S.)
1914 Mary K. Browne (U.S.)	1947 Louise Brough (U.S.)	1980 Chris Evert Lloyd (U.S.)
1915 Molla Bjurstedt (U.S.)	1948 Margaret O. du Pont (U.S.)	1981 Tracy Austin (U.S.)
1916 Molla Bjurstedt (U.S.)	1949 Margaret O. du Pont (U.S.)	1982 Chris Evert Lloyd (U.S.)
1917 Molla Bjurstedt (U.S.)	1950 Margaret O. du Pont (U.S.)	1983 Martina Navratilova (U.S.)
1918 Molla Bjurstedt (U.S.)	1951 Maureen Connolly (U.S.)	1984 Martina Navratilova (U.S.)
1919 Hazel H. Wightman (U.S.)	1952 Maureen Connolly (U.S.)	1985 Hana Mandlikova (Czech.)

U.S. OPEN MIXED DOUBLES CHAMPIONS

1892	Mabel E. Cahill-Clarence Hobart	1939	Alice Marble-Harry C. Hopman
1893	Ellen C. Roosevelt-Clarence Hobart	1940	Alice Marble-Robert L. Riggs
1894	Juliette P. Atkinson-Edwin P. Fischer	1941	Sarah Palfrey Cooke-John A. Kramer
1895	Juliette P. Atkinson-Edwin P. Fischer	1942	A. Louise Brough-F.R. Schroeder Jr.
1896	Juliette P. Atkinson-Edwin P. Fischer	1943	Margaret Osborne-William F. Talbert
1897	Laura Henson-D.L. Magruder	1944	Margaret Osborne-William F. Talbert
1898	Carrie B. Neely-Edwin P. Fischer	1945	Margaret Osborne-William F. Talbert
1899	Elizabeth J. Rastall-Albert L. Hoskins	1946	Margaret Osborne-William F. Talbert
1900	Margaret Hunnewell-Alfred Codman	1947	A. Louise Brough-John Bromwich
1901	Marion Jones-Raymond D. Little	1948	A. Louise Brough-Thomas P. Brown Jr.
1902	Elizabeth H. Moore-Wylie C. Grant	1949	A. Louise Brough-Eric Sturgess
1903	Helen Chapman-Harry F. Allen	1950	Margaret O. duPont-Kenneth McGregor
1904	Elizabeth H. Moore-Wylie C. Grant	1951	Doris Hart-Frank Sedgman
1905	Mr. and Mrs. Clarence Hobart	1952	Doris Hart-Frank Sedgman
1906	Sarah Coffin-Edward B. Dewhurst	1953	Doris Hart-E. Victor Seixas Jr.
1907	May Sayres-Wallace F. Johnson	1954	Doris Hart-E. Victor Seixas Jr.
1908	Edith E. Rotch-Nathaniel W. Niles	1955	Doris Hart-E. Victor Seixas Jr.
1909	Hazel V. Hotchkiss-Wallace F. Johnson	1956	Margaret O. duPont-Kenneth Rosewall
1910	Hazel V. Hotchkiss-J.R. Carpenter Jr.	1957	Althea Gibson-Kurt Nielson
1911	Hazel V. Hotchkiss-Wallace F. Johnson	1958	Margaret Osborne-Neale Fraser
1912	Mary K. Browne-R.N. Williams II	1959	Margaret Osborne duPont-Neale Fraser
1913	Mary K. Browne-Bill Tilden	1960	Margaret Osborne duPont-Neale Fraser
1914	Mary K. Browne-Bill Tilden	1961	Margaret Smith-Robert Mark
1915	Hazel H. Wightman-Harry C. Johnson	1962	Margaret Smith-Fred Stolle
1916	Eleonora Sears-Willis F. Davis	1963	Margaret Smith-Ken Fletcher
1917	Molla Bjurstedt-Irving C. Wright	1964	Margaret Smith-John Newcombe
1918	Hazel H. Wightman-Irving C. Wright	1965	Margaret Smith-Fred Stolle
1919	Marion Zinderstein-Vincent Richards	1966	Donna Floyd Fales-Owen Davidson
1920	Hazel H. Wightman-Wallace F. Johnson	1967	Billie Jean King-Owen Davidson
1921	Mary K. Browne-William Johnson	1968	Mary Ann Eisel-Peter Curtis
1922	Molla B. Mallory-Bill Tilden	1969	Margaret S. Court-Martin Riessen
1923	Molla B. Mallory-Bill Tilden	1970	Margaret S. Court-Martin Riessen
1924	Helen N. Wills-Vincent Richards	1971	Billie Jean King-Owen Davidson
1925	Kathleen McKane-John B. Hawkes	1972	Margaret S. Court-Martin Riessen
1926	Elizabeth Ryan-Jean Borotra	1973	Billie Jean King-Owen Davidson
1927	Eileen Bennett-Henri Cochet	1974	Pam Teeguarden-Geoff Masters
1928	Helen N. Wills-John B. Hawkes	1975	Rosemary Casals-Richard Stockton
1929	Betty Nuthall-George M. Lott Jr.	1976	Billie Jean King-Phil Dent
1930	Edith Cross-Wilmer L. Allison	1977	Betty Stove-Frew McMillan
1931	Betty Nuthall-George M. Lott Jr.	1978	Betty Stove-Frew McMillan
1932	Sarah Palfrey-Frederick Perry	1979	Greer Stevens-Bob Hewitt
1933	Elizabeth Ryan-H. Ellsworth Vines	1980	Wendy Turnbull-Martin Riessen
1934	Helen H. Jacobs-George M. Lott Jr.	1981	Anne Smith-Kevin Curren
1935	Sarah Palfrey Fabyan-Enrique Maier	1982	Anne Smith-Kevin Curren
1936	Alice Marble-C. Gene Mako	1983	Elizabeth Sayers-John Fitzgerald
1937	Sarah Palfrey Fabyan-J. Donald Budge	1984	Manuela Maleeva-Tom Gullikson
1938	Alice Marble-J. Donald Budge	1985	Martina Navratilova-Heinz Gunthardt

WIMBLEDON TENNIS CHAMPIONS

WIMBLEDON MEN'S SINGLES CHAMPIONS

1877	Spencer W. Gore (Britain)	1900	Reginald Doherty (Britain)	1926	Jean Borotra (France)
1878	P. Frank Hadow (Britain)	1901	Arthur W. Gore (Britain)	1927	Henri Cochet (France)
1879	J. T. Hartley (Britain)	1902	Hugh L. Doherty (Britain)	1928	René Lacoste (France)
1880	J. T. Hartley (Britain)	1903	Hugh L. Doherty (Britain)	1929	Henri Cochet (France)
1881	William Renshaw (Britain)	1904	Hugh L. Doherty (Britain)	1930	Bill Tilden (U.S.)
1882	William Renshaw (Britain)	1905	Hugh L. Doherty (Britain)	1931	Sid Wood (U.S.)
1883	William Renshaw (Britain)	1906	Hugh L. Doherty (Britain)	1932	Ellsworth Vines (U.S.)
1884	William Renshaw (Britain)	1907	Norman Brookes (Austr.)	1933	Jack Crawford (Australia)
1885	William Renshaw (Britain)	1908	Arthur W. Gore (Britain)	1934	Fred Perry (Britain)
1886	William Renshaw (Britain)	1909	Arthur W. Gore (Britain)	1935	Fred Perry (Britain)
1887	Herbert F. Lawford (Britain)	1910	Anthony F. Wilding (N.Z.)	1936	Fred Perry (Britain)
1888	Ernest Renshaw (Britain)	1911	Anthony F. Wilding (N.Z.)	1937	Don Budge (U.S.)
1889	William Renshaw (Britain)	1912	Anthony F. Wilding (N.Z.)	1938	Don Budge (U.S.)
1890	Willoughby J. Hamilton (Britain)	1913	Anthony F. Wilding (N.Z.)	1939	Bobby Riggs (U.S.)
1891	Wilfred Baddeley (Britain)	1914	Norman Brookes (Austr.)	1940–45	No matches
1892	Wilfred Baddeley (Britain)	1915–1918	No competition	1946	Yvon Petra (France)
1893	Joshua L. Pim (Britain)	1919	Gerald Patterson (Austr.)	1947	Jack Kramer (U.S.)
1894	Joshua L. Pim (Britain)	1920	Bill Tilden (U.S.)	1948	Bob Falkenburg (U.S.)
1895	Wilfred Baddeley (Britain)	1921	Bill Tilden (U.S.)	1949	Ted Schroeder (U.S.)
1896	Harold S. Mahony (Britain)	1922	Gerald Patterson (Australia)	1950	Budge Patty (U.S.)
1897	Reginald Doherty (Britain)	1923	Bill Johnston (U.S.)	1951	Dick Savitt (U.S.)
1898	Reginald Doherty (Britain)	1924	Jean Borotra (France)	1952	Frank Sedgman (Australia)
1899	Reginald Doherty (Britain)	1925	René Lacoste (France)	1953	Vic Seixas (U.S.)

WIMBLEDON TENNIS CHAMPIONS *(continued)*

1954	Jaroslav Drobny (Egypt)	1965	Roy Emerson (Australia)	1976	Bjorn Borg (Sweden)
1955	Tony Trabert (U.S.)	1966	Manuel Santana (Spain)	1977	Bjorn Borg (Sweden)
1956	Lew Hoad (Australia)	1967	John Newcombe (Australia)	1978	Bjorn Borg (Sweden)
1957	Lew Hoad (Australia)	1968	Rod Laver (Australia)	1979	Bjorn Borg (Sweden)
1958	Ashley Cooper (Australia)	1969	Rod Laver (Australia)	1980	Bjorn Borg (Sweden)
1959	Alex Olmedo (U.S.)	1970	John Newcombe (Australia)	1981	John McEnroe (U.S.)
1960	Neale Fraser (Australia)	1971	John Newcombe (Australia)	1982	Jimmy Connors (U.S.)
1961	Rod Laver (Australia)	1972	Stan Smith (U.S.)	1983	John McEnroe (U.S.)
1962	Rod Laver (Australia)	1973	Jan Kodes (Czech.)	1984	John McEnroe (U.S.)
1963	Chuck McKinley (U.S.)	1974	Jimmy Connors (U.S.)	1985	Boris Becker (W. Germany)
1964	Roy Emerson (Australia)	1975	Arthur Ashe (U.S.)		

WIMBLEDON WOMEN'S SINGLES CHAMPIONS

1884	Maud Watson (Britain)	1919	Suzanne Lenglen (France)	1955	Louise Brough (U.S.)
1885	Maud Watson (Britain)	1920	Suzanne Lenglen (France)	1956	Shirley Fry (U.S.)
1886	Blanche Bingley (Britain)	1921	Suzanne Lenglen (France)	1957	Althea Gibson (U.S.)
1887	Lottie Dod (Britain)	1922	Suzanne Lenglen (France)	1958	Althea Gibson (U.S.)
1888	Lottie Dod (Britain)	1923	Suzanne Lenglen (France)	1959	Maria Bueno (Brazil)
1889	Blanche Bingley Hillyard (Brit.)	1924	Kitty McKane (Britain)	1960	Maria Bueno (Brazil)
1890	L. Rice (Britain)	1925	Suzanne Lenglen (France)	1961	Angela Mortimer (Britain)
1891	Lottie Dod (Britain)	1926	Kitty McK. Godfree (Britain)	1962	Karen Hantze Susman (U.S.)
1892	Lottie Dod (Britain)	1927	Helen Wills (U.S.)	1963	Margaret Smith (Australia)
1894	Blanche Bingley Hillyard (Brit.)	1928	Helen Wills (U.S.)	1964	Maria Bueno (Brazil)
1895	Charlotte Cooper (Britain)	1929	Helen Wills (U.S.)	1965	Margaret Smith (Australia)
1896	Charlotte Cooper (Britain)	1930	Helen Wills Moody (U.S.)	1966	Billie Jean King (U.S.)
1897	Blanche Bingley Hillyard (Brit.)	1931	Cilly Aussen (Germany)	1967	Billie Jean King (U.S.)
1898	Charlotte Cooper (Britain)	1932	Helen Wills Moody (U.S.)	1968	Billie Jean King (U.S.)
1899	Blanche B. Hillyard (Brit.)	1933	Helen Wills Moody (U.S.)	1969	Ann Jones (Britain)
1900	Blanche B. Hillyard (Brit.)	1934	Dorothy Round (Britain)	1970	Margaret Smith Court (Australia)
1901	Charlotte Cooper Sterry (Brit.)	1935	Helen Wills Moody (U.S.)	1971	Evonne Goolagong (Australia)
1902	M. E. Robb (Britain)	1936	Helen Hull Jacobs (U.S.)	1972	Billie Jean King (U.S.)
1903	Dorothy K. Douglass (Brit.)	1937	Dorothy Round (Britain)	1973	Billie Jean King (U.S.)
1904	Dorothy K. Douglass (Brit.)	1938	Helen Wills Moody (U.S.)	1974	Chris Evert (U.S.)
1905	May G. Sutton (U.S.)	1939	Alice Marble (U.S.)	1975	Billie Jean King (U.S.)
1906	Dorothy K. Douglass (Britain)	1940–45	No matches	1976	Chris Evert (U.S.)
1907	May G. Sutton (U.S.)	1946	Pauline Betz (U.S.)	1977	Virginia Wade (Britain)
1908	Charlotte Cooper Sterry (Brit.)	1947	Margaret Osborne (U.S.)	1978	Martina Navratilova (U.S.)
1909	Dorothea P. Boothby (Brit.)	1948	Louise Brough (U.S.)	1979	Martina Navratilova (U.S.)
1910	Dorothy D. Chambers (Brit.)	1949	Louise Brough (U.S.)	1980	Yvonne Goolagong (Australia)
1911	Dorothy D. Chambers (Brit.)	1950	Louise Brough (U.S.)	1981	Chris Evert Lloyd (U.S.)
1912	Ethel W. Larcombe (Brit.)	1951	Doris Hart (U.S.)	1982	Martina Navratilova (U.S.)
1913	Dorothy D. Chambers (Brit.)	1952	Maureen Connolly (U.S.)	1983	Martina Navratilova (U.S.)
1914	Dorothy D. Chambers (Brit.)	1953	Maureen Connolly (U.S.)	1984	Martina Navratilova (U.S.)
1915-18	No competition	1954	Maureen Connolly (U.S.)	1985	Martina Navratilova (U.S.)

DAVIS CUP—MEN'S TEAM TENNIS

The most highly prized trophy of international men's team tennis, the Davis Cup, was put up in 1900 by Dwight F. Davis, an outstanding sportsman and U.S. public official.

American men's tennis teams have been awarded the trophy oftener than those of any other country, winning a total of 28 final challenge rounds.

DAVIS CUP CHALLENGE ROUND

YEAR	WINNER	LOSER	SCORE	YEAR	WINNER	LOSER	SCORE
1900	United States ..	England	5–0	1923	United States ..	Australasia	4–1
1902	United States ..	England	3–2	1924	United States ..	Australasia	5–0
1903	England	United States ..	4–1	1925	United States ..	France	5–0
1904	England	Belgium	5–0	1926	United States ..	France	4–1
1905	England	United States ..	5–0	1927	France	United States ..	3–2
1906	England	United States ..	5–0	1928	France	United States ..	4–1
1907	Australia	England	3–2	1929	France	United States ..	3–2
1908	Australia	United States ..	3–2	1930	France	United States ..	4–1
1909	Australasia	United States ..	5–0	1931	France	England	3–2
1910	Not held	—	—	1932	France	United States ..	3–2
1911	Australasia	United States ..	5–0	1933	England	France	3–2
1912	England	Australasia	3–2	1934	England	United States ..	4–1
1913	United States ..	England	3–2	1935	England	United States ..	5–0
1914	Australasia	United States ..	3–2	1936	England	Australia	3–2
1915–18	Not held	—	—	1937	United States ..	England	4–1
1919	Australasia	England	4–1	1938	United States ..	Australia	3–2
1920	United States ..	Australasia	5–0	1939	Australia	United States ..	3–2
1921	United States ..	Japan	5–0	1940–45	Not held	—	—
1922	United States ..	Australasia	4–1	1946	United States ..	Australia	5–0

DAVIS CUP *(continued)*

YEAR	WINNER	LOSER	SCORE	YEAR	WINNER	LOSER	SCORE
1947	United States ..	Australia	4–1	1966	Australia	India..........	4–1
1948	United States ..	Australia	5–0	1967	Australia	Spain	4–1
1949	United States ..	Australia	4–1	1968	United States ..	Australia	4–1
1950	Australia	United States ..	4–1	1969	United States ..	Romania	5–0
1951	Australia	United States ..	3–2	1970	United States ..	West Germany .	5–0
1952	Australia	United States ..	4–1	1971	United States ..	Romania	3–2
1953	Australia	United States ..	3–2	1972	United States ..	Romania	3–2
1954	United States ..	Australia	3–2	1973	Australia	United States ..	5–0
1955	Australia	United States ..	5–0	1974	South Africa ...	India[1]	—
1956	Australia	United States ..	5–0	1975	Sweden	Czechoslovakia	3–2
1957	Australia	United States ..	3–2	1976	Italy	Chile	4–1
1958	United States...	Australia	3–2	1977	Australia	Italy	4–1
1959	Australia	United States ..	3–2	1978	United States ..	Britain	4–1
1960	Australia	Italy	4–1	1979	United States ..	Italy	5–0
1961	Australia	Italy	5–0	1980	Czechoslovakia	Italy	4–1
1962	Australia	Mexico	5–0	1981	United States ..	Argentina	4–1
1963	United States ..	Australia	3–2	1982	United States ..	France	4–1
1964	Australia	United States ..	3–2	1983	Australia	Sweden	3–2
1965	Australia	Spain	4–1	1984	Sweden	United States ..	4–1

WIGHTMAN CUP—WOMEN'S TEAM TENNIS

Donated in 1923 by Mrs. Hazel Wightman, an American tennis champion and socialite, the Wightman Cup is the premier prize in women's international competition. Teams from the U.S. and Britain compete for the trophy. The site alternates between the two countries.

YEAR	WINNER	SCORE	YEAR	WINNER	SCORE	YEAR	WINNER	SCORE
1923	United States	7–0	1948	United States	6–1	1968	Britain	4–3
1924	Britain	6–1	1949	United States	7–0	1969	United States	5–2
1925	Britain	4–3	1950	United States	7–0	1970	United States	4–3
1926	United States	4–3	1951	United States	6–1	1971	United States	4–3
1927	United States	5–2	1952	United States	7–0	1972	United States	5–2
1928	Britain	4–3	1953	United States	7–0	1973	United States	5–2
1929	United States	4–3	1954	United States	6–0[2]	1974	Britain	6–1
1930	Britain	4–3	1955	United States	6–1	1975	Britain	5–2
1931	United States	5–2	1956	United States	5–2	1976	United States	5–2
1932	United States	4–3	1957	United States	6–1	1977	United States	7–0
1933	United States	4–3	1958	Britain	4–3	1978	Britain	4–3
1934	United States	5–2	1959	United States	4–3	1979	United States	7–0
1935	United States	4–3	1960	Britain	4–3	1980	United States	5–2
1936	United States	4–3	1961	United States	6–1	1981	United States	7–0
1937	United States	6–1	1962	United States	4–3	1982	United States	6–1
1938	United States	5–2	1963	United States	6–1	1983	United States	6–1
1939	United States	5–2	1964	United States	5–2	1984	United States	5–2
1940–45	Not held	—	1965	United States	5–2			
1946	United States	7–0	1966	United States	4–3			
1947	United States	7–0	1967	United States	6–1			

[1] India defaulted in protest against South Africa's racial policies. [2] One doubles match was not played because of rain.

TRACK AND FIELD

WORLD OUTDOOR TRACK AND FIELD RECORDS: MEN

EVENT	RECORD	RECORD HOLDER	NATION	DATE	SITE
RUNNING					
1 Mile	3:46.31	Steve Cram	Britain	7-27-85	Oslo, Norway
1 Hour	20,944 meters[1]	Jos Hermens	Netherlands ..	5-1-76	Arnhem, Netherlands
100 Meters	0:09.93	Calvin Smith	United States .	7-3-83	Colorado Springs, Colo.
200 Meters	0:19.72	Pietro Mennea........	Italy	9-12-79	Mexico City, Mexico
200 Meters (turn)	0:19.8	Donald Quarrie	Jamaica	8-3-71	Cali, Colombia
400 Meters	0:43.86	Lee Evans	United States .	10-18-68	Mexico City, Mexico
600 Meters	1:14.3	Lee Evans............	United States .	8-31-68	Lake Tahoe, California
800 Meters	1:41.73	Sebastian Coe	Britain	6-10-81	Florence, Italy
1,000 Meters ...	2:12.18	Sebastian Coe	Britain	7-11-81	Oslo, Norway
1,500 Meters ...	3:29.45	Said Aouita	Morocco	8-23-85	Berlin, West Germany
2,000 Meters	4:51.39	Steve Cram	Britain	8-4-85	Budapest, Hungary
3,000 Meters ...	7:32.1	Henry Rono	Kenya	6-27-78	Oslo, Norway
3,000 Meters[2] ...	8:05.4	Henry Rono	Kenya	5-13-78	Seattle, Washington
5,000 Meters ...	13:00.40	Said Aouita	Morocco	7-27-85	Oslo, Norway
10,000 Meters...	27:13.81	Fernando Mamede	Portugal......	7-2-84	Stockholm, Sweden
20,000 Meters...	57:24.2	Jos Hermens	Netherlands ..	5-1-76	Arnhem, Netherlands
25,000 Meters...	1:13:55.8	Toshiko Seko	Japan........	3-22-81	Christchurch, New Zealand
30,000 Meters...	1:29:18.8	Toshiko Seko	Japan........	3-22-81	Christchurch, New Zealand
Marathon	2:07:12	Carlos Lopes	Portugal......	4-27-85	Rotterdam, Netherlands

[1] 13 miles, 24 yards. [2] Steeplechase.

WORLD OUTDOOR TRACK AND FIELD RECORDS: MEN (continued)

EVENT	RECORD	RECORD HOLDER	NATION	DATE	SITE
RELAYS					
400 Meters	0:37.83	United States team ...	United States .	8–11–84	Los Angeles, California
800 Meters	1:20.26	So. California	United States .	5–27–78	Tempe, Arizona
1,600 Meters	2:56.16	United States team ...	United States .	10–20–68	Mexico City, Mexico
3,200 Meters	7:03.89	British team..........	Britain	8–30–82	London, England
6,000 Meters	14:38.8	West German team ...	West Germany	8–17–77	Cologne, West Germany
HURDLES					
110 Meters	0:12.93	Renaldo Nehemiah	United States .	8–19–81	Zurich, Switzerland
400 Meters	0:47.02	Edwin Moses	United States .	8–31–83	Koblenz, West Germany
WALKING					
20 Kilometers ...	1:18:40.0	Ernesto Canto	Mexico	5–5–84	Bergen, Norway
30 Kilometers ...	2:06:27	Maurizio Damilano	Italy	5–5–85	S.Donato, Italy
50 Kilometers ...	3:41:38.4	Raul Gonzalez	Mexico	5–25–79	Fana, Norway
2 Hours	28,165 meters[1]	Jose Marin	Spain	8–4–79	Barcelona, Spain
JUMPING					
High Jump	7' 10¾"	Igor Paklin	Soviet Union ..	9–4–85	Kobe, Japan
Long Jump......	29' 2½"	Bob Beamon	United States ..	10–18–68	Mexico City, Mexico
Triple Jump	58' 11½"	Willie Banks	United States .	6–16–85	Indianapolis, Ind.
Pole Vault.......	19' 8¼"	Sergei Bubka	Soviet Union ..	7–14–85	Paris, France
THROWING					
Shot	72' 10¾"	Udo Beyer	East Germany .	6–25–83	Los Angeles, Calif.
Discus.........	235' 9"	Yuriy Dumchev	Soviet Union ..	5–29–83	Moscow, Soviet Union
Hammer........	283' 3"	Yuri Sedykh	Soviet Union ..	7–3–84	Cork, Ireland
Javelin.........	343' 10"	Uwe Hohn	East Germany .	7–20–84	Berlin, East Germany
DECATHLON	8,798 pts.	Jurgen Hingsen	West Germany	6–9–84	Mannheim, West Germany

OUTDOOR AMERICAN RECORDS: MEN

EVENT	RECORD	RECORD HOLDER	NATION	DATE	SITE
RUNNING					
1 Mile	3:47.69	Steve Scott	United States .	7–7–82	Oslo, Norway
1 Hour	20,547 meters[2]	Bill Rodgers	United States .	8–9–77	Boston, Massachusetts
100 Meters	9.93	Calvin Smith	United States .	7–3–83	Colorado Springs, Colo.
200 Meters	19.75	Carl Lewis	United States .	6–19–83	Indianapolis, Indiana
400 Meters	43.86	Lee Evans...........	United States .	10–18–68	Mexico City, Mexico
800 Meters	1:42.96	Johnny Gray	United States .	8–29–84	Koblenz, West Germany
1,000 Meters	2:13.9	Rick Wohlhuter	United States .	7–30–74	Oslo, Norway
1,500 Meters	3:31.96	Steve Scott	United States .	8–26–81	Koblenz, West Germany
2,000 Meters	4:54.71	Steve Scott	United States .	8–31–82	Ingelheim, West Germany
3,000 Meters	7:35.84	Doug Padilla	United States .	7–9–83	Oslo, Norway
3,000 Meters[3] ...	8:12.37	Henry Marsh	United States .	8–17–83	Berlin, West Germany
5,000 Meters	13:01.15	Sydney Maree	United States .	7–27–85	Oslo, Norway
10,000 Meters...	27:25.61	Alberto Salazar	United States .	6–26–82	Oslo, Norway
15,000 Meters...	43:39.8	Bill Rodgers	United States .	8–9–77	Boston, Massachusetts
20,000 Meters...	58:15.0	Bill Rodgers	United States .	8–9–77	Boston, Massachusetts
HURDLES					
110 Meters	12.93	Renaldo Nehemiah	United States .	8–19–81	Zurich, Switzerland
400 Meters	47.02	Edwin Moses	United States .	8–31–83	Koblenz, West Germany
WALKING					
20 Kilometers ...	1:25:29.3	Marco Evoniuk	United States .	5–15–82	Softeland, Norway
30 Kilometers ...	2:23:14	Goetz Klopfer	United States .	11–15–70	Seattle, Washington
50 Kilometers ...	4:12:45.0	Dan O'Connor	United States .	11–19–83	Irvine, California
RELAYS					
400 Meters	0:37.83	U.S. Olympic team ...	United States .	8–11–84	Los Angeles, California
800 Meters	1:20.26	So. California team....	United States .	5–27–78	Tempe, Arizona
1,600 Meters	2:56.16	U.S. Olympic team	United States .	10–20–68	Mexico City, Mexico
3,200 Meters	7:08.96	Arizona State team ...	United States .	4–7–84	Tempe, Arizona
6,000 Meters ...	14:46.3	U.S. team	United States .	6–24–79	Bourges, France
JUMPING					
High Jump	7' 8½"	Jim Howard	United States .	5–25–85	Houston, Texas
Long Jump......	29' 2½"	Bob Beamon	United States .	10–18–68	Mexico City, Mexico
Triple Jump	58' 11½"	Willie Banks	United States .	6–16–85	Indianapolis, Ind.
Pole Vault.......	19' 2¼"	Joe Dial	United States .	5–19–85	Norman, Oklahoma
THROWING					
Shot	72' 9¾"	Brian Oldfield	United States .	5–26–84	San Jose, California
Discus.........	237' 4"	Ben Plucknett	United States .	7–7–81	Stockholm, Sweden
Hammer........	253' 5"	Jud Logan	United States .	5–5–85	Columbus, Ohio
Javelin.........	327' 2"	Tom Petranoff	United States .	5–15–83	Los Angeles, California
DECATHLON ...	8,617 pts.	Bruce Jenner	United States .	7–29/30–76	Montreal, Canada

[1] 17 miles, 881 yards. [2] 12 miles, 1,351 yards. [3] Steeplechase.

WORLD OUTDOOR TRACK AND FIELD RECORDS: WOMEN

EVENT	RECORD	RECORD HOLDER	NATION	DATE	SITE
RUNNING					
60 Meters.......	0:07.02	Betty Cuthbert	Australia	2-27-60	Sydney, Australia
100 Meters	0:10.76	Evelyn Ashford	United States	8-22-84	Zurich, Switzerland
200 Meters	0:21.71	Marita Koch..........	East Germany .	6-10-79	Berlin, East Germany
400 Meters	0:47.0	Marita Koch..........	East Germany .	10-6-85	Canberra, Australia
800 Meters	1:53.28	Jarmila Kratochvilova .	Czechoslovakia	7-26-83	Munich, West Germany
1,000 Meters		Tatyana Providokhina .	Soviet Union ..	8-20-78	Podolsk, Soviet Union
1,500 Meters	3:52.47	Tatyana Kazankina....	Soviet Union ..	8-13-80	Zurich, Switzerland
2,000 Meters	5:28.72	Tatyana Kazankina....	Soviet Union ..	8-4-84	Moscow, Soviet Union
1 Mile	4:16.71	Mary Decker Slaney ...	United States .	8-21-85	Zurich, Switzerland
3,000 Meters	8:22.72	Tatyana Kazankina....	Soviet Union ..	8-26-84	Leningrad, Soviet Union
5,000 Meters	14:48.07	Zola Budd	Britain	8-26-85	London, England
10,000 Meters ...	30:59.42	Ingrid Kristiansen	Norway.......	7-27-85	Oslo, Norway
Marathon	2:21:06	Ingrid Kristiansen	Norway.......	4-21-85	London, England
HURDLES					
100 Meters	0:12.36	Grazyna Rabsztyn ...	Poland	6-13-80	Warsaw, Poland
200 Meters	0:25.70	Pamela Ryan	Australia	11-25-71	Melbourne, Australia
400 Meters	0:53.58	Margarita Ponomaryeva	Soviet Union ..	6-22-84	Kiev, Soviet Union
JUMPING					
High Jump	6' 9½"	Lyudmila Andonova ...	Bulgaria	7-20-84	Berlin, East Germany
Long Jump......	24' 4½"	Anisoara Cusmir	Romania	6-4-83	Bucharest, Romania
THROWING					
Shot	73' 11"	Natalya Lisovskaya....	Soviet Union ..	5-27-84	Sochi, Soviet Union
Discus..........	244' 7"	Zdenka Silhava	Czechoslovakia	8-26-84	Nitra, Czechoslovakia
Javelin	246' 11"	Petra Felke	East Germany .	6-4-85	Schwerin, East Germany
PENTATHLON ..	5,083 pts.	Nadyezhda Tkachenko	Soviet Union ..	7-24-80	Moscow, Soviet Union
HEPTATHLON ..	6,867 pts.	Sabine Paetz	East Germany .	5-6-84	Potsdam, East Germany
RUNNING RELAYS					
400 Meters	0:41.37	East German team	East Germany .	10-6-85	Canberra, Australia
800 Meters	1:28.15	East German team	East Germany .	8-9-80	Jena, East Germany
1,600 Meters....	3:15.92	East German Team ...	East Germany .	6-3-84	Erfurt, East Germany
3,200 Meters....	7:50.17	Soviet team	Soviet Union ..	8-5-84	Moscow, Soviet Union
RACE WALKING					
5,000 Meters....	21:36.20	Olga Krishtop	Soviet Union ..	8-4-84	Penza, Soviet Union
10,000 Meters ...	45:39.5	Yan Hong	China	5-13-84	Copenhagen, Denmark

OUTDOOR AMERICAN RECORDS: WOMEN

EVENT	RECORD	RECORD HOLDER	NATION	DATE	SITE
RUNNING					
60 Meters.......	0:07.30	Barbara Ferrell	United States	8-25-68	Walnut, California
100 Meters	0:10.76	Evelyn Ashford	United States	8-22-84	Zurich, Switzerland
200 Meters	0:21.81	Valerie Brisco-Hooks ..	United States	8-9-84	Los Angeles, California
400 Meters	0:48.43	Valerie Brisco-Hooks ..	United States	8-6-84	Los Angeles, California
800 Meters	1:56.90	Mary Decker Slaney ...	United States	8-16-85	Zurich, Switzerland
1,500 Meters	3:57.12	Mary Decker	United States	7-26-83	Stockholm, Sweden
1 Mile	4:16.71	Mary Decker Slaney ...	United States	8-21-85	Zurich, Switzerland
3 Miles	15:04.10	Kathy Mills...........	United States	5-26-78	Knoxville, Tennessee
2,000 Meters	5:38.9	Mary Decker	United States	7-7-82	Oslo, Norway
3,000 Meters	8:29.71	Mary Decker	United States	7-7-82	Oslo, Norway
5,000 Meters	15:06.53	Mary Decker Slaney ...	United States	6-1-85	Eugene, Oregon
10,000 Meters ...	31:35.30	Mary Decker	United States	7-17-82	Eugene, Oregon
Marathon	2:22:43	Joan Benoit	United States	4-18-83	Boston, Massachusetts
HURDLES					
100 Meters	0:12.79	Stephanie Hightower ..	United States	7-10-82	Karl Marx Stadt, E. Germany
200 Meters	0:26.10	Pat Hawkins	United States	7-10-71	Bakersfield, California
400 Meters	0:54.66	Latanya Sheffield	United States	5-31-85	Austin, Texas
RELAYS					
400 Meters	0:41.61	United States team ...	United States	7-3-83	Colorado Springs, Colorado
800 Meters	1:32.60	United States team ...	United States	6-24-79	Bourges, France
1,600 Meters....	3:18.29	United States team ...	United States	8-11-84	Los Angeles, California
3,200 Meters....	8:17.09	Athletics West team ...	United States	4-24-83	Walnut, California

OUTDOOR AMERICAN RECORDS: WOMEN (continued)

EVENT	RECORD	RECORD HOLDER	NATION	DATE	SITE
RACE WALKING					
1,500 Meters	6:46.6	Lisa Metheny	United States	6-28-75	White Plains, New York
1 Mile	7:20.1	Sue Brodock	United States	2-2-74	Los Angeles, California
5,000 Meters	23:19.1	Sue Brodock	United States	6-13-80	Walnut, California
10,000 Meters . . .	50:32.8	Sue Brodock	United States	6-17-79	Walnut, California
JUMPING					
High Jump	6' 7"	Louise Ritter	United States	9-1-83	Rome, Italy
Long Jump	22' 11¾"	Jodi Anderson	United States	6-28-80	Eugene, Oregon
THROWING					
Shot	62' 9¼"	Ramona Pagel	United States	5-26-85	Los Angeles, California
Discus	213' 11"	Leslie Deniz	United States	4-7-84	Tempe, Arizona
Javelin	227' 5"	Kate Schmidt	United States	9-10-77	Pacific Palisades, California
HEPTATHLON . .	6,714 pts.	Jane Frederick	United States	9-16-84	Talence, France

NCAA MEN'S OUTDOOR TRACK TEAM CHAMPIONSHIPS 1921–1985

1921 Illinois	1935 Southern Calif.	1949 Southern Calif.	1963 Southern Calif.	1976 Southern Calif.
1922 California	1936 Southern Calif.	1950 Southern Calif.	1964 Oregon	1977 Arizona State
1923 Michigan	1937 Southern Calif.	1951 Southern Calif.	1965 Oregon, So. Calif.	1978 Southern Calif.
1924 No meet	1938 Southern Calif.	1952 Southern Calif.	1966 UCLA	1979 Texas-El Paso
1925 Stanford [1]	1939 Southern Calif.	1953 Southern Calif.	1967 Southern Calif.	1980 Texas-El Paso
1926 Southern Calif. [1]	1940 Southern Calif.	1954 Southern Calif.	1968 Southern Calif.	1981 Texas-El Paso
1927 Illinois [1]	1941 Southern Calif.	1955 Southern Calif.	1969 San Jose State	1982 Texas-El Paso
1928 Stanford	1942 Southern Calif.	1956 UCLA	1970 Brigham Young,	1983 SMU
1929 Ohio State	1943 Southern Calif.	1957 Villanova	Kansas, Oregon,	1984 Oregon
1930 Southern Calif.	1944 Illinois	1958 Southern Calif.	1971 UCLA	1985 Arkansas
1931 Southern Calif.	1945 Navy	1959 Kansas	1972 UCLA	
1932 Indiana	1946 Illinois	1960 Kansas	1973 UCLA	
1933 Louisiana State	1947 Illinois	1961 Southern Calif.	1974 Tennessee	
1934 Stanford	1948 Minnesota	1962 Oregon	1975 Texas-El Paso	

[1] Unofficial.

NCAA WOMEN'S FIRST OUTDOOR TRACK TEAM CHAMPIONSHIP: 1985

CHAMPION	POINTS	RUNNER-UP	POINTS
Oregon	52	Florida State, Louisiana State	46

VOLLEYBALL

NCAA VOLLEYBALL MEN'S TEAM CHAMPIONSHIPS

Year	Champion	Score	Runner-Up	Host or Site	Year	Champion	Score	Runner-Up	Host or Site
1970	UCLA	3-0	Long Beach St.	UCLA	1978	Pepperdine	3-2	UCLA	Ohio State
1971	UCLA	3-0	Cal-Santa Barb.	UCLA	1979	UCLA	3-1	Southern Cal	UCLA
1972	UCLA	3-2	San Diego St.	Ball State	1980	Southern Cal	3-1	UCLA	Ball State
1973	San Diego St.	3-1	Long Beach St.	San Diego St.	1981	UCLA	3-2	Southern Cal	Cal-Santa Barb.
1974	UCLA	3-2	Cal-Santa Barb.	Cal-Santa Barb.	1982	UCLA	3-0	Penn State	Penn State
1975	UCLA	3-1	Cal-Santa Barb.	UCLA	1983	UCLA	3-0	Pepperdine	Ohio State
1976	UCLA	3-0	Pepperdine	Ball State	1984	UCLA	3-1	Pepperdine	UCLA
1977	Southern Cal	3-1	Ohio State	UCLA	1985	Pepperdine	3-1	Southern Cal	Los Angeles

NCAA VOLLEYBALL WOMEN'S TEAM CHAMPIONSHIPS

Year	Champion	Score	Runner-Up	Host or Site	Year	Champion	Score	Runner-Up	Host or Site
1981	Southern Cal	3-2	UCLA	UCLA	1983	Hawaii	3-0	UCLA	Kentucky
1982	Hawaii	3-2	Southern Cal	Pacific	1984	UCLA	3-2	Stanford	UCLA

WATER POLO

NCAA WATER POLO MEN'S TEAM CHAMPIONSHIPS

Year	Champion	Score	Runner-Up	Host or Site	Year	Champion	Score	Runner-Up	Host or Site
1969	UCLA	5-2	California	Long Beach St.	1977	California	8-6	California-Irvine	Brown
1970	California-Irvine	7-6*	UCLA	Long Beach St.	1978	Stanford	7-6	California	Long Beach St.
1971	UCLA	5-3	San Jose St.	Long Beach St.	1979	Cal-Santa Barb.	11-3	UCLA	Long Beach St.
1972	UCLA	10-5	California-Irvine	New Mexico	1980	Stanford	8-6	California	Long Beach St.
1973	California	8-4	California-Irvine	Long Beach St.	1981	Stanford	17-6	Long Beach St.	Long Beach St.
1974	California	7-6	California-Irvine	Long Beach St.	1982	California-Irvine	7-4	Stanford	Long Beach St.
1975	California	9-8	California-Irvine	Long Beach St.	1983	California	10-7	Southern Cal	Long Beach St.
1976	Stanford	13-12	UCLA	Long Beach St.	1984	California	9-8	Stanford	Long Beach St.

* three overtimes.

WEIGHTLIFTING

U.S. WEIGHTLIFTING FEDERATION NATIONAL CHAMPIONSHIPS

52 KILOGRAMS (114½ POUNDS)
1983 Dirk Yasko, 172.5 kg.	1984 Brian Okada, 205 kg.	1985 Stephen Bartlett, 170 kg.

56 KILOGRAMS (123 POUNDS)
1983 Ron Crawley, 200.0 kg.	1984 Albert Hood, 232.5 kg.	1984 Brad Wickersham, 197.5 kg.

60 KILOGRAMS (132 POUNDS)
1983 Brian Miyamoto, 235.0 kg.	1984 Phil Sanderson, 235 kg.	1985 Brian Miyamoto, 230 kg.

67.5 KILOGRAMS (148 POUNDS)
1983 Michael Jacques, 287.5 kg.	1984 Don Abrahamson, 275 kg	1985 Michael Jacques, 290 kg.

75 KILOGRAMS (165 POUNDS)
1983 Cal Schake, 320.0 kg.	1984 Chuck Jambliter, 300 kg.	1985 John Orlando, 280 kg.

82.5 KILOGRAMS (181 POUNDS)
1983 Curt White, 355.0 kg.	1984 Mark Levell, 310 kg.	1985 Arn Kritsky, 325 kg.

90 KILOGRAMS (198 POUNDS)
1983 Michael Cohen, 352.5 kg.	1984 Kevin Winter, 347.5 kg.	1985 Curt White, 350 kg.

100 KILOGRAMS (220 POUNDS)
1983 Ken Clark, 370.0 kg.	1984 Ken Clark, 360 kg.	1985 Ken Clark, 355 kg.

110 KILOGRAMS (242 POUNDS)
1983 Jeff Michaels, 407.5 kg.	1984 Guy Carlton, 362.5 kg.	1985 Jeff Michels, 377.5 kg.

SUPERHEAVYWEIGHT (+ 242 POUNDS)
1983 Mario Martinez, 377.5 kg.	1984 Mario Martinez, 400 kg.	1985 Mario Martinez, 395 kg.

U.S. WEIGHTLIFTING FEDERATION WOMEN'S NATIONAL CHAMPIONSHIPS

44 KILOGRAMS (97 POUNDS)
1984 DeAnna Hammock, 85 kg.
1985 DeAnna Hammock, 90 kg.

48 KILOGRAMS (105½ POUNDS)
1984 Mary Carr, 117.5 kg.
1985 Rachel Silverman, 120 kg.

52 KILOGRAMS (114½ POUNDS)
1984 Rachel Silverman, 125 kg.
1985 Michele Evris, 145 kg.

56 KILOGRAMS (123¼ POUNDS)
1984 Colleene Colley, 157.5 kg.
1985 Colleene Colley, 135 kg.

60 KILOGRAMS (132¼ POUNDS)
1984 Jane Camp, 155 kg.
1985 Giselle Shepatin, 140 kg.

67.5 KILOGRAMS (148¾ POUNDS)
1984 Judy Glenney, 167.5 kg.
1985 Glenda Gord, 162.5 kg.

75 KILOGRAMS (165¼ POUNDS)
1984 Jody Anderson, 170 kg.
1985 Ann McKinnon, 135 kg.

82.5 KILOGRAMS (181¾ POUNDS)
1984 Benita Carswell, 160 kg.
1985 Carol Cady, 192.5 kg.

+82.5 KILOGRAMS (+181¾ POUNDS)
1984 Karyn Tarter, 202.5 kg.
1985 Karyn Tarter 220 kg.

WRESTLING

NATIONAL COLLEGIATE ATHLETIC ASSOCIATION WRESTLING CHAMPIONSHIPS

NCAA TEAM CHAMPIONSHIPS

1928–31	Oklahoma St.	1942	Oklahoma St.	1953	Penn State	1964	Oklahoma St.	1975	Iowa
1932	Indiana	1943	Oklahoma St.	1954	Oklahoma St.	1965	Iowa State	1976	Iowa
1933(tie)	Iowa State;	1944	Oklahoma St.	1955	Oklahoma St.	1966	Oklahoma St.	1977	Iowa State
	Oklahoma St.	1945	Oklahoma St.	1956	Oklahoma St.	1967	Michigan St.	1978	Iowa
1934–35	Oklahoma St.	1946	Oklahoma St.	1957	Oklahoma	1968	Oklahoma St.	1979	Iowa
1936	Oklahoma	1947	Cornell Col.	1958	Oklahoma St.	1969	Oklahoma St.	1980	Iowa
1937	Oklahoma St.	1948	Oklahoma St.	1959	Oklahoma St.	1970	Iowa State	1981	Iowa
1938	Oklahoma St.	1949	Oklahoma St.	1960	Oklahoma	1971	Oklahoma St.	1982	Iowa
1939	Oklahoma St.	1950	No. Iowa	1961	Oklahoma St.	1972	Iowa State	1983	Iowa
1940	Oklahoma St.	1951	Oklahoma	1962	Oklahoma St.	1973	Iowa State	1984	Iowa
1941	Oklahoma St.	1952	Oklahoma	1963	Oklahoma	1974	Oklahoma	1985	Iowa

NCAA INDIVIDUAL WRESTLING CHAMPIONS: 1985

118 Pounds	Ricky Bonomo, Bloomsburg	158 Pounds	Marty Kistler, Iowa
126 Pounds	Barry Davis, Iowa	167 Pounds	Chris Edmond, Tennessee
134 Pounds	Jim Jordan, Wisconsin	177 Pounds	Melvin Douglas, Oklahoma
142 Pounds	Joe Gibbons, Iowa State	190 Pounds	Dan Chaid, Oklahoma
150 Pounds	Eddie Urbano, Arizona State	Heavyweight	Bill Hyman, Temple

YACHTING

THE AMERICA'S CUP RACES

The 25th challenge for the America's Cup in 1983 was won by *Australia II,* the first foreign yacht to capture the cup since the series began in 1851. The Australian entry, skippered by John Bertrand, defeated the U.S. entry *Liberty,* 4 races to 3, off Newport, R.I.

The next America's Cup series will start on Jan. 31, 1987, off Fremantle in western Australia.

A feature of the London Exhibition of 1851 was a 58-mile yacht race around the Isle of Wight. Among the entries was a 100-foot schooner from the United States, named the *America* and sponsored by members of the New York Yacht Club. The *America* took the race, defeating 14 English cutters and schooners, and winning a trophy called the Hundred-Guineas Cup.

The *America* was sold and left in England, but the cup was brought back to the U.S. and presented to the New York Yacht Club. Used as a trophy for international yacht racing, it became known as the America's Cup.

The first international challenge race took place in 1870 and set a pattern that is still followed. In the first contest the America's Cup was successfully defended, as were successive challenges over the years.

Specifications for yachts in America's Cup races have undergone several changes since the first race in 1851. The race in 1881 was restricted to sloop-rigged craft. Since 1956 only 12-meter (39.4-foot) sloops have been eligible to compete.

YEAR	WINNING YACHT	SPONSOR	RESULTS	LOSING YACHT	SPONSOR
1851	America, U.S.....	John C. Stevens	1 race to 0	Aurora...........	T. Le Marchant, England
1870	Magic, U.S......	Franklin Osgood	1 race to 0	Cambria[1]........	James Ashbury, England
1871	Columbia[2], U.S...	Franklin Osgood	2 races to 0	Livonia...........	James Ashbury, England
	Sappho[2], U.S...	William P. Douglass	2 races to 0		
1876	Madeleine, U.S. ..	John S. Dickerson	2 races to 0	Countess of Dufferin........	Charles Gifford Canada
1881	Mischief, U.S.....	J.R. Busk	2 races to 0	Atlanta	Alexander Cuthbert, Canada
1885	Puritan, U.S......	J.M. Forbes, Charles Paine	2 races to 0	Genesta...........	Sir Richard Sutton, England
1886	Mayflower, U.S....	Charles Paine	2 races to 0	Galatea...........	William Henn, England
1887	Volunteer, U.S....	Charles Paine	2 races to 0	Thistle	James Bell, England
1893	Vigilant, U.S.	Oliver Iselin	3 races to 0	Valkyrie II	Lord Dunraven, England
1895	Defender, U.S. ...	Oliver Iselin, E.D. Morgan, W.K. Vanderbilt	3 races to 0	Valkyrie III........	Lord Dunraven, Lord Lonsdale, Lord Wolverton, England
1899	Columbia, U.S....	Oliver Iselin, J.P. Morgan	3 races to 0	Shamrock I.......	Sir Thomas Lipton, Ireland
1901	Columbia, U.S....	E.D. Morgan	3 races to 0	Shamrock II	Sir Thomas Lipton, Ireland
1903	Reliance, U.S.	Cornelius Vanderbilt	3 races to 0	Shamrock III......	Sir Thomas Lipton, Ireland
1920	Resolute, U.S. ...	Harry Walters	3 races to 2	Shamrock IV......	Sir Thomas Lipton, Ireland
1930	Enterprise, U.S. ..	Harold S. Vanderbilt	4 races to 0	Shamrock V	Sir Thomas Lipton, Ireland
1934	Rainbow, U.S.....	Harold S. Vanderbilt	4 races to 2	Endeavour	T.O.M. Sopwith, England
1937	Ranger, U.S......	Harold S. Vanderbilt	4 races to 0	Endeavour II......	T.O.M. Sopwith, England
1958	Columbia, U.S....	Henry Sears	4 races to 0	Sceptre..........	Hugh Goodson, England
1962	Weatherly, U.S. ..	Henry Mercer	4 races to 1	Gretel	Sir Frank Packer, Australia
1964	Constellation, U.S.	Walter Gubelmann	4 races to 0	Sovereign	Anthony Boyden, England
1967	Intrepid, U.S.	N.Y. Yacht Club's Intrepid Syndicate	4 races to 0	Dame Pattie	Royal Sydney Yacht Squadron's Syndicate, Australia
1970	Intrepid, U.S.	N.Y. Yacht Club's Intrepid Syndicate	4 races to 1	Gretel II	Sir Frank Packer, Australia
1974	Courageous, U.S..	N.Y. Yacht Club's Courageous Syndicate	4 races to 0	Southern Cross ...	Royal Perth Y.C. Challenger Syndicate, Australia
1977	Courageous, U.S..	Kings Point Maritime Acad. Synd.	4 races to 0	Australia	Sun City Yacht Club, Australia
1980	Freedom, U.S. ...	Maritime College at Fort Schuyler Found.	4 races to 1	Australia	Sun City Yacht Club, Australia
1983	Australia II, Australia	Royal Perth Yacht Club, Australia	4 races to 3	Liberty, U.S.	Maritime College at Ft. Schuyler Found.

[1] *Cambria,* the only English schooner in the race, finished tenth in a field of 24.
[2] After winning the first two races, the *Columbia* was disabled. *Sappho* substituted and won the fourth and fifth races.

UNITED STATES YACHT RACING UNION CHAMPIONSHIPS

MALLORY CUP—MEN		ADAMS CUP—WOMEN	
1976	David J. Crockett, Los Alamitos, California	1976	Ellen Gerloff, Galveston, Texas
1977	Marvin Beckman, Houston, Texas	1977	Cindy Stieffel, Bay Waveland, Missouri
1978	Glenn Darden, Fort Worth, Texas	1978	Bonnie Shore, Newport, Rhode Island
1979	Glenn Darden, Fort Worth, Texas	1979	Allison Jolly, St. Petersburg, Florida
1980	Dave Ullman, Corona del Mar, California	1980	Judy McKinney, Bay St. Louis, Mississippi
1981	Mark Foster, Corpus Christi, Texas	1981	Ann Boyd Sloger, Charleston, South Carolina
1982	Mark Gollison, Long Beach, California	1982	Heidi Backus, Corpus Christi, Texas
1983	Peter Coleman, Larchmont, N.Y.	1983	Martha S. Altreuter, Marblehead, Mass.
1984	Marc Eagan, Bay St. Louis, Miss.	1984	Betsy Gelenitis, Metedeconk, N.J.
1985	Scott Young, Austin, Texas	1985	Cory Fischer, Annapolis, MD

States of the United States

A stamp for international airmail honoring Junipero Serra (1713-84) was issued in San Diego, Calif., on Aug. 22. Born on the Spanish island of Mallorca, Serra went to Mexico with other Franciscan friars in 1750. He founded the first Roman Catholic mission in what is now San Diego on July 16, 1769.

HIGHLIGHTS: 1985

DRINKING AGE LAWS
At the beginning of 1985 only 23 of the 50 states had laws establishing the minimum drinking age at 21. In the face of a federal law signed by President Reagan in 1984 that will cut federal highway funds for states that do not pass such legislation, 12 more states had adopted the 21-year minimum by mid-1985: Alabama, Connecticut, Georgia, Kansas, Maine, Massachusetts, Mississippi, New Hampshire, New York, North Carolina, Texas, and Wisconsin.

Nine state legislatures voted down legislation to raise the drinking age minimum to 21: Colorado, Hawaii, Idaho, Iowa, Minnesota, South Dakota, Vermont, West Virginia, and Wyoming. Montana set a public referendum on the issue for November 1986.

Idaho, South Dakota, and Wyoming joined in a suit challenging the constitutionality of the federal government's attempt to force them to adopt age-21 drinking laws.

LURING TOURISTS
Many state governments increased the amounts spent in an effort to lure tourists into their states. Illinois was the leader, budgeting $14.4 to promote tourism. Other states with large tourism budgets were New York $12 million, Massachusetts $10.5 million, Alaska $9.2 million, Florida $9.2 million, Michigan $9 million, Pennsylvania $7.8 million, Tennessee $7.2 million, California $5.7 million, New Jersey $5.5 million, Ohio $5.5 million, South Carolina $5.4 million, and Virginia $5.3 million.

MORE BLACK LEGISLATORS
The Joint Center for Political Studies reported that in the 10-year period from 1974 to 1984 the number of blacks elected to state legislatures increased by more than 60%—rising from 236 in 1974 to 382 in 1984. Georgia has the largest number, 26, followed by Alabama and Maryland, each with 24.

FEDERAL EXPENDITURES
According to a study released by State Policy Research Inc. there is great disparity among the states in how much they benefit from federal expenditures.

HIGHLIGHTS: 1985 *(continued)*

The study considered on a state by state basis how much each gained or lost when the state's contribution in federal taxes was subtracted from the amount spent by the federal government in the state.

New Mexico gained the most with an average of $1,983 per capita. Missouri was second with $1,377 per capita. The remainder of the top 10 gainers were Virginia $1,368, Mississippi $1,276, Hawaii $1,221, Maryland $1,023, Utah $802, Alabama $726, Maine $684, and South Dakota $667.

At the other end of the scale, 20 states showed a per capita deficit—paying more in federal taxes than the amount received in

federal expenditures. Illinois had a $1,161 per capita deficit. New Jersey was next with a loss of $1,013 per capita. Others in the bottom 10 showing per capita losses were Texas $703, Wyoming $626, Michigan $619, Delaware $593, Iowa $500, Wisconsin $485, Ohio $484, and Oklahoma $377.

California, which received the largest amount of federal expenditures in 1984 with $91.7 billion, showed a per capita gain of $395. On the other hand, New York, which received the second largest amount of federal expenditures, $53.3 billion, paid to the federal government more than it received—an average loss of $232 per capita.

25 LARGEST STATES IN AREA

RANK	STATE	SQUARE MILES
1	Alaska	591,004
2	Texas	266,807
3	California	158,706
4	Montana	147,046
5	New Mexico	121,593
6	Arizona	114,000
7	Nevada	110,561
8	Colorado	104,091
9	Wyoming	97,809
10	Oregon	97,073
11	Utah	84,899
12	Minnesota	84,402
13	Idaho	83,564
14	Kansas	82,277
15	Nebraska	77,355
16	South Dakota	77,116
17	North Dakota	70,702
18	Oklahoma	69,956
19	Missouri	69,697
20	Washington	68,139
21	Georgia	58,910
22	Florida	58,664
23	Michigan	58,527
24	Illinois	56,345
25	Iowa	56,275

25 SMALLEST STATES IN AREA

RANK	STATE	SQUARE MILES
50	Rhode Island	1,212
49	Delaware	2,044
48	Connecticut	5,018
47	Hawaii	6,471
46	New Jersey	7,787
45	Massachusetts	8,284
44	New Hampshire	9,279
43	Vermont	9,614
42	Maryland	10,460
41	West Virginia	24,231
40	South Carolina	31,113
39	Maine	33,265
38	Indiana	36,185
37	Kentucky	40,409
36	Virginia	40,767
35	Ohio	41,330
34	Tennessee	42,144
33	Pennsylvania	45,308
32	Mississippi	47,689
31	Louisiana	47,752
30	New York	49,108
29	Alabama	51,705
28	North Carolina	52,669
27	Arkansas	53,187
26	Wisconsin	56,153

25 LARGEST STATES IN POPULATION

RANK	STATE	POPULATION[1]
1	California	25,622,000
2	New York	17,735,000
3	Texas	15,989,000
4	Pennsylvania	11,901,000
5	Illinois	11,511,000
6	Florida	10,976,000
7	Ohio	10,752,000
8	Michigan	9,075,000
9	New Jersey	7,515,000
10	North Carolina	6,165,000
11	Georgia	5,837,000
12	Massachusetts	5,798,000
13	Virginia	5,636,000
14	Indiana	5,498,000
15	Missouri	5,008,000
16	Wisconsin	4,766,000
17	Tennessee	4,717,000
18	Louisiana	4,462,000
19	Maryland	4,349,000
19	Washington	4,349,000
21	Minnesota	4,162,000
22	Alabama	3,990,000
23	Kentucky	3,723,000
24	South Carolina	3,300,000
25	Oklahoma	3,298,000

25 SMALLEST STATES IN POPULATION

RANK	STATE	POPULATION[1]
50	Alaska	500,000
49	Wyoming	511,000
48	Vermont	530,000
47	Delaware	613,000
46	North Dakota	686,000
45	South Dakota	706,000
44	Montana	824,000
43	Nevada	911,000
42	Rhode Island	962,000
41	New Hampshire	977,000
40	Idaho	1,001,000
39	Hawaii	1,039,000
38	Maine	1,156,000
37	New Mexico	1,424,000
36	Nebraska	1,606,000
35	Utah	1,652,000
34	West Virginia	1,952,000
33	Arkansas	2,349,000
32	Kansas	2,438,000
31	Mississippi	2,598,000
30	Oregon	2,674,000
29	Iowa	2,910,000
28	Arizona	3,053,000
27	Connecticut	3,154,000
26	Colorado	3,178,000

[1] July 1, 1984 Census Bureau estimates.

U.S. STATES AND TERRITORIES—Important Facts: 1986

	AREA Sq. Mi.	POPULATION[1] Total	Density	GOVERNOR Name	Party	Term Years	Term Expires	LEGISLATURE Senate Majority Party	House Majority Party
Alabama	51,705	3,990,000	77.2	George C. Wallace	D	4	Jan. '87	Democratic	Democratic
Alaska	591,004	500,000	0.8	William Sheffield	D	4	Dec. '86	Republican	Democratic
Arizona	114,000	3,053,000	26.8	Bruce Babbitt	D	4	Jan. '87	Democratic	Republican
Arkansas	53,187	2,349,000	43.8	Bill Clinton	D	2	Jan. '87	Democratic	Democratic
California	158,706	25,622,000	161.4	George Deukmejian	R	4	Jan. '87	Democratic	Democratic
Colorado	104,091	3,178,000	30.5	Richard D. Lamm	D	4	Jan. '87	Republican	Republican
Connecticut	5,018	3,154,000	628.5	William A. O'Neill	D	4	Jan. '87	Republican	Republican
Delaware	2,044	613,000	299.9	Michael N. Castle	R	4	Jan. '89	Democratic	Republican
Florida	58,664	10,976,000	187.1	Robert Graham	D	4	Jan. '87	Democratic	Democratic
Georgia	58,910	5,837,000	99.1	Joe Frank Harris	D	4	Jan. '87	Democratic	Democratic
Hawaii	6,471	1,039,000	160.6	George R. Ariyoshi	D	4	Dec. '86	Democratic	Democratic
Idaho	83,564	1,001,000	12.0	John V. Evans	D	4	Jan. '87	Republican	Republican
Illinois	56,345	11,511,000	204.3	James R. Thompson	R	4	Jan. '87	Democratic	Democratic
Indiana	36,185	5,498,000	151.9	Robert D. Orr	R	4	Jan. '89	Republican	Republican
Iowa	56,275	2,910,000	51.7	Terry Branstad	R	4	Jan. '87	Democratic	Democratic
Kansas	82,277	2,438,000	29.6	John W. Carlin	D	4	Jan. '87	Republican	Republican
Kentucky	40,409	3,723,000	92.1	Martha L. Collins	D	4	Dec. '87	Democratic	Democratic
Louisiana	47,752	4,462,000	93.4	Edwin W. Edwards	D	4	Mar. '88	Democratic	Democratic
Maine	33,265	1,156,000	34.8	Joseph E. Brennan	D	4	Jan. '87	Democratic	Democratic
Maryland	10,460	4,349,000	415.8	Harold R. Hughes	D	4	Jan. '87	Democratic	Democratic
Massachusetts	8,284	5,798,000	699.9	Michael S. Dukakis	D	4	Jan. '87	Democratic	Democratic
Michigan	58,527	9,075,000	155.1	James J. Blanchard	D	4	Jan. '87	Republican	Democratic
Minnesota	84,402	4,162,000	49.3	Rudy Perpich	D	4	Jan. '87	Democratic	Republican
Mississippi	47,689	2,598,000	54.5	Bill Allain	D	4	Jan. '88	Democratic	Democratic
Missouri	69,697	5,008,000	71.8	John Ashcroft	R	4	Jan. '89	Democratic	Democratic
Montana	147,046	824,000	5.6	Ted Schwinden	D	4	Jan. '89	Democratic	Tie
Nebraska	77,355	1,606,000	20.8	Bob Kerrey	D	4	Jan. '87	Nonpartisan	—
Nevada	110,561	911,000	8.2	Richard H. Bryan	D	4	Jan. '87	Democratic	Republican
New Hampshire	9,279	977,000	105.3	John H. Sununu	R	2	Jan. '87	Republican	Democratic
New Jersey	7,787	7,515,000	965.1	Thomas H. Kean	R	4	Jan. '86	Democratic	Democratic
New Mexico	121,593	1,424,000	11.7	Toney Anaya	D	4	Jan. '87	Democratic	Democratic
New York	49,108	17,735,000	361.1	Mario M. Cuomo	D	4	Jan. '87	Republican	Democratic
North Carolina	52,669	6,165,000	117.1	James G. Martin	R	4	Jan. '89	Democratic	Democratic
North Dakota	70,702	686,000	9.7	George Sinner	D	4	Jan. '89	Republican	Republican
Ohio	41,330	10,752,000	260.2	Richard F. Celeste	D	4	Jan. '87	Republican	Democratic
Oklahoma	69,956	3,298,000	47.1	George Nigh	D	4	Jan. '87	Democratic	Democratic
Oregon	97,073	2,674,000	27.5	Victor Atiyeh	R	4	Jan. '87	Democratic	Democratic
Pennsylvania	45,308	11,901,000	262.7	Richard L. Thornburgh	R	4	Jan. '87	Republican	Democratic
Rhode Island	1,212	962,000	793.7	Edward Diprete	R	2	Jan. '87	Democratic	Democratic
South Carolina	31,113	3,300,000	106.1	Richard W. Riley	D	4	Jan. '87	Democratic	Democratic
South Dakota	77,116	706,000	9.2	William J. Janklow	R	4	Jan. '87	Republican	Republican
Tennessee	42,144	4,717,000	111.9	Lamar Alexander	R	4	Jan. '87	Democratic	Democratic
Texas	266,807	15,989,000	59.9	Mark White	D	4	Jan. '87	Democratic	Democratic
Utah	84,899	1,652,000	19.5	Norman H. Bangerter	R	4	Jan. '89	Republican	Republican
Vermont	9,614	530,000	55.1	Madeline M. Kunin	D	2	Jan. '87	Democratic	Democratic
Virginia	40,767	5,636,000	138.2	Charles S. Robb	D	4	Jan. '86	Democratic	Democratic
Washington	68,139	4,349,000	63.8	Booth Gardner	D	4	Jan. '89	Democratic	Democratic
West Virginia	24,231	1,952,000	80.6	Arch A. Moore Jr.	R	4	Jan. '89	Democratic	Democratic
Wisconsin	56,153	4,766,000	84.9	Anthony S. Earl	D	4	Jan. '87	Democratic	Democratic
Wyoming	97,809	511,000	5.2	Ed Herschler	D	4	Jan. '87	Republican	Republican
Dist. of Columbia	69	623,000	9,029.0	Marion Barry [2]	D	4	Jan. '87	Democratic	—
Am. Samoa	77	34,500	448.1	A.P. Lutali	—	4	Jan. '89	Nonpartisan	Nonpartisan
Guam	209	116,400	556.9	Ricardo Bordallo	D	4	Jan. '87	Democratic	—
No. Marianas	184	18,200	98.9	Pedro P. Tenorio	—	4	Jan. '86	—	—
Puerto Rico	3,515	3,267,000	929.4	R. Hernandez-Colon	—	4	Jan. '89	Pop. Dem.[4]	Pop. Dem.[4]
Virgin Islands	132	103,800	786.4	Juan Luis	I	4	Jan. '87	—	Democratic

[1] July 1, 1984, Bureau of Census estimates. [2] Mayor. [3] New Progressive Party. [4] Popular Democratic Party.

FEDERAL EXPENDITURES[1] BY STATE AND TERRITORY

Source: U.S. Department of Commerce, Bureau of the Census

State and territory	Total Federal expenditures				Federal Grants to State and local governments			
	1984	1983	1982	1981	1984	1983	1982	1981
United States, Total	$724,749	$694,568	$603,683	$562,219	$97,209	$92,693	$88,221	$94,806
Alabama......................	11,444	10,814	9,668	9,112	1,532	1,470	1,429	1,493
Alaska.......................	2,322	2,060	1,868	2,009	616	541	422	448
Arizona......................	9,174	8,171	7,465	6,767	990	845	799	864
Arkansas	6,088	6,095	5,100	4,737	946	901	844	887
California....................	91,713	86,365	74,964	67,040	9,799	9,207	9,016	10,008
Colorado	9,165	8,903	7,613	7,156	1,176	1,058	967	1,022
Connecticut..................	12,791	12,104	11,967	10,094	1,221	1,189	1,120	1,180
Delaware	1,635	1,569	1,491	1,450	299	307	279	314
District of Columbia..........	12,866	12,115	10,807	12,179	1,382	1,355	1,295	1,417
Florida	33,224	32,577	28,420	25,498	2,784	2,817	2,859	2,868
Georgia......................	15,915	14,801	12,766	11,759	2,214	2,109	2,185	2,169
Hawaii.......................	4,232	4,055	3,433	3,743	459	457	408	443
Idaho........................	2,497	2,399	2,098	1,905	413	380	350	361
Illinois......................	25,506	25,982	22,305	21,391	4,304	4,189	4,103	4,610
Indiana......................	13,037	12,085	10,613	9,792	1,760	1,611	1,558	1,729
Iowa	6,332	6,549	5,196	4,746	1,091	981	893	961
Kansas	8,158	7,127	6,334	5,360	805	763	706	774
Kentucky	9,369	8,853	7,747	7,161	1,590	1,488	1,424	1,433
Louisiana	10,693	10,329	9,575	10,106	1,776	1,710	1,591	1,730
Maine	3,341	3,075	3,100	2,644	590	575	527	536
Maryland	18,783	18,036	15,065	13,951	1,697	1,790	1,793	1,890
Massachusetts	21,422	20,252	17,313	15,919	2,634	2,898	2,745	2,889
Michigan	20,297	19,995	17,966	17,614	3,776	3,612	3,634	4,108
Minnesota	10,591	10,126	8,560	8,040	1,865	1,765	1,769	1,774
Mississippi..................	8,278	7,716	6,562	6,327	1,176	1,100	1,091	1,098
Missouri.....................	20,335	19,054	15,955	14,578	1,775	1,675	1,652	1,663
Montana.....................	2,377	2,206	1,782	1,703	532	477	382	449
Nebraska	4,119	4,109	3,324	3,034	637	575	524	517
Nevada	2,807	2,608	2,215	2,108	340	356	346	351
New Hampshire	2,904	2,680	2,368	2,138	368	352	317	306
New Jersey	20,433	18,563	16,619	15,310	2,871	2,812	2,718	2,891
New Mexico	6,131	5,375	5,142	4,880	863	676	727	716
New York	53,298	50,105	43,685	41,420	10,268	10,031	9,288	10,374
North Carolina...............	13,626	12,874	11,527	10,792	1,929	1,878	1,852	1,909
North Dakota.................	2,276	2,130	1,563	1,439	454	372	301	318
Ohio	25,670	26,237	23,232	21,096	4,044	3,642	3,612	3,725
Oklahoma	8,404	7,782	6,952	6,764	1,167	1,075	991	1,043
Oregon	6,545	6,212	5,510	5,040	1,246	1,161	1,168	1,175
Pennsylvania.................	32,413	33,290	28,431	26,301	4,667	4,817	4,629	4,887
Rhode Island	2,982	2,825	2,538	2,496	548	486	471	482
South Carolina...............	8,947	8,352	7,371	6,782	1,169	1,113	1,043	1,009
South Dakota.................	2,056	1,927	1,601	1,506	436	361	325	356
Tennessee	13,610	12,521	11,359	10,540	1,885	1,687	1,607	1,910
Texas	39,275	36,957	32,064	31,600	4,136	3,805	3,725	4,146
Utah	4,840	4,139	3,710	3,335	708	622	605	593
Vermont.....................	1,394	1,339	1,155	1,069	331	312	271	279
Virginia......................	24,251	25,257	21,865	18,650	1,628	1,665	1,623	1,862
Washington	14,812	15,279	13,010	12,184	1,698	1,537	1,580	1,772
West Virginia.................	4,825	4,731	3,997	3,995	819	840	772	941
Wisconsin....................	10,853	10,552	8,880	8,680	2,064	1,904	1,894	2,299
Wyoming	1,472	1,229	1,048	1,527	556	426	349	321
American Samoa	61	47	14	9	47	37	—	—
Guam	768	407	843	755	89	63	72	—
Northern Marianas............	103	46	1	1	44	43	—	—
Puerto Rico	5,403	4,746	4,617	4,110	2,231	2,111	1,397	1,352
Trust Territory	182	180	181	56	162	170	101	—
Virgin Islands	407	177	280	570	137	91	116	154

[1] In $ millions (add 000,000). Data for fiscal years.

ALABAMA

Area: 51,705 square miles; 133,913 sq. km.
Population: 3,990,000 (1984); 3,893,978 (1980).
Capital: Montgomery.
Flower: Camellia. **Tree:** Southern (longleaf) pine.
Bird: Yellowhammer. **Nickname:** The Heart of Dixie.
Stone: Marble. **Mineral:** Hematite. **Fish:** Tarpon.
Song: *Alabama.* **Motto:** We Dare Defend Our Rights.
Flag: Diagonal red cross on white field.
Leading Industries: Manufacturing (iron, steel, aluminum, chemicals, paper), agriculture (poultry, dairy products, beef cattle, cotton, peanuts, pecans), mining (coal, iron ore, petroleum).
Climate (Montgomery): *Normal temperatures:* Jan. high 58°F., low 37°F.; July high 89°F., low 69°F. *Normal yearly precipitation:* 50" (water). *Record snowstorm:* 11" in December 1886.
Recreation Areas: National forests, 4; state parks and recreation areas, 20; Gulf Coast beaches.
Points of Interest: George C. Marshall Space Flight Center (Huntsville); Horseshoe Bend National Memorial Park; Russell Cave National Monument; White House of Confederacy in Montgomery; battleship USS *Alabama* in Mobile Bay.

KEY EVENTS IN ALABAMA

1519 Mobile Bay believed to have been discovered by Spanish explorer Alonso Álvarez de Piñeda.
1702 French settlement at Fort Louis founded; colony moves in 1711 to present site of Mobile, Ala.
1763 Britain wins region from France.
1783 Spain acquires southern Alabama from Britain, while U.S. receives northern Alabama.
1795 U.S. obtains rest of Alabama except Mobile from Spain in Treaty of San Lorenzo.
1813 (April 15) U.S. captures Mobile from Spain.
1814 (March 27) Battle of Horseshoe Bend: Gen. Andrew Jackson defeats Creek Indians.
1817 (March 3) Territory of Alabama organized.
1819 (Dec. 14) Alabama becomes 22d U.S. state.
1861 First capital of Confederacy at Montgomery.
1861 (Jan. 11) Alabama secedes from Union.
1864 (Aug. 5–23) Battle of Mobile Bay: Union Adm. David Farragut conquers Mobile's forts.
1868 (June 25) Alabama readmitted to Union.
1880 Iron and steel industry begins growth at Birmingham with opening of first blast furnace.
1944 State's first oil well produces at Gilbertown.
1949 Space research center established at Huntsville.
1955 Black civil-rights crusade by Rev. Martin Luther King Jr. begins bus boycott in Montgomery.
1961–76 Confederate flag flown above U.S. flag on state capitol.
1983 George C. Wallace becomes state's first four-term governor; served 1963–67, 1971–79.
1984 State population grows 2.5% since 1980.

ALASKA

Area: 591,004 square miles; 1,530,693 sq. km.
Population: 500,000 (1984); 401,851 (1980).
Capital: Juneau.
Flower: Forget-me-not. **Tree:** Sitka spruce. **Bird:** Willow ptarmigan. **Gem:** Jade. **Fish:** King salmon. **Song:** *Alaska's Flag.* **Nickname:** The Last Frontier. **Motto:** North to the Future.
Flag: Blue field with 7 gold stars on left representing Big Dipper and one on right representing Polaris.
Leading Industries: Government, mining (petroleum, gold, coal), food processing, forestry, agriculture (dairy products, poultry, cattle, hogs, sheep, potatoes, barley, oats, vegetables), tourism.
Climate (Fairbanks): *Normal temperatures:* Jan. high −2.2°F., low −22°F.; July high 72°F., low 50°F. *Normal yearly precipitation:* 11" (water). *Record*

snowstorm: 20.1" in February 1966.
Recreation Areas: National parks, 8; national forests, 2; state parks and recreation areas, 64.
Points of Interest: Mt. McKinley, in Denali National Park; Mendenhall Glacier (in North Tongass National Forest); Glacier Bay and Katmai national parks; Sitka National Historical Park; Klondike Gold Rush National Historical Park; Russian-era relics in Ketchikan and Sitka; Eskimo villages.

KEY EVENTS IN ALASKA

1741 Alaska discovered by Danish sea captain Vitus Bering, exploring for Russia.
1784 (Aug. 14) First Russian settlement established on Kodiak Island by fur trader Grigori Shelekhov.
1867 (Oct. 18) U.S. acquires Alaska from Russia for $7.2 million.
1896–99 Discoveries of gold bring rush of prospectors to Klondike and Alaska.
1912 (Aug. 24) Territory of Alaska organized.
1942 (June 12) Japan invades and occupies Attu Island in Aleutians; later takes Kiska and Agattu.
1943 (May 11–30) U.S. troops recapture Attu; reoccupy Kiska on Aug. 15.
1959 (Jan. 3) Alaska becomes 49th U.S. state.
1964 (March 27) Severe earthquake in south central Alaska kills 131 persons, causes widespread damage.
1968 Discovery of oil at Prudhoe Bay, believed largest oil reserve in world.
1975 (May 27) Alaska becomes first state to legalize use of marijuana in ruling by state court.
1976 Voters approve moving state capital.
1977 Trans-Alaska pipeline completed at cost of $7.7 billion; oil flows south 799 miles from Prudhoe Bay to Valdez at rate of 1.2 million barrels a day.
1978 (Dec. 1) About 56 million acres of land made into 17 national monuments by President Carter.
1980 (April 27) Time zone shift moves Juneau and nearby area to north into Yukon Time Zone.
1980 State income tax abolished; $185 million already collected is refunded to taxpayers; state government grows rich with 12.5% royalty on oil production.
1982 State distributes $1,000 to each resident from oil income.
1982 Voters reject moving state capital to Willow.
1983 (Oct. 30) Time zone shift: Entire state, except for westernmost Aleutian Islands, moved to Yukon Time Zone, 1 hour earlier than Pacific Time Zone.
1984 State population grows 24.4% since 1980, fastest growth rate in U.S.

ARIZONA

Area: 114,000 square miles; 295,259 sq. km.
Population: 3,053,000 (1984); 2,718,425 (1980).
Capital: Phoenix.
Flower: Saguaro cactus blossom. **Tree:** Palo verde. **Bird:** Cactus wren. **Gemstone:** Turquoise. **Song:** *Arizona.*
Nickname: The Grand Canyon State.
Motto: *Ditat Deus* (God Enriches).
Flag: Copper-colored star centered on radiating red and yellow stripes above horizontal blue stripe.
Leading Industries: Manufacturing (machinery, smelting, metal products), mining (copper, molybdenum, gold, silver, zinc), agriculture (beef cattle, cotton, lettuce, dairy products, sheep, vegetables, fruits), tourism.
Climate (Phoenix): *Normal temperatures:* Jan. high 65°F., low 38°F.; July high 102°F., low 78°F. *Normal yearly precipitation:* 7" (water). *Record snowstorm:* 1" in January 1937.
Recreation Areas: National parks, 2; national forests, 7; national recreation area, 1; state parks and recreation areas, 11.
Points of Interest: Grand Canyon and Petrified Forest national parks; Monument Valley; Painted Desert;

ARIZONA *(continued)*

Indian reservations; Tombstone; Fort Apache: numerous national monuments (including Chiricahua, Saguaro, Organ Pipe Cactus, Pipe Spring, Canyon de Chelly, Navajo, Casa Grande Ruins, Hohokam Pima, Montezuma Castle, Tonto, Tumacacori, Tuzigoot, Walnut Canyon, Wupatki, Sunset Crater, and Marble Canyon); Oak Creek Canyon (in Coconino National Forest); Fort Bowie and Hubbell Trading Post national historical parks; Kitt Peak National Observatory.

KEY EVENTS IN ARIZONA

1539–40 Arizona explored for Spain: Marcos de Niza (1539); Francisco de Coronado (1540).
1690s Roman Catholic missions founded in Arizona by Spanish Jesuit priest Eusebio Kino.
1776 Fort Tucson established by Spaniards.
1848 U.S. acquires Arizona in Mexican War.
1853 Southern Arizona obtained from Mexico in Gadsden Purchase.
1863 Navajo Indians subdued by Kit Carson leading 400 troops against stronghold in Canyon de Chelly.
1863 (Feb. 24) Arizona Territory created.
1871–86 Apache War: Chief Geronimo captured.
1912 (Feb. 14) Arizona becomes 48th U.S. state.
1948 Indians win right to vote in Arizona.
1973 Biggest dam in world completed: New Cornelia Tailings Dam, near Ajo, containing 274,026,000 cubic yards of material, 98 feet high, 6.7 miles long.
1983 Arizona moves ahead of Iowa to rank 28th in population among the states.
1983 First new county (La Paz) created since statehood achieved in 1912.
1984 State population grows 12.3% since 1980.

ARKANSAS

Area: 53,187 square miles; 137,753 sq. km.
Population: 2,349,000 (1984); 2,286,419 (1980).
Capital: Little Rock.
Flower: Apple blossom. **Tree:** Pine. **Bird:** Mockingbird. **Stone:** Diamond. **Song:** *Arkansas.*
Nickname: The Land of Opportunity.
Motto: *Regnat Populus* (The People Rule).
Flag: Star-studded white diamond on red field.
Leading Industries: Food processing, manufacturing (machinery, appliances, paper), agriculture (soybeans, cotton, rice, poultry, beef cattle, dairy products), mining (petroleum, bauxite, bromine).
Climate (Little Rock): *Normal temperatures:* Jan. high 50° F., low 29° F.; July high 93° F., low 70° F. *Normal yearly precipitation:* 49″ (water). *Record snowstorm:* 13″ in January 1893.
Recreation Areas: National park, 1; national forests, 3; state parks and recreation areas, 34.
Points of Interest: Hot Springs National Park; Pea Ridge National Military Park; Arkansas Territorial Capitol Restoration (Little Rock); Fort Smith National Historic Site; Arkansas Post National Memorial; Buffalo National River; Crater of Diamonds mine near Murfreesboro; Dogpatch U.S.A., amusement park near Harrison.

KEY EVENTS IN ARKANSAS

1541 Arkansas region explored by Hernando de Soto of Spain, discoverer of Mississippi River.
1686 Arkansas Post established as fort by French explorer Henri de Tonti.
1803 U.S. acquires area in Louisiana Purchase.
1819 (March 2) Territory of Arkansas organized.
1836 (June 15) Arkansas becomes 25th U.S. state.
1861 (May 6) Arkansas secedes from Union.
1862 (March 7–8) Battle of Pea Ridge: Union troops defeat Confederate army.
1868 (June 22) Arkansas readmitted to Union.

1887 Bauxite discovered near Little Rock.
1906 Only diamond deposit in North America found near Murfreesboro.
1921 Oil production begins in El Dorado field.
1957 (Sept. 24–Nov. 27) President Eisenhower sends federal troops into Little Rock to enforce school racial desegregation barred by Gov. Orval Faubus.
1984 Population grows 2.7% since 1980.

CALIFORNIA

Area: 158,706 square miles; 411,047 sq. km.
Population: 25,622,000 (1984); 23,667,837 (1980).
Capital: Sacramento.
Flower: Golden poppy. **Tree:** California redwood. **Bird:** California valley quail. **Stone:** Serpentine. **Mineral:** Native gold. **Animal:** California grizzly bear. **Fish:** California golden trout. **Reptile:** California desert tortoise. **Insect:** California dog-face butterfly. **Marine mammal:** California gray whale. **Fossil:** Saber-toothed cat. **Song:** *I Love You, California.* **Nickname:** The Golden State. **Motto:** *Eureka* (I Have Found It).
Flag: Bear and red star on white field above "California Republic " with red stripe at bottom.
Leading Industries: Manufacturing (aircraft, automobiles, electronic equipment, appliances, weapons, steel, chemicals), food processing, agriculture (beef cattle, dairying, sheep, grain, fruits, vegetables, nuts), mining (petroleum, natural gas, boron, gold), tourism.
Climate (Sacramento): *Normal temperatures:* Jan. high 53° F., low 37° F.; July high 93° F., low 58° F. *Normal yearly precipitation:* 17″ (water). *Record snowstorm:* 7.24″ in April 1880.
Recreation Areas: National parks, 5; national forests, 22; national seashore, 1; national recreation areas, 2; state parks and recreation areas, 186; many beaches.
Points of Interest: Yosemite, Kings Canyon, Sequoia, Lassen Volcanic, and Redwood national parks; Cabrillo, Channel Islands, Death Valley, Devils Postpile, Joshua Tree, Pinnacles, Lava Beds, and Muir Woods national monuments; Mt. Wilson Observatory, Disneyland, and Hollywood in Los Angeles area; Civic Center and Golden Gate Bridge and Park in San Francisco; San Simeon State Park; Point Reyes National Seashore.

KEY EVENTS IN CALIFORNIA

1542 California coast explored for Spain by Juan Rodríguez Cabrillo.
1769 First Spanish fort and mission in California established at San Diego.
1826 First American explorer reaches California by land: Jedediah Strong Smith.
1846–48 U.S. troops capture California.
1848 (Jan. 24) Gold discovered at Sutter's Mill by James W. Marshall, starting gold rush to California.
1850 (Sept. 9) California becomes 31st U.S. state.
1906 (April 18) Severe earthquake destroys most of San Francisco, killing 700 persons.
1911 First movie studio built in Hollywood.
1963 California tops New York to become largest state in population.
1968 Highest dam in U.S. built on Feather River near Oroville, 770 feet high.
1971 (Feb. 9) Earthquake in southern California kills 64 persons, causes $500 million damage.
1976 Nation's first right-to-die law approved.
1976–77 Drought causes $3 billion in farm losses.
1977 First woman appointed as state chief justice: Rose Elizabeth Bird.
1978 Voters approve Proposition 13, cutting property taxes about 60%.
1981 Fruit fly infestation threatens state's agricultural production; controlled by spraying.
1984 Population grows 8.3% since 1980.

COLORADO

Area: 104,090 square miles; 269,594 sq. km.
Population: 3,178,000 (1984); 2,889,964 (1980).
Capital: Denver.
Flower: Rocky Mountain columbine.
Tree: Colorado blue spruce.
Bird: Lark bunting. **Stone:** Aquamarine.
Animal: Rocky Mountain bighorn sheep.
Song: *Where the Columbines Grow.*
Motto: *Nil Sine Numine* (Nothing Without Providence).
Flag: Red "C" enclosing gold ball against blue, white, and blue stripes. **Nickname:** The Centennial State.
Leading Industries: Food processing, manufacturing (metal products, machinery), agriculture (beef cattle, sheep, dairy products, wheat, corn; sugar beets), tourism, mining (petroleum, molybdenum, coal, lead).
Climate (Denver): *Normal temperatures:* Jan. high 44° F., low 16° F.; July high 87° F., low 59° F. *Normal yearly precipitation:* 16" (water). *Record snowstorm:* 23" in April 1885.
Recreation Areas: National parks, 2; national forests, 12; national recreation areas, 2; state parks and recreation areas, 26.
Points of Interest: Rocky Mountain and Mesa Verde national parks; Dinosaur, Colorado, Black Canyon of Gunnison, Florissant Fossil Beds, Hovenweep, Yucca House, and Great Sand Dunes national monuments; Pikes Peak; Garden of the Gods; U.S. Air Force Academy; Durango-Silverton narrow-gauge railway; Central City; Aspen resort area; Bent's Old Fort National Historic Site.

KEY EVENTS IN COLORADO

1706 Colorado claimed for Spain by Juan de Ulibarri.
1803 U.S. acquires eastern Colorado in Louisiana Purchase.
1806 Colorado explored by Lt. Zebulon M. Pike, who discovers Pikes Peak.
1833 First permanent American settlement established at Bent's Fort, near present-day La Junta.
1845 Central Colorado acquired by U.S. with admission of Texas as state.
1848 Western Colorado obtained in Mexican War.
1858 Discovery of gold by Green Russell on Cherry Creek near present-day Denver begins gold rush.
1861 (Feb. 28) Territory of Colorado organized.
1864 Sand Creek Massacre: Settlers attack and kill hundreds of Cheyenne Indians.
1870 Railroads link Colorado with eastern states.
1875 Rich silver deposits discovered.
1876 (Aug. 1) Colorado becomes 38th U.S. state.
1891 Gold discovered at Cripple Creek.
1934–35 Drought develops "dust bowl" in eastern Colorado, causing abandonment of farms.
1974 Dwight D. Eisenhower 1.7-mile automobile tunnel completed through Rocky Mountains west of Denver, longest auto tunnel in U.S.
1976 Nation's first sunset law approved to disband agencies that do not serve public.
1977 Gem-quality diamonds discovered in northeastern Colorado.
1983 Becomes 26th most populous state.
1984 Population increases 10% since 1980.

CONNECTICUT

Area: 5,018 square miles; 12,997 sq. km.
Population: 3,154,000 (1984); 3,107,576 (1980).
Capital: Hartford.
Flower: Mountain laurel. **Tree:** White oak. **Mineral:** Garnet. **Insect:** Praying mantis. **Animal:** Sperm whale.
Bird: American robin. **Nickname:** Constitution State.
Song: *Yankee Doodle.*

Motto: *Qui Transtulit Sustinet* (He Who Transplanted Still Sustains).
Flag: State seal centered on blue field.
Leading Industries: Manufacturing (aircraft, machinery, metal products), tourism, agriculture (dairy products, poultry, tobacco).
Climate (Hartford): *Normal temperatures:* Jan. high 33° F., low 16° F.; July high 84° F., low 61° F. *Normal yearly precipitation:* 43" (water). *Record snowstorm:* 19" in February 1949.
Recreation Areas: State parks and recreation areas, 9; Long Island Sound beaches.
Points of Interest: Mystic Seaport Museum of Maritime America; Yale University (New Haven); Nathan Hale Homestead (South Coventry); Wadsworth Athenaeum, Harriet Beecher Stowe House, State Capitol, and Mark Twain Memorial (Hartford). U.S. Coast Guard Academy (New London); U.S. Navy submarine base (Groton); American Shakespeare Festival Theater (Stratford).

KEY EVENTS IN CONNECTICUT

1614 Connecticut region claimed for Netherlands by Adriaen Block.
1633 Dutch build fort at site of Hartford.
1633 English colonists from Massachusetts settle Windsor.
1636–37 Pequot War: Colonists slaughter Pequot Indians near Mystic and Fairfield.
1639 (Jan. 24) Connecticut colony organized under Fundamental Orders, unifying early settlements.
1662 (May 3) Royal charter granted Connecticut: serves as constitution until 1818.
1665 Connecticut expanded, unifying with New Haven colony.
1687 Colonists save charter by hiding it in Charter Oak at Hartford to prevent being ruled by British governor of New England Sir Edmund Andros.
1776 (June 14) Independence from Britain approved in resolution by Connecticut assembly.
1788 (Jan. 9) Connecticut becomes 5th U.S. state, ratifying U.S. Constitution.
1794 Eli Whitney begins manufacture of cotton gins at New Haven; starts mass production of firearms with interchangeable parts in 1798.
1960 (Oct. 1) County governments abolished.
1974 (Nov. 5) Connecticut elects first woman governor: Ella T. Grasso; first woman governor in U.S. who was not wife or widow of preceding governor.
1977 Reorganization plan adopted by legislature reduces 256 state agencies and commissions to 23.
1984 Population increases 1.5% since 1980.

DELAWARE

Area: 2,044 square miles; 5,295 sq. km.
Population: 613,000 (1984); 594,338 (1980).
Capital: Dover.
Flower: Peach blossom.
Tree: American holly.
Bird: Blue hen chicken.
Song: *Our Delaware.*
Nickname: The First State.
Motto: Liberty and Independence.
Flag: Blue field with centered state seal in yellow diamond above date Delaware ratified U.S. Constitution (Dec. 7, 1787).
Leading Industries: Manufacturing (chemicals, plastics, leather products), food processing, agriculture (poultry, dairy products, corn, hogs, beef cattle, soybeans).
Climate (Wilmington): *Normal temperatures:* Jan. high 40° F., low 23° F.; July high 86° F., low 66° F. *Normal yearly precipitation:* 40" (water). *Record rainfall* in 24 hours: 6.5" in August 1945.

DELAWARE (continued)

Recreation Areas: State parks with recreation areas, 9; Rehoboth, Bethany, Dewey, and Fenwick Island beaches.

Points of Interest: Henry Francis du Pont Winterthur Museum (near Wilmington); several historic towns, including New Castle, Dover, Odessa.

KEY EVENTS IN DELAWARE

1609 Delaware Bay discovered for Dutch by Henry Hudson.

1631 First Dutch colonists settle at Zwaanendael (near Lewes).

1638 Swedish colonists found New Sweden; establish Fort Christina at Wilmington; led by Peter Minuit.

1655 New Sweden captured by Dutch led by Peter Stuyvesant.

1664 England makes Delaware part of colony of New York.

1682 Delaware region made part of Pennsylvania colony.

1704 Separate Delaware legislature granted by Pennsylvania.

1776 (Sept. 20) First state constitution adopted.

1777 (Sept. 3) Battle of Coochs Bridge: British defeat Americans in Revolutionary War battle.

1787 (Dec. 7) Delaware becomes first U.S. state, ratifying U.S. Constitution.

1802 Gunpowder manufacturing plant established by Eleuthère Irénée du Pont near Wilmington.

1861–65 In Civil War, although slave state, Delaware fights on side of Union.

1951 Delaware Memorial Bridge completed across Delaware River at Wilmington; second span opened in 1968.

1963 Delaware Turnpike opens, completing superhighway from Boston to Washington, D.C.

1984 Population grows 3.1% since 1980.

FLORIDA

Area: 58,664 square miles; 151,938 sq. km.
Population: 10,976,000 (1984); 9,746,421 (1980).
Capital: Tallahassee.
Flower: Orange blossom.
Tree: Sabal palmetto palm.
Bird: Mockingbird.
Saltwater fish: Atlantic sailfish.
Saltwater mammal: Dolphin.
Gem: Moonstone.
Shell: Horse conch.
Song: *Swanee River.* **Beverage:** Orange juice.
Nickname: The Sunshine State.
Motto: In God We Trust.
Flag: Centered state seal and diagonal red bars on white field.
Leading Industries: Tourism, manufacturing (chemicals, metal products, transportation equipment, missiles), food processing, agriculture (fruits, nuts, vegetables, tobacco, beef cattle, dairy products), mining (phosphates).
Climate (Miami): *Normal temperatures:* Jan. high 76° F., low 59° F.; July high 89° F., low 76° F. *Normal yearly precipitation:* 60" (water). *Record snowstorm (Jacksonville):* 1.9" in February 1899.
Recreation Areas: National park, 1; national forests, 3; national seashore, 1; state parks and recreation areas, 103; numerous beaches.
Points of Interest: Everglades National Park; Biscayne, Castillo de San Marcos, Fort Jefferson, and Fort Matanzas national monuments; Fort Caroline National Memorial near St. Augustine; Marineland; Silver Springs; Ringling museums (Sarasota); Cypress Gardens (near Winter Haven); Kennedy Space Center, Cape Canaveral; Walt Disney World; Miami Beach;

Gulf Islands National Seashore.

KEY EVENTS IN FLORIDA

1513 (April 2) Florida discovered, named, and claimed for Spain by Juan Ponce de Léon.

1564 French Huguenot colonists establish Fort Caroline on St. Johns River near Jacksonville.

1565 (Sept. 8) Spaniards found St. Augustine.

1565 (Sept. 20) Spaniards under Pedro Menéndez de Avilés capture Fort Caroline, massacring French.

1763–83 Britain wins Florida in Seven Years War, but loses it back to Spain in Revolutionary War.

1810 (Oct. 27) U.S. annexes West Florida from Spain.

1814 (Nov. 7) Pensacola captured by Gen. Andrew Jackson.

1818 (April–May) East Florida captured from Spain by Gen. Jackson during First Seminole War.

1821 (Feb. 22) East Florida acquired by U.S. from Spain for $5 million in Adams-Onís Treaty (signed on Feb. 22, 1819).

1822 (March 30) Territory of Florida organized.

1835–43 Second Seminole War fought by settlers, ending with removal of Indians west of Mississippi.

1845 (March 3) Florida becomes 27th U.S. state.

1861 (Jan. 10) Florida secedes from Union.

1868 (June 25) Florida readmitted to Union.

1906 State drains Everglades near Fort Lauderdale.

1912–15 Miami Beach created as resort by Carl Fisher.

1938 Overseas Highway links Key West to mainland.

1969 First men to land on Moon launched in *Apollo 11* from Cape Canaveral.

1977 (January) Cold wave causes $385 million in agricultural losses; throws 50,000 out of work.

1982 Overseas Highway to Key West rebuilt at cost of $238 million.

1984 Becomes 6th most populous state.

1984 Population grows 12.6% since 1980.

GEORGIA

Area: 58,910 square miles; 152,575 sq. km.
Population: 5,387,000 (1984); 5,463,087 (1980).
Capital: Atlanta.
Flower: Cherokee rose.
Tree: Live oak.
Bird: Brown thrasher.
Fish: Largemouth bass.
Song: *Georgia on My Mind.*
Nickname: The Empire State of the South.
Motto: Wisdom, Justice, and Moderation.
Flag: State seal on blue bar, with Confederate flag on right.
Leading Industries: Manufacturing (textiles, aircraft, automobiles), food processing, forestry, agriculture (poultry, beef cattle, hogs, peanuts, tobacco, corn, cotton), mining (kaolin, barite, bauxite).
Climate (Atlanta): *Normal temperatures:* Jan. high 51° F., low 33° F.; July high 87° F., low 69° F. *Normal yearly precipitation:* 48" (water). *Record snowstorm:* 5.67" in February 1961.
Recreation Areas: National forests, 2; state parks and recreation areas, 70.
Points of Interest: Okefenokee National Wildlife Refuge; Andersonville National Historic Site; Chickamauga and Chattanooga National Military Park; Little White House (Warm Springs); Sea Island; Stone Mountain; Fort Frederica, Fort Pulaski, and Ocmulgee national monuments; Kennesaw Mountain National Battlefield Park; Cumberland Island National Seashore.

KEY EVENTS IN GEORGIA

1732 (June 9) Royal charter for Georgia granted to

Gen. James Edward Oglethorpe by King George II.
1733 (Feb. 12) First permanent settlement established by Oglethorpe at site of Savannah.
1742 (July) Battle of Bloody Marsh: Oglethorpe defeats Spanish invasion at Fort Frederica on St. Simons Island.
1753 Georgia becomes royal colony.
1776 (Jan. 18) Patriots imprison last royal governor.
1777 (Feb. 5) First state constitution adopted.
1778 (Dec. 29) British capture and hold Savannah until July 11, 1782.
1788 (Jan. 2) Georgia becomes 4th U.S. state, ratifying U.S. Constitution.
1793 Eli Whitney invents cotton gin near Savannah.
1795 Yazoo Fraud: Speculators bribe legislature to sell about 50,000 square miles of western land.
1838 Cherokees forced to move to Oklahoma.
1861 (Jan. 19) Georgia secedes, joins Confederacy.
1864 (Nov. 14–Dec. 22) March to the Sea: Union Gen. William T. Sherman burns Atlanta, destroys 60-mile-wide path to coast, captures Savannah.
1870 (July 15) Georgia readmitted to Union.
1943 First state to give vote to 18-year-olds.
1961 (Aug. 30) Atlanta begins to end segregation of public schools under court order.
1972 State government reorganized by Gov. Jimmy Carter, reducing agencies from 300 to 22 departments.
1973 First black mayor of Atlanta elected: Maynard H. Jackson Jr.
1984 Becomes 11th most populous state.
1984 Population increases 6.8% since 1980.

HAWAII

Area: 6,471 square miles; 16,759 sq. km.
Population: 1,039,000 (1984); 964,691 (1980).
Capital: Honolulu.
Flower: Hibiscus. **Tree:** Candlenut. **Bird:** Hawaiian goose. **Fish:** Humuhumu-nukunuku-a-pua'a.
Song: *Hawaii Ponoi.* **Nickname:** The Aloha State.
Motto: *Ua Mau Ke Ea O Ka Aina I Ka Pono* (The Life of the Land Is Perpetuated in Righteousness).
Flag: Alternating white, red, and blue stripes, with Union Jack in upper left.
Leading Industries: Tourism, military installations, food processing, agriculture (sugarcane, pineapples, beef cattle, coffee).
Climate (Honolulu): *Normal temperatures:* Jan. high 79 ° F., low 65 ° F.; July high 87 ° F., low 73 ° F. *Normal yearly rain:* 23". *Record rainfall in 24 hours:* 17.07" in March 1958.
Recreation Areas: National parks, 2; state parks and recreation areas, 46; many fine beaches.
Points of Interest: Hawaii Volcanoes National Park (Hawaii) and Haleakala National Park (Maui); City of Refuge National Historical Park (Hawaii); Polynesian Cultural Center (Oahu, near Laie); Waimea Canyon (Kauai); USS *Arizona* Memorial (Pearl Harbor); Iolani Palace, Bishop Museum, and the Waikiki area (all in Honolulu); Nuuanu Pali (near Honolulu); Puukohola Heiau National Historic Site (Hawaii).

KEY EVENTS IN HAWAII

1778 (Jan. 18) British Capt. James Cook discovers Hawaiian Islands, naming them Sandwich Islands.
1795 Hawaii unified by King Kamehameha I.
1820 Protestant missionaries from New England led by Hiram Bingham begin converting Hawaiians.
1893 (Jan. 17) Queen Liliuokalani deposed.
1894 (July 4) Republic of Hawaii established with Sanford B. Dole as president.
1898 (Aug. 12) U.S. annexes Hawaii.
1900 (June 14) Territory of Hawaii organized.
1941 (Dec. 7) Japanese attack Pearl Harbor.
1959 (Aug. 21) Hawaii becomes 50th U.S. state.

1981 First woman mayor of Honolulu, Eileen Anderson, takes office on Jan. 2.
1983 Population tops 1 million for first time.
1984 Population increases 7.7% since 1980.

IDAHO

Area: 83,564 square miles; 216,431 sq. km.
Population: 1,001,000 (1984); 944,038 (1980).
Capital: Boise.
Flower: Syringa. **Tree:** White pine.
Bird: Mountain bluebird.
Horse: Appaloosa. **Gemstone:** Star garnet.
Song: *Here We Have Idaho.*
Nickname: The Gem State.
Motto: *Esto Perpetua* (It Is Perpetual).
Flag: State seal and inscription "State of Idaho" centered on blue field.
Leading Industries: Agriculture (potatoes, wheat, barley, beans, hay, sugar beets, beef cattle, sheep, dairy products), food processing, forestry, mining (silver, lead, zinc, copper).
Climate (Boise): *Normal temperatures:* Jan. high 37 ° F., low 21 ° F.; July high 91 ° F., low 59 ° F. *Normal yearly precipitation:* 11.5" (water). *Record snowstorm:* 17" in December 1884.
Recreation Areas: National park, 1; national forests, 15; state parks and recreation areas, 19.
Points of Interest: Yellowstone National Park; Hells Canyon–Seven Devils scenic area; Sun Valley resort area; Shoshone Falls (near Twin Falls); Craters of the Moon National Monument; Nez Percé National Historical Park.

KEY EVENTS IN IDAHO

1805 Idaho explored by Lewis and Clark.
1846 (Aug. 5) Idaho acquired by U.S. as Oregon Treaty with Britain becomes effective.
1860 First permanent settlement established by Mormons at Franklin.
1860 (Sept. 30) Gold discovered on Orofino Creek.
1863 (March 4) Territory of Idaho established.
1877–79 Battles between U.S. troops and Nez Percé, Bannock, and Sheepeater Indians.
1880 Railroad completed to southeastern Idaho.
1890 (July 3) Idaho becomes 43d U.S. state.
1951 (Dec. 20) First electricity generated with atomic power near Idaho Falls.
1959–68 Three hydroelectric plants built on Snake River, providing over 1 million kilowatts.
1975 Snake River project opens 469-mile navigable waterway from Lewiston, Idaho, to Astoria, Oregon.
1976 (June 5) 300-foot-high Teton Dam collapses, causing 11 deaths and $1 billion in damage.
1984 Population tops 1 million for first time.
1984 Population increases 6% since 1980.

ILLINOIS

Area: 56,345 square miles; 145,933 sq. km.
Population: 11,511,000 (1984); 11,427,414 (1980).
Capital: Springfield.
Flower: Native violet. **Tree:** White oak.
Bird: Cardinal.
Mineral: Fluorite.
Insect: Monarch butterfly.
Song: *Illinois.*
Nickname: The Prairie State.
Motto: State Sovereignty–National Union.
Flag: State seal and "Illinois" centered on white field.
Leading Industries: Manufacturing (machinery, appliances, iron and steel, construction materials), food processing, agriculture (corn, hogs, oats, beef cattle, poultry, dairy products, soybeans, fruits), mining (coal, petroleum).

ILLINOIS (continued)

Climate (Chicago): *Normal temperatures:* Jan. high 32 ° F., low 17 ° F.; July high 84 ° F., low 65 ° F. *Normal yearly precipitation:* 34″ (water). *Record snowstorm:* 19.8″ in January 1967.

Recreation Areas: National forest, 1; state parks and recreation areas, 144; Lake Michigan beach and boating areas.

Points of Interest: Dickson Mounds Indian burial ground (near Lewistown); New Salem restoration; homestead and mansion of Joseph Smith (Nauvoo); Lincoln's home and burial place (Springfield). *In Chicago:* Art Institute; Field Museum; Museum of Science and Industry; Shedd Aquarium; Adler Planetarium; Merchandise Mart; Chicago Portage National Historic Site.

KEY EVENTS IN ILLINOIS

1673 **Illinois explored** by Louis Joliet and Jesuit priest Jacques Marquette for France.
1675 **Roman Catholic mission founded** at Kaskaskia, near present-day Utica, by Father Marquette.
1699 **French settlers** establish first permanent town at Cahokia, near present-day East St. Louis.
1763 **Britain obtains** region in settlement of French and Indian War.
1778 **George Rogers Clark** captures Kaskaskia and Cahokia during American Revolutionary War.
1787 **Region becomes** part of Northwest Territory.
1809 **(Feb. 3)** **Territory of Illinois** organized.
1812 **(Aug. 15–16)** In War of 1812 Britain's Indian allies massacre U.S. troops and settlers at Fort Dearborn, at site of present-day Chicago.
1818 **(Dec. 3)** **Illinois becomes 21st U.S. state.**
1832 **(April 6–Aug. 2)** **Black Hawk War** fought by settlers and Indians along Mississippi River.
1844 **(June 27)** **Carthage mob kills Joseph Smith,** founder of Mormon church, and his brother Hyrum.
1848 **Illinois and Michigan Canal** completed, linking Great Lakes to Mississippi River.
1855 **Railroad links** Chicago to East Coast.
1871 **(Oct. 8–9)** **Fire destroys most of Chicago,** killing 300 persons.
1942 **(Dec. 2)** **Atomic Age begins** with first successful nuclear chain reaction achieved in Chicago.
1973 **World's tallest building** completed in Chicago: 1,454-foot Sears Tower.
1977 **State legislature tied up 6 weeks** as record 186 roll calls are taken in choosing senate president.
1984 **Population grows** only 0.7% since 1980.

INDIANA

Area: 36,185 square miles; 93,720 sq. km.
Population: 5,498,000 (1984); 5,490,260 (1980).
Capital: Indianapolis.
Flower: Peony.
Tree: Tulip poplar.
Bird: Cardinal.
Stone: Limestone.
Song: *On the Banks of the Wabash, Far Away.*
Nickname: The Hoosier State.
Motto: Crossroads of America.
Flag: Gold torch with 19 gold stars on blue field.
Leading Industries: Manufacturing (machinery, appliances, steel, transportation equipment), agriculture (corn, hogs, soybeans, tomatoes, wheat, sheep, poultry, dairy products), mining (coal, natural gas, petroleum).
Climate (Indianapolis): *Normal temperatures:* Jan. high 36 ° F., low 20 ° F.; July high 85 ° F., low 65 ° F. *Normal yearly precipitation:* 39″ (water). *Record snowstorm:* 6.4″ on Feb. 24, 1974.
Recreation Areas: National forest, 1; national lakeshore, 1; state park and recreation areas, 22.

Points of Interest: Prehistoric Indian mounds; Indiana Dunes National Lakeshore; mineral springs at French Lick; Motor Speedway (Indianapolis); Lincoln Boyhood National Memorial (near Lincoln City); George Rogers Clark National Historical Park.

KEY EVENTS IN INDIANA

1679–80 **Indiana explored** for France by Robert Cavelier, Sieur de La Salle.
1731–33 **French settlers** establish Vincennes.
1763 **Britain wins region** in French and Indian War.
1779 **(Feb. 24)** **George Rogers Clark captures Vincennes** from British in Revolutionary War.
1787 **Becomes part** of Northwest Territory.
1800 **(May 7)** **Indiana Territory** organized.
1811 **(Nov. 7)** **Battle of Tippecanoe:** Shawnees defeated near present-day Lafayette by Gen. William H. Harrison, then governor of Indiana Territory and later President of the United States.
1816 **(Dec. 11)** **Indiana becomes 19th U.S. state.**
1861–65 In Civil War Indiana supports Union with about 200,000 soldiers.
1906 **Gary established** as steelmaking center.
1911 **First Memorial Day 500-mile auto race** held at Indianapolis.
1913 **(March 25–27)** **Floods** in Indiana and Ohio kill 732 persons, cause over $180 million in damage.
1956 **Indiana Turnpike** opened.
1963 **Studebaker Corporation** ends auto production at South Bend; began as wagonmaker in 1852.
1984 **Population increases** only 0.1% since 1980; state remains 14th in rank.

IOWA

Area: 56,275 square miles; 145,752 sq. km.
Population: 2,910,000 (1984); 2,913,808 (1980).
Capital: Des Moines.
Flower: Wild rose.
Tree: Oak.
Bird: Eastern goldfinch.
Stone: Geode.
Song: *The Song of Iowa.*
Nickname: The Hawkeye State.
Motto: Our Liberties We Prize and Our Rights We Will Maintain.
Flag: Blue, white, and red bars, with eagle and "Iowa" in larger white bar.
Leading Industries: Agriculture (beef cattle, hogs, corn, dairy products, poultry, soybeans, oats, hay), manufacturing (machinery, chemicals), food processing.
Climate (Des Moines): *Normal temperatures:* Jan. high 28 ° F., low 11 ° F.; July high 85 ° F.; low 65 ° F. *Normal yearly precipitation:* 31″ (water). *Record snowstorm:* 19.8″ in January 1942.
Recreation Areas and State Parks: 92.
Points of Interest: Herbert Hoover National Historic Site (West Branch); Amana Colonies; Fort Dodge Historical Museum, Fort, and Stockade; Effigy Mounds National Monument; Grotto of the Redemption (West Bend).

KEY EVENTS IN IOWA

1682 **Iowa region claimed** for France.
1762 **Region ceded** to Spain by France.
1788 **First settler,** French-Canadian Julien Dubuque, begins mining lead near present-day Dubuque.
1803 **U.S. acquires** region in Louisiana Purchase.
1808 **Fort Madison** established by U.S. Army.
1838 **(June 12)** **Territory of Iowa** organized.
1846 **(Dec. 28)** **Iowa becomes 29th U.S. state.**
1857 **Des Moines** becomes state capital.
1867 **Railroad completed** west to Council Bluffs.
1929–35 **During Great Depression** more than half of

Iowa's farmers lose land by mortgage foreclosures.
1960 Majority of state's people live in cities and towns for first time.
1984 Population decreases by 0.1% since 1980; one of three states that lost population since 1980.

KANSAS

Area: 82,277 square miles; 213,097 sq. km.
Population: 2,438,000 (1984); 2,364,236 (1980).
Capital: Topeka.
Flower: Native sunflower. **Tree:** Cottonwood.
Bird: Western meadowlark.
Animal: American buffalo.
Insect: Honeybee.
Song: *Home on the Range.*
Nickname: The Sunflower State.
Motto: *Ad Astra per Aspera* (To the Stars Through Difficulties).
Flag: Sunflower atop state seal on blue field.
Leading Industries: Manufacturing (aircraft, railroad equipment, chemicals, machinery), food processing, agriculture (beef cattle, wheat, hogs, sorghum grains, corn), mining (petroleum, natural gas, helium).
Climate (Topeka): *Normal temperatures:* Jan. high 38 ° F., low 18 ° F.; July high 89 ° F., low 67 ° F. *Normal yearly precipitation:* 35″ (water). *Record snowstorm:* 18.7″ on Feb. 27–28, 1900.
Recreation Areas: State parks and recreation areas, 29.
Points of Interest: Fort Larned and Fort Scott national historic sites; Hollenberg Pony Express Station; Fort Leavenworth; Eisenhower Library and boyhood home (Abilene); 1870s restoration of Dodge City; Kansas State Historical Society and Museum (Topeka); Museum of Art (Lawrence); John Brown Memorial State Park (Osawatomie).

KEY EVENTS IN KANSAS

1541 Region explored for Spain by Francisco de Coronado.
1682 Kansas region claimed for France.
1803 U.S. acquires Kansas in Louisiana Purchase.
1806 Kansas explored by U.S. Lt. Zebulon Pike.
1821 Santa Fe Trail route across Kansas pioneered by William Becknell.
1827 First permanent settlement: Fort Leavenworth.
1854 (May 30) Territory of Kansas created, setting off guerrilla warfare between proslavery and antislavery factions seeking to control government.
1860 (July 19) First railroad reaches Kansas.
1861 (Jan. 29) Kansas becomes 34th U.S. state.
1863 (Aug. 21) Lawrence burned and 150 settlers killed by Confederate guerrillas led by William C. Quantrill.
1865–80 Over 3,000 miles of railroad open across Kansas, making such towns as Abilene cattle-shipping centers for trail drives from Texas.
1870s Mennonite settlers introduce winter wheat, making Kansas leading wheat producer.
1892 Petroleum discovered near Neodesha.
1919 First airplane factory opens in Wichita; city becomes leading plane manufacturer in nation.
1934–35 Drought develops "dust bowl" in southwestern Kansas, driving many farmers from homes.
1984 Population grows 3.1% since 1980.

KENTUCKY

Area: 40,409 square miles; 104,660 sq. km.
Population: 3,723,000 (1984); 3,660,257 (1980).
Capital: Frankfort.
Flower: Goldenrod.
Tree: Coffee tree.
Bird: Cardinal.
Song: *My Old Kentucky Home.*

Nickname: The Bluegrass State.
Motto: United We Stand, Divided We Fall.
Flag: State seal on blue field.
Leading Industries: Manufacturing and processing (machinery, food, tobacco products, chemicals), distilling (bourbon whisky), agriculture (beef cattle, dairy products, tobacco, corn, hay, hogs, poultry, horses), mining (coal, petroleum, gas).
Climate (Louisville): *Normal temperatures:* Jan. high 42 ° F., low 25 ° F.; July high 87 ° F., low 66 ° F. *Normal yearly precipitation:* 43″ (water). *Record snowstorm:* 15″ in December 1917.
Recreation Areas: National park, 1; national forests, 2; state parks and recreation areas, 48.
Points of Interest: Mammoth Cave National Park; Kentucky Woodlands National Wildlife Refuge; Abraham Lincoln Birthplace National Historical Site (near Hodgenville); Cumberland Gap National Historical Park; Bluegrass region (around Lexington); Churchill Downs (Louisville); My Old Kentucky Home (Bardstown); Constitution Square restoration (Danville).

KEY EVENTS IN KENTUCKY

1750 Cumberland Gap pass in Appalachian Mountains discovered by Thomas Walker.
1774 First permanent settlement established at Harrodsburg by James Harrod.
1775 Daniel Boone blazes Wilderness Road through Cumberland Gap; established Boonesborough on Kentucky River.
1792 (June 1) Kentucky becomes 15th U.S. state.
1798 (Nov. 16) Kentucky Resolution written by Thomas Jefferson adopted by state legislature declaring federal Alien and Sedition Acts unconstitutional.
1800 (July) "Great revival" of religion begins with huge camp meeting at Gaspar River.
1815 First steamboat reaches Louisville from New Orleans.
1861–65 In Civil War Kentucky remains in Union despite opposition by state's slave owners; battles fought in Kentucky at Mill Springs on Jan. 19, 1862, at Richmond on Aug. 30, 1862, and at Perryville on Oct. 8, 1862.
1875 First Kentucky Derby horse race run at Louisville.
1984 State population grows 1.7% since 1980; lowest growth rate in East South Central states.

LOUISIANA

Area: 47,752 square miles; 123,676 sq. km.
Population: 4,462,000 (1984); 4,206,098 (1980).
Capital: Baton Rouge.
Flower: Magnolia.
Tree: Cypress.
Bird: Eastern brown pelican.
Songs: *Give Me Louisiana* and *You Are My Sunshine.*
Nickname: The Pelican State.
Motto: Union, Justice and Confidence.
Flag: Pelican atop state motto on blue field.
Leading Industries: Mining (petroleum, natural gas, salt, sulfur), manufacturing (chemicals, metal products), food processing, forestry, agriculture (beef cattle, poultry, cotton, rice, sugarcane, soybeans), services, fishing.
Climate (New Orleans): *Normal temperatures:* Jan. high 62 ° F., low 44 ° F.; July high 90 ° F., low 73 ° F. *Normal yearly precipitation:* 57″ (water). *Record snowstorm:* 8.2″ February 1895.
Recreation Areas: National forest, 1; state park and recreation areas, 31.
Points of Interest: New Orleans, including French Quarter, Superdome; plantation homes near Natchitoches and New Iberia; Cajun country (in Mississippi River delta region); Chalmette National Historical

LOUISIANA *(continued)*
Park; Evangeline Oak in St. Martinville; Live Oak Gardens on Jefferson Island.

KEY EVENTS IN LOUISIANA

1541 Hernando de Soto explores part of region, discovering Mississippi River for Spain.

1682 (April 9) Region claimed for France by Robert Cavelier, Sieur de La Salle.

1714 First permanent French settlement: Natchitoches.

1718 New Orleans founded by Jean Baptiste le Moyne, Sieur de Bienville.

1762 (Nov. 3) Spain acquires Louisiana.

1800 France regains Louisiana from Spain.

1803 (Dec. 20) U.S. takes formal possession of most of Louisiana after purchase from France.

1804 (March 26) Region organized by U.S. as Territory of Orleans.

1810 (Oct. 27) U.S. annexes West Feliciana District (Baton Rouge) from Spain after uprising by Americans captures area.

1812 (April 30) Louisiana becomes 18th U.S. state.

1815 (Jan. 8) Battle of New Orleans: Gen. Andrew Jackson defeats larger British army; neither side aware treaty already signed ending War of 1812.

1840 New Orleans becomes second-largest U.S. port as result of steamboat traffic on Mississippi River.

1861 (Jan. 26) Louisiana secedes from Union, joins Confederacy.

1862 (May 1) New Orleans surrenders to Union forces after Adm. David Farragut bombards its forts.

1868 (June 25) Louisiana readmitted to Union.

1877 (April 20) Reconstruction ends with withdrawal of federal troops.

1879 New Orleans becomes ocean port with dredging of Mississippi River channel by U.S. Army.

1901 Petroleum discovered near Jennings and White Castle.

1927 Mississippi River flood drives 300,000 persons from homes, causes huge property losses.

1935 (Sept. 8) Assassination in Baton Rouge of U.S. Sen. Huey P. Long, political boss of state.

1975 (Jan. 1) New constitution becomes effective, ending property taxes for homes of $30,000 or less.

1980 (March 10) First Republican governor in 103 years, David C. Treen, sworn in.

1983 (July 5) Racial designation law repealed: 1970 law had defined as black anyone with more than one thirty-second Negro blood.

1984 Population grows 6.1% since 1980; state remains 18th most populous.

MAINE

Area: 33,265 square miles; 86,156 sq. km.
Population: 1,156,000 (1984); 1,125,030 (1980).
Capital: Augusta.
Flower: White pine cone and tassel. **Tree:** Eastern white pine. **Bird:** Chickadee. **Insect:** Honeybee. **Mineral:** Tourmaline. **Fish:** Landlocked salmon.
Song: *State of Maine Song.*
Nickname: The Pine Tree State.
Motto: *Dirigo* (I Direct).
Flag: State seal centered on blue field.
Leading Industries: Manufacturing (paper, leather products, lumber), food processing, agriculture (poultry, dairy products, potatoes, oats, corn, vegetables, fruits), fishing.
Climate (Portland): *Normal temperatures:* Jan. high 31° F., low 12° F.; July high 79° F., low 57° F. *Normal yearly precipitation:* 41" (water). *Record snowstorm:* 23.3" in January 1935.
Recreation Areas: National park, 1; national forest, 1; state parks and recreation areas, 39.
Points of Interest: Bar Harbor; Acadia National Park; Allagash National Wilderness Waterway; Baxter State Park; Wadsworth-Longfellow House (Portland); Roosevelt Campobello International Park; Saint Croix Island National Monument; Old Gaol Museum (York).

KEY EVENTS IN MAINE

1498 John Cabot explores Maine coast.

1604 First French colony established at Saint Croix Island by Pierre du Guast, Sieur de Monts.

1607 First English colony founded on Kennebec River by George Popham and Raleigh Gilbert (abandoned 1608).

1622 (Aug. 10) Maine and New Hampshire granted to Sir Ferdinando Gorges and John Mason.

1623 First English settlements established.

1629 Region divided by Gorges and Mason with Gorges keeping Maine.

1677 (March 13) Massachusetts gains title to Maine by purchase for about $6,000.

1775 (June 12) First naval action of Revolutionary War: Patriots capture British sloop *Margaretta* off Machias, Me.

1775 (Oct. 18) British burn Falmouth (now Portland).

1814 In War of 1812, Eastport and eastern Maine captured and occupied by British.

1820 (March 15) Maine becomes 23d U.S. state as part of Missouri Compromise.

1838–39 Aroostook War: Militia of Maine and New Brunswick prepare to fight in boundary dispute.

1842 (Aug. 9) Webster-Ashburton Treaty signed, settling Maine's boundary with Canada.

1851 First state prohibition law enacted.

1948 First woman elected by Maine to U.S. Senate: Margaret Chase Smith.

1958 First Democrat elected to U.S. Senate by popular vote in Maine: Edmund S. Muskie.

1972 Penobscot and Passamaquoddy Indians file suit asking $300 million in damages because over 12 million acres of their land were seized illegally.

1974 First Maine governor independent of both major political parties elected: James B. Longley.

1977 Legal age raised to 20 from 18 for drinking alcoholic beverages.

1984 Population grows 2.8% since 1980.

MARYLAND

Area: 10,460 square miles; 27,092 sq. km.
Population: 4,349,000 (1984); 4,216,941 (1980).
Capital: Annapolis.
Flower: Black-eyed Susan.
Tree: White oak.
Bird: Baltimore oriole.
Animal: Chesapeake Bay retriever. **Fish:** Striped bass.
Song: *Maryland, My Maryland.*
Nickname: The Old Line State.
Motto: *Fatti Maschii, Parole Femine* (Manly Deeds, Womanly Words).
Flag: Geometric black-and-gold pattern in top left and bottom right quarters; red and white ornate crosses in other quarters.
Leading Industries: Manufacturing (steel, metal products, transportation equipment, appliances, machinery), agriculture (poultry, dairy products, corn, tobacco, soybeans), mining (stone, coal, clay), fishing.
Climate (Baltimore): *Normal temperatures:* Jan. high 42° F., low 25° F.; July high 87° F., low 67° F. *Normal yearly precipitation:* 41" (water). *Record snowstorm:* 24.5" in January 1922.
Recreation Areas: National seashore, 1; state parks and recreation areas, 49; Atlantic Ocean and Chesapeake Bay resorts.
Points of Interest: Fort McHenry National Monument; Harpers Ferry and Chesapeake and Ohio Canal national historical parks; Hampton National Historic Site; Antietam National Battlefield Site and National

Cemetery; U.S. Naval Academy (Annapolis); Assateague Island National Seashore; Catoctin Mountain and Piscataway parks; George Washington Memorial Parkway; Barbara Fritchie House in Frederick; St. Marys City restoration near Leonardtown; USS *Constellation* at Baltimore.

KEY EVENTS IN MARYLAND

1608 Chesapeake Bay explored for England by John Smith.

1631 First English settlement established by William Claiborne of Virginia on Kent Island.

1632 (June 30) Maryland colony charter granted to Cecil Calvert, 2d Lord Baltimore, by King Charles I.

1634 (March 25) English Roman Catholics land on St. Clements (now Blakistone) Island, establishing St. Marys City as capital of colony.

1649 (April 21) Religious freedom granted all Christians in Toleration Act approved by legislature.

1654–58 Revolt by Puritans led by William Claiborne takes over government, ending toleration.

1691–1715 Colonial governors appointed by British crown; Church of England established (1692), with Catholics forbidden right to vote or hold office.

1715 Calvert family regains control of colony under 4th Lord Baltimore, who renounces Catholicism.

1767. Mason and Dixon Line established as boundary between Maryland and Pennsylvania.

1774 (Oct. 19) Patriots burn British tea ship *Peggy Stewart* in Annapolis Harbor.

1776 (Nov. 9) First state constitution adopted.

1788 (April 28) Maryland becomes 7th U.S. state, ratifying U.S. Constitution.

1814 (Aug. 24) Battle of Bladensburg: British defeat U.S. forces in War of 1812.

1814 (Sept. 12–14) British unsuccessfully try to capture Baltimore; bombardment of Fort McHenry inspires Francis Scott Key to write *The Star-Spangled Banner.*

1828–50 Chesapeake and Ohio Canal built.

1829 Chesapeake and Delaware Canal completed.

1844 (May 24) First telegraph line opens between Baltimore and Washington, D.C.

1845 U.S. Naval Academy founded at Annapolis.

1861–65 In Civil War, although slave state, Maryland remains in Union; battles include Antietam (Sept. 17, 1862) and Monocacy (July 9, 1864).

1938 First state income tax adopted.

1952 Chesapeake Bay Bridge connects eastern and western Maryland; parallel span completed in 1973.

1977 Gov. Marvin Mandel convicted of fraud; sentenced to 4 years in jail.

1984 Population grows only 3.1% since 1980; state remains 19th in rank.

MASSACHUSETTS

Area: 8,284 square miles; 21,456 sq. km.
Population: 5,798,000 (1984); 5,737,081 (1980).
Capital: Boston.
Flower: Mayflower. **Tree:** American elm. **Bird:** Chickadee. **Fish:** Cod. **Song:** *All Hail to Massachusetts.* **Nickname:** The Bay State. **Motto:** *Ense Petit Placidam Sub Libertate Quietem* (By the Sword We Seek Peace, but Peace Only Under Liberty).
Flag: State coat of arms centered on white field.
Leading Industries: Manufacturing (machinery, appliances, printing, metal products), agriculture (dairy products, flowers, shrubs, poultry, beef cattle, hogs, hay, vegetables, tobacco).
Climate (Boston): *Normal temperatures:* Jan. high 36° F., low 23° F.; July high 81° F., low 65° F. *Normal yearly precipitation:* 43″ (water). *Record snowstorm:* 19.4″ in February 1958.
Recreation Areas: National seashore, 1; state parks and

recreation areas, 68.
Points of Interest: Adams, Dorchester Heights, John F. Kennedy Birthplace, Longfellow, Salem Maritime, and Saugus Iron Works national historic sites; Minute Man National Historical Park between Lexington and Concord; Bunker Hill Memorial; Cape Cod National Seashore; Nantucket; Martha's Vineyard; Berkshire Music Festival; Salem; reconstruction of first Pilgrim village at Plymouth; Old Sturbridge Village; Basketball Hall of Fame (Springfield); *In Boston:* Old North Church, Old State House, Custom House, Quincy Market, Faneuil Hall, USS *Constitution,* and Paul Revere's House.

KEY EVENTS IN MASSACHUSETTS

c.1000 Coast believed explored by Vikings led by Leif Ericson.

1498 John Cabot explores coast for England.

1620 (Dec. 26) Pilgrims land, founding Plymouth Colony.

1628 (Sept. 6) Puritans found Salem under leadership of John Endecott, forerunner of Massachusetts Bay Colony (given royal charter March 14, 1629).

1630 (Sept. 17) Boston founded; becomes capital of Massachusetts Bay Colony in 1632.

1636 (Oct. 28) Harvard College founded.

1636–37 War fought against Pequot Indians.

1675–78 King Philip's War: Many settlers killed fighting Wampanoag Indians and their allies.

1684 (Oct. 18) Massachusetts Bay Colony charter annulled by English court.

1689 (April 18) Revolt in Boston overthrows royal governor of New England Sir Edmund Andros.

1689–1763 Massachusetts colonists take major role in French and Indian War.

1691 (Oct. 17) New royal charter for Massachusetts incorporates Plymouth and Maine in colony.

1692 Witchcraft trials result in execution of 20 persons as witches.

1775 (April 19) Revolutionary War begins with Battles of Lexington and Concord.

1775 (June 17) Battle of Bunker Hill: British defeat Massachusetts militia, but with heavy losses.

1776 (March 17) British evacuate Boston by sea after victorious 9-month siege by Continental Army.

1780 (June 15) First state constitution, written by John Adams, becomes effective; first ratified by popular referendum.

1786–87 Shays' Rebellion put down by militia.

1788 (Feb. 6) Massachusetts becomes 6th U.S. state, ratifying U.S. Constitution.

1837 (June 29) State board of education established with Horace Mann as secretary.

1853 (May 17) Labor law adopted reducing hours of work per day from 12 to 10 beginning Oct. 1, 1854.

1914 Cape Cod Canal opens.

1919 Gov. Calvin Coolidge calls out national guard to break Boston police strike.

1966 First black U.S. senator elected in U.S. since Reconstruction era: Edward W. Brooke.

1977 Islands of Martha's Vineyard and Nantucket vote to secede from state because of redistricting that would eliminate their representation in legislature.

1980 Voters approve $1.5 billion property tax cut; measure limits property tax to 2.5% of market value.

1983 (March 26) Ban on Sunday store sales ends; result of 1982 legislation.

1984 Population grows only 1.1% since 1980.

MICHIGAN

Area: 58,527 square miles; 151,844 sq. km.
Population: 9,075,000 (1984); 9,262,070 (1980).
Capital: Lansing.
Flower: Apple blossom.

MICHIGAN *(continued)*
Tree: White pine.
Bird: Robin. **Fish:** Trout.
Stone: Petoskey stone.
Gem: Chlorastrolite.
Song: *Michigan, My Michigan.*
Nickname: The Wolverine State.
Motto: *Si Quaeris Peninsulam Amoenam Circumspice* (If You Seek a Pleasant Peninsula, Look About You).
Flag: State coat of arms centered on blue field.
Leading Industries: Manufacturing (automobiles, machinery, metal products, chemicals), food processing, agriculture (dairy products, beef cattle, hogs, poultry, fruits, vegetables, corn, potatoes, soybeans, sugar beets), mining (iron ore, copper, salt, petroleum, natural gas), tourism.
Climate (Detroit): *Normal temperatures:* Jan. high 32 ° F., low 17 ° F.; July high 83 ° F., low 61 ° F. *Normal yearly precipitation:* 32″ (water). *Record snowstorm:* 19.2″ on Dec. 1–2, 1974.
Recreation Areas: National park, 1; national forests, 4; national lakeshores, 2; state parks and recreation areas, 78.
Points of Interest: Pictured Rocks and Sleeping Bear Dunes national lakeshore; Isle Royale National Park; Mackinac Island; Greenfield Village (Dearborn); Cook Nuclear Center (Bridgman); Detroit Zoological Park (Royal Oak); automobile plants in Dearborn, Detroit, Flint, Lansing, Pontiac; Soo Canals, Sault Ste. Marie.

KEY EVENTS IN MICHIGAN

c.1620 **Michigan explored for France** by Etienne Brulé.
1668 **First permanent French settlement** founded at Sault Ste. Marie by Father Jacques Marquette.
1763 **Britain wins region** in French and Indian War.
1783 **U.S. acquires region** in Revolutionary War, but British retain Detroit and other posts until 1796.
1787 **Region becomes part of Northwest Territory;** made part of Indiana Territory in 1800–03.
1805 **(Jan. 11) Michigan Territory organized.**
1812 **(Aug. 16) In War of 1812** Detroit and U.S. army of 2,000 surrendered to British by territorial governor, Gen. William Hull; British troops remain on Michigan's Drummond Island until 1828.
1818 **First steamboat on Lake Erie** reaches Detroit.
1837 **(Jan. 26) Michigan becomes 26th U.S. state.**
1854 **(July 6) New Republican Party** given name at state convention in Jackson, Mich.
1855 **First Soo Canal** completed at Sault Ste. Marie, linking Lake Superior and Lake Huron.
1899 **First automobile manufacturing company** founded in Detroit by Ransom E. Olds.
1935–37 **United Automobile Workers union** uses sit-down strikes to obtain collective bargaining contracts.
1957 **Straits of Mackinac bridge** opens.
1967 **State income tax** adopted.
1980–82 **Slump in auto production** brings state highest unemployment rate in nation with over 15% jobless.
1984 **Population decreases** by 2.0% since 1980, with highest decline among states.

MINNESOTA

Area: 84,402 square miles; 218,600 sq. km.
Population: 4,162,000 (1964); 4,075,970 (1980).
Capital: St. Paul.
Flower: Pink and white lady's-slipper.
Tree: Red pine. **Grain:** Wild rice.
Bird: Common loon.
Gemstone: Lake Superior agate. **Fish:** Walleye.
Song: *Hail! Minnesota.*
Nickname: The North Star State.

Motto: *L'Etoile du Nord* (The Star of the North).
Flag: State seal and gold stars on blue field.
Leading Industries: Manufacturing (paper, automobiles, printing, lumber), food processing, agriculture (beef cattle, hogs, turkeys, poultry, sheep, dairy products, oats, corn, hay, flaxseed, potatoes, soybeans, sugar beets), mining (iron ore, taconite).
Climate (Minneapolis–St. Paul): *Normal temperatures:* Jan. high 21 ° F., low 3 ° F.; July high 82 ° F., low 61 ° F. *Normal annual precipitation:* 26″ (water). *Record snowstorm:* 16.2″ in November 1940.
Recreation Areas: National park, 1; national forests, 2; state parks and recreation areas, 98.
Points of Interest: Voyageurs National Park; North Shore Drive; Pipestone and Grand Portage national monuments; St. Croix and Lower St. Croix national scenic riverways; Lumbertown restoration in Brainerd. *In Minneapolis:* Institute of Arts; Walker Art Center; Minnehaha Park; Tyrone Guthrie Theater.

KEY EVENTS IN MINNESOTA

1679 **Region explored and claimed for France** by Daniel Greysolon, Sieur Duluth.
1680 **Falls of St. Anthony** at present-day Minneapolis named by Belgian missionary Louis Hennepin.
1762 **Spain acquires western Minnesota** from France.
1763 **Britain obtains eastern Minnesota** from France.
1783 **U.S. acquires eastern Minnesota** from Britain.
1800 **France obtains western Minnesota** from Spain.
1803 **U.S. acquires western Minnesota** from France in Louisiana Purchase.
1805–06 **Region explored** by U.S. Lt. Zebulon M. Pike.
1818 **(Oct. 20) Northern Minnesota** ceded to U.S. by Britain.
1820–22 **Fort Snelling** built by U.S. Army just south of present-day Minneapolis (first called Fort St. Anthony, renamed Fort Snelling in 1825).
1823 **First Mississippi River steamboat** reaches Fort Snelling from St. Louis.
1832 **Lake Itasca,** source of Mississippi River, discovered by Henry R. Schoolcraft.
1849 **(March 3) Territory of Minnesota** organized.
1858 **(May 11) Minnesota becomes 32d U.S. state.**
1862 **Sioux Indian uprising** led by Chief Little Crow kills hundreds of settlers.
1890 **Rich iron-ore deposits** discovered in Mesabi Range.
1894 **(Sept. 1) Forest fire** destroys towns of Hinkley and Sandstone, killing 418 persons.
1918 **(Oct. 13–15) Forest fire** in Carlton and St. Louis counties kills over 400 persons.
1955 **Taconite processing plant** opens at Silver Bay to extract iron from low-grade taconite ore.
1981 **14,000 State employees strike** for 22 days to win wage increase.
1984 **Population grows** 2.1% since 1980.

MISSISSIPPI

Area: 47,689 square miles; 123,515 sq. km.
Population: 2,598,000 (1984); 2,520,631 (1980).
Capital: Jackson.
Flower: Magnolia. **Tree:** Magnolia.
Bird: Mockingbird.
Song: *Go, Mississippi.*
Nickname: The Magnolia State.
Motto: *Virtute et Armis* (By Valor and Arms).
Flag: Red, white, and blue stripes, with Confederate flag in upper left.
Leading Industries: Manufacturing (clothing, lumber, chemicals, appliances), food processing, agriculture (cotton, rice, soybeans, livestock feed, beef cattle, dairy products, poultry), mining (petroleum, gas).

Climate (Jackson): *Normal temperatures:* Jan. high 58 ° F., low 36 ° F.; July high 93 ° F., low 71 ° F. *Normal annual precipitation:* 49" (water). *Record snowstorm:* 10.6" in January 1940.

Recreation Areas: National seashore, 1; national forests, 6; state parks and recreation areas, 18.

Points of Interest: Gulf Islands National Seashore; Vicksburg National Military Park; Tupelo National Battlefield; Brices Cross Roads National Battlefield Site; Jefferson Davis' homes at *Rosemont* near Woodville and *Beauvoir* at Biloxi; antebellum homes and gardens of Natchez; Old Spanish Trail; Gulf Coast beaches.

KEY EVENTS IN MISSISSIPPI

1540–41 Region explored for Spain by Hernando de Soto, who discovered Mississippi River.

1682 (April 9) Region claimed for France.

1699 (May) French found first settlement at Old Biloxi (now Ocean Springs).

1736 (May) Battle of Ackia: French defeated in attempt to destroy Chickasaw Indian fort in northeastern Mississippi, preventing French conquest of Mississippi Valley.

1763 Britain acquires region in French and Indian War.

1783 U.S. acquires northern Mississippi in Revolutionary War; Spain obtains southern Mississippi as part of West Florida.

1795 U.S. obtains part of Mississippi between 31st and 32d parallels of latitude from Spain.

1798 (April 7) Territory of Mississippi organized.

1810 (Oct. 27) U.S. annexes West Florida from Spain, including what is now southern Mississippi.

1817 (Dec. 10) Mississippi becomes 20th U.S. state.

1861 (Jan. 9) Mississippi joins Confederacy.

1861–65 In Civil War Biloxi captured by Union Navy on Dec. 31, 1861; Natchez surrenders on Sept. 10, 1862; many battles in state including Vicksburg, which surrendered on July 4, 1863, Brices Cross Roads on June 10, 1864, and Tupelo on July 14, 1864.

1870 (Feb. 17) Mississippi readmitted to Union.

1927 Mississippi River flood drives 100,000 persons from their homes, causes vast property damage.

1939 Petroleum discovered near Tinsley.

1940–60 Population declines in Mississippi.

1969 First black mayor elected since Reconstruction era, in Fayette: Charles Evers.

1984 Population grows 3.1% since 1980.

MISSOURI

Area: 69,697 square miles; 180,515 sq. km.
Population: 5,008,000 (1984); 4,916,759 (1980).
Capital: Jefferson City.
Flower: Hawthorn.
Tree: Dogwood.
Bird: Bluebird.
Stone: Mozarkite.
Song: *Missouri Waltz.*
Nickname: The Show-Me State.
Motto: *Salus Populi Suprema Lex Esto* (The Welfare of the People Shall Be the Supreme Law).
Flag: State seal centered on red, white, and blue stripes.
Leading Industries: Manufacturing (transportation equipment, chemicals, machinery), food processing, agriculture (dairy products, beef cattle, hogs, sheep, poultry, horses, soybeans, corn, cotton, wheat), mining (lead, clay, barite).
Climate (St. Louis): *Normal temperatures:* Jan. high 40 ° F., low 23 ° F.; July high 88 ° F., low 69 ° F. *Normal yearly precipitation:* 36" (water). *Record snowstorm:* 20.4" in March 1890.
Recreation Areas: Scenic riverway, 1; national forests,

2; state parks and recreation areas, 53.

Points of Interest: Mark Twain's boyhood home and Mark Twain Cave (Hannibal); Harry S. Truman Library and Museum (Independence); house where Jesse James was killed (St. Joseph); George Washington Carver National Monument near Diamond Grove; Winston Churchill Memorial and Library in Fulton; Silver Dollar City reconstruction near Branson; Wilson's Creek National Battlefield; Jefferson National Expansion Memorial National Historic Site (St. Louis); Ozark National Scenic Riverways; Lake of the Ozarks; Meramec Caverns near Stanton.

KEY EVENTS IN MISSOURI

1673 Mouth of Missouri River discovered by French explorers Louis Joliet and Jacques Marquette.

1682 (April 9) Missouri region claimed for France.

1735 First permanent settlement established at Sainte Genevieve by settlers from Kaskaskia, Ill.

1762 Spain acquires region from France.

1764 (Feb. 15) St. Louis founded by Pierre Laclede Liguest and René Auguste Chouteau.

1800 France regains region from Spain.

1803 U.S. acquires Missouri in Louisiana Purchase.

1812 (June 4) Territory of Missouri organized.

1817 (Aug. 2) Steamboat *General Pike* ascends Mississippi River to St. Louis.

1821 Kansas City established as fur trading post.

1821 (Aug. 10) Missouri becomes 24th U.S. state.

1854–65 Border warfare with Kansas as proslavery Missourians attack antislavery Kansans.

1859 First railroad crosses state.

1861–65 In Civil War Gov. Claiborne F. Jackson leads state militia in battles with Union forces; Union troops gain control of state in series of battles, but guerrilla warfare continues.

1874 (July 4) Eads Bridge opened across Mississippi River at St. Louis, longest steel-arch bridge of day.

1882 (April 3) Outlaw Jesse James slain by member of his gang in St. Joseph.

1904 World's Fair and Olympic Games held at St. Louis.

1931 Bagnell Dam completed, forming Lake of Ozarks.

1957 Truman Library opens at Independence.

1984 Population grows only 1.9% since 1980.

MONTANA

Area: 147,046 square miles; 380,846 sq. km.
Population: 824,000 (1984); 786,690 (1980).
Capital: Helena.
Flower: Bitterroot.
Tree: Ponderosa pine. **Bird:** Western meadowlark.
Stones: Sapphire and agate. **Fish:** Blackspotted cutthroat trout. **Grass:** Bluebunch wheatgrass.
Song: *Montana.*
Nicknames: The Treasure State; Big Sky Country.
Motto: *Oro y Plata* (Gold and Silver).
Flag: State seal centered on blue field.
Leading Industries: Agriculture (beef cattle, sheep, wheat) forestry, food and mineral processing, mining (petroleum, copper, gold, silver), tourism.
Climate (Helena): *Normal temperatures:* Jan. high 28 ° F., low 8 ° F.; July high 84 ° F., low 52 ° F. *Normal yearly precipitation:* 11" (water). *Record snowstorm:* 21.5" in November 1959.
Recreation Areas: National parks, 2; national forests, 11; national recreation area, 1; state parks and recreation areas, 177.
Points of Interest: Glacier National Park; Yellowstone National Park (which extends into Wyoming and Idaho); Custer Battlefield National Monument; Big Hole National Battlefield; Virginia City; Gallery '85 (Billings); Museum of the Plains Indians (Brown-

MONTANA *(continued)*

ing); Fort Union Trading Post and Grant-Kohr's Ranch national historic sites; Bighorn Canyon National Recreation Area.

KEY EVENTS IN MONTANA

1742–43 Region explored for France by François and Louis-Joseph de La Vérendrye.

1803 U.S. acquires eastern Montana in Louisiana Purchase.

1805–06 Region explored for U.S. by Meriwether Lewis and William Clark.

c.1807 First trading post established by Emanuel Lisa at junction of Bighorn and Yellowstone rivers.

1818 (Oct. 20) Northern boundary of Montana established in treaty with Britain.

1829 Fort Union trading post built for American Fur Company by Kenneth McKenzie near junction of Missouri and Yellowstone rivers.

1846 First permanent settlement established at Fort Benton on Missouri River by Alexander Culbertson.

1846 (Aug. 5) Western Montana obtained from Britain in Oregon Treaty.

1852 Gold discovered in what is now Deer Lodge County by Francis Finlay.

1860 (July 2) First steamboats reach Fort Benton.

1864 (May 26) Territory of Montana organized.

1876 (June 25) Massacre of George Custer and his troops by Sioux Indians in Battle of Little Bighorn.

1877 (Oct. 5) Chief Joseph surrenders to Col. Nelson A. Miles, ending Nez Percé War.

1882 Copper discovered at Anaconda.

1883 (Sept. 8) Railroad completed across Montana.

1889 (Nov. 8) Montana becomes 41st U.S. state.

1916 First woman elected to U.S. Congress: Jeannette Rankin.

1940 Fort Peck Dam completed on Missouri River, largest earth-fill dam in U.S.

1951 Oil wells begin production in Williston Basin.

1975 Libby Dam power project on Kootenai River begins operation.

1984 Population grows 4.7% since 1980.

NEBRASKA

Area: 77,355 square miles; 200,349 sq. km.
Population: 1,606,000 (1984); 1,569,825 (1980).
Capital: Lincoln.
Flower: Goldenrod.
Tree: Cottonwood.
Bird: Western meadowlark.
Gemstone: Blue agate. **Fossil:** Mammoth.
Grass: Little blue stem. **Insect:** Honeybee.
Rock: Chalcedony stone.
Song: *Beautiful Nebraska.*
Nickname: The Cornhusker State.
Motto: Equality Before the Law.
Flag: State seal centered on blue field.
Leading Industries: Agriculture (beef cattle, corn, hogs, wheat), meat-packing, milling, manufacturing.
Climate (Omaha): *Normal temperatures:* Jan. high 33° F., low 12° F.; July high 89° F., low 66° F. *Normal yearly precipitation:* 30″ (water). *Record snowstorm:* 29.2″ in March 1912.
Recreation Areas: National forests, 2; state parks and recreation areas, 93.
Points of Interest: Agate Fossil Beds, Homestead, and Scotts Bluff national monuments; Chimney Rock National Historic Site; re-created pioneer village at Minden; Boys Town near Omaha; Union stockyards in Omaha.

KEY EVENTS IN NEBRASKA

1700s French and Spanish explorers travel through parts of Nebraska.

1803 U.S. acquires Nebraska in Louisiana Purchase.

1804–06 Eastern Nebraska explored for U.S. by Meriwether Lewis and William Clark.

1812–13 Oregon Trail pioneered across Nebraska by fur trader Robert Stuart.

1819 Fort Atkinson built by U.S. Army north of present-day Omaha.

1823 First permanent settlement: Bellevue.

1848 Western Nebraska acquired in Mexican War.

1854 (May 30) Territory of Nebraska created.

1865 Construction of railroad across state begun.

1867 (March 1) Nebraska becomes 37th U.S. state.

1874–77 Plague of grasshoppers drives many farmers from state.

1934 Unicameral legislature established by amendment to state constitution; first meets in 1937.

1939 Oil discovered in southeastern Nebraska.

1966 Voters abolish state property tax; replaced with state sales and income taxes in 1967.

1984 Population increases 2.3% since 1980.

NEVADA

Area: 110,561 square miles; 286,351 sq. km.
Population: 911,000 (1984); 800,493 (1980).
Capital: Carson City.
Flower: Sagebrush.
Tree: Single-leaf piñon.
Bird: Mountain bluebird. **Animal:** Desert bighorn sheep. **Mineral:** Silver. **Grass:** Indian rice grass.
Song: *Home Means Nevada.*
Nickname: The Silver State.
Motto: All for Our Country.
Flag: Gold and green insignia in upper left on blue field.
Climate (Las Vegas): *Normal temperatures:* Jan. high 56° F., low 33° F.; July high 104° F., low 75° F. *Normal yearly precipitation:* 4″ (water). *Record snowstorm:* 9″ on Jan. 4–5, 1974.
Leading Industries: Gambling and tourism; mining and processing copper, mercury, gold, and silver; agriculture (beef cattle, sheep).
Recreation Areas: National forests, 4; national recreation area, 1; state parks and recreation areas, 16.
Points of Interest: Lehman Caves National Monument; Lake Tahoe area; Las Vegas; Reno; Virginia City; Liberty open-pit copper mine (near Ely); Lake Mead National Recreation Area; Hoover Dam.

KEY EVENTS IN NEVADA

1775–76 Spanish missionary Francisco Garcés crosses southern Nevada en route to California.

1825 Humboldt River discovered by fur trapper Peter Skeen Ogden of Hudson's Bay Company.

1830 Old Spanish Trail pioneered across Nevada from Santa Fe to Los Angeles by William Wolfskill.

1833 California Trail from Utah across Sierra Nevada mountains pioneered by Joseph R. Walker.

1848 U.S. acquires Nevada in Mexican War.

1849 First permanent settlement established at Mormon Station (now Genoa) by H.S. Beatie.

1850 Nevada included in new Utah Territory.

1859 (June 11) Rich Comstock silver lode discovered near Virginia City, starting rush of prospectors.

1861 (March 2) Territory of Nevada created.

1864 (Oct. 31) Nevada becomes 36th U.S. state.

1931 Nevada legalizes gambling; also reduces residence requirements for divorce to 6 weeks.

1936 Hoover Dam on Colorado River completed.

1951 Atomic weapons tests begun by U.S. government on Yucca Flats range northwest of Las Vegas.

1980 Nevada moves ahead of Montana to rank 43d in population.

1984 Second fastest growth rate among states increases population 13.8% since 1980.

NEW HAMPSHIRE

Area: 9,279 square miles; 24,031 sq. km.
Population: 977,000 (1984); 920,610 (1980).
Capital: Concord.
Flower: Purple lilac.
Tree: White birch.
Bird: Purple finch.
Song: *Old New Hampshire.*
Nickname: The Granite State.
Motto: Live Free or Die.
Flag: State seal centered on blue field.
Leading Industries: Manufacturing (machinery, paper, leather products), tourism, food processing, agriculture (dairying, poultry, beef cattle, fruits, vegetables).
Climate (Concord): *Normal temperatures:* Jan. high 31 ° F., low 10 ° F.; July high 83 ° F., low 57 ° F. *Normal yearly precipitation:* 36″ (water). *Record snowstorm:* 19″ in January 1944.
Recreation Areas: National forest, 1; state parks and recreation areas, 67.
Points of Interest: Lake Winnipesaukee; White Mountains; North Conway (resort); Portsmouth (old shipbuilding town); Saint-Gaudens National Historic Site (Cornish); President Franklin Pierce's homestead (Hillsboro); Daniel Webster's birthplace (near Salisbury); Mt. Washington cog railway; Profile Mountain at Franconia Notch.

KEY EVENTS IN NEW HAMPSHIRE

1603 Mouth of Piscataqua River explored for England by Martin Pring.
1622 (Aug. 10) Region of New Hampshire and Maine granted to John Mason and Sir Ferdinando Gorges by England.
1623 First English settlements established at what are now Rye and Dover.
1629 (Nov. 7) Region divided by Mason and Gorges, with Mason keeping New Hampshire.
1641 (Oct. 9) New Hampshire settlements unite with Massachusetts.
1675–76 Many settlers killed by Indian raids in King Philip's War.
1679 (Sept. 8) New Hampshire made separate royal colony.
1689–1763 In French and Indian War New Hampshire's settlements suffer many raids.
1774 (Dec. 11–12) Patriots capture British Fort William and Mary in Portsmouth, carrying off 100 barrels of gunpowder and 15 cannon.
1776 (Jan. 5) First state constitution adopted.
1776 (June 15) New Hampshire assembly votes for independence from Britain; state's delegates receive honor of being first to vote for Declaration of Independence in Continental Congress on July 4.
1788 (June 21) New Hampshire becomes 9th U.S. state; ratification puts U.S. Constitution into effect.
1803 First cotton textile factory in state built at New Ipswich.
1838 First railroad completed in state.
1852 State abolishes property ownership qualifications for elected state officials.
1963 New Hampshire becomes first state to adopt legal lottery as support for public education.
1978–79 Only state with neither income tax nor sales tax experiences boom as industries move in.
1984 Fastest growth among New England states increases population 6.1% since 1980.

NEW JERSEY

Area: 7,787 square miles; 20,169 sq. km.
Population: 7,515,000 (1984); 7,365,011 (1980).
Capital: Trenton.
Flower: Purple violet.
Tree: Red oak.
Bird: Eastern goldfinch.
Insect: Honeybee. **Animal:** horse.
Song (unofficial): *New Jersey Loyalty Song.*
Nickname: The Garden State.
Motto: Liberty and Prosperity.
Flag: State coat of arms on yellow field.
Leading Industries: Chemicals and pharmaceuticals, machinery, food processing, electronics, industrial research, agriculture (vegetables, dairying, poultry), tourism, gambling.
Climate (Newark): *Normal temperatures:* Jan. high 39 ° F., low 24 ° F.; July high 86 ° F., low 67 ° F. *Normal yearly precipitation:* 41″ (water). *Record snowstorm:* 26″ in December 1947.
Recreation Areas: State parks and recreation areas, 104; numerous beach resorts.
Points of Interest: Morristown National Historical Park; Edison National Historic Site (West Orange); restored colonial village of Batsto (in Wharton Tract State Forest); Walt Whitman House (Camden); Grover Cleveland Museum (Caldwell); Princeton University; Atlantic City boardwalk; Gateway National Recreation Area; Delaware Water Gap north of Columbia, N.J.

KEY EVENTS IN NEW JERSEY

1524 New Jersey coast explored for France by Giovanni da Verrazano.
1609 Delaware Bay and Sandy Hook Bay explored by Henry Hudson for Netherlands.
1623 Dutch establish Fort Nassau near present-day Gloucester.
1660 Dutch build first permanent settlement at Bergen, now in Jersey City.
1664 Dutch surrender New Jersey to England; English found first permanent settlement at Elizabethtown.
1665 New Jersey organized as English colony under Gov. Philip Carteret.
1676 New Jersey divided into two colonies: East Jersey owned by Sir George Carteret and West Jersey owned by William Penn and other Quakers.
1682 East Jersey also acquired by William Penn and other Quakers, but colony remains divided.
1702 (April 26) Proprietors of both Jerseys surrender government control to England's Queen Anne.
1702–38 New Jersey united with own legislature, but administered by royal governor of New York.
1738–76 New Jersey separated from New York with its own royal governor.
1776 (June 17) Patriots arrest royal Gov. William Franklin, son of Benjamin Franklin.
1776 (July 2) First state constitution adopted.
1776–81 In Revolutionary War many battles fought in New Jersey, including Trenton (1776), Princeton (1777), and Monmouth (1778).
1787 (Dec. 18) New Jersey becomes 3d U.S. state, ratifying U.S. Constitution.
1800 Women first vote in Elizabethtown.
1807 Law restricts voting rights to men.
1871 System of free public schools adopted.
1952 New Jersey Turnpike opens, linking New York City and Philadelphia by superhighway.
1976 State income tax adopted to finance public schools.
1978 Legal gambling casino opens in Atlantic City.
1983 Population grows only 2.0% since 1980.

NEW MEXICO

Area: 121,593 square miles; 314,923 sq. km.
Population: 1,424,000 (1984); 1,303,046 (1980).
Capital: Santa Fe.
Flower: Yucca.

NEW MEXICO (continued)

Tree: Piñon.
Bird: Roadrunner.
Gem: Turquoise.
Animal: Black bear.
Fish: Cutthroat trout.
Songs: *O, Fair New Mexico* and *Asi es Nuevo Mejico.*
Nickname: The Land of Enchantment.
Motto: *Crescit Eundo* (It Grows as It Goes).
Flag: Stylized red sun centered on yellow field.
Leading Industries: Mining (petroleum, natural gas, uranium, potash, copper), agriculture (beef cattle, sheep, cotton, vegetables, wheat), food processing, atomic research, forestry.
Climate (Albuquerque): *Normal temperatures:* Jan. high 47° F., low 24° F.; July high 92° F., low 65° F. *Normal yearly precipitation:* 8" (water). *Record snowstorm:* 14.2" in December 1958.
Recreation Areas: National park, 1; national forests, 7; state parks and recreation areas, 34.
Points of Interest: Carlsbad Caverns National Park; Aztec Ruins, Bandelier, Capulin Mountain, Chaco Canyon, El Morro, Fort Union, Fossil Butte, Gran Quivira, Pecos, White Sands, and Gila Cliff Dwellings national monuments; Taos and Acoma pueblos; Santa Fe; Intertribal Indian Ceremonial (Gallup); Bradbury Science Hall (Los Alamos); Gila Wilderness (near Silver City); Glorieta Battle Site (near Pecos).

KEY EVENTS IN NEW MEXICO

c.1528–39 Region explored for Spain by Alvar Núñez Cabeza de Vaca, Estéban, and Marcos de Niza.
1540–42 Spanish conquistador Francisco Vásquez de Coronado conquers Indian pueblos.
1598 First Spanish settlement established on Rio Grande River by Juan de Oñate.
1610 Santa Fe made capital of New Mexico.
1680 Revolt of Pueblo Indians led by Popé drives Spanish settlers out of New Mexico.
1692–96 Spanish rule restored by Diego de Vargas.
1821 Santa Fe Trail pioneered between New Mexico and Missouri by trader William Becknell.
1846–48 U.S. occupies and acquires New Mexico in Mexican War.
1850 (Sept. 9) Territory of New Mexico created.
1854 Southern New Mexico acquired from Mexico in Gadsden Purchase.
1861–62 Confederate troops from Texas capture New Mexico, but Union forces recapture territory; main battles at Apache Canyon and Glorieta Pass.
1862–65 Kit Carson leads New Mexican settlers in subduing Navajo and Apache Indians.
1867 (March 2) Peonage abolished by Congress.
1876–78 Lincoln County War among rival cattlemen ends after Gov. Lew Wallace declares martial law.
1878 (Nov. 30) Railroad reaches New Mexico.
1879–86 Apache Indians raid and massacre settlers until surrender of Chief Geronimo.
1881 Outlaw Billy the Kid killed by Sheriff Pat Garrett near Fort Sumner.
1912 (Jan. 6) New Mexico becomes 47th state.
1916 (March 9) Raid by Mexican bandit Pancho Villa on Columbus kills 17 persons; U.S. troops under Gen. John J. Pershing invade Mexico on March 15 in pursuit of Villa.
1945 (July 16) First atomic bomb successfully tested near Alamogordo.
1984 High growth rate increases population 9.3% since 1980.

NEW YORK

Area: 49,108 square miles; 127,189 sq. km.
Population: 17,735,000 (1984); 17,558,072 (1980).
Capital: Albany.

Flower: Rose.
Tree: Sugar maple.
Bird: Bluebird.
Animal: American beaver.
Fish: Brook trout.
Gem: Garnet. Fossil: Eurypterus remipes.
Nickname: The Empire State.
Motto: *Excelsior* (Ever Upward).
Flag: State coat of arms centered on blue field.
Leading Industries: Manufacturing (leading state), agriculture (dairy products, fruits, vegetables), mining (iron ore, petroleum, salt).
Climate (New York City): *Normal temperatures:* Jan. high 39° F., low 26° F.; July high 85° F., low 68° F. *Normal yearly precipitation:* 40" (water). *Record snowstorm:* 26.4" in December 1947.
Recreation Areas: National seashore, 1; state parks and recreation areas, 169.
Points of Interest: Castle Clinton, Fort Stanwix, and Statue of Liberty national monuments; Niagara Falls; Saratoga National Historical Park; U.S. Military Academy (West Point); national historic sites include homes of F. D. Roosevelt at Hyde Park, of Theodore Roosevelt in Oyster Bay and New York City, Vanderbilt mansion near Hyde Park, and St. Paul's Church; national memorials include General Grant's tomb and Federal Hall in New York City; Fort Ticonderoga; Baseball Hall of Fame (Cooperstown); Finger Lakes, Adirondacks, and Catskill areas; Fire Island National Seashore; Boscobel (Garrison); Gateway National Recreation Area; skyscrapers, museums, theaters, and parks in New York City.

KEY EVENTS IN NEW YORK

1524 New York Bay explored for France by Giovanni da Verrazano.
1609 (July) Northern New York explored and claimed for France by Samuel de Champlain.
1609 (Sept. 11–Oct. 4) Hudson River explored for Dutch by Henry Hudson.
1614 First Dutch trading post, Fort Nassau, built on Castle Island at present-day Albany.
1624 First permanent Dutch settlement established in New Netherland (New York) at Fort Orange (now Albany).
1625 New Amsterdam (New York City) founded by Dutch settlers; Manhattan Island purchased from Indians for about $24 in 1626.
1664 (Sept. 8) Dutch surrender New Amsterdam to English.
1673–74 Dutch reoccupy New York but return it to England in exchange for colony of Surinam in South America.
1683 (Oct. 30) Charter of liberties adopted; freedom of religion guaranteed; taxation to be permitted only by consent of voters.
1689–1763 French and Indian War: New York is battleground for frequent battles against French and their Indian allies.
1735 (Aug. 4) Freedom of press established in trial of John Peter Zenger on basis that truth is not libel.
1775–83 In Revolutionary War British occupy New York City in 1776–83; battles in state include Ticonderoga (1775), Long Island and White Plains (1776), Saratoga (1777), Stony Point (1779).
1777 (April 20) First state constitution adopted; written largely by John Jay.
1788 (July 26) New York becomes 11th U.S. state, ratifying U.S. Constitution.
1789–90 New York City serves as first capital of the United States under Constitution.
1812–14 In War of 1812 many battles fought in state.
1825 (Oct. 26) Erie Canal opens, connecting Hudson River with Great Lakes.
1827 (July 4) Slavery abolished in state.

1831 First railroad opens: Albany to Schenectady.
1832 Cholera kills 4,000 in New York City.
1863 (July 13–16) Riots in New York City protest Civil War draft, killing about 1,000 persons.
1883 (May 24) Brooklyn Bridge opens, longest suspension bridge of its day, with span of 1,595 feet.
1904 (Oct. 27) First subway completed in New York City.
1952 UN headquarters built in New York City.
1964 Verrazano-Narrows Bridge opens across New York Harbor from Brooklyn to Staten Island; suspension span, 4,260 feet.
1974 (April 5) New York City's highest building opens: twin-tower 1,353-foot World Trade Center.
1984 Population grows only 1.0% since 1980.

NORTH CAROLINA

Area: 52,669 square miles; 136,412 sq. km.
Population: 6,165,000 (1984); 5,881,385 (1980).
Capital: Raleigh.
Flower: Dogwood.
Tree: Pine.
Bird: Cardinal.
Mammal: Gray squirrel.
Fish: Channel bass.
Song: *The Old North State.*
Nickname: The Tar Heel State.
Motto: *Esse Quam Videri* (To Be Rather Than to Seem).
Flag: Blue bar to left has letters *NC* (separated by white star) in gold; red and white stripe to right.
Leading Industries: Manufacturing (leading state in textiles and tobacco products), agriculture (tobacco, corn, peanuts, soybeans, broiler chickens), forestry.
Climate (Charlotte): *Normal temperatures:* Jan. high 52 ° F., low 32 ° F.; July high 88 ° F., low 69 ° F. *Normal yearly precipitation:* 43″ (water). *Record snowstorm:* 14″ in February 1902.
Recreation Areas: National park, 1; national forests, 5; national seashores, 2; state parks and recreation areas, 19.
Points of Interest: Great Smoky National Park (partly in Tennessee); the Blue Ridge Parkway; Cape Hatteras National Seashore; Guilford Courthouse and Moores Creek national military parks; Carl Sandburg home (near Hendersonville) and Fort Raleigh national historic sites; Roanoke Island; Wright Brothers National Memorial (Kitty Hawk); Tryon Palace restoration (New Bern); Alamance Battlefield (Burlington); Biltmore Estate (near Asheville); Old Salem restoration (Winston-Salem).

KEY EVENTS IN NORTH CAROLINA

1524 Coast explored for France by Giovanni da Verrazano.
1585–87 English colonists sent by Sir Walter Raleigh unsuccessfully attempt twice to settle Roanoke Island.
1653 First permanent English colonists settle on Roanoke and Chowan rivers; led from Virginia by Roger Green.
1663–65 Carolina region granted to 8 proprietors by England's King Charles II; government established for northern part of region, called Albemarle County, with appointed governor and elected assembly.
1677–78 Culpeper's Rebellion: Colonists led by John Culpeper temporarily overthrow proprietary governor.
1691 Entire Carolina region begins to be ruled by proprietary governors from Charleston (now in S.C.).
1711–13 Tuscarora War: Hundreds of settlers slain in fighting with Tuscarora Indians.
1712 North Carolina separated from South Carolina with own governor.
1718 (Nov. 21) Pirate Blackbeard (Edward Teach) killed in battle near Ocracoke Island.
1729 (July 25) North Carolina becomes royal colony as King George II buys out proprietors.
1771 (May 16) Battle of Alamance: Militia led by Gov. William Tryon defeats uprising by western Regulators who protested lack of representation in legislature.
1775 (May 20) Mecklenburg Declaration of Independence said to have been adopted by patriots in Mecklenburg County.
1776 (April 12) First colony to instruct Continental Congress delegates to vote for independence.
1776 (Dec. 18) First state constitution adopted.
1776–81 In Revolutionary War major battles in state include Moores Creek Bridge (Feb. 27, 1776) and Guilford Courthouse (March 15, 1781).
1789 (Nov. 21) North Carolina becomes 12th U.S. state, ratifying U.S. Constitution.
1801–02 Gold discovered on Meadow Creek in Cabarrus County; state leads in gold production until 1850s.
1861 (May 20) State secedes, joins Confederacy.
1861–65 In Civil War many battles fought in state until surrender of Confederate Gen. Joseph E. Johnston to Union Gen. William T. Sherman near Durham (April 26, 1865).
1868 (June 25) State readmitted to Union.
1890 American Tobacco Company founded at Durham by James Buchanan Duke; cigarette manufacturing becomes leading industry in state.
1903 (Dec. 17) First airplane flight by Orville and Wilbur Wright at Kitty Hawk.
1980 North Carolina displaces Massachusetts as 10th-ranking state in population.
1984 Population grows 4.8% since 1980.

NORTH DAKOTA

Area: 70,702 square miles; 183,118 sq. km.
Population: 686,000 (1984); 652,717 (1980).
Capital: Bismarck.
Flower: Wild prairie rose.
Tree: American elm.
Bird: Western meadowlark.
Stone: Teredo petrified wood.
Fish: Northern pike.
Song: *North Dakota Hymn.*
March: *Spirit of the Land.*
Nicknames: The Sioux State; The Flickertail State.
Motto: Liberty and Union, Now and Forever, One and Inseparable.
Flag: Modified Seal of U.S. on blue field.
Leading Industries: Agriculture (wheat, flaxseed, barley, rye, beef cattle, sheep, hogs), food processing, mining (petroleum, lignite).
Climate (Bismarck): *Normal temperatures:* Jan. high 19 ° F., low –3 ° F.; July high 84 ° F., low 57 ° F. *Normal yearly precipitation:* 16″ (water). *Record snowstorm:* 15.5″ in March 1966.
Recreation Areas: State parks and recreation areas, 20.
Points of Interest: International Peace Garden (near Dunseith); Fort Union Trading Post (partly in Montana) National Historic Site; Theodore Roosevelt National Memorial Park; State Capitol (Bismarck); Fort Lincoln State Park (south of Mandan); Fort Abercrombie; Lake Sakakawea; Slant Village restoration (near Mandan); Badlands.

KEY EVENTS IN NORTH DAKOTA

1738 Region explored for France by Pierre Gaultier de Varennes, Sieur de La Vérendrye.
1803 U.S. acquires most of North Dakota in Louisiana Purchase from France.
1804–06 Region explored for U.S. by Meriwether Lewis and William Clark; Fort Mandan built 1804.
1812 First settlement established at Pembina by Scottish and Irish families from Canada.

NORTH DAKOTA (*continued*)

1818 Northeastern part of state acquired by U.S. by treaty with Britain.
1823 (Aug. 8) U.S. takes possession of Pembina.
1832 Missouri River steamboat reaches Fort Union.
1861 (March 2) Territory of Dakota created.
1863–64 Battles fought between U.S. troops and Sioux Indians.
1872 Bismarck founded.
1872 Construction begun on railroad across state.
1889 (Nov. 2) Becomes 39th U.S. state.
1912 First presidential preference primary held.
1914 Referendum process adopted.
1920 Recall procedure adopted.
1951 Petroleum discovered near Tioga.
1960 Garrison Dam completed, forming Lake Sakakawea.
1977 Bingo and lottery gambling legalized.
1981 (July 1) Blackjack gambling legalized in bars, restaurants and motels.
1984 Population grows 5.2% since 1980.

OHIO

Area: 41,330 square miles; 107,043 sq. km.
Population: 10,752,000 (1984); 10,797,624 (1980).
Capital: Columbus.
Flower: Scarlet carnation.
Tree: Buckeye.
Bird: Cardinal.
Insect: Ladybug.
Stone: Ohio flint. **Beverage:** Tomato juice.
Song: *Beautiful Ohio.*
Nickname: The Buckeye State.
Motto: With God, All Things Are Possible.
Flag: White-bordered red circle and blue stars on blue triangle to left; red and white stripes to right.
Leading Industries: Manufacturing (transportation equipment, machinery, metals, rubber products), agriculture (hogs, beef cattle, sheep, dairy products), mining (coal, petroleum).
Climate (Cleveland): *Normal temperatures:* Jan. high 33 ° F., low 20 ° F.; July high 82 ° F., low 61 ° F. *Normal yearly precipitation:* 35" (water). *Record snowstorm:* 17.4" in November 1913.
Recreation Areas: National forest, 1; state parks and recreation areas, 62.
Points of Interest: Mound City Group National Monument (Indian burial grounds); Perry's Victory International Peace Memorial; Presidents' homes: Grant (Point Pleasant), Taft (Cincinnati), Hayes (Fremont), Harding (Marion), and Garfield (Mentor); birthplace of Thomas A. Edison (Milan); Fort Recovery; Campus Martius Museum (Marietta); Pro Football Hall of Fame (Canton); Schoenbrunn village, New Philadelphia.

KEY EVENTS IN OHIO

1669–70 Region explored for France by Robert Cavelier, Sieur de La Salle.
1763 Britain wins region in French and Indian War.
1772 Moravian settlement at Schoenbrunn near present-day New Philadelphia; abandoned in 1776.
1780 (Aug. 6–8) Shawnee Indian villages of Chillicothe and Piqua destroyed by George Rogers Clark.
1782 (March 8) Massacre of 96 Christian Indians by frontiersmen at Gnadenhutten.
1782 (June 4–6) U.S. Col. William Crawford and 480 militia defeated by British and Indians near Upper Sandusky; Crawford tortured to death on June 11.
1783 Region acquired by U.S. in Revolutionary War.
1788 (April 7) First permanent settlement established at Marietta, capital of Northwest Territory.
1790–95 Severe fighting with Indians; major battle won by Maj. Gen. Anthony Wayne at Fallen Timbers near present-day Maumee (Aug. 20, 1794).

1803 (March 1) Ohio becomes 17th U.S. state.
1812–14 In War of 1812 frontier forts withstand sieges; Commodore Oliver H. Perry defeats British in Battle of Lake Erie (Sept. 10, 1813).
1832 Ohio and Erie Canal completed.
1845 Miami and Erie Canal connects Toledo and Cincinnati.
1852 Railroad reaches Cleveland from Pittsburgh.
1863 (July 26) Raiding Confederate Gen. John H. Morgan captured near New Lisbon.
1913 (March 25–27) Floods in Ohio and Indiana kill 732 persons, cause over $180 million in damage.
1967 First black mayor elected by major U.S. city: Carl B. Stokes, in Cleveland.
1971 State income tax adopted.
1984 Population decreases 0.4% since 1980.

OKLAHOMA

Area: 69,956 square miles; 181,185 sq. km.
Population: 3,298,000 (1984); 3,025,495 (1980).
Capital: Oklahoma City.
Flower: Mistletoe.
Tree: Redbud.
Bird: Scissor-tailed flycatcher.
Fish: White bass.
Stone: Barite rose (rose rock).
Animal: American buffalo.
Reptile: Mountain boomer lizard.
Song: *Oklahoma.*
Nickname: The Sooner State.
Motto: *Labor Omnia Vincit* (Labor Conquers All Things).
Flag: Symbols above "Oklahoma" on blue field.
Leading Industries: Manufacturing and food processing, oil refining, agriculture (beef cattle, wheat), oil and natural-gas mining.
Climate (Oklahoma City): *Normal temperatures:* Jan. high 48 ° F., low 26 ° F.; July high 93 ° F., low 70 ° F. *Normal yearly precipitation:* 31" (water). *Record snowstorm:* 11.3" in March 1924.
Recreation Areas: National park, 1; national forest, 1; national recreation area, 1; state parks and recreation areas, 76.
Points of Interest: Lake Texoma recreation area; Philbrook Art Center (Tulsa); Will Rogers Memorial (Claremore); Indian City (Andarko); Fort Sill Military Reservation (Lawton); National Cowboy Hall of Fame and Oklahoma Historical Society (Oklahoma City); Chickasaw National Recreation Area (formerly Platt National Park and Arbuckle National Recreation Area).

KEY EVENTS IN OKLAHOMA

1541 Region explored for Spain by Francisco Vásquez de Coronado.
1803 U.S. acquires most of Oklahoma in Louisiana Purchase from France.
1821 Santa Fe Trail pioneered across region by American trader William Becknell.
1823–42 Eastern Indian tribes forced to move to Oklahoma region, then known as Indian Territory.
1845 Western Panhandle region of Oklahoma acquired by U.S. with annexation of Texas.
1889 (April 22) U.S. opens part of Oklahoma to settlement; some 50,000 settlers rush in on first day.
1890 (May 2) Territory of Oklahoma created.
1893 (Sept. 16) Cherokee Outlet opened to settlement; 50,000 to 100,000 settlers rush into area.
1897 First major oil well produces at Bartlesville.
1907 (Nov. 16) Oklahoma becomes 46th U.S. state.
1934–35 Drought develops "dust bowl"; farmers abandon farms; "Okies" move to California.
1970 Arkansas River made navigable, turning Tulsa and Muskogee into important river ports.
1984 Population grows 9.0% since 1980.

OREGON

Area: 97,073 square miles; 251,417 sq. km.
Population: 2,674,000 (1984); 2,633,149 (1980).
Capital: Salem.
Flower: Oregon grape.
Tree: Douglas fir.
Bird: Western meadowlark.
Stone: Thunder egg.
Animal: Beaver.
Fish: Chinook salmon.
Song: *Oregon, My Oregon.*
Nickname: The Beaver State.
Motto: The Union.
Flag: State seal with "State of Oregon" above it on blue field.
Leading Industries: Lumbering and forestry, food processing, manufacturing, agriculture (beef cattle, dairy products, wheat, vegetables, fruits, nuts, flowers).
Climate (Portland): *Normal temperatures:* Jan. high 44 ° F., low 33 ° F.; July high 79 ° F., low 55 ° F. *Normal yearly precipitation:* 38″ (water). *Record snowstorm:* 16″ in January 1937.
Recreation Areas: National park, 1; national forests, 15; state parks and recreation areas, 235.
Points of Interest: Crater Lake National Park; Mt. Hood; Oregon Caves National Monument; Oregon Dunes; Cape Perpetua (in Siuslaw National Forest); Columbia River gorge between The Dalles and Troutdale; Bonneville Dam; Hells Canyon; Fort Clatsop National Memorial; McLoughlin House National Historic Site; Picture Gorge and John Day Fossil Beds near Dayville; Sea Lion Caves near Florence.

KEY EVENTS IN OREGON

1500s–1600s Spanish and English sailors sight coast; Sir Francis Drake in 1579.
1770s–1780s U.S. and British ships visit coast, trading with Indians for furs.
1792 (May 7) Columbia River discovered and named by U.S. Capt. Robert Gray, establishing U.S. claim to area.
1805 Fort Clatsop built by Meriwether Lewis and William Clark near mouth of Columbia River.
1811 Astoria established as first American settlement by fur trader John Jacob Astor.
1812–13 Oregon Trail pioneered to Missouri by fur trader Robert Stuart.
1818 (Oct. 20) U.S. and Britain sign convention agreeing on joint control of Oregon region; renewed in 1827.
1819 (Feb. 2) U.S. and Spain sign Adams-Onís Treaty: Spain gives up claim to Oregon region.
1825–46 Region controlled by Hudson's Bay Company's John McLoughlin; becomes known as "Father of Oregon."
1840s American settlers arrive by hundreds along Oregon Trail.
1846 (Aug. 5) Oregon Treaty goes into effect: Britain gives up claims to Oregon region.
1848 (Aug. 14) Territory of Oregon created.
1851–58 Indian Wars in eastern Oregon.
1859 (Feb. 14) Oregon becomes 33d U.S. state.
1877–78 Fighting by settlers with Nez Percé, Paiute, and Bannock Indians.
1902 (June 2) First statewide initiative and referendum law adopted.
1908 First statewide recall law adopted.
1912 Women given right to vote.
1937 Bonneville Dam completed on Columbia River.
1964 Worst floods in state's history.
1972 First environmental "bottle law" adopted, outlawing nonreturnable beverage containers.
1980 Oregon moves ahead of Mississippi to rank 30th in population among the states.
1984 Population grows 1.6% since 1980.

PENNSYLVANIA

Area: 45,308 square miles; 117,347 sq. km.
Population: 11,901,000 (1984); 11,864,751 (1980).
Capital: Harrisburg.
Flower: Mountain laurel.
Tree: Hemlock.
Bird: Ruffed grouse.
Dog: Great Dane.
Animal: Whitetail deer.
Fish: Brook trout. **Insect:** Firefly.
Nickname: The Keystone State.
Motto: Virtue, Liberty and Independence.
Flag: Gold-bordered blue field with state coat of arms flanked by horse on either side.
Leading Industries: Manufacturing (steel, machinery, metal products), agriculture (dairy products, beef cattle, poultry, corn, mushrooms), mining (coal, petroleum, natural gas).
Climate (Philadelphia): *Normal temperatures:* Jan. high 40 ° F., low 24 ° F.; July high 87 ° F., low 67 ° F. *Normal yearly precipitation:* 40″ (water). *Record snowstorm:* 21″ in December 1909.
Recreation Areas: National forest, 1; state parks and recreation areas, 152.
Points of Interest: Gettysburg National Military Park; Valley Forge National Historical Park; Independence National Historical Park (in Philadelphia); Delaware Water Gap National Recreation Area; Pennsylvania Dutch region; Fort Necessity National Battlefield; national historic sites include Eisenhower farm near Gettysburg, Gloria Dei Church, Hopewell Village (near Reading); national memorials include Benjamin Franklin, Johnstown Flood, and Thaddeus Kosciusko; Cloisters restoration in Ephrata. Oliver Hazard Perry's flagship *Niagara* from War of 1812 (at Erie); Pennsylvania Farm Museum of Landis Valley (near Lancaster).

KEY EVENTS IN PENNSYLVANIA

1609 (Aug. 28) Delaware Bay explored for Netherlands by Henry Hudson.
1643 First Swedish settlements established on Tinicum Island in Schuylkill River near present-day Philadelphia, and at Upland (now Chester).
1655 Dutch from New York capture New Sweden.
1664 England acquires region with capture of New York.
1681 Philadelphia surveyed and laid out by Thomas Holme as capital of Pennsylvania.
1681 (March 14) Pennsylvania granted to William Penn by King Charles II.
1682 (Oct. 29) William Penn arrives at Upland, renaming it Chester.
1754–63 French and Indian War: Begins with skirmish at Great Meadows, Pa., between Lt. Col. George Washington and French on May 28; Washington surrenders Fort Necessity, Pa., to French (July 4, 1754).
1755 (July 9) British Maj. Gen. Edward Braddock killed and army routed by French near Fort Duquesne (Pittsburgh).
1758 (Nov. 25) British capture Fort Duquesne; rename it Fort Pitt.
1763 Indian Chief Pontiac wages war on frontier settlers.
1775–83 In Revolutionary War Congress meets in Philadelphia for most of period; major battles in state include Brandywine and Germantown (1777); Army winters at Valley Forge (1777–78).
1776 (Sept. 28) First state constitution adopted at convention presided over by Benjamin Franklin.
1787 (Dec. 12) Pennsylvania becomes 2d U.S. state, ratifying U.S. Constitution.
1790–1800 Philadelphia serves as capital of U.S.
1792 State purchases triangle of land on Lake Erie.
1794 Whisky Rebellion in western Pennsylvania as

PENNSYLVANIA *(continued)*

farmers protest federal whisky taxes; put down by militia.

1795　First paved turnpike in U.S. completed from Philadelphia to Lancaster.

1811　(Oct. 29)　First Ohio River steamboat leaves Pittsburgh for New Orleans.

1829　First railroad begins operation.

1859　First successful oil well in U.S. drilled near Titusville by Edwin Drake.

1863　(July 1–3)　Battle of Gettysburg: Turning point of Civil War as Union army defeats invasion of Pennsylvania by Confederate army of Gen. Robert E. Lee.

1889　(May 31)　Flood caused by burst dam at Johnstown kills 2,209 persons.

1957　First full-scale atomic energy plant in U.S. to produce electricity opens at Shippingport.

1971　State income tax adopted.

1975　State drops from 3d to 4th in population rank among states.

1984　Population grows only 0.3% since 1980.

RHODE ISLAND

Area: 1,212 square miles; 3,140 sq. km.
Population: 962,000 (1984); 947,154 (1980).
Capital: Providence.
Flower: Violet.
Tree: Red maple.
Bird: Rhode Island red.
Rock: Cumberlandite.
Mineral: Bowenite.
Song: *Rhode Island.*
Nickname: Little Rhody.
Motto: Hope.
Flag: White field with gold anchor with state motto underneath, surrounded by 13 gold stars.
Leading Industries: Manufacturing (jewelry, silverware, textiles, machinery), food processing, agriculture (dairy products, vegetables, poultry).
Climate (Providence): *Normal temperatures:* Jan. high 36 ° F., low 21 ° F.; July high 81 ° F., low 63 ° F. *Normal yearly precipitation:* 43″ (water). *Record snowstorm:* 18.3″ in February 1961.
Recreation Areas: State parks and recreation areas, 85.
Points of Interest: Roger Williams National Memorial (Providence); Samuel Slater's Mill (Pawtucket); Touro Synagogue National Historic Site (Newport); Gilbert Stuart birthplace (North Kingstown); Gen. Nathanael Greene homestead (Coventry); Vanderbilt mansions (Newport); Block Island; Narragansett Pier.

KEY EVENTS IN RHODE ISLAND

1524　Narragansett Bay explored for France by Giovanni da Verrazano.

1614　Explored for Dutch by Adriaen Block.

1636　(June)　First English settlement established at Providence by Roger Williams, providing religious freedom.

1644　(March 14)　England grants patent for colony of Providence Plantations; four settlements in Rhode Island unite under this patent in 1647.

1663　(July 8)　Colony of Rhode Island and Providence Plantations granted new charter by King Charles II; charter remains state's constitution until 1843.

1675–76　King Philip's War: Many settlers killed in fighting with Indians; Wampanoag chief King Philip slain by settlers near present-day Bristol.

1772　(June 9)　Patriots destroy British revenue schooner *Gaspée* in Narragansett Bay.

1776　(May 4)　Independence from Britain declared by Rhode Island's legislature.

1776–79　British occupy Newport, defeating American-French effort to dislodge them in August 1778.

1787　State refuses to send delegates to U.S. Constitu-

tional Convention in Philadelphia.

1790　(May 29)　Rhode Island becomes 13th U.S. state, ratifying U.S. Constitution by narrow vote of 34 to 32.

1790　(Dec. 21)　First textile factory in U.S. begins operation at Pawtucket, built by Samuel Slater.

1842　Dorr's Rebellion: Thomas Dorr and followers set up own state government protesting property requirements for voting.

1870　Imprisonment for debt abolished.

1888　Property qualifications for voters abolished.

1969　Newport Bridge built across Narragansett Bay with 1,600-foot suspension span.

1983　State drops to 42d in population rank.

1984　Population grows only 1.6% since 1980.

SOUTH CAROLINA

Area: 31,113 square miles; 80,582 sq. km.
Population: 3,300,000 (1984); 3,122,814 (1980).
Capital: Columbia.
Flower: Carolina jessamine.
Tree: Palmetto.
Bird: Carolina wren.
Stone: Blue granite.
Song: *Carolina.*
Nickname: The Palmetto State.
Mottoes: *Animis Opibusque Parati* (Prepared in Mind and Resources) and *Dum Spiro Spero* (While I Breathe, I Hope).
Flag: Blue field with centered white palmetto and crescent in upper left corner.
Leading Industries: Manufacturing (textiles, chemicals, machinery), agriculture (tobacco, soybeans, cotton, beef cattle, hogs), forestry.
Climate (Columbia): *Normal temperatures:* Jan. high 57 ° F., low 34 ° F.; July high 92 ° F., low 70 ° F. *Normal yearly precipitation:* 46″ (water). *Record snowstorm:* 15.7″ in February 1973.
Recreation Areas: National forests, 2; state parks and recreation areas, 38; Atlantic beach resorts.
Points of Interest: Fort Sumter National Monument, Fort Moultrie, Fort Johnson, and aircraft carrier USS *Yorktown,* in Charleston Harbor; Cowpens National Battlefield; Kings Mountain National Military Park; Middleton, Magnolia, and Cypress gardens, Charleston; Brookgreen Gardens, Georgetown; Camden and Eutaw Springs battlefields; Hilton Head resorts.

KEY EVENTS IN SOUTH CAROLINA

1521　Coast explored for Spain by Francisco de Gordillo.

1526–27　Spaniards unsuccessfully try to found colony near present-day Georgetown; led by Lucas Vásquez de Ayllón.

1562–64　French Huguenots unsuccessfully try to colonize Parris Island near Port Royal.

1566–1650　Spaniards occupy Port Royal (which they call Santa Elena).

1663–65　Carolina region granted to eight proprietors by England's King Charles II.

1670　First English settlement established at Albemarle Point on west bank of Ashley River; in 1680 settlement (renamed Charles Town) moves across river; town renamed Charlestown in 1783.

1706　French-Spanish attack on Charles Town driven off.

1711–13　Indian war between settlers and Tuscaroras.

1712　South Carolina separated from North Carolina, each with own governor.

1715　About 400 settlers killed in war with Yamassee Indians.

1719　(Nov. 28)　Rebellion against proprietary government; colonists choose James Moore as governor.

1721　(May 29)　New royal governor takes office.

SOUTH CAROLINA (continued)

1729 (July 25) **South Carolina becomes royal colony** as King George II buys out 7 of 8 proprietors.
1775 (Sept. 15) **Last royal governor flees** to British warship.
1776 (March 26) **First temporary constitution** adopted; new constitution adopted March 19, 1778.
1776–81 **In Revolutionary War** state suffers extensive fighting; British attacks on Charles Town beaten back on June 28, 1776, and May 11–12, 1779; British capture Charles Town on May 12, 1780, after two-month siege; other major battles: Stono Ferry on June 20, 1779, Camden on Aug. 16, 1780, Kings Mountain on Oct. 7, 1780, Cowpens on Jan. 17, 1781, Hobkirk's Hill on April 25, 1781, and Eutaw Springs on Sept. 8, 1781.
1788 (May 23) **South Carolina becomes 8th U.S. state,** ratifying U.S. Constitution.
1832 (Nov. 24) **Ordinance of Nullification** adopted, forbidding collection of federal tariffs in state; repealed in 1833 after President Andrew Jackson threatens force.
1860 (Dec. 20) **First state to secede from Union.**
1861 (April 12) **Civil War begins** as South Carolina troops attack federal Fort Sumter in Charleston Harbor.
1861–65 **In Civil War** Charleston withstands Union siege from March 1863 to February 1865; in 1865 Union Gen. William T. Sherman marches across state destroying plantations and burning capital city Columbia.
1868 (June 25) **Readmitted to Union.**
1877 (March) **Federal troop occupation ends.**
1941 **Santee Dam completed,** providing hydroelectric power for Charleston area.
1953 **Huge $1.4 billion Savannah River plant** near Aiken begins production of atomic materials.
1975–79 **First elected Republican governor** since Reconstruction era: James B. Edwards.
1984 **Population increases** 5.7% since 1980.

SOUTH DAKOTA

Area: 77,116 square miles; 199,729 sq. km.
Population: 706,000 (1984); 690,768 (1980).
Capital: Pierre.
Flower: Pasqueflower.
Tree: Black Hills spruce.
Bird: Ringnecked pheasant.
Stone: Black Hills gold.
Animal: Coyote.
Song: *Hail, South Dakota.*
Nickname: The Coyote State.
Motto: Under God the People Rule.
Flag: Blue field with centered yellow sun encircled by "South Dakota the Sunshine State."
Leading Industries: Agriculture (beef cattle, hogs, sheep, wheat, corn, soybeans), food processing, mining (gold, uranium, petroleum), tourism.
Climate (Sioux Falls): *Normal temperatures:* Jan. high 25° F., low 4° F.; July high 85° F., low 62° F. *Normal yearly precipitation:* 25" (water). *Record snowstorm:* 26" on Feb. 17–18, 1962.
Recreation Areas: National park, 1; national forests, 2; state parks and recreation areas, 1.
Points of Interest: Black Hills region (including Wind Cave National Park, Mt. Rushmore National Memorial, and Jewel Cave National Monument); Badlands National Monument near Rapid City; Deadwood; Crazy Horse memorial near Custer; Corn Palace in Mitchell.

KEY EVENTS IN SOUTH DAKOTA

1743 (March 30) **Region claimed for France** by Louis-Joseph and François de La Vérendrye; plant lead plate at present-day Fort Pierre (plate discovered 1913).
1803 **U.S. acquires region** in Louisiana Purchase.
1804–06 **Region explored for U.S.** by Meriwether Lewis and William Clark.
1817 **Fort Pierre established** as fur trading post.

1831 **Missouri River steamboat** reaches Fort Pierre.
1861 (March 2) **Territory of Dakota** created.
1873 **Railroad** reaches capital at Yankton.
1874–75 **Gold discovered** in Black Hills.
1876 **Frontiersman Wild Bill Hickok** shot to death in Deadwood saloon.
1889 (Nov. 2) **Becomes 40th U.S. state.**
1890 (Dec. 29) **Wounded Knee Massacre** of 300 captive Sioux Indians by federal troops; last Indian war in West.
1930–40 **Drought, grasshoppers, and depression** bankrupt many farmers; about 50,000 leave state.
1963 **Oahe Dam** completed on Missouri River at Pierre.
1972 (June 9–10) **Flood at Rapid City** kills 242 persons.
1973 (Feb. 27–May 8) **Siege of Wounded Knee:** Indians occupy village to protest federal Indian policies.
1984 **Population grows** 2.2% since 1980, remains 45th in population rank.

TENNESSEE

Area: 42,144 square miles; 109,151 sq. km.
Population: 4,717,000 (1984); 4,591,120 (1980).
Capital: Nashville.
Flower: Iris.
Wildflower: Passionflower.
Tree: Tulip poplar.
Bird: Mockingbird.
Animal: Raccoon.
Stone: Agate. **Rock:** Limestone.
Songs: *When It's Iris Time in Tennessee; The Tennessee Waltz; My Homeland, Tennessee;* and *My Tennessee.*
Nickname: The Volunteer State.
Motto: Agriculture and Commerce.
Flag: Three white stars in white-bordered blue circle on red field, with narrow white bar and blue bar on right.
Leading Industries: Manufacturing (chemicals, electrical equipment, clothing), food processing, agriculture (dairy products, beef cattle, hogs, soybeans, tobacco, corn, cotton), mining (coal, zinc, phosphate).
Climate (Memphis): *Normal temperatures:* Jan. high 49° F., low 32° F.; July high 92° F., low 72° F. *Normal yearly precipitation:* 49" (water). *Record snowstorm:* 18" in March 1892.
Recreation Areas: National park, 1; national forest, 1; state parks and recreation areas, 37.
Points of Interest: Great Smoky Mountains National Park; Cumberland Gap National Historical Park; Rock City Gardens (on Lookout Mountain, near Chattanooga); Chickamauga and Chattanooga, Fort Donelson, and Shiloh national military parks; The Hermitage (home of Andrew Jackson, Nashville); Andrew Johnson National Historic Site (Greeneville); American Museum of Science & Energy (Oak Ridge); Stones River National Battlefield; Parthenon reproduction (Nashville); Grand Ole Opry House and Opryland entertainment park (near Nashville).

KEY EVENTS IN TENNESSEE

1540–41 **Region explored for Spain** by Hernando de Soto, discovering Mississippi River.
1673 **Eastern region explored for Virginia** by James Needham and Gabriel Arthur; western part for France by Louis Joliet and Jacques Marquette.
1682 **Region claimed for France** by Robert Cavelier, Sieur de La Salle, who builds Fort Prud'homme near present-day Memphis.
1763 **Britain acquires region** in French and Indian War, as part of colony of North Carolina.
1784–87 **State of Franklin** formed by settlers, electing John Sevier as governor; disbanded when region allowed to elect representatives to North Carolina legislature.
1790 (May 26) **Territory South of the River Ohio**

TENNESSEE *(continued)*

created; William Blount appointed governor (Aug. 7).
1796 (June 1) Tennessee becomes 16th U.S. state.
1797 (July 7) Tennessee's U.S. Sen. William Blount becomes first person impeached (for trying to stir Indian war against Spain); expelled by U.S. Senate; impeachment dismissed in 1799.
1818 (Oct. 19) Western Tennessee purchased from Chickasaw Indians in treaty negotiated by Gen. Andrew Jackson.
1857 (March 27) Memphis and Charleston Railroad completed from Atlantic Ocean to Mississippi River.
1861 (June 24) Governor proclaims secession after people vote June 8 to join Confederacy: east Tennessee supports Union; U.S. Sen. Andrew Johnson retains seat.
1861–65 In Civil War many battles fought in state, including Fort Henry, Fort Donelson, Shiloh, Stones River, Chattanooga, Franklin, and Nashville.
1866 (July 24) Tennessee becomes first Confederate state readmitted to Union.
1878–79 Yellow-fever epidemic kills over 5,000 persons in Memphis, over fourth of population.
1933 (May 18) Tennessee Valley Authority (TVA) created by Congress, providing cheap electric power.
1942 Oak Ridge atomic-energy plant built.
1968 (April 4) Assassination of black civil-rights leader Martin Luther King Jr. at Memphis.
1979 Gov. Ray Blanton removed from office after pardoning 52 prisoners; convicted in 1981 of 11 counts of extortion, fraud, and conspiracy.
1984 Population grows 2.7% since 1980.

TEXAS

Area: 266,807 square miles; 691,026 sq. km.
Population: 15,989,000 (1984); 14,227,574 (1980).
Capital: Austin.
Flower: Bluebonnet.
Tree: Pecan.
Bird: Mockingbird.
Gem: Topaz. **Stone:** Palmwood. **Grass:** Side oats grama. **Dish:** Chili.
Song: *Texas, Our Texas.*
Nickname: The Lone Star State.
Motto: Friendship.
Flag: Lone star on blue bar on left, with red and white stripes to right.
Leading Industries: Manufacturing (chemicals, transportation equipment, petroleum refining), food processing, mining (petroleum, natural gas, sulfur, salt), agriculture (beef cattle, grain, cotton, poultry, dairy products).
Climate (Houston): *Normal temperatures:* Jan. high 63 ° F., low 42 ° F.; July high 94 ° F., low 73 ° F. *Normal yearly precipitation:* 48" (water). *Record snowstorm:* 20" on Feb. 14–15, 1895.
Recreation Areas: National parks, 2; national forests, 4; national recreation areas, 2; national seashore, 1; state parks and recreation areas, 75.
Points of Interest: Padre Island National Seashore; Big Bend and Guadalupe Mountains national parks; Gulf Coast resort areas; Alamo (San Antonio); state capital (Austin); King Ranch (near Kingsville); Lyndon B. Johnson Space Center (Houston); Amistad and Lake Meredith national recreation areas; Alibates Quarries and Texas Panhandle Culture National Monument; national historic sites include Fort Davis, Lyndon B. Johnson ranch, San Jose Mission; Chamizal National Memorial; battleship USS *Texas* in Houston.

KEY EVENTS IN TEXAS

1519 Coast explored for Spain by Alonso Alvarez de Piñeda.
1682 First Spanish settlement established at Ysleta near present-day El Paso.

1685 French build Fort St. Louis at Matagorda Bay.
1821 Americans led by Stephen F. Austin settle along Brazos River in Mexican territory.
1836 (Feb. 23–March 6) Siege of Alamo: 187 Texans and frontiersmen fight to death against Mexicans.
1836 (March 2) Texas independence declared.
1836 (April 21) Battle of San Jacinto: Gen. Sam Houston defeats Mexicans; captures Mexican Gen. Antonio López de Santa Anna.
1836 (Oct. 22) Independent Republic of Texas installs Sam Houston as president.
1845 (Dec. 29) Texas becomes 28th U.S. state.
1846–48 Mexican War fought by U.S. and Mexico.
1861 (Feb. 23) Texans vote to secede; Gov. Sam Houston, who opposes secession, deposed March 20.
1861–65 In Civil War several battles fought in state; last Confederate army under Gen. Kirby Smith surrenders on May 26, 1865.
1866 Chisholm Trail for cattle drives pioneered by Jesse Chisholm from Texas to Kansas.
1870 (March 30) Texas readmitted to Union.
1900 (Sept. 8) Hurricane and tidal wave kills 6,000 persons at Galveston.
1901 Spindletop oil field opens near Beaumont.
1962 Space center built in Houston.
1963 (Nov. 22) President John F. Kennedy assassinated in Dallas.
1979 First Republican governor in 105 years takes office: William P. Clements Jr.
1984 Population grows 12.4% since 1980 with fifth highest growth rate among the states.

UTAH

Area: 84,899 square miles; 219,888 sq. km.
Population: 1,652,000 (1984); 1,461,037 (1980).
Capital: Salt Lake City.
Flower: Sego lily.
Tree: Blue spruce.
Bird: Sea gull.
Gem: Topaz.
Song: *Utah, We Love Thee.*
Nickname: The Beehive State.
Motto: Industry.
Flag: State seal in gold circle on blue field.
Leading Industries: Manufacturing (primary metals, transportation equipment, machinery), food processing, mining (copper, petroleum, gold, iron, lead, coal, uranium, zinc), agriculture (beef cattle, dairy products, hay, wheat, sugar beets, fruits, vegetables).
Climate (Salt Lake City): *Normal temperatures:* Jan. high 37 ° F., low 19 ° F.; July high 93 ° F., low 61 ° F. *Normal yearly precipitation:* 15" (water). *Record snowstorm:* 18.1" in December 1972.
Recreation Areas: National parks, 5; national forests, 9; national recreation area, 1; state parks and recreation areas, 44.
Points of Interest: Bryce Canyon, Zion, Canyonlands, Arches, and Capitol Reef national parks; Cedar Breaks, Natural Bridges, Rainbow Bridge, Hovenweep, Timpanogos Cave, and Dinosaur national monuments; Mormon Tabernacle (Salt Lake City); Great Salt Lake; Glen Canyon; Monument Valley; Flaming Gorge; Golden Spike National Historic Site; Glen Canyon National Recreation Area.

KEY EVENTS IN UTAH

1776 Region explored for Spain by Franciscan friars Silvestre Vélez de Escalante and Francisco Atanasio Domínguez.
1824–25 Great Salt Lake discovered by American frontiersman James Bridger.
1847 (July 21–24) Mormons reach Great Salt Lake under leadership of Brigham Young.

1848 Grasshopper plague wiped out by sea gulls.

1848 (Feb. 2) U.S. acquires Utah in treaty ending Mexican War.

1849 State of Deseret organized by Mormons.

1850 (Sept. 9) Territory of Utah created by Congress.

1857–58 Utah War: President Buchanan removes Brigham Young as territorial governor, sends federal troops to take control of Utah from Mormons.

1862 (July 1) Polygamy practiced by Mormons made crime by act of Congress; much trouble ensues for several decades as federal authorities seek to enforce law.

1869 (May 10) First transcontinental railroad completed with driving of golden spike at Promontory Point, Utah.

1890 (Oct. 6) Mormon Church renounces polygamy.

1894 (Sept. 7) Pardon and restoration of civil rights proclaimed by President Cleveland for persons disfranchised by antipolygamy laws.

1896 (Jan. 4) Utah becomes 45th U.S. state.

1916 First non-Mormon elected governor: Democrat Simon Bamberger.

1952 Uranium discovered near Moab.

1984 Population grows 13.0% since 1980.

VERMONT

Area: 9,614 square miles; 24,900 sq. km.
Population: 530,000 (1984); 511,456 (1980).
Capital: Montpelier.
Flower: Red clover.
Tree: Sugar maple.
Animal: Morgan horse. **Insect:** Honeybee.
Bird: Hermit thrush.
Song: *Hail, Vermont!*
Nickname: The Green Mountain State.
Motto: Freedom and Unity.
Flag: State coat of arms centered on blue field.
Climate (Burlington): *Normal temperatures:* Jan. high 26 ° F., low 8 ° F.; July high 81 ° F., low 59 ° F. *Normal yearly precipitation:* 33 ″ (water). *Record snowstorm:* 24.2 ″ in January 1934.
Leading Industries: Manufacturing (machinery, paper), food processing, tourism, agriculture (dairy products, poultry, potatoes, apples, maple sugar), mining (granite, marble).
Recreation Areas: National forest, 1; state parks and recreation areas, 72; winter sports areas, 5.
Points of Interest: Green Mountain National Forest; Lake Champlain; Bennington Battle Monument; Calvin Coolidge Homestead (Plymouth); Shelburne Museum; Marble Exhibit (Proctor).

KEY EVENTS IN VERMONT

1609 Region explored and claimed for France by Samuel de Champlain.

1666 First French settlement established at Fort Sainte Anne on Isle La Motte in Lake Champlain.

1724 First English settlers from Massachusetts establish Fort Dummer at present-day Brattleboro.

1749–64 New Hampshire grants land to settlers.

1763 Britain wins control of region in French and Indian War.

1764 (July 20) British crown rules New York, controls Vermont region; New York begins trying to force New Hampshire settlers in Vermont to give up land.

1770–75 Green Mountain Boys organize under Ethan Allen to drive out New York settlers.

1775 (May 10) Fort Ticonderoga captured by Green Mountain Boys led by Ethan Allen.

1777 (Jan. 15) Vermont settlers declare independence as republic called New Connecticut.

1777 (July 2–8) First constitution adopted, using name Vermont; abolishes slavery; provides universal male suffrage.

1777 (Aug. 16) Battle of Bennington: British defeated just west of Bennington in New York.

1790 (Oct. 28) New York gives up claims to Vermont upon payment of $30,000 by Vermont.

1791 (March 4) Vermont becomes 14th U.S. state.

1823 Champlain Canal opens, connecting Lake Champlain to Hudson River.

1848 First railroad begins operation in state.

1864 (Oct. 19) Confederate troops rob St. Albans banks of $200,000 and escape into Canada.

1963 First Democratic governor since 1854 takes office: Philip H. Hoff.

1982 State's "blue law" overturned by state supreme court, permitting stores to open on Sundays.

1984 State population grows 3.6% since 1980.

VIRGINIA

Area: 40,767 square miles; 105,585 sq. km.
Population: 5,636,000 (1984); 5,346,797 (1980).
Capital: Richmond.
Flower: Dogwood.
Tree: Dogwood.
Animal: Foxhound.
Bird: Cardinal. **Shell:** Oyster.
Song: *Carry Me Back to Old Virginia.*
Nickname: The Old Dominion.
Motto: *Sic Semper Tyrannis* (Thus Always to Tyrants).
Flag: State seal centered on blue field.
Leading Industries: Manufacturing (chemicals, tobacco products, electrical and electronic equipment), food processing, agriculture (tobacco, beef cattle), dairy products, hogs, horses, turkeys, corn, peanuts, soybeans), mining (coal).
Climate (Norfolk): *Normal temperatures:* Jan. high 49 ° F., low 32 ° F.; July high 87 ° F., low 70 ° F. *Normal yearly precipitation:* 45 ″ (water). *Record snowstorm:* 17.7 ″ in December 1892.
Recreation Areas: National park, 1; national forests, 2; national seashore, 1; state parks and recreation areas, 34.
Points of Interest: Shenandoah National Park; Assateague Island National Seashore; national monuments include Booker T. Washington birthplace (near Roanoke) and George Washington birthplace (in Westmoreland County); Fredericksburg and Spotsylvania National Military Park; Petersburg National Battlefield; Manassas and Richmond National Battlefield Parks; Arlington House, Robert E. Lee National Memorial; national cemeteries at Fredericksburg, Poplar Grove, and Yorktown; Prince William Forest; Wolf Trap Farm; Skyline Drive and Blue Ridge Parkway; Monticello; Williamsburg; Mount Vernon; Appomattox Court House, Cumberland Gap, and Colonial national historical parks (last includes Jamestown and Yorktown); Alexandria; Fredericksburg; Richmond; Stratford Hall; Berkeley Plantation.

KEY EVENTS IN VIRGINIA

1607 (May 13) English colony established at Jamestown.

1619 First black slaves in English colonies in America arrive at Jamestown on Dutch ship.

1619 (July 30) First representative legislature meets in America: Virginia's House of Burgesses.

1622 Indian uprising kills over 300 colonists.

1624 Virginia made royal colony by King James I.

1644 Indian raids massacre about 500 settlers.

1676 (Sept. 19) Nathaniel Bacon burns Jamestown in rebellion against royal governor.

1693 College of William and Mary chartered.

1754–63 French and Indian War: Virginia's George

VIRGINIA *(continued)*

Washington initiates conflict with French.

1775 (March 23) **Patrick Henry** appeals to patriots: "Give me liberty or give me death!"

1775 (June 8) **Royal governor** flees to British ship.

1776 (May 15) **Virginia directs delegates in Continental Congress** to vote for independence.

1776 (June 12) **Declaration of Rights** written by George Mason adopted by Virginia Convention; state constitution adopted on June 29, also written by Mason; Patrick Henry becomes first governor.

1776–81 In **Revolutionary War** Virginians drive off attacks by British in 1776; British invade Virginia (1780–81) but lose Battle of Yorktown as Gen. Charles Cornwallis' army surrenders (Oct. 19, 1781).

1788 (June 25) **Virginia becomes 10th U.S. state,** ratifying U.S. Constitution.

1798 (Dec. 24) **Virginia Resolution** by James Madison adopted by legislature, declaring Alien and Sedition Acts unconstitutional.

1831 (Aug. 13–23) **Slave uprising** led by Nat Turner; 57 whites and about 100 blacks killed; 20 blacks including Turner executed.

1861 (April 17) **Virginia secedes,** joins Confederacy; western Virginians remain loyal to Union, forming separate state of West Virginia in 1863.

1861–65 In **Civil War** Virginia is major battleground with scores of battles; Richmond serves as Confederate capital (May 1861–April 1865); war ends in Virginia with Lee's surrender to Grant at Appomattox Court House (April 9, 1865).

1870 (Jan. 16) **Virginia readmitted** to Union.

1873 **Railroad** built from Richmond to Ohio River.

1926 **Colonial Williamsburg restoration** begun by John D. Rockefeller Jr.

1969 **First Republican elected governor** since 1869: A. Linwood Holton.

1984 **State population increases** 5.4% since 1980; state remains 13th in population.

WASHINGTON

Area: 68,139 square miles; 176,478 sq. km.

Population: 4,349,000 (1984); 4,132,204 (1980).

Capital: Olympia.

Flower: Western rhododendron. **Tree:** Western hemlock.

Fish: Steelhead trout. **Bird:** Willow goldfinch.

Gem: Petrified wood.

Song: *Washington, My Home.*

Nickname: The Evergreen State.

Motto: *Alki* (By and By).

Flag: State seal centered on green field.

Leading Industries: Manufacturing (aircraft, ships, chemicals, paper, machinery), forestry, food processing, agriculture (wheat, potatoes, sugar beets, apples, beef cattle, dairy products, poultry).

Climate (Seattle): *Normal temperatures:* Jan. high 45°F., low 35°F.; July high 76°F., low 56°F. *Normal yearly precipitation:* 36″ (water). *Record snowstorm:* 21.5″ in February 1916.

Recreation Areas: National parks, 3; national forests, 9; national recreation areas, 3; state parks and recreation areas, 187.

Points of Interest: Mt. Rainier, Olympic, and North Cascades national parks; Grand Coulee Dam, Ross Lake, and Lake Chelan national recreation areas; Whitman Mission (west of Walla Walla) and Fort Vancouver national historic sites; San Juan Island National Historical Park; Pacific Science Center and Space Needle (Seattle).

KEY EVENTS IN WASHINGTON

1774 **Coast explored for Spain** by Juan Pérez.

1775 **Region claimed for Spain** by Bruno Heceta, who lands near mouth of Quinault River.

1792 (May 7) **Columbia River discovered** and named by American Capt. Robert Gray.

1792–94 **Coast surveyed for Britain** by Capt. George Vancouver.

1805–06 **Lewis and Clark** explore region along Columbia River and coastal area for U.S.

1810 **Trading post** built at present-day Spokane by Canadian explorer David Thompson.

1811 **First American settlement** at Okanogan by David Stuart for Pacific Fur Company.

1818 (Oct. 20) **U.S. and Britain** agree to joint control of region; treaty renewed in 1827.

1819 (Feb. 2) **Spain gives up claim to region** in Adams-Onís Treaty with U.S.

1824 **Russia gives up claim to region** in treaty with U.S.; ratified Jan. 12, 1825.

1825 **Vancouver founded** by Hudson's Bay Company's John McLoughlin, who controls region for next two decades.

1846 (Aug. 5) **Britain gives up claim to region** as Oregon Treaty goes into effect.

1847 (Nov. 29) **Cayuse Indians** massacre American missionaries Marcus and Narcissa Whitman and 11 other settlers near present-day Walla Walla, touching off Cayuse War; settlers destroy Indian villages.

1848 (Aug. 14) **Territory of Oregon** created, including present-day Washington.

1852 **Seattle** founded.

1853 (March 2) **Territory of Washington** created.

1855–59 **Yakima Indians** war with settlers in effort to protect their land.

1883 **Northern Pacific Railroad** completed between Washington and eastern United States.

1889 (Nov. 11) **Washington becomes 42d U.S. state.**

1917 **Canal completed** from Puget Sound to Lake Washington.

1941 **Grand Coulee Dam** begins operation on Columbia River, largest concrete dam and largest hydroelectric power plant in U.S.

1943 **Hanford Works** atomic-energy plant built.

1962 **Century 21 World's Fair** held at Seattle.

1974 **World's first environmental exposition,** Expo '74, held in Spokane.

1980 (May 18) **Mount St. Helens erupts;** 66 dead or missing; $1.6 billion in damage.

1984 **State population increases** 5.2% since 1980.

WEST VIRGINIA

Area: 24,231 square miles; 62,759 sq. km.

Population: 1,952,000 (1984); 1,950,258 (1980).

Capital: Charleston.

Flower: Big rhododendron. **Tree:** Sugar maple.

Bird: Cardinal. **Animal:** Black bear.

Fish: Brook trout.

Songs: *The West Virginia Hills; This Is My West Virginia;* and *West Virginia, My Home Sweet Home* (all official songs).

Nickname: The Mountain State.

Motto: *Montani Semper Liberi* (Mountaineers Are Always Free).

Flag: State coat of arms centered on blue-bordered white field.

Leading Industries: Manufacturing (chemicals, iron and steel, nickel, aluminum, glassware, pottery, machinery), mining (coal, natural gas, petroleum), agriculture (beef cattle, dairy products, poultry, fruits, corn).

Climate (Charleston): *Normal temperatures:* Jan. high 44°F., low 25°F.; July high 86°F., low 64°F. *Normal yearly precipitation:* 41″ (water). *Record snowstorm:* 15.1″ in November 1950.

Recreation Areas: National forests, 3; state parks and recreation areas, 34.

Points of Interest: Harpers Ferry and Chesapeake

and Ohio Canal national historical parks; White Sulphur Springs and Berkeley Springs resorts; National Radio Astronomy Observatory (Green Bank) Blennerhassett Island; scenic railroad at Cass; historic homes at Charles Town.

KEY EVENTS IN WEST VIRGINIA

1609–1863 West Virginia included in Virginia.
1726 First settler: Morgan Morgan builds cabin at Bunker Hill.
1727 German settlers from Pennsylvania found New Mecklenburg (now Shepherdstown).
1742 Coal discovered near present-day Racine.
1748 Harpers Ferry begins carrying passengers across Shenandoah River.
1754–63 French and Indian War: George Washington commands militia troops on Virginia's frontier, including what is now West Virginia.
1774 (Oct. 10) Battle of Point Pleasant: About 3,000 Virginia militia under Col. Andrew Lewis defeat 1,000 Shawnees led by Chief Cornstalk.
1775–83 In Revolutionary War Indians and British loyalists make many raids on settlers; last battle is attack on Fort Henry at present-day Wheeling (Sept. 11–13, 1782).
1859 (Oct. 16–18) John Brown seizes arsenal at Harpers Ferry; hanged at Charles Town on Dec. 2.
1860 Petroleum discovered at Burning Springs.
1861 (April 17) Opposition to secession voted by western delegates at Virginia Convention; West Virginians choose governor loyal to Union (June 20).
1861–65 Many Civil War battles take place.
1863 (June 20) Becomes 35th U.S. state.
1915 U.S. Supreme Court rules West Virginia owes Virginia over $12 million as part of state debt before Civil War; debt finally paid in 1939.
1921 Miners and owners battle in Logan County.
1950–70 Poor economic conditions cause 13% decline in population from 2,005,452 in 1950.
1965 (March) Appalachian Regional Redevelopment Act brings federal aid to revitalize economy.
1972 (Feb. 26) Flood caused by collapse of coal-waste dam at Buffalo Creek kills 118 persons.
1984 Population increases only 0.1% since 1980.

WISCONSIN

Area: 56,153 square miles; 145,435 sq. km.
Population: 4,766,000 (1984); 4,705,642 (1980).
Capital: Madison.
Flower: Wood violet.
Tree: Sugar maple.
Bird: Robin.
Rock: Red granite.
Mineral: Galena.
Animal: Badger. **Wildlife Animal:** White-tailed deer.
Domestic Animal: Dairy cow.
Symbol of Peace: Mourning dove.
Fish: Muskellunge.
Song: On, Wisconsin!
Nickname: The Badger State.
Motto: Forward.
Flag: State coat of arms centered on blue field.
Leading Industries: Manufacturing (machinery, automobiles, electrical equipment), food processing, forestry, agriculture (dairy products, beef cattle, hogs, hay, corn, poultry, vegetables, fruits).
Climate (Milwaukee): *Normal temperatures:* Jan. high 27 °F., low 11 °F.; July high 80 °F., low 59 °F. *Normal yearly precipitation:* 29 ″ (water). *Record snowstorm:* 20.3 ″ in February 1924.
Recreation Areas: National forests, 2; national scientific reserve, 1; national lakeshore, 1; state parks and recreation areas, 65.
Points of Interest: Apostle Islands National Lakeshore;

Ice Age National Scientific Reserve; Wolf, St. Croix, and Lower St. Croix national scenic riverways; Door County resort region; Wisconsin Dells; "Talie- sin," Frank Lloyd Wright's home and architectural school (Spring Green); Circus World Museum (Baraboo); Little Norway (near Mt. Horeb).

KEY EVENTS IN WISCONSIN

1634 Region explored for France by Jean Nicolet, landing at Green Bay.
1660–61 French trading post and Roman Catholic mission established near present-day Ashland.
1712–40 War between French and Fox Indians.
1763 Britain obtains region in settlement of French and Indian War.
1783 U.S. acquires region in Revolutionary War, but Britain does not turn over outposts to U.S. control until 1796.
1800–36 Region governed in turn as part of territories of Indiana, Illinois, and Michigan.
1820s American settlers begin mining lead.
1832 Black Hawk War: Settlers end power of Indians in Wisconsin.
1836 (April 20) Territory of Wisconsin created.
1837 Madison founded; becomes capital in 1838.
1848 (May 29) Wisconsin becomes 30th U.S. state.
1851 Railroad opens, Milwaukee-Waukesha.
1853 Capital punishment abolished.
1854 (Feb. 28) Formation of Republican Party first planned at meeting in Ripon.
1871 (Oct. 8–14) Forest fire kills about 800 persons, destroying village of Peshtigo.
1882 First hydroelectric power plant built on Fox River at Appleton.
1884 Ringling Brothers circus begins at Baraboo.
1911 First state income tax adopted.
1961 State sales tax adopted.
1977 (July 3–18) Illegal 15-day strike by 23,000 state workers wins higher pay.
1984 Population grows 1.3% since 1980.

WYOMING

Area: 97,809 square miles; 253,325 sq. km.
Population: 511,000 (1984); 469,557 (1980).
Capital: Cheyenne.
Flower: Indian paintbrush. **Tree:** Cottonwood.
Bird: Meadowlark. **Stone:** Jade. **Song:** Wyoming.
Nickname: Equality State. **Motto:** Equal Rights.
Flag: State seal and buffalo centered on red-and-white-bordered blue field.
Climate (Cheyenne): *Normal temperatures:* Jan. high 38 °F., low 15 °F.; July high 84 °F., low 55 °F. *Normal yearly precipitation:* 15 ″ (water). *Record snow storm:* 16.5 ″ in April 1955.
Leading Industries: Mining (petroleum, natural gas, coal, uranium), agriculture (beef cattle, sheep, beans, hay, sugar beets, wheat), food processing, tourism.
Recreation Areas: National parks, 2; national forests, 10; national recreation area, 1; state parks and recreation areas, 11.
Points of Interest: Grand Teton and Yellowstone national parks; Fort Laramie National Historic Site; Devils Tower and Fossil Butte national monuments; Buffalo Bill Historic Center (Cody); Flaming Gorge; Bighorn Canyon National Recreation Area.

KEY EVENTS IN WYOMING

1742–43 Believed first explored for France by Louis-Joseph and François de La Vérendrye.
1803 Region acquired in Louisiana Purchase.
1807 Yellowstone area explored by John Colter.
1833 Petroleum discovered in Wind River Basin by Capt. Benjamin de Bonneville.
1834 Fort William (later called Fort Laramie) built

WYOMING *(continued)*

by traders William Sublette and Robert Campbell.
1846–48 Western Wyoming obtained by U.S. in Oregon Treaty with Britain and in Mexican War.
1867 Cheyenne founded; first passenger train from Omaha reaches Cheyenne (Nov. 13, 1867).
1868 (July 25) Territory of Wyoming created.
1869 (Dec. 10) Women given right to vote and hold territorial offices.
1872 (March 1) Yellowstone becomes first national park in world.
1890 (July 10) Wyoming becomes 44th U.S. state; first to give women equal suffrage rights with men.

1892 Johnson County War: Cattlemen import gunmen from Texas to kill cattle rustlers.
1906 Devils Tower becomes first national monument.
1924 First woman elected governor in U.S.: Mrs. Nellie Tayloe Ross.
1951 Uranium discovered in Powder River region.
1960 First intercontinental ballistic missile (ICBM) base becomes operational near Cheyenne.
1978–80 Economic boom brings highest personal income gain in any state and lowest unemployment rate.
1984 High population growth of 8.9% since 1980; remains 49th in population rank among states.

U.S. TERRITORIES AND DEPENDENCIES

DISTRICT OF COLUMBIA (WASHINGTON, D.C.)

Area: 69 square miles; 178 sq. km.
Population: 623,000 (1984); 638,432 (1980).
National Capital: Washington, D.C.
Flower: American beauty rose.
Bird: Wood thrush. **Tree:** Scarlet oak.
Motto: *Justitia Omnibus* (Justice for All).
Flag: Two parallel horizontal red stripes on white field; three red stars above top red stripe.
Leading Industries: Government, tourism, service industries, manufacturing (printing and publishing).
Climate: *Normal temperatures:* Jan. high 44 °F., low 28 °F.; July high 88 °F., low 69 °F. *Normal yearly precipitation:* 39 ″ (water). *Record snowstorm:* 25 ″ in January 1922.
Points of Interest: White House, U.S. Capitol, Library of Congress, Supreme Court, U.S. Botanic Garden, Folger Shakespeare Library, Museum of African Art, Smithsonian Building, National Air and Space Museum, National Museum of History and Technology, National Gallery of Art, Hirshhorn Museum and Sculpture Garden, Freer Gallery of Art, National Collection of Fine Arts, National Portrait Gallery, Washington Monument, Lincoln Memorial, Jefferson Memorial, Ford's Theatre, Kennedy Center for the Performing Arts, National Zoological Park, Corcoran Gallery of Art; *in Arlington, Va.:* Pentagon, Arlington National Cemetery, Marine Corps War Memorial; *in Fairfax County, Va.:* Mount Vernon (George Washington's estate).

KEY EVENTS IN DISTRICT OF COLUMBIA

1751 Georgetown laid out in 80 city lots.
1788 (Dec. 23) Maryland cedes land for capital.
1789 (Dec. 3) Virginia cedes land for capital.
1790–91 Congress establishes district as seat of national government.
1791 (March 30) President George Washington proclaims boundaries of federal district.
1791 (Sept. 9) Washington chosen as name for city by federal commissioners.
1791–92 Plan for city designed by French engineer Pierre Charles L'Enfant.
1800 (Nov. 1) President John Adams moves into White House.
1800 (Nov. 21) Congress first meets in city.
1802 (May 3) Washington incorporated by Congress.
1814 (Aug. 24–25) In War of 1812 Washington captured and burned by British.
1820 (May 15) New charter provides for mayor elected by people.
1846 (July 9) Congress retrocedes 36 square miles of district to Virginia because of lack of growth.
1871 (Feb. 21) Congress repeals charters of Washington and Georgetown; forms territorial government with officials appointed by President.

1874 (June 20) Government by three commissioners appointed by President established by Congress.
1961 (April 3) Amendment 23 to U.S. Constitution proclaimed; enables residents to vote for President and Vice President; first vote in 1964.
1967 New district government established with commissioner (mayor) appointed by President.
1970 Nonvoting delegate to represent district in U.S. House of Representatives authorized.
1974 (May 7) New home-rule charter approved, giving residents right to elect mayor and council.
1975 (Jan. 2) First elected government since 1871 sworn in.
1976 First subway begins operation in new $5 billion rapid-transit system.
1977 Racial composition of population changes to 75% black from 55% in 1960.
1978 Congress approves proposed constitutional amendment to give district voting representation in congress.
1982 (Nov. 2) Voters approve constitution to make district 51st state: "New Columbia."
1984 Population decreases 2.4% since 1980, with higher loss rate than any state.

COMMONWEALTH OF PUERTO RICO

Area: 3,515 square miles; 9,104 sq. km.
Population: 3,267,000 (1983); 3,196,520 (1980).
Capital: San Juan, 434,849.
Other Cities: Bayamón, 196,206; Ponce, 189,046.
Nickname: Island of Enchantment.
Motto: *Joannes Est Nomen Ejus* (John Is His Name)
Animal: Lamb. **Reptile:** Coquí. **Song:** *La Borinqueña*.
Flag: Large white star on blue triangle next to staff; 3 red and 2 white horizontal stripes.
Leading Industries: Manufacturing (clothing, chemicals, electrical equipment, machinery), food processing, agriculture (sugarcane, coffee, tobacco, bananas, dairy products, poultry), tourism.
Climate (San Juan): *Normal temperatures:* Jan. high 82 °F., low 69 °F.; July high 87 °F., low 75 °F. *Normal yearly precipitation:* 60 ″. *Record rainstorm:* 10.55 ″ in December 1910.
Points of Interest: El Morro Fortress (San Juan), Art Museum (Ponce), Caribbean National Forest with El Yunque mountain, Luquillo Beach, Phosphorescent Bay, historic buildings in Old San Juan, beaches.

KEY EVENTS IN PUERTO RICO

1493 (Nov. 19) Christopher Columbus claims Puerto Rico for Spain; names it San Juan Bautista.
1508 Spanish settlers colonize island.
1513 Black slaves first imported.
1873 Slavery abolished by Spain.
1897 Spain grants autonomous government to Puerto Ricans led by Luis Muñoz Rivera.
1898 (July 25–Aug. 13) In Spanish-American War U.S. troops invade and conquer Spanish defenders.
1898 (Dec. 10) Spain cedes Puerto Rico to U.S.

PUERTO RICO *(continued)*
1899 (Aug. 8) Hurricane kills 3,369 persons.
1917 (March 2) Territory of Puerto Rico created by Jones Act, granting U.S. citizenship to Puerto Ricans.
1946 (July 25) First island-born governor: Jesús Toribio Piñero, appointed by President Truman.
1948 Luis Muñoz Marin becomes first elected governor (son of Luis Muñoz Rivera).
1952 (July 25) Puerto Rico becomes commonwealth with own constitution (adopted March 3, 1952).
1967 (July 23) Puerto Ricans vote by 60% majority to retain commonwealth status with U.S.: 39% vote for statehood; less than 1% vote for independence.
1979 U.S. Congress passes resolution favoring a popular vote in Puerto Rico to decide on statehood.
1980 Population grows 17.9% since 1970.
1982 (Jan. 12) President Reagan pledges support for Puerto Rican statehood if islanders want it.
1982 (Sept. 24) UN General Assembly votes 70–30 to uphold Puerto Rico's status, rejecting Cuban effort to label it as a U.S. colony.

U.S. VIRGIN ISLANDS

Area: 132 square miles; 342 sq. km.
Population: 103,800 (1983); 96,569 (1980).
Capital: Charlotte Amalie, 11,756 (on St. Thomas).
Islands: St. Thomas, 32 sq. mi.; St. Croix, 82 sq. mi.; St. John, 19 sq. mi.; about 60 small islets.
Nickname: American Paradise.
Territorial Flower: Yellow elder or yellow cedar.
Bird: Yellow breast. **Song:** *Virgin Islands March.*
Flag: Golden American eagle with shield on white field; eagle between blue letters V and I.
Leading Industries: Tourism, manufacturing (rum, refined bauxite, petroleum refining, textiles), agriculture (beef cattle, dairy products, poultry, vegetables, fruits, nuts).
Normal Temperatures: Year-round, 78° F.
Normal Yearly Rainfall: 40–60 inches.
Points of Interest: Virgin Islands National Park on St. John; St. Thomas and Christiansted national historic sites; Buck Island Reef National Monument; ruins of castles, forts, and plantations; beaches.

KEY EVENTS IN U.S. VIRGIN ISLANDS

1493 Islands discovered by Christopher Columbus.
1500s Spaniards kill or enslave Carib Indians.
1672 (May 25) First permanent settlement established on St. Croix by Danes led by Jorgen Iverson.
1716 St. John acquired by Denmark.
1733 St. Croix bought by Denmark from France.
1848 (July 3) Slavery abolished after slave revolt.
1917 (March 31) U.S. purchases islands from Denmark for $25 million; treaty signed Aug. 4, 1916.
1927 U.S. citizenship granted to islanders.
1954 Elected legislature established by Congress.
1956 National park established on St. John.
1958 First island-born governor: John D. Merwin, appointed by President Eisenhower.
1968 Islanders given right to elect governor.
1971 (Jan. 4) First elected governor takes office: Melvin Herbert Evans.
1979 (March 6) Voters reject home rule: In 5 to 4 vote, new constitution is rejected.
1981 (Nov. 3) Voters reject home-rule constitution by 7,157 to 4,821 in referendum.
1983 Population grows 7.5% since 1980.

AMERICAN SAMOA

Area: 77 square miles; 199 sq. km.
Population: 34,500 (1983); 32,297 (1980).
Capital: Pago Pago, 2,451.
Islands: Tutuila and Aunu'u, 53 sq. mi.; Ta'u, 17 sq. mi.; Ofu and Olosega, 4 sq. mi.; Swain's, 1.9 sq. mi. Rose, 0.4 sq. mi.

Flower: Paogo. **Tree:** Moso'oi. **Plant:** Ava.
Motto: *Samoa—Muamua le Atua* (In Samoa, God Is First).
Song: *Amerika Samoa.*
Flag: Blue field; white triangle bordered with red with apex at midpoint of staff; American eagle at right side of triangle.
Leading Industries: Tourism, fishing, tuna canning, handicrafts, agriculture (fruits, vegetables).
Languages: Samoan and English.
Normal Temperatures: Year-round, 70° to 86° F.
Normal Yearly Rainfall: 200 inches.
Points of Interest: Villages, beaches.

KEY EVENTS IN AMERICAN SAMOA

1722 Discovered by Dutch explorer Jacob Roggeveen.
1830 British missionaries begin converting islanders.
1839–40 Survey by U.S. Navy Lt. Charles Wilkes.
1872 U.S. Navy establishes naval base at Pago Pago.
1899 (Dec. 2) U.S. and Germany agree to divide Samoan Islands between them; Britain also signs agreement, withdrawing its claims to islands.
1900–04 Chiefs of islands cede them to U.S.; formally accepted by U.S. Congress on Feb. 20, 1929.
1925 Swain's and Rose islands annexed to American Samoa.
1900–51 U.S. Navy administers islands.
1951 U.S. Department of Interior takes over administration of islands.
1966 (Nov. 19) Constitution adopted by voters gives elected legislature taxing power.
1974 Islands declared drought disaster area.
1977 (Nov. 22) Voters for first time elect Samoa-born governor: Peter T. Coleman.
1983 Population grows 6.8% since 1980.

GUAM

Area: 209 square miles; 541 sq. km.
Population: 116,400 (1983); 105,979 (1980).
Capital: Agana, 881.
Flower: *Puti Tai Nobio* (Bougainvillea).
Bird: *Toto* (Fruit dove). **Animal:** Iguana. **Stone:** Latte.
Tree: *Ifit* (Intsiabijuga).
Song: *Stand Ye Guamanians.*
Nickname: Pearl of the Pacific.
Flag: Territorial seal on blue field bordered in red.
Leading Industries: Military installations, manufacturing (food, beverages, printing, watches, clothing), oil refining, construction, fishing, agriculture (vegetables, fruits, poultry, hogs, beef cattle), tourism.
Languages: Chamorro and English.
Normal Temperatures: Year-round, 71° to 87°F.
Normal Yearly Rainfall: 80–110 inches (mostly July through November).

KEY EVENTS IN GUAM

1521 Portuguese explorer Ferdinand Magellan believed to have visited Guam.
1668 Guam colonized by Spain.
1898 (Dec. 10) U.S. acquires Guam.
1899–1950 U.S. Navy administers Guam.
1941 (Dec. 7–13) Japan captures Guam.
1944 (July 21–Aug. 10) U.S. recaptures Guam.
1950 (Aug. 1) U.S. Territory of Guam created under U.S. Department of Interior; islanders become U.S. citizens; given right to elect own legislature.
1968 Right to elect own governor given Guam.
1976 (Sept. 4) Continued status as U.S. territory approved by voters 10,221 to 7,386.
1979 (Aug. 4) Voters reject proposed constitution by 5 to 1, demanding U.S. military give up much of the island's land to further economic development.
1982 (Sept. 7) Voters favor commonwealth status 3 to 1 over statehood in referendum.
1983 Population grows 9.8% since 1980.

COMMONWEALTH OF NORTHERN MARIANA ISLANDS

Area: *Land,* 184 square miles; 476.6 sq. km.
Population: 18,200 (1983); 16,780 (1980).
Capital: Susupe, Saipan, 7,967.
Islands: Saipan, Tinian, Rota, and 11 islets.
Legislature: 23 members.
Languages: English and Chamorro.
Leading Industries: Agriculture (coconuts); government; fishing.
Normal Temperatures: Year-round, 75 ° to 89 °F.

KEY EVENTS IN NORTHERN MARIANAS

1668 Spain colonizes Mariana Islands.
1899 Germany acquires Northern Marianas.
1947 (July 18) Northern Marianas included in U.S. Trust Territory of the Pacific Islands.
1975 (Feb. 15) U.S. signs agreement with representatives of Northern Marianas to make them U.S. commonwealth.
1976 (March 24) President Ford signs Northern Marianas Covenant establishing procedure to separate islands from Micronesia.
1976 (July 14) UN Trusteeship Council approves U.S. plan for Northern Marianas.
1978 (Jan. 9) Northern Marianas become U.S. commonwealth, pending end of trust territory; first elected governor, Carlos S. Camacho.
1982 (Jan. 9) Pedro P. Tenorio sworn in as governor for 4-year term; elected on Nov. 1, 1981.

TRUST TERRITORY OF THE PACIFIC ISLANDS

Including the many islands taken by U.S. military forces from Japan in World War II, the U.S. Trust Territory of the Pacific Islands was formally placed under American administration by the UN in 1947. The territory has been divided into four parts: (1) the Northern Marianas, a self-governing U.S. commonwealth; (2) the Federated States of Micronesia, whose capital is at Kolonia on Ponape and includes the island districts of Truk, Yap, and Kosrae of the Caroline group; (3) Belau (Palau Island) in the western Carolines, with its capital at Koror; and (4) the Marshall Islands, with its capital at Majuro.
Area: *Land,* 533 sq. mi. (1,380 sq. km.); *ocean,* 7,772 sq. mi. (20,129 sq. km.)
Population: 124,000 (1983); 116,149 (1980).
Administrative Center: Saipan in Mariana Islands.
Islands: 2,141 atolls and islands (96 inhabited).
Leading Industries: Agriculture (vegetables, fruits, poultry, copra), fishing, handicrafts.
Normal Temperatures: Year-round, 75 ° to 89 °F.
Government: High commissioner appointed by U.S.; congress of Micronesia elected by islanders.

KEY EVENTS

1885 Germany annexes Marshall Islands.
1899 Germany acquires Carolines from Spain.
1914 Japan seizes Micronesia in World War I.
1920 (Dec. 17) Japan receives League of Nations mandate over German possessions in Micronesia.
1944–45 U.S. captures Micronesia from Japan.
1946–58 U.S. test-explodes 64 nuclear weapons at Bikini and Enewetak atolls.
1947 (July 18) U.S. receives UN trusteeship over Pacific Islands.
1962 (May 7) U.S. Department of Interior given administration of entire territory.
1965 Elective congress of Micronesia established.
1975 (Nov. 8) Constitution for Federated States of Micronesia adopted.
1976 (July 14) UN Trusteeship Council approves U.S.

plan for self-government for Micronesia.
1978 (Jan. 9) Northern Marianas formally separated from Micronesia.
1978 (July 12) Micronesians vote to divide into three self-governing states.
1979 (May 1) Marshall Islands becomes separate self-governing nation.
1979 (May 10) Federated States of Micronesia established as self-governing state.
1979 (Nov. 27–Dec. 3) Majuro, capital of Marshall Islands, devastated by storm with 25-foot waves.
1980 (Jan. 14) U.S. signs agreement with Marshall Islands to grant limited independence.
1980 (April 8) Enewetak restored to former residents who were removed for U.S. A-bomb tests in 1940s.
1980 (July 9) Belau (Palau) voters ratify constitution providing self-rule.
1981 (Jan. 1) Belau becomes self-governing.
For other developments: See separate articles on nations Belau, Marshalls, and Micronesia.

U.S. ISLAND DEPENDENCIES

The United States also occupies or claims several other islands in the Caribbean Sea and the Pacific Ocean. Altogether these islands have an area of about 15 square miles and a total population of less than 5,000 persons. They include:
BAKER ISLAND lies in the Pacific Ocean about 1,650 miles southwest of Honolulu. Barren and uninhabited, it has an area of about 380 acres. Baker was claimed by the United States in 1857.
HOWLAND ISLAND, an uninhabited Pacific island, is about 40 miles north of Baker Island. It has an area of about 1 square mile.
JARVIS ISLAND, one of the Line Islands in the central Pacific Ocean, lies about 1,500 miles south of Honolulu. Its area is 1.66 square miles.
JOHNSTON AND SAND ISLANDS have an area of less than ½ square mile. About 800 miles southwest of Honolulu, the islands were annexed by the U.S. in 1858. The U.S. Navy built an airfield on Johnston Island in World War II, and the island was used for atomic-bomb tests in 1962.
KINGMAN REEF, about 9 miles long and 5 miles wide, is in the Line Islands about 920 miles south of Honolulu.
MIDWAY ISLANDS, about 1,150 miles northwest of Honolulu, have a population of about 2,200 and an area of about 2 square miles. The two islands are Sand Island and Eastern Island. Annexed by the U.S. in 1867, the islands are controlled by the U.S. Navy. The Battle of Midway on June 4, 1942, marked the turning point of World War II in the Pacific when a Japanese fleet attempting to capture the islands was defeated by a U.S. fleet.
NAVASSA ISLAND lies midway between Jamaica and Haiti in the West Indies. It is in the Jamaica Channel about 100 miles south of Cuba. It has an area of about 2 square miles.
PALMYRA ISLAND, one of the northernmost of the Line Islands, is about 1,000 miles south of Honolulu. It has an area of 4 square miles. It was annexed by Hawaii in 1862. It became the private possession of the Fullerd-Leo family of Hawaii. In 1979 the U.S. government reported plans to purchase the island and make it a dumping ground for radioactive waste materials.
WAKE ISLAND, about 2,300 miles west of Honolulu, has an area of 3 square miles and a population of 1,647. The U.S. claimed the island in 1899 for use as a station for the transpacific telegraph cable. In World War II, Japan captured Wake Island on Dec. 23, 1941, taking more than 1,600 Americans prisoner. Japan held the island until Sept. 4, 1945.

MAJOR SUPREME COURT DECISIONS: 1985

The Supreme Court completed its 1984–1985 term on July 2, generally rejecting positions held by President Reagan's administration on social and civil rights issues. The Court devoted special attention to emphasizing the necessity of preserving government neutrality toward religion. It also repeatedly rejected government restrictions on free speech.

Only 19 of the Court's 139 signed opinions were decided by a 1-vote margin. Fifty-nine of the opinions were unanimous.

Chief Justice Warren E. Burger irritated members of the legal profession who use television, radio, and newspapers to advertise their services. In a speech to the American Bar Association on July 7, he denounced advertising by lawyers.

"My advice to the public is never, never, never—under any circumstances, engage the services of a lawyer who advertises," he said.

Associate Justice Lewis Powell, 77, was absent from the Court during the first three months of 1985 while recovering from an operation for a cancerous prostate gland.

SCHOOL PRAYER OUTLAWED

An Alabama law that permitted public schools to establish a daily one-minute period for silent meditation or prayer was found unconstitutional by the Court in a 6-3 ruling on June 4.

The majority opinion, written by Associate Justice John Paul Stevens, said in part:

"Just as the right to speak and the right to refrain from speaking are complementary components of a broader concept of individual freedom of mind, so also the individual's freedom to choose his own creed is the counterpart of his right to refrain from accepting the creed established by the majority. At one time it was thought that this right merely proscribed the preference of one Christian sect over another, but would not require equal respect for the conscience of the infidel, the atheist, or the adherent of a non-Christian faith such as Mohammedism or Judaism.

"But when the underlying principle has been examined in the crucible of litigation, the Court has unambiguously concluded that the individual freedom of conscience protected by the First Amendment embraces the right to select any religious faith or none at all. This conclusion derives support not only from the interest in respecting the individu-

al's freedom of conscience, but also from the conviction that religious beliefs worthy of respect are the product of free and voluntary choice by the faithful, and from recognition of the fact that the political interest in forestalling intolerance extends beyond intolerance among Christian sects, or even intolerance among 'religions,' to encompass intolerance of the disbeliever and the uncertain. . . .

"The legislature enacted the law for the sole purpose of expressing the state's endorsement of prayer activities for one minute at the beginning of each school day. The addition of 'or voluntary prayer' indicates that the state intended to characterize prayer as a favored practice. Such an endorsement is not consistent with the established principle that the government must pursue a course of complete neutrality toward religion."

In a dissenting opinion, Chief Justice Burger wrote:

"Some who trouble to read the opinions in this care will find it ironic, perhaps even bizarre, that on the very day we heard arguments in this case, the Court's session opened with an invocation for divine protection. Across the park a few hundred yards away, the House of Representatives and the Senate regularly open each session with a prayer. These legislative prayers are not just one minute in duration, but are extended, thoughtful invocations and prayers for divine guidance. They are given, as they have been since 1789, by clergy appointed as official chaplains and paid from the Treasury of the United States. Congress has also provided chapels in the Capitol, at public expense, where members and others may pause for prayer, meditation, or a moment of silence.

"It makes no sense to say that Alabama has 'endorsed prayer' by merely enacting a new statute 'to specify expressly that voluntary prayer is one of the authorized activities during a moment of silence.' To suggest that a moment-of-silence statute that includes the word 'prayer' unconstitutionally endorses religion, while one that simply provides for a moment of silence does not, manifests not neutrality but hostility toward religion.

"For decades our opinions have stated that hostility toward any religion or toward all religions is as much forbidden by the Constitution as is an official establishment of religion. The Alabama legislature has no more 'endorsed' religion than a state or the Congress does when it provides for legisla-

tive chaplains, or than this Court does when it opens each session with an invocation to God."

PAROCHIAL SCHOOL AID BANNED

The Supreme Court ruled by 5-4 in two cases on July 1 that public schools cannot send teachers into parochial schools to provide special education.

Associate Justice William J. Brennan Jr. wrote the majority opinions, which were joined by Associate Justices Harry A. Blackmun, Thurgood Marshall, Lewis F. Powell Jr., and John Paul Stevens.

One case involved the Grand Rapids, Mich., public school system, and the other was concerned with a program conducted by the New York City public school system. Both programs sent public school teachers into parochial schools to provide remedial instruction for students. Hundreds of school districts throughout the nation have provided such services under terms of a federal law that requires public schools to provide remedial services for all students, including those who do not attend public schools.

In his opinion in the Grand Rapids case, Brennan wrote:

"Government promotes religion as effectively when it fosters a close identification of its powers and responsibilities with those of any—or all—religious denominations as when it attempts to inculcate specific religious doctrines. If this identification conveys a message of government endorsement or disapproval of religion, a core purpose of the Establishment Clause is violated.

"It follows that an important concern of the effects test is whether the symbolic union of church and state is sufficiently likely to be perceived by adherents as an endorsement and by the nonadherents as a disapproval, of their individual religious choices. The inquiry must be conducted with particular care when many of the citizens perceiving the governmental message are children in their formative years.

"In the programs challenged in this case, the religious school students spend their typical school day moving between religious school and 'public-school' classes. Both take place in the same religious-school building and both are largely composed of students who are adherents of the same denomination. In this environment, the students would be unlikely to discern the crucial difference between the classes.

"This effect—the symbolic union of government and religion in one sectarian enterprise—is an impermissible effect under the Establishment Clause."

SABBATH REST LAW OVERTURNED

In an 8-1 ruling on June 26, the Supreme Court ruled as unconstitutional a Connecticut law that gave employees the right not to work on their chosen Sabbath. Associate Justice William H. Rehnquist, the sole dissenter, did not write an opposing decision.

In the case Thornton v. Caldor, a department store employee, Donald Thornton, a Presbyterian, had brought suit under the state law, claiming he had been demoted after he told the store he no longer wished to work on Sunday.

Chief Justice Warren E. Burger wrote in the majority opinion:

"Government must guard against activity that impinges on religious freedom, and must take pains not to compel people to act in the name of any religion. ... a statute must not only have a secular purpose and not foster excessive entanglement of government with religion, its primary effect must not advance or inhibit religion.

"The Connecticut statute challenged here guarantees every employee, who 'states that a particular day of the week is observed as his Sabbath,' the right not to work on his chosen day. The state has thus decreed that those who observe a Sabbath any day of the week as a matter of religious conviction must be relieved of the duty to work on that day, no matter what burden or inconvenience this imposes on the employer or fellow workers. The statute arms Sabbath observers with an absolute and unqualified right not to work on whatever day they designate as their Sabbath.

"In essence, the Connecticut statute imposes on employers and employees an absolute duty to conform their business practices to the particular religious practices of the employee by enforcing observance of the Sabbath the employee unilaterally designates. The state thus commands that Sabbath religious concerns automatically control over all secular interests at the workplace; the statute takes no account of the convenience or interests of the employer or those of other employees who do not observe a Sabbath. The employer and others must adjust their affairs to the command of the state whenever the statute is invoked by an employee. ...

"Other employees who have strong and legitimate, but nonreligious reasons for wanting a weekend day off have no rights under the statute. For example, those employees who have earned the privilege through seniority to have weekend days off may be forced to surrender this privilege to the Sabbath observer; years of service and payment of 'dues' at the workplace simply cannot

compete with the sabbath observer's absolute right under the statute. Similarly, those employees who would like a weekend day off, because that is the only day their spouses are also not working, must take a back seat to the Sabbath observer. Finally, the statute allows for no consideration as to whether the employer has made reasonable accommodation proposals.'

"This unyielding weighting in favor of Sabbath observers over all other interests contravenes a fundamental principle of the Religion Clauses, so well articulated by Judge Learned Hand: 'The First Amendment . . . gives no one the right to insist that in pursuit of their own interests others must conform their conduct to his own religious necessities.'

"As such, the statute goes beyond having an incidental or remote effect of advancing religion. The statute has a primary effect that impermissibly advances a particular religious practice."

$10 LIMIT ON LEGAL FEES

In a 6-3 decision the Court upheld on June 28 a century-old law limiting to $10 the amount a lawyer can collect for representing a veteran in a dispute over veterans' benefits.

The law was adopted by Congress in 1864 to save veterans from paying large legal fees for help in filling out simple requests for benefits. In modern times, veterans needing legal assistance in disputes with the Veterans Administration have relied on help from national veterans organizations.

A federal district court in California had overturned the law, declaring that the $10 limit is "fundamentally unfair" to lawyers.

In writing the majority opinion, Associate Justice William H. Rehnquist said the law had been adopted to keep disputes over veterans' benefits "as informal and nonadversarial as possible." He then said, "The regular introduction of lawyers into the proceedings would be quite unlikely to further this goal."

Associate Justice John Paul Stevens, who dissented from the majority opinion, later told a lawyers' group: "One of the most disturbing features of the case is the suggestion that seems implicit in much of the opinion that, well, maybe you lawyers do more harm than good."

SHOOT TO KILL LIMITS

The Court in a 6-3 decision on March 27 overturned state laws that place no restrictions on the right of police to shoot to kill to prevent the escape of a criminal suspect. The case was one in which police in Memphis, Tenn., had shot to death an unarmed 15-year-old boy.

The majority opinion was written by Associate Justice Byron R. White. He said in part:

"Whenever an officer restrains the freedom of a person to walk away, he has seized that person. While it is not always clear just when minimal police interference becomes a seizure, there can be no question that apprehension by the use of deadly force is a seizure subject to the reasonableness of the Fourth Amendment.

"A police officer may arrest a person if he has probable cause to believe that person committed a crime. Petitioners argue that if this requirement is satisfied, the Fourth Amendment has nothing to say about how that seizure is made. This submission ignores the many cases in which this Court, by balancing the extent of the intrusion against the need for it, has examined the reasonableness of the manner in which a search of seizure is conducted. . . .

"Notwithstanding probable cause to seize a suspect, an officer may not always do so by killing him. The intrusiveness of a seizure by means of deadly force is unmatched. The suspect's fundamental interest in his own life need not be elaborated upon. The use of deadly force also frustrates the interest of the individual, and of society, in judicial determination of guilt and punishment. Against these interests are ranged governmental interests in effective law enforcement.

"The fact is that a majority of police departments in this country have forbidden the use of deadly force against nonviolent suspects.

"The use of deadly force to prevent the escape of all felony suspects, whatever the circumstances, is constitutionally unreasonable. It is not better that all felony suspects die than that they escape. Where the suspect poses no immediate threat to the officer and no threat to others, the harm resulting from the failing to apprehend him does not justify the use of deadly force to do so. It is no doubt unfortunate when a suspect who is in sight escapes, but the fact that the police arrive a little late or are a little slower afoot does not always justify killing the suspect. A police officer may not seize an unarmed, nondangerous suspect by shooting him dead. The Tennessee statute is unconstitutional insofar as it authorizes the use of deadly force against such fleeing suspects.

"It is not, however, unconstitutional on its face. Where the officer has probable cause to believe that the suspect poses a threat of serious physical harm, either to the officer or to others, it is not constitutionally unreasonable to prevent escape by using deadly force.

MAJOR COURT DECISIONS: 1985 *(continued)*

Thus, if the suspect threatens the officer with a weapon or there is probable cause to believe that he has committed a crime involving the infliction or threatened infliction of serious physical harm, deadly force may be used if necessary to prevent escape and if, where feasible, some warning has been given."

In a dissenting opinion, Associate Justice Sandra Day O'Connor said in part:

"Because burglary is a serious and dangerous felony, the public interest in the prevention and detection of the crime is of compelling importance. Where a police officer has probable cause to arrest a suspected burglar, the use of deadly force as a last resort might well be the only means of apprehending the suspect. With respect to a particular burglary, subsequent investigation simply cannot represent a substitute for immediate apprehension of the criminal suspect at the scene."

FORD COPYRIGHT SUSTAINED

The Court by a 6-3 decision on May 20, upheld the rights of copyright in the memoirs of former President Gerald R. Ford. In 1983 the U.S. Court of Appeals had ruled that the magazine *Nation* had not violated copyright by quoting from the book without permission prior to its official publication date in 1979. The Supreme Court overturned that ruling.

Associate Justice Sandra Day O'Connor wrote in the majority decision:

"In March 1979, an undisclosed source provided *Nation* magazine with the unpublished manuscript of *A Time to Heal: The Autobiography of Gerald R. Ford.* Working directly from the purloined manuscript, an editor of *Nation* produced a short piece entitled 'The Ford Memoir—Behind the Nixon Pardon'. . . .

"*Nation* effectively arrogated to itself the right of first publication, an important marketable subsidiary right. We find that this use of the copyrighted manuscript, even stripped to the verbatim quotes conceded by *Nation* to be copyrightable expression, was not a fair use within the meaning of the act."

LABOR UNION PENALTIES

Organized labor received a setback from the Supreme Court on June 27 with a 5-4 ruling that unions should not be allowed to penalize members who resign during or just prior to a strike.

The ruling upheld a decision by the National Labor Relations Board (NLRB) against the Pattern Makers' League of North America, a labor union of workers who make patterns for industrial metalwork. The NLRB had held that the union was guilty of an unfair labor practice when it fined 10 members who had resigned from the union during a strike in 1977.

The majority opinion of the Court was written by Associate Justice Lewis F. Powell Jr., who was joined by Chief Justice Burger and Associate Justices White, Rehnquist, and O'Connor. Powell wrote that the National Labor Relations Act guarantees employees "the right to refrain from any or all" collective bargaining activities.

Associate Justice Harry A. Blackmun wrote a dissenting opinion in which he said that the ruling "threatens the power to act collectively that is at the center of the act." He declared that the Court's action "improperly restricts a union's federally protected right to make and enforce its own rules, and at the same time traduces the broader aim of federal labor policy implicated by this right: to preserve the balance of power between labor and management by guaranteeing workers an effective right to strike."

Associate Justices Brennan and Marshall joined in Blakmun's dissent, while Associate Justice Stevens filed a separate brief dissent of his own.

FORCED RETIREMENT BARRED

In two unanimous decisions on June 17, the Court made it more difficult for employers to dismiss workers who reach a specific age.

In one case the Court upheld lower court decisions that Western Air Lines Inc. could not force flight engineers to retire when they reach the age of 60.

In the other case, the Court ruled that the city of Baltimore could not force firefighters to retire at age 55.

MOBILE HOMES CAN BE SEARCHED

The Court ruled 6-3 on May 13 that a motor home more nearly resembles an automobile than a home in regards to police search.

An automobile can be searched by the police without obtaining a search warrant, but a home cannot.

The decision applied only to mobile homes than can easily be driven away, not to mobile homes that are permanently located in a trailer park.

INDIAN TAX RIGHTS

In an 8-0 ruling on April 16, the Court upheld the right of the Navajo Indians to establish taxes on businesses operating on their reservation without obtaining approval of the federal government.

CIA SECRECY UPHELD

The Court ruled unanimously on April 16 that the Central Intelligence Agency (CIA) is exempt from disclosing sources of information in providing documents under the Freedom of Information Act.

HISTORIC SUPREME COURT DECISIONS

1803 Judicial Review—*Marbury v. Madison:* William Marbury was appointed a justice of the peace a few weeks before President John Adams' term expired. When the next administration refused to deliver his commission, Marbury petitioned the Court for a writ of mandamus to compel Secretary of State James Madison to issue a commission. The Court dismissed the case for lack of jurisdiction. Marbury had based his case on the Judiciary Act of 1789, which authorized the Court to take original jurisdiction over such controversies. Under Article III, Section 2 of the Constitution, Supreme Court jurisdiction over such matters begins at the appellate level. Therefore, the Judiciary Act was unconstitutional and void to the extent that it gave the Court powers implicitly denied by the Constitution.

Significance: It established the principle of "judicial review," whereby the Court has jurisdiction to pass on the constitutionality of legislative acts.

1816 Federal Questions—*Martin v. Hunter's Lessee:* This case dealt with land ownership in Virginia. The Virginia Court of Appeals ruled against Martin. On appeal to the Supreme Court, that decision was reversed. In 1821 the Supreme Court asserted in *Cohens v. Virginia* that it had power to review final decisions of state courts in criminal proceedings.

Significance: The two cases established the Court's appellate power when "federal questions" (involving the Constitution, a congressional statute, or a treaty) are involved. They established that one uniform interpretation will apply for "federal questions."

1819 Constitutional Interpretation—*McCulloch v. Maryland:* Congress chartered a federal bank in 1816 to control unregulated issuances of currency by state banks. Maryland then imposed a tax on notes issued by the U.S. Bank's Baltimore branch. The branch refused to pay, and Maryland sued to collect. At the same time it challenged congressional authority to charter a bank. The Court ruled that this was within the implied powers of government, that acts of Congress not expressly authorized are valid so long as they are "necessary and proper" to carrying out express grants of power. It declared further that federal instrumentalities are not subject to state taxes.

Significance: The decision sanctioned "loose," or liberal, interpretation of the Constitution.

1824 Regulation of Commerce—*Gibbons v. Ogden:* Aaron Ogden, part owner of a steamboat operation monopoly established by New York statute, challenged the right of Thomas Gibbons to operate a rival steamboat service between New Jersey and New York under federal license. The Court declared the New York statute unconstitutional because it clearly came in conflict with congressional power to regulate commerce.

Significance: It became the basis for the sweeping exercise of federal controls over commerce. It is significant also for its statement of "pre-emption": when Congress acts within its authorized powers, it can pass legislation to invalidate contradictory laws of the states.

1852 Local Powers—*Cooley v. Wardens of the Port of Philadelphia:* The case involved the constitutionality of a Pennsylvania statute regulating navigation in the Port of Philadelphia. Much of the traffic in and out of the harbor was interstate. In its ruling the Court noted that some commerce, although technically interstate, is essentially local in character. U.S. control is not really necessary, and until it is, states and municipalities are free to act according to local needs.

Significance: The decision reasserted the authority of the Court over state regulation of commerce, and ensured a national "common market" by stating that some matters are beyond state power.

1857 Slaves as Property—*Dred Scott v. Sanford:* Dred Scott, a Missouri slave, was at one time taken into free territory, where an Act of Congress (the Missouri Compromise) prohibited slavery. Several years after his return to Missouri, Scott sued for freedom, claiming he had acquired it through residence in free territory. The decision centered on two principles: first, that Scott, being a Negro, was not a U.S. citizen and therefore could not petition federal courts; second, that the Missouri Compromise was unconstitutional. Slaves were like any other property, the Court said, and under the 5th Amendment Congress could pass no law depriving citizens of their private property.

Significance: The decision, acclaimed in the South and bitterly denounced in the North, brought the nation another step closer to civil war.

1911 Business Regulation—*Standard Oil Co. of New Jersey v. United States:* The Sherman Act (1890) outlawed "every contract, combination in the form of trust or otherwise, or conspiracy in restraint of trade." In this case the Court said that the "rule of reason" must apply, and that "every" did not mean "all" but only "unreasonable" contracts or combinations or conspiracies in restraint of trade. Later (1932) the Court ruled in *United States v. Swift & Co.* that "mere size" is not an offense against the Sherman Act.

Significance: The Court's decisions permitted the growth of huge corporate enterprises in the U.S. by watering down the stringent provisions of the congressional statute.

1925 Bill of Rights Applied to States—*Gitlow v. New York:* Gitlow was prosecuted under New York's "criminal anarchy" statute, which made it a crime to advocate or teach the propriety of overthrowing the government by force and violence. The Supreme Court upheld Gitlow's state-court conviction, over objection that it violated Gitlow's rights of freedom of speech and the press. The Court assumed that those 1st Amendment provisions were also limitations on the states because they were "incorporated" in the 14th Amendment's "due process" clause.

Significance: For the first time a part of the Bill of Rights of the Constitution was made applicable to the states.

HISTORIC SUPREME COURT DECISIONS *(continued)*

1937 Regulation of Labor—*NLRB v. Jones & Laughlin Steel Corporation:* In upholding the National Labor Relations Board's authority to regulate industrial labor relations, the Court ruled that the U.S. government has jurisdiction over any dispute that will interfere with interstate commerce. The case grew out of a labor dispute in a Pennsylvania steel plant. Manufacturing, the Court ruled, was so closely linked to interstate commerce that its control was essential to "protect that commerce from burdens and obstructions."

Significance: The decision broadened the definition of interstate commerce to include all activities that would affect its flow, either directly or indirectly, and upheld the power of Congress to regulate industrial relations.

1954 Racial Segregation—*Brown v. Board of Education of Topeka:* In this case the Court set aside a Kansas statute authorizing segregation in primary schools. The decision declared that the "separate but equal" doctrine, established in *Plessy v. Ferguson* (1896), in fact denied equal protection under the 14th Amendment and was unconstitutional. The verdict directed lower courts to use their authority to implement desegregation of public elementary schools.

Significance: This was the first time the Court declared segregation unconstitutional. From the decision evolved a body of legislation and court action aimed at eradicating discrimination in schools, housing, employment, voting, and other areas.

1962 School Prayers—*Engel v. Vitale:* A non-denominational prayer written by the N.Y. State Board of Regents for voluntary recital in the public schools was ruled unconstitutional as a violation of the 1st Amendment, which provides that Congress "shall make no laws respecting an establishment of religion or prohibiting the free exercise thereof."

A year later, in *School District of Abbington Township v. Schempp,* the Court banned legislation requiring Bible reading and recitation of the Lord's Prayer in public schools on grounds that it tended to establish a state religion.

Significance: A state may not require promotion of a specific religion in public schools.

1962 One Man, One Vote—*Baker et al. v. Carr:* The Court ruled that federal courts have the power to review legislative apportionment. As a result of large population shifts, many legislative districts were unevenly drawn and voters were denied the right to "equal protection" guaranteed by the 14th Amendment. The Baker case led to a number of decisions in 1964 calling for reapportionment on a "one man, one vote" basis. *(Reynolds v. Sims* established this rule for state legislatures, and *Wesberry v. Sanders* did the same for congressional districts.)

Significance: Political districts, which often were drawn to favor rural areas, were ordered redrawn to give increased voting strength to city and suburban residents.

1964 Libel of Officials—*New York Times v. Sullivan:* The case revolved around a full-page advertisement placed in the *Times* by Dr. Martin Luther King Jr. and other civil-rights leaders. Many statements in the ad—charging that

Negroes in Montgomery, Ala., were being abused—proved false. Sullivan, a Montgomery city official, was subsequently awarded a $500,000 libel judgment. The Court reversed the judgment, ruling that criticism of official conduct cannot be termed libelous without showing actual malice.

Significance: The decision gave the news media greater freedom in reporting the news by limiting their liability for libel.

1966 Rights of Criminal Suspects—*Miranda v. Arizona:* The Court overturned the conviction of an Arizona man charged with rape and kidnapping, on grounds that his voluntary confession was obtained illegally. The decision invalidated any confessions or incriminating admissions unless the suspect is warned that he may remain silent, that anything he says may be held against him, that he has a right to have a lawyer present, and that if he cannot afford one, he is entitled to court-appointed counsel. If the suspect waives counsel and confesses, there is a "heavy burden" on the prosecution to show a waiver of rights.

Significance: The decision gives more protection to those accused of crimes.

1972 Death Penalty—*Furman v. Georgia:* The Supreme Court ruled in a 5–4 decision that the death penalty as it had been imposed by state courts was unconstitutional under the 8th and 14th Amendments.

Subsequently, in 1976, the Court ruled that the death penalty in and of itself was constitutional, upholding newly revised capital-punishment laws that provide separate consideration of sentencing after guilt had been determined.

In 1977 the Court decided that state legislatures cannot make the death penalty mandatory for the slaying of a police officer.

Significance: The decisions brought revision of capital-punishment laws to protect defendants' rights.

1972 Free Legal Counsel—*Argersinger v. Hamlin:* The Court decided that the state must provide free legal counsel for persons accused of crimes for which they may be imprisoned if they cannot afford to pay an attorney.

1973 Obscenity—*Miller v. California* and *Paris Adult Theatre I v. Slaton:* The Court redefined "obscenity," requiring a defendant prosecuted for obscenity to prove that the work as a whole shows "serious literary, artistic, political or scientific value." In addition, the Court ruled that the work must meet "contemporary community standards."

Significance: The decision gave states and local governments greater power to regulate works considered obscene.

1973 Abortion—*Roe v. Wade* and *Doe v. Bolton:* The Court overturned all state laws banning abortion during the first 6 months of pregnancy on grounds that it is a violation of the right of privacy stemming from the 14th Amendment.

Significance: The ruling broadened the rights of women in deciding whether or not to give birth to a child.

1980 New Life Forms Can Be Patented—*Diamond v. Chakrabarty:* Court recognized new science of genetic engineering, upholding patent for man-made microorganism.

UNITED STATES SUPREME COURT MEMBERS

JUSTICE (CHIEF JUSTICES IN BOLDFACE TYPE) AND STATE OF RESIDENCE	YEARS ON THE COURT	APPOINTED BY PRESIDENT:	BORN	DIED	POSITIONS BEFORE COURT APPOINTMENT
1. **John Jay** (N.Y.)	1789–95	Washington	1745	1829	President of Continental Congress; U.S. Secretary of State
2. John Rutledge (S.C.)[1]	1789–91	Washington	1739	1800	1st governor of South Carolina
3. William Cushing (Mass.)	1789–1810	Washington	1732	1810	Chief Judge, Supreme Judicial Court (Mass.)
4. James Wilson (Pa.)	1789–98	Washington	1742	1798	Private law practice
5. John Blair (Va.)	1789–96	Washington	1732	1800	State Appeals Court judge
6. James Iredell (N.C.)	1790–99	Washington	1751	1799	North Carolina Council of State
7. Thomas Johnson (Md.)	1791–93	Washington	1732	1819	Chief Judge, General Court of Maryland
8. William Paterson (N.J.)	1793–1806	Washington	1745	1806	Governor of New Jersey
9. **John Rutledge** (S.C.)[1]	1795	Washington	1739	1800	Chief Justice of South Carolina
10. Samuel Chase (Md.)	1796–1811	Washington	1741	1811	Chief Judge, General Court of Maryland
11. **Oliver Ellsworth** (Conn.)	1796–1800	Washington	1745	1807	U.S. Senator; helped write first Judiciary Act
12. Bushrod Washington (Va.)	1798–1829	John Adams	1762	1829	Private law practice
13. Alfred Moore (N.C.)	1799–1804	John Adams	1755	1810	State Superior Court judge
14. **John Marshall** (Va.)	1801–35	John Adams	1755	1835	U.S. Representative; U.S. Secretary of State
15. William Johnson (S.C.)	1804–34	Jefferson	1771	1834	Court of Common Pleas judge
16. Henry Brockholst Livingston (N.Y.)	1807–23	Jefferson	1757	1823	State Supreme Court justice
17. Thomas Todd (Ky.)	1807–26	Jefferson	1765	1826	Chief Justice, Kentucky Court of Appeals
18. Gabriel Duvall (Md.)	1812–35	Madison	1752	1844	Comptroller, U.S. Treasury
19. Joseph Story (Mass.)	1811–45	Madison	1779	1845	Massachusetts legislator
20. Smith Thompson (N.Y.)	1823–43	Monroe	1768	1843	U.S. Secretary of the Navy
21. Robert Trimble (Ky.)	1826–28	J.Q. Adams	1777	1828	U.S. District Court judge
22. John McLean (Ohio)	1829–61	Jackson	1785	1861	U.S. Postmaster General
23. Henry Baldwin (Pa.)	1830–44	Jackson	1780	1844	Private law practice
24. James Moore Wayne (Ga.)	1835–67	Jackson	1790	1867	U.S. Representative
25. **Roger Brooke Taney** (Md.)	1836–64	Jackson	1777	1864	U.S. Attorney General; private law practice
26. Philip Pendleton Barbour (Va.)	1836–41	Jackson	1783	1841	U.S. Circuit Court judge
27. John Catron (Tenn.)	1837–65	Jackson	1786	1865	Private law practice
28. John McKinley (Ala.)	1837–52	Van Buren	1780	1852	U.S. Senator-elect
29. Peter Vivian Daniel (Va.)	1841–60	Van Buren	1784	1860	U.S. District Court judge
30. Samuel Nelson (N.Y.)	1845–72	Tyler	1792	1873	Chief Justice, New York
31. Levi Woodbury (N.H.)	1845–51	Polk	1789	1851	U.S. Senator
32. Robert Cooper Grier (Pa.)	1846–70	Polk	1794	1870	State District Court judge
33. Benjamin Robbins Curtis (Mass.)	1851–57	Fillmore	1809	1874	Private law practice
34. John Archibald Campbell (Ala.)	1853–61	Pierce	1811	1889	Private law practice
35. Nathan Clifford (Maine)	1858–81	Buchanan	1803	1881	Private law practice
36. Noah Haynes Swayne (Ohio)	1862–81	Lincoln	1804	1884	Private law practice
37. Samuel Freeman Miller (Iowa)	1862–90	Lincoln	1816	1890	Private law practice
38. David Davis (Ill.)	1862–77	Lincoln	1815	1886	Judicial Circuit Court judge
39. Stephen Johnson Field (Calif.)	1863–97	Lincoln	1816	1899	State Superior Court judge
40. **Salmon Portland Chase** (Ohio)	1864–73	Lincoln	1808	1873	Governor of Ohio; U.S. Secretary of Treasury
41. William Strong (Pa.)	1870–80	Grant	1808	1895	Private law practice
42. Joseph P. Bradley (N.J.)	1870–92	Grant	1813	1892	Private law practice
43. Ward Hunt (N.Y.)	1873–82	Grant	1810	1886	N.Y. Commissioner of Appeals
44. **Morrison Remick Waite** (Ohio)	1874–88	Grant	1816	1888	President of Ohio Constitutional Convention
45. John Marshall Harlan (Ky.)	1877–1911	Hayes	1833	1911	Member, Louisiana Commission
46. William Burnham Woods (Ga.)	1881–87	Hayes	1824	1887	U.S. Circuit Court judge
47. Stanley Matthews (Ohio)	1881–89	Garfield	1824	1889	Private law practice
48. Horace Gray (Mass.)	1882–1902	Arthur	1828	1902	Chief Judge, Massachusetts
49. Samuel Blatchford (N.Y.)	1882–93	Arthur	1820	1893	U.S. Circuit Court judge
50. Lucius Quintus Cincinnatus Lamar (Miss.)	1888–93	Cleveland	1825	1893	U.S. Secretary of Interior
51. **Melville Weston Fuller** (Ill.)	1888–1910	Cleveland	1833	1910	State legislator; Chicago corporation lawyer
52. David Josiah Brewer (Kan.)	1890–1910	B. Harrison	1837	1910	U.S. Circuit Court judge

[1] Resigned as associate justice in 1791; was named Chief Justice in 1795, but Senate rejected nomination.

U.S. SUPREME COURT MEMBERS (continued)

JUSTICE (CHIEF JUSTICES IN BOLDFACE TYPE) AND STATE OF RESIDENCE	YEARS ON THE COURT	APPOINTED BY PRESIDENT:	BORN	DIED	POSITION BEFORE COURT APPOINTMENT
53. Henry Billings Brown (Mich.) ..	1891–1906	B. Harrison	1836	1913	U.S. District Court judge
54. George Shiras Jr. (Pa.)	1892–1903	B. Harrison	1832	1924	Private law practice
55. Howell Edmunds Jackson (Tenn.)	1893–95	B. Harrison	1832	1895	U.S. Circuit Court judge
56. **Edward Douglass White** [1] (La.)	1894–1921	Cleveland	1845	1921	U.S. Senator
57. Rufus Wheeler Peckham (N.Y.)	1896–1909	Cleveland	1838	1909	State Appeals Court judge
58. Joseph McKenna (Calif.)......	1898–1925	McKinley	1843	*1926	U.S. Attorney General
59. Oliver Wendell Holmes (Mass.)	1902–32	T. Roosevelt	1841	1935	Chief Justice, Massachusetts
60. William Rufus Day (Ohio)	1903–22	T. Roosevelt	1849	1923	U.S. Circuit Court judge
61. William Henry Moody (Mass.) .	1906–10	T. Roosevelt	1853	1917	U.S. Attorney General
62. Horace Harmon Lurton (Tenn.)	1910–14	Taft	1844	1914	U.S. Circuit Court judge
63. Charles Evans Hughes [2] (N.Y.)	1910–16	Taft	1862	1948	Governor of New York
64. Willis Van Devanter (Wyo.)	1911–37	Taft	1859	1941	U.S. Circuit Court judge
65. Joseph Rucker Lamar (Ga.) ...	1911–16	Taft	1857	1916	Private law practice
66. Mahlon Pitney (N.J.)	1912–22	Taft	1858	1924	State Supreme Court judge
67. James Clark McReynolds (Tenn.)	1914–41	Wilson	1862	1946	U.S. Attorney General
68. Louis Dembitz Brandeis (Mass.)	1916–39	Wilson	1856	1941	Private law practice
69. John Hessin Clarke (Ohio)	1916–22	Wilson	1857	1945	U.S. District Court judge
70. **William Howard Taft** (Ohio)	1921–30	Harding	1857	1930	27th U.S. President
71. George Sutherland (Utah)	1922–38	Harding	1862	1942	Private law practice
72. Pierce Butler (Minn.)	1922–39	Harding	1866	1939	Private law practice
73. Edward Terry Sanford (Tenn.) .	1923–30	Harding	1865	1930	U.S. District Court judge
74. **Harlan Fiske Stone** [1] (N.Y.).................	1925–46	Coolidge	1872	1946	U.S. Attorney General
75. **Charles Evans Hughes** (N.Y.) .	1930–41	Hoover	1862	1948	Judge, Permanent Court of International Justice
76. Owen Josephus Roberts (Pa.) .	1930–45	Hoover	1875	1955	Private law practice
77. Benjamin Nathan Cardozo (N.Y.)	1932–38	Hoover	1870	1938	State Appeals Court judge
78. Hugo Lafayette Black (Ala.) ...	1937–71	F. Roosevelt	1886	1971	U.S. Senator
79. Stanley Forman Reed (Ky.)....	1938–57	F. Roosevelt	1884	1980	U.S. Solicitor General
80. Felix Frankfurter (Mass.)	1939–62	F. Roosevelt	1882	1965	Professor of law
81. William Orville Douglas (Conn.)	1939–75	F. Roosevelt	1898	1980	Chairman of the SEC
82. Frank Murphy (Mich.)	1940–49	F. Roosevelt	1890	1949	U.S. Attorney General
83. James Francis Byrnes (S.C.) ..	1941–42	F. Roosevelt	1879	1972	U.S. Senator
84. Robert Houghwout Jackson (N.Y.)	1941–54	F. Roosevelt	1892	1954	U.S. Attorney General
85. Wiley Blount Rutledge (Iowa) ..	1943–49	F. Roosevelt	1894	1949	U.S. Circuit Court judge
86. Harold Hitz Burton (Ohio)	1945–58	Truman	1888	1964	U.S. Senator
87. **Frederick Moore Vinson** (Ky.).................	1946–53	Truman	1890	1953	U.S. Secretary of Treasury
88. Tom Campbell Clark (Texas) ..	1949–67	Truman	1899	1977	U.S. Attorney General
89. Sherman Minton (Ind.)	1949–56	Truman	1890	1965	U.S. Circuit Court judge
90. **Earl Warren** (Calif.)	1953–69	Eisenhower	1891	1974	Governor of California
91. John Marshall Harlan (N.Y.) ...	1955–71	Eisenhower	1899	1971	U.S. Circuit Court judge
92.*William Joseph Brennan Jr. (N.J.)	1956–	Eisenhower	1906	—	State Supreme Court judge
93. Charles Evans Whittaker (Mo.)	1957–62	Eisenhower	1901	1973	U.S. Circuit Court judge
94. Potter Stewart (Ohio)	1958–81	Eisenhower	1915	—	U.S. Circuit Court judge
95.*Byron Raymond White (Colo.)	1962–	Kennedy	1917	—	Deputy U.S. Attorney General
96. Arthur Joseph Goldberg (Ill.) ..	1962–65	Kennedy	1908	—	U.S. Secretary of Labor
97. Abe Fortas [3] (D.C.)	1965–69	L. Johnson	1910	1982	Private law practice
98.*Thurgood Marshall (N.Y.)	1967–	L. Johnson	1908	—	U.S. Solicitor General
99.***Warren Earl Burger** (Minn.)	1969–	Nixon	1907	—	U.S. Circuit Court judge
100.*Harry Andrew Blackmun (Minn.)	1970–	Nixon	1908	—	U.S. Circuit Court judge
101.*Lewis Franklin Powell Jr. (Va.)	1971–	Nixon	1907	—	Private law practice
102.*William Hubbs Rehnquist (Ariz.)	1971–	Nixon	1924	—	Asst. U.S. Attorney General
103.*John Paul Stevens (Ill.)	1975–	Ford	1920	—	U.S. Court of Appeals judge
104.*Sandra Day O'Connor (Ariz.)	1981–	Reagan	1930	—	Arizona Court of Appeals judge

* Current Court members. [1] Raised from Associate to Chief Justice: White, 1910 (by President Taft); Stone, 1941 (by President F. D. Roosevelt). [2] Resigned; later named Chief Justice in 1930. [3] Senate rejected nomination as Chief Justice.

Taxes

HIGHLIGHTS: 1985

TAX REFORM

President Reagan began a campaign on May 28 to reform the federal income tax code (see page 17). However, the President's illness and a congressional summer recess delayed action on the measure. As the year drew toward a close, many observers were not sure that Congress would act to adopt reforms in time for them to take effect in 1986.

The President declared that "the overwhelming majority of Americans are dissatisfied with the current tax system."

He said the present system is "unfair . . . too complicated . . . and impedes growth."

The centerpiece of the President's plan was a reduction and simplification of tax rates to a simple 3-bracket system:

—No taxes on taxable income up to $4,000.

—A 15% tax rate on taxable income from $4,000 to $29,000.

—A 25% tax rate on taxable income from $29,000 to $70,000.

—A 35% tax rate on taxable income more than $70,000.

The President's tax reform plan called for simplifying the complex system of itemized deductions, eliminating or curtailing more than 65 categories of preferential tax treatment.

Among the main deductions to be limited or eliminated were those for business meals and entertainment and for state and local taxes.

The main deductions to be retained in the President's tax plan were those for charitable contributions, for interest paid on mortgage loans for the taxpayer's principal residence, and preferential treatment for Social Security and veterans' disability payments.

Other features of the plan:

—Total taxes paid by individuals would be reduced by 7%.

—The personal exemption for each taxpayer and dependent would be increased to $2,000. This amount would be indexed to protect it from inflation.

—The earned income tax credit for the working poor would be increased and indexed to protect against inflation.

—The incentive for private saving by wage-earners through Individual Retirement Accounts (IRAs) would be expanded to afford the same benefit to spouses at home.

—More than half of all taxpayers would be relieved of the necessity of making out a tax return. The Internal Revenue Service would automatically sending a tax bill or a tax refund to those who chose.

—Virtually all persons at or below the poverty level would be freed from taxation.

—Unemployment and disability payments (with the exception of veterans' disability payments) would be treated as taxable income.

According to the U.S. Treasury Department, the President's plan was "revenue neutral"—increasing or decreasing revenues by no more than 1.5%.

The President proposed that the individual tax rates would become effective on July 1, 1986. Thus, the rates for tax withholding would change on that date. Tax returns for 1986 would reflect a blend of the old and new rates.

The Treasury Department estimated that over the next five years individuals would save $131.8 billion in tax payments and that this reduction in revenues would be largely made up with an additional $118.4 billion in taxes collected from corporations.

A study by a joint committee of congress released on July 25 estimated that in the 5-year period individuals would save $147.3 billion in taxes under the President's plan, while corporations would pay an additional $120.4 billion in taxes.

Both the House Ways and Means Committee and the Senate Finance Committee held extensive hearings in which they received testimony from supporters and opponents of tax reform.

IMPORTANT TAX DATES IN 1986

February 3—Employers must provide employees with a Statement of Wages Earned and Tax Withheld (Form W-2) for 1985.

February 3—Individuals should file an income tax return for 1985 and pay the tax due, if the last installment on their 1985 estimated income tax was not paid.

April 15—Individuals must file an income tax return for the calendar year 1985. Tax due must be paid in full with the return when filed.

April 15—Those required to do so must file a declaration of estimated income tax for 1986 and pay at least 25% of such tax.

June 16—Individuals must pay second installment of 1986 estimated income tax.

September 15—Individuals must pay third installment of 1986 estimated income tax.

January 15, 1987—Individuals must pay fourth installment of 1986 estimated income tax.

FILING YOUR FEDERAL INCOME TAX[1]

Source: Internal Revenue Service, U.S. Department of the Treasury

BLUE, PINK, AND GREEN FORMS

Taxpayers filing 1985 federal income tax returns have a choice of the blue form 1040 (the long form), the pink form 1040A (the short form), or the green form 1040EZ.

You can only use the pink short form if all your income is from salary, wages, tips, other employee compensation, and from dividends and interest.

If you have other sources of income or if you list deductions such as medical expenses, you must use the long blue form. However, you can claim child-care credit, IRA deduction, and two-earner couple deduction on form 1040A.

However, if you are single, claim only one exemption, have an income of $50,000 or less, and received no more than $400 in interest income, you can file the short green 1040EZ form.

You can claim a limited charitable deduction on the short pink or green forms.

WHAT INCOME IS TAXABLE

The following types of income are taxable: all wages and salaries, tips and gratuities, annuities, alimony, awards, back pay, bonuses, business income, commissions, compensations for personal services, dividends, fees, estate and trust income, gambling winnings, hobby income, illegal income, interest on savings, jury duty fees, partnership income, pensions, prizes, profits from sale or exchange of real estate or other property, rents, retirement pay, rewards, royalties, severance pay, and sick pay.

Also taxable, are Social Security benefits of individuals whose adjusted gross income (including tax-exempt interest income), combined with half of their Social Security benefits, exceeds $25,000. The limit is $32,000 for a married couple filing jointly.

INCOME NORMALLY NOT TAXABLE

The following income normally is not taxable and should not be reported on the U.S. tax return: Welfare payments; benefits paid by the Veterans Administration; dividends paid on veterans insurance; accident, health, and casualty insurance proceeds; disability and death payments; Federal Employees Compensation Act payments; gifts; bequests; inheritances; interest on municipal bonds; insurance proceeds paid because of death; mustering-out pay; Railroad Retirement Act pensions; rental allowances of clergymen; certain scholarship and fellowship grants; workers' compensation; cost-of-living allowances paid U.S. employees abroad; and Medicare or Medicaid reimbursements.

Also nontaxable are Social Security benefits of individuals whose adjusted gross incomes, combined with half of their Social Security benefits, are below $25,000. Married couples filing a joint return need not pay taxes on Social Security benefits if their combined adjusted gross income, including half of their Social Security benefits, is below $32,000.

WHO MUST FILE FEDERAL INCOME TAX RETURNS

No matter how low your income was during the year, you must file a return (1) *to get a refund* if income tax was withheld by your employer, or (2) if you qualify to receive up to $550 as an *earned income credit* (see next page).

No matter how young or how old you are, you must file a federal income tax return if you had as much income as one of the following amounts and meet the other specifications following that amount:

$400: if you received this much as net income from self-employment (such as operating your own lawn-mowing business).

$1,040: if you can be claimed as a dependent on your parent's return **and** have received this much in taxable dividends, interest, or other unearned income.

$1,040: if you are married **and** filing separately or are not living with your spouse at the end of the tax year.

$1,040: if you are entitled to exclude income from sources within U.S. possessions.

$3,430: if you are under 65 **and** you are single (or legally separated, divorced, or married living apart from your spouse for the entire year with a dependent child).

$4,470: if you are 65 or older **and** you are single (or as defined above).

$4,620: if you are under 65 **and** you are a qualifying widow or widower with a dependent child.

$5,660: if you are 65 or older **and** you are a qualifying widow or widower with a dependent child.

$5,660: if you are a married couple filing jointly **and** you both are under 65.

$6,700: if you are a married couple filing jointly **and** one of you is 65 or older.

$7,740: if you are a married couple filing jointly **and** you both are 65 or older.

[1] Based on federal income tax laws in effect on Oct. 1, 1985.

IRS WILL FIGURE OUT YOUR TAX

If you do not feel capable of figuring out how much tax you owe and do not wish to pay someone to do it for you, the Internal Revenue Service (IRS) now will calculate how much tax you owe and (1) send you a refund for overpayment or (2) a bill for underpayment.

Most taxpayers qualify for this service, although some do not.

The IRS will figure out your tax for you if you meet all five of these criteria: (1) Your adjusted gross income is $50,000 or less. (2) You do not itemize such deductions as medical expenses, taxes, charitable contributions, and so on. (3) All of your income must be from wages, salaries, tips, dividends, interest, pensions, and annuities. (4) You cannot use income averaging to reduce your taxable income. (5) You cannot use an exemption for money earned abroad.

SIMPLIFIED TAX TABLES

If you do not qualify to have the IRS figure out your tax, you will find that the tax tables that come with your income tax form have been made easier to use in finding how much tax you owe.

The term "standard deduction" was removed from the Internal Revenue Code by Congress when the Tax Reduction and Simplification Act of 1977 was passed. Instead, Congress replaced the term with "zero bracket amount," which is a flat amount of income on which no tax is paid as determined by your filing status.

The zero bracket amount has been taken into account in the tax tables so that you *do not* deduct it again in determining your tax.

The tax tables show that you pay **no tax:**

(1) If you file as a single person or head of household with no dependents and have an adjusted gross income of $3,430 or less.

(2) If you are married, file jointly with two exemptions, and have an adjusted gross income of $5,660 or less.

(3) If you are married, file separately with only your own exemption, and have an adjusted gross income of $2,810 or less.

The tax tables have been extended to higher amounts of income to enable more taxpayers to determine how much tax they owe merely by finding the tax in the tables.

The maximum income included in the tax tables is $50,000.

Additional computation using tax schedules is necessary for taxpayers with higher incomes, those using income averaging, or those in other special tax situations.

EARNED INCOME CREDIT

You may be entitled to a special payment or credit of up to $550, which you could receive as a refund check or as a credit applied against taxes you owe.

You are eligible for the credit if you meet all three of these tests: (1) Your adjusted gross income was less than $11,000; (2) Your earned income was more than $1 but was less than $11,000; (3) You paid more than half the cost of keeping up a home in the United States in which you and your dependent child lived.

The credit is equal to 11% of your earned income or your adjusted gross income up to a maximum credit of $550 for an income of $5,000. If your income is larger than $5,000, the credit is scaled down so that you receive a smaller and smaller credit until it reaches zero for an income of $11,000.

If you were married, to be eligible for the earned income credit you must file a joint return (unless you did not live with your spouse at all during the year but did pay over half the cost to maintain the household where the dependent child lived).

If you are eligible for the Earned Income Credit, the IRS also will figure out this credit for you if you write "EIC" and the name of the child that qualifies you for the credit on the line specified on your tax form.

Remember, to receive the credit, you *must* file a federal income tax return, even though your income was so small that otherwise you would not have to file.

PERSONAL EXEMPTIONS AND DEPENDENTS

You can claim exemptions for yourself and your dependents whether you use the pink short form 1040A or the blue long form 1040. Each exemption reduces by $1,040 the amount of your income on which you are taxed.

Your Own Exemptions. Whether you are married or single, you receive at least one exemption for yourself. If you are 65 or older, you can claim a *second* exemption for yourself. And if you are blind, you can claim a *third* exemption for yourself.

To claim the exemption for blindness, you must submit proof with your income tax form. If you are completely blind, submit a statement saying so.

If you partially blind, submit a statement from an eye physician or registered optometrist (1) that you cannot see over 20/200 with glasses, or (2) your field of view does not exceed 20 degrees.

Exemptions for Your Spouse. If you file a joint return with your spouse, your spouse is entitled to at least one exemption, a *second* exemption if 65 or older, and a *third* exemption if blind. Again, if a blindness exemption

YOUR FEDERAL INCOME TAX *(continued)*

for your spouse is claimed, proof should be submitted with the tax form.

If you were legally divorced or separated at the end of the tax year, you cannot take an exemption for your former spouse.

If your spouse died during the year and you did not remarry, you can still claim the exemptions that you could have taken for your spouse on the date of death.

Exemptions for Dependent Children. You can claim one additional exemption for each of your dependent children who live with you, listing their first names.

Even if your child who is 19 or younger had income of $1,040 or more and has to file a tax return, you can still claim an exemption if the child lived at your home and you paid over half of his or her support.

Even if your child is 19 or older, earns $1,040 or more, and does not live at home, you can claim him or her as an exemption if the child is enrolled as a full-time student during five months of the year and receives at least half his or her support from you.

Exemptions for Children of Divorced or Separated Parents. The parent who has custody of the child during most of the year usually can claim an exemption for the child.

However, the parent who does not have custody can claim the exemption for the child (1) if that parent gave at least $600 toward the child's support during the year and the divorce or separation agreement states he or she can take the exemption, *or* (2) if that parent gave $1,200 or more for the child's support during the year and the parent having custody cannot prove he or she provided more money for the child's support.

Exemptions for Other Dependents. You also can claim exemptions for other persons who are related to you or who lived in your home for the full year if you paid more than half their support and they received less than $1,040 income.

You can take an exemption for a dependent who died during the year if he or she met the tests for a dependent while alive.

You can obtain more information about dependent exemptions from the IRS booklet *Exemptions* (publication 501).

ADJUSTMENTS TO INCOME

The blue income tax form 1040 provides space where you can deduct certain expenses to determine what is called your *adjusted gross income.*

Moving Expenses. If you had to move at least 35 miles during the year for reasons connected with your job or business, you can deduct the cost of moving your family, furniture and other household goods and personal belong-ings. You also can deduct such related expenses as the cost of hunting for a new home, meals and lodging while living in temporary quarters for up to 30 days, and expenses in selling or renting your old home.

For more information, obtain the IRS booklet *Moving Expenses* (publication 521).

Employee Business Expenses. You can deduct the following expenses that were not paid by your employer: (1) *Travel and transportation,* including the cost of using your car in your work. Instead of figuring your actual automobile expenses, you can take a mileage rate of 20¢ a mile for the first 15,000 miles and 11¢ for each mile over 15,000, plus parking fees and tolls. (2) *Meals and lodging* expenses while you were temporarily away overnight on business from the area of your main place of work. (3) *Selling expenses,* if you are an outside salesperson who does all selling away from your employer's place of business. For more information, obtain IRS booklet *Travel, Entertainment, and Gift Expenses* (publication 463).

Payments to a Retirement Plan. You can deduct payments to an IRA retirement plan— up to $2,000 for an individual or $2,250 for a couple with a non-working spouse. No additional forms are required for IRA plans. See IRS booklets *Individual Retirement Arrangements* or *Self-Employed Retirement Plans* (publications 560 and 590).

Forfeited Interest Penalty. You can deduct a forfeited interest penalty that you have had to pay because you made a premature withdrawal from a time savings account. To do so, you must have included the interest payment you received as part of your gross income.

Alimony Paid. If you are divorced or legally separated from your spouse, you can deduct periodic payments of alimony or separate maintenance made under a court decree. You also can deduct payments made under a written separation agreement or decree for support entered into since 1954.

You *cannot deduct* lump-sum cash or property settlements, voluntary payments not made under a court order or written separation agreement, or amounts specified as child support.

The person *receiving* the alimony or separation payments must report them as taxable income.

Disability Income Exclusion. If you are under the age of 65 and totally disabled, you may be able to exclude up to $100 a week from your income. You must enclose a physician's certification of your total disability with your return.

For information on how to figure the amount of your disability income exclusion,

obtain IRS booklet *Disability Payments* (publication 522).

TAX CREDITS

You may be eligible for certain tax credits. These are amounts that are deducted directly from the taxes owed on your adjusted gross income.

Political Contributions. If you made contributions to political candidates or political organizations, you can claim a tax credit. The amount claimed cannot exceed half the amount you actually contributed and is limited to $50 on a single return or $100 on a joint return.

Credit for the Elderly. You may be able to claim this credit and reduce your tax by as much as $375 (if single) or $562.50 (if married filing jointly). To be eligible, you must be (1) 65 or older, *or* (2) under 65 but retired under a public retirement system. For more information, obtain IRS Schedules R and RP, or publication 524, *Credit for the Elderly*.

Credit for Child and Dependent Care Expenses. A taxpayer who pays for child care or care of a disabled dependent in order to be gainfully employed is eligible for a credit that can be deducted directly from taxes on blue form 1040 or 1040A. The credit amounts to up to 30% of eligible expenses for such care to a maximum of a $720 credit ($2,400 expenses) for one dependent or $960 to $1,440 for two or more ($4,800 expenses). A married couple can use this credit if one spouse works full-time and the other works part-time or is a full-time student.

Under certain circumstances payments to relatives for such care can be counted in calculating the tax credit.

For more information, see IRS Form 2441, *Credit for Child Care Expenses.*

Investment Credit. You may be eligible for this credit if you have invested in certain trade or business property. For more information, obtain IRS Form 3468, *Computations of Investment Credit.*

Foreign Tax Credit. If you paid income tax to a foreign country or U.S. possession, you can claim this credit.

Work Incentive Credit. An employer can claim a credit for the salaries and wages paid to employees hired under a Work Incentive (WIN) Program or to welfare recipients.

Jobs Credit. This is a credit for business employers who hire additional employees during the year.

Energy Credits. Homeowners and renters who, by December 31, 1985, have installed insulation, storm windows or other energy-conserving materials may qualify for a residential energy credit of up to 15% of the first $2,000 in costs, or a maximum credit of $300. A further credit of up to $4,000 is available for 40% of the first $10,000 spent on renewable energy sources using wind, solar, or geothermal energy.

ITEMIZED DEDUCTIONS

If you had certain expenses during the year, such as contributions to a church or large medical expenses, it may be to your advantage to itemize deductions on Schedule A of blue form 1040.

Medical and Dental Expenses. Medical and dental expenses that you actually paid during the year can be deducted in part from your income for tax purposes.

You can no longer deduct separately one-half (up to $150) of the amount you paid for insurance for medical or hospital care.

The medical expenses you claim for deduction can include those for yourself, your spouse, and any dependent who received over half his or her support from you. You may *not* include amounts repaid to you, or repaid to anyone else, by hospital, health, or accident insurance. To qualify as a deduction, your medical expenses must exceed 5% of your adjusted gross income.

Taxes. You can deduct state and local income taxes, real estate taxes, sales taxes, and personal property taxes.

You *cannot* deduct federal social security tax, federal excise taxes, gasoline taxes, fees for hunting and dog licenses, fees for car inspection or drivers' licenses, taxes you paid for another person, water taxes, or taxes on liquor, beer, wine, cigarettes, and tobacco.

Interest Expenses. You can deduct interest that you have paid on a mortgage or a loan, on a bank credit-card plan, on charge accounts, and on installment-plan purchases. There are limitations on the amount of interest you can deduct on interest expense paid or accrued on debts related to investment property.

Contributions. You can deduct gifts or donations made to organizations operated for religious, charitable, educational, scientific, or literary purposes, or to prevent cruelty to animals and children.

You *cannot* deduct gifts to relatives, friends, or other persons; to social clubs, labor unions, or chambers of commerce; or to foreign organizations, organizations operated for personal profit, or organizations whose purpose is to get people to vote for new laws or for changes in old laws.

Casualty or Theft Losses. You may be able to deduct part of your loss if you had property stolen or damaged by fire, storm, automobile accident, shipwreck, and so on. The first $100 of *each* casualty or theft loss of nonbusiness property in excess of insurance reimbursement is *not* deductible.

YOUR FEDERAL INCOME TAX *(continued)*

You can only deduct a casualty or theft loss to the extent it exceeds 10% of your adjusted gross income, plus $100.

For more information on tax policy concerning losses, obtain IRS booklet *Tax Information on Disasters, Casualties, and Thefts* (publication 547).

Adoption Expenses. You may deduct up to $1,500 for qualified expenses incurred to adopt a child with special needs (a child eligible for adoption assistance under the Social Security Act).

Other Deductions. A variety of other expenses may be claimed as deductible as follows:

Dues paid to unions, professional organizations, and chambers of commerce.

Expenses for education that helps you keep up or improve skills you must have in your present job, trade, or business. You *cannot* deduct expenses for education to meet the minimum requirements for your job, business, or trade; or for education that is part of a course of study that will lead to your getting a new trade or business.

Gambling losses to the extent of the amount that you won and reported as income.

Cost of safety equipment, small tools, and supplies used in your job.

Expenses relating to business or office use of your home.

Certain costs of business entertainment.

Fees paid to employment agencies.

TAX SAVINGS FOR HOMEOWNERS

If you own your own home, you usually can save on your income taxes by itemizing as deductions the interest on your mortgage and the local property taxes you must pay.

Any gain you realize on the sale or exchange of your home is not taxed at the time of sale if within 24 months before or after you buy and occupy another residence whose cost equals or exceeds the price of the old residence.

Additional time is allowed if you construct the new residence or if you were on active duty in the U.S. armed forces.

The tax is postponed; it is not forgiven.

If you are 55 or older you are entitled to a one-time exclusion of $125,000 in capital gains from the sale of your home.

For additional information, obtain IRS booklets *Tax Information for Homeowners* (publication 530) and *Tax Information on Selling or Buying Your Home* (publication 523).

INCOME AVERAGING

Certain taxpayers may benefit from a provision that provides for averaging of income.

Some persons with fluctuating incomes may be eligible to pay less tax through this provision.

If the income for a given year exceeds 140% of the average annual income for the three preceding years, and the excess is more than $3,000, the taxpayer may be eligible to use this provision in figuring his tax liability.

For more information, obtain IRS booklet *Income Averaging* (publication 506).

TAX EFFECT OF CAPITAL GAINS AND LOSSES

Usually, the tax on capital gains is less than the tax on ordinary income.

If the net gains from the sale or exchange of long-term capital assets (those held longer than six months if acquired after June 22, 1984) are greater than the net losses from the sale or exchange of capital assets held for a shorter time, a tax rate of 20% applies to the gain.

Net short-term capital losses (on assets held less than six months) can be used dollar-for-dollar to offset ordinary income, subject to limitations, while $2 of *net* long-term capital losses are required to reduce ordinary income by $1.

For example, if a taxpayer has an overall net short-term capital loss of $2,000, all $2,000 can be used to offset ordinary income. On the other hand, if a taxpayer had incurred a net long-term capital loss of $2,000, only $1,000 (2,000 x 50%) would be allowed as an offset to ordinary income. The additional $1,000 is permanently lost.

INCOME FROM DIVIDENDS OR INTEREST

Similar to interest paid on savings, dividends, are distributions of cash, property, services, or accommodations by a corporation to its stockholders.

Such payments are taxable income to the stockholder. Distributions other than cash are taxed at their fair market value.

The gross amount must be reported. However, the first $100 of qualified dividends and interest may be excluded from income by a single person on Form 1040 or 1040A. To qualify for exclusion, dividends must be from taxable domestic corporations.

Husbands and wives filing a joint return are permitted up to $200 exclusions for dividends or interest.

In addition to industrial, mercantile, and other commercial corporations, the exclusion applies to dividends on the capital stock of nonexempt cooperatives, stock of the Federal National Mortgage Association, the capital stock of building and loan associations (as distinct from dividends on deposits and withdrawable accounts), and similar organizations.

Some types of corporations whose dividends do not qualify are: foreign corporations, China Trade Act corporations, exempt farmers' cooperatives, real estate investment trusts, corporations doing business in U.S. possessions (under certain conditions), and a corporation that has elected not to be taxed as a corporation.

PRESERVE ADEQUATE RECORDS

Maintain proper records to prepare federal income tax returns correctly. These records, if complete, help ensure that you will pay only the proper tax. File and store in a safe place sales slips, invoices, receipts, canceled checks, paid bills, and other documents that are used as evidence of transactions.

Copies of returns filed by the taxpayer should also be kept. These are of help in preparing future returns and if it later becomes necessary to file a claim for refund.

WHERE TO FILE AND WHEN

Individual federal income tax returns may be filed anytime on or after January 1 of the year following the year of earnings, but no later than midnight April 15, if the calendar year is the basis for these earnings.

All taxpayers—those entitled to refunds as well as those who are not—should file their returns directly with the Internal Revenue Service center that serves their state (as indicated in the tax form instructions).

If the fiscal year is used, the return is due on or before the 15th day of the fourth month after the close of the particular fiscal or tax year. Returns submitted by mail must be postmarked on or before the due date.

Payment must be made at the time the return is filed. Interest is charged on taxes paid after their due date, even though an extension for filing may have been authorized. The rate of interest is changed every six months. It was 13% from January 1, 1985, to June 30, 1985, and 11% from July 1, 1985, to December 31, 1985.

A penalty of $1/2$% a month or part of a month to a maximum of 25% is imposed for failure to pay when due. Additional penalties are assessed for failure to file.

U.S. citizens abroad on the final filing date are allowed automatic extensions without application to June 15, 1986. Military personnel on duty outside the U.S. and Puerto Rico are allowed the same extension. Statements that the taxpayer was outside the U.S. on the due date must accompany the return.

When filing a return, you should use the preaddressed label (showing your name, address, and Social Security number) that you receive with the form 1040 or 1040A tax packages from IRS at the end of the year. Use of this label expedites processing and the issuance of any refund due.

Before filing your income tax return, make sure it is complete in every detail. It *must* include your complete name, Social Security number, amount of wages from all W-2 forms, total of personal exemptions, deductions (regardless of how computed), and signature (of both husband and wife if a joint return). Any error or omission can result in a processing delay and may slow a tax refund payment.

ESTIMATED TAX RETURN

Generally a person must declare and pay an estimated tax if total tax liability is expected to exceed the amount withheld by $400 or more. Your estimated tax payments (including withholding taxes paid) must be equal to the lesser of 80% of the tax shown on your return for the current tax year or 100% of last year's tax.

HISTORY OF THE U.S. INCOME TAX

The federal government first levied an income tax from 1862 to 1872 to help pay for the Civil War.

A new income tax law passed by Congress in 1894 was declared unconstitutional by the Supreme Court.

In 1909 the first corporate income tax law was approved by Congress.

In 1911 Wisconsin became the first state to levy an income tax on residents.

The 16th Amendment to the U.S. Constitution, adopted in 1913, made possible the present system of federal income taxes.

The first of the new income taxes began to be collected under the Underwood Tariff Act, which became law in October 1913.

Payroll taxes began in 1935, and pay-as-you-go wage deductions in 1944.

Exemptions for those who are blind or are senior citizens, as well as joint returns for married couples, took effect in 1948.

Today federal tax returns of all business and individual taxpayers in the United States are processed by computers. The system has three major features: (1) It provides a continuing updated multiple-year digest of each individual and business taxpayer's history in a master file. (2) Each taxpayer is identified in the master file by number—individuals by their social security number and businesses by their employer identification number. (3) The system centralizes processing operations in regional centers.

Individuals send their returns to one of 10 regional processing centers, where they are reviewed and remittances deposited. The center then transcribes pertinent information to the master file.

STATE INCOME TAX RATES AND EXEMPTIONS: 1985

Sources: Tax Foundation; Commerce Clearing House

Seven of the 50 states of the United States do not assess state taxes on personal incomes, including Alaska, Florida, Nevada, South Dakota, Texas, Washington, and Wyoming.

STATE	PERSONAL EXEMPTIONS			INDIVIDUAL RATES
	Single	Married	Dependent	
Alabama	$1,500	$ 3,000	$ 300	From 2% on 1st $1,000 to 5% on income over $6,000
Arizona	$1,834	$ 3,668	$1,100	From 2% on 1st $1,061 to 8% on income over $6,366
Arkansas	$17.50[1]	$ 35[1]	$ 6[1]	From 1% on 1st $2,999 to 7% on income over $25,000
California	$ 40[1]	$ 80[1]	$ 13[1]	From 1% on 1st $4,810 to 11% on income over $26,601
Colorado	$1,200	$ 2,400	$1,200	From 2.5% on 1st $1,420 to 8% on $14,151 or more; 2% surtax on intangible income over $15,000
Connecticut [2]	$ 100	$ 200	—	7% on capital gains; 6% on dividends and interest if income $50,000 to $59,999, rising to 13% if income over $100,000
Delaware	$ 800	$ 1,600	$ 800	From 1.3% on 1st $1,000 to 10.7% on income over $40,000
Dist. of Col.	$ 750	$ 1,500	$ 750	From 2% on 1st $1,000 to 11% on income over $25,000
Georgia	$1,500	$ 3,000	$ 700	From 1% on 1st $1,000 to 6% on income over $10,000
Hawaii	$1,000	$ 2,000	$1,000	From 2.25% on 1st $1,000 to 11% on income over $61,000
Idaho	$1,000	$ 2,000	$3,000	From 2% on 1st $1,000 to 7.5% on income over $5,000; each person (husband and wife filing jointly are deemed one person) filing return pays additional $10
Illinois	$1,000	$ 2,000	$1,000	3% on net income
Indiana	$1,000	$ 2,000	$ 500	3% of adjusted gross income
Iowa	$ 20[1]	$ 40[1]	$ 15[1]	From 0.5% on 1st $1,023 to 13% on income over $76,725
Kansas	$1,000	$ 2,000	$1,000	From 2% on 1st $2,000 to 9% on income over $25,000
Kentucky	$ 20[1]	$ 40[1]	$ 20[1]	From 2% on 1st $3,000 to 6% on income over $8,000
Louisiana	$4,500	$ 9,000	$1,000	From 2% on 1st $10,000 to 6% on income over $50,000
Maine	$1,000	$ 2,000	$1,000	From 1% on 1st $2,000 to 10% on income over $25,000
Maryland	$ 800	$ 1,600	$ 800	From 2% on 1st $1,000 to 5% on income over $3,000
Massachusetts	$2,200	$ 4,400	$ 700	Interest, dividends, net capital gains, 10%; earned and business income, 5%; additional surtax, 7.5%
Michigan	$1,500	$ 3,000	$1,500	All taxable income, 5.35%
Minnesota	$ 70	$ 140	$ 70	From 1.6% on 1st $690 to 16% on income over $37,921
Mississippi	$6,000	$ 9,500	$1,500	First $5,000, 3%; over $10,000, 5%
Missouri	$1,200	$ 2,400	$ 400	From 1.5% on 1st $1,000 to 6% on income over $9,000
Montana	$1,000	$ 2,000	$1,000	From 2% on 1st $1,300 to 11% on income over $43,900
Nebraska	$ 750	$ 1,500	$ 750	19% of federal income tax liability
New Hampshire	$ 600	$ 1,200	—	5% on income from interest and dividends
New Jersey	$1,000	$ 2,000	$1,000	2% on 1st $20,000; 3.5% on income over $50,000
New Mexico	$ 750	$ 1,500	$ 750	0.7% on 1st $2,000 to 7.8% on income over $100,000
New York	$ 800	$ 1,600	$ 800	From 2% on 1st $1,000 to 13.75% on income over $23,000
North Carolina	$1,100	$ 2,200	$ 800	From 3% on 1st $2,000 to 7% on income over $10,000
North Dakota	$ 750	$ 1,500	$ 750	From 2% on 1st $3,000 to 9% on income over $50,000
Ohio	$ 650	$ 1,300	$ 650	From 0.95% on 1st $5,000 to 9.5% on income over $100,000
Oklahoma	$1,000	$ 2,000	$1,000	From 0.5% on 1st $2,000 to 6% on income over $15,000
Oregon	$1,000	$ 2,000	$1,000	From 4.2% on 1st $500 to 10.8% on income over $5,000
Pennsylvania	—	—	—	2.35% on all taxable income
Rhode Island	$ 750	$ 1,500	$ 750	23.65% of federal income tax liability
South Carolina	$ 800	$ 1,600	$ 800	From 2% on 1st $2,019 to 7% on income over $10,093
Tennessee	—	—	—	On dividends and interest, 6%; on dividends from corporations having 75% of property taxable in state, 4%
Utah	$ 750	$ 1,500	$ 750	From 2.25% on 1st $1,500 to 7.75% on excess over $7,500
Vermont	—	—	—	26.5% of federal income tax liability
Virginia	$ 600	$ 1,200	$ 600	From 2% on 1st $3,000 to 5¾% on income over $12,000
West Virginia	$ 800	$ 1,600	$ 800	From 2.1% on 1st $2,000 to 13% on excess over $200,000
Wisconsin	$ 20[1]	$ 40[1]	$ 20[1]	From 3.4% on 1st $3,900 to 10% on income over $51,600

[1] Credit against tax. [2] Tax applies only to adjusted gross incomes of $20,000 or more; capital gains tax applies to gains of $200 and over for joint returns and $100 or over for singles.

STATE CORPORATE INCOME TAXES: 1985[1]

Source: Tax Foundation

Only 5 of the 50 states of the United States do not levy state corporation income taxes. These states are Nevada, South Dakota, Texas, Washington, and Wyoming.

STATE	RATE	SPECIAL CONDITIONS
Alabama [2]	5.0%	
Alaska	1st $10,000 — 1.0% Next $10,000 — 2.0% Next $10,000 — 3.0% Next $10,000 — 4.0%	Next $10,000 — 5.0% Next $10,000 — 9.0% Next $10,000 — 6.0% $90,000 or more — 9.4% Next $10,000 — 7.0% Next $10,000 — 8.0%
Arizona [2]	1st $1,000 — 2.5% 2d $1,000 — 4.0% 3d $1,000 — 5.0%	4th $1,000 — 6.5% 6th $1,000 — 9.0% 5th $1,000 — 8.0% Over $6,000 — 10.5%
Arkansas	1st $3,000 — 1.0% 2d $3,000 — 2.0% Next $5,000 — 3.0%	Next $14,000 — 5.0% Over $25,000 — 6.0%
California	9.6%	Financial corporations except banks allowed limited offset for personal property taxes and license fees. Minimum tax: $200
Colorado	5.0%	
Connecticut	11.5%	Additional tax of 3.1 mills per dollar of capital stock and surplus to the extent that it exceeds net income tax
Delaware	8.7%	
Dist. of Columbia	10.0%	Minimum tax: $100; surtax of 5%.
Florida	5.5%	Exemption of $5,000 of net income allowed each corporation
Georgia	6.0%	
Hawaii	$25,000 or less — 5.85% Over $25,000 — 6.435%	Capital gains, 3.08%
Idaho	7.7%	
Illinois	4.0%	Additional 2.5% on personal property replacement
Indiana	3.0%	Based on adjusted gross income; supplemental 4% based on net income
Iowa [2]	1st $25,000 — 6.0% Next $75,000 — 8.0% Next $150,000 — 10.0% Over $250,000 — 12.0%	Financial institutions franchise tax 5% of taxable net income
Kansas	4.5%	A 2.25% surtax imposed on taxable income over $25,000
Kentucky	$25,000 or less — 3.0% Next $25,000 — 4.0%	Next $50,000 — 5.0% Over $100,000 — 6.0%
Louisiana [2]	1st $25,000 — 4.0% 2d $25,000 — 5.0% Next $50,000 — 6.0%	Next $100,000 — 7.0% Over $200,000 — 8.0%
Maine	1st $25,000 — 3.5% Next $50,000 — 7.93%	Next $175,000 — 8.33% Over $250,000 — 8.93%
Maryland	7.0%	
Massachusetts	8.33%	Net income tax supplemented by a $2.60 per $1,000 levy on tangible property not subject to local taxes, plus 8.33% of net income or $228, whichever is greater. A 14% surtax is also imposed. Interstate corporations not subject to corporate income tax pay 4% of net income plus the 14% surtax
Michigan [3]	2.35%	
Minnesota	1st $25,000 — 6.0%	Over $25,000 — 12.0%
Mississippi	1st $5,000 — 3.0%	Next $5,000 — 4.0% Over $10,000 — 5.0%
Missouri [2,3]	5.0%	
Montana	6.75%	Minimum tax: $50, except $10 for small business corporations
Nebraska	1st $50,000 — 4.75%	Over $50,000 — 6.65%
New Hampshire	8.0%	A 13.5% surtax is levied for fiscal year 1985.
New Jersey	9.0%	Added tax on net worth
New Mexico	1st $1,000,000 — 4.8%	2d $1,000,000 — 6% Over $2 million — 7.2%
New York [3]	10.0%	Alternative computing methods used if tax yield is more. Minimum tax: $250. Surcharge is 20%
North Carolina	6.0%	
North Dakota [2]	1st $3,000 — 3.0% Next $5,000 — 4.5% Next $12,000 — 6.0%	Next $10,000 — 7.5% Next $20,000 — 9.0% Over $50,000 — 10.5%
Ohio [3]	1st $25,000 — 5.1% Over $25,000 — 9.2%	Alternative computing methods used if tax yield is more; Minimum tax $50
Oklahoma	4.0%	
Oregon	7.5%	
Pennsylvania	9.5%	
Rhode Island	8.0%	If yield is greater, tax is 40¢ on each $100 of net worth
South Carolina	6.0%	
Tennessee	6.0%	Additional tax on dividends and interest
Utah	5.0%	Minimum tax: $100
Vermont	1st $10,000 — 6.0% Next $15,000 — 7.2% Next $225,000 — 8.4% Over $250,000 — 9.0%	Minimum tax: $75
Virginia	6.0%	
West Virginia	$50,000 or less — 6.0% Over $50,000 — 7.0%	15% surtax imposed through June 30, 1985
Wisconsin	7.9%	

[1] All states levy special financial institutions tax based on net income or on value of shares of capital stock.
[2] Federal income tax is deductible in computing state tax. [3] Local taxes also imposed.

STATE TAX COLLECTIONS: WHERE THE MONEY COMES FROM [1]

Source: U.S. Department of Commerce, Bureau of the Census

STATE	TOTAL	LICENSES	INDI-VIDUAL INCOME	CORPO-RATE INCOME	PROPERTY	DEATH AND GIFT	SEVERANCE	MISC. TAXES[2]
All states	$196,795,039	$11,921,805	$58,942,227	$15,511,378	$3,861,655	$2,226,041	$7,248,943	$1,282,226
Alabama......	2,704,250	150,679	623,173	223,816	57,768	9,456	119,525	7,298
Alaska........	1,973,252	54,444	1,151	304,621	131,050	692	1,393,039	—
Arizona.......	2,525,812	161,653	528,275	197,363	127,757	12,535	—	—
Arkansas	1,541,361	110,043	434,021	106,241	4,682	7,850	27,125	4,238
California	25,617,718	908,311	9,238,455	3,218,856	1,041,682	115,669	—	17,475
Colorado......	2,132,825	125,807	763,627	87,721	5,757	10,567	30,009	4,913
Connecticut ...	3,086,003	140,114	278,682	401,801	12	109,393	—	37,559
Delaware	712,596	200,478	343,451	44,857	—	10,621	—	19,942
Florida	7,329,368	453,504	—	365,446	149,256	78,729	157,823	393,176
Georgia.......	3,954,615	125,618	1,465,773	315,960	15,377	13,716	—	11,286
Hawaii........	1,247,968	19,082	402,821	36,978	—	6,652	—	1,804
Idaho.........	687,244	68,547	227,763	25,374	233	2,807	1,247	—
Illinois	8,701,267	598,734	2,961,077	563,961	189,981	105,016	—	6,813
Indiana	4,043,446	152,983	1,214,975	129,939	20,154	42,419	1,521	—
Iowa..........	2,241,503	199,253	788,001	132,093	—	57,541	—	2,758
Kansas	1,789,628	115,828	567,469	136,665	24,117	30,071	116,990	—
Kentucky	2,798,662	146,467	710,474	198,261	229,616	42,831	210,704	866
Louisiana	3,131,667	219,939	407,101	262,100	2,753	40,020	792,087	—
Maine	920,273	72,226	261,956	52,004	14,692	13,271	—	1,546
Maryland	3,946,833	147,004	1,607,502	198,364	119,705	31,918	—	57,044
Massachusetts..	5,839,414	174,354	2,790,067	729,634	3,298	127,138	—	22,318
Michigan	8,568,674	405,207	3,383,794	1,289,915	166,119	61,290	73,313	4,571
Minnesota	5,077,158	290,781	2,316,365	305,498	4,205	17,922	74,085	26,439
Mississippi	1,740,692	151,422	260,061	110,196	672	8,555	102,956	—
Missouri	3,053,002	230,194	903,604	165,652	5,753	24,314	26	1,403
Montana	583,341	52,477	170,346	35,396	38,797	5,960	144,761	874
Nebraska	1,068,742	85,031	304,318	66,909	2,623	6,829	4,539	1,976
Nevada	861,115	97,121	—	—	32,271	—	83	—
New Hampshire	423,465	60,065	22,244	95,664	16,238	11,702	56	21,502
New Jersey ...	7,137,452	505,702	1,767,684	830,106	42,870	171,363	—	29,907
New Mexico ...	1,377,444	82,209	74,862	53,399	13,903	2,956	367,449	—
New York	18,817,736	740,689	9,373,945	1,524,619	—	259,140	—	239,881
North Carolina.	4,636,021	338,671	1,784,987	368,047	72,530	71,586	1,334	—
North Dakota..	684,399	58,133	73,951	43,712	1,867	2,525	199,553	—
Ohio	7,985,012	548,989	2,486,822	524,891	114,095	45,977	6,624	—
Oklahoma.....	2,661,981	260,720	657,831	97,223	—	31,667	703,738	11,709
Oregon	1,850,523	206,646	1,217,842	144,065	540	34,489	29,188	1,445
Pennsylvania ..	9,600,168	977,646	2,536,872	865,299	180,585	282,237	—	107,713
Rhode Island ..	809,986	30,642	285,141	59,274	6,287	10,079	—	2,126
South Carolina.	2,384,926	111,672	795,481	159,334	8,883	18,752	—	12,627
South Dakota..	358,773	30,823	—	17,881	—	10,635	8,910	—
Tennessee	2,511,631	250,843	54,723	226,242	—	37,107	3,335	40,018
Texas	9,829,191	1,130,297	—	—	22	97,544	2,218,760	—
Utah	1,196,687	53,250	386,052	45,035	373	3,121	38,416	—
Vermont	412,987	39,707	132,153	22,606	628	1,791	—	5,303
Virginia	4,064,368	247,017	1,760,732	242,706	31,347	26,299	1,424	58,818
Washington ...	4,542,268	234,985	—	—	690,597	20,236	31,148	104,125
West Virginia ..	1,713,819	89,606	394,690	92,173	1,363	18,292	—	4,036
Wisconsin.....	5,116,236	206,444	2,181,913	393,481	168,334	71,994	875	18,523
Wyoming	801,537	59,748	—	—	122,863	2,769	388,300	—

[1] In $ thousands (add 000) for fiscal year 1984.
[2] Document, stock transfer, and miscellaneous taxes.

SALES TAXES AND GROSS RECEIPTS TAXES[1]

General Sales Tax	Motor Fuels	Alcoholic Beverages	Tobacco Products	Insurance	Public Utilities	Pari-mutuels	Amusements	STATE
$62,563,602	$12,395,562	$2,899,986	$4,149,028	$3,973,688	$5,875,048	$739,391	$383,747	All states
735,318	253,053	90,262	69,700	80,626	236,081	—	64	Alabama
(X)	32,169	12,984	5,426	16,172	1,603	—	—	Alaska
1,140,734	193,299	25,499	41,475	49,369	37,187	10,591	—	Arizona
562,686	139,756	25,689	61,101	37,336	(X)	20,593	—	Arkansas
8,787,026	1,212,892	137,386	262,549	457,367	32,131	135,059	—	California
791,382	188,739	24,900	47,504	40,142	2,339	9,007	411	Colorado
1,339,110	197,507	31,144	88,040	82,272	257,633	60,612	12,927	...Connecticut
(X)	37,394	4,996	12,015	15,660	20,764	69	—	Delaware
3,980,949	617,252	395,505	277,925	149,747	149,577	116,354	2,500	Florida
1,361,598	372,751	105,820	85,402	81,314	(X)	—	—	Georgia
639,247	34,556	−209	19,949	27,529	59,559	—	—	Hawaii
241,819	79,821	7,143	10,234	17,895	2,413	442	—	Idaho
2,651,129	533,166	71,610	167,351	102,892	640,431	62,704	7,920	Illinois
1,969,547	331,636	36,667	77,282	66,267	(X)	—	56	Indiana
736,265	196,128	16,561	59,094	52,338	1,197	—	—	Iowa
518,907	143,362	42,022	45,836	46,548	996	—	817	Kansas
754,320	200,722	48,828	19,455	95,477	(X)	10,295	276	Kentucky
885,447	195,904	54,359	57,643	121,369	37,838	25,606	196	Louisiana
315,373	85,190	30,950	28,601	17,532	25,798	1,134	—	Maine
988,284	290,259	28,688	66,482	73,570	84,602	15,512	972	Maryland
1,248,045	274,916	83,762	169,999	134,937	(X)	36,828	11,8944	Massachusetts
2,273,137	564,998	98,114	126,688	99,241	(X)	22.287	—	Michigan
1,250,835	332,616	53,566	84,385	70,781	70,680	—	10	Minnesota
866,040	122,439	34,969	34,081	48,936	(X)	—	365	Mississippi
1,328,464	197,044	24,512	81,905	88,921	1,210	—	—	Missouri
(X)	79,230	14,760	12,622	19,516	6,973	153	—	Montana
374,541	129,981	13,559	29,250	28,312	1,599	9,317	2,201	Nebraska
411,413	71,610	13,187	17,487	30,462	2,804	56	181,309	Nevada
(X)	64,500	9,300	33,098	17,097	6,073	8,333	—	New Hampshire
2,054,059	301,160	59,327	217,214	112,696	872,402	9,705	153,302	...New Jersey
578,387	107,119	16,768	14,621	30,593	5,199	4,224	99	...New Mexico
3,900,395	422,232	171,568	440,000	247,089	1,031,734	106,337	1,173	New York
1,002,119	398,634	117,810	16,804	105,888	333,944	—	—	..North Carolina
204,342	53,754	6,362	13,000	10,058	9,994	—	—	..North Dakota
2,602,174	615,996	71,128	182,354	159,311	608,031	18,613	—	Ohio
456,679	145,453	39,626	77,457	100,307	14,005	—	—	Oklahoma
(X)	105,362	10,595	55,230	36,657	4,138	4,326	—	Oregon
2,720,628	598,533	132,367	242,717	187,066	511,126	20,577	199	.Pennsylvania
247,786	45,410	7,642	29,239	16,444	58,882	5,496	88	..Rhode Island
798,896	237,422	98,836	29,767	62,098	23,152	—	6,050	South Carolina
179,179	57,567	9,775	10,508	15,620	621	2,403	—	..South Dakota
1,356,733	290,029	60,711	77,735	76,813	28,596	—	413	Tennessee
3,803,548	515,494	284,804	340,272	362,460	296,213	—	361	Texas
529,091	87,947	13,488	12,855	24,569	2,490	—	—	Utah
81,097	36,968	14,335	12,734	8,173	14,168	925	—	Vermont
832,982	324,973	90,646	17,204	97,014	120,037	—	85	Virginia
2,725,534	338,610	104,421	99,303	56,456	126,173	10,645	35	...Washington
786,689	159,612	6,800	35,664	37,780	(X)	11,155	—	..West Virginia
1,374,566	343,897	44,963	126,714	49,288	134,655	—	24	Wisconsin
177,103	36,500	1,481	5,057	7,683	(X)	33	—	Wyoming

[1] Does not include miscellaneous Selective Sales taxes.
X Not applicable.

STATE EXPENDITURES: WHERE THE TAX MONEY GOES[1]

Source: U.S. Department of Commerce, Bureau of the Census

STATE	TOTAL[2]	EDU-CATION	PUBLIC WELFARE	HIGHWAYS	HOSPI-TALS	NATURAL RE-SOURCES	HEALTH	INSUR-ANCE TRUSTS[3]
All States	$334,019,136	$107,702,727	$57,544,499	$26,430,814	$14,914,997	$5,833,949	$9,010,726	$42,180,123
Alabama	5,220,496	2,197,274	552,671	514,477	334,894	94,341	127,799	458,022
Alaska	3,835,983	924,391	173,014	361,269	25,234	222,228	91,022	160,318
Arizona	3,589,486	1,552,791	266,464	373,405	113,958	50,753	67,937	365,992
Arkansas	2,487,836	945,490	391,984	291,745	109,516	68,421	62,574	233,551
California	42,493,210	13,921,646	10,000,112	1,835,727	1,062,943	962,486	1,211,711	6,001,139
Colorado......	4,061,778	1,573,381	586,879	323,094	203,366	78,791	95,187	576,207
Connecticut ...	4,427,351	1,075,092	842,247	267,621	306,400	36,660	87,807	533,675
Delaware	1,072,177	422,518	64,029	114,354	40,424	23,473	26,545	73,922
Florida	9,873,718	4,076,586	1,141,738	956,301	401,134	337,574	493,771	702,728
Georgia.......	6,563,235	2,561,427	1,011,453	778,092	289,575	135,242	230,672	550,246
Hawaii........	2,178,080	709,289	288,550	107,365	113,980	56,640	66,713	201,183
Idaho.........	1,245,388	423,104	121,114	160,099	29,962	54,786	36,477	175,668
Illinois........	15,003,880	4,262,278	3,193,161	1,254,911	469,811	139,134	320,005	2,735,182
Indiana	5,843,332	2,385,191	837,208	546,916	228,259	97,696	151,195	632,046
Iowa..........	4,157,238	1,575,272	629,561	496,572	258,473	77,762	42,183	439,574
Kansas	2,864,360	1,124,700	489,130	297,588	166,159	75,962	45,827	322,264
Kentucky	5,165,122	1,847,442	749,398	640,725	139,088	118,356	116,056	616,074
Louisiana	7,431,319	2,292,628	917,902	824,022	466,549	204,825	153,045	1,137,335
Maine	1,671,195	463,214	360,874	163,333	37,334	48,052	40,528	192,062
Maryland	6,921,024	1,797,089	1,024,227	759,845	492,707	103,177	197,869	726,535
Massachusetts	9,332,044	1,886,345	2,195,438	444,301	421,408	48,996	405,811	1,002,154
Michigan	14,789,362	3,815,896	3,535,777	878,963	754,746	146,762	577,166	2,301,597
Minnesota	6,495,649	2,058,177	1,196,838	600,412	310,947	163,989	90,145	669,799
Mississippi....	3,132,375	1,139,530	425,212	356,451	145,442	93,724	74,239	291,115
Missouri	4,780,214	1,753,145	805,680	495,501	268,893	106,055	128,557	453,986
Montana	1,263,305	384,070	151,517	168,297	30,432	64,772	38,116	170,785
Nebraska	1,806,700	606,093	285,411	272,434	106,397	68,790	63,199	84,830
Nevada	1,569,976	460,268	109,045	164,115	24,048	20,451	28,567	282,171
New Hampshire	1,109,030	225,789	164,833	142,639	40,597	14,529	46,259	74,573
New Jersey ...	11,764,456	2,895,702	1,873,873	642,517	459,410	144,127	181,907	1,518,313
New Mexico ...	2,692,239	1,098,558	217,763	324,900	111,958	49,246	79,289	168,255
New York	31,921,272	7,944,286	6,929,476	1,403,574	1,918,929	164,145	777,906	2,827,278
North Carolina..	7,231,806	3,124,452	851,486	625,123	367,935	152,350	201,600	804,290
North Dakota..	1,301,979	498,395	116,580	148,887	58,032	44,170	32,569	100,504
Ohio	15,900,597	4,630,704	2,698,014	1,103,157	717,902	131,532	564,701	3,667,477
Oklahoma.....	4,772,191	1,955,546	719,937	489,582	268,897	80,813	106,527	484,583
Oregon	4,356,447	1,131,185	444,066	344,337	173,571	114,259	80,035	731,366
Pennsylvania..	16,732,856	4,126,631	3,512,807	1,382,494	790,712	210,181	403,452	3,306,344
Rhode Island ..	1,707,511	440,728	377,333	58,578	101,294	10,442	56,803	212,375
South Carolina.	4,229,318	1,545,457	452,665	270,852	225,686	79,669	133,174	427,663
South Dakota..	858,527	242,338	114,906	128,203	23,900	43,669	24,326	39,211
Tennessee	4,578,341	1,650,903	695,339	519,657	223,932	70,349	148,223	516,480
Texas	15,796,491	7,441,919	1,924,401	1,564,518	904,559	246,329	295,865	1,681,005
Utah	2,303,907	1,029,287	252,971	196,225	93,515	54,094	56,600	249,041
Vermont	889,926	267,026	143,523	92,608	23,912	27,212	33,798	59,502
Virginia.......	6,746,574	2,435,962	863,513	779,217	522,939	63,959	184,440	437,458
Washington ...	7,907,602	2,993,309	935,740	717,071	207,507	191,916	199,441	1,319,427
West Virginia..	3,046,333	981,368	297,543	367,045	92,988	61,992	66,951	629,114
Wisconsin.....	7,632,876	2,477,181	1,536,109	478,021	206,643	132,850	232,245	676,367
Wyoming	1,263,044	331,781	74,987	203,674	28,105	46,218	24,892	159,337

[1] In $ thousands for fiscal year 1983. [2] Includes other expenditures not categorized. [3] Includes payments for employee retirement, unemployment compensation, workmen's compensation, and disability benefit social insurance programs.

STATE RETAIL SALES TAXES: 1985 [1]

Source: Tax Foundation

STATE	TAX	STATE	TAX	STATE	TAX	STATE	TAX
Alabama	4%	Indiana	5%	Nebraska	3.5%	South Carolina	5%
Alaska	—	Iowa	4%	Nevada	5.75%	South Dakota	4%
Arizona	5%	Kansas	3%	New Hampshire	—	Tennessee	5.5%
Arkansas	4%	Kentucky	5%	New Jersey	6%	Texas	4.125%
California	4.75%	Louisiana	4%	New Mexico	3.75%	Utah	4⅝%
Colorado	3%	Maine	5%	New York [2]	4%	Vermont	4%
Connecticut	7.5%	Maryland	5%	North Carolina	3%	Virginia	3%
Delaware	—	Massachusetts	5%	North Dakota	4%	Washington	6.5%
Florida	5%	Michigan	4%	Ohio	5%	West Virginia	5%
Georgia	3%	Minnesota	6%	Oklahoma	3%	Wisconsin	5%
Hawaii	4%	Mississippi	6%	Oregon	—	Wyoming	3%
Idaho	4%	Missouri	4.225%	Pennsylvania	6%	District of	
Illinois	5%	Montana	—	Rhode Island	6%	Columbia	6%

[1] Does not include local sales taxes, which are imposed in 33 states. [2] In New York City, 8¼%.

FEDERAL EXPENDITURES BY STATE

Source: U.S. Department of Commerce

The federal government in fiscal 1984 provided $97.2 billion in grants to state and local governments, $108.6 billion spent on salaries and wages, and $325.8 billion in direct payments to individuals.

California received the largest amount of federal expenditures—$91.7 billion. New York was second with $53.3 billion.

STATE	TOTAL*	PER CAPITA	STATE	TOTAL*	PER CAPITA	STATE	TOTAL*	PER CAPITA
Alabama	$11,444	$2,868.17	Louisiana	$10,693	$2,396.26	North Dakota	$ 2,276	$3,317.03
Alaska	2,322	4,642.17	Maine	3,341	2,891.07	Ohio	25,670	2,387.51
Arizona	9,174	3,005.21	Maryland	18,783	4,318.85	Oklahoma	8,404	2,548.52
Arkansas	6,088	2,591.67	Massachusetts	21,422	3,694.79	Oregon	6,545	2,447.62
California	91,713	3,579.46	Michigan	20,297	2,236.70	Pennsylvania	32,413	2,723.56
Colorado	9,165	2,883.86	Minnesota	10,591	2,544.82	Rhode Island	2,982	3,098.95
Connecticut	12,791	4,055.42	Mississippi	8,278	3,186.51	South Carolina	8,947	2,711.12
Delaware	1,635	2,667.75	Missouri	20,335	4,060.38	South Dakota	2,056	2,911.91
Florida	33,224	3,026.89	Montana	2,377	2,884.05	Tennessee	13,610	2,885.27
Georgia	15,915	2,726.37	Nebraska	4,119	2,564.91	Texas	39,275	2,456.36
Hawaii	4,232	4,072.89	Nevada	2,807	3,081.21	Utah	4,840	2,929.75
Idaho	2,497	2,493.89	New Hampshire	2,904	2,971.45	Vermont	1,394	2,631.19
Illinois	25,506	2,215.76	New Jersey	20,433	2,718.93	Virginia	24,251	4,302.98
Indiana	13,037	2,371.22	New Mexico	6,131	4,305.82	Washington	14,812	3,405.67
Iowa	6,332	2,176.18	New York	53,298	3,005.31	West Virginia	4,825	2,472.44
Kansas	8,158	3,345.97	North Carolina	13,626	2,210.28	Wisconsin	10,853	2,277.31
Kentucky	9,369	2,516.56				Wyoming	1,472	2,879.17

* In $ millions (add 000,000). For fiscal 1984.

STATE DEBTS

Source: U.S. Department of Commerce

The outstanding gross debt of the 50 states at the end of the 1983 fiscal year reached a new high—$167,289,946,000.

This debt averaged $716.88 per capita.

STATE	TOTAL DEBT*	DEBT PER CAPITA	STATE	TOTAL DEBT*	DEBT PER CAPITA	STATE	TOTAL DEBT*	DEBT PER CAPITA
Alabama	$2,339,606	$ 590.96	Louisiana	$5,244,181	$1,181.65	North Dakota	$ 381,830	$ 561.51
Alaska	4,665,456	9,739.99	Maine	1,073,010	936.31	Ohio	6,094,837	567.17
Arizona	558,627	188.53	Maryland	4,661,773	1,083.13	Oklahoma	1,331,290	403.67
Arkansas	650,995	279.64	Massachusetts	7,888,009	1,367.78	Oregon	6,589,036	2,475.22
California	12,071,209	479.51	Michigan	4,669,139	514.85	Pennsylvania	6,496,934	546.19
Colorado	1,150,530	366.53	Minnesota	2,761,480	666.38	Rhode Island	2,225,528	2,330.40
Connecticut	5,236,226	1,668.65	Mississippi	908,310	351.11	South Carolina	3,153,922	966.28
Delaware	1,562,169	2,577.84	Missouri	2,250,613	452.84	South Dakota	791,107	1,130.15
Florida	3,566,782	333.97	Montana	511,569	626.16	Tennessee	1,797,131	383.59
Georgia	1,844,100	321.72	Nebraska	387,355	242.55	Texas	3,028,877	192.63
Hawaii	2,320,186	2,268.02	Nevada	757,067	849.68	Utah	1,070,279	661.07
Idaho	448,342	453.33	New Hampshire	1,531,667	1,597.15	Vermont	764,745	1,456.66
Illinois	7,862,325	684.51	New Jersey	10,306,360	1,380.07	Virginia	2,666,034	480.37
Indiana	1,208,419	220.55	New Mexico	1,076,327	769.35	Washington	2,527,097	587.70
Iowa	594,381	204.61	New York	27,765,418	1,571.60	West Virginia	1,675,680	852.76
Kansas	379,435	156.47	North Carolina	1,622,561	266.78	Wisconsin	3,210,023	675.65
Kentucky	3,030,863	816.06				Wyoming	581,100	1,130.54

* In $ thousands (add 000).

CITY INCOME TAXES: 1985

Sources: Tax Foundation

Philadelphia has the distinction of levying the oldest and highest local income tax in effect today. Earlier efforts at such taxation, including one in Charleston, S.C., in the early 1800s, foundered on administrative difficulties.

Since the path-breaking Philadelphia enactment in 1939, however, about 4,000 localities in 11 states have followed suit. And authorizations have been granted (although no locality has acted) in Arkansas and Kansas.

In addition, a related levy has been imposed on employers: the local payroll tax, based on an employer's wage expenses. This has been enacted in Jersey City, Newark, N.J., Los Angeles, San Francisco, and four Oregon counties.

Despite first impressions from the table that follows, the local income tax is primarily a big-city phenomenon.

Most of the taxing jurisdictions are small, but this is because many—over 3,900—small towns and school districts in Ohio and Pennsylvania use the levy. Elsewhere the tax is typically used by large jurisdictions.

Nine of the 25 largest cities in the United States, including Washington, D.C., impose their own income taxes.

Few of these local taxes are really comparable to state or U.S. taxes, since most apply only to wages and salaries—"earned" income. However, those

levied by New York City, Baltimore, and cities in Michigan are closely linked, both in coverage and administration, to overlapping state taxes.

In the District of Columbia, it is similar to a state income tax.

Besides the roughly 40 million residents in localities levying income taxes, countless others who work in them but live elsewhere—commuters in Alabama, Delaware, Kentucky, Missouri, Ohio, and Pennsylvania—are subject to the levy.

Maryland's local taxes apply to residents only, as does the District of Columbia's tax.

Commuters in Michigan pay one-half the resident rates, while those in New York City pay sharply lower rates.

Where many localities in the same area tax income, special arrangements are necessary to avoid unfair treatment of those who work in one jurisdiction but live in another.

As the table below shows, local income taxes are essentially confined to the states in the Northeast and Middle Atlantic regions—with the exception of St. Louis and Kansas City, Mo., and eight places in Alabama, including Birmingham and Gadsden.

The table below, compiled by the Tax Foundation from Commerce Clearing House data, lists the rates in effect as of April 1, 1985, for all U.S. localities with income taxes.

CITY AND LOCAL INCOME TAXES AND RATES [1]

STATE AND LOCALITY	RATE	STATE AND LOCALITY	RATE	STATE AND LOCALITY	RATE
Alabama		**Michigan** (continued)		**Ohio** (continued)	
Birmingham	1.0%	Lansing	1.0%	Springfield	2.5%
Gadsden	2.0%	Pontiac	1.0%	Toledo	2.25%
6 cities		Saginaw	1.0%	Warren	1.5%
under 50,000	1.0–2.0%	10 cities		Youngstown	2.0%
		under 50,000	1.0%-2.0%	Over 400 cities	
Delaware				and villages	
Wilmington	1.25%	**Missouri**		under 50,000	0.25–2.5%
		Kansas City	1.0%		
Indiana		St. Louis	1.0%	**Pennsylvania**	
49 counties	0.2–1.0%			Abington Township	1.0%
		New York		Allentown	1.0%
Iowa		New York City [4]	0.9–4.3%	Altoona	1.0%
57 school districts [3]	2.0–17.75%	Yonkers [3]	15%	Bethlehem	1.0%
				Chester	1.0%
Kentucky		**Ohio**		Erie	1.0%
Covington	2.5%	Akron	2.0%	Harrisburg	1.0%
Lexington	2.0%	Canton	2.0%	Lancaster	1.0%
Louisville [2]	2.2%	Cincinnati	2.0%	Penn Hills	
Owensboro	1.0%	Cleveland	2.0%	Township	1.0%
65 cities		Cleveland Heights	2.0%	Philadelphia	4.96%
under 50,000	0.5–2.5%	Columbus	2.25%	Pittsburgh [5]	4.0%
8 counties	0.25–2.0%	Dayton	2.25%	Reading	1.0%
		Elyria	1.5%	Scranton [5]	3.5%
Maryland		Euclid	2.0%	Wilkes-Barre	2.5%
Baltimore [3]	50.0%	Hamilton	1.75%	York	1.0%
24 counties [3]	20.0–50.0%	Kettering	1.75%	Over 3,500	
		Lakewood	1.5%	other local	
Michigan		Lima	1.5%	jurisdictions	Up to 2.0%
Detroit	3.0%	Lorain	1.5%	**Washington, D.C.** [4]	2.0–11.0%
Flint	1.0%	Mansfield	1.0%		
Grand Rapids	1.0%	Parma	2.0%		

[1] Rates shown separately for cities of 50,000 or more. Where rates differ for resident and nonresident income, only resident rates are given. In Ohio and Pennsylvania cities, rates are the same. [2] Includes 0.75% additional tax imposed on residents of Louisville and Jefferson county for school purposes. [3] Percent of state income tax. [4] Resident income taxes are progressive. [5] Includes additional tax for school district.

Travel and Transportation

A stamp honoring the 1909 Stanley Steamer was issued by the U.S. Postal Service on April 3 in Kingfield, Maine, the hometown of Francis E. and Freelan O. Stanley, who first produced a steam-powered automobile in 1897. The stamp is part of a continuing transportation series that features early modes of transportation.

HIGHLIGHTS: 1985

TENNESSEE WINS SATURN
General Motors announced in July that its new $5 billion Saturn manufacturing plant would be located in Spring Hill, Tenn. The announcement ended months of visits by governors and mayors to GM headquarters as they offered millions of dollars in incentives to the automobile company in efforts to win for their own locality the huge plant with its 6,000 to 15,000 jobs.

The facility will build the Saturn subcompact car, GM's first new brand name automobile since World War I.

L.A. TOPS IN AUTO COSTS
The Hertz Corp. reported that a survey of major cities showed that Los Angeles is the most expensive place to own an automobile, registering an average cost per mile of 60.69 cents for a compact car. San Francisco was second with a cost of 58.16 cents per mile, and New York was third with 57.25 cents.

The remainder of the 10 most costly cities

for auto owners were Miami, 53.47 cents per mile; Chicago, 52.74 cents; Denver, 51.91 cents; St. Louis, 51.57 cents; Seattle, 50.58 cents; Houston, 49.31 cents; and Boston, 48.48 cents.

All 10 of these cities were higher than the average for the United States as a whole—45.67 cents per mile.

ROUTE 66: 1926-1985
U.S.66, the 2,200-mile highway from Chicago to California, faded into history in 1985 as it was decertified in June by the American Association of State Highway and Transportation Officials.

The highway, which was the subject of a popular song in the 1940s and a TV series in the 1960s, has been displaced by the new Interstate Highway System. It was first designated as U.S.66 in 1926.

ADDED NATIONAL HISTORIC LANDMARKS
Four presidential homes, two ships, and a

STATE PARKS

Source: National Association of State Park Directors

STATE	ACRES	STATE	ACRES	STATE	ACRES	STATE	ACRES
Alabama	48,027	Indiana	54,143	Nebraska	136,935	South Carolina	81,206
Alaska	3,000,000	Iowa	161,195	Nevada	152,964	South Dakota .	90,485
Arizona	33,841	Kansas	31,316	New Hampshire	70,979	Tennessee ...	166,548
Arkansas	44,235	Kentucky	42,813	New Jersey ...	290,353	Texas........	194,296
California	1,100,000	Louisiana	36,624	New Mexico ..	108,938	Utah.........	96,176
Colorado.....	159,693	Maine	66,451	New York	255,911	Vermont......	177,320
Connecticut ..	167,119	Maryland	217,327	North Carolina	120,335	Virginia	49,998
Delaware.....	10,129	Massachusetts	261,354	North Dakota .	15,259	Washington ..	220,000
Florida........	252,696	Michigan	247,737	Ohio.........	111,797	West Virginia .	149,951
Georgia	60,233	Minnesota....	182,143	Oklahoma	99,830	Wisconsin	120,792
Hawaii	20,534	Mississippi ...	20,542	Oregon	88,494	Wyoming.....	123,486
Idaho........	41,713	Missouri	97,670	Pennsylvania .	278,909		
Illinois	273,358	Montana	49,275	Rhode Island .	10,596		

Pullman car were among 11 new national historic landmarks designated by Secretary of the Interior Donald P. Hodel in May. The properties are:

Balclutha, a sailing ship in the National Maritime Museum at the Golden Gate National Recreation Area in California; built in 1886, it is the last square-rigged ship in San Francisco Bay.

Eureka, the last wooden side-wheel steamboat still afloat in the U.S.; at the National Maritime Museum in the Golden Gate National Recreation Area in California.

Governors Island in New York harbor, which was fortified before the War of 1812.

Harry S. Truman's farm home in Grandview, Mo., where he lived before World War I.

Hoover House in Palo Alto, Calif., designed by former First Lady Lou Henry Hoover, used as the Hoover family home from the 1920s to the 1940s.

Pension Building in Washington, D.C., built in 1835.

Prospect, home of Woodrow Wilson when he was president of Princeton University in New Jersey.

Pullman car Ferdinand Magellan in rail museum in Miami, Fla., which has been used by many Presidents.

Sayler's Creek Battlefield in Prince Edward County, Va., where Confederate Gen. Robert E. Lee fought his last battle before surrendering at Appomattox.

Ulysses S. Grant's boyhood home in Georgetown, Ohio.

Wayside, in Concord, Mass., where Nathaniel Hawthorne and Louisa May Alcott wrote some of their books.

CUMBERLAND GAP TUNNEL

Secretary of the Interior Hodel announced on May 16 he had approved construction of a $156 million highway tunnel to run under Cumberland Gap National Historic Park in Kentucky and Tennessee. He said the decision was made possible because the two states had agreed to be responsible for the annual maintenance costs of the tunnel, which have been estimated at $250,000.

The tunnel, which has been in the planning stage for a dozen years, would be 4,100 feet long. The project will involve the relocation of 4.2 miles of highway, removing the heavy traffic on U.S. route 25E from the park.

The federal government already has spent some $4.6 million on the project for planning and exploratory drilling.

LOXAHATCHEE RIVER

A 7.5-mile section of the Loxahatchee River in Florida was added to the National Wild and Scenic River System in May. The designated portion of the river extends from Riverbend Park in Palm Beach County to the southern boundary of Jonathan Dickinson State Park in Martin County.

The Loxahatchee became the 66th U.S. river to be included in the system, which was established in 1968 to protect the scenic qualities of waterways from commercial development.

REQUIRED USE OF SEAT BELTS

The first state law requiring automobile drivers and front seat passengers to buckle into seat belts went into effect in New York on Jan. 1, 1985. New Jersey became the second state to enforce a mandatory seat belt law on March 8, and Illinois followed on July 1.

The U.S. Department of Transportation has estimated that if all 50 states enforced such laws some 6,700 lives would be saved each year in automobile accidents.

AUTO SAFETY HOTLINE: 800-424-9393

You can phone this toll-free number day or night to report vehicle-safety problems and obtain vehicle-recall information from the National Highway Traffic Safety Administration.

HOW TO FIGURE OUT YOUR CAR'S MPG (MILES PER GALLON)

Source: General Services Administration

To check the miles-per-gallon (mpg) fuel economy of your automobile: (1) Fill your car with gasoline. (2) Write down the mileage shown on your car's odometer. (3) The next time you fill your car with gasoline, write down exactly how many gallons it takes. (4) Calculate how many miles you have gone since you last filled it. (5) Then use the following chart to discover how many miles per gallon your car gets. Locate (a) the number of gallons your car used in the row across the top of the table and (b) the number of miles it went in the left-hand column. The intersection of these two columns tells you the number of miles per gallon your car gets. For example, if it went 220 miles and used 15 gallons of gasoline, the table shows your car gets 14.7 mpg.

MILES	5	6	7	8	9	10	11	12	13	14	15	16	17	18	19	20	21	22	23	24	25
												NUMBER OF GALLONS OF GASOLINE USED (top row)									
100	20.0	16.7	14.3	12.5	11.1	10.0	9.1	8.3	7.7	7.1	6.7	6.3	5.9	5.6	5.3	5.0	4.8	4.5	4.3	4.2	4.0
110	22.0	18.3	15.7	13.8	12.2	11.0	10.0	9.2	8.5	7.9	7.3	6.9	6.5	6.1	5.8	5.5	5.2	5.0	4.8	4.6	4.4
120	24.0	20.0	17.1	15.0	13.3	12.0	10.9	10.0	9.2	8.6	8.0	7.5	7.1	6.7	6.3	6.0	5.7	5.5	5.2	5.0	4.8
130	26.0	21.7	18.6	16.3	14.4	13.0	11.8	10.8	10.0	9.3	8.7	8.1	7.6	7.2	6.8	6.5	6.2	5.9	5.7	5.4	5.2
140	28.0	23.3	20.0	17.5	15.6	14.0	12.7	11.7	10.8	10.0	9.3	8.8	8.2	7.8	7.4	7.0	6.7	6.4	6.1	5.8	5.6
150	30.0	25.0	21.4	18.8	16.7	15.0	13.6	12.5	11.5	10.7	10.0	9.4	8.8	8.3	7.9	7.5	7.1	6.8	6.5	6.3	6.0
160	32.0	26.7	22.9	20.0	17.8	16.0	14.5	13.3	12.3	11.4	10.7	10.0	9.4	8.9	8.4	8.0	7.6	7.3	7.0	6.7	6.4
170	34.0	28.3	24.3	21.3	18.9	17.0	15.5	14.2	13.1	12.1	11.3	10.6	10.0	9.4	8.9	8.5	8.1	7.7	7.4	7.1	6.8
180	36.0	30.0	25.7	22.5	20.0	18.0	16.4	15.0	13.8	12.9	12.0	11.3	10.6	10.0	9.5	9.0	8.6	8.2	7.8	7.5	7.2
190	38.0	31.7	27.1	23.8	21.1	19.0	17.3	15.8	14.6	13.6	12.7	11.9	11.2	10.6	10.0	9.5	9.0	8.6	8.3	7.9	7.6
200	40.0	33.3	28.6	25.0	22.2	20.0	18.2	16.7	15.4	14.3	13.3	12.5	11.8	11.1	10.5	10.0	9.5	9.1	8.7	8.3	8.0
210	42.9	35.0	30.0	26.3	23.3	21.0	19.1	17.5	16.2	15.0	14.0	13.1	12.4	11.7	11.1	10.5	10.0	9.5	9.1	8.8	8.4
220	44.0	36.7	31.4	27.5	24.4	22.0	20.0	18.3	16.9	15.7	14.7	13.8	12.9	12.2	11.6	11.0	10.5	10.0	9.6	9.2	8.8
230	46.0	38.3	32.9	28.8	25.6	23.0	20.9	19.2	17.7	16.4	15.3	14.4	13.5	12.8	12.1	11.5	11.0	10.5	10.0	9.6	9.2
240	48.0	40.0	34.3	30.0	26.7	24.0	21.8	20.0	18.5	17.1	16.0	15.0	14.1	13.3	12.6	12.0	11.4	10.9	10.4	10.0	9.6
250	50.0	41.7	35.7	31.3	27.8	25.0	22.7	20.8	19.2	17.9	16.7	15.6	14.7	13.9	13.2	12.5	11.9	11.4	10.9	10.4	10.0
260	52.0	43.3	37.1	32.5	28.9	26.0	23.6	21.7	20.0	18.6	17.3	16.3	15.3	14.4	13.7	13.0	12.4	11.8	11.3	10.8	10.4
270	54.0	45.0	38.6	33.8	30.0	27.0	24.5	22.5	20.8	19.3	18.0	16.9	15.9	15.0	14.2	13.5	12.9	12.3	11.7	11.3	10.8
280	56.0	46.7	40.0	35.0	31.1	28.0	25.5	23.3	21.5	20.0	18.7	17.5	16.5	15.6	14.7	14.0	13.3	12.7	12.2	11.7	11.2
290	58.0	48.3	41.4	36.3	32.2	29.0	26.4	24.2	22.3	20.7	19.3	18.1	17.1	16.1	15.3	14.5	13.8	13.2	12.6	12.1	11.6
300	60.0	50.0	42.9	37.5	33.3	30.0	27.3	25.0	23.1	21.4	20.0	18.8	17.6	16.7	15.8	15.0	14.3	13.6	13.0	12.5	12.0
310	62.0	51.7	44.3	38.7	34.4	31.0	28.2	25.8	23.8	22.1	20.7	19.4	18.2	17.2	16.3	15.5	14.7	14.1	13.5	12.9	12.4
320	64.0	53.3	45.7	40.0	35.6	32.0	29.1	26.7	24.6	22.9	21.3	20.0	18.8	17.8	16.8	16.0	15.2	14.5	13.9	13.3	12.6
330	66.0	55.0	47.1	41.3	36.7	33.0	30.0	27.5	25.4	23.6	22.0	20.6	19.4	18.3	17.4	16.5	15.7	15.0	14.3	13.7	13.2
340	68.0	56.7	48.6	42.5	37.8	34.0	30.9	28.3	26.2	24.3	22.7	21.3	20.0	18.9	17.9	17.0	16.2	15.5	14.8	14.2	13.6
350	70.0	58.3	50.0	43.7	38.9	35.0	31.8	29.2	26.9	25.0	23.3	21.9	20.6	19.4	18.4	17.5	16.7	15.9	15.2	14.6	14.0

WHAT IS THE YEARLY COST OF FUEL FOR YOUR CAR?

Based on an average of driving 12,000 miles per year, the following table shows the annual cost of your car's fuel. For example, if you pay $1.35 per gallon, and your car gets 20 mpg (miles per gallon) for 12,000 miles, then the annual cost of fuel for your car is $810.

MPG	$1.00	$1.05	$1.10	$1.15	$1.20	$1.25	$1.30	$1.35	$1.40	$1.45	$1.50	$1.55	$1.60	$1.65	$1.70	$1.75
							PRICE PER GALLON OF FUEL (top row)									
50	$240	$252	$264	$276	$288	$300	$312	$324	$336	$348	$360	$372	$384	$396	$408	$420
48	250	262	275	287	300	312	325	337	350	362	375	387	400	412	425	437
46	260	273	286	300	313	326	339	352	365	378	391	404	417	430	443	456
44	272	286	300	313	327	340	354	368	381	395	409	422	436	450	463	477
42	285	300	314	328	342	357	371	385	400	414	428	442	457	471	485	500
40	300	315	330	345	360	375	390	405	420	435	450	465	480	495	510	525
38	315	331	347	363	378	394	410	426	442	457	473	489	505	521	536	552
36	333	350	366	383	400	416	433	450	466	483	500	516	533	550	566	583
34	352	370	388	405	423	441	458	476	494	511	529	547	564	582	600	617
32	375	393	412	431	450	468	487	506	525	543	562	581	600	618	637	656
30	400	420	440	460	480	500	520	540	560	580	600	620	640	660	680	700
28	428	450	471	492	514	535	557	578	600	621	642	664	685	707	728	750
26	461	484	507	530	553	576	600	623	646	669	692	715	738	761	784	807
24	500	525	550	575	600	625	650	675	700	725	750	775	800	825	850	875
22	545	572	600	627	654	681	709	736	763	790	818	845	872	900	927	954
20	600	630	660	690	720	750	780	810	840	870	900	930	960	990	1,020	1,050
18	666	700	733	766	800	833	866	900	933	966	1,000	1,033	1,066	1,100	1,133	1,166
16	750	787	825	862	900	937	975	1,012	1,050	1,087	1,125	1,162	1,200	1,237	1,275	1,312
14	857	900	942	985	1,028	1,071	1,114	1,157	1,200	1,242	1,285	1,328	1,371	1,414	1,457	1,500
12	1,000	1,050	1,100	1,150	1,200	1,250	1,300	1,350	1,400	1,450	1,500	1,550	1,600	1,650	1,700	1,750
10	1,200	1,260	1,320	1,380	1,440	1,500	1,560	1,620	1,680	1,740	1,800	1,860	1,920	1,980	2,040	2,100

WORLD'S MAJOR ENGINEERING FEATS

STRUCTURE	LOCATION	FEATURES
Longest rail tunnel	Seikan, Japan	33.5 miles long (under construction)
Longest road tunnel	St. Gotthard, Switzerland	10.01 miles long (opens in 1980)
Longest water tunnel	Delaware Aqueduct, New York	85 miles long
Tallest dam	Rogun, Soviet Union	1,099 feet high, 2,165 feet long
Biggest dam	New Cornelia Tailings Dam, Arizona	Filled with 274,026,000 cu. yds. of material
Longest dam	Kiev, Soviet Union	33.6 miles long, 72 feet high
Tallest building	Sears Tower, Chicago, Illinois	110 stories, 1,454 feet high
Largest building	Boeing assembly building, Everett, Wash.	205,000,000 cubic feet of space
Tallest tower, with guy wires	KTHI–TV tower, Blanchard, North Dakota	2,063 feet high
Tallest tower, no guy wires	Canadian National Railways Tower, Toronto, Ontario, Canada	1,815 feet high
Longest single bridge span	Humber Bridge, Hull, England	4,626 feet long over River Humber
Highest bridge	Royal Gorge, Colorado	1,053 feet above water
Deepest mine	Carletonville, South Africa	13,000 feet deep gold mine
Deepest oil well	Beckham County, Oklahoma	30,050 feet deep
Great Pyramid of Cheops	Egypt	481 feet high, 755 feet square
Great Wall	China	1,500 miles long, 25 feet high

WORLD'S MAJOR TUNNELS

Source: Bridge Division, Federal Highway Administration

LENGTH	NAME	LOCATION	YEAR
HIGHWAY TUNNELS			
10.01 miles	St. Gotthard	Göschenen–Airolo, Switzerland	1980
8.7 miles	Arlberg Tunnel	Austria	1978
7.2 miles	Mont Blanc	France–Italy	1965
3.6 miles	Great St. Bernard	Italy–Switzerland	1964
3.1 miles	Viella	Pobla de Segur–Viella, Spain	1948
2.8 miles	Mersey	Liverpool, England	1934
2.1 miles	Kanmon	Yamaguchi–Fukuoka, Japan	1958
2.0 miles	Elbe River	Germany	1975
1.8 miles	Reboucas	Rio de Janeiro, Brazil	1967
1.73 miles	Brooklyn–Battery	Brooklyn–Manhattan, New York	1950
1.7 miles	Dwight D. Eisenhower	60 miles west of Denver, Colorado	1973; 1979
1.6 miles	Holland	New York–New Jersey	1927
1.6 miles	Salang	Afghanistan–Soviet Union	1964
1.6 miles	Lincoln, Center	New York–New Jersey	1937
1.5 miles	Lincoln, South	New York–New Jersey	1957
1.4 miles	Baltimore Harbor	Baltimore, Maryland	1957
1.4 miles	Lincoln, North	New York–New Jersey	1945
1.4 miles	Hampton Roads	Hampton–Norfolk, Virginia	1957; 1976
1.3 miles	Copperfield	Bingham Canyon, Utah	1939
1.2 miles	Queens–Midtown	Queens–Manhattan, New York	1940
1.2 miles	Ahmed Hamdi	Under Suez Canal, Suez, Egypt	1980
RAILROAD TUNNELS[1]			
33.5 miles	Seikan	Japan	UC
13.8 miles	Dai-Shimizu	Japan	1982
12.3 miles	Simplon No. I	Switzerland–Italy	1906
12.3 miles	Simplon No. II	Switzerland–Italy	1922
11.6 miles	Kanmon	Japan	1975
11.5 miles	Apennine	Italy	1934
9.9 miles	Rokko	Japan	1972
9.3 miles	Gotthard	Switzerland	1882
9.1 miles	Lötschberg	Switzerland	1913
8.6 miles	Hokuriku	Japan	1962
8.5 miles	Mont Cenis	France–Italy	1871
8.3 miles	Shin–shimizu	Japan	1967
8.2 miles	Furka	Switzerland	1982
7.8 miles	Cascade	Washington (U.S.)	1929
7.0 miles	Flathead	Montana (U.S.)	1970
7.0 miles	Kubiki	Japan	1969
6.7 miles	Lierasen	Norway	1973
6.4 miles	Arlberg	Austria	1884
6.2 miles	Moffat	Colorado (U.S.)	1928
6.0 miles	Shimizu	Japan	1931
5.6 miles	Kvineshei	Norway	1943
5.5 miles	Rimutaka	New Zealand	1955
SHIP TUNNEL			
4.3 miles	Rove	Rhone Canal, France	1927

UC = Under construction. [1] Subway tunnels not included.

WORLD'S TALLEST BUILDINGS AND FREE-STANDING TOWERS

FEET [1]	BUILDING AND LOCATION	FLOORS	FEET [1]	BUILDING AND LOCATION	FLOORS
1,821	CNR Tower, Toronto, Canada........	—	813	Chase Manhattan, New York City	60
1,454	Sears Tower [2], Chicago	110	808	Pan Am, New York City	59
1,350	World Trade Center [3], New York City ..	110	786	MLC Center, Sydney, Australia	68
1,250	Empire State [4], New York City	102	792	Woolworth, New York City	60
1,136	Standard Oil, Chicago	80	790	John Hancock Tower, Boston.........	60
1,107	John Hancock Center [5], Chicago	100	787	Sunshine 60, Tokyo, Japan	60
1,065	Centrepoint Tower, Sydney, Australia .	—	787	Moscow State U. [12], Soviet Union	32
1,002	Texas Commerce Tower, Houston, Texas	75	784	Commerce Court [13], Toronto	57
985	Allied Bank, Houston, Texas..........	71	780	Republic Bank, Houston, Texas	54
984	Eiffel Tower [6], Paris, France	—	778	Bank of America, San Francisco	52
936	First Canadian Place, Toronto, Canada	70	774	IDS Tower, Minneapolis..............	57
914	Citicorp Center, New York City	59	772	One Liberty Plaza, New York City	54
899	Transco Tower, Houston, Texas	64	764	One Penn Plaza, New York City	57
866	Chrysler [7], New York City	77	757	Palace of Culture, Warsaw, Poland ...	40
859	Water Tower Plaza, Chicago	74	750	Exxon Building, New York City	54
858	United Calif. Bank, Los Angeles	62	750	Prudential Tower, Boston	52
853	Transamerica Pyramid, San Francisco .	48	747	Detroit Plaza Hotel, Detroit	73
851	40 Wall Street [8], New York City	71	744	Interfirst Bank, Houston, Texas	55
850	RCA Building [9], New York City	70	743	U.S. Steel, New York City	50
844	First National Bank [10], Chicago	60	741	Citibank, New York City	57
841	U.S. Steel Building, Pittsburgh	64	740	Renaissance Center, Detroit........	70
826	60 Wall Street Tower [11], New York City	67	740	Dominion Bank, Toronto	56

[1] Height from sidewalk to roof, floors below ground not included. [2] 1,804 ft. with TV antenna. [3] Twin towers. [4] 1,454 ft. with TV antenna. [5] 1,451 ft. with TV antenna. [6] 1,052 ft. with TV antenna. [7] 1,046 ft. with spire. [8] 927 ft. with tower. [9] 885 ft. with tower. [10] 864 ft. with tower. [11] 950 ft. with tower. [12] 994 ft. with tower. [13] 942 ft. with tower.

WORLD'S MAJOR SHIP CANALS

Source: Defense Mapping Agency Hydrographic/Topographic Center

NAME	LOCATION	YEAR OPENED	LENGTH (in nautical miles)	WIDTH OF CHANNEL OR LOCKS	MINIMUM DEPTH	LOCKS
Cape Cod..............	U.S.A.: Buzzards Bay to Cape Cod Bay	1914	15.1	500 ft.	32 ft.	0
Chesapeake and Delaware	U.S.A.: Chesapeake Bay to Delaware River	1829	11.3	450 ft.	35 ft.	0
Corinth...............	Greece: Gulf of Corinth to Aegean	1893	2.6	69 ft.	26 ft.	0
Nord-Ostee Kanal	Germany: North Sea to Baltic Sea	1895	53.0	131 ft.	36 ft.	4
Manchester Ship	England: Mersey Estuary to city of Manchester	1894	31.0	80 ft.	29 ft.	10
North Sea	Netherlands: North Sea to Amsterdam	1876	13.0	164 ft.	49 ft.	3
Panama	Panama: Atlantic to Pacific	1914	44.6	110 ft.	40 ft.	12
St. Lawrence Seaway....	U.S.A.–Canada: Montreal to Lake Ontario	1959	164.0	80 ft.	27 ft.	7
Sault Ste. Marie	U.S.A.–Canada: Lake Huron to Lake Superior	1855	1.4	110 ft.	27 ft.	4
Suez	Egypt: Mediterranean Sea to Gulf of Suez	1869	104.3	525 ft.	61 ft.	0
Terneuzen Ghent	Netherlands–Belgium: Schelde River to Ghent	1827	17.3	131 ft.	44 ft.	3
Welland	Canada: Lake Ontario to Lake Erie	1932	27.0	80 ft.	27 ft.	8
White Sea—Baltic	Soviet Union: White Sea to Baltic Sea	1933	122.0	100 ft.	13 ft.	19

WORLD'S LONGEST BRIDGES

Source: Bridge Division, Federal Highway Administration

SUSPENSION BRIDGES

SPAN	BRIDGE	LOCATION	WATERWAY	OPENED
4,626 ft.	Humber...............	Hull, England	River Humber	1980
4,260 ft.	Verrazano-Narrows.....	Brooklyn to Staten Island, New York	New York Bay	1964
4,200 ft.	Golden Gate	San Francisco to Marin County, California...	San Francisco Bay .	1937
3,800 ft.	Mackinac	Michigan	Straits of Mackinac .	1957
3,524 ft.	Bosporus	Turkey	Bosporus	1973
3,500 ft.	George Washington	New York City to Fort Lee, New Jersey	Hudson River	1931
3,323 ft.	Salazar	Lisbon, Portugal	Tagus River	1966
3,300 ft.	Forth Road	Queensferry, Scotland	Firth of Forth	1964
3,240 ft.	Severn	Bristol, England, to Chepstow, Wales	River Severn	1966
2,871 ft.	Onaruto...............	Kobe–Naruto, Japan	Naruto Straits	1980

SUSPENSION BRIDGES (continued)

SPAN	BRIDGE	LOCATION	WATERWAY	YEAR
2,800 ft.	Tacoma Narrows II	Tacoma, Washington	Puget Sound	1950
2,526 ft.	In-no-Shima Bridge	In-no-Shima, Onomichi Imbari, Japan	Seto Island Sea	1982
2,336 ft.	Kanmon Straits	Kyushu to Honshu, Japan	Kanmon Straits	1973
2,336 ft.	Angostura	Ciudad Bolívar, Venezuela	Orinoco River	1967
2,310 ft.	Transbay	San Francisco to Oakland, California	San Francisco Bay	1936
2300 ft.	Bronx-Whitestone	Bronx to Whitestone, Queens, New York	East River	1939
2,190 ft.	Pierre-LaPorte	Quebec, Canada	St. Lawrence River	1970
2,150 ft.	Delaware Memorial	Wilmington, Delaware (twin spans)	Delaware River	1951;1968
2,150 ft.	Seaway Skyway	Ogdensburg, New York, to Prescott, Ontario	St. Lawrence River	1960
2,000 ft.	Walt Whitman	South Philadelphia, Pennsylvania	Delaware River	1957
2,000 ft.	Gas Pipe Line	Louisiana	Atchafalaya River	1951
1,995 ft.	Tancarville	Tancarville, France	Seine River	1959
1,969 ft.	New Lillebaelt	Denmark	Lillebaelt Straits	1970
1,850 ft.	Ambassador	Detroit, Michigan, to Windsor, Canada	Detroit River	1929
1,800 ft.	Throgs Neck	Bronx to Queens, New York	East River	1961
1,750 ft.	Benjamin Franklin	Philadelphia, Pennsylvania, to Camden, N.J.	Delaware River	1926
1,722 ft.	Skjomen	Norway	Skjervik-Grindjord	1972
1,722 ft.	Kvalsund	Stallogargo to Kvalsund, Hammerfest, Norway	Norwegian Sea	1977
1,640 ft.	Kleve-Emmerich	Kleve to Emmerich, West Germany	Rhine River	1965
1,632 ft.	Bear Mountain	Bear Mountain to Peekskill, New York	Hudson River	1924
1,600 ft.	Newport	Rhode Island	Narragansett Bay	1969
1,600 ft.	Chesapeake Bay	Sandy Point, Maryland	Chesapeake Bay	1952
1,600 ft.	Parallel Chesapeake Bay	Sandy Point, Maryland	Chesapeake Bay	1973
1,600 ft.	Williamsburg	Manhattan to Brooklyn, New York	East River	1903
1,595 ft.	Brooklyn	Manhattan to Brooklyn, New York	East River	1883

CABLE-STAYED BRIDGES

1,500 ft.	Second Hooghly	Calcutta, India	Hooghly River	UC
1,325 ft.	Saint Nazaire	Saint Nazaire, France	Loire River	1975
1,312 ft.	Puente de Rande	Vigo, Spain	Vigo River	1977
1,300 ft.	Dames Point	Jacksonville, Florida	St. Johns River	—
1,222 ft.	Luling	Luling, Louisiana	Mississippi River	1983
1,205 ft.	Düsseldorf-Flehe	Düsseldorf; West Germany	Rhine River	1979
1,200 ft.	Sunshine Skyway	Florida	Tampa Bay	1986
1,148 ft.	Duisburg	Duisburg, West Germany	Rhine River	1970
1,116 ft.	Mesopotamia	Mesopotamia, Argentina	Corrientas River	1972
1,102 ft.	Westgate	Melbourne to Victoria, Australia	Lower Yarra River	1977

CANTILEVER BRIDGES

1,800 ft.	Quebec	Quebec, Canada	St. Lawrence River	1917
1,710 ft.	Firth of Forth	Inch-Garvie to Queensferry, Scotland	Firth of Forth	1890
1,673 ft.	Nanko	Osaka to Amagasaki, Japan	Yodo River	1974
1,644 ft.	Commodore John Barry	Chester (Pa.) to Bridgeport (N.J.)	Delaware River	1974
1,575 ft.	Greater New Orleans[1]	New Orleans to Algiers, Louisiana	Mississippi River	1958
1,500 ft.	Howrah	Calcutta to Howrah, India	Hooghly River	1943
1,500 ft.	Parkersburg	Parkersburg, W. Va., to Belpre, Ohio	Ohio River	1976
1,400 ft.	Transbay (East Bay)	San Francisco to Oakland, California	San Francisco Bay	1936
1,235 ft.	Baton Rouge	Baton Rouge, Louisiana	Mississippi River	1968
1,212 ft.	Tappan Zee	Tarrytown, New York	Hudson River	1955
1,200 ft.	Longview	Longview, Washington	Columbia River	1930
1,182 ft.	Queensboro	Manhattan to Queens, New York	East River	1909

CONTINUOUS-TRUSS BRIDGES

1,232 ft.	Astoria-Megler	Astoria, Oregon, to Megler, Washington	Columbia River	1966
1,200 ft.	Patapsco River	Outer harbor, Baltimore, Maryland	Patapsco River	1976
1,088 ft.	Commodore Point	Jacksonville, Florida	St. Johns River	1967

CONCRETE-ARCH BRIDGES

1,280 ft.	Krk	Krk Island to mainland Yugoslavia	Adriatic Sea	1980
1,000 ft.	Gladesville	Sydney, Australia	Parramatta River	1964

FLOATING BRIDGES[2]

7,578 ft.	Evergreen Point	Seattle to North Bellevue, Washington	Lake Washington	1963
6,561 ft.	Lacey V. Murrow	Seattle, Washington, to Mercer Island	Lake Washington	1940
6,523 ft.	Hood Canal	Puget Sound, Washington	Hood Canal	1961

STEEL-ARCH BRIDGES

1,700 ft.	New River Gorge	Near Fayetteville, West Virginia	New River	1976
1,652 ft.	Kill van Kull	Port Richmond, New York, to Bayonne, N.J.	Kill van Kull	1931
1,650 ft.	Sydney Harbor	Sydney, Australia	Sydney Harbor	1932
1,255 ft.	Fremont	Portland, Oregon	Willamette River	1973
1,247 ft.	Orlik Reservoir	Czechoslovakia	Orlik Reservoir	1966
1,200 ft.	Port Mann	British Columbia, Canada	Fraser River	1964
1,128 ft.	Thatcher Ferry	Balboa, Panama Canal Zone	Panama Canal	1962
100 ft.	Trois Rivières	Trois Rivières, Quebec, Canada	St. Lawrence River	1967

allel bridges. [2] Floating length rather than span given for floating bridges. UC = Under construction.

U.S. MOTOR VEHICLE REGISTRATIONS

Source: Federal Highway Administration, U.S. Department of Transportation

STATE	AUTO-MOBILES 1983	TRUCKS 1983	MOTOR-CYCLES 1983	TOTAL MOTOR VEHICLES [1]			
				1975	1980	1982	1983
Alabama	2,271,950	864,316	72,039	2,492,785	2,938,108	3,039,460	3,144,769
Alaska	218,673	130,123	10,534	225,575	261,527	317,750	350,488
Arizona	1,634,258	650,709	88,712	1,459,492	1,916,753	2,215,549	2,289,476
Arkansas	941,393	500,358	23,768	1,283,321	1,573,718	1,481,366	1,445,471
California	13,935,390	3,797,926	695,816	13,890,670	16,873,117	17,130,403	17,766,759
Colorado	1,939,178	704,024	118,448	1,925,198	2,342,293	2,501,727	2,648,868
Connecticut	2,149,351	146,757	76,082	1,949,239	2,147,495	2,257,975	2,305,102
Delaware	342,205	82,996	10,634	350,992	397,127	414,764	426,803
District of Columbia	214,299	15,638	5,722	255,472	267,565	231,368	232,725
Florida	7,113,942	1,661,268	227,559	5,395,372	7,613,539	8,334,594	8,808,486
Georgia	3,132,514	1,061,017	105,033	3,210,973	3,818,438	3,915,819	4,207,708
Hawaii	557,879	54,927	8,005	462,011	569,802	586,386	616,415
Idaho	529,018	345,348	52,124	647,446	834,068	872,636	877,320
Illinois	5,929,783	1,561,330	232,624	6,343,875	7,476,832	7,241,982	7,513,118
Indiana	2,852,382	981,326	140,135	3,315,371	3,825,852	3,883,617	3,851,752
Iowa	1,764,651	707,397	238,700	2,099,336	2,329,465	2,345,805	2,479,118
Kansas	1,408,358	635,216	100,090	1,805,434	2,006,868	2,061,174	2,047,531
Kentucky	1,812,875	799,057	58,427	2,245,138	2,592,714	2,615,341	2,620,824
Louisiana	2,023,957	833,200	64,977	2,187,521	2,779,457	2,800,427	2,876,621
Maine	561,947	201,370	48,151	648,131	723,612	742,857	765,781
Maryland	2,516,084	484,589	74,267	2,422,724	2,802,896	2,893,425	3,011,109
Massachusetts	3,374,962	453,880	112,589	3,107,051	3,749,243	3,749,568	3,839,707
Michigan	5,024,521	1,249,193	231,900	5,545,460	6,488,070	6,250,289	6,294,849
Minnesota	2,407,373	857,870	171,474	2,524,517	3,091,126	3,278,425	3,282,157
Mississippi	1,189,446	363,168	29,068	1,376,510	1,576,774	1,593,021	1,560,277
Missouri	2,541,403	881,966	94,324	2,866,219	3,271,286	3,411,505	3,433,042
Montana	486,291	340,742	33,684	601,957	679,532	757,924	828,737
Nebraska	815,232	415,269	46,445	1,177,845	1,254,095	1,214,991	1,234,591
Nevada	527,232	201,566	21,535	463,835	654,667	709,966	730,451
New Hampshire	686,966	114,187	52,871	485,306	704,267	773,564	802,640
New Jersey	4,412,437	512,743	99,749	4,154,542	4,761,357	4,917,379	4,940,674
New Mexico	798,398	434,369	54,598	826,568	1,067,735	1,193,161	1,236,542
New York	7,357,044	1,024,802	199,707	7,591,359	8,001,546	8,234,857	8,416,503
North Carolina	3,461,818	1,111,010	116,057	3,689,569	4,531,848	4,583,305	4,603,381
North Dakota	390,331	273,455	32,134	550,827	626,932	653,026	665,691
Ohio	6,429,344	1,307,834	285,744	7,178,933	7,771,236	7,635,860	7,768,345
Oklahoma	1,757,739	999,771	130,252	2,112,733	2,582,999	2,779,800	2,769,058
Oregon	1,476,548	632,784	82,970	1,627,592	2,080,607	2,074,696	2,120,523
Pennsylvania	5,738,155	1,078,324	227,150	7,659,305	6,925,855	6,724,739	6,844,049
Rhode Island	518,803	78,010	26,783	562,641	622,928	586,060	598,338
South Carolina	1,578,316	467,402	36,117	1,772,362	1,995,993	1,974,742	2,057,795
South Dakota	390,543	236,761	39,255	520,896	601,241	615,386	629,458
Tennessee	2,904,367	621,417	79,821	2,725,569	3,271,345	3,381,216	3,537,012
Texas	8,159,008	3,482,625	322,903	8,396,489	10,474,816	11,387,833	11,695,478
Utah	735,930	337,215	67,252	844,974	992,495	1,038,411	1,074,284
Vermont	282,469	83,578	22,374	287,109	347,323	350,881	367,355
Virginia	3,328,903	551,992	81,030	3,250,861	3,626,280	3,705,347	3,894,060
Washington	2,360,117	968,144	138,787	2,539,764	3,225,262	3,236,854	3,338,333
West Virginia	906,519	385,222	31,881	966,009	1,319,915	1,141,936	1,295,165
Wisconsin	2,547,140	654,067	209,928	2,590,709	2,940,911	3,162,337	3,214,162
Wyoming	290,428	209,523	22,701	336,824	467,289	507,601	502,268
TOTAL	126,727,870	36,547,781	5,552,930	132,950,410	155,796,219	159,509,825	163,861,169

[1] Excludes motorcycles.

U.S. MOTOR VEHICLE STATISTICS

Source: National Safety Council

YEAR	MOTOR VEHICLES	DRIVERS	VEHICLE MILES TRAVELED	HIGHWAY DEATHS	HIGHWAY DEATH RATES (Per 100 million vehicle miles)	(Per 100,000 population)
1918–22 avg.	9,200,000	14,000,000	—	12,700	—	11.9
1923–27 avg.	19,700,000	29,000,000	120,000,000,000	21,800	18.20	18.7
1928–32 avg.	25,700,000	38,000,000	199,000,000,000	31,050	15.60	25.2
1935	26,500,000	39,000,000	229,000,000,000	36,369	15.91	28.6
1940	32,500,000	48,000,000	302,000,000,000	34,501	11.42	26.1
1945	31,000,000	46,000,000	250,000,000,000	28,076	11.22	21.2
1948	41,100,000	55,000,000	398,000,000,000	32,259	8.11	22.1
1949	44,700,000	59,300,000	424,000,000,000	31,701	7.47	21.3
1950	49,200,000	62,200,000	458,000,000,000	34,763	7.59	23.0
1952	53,300,000	66,800,000	514,000,000,000	37,794	7.36	24.3
1953	56,300,000	69,900,000	544,000,000,000	37,955	6.97	24.0
1954	58,600,000	72,200,000	562,000,000,000	35,586	6.33	22.1
1955	62,800,000	74,700,000	606,000,000,000	38,426	6.34	23.4
1956	65,200,000	77,900,000	631,000,000,000	39,628	6.28	23.7
1957	67,600,000	79,600,000	647,000,000,000	38,702	5.98	22.7
1958	68,800,000	81,500,000	665,000,000,000	36,981	5.56	21.3
1959	72,100,000	84,500,000	700,000,000,000	37,910	5.41	21.5
1960	74,500,000	87,400,000	719,000,000,000	38,137	5.31	21.2
1961	76,400,000	88,900,000	738,000,000,000	38,091	5.16	20.8
1962	79,700,000	92,000,000	767,000,000,000	40,804	5.32	22.0
1963	83,500,000	93,700,000	805,000,000,000	43,564	5.41	23.1
1964	87,300,000	95,600,000	847,000,000,000	47,700	5.63	25.0
1965	91,800,000	99,000,000	888,000,000,000	49,163	5.54	25.4
1966	95,900,000	101,000,000	930,000,000,000	53,041	5.70	27.1
1967	98,900,000	103,200,000	962,000,000,000	52,924	5.50	26.8
1968	103,100,000	105,400,000	1,016,000,000,000	55,862	5.40	27.5
1969	107,400,000	108,300,000	1,071,000,000,000	55,791	5.21	27.7
1970	111,200,000	111,500,000	1,120,000,000,000	54,633	4.88	26.8
1971	116,300,000	114,400,000	1,186,000,000,000	54,381	4.57	26.4
1972	122,300,000	118,400,000	1,268,000,000,000	56,278	4.43	27.0
1973	129,800,000	121,600,000	1,309,000,000,000	55,511	4.24	26.5
1974	134,900,000	125,600,000	1,290,000,000,000	46,402	3.59	22.0
1975	137,900,000	129,800,000	1,330,000,000,000	45,853	3.45	21.5
1976	143,500,000	133,800,000	1,412,000,000,000	47,038	3.33	22.0
1977	148,800,000	138,100,000	1,477,000,000,000	49,510	3.35	22.9
1978	153,600,000	140,800,000	1,548,000,000,000	52,411	3.39	24.0
1979	159,600,000	143,300,000	1,529,000,000,000	52,524	3.50	23.8
1980	161,600,000	145,000,000	1,521,000,000,000	53,172	3.50	23.4
1981	164,100,000	147,100,000	1,556,000,000,000	51,400	3.30	22.4
1982	165,300,000	150,300,000	1,592,000,000,000	46,000	2.89	19.8
1983	167,700,000	152,000,000	1,625,000,000,000	44,300	2.73	19.0
1984	174,200,000	157,300,000	1,727,000,000,000	46,200	2.68	19.6

INTERNATIONAL HIGHWAY AND TRAFFIC SIGNS

UNEVEN ROAD | DANGEROUS BEND | BEND | DOUBLE BEND | INTERSECTION | TRAFFIC CIRCLE | RAILWAY CROSSING: GATE

RAILWAY CROSSING: NO GATE | HILL (% = GRADIENT) | ROAD NARROWS | LIFT BRIDGE | MEN ON ROAD | SLIPPERY WHEN WET | PEDESTRIAN CROSSWALK

SLOW: CHILDREN | YIELD RIGHT OF WAY | NO LEFT TURN | DO NOT PASS | NO PARKING | MINIMUM SPEED | PARKING

U.S. STREETS, ROADS, HIGHWAYS, AND RAILROADS

Sources: U.S. Department of Transportation; Association of American Railroads

Of the 3,879,638 miles of U.S. streets, roads, and highways, 662,350 miles (17%) are streets and highways in urban areas. Only 1%, 43,028 miles, are part of the interstate system. Of those, 10,240 miles are in urban areas.

A total of 166,253 miles of track are operated in the United States by line-haul railroads with annual gross revenues of $50 million or more. This figure excludes track used by smaller lines and by switching and terminal companies.

STATE	U.S. INTERSTATE HIGHWAY SYSTEM MILEAGE[1]			NON-FEDERAL AID STREET AND HIGHWAY MILEAGE[1]		TOTAL STREETS & HIGHWAYS[1]	TRACK MILEAGE OPERATED BY LARGE RAILROADS[2]
	Rural	Urban	Total	Rural	Urban		
Alabama	639	191	830	55,815	10,788	87,598	4,114
Alaska	1,072	20	1,092	3,524	1,087	8,772	526
Arizona	1,021	123	1,144	59,930	6,917	76,334	1,758
Arkansas	419	122	541	57,484	5,868	77,053	2,682
California	1,443	938	2,381	88,037	45,671	174,036	6,521
Colorado	788	158	946	55,702	7,100	75,423	3,414
Connecticut	108	229	337	7,184	6,923	19,534	464
Delaware	—	41	41	2,837	1,064	5,280	220
District of Columbia	—	12	12	—	685	1,102	46
Florida	927	318	1,245	50,890	22,456	93,074	3,123
Georgia[1]	886	296	1,182	62,975	13,370	104,955	4,835
Hawaii	5	31	36	2,139	1,034	4,297	0
Idaho	536	71	607	58,893	1,570	68,447	2,233
Illinois	1,255	456	1,711	81,864	21,876	134,599	8,841
Indiana	854	259	1,113	59,767	11,838	91,736	5,204
Iowa	614	123	737	81,758	5,307	112,289	4,249
Kansas	654	154	808	92,982	6,290	132,265	7,636
Kentucky	579	159	738	50,616	4,985	69,150	3,286
Louisiana	519	167	686	35,201	9,698	58,010	3,103
Maine	282	31	313	14,854	1,400	21,953	46
Maryland	191	186	377	13,417	7,520	27,425	913
Massachusetts	172	390	562	10,013	13,189	33,796	1,084
Michigan	714	415	1,129	67,862	18,704	117,467	3,349
Minnesota	696	177	873	92,526	10,354	131,475	6,068
Mississippi	567	119	686	46,576	4,757	71,075	3,783
Missouri	824	308	1,132	78,916	11,388	118,713	5,818
Montana	1,089	46	1,135	58,077	1,831	71,553	3,414
Nebraska	444	38	482	68,628	3,180	91,961	4,736
Nevada	502	36	538	36,181	2,404	43,806	1,492
New Hampshire	164	43	207	9,782	1,477	14,545	409
New Jersey	128	253	381	8,860	16,102	33,871	1,377
New Mexico	913	87	1,000	41,412	3,491	54,127	2,060
New York	881	607	1,488	59,708	25,527	109,837	3,746
North Carolina	578	186	764	60,360	14,232	92,404	2,606
North Dakota	533	38	571	67,883	964	85,811	4,641
Ohio	880	666	1,546	65,356	19,884	112,252	6,561
Oklahoma	749	177	926	83,015	8,887	110,072	3,840
Oregon	585	133	718	112,177	5,875	133,469	2,941
Pennsylvania	1,186	338	1,524	70,104	19,083	115,601	6,200
Rhode Island	21	49	70	2,254	2,576	6,289	0
South Carolina	647	109	756	40,166	7,081	63,264	2,570
South Dakota	636	41	677	54,240	1,067	73,375	1,955
Tennessee	826	205	1,031	60,548	8,562	83,789	2,669
Texas	2,273	843	3,116	162,858	53,436	275,784	12,998
Utah	681	125	806	35,281	4,009	46,078	1,651
Vermont	302	18	320	9,794	549	13,994	102
Virginia	799	226	1,025	36,431	9,012	65,102	3,636
Washington	483	232	715	58,836	9,939	85,731	4,164
West Virginia	389	90	479	22,738	1,901	34,673	3,316
Wisconsin	466	111	577	74,182	9,984	108,225	3,860
Wyoming	868	49	917	30,610	941	38,170	1,993
Total	32,788	10,240	43,028	2,561,243	483,833	3,879,638	166,253

[1] 1983 data. [2] 1984 data.

UNITED STATES TRAVEL MAP

Interstate Highways ⬤ ━━━ Completed
━━━ Under Construction or Planned

🌲 National Parks
⬛ National Seashores, Lakeshores
⬤ Other Scenic Areas

HIGHWAY DISTANCES BETWEEN U. S. AND CANADIAN CITIES

Source: American Automobile Association. Distances in statute miles.

	Albuquerque, N.M.	Atlanta, Ga.	Boston, Mass.	Chicago, Ill.	Cleveland, Ohio	Dallas, Texas	Denver, Colo.	Detroit, Mich.	Houston, Texas	Las Vegas, Nev.	Los Angeles, Calif.	Memphis, Tenn.
Albuquerque, N.M. ...	—	1,424	2,248	1,351	1,616	670	449	1,572	1,016	573	802	1,010
Atlanta, Ga.	1,424	—	1,115	722	734	800	1,442	735	848	1,997	2,244	394
Baltimore, Md.	1,935	711	416	729	399	1,391	1,728	570	1,524	2,535	2,755	938
Birmingham, Ala. ...	1,251	149	1,264	662	738	651	1,288	739	717	1,894	2,076	241
Bismarck, N.D.	1,199	1,663	1,877	865	1,220	1,275	750	1,152	1,512	1,467	1,757	1,268
Boise, Idaho	961	2,293	2,804	1,795	2,110	1,657	851	1,772	1,977	775	943	1,898
Boston, Mass.	2,248	1,115	—	1,009	654	1,795	2,016	832	1,941	2,792	3,082	1,414
Buffalo, N.Y.	1,816	928	466	546	194	1,392	1,593	259	1,649	2,369	2,659	948
Charleston, S.C.	1,753	329	974	1,051	356	1,129	1,771	970	1,177	2,326	2,573	723
Charleston, W.Va. ...	1,567	557	823	487	260	1,357	1,360	438	1,405	2,136	2,369	591
Charlotte, N.C.	1,651	249	843	801	574	1,049	1,569	752	1,097	2,246	2,453	621
Cheyenne, Wyo.	551	1,544	2,018	1,009	1,324	908	102	1,296	1,145	878	1,163	1,151
Chicago, Ill.	1,351	722	1,009	—	355	933	1,047	287	1,341	1,823	2,113	583
Cincinnati, Ohio	1,404	470	896	285	264	986	1,197	265	1,248	1,973	2,214	490
Cleveland, Ohio	1,616	734	654	355	—	1,198	1,362	178	1,455	2,138	2,418	754
Dallas, Texas	670	800	1,795	933	1,198	—	806	1,154	237	1,243	1,425	453
Denver, Colo.	449	1,442	2,016	1,047	1,362	806	—	1,334	1,043	776	1,066	1,047
Des Moines, Iowa ...	992	985	1,331	362	677	748	685	649	985	1,461	1,751	625
Detroit, Mich.	1,572	735	832	287	178	1,154	1,334	—	1,456	2,110	2,400	755
El Paso, Texas	270	1,428	2,495	1,578	1,826	628	719	1,688	746	692	797	1,081
Grand Canyon, Ariz. .	409	1,833	2,657	1,760	2,025	1,079	676	1,981	1,307	336	573	1,419
Hartford, Conn.	2,210	914	101	949	594	1,694	1,940	772	2,132	2,732	2,967	1,253
Helena, Mont.	1,099	1,201	2,534	1,532	1,877	1,580	774	1,809	1,817	913	1,203	1,806
Houston, Texas	1,016	848	1,941	1,341	1,455	237	1,043	1,456	—	1,438	1,543	758
Indianapolis, Ind.....	1,495	578	975	177	321	877	1,088	277	1,285	1,564	2,097	501
Jackson, Miss.	1,087	383	1,498	795	966	417	1,267	967	546	1,660	1,842	212
Kansas City, Mo.	795	848	1,447	557	815	551	594	844	788	1,370	1,597	453
Las Vegas, Nev.	573	1,997	2,792	1,823	2,138	1,243	776	2,110	1,438	—	290	1,603
Little Rock, Ark.	1,092	532	1,552	721	892	315	997	871	552	1,465	1,694	138
Los Angeles, Calif. ..	802	2,244	3,082	2,113	2,418	1,425	1,066	2,400	1,543	290	—	1,832
Louisville, Ky.	1,510	432	998	290	366	841	1,103	367	1,146	1,879	2,112	388
Memphis, Tenn.	1,230	394	1,414	583	754	453	1,047	755	758	1,603	1,832	—
Miami, Fla.	2,018	688	1,571	1,410	1,342	1,348	2,130	1,423	1,274	2,629	2,773	1,057
Milwaukee, Wis.	1,442	813	1,100	91	446	1,024	1,138	378	1,432	1,914	2,102	674
Minn.–St. Paul, Minn.	1,257	1,152	1,439	430	785	1,013	941	717	1,250	1,717	2,007	823
Montreal, Quebec ...	2,217	1,281	325	932	697	1,805	1,917	583	2,039	2,693	2,983	1,338
New Orleans, La.	1,188	485	1,578	976	1,092	518	1,324	1,093	363	1,761	1,906	395
New York, N.Y.	2,029	896	219	831	476	1,576	1,822	654	2,014	2,614	2,849	1,135
Norfolk, Va.	2,007	605	650	917	600	1,405	1,790	868	1,453	2,580	2,809	977
Oklahoma City, Okla.	756	868	1,692	795	1,060	200	661	1,016	437	1,129	1,358	474
Omaha, Nebr.	893	1,042	1,514	505	820	654	542	792	891	1,318	1,608	647
Philadelphia, Pa.	2,033	809	318	809	454	1,489	1,826	632	1,622	2,535	2,816	1,036
Phoenix, Ariz.	460	1,884	2,708	1,811	2,070	1,032	909	2,032	1,150	288	393	1,470
Pittsburgh, Pa.	1,784	778	607	496	141	1,275	1,486	319	1,626	2,262	2,503	779
Portland, Maine	2,340	1,218	103	1,115	757	1,898	2,119	865	2,336	2,895	3,185	1,517
Portland, Oreg.	1,400	2,732	3,246	2,234	2,549	2,070	1,290	2,520	2,416	983	1,063	2,337
Providence, R.I.	2,277	1,081	49	1,016	661	1,590	1,975	724	2,199	2,799	3,034	1,320
Rapid City, S.D.	841	1,581	2,012	1,044	1,358	1,198	392	1,331	1,435	1,109	1,399	1,186
Richmond, Va.	1,898	541	551	818	500	1,341	1,691	769	1,389	2,467	2,745	913
Saint John, N.B.	2,695	1,573	458	1,538	1,112	2,253	2,474	1,189	2,399	3,250	3,589	1,872
St. Louis, Mo.	1,051	564	1,197	300	565	633	844	521	1,041	1,620	1,853	238
Salt Lake City, Utah .	617	1,949	2,420	1,451	1,766	1,287	507	1,738	1,633	431	721	1,554
San Antonio, Texas ..	830	1,038	2,068	1,206	1,471	273	961	1,427	190	1,252	1,357	726
San Francisco, Calif. .	1,091	2,515	3,174	2,205	2,520	1,761	1,261	2,492	1,968	670	425	2,101
Seattle, Wash.	1,460	2,793	3,123	2,114	2,469	2,130	1,350	2,401	2,476	1,158	1,174	2,408
Toronto, Ont.	1,810	973	562	525	290	1,392	1,572	238	1,694	2,348	2,638	993
Vancouver, B.C.	1,602	2,935	3,274	2,408	2,621	2,324	1,518	2,695	2,561	1,300	1,316	2,550
Washington, D.C.	1,896	672	443	753	398	1,352	1,689	576	1,485	2,496	2,716	899
Wichita, Kans.	714	1,024	1,650	760	1,018	358	518	1,047	595	1,287	1,516	630
Yellowstone Park, Wyo.	983	2,016	2,490	1,481	1,881	1,380	574	1,768	1,617	797	1,087	1,621

Miami, Fla.	Milwaukee, Wis.	Minn.–St. Paul, Minn.	New Orleans, La.	New York, N.Y.	Philadelphia, Pa.	Phoenix, Ariz.	St. Louis, Mo.	Salt Lake City, Utah	San Francisco, Calif.	Seattle, Wash.	Washington, D.C.	
2,018	1,442	1,257	1,188	2,029	2,033	460	1,051	617	1,091	1,460	1,896	..Albuquerque, N.M.
688	813	1,152	485	896	809	1,884	564	1,949	2,515	2,793	672	Atlanta, Ga.
1,167	820	1,159	1,161	197	98	2,420	884	2,207	2,961	2,867	39	Baltimore, Md.
816	753	1,064	354	1,045	923	1,683	504	1,795	2,342	2,638	786	Birmingham, Ala.
2,275	784	435	1,653	1,696	1,674	1,651	1,065	1,036	1,790	1,249	1,618	Bismarck, N.D.
2,981	1,784	1,579	2,149	2,586	2,564	1,063	1,695	344	649	499	2,512	Boise, Idaho
1,571	1,100	1,439	1,578	219	318	2,708	1,197	2,420	3,174	3,123	443	Boston, Mass.
1,536	637	979	1,286	405	419	2,264	759	1,997	2,751	2,660	420	Buffalo, N.Y.
625	1,142	1,433	814	755	668	2,213	893	2,278	2,844	3,122	531	Charleston, S.C.
1,082	578	917	1,042	604	517	2,061	516	1,867	2,621	2,711	380	...Charleston, W.Va.
768	892	1,265	734	612	525	2,133	725	2,076	2,764	2,920	♦ 388	Charlotte, N.C.
2,232	998	941	1,426	1,800	1,778	1,011	948	442	1,196	1,285	1,791	Cheyenne, Wyo.
1,410	91	430	978	831	809	1,811	300	1,451	2,205	2,114	753	Chicago, Ill.
1,158	376	715	955	677	602	1,858	353	1,704	2,458	2,399	523	Cincinnati, Ohio
1,342	446	785	1,092	476	454	2,070	565	1,766	2,520	2,469	398	Cleveland, Ohio
1,348	1,024	1,013	518	1,576	1,489	1,032	633	1,287	1,761	2,130	1,352	Dallas, Texas
2,130	1,138	941	1,324	1,822	1,826	909	844	507	1,261	1,350	1,689	Denver, Colo.
1,673	351	265	1,065	1,153	1,131	1,452	387	1,089	1,843	1,894	1,069	...Des Moines, Iowa
1,423	378	717	1,093	654	632	2,032	521	1,738	2,492	2,401	576	Detroit, Mich.
2,009	1,567	1,482	1,109	2,204	2,115	404	1,167	887	1,222	1,730	1,980	El Paso, Texas
2,427	1,712	1,617	1,597	2,498	2,502	225	1,460	600	868	1,443	2,046	.Grand Canyon, Ariz.
1,470	1,040	1,379	1,464	118	217	2,601	1,096	2,360	3,114	3,063	354	Hartford, Conn.
2,863	1,363	1,092	2,098	2,455	2,433	1,201	1,653	482	1,136	592	2,275	Helena, Mont.
1,274	1,432	1,250	363	2,014	1,622	1,150	1,041	1,633	1,968	2,476	1,485	Houston, Texas
1,266	268	607	922	734	670	1,749	244	1,595	2,349	2,291	631	Indianapolis, Ind.
969	886	1,035	183	1,279	1,157	1,449	495	1,704	2,178	2,547	1,020	Jackson, Miss.
1,510	548	462	841	1,228	1,205	1,255	250	1,036	1,790	1,944	1,095	Kansas City, Mo.
2,629	1,914	1,717	1,761	2,614	2,535	288	1,620	431	670	1,158	2,496	Las Vegas, Nev.
1,236	741	853	450	1,261	1,172	1,347	350	1,504	1,983	2,336	1,037	Little Rock, Ark.
2,773	2,102	2,007	1,906	2,849	2,816	393	1,853	721	425	1,174	2,716	...Los Angeles, Calif.
1,120	381	720	726	779	704	1,764	259	1,610	2,364	2,454	637	Louisville, Ky.
1,057	674	823	395	1,123	1,036	1,470	238	1,554	2,101	2,408	899	Memphis, Tenn.
	1,501	1,840	900	1,352	1,167	2,413	1,286	2,637	3,147	3,481	1,128	Miami, Fla.
1,501		349	1,069	922	900	1,902	391	1,440	2,194	2,033	844	Milwaukee, Wis.
1,840	349	—	1,218	1,261	1,239	1,717	540	1,251	2,005	1,684	1,183	Minn.–St. Paul, Minn.
1,698	913	1,140	1,676	385	484	2,615	1,104	2,383	3,075	2,742	609	Montreal, Quebec
900	1,069	1,218	—	1,346	1,259	1,513	678	1,805	2,279	2,648	1,122	New Orleans, La.
1,352	922	1,261	1,346	—	99	2,483	978	2,242	2,996	2,945	224	New York, N.Y.
1,052	1,008	1,347	1,090	432	345	2,489	946	2,297	3,051	3,141	208	Norfolk, Va.
1,572	886	813	718	1,473	1,450	1,016	495	1,168	1,647	2,011	1,391	Oklahoma City, Okla.
1,704	494	409	1,035	1,296	1,274	1,353	444	946	1,700	1,751	1,320	Omaha, Nebr.
1,167	900	1,239	1,259	99	—	2,493	955	2,220	2,835	3,025	137	Philadelphia, Pa.
2,413	1,902	1,717	1,513	2,552	2,493	—	1,505	719	817	1,446	2,389	Phoenix, Ariz.
1,303	587	926	1,263	388	313	2,147	642	1,907	2,661	2,610	251	Pittsburgh, Pa.
1,674	1,206	1,478	1,681	322	413	2,805	1,300	2,523	3,277	3,024	546	Portland, Maine
3,420	2,074	1,803	2,588	2,483	3,043	1,271	2,134	774	677	175	3,010	Portland, Oreg.
1,537	1,107	1,446	1,531	185	284	2,668	1,163	2,605	2,464	3,130	409	Providence, R.I.
2,243	922	573	1,574	1,835	1,813	1,301	983	678	1,432	1,212	1,859	Rapid City, S.D.
1,014	909	1,248	1,026	332	245	2,425	847	2,952	2,198	3,042	108	Richmond, Va.
2,029	1,662	1,746	2,036	677	776	3,150	1,655	2,927	3,681	3,349	901	Saint John, N.B.
1,286	391	540	678	978	955	1,505	—	1,351	2,105	2,195	845	St. Louis, Mo.
2,637	1,440	1,251	1,805	2,242	2,220	719	1,351	—	754	843	2,168	.Salt Lake City, Utah
1,464	1,300	1,336	553	1,849	1,762	964	906	1,447	1,782	2,290	1,625	.San Antonio, Texas
3,147	2,194	2,005	2,279	2,996	2,835	817	2,105	754	—	852	2,922	.San Francisco, Calif.
3,481	2,074	1,684	2,648	2,945	3,025	1,446	2,195	843	852	—	2,867	Seattle, Wash.
1,632	616	955	1,331	501	506	2,270	759	1,976	2,730	2,639	575	Toronto, Ont.
3,560	2,107	1,836	2,842	3,199	3,177	1,588	2,397	985	994	142	3,010	Vancouver, B.C.
1,128	844	1,183	1,122	224	137	2,389	845	2,168	2,922	2,867	—	Washington, D.C.
1,728	751	665	876	1,431	1,408	1,129	453	999	1,753	1,868	1,298	Wichita, Kans.
2,704	1,470	1,096	1,898	2,272	2,250	1,085	1,420	366	1,120	808	2,263	Yellowstone Park, Wyo.

NATIONAL PARK SYSTEM

The National Park Service of the U.S. Department of the Interior administers hundreds of park areas in the U.S.

The total recreation visits to the more than 335 areas in the National Park System in 1984 was 249,454,837. National Park Service officials reported 111,821 visits through the first six months of 1985. This compared with 103,538 in the first six months of 1984.

FIRST NATIONAL PARKS AND MONUMENTS

In the early 1800s western explorers John Colter and James Bridger visited the Yellowstone region and told of its wonders.

After an official surveying party visited the Yellowstone area in 1870, a campaign was mounted to save the scenic wonders for public enjoyment.

On March 1, 1872, Congress established Yellowstone as the first national park in the world. By 1900 four more national parks had been created: Kings Canyon (at first called General Grant), Mt. Rainier, Sequoia, and Yosemite.

Under a new law to protect land of scientific value, President Theodore Roosevelt named Devils Tower, Wyo., as the first national monument in 1906.

ESTABLISHMENT OF NATIONAL PARK SERVICE

The National Park Service was created by Congress in 1916 as a bureau in the Department of the Interior.

Under direction of Stephen T. Mather from 1916 to 1929, the National Park System grew to include 25 national parks, 32 national monuments, and a national memorial.

Since 1935 the secretary of the interior has

NATIONAL PARK SYSTEM AREAS

TYPE	AREA IN ACRES	NO.
National Battlefield Parks ...	8,169.18	3
National Battlefield Site	1.00	1
National Battlefields	12,249.29	10
National Capital Parks*	6,466.88	1
National Historic Sites	17,831.71	62
National Historical Parks	150,789.91	26
National Lakeshores	224,674.49	4
National Mall...............	146.35	1
National Memorials	7,995.69	23
National Military Parks	34,550.67	10
National Monuments	4,724,477.79	78
National Parks	47,971,576.97	48
National Parkways	163,225.55	4
National Preserves	21,106,349.55	12
National Recreation Areas ...	3,687,005.55	17
National Rivers	553,963.06	12
National Seashores	597,025.42	10
National Scenic Trails	126,858.04	3
Other Parks	32,076.78	11
White House	18.07	1
Total	**79,425,451.95**	**337**

* Contains 346 units.

been empowered to designate historic sites, but most are established by Congress.

ENTRANCE AND SERVICE FEES

Entrance fees varying from $1 to $3 are charged by the various parks and areas. The fee covers all passengers in the same car.

Anyone can purchase a "Golden Eagle Passport" for $10 that for a year provides unlimited admission to most national parklands for all passengers in one car.

Persons who are 62 or older or are permanently disabled can obtain a free "Golden Age" or "Golden Access" passport giving free admission to all national parklands and allowing a 50% discount on service fees.

Separate fees are charged within the national parklands for special services.

20 MOST VISITED NATIONAL PARKLAND AREAS: 1984

RANK	PARKLAND	LOCATION	VISITS
1	Golden Gate National Recreation Area	California..................................	16,731,706
2	Blue Ridge Parkway	Virginia-North Carolina	15,135,991
3	Natchez Trace Parkway	Mississippi-Tennessee-Alabama	13,478,261
4	Great Smoky Mountains National Park	North Carolina-Tennessee	8,508,390
5	George Washington Memorial Parkway	Virginia-Maryland	8,246,006
6	Gateway National Recreation Area	New York-New Jersey	7,881,106
7	National Capital Parks.......................	Washington, D.C.-Maryland	7,190,938
8	Lake Mead National Recreation Area	Arizona-Nevada	6,276,562
9	C & O Canal National Historical Park	Washington, D.C.-Maryland West Virginia	6,159,201
10	Gulf Islands National Seashore	Florida-Mississippi......................	5,803,384
11	Independence National Historical Park	Pennsylvania..........................	5,803,384
12	Cape Cod National Seashore	Massachusetts	4,560,713
13	Valley Forge National Historical Park	Pennsylvania..........................	3,957,742
14	Lincoln Memorial National Memorial	Washington, D.C.......................	3,812,471
15	Acadia National Park	Maine	3,734,763
16	J.F.K. Center for the Performing Arts	Washington, D.C.......................	3,219,681
17	Olympic National Park........................	Washington	2,759,011
18	Yosemite National Park.......................	California.............................	2,738,467
19	Colonial National Historical Park..............	Virginia	2,504,777
20	Vietnam Veteran's Memorial National Memorial ...	Washington, D.C.......................	2,303,690

TIPS FOR SAFE AND ENJOYABLE CAMPING

Outdoor living has certain hazards that can be avoided by all who take basic precautions.
Know the area. Be aware of potential land and water hazards. If you are camping in one of the national recreation areas, ask the park rangers for brochures, maps, and advice.
Watch your children. Your knowledge, experience, and wisdom cannot help a child who is beyond your reach and warning voice.
Keep distant from wild animals. Do not feed bears or other wildlife. All wild animals can be dangerous. Remember too that young animals are seldom abandoned and a very protective parent is probably nearby.
Dress properly. Even in the heat of summer it is often cool in the mountains or in caves. If you are hiking on rough terrain, be sure to wear sturdy boots or shoes.
Do not hike alone. Whether on a short hike or a month-long mountain climb, a companion may save your life in an emergency.
Know your own limits. Strenuous exertion in extremes of temperature or altitude can be dangerous if you are unaccustomed to sustained exercise.

When on backcountry camping trips, at least one member of your party should be an experienced outdoorsman.

Inform the park superintendent or ranger of your route, destination, and approximate time schedule.
If you hunt, do so only in areas where it is not prohibited. Hunting is prohibited, for example, in all national parks, national monuments, and national historical areas. The use of campgrounds in these areas as base camps for hunting outside park boundaries also is prohibited. Hunting is authorized, in accordance with state laws, in designated national recreation areas.
For camping information, write to Information Officer, Forest Service, Dept. of Agriculture, Washington, D.C. 20240; Technical Liaison Officer, Corps of Engineers, Dept. of the Army, Washington, D.C. 20315. "Camping in the National Park System" ($1.50)—order from Superintendent of Documents, Washington, D.C. 20402.

CAMPGROUNDS ON NATIONAL PARKLANDS

There are three classifications of camping sites:
Campground—Type A: Drinking water and sanitary facilities, including flush toilets and refuse cans, are furnished on a community basis. A typical campsite has parking space, fireplace, table and bench combination, and tent space.

There are Type A campgrounds at 32 of the 48 national parks. Parks with no Type A campgrounds are Biscayne, Canyonlands, Carlsbad Caverns, Channel Islands, Guadalupe Mountains, Isle Royale, North Cascades, Petrified Forest, Voyageurs, and all Alaska national parks except Denali.

Daily entrance fees range from $1 to $3 per car, and user fees range from $1 to $4 per night.

At most federal campgrounds, sites are assigned on a first-come, first-served basis.

Reservations may be made by mail at Cumberland Island and Point Reyes National Seashores; Acadia and Virgin Islands National Parks, Ozark National Scenic Riverways, and Dinosaur National Monument. Reservations through Ticketron are available for camping at Cape Hatteras National Seashore, Grand Canyon, Great Smoky Mountains, Rocky Mountain, Sequoia-Kings Canyon, Shenandoah, and Yosemite National Parks.
Camping Area—Type B: Relatively undeveloped sites regularly accessible by road or by trail. Facilities vary but tend to be minimal.
Group Camp—Type C: Areas used by organized groups, such as Boy Scouts and school groups. Each group space within a camp is provided with a large fireplace, several tables, and parking space for buses or a number of cars.

TYPE A CAMPGROUNDS IN ADDITION TO THOSE IN NATIONAL PARKS

Bandelier National Monument, N.M.	Glen Canyon National Recreation Area, Ariz.
Bighorn Canyon National Recreation Area, Mont.	
Blue Ridge Parkway, Va. and N.C.	Great Sand Dunes National Monument, Colo.
Buffalo National River, Ark.	Greenbelt Park, Md.
Canyon de Chelly National Monument, Ariz.	Gulf Islands National Seashore, Fla.-Miss.
Cape Hatteras National Seashore, N.C.	Hovenweep National Monument, Colo.
Catoctin Mountain Park, Md.	Joshua Tree National Monument, Calif.
Cedar Breaks National Monument, Utah	Lake Mead National Recreation Area, Nev.
Chaco Culture National Historical Park, N.M.	Lava Beds National Monument, Calif.
	Natchez Trace Parkway, Mo.
Chickasaw National Recreation Area, Okla.	Navajo National Monument, Ariz.
Chiricahua National Monument, Ariz.	Organ Pipe Cactus National Monument, Ariz.
Colorado National Monument, Colo.	Ozark National Scenic Riverways, Mo.
Coulee Dam National Recreation Area, Wash.	Padre Island National Seashore, Texas
Craters of the Moon National Mon., Ida.	Pinnacles National Monument, Calif.
Cumberland Gap National Historical Park, Ky.	Prince William Forest Park, Va.
Curecanti National Recreation Area, Colo.	Ross Lake National Recreation Area, Wash.
Death Valley National Monument, Calif.	Sleeping Bear Dunes National Lakeshore, Mich.
Devils Postpile National Monument, Calif.	Sunset Crater National Monument, Ariz.
Devils Tower National Monument, Wyo.	Whiskeytown National Recreation Area, Calif.
Dinosaur National Monument, Colo.	

GUIDE TO NATIONAL PARKLANDS

This guide provides brief descriptions of all 48 national parks as well as a variety of other national parklands noted as vacation attractions. Following this guide are tables listing all the parks and other areas administered by the National Park Service. Total acreages for each of the national parks and the other areas are included.

Acadia National Park. Located along the Maine coast, primarily on Mount Desert Island. The park contains campgrounds and trailer sites.

Apostle Islands National Lakeshore. A chain of islands off the coast of Wisconsin, in Lake Superior, and a stretch of mainland lakeshore along the Bayfield Peninsula. Scenic islands and a fine beach are this park's main attractions.

Arches National Park. Located in southeastern Utah, near the town of Moab. Huge, spectacular rock formations are this area's major feature. Campgrounds and trailer sites are in the park.

Assateague Island National Seashore. A 35-mile-long strip of barrier reef on the Atlantic coast of Maryland and Virginia. The park contains fine sand beaches, hiking trails, and good fishing sites. A herd of wild Chincoteague ponies inhabits the area. State campground near north end.

Badlands National Park. One of South Dakota's most popular attractions for its erosion-carved landscape, the park contains animal fossils 40 million years old. Prairie grasslands support bison, bighorn sheep, deer, and antelope.

Big Bend National Park. Located on the Texas-Mexico border some 320 miles east of El Paso, the nearest large city. This is an area of mountainous desert land and unusual geological formations along the Rio Grande. Fossils of prehistoric animals are commonly found in the area. Campsites, cabins, and motels are located in and around the park, available the year round.

Biscayne National Park. Located 20 miles southeast of Miami, Fla. Contains 25 miles of the only coral reef in North America. Access by boat only; camping permitted; no fresh water.

Bryce Canyon National Park. Located in southern Utah, about 50 miles from Cedar City. This park captures the flavor of the American West's colorful wilderness. Accommodations include tent and trailer sites, a lodge, and an inn.

Canaveral National Seashore. Lies on Florida's east coast just north of the Kennedy Space Center. Its 31 miles of waterfront are wild and undeveloped, with many bird species. Main visitor area is five-mile Playalinda Beach at the south end of the park.

Canyonlands National Park. A Utah park, this area surrounds the junction of the Colorado and Green rivers. There are water-sports facilities in the adjacent Glen Canyon National Recreation Area. Campsites open all year are located in the park.

Cape Cod National Seashore. Located on the southeastern tip of Massachusetts. A mecca for all water sports, this is an area of vast sand beaches, sand dunes, and salt marshes. The reservation adjoins towns where hotel, motel, and entertainment facilities abound.

Cape Hatteras National Seashore. Located on North Carolina's Outer Banks. Large, uncrowded beaches and fishing facilities are among this area's many assets. The park contains campsites. Hotels and motels are in several adjacent towns.

Cape Lookout National Seashore. In North Carolina, just south of Cape Hatteras, this area contains the ghost town of Portsmouth.

Capitol Reef National Park. Located in Utah, this park contains an abundance of rugged, colorful scenery. Accommodations include a motel, a guest ranch, and tent and trailer facilities.

Carlsbad Caverns National Park. Located in southeastern New Mexico, this is considered among the world's most spectacular natural caves. Guided tours are conducted through much of the 32 miles of explored caverns.

Channel Islands National Park. Includes several islands off southern California coast. Main attractions are flora and fauna. Access by boat only; camping permitted; no fresh water.

Crater Lake National Park. Located in southwest Oregon's Cascade Mountains. This park extends around a beautiful lake that fills an extinct volcano. Cottages, a hotel, and campgrounds are within the park.

Cumberland Island National Seashore. Located on the largest of Georgia's Golden Isles. Includes magnificent beaches, dunes, marshes, and lakes.

Denali National Park. A wide area of northern wilderness radiating from around Alaska's Mt. McKinley (20,320 feet), the highest peak in North America. Accommodations include campgrounds, trailer sites, and a hotel.

Everglades National Park. In southern Florida. This land of junglelike subtropical forests and swampland holds many rare species of subtropical flora and fauna. Numerous motels, cottages, and campsites are located in and around the park.

Fire Island National Seashore. A barrier island of fine Atlantic beach off Long Island's south shore. No camping facilities in the park. There are cottages and hotels in privately owned areas of Fire Island adjacent to the national seashore.

Gates of the Arctic National Park. Wilderness recreation lands near the Kobuk River in northern Alaska.

Glacier Bay National Park. Wilderness camping area in southeastern Alaska. Access by aircraft or boat only.

Glacier National Park. Located in northwestern Montana at the Canadian border. The park's chief attraction is its spectacular mountain scenery. Accommodations include campsites, cottages, and motels.

Grand Canyon National Park. The huge canyon, cutting through northwestern Arizona, was formed by the Colorado River. Camping and trailer sites as well as hotels and motels are located in and around the park.

Grand Teton National Park. Located in northwestern Wyoming, this park contains abundant camping, boating, and fishing facilities amid beautiful mountain scenery. Camping and trailer sites, hotels, and motels abound in and around the park.

Great Smoky Mountains National Park. Wooded highlands along the Tennessee–North Carolina border. This park offers extensive hiking and horse trails, with campsites along the way. A lodge and cottages are located in the park.

Guadalupe Mountains National Park. Located in far western Texas, this park is rich in geological interest and animal life, with more than 200 bird species. Carlsbad Caverns National Park in New Mexico is 34 miles away.

Gulf Islands National Seashore. Historic forts and sparkling white sand beaches near Pensacola, Fla., as well as Fort Massachusetts and primitive offshore islands in Mississippi, are included in the parkland. Facilities include campsites and boat trips from Biloxi and Gulfport to Ship Island.

Haleakala National Park. Located on Maui Island, Hawaii. Wild tropical gardens surround a volcano crater open to visitors. Volcano has not erupted for hundreds of years. Campsites and cabins are available for limited periods.

Hawaii Volcanoes National Park. Located on the island of Hawaii. This park is the site of several spectacularly smoldering active volcanoes. Campsites, cottages, and a hotel are situated within park grounds.

Hot Springs National Park. In Arkansas, adjacent to the city of Hot Springs. This attractive area is famed for its fine natural spring waters. Campgrounds and trailer sites inside the park are available the year round.

Indiana Dunes National Lakeshore. A fine stretch of sandy Lake Michigan beach between the towns of Gary and Michigan City, Ind.

Isle Royale National Park. A Michigan island in northern Lake Superior, located 15 miles from the Canadian shore. The island's woods are filled with wildlife, including wolves and moose. Accommodations include campsites, cabins, and a lodge in Rock Harbor.

Katmai National Park. Wilderness camping area in Alaska. Limited facilities include showers, stores, a lodge.

Kenai Fjords National Park. Located on Kenai Peninsula, Alaska. Limited camping available.

Kings Canyon National Park. Located in California's High Sierras. This is an area of mountain wilderness and includes a forest of giant sequoia trees. Horseback riding on trails. The park contains camping and trailer sites, as well as cabins and lodges.

Kobuk Valley National Park. Along Kobuk River in northern Alaska. Limited camping available.

Lake Clark National Park. Located in Alaska. Known for red salmon fishery watershed and habitat of caribou, Dall sheep, peregrine falcons.

Lassen Volcanic National Park. Located in northeastern California. An area of mountain wilderness, this park contains lakes, hot springs, and a volcano that was active as recently as 1921. Accommodations in and around the park, include campgrounds, cabins, and guest ranches.

Mammoth Cave National Park. A huge cavern in southwestern Kentucky, containing some 150 miles of passageways. Guided underground boat trips are a favorite attraction. Campgrounds,

trailer sites, motels, and hotels are situated in and around the park.

Mesa Verde National Park. Located in southwestern Colorado. The park's main attraction is a series of prehistoric cliff dwellings used by primitive Indian tribes some 1,500 years ago. Accommodations include campgrounds, cabins, and a lodge.

Mount Rainier National Park. Located near central Washington. This park radiates from around Mt. Rainier (14,410 feet), a dormant volcano. Also within the park is a massive system of glaciers. Accommodations include campgrounds, trailer sites, and inns.

North Cascades National Park. An area at the north end of the Cascade Range in north central Washington. This region of beautiful but rugged wilderness contains numerous active glaciers. Accommodations within the park are limited to campgrounds.

Obed Wild and Scenic River. Includes 46 miles of the Obed and Emory Rivers, Clear Creek, and Daddys Creek in eastern Tennessee.

Olympic National Park. Located on Washington's Olympic Peninsula, this park is divided into two areas. The inland area is predominantly rain forest surrounding Mt. Olympus. The coastal area, a section of rugged terrain along the Pacific shoreline, is a gathering place for marine birds and other wildlife. Accommodations include camping, trailer sites, and lodges.

Ozark National Scenic Riverways. Encompassing scenic Ozark hill country in southern Missouri along the Current and Jacks Fork rivers. It has 5 campgrounds.

Padre Island National Seashore. A 113-mile stretch of narrow island beach along the Texas Gulf Coast, near Corpus Christi. This park's main attractions are its sand beaches and fine fishing areas. Campsites are available, but primitive campers must bring their own fresh water.

Petrified Forest National Park. Located in northeastern Arizona. As its name denotes, this park holds numerous ancient trees that have turned to stone. There are no campgrounds.

Pictured Rocks National Lakeshore. Located in Michigan's northern peninsula on the Lake Superior shore. This park includes good beaches, scenic forest areas, and rugged sandstone cliffs. There are campgrounds in and around the park.

Point Reyes National Seashore. A stretch of Pacific beach and rugged coastal cliffs about 45 miles north of San Francisco. The area's main attractions are its fine beaches and offshore bird and sea-lion colonies. Accommodations include a small number of campsites.

Redwood National Park. Located along the northwest California coast. Forests of coastal redwoods contain the world's tallest trees. There are campsites in the park. There are nearby trailer sites and motels.

Rocky Mountain National Park. Located about 35 miles southwest of Fort Collins, in northern Colorado. This scenic mountainous area, located on the Continental Divide, contains good fishing and skiing facilities in their respective seasons. Campgrounds are available in the park.

Sequoia National Park. This High Sierra park in California contains giant sequoia groves; part of the John Muir Trail; and Mt. Whitney, the highest peak in the lower 48 states.

Shenandoah National Park. The park's Skyline Drive along Virginia's Blue Ridge Mountains meets the scenic Blue Ridge Parkway. Nature trails and conducted field trips are major attractions. The park has campgrounds and lodges.

Theodore Roosevelt National Park. This North Dakota park features scenic badlands along the Little Missouri River and part of President Theodore Roosevelt's Elkhorn Ranch.

Virgin Islands National Park. Located on St. John, in the U.S. Virgin Islands. This park features beautiful sand beaches and tropical gardens. Camping facilities are available.

Voyageurs National Park. Located in northern Minnesota on the Canadian border. Fishing is outstanding. Other attractions include hiking trails in the thickly forested parkland.

Wind Cave National Park. Located in South Dakota's Black Hills. This park includes interesting natural caverns and ancient Indian sites. There are campgrounds and trailer sites in the park, and motels in nearby towns.

Wrangell–St. Elias National Park. Wilderness recreation lands located in Alaska mountains.

Yellowstone National Park. Located where the borders of Wyoming, Montana, and Idaho meet. This area of spectacular scenery includes about 3,000 geysers and hot springs, as well as river canyons and waterfalls that cut through beautiful forests. Accommodations include campgrounds, trailer sites, and motels.

Yosemite National Park. Located in California's Sierra Nevadas. Majestic mountain country is broken by beautiful forested valleys. The park contains campgrounds, trailer sites, cabins, hotels, and lodges.

Zion National Park. Located in the extreme southwest of Utah. A land of unusual canyons and rock formations. There are campgrounds and two lodges in the park.

NATIONAL PARK SYSTEMS AREAS

TYPE OF AREA AND STATE	ACRES	TYPE OF AREA AND STATE	ACRES
NATIONAL BATTLEFIELD PARKS (3)		Hampton, Maryland	59.44
Kennesaw Mountain, Georgia	2,884.38	Hoover, Herbert, Iowa	186.80
Manassas, Virginia	4,513.29	Hopewell Village, Pennsylvania	848.06
Richmond, Virginia	771.41	Hubbell Trading Post, Arizona	160.09
		Jefferson National Expansion Memorial, Mo.	90.96
NATIONAL BATTLEFIELD SITE (1)		Johnson, Andrew, Tennessee	16.68
Brices Cross Roads, Mississippi	1.00	Kennedy, John F., Birthplace, Mass.	0.09
		King Jr., Martin Luther, Atlanta, Ga.	23.16
NATIONAL BATTLEFIELDS (10)		Knife River Indian Village, North Dakota	1,293.35
Antietam, Maryland	3,246.44	Lincoln, Abraham, Birthplace, Kentucky	116.50
Big Hole, Montana	655.61	Lincoln, Abraham, Home, Springfield, Illinois	12.28
Cowpens, South Carolina	841.56	Longfellow, Henry W., Massachusetts	1.98
Fort Necessity, Pennsylvania	902.80	Muir, John, California	8.90
Monocacy, Maryland	1,659.04	Ninety-Six, South Carolina	989.14
Moores Creek, North Carolina	86.52	Olmsted, Frederick Law, Brookline, Mass.	1.75
Petersburg, Virginia	2,735.38	O'Neill, Eugene, Alamo, Calif.	13.90
Stones River, Tennessee	330.86	Palo Alto Battlefield, Texas	50.00
Tupelo, Mississippi	1.00	Poe, Edgar Allan, Philadelphia, Pa.	0.52
Wilson's Creek, Missouri	1,749.91	Puukohola Heiau, Hawaii	77.71
		Roosevelt, Eleanor, New York	180.50
NATIONAL CAPITAL PARKS (1)		Roosevelt, Franklin D., Home, Hyde Park, N.Y.	290.34
Maryland-Virginia–D.C.	6,465.85	Roosevelt, Theodore, Birthplace, New York	0.11
		Roosevelt, Theodore, Inaugural, New York	1.03
NATIONAL HISTORIC SITES (62)		Sagamore Hill, New York	78.00
Adams, Massachusetts	9.82	Saint Gaudens, Augustus, New Hampshire	148.33
Allegheny Portage Railroad, Pennsylvania	1,134.91	Salem Maritime, Massachusetts	9.10
Andersonville, Georgia	475.72	San Juan, Puerto Rico	75.13
Barton, Clara, Maryland	8.59	Sandburg, Carl, Home, North Carolina	263.52
Bent's Old Fort, Colorado	800.00	Saugus Iron Works, Massachusetts	8.51
Christiansted, Virgin Islands	27.15	Sewall-Belmont House, Washington, D.C.	0.35
Edison, New Jersey	21.25	Springfield Armory, Massachusetts	54.93
Eisenhower, Pennsylvania	690.46	Stone, Thomas, Maryland	328.25
Ford's Theatre, Washington, D.C.	0.29	Taft, William H., Ohio	3.07
Fort Bowie, Arizona	1,000.00	Truman, Harry S, Missouri	0.86
Fort Davis, Texas	460.00	Tuskegee Institute, Alabama	74.39
Fort Laramie, Wyoming	832.46	Van Buren, Martin, New York	39.58
Fort Larned, Kansas	718.39	Vanderbilt Mansion, New York	211.65
Fort Point, California	29.00	Walker, Maggie L., Virginia	1.29
Fort Raleigh, North Carolina	157.27	Whitman Mission, Washington	98.15
Fort Scott, Kansas	10.69		
Fort Smith, Arkansas	73.36	**NATIONAL HISTORICAL PARKS (26)**	
Fort Union Trading Post, N.D.-Mont.	434.04	Appomattox Court House, Virginia	1,325.08
Fort Vancouver, Washington	208.89	Boston, Massachusetts	41.03
Friendship Hill, Point Marion, Pa.	674.56	Chaco Culture, New Mexico	33,977.82
Garfield, James A., Ohio	7.82	Chesapeake and Ohio Canal, Md.-W.Va.-D.C.	20,781.00
Golden Spike, Utah	2,735.28	Colonial, Virginia	9,315.39
Grant-Kohrs Ranch, Montana	1,498.89	Cumberland Gap, Ky.-Tenn.-Va.	20,274.42

NATIONAL PARK SYSTEM AREAS *(continued)*

TYPE OF AREA AND STATE	ACRES
NATIONAL HISTORICAL PARKS *(continued)*	
George Rogers Clark, Indiana	24.30
Harpers Ferry, West Virginia-Maryland-Va.	2,238.37
Independence, Pennsylvania	44.85
Kalaupapa, Hawaii	10,902.10
Kaloko-Honokohau, Hawaii	1,160.90
Klondike Gold Rush, Alaska-Washington	13,272.38
Lafitte, Jean, Louisiana	20,000.00
Lowell, Massachusetts	137.08
Lyndon B. Johnson, Texas	1,477.78
Minute Man, Massachusetts	748.81
Morristown, New Jersey	1,677.65
Nez Percé, Idaho	2,108.89
Puuhonua O Homaumau, Hawaii	181.80
San Antonio Missions, Texas	477.62
San Juan Island, Washington	1,751.99
Saratoga, New York	3,415.08
Sitka, Alaska	106.83
Valley Forge, Pennsylvania	3,464.70
War in the Pacific, Guam	1,957.89
Women's Rights, New York	4.99
NATIONAL LAKESHORES (4)	
Apostle Islands, Wisconsin	67,884.84
Indiana Dunes, Indiana	12,869.65
Pictured Rocks, Michigan	72,898.86
Sleeping Bear Dunes, Michigan	71,020.06
NATIONAL MALL	
Washington, D.C.	146.35
NATIONAL MEMORIALS (23)	
Arkansas Post, Arkansas	389.18
Arlington House, Robert E. Lee Mem., Va.	27.91
Chamizal, Texas	54.90
Coronado, Arizona	4,750.47
De Soto, Florida	26.84
Federal Hall, New York	0.45
Fort Caroline, Florida	138.39
Fort Clatsop, Oregon	125.20
General Grant, New York	0.76
Hamilton Grange, New York	0.71
Jefferson, Thomas, Mem., Washington, D.C.	18.36
Johnson, Lyndon B., Memorial Grove, Washington, D.C.	17.00
John F. Kennedy Center for the Performing Arts, Washington, D.C.	17.50
Johnstown Flood, Pennsylvania	163.47
Kosciuszko, Thaddeus, Pennsylvania	0.02
Lincoln Boyhood, Indiana	191.98
Lincoln Memorial, Washington, D.C.	163.63
Mount Rushmore, South Dakota	1,278.45
Theodore Roosevelt Island, Washington, D.C.	88.50
U.S.S. Arizona Memorial, Hawaii	0.00
Washington Monument, Washington, D.C.	106.01
Williams, Roger, Rhode Island	4.56
Wright Brothers, North Carolina	431.40
NATIONAL MILITARY PARKS (10)	
Chickamauga and Chattanooga, Ga.-Tenn.	8,102.54
Fort Donelson, Tennessee	536.09
Fredericksburg and Spotsylvania, Virginia	5,908.64
Gettysburg, Pennsylvania	3,865.11
Guilford Courthouse, North Carolina	220.25
Horseshoe Bend, Alabama	2,040.00
Kings Mountain, South Carolina	3,945.29
Pea Ridge, Arkansas	4,300.35
Shiloh, Tennessee	3,837.50
Vicksburg, Mississippi	1,619.70
NATIONAL MONUMENTS (78)	
Agate Fossil Beds, Nebraska	3,055.22

TYPE OF AREA AND STATE	ACRES
Alibates Flint Quarries and Texas Panhandle Culture, Texas	1,370.97
Aniakchak, Alaska	139,500.00
Aztec Ruins, New Mexico	27.14
Bandelier, New Mexico	36,916.89
Black Canyon of the Gunnison, Colorado	20,762.70
Buck Island Reef, Virgin Islands	880.00
Cabrillo, California	143.94
Canyon de Chelly, Arizona	83,840.00
Cape Krusenstern, Alaska	660,000.00
Capulin Mountain, New Mexico	775.38
Carver, George Washington, Missouri	210.00
Casa Grande, Arizona	472.50
Castillo de San Marcos, Florida	20.48
Castle Clinton, New York	1.00
Cedar Breaks, Utah	6,154.60
Chiricahua, Arizona	11,134.80
Colorado, Colorado	20,453.95
Congaree Swamp, South Carolina	15,138.25
Craters of the Moon, Idaho	53,545.05
Custer Battlefield, Montana	765.34
Death Valley, California-Nevada	2,067,627.68
Devils Postpile, California	798.46
Devils Tower, Wyoming	1,346.91
Dinosaur, Colorado-Utah	211,141.69
Effigy Mounds, Iowa	1,474.63
El Morro, New Mexico	1,278.72
Florissant Fossil Beds, Colorado	5,998.09
Fort Frederica, Georgia	213.72
Fort Jefferson, Florida	64,700.00
Fort Matanzas, Florida	298.51
Fort McHenry, Maryland	43.26
Fort Pulaski, Georgia	5,623.10
Fort Stanwix, New York	15.52
Fort Sumter, South Carolina	66.77
Fort Union, New Mexico	720.60
Fossil Butte, Wyoming	8,198.00
Gila Cliff Dwellings, New Mexico	533.13
Grand Portage, Minnesota	709.97
Great Sand Dunes, Colorado	38,662.18
Hohokam Pima, Arizona	1,690.00
Homestead, Nebraska	194.57
Hovenweep, Utah-Colorado	785.43
Jewel Cave, South Dakota	1,273.51
John Day Fossil Beds, Oregon	14,011.90
Joshua Tree, California	559,959.50
Lava Beds, California	46,559.87
Lehman Caves, Nevada	640.00
Montezuma Castle, Arizona	857.69
Mound City Group, Ohio	217.50
Muir Woods, California	553.55
Natural Bridges, Utah	7,791.00
Navajo, Arizona	360.00
Ocmulgee, Georgia	683.48
Oregon Caves, Oregon	487.98
Organ Pipe Cactus, Arizona	330,688.86
Pecos, New Mexico	364.80
Pinnacles, California	16,221.77
Pipe Spring, Arizona	40.00
Pipestone, Minnesota	281.78
Rainbow Bridge, Utah	160.00
Russell Cave, Alabama	310.45
Saguaro, Arizona	83,573.88
Saint Croix Island, Maine	35.39
Salinas, New Mexico	1,076.94
Scotts Bluff, Nebraska	2,997.08
Statue of Liberty, New York	58.38
Sunset Crater, Arizona	3,040.00
Timpanogos Cave, Utah	250.00
Tonto, Arizona	1,120.00
Tumacacori, Arizona	16.52
Tuzigoot, Arizona	809.30
Walnut Canyon, Arizona	2,249.46

NATIONAL PARK SYSTEM AREAS *(continued)*

TYPE OF AREA AND STATE	ACRES
NATIONAL MONUMENTS *(continued)*	
Washington, Booker T., Virginia	223.92
Washington, George, Birthplace, Virginia ..	538.23
White Sands, New Mexico	144,458.24
Wupatki Arizona	35,253.24
Yucca House, Colorado	10.00

NATIONAL PARKS (48)

Acadia, Maine.......................	39,706.91
Arches, Utah........................	73,378.98
Badlands, South Dakota	243,302.33
Big Bend, Texas	741,118.40
Biscayne, Florida	173,274.37
Bryce Canyon, Utah..................	35,835.08
Canyonlands, Utah	337,570.43
Capitol Reef, Utah	241,904.26
Carlsbad Caverns, New Mexico	46,755.33
Channel Islands, California	249,353.77
Crater Lake, Oregon	183,227.05
Denali, Alaska........................	4,700,000.00
Everglades, Florida	1,398,939.19
Gates of the Arctic, Alaska..............	7,500,000.00
Glacier, Montana	1,013,594.67
Glacier Bay, Alaska	3,225,197.95
Grand Canyon, Arizona.................	1,218,375.24
Grand Teton, Wyoming.................	310,520.94
Great Smoky Mountains, Tennessee- North Carolina	520,269.44
Guadalupe Mountains, Texas	76,293.06
Haleakala, Hawaii	28,655.25
Hawaii Volcanoes, Hawaii	229,177.03
Hot Springs Arkansas	5,823.54
Isle Royale, Michigan	571,790.11
Katmai, Alaska.......................	3,716,000.00
Kenai Fjords, Alaska	670,000.00
Kings Canyon, California	461,636.20
Kobuk Valley, Alaska..................	1,750,000.00
Lake Clark, Alaska	2,874,000.00
Lassen Volcanic, California	106,372.36
Mammoth Cave, Kentucky	52,369.60
Mesa Verde, Colorado..................	52,085.14
Mount Rainier, Washington	235,404.00
North Cascades, Washington	504,780.94
Olympic, Washington	914,576.46
Petrified Forest, Arizona	93,492.57
Redwood, California	110,178.03
Rocky Mountain, Colorado	265,192.86
Sequoia, California	402,487.83
Shenandoah, Virginia	195,072.00
Theodore Roosevelt, North Dakota	70,416.39
Virgin Islands, Virgin Islands	14,695.85
Voyageurs, Minnesota	217,892.01
Wind Cave, South Dakota	28,292.08
Wrangell-St. Elias, Alaska	8,945,000.00
Yellowstone, Wyoming-Montana-Idaho	2,219,822.70
Yosemite, California	761,170.18
Zion, Utah	146,551.10

NATIONAL PARKWAYS (4)

Blue Ridge, North Carolina-Virginia	82,117.37
George Washington Memorial, Virginia- Maryland	7,141.63
John D. Rockefeller Jr. Memorial Parkway, Wyoming..................	23,777.22
Natchez Trace, Tenn.-Ala.-Miss.	50,189.33

NATIONAL PRESERVES (12)

Aniakchak, Alaska	475,500.00
Bering Land Bridge, Alaska	2,770,000.00
Big Cypress, Florida	570,000.00
Big Thicket, Texas	85,849.55
Denali, Alaska.......................	1,330,000.00
Gates of the Arctic, Alaska.............	940,000.00

TYPE OF AREA AND STATE	ACRES
Glacier Bay, Alaska	55,000.00
Katmai, Alaska.......................	374,000.00
Lake Clark, Alaska....................	1,171,000.00
Noatack, Alaska......................	6,560,000.00
Wrangell-St. Elias, Alaska.............	4,255,000.00
Yukon-Charley Rivers, Alaska	2,520,000.00

NATIONAL RECREATION AREAS (17)

Amistad, Texas	57,292.44
Bighorn Canyon, Wyoming-Montana	120,277.86
Chattahoochee River, Georgia	8,699.00
Chickasaw, Oklahoma	952.91
Coulee Dam, Washington	100,390.31
Curecanti, Colorado	42,114.47
Cuyahoga Valley, Ohio	32,460.19
Delaware Water Gap, Pennsylvania-N.J. ...	66,696.79
Gateway, New York-New Jersey	26,310.93
Glen Canyon, Arizona-Utah	1,236,880.00
Golden Gate, California	72,815.04
Lake Chelan, Washington	61,890.07
Lake Mead, Arizona-Nevada	1,496,600.52
Lake Meredith, Texas	44,977.63
Ross Lake, Washington..................	117,574.09
Santa Monica Mountains, California	150,000.00
Whiskeytown-Shasta-Trinity, California	42,503.43

NATIONAL RIVERS (12)

Alagnak, Alaska	24,038.00
Big South Fork, Kentucky-Tennessee	122,960.00
Buffalo, Arkansas	94,221.00
Lower St. Croix, Minnesota-Wisconsin	9,465.14
Delaware, N.Y., Pennsylvania-New Jersey ...	1,973.33
Missouri National Recreational River, Neb., S.D.	—
New River Gorge, West Virginia	62,024.00
Obed, Tennessee	5,085.83
Ozark, Missouri	80,783.34
Rio Grande, Texas	9,600.00
St. Croix, Minnesota-Wisconsin	68,793.21
Upper Delaware, New York-Pennsylvania ..	75,000.00

NATIONAL SCENIC TRAIL (3)

Appalachian, Georgia to Maine (14 states) .	115,969.09
Natchez Trace, Miss.-Tenn.-Ala.	10,995.0
Potomac Heritage, Maryland-West Virginia-Virginia	—

NATIONAL SEASHORES (10)

Assateague Island, Maryland-Virginia	39,630.93
Canaveral, Florida	57,627.07
Cape Cod, Massachusetts	43,256.06
Cape Hatteras, North Carolina	30,319.43
Cape Lookout, North Carolina	28,414.74
Cumberland Island, Georgia	36,410.28
Fire Island, New York	19,578.55
Gulf Islands, Florida-Mississippi	139,775.46
Padre Island, Texas	130,696.83
Point Reyes, California	71,046.07

OTHER PARKS (11)

Catoctin Mountain, Maryland	5,770.22
Constitution Gardens, Wash. D.C.......	50.00
Douglass, Frederick, Home, Wash., D.C. ...	8.08
Fort Washington, Maryland	341.00
Greenbelt Park, Maryland	1,175.99
Perry's Victory and International Peace Memorial, Ohio.....................	25.38
Piscataway, Maryland	2,262.52
Prince William Forest, Virginia	18,571.55
Rock Creek Park, Washington, D.C.	1,754.37
Vietnam Veterans Memorial, Wash. D.C. ...	2.00
Wolf Trap Farm Park, Virginia	130.28

WHITE HOUSE

Washington, D.C.	18.07

U.S. NATIONAL FORESTS

Source: U.S. Department of Agriculture, Forest Service; data as of Sept. 30, 1984.

STATE AND FORESTS	GROSS ACRES	STATE AND FORESTS	GROSS ACRES	STATE AND FORESTS	GROSS ACRES	STATE AND FORESTS	GROSS ACRES
UNITED STATES		**FLORIDA**		**MONTANA** (cont.)		**SOUTH DAKOTA**	
Total Forest		Apalachicola[3]	632,000	Flathead[3,6]	2,628,705	Black Hills[1,2]	1,328,013
System	223,399,502	Choctawhatchee	675	Gallatin[3,4]	2,149,552	Custer[1]	77,833
ALABAMA		Ocala[2]	430,122	Helena[3]	1,162,602		
William B.		Osceola	161,814	Kaniksu[1,3]	489,752	**TENNESSEE**	
Bankhead[3]	348,917	**GEORGIA**		Kootenai[1,3]	2,097,950	Cherokee[1,2,3]	1,204,520
Conecuh	171,177	Chattahoochee[2,3]	1,571,790	Lewis & Clark[3]	1,999,212	**TEXAS**	
Talladega	727,154	Oconee	260,855	Lolo[3]	2,614,726	Angelina	402,231
Tuskegee	15,628	**IDAHO**		**NEBRASKA**		Davy Crockett	394,200
ALASKA		Bitterroot[1,3,4,6]	464,217	Samuel R. McKelvie	116,822	Sabine	442,705
Chugach	6,577,301	Boise[3,4,5,6]	2,959,719	Nebraska	229,599	Sam Houston	491,800
Tongass	17,441,114	Cache[1]	264,441	**NEVADA**		**UTAH**	
ARIZONA		Caribou[1]	1,067,409	Eldorado[1]	53	Ashley[1,4,5]	1,300,908
Apache[1,3,4]	1,226,686	Challis[3,4,5,6]	2,487,549	Humboldt[3]	2,680,449	Cache[1]	954,293
Coconino[3]	2,010,762	Clearwater[3,6]	1,765,545	Inyo[1]	62,348	Caribou[1]	8,940
Coronado[1,3]	1,782,238	Coeur d'Alene	806,523	Toiyabe[1]	2,681,447	Dixie[1]	1,967,187
Kaibab[2]	1,600,075	Kaniksu[1]	1,063,273	**NEW HAMPSHIRE**		Fishlake	1,525,686
Prescott[3]	1,407,596	Kootenai[1]	46,480	White Mountain[1,3]	798,063	Manti-LaSal[1]	1,310,645
Sitgreaves	884,481	Nezperce[3,4,5,6]	2,247,082	**NEW MEXICO**		Sawtooth[1]	92,404
Tonto[3]	2,969,514	Payette[3,4,5,6]	2,425,521	Apache[1,4]	650,219	Uinta[3]	889,208
ARKANSAS		St. Joe	1,074,637	Carson[3,6]	1,490,594	Wasatch[1,3,4]	1,024,321
Ouachita[1,2,3]	1,961,435	Salmon[4,6]	1,794,288	Cibola[3]	2,120,739	**VERMONT**	
Ozark[2,3]	1,496,920	Sawtooth[1,3,5]	1,805,654	Coronado[1]	71,541	Green Mountain[3]	629,019
St. Francis	29,729	Targhee[1]	1,355,419	Gila[3,4]	2,797,628	**VIRGINIA**	
CALIFORNIA		**ILLINOIS**		Lincoln[3]	1,271,066	George	
Angeles[3]	693,667	Shawnee	714,441	Santa Fe[3]	1,734,800	Washington[1,2]	1,638,575
Calaveras		**INDIANA**		**NEW YORK**		Jefferson[1,3,5]	1,585,896
Bigtree	380	Hoosier	644,139	Green Mountain	13,272	**WASHINGTON**	
Cleveland[3]	566,850	**KENTUCKY**		**NORTH CAROLINA**		Colville	1,021,071
Eldorado[1,3]	884,635	Daniel Boone[3]	1,360,776	Cherokee[1]	327	Gifford Pinchot[3]	1,379,298
Inyo[1,3]	1,843,591	Jefferson[3]	54,614	Croatan	308,226	Kaniksu[1]	293,463
Klamath[1,3,4]	1,886,725	**LOUISIANA**		Nantahala[3,6]	1,349,000	Mt. Baker[3]	1,312,120
Lassen[3]	1,374,945	Kisatchie[2]	1,022,703	Pisgah[2,3]	1,076,511	Okanogan[3]	1,536,961
Los Padres[3]	1,962,743	**MAINE**		Uwharrie	219,757	Olympic	715,751
Mendocino[3]	1,079,483	White		**OHIO**		Snoqualmie[3]	1,557,682
Modoc[3]	1,979,407	Mountain[1]	53,561	Wayne	832,147	Umatilla[1,3]	319,361
Plumas[6]	1,400,895	**MICHIGAN**		**OKLAHOMA**		Wenatchee[3]	1,904,259
Rogue River[1]	61,031	Hiawatha	1,281,637	Quachita[1]	412,912	**WEST VIRGINIA**	
San Bernardino[3]	818,999	Huron	694,097	**OREGON**		George	
Sequoia[2,3,4]	1,180,042	Manistee	1,331,673	Deschutes[3]	1,852,282	Washington[1]	157,568
Shasta[4,5]	1,634,602	Ottawa	1,559,892	Fremont[3]	1,710,570	Jefferson[1]	29,782
Sierra[3]	1,412,641	**MINNESOTA**		Klamath[1]	26,539	Monongahela[3,5]	1,650,951
Siskiyou[1]	39,666	Chippewa	1,599,649	Malheur[3]	1,540,754	**WISCONSIN**	
Six Rivers	1,118,247	Superior[3]	3,260,843	Mt. Hood[3]	1,108,554	Chequamegon[3,6]	1,049,347
Stanislaus[3,4]	1,090,543	**MISSISSIPPI**		Ochoco	978,547	Nicolet	973,403
Tahoe[3]	1,208,856	Bienville	382,821	Rogue River[1]	624,883	**WYOMING**	
Toiyabe[1,3]	694,987	De Soto	796,072	Siskiyou[1,3,6]	1,124,255	Ashley[1]	104,701
Trinity[3,4,5]	1,179,098	Delta	118,134	Siuslaw[5,7]	835,261	Bighorn[4]	1,115,160
COLORADO		Holly Springs	519,943	Umatilla[1,3]	1,189,747	Black Hills[1]	201,134
Arapaho[3]	1,157,008	Homochitto	373,497	Umpqua	1,029,351	Bridger[3]	1,744,631
Grand Mesa	351,707	Tombigbee	119,155	Wallowa[3,5,6]	1,064,634	Caribou[1]	9,612
Gunnison[3]	1,767,756	**MISSOURI**		Whitman[3,5]	1,311,545	Medicine Bow[2,3]	1,402,667
Manti-LaSal[1]	27,145	Mark Twain[3,6]	2,943,896	Willamette[3]	1,796,866	Shoshone[3,4]	2,466,587
Pike[3]	1,283,790	**MONTANA**		Winema[3]	1,086,116	Targhee[1]	333,473
Rio Grande[3]	1,960,466	Beaverhead[3]	2,198,806	**PENNSYLVANIA**		Teton[3]	1,694,947
Roosevelt[3]	1,082,567	Bitterroot[1,3]	1,189,610	Allegheny	742,693	Wasatch[1]	47,704
Routt[3]	1,248,154	Custer[1,3]	1,200,385	**SOUTH CAROLINA**		**PUERTO RICO**	
San Isabel	1,244,615	Deerlodge[3]	1,355,783	Francis Marion[2]	414,700	Caribbean	55,665
San Juan[3,4]	2,107,291			Sumter[3]	965,762		
Uncompahgre[4]	1,043,934						
White River[3]	2,090,246						

[1] Area within state boundaries; National Forest extends over two or more states. [2] Includes National Game Refuge. [3] Includes National Wilderness Area. [4] Includes Primitive Area. [5] Includes National Recreation Area. [6] Includes National Scenic River Area. [7] Includes National Scenic–Research Area.

RAILROAD HIGHLIGHTS: 1985

Oil Wagon 1890s
10.1 USA

An 1890s oil wagon, a predecessor of railroad tank cars and tanker trucks, was featured on this transportation series stamp issued in Oil Center, N.M., on April 18. Oil wagons, commonly pulled by two horses, were used to deliver oil as fuel for home heating, cooking stoves, and lanterns. The 10.1-cent denomination is used for bulk third-class mail presorted to the five-digit ZIP Code.

Congress debated who, if anyone, should be allowed to buy the government-controlled Consolidated Rail Corp. (Conrail), which carries freight over 14,000 miles of track in the Northeast states.

Secretary of Transportation Elizabeth Dole announced on Feb. 8 that she had chosen from among 16 bidders the offer of Norfolk Southern Corp. to pay $1.2 billion for the government's 85% interest in Conrail.

Labor unions strongly opposed the sale to Norfolk Southern, which carries freight in the Southern and Midwestern states over 18,000 miles of track, claiming jobs would be lost by the merger.

In testimony before the Senate Commerce Committee, Secretary Dole declared that sale of Conrail to Norfolk and Southern would assure "long-term rail service in the Northeast Region, true employment stability for Conrail's work force, and a very high level of confidence that Conrail will never again become a ward of the federal government."

She said that in addition to $1.2 billion in cash Norfolk Southern had agreed to surrender to the U.S. Treasury some $2.4 billion of tax benefits accumulated by Conrail.

The Senate Commerce Committee voted 12-5 on April 30 to approve the sale to Norfolk Southern.

Then on May 14 Morgan Stanley & Co. announced that it had assembled a group of 25 investors who were willing to match the Norfolk Southern cash offer. Morgan Stanley indicated that if successful in its bid, stock in Conrail would be offered for sale to the public within five years. Employees of Conrail, who own 15% of the railroad, would be permitted to retain their ownership under the Morgan Stanley plan.

Fearing that sale of Conrail to Norfolk Southern might result in higher freight rates and less service, a bipartisan group of legislators introduced legislation in Congress on June 26 to support the Morgan Stanley bid.

Federal Railroad Administrator John H. Riley released statistics that showed 1984 was the safest year the U.S. railroad industry ever had. He said the accident rate at grade crossings per million train-miles had decreased by 3.9%.

AVIATION HIGHLIGHTS: 1985

The historic *China Clipper* was honored with this 44-cent international airmail stamp issued on Feb. 15 in San Francisco. The plane made the first airmail flight across the Pacific Ocean in 1935 from San Francisco to Manila, Philippines, in 59 hours and 48 minutes. The *China Clipper* was one of three huge flying boats built for Pan American Airways by the Glen L. Martin Co.

TERRORISM COUNTERMEASURES

The Department of Transportation issued orders in June to tighten security at airports to curb terrorist hijackings and bombings.

Curbside checking of baggage was banned for international flights and more careful inspections of carry-on baggage was ordered.

Airlines can no longer accept baggage for checking at ticket counters except from ticketed passengers.

Any baggage to be carried that is not accompanied by a ticketed passenger must be physically inspected, X-rayed, or left behind.

On flights that carry both passengers and cargo, the airlines must inspect or X-ray the freight or mail, or hold it for 24 hours later than the flight to which it is originally assigned.

X-29 RESEARCH AIRCRAFT

The National Aeronautics and Space Administration (NASA) began a series of test flights of the X-29 high performance research aircraft that may point the way to tomorrow's airplanes. The forward-swept wing aircraft will be flown at speeds of about 400 mph at 30,000 feet in the first flights. In 1986 it will be tested at increased speeds of 1,000 mph or more at an altitude of 50,000 feet.

AVIATION HALL OF FAME

Four new members were inducted in 1985 into the National Aviation Hall of Fame in Dayton, Ohio. They were:

Gen. George Scratchley Brown (1918-78), who served in World War II and the Korean War, and was Chairman of the Joint Chiefs of Staff in 1974-78 during the Vietnam War.

Michael Collins (born 1930), astronaut, who was pilot of the command module Co-

lumbia in the Apollo-11 mission that landed the first astronauts on the Moon, and who later supervised the planning and construction of the National Air and Space Museum in Washington, D.C., as undersecretary of the Smithsonian Institution.

Carl Benjamin Eielson (1905-1929), who in 1928 became the first pilot to fly over both the Arctic Ocean and the continent of Antarctica.

John Paul Stapp (born 1910), an Army research scientist, who rode rocket sleds while testing the effects of high speed on the human body, pioneering the way to safe supersonic flight.

TWA SALE

Directors of Trans World Airlines Inc. (TWA) announced on June 13 that they had agreed to sell the airline to Texas Air Corporation for $793.5 million.

If completed, the deal could create an airline second only to United Airlines, because Texas Air already owns Continental Airlines and New York Air.

The merger was arranged in an effort to fend off an unwanted takeover by New York investor Carl C. Icahn.

However, in July Icahn continued to pursue his efforts to win control of the airline in partnership with the pilots union, whose members were said to own 20% of TWA's stock.

In August Icahn's persistence won out. He increased his offer to $24 a share, $1 more than Texas Air had bid and he and his associates also increased their stake in the airline to nearly 16 million shares, or more than 45% ownership.

BUSIEST U.S. AIRPORTS

Source: Federal Aviation Administration

At the beginning of 1984 the United States had 12,653 airports, 2,918 heliports, and 392 seaplane bases, and 66 stolports.

A total of 264,866 civil aircraft were registered in 1983, including 4,480 air carrier planes and 260,386 general aviation aircraft.

Following is a list of leading airports in the U.S. in 1984. For the 23d consecutive year Chicago's O'Hare International Airport ranked first. Leading airports for noncommercial operations include Van Nuys, Long Beach, and Santa Ana, Calif.

RANK AIRPORT	TOTAL TAKEOFFS & LANDINGS	TAKEOFFS AND LANDINGS BY TYPE OF OPERATION			
		Air Carrier	Air Taxi	General Aviation	Military
1. Chicago O'Hare Int'l	741,296	625,033	66,766	45,540	3,957
2. Atlanta International	689,482	547,112	101,051	39,747	1,572
3. Van Nuys	575,721	8	235	571,922	3,556
4. Los Angeles Int'l	550,756	329,475	147,356	69,008	4,917
5. Dallas/Ft. Worth Reg'l	524,564	409,278	91,784	22,720	782
6. Denver Stapleton Int'l	512,520	348,649	94,541	68,036	1,294
7. Santa Ana.....................	488,540	29,299	21,347	435,261	2,133
8. Long Beach	449,208	8,380	17,926	420,649	2,253
9. San Francisco	403,850	273,157	75,317	52,626	2,750
10. Phoenix Sky Harbor Int'l	399,298	196,239	56,109	138,964	7,986
11. St. Louis Int'l	395,906	260,583	71,791	55,263	8,269
12. Boston Logan	387,422	207,203	132,223	47,754	242
13. Anchorage Merrill	384,030	0	12,015	371,981	34
12. Oakland Int'l	379,192	65,193	39,297	273,558	1,144
15. Seattle Boeing	375,670	2,655	13,146	357,460	2,409
16. Newark	369,990	254,399	74,370	40,564	657
17. LaGuardia	365,118	246,739	81,634	36,269	476
18. San Jose Municipal	363,722	61,442	20,367	281,192	721
19. Denver Arapahoe Cnty.	362,777	0	1,029	360,753	995
20. John F. Kennedy Int'l	356,647	210,341	117,114	28,513	679
21. Pittsburgh Greater Int'l	355,632	211,036	94,927	41,815	7,854
22. Miami International	352,585	217,127	61,262	73,623	573
23. Philadelphia Int'l	344,709	144,028	124,585	74,694	1,402
24. Honolulu.....................	343,797	154,121	75,442	82,943	31,291
25. Washington Nat'l	340,682	191,479	63,533	85,253	417

WORLD GROWTH OF SCHEDULED AIRLINE TRAFFIC*

Source: International Civil Aviation Organization

YEAR	PASSENGERS CARRIED[1]	FREIGHT TONS CARRIED[1]	PASSENGER-MILES PERFORMED[1]	SEAT-MILES AVAILABLE[1]	PASSENGER LOAD FACTOR	TON-MILES PERFORMED[1]		
						Freight	Mail	Total (Passengers, baggage, Freight, Mail)
1970	383	6.7	286,000	522,000	55%	8,180	2,150	38,810
1971	411	7.4	307,000	568,000	54%	9,060	1,990	41,420
1972	450	8.0	348,000	609,000	57%	10,290	1,900	46,690
1973	489	9.0	384,000	667,000	58%	12,010	1,970	51,910
1974	514	9.5	408,000	688,000	59%	13,030	1,980	55,270
1975	534	9.6	433,000	733,000	59%	13,270	1,990	58,080
1976	576	10.3	475,000	789,000	60%	14,750	2,080	63,880
1977	610	11.0	508,000	836,000	61%	16,180	2,180	68,790
1978	679	11.7	582,000	902,000	65%	17,770	2,240	77,770
1979	754	12.1	659,000	999,000	66%	19,180	2,350	86,900
1980	748	12.1	677,000	1,071,000	63%	19,950	2,520	89,540
1981	752	11.9	695,000	1,091,000	64%	20,970	2,600	92,620
1982	764	12.6	710,000	1,114,000	64%	21,400	2,660	94,600
1983	795	13.2	738,000	1,148,000	64%	24,620	2,750	99,670
1984[2]	832	14.4	780,000	1,206,000	65%	27,010	2,950	107,930

[1] Millions. [2] Preliminary Estimates.

AVIATION WORLD RECORDS

Source: National Aeronautic Association, Washington, D.C., the United States representative of the Fédération Aeronautique Internationale (FAI), world governing body for aeronautical records.

JET AIRPLANE RECORDS

Jan. 10–11, 1962	Distance in Straight Line . Maj. Clyde P. Evely, USAF; Boeing B52-H, 8 engines Kadena, Okinawa, to Madrid, Spain	U.S.A.	12,532.28 miles (20,168.78 km.)
June 6–7, 1962	Distance over Closed Circuit . Capt. William Stevenson, USAF; Boeing B52-H Seymour-Johnson, North Carolina—Kindley, Bermuda— Sondrestrom, Greenland—Anchorage, Alaska—March Air Force Base, California—Key West, Florida—Seymour-Johnson, North Carolina	U.S.A.	11,336.92 miles (18,245.05 km.)
July 17, 1962	Altitude (launched from carrier plane) . Maj. Robert M. White, USAF; North American X-15-1 (NASA Aircraft) Edwards Air Force Base, California	U.S.A.	314,750 feet (95,935.99 meters)
July 28, 1976	Altitude in Horizontal Flight. Capt. Robert C. Helt, USAF; Lockheed SR-71; Beale AFB, Calif.	U.S.A.	85,068.997 feet (25,929.031 meters)
July 28, 1976	Speed over Straight Course (15/25 kilometers). Capt. Eldon W. Joersz, USAF; Lockheed SR-71; Beale AFB, Calif.	U.S.A.	2,193.16 mph (3,529.56 kph)
July 27, 1976	Speed over Closed Circuit . Maj. Adolphus H. Bledsoe Jr.; USAF, Lockheed SR-71 Beale Air Force Base, California	U.S.A.	2,092.294 mph (3,367.221 kph)
Sept. 1, 1974	New York to London, 3,490 miles . Maj. James V. Sullivan, USAF; SR-71, 1 hour, 54 min., 56.4 sec.	U.S.A.	1,806.964 mph (2,908.026 kph)
May 1–3, 1976	Speed Around World . Capt. Walter H. Mullikin; Boeing 747 jet airliner, 4 engines Course: New York—New Delhi—Tokyo—New York Elapsed time: 1 day, 22 hours, 50 seconds	U.S.A.	502.84 mph (809.24 kph)

PISTON ENGINE AIRPLANE RECORDS

Sept. 29, 1946	Distance in Straight Line . Cmdr. T.D. Davies, USN; Lockheed P2V-1 monoplane Pearce Field, Perth, Australia, to Port Columbus, Columbus, Ohio	U.S.A.	11,235.6 miles (18,081.99 km.)
Dec. 5–8, 1981	Distance in Closed Circuit . Jerry D. Mullens; BD-2 airplane, 10 360-C Continental engine Oklahoma City, Okla. to Jacksonville, Florida	U.S.A.	10,007 miles (16,104.0 km.)
Oct. 22, 1938	Altitude. Mario Pezzi; Caproni 161 Biplane; Montecelio, Italy	Italy	56,046 feet (17,083 meters)
Aug. 14, 1979	Speed over 3-Kilometer Course . Steve Hinton, P-51D Rolls-Royce-Griffin 3800 HP engine Tonopah, Nevada	U.S.A.	499.04 mph (803.138 kph)
April 9, 1951	Speed Over 15/25-Kilometer Course . Jacqueline Cochran; North American P-51 monoplane Near Indio, California	U.S.A.	464.374 mph (747.339 kph)
Nov. 4–9, 1977	Speed Around World (22,868.91 miles; 36,803.95 km.). Philander P. Claxton III and John L. Cink; Twin-engine Aero Star 601 Course: Los Angeles, Peoria, Gauder, Frankfurt, Teheran, Madras, Kota Kinabalu (Malaysia), Manila, Guam, Kwajalein Island, Wake Island, Honolulu, Los Angeles Elapsed time: 104 hours, 5 minutes, 30 seconds	U.S.A.	219.70 mph (353.57 kph)

HELICOPTER RECORDS

April 6–7, 1966	Distance in Straight Line . Robert G. Ferry; Hughes YOH6A helicopter Culver City, California, to Daytona Beach, Florida	U.S.A.	2,213.04 miles (3,561.55 km.)
June 21, 1972	Altitude. Jean Boulet; Alouette SA 315-001 "Lama"; Istres, France	France	40,820 feet (12,442 meters)
Sept. 21, 1978	Speed over 15/25-Kilometer Course . Gourguen Karapetyan; S-A-10 helicopter, Podmoskovnoye Aerodrome	U.S.S.R.	228.91 mph (368.4 kph)

BALLOON RECORDS

Nov. 9–12, 1981	Distance (transpacific). Crew: Ben Abruzzo, Larry Newman, Ron Clark, Rocky Aoki Balloon: Double Eagle V, helium-filled, 400,000 cu. ft. Course: Nagashima, Japan, to Covelo, Calif. Elapsed time: 84 hours, 31 minutes	U.S.A.	5,208.7 miles (8,384.5 km.)
Sept. 14–18, 1984	Distance and Duration (transatlantic) . Crew: Joe W. Kittinger Balloon: Rosie O'Grady's Peace Balloon, helium-filled Course: Caribou, Maine, to Montenotte, Italy Elapsed time: 83 hours, 45 minutes	U.S.A.	3,535 miles (5,689.03 km.)
May 4, 1961	Altitude. U.S. Navy Cmdr. Malcolm D. Ross in Lee Lewis Memorial over Gulf of Mexico	U.S.A.	113,739.9 feet (34,668 meters)

AIR DISTANCES IN THE UNITED STATES AND CANADA

Source: U. S. Civil Aeronautics Board. Distances in statute miles.

	Albuquerque, N.M.	Atlanta, Ga.	Boston, Mass.	Charleston, S.C.	Chicago, Ill.	Cincinnati, Ohio	Cleveland, Ohio	Dallas–Ft. Worth, Tx.	Denver, Colo.	Detroit, Mich.	Houston, Texas	Los Angeles, Calif.	Memphis, Tenn.
Albuquerque, N.M.	—	1,269	1,974	1,528	1,117	1,240	1,411	569	339	1,347	744	677	942
Atlanta, Ga.	1,269	—	946	259	606	373	554	721	1,208	595	689	1,946	332
Billings, Mont.	750	1,525	1,866	1,753	1,060	1,301	1,366	1,081	457	1,274	1,304	970	1,223
Birmingham, Ala.	1,138	134	1,050	392	584	396	604	597	1,091	625	562	1,815	211
Boston, Mass.	1,974	946	—	818	867	752	563	1,561	1,767	632	1,597	2,611	1,139
Buffalo, N.Y.	1,587	712	396	696	473	410	191	1,212	1,371	240	1,281	2,217	813
Charleston, S.C.	1,528	259	818	—	760	497	595	987	1,459	668	925	2,206	589
Charlotte, N.C.	1,450	227	727	168	599	335	430	936	1,348	500	913	2,125	512
Chicago, Ill.	1,117	606	867	760	—	264	316	802	901	235	925	1,745	491
Cincinnati, Ohio	1,240	373	752	497	264	—	221	811	1,081	230	871	1,900	403
Cleveland, Ohio	1,411	554	563	595	316	221	—	1,021	1,213	95	1,091	2,053	623
Columbus, Ohio	1,343	446	640	514	296	116	112	926	1,167	156	986	1,996	518
Dallas–Ft. Worth, Tx.	569	731	1,561	987	802	811	1,021	—	645	987	224	1,235	431
Dayton, Ohio	1,271	432	709	536	240	63	163	861	1,096	166	929	1,924	460
Denver, Colo.	339	1,208	1,767	1,459	901	1,081	1,213	645	—	1,135	864	849	880
Des Moines, Iowa	833	743	1,165	956	299	505	613	624	602	533	802	1,447	490
Detroit, Mich.	1,347	595	632	668	235	230	95	987	1,135	—	1,076	1,979	610
Hartford, Conn.	1,886	859	91	643	783	661	475	1,490	1,684	548	1,507	2,527	1,048
Houston, Texas	744	689	1,597	925	925	871	1,091	224	864	1,076	—	1,379	469
Indianapolis, Ind.	1,161	432	817	585	177	98	261	762	989	230	845	1,815	381
Jacksonville, Fla.	1,480	270	1,010	192	864	613	753	918	1,455	814	817	2,152	575
Kansas City, Mo.	717	693	1,257	931	403	540	695	460	543	630	643	1,363	393
Las Vegas, Nev.	487	1,747	2,381	2,005	1,514	1,678	1,825	1,056	616	1,749	1,222	236	1,416
Little Rock, Ark.	816	453	1,260	712	552	514	729	303	778	706	374	1,493	130
Los Angeles, Calif.	677	1,946	2,611	2,206	1,745	1,900	2,053	1,235	849	1,979	1,379	—	1,619
Louisville, Ky.	1,177	321	829	485	286	83	304	732	1,035	306	788	1,842	320
Memphis, Tenn.	942	332	1,139	589	491	403	623	431	880	610	469	1,619	—
Miami, Fla.	1,689	595	1,258	490	1,197	948	1,080	1,121	1,716	1,146	964	2,342	860
Milwaukee, Wis.	1,142	669	860	815	67	318	328	853	908	237	984	1,756	556
Minn.–St. Paul, Minn.	981	906	1,124	1,087	334	596	622	852	693	528	1,034	1,536	700
Montreal, Quebec	1,864	993	254	929	747	713	494	1,512	1,624	529	1,584	2,473	1,115
Nashville, Tenn.	1,123	214	943	439	409	230	448	631	1,023	457	657	1,797	200
New Orleans, La.	1,015	425	1,367	635	837	700	917	447	1,067	926	305	1,671	349
New York, N.Y.	1,825	760	187	636	740	589	425	1,391	1,638	509	1,417	2,475	964
Norfolk, Va.	1,702	516	468	351	717	485	435	1,212	1,564	529	1,201	2,371	782
Oklahoma City, Okla.	510	761	1,505	1,020	693	756	949	175	500	900	395	1,187	432
Omaha, Nebr.	725	821	1,282	1,048	416	614	730	583	485	651	781	1,330	538
Ottawa, Ontario	1,770	931	310	888	654	632	412	1,425	1,530	439	1,503	2,379	1,034
Philadelphia, Pa.	1,746	665	281	550	678	507	363	1,302	1,569	453	1,324	2,401	874
Phoenix, Ariz.	329	1,587	2,300	1,846	1,440	1,569	1,738	868	589	1,671	1,009	370	1,264
Pittsburgh, Pa.	1,486	526	496	524	412	256	105	1,066	1,302	201	1,117	2,136	652
Portland, Oreg.	1,111	2,172	2,537	2,411	1,739	1,975	2,046	1,616	985	1,953	1,825	834	1,854
Raleigh, N.C.	1,565	356	612	217	647	390	416	1,061	1,447	502	1,043	2,239	634
Rochester, N.Y.	1,643	749	343	717	528	461	244	1,265	1,425	296	1,332	2,272	863
St. Louis, Mo.	934	484	1,046	705	258	308	487	550	781	440	667	1,592	256
Salt Lake City, Utah	492	1,589	2,105	1,840	1,249	1,449	1,565	988	381	1,481	1,195	590	1,261
San Antonio, Texas	608	874	1,764	1,114	1,041	1,024	1,241	246	793	1,215	191	1,210	625
San Diego, Calif.	628	1,891	2,588	2,150	1,723	1,865	2,027	1,171	840	1,956	1,303	109	1,567
San Francisco, Calif.	896	2,139	2,704	2,395	1,846	2,036	2,161	1,465	956	2,079	1,635	337	1,807
Seattle, Wash.	1,179	2,181	2,496	2,415	1,720	1,964	2,021	1,660	1,019	1,927	1,874	954	1,870
Tampa, Fla.	1,497	406	1,185	371	1,012	773	927	928	1,513	983	787	2,158	656
Toronto, Ontario	1,554	739	446	744	437	413	193	1,199	1,328	214	1,280	2,176	812
Tulsa, Okla.	608	674	1,394	931	585	646	838	237	549	790	429	1,283	342
Vancouver, B.C.	1,290	2,248	2,514	2,475	1,764	2,014	2,057	1,754	1,110	1,962	1,971	1,080	1,943
Washington, D.C.	1,627	533	413	441	589	388	288	1,171	1,464	383	1,190	2,288	742
Wichita, Kans.	542	781	1,433	1,034	587	699	870	329	428	810	542	1,203	452
Winnipeg, Manitoba	1,130	1,299	1,354	1,467	707	971	945	1,174	793	850	1,378	1,540	1,089

Miami, Fla.	Milwaukee, Wis.	Minn.–St. Paul, Minn.	New Orleans, La.	New York, N.Y.	Oklahoma City, Okla.	Omaha, Nebr.	Philadelphia, Pa.	Portland, Oreg.	St. Louis, Mo.	Salt Lake City, Utah	San Francisco, Calif.	Seattle, Wash.	Washington, D.C.	
1,689	1,142	981	1,015	1,825	510	725	1,746	1,111	934	492	896	1,179	1,627	..Albuquerque, N.M.
595	669	906	425	760	761	821	665	2,172	484	1,589	2,139	2,181	533	Atlanta, Ga.
2,083	1,038	748	1,472	1,776	919	706	1,727	679	1,048	387	909	664	1,648	Billings, Mont.
661	650	854	321	866	631	732	772	2,064	410	1,471	2,013	2,079	638	...Birmingham, Ala.
1,258	860	1,124	1,367	187	1,505	1,282	281	2,537	1,046	2,105	2,704	2,496	413	Boston, Mass.
1,185	464	734	1,097	301	1,136	887	279	2,157	674	1,710	2,309	2,122	284	Buffalo, N.Y.
490	815	1,087	635	636	1,020	1,048	550	2,411	705	1,840	2,395	2,415	441	Charleston, S.C.
651	651	930	651	541	941	914	447	2,282	575	1,727	2,296	2,279	321	Charlotte, N.C.
1,197	67	334	837	740	693	416	678	1,739	258	1,249	1,846	1,720	589	Chicago, Ill.
948	318	596	700	589	756	614	507	1,975	308	1,449	2,036	1,964	388	Cincinnati, Ohio
1,080	328	622	917	425	949	730	363	2,046	487	1,565	2,161	2,021	288	Cleveland, Ohio
990	331	627	806	483	866	689	405	2,034	410	1,529	2,121	2,017	299	Columbus, Ohio
1,121	853	852	447	1,391	175	583	1,302	1,616	550	988	1,465	1,660	1,171	Dallas–Ft. Worth, Tx.
998	284	574	764	554	796	621	477	1,972	339	1,460	2,051	1,957	368	Dayton, Ohio
1,716	908	693	1,067	1,638	500	485	1,569	985	781	381	956	1,019	1,464	Denver, Colo.
1,327	311	232	818	1,038	474	117	972	1,471	259	955	1,549	1,464	874	...Des Moines, Iowa
1,146	237	528	926	509	900	651	453	1,953	440	1,481	2,079	1,927	383	Detroit, Mich.
1,194	780	1,050	1,279	106	1,415	1,199	196	2,470	957	2,026	2,625	2,431	326	Hartford, Conn.
964	984	1,034	305	1,417	395	781	1,324	1,825	667	1,195	1,635	1,874	1,190	Houston, Texas
1,021	238	503	708	664	689	517	587	1,877	229	1,355	1,944	1,866	476	...Indianapolis, Ind.
335	925	1,174	513	829	983	1,088	742	2,429	753	1,834	2,366	2,443	630	Jacksonville, Fla.
1,252	436	394	690	1,113	312	152	1,039	1,481	238	919	1,498	1,489	927	Kansas City, Mo.
2,175	1,524	1,300	1,500	2,248	986	1,099	2,176	763	1,372	368	414	866	2,066	Las Vegas, Nev.
942	613	703	346	1,088	308	495	999	1,759	296	1,155	1,689	1,782	868	Little Rock, Ark.
2,342	1,756	1,536	1,671	2,475	1,187	1,330	2,401	834	1,592	590	337	954	2,288	. Los Angeles, Calif.
911	348	603	621	662	685	582	576	1,950	254	1,408	1,989	1,944	451	Louisville, Ky.
860	556	700	349	964	432	538	874	1,854	256	1,261	1,807	1,870	742	Memphis, Tenn.
—	1,259	1,501	674	1,090	1,223	1,393	1,013	2,700	1,068	2,088	2,585	2,724	921	Miami, Fla.
1,259	—	297	903	746	736	426	690	1,718	317	1,246	1,845	1,694	612	Milwaukee, Wis.
1,501	297	—	1,040	1,028	695	282	980	1,426	448	991	1,589	1,399	908	Minn.–St. Paul, Minn.
1,404	723	949	1,393	333	1,429	1,147	394	2,333	969	1,941	2,538	2,284	489	...Montreal, Quebec
806	475	695	471	766	615	612	675	1,972	271	1,403	1,968	1,977	542	...Nashville, Tenn.
674	903	1,040	—	1,182	567	841	1,088	2,051	604	1,428	1,911	2,086	954	New Orleans, La.
1,090	746	1,028	1,182	—	1,345	1,155	94	2,454	892	1,989	2,586	2,421	228	New York, N.Y.
802	748	1,045	939	289	1,199	1,099	211	2,454	784	1,935	2,519	2,437	157	Norfolk, Va.
1,223	736	695	567	1,345	—	418	1,261	1,484	462	865	1,383	1,519	1,136	Oklahoma City, Okla.
1,393	426	282	841	1,155	418	—	1,088	1,368	342	839	1,433	1,367	988	Omaha, Nebr.
1,371	629	857	1,321	337	1,339	1,053	377	2,247	880	1,848	2,446	2,200	450	Ottawa, Ontario
1,013	690	980	1,088	94	1,261	1,088	—	2,406	813	1,926	2,521	2,378	134	Philadelphia, Pa.
1,972	1,460	1,276	1,301	2,153	833	1,037	2,075	1,009	1,262	507	651	1,106	1,956	Phoenix, Ariz.
1,013	431	726	918	340	1,010	821	267	2,148	553	1,659	2,253	2,124	183	Pittsburgh, Pa.
2,700	1,718	1,426	2,051	2,454	1,484	1,368	2,406	—	1,708	630	550	129	2,327	Portland, Oreg.
700	689	981	779	426	1,058	997	336	2,363	667	1,823	2,400	2,354	224	Raleigh, N.C.
1,204	518	783	1,142	264	1,190	942	257	2,203	729	1,762	2,361	2,166	289	Rochester, N.Y.
1,068	317	448	604	892	462	342	813	1,708	—	1,156	1,735	1,709	696	St. Louis, Mo.
2,088	1,246	991	1,428	1,989	865	839	1,926	630	1,156	—	599	689	1,827	.Salt Lake City, Utah
1,143	1,095	1,097	495	1,587	407	824	1,496	1,714	786	1,086	1,482	1,774	1,362	.San Antonio, Texas
2,267	1,739	1,532	1,599	2,446	1,136	1,313	2,369	933	1,557	626	447	1,050	2,253	..San Diego, Calif.
2,585	1,845	1,589	1,911	2,586	1,383	1,433	2,521	550	1,735	599	—	678	2,419	San Francisco, Calif.
2,724	1,694	1,399	2,086	2,421	1,519	1,367	2,378	129	1,709	689	678	—	2,306	Seattle, Wash.
204	1,075	1,307	487	1,005	1,023	1,190	920	2,497	869	1,887	2,392	2,520	810	Tampa, Fla.
1,234	420	679	1,110	366	1,114	846	347	2,097	654	1,660	2,260	2,060	346	Toronto, Ontario
1,168	631	616	538	1,235	111	352	1,151	1,532	351	926	1,465	1,558	1,028	Tulsa, Okla.
2,801	1,733	1,436	2,173	2,449	1,607	1,429	2,410	250	1,770	798	800	127	2,344	...Vancouver, B.C.
921	612	908	954	228	1,136	988	134	2,327	696	1,827	2,419	2,306	—	Washington, D.C.
1,295	622	545	670	1,283	156	265	1,204	1,406	392	808	1,364	1,430	1,087	Wichita, Kans.
1,893	654	394	1,421	1,303	1,002	597	1,275	1,212	841	951	1,505	1,154	1,231	.Winnipeg, Manitoba

AIR DISTANCES BETWEEN MAJOR WORLD AIRPORTS

Source: Defense Mapping Agency Aerospace Center. Distances in nautical miles.

	Bangkok	Berlin	Cairo	Cape Town	Caracas	Chicago	Hong Kong	Honolulu	Istanbul	Lima	London	Madrid	Melbourne
Aarhus, Denmark	4,715	244	1,801	5,417	4,465	3,632	4,736	6,121	1,164	5,924	488	1,103	8,675
Accra, Ghana	5,955	2,892	2,312	2,593	3,982	5,083	6,616	8,735	2,630	4,717	2,748	2,096	8,099
Amsterdam, Netherlands.	4,962	313	1,777	5,213	4,235	3,580	5,026	6,304	1,196	5,676	201	790	8,927
Anchorage, Alaska	5,220	3,946	5,339	9,111	4,647	2,473	4,408	2,413	4,688	5,547	3,902	4,502	6,713
Athens, Greece	4,283	984	603	4,306	5,054	4,742	4,623	7,261	300	6,357	1,307	1,278	8,060
Auckland, New Zealand ..	5,172	9,591	8,945	6,356	7,137	7,113	4,934	3,815	9,214	5,815	9,912	10,583	1,429
Baghdad, Iraq	3,274	1,766	682	4,271	6,092	5,589	3,716	7,304	871	7,368	2,221	2,313	7,032
Bangkok, Thailand	—	4,651	3,923	5,480	9,166	7,427	924	5,730	4,043	10,637	5,162	5,497	3,966
Beirut, Lebanon	3,714	1,476	305	4,162	5,666	5,305	4,138	7,419	535	6,929	1,883	1,900	7,437
Belgrade, Yugoslavia	4,413	543	1,026	4,712	4,847	4,344	4,638	6,846	440	6,225	921	1,086	8,313
Berlin, Germany	4,651	—	1,566	5,184	4,548	3,834	4,737	6,358	942	5,987	513	1,003	8,615
Bombay, India	1,628	3,402	2,348	4,438	7,847	6,999	2,327	6,972	2,605	9,031	3,899	4,066	5,289
Buenos Aires, Argentina .	9,123	6,432	6,396	3,727	2,757	4,869	9,965	6,569	6,611	1,700	6,000	5,432	6,278
Cairo, Egypt	3,923	1,566	—	3,899	5,520	5,343	4,397	7,682	664	6,723	1,909	1,812	7,526
Calais, France	5,084	433	1,816	5,157	4,193	3,530	5,157	6,349	1,264	5,554	96	672	9,047
Cape Town, South Africa .	5,480	5,184	3,899	—	5,542	7,398	6,404	10,025	4,517	5,289	5,209	4,617	5,577
Caracas, Venezuela......	9,166	4,548	5,520	5,542	—	2,178	8,835	5,232	5,253	1,480	4,036	3,785	8,451
Chicago, Illinois	7,427	3,834	5,343	7,398	2,178	—	6,768	3,688	4,771	3,283	3,436	3,652	8,399
Copenhagen, Denmark...	4,653	184	1,726	5,368	4,531	3,711	4,689	6,174	1,086	5,986	530	1,113	8,616
Denver, Colorado	7,293	4,413	5,968	8,114	2,668	784	6,496	2,913	5,353	3,463	4,071	4,366	7,621
Frankfurt, West Germany .	4,850	234	1,579	5,053	4,364	3,775	4,961	6,474	1,008	5,788	354	769	8,805
Helsinki, Finland	4,257	607	1,832	5,653	4,913	3,855	4,331	5,913	1,172	6,385	1,001	1,596	8,192
Hong Kong	924	4,737	4,397	6,404	8,835	6,768	—	4,824	4,345	9,916	5,218	5,695	3,982
Honolulu, Hawaii	5,730	6,358	7,682	10,025	5,232	3,688	4,824	—	7,058	5,165	6,289	6,841	4,785
Houston, Texas	8,023	4,621	6,099	7,493	1,966	805	7,245	3,392	5,552	2,723	4,202	4,351	7,821
Istanbul, Turkey	4,043	942	664	4,517	5,253	4,771	4,345	7,058	—	6,596	1,360	1,470	7,893
Karachi, Pakistan	2,002	2,930	1,925	4,479	7,389	6,572	2,585	6,995	2,140	8,646	3,428	3,605	5,757
Keflavik, Iceland	5,469	1,303	2,864	6,181	3,705	2,558	5,257	5,288	2,243	5,182	1,027	1,564	9,158
Kinshasa, Zaire	5,191	3,410	2,257	1,778	5,013	6,178	5,994	9,720	2,811	5,506	3,441	2,880	7,033
Leningrad, U.S.S.R.	4,093	714	1,782	5,642	5,076	3,995	4,078	5,930	1,132	6,548	1,146	1,716	8,033
Lima, Peru	10,637	5,987	6,723	5,289	1,480	3,283	9,916	5,165	6,596	—	5,476	5,140	7,013
Lisbon, Portugal	5,774	1,246	2,060	4,616	3,513	3,484	5,962	6,805	1,745	4,863	845	278	9,585
London, England	5,162	513	1,909	5,209	4,036	3,436	5,218	6,289	1,360	5,476	—	673	9,127
Madrid, Spain	5,497	1,003	1,812	4,617	3,785	3,652	5,695	6,841	1,470	5,140	673	—	9,334
Melbourne, Australia	3,966	8,615	7,526	5,577	8,451	8,399	3,982	4,785	7,893	7,013	9,127	9,334	—
Mexico City, Mexico	8,499	5,253	6,690	7,405	1,933	1,466	7,641	3,300	6,174	2,285	4,816	4,904	7,334
Montreal, Canada	7,238	3,251	4,725	6,896	2,116	650	6,726	4,270	4,177	3,443	2,825	3,007	9,030
Moscow, U.S.S.R........	3,822	869	1,572	5,467	5,355	4,318	3,869	6,112	962	6,818	1,359	1,852	7,781
Nairobi, Kenya	3,905	3,437	1,904	2,205	6,240	6,971	4,738	9,333	2,567	6,797	3,684	3,336	6,210
New Delhi, India........	1,578	3,130	2,383	5,003	7,675	6,504	2,042	6,445	2,466	9,061	3,642	3,926	5,494
New York, New York	7,526	3,448	4,879	6,775	1,833	644	7,013	4,331	4,359	3,153	3,000	3,119	9,016
Oslo, Norway	4,687	450	1,976	5,632	4,483	3,519	4,650	5,908	1,324	5,955	630	1,283	8,620
Panama City, Panama ...	12,176	5,072	6,189	6,106	740	2,020	8,766	4,575	5,857	1,268	4,567	4,408	7,873
Paris, France	5,105	477	1,734	5,023	4,113	3,610	5,213	6,481	1,214	5,533	197	557	9,056
Peking, China..........	1,779	3,984	4,078	6,997	7,766	5,717	1,071	4,398	3,829	8,974	4,415	4,984	4,903
Rabat, Morocco	5,776	1,406	1,948	4,310	3,577	3,732	6,043	7,107	1,736	4,864	1,081	414	9,416
Rio de Janeiro, Brazil	8,694	5,389	5,343	3,293	2,437	4,600	9,566	7,206	5,535	2,042	4,984	4,386	7,159
Rome, Italy	4,784	647	1,163	4,545	4,505	4,191	5,032	6,988	749	5,854	780	721	8,631
Saigon, Vietnam	400	5,016	4,323	5,670	9,469	7,546	813	5,475	4,434	10,584	5,524	5,882	3,608
St. Louis, Missouri	7,595	4,055	5,557	7,445	2,101	225	6,901	3,588	4,991	3,125	3,651	3,849	8,242
San Francisco, California .	6,888	4,933	6,495	8,909	3,383	1,605	6,009	2,084	5,844	3,911	4,665	5,052	6,827
Santiago, Chile	9,549	6,752	6,925	4,312	2,638	4,605	10,091	5,959	7,066	1,325	6,281	5,776	6,113
Seattle, Washington	6,474	4,400	5,951	8,877	3,548	1,495	5,640	2,326	5,294	4,300	4,172	4,615	7,106
Shanghai, China........	1,541	4,544	4,506	6,991	8,260	6,139	655	4,304	4,324	9,271	4,986	5,540	4,323
Shannon, Ireland	5,429	809	2,224	5,382	3,754	3,120	5,436	6,088	1,682	5,210	322	767	9,388
Singapore	775	5,363	4,460	5,220	9,910	8,132	1,389	5,836	4,678	10,163	5,876	6,147	3,256
Stockholm, Sweden	4,467	437	1,839	5,585	4,705	3,724	4,435	5,970	1,177	6,175	784	1,395	8,410
Teheran, Iran	2,952	1,899	1,058	4,551	6,357	5,648	3,348	7,013	1,106	7,688	2,389	2,575	6,798
Tokyo, Japan	2,476	4,837	5,174	7,948	7,657	5,480	1,555	3,350	4,857	8,366	5,192	5,828	4,387
Vienna, Austria	4,552	297	1,277	4,910	4,678	4,098	4,717	6,640	676	6,085	691	978	8,490
Warsaw, Poland	4,371	284	1,401	5,154	4,831	4,072	4,479	6,405	745	6,267	796	1,229	8,333
Washington, D.C.	7,645	3,631	5,064	6,866	1,774	532	7,092	4,206	4,543	3,041	3,185	3,302	8,850

Mexico City	Montreal	Moscow	New Delhi	New York	Paris	Peking	Rio de Janeiro	Rome	San Francisco	Singapore	Stockholm	Teheran	Tokyo	Vienna	Warsaw
5,065	3,063	895	3,229	3,272	546	3,929	5,464	873	4,695	5,447	299	2,058	4,728	540	441
5,800	4,478	3,511	4,578	4,443	2,587	6,389	3,047	2,269	6,681	6,244	3,329	3,359	7,470	2,687	2,981
4,979	2,981	1,162	3,443	3,166	235	4,238	5,150	701	4,756	5,676	613	2,201	5,043	521	597
3,284	2,721	3,780	4,965	2,943	4,089	3,443	7,073	4,577	1,754	5,794	3,563	4,913	3,013	4,229	4,003
6,102	4,126	1,217	2,707	4,287	1,134	4,128	5,238	580	5,914	4,891	1,308	1,332	5,156	688	865
5,917	7,761	8,754	6,748	7,672	10,027	5,617	6,631	9,953	5,663	4,546	9,191	8,114	4,759	9,643	9,377
7,019	5,017	1,393	1,714	5,212	2,083	3,422	6,019	1,599	6,500	3,857	1,884	382	4,534	1,531	1,518
8,499	7,238	3,822	1,578	7,526	5,105	1,779	8,694	4,784	6,888	775	4,467	2,952	2,476	4,552	4,371
6,698	4,706	1,332	2,151	4,882	1,726	3,782	5,627	1,200	6,357	4,290	1,684	790	4,873	1,207	1,268
5,736	3,743	933	2,845	3,921	776	4,020	5,334	397	5,475	5,075	878	1,515	4,981	251	443
5,253	3,251	869	3,130	3,448	477	3,984	5,389	647	4,933	5,363	437	1,899	4,837	297	284
8,454	6,536	2,727	613	6,778	3,789	2,576	7,250	3,349	7,306	2,113	3,368	1,514	3,641	3,220	3,123
3,984	4,872	7,280	8,531	4,590	5,963	10,414	1,077	6,014	5,606	8,577	6,783	7,444	9,914	6,384	6,657
6,690	4,725	1,572	2,383	4,879	1,734	4,078	5,343	1,163	6,495	4,460	1,839	1,058	5,174	1,277	1,401
4,911	2,920	1,292	3,557	3,096	136	4,371	5,019	695	4,749	5,793	743	2,297	5,169	597	714
7,405	6,896	5,467	5,003	6,775	5,023	6,997	3,293	4,545	8,909	5,220	5,585	4,551	7,948	4,910	5,154
1,933	2,116	5,355	7,675	1,833	4,113	7,766	2,437	4,505	3,383	9,910	4,705	6,357	7,657	4,678	4,831
1,466	650	4,318	6,504	644	3,610	5,717	4,600	4,191	1,605	8,132	3,724	5,648	5,480	4,098	4,072
5,145	3,143	836	3,159	3,351	560	3,897	5,488	828	4,769	5,381	284	1,980	4,716	474	361
1,254	1,412	4,761	6,716	1,425	4,256	5,516	5,090	4,845	831	7,881	4,230	6,104	5,057	4,695	4,622
5,166	3,172	1,096	3,312	3,351	256	4,217	5,155	517	4,953	5,549	647	2,039	5,067	337	486
5,316	3,341	474	2,824	3,578	1,045	3,415	5,973	1,208	4,723	5,004	221	1,796	4,235	791	509
7,641	6,726	3,869	2,042	7,013	5,213	1,071	9,566	5,032	6,009	1,389	4,451	3,348	1,555	4,717	4,479
3,300	4,270	6,112	6,445	4,331	6,481	4,398	7,206	6,988	2,084	5,836	5,970	7,013	3,350	6,640	6,405
663	1,377	5,123	7,277	1,233	4,369	6,252	4,360	4,938	1,421	8,631	4,526	6,451	5,803	4,876	4,865
6,174	4,177	962	2,466	4,359	1,214	3,829	5,535	749	5,844	4,678	1,177	1,106	4,857	676	745
8,035	6,086	2,272	578	6,321	3,318	2,632	7,030	2,886	7,027	2,555	2,907	1,044	3,746	2,749	2,653
4,008	2,019	1,798	4,127	2,254	1,223	4,279	5,286	1,795	3,654	6,238	1,172	3,098	4,786	1,588	1,519
6,885	5,558	3,772	4,065	5,541	3,252	6,088	3,577	2,769	7,762	5,325	3,818	3,133	7,218	3,141	3,396
5,459	3,491	324	2,663	3,731	1,174	3,279	6,101	1,271	4,817	4,841	378	1,664	4,125	852	556
2,285	3,443	6,818	9,061	3,153	5,533	8,974	2,042	5,854	3,911	10,163	6,175	7,688	8,366	6,085	6,267
4,686	2,835	2,107	4,203	2,926	777	5,227	4,153	996	4,937	6,422	1,611	2,850	6,036	1,248	1,487
4,816	2,825	1,359	3,642	3,000	197	4,415	4,984	780	4,665	5,876	784	2,389	5,192	691	796
4,904	3,007	1,852	3,926	3,119	557	4,984	4,386	721	5,052	6,147	1,395	2,575	5,828	978	1,229
7,334	9,030	7,781	5,494	9,016	9,056	4,903	7,159	8,631	6,827	3,256	8,410	6,798	4,387	8,490	8,333
—	2,003	5,782	7,926	1,817	4,974	6,726	4,135	5,529	1,635	8,972	5,178	7,105	6,120	5,499	5,505
2,003	—	3,814	6,099	290	2,993	5,655	4,411	3,566	2,206	7,998	3,189	5,112	5,628	3,501	3,503
5,782	3,814	—	2,358	4,052	1,345	3,138	6,221	1,297	5,108	4,558	657	1,344	4,057	900	623
8,006	6,322	3,430	2,927	6,391	3,490	4,988	4,828	2,906	8,349	4,037	3,741	2,357	6,086	3,141	3,301
7,926	6,099	2,358	—	6,360	3,563	2,062	7,597	3,210	6,698	2,239	3,015	1,377	3,170	3,000	2,846
1,817	290	4,052	6,360	—	3,158	5,942	4,159	3,717	2,248	8,288	3,416	5,329	5,887	3,686	3,708
4,968	2,973	883	3,241	3,196	731	3,804	5,608	1,088	4,521	5,433	226	2,139	4,563	740	580
1,302	2,197	5,818	8,175	1,912	4,671	7,733	2,856	5,119	2,884	10,149	5,161	6,945	7,339	5,240	5,354
4,974	2,993	1,345	3,563	3,158	—	4,452	4,929	590	4,860	5,801	840	2,275	5,273	570	741
6,726	5,655	3,138	2,062	5,942	4,452	—	9,353	4,410	5,139	2,417	3,632	3,043	1,131	4,035	3,760
4,878	3,084	2,237	4,198	3,154	971	5,375	3,988	1,012	5,216	6,382	1,807	2,826	6,239	1,344	1,615
4,135	4,411	6,221	7,597	4,159	4,929	9,353	—	4,943	5,739	8,509	5,762	6,399	10,024	5,322	5,602
5,529	3,566	1,297	3,210	3,717	590	4,410	4,943	—	5,444	5,427	1,075	1,854	5,353	420	716
8,446	7,436	4,173	1,972	7,726	5,475	1,830	8,947	5,172	6,812	588	4,810	3,348	2,334	4,929	4,738
1,242	843	4,543	6,718	776	3,824	5,862	4,536	4,402	1,508	8,278	3,948	5,872	5,564	4,317	4,294
1,635	2,206	5,108	6,698	2,248	4,860	5,139	5,739	5,444	—	7,343	4,674	6,406	4,486	5,227	5,099
3,549	4,718	7,619	9,140	4,429	6,276	10,271	1,586	6,413	5,132	8,866	7,054	7,982	9,299	6,751	7,002
2,027	1,985	4,529	6,137	2,105	4,368	4,699	5,975	4,943	590	7,016	4,118	5,818	4,176	4,697	4,551
6,989	6,145	3,690	2,298	6,427	5,016	581	8,848	4,942	5,360	2,040	4,203	3,451	961	4,586	4,312
4,494	2,506	1,609	3,931	2,678	491	4,573	4,862	1,078	4,387	6,157	981	2,702	5,275	1,012	1,091
8,972	7,998	4,558	2,239	8,288	5,801	2,417	8,509	5,427	7,343	—	5,210	3,573	2,860	5,237	5,080
5,178	3,189	657	3,015	3,416	840	3,632	5,762	1,075	4,674	5,210	—	1,927	4,434	678	444
7,105	5,112	1,344	1,377	5,329	2,275	3,043	6,399	1,854	6,406	3,573	1,927	—	4,158	1,707	1,627
6,120	5,628	4,057	3,170	5,887	5,273	1,131	10,024	5,353	4,486	2,860	4,434	4,158	—	4,949	4,657
5,499	3,501	900	3,000	3,686	570	4,035	5,322	420	5,227	5,287	678	1,707	4,949	—	298
5,505	3,503	623	2,846	3,708	741	3,760	5,602	716	5,099	5,080	444	1,627	4,657	298	—
1,632	423	4,224	6,521	186	3,343	6,024	4,148	3,902	2,123	8,397	3,592	5,508	5,910	3,870	3,890

OCEAN SHIPPING HIGHLIGHTS: 1985

The United States was in 8th place among leading merchant fleets of the world in 1984, according to statistics released by the U.S. Maritime Administration.

The number of privately owned U.S.-flag vessels on Jan. 1, 1985 totaled 492 of 20,939,000 deadweight tons (dwt.) compared to 538 of 21,569,000 one year earlier.

The U.S. statistics reflect the worldwide trend begun in the 1970s toward larger vessels. This trend established total tonnage rather than number of ships as a more meaningful international standard for ranking world merchant fleets.

The Liberian tanker *Seawise Giant*, built in Japan in 1976 is the world's largest ship, with a deadweight tonnage of 564,739 dwt. Its length of 1,504 feet 2 inches is more than five times the size of a football field.

The French tanker *Prairial*, completed in 1979, is the second largest vessel. It has a length of 1,359 feet 1 inch, a width of 206 feet 10 inches, and tonnage of 555,051 dwt.

The largest active passenger ship is the *Norway*, which can carry 2,400 passengers.

Liberia continued to boast the world's largest merchant fleet, attracting the registry of many American and Greek-owned vessels. However, few vessels under Liberian registry ever call at that nation's ports.

LEADING MERCHANT FLEETS OF THE WORLD

Source: U.S. Department of Commerce, Maritime Administration

1984 RANK	COUNTRY	SHIPS	DEADWEIGHT TONNAGE	1983 RANK	COUNTRY	SHIPS	DEADWEIGHT TONNAGE
1	Liberia	2,019	131,545,000	1	Liberia	2,220	146,124,000
2	Greece	2,454	68,612,000	2	Greece	2,893	74,629,000
3	Japan	1,712	61,191,000	3	Japan	1,770	63,192,000
4	Panama	3,290	57,781,000	4	Panama	2,725	45,820,000
5	Norway..........	529	32,470,000	5	Norway..........	600	38,809,000
6	Britain...........	685	27,251,000	6	Britain............	927	37,146,000
7	United States *	788	24,409,000	7	Soviet Union	2,449	21,886,000
8	Soviet Union	2,497	23,157,000	8	United States *	574	21,479,000
9	France	314	16,532,000	9	France	317	18,516,000
10	Italy..............	601	14,964,000	10	Italy..............	606	16,551,000
11	China	861	12,628,000	11	Spain..............	510	12,525,000
12	Singapore........	556	11,634,000	12	Singapore.........	592	11,932,000
13	Spain	511	10,765,000	13	China	750	10,945,000
14	South Korea.....	499	10,585,000	14	Germany, West	440	10,790,000
15	British Colonies ...	309	10,200,000	15	India	378	9,464,000

* Includes 250 U.S. government-owned ships of 2,840,000 DWT tons.

SEA DISTANCES BETWEEN MAJOR WORLD PORTS

Source: Defense Mapping Agency Hydrographic/Topographic Center. Distances in nautical miles.

MAJOR WORLD PORTS	AUCKLAND (New Zealand)	BOMBAY (India)	BUENOS AIRES (Argentina)	CAPE TOWN (South Africa)	COLOMBO (Sri Lanka)	HAMBURG (W. Germany)	HONG KONG	HONOLULU	ISTANBUL (Turkey)	LE HAVRE (France)	LISBON (Portugal)
AUCKLAND	—	7,088	6,186	7,153	6,229	11,602	5,060	3,820	10,189	11,170	10,707
BOMBAY	7,088	—	8,285	4,616	896	6,613	3,895	8,328	3,853	6,153	5,278
BUENOS AIRES	6,186	8,285	—	3,719	8,161	6,625	10,587	7,764	7,101	6,159	5,339
CAPE TOWN ...	7,153	4,616	3,719	—	4,398	6,431	6,917	10,649	6,184	5,986	5,134
COLOMBO	6,229	896	8,161	4,398	—	7,045	3,026	7,462	4,285	6,585	5,710
HAMBURG	11,602	6,613	6,625	6,431	7,045	—	10,029	9,790	3,425	511	1,369
HONG KONG ..	5,060	3,895	10,587	6,917	3,026	10,029	—	4,857	7,286	9,535	8,702
HONOLULU ...	3,820	8,328	7,764	10,649	7,462	9,790	4,857	—	10,857	9,336	8,881
ISTANBUL	10,189	3,853	7,101	6,184	4,285	3,425	7,286	10,857	—	2,982	2,107
LE HAVRE	11,170	6,153	6,159	5,986	6,585	511	9,535	9,336	2,982	—	909
LISBON	10,707	5,278	5,339	5,134	5,710	1,369	8,702	8,881	2,107	909	—
LIVERPOOL ...	11,107	6,258	6,246	6,069	6,690	1,014	9,692	9,370	3,061	560	1,007
MANILA	4,653	3,771	10,445	6,742	2,911	10,033	631	4,869	7,160	9,471	8,594
MELBOURNE ..	1,649	5,556	6,853	5,963	4,700	11,405	4,875	4,942	8,645	10,946	10,168
NEW ORLEANS	7,945	9,515	6,237	7,290	9,961	5,111	10,628	6,129	6,358	4,659	4,345
NEW YORK	8,529	8,173	5,871	6,786	8,633	3,747	11,212	6,703	5,005	3,293	2,978
PANAMA	6,511	9,300	5,385	5,385	9,775	5,105	9,195	4,680	6,172	4,651	4,152
PORT SAID	9,383	3,049	7,202	5,402	3,480	3,564	6,480	10,970	804	3,104	2,229
RIO DE JANEIRO	7,056	7,864	1,151	3,273	7,725	5,549	10,149	8,608	6,001	5,058	4,219
SAN FRANCISCO	5,680	9,794	7,582	9,753	8,934	8,350	6,044	2,091	9,417	7,896	7,441
SINGAPORE ...	5,017	2,441	9,283	5,603	1,581	8,582	1,454	5,899	5,822	8,139	7,247
VALPARAISO ..	5,247	10,281	2,826	5,711	9,986	7,721	10,218	5,919	8,788	7,267	6,812
YOKOHAMA ...	4,789	5,330	10,669	8,351	4,470	11,471	1,585	3,397	8,711	11,011	10,136

WORLD'S LARGEST MERCHANT SHIPS—THE SUPERTANKERS

Source: U.S. Department of Commerce, Maritime Administration

The world's largest merchant ships are all tankers. Three of the largest sail under the flag of France. Each is more than eight times larger in tonnage than Britain's passenger liner *Queen Elizabeth 2*.

SHIP	FLAG	YEAR BUILT	WHERE BUILT	DWT TONNAGE	OVERALL LENGTH	EXTREME WIDTH
1. Seawise Giant	Liberia	1976	Japan	564,739	1,504' 2"	225' 9"
2. Prairial	France	1979	France	555,051	1,359' 1"	206' 10"
3. Batillus	France	1976	France	553,662	1,359' 0"	206' 8"
4. Bellamya	France	1976	France	553,662	1,359' 0"	206' 8"
5. Esso Atlantic	Liberia	1977	Japan	516,893	1,334' 0"	233' 2"
6. Esso Pacific	Liberia	1977	Japan	516,423	1,334' 0"	233' 2"
7. King Alexander	Greece	1978	Sweden	491,120	1,194' 3"	259' 4"
8. Nissei Maru	Japan	1975	Japan	484,276	1,243' 1"	203' 6"
9. Globtik London	Britain	1973	Japan	483,933	1,243' 0"	203' 7"
10. Globtik Tokyo	Britain	1973	Japan	483,662	1,243' 0"	203' 7"

WORLD'S LARGEST PASSENGER SHIPS

Source: U.S. Department of Commerce, Maritime Administration

SHIP	FLAG	YEAR COMPLETED	PASSENGER CAPACITY	GROSS TONS	LENGTH OVERALL
1. Norway	Norway	1961	2,400	70,202	1,035' 2"
2. Queen Elizabeth 2	Britain	1968	1,970	67,140	963' 0"
3. Canberra	Britain	1961	2,400	44,807	818' 6"
4. Royal Princess	Britain	1984	1,200	44,348	757' 6"
5. Oriana	Britain	1960	2,217	41,920	804' 0"
6. Rotterdam	Netherlands	1959	1,499	37,783	748' 7"
7. Song of America	Norway	1982	1,575	37,584	689' 0"
8. Noordam	Netherlands	1983	1,374	33,930	704' 3"
9. Nieuw Amsterdam	Netherlands	1983	1,374	33,930	704' 3"
10. Europa	West Germany	1981	758	34,500	655' 10"
11. Eugenio C	Italy	1966	1,636	30,567	713' 3"
12. Royal Viking Star	Norway	1972	821	28,221	674' 1"
13. Costa Riviera	Italy	1963	1,700	28,137	700' 11"
14. Galileo	Italy	1963	1,700	28,084	700' 11"
15. Royal Viking Sea	Norway	1973	536	28,078	583' 2"
16. Royal Viking Sky	Norway	1973	536	28,078	583' 2"
17. Sea Princess	Britain	1966	840	27,670	660' 2"
18. Oceanic	Panama	1965	1,340	27,645	782' 3"
19. Stardancer	Bahamas	1982	1,607	26,747	602' 1"
20. Festivale	Panama	1961	730	26,632	760' 2"

LIVERPOOL (England)	MANILA (Philippines)	MELBOURNE (Australia)	NEW ORLEANS	NEW YORK	PANAMA	PORT SAID (Egypt)	RIO DE JANEIRO (Brazil)	SAN FRANCISCO	SINGAPORE	VALPARAISO (Chile)	YOKOHAMA (Japan)
11,107	4,653	1,649	7,945	8,529	6,511	9,383	7,056	5,680	5,017	5,247	4,789
6,258	3,771	5,556	9,515	8,173	9,300	3,049	7,864	9,794	2,441	10,281	5,330
6,246	10,445	6,853	6,237	5,871	5,385	7,202	1,151	7,582	9,283	2,826	10,669
6,069	6,742	5,963	7,290	6,786	6,472	5,402	3,273	9,753	5,603	5,711	8,351
6,690	2,911	4,700	9,961	8,633	9,775	3,480	7,725	8,934	1,581	9,986	4,470
1,014	10,033	11,405	5,111	3,747	5,105	3,564	5,549	8,350	8,582	7,721	11,471
9,692	631	4,875	10,628	11,212	9,195	6,480	10,149	6,044	1,454	10,218	1,585
9,370	4,869	4,942	6,129	6,703	4,680	10,970	8,608	2,091	5,899	5,919	3,397
3,061	7,160	8,645	6,358	5,005	6,172	804	6,001	9,417	5,822	8,788	8,715
560	9,471	10,946	4,659	3,293	4,651	3,104	5,058	7,896	8,139	7,267	11,011
1,007	8,594	10,168	4,345	2,978	4,152	2,229	4,219	7,441	7,247	6,812	10,136
—	9,557	11,053	4,693	3,283	4,641	3,209	5,143	7,930	8,227	7,302	11,085
9,557		4,515	10,809	11,388	9,370	6,348	10,001	6,299	1,330	9,710	1,758
11,053	4,515	—	9,372	9,946	7,951	7,842	8,212	6,970	3,844	6,185	4,896
4,693	10,809	9,372	—	1,721	1,564	6,491	5,136	4,678	11,497	4,049	9,115
3,283	11,388	9,946	1,721	—	2,018	5,137	4,770	5,263	10,158	4,634	9,700
4,641	9,370	7,951	1,564	2,018		6,294	4,284	3,245	10,529	2,616	7,680
3,209	6,348	7,842	6,491	5,137	6,294		6,123	9,539	5,035	8,910	7,924
5,143	10,001	8,212	5,136	4,770	4,284	6,123	—	7,573	8,846	3,670	11,567
7,930	6,299	6,970	4,678	5,263	3,245	9,539	7,573	—	7,350	5,140	4,536
8,227	1,330	3,844	11,497	10,158	10,529	5,035	8,846	7,350	—	9,902	2,880
7,302	9,710	6,185	4,049	4,634	2,616	8,910	3,670	5,140	9,902	—	9,280
11,085	1,758	4,896	9,115	9,700	7,680	7,924	11,567	4,536	2,880	9,280	—

WHAT YOU SHOULD KNOW ABOUT YOUR U.S. PASSPORT
Source: Passport Services, U.S. Department of State

A passport may be issued only to a U.S. citizen or to a person owing allegiance to the U.S. It is a travel document issued under the authority of the U.S. Secretary of State, attesting to the identity and nationality of the bearer.

Many countries require that visas issued by their consulates be stamped on a passport.

On Jan. 1, 1977, Passport Services began issuing a reduced-size passport more convenient to carry in a pocket or purse. The simplified format conforms to recommendations by the International Civil Aviation Organization (ICAO) for international standardization.

You should apply for a passport several months before your planned departure.

Application. A first-time passport application (DSP-11) must be presented in person before one of the following: (1) a Department of State passport agent, (2) a clerk of any federal court or state court of record or a judge or clerk of any probate court accepting applications, (3) a postal employee at a post office designated to accept passport applications, or (4) a U.S. consular or diplomatic officer abroad.

A person in the U.S. who has been issued a passport within the last 8 years, in his own name and after attaining 18 years of age, may obtain a new passport by filling out, signing, and mailing "Application for Passport by Mail" (Form DSP-82), which is available at offices accepting passport applications. He or she should enclose the previous passport, two identical signed photographs taken within the last 6 months, and the $35 passport fee, and address it to the nearest passport agency or to Passport Services in Washington, D.C.

Citizenship. An applicant must prove U.S. citizenship. Acceptable documents are a previous U.S. passport or certified birth certificate. If a birth certificate is unobtainable, secondary evidence will be considered, such as a baptismal certificate or hospital birth certificate. A naturalized citizen must present a naturalization certificate.

Identification documents submitted must bear the signature and description or photograph of the applicant. Acceptable documents may include a previous U.S. passport, a driver's license, or a governmental identification card.

Photographs. Two identical photographs, taken within 6 months of the date of application and identifying the applicant, must be presented with the application.

The photo may be in color or black and white and should be 2 x 2 inches in size. The person's face should measure from 1 to $1\frac{3}{8}$ inches from chin to top of head. Vending machine photographs are generally not acceptable.

It is no longer possible to include family members of any age in a U.S. passport. All persons are required to obtain individual passports in their own names.

Validity and Fees. An adult passport is valid for 10 years, and the passport of a minor under 18 years of age is valid for 5 years. The adult passport costs $35, the child's $20. An additional $7 fee is paid when the application is executed before an official, but is not required when the applicant applies by mail.

Offices. Passport agencies are located in Boston, Chicago, Honolulu, Houston, Los Angeles, Miami, New Orleans, New York, Philadelphia, San Francisco, Seattle, Stamford, and Washington, D.C.

Loss. Loss, theft, or destruction of a valid passport should be reported immediately to local police authorities and to Passport Services, Department of State, Washington, D.C. 20520, or, if overseas, to the nearest American embassy or consulate. A passport should be carefully guarded, as its loss could cause you unnecessary travel complications and expense.

CUSTOMS HINTS FOR RETURNING U.S. TRAVELERS
Source: U.S. Customs Service

When returning from foreign travel, a U.S. resident must declare to U.S. Customs, either orally or in writing, *all* articles acquired abroad and in his possession. Customs duty normally must be paid on most of these items.

Exemptions. You are allowed an exemption of $400 based on fair retail value of items where acquired. This duty-free exemption may include not more than 100 cigars or 200 cigarettes, and only one liter (33.8 fl. oz.) of alcoholic beverage, if you are 21 or older. Cuban tobacco products *brought directly from Cuba* may be included.

If you return directly or indirectly from the U.S. Virgin Islands, American Samoa, or Guam, your exemption is increased to $800, of which not more than $400 may be acquired elsewhere. Four liters of alcoholic beverages may be included if not more than one liter was acquired elsewhere.

If you have used the $400 resident exemption, the next $1,000 worth of items *you bring back with you* for your personal use or gifts are taxed at a flat rate of 10% (or 5% for articles from insular possessions). Articles that exceed the flat rate valuation are subject to various rates of duty as shown below.

If your purchases abroad exceed the resident exemption plus $1,000, then you must pay customs duties, such as the following:

Antiques: no duty if proof is provided that they are 100 or more years old.
Automobiles: 2.8%.
Books (foreign): free
Cameras: motion picture over $50 each, 5.3%; still cameras over $10 each, 5.3%; leather camera cases, 9.0%; lenses, 9.6%.
Candy: sweet chocolate bars, 5%; others, 7%.
Dolls and doll parts: 14.8%.
Drawings and paintings (original): free
Furniture: wood chairs, 6% to 6.9%; bentwood, 9.6%; other wood, 3.8%.
Jewelry: 9.3% to 27.5%.
Leather bags and pocketbooks: 6.9% to 10%.
Perfume: 4¢ per pound plus 6.3%.
Tape recorders: 4.7%.
Toys: 12.3%.

Rules Governing Exemptions. Except for articles acquired in the insular possessions, all articles must be with you at the time of your return. For-

CUSTOMS HINTS *(continued)*

eign purchases mailed or shipped home are subject to duty and tax. Articles purchased abroad and used during a journey must be declared. But articles acquired in the insular possessions need not accompany you. They may be sent from these islands and entered under the personal exemption or the flat rate of duty upon your return.

You must have been outside the U.S. at least 48 hours (unless entering from Mexico or the U.S. Virgin Islands) and have not claimed your customs exemption within 30 days.

Families traveling together may combine their exemptions to apply to the total value of all articles declared. Food, plants, and animals must meet U.S. Department of Agriculture or Public Health Service standards.

Duty-Free GSP Articles. Since Jan. 1, 1976, a wide range of articles have been admitted duty-free to the U.S. under the Generalized System of Preferences (GSP), designed to aid the economy of developing nations. Altogether 2,700 articles from liquor to cameras may be brought into the U.S. without paying customs duties if they were made in and purchased in any of 137 designated developing nations and dependencies.

Prohibited Articles. Certain items considered detrimental to the general welfare of the U.S. are prohibited entry by law, such as: narcotics; drugs containing narcotics in any amount; obscene articles, films, and publications; lottery tickets; wild birds or their feathers or eggs; liquor-filled candies; switchblade knives.

Restricted Articles. Firearms and ammunition are only admitted by specific authorization of the Bureau of Alcohol, Tobacco, and Firearms.

IMMUNIZATIONS REQUIRED OR RECOMMENDED FOR FOREIGN TRAVEL

Source: U.S. Public Health Service

According to the International Health Regulations adopted by the World Health Organization (WHO), under certain conditions a country may require travelers to present International Certificates of Vaccination against Cholera and Yellow Fever.

A traveler should contact the local health department at least four weeks before departure for vaccination requirements of countries to be visited.

No vaccinations are required to return to the United States.

Food and drink: Water may be safe in large cities commonly used by travelers. Chlorine treatment alone, however, may not kill some parasitic organisms. Boiling is the most reliable method to make water safe to drink. Travelers also may use tincture of iodine or water purification (hydroperiodide) tablets.

In areas where hygiene and sanitation are poor, travelers should eat only cooked food, or fruit peeled by the traveler, and avoid unpasteurized milk.

Travelers' diarrhea: Most cases of diarrhea require only replacement of fluids and salts lost in body fluids. A traveler should consult a physician rather than attempt self-medication if the condition is severe.

Malaria: Areas where malaria is known to exist include parts of Mexico, Haiti, Dominican Republic, Central and South America, Africa, the Middle East, Turkey, the Indian subcontinent, Southeast Asia, China, the Indonesian archipelago, and Oceania. Travelers to such areas should take prophylactic medication and avoid exposure to mosquitoes.

Diptheria, tetanus, pertussis, measles, mumps, rubella, and poliomyelitis are routinely administered in the United States, usually in childhood. Persons who do not have an adequate history of protection against these diseases should obtain immunizations.

Hepatitis, viral, type A: The risk of hepatitis-A appears small. Immune globulin is not routinely recommended for ordinary travel of less than 3 months that involves tourist routes. However, immune globulin is recommended for travelers who stay 3 or more months in tropical areas or countries where hepatitis-A is common.

Hepatitis B: The risk of hepatitis B virus (HBV) infection for international travelers is generally low. Primary factors to consider include the prevalence of HBV carriers in the local population and the extent of direct contact with blood (or secretions) or of intimate sexual contact with potentially infected persons. Travelers who have increased risk to both of these factors are candidates for HBV vaccines.

Typhoid fever: Vaccination is recommended for travelers to areas where there is a recognized risk of exposure to typhoid fever. It is transmitted by contaminated food and water. Typhoid is prevalent in many countries of Africa, Asia, and Central and South America.

Rabies: Preexposure vaccination is recommended for persons in high-risk groups such as those living in or visiting countries for prolonged periods where rabies is a constant threat.

Dengue fever: Dengue viruses are endemic in most of the tropical countries of Asia, Tahiti, Africa, many of the countries in the Caribbean, and in some Latin America countries. Travelers to endemic areas should take precautions to avoid mosquito bites.

Japanese encephalitis: Japanese encephalitis (JE) is a mosquito-borne viral encephalitis which occurs in epidemics during the summer months in some Asian countries. The risk to short-term travelers and persons who confine their travel to urban areas is low.

Yellow fever: Vaccination is recommended for travel to infected areas, usually parts of Africa and South America, and for travel outside urban areas in yellow fever endemic zones.

Cholera: Immunization is not routinely recommended for travelers to countries not requiring a cholera certificate. Cholera is acquired primarily from contaminated food and water.

Plague: Vaccination is not indicated for most travelers to countries reporting cases of plague if their travel is limited to urban areas with modern hotel accommodations.

Typhus fever: The threat of louse-borne typhus exists only in mountainous, highland, or other areas where a cold climate and other local conditions favor louse infestation. The risk for U.S. travelers is very low. Treatment with tetracycline or chloramphemicol is curative.

TOURIST DOCUMENTS FOR FOREIGN TRAVEL

Source: Passport Office, U.S. Department of State

When you travel to other countries, you must take with you certain documents in order to be allowed to visit them. Most countries require that you have a passport (see page 958). Some countries require that you obtain permission to visit them in advance of your arrival by getting a visa or tourist card from one of their consulates or their embassy in Washington. Some charge a fee.

To prove you are a tourist, many countries ask that you show them an air, rail, or ship ticket that will take you on to another country. Some countries also may insist that you prove you have enough funds to cover your expenses.

Some countries also require proof of immunization against some diseases. See page 959.

Americans visiting Canada, Mexico, and most Caribbean countries do not need a passport but must have proof of their citizenship with a birth certificate, voter's registration, or automobile driver's license.

Place	Documents	Fee	Limit	Place	Documents	Fee	Limit	Place	Documents	Fee	Limit
Afghanistan	PV	$14.00	3 m	Germany, East	PV	—	—	New Zealand	PO	No	30 d
Albania	S	—	—	Germany, West	P	No	3 m	Nicaragua	PV	No	—
Algeria	PV	$5.25	3 m	Ghana	PV	$8.00	14 d	Niger	PVO	$8.30	90 d
Andorra	P	No	3 m	Gibraltar	P	No	—	Nigeria	PVO	$2.55	3 m
Angola	S	—	—	Greece	P	No	3 m	Norway	P	No	3 m
Antigua	CO	—	6 m	Grenada	P	No	—	Oman	B	—	—
Argentina	PV	—	3 m	Guadeloupe	C	No	15 d	Pakistan	P	No	30 d
Australia	P	No	6 m	Guatemala	PCT	$1.00	6 m	Panama	PTO	No	4 y
Austria	P	No	3 m	Guinea	PV	—	—	Papua N. Guinea	PO	No	30 d
Azores	P	No	60 d	Guinea–Bissau	PV	—	—	Paraguay	P	No	90 d
Bahamas	CO	No	—	Guyana	PO	No	1 m	Peru	PO	—	90 d
Bahrain	PV	$20.00	—	Haiti	CT	$5.00	3 m	Philippines	PO	No	21 d
Bangladesh	PV	—	—	Honduras	PV	No	3 m	Poland	PV	$16.00	90 d
Barbados	CO	No	6 m	Hong Kong	PO	No	30 d	Portugal	P	No	60 d
Belgium	P	No	90 d	Hungary	PV	$10.00	30 d	Qatar	PV	No	6 m
Belize	CO	No	6 m	Iceland	P	No	3 m	Romania	PV	$13.00	3 d
Benin	PV	$8.00	7 d	India	P	$5.45	90 d	Rwanda	PV	$10.00	3 m
Bermuda	CO	No	—	Indonesia	P	—	2 m	St. Lucia	CO	No	6 m
Bhutan	P	—	—	Iran	PV	—	—	San Marino	P	—	3 m
Bolivia	P	No	90 d	Iraq	S	—	—	Saudi Arabia	PVO	—	72 h
Botswana	P	No	90 d	Ireland	PO	No	90 d	Senegal	PV	$5.10	3 m
Brazil	PVO	No	—	Israel	P	No	3 m	Seychelles	PO	—	—
Britain	P	No	—	Italy	P	No	3 m	Sierra Leone	PVO	$10.50	3 m
Brunei	P	No	—	Ivory Coast	PVO	No	3 m	Singapore	P	No	90 d
Bulgaria	PV	$14.00	2 m	Jamaica	CO	—	6 m	Somalia	PVO	$14.00	3 m
Burma	PVO	$4.85	1 w	Japan	PV	No	90 d	South Africa	PVO	No	1 y
Burundi	PV	$11.00	1 m	Jordan	PV	No	4 y	Soviet Union	PV	No	3 m
Cambodia	S	—	—	Kenya	PV	$6.10	6 m	Spain	P	No	6 m
Cameroon	PVO	$14.42	30d	Korea, North	PV	—	—	Sri Lanka	PO	—	1 m
Canada	C	No	—	Korea, South	PV	No	60 d	Sudan	PV	$25.63	3 m
Cape Verde	PV	$13.50	30 d	Kuwait	PV	No	1 m	Suriname	PV	$22.50	2 m
Central Africa	PV	No	—	Laos	PV	—	—	Swaziland	P	No	60 d
Chad	PVO	$6.25	3 m	Lebanon	PV	$40.00	6 m	Sweden	P	No	3 m
Chile	P	No	—	Lesotho	PV	No	20 d	Switzerland	P	No	3 m
China	PV	$7.00	—	Liberia	PV	$2.00	3 m	Syria	PV	$8.21	6 m
Colombia	PTO	—	90 d	Libya	S	—	—	Taiwan	PV	—	6 m
Congo	PV	—	—	Liechtenstein	P	No	3 m	Tanzania	PVO	$10.50	30 d
Costa Rica	P	No	6 m	Luxembourg	PO	No	3 m	Thailand	PO	No	15 d
Cuba	PV	$6.00	—	Madagascar	PV	$47.61	1 m	Togo	P	—	90 d
Cyprus	P	—	—	Malawi	P	No	1 y	Tonga	P	—	—
Czechoslovakia	PV	$12.00	5 m	Malaysia	P	No	3 m	Trinidad–Tobago	PO	No	2 m
Denmark	P	No	3 m	Maldives	P	—	—	Tunisia	P	No	4 m
Djibouti	PV	—	—	Mali	PV	$17.00	1 w	Turkey	P	No	3 m
Dominica	CO	No	6 m	Malta	P	No	3 m	Uganda	PV	$3.15	1 y
Dominican Rep.	PT	$5.00	60 d	Martinique	C	No	15 d	United Arab Em.	PVO	$15.00	2m
Ecuador	PO	No	—	Mauritania	PV	$10.00	3 m	Upper Volta			
Egypt	PV	$10.00	3 m	Mauritius	PV	No	—	(Burkinafaso)	PV	$2.00	3 m
El Salvador	C	—	—	Mexico	CT	No	3 m	Uruguay	P	No	3 m
Equat. Guinea	PV	—	—	Monaco	P	No	3 m	Venezuela	PVT	No	60 d
Ethiopia	PV	—	—	Mongolia	S	—	—	Vietnam	S	—	—
Fiji	PO	—	6 m	Morocco	P	No	3 m	Western Samoa	PO	No	30 d
Finland	P	No	3 m	Mozambique	S	—	—	Yemen, North	PV	$10.00	1 m
France	P	No	3 m	Nauru	P	—	—	Yugoslavia	PV	No	1 y
French Guiana	P	No	3 m	Nepal	PV	$10.00	3 m	Zaire	PV	$20.00	3 m
Gabon	PV	$15.00	—	Netherlands	PO	No	90 d	Zambia	PV	$3.51	6 m
Gambia	PV	$8.00	—	Neth. Antilles	CO	—	14 d	Zimbabwe	PO		

P = passport. V = visa. T = tourist card. C = proof of U.S. citizenship. O = onward ticket. S = special permission required. B = business visa only. d = days. m = months. y = years. h = hours. w = weeks.

United States

Clipper *Flying Cloud* 1852 USA 25

The clipper ship *Flying Cloud* is featured on a 25–cent postal card for use in international mail that was issued by the U.S. Postal Service on Feb. 27 at the Salem, Mass., Maritime National Historic Site. Launched at Boston on April 15, 1851, the *Flying Cloud* on its maiden voyage sailed to San Francisco via Cape Horn in a record 89 days. The *Flying Cloud* made its first voyage to China in 1852 as one of about 500 American clipper ships used in international trade in the 1840s and 1850s.

HIGHLIGHTS: 1985

The U.S. Bureau of the Census reported in August that civilian employment by the government (at the expense of taxpayers) is one of the fastest growing segments of the nation's economy. Altogether, more than 16.4 million persons work for federal, state, or local governments.

The only decrease in government employment since World War II came during the recession years of 1981–82, when the number of civilian government workers fell by 372,000. But that figure has been more than made up in the past two years with an increase of 595,000 workers added to government payrolls.

Data showed that from 1983 to 1984 federal government employment grew by 2.4%, an increase of 68,000 federal employees; state government employment rose 2.2% with 83,000 additional workers; and local government employment increased 2.7% with 252,000 added employees.

The Census Bureau said that government worker payrolls (excluding federal military payrolls) rose to $26.9 billion in 1984, an increase of 9.7% over the previous year.

Local governments average 337 full-time workers per 10,000 residents compared with 135 for state governments.

More than 52% of state and local government employees work in education, while 60% of federal civilian employees work in national defense, international relations, and the postal service.

States with the largest number of federal, state, and local government workers are: California with 1,763,000, New York with 1,306,000, Texas with 1,035,000, Illinois with 717,000, Ohio with 669,000, Pennsylva-

OUR GROWING POPULATION: 1790–2020

The continued growth of the United States population is shown in these figures from the Bureau of the Census. Populations from 1990 to 2020 are estimates.

YEAR	POPULATION	GROWTH	YEAR	POPULATION	GROWTH
1790	3,929,214	...	1910	92,407,000	21%
1800	5,308,483	35%	1920	106,461,000	15%
1810	7,239,881	36%	1930	123,188,000	15%
1820	9,638,453	33%	1940	132,288,000	7%
1830	12,866,020	33%	1950	151,718,000	14%
1840	17,069,453	32%	1960	180,007,000	18%
1850	23,191,876	35%	1970	204,335,000	13%
1860	31,443,321	35%	1980	226,548,861	11%
1870	39,818,449	26%	1990	249,203,000	10%
1880	50,155,783	25%	2000	267,461,600	18%
1890	62,947,714	25%	2010	283,141,000	6%
1900	76,094,000	20%	2020	296,339,000	5%

FACTS IN BRIEF ABOUT THE UNITED STATES

Area (50 states and the District of Columbia): 3,618,770 square miles; (plus Puerto Rico, territories, and possessions): 3,623,461 sq. mi.

Population (including armed forces overseas): 239,855,000 (Jan. 1, 1986, estimate); *density:* 66.3 persons per square mile; *distribution:* 73.7% urban, 26.3% rural; *median age:* 30.0 years; *sex:* 48.6% males, 51.4% females.

Chief Cities (1982 estimates): Washington, D.C., the national capital, 635,425; New York, 7,086,096; Los Angeles, 3,022,247; Chicago, 2,997,155; Houston, 1,725,617; Philadelphia, 1,665,382; Detroit, 1,138,717; Dallas, 943,848; San Diego, 915,916; Phoenix, 824,230; San Antonio, 819,021; Baltimore, 774,113.

Main Ethnic Groups: White, 83.1%; black, 11.7%; Spanish descent, 6.4%. .

Chief Religions: Protestantism, 66%; Roman Catholicism, 26%; Judaism, 3%.

Language: English (official).

Form of Government: Federal republic.

Chief of State: President Ronald Reagan, sworn in on Jan. 20, 1981, and on Jan. 20, 1985.

Legislature: Senate, 100 members; House of Representatives, 435 members.

Principal Manufactures: Machinery, cement, electricity, steel, paper, automobiles, aircraft, food, chemicals, electronic equipment.

Chief Crops: Wheat, barley, corn, cotton, hay, oats, potatoes, rice, rye, sorghum, soybeans, tobacco, citrus fruits, tomatoes.

Major Minerals: Coal, iron ore, copper, gold, uranium, lead, zinc, petroleum, natural gas.

States: *Largest,* Alaska (591,004 square miles); *smallest,* Rhode Island (1,212 square miles).

Counties: *Largest,* San Bernardino, Calif. (20,064 square miles); *smallest,* New York (Manhattan Island), N.Y. (22 square miles).

Extreme Points: *Northernmost,* Point Barrow, Alaska (71° 23′ N.); *southernmost,* Ka Lae, Hawaii (18°56′ N.); *easternmost,* West Quoddy Head, Me. (66°57′ W.); *westernmost,* Attu Island, Alaska (172°27′ E.).

Highest Mountain: Mt. McKinley, Alaska (20,320 feet).

Lowest Point: Death Valley, Calif. (−282 feet).

HIGHLIGHTS: 1985 *(continued)*

nia with 668,000, Florida with 641,000, Michigan with 582,000, New Jersey with 492,000, Virginia with 483,000, and North Carolina with 414,000.

States with the fewest number of federal, state, and local government workers are: Vermont with 35,000, Delaware with 42,000, Wyoming with 50,000, South Dakota with 58,000, Nevada with 59,000, Alaska with 60,000, North Dakota with 62,000, Rhode Island with 64,000, Idaho with 68,000, Montana with 69,000, New Hampshire with 72,000, Maine with 77,000, and Hawaii with 86,000.

States with the biggest payrolls for state and local government employees were: California with $2.581 billion, New York with $2.048 billion, Texas with $1.272 billion, Illinois with $923 million, Michigan with $835 million, Florida with $798 million, Pennsyl-

vania with $786 million, Ohio with $783 million, New Jersey with $674 million, Massachusetts with $456 million, North Carolina with $448 million, Virginia with $444 million, Wisconsin with $414 million, Georgia with $431 million, Maryland with $396 million, Washington with $396 million, Indiana with $385 million, Minnesota with $380 million, Louisiana with $344 million, Missouri with $335 million, and Tennessee with $315 million.

States with the smallest payrolls for state and local government were: Vermont with $38 million, South Dakota with $49 million; Delaware with $52 million, North Dakota with $61 million, New Hampshire with $62 million, Wyoming with $62 million, Idaho with $70 million, Montana with $75 million, Maine with $76 million, Nevada with $81 million, Rhode Island with $84 million, and Hawaii with $87 million.

OUR AGING POPULATION*

Source: U.S. Census Bureau

YEAR	TOTAL	55 TO 64 YEARS		65 TO 74 YEARS		75 TO 84 YEARS		85 AND OVER		65 AND OVER	
		Number	Percent	Number	Percent	Number	Percent	Number	Percent	Number	Percent
1900	76,303	4,009	5.3	2,189	2.9	772	1.0	123	0.2	3,084	4.0
1910	91,972	5,054	5.5	2,793	3.0	989	1.1	167	0.2	3,950	4.3
1920	105,711	6,532	6.2	3,464	3.3	1,259	1.2	210	0.2	4,933	4.7
1930	122,775	8,397	6.8	4,721	3.8	1,641	1.3	272	0.2	6,634	5.4
1940	131,669	10,572	8.0	6,375	4.8	2,278	1.7	365	0.3	9,019	6.8
1950	150,697	13,295	8.8	8,415	5.6	3,278	2.2	577	0.4	12,270	8.1
1960	179,323	15,572	8.7	10,997	6.1	4,633	2.6	929	0.5	16,560	9.2
1970	203,302	18,608	9.2	12,447	6.1	6,124	3.0	1,409	0.7	19,980	9.8
1980	226,505	21,700	9.6	15,578	6.9	7,727	3.4	2,240	1.0	25,544	11.3
1990	249,731	21,090	8.4	18,054	7.2	10,284	4.1	3,461	1.4	31,799	12.7
2000	267,990	23,779	8.9	17,693	6.6	12,207	4.6	5,136	1.9	35,036	13.1
2010	283,141	34,828	12.3	20,279	7.2	12,172	4.3	6,818	2.4	39,269	13.9
2020	296,339	40,243	13.6	29,769	10.0	14,280	4.8	7,337	2.5	51,386	17.3
2030	304,330	33,965	11.2	34,416	11.3	21,128	6.9	8,801	2.9	64,345	21.1
2040	307,952	34,664	11.3	29,168	9.5	24,529	8.0	12,946	4.2	66,643	21.6
2050	308,856	37,276	12.1	30,022	9.7	20,976	6.8	16,063	5.2	67,061	21.7

* All population figures in thousands (add 000).

POPULATION GROWTH OF THE UNITED STATES: 1790–2000
Source: U.S. Bureau of the Census

In its first census in 1790, the United States reported a population of 3,929,214. The totals for the individual states in 1790 were: Connecticut, 237,946; Delaware, 59,096; Georgia, 82,548; Kentucky, 73,677; Maine, 96,540; Maryland, 319,728; Massachusetts, 378,787; New Hampshire, 141,885; New Jersey, 184,139; New York, 340,120; North Carolina, 393,751; Pennsylvania, 434,373; Rhode Island, 68,825; South Carolina, 249,073; Tennessee, 35,691; Vermont, 82,425; Virginia, 691,737; West Virginia, 55,873. Population growth since 1790 is shown on the chart below.

	1850	1900	1950	1970	1980[1]	1990[2]	2000[2]
UNITED STATES .	23,191,876	76,212,168	151,325,798	203,302,031	226,548,861	249,203,000	267,461,600
Alabama	771,623	1,828,697	3,061,743	3,444,354	3,893,978	4,213,800	4,415,300
Alaska	—	63,592	128,643	302,583	401,851	522,100	630,700
Arizona	—	122,931	749,587	1,775,399	2,718,425	3,993,700	5,582,500
Arkansas	209,897	1,311,564	1,909,511	1,923,322	2,286,419	2,579,800	2,835,400
California........	92,597	1,485,053	10,586,223	19,971,069	23,667,837	27,525,600	30,613,100
Colorado	—	539,700	1,325,089	2,209,596	2,889,964	3,755,100	4,656,600
Connecticut	370,792	908,420	2,007,280	3,032,217	3,107,576	3,135,600	3,062,400
Delaware	91,532	184,735	318,085	548,104	594,338	629,800	638,200
District of Columbia	51,687	278,718	802,178	756,510	638,432	501,500	376,500
Florida	87,445	528,542	2,771,305	6,791,418	9,746,421	13,316,000	17,438,000
Georgia	906,185	2,216,331	3,444,578	4,587,930	5,463,087	6,174,600	6,708,200
Hawaii	—	154,001	499,794	769,913	964,691	1,138,100	1,277,700
Idaho	—	161,772	588,637	713,015	944,038	1,213,800	1,512,200
Illinois	851,470	4,821,550	8,712,176	11,110,285	11,427,414	11,502,500	11,187,500
Indiana..........	988,416	2,516,462	3,934,224	5,195,392	5,490,260	5,679,300	5,679,200
Iowa	192,214	2,231,853	2,621,073	2,825,368	2,913,808	2,983,300	2,972,100
Kansas	—	1,470,495	1,905,299	2,249,071	2,364,236	2,463,400	2,494,400
Kentucky	982,405	2,147,174	3,220,711	3,220,711	3,660,257	4,073,500	4,399,900
Louisiana	517,762	1,381,625	2,683,516	3,644,637	4,206,098	4,747,000	5,159,800
Maine	583,169	694,466	913,774	993,722	1,125,030	1,229,400	1,308,000
Maryland	583,034	1,188,044	2,343,001	3,923,897	4,216,941	4,491,100	4,581,900
Massachusetts ...	994,514	2,805,346	4,690,514	5,689,170	5,737,081	5,703,900	5,490,400
Michigan	397,654	2,420,982	6,371,766	8,881,826	9,262,070	9,394,300	9,207,600
Minnesota	6,077	1,751,394	2,982,483	3,806,103	4,075,970	4,358,400	4,489,400
Mississippi	606,528	1,551,270	2,178,914	2,216,994	2,520,631	2,761,400	2,939,200
Missouri.........	682,044	3,106,665	3,954,653	4,677,623	4,916,759	5,076,800	5,080,000
Montana	—	243,329	591,024	694,409	786,690	888,400	963,000
Nebraska........	—	1,066,300	1,325,510	1,485,333	1,569,825	1,639,800	1,661,900
Nevada	—	42,335	160,083	488,738	800,493	1,275,400	1,918,800
New Hampshire ..	317,976	411,588	553,242	737,681	920,610	1,138,800	1,363,500
New Jersey	489,555	1,883,669	4,835,329	7,171,112	7,365,011	7,513,100	7,427,600
New Mexico......	61,547	195,310	681,187	1,017,055	1,303,046	1,536,000	1,727,300
New York........	3,097,394	7,268,894	14,830,192	18,241,391	17,558,072	16,456,700	14,990,200
North Carolina ...	869,039	1,893,810	4,061,929	5,084,411	5,881,385	6,473,400	6,867,800
North Dakota	—	319,146	619,636	617,792	652,717	678,400	682,000
Ohio	1,980,329	4,157,545	7,946,627	10,657,423	10,797,624	10,763,100	10,356,800
Oklahoma	—	790,391	2,233,351	2,559,463	3,025,495	3,503,400	3,944,500
Oregon..........	12,093	413,536	1,521,341	2,091,533	2,633,149	3,318,600	4,025,300
Pennsylvania.....	2,311,786	6,302,115	10,498,012	11,800,766	11,864,751	11,720,400	11,207,600
Rhode Island.....	147,545	428,556	791,896	949,723	947,154	950,800	925,800
South Carolina ...	668,507	1,340,316	2,117,027	2,590,713	3,122,814	3,599,600	3,907,100
South Dakota	—	401,570	652,740	666,257	690,768	698,500	687,600
Tennessee.......	1,002,717	2,020,616	3,291,718	3,926,018	4,591,120	5,072,600	5,419,600
Texas	212,592	3,048,710	7,711,194	11,198,655	14,227,574	17,498,200	20,739,400
Utah	11,380	276,749	688,862	1,059,273	1,461,037	2,040,300	2,777,400
Vermont	314,120	343,641	377,747	444,732	511,456	574,600	625,000
Virginia	1,119,348	1,854,184	3,318,680	4,651,448	5,346,797	5,960,900	6,389,400
Washington	1,201	518,103	2,378,963	3,413,244	4,132,204	5,011,800	5,832,500
West Virginia	302,313	958,800	2,005,552	1,744,237	1,950,258	2,037,400	2,067,700
Wisconsin	305,391	2,069,042	3,434,575	4,417,821	4,705,642	5,032,700	5,215,500
Wyoming	—	92,531	290,529	332,416	469,557	701,300	1,002,200

[1] Official 1980 Census. [2] Estimates based on 1980 Census.

RACIAL POPULATION BY REGION AND STATE

Source: U.S. Census Bureau, 1980 Census

REGION AND STATE	TOTAL	WHITE	BLACK	SPANISH	ASIAN	INDIAN	ALL OTHER
New England	12,348,907	11,585,633	474,549	299,145	81,005	21,597	185,709
Maine	1,125,030	1,109,850	3,128	5,005	2,947	4,087	4,648
New Hampshire	920,610	910,099	3,990	5,587	2,929	1,352	2,240
Vermont	511,456	506,736	1,135	3,304	1,355	984	1,246
Massachusetts	5,737,081	5,362,836	221,279	141,043	49,501	7,743	95,678
Rhode Island	947,154	896,692	27,584	19,707	5,303	2,898	14,677
Connecticut	3,107,576	2,799,420	217,433	124,499	18,970	4,533	67,220
Middle Atlantic	36,787,834	30,740,655	4,373,882	2,305,144	478,753	57,441	1,136,059
New York	17,558,072	13,960,868	2,402,006	1,659,300	310,526	39,582	845,090
New Jersey	7,365,011	6,127,467	925,066	491,883	103,848	8,394	200,048
Pennsylvania	11,864,751	10,652,320	1,046,810	153,961	64,379	9,465	90,921
East North Central	41,683,010	36,150,455	4,548,546	1,067,944	302,984	105,907	574,325
Ohio	10,797,624	9,597,458	1,076,748	119,883	47,820	12,239	63,365
Indiana	5,490,260	5,004,394	414,785	87,047	20,557	7,836	42,652
Illinois	11,427,414	9,233,327	1,675,398	635,602	159,653	16,283	341,857
Michigan	9,262,070	7,872,241	1,199,023	162,440	56,790	40,050	93,974
Wisconsin	4,705,642	4,443,035	182,592	62,972	18,164	29,499	32,477
West North Central	17,184,083	16,044,344	788,549	208,601	87,006	142,486	121,068
Minnesota	4,075,970	3,935,770	53,344	32,123	26,536	35,016	25,304
Iowa	2,913,808	2,839,225	41,700	25,536	11,577	5,455	15,851
Missouri	4,916,759	4,345,521	514,276	51,653	23,096	12,321	21,472
North Dakota	652,717	625,577	2,568	3,902	1,979	20,158	2,455
South Dakota	690,768	639,669	2,144	4,023	1,738	44,968	2,249
Nebraska	1,569,825	1,490,381	48,390	28,025	7,002	9,195	14,857
Kansas	2,364,236	2,168,221	126,127	63,339	15,078	15,373	38,880
South Atlantic	36,960,473	28,659,351	7,651,969	1,194,172	260,636	118,726	268,441
Delaware	594,338	487,817	95,845	9,661	4,112	1,328	5,236
Maryland	4,216,941	3,158,838	958,150	64,746	64,278	8,021	27,688
District of Columbia	638,432	171,768	448,906	17,679	6,636	1,031	9,992
Virginia	5,346,797	4,229,798	1,008,668	79,868	66,209	9,454	32,689
West Virginia	1,950,258	1,874,751	65,051	12,707	5,194	1,610	3,038
North Carolina	5,881,385	4,457,507	1,318,857	56,667	21,176	64,652	19,574
South Carolina	3,122,814	2,147,224	948,623	33,426	11,834	5,757	8,382
Georgia	5,463,087	3,947,135	1,465,181	61,260	24,457	7,616	18,716
Florida	9,746,421	8,184,513	1,342,688	858,158	56,740	19,257	143,126
East South Central	14,665,986	11,702,269	2,868,960	119,513	41,079	22,477	31,638
Kentucky	3,660,257	3,379,006	259,477	27,406	9,970	3,610	8,714
Tennessee	4,591,120	3,835,452	725,942	34,077	13,963	5,104	10,659
Alabama	3,893,978	2,872,621	996,335	33,299	9,734	7,583	7,615
Mississippi	2,520,631	1,615,190	887,206	24,731	7,412	6,180	4,650
West South Central	23,745,586	18,598,726	3,526,858	3,160,281	168,107	231,027	1,222,098
Arkansas	2,286,419	1,890,322	373,768	17,904	6,740	9,428	6,177
Louisiana	4,206,098	2,912,172	1,238,241	99,134	23,779	12,065	19,643
Oklahoma	3,025,495	2,597,791	204,674	57,419	17,275	169,459	36,091
Texas	14,227,574	11,198,441	1,710,175	2,985,824	120,313	40,075	1,160,187
Mountain	11,373,250	9,961,018	268,790	1,442,909	98,433	364,381	680,163
Montana	786,690	740,148	1,786	9,974	2,503	37,270	4,983
Idaho	944,038	901,641	2,716	36,615	5,948	10,521	23,109
Wyoming	469,557	446,488	3,364	24,499	1,969	7,094	10,642
Colorado	2,889,964	2,571,498	101,703	339,717	29,916	18,068	168,779
New Mexico	1,303,046	977,587	24,020	477,222	6,825	106,119	188,343
Arizona	2,718,425	2,240,761	74,977	440,701	22,032	152,745	227,700
Utah	1,461,037	1,382,550	9,225	60,302	15,076	19,256	34,930
Nevada	800,493	700,345	50,999	53,879	14,164	13,308	21,677
Pacific	31,799,732	24,929,171	1,992,922	4,810,964	1,982,436	356,658	2,538,818
Washington	4,132,204	3,779,170	105,574	120,016	102,537	60,804	84,071
Oregon	2,633,149	2,490,610	37,060	65,847	34,775	27,314	43,346
California	23,667,837	18,030,893	1,819,281	4,544,331	1,253,818	201,369	2,362,541
Alaska	401,851	309,728	13,643	9,507	8,054	64,103	6,323
Hawaii	964,691	318,770	17,364	71,263	583,252	2,768	42,537
U.S. TOTAL	226,548,861	188,371,622	26,495,025	14,608,673	3,500,439	1,420,400	6,758,319

U.S. FEDERAL BUDGET FOR FISCAL 1986

President Reagan submitted to Congress on February 4, 1985, a budget with estimated outlays of $973.7 billion for fiscal year 1986—the period October 1, 1985, to September 30, 1986. The estimated receipts were $793.7 billion, leaving an estimated Federal budget deficit of $180.0 billion.

The Office of Management and Budget (OMB) issued revised estimates of the 1986 budget in April 1985, indicating outlays of $971.7 billion, receipts of $794.3 billion, and a deficit of $177.4 billion. For details of the revised April outlay estimates, see pages 966–967.

A comparison of the estimated outlays of the Federal Government for fiscal year 1986 with those for fiscal year 1985 reveals an increase of $17.8 billion.

Over the past decade budget outlays nearly tripled, increasing from $332.3 billion in 1975 to $953.9 billion in 1985.

The total Federal Government debt was estimated to reach $1,841.9 billion on September 30, 1985, or about $7,782 for each person in the U.S.

WHERE THE MONEY COMES FROM

In the fiscal 1986 budget submitted to Congress in February 1985, the OMB spelled out where the money for the budget comes from in terms of each dollar of estimated receipts:

Individual income taxes	37¢
Social insurance receipts (half from employees and half from employers)	30¢
Borrowing	18¢
Corporation income taxes	8¢
Excise taxes	3¢
Other receipts	4¢

WHERE THE MONEY GOES

The OMB also indicated the major areas of spending for fiscal 1986 in terms of each dollar of estimated outlays:

Direct benefit payments to individuals	41¢
National defense	29¢
Grants to states and localities	15¢
Net interest on debt	10¢
Other federal operations	5¢

THE FEDERAL BUDGET SYSTEM

Each year's federal budget represents the President's financial plan for operating the government for 12 months. The budget states how much money the President believes the federal government should spend during the fiscal year, where the revenues are to come from, and how much money is to be spent on each government program.

The budget, therefore, is an important tool for determining what the national priorities are to be during the next year.

By increasing or decreasing the amount of taxes to be collected and the amounts of money to be spent on various programs, the government can have an important effect on the entire economy of the nation because of the huge sums involved.

The budget, however, is merely a plan. The amount of money actually spent depends on appropriations and other legislation enacted by Congress. Therefore, whether the plan of the budget really is carried out is determined through the interaction of the President, the executive agencies, and Congress.

Under traditional procedures of the past, Congress did not generally vote on budget outlays directly. Instead, it would enact a variety of bills that permitted or required the government to spend money for specific programs. However, Congress passed budget-reform measures in 1974 to improve congressional control over federal spending.

The federal fiscal year historically was from July 1 to June 30. But beginning with fiscal 1977 the budget year became October 1 to September 30. Thus fiscal 1986 runs from Oct. 1, 1985, to Sept. 30, 1986.

THE BUDGET CYCLE

The federal budget cycle is a continuous process involving four phases:

1. Executive Submission: The President outlines his budget proposals to Congress in January each year, climaxing months of planning and analysis throughout the executive departments and agencies.

2. Congressional Authorizaton: Once Congress has the President's recommended budget, it can change programs, eliminate them, or add programs not requested by the President. It can decrease or increase the amounts recommended by the President to finance existing programs and proposed new ones.

Each September Congress is supposed to adopt a budget for the fiscal year that begins in October. Congress then cannot consider any legislation that would increase spending or decrease receipts from the adopted budget. However, Congress can adopt a new revised budget at any time.

3. Budget Execution and Control: Once approved, the budget becomes the basis for the operations of each department and agency during the fiscal year. Central control over most of the budget authority made available to the executive branch is maintained through a system of "apportioning" the authority.

4. Audit. The final step in the budget process is the audit. This involves the Office of Management and Budget in the executive branch and the General Accounting Office, which is responsible directly to Congress.

U.S. FEDERAL BUDGET OUTLAYS: FISCAL YEARS 1965–1986

Source: Office of Management and Budget; figures in $ millions (add 000,000).

	ACTUAL OUTLAYS						ESTIMATES[1]	
	1965	1970	1975	1980	1983	1984	1985	1986
NATIONAL DEFENSE:								
Department of Defense—Military:								
Military personnel[2]	$17,913	$29,032	$32,162	$40,897	$60,886	$64,158	$67,546	$72,798
Operation and maintenance	12,349	21,609	26,297	44,770	64,915	67,369	74,569	79,648
Procurement	11,839	21,584	16,042	29,021	53,624	61,879	69,706	83,045
Research & dev., test., evaluation	6,236	7,166	8,866	13,127	20,554	23,117	27,786	33,988
Military construction and other[3]	685	830	2,486	3,161	4,452	4,318	6,698	8,026
Atomic energy defense activities	1,620	1,415	1,506	2,878	5,171	6,120	6,991	7,700
Defense-related activities	−22	55	−850	142	301	453	533	464
Total outlays	50,620	81,692	86,509	133,995	209,903	227,413	253,830	285,669
INTERNATIONAL AFFAIRS:								
Foreign economic and financial assist.	3,357	2,341	3,134	3,626	3,955	4,478	5,523	5,278
International security assistance	1,599	1,094	2,535	4,763	6,613	7,924	10,177	9,213
Conduct of foreign affairs	336	398	659	1,366	1,766	1,882	2,130	2,420
Foreign information and exchange	224	235	348	534	602	682	941	1,041
International financial programs	−242	261	421	2,425	−1,089	910	190	47
Total outlays	5,273	4,330	7,097	12,714	11,848	15,876	18,962	17,998
GENERAL SCIENCE, SPACE, AND TECHNOLOGY:								
General science and basic research	789	947	1,038	1,381	1,644	1,849	2,116	2,237
Spaceflight	3,756	2,340	1,661	2,594	4,053	4,028	3,914	4,004
Space, science, applications, and tech.	1,017	853	958	1,346	1,486	1,687	1,890	2,144
Supporting space activities	261	370	334	512	751	754	819	900
Total outlays	5,823	4,511	3,991	5,832	7,935	8,317	8,740	9,285
ENERGY:								
Energy supply	602	856	2,446	8,363	6,135	3,252	3,074	1,814
Energy conservation	—	—	48	569	477	527	486	381
Emergency energy preparedness	—	—	33	342	1,855	2,518	1,849	416
Energy information, policy, regulation	97	142	389	882	886	790	750	736
Total outlays	699	997	2,916	10,156	9,353	7,086	6,158	3,346
NATURAL RESOURCES AND ENVIRONMENT:								
Water resources	1,546	1,514	2,608	4,223	3,904	4,068	4,289	3,511
Conservation and land management	341	376	655	1,043	1,503	1,302	979	718
Recreational resources	218	363	803	1,677	1,454	1,581	1,622	1,361
Pollution control and abatement	134	384	2,523	5,510	4,263	4,044	4,387	4,579
Other natural resources	292	428	757	1,405	1,548	1,595	1,744	1,660
Total outlays	2,531	3,065	7,346	13,858	12,672	12,591	13,020	11,829
AGRICULTURE:								
Farm income stabilization	3,551	4,589	2,160	7,441	21,323	11,877	18,449	11,527
Agricultural research and services	404	577	876	1,398	1,578	1,736	1,821	1,691
Total outlays	3,955	5,166	3,036	8,839	22,901	13,613	20,270	13,218
COMMERCE AND HOUSING CREDIT:								
Mortgage credit and deposit insurance	−108	94	5,966	5,602	3,880	3,766	2,159	−355
Postal Service	805	1,510	2,989	1,246	1,111	1,239	1,361	1,217
Other advancement of commerce	461	508	991	2,542	1,690	1,913	2,447	1,702
Total outlays	1,157	2,112	9,947	9,390	6,681	6,917	5,966	2,565
TRANSPORTATION:								
Ground transportation	4,105	4,678	7,027	15,274	14,265	16,158	17,676	17,766
Air transportation	941	1,408	2,387	3,723	4,000	4,415	4,966	5,175
Water transportation	717	895	1,430	2,229	2,969	3,010	3,176	2,792
Other transportation	—	26	74	104	99	85	123	127
Total outlays	5,763	7,008	10,918	21,329	21,334	23,669	25,941	25,860
COMMUNITY AND REGIONAL DEVELOPMENT:								
Community development	413	1,449	2,318	4,907	4,353	4,520	4,861	4,616
Area and regional development	648	685	1,607	4,303	3,208	3,034	3,414	2,817
Disaster relief and insurance	53	257	398	2,043	−1	119	326	−84
Total outlays	1,114	2,392	4,322	11,252	7,560	7,673	8,601	7,348

	ACTUAL OUTLAYS (in $ millions; add 000,000)						ESTIMATES [1]	
	1965	1970	1975	1980	1983	1984	1985	1986
EDUCATION, TRAINING, EMPLOYMENT AND SOCIAL SERVICES:								
Elementary, secondary and voc. educ.	$720	$2,895	$4,351	$6,908	$6,294	$6,520	$7,661	$7,670
Higher education	412	1,385	2,190	6,726	7,231	7,383	8,506	7,959
Research and general educ. aids	92	355	780	1,197	1,055	1,210	1,225	1,187
Training and employment	534	1,602	4,063	10,345	5,295	4,644	5,159	4,931
Other labor services	97	135	259	551	599	639	711	679
Social services	291	2,263	4,380	6,116	6,133	7,185	7,032	6,863
TOTAL OUTLAYS	2,146	8,634	16,022	31,843	26,606	27,579	30,295	29,288
HEALTH:								
Health care services	881	3,993	9,519	18,003	23,008	24,522	27,169	28,202
Health research	572	1,054	1,923	3,442	3,973	4,379	4,961	5,204
Educ. & trng. of health care work force	209	633	856	719	578	388	478	455
Consumer and occup. health and safety	130	226	632	1,006	1,081	1,129	1,196	1,059
TOTAL OUTLAYS	1,791	5,907	12,930	23,169	28,641	30,417	33,804	34,920
SOCIAL SECURITY AND MEDICARE:								
Social security	17,460	30,274	64,658	118,548	170,724	178,223	190,422	200,895
Medicare	—	6,213	12,875	32,090	52,588	57,540	65,553	67,685
TOTAL OUTLAYS	17,460	36,487	77,533	150,638	223,311	235,764	255,975	268,580
INCOME SECURITY:								
Gen. retirement and disability insur..	668	1,032	4,689	5,082	5,581	5,441	5,516	5,566
Fed. employee retire. & disability [4] ..	2,858	5,535	13,222	26,594	36,507	38,054	38,641	41,517
Unemployment compensation	2,570	3,359	13,459	18,023	31,464	18,421	17,472	16,694
Housing assistance	231	499	2,058	5,632	9,998	11,270	25,341	12,296
Food and nutrition assistance	299	960	6,643	14,016	17,952	18,055	18,664	18,194
Other income security	2,828	4,260	10,088	17,191	21,096	21,427	22,617	22,028
TOTAL OUTLAYS	9,455	15,645	50,160	86,539	122,598	112,668	128,251	116,295
VETERANS BENEFITS AND SERVICES:								
Income security for veterans	4,215	5,546	7,860	11,688	14,250	14,400	14,754	15,135
Veterans educ., training, and rehab..	58	1,015	4,593	2,342	1,625	1,359	1,283	903
Hospital and med. care for veterans.	1,270	1,800	3,665	6,515	8,272	8,861	9,621	9,994
Veterans housing	*	54	24	−23	3	244	358	−288
Other veterans benefits and services	180	263	458	665	696	751	823	817
TOTAL OUTLAYS	5,723	8,679	16,599	21,185	24,846	25,614	26,839	26,562
ADMINISTRATION OF JUSTICE:								
Federal law enforcement activities ..	332	570	1,349	2,237	2,887	3,205	3,681	3,610
Federal litigative and judicial activ...	146	245	550	1,347	1,627	1,825	2,192	2,066
Federal correctional activities	57	79	200	342	418	494	580	632
Criminal justice assistance	—	65	853	656	167	136	233	280
TOTAL OUTLAYS	535	958	2,951	4,582	5,099	5,660	6,686	6,587
GENERAL GOVERNMENT:								
Legislative functions	189	303	593	1,038	1,196	1,319	1,464	1,417
Executive direction and management	17	30	63	97	96	97	119	112
Central fiscal operations	637	915	1,891	2,614	3,053	3,254	3,522	3,095
General property and records manag.	624	551	429	327	196	201	376	182
Central personnel management	23	44	88	154	115	139	153	143
Other general government	39	121	424	569	768	557	586	390
Deductions for offsetting receipts...	−266	−177	−261	−351	−636	−513	−448	−504
TOTAL OUTLAYS	1,263	1,786	3,227	4,448	4,789	5,053	5,772	4,835
GENERAL PURPOSE FISCAL ASSISTANCE:								
General revenue sharing	—	—	6,130	6,835	4,620	4,573	4,617	1,168
Other general purpose fiscal assist..	238	535	1,055	1,747	1,831	2,197	1,934	1,629
TOTAL OUTLAYS	238	535	7,184	8,582	6,452	6,770	6,552	2,797
NET INTEREST:								
Interest on the public debt	11,346	19,304	32,665	74,781	128,619	153,822	178,795	197,095
Interest received by trust funds	−1,769	−3,934	−7,664	−12,045	−17,102	−20,354	−25,649	−29,036
Other interest	−986	−993	−1,756	−10,224	−21,743	−22,410	−23,564	−26,786
TOTAL OUTLAYS	8,591	14,376	23,244	52,512	89,774	111,058	129,582	141,272
UNDISTRIBUTED OFFSETTING RECEIPTS:								
Employer share, employee retirement [2]	−5,855	−8,445	−11,174	−15,842	−23,484	−25,263	−27,076	−29,082
Rents and royalties on Outer Continental Shelf	−53	−187	−2,428	−4,101	−10,491	−6,694	−5,399	−6,691
Sale of Conrail	—	—	—	—	—	—	—	−1,200
TOTAL OUTLAYS	−5,908	−8,632	−13,602	−19,942	−33,976	−31,957	−32,475	−36,973
ALLOWANCES [5]	...	...	...	...	...	...	1,131	399
TOTAL U.S. GOVT. OUTLAYS ...	$118,228	$195,649	$332,332	$590,920	$808,327	$851,781	$953,900	$971,679

* $500 thousand or less. [1] April Update of the 1986 Budget. [2] Beginning with 1985 Budget, reflects establishment of military retirement trust fund: prior years include accruals for military retirement. [3] Includes allowance for pay raises in 1986. [4] Includes cash payments to military retirees. [5] Includes allowances for civilian agency pay raises.

U.S. BUDGET AND FEDERAL DEBT: 1789–1986 [1]

Source: Office of Management and Budget; figures are in $ millions (add 000,000).

FISCAL YEAR	U.S. BUDGET RECEIPTS	U.S. BUDGET OUTLAYS	SURPLUS(+) OR DEFICIT(−)		GROSS DEBT AT END OF YEAR	FISCAL YEAR	U.S. BUDGET RECEIPTS	U.S. BUDGET OUTLAYS	SURPLUS(+) OR DEFICIT(−)	GROSS DEBT AT END OF YEAR
1789–91	$ 4	$ 4	$+	—	$ 77	1961	$ 94,388	$ 97,723	$− 3,335	$ 292,895
1800	11	11	+	—	83	1962	99,676	106,821	− 7,146	303,291
1810	9	8	+	1	48	1963	106,560	111,316	− 4,756	310,807
1820	18	18	−	—	90	1964	112,613	118,528	− 5,915	316,763
1830	25	15	+	10	39	1965	116,817	118,228	− 1,411	323,154
1840	19	24	−	5	5	1966	130,855	134,532	− 3,698	329,474
1850	44	40	+	4	63	1967	148,822	157,464	− 8,643	341,348
1860	56	63	−	7	65	1968	152,973	178,134	− 25,161	369,769
1870	411	310	+	101	2,436	1969	186,882	183,640	3,242	367,144
1880	334	268	+	66	2,091	1970	192,812	195,649	− 2,837	382,603
1890	403	318	+	85	1,122	1971	187,139	210,172	− 23,033	409,467
1900	567	521	+	46	1,263	1972	207,309	230,681	− 23,373	437,329
1905	544	567	−	23	1,132	1973	230,799	245,707	− 14,908	468,426
1910	676	694	−	18	1,147	1974	263,224	269,359	− 6,135	486,247
1915	683	746	−	63	1,191	1975	279,090	332,332	− 53,242	544,131
1920	6,649	6,358	+	291	24,299	1976	298,060	371,779	− 73,719	631,866
1925	3,641	2,924	+	717	20,516	1977	355,559	409,203	− 53,644	709,138
1930	4,058	3,320	+	738	16,185	1978	399,740	458,729	− 58,989	780,425
1935	3,706	6,497	−	2,791	28,701	1979	463,302	503,464	− 40,161	833,751
1940	6,548	9,468	−	2,920	50,696	1980	517,112	590,920	− 73,808	914,317
1945	45,159	92,712	−	47,553	260,123	1981	599,272	678,209	− 78,936	1,003,941
1950	39,443	42,562	−	3,119	256,853	1982	617,766	745,706	− 127,940	1,146,987
1955	65,451	68,444	−	2,993	274,366	1983	600,562	808,327	− 207,764	1,381,886
1957	79,990	76,578		3,412	272,353	1984	666,457	851,781	− 185,324	1,576,748
1958	79,636	82,405	−	2,769	279,693	1985 [2]	740,595	953,900	− 213,305	1,841,853
1959	79,249	92,098	−	12,849	287,767	1986 [2]	794,300	971,679	− 177,379	2,073,864
1960	92,492	92,191		301	290,862					

[1] For 1789–1939, administrative budget. [2] April 1985 estimates.

FEDERAL BUDGET RECEIPTS BY SOURCE: 1940–1986

Source: Office of Management and Budget; figures in $ millions (add 000,000).

SOURCE	COLLECTIONS								
	1940	1950	1960	1970	1980	1983	1984	1985[1]	1986[1]
Individual Income Taxes	$ 892	$15,755	$40,715	$90,412	$244,069	$288,938	$296,206	$331,142	$358,376
Corporation Income Taxes	1,197	10,449	21,494	32,829	64,600	37,022	56,893	69,539	76,183
Social Insurance Taxes and Contributions ...	1,785	4,338	14,683	44,367	157,803	208,994	241,651	267,139	288,723
Excise Taxes	1,977	7,550	11,676	15,705	24,329	35,300	37,361	36,907	34,973
Estate and Gift Taxes	353	698	1,606	3,644	6,389	6,053	6,010	5,944	5,345
Customs Duties	331	407	1,105	2,430	7,174	8,655	11,370	12,194	12,067
Miscellaneous Receipts	14	247	1,212	3,424	12,748	15,601	16,965	17,730	18,632
TOTAL RECEIPTS	$6,548	$39,443	$92,492	$192,812	$517,112	$600,562	$666,457	$740,595	$794,300

[1] 1985 and 1986 are April 1985 estimates.

COMPARISON OF FEDERAL RECEIPTS AND EXPENDITURES: 1975–1984 [1]

Federal Sector, National Income and Product Account (NIPA).
Source: U.S. Department of Commerce, *Survey of Current Business*; figures in $ billions (add 000,000,000).

	1975	1978	1979	1980	1981	1982	1983	1984
Federal government receipts........	$286.2	$431.6	$493.6	$540.8	$624.8	$616.7	$641.1	$704.7
Personal tax and nontax receipts ...	125.4	194.9	230.6	257.6	298.7	306.2	295.2	315.0
Corporate profits tax accruals	42.8	71.3	74.2	70.3	65.7	46.6	59.8	70.8
Indirect business tax and nontax accruals.	23.9	28.1	29.4	38.9	56.4	48.4	52.4	55.5
Contributions for social insurance ..	94.2	137.2	159.5	173.9	204.0	215.5	233.7	263.4
Federal government expenditures ...	$356.8	$461.0	$509.7	$602.1	$689.1	$764.9	$819.7	$880.5
Purchases of goods and services ...	123.1	153.6	168.3	197.0	228.9	258.9	269.7	295.4
Transfer payments	149.1	185.6	209.2	251.5	286.8	321.6	345.6	353.0
Grants-in-aid to state and local govts.	54.6	77.3	80.5	88.7	87.9	83.9	86.3	93.2
Net interest paid	23.2	35.2	42.4	53.4	73.3	84.4	94.2	116.7
Subsidies less current surplus of government enterprises	6.8	9.5	9.2	11.5	12.3	16.1	23.4	22.3
Deficit (−)	$−70.6	$−29.5	$−16.1	$−61.3	$−64.3	$−148.1	$−178.6	$−175.8

[1] Calendar years.

U.S. GOVERNMENT CIVILIAN EMPLOYEES

Source: Office of Personnel Management

The total number of civilian employees of the U.S. government increased by over 76,369 in the 12 months from June 1984 to June 1985.

Over one-third of the employees work for the Defense Department, which added about 28,000 civilian workers during the 12-month period.

The U.S. Postal Service employs about one-fourth of federal civilian workers.

	TOTAL [1]
TOTAL, ALL BRANCHES	**3,059,987***
LEGISLATIVE BRANCH	**40,788***
Congress	21,359
Architect of the Capitol	2,217*
General Accounting Office	5,505
Government Printing Office	5,448
Library of Congress	5,430
U.S. Tax Court	311
Congressional Budget Office	220*
Office of Technology Assessment	205
Botanic Garden	59*
Copyright Royalty Tribunal	6
JUDICIAL BRANCH	**17,938***
United States Courts	17,603
Supreme Court	335*
EXECUTIVE BRANCH	**3,001,261***
Executive Office of the President:	**1,567**
White House Office	367
White House Executive Residence	90
Office of the Vice President	18
Office of Management and Budget	608
Office of Administration	193
Domestic Policy Staff	35
National Security Council	58
Office of the U.S. Trade Representative	133
Council of Economic Advisers	33
Office of Science and Technology Policy	20
Council on Environmental Quality	12
Executive Departments:	**1,820,881**
State	25,642
Treasury	134,152
Defense	1,099,290
Army	408,056
Navy	351,862
Air Force	258,897
Defense Logistics Agency	51,866
Other Defense activities	28,609
Justice	63,902
Interior	79,856
Agriculture	122,528
Commerce	35,978
Labor	18,408
Health and Human Services	143,974
Housing and Urban Development	12,362
Transportation	62,794
Energy	16,998
Education	4,997
Independent Agencies:	**1,178,813***
ACTION	517
Advisory Commission on Intergovernmental Relations	32
Advisory Council on Historic Preservation	37
Alaska Natural Gas Transportation System	10
American Battle Monuments Commission	393

	TOTAL [1]
Independent Agencies (continued)	
Arms Control and Disarmament Agency	208
Board of Governors, Federal Reserve System	1,575
Commission on Civil Rights	225*
Commodity Futures Trading Comm.	516
Consumer Product Safety Commission	615
Environmental Protection Agency	13,890
Equal Employment Opportunity Comm.	3,253*
Export-Import Bank of the U.S.	386
Farm Credit Administration	318
Federal Communication Comm.	1,927
Federal Deposit Insurance Corp.	5,898*
Federal Election Commission	244
Federal Emergency Management Agency	2,972
Federal Home Loan Bank Board	1,543
Federal Labor Relations Authority	308*
Federal Maritime Commission	228
Federal Mediation and Conciliation Service	345
Federal Mine Safety and Health Review Commission	51
Federal Trade Commission	1,275
General Services Administration	25,977
Inter-American Foundation	73*
International Trade Commission	527
Interstate Commerce Commission	900
Merit Systems Protection Board	452
National Aeronautics and Space Administration	23,355
National Archives and Records Administration	3,163
National Capital Planning Commission	51
National Credit Union Administration	597
National Endowment for the Arts	301
National Endowment for the Humanities	273
National Labor Relations Board	2,614
National Mediation Board	55
National Science Foundation	1,270
National Transportation Safety Board	356
Navajo and Hopi Indian Relocation Commission	53
Nuclear Regulatory Commission	3,681
Occupational Safety and Health Review Commission	75
Office of Personnel Management	6,472
Panama Canal Commission	8,532
Peace Corps	1,155
Pennsylvania Ave. Development Corp.	35
Pension Benefit Guaranty Corporation	542
Postal Rate Commission	62
Railroad Retirement Board	1,683
Securities and Exchange Commission	1,917
Selective Service System	302
Small Business Administration	4,970
Smithsonian Institution	4,785
Soldiers' and Airmen's Home	1,061
Tennessee Valley Authority	33,421
U.S. Information Agency	8,808
U.S. International Development Cooperation Agency	5,178
U.S. Postal Service	752,126
Veterans Administration	246,945
Other boards and agencies (23)	345

* Preliminary data. [1] As of June 30, 1985. Excludes Central Intelligence Agency and National Security Agency.

U.S. GOVERNMENT AGENCIES AND DEPARTMENTS

The President is the administrative head of the executive branch of the government, which includes cabinet-level executive departments and independent agencies.

The cabinet functions at the pleasure of the President to advise him on matters of importance. The Vice President participates in all cabinet meetings. Others who regularly attend cabinet meetings include the heads of the executive departments, the counsel to the President, the special representative for trade negotiations, the director of the Office of Management and Budget, the U.S. ambassador to the UN, and presidential staff aides.

The President's salary is $200,000 a year plus $50,000 official allowance and $100,000 travel allowance.

EXECUTIVE OFFICE OF PRESIDENT REAGAN

This office consists of the individuals, agencies, and special commissions charged with aiding the President in carrying out the many activities incident to his office.

THE WHITE HOUSE OFFICE
1600 Pennsylvania Avenue, N.W., and Old
 Executive Office Building,
 Washington, D.C. 20500
Phone: (202) 456-1414

Assistants to the President:
Donald T. Regan, *Chief of Staff to the President*; James S. Brady, *Press Secretary*; Patrick J. Buchanan, *Director of Communications*; Mitchell E. Daniels, Jr., *Political and Intergovernmental Affairs*; Fred F. Elliott, *Director of Speechwriting*; Donald R. Fortier, *National Security Affairs*; Richard A. Hauser, *Deputy Counsel to the President*; William Henkel, *Director of the Presidential Advance Office*; Christopher Hicks, *Administration*; Charles D. Hobbs, *Policy Development*; Alfred H. Kingon, *Cabinet Secretary*; Alan M. Kranowitz, *Legislative Affairs (House)*; William B. Lacy, *Director, Office of Political Affairs*; John M. Poindexter Vice Admiral, USN, *National Security Affairs*; James S. Rosebush, *Deputy Assistant to the President*; Frederick J. Ryan, Jr., *Director of Presidential Appointments and Scheduling, Director of Private Sector Initiatives*; Karna Small, *National Security Affairs and Senior Director, Public Affairs, National Security Council*; Carlton E. Turner, *Drug Abuse Policy*; Pamela J. Turner, *Legislative Affairs (Senate)*; Robert H. Tuttle, *Director of Presidential Personnel*

Special Assistants to the President:
Ronald L. Alvarado, *Intergovernmental Affairs*; Carl A. Anderson, *Public Liaison*; Linda L. Arey, *Deputy Director of the Office of Public Liaison*; Haley Barbour, *Political Affairs*; Ralph C. Bledsoe, *Policy Development*; Melvin L. Bradley, *Policy Development*; Albert R. Brashear, *Deputy Press Secretary for Domestic Affairs*; Merlin P. Breaux, *Public Liaison*; Marshall J. Breger, *Public Liaison*; Andrew H. Card, Jr., *Intergovernmental Affairs*; James P. Covey, *National Security Affairs*; Kenneth E. DeGraffenreid, *National Security Affairs*; Edward P. Djerejian, *Deputy Press Secretary for Foreign Affairs*; Anthony Dolan, *Chief Speechwriter*; Thomas Donnelly, Jr., *Legislative Affairs*; Michael A. Driggs, *Policy Development*; Henry M. Gandy, *Legislative Affairs*; H. Lawrence Garrett, III, *Associate Counsel to the President*; Bryce L. Harlow, *Legislative Affairs*; Anne Higgins, *Director of Correspondence*; James L. Hooley, *Director of Presidential Advance*; John M. Hudson, *Legislative Affairs*

Deputy Assistants to the President:
Linda Chavez, *Director of the Office of Public Liaison*; David L. Chew, *Staff Secretary*; Thomas C. Dawson, *Executive Assistant to the Chief of Staff*; Bently T. Elliott, *Director of Speechwriting*;

Special Assistants to the President or Equivalent Positions:
Mary Jo Jacobi, *Public Liaison*; Nancy M. Kennedy, *Legislative Affairs*; James F. Kuhn, *Special Assistant to the President*; Ronald F. Lehman, *National Security Affairs*; Frederick D. McClure, *Legislative Affairs*; William F. Martin, *National Security Affairs*; John F. Matlock, Jr., *National Security Affairs*; Constantine C. Menges, *National Security Affairs*; Margaret Noonan, *Presidential Speechwriting*; Deborah K. Owen, *Associate Counsel to the President*; Richard Prendergast, *Legislative Affairs*; Walter Raymond, Jr., *National Security Affairs*; Nancy J. Risque, *Legislative Affairs*; John G. Roberts, Jr., *Associate Counsel to the President*; Robert R. Reilly, *Public Liaison*; William L. Roper, *Health Policy*; Peter H. Roussel, *Deputy Press Secretary*; Gaston J. Sigur, Jr., *National Security Affairs*; T. Burton Smith, M.D., *Physician to the President*; David B. Waller, *Senior Associate Counsel to the President*; Lyn M. Withey, *Legislative Affairs*

Chief of Protocol: Selwa Roosevelt
Personal Secretary to the President: Kathleen Osborne
Physician to the President: T. Burton Smith, M.D.
Chief Usher: Rex W. Scouten

EXECUTIVE OFFICE OF THE PRESIDENT *(cont.)*

CENTRAL INTELLIGENCE AGENCY (CIA)

Washington, D.C. 20505
Director: William J. Casey
Duties: To keep National Security Council informed on national-security matters; to coordinate intelligence from government agencies and from its agents in other countries. The CIA has no police or law-enforcement powers and no internal-security functions.

COUNCIL OF ECONOMIC ADVISERS (CEA)

Executive Office Building,
Washington, D.C. 20506
Established: 1946
Chairman: Beryl W. Sprinkel.
Members: Thomas Gale Moore, 1 vacancy
Duties: To analyze trends in the national economy; to appraise economic programs and policies of the federal government; to assist in the preparation of the President's economic reports to Congress.

COUNCIL ON ENVIRONMENTAL QUALITY

722 Jackson Place, N.W.,
Washington, D.C. 20006
Established: 1969
Chairman: A. Alan Hill
Duties: To develop and recommend national policies to promote environmental quality and to administer guidelines for the environmental impact statement process.

INTELLIGENCE OVERSIGHT BOARD

Executive Office Building,
Washington, D.C. 20500
Established: 1975
Chairman: W. Glenn Campbell
Membership: W. Glenn Campbell, Charles Jarvis Meyers, Charles Tyroler II
Duties: To review and assess foreign-intelligence activities and bring to the President's attention any abuses that might occur.

NATIONAL SECURITY COUNCIL

Executive Office Building,
Washington, D.C. 20506
Established: 1947
Director: Assistant to the President for National Security Affairs Robert C. McFarlane
Membership: The President, Vice President, Secretary of State, Secretary of Defense
Advisers: Chairman of the Joint Chiefs of Staff and director of the Central Intelligence Agency
Duties: To advise the President on national- security problems, formulating plans to promote the best interests of the United States in international relations.

OFFICE OF ADMINISTRATION

The White House,
Washington, D.C. 20500
Established: 1977
Director: Christopher Hicks
Purpose: To provide administrative services to the components of the Executive Office, including accounting and payroll, mail and messengers, library facilities, and computer facilities; to coordinate the zero-base budgeting system.

OFFICE OF MANAGEMENT AND BUDGET (OMB)

Executive Office Building,
Washington, D.C. 20503
Established: 1970
Director: James C. Miller 3d
Duties: To aid the President in the preparation and administration of the budget and make recommendations for the more efficient organization of the federal government.

OFFICE OF POLICY DEVELOPMENT

The White House,
Washington, D.C. 20500
Established: 1977
Director: John A. Svahn
Purpose: To administer the Presidential Domestic Policy Review System to coordinate the work of the departments and agencies in developing the administration's position on selected key domestic-policy issues.

OFFICE OF SCIENCE AND TECHNOLOGY POLICY

Executive Office Building,
Washington, D.C. 20506
Established: May 11, 1976
Director: George A. Keyworth II
Duties: To advise the President on science, engineering, and technology; to evaluate the overall federal-government efforts in science and technology.

OFFICE OF THE SPECIAL REPRESENTATIVE FOR TRADE NEGOTIATIONS

1800 G Street, N.W.,
Washington, D.C. 20506
Established: 1963
Special Representative for Trade Negotiations: Clayton Yeutter
Duties: To facilitate implementation of the trade-agreements program; to assist and advise the President in coordinating international trade policy; and to administer the negotiation and implementation of international trade agreements.

OFFICE OF THE VICE PRESIDENT

Executive Office Building,
Washington, D.C. 20501
Chief of Staff: Craig L. Fuller
Executive Functions: Participation in all cabinet meetings and meetings of the National Security Council; member of Board of Regents of the Smithsonian Institution; chairs executive committee that develops the President's long-term agenda.

PRESIDENT'S FOREIGN INTELLIGENCE ADVISORY BOARD

Executive Office Building
Washington, D.C. 20500
Established: 1981
Chairman: Anne L. Armstrong
Vice Chairman: Leo Cherne
Membership: 21 members
Duties: To assess the quality, quantity, and adequacy of intelligence collection and other intelligence activities.

CABINET-LEVEL EXECUTIVE DEPARTMENTS

AGRICULTURE, DEPARTMENT OF
14th Street and Independence Avenue, N.W.,
 Washington, D.C. 20250
Established: 1889 as an executive department
Secretary of Agriculture: John R. Block
Deputy Secretary: John R. Norton 3d
Administrator, Farmers Home Administration:
 Charles W. Shuman
Purpose: To carry out agricultural research, education, conservation, marketing, regulatory work, agricultural adjustment, and rural development. It also collects and distributes agricultural information.

COMMERCE, DEPARTMENT OF
14th Street and Constitution Avenue, N.W.,
 Washington, D.C. 20230
Established: 1913
Secretary: Malcolm Baldrige
Director of the Census: John G. Keane
Director, National Oceanic and Atmospheric Administration: John V. Byrne
Purpose: To promote full development of the economic resources of the U.S. It conducts censuses; disseminates commercial statistics; compiles nautical and aeronautical charts; establishes weights, measures, and standards; issues patents and registers trademarks; provides weather forecasting.

DEFENSE, DEPARTMENT OF
The Pentagon,
 Washington, D.C. 20301
Established: 1949
Secretary: Caspar W. Weinberger
Deputy Secretary: Willian Howard Taft IV
Functions: To defend the U.S. against all enemies; to ensure the security of the U.S. and areas vital to its interest.
Secretary of the Army: John O. Marsh Jr.
Secretary of the Navy: John F. Lehman
Secretary of the Air Force: Verne Orr

EDUCATION, DEPARTMENT OF
400 Maryland Ave., S.W.,
 Washington, D.C. 20202
Established: 1979
Secretary: William J. Bennett
Under Secretary: Gary L. Bauer
Purpose: To administer and coordinate federal education programs.
Commissioner, Rehabilitation Services Administration: George A. Conn

ENERGY, DEPARTMENT OF
1000 Independence Avenue, S.W.,
 Washington, D.C. 20585
Established: 1977
Secretary: John S. Herrington
Purpose: To carry out the national energy policy, including conservation, resource development and production, research, data management, and environmental protection and regulation related to energy.

Chairman, Federal Energy Regulatory Commission: Raymond J. O'Connor

HEALTH AND HUMAN SERVICES, DEPARTMENT OF
200 Independence Avenue, S.W.,
 Washington, D.C. 20201
Established: 1953 as Department of Health, Education, and Welfare; name changed 1979.
Secretary: Vacant
Under Secretary: Charles D. Baker
Purpose: To administer and coordinate federal activities in health and welfare.
Commissioner Food and Drug Administration: Dr. Frank E. Young
Commissioner on Aging: Lennie Marie Tolliver
Surgeon General, Public Health Service: Dr. C. Everett Koop
Director, National Institutes of Health: James B. Wyngaarden
Director, National Cancer Institute: Dr. Vincent T. DeVita Jr.
Commissioner of Social Security: Martha A. McSteen (Acting)

HOUSING AND URBAN DEVELOPMENT, DEPARTMENT OF
451 7th Street, N.W.,
 Washington, D.C. 20410
Established: 1965
Secretary: Samuel R. Pierce
Under Secretary: Lee Verstandig
Purpose: To administer housing and urban-development programs and offer technical aid to states, cities, and counties.

INTERIOR, DEPARTMENT OF THE
18th and C Streets, N.W.,
 Washington, D.C. 20240
Established: 1849
Secretary: Donald Paul Hodel
Under Secretary: Ann D. McLaughlin
Purpose: To formulate and administer programs for the conservation and development of natural resources. It supervises the Bureau of Mines, Geological Survey, Bureau of Indian Affairs, Bureau of Land Management, National Park Service, Fish and Wildlife Service, and Water and Power Resources Service.

JUSTICE, DEPARTMENT OF
Constitution Avenue and 10th Street, N.W.,
 Washington, D.C. 20530
Established: 1870
Attorney General: Edwin Meese 3d
Deputy Attorney General: D. Lowell Jensen
Director, Federal Bureau of Investigation: William A. Webster
Solicitor General: Rex E. Lee
Purpose: To provide means for enforcing federal laws, to furnish legal counsel in federal cases, and to construe the laws under which other departments act.

LABOR, DEPARTMENT OF

200 Constitution Avenue, N.W.,
Washington, D.C. 20210
Established: 1913
Secretary: William E. Brock 3d
Under Secretary: Dennis Whitfield
Purpose: To administer and enforce laws designed to advance the public interest by promoting the welfare of U.S. wage earners, improving their working conditions, and advancing their opportunities for profitable employment.

STATE, DEPARTMENT OF

2201 C Street, N.W.,
Washington, D.C. 20520
Established: 1789
Secretary: George P. Shultz
Deputy Secretary: Kenneth W. Dam
Administrator, Agency for International Development (AID): M. Peter McPherson
Purpose: The President, who has overall responsibility for U.S. foreign policy, looks to the Department of State for primary advice in formulating and executing that policy. The department's primary objective is to promote U.S. interest in international relations.

TRANSPORTATION, DEPARTMENT OF

400 7th Street, S.W.,
Washington, D.C. 20590
Established: 1966
Secretary: Elizabeth Dole
Deputy Secretary: James H. Burnley IV
Administrator, Federal Aviation Administration: Donald D. Enger
Administrator, Federal Highway Administration: Ray Barnhart
Administrator, Federal Railroad Administration: John H. Riley
Administrator, National Highway Safety Administration: Diane K. Steed
Purpose: To develop national policies to provide fast, safe, efficient, convenient, and economical transportation. It also directs the Federal Aviation Administration, St. Lawrence Seaway Development Corporation, and, in peacetime, the U.S. Coast Guard.

TREASURY, DEPARTMENT OF THE

15th Street and Pennsylvania Avenue, N.W.,
Washington, D.C. 20220
Established: 1789
Secretary: James A. Baker 3d
Deputy Secretary: Richard G. Darman
Treasurer of the U.S.: Katherine D. Ortega
Comptroller of the Currency: C. T. Conover
Commissioner, Internal Revenue Service: Roscoe L. Egger Jr.
Purpose: To manage national finances; provide coined and printed currency; maintain U.S. credit; represent the U.S. in international banking and monetary organizations; collect U.S. taxes through the Internal Revenue Service; and supervise the Secret Service.

INDEPENDENT AGENCIES OF THE U.S. GOVERNMENT

ACTION

806 Connecticut Avenue, N.W.,
Washington, D.C. 20525
Established: 1971
Director: Donna M. Alvarado
Deputy Director: Betty H. Brake
Activities: Coordinates citizen volunteer action programs, including the Peace Corps, VISTA, foster grandparents, and retired volunteers.

ARMS CONTROL AND DISARMAMENT AGENCY

Department of State Building,
Washington, D.C. 20451
Established: 1961
Director: Kenneth L. Adelman
Deputy Director: David F. Emery
Activities: Participates in nuclear-test-ban and general disarmament negotiations at Geneva and in the United Nations; conducts research on arms control and disarmament.

BOARD FOR INTERNATIONAL BROADCASTING

Department of State Building,
Washington, D.C. 20036
Established: 1973
Chairman: Malcolm Forbes Jr.
Activities: To provide assistance to Radio Free Europe and Radio Liberty and to encourage a flow of information to people of the communist nations of Europe.

COMMISSION OF FINE ARTS

708 Jackson Place, N.W.,
Washington, D.C. 20006
Established: 1910
Membership: Seven expert fine-arts judges
Chairman: J. Carter Brown
Activities: Advises, assists on matters relating to art, monuments, and public works.

COMMISSION ON CIVIL RIGHTS

1121 Vermont Avenue, N.W.,
Washington, D.C. 20425
Established: 1957
Chairman: Clarence M. Pendleton Jr.
Activities: Investigates complaints of persons being deprived of their civil rights because of race, color, religion, sex, or national origin.

COMMODITY FUTURES TRADING COMMISSION

2033 K Street N.W.,
Washington, D.C. 20581
Established: 1974
Chairman: Susan Meredith Phillips
Activities: Seeks to strengthen the regulation of futures trading and to bring under regulation all agricultural and other commodities that are traded on commodity exchanges, and to protect market users against abuses.

CONSUMER PRODUCT SAFETY COMMISSION

1111 18th Street, N.W.,
Washington, D.C. 20207
Established: Oct. 27, 1972
Chairman: Terrance M. Scanlon
Membership: Five members
Activities: Studies consumer-product safety; orders unsafe products taken off the market; establishes product-safety standards to reduce risks to consumers.

INDEPENDENT AGENCIES *(continued)*
ENVIRONMENTAL PROTECTION AGENCY (EPA)

401 M Street, S.W.,
 Washington, D.C. 20460
Established: 1970
Administrator: Lee M. Thomas
Deputy Administrator: A. James Barnes
Activities: To assure the protection of the environment by monitoring, regulating, abating, and controlling pollution of the environment on a systematic basis.

EQUAL EMPLOYMENT OPPORTUNITY COMMISSION (EEOC)

2401 E Street, N.W.,
 Washington, D.C. 20507
Established: 1965
Membership: Five members, appointed to 5-year terms by the President
Chairman: Clarence Thomas
Activities: Coordinates federal efforts to end discrimination in employment.

EXPORT-IMPORT BANK OF THE U.S.

811 Vermont Avenue, N.W.,
 Washington, D.C. 20571
Established: 1934
President: William H. Draper III
Activities: Aids in financing and facilitating trade between the U.S. and foreign countries.

FARM CREDIT ADMINISTRATION (FCA)

Federal Credit Building
1501 Farm Credit Drive
 McLean, VA 22102
Established: 1916
Governor: Donald E. Wilkinson
Activities: Supervises and coordinates a cooperative credit system for agriculture, providing long-term and short-term credits to farmers and their cooperative organizations.

FEDERAL COMMUNICATIONS COMMISSION (FCC)

1919 M Street, N.W.,
 Washington, D.C. 20554
Established: 1934
Membership: Five members, appointed to 7-year terms by the President.
Chairman: Mark S. Fowler
Activities: Regulates interstate and foreign commerce in communication by radio and wire to make available a rapid, efficient radio communication service at reasonable cost.

FEDERAL DEPOSIT INSURANCE CORPORATION (FDIC)

550 17th Street, N.W.,
 Washington, D.C. 20429
Established: 1933
Membership: The Board of Directors comprises three members. Two are appointed to 6-year terms by the President. The chairman is one of the presidential appointees. The Comptroller of the Currency serves ex-officio as the third member of the corporation.
Chairman: William M. Isaac
Activities: Insures the deposits of all banks entitled to benefits of insurance under the law, paying depositors of insured banks that close without adequate funds to meet claims against them; acts as a receiver for national banks placed in receivership and, under certain conditions, for state banks placed in receivership.

FEDERAL ELECTION COMMISSION

1325 K Street, N.W.,
 Washington, D.C. 20005
Established: 1975
Chairman: James W. McGarry
Activities: Enforces federal laws on election campaign financing.

FEDERAL EMERGENCY MANAGEMENT AGENCY

Federal Center Plaza
500 C Street, S.W.
 Washington, D.C. 20472
Established: 1979
Director: Julius W. Becton Jr.
Purpose: To oversee federal programs that assist areas and individuals affected by civil emergencies.

FEDERAL HOME LOAN BANK BOARD

1700 G Street, N.W.,
 Washington, D.C. 20552
Established: 1955
Chairman: Edwin J. Gray
Activities: Provides credit reserve for savings and home-financing institutions; supervises the Federal Home Loan Bank System, the Federal Savings and Loan System, and the Federal Savings and Loan Insurance Corporation.

FEDERAL MARITIME COMMISSION

1100 L Street, N.W.,
 Washington, D.C. 20573
Established: 1961
Membership: Five members, appointed to 4 year terms by the President.
Chairman: Edward V. Hickey Jr.
Activities: Regulates rates, fares, charges, classifications, tariffs, regulations, and practices of common carriers engaged in maritime commerce within U.S. jurisdiction.

FEDERAL MEDIATION AND CONCILIATION SERVICE

2100 K Street, N.W.,
 Washington, D.C. 20427
Established: 1947
Director: Kay McMurray
Activities: Assists in the solution of labor disputes affecting interstate commerce by offering conciliation and mediation services.

FEDERAL RESERVE SYSTEM

Board of Governors of the Federal Reserve System
20th Street and Constitution Avenue, N.W.,
 Washington, D.C. 20551
Established: 1913
Membership: The Board of Governors of the Federal Reserve System has seven members appointed by the President.
Chairman: Paul A. Volcker
Activities: Provides for establishment of Federal

Reserve Banks to furnish an elastic currency, to afford means of rediscounting commercial paper, and to establish effective supervision of banking in the United States.

FEDERAL SAVINGS AND LOAN INSURANCE CORPORATION (FSLIC)

1700 G Street, N.W.,
Washington, D.C. 20552
Established: 1934
Director: Paul O. Stearns
Activities: Insures each depositor's account in approved savings and loan associations; to prevent default of an insured institution, the corporation can make loans or purchase assets of the institution; income is from premiums paid by the insured institutions.

FEDERAL TRADE COMMISSION (FTC)

Pennsylvania Avenue at 6th Street, N.W.,
Washington, D.C. 20580
Established: 1915
Membership: Five members, appointed to 7-year terms by the President. Not more than three commissioners may be members of the same political party.
Chairman: Terry Calvini (Acting)
Activities: Promotes fair and free competition in interstate commerce by prevention of price fixing, boycotts, combinations in restraint of trade, and other practices; safeguards consumers from unfair advertising and sales techniques.

GENERAL SERVICES ADMINISTRATION (GSA)

18th and F Streets, N.W.,
Washington, D.C. 20405
Established: 1949
Administrator: Terence C. Golden
Activities: Manages government property and records, including the construction and operation of buildings, procurement and distribution of supplies, disposal of surplus property, management of traffic and communications, stockpiling of strategic and critical materials, and care of records.

INTER-AMERICAN FOUNDATION

1515 Wilson Blvd.,
Rosslyn, Va. 22209
Established: Dec. 30, 1969
Chairman: Victor Blanco
Purpose: Supports small-scale local social-development projects in Latin America.

INTERNATIONAL DEVELOPMENT COOPERATION AGENCY, U.S.

2201 C Street, N.W.,
Washington, D.C. 20520
Established: 1979
Director: M. Peter McPherson
Purpose: To consolidate policy direction of developing agencies and control budgets of various international development agencies.

INTERNATIONAL TRADE COMMISSION, U.S.

701 E Street, N.W.,
Washington, D.C. 20436
Established: 1916
Chairman: Paula Stern

Activities: Serves Congress and the President as an advisory, fact-finding agency on tariff, commercial policy, and foreign-trade matters.

INTERSTATE COMMERCE COMMISSION (ICC)

12th Street and Constitution Avenue, N.W.,
Washington, D.C. 20423
Established: 1887
Membership: Seven members
Chairman: Reese H. Taylor Jr.
Activities: Regulates interstate commerce, and foreign import and export commerce to the extent that it takes place in the United States.

NATIONAL AERONAUTICS AND SPACE ADMINISTRATION (NASA)

400 Maryland Avenue, S.W.,
Washington, D.C. 20546
Established: 1958
Administrator: James Montgomery Beggs
Activities: Conducts research on flight within and outside the Earth's atmosphere; develops, constructs, tests, and operates aeronautical and space vehicles.

NATIONAL CREDIT UNION ADMINISTRATION

1776 G Street, N.W.
Washington, D.C. 20456
Established: March 10, 1970
Chairman: Roger W. Jepsen
Activities: Regulates credit unions.

NATIONAL FOUNDATION ON THE ARTS AND HUMANITIES

1100 Pennsylvania Avenue, N.W.
Washington, D.C. 20506
Established: 1965
Chairman, National Endowment for the Arts: Francis S. M. Hodsoll
Chairman, National Endowment for the Humanities: Edward A. Curran
Purpose: To encourage and support national programs in the humanities and the arts. The Arts Endowment awards grants to groups (and some individuals) engaged in or concerned with the arts, awards grants-in-aid to assist state art agencies, and conducts special studies.

NATIONAL LABOR RELATIONS BOARD (NLRB)

1717 Pennsylvania Avenue, N.W.,
Washington, D.C. 20570
Established: 1935
Membership: Five members, appointed to 4-year terms by the President
Chairman: Donald L. Dotson
Activities: Prevents, through a variety of powers, unfair labor practices.

NATIONAL MEDIATION BOARD

1425 K Street, N.W.,
Washington, D.C. 20572
Established: 1934
Chairman: Walter C. Wallace
Activities: Mediates differences between the railroads and airlines on one hand and their employees on the other.

UNITED STATES 975

INDEPENDENT AGENCIES (continued)

NATIONAL SCIENCE FOUNDATION (NSF)
1800 G Street, N.W.,
 Washington, D.C. 20550
Established: 1950
Director: Eric Bloch
Purpose: Strengthens basic research and education in the sciences in the U.S.

NATIONAL TRANSPORTATION SAFETY BOARD
800 Independence Avenue, S.W.,
 Washington, D.C. 20594
Established: 1966
Chairman: James Eugene Burnett Jr.
Activities: Investigates major accidents in civil aviation, railroads, highways, pipelines, and ships; reports the facts and circumstances of accidents; and makes recommendations for legislation to prevent accidents.

NUCLEAR REGULATORY COMMISSION (NRC)
1717 H Street, N.W.,
 Washington, D.C. 20555
Established: Oct. 11, 1974
Chairman: Nunzio J. Palladino
Membership: Five members
Responsibilities: Took over duties of former Atomic Energy Commission (AEC) to regulate, license, and supervise the security and safety of peaceful uses of nuclear power.

OFFICE OF PERSONNEL MANAGEMENT
1900 E Street, N.W.,
 Washington, D.C. 20415
Established: 1979
Director: Constance Horner
Purpose: Administration of a merit system for federal-government employees.

OVERSEAS PRIVATE INVESTMENT CORPORATION
1129 20th Street, N.W.,
 Washington, D.C. 20527
Established: 1971
President: Craig A. Nalen
Purpose: To provide incentives (including insurance against loss by expropriation) for U.S. private investors in 90 developing nations.

POSTAL RATE COMMISSION
2000 L Street, N.W.,
 Washington, D.C. 20268
Established: Aug. 12, 1970
Chairman: Janet Dempsey Steiger
Activities: Holds hearings and submits recommendations to the Postal Service on postage rates, fees, and mail classifications.

POSTAL SERVICE, UNITED STATES
475 L'Enfant Plaza, S.W.,
 Washington, D.C. 20260
Established: 1970 (The U.S. Postal Service, which began operations July 1, 1971, replaced the cabinet-level Post Office Department established by Congress in 1872. The first Postal Service was created in 1775.)
Postmaster General: Paul N. Carlin
Activities: To provide postal services.

RAILROAD RETIREMENT BOARD
884 Rush Street
 Chicago, Ill. 60611
Established: 1935
Chairman: Robert A. Gielow

Purpose: Administers payment of retirement and disability annuities to railroad employees and their families.

SECURITIES AND EXCHANGE COMMISSION (SEC)
450 Fifth Street, N.W.
 Washington, D.C. 20549
Established: 1934
Membership: Five members, appointed by the President to 5-year terms. Only three may be members of the same political party.
Chairman: John S. R. Shad
Activities: Protects the interests of the public and investors against malpractices in securities and financial markets.

SMALL BUSINESS ADMINISTRATION (SBA)
1441 L Street, N.W.,
 Washington, D.C. 20416
Established: 1953
Administrator: James C. Sanders
Activities: Aids, counsels, and protects the interests of small business; ensures that small business concerns receive a fair proportion of government purchases and contracts, and of the sales of government property; makes loans to small business concerns, state and local development companies, and the victims of floods and disasters.

SMITHSONIAN INSTITUTION
1000 Jefferson Drive, S.W.,
 Washington, D.C. 20560
Established: 1846
Secretary of the Institution: Robert McC. Adams
Activities: Performs fundamental research; maintains library, theater, and museum facilities; engages in programs of national and international cooperative research.

TENNESSEE VALLEY AUTHORITY (TVA)
New Sprankle Building,
 Knoxville, Tenn. 37902
Capitol Hill Office Building
412 First Street, S.E.
 Washington, D.C. 20444
Established: 1933
Membership: Three-member Board of Directors appointed by the President.
Chairman: Charles H. Dean Jr.
Activities: Develops the Tennessee River system through construction of a series of dams; conducts forestry programs; assists in flood control; and is an important supplier of electricity to the surrounding region.

UNITED STATES INFORMATION AGENCY (USIA)
301 Fourth Street, S.W.
 Washington, D.C. 20547
Established: 1977
Director: Charles Z. Wick
Deputy Director: George Nesterczuk
Activities: Voice of America broadcasts to other countries and international educational and cultural-exchange activities

VETERANS ADMINISTRATION (VA)
Vermont Avenue and H Street, N.W.,
 Washington, D.C. 20420
Established: 1930
Administrator of Veterans Affairs: Harry N. Walters
Activities: Administers benefits for former members of the armed forces, their eligible dependents and beneficiaries.

Women's Rights

HIGHLIGHTS: 1985

UN WORLD CONFERENCE OF WOMEN

About 11,000 women from more than 100 nations congregated in Nairobi, Kenya, in July to conclude the United Nations' Decade for Women. Prior to the opening of the official conference on July 15 to 26, an informal 10-day "Forum '85" was held that included about a thousand small discussion groups and activities at which women voiced their concerns about a wide variety of topics.

Assistant UN Secretary General Leticia R. Shahani, 55, a Filipino diplomat, presided over the turbulent official meeting, which was called the Decade for Women Conference.

Maureen Reagan, daughter of President Reagan, headed the United States delegation, seeking to keep the conference focused on "unique problems of women" rather than on international political issues.

Although the sessions were marked with attacks by communist nations on U.S. foreign policy and a walkout by Arab delegates when an Israeli delegate addressed the conference, the representatives finally reached unanimous approval on a resolution that set goals for achievement in subsequent decades. The resolution called on governments to crack down on prostitution and to improve the economic position of women by funding child day care, by setting minimum wage standards, and by taking into account the non-paid work of women when calculating gross national product.

SMEAL AGAIN HEADS NOW

The National Organization for Women (NOW), the nation's largest feminist organization, held its 18th annual conference in New Orleans on July 19–21.

Eleanor Smeal, who had been president of NOW in 1977–82, campaigned to return as head of the organization to again lead a renewed campaign for the Equal Rights Amendment to the Constitution. She also promised to revitalize the organization with mass protests on such issues as efforts to limit women's rights to abortion.

Judy Goldsmith, NOW's president, sought reelection, declaring that NOW had been "devastated structurally and financially" by Smeal's campaign for the Equal Rights Amendment.

Smeal won the election on July 21 with 839 votes to Goldsmith's 703.

Black Heritage USA 22

U.S. Postal Service

Social activist and educator Mary McLeod Bethune (1875–1955) was honored with a commemorative stamp issued on March 5, in Washington, D.C., as the eighth in the Black Heritage USA series. In 1904 she founded a school for black girls in Daytona Beach, Fla., that grew to become the present Bethune-Cookman College. In 1936 she became the first black woman to head a federal agency when appointed director of the Division of Negro Affairs of the National Youth Administration.

A MISSISSIPPI FIRST

Alyce Clarke, 44, became the first black woman elected to the Mississippi legislature when she won a special election on March 19, defeating Sollie Norwood with 1,002 votes to 675.

WOMEN SWELL JAYCEE RANKS

Since the U.S. Supreme Court ruled in July 1984 that the Junior Chamber of Commerce (Jaycees) must admit women as members, more than 31,000 have joined, now making up about 12% of the membership. The largest number of women have joined the organization in Florida—3,563. California is second with 2,030, Michigan third with 1,973, and Texas fourth with 1,780.

Abigail Adams (1744-1818), the only woman whose husband (John Adams) and son (John Quincy Adams) both were President, was honored with a commemorative stamp issued on June 14 in Quincy, Mass.

COMPARABLE WORTH

Despite opposition at the federal level by the Reagan administration, proponents of comparable pay for comparable work made progress in 1985.

In May the Civil Service Employees Association won a 3-year contract with the New York state government that provides $34 million in raises to 50,000 women to achieve greater pay equity with men.

Earlier in May Los Angeles approved a union contract that provided $12 million in raises over three years to give clerks and librarians special raises to bring their salaries equal to those of men in such jobs as gardeners and maintenance workers.

ASIAN HEADS POLITICAL CAUCUS

The National Women's Political Caucus, a bipartisan organization that seeks to put more women in political office, held its national convention in Atlanta in June.

Geraldine Ferraro, the first women to run for Vice President as the candidate of a major party, was the convention's keynote speaker.

With the support of Ferraro, Philipine-born Irene Natividad, 36, was elected chairman of the organization, defeating Atlanta businesswoman Linda Hallenborg by a vote of 312 to 262.

Natividad, on leave as director of the Cen-

MISS AMERICA CONTEST WINNERS

Year	Winner	Year	Winner
1921	Margaret Gorman, Washington, D.C.	1958	Marilyn Van Derbur, Denver, Colorado
1922	Mary Campbell, Columbus, Ohio	1959	Mary Ann Mobley, Brandon, Mississippi
1923	Mary Campbell, Columbus, Ohio	1960	Lynda Lee Mead, Natchez, Mississippi
1924	Ruth Malcolmson, Philadelphia, Pennsylvania	1961	Nancy Fleming, Montague, Michigan
1925	Fay Lamphier, Oakland, California	1962	Maria Fletcher, Asheville, North Carolina
1926	Norma Smallwood, Tulsa, Oklahoma	1963	Jacquelyn Mayer, Sandusky, Ohio
1927	Lois Delaner, Joliet, Illinois	1964	Donna Axum, El Dorado, Arkansas
1933	Marion Bergeron, West Haven, Connecticut	1965	Vonda Kay Van Dyke, Phoenix, Arizona
1935	Henrietta Leaver, Pittsburgh, Pennsylvania	1966	Deborah Irene Bryant, Overland Park, Kansas
1936	Rose Coyle, Philadelphia, Pennsylvania	1967	Jane Anne Jayroe, Laverne, Oklahoma
1937	Bette Cooper, Bertrand Island, New Jersey	1968	Debra Dene Barnes, Moran, Kansas
1938	Marilyn Meseke, Marion, Ohio	1969	Judith Anne Ford, Belvidere, Illinois
1939	Patricia Donnelly, Detroit, Michigan	1970	Pamela Anne Eldred, Birmingham, Michigan
1940	Frances Marie Burke, Philadelphia, Pennsylvania	1971	Phyllis Ann George, Denton, Texas
		1972	Laurie Lee Schaefer, Columbus, Ohio
1941	Rosemary LaPlanche, Los Angeles, California	1973	Terry Anne Meeuwsen, DePere, Wisconsin
1942	Jo-Caroll Dennison, Tyler, Texas	1974	Rebecca Ann King, Denver, Colorado
1943	Jean Bartel, Los Angeles, California	1975	Shirley Cothran, Fort Worth, Texas
1944	Venus Ramey, Washington, D.C.	1976	Tawney Elaine Godin, Yonkers, N.Y.
1945	Bess Myerson, New York City, N.Y.	1977	Dorothy Kathleen Benham, Edina, Minnesota
1946	Marilyn Buferd, Los Angeles, California	1978	Susan Perkins, Columbus, Ohio
1947	Barbara Walker, Memphis, Tennessee	1979	Kylene Baker, Galax, Virginia
1948	BeBe Shopp, Hopkins, Minnesota	1980	Cheryl Prewitt, Ackerman, Mississippi
1949	Jacque Mercer, Litchfield, Arizona	1981	Susan Powell, Elk City, Oklahoma
1951	Yolande Betbeze, Mobile, Alabama	1982	Elizabeth Ward, Russellville, Arkansas
1952	Coleen Kay Hutchins, Salt Lake City, Utah	1983	Debra Maffett, Anaheim, California
1953	Neva Jane Langley, Macon, Georgia	1984	Vanessa Williams, Milwood, New York (resigned)
1954	Evelyn Margaret Ay, Ephrata, Pennsylvania		
1955	Lee Meriwether, San Francisco, California		Suzette Charles, Mays Landing, New Jersey
1956	Sharon Ritchie, Denver, Colorado	1985	Sharlene Wells, Salt Lake City, Utah
1957	Marian McKnight, Manning, South Carolina	1986	Susan Akin, Meridan, Mississippi

NATION'S 100 LEADING BLACK WOMEN

The nations 100 leading black business and professional women were named in 1985 by Delta Sigma Theta Sorority. The women were selected by the sorority on the basis of professional achievement, community service, and financial success.

Lois K. Alexander, New York City	Dr. Shirley A. Jackson, Murry Hill, N.J.
Sharon Giles-Alexander, East Orange, N.J.	Elaine B. Jenkins, Washington, D.C.
Dr. Adrienne Bailey, New York City	Joan Johnson, Chicago
Rev. Willie T. Barrow, Chicago	Caroline R. Jones, New York City
Mary Bell, Detroit	Dr. Edith Irby Jones, Houston
Dr. Mary Frances Berry, Washington, D.C.	Arthenia L. Joyner, Tampa, Fla.
Dr. Jacqueline M. Bontemps, Hampton, Va.	Inez Y. Kaiser, Kansas City
Dr. Arnita Boswell, Chicago	Dr. Yvonne Kennedy, Mobile, Ala.
Barbara Bowles, Northbrook, Ill.	Coretta Scott King, Atlanta
Gwendolyn Brooks, Chicago	Dr. Ruth E. King, Wheaton, Md.
Dr. Hazel W. Johnson-Brown, Washington, D.C.	Jewel LaFontant, Chicago
Jane Smith Browning, Atlanta	Louise Q. Lawson, Chicago
Dorothy Brunson, Baltimore, Md.	Dr. Ruth B. Love, Chicago
Faye Bryant, Houston	Dr. Julianne Malveaux, San Francisco
Dr. Selma H. Burke, New Hope, Pa.	Joel P. Martin, New York City
Barbara Burrell, Chicago	Dr. JoAnn Matory, Chicago
Dr. Margaret Burroughs, Chicago	Dorothy McConner, Chicago
Brig. Gen. Sherian G. Cadoria, Washington, D.C.	Floretta Dukes McKenzie, Washington, D.C.
Dr. Alexa Canady, Detroit	Dr. Sybil Collins Mobley, Tallahassee, Fla.
Hortense Canady, Lansing, Mich.	Linda Bates-Parker, Cincinnati, Ohio
Dr. Donnie E. Cannon, Tulsa, Okla.	Rosa L. Parks, Detroit
Sheila Wheatley Clark, Houston	Ethel Payne, Washington, D.C.
Dr. Constance E. Clayton, Philadelphia	Dr. Evelyn Sears Peevy, Norfolk, Va.
Isabell P. Cottrell, Dallas	Dr. Rejesta V. Perry, St. Louis
JoAnn Charleston, Lorain, Ohio	Marion B. Phillipps, Washington, D.C.
Xerona Clayton, Atlanta	Ernesta Procope, New York City
Dr. Jewel Plummer-Cobb, Fullerton, Calif.	Barbara Proctor, Chicago
Rev. Johnnie Colemon, Chicago	Dr. Marie A. Jackson-Randolph, Detroit
Helen J. Collins, Atlanta	Burnella H. Jackson-Ranson, Atlanta
Marva Collins, Chicago	Pastor Ernestine Reems, Oakland, Calif.
Ruell Cone, Atlanta	Lois D. Rice, Washington, D.C.
Gloria D. Cooke, Chicago	Lillian Roberts, New York City
Helen B. Dean, Wellesly, Mass.	Jacqueline Robinson, Washington, D.C.
Dr. Yvonne V. Delk, New York City	Rachel Robinson, New York City
Dr. Helen G. Edmonds, Cambridge, Mass.	Wilma Rudolph, Indianapolis, Ind.
Dr. Edith V. Francis, Trenton, N.J.	Dr. Claytie D. Searcy, Dallas
Frankie M. Freeman, St. Louis	Patricia Walker Shaw, Memphis
Mary Hatwood Futrell, Washington, D.C.	Naomi Sims, New York City
Bettiann Gardner, Chicago	Thelma Smith, Chicago
Charlayne Hunter-Gault, New York City	Dr. Eunice F. Stanfield, Dallas
Frankie J. Gillette, San Francisco	Rev. Imagene Bigham-Stewart, Washington, D.C.
Sharon Gist Gilliam, Chicago	Susan L. Taylor, New York City
Clara Hale, New York City	Doris J. Turner, Warren, Mich.
Wilhelmina E. Holliday-Hayes, New York City	Phyllis Tucker-Vinson, Los Angeles
Dorothy I. Height, Alexandria, Va.	Lennetta Wells, Chicago
Erma Lois Henderson, Detroit	Rita P. Wilson, Brookfield, Wis.
Arnette Hubbard, Chicago	Constance Woodruff, West Orange, N.J.
Marilyn F. Hubbard, Detroit	Dr. Geraldine P. Woods, Los Angeles
Jean Blackwell-Hutson, New York City	Addie Wyatt, Chicago
Dr. Velma H. Jackson, Baton Rouge, La.	Margaret B. Young, New York City

ter for Continuing Education at William Paterson College in Wayne, N.J., described herself a member of "a minority group perceived as invisible." She said her election demonstrated that "this organization specifically and the women's movement in general must be open to all kinds of women."

When asked by a reporter if she believed the women's movement was losing its steam, Natividad replied: "Look where we are today. . . . We have 1,096 women state legislators, compared to 771 fourteen years ago. . . . Does this look like a movement that's on hold or being eroded?"

IMPORTANT DATES IN THE HISTORY OF AMERICAN WOMEN

1773 First play by American woman playwright: *The Adulateur,* a satire by Mercy Otis Warren (1728–1814).

1774–83 First American woman secret agent abroad: Patience Lovell Wright (1725–26), who sent back secret reports while doing wax sculp-

tures of George III and others in London.

1779 First woman to fight as a uniformed U.S. soldier (disguised as a man): Deborah Sampson (1760–1827), who was wounded twice.

1790 Publication of first popular novel by an American woman: *Charlotte Temple* by Susanna

HISTORY OF AMERICAN WOMEN *(continued)*
Haswell Rowson (c.1762–1824).

1800 Women first vote in local election in Elizabethtown, N.J.

1821 First college-level school for women: the Troy (N.Y.) Female Seminary, founded by Emma Willard (1787–1870).

1824 First strike by women workers at Pawtucket, R.I., weaving mill.

1830 First major women's magazine: *Lady's Book* (later *Godey's Lady's Book*).

1835 Oberlin College in Ohio admits women, becoming first coeducational college; awards first degrees to women in 1841.

1836 First American stage actress to become a star: Charlotte Cushman (1816–76) debuts in New York City as Lady Macbeth.

1836–37 First permanent women's colleges founded: Georgia Female College at Macon, Ga. (later Wesleyan College) and Mt. Holyoke Female Seminary at South Hadley, Mass. (later Mt. Holyoke College).

1847 First American woman astronomer discovers a comet: Maria Mitchell (1818–89).

1848 Married women given right to own real estate in own name by New York legislature.

1848 (July 19–20) First women's rights convention held in Seneca Falls, N.Y.; planned by Elizabeth Cady Stanton (1815–1902) and Lucretia C. Mott (1793–1880).

1849 First woman doctor granted M.D. degree by medical school at Geneva N.Y.: Elizabeth Blackwell (1821–1910).

1850 Founding of first school of medicine for women: Women's College of Pennsylvania.

1852 Publication of first bestselling reform novel by a woman: *Uncle Tom's Cabin* by Harriet Beecher Stowe (1811–96).

1861 First superintendent of women nurses appointed for Union forces in Civil War: Dorothea Lynde Dix (1802–87).

1862 An 8-hour-day law for women and children workers enacted by Wisconsin legislature.

1869 First law giving women right to vote and hold office by Wyoming territorial legislature.

1869 National American Woman Suffrage Association founded; Susan B. Anthony (1820–1906) served as president from 1892 to 1900.

1870 (Aug. 1) Women vote in territorial election for first time in Utah.

1874 National Woman's Christian Temperance Union (WCTU) founded in Cleveland, Ohio.

1881 American Red Cross organized by Clara Barton (1821–1912).

1883 First international organization for women, World's Woman's Christian Temperance Union, founded by Frances E. Willard (1839–98).

1887 First woman mayor elected: Susanna Madora Salter (1860–1961) in Argonia, Kan.

1889 Woman reporter sets record for trip around the world in 72 days, 6 hours, and 11 minutes: Nellie Bly (1867?–1922).

1890 Wyoming provides equal voting rights for women in its constitution.

1895 First American woman interpretive dancer debuts in New York City: Isadora Duncan (1878–1927).

1910 Congress passes Mann Act: forbids interstate transport of women for immoral purposes.

1912 First minimum-wage act for women and children enacted in Massachusetts.

1913 First woman movie star: Pearl White (1889–1938) in the serial *Perils of Pauline.*

1916 First woman elected to Congress: Jeannette Rankin (1880–1973), U.S. representative from Montana; the only member of Congress to vote against U.S. declarations of war both in World War I and World War II.

1918 Woman-in-Industry Service established in U.S. Department of Labor as first agency for women; became Women's Bureau in 1920.

1920 (Aug. 26) Women win right to vote in national elections for first time with proclamation of Amendment 19 to the United States Constitution.

1922 First woman appointed U.S. senator: Rebecca Latimer Felton (1835–1930; D-Ga.) attended sessions on only two days.

1924 First woman elected state governor in Wyoming: Nellie Tayloe Ross (1876–1977).

1931 First American woman to win the Nobel Peace Prize: Jane Addams (1860–1935).

1932 First woman pilot to solo across the Atlantic Ocean from Newfoundland to Ireland: Amelia Earhart (1897–1937).

1932 (Jan. 12) First woman elected to U.S. Senate: Hattie Wyatt Caraway (1878–1950) was reelected to full 6-year terms in 1932 and 1938.

1933 First woman appointed as member of presidential cabinet: Frances Perkins (1882–1965), secretary of labor under President Franklin D. Roosevelt in 1933–45.

1938 First American woman to win the Nobel Prize for Literature: Pearl S. Buck (1892–1973).

1955 First American black woman opera star debuts at New York City's Metropolitan Opera: Marian Anderson (born 1902).

1964 Job discrimination against women forbidden by U.S. Civil Rights Act.

1966 National Organization for Women (NOW) founded by Betty Friedan as leading organization in women's liberation movement.

1972 Equal rights for women amendment to U.S. Constitution approved by Congress and sent to states for ratification.

1973 (Jan. 22) Supreme Court orders repeal of abortion laws in 46 states; rules that women must be allowed to receive abortions on demand during first 6 months of pregnancy.

1974 (June 3) Supreme Court rules for first time that employers must pay women equal wages for same work as men.

1978 (Nov. 1) First women report for sea duty aboard U.S. Navy noncombat ships.

1980 (May) U.S. military service academies graduate women officers for first time.

1981 (Sept. 25) First woman justice of U.S. Supreme Court, Sandra Day O'Connor, sworn in.

1982 (June 30) Equal Rights Amendment defeated; ratified by only 35 states.

1983 (Sept. 17) First black Miss America named: Vanessa Williams, of Millwood, N.Y., honored.

1984 First woman to run on national ticket of major political party: Rep. Geraldine A. Ferraro (D-N.Y.) runs as candidate for Vice President on Democratic ticket headed by former Vice President Walter Mondale as candidate for President.

Deaths

Persons who died in 1985 are listed below and on the following pages. Some gained such fame that their names are instantly recognizable. Others are included because of noteworthy activities or achievements in their lifetimes, even though their names are less well known.

Ben Abruzzo, 54, balloonist; aboard first balloon to cross Atlantic in 1978 and first to cross Pacific in 1981: killed in private plane crash with his wife and four others near Albuquerque, N.M., on Feb. 11.

Tom Adams, 53, prime minister of Barbados since 1976: in Bridgetown, Barbados, on March 11.

Dawn Addams, 54, British actress; best-known role as leading lady in Charlie Chaplin's film *A King in New York* (1957): in London on May 7.

Evelyn Ankers, 67, actress; heroine in scores of "B" adventure movies in 1930s and 1940s: in Haiku, Hawaii, on Aug. 29.

Leslie Cornelius Arends, 89, U.S. representative (R-Ill.) in 1935–74; Republican whip in House in 1943–74; in Naples, Fla., on July 16.

Laura Ashley, 60, British fabric and clothing designer who built multi-million dollar business with her designs: in Coventry, England, on Sept. 17.

Frank H. Bartholomew, 86, war correspondent in World War II who became president of United Press International (UPI) news agency in 1955–62 and chairman in 1962–72: in Sonoma, Calif., on March 26.

Charita Bauer, 62, actress; best known for role of Bertha Bauer that she played for nearly 40 years in daytime radio and TV serial *The Guiding Light:* in New York City on Feb. 28.

Herbert Bayer, 85, Austrian-born painter and designer, noted as one of major artists of Germany's Bauhaus school of 1920s; helped develop Aspen, Colo., as cultural center: in Montecito, Calif., on Sept. 30.

James Beard, 81, chef and cookbook author: in New York City on Jan. 23.

Julian Beck, 60, avant-garde theater producer and social activist; with wife Judith Malina founded Living Theater troupe in 1947; in New York City on Sept. 14.

Alvah Bessie, 81, screenwriter: one of "Hollywood 10" jailed in 1950 for refusing to answer questions by House Un-American Activities Committee; blacklisted, he never

again obtained work as screenwriter: in Terra Linda, Calif., on July 21.

Eugene Carson Blake, 78, Protestant church official: general secretary of World Council of Churches in 1966–72: in Stamford, Conn., on July 31.

Sarah Gibson Blanding, 86, first woman president of Vassar College in 1946–64: in Newtown, Pa., on March 3.

Roger M. Blough, 81, chairman of U.S. Steel Corp. in 1955–69; was forced by President Kennedy in 1962 to rescind steel price increase to hold line against inflation: in Hawley, Pa., on Oct. 8.

Heinrich Theodore Böll, 67, German novelist; won Nobel Literature Prize in 1972: in West Germany on July 16.

Eva Kelly Bowring, 92, U.S. senator (R-Neb.) in 1954: in Gordon, Neb., on Jan. 8.

W. A. (Tony) Boyle, 83, convicted union leader; president United Mine Workers (UMW) in 1963–72; sentenced to life in prison for planning 1969 murder of union opponent Joseph Yablonski and his family: in Wilkes-Barre, Pa., on May 31.

Scott Brady (Jerry Tierney), 60, star of Western movies in 1950s: in Woodland Hills, Calif., on April 17.

Louise Brooks, 78, silent film actress; acclaimed by critics for role of Lulu in 1929 German film *Pandora's Box;* her memoirs were published in 1982 as *Lulu in Hollywood:* in Rochester, N.Y., on Aug. 8.

Carter Brown, 61, Australian mystery writer of more than 270 books: in Sydney, Australia, on May 5.

Yul Brynner, 65, actor; won Oscar as best actor in 1956 as king of Siam in musical *The King and I;* played role 4,625 times on stage; in New York City on Oct. 10.

Sir F. Macfarlane Burnet, 85, Australian microbiologist and virologist; shared 1960 Nobel Prize for Medicine for discovery of acquired immunological tolerance: in Melbourne, Australia, on Aug. 31.

Forbes Burnham, 62, president of Guyana since 1980: in Georgetown, Guyana, on Aug. 6.

Eveline M. Burns, 85, British-born economist; helped develop Social Security Act of 1935: in Newton, Pa., on Sept. 2.

Abe Burrows, 74, playwright and director; co-winner of 1962 Pulitzer Prize with composer Frank Loesser for their musical *How to Succeed in Business Without Really Trying:* in New York City on May 17.

John W. Byrnes, 71, U.S. representative (R-

982 DEATHS

DEATHS: 1985 *(continued)*
Wis.) in 1945–73: in Marshfield, Wis., on Jan. 12

Taylor Caldwell, 84, author of many best-selling novels since 1938, including *Captains and Kings,* which was adapted for TV mini-series: in Greenwich, Conn., on Aug. 30.
Italo Calvino, 61, Italian novelist and author of folk tales; his *Mr. Palomar* was published in the United States in 1985: in Siena, Italy, on Sept. 19.
Roderick W. Cameron, 71, author of many books on travel and history: in Menerbes, France, on Sept. 18.
John Edwin Canaday, 78, art critic of *New York Times* in 1959–76: in New York City on July 19.
Marc Chagall, 97, Russian-born expressionist painter: two of his huge murals that decorate New York City's Metropolitan Opera in Lincoln Center: in St. Paul de Vence, France, on March 28.
George Chandler, 86, actor; succeeded Ronald Regan as president of Screen Actors Guild in 1960: in Los Angeles on June 10.
Grand Duchess Charlotte, 89, Luxembourg ruler in 1919–64: in Luxembourg on July 9.
Konstantin U. Chernenko, 73, president of the Soviet Union: See page 13.
Ina Claire, 92, stage and screen actress of 1920s to 1950s; played Duchess Swana in Greta Garbo film *Ninotchka* (1939): in San Francisco on Feb. 21.
Charles R. Clason, 94, U.S. representative (R-Mass.) in 1937–49: in Springfield, Mass., on July 7.
Earle C. Clements, 88, U.S. senator (D-Ky.) in 1951–57; governor of Kentucky in 1947–50: in Morganfield, Ky., on March 12.
Larry Clinton, 75, composer and bandleader; best-known song was *The Dipsy Doodle* (1937): in Tucson, Ariz., on May 2.
Sidney Clute, 69, actor known for role of Detective Paul LaGuardia on TV series *Cagney & Lacey:* in Santa Monica, Calif., on Oct. 2.
Lester Cole, 81, screenwriter; one of "Hollywood 10" jailed in 1950 for contempt of Congress for refusing to testify about communist infiltration of movie unions; blacklisted by movie studios, had to work at other jobs: in San Francisco on Aug. 15.
Charles Collingwood, 68, CBS News radio and TV correspondent since World War II: in New York City on Oct. 3.
J. Fred Coots, 87, composer; one of best known tunes is *Santa Claus is Coming to Town:* in New York City on April 8.
Gardner Cowles, Jr., 82, co-founder of popular picture magazine *Look* that he headed from 1937 until it ceased publication in

1971: in Southampton, N.Y., on July 8.
Barry Crane, 57, TV director and master bridge tournament player: beaten to death by unknown person in his home in Studio City, Calif., on July 5.
Archibald M. Crossley, 88, pioneer in public opinion polls: in Princeton, N.J., on May 1.
Ramon Ernesto Cruz, 82, elected president of Honduras in 1971–72, overthrown in military coup: in Honduras on Aug. 6.
Jose Cubero, 21, Spanish matador: killed by bull in bullring near Madrid on Aug. 30.
Gen. Robert E. Cushman Jr., 70, commandant of U.S. Marine Corps in 1972–75: in Fort Washington, Md., on Jan. 2.

Neil Davis, 51, NBC news correspondent: killed by tank fire during coup attempt in Bangkok, Thailand, on Sept. 9.
Jeanine Deckers, 52, Belgian "Singing Nun" who recorded song *Dominique* (1963); left Dominican order in 1966 after movie *The Singing Nun* (1966) told her story: joint suicide with woman friend in Wavres, Belgium, on April 1.
Johnny Desmond (Giovanni de Simone), 65, singer and actor; best known for recordings, such as *C'est si Bon* and *The Yellow Rose of Texas:* in Los Angeles on Sept. 6.
James A. Dewar, 88, invented mass-produced pasteries called Twinkies in 1930: in Chicago on June 30.
Selma Diamond, 64, comedic actress and writer; best known for role as court matron Selma Hacker on TV series *Night Court:* in Los Angeles on May 14.
Dame Bridget D'Oyly Carte, 77, British director of Gilbert and Sullivan operetta troupe D'Oyly Carte Opera Co. in 1948–82; was granddaughter of troupe's founder: in Chalfonte St. Giles, England, on May 2.
Jean Dubuffet, 83, French surrealist painter and sculptor; his sculpture *Group of Four Trees* (1972) stands 42 feet high in Chase Manhattan Plaza in New York City: in Paris on May 12.

Milton Stover Eisenhower, 85, educator and brother of President Dwight D. Eisenhower; president of Kansas State University in 1943–50, Pennsylvania State University in 1950–56, and Johns Hopkins University in 1956–67 and 1971–72: in Baltimore, Md., on May 2.
John F. Enders, 88, virologist; awarded Nobel Prize for Medicine in 1954 for discovery of way to grow polio virus; helped develop vaccine for measles in 1963: in Waterford, Conn., on Sept. 8.
Tage Erlander, 84, Socialist prime minister of Sweden in 1946–69: in Huddinge, Sweden, on June 21.

Sam J. Ervin, Jr., 88, U.S. senator (D-N.C.) in 1954–74; won chairman of Senate committee that held TV hearings on Watergate scandal, leading to resignation of President Nixon: in Winston-Salem, N.C., on April 23.

Philip D. Estridge, 47, head of task force that developed IBM's Personal Computer unveiled in 1981: killed with his wife and five other IBM executives in Delta Airlines crash in Dallas, Tex., on Aug. 2.

Frank Faylen, 79, actor best known for role on TV series *The Many Loves of Dobie Gillis* as Dobie's long-suffering father: in Burbank, Calif., on Aug. 2.

Paul J. Flory, 75, chemist; won 1974 Nobel Prize for Chemistry for analytical studies of long-chain molecules that led to development of many plastics and synthetic materials: in Big Sur Calif., on Sept. 9.

Phil Foster (Fivel Feldman), 72, comedian; best-known for role on TV series *Laverne and Shirley* as father of Laverne: in Palm Desert, Calif., on July 8.

Jane Frazee (Mary Jane Frehse), 67, actress and singer in 40 films in 1940s and 1950s: in Newport Beach, Calif., on Sept. 6.

Rudi Gernreich, 62, fashion designer introduced topless bathing suits for women in 1964: in Los Angeles on April 21.

Ruth Gordon, 88, stage and movie actress; won 1968 Oscar for best supporting actress as witch in *Rosemary's Baby:* in Edgartown, Mass., on Aug. 28.

Jess Gorkin, 71, editor of *Parade* magazine in 1949-78: in Longboat Key, Fla., on Feb. 19.

Manfred Gottfried, 85, first writer hired by Henry Luce in 1922 on founding of *Time* magazine; remained with *Time* throughout career, serving in all its top editorial positions: in Falmouth, Mass., on Sept. 19.

Chester Gould, 84, cartoonist; created *Dick Tracy* detective comic strip in 1931: in Woodstock, Ill., on May 11.

Richard Greene, 66, British actor; best known for role of Robin Hood on long-running 1950s TV series *The Adventures of Robin Hood:* in London on June 1.

Mikhail Gromov, 85, Soviet aviator who made nonstop Moscow to San Jacinto, Calif., flight in 1937: in Moscow on Jan. 22.

Johnny Guarnieri, 67, jazz pianist and harpsichordist: in Livingston, N.J., on Jan. 7.

John Chandler Gurney, 88, U.S. senator (R-S.D.) in 1939-51: in Yankton, S.D., on March 9.

Margaret Hamilton, 82, character actress known for role as Wicked Witch of West in movie *The Wizard of Oz* (1939): in Salisbury, Conn., on May 16.

Mark W. Hannaford, 60, U.S. representative (D-Calif.) in 1975-79: in Lakewood, Calif., on June 2.

Sir Alister Hardy, 89, British marine biologist; won prestigious 1985 Templeton Prize for Progress in Religion: in Oxford, England, on May 23.

Patricia Roberts Harris, 60, first black woman cabinet officer, serving President Carter as Secretary of Housing and Urban Development in 1977–79 and as Secretary of Health, Education, and Welfare in 1979–81: in Washington, D.C., on March 23.

Henry Hathaway, 86, director of over 60 movies from *Lives of a Bengal Lancer* (1935) to *True Grit* (1969): in Los Angeles on Feb. 11.

Louis Hayward, 75, South African-born film and TV actor; in *The Saint in New York* (1938) was first to play author Leslie Charteris' Robin-Hood-of-crime character; in Palm Springs, Calif., on Feb. 21.

John Holt, 62, teacher and writer; his book *How Children Fail* in 1964 helped spark reevaluation of teaching methods in 1960s: in Boston, Mass., on Sept. 14.

Rock Hudson, 59, movie star who acted in 62 films and TV series *Dynasty* and *McMillan & Wife;* his disclosure in July 1985 that he suffered from fatal disease AIDS focused public attention on need for more research on AIDS: in Los Angeles on Oct. 2.

Sarah Tilghman Hughes, 88, federal district judge who swore in President Lyndon B. Johnson in Dallas, Tex., after assassination of President John F. Kennedy: in Dallas on April 23.

Edward Hutchinson, 70, U.S. representative (R-Mich) in 1963-77; was senior Republican on House Judiciary Committee that voted for impeachment of President Nixon: in Naples, Fla., on July 22.

Sam Jaffe, 55, TV news reporter for CBS in 1955–61 and ABC in 1961–69: in Bethesda, Md., on Feb. 8.

Serge Jaroff, 89, founder and director of Don Cossack Russian Male Chorus in 1920s to 1960s: in Lakewood, N.J., on Oct. 5.

William Ezra Jenner, 76, U.S. senator (R-Ind.) in 1944–45 and 1947–59: in Bedford, Ind., on March 9.

Jonathan (Jo) Jones, 73, jazz drummer with Count Basie's first band in 1935–48: in New York City on Sept. 3.

Joseph Rudolph (Philly Joe) Jones, 62, jazz drummer with Miles Davis' quintet in 1950s: in Philadelphia on Aug. 30.

Leatrice Joy (Leatrice Joy Zeidler), 91, actress in silent movies; married to actor John

Gilbert: in New York City on May 13.

Anton Karas, 78, Austrian composer and zither player; best known for composition and playing of theme of movie *The Third Man* (1949): in Vienna on Jan. 10.

Charles (Commando) Kelly, 64, first enlisted man awarded Medal of Honor in World War II for exploits in Italy in 1943: in Pittsburgh, Pa., on Jan. 11.

Frank M. Kinard, 70, member of Pro Football Hall of Fame; first all-American from University of Mississippi: in Jackson, Miss., on Sept. 7.

Wayne King, 84, saxophonist and big band leader in 1920s to 1940s; known as "Waltz King" for his featuring of waltzes: in Phoenix, Ariz., on July 16.

Leon Klinghoffer, 69, partially-paralyzed New York retiree: killed by Palestinian hijackers and thrown overboard with wheelchair from Mediterranean cruise ship *Achille Lauro* on Oct. 8.

Stanley Kresge, 85, philanthropist heir to S.S. Kresge dime store fortune: in Detroit on June 30.

Simon Kuznets, 84, economist; won Nobel Economics Prize in 1971 for developing way to calculate nation's gross national product (GNP): in Cambridge, Mass., on July 9.

Kay Kyser (James King Kern Kyser), 79, bandleader of 1930s–1940s, known as "Old Perfessor of Kollege of Musical Knowledge:" in Chapel Hill, N.C., on July 23.

Harold Lang, 64, ballet star in 1940s to 1950s: in Chico, Calif., on July 26.

William Latch, 35, NBC news correspondent: killed by tank fire during coup attempt in Bangkok, Thailand, on Sept. 9.

Henry Cabot Lodge Jr., 82, U.S. senator (R-Mass) in 1937–44 and 1947–53; U.S. ambassador to UN in 1953–60; unsuccessful candidate for Vice President as running mate of Richard Nixon in 1960: in Beverly, Mass., on Feb. 27.

Gillis W. Long, 61, U.S. representative (D-La.) in 1963–65 and 1973–85: in Washington, D.C., on Jan. 20.

Helen MacInnes, 77, Scottish-born author of best-selling spy novels: in New York City on Sept. 30.

Albert Maltz, 76, screenwriter and novelist; one of "Hollywood 10" jailed in 1950 for refusing to answer questions of House Un-American Activities Committee; blacklisted, he wrote film scripts under pseudonyms: in Los Angeles on April 26.

Lt. Gen. Richard C. Mangrum, 78, former assistant commandant of U.S. Marine Corps;

combat pilot in World War II and Korean War; in Southern Pines, N.C., on Sept. 28.

Margo (Margo Albert), 68, Mexican-born film actress; wife of actor Eddie Albert; niece of bandleader Xavier Cugat: in Pacific Palisades, Calif., on July 17.

J. Willard Marriott, 84, founder of Marriott Corp. which he built from root beer stand in Washington, D.C., in 1927 into multi-billion dollar hotel and restaurant business: in Wolfeboro, N.H., on Aug. 13.

Johnny Marks, 75, songwriter; best known for his *Rudolph the Red-Nosed Reindeer:* in New York City on Sept. 3.

Fred Marshall, 79, U.S. representative (D-Minn.) in 1949–63: in Litchfield, Minn., on June 5.

John Martin, 91, first fulltime dance critic for *New York Times* in 1927–62: in Saratoga, N.Y., on May 19.

Robert K. McCormick, 74, NBC radio and TV news reporter: in New York City on Sept. 4.

Gen. Emilio Garrastazu Medici, 79, dictatorial president of Brazil in 1969–74: in Rio de Janeiro on Oct. 9.

Arnold Ray Miller, 62, disabled coal miner who wrested control of United Mine Workers (UMW) from entrenched leadership to become president of UMW in 1972–79: in Charleston, W.Va., on July 12.

Marvin Miller (Marvin Mueller), 71, actor; known for role of Michael Anthony in 1950s TV series *The Millionaire:* in Santa Monica, Calif., on Feb. 8.

Ewen Montagu, 84, leader of British counterspy group in World War II that misled Germans into belief Sardinia and Greece would be main landing spots for Allied forces instead of Sicily; wrote best-selling *The Man Who Never Was* (1953) about operation: in London on July 19.

Paull Murray, 74, first black woman to become Episcopal priest (1971): in Pittsburgh, Pa., on July 1.

Clarence Nash, 80, first voice of Donald Duck in more than 150 Walt Disney cartoon films: in Burbank, Calif., on Feb. 20.

Robert Nathan, 91, best-selling author of about 50 books; best known novel *Portrait of Jennie* (1940): in Los Angeles on May 25.

Tancredo de Almeida Neves, 75, elected on Jan. 15, 1985, as first civilian president of Brazil in 21 years, but fatal illness prevented his being sworn into office: in Sao Paulo, Brazil, on April 21.

Lloyd Nolan, 83, actor who won awards for his stage and TV roles as Captain Queeg in *The Caine Mutiny Court Martial:* in Los Angeles on Sept. 27.

John Ringling North, 81, head of Ringling

Brothers and Barnum & Bailey Circus for most of 1937–67: in Belgium on June 4.

Edmond O'Brien, 69, film actor; won 1955 Oscar as best supporting actor in *The Barefoot Contessa:* in Inglewood, Calif., on May 9.

George O'Brien, 86, actor in many Western movies from 1920s to 1960s: in Broken Arrow, Okla., on Sept. 4.

J. Pat O'Malley, 80, Irish-born actor; appeared in many movies and TV series: in San Juan Capistrano, Calif., on Feb. 27.

Eugene Ormandy, 85, Hungarian-born conductor; director of Philadelphia Orchestra in 1936–80: in Philadelphia on March 12.

Bonaro W. Overstreet, 82, author, psychologist, lecturer; with husband Harry A. Overstreet wrote many books, such as *Mind Alive:* in Arlington, Va., on Sept. 10.

Harold Peary (Harrold Jese Pereira de Faria), 76, actor best known as star of 1941–50 radio series *The Great Gildersleeve:* in Torrance, Calif., on March 30.

Sir (Isaac) James Pitman, 84, Conservative member of British parliament in 1945–64; promoted teaching of reading with i.t.a. (initial teaching alphabet), 42-character phonetic alphabet; grandson of inventor of Pitman shorthand system: in England on Sept. 1.

George Polya, 97, mathematician; professor emeritus of Stanford University; author of best-selling *How to Solve It:* in Palo Alto, Calif., on Sept. 7.

Antonio Cardinal Poma, 75, head of Roman Catholic Church in Italy: in Bologna, Italy, on Sept. 25.

Rodney Robert Porter, 67, British biochemist who won Nobel Prize for Medicine in 1972 for determining chemical structure of antibodies: killed in auto accident in Winchester, England, on Sept. 7.

Nathan Pritikin, 69, author of best-selling diet books: suicide in Albany, N.Y., on Feb. 21.

Ida Pruitt, 96, social worker, as chief of social services at Peking Union Medical College Hospital in 1921–39, trained China's first social workers; born in China, her autobiography in 1978 was titled *A China Childhood:* in Philadelphia on July 24.

Karen Ann Quinlan, 31, woman who had existed in coma since 1975; her parents won landmark court decision in 1976 allowing her to be disconnected from respirator, but she continued to live: in Morris Plains, N.J., on June 11.

Sir Michael Redgrave, 77, British stage and film actor; father of actresses Lynn and Vanessa Redgrave: in Denham, England, on March 21.

Charles F. Richter, 85, seismologist who developed Richter scale to measure power of earthquakes: in Pasadena, Calif., on Sept. 30.

Nelson Riddle, 64, composer; won Academy Award in 1975 for score of movie *The Great Gatsby:* in Los Angeles on Oct. 6.

Julian B. Robinson, 86, mathematician; first woman elected to National Academy of Science in 1976: in Oakland, Calif., on July 30.

Leonard M. Ross, 39, child prodigy who at ages of 10 and 11 won $164,000 on 1950s TV quiz shows; as adult, after receiving law degree from Yale, believed he never lived up to potential: apparent suicide in Santa Clara, Calif., on May 1.

Morrie Ryskind, 89, playwright; shared 1932 Pulitzer Prize for Drama with George S. Kaufman and Ira Gershwin for musical *Of Thee I Sing:* in Washington, D.C., on Aug. 24.

Charles W. Sandman, Jr., 63, U.S. representative (R-N.J.) in 1967–75; strongly supported President Nixon in televised Watergate impeachment hearings in 1974: in Cape May Courthouse, N.J., on Aug. 26.

Giorgio Santelli, 87, Italian-born fencing master; coached U.S. Olympic fencing teams in 1928–52; in Teaneck, N.J., on Oct. 8.

Elias Sarkis, 60, Christian president of Lebanon in 1976–82: in Paris, France, on June 27.

Abdus Sattar, 79, only civilian elected president of Bangladesh, who was ousted by military coup in 1982 after five months in office: in Dhaka, Bangladesh, on Oct. 5.

George Savalas, 58, actor with brother Telly on TV's *Kojak* series: in Los Angeles on Oct. 2.

John Scarne, 82, authority on gambling; wrote *Scarne's Complete Guide to Gambling* (1961): in Englewood, N.J., on July 7.

Martha Schlamme, 60, Austrian-born singer best known for performance of songs of Kurt Weill: in New York City on Oct. 6.

Alexander Scourby, 71, actor and narrator of documentaries: in Boston on Feb. 23.

Roger Huntington Sessions, 88, composer; won 1982 Pulitzer Prize for *Concerts for Orchestra:* in Princeton, N.J., on March 16.

Joseph C. (Mickey) Shaughnessy, 64, comic actor who appeared in about 40 films: in Cape May Court House, N.J., on July 23.

Simone Signoret, 64, French actress who won 1950 Oscar as best actress for role in *Room at the Top:* in France on Sept. 30.

John (Zoot) Sims, 59, jazz saxophonist: in New York City on March 23.

Eric Sloane, 80, painter, illustrator, and author; in 1980 painted 6-story-high mural for National Air and Space Museum in Wash-

DEATHS: 1985 *(continued)*

ington, D.C.: in New York City on March 6.

Muriel Smith, 62, singer and actress who was first to play lead role in musical *Carmen Jones* on Broadway in 1943: in Richmond, Va., on Sept. 13.

Samantha Smith, 13, schoolgirl who visted Soviet Union in 1983 at invitation of Soviet leader Yuri Andropov because of letter she had written to him expressing fear of nuclear war: killed with her father and 6 others in crash of commuter airliner near Auburn, Me., on Aug. 26.

John W. Snyder, 90, U.S. secretary of the treasury in 1946–1953 under President Truman: on Seabrook Island, S.C., on Oct. 8.

Gale Sondergaard, 86, stage and movie actress; won 1936 Oscar for best supporting actress in *Anthony Adverse;* her husband, Herbert Biberman, was one of "Hollywood 10" jailed in 1950 for refusing to testify in congressional investigation into communist infiltration of movie industry; she too refused to testify before House Committee on Un-American Activities in 1951; blacklisted, she obtained no roles in film until 1969: in Woodland Hills, Calif., on Aug. 14.

Robert D. Stethem, 23, U.S. Navy diver: killed by Arab hijackers of TWA jet airliner in Beirut, Lebanon, on June 14.

Aaron Marc Stein, 79, mystery writer; awarded Grand Master Edgar award of Mystery Writers of America in 1979 for his life work: in New York City on Aug. 29.

Jock Stein, 62, manager of Scotland's national soccer team: of heart attack at World Cup qualifying game between Scotland and Wales in Cardiff, Wales, on Sept. 10.

E. J. Wallace Sterling, 78, President of Stanford University in 1949–68: in Woodside, Calif., on July 1.

Gabor Szego, 90, Hungarian-born mathematician; headed department of mathematics at Stanford University in 1938–60: in Palo Alto, Calif., on Aug. 7.

Yoshiuki Takada, 31, avant-garde Japanese dancer: killed when rope broke during dance "Jomon Sho" while he and other dancers were suspended upside down from roof of Mutual Life Building in Seattle, Wash., on Sept. 10.

Vic Tanny (Victor Iannidinardo), 73, physical fitness expert who opened about 100 health clubs throughout nation: in Tampa, Fla., on June 11.

John-Michael Tebelak, 36, author of the 1970s hit musical *Godspell:* in New York City on April 2.

Luther Terry, 73, physician; as surgeon general of U.S. in 1961–65 led in linking tobacco smoking to lung cancer and heart disease: in Philadelphia on March 29.

Mims Thomason, 74, president of United Press International (UPI) wire news service in 1962–76 and its chairman in 1972–74: in Greenwich, Conn., on July 26.

Harold H. Velde, 75, U.S. representative (R-Ill.) in 1949–57; chairman of House Un-American Activities Committee in 1953–55: in Sun City, Ariz., on Sept. 1.

Joe Walker, 92, pioneer movie carmeraman; member of Motion Picture Hall of Fame; awarded honorary Oscar in 1982: in Las Vegas, Nev., on Aug. 1.

Lynd Ward, 80, illustrator; won Caldecott Medal in 1952 for children's book *The Biggest Bear:* in Reston, Va., on June 28.

Orson Welles, 70, innovative actor and director; won fame at age 23 in 1938 with realistic radio production *War of the Worlds,* causing listeners to panic and flee from their homes to escape his fictional invasion of U.S. by Martians; starred in, wrote, and directed classic film *Citizen Kane* in 1941: in Los Angeles on Oct. 10.

E. B. White, 86, author, known to parents and children for his books *Stuart Little* and *Charlotte's Web* and to writers for his *Elements of Style:* in North Brooklin, Me., on Oct. 1.

Charles (Cootie) Williams, 77, jazz trumpet player; last survivor of Duke Ellington's 1920s band: in New York City on Sept. 15.

Grant Williams, 54, film and TV actor; starred in movie *The Incredible Shrinking Man:* in Los Angeles, Calif., on July 28.

Tex Williams, 68, country-western singer; one of best-known hits *Smoke! Smoke! Smoke! (that Cigarette);* in Newhall, Calif., on Oct. 11.

Tom Williams, 99, Canadian flying ace in World War I whose pilot's certificate was signed by airplane inventor Orville Wright: in Woodstock, Ont., on July 25.

Olgivanna Lloyd Wright, 87, widow of architect Frank Lloyd Wright: in Scottsdale, Ariz., on March 1.

Richard Yardumian, 68, composer; best known for *Armenian Suite* (1954): in Bryn Athyn, Pa., on Aug. 15.

Gen. Aleksei A. Yepishev, 77, chief political commissar of Soviet armed forces since 1962: in Moscow on Sept. 15.

Sir Muhammad Zafrullah Khan, 92, first foreign minister of Pakistan in 1947–1954: in Islamabad, Pakistan, on Sept. 1.

Efrem Zimbalist, 95, Russian-born concert violinist; father of actor Efrem Zimbalist Jr.: in Reno, Nev., on Feb. 22.

Index